Mobil 1999
TRAVEL GUIDE®

Northeast

**CONNECTICUT • MAINE
MASSACHUSETTS • NEW HAMPSHIRE • NEW YORK
RHODE ISLAND • VERMONT**

**NEW BRUNSWICK • NOVA SCOTIA • ONTARIO
PRINCE EDWARD ISLAND • QUEBEC**

Fodor's Travel Publications, Inc.

Guide Staff

General Manager: Diane E. Connolly
Editorial/Inspection Coordinator: Doug Weinstein
Inspection Assistant: Brenda Piszczek
Editorial Assistants: Sheila Connolly, Susanne Ochs, Julie Raio, Kathleen Rose,
  Elizabeth Schwar
Creative Director: Fabrizio La Rocca
Cover Design: Chermayeff & Geismar Inc.
Cover Photograph: Peter Guttman

Acknowledgments

We gratefully acknowledge the help of our more than 100 field representatives for their efficient and perceptive inspection of every lodging and dining establishment listed; the establishments' proprietors for their cooperation in showing their facilities and providing information about them; the many users of previous editions of the *Mobil Travel Guide* who have taken the time to share their experiences; and for their time and information, the thousands of chambers of commerce, convention and visitors bureaus, city, state, and provincial tourism offices, and government agencies who assisted in our research.

Mobil

Copyright

Published in 1999 by Fodor's Travel Publications, Inc.
201 E. 50th St.
New York, NY 10022

Northeast
ISBN 0-679-00196-4
ISSN 1040-1075

Printed in the United States of America
10 9 8 7 6 5 4 3 2 1

Contents

Northeast

Maps

Larger, more detailed maps are available at many Mobil service stations

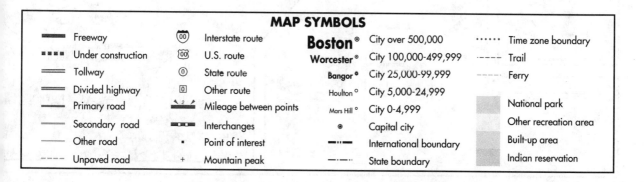

MAP SYMBOLS

Freeway	Interstate route	**Boston** ®	City over 500,000	Time zone boundary
Under construction	U.S. route	**Worcester** ®	City 100,000-499,999	Trail
Tollway	State route	**Bangor** ®	City 25,000-99,999	Ferry
Divided highway	Other route	Houlton °	City 5,000-24,999	
Primary road	Mileage between points	Mars Hill °	City 0-4,999	National park
Secondary road	Interchanges	®	Capital city	Other recreation area
Other road	Point of interest		International boundary	Built-up area
Unpaved road	+ Mountain peak		State boundary	Indian reservation

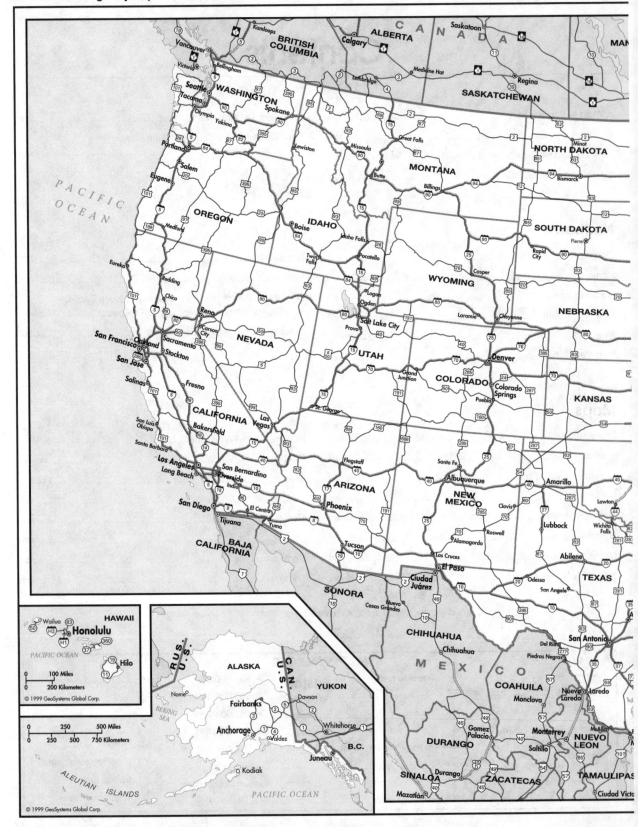

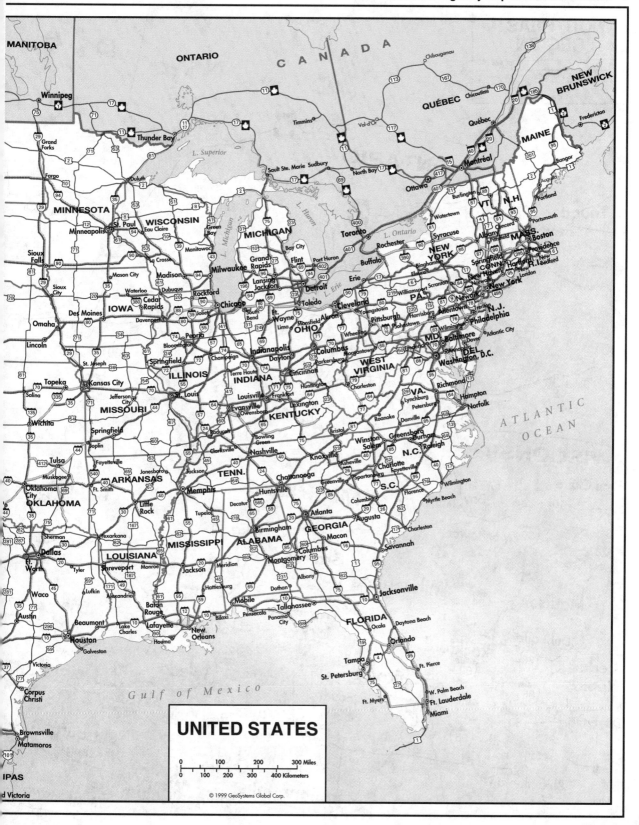

UNITED STATES

0   100   200   300 Miles
0   100   200   300   400 Kilometers

© 1999 GeoSystems Global Corp.

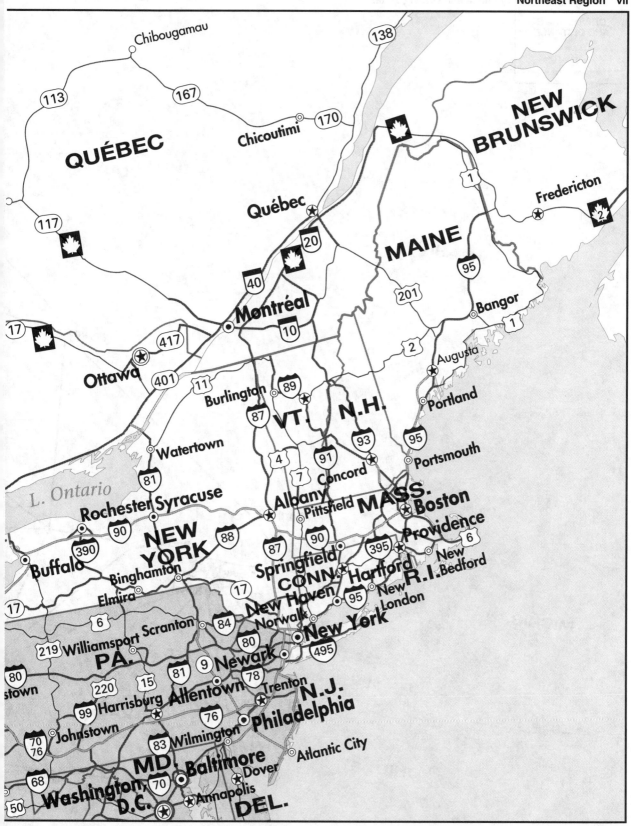

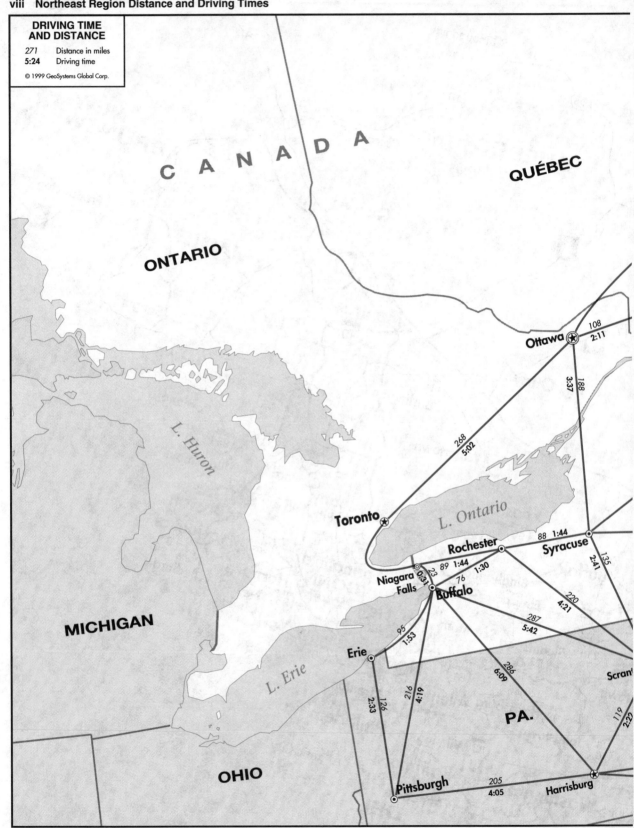

**DRIVING TIME
AND DISTANCE**

271   Distance in miles
5:24   Driving time

© 1999 GeoSystems Global Corp.

C A N A D A

QUÉBEC

ONTARIO

Ottawa   108
2:11

188
3:37

268
5:02

L. Huron

Toronto   L. Ontario

Rochester   88 1:44
Syracuse

89 1:44   1:30
135
2:41

Niagara   23
Falls   0:31   76

Buffalo   220
4:21

287
5:42

MICHIGAN

95
1:53

286
6:09

Scrant

Erie

L. Erie   126
2:33   216
4:19   119
2:2

PA.

OHIO

Pittsburgh   205
4:05   Harrisburg

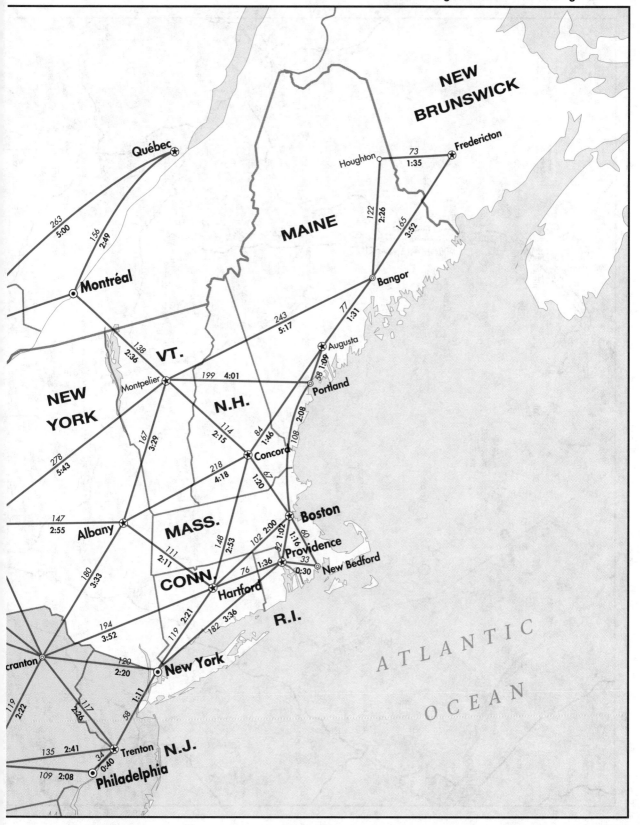

Québec

NEW BRUNSWICK

263
5:00

156
2:49

Houghton   73   Fredericton
            1:35

122
2:26

165
3:52

MAINE

Montréal

138
2:36

VT.

243
5:17

Bangor

77
1:31

199   4:01

Montpelier

NEW YORK

N.H.

Augusta
38 1:09

Portland

167
3:29

114
2:15

84
1:46

108
2:08

278
5:43

Concord

218
4:18

67
1:20

147
2:55

Albany

MASS.

Boston

102 2:00
62 1:01
1:16

180
3:33

111
2:11

148
2:53

Providence

33
0:30   New Bedford

CONN.

76   1:36
Hartford

60

194
3:52

119   2:21

182   3:36

R.I.

Scranton

120
2:20

New York

ATLANTIC

119
2:22

117
2:26

58
1:11

OCEAN

135   2:41

Trenton   N.J.
34
0:40

109   2:08

Philadelphia

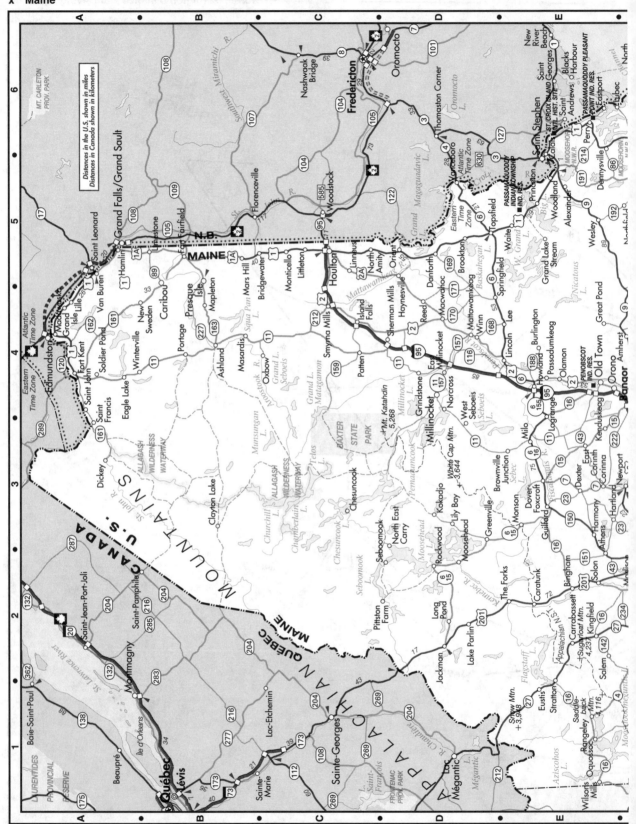

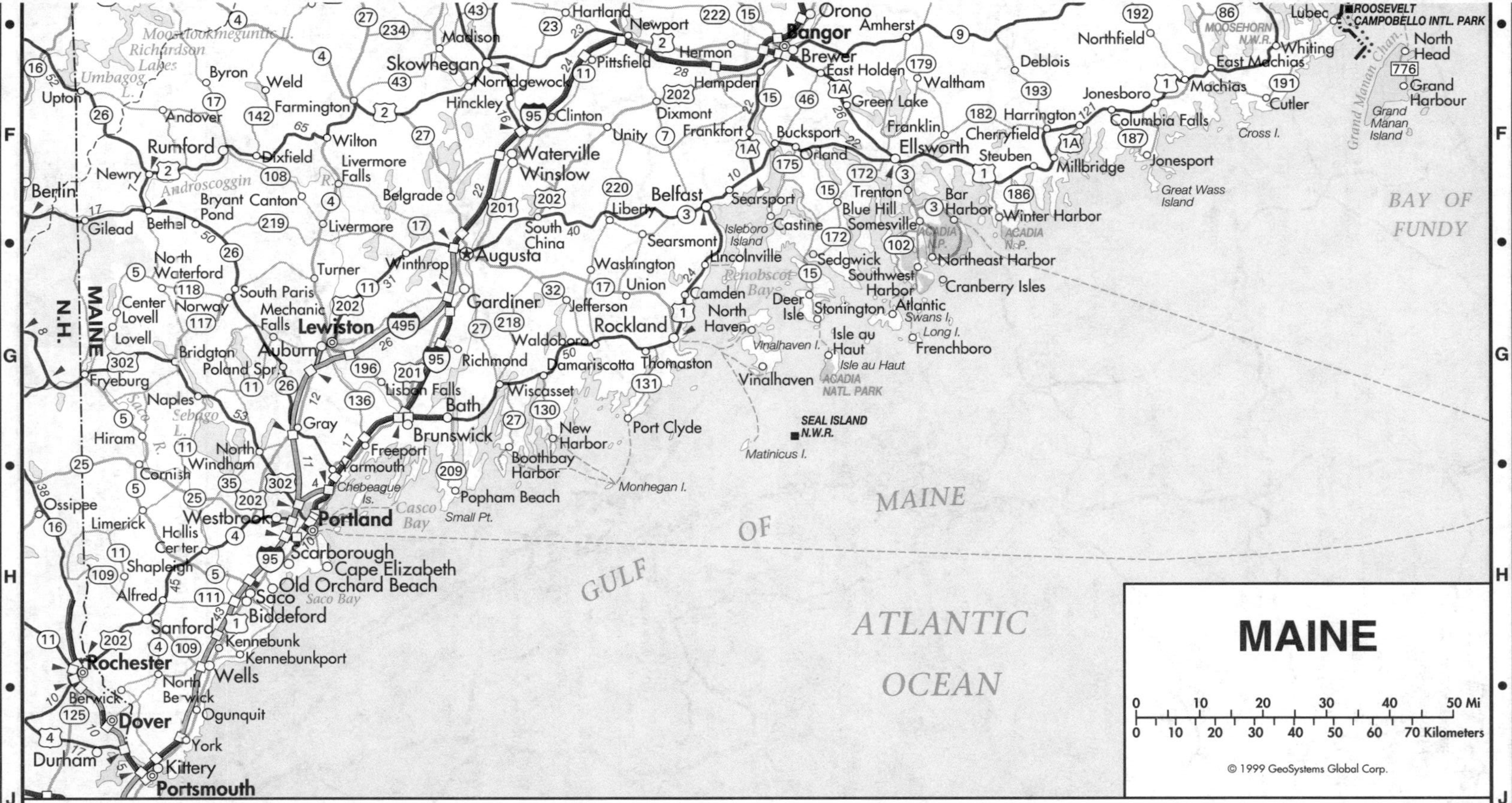

MAINE

© 1999 GeoSystems Global Corp.

Scale:
0 10 20 30 40 50 Mi
0 10 20 30 40 50 60 70 Kilometers

Map labels include: BAY OF FUNDY · GULF OF MAINE · ATLANTIC OCEAN · STATE OF MAINE · MAINE / N.H. · ACADIA NATL. PARK · ROOSEVELT CAMPOBELLO INTL. PARK · SEAL ISLAND N.W.R. · MOOSEHORN N.W.R. · Grand Manan Island · Casco Bay · Penobscot Bay · Androscoggin R. · Kennebec R. · Umbagog L. · Richardson L. · Moosehead L. · Sebago L.

PARTIAL INDEX TO
CITIES AND TOWNS

Auburn	G-2
Augusta	G-2
Bailey Island	H-2
Bangor	F-4
Bar Harbor	F-4
Bath	G-2
Belfast	F-3
Bethel	F-1
Bingham	E-2
Blue Hill	F-4
Boothbay Harbor	G-3
Brewer	F-4
Bridgton	G-1
Brunswick	G-2
Bucksport	F-4
Calais	E-6
Camden	F-3
Cape Elizabeth	H-2
Caribou	B-5
Castine	F-4
Center Lovell	G-1
Cranberry Isles	G-4
Damariscotta	G-3
Deer Isle	G-4
Dover-Foxcroft	E-3
Eagle Lake	J-1
East Millinocket	D-4
Eastport	E-6
Ellsworth	F-4
Farmington	F-2
Fort Kent	J-1
Freeport	G-2
Gardiner	G-2
Greenville	D-3
Hampden	F-4
Houlton	B-5
Jackman	D-2
Jonesport	F-5
Kennebunk	H-1
Kennebunkport	H-1
Kingfield	E-2
Kittery	J-1
Lewiston	G-2
Lincoln	E-4
Lisbon Falls	G-2
Lubec	E-6
Machias	E-5
Madawaska	J-1
Millinocket	D-4
Milo	E-3
Newport	F-3
Northeast Harbor	G-4
Norway	G-1
Ogunquit	H-1
Old Orchard Beach	H-2
Old Town	F-4
Orono	F-4
Patten	D-4
Poland Spring	G-2
Portland	H-2
Presque Isle	C-5
Rangeley	E-1
Rockland	G-3
Rockwood	D-2
Rumford	F-1
Saco	H-1
Sanford	H-1
Scarborough	H-2
Searsport	F-3
Skowhegan	F-2
South Paris	G-1
Southwest Harbor	G-4
Stonington	G-4
Vinalhaven	G-4
Waterville	F-3
Wells	H-1
Westbrook	H-2
Winslow	F-3
Winthrop	G-2
Wiscasset	G-2
Yarmouth	H-2
York	J-1

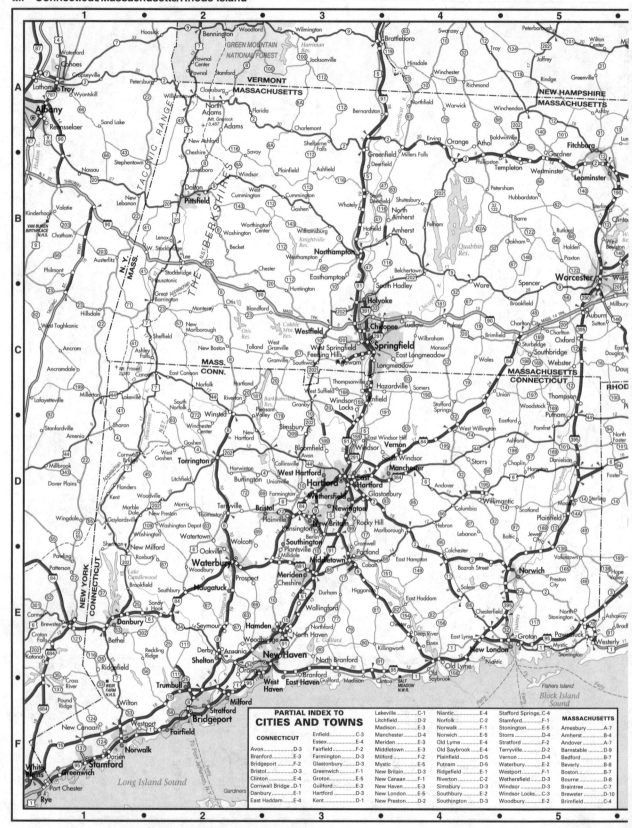

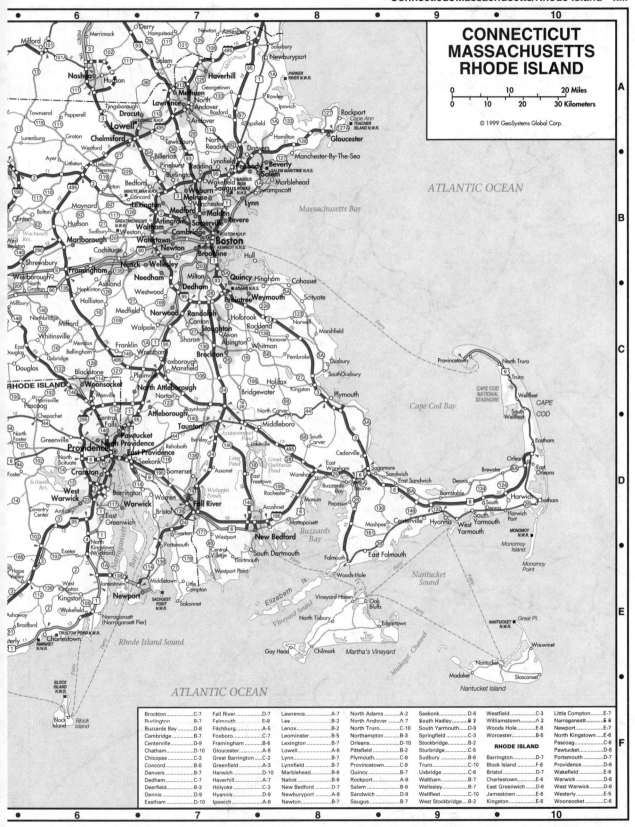

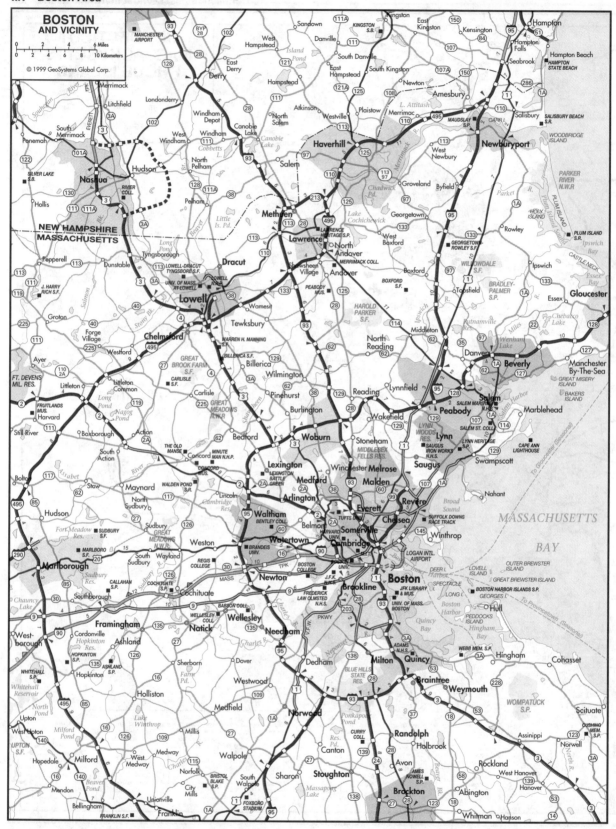

BOSTON
AND VICINITY

© 1999 GeoSystems Global Corp.

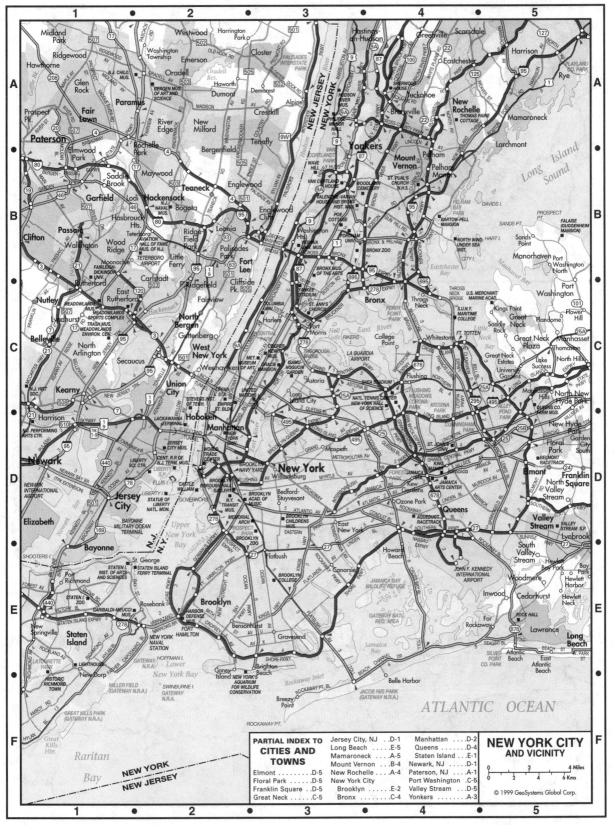

NEW YORK CITY AND VICINITY

© 1999 GeoSystems Global Corp.

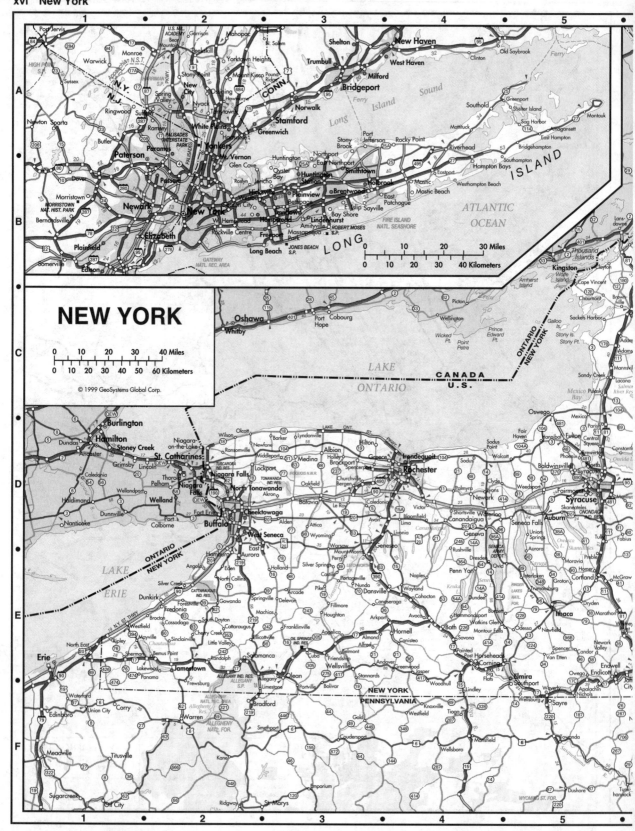

NEW YORK

© 1999 GeoSystems Global Corp.

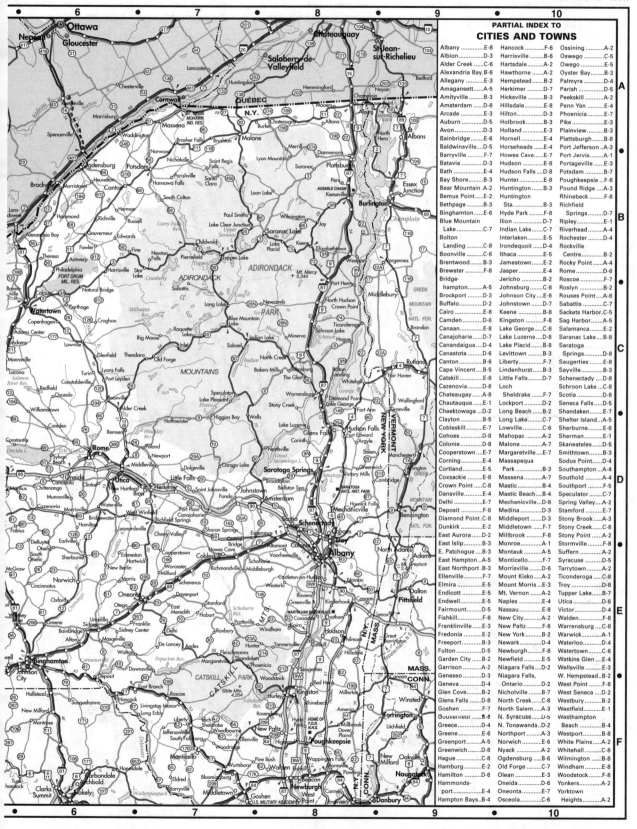

PARTIAL INDEX TO CITIES AND TOWNS

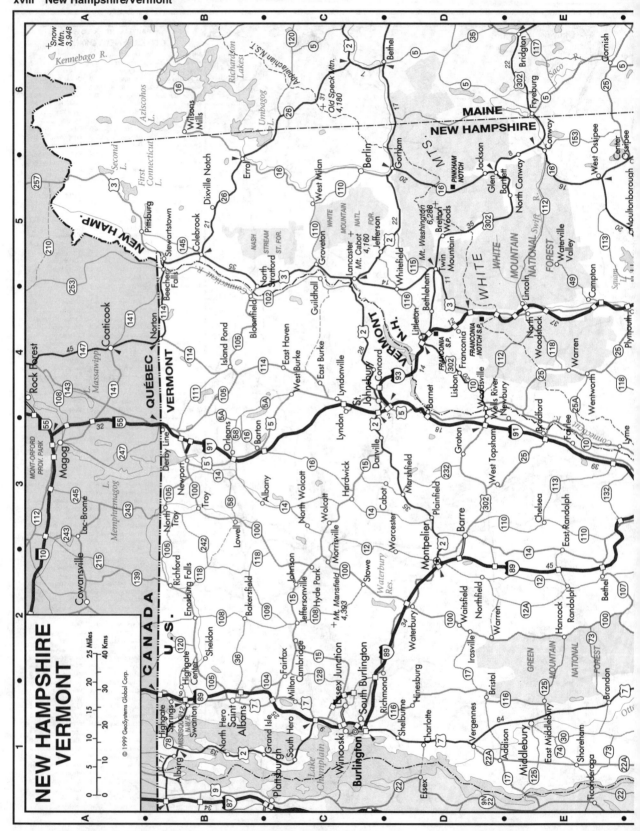

NEW HAMPSHIRE
VERMONT

25 Miles
40 Kms

© 1999 GeoSystems Global Corp.

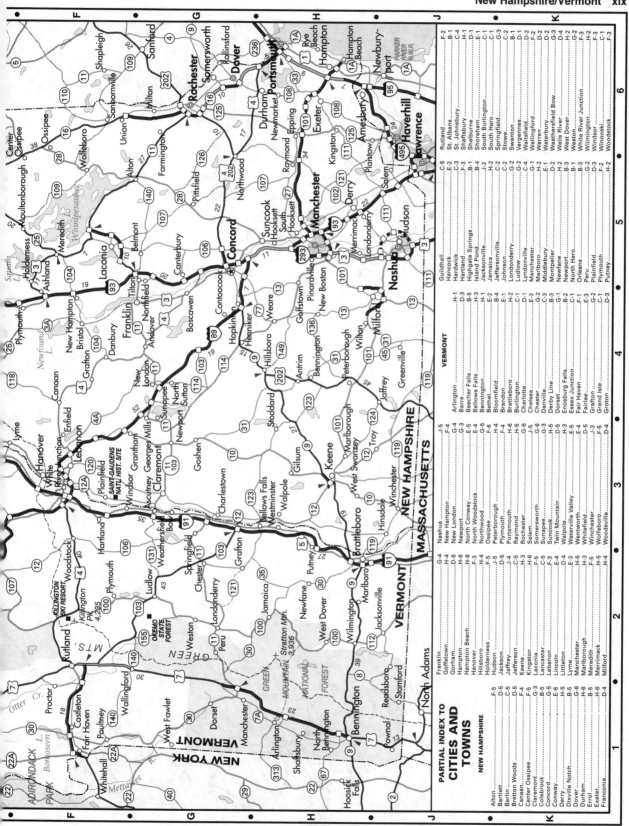

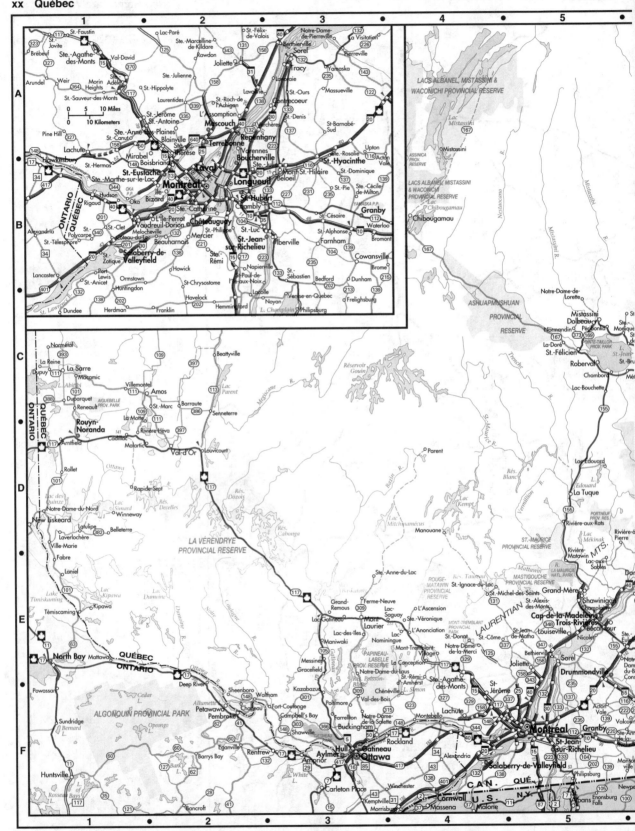

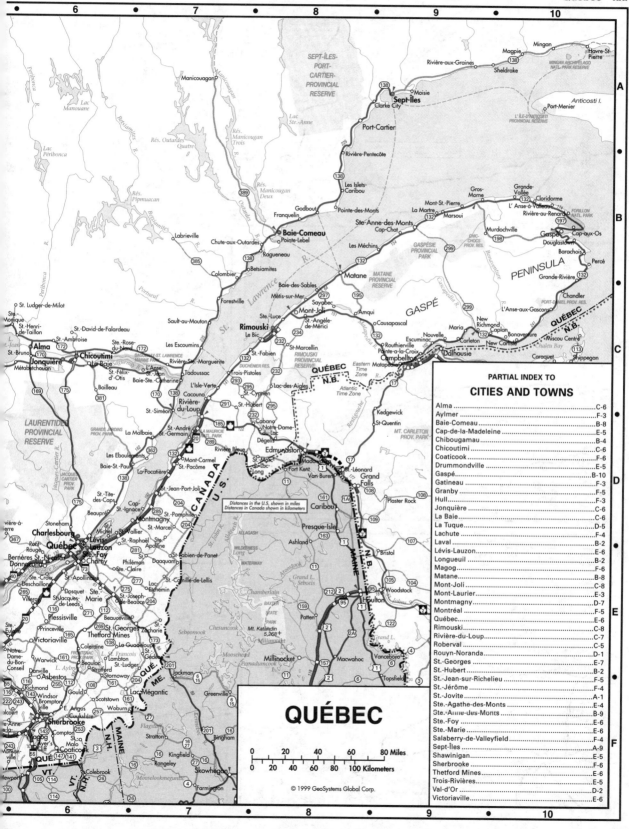

QUÉBEC

Distances in the U.S. shown in miles
Distances in Canada shown in kilometers

| 0 | 20 | 40 | 60 | 80 Miles |

| 0 | 20 | 40 | 60 | 80 | 100 Kilometers |

© 1999 GeoSystems Global Corp.

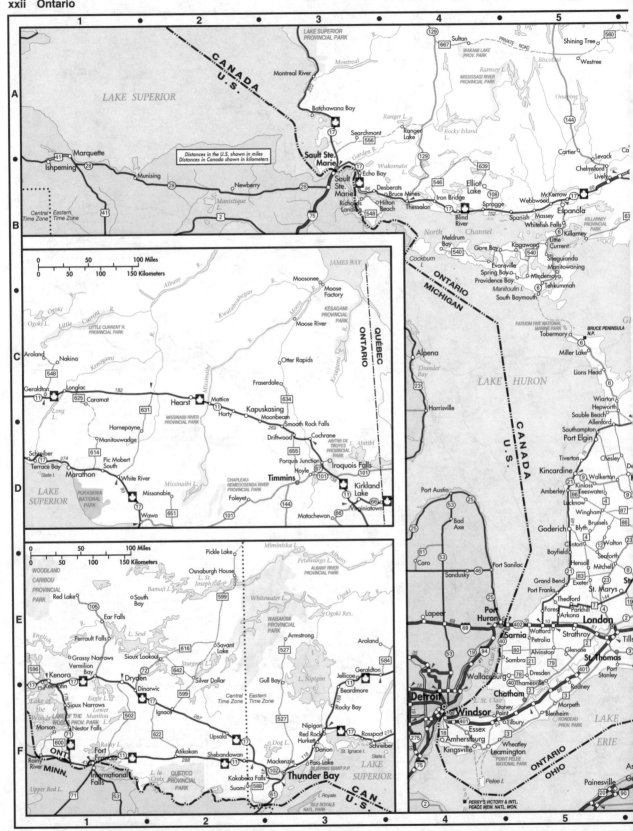

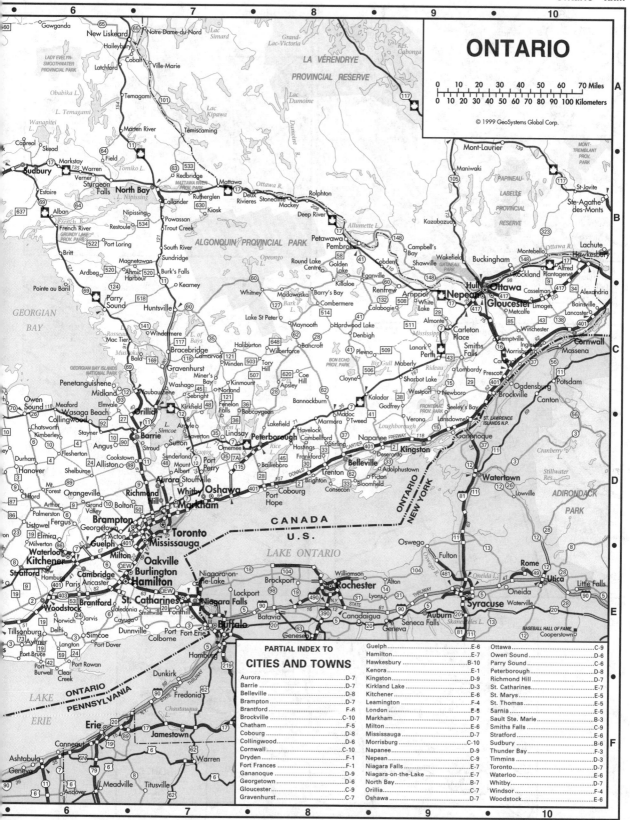

ONTARIO

0 10 20 30 40 50 60 70 Miles
0 10 20 30 40 50 60 70 80 90 100 Kilometers

© 1999 GeoSystems Global Corp.

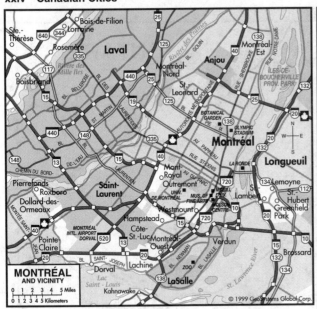

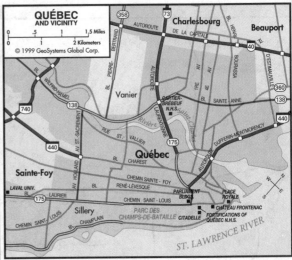

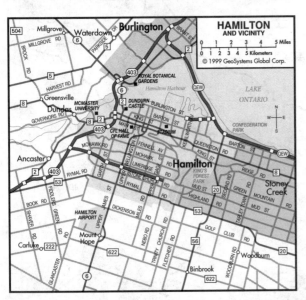

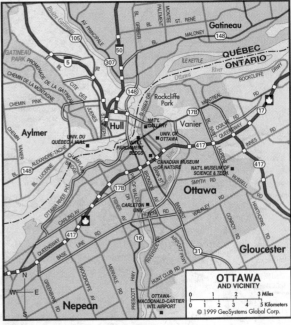

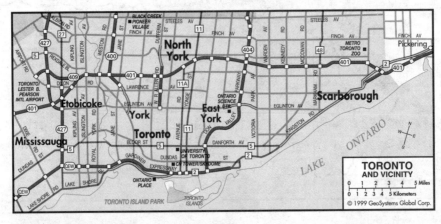

Travel first class.

Before a long trip,
it's always smart to stop at Mobil.

On its ten-year, billion-mile mission, the International Space Station won't make pit stops, and its air system can't ever break down. So the grease for its fans and motors isn't a detail. It had to pass nearly as many tests as astronauts do, and in the end a Mobil synthetic won the job. What excites us is that we didn't create this grease for outer space. You can buy the same stuff (Mobilith SHC® 220) for your bicycle, bus or paper mill. Which, to us, shows the value of how we do research, trying to make things better than necessary. Nobody asked us to develop synthetic lubes, but we pursued it because that's how real innovation works. You aim to exceed present-day expectations so that when the future arrives, you're already there. To learn more, visit www.mobil.com.

Mobil® The energy
to make a difference.™

A Word to Our Readers

Whether you're going on an extended family vacation, a weekend getaway, or a business trip, you need good, solid information on where to stay and eat and what to see and do. It would be nice if you could take a corps of well-seasoned travelers with you to suggest lodgings and activities, or ask a local restaurant critic for advice on dining spots, but since these options are rarely practical, the *Mobil Travel Guide* is the next best thing. It puts a huge database of information at your disposal and provides the value judgments and advice you need to use that information to its fullest.

Published by Fodor's Travel Publications, Inc., in collaboration with Mobil Corporation, the sponsor since 1958, these books contain the most comprehensive, up-to-date information possible on each region. In fact, listings are revised and ratings reviewed annually, based on inspection reports from our field representatives, evaluation by senior staff, and comments from more than 100,000 readers. These incredible data are then used to develop the *Mobil Travel Guide*'s impartial quality ratings, indicated by stars, which Americans have trusted for decades.

Space limitations make it impossible for us to include every fine hotel and restaurant, so we have picked a representative group, all above-average for their type. There's no charge to any establishment for inclusion, and only places that meet our standards are chosen. Because travelers' needs differ, we make every effort to select a variety of establishments and provide the information to decide what's right for you. If you're looking for a lodging at a certain price or location, or even one that offers 24-hour room service, you'll find the answers you need at your fingertips. Take a minute to read the next section, How to Use This Book; it'll make finding the information you want a breeze.

Also look at Making the Most of Your Trip, the section that follows. It's full of tips from savvy travelers that can help you save money, stay safe, and get around more easily—the keys to making any trip a success.

Of course, the passage of time means that some establishments will close, change hands, remodel, improve, or go downhill. Though every effort has been made to ensure the accuracy of all information when it was printed, change is inevitable. Always call and confirm that a place is open and that it has the features you want. Whatever your experiences at any of the establishments we list—and we hope they're terrific—or if you have general comments about our guide, we'd love to hear from you. Use the convenient card near the end of this book, or drop us a line at the *Mobil Travel Guide,* 3225 Gallows Rd., Suite 7D 0407, Fairfax, VA 22037 or www.mobil.com/travel.

So pack this book in your suitcase or toss it next to you on the front seat. If it gets dog-eared, so much the better. We here at the *Mobil Travel Guide* wish you a safe and successful trip.

Bon voyage and happy driving,

THE EDITORS

Welcome

For over 40 years, the *Mobil Travel Guide* has provided travelers in North America with reliable advice on finding good value, quality service, and the attractions that give a destination its special character. During this time, our teams of culinary and hospitality experts have worked hard to develop objective and exacting standards. In so doing, they seek to fully meet the desires and expectations of a broad range of customers.

At Mobil, we demonstrate the energy to make a difference through a commitment to excellence that allows us to bring the best service and products to the people we serve. We believe that the ability to respond to and anticipate customers' needs is what distinguishes good companies from truly great ones.

It is our hope, whether your travels are for business or leisure, over a long distance or a short one, that this book will be your companion, dependably guiding you to quality and value in lodging and dining.

Finally, I ask that you help us improve the guides. Please take the time to fill out the customer feedback form at the back of this book or contact us on the Internet at www.mobil.com/travel.

Lucio A. Noto

Lucio A. Noto
Chairman and
Chief Executive Officer
Mobil Corporation

How to Use This Book

The *Mobil Travel Guide* is easy to use. Each state chapter begins with a general introduction that both provides a general geographical and historical orientation to the state and covers basic statewide tourist information, from state recreation areas to seat-belt laws. The balance of each chapter is devoted to the travel destinations within the state—cities and towns, state and national parks, and tourist regions—which, like the states themselves, are arranged alphabetically.

What follows is an explanation of the wealth of information you'll find within those travel destinations—information on the area, on things to see and do there, and on where to stay and eat.

Maps and Map Coordinates

The first thing you'll notice is that next to each destination is a set of map coordinates. These refer to the appropriate state map in the front of this book. In addition, there are maps of selected larger cities in the front section as well as maps of key neighborhoods within the sections on the cities themselves.

Destination Information

Because many travel destinations are so close to other cities and towns where visitors might find additional attractions, accommodations, and restaurants, cross-references to those places are included whenever possible. Also listed are addresses and phone numbers for travel-information resources—usually the local chamber of commerce or office of tourism—as well as pertinent vital statistics and a brief introduction to the area.

What to See and Do

More than 11,000 museums, art galleries, amusement parks, universities, historic sites and houses, plantations, churches, state parks, ski areas, and other attractions are described in the *Mobil Travel Guide*. A white star on a black background ★ signals that the attraction is one of the best in the state. Since municipal parks, public tennis courts, swimming pools, and small educational institutions are common to most towns, they are generally excluded.

Following the attraction's description are the months and days it's open, address/location and phone number, and admission costs (see the inside front cover for an explanation of the cost symbols). Note that directions are given from the center of the town under which the attraction is listed, which may not necessarily be the town in which the attraction is located. Zip codes are listed only if they differ from those given for the town.

Events

Events—categorized as annual, seasonal, or special—are highlighted. An annual event is one that's held every year for a period of usually no longer than a week to 10 days; festivals and fairs are typical entries. A seasonal event is one that may or may not be annual and that is held for a number of weeks or months in the year, such as horse racing, summer theater, concert or opera festivals, and professional sports. Special event listings occur infrequently and mark a certain date or event, such as a centennial or other commemorative celebration.

Major Cities

Additional information on airports and transportation, suburbs, and neighborhoods, including a list of restaurants by neighborhood, may be included for large cities.

Lodging and Restaurant Listings

ORGANIZATION

For both lodgings and restaurants, when a property is in a town that does not have its own heading, the listing appears under the town nearest its location with the address and town in parentheses immediately after the establishment name. In large cities, lodgings located within 5 miles of major, commercial airports are listed under a separate "Airport" heading, following the city listings.

LODGING CLASSIFICATIONS

Each property is classified by type according to the characteristics below. Because the following features and services are found at most motels, lodges, motor hotels, and hotels, they are not shown in those listings:

- Year-round operation with a single rate structure unless otherwise quoted
- European plan (meals not included in room rate)
- Bathroom with tub and/or shower in each room
- Air-conditioned/heated, often with individual room control
- Cots
- Daily maid service
- Phones in rooms
- Elevators

Motels and Lodges. Accommodations are in low-rise structures with rooms easily accessible to parking (usually free). Properties have outdoor room entry and small, functional lobbies. Service is often limited, and dining may not be offered in lower-rated motels and lodges. Shops and businesses are found only in higher-rated properties, as are bellhops, room service, and restaurants serving three meals daily.

Lodges differ from motels primarily in their emphasis on outdoor recreational activities and in location. They are often found in resort and rural areas rather than in major cities or along highways.

Motor Hotels. Offering the convenience of motels along with many of the features of hotels, motor hotels range from low-rise structures offering limited services to multistory buildings with a wide range of services and facilities. Multiple building entrances, elevators, inside hallways, and parking areas (generally free) near access doors are some of the features of a motor hotel. Lobbies offer sitting areas and 24-hour desk and switchboard services. Often bellhop and valet services as well as restaurants serving three meals a day are found. Expanded recreational facilities and more than one restaurant are available in higher-rated properties.

The distinction between motor hotels and hotels in metropolitan areas is minor.

Hotels. To be categorized as a hotel, an establishment must have most of the following facilities and services: multiple floors, a restaurant and/or coffee shop, elevators, room service, bellhops, a spacious lobby, and recreational facilities. In addition, the following features and services not shown in listings are also found:

- Valet service (one-day laundry/cleaning service)
- Room service during hours restaurant is open
- Bellhops
- Some oversize beds

Resorts. These specialize in stays of three days or more and usually offer American Plan and/or housekeeping accommodations. Their emphasis is on recreational facilities, and a social

director is often available. Food services are of primary importance, and guests must be able to eat three meals a day on the premises, either in restaurants or by having access to an on-site grocery store and preparing their own meals.

Inns. Frequently thought of as a small hotel, an inn is a place of homelike comfort and warm hospitality. It is often a structure of historic significance, with an equally interesting setting. Meals are a special occasion, and refreshments are frequently served in late afternoon. Rooms are usually individually decorated, often with antiques or furnishings representative of the locale. Phones, bathrooms, and TVs may not be available in every room.

Guest Ranches. Like resorts, guest ranches specialize in stays of three days or more. Guest ranches also offer meal plans and extensive outdoor activities. Horseback riding is usually a feature; there are stables and trails on the ranch property, and trail rides and daily instruction are part of the program. Many guest ranches are working ranches, ranging from casual to rustic, and guests are encouraged to participate in ranch life. Eating is often family-style and may also include cookouts. Western saddles are assumed; phone ahead to inquire about English saddle availability.

Cottage Colonies. These are housekeeping cottages and cabins that are usually found in recreational areas. Any dining or recreational facilities are noted in our listing.

DINING CLASSIFICATIONS

Restaurants. Most dining establishments fall into this category. All have a full kitchen and offer table service and a complete menu. Parking on or near the premises, in a lot or garage, is assumed. When a property offers valet or other special parking features, or when only street parking is available, it is noted in the listing.

Unrated Dining Spots. These places, listed after Restaurants in many cities, are chosen for their unique atmosphere, specialized menu, or local flavor. They include delis, ice-cream parlors, cafeterias, tearooms, and pizzerias. Because they may not have a full kitchen or table service, they are not given a *Mobil Travel Guide* rating. Often they offer extraordinary value and quick service.

QUALITY RATINGS

The *Mobil Travel Guide* has been rating lodgings and restaurants on a national basis since the first edition was published in 1958. For years the guide was the only source of such ratings, and it remains among the few guidebooks to rate restaurants across the country.

All listed establishments were inspected by experienced field representatives or evaluated by a senior staff member. Ratings are based upon their detailed inspection reports of the individual properties, on written evaluations of staff members who stay and dine anonymously, and on an extensive review of comments from our readers.

You'll find a key to the rating categories, ★ through ★★★★★, on the inside front cover. All establishments in the book are recommended. Even a ★ place is above average, usually providing a basic, informal experience. Rating categories reflect both the features the property offers and its quality in relation to similar establishments.

For example, lodging ratings take into account the number and quality of facilities and services, the luxury of appointments, and the attitude and professionalism of staff and management. A ★ establishment provides a comfortable night's lodging. A ★★ property offers more than a facility that rates one star, and the decor is well planned and integrated. Establishments that rate ★★★ are professionally managed and staffed and often beautifully appointed; the lodging experience is truly excellent and the range of facilities is extensive. Properties that have been given ★★★★ not only offer many services but also have their own style and personality; they are luxurious, creatively decorated, and superbly maintained. The ★★★★★ properties are among the best in North America, superb in every respect and entirely memorable, year in and year out.

Restaurant evaluations reflect the quality of the food and the ingredients, preparation, and presentation as well as service levels and the property's decor and ambience. A restaurant that has fairly simple goals for menu and decor but that achieves those goals superbly might receive the same number of stars as a restaurant with somewhat loftier ambitions but whose execution falls somewhat short of the mark. In general, ★ indicates a restaurant that's a good choice in its area, usually fairly simple and perhaps catering to a clientele of locals and families; ★★ denotes restaurants that are more highly recommended in their area; ★★★ restaurants are of national caliber, with professional and attentive service and a skilled chef in the kitchen; ★★★★ reflects superb dining choices, where remarkable food is served in equally remarkable surroundings; and ★★★★★ represents that rarefied group of the best restaurants in the country, where in addition to near perfection in every detail, there's that special something extra that makes for an unforgettable dining experience.

A list of the four-star and five-star establishments in this region is located just before the state listings.

Each rating is reviewed annually and each establishment must work to maintain its rating (or improve it). Every effort is made to assure that ratings are fair and accurate; the designated ratings are published purely as an aid to travelers.

In general, properties that are very new or have recently undergone major management changes are considered difficult to assess fairly and are often listed without ratings.

Good Value Check Mark. In all locales, you'll find a wide range of lodging and dining establishments with a ✔ in front of a star rating. This indicates an unusually good value at economical prices as follows:

In Major Cities and Resort Areas

Lodging: average $105–$125 per night for singles; average $115–$140 per night for doubles

Restaurants: average $25 for a complete lunch; average $40 for a complete dinner, exclusive of beverages and gratuities

Local Area Listings

Lodging: average $50–$60 per night for singles; average $60–$75 per night for doubles

Restaurants: average $12 for a complete lunch; average $20 for a complete dinner, exclusive of beverages and gratuities

LODGINGS

Each listing gives the name, address, directions (when there is no street address), neighborhood and/or directions from downtown (in major cities), phone number (local and 800), fax number, number and type of rooms available, room rates, and seasons open (if not year-round). Also included are details on recreational and dining facilities on property or nearby, the presence of a luxury level, and credit-card information. A key to the symbols at the end of each listing is on the inside front cover. (Note that Mobil Corporation credit cards cannot be used for payment of meals and room charges.)

All prices quoted in the *Mobil Travel Guide* publications are expected to be in effect at the time of publication and during the entire year; however, prices cannot be guaranteed. In some localities there may be short-term price variations because of special events or holidays. Whenever possible, these price changes are noted. Certain resorts have complicated rate structures that vary with the time of year; always confirm listed rates when you make your plans.

RESTAURANTS

Each listing gives the name, address, directions (when there is no street address), neighborhood and/or directions from downtown (in major cities), phone number, hours and days of operation (if not open daily year-round), reservation policy, cuisine (if other than American), price range for each meal served, children's meals (if offered), specialties, and credit card information. Additionally, special features such as chef ownership, ambience, and entertainment are noted. By carefully reading the detailed restaurant information and comparing prices, you can easily determine whether the restaurant is formal and elegant or informal and comfortable for families.

TERMS AND ABBREVIATIONS IN LISTINGS

A la carte entrees With a price, refers to the cost of entrees/main dishes only that are not accompanied by side dishes.

AP American plan (lodging plus all meals).

Bar Liquor, wine, and beer are served in a bar or cocktail lounge and usually with meals unless otherwise indicated (e.g., "wine, beer").

Business center The property has a designated area accessible to all guests with business services.

Business servs avail

The property can perform/arrange at least two of the following services for a guest: audiovisual equipment rental, binding, computer rental, faxing, messenger services, modem availability, notary service, obtaining office supplies, photocopying, shipping, and typing.

Cable Standard cable service; "premium" indicates that HBO, Disney, Showtime, or similar services are available.

Ck-in, ck-out Check-in time, check-out time.

Coin lndry Self-service laundry.

Complete meal Soup and/or salad, entree, and dessert, plus nonalcoholic beverage.

Continental bkfst Usually coffee and a roll or doughnut.

Cr cds: A, American Express; C, Carte Blanche; D, Diners Club; DS, Discover; ER, enRoute; JCB, Japanese Credit Bureau; MC, MasterCard; V, Visa.

D Followed by a price, indicates room rate for a "double"—two people in one room in one or two beds (the charge may be higher for two double beds).

Downhill/x-country ski Downhill and/or cross-country skiing within 20 miles of property.

Each addl Extra charge for each additional person beyond the stated number of persons at a reduced price.

Early-bird dinner A meal served at specified hours, typically around 4:30–6:30 pm.

Exc Except.

Exercise equipt Two or more pieces of exercise equipment on the premises.

Exercise rm Both exercise equipment and room, with an instructor on the premises.

Fax Facsimile machines available to all guests.

Golf privileges Privileges at a course within 10 miles

Hols Holidays

In-rm modem link Every guest room has a connection for a modem that's separate from the phone line.

Kit. or kits. A kitchen or kitchenette that contains stove or microwave, sink, and refrigerator and that is either part of the room or a separate room. If the kitchen is not fully equipped, the listing will indicate "no equipt" or "some equipt".

Luxury level A special section of a lodging, covering at least an entire floor, that offers increased luxury accommodations. Management must provide no less than three of these four services: separate check-in and check-out, concierge, private lounge, and private elevator service (key access). Complimentary breakfast and snacks are commonly offered.

MAP Modified American plan (lodging plus two meals).

Movies Prerecorded videos are available for rental.

No cr cds accepted No credit cards are accepted.

No elvtr In hotels with more than two stories, it's assumed there are elevators; only their absence is noted.

No phones Phones, too, are assumed; only their absence is noted.

Parking There is a parking lot on the premises.

Private club A cocktail lounge or bar available to members and their guests. In motels and hotels where these clubs exist, registered guests can usually use the club as guests of the management; the same is frequently true of restaurants.

Prix fixe A full meal for a stated price; usually one price is quoted.

Res Reservations.

S Followed by a price, indicates room rate for a "single," i.e., one person.

Semi-a la carte Meals include vegetable, salad, soup, appetizer, or other accompaniments to the main dish.

Serv bar A service bar, where drinks are prepared for dining patrons only.

Serv charge Service charge is the amount added to the restaurant check in lieu of a tip.

Table d'hôte A full meal for a stated price, dependent upon entree selection; no a la carte options are available.

Tennis privileges Privileges at tennis courts within 5 miles.

TV Indicates color television.

Under certain age free Children under that age are not charged for if staying in room with a parent.

Valet parking An attendant is available to park and retrieve a car.

VCR VCRs in all guest rooms.

VCR avail VCRs are available for hookup in guest rooms.

Special Information for Travelers with Disabilities

The *Mobil Travel Guide* symbol D shown in accommodation and restaurant listings indicates establishments that are at least partially accessible to people with mobility problems.

The *Mobil Travel Guide* criteria for accessibility are unique to our publication. Please do not confuse them with the universal symbol for wheelchair accessibility. When the D symbol appears following a listing, the establishment is equipped with facilities to accommodate people using wheelchairs or crutches or otherwise needing easy access to doorways and rest rooms. Travelers with severe mobility problems or with hearing or visual impairments may or may not find facilities they need. Always phone ahead to make sure that an establishment can meet your needs.

All lodgings bearing our D symbol have the following facilities:

- ISA-designated parking near access ramps
- Level or ramped entryways to building
- Swinging building entryway doors minimum 3'0"
- Public rest rooms on main level with space to operate a wheelchair; handrails at commode areas
- Elevators equipped with grab bars and lowered control buttons
- Restaurants with accessible doorways; rest rooms with space to operate wheelchair; handrails at commode areas
- Minimum 3'0" width entryway to guest rooms

- Low-pile carpet in rooms
- Telephone at bedside and in bathroom
- Bed placed at wheelchair height
- Minimum 3′0″ width doorway to bathroom
- Bath with open sink—no cabinet; room to operate wheelchair
- Handrails at commode areas; tub handrails
- Wheelchair accessible peephole in room entry door
- Wheelchair accessible closet rods and shelves

All restaurants bearing our D symbol offer the following facilities:

- ISA-designated parking beside access ramps
- Level or ramped front entryways to building
- Tables to accommodate wheelchairs
- Main-floor rest rooms; minimum 3′0″ width entryway

- Rest rooms with space to operate wheelchair; handrails at commode areas

In general, the newest properties are apt to impose the fewest barriers.

To get the kind of service you need and have a right to expect, do not hesitate when making a reservation to question the management in detail about the availability of accessible rooms, parking, entrances, restaurants, lounges, or any other facilities that are important to you, and confirm what is meant by "accessible." Some guests with mobility impairments report that lodging establishments' housekeeping and maintenance departments are most helpful in describing barriers. Also inquire about any special equipment, transportation, or services you may need.

Making the Most of Your Trip

A few diehard souls might fondly remember the trip where the car broke down and they were stranded for a week, or the vacation that cost twice what it was supposed to. For most travelers, though, the best trips are those that are safe, smooth, and within their budget. To help you make your trip the best it can be, we've assembled a few tips and resources.

Saving Money

ON LODGING

After you've seen the published rates, it's time to look for discounts. Many hotels and motels offer them—for senior citizens, business travelers, families, you name it. It never hurts to ask—politely, that is. Sometimes, especially in late afternoon, desk clerks are instructed to fill beds, and you might be offered a lower rate, or a nicer room, to entice you to stay. Look for bargains on stays over multiple nights, in the off-season, and on weekdays or weekends (depending on location). Many hotels in major metropolitan areas, for example, have special weekend package plans, which offer considerable savings on rooms and may include breakfast, cocktails, and meal discounts. Prices change frequently throughout the year, so phone ahead.

Another way to save money is to choose accommodations that give you more than just a standard room. Rooms with kitchen facilities enable you to cook some meals for yourself, reducing restaurant costs. A suite might save money for two couples traveling together. Even hotel luxury levels can provide good value, as many include breakfast or cocktails in the price of the room.

State and city sales taxes as well as special room taxes can increase your room rates as much as 25% per day. We are unable to bring this specific information into the listings, but we strongly urge that you ask about these taxes when placing reservations in order to understand the total price to you.

Watch out for telephone-usage charges that hotels frequently impose on long-distance calls, credit-card calls, and other phone calls—even those that go unanswered. Before phoning from your room, read the information given to you at check-in, and then be sure to read your bill carefully before checking out. You won't be expected to pay for charges that weren't spelled out. (On the other hand, it's not unusual for a hotel to bill you for your calls after you return home.) Consider using public telephones in hotel lobbies; the savings may outweigh the inconvenience.

ON DINING

There are several ways to get a less-expensive meal at a more-expensive restaurant. Early-bird dinners are popular in many parts of the country and offer considerable savings. If you're interested in sampling a ★★★★ or ★★★★★ establishment, consider going at lunchtime. While the prices then are probably relatively high, they may be half of those at dinner and come with the same ambience, service, and cuisine.

PARK PASSES

While many national parks, monuments, seashores, historic sites, and recreation areas may be used free of charge, others charge an entrance fee (ranging from $1 to $5 per person to $5 to $15 per carload) and/or a "use fee" for special services and facilities. If you plan to make several visits to federal recreation areas, consider one of the following National Park Service money-saving programs:

Park Pass. This is an annual entrance permit to a specific unit in the National Park Service system that normally charges an entrance fee. The pass admits the permit holder and any accompanying passengers in a private noncommercial vehicle or, in the case of walk-in facilities, the holder's spouse, children, and parents. It is valid for entrance fees only. A Park Pass may be purchased in person or by mail from the National Park Service unit at which the pass will be honored. The cost is $15 to $20, depending upon the area.

Golden Eagle Passport. This pass, available to people who are between 17 and 61, entitles the purchaser and accompanying passengers in a private noncommercial vehicle to enter any outdoor NPS unit that charges an entrance fee and admits the purchaser and family to most walk-in fee-charging areas. Like the Park Pass, it is good for one year and does not cover use fees. It may be purchased from the National Park Service, Office of Public Inquiries, Room 1013, US Department of the Interior, 18th and C Sts NW, Washington, DC 20240, phone 202/208–4747; at any of the 10 regional offices throughout the country; and at any NPS area that charges a fee. The cost is $50.

Golden Age Passport. Available to citizens and permanent residents of the United States 62 years or older, this is a lifetime entrance permit to fee-charging recreation areas. The fee exemption extends to those accompanying the permit holder in a private noncommercial vehicle or, in the case of walk-in facilities, to the holder's spouse and children. The passport also entitles the holder to a 50% discount on use fees charged in park areas but not to fees charged by concessionaires. Golden Age Passports must be obtained in person. The applicant must show proof of age, i.e., a driver's license, birth certificate, or signed affidavit attesting to age (Medicare cards are not acceptable proof). Passports are available at most park service units where they're used, at National Park Service headquarters (see above), at park system regional offices, at National Forest Supervisors' offices, and at most Ranger Station offices. The cost is $10.

Golden Access Passport. Issued to citizens and permanent residents of the United States who are physically disabled or visually impaired, this passport is a free lifetime entrance permit to fee-charging recreation areas. The fee exemption extends to those accompanying the permit holder in a private noncommercial vehicle or, in the case of walk-in facilities, to the holder's spouse and children. The passport also entitles the holder to a 50% discount on use fees charged in park areas but not to fees charged by concessionaires. Golden Access Passports must be obtained in person. Proof of eligibility to receive federal benefits is required (under programs such as Disability Retirement, Compensation for Military Service-Connected Disability, Coal Mine Safety and Health Act, etc.), or an affidavit must be signed attesting to eligibility. These passports are available at the same outlets as Golden Age Passports.

FOR SENIOR CITIZENS

Look for the senior-citizen discount symbol in the lodging and restaurant listings. Always call ahead to confirm that the discount is being offered, and be sure to carry proof of age. At places not listed in the book, it never hurts to ask if a senior-citizen discount is offered. Additional information for mature travelers is available from: the American Association of Retired Persons (AARP), 601 E St NW, Washington, DC 20049, phone 202/434–2277.

Tipping

Tipping is an expression of appreciation for good service, and often service workers rely on tips as a significant part of their income. However, you never need to tip if service is poor.

IN HOTELS

Doormen in major city hotels are usually given $1 for getting you a cab. Bellhops expect $1 per bag, usually $2 if you have only one bag. Concierges are tipped according to the service they perform. It's not mandatory to tip when you've asked for suggestions on sightseeing or restaurants or help in making reservations for dining. However, when a concierge books you a table at a restaurant known to be difficult to get into, a gratuity of $5 is appropriate. For obtaining theater or sporting event tickets, $5–$10 is expected. Maids, often overlooked by guests, may be tipped $1–$2 per day of stay.

AT RESTAURANTS

Coffee shop and counter service wait staff are usually given 8%–10% of the bill. In full-service restaurants, tip 15% of the bill, before sales tax. In fine restaurants, where the staff is large and shares the gratuity, 18%–20% for the waiter is appropriate. In most cases, tip the maitre d' only if service has been extraordinary and only on the way out; $20 is the minimum in upscale properties in major metropolitan areas. If there is a wine steward, tip him or her at least $5 a bottle, more if the wine was decanted or if the bottle was very expensive. If your busboy has been unusually attentive, $2 pressed into his hand on departure is a nice gesture. An increasing number of restaurants automatically add a service charge to the bill in lieu of a gratuity. Before tipping, carefully review your check.

AT AIRPORTS

Curbside luggage handlers expect $1 per bag. Car-rental shuttle drivers who help with your luggage appreciate a $1 or $2 tip.

Staying Safe

The best way to deal with emergencies is to be prepared enough to avoid them. However, unforeseen situations do happen, and you can prepare for them.

IN YOUR CAR

Before your trip, make sure your car has been serviced and is in good working order. Change the oil, check the battery and belts, and make sure tires are inflated properly (this can also improve gas mileage). Other inspections recommended by the car's manufacturer should be made, too.

Next, be sure you have the tools and equipment to deal with a routine breakdown: jack, spare tire, lug wrench, repair kit, emergency tools, jumper cables, spare fan belt, auto fuses, flares and/or reflectors, flashlights, first-aid kit, and, in winter, a windshield scraper and shovel.

Bring all appropriate and up-to-date documentation—licenses, registration, and insurance cards—and know what's covered by your insurance. Also bring an extra set of keys, just in case.

En route, always buckle up!

If your car does break down, get out of traffic as soon as possible—pull well off the road. Raise the hood and turn on your emergency flashers or tie a white cloth to the roadside door handle or antenna. Stay near your car. Use flares or reflectors to keep your car from being hit.

IN YOUR LODGING

Chances are slim that you will encounter a hotel or motel fire. The ▲ in a listing indicates that there were smoke detectors and/or sprinkler systems in the rooms we inspected. Once you've checked in, make sure that any smoke detector in your room is working properly. Ascertain the locations of fire extinguishers and at least two fire exits. Never use an elevator in a fire.

For personal security, use the peephole in your room's door.

PROTECTING AGAINST THEFT

To guard against theft wherever you go, don't bring any more of value than you need. If you do bring valuables, leave them at your hotel rather than in your car, and if you have something very expensive, lock it in a safe. Many hotels have one in each room; others will store your valuables in the hotel's safe. And of course, don't carry more money than you need; use traveler's checks and credit cards, or visit cash machines.

For Travelers with Disabilities

A number of publications can provide assistance. Fodor's *Great American Vacations for Travelers with Disabilities* ($19.50) covers 38 top U.S. travel destinations, including parks, cities, and popular tourist regions. It's available from bookstores or by calling 800/533–6478. The most complete listing of published material for travelers with disabilities is available from *The Disability Bookshop*, Twin Peaks Press, Box 129, Vancouver, WA 98666, phone 360/694–2462. A comprehensive guidebook to the national parks is *Easy Access to National Parks: The Sierra Club Guide for People with Disabilities* ($16), distributed by Random House.

The Reference Section of the National Library Service for the Blind and Physically Handicapped (Library of Congress, Washington, DC 20542, phone 202/707–9275 or 202/707–5100) provides information and resources for persons with mobility problems and hearing and vision impairments, as well as information about the NLS talking-book program (or visit your local library).

Traveling to Canada

Citizens of the United States do not need visas to enter Canada, but proof of citizenship—passport, birth certificate, or voter registration card—is required. A driver's license is not acceptable. Naturalized citizens will need their naturalization certificates or their U.S. passport to reenter the United States. Children under 18 who are traveling on their own should carry a letter from a parent or guardian giving them permission to travel in Canada.

Travelers entering Canada in automobiles licensed in the United States may tour the provinces for up to three months without fee. Drivers are advised to carry their motor vehicle registration card and, if the car is not registered in the driver's name, a letter from the registered owner authorizing use of the vehicle. If the car is rented, carry a copy of the rental contract stipulating use in Canada. For your protection, ask your car insurer for a Canadian Non-resident Interprovince Motor Vehicle Liability Insurance Card. This card ensures that your insurance company will meet minimum insurance requirements in Canada.

The use of seat belts by drivers and passengers is compulsory in all provinces. A permit is required for the use of citizens' band radios. Rabies vaccination certificates are required for dogs or cats.

No handguns may be brought into Canada. If you plan to hunt, sporting rifles and shotguns plus 200 rounds of ammunition per person will be admitted duty-free. Hunting and fishing licenses must be obtained from the appropriate province. Each province has its own regulations concerning the transportation of firearms.

The Canadian dollar's rate of exchange with the U.S. dollar varies; contact your local bank for the latest figures. Since customs regulations can change, it's recommended that you contact the Canadian consulate or embassy in your area. Offices are located in Atlanta, Boston, Buffalo, Chicago, Dallas, Detroit, Los Angeles, Minneapolis, New York City, Seattle, and Washington, DC. For the most current and detailed listing of regulations and sources, ask for the annually revised brochure "Canada: Travel Information," which is available upon request.

Important Toll-Free Numbers

and On-Line Information

HOTELS AND MOTELS

Adam's Mark 800/444–2326
Web www.adamsmark.com
Best Western .... 800/528–1234, TDD 800/528–2222
Web www.bestwestern.com
Budgetel Inns 800/428–3438
Web www.budgetel.com
Budget Host 800/283–4678
Clarion 800/252–7466
Web www.clarioninn.com
Comfort 800/228–5150
Web www.comfortinn.com
Courtyard by Marriott 800/321–2211
Web www.courtyard.com
Days Inn 800/325–2525
Web www.travelweb.com/daysinn.html
Doubletree 800/528–0444
Web www.doubletreehotels.com
Drury Inns 800/325–8300
Web www.drury-inn.com
Econo Lodge 800/446–6900
Web www.hotelchoice.com
Embassy Suites 800/362–2779
Web www.embassy-suites.com
Exel Inns of America 800/356–8013
Fairfield Inn by Marriott 800/228–2800
Web www.marriott.com
Fairmont Hotels 800/527–4727
Forte 800/225–5843
Four Seasons 800/332–3442
Web www.fourseasons.com
Friendship Inns 800/453–4511
Web www.hotelchoice.com
Hampton Inn 800/426–7866
Web www.hampton-inn.com
Hilton .... 800/445–8667, TDD 800/368–1133
Web www.hilton.com
Holiday Inn .... 800/465–4329, TDD 800/238–5544
Web www.holiday-inn.com
Howard Johnson .... 800/654–4656, TDD 800/654–8442
Web www.hojo.com
Hyatt & Resorts 800/233–1234
Web www.hyatt.com
Inns of America 800/826–0778
Inter-Continental 800/327–0200
Web www.interconti.com
La Quinta .... 800/531–5900, TDD 800/426–3101
Web www.laquinta.com
Loews 800/235–6397
Web www.loewshotels.com
Marriott 800/228–9290
Web www.marriott.com
Master Hosts Inns 800/251–1962

Meridien 800/225–5843
Motel 6 .... 800/466–8356
Nikko International 800/645–5687
Web www.hotelnikko.com
Omni 800/843–6664
Web www.omnirosen.com
Quality Inn 800/228–5151
Web www.qualityinn.com
Radisson 800/333–3333
Web www.radisson.com
Ramada .... 800/228–2828, TDD 800/228–3232
Web www.ramada.com/ramada.html
Red Carpet/Scottish Inns 800/251–1962
Red Lion 800/547–8010
Web www.travelweb.com/travelweb/rl/common/redlion.html
Red Roof Inn 800/843–7663
Web www.redroof.com
Renaissance 800/468–3571
Web www.niagara.com/nf.renaissance
Residence Inn by Marriott 800/331–3131
Web www.marriott.com
Ritz-Carlton 800/241–3333
Web www.ritzcarlton.com
Rodeway 800/228–2000
Web www.rodeway.com
Sheraton 800/325–3535
Web www.sheraton.com
Shilo Inn 800/222–2244
Signature Inns 800/822–5252
Web www.signature-inns.com
Sleep Inn 800/221–2222
Web www.sleepinn.com
Super 8 .... 800/848–8888
Web www.super8motels.com/super8.html
Susse Chalet 800/258–1980
Web www.sussechalet.com
Travelodge/Viscount 800/255–3050
Web www.travelodge.com
Vagabond 800/522–1555
Westin Hotels & Resorts 800/937-8461
Web www.westin.com
Wyndham Hotels & Resorts 800/996-3426
Web www.travelweb.com

AIRLINES

Air Canada 800/776–3000
Web www.aircanada.ca
Alaska 800/426–0333
Web www.alaska-air.com/home.html
American 800/433–7300
Web www.americanair.com/aahome/aahome.html
America West 800/235–9292
Web www.americawest.com

British Airways 800/247–9297
Web www.british-airways.com
Canadian 800/426–7000
Web www.cdair.ca
Continental 800/525–0280
Web www.flycontinental.com
Delta 800/221–1212
Web www.delta-air.com
IslandAir 800/323–3345
Mesa 800/637–2247
Northwest 800/225–2525
Web www.nwa.com
SkyWest 800/453–9417
Southwest 800/435–9792
Web www.iflyswa.com
TWA 800/221–2000
Web www.twa.com
United 800/241–6522
Web www.ual.com
USAir..800/428–4322
Web www.usair.com

TRAINS

Amtrak 800/872–7245
Web www.amtrak.com

BUSES

Greyhound 800/231–2222
Web www.greyhound.com

CAR RENTALS

Advantage...800/777–5500
Alamo 800/327–9633
Web www.goalamo.com
Allstate 800/634–6186
Avis 800/331–1212
Web www.avis.com
Budget 800/527–0700
Web www.budgetrentacar.com
Dollar..800/800–4000
Web www.dollarcar.com
Enterprise 800/325–8007
Web www.pickenterprise.com
Hertz 800/654–3131
Web www.hertz.com
National 800/328–4567
Web www.nationalcar.com
Payless 800/237–2804
Rent-A-Wreck 800/535–1391
Web www.rent-a-wreck.com
Sears 800/527–0770
Thrifty 800/367–2277
Web www.thrifty.com

Four-Star and Five-Star Establishments
in the Northeast

CONNECTICUT

★★★★★ Lodging
Mayflower Inn, *Washington*

★★★★ Lodging
Inn at National Hall, *Westport*

★★★★ Restaurant
Jean-Louis, *Greenwich*

MAINE

★★★★ Lodgings
Bar Harbor Hotel-Bluenose Inn, *Bar Harbor*
Captain Lord Mansion, *Kennebunkport*
Inn at Harbor Head, *Kennebunkport*
Lodge at Moosehead Lake, *Greenville*

★★★★ Restaurant
White Barn, *Kennebunkport*

MASSACHUSETTS

★★★★ Lodgings
Blantyre, *Lenox*
Boston Harbor Hotel, *Boston*
The Eliot, *Boston*
Four Seasons, *Boston*
The Ritz-Carlton, *Boston*
The Wauwinet, *Nantucket Island*
Wequassett Inn, *Chatham*

★★★★ Restaurants
Aujourd'hui (Four Seasons), *Boston*
Biba, *Boston*
Blantyre, *Lenox*
Chillingsworth, *Brewster*
Hamersley's Bistro, *Boston*
L'Espalier, *Boston*
Wheatleigh, *Lenox*

NEW HAMPSHIRE

★★★★ Lodging
The Balsams, *Dixville Notch*

NEW YORK

★★★★★ Lodgings
Carlyle, *Manhattan*

Four Seasons, *Manhattan*
The Point, *Saranac Lake*
The St Regis Hotel, *Manhattan*
Trump International Hotel & Tower, *Manhattan*

★★★★★ Restaurants
Chanterelle, *Manhattan*
Jean Georges, *Manhattan*
Le Cirque 2000, *Manhattan*
Les Célébrités, *Manhattan*
Lespinasse, *Manhattan*

★★★★ Lodgings
Essex House Hotel Nikko New York, *Manhattan*
Lake Placid Lodge, *Lake Placid*
Lowell, *Manhattan*
Millenium Hilton, *Manhattan*
The New York Palace, *Manhattan*
Old Chatham Sheepherding Company Inn, *Canaan*
The Pierre, *Manhattan*
The Plaza Hotel, *Manhattan*
Plaza Athénée, *Manhattan*
Regal U.N. Plaza Hotel, *Manhattan*
The Regency Hotel, *Manhattan*
Rose Inn, *Ithaca*
The Stanhope, *Manhattan*
Waldorf-Astoria & Waldorf Towers, *Manhattan*

★★★★ Restaurants
Aquavit, *Manhattan*
Aureole, *Manhattan*
Aubergine, *Hillsdale*
Barbetta, *Manhattan*
David Ruggerio, *Manhattan*
Fifty Seven Fifty Seven, *Manhattan*
The Four Seasons, *Manhattan*
Gotham Bar and Grill, *Manhattan*
Gramercy Tavern, *Manhattan*
Harralds, *Fishkill*
Hudson River Club, *Manhattan*
La Caravelle, *Manhattan*
La Côte Basque, *Manhattan*
La Panetiere, *White Plains*

Le Bernardin, *Manhattan*
Lutéce, *Manhattan*
March, *Manhattan*
Nobu, *Manhattan*
Otabe, *Manhattan*
Parioli Romanissimo, *Manhattan*
Patria, *Manhattan*
Peacock Alley, *Manhattan*
Rainbow Room, *Manhattan*
San Domenico, *Manhattan*
Xavier's, *Garrison*
Windows on the World, *Manhattan*

VERMONT

★★★★★ Lodging
Twin Farms, *Woodstock*

★★★★ Lodgings
Governor's, *Ludlow*
Rabbit Hill, *St Johnsbury*
Topnotch at Stowe, *Stowe*
Woodstock Inn, *Woodstock*

★★★★ Restaurant
Hemingway's, *Killington*

EASTERN CANADA

★★★★★ Restaurants
The Beaver Club, *Montréal*
Nuances, *Montréal*

★★★★ Lodgings
Four Seasons, *Toronto*
Inter-Continental, *Toronto*
King Edward, *Toronto*
Kingsbrae Arms, *St Andrews*
Loews Hôtel Vogue, *Montréal*
The Ritz-Carlton, Montréal, *Montréal*

★★★★ Restaurants
Centro Grill, *Toronto*
La Marée, *Montréal*
North 44 Degrees, *Toronto*
Scaramouche, *Toronto*
Truffles, *Toronto*

Connecticut

Population: 3,287,116
Land area: 4,872 square miles
Elevation: 0-2,380 feet
Highest point: Mount Frissel (Litchfield County)
Entered Union: Fifth of original 13 states (January 9, 1788)
Capital: Hartford
Motto: He who transplanted, still sustains
Nickname: Constitution State
State flower: Mountain laurel
State bird: American robin
State tree: White oak
Time zone: Eastern
Web: www.state.ct.us/tourism/

Connecticut is a state of beautiful hills and lakes and lovely old towns with white church steeples rising above green commons. It is also a state with a tradition of high technical achievement and fine machining. Old houses and buildings enchant the visitor; a re-creation of the life of the old sailing ship days at Mystic Seaport leads the traveler back to times long gone.

Adriaen Block sailed into the Connecticut River in 1614. This great river splits Massachusetts and Connecticut and separates Vermont from New Hampshire. It was the river by which Connecticut's first settlers, coming from Massachusetts in 1633, settled in Hartford, Windsor and Wethersfield. These three towns created a practical constitution called the Fundamental Orders, by which a powerful "General Court" exercised both judicial and legislative duties. The Royal Charter of 1662 was so liberal that Sir Edmund Andros, governor of New England, tried to seize it (1687). To save it, citizens hid the charter in the Charter Oak, which once stood in Hartford.

Poultry, dairy products and tobacco are the state's most important agricultural products; forest products, nursery stock, and fruit and vegetable produce follow in importance. Aircraft engines, helicopters, hardware, tools, nuclear submarines and machinery are the principal manufactured products. The home offices of more than 40 insurance companies are located in the state.

When to Go/Climate

Connecticut's climate is the mildest of all the New England states. Coastal breezes help keep the humidity manageable and mud season (between winter and spring, when topsoil thaws and lower earth remains frozen) is shorter here than in other New England states.

AVERAGE HIGH/LOW TEMPERATURES (°F)

BRIDGEPORT

Jan 29/22	**May** 59/50	**Sept** 66/58
Feb 31/23	**June** 68/59	**Oct** 56/47
Mar 39/31	**July** 74/66	**Nov** 46/38
Apr 49/40	**Aug** 73/65	**Dec** 35/28

HARTFORD

Jan 25/16	**May** 60/48	**Sept** 64/52
Feb 28/19	**June** 69/57	**Oct** 53/41
Mar 38/28	**July** 74/62	**Nov** 42/33
Apr 49/38	**Aug** 72/60	**Dec** 30/21

Parks and Recreation Finder

Directions to and information about the parks and recreation areas below are given under their respective town/city sections. Please refer to those sections for details.

STATE PARK AND RECREATION AREAS

Key to abbreviations: I.P. = Interstate Park; S.A.P. = State Archaeological Park; S.B. = State Beach; S.C. = State Conservation Area; S.C.P. = State Conservation Park; S.Cp. = State Campground; S.F. = State Forest; S.G. = State Garden; S.H.A. = State Historic Area; S.H.P. = State Historic Park; S.H.S. = State Historic Site; S.M.P. = State Marine Park; S.N.A. = State Natural Area; S.P. = State Park; S.P.C. = State Public Campground; S.R. = State Reserve; S.R.A. = State Recreation Area; S.Res. = State Reservoir; S.Res.P = State Resort Park; S.R.P. = State Rustic Park.

Place Name	Listed Under
Campbell Falls S.P.	NORFOLK
Chatfield Hollow S.P.	CLINTON
Dennis Hill S.P.	NORFOLK
Hammonasset Beach S.P.	MADISON
Hatstack Mt S.P.	NORFOLK
Housatonic Meadows S.P.	CORNWALL BRIDGE
Kent Falls S.P.	KENT
Kettletown S.P.	SOUTHBURY
Lake Waramaug S.P.	NEW PRESTON

Macedonia Brook S.P.	KENT
Rocky Neck S.P.	OLD LYME
Southford Falls S.P.	SOUTHBURY
Squantz Pond S.P.	DANBURY
Wadsworth Falls S.P.	MIDDLETOWN

Water-related activities, hiking, riding, various other sports, picnicking and visitor centers, as well as camping, are available in some of these areas. There are 32 state forests and 92 state parks inland and on the shore. A parking fee ($4-$12) is charged at many of these. Camping, mid-April-September; shore parks $12/site/night; inland parks with swimming $10/site/night; inland parks without swimming $9/site/night; additional charge per person for groups larger than 4 persons. Two- to three-week limit, mid-April-September; three-day limit, October-December. No camping January-mid-April; selected parks allow camping October-December. Forms for reservations for stays of more than two days may be obtained after January 15 by writing to the address in Hartford; these reservations should then be mailed to the park itself; no reservations by phone. Parks and forests are open all year, 8 am-sunset. Most shore parks allow all-night fishing (with permit). Inland swimming areas are open 8 am-sunset. No pets allowed in state park campgrounds. For further information, reservations and regulations contact Dept of Environmental Protection, Bureau of Outdoor Recreation, 79 Elm St, Hartford 06106; 860/424-3200.

SKI AREAS

Place Name	Listed Under
Mohawk Mt Ski Area	CORNWALL BRIDGE
Mt Southington Ski Area	MERIDEN
Powder Ridge Ski Area	MIDDLETOWN
Ski Sundown	AVON

FISHING & HUNTING

Hunting license: nonresident, $42 (firearms). Archery permit (incl big and small game): nonresident, $44. Deer permit: nonresident, $30 (firearms). Fishing license: nonresident, season, $25; 3-day, $8. Combination firearm hunting, fishing license: nonresident, $55. Further information, including the latest regulations, can be obtained from Dept of Environmental Protection, Licensing and Revenue, 79 Elm St, Hartford 06106; 860/424-3105.

Driving Information

Safety belts are mandatory for all persons in front seat of vehicle. Children under 4 years must be in an approved passenger restraint anywhere in vehicle: ages 1-3 may use a regulation safety belt; under age 1 must use an approved safety seat. For further information phone 860/666-4343.

INTERSTATE HIGHWAY SYSTEM

The following alphabetical listing of Connecticut towns in *Mobil Travel Guide* shows that these cities are within 10 miles of the indicated interstate highways. A highway map, however, should be checked for the nearest exit.

Highway number	Cities/Towns within 10 miles
Interstate 84:	Danbury, Farmington, Hartford, Manchester, Southbury, Stafford Springs, Vernon, Waterbury.
Interstate 91:	Enfield, Hartford, Meriden, Middletown, New Haven, Wethersfield, Windsor, Windsor Locks.
Interstate 95:	Branford, Bridgeport, Clinton, Fairfield, Greenwich, Groton, Guilford, Madison, Milford, Mystic, New Haven, New London, Norwalk, Old Saybrook, Stamford, Stonington, Stratford, Westport.
Interstate 395:	Groton, New London, Norwich, Plainfield, Putnam.

Additional Visitor Information

Pamphlets, maps and booklets, including the Connecticut Vacation Guide, are available to tourists by contacting the State of Connecticut, Department of Economic and Community Development, 505 Hudson St, Hartford 06106; 800/282-6863. In addition, *Connecticut*—a monthly magazine published by Communications Intl, 789 Reservoir Ave, Bridgeport 06606—gives a listing of activities around the state; available by subscription or at newsstands.

Connecticut tourism information centers also provide useful information: on I-95 southbound at North Stonington, northbound at Darien, northbound at Westbrook (seasonal); on I-84 eastbound at Danbury, eastbound at Southington (seasonal), westbound at Willington; on I-91 northbound at Middletown, southbound at Wallingford; on Merritt Parkway (CT 15) northbound at Greenwich (seasonal). Also, several privately operated tourism centers are located throughout the state.

Avon (D-3)

(See also Bristol, Farmington, Hartford, Wethersfield)

Pop 13,937 **Elev** 202 ft **Area code** 860 **Zip** 06001 **E-mail** ctfuntour@aol.com **Web** www.travelfile.com/get/ghtd
Information Greater Hartford Tourism District, 234 Murphy Rd, Hartford 06114; 860/244-8181 or 800/793-4480.

What to See and Do

Farmington Valley Arts Center. 20 studios, located in historic stone explosives plant, occupied by artists and artisans and open to public at artist's discretion. Fisher Gallery and Shop featuring guest curated exhibitions and a juried collection of handmade crafts, gifts and artwork. (Jan-Oct, Wed-Sat, Sun afternoons; Nov-Dec, daily; closed most hols) 25 Arts Center Lane, Avon Park North, off US 44. Phone 860/678-1867. **Free.**

Roaring Brook Nature Center. This 112-acre wildlife refuge has interpretive building with seasonal natural history exhibits, wildlife observation area; 6 mi of marked trails. Gift shop. (Sept-June, daily exc Mon; rest of yr, daily; closed some major hols) 1½ mi N of US 44, at 70 Gracey Rd in Canton. Phone 860/693-0263. **¢¢**

Ski Sundown. 3 triple chairlifts; Pomalift; snowmaking; school, patrol, rentals, half-day rate; bar, snack bar. 15 trails. Longest run 1 mi; vertical drop 625 ft. (Dec-Mar, daily) 6 mi W via CT 44, then 1½ mi NE on CT 219, in New Hartford. Phone 860/379-9851 or 860/379-SNOW (snow conditions). **¢¢¢¢¢**

Motel

★ ★ ★ **AVON OLD FARMS HOTEL.** *E at jct US 44 & CT 10.* 860/677-1651; FAX 860/677-0364. 160 rms, 3 story. S, D $89-$129; suites $160-$260; under 18 free. Crib free. Pet accepted, some restrictions. TV; cable, VCR avail. Pool. Complimentary continental bkfst. Restaurant 6:30-10 am, 11:30 am-2 pm, 5-9 pm; Sun 7 am-1 pm. Rm serv. Ck-out noon. Meeting rms. Business servs avail. Valet serv. Beauty shop. Exercise equipt; sauna. Cr cds: A, C, D, DS, MC, V.

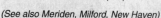

Restaurants

★ ★ ★ **AVON OLD FARMS INN.** *E at jct US 44 & CT 10, 5 mi off I-84.* 860/677-2818. E-mail avonoldfarmsinn@imagine.com; web www.avonoldfarminn.com. Own baking. Hrs: noon-9:30 pm; Fri to 10 pm; Sat to 10:30 pm; Sun 5:30-8:30 pm; Sun brunch 10 am-2:30 pm. Res required. Bar. Semi-a la carte: lunch $6.95-$13.95, dinner $18.95-$26.95. Sun brunch $15.95. Child's meals. Entertainment. 1757 stagecoach stop. Cr cds: A, C, D, DS, MC, V.

★ ★ **DAKOTA.** *225 W Main St.* 860/677-4311. Specializes in steak, seafood. Salad bar. Hrs: 5-10 pm; Fri to 11 pm; Sat 4-11 pm; Sun 4-10 pm. Res accepted. Bar. A la carte entrees: dinner $9.95-$23.95. Child's meals. Casual, rustic atmosphere with a touch of Southwestern decor. Cr cds: A, D, DS, MC, V.

[D]

Branford (E-3)

(See also Meriden, Milford, New Haven)

Settled 1644 **Pop** 27,603 **Elev** 49 ft **Area code** 203 **Zip** 06405 **E-mail** crvsvc@cttourism.org **Web** www.cttourism.org
Information CT River Valley & Shoreline Visitors Council, 393 Main St, Middletown 06457; 860/347-0028 or 800/486-3346.

Once a busy shipping center, Branford has become a residential and industrial suburb of New Haven. The community's bays and beaches attract many summertime vacationers. Branford's large green, dating from colonial days, is surrounded by public buildings.

What to See and Do

Harrison House (ca 1725). Classic colonial saltbox restored by J. Frederick Kelly, an early 20th-century architect; stone chimney, herb garden, period furnishings and farm implements. (June-Sept, Thurs-Sat mid-late afternoon; also by appt) 124 Main St. Phone 203/488-4828 or 203/488-2126. **Free.**

Thimble Islands Cruise. Legends of treasures hidden by Captain Kidd, along with picturesque shores and vegetation, have for more than 250 yrs lured people to these 20 to 30 rocky islets in Long Island Sound. Narrated tours (30-45 min) leave hrly aboard the *Volsunga III.* (May-Oct, daily exc Mon) Res required. Departs from Stony Creek Dock. Phone 203/481-3345 or 203/488-9978. **¢¢¢**

Motel

★ ★ **DAYS INN.** *375 E Main St (US 1).* 203/488-8314; FAX 203/483-6885; res: 800/255-9296. 74 rms, 2 story. S $75-$80; D $90-$99; each addl $10; suites $245; under 16 free. Crib free. Pet accepted; $10. TV; cable (premium), VCR avail. Pool. Complimentary continental bkfst. Coffee in rms. Restaurant 7 am-2 pm; Sat, Sun to noon. Ck-out 11 am. Valet serv. Meeting rms. Business center. Gift shop. Barber, beauty shop. Refrigerators avail. Cr cds: A, C, D, DS, ER, JCB, MC, V.

[D]

Bridgeport (F-2)

(See also Fairfield, Milford, Norwalk, Stratford, Westport)

Settled 1639 **Pop** 141,686 **Elev** 20 ft **Area code** 203 **E-mail** info@brbc.org
Information Chamber of Commerce, 10 Middle St, 14th flr, 06604; 203/335-3800.

An important manufacturing city, Bridgeport is home to dozens of well-known companies that produce a highly diversified array of manufactured products. The University of Bridgeport (1927) is also located in the city.

Bridgeport's most famous resident was probably P.T. Barnum. The city's most famous son was 28-inch Charles S. Stratton, who was promoted by Barnum as General Tom Thumb. There was a time when train passengers in and out of Bridgeport occasionally saw elephants hitched to plows; the elephants, of course, were from Barnum's winter quarters. As well as running the "Greatest Show on Earth," Barnum was for a time the mayor of Bridgeport.

What to See and Do

Beardsley Zoological Gardens. This 30-acre zoo, the state's only, houses more than 200 animals; Siberian tiger exhibit; farmyard; concession; gift shop. (Daily; closed Jan 1, Thanksgiving, Dec 25) Noble Ave,

Beardsley Park, off I-95 exit 27A. Phone 203/576-8082. Zoo ¢¢; Park entrance fee per vehicle ¢¢

Captain's Cove Seaport. Replica of the HMS *Rose*, the British warship that triggered the founding of the American Navy during the Revolutionary War. Marina; shops, restaurant, fish market. (Schedule varies) 1 Bostwick Ave, I-95 exit 26. Phone 203/335-1433. HMS *Rose* ¢¢

Discovery Museum. Planetarium; films; approx 120 hands-on science and art exhibits; children's museum; Challenger Learning Center; changing art exhibits; lectures, demonstrations and workshops. (Daily exc Mon; closed Labor Day, Thanksgiving, Dec 25) 4450 Park Ave, off Merritt Pkwy, exit 47. Phone 203/372-3521. ¢¢¢

Ferry to Port Jefferson, L.I. Car and passenger service across Long Island Sound (1 hr, 20 min). (Daily) Union Square Dock, at foot of State St. Phone 203/367-3043or 516/473-0286. One way, individual ¢¢¢¢

Statue of Tom Thumb. Life-size statue on 10-ft base. Mountain Grove Cemetery, North Ave & Dewey St.

⭐ **The Barnum Museum.** Houses memorabilia from P.T. Barnum's life and circus career, including artifacts relating to Barnum's legendary discoveries, Gen Tom Thumb and Jenny Lind; scale model of 3-ring circus; displays of Victorian Bridgeport; changing exhibits; art gallery. (Daily exc Mon; closed most hols) 820 Main St. Phone 203/331-9881. ¢¢

Seasonal Event

Barnum Festival. Commemorates the life of P.T. Barnum. Phone 203/367-8495. Early July.

Hotels

⭐ ⭐ **HOLIDAY INN.** *1070 Main St (06604). 203/334-1234; FAX 203/367-1985.* 234 rms, 9 story. S $79-$119; D $89-$129; each addl $10; suites $179-$450; under 16 free; family, wkend rates. Crib free. Pet accepted, some restrictions. TV; cable. Indoor/outdoor pool. Restaurant 6 am-10 pm. Bar 4 pm-midnight. Ck-out noon. Meeting rms. Business center. In-rm modem link. Free covered parking. Free airport, RR station, bus depot transportation. Exercise equipt. Refrigerator in some suites. Atrium; waterfall. Beach 4 blks. Cr cds: A, C, D, DS, JCB, MC, V.

D 🏊 🛥 🏋 🐾 🐾 SC 🚶

⭐ ⭐ **MARRIOTT TRUMBULL.** *(180 Hawley Lane, Trumbull 06611) N via CT 8/25 to CT 15 (Merritt Pkwy) exit 51S, 3 blks S to Hawley Lane. 203/378-1400; FAX 203/375-0632.* 320 rms, 5 story. S $144-$189; D $164-$209; each addl $20; suites $300-$400; under 18 free; wkend rates. Crib free. TV; cable (premium), VCR avail. 2 pools, 1 indoor; whirlpool, poolside serv. Coffee in rms. Restaurants 6:30 am-11 pm. Bars 11-1 am; entertainment. Ck-out noon. Convention facilities. Business center. In-rm modem link. Gift shop. Exercise equipt; sauna. Some refrigerators. Cr cds: A, C, D, DS, ER, JCB, MC, V.

D 🏊 🏋 🐾 🐾 SC 🚶

Restaurant

⭐ **BLACK ROCK CASTLE.** *2895 Fairfield Ave (06605). 203/336-3990.* Irish menu. Specialties: flaming Irish whiskey steak, beef. Hrs: 11:30 am-2:30 pm, 5-10 pm; Fri, Sat to 11 pm. Closed Jan 1, Dec 25. Res accepted. A la carte entrees: lunch $4.95-$6.95, dinner $9.95-$16.95. Child's meals. Entertainment Wed-Sun. Valet parking. Castle motif; dining beneath tower. Cr cds: A, DS, MC, V.

Bristol (D-3)

(See also Meriden, New Britain, Waterbury)

Settled 1727 **Pop** 60,640 **Elev** 289 ft **Area code** 860 **Zip** 06010 **E-mail** gbcc@usa.net **Web** www.chamber.bristol.ct.us

Information Greater Bristol Chamber of Commerce, 10 Main St, phone 860/584-4718; or the Litchfield Hills Travel Council, PO Box 1776, Marbledale 06777, phone 860/868-2214.

Gideon Roberts began making and selling clocks here in 1790. Bristol has since been famous for clocks—particularly for Sessions and Ingraham. Today Bristol is also the home of Associated Spring Corporation, Dana Corp/Warner Electric, Theis Precision Steel and ESPN, the nation's first all-sports cable television network.

What to See and Do

American Clock and Watch Museum. More than 3,000 timepieces; exhibits and video show on history of clock and watch manufacturing located in historic house built 1801. Also award-winning sundial garden; bookshop. (Apr-Nov, daily; closed Thanksgiving) 100 Maple St. Phone 860/583-6070. ¢¢

Burlington Trout Hatchery. Hatchery building houses incubators and tanks; development of trout from egg to fish. (Daily) 10 mi N via CT 69, then approx 1 mi E on CT 4 to Belden Rd, in Burlington. Phone 860/673-2340. **Free.**

H.C. Barnes Memorial Nature Center. Self-guiding trails through 70-acre preserve. Interpretive building features ecological and animal displays. (Sat, also Wed-Fri & Sun afternoons) Trails (daily; closed most hols) 175 Shrub Rd, 3 mi N on CT 69. Phone 860/589-6082. ¢

Lake Compounce Theme Park. One of the oldest continuously operating amusement parks in the nation. Over 25 wet & dry attractions including roller coasters, white water raft ride, vintage trolley, bumper cars and 1911 carousel. Special events. (June-Aug, daily exc Tues; Sept, wkends) 822 Lake Ave. Phone 860/583-3631. All-day ride pass ¢¢¢¢

Lock Museum of America. Antique locks, displays on lock history and design. (May-Oct, daily exc Mon, limited hrs) 3½ mi NW on CT 72, then W ¾mi on US 6 to 130 Main St in Terryville. Phone 860/589-6359. ¢¢ 2 blks W is

Eli Terry, Jr Waterwheel. Built in the early 1840s, this 20-ft diameter, rack and pinion, breast-type wheel is an excellent example of the type of waterwheel used to supply power to industrial buildings during this period. 160 Main St.

New England Carousel Museum. Displays over 300 carved, wooden antique carousel figures, including two chariots. Restoration workshop on view. (Apr-Oct, Mon-Sat, also Sun afternoons; rest of yr, Wed-Sat, also Sun afternoons; closed some major hols) 95 Riverside Ave. Phone 860/585-5411. ¢¢

Annual Events

Balloons Over Bristol. Bristol Eastern High School. More than 60 hot-air balloons from around the country gather to participate in 3-day event; carnival, crafts fair, food booths. Phone 860/584-4718. Memorial Day wkend.

Chrysanthemum Festival. Music, art, theater, hayrides, picking pumpkins, parades and dances, Historical Society tours. Phone 860/584-4718. Late Sept.

Inn

⭐ ⭐ ⭐ **CHIMNEY CREST MANOR.** *5 Founders Dr. 860/582-4219; FAX 860/584-5903.* 6 units, 3 story, 4 suites. S, D $85-$150; each addl $15. Closed Dec 24 & 25. Crib free. TV; cable (premium), VCR avail. Complimentary full bkfst. Ck-out 11 am, ck-in 3 pm. Framed artwork, beamed ceilings in 32-rm Tudor-style mansion (1930). Library; sun rm. Totally nonsmoking. Cr cds: A, MC, V.

Clinton (E-4)

(See also Essex, Guilford, Madison, New Haven, Old Saybrook)

Settled 1663 **Pop** 12,767 **Elev** 25 ft **Area code** 860 **Zip** 06413 **E-mail** chamber@ClintonCT.com **Web** www.ClintonCT.com
Information Chamber of Commerce, 50 E Main St, PO Box 334, phone 860/669-3889; or the Connecticut Valley Tourism Commission, 393 Main St, Middletown 06457, phone 860/669-3889.

What to See and Do

Chamard Vinyards. A 15-acre vineyard and winery offering Chardonnay, Pinot Noir, Merlot and other varieties. Tours and tastings (Wed-Sat). 115 Cow Hill Rd. Phone 860/664-0299 or 800/371-1609. **Free.**

Chatfield Hollow State Park. Approx 550 acres situated in a heavily wooded hollow with fine fall scenery and natural caves that once provided shelter for Native Americans. Pond swimming; fishing. Hiking. Ice skating. Picnicking, concessions. Standard hrs, fees. 7 mi NW via CT 80 & 81, on N Branford Rd in Killingworth. Phone 860/663-2030. ¢¢¢

Stanton House (1789). Thirteen-rm house connected to general store; original site of first classroom of Yale Univ. Period furnishings; antique American and Staffordshire dinnerware; weapon collection; bed used by Marquis de Lafayette during 1824 visit. (June-Sept, daily exc Mon) 63 E Main St. Phone 860/669-2132. **Free.**

Motel

✔★ **CLINTON.** *163 E Main St. 860/669-8850; FAX 860/669-3849.* 15 rms. Mid-June-mid-Sept: S, D $36-$82; lower rates rest of yr. Crib free. TV; cable, VCR avail. Pool. Restaurant nearby. Ck-out 11 am. Lawn games. Refrigerators. Cr cds: A, C, D, DS, MC, V.

Restaurant

★ **LOG CABIN RESTAURANT & LOUNGE.** *232 Boston Post Rd. 860/669-6253.* Italian, Amer menu. Specializes in seafood, steak, pasta. Hrs: 11:30 am-10 pm. Closed Dec 25. Res accepted. Bar. Semi-a la carte: lunch $4.95-$7.95, dinner $10.95-$18.95. Child's meals. Fireplace. Log cabin decor. Cr cds: A, D, DS, MC, V.

Cornwall Bridge (D-1)

(See also Kent)

Pop 450 (est) **Elev** 445 ft **Area code** 860 **Zip** 06754
Information Litchfield Hills Travel Council, PO Box 968, Litchfield 06759; 860/567-4506.

The small central valley containing the villages of Cornwall, West Cornwall and Cornwall Bridge was avoided by early settlers because its heavy stand of pine made the clearing of land difficult.

What to See and Do

Covered bridge. Designed by Ithiel Town, in continuous service since 1837. 4 mi N via US 7 to CT 128 near West Cornwall, at Housatonic River. **Free.**

Housatonic Meadows State Park. A 452-acre park bordering the Housatonic River. Fishing; boating, canoeing. Picnicking. Camping (dump station). No pets. Standard hrs, fees. 1 mi N on US 7. Phone 860/672-6772 (May-Sept) or 860/927-3238. **Free.**

Mohawk Mt Ski Area. More than 20 trails and slopes, most with snowmaking; triple, 4 double chairlifts; patrol, school, rentals; cafeteria. Longest run 1 1/4mi; vertical drop 640 ft. (Late Nov-early Apr, daily; closed Dec 25) More than 40 mi of cross-country trails. Night skiing (exc Sun). 4 mi NE on CT 4, S on CT 128, on Great Hollow Rd in Mohawk Mt State Park. Phone 860/672-6100 (snow conditions), 860/672-6464 or 800/895-5222. ¢¢¢¢

Sharon Audubon Center. National Audubon Society wildlife sanctuary (684 acres) includes nature center, 11 mi of walking trails, self-guided tours, herb and wildflower garden, gift/bookstore. Grounds (daily). Nature center, store (daily; closed major hols). Approx 8 mi NW on CT 4 near Sharon. Phone 860/364-0520. ¢¢

Inn

★ **CORNWALL INN.** *270 Kent Rd (US 7). 860/672-6884; res: 800/786-6884.* 13 rms, 2 story, 1 suite. No rm phones. S, D $50-$110; each addl $10; suite $150; under 5 free. Crib free. Pet accepted, some restrictions. TV in some rms, also in sitting rm. Pool. Complimentary continental bkfst. Dining rm 6-9 pm Thurs-Mon; res required. Bar 5-10 pm. Ck-out 11 am, ck-in 2 pm. Bellhop. Bus depot transportation. Downhill ski 5 mi; x-country ski 1/4 mi. Picnic tables. Restored 19th-century country inn; antiques. Cr cds: A, DS, MC, V.

Danbury (E-1)

(See also Southbury, Woodbury)

Settled 1685 **Pop** 65,585 **Elev** 378 ft **Area code** 203 **Web** www.housatonic.org
Information Housatonic Valley Tourism Commission, 30 Main St, PO Box 406, 06813; 203/743-0546 or 800/841-4488 outside CT.

Danbury, which was settled by eight Norwalk families seeking fertile land, played an important role during the American Revolution as a supply depot and site of a military hospital for the Continental Army. After the war and until the 1950s, the community was the center of the hat industry. Zadoc Benedict is credited with the first factory in 1790, making three hats a day.

What to See and Do

Candlewood Lake. Connecticut's largest lake, more than 14 mi long and with more than 60 mi of shoreline, extends one finger into Danbury. Swimming; fishing; boating. Picnicking, concession. Fees for some activities. 2 mi NW on CT 37, then E on Hayestown Ave to E Hayestown Rd. Phone 203/354-6928. On the W shore are Pootatuck State Forest and

Squantz Pond State Park. More than 170 acres. Freshwater swimming, scuba diving; fishing; boating (7 1/2 hp limit), canoeing (rentals). Hiking, biking. Picnicking; concessions. No pets. Standard hrs, fees. 10 mi N on CT 37 & 39 in New Fairfield. Phone 203/797-4165. ¢¢¢

Scott-Fanton Museum. Includes Rider House (1785), period furnishings, New England memorabilia; Dodd Shop (ca 1790), historical display of hat industry; Huntington Hall, changing exhibits and research library. (Wed-Sun afternoons; closed hols) 43 Main St. Phone 203/743-5200. **Donation.**

Annual Event

Taste O' Danbury. Phone 203/790-6970. Sept.

Seasonal Event

Charles Ives Center for the Arts. At Westside campus, Western Connecticut State University, on Mill Plain Rd. Outdoor classical, country, folk, jazz and pop concerts. Fri-Sun. Phone 203/837-9226. July-Sept.

Motels

★ ★ **BEST WESTERN STONY HILL INN.** (46 Stony Hill Rd, Bethel 06801) 1¼ mi E on US 6 exit 8, between I-84 exits 8 & 9. 203/743-5533; FAX 203/743-4958. 36 rms, 4 kits. May-Oct: S $90; D $94; each addl $8; kit. units $100; under 12 free; lower rates rest of yr. Crib $10. TV; cable (premium). Pool. Playground. Complimentary continental bkfst. Restaurant 11:30 am-2 pm, 5-9:30 pm; Fri from 5 pm; Sat to 10 pm; Sun 10:30 am-2:30 pm. Bar; pianist Fri, Sat. Ck-out 11 am. Coin lndry. Meeting rms. Golf pro, driving range. Health club privileges. Extensive grounds; pond. Cr cds: A, C, D, DS, MC, V.

[D] [符] [≈] [⊠] [▲] [SC]

★ ★ **RAMADA INN.** exit 8 on I-84 (06810), 1½ mi NE at exit 8. 203/792-3800; FAX 203/730-1899. 181 rms, 2-5 story. S $79-$145; D $79-$155; each addl $15; under 16 free; wknd rates. Pet accepted, some restrictions. TV; cable (premium). Coffee in rms. Restaurant 6:30 am-10:30 pm; Fri to 11 pm; hrs vary wkends. Rm serv. Bar 11-1 am. Ck-out 11 am. Coin lndry. Meeting rms. Business servs avail. In-rm modem link. Valet serv. Health club privileges. Refrigerators, microwaves avail. Cr cds: A, C, D, DS, ER, JCB, MC, V.

[D] [➤] [≈] [⊠] [▲] [SC]

Motor Hotels

★ ★ **BEST WESTERN BERKSHIRE MOTOR INN.** (11 US 6, Bethel 06801) I-84 exit 8. 203/744-3200; FAX 203/744-3979. 69 rms, 3 story. May-Oct: S $80-$90; D $84-$94; each addl $8; under 12 free; higher rates: Special Olympics, Dec 31; lower rates rest of yr. Crib $10. TV; cable (premium). Complimentary continental bkfst. Restaurant nearby. Ck-out 11 am. Meeting rms. Business servs avail. In-rm modem link. Health club privileges. Playground. Microwaves avail. Cr cds: A, C, D, DS, MC, V.

[D] [⊠] [▲] [SC]

★ ★ **HOLIDAY INN.** 80 Newtown Rd (06810), I-84 exit 8. 203/792-4000; FAX 203/797-0810. 114 rms, 4 story. Apr-Dec: S, D $104-$109; suites $109-$114; under 18 free; lower rates rest of yr. Crib free. Pet accepted. TV; cable (premium). VCR avail (movies). Pool; poolside serv. Complimentary coffee in rms. Restaurant 6 am-midnight. Rm serv 24 hrs. Bar noon-2 am. Ck-out noon. Meeting rms. Business servs avail. In-rm modem link. Bellhops. Valet serv. Shopping arcade. Free airport transportation. Health club privileges. Some refrigerators; microwaves avail. Cr cds: A, C, D, DS, JCB, MC, V.

[D] [➤] [≈] [⊠] [▲] [SC]

Hotels

★ ★ **ETHAN ALLEN INN.** 21 Lake Ave (06811), I-84 exit 4, 1 blk W. 203/744-1776; FAX 203/791-9673; res: 800/742-1776. E-mail eallen-inn@aol.com. 195 rms, 6 story. S $108-$115; D $123-$130; each addl $15; suites $113-$130; under 17 free; wknd rates. TV; cable (premium). Pool. Restaurant 6:30-10 am, noon-2 pm, 5-10 pm; Sat, Sun 7:30 am-2 pm. Bar 4 pm-1 am, wkends from 11:30 am. Ck-out noon. Coin lndry. Meeting rms. Business center. In-rm modem link. Free RR station, bus depot transportation. Airport transportation. Exercise equipt; sauna. Microwaves avail. Owned by Ethan Allen Furniture Co. Cr cds: A, D, DS, MC, V.

[D] [≈] [⊀] [✈] [⊠] [▲] [SC] [✦]

★ ★ ★ **HILTON AND TOWERS.** 18 Old Ridgebury Rd (06810), I-84 E, exit 2A. 203/794-0600; FAX 203/798-2709. 242 rms, 10 story. S, D $125-$195; each addl $15; family, wknd rates. Crib free. Pet accepted, some restrictions. TV; cable (premium), VCR (movies). Indoor pool; whirlpool, poolside serv. Restaurant 6:30 am-10 pm. Bar 11-2 am; entertainment. Ck-out noon. Meeting rms. Business center. In-rm modem link. Coin lndry. Lighted tennis. Exercise equipt; sauna. Health club privileges. Microwaves avail. Cr cds: A, C, D, DS, ER, JCB, MC, V.

[D] [➤] [🏃] [≈] [⊀] [⊠] [▲] [SC] [✦]

Inn

★ ★ **HOMESTEAD.** (5 Elm St, New Milford 06776) 13 mi N on US 7. 860/354-4080; FAX 860/354-7046. 8 rms in 2-story inn, 6 motel rms. S $72-$81; D $80-$103; each addl $10; family rates. Crib free. TV; cable, VCR avail. Complimentary continental bkfst. Restaurant nearby. Ck-out 11 am, ck-in 2 pm. Business servs avail. In-rm modem link. Health club privileges. Microwaves avail. Inn built 1853; many rms furnished with country antiques. Cr cds: A, C, D, DS, MC, V.

[⊠] [▲]

Restaurants

★ ★ **CIAO CAFE AND WINE BAR.** 2B Ives St (06810). 203/791-0404. Italian menu. Specialties: veal Christine, rigatoni with tortanella cheese. Hrs: 11 am-10 pm; Fri, Sat to 11 pm; Sun brunch to 2 pm. Closed Labor Day, Dec 25. Res accepted. A la carte entrees: lunch $5.95-$8.95, dinner $8.75-$16.95. Sun brunch $7.95. Outdoor dining. Contemporary decor. Cr cds: A, MC, V.

[D] [⊰]

★ **THE HEARTH.** (US 7, Brookfield 06804) NE via I-84 to exit 7, 5 mi N on US 7. 203/775-3360. Specializes in open-hearth steak, seafood. Hrs: noon-2:30 pm, 5-9 pm; Fri, Sat 5-9:30 pm; Sun 1-8 pm. Closed Mon; Thanksgiving, Dec 24, 25; Feb. Serv bar. Semi-a la carte: lunch $4.75-$7, dinner $8.95-$22.95. Complete meals: dinner $11.50-$23. Child's meals. Open-hearth cooking in center of restaurant. Cr cds: A, DS, MC, V.

[D] [⊰]

★ ★ **TWO STEPS DOWNTOWN GRILLE.** 5 Ives St (06810), I-84 exit 5. 203/794-0032. Southwestern, Amer menu. Specialties: fajitas, baby back ribs. Hrs: 11 am-10 pm; wkends to midnight; Sun brunch 10 am-2 pm. Closed Labor Day, Dec 25. Res accepted. Bar. Semi-a la carte: lunch $5.95-$7.95, dinner $7.95-$15.95. Sun brunch $7.95. Child's meals. Outdoor dining. Former firehouse; lower level has Western decor. Cr cds: A, MC, V.

[D] [⊰]

East Haddam (E-4)

(See also Essex, Middletown)

Pop 6,676 **Elev** 35 ft **Area code** 860 **Zip** 06423 **E-mail** crvsvc@cttourism.org **Web** www.cttourism.org

Information CT River Valley & Shoreline Visitors Council, 393 Main St, Middletown 06457; 860/347-0028 or 800/486-3346.

Crossing the Connecticut River to Haddam is the longest remaining swinging bridge in New England.

What to See and Do

Amasa Day House (1816). Period furnishings include some pieces owned by 3 generations of the Day family; stenciled floors and stairs. (June-Labor

Day, Fri-Sun) 4 mi N on CT 149 at jct CT 151 in Moodus. Phone 860/873-8144 or 860/247-8996. ¢¢

Gillette Castle State Park. The 184-acre park surrounds a 24-rm castle built by turn-of-the-century actor/playwright William Gillette; medieval German design with dramatically decorated rms. (Late May-mid-Oct, daily; mid-Oct-mid-Dec, Sat & Sun) Picnicking & hiking trails in the surrounding park. Standard hrs. 4 mi SE via local roads to 67 River Rd. Phone 860/526-2336. Castle ¢¢

Goodspeed Opera House. Home of the American Musical Theatre (1876). Performances of American musicals (Apr-Dec, Wed-Sun eves, matinees Wed, Sat & Sun) Guided tours (June-Sept, Mon & Sat; fee). On CT 82 at East Haddam Bridge. For schedule, res phone 860/873-8668. Tours ¢

Nathan Hale Schoolhouse. One-rm school where the American Revolutionary patriot taught during winter of 1773; period furnishings, memorabilia. Church has bell said to have been cast in Spain in A.D. 815. (Memorial Day-Labor Day, Sat, Sun & hols, limited hrs) Main St (CT 149), at rear of St Stephen's Church. Phone 860/873-9547 (church). **Free.**

Sightseeing.

Camelot Cruises, Inc. Offers Connecticut River cruises, Long Island cruises, Murder Mystery cruises and evening music excursions. Long Island cruises (mid-June-Labor Day, daily; after Labor Day-mid-Oct, Sun). Murder Mystery cruises (Mar-Dec, Fri & Sat eves). W on CT 82, across river at Marine Park in Haddam. Phone 860/345-8591. ¢¢¢¢¢

Eagle Aviation. Scenic airplane rides over the Connecticut River Valley. (Daily; closed Dec 25-Jan 8) Goodspeed Airport & Seaplane Base, Goodspeed Landing, Lumberyard Rd. Phone 860/873-8568 or 860/873-8658. ¢¢¢¢¢

Inn

★ ★ **BISHOPSGATE.** 7 Norwich Rd. 860/873-1677; FAX 860/873-3898. E-mail ctkagel@bishopsgate.com; web www.bishopsgate.com. 6 rms, 2 story. S, D $95-$150; each addl $15; suite $150. Children over 5 yrs only. Complimentary full bkfst; afternoon refreshments. Restaurant nearby. Ck-out 11 am, ck-in 2 pm. RR station transportation. Near Connecticut River. Colonial house (1818) furnished with period pieces. Cr cds: MC, V.

Enfield (C-3)

(See also Windsor Locks; also see Holyoke & Springfield, MA)

Settled 1680 **Pop** 45,532 **Elev** 150 ft **Area code** 860 **Zip** 06082 **E-mail** Eileen@cnctb.org **Web** www.cnctb.org

Information Connecticut North Central Tourism Bureau, 111 Hazard Ave; 860/763-2578 or 800/248-8283.

Located on the Connecticut River, Enfield was an important embarking point for flat-bottom boats transporting wares to Springfield, Massachusetts in the 18th century. The Enfield Society for the Detection of Horse Thieves and Robbers was founded here over a century ago. Jonathan Edwards, the famous theologian, delivered his fire and brimstone sermon "Sinners in the Hands of an Angry God" here in 1741.

What to See and Do

Martha A. Parsons House (1782). Constructed on land put aside for use by parsons or ministers, this house holds 180 yrs' worth of antiques collected by the Parsons family; tables brought from West Indies, George Washington memorial wallpaper. (May-Oct, Sun afternoons or by appt) 1387 Enfield St. Phone 860/745-6064. **Free.**

Old Town Hall (Purple Heart Museum). Includes inventions of the Shakers, a religious sect that observed a doctrine of celibacy, common property and community living; medals and service memorabilia, 46-star flag; local

historical displays and artifacts. (May-Oct, Sun afternoons or by appt) 1294 Enfield St. Phone 860/745-1729. **Free.**

Motel

✔ ★ **RED ROOF INN.** 5 Hazard Ave. 860/741-2571; FAX 860/741-2576. 109 rms, 2 story. S $34.99-$42.99; D $39.99-$46.99; under 18 free. Crib free. Pet accepted. TV; cable (premium). Restaurant adj 6:30-12:30 am. Ck-out noon. Business servs avail. In-rm modem link. X-country ski 15 mi. Cr cds: A, C, D, DS, MC, V.

Hotel

★ ★ ★ **HARLEY.** 1 Bright Meadow Blvd. 860/741-2211; FAX 860/741-2210. Web www.harleyhotels.com. 181 rms, 6 story. S $104-$114; D $114-$124; each addl $10; under 18 free; wkend rates. Crib free. TV; cable (premium), VCR avail. 2 pools, 1 indoor; whirlpool, lifeguard (summer wknds). Restaurant 6:30 am-2 pm, 5:30-10 pm; Sat, Sun from 7 am. Bar 11 am-midnight; Sun to 11 pm; entertainment. Ck-out 11 am. Meeting rms. Business servs avail. In-rm modem link. Concierge. Free airport, RR station, bus depot transportation. Lighted tennis. Exercise equipt; sauna. Health club privileges. Game rm. Lawn games. Some in-rm steam baths. Picnic area. Cr cds: A, C, D, DS, MC, V.

Essex (E-4)

(See also Clinton, East Haddam, Middletown, Old Lyme, Old Saybrook)

Pop 5,904 **Elev** 100 ft **Area code** 860 **Zip** 06426 **E-mail** crvsvc@cttourism.org **Web** www.cttourism.org

Information CT River Valley & Shoreline Visitors Council, 393 Main St, Middletown, 06457; 860/347-0028 or 800/486-3346.

What to See and Do

Connecticut River Museum. Displays include full-rigged ship models; navigation instruments; full-size reproduction of world's first submarine. Waterfront park adj. (Daily exc Mon; closed major hols) At foot of Main St at river. Phone 860/767-8269. ¢¢

Valley Railroad. Scenic 12-mi steam train excursion along Connecticut River to Chester; can opt to connect with a riverboat for 1-hr Connecticut River cruise (addl fare). Cruise passengers are returned to Essex via later connecting trains. Turn-of-the-century equipment. (Early May-late Oct, days vary; also Christmas trips) 1 Railroad Ave. Phone 860/767-0103. Train ¢¢¢; Train and cruise ¢¢¢¢¢

Annual Event

Ancient Fife & Drum Corp Muster and Parade. 2½ mi N via CT 9, at Devitt's Field, Main St, in Deep River. Approx 60 fife & drum corps recall Revolutionary War period; displays. 3rd Sat July.

Inns

★ ★ ★ **COPPER BEECH.** (46 Main St, Ivoryton 06442) W off CT 9 exit 3. 860/767-0330; FAX 860/767-7840. Web www.copperbeechinn.com. 13 rms, 2 story. D $110-$180. Children over 8 yrs only. Closed 1st wk Jan, Dec 24 & 25. TV. Complimentary buffet bkfst. Restaurant (see COPPER BEECH INN). Ck-out 11 am. Whirlpools. Restored Victorian building (1889), once residence of prominent ivory importer; on 7 acres of wooded countryside, terraced gardens. Totally nonsmoking. Cr cds: A, C, D, MC, V.

★★ **GRISWOLD.** *36 Main St. 860/767-1776; FAX 860/767-0481.* E-mail griswoldinn@snet.net. 30 rms, 3 story. S, D $90-$185; each addl $10. Crib $10. TV in sitting rm. Complimentary continental bkfst. Restaurant (see GRISWOLD INN). Ck-out 11 am, ck-in 2 pm. Business servs avail. Inn since 1776. Fireplace in spacious library. Many antiques. Near Connecticut River. Cr cds: A, MC, V.

⊡ 🏊 🖐

Restaurants

★★ **CHART HOUSE.** *(W Main St, Chester 06412) 5 mi NW on CT 9 exit 6, E on Main St, near Good Speed Theater. 860/526-9898.* Specializes in seafood, prime rib, steak. Hrs: 5-9:30 pm; Fri to 10 pm; Sat to 10:30 pm; Sun 4-9 pm. Res accepted. Semi-a la carte: dinner $13.95-$23.95. Child's meals. Outdoor lounge. In coverted 19th-century mill with wheels & belts overhead. Overlooks waterfall, brook, covered walking bridge. Cr cds: A, C, D, DS, MC, V.

⊡

★★★ **COPPER BEECH INN.** *(See Copper Beech Inn) 860/767-0330.* French country menu. Specialties: bouillabaisse, breast of duck, veal. Own baking. Hrs: 5:30-8 pm; Fri, Sat to 9 pm; Sun 1-7 pm. Closed Mon, Tues (Jan-Mar); Jan 1, Dec 24, 25. Res accepted; required Sat. Serv bar. A la carte entrees: dinner $20.75-$26.25. In restored Victorian building (1889), once residence of prominent ivory importer. Jacket. Totally nonsmoking. Cr cds: A, C, D, MC, V.

⊡

★★★ **GRISWOLD INN.** *(See Griswold Inn) 860/767-1776.* Specializes in prime rib, local seafood, game (winter). Own sausage. Hrs: 11:45 am-3 pm; Fri, Sat 11:30 am-3 pm, 5-10 pm; Sun 4:30-9 pm; Sun brunch 11 am-2:30 pm. Closed Dec 24 eve, 25. Res accepted. Bar 11-1 am; Fri, Sat to 2 am. Semi-a la carte: lunch $6.95-$12.95, dinner $12.95-$22.95. Sun brunch $12.95. Child's meals. Entertainment, banjo concerts Fri & Sun, jazz pianist Sat. 1776 inn. Family-owned. Cr cds: A, MC, V.

★★ **STEVE'S CENTERBROOK CAFE.** *(78 Main St, Centerbrook) E of CT 9 exit 3. 860/767-1277.* European, Amer menu. Specializes in grill items, pasta. Hrs: 5:30-9 pm. Closed Mon. Res accepted. Bar. A la carte entrees: dinner $15.95-$19.50. Victorian house; country decor. Totally nonsmoking. Cr cds: A, MC, V.

⊡

Fairfield (F-2)

(See also Bridgeport, Milford, Norwalk, Stamford, Stratford)

Settled 1639 **Pop** 53,418 **Elev** 15 ft **Area code** 203
Information Chamber of Commerce, 1597 Post Rd, 06430; 203/255-1011.

A small band of colonists led by Roger Ludlowe settled Fairfield two years after the Pequot were subdued in the Great Swamp Fight. In 1779 British troops under General Tyron marched into the area and requested that the people submit to royal authority. When this was refused, the village was put to the torch.

What to See and Do

Connecticut Audubon Society Birdcraft Museum and Sanctuary. Established in 1914, this vest-pocket, six-acre sanctuary houses natural history museum with wildlife displays, dinosaur footprints and observational beehive; trails, ponds. (Sat-Sun, limited hrs) 314 Unquowa Rd. Phone 203/259-0416.   **Free.**

Connecticut Audubon Society Fairfield Nature Center and Larsen Sanctuary. Center features Connecticut wildlife and flora, solar green-house, natural history library, nature store. (Tues-Sat; also Sun in spring, fall; closed major hols) **Donation.** Adj is 160-acre sanctuary with 6 mi of trails through woodlands, meadows, ponds, streams. (Daily) Trail for the disabled. 2325 Burr St. Phone 203/259-6305. Sanctuary ¢

Fairfield Historical Society. Museum with permanent displays of furniture, paintings, maritime memorabilia, dolls, toys, farm implements, clocks; changing exhibits of history, costumes, decorative arts; genealogical and research library. (Daily; closed major hols) 636 Old Post Rd. Phone 203/259-1598.   ¢¢

Ogden House (ca 1750). Maintained by the Fairfield Historical Society, this 18th-century saltbox farmhouse, with authentic furnishings, has been restored to the time of its building by David and Jane Ogden; mid-18th-century kitchen garden. (Mid-May-mid-Oct, Thurs & Sun; other times by appt) 1520 Bronson Rd. Phone 203/259-1598.   ¢¢

Annual Events

Garlicfest. Notre Dame Catholic High School, 220 Jefferson St. Vendors prepare international array of garlic-seasoned cuisine. Sales, entertainment. Phone 203/372-6521. 3 days early May.

Dogwood Festival. At Greenfield Hill Congregational Church, 1045 Old Academy Rd. Herbs, plants; arts & crafts; walking tours, music programs; food. Phone 203/259-5596. Early or mid-May.

Chamber Arts & Crafts Festival. On Sherman Green. Phone 203/255-1011. Mid-June.

Motel

★ **FAIRFIELD MOTOR INN.** *417 Post Rd (06430). 203/255-0491; FAX 203/255-2073; res: 800/257-0496.* 80 rms, 2 story. S $68.50; D $75.50; each addl $10; under 15 free. Crib $10. TV; cable (premium). Pool. Restaurant noon-9 pm. Bar to 1 am; entertainment. Ck-out 11 am. Meeting rms. In-rm modem link. Cr cds: A, C, D, MC, V.

🏊 ⟋ 🖐 🐾 SC

Farmington (D-3)

(See also Bristol, Hartford, New Britain, Wethersfield)

Settled 1640 **Pop** 20,608 **Elev** 245 ft **Area code** 860 **Zip** 06032 **E-mail** ctfuntour@aol.com **Web** www.travelfile.com/get/ghtd
Information Greater Hartford Tourism District, 234 Murphy Rd, Hartford 06114; 860/244-8181 or 800/793-4480.

In 1802 and 1803, 15,000 yards of linen cloth were loomed in Farmington, and 2,500 hats were made in a shop on Hatter's Lane. There were silversmiths, tinsmiths, cabinetmakers, clockmakers and carriage builders. Today Farmington is a beautiful community—one of New England's museum pieces. It is also the home of Miss Porter's School (1844), a well-known private preparatory school for girls.

What to See and Do

Hill-Stead Museum (1901). Colonial revival-style country house designed by Theodate Pope in collaboration with McKim, Mead and White for industrialist A.A. Pope; contains Pope's collection of French impressionist paintings and decorative arts. Set on 152 acres, which includes a sunken garden. One-hr tours. (Daily exc Mon) 35 Mountain Rd. Phone 860/677-9064.   ¢¢¢

Stanley-Whitman House (ca 1720). This is one of the finest early 18th-century houses in the US; period furniture, local artifacts; changing displays; 18th-century herb and flower gardens. (May-Oct, Wed-Sun afternoons; Nov-Apr, Sun afternoons, also by appt) 37 High St. Phone 860/677-9222.   ¢¢

Annual Event

Farmington Antiques Weekend. Polo Grounds. One of the largest antique events in Connecticut; approx 600 dealers. Phone 860/871-7914. Mid-June.

Motels

★ ★ **CENTENNIAL INN.** 5 Spring Lane. 860/677-4647; FAX 860/676-0685; res: 800/852-2052. E-mail jill@centennialinn.com; web www.centennialinn.com. 112 kit. suites, 2 story. S, D $119-$209; family, wkend rates. Crib free. Pet accepted. TV; cable (premium), VCR (movies $4). Pool; whirlpool. Complimentary continental bkfst. Complimentary coffee in rms. Ck-out noon. Coin lndry. Meeting rms. Business center. In-rm modem link. Downhill ski 15 mi. Exercise equipt. Fireplaces. Balconies. Grills. On 12 wooded acres. Cr cds: A, C, D, DS, MC, V.

★ ★ **FARMINGTON INN.** 827 Farmington Ave, I-84 exit 39 to CT 4. 860/677-2821; FAX 860/677-8332, ext. 232; res: 800/648-9804. 72 rms, 2 story. S D $89-$119; each addl $10; suites $109-$149; under 16 free. Crib free. Pet accepted. TV; cable (premium), VCR avail. Complimentary continental bkfst. Ck-out 11 am. Meeting rms. Business servs avail. In-rm modem link. Sundries. Tennis privileges. Golf privileges. X-country ski 1½ mi. Health club privileges. Cr cds: A, C, D, DS, MC, V.

Hotel

★ ★ ★ **MARRIOTT.** 15 Farm Springs Rd, in Farm Springs Office Complex. 860/678-1000; FAX 860/677-8849. 381 rms, 4 story. S, D $79-$145; suites $250-$500; studio rms $145; under 18 free; wkend rates. TV; cable (premium), VCR avail. 2 pools, 1 indoor; whirlpool, poolside serv. Restaurant 6:30 am-midnight. Bar 11:30-1 am; Fri, Sat to 2 am; Sun to midnight; entertainment. Ck-out noon. Coin lndry. Convention facilities. Business center. In-rm modem link. Gift shop. 2 tennis courts. Downhill ski 15 mi. Exercise equipt. Game rm. Lawn games. Some bathrm phones. Refrigerator in some suites. Private patios, balconies. Luxury level. Cr cds: A, C, D, DS, ER, JCB, MC, V.

Inn

★ ★ ★ **BARNEY HOUSE.** 11 Mountain Spring Rd. 860/674-2796; FAX 860/677-7259. 6 rms, 3 story. S $100; D $115; each addl $10; under 6 free; wkly rates. Crib $10. TV; cable, VCR avail (movies). Heated pool. Complimentary continental bkfst. Ck-out 11 am, ck-in 3:30 pm. Luggage handling. Business servs avail. Tennis. 18-hole golf privileges, pro, putting green, driving range. Downhill ski 10 mi; x-country ski 5 mi. Health club privileges. Country estate built in 1832; many fireplaces framed with Dutch or Persian tiles. Totally nonsmoking. Cr cds: A, MC, V.

Restaurants

★ ★ **APRICOT'S.** 1593 Farmington Ave. 860/673-5405. Specializes in fresh seafood. Hrs: 11:30 am-2:30 pm, 6-10 pm; Sun 5:30-9 pm; Sun brunch 11:30 am-2:30 pm. Res required. Bar to 1 am. A la carte entrees: lunch $7-$12, dinner $15-$28. Sun brunch $7-$14.95. Child's meals. Pianist Wed-Sat. Patio dining. Converted trolley house. Cr cds: A, C, D, MC, V.

★ **STONEWELL.** 354 Colt Hwy (CT 6). 860/677-8855. Specializes in seafood, steak. Hrs: 11:30 am-3 pm, 5-9 pm; Wed, Thurs to 10 pm; Fri to 11 pm; Sat 11:30 am-11 pm; Sun 3-9 pm; Sun brunch 11 am-3 pm. Closed July 4, Dec 25. Res accepted. Bar to 1 am; Fri, Sat to 2 am.

Semi-a la carte: lunch $4.95-$11.95, dinner $6.25-$17.95. Sun brunch $12.95. Child's meals. Fri, Sat sing-along. Large stone fireplace. Informal atmosphere. Cr cds: A, D, MC, V.

★ ★ **THE WHITMAN.** 1125 Farmington Ave (CT 4). 860/678-9217. Specializes in seafood, veal. Hrs: 11:30 am-3 pm, 5-9 pm; Fri, Sat to 10 pm; Sun 5-9 pm; Sun brunch 10 am-3 pm. Closed Dec 25. Res accepted. Bar. Semi-a la carte: lunch $3.95-$9.95, dinner $11.95-$22.95. Sun brunch $16.95. Child's meals. Pianist Sun brunch; entertainment Fri. Cr cds: A, D, DS, MC, V.

Glastonbury

(see Hartford)

Greenwich (F-1)

(See also Norwalk, Stamford; also see Mt Kisco & White Plains, NY)

Settled 1640 **Pop** 58,441 **Elev** 71 ft **Area code** 203
Information Chamber of Commerce, 21 W Putnam Ave, 06830; 203/869-3500.

Greenwich (GREN-itch) is on the New York state line just 28 miles from Times Square. Behind the city's old New England facade, community leaders continue searching for ways to preserve 18th-century charm in the face of present-day economic, political and social problems.

What to See and Do

Audubon Center in Greenwich. This 485-acre sanctuary includes self-guided nature trail and 8-mi hiking trail; interpretive building with exhibits. Resident workshop for adults. (Daily exc Mon; closed hols, hol wkends) 613 Riversville Rd, 8 mi NW. Phone 203/869-5272. ¢¢

Bruce Museum. Arts and sciences museum features exhibits, lectures, concerts and educational programs. (Tues-Sat) 1 Museum Dr. Phone 203/869-0376. ¢¢

Bush-Holley House (1732). Headquarters of the Historical Society of the Town of Greenwich. Residence of a successful 18th-century farmer, it became the site of the Cos Cob art colony at the turn of the century. Exhibits include late 18th-century Connecticut furniture; paintings by Childe Hassam, Elmer Livingston MacRae, John Henry Twachtman; sculptures by John Rogers; pottery by Leon Volkmar. (Tues-Fri & Sun, afternoons; closed some major hols) S off US 1, at 39 Strickland Rd in Cos Cob. Phone 203/869-6899. ¢¢

Putnam Cottage/Knapp Tavern (ca 1690). Near this tavern, Revolutionary General Israel Putnam made a daring escape from the Redcoats in 1779; museum exhibits; rare scalloped shingles; herb garden, restored barn on grounds. (Sun, Wed & Fri; also by appt) 243 E Putnam Ave. Phone 203/869-9697. ¢

Hotel

★ ★ ★ **HYATT REGENCY.** (1800 E Putnam Ave, Old Greenwich 06870) NE via I-95 exit 5, then E on US 1. 203/637-1234; FAX 203/637-2940. Web www.travelweb.com/hyatt. 374 rms, 4 story. S $219-$275; D $254-$280; each addl $25; suites $325-$850; under 18 free; wkend rates. TV; cable (premium), VCR avail. Indoor pool; whirlpool. Restaurant 6:30 am-11 pm. Rm serv 6-1 am. Bar 11:30 am-midnight; Fri, Sat to 1 am. Ck-out noon. Convention facilities. Business center. In-rm modem link. Gift shop. Exercise equipt; sauna, steam rm. Health club privileges. 4-story atrium; skylights; garden paths & waterways. Luxury level. Cr cds: A, C, D, DS, ER, JCB, MC, V.

Inns

★ ★ **HARBOR HOUSE.** (165 Shore Rd, Old Greenwich 06870) I-95 exit 5, E on US 1, S on Sound Beach Ave, W on Shore Rd. 203/637-0145; FAX 203/698-0943. Web www.hhinn.com. 23 rms, 6 share bath, 3 story. No elvtr. S, D $99-$179. Crib free. TV; VCR (movies). Complimentary continental bkfst. Complimentary coffee in rms. Restaurant nearby. Ck-out 11 am, ck-in 2 pm. Meeting rm. Business servs avail. In-rm modem link. Health club privileges. Refrigerators. Picnic tables. Totally nonsmoking. Cr cds: A, MC, V.

★ ★ **HOMESTEAD INN.** 420 Field Point Rd (06830). 203/869-7500; FAX 203/869-7502. 23 rms. S $95-$195; D $130-$195. Children over 12 yrs only. TV; cable, VCR. Restaurant (see THOMAS HENKELMANN). Bar 11:30 am-midnight. Ck-out noon, ck-in 3 pm. Meeting rm. Business servs avail. Private patios, verandas. Wraparound porch. Built 1799; antiques. Extensive grounds. Cr cds: A, MC, V.

★ ★ **STANTON HOUSE.** 76 Maple Ave (06830). 203/869-2110; FAX 203/629-2116. 22 rms, 2 share bath, 3 story. S, D $89-$179; each addl $20. TV; cable. Pool. Complimentary continental bkfst. Ck-out 11 am, ck-in 2 pm. Business servs avail. Health club privileges. Some refrigerators. Built 1900; antiques. Totally nonsmoking. Cr cds: A, D, DS, MC, V.

Restaurants

★ ★ ★ **JEAN-LOUIS.** 61 Lewis St (06830), corner of Greenwich Ave & Lewis St, downtown. 203/622-8450. Bernadaut Limoges china and crisp, white tablecloths with lace underskirts complement extraordinary food, carefully served. French menu. Specializes in seafood, poultry. Own baking. Hrs: 6-9 pm. Closed Sun. Res accepted. Wine cellar. A la carte entrees: dinner $25-$30. Menu degùstation: dinner $68. Street parking. Jacket. Cr cds: A, C, D, MC, V.

★ ★ **TERRA RISTORANTE ITALIANO.** 156 Greenwich Ave (06830). 203/629-5222. Italian menu. Specialty: wood-fired pizza. Hrs: noon-2:30 pm, 5:30-10 pm; Fri, Sat to 10:30 pm; Sun 5:30-9:30 pm. Closed some major hols. Res accepted. Wine, beer. A la carte entrees: lunch $4-$25, dinner $13-$29. Outdoor dining. Italian villa decor; arched ceiling with original frescoes. Cr cds: A, D, MC, V.

★ ★ **THOMAS HENKELMANN.** (See Homestead Inn) 203/869-7500. Contemporary French menu. Specializes in veal, game, seafood. Own baking. Hrs: 7-9:30 am, noon-2:30 pm, 6-9:30 pm; Fri to 10 pm; Sat 8-10 am, 6-10 pm; Sun 8-10 am, 12:30-3 pm, 6-10 pm. Closed Jan 1, Labor Day. Res accepted. Bar. Wine cellar. Semi-a la carte: bkfst $10.50-$16, lunch $15-$23, dinner $26-$34. Valet parking (dinner). Porch; overlooks garden. Fireplaces. Jacket (dinner). Cr cds: A, MC, V.

★ **TUCSON CAFE.** 130 E Putnam Ave (06830), I-95 exit 4 to US 1 S. 203/661-2483. Southwestern menu. Specializes in chicken fajitas, quesadillas, innovative Southwestern dishes. Hrs: 11:30 am-3 pm, 5:30-11 pm; Fri, Sat to midnight. Closed Easter, Thanksgiving, Dec 25. Res accepted. Bar. Semi-a la carte: lunch $7.50-$13.50, dinner $8.50-$22. Sun brunch $6.50-$12. Jazz Wed. Parking. Outdoor dining. Skylight. Native American artwork. Cr cds: A, D, MC, V.

Groton (E-5)

(See also Mystic, New London, Norwich)

Settled 1705 **Pop** 9,837 **Elev** 90 ft **Area code** 860 **Zip** 06340 **E-mail** more2see@aol.com **Web** www.mysticmore.com

Information Connecticut's Mystic & More, 470 Bank St, PO Box 89, New London 06320; 860/444-2206 or 800/TO-ENJOY outside CT.

Groton is the home of a huge US naval submarine base. It is also the place where the Electric Boat Division of the General Dynamics Corp, world's largest private builder of submarines, built the first diesel-powered submarine (1912) and the first nuclear-powered submarine, *Nautilus* (1955). Pfizer Inc operates one of the largest antibiotic plants in the world and maintains a research laboratory here.

What to See and Do

Charter fishing trips. Several companies offer full- and 1/2-day saltwater fishing trips both for small and large groups. Phone 800/TO-ENJOY for details.

Ft Griswold Battlefield State Park. Includes 135-ft monument to 88 Revolutionary soldiers slain here in 1781 by British troops under the command of Benedict Arnold. Park (daily). Monument and museum (Memorial Day-Labor Day, daily; Labor Day-Columbus Day, Sat & Sun). 1 1/2 mi S of US 1 on Monument St & Park Ave. Phone 860/449-6877 or 860/445-1729. **Free.**

Oceanographic cruise. A 2 1/2-hr educational cruise on Long Island Sound aboard marine research vessels *Enviro-lab II* and *Enviro-lab III*. Opportunity to use nets and scientific instruments to explore marine environment first hand. (June-Aug) Avery Point. Phone 800/364-8472. ¢¢¢

Historic Ship *Nautilus* & **Submarine Force Museum.** Permanent home for *Nautilus*, world's first nuclear-powered submarine. Self-guided, audio tour; museum exhibits depicting history of the US Submarine Force; working periscopes; authentic submarine control rm; 4 mini-subs; minitheaters. Picnicking. (Spring-fall, daily; winter, daily exc Tues; closed Jan 1, Thanksgiving, Dec 25, also 1 wk early May & early Dec) 2 mi N on CT 12 at Crystal Lake Rd. Phone 860/694-3174 or 800/343-0079. **Free.**

Motels

✔ ★ ★ **CLARION INN.** 156 Kings Hwy. 860/446-0660; FAX 860/445-4082. 69 rms, 2 story, 34 kits. July-Oct: S, D, kit. units $76-$139; each addl $10; suites $89-$179; under 18 free; lower rates rest of yr. Crib free. TV; cable (premium). Indoor pool; whirlpool. Restaurant 6 am-10 pm; wkends from 7 am. Rm serv. Bar 11-1 am. Ck-out 11 am. Coin lndry. Meeting rms. Business servs avail. Valet serv. Barber, beauty shop. Exercise equipt; sauna. Game rm. Many refrigerators; some wet bars. Balconies. Picnic tables, grills. Cr cds: A, C, D, DS, MC, V.

★ ★ **QUALITY INN.** 404 Bridge St. 860/445-8141. 106 rms, 3 story. No elvtr. Late May-late Oct: S, D $90-$130; each addl $10; under 18 free; monthly rates; lower rates rest of yr. Crib free. TV; cable (premium). Pool. Restaurant hrs vary. Bar noon-midnight. Ck-out 11 am. Meeting rms. Business center. Exercise equipt. Refrigerators avail. Cr cds: A, C, D, DS, JCB, MC, V.

Guilford (E-3)

(See also Branford, Clinton, Madison, New Haven)

Founded 1639 **Pop** 19,848 **Elev** 20 ft **Area code** 203 **Zip** 06437
Information Destination Guilford, 115 State Square, Dept MOB; 203/453-9677.

Guilford was settled by a group of Puritans who followed Rev. Henry Whitfield here from England. One of the residents, Samuel Hill, gave rise to the expression "run like Sam Hill" when he repeatedly ran for political office.

What to See and Do

Henry Whitfield State Museum (1639). One of the oldest houses in the state and among the oldest of stone houses in New England. Restored with 17th- and 18th-century furnishings; exhibits; herb garden. Gift shop. (Wed-Sun; closed hols) 1/2 mi S on Whitfield St. Phone 203/453-2457. **¢¢**

Hyland House (1660). Restored and furnished in 17th-century period, herb garden; guided tours. (Early June-Oct, daily exc Mon) A map of historic houses in Guilford avail. 84 Boston St. Phone 203/453-9477. **¢**

Thomas Griswold House Museum (ca 1775). Fine example of a saltbox house; costumes of 1800s, changing historical exhibits, period gardens, restored working blacksmith shop. (Early June-Oct, daily exc Mon; winter by appt) 171 Boston St. Phone 203/453-3176 or 203/453-5517. **¢**

Motel

✔★ TOWER. *320 Boston Post Rd (US 1). 203/453-9069.* 14 kit. units. May-Oct: S $55; D $69; each addl $10; under 12 free; lower rates rest of yr. Crib free. TV; cable (premium). Coffee in rms. Restaurant nearby. Ck-out 11 am. Lawn games. Cr cds: A, MC, V.

🛇 🐾 **SC**

Restaurants

★ BISTRO ON THE GREEN. *25 Whitfield St. 203/458-9059.* Continental menu. Specializes in vegetarian pita, poached salmon filet, fresh seafood. Hrs: 10 am-5 pm; Tues-Fri to 10 pm; Sat 8 am-10 pm; Sun 8 am-4 pm; Sun brunch to 4 pm. Closed most major hols. Res accepted. Serv bar. A la carte entrees: bkfst $2.95-$11.95, lunch $3.75-$7.75, dinner $8.95-$18.95. Sun brunch $3.95-$8.95. Child's meals. Outdoor dining. Victorian bistro. Totally nonsmoking. Cr cds: MC, V.

✔★★ SACHEM COUNTRY HOUSE. *Goose Lane, at I-95 exit 59. 203/453-5261.* Specializes in seafood, prime rib. Hrs: 4-9 pm; Fri to 10 pm; Sat 5-10 pm; Sun 11 am-7:30 pm; Sun brunch to 2:30 pm. Res required Fri, Sat. Semi-a la carte: dinner $10.95-$14.95. Sun brunch $12.95. Child's meals. In 18th-century house; fireplace. Family-owned. Cr cds: A, MC, V.

Hartford (D-3)

(See also Avon, Farmington, Wethersfield)

Settled 1633 **Pop** 139,739 **Elev** 50 ft **Area code** 860 **E-mail** ghcvb@connix.com **Web** www.grhartfordcvb.com
Information Greater Hartford Convention & Visitors Bureau, One Civic Center Plaza, Ste 300, 06103; 860/728-6789 or 800/446-7811 (outside CT).

The capital of Connecticut and a major industrial and cultural center on the Connecticut River, Hartford is headquarters for many of the nation's insurance companies.

Roots of American democracy are deep in Hartford's history. The city was made virtually independent in 1662 by Charles II, but an attempt was made by Sir Edmund Andros, governor of New England, to seize its charter. The document was hidden by Joseph Wadsworth in a hollow tree since known as the Charter Oak. The tree was blown down in 1856; a plaque on Charter Oak Avenue marks the spot.

Hartford has what is said to be the oldest continuously published newspaper in the United States, the *Courant.* Founded in 1764, it became a daily in 1837. Trinity College (1823), the American School for the Deaf, Connecticut Institute for the Blind and the Institute of Living (for mental illness) are located in the city.

Transportation

Hartford Bradley Intl Airport: Information 860/627-3000; lost and found 860/627-3340; weather 860/936-1212; cash machines, Terminal B, Concourse A.

Car Rental Agencies: See IMPORTANT TOLL-FREE NUMBERS.

Public Transportation: Buses (Connecticut Transit), phone 860/525-9181.

Rail Passenger Service: Amtrak 800/872-7245.

What to See and Do

Bushnell Park. The 41-acre park contains 150 varieties of trees and a restored 1914 carousel (schedule varies; fee); concerts & special events (spring-fall). Downtown, between Jewell, Elm & Trinity Sts. Phone 860/246-7739. **Free.**

Butler-McCook Homestead (1782). Preserved house, occupied by 4 generations of one family (1782-1971), has possesions dating back 200 yrs; collection of Victorian toys; Japanese armor; Victorian garden. (Mid-May-mid-Oct, Tues, Thurs & Sun afternoons; closed hols) 396 Main St. Phone 860/522-1806 or 860/247-8996. **¢¢**

Center Church and Ancient Burying Ground. Church (1807) is patterned after London's St Martin-in-the-Fields, with Tiffany stained-glass windows. Cemetery contains markers dating back to 1640. Main & Gold Sts.

Connecticut Audubon Society Holland Brook Nature Center. On 38 acres adj to Connecticut River, the center features a variety of natural history exhibits including discovery rm. Nature store; many activities. (Daily exc Mon; closed most hols, Dec 25-Jan 1) 5 mi SE via CT 2 at 1361 S Main St, in Glastonbury. Phone 860/633-8402. Discovery rm **¢**

Connecticut Historical Society. Library contains more than 2 million books and manuscripts (Memorial Day-Labor Day, Tues-Fri; rest of yr, Tues-Sat; closed major hols). Museum has 9 galleries featuring permanent and changing exhibits on state history (Memorial Day-Labor Day, Tues-Fri, Sun afternoons; rest of yr, Tues-Sun afternoons; closed major hols). 1 Elizabeth St. Phone 860/236-5621. **¢¢¢**

Elizabeth Park. Public gardens feature 900 varieties of roses and more than 14,000 other plants; first municipal rose garden in country; greenhouses (all yr). Outdoor concerts in summer; ice-skating in winter. (Daily) Prospect & Asylum Aves. Phone 860/722-6490. **Free.**

Harriet Beecher Stowe House (1871). The restored Victorian cottage of the author of *Uncle Tom's Cabin* contains original furniture, memorabilia. Tours. (Tues-Sat, also Sun afternoons; also Mon June-Columbus Day & Dec) 73 Forest St. Phone 860/525-9317. ¢¢¢

Mark Twain House (1874). *Tom Sawyer, Huckleberry Finn* and other books were published while Samuel Clemens (Mark Twain) lived in this 3-story Victorian mansion featuring the decorative work of Charles Comfort Tiffany and the Associated Artists; Tiffany-glass light fixtures, windows and Tiffany-designed stencilwork in gold and silver leaf. Tours. (Tues-Sat, also Sun afternoons; also Mon June-Columbus Day & Dec) 351 Farmington Ave. Phone 860/525-9317. ¢¢¢

Noah Webster Foundation and Historical Society. This 18th-century homestead was birthplace of America's first lexicographer, writer of the *Blue-Backed Speller* (1783) and the *American Dictionary* (1828). Period furnishings, memorabilia; costumed guides; period gardens. (Daily exc Wed; closed hols) 227 S Main St in West Hartford. Phone 860/521-5362. ¢¢

Old State House (1796). Oldest state house in nation, designed by Charles Bulfinch; restored Senate chamber with Gilbert Stuart portrait of Washington; displays and rotating exhibitions. Tourist information center; museum shop. Guided tours by appt. (Daily; closed hols) 800 Main St. Phone 860/522-6766. **Free.**

Raymond E. Baldwin Museum of Connecticut History. Exhibits include Colt Collection of Firearms; Connecticut artifacts, including original 1662 Royal Charter; portraits of Connecticut's governors. Library features law, social sciences, history, genealogy collections and official state archives. (Mon-Fri; closed state hols) Connecticut State Library, 231 Capitol Ave, opp Capitol. Phone 860/566-4777. **Free.**

Science Museum of Connecticut. Computer lab; mini-zoo; physical sciences discovery rm; walk-in replica of sperm whale; hands-on aquarium; "KaleidoSight," a giant walk-in kaleidoscope; planetarium shows; changing exhibits. (Tues-Sat, also Sun afternoons, also Mon during summer; closed most major hols) 950 Trout Brook Dr in West Hartford. Phone 860/231-2824. ¢¢¢

Sightseeing tours.

Heritage Trails Sightseeing. Guided and narrated tours of Hartford. (Daily) Phone 860/677-8867. ¢¢¢¢

Hartford on Tour. One- and two-hr walking tours of various historic neighborhoods. (May-July & Sept-Oct, Sat & Sun) Phone 860/525-0279. ¢¢

Connecticut River Cruise. The *Lady Fenwick,* a reproduction of an 1850s steam yacht, makes 1-2½-hr trips on the Connecticut River. (Memorial Day-Labor Day, daily; after Labor Day-Oct, Fri-Sun) Departs from Charter Oak Landing. Phone 860/526-4954. ¢¢¢

State Capitol (1879). Guided tours (1 hr) of the restored, gold-domed capitol building and the contemporary legislative office building (Apr-Oct, daily exc Sun; rest of yr, Mon-Fri; closed hols, also Dec 25-Jan 1); includes historical displays. 210 Capitol Ave, at Trinity St. Phone 860/240-0222. **Free.**

Talcott Mt State Park. The 557-acre park features the 165-ft Heublein Tower, on mountaintop 1,000 ft above Farmington River; considered best view in state. (3rd Sat Apr-Labor Day, Thurs-Sun; after Labor Day-1st wkend Nov, daily) Picnicking, shelters. 8 mi NW via US 44, off CT 185, near Simsbury. Phone 860/677-0662.

University of Hartford (1877). (7,600 students) Independent institution on 300-acre campus. Many free concerts, operas, lectures and art exhibits. 4 mi W, at 300 Bloomfield Ave in West Hartford. Phone 860/768-4100. Located here is

Museum of American Political Life. Exhibits include life-size mannequins re-creating political marches from 1830s-1960s; 70-ft wall of historical pictures and images; political television commercials since 1952. (Tues-Sun afternoons; closed major hols) In the Harry Jack Gray Center. Phone 860/768-4090. **Free.**

★ **Wadsworth Atheneum.** One of nation's oldest continuously operating public art museums with more than 40,000 works of art, spanning 5,000 yrs; 15th-20th-century paintings, American furniture, sculpture, porcelains, English and American silver, the Amistad Collection of African-American

art; changing contemporary exhibits. (Daily exc Mon; closed hols) Free admission Thurs & Sat morning. 600 Main St. Phone 860/278-2670 or 860/278-2670 (recording). ¢¢¢

Annual Events

Taste of Hartford. Main St, downtown. Four-day event features specialties of more than 50 area restaurants; continuous entertainment. Phone 860/728-3089. Mid-June.

Riverfest. Celebration of America's independence and the Connecticut River. Family entertainment, concerts, food, fireworks display over river. Phone 860/293-0131. Early July.

Mark Twain Days. Celebration of Twain's legacy and Hartford's cultural heritage with more than 100 events. Concerts, riverboat rides, medieval jousting, tours of Twain House, entertainment. Phone 860/247-0998. Wkend mid-July.

Christmas Crafts Expo I & II. Hartford Civic Center. Exhibits and demonstrations of traditional and contemporary craft media. Phone 860/693-6335. 1st & 2nd wkends Dec.

City Neighborhoods

Many of the restaurants, unrated dining establishments and some lodgings listed under Hartford include neighborhoods as well as exact street addresses. Geographic descriptions of these areas are given, followed by a table of restaurants arranged by neighborhood.

Civic Center District: South of Church St, west of Main St, north of Elm St and east of Union Place.

Franklin Ave Area: South of Southern Downtown; along Franklin Ave between Maple Ave on the north and Victoria Rd on the south.

Southern Downtown: Area east and south of Civic Center District; south of State St, west of Prospect St and Charter Oak Place and north of Wyllys St.

HARTFORD RESTAURANTS BY NEIGHBORHOOD AREAS

(For full description, see alphabetical listings under Restaurants)

CIVIC CENTER DISTRICT
Gaetano's. 1 Civic Center Plaza
Hot Tomatoes. 1 Union Place

FRANKLIN AVE AREA
Carbone's Ristorante. 588 Franklin Ave

SOUTHERN DOWNTOWN
Max Downtown. 205 Main St
Peppercorn's Grill. 357 Main St

Note: When a listing is located in a town that does not have its own city heading, it will appear under the city nearest to its location. In these cases, the address and town appear in parenthesis immediately following the name of the establishment.

Motor Hotels

★ ★ **HOLIDAY INN.** *363 Roberts St (06108), I-84, exit 58, east of downtown.* 860/528-9611; FAX 860/289-0270. 130 rms, 5 story. S, D $65-$85; under 18 free; wkend rates. Crib free. Pet accepted. TV; cable (premium). Indoor pool. Complimentary coffee in rms. Restaurant 6 am-10 pm. Rm serv. Bar 4 pm-midnight. Ck-out noon. Coin lndry. Meeting rms. Business servs avail. In-rm modem link. Valet serv. Exercise equipt. Some refrigerators. Cr cds: A, C, D, DS, ER, JCB, MC, V.

D ⊱ ≈ ✈ ⚓ ➷ SC

★ ★ **RAMADA INN.** *(100 East River Dr, East Hartford 06108) S via I-91 exit 3 to Pitkin, I-84 exit 53.* 860/528-9703; FAX 860/289-4728. 199 rms, 8 story. S $59-$119; D $65-$129; each addl $10; suites $150-$200; under 18 free; wkend rates. Crib free. Pet accepted. TV; cable (premium). Indoor pool. Playground. Restaurant 6:30 am-2 pm, 5-10 pm. Rm serv. Bar. Ck-out 11 am. Coin lndry. Meeting rms. Business servs avail. In-rm modem link. Valet serv. Health club privileges. Cr cds: A, C, D, DS, ER, JCB, MC, V.

D ✍ ✈ ≋ ⊠ 🔥 SC

Hotels

★ ★ ★ **THE GOODWIN.** *One Haynes St (06103), opp Hartford Civic Center at Goodwin Square.* 860/246-7500; FAX 860/247-4576; res: 800/922-5006. 124 rms, 6 story. D $131-$163; suites $228-$786; children free; wkend rates & packages. Crib free. Garage, valet parking $13. TV; cable (premium), VCR avail. Restaurant 6:30 am-10:30 pm. Rm serv 6 am-midnight. Bar 11-1 am. Ck-out noon. Meeting rms. Business servs avail. In-rm modem link. Concierge. Exercise equipt. Bathrm phones; some fireplaces. Refrigerators avail. Small, European-style luxury hotel in red-brick, Queen Anne-style building (1881) built for J.P. Morgan; 19th-century paintings and replicas of sailing ships. Cr cds: A, C, D, DS, JCB, MC, V.

D ✈ ≋ 🔥 SC

★ ★ **HOLIDAY INN-DOWNTOWN.** *50 Morgan St (06120), at jct I-84 exit 52 & I-91 exit 32, in Civic Center District.* 860/549-2400; FAX 860/527-2746. 342 rms, 18 story. S $79.95-$119.95; D $89.95-$129.95; each addl $10; suites $225; under 18 free; wkend rates. Crib free. Pet accepted. TV; cable (premium), VCR avail. Pool; poolside serv. Restaurant 6:30 am-10 pm. Bar 4 pm-2 am. Ck-out noon. Convention facilities. Business center. In-rm modem link. Free airport transportation. Exercise equipt. Cr cds: A, C, D, DS, JCB, MC, V.

D ✍ ≋ ✈ ⊠ 🔥 SC ⚒

★ **RAMADA INN-CAPITOL HILL.** *440 Asylum St (06103), opp State Capitol Building, in Civic Center District.* 860/246-6591; FAX 860/728-1382. 96 rms, 9 story. S $49-$65; D $55-$65; each addl $10. Crib free. Pet accepted, some restrictions. TV; cable (premium). Ck-out noon. Business servs avail. Free valet parking. Cr cds: A, C, D, DS, MC, V.

D ✍ ≋ 🔥 SC

★ ★ ★ **SHERATON.** *315 Trumbull St (06103), at Civic Center Plaza.* 860/728-5151; FAX 860/240-7247. E-mail dan_riss@ihsheraton.com; web www.hartforddowntown.com/sheraton.html. 388 rms, 22 story. S, D $120; each addl $15; suites $250-$600; under 17 free; wkend, hol rates. Crib free. Garage parking $10. TV; cable (premium), VCR avail. Indoor pool; whirlpool. Coffee in rms. Restaurant 6:30 am-11 pm. Bar. Ck-out noon. Convention facilities. Business servs avail. In-rm modem link. Exercise equipt; sauna. Civic Center Plaza adj; shops. Cr cds: A, C, D, DS, ER, JCB, MC, V.

D ≋ ✈ ⊠ 🔥 SC

Restaurants

✔★ ★ **BUTTERFLY.** *(831 Farmington Ave, West Hartford 06119) W on Farmington Ave.* 860/236-2816. Chinese menu. Specializes in Szechwan cuisine. Hrs: 11:30 am-10 pm; Fri, Sat to 11 pm; Sun brunch to 4 pm. Closed Thanksgiving. Res accepted. Bar. A la carte entrees: lunch $5.50-$6.95, dinner $5.95-$14.95. Sun brunch $12.95. Parking. Contemporary decor. Cr cds: A, D, DS, MC, V.

D �«

★ ★ ★ **CARBONE'S RISTORANTE.** *588 Franklin Ave (06114), in Franklin Ave Area.* 860/296-9646. Italian menu. Specialties: fettucine carbonara, vitello cuscinetto. Own baking, desserts. Hrs: 11:30 am-2 pm, 5-9:30 pm; Sat from 5 pm. Closed Sun; major hols. Res accepted. Bar. Semi-a la carte: lunch $8-$11, dinner $12-$20. Parking. Tableside preparation. Family-owned. Cr cds: A, D, MC, V.

D ➺ ♥

★ ★ **GAETANO'S.** *1 Civic Center Plaza, in Civic Center District.* 860/249-1629. Northern Italian menu. Specializes in veal, chicken, pasta. Own baking. Hrs: 11:30 am-2 pm, 5-10 pm. Closed Sun; major hols. Res

accepted. Bar. Wine cellar. A la carte entrees: lunch $7.95-$11.25, dinner $12-$20. Parking. Tableside preparation. Cr cds: A, D, MC, V.

D ➺

★ **HOT TOMATOES.** *1 Union Place, in Civic Center District.* 860/249-5100. Italian menu. Specializes in pasta, veal. Hrs: 11:30 am-2:30 pm, 5:30-9:30 pm; Fri, Sat to 10:30 pm; Sun, Mon 5:30-9 pm. Res accepted. Bar. A la carte entrees: lunch $6.95-$8.95, dinner $8.95-$18.95. Outdoor dining. Cr cds: A, C, D, MC, V.

D

★ ★ **MAX DOWNTOWN.** *205 Main St, in Southern Downtown.* 860/522-2530. Specializes in black Angus beef, stone pies. Hrs: 11:30 am-2:30 pm, 5-10 pm; Fri to 11 pm; Sat 5-11 pm; Sun 5-9 pm. Closed most major hols. Res accepted. Bar. A la carte entrees: lunch $6.95-$9.95, dinner $9.95-$23. Child's meals. Intimate bistro atmosphere. Cr cds: A, D, MC, V.

D ➺

★ ★ **PEPPERCORN'S GRILL.** *357 Main St (06106), in Southern Downtown.* 860/547-1714. Italian menu. Specialties: orange ravioli, veal chops, osso bucco. Hrs: 11:30 am-2:30 pm, 5-10 pm; Thurs to 10:30 pm; Fri to 11:30 pm; Sat 5-11:30 pm. Closed Sun; major hols. Res accepted. Bar. A la carte entrees: lunch $6.95-$16.95, dinner $16.95-$45. Child's meals. Parking. Contemporary bistro atmosphere. Cr cds: A, D, MC, V.

D

Kent (D-1)

(See also Cornwall Bridge, New Preston)

Pop 2,918 **Elev** 395 ft **Area code** 860 **Zip** 06757
Information Litchfield Hills Travel Council, PO Box 968, Litchfield 06759; 860/567-4506.

Kent, a small community near the western border of Connecticut, has become an art and antique center. Home to a large art colony, the surrounding area is characterized by massive hills that overlook the plain of the Housatonic River. The village of Kent was incorporated in 1738, after the tract of land was sold in a public auction. Although early development was based on agriculture, by the middle of the 19th century Kent was a booming industrial village with three iron furnaces operating in the area.

What to See and Do

Kent Falls State Park. This 295-acre park is beautiful in spring when the stream is high and in fall when leaves are changing; 200-ft cascading waterfall. Stream fishing. Hiking. Picnicking. Standard fees. (Daily) 5 mi N on US 7. Phone 860/927-4100 or 860/927-3238.

Macedonia Brook State Park. These 2,300 acres provide one of the state's finest nature study areas, as well as views of the Catskills and Taconic mountains. Trout-stocked stream fishing. Hiking. Picnicking. Camping (late Apr-Sept) on 84 sites in open and wooded settings. Standard fees. (Daily) 2 mi E on CT 341, N on Macedonia Brook Rd. Phone 860/927-4100 or 860/927-3238. **Free.**

Sloane-Stanley Museum and Kent Furnace. New England barn houses Eric Sloane's collection of early American tools, re-creation of his studio, artifacts, works; on site of old Kent furnace (1826); video presentation. (Mid-May-Oct, Wed-Sun) 1 mi N on US 7. Phone 860/927-3849 or 860/566-3005. ¢¢

Annual Event

Fall Festival. 1 mi N on US 7, on grounds of the Connecticut Antique Machinery Museum. Exhibits include steam and traction engines, road roller (ca 1910), windmill; threshers; broom making, shingle sawing; antique cars, steamboats, tractors and trucks. Phone 860/927-0050. Late Sept.

Inn

★ ★ **FIFE 'N DRUM.** *Rte 7, on Main St.* 860/927-3509; *FAX 860/927-4595.* 8 rms. Apr-Oct: D $95-$110; each addl $12.50; lower rates rest of yr. TV. Complimentary coffee. Restaurant (see FIFE 'N DRUM). Rm serv. Bar 11:30 am-11 pm; wkends to midnight; entertainment. Ck-out 11 am, ck-in 2 pm. Gift shop. Downhill/x-country ski 11 mi. Balconies. Cr cds: A, MC, V.

Restaurant

★ ★ ★ **FIFE 'N DRUM.** *(See Fife 'n Drum Inn)* 860/927-3509. Continental menu. Specialties: roast duckling, filet mignon au poivre, sweetbreads. Own baking. Hrs: 11:30 am-3 pm, 5:30-9:30 pm; Fri to 10 pm, Sat to 10:30 pm; Sun brunch to 3 pm. Closed Tues; Dec 25. Res accepted. Bar; Fri, Sat to midnight. Wine cellar. Semi-a la carte: lunch $4.50-$7.95, dinner $8.95-$24.50. Sun brunch $15.95. Child's meals. Entertainment. Cr cds: A, MC, V.

Lakeville (C-1)

(See also Cornwall Bridge, Norfolk)

Settled 1740 **Pop** 1,800 (est) **Elev** 764 ft **Area code** 860 **Zip** 06039
Information Litchfield Hills Travel Council, PO Box 968, Litchfield 06759; 860/567-4506.

Lakeville, located on Lake Wononscopomuc in the Litchfield Hills area, developed around a major blast furnace once owned by Ethan Allen. The furnace and nearby metals foundry cast many of the weapons used in the Revolutionary War as well as the guns for the USS *Constellation.* When the furnace was torn down in 1843, the first knife manufacturing facility was erected there. Nearby is the famous Hotchkiss School, a coed prep school.

What to See and Do

Holley House. Museums of 18th and 19th-century history include 1768 iron-master's home with 1808 Classical-revival wing; Holley Mfg Co pocketknife exhibit from 1876; hands-on 1870s kitchen exhibit illustrating the debate over women's roles. 1876 Living History Tours (4 tours daily). (Mid-June-mid-Oct, Sat, Sun & hol afternoons; also by appt) Main St at Millerton Rd. Phone 860/435-2878. Tours ¢¢ Also here is

Salisbury Cannon Museum. Hands-on exhibits illustrate contributions of local iron industry to American Revolution. Includes ice house, cutting tools, outhouse, 19th-century heritage gardens and Nature’s Medicine Cabinet exhibit. Same hrs as Holley House. **Free.**

Annual Event

Grand Prix at Lime Rock. Phone 800/RACE-LRP. Memorial Day wkend.

Seasonal Events

Sports car racing. Lime Rock Park, 2 mi S on CT 41, then 4 mi E on CT 112, at jct US 7. Sat & Mon hols. Phone 800/RACE-LRP.

Music Mountain Summer Music Festival. On Music Mt, 5 mi NE via US 44, 3 mi S on CT 126 to Falls Village, then 2½ mi E on CT 126 to top of Music Mt Rd. Performances by known ensembles and guest artists; also jazz series. Sat, Sun. Phone 860/824-7126 (box office). Mid-June-early Sept.

Motels

✔ ★ ★ **INN AT IRON MASTERS.** *229 Main St, on US 44, ½ mi W of CT 41.* 860/435-9844; *FAX 860/435-2254.* Web www.innatironmasters.com. 28 rms. Apr-Nov: S $85-$125; D $95-$135; each addl $15; under 15 free; lower rates rest of yr. Crib free. Pet accepted, some restrictions. TV; cable. Heated pool. Continental bkfst. Coffee in rms. Restaurant 11 am-9 pm; Thurs-Sat to 10 pm. Bar. Ck-out 11 am. Cr cds: A, MC, V.

★ **SHARON MOTOR LODGE.** *(CT 41, Sharon 06069)* 7 mi S on CT 41. 860/364-0036; *FAX 860/364-0462.* 22 rms. May-Oct: S, D $69-$125; lower rates rest of yr. Crib $10. TV; cable. Pool. Restaurant opp 7:30 am-10:30 pm. Ck-out 11 am. Business servs avail. Downhill/x-country ski 10 mi. Cr cds: A, DS, MC, V.

Inns

★ ★ **RAGAMONT INN.** *(10 Main St, Salisbury 06068)* 1 mi N on US 44, at jct CT 41. 860/435-2372. 10 rms, 2 story. 7 rms with A/C. No rm phones. S $60-$95; D $70-$105; each addl $10; under 5 free. Closed Nov-May. TV in some rms; cable. Restaurant (see RAGAMONT INN). Ck-out 11 am, ck-in 2 pm. Built in 1830; country inn atmosphere with antiques. No cr cds accepted.

★ ★ **WAKE ROBIN.** *104 Sharon Rd (Rt 41), ¼ mi S on CT 41.* 860/435-2515; *FAX 860/435-2000.* E-mail info@wake-robin-inn.com; web www.wake-robin-inn.com. 39 rms, 2 story. Apr-Nov: S, D $95-$250; each addl $10; lower rates rest of yr. Crib free. Pet accepted. TV; cable (premium). Ck-out noon, ck-in 2 pm. Former girls school (1896); antiques. Library, sitting rm. On hill. Cr cds: A, MC, V.

Resort

★ ★ ★ **INTERLAKEN INN.** *74 Interlaken Rd, 2½ mi SW on CT 112.* 860/435-9878; *FAX 860/435-2980.* E-mail intrlakn@licom. 80 rms, 2 story. May-Oct: S, D $99-$165; each addl $15; suites $265; higher rates special events; lower rates rest of yr. Crib $10. Pet accepted. TV; cable (premium), VCR (movies). Heated pool. Restaurant 7 am-9 pm; Fri, Sat to 10 pm. Rm serv. Ck-out noon, ck-in 3 pm. Meeting rms. Business servs avail. In-rm modem link. Valet serv. Tennis. 9-hole golf, pro. Rowboats, canoes, sailboats, paddleboats. Lawn games. Rec rm. Exercise equipt; sauna. Refrigerator avail. Balconies. Cr cds: A, MC, V.

Restaurant

★ ★ ★ **RAGAMONT INN.** *(See Ragamont Inn)* 860/435-2372. European menu. Specializes in Swiss dishes, fresh fish in season, veal dishes. Own baking. Hrs: 5:30-9 pm; Fri to 10 pm; Sat 6-10 pm; Sun 11:30 am-2 pm, 5-9 pm. Closed Mon, Tues; also Nov-May. Res accepted. Bar. Semi-a la carte: dinner $16-$22. Child's meals. Parking. Covered patio dining. Early Amer decor in 1830 inn; fireplaces. Family-owned. No cr cds accepted.

Litchfield (D-2)

(See also Bristol, Cornwall Bridge)

Settled 1720 **Pop** 8,365 **Elev** 1,085 ft **Area code** 860 **Zip** 06759
InformationLitchfield Travel Council, PO Box 968; 860/567-4506.

Litchfield has preserved a semblance of the 18th century through both its many early houses and its air of peace and quiet. Because the railroads laid their main lines below in the valley, industry largely bypassed Litchfield. The Rev. Henry Ward Beecher and his sister, Harriet Beecher Stowe, author of *Uncle Tom's Cabin*, grew up in Litchfield. Tapping Reeve established the first law school in the country here in the late 18th century.

What to See and Do

Haight Vineyard and Winery. First Connecticut winery; one of the few to grow vinifera grapes in New England. Tours, tastings; vineyard walk, picnic tables; gift shop. (Daily; closed some major hols) Chestnut Hill Rd. Phone 860/567-4045. **Free.**

Litchfield Historical Society Museum. Exhibits include American fine and decorative arts and county historical displays; research library, changing exhibits, video presentation. (Apr-mid-Nov, daily exc Mon; closed major hols) On the Green, at jct East & South Sts. Phone 860/567-4501. **¢**

Tapping Reeve House (1773) **and Law School** (1784). Period furnishings in house used as America's first law school; graduates included Aaron Burr and John C. Calhoun; garden. (June-mid-Oct, daily exc Mon; closed July 4, Labor Day) South St. Phone 860/567-4501. **¢**

Topsmead State Forest. This 511-acre forest includes an English-Tudor mansion overlooking a 40-acre wildlife preserve. Tours of mansion (June-Oct, phone for schedule). Nature trail, hiking. Picnicking. 1 mi E, off CT 118, E Litchfield Rd to Buell Rd. Phone 860/567-5694 or 860/485-0226. **Free.**

White Memorial Foundation, Inc. The 4,000-acre conservation area is contiguous with part of Bantam Lake shoreline (largest natural lake in the state), the Bantam River and several small streams and ponds. Rolling woodland has wide variety of trees, flowers, ferns, mosses, 35 mi of trails; woodland birds, both nesting and in migration; and other woodland animals. The Conservation Center has displays and exhibits, extensive nature library with children's rm (daily; fee). Swimming; fishing, boating. Hiking trails, including "trail of the senses." Cross-country skiing. Camping. 2½ mi W on US 202. For schedule and fee information, phone 860/567-0857.

Annual Event

Open House Tour. Tour of Litchfield's historic homes, special exhibits, tea & luncheon. Phone 860/567-9423. Early July.

Inns

★★ **LITCHFIELD INN.** *US 202. 860/567-4503; FAX 860/567-5358; res: 800/499-3444.* 32 rms, 2 story. Apr-Oct: S $90-$100; D $100-$150; each addl $10; under 12 free; lower rates rest of yr. Crib free. TV; cable (premium), VCR. Complimentary continental bkfst. Restaurant 6:30-10 am, noon-3 pm, 5:30-9 pm. Rm serv. Bar noon-closing. Ck-out noon. Meeting rms. Business servs avail. In-rm modem link. Downhill ski 20 mi; x-country ski 5 mi. Game rm. Lawn games. Some refrigerators. Picnic tables. Country inn with theme rms such as "The Lace Room" and "The Presidential Quarters." Cr cds: A, MC, V.

★★ **TOLLGATE HILL.** *Rte 202, Box 1339, at Tollgate Rd, 2½ mi NE of the Green on US 202. 860/567-4545; FAX 860/563-8397; res: 800/445-3903.* 20 rms. Mid-May-Dec: S, D $110-$175; each addl $15; lower rates rest of yr. Pet accepted. TV; cable (premium). Complimentary continental bkfst. Restaurant (see TOLLGATE HILL). Rm serv. Bar; enter-

tainment Sat, Sun. Ck-out 11 am. Business servs avail. Airport transportation. Some fireplaces. Restored historic mansion (1745) originally a way station for travelers, relocated to present site. 18th-century paneled walls, corner cupboards, antique furniture, fireplace. Re-creation of colonial ballroom with fiddler's loft. Cr cds: A, D, DS, MC, V.

Restaurants

★★ **GRAPPA.** *26 Commons Dr. 860/567-1616.* Italian Mediterranean menu. Specializes in free-range chicken, salmon, gourmet pizzas. Hrs: 5-10 pm; Fri to 11 pm; Sat, Sun noon-11 pm. Closed Mon; Jan 1. Bar. Semi-a la carte: lunch, dinner $9.95-$15. Child's meals. Parking. Outdoor dining. Festive atmosphere; mirrors line walls of one dining rm. Totally nonsmoking. No cr cds accepted.

D

★★★ **TOLLGATE HILL.** *(See Tollgate Hill Inn) 860/567-4545.* Specializes in fresh fish, shellfish pie, seasonal foods. Hrs: noon-3 pm, 5:30-9:30 pm; Fri, Sat to 10:30 pm; Sun brunch noon-3 pm. Closed Tues Jan-June. Res accepted. Bar to midnight. Wine cellar. Semi-a la carte: lunch $7-$11, dinner $18-$23. Entertainment Sat. Outdoor dining. A historic way station (1745). Early Amer decor; fireplaces. Cr cds: A, D, DS, MC, V.

D

★★ **THE VILLAGE.** *25 West St, on the Green. 860/567-8307.* Continental menu. Specializes in fresh seafood, steak. Hrs: 11:30 am-9 pm; Fri, Sat to 10 pm; Sun brunch 11:30 am-3:30 pm. Closed Dec 25. Res accepted. Bar. A la carte entrees: lunch $6-$10, dinner $12-$20. Sun brunch $8-$12. Child's meals. Overlooks village green. Cr cds: A, MC, V.

★★★ **WEST STREET GRILL.** *43 West St. 860/567-3885.* Contemporary Amer menu. Hrs: 11:30 am-3 pm, 5:30-9 pm; wkends 11:30 am-4 pm, 5:30-10 pm. Closed Dec 25. Res accepted; required Fri, Sat. Bar. Wine cellar. A la carte entrees: lunch $4.95-$14.95, dinner $6.95-$25.95. Child's meals. Contemporary black & white decor. Cr cds: A, MC, V.

D

Madison (E-3)

(See also Branford, Clinton, Guilford, New Haven)

Settled 1649 **Pop** 15,485 **Elev** 22 ft **Area code** 203 **Zip** 06443 **E-mail** Chamber@MadisonCT.com **Web** MadisonCT.com

Information Chamber of Commerce, 22 Scotland Ave, PO Box 706, phone 203/245-7394; also the Tourism Office, 22 School St, phone 203/245-5659.

What to See and Do

Allis-Bushnell House and Museum (ca 1785). Period rms with four-corner fireplaces; doctor's office and equipment; exhibits of costumes, dolls, household implements; original paneling; herb garden. (Early June-Labor Day, Wed, Fri & Sat, limited hrs; other times by appt) 853 Boston Post Rd. Phone 203/245-4567. **Donation.**

Deacon John Grave House. Frame garrison colonial house (1685). (Memorial Day-Labor Day, daily exc Mon; spring & fall, wkends only) Academy & School Sts. Phone 203/245-4798. **Donation.**

Hammonasset Beach State Park. More than 900 acres with 2-mi beach on Long Island Sound. Saltwater swimming, scuba diving; fishing; boating. Hiking. Picnicking (shelters). Camping. Nature Center. Standard fees. 1 mi S of I-95 exit 62. Phone 203/245-1817.

Motel

★ ★ **MADISON BEACH HOTEL.** *944 W Wharf Rd.* 203/245-1404; FAX 203/245-0410. 35 rms, 4 story. No elvtr. May-Oct: S $85-$125; D $95-$140; each addl $10; suites $150-$225; under 18 free; wkly rates; lower rates Mar-mid-May, Oct-Dec. Closed Jan-Feb. TV; cable (premium). Complimentary continental bkfst. Restaurant 11:30 am-3 pm, 5:30-10 pm. Bar to 1 am; entertainment Fri, Sat. Ck-out 11 am. Meeting rms. Business servs avail. Lawn games. Some refrigerators. Many balconies. On ocean. Cr cds: A, D, DS, MC, V.

D ⚑ 🔥 SC

Restaurants

★ ★ ★ **CAFE ALLEGRA.** *725 Boston Post Rd.* 203/245-7773. Continental menu. Specializes in regional and international dishes. Hrs: 11:30 am-10 pm; Sun brunch to 4 pm. Closed Jan 1, Dec 25. Res accepted. Bar. Wine cellar. A la carte entrees: lunch $5.95-$9.95, dinner $13.95-$21.95. Sun brunch $14.95. Child's meals. Pianist, harpist Sun. Outdoor dining. Garden atmosphere; 3 dining rms. Cr cds: A, D, DS, MC, V.

D

✔ ★ ★ **FRIENDS & COMPANY.** *11 Boston Post Rd.* 203/245-0462. Specializes in fresh seafood, steak, seasonal dishes. Own baking, desserts. Hrs: noon-2:30 pm, 5-10 pm; Fri to 11 pm; Sat 5-11 pm; Sun 4:30-9 pm; early-bird dinner Sun-Fri 5-6 pm; Sun brunch 11 am-2:30 pm. Closed Thanksgiving, Dec 25; also last Mon June. Bar. Semi-a la carte: lunch $5.75-$8.95, dinner $5.75-$15.50. Sun brunch $5.75-$8.75. Child's meals. Totally nonsmoking. Cr cds: A, DS, MC, V.

D

Manchester (D-4)

(See also Hartford, Storrs, Windsor)

Settled 1672 **Pop** 51,618 **Elev** 272 ft **Area code** 860 **Zip** 06040 **E-mail** ctfuntour@aol.com **Web** www.travelfile.com/get/ghtd
Information Greater Hartford Tourism District, 234 Murphy Rd, Hartford 06114; 860/244-8181 or 800/793-4480.

The "city of village charm" has the peaceful air of another era, with great trees and 18th-century houses. Manchester, once the silk capital of the western world, is still a major manufacturing center with more than 100 industries—many more than a century old.

What to See and Do

Cheney Homestead (ca 1780). Birthplace of the brothers that launched the state's once-promising silk industry; built by Timothy Cheney, clockmaker. Paintings and etchings, early 19th-century furniture; replica of schoolhouse. (Limited hrs) 106 Hartford Rd. Phone 860/643-5588. ¢

Connecticut Firemen's Historical Society Fire Museum. Located in 1901 firehouse, this museum exhibits antique fire fighting equipment and memorabilia; leather fire buckets, hoses and helmets, hand-pulled engines, horse-drawn hose wagon, old prints and lithographs. (Mid-Apr-mid-Nov, Fri-Sun) 230 Pine St. Phone 860/649-9436. **Donation.**

Lutz Children's Museum. Houses participatory exhibits on natural and physical science, art, ethnology and history; live animal exhibit; outdoor "playscape" area. (Daily exc Mon; closed hols) 247 S Main St. Phone 860/643-0949. ¢¢

Oak Grove Nature Center. More than 50 acres of woods, fields, stream, pond; trails. (Daily) Oak Grove St. Phone 860/647-3321. **Free.**

Wickham Park. More than 200 acres with gardens, including Oriental, woods, ponds; log cabin (refreshments wkends); playgrounds, picnic areas; aviary and small zoo; tennis courts, softball fields (Apr-Oct, daily).

1329 W Middle Tpke, entrance on US 44, off I-84 exit 60. Phone 860/528-0856. Parking fee ¢

Motels

★ ★ **CLARION SUITES INN.** *191 Spencer St.* 860/643-5811; FAX 860/643-5811. 104 kit. suites, 2 story. S, D $99-$139; under 16 free; wkend rates. Crib free. Pet accepted; $250 refundable & $10/day. TV; cable, VCR. Heated pool; whirlpool. Complimentary full bkfst. Complimentary coffee in rms. Restaurant adj 6:30 am-midnight. Ck-out noon. Coin lndry. Meeting rms. Business servs avail. Sundries. Gift shop. Grocery store. Drug store. Valet serv. Free airport, RR station transportation. Downhill/x-country ski 20 mi. Exercise equipt. Lawn games. Balconies. Cr cds: A, C, D, DS, ER, MC, V.

D ✔ ≍ ⊼ 🏊 ⏃ 🗶 🔥 SC

★ ★ **CONNECTICUT MOTOR LODGE.** *400 Tolland Tpke, at I-84 exit 63.* 860/643-1555; FAX 860/643-1881. 31 rms. S $40-$45; D $55-$65; each addl $5. Crib $5. TV; cable. Restaurant adj 7 am-11 pm. Ck-out 11 am. Cr cds: A, C, D, DS, JCB, MC, V.

🗶 🗶 🔥 SC

★ **MANCHESTER VILLAGE MOTOR INN.** *100 E Center St.* 860/646-2300; FAX 860/649-6499; res: 800/487-6499. 44 rms, 2 story. S $39.95-$49.50; D $49.50-$57.50; each addl $5; under 18 free. Crib free. Pet accepted. TV; cable (premium), VCR (movies). Complimentary coffee in lobby. Restaurant opp 6:30 am-9 pm. Ck-out 11 am. Business servs avail. Sundries. Balconies. Picnic tables. Cr cds: A, C, D, DS, MC, V.

✔ 🗶 🔥 SC

Restaurants

★ ★ ★ **CAVEY'S FRENCH RESTAURANT.** *45 E Center St.* 860/643-2751. French menu. Own baking. Hrs: 6-10 pm. Closed Sun, Mon; major hols. Res accepted; required Sat. Bar. Wine cellar. A la carte entrees: dinner $19-$27. Prix fixe: dinner from $55. Parts of building from old mansions. Cr cds: A, MC, V.

★ ★ ★ **CAVEY'S ITALIAN RESTAURANT.** *45 E Center St.* 860/643-2751. Northern Italian menu. Hrs: 11:30 am-2:30 pm, 5:30-9:30 pm; Fri to 10 pm; Sat noon-2:30 pm, 5:30-10 pm. Closed Sun, Mon; major hols. Res accepted; required Sat. Bar. A la carte entrees: lunch $8-$12, dinner $13-$19. Entertainment Fri, Sat. Country Mediterranean decor. Family-owned since 1933. Cr cds: A, MC, V.

D

Meriden (E-3)

(See also Hartford, Middletown, New Haven)

Settled 1661 **Pop** 59,479 **Elev** 144 ft **Area code** 203 **Zip** 06450 **Web** www.mayormeriden.com
Information City Hall, Mayor's Office, 142 E Main St; 203/630-4000.

Located in the heart of the central Connecticut Valley, Meriden was named after Meriden Farm, Warwickshire, England. Once called the "silver city of the world" because its principal business was the manufacture of silver products, Meriden now has a broad industrial base.

What to See and Do

Castle Craig Tower. Road leads to tower atop East Peak, site of Easter sunrise services. (May-Oct) In Hubbard Park, 2 mi W on I-691/CT 66.

Mt Southington Ski Area. Triple, double chairlifts, 3 T-bars, J-bar; snowmaking, patrol, school, rentals; cafeteria, lounge. 12 trails; longest run approx 1 mi; vertical drop 425 ft. Night skiing. (Dec-Mar, daily) Approx 10 mi W; 1/2 mi W of I-84 exit 30, at Mt Vernon Rd in Southington. Phone 203/628-0954 or 800/982-6828 (CT) for snow conditions. ¢¢¢¢¢

Solomon Goffe House (1711). Gambrel-roofed house features period furnishings, artifacts. Costumed guides. (July-Aug, Sat & Sun; rest of yr, 1st Sun of month) 677 N Colony St. Phone 203/634-9088. ¢

Annual Events

Daffodil Festival. Hubbard Park, W Main St. Approx 500,000 daffodils in bloom; various events. Mid-Apr.

Apple Harvest Festival. 3 mi S on CT 120, in Southington, on Town Green. Street festival celebrating local apple harvest. Carnival, arts & crafts, parade, road race, food booths, entertainment. Phone 860/628-8036. 7 days early Oct.

Motels

★ **HAMPTON INN.** *10 Bee St, I-91 N exit 16, I-91 S exit 17.* 203/235-5154; FAX 203/235-7139. 125 rms, 4 story. S, D $75-$85; under 18 free; wkend rates. Crib free. TV; cable (premium). Complimentary continental bkfst. Coffee in rms. Restaurant nearby. Ck-out noon. Meeting rms. Business servs avail. In-rm modem link. Cr cds: A, C, D, DS, MC, V.

D ◨ ⚓ SC

✔★ ★ **HOLIDAY INN EXPRESS.** *(120 Laning St, Southington 06489)* 6 mi N on CT 10 to Laning St, 2 blks N of I-84 exit 32. 860/276-0736; FAX 860/276-9405. 122 rms, 3 story. May-Oct: S $59-$69; D $64-$74; each addl $6; under 18 free; lower rates rest of yr. Crib free. TV; cable, VCR avail. Pool. Complimentary continental bkfst. Restaurant adj 11:30 am-10 pm. Ck-out 11 am. Meeting rms. Business servs avail. In-rm modem link. Valet serv. Downhill ski 5 mi. Exercise equipt. Some refrigerators. Cr cds: A, C, D, DS, ER, JCB, MC, V.

D ≋ ⚓ ✕ ⊠ ⚒ SC

Motor Hotel

★ ★ ★ **RAMADA.** *275 Research Pkwy.* 203/238-2380; FAX 203/238-3172. 150 rms, 6 story. S $69-$149; D $79-$159; each addl (after 3rd person) $10; suites $150-$200; under 18 free; wkend rates; higher rates college graduation. Crib free. TV; cable (premium), VCR avail. Indoor pool; poolside serv. Complimentary coffee in rms. Restaurant 6:30 am-10 pm. Rm serv. Bar 11-1 am; entertainment. Ck-out noon. Coin lndry. Meeting rms. Business center. Bellhops. Valet serv. Free RR station transportation. Downhill ski 10 mi. Exercise equipt; sauna. Refrigerator, wet bar in suites. Cr cds: A, C, D, DS, JCB, MC, V.

D ✕ ≋ ✕ ⊠ ⚒ SC ⚞

Restaurant

✔★ ★ **BRANNIGAN'S.** *(176 Laning St, Southington 06489)* S on CT 10. 860/621-9311. Specializes in barbecue ribs, seafood. Hrs: 11:30 am-midnight; Sun brunch 11 am-2:30 pm. Closed Memorial Day, Dec 25. Res accepted. Bar. Semi-a la carte: lunch $4.95-$8.95, dinner $4.95-$15.95. Sun brunch $10.95. Child's meals. Cr cds: A, D, MC, V.

D ⊠

Middletown (E-3)

(See also Hartford, Meriden)

Settled 1650 **Pop** 42,762 **Elev** 51 ft **Area code** 860 **Zip** 06457 **E-mail** crvsvc@cttourism.org; **Web** www.cttourism.org

Information CT Valley Tourism Commission, 393 Main St; 860/347-0028 or 800/486-3346.

On the Connecticut River between Hartford and New Haven, Middletown was once an important shipping point for trade with the West Indies. The first official pistol-maker to the United States Government, Simeon North, had his factory here in 1799. Today Middletown boasts diversified industry and one of the longest and widest main streets in New England.

What to See and Do

Powder Ridge Ski Area. Quad, 3 chairlifts, handletow; patrol, school, rentals; snowmaking; bar, restaurant, cafeteria; nursery. 14 trails; vertical drop 500 ft. (Nov-Apr, daily) 5 mi SW off CT 147, on Powder Hill Rd in Middlefield. Phone 860/349-3454. ¢¢¢¢¢

Wadsworth Falls State Park. These 285 acres surround Wadsworth Falls and lookout. Pond swimming, stream fishing. Hiking along wooded area with mountain laurel display. Picnicking. Beautiful waterfall with overlook. Standard hrs, fees. 3 mi SW off CT 66, on CT 157. Phone 860/566-2304.

Annual Event

Durham Fair. Fairgrounds, in Durham on CT 17. State's largest agricultural fair. Phone 860/349-9495. Last wkend Sept.

Motels

★ ★ **COMFORT INN.** *(111 Berlin Rd (CT 372), Cromwell 06416)* 4 mi N on CT 372, E of I-91 exit 21. 860/635-4100; FAX 860/632-9546. 77 rms, 4 story. S $54; D $61; each addl $6; under 18 free. Crib free. Pet accepted; $75 refundable. TV; VCR avail. Swimming privileges. Complimentary continental bkfst. Restaurant opp 5:30 am-10 pm. Ck-out 11 am. Health club privileges. Cr cds: A, C, D, DS, ER, JCB, MC, V.

D ◨ ⚓ ⊠ SC

★ ★ **HOLIDAY INN.** *(4 Sebethe Dr, Cromwell 06416)* just W of I-91 exit 21. 860/635-1001; FAX 860/635-0684. 145 rms, 3 story. S $79-$139; D $89-$149; each addl $10; suites $149; under 18 free; wkend rates. Crib free. TV; cable (premium). Indoor pool. Restaurant 6 am-10 pm. Rm serv. Bar. Ck-out 11 am. Coin lndry. Meeting rms. Business servs avail. In-rm modem link. Valet serv. Sundries. Airport transportation. Exercise equipt; sauna. Health club privileges. Lawn games. Picnic tables. Cr cds: A, C, D, DS, JCB, MC, V.

D ≋ ✕ ⊠ ⚒ SC

Motor Hotel

★ ★ ★ **RADISSON HOTEL & CONFERENCE CENTER.** *(100 Berlin Rd, CT 372, Cromwell 06416)* 4 mi N on CT 72, E of I-91 exit 21. 860/635-2000; FAX 860/635-6970. Web www.radisson.com. 211 rms, 4 story. S $69-$99; D $79-$109; suites $195-$350; under 18 free; wkend rates. Crib free. TV; cable, VCR avail. Indoor pool; whirlpool, poolside serv. Coffee in rms. Restaurants 6:30 am-10:30 pm. Rm serv. Bar noon-1 am; entertainment Sat. Ck-out noon. Meeting rms. Business servs avail. In-rm modem link. Gift shop. Exercise equipt; sauna. Some bathrm phones. Cr cds: A, C, D, DS, ER, JCB, MC, V.

D ≋ ✕ ⊠ ⚒ SC

Milford (F-2)

(See also Bridgeport, Fairfield, New Haven, Stratford)

Settled 1639 **Pop** 49,938 **Elev** 89 ft **Area code** 203 **Zip** 06460 **E-mail** mail@newhavencvb.org **Web** www.newhavencvb.org or www.milfordct.com
Information Greater New Haven Convention and Visitors Bureau, 59 Elm St, 1st flr, New Haven 06510; 203/777-8550or 800/332-STAY.

What to See and Do

Milford Historical Society Wharf Lane Complex. Three historical houses including Eells-Stow House (ca 1700), believed to be oldest house in Milford and featuring unusual "dog sled" stairway; Stockade House (ca 1780), first house built outside the city's early stockade; and Bryan-Downs House (ca 1785), 2-story early American structure housing more than 400 Native American artifacts spanning more than 10,000 yrs. (Memorial Day-Columbus Day, Sun; also by appt) 34 High St. Phone 203/874-2664. ¢

Milford Jai-Alai. Parimutuel wagering. Restaurant. (Tues-Sat eves; matinees Tues, Wed, Sat & Sun) 311 Old Gate Lane, off I-95 exit 40. For schedule information, phone 203/877-4242.

Annual Event

Oyster Festival. Milford Center, town green. Arts & crafts exhibits, races, boat tours; games; food; entertainment. Phone 203/878-4225. Mid-Aug.

Motel

★ ★ **HAMPTON INN.** *129 Plains Rd. 203/874-4400; FAX 203/874-5348.* 148 rms, 3 story. S $62-$72; D $67-$77; under 18 free. TV; cable (premium). Continental bkfst. Ck-out noon. Coin lndry. Meeting rms. Business servs avail. Valet serv. Some refrigerators. Cr cds: A, C, D, DS, MC, V.

 D ⤢ ⚲ ⧖ SC

Restaurants

★ **ALDARIO'S.** *240 Naugatuck Ave. 203/874-6096.* E-mail sante123@aol.com; web www.aldarios.com. Italian menu. Specializes in seafood, veal. Salad bar (lunch). Hrs: 11:30 am-2 pm, 4:30-10 pm. Closed Mon; some major hols. Res accepted. Bar. Semi-a la carte: lunch $4.50-$9.95, dinner $8.95-$16.95. Child's meals. Family-owned. Cr cds: A, C, D, DS, MC, V.

D ⤢

★ ★ **THE GATHERING.** *989 Boston Post Rd (US 1). 203/878-6537.* Specializes in fresh fish, steak, prime rib. Salad bar. Hrs: 4:30-9:30 pm; Fri, Sat to 10 pm; Sun to 9 pm; Sun brunch 11 am-2:30 pm. Closed Dec 25. Res accepted. Bar 4-11:30 pm; Thurs to midnight; Fri, Sat to 2 am. Semi-a la carte: dinner $9.95-$16.95. Child's meals. Colonial decor. Family-owned. Cr cds: A, MC, V.

D

★ ★ **SCRIBNER'S.** *31 Village Rd. 203/878-7019.* Specializes in exotic fish, fresh seafood, Angus beef. Hrs: 11:30 am-2:30 pm, 5 pm-closing. Closed most major hols. Res accepted. Bar. Semi-a la carte: lunch $4.95-$8.95, dinner $17.95-$26.95. Child's meals. Casual dining. Nautical decor. Cr cds: A, MC, V.

D

Mystic (E-5)

(See also Groton, New London, Norwich, Stonington)

Settled 1654 **Pop** 2,618 **Elev** 16 ft **Area code** 860 **Zip** 06355 **E-mail** more2see@aol.com **Web** www.mysticmore.com
Information Tourist Information Center, Building 1D, Olde Mistick Village, phone 860/536-1641; or Connecticut's Mystic & More, 470 Bank St, PO Box 89, New London 06320, phone 860/444-2206 or 800/222-6783 (outside CT).

The community of Mystic, divided by the Mystic River, was a shipbuilding and whaling center from the 17th to the 19th centuries. It derives its name from the Pequot, "Mistuket."

What to See and Do

Denison Homestead (1717). Restored in the style of 5 eras (18th-mid-20th centuries); furnished with heirlooms of 11 generations of a single family. Guided tour (mid-May-mid-Oct, afternoons exc Tues; rest of yr, by appt). 2 mi E of I-95 exit 90, on Pequotsepos Rd. Phone 860/536-9248. ¢¢

Denison Pequotsepos Nature Center. An environmental education center and natural history museum active in wildlife rehabilitation. The 125-acre sanctuary has over 7 mi of trails; family nature walks, films, lectures. (Daily; closed major hols) 2 mi NE of I-95 exit 90, on Pequotsepos Rd. Phone 860/536-1216. ¢¢

Mystic Marinelife Aquarium. Exhibits feature more than 6,000 live specimens from all waters of the world; demonstrations with dolphins, sea lions and the only whales in New England; Seal Island, outdoor exhibit of seals and sea lions in natural settings; penguin pavilion. (Daily; closed Jan 1, Thanksgiving, Dec, also last full wk Jan) 55 Coogan Blvd. Phone 860/536-3323. ¢¢¢

★ **Mystic Seaport.** This 17-acre complex is the nation's largest maritime museum, dedicated to preservation of 19th-century maritime history. Visitors may board the 1841 wooden whaleship *Charles W. Morgan,* square-rigged ship *Joseph Conrad* or fishing schooner *L.A. Dunton.* Collection also includes some 400 smaller vessels; representative seaport community with historic homes and waterfront industries, some staff in 19th-century costume; exhibits, demonstrations, working shipyard; children's museum, planetarium (fee), 1908 steamboat cruises (May-Oct, daily; fee); restaurants; shopping; special events throughout the yr. (Daily; closed Dec 25) 75 Greenmanville Ave (CT 27), 1 mi S of I-95 exit 90. Phone 860/572-5315. ¢¢¢¢¢

Olde Mistick Village. More than 60 shops and restaurants in 1720s-style New England village, on 22 acres; duck pond, millwheel, waterfalls; entertainment, carillon (May-Oct, Sat & Sun). Village (daily). Coogan Blvd & CT 27. Phone 860/536-4941. **Free.**

Annual Event

Lobsterfest. Mystic Seaport. Outdoor food festival. Phone 860/572-5315. Late May.

Motels

★ ★ **COMFORT INN.** *48 Whitehall Ave (CT 27), I-95, exit 90. 860/572-8531; FAX 860/572-9358.* 120 rms, 2 story. May-Oct: S, D $79-$139; each addl $10; under 17 free; lower rates rest of yr. Crib free. TV; cable. Complimentary continental bkfst. Restaurant nearby. Ck-out 11 am. Meeting rms. Business servs avail. Valet serv. Exercise equipt. Cr cds: A, D, DS, JCB, MC, V.

D ⚷ ⚲ ⧖ SC

★ ★ **DAYS INN.** *55 Whitehall Ave. 860/572-0574; FAX 860/572-1164.* 122 rms, 2 story. Mid-May-mid-Oct: S, D $79-$139; each addl $10; under 18 free; lower rates rest of yr. Crib free. TV; cable. Pool. Playground. Coffee in rms. Restaurant 6 am-9 pm; Fri, Sat to 10 pm. Rm serv. Ck-out

11 am. Meeting rms. Business servs avail. In-rm modem link. Valet serv. Airport transportation. Health club privileges. Refrigerators avail. Cr cds: A, C, D, DS, JCB, MC, V.

D ⊠ ⊠ ⊠ SC

★ ★ ★ **INN AT MYSTIC.** *US 1 & CT 27, 2 mi S of I-95 exit 90.* 860/536-9604; FAX 860/572-1635; res: 800/237-2415. 67 rms, 2 story. May-Oct: S, D $100-$235; each addl $10; under 18 free; lower rates rest of yr. Crib $10. TV; cable (premium), VCR avail. Heated pool; whirlpool. Complimentary afternoon tea. Restaurant (see FLOOD TIDE). Rm serv. Bar. Ck-out 11 am. Meeting rm. Business servs avail. Tennis. Some in-rm whirlpools, fireplaces. Some private patios, balconies. Formal gardens. Long Island Sound ¼ mi. Cr cds: A, D, DS, MC, V.

D ⊠ ⊠ ⊠ ⊠ ⊠ ⊠ SC

Motor Hotels

★ ★ ★ **HILTON.** *20 Coogan Blvd.* 860/572-0731; res: 800/826-8699; FAX 860/572-0328. 184 rms, 4 story. S, D $115-250; each addl $20; suites $295-$825; family rates. Crib free. TV; cable (premium). Indoor pool. Supervised child's activities wkends; also July, Aug. Restaurant 6:30 am-10 pm. Rm serv. Bar 11-1 am; entertainment Fri, Sat. Ck-out 11 am. Lndry. Meeting rms. Business servs avail. In-rm modem link. Free valet parking. Bellhops. Tennis privileges. Exercise equipt. Refrigerators avail. Cr cds: A, C, D, DS, MC, V.

D ⊠ ⊠ ⊠ ⊠ ⊠ SC

★ ★ ★ **TWO TREES AT FOXWOODS.** *(240 Lantern Hill Dr, Ledyard 06339)* E on I-95 to exit 92, NW on CT 2. 860/885-3000; FAX 860/885-4050; res: 800/FOXWOOD. 280 rms, 3 story, 60 suites. Late June-early Sept: S, D $150; each addl $20; suites $175; under 18 free; package plans; lower rates rest of yr. Crib $10. TV; cable (premium), VCR avail. Indoor pool; whirlpool. Complimentary continental bkfst. Restaurant 11:30 am-10 pm. Ck-out noon. Business servs avail. Bellhops. Health club privileges. Refrigerators. Foxwoods Casino adj. Cr cds: A, DS, MC, V.

D ⊠ ⊠ ⊠ SC

Hotel

★ ★ ★ **FOXWOODS RESORT.** *(CT 2, Ledyard 06339)* E on I-95, exit 92, approx 8 mi W on CT 2. 860/312-3000; FAX 860/312-4040; res: 800/369-9663. 312 rms, 6 story, 40 suites. July-early Sept: S, D $200; each addl $20; suites $275; under 18 free; lower rates rest of yr. Crib $10. TV; cable (premium), VCR avail. Indoor pool; whirlpool, lifeguard. Restaurants open 24 hrs. Bar 11-1:30 am; entertainment. Ck-out noon. Meeting rms. Business servs avail. In-rm modem link. Concierge. Shopping arcade. Barber, beauty shop. Free garage, valet parking. Exercise rm. Some refrigerators. Connected to casino. Cr cds: A, DS, MC, V.

D ⊠ ⊠ ⊠ ⊠ SC

Inns

★ **APPLEWOOD FARMS.** *(528 Colonel Ledyard, Ledyard 06339)* I-95, exit 89, N to CT 184, W to Col Ledyard Hwy. 860/536-2022; FAX 860/536-6015. E-mail betz@snet.net; web www.visitmystic.com/applewoodfarmsinn. 5 rms, 3 with shower only, 2 story, 1 suite. No rm phones. S, D $115-$250, each addl $25; suite $250; wkly rates; wkends (2-day min), hols (3-day min). Children over 8 yrs only. Pet accepted, some restrictions. Complimentary full bkfst; afternoon refreshments. Ck-out 11 am, ck-in 3 pm. Luggage handling. Picnic tables. Putting green. Whirlpool. House built 1826, once used as town hall; many fireplaces, Colonial atmosphere. Cr cds: A, DS, MC, V.

⊠ ⊠ ⊠

★ ★ **OLD MYSTIC INN.** *(06372).* 1½ mi N on CT 27, then right at stop sign. 860/572-9422; FAX 860/572-9954. E-mail omysticinn@aol.com; web www.visitmystic.com/oldmysticinn. 8 rms, 2 story. No rm phones. May-mid-Oct: S, D $115-$145; each addl $30-$40; higher rates: wkends, hols (2-day min); lower rates rest of yr. TV in sitting rm;

cable. Complimentary afternoon refreshments. Ck-out 11 am, ck-in 2 pm. Business servs avail. In-rm modem link. Lawn games. Picnic tables. Built 1794; early American decor. Cr cds: A, MC, V.

D ⊠ ⊠

★ ★ ★ **PALMER INN.** *(25 Church St, Noank 06340)* 3 mi S via CT 215. 860/572-9000. 6 rms, 5 A/C, 3 story. No rm phones. S, D $115-$225. Children over 16 yrs only. Complimentary continental bkfst; afternoon refreshments. Setups. Ck-out 11 am, ck-in 2-6 pm. Near ocean. Mansion built 1907; antiques, stained-glass. Totally nonsmoking. Cr cds: A, DS, MC, V.

⊠ ⊠

★ ★ **RED BROOK.** *(Old Mystic 06372)* 3 mi N on CT 27 to Ct 184, W ½ mi to inn. 860/572-0349. E-mail rkeyes1667@aol.com. 11 rms, 8 A/C, 2 story. No rm phones. S, D $105-$169. Advance payment required. Crib free. TV; cable. Complimentary full bkfst. Restaurants nearby. Ck-out 11 am, ck-in noon. Concierge serv. Fireplaces in 7 rms. Two colonial buildings (ca 1740 and ca 1770) furnished with period antiques. Totally nonsmoking. Cr cds: A, DS, MC, V.

⊠ ⊠

★ ★ **THE WHALER'S.** *20 E Main St.* 860/536-1506; FAX 860/572-1250; res: 800/243-2588. 41 rms, 18 with shower only, 2 story. May-late Oct: S $99-$105; D $119-$139; suite $175-$210; each addl $10; under 18 free; lower rates rest of yr. Crib $5. TV; cable. Dining rm 11:30 am-9 pm. Ck-out 11 am, ck-in 2 pm. Business servs avail. In-rm modem link. Balconies. Built 1865; colonial decor. Cr cds: A, MC, V.

D ⊠ ⊠

Restaurants

★ ★ ★ **FLOOD TIDE.** *(See Inn At Mystic)* 860/536-8140. Web www.innatmystic.com. Continental menu. Specialties: beef Wellington, châteaubriand, Caesar salad. Hrs: 7-10:30 am, 11:30 am-2 pm, 5:30-9:30 pm; Fri, Sat to 10 pm; Sun 7 am-2 pm, 5:30-9 pm; Sun brunch 11 am-2 pm. Res required. Bar. Wine list. A la carte entrees: bkfst $2-$10, lunch $5.95-$19.95, dinner $13.95-$25.95. Buffet: bkfst $8.95, lunch $11.95. Sun brunch $15.95. Child's meals. Pianist evenings. Parking. Outdoor dining. Nautical decor; elegant dining with view of sea. Cr cds: A, C, D, DS, MC, V.

D

★ ★ **J.P. DANIELS.** *(CT 27 & 184, Old Mystic)* ½ mi N on CT 184. 860/572-9564. Web www.synderblox.com/j.p.daniels. Continental menu. Specializes in veal, seafood. Hrs: 5-9 pm; Fri, Sat to 9:30 pm; Sun brunch 11 am-2 pm. Closed Dec 24, 25. Res accepted. Bar. Wine list. Semi-a la carte: dinner $8.95-$17.95. Sun brunch $13.95. Child's meals. Parking. Elegant dining in relaxed country setting. Totally nonsmoking. Cr cds: A, DS, MC, V.

D

★ **MYSTIC PIZZA.** *56 W Main St.* 860/536-3737. Web www.mystic-pizza.com. Specializes in pizza, pasta. Hrs: 10 am-midnight. Closed Easter, Thanksgiving, Dec 25. Wine, beer. A la carte entrees: lunch $2-$8.75, dinner $2-$9.25. Child's meals. Parking. Popular pizza parlor immortalized in the Julia Roberts film by the same name. Family-owned. Cr cds: DS, MC, V.

D SC

★ ★ **SEAMAN'S INNE.** *105 Greenmanville Ave.* 860/536-9649. Specializes in primo rib, fresh Atlantic seafood. Hrs: 11:30 am-9 pm; Fri to 10 pm; Sat, Sun 11 am-10 pm; Sun brunch 10:30 am-2 pm. Closed Dec 25. Res accepted. Bar. Semi-a la carte: lunch $4.95-$9.95, dinner $10.95-$18.95. Sun brunch $9.95. Child's meals. Family entertainment Wed-Sun. 19th-century sea captain's house decor; overlooks river. Cr cds: A, MC, V.

D

★ **STEAK LOFT.** *Olde Mistick Village, 2 mi N on CT 27.* 860/536-2661. E-mail steakloft@aol.com; web www.visitmystic.com/

steakloft. Specializes in steak, seafood. Salad bar. Hrs: 11:30 am-10:30 pm. Closed Thanksgiving, Dec 25. Bar to 1 am. Semi-a la carte: lunch $3-$12, dinner $11-20. Child's meals. Entertainment Wed-Sun. Parking. Casual New England atmosphere. Cr cds: A, DS, MC, V.

New Britain (D-3)

(See also Hartford, Meriden, Wethersfield)

Settled 1686 **Pop** 75,491 **Elev** 179 ft **Area code** 860 **Web** www.newbritainchamber.org
Information Chamber of Commerce, 1 Court St, 06051, phone 860/229-1665; or the Central Connecticut Tourism District, 1 Enterprise Grove Plaza, 06051, phone 860/225-3901.

This is the "hardware city." Production of sleigh bells and farm tools began about 1800, followed by locks and saddlery hardware. Many tool, hardware and machinery manufacturers, including The Stanley Works, organized in 1843, are headquartered in New Britain.

What to See and Do

Central Connecticut State University (1849). (14,000 students) On campus is Copernican Planetarium and Observatory, featuring one of the largest public telescopes in the US; planetarium shows (Fri, Sat; children's shows Sat; phone for schedule). Also on campus is college theater and art gallery. 1615 Stanley St. Phone 860/827-7000. Planetarium shows ¢¢

Hungerford Outdoor Education Center. Outdoor animal areas, trails, gardens, pond, exhibits of natural history, nutrition and energy; picnicking. (Apr-Oct, daily exc Mon; rest of yr, Tues-Sat) Approx 3 mi S via CT 372, at 191 Farmington Ave in Kensington. Phone 860/827-9064. ¢

New Britain Museum of American Art. Works by outstanding American artists from 1740 to the present; works by Whistler, Church, Sargent, Wyeth; Thomas Hart Benton murals; Sanford Low Collection of American illustrations; Charles and Elizabeth Buchanan Collection of American impressionists. (Tues-Sun afternoons; closed most hols) 56 Lexington St. Phone 860/229-0257. **Free.**

New Britain Youth Museum. Exhibits of Americana, cultures of other nations, circus miniatures, dolls, hands-on displays. (Tues-Fri) 30 High St. Phone 860/225-3020. **Free.**

Annual Events

Main Street, USA. Street festival featuring wide variety of ethnic foods, entertainment, rides, arts & crafts. Phone 860/225-3901. 2nd Sat June.

Dozynki Polish Harvest Festival. Broad St. Street dancing; polka bands; cultural displays; beer, singing, ethnic food; pony & hayrides; Polish arts & crafts. Phone 860/225-3901. 3rd wkend Sept.

Seasonal Event

Baseball. New Britain Rock Cats (AA team). New Britain Stadium, Willowbrook Park. Phone 860/224-8383. Mid-Apr-Sept.

Motor Hotel

✔★★ **RAMADA INN.** *65 Columbus Blvd (06051). 860/224-9161; FAX 860/224-1796.* 119 rms, 6 story. S, D $45-$95; each addl $10; suites $125; under 19 free; wkend plans. Crib free. Pet accepted, some restrictions; $10. TV; cable (premium), VCR avail. Ck-out noon. Coin lndry. Meeting rms. Business servs avail. Airport transportation. Garage parking. Downhill ski 5 mi. Cr cds: A, C, D, DS, JCB, MC, V.

D ✔ ✕ ✕ ✕ SC

Restaurant

★ **EAST SIDE.** *131 Dwight St. 860/223-1188.* German, Amer menu. Specializes in German dishes, baked shrimp, steak. Hrs: 11:30 am-2:30 pm, 4:30-10 pm; Sun noon-8 pm. Closed Mon; July 4, Dec 25. Res accepted. Bar to 10 pm. Semi-a la carte: lunch $4.95-$9.95, dinner $10.95-$16.95. Child's meals. European atmosphere. Family-owned. Cr cds: MC, V.

D

New Canaan (F-1)

(See also Norwalk, Stamford)

Founded 1801 **Pop** 17,864 **Elev** 300 ft **Area code** 203 **Zip** 06840
Information Chamber of Commerce, 111 Elm St; 203/966-2004.

New Canaan was settled in 1731 as Canaan Parish, a church society encompassing parts of Norwalk and Stamford. A quiet residential community situated on high ridges, New Canaan has retained its rural character despite its proximity to industrial areas.

What to See and Do

New Canaan Historical Society. The First Town House (original town hall) has costume museum, library and Cody Drugstore (1845), a restoration of the town's first pharmacy; on grounds of Hanford-Silliman House Museum (ca 1765) are a tool museum, hand press, one-room schoolhouse and sculptor John Roger's studio and museum. (Town House, Tues-Sat; other buildings Wed, Thurs & Sun, limited afternoon hrs; closed hols) 13 Oenoke Ridge Rd. Phone 203/966-1776. ¢¢

New Canaan Nature Center. More than 40 acres of woodland, ponds and meadows; discovery center with hands-on exhibits; suburban ecology exhibits; solar greenhouse; cider house & maple sugar shed; herb and wildflower gardens; trails, marsh boardwalk; animals. Grounds (daily). Buildings (daily exc Mon; closed some hols). 144 Oenoke Ridge Rd. Phone 203/966-9577. **Free.**

Silvermine Guild Arts Center. Art center in rustic six-acre setting has a school of the arts and three galleries with changing exhibits by member artists and artisans; invitational and juried exhibitions; many educational events and programs. (Daily exc Mon; closed Jan 1, Thanksgiving, Dec 25) 1037 Silvermine Rd. Phone 203/966-5617 (galleries) or 203/966-5618 (programs). **Free.**

Inn

★★★ **ROGER SHERMAN.** *195 Oenoke Ridge, I-95 exit 12, N on CT 124 (Oenoke Ridge Rd). 203/966-4541; FAX 203/966-0503.* Web www.rogershermaninn.com. 18 rms, 2 story. S $85-$105; D $110-$175; each addl $20. TV; cable. Complimentary continental bkfst. Dining rm noon-2 pm, 6-9:30 pm. Ck-out 11 am, ck-in 2-6 pm. Business servs avail. Some fireplaces. Colonial inn (ca 1740); antiques. Cr cds: A, C, D, MC, V.

D ✕ ✕

New Haven (E-3)

(See also Branford, Milford)

Settled 1638 **Pop** 130,474 **Elev** 25 ft **Area code** 203 **E-mail** mail@newhavencvb.org **Web** www.newhavencvb.org or www.cityofnewhaven.com
Information Greater New Haven Convention & Visitors Bureau, 59 Elm St, 1st flr, 06510; 203/777-8550 or 800/332-STAY.

New Haven is only 75 miles from New York City, but it is typically New England. Its colorful history is built into the stones and timbers of the area. Here Eli Whitney worked out the principle of interchangeable parts for mass production. Around the corner, Nathan Hale roomed as a student, not far from where Noah Webster compiled the first dictionary. Besides all this, Yale University puts New Haven on any list of the world's cultural centers.

Northwest of New Haven is a 400-foot red sandstone cliff called West Rock. In 1661 three Cromwellian judges, who had ordered Charles I beheaded, took refuge here from the soldiers of Charles II.

What to See and Do

Amistad Memorial. This 14-ft bronze relief sculpture is a unique 3-sided form. Each side depicts a significant episode of the life of Joseph Cinque, one of 50 Africans kidnapped from Sierra Leone and slated for sale in Cuba in 1839. After secretly rerouting the slave ship to Long Island Sound, the battle for the would-be slaves' freedom ensued in New Haven. Two years later, their victory was complete. Ed Hamilton sculpted this important piece. In front of City Hall. 165 Church St.

East Rock Park. City's largest park includes Pardee Rose Gardens, bird sanctuary, hiking trails, athletic fields, tennis courts, picnic grounds. Excellent view of harbor and Long Island Sound. (Apr-Oct, daily; rest of yr, Sat, Sun & hols) 1 mi NE at foot of Orange St, on E Rock Rd. Phone 203/946-6086. **Free.**

Ft Hale Park and Restoration. Here Federal guns kept British warships out of the harbor in 1812. Old Black Rock Ft, from Revolutionary War days, has been restored, and archaeological excavations are in progress. Ft Nathan Hale, from Civil War era, also has been reconstructed. Both offer spectacular views of the harbor. Picnicking. Guided tours (Memorial Day-Labor Day, daily). 4 mi SE on Woodward Ave. Phone 203/787-8790. **Free.**

Grove Street Cemetery. First cemetery in the US divided into family plots. Buried here are Noah Webster, Charles Goodyear, Eli Whitney and many early settlers of the area. Grove & Prospect Sts. **Free.**

Historic New Haven Harbor & Long Island Sound Cruises. Afternoon cruises on Long Island Sound aboard the MV *Liberty Belle*, highlighted by comments on historical landmarks and maritime history; also Moonlight Music cruises with live band as well as Murder Mystery cruises. (June-mid-Oct; Long Island Sound cruises, daily; Moonlight Music cruises Fri & Sat) Departs from Long Wharf Pier, I-95 exit 46. Phone 203/562-4163. ¢¢¢-¢¢¢¢

Lighthouse Point. This 82-acre park on Long Island Sound has lighthouse built in 1840; restored antique carousel (fee); bird sanctuary. Beach, bathhouse, playfield, picnic facilities, boat ramp. (Daily) Parking fee (Memorial Day-Labor Day only). End of Lighthouse Rd, 5 mi SE off I-95, exit 50. Phone 203/946-8027. ¢¢

New Haven Colony Historical Society Museum. Museum of local history; special exhibits; also research library (fee). (Daily exc Mon; closed major hols) 114 Whitney Ave, at Trumbull St. Phone 203/562-4183. ¢

Pardee-Morris House (1750). Built in 18th century, burned by the British in 1779, then rebuilt in 1780 around surviving masonry; American period furnishings; kitchen garden. (June-Aug, Sat & Sun) 325 Lighthouse Rd, S of I-95 exit 50. Phone 203/562-4183. ¢

Shore Line Trolley Museum. Collection of trolley, interurban, and rapid-transit cars from 15 states and Canada. A National Historic Site. Cars on display include pre-1900 trolleys (1893, 1899), the first commercially-pro-duced electric locomotive (1888), and a trolley parlor car. Exhibits on electric railways. Scenic trolley ride in authentic, restored cars; operator narrates on tour of display buildings and restoration shop; trolleys depart every 30 min (inquire for schedule). Picnic grove (May-Oct); gift shop; special events. (Memorial Day-Labor Day, daily; May & after Labor Day-Oct, wkends & some hols; Apr & early- to late-Nov, Sun only; wkend after Thanksgiving-wkend prior to Dec 25, Sat & Sun) 5 mi E via I-95 exit 51 or 52, at 17 River St in East Haven. Phone 203/467-6927. ¢¢¢

Shubert Performing Arts Center. Full-service performing arts venue opened in 1914. Known as the "Birthplace of the Nation's Greatest Hits." Home to dance, musical, comedy and dramatic performances. (Sept-May) 247 College St. For schedule and fees, phone 203/562-5666 or 800/228-6622.

The Green. In 1638 these 16 acres were laid out, making New Haven the first planned city in America. On the town common are 3 churches—United (1813), Trinity Episcopal (1814) and Center Congregational (1813), which is one of the masterpieces of American Georgian architecture. **Free.**

West Rock Nature Center. Nature center features native Connecticut wildlife in outdoor bird and mammal sections; indoor nature house with reptiles and other displays. Hiking trails; picnic areas. (Mon-Fri; closed hols) On Wintergreen Ave, 1 mi N of Southern Connecticut State Univ. Phone 203/946-8016. **Free.**

★ **Yale University** (1701). (10,000 students) Founded by 10 Connecticut ministers and named for Elihu Yale, an early donor to the school. In September 1969, the undergraduate school became coeducational. In center of city. Phone 203/432-2300. Of special interest are

The Old Campus. Nathan Hale (class of 1773) roomed. One-hr guided walking tours (Mon-Fri, one tour morning, one tour afternoon; Sat, Sun, one tour afternoon). Inquire at Visitor Information Office, 149 Elm St; 203/432-2300. **Free.**

Yale Art Gallery. Collections include Italian Renaissance paintings, American paintings and decorative arts, ancient art, African sculpture, Near and Far Eastern art, and European paintings from the 13th-20th centuries. (Tues-Sat, also Sun afternoons; closed some major hols, also Aug) 1111 Chapel St at York St. Phone 203/432-0600. **Free.**

Sterling Memorial and Beinecke Rare Book and Manuscript Libraries. Exhibits of famous collections, Gutenberg Bible. Sterling: (June-Aug, daily exc Sun; rest of yr, daily; closed most hols). Beinecke: (Sept-July, daily exc Sun; Aug, Mon-Fri; closed most hols). Best approach is from College St via Cross Campus Walk, on High St. Phone 203/432-2798 (Sterling) or 203/432-2977 (Beinecke). **Free.**

Collection of Musical Instruments. Total holdings of 850 musical instruments; permanent displays and changing exhibits; lectures, concerts, special events. (Sept-May, Tues-Thurs afternoons; June, Tues & Thurs afternoons; closed hols, also school breaks, July & Aug) Under 14 only with adult. 15 Hillhouse Ave. Phone 203/432-0822. ¢

Peabody Museum of Natural History. Exhibits on mammals, invertebrate life, Plains and Connecticut Native Americans, meteorites, minerals & rocks, birds of Connecticut; several life-size dinosaur exhibits including a brontosaurus (60-ft long) reconstructed from original fossil material; dioramas of North American flora and fauna; wkend films (free). (Daily; closed some major hols) Free admission Mon-Fri late afternoon. 170 Whitney Ave at Sachem St. Phone 203/432-5050 (recording). ¢¢

Yale Center for British Art. British paintings, prints, drawings, sculpture and rare books from Elizabethan period to present. Reference library and photo archive. Lectures, tours, films, concerts. (Daily exc Mon; closed some major hols) 1080 Chapel St. Phone 203/432-2800. **Free.**

Yale Bowl. An Ivy League football mecca. 2 mi W on Chapel St.

Annual Events

Powder House Day. Marks anniversary of the demand made upon the First Selectman in 1775 by Captain Benedict Arnold for the keys to the Powder House (arsenal). Having obtained the ammunition, Arnold marched his company to Boston to take part in the rebellion. The present governor's footguard appears in authentic Revolutionary War garb to join in ceremonies that are held on the Green. Phone 203/784-8615. Late Apr or early May.

International Festival of Arts and Ideas. Celebration of the arts and humanities. 195 Church St. Phone 888/ART-IDEA. Late June.

Pilot Pen International Tennis Tournament. Connecticut Tennis Center, near Yale Bowl. Championship Series on the ATP tour. Phone 888-99-PILOT. Mid-Aug.

Downtown Summertime Street Festival. Downtown, along Chapel St. Phone 203/946-7821. Mid-Aug.

Seasonal Events

Long Wharf Theatre. 222 Sargent Dr, at I-95 exit 46. Features new plays as well as classics. Phone 203/787-4282 (box office). Nightly exc Mon, Sept-June.

New Haven Symphony Orchestra. Woolsey Hall, College & Grove Sts. Series of concerts by leading artists. Phone 203/776-1444. Oct-mid-Apr.

Yale Repertory Theater. 222 York St. Phone 203/432-1234. Oct-May.

Motel

★ ★ **RESIDENCE INN BY MARRIOTT.** *3 Long Wharf Dr (06511).* 203/777-5337. 112 kit. suites, 2 story. S, D $130-$140. Crib avail. TV; cable (premium); whirlpool. Complimentary continental bkfst. Complimentary coffee in rms. Restaurant nearby. Ck-out noon. Coin lndry. Meeting rms. Business servs avail. In-rm modem link. Valet serv. Free airport transportation. Health club privileges. Stone fireplace in lobby. Cr cds: A, D, DS, MC, V.

Motor Hotels

★ ★ **THE COLONY.** *1157 Chapel St (06511-4892).* 203/776-1234; FAX 203/772-3929; res: 800/458-8810. 86 rms, 4 story. May-Oct: S $88-$98; D $98-$108; each addl $10; suites $195; kit. units $450; under 12 free; higher rates Yale events. Crib free. Parking $4. TV; cable. Restaurant 6:30 am-10 pm. Rm serv. Ck-out noon. Business servs avail. In-rm modem link. Concierge. Bellhops. Free airport, RR station transportation. Refrigerators avail. Within walking distance of Yale theaters. Cr cds: A, C, D, MC, V.

✔★ **HOLIDAY INN.** *30 Whalley Ave (06511), adj to Yale Univ.* 203/777-6221; FAX 203/772-1089. 160 rms, 8 story. S, D $90-$105; under 18 free; higher rates Yale special events. Crib free. TV; cable (premium). Pool. Coffee in rms. Restaurant 6 am-2 pm, 5-10 pm. Rm serv. Bar 5 pm-midnight. Ck-out noon. Meeting rms. Business servs avail. In-rm modem link. Bellhops. Valet serv. Cr cds: A, C, D, DS, JCB, MC, V.

Inn

★ ★ ★ **THREE CHIMNEYS.** *1201 Chapel St (06511).* 203/789-1201; res: 800/443-1554; FAX 203/776-7363. E-mail chimneysnn@ aol.com; www.the.ultranet.com/chimney3/. 10 rms, 3 story. S, D $160; each addl $20. TV; cable (premium); VCR avail. Complimentary full bkfst; afternoon refreshments. Restaurant nearby. Concierge serv. Ck-out 11 am, ck-in 3 pm. Business servs avail. Restored Victorian mansion (ca 1870). Rms individualy furnished with antiques and period pieces. Cr cds: A, DS, MC, V.

Restaurants

★ ★ **500 BLAKE ST.** *(500 Blake St, Westville 06515)* Merritt Pkwy (US 15) exit 59. 203/387-0500. Italian, Amer menu. Specializes in

fresh fish, Italian dishes. Hrs: 11:30 am-midnight; Sun to 9 pm; Sun brunch 11 am-3 pm. Closed legal hols. Res accepted. Bar. A la carte entrees: lunch $6.95-$19.95, dinner $14.95-$29.95. Sun brunch $19.95. Pianist. Turn-of-century decor, antiques. Cr cds: A, D, DS, MC, V.

★ **INDIOCHINE PAVILLION.** *1180 Chapel St (06511).* 203/865-5033. Vietnamese menu. Specialties: spicy chicken, Saigon noodle soup, Saigon sound pancakes. Hrs: noon-2:30 pm, 5:30-9:30 pm; Sat from 5:30 pm; Sun 5-9 pm. Closed Mon; major hols. Res accepted. Serv bar. Semi-a la carte: lunch $4.95-$6.95, dinner $8.75-$17.95. Storefront restaurant; Asian paintings. Cr cds: A, D, MC, V.

★ ★ **LA MIRAGE.** *(111 Scrub Oak Rd, North Haven)* N on I-91 exit 13, 1¹/₂ mi S on Scrub Oak Rd. 203/239-1961. Specializes in baked stuffed shrimp, prime rib. Hrs: 5:30-10 pm; Sun to 7 pm. Closed Mon-Thurs; July 4, Dec 25. Res accepted. Bar. Semi-a la carte: dinner $10.95-$18.95. Family-owned. Cr cds: A, MC, V.

New London (E-5)

(See also Groton, Mystic, Norwich, Stonington)

Settled 1646 **Pop** 28,540 **Elev** 33 ft **Area code** 860 **Zip** 06320 **E-mail** more2see@aol.com **Web** www.mysticmore.com

Information Connecticut's Mystic & More, 470 Bank St, PO Box 89; 860/444-2206 or 800/222-6783.

New London is a seagoing community and always has been; it has one of the finest deep-water ports on the Atlantic coast. From the first days of the republic into the 20th century, whalers brought fortunes home to New London. Townspeople still welcome all ships—submarines, cutters, yachts, cruisers. Today the city's manufacturing industries include turbines, steel fabrication, high-tech products, medicines, electronics and other products.

What to See and Do

Eugene O'Neill Theater Center. Complex includes National Playwrights Conference, National Critics Institute, National Music Theater Conference, National Puppetry Conference, National Theater Institute. Staged readings of new plays and musicals during summer at Barn Theater, Amphitheater and Instant Theater (June-Aug). W via US 1, at 305 Great Neck Rd in Waterford. Phone 860/443-5378.

Ferries. Most operate yr-round.

New London-Orient Point, NY. Five auto ferries make 1¹/₂-hr trip across Long Island Sound. High-speed passenger ferry makes a 40-min trip daily. (Daily; no trip Dec 25) Departs from 2 Ferry St. Advance res required for vehicles. For information phone 860/443-7394. ¢¢¢¢-¢¢¢¢¢

New London-Block Island, RI. Auto ferry makes 2-hr crossing; one round-trip (mid-June-Labor Day). Phone 860/442-9553. (See BLOCK ISLAND, RI) Individuals, vehicles ¢¢¢¢¢

New London-Fishers Island, NY. Auto ferries *Race Point* and *Munnatawket* make crossing to Fishers Island; several departures daily. Departs from New London Pier, foot of State St. Phone 860/443-6851 or 516/788-7463. One way: pedestrian ¢¢; vehicle & driver ¢¢¢¢

Joshua Hempsted House (1678). Oldest house in city; restored, 17th- and 18th-century furnishings; Hempsted family diary detailing life in the house during colonial times. (Mid-May-mid-Oct, Tues-Sun afternoons) 11 Hempstead St. Phone 860/443-7949 or 860/247-8996. ¢¢ Admission includes

Nathaniel Hempsted House (1759). One of two surviving examples of mid-18th-century cut-stone architecture in state. Stone exterior bake oven, 7 rms with period furnishings. (Mid-May-mid-Oct, Tues-Sun afternoons) Phone 860/443-7949 or 860/247-8996.

Lyman Allyn Art Museum. Colonial silver; 18th- and 19th-century furniture; collection of dolls, doll houses; American and European paintings; Oriental and primitive art. (Daily exc Mon; closed hols) 625 Williams St. Phone 860/443-2545. ¢¢

Monte Cristo Cottage. Restored boyhood home of playwright and Nobel prize winner Eugene O'Neill; houses research library and memorabilia. Multimedia presentation. Literary readings. (Labor Day-Memorial Day, Mon-Fri afternoons) 325 Pequot Ave. Phone 860/443-0051 or 860/443-5378. ¢¢

Ocean Beach Park. Swimming in ocean, olympic-size pool; waterslide; sheltered pavilion, boardwalk, picnic area, concessions; miniature golf, novelty shop; amusement arcade, entertainment. (Sat before Memorial Day-Labor Day, daily; arcade open all yr) 3 mi S on Ocean Ave, on Long Island Sound. Phone 800/510-7263. Per vehicle ¢¢¢

Science Center of Eastern Connecticut. Regional science museum located on 415-acre Connecticut Arboretum with trees and shrubs native to the area (daily). Major exhibit on eastern Connecticut's natural and cultural history entitled "Time and the River: The Story of Land & People in the Thames River Basin"; workshops & courses; field trips, special programs; nature trail, herb garden; museum shop. (Daily exc Mon; closed major hols) 33 Gallows Lane, N of I-95 exit 83. Phone 860/442-0391. ¢¢

Shaw Perkins Mansion (1756). Naval HQ for state during Revolution; genealogical and historical library. Unique paneled cement fireplace walls. 305 Bank St. For schedule information phone 860/443-1209. ¢

Sunbeam Fleet Nature Cruises. Trips to observe humpback, minke, finback and other whales and schools of dolphins and porpoises from aboard the 100-ft *Sunbeam Express*; naturalist will answer questions. (July-Aug, days vary) Also cruises to view bald eagles and seals (Jan-Feb). Res suggested. Departs from dock near Niantic River bridge in Waterford, W via I-95 exit 74, S on CT 156, left on CT 156 to first dock on left past bridge. Phone 860/443-7259. ¢¢¢¢¢

US Coast Guard Academy (1876). (800 cadets) Visitors' Pavilion with multimedia show (May-Oct, daily). US Coast Guard Museum (daily; closed some hols). Cadet parade-reviews (fall, spring, usually Fri). Barque *Eagle*, 295 ft, open to visitors (Fri-Sun, when in port; limited hrs); photography permitted. Mohegan Ave, 1 mi N on I-95 exit 83. Phone 860/444-8270. **Free.**

Ye Antientiest Burial Ground (1653). Huntington St. **Free.**

Ye Olde Towne Mill (1650). Built for John Winthrop Jr, founder of New London and Connecticut's sixth governor; restored 1981; overshot waterwheel (closed to public). Mill St & State Pier Rd, under Gold Star Bridge.

Annual Events

Connecticut Storytelling Festival. Connecticut College. Nationally acclaimed artists; workshops, concerts. Phone 860/439-2764. Late Apr.

Sail Festival. City Pier. Phone 860/443-8331. 1 wkend July.

Motels

✔★ **CONNECTICUT YANKEE INN.** *(I-95 & CT 161, Niantic 06357) 6 mi S on I-95 exit 74, at jct CT 161. 860/739-5483; FAX 860/739-4877; res: 800/942-8466.* 50 rms, 2 story. July-Labor Day: S $45-$120; D $55-$120; each addl $10; under 17 free; lower rates rest of yr. Crib free. TV; cable (premium). Pool. Complimentary bkfst. Ck-out 11 am. Meeting rms. Business servs avail. In-rm modem link. Valet serv. Game rm. Health club privileges. Beach privileges. Cr cds: A, C, D, DS, MC, V.

★ **NIANTIC INN.** *(345 Main St, Niantic 06357) I-95 exit 72, approx 3 mi W on CT 156. 860/739-5451; FAX 860/691-1488.* 24 suites, 3 story. Mid-May-late Oct: suites $145; each addl $30; under 12 free; lower rates rest of yr. Crib free. TV; cable. Complimentary coffee in rms. Restaurant nearby. Ck-out 11 am. Business servs avail. Refrigerators. Picnic tables. Swimming beach opp. Cr cds: A, D, DS, MC, V.

★ **RED ROOF INN.** *707 Colman St, I-95, exit 82A. 860/444-0001; FAX 860/443-7154.* 108 rms, 2 story. May-Oct: S $39.99-$57; D $34.99-$77; each addl $5; under 18 free; higher rates special events; lower rates rest of yr. Pet accepted. TV; cable (premium), VCR avail. Complimentary coffee in lobby. Restaurant nearby. Ck-out noon. Meeting rms. Business servs avail. In-rm modem link. Cr cds: A, C, D, DS, MC, V.

★ **STARLIGHT MOTOR INN.** *(256 Flanders Rd, Niantic 06357) 6 mi S on I-95 exit 74, at jct CT 161. 860/739-5462; FAX 860/739-0567.* 48 rms, 2 story. May-Sept: S, D $44-$99; lower rates rest of yr. TV; cable (premium), VCR avail. Pool. Restaurant nearby. Cr cds: A, C, D, DS, MC, V.

Motor Hotel

★ ★ ★ **RADISSON.** *35 Governor Winthrop Blvd, I-95 exit 83N. 860/443-7000; FAX 860/443-1239.* 120 rms, 5 story. S, D $65-$155; each addl $20; suites $75-$155; under 18 free; wknd packages. Crib free. TV; cable (premium). Indoor pool; whirlpool. Restaurant 6:30 am-9 pm. Rm serv. Bar 11-1 am. Ck-out noon. Meeting rms. Business center. In-rm modem link. Bellhops. Valet serv. Sundries. Free airport, RR station, bus depot transportation. Lighted tennis privileges. Health club privileges. Refrigerator, wet bar in most suites. Cr cds: A, C, D, DS, ER, MC, V.

Inn

★ ★ **QUEEN ANNE INN.** *265 Williams St. 860/447-2600; FAX 860/443-0857; res: 800/347-8818.* E-mail burbacks@aol.com; web www .visitmystic.com/queenanneinn. 10 rms, 2 share bath, 7 with shower only, 3 story, 1 kit. suite. Some rm phones. S $84-$160; D $89-$175; each addl $25; kit. suite $185; 2-day min wkends, May-Sept. Children over 12 yrs only. TV in some rms; cable. Complimentary full bkfst. Ck-out 11 am, ck-in 3-9 pm. Queen Anne Victorian built in 1903. Turn-of-the-century art and antiques. Totally nonsmoking. Cr cds: A, C, D, DS, MC, V.

Restaurant

★ **CONSTANTINE'S.** *(252 Main St, Niantic 06357) 5 mi W on CT 156. 860/739-2848.* Specializes in fresh seafood. Hrs: 11:30 am-9 pm; wkends to 10 pm; summer hrs vary. Closed Mon; Thanksgiving, Dec 25. Bar to 1 am. Semi-a la carte: lunch $2-$8.50, dinner $6.95-$20.95. Child's meals. View of Long Island Sound. Family-owned. Cr cds: A, DS, MC, V.

New Preston (D-2)

(See also Cornwall Bridge, Kent)

Pop 1,217 **Elev** 700 ft **Area code** 860 **Zip** 06777

Information Litchfield Hills Travel Council, PO Box 968, Litchfield 06759; 860/567-4506.

What to See and Do

Historical Museum of Gunn Memorial Library. House built 1781; contains collections & exhibits on area history; paintings, furnishings, gowns, dolls, dollhouses and tools. (Thurs-Sun afternoons) 4 mi SW via CT 47 at jct Wykeham Rd, on the green in Washington. Phone 860/868-7756. **Free.**

Lake Waramaug State Park. Swimming, fishing, scuba diving; field sports, hiking; ice-skating; camping; picnicking. Standard hrs, fees. 5 mi N on Lake Waramaug Rd (CT 478). Phone 860/868-2592 or 860/868-0220 (camping). (See ANNUAL EVENT)

 The Institute for American Indian Studies. A museum of Northeastern Woodland Indian artifacts with permanent exhibit hall. Exhibits include changing Native American art displays; also a replicated indoor longhouse, outdoor replicated Algonkian village, simulated archaeological site and nature trail. Special programs. (Apr-Dec, daily; rest of yr, Wed-Sun; closed some major hols) 4 mi SW via CT 47 to CT 199S, then 1½ mi to Curtis Rd in Washington. Phone 860/868-0518.   ¢¢

Annual Event

Women's National Rowing Regatta. Lake Waramaug State Park. Mid-May.

Inns

★ ★ ★ **BOULDERS.** *E Shore Rd (CT 45), 1½ mi N on East Shore Rd (CT 45). 860/868-0541; FAX 203/868-1925.* 6 rms in inn, 2 story, 8 rms in cottages, 3 rms in carriage house. MAP: S $200-$300; D $250-$350; each addl $50. Restaurant (see BOULDERS). Bar. Ck-out 11:30 am. Business servs avail. In-rm modem link. Tennis. Downhill ski 20 mi; x-country ski 5 mi. Rec rm. Refrigerators, fireplace in cottages and carriage house. Balconies. Canoes, rowboats, sailboats, paddleboats. Bicycles. Hiking. Private beach on lake. Cr cds: A, MC, V.

✓ ★ **HOPKINS.** *22 Hopkins Rd, 2 mi N on CT 45, ½ mi W. 860/868-7295; FAX 860/868-7464.* 11 rms, 2 share bath, 3 story. No A/C. No rm phones. Apr-Dec: S, D $67-$150; each addl $7. Closed rest of yr. Restaurant (see HOPKINS INN). Bar. Ck-out 11 am, ck-in 1 pm. Lake Waramaug opp., private beach. Established 1847. Cr cds: A, MC, V.

Restaurants

★ ★ ★ **BOULDERS.** *(See Boulders Inn) 860/868-0541; FAX 860/868-1925.* E-mail boulders@bouldersinn.com; web www.bouldersinn.com. Own baking. Hrs: 6-8 pm; Fri, Sat to 9 pm; Sun 5-8 pm. Closed Dec 25; also Mon & Tues (winter), Tues (summer). Res accepted; required wkends. Serv bar. A la carte entrees: dinner $17.50-$24. Outdoor dining. In turn-of-the-century summer home. Cr cds: A, MC, V.

★ ★ **HOPKINS INN.** *(See Hopkins Inn) 860/868-7295.* Continental menu. Specialties: roast duck à l'orange, sweetbreads, Wienerschnitzel. Hrs: noon-2 pm, 6-9 pm; Fri to 10 pm; Sat 5:30-10 pm; Sun 12:30-8:30 pm; Apr, Nov, Dec 6-9 pm, wkend hrs vary. Closed Mon; also Jan-Mar. Res accepted. Bar. Semi-a la carte: lunch $10-$14, dinner $18-$21. Child's meals. Terrace dining. In old inn on hill overlooking lake. Cr cds: A, MC, V.

★ ★ **LE BON COIN.** *On US 202. 860/868-7763.* Country French menu. Specializes in sweetbreads, Dover sole. Hrs: noon-2 pm, 6-9 pm; Sat to 10 pm; Sun 5-9 pm. Closed Tues, Wed; Jan 1, Memorial Day, Dec 25. Res accepted. Bar. Wine list. A la carte entrees: lunch $4.75-$10, dinner $12.75-$19. Child's meals. Country French atmosphere. Cr cds: MC, V.

Niantic

(see New London)

Norfolk (C-2)

(See also Lakeville, Riverton)

Founded 1758 **Pop** 2,060 **Elev** 1,230 ft **Area code** 860 **Zip** 06058
Information Litchfield Hills Travel Council, PO Box 968, Litchfield 06759; 860/567-4506.

What to See and Do

Historical Museum. Located in former Norfolk Academy (1840). Exhibits on history of Norfolk including displays of a country store and post office as well as a children's rm with an 1879 doll house. (Late May-mid-Oct, Sat & Sun; rest of yr, by appt) On the green. Phone 860/542-5761.   **Free.**

State parks.

Haystack Mountain. A 34-ft-high stone tower at the summit, 1,716 ft above sea level, provides an excellent view of Long Island Sound, the Berkshires and peaks in New York. A ½-mi trail leads from parking lot to tower. Picnicking; hiking. 1 mi N on CT 272. Phone 860/482-1817. **Free.**

Campbell Falls. Winding trails through woodland composed of many splashing cascades; focal point is Campbell Falls. Fishing, hiking, picnicking. 6 mi N on CT 272. Phone 860/482-1817.   **Free.**

Dennis Hill. A unique summit pavilion (formerly a summer residence) is located at an elevation of 1,627 ft, providing a panoramic view of the Litchfield Hills and beyond. Picnicking; hiking; cross-country skiing. 2 mi S on CT 272. Phone 860/482-1817.   **Free.**

Seasonal Event

Norfolk Chamber Music Festival. Musical performances Fri, Sat evenings in acoustically superb 1906 Music Shed located on grounds of 19th-century estate; also picnicking, indoor performances and art gallery before concerts; informal chamber music recitals Thurs & Sat. E.B. Stoeckel Estate at jct US 44, CT 272. Phone 860/542-3000 (June-Oct), phone 203/432-1966. (rest of yr). Mid-June-mid-Sept.

Inn

✓ ★ **MOUNTAIN VIEW.** *¼ mi S on CT 272, off US 44. 860/542-6991; FAX 860/542-5689.* E-mail mvinn@snet.net; web www.mvinn.com. 7 rms, 6 with bath, 2 story. No A/C. S, D $60-$120; each addl $10; family rates. Crib free. Complimentary full bkfst. Restaurant (see MOUNTAIN VIEW INN). Bar. Ck-out noon. Downhill ski 20 mi; x-country ski 2 mi. Lawn games. Victorian building (1880s); turn-of-the-century decor, antiques; 4 fireplaces. Cr cds: A, DS, MC, V.

Restaurant

★ ★ **MOUNTAIN VIEW INN.** *(See Mountain View Inn) 860/542-6991.* E-mail mvinn@snet.net; web www.mvinn.com. Continental menu. Own soups, desserts. Hrs: Fri, Sat 5-9 pm. Closed Sun-Thurs; also Nov-June. Res accepted. Semi-a la carte: dinner $13-$21. Child's meals. Victorian country inn (ca 1880). Cr cds: A, DS, MC, V.

Norwalk (F-1)

(See also Bridgeport, Fairfield, Greenwich, Stamford)

Founded 1651 **Pop** 78,331 **Elev** 42 ft **Area code** 203
Information Coastal Fairfield County Tourism District, 297 West Ave, 06850; 203/854-7925 or 800/866-7925.

Norwalk's growth was heavily influenced by Long Island Sound. The city evolved rapidly from an agriculturally based community to a major seaport, then to a manufacturing center known for high-fashion hats, corsets and clocks. The Sound still plays an important part in Norwalk's development, providing beauty, recreation and, of course, oysters.

What to See and Do

Charter fishing trips. Several companies offer full- and half-day saltwater fishing excursions. Contact the Coastal Fairfield County Tourism District for details.

Ferry to Sheffield Island Lighthouse. *Island Girl* departs from Hope Dock, jct Washington and N Water St, in South Norwalk. Ferry through Norwalk Harbor to historic lighthouse (1868) on three-acre island. Tour. Picnicking. (Memorial Day-June, wkends; July-Labor Day, daily) Phone 203/838-9444. Round trip ¢¢¢

Historic South Norwalk (SoNo). Nineteenth-century waterfront neighborhood on National Register featuring historical buildings, unique shops, art galleries and restaurants. 1 mi SE via I-95 exit 14N/15S, bounded by Washington, Water, N & S Main Sts, in South Norwalk. Phone 800/866-7925.

Lockwood-Mathews Mansion Museum (1864-1868). Fifty-room Victorian mansion built by financier LeGrand Lockwood; 42-ft skylit rotunda, ornamented doors and carved marble, inlaid woodwork throughout, period furnishings, musical boxes and mechanical music exhibit; 1-hr guided tour. Victorian Ice-Cream Social (mid-July) and Antiques Show (late Oct). (Tues-Fri & Sun, limited hrs; July & Aug, also Sat; closed major hols, also mid-Dec-Feb) 295 West Ave. Phone 203/838-1434. ¢¢¢

Maritime Aquarium at Norwalk. Hands-on maritime museum featuring shark touch tank and harbor seal pool; 125 species, touch tanks, films on IMAX screen; boat building exhibit. Guided harbor study tours. (Daily; closed Thanksgiving, Dec 25) 2 mi S via I-95 exit 14N or 15S, at 10 N Water St. Phone 203/852-0700, ext 206. ¢¢¢

Mill Hill Historic Park. Complex of historic early American buildings include the Town House Museum (ca 1835), Fitch House Law Office (ca 1740) and schoolhouse (1826); also old cemetery. (May-Oct, Sun) Wall St & East Ave. Phone 203/846-0525. **Free.**

St Paul's-on-the-Green. This 14th-century-style Gothic church contains the Seabury Altar; medieval stained glass; exquisite needlepoint. Antique organ. Also here is colonial cemetery. (Daily by appt) 60 East Ave. Phone 203/847-2806. **Free.**

WPA Murals. America's largest collection of Works Progress Administration murals depict life in southeastern Fairfield County in the 1930s. (Mon-Fri; closed hols) City Hall, 125 East Ave (parking entrance, Sunset Hill Ave). Phone 203/854-7702 or 203/866-0202. **Free.**

Annual Events

Norwalk Harbor Splash. South Norwalk. Regatta, harbor tours, music. Phone 800/866-7925. Mid-May.

Round Hill Scottish Games. Cranbury Park. Heritage celebration with Highland dancing, pipe bands, caber tossing, clan tents, Scottish and American food. Phone 203/324-1094. Late June or early July.

SoNo Arts Celebration. Washington St, in Historic South Norwalk. Juried crafts, kinetic sculpture race, entertainment, concessions, block party. 1st wkend Aug.

Oyster Festival. Veteran's Park, East Norwalk. Three-day event featuring entertainment, boat rides, concessions. Phone 203/854-7825. Wkend after Labor Day.

International In-water Boat Show. Cove Marina, Calf Pasture Beach Rd. Phone 212/922-1212. Mid-Sept.

Motor Hotels

✔★★★ **CLUB HOTEL BY DOUBLETREE.** *789 Connecticut Ave (06854).* 203/853-3477; FAX 203/855-9404. 268 rms, 8 story. S, D $169; each addl $10; under 18 free; wkend rates. Crib free. TV; cable (premium). Indoor pool. Coffee in rms. Restaurant 6 am-11 pm. Bar 5 pm-midnight. Ck-out noon. Meeting rms. Business center. In-rm modem link. Exercise equipt. Covered parking. Cr cds: A, C, D, DS, JCB, MC, V.

 D ⛱ ✗ ⊠ 🐾 SC 🎿

★★ **FOUR POINTS BY SHERATON.** *426 Main Ave (06851).* 203/849-9828; FAX 203/846-6925. 127 rms, 4 story. S, D $169; each addl $10; under 18 free; wkend rates. Crib free. TV; cable (premium). Coffee in rms. Restaurant 7 am-10 pm. Bar. Ck-out noon. Coin lndry. Meeting rms. Business servs avail. Sundries. Exercise equipt. Health club privileges. Cr cds: A, C, D, DS, MC, V.

D ✗ ⊠ 🐾 SC

Inn

★★ **SILVERMINE TAVERN.** *194 Perry Ave (06850), at jct Silvermine Ave.* 203/847-4558; FAX 203/847-9171. 10 rms, 2 story. No rm phones. S $75; D $99-$125; higher rates wkends. Closed Dec 25; also Tues Sept-May. Complimentary continental bkfst. Restaurant (see SILVERMINE TAVERN). Bar noon-10 pm. Ck-out 11 am. Meeting rms. Business servs avail. Some balconies. On river. Country inn (1767); antiques. Cr cds: A, C, D, MC, V.

 🐾

Restaurants

★★ **MESON GALICIA.** *10 Wall St (06850).* 203/866-8800. Spanish menu. Specializes in seafood, duckling, lamb. Hrs: noon-2:30 pm, 6-9:30 pm; Fri to 10:30 pm; Sat 6-10:30 pm; Sun 6-9 pm. Closed Mon; most major hols. Res accepted; required Fri, Sat. Bar. A la carte entrees: lunch $9-$16, dinner $17.50-$25. Outdoor dining. Bldg once a trolley barn (1800s). Totally nonsmoking. Cr cds: A, C, D, DS, MC, V.

D

★★ **SILVERMINE TAVERN.** *(See Silvermine Tavern Inn)* 203/847-4558. Specializes in New England fare, fresh seafood. Hrs: noon-3 pm, 6-9 pm; Sun 3-9 pm; Sun brunch 11 am-2:30 pm. Closed Dec 25; also Tues. Res accepted. Bar. Semi-a la carte: lunch $6.50-$11.95, dinner $15.50-$24.95. Buffet: dinner (Thurs) $17.50. Sun brunch $18.50. Child's meals. Outdoor dining. 18th-century colonial tavern overlooking mill pond; antiques. Country store opp. Family-owned. Cr cds: A, C, D, MC, V.

Norwich (E-5)

(See also Groton, New London)

Settled 1659 **Pop** 37,391 **Elev** 52 ft **Area code** 860 **Zip** 06360 **E-mail** more2see@aol.com **Web** www.mysticmore.com
Information Connecticut's Mystic and More!, 470 Bank St, PO Box 89, New London 06320; 860/444-2206 or 800/863-6569 outside CT.

Norwich was one of the first cities chartered in Connecticut. Since the end of the 18th century it has been a leader in the industrial development of the state. Here the colony's first paper mill was opened in 1766 and the first cut nails in America were made in 1772. Cotton spinning began about 1790.

There are three distinct sections: NorwichTown to the northwest, a living museum of the past; the business section near the Thames docks; and a central residential section with many 19th-century homes.

What to See and Do

Indian Leap. The falls was a favorite resort and outpost of the Mohegan. Legend has it that a band of Narragansetts, during the Battle of Great Plains in 1643, fled from pursuing Mohegans. As they came upon the falls, many were forced to jump off the cliffs and into the chasm below, hence the name. Can be viewed from the Monroe St footbridge. Yantic Falls off Yantic St. **Free.**

Leffingwell Inn (1675). Scene of Revolutionary War councils. Museum; period rms. (Mid-May-Labor Day, daily exc Mon; rest of yr, by appt) 348 Washington St at CT Tpke exit 81E. Phone 860/889-9440. **¢¢**

Mohegan Park and Memorial Rose Garden. Picnic and play area; swimming area (June-Labor Day, daily). Rose garden; best time to visit, June-Sept. (Daily) Entrances on Judd Rd & Rockwell St. Phone 860/823-3759. **Free.**

Native American Burial Grounds. Resting place of Uncas, chief of the Mohegan (more popularly known as Mohicans) who gave the original land for the settlement of Norwich. Sachem St, off CT 32.

Slater Memorial Museum & Converse Art Gallery. Roman and Greek casts; Vanderpoel Collection of Oriental Art; 17th-20th-century American art and furnishings; changing exhibits. (Sept-June, daily; rest of yr, daily exc Mon; closed hols) Approx 1 mi N via I-395 exit 81E, on campus of Norwich Free Academy, 108 Crescent St. Phone 860/887-2506. **Donation.**

Tantaquidgeon Indian Museum. Works of Mohegan and other New England tribes, past and present; also displays of Southeast, Southwest and Northern Plains Native Americans. (May-Oct, daily exc Mon) 5 mi S on CT 32, at 1819 Norwich-New London Tpke, in Uncasville. Phone 860/848-9145. **Donation.**

The Old Burying Ground. Burial place of many Revolutionary War soldiers, including French soldiers; also Samuel Huntington, signer of the Declaration of Independence. Entrance from E Town St ; brochure avail at Cemetery Lane entrance.

Annual Events

Chelsea Street Festival. Chelsea district. Fine arts, entertainment, hay rides, children's events. Phone 860/887-2789. 3rd Sat May.

Blue Grass Festival. Strawberry Park. Phone 860/886-1944. Late May.

Rose-Arts Festival. Broadway & Washington Sts. Crowning of Rose Queen; arts & crafts shows; children's activities; entertainment; international food festival; flower competition; golf tournament; bicycle and road races. 10 days late June-early July.

Harbor Day. Brown Memorial Park, at waterfront. Raft race; boat rides; dunking booth; arts & crafts; entertainment. Phone 860/886-1463. Late Aug.

Historic Norwichtown Days. Norwichtown Green. Living history events, crafts, parade. Phone 860/887-2808. 2nd wkend Sept.

Motor Hotel

★ ★ **RAMADA HOTEL.** 10 Laura Blvd. 860/889-5201; FAX 860/889-1767. 127 rms, 6 story. Mid-May-mid-Oct: S $95-$145; D $105-$165; each addl $10-$15; suites $200; under 18 free; package plans; lower rates rest of yr. TV; cable (premium). Indoor pool. Restaurant 6:30 am-10 pm. Rm serv. Bar 4 pm-midnight. Ck-out 11 am. Meeting rms. In-rm modem link. Valet serv. Sundries. Some bathrm phones. Private patios, balconies. Cr cds: A, C, D, DS, MC, V.

Inn

★ ★ ★ **NORWICH INN & SPA.** 607 W Thames St (CT 32). 860/886-2401; FAX 860/886-9483; res: 800/ASK-4SPA. 65 rms in inn, 3 story, 70 villas. May-Oct: S, D $130-$150; suites $165-$245; lower rates rest of yr. TV; cable, VCR avail (movies). 2 pools; whirlpool. Restaurant (see PRINCE OF WALES). Bar 4 pm-midnight; Fri, Sat to 1 am; entertainment Fri, Sat. Ck-out noon. Meeting rms. Business center. Concierge serv. RR station transportation. Lighted tennis, pro. Exercise rm; sauna. Massage. Lawn games. Built in 1929 as gathering place for prominent persons. Cr cds: A, D, MC, V.

Restaurant

★ ★ **PRINCE OF WALES.** (See Norwich Inn & Spa) 860/886-2401. Specializes in classic New England menu and spa cuisine. Own baking, desserts. Hrs: 7-10 am, noon-2 pm, 6:30-9:30 pm; Fri, Sat to 10:30 pm; Sun brunch noon-3 pm. Res accepted. Bar 4 pm-midnight. Bkfst buffet $12.95. A la carte entrees: lunch $10.95-$14.95; dinner $16.95-$28.95. Sun brunch $15.95. Outdoor dining. Georgian colonial decor; antiques. Totally nonsmoking. Cr cds: A, D, DS, JCB, MC, V.

D

Old Lyme (E-4)

(See also Essex, New London, Old Saybrook)

Settled 1665 **Pop** 6,535 **Elev** 17 ft **Area code** 860 **Zip** 06371 **E-mail** more2see@aol.com **Web** www.mysticmore.com

Information Connecticut's Mystic and More!, 470 Bank St, PO Box 89, New London 06320; 860/444-2206 or 800/863-6569.

Once, long ago, they say a sea captain lived in every house in Old Lyme. Fortunately a good many of the houses are still standing on the tree-lined streets of this sleepy old village. Named for Lyme Regis, England, it is a summer resort and an artists colony, one of the first on the coast.

What to See and Do

Florence Griswold Museum. (1817). Stately late-Georgian mansion that housed America's most celebrated art colony at the turn of the century. Paintings by Willard Metcalf, Childe Hassam and other artists of the colony; exhibits of 18th- & 19th-century New England furnishings and decorative arts. (June-Nov, Tues-Sat, also Sun afternoons; rest of yr, Wed-Sun afternoons; closed some major hols) 96 Lyme St, 1 blk W off CT Tpke exit 70. Phone 860/434-5542. **¢¢**

Rocky Neck State Park. Approx 560 acres with1/2-mi frontage on Long Island Sound. Saltwater swimming, scuba diving; fishing. Hiking. Picnicking (shelters, concessions). Camping. Standard hrs, fees. 6 mi E via I-95 exit 72, on CT 156 in East Lyme. Phone 860/739-5471.

Inns

✔★ ★ ★ **BEE AND THISTLE INN.** 100 Lyme St. 860/434-1667; FAX 860/434-3402; res: 800/622-4946. E-mail info@beeandthistle-inn.com; web www.beeandthistleinn.com. 11 rms, 3 story, 1 cottage. S $75-$150; D $75-$155; each addl $15; cottage $210. Children over 12 yrs only. Closed 2 wks Jan. TV in cottage. Restaurant (see BEE AND THISTLE INN). Rm serv 8:30-10 am. Bar noon-11 pm; guitarist Fri, harpist Sat. Ck-out 11 am, ck-in 2 pm; cottage: ck-out noon, ck-in 3 pm. Picnic tables. Colonial house (1756); antique furniture. 5 acres on river. Cr cds: A, D, DS, MC, V.

★ ★ ★ **OLD LYME.** *85 Lyme St. 860/434-2600; FAX 860/434-5352; res: 800/434-5352.* E-mail olinn@aol.com; web www.oldlyme-inn.com. 13 rms, 2 story. S $86-$133; D $99-$158. Pet accepted. TV; VCR avail. Complimentary continental bkfst. Restaurant (see OLD LYME INN). Bar. Ck-out noon, ck-in 3-11 pm. Business center. Built 1850, former farm; antiques, murals. Ocean ½ mi. Cr cds: A, C, D, DS, MC, V.

Restaurants

★ ★ ★ **BEE AND THISTLE INN.** *(See Bee And Thistle Inn) 860/434-1667.* E-mail info@beeandthistleinn.com; web www.beeandthistleinn.com. Changing menu. Hrs: 8-10 am, 11:30 am-2 pm, 6-9:30 pm; Sun 8-9:30 am, 5:30-9:30 pm; Sun brunch 11 am-2 pm. Afternoon tea (Nov-Apr) Mon, Wed & Thurs 3:30-5 pm. Closed Tues; Dec 24 evening-Dec 25; also 2 wks Jan. Res accepted. Bar. A la carte entrees: bkfst $3.50-$7, lunch $8.95-$12, dinner $19-$28. Sun brunch $10.95-$15. Guitar duo Fri; harpist Sat. In colonial house (1756); 4 fireplaces. Cr cds: A, D, MC, V.

★ ★ ★ **OLD LYME INN.** *(See Old Lyme Inn) 860/434-2600.* E-mail olinn@aol.com; web www.oldlymeinn.com. Own baking. Hrs: noon-2 pm, 6-9 pm; Sun 11 am-9 pm; Sun brunch to 3 pm. Res accepted. Bar. Wine list. Semi-a la carte: lunch $6.95-$10.95, dinner $19.95-$27.95. Jazz guitarist Fri, Sat. Restored 1850 home; 3 fireplaces; many antiques; murals by local artist. In historic district. Cr cds: A, C, D, DS, MC, V.

Old Saybrook (E-4)

(See also Clinton, Essex, New London, Old Lyme)

Settled 1635 **Pop** 9,552 **Elev** 31 ft **Area code** 860 **Zip** 06475 **E-mail** sybrk.chmbr.cmmrce@snet.net; **Web** www.oldsaybrook.ct.com

Information Chamber of Commerce, 146 Main St, PO Box 625, phone 860/388-3266; or the Connecticut Valley Tourism Commission, 393 Main St, Middletown 06457, phone 860/347-0028.

Old Saybrook, at the mouth of the Connecticut River, is popular with summer vacationers. It is the third-oldest named community in Connecticut and is the oldest officially chartered town in the state. It was also the original site of Yale College until 1716.

What to See and Do

Ft Saybrook Monument Park. Nearly 18-acre park with remains of Ft Saybrook, first military fortification in the state; picnicking. (Daily) On College St, at Saybrook Point. **Free.**

Gen William Hart House (1767). Provincial Georgian-style, colonial residence of well-to-do New England merchant & politician; features include 8 corner fireplaces, one of which is decorated with Sadler & Green transfer-print tiles illustrating Aesop's Fables; original wainscotting; Federal-style pieces, several of which are Hart family items; antique furniture, costumes, artifacts; on grounds are re-created colonial gardens, including award-winning herb garden. (Mid-June-mid-Sept, Fri-Sun, limited hrs) 350 Main St. Phone 860/388-2622. **Donation.**

Annual Events

Arts & Crafts Show. Town Green, Main St. More than 200 artists and craftspersons exhibiting. Phone 860/388-3266. Last full wkend July.

Christmas Torchlight Parade. Over 40 fife & drum corps march down Main St. 2nd Sat Dec.

Motels

 ★ ★ **HERITAGE MOTOR INN.** *1500 Boston Post Rd. 860/388-3743.* 12 rms. Mid-May-mid-Oct: S, D $58-$85; each addl $5; suites $140; lower rates rest of yr. Crib free. TV; cable. Pool. Restaurant nearby. Ck-out 11 am. Some refrigerators. Beach privileges. Connected to Nathaniel Bushnell House (1755). Cr cds: A, DS, MC, V.

★ **SANDPIPER MOTOR INN.** *1750 Boston Post Rd, I-95 exit 66. 860/399-7973; FAX 860/399-7387; res: 800/323-7973.* 44 rms, 3 story. Mid-May-Oct: S, D $85-$140; each addl $6; under 12 free; lower rates rest of yr. Crib free. TV; cable, VCR avail. Pool. Complimentary continental bkfst. Restaurant adj. Ck-out 11 am. Meeting rm. In-rm modem link. Some refrigerators. Picnic tables, grills. Near Long Island Sound. Cr cds: A, C, D, DS, MC, V.

Motor Hotel

★ ★ ★ **SAYBROOK POINT INN.** *2 Bridge St. 860/395-2000; FAX 860/388-1504; res: 800/243-0212 (exc CT).* 62 rms, 3 story, 7 suites. May-Oct: S, D $179-$259; suites $299-$495; under 12 free; lower rates rest of yr. Crib avail. TV; cable, VCR avail (movies). 2 pools, 1 indoor; whirlpool. Restaurant 8 am-9 pm. Rm serv. Bar noon-1 am. Ck-out noon. Coin lndry. Meeting rms. Business servs avail. In-rm modem link. Bellhops. Valet serv. Concierge. Gift shop. RR station transportation. Exercise rm; sauna. Touring bicycles. Health club privileges. Refrigerators, wet bars. Balconies. Cr cds: A, C, D, DS, MC, V.

Resort

★ ★ ★ **WATER'S EDGE.** *(1525 Boston Post Rd, Westbrook 06498) 5 mi W on US 1. 860/399-5901; FAX 860/399-6172; res: 800/222-5901 (exc CT).* 32 rms in hotel, 1-3 story, 66 villas. May-Oct: S, D $135-$280; villas $200-$280; wkly rates; lower rates rest of yr. Crib free. TV; cable; VCR in villas. 2 pools, 1 indoor; whirlpool. Supervised child's activities (May-Sept); ages 4-12. Dining rm (public by res) 7-10 am, 11:30 am-2:30 pm, 5-9 pm; Sun 8 am-9 pm. Rm serv. Bar noon-1 am; Fri, Sat to 2 am; Sun to 11 pm. Ck-out noon, ck-in 3 pm. Business servs avail. In-rm modem link. Grocery, package store ¼ mi. Bellhops. Valet serv. Tennis. Downhill ski 20 mi. Exercise equipt; sauna. Bicycles. Lawn games. Soc dir. Game rm. Fishing guides. Fireplaces. Refrigerator in villas. Balconies. Sitting rm in main lodge. On Long Island Sound. Private beach. Cr cds: A, C, D, DS, MC, V.

Restaurants

★ ★ **ALEIA'S.** *(1687 Boston Post Rd, Westbrook 06498) 5 mi W on US 1, exit 65. 860/399-5050.* Web www.aleias.com. Mediterranean menu. Specializes in fish, pasta, steak. Hrs: 5:30-9 pm; Fri, Sat to 10 pm. Closed Mon. Res accepted. Bar. Semi-a la carte: dinner $13.50-$19.95. Child's meals. Pianist Fri, Sat. Outdoor dining. Bistro atmosphere. Cr cds: A, MC, V.

★ ★ **DOCK & DINE.** *College St, S on Main St to the water. 860/388-4665.* Specializes in fresh seafood, steak, ribs. E-mail dockdirect @aol.com. Hrs: 11:30 am-10 pm; Sun from noon; winter to 9 pm. Closed Mon, Tues (mid-Oct- mid-Apr); Thanksgiving, Dec 24, 25. Res accepted. Bar. Semi-a la carte: lunch $5.95-$10.95, dinner $11.95-$21.95. Child's meals. Entertainment Fri-Sun (summer). View of Sound, dock. Cr cds: A, DS, MC, V.

★ **SAYBROOK FISH HOUSE.** *99 Essex Rd. 860/388-4836.* Web www.saybrookfishhouse.com. Specializes in fresh seafood. Hrs: 11:45 am-9:30 pm; Fri, Sat to 10:30 pm; Sun noon-9 pm; early-bird dinner Mon-Fri 4:30-6 pm, Sat 4-5:30 pm, Sun noon-9 pm. Closed Thanksgiving, Dec 25. Bar. Semi-a la carte: lunch $4.95-$8.95, dinner $11.95-$19.95. Child's meals. Tables covered with brown packing paper. Cr cds: A, D, DS, MC, V.

D SC ⌐

Plainfield (D-5)

(See also Norwich, Putnam)

Settled 1689 **Pop** 14,363 **Elev** 203 ft **Area code** 860 **Zip** 06374 **E-mail** quietcorner@snet.net; **Web** www.webtravels.com/quietcorner

Information Northeast Connecticut Visitors District, PO Box 598, Putnam 06260; 860/928-1228 or 888/628-1228.

What to See and Do

Plainfield Greyhound Park. Parimutuel betting. Restaurant, bar. No minors. Races every 15 min. (All yr; phone for schedule) I-395 exit 87, on Lathrop Rd. Phone 860/564-3391. ¢¢

Prudence Crandall House. Site of New England's first academy for black girls (1833-1834). Restored 2-story frame building with changing exhibits, period furnishings; research library. Gift shop. (Wed-Sun; closed Thanksgiving; also mid-Dec-mid-Jan) W on CT 14A at jct CT 169 in Canterbury. Phone 860/546-9916. ¢

Quinebaug Valley Trout Hatchery. A 1,200-acre hatchery for brook, brown and rainbow trout. Exhibits and displays (daily). Fishing by permit only (Mar-May, wkends and hols). Trout Hatchery Rd, at end of Cady Lane, in Central Village. Phone 860/564-7542. **Free.**

Motels

✔★ **PLAINFIELD.** *(Box 101, RR 2, Moosup 06354) on CT 14 at I-395 exit 89. 860/564-2791; FAX 860/564-4647.* 35 rms. S, D $42-$59; each addl $10. Crib $10. Pet accepted, some restrictions; $7. TV; cable (premium). Pool. Restaurant adj 5:30 am-9 pm; wkends 24 hrs. Ck-out noon. Coin lndry. Business servs avail. Sundries. Picnic tables, grills. Cr cds: A, C, D, DS, MC, V.

D ✔ ≈ ⋈ ⋈

★ **PLAINFIELD YANKEE MOTOR INN.** *Lathrop Rd, I-395 exit 87. 860/564-4021; res: 800/847-5689 (exc CT), 800/523-7549 (CT).* 48 rms, 2 story. Late May-mid-Oct: S $69; D $75; each addl $10; under 18 free; wkly rates; lower rates rest of yr. Crib $10. TV; cable (premium). Ck-out 11 am. Meeting rms. Business servs avail. Health club privileges. Refrigerators avail. Picnic tables. Cr cds: A, C, D, DS, MC, V.

⋈ ⋈ SC

Putnam (D-5)

(See also Plainfield)

Pop 9,031 **Elev** 290 ft **Area code** 860 **Zip** 06260 **E-mail** quietcorner@snet.net; **Web** www.webtravels.com/quietcorner

Information Northeast Connecticut Visitors District, PO Box 598; 860/928-1228 or 888/628-1228.

Named for Revolutionary War hero Israel Putnam, this town is situated on four small hills. Because it was located at Cargill Falls on the Quinebaug River and a railroad station served as a connecting point between New York and Boston, Putnam at one time ranked eighth in New England in the volume of freight handled.

What to See and Do

⭐ **Roseland Cottage** (1846). Influential abolitionist publisher Henry C. Bowen's summer home. One of the most important surviving examples of a Gothic-revival "cottage," complete with period furnishings. Located on Woodstock Hill with its bright pink exterior and picturesque profile, it stands in contrast to the otherwise colonial character of this New England village. Surrounded by original outbuildings, including one of the oldest indoor bowling alleys in the country; aviary. Boasts one of the oldest parterre gardens in New England, edged by 1,800 ft of dwarf boxwood. Presidents Grant, Hayes, Harrison and McKinley attended Bowen's celebrated Fourth of July parties here. (June-mid-Oct, Wed-Sun; closed some hols) 7 mi NW via CT 171 & 169 in Woodstock. Phone 860/928-4074. ¢¢

Motel

★★ **KING'S INN.** *5 Heritage Rd, I-395 exit 96. 860/928-7961; FAX 860/963-2463; res: 800/541-7304.* 41 rms, 1-2 story. S $62-$72; D $68-$78; each addl $8; under 12 free; wkly rates. Crib free. Pet accepted. TV; cable (premium), VCR avail. Pool. Complimentary continental bkfst. Restaurant 11 am-10 pm; Fri, Sat to 10:30 pm. Bar. Ck-out 11 am. Meeting rms. Business servs avail. On pond; gazebo. Cr cds: A, C, D, DS, MC, V.

✔ ✔ ≈ ⋈ ⋈ SC

Inn

★★★ **INN AT WOODSTOCK HILL.** *(94 Plaine Hill Rd, Woodstock 06267) W on CT 171 to CT 169, then 1 mi N on CT 169. 860/928-0528; FAX 860/928-3236.* E-mail innwood@snet.net; web www.webtravels.com/woodstockhill. 22 rms, 3 story, 7 suites. May-Oct: S $82-$145; D $90-$155; each addl $12; suites $100-$155; lower rates rest of yr. TV; cable (premium), VCR avail. Complimentary continental bkfst. Restaurant 11 am-2 pm, 5:30-9 pm; Sun to 7:30 pm; closed Mon. Limited rm serv. Bar. Ck-out 11 am, ck-in 2 pm. Business servs avail. Concierge serv. Lawn games. Fireplaces. Library, sitting rm. Historic building (1815). Cr cds: DS, MC, V.

D ⋈ ⋈

Ridgefield (E-1)

(See also Danbury, New Canaan, Norwalk, Stamford)

Settled 1709 **Pop** 20,919 **Elev** 749 ft **Area code** 203 **Zip** 06877 **E-mail** chamber@ridgefield-ct.com; **Web** www.ridgefield.net

Information Chamber of Commerce, 9 Bailey Ave, PO Box 191, phone 203/438-5992 or 800/FUN-1708; or Housatonic Valley Tourism Commission, Box 406, 72 West St, Danbury 06813, phone 203/743-0546 or 800/841-4488 (outside CT).

Ridgefield is unusual among communities settled in the 19th century because it has a main street of boulevard width—99 feet lined with tree-shaded houses. On this street in 1777, Benedict Arnold (still a revolutionary) set up barricades and fought the Battle of Ridgefield against General Tyron.

What to See and Do

Aldrich Museum of Contemporary Art. Changing exhibits; sculpture garden (daily; free). Museum (Tues-Sun afternoons). 258 Main St. Phone 203/438-4519. ¢¢

Keeler Tavern. Restored 18th-century tavern, stagecoach stop, home. Once Revolutionary patriot HQ; British cannonball still embedded in wall. Summer home of architect Cass Gilbert. Period furnishings; gardens; tours; museum shop. (Wed, Sat & Sun afternoons; closed Jan) 132 Main St. Phone 203/438-5485. ¢¢

Inns

★ ★ ★ **THE ELMS INN.** *500 Main St (CT 35). 203/438-2541; FAX 203/438-2541, ext. 101.* 20 rms, 2-3 story. No elvtr. S $110-$165; D $120-$175; each addl $15; suites $175. Crib free. TV; cable (premium). Complimentary continental bkfst. Restaurant (see THE ELMS). Bar. Ck-out noon. X-country ski 10 mi. Built in 1760s; in 1799 became inn. Four-poster beds in some rms. Fireplaces in public rms. Cr cds: A, C, D, MC, V.

★ ★ **STONEHENGE.** *35 Stonehenge Rd, 1 mi S of jct CT 35 & US 7. 203/438-6511; FAX 203/438-2478.* 16 rms, 2 story. S $90-$160; D $120-$200; each addl $10; suites $200. Crib avail. TV; cable. Complimentary continental bkfst. Restaurant (see STONEHENGE). Bar 6-11 pm. Ck-out 11 am. Pond with geese. Cr cds: A, MC, V.

★ ★ ★ **WEST LANE.** *22 West Lane. 203/438-7323.* Web www.innbook.com. 18 rms, 3 story, 4 kits. No elvtr. S, D $115-$170. Crib free. TV; cable, VCR avail. Complimentary continental bkfst. Ck-out 11 am. Meeting rm. Business servs avail. In-rm modem link. Heated towel racks; some fireplaces. Each rm individually decorated. Mid-1800s architecture. Cr cds: A, D, MC, V.

Restaurants

★ ★ ★ **THE ELMS.** *(See The Elms Inn) 203/438-9206.* Specializes in game, lobster, seafood. Own baking. Hrs: 11:30 am-9:30 pm. Res required dinner. Closed Easter, Dec 25. Bar. Wine cellar. Semi-a la carte: lunch $7.95-$14.95, dinner $23-$27. Child's meals. Patio dining. Oldest continuously run inn in Ridgefield; established 1799. Family-owned. Cr cds: A, C, D, MC, V.

★ ★ **STONEHENGE.** *(See Stonehenge Inn) 203/438-6511.* Continental menu. Specializes in fresh brook trout, rack of lamb, game. Own baking. Hrs: 6-9 pm; Sat to 9:30 pm; Sun 4-8 pm; Sun brunch noon-2:30 pm. Closed Mon. Res accepted; required wkends. Wine cellar. Semi-a la carte: dinner $14-$28. Complete meals: dinner $46. Sun brunch $26. Valet parking. Restored home (1853) near pond. Cr cds: A, MC, V.

D

Riverton (C-2)

(See also Hartford, Norfolk)

Pop 500 (est) **Elev** 505 ft **Area code** 860 **Zip** 06065
Information Litchfield Hills Travel Council, PO Box 968, Litchfield 06759; 860/567-4506.

Lambert Hitchcock, one of America's greatest chairmakers, built his original chair factory here in 1826. His famous stenciled chairs and cabinet furniture are now prized pieces. The old factory is still in operation, and some antiques are on display. Today, the grand colonial houses and tree-lined streets of this New England village are filled with emporiums and shops.

What to See and Do

Hitchcock Museum. Collection of original 18th-century furnishings by Hitchcock and others, displayed in historic church (1829). (Apr-Dec, Thurs-Sun) CT 20, center of village. Phone 860/738-4950. **Donation.**

Solomon Rockwell House (1813). Antebellum house built by early industrialist; Hitchcock chairs, antique clocks, Revolutionary & Civil War memorabilia, wedding gown collection, melodeon. (June-Oct, Thurs-Sun

afternoons) 3 mi SW on CT 20, 2 mi S on CT 8, at 225 Prospect St in Winsted. Phone 860/379-8433. ¢

Annual Event

Riverton Fair. 1800s country village fair, held since 1909; chopping, sawing & pie-eating competitions, displays, art & crafts, entertainment. 2nd wkend Oct.

Simsbury (D-3)

(See also Avon, Farmington, Hartford)

Settled 1660 **Pop** 22,023 **Elev** 181 ft **Area code** 860 **Zip** 06070 **E-mail** ghcvb@connix.com; **Web** www.grhartfordcvb.com
Information Greater Hartford Tourism District, 1 Civic Center Plaza, Hartford 06103; 860/728-6789 or 800/446-7811.

Hopmeadow Street, in this characteristic New England village, is so named because hops were grown in the area to supply early distillers. Simsbury's handsome Congregational Church was built in 1830.

After it was founded, Simsbury developed steadily until 1676, when the settlers fled in terror during King Philip's War. Scouts returning three days later found the settlement in ashes. Soon the village was reconstructed and activity was again stimulated by the discovery of copper at East Granby (then part of Simsbury).

What to See and Do

Massacoh Plantation-Simsbury Historic Center. Restored Victorian carriage house. Furnished buildings and exhibits represent 3 centuries of community life; industrial and agricultural tools; old meetinghouse, ice-house; first copper coins struck in America (1737). Tours. (Sun-Fri afternoons) 800 Hopmeadow St. Phone 860/658-2500. ¢¢¢

Simsbury Farms. Recreational facility covering 300 acres; picnicking, ice-skating, tennis, swimming, golf, cross-country skiing, nature and family fitness trails, volleyball, paddle tennis. (Daily; some activities seasonal) Fees for most activities. 100 Old Farms Rd. Phone 860/658-3836 or 860/658-3200.

Motels

✔★ **IRON HORSE INN.** *969 Hopmeadow St. 860/658-2216; FAX 860/651-0822; res: 800/245-9938 (CT).* 27 kit. units (no ovens), 2 story. S $73; D $83; under 12 free; wkly rates. Crib free. Pet accepted; $15. TV; cable. Pool; sauna. Complimentary continental bkfst. Restaurant nearby. Ck-out 11 am. Coin lndry. In-rm modem link. Bathrm phones; refrigerators. Balconies. Picnic tables. Cr cds: A, MC, V.

★ ★ **SIMSBURY INN.** *397 Hopmeadow St. 860/651-5700; FAX 860/651-8024; res: 800/634-2719.* 98 rms, 4 story. S, D $139; suites $200-$400; under 18 free; wkend rates. Crib free. TV; cable, VCR avail. Indoor pool; whirlpool. Complimentary continental bkfst. Restaurant 6:30 am-9:30 pm. Bar. Ck-out 11 am. Meeting rms. Business servs avail. In-rm modem link. Bellhops. Free airport, RR station transportation. Tennis. 18-hole golf privileges, pro, putting green. Downhill/x-country ski 15 mi. Exercise equipt; sauna. Lawn games. Refrigerators. Traditional New England country inn atmosphere. Cr cds: A, D, DS, MC, V.

Inn

★ ★ **SIMSBURY 1820 HOUSE.** *731 Hopmeadow St. 860/658-7658; FAX 860/651-0724.* 32 rms, 3 story. S, D $115-$185; each addl $10. TV. Complimentary continental bkfst. Restaurant 5:30-8:30 pm. Ck-out 11 am, ck-in 3 pm. Business servs avail. Private patios, balconies. Built 1820; antiques. Veranda. Cr cds: A, D, DS, MC, V.

Restaurants

★ ★ **CHART HOUSE.** *(4 Hartford Rd, Weatoque) 2 mi S on CT 10, at jct CT 185. 860/658-1118.* Specializes in steak, prime rib, fresh seafood. Own dressings. Hrs: 5-10 pm; Fri, Sat to 11 pm; Sun 4-9 pm; early-bird dinner 5-6:30 pm. Res accepted. Bar. Semi-a la carte: dinner $14-$32. Child's meals. Former tavern (1780); period furnishings, antiques. Cr cds: A, C, D, DS, MC, V.

✔★ **ONE-WAY FARE.** *4 Railroad St. 860/658-4477.* Specializes in chili, homemade soups, hamburgers. Hrs: 11:30 am-midnight; Fri, Sat to 1 am; Sun brunch 10:30 am-3 pm. Closed Labor Day, Thanksgiving, Dec 25. Bar. Semi-a la carte: lunch, dinner $4.50-$16.50. Sun brunch $3.95-$16.50. Outdoor dining. Old brick RR station (1874); RR memorabilia. Cr cds: A, D, MC, V.

Southbury (E-2)

(See also Danbury, Waterbury, Woodbury)

Settled 1673 **Pop** 15,818 **Elev** 257 ft **Area code** 203 **Zip** 06488
Information Litchfield Hills Travel Council, PO Box 968, Litchfield 06759; 860/567-4506.

What to See and Do

Bullet Hill Schoolhouse. One of the oldest school buildings in the country, estimated to have been built in 1789, in use until 1942; some experts believe it antedates the Revolutionary War; early schooling exhibits. (April-May, limited hours; rest of yr, by appt) 1/2 mi E of I-84 exit 15, on US 6. Phone 203/264-8781. **Donation.**

State parks.

  Southford Falls. Approx 120 acres. Former site of Diamond Match Co. Stream and pond fishing; ice-skating; bridle trail nearby; scenic hiking along Eight Mile River; picnicking. (Daily) 4 mi SE via CT 67 & 188. Phone 203/264-5169. ¢

  Kettletown. The name of this park is derived from the time when settlers first arrived and purchased this tract of land from the Native Americans for one brass kettle. Swimming, fishing. Hiking. Sports field. Picnicking. Camping. Nature trail for the disabled. Standard hrs, fees. 5 mi S via I-84, exit 15. Phone 203/264-5169.

Motor Hotel

★ ★ **HILTON.** *1284 Strongtown Rd. 203/598-7600; FAX 203/598-0837.* 198 rms, 3 story. S $95-$140; suites $125-$315; under 12 free; ski plans; wkend, hol rates. Crib free. Pet accepted. TV; cable (premium), VCR avail. Indoor pool; whirlpool, poolside serv. Coffee in rms. Restaurant 6:30 am-10:30 pm. Rm serv. Bar. Ck-out noon. Convention facilities. Business servs avail. In-rm modem link. Bellhops. Valet serv. Sundries. Exercise equipt; sauna. Cr cds: A, C, D, DS, MC, V.

Restaurant

★ ★ **TARTUFO.** *900 Main St S. 203/262-8001.* Northern Italian menu. Specialties: fettuccine with truffles, risotto alla Piemontese. Hrs: noon-2:30 pm, 5-9 pm; Thurs, Fri to 10 pm; Sat 6-10 pm; Sun 5-8 pm; Sun brunch noon-2:30 pm. Closed some major hols. Res accepted. Bar. A la

carte entrees: lunch $6.50-$14, dinner $14.95-$23. Sun brunch $18.95. Child's meals. Jazz Thurs-Sat. Country setting. Cr cds: A, D, MC, V.

Southington
(see Meriden)

Stafford Springs (C-4)

(See also Enfield, Storrs, Windsor; also see Springfield, MA)

Settled 1719 **Pop** 4,100 **Elev** 591 ft **Area code** 860 **Zip** 06076
Information Connecticut Northcentral Tourism & Visitors Bureau, 111 Hazard Ave, Enfield 06082; 860/763-2578 or 800/248-8283.

Stafford Springs is known for its production of woolen fabrics, printed circuits and industrial filters.

What to See and Do

Civilian Conservation Corps Museum. New Deal program devoted to state and national parks is commemorated. Video and photograph exhibits; equipment and uniforms; camp memorabilia. (Late May-Aug afternoons) 166 Chestnut Hill Rd (CT 190). Phone 860/684-3430. **Donation.**

Mineral Springs. Located here are the springs that gave the town its name. In 1771, John Adams, future president of the United States, came to bathe in the springs after hearing of their healing effects. Spring St, between Grace Episcopal Church and the library. **Free.**

Seasonal Event

Stafford Motor Speedway. CT 140W. A 1/2-mi paved oval track for stock car racing. Phone 860/684-2783. Apr-Sept.

Restaurant

★ ★ ★ **CHEZ PIERRE.** *111 W Main St. 860/684-5826.* Classic French menu. Specialties: noisettes d'agneau rivoli, cassoulet de Castelnaudary, grenadin de veau au romarin. Own baking. Hrs: 5-11 pm. Closed Sun-Thurs June-Aug; also Mon-Thurs Sept-May. Res accepted. Bar. A la carte entrees: dinner $21-$22.50. Prix fixe: dinner $28.25-$31.25. French country inn decor; hand-painted murals. In 1830 house. Cr cds: A, DS, MC, V.

Stamford (F-1)

(See also Greenwich, New Canaan, Norwalk)

Settled 1641 **Pop** 108,056 **Elev** 10 ft **Area code** 203
Information Greater Stamford Convention & Visitors Bureau, One Landmark Square, 06902; 203/359-4761.

Stamford is a corporate headquarters, manufacturing and research center as well as a residential suburb of New York City. More than 20 Fortune 500 corporations are located in this area. An assortment of marinas and beaches provide recreation on Long Island Sound.

What to See and Do

First Presbyterian Church (1958). Contemporary building shaped like a fish, designed by Wallace Harrison; glass by Gabriel Loire of Chartres,

France; 56-bell carillon tower (1968), summer concerts (July, Thurs night, Sun morning; June & Aug, Sun morning). 1101 Bedford St. Phone 203/324-9522. **Free.**

University of Connecticut-Bartlett Arboretum. Collections of dwarf conifers, rhododendrons, azaleas, wildflowers, perrenials and witches brooms; ecology trails and swamp walk are within the natural woodlands surrounding the gardens. Grounds (daily). 151 Brookdale Rd, off High Ridge Rd, 1 mi N of Merritt Pkwy (CT 15) exit 35. Phone 203/322-6971. **Free.**

Whitney Museum of American Art at Champion. Local branch of Whitney Museum of New York offers changing exhibits, gallery talks (Tues, Thurs & Sat), concerts & other related programs and activities. (Tues-Sat) Atlantic St & Tresser Blvd, downtown. Phone 203/358-7630 or 203/358-7652. **Free.**

Annual Event

Festival of Arts. Mill River Park. Various exhibits of performing and visual arts. Late June.

Motel

✔★ SUPER 8. 32 Grenhart Rd (06902), I-95 exit 6. 203/324-8887. 99 rms, 4 story. S $52.88; D $61.88; each addl $5; under 12 free; wkly rates; higher rates special events. Crib avail. TV; cable (premium), VCR avail. Complimentary continental bkfst. Restaurant nearby. Ck-out 1 pm. Refrigerators, microwaves avail. Cr cds: A, C, D, DS, ER, JCB, MC, V.

Hotels

★ ★ ★ HOLIDAY INN SELECT. 700 Main St (06901), I-95 exit 8. 203/358-8400; FAX 203/358-8872. Web www.holiday-inn.com. 385 rms, 10 story. S, D $99-$139; suites $400-$500; under 12 free; wkend rates. Crib free. TV; cable (premium), VCR avail. Indoor pool. Coffee in rms. Restaurants 6-11 am, 5-11 pm. Bar noon-midnight; wkends to 1:30 am. Ck-out noon. Coin lndry. Convention facilities. Business center. Gift shop. Garage. Free RR station transportation. Exercise equipt. Health club privileges. Some refrigerators. Microwaves avail. Luxury level. Cr cds: A, C, D, DS, JCB, MC, V.

★ ★ ★ MARRIOTT. 2 Stamford Forum (06901). 203/357-9555; FAX 203/357-6897. 506 rms, 17 story. S, D $145-$164; each addl $10; suites $250-$440; wkend rates. Crib free. Covered parking $3/day. TV; cable (premium), VCR avail. Indoor/outdoor pool; whirlpool, poolside serv. Restaurant 6:30 am-2 pm, 5-10 pm; Sat, Sun 7 am-10 pm. Bars; entertainment. Ck-out noon. Coin lndry. Convention facilities. Business center. In-rm modem link. Gift shop. Beauty shop. Exercise rm; sauna, steam rm. Game rm. Luxury level. Cr cds: A, C, D, DS, JCB, MC, V.

★ ★ ★ SHERATON. 2701 Summer St (06905). 203/359-1300; FAX 203/348-7937. 445 rms, 5 story. S, D $185-$220; each addl $30; suites $179-$300; under 18 free; wkend rates. Crib free. TV; cable (premium), VCR avail. Heated pool; whirlpool. Restaurant 6:30 am-11 pm. Bar noon-midnight. Ck-out noon. Coin lndry. Convention facilities. Business center. Beauty shop. Exercise rm; sauna. Some refrigerators; microwaves avail. 5-story atrium lobby. Cr cds: A, C, D, DS, ER, MC, V.

★ ★ STAMFORD SUITES. 720 Bedford St (06901), I-95 exit 7. 203/359-7300; FAX 203/359-7304. E-mail sales@stamford.newcastle hotels.com; web www.stamfordsuites.com. 42 suites, 8 story. Suites $259-$299; under 16 free; wkly, wkend, hol, monthly rates. Crib free. TV; cable (premium). Complimentary continental bkfst. Restaurants nearby. No rm serv. Ck-out 11 am. Business center. In-rm modem link. No bellhops. Free garage parking. Health club privileges. Bathrm phones, in-rm whirlpools, refrigerators, microwaves, minibars. Cr cds: A, C, D, DS, MC, V.

★ ★ ★ WESTIN. 1 First Stamford Place (06902), I-95 exit 7 N. 203/967-2222; FAX 203/967-3475. Web www.ittsheraton.com. 480 rms, 10 story. S, D $145; each addl $20; suites $200-$500; wkend rates. Crib free. Garage: self-park free, valet parking $6. TV; cable (premium), VCR avail. Indoor pool; whirlpool, poolside serv. Coffee in rms. Restaurants 6 am-10:30 pm. Bar 11:30-1:00 am. Ck-out noon. Convention facilities. Business center. In-rm modem link. Concierge. Gift shop. Tennis. Exercise equipt. Health club privileges. Some bathrm phones; microwaves avail. Cr cds: A, C, D, DS, ER, JCB, MC, V.

Restaurants

★ ★ ★ AMADEUS. 201 Summer St (06901), I-95 exit 7. 203/348-7775. E-mail gwamadeus@aol.com; web www.connmart.com/amadeus. Continental menu. Specialties: Vienna schnitzel, New Zealand rack of lamb. Hrs: noon-2:30 pm, 5:30-9:30 pm; Fri to 10 pm; Sat 5-11 pm; Sun 5-9 pm. Closed some major hols; also Sun June-Aug. Res accepted. Bar. Wine list. Semi-a la carte: lunch $9-$13.50, dinner $16.75-$26. Pianist evenings. Viennese atmosphere. Jacket. Cr cds: A, C, D, DS, MC, V.

★ CRAB SHELL. 46 Southfield Ave (06902), at Stamford Landing. 203/967-7229. Web www.mv.com/users/lindaknight/crabshell. Specializes in grilled seafood, Maryland blue crab, ribs. Hrs: 11:30 am-3 pm, 5-10 pm; Fri to 11 pm; Sat noon-11 pm; Sun noon-9:30 pm. Bar. Semi-a la carte: lunch $6.95-$12.95, dinner $8.95-$29.95. Child's meals. Parking. Entertainment. Waterfront dining. Cr cds: A, D, DS, MC, V.

★ ★ GIOVANNI'S. 1297 Long Ridge Rd (06903), S on Merritt Pkwy, exit 34, E at stoplight. 203/322-8870. Web www.giovannis.com. Specializes in steak & chops, seafood. Own pasta. Hrs: 11:30 am-3 pm, 4:30-10 pm; Sat 4:30-10:30 pm; Sun noon-9 pm. Closed Thanksgiving, Dec 25. Bar. Semi-a la carte: lunch $6-$11, dinner $12-$27.95. Child's meals. Three dining rms with semi-formal atmosphere; lobster tank in lobby. Family-owned. Cr cds: A, C, D, DS.

★ ★ IL FALCO. 59 Broad St (06902), I-95 exit 7. 203/327-0002. Italian menu. Specializes in pasta, veal, fresh seafood. Hrs: noon-3 pm, 5:30-10:30 pm; Fri to 11 pm; Sat 5:30-11 pm. Closed Sun; some major hols. Res accepted. Bar. A la carte entrees: lunch $9.50-$15.50, dinner $11.50-$22. Parking. Pleasant atmosphere. Cr cds: A, C, D, DS, MC, V.

★ ★ KATHLEEN'S. 25 Bank St (06901), I-95S, exit 8, W on Atlantic, W on Main, W on Bank. 203/323-7785. Web www.diners-grapevine.com/kathleen. Contemporary Amer menu. Specializes in seafood. Own pastries, pasta. Hrs: 11:30 am-3 pm, 5:30-10 pm; Fri to 11 pm; Sat 5:30- 11 pm. Closed Sun; most major hols. Res accepted. Bar. Semi-a la carte: lunch $6.75-$15.99, dinner $15.25-$24. Outdoor dining. Contemporary decor; wine bottle motif. Cr cds: A, C, D, DS, MC, V.

★ ★ LA BRETAGNE. 2010 W Main St (US 1) (06902), I-95 exit 5. 203/324-9539. Country French menu. Specializes in seafood, veal, duck. Hrs: noon-2:30 pm, 6-9:30 pm; Fri, Sat to 10 pm. Closed Sun; most major hols. Res accepted; required Sat. Bar. Semi-a la carte: lunch $9-$18, dinner $21-$28. Child's meals. Parking. Cr cds: A, C, D, MC, V.

★ ★ LA HACIENDA. 222 Summer St, I-95 exit 8. 203/324-0577. Mexican menu. Specializes in fresh fish, game. Hrs: 11:30 am-2:30

pm, 5-10 pm; Fri to 11:30 pm; Sat noon-11:30 pm; Sun 1-9:30 pm. Closed Thanksgiving, Dec 25. Res accepted. Bar. Semi-a la carte: lunch $8.95-$14.95, dinner $10.95-$17.95. Parking. Outdoor dining. Multi-level dining. Southwestern decor. Cr cds: A, D, MC, V.

✔★ **MEERA, CUISINE OF INDIA.** *227 Summer St (06901), I-95 N exit 8.* 203/975-0479. Indian menu. Specializes in tandoor chicken, chicken tikka kebab. Salad bar. Hrs: 11:45 am-2:30 pm, 5:30-10 pm; Fri to 11 pm; Sat 5-11 pm. Res accepted. Bar. A la carte entrees: lunch, dinner $5-$12.95. Lunch buffet $8.95. Indian decor. Cr cds: A, C, D, MC, V.

Stonington (E-5)

(See also Groton, Norwich, Mystic, New London, Old Lyme, Old Saybrook; also see Westerly, RI)

Settled 1649 **Pop** 16,919 **Elev** 7 ft **Area code** 860 **Zip** 06378 **E-mail** more2see@aol.com **Web** www.mysticmore.com
Information Connecticut's Mystic and More!, 470 Bank St, PO Box 89, New London 06320; 860/444-2206 or 800/863-6569 outside CT.

Until their defeat at Mystic Fort in 1637, the Pequot dominated the area around Stonington. In 1649, the first European settlers came here from Rehoboth, Massachusetts. Connecticut and Massachusetts both claimed ownership of the territory. In 1662, permanent control was granted to Connecticut by charter from King Charles II. Three years later the area was officially called Mystic, and in 1666 the name was changed to Stonington (which includes Stonington Borough).

The conclusion of the King Philip War in 1676 effectively ended the Native American threat in southern New England. The local economy, based on farming, shipping and manufacturing, thrived. Prior to the Civil War, whaling and sealing expeditions left Stonington's port at regular intervals. After the war, maritime interests flourished, as Stonington served as the connecting point for rail and steamer service to New York City. Today this maritime heritage is represented by a commercial fishing fleet and recreational boating.

What to See and Do

Old Lighthouse Museum. First government-operated lighthouse in Connecticut (1823); exhibits include Stonington-made firearms, stoneware; ship models, whaling gear; China trade objects; folk art; local artifacts. Children's gallery. Visitors can climb the tower for a panoramic view of Long Island Sound. (May-June & Sept-Oct, daily exc Mon; July-Aug, daily; rest of yr, by appt) 7 Water St. Phone 860/535-1440 (summer) or 860/535-1492 (winter). ¢

Inn

★ ★ **RANDALL'S ORDINARY.** *(CT 2, North Stonington 06359) N of I-95 exit 92.* 860/599-4540; FAX 860/599-3308. 15 units in 2 bldgs, 2 story, 1 suite. Many rm phones. S, D, suite $75-$195; each addl $10. TV in most rms; cable (premium). Complimentary continental bkfst. Dining rm 7-11 am, noon-2 pm, 7-10 pm. Ck-out 11 am, ck-in 2 pm. Business servs avail. X-country ski on site. Lawn games. Picnic tables. Historic buildings (1685 & 1819); many antiques; 3 dining rms, each with fireplace. Rural setting; 200 acres with barn and some farm animals. Cr cds: A, MC, V.

Storrs (D-4)

(See also Hartford, Manchester, Stafford Springs)

Pop 12,198 **Elev** 600 ft **Area code** 860 **Zip** 06268 **E-mail** quietcorner@snet.net; **Web** www.webtravels.com/quietcorner
Information Northeast Connecticut Visitors District, PO Box 598, Putnam 06260; 860/928-1228 or 888/628-1228.

What to See and Do

Ballard Institute and Museum of Puppetry. Features changing exhibits from collection of over 2,000 puppets. Gives visitors appreciation of puppetry as artform. (Mid-Apr-mid-Nov, Fri & Sat) 6 Boum Pl. Phone 860/468-4605. **Free.**

Caprilands Herb Farm. More than 30 different theme gardens using herbs, spices and wild grasses; 18th-century farm building; lunchtime lectures (Apr-Dec; fee). Tea program (Sun). Basket & bookshops. (Daily) 8 mi SW via US 44 to 534 Silver St in Coventry. Phone 860/742-7244. **Free.**

Nathan Hale Homestead (1776). Country-Georgian-style structure built by Nathan's father, Richard. Restored; many original furnishings. (Mid-May-mid-Oct, afternoons) 8 mi SW via US 44 to 2299 South St in Coventry. Phone 860/742-6917 or 860/247-8996. **¢¢**

University of Connecticut (1881). (26,200 students) On campus are state's largest public research library, art galleries, museums, animal barns, biological and floricultural greenhouses (tours; free). (See SEASONAL EVENT) SE on I-84 exit 68, then S on CT 195. Phone 860/486-3530 or 860/486-2000; for campus tours phone 860/486-4866. Also here are

William Benton Museum of Art. Permanent collection including American and European paintings, sculpture, prints and drawings; changing exhibits. (Tues-Sun; closed hols & between exhibitions) 245 Glenbrook Rd. Phone 860/486-4520. **Free.**

Connecticut State Museum of Natural History. Exhibits on Native Americans, mounted birds of prey, honey bees, sharks, minerals. (Thurs-Mon, afternoons) Wilbur Cross Bldg. Phone 860/486-4460. **Free.**

Seasonal Event

Connecticut Repertory Theatre. Univ of Connecticut, Harriet S. Jorgensen Theatre. Musicals, comedies and dramas. Nightly. Phone 860/486-4226. July & Sept-May exc Jan.

Stratford (F-2)

(See also Bridgeport, Fairfield, Milford, Norwalk)

Settled 1639 **Pop** 49,389 **Elev** 25 ft **Area code** 203 **Zip** 06497 **E-mail** info@brbc.org
Information Chamber of Commerce, 10 Middle St, PO Box 999, 06601-0999; 203/335-3800.

A fine port on the Housatonic River, Stratford has been a hub of shipbuilding and industry for more than three centuries.

What to See and Do

Boothe Memorial Park. Former Boothe homestead (1663-1949) on 30 acres; unusual, historical buildings; Boothe home and carriage house (mid-May-late Oct, daily exc Mon), Americana Museum, blacksmith shop, architecturally eccentric "technocratic cathedral"; flower gardens, rose garden, picnicking, playgrounds. Park (daily). Other buildings (Memorial Day-late Oct, daily) Main St. Phone 203/381-2068 or 203/385-4085. **Free.**

Captain David Judson House (ca 1750). Restored and furnished colonial house; period furnishings and crafts, slave quarters, tool display; local history exhibits. (Late May-Oct, Wed, Sat, Sun; closed Memorial Day, July 4) 967 Academy Hill. Phone 203/378-0630. ¢ Admission includes

Catharine B. Mitchell Museum. Changing and permanent exhibits depict history of the Stratford area 1639-1830; local memorabilia. (Same hrs as Judson House)

Motel

✔★ **HONEY SPOT LODGE.** *360 Honeyspot Rd.* 203/375-5666; *FAX* 203/278-1509. 93 rms, 2 story. S $32.95-$55; D $39.95-$60; each addl $8; under 18 free. Crib avail. TV; cable (premium). Pool. Ck-out noon. Meeting rms. Business servs avail. Cr cds: A, C, D, DS, MC, V.

[icons]

Hotel

★ ★ **RAMADA INN.** *225 Lordship Blvd, near Igor I. Sikorsky Memorial Airport.* 203/375-8866; *FAX* 203/375-2482. 145 rms, 6 story. S, D $85-$100; each addl $10; under 18 free; wkend rates. Crib free. TV; cable (premium). Indoor pool. Restaurant 6:30 am-2 pm, 5-10 pm; Sun 7 am-9 pm. Bar. Ck-out noon. Meeting rms. Business servs avail. Free airport, RR station, bus depot transportation. Health club privileges. Cr cds: A, C, D, DS, JCB, MC, V.

[icons]

Terryville

(see Bristol)

Vernon (D-4)

(See also Hartford, Manchester, Windsor)

Pop 29,841 **Elev** 350 ft **Area code** 860 **Zip** 06066 **E-mail** ctfuntour@aol.com; **Web** www.travelfile.com/get/ghtd
Information Greater Hartford Tourism District, 234 Murphy Rd, Hartford 06114; 860/244-8181 or 800/793-4480.

Motel

★ ★ **QUALITY INN & CONFERENCE CENTER.** *51 Hartford Tpke.* 860/646-5700; *FAX* 860/646-0202. 127 rms, 2 story. S $49.95-$79; D $79-$125; under 18 free. Crib free. TV; cable (premium). Pool. Continental bkfst. Restaurant 11:30 am-10 pm; Sat, Sun, hols 7 am-11 pm. Rm serv 11:30 am-9 pm; Sun from noon. Bar 11:30 am-midnight; Fri, Sat to 1 am. Ck-out 11 am. Coin lndry. Meeting rms. Business servs avail. In-rm modem link. Valet serv. Sundries. Par-3 golf; miniature golf. Health club privileges. Game rm. Refrigerators. Cr cds: A, C, D, DS, MC, V.

[icons]

Inns

★ **CUMON INN.** *(130 Buckland Rd, South Windsor 06074)* 1/2 mi N of I-84 exit 62. 860/644-8486; *FAX* 800/286-6646. 8 rms, 6 share bath, 2 story. No rm phones. S, D $50-$100. Complimentary full bkfst. Ck-out 11 am, ck-in 2 pm. Free airport transportation. Reproduction of colonial salt box structure. Antiques; library. On working farm. No cr cds accepted.

★ ★ **TOLLAND INN.** *(63 Tolland Green, Tolland 06084-0717)* approx 3/4 mi N on I-84, exit 68, N on CT 195. 860/872-0800; *FAX*

860/870-7958. E-mail tollinn@ntplx.net. 7 rms, 4 with shower only, 2 story, 2 suites. No rm phones. S $60-$120; D $70-$130; suites $110-$130; wkly rates; wkends May & Oct (2-day min). Children over 10 yrs only. TV; VCR. Complimentary full bkfst. Ck-out 11 am, ck-in 4-9 pm. Concierge serv. Luggage handling. X-country ski 7 mi. Refrigerators. Picnic tables. New England inn built 1800; handcrafted furniture. Totally nonsmoking. Cr cds: A, C, D, DS, MC, V.

[icons]

Restaurant

✔★ **REIN'S NEW YORK STYLE DELI.** *435 Hartford Tpke.* 860/875-1344. New York-style delicatessen. Specializes in corned beef, lox & bagels, pastrami. Hrs: 7 am-midnight. Bar. Semi-a la carte: bkfst, lunch, dinner $3.75-$8.95. Child's meals. Cr cds: A, MC, V.

[icon]

Washington

Area code 860

Inn

★ ★ ★ ★ ★ **MAYFLOWER INN.** *CT 47 (06793), 4 mi W.* 860/868-9466; *FAX* 860/868-1497. This idyllic retreat in the Litchfield Hills of western Connecticut was restored in 1992 to look like a generations-old elegant country estate. There's fine dining on site, and guest rooms are large, some with balconies and fireplaces and all with views of the magnificent manicured gardens ablaze with flowers in season. 25 rms in 3 bldgs, 2-3 story, 7 suites. S, D $290-$430; each addl (1 addl max) $50; suites $450-$690; 2-3-day min wkends. Children over 12 yrs only. Valet parking wkends. TV; cable (premium), VCR avail (movies). Heated pool. Dining rm 7:30-11 am, noon-2 pm; dinner (public by res) 6-9 pm. Rm serv 24 hrs. Ck-out 1 pm, ck-in 3 pm. Meeting rms. Business servs avail. In-rm modem link. Luggage handling. Sundries. Gift shop. Tennis, pro. 9-hole golf privileges. Extensive exercise rm; sauna, steam rm. Massage. Game rm. Refrigerators, minibars. Balconies. Totally nonsmoking. Cr cds: A, MC, V.

[icons]

Waterbury (E-2)

(See also Bristol, Meriden, New Britain)

Settled 1674 **Pop** 108,961 **Elev** 290 ft **Area code** 203 **E-mail** wrcvb@compuserve.com
Information Waterbury Region Convention & Visitors Bureau, 21 Church St, 06702-2106; 203/597-9527.

Waterbury, fourth-largest city in Connecticut, was once an important manufacturing center for brass related products. Today, high-technology manufacturing and the banking industry dominate the economy. Waterbury's location near major highways provides quick and direct access to all Eastern cities.

What to See and Do

Brass Mill Center. Over 1 million-sq-ft indoor mall with many shops, food court, and 12-screen movie theater. (Daily) I-84 exit 22 or 23, at 495 Union St. Phone 203/755-5003

Mattatuck Museum. Industrial history exhibit, decorative arts, period rms, paintings and prints by Connecticut artists. (July-Aug, Tues-Sat; rest of yr, daily exc Mon; closed hols) 144 W Main St. Phone 203/753-0381. **Free.**

Quassy Amusement Park. More than 30 different rides and activities set against Lake Quassapaug; miniature golf; petting zoo; beach, swimming, boating; picnicking, concession. (Late May-Labor Day, daily; Apr-late May, after Labor Day-Oct, wkends) 5 mi W on I-84 exit 17, on CT 64 in Middlebury. Phone 203/758-2913. All-day pass ¢¢¢; Parking fee ¢¢

Motel

✔★ **KNIGHTS INN.** 2636 S Main St (06706), I-84 exit 19 to CT 8 exit 29. 203/756-7961; FAX 203/754-6642. 84 rms, 2 story. S $39.95-$45.95; D $45.95-$55.95; each addl $8; under 18 free. Crib free. Pet accepted; $8. TV; cable (premium). Pool. Restaurant open 24 hrs. Ck-out 11 am. Meeting rms. Business center. Valet serv. Sundries. Balconies. Cr cds: A, C, D, DS, MC, V.

⬜🏊🛏🔀 SC 🏃

Motor Hotel

★ ★ **FOUR POINTS BY SHERATON.** 3580 E Main St (06705). 203/573-1000; FAX 203/573-1349. E-mail sales@waterbury.newcastle hotels.com; web www.fourpointshotels.com. 279 rms, 4 story. S, D $75-$129; under 18 free; wkend rates. Crib free. TV; cable (premium). Indoor pool; whirlpool. Restaurant 6:30 am-11 pm. Rm serv. Sports bar. Ck-out noon. Convention facilities. Business servs avail. In-rm modem link. Bellhops. Sundries. Valet serv. Exercise equipt; sauna, steam rm. Some refrigerators. Balconies. Cr cds: A, D, DS, MC, V.

⬜🏊🏃🛏🔥 SC

Inn

★ ★ **HOUSE ON THE HILL.** 92 Woodlawn Terrace (06710-1929). 203/757-9901. 4 suites, 3 story, 1 kit. unit. 1 rm with A/C. Suites $100-$150; kit. unit $100; wkly rates; wkends, hols (2-day min). TV; cable. Complimentary full bkfst. Coffee in rms. Ck-out 11 am, ck-in 3-6 pm. Luggage handling. Concierge serv. Free RR station, bus depot transportation. Lawn games. Some refrigerators. Historic mansion built in 1888; library, gardens, many fireplaces. Totally nonsmoking. No cr cds accepted.

🔀🔥

Restaurant

★ **SEAFOOD PEDDLER.** 689 Wolcott St. 203/597-9466. Italian, Amer menu. Specializes in seafood, pasta. Oyster bar. Hrs: 11:30 am-10 pm; Fri, Sat to 11 pm. Closed Thanksgiving, Dec 25. Res accepted. Bar. Semi-a la carte: lunch $3.99-$7.99, dinner $7.99-$19.99. Child's meals. Cr cds: A, DS, MC, V.

⬜

Westport (F-1)

(See also Bridgeport, Fairfield, Norwalk, Stamford)

Settled 1648 **Pop** 24,410 **Elev** 78 ft **Area code** 203 **Zip** 06880 **E-mail** wcc@webquill.com **Web** www.bcnnews.com/westport//chamber
Information Chamber of Commerce, 180 Post Rd E, PO Box 30; 203/227-9234.

Westport is a fashionable community on Long Island Sound 45 miles from New York City. Well-known writers and many successful actors, illustrators and corporate and advertising executives make their homes here. Westport is surrounded by wooded hills and has three municipal beaches and a state park on the Sound.

Annual Events

Westport Handcrafts Fair. Staples High School Field House. Features 100 crafts artisans. Phone 203/227-9318. Memorial Day wkend.

Antique Dealers Outdoor Show and Sale. Phone 203/227-9234. Early Sept.

Seasonal Events

Westport Country Playhouse. 25 Powers Court, on Post Rd E. Broadway and pre-Broadway presentations by professional companies. Nightly exc Sun; matinees Wed & Sat; children's shows Fri. Phone 203/227-4177. Mid-June-mid-Sept.

Levitt Pavilion for the Performing Arts. Jesup Green, on the Saugatuck River. Nightly free outdoor performances of classical, jazz, pop, rock; dance, children's series. Phone 203/226-7600. Late June-late Aug.

Motor Hotel

★ ★ **WESTPORT INN.** 1595 Post Rd E (US 1). 203/259-5236; FAX 203/254-8439; res: 800/446-8997. 116 rms, 2 story. S $103-$149; D $109-$159; each addl $10; suites $210-$285; under 18 free. Crib free. TV; cable (premium), VCR avail (movies). Indoor pool; whirlpool. Coffee in rms. Restaurant 7-11 am, 6-10 pm. Rm serv. Bar. Meeting rms. Bellhops. Sundries. Exercise equipt; sauna. Game rm. Bathrm phone, wetbar, refrigerator in suites. Cr cds: A, D, DS, MC, V.

⬜🏊🏃🛏🔥 SC

Inns

★ ★ **THE INN AT LONGSHORE.** 260 S Compo Rd. 203/226-3316; FAX 203/226-5723. 10 rms, 3 story, 3 suites. Apr-Oct: S $110; D $150; suites $175; lower rates rest of yr. Crib $15. TV; cable. Pool. Playground. Complimentary coffee in rms. Complimentary continental bkfst. Restaurant 11:30 am-2:30 pm, 5:30-11 pm. Ck-out noon, ck-in 3 pm. Business servs avail. Lighted tennis. 18-hole golf, greens fee $22, pro, putting green, driving range. Built as a private estate in 1890; overlooks Long Island Sound. Cr cds: A, MC, V.

🏃🧍🏊🐟🔥

★ ★ ★ **INN AT NATIONAL HALL.** 2 Post Road W. 203/221-1351; FAX 203/221-0276; res: 800/628-4255. In a historic district on the Saugatuck River, this European manor-style house built in 1873 combines old-world elegance with modern convenience. 15 rms, 3 story, 7 suites. S, D $195-$395; each addl $15; suites $425-$575; 2-day min wkends June-Nov. Crib free. TV; cable (premium), VCR (movies). Complimentary continental bkfst; refreshments in rms. Restaurant noon-2 pm, 6-10 pm. Rm serv. Ck-out 11:30 am, ck-in 3 pm. Business servs avail. Luggage handling. Concierge serv. Health club privileges. Refrigerators. Totally nonsmoking. Cr cds: A, D, MC, V.

🔀🔥

Restaurants

★ ★ **CAFE CHRISTINA.** 1 Main St. 203/221-7950. Continental menu. Specializes in fresh pasta. Hrs: 11:45 am-2:30 pm, 5:45-9:45 pm; Fri, Sat to 10:30 pm; Sun 11:45 am-3 pm (brunch), 5:45-9:45 pm. Closed Thanksgiving, Dec 25. Res accepted; required Fri, Sat. Serv bar. A la carte entrees: lunch, Sun brunch $8.50-$16, dinner $15.50-$24.50. Complete meals: dinner (exc Sat) $25.50. Child's meals. Pianist Wed-Fri evenings; jazz Sun brunch. Parking. Outdoor dining. Once section of Westport Library; original murals. Totally nonsmoking Fri, Sat evenings. Cr cds: A, C, D, MC, V.

⬜

★ ★ **COBB'S MILL INN.** (CT 57, Weston) NW on CT 57, 4 mi N of Merritt Pkwy (CT 15). 203/227-7221. Specializes in steak, chops, seafood. Hrs: 11:30 am-2:30 pm, 5-9 pm; Fri, Sat 6-10 pm; early-bird dinner Mon-Thurs 5-6:30 pm. Res accepted. Bar. A la carte entrees: lunch

$6-$11, dinner $19-$27. Valet parking. In 200-yr-old grist and lumber mill; colonial decor, pewter display. Overlooks waterfall, lake. Cr cds: A, C, D, DS, MC, V.

★ **CONNOLLY'S.** *221 Post Rd W, in Westbank Shopping Ctr. 203/226-5591.* Specializes in seafood, steak. Salad bar. Hrs: 11:30 am-9:30 pm; Fri, Sat to 10 pm; Sun 5-9 pm. Closed major hols. Bar. Semi-a la carte: lunch $4.50-$10.95, dinner $5.50-$18.95. Child's meals. Outdoor dining. Cr cds: A, D, DS, MC, V.

★ ★ **NISTICO'S RED BARN.** *On CT 33, at Merritt Pkwy (CT 15) exit 41. 203/222-9549.* Continental menu. Specializes in live Maine lobster, rack of lamb, prime rib. Hrs: 11:30 am-2:15 pm, 5-10 pm; Sun from 5 pm; Sun brunch sittings 11:30 am & 1:30 pm. Closed Dec 24-25. Res accepted. Serv bar. Semi-a la carte: lunch $5.95-$12.95, dinner $14.95-$29.95. Sun brunch $16.95. Child's meals. Pianist Fri, Sat. Valet parking Sat. Outdoor dining. Cr cds: A, C, D, DS, MC, V.

★ ★ **PROMIS.** *1563 Post Rd E. 203/256-3309.* Specialties: buttermilk-fried chicken, Louisiana-style crab & crawfish cakes. Hrs: noon-2:30 pm, 6-10 pm; Fri to 10:30 pm; Sat 6-10:30 pm; Sun 5-9 pm. Closed most major hols. Res accepted. Bar. A la carte entrees: lunch $4.50-$12, dinner $14-$22. Child's meals. Jazz duo Fri, Sat. Parking. Outdoor dining. Ceiling murals; upbeat atmosphere. Totally nonsmoking. Cr cds: A, D, DS, MC, V.

D

Wethersfield (D-3)

(See also Avon, Hartford, Windsor)

Settled 1634 **Pop** 25,651 **Elev** 45 ft **Area code** 860 **Zip** 06109 **Web** www.westhist.org
Information Wethersfield Historical Society, 150 Main St; 860/529-7656.

Wethersfield, "the most ancient towne in Connecticut," has a rich heritage. Settled by a group of Massachusetts colonists, it became the commercial center of the Connecticut River communities and an important post in the trade between the American colonies and the West Indies. Agriculture, especially corn, rye and, later, the famous red onion, was the source of Wethersfield's trade. During the Revolutionary War years, notable figures, such as George Washington and Count de Rochambeau, came to Wethersfield and decided upon plans that became part of US history. Many existing buildings date from the Revolutionary War.

With the birth and development of the railroad and the shift of trade to the coastal villages, Wethersfield's importance as an industrial and commercial center declined.

What to See and Do

Buttolph-Williams House (ca 1700). Restored building contains fine collection of pewter, delft, fabrics, period furniture. (May-Oct, daily exc Tues, limited hrs) 249 Broad St, at Marsh St. Phone 860/529-0460, 860/529-0612 or 860/247-8996. ¢

★ **Dinosaur State Park.** While excavating the site of a new building, a stone slab bearing the 3-toed tracks of dinosaurs, which roamed the area 200 million yrs ago, was discovered. Construction was halted, and a 65-acre area was designated a state park. Eventually more than 2,000 prints were unearthed. A geodesic dome was set up over parts of the trackway to protect the find. Visitors are able to examine the crisscrossing tracks and view a skeletal cast and life-size models of the area's prehistoric inhabitants. Nature trails; picnicking. Exhibit center (daily exc Mon; closed Jan 1, Thanksgiving, Dec 25). Park (daily). 3 mi S via I-91 exit 23, off West St in Rocky Hill. Phone 860/529-8423. ¢

First Church of Christ, Congregational United Church of Christ. Church established 1635; the Meetinghouse (1761; restored 1973) is the third one to stand on or near this site. (Mon-Fri; also by appt) Main & Marsh Sts. Phone 860/529-1575. **Free.**

Hurlburt-Dunham House. Georgian house updated in Italianate style. Rich in decoration, including original Rococo Revival wallpapers, painted ceilings and a varied collection of furniture. (Mid-Mar-mid-May, mid-Oct-Dec 25, Sat & Sun; mid-May-mid-Oct, Thurs-Sun) 212 Main St. Phone 860/529-7656. ¢¢

Webb-Deane-Stevens Museum. Consists of three 18th-century houses that stand at the center of old Wethersfield: the Joseph Webb house (1752), the Silas Deane house (1766) and the Isaac Stevens house (1788). The houses have been restored and are furnished with objects to reflect the different ways of life of their owners—a merchant, a diplomat and a tradesman; also flower & herb gardens. (May-Oct, daily exc Tues; rest of yr, Fri-Sun) 211 Main St. Phone 860/529-0612. Combination ticket ¢¢¢

Wethersfield Museum. Changing exhibit galleries; permanent Wethersfield exhibit. (Daily exc Mon) Keeney Memorial Cultural Center, 200 Main St. Phone 860/529-7161. ¢

Motor Hotel

✔ ★ ★ **RAMADA INN.** *1330 Silas Deane Hwy. 860/563-2311.* 112 rms, 4 story. S, D $42-$59; under 18 free. Crib free. Pet accepted. TV; cable (premium), VCR avail. Complimentary continental bkfst. Restaurant adj 11 am-10 pm. Bar; entertainment Fri, Sat. Ck-out noon. Coin lndry. Meeting rms. Business servs avail. In-rm modem link. Downhill ski 20 mi. Health club privileges. Some in-rm whirlpools. Cr cds: A, C, D, DS, MC, V.

Windsor (D-3)

(See also Enfield, Hartford, Manchester)

Settled 1633 **Pop** 27,817 **Elev** 57 ft **Area code** 860 **Zip** 06095
Information Chamber of Commerce, 261 Broad St, PO Box 9, 06095-0009, phone 860/688-5165; or the Tobacco Valley Convention & Visitors District, 111 Hazard Ave, Enfield 06082, phone 860/763-2578.

Windsor was first settled by members of an expeditionary group from the original Plymouth Colony. A farming center since the 17th century, it is only nine miles north of Hartford. The village is divided by the Farmington River; there is a green and many colonial houses on each side of the river.

What to See and Do

Connecticut Trolley Museum. Unlimited 3-mi ride on vintage trolleys; static displays. (Memorial Day-Labor Day, daily; rest of yr, wkends) 58 North Rd. Phone 860/627-6540. ¢¢¢

Oliver Ellsworth Homestead (1781). Home of one of five men who drafted the Constitution; third Chief Justice of the US and one of the first senators from Connecticut; Washington and Adams visited the house. Restored to period; many original Ellsworth furnishings. (May-Oct, Tues, Wed, Sat) 778 Palisado Ave. Phone 860/688-8717. ¢¢

The First Church in Windsor (1630). (United Church of Christ Congregational) Classic Georgian-style architecture (1794); cemetery (1644) adjacent. Request key at church office, 107 Palisado Ave. (Daily) 75 Palisado Ave. Phone 860/688-7229. **Free.**

Windsor Historical Society. Walking tours of the Lt. Walter Fyler House (1640) and the Dr. Hezekiah Chaffee House (1765); period costumes and furnishings; Puritan cemetery. (Apr-Oct, Tues-Sat; Nov-Mar, Mon-Fri) 96 Palisado Ave. Phone 860/688-3813. ¢¢

Motels

★ ★ **COURTYARD BY MARRIOTT.** *1 Day Hill Rd. 860/683-0022; FAX 860/683-1072.* 149 rms, 2 story. S, D $119; suites $139; wkend rates. Crib free. TV; cable (premium), VCR avail. Indoor pool; whirlpool. Complimentary coffee in rms. Restaurant 6:30-10:30 am, 5-10 pm; Sat-

Sun 7-11 am, 5-10 pm. Ck-out 1 pm. Coin lndry. Meeting rms. Business servs avail. In-rm modem link. Valet serv. Sundries. Exercise equipt. Game rm. Refrigerator in suites. Balconies. Marble courtyard, gazebo. Cr cds: A, C, D, DS, MC, V.

⬚ 🏊 🏋 🛶 🔥 SC

★ ★ **RESIDENCE INN BY MARRIOTT.** *100 Dunfey Lane.* *860/688-7474; FAX 860/683-8457.* Web www.residenceinn.com. 96 kit. suites, 2 story. S, D $129-$159. Crib avail. Pet accepted; $100. TV; cable (premium), VCR avail. Pool; whirlpool. Complimentary continental bkfst. Complimentary coffee in rms. Ck-out noon. Coin lndry. Meeting rm. Business servs avail. In-rm modem link. Valet serv. Free airport transportation. Lawn games. Some fireplaces. Picnic tables, grill. Cr cds: A, C, D, DS, JCB, MC, V.

⬚ 🐾 🏊 🛶 🔥 SC

Windsor Locks (C-3)

(See also Enfield, Hartford, Windsor; also see Springfield, MA)

Pop 12,358 **Elev** 80 ft **Area code** 860 **Zip** 06096
Information Chamber of Commerce, PO Box 257; 860/623-9319.

What to See and Do

New England Air Museum. One of the largest and most comprehensive collections of aircraft and aeronautical memorabilia in the world. More than 80 aircraft on display including bombers, fighters, helicopters and gliders dating from 1909-present era; movies; jet fighter cockpit simulator. Tour guides. (Daily; closed Thanksgiving, Dec 25) Adj to Bradley International Airport, 3 mi SW via I-91 exit 40, W on CT 20 to CT 75, follow signs. Phone 860/623-3305. ¢¢¢

Noden-Reed House & Barn. Housed in 1840 house and 1825 barn are antique sleigh bed, 1871 taffeta evening dress, 1884 wedding dress, antique quilts, kitchen utensils, 1880s newspapers and periodicals. (May-Oct, Sun afternoons) 58 West St. Phone 860/627-9212. **Free.**

Old New Gate Prison. Site of a copper mine (1707) converted to Revolutionary prison for Tories (1775-1782) and a state prison (until 1827); self-guided tour of underground caverns where prisoners lived. (Mid-May-Oct, Wed-Sun) 8 mi W on US 91 to exit 40; in East Granby at jct Newgate Rd and CT 120. Phone 860/653-3563 or 860/566-3005. ¢¢

Trolley Museum. Exhibits include more than 50 antique trolley cars from 1894-1949; operating trolleys take visitors on 3-mi ride through countryside; electric passenger trains also operate some wkends. (Memorial Day-Labor Day, daily; rest of yr, Sat, Sun & hols; closed Thanksgiving, Dec 25) In East Windsor at 58 North Rd (CT 140); from Windsor Locks proceed NE on I-91 to exit 45, then ³/₄ mi E on CT 140 *(for clarification of directions, phone ahead).* Phone 860/627-6540. ¢¢¢ On grounds is

Connecticut Fire Museum. Collection of fire engines and antique motorcoaches from 1856-1954. (June-Aug, daily; Apr-May & Sept-Oct, Sat & Sun) Phone 860/623-4732. ¢

Motel

★ ★ **HOMEWOOD SUITES.** *65 Ella Grasso Tpke, near Hartford Bradley Intl Airport. 860/627-8463; FAX 860/627-9313.* 132 kit. suites, 2-3 story. S, D $99-$140. Crib free. Pet accepted, some restrictions; $10. TV; cable, VCR (movies). Pool. Complimentary continental bkfst. Complimentary coffee in rms. Restaurant nearby. Ck-out noon. Coin lndry. Business center. In-rm modem link. Valet serv. Sundries. Gift shop. Free airport, RR station transportation. Exercise equipt. Lawn games. Picnic tables. Cr cds: A, C, D, DS, MC, V.

⬚ 🐾 🏊 🏋 ✈ 🛶 🔥 SC 🚶

Motor Hotel

★ ★ **DOUBLETREE.** *16 Ella Grasso Tpke, near Hartford Bradley Intl Airport. 860/627-5171; FAX 860/627-7029.* 200 rms, 5 story. S, D $69-$119; each addl $10; suites $150-$195; under 18 free; wkend rates; higher rates Dec 31. Crib avail. TV; cable (premium), VCR avail. Indoor pool; whirlpool. Restaurant 6:30 am-10 pm. Rm serv. Bar 4-11 pm. Ck-out noon. Coin lndry. Meeting rms. Business servs avail. Bellhops. Valet serv. Free airport, RR station transportation. Exercise equipt; sauna. Game rm. Cr cds: A, C, D, DS, ER, JCB, MC, V.

⬚ 🏊 ✈ 🛶 🔥 SC

Hotel

★ ★ ★ **SHERATON.** *1 Bradley Intl Airport, at Hartford Bradley Intl Airport. 860/627-5311; FAX 860/627-9348.* 237 rms, 8 story. Sept-June: S, D $85-$153; each addl $15; suites $225-$300; under 5 free; lower rates rest of yr. Crib free. Pet accepted, some restrictions. Free garage parking. TV; cable (premium), VCR avail. Indoor pool. Complimentary coffee in rms. Restaurant 6:30 am-10 pm. Bar 11 am-midnight; entertainment Tues-Thurs. Ck-out noon. Meeting rms. Business servs avail. Concierge. Free RR station transportation. Exercise equipt; sauna. Cr cds: A, D, MC, V.

⬚ 🐾 🏊 ✈ 🏋 🛶 🔥 SC

Woodbury (E-2)

(See also Bristol, Danbury, Waterbury)

Pop 1,290 **Elev** 264 ft **Area code** 203 **Zip** 06798
Information Litchfield Hills Travel Council, PO Box 968, Litchfield 06759; 860/567-4506.

What to See and Do

Flanders Nature Center. Large conservation area with woodland hiking trails, wildlife marshes; wildflower trails. Self-guided tour; special events including maple syrup demonstration (Mar). (Daily) Church Hill & Flanders Rd. Phone 203/263-3711. **Free.**

Glebe House and Gertrude Jekyll Garden (ca 1770). Minister's farmhouse or *glebe,* where Samuel Seabury was elected America's first Episcopal bishop in 1783; restored with 18th-century furnishings, original paneling; garden designed by Gertrude Jekyll. (Apr-Nov, Wed-Sun afternoons; rest of yr, by appt) On Hollow Rd off US 6. Phone 203/263-2855. ¢¢

Inn

★ **CURTIS HOUSE.** *506 Main St S. 203/263-2101.* 18 rms, 12 with bath, 12 A/C, 3 story. S $33.60-$72; D $61.60-$123.20; each addl $10. TV in most rms; cable (premium). Restaurant (see CURTIS HOUSE). Bar. Ck-out 11 am, ck-in 1 pm. Downhill/x-country ski 5 mi. Oldest inn in state (1754). Cr cds: DS, MC, V.

🐾 🛶

Restaurants

★ ★ **CAROLE PECK'S GOOD NEWS CAFE.** *694 Main St S. 203/266-4663.* Specialties: wok-seared shrimp, free-range rotisserie chicken. Hrs: 11:30 am-10 pm. Closed Tues; some major hols. Res accepted. Bar. A la carte entrees: lunch $5.95-$9.95, dinner $11.50-$20.

Child's meals. Jazz Sat. Outdoor dining. Modern cafe with changing artwork. Cr cds: A, D, MC, V.

D

★ **CURTIS HOUSE.** *(See Curtis House Inn)* 203/263-2101. Hrs: noon-2 pm, 5-8:30 pm; Mon from 5 pm; Sun noon-8 pm. Closed Dec 25. Res accepted major hols. Bar to 10 pm. Complete meals: lunch $7.50-$11.50, dinner $13.50-$20. Child's meals. 3 dining rms. Family-owned. Cr cds: DS, MC, V.

D

Maine

> **Population:** 1,227,928
> **Land area:** 30,995 square miles
> **Elevation:** 0-5,268 feet
> **Highest point:** Mt Katahdin (Piscataquis County)
> **Entered Union:** March 15, 1820 (23rd state)
> **Capital:** Augusta
> **Motto:** I lead
> **Nickname:** Pine Tree State
> **State flower:** Pine cone and tassel
> **State bird:** Chickadee
> **State tree:** Eastern white pine
> **State fair:** Mid-August 1999, in Skowhegan
> **Time zone:** Eastern
> **Web:** www.visitmaine.com

Here are the highest tides (28 feet in Passamaquoddy Bay), the tastiest potatoes and the tartest conversation in the country. Flat Yankee twang and the patois of French Canadians make Maine's speech as salty as its sea. Hunters, anglers, canoeists and campers appreciate its 6,000 lakes and ponds, and summer vacationers enjoy its 3,500 miles of seacoast even though the water is a bit chilly.

Downeasters brag about the state's temperature range from -46° to 105°F as well as its famous lobsters. Paper and allied products are the chief manufactured products; machine tools, electronic components and other metal products are important. Food canning and freezing are major industries. Potatoes, blueberries, poultry, eggs, dairy products and apples are leading farm crops.

Maine's first settlement (1604) was on St Croix Island; it lasted one winter. Another early settlement was established near Pemaquid Point. The short-lived Popham Colony, at the mouth of the Kennebec River, built America's first transatlantic trader, the *Virginia*, in 1607. Until 1819 Maine was a part of Massachusetts. It was admitted to the Union in 1820.

Most of Maine's 17.6 million acres of forest land is open to public recreational use including more than 580,000 acres owned by the state. For more information about recreational use of public and private forest land, contact the Maine Bureau of Public Lands, 207/287-3061, or the Maine Forest Service at 207/287-2791.

When to Go/Climate

Maine is a large state affected by several different weather patterns. Coastal temperatures are more moderate than inland temperatures, and fog is common in spring and fall. In general, winters are cold and snowy. Summers are filled with warm, sunny days and cool, clear nights. Fall's famous "nor'easters" can bring high tides, gale-force winds and huge amounts of rain to the coastal areas.

AVERAGE HIGH/LOW TEMPERATURES (°F)

CARIBOU

Jan 19/-2	**May** 62/40	**Sept** 64/43
Feb 23/7	**June** 72/49	**Oct** 52/34
Mar 34/15	**July** 77/55	**Nov** 38/24
Apr 47/29	**Aug** 74/52	**Dec** 24/6

PORTLAND

Jan 30/11	**May** 63/43	**Sept** 69/49
Feb 33/14	**June** 73/52	**Oct** 59/38
Mar 41/25	**July** 79/58	**Nov** 47/30
Apr 52/34	**Aug** 77/57	**Dec** 35/18

Parks and Recreation Finder

Directions to and information about the parks and recreation areas below are given under their respective town/city sections. Please refer to those sections for details.

NATIONAL PARK AND RECREATION AREAS

Key to abbreviations: I.H.S. = International Historic Site; I.P.M.=International Peace Memorial; N.B. = National Battlefield; N.B.P. National Battlefield Park; N.B.C. = National Battlefield & Cemetery; N.C. = National Conservation Area; N.E.M. = National Expansion Memorial; N.F. = National Forest; N.G. = National Grassland; N.H. = National Historical Park; N.H.C. = National Heritage Corridor; N.H.S. National Historic Site; N.L. = National Lakeshore; N.M. = National Monument; N.M.P. National Military Park; N.Mem. = National Memorial; N.P. = National Park; N.Pres. = National Preserve; N.R. = National Recreational Area; N.R.R. = National Recreational River; N.Riv. = National River; N.S. = National Seashore; N.S.R. = National Scenic Riverway; N.S.T. = National Scenic Trail; N.Sc. = National Scientific Reserve; N.V.M. = National Volcanic Monument.

CALENDAR HIGHLIGHTS

FEBRUARY

Kennebunk Winter Carnival (Kennebunk). Snow sculpture contests, snow palace moonwalk, magic show, ice-skating party, chili & chowder contests, children's events. Phone 207/985-6890.

MAY

Maine State Parade (Lewiston). Downtown Lewiston & Auburn. Maine's largest parade; over 30,000 people represent 60 communities. Phone Androscoggin County Chamber of Commerce, 207/783-2249; or 207/784-0599.

JUNE

Windjammer Days (Boothbay Harbor). Old schooners that formerly sailed the trade routes and now cruise the Maine coast sail en masse into harbor. Waterfront food court, entertainment, street parade, children's activities. Phone 207/633-2353.

JULY

Great Whatever Family Festival Week (Augusta). More than 60 events including tournaments, carnival, barbecue, parade and fireworks. Festivities culminate with the canoe and kayak regatta on the Kennebec River between Augusta and Gardiner. There are also canoe and kayak races. Phone Kennebec Valley Chamber of Commerce, 207/623-4559.

Bangor Fair (Bangor). One of the country's oldest fairs. Horse racing, exhibits, stage shows. Phone 207/942-9000.

Festival de Joie (Lewiston). Central Maine Civic Center. Celebration of Lewiston and Auburn's Franco-American heritage. Features ethnic song, dance, cultural activities, traditional foods. Phone Androscoggin County Chamber of Commerce, 207/783-2249.

Schooner Days & North Atlantic Blues Festival (Rockland). Three-day festival celebrating Maine's maritime heritage; features Parade of Schooners, arts, entertainment, concessions, fireworks; blues bands & club crawl. Phone 207/596-0376.

AUGUST

Maine Lobster Festival (Rockland). A 5-day event centered around Maine's chief marine creature, with a huge tent cafeteria serving lobster and other seafood. Parade, harbor cruises, maritime displays, bands, entertainment. Phone 207/596-0376.

Skowhegan State Fair (Skowhegan). One of the oldest fairs in the country (1818). Mile-long midway, stage shows, harness racing; contests, exhibits. Phone 207/474-2947.

DECEMBER

Christmas by the Sea (Camden). Celebration of holiday season with musical entertainment, horse-drawn wagon rides, Holiday House Tour, Santa's arrival by lobsterboat. Phone 207/236-4404.

Place Name	Listed Under
Acadia N.P.	same
St Croix Island I.H.S.	CALAIS
White Mountain N.F.	BETHEL

STATE PARK AND RECREATION AREAS

Key to abbreviations: I.P. = Interstate Park; S.A.P. = State Archaeological Park; S.B. = State Beach; S.C. = State Conservation Area; S.C.P. = State Conservation Park; S.Cp. = State Campground; S.F. = State Forest; S.G. = State Garden; S.H.A. = State Historic Area; S.H.P. = State Historic Park; S.H.S. = State Historic Site; S.M.P. = State Marine Park; S.N.A. = State Natural Area; S.P. = State Park; S.P.C. = State Public Campground; S.R. = State Reserve; S.R.A. = State Recreation Area; S.Res. = State Reservoir; S.Res.P. = State Resort Park; S.R.P. = State Rustic Park.

Place Name	Listed Under
Aroostook S.P.	PRESQUE ISLE
Baxter S.P.	same
Camden Hills S.P.	CAMDEN
Cobscook Bay S.P.	MACHIAS
Crescent Beach S.P.	PORTLAND
Ferry Beach S.P.	SACO
Fort O’Brien Memorial S.P.	MACHIAS
Lake St George S.P.	BELFAST
Lamoine S.P.	ELLSWORTH
Lily Bay S.P.	GREENVILLE
Mt Blue S.P.	RUMFORD
Popham Beach S.P.	BATH
Rangeley Lake S.P.	RANGELEY
Reid S.P.	BATH
Roque Bluffs S.P.	MACHIAS
Sebago Lake S.P.	SEBAGO LAKE
Two Lights S.P.	PORTLAND

Water-related activities, hiking, biking, various other sports, picnicking and visitor centers, as well as camping, are available in many of these areas. Most state parks and historic sites are open seasonally, 9 am-sunset; Popham Beach, John Paul Jones Memorial and Reid are open year round. Most areas have day-use and/or parking fees, $1-$2.50/person; annual pass, $40/family, $20/individual. Camping May-Oct (areas vary), nonresidents $11-$17/site, residents $9-$13/site; reservation fee $2/night. Camping reservations may be made by mail to the Bureau of Parks and Lands, Station #22, Augusta 04333, Attn Reservation Clerk; in person at the office of the Bureau of Parks and Lands in Augusta; by phone, 207/287-3824 or 800/332-1501(ME). Maine historic sites fee $1.50-$2. Pets on leash only in most parks. No dogs on beaches (or at Sebago Lake campground). For information contact the Bureau of Parks and Lands, Maine Dept of Conservation, State House Station #22, Augusta 04333; 207/287-3821.

SKI AREAS

Place Name	Listed Under
Camden Snow Bowl	CAMDEN
Carter's X-C Ski Center	BETHEL
Lonesome Pine Trails	FORT KENT
Lost Valley Ski Area	AUBURN
Moosehead Resort on Big Squaw Mountain	GREENVILLE
Mt Jefferson Ski Area	LINCOLN
Saddleback Ski & Summer Lake Preserve	RANGELEY
Shawnee Peak at Pleasant Mt Ski Area	BRIDGTON
Sugarloaf/USA Ski Area	KINGFIELD
Sunday River Ski Resort	BETHEL

FISHING & HUNTING

Nonresident fishing license: $51; 12-15 years, $8; 15-day license, $39; 7-day license, $35; 3-day license, $22; 1-day license, $10. Nonresident hunting license for birds and animals except deer, bear, turkey, moose, bobcat and raccoon: $56; including all legal game species: $86. More detailed information on the state's regulations is available in the brochures *Maine Hunting and Trapping Laws* and *Maine Open Water Fishing Laws* from the Maine Fish and Wildlife Dept, Station 41, 284 State St, Augusta 04333; 207/287-8000.

Driving Information

Every person must be in an approved passenger restraint anywhere in vehicle: children under age 4 must use an approved safety seat. For further information phone 207/287-3311.

INTERSTATE HIGHWAY SYSTEM

The following alphabetical listing of Maine towns in *Mobil Travel Guide* shows that these cities are within 10 miles of the indicated interstate highway. A highway map, however, should be checked for the nearest exit.

Highway Number	Cities/Towns within 10 miles
Interstate 95	Augusta, Bangor, Bath, Biddeford, Brunswick, Freeport, Houlton, Kennebunk, Kittery, Lincoln, Millinocket, Newport, Ogunquit, Old Orchard Beach, Orono, Portland, Saco, Scarborough, Waterville, Wells, Yarmouth, York.

Additional Visitor Information

The Maine Publicity Bureau (PO Box 2300, Hallowell 04347, phone 207/623-0363 or 888/624-6345) publishes many pamphlets and brochures for distribution, including *Exploring Maine* and *Maine Invites You*.

The pulp and paper industry mills throughout Maine offer tours of their woodlands and manufacturing facilities at various times of the year. For further information contact the Paper Industry Information Office, 104 Sewall St, PO Box 5670, Augusta 04332; 207/622-3166.

There are eight official information service centers in Maine; visitors who stop by will find information and brochures most helpful in planning stops to points of interest. Their locations are as follows: in Bethel, on US 2; at Kittery, between I-95 & US 1; in Fryeburg (summer only), on US 302; in Calais, on Union St, off US 1; in Hampden, on I-95N at mile marker 169, on I-95S between mile markers 171 & 172; in Houlton, on Ludlow Rd; in Yarmouth, between I-95 exit 17 & US 1.

Acadia National Park (F-4 - G-4)

(See also Bar Harbor, Northeast Harbor, Southwest Harbor)

(On Mt Desert Island, S and W of Bar Harbor; entrance off ME 3)

Waves crashing against a rocky coastline, thick woodlands abundant with wildlife and mountains scraping the sky—this, Acadia National Park, is the Maine of storybooks. Occupying nearly half of Mt Desert Island, with smaller areas on Isle au Haut, Little Cranberry Island (see CRANBERRY ISLES), Baker Island, Little Moose Island and part of the mainland at Schoodic Point, Acadia amazes visitors. It is a sea-lashed granite coastal area of forested valleys, lakes and mountains, all created by the force of the glaciers. At 40,000 acres, Acadia is small compared to other national parks; however, it is one of the most visited national parks in the US, and the only national park in the northeastern United States. A 27-mile loop road connects the park's eastern sights on Mt Desert Island, and ferry services take travelers to some of the smaller islands. Visitors can explore 1,530-foot Cadillac Mountain, the highest point on the Atlantic Coast of the US; watch waves crash against Thunder Hole, creating a thunderous boom; or swim in the ocean at various coastal beaches. A road to the summit of Cadillac provides views of Frenchman, Blue Hill and Penobscot bays.

Mt Desert Island was named by the French explorer Samuel de Champlain in 1604. Shortly thereafter French Jesuit missionaries settled here until driven off by an armed vessel from Virginia. This was the first act of overt warfare between France and England for control of North America. Until 1713, the island was a part of French Acadia. It was not until after the Revolutionary War that it was extensively settled. In 1916, a portion of the area was proclaimed Sieur de Monts National Monument. It was changed to Lafayette National Park in 1919, and finally, in 1929, it was enlarged and renamed Acadia National Park.

Like all national parks, Acadia is a wildlife sanctuary. Fir, pine, spruce, many hardwoods and hundreds of varieties of wildflowers thrive. Nature lovers will be delighted with the more than 120 miles of trails; park rangers take visitors on various walks and cruises, pointing out and explaining the natural, cultural and historical features of the park. Forty-five miles of carriage roads offer bicyclists scenic rides through Acadia. Copies of ranger-led programs and trail maps are available at the visitor center.

There is saltwater swimming at Sand Beach and freshwater swimming at Echo Lake. Snowmobiles are allowed in some areas and cross-country skiing is available. Most facilities are open Memorial Day-September, however, portions of the park are open year round; picnic grounds are open May-October. Limited camping is available at two park campgrounds: Blackwoods, open year round, requires reservations from mid-June-mid-September; Seawall, open late May-late September, is on a first-come, first-served basis. The park headquarters, 2¹/₂ mi W of Bar Harbor (see) on ME 233 provides visitor information (Nov-Apr, daily; closed Jan 1, Thanksgiving, Dec 24, 25). For further information contact the Superintendent, PO Box 177, Bar Harbor 04609; 207/288-3338. Golden Eagle, Golden Age and Golden Access passports accepted (see MAKING THE MOST OF YOUR TRIP). Park entrance fee (subject to change) ¢¢; Per vehicle ¢¢¢ In the park are

Visitor Center. 3 mi NW of Bar Harbor at Hulls Cove. (May-Oct, daily)

The Robert Abbe Museum. Exhibits feature Native American prehistoric and ethnographic artifacts. (Mid-May-Oct, daily) At Sieur de Monts Spring. Phone 207/288-3519. ¢

Islesford Historical Museum. In Islesford, on Little Cranberry Island, 2 mi S of Seal Harbor, a ¹/₂-hr boat trip from Northeast Harbor. (See CRANBERRY ISLES) **Free.**

Isle au Haut (EEL-oh-HO). Mountains rise more than 540 feet on this island of forested shores and cobblestone beaches; hiking trails; small primitive campground (advance mail reservations; phone 207/288-3338for reservation form). A ferry from Stonington (see DEER ISLE) takes visitors on the 45-min trip to island (daily exc Sun; no hols; fee).

Ferry Service. Connects Islesford, Great Cranberry Island and Northeast Harbor on a regular schedule all yr. Phone 207/244-3575. ¢¢¢

Park tours. Narrated sightseeing trips through the park. Buses leave Main St, Bar Harbor. (June-early Oct) For tickets and information on tour schedules and fees contact Testa's Cafe, 53 Main St, Bar Harbor, phone 207/288-3327. ¢¢¢

Naturalist Sea Cruises. Marine life and history of the area are explained. Cruises visit Frenchman Bay (phone 207/288-3322), Islesford (phone 207/276-5352) and Baker Island (phone 207/276-3717). (Daily during summer season, schedules vary; phone for fees)

Auto Tape Tours. A scenic, 56-mile self-guided tour gives a mile-by-mile description of points of interest, history and geology of the park. Tape available May-Oct at visitor center. Cassette player and tape rental, deposit required; or tape may be purchased. ¢¢¢-¢¢¢¢¢

Allagash Wilderness Waterway (A-3 - C-3)

(See also Fort Kent)

In 1970 the Allagash River was designated a national wild river. Stretching 95 miles through 200,000 acres of lakes, rivers and timberland in Maine's northern wilderness, this waterway is a favorite of canoeists. A good put-in point is Chamberlain Thoroughfare at the junction of Chamberlain and Telos lakes. The trip ends at Allagash Village, eight miles north of Allagash Falls, near the Canadian border, where the Allagash flows into the St John River. Some canoe experience is necessary before attempting the entire trip as high winds can be a problem on the lakes and, depending on the level of the Allagash, the rapids can be dangerous.

Registration is required upon entering and leaving the waterway; rangers at Allagash Lake, Chamberlain Thoroughfare, Eagle Lake, Churchill Dam, Long Lake Thoroughfare and the Michaud Farm. Supplies & canoes must be brought in; gasoline is not available. There are restrictions regarding the size of parties using the waterway, as well as watercraft permitted. Numerous primitive campsites accessible only by water are scattered along the waterway (mid-May-mid-Oct). Campsite fee per person, per night ¢¢

For further information and rules contact the Bureau of Parks & Lands, Maine Department of Conservation, Northern Regional Office, BMHi Complex, Bldg H, 106 Hogan Rd, Bangor, 04401; 207/941-4014.

Auburn (G-2)

(See also Lewiston)

Settled 1797 **Pop** 24,309 **Elev** 188 ft **Area code** 207 **Zip** 04210 **E-mail** info@androscoggincounty.com **Web** www.androscoggincounty.com
Information Androscoggin County Chamber of Commerce, 179 Lisbon, PO Box 59, Lewiston 04243-0059; 207/783-2249.

Auburn, together with its sister city Lewiston, make up an important manufacturing center. In 1836, the first organized shoe company was started here. The Minot Shoe Company prospered, selling more than $6 million in shoes by 1900, and becoming the fifth-largest shoe company in the US by 1920. When the depression hit, the company suffered a severe blow. The city continued to expand, however, and today Auburn is one of the largest cities in the state.

What to See and Do

Androscoggin Historical Society Library and Museum. Exhibits trace local, county and state history. (Wed-Fri; closed hols) Museum; library. County Bldg, 2 Turner St at Court St. Phone 207/784-0586. **Free.**

Norlands Living History Center. Life as it was lived a century ago; clothing, customs. Yr-round working farm with oxen, horses, cows, crops and seasonal activities. Features 19th-century Victorian home of Washburn family; school, library, church, farmer's cottage, barn. Tours (Aug, daily). Picnicking. (See ANNUAL EVENTS) 25 mi N just off ME 4, in Livermore. Phone 207/897-4366. Tours ¢¢

Skiing. Lost Valley Ski Area. 2 double chairlifts, T-bar; snowmaking; patrol, school, rentals; bar, restaurant. (Dec-mid-Mar, daily) Follow signs off ME 11. Phone 207/784-1561. ¢¢¢¢¢

Annual Events

Maple Days. Norlands Living History Center. Mid-Mar.

Heritage Days. Norlands Living History Center. Thurs-Sun, last wkend June.

Autumn Celebration. Norlands Living History Center. Sept.

Augusta (G-2)

(See also Waterville)

Settled 1628 **Pop** 21,325 **Elev** 153 ft **Area code** 207 **Zip** 04330 **E-mail** kvcc@mint.net **Web** www.augustamaine.com
Information Kennebec Valley Chamber of Commerce, University Dr, PO Box E, 04332-0192; 207/623-4559.

Augusta, the capital of Maine, began in 1628 when men from Plymouth established a trading post on the site of Cushnoc, a Native American village. From there, Fort Western was built in 1754 to protect settlers against Native American raids, and the settlement grew. Today, 39 miles from the sea, Augusta is at the head of navigation on the Kennebec River; some of the town's leading industries include steel and food processing and service-related industries.

What to See and Do

Old Ft Western. Ft complex built in 1754 by Boston merchants; main house and reproduction blockhouse, watchboxes and palisade. Costumed staff interprets 18th-century life on the Kennebec River. (Mid-June-Labor Day, daily; after Labor Day-Columbus Day, Sat & Sun, limited hrs) City Center Plaza, 16 Cony St. Phone 207/626-2385. ¢¢

State House (1829-1832). The original design for this impressive building was by Charles Bulfinch (architect of the Massachusetts State House). Remodeled and enlarged (1909-1910), it rises majestically above Capitol Park and the Kennebec River. On its 185-ft dome is a statue, designed by W. Clark Noble, of a classically robed woman bearing a pine bough torch. (Daily; closed hols) State & Capitol Sts. Phone 207/287-2301. **Free.** Also here are

> **Maine State Museum.** Exhibits of Maine's natural environment, prehistory, social history and manufacturing heritage. "This Land Called Maine" features 5 natural history scenes as well as a presentation of 40 spectacular gems and gem minerals found in Maine. "Made in Maine" presents 19th-century products and manufacturing technologies and includes a water-powered woodworking mill, a 2-story textile factory and more than 1,000 Maine-made objects. Other exhibits examine the early economic activities of agriculture, fishing, granite quarrying, ice harvesting, lumbering and shipbuilding. Also featured are a display of military, political and geographical artifacts relating to the formation of the state of Maine as well as an exhibition of early 19th-century wall decoration. Gift shop. (Daily; closed Jan 1, Easter, Thanksgiving, Dec 25) Phone 207/287-2301. **Free.**

> **Blaine House** (1833). House of James G. Blaine, Speaker of the US House of Representatives and 1884 presidential candidate. Since 1919, this 28-rm house has been official residence of Maine's governors. Originally built in Federal style, it was remodeled several times and today appears semi-colonial. Tours (Tues-Thurs, limited hrs; closed hols). State & Capitol Sts. Phone 207/287-2301. **Free.**

Annual Event

Great Whatever Family Festival Week. Augusta/Gardiner area. More than 60 events including tournaments, carnival, barbecue, parade and fireworks. Festivities culminate with the canoe and kayak regatta on the Kennebec River between Augusta and Gardiner. There are also canoe and kayak races. Contact Chamber of Commerce. 10 days late June-early July.

Motels

★★ **AUGUSTA.** *390 Western Ave.* 207/622-6371; FAX 207/621-0349. 98 rms, 30 kit. suites, 2 story. Mid-June-late Oct: S, D $89-$169; each addl $10; under 18 free; lower rates rest of yr. Pet accepted. TV; cable (premium). Pool; wading pool. Complimentary continental bkfst. Coffee in rms. Restaurant 6 am-2 pm, 4 pm-1 am. Bar. Ck-out 11 am. Coin lndry. Meeting rms. Business servs avail. Valet serv. Microwaves avail. Cr cds: A, C, D, DS, MC, V.

[D] [icons] SC

★★★ **BEST WESTERN SENATOR INN.** *284 Western Ave, at I-95 exit 30.* 207/622-5804. 103 rms, 1-2 story. July-Aug: S $79-$99; D $89-$109; each addl $9; suites $149-$189; under 18 free; lower rates rest of yr. Crib free. Pet accepted, some restrictions; $50. TV; cable (premium), VCR avail (movies). 2 heated pools, 1 indoor. Playground. Complimentary full bkfst. Complimentary coffee in rms. Restaurant 6:30 am-10 pm. Rm serv. Bar to 1 am. Ck-out noon. Coin lndry. Meeting rms. Business servs avail. In-rm modem link. Sundries. Exercise rm; sauna. Massage. Indoor putting green. Game rm. Some refrigerators, fireplaces. Picnic tables. Cr cds: A, C, D, DS, MC, V.

[D] [icons] SC

★★ **COMFORT INN.** *281 Civic Center Dr (ME 27).* 207/623-1000; FAX 207/623-3505. E-mail hotelsaug@aol.com. 99 rms, 3 story. Late June-mid-Oct: S, D $89-$139; each addl $10; under 18 free; higher rates camp wkends; lower rates rest of yr. Crib free. TV; cable (premium). Indoor pool; wading pool, whirlpool. Complimentary continental bkfst. Restaurant 11 am-10 pm. Bar. Ck-out 11 am. Meeting rms. Business servs avail. Valet serv. X-country ski 10 mi. Exercise equipt; sauna. Cr cds: A, C, D, DS, MC, V.

★ **MOTEL 6.** *18 Edison Dr. 207/622-0000; FAX 207/622-1048.* 68 rms, 2 story. Late June-Sept: S $32.99; D $38.99; each addl $3; under 18 free. Crib free. Pet accepted, some restrictions. TV; cable (premium). Complimentary coffee in lobby. Restaurant nearby. Ck-out noon. Coin lndry. Cr cds: A, D, DS, MC, V.

✔★★ **SUSSE CHALET GUEST LODGE.** *On Whitten Rd, just off ME Tpke, Augusta-Winthrop exit. 207/622-3776; res: 800/524-2538; FAX 207/622-3778.* Web www.sussechalet.com. 59 rms, 8 kit, 2 story. S $45.70-$51.70; D $47.70-$67.70; kit $63.70-$80.70. Crib $5. TV; cable (premium). Heated pool. Complimentary continental bkfst. Restaurant nearby. Ck-out 11 am. Coin lndry. Meeting rm. Business servs avail. Cr cds: A, C, D, DS, MC, V.

Inn

★★ **WINGS HILL.** *(ME 27, Belgrade Lakes 04918) I-95 exit 31B, 15 mi N on ME 27. 207/495-2400; res: 800/509-4647.* 9 rms, 5 with shower only, 2 story. No A/C. No rm phones. June-Sept: S, D $95; each addl $20; ski plans; wkend rates (2-day min); lower rates rest of yr. TV in common rm; cable, VCR avail. Complimentary full bkfst. Restaurant nearby. Ck-out 11 am, ck-in 2-6 pm. Some balconies. Renovated farmhouse built 1800; antique quilts. Totally nonsmoking. Cr cds: MC, V.

Bailey Island (H-2)

(See also Brunswick)

Pop (est) **Elev** 20 ft **Area code** 207 **Zip** 04003 **E-mail** ccbbr@horton.col.k12.me.us **Web** www.midcoastmaine.com

Information Chamber of Commerce of the Bath-Brunswick Region, 59 Pleasant St, Brunswick 04011; 207/725-8797.

At the terminus of ME 24 South, along the northern shore of Casco Bay, lies Bailey Island, the most popular of the 365 Calendar Islands. Together with Orr's Island, to which it is connected by a cribstone bridge, Bailey is a resort and fishing center. Originally called Newwaggin by an early trader from Kittery, Bailey Island was renamed after Deacon Timothy Bailey of Massachusetts, who claimed the land for himself and banished early settlers. Bailey Island and Orr's Island partially enclose an arm of Casco Bay called Harpswell Sound—the locale of John Whittier's poem "The Dead Ship of Harpswell" and of Harriet Beecher Stowe's "Pearl of Orr's Island."

What to See and Do

Bailey Island Cribstone Bridge. Unique construction of uncemented granite blocks laid honeycomb fashion, allowing the tides to flow through. On ME 24 S, over Will Straits.   **Free.**

Giant Staircase. Natural rock formation dropping 200 ft in steps to ocean. Scenic overlook area. Washington St.   **Free.**

Motels

★ **BAILEY ISLAND.** *on ME 24. 207/833-2886.* 11 rms, 2 story. 1 kit. No A/C. No rm phones. Mid-June-early Oct: D $95; each addl $10; under 10 free; lower rates May-mid-June, Oct. Closed rest of yr. Crib

free. TV; cable. Complimentary continental bkfst. Ck-out 11 am. Picnic tables. Balconies. On ocean. Totally nonsmoking. Cr cds: MC, V.

★ **COOK'S ISLAND VIEW.** *on ME 24. 207/833-7780.* 18 rms, 3 kits. No A/C. July-Labor Day, hol wkends: D $80; kit. units $15 addl; under 18 free; lower rates after Memorial Day-June, after Labor Day-Oct. Closed rest of yr. Pet accepted, some restrictions. TV; cable. Pool. Restaurant nearby. Ck-out 11 am. Cr cds: A, MC, V.

Inn

★★ **LOG CABIN.** *ME 24. 207/833-5546; FAX 207/833-7858.* E-mail info@logcabin-maine.com; web www.logcabin-maine.com. 8 rms, 2 with shower only, 1 suite, 4 kit. units. Memorial Day-Labor Day: S, D $109-$199; each addl $19.95; suite $199; kit. units $125-$145; wkly rates; hols 2-day min; lower rates rest of yr. Closed Nov-Mar. TV; cable, VCR (movies). Complimentary full bkfst. Complimentary coffee in rms. Restaurant 5-8 pm. Ck-out 11 am, ck-in 3 pm. Business servs avail. Gift shop. Refrigerators; some in-rm whirlpools, fireplaces. Balconies. Built in 1940s. Log cabin; panoramic view of bay, islands. Totally nonsmoking. Cr cds: A, DS, MC, V.

Restaurant

★ **COOK'S LOBSTER HOUSE.** *On Garrison Cove Rd, just off ME 24. 207/833-2818.* Web www.milepost.org/co/cookslobster. Specializes in baked stuffed lobster, shore dinners, steak. Raw bar. Hrs: 11:30 am-9 pm; mid-June-Aug to 10 pm. No A/C. Bar. Semi-a la carte: lunch $2.95-$9.95, dinner $9.25-$26.95. Child's meals. Outdoor dining. Dockage. Family-owned. Cr cds: DS, MC, V.

Bangor (F-4)

Settled 1769 **Pop** 33,181 **Elev** 61 ft **Area code** 207 **Zip** 04401 **E-mail** chamber@bangorregion.com **Web** www.bangorregion.com

Information Bangor Region Chamber of Commerce, 519 Main St, PO Box 1443; 207/947-0307.

In 1604, Samuel de Champlain sailed up the Penobscot River to the area that was to become Bangor and reported that the country was "most pleasant and agreeable," the hunting good and the oak trees impressive. As the area grew, these things remained true. Begun as a harbor town, as did many of Maine's coastal areas, Bangor turned to lumber when the railroads picked up much of the shipping business. In 1842, it became the second-largest lumber port in the country.

Bangor received its name by mistake. An early settler, Reverend Seth Noble, was sent to register the new town under its chosen name of Sunbury; however, when officials asked Noble for the name, he thought they were asking him for the name of a tune he was humming, and replied "Bangor" instead. Today, the city is the third-largest in Maine and a trading and distribution center.

What to See and Do

Bangor Historical Museum (Thomas A. Hill House, 1834). Tour of first floor of Greek-revival house; second-floor gallery features changing exhibits. (June-mid-Sept, Mon-Fri & Sun afternoons; Mar-May & mid-Sept-Dec, Tues-Fri afternoons) 159 Union St, at High St. Phone 207/942-5766.   ¢

Cole Land Transportation Museum. Exhibits on more than 200 vehicles including vintage cars, horse-drawn logging sleds and fire engines. Historic photographs of Maine also on display. (May-early Nov, daily) 405 Perry Rd. Phone 207/990-3600. ¢

Monument to Paul Bunyan. A 31-ft-tall statue commemorating the legendary lumberjack. Main St, in Bass Park. **Free.**

Annual Events

Kenduskeag Stream Canoe Race. Phone 207/947-1018. Mid-Apr.

Bangor Fair. One of country's oldest. Horse racing, exhibits, stage shows. Phone 207/942-9000. Late June-1st wk Aug.

Seasonal Events

Harness racing. Bass Park. Phone 207/866-7650. June-July.

Band concerts. Paul Bunyan Park. Phone 207/947-1018. Tues eves, July-Aug.

Motels

★ ★ ★ **BEST WESTERN WHITE HOUSE.** *155 Littlefield Ave, W at I95 exit 44.* 207/862-3737; FAX 207/862-6465. 66 rms, 3 story. May-Oct: S $59-$74; D $64-$74; each addl $5; family rm $79-$99; under 12 free; lower rates rest of yr. Crib $3. Pet accepted. TV; cable, VCR avail (movies). Heated pool; sauna. Complimentary continental bkfst. Complimentary coffee in rms. Restaurant adj open 24 hrs. Bar 4 pm-1 am. Ck-out 11 am. Coin lndry. Business servs avail. In-rm modem link. Sundries. Downhill/x-country ski 4 mi. Lawn games. Refrigerators avail. Picnic tables. Cr cds: A, C, D, DS, ER, MC, V.

⟦🐾⟧ ⟦🏊⟧ ⟦⛷⟧ ⟦🔥⟧ ⟦SC⟧

★ ★ **COMFORT INN.** *750 Hogan Rd.* 207/942-7899; res: 800/338-9966; FAX 207/942-6463. E-mail comfort@midmaine.com; web www.placestostay.com. 96 rms, 2 story. Mid-June-Oct: S $49-$89; D $59-$99; each addl $5; under 19 free; lower rates rest of yr. Crib free. Pet accepted; $6. TV; cable (premium). Pool. Complimentary continental bkfst. Complimentary coffee in rms. Ck-out noon. Meeting rms. Business servs avail. Sundries. Free airport transportation. Game rm. Exercise equipt. X-country ski 10 mi. Shopping mall adj. Cr cds: A, C, D, DS, ER, MC, V.

⟦D⟧ ⟦🐾⟧ ⟦🏊⟧ ⟦⛷⟧ ⟦✗⟧ ⟦⛷⟧ ⟦🔥⟧ ⟦SC⟧

★ ★ **DAYS INN.** *250 Odlin Rd.* 207/942-8272; res: 800/835-4667; FAX 207/942-1382. E-mail daysinn@midmaine.com; web www.placestostay.com/bangor-daysinn/. 101 rms, 2 story. July-Oct: S $50-$65; D $55-$85; each addl $6; under 12 free; lower rates rest of yr. Crib free. Pet accepted; $6. TV; cable (premium), VCR avail. Indoor pool; whirlpool. Complimentary continental bkfst. Restaurant adj 11-1 am. Rm serv. Ck-out 11 am. Business servs avail. In-rm modem link. Sundries. Free airport transportation. Downhill/x-country ski 12 mi. Game rm. Cr cds: A, C, D, DS, ER, JCB, MC, V.

⟦D⟧ ⟦🐾⟧ ⟦🏊⟧ ⟦⛷⟧ ⟦⛷⟧ ⟦🔥⟧ ⟦SC⟧

✔★ **ECONO LODGE.** *327 Odlin Rd.* 207/945-0111; FAX 207/942-8856. E-mail econolodge@midmaine.com. 128 rms, 4 story. S $29.95-$65.95; D $39.95-$85.95; under 19 free. Crib free. Pet accepted. TV; cable (premium). Complimentary coffee in lobby. Ck-out 11 am. Coin lndry. Business servs avail. In-rm modem link. Downhill/x-country ski 7 mi. Some refrigerators, microwaves. Cr cds: A, D, DS, MC, V.

⟦D⟧ ⟦🐾⟧ ⟦🏊⟧ ⟦⛷⟧ ⟦🔥⟧ ⟦SC⟧

★ ★ **FAIRFIELD INN BY MARRIOTT.** *300 Odlin Rd, I-95 exit 45-B.* 207/990-0001; FAX 207/990-0917. Web www.acadia.net/fairfield. 153 rms, 3 story. Mid-June-mid-Oct: S, D $49.95-$84.95; each addl $3; under 18 free; lower rates rest of yr. Crib free. TV; cable (premium). Indoor pool; whirlpool. Complimentary continental bkfst. Restaurant adj 6 am-10 pm. Ck-out noon. Coin lndry. Meeting rm. Business servs avail. In-rm modem link. Downhill ski 7 mi; x-country ski 5 mi. Exercise equipt; sauna. Cr cds: A, C, D, DS, MC, V.

⟦D⟧ ⟦🏊⟧ ⟦⛷⟧ ⟦✗⟧ ⟦⛷⟧ ⟦🔥⟧ ⟦SC⟧

★ ★ ★ **HOLIDAY INN-CIVIC CENTER.** *500 Main St.* 207/947-8651; res: 800/799-8651; FAX 207/942-2848. E-mail hibgrms@acadia.net; web www.maineguide.com/bangor/holidayinn. 122 rms, 2-4 story. May-Oct: S, D $84; suites $115-$200; under 19 free; lower rates rest of yr. Crib free. Pet accepted. TV; cable (premium). Pool. Complimentary coffee in rms. Restaurant 6:30 am-1:30 pm, 5-10 pm. Rm serv. Bar 3:30 pm-1 am; entertainment Tues-Sat. Ck-out noon. Coin lndry. Meeting rms. Business servs avail. In-rm modem link. Valet serv. Sundries. Free airport transportation. Health club privileges. Some bathrm phones. Opp Civic Center. Cr cds: A, C, D, DS, JCB, MC, V.

⟦D⟧ ⟦🐾⟧ ⟦🏊⟧ ⟦⛷⟧ ⟦🔥⟧ ⟦SC⟧

★ **PENOBSCOT INN.** *570 Main St.* 207/947-0566. Web www.visionwork.com/penobscot-inn. 50 rms, 2 story. June-Oct: S $59-$69; D $64-$74; each addl $5; under 12 free; lower rates rest of yr. Crib free. Pet accepted. TV; cable. Restaurant 7 am-10 pm; Sun to 9 pm. Bar 11-1 am. Ck-out 11 am. Business servs avail. Sundries. Cr cds: A, D, DS, MC, V.

⟦🐾⟧ ⟦⛷⟧ ⟦🔥⟧ ⟦SC⟧

Motor Hotel

★ ★ ★ **HOLIDAY INN.** *404 Odlin Rd, 3 mi W on I-395, near Intl Airport.* 207/947-0101; res: 800/914-0101; FAX 207/947-7619. E-mail hibgr_or@acadia.net. 207 rms, 3 story. July-Oct: S $65-$80; D $75-$90; each addl $10; under 19 free; lower rates rest of yr. Crib free. Pet accepted. TV; cable (premium), VCR avail. 2 pools; 1 indoor, whirlpool. Complimentary coffee in rms. Restaurant 6:30 am-1:30 pm, 5-10 pm. Rm serv. Bar noon-1 am; entertainment. Ck-out noon. Coin lndry. Meeting rms. Business servs avail. In-rm modem link. Sundries. Valet serv. Free airport transportation. Downhill ski 15 mi; x-country ski 10 mi. Health club privileges. Some refrigerators. Cr cds: A, C, D, DS, JCB, MC, V.

⟦D⟧ ⟦🐾⟧ ⟦🏊⟧ ⟦⛷⟧ ⟦✗⟧ ⟦⛷⟧ ⟦🔥⟧ ⟦SC⟧

Hotel

★ ★ ★ **FOUR POINTS BY SHERATON.** *308 Godfrey Blvd, at Intl Airport.* 207/947-6721; res: 800/228-4609; FAX 207/941-9761. 101 rms, 9 story. S, D $98-$155; each addl $15; under 18 free. Crib free. Pet accepted. TV; cable (premium). Pool. Complimentary coffee in rms. Restaurant 6 am-2:30 pm, 5-11 pm. Bar 2 pm-midnight. Ck-out noon. Meeting rms. Business center. In-rm modem link. Gift shop. Validated parking. Airport transportation. Downhill/x-country ski 7 mi. Exercise equipt. Enclosed walkway to airport. Cr cds: A, C, D, DS, MC, V.

⟦🐾⟧ ⟦🏊⟧ ⟦⛷⟧ ⟦✗⟧ ⟦✗⟧ ⟦⛷⟧ ⟦🔥⟧ ⟦SC⟧ ⟦🚶⟧

Inns

★ ★ **LUCERNE.** *(, East Holden 04429) 11 mi E on US 1A.* 207/843-5123; FAX 207/843-6138; res: 800/325-5123. E-mail info@lucerneinn.com. 25 rms, 3 story. July-Oct: S, D $99-$159; each addl $15; package plans; lower rates rest of yr. TV; cable (premium). Pool. Complimentary continental bkfst. Dining rm 5-9 pm; Sun brunch 9 am-1 pm. Rm serv. Ck-out 11 am, ck-in 2 pm. Meeting rm. Business servs avail. Downhill/x-country ski 20 mi. Fireplaces. Colonial-style farmhouse and connecting stable, established as inn in 1814; antiques. Gazebo. On hill overlooking Phillips Lake. Cr cds: A, MC, V.

⟦D⟧ ⟦⛷⟧ ⟦🏊⟧ ⟦⛷⟧ ⟦🔥⟧

✔★ **PHENIX INN AT WEST MARKET SQUARE.** *20 Broad St, in West Market Square.* 207/947-0411; FAX 207/947-0255. Web www.maineguide.com/bangor/phenixinn/rooms.html. 32 rms, 4 story. July-late-Oct: S, D $75-$150; lower rates rest of yr. Crib free. Pet accepted. TV; cable, VCR avail. Complimentary continental bkfst. Restaurant adj 7 am-midnight. Ck-out noon, ck-in 1 pm. Guest lndry. Meeting rm. Business servs avail. Exercise equipt. Refrigerator avail. Restored commercial building (1873) located in West Market Square; furnished with antique reproductions. Near river. Cr cds: A, C, D, DS, MC, V.

Restaurants

★ **CAPTAIN NICK'S SEAFOOD HOUSE.** *1165 Union St.* *207/942-6444.* Specializes in lobster, seafood, local dishes. Hrs: 11 am-10 pm; wkends to 11 pm. Closed Thanksgiving, Dec 25. Res accepted. Bar. Semi-a la carte: lunch $3.50-$7.25, dinner $6.95-$17.95. Child's meals. Cr cds: A, DS, MC, V.

★ ★ **GREENHOUSE.** *193 Broad St, on 2nd fl of Helm Mall.* *207/945-4040.* Specializes in seafood, prime rib, lamb. Own desserts. Hrs: 11:30 am-9 pm; Sat from 4 pm. Closed Sun, Mon; Dec 25. Res accepted. Bar. Semi-a la carte: lunch $4-$9, dinner $10-$18. Child's meals. Glass-walled dining rms. Cr cds: A, MC, V.

★ ★ **MILLER'S.** *427 Main St.* *207/945-5663.* Specializes in prime rib, fresh seafood, rotisserie chicken. Extensive salad bar. Dessert bar. Own baking. Hrs: 11 am-10 pm; Sun 10:30 am-9 pm; Sun brunch to noon. Closed Dec 25. Res accepted. Semi-a la carte: lunch $3.95-$7.50, dinner $8.95-$21.95. Sun brunch $6.95. Child's meals. 2 separate dining areas. Family-owned. Cr cds: A, DS, MC, V.

★ ★ **PILOTS GRILL.** *1528 Hammond St.* *207/942-6325.* Specialties: baked stuffed lobster, baked haddock, prime rib. Own desserts. Hrs: 11:30 am-2 pm, 5-9 pm; Sun 11:30 am-9 pm. Closed July 4, Dec 25. Res accepted. Bar. Semi-a la carte: lunch $5.95-$9.95, dinner $8.95-$19.95. Child's meals. Family-owned since 1940. Cr cds: A, C, D, DS, MC, V.

Bar Harbor (F-4)

(See also Cranberry Isles, Northeast Harbor, Southwest Harbor)

Pop 2,768 **Elev** 20 ft **Area code** 207 **Zip** 04609 **E-mail** bhcc@acadia.net **Web** www.acadia.net/bhcc

Information Chamber of Commerce, 93 Cottage St, PO Box 158; 207/288-5103 or 800/288-5013.

Bar Harbor, the largest village on Mt Desert Island, has a summer population of as many as 20,000 and is headquarters for the surrounding summer resort area. The island, which includes most of Acadia National Park, is mainly rugged granite, forested and flowered, with many bays and inlets where sailing is popular. In the mid-1800s, socially prominent figures, including publisher Joseph Pulitzer, had elaborate summer cottages built on the island. The era of elegance ebbed, however, with the Great Depression, World War II and the "Great Fire of 1947," which destroyed many of the estates and scorched more than 17,000 acres. As a result, the forests in the area now have younger, more varied trees bearing red, yellow and orange leaves instead of just evergreens.

What to See and Do

✪ **Acadia National Park** (see). Borders town on W & S. HQ 2½ mi W on ME 233. Phone 207/288-3338. ¢¢

Bar Harbor Historical Society Museum. Collection of early photographs of hotels, summer cottages and Green Mt cog RR; hotel registers from the early to late 1800s; maps, scrapbook of the 1947 fire. (Mid-June-Oct, daily exc Sun; closed hols) 34 Mt Desert St, Jesup Memorial Library. Phone 207/288-4245. **Free.**

Bar Harbor Whale Watch Co. Offers variety of cruises aboard catamaran *Friendship V* or *MV Seal* to view whales, seal, puffin, osprey, lobster and more. Also nature cruises and fishing trips. Cruises vary in length & destination. (May-Oct, daily) Depart from Bluenose Ferry Terminal, 1 mi N on ME 3. For fees and schedule, phone 207/288-2386 or 800/WHALES-4.

Ferry service to Yarmouth, Nova Scotia. Passenger and car carrier *Bluenose* makes 6-hr trips (cabins avail). For res, schedule phone 888/249-7245. ¢¢¢¢¢

Fishing. Fresh water in many lakes and streams (check regulations, obtain license). Salt water off coast; commercial boat operators will arrange trips.

Natural History Museum. More than 50 exhibits depicting animals in their natural settings; 22-ft Minke whale skeleton. Interpretive programs; evening lectures in summer (Wed). (June-Labor Day, daily; rest of yr, by appt) Eden St. In historic Turrets Bldg on College of the Atlantic waterfront campus. Phone 207/288-5015. ¢¢

Oceanarium-Bar Harbor. An extension of the Mt Desert Oceanarium in Southwest Harbor (see); features include harbor seals, salt-marsh walks, viewing tower; also lobster museum with hands-on exhibits. (Mid-May-mid-Oct, daily exc Sun) 9 mi N on ME 3. Phone 207/288-5005. ¢¢ Also included is the

Lobster Hatchery. Young lobsters are hatched from eggs to ½inch in length, then returned to ocean to supplement supply; guides narrate process. (Mid-May-mid-Oct, daily exc Sun)

The Abbe Museum. Collection of Native American artifacts. (May-Oct) ME 3 S to Sieur de Monts exit. Phone 207/288-3519. ¢

The Jackson Laboratory. An internationally known mammalian genetics laboratory conducting research relevant to cancer, diabetes, AIDS, heart disease, blood disorders, birth defects, aging and normal growth and development. Audiovisual and lecture programs (early-June-late Aug, Tues & Thurs afternoons; closed 1 wk late July & 1 wk mid-Aug). 2 mi S on ME 3. Phone 207/288-3371. **Free.**

Annual Events

Celebrate Bar Harbor. Mid-June.

Art Exhibit. Village Green. 3rd wkend in July & Aug.

Motels

★ ★ **ACADIA INN.** *98 Eden St (ME 3).* *207/288-3500;* FAX *207/288-8424;* res: *800/638-3636.* E-mail acadiain@acadia.net; web www.acadiainn.com. 95 rms, 3 story. Late June-Aug: S, D $109-$145; under 10 free; lower rates early Apr-late June, Sept-mid-Nov. Closed rest of yr. Crib free. TV; cable (premium). Pool; whirlpool. Playground. Complimentary continental bkfst. Restaurant nearby. Ck-out 11 am. Coin lndry. Meeting rms. Business servs avail. In-rm modem link. Gift shop. Refrigerators avail. Picnic tables. Cr cds: A, C, DS, MC, V.

★ ★ **ATLANTIC EYRIE LODGE.** *6 Norman Rd.* *207/288-9786;* FAX *207/288-8500;* res: *800/422-2883.* Web www.barharbor.com/eyrie. 58 rms, 5 story. July-Labor Day: S, D $99-$153; each addl $10; suites, kit. units $184; under 7 free; lower rates late May-June, after Labor Day-mid-Oct. Closed rest of yr. Crib free. TV; cable. Pool. Complimentary continental bkfst. Restaurant nearby. Ck-out 11 am. Coin lndry. Meeting rms. Business servs avail. Refrigerators avail. Private patios, balconies. Picnic tables. Cr cds: A, MC, V.

★ ★ **BAR HARBOR.** *100 Eden St.* *207/288-3453;* FAX *207/288-3598;* res: *800/388-3453.* E-mail bhmotel@acadia.net; web www.acadia.net/bhmotel/. 70 rms, 16 suites. July-Aug: S, D $104; each addl $8; suites $137; under 13 free; lower rates mid-May-June, Sept-mid-Oct. Closed rest of yr. Crib free. TV; cable. Heated pool. Playground. Complimentary coffee in lobby. Restaurant adj 11:30 am-11 pm. Ck-out 11 am. Business servs avail. Refrigerators. Picnic tables. Cr cds: DS, MC, V.

★ ★ ★ **BAR HARBOR INN.** *Newport Dr. 207/288-3351; FAX 207/288-5296; res: 800/248-3351.* E-mail bhinn@acadia.net; web www.barharborinn.com. 153 rms, 2 story. July-Aug: S, D $139-$279; each addl $15; suites (to 4 persons) $310-$395; under 16 free; lower rates Apr-June, Sept-Nov. Crib $15. TV; cable (premium), VCR avail (movies). Heated pool; poolside serv. Complimentary continental bkfst. Coffee in rms. Restaurant (see READING ROOM). Rm serv. Bar 11:30 am-closing. Ck-out 11 am. Meeting rms. Business servs avail. Bellhops. Valet parking. Sundries. Gift shop. Golf privileges. Exercise equipt. Health club privileges. Some refrigerators, minibars. Some balconies. On beach. Pier; sailing cruises on 19th-century replica schooner. Cr cds: A, D, DS, MC, V.

★ ★ **BEST WESTERN INN.** *4 mi W on ME 3. 207/288-5823; res: 800/258-1234; FAX 207/288-9827.* 68 rms. July-mid-Sept: S $98; D $105; each addl $10; under 12 free; lower rates May-June, Sept-Oct. Crib $5. TV; cable (premium). Heated pool. Complimentary continental bkfst. Ck-out 11 am. Coin lndry. Some refrigerators. Cr cds: A, C, D, DS, MC, V.

✔ ★ **CADILLAC MOTOR INN.** *336 Main St. 207/288-3831; res: 888/207-2593; FAX 207/288-9370.* E-mail cadillac@acadia.net; web www.acadia.net/cadillac. 49 rms, 1-2 story, 5 suites, 18 kits. 22 A/C. July-Labor Day: S, D $64-$98; each addl $10; suites $125-$150; kit. units $69-$150; under 13 free; lower rates May-June, after Labor Day-Oct. Closed rest of yr. Crib $10. TV; cable (premium). Complimentary coffee in lobby. Restaurant nearby. Ck-out 11 am. Coin lndry. Some fireplaces. Balconies. Picnic tables. Cr cds: D, DS, MC, V.

★ ★ **CROMWELL HARBOR.** *359 Main St. 207/288-3201; res: 800/544-3201.* Web www.acadia.net/cromwellharbormotel. 25 rms, 9 A/C. Mid-July-Aug: S, D $80-$115; each addl $10; lower rates rest of yr. TV; cable (premium). Heated pool. Restaurant nearby. Ck-out 11 am. Some refrigerators, microwaves. Picnic tables. Cr cds: MC, V.

★ ★ **DREAMWOOD PINES.** *RR 1, Box 1100, 4 mi N on ME 3. 207/288-9717; FAX 207/288-4194.* 22 rms, 5 kit. units. July-Aug: S, D $74-$98; each addl $8; kit. units $98-$158; lower rates May-June, Sept-late Oct. Closed rest of yr. Crib $6. TV; cable (premium). Heated pool. Complimentary coffee in rms. Restaurant adj 6 am-8 pm. Ck-out 11 am. Picnic tables, grills. Wooded grounds. Cr cds: DS, MC, V.

★ **EDENBROOK.** *96 Eden St (ME 3). 207/288-4975; res: 800/323-7819.* Web www.acadia.net.edenbrook/office.html. 47 rms in 4 bldgs, 1-2 story, July-Aug: S, D $65-$85; each addl $5; lower rates late May-June, Sept-late Oct. Closed rest of yr. Crib $5. TV; cable. Complimentary coffee in rms. Ck-out 11 am. Some refrigerators. Some balconies. Cr cds: A, DS, MC, V.

★ **EDGEWATER.** *(Old Bar Harbor Rd, Salisbury Cove) Salisbury Cove, 5 mi W on ME 3. 207/288-3491; res: 888/310-9920.* Web www.sourcemaine.com/edgewatr. 23 units, 1-2 story, 8 motel rms, 4 kits. 11 kit. cottages, 4 apts (2-bedrm). July-Labor Day: S, D $97; kits. $107; each addl $10; kit. cottages, apts $78-$130; wkly rates; lower rates mid-Apr-June, early Sept-Oct. Closed rest of yr. TV; cable (premium). Complimentary coffee in lobby. Ck-out 11 am. Coin lndry. Refrigerators; some fireplaces. Patios, balconies. Picnic tables, grills. On Frenchman Bay; swimming beach. Cr cds: MC, V.

★ ★ **GOLDEN ANCHOR INN.** *55 West St. 207/288-5033; FAX 207/288-4577; res: 800/328-5033.* 88 rms, 4 kit. units, 2 story. July-early Sept: S, D $110-$185; each addl $10; under 5 free, 5-12 $2.50; lower rates Apr-June, early Sept-Oct. Closed rest of yr. Crib free. TV; cable. Heated pool; whirlpool. Complimentary bkfst buffet in season. Restaurant 7 am-10 pm. Rm serv 1-9 pm. Bar from noon. Ck-out 11 am. Business servs avail.

In-rm modem link. Balconies. On ocean. Private pier, dockage; whale watching cruises in season. Cr cds: C, D, DS, MC, V.

✔ ★ **HIGGINS HOLIDAY.** *43 Holland Ave. 207/288-3829; res: 800/345-0305.* E-mail cooper@midmaine.com; web www.mainetravel-guide.com. 25 rms, 7 kit. units, 1-2 story. Some A/C. July-Labor Day: S, D $79-$110; each addl $5; kit. units $96-$150; wkly rates kit. units; lower rates mid-May-June, Labor Day-Oct. Closed rest of yr. Crib $5. TV; cable. Complimentary coffee in rms. Restaurant nearby. Ck-out 11 am. Cr cds: DS, MC, V.

✔ ★ **HIGH SEAS.** *RR 1, Box 1085, 4 mi N on ME 3. 207/288-5836; res: 800/959-5836.* 34 rms. July-Aug: S, D $68-$98; under 12 free; lower rates May-June, Sept-mid-Oct. Closed rest of yr. Crib $2. TV; cable. Heated pool. Restaurant 6 am-9 pm. Ck-out 11 am. Refrigerators avail. Cr cds: DS, MC, V.

★ **MAINE STREET.** *315 Main St. 207/288-3188; FAX 207/288-2317; res: 800/333-3188.* 44 rms, 1-2 story. July-Aug: S, D $88-$98; each addl $10; under 16 free; lower rates Apr-June, Sept-Oct. Closed rest of yr. Crib $10. TV; cable (premium). Restaurant adj from 11 am. Ck-out 11 am. Business servs avail. Cr cds: DS, MC, V.

★ ★ **PARK ENTRANCE.** *RR 2, Box 180, Hamor Ave, 2½ mi N just off ME 3, adj Acadia Park entrance. 207/288-9703; res: 800/288-9703.* Web www.acadia.net/parkentrance. 58 rms, 24 A/C, 2 story, 6 kits. (5 no ovens). Aug: S, D $134-$179; kit. units $199-$299; under 18 free; lower rates early May-July, Sept-late Oct. Closed rest of yr. Crib $6. TV; cable (premium). Heated pool; whirlpool. Complimentary coffee in rms. Restaurant nearby. Ck-out 11 am. Business servs avail. Lawn games. Refrigerators avail. Private patios, balconies. Picnic tables, grills. Overlooks bay, beach. Mooring, dock; fishing pier. Cr cds: MC, V.

★ ★ **QUALITY INN.** *ME 3 and Mt Desert St. 207/288-5403; FAX 207/288-5473; res: 800/282-5403.* E-mail quality@acadia.net; web www.acadia.net/quality. 77 rms, 2 story, 10 kits. Late June-Aug: S, D $99-$149; each addl $10; kits. (3-day min) $149; under 19 free; lower rates late Apr-late June, Sept-late Oct. Closed rest of yr. Crib free. TV; cable. Heated pool; whirlpool. Complimentary coffee in rms. Restaurant opp 7-10:30 am, 4:30-9 pm. Ck-out 11 am. Coin lndry. Business servs avail. Sundries. Gift shop. Refrigerators avail. Balconies. Picnic tables, grill. 4 blks to ocean. Totally nonsmoking. Cr cds: A, D, DS, MC, V.

★ **VILLAGER.** *207 Main St. 207/288-3211; FAX 207/288-2270.* E-mail villager@acadia.net; web www.acadia.net/villager. 52 rms, 2 story. July-Aug: S, D $79-$98; each addl $10; under 11 free; lower rates May-June, Sept-late Oct. Closed rest of yr. Crib $5. TV; cable. Heated pool. Complimentary coffee in lobby. Restaurant nearby. Ck-out 11 am. Cr cds: A, MC, V.

★ ★ **WONDER VIEW INN.** *50 Eden St. 207/288-3358; res: 888/439-8439; FAX 207/288-2005.* E-mail wonderview@acadia.net; web www.wonderviewinn.com. 79 rms, 10 with shower only, 26 A/C, 1-2 story. July-Labor Day: S $87; D $87-$130; each addl $10; under 12 free; lower rates early May-June, Labor Day-Oct. Closed rest of yr. Crib $10. TV; cable. Pool. Complimentary coffee in lobby. Restaurant 7-10 am, 5-9 pm. Bar trom 5 pm. Ck-out 11 am. Business servs avail. Refrigerator avail. Balconies. Picnic tables. Cr cds: A, DS, MC, V.

Motor Hotels

★ ★ ★ **BAR HARBOR HOTEL-BLUENOSE INN.** *90 Eden St. 207/288-3348; FAX 207/288-2183; res: 800/445-4077 (exc ME), 800/531-5523 (ME).* Web www.acadia.net/bluenose. This service-oriented property has a premiere location atop a granite-terraced hillside that provides beautiful views of Frenchman Bay. Two elegant guest buildings, Mizzentop and Stenna Nordica, offer a number of amenities and services. 97 rms, 3-4 story, 48 suites. July-Aug: S, D $138-$258; suites $268; each addl $25; lower rates May-June, Sept-Oct. Closed rest of yr. TV; cable (premium), VCR avail. 2 heated pools, 1 indoor; whirlpool. Complimentary coffee in rms. Restaurant 7-11 am, 6-9:30 pm. Rm serv. Bar 5-11 pm. Ck-out 11 am. Coin lndry. Meeting rm. Business servs avail. Bellhops. Gift shop. Tennis privileges, pro. 18-hole golf privileges. Exercise equipt. Refrigerators; many fireplaces, bathrm phones. Balconies. Ocean view. Totally nonsmoking. Cr cds: MC, V.

★ ★ ★ **HOLIDAY INN SUNSPREE.** *123 Eden St. 207/288-9723; res: 800/234-6835; FAX 207/288-3089.* 221 rms, 4 story. Late June-late Aug: S, D $165-$205; suites, kit. units $250-$500; under 19 free; lower rates May-late June, late Aug-late Oct. Closed rest of yr. Crib avail. TV; cable. Heated pool; poolside serv. Supervised child's activities (July-Aug). Coffee in rms. Restaurant 6:30 am-10 pm; hrs vary off season. Rm serv. Bar 11 am-midnight. Ck-out noon. Meeting rms. Business servs avail. Bellhops. Gift shop. Lighted tennis. Putting green. Lawn games. Exercise equipt; sauna. Refrigerators. Balconies. On ocean; marina, dockage. Whale watch tours. Cr cds: A, C, D, DS, ER, JCB, MC, V.

Hotel

★ ★ ★ **BAYVIEW HOTEL & INN.** *111 Eden St. 207/288-5861; FAX 207/288-3173; res: 800/356-3585.* Web www.barharbor.com/bayview. 39 rms, 2-3 story, 7 kit. town homes. No elvtr. Late June-Labor Day: S, D $110-$275; each addl $20; ages 12-18 $10; under 12 free; town homes $390-$440; lower rates mid-May-late June, Labor Day-late Oct. Closed rest of yr. TV; cable (premium), VCR avail. Heated pool; poolside serv. Complimentary bkfst buffet; afternoon refreshments. Restaurant 7-10 am; 5-8:30 pm. Bar 11-1 am. Ck-out 11 am. Meeting rms. Business servs avail. Airport transportation. Lighted tennis privileges. Exercise equipt. Massage. Lawn games. Whirlpool in town homes. Private patios, balconies. Situated on 8 wooded acres with water frontage on Frenchmen Bay. Former estate; Georgian country house furnished with antiques. Fireplaces. Library. Gardens. Cr cds: A, C, D, MC, V.

Inns

★ ★ ★ **BAY LEDGE.** *1385 Sandpoint Rd. 207/288-4204; FAX 207/288-5573. E-mail bayledge@downeastnet.com; web www.maineguide.com/barharbor/bayledge.* 10 rms, 2 story. No A/C. No rm phones. Mid-June-mid-Oct: S, D $135-$250; each addl $25; lower rates May-mid-June, Oct. Closed rest of yr. Children over 15 yrs only. TV in sitting rm; cable, VCR (free movies). Heated pool. Complimentary full bkfst; afternoon refreshments. Ck-out 11 am, ck-in 3 pm. Sauna, steam rm. Some in-rm whirlpools. Built 1907; antiques, country decor. Atop rocky hill overlooking Frenchman Bay; surrounded by pine forest. Near Acadia National Park. Totally nonsmoking. Cr cds: MC, V.

★ ★ **BLACK FRIAR.** *10 Summer St, off Cottage St. 207/288-5091; FAX 207/288-4197. E-mail blackfriar@acadia.net; web www.blackfriar.com.* 7 rms, 3 story. No rm phones. Mid-June-Columbus Day: S, D $90-$145; lower rates May-mid-June, Columbus Day-Nov. Children over 12 yrs only. TV in sun rm; VCR avail (free movies). Complimentary full bkfst; afternoon refreshments. Ck-out 11 am, ck-in after 4 pm. Victorian decor; antiques. Totally nonsmoking. Cr cds: DS, MC, V.

★ ★ **CANTERBURY COTTAGE.** *12 Roberts St. 207/288-2112; FAX 207/288-5681. E-mail canterbury@acadia.net; web www.acadia.net/cantebury.* 4 rms, 3 with shower only, 2 story. No A/C. No rm phones. Mid-June-mid-Oct: S, D $85-$100; each addl $15; hols 2-day min (in season); lower rates rest of yr. Children over 8 yrs only. Cable TV in common rm; VCR. Complimentary full bkfst; afternoon refreshments. Restaurant nearby. Ck-out 11 am, ck-in 2 pm. Built in 1900. Totally nonsmoking. Cr cds: MC, V.

★ ★ ★ **CASTLEMAINE.** *39 Holland Ave. 207/288-4563; FAX 207/288-4525; res: 800/338-4563.* Web www.acadia.net/castle. 17 rms, 3 story, 4 suites. No rm phones. July-Aug: S, D $98-$175; each addl $25; suites $155-$175; lower rates May-June, Sept-Oct. Closed rest of yr. TV; cable, VCR (movies $2). Complimentary continental bkfst. Restaurant nearby. Ck-out 11 am, ck-in 2 pm. Some refrigerators, whirlpools; many fireplaces. Many balconies. Rambling, Victorian-style house (1886), once the summer residence of Austro-Hungarian ambassador; parlor, antiques. Totally nonsmoking. Cr cds: MC, V.

★ ★ ★ **CLEFTSTONE MANOR.** *92 Eden St. 207/288-4951; res: 888/288-4951; FAX 207/288-2089. E-mail cleftstone@acadia.net; web www.cleftstone.com.* 16 rms, 3 story. No rm phones. Mid-June-Oct: D $100-$185; lower rates May-mid-June. Closed rest of yr. Children over 8 yrs only. Complimentary full bkfst; afternoon, evening refreshments. Ck-out 11 am, ck-in 3 pm. Some fireplaces, balconies. Victorian mansion (1894) once owned by Blair family of Washington, DC. Antiques. Victorian gardens. Totally nonsmoking. Cr cds: DS, MC, V.

★ ★ **GRAYCOTE.** *40 Holland Ave. 207/288-3044; FAX 207/288-2719. E-mail graycote@acadia.net; web www.graycoteinn.com.* 12 rms, 3 story, 2 suites. Some A/C. No rm phones. Mid-June-Columbus Day: S, D $95-$155; suites $200; each addl $20; lower rates rest of yr. Children over 9 yrs only. TV in suites. Complimentary full bkfst; afternoon refreshments. Ck-out 10:30 am, ck-in 3 pm. Some balconies. Near ocean. Restored 19th-century Victorian cottage; 5 fireplaces, antiques, parlor. Totally nonsmoking. Cr cds: A, DS, MC, V.

★ ★ **HATFIELD BED & BREAKFAST.** *20 Roberts Ave. 207/288-9655; FAX 207/288-0360. E-mail hatfield@hatfieldinn.com; web www.hatfieldinn.com.* 6 rms, 2 share bath, 3 with shower only, 3 story. No A/C. No elvtr. No rm phones. Mid-June-Columbus Day: S, D $75-$110; each addl $20; July-Aug (2-day min); lower rates rest of yr. Children over 9 yrs only. Complimentary full bkfst; afternoon refreshments. Restaurant nearby. Ck-out 11 am, ck-in 2 pm. Luggage handling. X-country ski 1 mi. Built in 1895; antiques. Totally nonsmoking. Cr cds: MC, V.

★ ★ **HEARTHSIDE.** *7 High St. 207/288-4533; FAX 207/288-9818. E-mail hearth@acadia.net; web www.hearthsideinn.com.* 9 rms, 4 with shower only, 3 story. No rm phones. Mid-June-mid-Oct: S, D $90-$135; lower rates rest of yr. Children over 10 yrs only. Complimentary full bkfst. Restaurant nearby. Ck-out 11 am, ck-in 1 pm. X-country ski 5 mi. Some in-rm whirlpools, fireplaces. Former doctor's house (1907); antiques. Parlor. Totally nonsmoking. Cr cds: DS, MC, V.

★ ★ ★ **MANOR HOUSE.** *106 West St. 207/288-3759; FAX 207/288-2974; res: 800/437-0088.* Web www.acadia.net/manorhouse. 14 rms, 7 A/C, 3 story, 5 suites, 2 cottages. No rm phones. July-Columbus Day: D $95-$155; each addl $20; suites $105-$175; lower rates mid-April-June, after Columbus Day-mid-Nov. Closed rest of yr. Children over 10 yrs only. TV in sitting rm, cottages; cable. Complimentary full bkfst; afternoon refreshments. Restaurant nearby. Ck-out 10:30 am, ck-in 3 pm. Lawn games. Picnic tables. Near ocean. Restored historic Victorian mansion (1887); period antiques, library. Some fireplaces. Totally nonsmoking. Cr cds: A, DS, MC, V.

★ ★ **MAPLES INN.** *16 Roberts Ave. 207/288-3443; FAX 207/288-0356.* E-mail maplesinn@acadia.net; web www.acadia.net/maples. 6 rms, 3 story, 1 suite. 1 A/C. No rm phones. Mid-June-mid-Oct: S, D $90-$120; each addl $15; suite $150; higher rates Memorial Day wkend; lower rates mid-Apr-mid-June, mid-Oct-early Dec. Closed rest of yr. Children over 8 yrs only. Complimentary full bkfst. Restaurant nearby. Ck-out 11 am, ck-in 2 pm. X-country ski 5 mi. Some fireplaces. Balconies. Restored, turn-of-the-century Victorian inn. Totally nonsmoking. Cr cds: DS, MC, V.

★ ★ ★ **MIRA MONTE.** *69 Mt Desert St. 207/288-4263; FAX 207/288-3115; res: 800/553-5109.* E-mail mburns@acadia.net; web www.miramonte.com. 16 rms in 2 bldgs, 2 story, 2 suites. Mid-June-mid-Oct: S, D $135-$160; each addl $15; suites $205; lower rates May-mid-June. Closed rest of yr. TV; cable. Complimentary full bkfst buffet; afternoon refreshments. Restaurant nearby. Ck-out 11 am, ck-in 2 pm. Business servs avail. Lawn games. Many fireplaces. Balconies. Restored Victorian home (1864) on 2½ acres; wrap-around porch, two formal gardens, library, period furnishings. Totally nonsmoking. Cr cds: A, DS, MC, V.

★ ★ **RIDGEWAY.** *11 High St. 207/288-9682; res: 800/360-5226.* Web www.maineguide.com/barharbor/ridgeway. 5 rms, 1 with shower only, 3 story. No A/C. No rm phones. Mid-June-Columbus Day: S, D $100-$110; each addl $15; suites $125-$150; lower rates May-mid-June, Columbus Day-late Oct. Closed rest of yr. Children over 8 yrs only. Complimentary full bkfst; afternoon refreshments. Restaurant nearby. Ck-out 11 am, ck-in 3 pm. 2 blks from ocean. Built 1884; many antiques. Fireplace in parlor and dining rm. Totally nonsmoking. Cr cds: MC, V.

★ ★ **STRATFORD HOUSE.** *45 Mt Desert St. 207/288-5189; FAX 207/288-5181.* E-mail stratford@maine.com; web www.portland.maine.com/people/stratford. 10 rms, 2 share bath, 3 story. July-mid-Sept: S, D $75-$150; each addl $15; under 5 free; lower rates mid-May-June, mid-Sept-mid-Oct. Closed rest of yr. TV, 5 B&W. Complimentary continental bkfst. Ck-out 11 am, ck-in 1 pm. Fireplaces. Music rm. Built by publisher of Louisa May Alcott's Little Women (1900); English Tudor design modeled after Shakespeare's house in Stratford-on-Avon, original Jacobean furniture. Totally nonsmoking. Cr cds: A, MC, V.

★ ★ ★ **THORNHEDGE.** *47 Mt Desert St. 207/288-5398; res: 877/288-5395.* 13 rms, 3 story. 1 A/C. Mid-June-mid-Oct: S, D $80-$140; lower rates mid-May-mid-June. Closed rest of yr. TV; cable. Continental bkfst; evening refreshments. Ck-out 11 am, ck-in noon. Some fireplaces. Queen Anne-style structure built by publisher of Louisa May Alcott's Little Women as a summer cottage (1900). Totally nonsmoking. Cr cds: MC, V.

Cottage Colony

✔★ **EMERY'S COTTAGES ON THE SHORE.** *Box 172, Sand Point Rd, 4 mi NE off ME 3. 207/288-3432.* E-mail emerycottages@acadia.net; web www.acadia.net/emerycottages. 21 cottages, 13 kits. (oven in 6). No A/C. No rm phones. Late June-Labor Day: D $70-$84; kit. units $90-$110; wkly rates; lower rates early May-late June, Labor Day-Oct. Closed rest of yr. Crib free. TV; cable (premium). Complimentary coffee. Ck-out 10 am, ck-in 2 pm. Coin lndry. Refrigerators. Picnic tables, grills. On Frenchman Bay. Cr cds: A, DS, MC, V.

Restaurants

★ ★ **124 COTTAGE STREET.** *124 Cottage St. 207/288-4383.* E-mail cottage124@acadia.net. Continental menu. Specializes in fresh fish, desserts. Salad bar. Hrs: 5-10 pm; early-bird dinner 5-6 pm. Closed Nov-May. Res accepted. Bar. Semi-a la carte: dinner $8.95-$18.95.

Child's meals. Outdoor dining. In restored, turn-of-the-century cottage. Cr cds: A, MC, V.

✔★ **DOCKSIDER TOO.** *131 Cottage St. 207/288-9093.* Specializes in fresh seafood, pasta. Hrs: 11 am-9 pm; early-bird dinner 11 am-6 pm. Closed mid-Oct-mid-May. Res accepted. No A/C. Wine, beer. Semi-a la carte: lunch, dinner $2.25-$17.95. Child's meals. Parking. Outdoor dining. Casual dining. Cr cds: DS, MC, V.

★ ★ **DUFFY'S QUARTERDECK.** *1 Main St. 207/288-5292.* Specialties: lobster crêpe à la Reine, sole Marguery hollandaise au supreme. Hrs: 11 am-10 pm; early-bird dinner 4-6 pm. Closed Nov-Apr. Serv bar. Semi-a la carte: lunch $3.95-$10.95, dinner $10.95-$19.95. Outdoor dining. Totally nonsmoking. Cr cds: A, D, DS, MC, V.

✔★ **FREDDIE'S ROUTE 66.** *21 Cottage St. 207/288-3708.* Specializes in prime rib, lobster, roast pork. Hrs: 4:30-10 pm; early-bird dinner 4:30-6 pm. Closed mid-Oct-mid-May. Res accepted. Bar. Semi-a la carte: dinner $7.95-$15.95. Child's meals. 1950s-theme decor. Family-owned. Cr cds: A, DS, MC, V.

★ ★ ★ **GEORGE'S.** *7 Stephens Lane, off Main St, behind 1st Natl Bank. 207/288-4505.* Mediterranean menu. Specializes in grilled fish, lobster, lamb. Own baking. Hrs: 5:30-10 pm; hrs vary after Labor Day. Closed Nov-Memorial Day. Res accepted. No A/C. Bar. Wine list. Semi-a la carte: dinner $12-$24. Prix fixe: dinner $33-$36. Child's meals. Pianist or guitarist Wed-Sat. Outdoor dining. In restored mid-1800s home; near ocean. Totally nonsmoking. Cr cds: A, C, D, DS, MC, V.

★ **ISLAND CHOWDER HOUSE.** *38 Cottage St. 207/288-4905.* Specializes in lobster, chowder. Own desserts. Hrs: 11 am-10 pm; early-bird dinner 11 am-6 pm. Closed Nov-Apr. Res accepted. Bar. Semi-a la carte: lunch $4.29-$9.99, dinner $8.99-$19.99. Child's meals. Pub decor with model train operating in dining rm. Cr cds: A, DS, MC, V.

★ ★ **MAGGIE'S CLASSIC SCALES.** *6 Summer St. 207/288-9007.* E-mail moc@acadia.net. Specializes in fresh local seafood. Own desserts. Hrs: 5-10 pm. Closed late Oct-Memorial Day. Res accepted. Serv bar. Semi-a la carte: dinner $7.95-$19.95. Totally nonsmoking. Cr cds: DS, MC, V.

✔★ **MIGUEL'S.** *51 Rodick St. 207/288-5117.* Mexican menu. Specializes in tostadas, enchiladas, fajitas. Hrs: 5-10 pm. Closed mid-Nov-Mar. Bar. Complete meals: dinner $5.95-$13.95. Child's meals. Outdoor dining. Mexican atmosphere; artifacts, tiled floors. Braille menu. Cr cds: MC, V.

★ ★ ★ **READING ROOM.** *(See Bar Harbor Inn Motel) 207/288-3351.* E-mail bhinn@acadia.net; web www.barharborinn.com. Specializes in fresh local seafood. Own baking. Hrs: 7-10:30 am, 5:30-9:30 pm; Sun brunch 11:30 am-2:30 pm. Closed mid-Nov-Easter. Res accepted. Bar from 4:30 pm. Wine list. A la carte entrees: bkfst $1.50-$4.95. Buffet: bkfst $8.95. Semi-a la carte: dinner $15.95-$24.95. Sun brunch $14.95. Child's meals. Pianist or harpist. Valet parking. Panoramic view of harbor and docks. Cr cds: A, D, DS, MC, V.

★ ★ **RHINEHART DINING PAVILION.** *On Highbrook Rd, off Eden St. 207/288-5663.* Specializes in prime rib, seafood. Hrs: 7-10 am, 5-9 pm. Closed Nov-Apr. Bar. Buffet: bkfst $7. Semi-a la carte: dinner $10.95-$19.95. Child's meals. Parking. Octagonal building on hill; overlooks harbor. Cr cds: DS, MC, V.

Unrated Dining Spot

FISHERMAN'S LANDING. *35 West St. 207/288-4632.* Specializes in lobster, seafood. Hrs: noon-9 pm. Closed Oct-May. No A/C. Bar. Semi-a la carte: lunch, dinner $1.50-$9. Outdoor deck dining. Built over water. Lobster tanks; select own lobster. Blackboard menu. Family-owned. Cr cds: MC, V.

D

Bath (G-2)

(See also Boothbay Harbor, Brunswick, Freeport)

Pop 9,799 **Elev** 13 ft **Area code** 207 **Zip** 04530 **E-mail** ccbbr@horton.col.k12.me.us **Web** www.midcoastmaine.com
InformationChamber of Commerce of the Bath-Brunswick Region, 45 Front St; 207/443-9751 or 207/725-8797.

For more than two centuries Bath has been a shipbuilding center on the west bank of the Kennebec River. The Bath Iron Works, which dates back to 1833, began building ships in 1889. It has produced destroyers, cruisers, a battleship, pleasure craft and steamers, and now also produces patrol frigates. Altogether, Bath has launched more than 4,000 ships from its shores, and launching a ship today is still a great event.

Many fine old mansions, built when Bath was a great seaport, still stand. A restored 19th-century business district, waterfront park and public landing are also part of the city.

What to See and Do

Ft Popham Memorial. Construction of the fort began in 1861. Never finished, it was garrisoned in 1865-1866 and remains an impressive masonry structure with gun emplacements. Picnic tables (no garbage receptacles). (May-Sept, daily) 16 mi S on ME 209 in Popham Beach. Phone 207/389-1335 or 207/287-3821.   **Free.**

Maine Maritime Museum and Shipyard. Maritime History Bldg has exhibits of models, navigational instruments, scrimshaw, macramé, seafaring crafts and memorabilia, paintings. Tours of original shipyard buildings, demonstrations of seafaring techniques (seasonal); waterfront picnic area and playground. Museum shop. (Daily; closed Jan 1, Thanksgiving, Dec 25) 243 Washington St, 2 mi S of US 1, located on Kennebec River. Phone 207/443-1316.   **¢¢¢**

Popham Colony. A picturesque drive. In 1607 the first American vessel, the *Virginia,* was built here by colonists who shortly thereafter returned to England, many of them in the ship they had built. On the hilltop nearby is Ft Baldwin, built during World War I. A 70-ft tower offers a panoramic view of the coast and the Kennebec River. 16 mi S on ME 209 on Sabino Head. **Free.**

State parks.

  Popham Beach. Swimming, tidal pools (mid-Apr-Nov); surfing; fishing; picnicking. (Daily) Standard fees. 12 mi S on ME 209. Phone 207/389-1335.   **¢**

  Reid. Swimming, saltwater lagoon, bathhouse; fishing. Picnic facilities, concession. (Daily) Standard fees. 1 mi E on US 1 to Woolwich, then 13 mi SE on ME 127 to Georgetown, then SE. Phone 207/371-2303.   **¢¢**

Motel

  ★ ★ HOLIDAY INN. *139 Western Ave.* 207/443-9741; *FAX* 207/442-8281. E-mail hibath@aol.com; web www.holiday-inn.com/bthme. 141 rms, 3 story. Late June-early Oct: S, D $85-$119; each addl $10; under 19 free; lower rates rest of yr. Crib free. Pet accepted. TV; cable, premium. Heated pool; whirlpool. Complimentary coffee in rms. Restaurant 6 am-2 pm, 5-10 pm. Bar 11-1 am; Sun from noon; entertainment Wed-Sun. Ck-out noon. Meeting rm. Business servs avail. In-rm modem link. Valet serv. Sundries. Coin lndry. Exercise equipt; sauna. Refrigerators. Cr cds: A, C, D, DS, ER, JCB, MC, V.

D 🛥 ≋ ✕ 🏊 🐾 **SC**

Inns

  ✔★ ★ **FAIRHAVEN.** *North Bath Rd, 1¹/₂ mi N on High St to Whiskeag Rd, left onto Whiskeag Rd to North Bath Rd.* 207/443-4391; *res: 888/443-4391; FAX 207/443-6412.* E-mail fairhvn@gwi.net; web www.mainecoast.com/fairhaveninn. 8 rms, 2 share bath, 2 story. No A/C. No rm phones. Mid-May-Oct: S $60-$80; D $80-$120; each addl $15; wkly rates; lower rates rest of yr. Crib free. Complimentary full bkfst. Ck-out 11 am, ck-in 4-6 pm. Meeting rms. X-country ski on site. Picnic tables. Federalist house (1790) with tavern rm, library, antique & country furnishings; on 16 acres on Kennebec River. Cr cds: DS, MC, V.

🛥 🏂 🐾

  ✔★ ★ ★ **GALEN C. MOSES HOUSE.** *1009 Washington St.* 207/442-8771; *res: 888/442-8771.* E-mail galenmoses@clinic.net; web www.galenmoses.com. 4 rms, 2 shower only. No A/C. No rm phones. Mid-May-Oct: S, D $69-$99; wkends 2-day min (in season); lower rates rest of yr. Children over 12 yrs only. Cable TV in common rm, VCR avail (movies). Complimentary full bkfst; afternoon refreshments. Ck-out 11 am, ck-in 3-8 pm. Picnic tables, grills. Built in 1874; antiques. Italian bldg with Victorian interior; stained glass windows. Totally nonsmoking. Cr cds: MC, V.

🏂 🐾

Restaurants

  ★ ★ **KRISTINA'S.** *160 Centre St.* 207/442-8577. Hrs: 8 am-9 pm (July-Labor Day); Sat, Sun brunch 9 am-2 pm. Varied hrs off season. Closed Thanksgiving, Dec 25; also Jan, Mon off season. Res accepted. Bar. Semi-a la carte: bkfst $3.25-$7.50, lunch $4.95-$8.95, dinner $10.95-$15.95. Sat, Sun brunch $3.50-$9.25. Child's meals. Patio dining. Bakery on premises. Cr cds: DS, MC, V.

D

  ★ **TASTE OF MAINE.** *(US 1, Woolwich 04579) 1 mi N on US 1.* 207/443-4554. Specializes in lobster, seafood, steak. Hrs: 11 am-9 pm. Serv bar. Semi-a la carte entrees: lunch, dinner $2.95-$24.95. Child's meals. Gift shop. Outdoor dining. Overlooks fork of Kennebec River. Cr cds: A, DS, MC, V.

D **SC**

Baxter State Park (C-3)

(See also Millinocket)

(18 mi NW of Millinocket via park roads)

While serving as a legislator and as governor of Maine, Percival P. Baxter urged creation of a wilderness park around Mt Katahdin—Maine's highest peak (5,267 feet). Rebuffed but not defeated, Baxter bought the land with his own money and deeded to the state of Maine a 201,018-acre park "to be forever left in its natural, wild state." The park can be reached from Greenville via paper company roads, Millinocket via ME 157 or from Patten via ME 159.

The Park Authority operates the following campgrounds: Katahdin Stream, Abol and Nesowadnehunk, Roaring Brook (Roaring Brook Road), Chimney Pond (by trail 3.3 miles beyond Roaring Brook), Russell Pond (Wassataquoik Valley, 7 miles by trail beyond Roaring Brook), South Branch Pond (at outlet of Lower South Branch Pond), Trout Brook Farm (Trout Brook Crossing). There are cabins ($17/person/night) at Daicey Pond off Nesowadnehunk Road and at Kidney Pond. All areas except Chimney, Kidney & Daicey ponds have tent space, and all areas except Trout Brook Farm, Kidney & Daicey ponds have lean-tos; ($6/person/night), water (unprotected, should be purified) and primitive facilities (no indoor plumbing, no running water; some springs); bunkhouses ($7/night) at some campgrounds. Under age 7 free throughout the park.

Reservations should be made by mail (and paid in full) in advance. For detailed information contact the Reservation Clerk, Baxter State Park, 64 Balsam Dr, Millinocket 04462. Swimming, fishing; canoes for rent at Russell Pond, South Branch Pond, Daicey Pond, Kidney Pond and Trout Brook farm.

The park is open for camping mid-May-mid-Oct. No pets or motorcycles are permitted. Vehicles exceeding 7 feet wide, 9 feet high or 22 feet long will not be admitted. For further information contact Park Manager, 64 Balsam Dr, Millinocket 04462; 207/723-5140. Nonresident vehicle fee ¢¢¢

Belfast (F-3)

(See also Bucksport, Camden, Searsport)

Settled 1770 **Pop** 6,355 **Elev** 103 ft **Area code** 207 **Zip** 04915
Information Chamber of Commerce, 29 Front St, PO Box 58; 207/338-5900.

Belfast, named for the city in Northern Ireland, was settled in 1770 by Irish and Scottish immigrants. An old seaport on the west shore of Penobscot Bay, Belfast is also a hub of small boat traffic to the bay islands. It is the seat of Waldo County, with sardine canneries, potato processing, window making and printing as its major industries.

What to See and Do

Lake St George State Park. More than 360 acres. Swimming, bathhouse, lifeguard; fishing; boating (ramp, rentals). Snowmobiling permitted. Picnicking; camping. (Mid-May-mid-Oct) Standard fees. 19 mi W on ME 3, near Montville. Phone 207/589-4255.

Annual Event

Belfast Bay Festival. City Park. Parade, concerts, carnival. Phone 207/338-5900. July.

Motels

★ ★ **BELFAST HARBOR INN.** *1/2 mi N on US 1. 207/338-2740; FAX 207/338-5205; res: 800/545-8576.* E-mail stay@belfastharborinn.com; web www.belfastharborinn.com. 61 rms, 2 story. July-Aug: S, D $74-$89; each addl $10; under 12 free; wkly rates; lower rates rest of yr. Crib free. Pet accepted; $5. TV; cable (premium). Pool. Complimentary continental bkfst. Restaurant 11 am-9 pm. Ck-out 11 am. Meeting rm. Business servs avail. Downhill/x-country ski 15 mi. Balconies. Picnic tables. Overlooks Penobscot Bay. Cr cds: A, DS, MC, V.

  SC

★ **GULL.** *3 mi N on US 1. 207/338-4030.* 14 rms, 2 story. July-Labor Day: S, D $59-$68; each addl $5, under 12 $3; lower rates rest of yr. Crib $5. Pet accepted, some restrictions. TV; cable. Restaurant nearby. Ck-out 11 am. Overlooks bay. Cr cds: MC, V.

SC

★ **WONDERVIEW COTTAGES.** *Searsport Ave, 3 mi NE on US 1, ME 3. 207/338-1455.* E-mail wondercottages@acadia.net; web www.maineguide.com/belfast/wonderview. 20 kit. cottages, 1 condo. No A/C. July-Labor Day, wkly: kit. cottages for 2-6, $475-$850; lower rates Apr-June, Sept-late Oct. Closed rest of yr. Crib free. Pet accepted. TV; cable. Playground. Restaurant nearby. Ck-out 10:30 am. Lawn games. Fireplaces. Screened porches. Picnic tables, grills. Private beach on Penobscot Bay. Cr cds: DS, MC, V.

Inn

★ ★ **BELFAST BAY MEADOWS.** *192 Northport Ave, S on US 1. 207/338-5715; res: 800/335-2370.* E-mail bbmi@acadia.net; web www.maineguide.com/belfast/baymeadows. 20 rms, 1-3 story. July-Aug: S, D $85-$165; each addl $15; lower rates rest of yr. Crib free. Pet accepted. TV in some rms, sitting rm; cable, VCR avail (free movies). Playground. Complimentary full bkfst. Ck-out 11 am, ck-in 3:30-6:30 pm. Meeting rm. Business servs avail. Refrigerators avail. Turn-of-the-century country inn; antiques. Overlooks bay. Totally nonsmoking. Cr cds: A, DS, MC, V.

Restaurants

✔★ **90 MAIN.** *92 Main St. 207/338-1106.* Specializes in fresh seafood, lobster, vegetarian/macrobiotic dishes. Hrs: 11 am-4 pm, 5-10 pm; Sun brunch 9 am-3 pm. Closed Thanksgiving, Dec 25. No A/C. Bar to 1 am. Semi-a la carte: lunch $3.95-$8, dinner $6-$15. Sun brunch $3.95-$5.95. Child's meals. Entertainment Fri. Outdoor dining. Bakery on premises. Local artwork on display. Totally nonsmoking. Cr cds: A, DS, MC, V.

✔★ ★ **DARBY'S.** *155 High St. 207/338-2339.* Eclectic menu. Specialties: pad thai, Mahogany duck. Own desserts. Hrs: 11 am-3:30 pm, 5-9:30 pm. Closed Easter, Dec 25. Res accepted. Bar. Semi-a la carte: lunch $3.95-$10.95, dinner $6.95-$16.95. Child's meals. Street parking. Cr cds: DS, MC, V.

★ ★ **THE MAINE CHOWDER HOUSE.** *Searsport Ave (US 1). 207/338-5225.* Specializes in fresh local seafood, steaks. Hrs: 11 am-9 pm. Closed Thanksgiving, Dec 25. Res accepted. Bar from 4 pm. Semi-a la carte: lunch, dinner $3.95-$26.95. Child's meals. Entertainment Thurs & Sun (in-season). Parking. Outdoor dining. Cr cds: DS, MC, V.

Bethel (F-1)

Settled 1774 **Pop** 2,329 **Elev** 700 ft **Area code** 207 **Zip** 04217 **E-mail** bethelcc@nxi.com
Information Chamber of Commerce, PO Box 439; 207/824-2282 or 800/442-5826 (reservations).

Bethel, on both banks of the winding Androscoggin River, is built on the rolling Oxford Hills and is backed by the rough foothills of the White Mountains. In addition to being a year-round resort, it's an educational and wood products center. One of Maine's leading preparatory schools, Gould Academy (founded 1836), is located here.

What to See and Do

Dr. Moses Mason House Museum (1813). Restored home of prominent congressman who served during administration of Andrew Jackson. Antique furnishings, early American murals. (July-Labor Day, Sat & Sun afternoons; rest of yr, Mon-Fri, also by appt) Broad St, in National Historic District. Phone 207/824-2908. ¢

Grafton Notch State Park. The Appalachian Trail passes through the notch; interpretive displays, scenic view, picnicking; fishing. (Memorial Day-mid-Oct) Approx 9 mi NW via US 2, ME 26. Phone 207/824-2912. ¢

Skiing.

Carter's X-C Ski Center. 1,000 acres with 65 km of groomed cross-country trails. Rentals, lessons; lounge, shop; 2 lodges. (May-Oct, daily) Middle Intervale Rd. Phone 207/539-4848. ¢¢

Sunday River Ski Resort. 9 quad, 4 triple, 2 double chairlifts (including 4 high-speed detachables, 1 surface lift); patrol, school, rentals, ski shop; snowmaking; cafeterias, restaurants; bars. 126 runs; longest run 3 mi; vertical drop 2,340 ft. (Early Oct-mid-May, daily) 112 cross-country trails adj. Mountain biking (late June-Labor Day, daily; Labor Day-late Oct, wkends). 6 mi NE on US 2. Phone 207/824-3000 or 800/543-2SKI (reservations).   ¢¢¢¢¢

Swimming, picnicking, camping, boating, fishing. Songo Lake in Bethel; Christopher Lake in Bryant Pond; North and South ponds in Locke Mills; Littlefield beaches and Stony Brook campgrounds. E on ME 26.

White Mt National Forest (see under NEW HAMPSHIRE). More than 49,000 acres of this forest extend into Maine SW of here. Birches and sugar maples turn fall into a season of breathtaking color. Fishing. Hiking, rock hounding. Camping (fee). For information contact the Supervisor, 719 Main St, PO Box 638, Laconia, NH 03247, phone 603/528-8721; or the Evans Notch Ranger District office in Bethel, phone 207/824-2134.   **Free.**

Motels

✔★ **INN AT THE ROSTAY.** *186 Mayville Rd (US 2). 207/824-3111.* 18 rms, 10 with shower only. No A/C. No rm phones. Mid-Dec-mid-Apr: S $45-$55; D $55-$85; each addl $5; under 12 free; lower rates rest of yr. TV; cable. Restaurant opp open 24 hrs. Ck-out 11 am. Downhill ski 5 mi; x-country ski 4 mi. Some refrigerators, microwaves. Some balconies. Cr cds: A, DS, MC, V.

 ✎ ⬚ ⬚ 🔥 ⬚

✔★★ **NORSEMAN INN AND MOTEL.** *134 Mayville Rd. 207/824-2002; FAX 207/824-6046.* Web www.nettx.com/norseman.html. 31 rms, 22 A/C, 2 story. No rm phones. S $39-$89; D $49-$99; each addl $10; higher rates: hol wkends, fall foliage, winter. Crib free. TV; cable. Complimentary continental bkfst. Restaurant opp 7 am-9 pm. Ck-out 10:30 am. Coin lndry. Downhill ski 5 mi; x-country ski on site. Game rm. Lawn games. Some balconies. Picnic tables. Cr cds: DS, MC, V.

⬚ ✎ ⬚ 🔥 ⬚ SC

★★ **RIVER VIEW.** *357 Mayville Rd, 2 mi NE on US 2 (ME 5/26). 207/824-2808; FAX 207/824-6808.* E-mail rview@nxi.com. 32 kit. units (2-bedrm). Mid-Dec-mid-Apr: D $89-$139; each addl $20; suites $150-$250; 2-day min; higher rates hols; lower rates rest of yr. TV; cable (premium). Indoor pool; whirlpool. Playground. Ck-out 10 am. Tennis. Downhill ski 4 mi; x-country ski 3 mi. Sauna. Game rm. Lawn games. Picnic tables, grills. On river. Cr cds: A, DS, MC, V.

✎ 🏃 ⬚ ⬚ 🔥

Hotel

★★★ **GRAND SUMMIT HOTEL & CONFERENCE CENTER.** *PO Box 450, 4 mi N on US 2, follow Sunday River signs. 207/824-3500; FAX 207/824-3993.* 230 rms, 4 story, 150 kit. units. Mid-Dec-mid-Apr: S, D $95-$229; each addl $10; kits. $95-$440; family, wkend, hol, wkly rates; ski plan; lower rates rest of yr. Crib $10. TV; cable, VCR avail. Heated pool; whirlpool, poolside serv. Supervised child's activities (mid-Dec-Apr); ages 6 wks-12 yrs. Restaurant 7-11 am, noon-3 pm, 5-10 pm. Bar; entertainment (in season). Ck-out 10:30 am. Coin lndry. Meeting rms. Business servs avail. Valet serv. Concierge. Gift shop. Lighted tennis. 18-hole golf privileges. Downhill/x-country ski on site. Exercise equipt; sauna. Game rm. Microwaves avail. Lawn games. Some balconies. Cr cds: A, DS, MC, V.

⬚ ➾ ✎ 🏃 ⬚ ⬚ 🔥 ⬚

Inn

★★ **BRIAR LEA B & B.** *150 Mayville Rd, 1 mi N on US 2 at jct ME 26. 207/824-4717; FAX 207/824-7121.* E-mail briarlea@megalink.com; web www.nettex.com/briarlea. 7 rms, 3 with shower only. No A/C. No rm phones. Jan-Apr, mid-Sept-mid-Oct: S $79; D $89-$99; each addl $15; ski plans; wkends, hols (2-day min); higher rates major hols; lower rates rest of yr. Crib $15. Pet accepted, some restrictions. TV in common rm; cable,

VCR avail. Complimentary full bkfst. Restaurant 6:30-11 am, 5-9:30 pm; Sun to noon. Ck-out 11 am, ck-in 4 pm. Downhill ski 5 mi; x-country ski on site. Built in 1850s; farmhouse atmosphere; antiques. Cr cds: A, MC, V.

➾ ✎ ⬚ ⬚ SC

Resort

★★ **BETHEL INN & COUNTRY CLUB.** *On the town common, at jct US 2, ME 5, 26, 35. 207/824-2175; FAX 207/824-2233; res: 800/654-0125.* E-mail connorsa@nxi.com; web www.bethelinn.com. 60 rms in 5-bldg complex, 40 2-bedrm townhouses. No A/C. May-Oct, Dec-Mar: S $79-$129/person; each addl $55; MAP: suites $90-$175; EP: townhouses $79-$129/person; lower rates rest of yr. Pet accepted. TV; cable, VCR avail. Heated pool; whirlpool, poolside serv. Supervised child's activities (July 7-Labor Day); ages 5-12. Dining rm 7:30-9:30 am, 11:30 am-3 pm, 5:30-9 pm. Bars; entertainment. Ck-out 11 am, ck-in 2 pm. Meeting rms. Business servs avail. Gift shop. Tennis. 18-hole golf, greens fee $35-$40, pro, putting green, driving range. Canoes, sailboats. Downhill ski 7 mi; x-country ski on site. Exercise equipt; saunas. Massage. Lawn games. Cr cds: A, C, D, DS, MC, V.

⬚ ➾ ✎ 🏃 ⬚ ✎ 🏃 ⬚ 🔥

Restaurant

✔★ **MOTHERS.** *On Upper Main St. 207/824-2589.* Specializes in seafood, chicken, pasta. Own soups. Hrs: 11:30 am-9:30 pm; hrs vary off season. Closed Thanksgiving, Dec 24, 25. Serv bar. Semi-a la carte: lunch $4.50-$14.50, dinner $6.50-$19. Child's meals. Parking. Outdoor dining. Gothic gingerbread-style house (late 1800s); antiques. Cr cds: MC, V.

🏃

Bingham (E-2)

(See also Skowhegan)

Settled 1785 **Pop** 1,071 **Elev** 371 ft **Area code** 207 **Zip** 04920

What to See and Do

Wilderness Expeditions. Guided raft trips on the Kennebec, Penobscot and Dead rivers; also canoe outfitting, guided kayaking and ski tours. (May-Sept, daily) Phone 207/534-7305 or 800/825-9453.   ¢¢¢¢¢

Motel

✔★ **BINGHAM MOTOR INN.** *US 201, 1 mi S on US 201. 207/672-4135; FAX 207/672-4138.* 20 rms, 4 kits. July-Labor Day, hunting season: S $45.95; D $57.95; each addl $5; kit. units $5 addl; wkly; lower rates rest of yr. Crib $5. Pet accepted, some restrictions. TV; cable. Pool. Restaurant nearby. Ck-out 10 am. Downhill ski 3 mi. Lawn games. Some refrigerators. Picnic tables. Cr cds: MC, V.

⬚ ➾ ✎ ⬚

Blue Hill (F-4)

(See also Bar Harbor, Ellsworth)

Settled 1722 **Pop** 1,941 **Elev** 40 ft **Area code** 207 **Zip** 04614
Information Office of the Town Clerk, PO Box 433; 207/374-2281 or -5741.

Named for a nearby hill that gives a beautiful view of Mt Desert Island, Blue Hill changed from a thriving seaport to a summer colony known for its crafts and antiques. Mary Ellen Chase, born here in 1887, wrote about Blue Hill in *A Goodly Heritage* and *Mary Peters.*

What to See and Do

Holt House. One of the oldest houses in Blue Hill; now home of the Blue Hill Historical Society. Memorabilia. (July-Aug, Tues & Fri afternoons; closed hols) For further information contact the town clerk. ¢

Parson Fisher House (1814). House designed and built by town's first minister, who also made most of his own furniture and household articles; paintings and woodcuts by the minister; memorabilia. (July-mid-Oct, Mon-Sat afternoons) On ME 15. Phone 207/374-2844.   ¢¢

Rackliffe Pottery. Family manufactures wheel-thrown dinnerware from native red-firing clay. Open workshop. (July-Aug, daily; rest of yr, daily exc Sun; closed hols) Ellsworth Rd. Phone 207/374-2297.   **Free.**

Rowantrees Pottery. Manufactures functional pottery and wheel-thrown handcrafted dinnerware; 10- to 15-min tours. (June-Sept, daily; rest of yr, Mon-Fri; closed hols) Union St. Phone 207/374-5535.   **Free.**

Wooden Boat School. (Daily) Naskeag Rd & Brooklyn. Phone 207/359-4651.

Annual Event

Blue Hill Fair. Sheep dog trials, agriculture & livestock exhibits; midway, harness racing, crafts. 5 days Labor Day wkend.

Motel

✔★★ **HERITAGE MOTOR INN.** *Ellsworth Rd, ½ mi E on ME 172.* 207/374-5646. 23 rms, 2 story. No A/C. July-Labor Day: S, D $85; each addl $8; kit. unit $115; lower rates rest of yr. Crib $5. TV; cable. Complimentary coffee in rms. Restaurant nearby. Ck-out 11 am. On hillside, overlooking bay. Cr cds: MC, V.

Inn

★★★ **BLUE HILL.** *Union St, W on ME 177.* 207/374-2844; FAX 207/374-2829; res: 800/826-7415. E-mail bluhilin@downeast.net; web www.bluehillinn.com. 12 rms, 3 story. 3 A/C. MAP, July-mid-Oct: S $130-$150; D $150-$260; each addl $50; lower rates rest of yr. Closed mid-May-June, Nov. Closed rest of yr. Complimentary coffee; afternoon refreshments. Dining rm 8-9:30 am, dinner sitting 7 pm (public by res only); closed Mon, Tues. Ck-out 10:30 am, ck-in 2-5 pm. Airport transportation. Fireplaces. Inn since 1840. Antiques. Flower garden. Totally nonsmoking. Cr cds: DS, MC, V.

Restaurant

★★ **JONATHAN'S.** *Main St.* 207/374-5226. Specialties: braised lamb shank, poached Atlantic salmon. Hrs: 5-9:30 pm; off-season hrs vary. Closed Mon (off-season); also most major hols. Res accepted. Liquor, wine, beer. A la carte entrees: dinner $16-$19.50. Street parking. Totally nonsmoking. Cr cds: MC, V.

Boothbay Harbor (G-3)

(See also Damariscotta, Wiscasset)

Pop 1,267 **Elev** 16 ft **Area code** 207 **Zip** 04538 **E-mail** seamaine@boothbayharbor.com **Web** www.boothbayharbor.com
Information Boothbay Harbor Region Chamber of Commerce, PO Box 356; 207/633-2353 or 800/266-8422.

Native Americans were paid 20 beaver pelts for the area encompassing Boothbay Harbor. Today, its protected harbor, a haven for boatmen, is the scene of well-attended regattas several times a summer. Boothbay Harbor, on the peninsula between the Sheepscot and Damariscotta rivers, shares the peninsula and adjacent islands with a dozen other communities, including Boothbay (settled 1630), of which it was once a part.

What to See and Do

Boat trips.

Balmy Days. Makes trips to Monhegan Island (see) with 4-hr stopover. (June-Sept, daily) Pier 8, Commercial St. Phone 207/633-2284.   ¢¢¢¢¢

Cap'n Fish's Boat Trips and Deep Sea Fishing. Boats make varied excursions: 1¼-3-hr trips; fishing cruises; lobster hauling, puffin, seal and whale watches; scenic, sunset & cocktail cruises; fall foliage and Kennebec River trips; charters. (Mid-May-Oct; days vary) Pier 1. Phone 207/633-3244 or 207/633-2626.   ¢¢¢-¢¢¢¢¢

Novelty. One-hr harbor cruises with stop at Squirrel Island; Night Lights cruises (July-Aug, Tues-Sat). Harbor cruises (Apr-Oct, daily exc Sat). Pier 8, Commercial St. Phone 207/633-2284.   ¢¢¢

Boothbay Railway Village. Historical Maine exhibits of rural life, railroads and antique autos and trucks. Rides on a coal-fired, narrow-guage steam train to an antique vehicle display. Also on exhibit on 8 acres are displays of early fire equipment, a general store, a one-rm schoolhouse and 2 restored RR stations. (Mid-June-mid-Oct, daily) 1 mi N of Boothbay Center on ME 27. Phone 207/633-4727.   ¢¢

Boothbay Region Historical Society Museum. Artifacts of Boothbay Region. (July-Labor Day, Wed, Fri, Sat; rest of yr, Sat only) 70 Oak St. **Donation.**

Fishing. In inland waters, Golf Course Brook, Adams, W Harbor and Knickerbocker ponds in Boothbay; Meadow Brook in E Boothbay. Ocean fishing from harbor docks. Boat rentals; deep-sea fishing.

Picnicking. Boothbay Region Lobstermen's Cooperative, Atlantic Ave. Lobsterman's Wharf, E Boothbay. Robinson's Wharf, ME 27 at bridge, Southport. Boiled lobsters and steamed clams, snacks avail.

Annual Events

Fisherman's Festival. Phone 207/633-2353. Mid-Apr.

Windjammer Days. Old schooners that formerly sailed the trade routes and now cruise the Maine coast sail en masse into harbor. Waterfront food court, entertainment, street parade, children's activities. Phone 207/633-2353. Late June.

Antique Show. Phone 207/633-4727. 3rd wkend July.

Fall Foliage Festival. Foliage drives, harvest suppers, boat trips, country fair. Phone 207/633-4743. Columbus Day wkend.

Harbor Lights Festival. Craft fair, lighted boat parade. Phone 207/633-2353. 1st Sat Dec.

Motels

★★★ **BROWN BROS WHARF.** *121 Atlantic Ave, 1 mi SE.* 207/633-5440; FAX 207/633-2953; res: 800/334-8110. Web www.brownswharfinn.com. 70 rms, 3 story. No elvtr. Late June-Labor Day: D $109-$149; each addl $10; kit. unit $30 addl; kit. apts $50 addl; lower rates May-mid-June, Labor Day-Oct. Closed rest of yr. Crib free. TV; cable.

Restaurant 8-10 am, 5:30-8:30 pm. Bar to 9:30 pm in season. Ck-out 11 am. Coin lndry. Meeting rm. Business servs avail. Balconies. All rms with harbor view. Dockage; marina; trolley stop (in season). Cr cds: A, MC, V.

⊡ 🖙 ⊠ 🔥

★ ★ **CAP'N FISH'S.** *65 Atlantic Ave. 207/633-6605; FAX 207/633-6239; res: 800/633-0860.* Web www.sourcemaine.com/capmotel. 54 rms, 2 story, 2 kit. Mid-June-Sept: D $75-$95; each addl $8; kit. unit $110; lower rates mid-May-mid-June & Oct. Closed rest of yr. Crib free. TV; cable. Restaurant 7-9 am. Ck-out 11 am. Business servs avail. Some refrigerators. Picnic tables. On harbor, dockage. Cruises, whale-watching avail. Cr cds: A, MC, V.

⊡ ⊠ 🔥

★ ★ **FISHERMAN'S WHARF INN.** *Pier 6 at 22 Commercial St. 207/633-5090; FAX 207/633-5092; res: 800/628-6872.* E-mail fishermanswharf@clinic.net; web www.fishermanswharfinn.com. 54 rms, 2-3 story. No elvtr. Mid-July-mid-Aug: D $90-$170; each addl $5; suites $120-$170; lower rates mid-May-mid-July, Mid-Aug-Oct. Closed rest of yr. Crib $5. TV; cable (premium). Complimentary continental bkfst. Restaurant (see FISHERMAN'S WHARF INN). Bar 11 am-11 pm. Ck-out 11 am. Business servs avail. Gift shop. Valet parking. Balconies. On wharf overlooking harbor; pickup point for boat tour, whale watch. Cr cds: A, C, D, DS, MC, V.

⊡ 🖙 ⊠ 🔥

✔ ★ **FLAGSHIP MOTOR INN.** *200 Townsend Ave (ME 27). 207/633-5094; FAX 207/633-7055; res: 800/660-5094 (ME).* E-mail flagship@clinic.net; web www.maineguide.com/boothbay/flagship. 84 rms, 2 story. Mid-July-Labor Day: D $70; each addl $10; under 13 free; lower rates rest of yr. Crib $5. TV; cable. Pool. Restaurant 6 am-9 pm. Bar 4-11 pm. Ck-out 11 am. Balconies. Cr cds: A, DS, MC, V.

⊠ ⊠ 🔥

✔ ★ **HILLSIDE ACRES.** *(Adams Pond Rd, Boothbay 04537) 1½ mi N on Adams Rd, off ME 27. 207/633-3411.* 14 units, 2 share bath, 1-2 story, 7 kit. units, 7 cottages. No A/C. No rm phones. July-Aug: S, D $40-$75; kit. cottages $63-$75; cottages $57; wkly rates; lower rates rest of yr. Crib free. Pet accepted. TV; cable. Pool. Complimentary continental bkfst (mid-June-Labor Day). Ck-out 10:30 am. Picnic tables, grills. Cr cds: MC, V.

✔ ⊠ ⊠ 🔥

★ ★ **HOWARD HOUSE.** *347 Townsend Ave (ME 27), 1 mi N on ME 27. 207/633-3933; FAX 207/633-6244.* 14 rms, 2 story. No A/C. No rm phones. Late June-Labor Day: D $72-$86; each addl $15; lower rates rest of yr. TV; cable. Complimentary bkfst buffet (Memorial Day-Oct). Restaurant nearby. Ck-out 11 am. Balconies. Country, chalet-style building in wooded area. No cr cds accepted.

⊡ ⊠ 🔥

★ ★ **LAWNMEER INN.** *(Box 505, West Boothbay Harbor 04575) 2½ mi S on ME 27. 207/633-2544; FAX 207/633-3037; res: 800/633-7645.* E-mail cooncat@lawnmeerinn.com; web www.lawnmeerinn.com. 35 rms, 1-2 story. Some A/C. July-Labor Day: D $88-$140; each addl $25; lower rates: mid-May-June, wkdays after Labor Day-mid-Oct. Closed rest of yr. Pet accepted; $10. TV; cable. Restaurant 7:30-10 am, 6-9 pm. Bar 5:30-9 pm. Ck-out 11 am. Lawn games. Balconies. Built 1898. On inlet; dock. Cr cds: MC, V.

✔ ⊠ 🔥

✔ ★ **LEEWARD VILLAGE.** *(HCR 65, Box 776, East Boothbay 04544) 3½ mi E on ME 96. 207/633-3681; res: 888/817-9907.* E-mail leeward@gwi.net; web www.gwi.net/~leeward. 26 units, 1-2 story, 20 kit. units, 8 cottages. No A/C. No rm phones. Late June-late Aug: S, D $75; kit. units $80; kit. cottages $70-$100; lower rates mid-May-late June, late Aug-mid-Oct. Closed rest of yr. Crib $5. Pet accepted, some restrictions; $10. TV; cable. Playground. Ck-out 10 am. Coin lndry. Lawn games. Refrigerators. Balconies. Picnic tables, grills. On ocean; dockage; swimming beach. Cr cds: MC, V.

⊡ ✔ 🖙 ⊠ 🔥

★ ★ ★ **OCEAN GATE.** *(West Southport 04576) 2½ mi SW on ME 27. 207/633-3321; FAX 207/633-9968; res: 800/221-5924.* E-mail ogate@oceangateinn.com; web www.oceangateinn.com. 67 rms, 1-2 story. 15 A/C. July-Aug: S, D, kit. units $110-$145; each addl $15; suites for 2-4 $160-$190; kit. cottages for 2-8, $1,800/wk; under 12 free; lower rates mid-May-June, Sept-mid-Oct. Closed rest of yr. Crib $5. TV; cable. Heated pool; whirlpool. Playground. Complimentary full bkfst. Complimentary coffee in rms. Ck-out 11 am. Coin lndry. Tennis. Exercise equipt. Refrigerators avail. Lawn games. Private porch on most rms. On 85 wooded-acres. On ocean; dock, boats avail. View of harbor. Cr cds: MC, V.

⊡ 🖙 🌊 ≋ 🏂 ⊠ 🔥

★ ★ **THE PINES.** *Box 693, Sunset Rd, 1¼ mi SE, off Atlantic Ave. 207/633-4555.* 29 rms. No A/C. July-Aug: S $70; D $80; each addl $6; lower rates May-June, after Sept-mid-Oct. Closed rest of yr. Crib free. Pet accepted. TV; cable. Heated pool. Playground. Ck-out 11 am. Tennis. Lawn games. Refrigerators. Balconies, decks. In wooded area; view of harbor. Cr cds: DS, MC, V.

✔ 🏂 ≋ 🔥

★ **SEAGATE.** *138 Townsend Ave (ME 27). 207/633-3900; FAX 207/633-3998; res: 800/633-1707.* E-mail walshcon@lincoln.midcoast.com; web www.maineguide.com/boothbay/seagate. 25 rms, 4 kit. units. Mid-June-mid-Oct: S, D $70-$90; each addl $5; under 13 free; lower rates Apr-mid-June. Closed rest of yr. Crib $5. TV; cable. Continental bkfst. Restaurant nearby. Ck-out 11 am. Refrigerators. Picnic tables. Cr cds: A, DS, MC, V.

⊡ ⊠ 🔥

★ ★ **SMUGGLERS COVE INN.** *ME 96 (04544), 4¼ mi E on ME 96. 207/633-2800; FAX 207/633-5926; res: 800/633-3008.* E-mail pdan@msn.com. 60 units, 2 story, 6 kit. units (most without ovens). No A/C. Late June-Labor Day: S, D $60-$140; each addl $10; kit. units $85-$140; under 12 free; wkly rates; lower rates after Labor Day-mid-Oct. Closed rest of yr. Crib $10. Pet accepted, some restrictions; $50 deposit, refundable. TV; cable. Heated pool. Restaurant 8-10:30 am, 6-9:30 pm. Bar from 5:30 pm. Ck-out 11 am. Business servs avail. Balconies. On ocean; swimming beach. Cr cds: A, DS, MC, V.

✔ 🖙 ≋ 🏂 SC

★ **TOPSIDE.** *McKown Hill, atop McKnown Hill, 1 blk off ME 27. 207/633-5404.* 7 rms, 17 motel rms, 2-3 story, 2 kit. suites. No A/C. No elvtr. July-Aug: D $70-$150; each addl $10; under 8 free; lower rates late May-June, after Labor Day-mid-Oct. Closed rest of yr. Crib free. TV in motel rms; cable. Complimentary continental bkfst. Coffee in rms. Restaurant nearby. Ck-out 11 am. Lawn games. Refrigerator in motel rms. View of bay, harbor. Cr cds: DS, MC, V.

⊠ 🔥

★ ★ ★ **TUGBOAT INN.** *80 Commercial St. 207/633-4434; FAX 207/633-7107; res: 800/248-2628.* 64 rms, 1-2 story, 2 kit. Late June-early Sept: D $115-$160; each addl $10; suites $160-$195; under 16 free; lower rates late Mar-late June, early Sept-Nov. Closed rest of yr. Crib $10. TV; cable (premium). Restaurant 7:30-10 am, 11:30 am-2:30 pm, 5:30-9 pm. Bar noon-11:30 pm; entertainment (seasonal). Ck-out 11 am. Coin lndry. Meeting rm. Business servs avail. Valet parking in season. Refrigerators avail. Balconies. On pier overlooking harbor; marina; dockage, mooring avail. Cr cds: A, DS, MC, V.

⊡ 🖙 ⊠ 🔥

Inns

★ ★ **ADMIRAL'S QUARTERS.** *71 Commercial St. 207/633-2474; FAX 207/633-5904.* E-mail loon@admiralsquartersinn.com; web www.admiralsquartersinn.com. 6 rms, 2 with shower only, 4 suites. No A/C. Late June-Columbus Day: S, D $105-$115; each addl $20; suites $105-$135; lower rates rest of yr. Closed mid-Dec-mid-Feb. Children over 12 yrs only. TV; cable. Complimentary full bkfst; afternoon refreshments. Restaurant opp 7 am-9 pm. Ck-out 11 am, ck-in 2-6 pm. Luggage handling.

Gift shop. Coin lndry. Balconies. Picnic tables. Opp ocean; overlooks harbor. Built in 1830; antiques. Totally nonsmoking. Cr cds: DS, MC, V.

★ ★ **THE ANCHOR WATCH.** *9 Eames Rd.* 207/633-7565. E-mail diane@lincoln.midcoast.com; web www.maineguide.com/boothbay/anchorwatch. 5 rms, 3 with shower only, some A/C, 3 story. No rm phones. Mid-June-Oct: S, D $99-$129; each addl $20; lower rates rest of yr. Children over 9 yrs only. TV in sitting rm; cable, VCR (movies). Complimentary full bkfst. Restaurant nearby. Ck-out 11 am, ck-in 2 pm. Whirlpool in 1 rm. Ocean views. Cruises avail. Totally nonsmoking. Cr cds: DS, MC, V.

★ **CAPTAIN SAWYER'S PLACE.** *55 Commercial St.* 207/633-2290. 10 rms, 2 story. No A/C. No rm phones. July-Labor Day: D $65-$95; each addl $10; lower rates rest of yr. TV; cable. Complimentary continental bkfst. Restaurant nearby. Ck-out 11 am, ck-in 2 pm. Balconies. Former sea captain's home (1877). Sitting rm. Opp harbor. Totally nonsmoking. Cr cds: MC, V.

★ ★ **FIVE GABLES.** *(Murray Hill Rd, East Boothbay 04544)* 3¹/₂ mi E on ME 96. 207/633-4551; res: 800/451-5048. E-mail info@fivegablesinn.com; web www.fivegablesinn.com. 15 rms, 10 with shower only, 3 story. No A/C. No elvtr. Mid-May-Oct: S, D $100-$165; each addl $25; lower rates rest of yr. Children over 11 yrs only. Complimentary full bkfst; afternoon refreshments. Restaurant nearby. Ck-out 11 am, ck-in 2 pm. Some fireplaces. Opp ocean. Built in 1890; Victorian decor, antiques. Totally nonsmoking. Cr cds: MC, V.

★ ★ **HARBOUR TOWNE.** *71 Townsend Ave (ME 27).* 207/633-4300; res: 800/722-4240. E-mail mainco@gwi.net; web www.acadia.net/harbourtowneinn. 12 rms, 3 story, 7 kits. No A/C. Memorial Day-Oct: S, D $99-$175; suite $275; each addl $25; kits. $129-$175; lower rates rest of yr. Crib $25. TV; cable. Complimentary continental bkfst; afternoon refreshments. Restaurant nearby. Ck-out 10 am, ck-in 3:30 pm. Balconies. On harbor. Totally nonsmoking. Cr cds: A, DS, MC, V.

★ ★ **KENNISTON HILL.** *ME 27 (04537).* 207/633-2159; res: 800/992-2915 (exc ME). E-mail innkeeper@maine.com; web www.maine.com/innkeeper/. 10 rms, 7 with shower only, 1-2 story. No A/C. No rm phones. Mid-June-Oct: D $69-$110; each addl $25; lower rates rest of yr. Children over 10 yrs only. Complimentary full bkfst; afternoon refreshments. Ck-out 11 am, ck-in 3 pm. Some fireplaces. Restored Colonial-style farmhouse (1786); antiques. Totally nonsmoking. Cr cds: DS, MC, V.

★ ★ **OCEAN POINT.** *(Shore Rd, East Boothbay 04544)* 6¹/₂ mi SE on ME 96 at Ocean Point. 207/633-4200; res: 800/552-5554. E-mail opi@oceanpointinn.com; web www.oceanpointinn.com. 61 units, 1-2 story, 50 rms in 5 bldgs, 6 cottage units; 5 kit. units. Some A/C. Late June-early Sept: S, D $96-$160; each addl $10; cottage units $91-$136; kit. units. $925-$1,020/wk; under 13, $5 (cottages only); hol wkends (3-day min); lower rates late May-late June, early Sept-mid-Oct. Closed rest of yr. Crib $5. TV; cable. Heated pool. Dining rm (in season) 7:30-10 am, 6-9 pm; closed Sun, early Sept-mid-Oct. Bar 5-10 pm. Ck-out 11 am, ck-in 3 pm. Refrigerators. Some balconies; porch on cottages. On peninsula at entrance to Linekin Bay. Cr cds: A, DS, MC, V.

Resort

★ ★ ★ **SPRUCE POINT INN.** *Spuce Point, 1¹/₂ mi SE off ME 27.* 207/633-4152; FAX 207/633-7138; res: 800/553-0289. E-mail thepoint@sprucepointinn.com; web www.sprucepointinn.com. 75 units, 1-3 story, 9 rms in inn, 27 suites, 45 rms in cottages (1-3 bedrm), 4 rms in condos (2-3 bedrm). A/C in suites. July-Aug, MAP: cottage units $132-

$174/person; each addl (exc cottages) $59; suites $184-$198; MAP: condo units $365-$532; family rates; lower rates late May-June, Sept-mid-Oct. Closed rest of yr. TV; cable, VCR avail. 2 pools, 1 saltwater; whirlpool. Playground. Dining rm 7:30-9:30 am, 6-9 pm. Box lunches, lobster cookouts. Bar 5 pm-midnight. Ck-out 11 am, ck-in 3 pm. Meeting rms. Business servs avail. Tennis. Putting green. Exercise equipt. Massage. Dock, yacht moorings; sunset cruise sail. Lawn games. Entertainment; movies. Rec rm. Library. Some in-rm whirlpools. Located on 100-acre wooded peninsula; ocean view. Cr cds: A, DS, MC, V.

Restaurants

★ **ANDREWS' HARBORSIDE.** *12 Bridge St, at W end of footbridge.* 207/633-4074. Specializes in seafood, cinnamon rolls. Own soups, desserts. Hrs: 7:30-11 am, 11:30 am-3 pm, 5:30-9 pm; wkends to 9:30 pm. Closed mid-Oct-Apr. Serv bar. Semi-a la carte: bkfst $2.25-$6.25, lunch $3.95-$10.95, dinner $9.95-$16.95. Child's meals. Overlooks harbor. Cr cds: D, DS, MC, V.

✔★ **CHINA BY THE SEA.** *36 McKown St.* 207/633-4449. Chinese menu. Hrs: 11 am-10 pm. Closed Thanksgiving, Dec 25. Res accepted. Serv bar. Semi-a la carte: lunch, dinner $4.50-$14.95. Outdoor dining. Overlooks harbor. Cr cds: A, DS, MC, V.

✔★ **EBB TIDE.** *43 Commercial St.* 207/633-5692. Specializes in seafood, omelettes. Own desserts. Hrs: 6:30 am-9 pm; Fri, Sat to 9:30 pm; hrs vary off season. Closed Dec 25. Semi-a la carte: bkfst $3-$5.50, lunch $3-$12.95, dinner $7-$12.95. Child's meals. Totally nonsmoking. No cr cds accepted.

★ ★ **FISHERMAN'S WHARF INN.** *(See Fisherman's Wharf Inn Motel)* 207/633-5090. Specializes in seafood. Hrs: 11:30 am-9 pm; wkends to 9:30 pm. Closed mid-Oct-mid-May. Bar 11 am-11 pm. Semi-a la carte: lunch, dinner $6-$27. Valet parking. Outdoor dining. Scenic murals. Waterfront view. Family-owned. Cr cds: A, C, D, DS, MC, V.

Bridgton (G-1)

(See also Poland Spring, Sebago Lake)

Pop 2,195 **Elev** 494 ft **Area code** 207 **Zip** 04009

Information Bridgton Lakes Chamber of Commerce, PO Box 236M; 207/647-3472.

Primarily a resort, this community between Long and Highland lakes is within easy reach of Pleasant Mountain (2,007 feet), a recreational area that offers skiing as well as a magnificent view of 50 lakes. Bridgton also has many unique craft and antique shops located within a two-mile radius of the town center.

What to See and Do

Gibbs Avenue Museum. HQ of Bridgton Historical Society. Permanent exhibits include narrow-guage RR memorabilia; Civil War artifacts; Sears "horseless carriage" (1911). Special summer exhibits. Genealogy research facility includes Bridgton and Saw River RR documents. (Sept-June, Tues & Thurs; rest of yr, Tues-Fri; closed some hols) Gibbs Ave. Phone 207/647-3699. ¢

Shawnee Peak at Pleasant Mt Ski Area. Triple, 3 double chairlifts; snowmaking, school, rentals, patrol; nursery; restaurant, cafeteria, bar. Longest run 1¹/₂ mi; vertical drop 1,350 ft. Night skiing. (Late Nov-early Apr, daily) 6 mi W, off US 302. Phone 207/647-8444. ¢¢¢¢¢

Annual Event

Quilt Show. Town hall. New and old quilts; demonstrations. Contact Chamber of Commerce. Mid-July.

Inn

★ ★ ★ **INN AT LONG LAKE.** *(Lakehouse Rd, Naples 04055) S on US 302, at jct ME 11.* 207/693-6226; *res:* 800/437-0328. 16 rms, 4 story. No elvtr. July-Labor Day: S, D $95-$120; suites $150; mid-wk rates; lower rates Apr-June, Labor Day-Dec. Closed rest of yr. TV. Complimentary continental bkfst. Restaurant opp 8 am-8 pm (summer). Ck-out 11 am, ck-in 3 pm. Built 1906; stone fireplace. Near lake. Totally nonsmoking. Cr cds: DS, MC, V.

Restaurant

★ **BLACK HORSE TAVERN.** *8 Portland Rd (04099).* 207/647-5300. Specializes in ribs, steak, fresh seafood. Hrs: 11 am-10 pm; Sun 9 am-9 pm; Sun brunch 9 am-3 pm; hrs may vary off season. Closed Thanksgiving, Dec 25. Bar. Semi-a la carte: lunch $3.95-$7.95, dinner $5.95-$19.95. Sun brunch $1.50-$5.95. Child's meals. In restored homestead. Equestrian motif; saddles, bridles, harnesses on display. Cr cds: DS, MC, V.

Brunswick (G-2) 🐎

(See also Bailey Island)

Settled 1628 **Pop** 20,906 **Elev** 67 ft **Area code** 207 **Zip** 04011 **E-mail** ccbbr@horton.col.k12.me.us **Web** www.midcoastmaine.com

Information Chamber of Commerce of the Bath-Brunswick Region, 59 Pleasant St; 207/725-8797.

Once a lumbering center and later a mill town, Brunswick is now mainly concerned with trade, health care and education; it is the home of Bowdoin College and Brunswick Naval Air Station. The city lies northeast of a summer resort area on the shores and islands of Casco Bay. Magnificent Federalist mansions along Federal Street and Park Row remind visitors of Brunswick's past.

What to See and Do

Bowdoin College (1794). (1,500 students) Nathaniel Hawthorne, Henry Wadsworth Longfellow, Robert Peary, Franklin Pierce and Joan Benoit Samuelson graduated from here. Tours. Maine St. Phone 207/725-3000. On campus are

Museum of Art. Portraits by Stuart, Feke and Copley; paintings by Homer and Eakins; Greek and Roman vases and sculpture. (Daily exc Mon; closed hols) Walker Art Bldg. Phone 207/725-3275. **Free.**

Peary-MacMillan Arctic Museum. Exhibits relating to Arctic exploration, ecology, and Inuit (Eskimo) culture. (Daily exc Mon; closed hols) Hubbard Hall. Phone 207/725-3416. **Free.**

Pejepscot Historical Society Museum. Regional historical museum housed in an 1858 sea captain's home; changing exhibits, research facilities. (Memorial Day-Labor Day, daily exc Sun; rest of yr, Mon-Fri; closed hols) 159 Park Row. Phone 207/729-6606. **Free.** The Society also operates

Skolfield-Whittier House. An 18-rm Victorian structure last occupied in 1925; furnishings and housewares of 3 generations. Guided tours. (Memorial Day-Labor Day, Tues-Sat; closed hols) 161 Park Row. ¢¢ Combination ticket with Chamberlain Museum ¢¢¢

Joshua L. Chamberlain Museum. Former residence of Maine's greatest Civil War hero, 4-term Governor of Maine and president of Bowdoin

College. Guided tours. (Memorial Day-Labor Day, Tues-Sat; closed hols) 226 Maine St. ¢¢ Combination ticket with Skolfield-Whittier House ¢¢¢

Thomas Point Beach. Swimming, lifeguard. Picnicking, tables, fireplaces. Snack bar; gift shop, arcade, playground; camping (fee). (Memorial Day-Labor Day, daily) Off ME 24, at Cook's Corner. Phone 207/725-6009.

Annual Events

Topsham Fair. N via ME 24 in Topsham. Entertainment, arts & crafts. Phone 207/725-2735. 7 days early Aug.

Bluegrass Festival. At Thomas Point Beach. Phone 207/725-6009. Labor Day wkend.

Seasonal Events

Maine State Music Theater. Pickard Theater, Bowdoin College campus. Broadway musicals by professional cast. Tues-Sat eves; Wed, Fri, Sun matinees. Phone 207/725-8769. Mid-June-Aug.

Bowdoin Summer Music Festival and School. Brunswick High School & Bowdoin College campus. Chamber music, concert series. Phone 207/725-3322. Fri eves, late June-Aug.

Music on the Mall. Downtown. Free outdoor family concert series. Phone 207/725-8797. Wed eves, July & Aug.

Motels

★ **ATRIUM INN & CONVENTION CENTER.** *21 Gurnet Rd (ME 24).* 207/729-5555; *FAX* 207/729-5149. 186 rms, 3 story. July-Aug: S, D $74-$86; each addl $10; suites $125; under 19 free; lower rates rest of yr. Crib free. Pet accepted. TV; cable, VCR (movies $2.95). Indoor pool; wading pool, whirlpool. Complimentary coffee in lobby. Restaurant 6 am-10 pm. Rm serv. Bar to midnight. Ck-out noon. Meeting rms. Business servs avail. Sundries. Coin lndry. Exercise equipt; sauna. Game rm. Lawn games. Refrigerators. Cr cds: A, C, D, DS, MC, V.

★ ★ **COMFORT INN.** *199 Pleasant St (US 1).* 207/729-1129; *FAX* 207/725-8310. 80 rms, 2 story. May-Oct: S, D $80-$89; each addl $7; under 18 free; lower rates rest of yr. Crib free. TV; cable (premium). Complimentary continental bkfst. Restaurant nearby. Ck-out 11 am. Business servs avail. Valet serv Mon-Fri. Cr cds: A, C, D, DS, JCB, MC, V.

★ **ECONO LODGE.** *215 Pleasant St (US 1), 2 mi S on US 1 at jct I-95.* 207/729-9991; *res:* 800/654-9991; *FAX* 207/721-0413. 29 rms, 1-2 story. July-Labor Day: D $76-$83; each addl $7; lower rates rest of yr. Crib $3. TV; cable. Pool. Complimentary coffee in lobby. Restaurant nearby. Ck-out 11 am. Coin lndry. Business servs avail. Sundries. Cr cds: A, C, D, DS, JCB, MC, V.

✔★ **SUPER 8.** *224 Bath Rd.* 207/725-8883; *FAX* 207/729-8766. 71 rms. June-Oct: S $65.88; D $69.88; each addl $5; suite $92.82; under 16 free; higher rates: graduation, local festivals; lower rates rest of yr. Crib free. TV; cable, VCR avail (movies). Complimentary continental bkfst. Restaurant opp 10 am-10 pm. Ck-out 11 am. Picnic tables. Cr cds: A, D, DS, JCB, MC, V.

✔★ **VIKING MOTOR INN.** *287 Bath Rd.* 207/729-6661; *FAX* 207/729-6661, ext. 40; *res:* 800/429-6661. 28 rms, 10 kit. units. July-Oct: S, D $59-$89; each addl $5; under 12 free; wkly rates off season; lower rates rest of yr. Pet accepted, some restrictions; fee. TV; cable. Pool. Playground. Ck-out 10 am. Lawn games. Refrigerators, microwaves avail. Picnic tables, grill. Cr cds: A, D, DS, MC, V.

Inn

★ ★ ★ **CAPTAIN DANIEL STONE.** *10 Water St. 207/725-9898; res: 800/267-0525; FAX 207/725-9898.* E-mail cdsi@netquarters.net; web www.netquarters.net/cdsi. 34 rms, 3 story, 4 suites. Mid-July-mid-Sept: S, D $125-$145; each addl $10; suites $175-$210; lower rates rest of yr. Crib free. TV; cable, VCR (movies). Complimentary continental bkfst. Dining rm 11:30 am-2 pm, 5-9 pm. Bar 4-10 pm. Ck-out 11 am, ck-in 4 pm. Business servs avail. Bathrm phones; some in-rm whirlpools. Balconies. Antiques. Screened veranda. Former sea captain's house (1819). Cr cds: A, D, MC, V.

D ⬛ ⬛ SC

Restaurant

✔★ ★ **GREAT IMPASTA.** *42 Maine St. 207/729-5858.* Specializes in pasta, veal. Hrs: 11 am-9 pm; Fri, Sat to 10 pm; Sun 5-9 pm. Closed Thanksgiving, Dec 25. Italian menu. Serv bar. Semi-a la carte: lunch $3.95-$6.95, dinner $7.95-$12.95. Totally nonsmoking. Cr cds: A, DS, MC, V.

Bucksport (F-4)

(See also Bangor, Belfast, Ellsworth)

Settled 1762 **Pop** 4,825 **Elev** 43 ft **Area code** 207 **Zip** 04416 **E-mail** chamber@bangorregion.com **Web** www.bangorregion.com

Information Bangor Region Chamber of Commerce, 519 Main St, PO Box 1443, Bangor 04401; 207/947-0307.

Although originally settled in 1762, the Penobscot valley town of Bucksport was so thoroughly burned by the British in 1779 that it was not resettled until 1812. On the east bank of the Penobscot River, Bucksport is a shopping center for the area, but is primarily an industrial town with an emphasis on paper manufacturing. The Waldo Hancock Bridge crosses the Penobscot to Verona Island.

What to See and Do

Accursed Tombstone. Granite obelisk over grave of founder Jonathan Buck bears an indelible mark in the shape of a woman's leg—said to have been put there by a witch whom he had hanged. Buck Cemetery, Main & Hinks Sts, near Verona Island Bridge. **Free.**

Ft Knox State Park. Consists of 124 acres around huge granite fort started in 1844 and used as a defense in the Aroostook War. Structure includes spiral staircases. Hiking. Picnicking. Interpretive displays. Tours (Aug, Sept). (May-Oct) Standard fees. S on US 1 across Waldo Hancock Bridge. Phone 207/469-7719. **¢¢**

Ft Point State Park. Ocean view. Fishing. Picnicking. (Memorial Day-Labor Day) Standard fees. 8 mi S on US 1. Phone 207/469-6818. **¢**

Jed Prouty Tavern. A 1798 hostelry once a stopping place on a stagecoach run. Famous guests were Presidents Martin Van Buren, Andrew Jackson, William Henry Harrison and John Tyler. Admiral Peary also lodged here while a ship for one of his Arctic expeditions was built nearby. (Daily; closed Dec 25) 52-54 Main St. Phone 207/469-3113 or 207/469-7972. **Free.**

Northeast Historic Film. The Alamo Theatre (1916) houses museum, theater, store and archives of northern New England film and video. Exhibits present 100 yrs of moviegoing, from nickelodeons to mall cinemas. Video & film presentations interpret regional culture. (Oct-May, Mon-Fri; rest of yr, daily exc Sun) 379 Main St. Phone 207/469-0924. **Free.**

Wilson Museum. Prehistoric, historic, geologic and art exhibits (late May-Sept, Tues-Sun, also hols). On grounds are John Perkins House (1763-1783), Hearse House, Blacksmith Shop (July-Aug, Wed & Sun). 18 mi S via ME 175, 166 in Castine. Phone 207/326-8753. Museum **Free;** Perkins House **¢¢**

Motels

★ ★ **BEST WESTERN JED PROUTY.** *53 Maim St. 207/469-3113; FAX 207/469-3113.* 40 rms, 2-4 story. July-Oct: S $89; D $99; each addl $10; suites $125; under 12 free; lower rates rest of yr. Pet accepted, some restrictions. TV; cable. Restaurant opp 5:30-9:30 pm. Ck-out 11 am. Business servs avail. In-rm modem link. On Penobscot River. Cr cds: A, C, D, DS, MC, V.

⬛ ⬛ ⬛ ⬛ SC

✔★ **BUCKSPORT MOTOR INN.** *151 Main St, 1/2 mi NE on US 1 (ME 3). 207/469-3111; FAX 207/469-6822; res: 800/626-9734.* E-mail bucksprt@aol.com. 24 rms, some A/C. Aug: S $55; D $60; each addl $5; lower rates rest of yr. Pet accepted. TV; cable. Complimentary coffee in rms. Restaurant nearby. Ck-out 11 am. Cr cds: A, DS, MC, V.

⬛ ⬛ ⬛ SC

Inns

★ ★ **CASTINE.** *(Main St, Castine 04421) 2 mi N on US 1, then 16 mi SE on ME 175 & ME 166. 207/326-4365; FAX 207/326-4570.* E-mail relax@castineinn.com; web www.castineinn.com. 19 rms, 4 suites, 3 story. No A/C. No rm phones. Memorial Day-Columbus Day: D $85-$130; each addl $20; suites $135-$210; lower rates May-Memorial Day, after Columbus Day-mid-Dec. Closed rest of yr. Children over 8 yrs only. Complimentary full bkfst. Dining rm 8-9:30 am, 5:30-8:30 pm. Bar 5-10 pm. Ck-out 11 am, ck-in 3 pm. Business servs avail. Built 1898; sitting rm with wood-burning fireplace. Many rms with harbor view; perennial and rose gardens. Totally nonsmoking. Cr cds: MC, V.

⬛

★ ★ **PENTAGÖET.** *(Main St, Castine 04421) 2 mi NE on US 1 to ME 175, then 16 mi S on ME 166 to Castine, at jct Main & Perkins Sts. 207/326-8616; FAX 207/326-9382; res: 800/845-1701 (exc ME).* E-mail penagoet@hypernet.com; web www.pentagoet.com. 16 rms in 2 bldgs, 3 story. No A/C. No rm phones. Late-May-mid-Oct: D $99-$129. Closed rest of yr. Complimentary full bkfst; afternoon refreshments. Ck-out 10:30 am, ck-in 2-6 pm. Street parking. Victorian main building (1894) with smaller, colonial annex (ca 1770); library/sitting rm, antiques, period furnishings. Landscaped gardens. Totally nonsmoking. Cr cds: MC, V.

⬛ ⬛

Restaurant

★ ★ **L'ERMITAGE.** *219 Main St. 207/469-3361.* Continental menu. Specialties: steak au poivre, steak chasseur, shrimp Arlesienne. Own desserts. Hrs: 5:30-9 pm. Closed Mon, Tues; also 1st 2 wks Apr. Res accepted. No A/C. Serv Bar. Wine list. Semi-a la carte: dinner $12.95-$19.95. Guest rms avail. Cr cds: A, DS, MC, V.

Calais (E-6)

Settled 1770 **Pop** 3,963 **Elev** 19 ft **Area code** 207 **Zip** 04619 **E-mail** calcham@nemaine.com **Web** www.mainerec.com/calais.html

Information Calais Regional Chamber of Commerce, PO Box 368; 207/454-2308 or 800/377-9748.

International cooperation is rarely as warm and helpful as it is between Calais (KAL-iss) and St Stephen, New Brunswick, just across the St Croix River in Canada. Because of an early closing law in St Stephen, Canadians stroll over to the US for a nightcap, and fire engines and ambulances cross the International Bridge in both directions as needed. (For Border Crossing Regulations, see MAKING THE MOST OF YOUR TRIP.) **Note:** New Brunswick is on Atlantic Time, one hour ahead of Eastern Standard Time.

Calais has a unique distinction—it is located exactly halfway between the North Pole and the Equator. The 45th Parallel passes a few miles south of town; a marker on US 1 near Perry indicates the spot. Bass, togue, trout and salmon fishing is available in many lakes and streams in Calais, and there is swimming at Meddybemps Lake, 13 miles north on ME 191.

What to See and Do

Moosehorn National Wildlife Refuge. Glacial terrain with forests, valleys, lakes, bogs and marshes. Abundant wildlife. Hiking, fishing, hunting, cross-country skiing, bird-watching. (Daily) 4 mi N via US 1, on Charlotte Rd. Contact Refuge Manager, PO Box 1077; 207/454-7161. **Free.**

St Croix Island International Historic Site. In 1604 French explorers Sieur de Monts and Samuel de Champlain, leading a group of approx 75 men, selected this as the site of the first attempted European settlement on the Atlantic Coast north of Florida. Information shelter; no facilities. (Daily) 8 mi S via US 1, opp Red Beach in St Croix River; accessible only by boat. Phone 207/288-3338. **Free.**

Annual Event

International Festival Week. Celebration of friendship between Calais and St Stephen, New Brunswick; entertainment, concessions, contests, fireworks, parade. Early Aug.

Motels

✓★ **HESLIN'S.** *Rte 1, Box 111, 5 mi S on US 1. 207/454-3762; FAX 207/454-0148.* 15 motel rms, 9 cottages. No cottage phones. S $48; D $58-$62; each addl $5; cottages $48-$80; kit. cottages $80-$100; under 12 free; wkly rates. Closed Dec-Apr. Crib $5. TV; cable. Heated pool; wading pool. Complimentary coffee in rms. Restaurant 5-9 pm. Bar. Ck-out 10 am. Meeting rm. View of St Croix River & Canada. Cr cds: MC, V.

★ **INTERNATIONAL.** *276 Main St. 207/454-7515; FAX 207/454-3396; res: 800/336-7515.* 61 rms. June-Sept: D $70; each addl $5; studio rms $80; suites $90; lower rates rest of yr. TV; cable. Complimentary coffee in rms. Restaurant adj 6 am-10 pm. Ck-out 11 am. Business servs avail. Cr cds: A, C, D, DS, MC, V.

★ ★ **REDCLYFFE SHORE MOTOR INN.** *(Rte 1 Box 53 (US 1), Robbinston 04671) 12 mi S on US 1. 207/454-3270; FAX 207/454-8723.* 17 rms. S, D $62-$73; each addl $5. Closed Dec-Apr. TV; cable (premium). Complimentary coffee in rms. Restaurant 5-9 pm. Ck-out 10 am. Victorian-Gothic building (1863); on bluff overlooking St Croix River, Passamaquoddy Bay. Cr cds: A, DS, MC, V.

Restaurant

✓★ **WICKACHEE.** *282 Main St. 207/454-3400.* Specializes in steak, seafood. Salad bar. Hrs: 6 am-10 pm. Closed Dec 25. Res accepted. Beer, wine. Semi-a la carte: bkfst $1.75-$4, lunch $2.50-$8.95, dinner $6.95-$13.95. Child's meals. Cr cds: MC, V.

Camden (G-3)

(See also Belfast, Rockland)

Pop 5,060 **Elev** 33 ft **Area code** 207 **Zip** 04843 **E-mail** chamber@camdenme.org **Web** www.camdenme.org
Information Camden-Rockport-Lincolnville Chamber of Commerce, Public Landing, PO Box 919; 207/236-4404.

Camden's unique setting—where the mountains meet the sea—makes it a popular four-season resort area. Recreational activities include boat cruises and boat rentals, swimming, fishing, camping, hiking and picnicking, as well as winter activities. The poet Edna St Vincent Millay began her career in Camden.

What to See and Do

Bay Chamber Concerts. Classical music performances by Vermeer Quartet and guest artists (July & Aug, Thurs & Fri eves). Jazz musicians perform Sept-June (one show each month). Rockport Opera House, Central St in Rockport. Phone 207/236-2823 for schedule and ticket information.

Camden Hills State Park. Maine's third-largest state park, surrounding 1,380-ft Mt Megunticook. Road leads to Mt Battie (800 ft). Spectacular view of coast. Hiking. Picnic facilities. Camping (dump station). (Memorial Day-Columbus Day) Standard fees. 2 mi NE on US 1. Phone 207/236-3109.

Conway Homestead-Cramer Museum. Authentically restored 18th-century farmhouse. Collection of carriages, sleighs and farm implements in old barn; blacksmith shop, privy and herb garden. Mary Meeker Cramer Museum contains paintings, ship models, quilts; costumes, documents and other memorabilia; changing exhibits. (July-Aug, Tues-Fri) On US 1, near city limits. Phone 207/236-2257. ¢

Kelmscott Farm. Working farm established to conserve rare and endangered breeds of farm livestock, including Cotswold sheep, Nigerian dwarf goats, Kerry cattle and Gloucestershire Old Spots pigs. Educational demonstrations. Farm tours (Labor Day-Memorial Day, by appt). Museum and gift shop. Picnic area. Special events throughout the yr. (Daily exc Mon) N on ME 52, in Lincolnville. Phone 207/763-4088. ¢¢

Maine State Ferry Service. 20-min trip to Islesboro (Dark Harbor) on *Margaret Chase Smith.* (Mid-May-late Oct, wkdays, 9 trips; Sun, 8 trips; rest of yr, 6 trips daily) 6 mi N on US 1 in Lincolnville Beach. For schedule information phone 207/789-5611 or 207/624-7777. ¢¢

Sailing trips. Old-time schooners leave from Camden and Rockport Harbors for ½- to 6-day trips along the coast of Maine. (May-Oct) For further information, rates, schedules or res, contact the individual companies.

Appledore. Lily Pond Dr; phone 207/236-8353.

Angelique. PO Box 736; phone 800/282-9989.

Maine Windjammer Cruises. PO Box 617; phone 207/236-2938.

Olad & Northwind. PO Box 432; phone 207/236-2323.

Schooner *Lewis R. French.* PO Box 992; phone 800/469-4635.

Schooner *Mary Day.* PO Box 798M; phone 800/992-2218.

Schooner *Roseway.* PO Box 696X; phone 800/255-4449.

Schooner *Surprise.* PO Box 450; phone 207/236-4687.

Schooner *Timberwind.* PO Box 247, Rockport 04856; phone 207/236-3639 or 800/759-9250.

Schooner Yacht *Wendameen.* PO Box 252; phone 207/594-1751.

Windhorse. PO Box 898, Rockport; phone 800/777-1554.

Sightseeing cruises on Penobscot Bay. Cruises (1-4 hrs) leave from public landing. Contact Chamber of Commerce, phone 207/236-4404. ¢¢¢¢¢

Skiing. Camden Snow Bowl. Double chairlift, 2 T-bars; patrol, school, rentals; toboggan chute and rentals; snowboarding; snowmaking; snack bar, lodge. (Mid-Dec-mid-Mar, daily) S on US 1 to John St to Hosmer Pond Rd. Phone 207/236-3438 or 207/236-4418 (snow conditions). ¢¢¢¢¢

Annual Events

Garden Club Open House Day. Tour of homes and gardens (fee). Contact Chamber of Commerce. 3rd Thurs July.

Windjammer Weekend. Celebration of windjammer industry; fireworks. Phone 207/236-4404. Labor Day wkend.

Christmas by the Sea. Celebration of holiday season with musical entertainment, horse-drawn wagon rides, Holiday House Tour, Santa’s arrival by lobsterboat. Phone 207/236-4404. 1st wkend Dec.

Seasonal Event

Camden Opera House. Elm St. Theater with musical and theatrical performances and concerts. Phone 207/236-4404. July-Aug.

Motels

★ ★ **BEST WESTERN CAMDEN RIVER HOUSE.** *11 Tannery Lane.* 207/236-0500; res: 800/755-7483; FAX 207/236-4711. E-mail riverhouse@acadia.net; web www.camdenmaine.com. 35 rms, 3 story. Mid-July-Labor Day: S, D $149-$199; under 17 free; lower rates rest of yr. Crib free. TV; cable (premium), VCR avail. Indoor pool; whirlpool. Complimentary continental bkfst. Restaurant nearby. Ck-out 11 am. Meeting rms. Business servs avail. In-rm modem link. Sundries. Downhill/x-country ski 5 mi. Exercise equipt. Some refrigerators; many microwaves. Cr cds: A, C, D, DS, JCB, MC, V.

★ ★ ★ **BLACK HORSE INN.** *(Atlantic Hwy (US 1), Lincolnville Beach)* 4 mi N on US 1. 207/236-6800; FAX 207/236-6509; res: 800/374-9085. Web www.midcoast.com/mblkhorse. 21 rms, 2 story. Mid-June-mid-Oct: S, D $85-$135; under 13 free; lower rates rest of yr. Crib $5. TV; cable. Restaurant 7-10 am, 5-9 pm; Sun to 10 am; closed Mon-Wed. Ck-out 11 am. Business servs avail. Downhill ski 6 mi, x-country ski 2 mi. Some refrigerators. Borders Camden Hills State Park. Totally nonsmoking. Cr cds: A, DS, MC, V.

★ ★ **CEDAR CREST.** *115 Elm St.* 207/236-4839; FAX 207/236-6719; res: 800/422-4964. Web www.sourcemaine.com/ccrest. 37 rms, 1-2 story. July-Labor Day: D $99-$125; each addl $10; lower rates May-June, Labor Day-Oct. Closed Nov-Apr. Crib free. TV; cable. Playground. Restaurant 6 am-noon; closed Mon. Ck-out 11 am. Coin lndry. Some refrigerators. Balconies. Cr cds: A, C, D, DS, MC, V.

★ ★ **GLENMOOR BY THE SEA.** *(US Rte 1, Lincolnville)* 4 mi N on US 1 in Lincolnville. 207/236-3466; FAX 207/236-7043; res: 800/439-3541. Web www.maineguide.com/camden/glenmoor. 22 units, 7 cottages, 1 kit. unit. Early July-Aug: D $109-$169; each addl $10; cottages $129-$225; under 19 free; lower rates mid-May-early July, Sept-early Nov. Closed rest of yr. Crib $5. TV; cable, VCR avail. Heated pool. Complimentary continental bkfst. Ck-out 11 am. Tennis. Refrigerators avail. Balconies. Sun deck. On ocean. Totally nonsmoking. Cr cds: A, MC, V.

★ ★ **MOUNT BATTIE.** *(US 1, Lincolnville Beach 04849)* 4 mi N on US 1. 207/236-3870; FAX 207/230-0068; res: 800/224-3870. E-mail mtbattie@acadia.net; web www.acadia.net/~mtbattie. 21 rms. July-mid-Oct: S, D $65-$115; each addl $15; lower rates May-June & mid-Oct-early Nov. Closed rest of yr. Crib $5. TV; cable. Complimentary continental bkfst. Complimentary coffee in rms. Ck-out 11 am. Business servs avail. Refrigerators. Picnic tables, sundeck, gazebo, grill. Totally nonsmoking. Cr cds: A, DS, MC, V.

✔★ ★ **SNOW HILL LODGE.** *(Atlantic Hwy (US 1), Lincolnville Beach 04849)* 4½ mi N on US 1. 207/236-3452; FAX 207/236-8052; res: 800/476-4775. E-mail theview@midcoast.com; web www.midcoast.com/~theview. 30 rms, 1-2 story. No A/C. Mid-June-late-Oct: D $40-$95; each addl $10; lower rates rest of yr. Crib $6. TV; cable. Restaurant 7-10 am. Ck-out 10:30 am. Downhill/x-country ski 4 mi. Lawn games. Picnic tables, grills. Tree-shaded grounds. View of bay. Cr cds: A, DS, MC, V.

✔★ **SUNRISE MOTOR COURT.** *(US 1, Lincolnville Beach 04849)* 5 mi N on US 1. 207/236-3191. 13 cottages, shower only. No A/C. No rm phones. July-Labor Day: S, D $49-$69; each addl $10; lower rates Memorial Day-June & Labor Day-Columbus Day. Closed rest of yr. TV; cable. Complimentary continental bkfst. Ck-out 10 am. Picnic tables. View of bay. Totally nonsmoking. Cr cds: DS, MC, V.

Lodge

★ ★ **LODGE AT CAMDEN HILLS.** US 1, 1 mi N on US 1. 207/236-8478; FAX 207/236-7163; res: 800/832-7058. E-mail lodge@acadia.net; web www.acadia.net/lodge. 23 units. D $99-$139; each addl $15; suites, kit. units $159-$199; under 16 free; wkly rates. Crib free. TV; cable, VCR avail. Complimentary coffee in rms. Restaurant nearby. Ck-out 11 am, ck-in 3 pm. Business servs avail. In-rm modem link. Downhill/x-country ski 5 mi. Refrigerators; some in-rm whirlpools, fireplaces, microwaves. Quiet, wooded setting. View of bay. Totally nonsmoking. Cr cds: A, DS, MC, V.

Inns

★ ★ ★ **BLUE HARBOR HOUSE.** *67 Elm St.* 207/236-3196; FAX 207/236-6523; res: 800/248-3196. E-mail balidog@midcoast.com; web www.blueharborhouse.com. 10 units, 2 story, 2 suites, 2 kits. Some A/C. D $85-$125; each addl $30; suites, kit. units $145; MAP avail. Crib free. TV in some rms; cable, VCR. Complimentary full bkfst. Restaurant nearby. Ck-out 11 am, ck-in 2-6 pm. Downhill/x-country ski 4 mi. Restored New England Cape (1810); country antiques, hand-fashioned quilts, sun porch. Totally nonsmoking. Cr cds: A, DS, MC, V.

★ ★ ★ **DARK HARBOR HOUSE.** *(117 Wharf Landing W, Islesboro 04848)* 6 mi N on US 1 to Lincolnville, ferry across Penobscot Bay to Islesboro Island, Ferry Road, right at next 2 intersections, 2 mi S to Dark Harbor. 207/734-6669; FAX 207/734-6938. 11 rms, 2-3 story, 3 suites. Some A/C. No rm phones. May-Oct: D, suites $115-$275; each addl $15. Closed rest of yr. Adults only. Complimentary full bkfst. Dining rm (by res only) 5:30-8:30 pm. Serv bar. Ck-out 11 am, ck-in 1:30 pm. Some fireplaces. Many private porches, balconies. Georgian-revival summer mansion (1896) with double staircase, wide veranda, library/sitting rm, antiques. Bicycles. Totally nonsmoking. Cr cds: MC, V.

✔★ ★ **THE ELMS.** *84 Elm St.* 207/236-6250; res: 800/755-3567; FAX 207/236-7330. E-mail theelms@midcoast.com; web www.midcoast.com/~theelms. 6 rms, 1 with A/C, 3 with shower only, 3 story. No elvtr. Mid-June-mid-Oct: S, D $85-$95; each addl $30; package plans; lower rates rest of yr. Children over 9 yrs only. Complimentary full bkfst; afternoon refreshments. Restaurant nearby. Ck-out 10:30 am, ck-in 3-6 pm. In-rm modem link. Downhill/x-country ski 3 mi. Lawn games. Built in 1806; lighthouse theme. Federal-style home; fireplace in parlor, sun deck. Totally nonsmoking. Cr cds: DS, MC, V.

★ ★ ★ **THE HAWTHORN INN.** *9 High St (US 1).* 207/236-8842; FAX 207/236-6181. E-mail hawthorn@midcoast.com; web www.camden-inn.com. 10 units in 2 bldgs, 2 story. No A/C. Mid-June-mid-Oct: S, D $100-$195; each addl $30; lower rates rest of yr. Closed Jan. Children over

12 yrs only. TV; cable, VCR avail (free movies). Complimentary full bkfst; afternoon refreshments. Restaurant nearby. Ck-out 11 am, ck-in 3 pm. Downhill/x-country ski 5 mi. Some fireplaces. Balconies. Victorian mansion (1894) built by wealthy coal merchant; turret, original stained-glass panels. Carriage house adj. View of harbor. Totally nonsmoking. Cr cds: A, MC, V.

★ ★ ★ **INN AT SUNRISE POINT.** (Sunrise Point Rd, Lincolnville) 4 mi N on US 1. 207/236-7716; FAX 207/236-0820; res: 800/435-6278. E-mail info@sunrisepoint.com; web www.sunrisepoint.com. 7 rms, 2 story. No A/C. July, Aug, Oct: D $160-$350; lower rates Memorial Day-June, Sept. Closed rest of yr. Children over 16 yrs only. TV; cable, VCR (free movies). Complimentary full bkfst; afternoon refreshments. Ck-out 11 am, ck-in 3 pm. In-rm modem link. Sundries. Refrigerators, fireplaces. Whirlpools in cottages. Four-acre estate situated along Penobscot Bay; glass conservatory. Totally nonsmoking. Cr cds: A, MC, V.

✔ ★ ★ **MAINE STAY.** 22 High St, on US 1. 207/236-9636; FAX 207/236-0621. E-mail mainstay@midcoast.com; web www.mainestay.com. 8 rms, 5 with shower only, 3 story. No A/C. Rm phones avail. June-late Oct: D $100-$145; lower rates rest of yr. Children over 10 yrs only. TV in sitting rm, some rms; cable, VCR (free movies). Complimentary full bkfst. Coffee & tea in library. Restaurant nearby. Ck-out 11 am, ck-in 2 pm. Business servs avail. Luggage handling. Downhill/x-country ski 4 mi. Some fireplaces. Picnic tables. Farm house built 1802; barn & carriage house. Antiques include a 17th-century samurai chest. Totally nonsmoking. Cr cds: A, MC, V.

★ ★ ★ **NORUMBEGA.** 61 High St (US 1). 207/236-4646; FAX 207/236-0824. E-mail norumbeg@acadia.com; web www.acadia.net/norumbega. 13 rms, 1 A/C, 4 story, 2 suites. No A/C. July-mid-Oct: D $155-$325; each addl $35; suites $375-$450; lower rates rest of yr. Children over 7 yrs only. TV in some rms; cable, VCR in suites. Complimentary full bkfst; afternoon refreshments. Restaurant nearby. Ck-out 11 am, ck-in 3 pm. Business servs avail. In-rm modem link. Downhill/x-country ski 4 mi. Lawn games. Some fireplaces. Balconies. Stone castle (1886); hand-carved oak woodwork, baby grand piano, antique billiard table, library within turret. Built by inventor of duplex telegraphy. Murder mystery wknds. Totally nonsmoking. Cr cds: A, DS, MC, V.

★ ★ **VICTORIAN BY THE SEA.** (Sea View Dr, Lincolnville 04849) 5 mi N on US 1. 207/236-3785; FAX 207/236-0017; res: 800/382-9817. E-mail victbb@midcoast.com; web www.midcoast.com/~victbb. 7 rms, 2 with shower only, 1 A/C, 3 story. Mid-June-mid-Oct: S, D $135-$150; each addl $20; suites $205; wkly rates; 2-day min wknds in season; lower rates rest of yr. Children over 11 yrs only. Complimentary full bkfst; afternoon refreshments. Ck-out 11 am, ck-in 3 pm. Luggage handling. Downhill/x-country ski 7 mi. Lawn games. Many fireplaces. Some balconies. Antiques. Victorian summer cottage built in 1881. Totally nonsmoking. Cr cds: A, MC, V.

★ ★ **WHITEHALL.** 52 High St (US 1). 207/236-3391; FAX 207/236-4427; res: 800/789-6565. E-mail stay@whitehall-inn.com; web www.whitehall-inn.com. 50 rms in 3 bldgs, most with bath, 2-3 story. No A/C. MAP, July-mid-Oct: S $85-$100; D $140-$180; each addl $45; under 14, $35; EP avail; lower rates Memorial Day-June. Closed rest of yr. Serv charge 15%. Crib $10. TV; cable in lobby. Afternoon refreshments. Restaurant (see WHITEHALL DINING ROOM). Bar. Ck-out 11 am, ck-in after 3 pm. Meeting rm. Business servs avail. Tennis. Health club privileges. Lawn games. Spacious old resort inn (1834); poet Edna St Vincent Millay gave a reading here in 1912. Garden with patio. Cr cds: A, MC, V.

★ ★ ★ **WINDWARD HOUSE.** 6 High St. 207/236-9656; FAX 207/230-0433. E-mail bnb@windwardhouse.com; web www.windwardhouse.com. 8 rms, 5 with shower only, 3 story. No A/C. No rm phones. Memorial Day-mid-Oct: S, D $105-$175; lower rates rest of yr. Children over 12 yrs only. Complimentary full bkfst; afternoon refreshments. Res-

taurant nearby. Ck-out 11 am, ck-in 3 pm. Downhill/x-country ski 5 mi. Some fireplaces. Picnic tables. Built in 1854; some antiques. Totally nonsmoking. Cr cds: MC, V.

Restaurants

★ ★ **THE HELM.** (Commercial St, Rockport 04856) 1½ mi S on US 1. 207/236-4337. French, Amer menu. Specialties: French onion soup, steak au poivre, fresh seafood. Salad bar. Own desserts. Hrs: 11:30 am-8:30 pm; July-Labor Day to 9 pm. Closed mid-Dec-early Apr. Res accepted. Bar. Semi-a la carte: lunch, dinner $7-$17. Child's meals. Parking. Cr cds: DS, MC, V.

✔ ★ ★ **LOBSTER POUND.** (PO Box 118, Lincolnville 04849) 6 mi N on US 1. 207/789-5550. Specializes in seafood, turkey, steak. Own desserts. Hrs: 11:30 am-9 pm. Closed Nov-Apr. Res accepted. Serv bar. Semi-a la carte: lunch, dinner $4.95-$13.95. Complete meals: dinner $9.95-$34.95. Child's meals. Parking. Lobster tanks. Outdoor dining. Fireplace. Gift shop. Overlooks Penobscot Bay. Family-owned. Cr cds: A, C, D, DS, MC, V.

★ ★ **PETER OTT'S.** 16 Bayview St. 207/236-4032. Specializes in local seafood, black Angus beef. Own desserts. Salad bar. Hrs: 5:30-9:30 pm; July-Aug to 10 pm. Closed Jan 1, Dec 25; also Mon mid-Sept-mid-May. Bar 5-11 pm. Semi-a la carte: dinner $7.95-$22.95. Child's meals. Harbor view. Totally nonsmoking. Cr cds: MC, V.

★ ★ **WATERFRONT.** Bayview St. 207/236-3747. Specializes in seafood. Own desserts. Hrs: 11:30 am-9:30 pm; June-Aug to 10 pm. Closed Thanksgiving, Dec 25. No A/C. Bar. Semi-a la carte: lunch $5.95-$13.95, dinner $12.95-$21.95. Child's meals. Parking. Outdoor dining. On harbor. Cr cds: A, MC, V.

★ ★ ★ **WHITEHALL DINING ROOM.** (See Whitehall Inn) 207/236-3391. E-mail stay@whitehall-inn.com; web www.whitehall-inn.com. Regional menu. Specializes in seafood, beef, vegetarian specials. Own baking, desserts. Hrs: 8-9:30 am, 6-8:30 pm. Closed mid-Oct-mid-June. No A/C. Bar. Wine list. Semi-a la carte: bkfst $7.95, dinner $15-$18. Child's meals. Cr cds: A, MC, V.

Caribou (B-5)

(See also Presque Isle)

Pop 9,415 **Elev** 442 ft **Area code** 207 **Zip** 04736 **E-mail** caribouc@mfx.net **Web** www.mainerec.com/caribou.html
Information Chamber of Commerce, 111 High St; 207/498-6156.

Caribou, the nation's northeasternmost city, is primarily an agricultural area but has become diversified in manufacturing. Located here are a food processing plant, a paper bag manufacturing plant and an electronics manufacturing plant. Swimming, fishing, boating, camping and hunting are available in the many lakes located 20 miles northwest on ME 161.

What to See and Do

Caribou Historical Center. Museum housing history of northern Maine. (June-Aug, Tues-Sat; rest of yr, by appt) 3 mi S on US 1. Phone 207/498-2556. **Donation.**

Nylander Museum. Fossils, rocks, minerals, butterflies and shells collected by Olof Nylander, Swedish-born geologist and naturalist; early man artifacts; changing exhibits. Gift shop. (Memorial Day-Labor Day, Wed-Sun; rest of yr, wkends & by appt) 393 Main St, ¼ mi S on ME 161. Phone 207/493-4209. **Free.**

Rosie O'Grady's Balloon of Peace **Monument.** Honoring Col. Joe W. Kittinger Jr., who in 1984 was the first balloonist to fly solo across the Atlantic Ocean, breaking distance record set earlier by the *Double Eagle II* flight. 2 mi S on S Main St. **Free.**

Annual Event

Winter Carnival. Phone 207/498-6156. Feb.

Motels

★ ★ ★ **CARIBOU INN & CONVENTION CENTER.** *19 Main St, 2 mi S at US 1 & ME 164.* 207/498-3733; FAX 207/498-3149; res: 800/235-0466. Web www.mainerec.com/cnvntr.html. 73 rms, 3 story. No elvtr. S, D $56-$80; suites $98-$106; each addl $8; under 12 free. Crib free. TV; cable (premium), VCR avail. Indoor pool; whirlpool. Restaurant 6 am-2 pm, 5-9 pm; Sat 7 am-2 pm, 5-9 pm; Sun 7 am-2 pm, 4-8 pm. Rm serv. Bar 5 pm-midnight; entertainment Fri, Sat. Ck-out 11 am. Coin lndry. Meeting rms. Business servs avail. Free airport transportation. X-country ski 1/2 mi. Exercise rm; sauna. Health club privileges. Game rm. Rec rm. Refrigerators, minibars. Some balconies. Cr cds: A, C, D, DS, MC, V.

☐ ☐ ☐ ☐ ☐ ☐ SC

✔ ★ ★ **CROWN PARK INN.** *at jct ME 89 & US 1.* 207/493-3311; FAX 207/493-3311, ext. 303. 60 rms, 2 story. S, D $50-$58; each addl $10; under 18 free. Crib $7. TV; cable, VCR avail (movies). Complimentary continental bkfst. Restaurant nearby. Bar 4 pm-1 am. Ck-out 11 am. Coin lndry. Meeting rm. Business servs avail. In-rm modem link. Exercise equipt. Some refrigerators. Cr cds: A, C, D, DS, MC, V.

☐ ☐ ☐ SC

Restaurants

✔ ★ **JADE PALACE.** *Box 1032, on US 1, in Skyway Plaza Mall.* 207/498-3648. Chinese, Amer menu. Specialties: sizzling imperial steak, flaming Hawaiian duck, seafood. Hrs: 11 am-10 pm; wkends to 11 pm. Closed Thanksgiving. Res accepted. Bar. Semi-a la carte: lunch $1.95-$5.55, dinner $4.55-$12.95. Buffet: lunch $5.95, Sun $7.95. Cr cds: A, DS, MC, V.

☐

★ **RENO'S.** *117 Sweden St.* 207/496-5331. Italian, Amer menu. Specializes in pizza, sandwiches, fish. Salad bar. Hrs: 5 am-11 pm; Sun 6 am-10 pm. Closed Memorial Day, Thanksgiving, Dec 25. Semi-a la carte: bkfst 95¢-$5, lunch $2.50-$7.95, dinner $2.50-$9. Child's meals. Cr cds: MC, V.

☐ ☐

Center Lovell (G-1)

Pop 100 (est) **Elev** 532 ft **Area code** 207 **Zip** 04016

This community on Kezar Lake is close to the New Hampshire border and the recreational opportunities of the White Mountain National Forest (see BETHEL). The surrounding region is rich in gems and minerals.

Inns

★ ★ ★ **ADMIRAL PEARY HOUSE.** *(9 Elm St, Fryeburg 04037) 15 mi S on ME 5, W on US 302.* 207/935-3365; res: 800/237-8080. E-mail admpeary@nxi.com; web www.mountwashingtonvalley.com/admiralpeary house. 6 rms, 3 story. No rm phones. S $55-$108; D $70-$128; ski package; higher rates fall foliage; lower rates winter. TV in sitting rm; cable. Complimentary full bkfst. Restaurant nearby. Ck-out 11 am, ck-in 3 pm. Free airport transportation. Tennis. Bicycles. Downhill ski 8 mi; x-country

ski on site. Billiard rm. Whirlpool. Bicycles. Home of Arctic explorer Robert E. Peary (1865). Extensive library. Totally nonsmoking. Cr cds: A, MC, V.

☐ ☐ ☐ ☐

★ ★ **OXFORD HOUSE.** *(105 Main St, Fryeburg 04037) 15 mi S on ME 5, W on US 302.* 207/935-3442; FAX 207/935-7046; res: 800/261-7206. E-mail oxford@nxi.com; web www.mountwashingtonvalley.com/ox fordhouse/. 5 rms, 3 story. No rm phones. D $80-$125; each addl $15. TV in some rms, sitting rm; cable. Complimentary full bkfst. Restaurant (see OXFORD HOUSE INN). Ck-out 11 am, ck-in 1 pm. Downhill ski 8 mi; x-country ski on site. Historic house (1913); antiques, verandah. Totally nonsmoking. Cr cds: A, C, D, DS, MC, V.

☐ ☐ ☐

Resort

★ ★ **QUISISANA.** *1 mi W of ME 5 on Pleasant Point Rd.* 207/925-3500; FAX 207/925-1004. 16 rms in 2 lodges, 38 cottages (1-3 bedrm). No A/C. AP, mid-June-Aug: S $165-$265; D $230-$320; each addl $80; July-Aug (1-wk min). Closed rest of yr. Crib free. Dining rm. Box lunches. Ck-out 11 am, ck-in 2 pm. Tennis. Private sand beaches. Waterskiing. Boats, motors; rowboats, canoes. Fishing guides. Windsurfing. Lawn games. Musicals, operas, concerts performed by staff (music students). Game rm. Rec rms. Dancing. Units vary. Refrigerators, fireplaces. Porch in cottages. Lake sightseeing tours. On Lake Kezar in foothills of White Mts. No cr cds accepted.

☐ ☐ ☐

Restaurant

★ ★ **OXFORD HOUSE INN.** *(See Oxford House Inn)* 207/935-3442. E-mail oxford@nxi.com; web www.mountwashingtonvalley.com/ox fordhouse/. Specializes in fresh seafood, sautéed dishes. Hrs: 6-9 pm. Closed Dec 24-25; also Mon-Wed winter & spring. Res required. Bar. Semi-a la carte: dinner $17-$22. Child's meals. Outdoor dining on screened porch. Fireplace. View of mountains. Totally nonsmoking. Cr cds: A, D, DS, MC, V.

Chebeague Islands (H-2)

Pop 300 (est) **Elev** 40 ft **Area code** 207 **Zip** 04017

Little Chebeague (sha-BEEG) and Great Chebeague islands, off the coast of Portland in Casco Bay, were at one time a favorite camping spot of various tribes. The Native Americans had a penchant for clams; the first European settlers thus found heaps of clamshells scattered across the land. Those shells were later used to pave many of the islands' roads, some of which still exist today.

Great Chebeague, six miles long and approximately three miles wide, is connected to Little Chebeague at low tide by a sandbar. There are various locations for swimming. Additionally, both islands lend themselves well to exploring on foot or bicycle. At one time, Great Chebeague was home to a bustling fishing and shipbuilding community, and it was a quarrying center in the late 1700s. Today, it welcomes hundreds of visitors every summer.

What to See and Do

Ferry service from mainland.

Chebeague Transportation. From Cousins Island, near Yarmouth; 15-min crossing. (Daily) Off-site parking with shuttle to ferry (phone for directions). Phone 207/846-3700. Round trip ¢¢¢

Casco Bay Lines. From Portland, Commercial & Franklin Sts; 1-hr crossing. (Daily) Phone 207/774-7871. Round trip ¢¢¢

Cranberry Isles (G-4)

(See also Bar Harbor, Northeast Harbor, Southwest Harbor)

Pop 189 **Elev** 20 ft **Area code** 207 **Zip** 04625

The Cranberry Isles, named because of the rich, red cranberry bogs that once covered Great Cranberry Isle, lie off the southeast coast of Mt Desert Island. There are five islands in the group: Little and Great Cranberry, Sutton, Bear and Baker. Great Cranberry, the largest, covers about 900 acres. Baker Island is part of Acadia National Park, and Sutton is privately owned. In 1830, the islands petitioned the state to separate from Mt Desert Island. In the late 1800s, the area was a thriving fishing and herring community.

What to See and Do

⊠ **Acadia National Park** (see). N on Mt Desert Island.

Ferry service. Ferry connects Little Cranberry and Great Cranberry with Northeast Harbor (see) on Mt Desert Island; 3-mi, 30-min crossing. (Summer, daily; rest of yr, varied schedule) Phone 207/244-3575. ¢¢¢

Islesford Historical Museum. Exhibits on local island history from 1604. (July-Aug, daily; Sept, by appt) Islesford, on Little Cranberry Island. Phone 207/244-9224. **Free.**

Damariscotta (G-3)

(See also Boothbay Harbor, Wiscasset)

Settled 1730 **Pop** 1,811 **Elev** 69 ft **Area code** 207 **Zip** 04543

Information Chamber of Commerce, PO Box 13; 207/563-8340.

Damariscotta, whose name is an Abenaki word meaning "river of many fishes," has a number of colonial, Greek-revival and pre-Civil War houses. With the neighboring city of Newcastle across the Damariscotta River, this is a trading center for a seaside resort region extending to Pemaquid Point and Christmas Cove.

What to See and Do

Chapman-Hall House (1754). Restored house with original whitewash kitchen, period furniture; local shipbuilding exhibition. (July-early Sept, daily exc Sun) Main & Church Sts. ¢

Colonial Pemaquid State Memorial. Excavations have uncovered foundations of jail, tavern, private homes. Fishing, boat ramp; picnicking; free parking. (Memorial Day-Labor Day, daily) Standard fees. 14 mi S via ME 130, in New Harbor. Phone 207/677-2423. Also here is

Ft William Henry State Memorial. Reconstructed 1692 fort tower; museum contains relics, portraits, maps and copies of Native American deeds (fee).

⊠ **Pemaquid Point Lighthouse Park.** Includes 1827 lighthouse that towers above the pounding surf (not open to public); Fishermen's Museum housed in old lightkeeper's dwelling (donation); art gallery; some recreational facilities. Fishermen's Museum (Memorial Day-Columbus Day, daily; rest of yr by appt). 15 mi S at end of ME 130 on Pemaquid Point. Phone 207/677-2494 or 207/677-2726. Park ¢

St Patrick's Church (1808). Early Federal architecture; Revere bell in steeple; one of the oldest surviving Catholic churches in New England. W to Newcastle, then 2 mi N off US 1. Phone 207/563-3240.

Swimming. Pemaquid Beach, N of lighthouse.

Motel

★ ★ **OYSTER SHELL RESORT.** *1½ mi N on US 1 Business.* 207/563-3747; FAX 207/563-3747; res: 800/874-3747 (exc ME). E-mail

oystrshl@lincoln.midcoast.com; web www.lincoln.midcoast.com/~oystrshl/. 18 kit. suites, 4 story. No elvtr. July-Labor Day: S, D $95-$119; under 12 free; lower rates rest of yr. Crib free. TV; cable (premium). Heated pool. Complimentary coffee in rms. Restaurant nearby. Ck-out 11 am. X-country ski 2 mi. Microwaves. Balconies. Overlooks salt water bay. Totally nonsmoking. Cr cds: A, MC, V.

Inns

★ ★ ★ **BRADLEY INN.** *(3063 Bristol Rd, New Harbor 04554)* 207/677-2105; FAX 207/677-3367; res: 800/942-5560. E-mail bradley@lincoln.midcoast.com; web www.lincoln.midcoast.com/~bradley. 16 rms, 5 with shower only, 3 story. No A/C. June-Oct: S, D $125-$195; each addl $25; suites $140-$185; lower rates rest of yr. Crib avail. TV in parlor; cable. Complimentary full bkfst; afternoon refreshments. Restaurant 6-9 pm. Ck-out 11 am, ck-in 2-6 pm. Luggage handling. Bicycles. Lawn games. Some fireplaces. Built by a sea captain for his new bride in 1880. Near Pemaquid Lighthouse. Cr cds: A, MC, V.

★ ★ **BRANNON-BUNKER.** *(349 ME 129, Walpole 04573) 4½ mi S on ME 129.* 207/563-5941; res: 800/563-9225. E-mail brbnkinn@lincoln.midcoast.com. 8 rms, 2 share bath, 2 story, 3 kits. No A/C. No rm phones. S $55-$70; D, kit. units $70-$120. TV in sitting rm; VCR avail (free movies). Complimentary continental bkfst. Ck-out 11 am, ck-in 2 pm. Former barn & carriage house (1820s); antiques. WWI memorabilia. On river. Totally nonsmoking. Cr cds: A, MC, V.

★ ★ **DOWN EASTER.** *222 Bristol Rd.* 207/563-5332. 22 rms, 2 story. No A/C. No rm phones. Memorial Day-Oct: S $63.50; D $70-$80; each addl $10; under 16 free. Closed rest of yr. TV. Complimentary continental bkfst. Restaurant 6:30-10 am, 11 am-3 pm, 5-9 pm. Ck-out 11 am, ck-in 2 pm. Antiques. Lawn games. Greek-revival farmhouse (1785); built by a ship chandler whose ancestors were among the first settlers of Bristol. Cr cds: MC, V.

★ ★ ★ **NEWCASTLE.** *(River Rd, Newcastle 04553) SW on US 1 Business (Main St) across bridge, follow left to River Rd, ½ mi E of US 1.* 207/563-5685; FAX 207/563-6877; res: 800/832-8669 (exc ME). E-mail innkeep@newcastleinn.com; web www.newcastleinn.com. 15 rms, some A/C, 3 story. No rm phones. S, D $125-$225; lower rates rest of yr. Children over 12 yrs only. TV in sitting rm; cable. Dining rm 8-9 am, 5:30-7:30 pm. Bar. Ck-out 11 am, ck-in 3 pm. X-country ski 3 mi. Some fireplaces, in-rm whirlpools. Dormered, clapboard, Federal-style inn (1850); library, antiques. Overlooks Damariscotta River. Totally nonsmoking. Cr cds: A, MC, V.

Restaurant

✔★ ★ **BACKSTREET.** *Elm St Plaza.* 207/563-5666. Specializes in seafood, vegetarian dishes. Own desserts. Hrs: 11:30 am-9 pm; Jul-Aug to 9:30 pm. Closed Jan 1, Thanksgiving, Dec 25; Wed Nov-Apr. Bar. Semi-a la carte: lunch $3.95-$13.95, dinner $8.95-$20.95. Child's meals. On river; scenic view. Cr cds: DS, MC, V.

Deer Isle (G-4)

Settled 1762 **Pop** Deer Isle 1,829; Stonington 1,252 **Elev** 23 ft **Area code** 207 **Zip** 04627 **E-mail** deerisle@acadia.net **Web** www.acadia.net/deerisle
Information Deer Isle/Stonington Chamber of Commerce, PO Box 459, Stonington 04681; 207/348-6124 in season.

A bridge over Eggemoggin Reach connects these islands with the mainland. There are two major villages here—Deer Isle (the older) and Stonington. Lobster fishing and tourism are the backbone of the economy, and Stonington also cans sardines. Fishing, sailing, tennis and golf are available in the area.

What to See and Do

Isle au Haut (EEL-oh-HO). Reached by ferry from Stonington. Much of this island—with hills more than 500 ft tall, forested shores and cobblestone beaches—is in Acadia National Park (see).

Isle au Haut Ferry Service. Service to the island and excursion trips avail. For schedule and fees phone 207/367-5193.

Inn

★ ★ ★ **PILGRIM'S.** On ME 15. 207/348-6615; FAX 207/348-7769. Web www.pilgrimsinn.com. 15 rms, 3 share bath, 4 story. No A/C. MAP, July & Aug: D $160-$180; each addl $65; kit. cottage $215; wkly rates; lower rates mid-May-June & Sept-late Oct. Serv charge 15%. Closed rest of yr. Dining rm 8-9 am, 7 pm (one sitting; by res only). Honor bar. Ck-out 11 am, ck-in 1-5 pm. Gift shop. Fireplaces in library/sitting rm. Antiques. On ocean. Built 1793. Cr cds: MC, V.

Resort

★ ★ **GOOSE COVE LODGE.** (Goose Cove Rd, Sunset 04683) 3 mi S on Sunset Rd, then 1 1/2 mi W on Goose Cove Rd. 207/348-2508; res: 800/728-1963; FAX 207/348-2624. E-mail goosecove@hypernet.com; web www.hypernet.com/goosecove.html. 23 units in cabins & lodge, 2 suites, 10 kit. units. No A/C. MAP, late June-Labor Day (2-day min): S $85-$143/person; lower rates May-late June, Labor Day-mid-Oct. Closed rest of yr. Serv charge 15%. Crib avail. Playground. Free supervised child's activities. Sitting (public by res): lunch 11:30-3:30; dinner 5:30, 6:30, 7:30 pm. Box lunches, lobster cookouts. Ck-out 10:30 am, ck-in 3 pm. Business servs avail. Gift shop. Grocery, coin lndry 2 mi. Tennis privileges. Golf privileges. Private beach. Boats, sailboats, canoes, kayaks. Bicycles. Nature trails. Lawn games. Rec rm. Entertainment. Refrigerators; many fireplaces. Sun decks. Library with over 1,000 volumes. Rustic atmosphere. View of cove; on 21 acres. Cr cds: A, DS, MC, V.

Eastport (E-6)

(See also Lubec)

Settled 1780 **Pop** 1,965 **Elev** 60 ft **Area code** 207 **Zip** 04631 **E-mail** eastportcc@nemaine.com **Web** www.nemaine.com/eastportcc
Information Chamber of Commerce, PO Box 254; 207/853-4644.

At the southern end of Passamaquoddy Bay, Eastport is a community with 150-year-old houses and ancient elms. The average tide at Eastport is approximately 18 feet, but tides up to 25 feet have been recorded here. Eastport was the site of one of the country's first tide-powered electric generating projects, and though never completed, it resulted in the con-

struction of two tidal dams. The city also boasts of being the nation's salmonid aquaculture capital, where millions of salmon and trout are raised in pens in the chilly off-shore waters.

What to See and Do

Barracks Museum. This 1822 building once served as the officers' barracks for a nearby fort, which was held by British troops during the War of 1812. Museum. (Memorial Day-Labor Day, Tues-Sat afternoons) 74 Washington St. **Free.**

Ferry to Deer Island, New Brunswick. A 20-min trip; camping, picnicking on Deer Island. (June-Sept, daily) For schedules, fees inquire locally. (For Border Crossing Regulations, see MAKING THE MOST OF YOUR TRIP.) ¢¢

Fishing. Pollock, cod, flounder and others caught from wharves. Charter boats avail for deep-sea fishing in sheltered waters.

Old Sow **Whirlpool.** One of largest in Western Hemisphere; most active 3 hrs before high tide. Between Dog & Deer islands. **Free.**

Passamaquoddy Indian Reservation. Champlain, in 1604, was the first European to encounter members of this Algonquin tribe. Festivals and ceremonies throughout the yr (see ANNUAL EVENT). About 5 mi N on ME 190 at Pleasant Point. Phone 207/853-2551. **Free.**

Whale-watching trips. Boat excursions during the summer to view whales in the bay.

Annual Event

Indian Festival. At Passamaquoddy Indian Reservation. Ceremonies, fireworks, traditional celebrations. 2nd wkend Aug.

Salmon Festival. Tours of aquaculture pens; music, crafts, educational displays; farm-raised Atlantic salmon dinners. Phone 207/853-4644. Sun after Labor Day.

Motels

★ ★ **MOTEL EAST.** 23 A Water St. 207/853-4747; FAX 207/853-4747. E-mail eastportcc@nemaine.com; web www.ne-maine.com/eastportcc. 14 rms, 2 story. No A/C. No elvtr. S, D $80-$95; each addl $10; under 18 free. TV; cable. Complimentary coffee in rms. Restaurant adj. Ck-out 11 am. Business servs avail. Many refrigerators, microwaves. Many balconies. Picnic tables. On ocean. Cr cds: A, C, D, DS, ER, MC, V.

★ **SEAVIEW.** 16 Norwood Rd (ME 190), E on ME 190. 207/853-4471. 13 units, 12 with shower only, 9 kit. cottages. No A/C. No rm phones. Mid-May-mid-Oct: S, D $39; cottages $45-$55; wkly rates. Closed rest of yr. Crib free. TV; cable. Playground. Restaurant 6:30-10:30 am. Ck-out 10:30 am. Coin lndry. Gift shop. Rec rm. Lawn games. Picnic tables. On ocean, overlooking bay. Cr cds: DS, MC, V.

Inns

★ ★ **TODD HOUSE.** 1 Capen Ave. 207/853-2328. 8 rms, 6 share bath, 2 story, 2 kits. No A/C. No rm phones. D $45-$80; each addl $5-$10; under 5 free; wkly rates. Pet accepted. TV in most rms; cable. Complimentary continental bkfst. Restaurant nearby. Ck-out 11 am, ck-in 2 pm. Picnic tables, grill. This authentic New England Cape once housed soldiers during the War of 1812. Period antiques; original chimney. Near ocean; view of bay. Cr cds: MC, V.

✔★ ★ **WESTON HOUSE.** 26 Boynton St. 207/853-2907; res: 800/853-2907. Web www.virtualcities.com. 5 rms, 2 share baths. No A/C. S, D $50-$75; each addl $15. Complimentary full bkfst; afternoon refreshments. Restaurant nearby. Ck-out 11 am, ck-in 1 pm. Lawn games. Picnic tables. Restored 19th-century residence; sitting rm with tin ceiling. No cr cds accepted.

Ellsworth (F-4)

(See also Bar Harbor)

Settled 1763 **Pop** 5,975 **Elev** 100 ft **Area code** 207 **Zip** 04605 **E-mail** eacc@acadia.net **Web** www.acadia.net/eacc

Information Chamber of Commerce, 163 High St, PO Box 267; 207/667-5584 or 207/667-2617.

This is the shire town and trading center for Hancock County—which includes some of the country's choicest resort territory, including Bar Harbor. In the beginning of the 19th century, Ellsworth was the second biggest lumber shipping port in the world. Its business district was destroyed by fire in 1933, but was handsomely rebuilt, contrasting with the old residential streets.

What to See and Do

John Black Mansion (ca 1820). Georgian house built by a local landowner; antiques. Garden; carriage house with old carriages and sleighs. (June-mid-Oct, daily exc Sun) W Main St. Phone 207/667-8671. ¢¢

Lamoine State Park. A 55-acre recreation area around beach on Frenchman Bay. Fishing; boating (ramp); picnicking, camping. (Memorial Day-mid-Oct, daily) Standard fees. 8 mi SE on ME 184. Phone 207/667-4778. ¢

Stanwood Sanctuary (Birdsacre) and Homestead Museum. Trails, ponds and picnic areas on 130-acre site. Collections include mounted birds, nests and eggs. Wildlife rehabilitation center with shelters for injured birds, including hawks and owls. Museum was home of pioneer ornithologist, photographer and writer Cordelia Stanwood (1865-1958). Sanctuary and rehabilitation center (daily; free); museum (mid-June-mid-Oct, daily). Gift shop. On Bar Harbor Rd (ME 3). Phone 207/667-8460. Tours of museum ¢¢

Motels

★ ★ **COLONIAL TRAVELODGE.** *Bar Harbor Rd. 207/667-5548; FAX 207/667-5549.* E-mail colonial@acadia.net; web www.acadia.net/colonial. 68 rms, 2 story, 18 kit. units. July-Aug: S $68; D $78-$94; each addl $6; suites $125; kit. units $78-$94; under 17 free; wkly rates; lower rates rest of yr. Crib $6. Pet accepted. TV. Indoor pool; whirlpool. Complimentary continental bkfst (June-Sept). Complimentary coffee in rms. Restaurant 11 am-9 pm. Ck-out 11 am. Business servs avail. X-country ski 15 mi. Health club privileges. Refrigerator avail. Balconies. Picnic tables. Cr cds: A, DS, MC, V.

✔★ **ELLSWORTH.** *24 High St. 207/667-4424; FAX 207/667-6942.* 16 rms, many with shower only, 1-2 story. Some A/C. July-Labor Day: S $44-$48; D $46-$58; each addl $8; lower rates rest of yr. Crib $4. TV; cable. Pool. Restaurant nearby. Ck-out 10 am. Cr cds: MC, V.

★ ★ ★ **HOLIDAY INN.** *215 High St, US 1 and ME 3. 207/667-9341; res: 800/401-9341; FAX 207/667-7294.* E-mail hielwme@acadia.net; web www.holidayinnellsworth.com. 103 rms, 2 story. July-Aug: S $109-$119; D $119-$129; each addl $10; under 19 free; lower rates rest of yr. Crib free. Pet accepted. TV; cable, premium. Indoor pool; whirlpool, poolside serv. Complimentary coffee in rms. Restaurant 7-11 am, 5-10 pm. Rm serv. Bar 4 pm-1 am. Ck-out noon. Coin lndry. Meeting rms. Business servs avail. In-rm modem link. Sundries. Indoor tennis.

X-country ski 15 mi. Exercise equipt; sauna. Near river. Cr cds: A, C, D, DS, MC, V.

✔★ **HOMESTEAD.** *RR 3 Box 198 (US 1), 1 mi W on US 1 (ME 3). 207/667-8193; FAX 207/667-8193.* 14 rms, some A/C. July-Aug: S $47-$52; D $48-$62; each addl $5; under 12 free; lower rates mid-May-June, Sept-mid-Oct. Closed rest of yr. TV; cable. Complimentary coffee in lobby. Ck-out 11 am. Some refrigerators. Totally nonsmoking. Cr cds: A, DS, MC, V.

★ ★ **TWILITE.** *1 mi W on US 1 (ME 3). 207/667-8165; FAX 207/667-0289; res: 800/395-5097.* E-mail twilite@ct1.com; web www.acadia.net/twilite. 22 rms, some A/C. July-Labor Day: S, D $64-$74; each addl $5; lower rates rest of yr. Crib free. Pet accepted; $5. TV; cable, VCR avail. Complimentary continental bkfst. Ck-out 10 am. Some refrigerators. Picnic table, grill. Cr cds: A, D, DS, MC, V.

Restaurants

★ ★ **ARMANDO'S.** *(Hancock 04640) 7 mi NE on US 1. 207/422-3151.* Specializes in pasta, seafood. Hrs: 5-9 pm. Closed Jan 1, Easter, Dec 25; also Sun-Mon in summer, Sun-Thurs in winter. Res accepted. Italian menu. No A/C. Bar. Semi-a la carte: dinner $8.95-$16.95. Two-sided, stone fireplaces. Cr cds: MC, V.

✔★ **HILLTOP HOUSE.** *Bar Harbor Rd, 1 mi S on ME 3. 207/667-9368.* E-mail htop@acadia.net. Specializes in steak, seafood, pizza. Own baking. Hrs: 11 am-9:30 pm. Closed Jan 1, Thanksgiving, Dec 25. Bar. Semi-a la carte: lunch $2.25-$9.95, dinner $4.25-$16.95. Child's meals. Cr cds: A, DS, MC, V.

Fort Kent (A-4)

(See also Edmundston, NB, Canada)

Settled 1829 **Pop** 4,268 **Elev** 530 ft **Area code** 207 **Zip** 04743 **E-mail** seefkme@shire.sjv.net **Web** www.sjv.net/seefkme

Information Chamber of Commerce, PO Box 430; 207/834-5354 or 800/733-3563.

Fort Kent, at the northern end of famous US 1 (the other end is at Key West, Florida), is the chief community of Maine's "far north." A bridge across the St John River leads to Clair, New Brunswick. (For Border Crossing Regulations, see MAKING THE MOST OF YOUR TRIP.) The town is a lumbering, farming, hunting and fishing center, and canoeing, downhill and cross-country skiing and snowmobiling are popular here. A campus of the University of Maine is located here.

What to See and Do

Canoeing. Ft Kent is the downstream terminus of the St John-Allagash canoe trip, which starts at E Seboomook on Moosehead Lake, 156 mi and 6 portages away. (See ALLAGASH WILDERNESS WATERWAY)

Cross-country skiing. 11½ mi of scenic intermediate and advanced trails. **Free.**

Fishing. Guides, boats and gear avail for short or long expeditions up the Fish River chain of lakes for salmon or trout; St John or Allagash rivers for trout.

Ft Kent Block House. Built in 1839, during the Aroostook Bloodless War with Britain, used for training exercises and as a guard post. Restored; antique hand tools in museum; interpretive displays. Picnicking. (Memorial

Day-Labor Day, daily) N edge of town. Phone 207/834-3866 or 207/764-2040. **Free.**

Ft Kent Historical Society Museum and Gardens. Former Bangor and Aroostook RR station, built in early 1900s, now houses historical museum. (Usually last 2 wks June-1st wk Aug, Tues-Sat) 54 W Main St. For further information contact the Chamber of Commerce.

Skiing. Lonesome Pine Trails. 13 trails, 2,300-ft slope with 500-ft drop; beginners slope and tow; rope tow, T-bar; school, patrol, lodge, concession. (Dec-Apr, Wed & Fri-Sun, also hols) Forest Ave. Phone 207/834-5202. ¢¢¢¢

Annual Event

Can Am Crown Sled Dog Races. Late Feb-early Mar.

Freeport (G-2)

(See also Bath, Brunswick, Yarmouth)

Pop 6,905 **Elev** 130 ft **Area code** 207 **Zip** 04032 **E-mail** freeportcc@maine.com **Web** www.freeportusa.com

Information Freeport Merchants Association, Hose Tower Information Center, 23 Depot St, PO Box 452MTG; 207/865-1212 or 800/865-1994.

It was in Freeport that legislators signed papers granting Maine independence from Massachusetts and, eventually, its statehood. The town is home to the renowned L.L. Bean clothing and sporting goods store; its major industries include retail, tourism, crabbing and crabmeat packing.

What to See and Do

Atlantic Seal **Cruises.** Cruises aboard 40-ft, 28-passenger vessel on Casco Bay to Eagle Island and Robert E. Peary house museum; also seal- and bird-watching trips, fall foliage sightseeing cruises. (Schedules vary) Tickets must be purchased at Main St office, S Freeport. Depart from Town Wharf, foot of Main St in S Freeport, 2 mi S on S Freeport Rd. Phone 207/865-6112. ¢¢¢¢

⭐**Factory outlet stores.** Freeport is home to more than 120 outlet stores and centers that offer brand-name merchandise at discounted prices, including the famous L.L. Bean clothing and sporting goods store, which stays open 24 hrs a day. For a list of outlet stores contact the Freeport Merchants Association.

Mast Landing Sanctuary. A 140-acre area maintained by the Maine Audubon Society. Hiking, cross-country skiing. (Daily) Upper Mast Landing Rd, 1 1/2 mi E. Phone 207/781-2330. **Free.**

Winslow Memorial Park. Campground with swimming, boating (fee), cross-country skiing; picnicking. (Schedule varies) Staples Point, 5 mi S off US 1, I-95. Phone 207/865-4198. ¢

Motels

⭐ **CASCO BAY INN.** *317 US 1S. 207/865-4925; res: 800/570-4970.* 30 rms, 2 story. July-mid-Oct: S, D $74-$89; each addl $7; lower rates mid-Apr-June, mid-Oct-mid-Dec. Closed rest of yr. TV; cable. Continental bkfst. Restaurant nearby. Ck-out 11 am. Totally nonsmoking. Cr cds: A, DS, MC, V.

D 🐾 🚫 🐾

⭐ ⭐ **COASTLINE INN.** *209 US 1S. 207/865-3777; FAX 207/865-4678; res: 800/470-9494.* Web coastlineinn.com. 108 rms in 3 bldgs, 2 story. July-Oct: S $89.95; D $99.95; under 12 free; wkly rates (off season); lower rates rest of yr. TV; cable (premium), VCR avail. Pet accepted, some restrictions. Complimentary continental bkfst. Coffee in rms. Restaurant nearby. Ck-out 11 am. Coin lndry. Balconies. Picnic tables, grills. Cr cds: A, DS, JCB, MC, V.

D 🐾 🚫 🐾 SC

⭐ ⭐ **FREEPORT INN AND CAFE.** *335 US 1S, exit 17 off I-95. 207/865-3106; FAX 207/865-6364; res: 800/998-2583.* E-mail freeport@maineinns.com; web www.freeportinn.com. 80 rms, 3 story. No elvtr. May-Oct: S, D $70-$120; each addl $10; lower rates rest of yr. Crib $10. Pet accepted, some restrictions. TV; cable. Pool. Restaurant 6 am-9 pm; to 8 pm off season. Ck-out 11 am. Meeting rms. Business servs avail. In-rm modem link. Valet serv. Lawn games. Balconies. Picnic tables. On 25 acres; river; canoe. Some refrigerators. Cr cds: A, C, D, DS, MC, V.

D 🐾 🐾 🚫 🐾 🐾

Inns

⭐ ⭐ **181 MAIN STREET.** *181 Main St (US 1). 207/865-1226; res: 800/235-9750.* E-mail bb181main@aol.com; web mem bers.aol.com/bb181main/index.htm. 7 rms, 2 story. 4 A/C. No rm phones. Memorial Day-Oct: S $85; D $110; lower rates rest of yr. Children over 14 yrs only. TV in sitting rm; cable, VCR. Pool. Complimentary full bkfst. Restaurant nearby. Ck-out 11 am, ck-in 3-7 pm. X-country ski 2 mi. Antiques. Library. Restored Greek-revival cape (ca 1840); Colonial furnishings. Totally nonsmoking. Cr cds: MC, V.

🐾 🚫 🐾 🐾

⭐ ⭐ **ATLANTIC SEAL.** *(25 Main St, South Freeport 04078) 2 mi S on US 1 to Pine St, Pine St to Main St. 207/865-6112.* 3 rms, 1 with shower only, 2 story. No rm phones. May-Nov: D $95-$135; each addl $10-$15; hols (2-day min); lower rates rest of yr. TV; cable, VCR avail (free movies). Complimentary full bkfst. Restaurant nearby. Ck-out 11 am, ck-in 3 pm. X-country ski 2 mi. Bicycles. Built 1850; many antiques. Nautical theme. Dockage. Rowboats. Cruises avail. Totally nonsmoking. Cr cds: MC, V.

🐾 🚫 🐾

⭐ ⭐ **BAGLEY HOUSE.** *(1290 Royalsborough Rd, Durham 04222) I-95 exit 20, then 6 mi N on ME 136. 207/865-6566; FAX 207/353-5878; res: 800/765-1772.* Web members.aol.com/bedandbrk/bagley. 8 rms, 2 story. No A/C. No rm phones. Early July-Oct: S, D $100-$125; each addl $25; lower rates rest of yr. Complimentary full bkfst; afternoon refreshments. Ck-out 11 am, ck-in 3 pm. Meeting rm. X-country ski on site. Some fireplaces. Picnic tables. Antiques. Library. Restored country inn (1772); hand-hewn wood beams, wide pine floors, original beehive oven. Totally nonsmoking. Cr cds: A, DS, JCB, MC, V.

D 🐾 🚫 🐾

⭐ ⭐ **BREWSTER HOUSE.** *180 Main St. 207/865-4121; FAX 207/865-4221; res: 800/865-0822.* Web members.aol.com/bedandbrk/brewster. 7 rms, 1 with shower only, 3 story. No rm phones. Memorial Day-Oct: S, D $110; each addl $15; suites $125; lower rates rest of yr. Children over 7 yrs only. TV in sitting rm; cable. Complimentary full bkfst. Restaurant nearby. Ck-out 11 am, ck-in 3 pm. Built in 1888; antiques. Totally nonsmoking. Cr cds: DS, MC, V.

🚫 🐾

⭐ ⭐ ⭐ **HARRASEEKET.** *162 Main St (US 1). 207/865-9377; FAX 207/865-1684; res: 800/342-6423.* E-mail harraseeke@aol.com; web www.harraseeket.com. 84 rms, 3 story. Late May-Oct: S, D $140-$185; each addl $20; suites $225; under 6 free; lower rates rest of yr. Crib $5. TV; cable, VCR avail. Indoor pool. Complimentary full bkfst. Dining rm (see THE MAINE DINING ROOM). Rm serv. Bar. Ck-out 11 am, ck-in 3 pm. Meeting rms. Business servs avail. In-rm modem link. Luggage handling. Gift shop. Airport transportation. X-country ski 8 mi. Exercise equipt. Some in-rm whirlpools, fireplaces. Consists of 3 structures: Federalist house (1798), early Victorian house (1850) modern, colonial-style inn; drawing rm, antiques. On 5 acres. Cr cds: A, C, D, DS, ER, JCB, MC, V.

D 🐾 🚫 🐾 🐾 🐾

⭐ ⭐ **KENDALL TAVERN.** *213 Main St (US 1). 207/865-1338; FAX 207/865-3544; res: 800/341-9572.* Web nettx.com/kendalltavern. 7 rms, 3 story. No A/C. No rm phones. Memorial Day-Oct: S, D $100-$125; each addl $20; lower rates rest of yr. TV in sitting rm; cable. Complimentary full bkfst. Restaurant nearby. Ck-out 11 am, ck-in 3 pm. Whirlpool. X-country ski 2 mi. Restored New England farmhouse (ca 1850); antiques. Totally nonsmoking. Cr cds: A, DS, MC, V.

★ ★ **WHITE CEDAR.** *178 Main St. 207/865-9099; res: 800/853-1269.* Web www.members.ad.com/bedandbrk/cedar. 7 rms, 6 with shower only, 2 story. No rm phones. July-Oct, wkends in June, Nov, Dec: S, D $95-$130; each addl $15; lower rates rest of yr. Children over 11 yrs only. TV in sitting rm; cable. Complimentary full bkfst. Restaurant adj 11 am-10 pm. Ck-out 11 am, ck-in 3 pm. Luggage handling. Former home of Arctic explorer Donald MacMillan. Totally nonsmoking. Cr cds: A, DS, MC, V.

Restaurants

✔★ **CORSICAN.** *9 Mechanic St. 207/865-9421.* Web www.dinefreeport.com. Italian, Amer menu. Specialties: pesto & tomato pizza, vegetable lasagne, calzones. Hrs: 11 am-9 pm. Closed Jan 1, Thanksgiving, Dec 25. Beer, wine. Semi-a la carte: lunch $4-$9.95, dinner $4-$14.95. Totally nonsmoking. Cr cds: MC, V.

✔★ **GRITTY McDUFF'S.** *183 Lower Main St (US 1). 207/865-4321.* E-mail gritty@grittys.com; web www.grittys.com. Specializes in seafood, pizza. Hrs: 11:30-1 am. Res accepted. Bar. Semi-a la carte: lunch, dinner $4.25-$12.50. Child's meals. Outdoor dining. Casual decor. Cr cds: A, DS, MC, V.

★ ★ **JAMESON TAVERN.** *115 Main St (US 1). 207/865-4196.* Specializes in seafood, steak. Hrs: 11 am-2:30 pm, 5-10 pm. Closed Dec 25. Res accepted. Bar to 11 pm. Semi-a la carte: lunch $4.95-$9.50, dinner $10.25-$21.95. Child's meals. Parking. Patio dining. Historic tavern (1779); final papers separating Maine from the Commonwealth of Massachusetts were signed here. Cr cds: A, C, D, DS, MC, V.

♥

✔★ **LOBSTER COOKER.** *39 Main St (US 1). 207/865-4349.* Specializes in fresh crab & lobster rolls, chowder. Hrs: 11 am-9 pm. No A/C. Wine, beer. A la carte entrees: lunch, dinner $2.95-$12.95. Parking. Outdoor dining. Lobster tank. Historic building (1816). No cr cds accepted.

★ ★ ★ **THE MAINE DINING ROOM.** *(See Harraseeket Inn)* 207/865-1085. E-mail harraseeke@aol.com; web www.harraseeket.com. Regional menu. Hrs: 11:30 am-10 pm. Res accepted. Bar to 10 pm. Wine cellar. Semi-a la carte: lunch $5.95-$16.95, dinner $13-$26. Complete meals for 2: dinner $36-$52.50. Child's meals. Parking. Own baking. Outdoor dining. Colonial decor; some antiques. Totally nonsmoking. Cr cds: A, C, D, DS, ER, JCB, MC, V.

★ **OCEAN FARMS.** *23 Main St. 207/865-3101.* Specializes in seafood, steak. Hrs: 11 am-10 pm; hrs vary off season. Closed Easter, Thanksgiving, Dec 25. Res accepted. Serv bar. Semi-a la carte: lunch $3-$20, dinner $4.95-$25. Child's meals. Parking. Patio dining. Cr cds: A, DS, MC, V.

Greenville (D-3)

Settled 1824 **Pop** 1,884 **Elev** 1,038 ft **Area code** 207 **Zip** 04441 **E-mail** moose@moosehead.net **Web** www.moosehead.net/moose/chamber.html
Information Moosehead Lake Region Chamber of Commerce, PO Box 581; 207/695-2702 or -2026.

Greenville is a starting point for trips into the Moosehead Lake region (see). Until it was incorporated in 1836, it was known as Haskell, in honor of its founder Nathaniel Haskell.

What to See and Do

Baxter State Park (see). Approx 45 mi NE via private paper company roads.

Lily Bay State Park. A 924-acre park on Moosehead Lake. Swimming, fishing, boating (ramp). Picnicking. Camping (dump station). (Mid-May-mid-Oct) Snowmobiling permitted. Standard fees. 8 mi N via local roads, near Beaver Cove. Phone 207/695-2700 (seasonal).

Moosehead Marine Museum. On steamboat *Katahdin,* berthed in East Cove. Exhibits of the steamboat era and the Kineo Hotel; cruises avail. (July-Labor Day, daily; mid-May-June & rest of Sept, Sat & Sun) Phone 207/695-2716. Cruises ¢¢¢¢¢

Skiing. Moosehead Resort on Big Squaw Mountain. Double, triple chairlifts, T-bar, pony lift; novice-to-expert trails; rentals, school, patrol, snowmaking; cafeteria, restaurant, bar; nursery; lodge. Longest run 2¹/₂ mi; vertical drop 1,750 ft. (Late Nov-Apr, daily) Cross-country trails. Chairlift rides (June-mid-Oct; fee). 5 mi NW on ME 6/15, then 2 mi W on access road. For further information contact the Chamber of Commerce.

Annual Event

Moose Mainea. Various locations around Greenville. Celebration honoring the moose. Canoe race, rowing regatta, fly-fishing championship, Tour de Moose bike race. Family Fun Day with parade, crafts, entertainment. Moose-sighting tours. Phone 207/695-2702. Mid-May-mid-June.

Motels

★ **CHALET MOOSEHEAD LAKEFRONT.** *(, Greenville Junction 04442)* 1 mi W, just off ME 6/15. 207/695-2950; res: 800/290-3645. 15 rms, 8 kit. units (no ovens); 2-story motel unit, 2 kit. cottages. No A/C. Late June-early Sept, also Memorial Day, Columbus Day wkends: S, D $65; each addl $10; cottages $80-$100; kit. units $72; under 5 free; lower rates rest of yr. Pet accepted; $10. TV; cable (premium). Complimentary coffee in lobby. Restaurant nearby. Ck-out 10 am. Boat rentals. Seaplane rides nearby. Lawn games. Picnic tables, grills. On Moosehead Lake; dockage, canoes, paddleboats. Cr cds: A, DS, MC, V.

★ **GREENWOOD.** *(Rt 15 Rockwood Rd, Greenville Junction 04442)* 3 mi NW on ME 6/15. 207/695-3321; FAX 207/695-2122; res: 800/477-4386 (US & CAN). 16 rms, 2 story. Mid-May-mid-Sept: S $55; D $55-75; each addl $5; hunting plans; lower rates rest of yr. Crib free. Pet accepted; $5. TV; cable (premium). Pool. Complimentary continental bkfst. Complimentary coffee in rms. Restaurant nearby. Ck-out 10:30 am. Meeting rm. Business servs avail. 9-hole golf privileges. Downhill/x-country ski 3 mi. Hiking trails. Lawn games. Refrigerators. Picnic tables, grills. Cr cds: A, C, D, DS, MC, V.

✔★ **INDIAN HILL.** *ME 15, 1/2 mi S on ME 6/15. 207/695-2623; FAX 207/695-2950; res: 800/771-4620.* 15 rms. No A/C. May-Oct: S, D $58; each addl $10; lower rates rest of yr. TV; cable (premium). Complimentary coffee in lobby. Restaurant nearby. Ck-out 10:30 am. Gift shop. View of Moosehead Lake, mountains. Cr cds: A, DS, MC, V.

★ **KINEO VIEW MOTOR LODGE.** *2 mi S on ME 15/6. 207/695-4470; FAX 207/695-4656; res: 800/659-8439.* Web www.maine guide.com/moosehead/kineo.html. 12 rms, 2 story. No A/C. Memorial Day-mid-Oct: D $65-$75; each addl $5; under 13 free; wkly rates; lower rates rest of yr. Pet accepted; $5. TV. Whirlpool. Complimentary continental bkfst in season. Ck-out 10:30 am. Downhill ski 9 mi; x-country ski on site. Game rm. Lawn games. Balconies. Picnic tables. Lake views. Cr cds: A, DS, MC, V.

Inns

★ ★ **GREENVILLE.** *Norris St. 207/695-2206; res: 888/695-6000; FAX 207/695-0335.* E-mail gvlinn@moosehead.net; web www.greenvilleinn.com. 5 rms, 3 story, 1 suite, 6 cottages. No rm phones. Late June-mid Oct: S, D $115-$148; each addl $20; suite $195; lower rates rest of yr. Complimentary continental bkfst. Dining rm May-Oct 6-9 pm. Bar 5-11 pm. Ck-out 11 am, ck-in 3 pm. TV in some rms, cottages; cable. Downhill/x-country ski 8 mi. Some refrigerators, fireplaces. Former lumber baron residence (1895); cherrywood, mahogany antiques. Porches with view of mountains, lake; flower gardens. Cr cds: DS, MC, V.

★ ★ ★ **LODGE AT MOOSEHEAD LAKE.** *Lily Bay Rd, 2 mi N. 207/695-4400; FAX 207/695-2281.* E-mail lodge@moosehead.net; web www.lodgeatmooseheadlake.com. This 1918 inn features a seafaring theme throughout; rooms are individually decorated with hand-carved furnishings and regional craftwork. The dining room and common areas afford spectacular views of Moosehead Lake and Squaw Mountain. 8 rms, 3 suites, 2 story. No rm phones. S, D $175-$395; MAP avail. Adults only. TV; cable, VCR (movies). Complimentary full bkfst; afternoon refreshments. Coffee in rms. Ck-out 11 am, ck-in 3 pm. Luggage handling. Concierge serv. Business servs avail. Downhill ski 10 mi; x-country ski opp. Lawn games. Fireplaces, whirlpools. Totally nonsmoking. Cr cds: DS, MC, V.

Restaurant

★ ★ **CANGIANO'S.** *ME 15N (04442), 2 mi N. 207/695-3314.* Italian menu. Specializes in fresh seafood. Own desserts. Hrs: 11:30 am-9 pm. Closed Dec 25. Res accepted. Serv bar. Semi-a la carte: dinner $8.95-$14.95. Child's meals. Cr cds: A, DS, MC, V.

Houlton (C-5)

Settled 1805 **Pop** 6,613 **Elev** 366 ft **Area code** 207 **Zip** 04730 **E-mail** chamber@houlton.com **Web** www.mainerec.com/houlton.html

Information Greater Houlton Chamber of Commerce, 109 Main St; 207/532-4216.

Houlton prospered first from lumber, then from the famous Maine potatoes. It is young by New England standards, but was the first town settled in Aroostook County. Industries include woodworking, wood chip and waferboard factories. It is two miles from the Canadian border and a major port of entry. Swimming is available at Nickerson Lake. Fishing is available in several nearby lakes. (For Border Crossing Regulations, see MAKING THE MOST OF YOUR TRIP.)

What to See and Do

Aroostook Historical and Art Museum. Pioneer exhibits, local historical items including model and artifacts from Hancock Barracks, memorabilia from the now closed Ricker College. (By appt) 109 Main St. Phone 207/532-4216. **Free.**

Hancock Barracks. Second northernmost Federal outpost in the country; manned by troops from 1828-1846. Garrison Hill, 1 mi E on US 2. **Free.**

Market Square Historic District. These historic 1890s buildings show a high degree of design artistry. Contact Chamber of Commerce for walking tour maps. Main St between Kendall & Broadway. **Free.**

Museum of Vintage Fashions. Contains 17 rms of men's, women's and children's vintage fashions. Dress-makers shop, hat boutique, bridal rm, haberdashery. (June-early Oct, Mon-Thurs, also Fri-Sun by appt only) 25 mi SW via US 2 to Island Falls, on Sherrnan St. Phone 207/463-2404 or 207/862-3797. **Donation.**

Annual Events

Meduxnekeag River Canoe Race. Mid- or late Apr.

Houlton Fair. Entertainment, concessions, rides. Early July.

Houlton Potato Feast Days. Last full wkend Aug.

Motels

✔ ★ ★ **IVEY'S.** *Box 241, I-95 exit 62, on US 1. 207/532-4206; res: 800/244-4206.* Web www.mainerec.com/ivey.html. 24 rms. June-mid-Oct: S $48-$64; D $64-$68; each addl $8; lower rates rest of yr. Crib $8. TV; cable (premium). Complimentary coffee in rms. Restaurant adj open 24 hrs. Bar 4 pm-midnight. Ck-out 11 am. Meeting rms. Business servs avail. Health club privileges. Refrigerators. Cr cds: A, C, D, DS, MC, V.

★ **SCOTTISH INNS.** *RFD #4 Box 450 (Bangor Rd), 1 mi S on US 2A. 207/532-2236; FAX 207/532-9893.* 43 rms. May-mid-Nov: S, D $44-$48; each addl $6; lower rates rest of yr. Crib $6. Pet accepted; $6. TV; cable (premium). Complimentary coffee in lobby. Restaurant nearby. Ck-out 11 am. Business servs avail. Refrigerators. Cr cds: A, DS, MC, V.

★ ★ **SHIRETOWN.** *Rte 3, Box 30, on North Rd, 1 mi N of US 1, just N of I-95 exit 62. 207/532-9421; FAX 207/532-3390; res: 800/441-9421.* 51 rms. June-mid Oct: S, D $60-$62; each addl $10; suites $72; kit. units $72. Crib $7. TV; cable (premium). Indoor pool. Complimentary coffee in lobby. Restaurant 5-10 pm. Bar to 1 am. Ck-out 11 am. Coin lndry. Meeting rms. Business servs avail. Tennis. Exercise equipt. Refrigerators. Cr cds: A, D, DS, MC, V.

★ **STARDUST.** *US 1, 2 mi N. 207/532-6538; FAX 207/532-9130; res: 800/437-8406.* 11 rms. May-Sept: S $40; D $40-$50; each addl $5; lower rates rest of yr. TV; cable (premium). Ck-out 11 am. Cr cds: DS, MC, V.

Kennebunk (H-1)

(See also Kennebunkport, Old Orchard Beach, Portland, Saco)

Settled 1650 **Pop** 8,004 **Elev** 50 ft **Area code** 207 **Zip** 04043 **E-mail** kkcc@maine.org **Web** www.kkcc.maine.org

Information Chamber of Commerce, 17 Western Ave, ME 9-Lower Village, PO Box 740; 207/967-0857.

The original settlement that was to become Kennebunk was at one time a part of Wells. When Maine separated from Massachusetts in 1820, Kennebunk separated from Wells. Once a shipbuilding community on the Mousam and Kennebunk rivers, Kennebunk today is the principal business center of a summer resort area that includes Kennebunkport (see) and Kennebunk Beach.

What to See and Do

Brick Store Museum. A block of restored 19th-century buildings including William Lord's Brick Store (1825); exhibits of fine and decorative arts, historical and maritime collections. (Tues-Sat; closed hols) 117 Main St, US 1, opp library. Phone 207/985-4802. ¢¢

Taylor-Barry House (ca 1803). Sea captain's Federal-period house with furniture, stenciled hallway; 20th-century artist's studio. (June-Sept, Tues-Fri afternoons) 24 Summer St. Phone 207/985-4802. ¢¢

Annual Event

Winter Carnival. Snow sculpture contests, snow palace moonwalk, magic show, ice-skating party, chili & chowder contests, children's events. Phone 207/985-6890. Feb.

Motels

★ ★ **ECONO LODGE.** *55 York St. 207/985-6100; res: 800/336-5634.* 46 rms, 2 story. July-mid Oct: S, D $99-$149; each addl $10; under 18 free; lower rates rest of yr. Crib $10. TV; cable. Pool. Complimentary continental bkfst. Complimentary coffee in rms. Ck-out 11 am. Balconies. Some refrigerators; microwaves avail. Cr cds: A, D, DS, JCB, MC, V.

D ≋ ⊠ ⚓ SC

✔★ **TURNPIKE.** *77 Old Alewive Rd, at ME Turnpike exit 3 N. 207/985-4404.* 25 rms, 2 story. Mid-June-early Sept: S, D $65.50; each addl $5; lower rates rest of yr. Crib $5. TV; cable. Complimentary coffee in rms. Ck-out 11 am. Refrigerators. Picnic tables. Cr cds: MC, V.

⊠ ⚓ SC

Inns

★ ★ **ARUNDEL MEADOWS.** *1024 Portland Rd, 2 mi N on US 1 in Arundel. 207/985-3770.* Web www.biddeford.com/arundel_meadows-inn. 7 rms, 2 story, 2 suites. No rm phones. June-Oct: S, D $75-$95; each addl $20; suites $100-$125; wkly rates; lower rates rest of yr. Children over 11 yrs only. TV in some rms; cable. Complimentary full bkfst. Ck-out 11 am, ck-in 2 pm. Some fireplaces. Picnic tables, grills. Sitting rm. Restored farmhouse (1827); artwork, antiques, garden. Totally nonsmoking. Cr cds: MC, V.

⊠ ⚓

★ ★ **KENNEBUNK INN 1799.** *45 Main St (US 1). 207/985-3351; FAX 207/985-8865.* 28 rms, 3 story, 4 suites. Some rm phones. Mid-June-late Oct: D $100-$115; each addl $10; suites $160; under 5 free; lower rates rest of yr. Crib $10. Pet accepted. TV in some rms, sitting rm; cable. Complimentary continental bkfst. Dining rm (see THE KENNE-BUNK INN). Ck-out 11 am, ck-in 3 pm. Business servs avail. Built 1799; turn-of-the-century decor, antiques, library. Cr cds: A, DS, MC, V.

✔ ⊠ ⚓

★ ★ ★ **SUNDIAL INN.** *211 Beach Ave. 207/967-3850; FAX 207/967-4719.* E-mail sundial@gwi.net; web www.vrmedia.com/sundial/. 34 rms, 2-4 story. Late June-early Sept: S, D $115-$195; each addl $25; 3-day min high-season, hols; lower rates rest of yr. TV; cable. Complimentary continental bkfst. Ck-out 11 am, ck-in 2 pm. Built circa 1890; period antiques, gardens. Overlooks ocean, swimming beach. Totally nonsmoking. Cr cds: A, C, D, DS, MC, V.

D ✔ ⊠ ⚓

Restaurants

✔★ ★ ★ **GRISSINI.** *27 Western Ave. 207/967-2211.* Specializes in fresh pasta, wood-oven pizza. Hrs: 5:30-9:30 pm; Sat from 5 pm; off-season hrs vary. Closed Thanksgiving. Res accepted. Northern Italian menu. Bar. Wine list. Semi-a la carte: dinner $10.95-$17.95. Child's meals. Parking. Outdoor dining. Totally nonsmoking. Cr cds: A, MC, V.

D

★ ★ **THE KENNEBUNK INN.** *(See Kennebunk Inn 1799) 207/985-3351.* Contemporary Amer menu. Specialties: grilled loin of lamb, flaming crème brulee. Hrs: 5-9:30 pm. Closed Dec 25. Res accepted. Bar from 4 pm. Semi-a la carte: dinner $11-$19. Child's meals. Parking. Outdoor dining. Inn built 1799; stained glass windows. Totally nonsmoking. Cr cds: A, DS, MC, V.

★ ★ ★ **SALTMARSH TAVERN.** *46 Western Ave (ME 9), in Lower Village. 207/967-4500.* E-mail jonhill@cybertours.com. Hrs: 6 pm-closing. Closed Mon (off-season); Dec 25. Res accepted. No A/C. Eclectic menu.

Bar. Wine list. Semi-a la carte: dinner $18.95-$26.95. Child's meals. Specializes in seafood, lamb, duckling. Piano bar. Early 1800s barn. Original artwork. Cr cds: A, DS, MC, V.

D

★ ★ ★ **WINDOWS ON THE WATER.** *12 Chase Hill Rd, E on ME 35 to Chase Hill Rd. 207/967-3313.* E-mail jphughes@biddeford.com; web www.biddeford.com/wow. Regional Amer menu. Specializes in lobster. Hrs: 11:45 am-2:30 pm, 5:30-9:30 pm. Closed Dec 25. Res accepted. Serv bar. Wine list. Semi-a la carte: lunch $6.90-$12.90, dinner $12.90-$25.90. Child's meals. Outdoor dining. Contemporary decor with views of river and marina; open kitchen. Totally nonsmoking. Cr cds: A, D, DS, MC, V.

Kennebunkport (H-1)

(See also Kennebunk, Old Orchard Beach, Portland, Saco)

Settled 1629 **Pop** 3,356 **Elev** 20 ft **Area code** 207 **Zip** 04046 **E-mail** kkcc@maine.org **Web** www.kkcc.maine.org
Information Chamber of Commerce, 17 Western Ave, ME 9-Lower Village, PO Box 740, Kennebunk 04043; 207/967-0857.

At the mouth of the Kennebunk River, this coastal town is a summer and winter resort, as well as an art and literary colony. It was the home of author Kenneth Roberts and the scene of his novel *Arundel*. During the Bush administration, the town achieved fame as the summer residence of the 41st President.

What to See and Do

Architectural Walking Tour. Tours of historic district (June-Sept, Thurs) Phone 207/985-4802. ¢¢

School House (1899). HQ of the Kennebunkport Historical Society. Houses collections of genealogy, photographs, maritime history and many artifacts and documents on Kennebunkport's history. (Wed-Fri afternoons) 135 North St. Phone 207/967-2751. **Free.**

Seashore Trolley Museum. Approx 200 antique streetcars from US and abroad; special events. (Late May-mid-Oct, daily) 3½ mi N on Log Cabin Rd (North St). Phone 207/967-2800 or 207/967-2712. ¢¢¢

Swimming. Colony Beach and Goose Rocks Beach.

The Nott House (1853). Greek-revival house with original wallpaper and furnishings from the Perkins-Nott family. Tours. (June-mid-Oct, Tues-Fri afternoons) 8 Maine St. Phone 207/967-2751. ¢¢

Motels

★ ★ **CAPE ARUNDEL INN.** *208 Ocean Ave, between Spouting Rock & Blowing Cave, 2½ mi S. 207/967-2125; FAX 207/967-1199.* Web www.caparundelinn.com. 7 inn rms, 6 motel rms. No A/C. Mid-June-late-Oct: inn rms $145-$180; motel rms $175; each addl $20; lower rates late-Apr-mid-June, late-Oct-mid-Dec. Closed rest of yr. TV in motel rms; cable. Complimentary continental bkfst. Restaurant 6-9 pm. Ck-out 11 am. Balconies on motel rms. Victorian-style inn (1890); turn-of-the-century decor. Overlooks seacoast. Totally nonsmoking. Cr cds: A, DS, MC, V.

⊠ ⚓

★ ★ **RHUMB LINE MOTOR LODGE.** *Ocean Ave, 3 mi SE. 207/967-5457; FAX 207/967-4418; res: 800/337-4862.* E-mail rhum bline@rhumblinemaine.com; web www.rhumblinemaine.com. 59 units, 1-3 story. No elvtr. July-Aug: S, D $118-$139; suites $125-$145; under 12 free; wkly rates; lower rates rest of yr. Crib free. TV; cable. 2 pools, 1 indoor; whirlpool. Complimentary continental bkfst. Bar to 8 pm (in season). Ck-out 11 am. Meeting rms. Business servs avail. Exercise equipt; sauna. Refrigerators. Balconies. Picnic tables. Secluded woodland location. On trolley route. Cr cds: A, MC, V.

D ≋ ✈ ⊠ ⚓ SC

★ ★ **SEASIDE.** *Gooch's Beach, 3/4 mi S on ME 35.* 207/967-4461; FAX 207/967-1135. Web www.kennebunkbeach.com. 22 rms, 1-2 story, 10 kit. cottages (1-wk min). No A/C. July-late Aug: S, D $119-$188; lower rates rest of yr. Cottages closed Nov-Apr. Crib avail. Pet accepted, some restrictions; $50 refundable. TV; cable. Playground. Ck-out 11 am. Coin lndry. Lawn games. Refrigerators. Private patios, balconies. Private beach; boat ramps. Cr cds: A, MC, V.

⊡ 🏄 ☞ ⊠ ⚑

★ ★ **VILLAGE COVE INN.** *29 S Maine St, 1/2 mi SE.* 207/967-3993; FAX 207/967-3164; res: 800/879-5778 (exc ME). E-mail info@villagecoveinn.com; web www.villagecoveinn.com. 32 rms, 1-2 story. July-Aug: S, D $129-$179; each addl $25; under 12 free; lower rates rest of yr. Crib $20. TV; cable. 2 pools, 1 indoor; poolside serv in season. Complimentary full bkfst. Restaurant 7:30-10 am, 5:30-9:30 pm; varied hrs off season. Bar 11:30 am-closing, off-season from 4:30 pm; entertainment wkends. Ck-out 11 am. Meeting rms. Business servs avail. Refrigerators. Totally nonsmoking. Cr cds: A, DS, MC, V.

⊡ ⊠ ⊠ ⚑

★ ★ **YACHTSMAN.** *Ocean Ave, 1/4 mi to Dock Square.* 207/967-2511; FAX 207/967-5056; res: 800/992-2487. E-mail yachtsman@kport.com; web www.kport.com/yachtsman. 29 rms. Some A/C. July-early Sept: D $139-$175; each addl $15; lower rates May-June, early Sept-Oct. Closed rest of yr. TV; cable (premium). Complimentary continental bkfst. Restaurant opp 8 am-8 pm. Ck-out 11 am. Business servs avail. Refrigerators. Patios. Picnic tables; grill. On river; marina, dockage. Cr cds: A, MC, V.

⊠ ⚑

Motor Hotels

★ ★ ★ **NONANTUM RESORT.** *95 Ocean Ave, 3/4 mi S, 1/2 mi S of ME 9.* 207/967-4050; FAX 207/967-8451; res: 800/552-5651. E-mail nonantum@nonantumresort.com; web www.nonantumresort.com. 116 rms, 26 kit units, 3-4 story. Late May-early Sept: S, D $129-$229; each addl $10; lower rates Apr-late May, early Sept-Nov. Closed rest of yr. TV; cable. Heated pool; poolside serv. Restaurant 7:30-10:30 am, 6-9 pm. Bar; entertainment (in season). Ck-out 11 am. Meeting rm. Business servs avail. Bellhops. Lawn games. Some refrigerators, microwaves. Picnic tables. One of oldest operating inns in state. On Kennebunk River; dockage. Lighthouse. Cr cds: A, C, D, DS, JCB, MC, V.

⊡ ☞ ⊠ ⊠ ⚑ SC

🚭★ ★ **SHAWMUT OCEAN RESORT.** *Box 431, 3 mi E on Ocean Ave to Turbat's Creek Rd.* 207/967-3931; FAX 207/967-4158; res: 800/876-3931. E-mail shawmutreservations@juno.com. 82 rms, some A/C, 2 suites, 1-3 story, 37 kits. No elvtr. July-Aug: S, D $99-$169; MAP avail; wkend packages; lower rates rest of yr. Crib $10. TV; cable. Saltwater pool; poolside serv. Complimentary full bkfst. Restaurant 8-10:30 am, noon-2:30 pm, 6-10 pm. Bar 11:30-1 am; entertainment wkends. Ck-out 11 am. Meeting rms. Business servs avail. Gift shop. Town transportation by trolley. Tennis privileges, pro. 18-hole golf privileges. Lawn games. Private patios, balconies. Picnic tables. Historic inn (1913) located on more than 20 acres along ocean. Cr cds: A, C, D, DS, MC, V.

⊡ ☞ 🏃 ⌖ ⊠ ⊠ ⚑ SC

Inns

★ **AUSTIN'S INN TOWN HOTEL.** *28 Dock Square.* 207/967-4241; res: 800/227-3809. 14 rms, 3 story, 2 suites, 2 kits. No rm phones. Mid-June-mid-Oct: S, D $54-$149; each addl $15; suites $99-$198; kit. units $99-$198; mid-wk rates; lower rates Apr-mid-June, mid-late Oct. Closed rest of yr. Crib free. TV; cable (premium). Restaurant nearby. Ck-out 11 am, ck-in 1 pm. Gift shop. In historic district on Kennebunk River. Cr cds: DS, MC, V.

⚑

★ ★ **BREAKWATER INN.** *1 mi S on Ocean Ave.* 207/967-3118. 20 rms in 2 houses, 2 with shower only, 3-4 story, 2 suites. No elvtr. No rm phones. Late June-Labor Day: D $90-$150; suites $115; wkly rates; lower rates Labor Day-late Oct & May-late June. Closed rest of yr. Crib free. TV; cable. Complimentary continental bkfst. Restaurant (see BREAKWATER INN). Ck-out 11 am, ck-in 2 pm. Many refrigerators; some balconies. Built 1883. Located at mouth of Kennebunkport Harbor; views of Atlantic, harbor. Cr cds: A, MC, V.

⊠ ⚑

★ ★ ★ **BUFFLEHEAD COVE.** *Bufflehead Cove Rd, S on ME 35.* 207/967-3879. Web www.buffleheadcove.com. 5 rms, 3 with shower only, 2 story. No rm phones. Late June-late Oct: S, D $135-$250; 2-day min in season; open wkends only Jan-Mar. Children over 11 yrs only. Complimentary full bkfst; afternoon refreshments. Ck-out 11 am, ck-in 3 pm. Concierge serv. Many fireplaces. Balconies. Picnic tables. On river, swimming. Secluded late 19th-century shingle cottage on Kennebunk River. Riverboats avail. Totally nonsmoking. Cr cds: DS, MC, V.

☞ ⊠ ⚑

★ ★ ★ **CAPTAIN FAIRFIELD.** *8 Pleasant St, at Village Green.* 207/967-4454; FAX 207/967-8537; res: 800/322-1928. E-mail chefctennis@int.usa.com; web www.captain-fairfield.com. 9 rms, 2 story. 6 A/C. No rm phones. Mid-June-mid-Oct: S, D $125-$225; each addl $25; lower rates rest of yr. Children over 6 yrs only. TV in sitting rm; cable, VCR avail. Complimentary full bkfst; afternoon refreshments. Restaurant nearby. Ck-out 11 am, ck-in 3 pm. Business servs avail. Some fireplaces. Federal-style mansion (1813); former sea captain's residence. Overlooks Village Green. Totally nonsmoking. Cr cds: A, D, DS, MC, V.

⊠ ⚑

★ ★ ★ **CAPTAIN JEFFERDS.** *5 Pearl St, 5 blks S on Ocean Ave, left at River Green, then left at next corner.* 207/967-2311; res: 800/839-6844; FAX 207/967-0721. E-mail captjeff@captainjefferdsinn.com; web www.captainjefferdsinn.com. 16 rms, 3 story, 1 kit. suite in attached carriage house. Most A/C. No rm phones. Memorial Day-Oct: S, D $105-$240; each addl $20; lower rates rest of yr. Closed last 2 wks Dec. Children over 7 yrs only. Pet accepted; $20. TV in sitting rm; VCR avail. Complimentary full bkfst; afternoon refreshments. Restaurant nearby. Ck-out 11 am, ck-in 3 pm. Some fireplaces. Federal-style house (1804) built by a merchant sea captain. Solarium; antique furnishings. Near harbor. Totally nonsmoking. Cr cds: A, MC, V.

☞ ⊠ ⚑

★ ★ ★ **CAPTAIN LORD MANSION.** *6 Pleasant St, 1 blk E of Ocean Ave, at jct Pleasant & Green Sts.* 207/967-3141; FAX 207/967-3172. E-mail captain@biddeford.com; web www.captainlord.com. This Federal-style building (1812) was the former residence of a shipbuilder and is decorated with antique furnishings. A cupola overlooks the river. 16 rms, 3 story. May-Dec: D $159-$299; each addl $25; suite $399; 2-day min wkends, 3-day min hol wkends; lower rates rest of yr. Children over 5 yrs only. Complimentary full bkfst; afternoon refreshments. Restaurant nearby. Ck-out 11 am, ck-in after 3 pm. Meeting rms. Business servs avail. Gift shop. Many fireplaces; some refrigerators. Totally nonsmoking. Cr cds: DS, MC, V.

⊠ ⚑

🚭★ ★ **ENGLISH MEADOWS.** *(141 Port Rd, Kennebunk 04043)* I-95 (ME Tpke) exit 3, then 5 mi S on ME 35. 207/967-5766; res: 800/272-0698. 12 rms, 2 share bath, 3 story, 2 kit. units. 3 A/C. No rm phones. Mid-June-Oct: D $95-$125; each addl $20; kit. units $145; wkly rates; lower rates rest of yr. Closed Jan. TV in living rm & kit. units; cable. Complimentary full bkfst; afternoon refreshments. Restaurant nearby. Ck-out 11 am, ck-in 3 pm. Victorian farmhouse (1860) and attached carriage house; library/sitting rm, antiques. Totally nonsmoking. Cr cds: A, MC, V.

⊠ ⚑

★ ★ ★ **INN AT HARBOR HEAD.** *41 Pier Rd, at Cape Porpoise Harbor.* 207/967-5564; FAX 207/967-1294. Web www.harborhead.com. A restored farmhouse, this inn has antiques, hand-painted murals, a deck overlooking the harbor, a private wharf and ocean swimming. 4 rms, 2 story, 2 suites. Rm phones avail. Memorial Day-mid-Oct: S, D $190-$195; suites $290-$295; lower rates rest of yr. Children over 12 yrs only. Complimentary full bkfst; afternoon refreshments. Ck-out 11 am, ck-in 3 pm. Balconies. Private beach. Totally nonsmoking. Cr cds: MC, V.

★ ★ ★ **KENNEBUNKPORT INN.** *1 Dock Square, at Dock Square.* 207/967-2621; FAX 207/967-3705; res: 800/248-2621. Web www.thekennebunkportinn.com. 34 rms, 2-3 story. Late June-Oct: D $89.50-$249; each addl $12; MAP avail; summer & hol wkends (3-day min), spring, fall wkends (2-day min); lower rates rest of yr. Crib $12. TV; cable. Pool. Outdoor lunch noon-2:30 pm; Dining rm 8-10 am, 6-9 pm (May-Oct). Bar 5 pm-1 am; pianist in season. Ck-out 11 am, ck-in 3 pm. Business servs avail. Victorian mansion (1899) built by wealthy tea and coffee merchant, renovated to an inn (1926); lounge/sitting rm, antiques. Cr cds: A, MC, V.

★ ★ ★ **MAINE STAY INN & COTTAGES.** *34 Maine St.* 207/967-2117; FAX 207/967-8757; res: 800/950-2117. E-mail innkeeper@mainestayinn.com; web www.mainestayinn.com. 17 rms, 1-2 story, 11 cottages, some kits. No rm phones. Late June-mid-Oct: S, D, cottages $125-$205; each addl $10-$20; suites $195-$215; higher rates Christmas, prelude wkends; lower rates rest of yr. Crib $15. TV; cable, some VCRs. Complimentary full bkfst; afternoon refreshments. Ck-out 11 am, ck-in 3 pm. Meeting rm. Business servs avail. Some refrigerators, fireplaces. Picnic tables, grills. Playground. Near harbor, beach. In historic preservation district. Built 1860. Antique furnishings. Totally nonsmoking. Cr cds: A, MC, V.

★ ★ ★ **OLD FORT.** *8 Old Fort Ave, S on Ocean Ave to Old Fort Ave.* 207/967-5353; FAX 207/967-4547; res: 800/828-3678. E-mail oldfort@cybertours.com; web www.oldfortinn.com. 16 rms, 2 story. Mid-June-Oct: D $140-$295; each addl $25; wkends, July-Labor Day (2-day min); hol wkends (3-day min); lower rates mid-Apr-mid-June & Nov-mid-Dec. Closed rest of yr. TV; cable. Heated pool. Complimentary full bkfst. Coffee in rms. Restaurant nearby. Ck-out 11 am, ck-in 2 pm. Coin lndry. Meeting rm. Business servs avail. Tennis. Lawn games. Refrigerators, microwaves. Some fireplaces. Antique shop. 1880 carriage house converted to inn; early Amer decor. Extensive grounds. Totally nonsmoking. Cr cds: A, DS, MC, V.

★ ★ **SCHOONERS INN.** *127 Ocean Ave.* 207/967-5333; FAX 207/967-2040. Web www.schoonersinn.com. 17 rms, 3 story. Mid-June-mid-Oct: S, D $135-$175; each addl $10; suite $250; under 12 free; wkends (2-day min); higher rates hols; lower rates rest of yr. Crib $10. TV; cable (premium), VCR avail. Complimentary continental bkfst. Restaurant 7 am-2 pm. Rm serv. Ck-out 11 am, ck-in 3 pm. Business servs avail. Luggage handling. Concierge serv. Gift shop. Refrigerators. Some balconies. On river with views of Atlantic Ocean. Cr cds: A, MC, V.

★ ★ **THE TIDES INN BY-THE-SEA.** *252 Kings Hwy, ME 9 to Dyke Rd, left at end to inn.* 207/967-3757; FAX 207/967-5183. 25 rms, 4 share bath, 3 with shower only, 3 story, 3 kits. No A/C. No rm phones. Mid-June-Labor Day (3-day min wkends): D $165-$225; kit. units $1,200-$2,600/wk; lower rates mid-May-mid-June & Labor Day-Columbus Day. Closed rest of yr. Crib $20. TV in lobby, some rms. Dining rm (see THE BELVIDERE ROOM AT THE TIDES INN). Ck-out 10:30 am, ck-in 3 pm. Swimming beach. Built as inn 1899; antiques. Original guest book on display; signatures include T. Roosevelt and Arthur Conan Doyle. Cr cds: A, MC, V.

★ ★ ★ **WHITE BARN.** *(37 Beach St, Kennebunk)* 207/967-2321; FAX 207/967-1100. E-mail innkeeper@whitebarninn.com; web www.whitebarninn.com. 25 rms, 1-3 story, 9 suites. May-Oct: S, D $199-$260; suites $295-$425; 2-day min wkends, 3-day min hols; lower rates rest of yr. Children over 12 yrs only. TV avail; cable. Heated pool. Complimentary continental bkfst; afternoon refreshments. Restaurant (see WHITE BARN). Rm serv. Ck-out 11 am, ck-in 3 pm. Concierge serv. Luggage handling. Golf privileges. Bicycles, canoes. Some fireplaces, in-rm whirl-

pools. Restored 1820s farmhouse with barn & carriage house; many antiques. Perennial, herb & vegetable gardens. Cr cds: A, MC, V.

Resort

★ ★ ★ **THE COLONY HOTEL.** *Ocean Ave & King's Hwy.* 207/967-3331; FAX 207/967-8738; res: 800/552-2363. E-mail info-me@thecolonyhotel.com; web www.thecolonyhotel.com/maine. 125 rms in hotel, annex and motel, 2-4 story. No A/C. July-early Sept (wkends 2-day min in hotel), MAP: D $175-$375; each addl $30; EP avail off season; lower rates mid-May-June, Sept-late Oct. Closed rest of yr. Crib free. Pet accepted; $22. TV in some rms. Heated saltwater pool. Dining rm 7:30-9:30 am, 6:30-8:30 pm; Sun brunch 11 am-2 pm; poolside lunches in season. Rm serv. Bar. Ck-out 11 am, ck-in 3 pm. Meeting rms. Business servs avail. In-rm modem link. Bellhops. Gift shop. Tennis privileges. Golf privileges. Putting green. Private beach. Bicycles. Lawn games. Soc dir in summer; entertainment; movies. On trolley route. Spacious grounds; on ocean peninsula. Family-operated since 1948. Totally nonsmoking. Cr cds: A, D, MC, V.

Restaurants

✔ ★ **ALISSON'S.** *5 Dock Sq.* 207/967-4841. E-mail alissons@cybertours.com. Seafood menu. Specialty: extra-long lobster roll. Hrs: 11 am-11 pm; to 10 pm off season. Closed Thanksgiving, Dec 25. Bar to 1 am. Semi-a la carte: lunch $5-$8, dinner $11-$16. Child's meals. Two store-front rms; 2nd flr overlooks Dock Square. Family-owned. Cr cds: A, DS, MC, V.

★ ★ **ARUNDEL WHARF.** *43 Ocean Ave.* 207/967-3444. Specializes in seafood. Hrs: 11:30 am-10 pm. Closed Nov-Mar. Res accepted. Bar. Semi-a la carte: lunch $4-$15, dinner $13-$25. Outdoor dining overlooking Kennebunkport River, marina. Fireplace. Cr cds: A, C, D, DS, MC, V.

✔ ★ **BARTLEY'S DOCKSIDE.** *ME 9, by the bridge.* 207/967-5050. E-mail bart@int-usa.net; web www.int-usa.net/bartley/. Specialties: seafood-stuffed haddock, bouillabaisse, blueberry pie. Hrs: 11 am-10 pm. Closed mid Dec-Apr. Res accepted. Serv bar. Semi-a la carte: lunch $2.95-$14.95, dinner $6.50-$23.95. Child's meals. Parking. Outdoor dining. View of water. Family owned. Cr cds: A, C, D, DS, MC, V.

★ ★ **THE BELVIDERE ROOM AT THE TIDES INN.** *(See The Tides Inn By-The-Sea)* 207/967-3757. Regional Amer menu. Specialties: lobster burrito, wild game, shellfish ragout. Own baking, ice cream. Hrs: 8-10:30 am, 5-9:30 pm. Closed mid-Oct-mid-May. Res accepted (dinner). Bar 5 pm-midnight. Wine list. Semi-a la carte: bkfst $3.95-$7.95, dinner $16.95-$27.95. Child's meals. In historic inn. View of beach and ocean; antique china; player piano. Family-owned. Totally nonsmoking. Cr cds: A, MC, V.

★ ★ **BREAKWATER INN.** *(See Breakwater Inn)* 207/967-3118. Specializes in lobster, fresh seafood. Own desserts. Hrs: 5:30-9 pm early May-late Oct. Closed rest of yr. Res accepted. No A/C. Bar. Semi-a la carte: dinner $13.95. Child's meals. Parking. Built 1883 as guest house; view of river, ocean. Cr cds: A, MC, V.

★ ★ **MABEL'S LOBSTER CLAW.** *124 Ocean Ave.* 207/967-2562. Specialties: lobster Savannah, baked stuffed lobster. Own desserts. Hrs: 11:30 am-3 pm, 5-10 pm. Closed early Nov-Apr. Res accepted. Serv bar. Semi-a la carte: lunch $5-$9, dinner $12.95-$24. Child's meals. Outdoor dining. Family-owned. Totally nonsmoking. Cr cds: A, MC, V.

★ ★ ★ **SEASCAPES.** *(77 Pier Rd, Cape Porpoise) 2 mi NE off ME 9, on Pier.* 207/967-8500. Web www.seascapes.com. Mediterranean, Pacific rim cuisine. Specialties: medallions of roasted lobster, Christina's shrimp, sugar cane-planked seafood grille. Hrs: 11:30 am-9 pm; Fri, Sat to 10 pm. Closed Nov-mid-Apr. Res accepted. Serv bar. Wine list. Semi-a la carte: lunch $7.95-$14.95, dinner $19.95-$26.95. Pianist Wed-Sun in season. Parking. Situated over tidal harbor. Cr cds: A, C, D, DS, MC, V.

★ ★ ★ ★ **WHITE BARN.** *(See White Barn Inn) 207/967-2321.* In a Maine coastal resort, lobster is expected, but not haute cuisine this imaginative. The prix-fixe dinner menu includes the best seafood, fowl and meat of the season in generous portions. The restored stable features original timber, art and antiques with a view of the flower garden. Specializes in fresh Maine seafood, seasonal game. Hrs: 6-9 pm. Closed Jan-mid-Feb. Res accepted. Bar. Wine cellar. Complete meals: 4-course dinner $62. Pianist. Cr cds: A, MC, V.

Kingfield (E-2)

Pop 1,114 **Elev** 560 ft **Area code** 207 **Zip** 04947

On a narrow intervale in the valley of the Carrabassett River, Kingfield once had several lumber mills. The town was named after William King, Maine's first governor, and was the birthplace of F.E. and F.O. Stanley, the twins who developed the Stanley Steamer. There is good canoeing, hiking, trout fishing and hunting in nearby areas.

What to See and Do

Carrabassett Valley Ski Touring Center. Approx 50 mi of ski touring trails. Center offers lunch (daily); school, rentals; skating rink (fee), rentals; trail information area; shop. (Early Dec-late Apr, daily) Half-day rates. 15 mi N via ME 16/27. Phone 207/237-2000. ¢¢¢¢¢

Sugarloaf/USA Ski Area. 2 quad, triple, 8 double chairlifts; T-bar; school, patrol, rentals; snowmaking; lodge; restaurants, coffee shop, cafeteria, bars; nursery; bank, health club, shops. 6 Olympic runs, 45 mi of trails; longest run 3½ mi; vertical drop 2,820 ft. (Early Nov-May, daily) 65 mi of cross-country trails. 15 mi N on ME 16/27. Phone 207/237-2000 or 800/THE-LOAF (res only). ¢¢¢¢¢

Motor Hotel

★ ★ ★ **GRAND SUMMIT.** *Carrabassett Valley, 16 mi N, 2 mi SW of ME 27 on Sugarloaf Mt. 207/237-2222; FAX 207/237-2874; res: 800/527-9879.* E-mail smhotel@somtel.com; web www.sugarloaf-hotel.com. 119 rms, 6 story. No A/C. Late Dec-Mar: D $90-$180; suites, kit. units (1-2-bedrm) $130-$300; family rates; tennis, golf, ski, rafting packages; lower rates rest of yr. Crib free. TV; cable (premium), VCR (movies $3). Restaurant 7-10 am, 6-9 pm. Bar 4 pm-1 am. Ck-out 10 am. Coin lndry. Meeting rms. Business servs avail. Bellhops. Valet serv. Concierge (in season). Sundries. Gift shop. Tennis. 18-hole golf, greens fee $76, pro, putting green. Downhill/x-country ski on site. Exercise rm; sauna. Massage. Whirlpool. Game rm. Refrigerators, wet bars. At base of slopes. Cr cds: A, D, DS, MC, V.

⊡ ⤼ 👤👣 🏊 🎿 🔥 🐾 SC

Inn

✔★ ★ **HERBERT.** *Main St. 207/265-2000; FAX 207/265-4594; res: 800/843-4372.* E-mail herbert@somtel.com; web www.byme.com/theherbert. 33 rms, 3 story, 4 suites. No A/C. No rm phones. Dec 25-Mar: S $38-$65; D $60-$95; each addl $10; suites $90-$150; under 12 free; MAP avail; wkly rates; package plans; lower rates rest of yr. Crib free. Pet accepted. TV in sitting rm. Complimentary continental bkfst. Dining rm (public by res) 5:30-9 pm. Rm serv. Ck-out 11 am, ck in noon. Gift shop. Downhill/x-country ski 14 mi. Massage. In-rm whirlpools. Built 1917; antiques, elaborate fumed oak woodwork. On river. Cr cds: A, D, DS, MC, V.

🐾 ⤼ 🎿 🐾 SC

Resort

★ ★ **SUGARLOAF INN.** *Carrabassett Valley, 16 mi N, 2 mi SW of ME 27 on Sugarloaf Mt. 207/237-2000; FAX 207/237-3773; res: 800/843-5623.* E-mail info@sugarloaf.com; web www.sugarloaf.com. 42 rms, 325 condominiums, 2-5 bedrm, 3-4 story. A/C in inn, some condos. EP, Dec 25-Mar: D $89-$185; studio $110-$208; 2-5 bedrm $158-$526; under 12 free; higher rates hols; lower rates rest of yr. Crib $11. TV; cable. 2 pools, 1 indoor; whirlpool. Dining rm 7-10 am, 6-9 pm; hrs vary summer. Bar. Ck-out 11 am, ck-in 4 pm. Meeting rms. Tennis. Golf. Downhill ski on site; x-country ski adj. Exercise rm; sauna, steam rm. Massage. Fishing, hiking, whitewater rafting. Mountain bike rentals, guides. Lawn games. Cr cds: A, DS, MC, V.

⊡ ⤼ 👤👣 🏊 🎿 🔥 🐾

Restaurant

✔★ ★ **LONGFELLOW'S.** *Main St (ME 27). 207/265-4394.* Continental menu. Specializes in prime rib, seafood, chicken, beef. Hrs: 11 am-9 pm; wkends to 9:30 pm. Res accepted. Semi-a la carte: lunch $2.95-$6.75, dinner $5.50-$13.50. Child's meals. Outdoor dining overlooking river. One of town's oldest buildings (1860s). Cr cds: MC, V.

Kittery (J-1)

(See also York; also see Portsmouth, NH)

Settled 1623 **Pop** 9,372 **Elev** 22 ft **Area code** 207 **Zip** 03904 **E-mail** info@kittery-eliot-chamber.org **Web** kittery-eliot-chamber.org

Information Chamber of Commerce, US 1, PO Box 526; 207/439-7545 or 800/639-9645.

This old sea community has built ships since its early days. Kittery men built the *Ranger,* which sailed to France under John Paul Jones with the news of Burgoyne's surrender. Across the Piscataqua River from Portsmouth, NH, Kittery is the home of the Portsmouth Naval Shipyard, which sprawls over islands on the Maine side of the river.

What to See and Do

Factory Outlet Stores. Approx 120 outlet stores can be found throughout Kittery. For a complete listing, contact the Chamber of Commerce.

Ft Foster Park. A 92-acre park with picnicking, pavilion; beach; baseball field; fishing pier. Cross-country skiing in winter. (June-Aug, daily; May & Sept, Sat & Sun) Entrance fee per individual and per vehicle. NE via ME 103 to Gerrish Island. Phone 207/439-3800.

Ft McClary Memorial. Restored hexagonal blockhouse on site of 1809 fort. Interpretive displays; picnicking. (Memorial Day-Labor Day, daily) For further information contact the Chamber of Commerce. 3½ mi E of US 1 in Kittery Point. **Free.**

Hamilton House (ca 1785). This Georgian house, situated overlooking the Salmon Falls River, was redecorated at the turn of the century with a mixture of antiques, painted murals and country furnishings to create an interpretation of America's Colonial past. Perennial garden, flowering trees & shrubs and garden cottage. Tours. (June-mid-Oct, Tues, Thurs, Sat & Sun afternoons) N on I-95 to ME 236, then approx 10 mi NW to Vaughan Lane in South Berwick. Phone 207/384-5269. ¢¢

John Paul Jones State Memorial. Memorial to the sailors and soldiers of Maine. Hiking. (Daily) River bank, E side of US 1 at entrance to Kittery. **Free.**

Kittery Historical and Naval Museum. Exhibits portray history of US Navy and Kittery—Maine's oldest incorporated town—as well as southern Maine's maritime heritage. (June-Oct, Mon-Fri; rest of yr, Fri & by appt) Rogers Rd, off US 1 by Rotary at ME 236. Phone 207/439-3080. ¢¢

Sarah Orne Jewett House (1774). Novelist Sarah Orne Jewett spent most of her life in this fine Georgian residence. Interior restored to recreate the appearance of the house during her time (1849-1909). Contains some original 18th- and 19th-century wallpaper; fine paneling. Her own bedroom-study has been left as she arranged it. (June-mid-Oct, Tues, Thurs, Sat & Sun) N on I-95 to ME 236, then approx 10 mi NW to 5 Portland St in South Berwick. Phone 207/384-2454. ¢¢

Motels

★★ **COACHMAN MOTOR INN.** *380 US 1, adj Kittery Outlet Mall.* 207/439-4434; FAX 207/439-6757; res: 800/824-6183. 43 rms, 2 story. July-Aug: S $103; D $109; each addl $10; package plans off-season; lower rates rest of yr. Crib free. TV; cable (premium). Pool. Complimentary continental bkfst. Restaurant nearby. Ck-out 11 am. Business servs avail. Sundries. Cr cds: A, DS, MC, V.

⬚ ⬚ ⬚ SC

★★ **DAYS INN KITTERY/PORTSMOUTH.** *2 Gorges Rd, US 1 Bypass S.* 207/439-5555. 108 rms, 1-3 story. Late June-early Sept: S $89.90; D $94.90; each addl $6; under 18 free; package plans off-season; lower rates rest of yr. Crib free. TV; cable (premium); VCR avail (movies). Indoor pool; sauna. Restaurant 7-11 am, 5-9 pm; off-season hrs vary. Bar 5 pm-midnight. Ck-out 11 am. Coin lndry. Meeting rms. Business servs avail. Valet serv. Sundries. Refrigerators, microwaves avail. Cr cds: A, D, DS, MC, V.

D ⬚ ⬚ ⬚ SC

Restaurants

✔★ **CAP'N SIMEON'S GALLEY.** *(90 Pepperrell Rd (ME 103), Kittery Point 03905)* 207/439-3655. Specializes in fresh seafood, steak, chicken. Hrs: 11 am-10 pm; Sun brunch 10 am-2 pm; off-season hrs vary. Closed Thanksgiving, Dec 25; also Tues (off season). Res accepted. Bar Thurs-Sat 4 pm-midnight. Semi-a la carte: lunch $2.95-$8.95, dinner $6.95-$14.25. Sun brunch $1.99-$5.95. Nautical decor. Original hand-hewn beams from 17th-century boathouse; views of pier, lighthouses. Cr cds: A, DS, JCB, MC, V.

D SC

★★ **WARREN'S LOBSTER HOUSE.** *US 1.* 207/439-1630. Web www.lobsterhouse.com. Specializes in lobster Thermidor, fresh seafood. Salad bar. Own baking. Hrs: 11:30 am-9 pm; Fri, Sat to 10 pm; Sun brunch 11 am-2 pm. Hrs vary off season. Closed Jan 1, Dec 24-25. Bar. Semi-a la carte: lunch $4.50-$9.95, dinner $9.95-$15.95. Sun brunch $10.95. Child's meals. Nautical decor. Outdoor dining. View of waterfront. Cr cds: A, MC, V.

D ⬚

Lewiston (G-2)

(See also Auburn)

Settled 1770 **Pop** 39,757 **Elev** 210 ft **Area code** 207 **E-mail** info@androscoggincounty.com **Web** www.androscoggincounty.com

Information Androscoggin County Chamber of Commerce, 179 Lisbon St, PO Box 59, 04243-0059; 207/783-2249.

Maine's second-largest city is 30 miles up the Androscoggin River from the sea, directly across the river from its sister city of Auburn (see). Known as the Twin Cities, both are strong manufacturing and service-oriented communities. Lewiston was the first of the two cities to harness the water power of the Androscoggin Falls; however, both cities have benefitted from the river.

What to See and Do

Bates College (1855). (1,500 students) New England's oldest and the nation's second-oldest coeducational institution of higher learning; originally the Maine State Seminary, it was renamed after a prominent Boston investor. Liberal arts and sciences. On its well-landscaped campus is the Edmund S. Muskie Archives (1936 alumnus and former Senator and US Secretary of State) and a beautiful chapel containing a hand-crafted tracker-action organ. College St & Campus Ave. Phone 207/786-6255 or 207/786-6330. Also on campus are

Olin Arts Center. Multilevel facility overlooking campus lake houses a concert hall and a Museum of Art that contains a variety of changing and permanent exhibits (daily exc Mon; closed hols; free). Phone 207/786-6158 (museum) or 207/785-6135 (center).

Mt David. A 340-ft rocky hill offering a view of Lewiston, the Androscoggin Valley and the Presidential Range of the White Mts to the west.

Annual Events

Maine State Parade. Downtown Lewiston & Auburn. Maine's largest parade; over 30,000 people representing 60 communities. Televised statewide. Phone 207/784-0599. 1st wkend May.

Lewiston-Auburn Garden Tour. Tour of 6 gardens in the area. Ticket purchase required. Phone 207/782-1403. July.

Festival de Joie. Central Maine Civic Center. Celebration of Lewiston & Auburn's Franco-American heritage. Features ethnic song, dance, cultural activities, traditional foods. July.

Motels

✔★ **CHALET.** *1243 Lisbon St (04240).* 207/784-0600; FAX 207/786-4214; res: 800/733-7787. 74 units, 2-3 story, 8 suites, 7 kit. units (some equipt). No elvtr. Mid-May-mid-Nov: S $36; D $40-$45; each addl $5; suites $60-$85; kit. units $5 addl; under 13 free; lower rates rest of yr. Crib $5. TV; cable (premium). Indoor pool; whirlpool. Restaurant 6-11 am. Bar 4 pm-midnight. Ck-out 11 am. Coin lndry. Downhill/x-country ski 15 mi. Exercise equipt; sauna. Refrigerators avail. Picnic tables, grills. Cr cds: A, C, D, DS, MC, V.

D ⬚ ⬚ ⬚ ⬚ ⬚ SC

✔★ **SUPER 8.** *1440 Lisbon St (04240).* 207/784-8882; FAX 207/784-1778. 49 rms. July-Sept: S $40.88-$43.88; D $55.88; each addl $6; under 12 free; lower rates rest of yr. Crib free. TV; cable, VCR avail (movies). Complimentary continental bkfst. Restaurant nearby. Ck-out 11 am. Downhill/x-country ski 15 mi. Cr cds: A, C, D, DS, MC, V.

D ⬚ ⬚ ⬚ SC

Motor Hotel

★★★ **RAMADA INN.** *490 Pleasant St (04240).* 207/784-2331; FAX 207/784-2332. 117 rms, 2 story. Mid-May-mid-Oct: S $74.90; D $89-$99; each addl $10; suites $149; studio rms $79-$99; under 18 free. Crib free. TV; cable. Indoor pool; whirlpool. Complimentary bkfst buffet. Coffee in rms. Restaurant 7 am-1:30 pm, 5-10 pm. Bar 11-1 am; entertainment. Ck-out 11 am. Coin lndry. Meeting rms. Business center. In-rm modem link. Gift shop. Downhill ski 10 mi. Exercise equipt; sauna. Cr cds: A, C, D, DS, MC, V.

 ⬚ ⬚ ⬚ ⬚ ⬚ SC ⬚

Lincoln (E-4)

Pop 5,587 **Elev** 180 ft **Area code** 207 **Zip** 04457 **Web** www.mainerec.com/linchome.html
Information Chamber of Commerce, 75 Main St, PO Box 164; 207/794-8065 or 800/794-8065.

What to See and Do

Mt Jefferson Ski Area. Novice, intermediate and expert trails; T-bar, rope tow; patrol, school, rentals; lodge, concession. Longest run 0.7 mi, vertical drop 432 ft. (Jan-Mar, Tues, Wed, Sat & Sun; daily during school vacations) 12 mi NE via ME 6 in Lee. Phone 207/738-2377. ¢¢¢¢

Motels

★ **BRIARWOOD MOTOR INN.** *outer W Broadway, 1 mi S. 207/794-6731; res: 800/734-6731 (ME only).* 24 rms, 2 story. July-Aug: S $55; D $60; each addl $5; lower rates rest of yr. Crib $5. Pet accepted. TV; cable (premium). Complimentary coffee in lobby. Restaurant nearby. Ck-out 11 am. Downhill ski 11 mi; x-country ski 2 mi. Refrigerators avail. Cr cds: A, DS, MC, V.

↙★ **LINCOLN HOUSE.** *85 Main St. 207/794-3096; FAX 207/794-9059.* 19 rms. June-mid-Sept: S $40; D $44-$52; each addl $5; under 13 free; lower rates rest of yr. Pet accepted, some restrictions; $5. TV; cable. Ck-out 11 am. Business servs avail. Valet serv. Restaurant nearby. Downhill ski 12 mi. Refrigerators, microwaves avail. Cr cds: A, DS, MC, V.

Lubec (E-6)

(See also Eastport)

Pop 1,853 **Elev** 20 ft **Area code** 207 **Zip** 04652

Quoddy Head State Park, the easternmost point in the US, is located in Lubec. There is a lighthouse here, as well as the Franklin D. Roosevelt Memorial Bridge, which stretches over Lubec Narrows to Campobello Island. Herring smoking and sardine packing are local industries.

What to See and Do

Roosevelt Campobello International Park. Canadian property jointly maintained by Canada and US. Approx 2,800 acres include the 11-acre estate where Franklin D. Roosevelt had his summer home and was stricken with poliomyelitis. Self-guided tours of 34-rm house, interpretive guides avail; films shown in visitor center; picnic sites in natural area; observation platforms and interpretive panels at Friar's Head; vistas. No camping. (Sat before Memorial Day-Columbus Day, daily) 1 1/2 mi E off ME 189 on Campobello Island. Phone 506/752-2922. **Free.**

Motel

↙★ **EASTLAND.** *ME 189, 4 mi W. 207/733-5501; FAX 207/733-2932.* E-mail eastland@nemaine.com. 20 rms. Some A/C. Mid-June-Oct: S $38-$45; D $52-$62; each addl $4; under 17, $2; lower rates rest of yr. Crib free. Pet accepted; $3. TV; cable (premium). Ck-out 10 am. Complimentary coffee in lobby. Airport for small planes adj. Cr cds: DS, MC, V.

Inns

★★ **HOME PORT.** *45 Main St. 207/733-2077; res: 800/457-2077.* E-mail carmant@nemaine.com. 7 rms, 2 story. No rm phones. Memorial Day-mid-Oct: S, D $60-$80; each addl $10. Closed rest of yr. TV in sitting rm; VCR avail. Complimentary continental bkfst. Restaurant (see HOME PORT INN). Ck-out 10 am, ck-in 2 pm. Gift shop. Picnic tables. Built 1880; antiques, library. Totally nonsmoking. Cr cds: DS, MC, V.

★★ **OWEN HOUSE.** *(Welshpool, Campobello, New Brunswick, CAN E0G 3H0) 2 mi from International Bridge. 506/752-2977.* 9 rms, 4 share bath, 3 story. No rm phones. Memorial Day-mid-Oct: S, D $60-$83; each addl $15. Closed rest of yr. TV in sitting rm. Complimentary full bkfst. Restaurant nearby. Ck-out 11 am, ck-in noon. Built by son of first settler of Campobello Island. On ocean. Totally nonsmoking. Cr cds: V.

Restaurant

★★ **HOME PORT INN.** *(See Home Port Inn) 207/733-2077.* E-mail carmant@nemaine.com. Specializes in seafood, beef, chicken. Hrs: 5-8 pm. Closed mid-Oct-Memorial Day. Res accepted. No A/C. Wine, beer. Semi-a la carte: dinner $8.99-$14.99. Child's meals. Parking. Dining rm of inn; many antiques displayed. Totally nonsmoking. Cr cds: DS, MC, V.

Machias (F-5)

(See also Lubec)

Settled 1763 **Pop** 2,569 **Elev** 70 ft **Area code** 207 **Zip** 04654
Information Machias Bay Area Chamber of Commerce, PO Box 606; 207/255-4402.

For almost a hundred years before 1750, Machias (muh-CHY-as) was the headquarters for a number of pirates including Samuel Bellamy, called the Robin Hood of Atlantic pirates. After pirating abated, Machias became a hotbed of Revolutionary fervor. Off Machiasport, downriver, the British schooner *Margaretta* was captured (June, 1775) in the first naval engagement of the war. Today the area is noted particularly for hunting, fishing and nature trails. Bear, deer, puffins, salmon and striped bass abound nearby. The University of Maine has a branch in Machias.

What to See and Do

Burnham Tavern Museum (1770). Memorabilia from 1770-1830. (June-Sept, Mon-Fri; rest of yr, by appt) Main St, just off US 1 on ME 192. Phone 207/255-4432. ¢

Ruggles House (1820). This home exhibits Adam-style architecture and unusual "flying" staircase. Intricate wood carving; period furnishings. (June-mid-Oct, daily) 20 mi S on US 1, then 1/4 mi off US 1 in Columbia Falls. Phone 207/483-4637 or 207/546-7903. ¢

State parks.

Fort O'Brien Memorial. Remains of a fort commanding the harbor, commissioned by Washington in 1775. Hiking. Picnicking. (Memorial Day-Labor Day, daily) 5 mi E on ME 92. **Free.**

Cobscook Bay. Fishing, boating (ramp). Hiking. Picnicking. Snowmobiling permitted. Camping (dump station). (Mid-May-mid-Oct, daily) Standard fees. 20 mi NE on US 1 near Whiting. Phone 207/726-4412. ¢

Roque Bluffs. Oceanfront pebble beach; freshwater pond. Swimming, fishing; picnicking. (Mid-May-mid-Oct, daily) 7 mi S, off US 1. Phone 207/255-3475. ¢

Annual Event

Wild Blueberry Festival. 3rd wkend Aug.

Motels

★ **BLUEBIRD.** *Rte 1, Box 45, 1 mi W on US 1. 207/255-3332.* 40 rms. Mid-June-mid-Sept: S $50; D $56; each addl $4; lower rates rest of yr. Crib free. Pet accepted. TV; cable. Ck-out 11 am. Cr cds: A, C, MC, V.

D 🐾 ⊠ 🔥 SC

✔★ **MAINELAND.** *(Rte 1, Box 177, East Machias 04630) 1 mi E on US 1. 207/255-3334.* 30 rms, 18 A/C. June-mid-Sept: S $45-$55; each addl $5; lower rates rest of yr. Pet accepted, some restrictions. TV; cable. Complimentary coffee in rms. Restaurant adj 11 am-8 pm. Ck-out 11 am. Some refrigerators; microwaves avail. Picnic tables. Cr cds: A, C, D, DS, MC, V.

🐾 ⊠ 🔥

Millinocket (D-4)

Pop 6,956 **Elev** 350 ft **Area code** 207 **Zip** 04462 **E-mail** kacc@agate.net **Web** www.mainerec.com/millhome.html

Information Katahdin Area Chamber of Commerce, 1029 Central St; 207/723-4443.

What to See and Do

Baxter State Park (see). 18 mi NW via state park road. Phone 207/723-5140.

Motels

★★ **ATRIUM.** *740 Central St. 207/723-4555.* 82 rms, 3 story, 10 suites. June-Oct: S $65-$75; D $70-$80; each addl $5; suites $90; under 18 free; ski plans; lower rates rest of yr. Crib free. Pet accepted. TV; cable, VCR avail. Indoor pool; wading pool, whirlpool. Playground. Complimentary bkfst buffet. Restaurant nearby. Bar 4 pm-midnight. Ck-out noon. Coin lndry. Meeting rms. Sundries. X-country ski 10 mi. Exercise equipt. Rec rm. Some refrigerators; microwaves avail; bathrm phone, wet bar in suites. Cr cds: A, D, DS, MC, V.

D 🐾 ⊠ ⊠ 🎿 ⊠ 🔥

★★ **BEST WESTERN HERITAGE.** *935 Central St. 207/723-9777; FAX 207/723-9777, ext. 284.* 49 rms, 2 story. June-Aug: S $69; D $79; each addl $10; under 12 free; lower rates rest of yr. Crib free. Pet accepted, some restrictions. TV; cable. Complimentary continental bkfst. Restaurant 4-10 pm. Bar. Ck-out 11 am. Meeting rm. Business servs avail. Sundries. Exercise equipt. Whirlpools. Refrigerators avail. Cr cds: A, D, DS, MC, V.

D 🐾 🎿 ⊠ 🔥 SC

✔★ **PAMOLA MOTOR LODGE.** *973 Central St. 207/723-9746; FAX 207/723-9746, ext. 63.* 29 rms, 1-2 story, 3 kits. Mid-May-mid-Oct: S $39; D $54; each addl $6; under 18 free; lower rates rest of yr. Crib free. TV; cable. Pool; whirlpool. Complimentary continental bkfst. Restaurant 11 am-9 pm. Bar 4 pm-1 am; entertainment Fri, Sat. Ck-out 11 am. Business servs avail. Game rm. Some balconies. Cr cds: A, D, DS, MC, V.

⊠ ⊠ 🔥 SC

Monhegan Island (H-3)

(See also Boothbay Harbor, Damariscotta, Rockland)

Settled 1720 **Pop** 88 **Elev** 50 ft **Area code** 207 **Zip** 04852

Monhegan Plantation, nine miles out to sea, approximately two miles long and one mile wide, is profitably devoted to lobsters and summer visitors. Rockwell Kent and Milton Burns were among the first of many artists to summer here. Today, the warm-weather population is about 20 times the year-round number. There is more work in winter: by special law, lobsters may be trapped in Monhegan waters only from January to June. This gives them the other six months to fatten. Monhegan lobsters thus command the highest prices.

Leif Ericson may have landed on Monhegan Island in A.D. 1000. In its early years, Monhegan Island was a landmark for sailors, and by 1611 it was well known as a general headquarters for European fishermen, traders and explorers. For a time, the island was a pirate den. Small compared to other Maine islands, Monhegan is a land of contrasts. On one side of the island sheer cliffs drop 150 feet to the ocean below, while on the other side, Cathedral Woods offers visitors a serene haven.

What to See and Do

Boat and ferry service.

Ferry from Port Clyde. *Laura B* makes 11-mi journey (1 hr, 10 min) from Muscongus Bay. (July-Oct, 2-3 trips daily; May-June, 1 trip daily; rest of year, Mon, Wed, Fri,; no trips hols) No cars permitted; res required. Foot of ME 131. Phone 207/372-8848. ¢¢¢¢¢

Trips from Boothbay Harbor. *Balmy Days* makes trips from mainland (see BOOTHBAY HARBOR). (June-Sept, daily) Phone 207/633-2284. ¢¢¢¢¢

✖ **Monhegan Lighthouse.** Historic lighthouse has been in operation since 1824; automated since 1959. Magnificient views. **Free.**

Moosehead Lake (D-2)

(See also Greenville, Rockwood)

E-mail moose@moosehead.net **Web** www.moosehead.net/moose/chamber.html

Information Moosehead Lake Region Chamber of Commerce, PO Box 581, Greenville 04441; 207/695-2702 or 207/695-2026.

(N of Greenville; approx 32 mi E of Jackman)

The largest of Maine's countless lakes, Moosehead is also the center for the state's wilderness sports. The source of the Kennebec River, Moosehead Lake is 40 miles long and 20 miles wide, with many bays, islands, ponds, rivers and brooks surrounding it. Its waters are good for ice-fishing in the winter, and trout, landlocked salmon and togue can be caught in the summer. The lake is located in the heart of Maine's North Woods. Here is the largest moose population in the continental US. Moose can best be seen in the early morning or at dusk. Being placid creatures, the moose allow watchers plenty of time to snap pictures. It is possible to hunt moose in northern Maine in season, but only by permit granted through a lottery.

Greenville (see), at the southern tip of the lake, is headquarters for moose-watching, hunting, fishing, camping, whitewater rafting, canoeing, hiking, snowmobiling and cross-country and alpine skiing. The town has an airport with two runways, one 3,000 feet long. Other communities around Moosehead Lake include Rockwood, Kokadjo and Greenville Junction.

Newport (F-3)

(See also Skowhegan)

Pop 3,036 **Elev** 202 ft **Area code** 207 **Zip** 04953

Motel

✔★ ★ **LOVLEY'S.** *RFD 2, ¹/₂ mi W at jct US 2, ME 11/100, just N of I-95 Newport-Detroit exit 39.* 207/368-4311; res: 800/666-6760. 63 rms, 1-2 story, 3 kits. (no ovens, equipt). June-Nov: S $29.70-$49.90; D $39.90-$89.90; each addl $5; kit. units $8 addl; lower rates rest of yr. Crib $8. Pet accepted. TV; cable (premium). Heated pool; whirlpool. Complimentary coffee in rms. Restaurant nearby. Ck-out 11 am. Coin lndry. Business servs avail. Lawn games, gliders. Picnic tables. Cr cds: A, DS, MC, V.

Inn

✔★ ★ **BREWSTER INN.** *(37 Zion's Hill Rd, Dexter 04930) 14 mi N on ME 7 to Main St.* 207/924-3130. E-mail brewster@nconline.net; web www.bbonline.com/me/brewsterinn. 7 rms, 3 with shower only, 2 story, 2 suites. No rm phones. S, D $59-$69; each addl $10; suites $79-$89; wkly rates. Crib free. TV; cable, VCR avail. Complimentary full bkfst; afternoon refreshments. Restaurant nearby. Ck-out 11 am, ck-in 3 pm. Luggage handling. Downhill ski 15 mi. Some fireplaces; refrigerators avail. Built in 1935; original fixtures. Totally nonsmoking. Cr cds: MC, V.

Restaurant

✔★ **LOG CABIN DINER.** *(US 2, East Newport) 3 mi E on ME 2 & 100.* 207/368-4551. Specializes in steak, seafood. Own desserts. Hrs: 6 am-9 pm; Sun 7 am-8 pm. Closed Dec-Mar. Semi-a la carte: bkfst, lunch, dinner $1.95-$14.95. Child's meals. Family-owned. Cr cds: DS, MC, V.

Northeast Harbor (G-4)

(See also Bar Harbor)

Pop 650 (est) **Elev** 80 ft **Area code** 207 **Zip** 04662

This coastal village is located on Mt Desert Island, a land of rocky coast-lines, forests and lakes. The island is reached from the mainland by a short bridge.

What to See and Do

Acadia National Park (see). N via ME 3.

Ferry Service. Connects Northeast Harbor with the Cranberry Isles (see); 3-mi, 30-min crossing. (Summer, daily; rest of yr, schedule varies) Phone 207/244-3575. ¢¢¢

Motel

★ ★ **KIMBALL TERRACE INN.** *10 Huntington Rd, 2 blks SE of ME 3.* 207/276-3383; FAX 207/276-4102; res: 800/454-6225. E-mail kimballterrace@acadia.net; web www.acadia.net/kimball. 70 rms, 2-3 story. No A/C. July-Labor Day: S, D $109-$135; each addl $10; under 6 free; lower rates Apr-June, Labor Day-Oct; closed rest of yr. Crib $5. TV; cable (premium). Pool. Restaurant 7 am-9 pm. Rm serv. Ck-out 11 am. Meeting rms. Business servs avail. Gift shop. Tennis adj. Balconies. Overlooks harbor. Cr cds: A, DS, MC, V.

Inns

★ ★ **ASTICOU.** *1 mi NE on ME 3, 198.* 207/276-3344; FAX 207/276-3373; res: 800/258-3373. Web www.asticou.com. 33 rms in inn, 14 rms in 5 cottages, 7 kits. (no ovens). No A/C. Mid-June-mid-Sept, MAP: S $200-$255; D $264-$350; each addl $66.50; suites $299-$364; EP avail. Closed rest of yr. TV in game rm. Heated pool. Dining rm 7:30-9:30 am, 11:30 am-10 pm. Rm serv. Bar noon-11 pm; entertainment. Ck-in 3 pm, ck-out 11 am. Business servs avail. Luggage handling. Valet serv. Concierge serv. Tennis. Massage. Renovated country inn (1883). At head of harbor, public dock adj. Cr cds: MC, V.

★ ★ **MAISON SUISSE.** *144 Main St.* 207/276-5223; res: 800/624-7668. E-mail maison@acadia.net; web www.acadia.net/maison. 10 rms, 2 story, 4 suites. No A/C. Mid-July-Aug: S, D $125-$175; each addl $10-$15; suites $195-$245; under 2 free; lower rates May-mid-July & Sept-Oct. Closed rest of yr. Crib $5. TV; cable. Complimentary full bkfst. Restaurant opp 6:30 am-9 pm. Ck-out 11 am, ck-in 3-7 pm. Near ocean. Restored, shingle-style summer cottage (1892); once a speakeasy during Prohibition; library, antiques, gardens. Totally nonsmoking. Cr cds: A, MC, V.

Restaurants

★ **DOCKSIDER.** *14 Sea St.* 207/276-3965. Specializes in seafood. Hrs: 11 am-9 pm; hrs vary spring & fall. Closed mid-Oct-mid-May. No A/C. Beer, wine. Semi-a la carte: lunch, dinner $1.95-$16.95. Child's meals. Outdoor dining. Rustic nautical decor. Cr cds: DS, MC, V.

✔★ ★ **JORDAN POND HOUSE.** *(5 mi N on Park Loop Rd, Seal Harbor) on grounds of Acadia Natl Park.* 207/276-3316. E-mail arcadia@arcadia.net; web www.jordanpond.com. Hrs: 11:30 am-9 pm; hrs vary off season. Closed Nov-late May. Res accepted. No A/C. Serv bar. Semi-a la carte: lunch, dinner $6.50-$16. Child's meals. Specializes in homemade ice cream, popovers. Outdoor dining. Cr cds: A, DS, MC, V.

Norway (G-1)

(See also Poland Spring)

Pop 4,754 **Elev** 383 ft **Area code** 207 **Zip** 04268
Information Oxford Hills Chamber of Commerce, PO Box 167, South Paris 04281; 207/743-2281.

What to See and Do

Pennesseewasee Lake. This 7-mi-long lake, covering 922 acres, received its name from the Native American words meaning "sweet water." Swimming, beaches, waterskiing; fishing for brown trout, bass and perch; boating (marina, rentals, launch). Ice-skating. Contact Chamber of Commerce. W of town. **Free.**

Motel

★ **GOODWIN'S.** *(191 Main St, South Paris 04281) ¹/₂ mi W on ME 26.* 207/743-5121; res: 800/424-8803 (exc ME). 24 rms. S $40; D $48; under 12 free; higher rates special events. Pet accepted. TV; cable.

Restaurant nearby. Ck-out 11 am. Downhill/x-country ski 6 mi. Some refrigerators. Two family units. Cr cds: A, C, D, DS, MC, V.

Inn

★ ★ ★ **WATERFORD.** *(Box 149, Waterford 04088) 8 mi W via ME 118, then S on ME 37 to Chadbourne Rd.* 207/583-4037. 9 rms, 2 share bath, 2 story. No rm phones. S, D $75-$100; each addl $29. Closed Apr. Pet accepted: $10. Complimentary full bkfst. Dining rm 8-9:30 am, 5-9 pm. Ck-out 11 am, ck-in 2 pm. Downhill ski 20 mi; x-country ski on site. Lawn games. Private patios, balconies. Built 1825; antiques. Parlor, library. Extensive grounds; flower gardens. Cr cds: A.

Restaurants

✔★ **BARJO.** *210 Main St.* 207/743-5784. Specialties: marinated sirloin tips, homemade chicken pie. Salad bar. Hrs: 11 am-2 pm, 4-7 pm; Fri, Sat to 8 pm. Semi-a la carte: lunch $3.50-$8.95, dinner $4.95-$8.95. No cr cds accepted.

★ ★ **MAURICE.** *(109 Main St, South Paris 04281) 1 mi N on ME 26.* 207/743-2532. French menu. Specialties: escalope de veau flambé, roast duck á l' orange. Own desserts. Hrs: 11:30 am-1:30 pm, 4:30-9 pm; Sat from 4:30 pm; Sun brunch 11 am-2 pm. Closed Thanksgiving, Dec 24, 25. Res accepted. Serv bar. Semi-a la carte: lunch $3-$9.95, dinner $10.95-$16.95. Sun brunch $3-$9.95. Cr cds: A, C, D, DS, MC, V.

Ogunquit (J-1)

(See also Kennebunk, Kittery, Wells, York)

Pop 974 **Elev** 40 ft **Area code** 207 **Zip** 03907 **Web** www.Ogunquit.org
Information Chamber of Commerce, PO Box 2289; 207/646-2939.

Here Maine's "stern and rockbound coast" becomes a sunny strand—a great white beach stretching three miles, with gentle (though sometimes chilly) surf. The Ogunquit public beach is one of the finest on the Atlantic. Marine views, with the picturesque little harbor of Perkins Cove, have attracted a substantial art colony.

What to See and Do

Marginal Way. A beautiful and unusual walk along the cliffs overlooking the ocean, with tidepools at the water's edge.

Ogunquit Museum of American Art. Twentieth-century American sculpture and painting. (July-mid-Sept, daily) 183 Shore Rd, at Narrow Cove. Phone 207/646-4909. **Free.**

Seasonal Event

Ogunquit Playhouse. 1 mi S on US 1. Established in the early 1930s. Top plays and musicals with professional actors. Phone 207/646-5511 (seasonal). Late June-Labor Day wkend.

Motels

★ ★ ★ **ANCHORAGE BY THE SEA.** *55 Shore Rd, on Marginal Way.* 207/646-9384; FAX 207/646-6256. Web www.source-maine.com/travel/maine. 212 rms, 2-3 story. July-Aug: S, D $135-$200; each addl $15; kit. units $175-$250; July, Aug (3-7 day min); higher rates July 4 wkend; lower rates rest of yr. Crib $15. TV; cable. 2 pools, 1 indoor; wading pool, whirlpool, sauna. Complimentary continental bkfst Nov-Apr. Restaurant 7 am-7 pm; Oct-late May hrs vary. Ck-out 11 am. Meeting rm. Business servs avail. Bellhops. Sundries. Golf privileges. Health club

privileges. Refrigerators; some fireplaces. Balconies. Gazebos. Overlooking ocean. On trolley route. Cr cds: DS, MC, V.

★ ★ **THE BEACHMERE INN.** *12 Beachmere Place.* 207/646-2021; FAX 207/646-2231; res: 800/336-3983. E-mail info@beachmere-inn.com; web www.beachmereinn.com. 54 units in inn, motel & cottages, 52 with bath, 2-3 story, 51 kits. Mid-June-Labor Day: D $100-$195; each addl $10; spring, fall plans; lower rates late Mar-mid-June, after Labor Day-mid-Dec. Closed rest of yr. Crib $5. TV; cable, VCR (free movies). Playground. Complimentary continental bkfst. Restaurant nearby. Ck-out 11 am. Business servs avail. 9-hole golf privileges. Many microwaves; some fireplaces. Private patios, balconies. Picnic tables, grills. Victorian-style inn (1889). On ocean, swimming beach. Cr cds: A, C, D, DS, MC, V.

★ **BRIARBROOK MOTOR INN.** *42 US 1.* 207/646-7571. Web www.briarbrook.com. 18 rms, 2 kit. units. Late June-Labor Day: D $82-$89; each addl $12; under 13, $10; kit. units $695/wk; lower rates mid-Apr-late June, after Labor Day-Oct. Closed rest of yr. Crib $9. TV; cable. Heated pool. Complimentary coffee in lobby. Restaurant adj 7 am-10 pm. Ck-out 11 am. Refrigerators. Picnic tables. On trolley route. Ogunquit Playhouse adj. Cr cds: A, DS, MC, V.

★ ★ **COLONIAL VILLAGE RESORT.** *266 US 1, 1/2 mi N on US 1.* 207/646-2794; FAX 207/646-2463; res: 800/422-3341. E-mail tooey@cybertours.com; web www.cybertours.com/~tooey. 67 rms, 1-2 story, 29 suites, 24 kit. units (no ovens), 4 kit. cottages (2-bedrm). July-Aug, motel (3-day min in season): D, kit. units $109-$140; each addl $15; suites $135-$173; kit. cottages for 2-4, (1-wk min July-Labor Day) $950/wk; lower rates early Apr-June, Sept-mid-Dec. Closed rest of yr. Crib $10. No maid serv in cottages. TV; cable, VCR avail (movies). 2 pools, 1 indoor; whirlpools. Complimentary continental bkfst. Restaurant nearby. Ck-out 11 am. Coin lndry. Tennis. Game rm. Private deck on cottages. Rowboats. Picnic tables, grills. On Tidal River. Cr cds: DS, MC, V.

★ ★ **COUNTRY SQUIRE.** *56 US 1, US 1 & Bourne's Lane.* 207/646-3162; FAX 207/641-2365. 35 rms, 1-2 story. Some rm phones. Late June-Labor Day: S, D $86-$100; each addl $10; under 12, $5; higher rates hols; lower rates late Apr-late June, after Labor Day-mid-Oct. Closed rest of yr. TV; cable. Pool. Complimentary continental bkfst. Restaurant adj 7 am-9 pm. Ck-out 11 am. Refrigerators. Balconies. On trolley route. Cr cds: A, MC, V.

★ ★ ★ **GORGES GRANT.** *239 US 1 (Old King's Hwy), 1/2 mi N on US 1.* 207/646-7003; FAX 207/646-0660; res: 800/646-5001. E-mail gorgesgrant@ogunquit.com; web www.ogunquit.com. 81 rms. Mid-July-Aug: S, D $119-$169; each addl $12; lower rates early-Apr-mid July, Sept-mid-Dec. Closed rest of yr. Crib free. TV; cable (premium). 2 heated pools, 1 indoor; whirlpool, poolside serv. Complimentary coffee in lobby. Restaurant 6:30-11 am, 5-9 pm in season. Ck-out 11 am. Meeting rms. Business servs avail. Golf privileges. Exercise equipt. Refrigerators; some wet bars. Cr cds: A, C, D, DS, MC, V.

★ ★ **JUNIPER HILL INN.** *196 US 1.* 207/646-4501; FAX 207/646-4595; res: 800/646-4544. E-mail juniperhill@ogunquit.com; web www.ogunquit.com. 100 rms, 2 story. July-Aug: S, D $119-$169; each addl $10-$12; higher rates hol wkends; lower rates rest of yr. Crib free. TV; cable (premium). 3 heated pools, 1 indoor; whirlpool. Complimentary coffee in lobby. Restaurant opp 11 am-9 pm. Ck-out 11 am. Coin lndry. Business servs avail. Golf privileges. Exercise equipt; sauna. Refrigerators. Balconies. Garden. Cr cds: A, C, D, DS, MC, V.

★ ★ **THE MILESTONE.** *333 US 1.* 207/646-4562; res: 800/646-6453; FAX 207/646-1739. E-mail milestone@ogunquit.com; web www.ogunquit.com/milestone/. 70 rms, 1-3 story. No elvtr. Mid-July-Aug:

S, D $99-$144; each addl $12; higher rates hols; lower rates rest of yr. Closed Nov-Mar. Crib free. TV; cable (premium). Complimentary coffee in lobby. Restaurant opp 6 am-10 pm. Exercise equipt. Heated pool. Refrigerators. Many balconies. Cr cds: A, C, D, DS, MC, V.

★ **NORSEMAN MOTOR INN.** *41 Beach St, 2 blks E at beach. 207/646-7024; FAX 207/646-0655; res: 800/822-7024.* E-mail norseman-resorts@cybertours.com; web www.norsemanresorts.com. 94 rms, 1-3 story. No elvtr. Early July-late Aug: S, D $95-$185; each addl $15; lower rates early Apr-early June, late Aug-Oct. Closed rest of yr. Crib free. TV; cable. Restaurant 6:30 am-11 pm; off-season to 9 pm. Ck-out 11 am. Bellhops. Sundries. Many refrigerators. Private patios, balconies, decks. Rms vary. On beach. Cr cds: A, DS, MC, V.

★★ **PINK BLOSSOMS.** *66 Shore Rd. 207/646-7397; res: 800/228-7465.* E-mail pinkb@concentric.net; web www.pinkb.com. 37 kit. units, 8 with shower only, 2 story. July-Aug (5-7-day min): kit. units $125-$240; under 6 free; lower rates May-June, Sept-late-Oct. Closed rest of yr. Crib free. TV; cable. Heated pool. Restaurant nearby. Ck-out 11 am. Tennis. Golf privileges. Lawn games. Refrigerators, microwaves. Balconies. Picnic tables, grills. Cr cds: MC, V.

★★ **RIVERSIDE.** *159 Shore Rd, 1 mi S on Shore Rd at Perkins Cove. 207/646-2741; FAX 207/646-0216.* E-mail rvrsyd@aol.com. 38 rms, 2 story. Late June-Labor Day (3-day min): D $125-$145; each addl $10; lower rates late Apr-late June, after Labor Day-late Oct. Closed rest of yr. Crib $10. TV; cable. Complimentary continental bkfst. Ck-out 11 am. Lawn games. Refrigerators. Balconies. Overlooks Perkins Cove. Cr cds: MC, V.

★★ **SEA CHAMBERS MOTOR LODGE.** *25 Shore Rd. 207/646-9311; FAX 207/646-0938.* E-mail info@seachambers.com; web seachambers.com. 43 rms, 2-3 story. No elvtr. Mid-June-Aug (4-day min July-Aug; 3-day min some hol wkends): S, D $118-174; each addl $15; lower rates Apr-mid-June, Sept-mid-Dec. Closed mid-Dec-Mar. Crib free. TV; cable. Heated pool. Complimentary continental bkfst. Ck-out 11 am. Business servs avail. Bellhops. Tennis. Golf privileges. Health club privileges. Refrigerators. Most rms with ocean view. Sun decks. Cr cds: A, DS, MC, V.

✔★★ **SEA VIEW.** *US 1, 1/4 mi N on US 1. 207/646-7064; FAX 207/646-7064.* 40 rms, 2-3 story. No elvtr. July-Aug: S, D $79-$139; each addl $10; higher rates major hols; lower rates rest of yr. Crib free. TV; cable (premium). Heated pool; whirlpool. Complimentary coffee. Restaurant nearby. Ck-out 11 am. Meeting rm. Exercise equipt. Refrigerators. Cr cds: A, D, DS, MC, V.

★★ **SPARHAWK.** *41 Shore Rd, 1/4 mi SE. 207/646-5562.* 82 rms, 2-3 story. No elvtr. Late June-mid Aug (1-wk min): D $150-$160; each addl $15; suites $160-$180; kit. units $170-$225; lower rates mid-Apr-late June, late Aug-late Oct; hol wkends (3-day min). Closed rest of yr. Crib $5. TV; cable (premium). Heated pool. Complimentary continental bkfst. Restaurant nearby. Ck-out 11 am. Luggage handling. Tennis. Golf privileges. Lawn games. Health club privileges. Refrigerators. Balconies. Ocean view. On trolley route. Cr cds: MC, V.

★ **STAGE RUN.** *238 US 1. 207/046-4823; FAX 207/641-2884.* E-mail stagerun@cybertours.com; web www.inettravel.com. 24 rms, 2 story. July-Labor Day: S, D $89-$129; lower rates early Apr-June, early Sept-Oct. Closed rest of yr. Crib $10. TV; cable; VCR avail. Heated pool. Restaurant opp 6 am-9 pm. Ck-out 11 am. Refrigerators. Balconies. Near ocean, swimming beach. Cr cds: DS, MC, V.

★★ **TERRACE BY THE SEA.** *11 Wharf Lane. 207/646-3232.* Web www.terracebythesea.com. 36 rms, 1-2 story, 7 kits. Mid-June-Labor Day: D $110-$169; each addl $20; lower rates May-mid-June, after Labor Day-Oct. Closed rest of yr. Crib free. TV; cable. Heated pool. Complimentary continental bkfst. Restaurant nearby. Ck-out 11 am. Refrigerators. Balconies. On ocean. No cr cds accepted.

★★ **TOWNE LYNE.** *US Rt 1 N, 1 1/2 mi N on US 1. 207/646-2955.* 20 rms. Late June-Labor Day (2-day min hol wkends): D $90-$110; each addl $10; kit. unit $90-$120; lower rates Apr-late June, after Labor Day-mid Nov. Closed rest of yr. TV; cable. Complimentary coffee in rms. Restaurant nearby. Ck-out 11 am. Refrigerators avail. Some rms with screened porch overlook river. Cr cds: A, DS, MC, V.

Hotel

★★ **THE GRAND.** *108 Shore Rd. 207/646-1231.* E-mail info@thegrandhotel.com; web www.thegrandhotel.com. 28 suites, 3 story. Late June-early Sept (2-day min wkdays, 3-day min wkends): S, D $150-$200; lower rates mid-Apr-late June, early Sept-mid-Nov. Closed rest of yr. Crib $10. TV; cable; VCR (movies $4.50). Indoor pool. Complimentary continental bkfst. No rm serv. Restaurant adj 7 am-10 pm. Ck-out 11 am. Refrigerators. Balconies. Cr cds: A, DS, MC, V.

Inns

★ **ABOVE TIDE.** *26 Beach St. 207/646-7454.* Web www.abovetideinn.com. 9 rms, 7 with shower only, 2 story. No rm phones. Mid-June-mid-Sept (3-day min): S, D $125-$160; each addl $20; lower rates mid-Sept-mid-Oct, mid-May-mid-June. Closed rest of yr. TV; cable. Complimentary continental bkfst. Restaurant nearby. Ck-out 11 am, ck-in 2 pm. Massage. Refrigerators. Balconies. Sun deck. Situated on pilings over river; ocean, dune views. Cr cds: MC, V.

★★ **HARTWELL HOUSE.** *118 Shore Rd. 207/646-7210; FAX 207/646-6032.* E-mail hartwell@cybertours.com; web hartwellhouse-inn.com. 16 rms, 2 story, 3 suites, 2 kits. June-mid-Sept: S, D $125-$190; kits $750-$850; spring, fall packages; lower rates rest of yr. Children over 14 yrs only. TV in parlor; cable. Complimentary full bkfst; afternoon refreshments. Ck-out 11 am, ck-in 3 pm. Meeting rms. Restaurant nearby. Golf privileges. Private patios, balconies. Antiques. Cr cds: A, DS, MC, V.

★★ **PINE HILL INN.** *14 Pine Hill Rd S. 207/361-1004; FAX 207/361-1815.* 6 units, 4 with shower only, 1-2 story, 2-bdrm kit. cottage. No rm phones. Late June-Labor Day: S, D $90-$115; kit. cottage $100; wkly rates cottage; 3-day min cottage; lower rates rest of yr. Children over 12 yrs only in inn rms. TV in cottage, sitting rm; cable. Complimentary full bkfst (inn rms only). Ck-out 11 am, ck-in 4-6 pm. Turn-of-the-century cottage with sun porch. Short walk to ocean. Totally nonsmoking. Cr cds: A, MC, V.

Restaurants

★★★ **98 PROVENCE.** *104 Shore Rd. 207/646-9898.* French Provençale menu. Specializes in fresh local seafood, venison, lamb. Own desserts, ice cream. Hrs: 5:30-9:30 pm. Closed Tues; also mid-Dec-mid-Apr. Res accepted. Bar. Wine list. Semi-a la carte: dinner $20-$40. Intimate dining in country-French atmosphere; antiques and china displayed. Totally nonsmoking. Cr cds: A, MC, V.

★★★ **ARROWS.** *Berwick Rd. 207/361-1100.* Contemporary Amer menu. Specialty: house-cured prosciutto. Own baking, pastas. Hrs:

6-9 pm. Closed Mon; also late Nov-late Apr. Res accepted. Bar. Wine cellar. Semi-a la carte: dinner $29.95-$35.95. Valet parking. Renovated 1765 farmhouse; original plank floors, antiques, fresh flowers. Expansive windows overlook more than three acres of perennial, herb and vegetable gardens. Cr cds: MC, V.

★ **BARNACLE BILLY'S.** *Perkins Cove, 1 mi E of US 1 at Perkins Cove.* 207/646-5575. E-mail info@barnbilly.com; web barnbilly.com. Specializes in boiled lobster, steamed clams, barbecued chicken. Hrs: 11 am-10 pm; hrs vary mid-Apr-mid-June, mid-Sept-mid-Oct. Closed mid-Oct-mid-Apr; also Mon-Thurs mid-Apr-early-May. Serv bar. Semi-a la carte: lunch from $5, dinner $7.50-$20. Valet parking in season. Outdoor dining on decks over water. Lobster tank. Fireplaces; nautical decor. Family-owned. Cr cds: A, MC, V.

✔★ **BILLY'S, ETC.** *Oarweed Cove Rd, 1 mi S on Shore Rd, in Perkin's Cove area.* 207/646-4711. E-mail info@barnbilly.com; web www.barnbilly.com. Specializes in fresh seafood, lobster, steak. Hrs: noon-9 pm. Closed Nov-early May. Bar. Semi-a la carte: lunch, dinner $4.95-$19.95. Child's meals. Valet parking. Outdoor dining. Views of river and gardens. Totally nonsmoking. Cr cds: A, MC, V.

 D

★ ★ **CLAY HILL FARM.** *(226 Clay Hill Rd, Cape Neddick) ¹/4 mi S on US 1, then 2 mi W on Agamenticus Rd.* 207/361-2272. E-mail info@clayhillfarm.com; web www.clayhillfarm.com. Specializes in prime rib, fresh seafood. Own pastries. Hrs: 5:30-9 pm. Closed Mon-Wed Nov-Apr. Res accepted. Bar to 9 pm. Wine cellar. Semi-a la carte: dinner $12-$24. Pianist Wed-Sat (in season), Fri-Sat (off season). Valet parking. Fireplace. Historic farmhouse (1780) in country setting; antiques, herb garden, bird sanctuary. Cr cds: A, DS, MC, V.

D

★ ★ **GYPSY SWEETHEARTS.** *10 Shore Rd.* 207/646-7021. E-mail gypsy@cybertours.com; web www.gypsysweethearts.com. Contemporary Amer menu. Specialties: shrimp margarita, almond-crusted haddock, East Coast crab cakes. Own desserts. Hrs: 5:30-close; Sat, Sun also 7:30 am-noon; early-bird dinner to 6 pm. Closed Nov-early Apr. Res accepted. Bar to 1 am. Semi-a la carte: dinner $13.95-$22.95. Child's meals. Converted early-1800s home with original decor, perennial gardens, enclosed sunporch. Family-owned. Totally nonsmoking. Cr cds: A, DS, MC, V.

★ ★ **HURRICANE.** *52 Oarweed Cove Rd, ¹/2 mi S on Shore Rd, in Perkin's Cove area.* 207/646-6348. E-mail hurricane@perkinscove.com; web perkinscove.com. Contemporary Amer menu. Specialties: rack of lamb, baked stuffed lobster, roasted vegetable lasagna. Own desserts. Hrs: 11:30 am-4 pm, 5:30-10:30 pm; Sun brunch Oct-May to 4 pm; winter hrs vary. Closed Thanksgiving, Dec 25. Res accepted; required dinner (May-Sept). Bar. Semi-a la carte: lunch $7-$15, dinner $14-$26. Sun brunch $7-$15. Jazz Sun brunch Oct-May. Limited parking. Panoramic views of ocean. Cr cds: A, D, DS, MC, V.

★ ★ ★ **JONATHAN'S.** *2 Bourne Lane.* 207/646-4777. Continental menu. Specializes in seafood, beef, chicken. Own baking. Hrs: 5-11 pm; Oct-June 5:30-9 pm. Res accepted. Bar 5-11 pm. Wine cellar. Semi-a la carte: dinner $14.50-$21.95. Child's meals. Pianist Wed-Sat. Parking. Aquarium; tropical fish. Doll collection. Herb & country rock gardens. Cr cds: A, D, DS, MC, V.

D

★ **OARWEED.** *Oarweed Rd, Perkins Cove.* 207/646-4022. E-mail oarweed@cybertours.com; web www.oarweed.com. Specializes in lobster, lobster rolls, chowder. Hrs: 11 am-9 pm. Closed mid-Oct-Apr. No A/C. Serv bar. Semi-a la carte: lunch, dinner $3.95-$19.95. Child's meals. Parking. Outdoor dining. View of ocean. Cr cds: A, DS, MC, V.

★ **OGUNQUIT LOBSTER POUND.** *256 US 1.* 207/646-2516. Specializes in boiled lobster; select your own. Hrs: May-Columbus Day: 4:30-9:30 pm. Closed rest of yr. Bar. Semi-a la carte: dinner $5.95-$25. Parking. New England decor; fireplaces. Outdoor pine grove dining. Family-owned. Cr cds: A, DS, MC, V.

★ ★ ★ **OLD VILLAGE INN.** *30 Main St.* 207/646-7088. Specializes in local seafood, duckling, beef. Hrs: 5:30-9:30 pm; wkends, hols also 8-11:30 am (Sept-June only). Closed Dec 25. Bar. Wine list. Semi-a la carte: bkfst $3.95-$6.95, dinner $12.95-$22.95. Child's meals. Town's oldest commercial building (1833). Guest rms avail. Cr cds: A, DS, MC, V.

★ ★ **POOR RICHARD'S TAVERN.** *2 Pine Hill Rd, 1 mi S on Shore Rd to Pine Hill Rd.* 207/646-4722. Regional Amer menu. Specialties: Yankee pot roast, lobster-stuffed filet of sole. Hrs: 5:30-9 pm. Closed Sun; also Dec-Mar. Res accepted. Bar. Semi-a la carte: dinner $12-$24. Valet parking. Outdoor dining. 1780 inn with orginal hand-hewn beams, brick fireplace, antiques. Cr cds: A, MC, V.

Old Orchard Beach (H-2)

(See also Portland, Saco)

Settled 1630 **Pop** 7,789 **Elev** 40 ft **Area code** 207 **Zip** 04064 **E-mail** famlyfun@oldorchardbeach.com **Web** www.oldorchardbeachmaine.com
Information Chamber of Commerce, PO Box 600; 207/934-2500 or 800/365-9386.

This popular beach resort, 12 miles south of Portland, is one of the long-time favorites on the Maine Coast. It has a crescent beach 7 miles long and about 700 feet wide—which in rocky Maine is a good deal of beach. In summer it is the vacation destination of thousands.

What to See and Do

Palace Playland. Amusement park featuring restored 1906 carousel, arcade, games, rides, water slide; concessions. (Late June-Labor Day, daily; Memorial Day-late June, wkends) Fee for individual attractions or one-price daily pass. Off ME 5, on beachfront. Phone 207/934-2001. One-price pass ¢¢¢¢¢

The Pier. Extends 475 ft into the harbor; features shops, boutiques, restaurant. (May-Sept, daily)

Motels

★ **CAROLINA.** *1 Roussin St, ¹/2 blk E of Grand Ave (ME 9).* 207/934-4476. 34 kit. units (no ovens), 2 story. No A/C. Late June-early Sept: S, D $115-$150; each addl $8; lower rates May-late June, early Sept-Oct. Closed rest of yr. Crib free. TV; cable. Heated pool. Restaurant 8 am-8 pm. Ck-out 10 am. Some private balconies. On ocean. Cr cds: A, DS, MC, V.

★ ★ **THE EDGEWATER.** *57 W Grand Ave (ME 9).* 207/934-2221; FAX 207/934-3731; res: 800/203-2034. E-mail edgelamb@janelle.com; web www.janelle.com. 35 rms, 2 story, 5 kits. (no ovens). Late June-mid-Aug, Labor Day wkend: S, D $99-$149; each addl $8; under 12 free; lower rates mid-Mar-late June, after Labor Day-mid-Nov. Closed rest of yr. TV; cable. Heated pool. Complimentary coffee in lobby. Restaurant adj 7:30 am-noon, 5-10 pm. Ck-out 11 am. Meeting rm. In-rm modem link. Refrigerators, microwaves. Sun deck. On ocean. Cr cds: A, DS, MC, V.

✔★ **FLAGSHIP.** *54 W Grand Ave (ME 9), 54 W Grand Ave (ME 9).* 207/934-4866; res: 800/486-1681. 27 rms, 24 A/C, 2 story, 8 suites, 1 cottage. July-Labor Day: D $79-$105, suites $89-$110; each addl $8; under 12 free; lower rates mid-May-June, after Labor Day-mid-Oct. Closed rest of yr. Crib free. Pet accepted, some restrictions. TV; cable. Pool. Complimentary coffee in lobby. Restaurant opp 7-11 am, 5-10 pm. Ck-out 11 am. Refrigerators. Balconies. Picnic tables. Opp ocean; beach. Cr cds: A, DS, MC, V.

★ ★ **FRIENDSHIP MOTOR INN.** *167 E Grand Ave (ME 9). 207/934-4644; FAX 207/934-7592; res: 800/969-7100.* 71 suites (2-rm), 6 kit. units, some A/C, 2 story. Mid-June-Labor Day: S, D $95-$135; each addl $8; lower rates Apr-mid-June, after Labor Day-Nov. Closed rest of yr. Crib free. TV; cable (premium), VCR avail. Heated pool. Complimentary coffee in lobby. Restaurant nearby. Ck-out 10 am. Coin lndry. Sundries. Refrigerators, microwaves. Balconies. On ocean. Cr cds: A, DS, MC, V.

⊅ ⊠ ⊠ 🔥

✔★ **GRAND BEACH INN.** *198 E Grand Ave (ME 9). 207/934-3435; res: 800/926-3242.* E-mail gbi@int.usa.net. 87 units, 2-3 story, 37 kits. No elvtr. July-early Sept: S, D $89-$139; suites, kit. units $149-$179; under 13 free; lower rates rest of yr. Closed rest of yr. Crib $10. Pet accepted, some restrictions. TV; cable. Heated pool. Playground. Restaurant 7-11 am. Ck-out 10 am. Coin lndry. Balconies. Picnic tables, grills. Cr cds: A, DS, MC, V.

🐾 ⊠ ⊠ 🔥

★ **GULL.** *89 W Grand Ave (ME 9). 207/934-4321; FAX 207/934-1742.* 21 kit. units, 2 story, 4 kit. cottages. Late-June-Labor Day: D $75-$115; each addl $10; kit. cottages (2-bedrm) June-Sept $750/wk; lower rates May-late-June, Labor Day-early Oct. Closed rest of yr. Crib $5. TV; cable. Heated pool. Restaurant nearby. Ck-out 10 am. Private patios, balconies. Picnic tables, grills. Cr cds: DS, MC, V.

⊠ ⊠ 🔥 SC

★ ★ **HORIZON.** *2 Atlantic Ave. 207/934-2323; res: 888/550-1745.* 14 kit. suites (2-rm), 3 story. Late June-mid-Aug: D $80-$100; each addl $5; lower rates rest of yr. Closed Nov-Mar. Crib free. TV; cable. Restaurant nearby. Ck-out 10 am. Coin lndry. On ocean. Cr cds: A, MC, V.

🐾 🔥

✔★ **ISLAND VIEW.** *174 E Grand Ave (ME 9). 207/934-4262;* E-mail islandview@int-usa.net; web islandview. rms, 1-3 story. No elvtr. Late June-mid-Aug: D $65-$95; under 12 free; each addl $5; lower rates rest of yr. Crib free. TV; cable, VCR avail (movies). Pool. Complimentary coffee in rms. Restaurant nearby. Ck-out 10 am. Refrigerators. Balconies. Opp beach. Cr cds: A, DS, MC, V.

⊠ 🔥

✔★ **NEPTUNE.** *82 E Grand Ave (04064-2903). 207/934-5753; res: 800/624-6786.* 16 kit. units, A/C in suites, 3 story, 12 suites. July-late Aug: S, D $65; each addl $10; suites $95; under 16 free; wkly rates; lower rates rest of yr. Crib free. TV; cable. Complimentary coffee in lobby. Restaurant nearby. Ck-out 10 am. Balconies. Picnic tables, grills. Cr cds: DS, MC, V.

⊠ 🐾 SC

★ ★ **ROYAL ANCHOR.** *201 E Grand Ave (ME 9). 207/934-4521; FAX 207/934-4521; res: 800/934-4521.* Web www.nettx.com/royal-anchor. 40 rms, 3 story. No A/C. No elvtr. Late June-late Aug: S, D $105-$145; each addl $10-$15; lower rates May-late June & late Aug-mid-Oct. Closed rest of yr. Crib free. TV; cable, VCR avail. Heated pool. Complimentary continental bkfst. Ck-out 10:30 am. Coin lndry. Tennis. Refrigerators, microwaves. Many private patios, balconies. On ocean. Cr cds: A, D, DS, MC, V.

🐾 🏊 ⊠ ⊠ 🔥

★ **SANDPIPER.** *2 Cleaves St, at beachfront, 1/2 blk from Grand Ave (ME 9). 207/934-2733; res: 800/611-9921.* 22 rms, 2 story, 10 kits. Early July-Aug: S, D $85-$115; each addl $5; varied lower rates rest of yr. Crib $5. TV; cable. Complimentary continental bkfst. Restaurant nearby. Ck-out 10 am. Refrigerators. Picnic tables, grills. On beach; sun terrace. Cr cds: A, MC, V.

🔥

★ **SEA CLIFF HOUSE.** *2 Sea Cliff Ave. 207/934-4874; FAX 207/934-1445; res: 800/326-4589.* 35 rms, 2-3 story, 22 kit. suites (2-rm). July-Aug: D $89-$125; each addl $10; lower rates rest of yr. Crib $5. TV; cable, VCR avail. Heated pool. Complimentary coffee in rms. Restaurant

nearby. Ck-out 10 am. Refrigerators. Balconies. On ocean, beach. Cr cds: A, DS, MC, V.

⊠ 🔥

★ **SKYLARK.** *8 Brown St. 207/934-4235.* E-mail skylark@customnet.com. 22 rms, 3 story, 3 kit. suites (2-bedrm), 19 kit. units (no ovens). Mid-July-mid-Aug: S, D, kit. units $104-$120; kit. suites $160-$180; wkly rates late June-late Aug; lower rates Apr-mid-July, mid-Aug-Oct. Closed rest of yr. Crib free. TV; cable (premium). Complimentary coffee in lobby. Restaurant nearby. Ck-out 11 am. Coin lndry. Picnic tables, grill. On ocean. Cr cds: A, DS, MC, V.

🔥

Inn

✔★ ★ **ATLANTIC BIRCHES.** *20 Portland Ave. 207/934-5295; res: 888/934-5295; FAX 207/934-3781.* E-mail cbolduc@gwi.net; web www.mnetwork.com/atlanticbirches. 10 rms, 3 A/C, 2 kit. units (no oven), 2-3 story. No rm phones. Early July-Labor Day: S, D $75-$95; each addl $10; family rates; lower rates rest of yr. Crib free. TV in sitting rm; cable, VCR avail (movies free). Pool. Playground. Complimentary continental bkfst. Restaurant nearby. Ck-out 11 am, ck-in 2 pm. Picnic tables, grills. Restored Victorian house. Swimming beach nearby. Totally nonsmoking. Cr cds: A, D, DS, MC, V.

⊠ ⊠ 🔥

Orono (E-4)

Settled 1774 **Pop** 10,573 **Elev** 80 ft **Area code** 207 **Zip** 04473 **E-mail** chamber@bangorregion.com **Web** www.bangorregion.com

Information Bangor Region Chamber of Commerce, 519 Main St, PO Box 1443, Bangor 04401; 207/947-0307.

The Penobscot River flows through this valley town, which was named for a Native American chief called Joseph Orono (OR-a-no). The "Maine Stein Song" was popularized here in the 1930s by Rudy Vallee.

What to See and Do

University of Maine-Orono. (1865). (11,500 students) This is the largest of 7 campuses of the University of Maine system. On campus is Jordan Planetarium (shows; phone 207/581-1341), Hutchins Concert Hall, ornamental and botanical gardens and the largest library in the state. Main St & College Ave. Phone 207/581-1110. Also on campus is

Hudson Museum. Exhibits relating to history and anthropology. (Daily exc Mon) At Maine Center for the Arts. Phone 207/581-1901. **Free.**

Motels

★ ★ **BEST WESTERN BLACK BEAR INN.** *4 Godfrey Dr, I-95 exit 51. 207/866-7120; FAX 207/866-7433.* 68 rms, 3 story. July-Oct: S $75; D $80; each addl $5; suites $109-$119; under 12 free; lower rates rest of yr. Pet accepted. TV; cable (premium), VCR avail. Complimentary continental bkfst. Complimentary coffee in rms. Restaurant 5-8 pm; closed Sun. Ck-out 11 am. Meeting rms. Business center. Exercise equipt; sauna. Microwaves avail. Cr cds: A, C, D, DS, MC, V.

⊅ 🐾 ✈ ⊠ 🔥 SC 🚶

✔★ **MILFORD MOTEL ON THE RIVER.** *(154 Main St (US 2), Milford 04461) US 95 exit 51, US 2A to US 2. 207/827-3200; res: 800/282-3330.* E-mail milford@mint.net; web www.mint.net/milford.motel. 22 rms, 2 with shower only, 2 story, 8 suites. Mid-June-Aug: S $49; D $59-$69; suites $84; under 18 free; wkly rates; lower rates rest of yr. Crib free. Pet accepted. TV; cable (premium). Complimentary coffee in rms. Restaurant nearby. Ck-out 10 am. Coin lndry. Refrigerators. Some balconies. Picnic tables. On river. Cr cds: A, DS, MC, V.

✔★ ★ **UNIVERSITY MOTOR INN.** *5 College Ave. 207/866-4921; FAX 207/866-4550; res: 800/321-4921.* 48 rms, 2 story. June-Sept: S $48; D $58; each addl $4-$6; under 13 free; higher rates: Univ ME graduation, homecoming; lower rates rest of yr. Crib free. Pet accepted. TV; cable. Pool. Complimentary continental bkfst. Ck-out 11 am. Private patios, balconies. Cr cds: A, C, D, DS, MC, V.

Restaurant

✔★ ★ **MARGARITA'S.** *15 Mill St. 207/866-4863.* Mexican menu. Hrs: 4-10 pm; Fri-Sun noon-10:30 pm. Bar to 12:30 am. A la carte entrees: dinner $3.25-$12.95. Child's meals. Cr cds: A, DS, MC, V.

Poland Spring (G-2)

(See also Auburn, Bridgton, Norway, Sebago Lake)

Settled 1768 **Pop** 200 (est) **Elev** 500 ft **Area code** 207 **Zip** 04274

The Poland Spring Inn, once New England's largest private resort (5,000 acres), stands on a rise near the mineral spring that has made it famous since 1844. Actually, the hotel had even earlier beginnings with the Mansion House built in 1794 by the Ricker brothers. In 1974 the original inn burned and was replaced by a smaller hotel.

What to See and Do

Shaker Museum. Shaker furniture, folk and decorative arts, textiles, tin and woodenware; early American tools and farm implements displayed. Guided tours of buildings in this last active Shaker community include Meetinghouse (1794), Ministry Shop (1839), Boys' Shop (1850), Sisters' Shop (1821) and Spin House (1816). Workshops, demonstrations, concerts and other special events. Extensive research library (Tues-Thurs, by appt only). (Memorial Day-Columbus Day, daily exc Sun) 1 mi S on ME 26. Phone 207/926-4597. Tour ¢¢

Portland (H-2)

(See also Old Orchard Beach, Scarborough, Yarmouth)

Settled 1632 **Pop** 64,358 **Elev** 50 ft **Area code** 207 **Web** www.visitportland.com
Information Convention & Visitors Bureau of Greater Portland, 305 Commercial St, 04101; 207/772-5800.

Maine's largest city is on beautiful Casco Bay, dotted with islands popular with summer visitors. Not far from the North Atlantic fishing waters, it leads Maine in this industry. Shipping is also important. It is a city of fine elms, stately old homes, historic churches and charming streets.

Portland was raided by Native Americans several times before the Revolution. In 1775 it was bombarded by the British, who afterward burned the town. Another fire, in 1866, wiped out large sections of the city. Longfellow remarked that the ruins reminded him of Pompeii.

What to See and Do

Boat trips. Cruises along Casco Bay, some with stops at individual islands or other locations; special charters also avail. Most cruises (May-Oct). For further information, rates, schedules or fees contact the individual companies.

Bay View Cruises. Fisherman's Wharf, 184 Commercial St, 04101; phone 207/761-0496.

Casco Bay Lines. PO Box 4656 DTS, 04112; phone 207/774-7871.

Eagle Tours Inc. 19 Pilot Point Rd, Cape Elizabeth 04107; phone 207/774-6498.

Olde Port Mariner Fleet, Inc. PO Box 1084, 04104; phone 207/775-0727.

Palawan Sailing. PO Box 9715-240, 04104; phone 207/773-2163.

M/S *Scotia Prince.* A 1,500-passenger cruise ferry leaves nightly for 11-hr crossing to Yarmouth, Nova Scotia. (May-Oct) Staterooms avail. Phone 207/775-5616, 800/341-7540 or 800/482-0955 (ME). ¢¢¢¢¢

Children's Museum of Maine. Hands-on museum where interactive exhibits allow children to become a Maine lobsterman, storekeeper, computer expert or astronaut. (Daily) 142 Free St. Phone 207/828-1234. ¢

Maine Historical Society. Research library for Maine history and genealogy. (Tues-Fri, 2nd & 4th Sat of each month; closed hols) Phone 207/774-1822. ¢¢

Old Port Exchange. A charming collection of shops and restaurants located in 19th-century, brick buildings built after the fire of 1866. Between Exchange & Pearl Sts, extending 5 blks from waterfront to Congress St.

Portland Museum of Art. Collections of American and European painting, sculpture, prints and decorative art; State of Maine Collection with works by artists from and associated with Maine; John Whitney Payson Collection (Renoir, Monet, Picasso and others). Free admission Sat mornings. (Apr-Oct, Tues-Sun; Nov-Mar, Wed-Sun; closed hols) 7 Congress Square. Phone 207/775-6148or 207/773-ARTS (recording). ¢¢

Southworth Planetarium. Astronomy programs, laser light concerts, children's shows. (Fri & Sat; addl shows summer months) 96 Falmouth St. For schedule phone 207/780-4249. ¢¢¢

State parks.

Two Lights. Approx 40 acres along Atlantic Ocean. Fishing. Picnicking. (Mid-Apr-Nov) Standard fees. 9 mi SE off ME 77 in Cape Elizabeth. Phone 207/799-5871.

Crescent Beach. Swimming, sand beach, bathhouse; fishing. Picnicking, playground, concession. (Memorial Day-Sept) Standard fees. 10 mi SE on ME 77 in Cape Elizabeth. Phone 207/799-5871 (seasonal).

Tate House (1755). Georgian structure built by George Tate, mast agent for the British Navy. Furnished and decorated in the period of Tate's residence, 1755-1800; 18th-century herb gardens. (July-mid-Sept, daily exc Mon; mid-May-June & mid-Sept-mid-Oct, by appt only; closed July 4, Labor Day) 1270 Westbrook St. Phone 207/774-9781. ¢¢

The Museum at Portland Headlight (1791). Said to be first lighthouse authorized by the US and oldest lighthouse in continuous use; erected on orders from George Washington. (June-Oct, daily; Nov-Dec & Apr-May, wkends) 1000 Shore Rd, in Ft Williams Park, Cape Elizabeth. Phone 207/799-2661. ¢

University of Southern Maine (1878). (10,500 students) One of the 7 units of the Univ of Maine system. Special shows are held periodically in the univ planetarium and in the art gallery. Also theatrical and musical events. Portland campus, off I-295 exit 6; Gorham campus, jct ME 25 & College Ave. Phone 207/780-4500 (special events) or 207/780-4200.

Victoria Mansion (1858). One of the finest examples of 19th-century architecture surviving in the US. Opulent Victorian interior includes frescoes, carved woodwork and stained and etched glass. (June-Labor Day wkend, Wed-Sun, also Tues afternoons; wkend after Labor Day-Columbus Day, Fri-Sun; closed July 4, Labor Day) 109 Danforth St at Park St. Phone 207/772-4841. ¢¢

Wadsworth-Longfellow House (1785). Boyhood home of Henry Wadsworth Longfellow. Built by the poet's grandfather, General Peleg Wadsworth, it is maintained by the Maine Historical Society. Contains furnishings, portraits and personal possessions of the family. (June-mid-Oct, Tues-Sat; closed July 4, Labor Day) 487 Congress St. Phone 207/772-1807 or 207/774-1822. ¢¢

Annual Events

Old Port Festival. Exchange St. Phone 207/772-6828. Early June.

Sidewalk Art Show. Exhibits extend along Congress St from Congress Sq to Monument Sq. Phone 207/828-6666. 3rd Sat Aug.

New Year's Eve Portland. Fifteen indoor and many outdoor locations. More than 90 performances, mid-afternoon to midnight; a city-wide, nonalcoholic celebration with parade and fireworks. Phone 207/772-9012. Dec 31.

Seasonal Event

Outdoor summer concerts. Deering Oaks Park. Phone 207/874-8793. Tues afternoons-Thurs eves, late June-Aug.

Motels

✔★★ **BEST WESTERN MERRY MANOR INN.** (700 Main St, South Portland 04106) 3 1/2 mi S on US 1, 2 mi off ME Tpke exit 7. 207/774-6151; FAX 207/871-0537. Web www.bestwestern.com/thisco/20015. 151 rms, 1-3 story. No elvtr. June-late Oct: S $109.95; D $119.95; each addl $10; under 12 free; lower rates rest of yr. Crib $3. Pet accepted. TV; cable (premium), VCR avail (movies). Heated pool. Coffee in rms. Restaurant 6 am-10 pm. Ck-out 11 am. Coin lndry. Business servs avail. In-rm modem link. Valet serv. Health club privileges. Some refrigerators; microwaves avail. Cr cds: A, C, D, DS, MC, V.

D 🐾 ≈ 🏂 🔥 SC

★★ **COMFORT INN.** (90 Maine Mall Rd, South Portland 04106) 2 mi S at ME Tpke exit 7, near Intl Jetport. 207/775-0409; res: 800/368-6485; FAX 207/775-1755. 128 rms, 3 story. Mid-June-Oct: S, D $119-$149.95; each addl $5; under 19 free; lower rates rest of yr. Crib free. TV; cable (premium). Heated pool. Complimentary continental bkfst. Coffee in rms. Restaurant nearby. Ck-out 11 am. Coin lndry. Business servs avail. In-rm modem link. Valet serv. Free airport transportation. Health club privileges. Some refrigerators. Cr cds: A, D, DS, MC, V.

D ≈ ✈ 🏂 🔥 SC

★★ **HAMPTON INN.** (171 Philbrook Ave, South Portland 04106) S on I-295 exit 1 to Maine Mall Rd, then right to Philbrook Ave, near Intl Jetport. 207/773-4400; FAX 207/773-6786. E-mail hinn0886@aol.com; web maineguide.com/portland/hampton/. 118 rms, 4 story. Mid-June-late Oct: S $99; D $109; under 19 free; wkly rates; lower rates rest of yr. Crib free. TV; cable (premium). Complimentary continental bkfst. Restaurant nearby. Ck-out noon. Business servs avail. Sundries. Free airport transportation. Refrigerators, microwaves avail. Maine Mall opp. Cr cds: A, C, D, DS, MC, V.

D ✈ 🏂 🔥 SC

★★★ **HOLIDAY INN BY THE BAY.** 88 Spring St (04101). 207/775-2311; FAX 207/761-8224; res: 800/345-5050. E-mail sales@innbythebay.com; web www.innbythebay.com. 239 rms, 12-14 story. Mid-June-Oct: S $132-$147; D $142-$170; each addl $10; under 20 free; lower rates rest of yr. Crib free. TV; cable (premium). Indoor pool; poolside serv. Complimentary coffee in rms. Restaurant 6:30 am-2:30 pm, 5:30-10 pm. Rm serv. Bar 11-1 am; entertainment Fri, Sat. Ck-out noon. Coin lndry. Meeting rms. Business servs avail. In-rm modem link. Bellhops. Valet serv. Gift shop. Free garage parking. Free airport transportation. Tennis privileges. Golf privileges. Exercise equipt; sauna. Some rms overlook harbor. Cr cds: A, C, D, DS, JCB, MC, V.

D 🏋 🎾 ≈ ✈ 🏂 🔥 SC

★★★ **HOLIDAY INN WEST.** 81 Riverside St (04103-1098), I-95 exit 8. 207/774-5601; FAX 207/774-2103. Web www.portlandholiday-inn.com. 200 rms, 2 story. July-Oct: S, D $108-$129; under 20 free; lower rates rest of yr. Crib free. TV; cable (premium). Heated pool; whirlpool, poolside serv. Complimentary coffee in rms. Restaurant 6 am-2 pm, 5-10 pm. Rm serv. Bar 11:30-1 am; Sun from noon. Ck-out noon. Coin lndry. Meeting rms. Business servs avail. In-rm modem link. Bellhops. Sundries.

Free airport transportation. Exercise equipt; sauna. Refrigerators avail. Picnic tables. Cr cds: A, D, DS, JCB, MC, V.

D ≈ ✈ 🏂 🔥 SC

★★ **HOWARD JOHNSON.** 155 Riverside St (04103), ME Tpke exit 8. 207/774-5861; FAX 207/774-5861. 119 rms, 3 story. July-mid-Oct: S, D $95-$120; each addl $10; under 18 free; lower rates rest of yr. Crib free. Pet accepted; $50 deposit. TV; cable (premium). Indoor pool; whirlpool. Coffee in rms. Restaurant 7 am-10 pm. Rm serv. Bar noon-1 am; entertainment Fri, Sat. Ck-out noon. Coin lndry. Meeting rms. Business servs avail. Bellhops. Valet serv. Sundries. Free airport transportation. Exercise equipt. Some in-rm whirlpools, microwaves. Some private patios, balconies. Cr cds: A, C, D, DS, ER, JCB, MC, V.

D 🐾 ≈ ✈ 🏂 🔥 SC

✔★ **SUSSE CHALET.** 1200 Brighton Ave (04102). 207/774-6101; FAX 207/772-8697. 132 rms, 2 story. July-Oct: S $59.70; D $69.70-$79.70; under 19 free; lower rates rest of yr. Crib free. TV; cable (premium). Pool. Complimentary continental bkfst. Restaurant adj open 24 hrs. Ck-out 11 am. In-rm modem link. Cr cds: A, C, D, DS, MC, V.

D ≈ 🏂 🔥 SC

Motor Hotels

★★★ **INN BY THE SEA.** (40 Bowery Beach Rd, Cape Elizabeth 04107) 6 mi SE on ME 77. 207/799-3134; FAX 207/799-4779; res: 800/888-4287. E-mail innmaine@aol.com; web www.innbythesea.com. 43 kit. suites, 3 story. No A/C. July-Aug: S, D $180-$420; package plans off-season; lower rates rest of yr. Pet accepted. TV; cable (premium), VCR (movies). Heated pool; poolside serv. Coffee in rms. Restaurant 7:30 am-9:30 pm. Rm serv. Ck-out noon. Meeting rms. Business servs avail. In-rm modem link. Bellhops. Concierge. Lighted tennis. Lawn games. Bicycles. Health club privileges. Bathrm phones. Balconies, decks. Picnic tables. On ocean; access to swimming beach. Totally nonsmoking. Cr cds: A, DS, MC, V.

D 🐾 🎾 ≈ 🎣 ✈ 🏂 🔥 SC

★★★ **MARRIOTT AT SABLE OAKS.** (200 Sable Oaks Dr, South Portland 04106) 4 mi S on I-295 exit 1, W to Maine Mall Rd, N to Running Hill Rd, then W. 207/871-8000; FAX 207/871-7971. 227 rms, 6 story. Late May-early Nov: S, D $129-$159; suites $125-$300; lower rates rest of yr. Crib free. Pet accepted, some restrictions. TV; cable (premium), VCR avail. Indoor pool; whirlpool, poolside serv. Complimentary coffee in rms. Restaurant 6:30 am-11 pm. Rm serv. Bar noon-1 am. Ck-out noon. Meeting rms. Business servs avail. In-rm modem link. Bellhops. Valet serv. Gift shop. Exercise equipt; sauna. Cr cds: A, C, D, DS, ER, JCB, MC, V.

D 🐾 ≈ 🏋 🏂 🔥 SC

Hotels

★★★ **EMBASSY SUITES.** 1050 Westbrook St (04102), opp Intl Jetport. 207/775-2200; res: 800/753-8767; FAX 207/775-4052. E-mail embassy@embassysuitesportland.com; web www.embassysuitesportland.com. 119 suites, 6 story. June-Oct: suites $159-$299; each addl $10; under 18 free; off-season packages; lower rates rest of yr. Crib free. TV; cable (premium), VCR (movies $8). Indoor pool. Complimentary full bkfst. Coffee in rms. Restaurant 6:30 am-9:30 pm. Bar noon-11 pm. Ck-out noon. Coin lndry. Meeting rms. Business servs avail. In-rm modem link. Free airport transportation. Tennis privileges. Exercise equipt; sauna. Refrigerators, microwaves. Cr cds: A, C, D, DS, ER, JCB, MC, V.

D 🎾 ≈ ✈ 🏂 🔥

★★★ **PORTLAND REGENCY.** 20 Milk St (04101), in Old Port Exchange area. 207/774-4200; FAX 207/775-2150; res: 800/727-3436. Web www.theregency.com. 95 rms, 4 story, 10 suites. Early July-late Oct: S, D $169-$199; each addl $10; suites $209-$249; wkend rates off-season; lower rates rest of yr. Crib free. Valet parking $5. TV; cable (premium), VCR avail. Complimentary coffee in rms. Restaurant 6:30 am-9:30 pm; Sat, Sun from 7 am. Bar 11:30 am-midnight. Ck-out noon. Meeting rms. Business servs avail. In-rm modem link. Concierge. Free airport transportation. Exercise rm; sauna. Massage. Whirlpool. Bathrm phones, minibars. Small, European-style hotel in refurbished, brick armory building (1895). Cr cds: A, C, D, DS, MC, V.

⊡🏋️🏊🎿🔥🛶

★ ★ **RADISSON EASTLAND.** *157 High St (04101). 207/775-5411; FAX 207/775-2872.* Web www.radisson.com. 204 rms, 12 story. June-Oct: S, D $119-$139; each addl $15; suites $275-$350; under 18 free; lower rates rest of yr. Crib free. Garage parking, fee. TV; VCR, cable (premium). Complimentary coffee in rms. Restaurant 6:30 am-2 pm, 5:30-9 pm; Fri, Sat to 10 pm. Bar 5 pm-1 am; entertainment wkends. Ck-out noon. Meeting rms. Business center. Concierge. Gift shop. Free airport transportation. Exercise equipt; sauna. Refrigerator avail. Cr cds: A, C, D, DS, ER, MC, V.

⊡🏋️🎿🔥SC🎿

★ ★ **SHERATON TARA.** *(363 Maine Mall Rd, South Portland 04106) 4 mi S at ME Tpke exit 7, near Intl Jetport. 207/775-6161; FAX 207/775-0196.* Web www.ittsheraton.com. 220 rms, 7-9 story. Late June-Oct: S, D $139-$203; each addl $10; under 18 free; lower rates rest of yr. Crib free. TV; cable (premium). Indoor pool. Complimentary coffee in rms. Restaurant 6:30 am-11 am, 11:30 am-midnight. Ck-out noon. Meeting rms. Business servs avail. In-rm modem link. Free airport transportation. Exercise rm; sauna. Refrigerators, microwaves avail. Cr cds: A, C, D, DS, ER, MC, V.

⊡🏊🏋️🎿🔥SC

Inns

★ ★ **INN AT ST JOHN.** *939 Congress St (04102), near Intl Airport. 207/773-6481; res: 800/636-9127; FAX 207/756-7629.* Web www.innatstjohn.com. 32 rms, 16 share bath, 4 with shower only, 4 story. Some A/C. No elvtr. July-Oct: S, D $49-$134; each addl $6; under 13 free; lower rates rest of yr. Crib free. Pet accepted. TV; cable (premium). Complimentary continental bkfst. Complimentary coffee in rms. Restaurant nearby. Ck-out 11 am, ck-in varies. Business servs avail. Coin lndry. Free airport, bus depot transportation. Refrigerators, microwaves avail. Built in 1896; European motif, antiques. Cr cds: A, C, D, DS, MC, V.

🐾🎿🔥

★ ★ **INN ON CARLETON.** *46 Carleton St (04102). 207/775-1910; FAX 207/761-0956; res: 800/639-1779.* Web www.innoncarleton.com. 7 rms, 3 share bath, 2 with shower only, 3 story, 1 suite. No rm phones. June-Oct: S $65; D $115-$155; each addl $15; suite $225; hols (2-day min); lower rates rest of yr. Children over 8 yrs only. Complimentary full bkfst. Restaurant nearby. Ck-out 11 am, ck-in 4-6:30 pm. Business servs avail. Brick townhouse built 1869; Victorian antiques. Totally nonsmoking. Cr cds: DS, MC, V.

🎿🔥

★ ★ **POMEGRANATE.** *49 Neal St (04102). 207/772-1006; FAX 207/773-4426; res: 800/356-0408.* Web www.innbook.com/pome.html. 8 rms, 4 with shower only, 3 story. Memorial Day-Oct: S, D $135-$175; wkends, hols (2-day min); lower rates rest of yr. Children over 16 yrs only. TV; cable. Complimentary full bkfst. Ck-out 11 am, ck-in 4-6 pm. Street parking. Some in-rm fireplaces. Colonial-revival house built 1884; antiques, art collection. Totally nonsmoking. Cr cds: A, DS, MC, V.

⊡🎿🔥

Resort

★ ★ ★ **BLACK POINT INN.** *(510 Black Point Rd, Prouts Neck 04074) 4 mi S on US 1, then 4 mi SE on ME 207. 207/883-2500; FAX 207/883-9976; res: 800/258-0003.* E-mail bpi@nlis.net; web www.black-pointinn.com. 65 rms in inn, 25 units in 4 cottages. MAP, July-Aug: S $220-$260; D $300-$450; each addl $75; suites $400-$450; lower rates May-mid-June, late Oct-Nov. Closed rest of yr. Children over 8 yrs only mid-July-mid-Aug. Serv charge 15%. Crib free. TV; cable (premium), VCR avail (movies). 2 pools, 1 indoor, 1 heated; whirlpools, poolside serv, lifeguard in season. Dining rm (public by res) 8-11 am, noon-5 pm, 6-9 pm.

Rm serv. Bar noon-1 am. Ck-out noon, ck-in 3 pm. Meeting rms. Business servs avail. In-rm modem link. Bellhops. Valet serv. Concierge. Gift shop. Barber, beauty shop. Airport transportation. Tennis privileges. 18-hole golf privileges. Bicycles. Exercise rm; sauna. Massage. Lawn games. Many bathrm phones; some balconies. Private beach. 1878 inn; antiques. Secluded grounds on ocean; rose garden. Cr cds: A, DS, MC, V.

⊡🛥️⛷️🎾🏊🏋️🎿🔥

Restaurants

★ ★ ★ **BACK BAY GRILL.** *65 Portland St (04101). 207/772-8833.* E-mail joel@backbaygrill.com; web www.backbaygrill.com. Specializes in fresh seafood, grilled dishes, creme brulee. Own baking. Hrs: 5:30-9:30 pm; Fri, Sat to 10 pm. Closed Sun; some major hols. Res accepted. Serv bar. Wine cellar. Semi-a la carte: dinner $14.95-$24.95. In restored pharmacy (1888). Totally nonsmoking. Cr cds: A, C, D, DS, MC, V.

⊡

★ ★ **BOONE'S.** *6 Custom House Wharf (04112), off Commercial St. 207/774-5725.* Specializes in shore dinners, seafood, steak. Hrs: 11 am-9 pm. Closed Thanksgiving, Dec 25. Bar. Semi-a la carte: lunch $4.50-$8.95, dinner $9.95-$19.95. Child's meals. Parking. Outdoor dining. Fishing port atmosphere; built on wharf. Established in 1898. Cr cds: A, C, D, DS, MC, V.

★ ★ **DI MILLO'S FLOATING RESTAURANT.** *25 Long Wharf (04101). 207/772-2216.* Web www.dimillo.com. Specializes in seafood, steak, lobster. Hrs: 11 am-11 pm. Closed Thanksgiving, Dec 25. Bar to 1 am. Semi-a la carte: lunch $3.75-$11.95, dinner $9.95-$24.95. Child's meals. Parking. Outdoor dining. Nautical decor; located on waterfront in a converted ferry boat. Family-owned. Cr cds: A, C, D, DS, MC, V.

⊡🛶

✔ ★ ★ **F. PARKER REIDY'S.** *83 Exchange St (04101), in Old Port Exchange area. 207/773-4731.* Specializes in fresh fish, seafood, steak. Hrs: 11:30 am-11 pm; Fri, Sat to 12:30 am; Sun 4:30-11 pm. Closed July 4, Thanksgiving, Dec 25. Res accepted. Bar. Semi-a la carte: lunch $3-$9, dinner $7.95-$16. Child's meals. Originally Portland Savings Bank (1866). Cr cds: A, D, DS, MC, V.

🛶

✔ ★ ★ **FORE STREET.** *288 Fore St (04101). 207/775-2717.* Specialties: spit-roasted pork, applewood-grilled steaks, wood-baked seafood. Own desserts. Hrs: 5:30-10 pm; Fri, Sat to 10:30 pm; Sun to 9:30 pm. Closed some major hols. Res accepted. Bar to midnight. Wine list. Semi-a la carte: dinner $10.95-$21.95. Child's meals. Converted 1930s oil tank garage; unique decor with copper and steel tables, poured-concrete bar; view of harbor and ferry terminal. Totally nonsmoking. Cr cds: A, MC, V.

⊡

★ **NEWICK'S SEAFOOD.** *(740 Broadway, South Portland 04106) S on US 295 to exit 3, then S to Broadway. 207/799-3090.* Web www.newicks.com. Specializes in seafood fresh. Hrs: 11:30 am-8 pm; Fri, Sat to 9 pm. Closed Mon; Thanksgiving, Dec 25. Bar. Semi-a la carte: lunch, dinner $5.25-$19.95. Child's meals. Parking. Seafood market on premises. Casual dining. Cr cds: A, DS, MC, V.

⊡🛶

✔ ★ ★ **RIBOLLITA.** *41 Middle St (04101). 207/774-2972.* Northern Italian & Tuscan menu. Specialty: risotto. Hrs: from 5 pm. Closed Sun; also most major hols. Res accepted. Semi-a la carte: dinner $9.50-$16.50. Child's meals. Street parking. Outdoor dining. Totally nonsmoking. Cr cds: MC, V.

★ ★ ★ **THE ROMA.** *769 Congress St (04102). 207/773-9873.* Continental menu. Specializes in lobster, fresh seafood, Northern Italian dishes. Own desserts. Hrs: 11:30 am-2 pm, 5-9 pm; Sat from 5 pm; Sun 5-8 pm. Closed Memorial Day, Labor Day, Dec 25; also Sun Dec-May. Res accepted. Bar to 1 am. Semi-a la carte: lunch $4.95-$9.95, dinner $9.95-

$16.95. Child's meals. Parking. Fireplaces. Victorian mansion (ca 1885). Cr cds: A, DS, MC, V.

★ ★ **SEA DOG BREWING COMPANY.** *(215 Foreside Rd, Falmouth 04105)* N on ME Tpke exit 9 in Falmouth Foreside, off ME 88. 207/781-0988. Web www.seadogbrewing.com. Specializes in seafood, lobster. Hrs: 11:30 am-2 pm, 5-9 pm; Fri, Sat 11:30 am-3 pm, 5-9:30 pm. Closed Dec 25. Res accepted. Bar. Semi-a la carte: lunch, dinner $6.95-$19.95. Parking. Outdoor dining. On pier at waterfront; dockage. Cr cds: A, DS, MC, V.

✔★ ★ **SEAMEN'S CLUB.** 375 Fore St (04112), in Old Port Exchange area. 207/774-7777. Specializes in fresh chowder, seafood, baked Indian pudding. Own desserts. Hrs: 11 am-10 pm; Sat, Sun brunch all day. Closed Dec 25. Res accepted. Bar to 1 am. Semi-a la carte: lunch $3.95-$12.95, dinner $5.95-$18.95. Sat, Sun brunch $2.95-$7.95. Child's meals. Entertainment Fri, Sat. Gothic-style building (1866); overlooking harbor. Cr cds: C, D, DS, MC, V.

✔★ ★ **STREET & CO.** 33 Wharf St (04101). 207/775-0887. Mediterranean seafood menu. Specialties: lobster diavolo, scallops in pernod & cream, shrimp over linguini with tomato caper sauce. Hrs: 5:30-9:30 pm; Fri, Sat to 10 pm. Closed Jan 1, Dec 24, 25. Res accepted. Bar. Semi-a la carte: dinner $12.95-$19.95. Street parking. Outdoor dining. 19th century commercial bldg with original floor woodwork. Open kitchen. Cr cds: A, MC, V.

★ ★ **VALLE'S STEAK HOUSE.** 1140 Brighton Ave (04102), at ME Tpke exit 8. 207/774-4551. Specializes in seafood, steak. Hrs: 11 am-10 pm; Fri, Sat to 11 pm. Res accepted. Bar to midnight; Fri, Sat to 1 am. Semi-a la carte: lunch $3.95-$7.95, dinner $7.95-$14.95. Child's meals. Entertainment Fri, Sat. Parking. Family-owned. Cr cds: A, DS, MC, V.

✔★ ★ **VILLAGE CAFE.** 112 Newbury St (04101), near Old Port Exchange area. 207/772-5320. Italian, Amer menu. Specializes in fried clams, lobster, veal, steak. Hrs: 11 am-10 pm; Fri, Sat to 11 pm; Sun 11:30 am-9:30 pm. Closed Thanksgiving, Dec 25. Bar. Semi-a la carte: lunch $4.25-$8.75, dinner $6.75-$24.95. Child's meals. Parking. Family-owned. Cr cds: A, DS, MC, V.

✔★ ★ **WALTER'S CAFE.** 15 Exchange St (04101). 207/871-9258. Web www.walterscafe.com. Contemporary Amer menu. Specialties: lobster with angel hair pasta, crazy chicken. Own baking. Hrs: 11 am-3 pm, 5-9 pm; Sun from 5 pm. Closed Jan 1, Dec 25; also 1st Sat in May. Bar. Semi-a la carte: lunch $6.95-$12.95, dinner $11.95-$17.95. Street parking. Mid-1800s commercial bldg with much original interior; three dining areas on two levels. Totally nonsmoking. Cr cds: A, MC, V.

Presque Isle (B-5)

(See also Caribou)

Settled 1820 **Pop** 10,550 **Elev** 446 ft **Area code** 207 **Zip** 04769 **E-mail** piacc@agate.net **Web** www.mainerec.com/pimaine.html

Information Presque Isle Area Chamber of Commerce, PO Box 672; 207/764-6561 or 800/764-7420.

Commercial and industrial center of Aroostook County, this city is famous for its potatoes. A deactivated air base nearby is now a vocational school and industrial park.

What to See and Do

Aroostook Farm—Maine Agricultural Experiment Station. Approx 375 acres operated by Univ of Maine; experiments to improve growing and marketing of potatoes and grain. (Mon-Fri; closed hols) Houlton Rd, 2 mi S on US 1. Phone 207/762-8281. **Free.**

Aroostook State Park. 577 acres. Swimming, bathhouse; fishing; boating (rentals, ramp on Echo Lake). Hiking. Cross-country trails. Picnicking. Camping. (Mid-May-mid-Oct, daily) Snowmobiling permitted. Standard fees. 4 mi S on US 1, then W. Phone 207/768-8341.

Double Eagle II Launch Site Monument. Double Eagle II, the first balloon to travel across the Atlantic Ocean, was launched from this site in 1978. Spragueville Rd, 4 mi S on US 1, then W. **Free.**

University of Maine at Presque Isle (1903). (1,500 students) During the summer there is the Pioneer Playhouse and an Elderhostel program. In winter, the business bkfst program, theater productions and a number of other cultural and educational events are open to the public. US 1. Phone 207/768-9400.

Annual Events

Spudland Open Amateur Golf Tournament. Presque Isle Country Club. Mid-July.

Northern Maine Fair. Midway, harness racing, entertainment. 1st full wk Aug.

Motels

✔★ **BUDGET TRAVELER.** 71 Main St, on Houlton Rd. 207/769-0111; FAX 207/764-6836; res: 800/958-0111. E-mail budgeth@bangornews.infi.net. 53 rms, 6 kit, 2 story. S $29.95; D $35.95-$49.95; each addl $5; under 12 free. Crib $6. TV; cable, VCR avail (movies). Complimentary continental bkfst. Restaurant nearby. Ck-out 11 am. Coin lndry. Business servs avail. Free airport transportation. Refrigerators; microwaves avail. Cr cds: A, C, D, DS, MC, V.

★ **NORTHERN LIGHTS.** 72 Houlton Rd. 207/764-4441. 14 rms. S $26.95; D $39.95; each addl $5; under 12 free. Crib $5. Pet accepted; $10. TV; cable. Morning coffee. Ck-out 11 am. Cr cds: A, DS, MC, V.

Rangeley (E-1)

Settled 1825 **Pop** 1,063 **Elev** 1,545 ft **Area code** 207 **Zip** 04970 **E-mail** mtlakes@rangeley.org **Web** www.rangeleymaine.com

Information Chamber of Commerce, PO Box 317; 207/864-5364 or 800/MT-LAKES (reservations).

Within 10 miles of Rangeley there are 40 lakes and ponds. The six lakes that form the Rangeley chain—Rangeley, Cupsuptic, Mooselookmeguntic, Aziscoos, Upper Richardson and Lower Richardson—spread over a wide area and give rise to the Androscoggin River. Some of Maine's highest mountains rise beside the lakes. The development of ski and snowmobiling areas has turned this summer vacation spot into a year-round resort.

What to See and Do

Camping. Several designated public camp and picnic sites; wilderness sites on islands.

Fishing. Boats for rent; licensed guides. The lakes are stocked with square-tailed trout and landlocked salmon.

Rangeley Lake State Park. More than 690 acres on Rangeley Lake. Swimming, fishing, boating (ramp, floating docks). Snowmobiling permitted. Picnicking. Camping (dump station). (May-Oct) Standard fees. 4 mi S on ME 4, then 5 mi W via local road. Phone 207/864-3858.

Saddleback Ski & Summer Lake Preserve. Two double chairlifts, 3 T-bars; rentals, school, patrol; snowmaking; cafeteria, bar; nursery, lodge. Longest run 2.5 mi; vertical drop 1,830 ft. (Late Nov-mid-Apr, daily) Cross-country trails. 7 mi E off ME 4. Phone 207/864-5671 or 207/864-3380 (snow conditions). ¢¢¢¢

Swimming, boating. Several public beaches and docks on lakefront. Rangeley Lakeside Park on lakeshore has public swimming, picnicking areas.

Wilhelm Reich Museum. Unusual stone building housing scientific equipment, paintings and other memorabilia of this physician-scientist; slide presentation, nature trail, discovery rm. (July-Aug, daily exc Mon; Sept, Sun only) Dodge Pond Rd, 4 mi W off ME 4. Phone 207/864-3443. ¢¢

Annual Events

Sled Dog Race. Teams from eastern US and Canada compete in 20-mi race. Phone 207/864-5364. 1st wkend Mar.

Logging Museum Field Days. Logging competitions, Miss Woodchip contest, parade, logging demonstrations. Phone 207/864-5595. Last wkend July.

Lodge

★ ★ **COUNTRY CLUB INN.** *Country Club Dr, 2¹/₂ mi N, off ME 4/16.* 207/864-3831. E-mail ccinn@tdstelme.net; web www.rangeley-maine/ccinn. 10 rms in 2 story inn; 9 rms in motel. No A/C. Late May-mid-Oct, late Dec-Mar, MAP: S $114; D $72-$77/person; golf plans; EP avail. Closed Apr, Nov. Serv charge 15%. Crib $5. TV in lobby. Pool. Dining rm 7:30-9 am, 6:30-8 pm. Box lunches. Bar. Ck-out 10:30 am, ck-in 1 pm. Grocery, coin lndry 2¹/₂ mi. Free airport transportation. Boat; waterskiing 1¹/₂ mi. Downhill/x-country ski 7 mi. Lawn games. Scenic view of mountains, lake. Cr cds: A, DS, MC, V.

Inn

★ ★ ★ **RANGELEY.** *51 Main St (Rt 4).* 207/864-3341; FAX 207/864-3634; res: 800/666-3687. E-mail rangeinn@rangeley.org; web www.rangeleyinn.com. 50 units, 15 motel rms, 3 kits. No A/C. July-mid-Oct, hol wks, winter wkends: S, D $69-$119; each addl $6; kit. units for 2-6, $89-$109; lower rates rest of yr. Crib $6. TV; cable in motel rms, sitting rm, VCR in sitting rm (movies). Restaurant (see RANGELEY INN). Bar 4 pm-1 am; entertainment wkends. Ck-out 11 am. Meeting rms. Downhill/x-country ski 7 mi. Snowmobile trail. Some in-rm whirlpools, fireplaces. On pond. Cr cds: A, DS, MC, V.

Restaurants

✔★ **PEOPLE'S CHOICE.** *Main St (ME 4), 1 mi N on ME 4/16.* 207/864-5220. Specializes in fresh seafood. Own baking. Salad bar. Hrs: 6 am-9 pm. Closed Thanksgiving, Dec 25. Res accepted. Bar 11 am-midnight. Semi-a la carte: bkfst $2-$7, lunch $3-$9, dinner $7-$15. Child's meals. Entertainment wkends. Chainsaw-carved lumberjack on display. Cr cds: A, DS, MC, V.

★ ★ **RANGELEY INN.** *(See Rangeley Inn)* 207/864-3341. E-mail rangeinn@rangeley.org; web www.rangeleyinn.com. Continental menu. Specializes in fresh seafood, rack of lamb, filet mignon. Own baking. Hrs: 7:30-10 am, 6-9 pm. Closed Dec 25; also Apr-May. Res accepted. Bar. Wine list. Semi-a la carte: bkfst $3-$7, dinner $12.95-$28.95. Child's meals. Elegant decor; oak woodwork, brass chandeliers, tin ceiling. Outdoor dining. Totally nonsmoking. Cr cds: A, DS, MC, V.

Rockland (G-3)

Settled 1770 **Pop** 7,972 **Elev** 35 ft **Area code** 207 **Zip** 04841 **E-mail** rtacc@midcoast.com **Web** www.midcoast.com/~rtacc

Information Rockland-Thomaston Area Chamber of Commerce, PO Box 508; 207/596-0376 or 800/562-2529.

This town on Penobscot Bay is the banking and commercial center of the region and seat of Knox County. It is also the birthplace of the poet Edna St Vincent Millay. Its economy is geared to the resort trade, but there is commercial fishing and light industry. It is the railhead for the whole bay. Supplies for boats, public landing and guest moorings are here.

What to See and Do

Farnsworth Art Museum and Wyeth Center. Cultural and educational center for the region. Collection of over 6,000 works of 18th-20th-century American art. Center houses personal collection of Wyeth family art and archival material. (June-Sept, daily; rest of yr, daily exc Mon) 325 Main St. Phone 207/596-6457. ¢¢¢ Included in admission and adj is

Farnsworth Homestead. 19th-century Victorian mansion with period furniture. (June-Sept, daily)

Fisherman's Memorial Pier & Chamber of Commerce. Public landing, Harbor Park. **Free.**

Maine State Ferry Service. Ferries make 15-mi (1 hr, 15 min) trip to Vinalhaven and 12¹/₂-mi (1 hr, 10 min) trip to North Haven. (All-yr, 2-3 trips daily) Also 23-mi (2 hr, 15 min) trip to Matinicus Island once a month. 517A Main St. For schedule and fee information, phone 207/596-2202.

Owls Head Transportation Museum. Working display of antique cars, airplanes and 100-ton steam engine. (Daily) 2 mi S via ME 73, in Owls Head. Phone 207/594-4418. ¢¢

Sailing trips.

Coasting schooners *Isaac H. Evans, American Eagle & Heritage.* Three- & six-day cruises (late May-mid-Oct). Phone 207/594-8007 or 800/648-4544 (exc ME). ¢¢¢¢

Schooner *J. & E. Riggin.* Wk-long cruises (June-Sept). Phone 207/594-1875 or 800/869-0604. ¢¢¢¢¢

Schooner *Stephen Taber* **& Motor Yacht** *Pauline.* Three- and six-day cruises through Penebscot, Casco, Blue Hill and Frenchman Bay. (Late May-mid-Oct) Phone 207/236-3520 or 800/999-7352. ¢¢¢¢

For information on other cruises contact the Chamber of Commerce.

Shore Village Museum (Maine's Lighthouse Museum). A large collection of lighthouse lenses and artifacts; Civil War collection. Museum shop. (June-mid-Oct, daily; rest of yr, by appt) 104 Limerock St. Phone 207/594-0311. **Free.**

Annual Events

Schooner Days & North Atlantic Blues Festival. Three-day festival celebrating Maine's maritime heritage, featuring Parade of Schooners, arts, entertainment, concessions, fireworks; blues bands & club crawl. Phone 207/596-0376. Wkend after July 4.

Maine Lobster Festival. A 5-day event centered on Maine's chief marine creature, with a huge tent cafeteria serving lobster and other seafood. Parade, harbor cruises, maritime displays, bands, entertainment. Phone 207/596-0376. 1st wkend Aug.

Motels

★ ★ **GLEN COVE.** *(Glen Cove 04846)* 3 mi N on US 1. 207/594-4062; res: 800/453-6268. 34 rms, 1-2 story. July-Aug: S, D $79-$119; each addl $10; lower rates rest of yr. Closed Feb. Crib free. TV; cable. Heated pool. Complimentary coffee in lobby. Restaurant nearby.

Ck-out 11 am. Refrigerators. Overlooks Penobscot Bay. Cr cds: A, DS, MC, V.

★ **NAVIGATOR MOTOR INN.** *520 Main St, across from State Ferry terminal.* 207/594-2131; FAX 207/594-7763; res: 800/545-8026. 81 rms, 4-5 story, 6 kits. Mid-June-Aug: D $70-$99; each addl $10; under 16 free; lower rates rest of yr. Pet accepted, some restrictions. TV; cable. Restaurant 6:30 am-2 pm, 5:30-9:30 pm. Rm serv. Bar 11-1 am. Ck-out 11 am. Coin lndry. Meeting rms. Business servs avail. Downhill ski 10 mi; x-country ski 2 mi. Refrigerators; microwaves avail. Balconies. Near ocean. Cr cds: A, D, DS, MC, V.

✔★ **WHITE GATES.** *(700 Commercial St (US 1), Rockport 04856)* 4 mi N on US 1. 207/594-4625. 15 rms. Early July-Sept: S $62; D $62-$72; each addl $4; lower rates May-early July & Oct. Closed rest of yr. Crib $4. TV; cable. Complimentary continental bkfst. Restaurant nearby. Ck-out 11 am. Some refrigerators. Cr cds: A, MC, V.

Inns

★ ★ ★ **CAPT. LINDSEY HOUSE INN.** *5 Lindsey St.* 207/596-7950; res: 800/523-2145; FAX 207/596-2758. E-mail lindsey@midcoast.com. 9 rms, 3 story. No elvtr. Mid-June-early Sept: S, D $95-$160; each addl $45; wkends 2-day min (in season); lower rates rest of yr. Children over 10 yrs only. TV; cable. Complimentary continental bkfst; afternoon refreshments. Restaurant 11 am-10 pm. Ck-out 11 am, ck-in 3 pm. In-rm modem link. Luggage handling. Street parking. Downhill/x-country ski 10 mi. Built in 1830. Antiques; 1920s walk-in safe. Totally nonsmoking. Cr cds: A, DS, MC, V.

✔★ ★ **CRAIGNAIR INN.** *(533 Clark Island Rd, Spruce Head 04859)* 5 mi S on US 1, exit ME 131 S. 207/594-7644; res: 800/320-9997; FAX 207/596-7124. E-mail craignar@midcoast.com; web www.midcoast.com/~craignar/. 24 rms, 16 share bath, 2-3 story. No A/C. June-Sept: S $55; D $88-$115; each addl $17; under 6 free; wkly rates; hols, wkends (2-day min); lower rates rest of yr. Crib $5. Pet accepted, some restrictions; $3.50/day. Cable TV in common rm, VCR avail (movies). Complimentary full bkfst; afternoon refreshments. Restaurant 8-9 am, 11 am-1:30 pm, 5:30-9 pm. Rm serv. Ck-out 11 am, ck-in 2 pm. Business servs avail. Luggage handling. Downhill/x-country ski 15 mi. On ocean. Built in 1930; boarding house converted to an inn in 1947. Antiques. Totally nonsmoking. Cr cds: A, MC, V.

★ ★ **LAKESHORE INN.** *184 Lakeview Dr.* 207/594-4209; FAX 207/596-6407. E-mail lakeshore@midcoast.com; web www.midcoast.com/~lakeshore. 4 rms, 1 with shower only, 2 story. S, D $115-$125; each addl $20; wkends July-Aug (2-day min); special events (3-day min). Children over 9 yrs only. TV; VCR (movies) in sunroom. Complimentary full bkfst. Whirlpool. Ck-out 11 am, ck-in 3 pm. Downhill ski 6 mi; x-country ski 3 mi. Balconies. Colonial New England farmhouse built in 1767. Totally nonsmoking. Cr cds: MC, V.

Resort

★ ★ ★ **SAMOSET.** *(220 Warrenton St, Rockport 04856)* ½ mi N on US 1, then E on Waldo Ave. 207/594-2511; FAX 207/594-0722; res: 800/341-1650 (exc ME). E-mail info@samoset.com; web www.samoset.com. 150 rms, 4 story. Early July-early Sept: S $195-$230; D $217-$265; each addl $20; suites from $290; under 16 free; ski, golf, tennis plans; lower rates rest of yr. Crib free. TV; cable (premium). 2 pools, 1 indoor; whirlpool, poolside serv. Playground. Supervised child's activities. Coffee in rms. Dining rm 7 am-9 pm. Bar 11:30-1 am; entertainment. Ck-out noon, ck-in after 3 pm. Meeting rms. Business servs avail. In-rm modem link. Valet serv. Concierge. Gift shop. Sports dir. Tennis. Racquet-

ball. 18-hole golf, putting green, driving range, pro, pro shop. Sailing. Dockage in season. Downhill ski 10 mi; x-country ski on site. Fitness trails. Lawn games. Movies. Game rm. Exercise rm; saunas. Massage. Private patios, balconies. Clambakes. On bay. Cr cds: A, C, D, DS, MC, V.

Restaurant

★ **HARBOR VIEW.** *(Thomaston Landing, Thomaston 04861)* 207/354-8173. Specializes in pasta, seafood. Hrs: 11:30 am-10 pm. Closed Thanksgiving, Dec 25; also Sun & Mon Nov-Apr. No A/C. Bar. Semi-a la carte: lunch $6.75-$12.95, dinner $9.95-$17.95. Parking. Antiques. Outdoor dining. View of harbor. Cr cds: A, DS, MC, V.

Rockwood (D-2)

Pop 190 (est) **Elev** 1,050 ft **Area code** 207 **Zip** 04478

What to See and Do

Moosehead Lake (see). E & S of town.

Raft trips.

Northern Outdoors, Inc. Specializes in outdoor adventures including whitewater rafting on Maine's Kennebec, Penobscot and Dead rivers (May-Oct). Also snowmobiling (rentals), hunting and resort facilities. Rock climbing, freshwater kayak touring. Phone 207/663-4466 or 800/765-RAFT. ¢¢¢¢¢

Wilderness Expeditions, Inc. Whitewater rafting on the Kennebec, Penobscot and Dead rivers; also canoe trips and ski tours. (May-Sept, daily) Phone 207/534-2242, 207/534-7305 or 800/825-9453. ¢¢¢¢¢

Motel

✔★ **MOOSEHEAD.** *On ME 6, 15.* 207/534-7787. Web www.maine guide.com/moosehead/motel. 27 rms, 11 A/C, 4 kit. units, 2 story. No rm phones. S, D $47-$56; kit. units $60-$75; each addl $5; family units $60-$75; hunters' plan. TV, some B/W. Restaurant 7-10 am, 5-8 pm; closed Apr, Dec. Ck-out 11 am. Private docks; canoes, boats, motorboats; fishing, hunting guides. Picnic tables, grill. Plane rides avail. Moosehead Lake opp, boat tour. Cr cds: A, DS, MC, V.

Resort

★ **THE BIRCHES.** *2 mi NE of ME 6/15.* 207/534-7305; FAX 207/534-8835; res: 800/825-9453. E-mail wwld@aol.com; web www.birches.com. 3 rms in main lodge, shared baths; 17 kit. cottages, shower only. No A/C. AP, May-Nov: S $105; D $65/person; wkly rates; housekeeping plan (no maid serv) $550-$750/wk (4 people); lower rates rest of yr. Pet accepted; $5. Dining rm 7-10 am, 6-9 pm; also 11 am-3 pm in season. Box lunches. Bar. Ck-out 10 am, ck-in 3 pm. Business servs avail. Gift shop. Grocery, package store 2 mi. Private beach. Marina, dockage. Boats, motors; canoes, sailboats. Canoe, rafting trips. Moose-watching cruises. Downhill ski 15 mi; x-country ski on site. Ski, kayak, snowmobile rentals. Bicycles. Sauna. Whirlpool. Fishing guides; clean/store area. Rustic log cabins. On Moosehead Lake. Cr cds: A, DS, MC, V.

Rumford (F-1)

(See also Bethel)

Settled 1774 **Pop** 7,078 **Elev** 505 ft **Area code** 207 **Zip** 04276 **E-mail** rvcc@agate.net **Web** www.agate.net/~rvcc

Information River Valley Chamber of Commerce, PO Drawer 598; 207/364-3241.

This papermill town is located in the valley of the Oxford Hills, where the Ellis, Swift and Concord rivers flow into the Androscoggin. The spectacular Penacook Falls of the Androscoggin are right in town. Rumford serves as a year-round resort area.

What to See and Do

Mt Blue State Park. Recreation areas on Lake Webb include swimming, bathhouse, lifeguard; fishing; boating (ramp, rentals). Hiking trail to Mt Blue. Cross-country skiing, snowmobiling permitted. Picnicking. Camping (dump station). (Memorial Day-Labor Day) Standard fees. 4 mi E on US 2 to Dixfield, then 14 mi N on ME 142 in Weld. Phone 207/585-2347.

Motels

✔★ ★ **BLUE IRIS.** *Box 127 (04278), 5 mi W on US 2.* 207/364-4495. 14 rms, 5 kit. units. S $30; D $38-$45; each addl $7; kit. units $45-$70; family, wkly rates; ski plans. TV; cable. Pool. Restaurant nearby. Ck-out 10 am. Downhill/x-country ski 5 mi. Balconies. Picnic tables. On river. Cr cds: A, MC, V.

★ **LINNELL.** *Rte 2, 2 mi W just off US 2.* 207/364-4511; *FAX* 207/369-0800; *res:* 800/446-9038. 50 rms, 1-2 story. S $44-$55; D $49-$60; each addl $5; kit. units $55-$60; under 12 free. Crib free. Pet accepted; $5. TV; cable. Complimentary continental bkfst. Ck-out 11 am. Coin lndry. Meeting rms. Business servs avail. Downhill/x-country ski 3 mi. Many refrigerators. Some balconies. Picnic tables. Cr cds: A, D, DS, MC, V.

D ✔ ✉ ✉ ✉ 🔥 SC

★ ★ **MADISON MOTOR INN.** *PO Box 398, Rte 2, 4 mi W on US 2.* 207/364-7973; *FAX* 207/369-0341; *res:* 800/258-6234. 60 rms, 38 A/C, 2 story. S $65; D $85-$95; each addl $15; kit. units $95-$125; under 12 free. Crib free. Pet accepted. TV; cable, VCR avail (movies). Pool; whirlpool. Restaurant 6-10 am, 5-9 pm. Bar 4-10 pm. Ck-out 11 am. Meeting rms. Business servs avail. Downhill/x-country ski 10 mi. Exercise rm; sauna. Lawn games. Refrigerators. Balconies. On river; boats, canoes. Cr cds: A, C, D, DS, MC, V.

D ✔ ✉ ✉ ✉ ✕ ✉ 🔥 SC

Saco (H-1)

(See also Old Orchard Beach, Portland)

Settled 1631 **Pop** 15,181 **Elev** 60 ft **Area code** 207 **Zip** 04072 **E-mail** chamber@int-usa.net **Web** www.biddefordsacomaine.com

Information Biddeford/Saco Chamber of Commerce, 110 Main St, Ste 1202, Saco 04072; 207/282-1567.

Saco, on the east bank of the Saco River, facing its twin city Biddeford, was originally called Pepperellboro, until its named was changed in 1805. The city has diversified industry, including a machine and metalworking plant. Saco is home to the University of Maine system and is only four miles from the ocean.

What to See and Do

Aquaboggan Water Park. More than 40 acres of water and land attractions, including 5 water slides, wave pool, children's pool, "aquasaucer," games, miniature golf, bumper boats, race cars. Picnicking. (May-Sept, daily) 4 mi N on US 1. Phone 207/282-3112. ¢¢¢¢¢

Dyer Library & York Institute Museum. Public library has arts and cultural programs. Museum features local history, decorative and fine art; American paintings, ceramics, glass, clocks and furniture; changing exhibits. (Tues-Sat) 371 Main St, on US 1. Phone 207/283-3861 or 207/282-3031. ¢

Ferry Beach State Park. Beach, swimming, picnicking, nature & cross-country trails. (Memorial Day-Labor Day, daily) Standard fees. 3½ mi N via ME 9. Phone 207/283-0067.

Funtown USA. Theme park featuring adult and kiddie rides; log flume ride; Excalibur wooden roller coaster; Grand Prix Racers; games. Picnicking. (Mid-June-Sept, daily; early May-mid-June, wkends) 2 mi NE on US 1. Phone 207/284-5139 or 207/284-7113. ¢¢¢¢

Maine Aquarium. More than 150 forms of marine life, including seals, penquins, electric eels, sharks and tropical fish. Touch tanks. Remote-controlled miniature boats. Petting zoo. Snack bar. Picnicking. (Daily) 1½ mi N on US 1. Phone 207/284-4511. ¢¢¢

Motels

★ **CLASSIC.** *21 Ocean Park Rd (ME 5).* 207/282-5569; *res:* 800/290-3909. Web www.classicmotel.com. 17 rms, 2 story, 15 kits. (no ovens). Mid-June-Labor Day: S $80; D $85; each addl $10; under 13 $5; lower rates rest of yr. TV; cable. Indoor pool; whirlpool. Complimentary continental bkfst. Restaurant nearby. Ck-out 11 am. In-rm modem link. Many refrigerators. Balconies. Picnic tables. Cr cds: A, DS, MC, V.

✉ 🔥

★ ★ **EASTVIEW.** *924 Portland Rd (US 1), 3 mi N.* 207/282-2362. 22 rms. Late June-Labor Day: S $65; D $70; each addl $5; under 12 free; lower rates May-late June, after Labor Day-late Oct. Closed rest of yr. TV; cable. Pool. Restaurant opp 8 am-10 pm. Ck-out 10 am. Lawn games. Some refrigerators. Cr cds: A, DS, MC, V.

✉ ✉ 🔥

✔★ **SUNRISE.** *962 Portland Rd (US 1).* 207/283-3883; *FAX* 207/284-8888; *res:* 800/467-8674. Web www.sunrisemotel.com. 30 rms, 1-2 story, 6 kit. cottages. July-Aug: D $60-$75; each addl $8; suites, cottages $50-$75; wkly rates; lower rates rest of yr. Crib free. TV; cable (premium). Heated pool. Playground. Complimentary continental bkfst. Ck-out 10 am. Coin lndry. Business servs avail. Sundries. Lawn games. Refrigerators, microwaves avail. Balconies. Picnic tables, grills. Cr cds: A, DS, MC, V.

D ✉ 🔥 SC

Restaurant

✔★ ★ **CASCADE INN.** *941 Portland Rd (US 1), at Cascade Rd.* 207/283-3271. Specializes in steak, seafood. Hrs: 8 am-10 pm; off-season 11 am-9 pm; Sun brunch 9 am-1 pm. Bar. Semi-a la carte: bkfst buffet $4.95-$5.95, lunch $3.99-$9.95, dinner $5.25-$14.95. Sun brunch $3.95-$5.95. Child's meals. Fireplaces. Cr cds: DS, MC, V.

D

Scarborough (H-2)

(See also Portland)

Pop 12,518 **Elev** 17 ft **Area code** 207 **Zip** 04074 **Web** www.visitportland.com
Information Convention & Visitors Bureau of Greater Portland, 305 Commercial St, Portland 04101; 207/772-5800.

Scarborough contains some industry, but it is primarily a farming community and has been for more than 300 years. It is also a bustling tourist town during the summer months as vacationers flock to nearby beaches and resorts. The first Anglican church in Maine is here, as is painter Winslow Homer's studio, now a National Landmark.

What to See and Do

Scarborough Marsh Nature Center. Miles of nature and waterway trails through marshland area; canoe tours, special programs (fee). (Mid-June-Labor Day, daily) Phone 207/883-5100 or 207/781-2330. **Free.**

Seasonal Event

Harness racing. On US 1, ME Tpke exit 6. Scarborough Downs. Evenings and matinees. Phone 207/883-4331. Apr-Nov.

Motels

★★ **FAIRFIELD INN BY MARRIOTT.** *2 Cummings Rd.* 207/883-0300; FAX 207/883-0300. Web www.fairfieldinn.com. 120 rms, 3 story. Mid-July-Sept: S $99; D $119; under 18 free; lower rates rest of yr. Crib free. TV; cable (premium). Heated pool. Complimentary continental bkfst. Ck-out noon. Meeting rms. Business servs avail. In-rm modem link. Sundries. Refrigerators. Cr cds: A, C, D, DS, MC, V.

[D] [≈] [✈] [🔥] [SC]

★★ **HOLIDAY HOUSE INN & MOTEL.** *106 E Grand Ave.* 207/883-4417. 16 rms in motel, 8 rms in inn, 1 A/C. Late June-Labor Day: D $100-$130; each addl $10; lower rates mid-May-mid-June, after Labor Day-Oct. Closed rest of yr. Crib $10. Adults only in inn. TV; cable. Restaurant nearby. Ck-out 10:30 am. Refrigerators. Picnic tables. Ceiling fans. Utility kit. 8 am-4:30 pm. On ocean; sun deck. Cr cds: A, MC, V.

[✈] [🔥]

★ **LIGHTHOUSE.** *366 Pine Point Rd.* 207/883-3213; res: 800/780-4912. No A/C. July-Aug: S, D $90-$150; each addl $10-$20; lower rates mid-May-June, Sept-mid-Oct. Closed rest of yr. Crib free. TV; cable. Restaurant opp 7:30-11:30 am, 5-9 pm. Ck-out 10 am. Balconies. Picnic tables. On ocean; swimming beach. Cr cds: A, DS, MC, V.

[🚭] [✈] [🔥] [SC]

★ **MILLBROOK.** *321 US 1.* 207/883-6004; FAX 207/883-3036; res: 800/371-6005 (ME only). 15 rms, 2 story. Early July-late Aug: S, D $80; each addl $7.50; lower rates rest of yr. Crib $3. TV; cable (premium). Ck-out 11 am. Some balconies. Picnic tables. Cr cds: A, DS, MC, V.

[D] [✈] [🔥]

Restaurant

★ **MARSHVIEW.** *578 Portland Rd, 3 mi S on US 1, SE of ME Tpke exits 6, 7.* 207/883-3401. Specializes in Italian dishes, seafood. Hrs: 11 am-10 pm; wkends from 8 am; hrs vary off-season. Serv bar. Semi-a la carte: bkfst $2.50-$5.95, lunch $3.95-$9.25, dinner $7.95-$21.95. Child's meals. Cr cds: A, C, D, DS, MC, V.

[D] [↵]

Searsport (F-3)

(See also Belfast, Bucksport)

Settled 1770 **Pop** 2,603 **Elev** 60 ft **Area code** 207 **Zip** 04974
Information Chamber of Commerce, Main St, PO Box 139; 207/548-6510.

On the quiet upper reaches of Penobscot Bay, this is an old seafaring town. In the 1870s at least 10 percent of the captains of the US Merchant Marines lived here. Sea terminal of the Bangor and Aroostook Railway, Searsport ships potatoes and newsprint. This village abounds with antique shops and is sometimes referred to as the "antique capital of Maine."

What to See and Do

Fishing, boating on bay. Town maintains wharf and boat landing, beachside park.

Penobscot Marine Museum. Old Town Hall (1845), Merithew House (ca 1860), Fowler-True-Ross House (1825), Phillips Library and Carver Memorial Gallery. Ship models, marine paintings, American and Oriental furnishings. (Memorial Day wkend-mid-Oct, daily) Church St, off US 1. Phone 207/548-2529. **¢¢¢**

Motel

★ **YARDARM.** *172 E Main St, 1 mi NE.* 207/548-2404; res: 888/676-8006. E-mail yardarm@searsportmaine.com; web www.searsportmaine.com. 18 rms. No A/C. Late June-late Sept: S, D $45-$75; each addl $5-$7; under 13 free; lower rates May-late June, late Sept-Oct. Closed rest of yr. Crib $4. TV; cable. Complimentary continental bkfst. Ck-out 11 am. Refrigerators avail. Cr cds: DS, MC, V.

[✈] [🔥]

Inns

★★ **BRASS LANTERN.** *81 W Main St (US 1).* 207/548-0150; res: 800/691-0150. E-mail brasslan@agate.net; web www.agate.net/~brasslan/brasslantern.html. 5 rms, 4 with shower only, 2 story. No A/C. No rm phones. Mid-May-Oct: S, D $75-$90; each addl $20; lower rates rest of yr. Children over 11 yrs only. TV in sitting rm; cable, VCR. Complimentary full bkfst; afternoon refreshments. Restaurant nearby. Ck-out 11 am, ck-in 4 pm. Downhill/x-country ski 20 mi. Captain's house built 1850. Totally nonsmoking. Cr cds: DS, MC, V.

[🚭] [✈] [🔥]

✔★★ **THE HICHBORN INN.** *(Church St, Stockton Springs 04981) 4 mi N on US 1, exit Main St.* 207/567-4183; res: 800/346-1522. Web members.aol.com/hichborn. 4 rms, 2 share bath. A/C avail. No rm phones. Late May-early Nov: S, D $60-$95; package plans; lower rates rest of yr. Children over 12 yrs only. Complimentary full bkfst; afternoon refreshments. Restaurant nearby. Ck-out noon, ck-in 4 pm. Downhill/x-country ski 20 mi. Built in 1850. Victorian Italianate bldg in original condition; period antiques. Totally nonsmoking. No cr cds accepted.

[🚭] [✈] [🔥]

✔★★ **HOMEPORT.** *121 E Main St (US 1/ME 3).* 207/548-2259; FAX 978/443-6682; res: 800/742-5814. E-mail hportinn@acadia.net; web www.bnbcity.com/inns/20015. 10 rms, 3 share bath, 2 story, 3 kit. cottage. No A/C. No rm phones. May-Oct: S $35-$45; D $55-$90; each addl $20; kit. cottage $600-$750/wk; wkly rates; lower rates rest of yr. TV in sitting rm; cable, VCR. Complimentary full bkfst. Restaurant nearby. Ck-out 11 am, ck-in 1 pm. Downhill/x-country ski 20 mi. Lawn games. Balconies. Former sea captain's house (1863); antiques. Library, family rm. View of bay. Cr cds: A, DS, ER, MC, V.

[🚭] [✈] [🔥] [SC]

Restaurant

★ ★ **NICKERSON TAVERN.** *E Main St (US 1/ME 3). 207/548-2220.* Specializes in fresh seafood, roast duck. Hrs: 5:30-9 pm. Closed Mon; also Dec-Mar. Res accepted. Serv bar. Wine list. Semi-a la carte: dinner $14.95-$19.95. In former sea captain's home (1838). Cr cds: MC, V.

Sebago Lake (G-1)

(See also Bridgton, Poland Spring)

Area code 207

Information Bridgton Lakes Region Chamber of Commerce, PO Box 236-G, Bridgton 04009; 207/647-3472.

Second-largest of Maine's lakes, this is perhaps the most popular, partly because of its proximity to Portland. About 12 miles long and 8 miles wide, it lies among wooded hills. Boats can run a total of more than 40 miles from the south end of Sebago Lake, through the Songo River to the north end of Long Lake. Numerous resort communities are hidden in the trees along the shores. Sebago, home of the landlocked salmon *(Salmo sebago)*, is also stocked with lake trout.

What to See and Do

Marrett House and Garden (1789). Built in Georgian style, but later enlarged and remodeled in the Greek-revival fashion; period furnishings; farm implements. Coin from Portland banks was stored here during the War of 1812, when it was thought that the British would take Portland. Perennial and herb garden. Tours (mid-June-Aug, Tues, Thurs, Sat & Sun). Approx 2 mi S on ME 25 to center of Standish. Phone 207/642-3032 or 617/227-3956. ¢¢

Sebago Lake State Park. A 1,300-acre area. Extensive sand beaches, bathhouse, lifeguards; fishing, boating (rentals, ramps). Picnicking, concession. Camping (dump station). No pets. (May-mid-Oct, daily) Standard fees. 2 mi S of Naples off ME 11/114. Phone 207/693-6231 or 207/693-6613 (campground).

The Jones Museum of Glass and Ceramics. A decorative arts museum significant for its collection of both glass and ceramics. More than 7,000 pieces from early times to present. Changing exhibits; gallery tours, library, museum shop. (Mid-May-mid-Nov, daily) 5 mi NW via ME 114 & 107 on Douglas Hill in Sebago. Phone 207/787-3370. ¢¢

Motel

✔★ **SUBURBAN PINES.** *(322 Roosevelt Trail, Windham 04062)* Approx 7 mi S on US 302. 207/892-4834. 25 rms, 11 kits, 1-3 story. June-Oct: S, D $50-$60; suites $75-$85; under 12 free; lower rates rest of yr. Pet accepted; $50 deposit. TV; cable. Complimentary coffee. Ck-out 11 am. Coin lndry. Picnic table, grill. Maine state picnic area opp. Cr cds: DS, MC, V.

Resort

★ ★ ★ **MIGIS LODGE.** *(South Casco 04077)* 8 mi N on US 302. 207/655-4524; FAX 207/655-2054. E-mail migis@migis.com; web www.migis.com. 6 rms in lodge, 2 story, 52 units in 30 cottages. AP, late-June-mid-Sept: D $160-$200/person; lower rates June & mid-Sept-Columbus Day wkend. Closed rest of yr. TV; cable. Playground. Supervised child's activities. Dining rm 8-9:30 am, 12:30-1:30 pm, 6:30-8 pm; jacket (dinner). Rm serv. Box lunches, island cookouts, lakeside Sat buffet, outdoor Sun bkfst, lobster bakes. Serv bar. Ck-out noon, ck-in anytime. Meeting rms. Sundries. Valet serv. Airport, bus depot transportation. Ten-

nis. Golf privileges. Exercise rm. Private sand beaches. Waterskiing, instruction. Motorboats, sailboats, canoes, rowboats, pedalboats, boat trips; dockage. Lawn games. Hiking trails. Rec rm. Entertainment evenings. Refrigerators, wet bars, fireplaces. Porches. Library. On 97 acres; 3,500 ft of lakefront. No cr cds accepted.

Restaurants

✔★ ★ **BARNHOUSE TAVERN.** *Box 61 ME 35 North Windham (04062), on ME 35, at jct US 302.* 207/892-2221. Specialties: seafood casserole, baked stuffed haddock, steak. Hrs: 11 am-10 pm. Closed Dec 25. Res accepted. Bar to 12:30 am. Semi-a la carte: lunch $3.95-$8.95, dinner $7.95-$18.95. Entertainment Thurs-Sat. Outdoor dining. Authentically restored post-and-beam barn and farmhouse (1872); country atmosphere, loft dining. Cr cds: A, DS, MC, V.

★ ★ **OLDE HOUSE.** *(Rte 85, Raymond 04071) 1 mi N of US 302, on Rte 85.* 207/655-7841. Specialties: beef Wellington, lemon chicken, duck. Own baking. Hrs: 5-10 pm. Res accepted; required hols. Serv bar. Wine list. Semi-a la carte: dinner $15.95-$22.95. Child's meals. Historic (1790) home; victorian decor, antiques. Cr cds: MC, V.

Skowhegan (F-2)

(See also Newport, Waterville)

Settled 1771 **Pop** 8,725 **Elev** 175 ft **Area code** 207 **Zip** 04976 **E-mail** skowman@skowman.sdi.agate.net
Information Chamber of Commerce, PO Box 326; 207/474-3621 or 800/426-8713.

Skowhegan, on the Kennebec River, is surrounded by beautiful lakes. Shoes, paper pulp and other wood products are made here. In the village's center stands a 12-ton, 62-foot high Native American carved of native pine by Bernard Langlais. Skowhegan is the birthplace of Margaret Chase Smith, who served three terms in the US House of Representatives and four terms in the Senate.

What to See and Do

History House (1839). Old household furnishings; museum contains books, china, dolls and documents. (Mid-June-mid-Sept, Tues-Fri afternoons) Elm St, on the Kennebec River. Phone 207/474-6632. ¢

Annual Events

Skowhegan State Fair. One of oldest in country (1818). 1=mi-long midway, stage shows, harness racing; contests, exhibits. Phone 207/474-2947. Mid-Aug.

Skowhegan Log Days. Parade, fireworks, pig roast, lobster bake, golf tournament, amateur and professional competitions, bean dinner. Commemorates last log drive on Kennebec River. Phone 207/474-3621. Last full wk Aug.

Motels

✔★ ★ **BELMONT.** *425 Madison Ave.* 207/474-8315; res: 800/235-6669. 36 rms. July-Oct: S $50; D $65; each addl $5; suites $110-$130; higher rates: State Fair, special events; lower rates rest of yr. TV; cable (premium). Pool. Restaurants nearby. Ck-out 11 am. Sundries. Downhill ski 5 mi; x-country ski 1 mi. Lawn games. Refrigerators avail. Picnic tables. Cr cds: A, D, DS, MC, V.

★ ★ **TOWNE.** *248 Madison Ave. 207/474-5151; FAX 207/474-6407; res: 800/843-4405.* 33 rms, 1-2 story, 7 kits. July-Oct: S, D $60-$68; each addl $6; kit. units $72-$78; higher rates: state fair, racing; lower rates rest of yr. TV; cable (premium). Pool. Complimentary continental bkfst. Restaurant nearby. Ck-out 11 am. Coin lndry. Downhill/x-country ski 6 mi. Cr cds: A, DS, MC, V.

Restaurants

✔★ ★ **CANDLELIGHT.** *Madison Ave & Water St. 207/474-9724.* Specializes in beef, seafood. Own baking. Hrs: 11 am-9 pm; Sun brunch 11 am-2 pm. Closed Dec 25. Res accepted. Bar. Semi-a la carte: lunch $1.50-$7.25, dinner $7.95-$14.95. Child's meals. Salad bar. Parking. Cr cds: A, D, DS, MC, V.

★ ★ **HERITAGE HOUSE.** *260 Madison Ave. 207/474-5100.* Specializes in fresh seafood, steak, vegetables. Hrs: 11:30 am-2 pm, 5-9 pm; Fri, Sat 5-10 pm. Closed July 4, Dec 25. Res accepted. Bar. Semi-a la carte: lunch $3.95-$6.95, dinner $7.95-$15. Child's meals. Restored home; oak staircase. Cr cds: A, MC, V.

Southwest Harbor (G-4)

(See also Bar Harbor, Cranberry Isles)

Pop 1,952 **Elev** 50 ft **Area code** 207 **Zip** 04679 **E-mail** swhtrcoc@acadia.net **Web** www.acadia.net/swhtrcoc

Information Chamber of Commerce, PO Box 1143; 207/244-9264 or 800/423-9264.

This is a prosperous, working seacoast village on Mt Desert Island. There are lobster wharves, where visitors can watch about 70 fishermen bring their catch, and many shops where boats are constructed. Visitors may rent sail and power boats in Southwest Harbor to explore the coves and islands; hiking trails and quiet harbors offer relaxation.

What to See and Do

Acadia National Park (see). W, N & E of village.

Cranberry Cove Boating Co. Cruise to Cranberry Islands. See native wildlife and learn island history. Six departures daily. (Mid-June-mid-Sept, daily) Departs Upper Town Dock. For schedule phone 207/244-5882. ¢¢

Maine State Ferry Service. Ferry makes 6-mi (40 min) trip to Swans Island and 8¼-mi (50 min) trip to Frenchboro (limited schedule). Swans Island (all-yr, 1-6 trips daily). 4 mi S on ME 102 & ME 102A, in Bass Harbor. For schedule and fee information, phone 207/244-3254 (Bass Harbor) or 207/526-4273.

Mt Desert Oceanarium. More than 20 tanks with Gulf of Maine marine creatures. Touch tank permits animals to be picked up. Exhibits on tides, seawater, plankton, fishing gear, weather. Inquire for information on special events. (Mid-May-mid-Oct, daily exc Sun) Clark Point Rd. Phone 207/244-7330. ¢¢

Wendell Gilley Museum. Art and natural history museum featuring collection of bird carvings by local artist Wendell Gilley; changing exhibits of local and historical art; films. (June-Oct, daily exc Mon; May & Nov-Dec, Fri-Sun) Main St & Herrick Rd. Phone 207/244-7555. ¢¢

Motor Hotel

★ ★ **CLAREMONT HOTEL.** *Claremount Rd. 207/244-5036; FAX 207/244-3512; res: 800/244-5036.* Web www.acadia.net/claremont. 45 units, 1-4 story, 14 kit. cottages. No A/C. July-early Sept: S, D $145-

$210; each addl $20-$50; kit. cottages $165-$205; wkly rates; lower rates Memorial Day-June, early Sept-Oct. Closed rest of yr. Crib $10. Supervised child's activities (July-Aug). Restaurant 8-10 am, 6-9 pm. Rm serv in hotel. Bar 5-9 pm. Ck-out 11:30 am. Meeting rms. Business servs avail. Bellhops. Tennis. Lawn games. Picnic tables. Restored New England resort hotel situated on five wooded acres; beach access. Dockage. No cr cds accepted.

Inns

✔★ ★ **HARBOUR WOODS INN & COTTAGES.** *410 Main St. 207/244-5388; FAX 207/244-7156.* E-mail harbourwoods@acadia.net; web www.acadia.net/harbourwoods. 14 rms, 11 with shower only, 1-2 story, 9 kit. units. No A/C. Some rm phones. July-Aug: S, D $95-$115; each addl $15; kit. units $79-$95; wkly rates; July-Aug (2-3 day min); lower rates rest of yr. TV; cable, VCR avail (movies). Complimentary continental bkfst (inn). Restaurant nearby. Ck-out 11 am, ck-in 3-6 pm. Coin lndry. X-country ski 5 mi. Pool. Many refrigerators. Picnic tables. Opp harbor. Built in 1840; 19th century farmhouse. Totally nonsmoking. Cr cds: DS, MC, V.

★ ★ **KINGSLEIGH.** *373 Main St. 207/244-5302; FAX 207/244-7691.* Web www.kingsleighinn.com. 8 rms, 3 story. No rm phones. July-mid-Oct: D $90-$125; each addl $15; suite $175; lower rates rest of yr. Children over 11 yrs only. TV in suite; cable. Complimentary full bkfst. Restaurant nearby. Ck-out 11 am, ck-in 3 pm. Built 1904; library, antiques, wrap-around porch. Near ocean; overlooks harbor. Totally nonsmoking. Cr cds: MC, V.

★ ★ **THE LAMB'S EAR.** *60 Clark Point Rd. 207/244-9828; FAX 207/244-9924.* Web www.acadia.net/lambsear. 8 rms, 2 with shower only, 2 story. No A/C. No rm phones. Mid-June-mid-Oct: S, D $85-$165; each addl $25; lower rates May-mid-June. Closed rest of yr. Children over 8 yrs only. TV in some rms; cable. Complimentary bkfst buffet; afternoon refreshments. Restaurant nearby. Ck-out 10:30 am, ck-in 2-6 pm. Captain's house (1857); deck with harbor view. Some in-rm whirlpools, fireplaces. Totally nonsmoking. Cr cds: A, DS, MC, V.

✔★ ★ **MOORINGS.** *Shore Rd, 2 mi E, on Shore Rd. 207/244-5523; res: 800/596-5523.* E-mail mansell@downeast.net; web www.downeast.net/com/mansell/mansell.html. 10 rms in inn, 3 motel rms, 9 kits., 3 kit. cottages. No A/C. July-mid-Sept: S $55; D $65-$85; each addl $10; suites $85; kit. cottages $100; lower rates May-June, mid-Sept-Oct. Closed rest of yr. Crib free. TV in sitting rm; VCR avail. Complimentary continental bkfst. Restaurant nearby. Ck-out 11 am, ck-in 3 pm. Fireplace in cottages. Balconies, private screened decks. Picnic tables, grills. Bicycles, canoes, kayaks avail. Sections of inn date to 1784; nautical motif. On waterfront; private beach, dock, launching ramp. No cr cds accepted.

Restaurant

★ **SEAWALL DINING ROOM.** *566 Seawall Rd, 3½ mi E on ME 102A. 207/244-3020.* Specializes in seafood, baked stuffed lobster. Own desserts. Hrs: 11:30 am-9 pm; July-Labor Day to 10 pm. Closed Dec-Apr. Res accepted. No A/C. Semi-a la carte: lunch, dinner $3.25-$18. Child's meals. Family-owned. Cr cds: A, D, DS, MC, V.

Unrated Dining Spot

BEAL'S LOBSTER PIER. *Clark Point Rd. 207/244-3202.* E-mail beals@acadia.net. Specializes in fresh seafood, steamed lobster. Hrs: 9 am-8 pm; hrs vary off-season. Closed July 4. No A/C. Wine, beer. A la carte entrees: lunch, dinner $10-$20. All dining outdoors on working wharf overlooking Southwest Harbor. Lobsters boiled to order; self-service. Menu boards. Family-owned since 1930. Cr cds: A, DS, MC, V.

Waterville (F-3)

(See also Augusta)

Settled 1754 **Pop** 17,173 **Elev** 113 ft **Area code** 207 **Zip** 04901 **E-mail** mmcc@mint.net **Web** www.mid-mainechamber.com

Information Mid-Maine Chamber of Commerce, One Post Office Square, PO Box 142, 04903; 207/873-3315.

A large Native American village once occupied the west bank of the Kennebec River where many of Waterville's factories now stand. An important industrial town, Waterville is the center of the Belgrade and China lakes resort area. Manufactured goods include men's and women's shirts, paper and molded pulp products and woolens.

What to See and Do

Colby College (1813). (1,700 students) This 714-acre campus includes an art museum in the Bixler Art and Music Center (daily; closed hols; free), a Walcker organ designed by Albert Schweitzer in Lorimer Chapel and books, manuscripts and letters of Maine authors Edwin Arlington Robinson and Sarah Jewett in the Miller Library (Mon-Fri; closed hols; free). Mayflower Hill Dr, 2 mi W, 1/2 mi E of I-95. Phone 207/872-3000.

Old Ft Halifax (1754). Blockhouse. Bridge over Kennebec gives view of Ticonic Falls. (Memorial Day-Labor Day, daily) 1 mi E on US 201, on Bay St in Winslow, on E bank of Kennebec River.   **Free.**

Redington Museum (1814). Waterville Historical Society collection includes 18th- and 19th-century furnishings, manuscripts, Civil War and Native American relics; historical library; children's rm; apothecary museum. (Mid-May-Sept, Tues-Sat) 64 Silver St. Phone 207/872-9439.   ¢¢

Two-Cent Footbridge. One of the few remaining former toll footbridges in the US. Front St.   **Free.**

Seasonal Event

New England Music Camp. 5 mi W on ME 137 to Oakland, then 4 mi S on ME 23; on Pond Rd. Faculty and student concerts, Sun; faculty concerts, Wed; student recitals, Fri. Phone 207/465-3025. Late June-late Aug.

Motels

✔★ **ATRIUM.** 332 Main St. 207/873-2777; FAX 207/872-2838. 102 rms, 4 story. July-Sept: S $51-$60; D $61-$86; each addl $10; under 18 free; lower rates rest of yr. Crib free. Pet accepted. TV; cable. Indoor pool; wading pool. Complimentary continental bkfst. Ck-out noon. Coin Indry. Meeting rm. Business servs avail. Valet serv. Sundries. Exercise equipt; sauna. Rec rm. Some refrigerators; microwaves avail. Cr cds: A, D, DS, MC, V.

★★ **BEST WESTERN.** 356 Main St, at I-95 exit 34 (Main St). 207/873-3335; FAX 207/873-3335. E-mail pdaigle@uninet.net; web www.bestwestern.com/thisco/bw/20018/20018_b.html. 86 rms, 2 story. July-Oct: S, D $90-$100; each addl $10; under 18 free; higher rates Colby graduation wkend; lower rates rest of yr. Crib $3. Pet accepted. TV; cable. VCR avail (movies). Pool. Coffee in rms. Restaurant 6 am-10 pm. Bar. Ck-out noon. Meeting rms. Business servs avail. Valet serv. Health club privileges. Sundries. Refrigerators, microwaves avail. Cr cds: A, C, D, DS, JCB, MC, V.

★★★ **HOLIDAY INN.** 375 Main St. 207/873-0111; FAX 207/872-2310. E-mail hiwvlme@mint.net; web www.acadia.net/hiwat-cm. 138 rms, 3 story. May-Oct: S $85; D $95; each addl $10; suite $150; under 19 free; lower rates rest of yr. Crib free. Pet accepted. TV; cable (premium), VCR avail. Indoor pool; whirlpool. Complimentary coffee in rms. Restaurant 6 am-2 pm, 5-10 pm. Rm serv. Bar 11-1 am. Ck-out noon. Coin Indry. Meeting rms. Business servs avail. In-rm modem link. Sundries. Exercise equipt; sauna. Refrigerators, microwaves avail. Cr cds: A, C, D, DS, JCB, MC, V.

Restaurants

★★ **JOHN MARTIN'S MANOR.** 54 College Ave. 207/873-5676. Specializes in prime rib, popovers, seafood. Salad bar. Hrs: 11 am-9 pm; Sun 11:30 am-8 pm; early-bird dinner Mon-Fri 4-5:30 pm. Closed Dec 25. Res accepted. Bar 4:30 pm-1 am. Semi-a la carte: lunch $3.95-$7.45, dinner $6.95-$15.95. Child's meals. Cr cds: A, C, D, DS, ER, MC, V.

★ **WEATHERVANE.** 470 Kennedy Memorial Dr, at I-95 exit 33. 207/873-4522. Specializes in seafood. Raw bar. Hrs: 11 am-9:30 pm. Closed Thanksgiving, Dec 24, 25. Serv bar. A la carte entrees: lunch $1.99-$10.95, dinner $6-$19.95. Child's meals. Fireplaces. Cr cds: MC, V.

Unrated Dining Spot

BIG G'S DELI. (Outer Benton Dr, Winslow) 2 mi NE on Benton Ave. 207/873-7808. Specializes in sandwiches, bkfst dishes. Deli with self serv. Hrs: 6 am-8 pm. Semi-a la carte: bkfst $3-$5, lunch, dinner $5-$9. Child's meals. Paintings of entertainers. No cr cds accepted.

Wells (H-1)

(See also Kennebunk, Ogunquit, York)

Settled 1640 **Pop** 7,778 **Elev** 70 ft **Area code** 207 **Zip** 04090 **E-mail** wellschamber@wellschamber.org **Web** www.wellschamber.org

Information Chamber of Commerce, PO Box 356; 207/646-2451.

One of the oldest English settlements in Maine, Wells includes Moody, Wells Beach and Drake's Island. It was largely a farming center, with some commercial fishing, until the resort trade began in the 20th century. Charter boats, surf casting and pier fishing attract fishermen; seven miles of beaches entice swimmers.

What to See and Do

☑ **Rachel Carson National Wildlife Refuge.** Approx 4,500 acres of salt marsh and coastal edge habitat; more than 230 species of birds may be observed during the yr. Visitor center; 1-mi interpretive nature trail. (All yr, sunrise-sunset) Located along coastline between Kittery Point and Cape Elizabeth; visitor center 3 mi NE on ME 9. Phone 207/646-9226.   **Free.**

Wells Auto Museum. Approx 80 antique cars dating from 1900 trace progress of the automotive industry. Also displayed is a collection of nickelodeons, picture machines and antique arcade games to play. (Memorial Day wkend-Columbus Day wkend, daily) US 1. Phone 207/646-9064.   ¢¢

Wells Natural Estuarine Research Reserve. Approx 1,600 acres of fields, forest, wetlands and beach. Laudholm Farm serves as visitor center. Programs on coastal ecology and stewardship, exhibits and tours. Reserve (daily). Visitors center (May-Oct, daily; rest of yr, Mon-Fri). 1 1/2 mi N of Wells Corner on ME 1. Phone 207/646-1555.   **Free.**

Motels

★ ★ **ATLANTIC MOTOR INN.** *37 Atlantic Ave, 2 mi S on US 1, then E on Mile Rd to Atlantic Ave.* 207/646-7061; FAX 207/641-0607; res: 800/727-7061. E-mail ami@cybertours.com; web nettx.com. 35 rms, 3 story. No elvtr. Early July-late Aug: S, D $129-$169; each addl $15; suites $149; higher rates hol wkends; lower rates Apr-early July, late Aug-Oct. Closed rest of yr. Crib $10. TV; cable. Heated pool. Restaurant nearby. Ck-out 11 am. Refrigerators, microwaves avail. Balconies. On beach. Cr cds: A, DS, MC, V.

★ ★ **GARRISON SUITES.** *1099 Post Rd (US 1).* 207/646-3497; res: 800/646-3497. E-mail garrison@cybertours.com; web www.chicka-dee.com/garrison. 47 units, 13 cottages (shower only in 10 cottages). July-Aug (2-day min): S, D $79; kits. (3-day min) $89; suites $115; kit. cottages $625-$725 wkly; lower rates May-June, Sept-Oct; off season packages. Closed rest of yr. Crib $10, $30/wk. TV; cable. VCR avail. Heated pool; whirlpool. Playground. Complimentary coffee in rms. Restaurant opp 7 am-11 pm. Ck-out 11 am. Lawn games. Refrigerators, microwaves. Picnic tables. Grills. Cr cds: MC, V.

★ **LAFAYETTE'S OCEAN FRONT.** *(393 Mile Rd, Wells Beach)* S on US 1, E on Mile Rd. 207/646-2831; FAX 207/646-6770. Web www.visionwork.com/ocean-front/. 128 rms, 15 with shower only, 2-3 story. Early July-Labor Day: S, D $80-$150; kit. units $115-$150; family rates; in-season and hols (2-5 day min); lower rates rest of yr. Crib $10. TV; cable. Restaurant adj 7 am-10 pm. Ck-out 11 am. Meeting rms. Business servs avail. Sundries. Coin lndry. Indoor pool; whirlpool. Refrigerators. Many balconies. On beach. Cr cds: DS, MC, V.

✔ ★ **NE'R BEACH.** *(US 1, Moody 04054) 2 mi S on US 1.* 207/646-2636. 47 rms, 1-2 story, 21 kits. Late June-Aug: S, D $49-$99; kit. units $89-$139; wkly rates for kit. units; lower rates Apr-late June, after Labor Day-mid-Nov. Closed rest of yr. Crib $7. Pet accepted. TV; cable. Heated pool. Playground. Restaurant nearby. Ck-out 11 am. Lawn games. Refrigerators avail. Picnic tables. Cr cds: A, DS, MC, V.

★ **SEA MIST RESORT.** *733 Post Rd, on US 1, at ME 9B.* 207/646-6044; FAX 207/646-2199; res: 800/448-0925. 68 rms, 2 story. July-Labor Day: D $85-$95; wkly rates; lower rates Apr-June, Labor Day-early Dec. Closed rest of yr. Crib $5. TV; cable. Indoor pool; whirlpool. Playground. Restaurant nearby. Ck-out 10 am. Lawn games. Refrigerators, microwaves. Balconies. Picnic tables, grills. Cr cds: DS, MC, V.

★ ★ **SEAGULL MOTOR INN.** *1413 Post Rd (US 1), ¼ mi S on US 1, 2¼ mi SE of ME Tpke exit 2.* 207/646-5164; res: 800/573-2485; FAX 207/646-5164. 24 motel rms, 24 cottages, 21 kits. (oven in 9). No A/C in cottages. July-Aug: D $84-$95 each addl $12; kit. cottages for 2-4, $475-$750/wk; lower rates mid-Apr-June, Sept-mid-Oct. Closed rest of yr. Crib $3. TV; cable. Heated pool; whirlpool. Playground. Ck-out 11 am. 9-hole par 3 golf. Lawn games. Refrigerators; some microwaves in cottages. Screened porch on cottages. Picnic tables. Spacious grounds. Ocean view. Cr cds: A, C, D, DS, MC, V.

✔ ★ **SUPER 8.** *(820 Main St, Sanford 04073) approx 9 mi N on ME 109.* 207/324-8823; FAX 207/324-8782. 49 rms, 2 story. Apr-Sept: S $43.88-$46.88; D $55.88-$60.88; each addl $5; under 13 free; lower rates rest of yr. Crib free. TV; cable. VCR avail (movies). Complimentary coffee in lobby. Ck-out 11 am. Business servs avail. Refrigerator, microwave avail. Cr cds: A, D, DS, JCB, MC, V.

★ **VILLAGE GREEN MOTEL & COTTAGES.** *773 Post Rd, 2 mi S on US 1.* 207/646-3285; FAX 207/646-4889. 18 units, 10 rms in motel, 1-2 story, 8 kit. cottages; 11 A/C. No rm phones. July-Aug: S, D $72-$90;

each addl $10; cottages $485-$650/wk; lower rates mid-Apr-June, Sept-mid-Oct. Closed rest of yr. Crib $5. TV; cable. Heated pool. Restaurant nearby. Lawn games. Refrigerators. Screened porch on cottages. Picnic tables. Cr cds: A, DS, MC, V.

✔ ★ **WATERCREST COTTAGES & MOTEL.** *1277 Post Rd (US 1), ½ mi S on US 1, 1½ mi SE of ME Tpke exit 2.* 207/646-2202; FAX 207/646-7067; res: 800/847-4693. E-mail wcrest@cybertours.com; web www.watercrestcottages.com. 9 motel rms, 4 kits., 50 kit. cottages. July-late Aug, hol wkends: S, D $64-$74; each addl $10; cottages for 2-8 (late June-Labor Day, 1-wk min) $435-$735/wk; lower rates May-June, late Aug-mid-Oct. Closed rest of yr. Crib free. Pet accepted, some restrictions. TV; cable, VCR avail (free movies). Heated pool; whirlpool. Playground. Restaurant nearby. Ck-out 11 am; cottages 10 am. Coin lndry. Lawn games. Exercise equipt. Microwaves in cottages. Picnic tables, grills. Screened porch on cottages. Cr cds: DS, MC, V.

★ **WELLS-MOODY.** *(119 Post Rd, Moody 04054) 2½ mi S on US 1.* 207/646-5601. 24 rms. Memorial Day-Labor Day: S, D $69-$99; each addl $10; 2-day min; lower rates mid-Apr-Memorial Day, Labor Day-mid-Oct. Closed rest of yr. TV; cable. Pool. Restaurant opp 6 am-11 pm. Ck-out 11 am. Refrigerators. Picnic tables. Cr cds: DS, MC, V.

Motor Hotel

★ ★ ★ **VILLAGE BY THE SEA.** *US 1S.* 207/646-1100; FAX 207/646-1401; res: 800/444-8862. Web www.vbts.com. 73 kit. units, 3-4 story. No elvtr. Early July-early Sept (2-day min): kit. units (up to 4) $140-$165; each addl $10; under 12 free; wkly rates; higher rates hols; lower rates rest of yr. Crib $10. TV; cable, VCR avail (movies $3.50). 2 heated pools, 1 indoor. Restaurant nearby. Ck-out 10 am. Coin lndry. Meeting rms. Sundries. Health club privileges. Balconies. Picnic tables, grills. Wildlife refuge adj. On trolley route. Cr cds: A, D, DS, MC, V.

Restaurants

★ ★ **THE GREY GULL.** *475 Webhannet Dr.* 207/646-7501. Specializes in seafood, beef. Hrs: 5-9 pm; Sun brunch (mid-Sept-mid-June) 9 am-1 pm. Closed Mon-Wed mid-Dec-mid Mar. Res accepted. Bar. Semi-a la carte: dinner $10.95-$22.95. Sun brunch $4-$13. Child's meals. Classical guitarist Sun, Irish entertainment Tues. Valet parking (in season). A 19th-century inn located on ocean. Guest rms avail. Cr cds: A, DS, MC, V.

✔ ★ **HAYLOFT.** *(US 1, Moody 04054) 2½ mi S on US 1 (Post Rd).* 207/646-4400. Specializes in broasted chicken, Maine seafood, Angus beef. Hrs: 11 am-9:30 pm. Closed wk before Dec 25. Serv bar. Semi-a la carte: lunch $3.95-$7.95, dinner $6.95-$19.95. Child's meals. Country farm decor. Cr cds: A, DS, MC, V.

★ ★ **LITCHFIELD'S.** *2135 Post Rd (US 1), 1 mi N on US 1.* 207/646-5711. Specializes in seafood, steak, pasta. Own desserts. Raw bar. Hrs: 11:30 am-3 pm, 5-9:30 pm; winter months to 9 pm; Sunday brunch 11 am-3 pm. Closed Dec 25. Res accepted. Bar to 11:30 pm. Semi-a la carte: lunch $4.95-$10.95, dinner $4-$35. Child's meals. Pianist. Parking. Cr cds: A, D, DS, MC, V.

★ ★ **LORD'S HARBORSIDE.** *352 Harbor Rd, at harbor.* 207/646-2651. Specializes in fresh seafood, chowders, lobster. Hrs: noon-9 pm; varied hrs off season. Closed Tues; also mid-Oct-Apr. No A/C. Serv bar. Semi-a la carte: lunch, dinner $4.95-$19.95. Child's meals. Parking. Nautical dining rm overlooking harbor. Family-owned. Cr cds: MC, V.

✔★ **MAINE DINER.** 2265 Post Rd, 1³/4 mi N on US 1. 207/646-4441. E-mail eat@mainediner.com; web www.mainediner.com. Specializes in homemade chowders, lobster pie. Own desserts. Hrs: 7 am-9:30 pm; Columbus Day-Memorial Day to 8 pm. Closed Thanksgiving, Dec 25. Wine, beer. Semi-a la carte: bkfst $1.35-$7.95, lunch $2.50-$9.95, dinner $5.95-$13.95. Child's meals. Traditional diner decor; bkfst avail all day. Totally nonsmoking. Cr cds: DS, MC, V.

★★ **THE STEAKHOUSE.** 1205 Post Rd (US 1), 1 mi S. 207/646-4200. Specializes in steak, seafood. Hrs: 4:30-9 pm. Closed Mon; also mid-Dec-Mar. Serv bar. Semi-a la carte: dinner $7.95-$18.95. Child's meals. Parking. Antique farm implements and ship models displayed. Cr cds: D, MC, V.

Wiscasset (G-2)

(See also Bath, Boothbay Harbor, Damariscotta)

Settled 1653 **Pop** 3,339 **Elev** 50 ft **Area code** 207 **Zip** 04578

Many artists and writers live here in beautiful old houses put up in the golden days of clipper ship barons and sea captains. Chiefly a summer resort area centered around its harbor, Wiscasset is half as populous as it was in 1850. Its pictorial charm is extraordinary even on the picturesque Maine coast. A noted sight in Wiscasset are the remains of two ancient wooden schooners, which were hauled into the harbor in 1932.

What to See and Do

Lincoln County Museum & Old Jail. First penitentiary built in the District of Maine (1809-1811). Jailer's house has changing exhibits, relics of Lincoln County. (July & Aug, daily exc Mon) Federal St, ME 218. Phone 207/882-6817. ¢

Maine Art Gallery. Exhibits by Maine artists. (Mid-May-early-Oct, daily exc Mon; rest of yr Thurs-Sun) Warren St, in Old Academy Bldg (1807). Phone 207/882-7511. **Donation.**

Musical Wonder House-Music Museum (1852). Talking machines, antique musical boxes, player pianos shown and played in historical settings; antique furnishings; gift shop. (Late May-mid-Oct, daily) 18 High St. Phone 207/882-7163 or 800/336-3725. ¢¢¢-¢¢¢¢¢

Nickels-Sortwell House (1807). Classic Federal-style elegance. Built for a shipmaster in the lumber trade, William Nickels, it was used as a hotel between 1820 and 1900. The mansion was then bought by Mayor Alvin Sortwell of Cambridge, Massachusetts, as a private home. Graceful elliptical stairway; many Sortwell family furnishings; restored garden. (June-mid-Oct, Wed-Sun) 121 Main St at Federal St, US 1. Phone 207/882-6218 or 617/227-3956. ¢¢

Pownalborough Court House (1761). Oldest pre-Revolutionary court house in Maine. Three-story building houses furnished courtrm, judges’ chambers, spinning rm, tavern, bedrms, parlor and kitchen. Nature trails along river; picnic areas; Revolutionary cemetery. (Wed-Sat; July & Aug also Sun afternoon) 8 mi N on ME 27, then 3 mi S on ME 128 in Dresden, bordering Kennebec River. Phone 207/882-6817. ¢¢

Motels

★★★ **COD COVE INN.** (Edgecomb 04556) Jct US 1 & ME 27. 207/882-9586; FAX 207/882-9294; res: 800/882-9586 (exc ME). Web www.mainesource.com/codcove. 30 rms, 2 story, 1 cottage. July-Labor Day: S, D $115-$175; suite $175; each addl $10; higher rates Columbus Day wkend; lower rates mid-Apr-June, Labor Day-late Oct. TV; cable.

Heated pool; whirlpool. Complimentary continental bkfst. Restaurant opp 6-9 am. Ck-out 11:30 am. Meeting rms. Business servs avail. In-rm modem link. Refrigerators; some fireplaces. Balconies. Colonial-style building. Overlooks bay. Cr cds: A, MC, V.

✔★ **WISCASSET MOTOR LODGE.** 596 Bath Rd, 3 mi S on US 1. 207/882-7137; res: 800/732-8168. 22 rms, 2 story, 6 cabins. Some A/C. July-Labor Day: S, D $39-$68; each addl $8; lower rates Apr-June & after Labor Day-Oct. Closed rest of yr. Crib $5. TV; cable. Complimentary continental bkfst (July-Labor Day). Ck-out 11 am. Cr cds: DS, MC, V.

Inn

★★ **SQUIRE TARBOX INN.** 1181 Main Rd, Westport Island, US 1 to ME 144, then 8 mi S. 207/882-7693; FAX 207/882-7107. E-mail squiretarbox@ime.net. 11 rms, 6 A/C, 2 story. No rm phones. Mid-July-Oct: S $105; D $106-$175; each addl $30; MAP avail; lower rates May-mid-July. Closed rest of yr. Complimentary full bkfst. Dining rm (public by res): sitting 6 pm. Ck-out 11 am, ck-in 2 pm. Dock, rowboat, bicycles. Restored 18th-century farmhouse situated on working dairy goat farm; antiques; library; some fireplaces. Some rms in former stable area. Guests may view dairy operations. Totally nonsmoking. Cr cds: A, DS, MC, V.

Cottage Colony

✔★ **BAY VIEW INN & COTTAGES.** (179 US 1, Edgecomb 04556) 1/2 mi N on US 1. 207/882-6911; res: 800/530-2445. Web www.sourcemaine.com/bayview. 14 rms, 11 with shower only. No A/C. No rm phones. July-Labor Day: cottages $65-$85, kit. cottages $75-$85; each addl $10; wkly rates; lower rates rest of yr. Crib free. Pet accepted; $5. TV; cable. Complimentary coffee in lobby. Restaurant nearby. Ck-out 11 am. Pool. Refrigerators avail. Picnic tables, grills. Cr cds: DS, MC, V.

Restaurant

★★ **LE GARAGE.** Water St, 1 blk S of US 1. 207/882-5409. Specialities: char-broiled marinated lamb, broiled seafood platter, chicken pie. Own baking. Hrs: 11:30 am-3 pm, 5-9:30 pm; Sun 11 am-9 pm. Closed Jan; major hols. Res accepted. No A/C. Bar. Semi-a la carte: lunch $3.95-$18.95, dinner $7.95-$18.25. View of bay. Cr cds: MC, V.

Yarmouth (H-2)

(See also Brunswick, Freeport, Portland)

Settled 1636 **Pop** 7,862 **Elev** 100 ft **Area code** 207 **Zip** 04096 **E-mail** ycc@omnisystem.com **Web** www.omnisystem.com/yarmouth/chamber/ **Information** Chamber of Commerce, 158 Main St; 207/846-3984.

Yarmouth is a quaint New England village 10 miles north of Portland (see) on US 1. There are many well maintained older homes and specialty shops. It is linked by a bridge to Cousins Island in the bay.

What to See and Do

Yarmouth Historical Society Museum. Two galleries with changing exhibits of local and maritime history, fine and decorative arts. Local history research rm; historical lecture series. (July-Aug, Mon-Fri afternoons; rest of yr, Tues-Sat) 3rd floor, Merrill Memorial Library, Main St. Phone 207/846-6259. **Free.**

Old Ledge School (1738). Restored one-rm schoolhouse. (By appt) W Main St. Phone 207/846-6259.   **Free.**

Annual Event

Clam Festival. Celebration of soft-shelled clam. Arts & crafts, entertainment, parade, fireworks. 3rd wkend July.

Restaurant

★ ★ **THE CANNERY.** *ME 88 at Lower Falls Landing.* 207/846-1226. Specializes in fresh local seafood. Hrs: 11:30 am-9 pm; Fri, Sat to 9:30 pm. Closed Thanksgiving, Dec 25. Bar. Semi-a la carte: lunch $6.95-$12.95, dinner $10.95-$17.95. Child's meals. Outdoor dining. View of river, marina. Nautical decor. Cr cds: A, MC, V.

[D]

York (J-1)

(See also Kittery, Ogunquit, Wells)

Settled 1624 **Pop** 9,818 **Elev** 60 ft **Area code** 207 **Zip** 03909 **E-mail** york@gwi.net **Web** www.yorkme.org

Information The Yorks Chamber of Commerce, 599 US 1, PO Box 417; 207/363-4422.

Originally named Agamenticus by the Plymouth Company, which settled the area in 1624, the settlement was chartered as a city—the first in America—in 1641 and renamed Gorgeanna. Following a reorganization in 1652, the "city" in the wilderness took the name York. The present-day York area includes York Village, York Harbor, York Beach and Cape Neddick.

What to See and Do

⭐ **Old York Historical Society.** Tours of 7 buildings dating from the early 1700s. (Mid-June-Sept, Tues-Sun) Visitor orientation and tickets at Jefferds Tavern. Administration Office houses museum offices (Mon-Fri) and historical and research library (phone for hours). On US 1A next to Old Gaol. Phone 207/363-4974. Per building   ¢;   Combination ticket   ¢¢¢

Jefferds Tavern and Schoolhouse. Built by Capt Samuel Jefferds in 1750 and furnished as a tavern in coastal Maine in the late 18th century; used as an orientation center & educational facility. Schoolhouse adj is probably the state's oldest surviving one-rm schoolhouse; contains exhibit on one-rm schooling in Maine.

Emerson-Wilcox House. Built in 1742, with later additions. Served at various times as a general store, tavern and post office as well as the home of 2 of the town's prominent early families. Now contains a series of period rms dating from 1750; antique furnishings.

Old Gaol. Built in 1719 with 18th-century additions. One of the oldest English public buildings in the US, it was used as a jail until 1860. Has dungeons and cells for felons and debtors, as well as galleries of local historical artifacts, late 1800s photography exhibit. On US 1A.

Elizabeth Perkins House. Turn-of-the-century summer house on the banks of the York River, at Sewall's Bridge. Former home of a prominent York preservationist. The furnishings reflect the Colonial-revival period.

John Hancock Warehouse. Owned by John Hancock until 1794, this is one of the earliest surviving customs houses in Maine. Used now to interpret the maritime history of this coastal village. Lindsay Rd at York River.

George Marshall Store. Mid-19th-century general store houses local art exhibits. On Lindsay Rd at the York River.   **Free.**

Sayward-Wheeler House (1718). Home of the 18th-century merchant and civic leader Tory Jonathan Sayward. Tours. (June-mid-Oct, Sat & Sun) 79 Barrell Lane, 2 mi S in York Harbor. Phone 603/436-3205.   ¢¢

Annual Event

Harvest Fest. Juried crafts, ox-roast, colonial theme. Mid-Oct.

Motels

★ ★ **ANCHORAGE INN.** *(265 Long Beach Ave (US 1A), York Beach 03910)* 207/363-5112; FAX 207/363-6753. E-mail anchorage-inn.com; web www.anchorageinn.com. 179 rms, 3 story. Late June-Aug: S, D $119-$154; suites $195-$245; lower rates rest of yr. Crib $10. TV; cable. 3 pools; 2 indoor; whirlpool, poolside serv. Restaurant adj 7 am-9 pm. Bar. Ck-out 11 am. Meeting rms. Business servs avail. Golf privileges. Exercise equipt. Lawn game. Balconies. Refrigerators. Opp ocean. Cr cds: MC, V.

[D] [pool] [🏃] [✗] [🦎]

★ ★ **YORK COMMONS INN.** *362 US 1.* 207/363-8903; FAX 207/363-1130; res: 800/537-5515 (NY, NE only). 90 rms. Mid-June-mid-Oct: S, D $89-$99; each addl $5; under 18 free; lower rates rest of yr. Crib free. Pet accepted, some restrictions. TV; cable. Indoor pool. Complimentray complimentary bkfst. Complimentary coffee in rms. Restaurant opp 11 am-8 pm. Business servs avail. Sundries. Refrigerators, microwaves avail. Cr cds: A, D, DS, MC, V.

[D] [🐾] [pool] [✗] [🦎] [SC]

Motor Hotel

★ ★ ★ **STAGENECK INN.** *(22 Stageneck Rd, York Harbor 03911) 1 mi E on US 1A.* 207/363-3850; FAX 207/363-2221; res: 800/222-3238. E-mail stageneck@aol.com; web www.stageneck.com. 60 rms, 2-3 story. Mid-June-early Sept: S $160-$225; D $165-$230; each addl $10; under 13 free; wkends (3-day min); lower rates rest of yr; MAP avail off season. Crib $10. TV; cable, VCR avail (free movies). 2 pools, 1 indoor; whirlpool, poolside serv. Restaurant 7:30-10 am, noon-9 pm. Rm serv. Bar noon-midnight; pianist Fri, Sat. Ck-out 11 am. Coin lndry. Meeting rms. Business servs avail. Bellhops. Sundries. Tennis. 18-hole golf privileges. Exercise equipt; sauna. Game rm. Refrigerators. Balconies. On ocean; beach. Totally nonsmoking. Cr cds: A, DS, MC, V.

[D] [🐾] [🏃] [⛷] [pool] [🏃] [✗] [🦎] [🔥]

Inns

★ ★ **DOCKSIDE GUEST QUARTERS.** *Harris Island Rd, ME 103 to Harris Island Rd.* 207/363-2868; FAX 207/363-1977. E-mail info@docksidegq.com; web www.docksidegq.com. 25 rms, 4 with shower only, 2 share bath, 6 bldgs, 6 kits., 6 suites. No A/C. No rm phones. Mid-June-late-Sept: D $69-$128; each addl $10; kits. & suites $134-$174; under 12 free. July-Oct (2-day min); lower rates rest of yr. Open wkends only Nov-Apr. Crib free. TV; cable. Playground. Restaurant (see THE RESTAURANT AT DOCKSIDE). Ck-out 11 am, ck-in 3 pm. Concierge serv. Luggage handling. Lawn games. Balconies. Picnic tables, grills. On wooded island with views of harbor and ocean. Power boats, rowboats, bicycles. Totally nonsmoking. Cr cds: DS, MC, V.

[D] [🐾] [✗] [🔥]

★ ★ **EDWARD'S HARBORSIDE.** *(Stageneck Rd, York Harbor 03911) 1 mi E on UA 1A.* 207/363-3037; FAX 207/363-1544; res: 800/273-2686. 10 rms, 8 with shower only, 2 share bath, 3 story, 2 suites. July-Aug: D $90-$170; each addl $20; suites $210-$240; higher rates wkends; lower rates rest of yr. TV; cable. Complimentary continental bkfst; afternoon refreshments. Restaurant opp noon-9:30 pm. Ck-out 11 am, ck-in 3 pm. Luggage handling. Lawn games. Picnic tables. On ocean; swimming beach, dockage. Turn-of-century house with period furnishings. Totally nonsmoking. Cr cds: MC, V.

[🐾] [✗] [🔥]

✔★ **HOMESTEAD INN.** *(8 S Main St (US 1A), York Beach 03910) 4 mi E on US 1A.* 207/363-8952; FAX 207/363-8952. E-mail homestedbb@aol.com; web members.aol.com/homstedbb. 4 rms, 2 share bath, shower only, 3 story. No A/C. No elvtr. No rm phones. S, D $65; each addl $10; wkly rates. Closed Nov-Mar. Children over 12 yrs only. Complimentary continental bkfst. Restaurant nearby. Ck-out 11 am, ck-in 2 pm. Business servs avail. Opp beach. Built in 1905; former boarding house. Totally nonsmoking. No cr cds accepted.

★ ★ **YORK HARBOR INN.** *(US 1A, York Harbor 03911) 1 mi E on US 1A.* 207/363-5119; FAX 207/363-7151; res: 800/343-3869. E-mail garyinkeep@aol.com; web www.yorkharborinn.com. 33 rms, 23 with shower only, 2 story. Apr-Oct: D $109-$209; 2-day min most wkends; higher rates New Years Eve; lower rates rest of yr. Crib $10. TV; cable, VCR avail. Complimentary continental bkfst. Restaurant (see YORK HARBOR INN). Ck-out 11 am, ck-in 2:30 pm. Business servs avail. Golf privileges. Whirlpool. Balconies. Some fireplaces, bathrm phones. Ocean opp. Original section from 1637 is now sitting rm. Cr cds: A, C, D, ER, MC, V.

Restaurants

✔★ ★ ★ **CAPE NEDDICK INN.** *(1233 US 1, Cape Neddick 03902)* 207/363-2899. Web www.yorkme.org/dining/capeneddickinn.html. Contemporary Amer menu. Specializes in seafood, beef. Own baking. Hrs: 5:30-9:30 pm. Closed Dec 25. Res accepted. Bar. Wine list. Semi-a la carte: dinner $16-$27. Upscale country inn atmosphere; original artwork. Cr cds: DS, MC, V.

★ ★ **FAZIO'S.** *38 Woodbridge Rd.* 207/363-7019. E-mail fazios@fazios.com; web www.fazios.com. Italian menu. Specializes in fresh pasta. Hrs: 4-9 pm; Fri, Sat to 10 pm; early-bird dinner to 5:30 pm. Closed major hols. Bar. Semi-a la carte: dinner $6.50-$14.95. Child's meals. Outdoor dining. Mural of Italian street market; photos from '30s & '40s. Cr cds: A, DS, MC, V.

★ ★ **THE RESTAURANT AT DOCKSIDE.** *(See Dockside Guest Quarters)* 207/363-2722. E-mail info@docksidegq.com; web www.docksidegq.com. Specializes in Maine seafood, roast duckling. Salad bar. Hrs: 11:30 am-2 pm, 5:30-9 pm; hrs vary off season. Closed Mon; also Nov-Memorial Day. Res accepted. Bar. Semi-a la carte: lunch $5.50-$9.50, dinner $9.95-$19.95. Child's meals. Outdoor dining. Nautical decor; overlooks harbor and marina. Family-owned. Cr cds: DS, MC, V.

★ ★ **YORK HARBOR INN.** *(See York Harbor Inn)* 207/363-5119. E-mail garyinkeep@aol.com; web www.yorkharborinn.com. Hrs: 11:30 am-2:30 pm, 5:30-9:30 pm; Fri, Sat to 10 pm; Sun brunch 8:30 am-2:30 pm. Closed Mon-Thurs in Jan-mid-May. Res accepted Fri, Sat & Sun brunch. Continental menu. Bar 3:30 pm-12:30 am. Wine cellar. Semi-a la carte: lunch $4.95-$11.95, dinner $16.95-$24.95. Sun brunch $4.95-$11.95. Child's meals. Specializes in seafood, lobster. Ocean and harbor views. Totally nonsmoking. Cr cds: A, C, D, ER, MC, V.

Massachusetts

Population: 6,016,425
Land area: 7,826 square miles
Elevation: 0-3,491 feet
Highest point: Mt Greylock (Berkshire County)
Entered Union: Sixth of original 13 states (February 6, 1788)
Capital: Boston
Motto: By the sword we seek peace, but peace only under liberty
Nickname: Bay State
State flower: Mayflower
State bird: Chickadee
State tree: American elm
Time zone: Eastern
Web: www.mass-vacation.com

Leif Ericson—or even a French or Spanish fisherman—may have originally discovered the Cape Cod coast. However, the first recorded visit of a European to Massachusetts was that of John Cabot in 1497. Not until the Pilgrims landed at Provincetown and settled at Plymouth was there a permanent settlement north of Virginia. Ten years later, Boston was founded with the arrival of John Winthrop and his group of Puritans.

Native American wars plagued Massachusetts until the 1680s, after which the people experienced a relatively peaceful period combined with a fast-growing, mostly agricultural economy. In the 1760s, opposition to British taxation without representation exploded into the American Revolution. It began in Massachusetts, and from here, the American tradition of freedom and justice spread around the world. The Constitution of Massachusetts is the oldest written constitution still in effect. The New England town meeting, a basic democratic institution, still governs most of its towns. It had a child labor law in 1836, a law legalizing trade unions in 1842 and the first minimum wage law for women and children.

Massachusetts proved to be fertile ground for intellectual ideas and activities. In the early 19th century, Emerson, Thoreau and their followers expounded the Transcendentalist theory of the innate nobilty of man and the doctrine of individual expression, which exerted a major influence on American thought, then and now. Social improvement was sought through colonies of idealists, many of which hoped to prove that sharing labor and the fruits of labor were the means to a just society. Dorothea Dix crusaded on behalf of the mentally disturbed, and Horace Mann promoted universal education. In 1831, William Lloyd Garrison, an ardent abolitionist, founded his weekly, *The Liberator*. Massachusetts was the heartland of the Abolitionist movement and her soldiers fought in the Civil War because they were convinced it was a war against slavery.

Massachusetts was also an important center during the Industrial Revolution. After the Civil War the earlier success of the textile mills, like those in Lowell, generated scores of drab, hastily built, industrial towns. Now these towns are being replaced by modern plants with landscaped grounds. Modern industry is as much a part of Massachusetts as the quiet sandy beaches of Cape Cod, with their bayberry and beach plum bushes.

Massachusetts has also been home to several generations of the politically prominent Kennedy family. John F. Kennedy, 35th president of the United States, was born in the Boston suburb of Brookline, as were his younger brothers, Senators Robert and Edward.

The Bay State offers mountains, ocean swimming, camping, summer resorts, freshwater and saltwater fishing, and a variety of metropolitan cultural advantages. No other state in the Union can claim so much history in so small an area, for in Massachusetts each town or city has a part in the American story.

When to Go/Climate

Massachusetts enjoys a moderate climate with four distinct seasons. Cape Cod and the Islands offer milder temperatures than other parts of the state and rarely have snow, while windchill in Boston (the windiest city in the United States) can make temperatures feel well below zero and snow is not uncommon.

AVERAGE HIGH/LOW TEMPERATURES (°F)

BOSTON

Jan 36/22	**May** 67/50	**Sept** 73/57
Feb 38/23	**June** 76/60	**Oct** 63/47
Mar 46/31	**July** 82/65	**Nov** 52/38
Apr 56/40	**Aug** 80/64	**Dec** 40/27

WORCESTER

Jan 31/15	**May** 66/45	**Sept** 70/51
Feb 33/17	**June** 75/54	**Oot** 60/41
Mar 42/25	**July** 80/60	**Nov** 47/31
Apr 54/35	**Aug** 77/59	**Dec** 35/20

CALENDAR HIGHLIGHTS

APRIL

Boston Marathon (Boston). Famous 26-mile footrace from Hopkinton to Boston. Phone 617/236-1652.

Reenactment of Battle of Lexington and Concord (Lexington). Massachusetts Ave. Reenactment of opening battle of American Revolution; parade. Phone Lexington Historical Society, 781/862-1703.

Daffodil Festival (Nantucket Island). Festival is marked by over a million blooming daffodils. Parade of antique cars, prize for best tailgate picnic. Phone Chamber of Commerce, 508/228-1700.

JUNE

Hyannis Harbor Festival (Hyannis). Waterfront at Bismore Park. Coast Guard cutter tours, sailboat races, marine displays, food, entertainment. Phone 508/362-5230.

La Festa (North Adams). Ethnic festival, ethnic food, entertainment, events. Phone 413/66-FESTA.

JULY

Harborfest (Boston). Hatch Shell on the Esplanade. Concerts, chowder fest, children's activities; Boston Pops Orchestra, fireworks. Phone 617/227-1528.

Green River Music & Balloon Festival (Greenfield). Hot-air balloon launches, craft show, musical entertainment, food. Phone 413/733-5463.

SEPTEMBER

The "Big E" (Springfield). Largest fair in the Northeast; entertainment; exhibits; historic Avenue of States, Storrowton Village; horse show; agricultural events; "Better Living Center" exhibit. Phone 413/737-2443.

OCTOBER

Haunted Happenings (Salem). Various sites. Psychic festival, historical exhibits, haunted house, costume parade, contests, dances. Phone Salem Halloween Office, 508/744-0013.

NOVEMBER

Thanksgiving Week (Plymouth). Programs for various events may be obtained by contacting Destination Plymouth. Phone 508/747-7525 or 800/USA-1620.

DECEMBER

Stockbridge Main Street at Christmas (Stockbridge & West Stockbridge). Events include a re-creation of Norman Rockwell's painting. Holiday marketplace, concerts, house tour, silent auction, sleigh/hay rides, caroling. Phone 413/298-5200.

Parks and Recreation Finder

Directions to and information about the parks and recreation areas below are given under their respective town/city sections. Please refer to those sections for details.

NATIONAL PARK AND RECREATION AREAS

Key to abbreviations: I.H.S. = International Historic Site; I.P.M. = International Peace Memorial; N.B. = National Battlefield; N.B.P. = National Battlefield Park; N.B.C. = National Battlefield & Cemetery; N.C. = National Conservation Area; N.E.M. = National Expansion Memorial; N.F. = National Forest; N.G. = National Grassland; N.H. = National Historical Park; N.H.C. = National Heritage Corridor; N.H.S. = National Historic Site; N.L. = National Lakeshore; N.M. = National Monument; N.M.P. = National Military Park; N.Mem. = National Memorial; N.P. = National Park; N.Pres. = National Preserve; N.R. = National Recreational Area; N.R.R. = National Recreational River; N.Riv. = National River; N.S. = National Seashore; N.S.R. = National Scenic Riverway; N.S.T. = National Scenic Trail; N.Sc. = National Scientific Reserve; N.V.M. = National Volcanic Monument.

Place Name	Listed Under
Adams N.H.S.	QUINCY
Blackstone River Valley N.H.C.	WORCESTER
Boston African American N.H.S.	BOSTON
Boston N.H.	BOSTON
Cape Cod N.S.	same
Frederick Law Olmsted N.H.S.	BOSTON
John F. Kennedy N.H.S.	BOSTON
Longfellow N.H.S.	CAMBRIDGE
Lowell N.H.	LOWELL
Minute Man N.H.	CONCORD
Salem Maritime N.H.S.	SALEM
Saugus Iron Works N.H.S.	SAUGUS
Springfield Armory N.H.S.	SPRINGFIELD

STATE PARK AND RECREATION AREAS

Key to abbreviations: I.P. = Interstate Park; S.A.P. = State Archaeological park; S.B. = State Beach; S.C. = State Conservation Area; S.C.P. = State Conservation Park; S.Cp. = State Campground; S.F. = State Forest; S.G. = State Garden; S.H.A. = State Historic Area; S.H.P. = State Historic Park; S.H.S. = State Historic Site; S.M.P. = State Marine Park; S.N.A. = State Natural Area; S.P. = State Park; S.P.C. = State Public Campground; S.R. = State Reserve; S.R.A. = State Recreation Area; S.Res. = State Reservoir; S.Res.P. = State Resort Park; S.R.P. = State Rustic Park.

Place Name	Listed Under
Beartown S.F.	GREAT BARRINGTON
Brimfield S.F.	SPRINGFIELD
Fall River Heritage S.P.	FALL RIVER
Fort Phoenix Beach S.R.	NEW BEDFORD
Granville S.F.	SPRINGFIELD
Lowell Heritage S.P.	LOWELL
Mohawk Trail S.F.	NORTH ADAMS
Mt Greylock S.R.	NORTH ADAMS
Myles Standish S.F.	PLYMOUTH
Nickerson S.P.	BREWSTER
October Mountain State Forest	LEE
Savoy Mountain S.F.	NORTH ADAMS
Scusset Beach S.P.	SANDWICH
Shawme-Crowell S.F.	SANDWICH
Walden Pond S.R.	CONCORD

Water-related activities, hiking, riding, various other sports, picnicking and visitor centers, as well as camping, are available in many of these areas. Day-use areas (approx Memorial Day-Labor Day, some areas all yr): $2/car. Camping (approx mid-Apr-Oct, schedule may vary, phone ahead; 2-wk max, last Sat May-Sat before Labor Day at many parks): campsites $6-10/day; electricity $2/day. Pets on leash only in S.P.; no pets in bathing areas. Information available from Department of Environmental Management, Division of Forests & Parks, 617/727-3180.

SKI AREAS

Place Name	Listed Under
Bousquet Ski Area	PITTSFIELD
Brodie Mt Ski Area	PITTSFIELD
Butternut Basin Ski Area	GREAT BARRINGTON
Jiminy Peak Ski Area	GREAT BARRINGTON
Mt Tom Ski Area	HOLYOKE
Otis Ridge Ski Area	GREAT BARRINGTON

FISHING & HUNTING

Deep-sea and surf fishing are good; boats are available in most coastal towns. For information on saltwater fishing, contact Division of Marine Fisheries, phone 617/727-3193. Inland fishing is excellent in more than 500 streams and 3,000 ponds. Nonresident fishing license $37.50; 3-consecutive-day nonresident license $23.50. Nonresident hunting license: small game $65.50; big game $99.50. Inquire for trapping licenses. Fees subject to change. Licenses issued by town clerks, selected sporting good stores or from Division of Fisheries and Wildlife, phone 617/727-3151 or 800/ASK-FISH. Information on freshwater fishing, regulations and a guide to stocked trout waters and best bass ponds are also available from the Division of Fisheries and Wildlife.

Driving Information

Safety belts are mandatory for all persons. Children under 13 years must be in a federally approved child safety seat or safety belt anywhere in vehicle: it is recommended that children 40 lbs and under use a federally approved child safety seat and be placed in the back seat. For further information phone 617/624-5070 or 800/CAR-SAFE (MA).

INTERSTATE HIGHWAY SYSTEM

The following alphabetical listing of Massachusetts towns in *Mobil Travel Guide* shows that these cities are within 10 miles of the indicated Interstate highways. A highway map, however, should be checked for the nearest exit.

Highway number	Cities/Towns within 10 miles
Interstate 90:	Boston, Cambridge, Framingham, Great Barrington, Holyoke, Lee, Lenox, Natick, Newton, Pittsfield, Springfield, Stockbridge & West Stockbridge, Sturbridge, Sudbury Center, Waltham, Wellesley, Worcester.
Interstate 91:	Amherst, Deerfield, Greenfield, Holyoke, Northampton, Springfield.
Interstate 93:	Andover, Boston, Lawrence, Lowell.
Interstate 95:	Bedford, Boston, Burlington, Concord, Danvers, Dedham, Foxboro, Framingham, Lexington, Lynn, Lynnfield, Natick, Newton, Saugus, Sudbury Center, Waltham, Wellesley.

Additional Visitor Information

The Massachusetts Office of Travel and Tourism, 617/727-3201, has travel information. For a free *Massachusetts Getaway Guide* phone 800/447-MASS.

Many properties of the Society for the Preservation of New England Antiquities (SPNEA) are located in Massachusetts and neighboring states. For complete information on these properties contact the SPNEA Headquarters, 141 Cambridge St, Boston 02114; 617/227-3956. For information regarding the 71 properties owned and managed by The Trustees of Reservations, contact Box 563, Ipswich MA 01938; 508/356-4351.

Massachusetts has many statewide fairs, though none is considered the official state fair; contact the Massachusetts Dept of Agriculture, Division of Fairs, 617/727-3037.

There are several visitor centers located in Massachusetts; they are located on the MA Turnpike (daily, 9 am-6 pm) at Charlton (eastbound & westbound), Lee (eastbound), and Natick (eastbound); also I-95 at Mansfield, between exits 5 and 6 (northbound); and on MA 3 at Plymouth (southbound).

Amesbury (A-7)

(See also Haverhill, Newburyport)

Settled 1654 **Pop** 14,997 **Elev** 50 ft **Area code** 978 **Zip** 01913
Information Alliance for Amesbury, 5 Market Sq, 01913-2440; 978/388-3178.

In 1853, Jacob R. Huntington, "the Henry Ford of carriage-making," began a low-cost, high-quality carriage industry that became the economic backbone of Amesbury.

What to See and Do

Amesbury Sports Park. Winter snow tubing. Summer go-carts, golf range, miniature golf, bumper boats, volleyball park. Restaurant; lounge. (Daily; closed Easter, Thanksgiving, Dec 25) 12 Hunt Rd. ¢¢¢¢

Bartlett Museum (1870). Houses memorabilia of Amesbury's history dating from prehistoric days to the settlement and beyond. The Native American artifact collection, consisting of relics of local tribes, is considered one of the finest collections in the state. (Memorial Day-Labor Day, Wed-Sun afternoons; after Labor Day-Columbus Day, Sat & Sun) 270 Main St. Phone 978/388-4528. ¢

John Greenleaf Whittier Home. John Greenleaf Whittier lived here from 1836 until his death in 1892; 6 rms contain books, manuscripts, pictures and furniture; the Garden Room, where he wrote "Snow-Bound" and many other works, remains unchanged. (May-Oct, Tues-Sat) 86 Friend St. Phone 978/388-1337. ¢¢

Amherst (B-4)

Founded 1759 **Pop** 35,228 **Elev** 320 ft **Area code** 413 **Zip** 01002 **E-mail** aacc@crocker.com **Web** www.amherstcommon.com
Information Chamber of Commerce, 11 Spring St; 413/253-0700.

Amherst College, founded in 1821 to educate "promising but needy youths who wished to enter the Ministry," has educated several of the nation's leaders, including Calvin Coolidge and Henry Ward Beecher. Amherst is also the seat of the University of Massachusetts and of Hampshire College. This attractive, academic town was the home of three celebrated American poets: Emily Dickinson, Eugene Field and Robert Frost; Noah Webster also lived here.

What to See and Do

Amherst College (1821). (1,550 students) On the tree-shaded green in the middle of town. The Robert Frost Library owns approx half of Emily Dickinson's poems in manuscript and has a Robert Frost collection, as well as materials of Wordsworth, Eugene O'Neill and others. Phone 413/542-2000. Also on campus are

> **Pratt Museum of Geology** (1884). Some of the finest collections of dinosaur tracks, meteorites, minerals and fossils; also the world's largest mastodon skeleton. (Academic yr, daily; closed school hols) **Free.**

> **Mead Art Museum.** A notable art collection is housed here. (Sept-July, daily; Aug, by appt) **Free.**

Amherst History Museum. In 18th-century Strong House. House reflects changing tastes in local architecture and interior decoration; extensive collection of 18th- and 19th-century textiles and artifacts; gallery. (Mid-May-mid-Oct, Wed & Sat, afternoons) 18th-century herb and flower garden open to the public (spring-summer). 67 Amity St. Phone 413/256-0678. ¢¢

Emily Dickinson Homestead (1813). Birthplace and home of Emily Dickinson. Selected rms open for tours by appt (afternoons: May-Oct, Wed-

Sat; Mar-Apr & Nov-mid-Dec, Wed & Sat). 280 Main St. Phone 413/542-8161.   ¢¢

Hadley Farm Museum. Restored 1782 barn houses agricultural implements, tools and domestic items dating from 1700s; broom-making machines. (May-mid-Oct, daily exc Mon) 5 mi SW at jct MA 9, 47, at 147 Russell St in Hadley.   **Free.**

Jones Library. Building houses collections of the Amherst authors; an Emily Dickinson rm with some of Dickinson's personal articles, manuscripts and a model of her bedrm. Historical collection (daily exc Sun); library (Sept-May, daily; rest of yr, daily exc Sun; closed hols). 43 Amity St. Phone 413/256-4090.   **Free.**

National Yiddish Book Center. This 37,000-sq-ft, non-profit facility was developed by Aaron Lansky to preserve Yiddish literature and its history, and ensure its lasting legacy. Book Repository houses a core collection of 120,000 Yiddish books—the largest in the world—and 150,000 folios of rare Yiddish and Hebrew sheet music. Book Processing Center, shipping and receiving area, and Bibliography Center are all open for viewing as rare books are catalogued and shipped to libraries across the country. Vistors Center includes 3 exhibit halls, a kosher dairy kitchen, and educational story rails that introduce visitors to the books and the Center’s important work. Reading Room, Yiddish Resource Center, Yiddish Writers Garden. Also galleries for print, spoken and performing arts. Bookstore; museum store. (Daily exc Sat). MA 116, on campus of Hampshire College. Phone 800/535-3595.   **Free.**

University of Massachusetts (1863). (25,000 students) State's major facility of public higher education. More than 150 buildings on 1,200-acre campus. Tours (daily), phone 413/545-4237. N edge of town on MA 116. Visitors Center, phone 413/545-0306. Also here is

Fine Arts Center and Gallery. A variety of nationally and internationally known performances in theater, music and dance. Art gallery (daily). Performances (Sept-May). Phone 413/545-2511.

Seasonal Event

Maple sugaring. NW via MA 116 to Sunderland, then 2 mi N on MA 47. Visitors are welcome at maple camps, daily. Mount Toby Sugar House, phone 413/665-3127. Late Feb-Mar.

Motel

✔★ ★ **HOWARD JOHNSON.** *(401 Russell St, Hadley 01035)* MA 9 at jct MA 116. 413/586-0114; FAX 413/584-7163. 100 rms, 3 story. S $59-$109; D $69-$109; each addl $10; suites $79-$152; under 18 free; higher rates special events. Crib free. Pet accepted. TV; cable (premium). Pool. Complimentary bkfst. Ck-out noon. Meeting rm. Business servs avail. In-rm modem link. Downhill ski 16 mi; x-country ski 12 mi. Exercise equipt. Health club privileges. Private patios, balconies. Cr cds: A, C, D, DS, JCB, MC, V.

D ✔ ⊠ ≋ ✕ ⊠ 🔥 SC

Inns

★ ★ **ALLEN HOUSE VICTORIAN INN.** *599 Main St.* 413/253-5000; FAX 413/253-0846. E-mail allenhouse@webtv.net; web www.allenhouse.com. 7 rms, 5 with shower only, 2 story. Rm phones avail. Apr-Nov: S $55-$105; D $65-$135; each addl $10-$20; higher rates college events; lower rates rest of yr. Children over 8 yrs only. TV in sitting rm. Complimentary full bkfst; afternoon refreshments. Restaurant nearby. Ck-out 11 am, ck-in mid-afternoon. Queen Anne-style house built 1886; many antiques. Totally nonsmoking. Cr cds: DS, MC, V.

⊠ 🔥

★ ★ **LORD JEFFERY.** *30 Boltwood Ave.* 413/253-2576; FAX 413/256-6152. 50 rms, 4 story. S, D $69-$119.11; suites $109-$163. Crib $15. TV; cable. Bar. Ck-out 11 am, ck-in 3 pm. Downhill ski 18 mi; x-country ski 12 mi. Private patios, balconies. Cr cds: A, D, MC, V.

⊠ 🔥 SC

Andover & North Andover (A-7)

Settled ca 1643 **Pop** Andover: 29,151; North Andover: 22,792 **Elev** 164 ft **Area code** 978 **Zip** Andover: 01810; North Andover: 01845

Information Merrimack Valley Chamber of Commerce, 264 Essex St, Lawrence 01840-1496; 978/686-0900.

An attempt was made in Andover in the 19th century to surpass Japan's silk industry by growing mulberry trees on which silkworms feed. But Andover has had to be content with making electronic parts and woolen and rubber goods instead. Its true fame rests on Phillips Academy, the oldest incorporated school in the US, founded in 1778 by Samuel Phillips.

What to See and Do

Amos Blanchard House (1819) **and Barn Museum** (1818) **and Research Library** (1978). House features period rms; special local history exhibits; 17th-to-20th-century themes. Barn Museum features early farm equipment; household items; hand-pumped fire wagon. Library houses local history, genealogy and special collections. Guided tours (by appt). (Mon-Fri, also by appt; closed hols) 97 Main St. Phone 978/475-2236.   ¢

Phillips Academy (1778). (1,200 students) A coed residential school for grades 9-12. On 450 acres with 170 buildings, many of historical interest. The Cochran Sanctuary, a 65-acre landscaped area, has walking trails, a brook and 2 ponds. (Daily) Main St, MA 28. Phone 978/749-4000. Also on grounds are

Addison Gallery of American Art. More than 7,000 works, including paintings, sculpture & photographs. Changing exhibits. Ship model collection tracing era of sail through steam engine. (Sept-July, daily exc Mon; closed major hols) Phone 978/749-4016.   **Free.**

Robert S. Peabody Foundation for Archaeology. Exhibits on physical, cultural evolution of man; prehistoric archaeology of New England, New Mexico, Mexico, Canada. (Tues-Sat; closed major hols) Phillips & Main Sts. Phone 978/749-4490.   **Free.**

Stevens-Coolidge Place. House, interior and extensive gardens are maintained as they were in the early 20th century by diplomat John Gardener Coolidge and his wife, Helen Stevens Coolidge. Collection of Chinese porcelain, Irish and English cut glass, linens and clothing. Early American furnishings. House (late Apr-Oct, Sun afternoons). Gardens (daily; free). 137 Andover St, in North Andover. Phone 978/682-3580. House   ¢¢

Motor Hotels

★ ★ ★ **HOLIDAY INN.** *(4 Highwood Dr, Tewksbury 01876)* I-495 exit 39. 978/640-9000; FAX 978/640-0623. 237 rms, 5 story. S, D $119; under 18 free; wkend rates. TV; cable (premium). Complimentary coffee in rms. Restaurant 6:30 am-2 pm, 5-10 pm. Rm serv. Bar; entertainment Wed. Ck-out noon. Meeting rms. Business servs avail. In-rm modem link. Sundries. Exercise equipt; sauna. Indoor pool; whirlpool. Some refrigerators. Cr cds: A, C, D, DS, MC, V.

D ≋ ✕ ⊠ 🔥 SC

★ ★ ★ **MARRIOTT.** *(123 Old River Rd, Andover 01810)* 978/975-3600; FAX 978/975-2664. 293 rms, 5 story. S, D $175; under 18 free; family rates; package plans. Crib free. Pet accepted, some restrictions. TV; cable (premium), VCR avail (movies). Complimentary coffee in lobby. Restaurant 6:30 am-10 pm. Rm serv to 11 pm. Bar 5 pm-12:30 am; entertainment wkends. Ck-out noon. Convention facilities. Business servs avail. In-rm modem link. Bellhops. Valet serv. Sundries. Gift shop. Airport, RR station transportation. Exercise equipt; sauna. Indoor pool; whirlpool. Lawn games. Some refrigerators. Many balconies. Cr cds: A, C, D, DS, JCB, MC, V.

D ✔ ≋ ✕ ⊠ SC

★ ★ **RAMADA HOTEL-ROLLING GREEN.** *(311 Lowell St, Andover 01810) 2¹/₂ mi W on MA 133, 1 blk E of I-93 exit 43A.* 978/475-5400; FAX 978/470-1108. 179 rms, 2 story. S $99-$129; D $109-$139; each addl $12; suites $125-$250; under 18 free; group, wkend rates. Crib free. Pet accepted. TV; cable. 2 pools, 1 indoor; whirlpool. Restaurant 6:30 am-2 pm, 5-10 pm. Rm serv. Bar 11:30-1 am. Ck-out noon. Meeting rms. Business servs avail. Valet serv. Airport transportation. Indoor tennis, pro. 9-hole par 3 golf, greens fee $12-$14. Exercise equipt; sauna. Microwaves avail. Cr cds: A, C, D, DS, ER, JCB, MC, V.

✔ ★ **SUSSE CHALET.** *(1695 Andover St (MA 133), Tewksbury 01876) I-495 exit 39.* 978/640-0700; FAX 978/640-1175. Web www.sussechalet.com. 133 rms, 5 story. S, D $54.70-$68.70; each addl $7; under 18 free. TV; cable (premium). Complimentary continental bkfst. Restaurant adj 10 am-10 pm. Ck-out 11 am. In-rm modem link. Sundries. Coin lndry. Pool. Cr cds: A, C, D, DS, MC, V.

✔ ★ **TAGE INN.** *(131 River Rd, Andover 01810) 1 blk SW of I-93 exit 45.* 978/685-6200; FAX 978/794-9626; res: 800/322-TAGE. E-mail tageinn@tiac.net. 180 rms, 3 story. S $59.95; D $80; each addl $8; under 12 free. Crib free. TV; cable. Indoor pool; whirlpool. Complimentary continental bkfst. Restaurant 6:30-10 am, 5 pm-midnight; 7-11 am wkends. Ck-out noon. Meeting rms. Business servs avail. In-rm modem link. Valet serv. Lighted tennis. Exercise equipt. Some bathrm phones. Refrigerators avail. Cr cds: A, C, D, DS, MC, V.

Inn

★ ★ **ANDOVER.** *(Chapel Ave, Andover 01810) ³/₄ mi S on MA 28.* 978/475-5903; res: 800/242-5903; FAX 978/475-1053. 23 rms, 3 story. S $95; D $110; each addl $10; suites $140; under 12 free. Pet accepted, some restrictions. TV; VCR avail. Dining rm 7:30 am-9:45 pm. Rm serv. Bar 11:30 am-midnight. Ck-out noon. Meeting rms. Business center. In-rm modem link. Valet serv. Beauty shop. On campus of Phillips Academy. Cr cds: A, C, D, DS, MC, V.

Restaurant

★ **CHINA BLOSSOM.** *(946 Osgood, North Andover 01845) at MA 125 & Sutton St.* 978/682-2242. Chinese menu. Daily buffet. Hrs: 11:30 am-9:30 pm; Fri, Sat to midnight; Sun noon-9:30 pm. Closed Thanksgiving. Bar. A la carte: lunch, dinner $6.95-$26. Family-owned. Cr cds: A, C, D, DS, MC, V.

Barnstable (Cape Cod) (D-9)

(See also Hyannis, South Yarmouth)

Settled 1637 **Pop** 40,949 **Elev** 37 ft **Area code** 508 **Zip** 02630 **E-mail** info@capecodchamber.org **Web** www.capecodchamber.org

Information Cape Cod Chamber of Commerce, US 6 & MA 132, PO Box 790, Hyannis 02601-0790, 508/362-3225 or 888/33-CAPECOD.

Farmers first settled Barnstable because the marshes provided salt hay for cattle. Later the town prospered as a whaling and trading center, and when these industries declined, land development made it the political hub of the Cape. It is the seat of Barnstable County, which includes the entire Cape; like other Cape communities, it does a thriving resort business.

What to See and Do

Cape Cod Art Association Gallery. Changing exhibits, exhibitions by New England artists; demonstrations, lectures, classes. (Apr-Nov, daily, limited hrs; rest of yr, inquire for schedule) On MA 6A. Phone 508/362-2909. **Free.**

Donald G. Trayser Memorial Museum. Marine exhibits, scrimshaw, Barnstable silver, historic documents. (July-mid-Oct, Tues-Sat afternoons) In Old Custom House and Post Office, Main St on Cobb's Hill, MA 6A. Phone 508/362-2092. **Donation.**

Hyannis Whale Watcher Cruises. View whales aboard the *Whale Watcher*, a 297-passenger super-cruiser, custom designed and built specifically for whale watching. Naturalist on board will narrate. Cafe on board. (Apr-Oct, daily) Res necessary. Barnstable Harbor. Contact PO Box 254; phone 508/362-6088. ¢¢¢¢¢

Sturgis Library. Oldest library building (1644) in US has material on the Cape, including maritime history; genealogical records of Cape Cod families. Research fee for nonresidents. (Daily exc Sun; closed hols; limited hrs) On Main St, MA 6A. Phone 508/362-6636. ¢¢

West Parish Meetinghouse (1717). Said to be the oldest Congregational church in country; restored. Congregation established in London, 1616. Regular Sun services are held here all yr. Jct US 6, MA 149 in West Barnstable. **Free.**

Inns

★ ★ **ACWORTH INN.** *(4352 Old King's Hwy (MA 6A), Cummaquid 02637) 2 mi E on MA 6A.* 508/362-3330; FAX 508/375-0304; res: 800/362-6363. Web www.acworthinn.com. 4 rms, with shower only, 2 story, 1 suite. Some A/C. No rm phones. Late May-Oct: S, D $100-$125; each addl $20; suite $185; wkends, hols (2-day min); lower rates rest of yr. Children over 12 yrs only. TV in common rm; cable. Complimentary full bkfst. Restaurant nearby. Ck-out 11, ck-in 3-10 pm. Luggage handling. Concierge serv. Farmhouse built in 1860. Totally nonsmoking. Cr cds: A, DS, MC, V.

★ ★ **ASHLEY MANOR.** *3660 Olde Kings Hwy (MA 6A).* 508/362-8044; res: 888/535-2246; FAX 508/362-9927. E-mail ashleymn@capecod.net; web www.capecod.net/ashleymn. 6 rms, 2 story, 4 suites, 1 cottage. Phone avail. S, D $125-$180; suites $165-$180. Children over 14 yrs only. Complimentary full bkfst; afternoon refreshments. Complimentary coffee in rms. Ck-out 11 am, ck-in 2 pm. Tennis. Lawn games. Many fireplaces; some in-rm whirlpools. Library. Antiques. Restored early 18th-century inn on 2-acre estate. Cr cds: DS, JCB, MC, V.

★ ★ **BEECHWOOD.** *2839 Main St.* 508/362-6618; FAX 508/362-0298; res: 800/609-6618. E-mail bwdinn@virtualcapecod.com; web www.virtualcapecod.com/market/beechwood. 6 rms, 3 story. No rm phones. May-Oct: S, D $135-$175; each addl $20; lower rates rest of yr. Complimentary full bkfst; afternoon refreshments. Ck-out 11 am, ck-in 2 pm. Lawn games. Refrigerators; some fireplaces. Restored Victorian house (1853); veranda with rocking chairs, glider. Antique furnishings. Totally nonsmoking. Cr cds: A, DS, MC, V.

★ ★ **HONEYSUCKLE HILL.** *(591 Main St (MA 6A), West Barnstable 02668) 3 mi W on MA 6A.* 508/362-8418; res: 800/441-8418. Web www.bbonline.com/ma/honeysuckle/. 5 rms, 2 share bath, 2 with shower only, 2 story, 2 suites. S, D $115; suite $175; wkends, hols (2-day min). Children over 12 yrs only. Complimentary full bkfst. Restaurants nearby. Ck-out 11 am, ck-in 3 pm. Built in 1810; restored Victorian decor. Cr cds: A, DS, MC, V.

Restaurants

★ ★ **BARNSTABLE TAVERN & GRILLE.** *3176 Main St.* 508/362-2355. Specializes in black Angus beef, fresh native seafood, desserts. Hrs: 11:30 am-11:30 pm. Closed Dec 24, 25. Bar. Semi-a la carte: lunch $3.95-$10.95, dinner $10.95-$21.95. Child's meals. Entertainment. Outdoor dining. Inn and tavern since 1799. Cr cds: A, D, DS, MC, V.

★ ★ **HARBOR POINT.** *(Harbor Point Rd, Cummaquid)* 1¼ mi E. 508/362-2231. Specializes in fresh seafood, steak. Hrs: 11:30 am-10:30 pm; wkends to midnight; Sun brunch 11 am-3 pm. Closed Feb-Mar. Res accepted. Bar. Semi-a la carte: lunch $2.95-$10.95, dinner $15.95-$22.95. Sun brunch $10.95. Child's meals. Entertainment. Overlooking bay, marsh abundant with wildlife. Fountain. Cr cds: A, DS, MC, V.

★ ★ **MATTAKEESE WHARF.** *271 Mill Way, on Barnstable Harbor.* 508/362-4511. Specialties: bouillabaisse, baked stuffed shrimp, lobster. Own pasta. Hrs: 11:30 am-10 pm; Sun 11:30 am-9 pm; early-bird dinner Sun-Fri 4:30-6 pm; Sun brunch to 2:30 pm. Closed late Oct-early May. Res accepted. No A/C. Bar to 1 am. Semi-a la carte: lunch $5.25-$12, dinner $10.95-$19.95. Sun brunch $8.95. Child's meals. Entertainment wkends. Valet parking. View of boats in harbor; nautical motif. Family-owned. Cr cds: A, MC, V.

Bedford (B-7)

Pop 12,996 **Elev** 135 ft **Area code** 781 **Zip** 01730

Motel

★ **TRAVELODGE.** *285 Great Rd, exit 31B, 1 mi N of I-95 on MA 4/225.* 781/275-6120. 42 rms, 2 story. S $59-$79; D $69-$89; each addl $6; under 14 free. Crib $6. TV; cable. Pool. Complimentary coffee. Restaurant nearby. Ck-out 11 am. In-rm modem link. Balconies. Cr cds: A, D, DS, MC, V.

Motor Hotel

★ ★ **RAMADA INN.** *340 Great Rd.* 781/275-6700; FAX 781/275-3011. 99 rms, 3 story. Apr-Oct: S, D $69-$119; each addl $10; under 18 free; wkend, hol rates. Crib free. TV; cable (premium). Heated pool. Complimentary full bkfst. Complimentary coffee in rms. Restaurant 6:30-10:30 am, 5-9 pm; Sat 7-11 am, 5-9 pm; Sun 7 am-noon. Bar. Ck-out noon. Meeting rms. Business servs avail. Valet serv. Exercise equipt. Cr cds: A, C, D, DS, JCB, MC, V.

Hotel

★ ★ ★ **RENAISSANCE.** *44 Middlesex Tpke, MA 3 exit 26 to MA 62.* 781/275-5500; FAX 781/275-8956. 285 rms, 2-3 story. S, D $170-$210; suites $200-$225; wkend rates; under 18 free. Crib free. Pet accepted, some restrictions. TV; cable (premium), VCR avail. Indoor pool; whirlpool, poolside serv. Restaurant (see HAVILLAND'S GRILLE). Rm serv 24 hrs. Complimentary coffee delivered to rms. Bar 11:30-1 am; entertainment. Ck-out 1 pm. Convention facilities. Business center. In-rm modem link. Concierge. Indoor & outdoor tennis, pro. Exercise rm; sauna. Health club privileges. Refrigerators, minibars. On 24 wooded acres. Cr cds: A, C, D, DS, ER, JCB, MC, V.

Restaurant

★ ★ ★ **HAVILLAND'S GRILLE.** *(See Renaissance Hotel)* 781/275-5500. Specializes in Mediterranean cuisine featuring grilled seafood. Own baking. Hrs: 6:30 am-11 pm; Sat, Sun from 7:30 am. Closed Dec 25. Res accepted. Bar. Semi-a la carte: bkfst $4.95-$8.95, lunch $7-$14, dinner $10-$22. Child's meals. Valet parking. Totally nonsmoking. Cr cds: A, C, D, DS, ER, JCB, MC, V.

Berkshire Hills (B-2 - C-2)

E-mail bvb@berkshires.org **Web** www.berkshires.org

Information Berkshire Visitors Bureau, Berkshire Common, Pittsfield 01201; 413/443-9186or 800/237-5747.

This western Massachusetts resort area is just south of Vermont's Green Mountains, but has neither the ruggedness nor the lonesomeness of the range to its north. The highest peak, Mt Greylock (elevation: 3,491 feet), is cragless and serene. Farms and villages dot the landscape. The area is famous for its variety of accommodations, culture and recreation. There are also countless summer homes and camps for children by the lakes, ponds and brooks.

Berkshire County is about 45 miles long from north to south, and half that from east to west. It has 90 lakes and ponds, 90,000 acres of state forest, golf courses, ski areas, ski touring centers, numerous tennis facilities and campsites. The area first became famous when Nathaniel Hawthorne wrote *Tanglewood Tales*, and it has since become distinguished for its many summer cultural activities, including the Tanglewood Music Festival at Tanglewood (see LENOX) and the Berkshire Theatre Festival (see STOCKBRIDGE & WEST STOCKBRIDGE).

Beverly (B-8)

(See also Danvers)

Settled 1626 **Pop** 38,195 **Elev** 26 ft **Area code** 508 **Zip** 01915
InformationNorth Shore Chamber of Commerce, 5 Cherry Hill Dr, Danvers 01923; 508/774-8565.

When George Washington commissioned the first US naval vessel, the schooner *Hannah*, on September 5, 1775, at Glover's Wharf in Beverly, the town was already well established. In 1693, the local Puritan minister's wife, Mistress Hale, was accused of witchcraft. She was so far above reproach that the charge—and the hysteria—collapsed. Today, Beverly is a popular summer resort area. Saltwater fishing, boating and scuba diving are available near Glover's Wharf.

What to See and Do

Balch House (1636). One of the two oldest wood-frame houses in America. Born in 1579, John Balch came to America in 1623 as one of the first permanent settlers of Massachusetts Bay. (Mid-May-mid-Oct, Wed-Sun; closed hols) Inquire about combination ticket (includes Hale and Cabot houses). 448 Cabot St. Phone 508/922-1186. ¢¢

Cabot House (1781). HQ of Beverly Historical Society. Brick mansion of Revolutionary War privateer John Cabot, built a yr after it was written that "the Cabots of Beverly are now said to be by far the most wealthy in New England." Continental navy exhibit; period rms; portrait and primitive art collection; dolls; military and changing exhibits. (Wed-Sat) Inquire about combination ticket (includes Hale and Balch Houses). 117 Cabot St. Phone 508/922-1186. ¢¢

Hale House (1694). Built by the Rev John Hale, who was active in the witchcraft trials and whose own wife was accused of witchcraft. Rare wallpaper and furnishings show changes through the 18th & 19th centuries. (Mid-June-Labor Day, Fri-Sun afternoons; also by appt; closed hols) Inquire about combination ticket (includes Cabot and Balch Houses). 39 Hale St. Phone 508/922-1186. **¢¢**

"Le Grand David and his own Spectacular Magic Company." Resident stage magic company, New England's longest running theatrical attraction. This 2¼-hr stage magic production features magic, music, comedy and dance. 500 costumes, 2 dozen sets and backdrops; 50 magic illusions. (Sun) Additional performances at Larcom Theatre (1912), 13 Wallis St. Advance tickets recommended. Cabot Street Cinema Theatre (1920), 286 Cabot St. Phone 508/927-3677. **¢¢¢¢**

Wenham Museum. Doll collection representing cultures from 1500 B.C. to present; toy room, dollhouses; changing arts, crafts & antique exhibits. Claflin-Richards House (ca 1660) containing collections of quilts, costumes, fans; period furniture. Winslow Shoe Shop displays history of shoemaking; early ice-cutting tools; research library. (Daily; closed hols) 2 ½ mi N on MA 1A, at 132 Main St in Wenham. Phone 508/468-2377. **¢¢**

Seasonal Events

North Shore Music Theatre. 62 Dunham Rd, at MA 128N exit 19. Broadway musicals and plays; children's musicals; celebrity concerts. For schedule phone 508/922-8500. Late Apr-late Dec.

Band concerts. Lynch Park Bandshell Sun eve; downtown Ellis Square, Thurs eve. Late June-mid-Aug.

Restaurants

★ ★ **BEVERLY DEPOT.** *10 Park St, MA 62 Bridge St to end. 978/927-5402.* Specializes in fresh seafood, steak, prime rib. Salad bar. Hrs: 5-10 pm; Fri, Sat to 11 pm; Sun 4-9 pm. Bar. Semi-a la carte: dinner $9-$22. Child's meals. In 1800s train depot. Cr cds: A, C, D, DS, MC, V.

✔★ **COMMODORE.** *45 Enon St, 1A 3 mi N. 978/922-5590.* Hrs: 11:30 am-10 pm; Fri, Sat to 11 pm; Sun noon-9 pm. Closed Jan 1, July 4, Dec 25. Res accepted. Bar to 1 am. Semi-a la carte: lunch $4.75-$8.95, dinner $8.95-$15.95. Child's meals. Specializes in fresh seafood, prime rib. Own desserts. Entertainment Wed-Sat. Circular dining rm; colonial atmosphere, nautical motif. Operating old mill wheel, lighthouse tower. Chef-owned. Cr cds: A, C, D, DS, ER, JCB, MC, V.

Boston (B-7)

Founded 1630 **Pop** 574,283 **Elev** 0-330 ft **Area code** 617
Information Greater Boston Convention & Visitors Bureau, Prudential Tower, PO Box 990468, 02199; 617/536-4100 or 888/733-2678.

Suburbs Braintree, Burlington, Cambridge, Dedham, Framingham, Lexington, Lynn, Newton, Quincy, Saugus, Waltham, Wellesley. (See individual alphabetical listings.)

Greater Boston is a fascinating combination of the old and the new. It consists of 83 cities and towns in an area of 1,057 square miles with a total population of more than three million people. Boston proper is the hub of this busy complex, which many proper Bostonians still believe is the hub of the universe.

Boston is a haven for walkers; in fact, strolling along its streets is advised to get a true sense of this most European of all American cities. If you drive, a map is invaluable. Traffic is heavy. The streets (many of them narrow and one-way) run at odd angles; expressway traffic speeds.

Boston's wealth of historic sights makes it a must for all who are interested in America's past. John Winthrop and 800 colonists first settled in Charlestown, just north of the Charles River, and moved to Boston in 1630. Arriving too late to plant, 200 colonists died during the first winter,

mostly of starvation. In the spring, a ship arrived with provisions and the new Puritan commonwealth began to thrive and grow. Fisheries, fur trapping, lumbering and trading with Native Americans were the foundation of Boston's commerce. The port is still viable, with 250 wharves along 30 miles of berthing space.

The American Revolution began here in 1770. British troops fired on an angry mob, killing six in what has since been called the "Boston Massacre." In 1773, the Boston Tea Party dumped East Indian tea into the bay in a dramatic protest against restriction of colonial trade by British governors. Great Britain closed the port in retaliation. The course of history was set.

In April, 1775, British General Thomas Gage decided to march on Concord to capture military supplies and overwhelm the countryside. During the night of April 18-19, Paul Revere, William Dawes and Samuel Prescott spread the news to Lexington and Concord in a ride immortalized, somewhat inaccurately, by Henry Wadsworth Longfellow. The American Revolution had begun in earnest; the Battle of Bunker Hill followed the battles of Lexington and Concord. On March 17, 1776, General William Howe, commander of the British forces, evacuated the city.

Boston's list of distinguished native sons includes John Hancock, Samuel Adams, Paul Revere, Henry Ward Beecher, Edward Everett Hale, Ralph Waldo Emerson, William Lloyd Garrison, Oliver Wendell Holmes (father and son) and hundreds of others.

Mention Boston and many people will automatically think of the gentry of Beacon Hill, with their elegant homes and rigid social code. However, the Irish have long had a powerful influence in Boston's politics and personality, while a stroll down an Italian neighborhood on the North End will be like stepping back to the old country.

Boston today has managed to retain its heritage and charm while thriving in the modern age. Urban renewal and increased construction have reversed an almost 40-year slump that plagued Boston earlier this century. With more than 100 universities, colleges, trade and vocational schools in the area, Boston is a city as full of vigor and promise for the future as it is rich with the past.

Transportation

Car Rental Agencies: See IMPORTANT TOLL-FREE NUMBERS.

Public Transportation: Buses, subway & elevated trains (Massachusetts Bay Transportation Authority), visitor pass available, phone 617/722-3200.

Rail Passenger Service: Amtrak 800/872-7245.

Airport Information

Logan Intl Airport: Information 617/973-5500 or 800/235-6426; lost and found 617/561-1714; weather 617/936-1234; cash machines, Terminals A, B, C.

What to See and Do

Bell's Laboratory. Restored lab where telephone was born when Alexander Graham Bell first sent speech sounds electrically over a wire. Charts and instruments Bell used; first telephone switchboard; first commercial telephone. (Daily) New England Telephone Bldg, 185 Franklin St, in lobby. Phone 617/743-9800. **Free.**

Blue Hills Trailside Museum. Visitor center for the 5,700-acre Blue Hills Reservation. Deer, turkey, otter, snakes, owls and honeybees. Exhibit hall with natural science/history displays, including Native American wigwam; viewing tower. Activities include hikes, films, animal programs. Special events include maple sugaring (Mar); Hawks Wkend (Sept) and Honey Harvest (Oct). Visitor center & buildings (daily exc Mon; schedule may vary, phone ahead); grounds (daily). 8 mi S, MA 128 exit 2B (Milton), then 1/2 mi N on MA 138, next to Blue Hills Ski Area. Phone 617/333-0690. **¢¢**

Boston African American National Historic Site. Includes **African Meeting House.** Part of the Museum of Afro-American History. Built by free black Bostonians in 1806, building was an educational and religious center and site of founding of New England Anti-Slavery Society in 1832. (Memorial Day-Labor Day, Mon-Fri; rest of yr, by appt) 30-min tour (hrly on

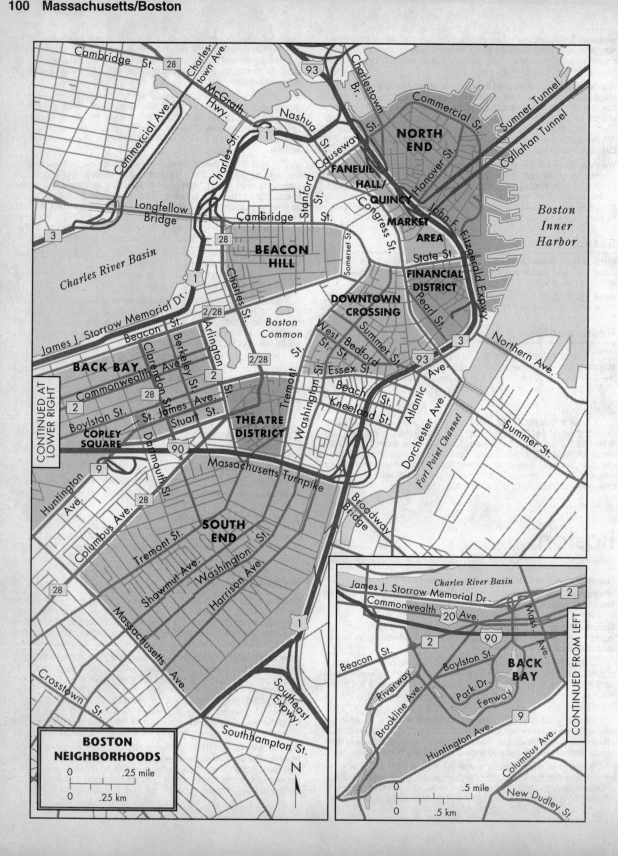

Cambridge St. 28
Charles-town Ave.
Commercial Ave.
McGrath Hwy.
Nashua
93
Charlestown Br.
Commercial St.
Sumner Tunnel
Callahan Tunnel
NORTH END
Charles St.
Longfellow Bridge
3
Charles River Basin
Cambridge St.
28
Somerset St.
Stanford St.
Causeway St.
Congress St.
FANEUIL HALL/ QUINCY MARKET AREA
Hanover St.
John F. Fitzgerald Expwy.
Boston Inner Harbor
BEACON HILL
State St.
FINANCIAL DISTRICT
James J. Storrow Memorial Dr.
1
Charles St.
Boston Common
DOWNTOWN CROSSING
Pearl St.
3
Northern Ave.
Beacon St.
Arlington St.
2/28
West St.
Summer St.
93
Berkeley St.
Clarendon Ave.
2/28
Bedford St.
Atlantic Ave.
BACK BAY
Commonwealth Ave.
28
St. James Ave.
Tremont St.
Washington St.
Essex St.
Beach St.
Kneeland St.
Dorchester Ave.
Summer St.
Fort Point Channel
2
Boylston St.
Stuart St.
THEATRE DISTRICT
COPLEY SQUARE
Darmouth St.
90
9
Massachusetts Turnpike
Huntington Ave.
Columbus Ave.
28
SOUTH END
Tremont St.
Shawmut Ave.
Washington St.
Harrison Ave.
Broadway Bridge
1
28
Massachusetts Ave.
Crosstown St.
Southeast Expwy.
Southhampton St.

CONTINUED AT LOWER RIGHT

BOSTON NEIGHBORHOODS
0 .25 mile
0 .25 km
N

Charles River Basin
James J. Storrow Memorial Dr.
Commonwealth 20 Ave.
2
90
Mass. Ave.
2
Beacon St.
2
Boylston St.
BACK BAY
Riverway
Brookline Ave.
Park Dr.
Fenway
9
Huntington Ave.
Columbus Ave.
New Dudley St.
CONTINUED FROM LEFT
0 .5 mile
0 .5 km

the hr) of Meeting House by museum staff. Smith Ct, off Joy St on Beacon Hill. Phone 617/742-5415. **Free.** Meeting House is starting point for the

Black Heritage Trail. Marked walking tour conducted by National Park Service, past sites in the Beacon Hill section that relate the history of 19th-century black Boston. Brochure and maps are at National Park Visitor Center, 46 Joy St, 2nd floor. Two-hr guided tours by National Park Service (by appt). Phone 617/742-5415. **Free.**

Boston College (1863). (14,500 students) 140 Commonwealth Ave, Chestnut Hill.On campus is

Bapst Library. English Collegiate Gothic building with fine stained glass. Rare books display; changing exhibits. (Summer, Mon-Fri; rest of yr, daily) Phone 617/552-3200. **Free.**

Boston Tea Party Ship and Museum. Atmosphere of the Boston Tea Party (1773) is recreated. Visitors may board the full-size working replica of the Tea Party Ship and throw tea chests overboard. Exhibits, artifacts, audiovisual presentations place the event in historical perspective; costumed tour guides. Complimentary tea served. (Daily) Congress St Bridge, on Harborwalk. Phone 617/338-1773. ¢¢¢

Boston University (1839). (28,000 students) Information center located at 771 Commonwealth Ave in the George Sherman Union (phone 617/353-2169); also located here is the George Sherman Union Gallery. Mugar Memorial Library houses papers of Dr. Martin Luther King, Jr, as well as those of Robert Frost, Isaac Asimov and other writers and artists. Boston University Art Gallery exhibits at the School for the Arts, 855 Commonwealth Ave. Commonwealth Ave near Kenmore Sq. Campus tours from the Admissions Office, 121 Bay State Rd; 617/353-2318.

Computer Museum. More than 125 hands-on exhibits allow visitors to explore the latest computer technologies. Films; computer animations; robot demonstrations; tours. Exhibits include a 2-story walk-through computer; history of computers from 1940 to present; the latest in personal computers, artificial intelligence, computer graphics and image processing. Museum offers programs, publications and archives, lectures, special events; gift shop. (Mid-June-Labor Day, daily; rest of yr, daily exc Mon) Museum Wharf, 300 Congress St. Phone 617/423-6758 or 617/426-2800, ext 329. ¢¢¢

Franklin Park Zoo. "Bird's World" indoor/outdoor aviary complex with natural habitats; African tropical forest; hilltop range with camels, antelopes, zebras, mouflon; children's zoo. (Daily; closed Jan 1, Thanksgiving, Dec 25) S on Jamaicaway, E on MA 203 in Dorchester. Phone 617/442-2002. ¢

Frederick Law Olmsted National Historic Site. Former home and office of the founder of landscape architecture in America. Site archives contain documentation of firm's work. Site also includes landscaped grounds designed by Olmsted. Guided tours. (Fri-Sun) 99 Warren St, in Brookline. Phone 617/566-1689. **Free.**

Gibson House Museum. Victorian townhouse with period furnishings. Tours (May-Oct, Wed-Sun afternoons; Nov-Apr, Sat & Sun; closed hols). 137 Beacon St. Phone 617/267-6338. ¢¢

Guided walking tours. Boston by Foot. 1¹/₂-hr architectural walking tours including the heart of Freedom Trail (Tues-Sat); Beacon Hill (daily, departures vary); Victorian Back Bay Tour (Fri & Sat); North End (Sat); children's tour (Sat-Mon, 1 departure daily); downtown Boston (Sun). All tours (May-Oct). Tour of the month each 4th Sun; custom tours. Contact 77 N Washington St, 02114; 617/367-2345 or -3766 (recording). ¢¢¢

Guild of Boston Artists. Changing exhibits of paintings, graphics and sculpture by New England artists. (Sept-June, Tues-Sat; closed Jan 1, Thanksgiving, Dec 25) 162 Newbury St. Phone 617/536-7660. **Free.**

Harborwalk. Blue line guides visitors from Old State House to New England Aquarium, ending at the Boston Tea Party Ship and Museum, forming a walking tour with many stops in between.

Harrison Gray Otis House (1796). Otis, a lawyer and statesman, built this first of three houses designed for him by Charles Bulfinch. A later move to Beacon Hill left this house as a rooming house for 100 yrs. Restored to reflect Boston taste and decoration of 1796-1820. Some family furnishings. Reflects the proportion and delicate detail Bulfinch introduced to Boston, strongly influencing the Federal style in New England. Museum. HQ for the Society for the Preservation of New England Antiquities; send stamped, self-addressed legal-size envelope to Society for guide to 22 historic

homes (02114). Tours (Wed-Sun). 141 Cambridge St, enter from Lynde St. Phone for schedule, 617/227-3956. ¢¢

Harvard Medical Area. One of the world's great centers of medicine. Huntington & Longwood Aves. Phone 617/432-1000.

Institute of Contemporary Art. Occupies a 19th-century Richardsonian-style building once used as a police station. Exhibits of contemporary art: painting, sculpture, video and photography. Docent-guided tours (Sat & Sun afternoons). Also film, video, music, dance, poetry, lectures and performance art in the ICA Theater. Gallery (Wed-Sun). Bookstore (daily). Free admission Thurs eve. 955 Boylston St, opp Prudential Center. Phone 617/266-5152. ¢¢¢

Isaac Royall House (1637). Originally built as a 4-rm farmhouse by John Winthrop, first governor of Bay State Colony; enlarged in 1732 by Isaac Royall. Example of early Georgian architecture; examples of Queen Anne, Chippendale and Hepplewhite furnishings. (May-Sept, Wed-Sun) ³/₄ mi S off I-93, at 15 George St in Medford. Phone 617/396-9032. ¢¢

Isabella Stewart Gardner Museum. This was the home of this patron of the arts from 1902 until her death in 1924. Paintings, sculpture and a flower display are in the enormous Venetian-style central courtyard, surrounded by 3 floors of galleries (daily exc Mon; closed most hols). Concerts (late Sept-May, Sat & Sun afternoons; fees). 280 The Fenway. Phone 617/734-1359 for concert information or 617/566-1401 for museum. ¢¢¢

John F. Kennedy National Historic Site. The birthplace and early childhood home of the nation's 35th president is restored in appearance to 1917, the year of his birth. Ranger-guided tours. (Wed-Sun; closed Jan 1, Thanksgiving, Dec 25) Golden Eagle Passport accepted (see MAKING THE MOST OF YOUR TRIP.). 83 Beals St, in Brookline. Phone 617/566-7937. ¢

★ **Museum at the John Fitzgerald Kennedy Library.** Designed by I.M. Pei, the library is considered one of the most beautiful contemporary works of architecture in the country. The library tower houses a collection of documents from the Kennedy administration as well as audiovisual programs designed to recreate the era. (Daily, closed Jan 1, Thanksgiving, Dec 25) Picnic facilities on oceanfront. 5 mi SE on I-93, off exit 15, at University of Massachusetts Columbia Point campus. Phone 617/929-4523. ¢¢¢

Museum of Fine Arts. Chinese, Japanese, Indian, Egyptian, Greek, Roman, European and American collections; also silver, period rms and musical instruments. Gallery lectures, films; library; children's programs; changing exhibits; restaurants; auditorium. (Daily; closed Thanksgiving, Dec 25) Free admission Wed, late afternoon-evening. 465 Huntington Ave. Phone 617/267-9300. ¢¢¢

Museum of Science. One of the finest and most modern science museums in the world, with many hands-on exhibits. "Seeing the Unseen," giant dinosaur model; "Human Body Discovery Space," health and environment displays; live animal, physical science and special effects demonstrations. Children's Discovery Room. Omnimax Theatre (fee). (Daily; closed Thanksgiving, Dec 25) Science Park, on Charles River Dam Bridge between Storrow Dr & Memorial Dr. Advance tickets recommended; phone 617/523-6664. Phone 617/723-2500. ¢¢¢ Also here is

Charles Hayden Planetarium. Shows approx 50 min. (Same hrs as museum) Children under 4 yrs not admitted. Phone 617/523-6664. Additional fee ¢¢¢

New England Aquarium. One of the largest cylindrical saltwater tanks in world, stocked with hundreds of specimens of marine life. Permanent exhibits include marine mammals, birds and reptiles. Freshwater gallery, marine life in American rivers, including exotic animals from the Amazon Basin area. Electric eel, turtles, and a 4,000-gallon replica of an Amazon rain forest. Adj is *The Discovery,* a barge where sea lion demonstrations are presented. (Daily; closed morning of Jan 1, Thanksgiving, Dec 25) Whale watches (mid-Apr-mid-Oct; fee; phone 617/673-5281 for res). Central Wharf. Phone 617/973-5200. ¢¢¢

Professional sports.

American League baseball (Boston Red Sox). Fenway Park, 4 Yawkey Way. Phone 617/267-9440.

NBA (Boston Celtics). Fleet Center, 1 Fleet Center Pl. Phone 617/523-6050.

NHL (Boston Bruins). Fleet Center, 1 Fleet Center Pl. Phone 617/624-1050.

Prudential Center. Complex of retail, civic, business, residential buildings on 32-acre site in Back Bay. Prudential Tower rises 52 stories (750 ft); restaurant. The Skywalk, an observation deck on the 50th floor, provides a 360° panoramic view and has temporary exhibits and displays. (Daily) 800 Boylston St, off MA Tpke. Phone 617/236-3318. Skywalk ¢¢

Shirley-Eustis House (1747). Built for royal governor William Shirley, restored to Federal-style of period when Gov William Eustis lived here (1818-1825). (June-Sept, Thurs-Sun afternoons) 33 Shirley St. Phone 617/442-2275. ¢¢

Shopping. Boston has many good department and specialty stores, grouped on downtown Washington and Tremont Sts and connecting streets. Wm Filene's Sons Co and Jordan Marsh are both excellent. Filene's Basement is famous and particularly fascinating for bargain-hunters. The Back Bay area, particularly on Newbury St, is also a shopper's haven, with numerous boutiques, art galleries and antique shops. Haymarket Square in the North End is an open-air farmers market good for shopping and photographing (Fri, Sat). Copley Place offers shoppers more than 100 stores among its retail, office, hotel and residential complex. Many wharves in the waterfront area now house shops and galleries.

Sightseeing tours.

Boston Tours. Escorted bus tours departing from suburban hotels and motels along I-95/MA 128. Also departures from metrowest suburban hotels in Natick/Framingham area. Tours follow Freedom Trail and include stops at Old North Church, "Old Ironsides," Faneuil Hall Marketplace and Cambridge. 6-hr tour (daily). 56 Williams St, in Waltham. For reservations, schedule and fee information phone 781/899-1454.

Brush Hill Tours. Fully lectured 3-hr bus tours of Boston/Cambridge (late Mar-mid-Nov); ½-day tours of Lexington/Concord, Salem/Marblehead (mid-June-Oct), and Plymouth (May-Oct); full-day tours of Cape Cod (including Provincetown) and Newport, RI (June-Sept). Also 1½-hr tours along Freedom Trail aboard the Beantown Trolleys. Departures from major downtown hotels, Copley Square and Boston Common (daily). For schedule & res, phone 617/236-2148 or 617/986-6100. ¢¢¢¢¢

Bay State Cruise Company. All-day sail to Provincetown and Cape Cod from Commonwealth Pier. 2½- & 3½-hr harbor and island cruises aboard *Spirit of Boston* highlighting adventure and history. (Mid-June-Labor Day, daily; May-mid-June & after Labor Day-Columbus Day, Sat & Sun only) Contact Bay State Cruise Company, Commonwealth Pier, World Trade Center; 617/457-1428. ¢¢¢¢¢

Symphony Hall. Home of Boston Symphony (late Sept-early May) and Boston Pops (May-mid-July, daily exc Mon). Huntington & Massachusetts Aves. Phone 617/266-1492.

The Bible Exhibit. Nondenominational exhibit; audiovisual activities; rare Biblical treasures; historical timeline; large plexiglass wall-map with lighted journeys of 6 Biblical figures; historic editions; children's story corner; exploring center for reference; film & slide program on the hr. (Wed-Sun; closed Jan 1, Thanksgiving, Dec 25) Belvidere St, opp Prudential Center, in Back Bay. Phone 617/450-3732. **Free.**

The Children's Museum. Participatory exhibits on science, disabilities; cultural diversity; computers and games; play activities. (July-Labor Day, daily; rest of yr, closed Mon exc school hols; closed Jan 1, Thanksgiving, Dec 25) 300 Congress St, near South Station, a short walk from Faneuil Hall. Phone 617/426-8855. ¢¢¢

⭐ **The Freedom Trail** is a walking tour through downtown Boston that passes 16 points of interest, plus other exhibits, monuments and shrines just off the trail, some of which are part of **Boston National Historical Park.** The trail is marked by signs and a red sidewalk line. Brochures are at the Greater Boston Convention & Visitors Bureau information centers at the Prudential Plaza (phone 617/536-4100) and on the Boston Common.

State House (1795). Designed by Charles Bulfinch, the nation's first professional architect, it has since had wings added to both sides. Inside are statues, paintings and other interesting materials. Hall of Flags on 2nd floor; House and Senate Chambers, State Library on 3rd floor. Tours (Mon-Fri; closed hols). Beacon St at head of Park St. Phone 617/727-3676. **Free.**

Park Street Church (1809). Often called "Brimstone Corner" because brimstone for gunpowder was stored here during the War of 1812. William Lloyd Garrison delivered his first antislavery address here in 1829. Tours. (July-Aug, Tues-Sat; Sun services all yr) 1 Park St. Phone 617/523-3383. **Free.**

Granary Burying Ground. Once the site of the town granary. The graves of John Hancock, Samuel Adams, Paul Revere, Benjamin Franklin's parents, many governors, another signer of the Declaration of Independence and the martyrs of the Boston Massacre are here. (Daily) Tremont St opp end of Bromfield St.

King's Chapel (1754). The first Anglican church in Boston (1686) became in 1786 the first Unitarian church in America. Adj is the King's Chapel Burying Ground. Tremont St at School St. **Free.**

Site of the first US free public school (1635). It was the Boston Public Latin School. School St opp Old City Hall. Across the street is

Statue of Benjamin Franklin (1856) by Richard S. Greenough. Continue W on School St to Parker House, a hotel where Ho Chi Minh and Malcolm X once worked as waiters.

Old South Meeting House (1729). This was the site of many important town meetings about the British, including those that sparked the Boston Tea Party. Multimedia exhibition depicts its 300-yr history. (Daily; closed Jan 1, Thanksgiving, Dec 24, 25) 310 Washington St. Phone 617/482-6439. ¢

Old State House (1713). Boston's oldest public building, the Old State House served as the seat of the Royal Governor and Colonial Legislature until the Revolution. The Boston Massacre took place outside the building on Mar 5, 1770. From the balcony, the Declaration of Independence was first proclaimed to the citizens of Boston. Houses permanent and changing exhibits related to Boston history (daily). Reference and photograph library at 15 State St (Mon-Fri; fee). 206 Washington St, at State St. Phone 617/720-3290. ¢¢

Site of the Boston Massacre. Marked by a circle of cobblestones in the pavement. 30 State St.

Faneuil (FAN'L) **Hall Marketplace.** Bostonian Peter Faneuil bequeathed this 2-story, bronze-domed building to the city in 1742 as a public meeting hall and marketplace. Called the "Cradle of Liberty" because it was the scene of mass meetings during the pre-Revolutionary period, the building and 2 other restored structures today house a bustling marketplace of more than 100 specialty shops, 20 restaurants and pubs and a variety of pushcarts and food stalls. Marketplace (daily). Adj is a military museum—the Ancient and Honorable Artillery Company Museum, chartered in 1638 as a school for officers. (Mon-Fri; closed hols) Merchants Row. Phone 617/523-1300 or 617/227-1638 (museum). **Free.**

Paul Revere House (ca 1680). This is the only 17th-century structure left in downtown Boston. It was from this house that the silversmith left for his historic ride on Apr 18, 1775. The interior features 17th- and 18th-century decorative arts and contains Revere artifacts and memorabilia. (Apr-Dec, daily; rest of yr, daily exc Mon) 19 North Sq. Phone 617/523-2338. ¢¢

Old North Church (1723). The oldest church building in Boston. From the steeple's highest window were hung 2 lanterns, sending Paul Revere on his historic ride to warn the militia in Lexington. (Daily) Also Sun services. 193 Salem St, at foot of Hull St. Phone 617/523-6676. **Donation.**

Copp's Hill Burying Ground. First burials date from 1660. During the Revolution, British cannon here were trained on Charlestown and Bunker Hill, across the Charles River. Rev Cotton Mather and Edmund Hart, builder of the US frigate *Constitution*, are buried here. (Daily) Hull & Snow Hill Sts.

Bunker Hill Monument. A 221-ft granite obelisk commemorates the Battle of Bunker Hill, which took place on June 17, 1775. Ranger-conducted battle talks (June-Oct, on the hr); musket firing demonstrations (mid-June-Labor Day, Wed-Sun). Spiral staircase (294 steps) to top of monument, no elevator. Four sides viewing Boston area. (Daily; closed Jan 1, Thanksgiving, Dec 25) Monument Sq, Charlestown, a few blks from the *Constitution*. Phone 617/242-5641. **Free.**

USS *Constitution.* "Old Ironsides," launched in 1797, was engaged in more than 40 battles without defeat. Oldest commissioned Navy ship afloat in world. 20-min tours. Museum with ship artifacts is adj. (Daily) Located in Charlestown Navy Yard, Boston National Historical Park. I-93: northbound, exit 25 and follow signs across Charlestown bridge; southbound, exit 28 to Sullivan Sq and follow signs. Phone 617/426-1812. **Free.**

The Mother Church, The First Church of Christ, Scientist. Tours. (Tues-Sat; also Sun after services; closed major hols) Christian Science Center, Huntington & Massachusetts Aves. Phone 617/450-3790. **Free.** Adj is

Christian Science Publishing Society *(The Christian Science Monitor).* Inquire about tours. Mapparium, a walk-through stained-glass globe, is here. (Tues-Sat; closed major hols) Bible exhibit (Wed-Sun; closed Jan, major hols). Massachusetts Ave at Clearway St. Phone 617/450-3790 or -3793. **Free.**

⭐ **Walking tour** through the Common, Public Garden & Beacon Hill. Start at Park & Tremont Sts, walk NW up the hill on Park St to the

State House. Walk W 2 blks to Walnut St, turn right 1 blk to Mt Vernon St.

Nichols House Museum (1804). Typical domestic architecture of Beacon Hill from its era; only home on Beacon Hill open to the public. Attributed to Charles Bulfinch; antique furnishings and art from America, Europe and the Orient from the 17th-early 19th centuries. Collection of Rose Standish Nichols, landscape designer and writer. (Tues-Sat) 55 Mt Vernon St. Phone for hrs, 617/227-6993. ¢¢ Continue W on Mt Vernon St to

Louisburg Square. This lovely little residential square with its central park is the ultimate in traditional Boston charm. Louisa May Alcott, William Dean Howells and other famous Bostonians have lived here. It is one of the most treasured spots in Boston. Christmas caroling is traditional here. Walk S on Willow St, turn left to Spruce St and follow it 1 blk to the

Boston Common. A 48-acre tract set aside in 1634 for a cow pasture and training field, and, by law, still available for these purposes. Free speech is honored here, and you may find groups discussing anything from atheism to zoology. At the far side of the Common is the

Boston Massacre Monument. Commemorates this 1770 event, which has been called the origin of the Revolution. At the SW corner of the Common is the

Central Burying Ground. The grave of Gilbert Stuart, the painter, is here; technically not a part of the Common, although in it. Proceed W, crossing Charles St, and enter the

Public Garden. Formal gardens, rare trees carefully labeled. Pond with the famous swan boats in summer and skating in winter (fee). Just W of the Public Garden is the

Back Bay area. Walk along Boylston St, S side of Public Garden, 2 blks to

Copley Square. Here is

Trinity Church (Episcopal) (1877). This Henry Hobson Richardson building, the inspiration of Phillips Brooks, was the noblest work of the architect. The interior was decorated by John LaFarge and has five of his windows as well as two by William Morris of England. Phillips Brooks, the ninth rector of Trinity Church, is known for his beautiful Christmas carol, "O' Little Town of Bethlehem." His statue, by Augustus Saint Gaudens, stands outside the North Transept of the Church. Daniel Chester French created Brooks' bust in the Baptistry. Phillips Brooks preached at Trinity Church for 22 yrs. Theodore Parker Ferris, one of the outstanding preachers of the 20th century, was the 15th rector of Trinity Church and preached here for 30 yrs. Phone 617/536-0944. Opp church is the

John Hancock Observatory. The observatory, considered the best place to see Boston, is located on the 60th floor of the John Hancock Tower. It offers a panoramic view of Boston and eastern Massachusetts and exciting multimedia exhibits of Boston, past and present. They include "Boston 1775," a sound and light show about Boston since revolutionary days; a taped narration by the late Walter Muir Whitehill,

architectural historian; and a lighted display of New England scenes. In addition, "Aviation Radio" allows visitors to tune in on the cross-talk between planes at Logan International's tower while viewing the action at the airport. (Daily; closed Thanksgiving, Dec 25) At Copley Square. Phone 617/572-6429. ¢¢ Nearby is the

Boston Public Library (1895). Italian Renaissance building by Charles McKim includes central courtyard and fountain. Mural decorations, bronze doors, sculpture. Contemporary addition (1972), by Philip Johnson, houses large circulating library, recordings and films. Film and author programs; exhibits. Central Library (daily exc Sun; schedule may vary, phone ahead) 666 Boylston St, at Copley Square. Phone 617/536-5400. **Free.**

"Whites of Their Eyes." Specially designed pavilion houses multimedia re-enactment of the Battle of Bunker Hill using life-size figures and eyewitness narratives. Audience "viewpoint" from atop Breed's Hill. Continuous 30-min shows. (Apr-Nov, daily; closed Thanksgiving) Bunker Hill Pavilion, 55 Constitution Rd, just W of the USS *Constitution* in Charlestown. Phone 617/241-7575. ¢¢

Annual Events

Patriots Day Celebration. 3rd Mon Apr.

Boston Marathon. Famous 26-mi footrace from Hopkinton to Boston. 3rd Mon Apr.

Bunker Hill Day. Mid-June.

Harborfest. Hatch Shell on the Esplanade. Boston Pops Orchestra, fireworks. July 1-6.

Esplanade Concerts. Musical programs by the Boston Pops in the Hatch Shell on the Esplanade. 2 wks July.

Charles River Regatta. 3rd Sun Oct.

First Night Celebration. Boston Common. Dec 31.

Additional Visitor Information

Literature and information is available at the Greater Boston Convention & Visitors Bureau, Prudential Tower, PO Box 990468, 02199; 617/536-4100, the Prudential Visitor Center and at the visitor information center on Tremont St, Boston Common (daily; closed Jan 1, Thanksgiving, Dec 25). The National Park Visitor Center (daily) at 15 State St also has helpful information. All have informative brochures with maps of the Freedom Trail and Black History Trail.

Bostix, located in Faneuil Hall Marketplace, offers half-price tickets for music, theater and dance performances on the day of performance; also provides cultural information and calender of events. (Daily exc Mon; closed Thanksgiving, Dec 25) Phone 617/723-5181 (recording).

City Neighborhoods

Many of the restaurants, unrated dining establishments and some lodgings listed under Boston include neighborhoods as well as exact street addresses. Geographic descriptions of these areas are given, followed by a table of restaurants arranged by neighborhood.

Back Bay: South of Memorial Dr along the Charles River Basin, west of Arlington St, north of Stuart St and Huntington Ave and east of Boston University campus and Brookline.

Beacon Hill: South of Cambridge St, west of Somerset St, north of Beacon St and east of Charles St.

Copley Square: South of Boylston St, west of Trinity Church (Trinity St), north of St James Ave and east of the Public Library (Dartmouth St).

Downtown Crossing Area: At intersection of Washington St and Winter and Summer Sts; area south of State St, north of Essex St, east of Tremont St and west of Congress St. **East of Downtown Crossing Area:** East of Congress St. **South of Downtown Crossing Area:** South of Essex St.

Faneuil Hall/Quincy Market Area: South and west of the John F. Fitzgerald Expy (I-93), north of State St and east of Congress St.

Financial District: South of State St, west of and north of the John F. Fitzgerald Expy (I-93) and east of Congress St.

North End: Bounded by Boston Harbor and the John F. Fitzgerald Expy (I-93).

South End: South of I-90, west of John F. Fitzgerald Expy (I-93), north of Massachusetts Ave and east of Columbus Ave.

Theatre District: South of Boylston St, west of Tremont St, north of I-90 and east of Arlington St.

BOSTON RESTAURANTS BY NEIGHBORHOOD AREAS

(For full description, see alphabetical listings under Restaurants)

BACK BAY
Anago (The Lenox Hotel). 65 Exeter St
Biba. 272 Boylston St
Bristol Lounge (Four Seasons Hotel). 200 Boylston St
Brown Sugar Cafe. 129 Jersey St
Cafe Louis. 234 Berkley St
The Capital Grille. 359 Newbury St
Casa Romero. 30 Gloucester St
Charley's. 284 Newbury St
Ciao Bella. 240A Newbury St
Clio (The Eliot Hotel). 370 A Commonwealth Ave
Davio's. 269 Newbury St
The Dining Room (The Ritz-Carlton, Boston Hotel). 15 Arlington St
Dubarry Restaurant Francais. 159 Newbury St
Grill 23. 161 Berkeley St
Kashmir. 279 Newbury St
L'espalier. 30 Gloucester St
Mercury. 116 Boylston St
Morton's Of Chicago. One Exeter Plaza
Pignoli. 79 Park Plaza
Small Planet Bar & Grill. 565 Boylston St
Tapeo. 266 Newbury St
Top Of The Hub. 800 Boylston St
Zinc. 35 Stanhope St

BEACON HILL
Cafe Marliave. 10 Bosworth St
Hungry I. 71½ Charles St
Lala Rokh. 97 Mt Vernon St
Library At The Hampshire House. 84 Beacon St
Ristorante Toscano. 47 Charles St

COPLEY SQUARE
Ambrosia. 116 Huntington Ave
Cafe Budapest (Copley Square Hotel). 90 Exeter St
The Oak Room (Fairmont Copley Plaza). 138 St James Ave
Palm (The Westin Copley Place Hotel). 200 Dartmouth St
Turner Fisheries (The Westin Copley Place Hotel). 10 Huntington Ave

DOWNTOWN CROSSING AREA
Anthony's Pier 4. 140 Northern Ave
Aujourd'hui (Four Seasons Hotel). 200 Boylston St
Ginza. 16 Hudson St
Locke Ober. Three Winter Place
Maison Robert. 45 School St
Parker's. (see Omni Parker House Hotel) 60 School St

FANEUIL HALL/QUINCY MARKET AREA
Bay Tower. 60 State St
Durgin Park. 30 N Market St
The Exchange. 148 Statet St
Plaza Iii. 101 S Faneuil Hall Marketplace
Seasons (Regal Bostonian Hotel). Faneuil Hall Marketplace
Tatsukichi. 189 State St
Tratorria Il Panino. 120 S Market
The Vault. 105 Water St
Ye Olde Union Oyster House. 41 Union St
Zuma's Tex Mex Cafe. 7 N Market St

FINANCIAL DISTRICT
Café Fleuri (Le Meridien Hotel). 250 Franklin St
Jimmy's Harborside. 242 Northern Ave
Julien (Le Meridien Hotel). 250 Franklin St
Rowes Wharf (Boston Harbor Hotel). 70 Rowes Wharf

NORTH END
Davide. 326 Commercial St
Filippo. 283 Causeway St
Mamma Maria. Three North Square
Marcuccio's. 125 Salem St
Ristorante Lucia. 415 Hanover St
Terramia. 98 Salem St

SOUTH END
Bob The Chef's. 604 Columbus Ave
Claremont Cafe. 535 Columbus Ave
Hamersley's Bistro. 553 Tremont St
Icarus. 3 Appleton St
La Bettola. 480 A Columbus Ave
Metropolis Cafe. 584 Tremont St
Mistral. 223 Columbus Ave
Truc. 560 Tremont

THEATRE DISTRICT
Galleria Italiana. 177 Tremont St
Jae's. 212 Stuart St
Kyoto Japanese Teppanyaki Steak House. 201 Stuart St

Note: When a listing is located in a town that does not have its own city heading, it will appear under the city nearest to its location. In these cases, the address and town appear in parenthesis immediately following the name of the establishment.

Motel

✔★ ★ **SUSSE CHALET.** *800 Morrissey Blvd (02122), I-93 exit 12, 3 mi S of Downtown Crossing Area.* 617/287-9100; FAX 617/265-9287. Web www.bostonhotel.com. 308 rms, 2-5 story. S $70.70-$115.70; D $77.70-$122.70; each addl $5; under 18 free. Crib $3. TV; cable (premium). Pool; lifeguard. Restaurant adj 6:30 am-10:30 pm. Ck-out 11 am. Coin lndry. Meeting rms. Business servs avail. In-rm modem link. Gift shop. Health club privileges. Game rm. Refrigerators, microwaves avail. Cr cds: A, C, D, DS, MC, V.

D ⇌ ⊗ 🖘 SC

Motor Hotel

✔★ ★ **HOLIDAY INN-AIRPORT.** *225 McClellan Hwy (02128), 1 mi N of Logan Intl Airport on Rte 1A.* 617/569-5250; FAX 617/569-5159. 356 rms, 12 story. S $119-$209; D $129-$219; each addl $10; under 18 free; lower rates off season. Crib free. TV; cable (premium). Pool. Coffee in rms. Restaurant 6-11:30 am, 5-10 pm. Bar 11-2 am. Ck-out noon. Meeting rms. Business servs avail. In-rm modem link. Gift shop. Free airport transportation. Exercise equipt. Microwaves avail. Cr cds: A, C, D, DS, JCB, MC, V.

D ⇌ ⊁ ✈ 🖘 SC

Hotels

★ ★ **BEST WESTERN BOSTON-THE INN AT LONGWOOD MEDICAL.** *342 Longwood Ave (02115), in Back Bay.* 617/731-4700; FAX 617/731-6273. E-mail innlwm@erols.com. 155 rms, 8 story. S $129-$250; D $139-$275; each addl $15; kits. $249; under 18 free. Crib free. Covered parking $14. TV; cable (premium). Restaurant 6:30-1 am. Bar. Ck-out noon. Meeting rms. In-rm modem link. Shopping arcade. Health club privileges. Cr cds: A, C, D, DS, ER, MC, V.

D 🖘 SC

★ ★ ★ **BOSTON HARBOR HOTEL.** *70 Rowes Wharf (02110), on the waterfront, in Financial District.* 617/439-7000; FAX 617/330-9450; res: 800/752-7077. Web www.bhh.com. Located on Boston's waterfront within walking distance of major sights, this property has a copper-domed observatory with views of Boston. Numerous objets d'art embellish the public areas. 230 rms, 16 story, 26 suites. S $195-$450; D $225-$485; each addl $50; suites $435-$1,600; under 18 free; wkend rates. Crib free. Pet accepted. Garage parking, valet $26; self-park $23. TV; cable (premium),

VCR avail. Indoor pool; whirlpool, poolside serv. Restaurant 6 am-midnight (also see ROWES WHARF). Rm serv 24 hrs. Bar 11:30-1 am. Ck-out 1 pm. Meeting rms. Business center. In-rm modem link. Concierge. Airport transportation. Exercise rm; sauna, steam rm. Extensive spa. Bathrm phones, minibars; microwaves avail. Balconies. Cr cds: A, C, D, DS, JCB, MC, V.

★ ★ **BOSTON PARK PLAZA HOTEL & TOWERS.** *64 Arlington St (02116), in Back Bay, opp Boston Public Garden.* 617/426-2000; FAX 617/426-5545; res: 800/225-2008. E-mail bpphsales@aol.com; web www.bpph.com. 960 rms, 15 story. S $189-$269; D $209-$289; each addl $20; suites $375-$1,500. Crib $10. Garage $23; valet. TV; cable (premium). Pool privileges. Restaurant 6:30 am-midnight. Bar 11-1:30 am. Ck-out noon. Convention facilities. Business center. In-rm modem link. Concierge. Shopping arcade. Barber, beauty shop. Exercise equipt. Health club privileges. Refrigerators. Cr cds: A, C, D, DS, ER, JCB, MC, V.

★ ★ ★ **THE COLONNADE.** *120 Huntington Ave (02116), in Back Bay, opp Hynes Convention Ctr, adj to Copley Plaza Shopping Ctr.* 617/424-7000; FAX 617/424-1717; res: 800/962-3030. 285 rms, 11 story. Sept-mid-Nov: S $495; D $515; suites $700-$1,400; under 12 free; wkly, wkend & hol rates; higher rates: marathon, graduation; lower rates rest of yr. Crib free. Pet accepted, some restrictions. Parking $22. TV; cable (premium), VCR avail. Pool (in season); poolside serv. Supervised child's activities (May-Sept); ages 8-13. Restaurant 6:30-1 am. Rm serv 24 hrs. Bar. Ck-out noon. Convention facilities. Business center. In-rm modem link. Concierge. Exercise equipt. Minibars; refrigerators avail. Cr cds: A, C, D, DS, ER, JCB, MC, V.

★ ★ **COPLEY SQUARE HOTEL.** *47 Huntington Ave (02116), in Copley Square, exit 22 off MA Turnpike.* 617/536-9000; FAX 617/236-0351; res: 800/225-7062. Web www.copleysquarehotel.com. 143 rms, 7 story. S, D $175-$225; each addl $20; suites $299-$345; under 17 free. Crib free. Garage $20. TV; cable (premium). Complimentary coffee in rms. Restaurants 7 am-11 pm (also see CAFE BUDAPEST). Bar 11:30-2 am. Ck-out noon. Meeting rms. Business servs avail. In-rm modem link. Concierge. Family-owned hotel; established 1891. Cr cds: A, C, D, DS, ER, JCB, MC, V.

★ ★ **DOUBLETREE GUEST SUITES.** *400 Soldiers Field Rd (02134), west of Back Bay, north of Brookline, I-90 exit Storrow Dr.* 617/783-0090; FAX 617/783-0897. 310 suites, 16 story. S, D $149-$289; each addl $20; under 18 free; wknd packages. Crib free. TV; cable (premium). Indoor pool; whirlpool. Complimentary coffee in rms. Restaurant 6:30 am-10 pm. Bar 11:30-12:45 am; entertainment Wed-Sat. Ck-out noon. Coin lndry. Convention facilities. Business center. In-rm modem link. Concierge. Exercise equipt; sauna. Game rm. Bathrm phones, refrigerators, minibars; some microwaves. Some private patios, balconies. On river. Cr cds: A, C, D, DS, ER, JCB, MC, V.

★ ★ ★ **THE ELIOT.** *370 Commonwealth Ave (02215), at Massachusetts Ave, in Back Bay.* 617/267-1607; FAX 617/536-9114; res: 800/44-ELIOT. E-mail hoteleliot@aol.com; web www.bostbest.com. The Eliot exudes the atmosphere of an elegant European hotel. Suites have marble baths and period furnishings. 95 kit. suites, 9 story. S $245-$265; D $248-$325; each addl $20; under 18 free. Crib free. Pet accepted, some restrictions. Valet parking $20. TV; cable (premium), VCR avail (movies). Restaurant (see CLIO). Ck-out noon. Meeting rms. Business center. In-rm modem link. Concierge. Health club privileges. Minibars; microwaves avail. Some balconies. Cr cds: A, D, MC, V.

★ ★ **FAIRMONT COPLEY PLAZA.** *138 St James Ave (02116), in Copley Square.* 617/267-5300; res: 800/527-4727; FAX 617/247-6681. E-mail fcpsales@aol.com; web www.fairmont.com. 379 rms, 7 story. S $259-$349; D $289-$379; each addl $30; suites $379-$1,500; under 18 free; package plans. Crib free. Pet accepted, some restrictions. Valet

parking $24. TV; cable (premium), VCR avail. Pool privileges. Restaurants (also see THE OAK ROOM). Rm serv 24 hrs. Bars 11:30-2 am; pianist. Ck-out 1 pm. Meeting rms. Business center. In-rm modem link. Concierge. Shopping arcade. Barber, beauty shop. Exercise equipt. Cr cds: A, C, D, DS, ER, JCB, MC, V.

★ ★ ★ **FOUR SEASONS.** *200 Boylston St (02116), in Boston Common, in Downtown Crossing Area.* 617/338-4400; FAX 617/423-0154. Web www.fshr.com. The Four Seasons Hotel is elegant, has a highly attentive staff and is eminently comfortable for leisure or work. Rooms are large and tastefully furnished, and most face the Boston Public Garden or an attactively business area behind it. 288 rms, 15 story. S, D $435-$565; each addl $40; suites $575-$3,500; under 18 free; wkend rates. Crib free. Pet accepted, some restrictions. Valet, garage parking $28. TV; cable (premium), VCR avail (movies). Indoor pool; whirlpool, poolside serv. Complimentary continental bkfst. Restaurants 7-12:30 am (also see AUJOURD'HUI and BRISTOL LOUNGE). Rm serv 24 hrs. Bar 11-2 am; entertainment. Ck-out 1 pm. Convention facilities. Business center. In-rm modem link. Concierge. Gift shop. Exercise rm; sauna. Massage. Bathrm phones, refrigerators. Cr cds: A, C, D, ER, JCB, MC, V.

★ ★ **HARBORSIDE HYATT CONFERENCE CENTER & HOTEL.** *101 Harborside Dr (02128), at Logan Intl Airport, on Boston Harbor.* 617/568-1234; FAX 617/568-6080. 270 rms, 14 story. S $230-$410; D $255-$435; suites $895. Crib free. TV; cable, VCR avail. Indoor pool; whirlpool. Coffee in rms. Restaurant 6 am-11 pm. Bar. Ck-out noon. Conference facilities. Business center. In-rm modem link. Free airport transportation. Exercise equipt; sauna. Refrigerator in suites. Adj to water shuttle. Cr cds: A, C, D, DS, ER, JCB, MC, V.

★ ★ **HILTON-BACK BAY.** *40 Dalton St (02115), in Back Bay adj to Hynes Convention Ctr.* 617/236-1100; FAX 617/267-8893. Web www.hilton.com/hotels/bosbhhf. 385 rms, 26 story. S $215-$280; D $235-$300; each addl $20; suites $450-$1,000; family rates; package plans. Pet accepted, some restrictions. Garage $17. TV; cable (premium). Indoor pool. Restaurant 7 am-midnight. Bar 5:30 pm-12:30 am. Ck-out noon. Convention facilities. Business center. In-rm modem link. Concierge. Gift shop. Exercise equipt. Some balconies. Cr cds: A, C, D, DS, ER, JCB, MC, V.

★ ★ **HOLIDAY INN-SELECT.** *5 Blossom St (02114), at Cambridge St at Govt Ctr.* 617/742-7630; FAX 617/742-4192. 303 rms, 14 story. Apr-Nov: S, D $199-$259; each addl $20; under 19 free; wkend rates; higher rates graduation wknds; lower rates rest of yr. Crib free. Garage $20. TV; cable (premium). Pool. Restaurant 6 am-11 pm. Bar. Ck-out noon. Coin lndry. Meeting rms. Business servs avail. In-rm modem link. Valet serv. Exercise equipt. Health club privileges. Overlooks Charles River. Luxury level. Cr cds: A, C, D, DS, JCB, MC, V.

★ ★ **LE MERIDIEN.** *250 Franklin St (02110), in Financial District.* 617/451-1900; FAX 617/423-2844. Web www.lemeridien.com. 326 rms, 9 story. S, D $295-$325; each addl $25; suites $400-$790; under 12 free; wkend rates. Crib free. Pet accepted, some restrictions. Valet parking $30. TV; cable (premium), VCR avail. Pool. Restaurants 7 am-10 pm (also see CAFÉ FLEURI and JULIEN). Rm serv 24 hrs. Bar 5 pm-1 am; pianist. Ck-out 1 pm. Meeting rms. Business center. In-rm modem link. Concierge. Exercise rm; sauna. Massage. Bathrm phones, minibars, refrigerators. Renaissance Revival bldg. Cr cds: A, C, D, DS, ER, JCB, MC, V.

★ ★ **THE LENOX.** *710 Boylston St (02116), near Copley Square.* 617/536-5300; FAX 617/266-0351; res: 800/225-7676. Web www.lenoxhotel.com. 212 rms, 11 story. S, D $275-$375; each addl $20; suites $500; under 18 free. Crib free. TV; cable, VCR avail. Restaurant (see ANAGO). Bars 11:30-1:30 am. Ck-out noon. Meeting rms. Business servs avail. In-rm modem link. Valet serv. Concierge. Airport transportation. Exercise equipt. Many decorative and wood-burning fireplaces. Cr cds: A, C, D, DS, ER, JCB, MC, V.

D ⊠ ⚐ ⊠ ⚒ SC

★ ★ ★ **MARRIOTT-COPLEY PLACE.** *110 Huntington Ave (02116), in Copley Square.* 617/236-5800; FAX 617/236-5885. 1,147 rms, 38 story. S, D $255; suites $400-$1,200; under 18 free. Crib free. Valet parking $24. TV; cable (premium), VCR avail (movies). Pool; whirlpool. Restaurant 6:30-1 am. Rm serv 24 hrs. Bar 11:30-2 am; entertainment. Ck-out noon. Convention facilities. Business center. In-rm modem link. Concierge. Shopping arcade. Exercise rm; sauna. Massage therapy. Game rm. Luxury level. Cr cds: A, C, D, DS, ER, JCB, MC, V.

D ⚐ ⊠ ⚐ ⊠ ⚒ SC ⚐

★ ★ ★ **MARRIOTT-LONG WHARF.** *296 State St (02109), on waterfront, in Faneuil Hall/Quincy Market Area.* 617/227-0800; FAX 617/227-2867. 400 rms, 7 story. S, D $210-$375; suites $375-$1,200; under 18 free; wkend rates. Crib free. Valet parking $27. TV; cable (premium), VCR avail (movies). Indoor pool; whirlpool; poolside serv. Coffee in rms. Restaurant 6:30-2 am. Bar. Ck-out noon. Coin lndry. Convention facilities. Business center. In-rm modem link. Gift shop. Exercise equipt; sauna. Luxury level. Cr cds: A, C, D, DS, ER, JCB, MC, V.

D ⚐ ⊠ ⚐ ⊠ ⚒ SC ⚐

★ ★ **OMNI PARKER HOUSE.** *60 School St (02108), 1 blk N of Boston Common, Downtown Crossing Area.* 617/227-8600; FAX 617/742-5729. Web www.omnihotels.com. 552 rms, 14 story. June, early Sept-mid-Nov: S, D $109-$205; suites $199-$225; under 18 free; wkend rates; lower rates rest of yr. Crib free. Garage $24. TV; cable (premium), VCR avail. Restaurant (see PARKER'S) Bar 6:30 am-midnight; entertainment exc Sun. Ck-out noon. Convention facilities. Business servs avail. In-rm modem link. Concierge. Gift shop. Health club privileges. Oldest continuously operating hotel in the US. Cr cds: A, C, D, DS, JCB, MC, V.

D ⊠ ⚒ SC

✔ ★ ★ **RADISSON.** *200 Stuart St (02116), in Theatre District.* 617/482-1800; FAX 617/451-2750. 356 rms, 24 story. S, D $128-$325; each addl $20; suites $230-$350; under 18 free. Crib free. Valet parking $5. TV; cable (premium). Indoor pool. Restaurant 6:30 am-10 pm; dining rm 11:30 am-11 pm, Sun noon-10 pm. Bar. Ck-out noon. Business servs avail. In-rm modem link. Gift shop. Exercise equipt. Cr cds: A, C, D, DS, ER, JCB, MC, V.

D ⊠ ⚐ ⚐ ⚒ SC

★ ★ **RAMADA-LOGAN AIRPORT.** *Logan Intl Airport (02128), on grounds of Logan Intl Airport.* 617/569-9300; FAX 617/569-3981. 516 rms, 14 story. S $129-$195; D $149-$245; each addl $20; suites $400; family, wkend rates. Crib free. Pet accepted, some restrictions. TV; cable (premium). Pool; poolside serv, lifeguard. Coffee in rms. Restaurant 5:30 am-10:30 pm. Bar 11-2 am. Ck-out 11 am. Convention facilities. Business center. In-rm modem link. Concierge. Free airport transportation. Exercise equipt. Many minibars. Cr cds: A, C, D, DS, ER, JCB, MC, V.

D ⚐ ⊠ ⚐ ✈ ⚐ ⚒ SC ⚐

★ ★ ★ **REGAL BOSTONIAN.** *9 Blackstone St N (02109), near Logan Intl Airport, in Faneuil Hall/Quincy Market Area.* 617/523-3600; res: 800/222-8888; FAX 617/523-2454. Web www.regal-hotels.com/boston. 201 rms, 7 story. S, D $245-$345; each addl $20; suites $450-$625; under 18 free; wkend rates. Valet parking $24. TV; cable (premium), VCR avail. Complimentary coffee in lobby. Restaurant (see SEASONS). Rm serv 24 hrs. Bar 2 pm-1 am; entertainment Tues-Sat. Ck-out 3 pm. Meeting rms. Business center. In-rm modem link. Concierge. Tennis privileges. Exercise equipt. Health club privileges. Bathrm phones, minibars; some in-rm whirlpools, fireplaces. Many balconies. 1 blk to harbor. Cr cds: A, C, D, DS, JCB, MC, V.

D ⚐ ⚐ ⊠ ⚐ ⚒ SC ⚐

★ ★ ★ ★ **THE RITZ-CARLTON, BOSTON.** *15 Arlington St (02117), at Newbury St, in Back Bay.* 617/536-5700; FAX 617/536-1335. This Boston institution is famous for its service and overall excellence. Rooms are traditionally furnished, and public spaces are tasteful and elegant. 278 rms, 17 story. S $260-$375; D $300-$415; each addl $20; 1-2 bedrm suites

$345-$1,495; under 12 free; wkend rates. Crib free. Pet accepted, some restrictions. Garage $22. TV; cable (premium), VCR avail (movies). Restaurants 6:30 am-midnight (also see THE DINING ROOM). Rm serv 24 hrs. Bar 11:30-1 am. Ck-out noon. Convention facilities. Business servs avail. In-rm modem link. Concierge. Barber. Airport transportation. Exercise equipt; sauna. Massage. Health club privileges. Bathrm phones, refrigerators; fireplace in suites. Overlooks Public Garden. Luxury level. Cr cds: A, C, D, DS, ER, JCB, MC, V.

D ⚐ ⊠ ⚐ ⚒

★ ★ ★ **SEAPORT.** *1 Seaport Ln (02210), east of Downtown Crossing Area.* 617/385-4000; res: 888/982-4683; FAX 617/385-4102. Web www.seaporthotel.com. 427 rms, 18 story. S $240-$315; D $265-$340; each addl $25; suites $500-$1500; under 12 free; package plans. Pet accepted, some restrictions. Valet parking $22; garage parking $18. TV; cable (premium), VCR avail. Complimentary coffee in rms. Restaurant 6:30-11 am, 11:30 am-2 pm, 5:30-11 pm. Bar 11-1 am. Ck-out 1 pm. Convention facilities. Business center. In-rm modem link. Concierge. Gift shop. Exercise rm; sauna. Massage. Indoor pool. Bathrm phones, minibars; refrigerators, microwaves, wet bars avail. On harbor. Luxury level. Totally nonsmoking. Cr cds: A, C, D, DS, ER, JCB, MC, V.

D ⚐ ⊠ ⚐ ⚒ SC ⚐

★ ★ ★ **SHERATON BOSTON HOTEL & TOWERS.** *39 Dalton St (02199), at Prudential Ctr, in Back Bay.* 617/236-2000; FAX 617/236-1702. Web www.sheraton.com. 1,181 rms, 29 story. D $189-$269; each addl $20; suites from $260; under 18 free; wkend rates. Crib free. Pet accepted. Garage $23; valet $24. TV; cable (premium). Indoor/outdoor pool; whirlpool. Coffee in rms. Restaurant 6:30-1:30 am. Bars 11:30-2 am; entertainment. Rm serv 24 hrs. Ck-out noon. Convention facilities. Business center. In-rm modem link. Gift shop. Exercise equipt. Luxury level. Cr cds: A, C, D, DS, ER, JCB, MC, V.

D ⚐ ⊠ ⚐ ⊠ ⚐ ⚒ SC ⚐

★ ★ ★ **SWISSÔTEL.** *1 Avenue de Lafayette (02111), in Financial District.* 617/451-2600; FAX 617/451-2198; res: 800/621-9200. 500 rms, 22 story. S, D $235-$260; each addl $25; under 16 free; wkend rates. Crib free. Pet accepted, some restrictions. Garage $24, valet parking $28. TV; cable (premium), VCR avail (movies). Indoor pool. Restaurant 7 am-11 pm. Rm serv 24 hrs. Bar 4 pm-1 am; entertainment. Ck-out noon. Convention facilities. Business center. In-rm modem link. Concierge. Gift shop. Exercise equipt; sauna. Health club privileges. Luxury level. Cr cds: A, C, D, DS, ER, JCB, MC, V.

D ⚐ ✈ ⊠ ⚐ ⊠ ⚐ ⚒ SC ⚐

★ ★ ★ **THE WESTIN COPLEY PLACE.** *10 Huntington Ave (02116), in Copley Square, I-90 Copley Sq exit.* 617/262-9600; FAX 617/424-7483. Web www.westin.com. 800 rms, 36 story. S $189-$280; D $219-$310; each addl $25; suites $400-$1,500; under 18 free. Crib free. Pet accepted, some restrictions. TV; cable (premium). Indoor pool; whirlpool. Coffee in rms. Restaurants (also see PALM and TURNER FISHERIES). Rm serv 24 hrs. Entertainment. Ck-out noon. Convention facilities. Business center. In-rm modem link. Concierge. Barber. Valet parking $24. Airport transportation. Exercise equipt; sauna. Health club privileges. Minibars. Copley Place shopping gallery across skybridge. Luxury level. Cr cds: A, C, D, DS, ER, JCB, MC, V.

D ⚐ ⚐ ⊠ ⚐ ⊠ ⚒ SC ⚐

★ ★ ★ **WYNDHAM-TREMONT HOUSE.** *275 Tremont St (02116), in Theatre District, 2 blks from Boston Common.* 617/426-1400; FAX 617/482-6730; res: 800/331-9998. 322 rms, 15 story. S, D $144-$250; each addl $10; under 18 free; wkend rates. Crib free. Valet parking $24. TV; cable (premium), VCR. Coffee in rms. Restaurant 6:30 am-11:30 pm. Bar noon-midnight; entertainment Thurs-Sun. Ck-out noon. Convention facilities. Business center. In-rm modem link. Concierge. Gift shop. Exercise equipt. Luxury level. Cr cds: A, C, D, DS, ER, JCB, MC, V.

D ⊠ ⚐ ⚒ SC ⚐

Inns

★ ★ **COPLEY INN.** *19 Garrison St (02116), in Back Bay.* 617/236-0300; FAX 617/536-0816; res: 800/232-0306. 21 kit. units, 4 with shower only, 4 story. May-Dec: S, D $95-$125; each addl $10; wkly rates; lower rates rest of yr. Crib free. TV; cable. Restaurant nearby. Ck-out 11 am, ck-in 9 am-8 pm. Brownstone built in 1880s. Cr cds: A, MC, V.

★ ★ **NEWBURY GUEST HOUSE.** 261 Newbury St (02116), in Back Bay, between Gloucester & Fairfield. 617/437-7666; FAX 617/262-4243; res: 800/437-7668. 32 rms, 4 story. Mar-Dec: S $85-$130; D $95-$140; each addl $10; under 3 free; higher rates: marathon, graduations. Parking $15. TV; cable. Complimentary continental bkfst. Ck-out noon, ck-in 3 pm. Sitting rm. Built 1882. Cr cds: A, C, D, DS, MC, V.

Restaurants

★ ★ ★ **AMBROSIA.** 116 Huntington Ave (02116), in Copley Square. 617/247-2400. French menu with Asian influence. Specialties: St Pierre fish imported from France, grilled meats, sushi. Hrs: 11:30 am-2 pm, 5:30-10 pm; Fri to 11 pm; Sat 5-11 pm; Sun 5-9 pm. Closed some major hols. Semi-a la carte: lunch $5-$12, dinner $16-$29. Valet parking (dinner). Spacious and elegant atmosphere. Cr cds: A, D, MC, V.

★ ★ ★ **ANAGO.** (See The Lenox Hotel) 617/266-6222. Contemporary Amer menu. Specialties: chilled shellfish platter, baked vegetable casserole, fire-roasted chicken. Hrs: 11:30 am-2 pm, 5:30-10 pm; Fri to 10:30 pm; Sat 5:30-10 pm; Sun 5:30-9 pm. Res accepted. Bar. Wine cellar. Semi-a la carte: lunch $9-$19, dinner $18-$33. Child's meals. Jazz Sun. Valet parking. Elegant dining. Totally nonsmoking. Cr cds: A, MC, V.

★ ★ **ANTHONY'S PIER 4.** 140 Northern Ave (02210), east of Downtown Crossing Area, adj to World Trade Center. 617/482-6262. Specializes in smoked salmon, lobster, bouillabaisse. Hrs: 11:30 am-11 pm; Sat from noon; Sun noon-10 pm. Closed Dec 25. Res accepted. Bar. Semi-a la carte: lunch $9.95-$26.95, dinner $13.95-$26.95. Parking. Outdoor dining. Nautical decor; view of city and Boston Harbor. Jacket in main dining rm. Family-owned. Cr cds: A, C, D, DS, ER, JCB, MC, V.

★ ★ ★ ★ **AUJOURD'HUI.** (See Four Seasons Hotel) 617/338-4400. If you're lucky enough to get a table near the broad windows, you can dine on regional specialties while gazing out on the Boston Public Garden. Menu changes seasonally. Own baking. Hrs: 6:30 am-2:30 pm, 5:30-10:30 pm; Sat 7 am-noon, 5:30-10:30 pm; Sun 7-11 am, 6-10:30 pm; Sun brunch 11:30 am-2:30 pm. Res accepted. Bar. Wine cellar. A la carte entrees: bkfst $14-$18, lunch $27-$32, dinner $52-$80. Degustation menu: dinner $56. Sun brunch $52. Child's meals. Valet parking. Jacket (dinner). Cr cds: A, C, D, ER, JCB, MC, V.

★ ★ ★ **BAY TOWER.** 60 State St (02109), 33rd floor, in Faneuil Hall/Quincy Market Area. 617/723-1666. Specializes in rack of lamb, sauteed Maine lobster, creative American cuisine. Hrs: 5:30-9:45 pm; Fri to 10:30; Sat to 10:15 pm. Closed Sun; Dec 25. Res accepted. Bar 4:30 pm-1 am; Fri, Sat to 2 am. Semi-a la carte: dinner $17-$33. Entertainment. Valet parking Fri, Sat. Harbor view. Parking. Jacket. Cr cds: A, C, D, DS, MC, V.

★ ★ ★ ★ **BIBA.** 272 Boylston St (02116), in Back Bay. 617/426-7878. This is a popular people-watching spot—both inside and out—from the huge windows in the downstairs bar. Striking art and vivid murals deck the dining room. The seasonal menu showcases fresh and innovative meals for affordable prices. Hrs: 11:30 am-2:30 pm, 5:30-10 pm; Fri to 11 pm; Sat 5:30-11 pm; Sun 11:30 am-3 pm, 5:30-10 pm. Closed some major hols. Res accepted. Bar. A la carte entrees: lunch $8-$16, dinner $12-$36. Valet parking. Cr cds: A, C, D, DS, MC, V.

★ ★ **BOB THE CHEF'S.** 604 Columbus Ave (02118), in the South End. 617/536-6204. Creole/Cajun menu. Specialties: chicken & ribs combo, Creole jambalaya, mustard-fried catfish. Hrs: 11:30 am-10 pm; Wed-Fri to midnight; Sat 11 am-midnight; Sun 11 am-10 pm; Sun brunch to 3:30 pm. Closed Mon; some major hols. Bar. Semi-a la carte: dinner $8.95-$13.95. Sun brunch $12.95. Jazz Thurs, Fri evening, Sun brunch. Bistro decor; intimate dining. Totally nonsmoking. Cr cds: A, MC, V.

★ ★ **BRISTOL LOUNGE.** (See Four Seasons Hotel) 617/338-4400. Contemporary Amer menu. Specializes in tapas, seasonal dishes. Own baking. Hrs: 11-1 am; Fri, Sat to 2 am; Sun 10 am-midnight; Sun brunch to 2 pm. Res accepted. Bar. Semi-a la carte: lunch $16-$26, dinner $26-$39. Sun brunch $35. Pianist, jazz duo. Valet parking. Art-deco decor with large windows overlooking Boston Gardens and flowered terrace. Cr cds: A, C, D, DS, ER, JCB, MC, V.

★ ★ **BROWN SUGAR CAFE.** 129 Jersey St (02115), 2 blks S of Fenway Park, near Back Bay. 617/266-2928. Web boston.sidewalk.com. Thai menu. Specialties: fisherman madness, mango curry, pad-Thai country style. Hrs: 11 am-3 pm, 4-10 pm; Fri, Sat to 11 pm. Closed Jan 1, July 4, Thanksgiving. Res accepted. Bar. Semi-a la carte: lunch $5.50-$7, dinner $8-$13. Parking. Outdoor dining. Thai decor. Totally nonsmoking. Cr cds: C, D, DS, MC, V.

★ ★ **CAFÉ FLEURI.** (See Le Meridien Hotel) 617/451-1900. French, Amer menu. Specialties: roasted cornish hen, swordfish stir fry, Boston clam chowder. Hrs: 7 am-10 pm; Sat, Sun from 7:30 am; Sun brunch 11 am-4 pm. Res accepted. Bar 11 am-10 pm. Semi-a la carte: bkfst $10.25-$17.95, lunch $15-$22, dinner $20-$25. Sun brunch $42. Child's meals. Jazz Sun. Valet parking. Totally nonsmoking. Cr cds: A, C, D, DS, JCB, MC, V.

★ ★ **CAFE BUDAPEST.** (See Copley Square Hotel) 617/266-1979. Hungarian, continental menu. Specialties: veal goulash, cherry soup, chicken paprikash. Own baking. Hrs: noon-3 pm, 5-10:30 pm; Fri, Sat to 11 pm; Sun 1-10:30 pm. Closed Jan 1, Dec 25; also wk of July 4. Res accepted. Bar. Semi-a la carte: lunch $14.50-$16.50, dinner $19.50-$33. Complete meals: dinner $42. Violin & piano Tues-Sat nights. Original paintings. Old World atmosphere. Family-owned. Jacket. Cr cds: A, C, D, DS, MC, V.

★ ★ ★ **CAFE LOUIS.** 234 Berkley St (02116), in Back Bay. 617/266-4680. Traditionally influenced Italian menu. Specializes in local seafood. Hrs: 11:30 am-3 pm, 5-10 pm. Closed Sun; most major hols. Beer. Wine cellar. A la carte entrees: lunch $9-$17, dinner $16-$32. Complete meals: dinner $59. Jazz in summer. Free valet parking. Outdoor dining. Contemporary cafe. Totally nonsmoking. Cr cds: A, MC, V.

★ ★ **CAFE MARLIAVE.** 10 Bosworth St (02108), in Beacon Hill. 617/542-1133. Italian menu. Specializes in fresh seafood, beef. Hrs: 11 am-10 pm. Closed some major hols. Res accepted. Bar. Semi-a la carte: lunch $5-$10.50, dinner $9-$22. Parking. Original artwork. Cr cds: A, D, MC, V.

★ ★ ★ **THE CAPITAL GRILLE.** 359 Newbury St (02115), in Back Bay. 617/262-8900. Steakhouse menu. Specialties: dry-aged 24 oz porterhouse steak, broiled lobster, shrimp scampi. Hrs: 5-10 pm; Thurs-Sat to 11 pm. Closed July 4. Res accepted. Bar from 4 pm. Wine cellar. A la carte entrees: dinner $16.95-$28.95. Valet parking. Cr cds: A, D, DS, MC, V.

★ ★ **CASA ROMERO.** 30 Gloucester St (02115), in Back Bay, enter on alley off Glouchester St. 617/536-4341. Web www.casaromero.com. Mexican menu. Specialties: marinated tenderloin of pork, giant shrimp in cilantro and tomatillos. Hrs: 5-10 pm; Fri, Sat to 11 pm. Closed Jan 1, July 4, Dec 25. Res accepted. Serv bar. Semi-a la carte: dinner

$12-$19.50. Outdoor dining. Authentic Mexican decor. Family-owned. Totally nonsmoking. Cr cds: DS, MC, V.

★ ★ **CHARLEY'S.** *284 Newbury St (02115), at Gloucester & Newbury, in Back Bay.* 617/266-3000. Specializes in fresh seafood, babyback ribs, steaks. Hrs: 11:30 am-11 pm; Fri, Sat 11 am-midnight. Res accepted. Bar 11:30-2 am. Semi-a la carte: lunch $5.99-$10.99, dinner $8.99-$22.95. Child's meals. Outdoor dining. Renovated Victorian school. Cr cds: A, D, DS, MC, V.

D ⌐

★ ★ **CIAO BELLA.** *240A Newbury St (02116), at Newbury & Fairfield, in Back Bay.* 617/536-2626. E-mail ciaobella@concierge.org; web www.concierge.org/ciaobella. Italian menu. Specializes in veal chops, swordfish chops, seafood. Hrs: 11:30 am-11 pm; Thurs-Sat to 11:45 pm; Sun brunch to 3:30 pm. Closed Thanksgiving, Dec 25. Res accepted. Bar. A la carte entrees: lunch $6.50-$14.95, dinner $8.95-$33.95. Sun brunch $4.95-$11.50. Valet parking (Tues-Sat evening). Outdoor dining. European decor. Cr cds: A, C, D, DS, MC, V.

★ **CLAREMONT CAFE.** *535 Columbus Ave (02118), in the South End.* 617/247-9001. Continental menu. Specializes in herb-roasted chicken, seafood, tapas. Hrs: 7:30 am-3 pm, 5:30-10 pm; Fri to 10:30 pm; Sat 8 am-10:30 pm; Sun 9 am-3 pm (brunch). Closed Mon; major hols. Semi-a la carte: bkfst $3.50-$9.95, lunch $4.95-$9.95, dinner $12.95-$21.95. Sun brunch $6.50-$10.95. Valet parking. Outdoor dining. Corner cafe with artwork by local artists. Totally nonsmoking. Cr cds: A, MC, V.

★ ★ ★ **CLIO.** *(See The Eliot Hotel)* 617/536-7200. Contemporary French, Amer menu. Specialties: seared day boat scallops, carmelized swordfish au poivre, aromatic glazed short ribs. Hrs: 6:30-10:30 am, 5:30-10 pm; Thurs to 10:30 pm; Sat 7-11 am, 5:30-10:30 pm; Sun 7 am-2 pm, 5:30-10 pm; Sun brunch 11:30 am-2 pm. Res accepted. Bar to 1 am. Wine list. A la carte entrees: bkfst $3-$16. Semi-a la carte: dinner $21-$34. Sun brunch $8-$16. Valet parking. Parisian-style supper club. Cr cds: A, C, D, MC, V.

D

★ ★ ★ **DAVIDE.** *326 Commercial St (02109), in the North End.* 617/227-5745. Northern Italian menu. Specialties: potato gnocchi, veal chop with fontina and prosciutto. Own pasta, ice cream. Hrs: 5-10 pm; Fri, Sat to 11 pm. Bar. A la carte entrees: dinner $14-$28. Valet parking. Cr cds: A, C, MC, V.

⌐

★ ★ **DAVIO'S.** *269 Newbury St (02116), in Back Bay.* 617/262-4810. Northern Italian menu. Specializes in veal chops, homemade pasta, pizza. Hrs: 11:30 am-10:30 pm; Fri, Sat to 11 pm; Sun to 10 pm. Closed Thanksgiving, Dec 25. Res accepted. Bar. Semi-a la carte: lunch $3.95-$12.95, dinner $3.95-$26.95. Child's meals. Valet parking (dinner). Outdoor dining. Cr cds: A, C, D, DS, MC, V.

★ ★ **THE DINING ROOM.** *(See The Ritz-Carlton, Boston Hotel)* 617/536-5700. Continental, regional menu. Hrs: 5:30-10 pm; Fri, Sat to 11 pm; Sat hrs vary in fall & winter; Sun brunch 10:45 am-2:30 pm. Closed Mon. Res accepted; required wkends. Bar. Wine cellar. Complete meals: lunch $29-$38, dinner $42-$55. A la carte entrees: dinner $29-$43. Sun brunch $47. Child's meals. Pianist. Valet parking. Jacket. Cr cds: A, C, D, DS, ER, JCB, MC, V.

D

★ ★ **DUBARRY RESTAURANT FRANCAIS.** *159 Newbury St (02116), in Back Bay.* 617/262-2445. French menu. Specialties: canard a l'orange, lapin dijonaise. Hrs: noon-2:30 pm, 5:30-10 pm; Sat 12:30-3 pm, 5:30-10 pm; Sun 5:30-9:30 pm. Closed Sun (summer); major hols. Res accepted. Wine. A la carte entrees: lunch $3.75-$17, dinner $14-$25. Child's meals. Outdoor dining. Casual dining. Original art. Family-owned. Cr cds: A, C, D, DS, MC, V.

D

🗸★ ★ **DURGIN PARK.** *30 N Market St (02109), in Faneuil Hall/Quincy Market Place.* 617/227-2038. Specializes in prime rib, Indian pudding, strawberry shortcake. Own soups. Hrs: 11:30 am-10 pm; Sun to 9 pm. Closed Dec 25. Bar to 2 am; entertainment. A la carte entrees: lunch $4.95-$16.95, dinner $5.95-$16.95. Near Faneuil Hall. Established 1826. Cr cds: A, D, DS, MC, V.

D ⌐

★ ★ **THE EXCHANGE.** *148 State St (02109), in Faneuil Hall/Quincy Market Area.* 617/726-7600. Contemporary Amer menu. Specialties: tournedos a la Neptune, slow braised chicken, rack of lamb. Hrs: 11:30 am-11 pm; Thurs, Fri to 1 am; Sat 5:30 pm-1 am. Closed Sun; also major hols. Res accepted. Bar. Semi-a la carte: lunch $6-$12, dinner $18-$25. Jazz Fri, Sat. Valet parking. Cr cds: A, C, D, DS, MC, V.

D

🗸★ ★ ★ **FILIPPO.** *283 Causeway St (02109), in North End.* 617/742-4143. Italian menu. Specialty: cappello del Contadino. Hrs: 11:30 am-10:30 pm; Sun from noon. Closed Thanksgiving, Dec 25. Res accepted. Bar. Wine list. Semi-a la carte: lunch $5.50-$8.50, dinner $12.95-$28.50. Child's meals. Valet parking (dinner). Italian decor with large murals. Cr cds: A, MC, V.

D

★ ★ **GALLERIA ITALIANA.** *177 Tremont St (02111), in Theatre District.* 617/423-2092. Regional Italian menu. Menu changes bimonthly. Hrs: 5:30-10 pm; Sun 4:30-9 pm. Closed most major hols. Res accepted. Wine, beer. Semi-a la carte: dinner $19-$28. Italian music Sun. Street parking. Classic trattoria decor. Cr cds: A, MC, V.

D

★ ★ ★ **GINZA.** *16 Hudson St (02111), Downtown Crossing Area.* 617/338-2261. Japanese menu. Specializes in maki special, sushi. Hrs: 11:30 am-2:30 pm; 5 pm-4 am; Sat 11:30 am-4 pm, 5 pm-4 am; Mon, Sun 11:30 am-4 pm, 5 pm-2 am. Res accepted. Wine, beer. Semi-a la carte: lunch $7.50-$11.75, dinner $12.50-$38.50. Upscale Japanese dining with sushi bar. Cr cds: A, MC, V.

D

★ ★ ★ **GRILL 23.** *161 Berkeley St (02116), at Stuart, in Back Bay.* 617/542-2255. Web www.grill23.com. Specializes in aged beef, New England seafood. Hrs: 5:30-10:30 pm; Fri, Sat to 11 pm. Closed major hols. Res accepted. Bar from 4:30 pm. A la carte entrees: $18.75-$26.75. Menu changes wkly. Valet parking. Open kitchen. 1920s decor. Former Salada Tea Bldg. Cr cds: A, C, D, DS, MC, V.

D ⌐

★ ★ ★ **HAMERSLEY'S BISTRO.** *553 Tremont St (02116), in South End.* 617/423-2700. Hamersley's includes a full bar and cafe area as well as a large dining room that's a bit more formal. The menu changes seasonally; the wine list is replete with offerings from France, Spain, Italy and California. French, Amer menu. Specialties: crispy duck confit, imported Dover sole, pan-roasted lobster. Hrs: 6-10 pm; Sat, Sun from 5:30 pm. Closed major hols. Bar. A la carte entrees: dinner $21-$30. Valet parking. Outdoor dining. Totally nonsmoking. Cr cds: A, D, DS, MC, V.

D

★ ★ ★ **HUNGRY I.** *71½ Charles St (02114), on Beacon Hill.* 617/227-3524. French country menu. Specialties: paté maison, venison au poivre. Hrs: 6-9:30 pm; Sat, Sun to 10 pm; Sat, Sun brunch 11 am-2 pm. Closed July 4, Thanksgiving, Dec 25. Res accepted. Serv bar. A la carte entrees: dinner $20-$30. Sun brunch $30. Patio dining Sun brunch only. 1840s house in historic district. Fireplaces. Cr cds: A, C, D, MC, V.

⌐

★ ★ ★ **ICARUS.** *3 Appleton St (02116), in the South End.* 617/426-1790. Specialties: grilled shrimp with mango and jalapeno sorbet, seared duck breast, game. Hrs: 6-10 pm; Fri, Sat to 11 pm. Closed most major hols. Res accepted; required wkends. Bar from 5:30 pm. Semi-a la carte: dinner $19-$29. Prix fixe: $39. Sun brunch $7-$12. Valet parking. Jazz Fri evening. Converted 1860s building. Cr cds: A, C, D, DS, MC, V.

★ ★ **JAE'S.** *212 Stuart St (02116), in Theatre District.* 617/451-7788. Specialties: sushi, pad Thai, okdol bibim bab. Hrs: 11:30 am-4 pm, 5-10:30 pm; Fri, Sat to 1 am; Sun noon-10 pm. Pan-Asian menu. Bar. Semi-a la carte: lunch $8.95-$9.95, dinner $7.95-$15.95. Street parking. Totally nonsmoking. Cr cds: A, D, DS, MC, V.

Ⓓ

★ ★ **JIMMY'S HARBORSIDE.** *242 Northern Ave (02210), E of World Trade Center, adj to Financial District.* 617/423-1000. Specializes in shrimp, lobster, broiled fish. Hrs: noon-9:30 pm; Sun 4-9 pm. Closed Dec 25. Res accepted. Bar. A la carte entrees: lunch $9-$22, dinner $10-$32. Child's meals. Valet parking. Nautical decor. Family-owned. Cr cds: A, C, D, DS, MC, V.

Ⓓ ⛴

★ ★ ★ **JULIEN.** *(See Le Meridien Hotel)* 617/451-1900. French, English menu. Specializes in seafood, lamb, breast of duck. Own baking. Hrs: noon-2 pm, 6-10 pm; Sat 6-10:30 pm; hrs vary July-Aug. Closed Sun; wk of July 4. Res accepted. Bar 5 pm-midnight. Wine list. A la carte entrees: lunch $14.50-$18.50, dinner $25-$34. Complete meals: lunch $25. Prix fixe: dinner $62. Pianist. Valet parking. Elegant surroundings; high carved-wood ceilings, crystal chandeliers. Former Federal Reserve Bank Bldg. Jacket. Cr cds: A, C, D, DS, JCB, MC, V.

Ⓓ ⛴

★ ★ **KASHMIR.** *279 Newbury St (02116), in Back Bay.* 617/536-1695. Indian menu. Specialties: tandoori tikki dal, tandoori duck kadahi, tandoori seafood masala. Hrs: 11 am-11 pm; Sun to 3 pm. Res accepted. Beer, wine. Buffet: lunch $8.95. A la carte entrees: dinner $12.95-$19.95. Complete meals: dinner $14.95-$39.95. Child's meals. Valet parking. Outdoor dining. Indian artifacts and decor. Jacket evenings. Cr cds: A, D, JCB, MC, V.

★ ★ **KYOTO JAPANESE TEPPANYAKI STEAK HOUSE.** *201 Stuart St (02116), in Theatre District.* 617/542-1166. Japanese menu. Specializes in teppan-yaki, sushi. Hrs: 4:30-11 pm; Fri, Sat to midnight; Mon to 10 pm; Sun 3-10 pm. Closed some major hols. Res accepted. Bar. Complete meals: dinner $12.95-$24.95. Child's meals. Parking. Japanese decor. Teppan-yaki grill. Cr cds: A, C, D, DS, JCB, MC, V.

Ⓓ ⛴

★ ★ ★ **L'ESPALIER.** *30 Gloucester St (02115), in Back Bay.* 617/262-3023. Elegance prevails in the three small dining rooms of this 19th-century Back Bay townhouse. Contemporary French menu. Specialties: grilled beef short ribs with black bean mango salsa, ragout of dayboat wolffish, pan-roasted free-range chicken in tamarind orange glaze with radishes. Own baking. Hrs: 6-10 pm. Closed Sun; most major hols. Res accepted. Bar. Wine cellar. Prix fixe: dinner $62. Menu dégustation (Mon-Fri): dinner $78/person. Valet parking. Daily menu. Totally nonsmoking. Cr cds: A, C, D, DS, MC, V.

★ ★ ★ **LA BETTOLA.** *480 A Columbus Ave (02118), in South End.* 617/236-5252. Italian, eclectic menu. Specializes in steak, pasta, chicken. Hrs: 5:30-11:30 pm; Sun to 10 pm. Closed most major hols. Res accepted. Bar. Wine list. Semi-a la carte: dinner $23-$35. Complete meals: dinner $41.50. Valet parking. Outdoor dining. Old Italy atmosphere. Cr cds: A, MC, V.

Ⓓ ⛴

★ ★ **LALA ROKH.** *97 Mt Vernon St (02108), on Beacon Hill.* 617/720-5511. Persian menu. Specializes in authentic Persian dishes. Own baking. Hrs: 5:30-10 pm. Closed some major hols. Res accepted. Wine. Semi-a la carte: dinner $14-$17. Several dining areas with authentic decor; Iranian art. Cr cds: A, D, MC, V.

Ⓓ

★ ★ **LIBRARY AT THE HAMPSHIRE HOUSE.** *84 Beacon St (02108), on Beacon Hill.* 617/227-9600. Hrs: 5-10:30 pm; July-Aug from 6 pm; Sun brunch 10:30 am-2:30 pm. Res accepted. Bar. A la carte entrees: dinner $18-$29. Sun brunch $12-$18. Pianist Fri, Sat, Sun brunch. Valet parking. In 1910 townhouse. Cr cds: A, C, D, MC, V.

Ⓓ ♥

★ ★ **LOCKE OBER.** *Three Winter Place (02108), Downtown Crossing Area.* 617/542-1340. Web www.lockeober.com. Continental menu. Specializes in Wienerschnitzel, baked lobster Savannah. Hrs: 11:30 am-10 pm; Sat from 5:30 pm. Closed Sun; major hols. Bar. Semi-a la carte: lunch $11.50-$20, dinner $22.75-$55. Built in 1875. Old World atmosphere. Jacket. Cr cds: A, C, D, DS, MC, V.

Ⓓ ⛴

★ ★ ★ **MAISON ROBERT.** *45 School St (02108), Downtown Crossing Area.* 617/227-3370. French menu. Specializes in rack of lamb, fresh seafood. Hrs: 11:30 am-2:30 pm, 5:30-10 pm; wkend hrs vary. Closed some major hols. Res accepted. Bar. Semi-a la carte: lunch $9-$22, dinner $17-$32. Valet parking. Outdoor dining in courtyard of former city hall. Jacket. Cr cds: A, C, D, MC, V.

Ⓓ ⛴

★ ★ ★ **MAMMA MARIA.** *Three North Square (02113), in the North End.* 617/523-0077. Italian menu. Menu changes seasonally. Hrs: 5-10 pm; Fri, Sat to 11 pm. Closed most major hols. Res accepted. Bar. A la carte entrees: dinner $18-$28. Valet parking. Private dining rms. Overlooks historic area; Paul Revere house across square. Cr cds: A, C, D, DS, MC, V.

Ⓓ

★ ★ ★ **MARCUCCIO'S.** *125 Salem St (02113), in the North End.* 617/723-1807. Italian menu. Specialties: sea bass with parsley sauce, calamari with black olive balsamic sauce, seared scallops with marjoram-walnut pesto. Hrs: 5-10 pm; Fri, Sat to 11 pm. Closed some major hols. Res accepted. Wine list. Semi-a la carte: dinner $16-$22. Complete meals: dinner $55-$65. Child's meals. Street parking. Totally nonsmoking. Cr cds: MC, V.

Ⓓ

★ ★ ★ **MERCURY.** *116 Boylston St (02116), in Back Bay.* 617/482-7799. Mediterranean menu. Specializes in seasonal Mediterranean dishes. Own baking. Hrs: 5:30-10 pm; Thurs-Sat to 11 pm. Closed Sun, Mon; some major hols. Res accepted. Bar 5 pm-2 am. Semi-a la carte: dinner $15-$19. Entertainment Wed-Sat. Valet parking. Chic bar atmosphere with ornate wood paneling, open kitchen. Cr cds: A, D, DS, MC, V.

Ⓓ ⛴

★ ★ ★ **METROPOLIS CAFE.** *584 Tremont St (02118), in the South End.* 617/247-2931. Eclectic Amer menu. Specialties: corn soup, sage and lavender roasted lamb, warm chocolate pudding cake with vanilla ice cream. Own pasta. Hrs: 5:30-10 pm; Thurs-Sat to 11 pm; Sat, Sun brunch 9 am-3 pm. Closed Jan 1, Thanksgiving, Dec 25. Res accepted. Bar. Wine list. Semi-a la carte: dinner $12.95-$18.95. Sat, Sun brunch $3.95-$6.95. Valet parking. Bistro decor with high ceilings, brass tables. Totally nonsmoking. Cr cds: A, D, MC, V.

★ ★ ★ **MISTRAL.** *223 Columbus Ave (02116), in the South End.* 617/867-9300. French, Mediterranean menu. Specialties: grilled portobello mushrooms, steamed black mussels, confit of duck & foie gras in brioche. Hrs: 5:30-11 pm. Closed Thanksgiving, Dec 25. Res accepted. Bar to midnight. Semi-a la carte: dinner $16-$35. Valet parking. Mediterranean garden atmosphere. Cr cds: A, C, D, DS, MC, V.

Ⓓ

★ ★ **MORTON'S OF CHICAGO.** *One Exeter Plaza (02116), at Boylston & Exeter, in Back Bay.* 617/266-5858; FAX 617/266-9521. Specializes in prime dry-aged beef, fresh seafood. Hrs: 5:30-11 pm; Sun 5-10 pm. Closed major hols. Res accepted. Bar. A la carte entrees: dinner $18.95-$29.95. Valet parking. Menu recited. Cr cds: A, C, D, MC, V.

Ⓓ ⛴

★ ★ ★ **THE OAK ROOM.** *(See Fairmont Copley Plaza Hotel)* 617/267-5300. Web www.fairmont.com. Specializes in steak, seafood. Own baking. Hrs: 5:30-10 pm; Fri, Sat to 11 pm. Res accepted. Bar 4:30 pm-1 am. A la carte entrees: dinner $18.95-$39.95. Complete meals: dinner $38-$68. Valet parking. Turn-of-the-century decor with carved moldings, crystal chandeliers. Cr cds: A, C, D, DS, ER, JCB, MC, V.

★ ★ ★ **OLIVES.** *(10 City Square, Charlestown 02129)* 617/242-1999. Country Mediterranean menu. Specialty: spit-roasted herb and garlic chicken. Own baking, pasta. Hrs: 5:30-10:15 pm; Sat 5-10:30 pm. Closed Sun; major hols. Bar. Wine list. Semi-a la carte: dinner $15.95-$28.95. Valet parking. Rustic European decor; large windows overlook square. Cr cds: A, D, MC, V.

D

★ ★ **PALM.** *(See The Westin Copley Place Hotel)* 617/867-9292. Specializes in steak, lobster, Italian dishes. Own baking. Hrs: 11:30 am-10:30 pm; Sat 5-11 pm; Sun 5-9:30 pm. Closed some major hols. Res accepted. Bar. A la carte entrees: lunch $8-$16, dinner $14-$32. Complete meals: lunch $10-$30, dinner $30-$50. Valet parking. Caricatures of regular clientele on walls. Family-owned since 1926. Cr cds: A, C, D, DS, MC, V.

★ ★ ★ **PARKER'S.** *(See Omni Parker House Hotel)*. 617/227-8600. Eclectic, continental menu. Specialties: Boston scrod, Boston cream pie. Salad bar. Hrs: 6:30-2 pm, 5:30-11 pm; Sat, Sun from 7 am. Res accepted. Bar 11-1 am. Semi-a la carte: bkfst $8-$10, lunch $10-$15, dinner $20-$30. Child's meals. Piano. Valet parking. Cr cds: A, C, D, DS, JCB, MC, V.

D **SC** **⊸**

★ ★ ★ **PIGNOLI.** *79 Park Plaza (02116), in Back Bay.* 617/338-7500. Contemporary Italian menu. Hrs: 11:30 am-2:30 pm, 5:30-10 pm; Fri, Sat to midnight; Sun from 5:30 pm. Bar. Semi-a la carte: lunch $8-$16, dinner $11-$32. Patio dining. Cr cds: A, C, D, DS, MC, V.

D

★ ★ **PLAZA III.** *101 S Faneuil Hall Marketplace (02109), in Faneuil Hall/Quincy Market Area.* 617/720-5570. Specializes in steaks, prime rib, fresh seafood. Hrs: 11 am-10 pm; Thurs-Sat to 11 pm; Sun from 10 am. Res accepted. Serv bar. A la carte entrees: lunch, dinner $7.50-$28.50. Outdoor dining. Cr cds: A, D, DS, MC, V.

D **⊸**

★ ★ ★ **PROVIDENCE.** *(1223 Beacon St, Brookline 02146) W on Commonwealth Ave to Beacon St.* 617/232-0300. Specialties: roast Long Island duckling, wood-grilled pork chop, bibb and watercress salad. Hrs: 5:30-10 pm; Fri, Sat to 11 pm; Sun to 9:30 pm; Sun brunch 11 am-2 pm. Closed Mon; Thanksgiving, Dec 25. Res accepted. Bar. A la carte entrees: dinner $16-$25. Sun brunch $17-$23. Child's meals. Valet parking. Ornate decor; marble pillars, decorated walls. Cr cds: A, C, D, MC, V.

D **SC**

★ ★ ★ **RISTORANTE LUCIA.** *415 Hanover St (02113), in North End.* 617/367-2353. Regional Italian menu. Specializes in linguini with seafood, homemade pasta, grilled veal chops. Hrs: 4-11 pm; Fri-Sun from 11:30 am. Closed Thanksgiving, Dec 25. Res accepted. Bar. Wine list. Semi-a la carte: lunch $4-$10, dinner $8.95-$17. Child's meals. Valet parking (dinner). Painted frescoes on walls and ceilings. Cr cds: A, MC, V.

D **⊸**

★ ★ **RISTORANTE TOSCANO.** *47 Charles St (02114), on Beacon Hill.* 617/723-4090. Northern Italian menu. Specializes in veal, fish, pasta. Hrs: 11:30 am-2:30 pm, 5:30-10 pm; Fri, Sat to 10:30 pm; Sun 11:30 am-3 pm, 5-9 pm. Closed some major hols. Res accepted. Bar. A la carte entrees: lunch $9-$20, dinner $18-$30. Valet parking (dinner). Authentic Italian decor. Cr cds: A.

D **⊸**

★ ★ ★ **ROWES WHARF.** *(See Boston Harbor Hotel)* 617/439-3995. Specialties: roast rack of Vermont lamb, Maine lobster sausage over lemon pasta, seared yellowfin tuna. Hrs: 6:30 am-10 pm; Sun brunch 10:30 am-2:30 pm. Res accepted. Bar 11:30-2 am. Wine cellar. A la carte entrees: bkfst $6-$11, lunch $11-$19, dinner $18-$30. Complete meals: dinner $45-$60. Sun brunch $45. Child's meals. Own baking. Valet parking. View of Boston Harbor. Jacket. Cr cds: A, C, D, DS, JCB, MC, V.

D **⊸** **♥**

★ ★ ★ **SEASONS.** *(See The Regal Bostonian Hotel)* 617/523-3600. Contemporary Amer menu. Specializes in roast duckling, seasonal dishes. Own baking, pasta. Hrs: 6:30-10:30 am, 11:30 am-2 pm, 6-10 pm; Sat 7 am-noon, 6-11 pm; Sun 7 am-noon. Res accepted. Bar. Extensive wine list. Semi-a la carte: bkfst $8-$16, lunch $10-$24, dinner $26-$37. Child's meals. Valet parking. Rooftop restaurant overlooks Faneuil Hall and city. Cr cds: A, C, D, JCB, MC, V.

D **⊸**

✔★ ★ **SMALL PLANET BAR & GRILL.** *565 Boylston St (02116), in Back Bay, opp Hancock Bldg.* 617/536-4477. Hrs: 11:30 am-midnight; Sun from 5 pm; Sun brunch 11 am-3 pm. Closed Thanksgiving, Dec 25. Bar. A la carte entrees: lunch $4.95-$9.95, dinner $8.95-$15.95. Colorful interior. Outdoor dining on Copley Square. Cr cds: A, C, D, DS, MC, V.

D **⊸**

★ ★ **TAPEO.** *266 Newbury St (02116), in Back Bay.* 617/267-4799. Web tapeo.com. Spanish menu. Specializes in tapas, paellas. Hrs: 5:30-10:30 pm; Thurs, Fri to 11:30 pm; Sat noon-11:30 pm; Sun noon-10:30 pm. Closed Thanksgiving, Dec 24, 25. Res accepted. Bar from 5 pm. A la carte entrees: lunch $2.50-$7.50, dinner $17-$22. Valet parking. Outdoor dining. Spanish decor; handpainted tile tapas bar, fireplaces. Cr cds: A, D, MC, V.

D

★ ★ **TATSUKICHI.** *189 State St (02109), in Faneuil Hall/Quincy Market Area.* 617/720-2468. Japanese menu. Specialties: kushiage, shabu shabu, sukiyaki. Hrs: 11:45 am-2:30 pm, 5-10 pm; Fri to 11 pm; Sat 5-11 pm. Closed Sun; also July 4, Thanksgiving, Dec 25. Res accepted. Bar 6 pm-1 am. Semi-a la carte: lunch $7-$10, dinner $14-$22. Street parking. Cr cds: A, C, D, DS, JCB, MC, V.

★ **TERRAMIA.** *98 Salem St (02113), in the North End.* 617/523-3112. Italian menu. Specialties: Maine lobster fritter, open-face seafood ravioli, roasted pork tenderloin in spicy prune sauce. Hrs: 5-10 pm; Fri to 10:30 pm; Sat 4-10:30 pm; Sun 1-10 pm. Closed some major hols. Res accepted. Wine, beer. Semi-a la carte: dinner $10.50-$27. Child's meals. Street parking. Totally nonsmoking. Cr cds: A, DS, MC, V.

D

★ ★ ★ **TOP OF THE HUB.** *800 Boylston St (02199), at top of Prudential Bldg, in Back Bay.* 617/536-1775. Web www.topofthehub.com. Hrs: 11:30 am-2:30 pm, 5:30-10 pm; Fri, Sat to 11 pm; Sun brunch 10 am-2:30 pm. Closed Dec 25. Res accepted. Bar. Wine list. A la carte entrees: lunch $6-$15, dinner $18-$30. Various jazz groups daily. Panoramic view of Charles River and downtown Boston. Cr cds: A, C, D, DS, MC, V.

D

★ **TRATORRIA IL PANINO.** *120 S Market (02109), in Faneuil Hall/Quincy Market Area.* 617/573-9700. Italian menu. Specialties: zuppe de pesce, il panino sandwich, lobster ravioli. Hrs: 11 am-11 pm. Closed Dec 25. Res accepted. Bar. Semi-a la carte: lunch $7.95-$13.95, dinner $10.95-$23.95. Jazz, blues Thurs-Sat. Street parking. Outdoor dining. Cr cds: A, D, MC, V.

D **⊸**

★ ★ **TRUC.** *560 Tremont (02118), in the South End.* 617/338-8070. French menu. Specializes in country French cuisine. Hrs: 6-10 pm; Fri, Sat to 10:30 pm; Sun (brunch) 11 am-2 pm, 6-9 pm. Closed Mon; also some major hols. Res accepted. Wine, beer. Semi-a la carte: dinner $19-$23. Sun brunch $8-$12. Valet parking. Totally nonsmoking. Cr cds: MC, V.

★ ★ **TURNER FISHERIES.** *(See The Westin Copley Place Hotel)* 617/424-7425. Seafood menu. Specialties: clam chowder, crab cakes, Oriental bamboo steamer basket. Hrs: 11 am-11 pm; Sun brunch to 2:30 pm. Res accepted. Bar. Semi-a la carte: lunch $9-$15, dinner $17-$27. Sun brunch $28.50. Child's meals. Jazz Tues-Sat. Valet parking. Cr cds: A, C, D, DS, MC, V.

D **SC** **⊸** **♥**

★ ★ **THE VAULT.** *105 Water St (02155), in Faneuil Hall/Quincy Market Area. 617/292-9966.* Web www.vaultbistro.com. Contemporary Amer menu. Specialties: pulled pork with jalapeño corn bread, steamed Maine lobster, steak & potatoes. Hrs: 11:30 am-2:30 pm, 5:30-11:30 pm; Sat 5:30-11:30 pm. Closed Sun; also July 4, Thanksgiving, Dec 25. Res accepted. Bar. A la carte entrees: dinner $15-$29. Street parking. Totally nonsmoking. Cr cds: A, C, D, DS, MC, V.

★ ★ **YE OLDE UNION OYSTER HOUSE.** *41 Union St (02108), in Faneuil Hall/Quincy Market Area. 617/227-2750.* Specializes in shore dinner, seafood platter. Hrs: 11 am-9:30 pm; Fri, Sat to 10 pm; Sun brunch 11 am-3 pm. Closed Thanksgiving, Dec 25. Res accepted. Bar. Semi-a la carte: lunch $7-$16, dinner $14.95-$25. Sun brunch $9.95. Child's meals. Valet parking (dinner). Historic oyster bar established 1826; originally a silk & dry goods shop (1742). Family-owned. Cr cds: A, C, D, DS, JCB, MC, V.

★ ★ ★ **ZINC.** *35 Stanhope St (02116), in Back Bay. 617/262-2323.* French menu. Specializes in fresh seafood. Hrs: 5:30-11:30 pm; Mon to 10 pm. Closed Sun. Res accepted. Bar to 2 am; Mon to midnight. Wine list. Semi-a la carte: dinner $21-$33. Valet parking. Inimate atmosphere; European bistro decor; menu changes daily. Cr cds: A, D, MC, V.

✔ ★ **ZUMA'S TEX MEX CAFE.** *7 N Market St (02109), in Faneuil Hall/Quincy Market Area. 617/367-9114.* Specializes in fajitas, enchiladas, neon margaritas. Hrs: 11:30 am-11 pm; Fri, Sat to midnight; Sun noon-10 pm. Closed Dec 25. Tex-Mex menu. Bar. Semi-a la carte: lunch, dinner $5-$12. Cr cds: A, C, D, DS, MC, V.

Unrated Dining Spot

RUBIN'S KOSHER DELICATESSEN. *(500 Harvard St, Brookline) W on Beacon St. 617/731-8787.* Kosher deli menu. Hrs: 10 am-8 pm; Fri 9 am-3 pm; Sun 9 am-8 pm. Closed Sat; Jewish hols. Semi-a la carte: lunch $3.50-$12, dinner $6.50-$15. Parking. Family-owned. Totally nonsmoking. No cr cds accepted.

Bourne (Cape Cod) (D-8)

(See also Buzzards Bay, Sandwich)

Settled 1627 **Pop** 16,064 **Elev** 19 ft **Area code** 508 **Zip** 02532 **E-mail** info@capecodchamber.org **Web** www.capecodchamber.org
Information Cape Cod Chamber of Commerce, US 6 & MA 132, PO Box 790, Hyannis 02601-0790; 508/362-3225or 888/33-CAPECOD.

Named for Jonathan Bourne, a successful whaling merchant, this town has had a variety of industries since its founding. Originally a center for herring fishing, the town turned to manufacturing stoves, kettles, and later, freight cars. Bourne's current prosperity is derived from cranberries and tourism.

What to See and Do

Aptucxet Trading Post. A replica of a 1627 trading post, which may have been the first of its kind in America. Native American artifacts; rune stone believed to be proof of visits to the area by the Phoenicians in 400 B.C.; artifacts in 2 rms. On grounds are herb garden, site of original spring, saltworks; RR station built for President Grover Cleveland for use at his Gray Gables home, his summer White House; Dutch-style windmill; picnic area adj to Cape Cod Canal. (July-Aug, daily; last 2 wkends May & June & Sept-mid-Oct, daily exc Mon) 24 Aptucxet Rd, off Shore Rd, ½ mi W of Bourne Bridge. Phone 508/759-9487. ¢

Bourne Scenic Park. Playground, picnicking; bike trails; swimming pool, bathhouse; recreation building; camping (fee); store. (Apr-Oct, daily) North bank of Cape Cod Canal. Phone 508/759-7873.

Industrial tour. Pairpoint Crystal Co. (est 1837). Handmade lead crystal ware, glassblowing demonstrations. Viewing (Mon-Fri). Store (daily). 851 Sandwich Rd (MA 6A), in Sagamore. Phone 508/888-2344. **Free.**

Braintree (C-7)

Settled 1634 **Pop** 33,836 **Elev** 90 ft **Area code** 617 **Zip** 02184 **Web** www.southshorechamber.org
Information South Shore Chamber of Commerce, 36 Miller Stile Rd, Quincy 02169; 617/479-1111.

What to See and Do

Abigail Adams House. Birthplace of Abigail Smith Adams (1744), daughter of a local clergyman, wife of President John Adams, mother of President John Quincy Adams. Period furnishings. (July-Labor Day, daily exc Mon) North & Norton Sts, 2 mi E in Weymouth. Phone 617/335-1849. ¢¢

General Sylvanus Thayer Birthplace (1720). Thayer, a soldier and educator, served as 5th Superintendent of West Point, 1817-1833. House contains 17th- & 18th-century furnishings, military exhibits and local historical displays. (Mid-Apr-mid-Oct, Sat & Sun afternoons, also by appt) 786 Washington St. Phone 617/848-1640. ¢¢ Adj is a

Reconstructed 18th-Century Barn. Houses farm equipment, ice cutting and wood tools; costumes; research library and genealogical records. (Mon-Fri; also by appt) **Free.**

Motels

✔ ★ ★ **DAYS INN.** *190 Wood Rd, MA 128 exit 6. 781/848-1260; res: 800/348-4667; FAX 781/848-9799.* 103 rms, 3 story. S $65-$80; D $75-$90; each addl $5; suites $150-$200; under 18 free. Crib free. Pet accepted, some restrictions. TV; cable (premium). Complimentary continental bkfst. Restaurant nearby. Ck-out 11 am. Meeting rm. Business servs avail. Valet serv. Microwaves avail. Boston tours. Cr cds: A, C, D, DS, MC, V.

★ ★ **HOLIDAY INN EXPRESS.** *(909 Hingham St, Rockland 02370) approx 10 mi S of MA 93 on MA 3, exit 14. 781/871-5660; FAX 781/871-7255.* 76 rms, 2 story. S $63-$72; D $70-$84; each addl $5; under 18 free. Pet accepted. TV. Continental bkfst. Coffee in rms. Ck-out 11 am. Free guest lndry. Meeting rm. Business servs avail. Health club privileges. Microwaves avail. Cr cds: A, C, D, DS, ER, JCB, MC, V.

Motor Hotels

★ ★ **HOLIDAY INN-RANDOLPH.** *(1374 N Main St, Randolph 02368)* ¼ *mi from MA 128, exit 5A. 781/961-1000; FAX 781/963-0089.* 158 rms, 4 story. S, D $85-$125; each addl $10; under 18 free; wkend rates. Crib free. TV; cable (premium). Pool; lifeguard. Restaurant 6:30 am-10 pm. Rm serv. Bar 11:30-2 am. Ck-out noon. Coin lndry. Meeting rms. Business servs avail. In-rm modem link. Bellhops. Valet serv. Sundries. Complimentary bus depot, RR, transportation. Microwaves avail. Cr cds: A, C, D, DS, MC, V.

★ ★ ★ **SHERATON.** *37 Forbes Rd, at MA 128 exit 6. 781/848-0600; FAX 781/843-9492.* 376 rms, 2-6 story. S, D $149-$209; each addl

$15; suites $189-$395; under 18 free; wkend rates. Crib free. TV; cable (premium). 2 pools, 1 indoor. Restaurant 6:30 am-11 pm. Rm serv. Bar; entertainment Tues-Sat. Ck-out noon. Meeting rms. In-rm modem link. Bellhops. Concierge. Sundries. Gift shop. Exercise rm; steam rm, sauna. Some bathrm phones. Cr cds: A, C, D, DS, ER, MC, V.

Restaurant

★★ **CAFFÉ BELLA.** *(19 Warren St (MA 139), Randolph 02368) 3 mi S on MA 28. 781/961-7729.* Italian menu. Specializes in grilled meats and seafood. Own baking, pasta. Menu changes seasonally. Hrs: 5-10 pm. Closed Sun; July 4, Thanksgiving, Dec 25. Bar. Semi-a la carte: dinner $12.50-$27.50. Mediterranean decor. Cr cds: A, D, MC, V.

Brewster (Cape Cod) (D-10)

Settled 1656 **Pop** 8,440 **Elev** 39 ft **Area code** 508 **Zip** 02631 **E-mail** info@capecodchamber.org **Web** www.capecodchamber.org

Information Cape Cod Chamber of Commerce, US 6 & MA 132, PO Box 790, Hyannis 02601-0790; 508/362-3225 or 888/33-CAPECOD.

What to See and Do

Cape Cod Museum of Natural History. Exhibits on wildlife and ecology of the area; art exhibits; library; lectures; films; nature trails; field walks; trips to Monomoy Island. Gift shop. (Daily; closed major hols) MA 6A, West Brewster. Phone 508/896-3867 or 800/479-3867. ¢¢

⭐ **New England Fire & History Museum.** This 6-building complex houses an extensive collection of fire-fighting equipment and includes the Arthur Fiedler Memorial Fire Collection; diorama of Chicago fire of 1871; engines dating from the Revolution to the 1930s; world's only 1929 Mercedes Benz fire engine; life-size reproduction of Ben Franklin's firehouse; 19th-century blacksmith shop; largest apothecary shop in the country contains 664 gold-leaf bottles of medicine; medicinal herb gardens; library; films; theater performances. Guided tours. Picnic area. (Memorial Day wkend-mid-Sept, daily; mid-Sept-Columbus Day, wkends) ½ mi W of MA 137 on MA 6A. Phone 508/896-5711. ¢¢

Nickerson State Park. Swimming; fishing; boating (ramp). Bicycling (Cape Cod Rail Trail). Picnicking. Camping (dump station). Standard fees. 3 mi E, off MA 6A. Phone 508/896-3491. **Free.**

Stoney Brook Mill. Museum upstairs includes historical exhibits, weaving. Corn grinding (July & Aug, Thurs-Sat afternoons). Old Grist Mill in West Brewster, on site of one of first gristmills in America. Phone 508/896-6745. **Free.**

Inns

★★★ **BRAMBLE INN.** *2019 Main St (MA 6A). 508/896-7644.* 8 rms, 2 story. No rm phones. Late May-mid-Oct: D $95-$125. Closed Jan-Apr. Children over 8 yrs only. TV in some rms; cable (premium). Complimentary full bkfst. Restaurant (see BRAMBLE INN). Ck-out 11 am, ck-in 2 pm. Two buildings (1849-1861); many antiques. Intimate, country atmosphere. Cr cds: A, DS, MC, V.

★★ **CAPTAIN FREEMAN.** *15 Breakwater Rd. 508/896-7481; FAX 508/896-5618; res: 800/843-4664.* E-mail visitus@capecod.net; web www.captfreemaninn.com. 12 rms, 6 A/C, 3 story. Some rm phones. Late-May-Oct: S, D $125-$250; wkly rates; lower rates rest of yr. Children over 10 yrs only. TV in some rms; VCR (free movies). Pool. Complimentary full bkfst. Restaurant nearby. Ck-out 11 am, ck-in 2 pm. Concierge serv.

Free airport, bus depot transportation. Game rm. Lawn games. Some fireplaces. Balconies. Antiques. Sitting rm. House built 1866. Totally non-smoking. Cr cds: A, MC, V.

★★★ **FARMHOUSE INN.** *716 Main St (MA 6A). 508/896-3910; FAX 508/896-4232; res: 800/892-3910.* E-mail bnbinn@capecod.net. 5 rms, some rms with shower only, some share bath, 2 story, 1 suite. No rm phones. Late May-Oct: D $110-$175; suite $220; lower rates rest of yr. Children over 16 only. TV; cable (premium). Heated pool; whirlpool. Complimentary full bkfst; afternoon refreshments. Ck-out 11 am, ck-in 3 pm. Business servs avail. Lawn games. Refrigerators. Balconies. Picnic tables. Built 1850; antiques and reproductions. Totally nonsmoking. Cr cds: A, C, D, DS, MC, V.

✔★★ **GREYLIN HOUSE.** *2311 Main St. 508/896-0004; FAX 508/896-0005; res: 800/233-6662.* Web www.capecodtravel.com/greylin. 5 rms, 2 story. June-Sept: S, D $65-$125; family, wkly rates; lower rates rest of yr. Children over 8 yrs only. Pet accepted. Complimentary full bkfst. Restaurant nearby. Ck-out 11 am, ck-in 2 pm. Refrigerators. Picnic tables. Built 1837; library/sitting rm; antiques. Totally nonsmoking. Cr cds: A, DS, MC, V.

★★★ **HIGH BREWSTER INN.** *964 Satucket Rd, W on Main St, left on Stony Brook Rd, left on Satucket Rd. 508/896-3636; FAX 508/896-3734; res: 800/203-2634.* 3 rms in main house, 2 story, 4 air-cooled kit. cottages. No rm phones in main house. Memorial Day-Labor Day: D $90-$110; kit. cottages $150-$210; under 16 free; wkly rates. Closed Jan-Mar. Crib free. Pet accepted, some restrictions; $25-$50. Complimentary continental bkfst. Restaurant (see HIGH BREWSTER INN). Rm serv. Ck-out 11 am, ck-in 3 pm. Lawn games. Antiques; library. Situated on 3 acres, house (1738) overlooks Lower Mill Pond. Adj is historic gristmill and herring run. Cr cds: A, MC, V.

★★ **INN AT THE EGG.** *1944 Old King's Hwy (MA 6A). 508/896-3123; FAX 508/896-6821; res: 800/259-8235.* Web www.innattheegg.com. 5 rms, 2 story. No rm phones. Mid-June-mid-Oct: D $89-$150; each addl $25; higher rates: hols, special events (3-day min); lower rates rest of yr. TV; cable (premium), VCR (free movies). Complimentary full bkfst; afternoon refreshments. Restaurant opp. Ck-out 10:30 am, ck-in 2 pm. Business servs avail. Lawn games. Balconies. Picnic tables, grills. Antiques; library/sitting rm. Formerly the First Parish Church parsonage. Totally nonsmoking. Cr cds: A, MC, V.

★★ **ISAIAH CLARK HOUSE.** *1187 Old King's Hwy (MA 6A). 508/896-2223; FAX 508/896-2138; res: 800/822-4001.* E-mail rgriffin@capecod.net; web www.isaiahclark.com. 7 rms, 2 story. Many rm phones. Late May-mid-Oct: D $98-$130; each addl $25; lower rates rest of yr. Children over 10 yrs only. TV in most rms; cable. Complimentary full bkfst; afternoon refreshments. Ck-out 11 am, ck-in 2 pm. Business servs avail. Concierge serv. Picnic tables. Antiques. Former sea captain's house (1780). Totally nonsmoking. Cr cds: A, DS, MC, V.

★★ **OLD SEA PINES.** *2553 Main St (MA 6A). 508/896-6114; FAX 508/896-7387.* E-mail seapines@c4.net; web www.oldseapinesinn.com. 23 rms, 18 with bath, 18 A/C, 3 story. No rm phones. June-Oct: S, D $55-$115; suite $155; each addl $20; lower rates rest of yr. Children over 8 yrs only exc in family suites. Complimentary full bkfst. Rm serv. Bkfst in bed avail. Serv bar 2-10 pm. Ck-out 11 am, ck-in 2 pm. Business servs avail. Some fireplaces. Antiques. Founded 1907 as School of Charm and Personality for Young Women. On 3½ acres. Totally nonsmoking. Cr cds: A, C, D, DS, MC, V.

★★ **PEPPER HOUSE.** *2062 Main St (MA 6A). 508/896-4389; FAX 508/896-5012.* E-mail pepper@capecod.net; web www.pepperhouseinn.com. 4 rms, 1 with shower only, 2 story. No rm phones. Late May-mid-Oct: S, D $109-$139; wkends (2-day-min in season); lower rates rest of yr. Children over 10 yrs only. TV; cable. Complimentary full bkfst; afternoon refreshments. Restaurant nearby. Ck-out 10:30 am, ck-in 2:30 pm. Luggage handling. Concierge serv. Some fireplaces. Picnic tables. Built in 1793; Federal Colonial style. Totally nonsmoking. Cr cds: A, MC, V.

★ ★ **RUDDY TURNSTONE INN.** *463 Main St (MA 6A).* 508/385-9871; FAX 508/385-5696; res: 800/654-1995. Web www.sun-sol.com/ruddyturnstone/. 5 rms, 1 with shower only, 2 story, 1 suite. No rm phones. Mid-June-mid-Oct: S, D $95-$120; suite $150; wkends, hols (2-3-day min); lower rates rest of yr. Children over 10 yrs only. Complimentary full bkfst. Ck-out 11 am, ck-in 1 pm. Luggage handling. Concierge serv. Lawn games. Picnic tables. Early 19th-century Cape Cod house; antique furnishings. Totally nonsmoking. Cr cds: MC, V.

Resort

★ ★ ★ **OCEAN EDGE.** *MA 6A, 2 1/2 mi E on MA 6A.* 508/896-9000; FAX 508/896-9123; res: 800/343-6074. E-mail oceanedge@ocean-edge.com; web www.oceanedge.com. 180 units, 2 story, 32 kit. villas. Apr-Oct: S, D $250-$350; suites $395-$500; cottages $475-$900; under 12 free; AP, MAP avail; wkly rates; golf, tennis plans; lower rates rest of yr. Crib $10. TV; cable, VCR avail (movies). 6 pools, 2 indoor; whirlpool; poolside serv, lifeguard. Playground. Supervised child's activities (June-Sept); ages 4-12. Dining rm 6 am-10 pm. Box lunches, snacks, picnics. Rm serv to midnight. Bar noon-1 am; entertainment. Ck-out 11 am, ck-in 3 pm. Grocery, package store 1 blk. Convention facilities. Business center. In-rm modem link. Bellhops. Valet serv. Airport transportation. Concierge. Gift shop. Sports dir. Tennis, pro. 18-hole golf, greens fee $68, pro, putting green, driving range. Swimming beach. Hiking. Bicycle rentals. Lawn games. Soc dir. Exercise equipt; sauna. Microwaves, bathrm phones. Balconies. On grounds of turn-of-the-century 380-acre estate fronting Cape Cod Bay; meeting rms in "English-manor" house (1912) with elaborate plasterwork, woodwork & paneling, fireplaces. Cr cds: A, C, D, DS, MC, V.

Restaurants

★ ★ ★ **BRAMBLE INN.** *(See Bramble Inn)* 508/896-7644; FAX 508/896-9332. Specialties: tenderloin of beef, rack of lamb, assorted seafood curry. Own baking. Hrs: 6-9 pm. Closed Mon-Wed off season; also Jan-Apr. Res accepted. Serv bar. Complete meals: dinner $42-$52. Parking. Built in 1861; 4 dining areas, including enclosed porch. Totally nonsmoking. Cr cds: A, DS, MC, V.

★ ★ ★ ★ **CHILLINGSWORTH.** *1 mi E of jct MA 6A & MA 124.* 508/896-3640. E-mail webchill@chillingsworth.com; web www.chillingsworth.com. Classical music accompanies meals at this 300-year-old property decorated in 18th-century style. Modern French menu. Daily changing menu emphasizing fresh native seafood, veal, pheasant. Own baking, pasta. Grows own herbs. Hrs: mid-June-mid-Sept, 2 dinner sittings: 6-6:30 pm & 9-9:30 pm; mid-May-mid-June & mid-Sept-Nov, wkends only; casual greenhouse lunches and dinners 11:30 am-2:30 pm & 6-9:30 pm; Sun brunch 11:30 am-2:30 pm. Off-season dinner, 1 sitting: 7-8 pm. Closed Mon; also Dec-mid-May. Res accepted. Bar. Wine list. Table d'hôte: 7-course dinner from $49.50. A la carte entrees: lunch from $7.50, dinner from $9.50. Sun brunch from $7.50. Outdoor dining. Guest rms avail. Cr cds: A, C, D, MC, V.

★ ★ ★ **HIGH BREWSTER INN.** *(See High Brewster Inn)* 508/896-3636. Specializes in fresh local seafood, beef, lamb. Hrs: 5:30-9 pm. Closed Dec-Mar. Res required. Complete meals: dinner $30-$50. Parking. Intimate atmosphere; 3 dining areas in 1738 structure; low ceilings, open

beams and wide plank floors; antiques. Colonial (1738) building and decor. Cr cds: A, MC, V.

★ ★ ★ **OLD MANSE INN.** *1861 Main St (US 6A).* 508/896-3149. Web www.oldmanseinn.com. Specialties: steamed lobster, braised lamb shank, lemon buttermilk pudding cake. Hrs: 5:30-10 pm. Closed Mon; Jan-Apr. Wine list. Semi-a la carte: dinner $14-$19. Parking. Two dining rms in early 19th-century inn; antiques. Romantic setting. Guest rms avail. Totally nonsmoking. Cr cds: A, DS, MC, V.

Brockton (C-7)

Settled 1700 **Pop** 92,788 **Elev** 112 ft **Area code** 508 **E-mail** info@metrosouthchamber.com **Web** www.metrosouthchamber.com
Information Metro South Chamber of Commerce, 60 School St, 02301; 508/586-0500.

Half of the Union Army in the Civil War marched in Brockton-made shoes. Known as the nation's "shoe capital" until this century, diverse manufacturing and service industries contribute to the city's economic base today. Brockton was home of boxing champions Rocky Marciano and "Marvelous Marvin" Hagler.

What to See and Do

Brockton Historical Society Museums. The Heritage Center, main building of the complex, consists of Shoe Museum, Fire Museum, and "The Homestead," an early Brockton shoemaker's home. "The Homestead" features exhibits on Thomas Edison, who electrified the first show factory in the world in Brockton in 1883, and former local shoemaker and undefeated world champion boxer, Rocky Marciano. (Sun afternoons or by appt) 216 N Pearl St. Phone 508/583-1039. ¢

Fuller Museum of Art. Permanent exhibits of 19th- & 20th-century American art; children's gallery; changing exhibits; lectures, gallery talks and tours. Museum (Tues-Sun afternoons; closed most major hols). 455 Oak St, on Porter's Pond. Phone 508/588-6000. ¢¢

Annual Event

Brockton Fair. Fairgrounds. Midway, agricultural exhibits, entertainment. Phone 508/586-8000. Early July.

Motels

✔★ **CARLTON HOUSE MOTOR INN.** *1005 Belmont St (02401), on MA 123 at jct MA 24, opp VA Hospital.* 508/588-3333. 64 rms, 2 story. S, D $49-$69; each addl $5; under 12 free. Crib free. TV; cable (premium). Pool. Restaurant 7 am-10 pm; Mon-Wed to 9 pm; Sun to noon. Rm serv. Bar 11-1 am; entertainment Thur-Sat. Ck-out noon. Meeting rms. Business servs avail. In-rm modem link. Sundries. Downhill ski 11 mi. Health club privileges. Cr cds: A, C, D, DS, MC, V.

★ ★ **HOLIDAY INN-BOSTON BROCKTON.** *195 Westgate Dr (02401), in Westgate Mall at jct MA 24, 27.* 508/588-6300; FAX 508/580-4384. 187 rms, 3 story. S $65-$95; D $75-$105; each addl $10; under 12 free. Crib free. TV; cable (premium). Indoor pool; whirlpool. Restaurant 6:30 am-2 pm, 5-10 pm. Rm serv. Bar 4 pm-midnight. Ck-out noon. Coin lndry. Meeting rms. Business servs avail. In-rm modem link. Bellhops. Exercise equipt; sauna. Cr cds: A, C, D, DS, JCB, MC, V.

Restaurant

✔★ **CHRISTO'S, INC.** *782 Crescent St (02402), adj to Eastside Shopping Plaza.* 508/588-4200. Specializes in steak, Greek salads. Hrs: 11 am-midnight. Closed Thanksgiving, Dec 25. Bar. Semi-a la carte: lunch $2.75-$6.95, dinner $5.95-$10.50. Family-owned. Cr cds: D, DS, MC, V.

D ➘

Burlington (B-7)

Settled 1641 **Pop** 23,302 **Elev** 218 ft **Area code** 617 **Zip** 01803

Motel

✔★ ★ **HOWARD JOHNSON.** *98 Middlesex Tpke, MA I-95 exit 32B.* 781/272-6550; FAX 781/229-8164. 132 rms, 3-4 story. S $84-$119; D $86-$109; each addl $8; under 18 free; wkend rates. Crib free. TV; cable (premium). Pool. Complimentary coffee in rms. Restaurant 7 am-11 pm. Rm servs 5-10 pm. Bar from 11 am. Ck-out noon. Coin lndry. Meeting rms. Business servs avail. In-rm modem link. Valet serv. Exercise equipt. Private patios, balconies. Cr cds: A, C, D, DS, ER, JCB, MC, V.

D ⚓ 🏋 ⚒ 🔥 SC

Motor Hotels

★ ★ **COURTYARD BY MARRIOTT.** *(240 Mishawum Rd, Woburn 01801) 5 mi E on I-95, exit 36.* 781/932-3200; FAX 781/935-6163. 121 rms, 3 story. S, D $139-$169; each addl $5; suites $159-$189; family rates; package plans. Crib avail. TV; cable (premium). Complimentary coffee in rms. Restaurant adj 11:30 am-11:30 pm. Bar 5-11 pm. Ck-out 1 pm. Meeting rms. Business servs avail. In-rm modem link. Valet serv. Sundries. Coin lndry. Airport, RR station transportation. Exercise equipt. Health club privileges. Pool. Cr cds: A, C, D, DS, MC, V.

D ⚓ 🏋 ⚒ 🔥 SC

★ ★ **HAMPTON INN.** *(315 Mishawum Rd, Woburn 01801) 5 mi E on I-95, exit 36.* 781/935-7666; FAX 781/933-6899. 99 rms, 5 story. S, D $79-$149; under 18 free; wkend rates. Crib free. Pet accepted. TV; cable (premium). Complimentary continental bkfst. Coffee in rms. Restaurant 10 am-11 pm. Rm serv noon-10 pm. Bar. Ck-out noon. Business servs avail. In-rm modem link. Valet serv. Sundries. Health club privileges. Some refrigerators. Cr cds: A, C, D, DS, MC, V.

D 🐾 ⚒ 🔥 SC

Hotel

★ ★ ★ **BOSTON MARRIOTT.** *One Mall Rd, MA 128/I-95 exit 33B.* 781/229-6565; FAX 781/229-7973. Web www.marriott.com. 419 rms, 9 story. S, D $159-$189; suites $250-$400; family rates wkends. TV; cable (premium). 2 pools, 1 indoor; whirlpool, poolside serv, lifeguard. Restaurant 6 am-10 pm; wkends from 7 am. Rm serv to midnight. Bar 4 pm-1 am; entertainment. Ck-out noon. Coin lndry. Convention facilities. Business servs avail. In-rm modem link. Concierge. Gift shop. Beauty shop. Exercise equipt; sauna. Massage. Game rm. Refrigerators avail. Luxury level. Cr cds: A, C, D, DS, ER, JCB, MC, V.

D ⚓ 🏋 ⚒ 🔥 SC

Restaurant

★ ★ **DANDELION GREEN.** *90 N Mall Rd, I-95 exit 32B.* 781/273-1616. Continental menu. Specializes in fresh seafood, steak. Salad bar. Hrs: 11:30 am-midnight. Closed some major hols. Res ac-

cepted. Bar. Semi-a la carte: lunch $5.95-$12.95, dinner $7.95-$29.95. Child's meals. Greenhouse decor. Cr cds: A, C, D, DS, MC, V.

D

Buzzards Bay (Cape Cod) (D-8)

Pop 3,250 **Elev** 10 ft **Area code** 508 **Zip** 02532 **E-mail** infor@capecodchamber.org **Web** www.capecodchamber.org

Information Cape Cod Chamber of Commerce, US 6 & MA 132, PO Box 790, Hyannis 02601-0790; 508/362-3225 or 888/33-CAPECOD.

Cape Cod is said to face "four seas": Buzzards Bay, Nantucket Sound, the Atlantic Ocean and Cape Cod Bay. There is a jagged, irregular shoreline here, dotted with hundreds of summer resorts, public and private beaches, yacht clubs and fishing piers.

The area of Buzzards Bay is at the west entrance to the Cape Cod Canal. Among the better-known towns on the mainland shore are Nonquit and South Yarmouth (see), west of New Bedford, and Fairhaven, Crescent Beach, Mattapoisett, Wareham and Onset, to the east. On the Cape side are Monument Beach, Pocasset, Silver Beach, West Falmouth, Woods Hole (see), and the string of Elizabeth Islands, which ends with Cuttyhunk.

What to See and Do

Cape Cod Canal Cruises. Cruises with historical narration. Also evening cocktail and entertainment cruises. (June-Oct, daily; May, Sat & Sun) 3 mi W via MA 6, 28, Onset Town Pier. Phone 508/295-3883. ¢¢¢

Porter Thermometer Museum. The world’s only thermometer museum houses an enormous collection of more than 2,700 of these instruments. (Daily) 49 Zarahemla Rd, just E of jct I-495 & I-195, in Onset. Phone 508/295-5504. **Free.**

Motel

✔★ **BAY MOTOR INN.** *223 Main St.* 508/759-3989; FAX 508/759-3199. E-mail bmotorinn@capecod.net; web www.cape-cod.com/baymotorinn/. 17 rms, 1-2 story, 3 kits. Mid-June-Labor Day: D $72-$99; each addl $10; kit. units $98-$110; wkly rates; lower rates Apr-mid-June, Labor Day-mid-Nov. Closed rest of yr. Crib $7. Pet accepted. TV; cable (premium). Pool. Complimentary coffee in lobby. Restaurant adj. Ck-out 11 am. Free bus depot transportation. Picnic tables, grills. Cr cds: A, DS, MC, V.

D 🐾 ⚓ 🔥 SC

Cambridge (B-7)

(See also Boston)

Settled 1630 **Pop** 95,802 **Elev** 40 ft **Area code** 617 **E-mail** ccinfo@cambcc.org **Web** www.cambcc.org/cambchmbr

Information Chamber of Commerce, 859 Massachusetts Ave, 02139; 617/876-4100.

Across the Charles River from Boston, Cambridge is world-famous for its educational institutions, but for the most part it is an industrial city. It is also known as a research center. It was named for Cambridge, England's famous university town.

What to See and Do

Christ Church (Episcopal) (1759). The oldest church building in Cambridge. It is a fine Georgian Colonial building designed by Peter Harrison. It was used as a colonial barracks during the Revolution. (Daily) Zero Garden St at the Common. Phone 617/876-0200. **Free.**

⭐ **Harvard University** (18,179 students). This magnificent university, America's oldest, was founded in 1636. Two yrs later, when a minister named John Harvard died and left half his estate and his considerable personal library, it was named for him. Includes Harvard and Radcliffe colleges as well as 10 graduate and professional schools. Harvard Yard, as the original campus is called, is tree-shaded and occupied by stately red-brick buildings. Harvard Square.In and around the yard are

Massachusetts Hall. Oldest building (1720) and architectural inspiration for the campus. **Free.**

Widener Library (1915). Has an enormous Corinthian portico; more than 3,000,000 books. Near it are Houghton, with a fine collection of rare books, and Lamont, the first undergraduate library in America. S side of Harvard Yard. **Free.**

University Hall (1813-1815). Designed by Charles Bulfinch, made of Chelmsford granite in contrast to the surrounding brick, and one of the Yard's most handsome buildings. **Free.**

Fogg Art Museum. European and American paintings, sculpture and decorative arts; drawings, prints, photographs; changing exhibits. (Daily; closed hols) Free admission Sat mornings. 32 Quincy St. Phone 617/495-9400. ¢¢

Harvard Museums of Cultural & Natural History. Contains four museums in one building, including Peabody Museum of Archaeology & Ethnology, Museum of Comparative Zoology, Botanical Museum and Mineralogical & Geological Museum. Exhibits range from pre-Columbian art to dinosaurs, rare gems, and the famous Blaschka glass flowers. Extensive research collections. (Daily; closed Jan 1, July 4, Thanksgiving, Dec 25) 26 Oxford St. Phone 617/495-1910 for general information; for guided tours and special programs phone 617/495-3045. ¢¢

The Houses of Harvard-Radcliffe are between Harvard Square and the Charles River and NE of Harvard Yard between Shepard & Linnaean Sts.

John F. Kennedy School of Government (1978). Contains library, classrooms, public affairs forum for lectures. 79 J.F.K. St, on the banks of the Charles River.

Information Center. Provides maps, brochures. (June-Aug, daily; rest of yr, daily exc Sun) Student-guided tours begin here. 1350 Massachusetts Ave. Phone 617/495-1573.

Longfellow National Historic Site. Georgian-style house built in 1759 was Washington's headquarters during the 1775-1776 siege of Boston, and Henry Wadsworth Longfellow's home from 1837 until his death in 1882. Longfellow taught at Harvard and his books are located here. (Daily; closed Jan 1, Thanksgiving, Dec 25) Golden Eagle Passport (see MAKING THE MOST OF YOUR TRIP). 105 Brattle St, ½ mi from Harvard. Phone 617/876-4491. ¢

Massachusetts Institute of Technology (1861). (9,500 students) One of the greatest science and engineering schools in the world. On the Charles River, the campus includes 135 acres of impressive neoclassic and modern buildings. Information center in the lobby of the main building, 77 Massachusetts Ave; guided tours, 2 departures (Mon-Fri). 77 Massachusetts Ave, at Memorial Dr. Information office, phone 617/253-4795.On campus are

MIT Museum. Collections and exhibits that interpret the Institute's social and educational history, developments in science and technology, and the interplay of technology and art. (Daily exc Mon; closed hols) 265 Massachusetts Ave. Phone 617/253-4444. ¢¢ Part of the museum, but in a separate building is

Hart Nautical Galleries. Shows ship and marine engineering development through displays of rigged merchant and naval ship models; changing exhibits. (Daily) 77 Massachusetts Ave. **Free.**

List Visual Arts Center at MIT. Changing exhibits of contemporary art. (Sept-June, daily; closed major hols; free) The MIT campus also has an outstanding permanent collection of outdoor sculpture, including works by Calder, Moore and Picasso, and significant architecture, including buildings by Aalto, Pei and Saarinen. Walking tour map at information center. Wiesner Bldg, 20 Ames St.

Radcliffe College (1879). (2,700 women) Coordinate institution with Harvard. Unique women's educational and scholarly resources include the Arthur and Elizabeth Schlesinger Library on the History of Women in America (at 3 James St). More than 850 major collections of history of women from 1800 to present. Admissions office at 8 Garden St. Phone 617/495-8601.

The Blacksmith House (1808). Home of Dexter Pratt, the village blacksmith made famous by Longfellow; now a bakery and coffee shop. (Daily; limited hrs; closed hols) 56 Brattle St. Phone 617/354-3036.

Motor Hotels

✔⭐ ★ **BEST WESTERN HOMESTEAD.** *220 Alewife Brook Pkwy (02138).* 617/491-8000; res: 800/491-4914; FAX 617/491-4932. Web www.bwhomestead.com/22025.html. 69 rms, 4 story. S $99-$199; D $109-$209; under 19 free. Crib $15. TV; cable (premium). Indoor pool; whirlpool. Complimentary continental bkfst. Restaurant adj 11:30 am-11:30 pm; Sun, Mon to 10:30 pm. Bar to 12:30 am. Ck-out noon. Meeting rm. Business servs avail. In-rm modem link. Health club privileges. Refrigerators avail. Cr cds: A, C, D, DS, ER, JCB, MC, V.

★ **HARVARD SQUARE HOTEL.** *110 Mt Auburn St (02138).* 617/864-5200; res: 800/458-5886; FAX 617/864-2409. 73 rms, 4 story. S, D $99-$199; under 17 free. Crib free. Garage parking $16. TV; cable (premium). Restaurant 7 am-9 pm. Ck-out 11 am. Business servs avail. In-rm modem link. Cr cds: A, C, D, DS, MC, V.

★ ★ ★ **THE INN AT HARVARD.** *1201 Massachusetts Ave (02138), 1 blk E of Harvard Square.* 617/491-2222; FAX 617/520-3711; res: 800/222-8733. Web www.theinnatharvard.com. 113 rms, 4 story. S, D $169-$299; suites $250-$550; under 17 free; higher rates commencement. Crib free. Valet parking $20. TV; cable (premium). Complimentary coffee in lobby. Restaurant 6:30-11 pm; Sat, Sun from 7 am. Rm serv. Bar. Ck-out noon. Meeting rms. Business servs avail. In-rm modem link. Bellhops. Concierge. Valet serv. Health club privileges. Cr cds: A, C, D, DS, MC, V.

Hotels

★ ★ ★ **CHARLES HOTEL IN HARVARD SQUARE.** *One Bennett St (02138), 1 blk S of Harvard Square.* 617/864-1200; FAX 617/864-5715; res: 800/882-1818. Web www.preferredhotels.com. 296 rms, 10 story. S, D $265-$329; each addl $20; suites $429-$1,500; under 18 free; wkend rates. Crib free. Pet accepted, some restrictions. Valet parking $16. TV; cable (premium), VCR avail (free movies). Indoor pool; whirlpool. Restaurants (see HENRIETTA'S TABLE and RIALTO). Rm serv 24 hrs. Bar noon-1 am; jazz. Ck-out 1 pm. Meeting rms. Business servs avail. In-rm modem link. Concierge. Beauty shop. Exercise rm; steam rm. Massage. Spa. Bathrm phones, minibars. On Charles River. Cr cds: A, C, D, JCB, MC, V.

★ ★ ★ **HOLIDAY INN-SOMERVILLE.** *(30 Washington St, Somerville 02143) I-93N exit Cambridge-Somerville, NE on MA 28.* 617/628-1000; FAX 617/628-0143. E-mail HIsomervil@aol.com. 184 rms, 9 story. S $145-$185; D $155-$205; each addl $10; under 19 free; wkend rates. Crib free. TV; cable (premium). Indoor pool; whirlpool, lifeguard. Restaurant 6:30 am-noon, 5-10 pm. Bar 11:30-1 am; Fri, Sat to 2 am. Ck-out noon. Coin lndry. Meeting rms. Business servs avail. In-rm modem link.

Sundries. Free parking. Exercise rm; sauna. Refrigerators avail. Cr cds: A, C, D, DS, ER, JCB, MC, V.

D ≈ ✗ ⤢ 🔥 SC

★ HOWARD JOHNSON. *777 Memorial Dr (02139). 617/492-7777; FAX 617/492-6038.* 201 rms, 16 story. S $90-$185; D $110-$225; each addl $10; under 18 free. Crib free. Pet accepted. TV; cable (premium). 5th-floor indoor pool. Restaurant 7-11 am, 5-10 pm. Bar 4 pm-2 am. Ck-out noon. Meeting rms. Business servs avail. In-rm modem link. Some refrigerators; microwaves avail. Some balconies. On river. Cr cds: A, C, D, DS, ER, JCB, MC, V.

🏊 ≈ 🐾 ✗ 🔥 SC

★ ★ HYATT REGENCY. *575 Memorial Dr (02139). 617/492-1234; FAX 617/491-6906.* Web www.hyatt.com. 469 rms, 16 story. S, D $159-$270; each addl $25; suites from $450; under 18 free; seasonal, wkend rates. Crib free. Garage $16. TV; cable (premium), VCR avail. Indoor pool; whirlpool. Restaurant 6:30 am-11 pm. Bar 11-1:30 am. Ck-out noon. Convention facilities. Business center. In-rm modem link. Concierge. Shopping arcade. Exercise equipt; sauna, steam rm. Refrigerators avail. Private patios, balconies. On river. Luxury level. Cr cds: A, C, D, DS, ER, JCB, MC, V.

D ≈ ✗ ⤢ 🔥 SC 🚶

★ ★ MARRIOTT. *2 Cambridge Ctr (02142). 617/494-6600; FAX 617/494-0036.* 431 rms, 26 story. Mar-Aug: S, D $229-$259; suites $400; under 18 free. Crib free. Covered valet parking $18. TV; cable (premium), VCR avail. Pool; whirlpool, poolside serv. Coffee in rms. Restaurant 6:30 am-11 pm. Bar noon-1 am; entertainment. Ck-out noon. Convention facilities. Business center. In-rm modem link. Coin Indry. Shopping arcade. Exercise equipt; sauna. Massage. Health club privileges. Some refrigerators; microwaves avail. Luxury level. Cr cds: A, D, DS, ER, JCB, MC, V.

D ≈ ✗ ⤢ 🔥 SC ⛷

★ ★ ROYAL SONESTA. *5 Cambridge Pkwy (02142). 617/491-3600; FAX 617/661-5956.* Web www.sonesta.com. 400 rms, 10 story. S, D $195-$325; each addl $25; suites $400-$850; under 18 free; wkend rates. Crib free. TV; cable (premium). Pool. Restaurant 6:30 am-11 pm. Rm serv to 1 am; Fri, Sat to 2 am. Bar 11-1 am. Ck-out noon. Convention facilities. Business servs avail. In-rm modem link. Concierge. Gift shop. Garage parking. Exercise rm. Massage. Health club privileges. Minibars; some bathrm phones. Most rms have view of Charles River and Boston. Cr cds: A, C, D, DS, ER, JCB, MC, V.

D ≈ ✗ ⤢ 🔥 SC

★ ★ SHERATON COMMANDER. *16 Garden St (02138), on Cambridge Common. 617/547-4800; FAX 617/868-8322.* 175 rms, 7 story. S $165-$279; D $185-$299; each addl $20; kit. suites $249-$770; under 17 free. Crib free. TV; cable (premium). Coffee in rms. Restaurant 6:30 am-10:30 pm. Bar noon-1 am. Ck-out noon. Meeting rms. Business servs avail. In-rm modem link. Concierge. Free parking. Exercise equipt. Some in-rm whirlpools, refrigerators. Cr cds: A, C, D, DS, JCB, MC, V.

D ✗ ⤢ 🔥 SC

Inn

★ ★ A CAMBRIDGE HOUSE. *2218 Massachusetts Ave (02140). 617/491-6300; FAX 617/868-2848; res: 800/232-9989.* E-mail innach@aol.com. Web www.acambridgehouse.com. 16 rms, 3 story. 4 share bath. S $99-$195; D $109-$275; each addl $40. TV; cable. Complimentary full bkfst; afternoon refreshments. Restaurant nearby. Ck-out noon, ck-in 3 pm. Business servs avail. In-rm modem link. Victorian house (1892) lavishly decorated in period style. Cr cds: A, D, DS, MC, V.

⤢ 🔥 SC

Restaurants

★ ★ BLUE ROOM. *1 Kendall Square (02139). 617/494-9034.* E-mail theblueroom@aol.com. Specializes in multi-ethnic dishes from around the world. Hrs: 5:30-10 pm; Fri, Sat to 11 pm; Sun brunch 11 am-2:30 pm. Closed July 4, Thanksgiving, Dec 24, 25. Res accepted. Bar. Semi-a la carte: dinner $16-$22. Sun brunch $16.95. Pianist Sun. Outdoor dining. Original artwork from local artists. Cr cds: A, D, DS, MC, V.

D

✔ ★ ★ BOMBAY CLUB. *57 JFK St (02138), Harvard Square. 617/661-8100.* E-mail sorabh@1x.netcom.com. Indian menu. Specializes in kebabs, breads. Hrs: 11:30 am-11 pm. Closed Thanksgiving, Dec 25. Res accepted. Bar. Buffet: lunch $7.95-$11.95. Semi-a la carte: lunch, dinner $6.95-$13.95. Sat, Sun brunch $11.95. Indian art. Totally nonsmoking. Cr cds: A, C, D, MC, V.

D

✔ ★ ★ ★ CAFÉ CELADOR. *5 Craigie Circle (02138). 617/661-4073.* Web www.bostonsidewalks.com. Northern Mediterranean, southern French menu. Seasonal specialties. Own ice cream. Hrs: 5:30-9:30 pm; Fri, Sat to 10 pm. Closed Sun, Mon; major hols. Res accepted. Wine, beer. A la carte entrees: dinner $15.50-$23. Totally nonsmoking. Cr cds: A, D, DS, MC, V.

★ ★ CHEZ HENRI. *1 Shepard St (02138). 617/354-8980.* French menu with Cuban influence. Specializes in chicken with tarragon vinegar. Hrs: 6-10 pm; Fri, Sat 5:30-11 pm; Sun to 9 pm; Sun brunch 11 am-2 pm (Sept-June). Closed Memorial Day, July 4. Bar to 1 am; Sun to 10 pm. A la carte entrees: dinner $14.95-$21.95. Complete meals: dinner $30. Sun brunch $5-$12. Cr cds: A, MC, V.

D

★ ★ COTTONWOOD CAFE. *1815 Massachusetts Ave (02140), in Porter Exchange Bldg. 617/661-7440.* Southwestern menu. Specializes in fresh pasta, fresh seafood, seasonal additions. Hrs: 11:45 am-3 pm, 5:30-10 pm; Fri, Sat to 10:30 pm; Sun 10:30 am-9 pm; winter hrs vary. Closed July 4, Dec 25. Res accepted. Bar. Semi-a la carte: lunch $4-$9, dinner $11-$20. Parking. Outdoor dining, open grill. Casual atmosphere, Southwestern decor. Cr cds: A, D, DS, MC, V.

D

★ ★ DALI. *(415 Washington St, Somerville 02143). 617/661-3254.* Spanish menu. Specializes in tapas, piedra. Hrs: 6-11 pm. Closed most major hols; also Dec 31. Bar. A la carte entrees: lunch $2.50-$7.50, dinner $14-$22. Street parking. Spanish decor. Cr cds: A, D, MC, V.

D ⤴

★ GRENDEL'S DEN. *89 Winthrop St (02138), on Harvard Square. 617/491-1160.* International menu. Specializes in fresh fish, vegetarian dishes, cheese fondue. Salad bar. Hrs: 11 am-11 pm; Fri, Sat to midnight. Closed Thanksgiving, Dec 24, 25. Bar. A la carte entrees: lunch, dinner $5-$12. Outdoor dining. Casual dining; busy atmosphere. Family-owned since 1971. Cr cds: A, DS, MC, V.

⤴

✔ ★ ★ THE HELMAND. *143 First St (02142). 617/492-4646.* Afghani menu. Specializes in authentic Afghani dishes. Own baking. Hrs: 5-10 pm; Fri, Sat to 11 pm. Closed Jan 1, Thanksgiving, Dec 25. Res accepted. Serv bar. Semi-a la carte: dinner $9.95-$16.95. Afghani decor with high ceilings. Totally nonsmoking. Cr cds: A, MC, V.

D

★ ★ HENRIETTA'S TABLE. *(See Charles Hotel In Harvard Square)* 617/661-5005. Regional Amer menu. Specialties: New England pot roast, chicken pot pie, fresh fish. Own baking, pasta. Hrs: 6:30-11 am, noon-3 pm, 5:30-10 pm; Fri to 11 pm; Sat 7 am-3 pm, 5:30-11 pm; Sun 7-10:30 am, noon-3 pm (brunch), 5:30-10 pm. Res accepted (exc Sat, Sun bkfst). Bar. Semi-a la carte: bkfst $6.50-$12, lunch $6.50-$12.50, dinner $10.50-$18.50. Sun brunch $32. Child's meals. Outdoor dining. Windows face courtyard; open kitchen; market on site. Cr cds: A, C, D, JCB, MC, V.

D

✔ ★ ★ LA GROCERIA RISTORANTE & PIZZERIA. *853 Main St (02139), off Central Sq. 617/876-4162.* Italian menu. Specializes in antipasto. Own pasta. Hrs: 11:30 am-10 pm; Fri to 11 pm; Sat 4-11 pm; Sun 1-10 pm; early-bird dinner 4-6:30 pm. Closed Jan 1, Thanksgiving, Dec 25.

Res accepted. Bar. Semi-a la carte: lunch $4.95-$8.95, dinner $9.95-$16.95. Child's meals. Valet parking wkends. Family-owned. Cr cds: A, C, D, DS, MC, V.

D ⊣

✔★ **REDBONES.** *(55 Chester St, Somerville 02144) 1 mi N off Massachusetts Ave at Davis Square.* 617/628-2200. Web www.redbonesbbq.com. Barbecue menu. Specializes in ribs. Hrs: 11:30-12:30 am. Closed Thanksgiving, Dec 25. Bar. Semi-a la carte: lunch $3.95-7.95, dinner $5.95-$14.95. Street parking. Southwestern decor. No cr cds accepted.

D ⊣

★ ★ ★ **RIALTO.** *(See Charles Hotel In Harvard Square)* 617/661-5050. Continental menu. Specializes in grilled sirloin, seasonal game, fresh seafood. Own baking, pasta. Hrs: 5:30-10 pm; Fri, Sat to 11 pm. Closed most major hols. Res accepted. Bar to 11 pm; Fri, Sat to midnight. Wine list. Semi-a la carte: dinner $19-$29. Validated parking. 1940s supper club atmosphere; original artwork. Cr cds: A, D, JCB, MC, V.

D

★ ★ ★ **SALAMANDER.** *1 Athenaeum (02142).* 617/225-2121. Web www.salamander-restaurant.com. Eclectic, contemporary menu. Hrs: 7:30 am-3:30 pm, 6-10:30 pm; Sat from 6 pm. Closed Sun; most major hols. Res accepted. Bar. Semi-a la carte: bkfst $3-$5, lunch $5-$9. A la carte entrees: dinner $20-$37.50. Child's meals. Parking. Converted factory bldg. Cr cds: A, D, DS, MC, V.

D

★ ★ ★ **SANDRINE'S.** *8 Holyoke St (02138).* 617/497-5300. Web www.bostonsidewalk.com. French menu. Specialties: choucroute, frog legs, tarte flambé. Hrs: 11:30 am-2:30 pm, 5:30-10 pm; Mon 5:30-10 pm; Fri, Sat to 10:30 pm; Sun 5:30-10 pm. Res accepted. Bar. Wine list. Semi-a la carte: lunch $6-$16, dinner $15-$30. Child's meals. Street parking. Classic bistro decor; casual dinng. Totally nonsmoking. Cr cds: A, MC, V.

D

★ ★ ★ **UPSTAIRS AT THE PUDDING.** *10 Holyoke St (02138), in Harvard Square, in Hasty Pudding Club.* 617/864-1933. Contemporary Mediterranean menu. Specializes in rack of lamb, hand-rolled pasta. Own desserts. Hrs: 11:30 am-2:30 pm, 6-10 pm; Sun brunch 11 am-2 pm. Closed Dec 25. Bar. A la carte entrees: lunch $8-$12, dinner $16-$30. Sun brunch $8-$14. Terrace dining. Located on 3rd floor of building (1885) housing famous Harvard College club, of which 5 Presidents were members; collection of century-old theater posters. Cr cds: A, D, MC, V.

D

Unrated Dining Spots

CREMALDI'S. *31 Putnam Ave.* 617/354-7969. Continental menu, grocery & delicatessen. Specialties: pesto, manicotti, veal Marsala. Own pasta, soups. Hrs: 10 am-7 pm. Closed Sun; July 4, Thanksgiving, Dec 25. Semi-a la carte: lunch $5-$10, dinner $6-$15. Outdoor dining. Cr cds: A, DS, MC, V.

EAST COAST GRILL. *1271 Cambridge St.* 617/491-6568. Specializes in grilled fish, barbecued beef & pork. Hrs: 5:30-10 pm; Fri, Sat to 10:30 pm. Closed Dec 25. A la carte entrees: dinner $12-$16. Cr cds: A, MC, V.

Cape Cod (C-9 - E-8)

E-mail Infor@capecodchamber.org **Web** www.capecodchamber.org
Information Cape Cod Chamber of Commerce, US 6 & MA 132, PO Box 790, Hyannis 02601-0790; 508/362-3225 or 888/33-CAPECOD.

The popularity of the automobile changed Cape Cod from a group of isolated fishing villages, big estates and cranberry bogs into one of the world's prime resort areas. The Cape's permanent population of about 201,000 witnesses the change each year with the arrival of nearly a half of a million summer people.

A great many motels have sprung up since the Second World War, and cottages line the beaches in some areas. Yet the villages have remained virtually unchanged. The long main streets of villages like Yarmouth Port and Brewster are still lined with old houses, some dating from the 17th century. The sea wind still blows across the moors below Truro and the woods of the Sandwich Hills.

The Cape is about 70 miles long and bent like an arm with its fist upraised. Buzzards Bay and the Cape Cod Canal are at the shoulder; Chatham and Nauset beach are at the elbow; and Provincetown is the fist. Since the Cape extends so far out toward the warm Gulf Stream (about 30 miles), its climate is notably gentler than that of the mainland; summers are cooler and winters milder. It has almost 560 miles of coastline, most of which is gleaming beach—the Cape being composed of sand rather than bedrock. As if to please every taste, many towns on the Cape have two coasts—the Nantucket Sound beaches with warm, calm waters; the Atlantic Ocean beaches with colder water and high breakers; or Cape Cod Bay with cool, calm waters. Inland woods are dotted with 365 clear freshwater ponds, known as kettle ponds.

Surf casting (day and night), small-boat and deep-sea fishing are major sports along the entire Cape coastline. At least a dozen varieties of game fish are found, including giant tuna.

This current summer gaiety belies the Cape's hardy pioneer history. It was in Provincetown harbor that the *Mayflower* first set anchor for the winter and the first party of Pilgrims went ashore. Eighteen years earlier, in 1602, Cape Cod was named by the English explorer Bartholomew Gosnold after the great schools of fish he saw in the bay.

The following towns, villages and special areas on Cape Cod are included in the *Mobil Travel Guide.* For full information on any one of them, see the individual alphabetical listing: Barnstable, Bourne, Brewster, Buzzards Bay, Cape Cod National Seashore, Centerville, Chatham, Dennis, Eastham, Falmouth, Harwich, Hyannis, Orleans, Provincetown, Sandwich, South Yarmouth, Truro & North Truro, Wellfleet, Woods Hole.

Cape Cod National Seashore (C-9 - D-10)

This recreation area consists of 44,600 acres, including submerged lands located offshore along the eastern part of Barnstable County. Headquarters are at South Wellfleet. Exhibits, interpretive programs at the Salt Pond Visitor Center in Eastham (Mid-Feb-Dec, daily; Jan-mid-Feb wkends only), phone 508/255-3421; Province Lands Visitor Center on Race Point Rd in Provincetown (mid-Apr-Nov, daily), phone 508/487-1256. Numerous private homes are within park boundaries. Hunting and fishing; bicycle trails, self-guiding nature trails; guided walks and evening programs in summer; swimming, lifeguards at designated areas (late June-Labor Day). Parking at beaches (fee); free after Labor Day. Buttonbush Trail has Braille trail markers. For further information contact the Superintendent, 99 Marconi Site, Wellfleet 02667; 508/349-3785.

Centerville (Cape Cod) (D-9)

(See also Hyannis)

Pop 9,190 **Elev** 40 ft **Area code** 508 **Zip** 02632 **E-mail** infor@capecodchamber.org **Web** www.capecodchamber.org
Information Cape Cod Chamber of Commerce, US 6 & MA 132, PO Box 790, Hyannis 02601-0790; 508/362-3225 or 888/33-CAPECOD.

What to See and Do

Centerville Historical Society Museum. Houses 14 exhibition rms interpreting Cape Cod's history, art, industry and domestic life. Displays include early American furniture, housewares, quilts; dolls, costumes; Crowell carved birds; Sandwich glass collection; marine rm; tool rm; research library. (June-mid-Sept, Wed-Sun; winter by appt) 513 Main St. Phone 508/775-0331. ¢¢

Osterville Historical Society Museum. Sea captain's house with 18th- and 19th-century furnishings; Sandwich glass, Chinese porcelain, majolica and Staffordshire pottery; doll collection. Special events throughout the summer. Boat-building museum, ship models; catboat *Cayugha* is on display. Restored Cammett House (ca 1730) is on grounds. (Mid-June-Sept, Thurs-Sun afternoons; other times by appt) 3 mi SW, at jct West Bay & Parker Rds in Osterville. Phone 508/428-5861. **Free.**

Motels

★ **CENTERVILLE CORNERS MOTOR LODGE.** *1338 Craigville Rd.* 508/775-7223; *FAX* 508/775-4147; *res:* 800/242-1137. E-mail komenda@capecod.com. 48 rms, 2 story. July-Labor Day: D $97-$125; each addl $10; kit. unit $95-$125; under 14 free; wkly rates; golf plan; lower rates rest of yr. Closed Dec-Apr. Crib $5. Pet accepted; $5. TV; cable. Indoor pool; sauna. Complimentary continental bkfst (in season). Complimentary coffee in rms. Ck-out 11 am. Lawn games. Picnic tables, grills. Cr cds: A, DS, MC, V.

★★ **TRADE WINDS INN.** *(780 Craigville Beach Rd, Craigville)* 1 mi E. 508/775-0365; *FAX* 508/790-1404. 46 rms, 2 story, 4 kits. Mid-June-Labor Day: S, D $109-$169; each addl $10; suites $190-$215; lower rates Apr-mid-June, after Labor Day-Oct. Closed rest of yr. TV; cable. Complimentary continental bkfst in season. Ck-out 11 am. Meeting rms. Putting green. Private patios, balconies. Private beach opp. Cr cds: A, MC, V.

Inn

✔★★ **ADAM'S TERRACE GARDENS.** *539 Main St.* 508/775-4707. Web www.virtualcapecod.com/market/adamsterrace. 7 rms, 5 with bath, 2 story. No A/C. No rm phones. Late-May-mid-Sept: S, D $75-$110; each addl $20; lower rates rest of yr. TV; cable. Complimentary full bkfst. Restaurant nearby. Ck-out 11 am, ck-in 3 pm. Patio. Built circa 1830. Antiques. Sitting rm. Totally nonsmoking. Cr cds: A, MC, V.

Restaurant

★★★ **REGATTA OF COTUIT.** *(4631 Falmouth Rd, Cotuit 02635)* 3 mi W on MA 28, just E of jct MA 130. 508/428-5715. Specialties: swordfish with scallion and lemon, lacquered duck, chocolate seduction cake. Menu changes frequently. Hrs: 5-10 pm. Res accepted. A la carte entrees: dinner $18-$26. 1790 Federal-style mansion house with 8 dining rms; early Amer decor; fireplaces; many antiques. Own herb garden. Cr cds: A, MC, V.

Unrated Dining Spot

WIMPY'S SEAFOOD CAFE & MARKET. *(752 Main St, Osterville 02655)* W on MA 28. 508/428-6300. Seafood menu. Specializes in local seafood, clambakes, lamb. Hrs: 11:30 am-10 pm; Sun brunch 11 am-2 pm; early-bird dinner 4-6 pm; hrs vary off-season. Closed Thanksgiving, Dec 24 (dinner), Dec 25. Res accepted. Bar. Semi-a la carte: lunch $6-$9, dinner $7-$19.95. Sun brunch $6.95-$10.95. Child's meals. Parking. Indoor atrium; garden & fountain. Fireplaces. Cr cds: C, D, DS, MC, V.

Chatham (Cape Cod) (D-10)

Settled 1656 **Pop** 6,579 **Elev** 46 ft **Area code** 508 **Zip** 02633 **E-mail** infor@capecodchamber.org **Web** www.capecodchamber.org
Information Chamber of Commerce, PO Box 793, phone 800/715-5567; or the Cape Cod Chamber of Commerce, US 6 & MA 132, PO Box 790, Hyannis 02601-0790, phone 508/362-3225 or 888/33-CAPECOD.

Chatham is among the Cape's fashionable shopping centers. Comfortable estates in the hilly country nearby look out on Pleasant Bay and Nantucket Sound. Monomoy Island, an unattached sand bar, stretches ten miles south into the sea. It was once a haunt of "moon-cussers"—beach pirates who lured vessels aground with false lights and then looted the wrecks.

What to See and Do

Gristmill (1797). (Daily) Shattuck Place, off Cross St, W shore of Mill Pond in Chase Park. Phone 508/945-5158. **Free.**

Monomoy National Wildlife Refuge. Wilderness area reached from Chatham (access by boat only, special regulations apply). Main St past Chatham Lighthouse, turn left onto Morris Island Rd, follow signs to HQ on Morris Island. Vista of Pleasant Bay, Monomoy Island & Atlantic Ocean. Surf fishing; more than 250 species of birds. No camping. (Daily) For further information contact Refuge Manager, Great Meadows NWR, Weir Hill Rd, Sudbury 01776; 508/945-0594 or 508/443-4661. **Free.**

Old Atwood House (1752). Chatham Historical Society. Memorabilia of Joseph C. Lincoln, Cape Cod novelist. Shell collection, murals by Alice Stallknecht, "Portrait of a New England Town." Stage Harbor Rd, 1/2 mi off MA 28. (Mid-June-Sept, Wed-Sat afternoons; schedule may vary, phone 508/945-2493 or Chamber of Commerce for information) ¢¢

Railroad Museum. Restored "country RR depot" houses scale models, photographs, RR memorabilia and relics; restored 1910 New York Central caboose. (Mid-June-mid-Sept, Tues-Sat) Depot Rd, off Main St, MA 28. **Donation.**

Seasonal Events

Monomoy Theatre. 776 Main St. Ohio Univ Players in comedies, musicals, dramas, classics. Phone 508/945-1589. Tues-Sat. Late June-late Aug.

Band Concerts. Kate Gould Park. Fri eve. Late June-early Sept.

Motels

✔★ **CHATHAM.** *1487 Main St.* 508/945-2630; *res:* 800/770-5545. Web www.virtualcapecod.com/chathammotel. 32 rms. July-mid-

Sept: S, D $90-$130; each addl $5; lower rates May-June, mid-Sept-Oct. Closed rest of yr. TV; cable (premium). Pool. Playground. Coffee in lobby. Restaurant nearby. Ck-out 11 am. Lawn games. Refrigerators. Picnic tables. In pine grove. Cr cds: MC, V.

★ ★ **CHATHAM TIDES.** *(394 Pleasant St, S Chatham 02659)* *1/2 mi S of MA 28 at foot of Pleasant St.* 508/432-0379; FAX 508/432-4289. Web www.allcapecod.com/chathamtides. 24 kit. units in motel & townhouses, suites avail. Some A/C. July-Aug: S, D $135-$155; each addl $20; kit. suites, townhouses $1,200-$1,650/wk; lower rates Sept-May. TV; cable. Ck-out 11 am. Some microwaves. Sun decks. On private beach. Cr cds: MC, V.

★ ★ ★ **DOLPHIN OF CHATHAM INN & MOTEL.** *352 Main St.* 508/945-0070; FAX 508/945-5945; res: 800/688-5900. Web www.dolphininn.com. 38 rms, 3 kits. Late June-early Sept: S, D $144-$219; each addl $15; suites $199-$229; kit. units $154; 2-bedrm kit. cottages $1,500/wk; lower rates rest of yr. TV; cable. Heated pool; whirlpool. Coffee in rms. Restaurant 8-11 am. Ck-out 10 am. Business servs avail. Some refrigerators, in-rm whirlpools; microwaves avail. Some private patios. Picnic tables, grills. Cr cds: A, C, D, DS, MC, V.

★ ★ **HAWTHORNE.** *196 Shore Rd, off MA 28.* 508/945-0372. Web www.virtualcapecod.com. 26 rms, 10 kits. Mid-June-mid-Sept: S, D $150, kit. units $140; cottage $275; each addl $15; lower rates mid May-mid-June, mid-Sept-Oct. Closed rest of yr. TV; cable. Restaurant nearby. Ck-out 11 am. Refrigerators; some microwaves. On private beach. Cr cds: A, MC, V.

★ **HIGHLANDER.** *946 Main St.* 508/945-9038; FAX 508/945-5731. E-mail highlandl@capecod.net. 28 rms. Late-June-early Sept: S, D $96; wkends (2-day min); hols (3-day min); lower rates rest of yr. Closed Dec-Apr. TV; cable. Complimentary coffee in rms. Restaurant nearby. Ck-out 10:30 am. 2 pools. Refrigerators. Picnic tables. Cr cds: DS, MC, V.

★ ★ **PLEASANT BAY VILLAGE.** *Box 772, 3 mi N on MA 28 in Chathamport.* 508/945-1133; FAX 508/945-9701; res: 800/547-1011. Web www.virtualcapecod.com/pleasantbayvillage. 58 rms, 20 kits., 10 suites (1-2 bedrm). Early June-Aug: S, D, kit. units $215-$245; each addl $15-$20; 1-bedrm suites $355; 2-bedrm suites (2-day min) $395-$415; lower rates mid-May-early June, Sept-mid-Oct. Closed rest of yr. Crib avail. TV; cable. Heated pool; poolside serv. Playground. Restaurant 8-11 am. Rm serv. Ck-out 11 am. Business servs avail. In-rm modem link. Sundries. Lawn games. Refrigerators, microwaves avail. On 6 landscaped acres. Extensive Chinese gardens; waterfall; ornamental pond. Cr cds: A, MC, V.

★ **SEAFARER.** *MA 28 & Ridgevale Rd.* 508/432-1739; res: 800/786-2772. Web www.seafarerofchatham.com. 20 rms, 7 kit. units. Mid-July-Aug: S, D $120-$150; each addl $15; kit. units $135-$155; wkends (2, 4 day min); higher rates Memorial Day, July 4th; lower rates rest of yr. TV; cable. Complimentary coffee in rms. Ck-out 11 am. Lawn games. Picnic tables. Cr cds: A, MC, V.

Inns

★ ★ **CAPTAIN'S HOUSE.** *371 Old Harbor Rd.* 508/945-0127; FAX 508/945-0866; res: 800/315-0728. E-mail capthous@capecod.net; web www.captainshouseinn.com. 19 rms, 3 with shower only, 2 story, 6 suites. Mid-May-Oct: S, D $135-$275; suites $200-$325; wkends (3-day min); lower rates rest of yr. TV in some rms; VCR. Complimentary full bkfst; afternoon refreshments. Restaurant nearby. Ck-out 11 am, ck-in 2 pm. Luggage handling. Concierge serv. Bicycles. Lawn games. Health club

privileges. Many in-rm whirlpools, fireplaces. Picnic tables. Greek-revival house built in 1839; Williamsburg-style antiques and period pieces decorate the inn. Totally nonsmoking. Cr cds: A, DS, MC, V.

★ ★ ★ **CHATHAM TOWN HOUSE INN.** *11 Library Lane, in Chatham Center.* 508/945-2180; FAX 508/945-3990; res: 800/242-2180. E-mail chathamthi@capecod.net; web www.chathamtownhouse.com. 27 rms, 2 1/2 story, 2 cottages. Late June-Sept, Columbus Day, Memorial Day: S, D $175-$300; each addl $25; cottages for 4 persons, $400; lower rates rest of yr. Crib free. TV; cable (premium). Heated pool; whirlpool, poolside serv (lunch). Complimentary full bkfst; afternoon refreshments. Ck-out noon, ck-in 3 pm. Refrigerators. Fireplace in cottages. Picnic tables. In Chatham historical district. Totally nonsmoking. Cr cds: A, C, D, DS, MC, V.

★ ★ ★ **CRANBERRY INN.** *359 Main St.* 508/945-9232; FAX 508/945-3769; res: 800/332-4667. Web www.capecod.com/cranberryinn. 18 rms, 2 story, 2 suites. Late June-early-Sept: S, D $165-$245; each addl $30; suites $220-$260; lower rates rest of yr. Children over 8 yrs only. TV; cable. Complimentary bkfst buffet; afternoon refreshments. Restaurant nearby. Ck-out 11 am, ck-in 2 pm. Library/sitting rm; antiques and reproduction furnishings. Some fireplaces, wet bars. Some balconies. Built in 1830. Inn has been in continuous operation for more than 150 yrs. Totally nonsmoking. Cr cds: A, DS, MC, V.

★ ★ ★ **MOSES NICKERSON HOUSE.** *364 Old Harbor Rd.* 508/945-5859; FAX 508/945-7087; res: 800/628-6972. E-mail tmnhi@capecod.net; web www.capecod.net/mosesnickersonhouse. 7 rms, 2 story. Late May-mid-Oct: S, D $129-$179; lower rates rest of yr. Children over 14 yrs only. TV avail. Complimentary full bkfst. Restaurant nearby. Ck-out 10:30 am, ck-in 2:30 pm. Lawn games. Antiques. Library/sitting rm. Built 1839. Totally nonsmoking. Cr cds: A, DS, MC, V.

✔ ★ **OLD HARBOR INN.** *22 Old Harbor Rd.* 508/945-4434; FAX 508/945-7665; res: 800/942-4434. 8 rms, 2 story. No rm phones. July-mid-Oct: D $115-$195; season special plans; lower rates rest of yr. Children over 14 yrs only. Complimentary bkfst buffet; afternoon refreshments. Restaurant nearby. Ck-out 11 am, ck-in 3 pm. Concierge serv. Gift shop. Built 1933; former residence of prominent doctor. Renovated and furnished with a blend of antiques and modern conveniences. Fireplace in parlor. Outside deck. Totally nonsmoking. Cr cds: A, C, D, DS, MC, V.

★ ★ **PORT FORTUNE INN.** *201 Main St.* 508/945-0792; res: 800/750-0792. E-mail portfor@capecod.net; web www.capecod.net/port fortune. 12 rms, 2 with shower only, 2 story. Mid-June-mid-Sept: S, D $130-$170; wkend, hols (2-3-day min); lower rates rest of yr. Children over 8 yrs only. TV in some rms; cable. Complimentary continental bkfst. Restaurant nearby. Ck-out 11 am, ck-in 2 pm. Opp beach. Built in 1910; antiques. Totally nonsmoking. Cr cds: A, MC, V.

★ ★ ★ **QUEEN ANNE.** *70 Queen Anne Rd.* 508/945-0394; FAX 508/945-4884; res: 800/545-4667. E-mail queenanne@capecod.net; web www.queenanneinn.com. 31 rms, 3 story. S, D $167-$275; each addl $25. Closed Jan. Crib free. TV; VCR avail. Heated pool; whirlpool. Complimentary continental bkfst. Restaurant (dinner only). Ck-out 11 am, ck-in 2 pm. Business servs avail. Tennis, pro. Lawn games. Antiques, handmade quilts. Many fireplaces; some in-rm whirlpools. Balconies. Built in 1840 for sea captain's daughter. Boats for excursions. Totally nonsmoking. Cr cds: A, DS, MC, V.

Resorts

★ ★ ★ **CHATHAM BARS INN.** *297 Shore Rd, Shore Rd at Seaview St. 508/945-0096; FAX 508/945-5491; res: 800/527-4884.* E-mail resrvcbi@chathambarsinn.com; web www.chathambarsinn.com. 41 rms in inn, 1-3 story, no elvtr, 28 cottages, 1-12 bedrm. Some A/C. Mid-June-mid-Sept: S, D $190-$410; suites $375-$1,000; lower rates rest of yr. Crib avail. TV; cable, VCR avail (free movies). Heated pool. Free supervised child's activities (Mid-June-Labor Day); ages 4-12. Dining rm 8 am-9 pm. Box lunches, clambakes in season. Rm serv. Bar noon-1 am, entertainment (in season). Ck-out 11 am, ck-in 3 pm. Meeting rms. Business servs avail. In-rm modem link. Bellhops. Valet serv. Concierge. Tennis, pro. Putting green. Exercise equipt. Complimentary boat shuttle. Lawn games. Rec rm. Many balconies. Spacious cottages. On 22 acres; private beach. Cr cds: A, D, MC, V.

D ⚬ ⚞ ⚟ ✕ ⚟ ⚟

★ ★ ★ ★ **WEQUASSETT INN.** *Pleasant Bay Rd, 5 mi NE on MA 28. 508/432-5400; FAX 508/432-5032; res: 800/225-7125 or 800/352-7169.* E-mail wequassett@wequassett.com; web www.wequassett.com. On 23 acres with gardens, the Wequassett Inn overlooks the bay. 104 rms, 1-2 story. Mid-Apr-mid-Nov: S, D $210-$350; suite $400-$500. Closed rest of yr. Crib free. TV; cable (premium), VCR. Heated pool; poolside serv. Supervised child's activities (in season); ages infant-12 yrs. Coffee in rms. Dining rm 7 am-10 pm. Rm serv. Ck-out 11 am, ck-in 3 pm. Business center. Valet serv. Gift shop. Airport, bus depot transportation. Tennis, pro. Golf privileges. Exercise rm. Massage. Refrigerators. Many private patios, balconies. Private beach. Sailboats, windsurfing, deep-sea fishing charters, whale-watching cruises. Cr cds: A, C, D, DS, MC, V.

D ⚟ ⚟ ⚟ ⚟ ✕ ⚟ ⚟ ⚟

Restaurants

★ ★ **CHATHAM SQUIRE.** *487 Main St. 508/945-0945.* E-mail squire@capecod.net. Specializes in local seafood. Raw bar. Hrs: 11:30 am-10:30 pm. Bar to 1 am. Semi-a la carte: lunch $4.95-$11.95, dinner $9.95-$21.95. Child's meals. Nautical decor. Cr cds: A, DS, MC, V.

D ⚟

★ ★ **CHRISTIAN'S.** *443 Main St. 508/945-3362.* Specializes in fresh local seafood, homemade meatloaf, oysters. Hrs: 5-10 pm. Bar to 1 am. Semi-a la carte: dinner $8-$20. Pianist. Outdoor dining. Two-level dining. Built 1819. Cr cds: A, DS, MC, V.

D ⚟

★ ★ **IMPUDENT OYSTER.** *15 Chatham Bars Ave. 508/945-3545.* Specializes in seafood. Hrs: 11:30 am-10 pm; Sun from noon. Res required. Bar to 1 am. Semi-a la carte: lunch $6.95-$12.95, dinner $14-$23. Child's meals. Cathedral ceilings, stained-glass windows. Cr cds: A, MC, V.

⚟

Chicopee
(see Springfield)

Concord (B-6)
(See Lexington, Sudbury Center)

Settled 1635 **Pop** 17,076 **Elev** 141 ft **Area code** 978 **Zip** 01742 **E-mail** conchamb@ma.ultranet.com **Web** www.ultranet.com/~pdurham/concordchamber
Information Chamber of Commerce, 2 Lexington Rd, in Wright Tavern, phone 978/369-3042; or visit the Heywood St Information Booth (Apr-Oct).

This town shares with Lexington the title of Birthplace of the Republic. But it was Ralph Waldo Emerson who saw to it that the shot fired "by the rude bridge" was indeed heard 'round the world.

The town's name arose because of the "peace and concord" between the settlers and the Native Americans in the 17th century. The famous Concord grape was developed here in 1849 by Ephraim Bull.

The town of Lincoln, adjoining Concord on the east, was the scene of a running battle with the Redcoats on their withdrawal toward Boston. Here the harassing fire of the Minutemen was perhaps most effective.

What to See and Do

Codman House (ca 1740). Originally a 2-story, L-shaped Georgian mansion. In 1797-1798 it was more than doubled in size by Federal merchant John Codman to imitate an English country residence. Family furnishings. Grounds have many unusual trees and plants; formal Italian garden. (June-mid-Oct, Wed-Sun afternoons) Codman Rd, 5 mi S of MA 2 via Bedford Rd in Lincoln. Phone 781/259-8843. ¢¢

Concord Free Public Library. Modern public library, historical collections of famous Concord authors. On display is a mantelpiece from the US Capitol (ca 1815). Also statues of Emerson and others by Daniel Chester French. (Nov-May, daily, limited hrs Sun; rest of yr, Mon-Sat) Main St at Sudbury Rd. Phone 978/371-6240. **Free.**

Concord Museum. Period rms and galleries of domestic artifacts and decorative arts chronicling history of Concord from Native American habitation to present. Exhibits include Ralph Waldo Emerson's study, Henry David Thoreau's belongings used at Walden Pond, and Revolutionary War relics, including Paul Revere's signal lantern. Self-guided tours. (Daily; closed Easter, Thanksgiving, Dec 25) 200 Lexington Rd. Phone 978/369-9609. ¢¢

DeCordova Museum & Sculpture Park. Contemporary art museum on 35 acres of parkland overlooking Flint's Pond; changing exhibits, lectures, films, special events. (Daily exc Mon) Concerts in summer (Sun). SE on Sandy Pond Rd in Lincoln. Phone 781/259-8355. ¢¢

Drumlin Farm Education Center. Demonstration farm with domestic and native wild animals and birds; gardens; hayrides; special events. (Tues-Sun & Mon hols; closed Jan 1, Thanksgiving, Dec 25) 2¹/₂ mi S on MA 126, then E on MA 117 (S Great Rd) in Lincoln. Phone 781/259-9807. ¢¢

Fruitlands Museums. Four museums, including the Fruitlands Farmhouse, the scene of Bronson Alcott's experiment in community life, which contains furniture, books and memorabilia of the Alcott family and the Transcendentalists; Shaker Museum, formerly in the Harvard Shaker Village, with furniture and handicrafts; Picture Gallery, with American primitive portraits and paintings by Hudson River School artists; American Indian Museum, with prehistoric artifacts and Native American art. Hiking trails with views west to Mt Wachusett and north to Mt Monadnock. Tearoom; gift shop. (Mid-May-mid-Oct, Tues-Sun & Mon hols) 102 Prospect Hill Rd.15 mi W via MA 2, exit 38A, in Harvard. Phone 978/456-9028. ¢¢¢

Great Meadows National Wildlife Refuge. Nature trails through wetland and upland woodland (daily). More than 200 bird species frequent this diverse habitat area. Nature trails, hiking, cross-country skiing, snowshoeing; canoeing and boating on Sudbury and Concord rivers (no rentals). Concord Unit, Dike Trail; Monsen Rd off MA 62, 1 mi E from Concord Center. Contact Refuge Manager, Weir Hill Rd, Sudbury 01776; 978/443-4661. **Free.**

Gropius House (1937-1938). Family home of architect Walter Gropius. First building he designed upon arrival in the US in 1937; blends New England traditions and Bauhaus principles of function and simplicity with New England's building materials and environment. Original furniture, artwork. (June-mid-Oct, Fri-Sun afternoons; rest of yr, Sat & Sun 1st full wkend of each month) 68 Baker Bridge Rd, SE in Lincoln. For information phone 781/259-8843 or 978/227-3956. ¢¢

Minute Man National Historical Park. North Bridge Unit, Monument St, contains famous Minuteman statue by Daniel Chester French and reconstructed North Bridge over Concord River. Interpretive talks are given. North Bridge Visitor Center at 174 Liberty St has exhibits, information, rest rms. (Daily; closed Jan 1, Thanksgiving, Dec 25) Battle Road Visitor Center, off MA 2A in Lexington, has exhibit rm, movie, and orientation program. (Mid-May-Oct, daily) Contact Superintendent, 174 Liberty St; 978/369-6993. **Free.**

Orchard House and School of Philosophy. Here Louisa May Alcott wrote *Little Women.* Alcott memorabilia. Guided tours. (Apr-Dec, daily; closed Easter, Thanksgiving, Dec 25, also early-mid-Jan) 399 Lexington Rd. Phone 978/369-4118. ¢¢

Ralph Waldo Emerson House. Ralph Waldo Emerson's home from 1835 to 1882. Original furnishings and family memorabilia; 30-min guided tours. (Mid-Apr-late Oct, Thurs-Sun, limited hrs Sun) 28 Cambridge Tpke, at Lexington Rd (MA 2A). Phone 978/369-2236. ¢¢

Sleepy Hollow Cemetery. The Alcotts, Ralph Waldo Emerson, Nathaniel Hawthorne, Margaret Sidney, Daniel Chester French and Henry David Thoreau are buried here. Bedford St, NE of square.

The Old Manse (1770). Parsonage of Concord's early ministers, including Rev William Emerson, Ralph Waldo Emerson's grandfather. Nathaniel Hawthorne lived here for a time and made it the setting for *Mosses from an Old Manse.* Original furnishings. (Mid-Apr-Oct, Mon-Sat, also Sun afternoons) Monument St at the North Bridge. Phone 978/369-3909. ¢¢

The Wayside. 19th-century authors Nathaniel Hawthorne, the Alcotts and Margaret Sidney, author of the *Five Little Peppers* books, lived here. Orientation program; 45-min tours (May-Oct) 455 Lexington Rd (MA 2A). Phone ahead for schedule, 978/369-6975.

⊠ **Walden Pond State Reservation.** Located in this 304-acre park is a replica of Thoreau's cabin; also trail to cairn that marks site of original cabin. Swimming, fishing; hiking trails; interpretive programs. (All yr, daylight hrs) Standard fees. 1/2 mi S of MA2 on MA 126. Phone 978/369-3254. Per vehicle ¢

Annual Event

Patriots' Day Parade. Events, reenactments. Mon nearest Apr 19 (or Sat if the 19th).

Motel

✔★ **BEST WESTERN.** *740 Elm St, I-495 exit 29, 7 mi E on MA 2. 978/369-6100; FAX 978/371-1656.* 106 rms, 2 story. S $79-$119; D $84-$129; each addl $10; under 18 free. Crib free. TV; cable (premium). Pool; whirlpool. Complimentary continental bkfst. Ck-out noon. Coin lndry. Meeting rms. Business servs avail. Valet serv. Downhill/x-country ski 3 1/2 mi. Exercise equipt. Balconies. Cr cds: A, C, D, DS, ER, JCB, MC, V.

D ⊠ ⊠ ⊠ ⊠ ⊠ SC

Motor Hotel

★★★ **HOLIDAY INN-BOXBOROUGH WOODS.** *(242 Adams Place, Boxborough 01719) MA 111 at I-495 exit 28. 978/263-8701; FAX 978/263-0518.* 143 rms, 2-3 story. S, D $119-$139; each addl $10; suites $199; under 18 free. Crib free. TV; cable (premium), VCR avail. Indoor pool. Coffee in rms. Restaurant 6:30 am-11 pm; Sat, Sun from 7 am. Rm serv. Bar 11 am-midnight. Ck-out noon. Meeting rms. Business servs avail. In-rm modem link. Valet serv. Sundries. Downhill/x-country ski 10 mi. Exercise equipt; sauna. Coin lndry. Lawn games. Refrigerators, micro-

waves avail. Private patios, balconies. Picnic tables. Cr cds: A, C, D, DS, ER, JCB, MC, V.

D ⊠ ⊠ ⊠ ⊠ ⊠ SC

Inns

★★ **COLONIAL.** *48 Monument Square. 978/369-9200; res: 800/370-9200; FAX 978/371-1533.* Web www.concordscolonialinn.com. 49 rms, 15 in main bldg (1716), 32 in Prescott wing (1960), 2 cottages. S, D $149-$185; each addl $10; cottages $250-$285; Crib $10. TV; cable (premium). Complimentary coffee. Restaurant (see COLONIAL INN). Bar; entertainment exc Mon. Ck-out 11 am, ck-in 2:30 pm. Meeting rms. Business servs avail. Luggage handling. Microwaves avail. Walden Pond 2 mi. Historically prominent guests noted. Cr cds: A, C, D, DS, MC, V.

D ⊠ ⊠

✔★★ **HAWTHORNE.** *462 Lexington Rd. 978/369-5610; FAX 978/287-4949.* E-mail reservations@concordmass.com; web www.concordmass.com. 7 rms, 2 story. No rm phones. S $110-$150; D $125-$210. Complimentary continental bkfst; afternoon refreshments. Ck-out 11 am, ck-in 3 pm. RR station transportation. X-country ski 2 mi. Microwaves avail. Antiques; original artwork. Library/sitting rm with fireplace. Totally nonsmoking. Cr cds: A, DS, MC, V.

⊠ ⊠ ⊠

Restaurants

★★ **AIGO BISTRO.** *84 Thoreau St. 978/371-1333.* Mediterranean menu. Specializes in seasonal entrees. Hrs: 11:30 am-2:30 pm, from 5:30 pm; Sun from 5 pm; early-bird dinner 5:30-6:30 pm Sun-Thurs. Closed major hols. Bar. Semi-a la carte: lunch $7-$11.50, dinner $16.50-$23.50. Street parking. Cr cds: A, C, D, DS, MC, V.

★★ **COLONIAL INN.** *(See Colonial Inn) 978/369-2373.* Continental menu. Specializes in fresh seafood, roast prime rib, regional specialties. Hrs: 7 am-10:30 pm. Sun brunch 10:30 am-2:30 pm. Bar noon-11 pm. Semi-a la carte: bkfst $1.85-$9, lunch $3.75-$12, dinner $14.95-$25.95. Sun brunch $20.95. Entertainment. Outdoor dining. Built in 1716; Henry David Thoreau's house. Cr cds: A, C, D, DS, MC, V.

D

Danvers (B-7)

(See also Beverly)

Settled 1636 **Pop** 24,174 **Elev** 48 ft **Area code** 508 **Zip** 01923 **Web** www.northshorechamber.org
Information North Shore Chamber of Commerce, #5 Cherry Hill Dr; 508/774-8565.

This small industrial town was once Salem Village—a community started by settlers from Salem looking for more farmland. In 1692, Danvers was the scene of some of the most severe witchcraft hysteria; twenty persons were put to death.

What to See and Do

Glen Magna Farms. A 20-rm mansion; 1790-1890 furnishings; Chamberlain gardens. Derby summer house was built by Samuel McIntire (1794); on the roof are 2 life-size carvings (reaper and milkmaid) by the Skillin brothers; reproduction of 1844 gazebo. Various special events and programs. (June-Sept, Tues & Thurs exc hols; also by appt) 2 mi N on US 1, then 1/4 mi E via Centre St to Ingersoll St. Phone 508/774-0516. ¢¢

Rebecca Nurse Homestead. The house (ca 1680), an excellent example of the New England saltbox, was the homestead of Rebecca Nurse, a saintly woman accused of and executed for witchcraft during the hysteria of 1692. House includes restored rms with furnishings from 17th & 18th centuries; outbuildings, a reproduction of the 1672 Salem Village Meeting-house and exhibit areas. (Mid-June-mid-Sept, daily exc Mon; mid-Sept-Oct, wkends; rest of yr, by appt; closed hols) 149 Pine St. Phone 508/774-8799. ¢¢

Witchcraft Victims' Memorial. Memorial includes names of those who died, as well as quotes from 8 victims. 176 Hobart St.

Annual Event

Danvers Family Festival. Exhibits, fireworks, races, music. Late June-early July.

Motels

★ ★ **COURTYARD BY MARRIOTT.** *275 Independence Way. 978/777-8630; FAX 978/777-7341.* Web www.courtyard.com. 122 rms, 3 story. Mid-Apr-mid-Nov: S, D $109-$129; suites $129-$149. Crib free. TV; cable (premium). Heated pool. Complimentary coffee in rms. Restaurant 6:30-10 pm; wkends from 7 am. Bar 5-10 pm. Coin lndry. Meeting rms. Business servs avail. In-rm modem link. Valet serv. Sundries. Exercise equipt. Refrigerator in suites; microwaves avail. Cr cds: A, C, D, DS, MC, V.

★ **DAYS INN.** *152 Endicott St. 978/777-1030; FAX 978/777-0264.* 129 rms, 2 story. May-Oct: S, D $69.95-$99.95; each addl $8; under 18 free; wkly, hol rates; lower rates rest of yr. Crib free. TV; cable (premium). Pool. Complimentary continental bkfst. Restaurant adj open 24 hrs. Ck-out 11 am. Coin lndry. Business servs avail. In-rm modem link. Sundries. Picnic tables. Cr cds: A, C, D, DS, MC, V.

★ ★ **RESIDENCE INN BY MARRIOTT.** *51 Newbury St (US 1N). 978/777-7171; FAX 978/774-7195.* Web www.residenceinn.com. 96 suites, 2 story. Suites $89-$189; wkly, wkend rates. Crib avail. Pet accepted, some restrictions. TV; cable. Pool. Complimentary continental bkst. Restaurant nearby. Ck-out noon. Coin lndry. Business servs avail. In-rm modem link. Valet serv. Lighted tennis. Exercise equipt. Sport court. Refrigerators, microwaves. Balconies. Picnic tables. Cr cds: A, C, D, DS, JCB, MC, V.

✔ ★ **SUPER 8.** *225 Newbury St (US 1N). 978/774-6500; FAX 978/762-6491.* 78 rms, 2 story, 11 kit. units. Mid-June-mid-Oct: S, D $56-$66; each addl $5; kit. units $79; under 16 free; lower rates rest of yr. Crib free. TV. Pool. Complimentary continental bkfst. Restaurant 11:30 am-10 pm. Bar to 12:30 am; entertainment Thurs-Sat. Ck-out 11 am. Meeting rms. Business servs avail. Microwaves avail. Cr cds: A, C, D, DS, MC, V.

Motor Hotel

★ ★ ★ **QUALITY INN KING'S GRANT INN.** *Trask Lane, N on MA 128 at exit 21. 978/774-6800; FAX 978/774-6502.* 125 rms, 2 story. S, D $99-$130; each addl $10; suite $250; under 18 free. Crib free. TV; cable (premium), VCR avail (movies). Indoor pool; whirlpool, poolside serv. Restaurant 7 am-10 pm. Rm serv. Bar; pianist Tues-Thurs, combo Fri-Sat. Ck-out 11 am. Meeting rms. Business servs avail. In-rm modem link. Sundries. Airport transportation. Health club privileges. Microwaves avail. Private patios, balconies. Indoor tropical garden. Cr cds: A, C, D, DS, ER, JCB, MC, V.

Hotel

★ ★ **SHERATON FERNCROFT RESORT.** *50 Ferncroft Rd, US 1 & I-95. 978/777-2500; FAX 978/750-7959; res: 800/544-2242.* 367 rms, 8 story. S, D $169-$260; each addl $15; suites $250-$800; under 18 free.

Crib free. TV; cable (premium), VCR avail. 2 pools, 1 indoor; whirlpool, poolside serv, lifeguard. Coffee in rms. Restaurant 6:30 am-11 pm. Bar 11-1 am. Ck-out 11 am. Meeting rms. Business center. In-rm modem link. Airport transportation. Gift shop. Lighted tennis, pro. 27-hole golf, pro, putting green, driving range. X-country ski on site. Exercise equipt. Lawn games. Refrigerators, microwaves avail. Private patios. Cr cds: A, C, D, DS, MC, V.

Restaurants

★ ★ ★ **THE HARDCOVER.** *15-A Newbury St (US 1N), at jct MA 114, enter from US 1 N. 978/774-1223.* Specializes in seafood, steak, prime rib. Salad bar. Hrs: 5-10 pm; Fri, Sat to 11 pm; Sun 4-9:30 pm. Bar. Wine cellar. Semi-a la carte: dinner $14.95-$29.95. Child's meals. Walls lined with books, rare prints, paintings. Fireplaces. Cr cds: A, C, D, DS, MC, V.

★ ★ **LEGAL SEA FOODS.** *(MA 128 & MA 114, Peabody 01960) S on MA 128, in Northshore Mall. 978/532-4500.* Specializes in seafood. Hrs: 11:30 am-10 pm; Fri, Sat to 10:30 pm; Sun to 9 pm. Closed Thanksgiving, Dec 25. Res accepted. Bar. Wine list. A la carte entrees: lunch $5.25-$11.95, dinner $10.95-$19.95. Child's meals. Totally non-smoking. Cr cds: A, C, D, DS, ER, JCB, MC, V.

Dedham (C-7)

Settled 1635 **Pop** 23,782 **Elev** 120 ft **Area code** 781 **Zip** 02026 **E-mail** infor@nvcc.com **Web** www.nvcc.com

Information Neponset Valley Chamber of Commerce, 190 Vanderbilt Ave, Suite 1, Norwood 02062-5047; 781/769-1126.

What to See and Do

Dedham Historical Society. Small but important collection of 16th-19th-century furniture; collection of work by silversmith Katharine Pratt; world's largest public collection of Dedham and Chelsea pottery; changing exhibits. Also 10,000-volume historical and genealogical library. (Tues-Fri, also some Sat; closed hols) 612 High St. Phone 781/326-1385. Museum ¢; Library ¢¢

Fairbanks House (1636). One of the oldest frame houses still standing in the US. Fine example of 17th-century architecture, furnished with Fairbanks family heirlooms; guided tours. (May-Oct, Tues-Sat, also Sun afternoons) 511 East St, at Eastern Ave, off US 1. Phone 781/326-1170. ¢¢

Motor Hotel

★ ★ **HOLIDAY INN.** *55 Ariadne Rd, jct US 1 & I-95 (MA 128), exit 15A. 781/329-1000; FAX 781/329-0903.* E-mail hidedham@gis.net; web www.holiday-inn.com/hotels/bosdh. 202 rms, 8 story. S, D $85-$125; each addl $5; under 19 free. Crib free. TV; cable. (premium). Heated pool; poolside serv, lifeguard. Restaurant 6:30 am-10 pm. Rm serv. Ck-out noon. Meeting rms. Business servs avail. In-rm modem link. Bellhops. Valet serv. Sundries. Exercise equipt. Microwaves avail. Cr cds: A, C, D, DS, ER, JCB, MC, V.

Hotel

★ ★ ★ **HILTON AT DEDHAM PLACE.** *25 Allied Dr, off I-95 exit 14. 781/329-7900; FAX 781/329-5552.* E-mail hilton@gis.net; web www.dedhamplace.hilton.com. 249 rms, 4 story. S $119-$245; D $134-$260; each addl $15; suites $400-$600; under 18 free; wkend rates. Crib free. Pet accepted. TV; cable (premium). Indoor pool; whirlpool, poolside serv (in season). Coffee in rms. Restaurant 6:30 am-10 pm. Bar 11-1 am; pianist. Ck-out noon. Meeting rms. Business center. In-rm modem link. Garage, valet parking. Lighted tennis. Exercise rm; sauna. Bathrm phones; refrigerators avail. Cr cds: A, C, D, DS, ER, JCB, MC, V.

Deerfield (B-3)

Settled 1669 **Pop** 5,018 (town); 600 (village) **Elev** 150 ft **Area code** 413 **Zip** 01342 **E-mail** grace@historic-deerfield.org **Web** www.historic-deerfield.org
Information Historic Deerfield, Inc, PO Box 321; 413/774-5581.

Twice destroyed by French and Native American attacks when it was the northwest frontier of New England, and almost forgotten by industry, Deerfield is noted for its unspoiled meadowland, beautiful houses and nationally famous boarding schools (Deerfield Academy, 1797, a coeducational preparatory school; the Bement School, a coeducational school; and Eaglebrook School for boys).

In 1675, the Bloody Brook Massacre (King Philip's War) crippled the settlement, which was then a struggling frontier outpost. In 1704 (Queen Anne's War), half of the resettled town was burned. Forty-nine inhabitants were killed, and more than 100 were captured and taken to Canada.

The village boasts that it has one of the most beautiful streets in America, known as just The Street, a mile-long stretch of 80 houses, many dating from the 18th and early 19th centuries.

What to See and Do

⭐ **Historic Deerfield, Inc.** Maintains 14 historic house museums (fee) furnished with collections of antique furniture, silver, ceramics, textiles. A 28,000-sq-ft Collections Study Center features changing exhibits and study-storage displays of portions of the museum's collections. Daily walking tours, meadow walk, antiques forums and workshops, special events wkends. Information Center is located at Hall Tavern, The Street. (Daily; closed Thanksgiving, Dec 24, 25) Phone 413/774-5581. Guided tours ¢¢¢¢

Memorial Hall Museum (1798). The first building of Deerfield Academy; contains colonial furnishings, Native American relics. (May-Oct, daily) Memorial St. Phone 413/774-7476. ¢¢

Inn

⭐⭐⭐ **THE DEERFIELD INN.** 81 Old Main St, The Street. 413/774-5587; FAX 413/773-8712; res: 800/926-3865. 23 rms, 2 story. S, D $141-$207. Crib $10. TV; cable. Complimentary afternoon refreshments. Restaurant (see DEERFIELD INN). Bar. Ck-out noon, ck-in 2 pm. Downhill ski 18 mi; x-country ski 11 mi. Antiques. Library. Built 1884. Totally nonsmoking. Cr cds: A, D, MC, V.

Restaurant

⭐⭐⭐ **DEERFIELD INN.** (See The Deerfield Inn) 413/774-5587. Specialties: fresh seafood, rack of lamb, veal dishes. Hrs: 7:30-9 am, noon-2 pm, 6-9 pm; Sat, Sun 7:30 am-10 pm, noon-2 pm, 6-9 pm. Closed Dec 25. Res accepted. Bar. Semi-a la carte: bkfst $7.50-$10.50, lunch $6-$12, dinner $20-$23. Afternoon tea 4-5 pm. Child's meals. Colonial decor. Built 1884. 14 museum houses nearby. Cr cds: A, D, MC, V.

Dennis (Cape Cod) (D-9)

Settled 1639 **Pop** 13,864 **Elev** 24 ft **Area code** 508 **Zip** 02638 **E-mail** denniscofc@aol.com **Web** www.dennischamber.com
Information Chamber of Commerce, PO Box 275, South Dennis 02660, phone 508/398-3568 or 800/243-9920; or the information booth at jct MA 28 & 134.

Dennis heads a group, often called "The Dennises," that includes Dennisport, East Dennis, South Dennis, West Dennis and Dennis. It was here, in 1816, that Henry Hall developed the commercial cultivation of cranberries. Swimming beaches are located throughout the area.

What to See and Do

Jericho House and Historical Center (1801). Period furniture. Barn museum contains old tools, household articles, model of salt works, photographs. (July-Aug, Wed & Fri) At jct Old Main St & Trotting Park Rds in West Dennis. **Donation.**

Josiah Dennis Manse (1736) **and Old West School House**(1770). Restored home of minister for whom town was named; antiques, Pilgrim chest, children's rm, spinning & weaving exhibit, maritime wing. (July-Aug, Tues & Thurs) 77 Nobscusset Rd. **Donation.**

Annual Event

Festival Week. Canoe and road races, antique car parade, craft fair, antique show. Late Aug.

Seasonal Event

Cape Playhouse. On MA 6A. Summer theater, daily exc Sun. Children's Theater (Fri mornings). Phone 508/385-3911 (box office) or 508/385-3838. Late June-Labor Day.

Motels

⭐⭐ **BREAKERS.** (61 Chase Ave, Dennisport 02639) 1 mi S of MA 28. 508/398-6905; FAX 508/398-7360; res: 800/540-6905 (MA). Web www.capecod.com/breakers. 40 rms, 2 story, 4 kits. Late June-Labor Day: S, D $100-$190; each addl $10; suites, kit. units $200-$350; lower rates May-late June, after Labor Day-mid-Oct. Closed rest of yr. Crib $10. TV; cable (premium). Heated pool. Continental bkfst. Restaurant nearby. Ck-out 11 am. Refrigerators; some microwaves. On beach. Cr cds: A, MC, V.

⭐⭐ **COLONIAL VILLAGE.** (426 Lower County Rd, Dennisport 02639) ½ mi S of MA 28. 508/398-2071; FAX 508/398-2071; res: 800/287-2071 (in 508 and 617 area codes). 49 rms, 1-2 story, 29 kits., 10 kit. cottages (4-rm, no A/C). July-Labor Day: S, D $94-$120; each addl $10; kit. units $105; kit. cottages $750/wk; each addl $60; lower rates mid-May-June, after Labor Day-mid-Oct. Closed rest of yr. TV; cable. 2 pools, 1 indoor; whirlpool, sauna. Restaurant nearby. Ck-out 11 am. Meeting rms. Fireplace, oven in cottages. Private beach. Cr cds: DS, MC, V.

⭐⭐ **CORSAIR OCEANFRONT.** (41 Chase Ave, Dennisport 02639) 1 mi S of MA 28. 508/398-2279; res: 800/201-1082. E-mail corsair@capecod.net; web www.virtualcapecod.com/market/corsair. 25 kit. units, 2 story. July-Aug: S, D $145-$225; each addl $10; suite $275; packages avail; higher rates hols; lower rates Apr-June, Sept-Nov. Closed rest of yr. TV; cable (premium), VCR avail. 2 pools, 1 indoor; whirlpool. Supervised child's activities (in season); ages 5-14. Complimentary continental bkfst (off season). Restaurant adj 8 am-9 pm (in season). Ck-out 11 am. Coin lndry. Lawn games. Microwaves avail. Enclosed sun deck. On private beach. Cr cds: A, MC, V.

★ ★ **CROSS RIP OCEANFRONT.** (33 Chase Ave, Dennisport 02639) 1 mi S of MA 28. 508/398-2279; res: 800/201-1082. E-mail corsair@capecod.net; web www.virtualcapecod.com/market/corsair. 22 rms, 2 story, 14 kits. July-Aug: S, D $95-$105; each addl $10; suites $165-$185; kit. units $135-$225; higher rates hols; packages avail; lower rates Apr-June, Sept-Nov. Closed rest of yr. TV; cable (premium), VCR avail. 2 pools, 1 indoor; whirlpool. Supervised child's activities. Continental bkfst. Restaurant adj 8 am-9 pm. Ck-out 11 am. Coin lndry. Refrigerators, microwaves avail. On beach. Cr cds: A, MC, V.

≈ 🔥 SC

✔★ **DENNIS WEST.** (691 Main St, West Dennis 02670) ¼ mi W of MA 134 on MA 28. 508/394-7434. 22 rms, 2 story. July-Labor Day: S $49-$56; D $55-$69; each addl $6-$10; lower rates rest of yr. Crib $7. TV; cable, VCR avail. Pool. Restaurant adj 7 am-2 pm. Ck-out 11 am. Refrigerators; microwaves avail. Cr cds: A, DS, MC, V.

≈ 🏊 🔥

★ ★ **EDGEWATER.** (95 Chase Ave, Dennisport 02639) 1 mi S of MA 28. 508/398-6922; FAX 508/760-3447. 86 rms, 1-2 story. July-Aug: S, D, kits. $90-$220; each addl $15; lower rates mid-Mar-June, Sept-mid-Nov. Closed rest of yr. TV; cable, VCR (movies). Indoor/outdoor pool; whirlpool. Restaurant adj 7-11 am. Ck-out 11 am. Meeting rm. Sundries. Putting green. Exercise equipt; sauna. Lawn games. Refrigerators, microwaves avail. Private patios, balconies. Ocean views from most rms. Cr cds: A, DS, MC, V.

🚣 ≈ 🎿 🔥

★ ★ **THE GARLANDS.** (117 Old Wharf Rd, Box 506, Dennisport 02639) 1 mi S of MA 28. 508/398-6987. 20 air-cooled kit. units, 2 story. July-Aug: 1-bedrm $122; 2-bedrm $110-$140; each addl $11; off-season package plans; lower rates mid-Apr-June, mid-Aug-mid-Oct. Closed rest of yr. Children over 5 yrs only. TV; cable. Restaurant nearby. Ck-out 10 am. Balconies. On ocean, beach. No cr cds accepted.

🚣 🔥

✔★ **HUNTSMAN.** (829 Main St, West Dennis 02670) ¼ mi W of MA 134 on MA 28. 508/394-5415; res: 800/628-0498. Web www.virtualcapecod.com. 27 rms, 2 story, 9 kits. Mid-June-early Sept: S $52-$59; D $61-$79; each addl $6-$10; kit. units $79; wkly rates; lower rates mid-Apr-mid-June, early Sept-Oct. Closed rest of yr. Crib $4. TV; cable. Pool. Complimentary coffee in lobby. Restaurant adj 7 am-2 pm. Ck-out 11 am. Lawn games. Refrigerators avail. Picnic tables, grills. Cr cds: MC, V.

≈ 🔥

★ ★ **LIGHTHOUSE INN.** (Box 128, West Dennis 02670) Lighthouse Rd, 1 mi S of MA 28. 508/398-2244; FAX 508/398-5658. E-mail inquire@lighthouseinn.com; web www.lighthouseinn.com. 63 rms in inn, motel, cottages, 15 A/C. MAP, late-May-mid-Oct: S $110; D $100-$117; each addl $35-$60; cottages to 6, $117-$140/person. Closed rest of yr. Crib free. TV; cable, VCR avail. Heated pool. Playground. Supervised child's activities (July-Aug); ages 3-10. Restaurant 8-9:15 am, noon-2 pm, 6-9 pm. Rm serv. Box lunches. Bar 11-1 am; entertainment. Ck-out 11 am. Meeting rms. Business center. Bellhops. Tennis. Miniature golf. Lawn games. Refrigerators. Large private beach. On ocean. Cr cds: MC, V.

D 🚣 🏊 ≈ 🔥 🎿

★ **SEA LORD.** (56 Chase Ave, Dennisport 02639) 1 mi S of MA 28. 508/398-6900; FAX 508/760-1901. Web www.svnsol.com/sealord/. 27 rms, 1-3 story. July-Aug: S, D $75-$89; kit units $75-$95; each addl $5; lower rates May-late-June, Sept-Oct. Closed rest of yr. Crib $3. TV; cable. Complimentary coffee. Ck-out 11 am. Some refrigerators. Balconies. Beach opp. Cr cds: DS, MC, V.

🎿 🔥

✔★ **SEA SHELL.** (45 Chase Ave, Dennisport 02639) 1 mi S of MA 28. 508/398-8965; res: 800/698-8965. 17 rms, 4 in guest house, 1-2 story, 5 kits. Some A/C. July-Labor Day: S, D $55-$195; each addl $15; kit. units $88-$190; lower rates rest of yr. Crib free. TV; cable. Complimentary continental bkfst in season. Restaurant adj 7 am-9:30 pm. Ck-out 11 am.

Refrigerators, microwaves avail. Balconies. Private beach. Sun deck. Cr cds: A, D, DS, MC, V.

🎿 🔥

✔★ ★ **SESUIT HARBOR.** (1421 Main St, East Dennis 02641) 2 mi E on MA 6A. 508/385-3326; res: 800/359-0097. Web www.capecod.net/sesuit. 20 rms, 1-2 story, 2 apts, 3 kits. Mid-June-mid-Sept: S, D $72-$99; each addl $12; children under 12 $6; apts $585-$765/wk; kits. $105; wkly rates; lower rates rest of yr. Crib free. TV; cable. Pool. Complimentary continental bkfst. Restaurant opp 6 am-2 pm. Ck-out 10:30 am. Business servs avail. In-rm modem link. Refrigerators avail. Some balconies. Picnic tables, grills. Cr cds: A, MC, V.

D ≈ 🎿 🔥

★ ★ **SOUNDINGS.** (79 Chase Ave, Dennisport 02639) 1 mi S of MA 28. 508/394-6561; FAX 508/394-7537. Web www.virtualcapecod/soundings. 102 rms, 1-2 story, 15 kits. Late June-Labor Day: S, D $110-$230; each addl $16; package plans; lower rates late Apr-late June, after Labor Day-mid-Oct. Closed rest of yr. TV; cable (premium). 2 pools, 1 indoor; poolside serv, sauna. Restaurant 7-11 am. Ck-out 11 am. Meeting rms. Business servs avail. In-rm modem link. Gift shop. Putting green. Refrigerators. Balconies. Sun decks. On 350-ft private beach. Cr cds: MC, V.

≈ 🔥

★ ★ **SPOUTER WHALE MOTOR INN.** (405 Old Wharf Rd, Dennisport 02639) 1 mi S of MA 28. 508/398-8010. E-mail spouter@capecod.net; web www.capecod.net/spouter. 38 rms in 2 bldgs, 2 story, 6 kits. Early July-early Sept: S, D $100-$160; each addl $15; lower rates Apr-early July, late Aug-late Oct. Closed rest of yr. TV; cable. Heated pool; whirlpool. Ck-out 11 am. Health club privileges. Refrigerators. Some private balconies. On ocean; private beach, beachside bkfst bar. Patio overlooking ocean. Totally nonsmoking. No cr cds accepted.

🚣 ≈ 🎿 🔥

★ ★ **THREE SEASONS.** (Box 188, Dennisport 02639) on Old Wharf Rd, 1 mi S of MA 28. 508/398-6091; FAX 508/398-3762. 63 rms, 2 story. Late June-Labor Day: D $115-$160; each addl $15; lower rates late May-late June, after Labor Day-Oct. Closed rest of yr. TV; cable. Restaurant 8 am-3 pm; 5-10 pm. Ck-out 11 am. Balconies. On private beach. Cr cds: DS, MC, V.

🚣 🔥

Inns

★ ★ **BY THE SEA GUESTS.** (57 Chase Ave, Dennisport 02639) 1 mi S of MA 28. 508/398-8685; FAX 508/398-0334; res: 800/447-9202. E-mail bythesea@capecod.net; web www.bytheseaguests.com. 12 rms, 3 story. 1 A/C. No rm phones. July-Aug: S, D $80-$135; each addl $15; lower rates May-June, Sept-Nov. Closed rest of yr. Crib $5. TV. Complimentary continental bkfst; afternoon refreshments. Restaurant adj 7 am-3 pm. Ck-out 11 am, ck-in 2 pm. Business servs avail. Concierge. Lawn games. Refrigerators. Picnic tables, grills. On private beach. Cr cds: A, C, D, MC, V.

🚣 ≈ 🔥

★ ★ **CAPTAIN NICKERSON.** (333 Main St, South Dennis 02660) approx 4 mi S on MA 134, W on Duck Pond Rd to Main St. 508/398-5966; res: 800/282-1619. E-mail captnick@capecod.net; web www.bbonline.com/ma/captnick. 7 rms, 2 share bath, 4 with shower only, 2 story. No rm phones. June-mid-Oct: S, D $75-$105; each addl $10; under 10 free; wkly rates; lower rates rest of yr. Crib $10-$15. TV in living rm; cable. Playground. Complimentary full bkfst. Ck-out 11 am, ck-in 3 pm. Luggage handling. Concierge serv. Bicycles. Lawn games. Picnic tables. Queen Anne-style house built in 1828. Totally nonsmoking. Cr cds: DS, MC, V.

🎿 🔥

✔★ ★ **FOUR CHIMNEYS.** 946 Main St (MA 6A). 508/385-6317; FAX 508/385-6285; res: 800/874-5502. E-mail chimneys4@aol.com; web www.virtualcapecod.com/fourchimneys. 8 air-cooled rms, 3 story. No rm phones. June-Sept: D $95-$140; wkly rates; lower rates Oct-May. Closed late Dec-mid-Feb. TV in sitting rm; cable (premium). Complimentary continental bkfst. Restaurant nearby. Ck-out 11 am, ck-in 3 pm. Lawn games. Balconies. Picnic tables. Opp lake. Former summer residence (1875); antiques. Cr cds: A, DS, MC, V.

★ ★ **ISAIAH HALL.** 152 Whig St. 508/385-9928; FAX 508/385-5879; res: 800/736-0160. E-mail isaiah@capecod.net; web www.virtual capecod.com/isaiahhall. 10 rms, 2 story. No rm phones. Mid-June-Labor Day: S, D $93-$128; each addl $15; suite $153; wkly rates; lower rates mid-Apr-mid-June, after Labor Day-mid-Oct. Closed rest of yr. Children over 7 yrs only. TV; VCR. Complimentary continental bkfst; afternoon refreshments. Restaurant nearby. Ck-out 11 am, ck-in 2 pm. Rec rm. Lawn games. Balconies. Picnic tables. Antiques. Library. Farmhouse built 1857. Totally nonsmoking. Cr cds: A, MC, V.

Restaurants

★ ★ **CAPTAIN WILLIAM'S HOUSE.** (106 Depot St, Dennisport 02639) 1/2 mi S of MA 28. 508/398-3910. Specializes in lobster, prime rib, fresh seafood, homemade pasta. Hrs: 4:30-10 pm; early-bird dinner 4:30-5:45 pm. Closed Jan-Mar. Res accepted. Bar. Semi-a la carte: dinner $12.95-$19.95. Child's meals. Sea captain's house (1820); colonial decor. Cr cds: A, D, DS, MC, V.

★ ★ **CHRISTINE'S.** (MA 28, West Dennis) 2 mi S on MA 134, 3 mi W on MA 28. 508/394-7333. Lebanese Amer menu. Specialties: chicken Christine, local seafood, Lebanese dishes. Hrs: 11:30 am-10 pm; Fri, Sat to 11 pm; early-bird dinner 4-6 pm; Sun brunch 10 am-2 pm. Res accepted. Bar to 1 am. Semi-a la carte: lunch $4.95-$6.95, dinner $8.95-$17.95. Sun brunch $9.95. Child's meals. Entertainment nightly in season; off season, wkends. Parking. Contemporary decor. Cr cds: A, D, DS, MC, V.

✔★ **DINO'S BY THE SEA.** (Chase Ave & Inman Rd, Dennisport) 1 mi S of MA 28. 508/398-8740. Specialties: lobster salad roll, health salad, Dino's plantation special. Own baking. Hrs: 7 am-3 pm. Closed mid-Oct-mid-May. Semi-a la carte: bkfst $3-$7, lunch $2.50-$10.95. Child's meals. Parking. Porch dining. Plate collection displayed. Family-owned. Cr cds: C, D, MC, V.

✔★ **THE MARSHSIDE.** (28 Bridge St, East Dennis 02641) 3 mi E on MA 6A to jct MA 134, left at light. 508/385-4010. Specializes in fresh seafood, lobster salad, homemade pies. Hrs: 7 am-9 pm; Sun brunch 8 am-3 pm. Closed Thanksgiving, Dec 25. Serv bar. Semi-a la carte: bkfst $2.95-$5.95, lunch $4.95-$7.95, dinner $6.95-$13.95. Sun brunch $2.95-$5.95. Child's meals. Cozy atmosphere; "knick-knacks," artificial flowers. Cr cds: A, D, DS, MC, V.

★ ★ ★ **RED PHEASANT INN.** 905 Main St (MA 6A). 508/385-2133. Specializes in salmon, rack of lamb, roast lobster. Hrs: 5-10 pm. Res accepted. Bar. A la carte entrees: dinner $15-$25. Valet parking. Once a barn (circa 1795); many antiques. Family-owned. Totally nonsmoking. Cr cds: DS, MC, V.

★ **ROYAL PALACE.** (369 MA 28/Main St, West Dennis) 2 mi S on MA 134, 3 mi W on MA 28. 508/398-6145. Chinese, Polynesian menu. Specializes in Cantonese & Mandarin dishes. Hrs: 4 pm-1 am. Res accepted. Bar. Semi-a la carte: dinner $6.50-$14.95. Parking. Cr cds: A, MC, V.

★ ★ **SCARGO CAFE.** 799 Rt 6A. 508/385-8200. E-mail scargo@capecod.net; web www.scargocafe.com. Continental menu. Specialties: chicken wildcat, mussels Ferdinand, grapenut custard. Hrs: 11 am-3 pm, 4:30-10 pm; early-bird dinner 4:30-5:30 pm. Closed Thanksgiving, Dec 25. Bar. Semi-a la carte: lunch $3.95-$10.95, dinner $9.95-$17.95. Child's meals. Parking. Former residence (1865); opp nation's oldest stock-company theater. Totally nonsmoking. Cr cds: A, DS, MC, V.

✔★ **SWAN RIVER.** (5 Lower County Rd, Dennisport 02639) 2 mi S on MA 134. 508/394-4466. Specialties: blackened fish-of-the-day, fried clams, fresh lobster. Hrs: noon-3 pm, 5-9:30 pm. Closed mid-Sept-late May. Res accepted. Bar to 11 pm. Semi-a la carte: lunch $5-$10, dinner $12-$16. Child's meals. Parking. Nautical decor; overlooks Swan River. Family-owned. Cr cds: A, MC, V.

Eastham (Cape Cod) (D-10)

(See also Orleans)

Settled 1644 **Pop** 4,462 **Elev** 48 ft **Area code** 508 **Zip** 02642 **E-mail** winstonsc@aol.com **Web** www.capecod.com/eastham/chamber

Information Chamber of Commerce, PO Box 1329, phone 508/240-7211 or 508/255-3444 (Summer only); or visit the Information Booth at MA 6 & Fort Hill.

On the bay side of the Cape, in what is now Eastham town, the Mayflower shore party met their first Native Americans—luckily, peaceful ones. Also in the town is a magnificent stretch of Nauset Beach, which was once a graveyard of ships. Nauset Light is an old friend of mariners.

What to See and Do

Eastham Historical Society. 1869 schoolhouse museum; Native American artifacts; farming and nautical implements. (July-Aug, Mon-Fri afternoons) Just off US 6. For hrs phone 508/255-0788. **Donation.** The society also maintains the

Swift-Daley House (1741). Cape Cod house contains period furniture, clothing, original hardware. (July-Aug, Mon-Fri afternoons or by appt) On US 6. For hrs phone 508/255-1766.   **Free.**

Eastham Windmill. Oldest windmill on the Cape (1680); restored in 1936. (Late June-Labor Day, daily) Windmill Green, in town center. **Donation.**

Motels

★ **BLUE DOLPHIN INN.** (US 6, North Eastham 02651) 3 mi N of Natl Seashore entrance. 508/255-1159; FAX 508/240-3676; res: 800/654-0504. E-mail bluedolphin@capecod.net; web www.cape-cod.net/bluedolphin.com. 49 rms. Mid-June-early Sept: S, D $75-$115; each addl $10; under 16 free; lower rates Apr-mid-June, early Sept-late Oct. Closed rest of yr. Crib $10. Pet accepted. TV; cable (premium). Pool; poolside serv. Restaurant 6:30 am-1 pm. Ck-out 11 am. Lawn games. Refrigerators. Private patios. On 7 wooded acres. Cr cds: A, MC, V.

★ ★ **CAPTAIN'S QUARTERS.** (US 6, North Eastham 02651) approx 2 mi N on US 6. 508/255-5686; FAX 508/240-0280; res: 800/327-7769. E-mail cqmcc@aol.com; web www.captains_quarters.com. 75 rms. Late-June-Labor Day: S, D $84-$105; each addl $8; lower rates mid-Apr-late-June, after Labor Day-mid-Nov. Closed rest of yr. Crib free. TV; cable. Heated pool. Complimentary continental bkfst. Restaurant nearby. Ck-out 11 am. Meeting rms. Tennis. Health club privileges. Lawn games. Bicycles. Refrigerators. Picnic tables, grill. Near beach. Cr cds: A, C, D, DS, MC, V.

★ **EAGLE WING.** *960 MA 6, 1¹/₂ mi S on MA 6. 508/240-5656; res: 800/278-5656; FAX 508/240-5657.* E-mail eaglewing@cape-cod.net; web www.sunsol.com/eaglewing. 19 rms. Late June-early Sept: D $89-$102; wkly rates; wkends (2-day min); hols (3-day min); higher rates July 4; lower rates rest of yr. Closed Nov-May. TV; cable (premium). Complimentary coffee in lobby. Pool. Refrigerators. Totally nonsmoking. Cr cds: DS, MC, V.

★ ★ **EASTHAM OCEAN VIEW.** *2470 US 6, 2¹/₂ mi N of Orleans Rotary. 508/255-1600; FAX 508/240-7104; res: 800/742-4133.* 31 rms, 2 story. Mid-June-Labor Day: S, D $85-$124; each addl $10; under 12 free; lower rates mid-Feb-mid-June & after Labor Day-Oct. Closed rest of yr. Crib $5. TV; cable. Heated pool. Complimentary coffee in rms. Restaurant nearby. Ck-out 11 am. Health club privileges. Refrigerators; microwaves avail. Ocean view. Cr cds: A, C, D, DS, MC, V.

★ ★ ★ **FOUR POINTS BY SHERATON.** *On US 6, ¹/₂ mi N of Eastham visitor center. 508/255-5000; FAX 508/240-1870.* E-mail sheraton@cape.com; web virtual-valley.com/fourpoints/. 107 rms, 2 story. July-Aug: S, D $147.90-$174; each addl $10; suites $225; under 18 free; MAP avail; lower rates rest of yr. Crib $5-$10. TV; cable (premium). 2 pools, 1 indoor; whirlpool, poolside serv. Restaurant 7-11 am, 6-9 pm. Rm serv. Bar to 11 pm. Ck-out 11 am. Meeting rms. Business servs avail. In-rm modem link. Tennis. Exercise equipt; sauna. Health club privileges. Game rm. Some refrigerators. Cr cds: A, C, D, DS, MC, V.

✔★ ★ **MIDWAY MOTEL & COTTAGES.** *(US 6, North Eastham 02651) 2¹/₂ mi N of Eastham visitor center. 508/255-3117; FAX 508/255-4235; res: 800/755-3117.* E-mail inquire@midwaymotel.com; web www.midwaymotel.com. 11 rms, 3 kits. Late June-Labor Day: D $82-$125; studio rms $90; 1-bedrm cottage $650/wk; 3-bedrm cottage $775/wk; lower rates Mar-late June, after Labor Day-Oct. Closed rest of yr. TV; cable (premium), VCR avail. Playground. Complimentary coffee. Restaurant nearby. Ck-out 11 am. Rec rm. Lawn games. Bicycle rentals. Refrigerators, microwaves. Picnic tables, grills. Cr cds: A, D, DS, MC, V.

★ **TOWN CRIER.** *US 6, ¹/₂ mi N of Eastham visitor center. 508/255-4000; FAX 508/255-7491; res: 800/932-1434 (exc MA), 800/872-8780 (MA).* E-mail joe111@msn.com; web www.capecod.com/towncrier. 36 rms. July-Labor Day: S, D $75-$95; each addl $8; lower rates rest of yr. TV; cable (premium). Indoor pool. Restaurant 7-11 am. Ck-out 11 am. Rec rm. Refrigerators. Cr cds: A, C, D, DS, MC, V.

★ ★ **VIKING SHORES.** *(North Eastham 02651) 3 mi N on US 6, at jct Nauset Rd. 508/255-3200; FAX 508/240-0205; res: 800/242-2131 (New England).* E-mail viking@cape.com; web vsp.cape.com/~viking. 40 rms. Mid-June-Labor Day: S, D $89-$98; each addl $8; under 12 free; wkly rates; lower rates mid-Apr-mid-June, after Labor Day-early Nov. Closed rest of yr. Crib free. TV; cable (premium). Heated pool. Complimentary continental bkfst. Restaurant adj. Ck-out 11 am. Meeting rm. Tennis. Lawn games. Refrigerators. Picnic tables, grills. Cr cds: A, DS, MC, V.

Inns

★ ★ **OVER LOOK.** *MA 6. 508/255-1886; FAX 508/240-0345.* E-mail winstonsc@aol.com; web www.overlookinn.com. 10 rms, 4 A/C, 3 story. Late June-mid-Sept: D $95-$165; lower rates rest of yr. Complimentary full bkfst; afternoon refreshments. Restaurant nearby. Ck-out 11 am,

ck-in 2 pm. Rec rm. Lawn games. Picnic tables. Health club privileges. 1869 sea captain's house; many antiques. Cr cds: A, C, D, DS, MC, V.

★ ★ **PENNY HOUSE.** *(Rte 6, Box 238, North Eastham 02651) On MA 6, ¹/₂ mi N of Eastham Center. 508/255-6632; FAX 508/255-4893; res: 800/554-1751.* E-mail pennyhouse@aol.com. 11 rms, 2 story. July-Aug: D $125-$185; lower rates rest of yr. Children over 8 yrs only. TV in parlor; cable (premium), VCR (free movies). Complimentary full bkfst; afternoon refreshments. Ck-out 11 am, ck-in 2 pm. Business servs avail. Lawn games. Former sea captain's house (1700); antiques. Audubon Society bird sanctuary, bicycle trails nearby. Totally nonsmoking. Cr cds: A, DS, MC, V.

Cottage Colony

✔★ **CRANBERRY COTTAGES.** *785 US 6, ³/₄ mi N of Orleans Rotary. 508/255-0602; res: 800/292-6631.* Web www.sunsol.com/cranberrycottages. 14 cottages, 7 kits. Some A/C. Late June-Labor Day: S, D $82-$87; each addl $10; 2-bedrm kit. cottages for 1-6, $650-$750/wk; lower rates rest of yr. Crib free. TV; cable (premium). Ck-out 10 am, ck-in 3 pm. Refrigerators; microwaves avail. Grill. Cape Cod cottages in shady grove. Cr cds: DS, MC, V.

Fall River *(D-7)*

(See also New Bedford; also see Providence, RI)

Settled 1656 **Pop** 92,703 **Elev** 200 ft **Area code** 508 **E-mail** ceo@frchamber.com **Web** www.frchamber.com

Information Fall River Area Chamber of Commerce, 200 Pocasset St,02721; 508/676-8226.

The city's name, adopted in 1834, was translated from the Native American "quequechan." In 1892, Fall River was the scene of one of the most famous murder trials in American history—that of Lizzie Borden, who was acquitted of the ax murders of her father and stepmother. Water power and cotton textiles built Fall River into one of the largest cotton manufacturers in the world, but its industry is now greatly diversified.

What to See and Do

★ **Battleship Cove.** Five historic naval ships of the WWII period. The submarine *Lionfish*, a WWII attack sub with all her equipment intact, and the battleship **USS *Massachusetts*** are open to visitors. The *Massachusetts*, commissioned in 1942, was active in the European and Pacific theaters of operation in the Second World War and now houses the state's official World War II & Gulf War Memorial; on board is a full-scale model of a Patriot missile. Also here are **PT Boat 796, PT Boat 617,** and the destroyer **USS *Joseph P. Kennedy, Jr.,*** which saw action in both the Korean and Vietnam conflicts and the Cuban missile blockade. The PT boats may be viewed from walkways. A landing craft (LCM) exhibit is located on the grounds. Gift shop; snack bar. (Daily; closed Jan 1, Thanksgiving, Dec 25) At jct MA 138, I-195. Phone 508/678-1100. ¢¢¢

Factory Outlet District. Fall River is an extensive factory outlet area. 657 Quarry St. Phone 508/675-5519 or 800/424-5519.

Fall River Heritage State Park. Nine acres on the riverfront; sailing. Visitor center (daily) has multimedia presentation on how Fall River developed into the greatest textile producer in the country; tourist information. (Daily; closed Jan 1, Dec 25) Davol St. Phone 508/675-5759. **Free.**

Fall River Historical Society. Historical displays in 16-rm Victorian mansion. Exhibits of toys, dolls, china and glassware, costumes; artifacts relating to the Lizzie Borden trial. Gift shop. (Apr-May, Sept-Dec, Tues-Fri; June-Aug, Tues-Fri, also Sat & Sun afternoons; closed hols) 451 Rock St. Phone 508/679-1071. ¢¢

Marine Museum. 103 ship models on display, including a 28-ft, 1-ton model of the *Titanic*, trace the growth of maritime steam power from the early 1800s to 1937; paintings, photographs, artifacts. (Summer, Mon-Fri, also wkend afternoons; winter, Wed-Fri, also wkend afternoons; closed Jan 1, Thanksgiving, Dec 25) 70 Water St. Phone 508/674-3533. ¢¢

St Anne's Church and Shrine (1906). Designed by Canadian architect Napoleon Bourassa, the upper church is constructed of Vermont blue marble; the lower church is of solid granite. In the upper church are stained-glass windows produced by E. Rault in Rennes, France, a "Casavant Freres" organ, and exceptional oak wood ornamentation in the vault of the ceiling. The shrine is in the lower church. S Main St, facing Kennedy Park. Phone 508/674-5651. **Free.**

Motel

★ ★ **QUALITY INN.** *(1878 Wilbur Ave, Somerset 02725) I-195 W, MA exit 4B; I-195E, MA exit 4.* 508/678-4545; FAX 508/678-9352. 107 rms, 2 story. Late May-Aug: S, D $60-$95; each addl $10; lower rates rest of yr; under 18 free. Crib free. Pet accepted, some restrictions. TV; cable (premium), VCR avail. Indoor/outdoor pool. Continental bkfst. Restaurant adj 6 am-10 pm. Ck-out noon. Coin lndry. Meeting rm. Business servs avail. In-rm modem link. Private patios, balconies. Cr cds: A, C, D, DS, JCB, MC, V.

D ⚟ 🏊 ⚡ 🐾 SC

Motor Hotel

★ ★ **HAMPTON INN.** *(53 Old Bedford Rd, Westport 02790) 6 mi E on I-195, exit 10.* 508/675-8500; FAX 508/675-0075. 133 rms, 4 story. Apr-Aug: S, D $69-$99; under 18 free; lower rates rest of yr. Crib free. TV; cable (premium), VCR avail (movies). Complimentary continental bkfst. Complimentary coffee in rms. Restaurant adj 11 am-10 pm. Ck-out noon. Meeting rms. Business servs avail. In-rm modem link. Sundries. Valet serv. Airport, RR station transportation. Lighted tennis. Exercise equipt; sauna. Whirlpool. Some refrigerators. Cr cds: A, D, DS, MC, V.

D 🏋 ✈ 🏊 🐾 SC

Restaurants

✔★ **McGOVERN'S.** 310 Shove St (02724). 508/679-5010. Italian, Amer menu. Specializes in seafood, steak. Hrs: 11 am-7 pm; Fri to 8 pm; Sat 7 am-9 pm; Sun 7 am-8 pm. Closed Mon; Dec 25. Res accepted. Semi-a la carte: bkfst $2-$3, lunch $4-$6, dinner $5-$12. Child's meals. Memorabilia from New England Steamship Line on walls. Family-owned. Cr cds: A, DS, MC, V.

D

★ ★ **WHITE'S OF WESTPORT.** (66 MA 6, Westport) 6 mi E on I-195 exit 9, at MA 6. 508/675-7185. Specializes in steak, ribs, seafood. Hrs: 11:30 am-9 pm; Fri, Sat to 10 pm; Sun from 9 am. Closed Dec 25. Res accepted. Bar to midnight. Semi-a la carte: lunch $4.95-$8.50, dinner $8.25-$14.95. Child's meals. Nautical decor; artifacts. Family-owned. Cr cds: A, C, D, DS, MC, V.

D

Falmouth (Cape Cod) (E-8)

Settled ca 1660 **Pop** 27,960 **Elev** 10 ft **Area code** 508 **Zip** 02540 **E-mail** info@capecodchamber.org **Web** www.capecodchamber.org

Information Cape Cod Chamber of Commerce, US 6 & MA 132, PO Box 790, Hyannis 02601-0790; 508/362-3225 or 888/33-CAPECOD.

What to See and Do

Ashumet Holly & Wildlife Sanctuary (Massachusetts Audobon Society). A 45-acre wildlife preserve with holly trail; herb garden; observation beehive. Trails open dawn to dusk. (Daily exc Mon) Ashumet Rd, off Currier Rd; just N of MA 151. ¢¢

Falmouth Historical Society Museums. Julia Wood House (1790) and **Conant House** (ca 1740). Whaling collection; period furniture; 19th-century paintings; glassware; silver; tools; costumes; widow's walk; memorial park; colonial garden. (Mid-June-mid-Sept, Mon-Fri; rest of yr, by appt) Katharine Lee Bates exhibit in Conant House honors author of "America the Beautiful." (Mid-June-mid-Sept, Mon-Fri) On village green. Phone 508/548-4857. ¢¢

Island Queen. Passenger boat trips to Martha's Vineyard; 600-passenger vessel. (Late May-mid-Oct) Phone 508/548-4800. ¢¢¢

Annual Event

Barnstable County Fair. 8 mi N on MA 151. Horse and dog shows; horse-pulling contest; exhibits. Phone 508/563-3200. Last wk July.

Seasonal Event

College Light Opera Co at Highfield Theatre. Off Depot Ave, MA 28. 9-wk season of musicals and operettas with full orchestra. Phone 508/548-0668 (after June 15). Daily exc Sun. Late June-Labor Day.

Motels

★ ★ **ADMIRALTY INN.** 51 Teaticket Hwy (MA 28) (02541). 508/548-4240; FAX 508/457-0537; res: 800/341-5700. E-mail motels@capecod.net; web www.capecod.net/vacation/. 98 rms, 3 story, 28 suites. Mid July-mid Aug: S, D $100-$120; suites $125-$150; under 12 free; hol rates; golf plans; higher rates: road race, hols; lower rates rest of yr. TV; cable (premium), VCR. 2 pools, 1 indoor; whirlpool, poolside serv. Supervised child's activities (seasonal); ages 5-12. Coffee in rms. Restaurant 4:30-10 pm; also Sat 6-10 am; Sun 8 am-1 pm. Bar 4:30 pm-1 am. Ck-out 11 am. Meeting rms. Business servs avail. Refrigerators, minibars. Cr cds: A, C, D, DS, MC, V.

D 🏊 🐾

★ ★ **BEST WESTERN MARINA TRADEWINDS.** Robbins Rd, 1 blk S of MA 28. 508/548-4300; res: 800/341-5700; FAX 508/548-6787. E-mail motels@capecod.net; web www.capecod.net/vacation/. 63 rms, 2 story, 18 suites, 11 kits. July-Aug: D $125; each addl $10; suites $140; kit. units $150-$205; wkly rates; lower rates Mar-June & Sept-Oct. Closed rest of yr. TV; cable (premium). Pool. Complimentary coffee in rms. Restaurant opp. Ck-out 11 am. Business servs avail. Refrigerators, wet bars. Balconies. Overlooks Falmouth Harbor. Cr cds: A, C, D, DS, MC, V.

🏊 🐾

✔★ **MARINER.** 555 Main St (MA 28). 508/548-1331; res: 800/233-2939. Web www.marinermotel.com. 30 rms. Late June-Labor Day: S, D $79-$109; each addl $4-$10; lower rates rest of yr. TV; cable, VCR avail. Pool. Complimentary coffee. Restaurant nearby. Ck-out 11 am. Refrigerators. Picnic tables. Walking distance to island ferry, village shopping. Cr cds: A, C, D, DS, MC, V.

 🏊 🚭 🐾

★ ★ **RAMADA INN-FALMOUTH SQUARE.** *40 N Main St. 508/457-0606; FAX 508/457-9694.* 72 rms, 2 story. July-Aug: S, D $139-$199; each addl $10; suites $179-$249; under 18 free; hol rates; higher rates some special events; lower rates rest of yr. Crib free. TV; cable, VCR (movies). Indoor pool. Restaurant 7 am-10 pm. Bar 11 am-10 pm. Ck-out 11 am. Meeting rms. Business center. In-rm modem link. Cr cds: A, C, D, DS, MC, V.

★ ★ **RED HORSE INN.** *28 Falmouth Heights Rd, 1 blk off MA 28. 508/548-0053; FAX 508/540-6563; res: 800/628-3811.* Web www.red-horseinn.com. 22 rms, 2 story. Last wkend June-Labor Day: S, D $122-$140; each addl $10; under 12, $5; lower rates May-last wkend June, after Labor Day-Nov. Closed rest of yr. TV; cable (premium). Pool. Restaurant opp open 24 hrs. Ck-out 11 am. In-rm modem link. Refrigerators. Cr cds: A, MC, V.

Inns

★ ★ **BEACH HOUSE.** *(10 Worcestor Ct, Falmouth Heights) E on MA 28. 508/457-0310; FAX 508/548-7895; res: 800/351-3426.* 8 rms, 6 with shower only, 2 story. No rm phones. S, D $115-$125; kit. units $135-$150; 2-3-day min wkends, hols. Closed Nov-May. Children over 12 yrs only. Pool. Complimentary continental bkfst. Restaurant nearby. Ck-out 11 am, ck-in 3-6 pm. Picnic tables. Hand-painted murals and furniture; unique theme rms. Totally nonsmoking. Cr cds: MC, V.

✔★ ★ ★ **CAPT. TOM LAWRENCE HOUSE.** *75 Locust St. 508/540-1445; FAX 508/457-1790; res: 800/266-8139.* E-mail capttom@cape-cod.net; web www.sunsol.com/captaintom/. 7 units, 2 story, 1 apt. No rm phones. Mid-June-mid-Oct: S, D $95-$135; each addl $30; apt $125-$200; Closed Jan. TV; cable. Complimentary full bkfst. Ck-out 11 am, ck-in 3 pm. Free bus depot transportation. Island ferry tickets avail. Antiques. Whaling captain's home (1861). Totally nonsmoking. Cr cds: MC, V.

✔★ ★ **ELM ARCH INN.** *26 Elm Arch Way, 1/4 blk S of MA 28. 508/548-0133.* 24 rms, 8 A/C, 12 baths, 2 story. No rm phones. Mid-June-mid-Oct: D $70-$90; each addl $8-$10; lower rates rest of yr. TV in some rms; cable (premium). Pool. Complimentary morning coffee in season. Restaurant nearby. Ck-out 11 am, ck-in after noon. Screened terrace. Built 1810; private residence of whaling captain. Bombarded by British in 1814; dining rm wall features cannonball hole. No cr cds accepted.

★ ★ ★ **GRAFTON.** *261 Grand Ave South. 508/540-8688; FAX 508/540-1861; res: 800/642-4069.* Web www.sunsol.com/graftoninn/. 11 air-cooled rms, 3 story. No rm phones. Mid-June-mid-Oct: D $105-$174; lower rates rest of yr. Children over 16 yrs only. TV; cable (premium). Complimentary full bkfst. Restaurant nearby. Ck-out 11 am, ck-in 2 pm. Free bus depot, ferry terminal transportation. Picnic tables. Former home of sea captain; built 1850. On Nantucket Sound. Totally nonsmoking. Cr cds: A, MC, V.

★ ★ **INN ON THE SOUND.** *313 Grand Ave (02541). 508/457-9666; FAX 508/457-9631; res: 800/564-9668.* Web www.falmouth-cape-cod.com/fww/inn.on.the.sound/. 10 air-cooled rms, 2 story. No rm phones. Late May-mid-Oct: D $95-$175; wkly rates; lower rates rest of yr. Children over 16 yrs only. TV; cable. Complimentary full bkfst. Restaurant nearby. Ck-out 11 am, ck-in 3-6 pm. Built 1880; antiques. Overlooking Vineyard Sound. Totally nonsmoking. Cr cds: A, DS, MC, V.

★ ★ **MOSTLY HALL.** *27 Main St (MA 28). 508/548-3786; FAX 508/457-1572; res: 800/682-0565.* E-mail mostlyhl@cape.com; web www.sunsol.com/mostlyhall. 6 rms, shower only, 3 story. No rm phones. May-Oct: S, D $125-$135; wkends, hols (2-, 3-day min); lower rates rest of

yr. Closed Jan. Children over 16 yrs only. TV in sitting rm. Complimentary full bkfst; afternoon refreshments. Restaurant nearby. Ck-out 11 am, ck-in 3 pm. Concierge serv. Bicycles. Greek-revival house built 1849; wrap-around porch, garden gazebo. Totally nonsmoking. Cr cds: A, DS, MC, V.

★ ★ ★ **PALMER HOUSE.** *81 Palmer Ave. 508/548-1230; FAX 508/540-1878; res: 800/472-2632.* 13 rms, 7 with shower only, 3 story, 1 suite. Mid-June-mid-Oct: S, D $90-$140; suite $165; higher rates wkends & hols (2-day min); lower rates rest of yr. Some TV. Complimentary full bkfst. Restaurant nearby. Ck-out 11 am, ck-in 3 pm. Business servs avail. Luggage handling. Concierge serv. Refrigerators; some in-rm whirlpools. Queen Anne-style inn built 1901; antiques. Totally nonsmoking. Cr cds: A, C, D, DS, MC, V.

★ ★ ★ **WILDFLOWER INN.** *167 Palmer Ave. 508/548-9524; res: 800/294-5459.* E-mail wldflr167@aol.com; web wildflower-inn.com. 6 rms, 3 story. No rm phones. May-Oct: S, D $120-$175; kit. units $150; wkly rates; 2-day min wkends, hols; lower rates rest of yr. TV; cable (premium). Complimentary full bkfst. Restaurant nearby. Ck-out 11 am, ck-in 3 pm. Luggage handling. Concierge serv. Game rm. Lawn games. Picnic tables. Built in 1898; wraparound porch. Totally nonsmoking. Cr cds: A, MC, V.

Resorts

★ ★ ★ **NEW SEABURY.** *(Grat Neck Rd, New Seabury 02649) 3 mi S of jct MA 28, 151, off Mashpee Rotary. 508/477-9111; FAX 508/477-9790; res: 800/999-9033.* 160 rms, some A/C, kits. Mid-June-Aug: S, D $210-$380; patio & pool villas $275-$380; lower rates rest of yr. Crib $10. TV; cable (premium), VCR (movies). Seaside freshwater pool; wading pool. Supervised child's activities (July-Aug). Dining rm 7 am-10 pm. Bar noon-1 am; entertainment in season. Ck-out 10 am, ck-in 4 pm. Grocery. Coin lndry. Convention facilities. Business center. In-rm modem link. Air-port transportation. Sports dir. 16 all-weather tennis courts, pro. Two 18-hole golf courses, pro, putting green, driving range. Miniature golf. Sailboats, wind surfing. Bike trails. Exercise rm. Trips to islands, whale watching, deep sea fishing avail. Private patios, balconies. On 2,300 acres. Cr cds: A, C, D, MC, V.

★ ★ **SEA CREST.** *(350 Quaker Rd at Old Silver Beach, North Falmouth 02556) 5 mi N on MA 28 exit 151. 508/540-9400; FAX 508/548-0556; res: 800/225-3110.* E-mail 74161.672@compuserve.com; web www.sumware.com/seacrest. 266 rms, 1-3 story. Mid-June-mid-Sept: S, D $160-$240; under 17 free; MAP avail; higher rates hols; lower rates rest of yr. Crib $12.50. TV; cable. 2 pools, 1 indoor; whirlpool; poolside serv, lifeguard. Playground. Free supervised child's activities (in season); ages over 3. Restaurant 7-10:30 am, 5:30-11 pm. Snack bar, deli. Rm serv. Bar 11:30-1 am; entertainment. Ck-out 11 am, ck-in 3 pm. Grocery, coin lndry, pkg store 1 mi. Convention facilities. Business center. In-rm modem link. Bellhops. Valet serv. Concierge. Gift shop. Sports dir. Tennis. Putting green. Swimming beach. Windsurfing. Lawn games. Soc dir. Game rm. Exercise equipt; sauna. Refrigerators. Balconies. Picnic tables. On ocean. Cr cds: A, D, DS, MC, V.

Restaurants

★ ★ ★ **COONAMESSETT INN.** *311 Gifford St. 508/548-2300.* E-mail cme.cathi@aol.com; web capecod.com/coonamessett. Specializes in New England seafood. Hrs: 11:30 am-10 pm; Sun brunch 11 am-2 pm. Res accepted. Bar to 1 am. Semi-a la carte: lunch $6-$16, dinner $16-$27. Sun brunch $4.95-$12.95. Entertainment in season. Valet parking. Built 1796. Cathedral ceiling. Large windows with view of pond. Tranquil setting. Family-owned. Cr cds: A, MC, V.

✔★ **FLYING BRIDGE.** *220 Scranton Ave. 508/548-2700.* E-mail cmi.cathi@aol.com; web capecodtravel.com/flyingbridge. Specializes in seafood. Hrs: 11:30 am-10 pm. Bar to 1 am. Semi-a la carte: lunch, dinner $5.95-$15.95. Child's meals. Entertainment Fri. Valet parking. Outdoor dining overlooking harbor. Cr cds: A, MC, V.

✔★ **GOLDEN SAILS.** *143 Main St. 508/548-3521.* Chinese menu. Specializes in Szechwan, Cantonese, Mandarin dishes. Hrs: 11:30-1 am; Fri, Sat noon-2 am; Sun noon-midnight. Closed Thanksgiving. Bar. A la carte entrees: lunch $4.25-$5.25, dinner $3.25-$13.50. Parking. Cr cds: A, MC, V.

★★★ **REGATTA OF FALMOUTH BY-THE-SEA.** *217 Clinton Ave, at Falmouth Harbor entrance, end of Scranton Ave. 508/548-5400.* French, Amer menu. Specialties: soft shell crab, roasted red pepper vinaigrette. Own desserts. Hrs: 4:30-10 pm. Closed Oct-Memorial Day. Res accepted. Wine list. A la carte entrees: dinner $17.50-$26. Parking. French decor; antiques. View of harbor & sound. Family-owned. Cr cds: A, MC, V.

Foxboro (C-7)

Settled 1704 **Pop** 14,637 **Elev** 280 ft **Area code** 508 **Zip** 02035 **E-mail** info@nvcc.com **Web** www.nvcc.com

Information Neponset Valley Chamber of Commerce, 190 Vanderbilt Ave, Ste 1, Norwood 02062; 781/769-1126.

What to See and Do

Professional sports.

NFL (New England Patriots). Foxboro Stadium, S on US 1. Phone 508/543-8200.

Motor Hotels

★★★ **COURTYARD BY MARRIOTT.** *35 Foxborough Blvd. 508/543-5222; FAX 508/543-0445.* 149 rms, 3 story. S, D $110; under 18 free. Crib avail. TV; cable (premium). Indoor pool; whirlpool. Complimentary coffee in rms. Restaurant 6:30-10 am. Bar 5-11 pm. Ck-out noon. Coin lndry. Meeting rms. Business servs avail. In-rm modem link. Valet serv. Exercise equipt. Balconies. Cr cds: A, C, D, DS, MC, V.

★★ **HOLIDAY INN.** *(31 Hampshire St, Mansfield 02048) 3 mi S on MA 140, off I-95 exit 7A, in Cabot Industrial Park. 508/339-2200; FAX 508/339-1040.* 202 rms, 2-3 story. S $99-$159; D $109-$169; each addl $10; suites $300; under 18 free; wkend rates. Crib free. TV; cable (premium), VCR avail. Indoor pool. Complimentary coffee in rms. Restaurant 6:30 am-10 pm. Rm serv. Bars 11:30-1 am; entertainment. Ck-out noon. Coin lndry. Meeting rms. Business servs avail. In-rm modem link. Bellhops. Lighted tennis. Exercise rm. Some in-rm whirlpools. Private patios, balconies. Cr cds: A, C, D, DS, ER, JCB, MC, V.

Restaurant

★★ **LAFAYETTE HOUSE.** *109 Washington St (US 1), 3 mi N of I-495 exit 14A, US 1. 508/543-5344.* Continental menu. Specializes in roast beef, seafood. Hrs: 11:45 am-9 pm; Fri, Sat to 10 pm. Bar to midnight. Semi-a la carte: lunch $5.95-$8.95, dinner $12.95-$19.95.

Child's meals. Historic colonial tavern built in 1784. Cr cds: A, C, D, DS, MC, V.

Framingham (B-6)

Settled 1650 **Pop** 64,989 **Elev** 165 ft **Area code** 508 **Zip** 01701

Framingham is an industrial, commercial and residential community. Framingham Centre, the original town, was bypassed by the railroad in the 19th century and is two miles north of downtown.

What to See and Do

Danforth Museum of Art. Six galleries, including a children's gallery; changing exhibits, special events; art reference library. (Wed-Sun afternoons; closed Aug & some major hols) 123 Union Ave. Phone 508/620-0050. ¢¢

Garden in the Woods. A 45-acre botanical garden and sanctuary. Exceptional collection of wildflowers and other native plants; variety of gardens and habitats. HQ of Northeast Wildflower Society. (Mid-June-Oct, daily exc Mon; mid-Apr-mid-June, daily) Guided walks (inquire for schedule). Visitor center; museum shop. 180 Hemenway Rd. Phone 508/877-6574 (recording). ¢¢¢

Hotel

★★ **SHERATON TARA.** *1657 Worcester Rd (MA 9), I-90 exit 12. 508/879-7200; FAX 508/875-7593.* 375 rms, 6 story. S $99-$180; D $109-$190; each addl $15; suites $165-$274; under 18 free. Crib free. TV; cable (premium), VCR avail. 2 pools, 1 indoor; whirlpool, poolside serv, lifeguard. Restaurant 6:30 am-2 pm, 5-10 pm. Bar 11-1 am; entertainment. Ck-out noon. Convention facilities. Business center. In-rm modem link. Gift shop. Exercise rm; sauna, steam rm. Bathrm phones; some in-rm whirlpools; microwaves avail. Cr cds: A, C, D, DS, ER, MC, V.

Gloucester (A-8)

Settled 1623 **Pop** 28,716 **Elev** 50 ft **Area code** 978 **Zip** 01930 **E-mail** cacc@shore.net **Web** www.cape-ann.com/cacc

Information Cape Ann Chamber of Commerce, 33 Commercial St; 978/283-1601 or 800/321-0133.

It is said that more than ten thousand Gloucester men have been lost at sea in the last three centuries—which emphasizes how closely the community has been linked with seafaring. Today it is still a leading fishing port—although the fast schooners made famous in *Captains Courageous* and countless romances have been replaced by diesel trawlers. Gloucester is also the center of an extensive summer resort area that includes the famous artists' colony of Rocky Neck.

What to See and Do

"Beauport," the Sleeper-McCann House (1907-1934). Henry Davis Sleeper, early 20th-century interior designer, began by building a 26-rm house, continually adding rms with the help of Halfdan Hanson, a Gloucester architect, until there were 40 rms; 25 are now on view, containing extraordinary collection of antique furniture, rugs, wallpapers, ceramics, glass; American and European decorative arts. Many artists, statesmen and businessmen were entertained here. (Mid-May-mid-Sept, Mon-Fri; mid-Sept-mid-Oct, daily) 75 Eastern Point Blvd. Phone 978/283-0800. ¢¢

Cape Ann Historical Museum. Paintings by Fitz Hugh Lane; decorative arts and furnishings; Federal-style house (ca 1805). Emphasis on Gloucester's fishing industry; fisheries/maritime galleries and changing exhibitions depict various aspects of Cape Ann's history. (Tues-Sat; closed most major hols, also Feb) 27 Pleasant St. Phone 978/283-0455. ¢¢

Gloucester Fisherman. Bronze statue by Leonard Craske, a memorial to fishermen lost at sea. On Stacy Blvd on the harbor.

Hammond Castle Museum (1926-1929). Built like a medieval castle by inventor Dr John Hays Hammond Jr; contains a rare collection of art objects. Great Hall contains pipe organ with 8,200 pipes; concerts (selected days throughout the yr). (Memorial Day-Labor Day, daily; after Labor Day-Columbus Day, Thurs-Sun; rest of yr, Sat & Sun; closed Jan 1, Thanksgiving, Dec 25). 80 Hesperus Ave, off MA 127. Schedule may vary, phone ahead; 978/283-2081. ¢¢

Sargent House Museum. Late 18th-century Georgian residence, built for Judith Sargent, an early feminist writer and sister of Governor Winthrop Sargent; also home of her second husband, John Murray, leader of Universalism. Period furniture, china, glass, silver, needlework, early American portraits, paintings by John Singer Sargent. (Memorial Day-Columbus Day, Fri-Mon; closed hols) 49 Middle St. Phone 978/281-2432. ¢

Annual Events

St Peter's Fiesta. A 4-day celebration with sports events, fireworks; procession; Blessing of the Fleet. Phone 978/283-1601. Last wkend June.

Waterfront Festival. Arts and crafts show, entertainment, food. Phone 978/283-1601. 3rd wkend Aug.

Schooner Festival. Races, parade of sail, maritime activities. Phone 978/283-1601. Labor Day wkend.

Seasonal Event

Whale Watching. Half-day trips, mornings and afternoons. Phone 978/283-1601. May-Oct.

Motels

★ **ATLANTIS OCEAN FRONT MOTOR INN.** *125 Atlantic Rd. 978/283-0014; res: 800/732-6313.* 40 rms, 2 story. No A/C. July-Aug: S, D $110-$130; under 12 free; lower rates Sept-Oct, Apr-June. Closed rest of yr. Crib $8. TV; cable. Heated pool. Ck-out noon. Refrigerators avail. Balconies. All rms with ocean view. Cr cds: A, MC, V.

🅳 〰 ⬜ SC

★ ★ **BEST WESTERN BASS ROCKS OCEAN INN.** *107 Atlantic Rd, in Bass Rocks. 978/283-7600; FAX 978/281-6489.* 48 rms, 2 story. Mid-June-Labor Day: S, D $130-$170; each addl $8; under 13 free; lower rates Apr-mid-June, after Labor Day-Nov. Closed rest of yr. TV; cable. VCR avail (movies $5). Heated pool. Complimentary bkfst buffet. Ck-out noon. Business servs avail. In-rm modem link. Rec rm. Balconies overlook ocean. Bicycles avail. Cr cds: A, C, D, DS, MC, V.

〰 🎿 ⬜ ⬜ 🔥 SC

★ **CAPTAIN'S LODGE.** *237 Eastern Ave, on Rte 127. 978/281-2420.* 47 rms, 7 kits. July-Sept: S, D $95; each addl $7; kit. units $102; lower rates rest of yr. Crib $7. TV; cable (premium). Heated pool. Restaurant 6 am-2 pm; Sat, Sun 7 am-noon. Ck-out 11 am. Tennis. Cr cds: A, C, D, DS, MC, V.

🅳 🎿 〰 ⬜ 🔥 SC

★ **VISTA.** *22 Thatcher Rd, MA 128N to exit 9, left on MA 127A. 978/281-3410.* 40 rms, 1-2 story, 20 kits. Late June-Labor Day: S, D, kit. units $100-$115; each addl $5; lower rates rest of yr. TV; cable (premium). Heated pool. Continental bkfst in summer. Restaurant nearby. Ck-out 11 am. Refrigerators avail. Private patios, balconies. Ocean opp, beach privileges. All rms with ocean view. Cr cds: A, MC, V.

🅳 〰 ⬜ 🔥

Inns

★ ★ **GEORGE FULLER HOUSE.** *(148 Main St, Essex 01929) W on MA 128, exit 15 to Main St (MA 133). 978/768-7766; FAX 978/768-6178; res: 800/477-0148.* 7 rms, 6 with shower only, 3 story, 3 suites. June-Oct: S, D $100-$155; each addl $15; under 6 free; lower rates rest of yr. TV; cable. Complimentary full bkfst. Restaurant nearby. Ck-out 11 am, ck-in 3-6 pm. In-rm modem link. Some balconies. Picnic table. An 1830 Federal-style house near the Essex River; antique furnishings. Totally nonsmoking. Cr cds: A, C, D, DS, MC, V.

⬜ 🔥

✔★ **THE MANOR.** *141 Essex Ave (MA 133). 978/283-0614.* 11 rms in 3-story manor, 4 share bath; 16 motel rms. Late June-early Sept: D $69-$110; lower rates Apr-late June, early Sept-Oct. Closed rest of yr. Crib $5. Pet accepted; $5. TV. Complimentary continental bkfst (in season). Restaurant nearby. Ck-out 11 am, ck-in 1 pm. Victorian manor house; sitting rm. Some rms overlook river. Cr cds: A, DS, MC, V.

🐾 ⬜ 🔥 SC

★ ★ **OCEAN VIEW INN.** *171 Atlantic Rd. 978/283-6200; FAX 978/283-1852; res: 800/315-7557 (exc MA), 800/283-6200 (MA).* E-mail oviar@shore.net; web www.oceanviewinnandresort.com. 63 rms, 3 story. May-Oct: S, D $69-$190; lower rates rest of yr. Crib $10. Pet accepted. TV; cable, VCR avail. 2 heated pools. Restaurants 7 am-9:30 pm. Ck-out 11 am, ck-in 2 pm. Meeting rms. Business servs avail. In-rm modem link. Luggage handling. Rec rm. Lawn games. Some balconies. On ocean. Several buildings have accommodations, including turn-of-the-century English manor house. Cr cds: A, C, D, DS, MC, V.

🅳 🐾 〰 ⬜ 🔥 SC

Restaurants

✔★ **CAMERON'S.** *206 Main St. 978/281-1331.* Specializes in native seafood, prime rib, Italian sautéed specialties. Hrs: 11 am-10 pm; Sat, Sun 8 am-10 pm. Closed Dec 25. Res accepted. Bar to 1 am. Semi-a la carte: lunch $3.95-$7.95, dinner $6.95-$12.95. Child's meals. Entertainment Wed-Sun. Family owned since 1936. Cr cds: A, DS, MC, V.

🅳

★ ★ **GLOUCESTER HOUSE.** *MA 127 at Waterfront, Seven Seas Wharf. 978/283-1812.* Specializes in seafood. Hrs: 11:30 am-10 pm; winter hrs vary. Closed Thanksgiving, Dec 25. Res accepted. Bar. A la carte entrees: lunch $5.95-$11.95, dinner $9.95-$21.95. Child's meals. Entertainment Thurs-Sun. Outdoor dining. Gift shop. Nautical decor; view of fishing harbor. Family-owned since 1958. Cr cds: A, C, D, DS, MC, V.

🅳

★ ★ **WHITE RAINBOW.** *65 Main St. 978/281-0017.* Continental menu. Specialties: Maui onion soup, sautéed lobster, seafood skewer. Hrs: 5:30-9:30 pm; Sat 6-10 pm. Closed Dec 24, 25; also Mon mid-Sept-June. Res accepted. Bar. Wine list. Semi-a la carte: dinner $17.95-$22.95. A la carte entrees: dinner $8.50-$11.95. In 1830 landmark building. Cr cds: A, C, D, DS, MC, V.

🅳

Great Barrington (C-2)

Settled 1726 **Pop** 7,725 **Elev** 721 ft **Area code** 413 **Zip** 01230 **E-mail** sbcoc@juno.com **Web** www.greatbarrington.org

Information Southern Berkshire Chamber of Commerce, 362 Main St; 413/528-1510 or 413/528-4006.

As early as 1774, the people of Great Barrington rose up against the King, seizing the courthouse. Today Great Barrington is the shopping center of the southern Berkshire resort country. Writer, professor and lawyer James

Weldon Johnson, cofounder of the NAACP, and W.E.B. du Bois, black author and editor, lived here. Another resident, the poet William Cullen Bryant, was the town clerk for 13 years.

What to See and Do

Beartown State Forest. Swimming; fishing, hunting; boating. Bridle, hiking trails. Snowmobiling; picnicking; camping. Standard fees. Approx 5 mi E on MA 23. Phone 413/528-0904.

Colonel Ashley House (1735). Elegance of home reflects Col. Ashley's prominent place in his society. One political meeting he held here produced the Sheffield Declaration, forerunner to Declaration of Independence. Period furnishings. Adj to Bartholowmew's Cobble. (July-Aug, Wed-Sun; Memorial Day-June & Sept-Columbus Day, wkends; also open Mon hols) 9 mi S via MA 7 & 7A to Ashley Falls, then 1/2 mi on Rannapo Rd to Cooper Hill Rd. Phone 413/229-8600. ¢¢

Skiing.

Butternut Basin. Triple, 5 double chairlifts, Pomalift, rope tow; patrol, school, rentals, snowmaking; nursery (wkends & hols after Dec 26); cafeterias; wine rm; electronically-timed slalom race course. Longest run 1.8 mi; vertical drop 1,000 ft. (Dec-Mar, daily) Also 7 mi of cross-country skiing; rentals. 2 mi E on MA 23. Phone 413/528-2000 or 800/438-SNOW. ¢¢¢¢

Otis Ridge. Double chairlift, T-bar, J-bar, 3 rope tows; patrol, school, rentals; snowmaking; cafeteria. Night skiing (Tues-Sat). Longest run 1 mi; vertical drop 400 ft. (Dec-Mar, daily) 16 mi E on MA 23. Phone 413/269-4444. ¢¢¢¢¢

Catamount. 7 mi W on NY 23 (see HILLSDALE, NY).

Annual Event

Berkshire Craft Fair. Monument Mt Regional High School. Juried fair with more than 100 artisans. Phone 413/528-3346, ext 28. Early Aug.

Motels

★ **BARRINGTON COURT.** *400 Stockbridge Rd, 1 mi N on US 7.* 413/528-2340. 23 rms, 2 story, 2 kit. suites. Late June-Labor Day: S, D $75-$115; each addl $5; kit. suites $175-$200; higher rates wkends in June-Aug (2-day min); lower rates rest of yr. Crib $10. TV; cable. Pool. Playground. Complimentary coffee in rms. Restaurant nearby. Ck-out 11 am. Downhill/x-country ski 2 mi. Lawn games. Refrigerators. Balconies. Cr cds: A, MC, V.

[symbols]

★ **LANTERN HOUSE.** *254 Stockbridge Rd.* 413/528-2350; res: 800/959-2350; FAX 413/528-0435. 14 rms. July-Aug: S, D $70-$140; wkends 3-day min; lower rates rest of yr. TV; cable, VCR avail. Complimentary coffee in lobby. Restaurant adj 6 am-10 pm. Pool. Cr cds: DS, MC, V.

[symbol]

✔★ **MONUMENT MOUNTAIN.** *249 Stockbridge Rd, 1 mi N on US 7.* 413/528-3272; FAX 413/528-3132. 18 rms. July-Oct: S, D $55-$115; each addl $5-$10; wkend rates; ski plans; lower rates rest of yr. TV; cable. Pool. Playground. Complimentary coffee in rms. Restaurant nearby. Ck-out 11 am. Business servs avail. Lighted tennis. Downhill/x-country ski 3 mi. Lawn games. Picnic tables, grills. 20 acres on river. Cr cds: A, C, D, DS, MC, V.

[symbols]

Inns

★★ **EGREMONT.** *(Old Sheffield Rd, South Egremont 01258) 3 mi SW off MA 23.* 413/528-2111; FAX 413/528-3284; res: 800/859-1780. Web www.egremontinn.com. 19 rms, 4 story. July-Aug (2-day min): S, D $90-$400; suites $125-$450; ski plans; lower rates rest of yr. Crib avail. TV in sitting rm. Pool. Complimentary continental bkfst. Dining rm 5:30-9:30 pm. Ck-out 11 am, ck-in 2 pm. Business servs avail. Tennis. Downhill/x-

country ski 3 mi. Antiques. Library/sitting rm. Some in-rm whirlpools. Sun porch. Built 1780; originally a stagecoach stop. Cr cds: A, DS, MC, V.

★★ **RACE BROOK LODGE.** *(864 S Under Mountain Rd, Sheffield 01257) Approx 9 mi S on MA 41.* 413/229-2916; res: 888/725-6343; FAX 413/229-6629. E-mail rblodge@bcn.net; web www.rblodge.com. 21 rms, some with shower only, 3 story. No rm phones. June-Aug: S, D $105-$145; each addl $15; under 5 free; min stay wkends (summer); lower rates rest of yr. Pet accepted, some restrictions. TV; cable in common rm. Complimentary full bkfst. Restaurant adj 5:30-9:30 pm. Bar. Ck-out 11 am, ck-in 2-3 pm. Meeting rm. Downhill/x-country ski 7 mi. Lawn games. Barn built in 1790s. Rustic decor. Totally nonsmoking. Cr cds: A, MC, V.

[symbols]

★★ **THORNEWOOD.** *453 Stockbridge Rd, Jct MA 7 & MA 183.* 413/528-3828; res: 800/854-1008; FAX 413/528-3307. Web www.thornewood.com. 10 rms, 2 story. June-Aug: S, D $75-$195; each addl $15; hol rates; higher rates: summer, foliage season; lower rates rest of yr. Children over 12 yrs only. TV; cable. Pool. Complimentary full bkfst. Restaurant (see SPENCER'S). Ck-out 11:30 am, ck-in 3 pm. Business servs avail. Downhill/x-country ski 2 mi. Antiques. Tap room. Built 1919. Cr cds: A, DS, MC, V.

[symbols]

★★★ **WINDFLOWER.** *684 S Egremont Rd, 3 mi W of US 7 on MA 23.* 413/528-2720; FAX 413/528-5147; res: 800/992-1993. E-mail wndflowr@windflowerinn.com; web www.windflowerinn.com. 13 rms. No rm phones. S, D $100-$170. Crib avail. TV. Pool. Complimentary full bkfst. Ck-out 11 am, ck-in 2 pm. Business servs avail. Downhill ski 4 mi; x-country ski adj. Rec rm. Some fireplaces. Many antiques. Golf course adj. On 10 acres. Cr cds: A.

[symbols]

Restaurants

★★★ **CASTLE STREET CAFE.** *10 Castle St.* 413/528-5244. Continental menu. Specializes in grilled fresh fish, grilled steak, pasta. Hrs: 5-9:30 pm; Fri, Sat to 10:30 pm. Closed Tues; Thanksgiving, Dec 25. Bar. Wine cellar. A la carte entrees: dinner $9-$22. Intimate, sophisticated bistro atmosphere. Entertainment. Totally nonsmoking. Cr cds: A, DS, MC, V.

[D symbol]

✔★ **JODI'S.** *327 Stockbridge Rd.* 413/528-6064. Italian menu. Specializes in fresh fish, fresh pasta, steaks. Hrs: 8 am-10 pm. Res accepted. Bar. Semi-a la carte: bkfst $1.95-$6.95, lunch $3.95-$8.95, dinner $12.95-$20.95. Child's meals. Entertainment wkends June-Oct. Porch dining. Antique decor, original 250-yr-old bldg, hardwood floors. Cr cds: A, C, D, DS, JCB, MC, V.

[D symbol]

★★ **JOHN ANDREWS.** *(MA 23, South Egremont 01258) 6 mi S on MA 23.* 413/528-3469. Specialties: napoleon of grilled shrimp, crisp duck confit. Hrs: 5-10 pm. Closed Wed Sept-June. Bar. Wine list. Semi-a la carte: dinner $13-$22. Child's meals. Outdoor dining. View of gardens. Cr cds: MC, V.

★★ **THE OLD MILL.** *(South Egremont 01258) 4 mi W on MA 23.* 413/528-1421. Continental, Amer menu. Specialties: fresh filet of salmon, baby rack of lamb, sautéed calves liver with smoked bacon. Hrs: 5-9:30 pm; Fri, Sat to 10:30 pm; Sun brunch 11 am-2 pm. Closed Mon; Thanksgiving, Dec 25. Bar. Semi-a la carte: dinner $16-$24. Sun brunch $7.50-$14. Child's meals. Parking. In grist mill. Built in 1978. Cr cds: A, D, MC, V.

★★ **THE PAINTED LADY.** *785 S Main St.* 413/528-1662. Continental menu. Specializes in fresh seafood, pasta, veal. Hrs: 5 pm-closing; Sun from 4 pm. Closed Dec 24, 25. Res accepted. Bar. Semi-a la carte:

dinner $12.95-$22.95. Child's meals. Formal, intimate dining in Victorian house. Cr cds: DS, MC, V.

★ ★ ★ **SPENCER'S.** *(See Thornewood Inn) 413/528-3828.* Continental, Amer menu. Specializes in fresh seafood, salads. Own desserts. Hrs: from 5 pm; Sun brunch 10:30 am-2 pm. Closed Tues; Jan 1; also Mon, Wed (Sept-mid-June). Res accepted. Bar. Wine cellar. A la carte entrees: dinner $15-$20. Sun brunch $14.95. Jazz Sat, Sun brunch. Parking. Outdoor dining. Family-owned since 1977. Totally nonsmoking. Cr cds: A, D, MC, V.

Unrated Dining Spot

MARTIN'S. *49 Railroad St. 413/528-5455.* Specializes in omelets, soups. Hrs: 6 am-3 pm. Closed Jan 1, Dec 25. Semi-a la carte: bkfst $2.85-$5.50, lunch $2.50-$5.50. Child's meals. Informal atmosphere. Totally nonsmoking. No cr cds accepted.

[D]

Greenfield (A-3)

Settled 1686 **Pop** 18,666 **Elev** 250 ft **Area code** 413 **Zip** 01301 **E-mail** fccc@valinet.com **Web** www.co.franklin.ma.us
Information Franklin County Chamber of Commerce, 395 Main St, Box 898; 413/773-5463.

The center of a prosperous agricultural area, Greenfield is also the home of many factories and a center for winter and summer sports, hunting and fishing. The first cutlery factory in America was established in Greenfield in the early 19th century.

What to See and Do

Northfield Mountain Recreation and Environmental Center. On site of Northeast Utilities Hydro Electric Pumped storage plant. Bus tours to the upper reservoir and underground powerhouse (May-Oct). Hiking, camping, riverboat ride and picnicking. (Dec-Mar, Mon-Fri; May-Oct, Wed-Sun) Fee for some activities. MA 63 in Northfield. Phone 413/659-3714.

Annual Events

Green River Music & Balloon Festival. Hot-air balloon launches, craft show, musical entertainment, food. Phone 413/773-5463. July.

Franklin County Fair. 4 days starting 1st Thurs after Labor Day.

Motel

✔★ ★ **HOWARD JOHNSON.** *125 Mohawk Trail (MA 2A), 1 blk E of I-91 exit 26. 413/774-2211; FAX 413/772-2637.* 100 rms, 2 story. S $54-$84; D $58-$94; each addl $10; under 18 free; higher rates: special events, some wkends; lower rates rest of yr. Crib free. TV. Pool. Coffee in rms. Restaurant 6 am-10 pm; Fri, Sat to 2 am. Bar 11-1 am. Ck-out noon. Meeting rms. Valet serv. Sundries. Putting green, miniature golf. Downhill ski 20 mi; x-country ski 12 mi. Private patios, balconies. Cr cds: A, C, D, DS, ER, JCB, MC, V.

[D] [symbols] [SC]

Restaurants

★ ★ **ANDIAMO.** *(Huckle Hill Rd, Bernardston 01337) 8 mi N on I-91, exit 28A. Follow signs to top of mountain. 413/648-9107.* Web san dri.com. Northern Italian menu. Specializes in veal, pasta, steaks. Hrs: 5-9 pm. Closed Dec 24, 25. Res accepted. Bar. Semi-a la carte: dinner $12.95-$22.95. Entertainment Fri, Sat. Dining in greenhouse-style rm. Cr cds: A, D, DS, MC, V.

 [D] [symbol]

✔★ ★ **FAMOUS BILL'S.** *30 Federal St at Ames St. 413/773-9230.* Specializes in lobster, prime rib, seafood. Own desserts. Hrs: 11 am-close; Mon from 4 pm. Res accepted. Bar. Semi-a la carte: lunch $3.75-$11.95, dinner $6.95-$17.95. Child's meals. Family-owned. Cr cds: MC, V.

[D] [SC]

★ ★ **HERM'S.** *91 Main St. 413/772-6300.* Specializes in seafood, chicken, steak. Hrs: 11 am-9:30 pm; Fri, Sat to 10:30 pm. Closed Sun; Thanksgiving, Dec 25. Res accepted. Bar. Semi-a la carte: lunch, dinner $6.95-$15.95. Child's meals. Cr cds: A, DS, MC, V.

[D] [SC]

Harwich (Cape Cod) (D-10)

Settled ca 1670 **Pop** 10,275 **Elev** 55 ft **Area code** 508 **Zip** 02646 **E-mail** info@capecodchamber.org **Web** www.capecodchamber.org
Information Harwich Chamber of Commerce, PO Box 34, phone 508/432-1600; or the Cape Cod Chamber of Commerce, US 6 & MA 132, PO Box 790, Hyannis 02601-0790, phone, 508/362-3225 or 888/33-CAPECOD.

Harwich, whose namesake in England was dubbed "Happy-Go-Lucky Harwich" by Queen Elizabeth, is one of those towns made famous in New England literature. It is "Harniss" in the Joseph C. Lincoln novels of Cape Cod. A local citizen, Jonathan Walker, was immortalized as "the man with the branded hand" in Whittier's poem about helping escaped slaves; Enoch Crosby of Harwich was the Harvey Birch of James Fenimore Cooper's novel *The Spy*. Today, summer people own three-quarters of the land.

What to See and Do

Brooks Free Library. Houses 24 John Rogers' figurines. (Daily exc Sun; closed hols) 739 Main St, Harwich Center. Phone 508/430-7562.   **Free.**

Harwich Historical Society. Includes Brooks Academy Bldg and Revolutionary War Powder House. Native American artifacts, marine exhibit, cranberry industry articles, early newspapers and photographs. Site of one of the first schools of navigation in US. (Usually mid-June-mid-Sept, Thurs-Sun; schedule may vary) 80 Parallel St, at Sisson Rd, in Harwich Center. Phone 508/362-3225.   **Free.**

Red River Beach. A fine Nantucket Sound swimming beach (water 68° to 72°F in summer). Off MA 28, S on Uncle Venies Rd in South Harwich. Sticker fee per wkday ¢¢;   Wkends & hols ¢¢¢

Saquatucket Municipal Marina. Boat ramp for launching small craft. (May-mid-Nov) Off MA 28 at 715 Main St. Phone 508/432-2562. Daily ¢¢¢

Annual Event

Cranberry Harvest Festival. Family Day, antique car show, music, arts and crafts, fireworks, carnival, parade. Phone 508/432-1600 or 800/441-3199. 1 wk mid-Sept.

Seasonal Event

Harwich Junior Theatre. Plays for the family and children through high-school age. Res required. (July-Aug, daily; Sept-June, monthly) Willow & Division Sts, West Harwich. For schedule phone 508/432-2002.

Motels

★ **COACHMAN MOTOR LODGE.** *(MA 28, Harwich Port) 1 mi E of Harwich Port on MA 28. 508/432-0707; res: 800/524-4265.* 28 rms.

July-Aug: D $98-$110 (2-day min); each addl $10; apt for 4-5, $735; package plans off-season; lower rates Sept-mid-Nov, May-July. Closed rest of yr. Crib free. TV; cable (premium). Pool. Restaurant 7 am-midnight. Ck-out 11 am. Refrigerators avail. Cr cds: A, D, MC, V.

✔✱ HANDKERCHIEF SHOALS. *(MA 28, South Harwich 02661) on MA 28 at Deep Hole Rd.* 508/432-2200. 26 rms. No A/C. Late June-Labor Day: S, D $70-$78; each addl $8; lower rates mid-Apr-late June, after Labor Day-Oct. Closed rest of yr. Crib free. TV; cable. Pool. Restaurant nearby. Ck-out 11 am. Lawn games. Refrigerators, microwaves. Cr cds: DS, MC, V.

✔✱ SEA HEATHER INN AT TROY COURT. *(28 Sea St, Harwich Port) 1 blk S of MA 28.* 508/432-1275; FAX 508/432-1275; res: 800/789-7809. E-mail wlean60964@aol.com; web www.virtualcape-cod.com/market/seaheather. 20 rms, 1-2 story. Mid-June-mid-Sept: S, D $95-$175; each addl $15; lower rates rest of yr. Children over 10 yrs only. TV; cable. Complimentary continental bkfst. Restaurant nearby. Ck-out 11 am. Lawn games. Some refrigerators, microwaves. Early Amer decor; porches, ocean view. Near beach. Totally nonsmoking. Cr cds: A, MC, V.

★ ★ SEADAR INN BY THE SEA. *(Bank St & Braddock Lane, Harwich Port) 2 blks S of MA 28.* 508/432-0264; FAX 508/430-1965. 20 rms, 1-2 story. No A/C. Late June-Labor Day: D $75-$115; each addl $15; lower rates late May-late June, after Labor Day-mid-Oct. Closed rest of yr. TV; cable, VCR. Complimentary continental bkfst. Restaurant nearby. Ck-out 11 am. Business servs avail. In-rm modem link. Bellhops. Lawn games. Some refrigerators. Picnic tables, grill. Near beach. Main bldg old Colonial house (1789); early Amer decor; some rms with bay windows, ocean view. Cr cds: A, MC, V.

★ ★ WYCHMERE VILLAGE. *(767 Main St, Harwich Port) ³/₄ mi E of Harwich Port on MA 28.* 508/432-1434; res: 800/432-1434. 25 units, 2 A/C, 11 kits. Mid-June-mid-Sept: D $75-$85; each addl $10; kit. units $90-$130; cottage with kit. for 4, $850/wk; lower rates rest of yr. Crib $10. TV; cable. Heated pool. Playground. Coffee in lobby. Restaurant opp 7 am-noon. Ck-out 11 am. Lawn games. Refrigerators. Picnic tables, grill. Cr cds: DS, MC, V.

Inns

★ ★ AUGUSTUS SNOW HOUSE. *(528 Main St, Harwich Port)* 508/430-0528; res: 800/320-0528; FAX 508/432-7995. E-mail snowhouse1@aol.com; web www.augustussnow.com. 5 rms, some A/C, 2 story. Late May-mid-Oct: S, D $145-$160; wkends (2-day min); lower rates rest of yr. Children over 12 yrs only. TV; cable. Complimentary full bkfst; afternoon refreshments. Restaurant nearby. Ck-out 11 am, ck-in 2 pm. Luggage handling. Concierge serv. Free airport transportation. Some in-rm whirlpools. Built in 1901; Victorian decor. Totally nonsmoking. Cr cds: A, DS, MC, V.

★ ★ CAPE COD CLADDAGH INN. *(77 Main St (Rt 28), West Harwich 02671) 2¹/₂ mi W on MA 28.* 508/432-9628; FAX 508/432-6039; res: 800/356-9628. E-mail claddagh@capecodonramp.com; web www.virtualcapecod.com/market/claddagh. 8 rms, 6 with shower only, 3 story, 4 suites. No rm phones. Memorial Day-mid-Oct: S, D $95-$120; each addl $25; suites $110; wkly rates. Closed Jan-Mar. TV; cable (premium). Pool. Complimentary full bkfst. Dining rm 11:30-1 am. Ck-out 10:30 am, ck-in 2 pm. Coin lndry. Parking. Refrigerators. Picnic tables. Former Baptist parsonage (ca 1900). Antiques. Cr cds: A, DS, MC, V.

★ ★ COUNTRY INN. *(86 Sisson Rd, Harwich Port) 1 mi S on MA 124.* 508/432-2769; res: 800/231-1722. Web www.virtualcape cod./

com/market.countryinn. 6 rms, 2 story. No rm phones. Memorial Day-Columbus Day: S, D $75-$110; each addl $15; lower rates rest of yr. TV. Pool. Complimentary continental bkfst. Dining rm (by res) 5-9 pm. Ck-out 11 am, ck-in 2 pm. Built in 1780; Colonial decor; antiques. On 6 acres. Use of private beach. Cr cds: A, MC, V.

★ ★ ★ DUNSCROFT BY THE SEA. *(24 Pilgrim Rd, Harwich Port) MA 39 S to MA 28, then E, right turn before Congregational church.* 508/432-0810; FAX 508/432-5134; res: 800/432-4345. E-mail alyce @capecod.net; web www.dunscroftbythesea.om. 8 rms, 2 story, 1 cottage. Late May-Oct: S, D $105-$225; each addl $25; kit. unit $165-$225; lower rates rest of yr. Children over 12 yrs only. Complimentary full bkfst. Restaurants nearby. Ck-out 11 am, ck-in 2 pm. Whirlpool. Library/sitting rm; antiques. Near mile-long beach on Nantucket Sound. Cr cds: A, MC, V.

Restaurants

★ ★ BISHOP'S TERRACE. *(Main St, West Harwich 02645) 2 mi W on MA 28.* 508/432-0253. Specializes in swordfish, prime rib, lobster. Hrs: 4:30-9:30 pm; Sun brunch 11:30 am-2 pm. Res accepted. Bar 4:30 pm-1 am. Semi-a la carte: dinner $5.95-$25. Sun brunch $11.95. Child's meals. Entertainment (in-season, Sat only off-season). Glass-enclosed terrace dining. Restored colonial house. Antiques. Cr cds: MC, V.

★ ★ L'ALOUETTE. *(787 MA 28, Harwich Port) 2 mi E on MA 28.* 508/430-0405. French menu. Own baking. Menu changes frequently. Hrs: 5-10 pm. Closed Mon; Dec 25; also Feb. Res required. Serv bar. A la carte entrees: dinner $15-$22. Intimate French atmosphere. Cr cds: A, D, DS, MC, V.

Haverhill (A-7)

Settled 1640 **Pop** 51,418 **Elev** 27 ft **Area code** 978 **E-mail** info@chamber.mva.net **Web** www.chamber.mva.net

Information Chamber of Commerce, 87 Winter St, 01830; 978/373-5663.

Haverhill is a thriving manufacturing and commercial center located along the Merrimack River. Long known for its role in the manufacture of women's shoes, Haverhill now boasts a highly diversified high-tech industrial base. The city features fine neighborhoods of early 19th-century homes. The Quaker poet John Greenleaf Whittier was born here.

A statue at Winter and Main streets commemorates the remarkable Hannah Dustin, who, according to legend, was kidnapped by Native Americans in March, 1697, and escaped with the scalps of ten of her captors.

What to See and Do

Haverhill Historical Society. Located in The Buttonwoods, an early 19th-century house. Period furnishings, china, glass, Hannah Dustin relics, memorabilia from turn-of-the-century theaters, Civil War artifacts and archaeological collection. Also on grounds is the John Ward House (1641), furnished with colonial items; and an 1850s shoe factory with displays. Guided tours. (Wed, Thurs, also Sat & Sun afternoons) 240 Water St, MA 97. Phone 978/374-4626. ¢¢

John Greenleaf Whittier Birthplace. Whittier family homestead since the 17th century, this is the setting of his best known poems, including "Snow-Bound," and "Barefoot Boy." His writing desk and mother's bedrm, built over a rock too large to move, are here. The house is furnished with original pieces and arranged as it would have appeared in his childhood. Grounds (69 acres) still actively farmed. (Daily exc Mon; closed Jan 1, Thanksgiving, Dec 25) 305 Whittier Rd, I-495 to exit 52, 1 mi E on MA 110. Limited hrs in winter, phone for schedule; 978/373-3979. ¢

Motels

✔★ ★ **BEST WESTERN-MERRIMACK VALLEY LODGE.** 401 Lowell Ave (08132), at jct MA 110, 113, off I-495 exit 49. 978/373-1511; res: 888/645-2025; FAX 978/373-1517. 127 rms, 3 story. Apr-Oct: S $49-$99; D $49-$109; under 18 free; higher rates special events. Crib free. Pet accepted, some restrictions. TV; cable (premium). Indoor pool; whirlpool. Complimentary continental bkfst. Coffee in rms. Restaurant adj. Ck-out 11 am. Meeting rms. Business center. In-rm modem link. Valet serv. Coin lndry. Airport transportation. Some refrigerators; microwaves avail. Some private patios. Cr cds: A, C, D, DS, MC, V.

★ ★ **COMFORT SUITES.** 106 Bank Rd (01832), I-495 exit 49. 508/374-7755; FAX 508/521-1894; res: 800/228-5150. 131 suites, 4 story. S, D $79-$129; each addl $10; under 18 free. Crib free. TV; cable (premium). Complimentary continental bkfst. Complimentary coffee in rms. Restaurant nearby. Ck-out noon. Coin lndry. Meeting rms. Business servs avail. In-rm modem link. Valet serv. Exercise equipt. Whirlpool. Refrigerators. Cr cds: A, C, D, DS, ER, JCB, MC, V.

Holyoke (C-3)

(See also South Hadley, Springfield)

Settled 1745 **Pop** 43,704 **Elev** 270 ft **Area code** 413 **Zip** 01040
Information Greater Holyoke Chamber of Commerce, 177 High St; 413/534-3376.

Captain Elizur Holyoke explored the Connecticut Valley as early as 1633. His name is preserved in a rich and bustling industrial city made possible with the development of the great river by an unusual set of power canals.

What to See and Do

Holyoke Heritage State Park. Canalside park; visitor center features cultural, environmental and recreational programs, slide show and exhibits on the region and on Holyoke's history as a planned city, its canals, industries and people. Mt Park Merry-Go-Round also here (Sat & Sun afternoons; expanded summer hrs). Restored train cars run periodically (fee); inquire for schedule. (Wed-Sun afternoons; schedule may vary, phone ahead; closed Jan 1) Between Appleton & Dwight Sts. Phone 413/534-1723. **Free.** Also on the site and adj is

Children's Museum. Participatory museum. Exhibits include papermaking, sand pendulum, bubble making, TV studio, tot lot, "Cityscape," and other changing exhibits. (Daily exc Mon) 444 Dwight St. Phone 413/536-KIDS. ¢¢

Mt Tom Ski Area & SummerSide. 13 slopes and trails; 3 double chairlifts, 2 T-bars, J-bar, halfpipe; snowmaking; school, patrol, ski shop, rentals; cafeteria, snack bar, restaurant. Longest run 3,600 ft; vertical drop 680 ft. (Mid-Dec-mid-Mar, daily) SummerSide includes wave pool, 4,000-ft alpine slide, 400-ft water slide, chairlift to 5-state view. (Mid-June-Labor Day, daily; Memorial Day-mid-June & early Sept-fall, wkends) 2 mi N on US 5 off I-91. Phone 413/536-0416. ¢¢¢¢-¢¢¢¢¢

Wistariahurst Museum. Victorian mansion, family home of noted silk manufacturer William Skinner. House highlights include interior architectural detail unique to late 19th and early 20th centuries, including a leather-paneled room, conservatory and music hall; period furniture, decorative arts. Textile and archival collections available for research scholars. Changing exhibits. Carriage house has collection of Native American materials and natural history. (Wed, Sat, Sun afternoons; schedule may vary) 238 Cabot St. Phone 413/534-2216. ¢

Motor Hotel

★ ★ **HOLIDAY INN CONFERENCE CENTER.** 245 Whiting Farms Rd, off I-91 exit 15. 413/534-3311; FAX 413/533-8443. 219 rms, 4 story. S $76-$80; D $86-$90; each addl $10; family rates; higher rates some college events. Crib free. Pet accepted; $25. TV; cable. Indoor pool; whirlpool, poolside serv. Restaurant 6:30 am-10 pm. Rm serv. Bar 11:30-2 am; entertainment Tues-Sat. Meeting rms. Bellhops. Concierge. Downhill ski 3 mi. Exercise equipt; sauna. Game rm. Luxury level. Cr cds: A, C, D, DS, JCB, MC, V.

Inn

✔★ **YANKEE PEDLAR.** 1866 Northampton (US 5), at jct US 202. 413/532-9494; FAX 413/536-8877. 28 rms in 4 houses, 4 kit. units. S, D $70-$125; wkly, monthly rates. Crib avail. TV; cable. Complimentary continental bkfst. Restaurant (see YANKEE PEDLAR). Bar 11:30 am-1 am; entertainment Thurs-Sat evenings. Ck-out 11 am, ck-in 2 pm. Health-club privileges. Cr cds: A, C, D, MC, V.

Restaurants

★ ★ ★ **DELANY HOUSE.** 5 mi N on MA 5 at Smith's Ferry. 413/532-1800. Specializes in fresh seafood, game. Own pastries & ice cream. Hrs: 5-9:30 pm; Fri, Sat to 10 pm; Sun 1-7 pm. Closed Jan 1, Dec 25. Res accepted. Bar 3:30-11 pm. Wine cellar. Semi-a la carte: dinner $12-$23. Child's meals. Valet parking. Patio dining. Late 18th-century furnishings. Cr cds: A, C, D, DS, MC, V.

D

★ ★ ★ **YANKEE PEDLAR.** (See Yankee Pedlar Inn) 413/532-9494. Specializes in fresh fish, veal, beef. Own baking. Hrs: 7 am-9 pm; Sat, Sun 7 am-10 pm; Sun brunch 10 am-2 pm. Closed Dec 25. Bar 11:30-1 am. Semi-a la carte: lunch $3.75-$12.50, dinner $8.95-$19.95. Sun brunch $13.95. Outdoor dining. Entertainment Thurs-Sat evenings. Cr cds: A, C, D, MC, V.

D

Hyannis (Cape Cod) (D-9)

(See also Martha's Vineyard, South Yarmouth)

Settled 1639 **Pop** 14,120 **Elev** 19 ft **Area code** 508 **Zip** 02601
Information Chamber of Commerce, 1481 Rte 132; 508/362-5230 or 800/FOR-HYNNIS.

Hyannis is the main vacation and transportation center of Cape Cod. Recreational facilities and specialty areas abound, including tennis courts, golf courses, arts and crafts galleries, theaters and antique shops. There are libraries, museums, the Kennedy Memorial and Compound. Candlemaking tours are available. Scheduled airliners and Amtrak stop here, and it is also a port for boat trips to Nantucket Island and Martha's Vineyard. More than six million people visit the village every year, and it is within an hour's drive of the many attractions on the Cape.

What to See and Do

Auto ferry service. Woods Hole, Martha's Vineyard and Nantucket Steamship Authority conducts trips to Nantucket from Hyannis (yr-round); departs from South St dock. For schedule, res phone 508/540-2022.

Hyannis-Nantucket or Martha's Vineyard Day Round Trip. (May-Oct) Also hrly sightseeing trips to Hyannis Port (late Apr-Oct, daily); all-day or

¹/₂-day deep-sea fishing excursions (late Apr-mid-Oct, daily). Hy-Line, Pier #1, Ocean St Dock. For schedule, information phone 508/778-2600. Harbor/sightseeing trips ¢¢¢; Fishing/ferry ¢¢¢¢¢

John F. Kennedy Hyannis Museum. Photographic exhibits focusing on President Kennedy's relationship with Cape Cod; 7-min video presentation. Gift shop. (Mon-Sat, also Sun afternoons) 397 Main St, in Old Town Hall. Phone 508/362-5230. ¢

John F. Kennedy Memorial. Circular fieldstone wall memorial 12 ft high with presidential seal, fountain and small pool honors late president who grew up nearby. Ocean St.

Swimming. Craigville Beach. SW of town center. **Sea St Beach.** Sea St. Overlooking Hyannis Port harbor, bathhouse. **Kalmus Park.** Ocean St, bathhouse. **Veteran's Park.** Ocean St. Picnicking at Kalmus and Veteran's Parks. Parking fee at all beaches.

Annual Event

Hyannis Harbor Festival. Waterfront at Bismore Park. Coast Guard cutter tours, sailboat races, marine displays, food, entertainment. Phone 508/362-5230 or 508/775-2201. Wkend early June.

Seasonal Event

Cape Cod Melody Tent. Summer musical theater in-the-round, daily; children's theater. 21 W Main St. Phone 508/775-9100. Wed morning, July-early Sept.

Motels

✔★ **BUDGET HOST.** MA 132, 1 blk W of jct MA 28, 132. 508/775-8910; FAX 508/775-6476. E-mail hymotel@capecodnet. 40 rms, 2 story, 8 kits. Late June-Labor Day: D $55-$85; each addl $10; under 17 free; lower rates rest of yr. Crib free. TV; cable (premium). Pool. Complimentary coffee in rms. Restaurant adj open 11:30 am-midnight. Ck-out 11 am. Refrigerators. Cr cds: A, C, D, DS, MC, V.

D ≈ ⊻ 🔥

★★ **CAPTAIN GOSNOLD HOUSE.** 230 Gosnold St. 508/775-9111. 36 units, 16 kits., 18 kit. cottages. Some A/C. Many rm phones. Late June-Labor Day: D $75; each addl $10; kit. units $95; cottages (1-3 bedrm) $150-$260; under 5 free; lower rates mid-Apr-mid-June, Labor Day-Nov. Closed rest of yr. Crib free. TV; cable, VCR avail (free movies). Pool; lifeguard. Playground. Restaurant nearby. Ck-out 10:30 am. Lawn games. Refrigerators, microwaves. Picnic tables, grills. Cr cds: MC, V.

≈ 🔥 SC

✔★ **COUNTRY LAKE.** 1545 Rte 132, Iyanough Rd, 2¹/₂ mi NW on MA 132, ³/₄ mi S of exit 6. 508/362-6455; FAX 508/362-8050. E-mail cllholtco@aol.com; web www.sunsul.com/countrylake. 20 rms, 5 kit. units (no ovens). Mid-June-early Sept: S, D $69-$99; kit. units $79-$99; lower rates mid-Apr-mid-June, early Sept-Oct. Closed rest of yr. Crib free. TV; cable. Heated pool. Ck-out 11 am. Refrigerators. Picnic tables, grills. On lake. Cr cds: A, DS, MC, V.

🏊 ≈ ⊻ 🔥 SC

★★ **DAYS INN.** 867 Iyanough Rd (MA 132). 508/771-6100; res: 800/368-4667; FAX 508/775-3011. Web www.sunsol.com/daysinn/. 99 rms, 2 story. June-Sept: S, D $120-$165; each addl $8; under 17 free; lower rates rest of yr. Crib free. TV; cable. 2 pools, 1 indoor; whirlpool, lifeguard. Complimentary continental bkfst. Restaurant opp open 24 hrs in season. Ck-out 11 am. In-rm modem link. Exercise equipt. Refrigerators. Balconies. Cr cds: A, C, D, DS, MC, V.

D ≈ ⊼ ⊻ 🔥 SC

★ **HOWARD JOHNSON.** 447 Main St, near Barnstable County Airport. 508/775-3000; FAX 508/771-1457; res: 800/446-4656. 39 rms, 2 story. July-Labor Day: S, D $95-$120; under 18 free; higher rates hol wkends; lower rates rest of yr. Crib $10. TV; cable. Indoor pool;

whirlpool. Restaurant 1-4 pm. Bar 10-1 am. Ck-out 11 am. Business servs avail. Refrigerators avail. Cr cds: A, D, DS, MC, V.

≈ ⊻ 🔥 SC

★★★ **INTERNATIONAL INN.** 662 Main St. 508/775-5600; FAX 508/775-3933. E-mail info@cuddles.com; web www.cuddles.com. 141 rms, 2 story. June-Sept: S, D $100; each addl $16; suites $140-$210; lower rates rest of yr. Crib $10. TV; cable, VCR. 2 pools, 1 indoor; lifeguard. Restaurant 7-11 am, 5-9 pm. Bar 5-10 pm. Ck-out 11 am. Business servs avail. In-rm modem link. Sauna. In-rm whirlpools; some bathrm phones. Cr cds: C, D, DS, MC, V.

D ≈ ⊻ 🔥

★★ **QUALITY INN.** 1470 MA 132. 508/771-4804; FAX 508/790-2336. 104 rms, 3 story. No elvtr. June-mid-Sept: S $108; D $118; under 18 free; higher rates wkends, hols; lower rates rest of yr. Crib free. TV; cable (premium). Indoor pool; whirlpool, lifeguard. Complimentary continental bkfst. Restaurant nearby. Ck-out noon. Meeting rms. Business servs avail. Sundries. Sauna. Health club privileges. Refrigerators, microwaves avail. Cr cds: A, C, D, DS, MC, V.

D ≈ ⊻ 🔥 SC

Motor Hotels

★★★ **FOUR POINTS BY SHERATON.** MA 132, 1 mi NW on MA 132, at Bearse's Way. 508/771-3000; FAX 508/771-6564; res: 800/843-8272. Web www.sheraton.com. 261 rms, 2 story. Memorial Day-Labor Day: S, D $99-$169; suites $275; wkend rates rest of yr. Crib free. TV; cable (premium), VCR avail. Heated pool; whirlpool. Coffee in rms. Restaurant 7 am-11:30 pm. Rm serv to 10 pm. Bar 11-1 am, Sun from noon; seasonal entertainment. Ck-out 11 am. Meeting rms. Business servs avail. In-rm modem link. Sundries. Gift shop. Airport transportation. Game rm. Tennis. Exercise equipt. Private patios, balconies. Cr cds: A, C, D, DS, MC, V.

D 🏃 ≈ ⊼ ✈ ⊻ 🔥 SC

★★ **HERITAGE HOUSE.** 259 Main St. 508/775-7000; FAX 508/778-5687; res: 800/352-7189. Web www.capeheritagehotel.com. 143 rms, 3 story. July 4-Labor Day: D $75-$125; each addl $12; under 16 free; package plans; lower rates rest of yr. Crib free. TV; cable (premium). 2 pools, 1 indoor; whirlpool, lifeguard. Restaurant 7-10 am. Ck-out 11 am. Meeting rms. Sauna. Balconies. Cr cds: A, C, D, DS, MC, V.

≈ ✈ ⊻ 🔥 SC

★★ **RAMADA.** 1127 US 132, MA 132. 508/775-1153; res: 800/676-0000; FAX 508/775-1169. E-mail info@ccrh.com; web www.ccrh.com. 196 rms, 2 story. July-Sept: S, D $99-$159; each addl $10; suites $119-$199; higher rates hols; lower rates rest of yr. Crib free. TV; cable. Indoor pool; lifeguard. Restaurant 7 am-10 pm. Rm serv. Bar noon-1 am. Ck-out 11 am. Meeting rms. Business servs avail. Concierge. Game rm. Balconies. Cr cds: A, C, D, DS, MC, V.

D ≈ ⊻ 🔥 SC

Inns

✔★★ **SEA BREEZE.** 397 Sea St. 508/771-7213; FAX 508/862-0663. E-mail seabreeze@capecod.net; web www.seabreezeinn.com. 14 rms, 2 cottages, 2 story. Mid-June-Labor Day: D $75-$110; each addl $10; kit. unit $69; cottages $95-$150; wkly rates; lower rates rest of yr. TV; cable. Complimentary continental bkfst. Restaurant nearby. Ck-out 10:30 am, ck-in 2:30 pm. Concierge. Microwaves avail. Picnic tables. Antiques. Sitting rm. Near beach; some rms with ocean view. Cr cds: A, DS, MC, V.

≈ 🔥

★★ **SIMMONS HOMESTEAD.** (288 Scudder Ave, Hyannis Port 02647) ¹/₂ mi W on Main St to Scudder Ave. 508/778-4999; FAX 508/790-1342; res: 800/637-1649. E-mail simmonsinn@aol.com; web www.capecod.com/simmonsinn. 14 rms, 2 story. No rm phones. May-Oct: D $150-$200; each addl $20; suite $300; wkly rates; lower rates rest of yr. Crib free. Pet accepted. TV in sitting rm; cable. Complimentary full bkfst.

Restaurant nearby. Ck-out 11 am, ck-in 1 pm. Business servs avail. Concierge. Lawn games. Rec rm. Bicycles. Health club privileges. Balconies. Restored sea captain's home built in 1820; some canopied beds, fireplaces. Unique decor; all rms have different animal themes. Library; antiques. Cr cds: A, DS, MC, V.

Resort

★ ★ ★ **SHERATON.** *35 Scudder Ave, W End Circle.* 508/775-7775; FAX 508/790-4221; res: 800/825-3535. Web www.sheraton.com. 224 rms, 2 story. June-Labor Day: S, D $119-$179; each addl $15; under 17 free; MAP avail; golf, wknd rates; lower rates rest of yr. Crib free. TV; cable. 2 pools, 1 indoor; whirlpool, lifeguard, poolside serv in season. Playground. Supervised child's activities (in season); ages 4-13. Coffee in rms. Dining rms 7-11 am, noon-3 pm, 5-10 pm. Snack bar. Rm serv. Bar 11-1 am. Ck-out 11 am, ck-in 4 pm. Meeting rms. Business center. In-rm modem link. Bellhops. Concierge. Gift shop. Spa. Airport transportation. Lighted tennis. 18-hole par 3 golf, greens fee $20-$30, pro, putting green. Lawn games. Soc dir; entertainment, movies. Game rm. Exercise rm; sauna, steam rm. Private patios, balconies. Picnic tables. Cr cds: A, C, D, DS, MC, V.

Restaurants

✔★ **DRAGON LITE.** *620 Main St.* 508/775-9494. Chinese menu. Specialties: beef and chicken Szechuan, coconut shrimp, Mongolian beef. Hrs: 11:30-1 am. Closed Thanksgiving. Res accepted. Bar. Semi-a la carte: lunch $4-$6, dinner $5-$15. Street parking. Chinese decor. Cr cds: A, D, MC, V.

★ **THE EGG & I.** *521 Main St.* 508/771-1596. Specializes in crow's nest eggs, original bkfsts. Hrs: 11-1 pm. Closed Dec-Feb; wkends only Mar, Nov. Res accepted. Semi-a la carte: bkfst $2-$10. Child's meals. Street parking. Family dining. Cr cds: A, C, D, DS, MC, V.

★ **THE ORIGINAL GOURMET BRUNCH.** *517 Main St.* 508/771-2558. Web www.capecod.com. Hrs: 7 am-3 pm. Closed Thanksgiving, Dec 25. Wine, beer. Semi-a la carte: bkfst, lunch $2.95-$8. Street parking. Casual dining spot. No cr cds accepted.

★ ★ **PADDOCK.** *W Main St at W End Rotary.* 508/775-7677. Web www.virtualcapecod.com/the paddock. Specializes in fresh local seafood, roast L.I. duckling. Hrs: 11:30 am-2:30 pm, 5-10 pm. Closed mid-Nov-Apr 1. Res accepted. Bar noon-1 am. Wine list. Semi-a la carte: lunch $4.95-$9.50, dinner $13.95-$24.95. Child's meals. Pianist. Valet parking. Victorian decor. Family-owned. Cr cds: A, D, MC, V.

★ ★ **PENGUINS SEA GRILL.** *331 Main St.* 508/775-2023. Specializes in seafood, wood-grilled meat, pasta. Hrs: 5-11 pm; winter to 10 pm. Closed Thanksgiving, Dec 25. Res accepted. Bar. Semi-a la carte: dinner $14-$19. Child's meals. Cr cds: A, C, D, DS, MC, V.

★ ★ **RISTORANTE BAROLO.** *297 North St.* 508/778-2878. Italian menu. Specialties: antipasti, chicken saltinbocca. Hrs: 4 pm-midnight. Closed Jan 1, Easter, Dec 25. Res required. Bar to 1 am. Semi-a la carte: dinner $7.95-$21.95. Outdoor dining. Italian decor. Cr cds: A, C, D, MC, V.

★ ★ **ROADHOUSE CAFE.** *488 South St, 2 mi W on South St.* 508/775-2386. Continental menu. Specializes in grilled veal chop, cioppino, thin-crust pizza. Hrs: 4-10 pm. Closed Dec 24, 25. Res accepted. Bar

to 1 am. Semi-a la carte: dinner $5.95-$22.95. Entertainment. Valet parking. In 1903 house. Cr cds: A, C, D, DS, MC, V.

✔★ **SAM DIEGO'S.** *950 Iyanough Rd (MA 132), 1 1/2 mi W on MA 132.* 508/771-8816. Mexican menu. Specialties: fajitas, enchiladas, barbecue baby-back ribs. Own baking. Hrs: 11:30 am-midnight. Closed Easter, Thanksgiving, Dec 25. Bar to 1 am. Semi-a la carte: lunch $2.95-$5.95, dinner $6.95-$12.95. Child's meals. Outdoor dining. Mexican decor. Cr cds: A, DS, MC, V.

✔★ **STARBUCK'S.** *645 MA 132.* 508/778-6767. Specializes in hamburgers, fish, Mexican dishes. Hrs: 11:30-1 am. Closed Dec 25. Res accepted. Bar. Semi-a la carte: lunch, dinner $5.95-$12.95. Child's meals. Entertainment. Parking. Outdoor dining. Coney Island beach house decor. Cr cds: A, C, D, DS, MC, V.

Unrated Dining Spot

BARBYANN'S. *120 Airport Rd.* 508/775-9795. Specializes in hamburgers, prime rib, seafood. Hrs: 11:30 am-11 pm; wkends from 11 am; Sun brunch 11 am-3 pm. Closed Thanksgiving, Dec 25. Bar. Semi-a la carte: lunch $3.95-$6.95, dinner $6.95-$12.95. Sun brunch $3.95-$6.95. Child's meals. Parking. Outdoor dining. Antique toys. Cr cds: A, C, D, DS, MC, V.

Ipswich (A-8)

(See also Boston, Gloucester)

Settled 1633 **Pop** 11,873 **Elev** 50 ft **Area code** 508 **Zip** 01938
Information Ipswich Visitors Center-Hall Haskell House, S Main St, next to Town Hall; 508/356-8540.

Ipswich is a summer resort town and home of the Ipswich clam; it has beaches nearby and a countryside of rolling woodland. Historically, Ipswich claims to have been the nation's first lacemaking town, the birthplace of the US hosiery industry and of the American independence movement. In 1687 the Reverend John Wise rose in a meeting and denounced taxation without representation. His target was the hated Sir Edmund Andros, the British Colonial governor.

Andros and the lace are gone, but Ipswich retains the aura of its past. Besides a fine green, it has nearly 50 houses built before 1725, many from the 17th century.

What to See and Do

Crane Beach. Among the best on the Atlantic coast; 5 mi of beach; lifeguards, bathhouses, refreshment stand, trail. (Daily) End of Argilla Rd, on Ipswich Bay. Phone 508/356-4354. Per vehicle ¢¢¢; Summer wkends ¢¢¢¢

The John Whipple House (1640). Contains 17th- and 18th-century furniture; garden. (May-mid-Oct, Wed-Sat, also Sun afternoons; closed hols) 53 S Main St, on MA 1A. Phone 508/356-2811. ¢¢ Opp is

John Heard House (1795). Bought as memorial to Thomas F. Waters, house has Chinese furnishings from the China sea trade. (Schedule same as Whipple House) 40 S Main St. Combination fee for both houses ¢¢

Annual Event

Old Ipswich Days. Arts and crafts exhibits, games, clambakes, entertainment. Late July.

Motel

★★ **COUNTRY GARDEN INN & MOTEL.** *(101 Main St, Rowley 01969) 3 mi N on MA 1A. 978/948-7773; res: 800/287-7773; FAX 978/948-7947.* E-mail reserve@gardenmotel.com; web www.countrygarden_motel.com. 19 rms, 12 with shower only, 1-3 story, 4 suites. No elvtr. May-Oct: S $65; D $75; each addl $15; suites $135; under 12 free; hols 2-day min; lower rates rest of yr. Children over 12 yrs only. Crib avail. TV; cable (premium), VCR avail (movies). Complimentary coffee in rms. Ck-out 10 am, ck-in after 1 pm. Business servs avail. X-country ski 2 mi. Lawn games. Some in-rm whirlpools, refrigerators, fireplaces. Picnic tables. Built in 1901. Cr cds: A, DS, MC, V.

Inn

★★★ **MILES RIVER COUNTRY INN.** *(823 Bay Rd (MA 1A), Hamilton 01936) 3 mi S on MA 1A. 978/468-7206.* E-mail milesriver@mediaone.net; web www.milesriver.com. 8 rms, 2 share bath, 2 with shower only, 3 story. No A/C. No elvtr. No rm phones. June-Oct: S, D $90-$165; each addl $15; suite $210; lower rates rest of yr. Crib $15. Complimentary full bkfst. Restaurant nearby. Ck-out 11 am, ck-in 3 pm. Many fireplaces. Built in 1790s; Colonial American decor, antiques. Totally nonsmoking. Cr cds: A, MC, V.

Restaurants

✔★★★ **1640 HART HOUSE.** *51 Linebrook Rd. 978/356-9411.* Web www.com/harthouse. Specialties: deep dish escargot, grilled boneless duck breast. Hrs: 11:30 am-3 pm, 4-9 pm; Fri to 10 pm; Sat 4-10 pm; early-bird dinner 4-6 pm. Closed Dec 25. Res accepted. Bar to midnight. Semi-a la carte: lunch $5-$11, dinner $10-$17. Child's meals. Entertainment Fri, Sat. Parking. Serving food since 1700s. Cr cds: A, DS, MC, V.

★ **MILLSTONE.** *108 County Rd (MA 1A), 1 mi S on MA 1A. 978/356-2772.* Specializes in seafood. Own baking. Hrs: 11:30 am-9 pm; Fri to 10 pm; Sat 7 am-10 pm; Sun 7 am-9 pm. Res accepted. Bar. Semi-a la carte: bkfst $2.95-$4.95, lunch $4.95-$7.95, dinner $6.50-$26.95. Child's meals. Cr cds: A, MC, V.

✔★★ **STEEP HILL GRILL.** *40 Essex Rd. 978/356-1121.* Eclectic menu. Specializes in seasonal cuisine. Hrs: 5-9:30 pm; Thurs-Sat to 10 pm. Closed Mon; also some major hols. Res accepted. Bar. Semi-a la carte: dinner $13.95-$17.95. Child's meals. Parking. Colonial tavern decor. Cr cds: A, D, DS, MC, V.

Lawrence (A-7)

Founded 1847 **Pop** 70,207 **Elev** 50 ft **Area code** 508
Information Chamber of Commerce, 264 Essex St, 01840; 508/686-0900.

Lawrence was founded by a group of Boston financiers to tap the water power of the Merrimack River for the textile industry. As textiles moved out, diversified industries have been attracted to the community.

What to See and Do

Lawrence Heritage State Park. Twenty-three acres in city center include restored Campagnone Common; canal and riverside esplanades. Visitor center in a restored worker's boardinghouse has participatory exhibits on the worker's experiences with industry in Lawrence and their contribution to the city's vitality. (Daily; closed Jan 1, Thanksgiving, Dec 25) Canal St. Phone 508/794-1655 or 508/685-2591. **Free.**

Motel

✔★★ **HAMPTON INN.** *224 Winthrop Ave (MA 114) (01843), I-495 exit 42A. 978/975-4050; FAX 978/687-7122.* 126 rms, 5 story. Aug-Oct: S, D $99; under 18 free; lower rates rest of yr. Crib free. TV; cable. Complimentary continental bkfst. Restaurant nearby. Ck-out noon. Meeting rm. Business servs avail. In-rm modem link. Exercise equipt. Refrigerators, microwaves avail. Cr cds: A, C, D, DS, ER, MC, V.

Restaurant

★★ **BISHOP'S.** *99 Hampshire at Lowell St (01840). 978/683-7143.* Middle Eastern, Amer menu. Specializes in lobster, roast beef, Arabic dishes. Hrs: 11:30 am-9:30 pm; Fri to 10 pm; Sat 4-10:30 pm; Sun 2-9 pm (July, Aug from 4 pm). Closed Thanksgiving, Dec 25. Bar to 1 am. Semi-a la carte: lunch $4.50-$9, dinner $11-$25. Entertainment Fri, Sat. Moorish, Mediterranean decor. Family-owned. Cr cds: A, C, D, DS, MC, V.

Lee (B-2)

Founded 1777 **Pop** 5,849 **Elev** 1,000 ft **Area code** 413 **Zip** 01238

Lee's major industry has been papermaking since the first years of the 19th century. Today, it is also a summer and ski resort area.

What to See and Do

October Mountain State Forest. Fine mountain scenery overlooking 16,000 acres. Hiking, hunting; snowmobiling. Camping on W side of forest. Standard fees. I-90 exit 2, US 20 westbound. Phone 413/243-1778.

Santarella "Tyringham's Gingerbread House." Former studio of sculptor Sir Henry Kitson, creator of the "Minuteman" statue in Lexington. Built in the early 1930s, the house's major element is the roof, which was designed to look like thatching and to represent the rolling hills of the Berkshires in autumn; the fronting rock pillars and the grottoes between them are fashioned after similar edifices in Europe; Santarella Sculpture garden. Exhibits include ceramics, glass, paintings, graphics, antiques, objets d'art; also changing exhibits. Sculpture garden with lily pond. (Late May-Oct, daily) 4 mi SE in Tyringham. Phone 413/243-0654. **¢¢**

Seasonal Event

Jacob's Pillow Dance Festival. Ted Shawn Theatre and Doris Duke Theatre, 8 mi E via US 20, on George Carter Rd in Becket. America's oldest and most prestigious dance festival includes performances by international dance companies. Performances Tues-Sat, some Sun. Phone 413/243-0745 (box office) or 413/637-1322 (info). Late June-Aug.

Motels

★★★ **BEST WESTERN-BLACK SWAN.** *435 Laurel St, 2 mi N on MA 20 at Laurel Lake. 413/243-2700.* E-mail blkswanma@aol.com; web www.travelweb.com/thisco/bw/22036/22036_b.html. 52 rms, 2 story. July-Aug: D $95-$180; suites $120-$215; higher rates wkends (2-day min); lower rates rest of yr. TV; cable, VCR (movies $6). Pool; sauna. Restaurant 5-9 pm. Bar. Ck-out 11 am. Meeting rm. Business center. In-rm modem link. Lawn games. Some refrigerators. Some balconies. Picnic tables. On lake. Cr cds: A, D, DS, MC, V.

★★ **PILGRIM.** *165 Housatonic St (US 20), ¼ mi N of MA Tpke exit 2. 413/243-1328; res: 888/537-5476; FAX 413/243-2339.* 37 rms, 1 & 2 story. July-Sept: S $85-$155; D $85-$195; each addl $7; under 12 free;

lower rates rest of yr. Crib $7. TV; cable. Pool. Complimentary coffee in lobby. Restaurant adj 6:30 am-midnight. Ck-out 11 am. Coin lndry. Business servs avail. Downhill ski 15 mi; x-country ski 5 mi. Refrigerators, microwaves avail. Balconies. Picnic tables. Cr cds: A, C, D, DS, MC, V.

Inns

★★★ **APPLEGATE.** *279 W Park St.* 413/243-4451; *FAX* 413/243-4451; *res:* 800/691-9012. E-mail applegate@taconic.net; web www.applegateinn.com. 6 rms, 2 with shower only, 2 story. No rm phones. June-Oct: S, D $115-$230; each addl $30; wkends, hols (3-day min); lower rates rest of yr. Children over 12 yrs only. TV in sitting rm. Pool. Complimentary continental bkfst. Restaurant nearby. Ck-out 11 am, ck-in 2 pm. Lawn games. Georgian Colonial built in 1920. Totally nonsmoking. Cr cds: DS, MC, V.

★★★ **CHAMBÉRY INN.** *199 Main St, corner of Main & Elm.* 413/243-2221; *FAX* 413/243-3600; *res:* 800/537-4321. E-mail innkeeper@berkshireinns.com; web www.berkshireinns.com. 9 rms, 3 story, 9 suites. July-Aug, Oct: S, D, suites $99-$265; each addl $25; 2- or 3-day min wkends; lower rates rest of yr. Over 18 yrs only. TV; cable. Restaurant adj 11:30 am-9 pm. Rm serv. Ck-out 11 am, ck-in 2 pm. Luggage handling. Business servs avail. Downhill ski 8 mi. In-rm whirlpools. Berkshires' oldest parochial school (built 1885); recently restored with custom Amish-crafted furnishings. Totally nonsmoking. Cr cds: A, DS, MC, V.

★★★ **DEVONFIELD.** *85 Stockbridge Rd, 1 mi W on Park St & Stockbridge Rd.* 413/243-3298; *FAX* 413/243-1360; *res:* 800/664-0880. E-mail innkeeper@devonfield.com; web www.devonfield.com. 10 rms, 3 story. June-Oct: D $110-$195; each addl $20; suites $155-$260; lower rates rest of yr; 3-day min wkends (July-Aug). Children over 10 yrs only. TV in some rms; cable. Heated pool. Complimentary full bkfst. Ck-out 11:30 am, ck-in 2 pm. Business servs avail. Tennis. Lawn games. Some fireplaces. Picnic tables. Built by Revolutionary War soldier; Federal-style rms with antique furnishings. Cr cds: A, DS, MC, V.

★★★ **FEDERAL HOUSE.** *(, South Lee 01260)* 3½ mi S on MA 102. 413/243-1824; *res:* 800/243-1824. 10 rms, 2 story. No rm phones. Memorial Day-Oct: S, D $95-$195; each addl $20; lower rates rest of yr. Children over 12 yrs only. Complimentary full bkfst. Restaurant (see FEDERAL HOUSE). Bar. Ck-out noon, ck-in 3 pm. Tennis privileges. Golf privileges. Built 1824. Cr cds: A, DS, MC, V.

★★★ **HISTORIC MERRELL.** *(1565 Pleasant St, South Lee 01260)* 3 mi S on MA 102. 413/243-1794; *res:* 800/243-1794. E-mail merry@bcn.net; web www.merrell-inn.com. 10 rms, 3 story. July-Oct: S $75-$155; D $85-$165; each addl $15; suite $135-$215; lower rates rest of yr. TV in some rms. Complimentary full bkfst. Ck-out 11 am, ck-in 2 pm. Downhill ski 10 mi; x-country ski 5 mi. Fireplaces. View of river. Historic New England inn (1794); English gardens. Cr cds: MC, V.

✔★★ **MORGAN HOUSE.** *33 Main St.* 413/243-0181; *res:* 888/243-0188. 11 rms, 6 share bath, 3 story. No rm phones. July-Oct: S, D $85-$160; each addl $15. Crib free. Complimentary full bkfst. Restaurant (see MORGAN HOUSE INN). Bar 11-1 am. Ck-out 11 am, ck-in 1 pm. Built 1817. Stagecoach inn (1853); antiques; country-style decor. Cr cds: A, D, DS, MC, V.

Restaurants

★★ **CORK 'N HEARTH.** *MA 20W.* 413/243-0535. Specializes in fresh seafood, veal, beef. Hrs: 5-9 pm. Closed Mon; Thanksgiving, Dec

24, 25. Res accepted. Bar 5-11 pm. Semi-a la carte: dinner $13.95-$18.95. Child's meals. 3 dining rms. Scenic view of lake. Cr cds: A, MC, V.

D

★★★ **FEDERAL HOUSE.** *(See Federal House Inn)* 413/243-1824. Specialties: black Angus sirloin, duck, fresh pasta. Own desserts. Hrs: 5:30-9 pm; off-season 6-8:30 pm, Sun 6-8 pm. Closed Mon, Tues; Dec 25. Res accepted. Bar. Prix fixe: dinner $38.50. Built 1824. Colonial decor; antiques. Cr cds: A, D, DS, MC, V.

★★ **MORGAN HOUSE INN.** *(See Morgan House Inn)* 413/243-0181. Contemporary Amer menu. Specialties: hazelnut-crusted rack of lamb, pork tenderloin with barbecue glaze, pan-seared salmon fillet. Hrs: 11:30 am-9:30 pm; Fri, Sat to 10 pm; Sun noon-9 pm; Sun brunch 10:30 am-2 pm. Closed Dec 25. Res accepted. Bar 11:30-1 am. Semi-a la carte: lunch $4.95-$9.95, dinner $12.95-$23.95. Sun brunch $9.95-$12.95. Child's meals. Colonial tavern-type inn since 1853. Cr cds: A, D, DS, MC, V.

✔★★ **SULLIVAN STATION.** *Railroad St.* 413/243-2082. Specializes in Boston baked scrod, steak, vegetarian dishes, homemade desserts. Hrs: noon-9 pm; winter hrs vary. Closed Thanksgiving, Dec 25; also 2 wks late Feb-early Mar. Res accepted. Bar. Semi-a la carte: lunch $4.95-$8.95, dinner $11.95-$18.95. Outdoor dining. Railroad memorabilia. Totally nonsmoking. Cr cds: A, DS, MC, V.

Lenox (B-2)

Settled ca 1750 **Pop** 5,069 **Elev** 1,200 ft **Area code** 413 **Zip** 01240 **Web** www.lenox.org
Information Chamber of Commerce, 65 Main St, PO Box 646; 413/637-3646.

This summer resort became world-famous for music when the Boston Symphony began its Berkshire Festival here in 1939. Nearby is Stockbridge Bowl, one of the prettiest lakes in the Berkshires.

What to See and Do

Edith Wharton Restoration (The Mount). Edith Wharton's summer estate; was planned from a book she coauthored in 1897, *The Decoration of Houses,* and built in 1902. This Classical-revival house is architecturally significant; ongoing restoration. On 49 acres, with gardens. Tour of house and gardens (late May-Labor Day, daily exc Mon; after Labor Day-late Oct, Sat & Sun). (See SEASONAL EVENTS) Plunkett St at S jct of US 7 & MA 7A. Phone 413/637-1899. ¢¢¢

Pleasant Valley Wildlife Sanctuary. Sanctuary of the Massachusetts Audubon Society. 1,200 acres with 7 mi of trails; beaver colony; office. (Daily exc Mon) Trailside Museum (May-Oct, daily exc Mon). No dogs. On West Mountain Rd, 1½ mi W of US 7/20. Phone 413/637-0320. ¢¢

Tanglewood. Where Nathaniel Hawthorne lived and wrote. Here he planned *Tanglewood Tales.* Many of the 210 acres, developed into a gentleman's estate by William Aspinwall Tappan, are in formal gardens. Well-known today as the summer home of the Boston Symphony Orchestra and the Tanglewood Music Center, the symphony's training academy for young musicians. (See SEASONAL EVENT) Grounds (daily; free exc during concerts). On West St, 1½ mi SW on MA 183. Phone 413/637-1600 (summer) or 617/266-1492 (rest of yr).

Main Gate Area. Friends of Tanglewood, box office, music and bookstore; cafeteria; gift shop.

Main House. Original mansion, now administrative building for Tanglewood Music Center. Excellent view of Lake Mahkeenac, Monument Mt.

Formal Gardens. Manicured hemlock hedges and lawn, tall pine. Picnicking.

Koussevitzky Music Shed (1938). The so-called "Shed," where Boston Symphony Orchestra concerts take place; holds 5,000.

Hawthorne Cottage. Replica of "Little Red House" where Hawthorne lived 1850-1851, now contains music studios, Hawthorne memorabilia. (Open before each festival concert.)

Chamber Music Hall. Small chamber music ensembles, lectures, seminars and large classes held here. Designed by Eliel Saarinen who also designed

Seiji Ozawa Concert Hall (1941). Festival chamber music programs, Tanglewood Music Center activities; seats 1,200.

Annual Events

Apple Squeeze Festival. Celebration of apple harvest; entertainment, food, music. Phone 413/637-3646. Usually 3rd wkend Sept.

House Tours of Historic Lenox. Phone 413/637-3646. Fall.

Seasonal Events

Shakespeare & Co. The Mount. Professional theater company performs plays by Shakespeare & Edith Wharton, as well as other events. Four stages, one outdoor. Daily exc Mon. Phone 413/637-3353. Late May-early Nov.

Tanglewood Music Festival. Tanglewood Boston Symphony Orchestra. Concerts, Fri & Sat eve and Sun afternoons. Inquire for other musical events. Phone 413/637-1940. July-Aug.

Motels

★ ★ **HOWARD JOHNSON.** 462 Pittsfield Rd (US 7/20). 413/442-4000; FAX 413/443-7954. 44 rms, 2 story, 6 suites. July-Aug: S, D $85-$215; suites $95-$215; under 18 free; wkends (2-3-day min); higher rates fall foliage; lower rates rest of yr. TV; cable. Pool. Complimentary continental bkfst. Restaurant adj 6 am-10 pm. Ck-out 11 am. Business center. Sundries. Many microwaves; some refrigerators. Cr cds: A, C, D, DS, MC, V.

★ ★ **THE LENOX.** Rts 7 & 20, US 7/20, 4 mi NE. 413/499-0324; FAX 413/499-5618. 17 rms. July-Aug: S, D $70-$125; each addl $10; under 12 free; wkly rates foliage season; varied lower rates rest of yr. Crib $5. TV; cable (premium). Pool. Complimentary coffee in lobby. Restaurant nearby. Ck-out 11 am. Business servs avail. Sundries. Downhill ski 1 mi. Picnic tables. Cr cds: A, C, D, DS, MC, V.

★ ★ **YANKEE.** 461 Pittsfield/Lenox Rd, 3 mi N on US 7/20. 413/499-3700; FAX 413/499-3634. Web www.berkshireinns.com. 61 rms, 1-2 story. July-Aug, Oct: S, D $69-$125 (wkdays); S, D $149-$199 (wkends); 3-day min wkends in season; lower rates rest of yr. Crib free. TV; cable. Heated pool. Playground. Continental bkfst. Coffee in rms. Restaurant nearby. Ck-out 11 am. Business center. Sundries. Downhill/x-country ski 1 mi. Some refrigerators, fireplaces; microwaves avail. Picnic tables. On 7½ acres with a pond. Cr cds: A, C, D, DS, MC, V.

Hotel

★ ★ ★ **CRANWELL.** 55 Lee Rd, 1/10 mi E of US 7/20. 413/637-1364; FAX 413/637-4364; res: 800/272-6935. Web www.cranwell.com. 93 rms in 7 bldgs, 2-3 story. Mid-June-Oct: S, D $199-$289; under 12 free; suites $289-$439; wkend rates; package plans; lower rates rest of yr. Crib free. TV; cable, VCR avail. Heated pool; poolside serv, lifeguard. Complimentary continental bkfst. Coffee in rms. Restaurant (see WYNDHURST). Bar; entertainment Fri, Sat. Ck-out 11 am. Meeting rms. Business servs avail. In-rm modem link. Tennis. 18-hole golf, greens fee $25-$85, pro, putting green, driving range, golf school. Downhill ski 7 mi; x-country ski on site. Exercise equipt. Some bathrm phones, fireplaces; microwaves avail. Balconies. Picnic tables. Heliport. Country Tudor mansion on 380 acres. Cr cds: A, D, DS, MC, V.

Inns

★ ★ **AMADEUS HOUSE INN.** 15 Cliffwood St. 413/637-4770; FAX 413/637-4484; res: 800/205-4770. E-mail info@amadeushouse.com. 8 rms, 2 share bath, 1 kit. suite. No A/C. Phone avail. July-Aug: S, D $70-$155; each addl $20; kit. suite (wkly) $900-$1,200. Children over 10 yrs only. Complimentary full bkfst. Restaurant nearby. Ck-out 11:30 am, ck-in 2 pm. Luggage handling. Business servs avail. Built in 1820; front porch, gardens and walkways. Totally nonsmoking. Cr cds: A, DS, MC, V.

★ ★ **APPLE TREE.** 10 Richmond Mt Rd. 413/637-1477; FAX 413/637-2528. E-mail reservations@appletree-inn.com; web www.appletree-inn.com. 35 rms, 2 share bath, 3 story, 2 suites. No rm phones. July-Aug: S, D $130-$210; suites $300; 3-day min wkends; some rms 5-day min; lower rates rest of yr. Crib free. TV in some rms; cable. Heated pool. Complimentary continental bkfst. Restaurant (see APPLE TREE). Ck-out 11:30 am, ck-in 2 pm. Luggage handling. Tennis. X-country ski 1 mi. Picnic tables. Built in 1885; situated on 22 hilltop acres. Cr cds: A, D, DS, MC, V.

★ ★ **BIRCHWOOD INN.** 7 Hubbard St. 413/637-2600; res: 800/524-1646. Web www.bbonline.com/ma/birchwood/. 12 rms, 8 with shower only, 2 share bath, 3 story, 2 kit. suites. July-Aug: S, D, kit. suites $90-$210; wkday rates; lower rates rest of yr. Children over 12 yrs only. TV in some rms; cable. Complimentary full bkfst. Restaurant adj 6-10 pm. Ck-out 11:30 am, ck-in 2 pm. Business servs avail. Downhill ski 5 mi; x-country ski adj. Built in 1767; many antiques, gardens. Totally nonsmoking. Cr cds: A, C, D, DS, MC, V.

★ ★ ★ ★ **BLANTYRE.** 16 Blantyre Rd, 1 mi E on MA 20; 3 mi W of I-90 (MA Tpke exit 2). 413/637-3556; FAX 413/637-4282. E-mail hide@blantyre.com; web www.blantyre.com. The facade of this 1902 mansion combines Norman and Tudor elements; the opulent interior is decorated in Regency style with ornamental plasterwork, oak paneling and antiques. The grounds are extensive and landscaped, punctuated with formal gardens and crossed by many walking trails. 23 rms in main house, carriage house & cottages, 2 story, 6 suites. Mid-May-mid-Nov: S, D $265-$475; each addl $50; suites $325-$675. Closed rest of yr. Children over 12 yrs only. TV; cable, VCR avail. Heated pool; whirlpool, poolside serv. Sauna. Complimentary continental bkfst; evening refreshments. Dining rm (see BLANTYRE). Rm serv 7 am-10 pm. Ck-out noon, ck-in 3 pm. Meeting rms. Business servs avail. In-rm modem link. Luggage handling. Valet serv. Airport, bus depot transportation. Tennis, pro. Formal croquet lawns, pro. Massage. Some fireplaces. Cr cds: A, C, D, MC, V.

★ ★ ★ **BROOK FARM.** 15 Hawthorne St. 413/637-3013; FAX 413/637-4715; res: 800/285-7638. E-mail innkeeper@brookfarm.com; web www.brookfarm.com. 12 rms, 3 story. July-Aug, hol wkends: S, D $115-$200; each addl $20; lower rates rest of yr. Children over 15 yrs only. Pool. Complimentary bkfst; afternoon refreshments. Ck-out noon, ck-in 3 pm. Business servs avail. Free bus depot transportation. Downhill ski 4 mi; x-country ski 1 mi. Picnic tables. Antiques. Library/sitting rm. Poetry readings Sat. Built 1870. Cr cds: DS, MC, V.

★ ★ **CANDLELIGHT.** 35 Walker St. 413/637-1555. E-mail innkeeper@candlelightinn-lenox.com; web www.candlelightinn-lenox.com. 8 rms, 3 story. No rm phones. July-Oct: D $145-$175; each addl $30; wkly rates; lower rates rest of yr. Children over 10 yrs only. TV in sitting rm. Complimentary continental bkfst. Dining rm noon-9.30 pm. Bar in season. Ck-out 11 am, ck-in 2 pm. Downhill ski 5 mi; x-country ski ½ mi. Built 1885. Cr cds: A, DS, MC, V.

★ ★ ★ **GABLES.** 81 Walker St. 413/637-3416; res: 800/382-9401. 18 rms, 3 story, 4 suites. No rm phones. Mid-June-Oct: S, D $90-$210; lower rates rest of yr. Children over 12 yrs only. TV; cable, VCR (free movies). Pool. Complimentary bkfst; afternoon refreshments. Restaurant nearby. Ck-out noon, ck-in 2 pm. Tennis. Downhill ski 5 mi; x-country ski 1/4 mi. Some fireplaces. Balconies. Picnic tables. Antiques. Library/sitting rm. Queen Anne-style house (1885), once the home of Edith Wharton. Cr cds: DS, MC, V.

★ ★ **GARDEN GABLES.** *141 Main St (MA 7A), downtown in historic district.* 413/637-0193; FAX 413/637-4554. E-mail gardeninn@aol.com; web www.lenoxinn.com. 18 rms, 2 story. June-Oct: D $110-$240; wkly rates; lower rates rest of yr. Children over 12 yrs only. TV in some rms. Pool. Complimentary full bkfst; afternoon refreshments. Restaurant nearby. Ck-out 11 am, ck-in 2 pm. Business center. In-rm modem link. Downhill ski 4 mi; x-country ski 1/4 mi. Fireplaces. Balconies. Picnic tables. Built 1780; antiques, books. Cr cds: A, DS, MC, V.

★ ★ **GATEWAYS.** *51 Walker St.* 413/637-2532; res: 888/492-9466; FAX 413/637-1432. E-mail gateways@berkshire.net; web www.gatewaysinn.com. 12 rms, 2 story. July-Oct: D $110-$260; suite $275-$400; lower rates rest of yr. Children over 12 yrs only. TV; cable. Continental bkfst. Restaurant (see GATEWAYS INN). Rm serv. Ck-out 11 am, ck-in 1 pm. Business servs avail. Downhill ski 5 mi; x-country ski 1/4 mi. Many fireplaces. Restored mansion (1912). Cr cds: A, D, DS, MC, V.

★ ★ **HILLTOP.** *174 Main St (MA 7A).* 413/637-1746. 6 rms, 2 story, 1 suite. June-Oct (2-3- day min): D $150-$240; suite $230-$340; wkly rates; lower rates rest of yr. Children over 12 yrs only. TV; cable. Complimentary continental bkfst; afternoon refreshments. Restaurant nearby. Ck-out 11 am, ck-in 2 pm. Luggage handling. Free bus depot transportation. Downhill ski 4 mi; x-country ski adj. Victorian inn; fireplaces in every rm. Many antiques. Gardens. Totally nonsmoking. Cr cds: A, D, DS, MC, V.

★ ★ ★ **KEMBLE INN.** *2 Kemble St.* 413/637-4113; res: 800/353-4113. Web www.kembleinn.com. 15 rms, 3 story. S, D, $85-$275; wkly rates. Children over 12 yrs only. TV; cable. Complimentary continental bkfst. Restaurant nearby. Ck-out 11 am, ck-in 2 pm. Fireplaces; some in-rm whirlpools. Panoramic mountain views; quiet, elegant atmosphere in restored mansion (1881). Totally nonsmoking. Cr cds: D, DS, MC, V.

★ ★ **ROOKWOOD.** *11 Old Stockbridge Rd.* 413/637-9750; FAX 413/637-1352; res: 800/223-9750. E-mail innkeepers@rookwoodinn.com; web www.rookwoodinn.com. 21 rms, 3 story, 2 suites. Phones in suites. Late June-Aug: D $110-$235; each addl $15; suite $250-$285; under 12 free; lower rates rest of yr. Crib free. TV in sitting rm and suites. Complimentary full bkfst; afternoon refreshments. Restaurant nearby. Ck-out 11 am, ck-in 3 pm. Bus depot transportation. Downhill ski 5 mi; x-country ski 1 mi. Fireplaces. Balconies. Victorian inn (1885) furnished with English antiques. Totally nonsmoking. Cr cds: A, C, D, DS, MC, V.

★ ★ **SUMMER WHITE HOUSE.** *17 Main St.* 413/637-4489. 6 rms. No rm phones. S, D $160-$175. Closed Dec-Apr. Children over 16 yrs only. TV; cable. Pool privileges. Complimentary continental bkfst. Coffee in library. Restaurant nearby. Ck-out 11 am, ck-in 2 pm. Mansion built 1885; original antiques. Totally nonsmoking. Cr cds: DS, MC, V.

✔★ ★ **VILLAGE INN.** *16 Church St, center of town.* 413/637-0020; FAX 413/637-9756; res: 800/253-0917. E-mail villinn@vgernet.net; web www.villageinn-lenox.com. 32 rms, 3 story. July-Aug, Oct: D $90-$225; each addl $20; MAP avail; wkly, wkend rates; ski plans; lower rates rest of yr. TV rm. Restaurant 8-10:30 am, 5:30-9 pm. Bar 5 pm-1 am. Ck-out 11 am, ck-in 1 pm. Downhill ski 4 mi; x-country ski 1 mi. Some whirlpools, fireplaces. Inn since 1775. Cr cds: A, D, DS, MC, V.

✔★ **WALKER HOUSE.** *64 Walker St.* 413/637-1271; FAX 413/637-2387; res: 800/235-3098. E-mail phoudek@vgernet.net; web www.walkerhouse.com. 8 rms, 2 story. No rm phones. Late June-early Sept: S, D $80-$190; each addl $5-$15; ski plans; lower rates rest of yr. Children over 12 yrs only. Pet accepted, some restrictions. TV in sitting rm; VCR avail. Complimentary continental bkfst. Restaurant opp 11 am-10 pm. Ck-out noon, ck-in 2 pm. Business servs avail. Downhill ski 6 mi; x-country ski 1/2 mi. Antiques. Library. Rms named after composers. Built 1804. Totally nonsmoking. No cr cds accepted.

★ ★ ★ **WHEATLEIGH.** *Hawthorne Rd.* 413/637-0610; FAX 413/637-4507. E-mail wheatleigh@taconic.net; web www.wheatleigh.com. 19 rms, 2 story. S, D $175-$625; 3-day min wkends (Tanglewood season & Oct). Children over 9 yrs only. TV; cable, VCR. Pool. Dining rm (see WHEATLEIGH). Rm serv. Ck-out noon, ck-in 3 pm. Business servs avail. Luggage handling. Concierge serv. Valet parking. Tennis, pro. Downhill ski 9 mi. Exercise equipt. Massage. Many fireplaces. Many balconies. Built in 1893; antiques, abstract sculptures. On 22 acres; mountain views. Cr cds: A, C, D, MC, V.

★ ★ **WHISTLER'S.** *5 Greenwood St (01246).* 413/637-0975; FAX 413/637-2190. E-mail rmears3246@aol.com. 14 rms, 2 story, 3 suites. July-Aug, Oct: D $90-$225; each addl $25; suites $160-$225; 3-day min summer; lower rates rest of yr. TV; cable; VCR avail. Complimentary full bkfst; afternoon refreshments. Restaurant nearby. Ck-out noon, ck-in 3 pm. Business servs avail. Free bus depot transportation. Downhill ski 5 mi; x-country ski 1/2 blk. Lawn games. Fireplaces. Picnic tables. Tudor-style mansion built 1820. Library. Music rm with Steinway grand piano, Louis XVI furniture. Cr cds: A, DS, MC, V.

Restaurants

★ ★ **APPLE TREE.** *(See Apple Tree Inn)* 413/637-1477. Continental menu. Specialties: fresh fish of the day, black Angus steak. Own baking. Hrs: 5:30-9 pm; July-Aug 5-9:30 pm; Sun brunch 10:30 am-2 pm. Closed Mon-Wed off-season. Res accepted. Bar. Semi-a la carte: dinner $12-$23. Parking. Outdoor dining. Round dining rm with hillside view. Totally nonsmoking. Cr cds: A, D, DS, MC, V.

★ ★ ★ ★ **BLANTYRE.** *(See Blantyre Inn)* 413/637-3556. This unique, castlelike Tudor mansion is set on 85 acres of meticulously sculpted ground. You choose from formal dining in the paneled dining room, a moire-walled Regency sitting room or the less-formal garden conservatory. Baking is done on the premises, and many entrees are prepared with fresh local New England ingredients. Contemporary French menu. Specializes in fresh game and seafood. Own baking, ice cream. Hrs: 6-9 pm; July-Aug also 12:30-1:45 pm. Closed Mon; also Nov-Apr. Res required. Serv bar. Wine cellar. Prix fixe: lunch (July-Aug) 2-course $32, 3-course $40; dinner $70. Serv charge 18%. Pianist, harpist (dinner). Valet parking. Outdoor dining (lunch). Jacket. Cr cds: A, C, D, MC, V.

★ ★ **CAFE LUCIA.** *80 Church St.* 413/637-2640. Italian menu. Specializes in veal, seafood, pasta. Hrs: 5:30-10 pm; hrs vary mid-Sept-May. Closed Mon; Easter, Thanksgiving, Dec 25; also Sun Nov-June. Res accepted. Serv bar. Semi-a la carte: dinner $13-$28. Outdoor dining. Cr cds: A, C, D, DS, MC, V.

✔★ **CAROL'S.** *8 Franklin St.* 413/637-8948. Specializes in bkfst; served all day. Hrs: 8 am-3 pm. Closed Tues, Wed (Sept-June); Thanksgiving, Dec 25. Semi-a la carte: bkfst, lunch $1.95-$6.50. Child's meals. No cr cds accepted.

★ ★ **CHURCH STREET CAFE.** *65 Church St.* 413/637-2745. Regional Amer menu. Specializes in seafood, crab cakes, grilled meat & fish. Hrs: 11:30 am-2 pm, 5:30-9 pm; Fri, Sat to 9:15 pm. Closed Jan 1, Thanksgiving, Dec 25; also Sun, Mon Nov-May. Res accepted. Bar.

Semi-a la carte: lunch $7.95-$13.95, dinner $16.95-$25.50. Outdoor dining. Bistro-style cafe; New England decor. Cr cds: MC, V.

D

★ ★ ★ **GATEWAYS INN.** *(See Gateways Inn) 413/637-2532.* New American menu. Specialties: escargot with gnocchi, rack of lamb Provençale, seasonal dishes. Hrs: 5-9 pm. Closed Mon, Tues in winter. Res accepted. Wine list. Semi-a la carte: dinner $18-$26. Parking. Outdoor dining. Cr cds: A, D, DS, MC, V.

★ ★ ★ **LENOX 218.** *218 Main St. 413/637-4218.* Web www.lenox218.com. Northern Italian, Amer menu. Specialties: Tuscan clam soup; New England seafood cakes; boneless breast of chicken with almonds, sesame and sunflower seeds. Hrs: 11:30 am-2:30 pm, 5-10 pm; Sun 10:30 am-9 pm; Sun brunch to 1:30 pm. Res accepted. Bar. Semi-a la carte: lunch $5.95-$8.95, dinner $12.95-$20.95. Sun brunch $11.95. Child's meals. Parking. Casual elegance; vaulted ceilings and skylights. Cr cds: A, C, D, DS, MC, V.

D

★ ★ **LENOX HOUSE.** *55 Pittsfield-Lenox Rd (US 7/20), 5 mi N of MA Tpke exit 2. 413/637-1341.* Web www.regionnet.com/colberk/lenoxhouse.html. Continental menu. Specializes in fresh fish, poultry, prime rib. Own baking. Hrs: 11:30 am-9:30 pm; Fri, Sat to 10 pm. Res accepted. Bar. Semi-a la carte: lunch $4.75-$9.95, dinner $10.95-$21.95. Parking. Totally nonsmoking. Cr cds: A, D, DS, MC, V.

D

✔★ **PANDA HOUSE.** *664 Pittsfield Rd, 4 mi N on MA 7. 413/499-0660.* Chinese menu. Specialties: General Tso's chicken, vegetarian paradise. Hrs: 11:30 am-10 pm; Fri, Sat to 11 pm; Sun brunch to 3 pm. Closed Thanksgiving, Dec 25. Res accepted. Bar. Semi-a la carte: lunch $4.75-$6.25, dinner $7.95-$15.95. Sun brunch $7.95. Parking. Oriental decor. Cr cds: A, DS, MC, V.

D

★ ★ ★ **WHEATLEIGH.** *(See Wheatleigh Inn) 413/637-0610.* An antique buffet, chandeliers and an ornate fireplace with candelabras highlight the elegant, formal atmosphere here. French menu. Menu changes daily. Hrs: 6-9 pm. Res required. Tasting menu: dinner $75. Own baking. Valet parking. Totally nonsmoking. Cr cds: A, C, D, MC, V.

★ ★ ★ **WYNDHURST.** *(See Cranwell Hotel) 413/637-1364.* Specializes in lamb, fresh fish, daily specialties. Own desserts. Sittings: 5-6:30 pm & 8-9:30 pm. Res accepted. Bar. Wine list. Semi-a la carte: dinner $16.50-$28. Child's meals. Entertainment Fri, Sat. Formal decor in Tudor mansion; ornately carved fireplace, original artwork. Totally nonsmoking. Cr cds: A, C, D, DS, MC, V.

Leominster (B-5)

Settled 1653 **Pop** 38,145 **Elev** 400 ft **Area code** 978 **Zip** 01453 **E-mail** chamber@massweb.org **Web** www.nc.massweb.org

Information Johnny Appleseed Visitor Center, 110 Erdman Way; 978/840-4300.

Leominster (LEMMINst'r) has retained the pronunciation of the English town for which it was named. Known at one time as "Comb City," in 1845 Leominster housed 24 factories manufacturing horn combs. It is the birthplace of "Johnny Appleseed"—John Chapman (1774-1845)—a devout Swedenborgian missionary who traveled throughout America on foot, planting apple orchards and the seeds of his faith. The National Plastics Center and Museum is located here.

Motels

✔★ **INN ON THE HILL.** *450 N Main St. 978/537-1661; FAX 978/840-3341; res: 800/357-0052.* 100 rms, 2 story. S, D $39-$49; each

addl $7; under 18 free; wkly rates. Crib free. Pet accepted, some restrictions; $20. TV; cable. Pool. Restaurant 6:30 am-11 pm. Rm serv. Bar 5:30-10 pm. Ck-out noon. Meeting rms. Sundries. Downhill/x-country ski 20 mi. Cr cds: A, C, D, DS, ER, JCB, MC, V.

D

★ ★ ★ **WESTMINSTER VILLAGE INN.** *(9 Village Inn Rd, Westminster 01473) 6 mi W on MA 2, exit 27. 978/874-2000; FAX 978/874-1753; res: 800/342-1905.* E-mail wvi@net; web www.washusetvillageinn.com. 74 rms, 2 story, 18 suites. S $89-$149; D $99-$159; each addl $10; suites, kit. units $129-$149; under 18 free; ski, golf plans. Crib free. Pet accepted. TV; cable. 2 pools, 1 indoor; poolside serv. Playground. Restaurant 6:30 am-9:30 pm. Ck-out 11 am. Meeting rms. Tennis. 18-hole golf privileges. Downhill/x-country ski 3 mi. Exercise equipt; sauna. Sitting rms with Colonial decor; extensive grounds. Cr cds: A, C, D, DS, MC, V.

D

Hotel

★ ★ ★ **FOUR POINTS BY SHERATON.** *99 Erdman Way, 1/4 mi N, at jct MA 2 & 12. 978/534-9000; FAX 978/534-0891.* 187 rms, 7 story. S $119-$130; D $134-$145; each addl $15; suites $130-$145; under 18 free. Crib free. TV; cable. Indoor pool. Complimentary continental bkfst Mon-Fri. Restaurant 6:30 am-10 pm. Bar 11:30-1 am. Ck-out noon. Meeting rms. Business center. In-rm modem link. Downhill ski 5 mi. Whirlpool. Cr cds: A, C, D, DS, MC, V.

D

Lexington (B-7)

(See also Concord)

Settled ca 1640 **Pop** 28,974 **Elev** 210 ft **Area code** 617 **Zip** 02173

Information Chamber of Commerce Visitors Center, 1875 Massachusetts Ave; 617/862-1450. The center, open daily, offers a diorama depicting the Battle of Lexington, and has a walking tour map.

Lexington is called the birthplace of American liberty. On its Green, April 19, 1775, eight Minutemen were killed in what is traditionally considered the first organized fight of the War for Independence. However, in 1908, the US Senate recognized the counterclaim of Point Pleasant, West Virginia as the first battle site. It is still possible to visualize the Battle of Lexington. Down the street came the British, 700 strong. To the right of the Green is the tavern the militia used as headquarters. It was here that 77 Minutemen lined up near the west end of the Green, facing down the Charlestown road. Nearby is a boulder with a plaque bearing the words of Captain John Parker, spoken just before the Redcoats opened fire: "Stand your ground. Don't fire unless fired upon. But if they mean to have a war, let it begin here!" It did—the fight then moved on to Concord.

What to See and Do

Battle Green. The Old Monument, the Minuteman Statue and the Boulder mark the line of the Minutemen, seven of whom are buried under the monument. At the center of town.

Lexington Historical Society. Revolutionary period houses. Guided tours. Phone 617/862-1703. Three-house combination ticket ¢¢¢

Hancock-Clarke House (1698). Here John Hancock and Samuel Adams were awakened by Paul Revere's alarm on Apr 18, 1775. Furniture, portraits, utensils; small museum. Fire engine exhibit in barn (by appt). (Mid-Apr-Oct, daily) 36 Hancock St. Phone 617/862-1703.

Buckman Tavern (1709). Minutemen assembled here before the battle. Period furnishings, portraits. (Mid-Apr-Oct, daily; Nov, wkends only) 1 Bedford St, facing the Battle Green. Phone 617/862-1703.

Munroe Tavern (1695). British hospital after the battle. George Washington dined here in 1789. Period furnishings, artifacts. (Mid-Apr-Oct, daily) 1332 Massachusetts Ave. Phone 617/862-1703.

Museum of Our National Heritage. Museum features exhibits on American history and culture, from its founding to the present; also history of Lexington and the American Revolution. (Daily) 33 Marrett Rd (MA 2A), at jct Massachusetts Ave. Phone 617/861-6559.   **Free.**

Annual Event

Reenactment of the Battle of Lexington and Concord. Massachusetts Ave. Reenactment of opening battle of American Revolution; parade. Patriots Day (Mon nearest Apr 19).

Motel

✔★ ★ **HOLIDAY INN EXPRESS.** *440 Bedford St, I-95 exit 31B. 781/861-0850; FAX 781/861-0821.* 204 rms, 2 story. S, D $69-$169; each addl $10; under 12 free. Crib free. TV; cable (premium). Heated pool; whirlpool. Complimentary continental bkfst. Ck-out noon. Coin lndry. Business servs avail. In-rm modem link. Valet serv. Health club privileges. Microwaves avail. Cr cds: A, C, D, DS, ER, JCB, MC, V.

D ≈ ⊠ 🛇 SC

Hotel

★ ★ ★ **SHERATON INN.** *727 Marrett Rd, exit 30 B off I 128/95. 781/862-8700; FAX 781/863-0404.* 119 rms, 2 story. S, D $149-$199; each addl $10; under 18 free; wkend rates. Crib free. TV; cable (premium). Pool; poolside serv, lifeguard. Coffee in rms. Restaurant 6:30 am-2:30 pm, 5-10 pm; Sat, Sun 8 am-noon. Bar 11:30 am-11:30 pm. Ck-out noon. Meeting rms. Business servs avail. In-rm modem link. Exercise equipt. Health club privileges. Some private patios, balconies. Picnic tables. Cr cds: A, C, D, DS, ER, MC, V.

D ≈ 🛇 ⊠ 🛇 SC

Lowell (A-6)

Settled 1655 **Pop** 103,439 **Elev** 102 ft **Area code** 978 **E-mail** chamber@glci.net **Web** www.greaterlowellchamber.org

Information Greater Lowell Chamber of Commerce, 77 Merrimack St, 01852; 978/459-8154.

In the 19th century, the powerful Merrimack River and its canals transformed Lowell from a handicraft to a textile industrial center. The Francis Floodgate, near Broadway and Clare streets, was called "Francis' Folly" when it was built in 1848, but it saved the city from flood in 1936. Restoration of the historic canal system is currently in progress.

What to See and Do

American Textile History Museum. Permanent exhibit, "Textiles in America," features 18th-20th-century textiles, artifacts and machinery in operation, showing the impact of the Industrial Revolution on labor. Collections of cloth samples, books, prints, photographs and pre-industrial tools may be seen by appt. Tours; activities. Library; education center. Restaurant; museum store. (Daily exc Mon; closed Jan 1, Thanksgiving, Dec 25) 491 Dutton St. Phone 978/441-0440.   ¢¢

Lowell Heritage State Park. Six miles of canals and associated linear parks and 2 mi of park on the bank of Merrimack River offers boating, boathouse; concert pavilion; interpretive programs. (Schedule varies; phone ahead) 500 Pawtucket Blvd. Phone 978/453-0592.   **Free.**

Lowell National Historical Park. Established to commemorate Lowell's unique legacy as the most important planned industrial city in America. The nation's first large-scale center for the mechanized production of cotton cloth, Lowell became a model for 19th-century industrial development.

Park includes mill buildings, 5.6-mi canal system. Visitor center at Market Mills, 246 Market St, includes audiovisual show and exhibits (daily; closed Jan 1, Thanksgiving, Dec 25). Free walking & trolley tours (winter & spring). Tours by barge and trolley (May-Columbus Day wkend; fee), reservations suggested. Downtown. For reservations and information contact Visitor Center, 246 Market St, 01852; 978/970-5000. Located here are

Patrick J. Mogan Cultural Center. Restored 1836 boarding house of the Boott Cotton Mills includes a re-created kitchen, keeper's rm, parlor and mill girls' bedrm; exhibits on working people, immigrants and labor history; also local history. (Winter, wkends; rest of yr, daily) 40 French St.   **Free.**

Boott Cotton Mills Museum. Industrial history museum with operating looms (ear plugs supplied). Interactive exhibits, video presentations. (Daily; closed Jan 1, Thanksgiving, Dec 25) At foot of John St.   ¢¢

New England Quilt Museum. Changing exhibits feature antique, traditional and contemporary quilts. Museum shop. (May-Nov, Tues-Sun; rest of yr, Tues-Sat; closed major hols) 18 Shattuck St. Phone 978/452-4207. ¢¢

University of MA-Lowell. (15,500 students) State-operated university formed by 1975 merger of Lowell Technological Institute (1895) and Lowell State College (1894). Music ensembles at Durgin Hall Performing Arts Center; for schedule and fees phone 978/934-4446. 1 University Ave. For general information phone 978/934-4000.

Whistler House Museum of Art. Birthplace of the painter James Abbott McNeill Whistler. Exhibits include several of his etchings. Collection of 19th- and early 20th-century American art. (May-Oct, Wed-Sun; Mar-Apr & Nov-Dec, Wed-Sat; closed major hols) 243 Worthen St. Phone 978/452-7641.   ¢

Annual Event

Lowell Folk Festival. Concerts, crafts & demonstrations, ethnic food, street parade. Last wkend July.

Motor Hotels

✔★ ★ **BEST WESTERN.** *(187 Chelmsford St, Chelmsford 01824) I-495 exit 34. 978/256-7511; res: 888/770-9992; FAX 978/250-1401.* 120 rms, 5 story. S $70-$85; D $75-$95; each addl $5; suites $95; under 18 free; wkend rates. Crib free. TV; cable (premium), VCR avail (movies). Pool; whirlpool; poolside serv. Complimentary coffee in rms. Restaurant adj 6-1 am. Ck-out noon. Meeting rms. Business sevs avail. In-rm modem link. Valet serv. Exercise equipt; sauna. Some refrigerators, minibars; microwaves avail. Some balconies. Cr cds: A, C, D, DS, JCB, MC, V.

D ≈ 🛇 ⊠ 🛇 SC

★ ★ **COURTYARD BY MARRIOTT.** *30 Industrial Ave E (01852), I-495 exit 35C to Lowell Connector. 978/458-7575; FAX 978/458-1302.* 120 rms, 3 story, 12 suites. S, D $99-$109; suites $129-$139; under 12 free; wkend rates. TV; cable (premium). Complimentary coffee in rms. Restaurant 6:30-10 am; Sat, Sun 7:30-11:30 am. Rm serv 5-10 pm. Bar Sun-Thurs 5-10 pm. Ck-out 1 pm. Meeting rms. Business servs avail. In-rm modem link. Valet serv. Sundries. Coin lndry. Airport transportation. Exercise equipt. Pool. Refrigerators avail. Cr cds: A, C, D, DS, MC, V.

D ≈ 🛇 ⊠ 🛇 SC

★ ★ ★ **RADISSON HERITAGE.** *(10 Independence Dr, Chelmsford 01824) ¼ mi S off I-495 exit 34. 978/256-0800; FAX 978/256-0750.* 214 rms, 5 story, 82 suites. S, D $129; each addl $10; suites $149; under 16 free; wkend rates. Crib free. TV; cable (premium), VCR in suites. Indoor pool. Restaurant 6:30 am-2 pm, 5-10 pm. Rm serv. Bar 11 am-midnight. Ck-out noon. Meeting rms. Business servs avail. In-rm modem link. Sundries. Exercise equipt; sauna. Rec rm. Bathrm phone, refrigerator in suites. Cr cds: A, C, D, DS, ER, JCB, MC, V.

D ≈ 🛇 ⊠ 🛇 SC

Hotels

★ ★ ★ **DOUBLETREE.** *50 Warren St (01852). 978/452-1200; FAX 978/453-4674.* 251 rms, 9 story. S, D $89-$129; suites $139-$250; under 18 free. Crib free. TV; cable (premium), VCR avail. Indoor pool; whirlpool, wading pool, poolside serv. Restaurant 6:30 am-10 pm. Bar. Ck-out 11 am. Coin lndry. Convention facilities. Business servs avail. In-rm modem link. Free garage parking. Exercise equipt; sauna. Cr cds: A, C, D, DS, MC, V.

★ ★ ★ **WESTFORD REGENCY.** *(219 Littleton Rd (MA 110), Westford 01886) 10 mi S on MA 110; 1/4 mi E of I-495 exit 32. 978/692-8200; FAX 978/692-7403; res: 800/543-7801 (exc MA), 800/543-7802 (MA).* 193 units, 4 story, 15 suites. S $114; D $140; each addl $8; suites $125-$235; under 18 free; wkend rates. Crib free. Pet accepted, some restrictions. TV; cable (premium). Indoor pool; whirlpool. Restaurant 7 am-10 pm. Bar 11-11 pm; entertainment. Ck-out noon. Convention facilities. Business servs avail. In-rm modem link. Exercise rm; sauna. Bathrm phones; some refrigerators. Atrium in lobby. Cr cds: A, C, D, DS, MC, V.

Restaurant

✔★ ★ ★ **COBBLESTONES.** *91 Dutton St (01852). 978/970-2282.* Eclectic menu. Specialties: chicken marsala, porterhouse steak, game specials. Hrs: 11:30 am-midnight. Closed Sun; Labor Day, Thanksgiving, Dec 25. Res accepted. Bar. Semi-a la carte: lunch $5.95-$7.95, dinner $10.95-$17.95. In restored 1859 building. Cr cds: A, D, DS, MC, V.

★ ★ ★ **LA BONICHE.** *143 Merrimack St (01852). 978/458-9473.* French menu. Specializes in homemade soups and pâtés, duck. Menu changes seasonally. Hrs: 11:30 am-2:30 pm, 5-9 pm; Fri to 9:30 pm; Sat 5-9:30 pm. Closed Sun, Mon; major hols. Res accepted. Bar. Semi-a la carte: lunch $6-$12, dinner $14-$21. Child's meals. Musicians Sat. French provincial decor with natural woodwork. Cr cds: A, MC, V.

★ ★ ★ **LUNA D'ORO.** *110 Gorham St (01852). 978/459-8666.* E-mail lunadoro@worldnet.att.net. Hrs: 11:30 am-2:30 pm, 5-10 pm; Sat 5-11 pm. Closed Mon, Sun; also major hols. Res accepted. Mediterranean menu. Bar. Wine cellar. Semi-a la carte: lunch $4.50-$9.95, dinner $14.95-$21.95. Specialties: vegetable entrees, seafood dishes, tapas. Parking. Casual bistro atmosphere. Cr cds: A, D, MC, V.

Lynn (B-7)

(See also Boston, Salem)

Settled 1629 **Pop** 81,245 **Elev** 30 ft **Area code** 781 **E-mail** staff@lynnchamber.com **Web** www.lynnchamber.com
Information Chamber of Commerce, 23 Central Ave, Suite 416, 01901; 781/592-2900.

Shoe manufacturing began as a home craft in Lynn as early as 1635. Today Lynn's industry is widely diversified. Founded here in 1883, General Electric is the biggest single enterprise. Lynn also has more than three miles of sandy beaches.

What to See and Do

Grand Army of the Republic Museum. Features Revolutionary War, Civil War, Spanish-American War & World War I weapons, artifacts and exhibits. (Mon-Fri by appt; closed hols) 58 Andrew St. Phone 781/477-7085. **Donation.**

Lynn Heritage State Park. Five-acre waterfront park; pedalboats; marina. (Daily; closed Jan 1, Dec 25) Visitor center (590 Washington St) with museum-quality exhibits from past to present, from hand-crafted shoes to high tech items; inquire for hrs. Lynnway. Phone 781/598-1974. **Free.**

Lynn Historical Society Museum/Library. 1836 house with period furnishings; museum wing with changing exhibits. Decorative arts, toys, tools, bicycles and photographs of Lynn. Library includes manuscripts and diaries from 1600s to present. Library (Mon-Fri; closed hols); museum tours (Mon-Sat, afternoons; closed hols). 125 Green St. Phone 781/592-2465. ¢¢

Lynn Woods Reservation. Wooded area consisting of 2,200 acres. Features walking trails, 18-hole golf course, historic dungeon rock (pirates cave), stone tower; picnic areas, playgrounds. (Daily)

Mary Baker Eddy Historical Home. Restored house where the founder of Christian Science lived from 1875-1882. (Mid-May-mid-Oct, Wed & Thurs) 12 Broad St. To arrange a tour phone 781/450-3790. **Free.**

Inn

★ ★ ★ **DIAMOND DISTRICT.** *142 Ocean St (01902), off Lynn Shore Drive at Wolcott. 781/599-4470; FAX 781/595-2200; res: 800/666-3076.* E-mail diamonddistrict@msn.com; web www.bbhost.com/diamond-district. 11 rms, 1 with shower only, 3 story. June-Oct: S, D $90-$235; each addl $20; under 3 free; lower rates rest of yr. Crib free. Pet accepted, some restrictions; $10. TV. Complimentary full bkfst. Restaurant nearby. Ck-out 11 am. Business servs avail. In-rm modem link. Gift shop. Health club privileges. Microwaves avail. Georgian-style residence built in 1911. Totally nonsmoking. Cr cds: A, C, D, DS, MC, V.

Lynnfield (B-7)

Settled 1639 **Pop** 11,274 **Elev** 98 ft **Area code** 617 **Zip** 01940

Hotel

★ ★ ★ **SHERATON COLONIAL.** *427 Walnut St, Just N of I-95, MA 128 exits 42, 43. 781/245-9300; FAX 781/245-0842.* 280 rms, 11 story. S $89-$169; D $89-$189; each addl $15; suites $275-$495; wkend rates. Crib free. TV; cable (premium), VCR avail. Indoor pool; whirlpool. Coffee in rms. Restaurant 6:30 am-10:30 pm. Ck-out 11 am. Convention facilities. In-rm modem link. Barber shop. Lighted tennis. 18-hole golf, pro, putting green, driving range. Exercise rm; sauna, steam rm. Some refrigerators; microwaves avail. Cr cds: A, C, D, DS, MC, V.

Restaurants

★ ★ ★ **KERNWOOD.** *55 Salem St. 781/245-4011.* New England menu. Specializes in seafood, prime beef. Hrs: 11 am-10 pm; Sun to 9 pm; early-bird dinner Mon-Fri 4:30-6:30 pm, Sat 4-6 pm. Closed July 4, Dec 25. Bar. Wine list. Semi-a la carte: lunch $4.95-$10.95, dinner $12-$19. Child's meals. Pianist exc Sun. Colonial atmosphere; open-hearth cooking. Family-owned. Cr cds: A, C, D, MC, V.

★ ★ ★ **TOWNE LYNE HOUSE.** *1/4 mi S on US 1, N of MA 128 exit 44 B. 781/592-6400.* Specializes in rack of lamb, stuffed breast of chicken, fresh seafood. Own baking. Hrs: 11:45 am-9 pm; Fri, Sat to 10 pm. Res accepted. Bar to 1 am. Semi-a la carte: lunch $5.95-$10.95, dinner $10.95-$20. Traditional colonial decor; built in 1800s. Overlooks Lake Suntaug. Cr cds: A, C, D, DS, MC, V.

Marblehead (B-8)

(See also Boston, Salem)

Settled 1629 **Pop** 19,971 **Elev** 65 ft **Area code** 617 **Zip** 01945 **E-mail** mcc@shore.net **Web** www.marbleheadchamber.org

InformationChamber of Commerce, 62 Pleasant St, PO Box 76; 617/631-2868.

A unique blend of old and new, Marblehead is situated on a peninsula 17 miles north of Boston. Originally named Marble Harbor by hardy fishermen from Cornwall and the Channel Islands in the 1600s, the town boasts a beautiful harbor and a number of busy boatyards. Pleasure craft anchor in this picturesque port each summer, and a record number of modern racing yachts participate in the annual Race Week. Beaches, boating, fishing, art exhibits, antique and curio shops—all combine to offer a choice of quiet relaxation or active recreation.

What to See and Do

Abbot Hall. Displays the original "Spirit of '76" painting and deed to town (1684) from the Nanepashemet. Museum, Marine Room. Gift shop. (Last wkend May-last wkend Oct, daily; rest of yr, Mon-Fri; closed winter hols) Town Hall, Washington Sq. Phone 617/631-0000. **Donation.**

Jeremiah Lee Mansion (1768). Marblehead Historical Society. Where Generals Glover, Lafayette and Washington were entertained. Georgian architecture; Marblehead history; antiques of the period, original wallpaper. (Mid-May-mid-Oct, daily; closed hols) 161 Washington St. Phone 617/631-1069. ¢¢

King Hooper Mansion (1728). Restored house with garden. Art exhibits. (Mon-Fri, also Sat & Sun afternoons; closed Jan 1, Dec 25) 8 Hooper St. Phone 617/631-2608. **Free.**

Seasonal Event

Sailing races. Phone 617/631-3100. Summer, Wed eve and wkends. Race Week 3rd wk July.

Inns

★ ★ **HARBOR LIGHT INN.** *58 Washington St.* 781/631-2186; FAX 781/631-2216. Web www.harborlightinn.com. 21 rms. S, D $95-$150; each addl $15; suites $160-$245. TV; cable (premium), VCR avail (free movies). Heated pool. Complimentary continental bkfst. Restaurant nearby. Ck-out 11 am, ck-in 1 pm. Business servs avail. In-rm modem link. Concierge serv. Airport transportation. Health club privileges. Antiques. Built 1712. Totally nonsmoking. Cr cds: A, MC, V.

✔★ ★ **MARBLEHEAD.** *264 Pleasant St (MA 114).* 781/639-9999; res: 800/399-5843; FAX 781/639-9996. Web www.marblehead-inn.com. 10 units, 3 story. S, D $119-$169; each addl $5. TV; cable (premium), VCR. Complimentary continental bkfst. Restaurants nearby. Ck-out 11 am, ck-in 3 pm. Guest lndry. Picnic tables. Refrigerators, microwaves. Antiques. Victorian inn (1872) near beach. Totally nonsmoking. Cr cds: A, MC, V.

★ ★ **THE SEAGULL INN.** *106 Harbor Ave.* 781/631-1893; FAX 781/631-3535. Web www.seagullinn.com. 6 rms, 1 with shower only, 2 story, 4 suites, 2 kit. units. May-Oct: suites, kit. units $100-$225; wkends 2-day min; lower rates rest of yr. Crib avail. Pet accepted. TV; cable, VCR (movies). Complimentary continental bkfst. Complimentary coffee in rms. Restaurant nearby. Ck-out 11 am, ck-in 2 pm. Business servs avail. Lawn games. Opp ocean. Built in 1880; turn-of-the-century atmosphere. Totally nonsmoking. Cr cds: MC, V.

★ ★ **SPRAY CLIFF.** *25 Spray Ave.* 781/631-6789; res: 800/626-1530; FAX 781/639-4563. E-mail spraycliff@aol.com; web www.marbleheadchmber.org/spraycliff. 7 rms, 4 with shower only, 3 story. No elvtr. No rm phones. May-Oct: S, D $175-$200; wkends (2-day min); lower rates rest of yr. Complimentary continental bkfst. Restaurant nearby. Ck-out 11 am, ck-in 3 pm. Some fireplaces. On ocean. Built in 1910. Cr cds: A, MC, V.

Restaurants

✔★ **THE KING'S ROOK.** *12 State St.* 781/631-9838. E-mail kings-rook@msn.com. Specializes in gourmet pizzas, sandwiches, salads. Hrs: noon-2:30 pm, 5:30-11:30 pm; Sat, Sun noon-11:30 pm. Closed Thanksgiving, Dec 25, Dec 31. Semi-a la carte: lunch, dinner $4.50-$7.50. Child's meals. Street parking. Family-owned since 1966. Cr cds: MC, V.

★ ★ **THE LANDING.** *Off Front St, 1 blk from Washington St.* 781/631-1878. Specializes in seafood. Hrs: 11:30 am-4 pm, 5-10 pm; Fri, Sat to 11 pm; Sun brunch 10:30 am-4 pm. Closed Thanksgiving, Dec 25. Bar. A la carte entrees: lunch $2.50-$19.95, dinner $9.95-$21.95. Sun brunch $2.95-$14.95. Child's meals. Entertainment Fri, Sun. Outdoor dining. Windows overlook beach and boating area. Family-owned. Cr cds: A, C, D, DS, MC, V.

★ ★ **PELLINO'S.** *261 Washington St.* 781/631-3344. Northern Italian menu. Specializes in pasta, seafood, chicken. Hrs: 5-10 pm; Fri, Sat to 10:30 pm. Closed Jan 1, Easter, Dec 25. Res required. Bar. Semi-a la carte: dinner $10.95-$17.95. Parking. Italian decor. Totally nonsmoking. Cr cds: A, DS, MC, V.

Martha's Vineyard (E-8 - E-9)

(See also Falmouth, Hyannis, Nantucket Island, Woods Hole)

Settled 1642 **Pop** 12,690 **Elev** 0-311 ft **Area code** 508 **E-mail** mvcc@vineyard.net **Web** www.mvy.com

Information Chamber of Commerce, Beach Rd, PO Box 1698, Vineyard Haven 02568; 508/693-0085.

This triangular island below the arm of Cape Cod combines moors, dunes, multicolored cliffs, flower-filled ravines, farmland and forest. It is less than 20 miles from west to east and 10 miles from north to south.

There was once a whaling fleet at the island, but Martha's Vineyard now devotes itself almost entirely to being a vacation playground, with summer houses that range from small cottages to elaborate mansions. The colonial atmosphere still survives in Vineyard Haven, the chief port, Oak Bluffs, Edgartown, West Tisbury, Gay Head and Chilmark.

Gay Head is one of the few Massachusetts towns in which many inhabitants are of Native American descent.

What to See and Do

Car/passenger boat trips.

Woods Hole, Martha's Vineyard & Nantucket Steamship Authority conducts round-trip service to Woods Hole (all yr, weather permitting). Phone 508/477-8600. ¢¢¢

Cape Island Express Lines. New Bedford-Martha's Vineyard Ferry. Daily passenger service (mid-May-mid-Oct) to New Bedford. One-way and same-day round trips avail. Also bus tours of the island. Schedule may vary; contact Cape Island Express Lines, PO Box 4095, New Bedford, 02741; phone 508/997-1688. Round-trip ¢¢¢¢

Island Queen. Daily round trips, Falmouth-Martha's Vineyard. (May-Oct) Phone 508/548-4800. Round trip ¢¢¢

Hyannis-Martha's Vineyard Day Round Trip. Passenger service from Hyannis (May-Oct). Phone 508/778-2600. ¢¢¢¢

Felix Neck Sanctuary. Approx 350 acres with woods, far-reaching salt marshes, pond with large variety of waterfowl, reptile pond, 6 mi of trails; barn; exhibit centers; library. (Daily) 3 mi out of Edgartown on the Vineyard Haven-Edgartown Rd. Phone 508/627-4850. ¢

Historic areas.

Oak Bluffs. In 1835 this Methodist community served as the site of annual summer camp meetings for church groups. As thousands attended these meetings, the communal tents gave way to family tents, which in turn became wooden cottages designed to look like tents. Today, visitors to the community may see these "Gingerbread Cottages of the Campground."

Edgartown. The island's first colonial settlement and county seat since 1642 is the location of stately white Greek-revival houses built by whaling captains. These have been carefully preserved and North Water St has a row of captains' houses unequaled anywhere.

Recreation. Swimming. Many sheltered beaches, among them public beaches at Menemsha, Oak Bluffs, Edgartown and Vineyard Haven. Surf swimming on south shore. **Tennis.** Public courts in Edgartown, Oak Bluffs, West Tisbury and Vineyard Haven. **Boat rentals** at Vineyard Haven , Oak Bluffs & Gay Head. **Fishing.** Good for striped bass, bonito, bluefish, weakfish. **Golf** at Farm Neck Club (phone 508/693-3057) and Mink Meadows (phone 508/693-0600). Bike, moped rentals avail.

⬛ **Vincent House.** Oldest known house on the island, built 1672. Carefully restored to allow visitors to see how buildings were constructed 300 yrs ago. Original brickwork, hardware and woodwork. (June-early Oct, daily; rest of yr, by appt) Main St in Edgartown. Phone 508/627-4440. **Free.** Also on Main St is

Old Whaling Church. Built in 1843, this is a fine example of Greek-revival architecture. Now a performing arts center with seating for 500. Phone 508/627-4442.

Seasonal Event

Striped Bass & Bluefish Derby. 2,000 entrants compete for cash and prizes. Includes boat, shore and flyrod divisions. Mid-Sept-mid-Oct.

Motels

★ ★ **COLONIAL INN.** *(38 N Water St, Edgartown 02539)* 508/627-4711; FAX 508/627-5904; res: 800/627-4701. E-mail www.ti ac.net/users/innmvy. 43 rms, 1-4 story. No elvtr. Memorial Day-mid-Sept: D $148-$245; each addl $15; under 16 free; wkly, hol rates; lower rates late Sept-Dec, mid-Apr-Memorial Day. Closed rest of yr. Crib free. TV; cable (premium), VCR avail (free movies). Complimentary continental bkfst. Restaurant 5:30 am-12:30 pm. Ck-out 11 am. Meeting rms. Business servs avail. In-rm modem link. Bellhops. Sundries. Shopping arcade. Barber. Some refrigerators. Balconies. Cr cds: A, MC, V.

Ⓓ 🔥

★ ★ **ISLAND INN.** *(Beach Rd, Oak Bluffs 02557)* 508/693-2002; FAX 508/693-7911; res: 800/462-0269. Web www.islandinn.com. 51 kit. units, 1-2 story. Mid-June-mid-Sept: $130-$295; lower rates rest of yr. Pet accepted. TV; cable. Pool. Restaurant 6-11 pm. Bar 4 pm-midnight. Ck-out 11 am. Coin lndry. Meeting rm. Business servs avail. In-rm modem link. Gift shop. Tennis, pro (in season). 18-hole golf adj, pro. Bicycle path adj. Near beach. Cr cds: A, C, D, DS, ER, JCB, MC, V.

Ⓓ 🧍 🏌 🌊 🔥 SC

★ ★ ★ **KELLEY HOUSE.** *(23 Kelley St, Edgartown 02539)* 508/627-7900; FAX 508/627-8142; res: 800/225-6005. 53 rms, 1-3 story. No elvtr. June-Sept: S, D $235-$495; each addl $20; suites, kit. units $285-$625; under 12 free; lower rates rest of yr. TV; cable (premium). Pool. Complimentary continental bkfst; afternoon refreshments. Ck-out 11 am. Meeting rms. Business servs avail. Bellhops. Concierge. Tennis privileges. Refrigerators. In operation since 1742. Rose gardens. Cr cds: A, C, D, JCB, MC, V.

🧍 🌊 ⊠ 🔥

Hotel

★ ★ ★ **HARBORVIEW.** *(131 N Water St, Edgartown 02539)* 508/627-7000; FAX 508/627-8417; res: 800/225-6005. Web www.harborview.com. 124 rms, 1-4 story, 14 kits. June-mid-Sept: D $225-$450; each addl $20; suites, kit. units $375-$625; under 12 free; lower rates rest of yr. TV; cable (premium). Heated pool; poolside serv. Restaurant (see COACH HOUSE). Bar 11 am-midnight. Ck-out 11 am. Meeting rms. Business servs avail. Concierge. Tennis. Refrigerators. Private patios, balconies. Beach opp. Overlooks harbor; view of lighthouse. In operation since 1891. Fieldstone fireplace in lobby. Extensive grounds and gardens. Cr cds: A, C, D, MC, V.

Ⓓ 🧍 🌊 ⊠ 🔥 SC

Inns

★ ★ **THE ARBOR.** *(222 Upper Main St, Edgartown 02539)* 508/627-8137. 10 air-cooled rms, 8 with bath, 2 story. No rm phones. Mid-June-Sept: D $110-$150; kit. cottage $700-$900/wk; lower rates May-mid-June, Oct. Closed rest of yr. Children over 12 yrs only. Complimentary continental bkfst; afternoon refreshments. Restaurant nearby. Ck-out 11 am, ck-in 2 pm. Concierge. Antique shop. Built 1880; antiques. Library/sitting rm. Cr cds: MC, V.

🔥

★ ★ **ASHLEY.** *(129 Main St, Edgartown 02539)* 508/627-9655; FAX 508/627-6629; res: 800/477-9655. Web www.vineyard.net/biz/ashleyinn. 10 rms, 3 story, 2 suites. Late June-late Sept: S, D $135-$265; suites $265; each addl $15; honeymoon packages; lower rates rest of yr. Children over 12 yrs only. TV; cable. Complimentary continental bkfst. Restaurant adj. Ck-out 11 am, ck-in 2 pm. Some refrigerators, fireplaces. Picnic tables. 1860 sea captain's house; antiques. Totally nonsmoking. Cr cds: MC, V.

⊠ ⊠ 🔥

★ **BEACH HOUSE.** *(Seaview & Pennacook Ave, Oak Bluffs 02557)* 508/693-3955. 9 rms, 3 story. No rm phones. July-Aug: S, D $135-$155; wkends, hols (3-day min); lower rates rest of yr. Children over 10 yrs only. TV. Complimentary continental bkfst. Ck-out 11 am, ck-in 1 pm. Luggage handling. Built in 1899; front porch. Opp ocean. Cr cds: A, C, D, DS, MC, V.

🖼 ⊠ 🔥

★ ★ ★ **BEACH PLUM.** *(North Rd, Menemsha 02552)* 508/645-9454; FAX 508/645-2801. Web www.beachpluminn.com. 11 rms, 2 story, 1 suite. Mid-June-mid-Sept: D $225-$300; suite $325; under 12 free; higher rates hols; lower rates rest of yr. Crib avail. TV; cable (premium), VCR (movies). Playground. Supervised child's activities; ages 3-12. Complimentary full bkfst. Restaurant (see BEACH PLUM INN). Ck-out 11 am, ck-in 2 pm. Business servs avail. In-rm modem link. Luggage handling. Concierge serv. Tennis. Lawn games. Balconies. Picnic tables. Built 1890 from salvage of shipwreck. Most rms with ocean view. Gardens. Cr cds: A, D, DS, MC, V.

🧍 🔥

★ ★ **CAPTAIN DEXTER HOUSE.** *(92 Main St, Vineyard Haven 02568)* 508/693-6564; FAX 508/693-8448. 8 rms, 3 story. 6 A/C. No rm phones. Memorial Day-Oct 1: D $115-$175; each addl $20; suite $175; lower rates rest of yr. Children over 12 yrs only. Complimentary continental bkfst; afternoon refreshments. Ck-out 11 am, ck-in 2 pm. Sitting garden. Some fireplaces. Old sea captain's home (1843); antiques. Totally nonsmoking. Cr cds: A, MC, V.

⊠ 🔥 SC

★ ★ **CAPTAIN DEXTER HOUSE.** *(35 Pease's Point Way, Edgartown 02539)* 508/627-7289; FAX 508/627-3328. Web www.mvy.com/captdexter. 11 rms, 10 A/C, 1 air-cooled, 2 story. No rm phones. June-Sept: S, D $135-$195; each addl $20; lower rates mid-Apr-May, Oct. Closed rest of yr. Complimentary continental bkfst; afternoon refreshments. Restaurant nearby. Ck-out 11 am, ck-in 2 pm. Traditional white clapboard house built in 1840 by a prominent merchant family; antiques; flower gardens. Totally nonsmoking. Cr cds: A, MC, V.

★ ★ **DAGGETT HOUSE.** (59 N Water St, Edgartown 02539) 508/627-4600; FAX 508/627-4611; res: 800/946-3400. Web www.mvweb.com/daggett. 31 rms in 4 bldgs, 2 story, 10 kits. May-Oct: S, D $150-$225; each addl $20; suites $155-$550; lower rates rest of yr. Crib free. TV; cable. Resturant 8-11 am, 5:30-9 pm; Sun brunch to 1 pm. Ck-out 11 am, ck-in 3 pm. Private pier. Gardens. Open hearth, antiques in dining rm, part of historic (1660) tavern. New England atmosphere. Totally nonsmoking. Cr cds: A, DS, MC, V.

★ ★ ★ **DOCKSIDE INN.** (Circuit Ave Ext, Oak Bluffs 02557) 508/693-2966; FAX 508/696-7293; res: 800/245-5979. E-mail inns@vineyard.net; web www.vineyard.net/inns. 22 rms, 3 story, 5 kit. suites. Mid-June-mid-Sept: S, D $130-$180; kit. suites $240-$350; family rates; 3-day min; lower rates mid-Sept-Nov, Apr-mid-June. Closed rest of yr. Crib free. TV; cable. Complimentary continental bkfst. Restaurant nearby. Ck-out 11 am, ck-in 2-7 pm. Luggage handling. Concierge serv. Business servs avail. In-rm modem link. Game rm. Refrigerators. Balconies. Colorful gingerbread-style inn opp docks. Totally nonsmoking. Cr cds: A, DS, MC, V.

★ ★ **EDGARTOWN.** (56 N Water St, Edgartown 02539) 508/627-4794; FAX 508/627-9420. Web www.vineyard.net/biz/edgartowninn. 12 rms in inn, 8 rms in 2 annexes, 1-3 story. Late May-late Sept: annex D $90-$185; inn S, D $125-$185; each addl $20; lower rates Oct, Apr-late-May. Closed rest of yr. TV in some rms, sitting rm. Dining rm 8-11 am. Ck-out 11 am, ck-in 2 pm. Historic (1798) sea captain's home. Inn since 1820; colonial furnishings & antiques in rms. No cr cds accepted.

★ ★ **GREENWOOD HOUSE.** (40 Greenwood Ave, Vineyard Haven 02568) 508/693-6150; FAX 508/696-8113; res: 800/525-9466. E-mail innkeeper@greenwoodhouse.com; web www.greenwoodhouse.com. 5 rms, 3 story. Mid-May-mid-Sept: S, D $169-$249; lower rates rest of yr. TV; cable. Complimentary full bkfst. Complimentary coffee in rms. Restaurant nearby. Ck-out 10 am, ck-in 2 pm. Business servs avail. In-rm modem link. Luggage handling. Concierge serv. Lawn games. Refrigerators. Built 1906. Totally nonsmoking. Cr cds: A, C, D, MC, V.

★ ★ ★ **HANOVER HOUSE.** (28 Edgartown Rd, Vineyard Haven 02568) 508/693-1066; FAX 508/696-6099; res: 800/339-1066. 15 rms, 4 with shower only, 2 story, 3 suites, 2 kit. units. No rm phones. Early June-mid-Sept: S, D $130-$185; suites, kit. units $185-$255; family, wkly rates; wkends (2-day min); lower rates rest of yr. TV; cable. Complimentary continental bkfst. Restaurant nearby. Ck-out 10 am, ck-in 2 pm. Business servs avail. Balconies. Built 1920; gardens, enclosed sitting porch. Totally nonsmoking. Cr cds: A, DS, MC, V.

✔ ★ ★ ★ **HOB KNOB.** (128 Main St, Edgartown 02539) 508/627-9510; FAX 508/627-4560; res: 800/696-2723. E-mail hobnob@vineyard.net; web www.hobnob.com. 16 rms, 3 story. Memorial Day-mid-Oct: S, D $185-$375; lower rates rest of yr. TV; cable. Complimentary full bkfst. Restaurant nearby. Ck-out 11 am, ck-in 2 pm. Meeting rm. Business servs avail. In-rm modem link. Concierge serv. Exercise equipt; sauna. Massage. Bicycle rental. Sun porch; garden. Inn built 1860; many antiques. Totally nonsmoking. Cr cds: A, MC, V.

★ ★ **LAMBERT'S COVE.** (Lambert's Cove Rd, Vineyard Haven 02568) 5 mi W on Lambert's Cove Rd. 508/693-2298; FAX 508/693-7890. 15 rms, 2 story. No rm phones. Late May-early Oct: D $145-$195; lower rates rest of yr. TV in sitting rm. Complimentary full bkfst. Dining rm (public by res) 6-9 pm. Ck-out 11 am, ck-in 2 pm. Tennis. Balconies. Picnic tables.

Secluded farmhouse (1790); many antiques. Gardens, apple orchard. Cr cds: A, MC, V.

★ ★ ★ **MARTHA'S PLACE.** (114 Main St, Vineyard Haven 02568) 508/693-0253. Web marthasplace.com. 7 rms, 3 with shower only, 2 story. No rm phones. June-Sept: S, D $175-$295; package plans; wkends 2-day min; special events 3-day min; higher rates special events; lower rates rest of yr. TV in some rms. Complimentary continental bkfst. Restaurant nearby. Ck-out 10 am, ck-in after noon. Business servs avail. Luggage handling. Valet serv. Some in-rm whirlpools. Balconies. Picnic tables, grills. Built in 1840; restored Greek-revival mansion. Totally nonsmoking. Cr cds: A, MC, V.

★ ★ ★ **THE OAK HOUSE.** (75 Seaview Ave, Oak Bluffs 02557). 508/693-4187; res: 800/245-5979. Web www.vineyard.net/inns. 10 rms, 9 with shower only, 3 story, 2 suites. No elvtr. Mid-June-mid-Sept: S, D $150-$190; suites $250-$260; lower rates rest of yr. Closed Mid-Oct-mid-May. Children over 10 yrs only. TV; cable, VCR avail. Complimentary continental bkfst; afternoon refreshments. Ck-out 11 am, ck-in 4 pm. Street parking. Some balconies. Picnic tables, grills. Opp beach. 1872 summer home for MA governor. Totally nonsmoking. Cr cds: A, DS, MC, V.

★ ★ **OUTERMOST INN.** (Lighthouse Rd, Gay Head 02535) 508/645-3511; FAX 508/645-3514. Web www.outermostinn.com. 7 rms, 2 story. No A/C. Mid-June-mid-Sept: S, D $240-$320; wkends (2-day min); lower rates mid-Apr-mid-June, mid-Sept-Oct. Children over 12 yrs only. TV. Complimentary full bkfst; afternoon refreshments. Dining rm 6-8 pm. Ck-out 11 am, ck-in 2 pm. Luggage handling. Concierge serv. Business servs avail. Balconies. Picnic tables. Picture windows provide excellent views of Vineyard Sound and Elizabeth Islands. Totally nonsmoking. Cr cds: A, DS, MC, V.

★ ★ **PEQUOT HOTEL.** (19 Pequot Ave, Oak Bluffs 02557). 508/693-5087; res: 800/947-8704; FAX 508/697-9413. Web www.mvy.com.pequot. 29 rms, 2 with shower only, 3 story. No rm phones. July-Aug: S, D $105-$195; kit. units $245-$385; wkday rates; higher rates July 4; lower rates rest of yr. Closed Nov-Apr. Crib $25. TV in some rms. Complimentary continental bkfst. Restaurant nearby. Ck-out 11 am, ck-in 3 pm. Street parking. Picnic tables. Built in 1920s. Cr cds: A, DS, MC, V.

★ ★ **POINT WAY.** (104 Main St, Edgartown 02539) 508/627-8633. 14 rms, 1-3 story. Late May-Oct: S, D $175-$325; each addl $25; suites $325; lower rates rest of yr. Pet accepted, some restrictions; $25. TV. Complimentary continental bkfst; afternoon refreshments. Ck-out 11 am, ck-in 2 pm. Lndry serv. Some balconies. Gardens. Totally nonsmoking. Cr cds: A, DS, MC, V.

★ ★ **SHIRETOWN.** (44 N Water St, Edgartown 02539) 508/627-3353; FAX 508/627-8478; res: 800/541-0090. 35 rms in 4 bldgs, 1-3 story. Some A/C. Mid-June-mid-Sept: S, D $129-$249; each addl $20; suites $179-$289; cottage $1,200-$1,800/wk; under 2 free; lower rates May-late-June, mid-Sept-mid-Oct. Closed rest of yr. TV; cable. Complimentary continental bkfst. Dining rm 11 am-2 pm, 5-10 pm. Bar 11-12:30 am. Ck-out 11 am, ck-in 2 pm. Business servs avail. Balconies. Sun decks. 18th-century whaling house. Cr cds: DS, MC, V.

★ ★ ★ **THORNCROFT.** (460 Main St, Vineyard Haven 02568) 508/693-3333; FAX 508/693-5419; res: 800/332-1236. Web www.thorncroft.com. 14 rms in 2 bldgs, 2 story. Mid-June-Labor Day: D $200-$450; lower rates rest of yr. TV; cable. Complimentary full bkfst; afternoon refreshments. Ck-out 11 am, ck-in 3-9 pm. Business servs avail. In-rm modem link. Luggage handling. Many fireplaces; some in-rm whirlpools.

Some balconies. 1918 bungalow; antiques. Totally nonsmoking. Cr cds: A, C, D, DS, ER, MC, V.

D ⊠ 🔥

Restaurants

★ ★ ★ BEACH PLUM INN. *(See Beach Plum Inn)* 508/645-9454. Specialties: roasted rack of lamb, local seafood, grilled lobster. Hrs: 8-11 am, 5:30-10 pm. Closed mid-Oct-mid-May. Res required (dinner). Semi-a la carte: bkfst $2-$9. A la carte entrees: dinner $26-$36. Complete meals: dinner $58. Pianist. Parking. Outdoor dining overlooking ocean. Totally nonsmoking. Cr cds: A, D, DS, MC, V.

D

★ ★ ★ COACH HOUSE. *(See Harborview Hotel)* 508/627-7000. New England cuisine. Specialties: crusty barbecued cod, whole steamed bass, lemon thyme lamb chops. Hrs: 7-11 am, noon-2 pm, 6-10 pm; Sun brunch 10 am-2 pm. Res accepted. Bar 11 am-11 pm. Wine cellar. A la carte entrees: bkfst $5.95-$10, lunch $7.95-$15, dinner $16.95-$32. Sun brunch $18.95. Child's meals. View of harbor. Totally nonsmoking. Cr cds: A, D, MC, V.

D

★ ★ HOME PORT. *(North Rd, Menemsha)* 508/645-2679. Specializes in seafood, lobster. Outdoor clam bar. Hrs: 5-10 pm. Closed mid-Oct-mid Apr. Res required. No A/C. Setups. Complete meals: dinner $16-$32. Child's meals. Parking. On harbor; scenic view; nautical atmosphere. Cr cds: MC, V.

D ⌐

★ ★ ★ L'ETOILE. *(S Summer St, Edgartown 02539) in Charlotte Inn.* 508/627-5187. Contemporary French menu. Specialties: foie gras, soft shell crabs, roasted rack of lamb. Hrs: 6:30-9:45 pm. Closed Jan-mid-Feb. Res required. Wine list. Prix fixe: dinner $58-$64. Outdoor dining. Enclosed garden room; many antiques. Jacket. Totally nonsmoking. Cr cds: A, MC, V.

D

★ ★ LE GRENIER. *(82 Main St, Vineyard Haven 02568)* 508/693-4906. French provincial menu. Specialties: lobster normande, steak au poivre, shrimp pernod. Hrs: 5:30-10 pm. Res accepted. A la carte entrees: dinner $18.95-$29.95. Street parking. Elegant bistro. Family-owned since 1979. Cr cds: A, C, D, DS, MC, V.

★ LOUIS' TISBURY CAFÉ. *(350 State Rd, Vineyard Haven 02568)* 508/693-3255. Web louis@vinyard.net. Italian, seafood menu. Specialties: eggplant parmesan, rack of lamb, pasta tomato cream shrimp. Hrs: 5:30-9 pm; Fri, Sat to 9:30 pm. Closed most major hols. Semi-a la carte: dinner $12.75-$24.95. Child's meals. Parking. Italian cafe style. Totally nonsmoking. Cr cds: A, DS, MC, V.

D

★ ★ NAVIGATOR. *(2 Lower Main St, Edgartown 02539)* 508/627-4320. Specializes in seafood. Hrs: 11-1 am. Closed mid-Oct-mid-May. Bar. A la carte entrees: lunch $5.95-$11.95. Semi-a la carte: dinner $19.95-$29.95. Child's meals. Outdoor dining. Overlooks harbor. Family-owned. Cr cds: A, C, D, DS, MC, V.

D

★ ★ ★ O'BRIEN'S. *(137 Upper Main, Edgartown 02539)* 508/627-5850. Web www.tiac.net/users/obriens. Specializes in chocolate cake, lobster, Angus steaks. Hrs: 6-11 pm. Closed Jan-Apr. Res accepted. Bar. Wine list. A la carte entrees: dinner $19.95-$32.95. Entertainment wknds. Valet parking. Patio dining. 3 dining rms, including wrap-around, enclosed porch; latticework. Cr cds: A, MC, V.

★ ★ ★ SAVOIR FAIRE. *(14 Church St, Edgartown 02539)* 508/627-9864. Specialties: grilled tuna, soft shell crabs, loster en brodo. Raw bar in summer. Hrs: 5:30-10 pm. Closed Nov-Mar. Res accepted. No

A/C. Bar. Wine cellar. Semi-a la carte: dinner $26-$32. Parking. Outdoor dining. Totally nonsmoking. Cr cds: MC, V.

D

★ ★ SQUARE RIGGER. *(Upper Main St, Edgartown 02539)* 508/627-9968. Specializes in seafood, grilled entrees, lobster. Hrs: 5:30-10 pm. Res accepted. Bar. A la carte entrees: dinner $14-$26. Child's meals. Parking. Open hearth kitchen in dining rm. Totally nonsmoking. Cr cds: A, MC, V.

D ♥

✔ ★ ★ THE WHARF. *(Lower Main St, Edgartown 02539)* 1 mi E on Main St. 508/627-9966. Specializes in fresh seafood, seafood Wellington pie, desserts. Hrs: 11:30 am-midnight. Closed Thanksgiving, Dec 24, 25. Res accepted. Bar. Semi-a la carte: lunch $5.95-$9.95, dinner $8.95-$17.95. Child's meals. Entertainment Wed-Sun. Cr cds: A, D, DS, MC, V.

D ♥

Nantucket Island (F-9 - E-10)

(See also Hyannis, Martha's Vineyard)

Settled 1659 **Pop** 6,012 **Elev** 0-108 ft **Area code** 508 **Zip** 02554 **Web** www.nantucketchamber.org

Information Chamber of Commerce, 48 Main St; 508/228-1700. General information may also be obtained at the Information Bureau, 25 Federal St; 508/228-1700.

This is not just an island; it is an experience. Nantucket Island is at once a popular resort and a living museum. Siasconset (SCON-set) and Nantucket Town remain quiet and charming despite heavy tourism. Nantucket, with 49 square miles of lovely beaches and green moors inland, is south of Cape Cod, 30 miles at sea. The island was the world's greatest whaling port from the late 17th century until New Bedford became dominant in the early 1800s. Whaling prosperity built the towns; tourism maintains them.

There is regular car ferry and passenger service from Hyannis. If you plan to take your car, make advance reservation by mail with the Woods Hole, Martha's Vineyard & Nantucket Steamship Authority, PO Box 284, Woods Hole 02543; 508/477-8600. A great variety of beaches, among them the Jetties, north of Nantucket Town (harbor), and Surfside, on the south shore of the island (surf), offer swimming. Tennis, golf, fishing, sailing, cycling can be arranged.

What to See and Do

Boat trips. Hyannis-Nantucket Day Round Trip. Summer passenger service from Hyannis. Phone 508/778-2600. ¢¢¢¢¢

⭐ **Main Street.** Paved with cobblestones, lined with elegant houses built by the whaling merchants and shaded by great elms, this is one of New England's most beautiful streets. The Nantucket Historical Association maintains the following attractions (June-Oct, daily; spring & fall, limited hrs). Phone 508/228-1894. **Note:** Some properties may be closed for renovation.

1800 House. Home of sheriff, early 19th century. Period home and furnishings; large, round cellar; kitchen garden. Mill St, off Pleasant St. ¢¢

Folger-Franklin Seat & Memorial Boulder. Birthplace site of Abiah Folger, mother of Benjamin Franklin. Madaket Rd, 1 mi from W end of Main St.

Hadwen House (1845). Greek-revival mansion; furnishings of whaling period; gardens. Main & Pleasant Sts. ¢¢

Jethro Coffin House (1686). Nantucket's oldest house. N on North Water to West Chester, left to Sunset Hill. ¢¢

Museum of Nantucket History (Macy Warehouse). Exhibits related to Nantucket history; diorama; craft demonstrations. Straight Wharf. ¢¢

Old Fire Hose Cart House (1886). Old-time firefighting equipment. Gardner St off Main St.   **Free.**

Old Gaol (1805). Unusual 2-story construction; used until 1933. Vestal St.   **Free.**

Old Windmill (1746). Built of wood from wrecked vessels with original machinery and grinding stones. Corn ground daily during summer. On Mill Hill, off Prospect St.   **¢**

Research Center. Ships' logs, diaries, charts and Nantucket photographs; library. (Mon-Fri) Broad St, next to Whaling Museum. For admission & research fees phone 508/228-1655.

Whaling Museum. Outstanding collection of relics from whaling days; whale skeleton, tryworks, scrimshaw, candle press. Broad St, near Steamboat Wharf.   **¢¢**

General pass for all the above   **¢¢¢**

Nantucket Maria Mitchell Association. Birthplace of first American woman astronomer; memorial observatory (1908). Scientific library has Nantucket historical documents, science journals and Mitchell family memorabilia. Natural science museum with local wildlife. Aquarium at 28 Washington St. (Mid-June-Aug, Tues-Sat; library also open rest of yr, Wed-Sat; closed July 4, Labor Day) 1 Vestal St. Phone 508/228-9198 or 508/228-0898 in summer. Combination ticket avail for museum, birthplace and aquarium.   **¢¢**

Sightseeing tours.

Barrett's Tours. Offers 1¹/₂-hr bus & van tours (Apr-Nov). Phone 508/228-0174.   **¢¢¢**

Gail's Tours. Narrated van tours (approx 1³/₄ hrs) of area. 3 tours daily. Res recommended. Depart from Information Center at Federal & Broad Sts; or phone for pick up at many guest houses. (Daily) Phone 508/257-6557.   **¢¢¢**

Annual Events

Daffodil Festival. Parade of antique cars, prize for best tailgate picnic. Last full wkend Apr.

Harborfest. 2nd wkend June.

Sand Castle Contest. 3rd Sun Aug.

Christmas Stroll. 1st Sat Dec.

Motels

★ ★ **HARBOR HOUSE.** *S Beach St.* 508/228-1500; *FAX* 508/228-7639; *res:* 800/475-2637. 113 rms, 2-3 story. No elvtr. Late June-mid-Sept: D $245-$285; each addl $20; package plans; lower rates rest of yr. TV; cable (premium). Heated pool; poolside serv. Restaurant 7:30-10 am, 11:30 am-10 pm. Rm serv in season. Bar noon-1 am; entertainment. Ck-out 11 am. Meeting rms. Business servs avail. In-rm modem link. Bellhops. Concierge. Private patios, balconies. Authentic reproductions of Colonial-period furnishings; some antiques. Extensive grounds, elaborate landscaping. Most rms with garden view. Public beach opp. Cr cds: A, C, D, DS, MC, V.

D 🏊 🛶 🔥 🐾 SC

★ ★ **NANTUCKET INN.** *27 Macy's Lane, near Memorial Airport.* 508/228-6900; *FAX* 508/228-9861; *res:* 800/321-8484. E-mail ackinn@nantucket.net. 100 rms, 1-2 story. June-Sept: S, D $130-$190; each addl $12; under 18 free; lower rates rest of yr. Pet accepted; $25. TV; cable. 2 pools, 1 indoor; whirlpool, lifeguard. Restaurant 7:30-10:30 am, noon-2 pm, 5:30-9 pm. Rm serv. Bars. Ck-out 11 am. Coin lndry. Meeting rms. Business servs avail. Bellhops. Sundries. Free airport transportation. Lighted tennis. Exercise equipt. Refrigerators. Cr cds: A, C, D, DS, MC, V.

D 🐾 🏌 ⛷ 🏊 🎾 ✈ 🐾

★ ★ **WHARF COTTAGES.** *New Whale St, on wharf, foot of Main St.* 508/228-4620; *FAX* 508/228-7197; *res:* 800/475-2637. 25 kit. cottages, 1-2 story. No A/C. Late May-Oct: kit. cottages $295-$575; wkly rates. Closed rest of yr. Crib free. TV; cable (premium). Restaurant nearby.

Ck-out 11 am. Coin lndry. Bellhops. Tennis privileges. Balconies. Picnic tables, grills. Dockage. Cr cds: A, C, D, DS, MC, V.

🐾 SC

Hotel

★ ★ ★ **WHITE ELEPHANT INN & COTTAGES.** *Easton St, 4 blks NE.* 508/228-2500; *FAX* 508/325-1195; *res:* 800/475-2637. 80 rms, most A/C, 1-3 story (no elvtr); suites in 15 cottages. Mid-June-mid-Sept: D $340-$590; each addl $20; cottages with kit. $425-$700; lower rates late-May-late-June, mid-Sept-mid-Oct. Closed rest of yr. Crib free. TV; cable (premium). Heated pool; whirlpool, poolside serv, lifeguard. Restaurant 7:30-10:30 am, noon-10 pm in season. Bar noon-1 am; entertainment. Ck-out 11 am. Meeting rm. Business servs avail. In-rm modem link. Concierge. Some private patios. Playground. Beach nearby; boat slips for guests only. On harbor; waterfront view from most inn rms. Cr cds: A, C, D, DS, MC, V.

D 🛶 🔥 SC

Inns

✔ ★ ★ **CARLISLE HOUSE.** *26 N Water St, in Historic District.* 508/228-0720. Web www.nantucket.net/lodging/carlisle. 14 rms, 5 share bath, 3 story. No rm phones. Mid-June-mid-Sept: S $75; D $95-$185; each addl $15; suites $250-$275; lower rates rest of yr. Children over 10 yrs only. Complimentary continental bkfst. Restaurant nearby. Ck-out 11 am, ck-in 2 pm. Street parking. Some fireplaces. Antiques. Library/sitting rm. Restored whaling captain's house (1765). Totally nonsmoking. Cr cds: A, MC, V.

🛶 🔥

★ **CARRIAGE HOUSE.** *5 Ray's Ct.* 508/228-0326. 7 rms, 2 story. No A/C. Mid-June-mid-Oct: S, D $120-$160; lower rates rest of yr. TV in sitting rm; cable. Complimentary continental bkfst. Restaurant nearby. Ck-out 11 am, ck-in 1 pm. Converted 1865 carriage house. Victorian decor. Garden terrace. Totally nonsmoking. No cr cds accepted.

🛶 🔥

★ ★ ★ **CENTERBOARD GUEST HOUSE.** *8 Chester St.* 508/228-9696. 7 rms, 3 story, 1 suite, 1 kit. Mid-June-mid-Oct: S, D $185; suite $325; lower rates rest of yr. TV. Complimentary continental bkfst. Restaurant nearby. Ck-out 11 am, ck-in 2 pm. In-rm modem link. Street parking. Refrigerators. Library/sitting rm, antiques. Restored Victorian residence (1885). Totally nonsmoking. Cr cds: A, MC, V.

🛶 🔥

★ ★ **CENTRE STREET INN.** *78 Centre St.* 508/228-0199; *FAX* 508/228-8676; *res:* 800/298-0199. E-mail inn@nantucket.net; web www.centrestreetinn.com. 13 rms, 6 share bath, 3 story. No rm phones. Late June-late Sept: S $75; D $95-$195; each addl $30; wkends, hols (3-day min); higher rates special hol events; lower rates May-late June, late Sept-mid-Dec. Closed rest of yr. Children over 8 yrs only. Complimentary continental bkfst. Ck-out 11 am, ck-in 3 pm. Luggage handling. Concierge serv. Refrigerator avail. Picnic tables. Colonial house built in 1742; some antiques. Totally nonsmoking. Cr cds: A, DS, MC, V.

🛶 🔥

★ ★ **COBBLESTONE.** *5 Ash St.* 508/228-1987; *FAX* 508/228-6698. 4 rms, 3 story, 1 suite. Mid-June-mid-Sept: D $125-$175; each addl $20; suite $250; higher rates Christmas Stroll; lower rates rest of yr. TV; cable. Complimentary bkfst. Restaurant nearby. Ck-out 11 am, ck-in 2 pm. Concierge. Lawn games. Picnic tables. Built 1725; antiques. Fireplace in library. Totally nonsmoking. Cr cds: MC, V.

🛶 🔥

★ **CORNER HOUSE.** *(49 Centre St, Nantucket)* 508/228-1530. Web www.cornerhousenantucket.com. 16 rms, 8 with shower only, 3 story, 2 suites. No rm phones. Mid-June-Late Sept: S, D $120-$195; D $195-$225; wkends (3-4 day min); lower rates rest of yr. Children over 8 yrs only. TV in most rms; cable (premium). Complimentary continental bkfst. Restaurant adj 6 am-11 pm. Ck-out 10:30 am, ck-in after 1 pm. Concierge serv. Street parking. Many refrigerators; microwave in suites. Built in 1790s as a father's wedding present for his daughter. Cr cds: A, MC, V.

[icon]

★ ★ **FOUR CHIMNEYS.** *38 Orange St. 508/228-1912; FAX 508/325-4864.* 10 rms, 8 with shower only, 3 story. No rm phones. Late May-mid-Oct: D $165-$275. Closed rest of yr. TV in sitting rm; cable. Complimentary continental bkfst; afternoon refreshments. Restaurant nearby. Ck-out 11 am, ck-in 1 pm. Luggage handling. Concierge serv. Built 1870 for sea captain; many antiques. Garden. Totally nonsmoking. Cr cds: A, MC, V.

[icons]

✔★ ★ ★ **JARED COFFIN HOUSE.** *29 Broad St, in Historic District. 508/228-2400; FAX 508/325-7752; res: 800/248-2405.* E-mail jchouse@nantucket.net; web www.nantucket.net/lodging/jchouse. 60 rms in 6 bldgs. Some A/C. Elvtr in main bldg. Late June-Sept: S $90-$150; D $160-$210; each addl $15; lower rates rest of yr. Crib $10. Pet accepted; $10. TV. Complimentary full bkfst. Restaurant (see JARED'S). Limited rm serv. Bar 11:30 am-11 pm. Ck-out 11 am, ck-in after 3 pm. Meeting rms. Business servs avail. In-rm modem link. Luggage handling. Concierge serv. Some refrigerators. Restored 1845 mansion; historical objets d'art. Cr cds: A, C, D, DS, MC, V.

[icons]

✔★ **MARTIN'S HOUSE.** *(Nantucket) 508/228-0678; FAX 508/325-4798.* E-mail martinn@nantucket.net; web nantucket.net/lodging/martinn. 13 rms, 4 share bath, 3 story. No A/C. No elvtr. No rm phones. Mid-June-mid-Oct: S $50-$65; D $65-$120; each addl $25; suites $170; under 7 free; lower rates rest of yr. Children over 7 yrs only. TV in common rm; cable (premium). Complimentary continental bkfst. Restaurant opp 6-10 pm. Ck-out 11 am, ck-in 2 pm. In-rm modem link. Luggage handling. Street parking. Built in 1803; antiques. Totally nonsmoking. Cr cds: A, MC, V.

[icon]

★ ★ **ROBERTS HOUSE.** *11 India St, in Historic District. 508/325-0750; FAX 508/325-4046; res: 800/992-2899.* E-mail RHInn@aol.com; web oneweb.com/nantucket/. 42 rms, 4 share bath, 3 story. Mid-June-mid-Oct: D $125-$275; each addl $40; under 12 free; package plans; lower rates rest of yr exc hols & some wkends. Crib $10. TV. Complimentary continental bkfst. Coffee in rms. Ck-out 11 am, ck-in after 2 pm. Concierge serv. Microwaves; some fireplaces. Built 1846; established 1883. Cr cds: DS, MC, V.

[icons]

★ ★ **SEVEN SEA STREET.** *7 Sea St, in Historic District. 508/228-3577; FAX 508/228-3578.* Web www.nantucket.net/lodging/seast7/. 11 rms, 2 story, 2 suites. July-Aug: S, D $155-$195; suites $235-$265; off-season package plans; higher rates Christmas stroll wkend; lower rates rest of yr. Children over 5 yrs only. TV; cable, VCR. Complimentary continental bkfst; afternoon refreshments. Restaurant nearby. Ck-out 11 am, ck-in 2 pm. Business servs avail. Whirlpool. Refrigerators. Picnic tables. Library/sitting rm. View of Nantucket Harbor. Totally nonsmoking. Cr cds: A, DS, MC, V.

[icons]

★ ★ **SHERBURNE.** *10 Gay St. 508/228-4425; FAX 508/228-8114.* Web www.nantucket.net/lodging/sherburne. 8 rms, 2 story. Mid-June-mid-Oct (3-day min): S, D $125-$235; each addl $25; higher rates: hols, special events; lower rates rest of yr. Children over 6 yrs only. Complimentary continental bkfst. Restaurant nearby. Ck-out 11 am, ck-in 2 pm. Concierge serv. Street parking. Built in 1835 as a silk factory; period antiques, fireplaced parlors. Totally nonsmoking. Cr cds: A, DS, MC, V.

[icons]

✔★ ★ **SHIPS INN.** *13 Fair St. 508/228-0040; FAX 508/228-6524.* 12 rms, 10 with bath. No A/C. Mid-May-mid-Oct: S $65-$90; D $145-$175; each addl $25. Closed rest of yr. Crib $10. TV. Complimentary continental

bkfst; afternoon refreshments. Dining rm 5:30-9:30 pm. Bar 4:30-10 pm. Ck-out 10:30 am, ck-in 2 pm. Refrigerators. Built in 1831 by sea captain; many original furnishings. Totally nonsmoking. Cr cds: A, DS, MC, V.

[icons]

★ ★ **TUCKERNUCK.** *60 Union St. 508/228-4886; FAX 508/228-4890; res: 800/228-4886.* 19 rms, 2-3 story. Mid-June-late-Sept: D $130-$165; each addl $20; suites $175-$240; higher rates: Memorial Day, Christmas stroll wkend; lower rates rest of yr. TV; cable (premium), VCR. Dining rm 8-11 am, 5:30-9:30 pm. Ck-out 11 am, ck-in 3 pm. Coin lndry. Business servs avail. Lawn games. Picnic tables. Library/sitting rm. Sun deck. View of Nantucket Harbor. Totally nonsmoking. Cr cds: A, MC, V.

[icons]

★ ★ ★ **THE WAUWINET.** *Wauwinet Rd (02584), 8 mi NE on Wauwinet Rd. 508/228-0145; FAX 508/325-0657; res: 800/426-8718.* E-mail email@wauwinet.com; web www.wauwinet.com. Guest rooms in this 1870 inn are done in a country style with pine antiques. 36 rms, 1-3 story, 4 suites. Mid-June-late Sept: S, D $320-$710; suites $610-$1,400; lower rates early May-mid-June, late Sept-Oct. Closed rest of yr. Crib free. TV; VCR (movies). Complimentary full bkfst; afternoon refreshments. Dining rm (see TOPPER'S). Rm serv to 9 pm. Ck-out 11 am, ck-in 4 pm. Business servs avail. In-rm modem link. Tennis, pro, pro shop. Rowboats & sailboats. Bicycles. Lawn games. Refrigerators avail. Some patios. Library. On ocean; swimming beach; complimentary harbor cruises. Totally nonsmoking. Cr cds: A, C, D, MC, V.

[icons]

Restaurants

★ ★ **21 FEDERAL.** *21 Federal St. 508/228-2121.* Specializes in seafood. Own baking, pasta. Menu changes daily. Hrs: 11:30-1 am. Closed Jan-Mar. Res accepted. Bar. A la carte entrees: lunch $10-$15, dinner $19-$29. Outdoor dining. Display of old prints, drawings. Cr cds: A, MC, V.

[icon]

★ ★ **AMERICAN SEASONS.** *80 Centre St. 508/228-7111.* Specialties: braised rabbit tostada, potato and thyme crusted sturgeon, homemade desserts. Hrs: 6-10 pm. Closed Jan-Apr. Res accepted. Bar. Semi-a la carte: dinner $16.50-$23.50. Outdoor dining. Popular spot features regional cuisine; decorated with country artifacts, hand-painted murals and gameboard tables. Cr cds: A, MC, V.

✔★ **ATLANTIC CAFE.** *15 S Water St, in Historic District, near wharf. 508/228-0570.* Specializes in seafood, hamburgers, Mexican dishes. Hrs: 11:30 am-midnight. Closed late Dec-early Jan. Bar. Semi-a la carte: lunch $5-$12, dinner $8-$21. Child's meals. Nautical decor; ship models. Cr cds: A, D, DS, MC, V.

[icon]

★ ★ **BOARDING HOUSE.** *12 Federal St. 508/228-9622.* Specialties: twin lobster tails, seared yellowfin tuna, pistachio-crusted chocolate finale. Hrs: noon-2 pm, 6-10 pm. Res accepted. Bar noon-1 am. A la carte entrees: lunch $6-$14, dinner $20-$32. Outdoor dining. Original art. Cr cds: A, MC, V.

[icon]

★ ★ **CAP'N TOBEY'S CHOWDER HOUSE.** *Straight Wharf, off Main St. 508/228-0836.* Specialties: Cap'n Tobey's clam chowder, Nantucket Bay scallops, Indian pudding. Salad bar. Hrs: 11-1 am. Closed mid-Oct-mid-May. Res accepted. Bar. Semi-a la carte: lunch $6.95-$9.95, dinner $12.95-$19.95. Child's meals. Nautical decor. Wharf view. Family-owned. Cr cds: A, D, DS, MC, V.

[icons]

★ ★ ★ **CHANTICLEER.** *9 New St (02564). 508/257-6231.* French menu. Specializes in fresh local seafood, lobster bisque, foie gras. Hrs: noon-2 pm, 6:30-9:30 pm. Closed Mon; also late Oct-mid-May. Res required. Bar. Wine cellar. A la carte entrees: lunch $15-$30, dinner $25-$60.

Prixe fixe: dinner $65. Parking. Garden dining. Elegant, romantic dining in four dining rms. View of flower and herb gardens, carousel. Cr cds: A, MC, V.

D

★ ★ ★ **CIOPPINO'S.** *20 Broad St.* *508/228-4622.* Continental menu. Specialties: cioppino, tournedos of beef with lobster topping, hazelnut salmon fillet. Hrs: 11:30-2:30 pm, 5:30-10 pm. Closed Nov-May. Res accepted. Bar. Wine cellar. A la carte entrees: lunch $8.50-$13.50, dinner $19.50-$36. Patio dining. 3 dining rms in turn-of-the-century house. Cr cds: D, DS, MC, V.

★ ★ ★ **CLUB CAR.** *1 Main St, off Straight Wharf.* *508/228-1101.* Continental menu. Specializes in rack of lamb, fresh seafood, veal. Hrs: 6-10 pm. Closed mid-Dec-mid-May. Res required. Bar 11:30-1 am; pianist. A la carte entrees: dinner $26-$40. In authentic railroad car; railroad memorabilia, photos. Turn-of-the-century decor. Cr cds: MC, V.

★ ★ **THE COMPANY OF THE CAULDRON.** *(5 India St, Nantucket)* *508/228-4016.* Web acktack@nantuket.net. Continental, Amer menu. Specializes in fresh fish. Own pasta. Sittings: 7 & 9 pm. Closed Mon; also Mid-Dec-May. Res accepted. Wine, beer. Complete meals: $46-$50. Harpist Wed, Fri, Sun. Street parking. Candlelight setting. Totally nonsmoking. Cr cds: MC, V.

D

★ ★ **INDIA HOUSE.** *37 India St.* *508/228-9043.* Specializes in lamb, swordfish, chocolate silk. Hrs: 6:30-9:30 pm; Sun brunch 9:30 am-12:30 pm. Closed Jan-Mar. Res accepted. Serv bar. A la carte entrees: dinner $15-$32. Sun brunch $16. Child's meals. Garden dining. 3 dining rms. Inn built 1803; overnight rms avail. Totally nonsmoking. Cr cds: A, DS, MC, V.

★ ★ ★ **JARED'S.** *(See Jared Coffin House Inn)* *508/228-2400.* Specializes in bay scallops, regional dishes. Hrs: 7:30-11 am, 6-9 pm. Res accepted. Tap rm 11:30 am-9:30 pm. Complete meals: bkfst $5.95-$8.95, dinner $19-$32. Child's meals. Outdoor dining June-Sept. Family-owned. Totally nonsmoking. Cr cds: A, C, D, DS, MC, V.

D

★ ★ ★ **LE LANGUEDOC.** *24 Broad St, in Historic District.* *508/228-2552.* Continental menu. Specializes in veal, lamb, fresh fish. Hrs: noon-2 pm (fall), 6-10 pm; Apr-early Sept from 6 pm. Closed Jan-Mar. Res accepted. Bar 6 pm-midnight. Semi-a la carte: lunch $8-$18, dinner $25-$35. Outdoor dining. Early 1800s building in heart of historic district. Cr cds: A, MC, V.

★ ★ **ROPE WALK.** *Straight Wharf.* *508/228-8886.* Specializes in fresh local seafood, homemade desserts. Hrs: 11:30-12:30 am. Closed mid-Oct-mid-May. No A/C. Bar. Semi-a la carte: lunch $7.50-$12, dinner $16.50-$26. Child's meals. Outdoor dining. Nautical artifacts. At end of wharf; view of harbor. Cr cds: MC, V.

D

★ **TAVERN AT HARBOR SQUARE.** *Straight Wharf, off Main St.* *508/228-1266.* Specializes in New England clam chowder, lobster, fresh seafood. Hrs: 11 am-9:30 pm. Closed mid-Oct-late May. No A/C. Bar to midnight. Semi-a la carte: lunch $6.95-$12, dinner $6.95-$21.95. Child's meals. Patio dining. Nautical decor. Wharf view. Cr cds: A, MC, V.

D

★ ★ ★ **TOPPER'S.** *(See The Wauwinet Inn)* *508/228-0145.* Specialties: lobster and crab cakes with smoked corn, jalapeno olives and mustard sauce; Nantucket lobster with asparagus, mushrooms and fettuccini; local seafood. Hrs: noon-2 pm, 6-9:30; Sun brunch 11 am-2 pm. Closed Nov-mid-May. Res accepted. Bar from noon. Wine list. A la carte entrees: lunch $19.50-$24, dinner $29-$52. Sun brunch $36. Child's meals. Valet parking. Outdoor dining (summer). Within country inn; pickled oak floors; folk art collection. View of Nantucket Bay. Totally nonsmoking. Cr cds: A, C, D, MC, V.

D

★ ★ **WEST CREEK CAFE.** *(11 W Creek Rd, Nantucket)* *508/228-4943.* Contemporary Amer menu. Specialties: sautéed crab fritter with Georgia peanut vinaigrette; roasted tenderloin with polenta fries & red wine sauce; seared salmon over oven roasted vegetable risotto & chive oil. Hrs: 6-9 pm; Fri, Sat to 9:30 pm. Closed Tues; also Jan 1, July 4, Dec 25. Res accepted. Bar. A la carte entrees: dinner $18-$26. Parking. Outdoor dining. Contemporary elegant cafe. Totally nonsmoking. Cr cds: MC, V.

D

Natick (B-6)

Pop 30,510 **Elev** 180 ft **Area code** 508 **Zip** 01760 **E-mail** chamber@metrowest.org **Web** www.metrowest.org

InformationMetroWest Chamber of Commerce, 1671 Worcester Rd, Suite 201, Framingham 01701; 508/879-5600.

This town was set aside as a plantation for the "Praying Indians" in 1650 at the request of Rev John Eliot. A missionary, he believed that he could promote brotherhood between Native Americans and settlers by converting them. After half a century, the Native Americans were crowded out by settlers.

Motel

✔ ★ ★ **TRAVELODGE.** *1350 Worcester Rd (MA 9).* *508/655-2222; res: 800/578-7878; FAX 508/655-7953.* E-mail sleepbr@banet.net. 68 rms, 2 story. S $79; D $89; each addl $5; under 18 free. Crib free. TV; cable (premium). Continental bkfst. Complimentary coffee in rms. Ck-out noon. Business servs avail. In-rm modem link. Cr cds: A, C, D, DS, ER, JCB, MC, V.

D ⊠ 🔥 SC

Motor Hotels

★ ★ ★ **CROWNE PLAZA.** *1360 Worcester Rd (MA 9).* *508/653-8800; FAX 508/653-1708.* 251 units, 7 story. S $99-$170; D $119-$190; suites $450; under 19 free; wkend rates. Crib free. TV; cable (premium), VCR avail (movies). Pool; whirlpool. Restaurant 6 am-5 pm; dining rm 5-10 pm. Bar 11-1 am. Ck-out noon. Convention facilities. Business servs avail. In-rm modem link. Concierge. Bellhops. Valet serv. Gift shop. Exercise equipt; sauna. Cr cds: A, C, D, DS, ER, JCB, MC, V.

D ⊠ 🍴 🏊 🔥 SC

✔ ★ ★ **HAMPTON INN.** *319 Speen St, MA 9 & Speen St; I-90 exit 13.* *508/653-5000; FAX 508/651-9733.* 190 rms, 7 story. S, D $90-$99. Crib free. TV; cable (premium). Complimentary continental bkfst. Ck-out noon. Meeting rms. Business servs avail. Exercise equipt. Some refrigerators. Cr cds: A, C, D, DS, MC, V.

D 🍴 ⊠ 🔥 SC

Inn

★ ★ **SHERBORN.** *(33 N Main St, Sherborn 01770) 3 mi S on MA 27.* *508/655-9521; res: 800/552-9742; FAX 508/655-5325.* 4 rms, 2 story. S, D $105-$140. Crib avail. Complimentary continental bkfst. Restaurant (see SHERBORN INN). Rm serv. Ck-out 11 am, ck-in 3 pm. Cr cds: A, MC, V.

D ⊠ 🔥

Restaurant

★ ★ **SHERBORN INN.** *(See Sherborn Inn)* *508/655-9521.* Contemporary Amer menu. Specializes in tenderloin of beef. Own baking. Hrs: 11:30 am-3 pm, 5-9:30 pm. Res accepted. Bar. Semi-a la carte: lunch

$4.95-$9.50, dinner $13-$24. Jazz Tues. Restored tavern decor. Cr cds: A, MC, V.

New Bedford (D-7)

Settled 1640 **Pop** 99,922 **Elev** 50 ft **Area code** 508 **Web** www.bristol-county.org

Information Bristol County Convention & Visitors Bureau, 70 N Second St, PO Box 976, 02741; 508/997-1250 or 800/288-6263.

Herman Melville, author of *Moby Dick,* said that the brave houses and flowery gardens of New Bedford were one and all harpooned and dragged up from the bottom of the sea. Whaling did in fact build this city. When oil was discovered in Pennsylvania in 1857, the world's greatest whaling port nearly became a ghost town. New Bedford scrapped the great fleet and became a major cotton textile center. More recently, it has thrived on widely diversified industries. New Bedford remains a major Atlantic deep-sea fishing port. The whaling atmosphere is preserved in local museums and monuments, while the Whaling National Historical Park celebrates the towns whaling legacy. In the County Street historic district many of the mansions built for sea captains and merchants still stand.

What to See and Do

Boat trips.

Cape Island Express Lines. New Bedford-Martha's Vineyard Ferry. Bus tours, car rentals on Martha's Vineyard. (Mid-May-mid-Oct, daily) Same-day round-trip and one-way trips avail. Schedule may vary, phone ahead. Contact Cape Island Express Lines, PO Box 4095, 02741; phone 508/997-1688. Round-trip ¢¢¢¢¢

New Bedford-Cuttyhunk Ferry. (Mid-June-mid-Sept, daily; rest of yr, varied schedule) Res suggested. Departs from Fisherman's Wharf, pier 3. Phone 508/992-1432. Round trip ¢¢¢¢¢

Buttonwood Park & Zoo. Greenhouse; ball fields, tennis courts, playground, picnic area, fitness circuit. Zoo exhibits include elephants, lions, deer, bears, buffalo; seal pool. (Apr-Nov, daily; rest of yr, wkends only) Rockdale Ave. Phone 508/991-6178 (zoo) or 508/991-6175. ¢

Children's Museum. Two floors of hands-on exhibits; 60 acres with nature trails, picnic areas. Special summer and wkend programs. (Daily exc Mon; closed major hols) From I-195 exit 12, left on US 6, first right (Tucker Rd), continue 4 mi to 4-way stop, left onto Gulf Rd in South Dartmouth. Phone 508/993-3361. ¢¢

Fort Phoenix Beach State Reservation. Swimming; fine view of harbor. Nearby is Fort Phoenix, a pre-Revolutionary fortification (open to the public). Off US 6 & I-95, E via US 6 to Fairhaven, then 1 mi S; follow signs. Phone 508/992-4524. Per vehicle ¢

New Bedford Whaling Museum. Features an 89-ft half-scale model of whaleship *Lagoda.* Galleries devoted to scrimshaw, local artists; murals of whales and whale skeleton; period rms and collections of antique toys, dolls, prints and ship models. Silent movie presentation (July & Aug). (Daily; closed Jan 1, Thanksgiving, Dec 25) 18 Johnny Cake Hill. Phone 508/997-0046. ¢¢

Rotch-Jones-Duff House and Garden Museum. Whaling era Greek-revival mansion (1834) and garden, has been maintained to reflect the lives of 3 families that lived in the house. (Oct-May, daily exc Mon; rest of yr, Mon-Sat, also Sun afternoons) Museum sponsors concerts & programs throughout the yr. Tours avail, inquire for schedule. Museum shop. 396 County St. Phone 508/997-1401. ¢¢

Seamen's Bethel (1832). "Whaleman's Chapel" referred to by Melville in *Moby Dick.* Prow-shaped pulpit later built to represent Melville's description. Also many cenotaphs dedicated to men lost at sea. Vespers 3rd Sun each month. (May-Columbus Day, Mon-Sat, also Sun afternoons; rest of yr, by appt) 15 Johnny Cake Hill. Phone 508/992-3295. **Donation.**

Annual Events

Feast of the Blessed Sacrament. Madeira Field, N end of town. Portuguese festival. 3 days usually beginning 1st wkend Aug.

Blessing of the Fleet. Waterfront. 3rd Sun Aug.

First Night New Bedford. Historic waterfront and downtown. Celebration of arts and culture; fireworks. Dec 31.

Motels

★ ★ **COMFORT INN.** *(171 Faunce Corner Rd, N Dartmouth 02747)* W via I-195, exit 12. 508/996-0800. E-mail comfort@ultranet.com; web www.s-t.com/comfortinn. 85 rms, 2 story. Late May-early Sept: S $65-$79; D $69-$89; each addl $5; under 18 free; lower rates rest of yr. Crib free. TV; cable (premium). Pool. Ck-out noon. Business center. In-rm modem link. Cr cds: A, C, D, DS, ER, JCB, MC, V.

D ⚊ ☇ 🐾 SC 🛟

✔★ ★ **DAYS INN.** 500 Hathaway Rd (02740), off I-195 at exit 13B, near Municipal Airport. 508/997-1231; FAX 508/984-7977. 153 rms, 3 story. S $64-$75; D $69-$82; each addl $5; under 12 free. Crib free. Pet accepted, some restrictions. TV; cable (premium). Indoor pool. Coffee in rms. Restaurant 7 am-11 pm. Rm serv. Bar 4 pm-midnight. Ck-out 11 am. Meeting rm. Business servs avail. In-rm modem link. Coin lndry. Free airport transportation. Golf course opp. Cr cds: A, C, D, DS, ER, JCB, MC, V.

D ⚘ ⚊ ✈ ☇ 🐾 SC

Restaurant

★ ★ **FREESTONE'S CITY GRILL.** 41 William St (02740). 508/993-7477. Specializes in fish chowder, seafood, specialty salads. Hrs: 11 am-11 pm; Sun noon-10 pm. Closed Labor Day, Thanksgiving, Dec 25. Res accepted. Bar. Semi-a la carte: lunch $4-$7, dinner $4-$18. Child's meals. Street parking. Renovated bank bldg (1877); interesting art objects. Cr cds: A, D, MC, V.

D

Newburyport (A-8)

Settled 1635 **Pop** 16,317 **Elev** 37 ft **Area code** 978 **Zip** 01950 **E-mail** chamber@newburyport.net **Web** www.newburyport.chamber.net

Information Greater Newburyport Chamber of Commerce & Industry, 29 State St; 978/462-6680.

Novelist John P. Marquand, who lived in Newburyport, said it "is not a museum piece although it sometimes looks it." High St is surely a museum of American Federalist architecture. Ship owners and captains built these great houses. The birthplace of the US Coast Guard, Newburyport lies at the mouth of the Merrimack River. The city's early prosperity came from shipping and shipbuilding. It is now a thriving year-round tourist destination.

What to See and Do

Coffin House (ca 1654). Developed in a series of enlargements, features 17th- & 18th-century kitchens, buttery and parlor with early 19th-century wallpaper; furnishings of 8 generations. Tours on the hr. (June-mid-Oct, Wed-Sun) 16 High Rd (US 1A). Phone 978/463-2057. ¢¢

Cushing House Museum (Historical Society of Old Newbury; ca 1810). A Federalist-style mansion, once the home of Caleb Cushing, first envoy to China from US. Museum houses collections of needlework, paperweights, toys, paintings, furniture, silver, clocks, china; library. Also shed, carriage house and 19th-century garden. (May-Oct, Tues-Sat; closed hols) 98 High St. Phone 978/462-2681. ¢¢

Custom House Maritime Museum. Collections of artifacts depicting maritime heritage of area; includes ship models, navigational instruments; decorative arts, library. (Apr-late Dec, Mon-Sat, also Sun afternoons) 25 Water St. Phone 978/462-8681. ¢¢

Parker River National Wildlife Refuge. Natural barrier beach formed by 6½ mi of beach and sand dunes is the home of many species of birds, mammals, reptiles, amphibians and plants; saltwater and freshwater marshes provide resting and feeding place for migratory birds on the Atlantic Flyway. Hiking, bicycling; waterfowl hunting; nature trail. (Daily) Closed to public when parking lots are full. 3 mi E on Plum Island. Contact Refuge Manager, Northern Blvd, Plum Island 01950; 978/465-5753. Pedestrians ¢; Per vehicle ¢¢

Annual Events

Spring Arts & Flower Festival. Downtown. Demonstrations, flower and garden show, crafts, exhibits. Sun, Mon of Memorial Day wkend.

Yankee Homecoming. Celebration includes parades, fireworks, exhibits; river cruises; sailboat and canoe races; craft show; lobster feeds. Last Sat July-1st Sun Aug.

Fall Harvest Festival. Downtown. Juried crafts, music, entertainment, food, baking contest. Sun, Mon of Columbus Day wkend.

Motel

✔★ **SUSSE CHALET.** *(35 Clarks Rd, Amesbury 01913) 3 mi N on I-95 exit 58B. 978/388-3400.* 105 rms, 4 story. S, D $69-$89; each addl $6; under 18 free; wkend rates. TV; cable (premium). Complimentary continental bkfst. Restaurant adj 6:30 am-11:30 pm. Ck-out 11 am. Meeting rms. Business servs avail. Health club privileges. Pool. Cr cds: A, D, DS, MC, V.

🅳 ⛌ ⛌ SC

Inns

★★ **CLARK CURRIER.** *45 Green St. 978/465-8363.* 8 rms, 3 story. May-mid-Jan: S, D $95-$155; lower rates rest of yr. TV in sitting rm. Complimentary bkfst buffet. Restaurant nearby. Ck-out 11 am, ck-in 3 pm. Bus depot transportation. Built in 1803 by a shipbuilder. Rms furnished with antiques. Garden with gazebo. Totally nonsmoking. Cr cds: A, DS, MC, V.

⛌ 🔥 SC

✔★★ **ESSEX STREET.** *7 Essex St. 978/465-3148; FAX 978/462-1907.* 19 rms, 3 story. June-Oct: S, D $85-$125; each addl $10; suites $155; kit. unit $175; townhouse $155; lower rates rest of yr. TV. Complimentary continental bkfst. Restaurant nearby. Ck-out 11 am, ck-in 2 pm. Some in-rm whirlpools. Built in 1801; fireplace. Cr cds: A, C, D, DS, MC, V.

⛌ 🔥

★ **GARRISON INN.** *11 Brown Square, off Pleasant St. 978/465-0910; FAX 978/465-4017.* 24 rms, 4 story. June-Oct: S, D $97.50-$107.50 each addl $10; town house $135-$175; lower rates rest of yr. Crib avail. TV; cable (premium), VCR avail. Restaurant (see DAVID'S). Supervised child's activities; ages 2-12. Bar; entertainment. Ck-out 11 am, ck-in 3 pm. Meeting rm. Business servs avail. In-rm modem link. Restored historic inn (1809). Cr cds: A, C, D, DS, MC, V.

🅳 ⛌ 🔥

✔★ **MORRILL PLACE.** *209 High St (MA 113). 978/462-2808; res: 888/594-4667; FAX 978/462-9966.* E-mail morrill@aol.com. 9 rms, 4 share bath, 3 story. No A/C. S, D $72-$95; each addl $10; EP avail; wkly rates. Pet accepted. TV rm; cable, VCR avail. Complimentary continental bkfst. Restaurant nearby. Ck-out noon, ck-in 4 pm. Tennis privileges. 18-hole golf privileges, pro. Built in 1806. Once owned by law partner of Daniel Webster; Webster was frequent visitor. Formal front parlor and library. No cr cds accepted.

🅳 ✈ 🎿 🏃 🔥

★★ **WINDSOR HOUSE.** *38 Federal St. 978/462-3778; FAX 978/465-3443.* E-mail tintagel@greennet.net. 4 rms, 3 story. S $99; D $135; each addl $35. Crib free. Pet accepted, some restrictions. TV in sitting rm; VCR. Complimentary full bkfst. Coffee in rms. Restaurant nearby. Ck-out 11 am, ck-in 4 pm. Meeting rm. Business servs avail. Microwaves avail. Federal mansion (1786) built by a lieutenant of the Continental Army for his wedding. Antiques. Totally nonsmoking. Cr cds: A, DS, MC, V.

🔙 ⛌ 🔥

Restaurants

✔★★ **CHEF'S HARVEST.** *38A Washington St. 978/463-1775.* Continental menu. Specializes in veal, fish, pasta. Hrs: 5-9 pm; Fri, Sat to 10 pm. Closed Tues; Easter, Dec 25. Res accepted. Semi-a la carte: dinner $5.75-$14.95. Child's meals. Street parking. Casual decor. Cr cds: A, D, DS, MC, V.

★★★ **DAVID'S.** *(See Garrison Inn) 978/462-8077.* Eclectic menu. Specializes in lobster, scallops, sweet potatoes. Own baking. Hrs: 5-9 pm; Fri, Sat to 10 pm. Closed Jan 1, Dec 24, 25. Res accepted. Bar. Wine list. Semi-a la carte: dinner $6.95-$24.50. Prix fixe: dinner $40-$54.50. Child's meals. Guitarist Thurs-Sat. Two distinct dining areas: formal dining rm with high ceiling and informal basement pub; separate menus. Cr cds: A, DS, MC, V.

🅳

★★★ **GLENN'S.** *44 Merrimas St. 978/465-3811.* Seafood menu. Menu changes daily. Hrs: 5:30-10 pm; Sat, Sun from 4 pm. Closed Mon; also major hols. Res accepted. Bar. Wine list. Semi-a la carte: dinner $18-$22. Child's meals. Wed, Thurs, Sun entertainment. Street parking. Bistro decor. Cr cds: A, C, D, DS, MC, V.

🅳

✔★ **THE GROG.** *13 Middle St. 978/465-8008.* Eclectic menu. Specializes in seafood. Hrs: 11:30-12:15 am. Closed Dec 25. Bar. Semi-a la carte: lunch, dinner $5.95-$14.95. Musicians Thurs-Sun. Tavern atmosphere. Family-owned. Cr cds: A, DS, MC, V.

🅳 ⇥

✔★ **JACOB MARLEY'S.** *23 Pleasant St. 978/465-5598.* Amer, fusion menu. Specializes in entree salads. Hrs: 11:30 am-11 pm; Sun from 10 am; Sun brunch 11 am-2 pm. Closed Dec 25. Bar to 1 am. Semi-a la carte: lunch, dinner $8.95-$13.95. Sun brunch $7.95-$10.95. Child's meals. Entertainment Tues, Sat, Sun. Restored mill; nautical objects. Cr cds: A, D, DS, MC, V.

🅳 ⇥

✔★★ **MICHAEL'S HARBORSIDE.** *MA1. 978/462-7785.* Seafood menu. Specializes in fresh seafood. Hrs: 11:30 am-3 pm, 5-9 pm; Sat to 10 pm; Sun noon-9 pm; winter hrs vary. Closed Thanksgiving, Dec 25. Bar. Semi-a la carte: lunch $5.95-$11.95, dinner $6.95-$15.95. Entertainment Sun (summer). Parking. Outdoor dining. Cr cds: A, MC, V.

🅳

★★★ **SCANDIA.** *25 State St. 978/462-6271.* Contemporary Amer menu. Specializes in seafood, game, vegetarian dishes. Hrs: 11:30 am-3 pm, 5-10 pm; Thurs-Sun from 8 am. Closed Thanksgiving, Dec 25. Res accepted. Bar. Semi-a la carte: lunch $3.25-$12, dinner $12-$17.95. Child's meals. Outdoor dining. Traditional, formal decor with large original oil paintings. Family-owned. Totally nonsmoking. Cr cds: A, MC, V.

★★★ **TEN CENTER STREET.** *10 Center St, 1 blk off Market Square. 978/462-6652.* Continental menu. Specializes in fresh seafood, veal, beef. Own baking. Hrs: 11:30 am-9:30 pm; Fri, Sat to 10:30 pm; Sun 11 am-10 pm; Sun brunch 11 am-3 pm. Res accepted. Bar to 1 am. A la carte entrees: lunch $5.95-$14.95, dinner $6.95-$22.95. Parking. Outdoor dining. In restored 1800s Federal-style house. Cr cds: A, C, D, DS, MC, V.

Newton (B-7)

(See also Boston)

Settled 1630 **Pop** 82,585 **Elev** 100 ft **Area code** 617 **Web** www.nnchamber.com

Information Chamber of Commerce, 199 Wells Ave, Ste 208, Newton Center 02159; 617/244-5300.

Newton, the "Garden City," is actually a city of 13 suburban neighborhoods that have maintained their individual identities. Of the 13, eight have "Newton" in their names: Newton, Newtonville, Newton Centre, Newton Corner, Newton Highlands, West Newton, Newton Upper Falls and Newton Lower Falls. Five colleges are located here: Boston College, Lasell College, Mount Ida College, Andover-Newton Theological School and Aquinas Junior College.

What to See and Do

Jackson Homestead (1809). Once a station on the Underground Railroad. Changing exhibits on Newton history; children's gallery; toys; textiles and tools. (July-Aug, Mon-Thurs; rest of yr, Mon-Thurs & Sun afternoons; closed hols) 527 Washington St. Phone 617/552-7238. ¢

Motel

★ **SUSSE CHALET.** *160 Boylston St (MA 9) (02167). 617/527-9000; FAX 617/527-4994.* 144 rms in 5 bldgs, 3-6 story. S, D $59.70-$116.70; under 18 free. Crib free. TV; cable (premium). Pool; lifeguard. Complimentary continental bkfst. Restaurant 11:30 am-11:30 pm. Bar to 12:30 am. Ck-out 11 am. In-rm modem link. Coin lndry. Shopping arcade. Barber, beauty shop. Cr cds: A, C, D, DS, MC, V.

Motor Hotels

★ ★ **HOLIDAY INN.** *399 Grove St (02162), I-95 (MA 128) exit 22. 617/969-5300; FAX 617/965-4280.* 192 rms, 7 story. S, D $99-$169; each addl $10; under 18 free; wkend rates. TV; cable (premium). Heated pool; poolside serv, lifeguard. Coffee in rms. Restaurant 6:30 am-2 pm, 5-10 pm. Rm serv. Bar 4 pm-12 am. Ck-out noon. Meeting rms. Business servs avail. In-rm modem link. Valet serv. Sundries. Exercise equipt. Refrigerators avail. Cr cds: A, C, D, DS, MC, V.

★ ★ ★ **MARRIOTT.** *2345 Commonwealth Ave (02166), I-95 Exit 24. 617/969-1000; FAX 617/527-6914.* 430 rms, 7 story. S, D $169; suites $300-$500; under 18 free; wkend rates; lower rates rest of yr. Crib free. Pet accepted, some restrictions. TV; cable (premium). 2 pools, 1 indoor; whirlpool; poolside serv, lifeguard. Playground. Restaurant 6:30 am-midnight. Rm serv. Bar; entertainment. Ck-out 1 pm. Coin lndry. Convention facilities. Business servs avail. In-rm modem link. Bellhops. Sundries. Barber. X-country ski 1 mi. Exercise equipt; sauna. Canoes. Game rm. Lawn games. Some private patios, balconies. Picnic tables. On Charles River. Luxury level. Cr cds: A, C, D, DS, ER, JCB, MC, V.

Hotels

★ ★ ★ **SHERATON.** *320 Washington St (02158), I-90 exit 17, in Gateway Center at Newton Corner. 617/969-3010; FAX 617/244-5894.* 272 rms, 12 story. S, D $109-$199; each addl $15; wkend rates. Crib free. TV; cable (premium). VCR avail. Indoor pool. Coffee in rms. Restaurant 7 am-10 pm. Bar. Ck-out 11 am. Meeting rms. Business servs avail. In-rm modem link. Bellhops. Exercise rm; sauna. Refrigerators, microwaves avail. Cr cds: A, C, D, DS, ER, MC, V.

★ ★ ★ **SHERATON.** *(100 Cabot St, Needham 02494) MA 128 at exit 19A. 781/444-1110; FAX 781/449-3945.* Web www.sheraton.eedham.com. 247 rms, 5 story, 48 suites. Mid-Apr-mid-Nov: S, D, suites $149-$229; each addl $15; under 18 free; wkend rates. TV; cable (premium). Indoor pool; poolside serv. Restaurant 6:30 am-10 pm. Bar 11:30-1 am, entertainment Thurs-Sat. Ck-out noon. Meeting rms. Business servs avail. Concierge. Garage parking. Gift shop. Exercise equipt; sauna. Health club privileges. Cr cds: A, C, D, DS, ER, MC, V.

Restaurants

★ ★ **LEGAL SEAFOODS.** *(43 Boylston St, Chestnut Hill 02167) 5 mi W on MA 9, in Chestnut Hill Shopping Mall. 617/277-7300.* Specialties: bluefish pâté, clam chowder, mussels au gratin. Hrs: 11 am-10 pm; Fri, Sat to 11 pm; Sun from noon. Closed Thanksgiving, Dec 25. Bar. Semi-a la carte: lunch $6.95-$13.95, dinner $9.95-$30.95. Child's meals. Fish market on premises. Family-owned. Totally nonsmoking. Cr cds: A, C, D, DS, JCB, MC, V.

★ ★ ★ **PILLAR HOUSE.** *(26 Quinobequin Rd, Newton Lower Falls 02462) at MA 16 & 128 (I-95) exit 21A. 617/969-6500.* Web www.pillarhouse.com. Specialties: lobster streudel, spit roasted rib of beef, crab cakes. Hrs: 5-9:30 pm; Fri to 10 pm. Closed Sat, Sun. Bar 4-11 pm. A la carte entrees: dinner $17-$30. Parking. In restored 1848 residence. Chef's table in kitchen (res only). Family-owned since 1952. Totally nonsmoking. Cr cds: A, C, D, DS, MC, V.

North Adams (A-2)

(See also Williamstown)

Settled 1745 **Pop** 16,797 **Elev** 707 ft **Area code** 413 **Zip** 01247

Information Northern Berkshire Chamber of Commerce, 40 Main St; 413/663-3735.

North Adams is an industrial community set in the beautiful four-season resort country of the northern Berkshires. Its factories make electronic components, textile machinery, wire, machine tools, paper boxes and other products. Susan B. Anthony was born in nearby Adams in 1820.

What to See and Do

Mohawk Trail State Forest. Spectacular scenery. Swimming; fishing; hiking, riding trails; winter sports. Picnicking. Camping; log cabins. Standard fees. E on MA 2, near Charlemont. Phone 413/339-5504. **Free.**

Mt Greylock State Reservation. Mt Greylock, highest point in state (3,491 ft), is here. War memorial tower at summit. Fishing; hunting; cross-country skiing, snowmobiles allowed. Picnicking. Lodge, snacks; campsites (mid-May-mid-Oct). Visitor center on Rockwell Rd in Lanesborough, off MA 7. Standard fees. 1 mi W on MA 2, then N on Notch Rd. Phone 413/499-4262. **Free.**

Natural Bridge State Park. A water-eroded marble bridge and rock formations, about 550 million yrs old, popularized by Nathaniel Hawthorne. Picnicking. (Mid-May-mid-Oct) 1¼ mi NE on MA 8. For hrs phone 413/663-6392. Per vehicle ¢¢

Savoy Mountain State Forest. Brilliant fall foliage. Swimming; fishing; boating (ramp). Hiking, riding trails; hunting; winter sports. Picnicking; camping, log cabins. Waterfall. Standard fees. E on MA 2, near Florida, MA. Phone 413/664-9567 or 413/663-8469. **Free.**

Western Gateway Heritage State Park. Restored freightyard with 6 buildings around a cobbled courtyard. Detailed historic exhibits on the construction of Hoosac Railroad Tunnel. (Daily; closed Jan 1, Easter,

Thanksgiving, Dec 25) Behind City Hall on MA 8. Phone 413/663-8059. **Donation.**

Annual Events

La Festa. Ethnic festival, ethnic food, entertainment, events. Phone 413/66-FESTA. 16 days beginning mid-June.

Fall Foliage Festival. Parade, entertainment, dancing, children's activities. Phone 413/663-3735. Late Sept-early Oct.

Northampton (B-3)

Settled 1673 **Pop** 29,289 **Elev** 140 ft **Area code** 413 **Zip** 01060

Information Chamber of Commerce, 62 State St, phone 413/584-1900; or the Tourist Information Center, 33 King St, phone 413/586-3178 (June-Oct).

When the famed concert singer Jenny Lind honeymooned in this town on the Connecticut River in 1852, she exclaimed, "Why, this is the paradise of America." But it was not always a peaceful town. Northampton was the scene of a frenzied religious revival movement in the first half of the 18th century. It stemmed from Jonathan Edwards, a Puritan divine who came to be regarded as the greatest preacher in New England. Later, the town was the home of President Calvin Coolidge. A granite memorial on the court house lawn honors Coolidge, who was once mayor. Clarke School for the Deaf is located here.

What to See and Do

Arcadia Nature Center and Wildlife Sanctuary, Massachusetts Audubon Society. 550 acres on migratory flyway; an ancient oxbow of the Connecticut River; self-guiding nature trails; observation tower; courses and programs. Grounds (daily exc Mon). 4 mi SW on MA 10, follow signs, in Northampton & Easthampton. Phone 413/584-3009. ¢¢

Calvin Coolidge Memorial Room. Displays of the late president's papers and correspondence; also books and articles on Coolidge. Memorabilia includes Native American headdress and beadwork given to him, Mrs Coolidge's needlework, photographs. (Mon-Wed; closed hols; schedule may vary, phone ahead) Forbes Library, 20 West St. Phone 413/584-8399. **Free.**

Historic Northampton Museum houses. All houses (Mar-Dec, Wed-Sun). Phone 413/584-6011. ¢¢

Damon House (1813). Permanent formal parlor exhibit (ca 1820).

Shepherd House (1798). Includes the lifetime collection of one Northampton family and focuses on family lifestyle at the turn of the 19th century.

Parsons House (ca 1730). Contains exhibits on local architecture.

Look Park. Miniature train and Christenson Zoo; boating; tennis; picnicking; playgrounds, ball fields; also here is Pines Theater (musical entertainment, children's theater & puppet programs, summer). Park (all yr). Fees for most facilities. 300 N Main St, NW off MA 9. Phone 413/584-5457. Per vehicle ¢

Smith College (1871). (2,700 women) The largest private liberal arts college for women in the US. On campus are Paradise Pond, named by Jenny Lind; Helen Hills Hills Chapel; William Allan Neilson Library with more than 1 million volumes; Center for the Performing Arts; Plant House and Botanical Gardens; Japanese Garden. On Elm St (MA 9). Phone 413/584-2700.Also here is

Museum of Art. A fine collection with emphasis on American and European art of the 19th and 20th centuries. (Sept-May, daily exc Mon; rest of yr, Tues-Sat; closed hols) Elm St (MA 9). **Free.**

⭐ **Words and Pictures Museum of Fine Sequential Art.** Displays of modern comic book art from 1970s to present. (Tues-Sun, afternoons) 140 Main St. Phone 413/586-8545. ¢¢

Annual Events

Eastern National Morgan Horse Show. Three-County Fairgrounds. Late July.

Three-County Fair. Agricultural exhibits, horse racing, parimutuel betting. Labor Day wk.

Seasonal Event

Maple sugaring. Visitors are welcome at many maple camps. Phone 413/584-1900. Mid-Mar-early Apr.

Motels

★ ★ **AUTUMN INN.** *259 Elm St. 413/584-7660; FAX 413/586-4808.* 30 rms, 2 story. Apr-Nov: S $68-$80; D $86-$106; each addl $6-$12; suites $110-$135; lower rates rest of yr. Crib free. TV; cable (premium). Pool. Restaurant 7-10 am, 11:30 am-2 pm; wkends 8-11 am. Bar. Ck-out 11 am. In-rm modem link. Downhill ski 5 mi; x-country ski 18 mi. Lawn games. Refrigerator in suites. Picnic table. Smith College opp. Cr cds: A, C, D, MC, V.

✔★ **DAYS INN.** *117 Conz St, off I-91 exit 18. 413/586-1500.* 59 rms, 2 story. S $39-$57; D $49-$69; each addl $10; under 18 free; higher rates: Smith College graduation, hols. Crib free. TV; cable. Pool. Complimentary coffee in lobby. Restaurant nearby. Ck-out noon. Downhill ski 7 mi. Cr cds: A, D, DS, MC, V.

★ ★ **INN AT NORTHAMPTON.** *1 Atwood Dr (01075), jct US 5 & I-91 exit 18. 413/586-1211; FAX 413/586-0630.* E-mail innnoho@java net.com. 124 rms, 2 story. S, D $75-$130; suites $130-$170. TV; cable. 2 pools, 1 indoor; wading pool, whirlpool, poolside serv. Restaurant 7-10:30 am, 5-9 pm; Mon to 10:30 am; Sat, Sun 7:30-11 am. Bar. Ck-out 11 am. Meeting rms. Valet serv. Sundries. Lighted tennis. Game rm. Balconies. Cr cds: A, DS, MC, V.

Hotel

★ ★ **HOTEL NORTHAMPTON & HISTORIC WIGGINS TAVERN.** *36 King St. 413/584-3100; FAX 413/584-9455.* 90 rms, 5 story. Sept-Oct: S, D $109-$160; each addl $12; suites $138-$290; under 12 free; higher rates special events; lower rates rest of yr. Crib free. TV; cable (premium). Restaurants 7-1 am. Bar. Ck-out noon. Meeting rms. Business center. Private patios, balconies. Cr cds: A, C, D, DS, MC, V.

Restaurant

★ ★ **EASTSIDE GRILL.** *19 Strong Ave. 413/586-3347.* E-mail esgrill@javanet.com. Specializes in seafood, steak. Hrs: 5-10 pm; Fri, Sat to 11 pm; Sun 4-9 pm. Closed Thanksgiving, Dec 25. Bar. Semi-a la carte: dinner $8.95-$14.95. New Orleans theme prints. Totally nonsmoking. Cr cds: A, MC, V.

North Truro

(see Truro & North Truro)

Orleans (Cape Cod) (D-10)

(See also Eastham)

Settled 1693 **Pop** 5,838 **Elev** 60 ft **Area code** 508 **Zip** 02653 **E-mail** info@capecodchamber.org **Web** www.capecodchamber.org

Information Cape Cod Chamber of Commerce, US 6 & MA 132, PO Box 790, Hyannis 02601-0790; 508/362-3225 or 888/33-CAPECOD.

Orleans supposedly was named in honor of the Duke of Orleans after the French Revolution. The settlers worked at shipping, fishing and salt production. Its history includes the dubious distinction of being the only town in America to have been fired upon by the Germans during World War I. The town is now a commercial hub for the summer resort colonies along the great stretch of Nauset Beach and the coves behind it. A cable station, which provided direct communication between Orleans and Brest, France, from 1897 to 1959, is restored to its original appearance and open to the public.

What to See and Do

Academy of Performing Arts. Theater presents comedies, drama, musicals, dance. Workshops for all ages. 120 Main St. Box office 508/255-1963.

French Cable Station Museum. Built in 1890 as American end of transatlantic cable from Brest, France. Original equipment for submarine cable communication on display. (July-Labor Day, Tues-Sat afternoons) MA 28 & Cove Rd. 508/240-1735.   ¢¢

Nauset Beach. One of the most spectacular ocean beaches on the Atlantic Coast is now within the boundaries of Cape Cod National Seashore (see). Swimming, surfing, fishing; lifeguards. Parking fee. About 3 mi E of US 6 on marked roads.

Motels

★ ★ **COVE.** on MA 28, near jct MA 6A. 508/255-1203; FAX 508/255-7736; res: 800/343-2233. 47 rms, 1-2 story. July-Aug: S, D $99-$179 (2-day min); each addl $10; kit. units $159-$179; lower rates rest of yr. Crib $10. TV; cable (premium), VCR. Heated pool. Coffee in rms. Restaurant nearby. Ck-out 11 am. Meeting rm. Business center. Lawn games. Refrigerators, microwaves. Picnic tables, grill. Sun deck. On town cove. Float boat rides avail. Cr cds: A, C, D, DS, MC, V.

★ **NAUSET KNOLL MOTOR LODGE.** (Box 642, East Orleans 02643) At Nauset Beach, 3 mi E of MA 28 at end of Beach Rd. 508/255-2364. 12 rms. No rm phones. Mid-June-early Sept: S, D $135; each addl $10; under 6 free; lower rates mid-Apr-mid-June, early Sept-late Oct. Closed rest of yr. Crib free. TV; cable. Ck-out 11 am. Picnic tables. Overlooks ocean, beach. Cr cds: MC, V.

★ ★ **OLDE TAVERN MOTEL & INN.** 151 MA 6A. 508/255-1565; res: 800/544-7705. Web capecodtravel.com/oldetavern. 29 rms. Late June-early Sept: S, D $80-$105; each addl $9; lower rates Apr-late June, early Sept-Nov. Closed rest of yr. Crib free. TV; cable (premium). Heated pool. Complimentary continental bkfst. Restaurant nearby. Ck-out 11 am. Refrigerators. 18 deck rms. Main building is a restored inn & tavern visited by Thoreau in 1849, Daniel Webster and other personalities of the day. Cr cds: A, DS, MC, V.

★ **RIDGEWOOD MOTEL & COTTAGES.** (10 Quanset Rd, South Orleans 02662) 2 mi S, jct MA 28 & 39. 508/255-0473. Web www.indigitweb.com/ridgewood. 18 units, some A/C, 6 cottages. No rm phones. Late June-Labor Day: S, D $69-$80; cottages $500-$610/wk;

lower rates rest of yr. Crib $10. TV. Pool. Playground. Complimentary continental bkfst. Ck-out 10 am. Lawn games. Many refrigerators. Picnic tables, grills. Totally nonsmoking. Cr cds: MC, V.

★ ★ **SEASHORE PARK MOTOR INN.** 24 Canal Rd, at US 6. 508/255-2500; FAX 508/240-2728; res: 800/772-6453. 62 rms, 2 story, 24 kits. Late-June-early Sept: S, D $99-$119; each addl $10; under 13 free; kit. units $109-$129; lower rates mid-Apr-late-June, early Sept-Oct. Closed rest of yr. TV; cable. 2 pools, 1 indoor; whirlpool, sauna. Complimentary continental bkfst. Restaurant adj 7 am-midnight. Ck-out 11 am. Business servs avail. Microwaves avail. Private patios, balconies. Sun deck. Totally nonsmoking. Cr cds: A, DS, MC, V.

★ ★ **SKAKET BEACH.** 203 Cranberry Hwy. 508/255-1020; FAX 508/255-6487; res: 800/835-0298. Web www.capecod.or leans.com./ska ketbeach. 46 rms, 1-2 story, 6 kits. 3rd wk June-early Sept: S, D $79-$156; each addl $9; lower rates Apr-mid-June, mid-Sept-Nov. Closed rest of yr. Crib free. Pet accepted, some restrictions; $9 (off season). TV; cable (premium). Heated pool. Complimentary continental bkfst. Restaurant nearby. Ck-out 11 am. Coin lndry. Lawn games. Refrigerators; microwaves avail. Picnic tables, grills. Cr cds: A, D, DS, MC, V.

Inns

★ ★ **THE PARSONAGE.** (202 Main St, East Orleans 02643) 508/255-8217; res: 888/422-8217; FAX 508/255-8216. E-mail inn keeper@par sonageinn.com; web www.parsonageinn.com. 8 rms, 2 story, 1 kit. unit. No rm phones. June-Labor Day: S, D $95-$125; each addl $10; kit. unit $125; lower rates rest of yr. Children over 6 yrs only. TV in some rms; cable. Complimentary full bkfst. Restaurants nearby. Ck-out 11 am, ck-in 2 pm. Antiques. Library/sitting rm. Originally a parsonage (1770) and cobbler's shop. Totally nonsmoking. Cr cds: A, MC, V.

✔★ ★ **SHIP'S KNEES INN.** (186 Beach Rd, East Orleans 02643) 3 mi E on Beach Rd; from MA 6 exit 12. 508/255-1312; FAX 508/240-1351. 19 air-cooled rms, 8 with bath, 2 story, 2 suites. Some A/C. No rm phones. July-Aug: D $65-$120; each addl $20; suites $110; lower rates rest of yr. Children over 12 yrs only. TV in some rms and in sitting rm; cable. Pool. Complimentary continental bkfst. Ck-out 10:30 am, ck-in 1 pm. Tennis. Picnic tables, grills. Restored sea captain's house (ca 1820); near ocean, beach. Rms individually decorated in nautical style; many antiques, some 4-poster beds. Some rms with ocean view. Totally nonsmoking. Cr cds: MC, V.

Restaurants

★ ★ **BARLEY NECK INN.** (5 Beach Rd, East Orleans 02643) 1½ mi E on Main St. 508/255-0212. E-mail barleynr@tial.net; web www.barleyneck.com. Continental menu. Specialties: trio salmon medallions, local swordfish steak, braised lamb shank. Hrs: 5-10 pm. Res accepted. Semi-a la carte: dinner $12-$20. Pianist. Four separate dining rms, both formal and informal; fireplaces, artwork. Cr cds: A, D, MC, V.

★ ★ ★ **CAPTAIN LINNELL HOUSE.** 137 Skaket Beach Rd, exit 12 off US 6 to West Rd (left). 508/255-3400. E-mail info@linnell.com; web www.linnell.com. Specializes in local seafood, rack of lamb. Own baking. Hrs: from 5 pm. Res accepted. Semi-a la carte: dinner $16.50-$26. Child's meals. Parking. Outdoor dining. Sea captain's 1840s mansion; oil paintings; gardens. Totally nonsmoking. Cr cds: A, MC, V.

✔★ **DOUBLE DRAGON.** Jct MA 6A & MA 28. 508/255-4100. Chinese, Polynesian menu. Specializes in Hunan and Cantonese cooking. Hrs: 11:30-2 am. Closed Thanksgiving. Serv bar. A la carte entrees: lunch

$3.50-$5.95, dinner $4.25-$12.95. Parking. Chinese decor. Cr cds: A, D, DS, MC, V.

★ **LOBSTER CLAW.** *On MA 6A. 508/255-1800.* Web www.capecod.com/lobclaw. Specializes in seafood, lobster, steak. Hrs: 11:30 am-9 pm; early-bird dinner 4-5:30 pm. Closed mid-Nov-Mar. No A/C. Bar. Semi-a la carte: lunch, dinner $4.95-$22.95. Child's meals. Parking. Nautical decor. Former cranberry packing factory. Family-owned. Cr cds: A, C, D, DS, MC, V.

★ ★ **NAUSET BEACH CLUB.** *(222 E Main St, East Orleans 02643)* 1/2 mi E on E Main St. *508/255-8547.* Regional Italian menu. Specializes in soups, salads. Own pasta. Hrs: 5:30-9 pm. Closed Sun, Mon off-season. Bar. Semi-a la carte: dinner $12-$19. Paper tablecloths invite guests to draw; crayons provided. Totally nonsmoking. Cr cds: A, C, D, DS, MC, V.

★ ★ **OLD JAILHOUSE TAVERN.** *28 West Rd, off MA 6A at Skaket Corners. 508/255-5245.* E-mail jailhouse@capecod.net. Specialties: prime rib, veal Orleans, seafood. Hrs: 11:30 am-midnight; Sun brunch 11 am-2:30 pm. Closed Thanksgiving, Dec 25. Bar to 1 am. Semi-a la carte: lunch $5.25-$10.95, dinner $12.95-$19.75. Parking. Part of old jailhouse. Cr cds: A, DS, MC, V.

Pittsfield (B-2)

(See also Berkshire Hills, Lenox, Stockbridge & West Stockbridge)

Settled 1743 **Pop** 48,622 **Elev** 1,039 ft **Area code** 413 **Zip** 01201 **E-mail** bvb@berkshires.org **Web** www.berkshires.org

Information Berkshire Visitors Bureau, Berkshire Common; 413/443-9186 or 800/237-5747.

Beautifully situated in the Berkshire Hills vacation area, this is also an old and important manufacturing center. It is the home of the Berkshire Life Insurance Co (chartered 1851) and of industries that make machinery, plastics, gauges and paper products.

What to See and Do

Arrowhead (1780). Herman Melville wrote *Moby Dick* while living here from 1850 to 1863; historical exhibits, furniture, costumes; gardens. Video presentation. Gift shop. HQ of Berkshire County Historical Society. (June-Labor Day, daily; after Labor Day-Oct, Thurs-Mon; rest of yr, by appt) 780 Holmes Rd. Phone 413/442-1793. ¢¢

Berkshire Museum. Museum of art, natural science and history, featuring American 19th- and 20th-century paintings; works by British, European masters; artifacts from ancient civilizations; exhibits on Berkshire County history; aquarium; changing exhibits; films, lectures, children's programs. (July-Aug, daily; rest of yr, daily exc Mon; closed hols) 39 South St (US 7). Phone 413/443-7171. ¢¢

Canoe Meadows Wildlife Sanctuary. 262 acres with 3 mi of trails, woods, open fields, ponds; bordering the Housatonic River. (Daily exc Mon) Holmes Rd. Phone 413/637-0320. ¢¢

Crane Museum. Exhibit of fine papermaking since 1801, emphasizing distinctive all-rag papers. (June-mid-Oct, Mon-Fri; closed hols) 5 mi E, on MA 9 in Dalton. Phone 413/684-2600. **Free.**

Hancock Shaker Village. An original Shaker site (1790-1960); now a living history museum of Shaker life, crafts and farming. Large collection of Shaker furniture and artifacts in 20 restored buildings, including the Round Stone Barn, set on 1,200 scenic acres in the Berkshires. Exhibits; seasonal craft demonstrations, Discovery Room activities, cafe; farm animals, heirloom herb and vegetable gardens; museum shop; picnicking. (Apr-Nov,

daily; Dec-Mar, by appt only) 5 mi W on US 20, at jct MA 41. Phone 413/443-0188. ¢¢¢¢

Skiing.

Bousquet. 2 double chairlifts, 2 rope tows; snowmaking, patrol, school, rentals; cafeteria, bar. Longest run 1 1/2 mi; vertical drop 750 ft. Night skiing. (Dec-Mar, daily) 2 mi S on US 7, then 1 mi W, on Dan Fox Dr. Phone 413/442-8316 or 413/442-2436 for snow conditions. ¢¢¢¢¢

Jiminy Peak. Triple, 3 double chairlifts, J-bar; patrol, school, rentals, restaurant, 2 cafeterias, bar, lodge. Longest run 2 mi; vertical drop 1,140 ft. (Thanksgiving-Apr 1, daily) Night skiing. Half-day rates. Also trout fishing; 18-hole miniature golf; Alpine slide and tennis center (Memorial Day-Labor Day); fee for activities. 9 mi N, then W, between US 7 & MA 43 on Corey Rd in Hancock. Phone 413/738-5500. ¢¢¢¢¢

Brodie Mt. 4 double chairlifts, 2 rope tows; patrol, school, rentals, snowmaking; bar, cafeteria, restaurant, nursery. (Nov-Mar, daily) Cross-country trails with rentals and instruction. Half-day rates. Tennis, racquetball, winter camping. 10 mi N on US 7 in New Ashford. Phone 413/443-4752. ¢¢¢¢

Seasonal Event

South Mountain Concerts. South St. 2 mi S on US 7, 20. Chamber music concerts. Box office phone 413/442-2106. Sun, Aug-Oct.

Motels

★ ★ **BEST WESTERN SPRINGS MOTOR INN.** *(US 7, New Ashford 01237)* 12 mi N on US 7 in New Ashford. *413/458-5945.* 40 rms, 1-2 story. July-Oct: S $51-$100; D $61-$113; each addl $10; under 12 free; lower rates rest of yr. Crib $10. TV; cable, VCR avail (movies). Heated pool. Complimentary coffee in rms. Restaurant 7 am-10 pm. Rm serv. Bar from 11:30 am; entertainment Sat. Ck-out 11:30 am. Meeting rms. Sundries. Tennis. Downhill/x-country ski opp. Game rm. Refrigerators avail. Some patios, balconies. Cr cds: A, C, D, DS, MC, V.

✔★ **TRAVELODGE.** *16 Cheshire Rd (MA 8N). 413/443-5661;* FAX 413/443-5866. 48 rms, 2 story. July-mid-Oct: S $65-$105; D $81-$120; each addl $6; under 17 free; lower rates rest of yr. Crib free. TV; cable. Complimentary coffee in rms. Restaurant opp 6 am-10 pm. Ck-out 11 am. Coin lndry. Meeting rm. Business servs avail. Downhill ski 5 mi; x-country ski 12 mi. Refrigerators. Picnic table. Cr cds: A, C, D, DS, MC, V.

Hotel

★ ★ ★ **CROWNE PLAZA.** *1 West St. 413/499-2000;* FAX 413/442-0449. 179 rms, 12 story. July-mid-Oct: S, D $120-$210; each addl $15; suites $295-$449; under 18 free; wkend rates; package plans; lower rates rest of yr. Crib free. TV; cable (premium). Indoor pool; whirlpool. Coffee in rms. Restaurant 6 am-11 pm. Bar 11:30-1 am. Ck-out noon. Meeting rms. Business servs avail. Beauty shop. Free covered parking. Shopping arcade. Exercise equipt; sauna. Health club privileges. Some refrigerators. Cr cds: A, C, D, DS, MC, V.

Resort

★ ★ **JIMINY PEAK.** *(Corey Rd, Hancock 01237)* 13 mi N on US 7, then 2 mi W on Brodie Mountain Rd. *413/738-5500; FAX 413/738-5513;* res: 800/882-8859. Web www.jiminypeak.com. 96 one-bedrm kit. suites, 3 story. S, D $95-$209; each addl $15; condos $275-$325; under 13 free; ski packages; wkly, monthly rates. Crib $5. TV; cable, VCR avail (movies $3). 2 pools, heated; whirlpool. Supervised child's activities (Dec-Mar). Dining rm 7:30 am-9 pm. Snack bar. Bar; entertainment wkends (seasonal). Ck-out 10:30 am, ck-in 4 pm. Coin lndry. Grocery 4 mi. Package store 5 mi. Meeting rms. Business servs avail. Sundries. Valet serv. Tennis courts.

Downhill ski on site. Hiking. Game rm. Exercise equipt; sauna. Alpine slide. Cr cds: A, C, D, DS, MC, V.

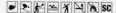

Restaurants

★ ★ **DAKOTA.** *1035 South St, 5 mi S on US 7/20. 413/499-7900.* Specializes in seafood, hand-cut aged prime beef. Salad bar. Hrs: 5-10 pm; Fri, Sat 4-11 pm; Sun 10 am-2 pm (brunch), 4-10 pm; early-bird dinner Mon-Fri 5-6 pm, Sat & Sun 4-5 pm. Closed Thanksgiving, Dec 25. Res accepted. Bar. Semi-a la carte: dinner $7.95-$19.95. Sun brunch $14.95. Child's meals. Rustic decor; Native American artifacts, mounted animals. Cr cds: A, D, DS, MC, V.

 D

✔ ★ ★ **GIOVANNI'S.** *1331 North St, US 7 N. 413/443-2441.* Italian, Amer menu. Specializes in veal, poultry, seafood. Hrs: noon-3 pm, 4:30-9 pm; Fri, Sat to 10 pm; Sun noon-8 pm. Closed July 4, Dec 25. Bar. Semi-a la carte: lunch $5.95-$8.95, dinner $7-$18.50. Child's meals. Italian prints. Cr cds: A, DS, MC, V.

D

★ ★ ★ **THE SPRINGS.** *(US 7, New Ashford 01237) 12 mi N on US 7. 413/458-3465.* Continental menu. Specialties: steak Diana, veal Oscar, Boston scrod Hammann. Own baking. Hrs: 11:30 am-10 pm; Sun 9 am-9 pm; early-bird dinner Mon-Fri 4-6 pm; Sun brunch 9 am-1 pm. Closed Dec 25. Res accepted. Bar. Wine cellar. Semi-a la carte: lunch $5.50-$10.25, dinner $11.50-$18. Sun brunch $12.95. Child's meals. Old World decor. Cr cds: A, C, D, DS, MC, V.

D

Plymouth (C-8)

Settled 1620 **Pop** 45,608 **Elev** 50 ft **Area code** 508 **Zip** 02360 **E-mail** info@visit-plymouth.com **Web** www.visit-plymouth.com

Information Destination Plymouth, 225 Water St, Suite 202; 508/747-7525 or 800/USA-1620.

On December 21, 1620, 102 men, women and children arrived on the *Mayflower* to found the first permanent European settlement north of Virginia. Although plagued by exposure, cold, hunger and disease during the terrible first winter, the colony was firmly established by the next year. Plymouth Rock lies under an imposing granite colonnade, marking the traditional place of landing.

Plymouth now combines a summer resort, beaches, a harbor full of pleasure craft, an active fishing town and a remarkable series of restorations of the original town.

What to See and Do

Burial Hill. Governor Bradford is buried here. Just W of Town Square.

Cole's Hill. Here Pilgrims who died during the first winter were secretly buried. Across the street from Plymouth Rock.

Cranberry World. Visitors Center with exhibits of the history and cultivation of the cranberry. ¹/₂-hr self-guided tours; guided tours by appt. (May-Nov, daily) 225 Water St. Phone 508/747-2350. **Free.**

Harlow Old Fort House (1677). Pilgrim household crafts; spinning, weaving & candle-dipping demonstrations; herb garden. (July-Oct, Wed-Sat) 119 Sandwich St. Phone 508/746-9497. **¢¢**

Hedge House (1809). Period furnishings, special exhibits. (June-Oct, Wed-Sat) 126 Water St, opp Town Wharf. Phone 508/746-0012. **¢¢**

Howland House (1666). Restored Pilgrim house has 17th- and 18th-century furnishings. (Memorial Day-mid-Oct, Mon-Sat, also Sun afternoons & Thanksgiving) 33 Sandwich St. Phone 508/746-9590. **¢¢**

Mayflower Society House Museum. National HQ of the General Society of Mayflower Descendants. House built in 1754; 9 rms with 17th- & 18th-century furnishings. Formal garden. (July-Labor Day, daily; Memorial Day wkend-June & early Sept-Oct, Fri-Sun) 4 Winslow St, off North St. Phone 508/746-2590. **¢¢**

Myles Standish State Forest. Approx 15,000 acres. Swimming, bathhouse; fishing; boating, hiking and bicycle trails; riding; hunting; winter sports; picnicking (fee); camping (fee; dump station). S on MA 3, exit 5, Long Pond. Phone 508/866-2526.

National Monument to the Forefathers. Built between 1859 and 1889 (at a cost of $155,000) to depict the virtues of the Pilgrims. At 81 ft, it is the tallest solid granite monument in the US. (May-Oct, daily) Allerton St. Phone 508/746-1790. **Free.**

Pilgrim Hall Museum (1824). Decorative arts and possessions of first Pilgrims and their descendants; includes furniture, household items, ceramics; only known portrait of a Mayflower passenger. (Daily; closed Jan 1, Dec 25) 75 Court St, on MA 3A. Phone 508/746-1620. **¢¢**

 Plimoth Plantation. Living history museum re-creates day-to-day life in 17th-century Plymouth. All exhibits (Apr-Nov, daily). 3 mi S on MA 3A. Phone 508/746-1622. General admission ticket (includes *Mayflower II*) **¢¢¢¢**

Visitor Center. Provides visitors with introduction to this unique museum. Orientation program includes 12-min multi-image screen presentation. Exhibits; educational services; museum shop; restaurants, picnic area.

1627 Pilgrim Village. Fort-Meetinghouse and 14 houses. Costumed people portray actual residents of Plymouth and re-create life in an early farming community.

Hobbamock's (Wampanoag) Homesite. A large bark-covered house representing Hobbamock's dwelling as well as specially crafted tools and artifacts, depict the domestic environment of the Wampanoag culture. Staff members explain this rich heritage from a modern day perspective.

Mayflower II. This 90-ft bark, a full-size reproduction of the type of ship that carried the Pilgrims, was built in England and sailed to America in 1957. Costumed men and women portray crewmen and passengers who made the 1620 voyage. At State Pier, on Water St. **¢¢¢**

Plymouth Colony Winery. Grape growing area, working cranberry bogs, picnic areas. Tour, winetasting. Watch cranberry harvest activities in fall (usually last wkend Sept). Winery (Apr-late Dec, daily; Mar, Fri-Sun; also hols). US 44W, left on Pinewood Rd. Phone 508/747-3334. **Free.**

Plymouth Harbor Cruises. One-hr cruises of historic harbor aboard *Pilgrim Belle*, a Mississippi-style paddlewheeler. (Mid-May-Mid-Oct, daily) Departs from State Pier . Phone 508/747-2400 for schedule. **¢¢¢**

Plymouth National Wax Museum. Pilgrim story told through narrations and animation; includes 26 life-size scenes and more than 180 figures. (Mar-Nov, daily) 16 Carver St. Phone 508/746-6468. **¢¢**

Plymouth Rock. Water St, on the harbor.

Provincetown Ferry. Round-trip passenger ferry departs State Pier in the morning, returns in evening. (Mid-June-Labor Day, daily; May-Mid-June & after Labor Day-Oct, wkends) Phone 508/747-2400. **¢¢¢¢¢**

Richard Sparrow House (1640). Plymouth's oldest restored home; craft gallery, pottery made on premises. (Memorial Day wkend-Thanksgiving, daily exc Wed; gallery open through late Dec) 42 Summer St. Phone 508/747-1240. **¢**

Site of First Houses. Marked by tablets. On Leyden St, off Water St.

Splashdown Amphibious Tours. One-hr tours of historic Plymouth-half on land, half on water. Hrly departures from Harbor Place and Village Landing. (Mid-Apr-late Oct, daily) Phone 508/747-7658. **¢¢¢¢**

Spooner House (1747). Occupied by Spooner family for 5 generations and furnished with their heirlooms. Collections of Oriental export wares, period furniture. (June-Oct, Wed-Sat) 27 North St. Phone 508/746-0012. **¢¢**

Supersports Family Fun Park. Rides, games, sports, mini-golf, bumper boats. (Daily, call for off-season hours; closed Dec 25) W of Plymoth historical area, 108 N Main St, jct MA 58 & 44, in Carver. Phone 508/866-9655. ¢¢¢-¢¢¢¢

Swimming. Six public bathing beaches.

Village Landing Marketplace. Modeled after colonial marketplace; contains a restaurant and specialty shops. Overlooks historic Plymouth Harbor. 170 Water St, near jct US 44 & MA 3A.

Whale watching. Four-hr trip to Stellwagen Bank to view world’s largest mammals. (Early May-mid-Oct, daily; early Apr-early May & mid-Oct-early Nov, wkends) For departure times and locations, phone 508/746-2643. ¢¢¢¢¢

Annual Events

Destination Plymouth Sprint Triathlon. Myles Standish State Forest (see). National Championship qualifier includes 1/2 mi swim, 12-mi bike ride and 4-mi run. 800/USA-1620. July.

Pilgrim's Progress. A reenactment of Pilgrims going to church, from Cole's Hill to Burial Hill. Each Fri in Aug; also Thanksgiving.

Autumnal Feasting. Plimoth Plantation's 1627 Pilgrim Village. A harvest celebration with Dutch colonists from Fort Amsterdam re-creating a 17th-century event. Activities, feasting, games. Phone 508/742-1622. Columbus Day wkend.

Thanksgiving Week. Programs for various events may be obtained by contacting Destination Plymouth. Phone 508/747-7525 or 800/USA-1620. Nov (starts Thanksgiving wkend).

Motels

★ **BLUE SPRUCE.** *710 State Rd (MA 3A), 6½ mi S on MA 3A. 508/224-3990; FAX 508/224-2279; res: 800/370-7080.* 28 rms, 4 townhouses. June-Aug: S, D $58-$76; each addl $6; townhouses $165-$189; lower rates rest of yr. Crib free. Pool. Restaurant nearby. Ck-out 11 am. Business servs avail. In-rm modem link. Lawn games. Refrigerators. Cr cds: A, C, D, DS, MC, V.

D ⚊ ⊠ 🖎 SC

✔★ **COLD SPRING.** *188 Court St. 508/746-2222; FAX 508/746-2744.* 31 rms. Late Mar-late Nov: S, D $59-$89; each addl $5. Closed rest of yr. Crib $5. TV; cable (premium). Complimentary continental bkfst (in season). Restaurant nearby. Ck-out 11 am. Business servs avail. Cr cds: A, DS, MC, V.

⊠ 🖎

★ **GOVERNOR BRADFORD MOTOR INN.** *98 Water St. 508/746-6200; FAX 508/747-3032; res: 800/332-1620.* 94 rms, 3 story. July-Oct: S, D $82-$130; each addl $10; under 14 free; lower rates rest of yr. Crib free. TV; cable (premium), VCR avail (movies). Heated pool. Complimentary coffee in rms. Restaurant adj 11:30 am-11:30 pm. Ck-out 11 am. Refrigerators. On waterfront. Cr cds: A, C, D, DS, ER, MC, V.

⊠ ⊠ 🖎 SC

★★ **PILGRIM SANDS.** *150 Warren Ave, 2½ mi SE on MA 3A. 508/747-0900; FAX 508/746-8066; res: 800/729-7263.* E-mail the beach@pilgrimsands.com; web www.pilgrimsands.com. 64 rms, 2 story. Mid-June-Labor Day: S, D $98-$130; each addl $8; lower rates rest of yr. Crib free. TV; cable (premium). 2 pools, 1 indoor; whirlpool. Continental bkfst. Ck-out 11 am. Many refrigerators. Private beach. Cr cds: A, C, D, DS, MC, V.

D 🗗 ⊠ 🖎

✔★ **SLEEPY PILGRIM.** *182 Court St. 508/746-1962; res: 877/776-6835; FAX 508/746-0203.* E-mail frontdesk@sleepypilgrim.com; web www.sleepypilgrim.com. 16 rms. Mid-June-late Oct: S $64; D $79; each addl $10; lower rates Apr-mid-June, late Oct-Thanksgiving. Closed rest of yr. Crib $5. TV; cable. Complimentary continental bkfst in season. Restaurant nearby. Ck-out 10 am. Picnic tables, grills. Cr cds: A, DS, MC, V.

D ⊠ 🖎

Motor Hotel

★★ **JOHN CARVER INN.** *25 Summer St, at Market St, opp town brook in historic district. 508/746-7100; FAX 508/746-8299; res: 800/274-1620.* 79 rms, 3 story. Sept-Oct: S, D $65-$105; each addl $10; under 19 free; MAP avail; package plans. Crib free. TV; cable. Pool. Restaurant (see HEARTH & KETTLE). Rm serv. Bar to midnight. Ck-out 11 am. Laundry serv. Meeting rms. Business servs avail. Gift shop. Health club privileges. Cr cds: A, C, D, DS, MC, V.

D ⚊ ⊠ 🖎 SC

Hotel

★★★ **SHERATON INN PLYMOUTH AT VILLAGE LANDING.** *180 Water St. 508/747-4900; FAX 508/746-2609.* Web www.sheratonplymouth.com. 175 rms, 4 story. June-Oct: S, D $150-$165; each addl $15; suites $230; under 18 free; wkend rates; lower rates rest of yr. Crib free. TV; cable (premium), VCR avail. Indoor pool; poolside serv. Restaurant 6:30 am-2 pm, 5-10 pm. Bar; entertainment Fri-Sat. Ck-out 11 am. Meeting rms. Business servs avail. In-rm modem link. Exercise equipt. Some bathrm phones. Some balconies. Some rms with ocean view. Cr cds: A, C, D, DS, ER, JCB, MC, V.

D ⚊ 🖾 ⊠ 🖎 SC

Inn

★★ **THE MABBETT HOUSE.** *7 Cushman St. 508/830-1911; FAX 508/830-9775; res: 800/572-7829.* E-mail bill@mabbett.com; web www.mabbetthouse.com. 3 rms, 2 story. No rm phones. S, D $90-$110. Children over 12 yrs only. TV in lobby. Complimentary full bkfst. Restaurant nearby. Ck-out 11 am. Game rm. Colonial-revival house; artifacts collected from world travels. Totally nonsmoking. Cr cds: A, MC, V.

⊠ 🖎

Restaurants

✔★ **HEARTH & KETTLE.** *(See John Carver Inn) 508/746-7100.* Specializes in fresh seafood. Hrs: 7 am-10 pm; early-bird dinner noon-6 pm. Closed Dec 25. Res accepted. Bar. Semi-a la carte entrees: bkfst $3.99-$5.99, lunch $3.99-$7.99, dinner $8.99-$14.99. Child's meals. Servers dressed in Colonial attire. Cr cds: A, C, D, DS, MC, V.

D

✔★★ **McGRATH'S.** *Water St, 1 blk E of MA 3A. 508/746-9751.* Specializes in seafood, prime rib. Hrs: 11:30 am-10 pm; Sun to 9 pm. Closed Thanksgiving, Dec 25. Res accepted. Bar to 1 am. Semi-a la carte: lunch, dinner $4.95-$14.95. Child's meals. Ocean view. Family-owned. Cr cds: A, D, DS, MC, V.

D

Provincetown (Cape Cod) (C-9)

(See also Cape Cod National Seashore)

Settled ca 1700 **Pop** 3,561 **Elev** 40 ft **Area code** 508 **Zip** 02657 **E-mail** info@ptownchamber.com **Web** www.capecodaccess.com/provincetownchamber
Information Chamber of Commerce, 307 Commercial St, PO Box 1017; 508/487-3424.

Provincetown is a startling mixture of heroic past and easygoing present. The Provincetown area may have been explored by Leif Ericson in A.D. 1004. It is certain that the *Mayflower* anchored first in Provincetown Harbor while the Mayflower Compact, setting up the colony's government, was signed aboard the ship. Provincetown was where the first party of Pilgrims came ashore. A bronze tablet at Commercial St and Beach Hwy marks the site of the Pilgrims' first landing. The city attracts many tourists who come each summer to explore the narrow streets and rows of picturesque old houses.

What to See and Do

Expedition Whydah's Sea Lab & Learning Center. Archaeological site of sunken pirate ship *Whydah*, struck by storms in 1717. Learn about recovery of the ship's pirate treasure, the lives and deaths of pirates and the history of the ship and its passengers. (Apr-mid-Oct, daily; mid-Oct-Dec, wkends & school hols) 16 MacMillan Wharf. Phone 508/487-7955. ¢¢

⭐ Pilgrim Monument & Museum. A 252-ft granite tower commemorating the Pilgrims' 1620 landing in the New World; provides an excellent view. (Summer, daily; phone ahead rest of yr) High Pole Hill, off Winslow St. Phone 508/487-1310.   ¢¢   Admission includes

Provincetown Museum. Exhibits include whaling equipment, scrimshaw, ship models, artifacts from shipwrecks; Pilgrim Room with scale model diorama of the merchant ship *Mayflower;* Donald MacMillan's Arctic exhibit; antique fire engine and firefighting equipment; theater history display. (Summer, daily; phone ahead rest of yr) Phone 508/487-1310.

Provincetown Art Association & Museum. Changing exhibits; museum store. (Late May-Oct, daily; rest of yr, wkends) 460 Commercial St. Phone 508/487-1750.   ¢

Recreation. Swimming at surrounding beaches, including town beach, W of the village, Herring Cove and Race Point, on the ocean side. Tennis, cruises, beach buggy tours and fishing avail.

Town Wharf (MacMillan Wharf). Off Commercial St at Standish St. Center of maritime activity.Also here is

Portuguese Princess **Whale Watch.** 100-ft boats offer 3½-hr narrated whale watching excursions. Naturalist aboard. (Apr-Oct, daily) Phone 508/487-2651 or 800/442-3188 (New England). ¢¢¢¢¢

Whale Watching. Offers 3½-4-hr trips (mid-Apr-Oct, daily). Research scientists from the Provincetown Center for Coastal Studies are aboard each trip to lecture on the history of the whales being viewed. Dolphin Fleet of Provincetown. For info and res, phone 508/349-1900 or 800/826-9300. ¢¢¢¢¢

Annual Event

Portuguese Festival. Parades, concerts; dance, ethnic food court, children’s games; fireworks. Culminates with blessing of the fleet (Sun). Last wk June.

Motels

★ ★ BEST WESTERN CHATEAU MOTOR INN. 105 Bradford St W. 508/487-1286; res: 800/528-1234; FAX 508/487-3557. E-mail chateau@capecod.net; web www.bwprovincetown.com. 55 rms, 1-2 story. Late June-Labor Day: S, D $130-$200; each addl $20; under 18 free; higher rates hols; lower rates May-late June, after Labor Day-Oct. Closed rest of yr. Crib $5. TV; cable (premium). Heated pool. Complimentary continental bkfst. Restaurant nearby. Ck-out 11 am. Business servs avail. In-rm modem link. Some refrigerators. Some balconies. Harbor view. Cr cds: A, C, D, DS, MC, V.

★ ★ BEST WESTERN TIDES BEACHFRONT. 837 Commercial St. 508/487-1045; res: 800/528-1234; FAX 508/487-1621. E-mail tides@capecod.net; web www.bwprovincetown.com. 64 rms, 1-2 story. Mid-June-early Sept: S, D $129-$179; suites $199-$249; lower rates mid-May-mid-June, early Sept-mid-Oct. Closed rest of yr. TV; cable (premium). Heated pool. Restaurant 7 am-3 pm. Ck-out 11 am. Coin lndry. Business

servs avail. In-rm modem link. Some refrigerators. Some balconies. On private beach. Cr cds: A, C, D, DS, JCB, MC, V.

✔ ★ ★ BLUE SEA. (696 Shore Rd, Norht Truro) 1¾ mi E on MA 6A. 508/487-1041. Web www.virtualcapecod.com/bluesea. 43 rms, 1-2 story. July-Aug: S, D $97-$127; each addl $10; kit. units $650-$920/wk; lower rates Sept-Oct, May-June. Closed rest of yr. Crib $10. TV. Indoor pool; whirlpool. Coffee in lobby. Ck-out 10 am. Coin lndry. In-rm modem link. Refrigerators. Balconies. Picnic tables, grills. On ocean; swimming beach. Cr cds: MC, V.

★ ★ BRADFORD HOUSE. 41 Bradford St. 508/487-0173; FAX 508/487-0173. 19 rms, 3 story. No elvtr. No rm phones. July-Aug: S $100; D $110-$150; each addl $25; lower rates rest of yr. TV; cable. Complimentary continental bkfst. Restaurant nearby. Ck-out 11 am. Concierge. Refrigerators. Built 1888. Cr cds: A, MC, V.

★ ★ MASTHEAD MOTEL AND COTTAGES. 31 Commercial St. 508/487-0523; FAX 508/487-9251; res: 800/395-5095. Web www.cape cod.com/masthead. 10 rms, 2 share bath, 4 cottages, 7 apts, 2 story. July-Labor Day, motel rms: S, D $63-$188; each addl $20; kit. apts $893/wk; kit. cottages (1-wk min) $1,200-$1,850/wk; under 12 free (limit 2); lower rates rest of yr. Crib free. TV; cable, VCRs in cottages. Restaurant nearby. Ck-out 11 am, cottages 10 am. Refrigerators, microwaves. 450-ft sun deck on water. Picnic tables; grills. On private beach. In-shore & deep water moorings, launch serv. Cr cds: A, C, D, DS, MC, V.

★ ★ PROVINCETOWN INN. 1 Commercial St. 508/487-9500; FAX 508/487-2911; res: 800/942-5388 (New England). E-mail ptowninn@tiac.net; web www.provincetown.com/ptowninn. 100 rms, 1-2 story. July-Aug: S, D $119-$174; each addl $12.50; under 14 free; wkly rates; whale package plans; higher rates hols; lower rates rest of yr. TV; cable. Heated pool. Complimentary continental bkfst. Restaurant 6-9 pm. Bar 4 pm-midnight. Ck-out 11 am. Meeting rms. Business servs avail. Sundries. Gift shop. Picnic tables. Ocean view. Private beach. Cr cds: MC, V.

★ ★ SHIP'S BELL INN. 586 Commercial St. 508/487-1674; FAX 508/487-1675. 20 units, 1-2 story, 7 kit. studios, 3 kit. apts. No A/C. July-Aug: S, D $80; kit. studios $110-$140; kit. apts $140-$190; wkly rates; package plans; lower rates late Apr-June, Sept-Oct. Closed rest of yr. Crib $15. TV; cable. Ck-out 10 am. Microwaves avail. Balconies. Picnic tables. Private beach opp. Cr cds: A, DS, MC, V.

Inns

★ ★ ★ BRADFORD GARDENS. 178 Bradford St. 508/487-1616; FAX 508/487-5596; res: 800/432-2334. E-mail bradgard@capecod.net; web www.ptownlib.com/bradford.htm/. 8 rms, 5 A/C, 1-2 story, 4 cottages, 5 townhouses. July: S, D $116-$138; each addl $20; cottages $115-$165; townhouses $135-$185; lower rates rest of yr. TV; cable, VCR (free movies). Complimentary full bkfst. Restaurant nearby. Ck-out 11 am, ck-in 3 pm. Fireplaces; microwaves avail. Built 1820. Cr cds: A, MC, V.

★ ★ FAIRBANKS. 90 Bradford St. 508/487-0386; FAX 508/487-3540; res: 800/324-7265. E-mail fairbank@capecod.net; web www.provincetown.com. 14 rms, 11 with bath, 2 story. No rm phones. July-Aug: S, D $89-$175; higher rates hols; lower rates rest of yr. Children over 15 yrs only. TV; cable (premium). Complimentary continental bkfst. Restaurant nearby. Ck-out 11 am, ck-in 2 pm. Concierge. Balconies. Picnic tables, grills. Antiques. Built 1776; courtyard. Totally nonsmoking. Cr cds: A, MC, V.

✔★ ★ **SOMERSET HOUSE.** *378 Commercial St. 508/487-0383; FAX 508/487-4746; res: 800/575-1850.* E-mail somerset@somerset houseinn.com; web www.somersethouseinn.com. 13 rms, 10 with bath, 2-3 story. No A/C. Mid-June-Mid-Sept: S, D $75-$130; each addl $20; wkly rates; lower rates rest of yr. TV; cable. Complimentary continental bkfst. Restaurant nearby. Ck-out 11 am, ck-in 3 pm. Refrigerators. Opp beach. Restored 1850s house. Totally nonsmoking. Cr cds: MC, V.

★ ★ **WATERMARK.** *603 Commercial St. 508/487-0165; FAX 508/487-2383; res: 800/734-0165 (MA).* 10 suites, 2 story. July-Aug: suites $135-$290 (1-wk min); each addl $10-$20; wkly rates; lower rates rest of yr. TV; cable. Restaurant nearby. Ck-out 11 am, ck-in 3 pm. Business servs avail. In-rm modem link. Microwaves. Private patios, balconies. On beach. Cr cds: A, MC, V.

✔★ ★ **WATERSHIP INN.** *7 Winthrop St. 508/487-0094; res: 800/330-9413.* Web cimarron.net/usa/ma/watership. 15 rms, 3 story. Some A/C. No rm phones. Mid-June-mid-Sept: S, D $85-$193; each addl $20; 2-bedrm condo $1,210/wk; wkly rates. TV. Complimentary continental bkfst. Restaurant nearby. Ck-out 11:30 am, ck-in 2 pm. Lawn games. Picnic tables, grills. Antiques. Library/sitting rm. Built 1820. Cr cds: A, DS, MC, V.

★ ★ **WHITE WIND INN.** *174 Commercial St, near Municipal Airport. 508/487-1526; FAX 508/487-3985.* E-mail wwinn@capecod.net; web www.nj-marketplace.com/winn. 11 rms, 7 A/C, 4 air-cooled, 8 with shower only, 3 story. No elvtr. No rm phones. Late May-mid-Sept: S, D $115-$190; wkend, wkly rates; wkends, hols (2-day min); higher rates hols; lower rates rest of yr. Pet accepted. TV; cable, VCR avail (movies). Complimentary continental bkfst. Restaurant nearby. Ck-out 11 am, ck-in 2 pm. Luggage handling. Concierge serv. Refrigerators; some fireplaces. Some balconies. Picnic tables. Opp harbor. Built in 1845; former shipbuilder's home. Totally nonsmoking. Cr cds: A, MC, V.

Restaurants

★ ★ **CAFE EDWIGE.** *333 Commercial St. 508/487-2008.* Specialties: stir-fry tofu, crab cakes, native littleneck clams. Hrs: 8 am-1 pm, 6-11 pm. Closed Oct 31; also late May. Res accepted (dinner). No A/C. Serv bar. Semi-a la carte: bkfst $5-$10, dinner $10-$20. Street parking. Outdoor dining. Cathedral ceilings, skylights. Totally nonsmoking. Cr cds: A, D, MC, V.

★ ★ **DANCING LOBSTER.** *463 Commercial St, 12 blks E on Commercial St. 508/487-0900.* Mediterranean menu. Specialties: Venetian fish soup, crab ravioli, Provençal seafood stew. Hrs: 6-11 pm. Closed Mon; also Dec-May. Res accepted. Bar to 1 am. A la carte entrees: dinner $9.95-$18.95. On beach; harbor views. Cr cds: MC, V.

★ ★ **FRONT STREET.** *230 Commercial St. 508/487-9715.* E-mail frontst@capecod.net; web www.capecod.net/frontstreet. Italian, continental menu. Specialties: rack of lamb, tea-smoked duck, chocolate oblivion purse. Own desserts. Hrs: 6-10:30 pm. Closed Jan-Apr. Res accepted. Bar to 1 am. Semi-a la carte: dinner $12-$21. Street parking. Local artwork displayed. Totally nonsmoking. Cr cds: A, DS, MC, V.

★ ★ **LOBSTER POT.** *321 Commercial St. 508/487-0842.* E-mail lpot@wn.net; web www.provincetown.com/lobsterpot. Specialties: chowder, bouillabaisse, clambake. Hrs: 11:30 am-10 pm. Closed Jan. Bar to 1 am. Semi-a la carte: lunch $7-$12, dinner $10-$17. Lobster & chowder market on premises. Overlooks Cape Cod Bay. Cr cds: A, C, D, DS, MC, V.

★ **THE MOORS.** *5 Bradford St W. 508/487-0840.* Portuguese, Amer menu. Specialties: espada cozida, porco em pau, kale soup. Hrs: noon-3 pm, 5-10 pm; wkend to 10:30 pm; early-bird dinner Mon-Fri 5:30-6:30 pm. Closed late Nov-Mar. Res accepted. Bar 5 pm-midnight.

Semi-a la carte: lunch $3.95-$8.95, dinner $11.95-$19.95. Child's meals. Parking. Pianist. Nautical decor. Family-owned. Cr cds: A, C, D, DS, MC, V.

★ ★ **NAPI'S.** *7 Freeman St, 1 blk N of Commercial St. 508/487-1145.* Continental menu. Specialties: bouillabaisse, shrimp Santa Fe, banana decadence. Extensive vegetarian selections. Hrs: 5-10 pm; early-bird dinner 5-6 pm. Res accepted. Bar to 1 am. Semi-a la carte: dinner $12.95-$22.95. Child's meals. Parking. Gathering place of artists and craftsmen. Large collection of art in various media, including paintings, sculpture, stained glass, graphics, ceramics and crafts. Cr cds: A, D, DS, MC, V.

✔★ ★ **PROVINCETOWN FERRY.** *177 Commercial St. 508/487-0120.* Specializes in seafood, prime rib. Hrs: 6 pm-1 am. Closed late Oct-Apr. Bar. Semi-a la carte: lunch, dinner $13-$22. Harbor view. Cr cds: A, MC, V.

★ **PUCCI'S HARBORSIDE.** *539 Commercial St. 508/487-1964.* Specializes in hot, spicy chicken wings, grilled seafood. Hrs: 11:30 am-3 pm, 5 pm-1 am. Closed Nov-mid-Apr. Res accepted. No A/C. Bar. Semi-a la carte: lunch $4-$10, dinner $8-$16. Cr cds: A, MC, V.

★ ★ ★ **RED INN.** *15 Commercial St. 508/487-0050.* Continental menu. Specializes in fresh local seafood & meats. Own desserts. Hrs: 11 am-10 pm; Sun brunch 10 am-3 pm; Jan-May: wkends only. Closed Dec 25. Res accepted. Serv bar. Semi-a la carte: lunch $6.95-$19.95, dinner $19-$24.95. Sun brunch $9-$15. Parking. Three dining rms in restored colonial building. Many antiques. View of Cape Cod Bay. Cr cds: A, DS, MC, V.

★ ★ **SAL'S PLACE.** *99 Commercial St. 508/487-1279.* Southern Italian menu. Specialties: steak pizzaiola, grilled shrimp, mousse pie. Hrs: 6-10 pm. Closed Nov-Apr. Res accepted. Serv bar. A la carte entrees: dinner $10-$19. Child's meals. Outdoor dining. Southern Italian decor; ocean view. Cr cds: MC, V.

Quincy (B-7)

(See also Boston)

Settled 1625 **Pop** 84,985 **Elev** 20 ft **Area code** 617

Information Tourism and Visitors Bureau, 1250 Hancock St, Suite 802 N, 02169; 617/847-1454 or 888/232-6737.

Boston's neighbor to the south, Quincy (QUIN-zee) was the home of the Adamses, a great American family whose fame dates from colonial days. Family members include the second and sixth presidents—John Adams and his son, John Quincy Adams. John Hancock, first signer of the Declaration of Independence, was born here. George Bush, the 41st president, was born in nearby Milton.

Thomas Morton, an early settler, held May Day rites at Merrymount (a section of Quincy) in 1627 and was shipped back to England for selling firearms and "firewater" to the Native Americans.

What to See and Do

✪ **Adams National Historic Sites Visitor Center.** Administered by the National Park Service. Tickets to sites can be purchased here *only*. (Mid-Apr-mid-Nov, daily) Golden Eagle Passport accepted (see MAKING THE MOST OF YOUR TRIP). 1250 Hancock St. Phone 617/770-1175. Combination ticket ¢ Includes

The Adams National Historic Site. The house (1731), bought in 1787 by John Adams, was given as a national site by the Adams family in 1946. Original furnishings. 135 Adams St, off Furnace Brook Parkway.

John Adams and John Quincy Adams Birthplaces. Two 17th-century saltbox houses. The elder Adams was born and raised at 133 Franklin St; his son was born in the other house. While living here, Abigail Adams wrote many of her famous letters to her husband, John Adams, when he was serving in the Continental Congress in Philadelphia and as an arbitrator for peace with Great Britain in Paris. Guided tours. 133 & 141 Franklin St.

Josiah Quincy House (1770). Built on 1635 land grant, this fine Georgian house originally had a view across Quincy Bay to Boston Harbor; was surrounded by outbuildings and much agricultural land. Long the home of the Quincy family; furnished with family heirlooms and memorabilia. Period wall paneling, fireplaces surrounded by English tiles. Tours on the hr. (June-mid-Oct, Tues, Thurs, Sat & Sun afternoons) 20 Muirhead St in Wollaston. Phone 617/227-3956. ¢¢

Quincy Historical Society. Museum of regional history; library. (Daily exc Sun) Adams Academy Bldg, 8 Adams St. Phone 617/773-1144. ¢

Quincy Homestead. Four generations of Quincys lived here, including Dorothy Quincy, wife of John Hancock. Two rms built in 1686, rest of house dates from the 18th century; period furnishings; herb garden. (May-Oct, Wed-Sun) 1010 Hancock St, at Butler Rd. Phone 617/472-5117. ¢¢

United First Parish Church (1828). Only church in US where 2 presidents and their wives are entombed: John Adams and John Quincy Adams and their wives. Tours (late Apr-mid-Nov, Mon-Sat & Sun afternoons) 1306 Hancock St, at Washington St. Phone 617/773-1290. ¢

Annual Events

Quincy Bay Race Week. Sailing regatta, marine parades, fireworks. July.

South Shore Christmas Festival. Includes parade with floats. Sun after Thanksgiving.

Seasonal Event

Summerfest. Concerts on the Green, Ruth Gordon Amphitheatre. Wed, mid-June-Aug.

Rockport (A-8)

Settled 1690 **Pop** 7,482 **Elev** 77 ft **Area code** 978 **Zip** 01966 **E-mail** info@rockportusa.com **Web** www.rockportusa.com

Information Chamber of Commerce, PO Box 67M, 978/546-6575 or 888/726-3922.

Rockport is a year-round artists' colony. A weather-beaten shanty on one of the wharves has been the subject of so many paintings that it is called "Motif No. 1."

Studios, galleries, summer places, estates and cottages dot the shore of Cape Ann from Eastern Point southeast of Gloucester all the way to Annisquam.

What to See and Do

Old Castle (1715). A fine example of early 18th-century architecture and exhibits. (July-Labor Day, daily; rest of yr, by appt) Granite & Curtis Sts, Pigeon Cove. Phone 978/546-9533 or 978/546-6821. **Donation.**

Rockport Art Association. Changing exhibits of paintings, sculpture and graphics by 250 artist members. Special events include concerts (see ANNUAL EVENTS), lectures, artist demonstrations. (Daily; closed Thanksgiving, Dec 25-Jan 1) 12 Main St. Phone 978/546-6604. **Free.**

Sandy Bay Historical Society & Museums. Early American and 19th-century rms and objects, exhibits on fishing, granite industry, the Atlantic cable and a children's rm in 1832 home constructed of granite. (July-Labor Day, daily; rest of yr, by appt) 40 King St, near RR station. Phone 978/546-9533 or 978/546-6821. **Donation.**

Sightseeing tours & boat cruises. Contact the Chamber of Commerce for a list of companies offering sightseeing, fishing and boat tours.

The Paper House. Newspapers were used in the construction of the house and furniture. (July-Aug, daily; rest of yr, by appt) 52 Pigeon Hill St. Phone 978/546-2629. ¢

Annual Event

Rockport Chamber Music Festival. Phone 978/546-7391. 4 wkends June or July.

Motels

★ **CAPTAIN'S BOUNTY MOTOR INN.** *1 Beach St. 978/546-9557.* Web www.cape-ann.com. 24 rms, 3 story, 9 kits. No A/C. No elvtr. Mid-June-Labor Day: S, D $102-$117; each addl $10; suites $127; kit. units $110; lower rates Apr-mid-June, after Labor Day-late Oct. Closed rest of yr. TV; cable. Restaurant nearby. Ck-out 11 am. Microwaves avail. On beach; lifeguard. Cr cds: DS, MC, V.

★ **EAGLE HOUSE.** *8 Cleaves St. 978/546-6292; FAX 978/546-1136.* 15 rms, 2 story, 2 kit. units. Mid-June-Labor Day: S, D $79-$84; each addl $7; kit. units $89; higher rates: Memorial Day, Columbus Day; lower rates May-mid-June, after Labor Day-mid-Oct. Closed rest of yr. TV; cable (premium). Restaurant adj 6:30 am-11 pm. Ck-out 11 am. Refrigerators. Some balconies. Picnic tables. Beach opp. Cr cds: A, DS, MC, V.

★ **PEG LEG.** *10 Beach St. 978/546-6945; FAX 978/546-5157.* 15 rms, 2 story. No A/C. Late June-Labor Day: S, D $125-$135; each addl $10; under 6 free; wkends (2-day min); hols (3-day min); lower rates rest of yr. Closed Nov-mid-Apr. TV; cable (premium). Restaurant adj 7 am-9 pm. Ck-out 11 am. Opp swimming beach. Cr cds: DS, MC, V.

★ ★ ★ **SANDY BAY MOTOR INN.** *173 Main St. 978/546-7155; FAX 978/546-9131; res: 800/437-7155.* 80 rms, 2 story, 23 kits. Late June-Labor Day: S, D $98-$142; each addl $8; family rates; lower rates rest of yr. Crib free. Pet accepted, some restrictions; deposit. TV; cable (premium), VCR avail. Indoor pool; whirlpool, sauna. Restaurant 7-11 am; wkends, hols to noon. Ck-out 11 am. Coin lndry. Meeting rms. Business servs avail. In-rm modem link. Free RR station transportation. Tennis. Putting green. Refrigerators avail. Cr cds: A, MC, V.

★ ★ **TURKS HEAD MOTOR INN.** *151 South St, 1½ mi S on MA 127A. 978/546-3436.* Web www.rockportusa.com. 28 rms, 2 story. Mid-June-Labor Day: S, D $95; each addl $6; lower rates Apr-mid-June, after Labor Day-mid-Oct. Closed rest of yr. TV; cable. Indoor pool. Restaurant 6:30-11 am; Sun to noon. Ck-out 11 am. 2 beaches nearby. Cr cds: A, DS, MC, V.

Inns

★ ★ ★ **ADDISON CHOATE INN.** *49 Broadway. 978/546-7543; res: 800/245-7543; FAX 978/546-7638.* Web www.cape-ann.com/addison-choate. 8 rms, 2 with shower only, 3 story, 3 suites; 1 guest house. Some A/C. No elvtr. No rm phones. Children over 11 yrs only. Late June-late Sept: S, D $95; suites $140. TV in common rm; cable, VCR avail (movies). Complimentary continental bkfst. Restaurant nearby. Ck-out 11 am, ck-in 3 pm. Business servs avail. Free RR station transportation. Pool. Built in 1851; antiques. Totally nonsmoking. Cr cds: MC, V.

✔★ ★ **INN ON COVE HILL.** *37 Mt Pleasant St. 978/546-2701; res: 888/546-2701.* 11 rms, 9 with bath, 3 story. No rm phones. S, D $50-$110; each addl $25. Closed mid-Oct-mid-Apr. TV; cable. Complimentary continental bkfst. Restaurant nearby. Ck-out 11 am, ck-in 2 pm. Free RR station transportation. Built 1791 from proceeds of pirates' gold found nearby. Period furnishings; antiques. Near wharf, yacht club. Totally nonsmoking. Cr cds: MC, V.

★ ★ **LINDEN TREE INN.** *26 King St. 978/546-2494; res: 800/865-2122.* E-mail ltree@shore.net; web www.shore.net/~ltree. 18 rms, 2 with shower only, 3 story, 4 kit. units, 10 A/C. No rm phones. Mid-June-early Sept (2-day min): S $70; D $99-$109; each addl $15; kit. units $105; under 4 free; lower rates rest of yr. Closed 2 wks Jan. TV in some rms; cable, VCR avail (movies). Complimentary continental bkfst. Complimentary coffee in rms. Restaurant nearby. Ck-out 11 am, ck-in 2 pm. Business servs avail. Microwaves avail. Some balconies. Picnic tables. Cr cds: MC, V.

★ ★ **PEG LEG INN.** *2 King St, MA 128, Rte 127 to 5 corners. 978/546-2352; res: 800/346-2352.* Web www.cape-ann.com. 33 rms in 5 houses. Mid-June-Labor Day: S, D $85-$140; each addl $10; hol wkends (3-day min); lower rates Apr-mid-June, wkdays after Labor Day-Oct. Closed rest of yr. TV. Complimentary continental bkfst. Restaurant (see PEG LEG). Ck-out 11 am, ck-in 2 pm. 6 sun decks. Totally nonsmoking. Cr cds: A, MC, V.

★ ★ ★ **RALPH WALDO EMERSON INN.** *(Phillips Ave, Pigeon Cove)* 1½ mi N on MA 127. 978/546-6321; FAX 978/546-7043. E-mail emerson@cove.com. 36 rms, 4 story. July-Labor Day: S $90-$135; D $100-$145; each addl $7; suites $100-$145; lower rates Apr, Nov. Closed rest of yr. Crib $7. TV in lounge. Sauna. Heated saltwater pool; whirlpool. Dining rm 8-11 am, 6-9 pm. Rm serv. Ck-out noon, ck-in after 1 pm. Coin lndry. Meeting rms. Business servs avail. In-rm modem link. Luggage handling. Free RR station transportation. Lawn games. Spa, massage. Sun deck. Older inn; Victorian decor. Many rms with ocean view. Cr cds: DS, MC, V.

★ ★ **ROCKY SHORES.** *65 Eden Rd, 1½ mi S on MA 127A to Eden Rd. 978/546-2823; res: 800/348-4003.* 11 rms, 1 A/C, 3 story. Mid-Apr-mid-Oct: D $84-$121; each addl $10. Closed rest of yr. TV; cable. Complimentary full bkfst. Ck-out 11 am, ck-in 3 pm. Antiques. Mansion built 1905. Overlooks ocean. Cr cds: A, MC, V.

★ ★ ★ **SEACREST MANOR.** *99 Marmion Way, just off MA 127A. 978/546-2211.* Web www.rockportusa.com/seacrestmanor. 8 rms, 6 with bath, 2 story. No A/C. May-Oct (2-day min): S $88-$136; D $98-$146; lower rates Apr, Nov; hol wkends (3-day min). Closed rest of yr. TV; cable. Complimentary full bkfst; afternoon refreshments. Dining rm (inn guests only) 7:30-9:30 am. Ck-out 11 am, ck-in after 2 pm. RR station transportation. Bicycles. Lawn games. Library, living rm. Garden. View of ocean. Totally nonsmoking. No cr cds accepted.

✔★ **SEAFARER INN.** *50 Marmion Way. 978/546-6248; res: 800/394-9394.* Web www.rockportusa.com/seafarer. 5 rms, 2 suites. No A/C. No rm phones. Mid-June-mid-Oct: D $75-$110; suites $160; kit. units $95; lower rates rest of yr. TV. Complimentary continental bkfst. Ck-out 11 am, ck-in 3 pm. On Gap Cove; all rms overlook ocean. 100-yr-old bldg. Totally nonsmoking. Cr cds: MC, V.

★ ★ ★ **SEAWARD.** *44 Marmion Way, 1 mi S of Rockport Center on ocean. 978/546-3471; 800 877/473-2927.* E-mail info@seawardinn.com; web www.seawardinn.com. 38 rms, 3 story, 9 cottages. No A/C. Mid-May-Oct: D $119-$225; each addl $20; under 3 free. Crib free. TV. Natural spring-fed swimming pond. Complimentary full bkfst. Dining rm 8-10 am,

5-9 pm. Ck-out 11 am, ck-in 2 pm. Business servs avail. Luggage handling. Airport transportation. Free RR station transportation. Lawn games. Refrigerators, microwaves avail. Bird sanctuary. Vegetable & herb garden. On 5 acres. Ocean opp. Cr cds: A, DS, MC, V.

★ ★ **TUCK INN.** *17 High St. 978/546-7260; res: 800/789-7260.* E-mail tuckinn@shore.net; web www.rockportusa.com. 13 rms, 6 with shower only, 2 story, 1 suite, 1 apt, 1 studio apt. No rm phones. July-mid-Oct: S, D $75-$95; suite $115; family, wkly rates; lower rates rest of yr. TV; cable. Pool. Complimentary continental bkfst. Restaurant nearby. Ck-out 11 am, ck-in 2-9 pm. Colonial house built in 1790; within walking distance to downtown, beach. Cr cds: MC, V.

★ ★ ★ **YANKEE CLIPPER INN.** *(96 Granite St, Pigeon Cove) 5 mi N on MA 127 at MA 128. 978/546-3407; FAX 978/546-9730; res: 800/545-3699.* 26 rms in 3 bldgs, 2-3 story, 3-bedrm villa. Late May-late Oct: S, D $99-$269; each addl $25; MAP avail; lower rates late Oct-Dec, Mar-late May. Closed rest of yr. TV; cable, VCR avail (movies). Saltwater pool. Complimentary bkfst. Dining rm (see VERANDA). Ck-out 11 am. Business servs avail. Airport, RR station transportation. Some in-rm whirlpools. Movies, slides. Rms vary; some antiques. Sun porches. Terraced gardens overlook ocean. Totally nonsmoking. Cr cds: A, DS, MC, V.

Restaurants

★ **BRACKETT'S OCEANVIEW.** *27 Main St. 978/546-2797.* Specializes in seafood. Hrs: 11:30 am-2:30 pm, 5-8:30 pm. Closed Nov-mid-Mar. Semi-a la carte: lunch $3.75-$11.95, dinner $7.95-$16.95. Informal family dining. Cr cds: A, C, D, DS, MC, V.

✔★ ★ **PEG LEG.** *(See Peg Leg Inn) 978/546-3038.* Specializes in baked stuffed shrimp, steak, duck. Hrs: 5:30-9 pm; Sun noon-8:30 pm. Closed Nov-mid-Apr. Semi-a la carte: dinner $9.95-$21.95. Outdoor dining. Greenhouse dining rm (in season). Ocean view. Cr cds: A, D, MC, V.

★ ★ ★ **VERANDA.** *(See Yankee Clipper Inn) 978/546-7795.* Regional Amer menu. Specialties: grilled salmon, garlic-roasted duck. Own baking, pasta. Hrs: 7:30-10:30 am, 5:30-9 pm. Closed Jan, Feb. Res required. Semi-a la carte: bkfst $8.50, dinner $12-$22. Enclosed porch overlooks ocean. Cr cds: A, DS, MC, V.

Salem (B-8)

(See Beverly, Danvers, Lynn, Marblehead)

Settled 1626 **Pop** 38,091 **Elev** 9 ft **Area code** 978 **Zip** 01970
Information Chamber of Commerce, 32 Derby Square; 978/744-0004.

In old Salem the story of early New England life is told with bricks, clapboards, carvings and gravestones. The town had two native geniuses to immortalize it: Samuel McIntire (1757-1811), master builder, and Nathaniel Hawthorne (1804-1864), author. History is charmingly entangled with the people and events of Hawthorne's novels. Reality, however, could be far from charming. In the witchcraft panic of 1692, 19 persons were hanged on Gallows Hill, another "pressed" to death; at least two others died in jail. Gallows Hill is still here; so is the house of one of the trial judges.

Early in the 18th century, Salem shipbuilding and allied industries were thriving. Salem was a major port. The Revolution turned commerce into privateering. Then began the fabulous China trade and Salem's heyday. The captains came home, and Sam McIntire built splendid houses for them that still stand. Shipping declined after 1812. Salem turned to industry, which, together with tourism, is the present-day economic base.

What to See and Do

Chestnut Street. Architecturally, one of the most beautiful streets in America; laid out in 1796.

✪ **House of Seven Gables** (1668). Said to be the setting for Nathaniel Hawthorne's classic novel. Audiovisual introduction and guided tours of the "Gables" and Hawthorne's birthplace (1750). On grounds are the Hathaway House (1682) and the Retire Becket House (1655), now the Museum Shop. Garden cafe (seasonal). (Daily; closed Thanksgiving, Dec 25; also first 2 wks Jan) 54 Turner St, off Derby St on Salem Harbor. Phone 978/744-0991. ¢¢¢

Peabody Museum & Essex Institute. Peabody Museum founded by sea captains in 1799 features 5 world-famous collections in 30 galleries. Large collections of marine art, Asian export art. Essex Institute features historical interpretations of area. Peabody Museum (daily; closed Jan 1, Thanksgiving, Dec 25). Essex Institute (Daily) East India Square. Phone 978/745-9500. ¢¢¢ Admission includes

    Gardner-Pingree House (1804). Designed by McIntire; restored and handsomely furnished. (June-Oct, daily; rest of yr, Sat-Sun & hols) 128 Essex St.

    John Ward House (1684). 17th-century furnishings. (June-Oct, daily; rest of yr, Sat-Sun & hols) Behind Essex Institute.

    Crowninshield-Bentley House (1727). Rev. William Bentley, minister and diarist, lived here 1791-1819. Period furnishings. (June-Oct, daily; rest of yr, Sat, Sun & hols) Essex St & Hawthorne Blvd.

Peirce-Nichols House (1782). One of the finest examples of McIntire's architectural genius; authentically furnished. (By appt only) 80 Federal St. Phone 978/745-9500.

Pickering Wharf. Six-acre commercial and residential village by the sea includes shops, restaurants, marina. Adj to Salem Maritime National Historic Site.

Pioneer Village: Salem In 1630. Reproduction of early Puritan settlement, including dugouts, wigwams, thatched cottages; animals; costumed interpreters; craft demonstrations. Guided tours. (Last wknd May-Oct, daily) Forest River Park, off West St. Phone 978/744-0991 or 978/745-0525. ¢¢

Ropes Mansion and Garden (late 1720s). Gambrel-roofed, Georgian & Colonial mansion; restored and furnished with period pieces. The garden (laid out 1912) is nationally known for its beauty and variety. (June-Oct, daily; limited hrs Sun) 318 Essex St. Phone 978/745-9500. ¢¢

✪ **Salem Maritime National Historic Site.** Nine acres of historic waterfront. Self-guided and guided tours. For guided tours, res contact the Orientation Center, Central Wharf Warehouse, 174 Derby St; 978/740-1660. **Free.** Site includes

    Visitor Information. In Central Wharf Warehouse and downtown visitor center at Museum Place, Essex St.

    Derby Wharf. Once a center of Salem shipping (1760-1810). Off Derby St.

    Custom House (1819). Restored offices. (Daily; closed Jan 1, Thanksgiving, Dec 25) Derby St, opp wharf. Adj are

    Scale House (1829) and **Bonded Warehouse** (1819). Site of 19th-century customs operations. (Apr-Oct, daily)

    Derby House (1761-62). Home of maritime merchant Elias Hasket Derby, the country's first millionaire. In back are the Derby House Gardens, featuring roses, herbs and 19th-century flowers. Inquire at Central Wharf Warehouse for tour information.

    Narbonne House. 17th-century house with archaeological exhibits. Inquire at Central Wharf Warehouse for tour information.

    West India Goods Store (1800). Coffee, teas, spices and goods for sale. (Daily; closed Jan 1, Thanksgiving, Dec 25) 164 Derby St.

Salem State College (1854). (9,300 students) 352 Lafayette St. Phone 978/741-6000. On campus are

    Chronicle of Salem. Mural, 60 ft by 30 ft, depicts Salem history from settlement to present in 50 sequences. (Mon-Fri; closed hols) Meier Hall. **Free.**

Main Stage Auditorium. This 750-seat theater presents musical and dramatic productions (Sept-Apr). Inquire for schedule, fees. Phone 978/744-3700.

Winfisky Art Gallery. Photographs, paintings, graphics and sculpture by national and local artists. (Sept-May, Mon-Fri) **Free.**

Library Gallery. Art exhibits by local and national artists. (Daily exc Sun) **Free.**

Salem Witch Museum. Multimedia presentation reenacting the witch hysteria of 1692. (Daily; closed Jan 1, Thanksgiving, Dec 25) Washington Sq. Phone 978/744-1692. ¢¢

Stephen Phillips Memorial Trust House (1804). Federal-style mansion with McIntire mantels and woodwork. Furnishings, rugs, porcelains reflect the merchant and seafaring past of the Phillips family. Also carriage barn with carriages and antique automobiles. (Late May-mid-Oct, daily exc Sun) 34 Chestnut St. Phone 978/744-0440. ¢

Witch Dungeon Museum. Reenactment of witch trial of Sarah Good by professional actresses; tour through re-created dungeon where accused witches awaited trial; original artifacts. (May-Nov, daily) 16 Lynde St. Phone 978/741-3570. ¢¢

Witch House (1642). Home of witchcraft trial judge Jonathan Corwin. Some of the accused witches may have been examined here. (Mid-Mar-early Dec, daily) 310½ Essex St. Phone 978/744-0180. ¢¢

Annual Events

Heritage Days Celebration. Band concerts, parade, exhibits, ethnic festivals. Mid-Aug.

Haunted Happenings. Various sites. Psychic festival, historical exhibits, haunted house, costume parade, contests, dances. Starts wknd before and includes Halloween.

Hotel

★ ★ **HAWTHORNE.** *18 Washington Sq W, Rte 1A N, on the Common.* 978/744-4080; FAX 978/745-9842; res: 800/729-7829. E-mail info@hawthornehotel.com; web www.hawthornehotel.com. 89 rms, 6 story. July-Oct: S $125-$154; D $125-$172; each addl $12; suites $285; under 18 free; lower rates rest of yr. Crib free. Pet accepted; $15. TV; cable (premium). Restaurant 6:30-11 pm; Sat, Sun from 7 am. Ck-out 11 am. Meeting rms. Business servs avail. In-rm modem link. Lndry serv. Exercise equipt. Health club privileges. Cr cds: A, C, D, DS, MC, V.

🖢 🏋 🛏 🛏 SC

Inns

✔★ **COACH HOUSE.** *284 Lafayette St, on MA1A & 114.* 978/744-4092; res: 800/688-8689. Web www.salemweb.com/biz/coach-house. 11 rms, 9 with bath, 9 A/C, 3 story. No rm phones. Apr-Nov: S, D $75-$92; each addl $20; suites $78-$105; lower rates rest of yr. Crib free. TV. Complimentary continental bkfst. Restaurant nearby. Ck-out 11 am, ck-in 3 pm. Microwaves avail. Built 1879; many antiques. Totally nonsmoking. Cr cds: A, MC, V.

🖂 🛏

★ ★ ★ **SALEM INN.** *7 Summer St (MA 114).* 978/741-0680; FAX 978/744-8924; res: 800/446-2995. Web www.salemweb.com/biz/saleminn. 33 units, 4 story, 5 suites, 6 kits. No elvtr. S, D $109-$189; each addl $15; suites $169-$199. Pet accepted. TV; cable (premium). Complimentary continental bkfst. Ck-out 11 am, ck-in 3 pm. Meeting rm. Business servs avail. In-rm modem link. Many fireplaces; some in-rm whirlpools. Brick patio, rose garden. Sea captain's house (1834); on Salem's Heritage trail; many antiques. Cr cds: A, C, D, DS, JCB, MC, V.

D 🖢 🛏 🛏

Restaurants

★ **CHASE HOUSE.** *Pickering Wharf.* 978/744-0000. Specializes in seafood. Hrs: 11:30 am-11 pm. Closed Thanksgiving, Dec 25. Bar. Semi-a la carte: lunch $5.50-$10.95, dinner $8.50-$17.95. Child's meals. Entertainment wkends. Outdoor dining. Cr cds: A, D, DS, MC, V.

[D] [⊐]

★ ★ **THE GRAPEVINE.** *26 Congress St.* 978/745-9335. E-mail gvine@shore.net; web www.shore.net/~gvineamericangrill/italian. Italian, Amer menu. Specializes in pasta, vegetarian entrees, chicken. Hrs: 5:30-10 pm; Wed-Fri 11:30 am-2:30 pm, 5:30-10 pm. Closed some major hols; also Super Bowl Sun. Res accepted. Bar to 1 am. Semi-a la carte: lunch $8-$12, dinner $13-$22. Parking. Outdoor dining. Eclectic deco dining rm. Cr cds: A, DS, MC, V.

[D]

✔★ ★ **LYCEUM BAR & GRILL.** *43 Church St.* 978/745-7665. Specializes in grilled food. Own baking. Hrs: 11:30 am-3 pm, 5:30-10 pm; Sat from 5:30 pm; Sun brunch 11 am-3 pm. Closed Thanksgiving, Dec 25. Res accepted. Bar to 1 am. Semi-a la carte: lunch $5.95-$9.95, dinner $13.95-$18.95. Sun brunch $3.95-$8.95. Built in 1830. Alexander Graham Bell presented the first demonstrations of long distance telephone conversations here in 1877. Cr cds: A, JCB, MC, V.

[D] [⊐]

★ ★ **RED RAVEN'S HAVANA.** *90 Washington St.* 978/740-3888. Eclectic menu. Specialties: roasted mussels, smoked salmon. Hrs: 5:30-10 pm. Closed Mon, Sun; also most major hols. Res accepted. Bar to 1 am. Wine list. Semi-a la carte: dinner $14.95-$22.95. Street parking. Turn-of-the-century Victorian decor; paintings. Cr cds: A, MC, V.

[D] [♥]

★ **VICTORIA STATION.** *86 Wharf St.* 978/745-3400. Specializes in prime rib, seafood. Salad bar. Hrs: 11:30 am-10 pm; Fri, Sat to 11 pm. Closed Dec 25. Res accepted. Bar. Semi-a la carte: lunch $5.25-$9.95, dinner $8.95-$19.95. Child's meals. Outdoor dining. Overlooks harbor. Cr cds: A, C, D, DS, MC, V.

[D] [⊐]

Sandwich (Cape Cod) (D-9)

Settled 1637 **Pop** 15,489 **Elev** 20 ft **Area code** 508 **Zip** 02563
Information Cape Cod Canal Region Chamber of Commerce, 70 Main St, Buzzards Bay 02532; 508/759-6000.

The first town to be settled on Cape Cod, Sandwich made the glass that bears its name. This pressed glass was America's greatest contribution to the glass industry.

What to See and Do

✪ **Heritage Plantation.** 1899-mid-1930s autos including a restored and rebuilt 1931 Duesenberg Model J. Tourer built for Gary Cooper, a 1908 white steamer, and the first official presidential car, which was used by President Taft. The Military Museum houses the Lilly collection of miniature soldiers and antique firearms. Art Museum has Early American collections of scrimshaw and weather vanes, trade signs and primitive paintings include large Currier & Ives collection; jitney rides (free); ride on restored 1912 carousel; windmill (1800); entertainment (summer). Extensive rhododendron plantings on this 76-acre site. Changing exhibits. Cafe and garden shop. (Mid-May-late Oct, daily) Picnic area opp main parking lot. Grove & Pine Sts. Phone 508/888-3300. ¢¢¢

Hoxie House & Dexter Gristmill. Restored mid-17th-century buildings. House, operating mill; stone-ground corn meal sold. (Mid-June-mid-Oct, daily) Water St. Phone 508/888-1173. ¢;   Combination ticket ¢¢

Sandwich Glass Museum. Internationally renowned collection of exquisite Sandwich Glass (ca 1825-1888). (Apr-Oct, daily; phone for off-season hrs) 129 Main St. Phone 508/888-0251. ¢¢

State parks.

Scusset Beach. Swimming beach; fishing pier; camping (fee). Standard fees. 3 mi NW on MA 6A across canal, then 2 mi E at jct MA 3 & US 6. Phone 508/362-3225. Day use parking (per vehicle) ¢¢

Shawme-Crowell State Forest. Approx 2,700 acres. Primitive camping. Standard fees. 3 mi W on MA 130, off US 6. Phone 508/888-0351.

Yesteryears Doll and Miniature Museum. Old First Parish Meeting House (1638) houses antique costumed dolls. (Mid-May-Oct, daily exc Sun) Main & River Sts. Phone 508/888-1711. ¢¢

Motels

★ **COUNTRY ACRES.** *187 MA 6A.* 508/888-2878; res: 888/860-8650; FAX 508/888-8511. Web www.sunsol.com/countryacres/. 17 rms, 1 cottage. Late June-Labor Day: S, D $65-$85; each addl $8; lower rates rest of yr. Crib $8. TV; cable (premium). Pool. Ck-out 11 am. Lawn games. Refrigerators. Cr cds: A, C, D, DS, MC, V.

[≈][⊠][🔥]

✔★ ★ **EARL OF SANDWICH MOTOR MANOR.** *(378 MA 6A, East Sandwich 02537)* 2½ mi E on MA 6A. 508/888-1415; res: 800/442-3275. 24 rms. Late June-early Sept: S, D $65-$89; each addl $10; lower rates rest of yr. Crib $5. Pet accepted. TV. Complimentary continental bkfst. Restaurant nearby. Ck-out 11 am. Tudor motif. Cr cds: A, C, D, DS, MC, V.

[D][🐾][⊠][🔥]

★ **OLD COLONY.** *(436 6A, East Sandwich 02537)* 508/888-9716; res: 800/786-9716. E-mail jirenec@aol.com; web www.sunsol.com/old.colony/. 10 rms. Late June-Labor Day: S, D $69-$84; under 12 free; higher rates: hols (2-day min), mid-May-mid-June; lower rates mid-Sept-Nov, Mar-mid-May. Crib free. TV; cable. Pool. Playground. Complimentary continental bkfst. Restaurant nearby. Ck-out 11 am. Lawn games. Refrigerators. Picnic tables. Cr cds: A, DS, MC, V.

[≈][🔥]

★ **SANDWICH MOTOR LODGE.** *(54 Rte 6A, East Sandwich)* 508/888-2275; FAX 508/888-8102; res: 800/282-5353. 68 rms, 2 story, 33 suites, 4 kit. units. July-Aug: D $109; each addl $10; suites $129; kit. units $450/wk; lower rates rest of yr. Crib $5. Pet accepted; $15. TV; cable (premium), VCR avail. 2 pools, 1 indoor; whirlpool. Complimentary continental bkfst. Restaurant adj 11:30 am-9 pm. Ck-out 11 am. Coin lndry. Meeting rms. Game rm. Refrigerators, wet bars. Cr cds: A, D, DS, MC, V.

[D][🐾][≈][⊠][🌊][SC]

★ **SANDY NECK.** *(669 MA 6A, East Sandwich 02537)* 5½ mi E on MA 6A. 508/362-3992; FAX 508/362-5170; res: 800/564-3992. E-mail snmotel@capecod.net; web www.sunsol.com/sandyneck/. 12 rms. Mid-June-Labor Day: S, D $79-$89; each addl $10; lower rates Feb-mid-June & after Labor Day-Dec. Closed rest of yr. Crib free. TV; cable (premium). Complimentary coffee. Restaurant nearby. Ck-out 11 am. Refrigerators. Cr cds: A, C, D, DS, MC, V.

[≈][🔥]

★ ★ **SHADY NOOK INN.** *MA 6A.* 508/888-0409; FAX 508/888-4039; res: 800/338-5208. E-mail thenook@capecod.net; web www.capecod.net/shadynook/nook.html. 30 rms, 7 kits. Mid-June-Labor Day: S, D $89-$95; each addl $8; suites $110-$150; lower rates rest of yr. TV; cable (premium). Heated pool. Restaurant nearby. Ck-out 11 am. Guest lndry. In-rm modem link. Refrigerators. Cr cds: A, C, D, DS, MC, V.

[≈][⊠][🔥]

★ ★ **SPRING HILL MOTOR LODGE.** *(351 MA 6A, East Sandwich 02537) 2¹/₂ mi E. 508/888-1456; FAX 508/833-1556; res: 800/647-2514.* E-mail raldhurs@capecod.net; web www.sunsol .com/springhill/. 24 rms, 2 kit. units. Late June-Labor Day: S, D $95-$115; each addl $10; kit. units $155; lower rates rest of yr. Crib $10. TV; cable (premium). Heated pool. Coffee in rms. Restaurant nearby. Ck-out 11 am. Tennis. Picnic tables. Refrigerators. Cr cds: A, C, D, DS, MC, V.

Inns

★ ★ ★ **BAY BEACH.** *1-3 Bay Beach Lane. 508/888-8813; FAX 508/888-5416; res: 800/475-6398.* 6 rms, 3 story. S, D $175-$240. Closed Nov-mid-May. Children over 16 yrs only. TV; cable (premium). Complimentary full bkfst; afternoon refreshments. Restaurant nearby. Ck-out noon, ck-in 2-6 pm. Luggage handling. Concierge serv. Exercise equipt. Refrigerators. Balconies. Grey weathered clapboard houses with extensive gardens. On beach. Totally nonsmoking. Cr cds: MC, V.

★ ★ **BELFRY INNE & BISTRO.** *8 Jarves St. 508/888-8550; res: 800/844-4542; FAX 508/888-3922.* E-mail info@belfryinn.com; web www.belfryinn.com. 9 air-cooled rms, 3 with shower only, 3 story. No elvtr. Late May-mid-Oct: S, D $85-$165; package plans; wkends, hols (2-day min); lower rates rest of yr. Children over 10 yrs only. TV in common rm; cable (premium), VCR avail (movies). Complimentary full bkfst; afternoon refreshments. Restaurant 5-11 pm. Rm serv 24 hrs. Ck-out 11 am, ck-in 3 pm. Business center. In-rm modem link. Valet serv. Concierge serv. Lawn games. Some in-rm whirlpools, fireplaces. Some balconies. Former rectory built 1882; belfrey access. Totally nonsmoking. Cr cds: A, MC, V.

✔★ ★ **CAPTAIN EZRA NYE HOUSE.** *152 Main St. 508/888-6142; FAX 508/833-2897; res: 800/388-2278.* E-mail captnye@aol.com; web captainezranyehouse.com. 6 rms, 2 story. No A/C. No rm phones. June-Oct: S, D $90-$110; suite $110; wkly rates; lower rates rest of yr. Children over 10 yrs only. TV in sitting rm, suite; cable. Complimentary full bkfst. Restaurant nearby. Ck-out 11 am, ck-in 2 pm. Business servs avail. Built 1829; antiques. Totally nonsmoking. Cr cds: A, DS, JCB, MC, V.

★ ★ ★ **DAN'L WEBSTER INN.** *149 Main St. 508/888-3622; FAX 508/888-5156; res: 800/444-3566.* Web www.danlwebsterinn.com. 47 rms, 1-3 story. Late May-Oct: S, D $139-$179; each addl $10; suites $209-$335; under 12 free; MAP avail, addl $44/person; lower rates rest of yr. Crib free. TV; cable (premium). Pool. Dining rm (see DAN'L WEBSTER INN). Rm serv. Bar noon-1 am; entertainment. Ck-out 11 am, ck-in 3 pm. Meeting rms. Business center. In-rm modem link. Luggage handling. Health club privileges. Some fireplaces. Whirlpool in suites. Modeled on an 18th-century house. Cr cds: A, C, D, DS, MC, V.

★ ★ **DUNBAR HOUSE.** *1 Water St, at Tupper Rd. 508/833-2485; FAX 508/833-4713.* E-mail dunbar@capecod.net. 3 rms, 2 with shower only, 2 story. No A/C. No rm phones. May-Oct: D $85-$95; lower rates rest of yr. Crib $5. TV in sitting rms; cable. Complimentary full bkfst; afternoon refreshments. Restaurant nearby. Ck-out 11 am, ck-in 3 pm. Luggage handling. Concierge serv. Gift shop. Picnic tables. Colonial house built 1741; overlooking Shawme Pond. Tea rm. Some fireplaces. Totally nonsmoking. Cr cds: DS, MC, V.

★ ★ ★ **ISAIAH JONES HOMESTEAD.** *165 Main St. 508/888-9115; FAX 508/888-9648; res: 800/526-1625.* Web www.sunsol.com/isaiahjones. 5 rms, 2 with shower only, 2 story. No A/C. No rm phones. Mid-May-late Oct: D $95-$155; wkend rates; lower rates rest of yr. Children over 12 yrs only. TV in sitting rm; cable. Complimentary full bkfst; afternoon refreshments. Restaurant nearby. Ck-out 11 am, ck-in 3-6 pm. Luggage handling. Concierge serv. Some in-rm whirlpools. Picnic tables.

Restored Victorian house built 1849; many antiques. Totally nonsmoking. Cr cds: A, DS, MC, V.

★ ★ **THE VILLAGE INN.** *4 Jarves St. 508/833-0363; FAX 508/833-2063; res: 800/922-9989.* E-mail capecodinn@aol.com; web www.capecodinn.com. 8 rms, 2 share bath, 3 story. No A/C. No rm phones. June-Oct: D $85-$115; wkends (2-day min); lower rates Nov-May. Children over 8 yrs only. Complimentary full bkfst; afternoon refreshments. Restaurant nearby. Ck-out 11 am, ck-in 3-6 pm. Federal-style house (1837) with wrap-around porch, gardens. Many antique furnishings. Totally nonsmoking. Cr cds: A, DS, MC, V.

Restaurants

★ **BOBBY BYRNE'S.** *MA 6A, in Stop and Shop Plaza Shopping Center. 508/888-6088.* Specializes in steak, seafood, pasta. Hrs: 11 am-11 pm; early-bird dinner 4-6 pm. Closed Thanksgiving, Dec 25. Bar to 1 am. Semi-a la carte: lunch $4.95-$7.95, dinner $6.95-$10.50. Child's meals. Family-owned. Cr cds: A, DS, MC, V.

★ ★ **THE BRIDGE.** *(21 MA 6A, Sagamore 02561) 2 mi W on MA 6A. 508/888-8144.* Specializes in Yankee pot roast, fresh scrod, grape nut custard pudding. Hrs: 11:30 am-9:30 pm; wkends from noon. Closed Thanksgiving, Dec 25. Res accepted. Bar. Semi-a la carte: lunch $1.95-$7.95, dinner $8.95-$16.95. Child's meals. Family-owned since 1953. Cr cds: C, D, DS, MC, V.

★ ★ ★ **DAN'L WEBSTER INN.** *(See Dan'l Webster Inn) 508/888-3623.* Web www.danlwebsterinn.com. Specializes in seafood, chicken, veal. Own baking. Hrs: 8 am-10 pm; Sun brunch noon-2:30 pm; early-bird dinner 4:30-5:30 pm. Res accepted. Bar. Wine cellar. Semi-a la carte: bkfst $3.50-$6.95, lunch $5.25-$11.95, dinner $10.95-$23.95. Sun brunch $7-$12.95. Child's meals. Pianist. Valet parking. Conservatory dining overlooks garden. Authentic reproduction of 1700s house. Several dining rms; some with fireplace. Cr cds: A, C, D, DS, MC, V.

✔★ **HORIZON'S.** *98 Town Neck Rd. 508/888-6166.* Specializes in fresh seafood, clam bakes, steaks. Hrs: 11:30 am-midnight. Closed Nov-Apr. No A/C. Bar. Semi-a la carte: lunch $4.95-$7.95, dinner $6.95-$13.95. Child's meals. Entertainment Sat. Outdoor dining. Overlooks Cape Cod Bay. Cr cds: A, DS, MC, V.

Saugus (B-7)

(See also Boston)

Settled 1630 **Pop** 25,549 **Elev** 21 ft **Area code** 781 **Zip** 01906

Saugus is the birthplace of the American steel industry. The first ironworks were built here in 1646.

What to See and Do

Saugus Iron Works National Historic Site. Commemorates America's first successful integrated ironworks. Reconstructed furnace, forge, mill on original foundations; furnished 17th-century house; museum; working blacksmith shop; 7 working waterwheels; guided tours and demonstrations (Apr-Oct); film. (Daily; closed Jan 1, Thanksgiving, Dec 25) Contact the National Park Service, Saugus Iron Works National Historic Site, 244 Central St; 781/233-0050.   **Free.**

Restaurants

✔★ ★ ★ **DONATELLO.** *44 Broadway. 781/233-9975.* Specializes in regional Italian cuisine. Hrs: 11:30 am-10:30 pm; Sat to 11:30 pm; Sun from 3:30 pm. Closed July 4, Thanksgiving, Dec 24. Res accepted. Bar. Semi-a la carte: lunch $6-$10, dinner $5.50-$19.95. Own pasta. Valet parking. Italian decor. Totally nonsmoking. Cr cds: A, C, D, MC, V.

 D SC

✔★ ★ **HILLTOP STEAK HOUSE.** *855 Broadway, Rte 1, S on US1. 781/233-7700.* Specializes in beef, seafood. Hrs: 11 am-10 pm; Fri, Sat to 11 pm. Closed Thanksgiving, Dec 25. Bar. Semi-a la carte: lunch $5.99-$9.95, dinner $7.99-$22.99. Child's meals. Cr cds: A, DS, MC, V.

D ⛵

Seekonk
(see Providence, RI)

Sheffield
(see Great Barrington)

South Hadley (B-3)
(See also Amherst, Holyoke)

Settled ca 1660 **Pop** 13,600 (est) **Elev** 257 ft **Area code** 413 **Zip** 01075
Information Chamber of Commerce, 10 Harwich Place; 413/532-6451.

Nestled on the banks of the Connecticut River, South Hadley was incorporated as a town in 1775. Twenty years later the first navigable canal in the United States began operation here. The town remained a busy shipping center until 1847, when the coming of the railroad made shipping by river unprofitable. Still visible in spots, the canal is being restored.

What to See and Do

Mount Holyoke College (1837). (1,950 women) Campus tours (inquire for schedule). College St. Phone 413/538-2000. On grounds are

Mount Holyoke College Art Museum. Small but choice permanent collection of paintings, drawings, prints and sculpture; also special exhibitions. (Tues-Fri, also Sat & Sun afternoons; closed college hols) Phone 413/538-2245. **Free.**

Joseph Allen Skinner Museum. Housed in a small Congregational church (1846). Collection of Early American furnishings, decorative arts; one-rm schoolhouse. (May-Oct, Wed & Sun, afternoons) MA 116. Phone 413/538-2085. **Free.**

Talcott Arboretum. Campus features variety of trees and plantings; Japanese meditation, wildflower and formal perennial gardens; greenhouse complex has collections of exotic plants; flower show (Mar); tours by appt. (Mon-Fri, also Sat & Sun afternoons; closed hols) Phone 413/538-2199. **Free.**

Old Firehouse Museum. Served as a firehouse 1888-1974; features firefighting equipment, Native American artifacts, items relating to local history and South Hadley Canal. (June-Sept, Wed & Sun; schedule may vary, phone ahead or contact Chamber of Commerce) 2 N Main St. Phone 413/536-4970. **Free.**

Annual Event

Women's Regatta. Brunelle's Marina. Oct.

South Yarmouth (Cape Cod) (D-9)
(See also Hyannis)

Pop 10,358 **Elev** 20 ft **Area code** 508 **Zip** 02664 **E-mail** info@capecodchamber.org **Web** www.capecodchamber.org
Information Yarmouth Area Chamber of Commerce, PO Box 479; 800/732-1008 or the Cape Cod Chamber of Commerce, US 6 & MA 132, PO Box 790, Hyannis 02601-0790; 508/362-3225 or 888/33-CAPECOD.

Much of the area of the Yarmouths developed on the strength of seafaring and fishing in the first half of the 19th century. South Yarmouth is actually a village within the town of Yarmouth. Well-preserved old houses line Main St to the north in Yarmouth Port, architecturally among the choicest communities in Massachusetts. Bass River, to the south, also contains many fine estates.

What to See and Do

Captain Bangs Hallet House. Early 19th-century sea captain's home. (June-Sept, Wed-Fri & Sun afternoons; rest of yr, by appt) Botanic trails (all yr; donation). Gate house (June-mid-Sept, daily). Off MA 6A, near Yarmouth Port Post Office. Phone 508/362-3021. ¢¢

Swimming. Nantucket Sound and bayside beaches. Parking fee.

Winslow Crocker House (ca 1780). Georgian house adorned with 17th-, 18th- and 19th-century furnishings collected in early 20th century. Includes furniture made by New England craftsmen in the colonial and Federal periods; hooked rugs, ceramics, pewter. (June-mid-Oct, Tues, Thurs, Sat & Sun) On Old King's Hwy, US 6A, in Yarmouth Port. Phone 508/362-4385. ¢¢

Motels

★★ **ALL SEASONS MOTOR INN.** *1199 Main St (MA 28). 508/394-7600; FAX 508/398-7160; res: 800/527-0359.* Web www.allseasons.com. 114 rms, 2 story. July-early Sept: S, D $85-$105; each addl $5; lower rates rest of yr. Crib $5. TV; cable (premium), VCR (movies). Indoor/outdoor pool; whirlpool. Playground. Restaurant 7:30-11 am, noon-3 pm (in season). Ck-out 11 am. Coin lndry. Business servs avail. Exercise equipt; sauna. Game rm. Refrigerators. Private patios, balconies. Picnic tables. Cr cds: A, C, D, DS, MC, V.

 D ⛵ 🖈 ⛵ 🔥

✔★ ★ **AMERICANA HOLIDAY.** *(99 Main (MA 28), West Yarmouth 02673) 2 mi W on MA 28. 508/775-5511; FAX 508/790-0597; res: 800/445-4497 (MA), 800/367-3319 (New England).* E-mail americana@all-season.com; web www.americanaholiday.com. 153 rms, 2 story. Late June-Labor Day: S, D $59-$69; each addl $5; suites $85-$105; lower rates Mar-late June, after Labor Day-Oct. Closed rest of yr. Crib free. TV; cable. 3 pools, 1 indoor; whirlpool. Playground. Complimentary coffee. Restaurant nearby. Ck-out 11 am. Putting green. Sauna. Game rm. Lawn games. Refrigerators. Cr cds: A, C, D, DS, MC, V.

D ⛵ ⛵ 🔥

✔★ **BASS RIVER.** *(891 MA 28, Bass River) 1/2 mi W on MA 28. 508/398-2488.* 20 rms, 4 kits. July-Aug: S $56; D $58; each addl $6; kit. units $60-$64; wkly rates; lower rates rest of yr. Crib $4. TV; cable. Pool. Restaurant nearby. Ck-out 11 am. Lawn games. Some refrigerators. Picnic tables, grills. Cr cds: A, MC, V.

⛵ ⛵ 🔥 SC

★ **BEACH 'N TOWNE.** *1261 MA 28, 1/4 mi W of Bass River Bridge. 508/398-2311; res: 800/987-8556.* 21 rms. Late June-late Aug: S, D $60-$67; each addl $5-$7; lower rates Feb-late June, late Aug-Dec. Closed rest of yr. Crib free. TV; cable. Pool. Playground. Coffee in lobby.

Restaurant nearby. Ck-out 11 am. Lawn games. Refrigerators. Picnic tables, grills. Library. Cr cds: A, DS, MC, V.

⌘ ⌘ ⌘

★ ★ ★ **BEST WESTERN BLUE WATER RESORT.** *(291 South Shore Dr, South Yarmouth)* 1½ *mi SW off MA 28. 508/398-2288; FAX 508/398-1010; res: 800/367-9393.* E-mail bluewater@redjacketinns.com; web www.redjacketinns.com/bluewater. 113 rms, 1-2 story. Late June-Labor Day: D $168-$265; each addl $10; lower rates rest of yr. Crib $5. TV; cable. 2 pools, 1 indoor; whirlpool, poolside serv. Free supervised child's activities (July-Labor Day); ages 6-15. Restaurant 7:30-11 am, noon-2 pm; off-season wkend dinner only. Bar noon-1 am; entertainment Fri, Sat. Ck-out 11 am. Meeting rms. Business servs avail. Bellhops. Sundries. Tennis. Putting green. Sauna. Lawn games. Sun decks. Microwaves avail. On 600-ft private ocean beach. Cr cds: DS, MC, V.

⌘ ⌘ ⌘ ⌘ ⌘ SC

★ ★ **BEST WESTERN-BLUE ROCK MOTOR INN.** *39 Todd Rd, 1 mi N off MA 28, off High Bank Rd. 508/398-6962; FAX 508/398-1830.* E-mail bluerock@redjacketinns.com; web www.redjacketinns.com/bluerock. 45 rms, 1-2 story. Late June-Labor Day (2-day min wkends): S, D $105-$150; each addl $10; under 12 free; golf plan; lower rates Apr-late June, after Labor Day-late Oct. Closed rest of yr. Crib free. TV; cable. Heated pool; whirlpool. Restaurant 7 am-2:30 pm. Bar 11 am-7 pm. Ck-out 11 am. Meeting rm. Business servs avail. Tennis. 18-hole, par 3 golf, pro, greens fee $31, putting greens. Refrigerators. Private patios, balconies. Overlooks golf course. Cr cds: A, D, DS, MC, V.

⌘ ⌘ ⌘ ⌘ ⌘

✔★ **CAPE SOJOURN.** *(149 Main St, West Yarmouth 02673)* 3½ *mi W on MA 28. 508/775-3825; FAX 508/778-2870; res: 800/882-8995.* E-mail sojourn@capecod.net; web www.capecod.net/capesojourn. 68 rms, 2 story. Late June-Aug: S, D $58-$78; higher rates special events; lower rates late Apr-late June, Sept-Oct. Closed rest of yr. Crib $6. TV; cable (premium). 2 pools, 1 indoor; whirlpool. Complimentary continental bkfst. Restaurant nearby. Ck-out 11 am. Excercise equipt. Rec rm. Microwaves avail. Cr cds: A, DS, MC, V.

⌘ ⌘ ⌘ ⌘ ⌘

★ **CAPTAIN JONATHAN.** *1237 MA 28, 1 mi W of Bass River Bridge. 508/398-3480; res: 800/342-3480.* 21 rms, 2 story. July-Aug: S, D $63-$68; each addl $5; cottage $700-$750/wk; under 12 free; wkly rates; higher rates hols; lower rates rest of yr. Crib free. TV; cable. Pool. Playground. Complimentary continental bkfst. Restaurant nearby. Ck-out 11 am. Lawn games. Microwaves avail. Picnic tables. Cr cds: A, C, D, DS, MC, V.

⌘ ⌘ ⌘

★ **CAVALIER MOTOR LODGE & RESORT.** *(881 Main St (MA 28), Bass River)* ½ *mi W on MA 28. 508/394-6575; FAX 508/394-6578; res: 800/545-3536.* 66 rms, 46 A/C, 1-2 story. July-Aug: S, D $59-$99; each addl $7; kit. units $600-$975; golf plans off season; lower rates late Mar-mid-June, Sept-Oct. Closed rest of yr. TV; cable, VCR avail (movies). Indoor/outdoor pool; wading pool, whirlpool, sauna. Playground. Putting green. Lawn games. Game rm. Refrigerators, microwaves avail. Grills. Cr cds: A, DS, MC, V.

⌘ ⌘ ⌘

★ ★ **FLAGSHIP MOTOR INN.** *(343 Main St, West Yarmouth 02673)* 2 *mi W on MA 28. 508/775-5155; FAX 508/790-8255; res: 800/676-0000 (MA).* 138 rms, 2 story. July-Aug: D $65-$99; each addl $10; suites $75-$119; under 18 free; lower rates May-June, Sept-Oct. Crib free. TV; cable. 2 pools, 1 indoor; whirlpool. Playground. Ck-out 11 am. Meeting rms. Business servs avail. In-rm modom link. Sauna. Game rm. Many refrigerators. Balconies. Cr cds: A, D, DS, MC, V.

⌘ ⌘ ⌘ ⌘

★ ★ **GULL WING SUITES.** *822 Main St (MA 28). 508/394-9300; FAX 508/394-1190; res: 800/676-0000.* 136 suites, 2 story. July-Labor Day: suites $105-$130; package plans; lower rates rest of yr. Crib avail. TV; cable (premium). 2 pools, 1 indoor; whirlpool, saunas. Restau-

rant nearby. Ck-out 11 am. Meeting rms. Business servs avail. Game rm. Refrigerators, wet bars. Balconies. Cr cds: A, D, DS, MC, V.

⌘ ⌘ ⌘ ⌘ SC

✔★ **HUNTERS GREEN.** *(553 Main St, West Yarmouth 02673)* 2 *mi W on MA 28. 508/771-1169; res: 800/334-3220.* 74 rms, 2 story. Late June-Labor Day: S, D $54-$64; each addl $6; lower rates mid-Apr-late June, after Labor Day-Oct. Closed rest of yr. Crib $6. TV; cable (premium). Indoor/outdoor pool; whirlpool. Restaurant nearby. Ck-out 11 am. Lawn games. Picnic tables. Cr cds: A, DS, MC, V.

⌘ ⌘ ⌘

★ ★ **MARINER MOTOR LODGE.** *(573 Main St, West Yarmouth 02673)* 2 *mi W on MA 28. 508/771-7887; FAX 508/771-2811; res: 800/445-4050.* Web www.mariner-capecod.com. 100 rms, 2 story. S, D $69-$95; under 18 free. Crib $5. TV; cable (premium). 2 heated pools, 1 indoor; whirlpool. Continental bkfst off-season. Restaurant nearby. Ck-out 11 am. Meeting rm. Business servs avail. Sauna. Game rm. Refrigerators. Cr cds: A, DS, MC, V.

⌘ ⌘ ⌘ ⌘ SC

★ ★ **OCEAN MIST.** *97 South Shore Dr,* ½ *mi S of MA 28. 508/398-2633; FAX 508/760-3151; res: 800/248-6478.* E-mail mist@capecod.net; web www.capecod.com/oceanmist. 63 units, 2 story, 32 loft suites, 21 kit. units. July-Aug: D $179; suites $229-$269; kit. units $179-$219; under 15 free; lower rates Sept-Dec & Feb-June. Closed Jan. Crib $10. TV; cable, VCR avail (movies). Indoor pool; whirlpool. Bkfst avail. Complimentary coffee. Ck-out 11 am. Coin lndry. Business servs avail. Refrigerators, wet bars. On ocean; swimming beach. Cr cds: A, DS, MC, V.

⌘ ⌘ ⌘

★ ★ ★ **RED JACKET BEACH RESORT.** *(1 South Shore Dr, Bass River)* Approx ½ *mi S of MA 28 to Seaview Ave. 508/398-6941; FAX 508/398-1214; res: 800/672-0500.* 150 rms, 1-2 story, 13 cottages. Late June-Labor Day: S, D $160-$250; each addl $10; 2-4 bedrm cottages $200-$2,800/wk; lower rates Apr-late June, after Labor Day-late Oct. Closed rest of yr. Crib free. TV; cable. 2 pools, 1 indoor; whirlpool, poolside serv. Supervised child's activities (July-Labor Day); ages 4-12. Restaurant 7:30-11 am, noon-3 pm; also 6-9:30 pm in season. Rm serv. Bar noon-midnight. Ck-out 11 am. Coin lndry. Meeting rms. Business servs avail. Bellhops. Sundries. Tennis. Putting green. Exercise equipt; sauna. Sailing. Game rm. Lawn games. Refrigerators, microwaves avail. Private patios, balconies. On ocean, beach. Cr cds: A, MC, V.

⌘ ⌘ ⌘ ⌘ ⌘ ⌘ ⌘

★ ★ **RIVIERA BEACH RESORT.** *327 South Shore Dr, 1½ mi off MA 28. 508/398-2273; FAX 508/398-1202; res: 800/CAPE-COD.* E-mail riviera@capecod.net; web redjacketinns.com/riviera. 125 rms, 2 story. July-early Sept: D $160-$275; each addl $10; lower rates mid-Apr-June, early Sept-late Oct. Closed rest of yr. Crib free. TV; cable, VCR avail (movies). 2 pools, 1 indoor; whirlpool. Free supervised child's activities (July-Labor Day); ages 4-11. Restaurant 7:30-11 am, noon-2 pm. Bar noon-8 pm. Ck-out 11 am. Bellhops. Sailing, waterbikes, sailboards in season. Lawn games. Refrigerators. Some in-rm whirlpools. Balconies. Sun decks. On 415-ft private beach. Cr cds: A, MC, V.

⌘ ⌘ ⌘ ⌘ ⌘ ⌘

★ ★ **TIDEWATER.** *(135 Main St, West Yarmouth 02673)* 3½ *mi W on Main St (MA 28). 508/775-6322; FAX 508/778-5105; res: 800/338-6322.* E-mail tidewater@capecod.net; web www.capecod.net/tidewater/. 101 rms, 1-2 story. July-Aug: S, D $82-$101; each addl $6; under 12 free; golf plans; higher rates: Memorial Day, Labor Day, Columbus Day; lower rates rest of yr. Crib $5. TV; cable. 2 pools, 1 indoor; whirlpool. Playground. Complimentary coffee in lobby. Restaurant nearby. Ck-out 11 am. Sauna. Game rm. Lawn games. Refrigerators. Balconies. Picnic tables. On 4 acres; view of Mill Creek Bay. Cr cds: A, DS, MC, V.

⌘ ⌘ ⌘ ⌘ SC

Inns

★ ★ ★ **CAPTAIN FARRIS HOUSE.** *308 Old Main St. 508/760-2818; FAX 508/398-1262; res: 800/350-9477.* E-mail farris@cape.com; web www.captainfarriscapecod.com. 8 rms, 4 suites. 6 A/C. Late May-mid-Oct: S, D $95-$140; suites $155-$185; wkends (2-day min); lower rates rest of yr. Children over 10 yrs only. TV; cable, VCR. Complimentary full bkfst; afternoon refreshments. Dining rm by res. Ck-out 11 am, ck-in 2 pm. Business servs avail. In-rm modem link. Luggage handling. Concierge serv. Lawn games. Whirlpools. Refrigerators, fireplaces. Balconies. Two buildings (1825 & 1845). Many antiques. Near Bass River. Cr cds: A, MC, V.

★ ★ **COLONIAL HOUSE.** *(Old Kings Hwy (MA 6A), Yarmouth Port 02675) 508/362-4348; FAX 508/362-8034; res: 800/999-3416.* 21 rms, 3 story. July-mid-Oct, S, D $85-$95; each addl $10; higher rates hol wkends; lower rates rest of yr. Crib $5. Pet accepted, some restrictions. TV; VCR avail. Indoor pool; whirlpool. Complimentary bkfst. Dining rm 11:30 am-2:30 pm, 4-9 pm. Bar to 1 am. Ck-out noon, ck-in 2 pm. Meeting rm. Business center. In-rm modem link. Massage. Lawn games. Old mansion (1730s); many antiques, handmade afghans. Cr cds: A, C, DS, ER, MC, V.

★ ★ ★ **LIBERTY HILL.** *(77 MA 6A, Yarmouth Port 02675) 508/362-3976; FAX 508/362-6485; res: 800/821-3977.* E-mail libertyh@capecod.net; web www.capecod.net/libertyhillinn. 9 rms, 3 story. No rm phones. Memorial Day-Columbus Day: D $100-$170; each addl $20; higher rates Presidents' Day; lower rates rest of yr. Crib $8. TV. Complimentary full bkfst. Restaurant nearby. Ck-out 11 am, ck-in 3 pm. Concierge. Free airport transportation. Antiques. Greek-revival mansion built 1825 for ship builder. Sitting rm furnished with early-American pieces. Totally nonsmoking. Cr cds: A, MC, V.

★ ★ **MANOR HOUSE.** *(57 Maine Ave, West Yarmouth 02673) 2 mi W on MA 28. 508/771-3433; FAX 508/790-1186; res: 800/962-6679.* E-mail manorhse@capecod.net; web www.capecod.net/manorhouse. 7 rms, 2 with shower only, 2 story. No rm phones. Mid-May-Oct: S, D $78-$138; wkly rates; wkends, hols (2-day min); lower rates rest of yr. Children over 12 yrs only. Complimentary full bkfst. Ck-out 11 am, ck-in 3-8 pm. Luggage handling. Concierge serv. Lawn games. Picnic tables. Beach house built in 1920s. Totally nonsmoking. Cr cds: A, MC, V.

Restaurants

★ ★ **AARDVARK CAFE.** *(134 Main St, Yarmouth Port) on MA 6A. 508/362-9866.* Specialties: free-range chicken breast grilled and spice rubbed, quiche of the day, fresh grilled Maine salmon with spicy Thai noodles. Own baking. Hrs: 7:30 am-9 pm. Sun brunch 9 am-3 pm. Bar. Semi-a la carte: bkfst $3-$6, lunch $3-$7.50, dinner $11-$23. Sun brunch $3-$8. Parking. In old sea captain's house (1840) with gables & gingerbread ornamentation. Casual decor. Totally nonsmoking. Cr cds: A, D, DS, MC, V.

★ ★ **ABBICCI.** *(43 Main St, Yarmouth Port) on MA 6A. 508/362-3501.* Italian menu. Specializes in authentic Italian cuisine, local seafood, desserts. Hrs: 11:30 am-2:30 pm, 5-10 pm. Res accepted. Bar. Semi-a la carte: lunch $6.95-$11.95, dinner $10.95-$23.95. Parking. Country inn atmosphere. Cr cds: A, D, DS, MC, V.

★ ★ **INAHO.** *(157 MA 6A, Yarmouth Port 02675) 1½ mi N on Union St to Main St (MA 6), W ½ mi. 508/362-5522.* Japanese menu. Specializes in tempura, teriyaki, sushi. Hrs: 5-10 pm. Closed Mon; Easter, Thanksgiving, Dec 25. Res accepted. Serv bar. Semi-a la carte: dinner $12-$22. Japanese decor; sushi bar. Totally nonsmoking. Cr cds: MC, V.

★ ★ **RIVERWAY LOBSTER HOUSE.** *MA 28, 1 blk W of Bass River Bridge. 508/398-2172.* Specializes in lobster, seafood. Hrs: 4:30-10 pm; Sun from noon; early-bird dinner Mon-Thurs 4:30-6:30 pm, Fri-Sat to 6 pm. Closed Dec 25. Res accepted. Bar. Semi-a la carte: dinner $8.50-$18. Child's meals. Parking. 2 fireplaces. Family-owned. Cr cds: A, C, D, DS, MC, V.

★ **SKIPPER RESTAURANT & LOOKOUT LOUNGE.** *152 South Shore Dr, 1 mi E off MA 28, S on Seaview Ave. 508/394-7406.* Specializes in seafood, steak. Hrs: 11:30-1 am; Sun from 8 am; early-bird dinner 4:30-6 pm. Closed Oct-Mar. A/C upstairs only. Bar. Semi-a la carte: bkfst $1.99-$5.95, lunch $3.95-$9.95, dinner $8.95-$18.95. Child's meals. Parking. Nautical motif. Scenic view of Nantucket Sound. Cr cds: A, C, D, DS, MC, V.

★ ★ **YARMOUTH HOUSE.** *(335 Main St, W Yarmouth 02673) 3 mi W on MA 28. 508/771-5154.* Specializes in seafood, beef, chicken, stir-fry. Hrs: 11:30 am-11 pm; early-bird dinner 3-6 pm. Closed Dec 25. Res accepted. Bar. A la carte entrees: lunch $3.95-$11.95, dinner $8.95-$18.95. Child's meals. Parking. 3 dining rms; working water wheel. Cr cds: A, C, D, DS, MC, V.

Springfield (C-3)

(See also Holyoke)

Settled 1636 **Pop** 156,983 **Elev** 70 ft **Area code** 413
Information Greater Springfield Convention & Visitors Bureau, 1500 Main St, PO Box 15589, 01115-5589; 413/787-1548 or 800/723-1548.

Established under the leadership of William Pynchon of Springfield, England, this is now a major unit in the Connecticut River industrial empire. Springfield is also a cultural center with a fine library, museums and a symphony orchestra, and is the home of Springfield College.

Transportation

Hartford Bradley Intl Airport: Information 860/292-2000; weather 860/627-3440; cash machines, Terminals A and B.

Car Rental Agencies: See IMPORTANT TOLL-FREE NUMBERS.

Public Transportation: Pioneer Valley Transit Authority, phone 413/781-PVTA.

Rail Passenger Service: Amtrak 800/872-7245.

What to See and Do

Basketball Hall of Fame. Exhibits on the game and its teams and players; shrine to the sport invented here in 1891 by Dr. James Naismith. Historic items on display; free movies; video highlights of great games; life-size, action blow-ups of Hall of Famers. Major features include: "Hoopla," a 22-min film; and "The Spalding Shoot-Out," the most popular participatory attraction, which allows visitors to try their skill at scoring a basket of varying heights while on a moving sidewalk. (Daily; closed Jan 1, Thanksgiving, Dec 25) 1150 W Columbus Ave, adj to I-91. Phone 413/781-6500. ¢¢¢

Forest Park. On 735 acres. Nature trails, tennis, swimming pool. Picnicking, playgrounds, ball fields. Zoo (Apr-Oct, daily; rest of yr, Sat & Sun; fee). Duck ponds. Pony rides, train rides (fee for both). Park (all yr). MA 83 off I-91. Phone 413/787-6461 (park) or 413/733-2251 (zoo). Park ¢¢

Indian Motocycle Museum. Part of the vast complex where Indian motorcycles were made until 1953. On display are historical cycles and other American-made machines; photographs; extensive collection of toy motorcycles; other Native American products, including an early snowmobile and a 1928 roadster. (Daily; closed Jan 1, Thanksgiving, Dec 25) 33 Hendee St. Phone 413/737-2624. ¢¢

Laughing Brook Education Center and Wildlife Sanctuary. Woodlands and wetlands, 354 acres. Former house (1782) of children's author and storyteller Thornton W. Burgess. Live animal exhibits of wildlife native to New England. Observation areas of pond, field and forest habitats. 4½ mi of walking trails; picnic area. (Tues-Sun; also Mon hols; closed Jan 1, Thanksgiving, Dec 25) 793 Main St, 7 mi SE in Hampden. Phone 413/566-8034. ¢¢

Municipal Group. Includes renovated Symphony Hall, which together with the Springfield Civic Center offers a performing arts complex presenting a variety of concerts, theater, children's productions, dance and sporting events and industrial shows; 300-ft campanile, modeled after the bell tower in the Piazza San Marco of Venice. NW side of Court Sq.

Riverside Park. Amusement park, rides, roller coasters; children's area; games & arcades; shows; restaurants. (June-Labor Day, daily; Apr, May & Sept, wkends only) 5 mi W via MA 57 & MA 159S in Agawam. Phone 413/786-9300. ¢¢¢¢

Springfield Armory National Historic Site. US armory (1794-1968) contains one of the largest collections of military small arms in the world. Exhibits include "Organ of Guns," made famous by Longfellow's poem "The Arsenal at Springfield." Film, video presentations. (Memorial Day-Labor Day, daily; rest of yr, daily exc Mon; closed Jan 1, Thanksgiving, Dec 25) Old Armory Square Green, Federal & State Sts. Phone 413/734-8551. **Free.**

Springfield Library and Museums. Includes **George Walter Vincent Smith Art Museum.** Italian Renaissance building housing collection of Oriental armor, arms, jade, bronzes and rugs; 19th-century American paintings, sculpture. (Thurs-Sun) State & Chestnut Sts. Phone 413/263-6800. **Connecticut River Valley Historical Museum** with genealogy and local history library; period rms. (Thurs-Sun) Phone 413/263-6800. **Museum of Fine Arts** has 20 galleries including outstanding collection of American and European works. (Thurs-Sun) Phone 413/263-6800. **Science Museum** has an exploration center, early aviation exhibit, aquarium, planetarium (fee), African hall, dinosaur hall. (Thurs-Sun) Phone 413/263-6800. Above buildings all closed major hols. Planetarium shows (Thurs, Sat & Sun). Library (fall-spring, daily exc Sun; summer, Mon-Fri; closed major hols). Inclusive admission ¢¢

State forests.

Brimfield. Swimming; trout fishing from shore (stocked). Hiking. Picnicking. Standard fees. 24 mi E on US 20, then SE near Brimfield. Phone 413/245-9966. Per vehicle ¢

Granville. Scenic gorge, laurel display. Swimming; fishing. Hiking. Picnicking. Camping. Standard fees. 22 mi W off MA 57. Phone 413/357-6611.

Storrowton Village. A group of restored Early American buildings: meetinghouse, schoolhouse, blacksmith shop and homes. Old-fashioned herb garden. Dining (see RESTAURANTS). Guided tours (June-Labor Day, Mon-Sat; rest of yr, by appt; closed hols). Eastern States Exposition, 1305 Memorial Ave, on MA 147 in West Springfield. Phone 413/787-0136. ¢¢

Annual Events

World's Largest Pancake Breakfast. A battle with Battle Creek, Michigan, to see who can serve the "world's largest breakfast." Features pancake bkfst served at a 4-blk-long table. Phone 413/733-3800. Sat closest to May 14.

Taste of Springfield. Phone 413/733-3800. Wed-Sun, mid-June.

Indian Day. Indian Motocycle Museum. Gathering of owners and those interested in Indian motorcycles and memorabilia. Phone 413/737-2624. 3rd Sun July.

Glendi Greek Celebration. Greek folk dances, observance of doctrine and ritual festivities, Greek foods, art exhibits, street dancing. Early Sept.

Eastern States Exposition (The Big E). 1305 Memorial Ave, on MA 147 in West Springfield. Largest fair in the Northeast; entertainment, exhibits; historic Avenue of States, Storrowton Village; horse show; agricultural events; "Better Living Center" exhibit. Phone 413/737-2443. 17 days Sept.

Hall of Fame Tip-off Classic. At Springfield Civic Center, 1277 Main St. Official opening game of the collegiate basketball season with 2 of the nation's top teams. Phone 413/781-6500. Mid-Nov.

Motels

★ ★ **COMFORT INN AT THE PARWICK CENTRE.** *(450 Memorial Dr, Chicopee 01020) off MA Tpke (I-90) exit 5, on Rte 33. 413/739-7311; FAX 413/594-5005.* 100 rms, 3 story. S $54-$73; D $61-$80; each addl $7; under 18 free. Crib free. TV; cable (premium). Restaurant 5-10 pm. Bar; entertainment Thurs-Mon. Ck-out 11 am. Coin lndry. Meeting rms. Business servs avail. Valet serv. Cr cds: A, C, D, DS, JCB, MC, V.

D ⊠ 🔥 SC

✔ ★ **DAYS INN.** *(437 Riverdale St, West Springfield 01089) Off I-91 exit 13B. 413/785-5365; FAX 413/732-7017.* 84 rms. S $38-$58; D $45-$65; each addl $10; higher rates special events. Crib free. TV. Pool. Complimentary continental bkfst. Restaurant nearby. Ck-out 11 am. Meeting rms. Downhill ski 9 mi. Cr cds: A, D, DS, MC, V.

D 🏊 ≋ ⊠ 🔥 SC

★ ★ **HAMPTON INN.** *(1011 Riverdale St, West Springfield 01089) on US 5, ¼ mi S of MA Tpke (I-90) exit 4 or N of I-91 exit 13B. 413/732-1300; FAX 413/732-9883.* 126 rms, 4 story. S, D $70; under 18 free. Crib free. TV; cable (premium), VCR avail. Pool. Complimentary continental bkfst. Ck-out noon. Meeting rms. Business servs avail. In-rm modem link. Sundries. Downhill/x-country ski 6 mi. Health club privileges. Cr cds: A, C, D, DS, MC, V.

D 🏊 ≋ ⊠ 🔥 SC

Hotels

★ ★ **HOLIDAY INN.** *711 Dwight St (01104). 413/781-0900; FAX 413/785-1410.* 245 rms, 12 story. S $85-$110; D $95-$120; suites $130-$210; under 19 free; wkend, family rates. Pet accepted; $25. TV; cable. Indoor pool; whirlpool. Restaurant 6:30 am-2 pm, 5-10 pm. Bar from 4:30 pm; Sat, Sun from noon. Ck-out noon. Meeting rm. Downhill/x-country ski 10 mi. Exercise equipt. Game rm. Some refrigerators. Cr cds: A, C, D, DS, ER, JCB, MC, V.

D 🐾 🏊 ≋ 🍴 ⊠ 🔥 SC

★ ★ ★ **MARRIOTT.** *Corner Boland & Columbus Ave (01115), at I-91 Springfield Center exit. 413/781-7111; FAX 413/731-8932.* 265 rms, 16 story. S $99-$115; D $139-$149; each addl $10; suites $275; under 18 free; wkend package plans. Crib free. TV. Indoor pool; whirlpool, poolside serv. Complimentary coffee in lobby. Restaurant 6:30 am-11 pm. Bars 11:30-2 am; entertainment. Ck-out 1 pm. Meeting rms. Shopping arcade. Barber, beauty shop. Airport transportation. Downhill/x-country ski 15 mi. Exercise equipt; sauna. Some refrigerators. Luxury level. Cr cds: A, C, D, DS, ER, JCB, MC, V.

D 🏊 ≋ 🍴 ⊠ 🔥 SC

★ ★ ★ **SHERATON SPRINGFIELD MONARCH PLACE.** *1 Monarch Place (01104). 413/781-1010; FAX 413/734-3249.* E-mail sheraton@javanet.com; web sheraton-springfield.com. 304 rms, 12 story. S, D $89-$139; suites $149-$169; under 18 free; wkend rates. Crib free. Garage $7.95; valet. TV; cable (premium). Indoor pool; whirlpool, poolside serv. Restaurant 6:30 am-11 pm. Bar 11:30-2 am; entertainment Fri, Sat. Ck-out noon. Convention facilities. Business center. Shopping arcade. Airport transportation. Exercise rm; sauna, steam rm. Bathrm phones. Cr cds: A, C, D, DS, MC, V.

D ≋ 🍴 ⊠ 🔥 SC 🎿

Restaurants

★ ★ ★ **HOFBRAUHAUS.** *(1105 Main St, West Springfield 01089) off MA Tpke (I-90) exit 4, S on US 5, then W on MA 147. 413/737-4905.* German, Amer menu. Specialties: lobster, Wienerschnitzel, rack of lamb. Hrs: 11:30 am-midnight; Mon 5:30-9 pm; Tues-Fri to 9 pm; Sat 5 pm-midnight. Closed Dec 25. Res accepted. Bar 11 am-midnight. Semi-a la carte: lunch $2.75-$13, dinner $10.25-$30. Child's meals. Parking. Tableside cooking. Bavarian atmosphere; antiques. Cr cds: A, D, DS, MC, V.

✔★ **IVANHOE.** *(1422 Elm St, West Springfield) I-91 exit 13 B, on US 5.* 413/736-4881. Continental menu. Specializes in prime rib, fresh seafood. Salad bar. Hrs: 11:30 am-10:30 pm; Mon to 9 pm; Tues to 10 pm; Sat from 4 pm; Sun 10 am-9 pm; Sun brunch to 3 pm. Closed Dec 25. Bar; Fri & Sat to 1 am. Semi-a la carte: lunch $3.95-$8.95, dinner $9.95-$15.95. Lunch buffet $5.75. Sun brunch $11.95. Child's meals. Parking. Contemporary decor. Casual atmosphere. Cr cds: A, C, D, DS, MC, V.

★★ **MONTE CARLO.** *(1020 Memorial Ave, West Springfield 01089) 1 mi W of I-91, opp exposition grounds.* 413/734-6431. Specialties: beef Marsala, veal Francaise, pasta. Hrs: 11:30 am-9 pm; Fri to 10 pm; Sat 4-10 pm; Sun from 4 pm. Closed Mon; Dec 25. Res accepted. Bar. Semi-a la carte: lunch $4.95-$8.95, dinner $8.95-$16.95. Child's meals. Family-owned. Cr cds: A, C, D, DS, MC, V.

★★★ **OLD STORROWTON TAVERN.** *(1305 Memorial Ave, West Springfield) 2 mi W on MA 147, in Eastern States Exposition.* 413/732-4188. Continental menu. Specializes in seafood, veal & beef dishes. Own baking. Hrs: 11:30 am-2:30 pm, 5-8:30 pm; Sat 11:30 am-4 pm, 5-9 pm. Res required. Closed Sun; Jan 1, Dec 25. Bar. Semi-a la carte: lunch $5.75-$12, dinner $12-$22. Outdoor dining. Part of restored colonial village. Cr cds: A, C, DS, MC, V.

★★ **STUDENT PRINCE AND FORT.** *8 Fort St (01103).* 413/734-7475. German, Amer menu. Specialties: jägerschnitzel, sauerbraten. Hrs: 11 am-11 pm; Sun noon-10 pm. Res accepted. Bar; imported draft beer. Semi-a la carte: lunch $4.50-$10, dinner $8.50-$24. Child's meals. Large collection of German beer steins. Family-owned. Cr cds: A, C, D, DS, MC, V.

Stockbridge & West Stockbridge (B-2)

(See also Lenox, Pittsfield)

Settled 1734 **Pop** 2,408 & 1,483 **Elev** 842 & 901 ft **Area code** 413 **Zip** Stockbridge, 01262; West Stockbridge, 01266 **Web** www.stockbridgechamber.org
Information Stockbridge Chamber of Commerce, Box 224, 413/298-5200; or visit the Information Booth, Main St.

Established as a mission, Stockbridge was for many years a center for teaching the Mahican. The first preacher was John Sergeant. Jonathan Edwards also taught at Stockbridge. The town is now mainly a summer resort but still has many features and attractions open year round. West Stockbridge is a completely restored market village. Its Main St is lined with well-kept storefronts, renovated in the style of the 1800s, featuring stained glass, antiques and hand-crafted articles.

What to See and Do

Berkshire Botanical Garden. 15-acre botanical garden; perennials, shrubs, trees, antique roses, ponds; wildflower exhibit, herb, vegetable gardens; solar, semi-tropical & demonstration greenhouses. Garden shop. Herb products. Special events, lectures. Picnicking. (May-Oct, daily) 2 mi NW, at jct MA 102, 183 in Stockbridge. Phone 413/298-3926. ¢¢

Chesterwood. Early 20th-century summer residence and studio of Daniel Chester French, sculptor of the Minute Man statue in Concord and of Lincoln in the Memorial in Washington, DC. Also museum; gardens,

woodland walk; guided tours. A property of the National Trust for Historic Preservation. (May-Oct, daily) 2 mi S of jct MA 102 & MA 183, in Stockbridge. Phone 413/298-3579. ¢¢¢

Children's Chimes Bell Tower (1878). Erected by David Dudley Field, prominent lawyer, as a memorial to his grandchildren. Carillon concerts (June-Aug, daily). Main St in Stockbridge.

Merwin House "Tranquility" (ca 1825). Brick house in late Federal period; enlarged with "shingle"-style wing at end of 19th century. European and American furniture and decorative arts. (June-mid-Oct, Tues, Thurs, Sat & Sun) 14 Main St, in Stockbridge. Phone 413/298-4703. ¢¢

Mission House (1739). House built in 1739 for the missionary Rev. John Sergeant and his wife, Abigail Williams; now a museum of colonial life. Collection of colonial antiques; Native American museum; gardens and orchard. Guided tours. (Memorial Day wkend-Columbus Day wkend, daily) Main & Sergeant Sts in Stockbridge, on MA 102. Phone 413/298-3239. ¢¢

Naumkeag. Stanford White designed this Norman-style "Berkshire cottage" (1886); interior has antiques, Oriental rugs, collection of Chinese export porcelain. Gardens include terraces of tree peonies, fountains, Chinese garden and birch walk. Guided tours. (Memorial Day wkend-Columbus wkend, daily) Prospect Hill in Stockbridge. Phone 413/298-3239. Gardens ¢¢; House & gardens ¢¢¢

★ **Norman Rockwell Museum.** Maintains and exhibits the nation's largest collection of original art by Norman Rockwell. (Daily; closed Jan 1, Thanksgiving, Dec 25) MA 183, in Stockbridge. Phone 413/298-4100. ¢¢¢

Annual Events

Harvest Festival. Berkshire Botanical Garden. Celebrates beginning of harvest and foliage season in the Berkshire Hills. Phone 413/298-3926. 1st wkend Oct.

Stockbridge Main Street at Christmas. Events include a re-creation of Norman Rockwell's painting. Holiday marketplace, concerts, house tour, silent auction, sleigh/hay rides, caroling. Phone 413/298-5200. 1st wkend Dec.

Seasonal Event

Berkshire Theatre Festival. Berkshire Playhouse. E Main St, in Stockbridge, entrance from US 7, MA 102. Summer theater (Mon-Sat); Unicorn Theater presents new and experimental plays (Mon-Sat in season); children's theater (July-Aug, Thurs-Sat). Phone 413/298-5576. Late June-late Aug.

Inns

★★★ **INN AT STOCKBRIDGE.** *(US 7, Stockbridge 01262)* approx 1 mi N on US 7. 413/298-3337; FAX 413/298-3406. E-mail innkeeper@stockbridgeinn.com; web www.stockbridgeinn.com. 12 rms, 2 story. June-Oct: S $100-$125, D $180-$260; each addl $30; wkend pkgs; lower rates rest of yr. Children over 12 yrs only. TV; VCR avail. Pool. Complimentary full bkfst; afternoon refreshments. Ck-out 11 am, ck-in 2 pm. Business servs avail. 1906 building on 12-acre estate. Totally non-smoking. Cr cds: A, DS, MC, V.

✔★★★ **THE RED LION.** *(30 Main St, Stockbridge 01262)* 413/298-5545; FAX 413/298-5130. E-mail innkeeper@redlioninn.com; web www.redlioninn.com. 110 rms, 94 with bath. Mid-May-Oct: S, D $85-$165; each addl $20; suites $250-$400; lower rates rest of yr. TV; cable, VCR. Pool. Restaurant (see THE RED LION). Rm serv. Bars 11:30-1 am; entertainment. Ck-out noon, ck-in 3 pm. Meeting rms. Business servs avail. Luggage handling. Gift shop. Free train, bus station transportation. Tennis privileges. Golf privileges. Exercise equipt. Massage. Some refrigerators, microwaves in suites. Collection of antiques, china. Historic resort inn, established 1773. Victorian decor. Cr cds: A, C, D, DS, MC, V.

★ ★ ★ **TAGGART HOUSE.** *(18 Main St, Stockbridge 01262)* *413/298-4303.* E-mail info@taggarthouse.com; web www.tag garthouse.com. 4 rms. No rm phones. July-Aug: S $235-$295; D $275-$355; wkends 2-3 day min; lower rates rest of yr. Closed Jan-Apr. Children over 18 yrs only. Complimentary full bkfst. Restaurant adj 8 am-10 pm. Ck-out 11:30 am, ck-in 3 pm. In-rm modem link. Luggage handling. Tennis privileges. Game rm. Built in late 1800s; country manor house. Totally nonsmoking. Cr cds: A, C, D, DS, MC, V.

★ ★ ★ **WILLIAMSVILLE.** *(MA 41, West Stockbridge 01266)* 5 mi S on MA 41, 5 mi S of MA Tpke exit 1. 413/274-6118; FAX 413/274-3539. E-mail williamsville@tacoma.net; web www.williamsvilleinn.com. 16 rms, 1-3 story. No rm phones. July-Oct: S, D $140-$150; each addl $20; suite $185; lower rates rest of yr. Pool. Complimentary full bkfst. Restaurant (see WILLIAMSVILLE INN). Bar from 5 pm. Ck-out 11 am, ck-in 2 pm. Meeting rms. Tennis. Downhill/x-country ski 8 mi. Lawn games. Built 1797. Sculpture garden. Cr cds: A, MC, V.

Restaurants

✔★ ★ **MICHAEL'S.** *(9 Elm St, Stockbridge 01262)* 413/298-3530. Continental menu. Specializes in hamburgers, New England clam chowder, fettuccini Alfredo. Hrs: 11:30 am-midnight. Closed Dec 25. Res accepted. Bar. Semi-a la carte: lunch $4.95-$7.95, dinner $8.95-$16.95. Child's meals (dinner). Cr cds: A, D, MC, V.

D

★ ★ ★ **THE RED LION.** *(See The Red Lion Inn)* 413/298-5545. Contemporary New England menu. Specializes in fresh seafood, New England clam chowder, roast prime rib of beef. Hrs: 7:30-10:30 am, noon-2:30 pm, 5:30-9:30 pm; extended hrs in season. Res accepted. Bar noon-1 am. Semi-a la carte: bkfst $5-$12, lunch $8-$15, dinner $17.50-$24. Child's meals. Pianist wkends. Parking. Outdoor dining. Jacket. Cr cds: A, C, D, DS, MC, V.

D

★ ★ **SHAKER MILL.** *(5 Albany Rd, West Stockbridge 01266)* 6 blks W on MA 102. 413/232-0100. Continental menu. Specializes in fresh pasta, grilled meat. Hrs: 11:30 am-10 pm; Sun brunch to 2 pm. Res accepted. Bar. Semi-a la carte: lunch $5.50-$9.95, dinner $7.95-$16.95. Sun brunch $14.95. Child's meals. Parking. Outdoor dining. Cr cds: A, MC, V.

D

★ ★ **TRUC ORIENT EXPRESS.** *(3 Harris St, West Stockbridge 01266)* 5 mi NW on MA 102. 413/232-4204. Vietnamese menu. Specializes in Banh Xeo (pancake stuffed with shrimp and pork). Hrs: 11 am-9 pm; wkends to 10 pm. Closed Thanksgiving, Dec 25; also Tues, Nov-Apr. Res accepted. Bar. A la carte entrees: lunch $7.50-$11, dinner $11.50-$17. Parking. Outdoor dining. Cr cds: A, DS, MC, V.

D

★ ★ ★ **WILLIAMSVILLE INN.** *(See Williamsville Inn)* 413/274-6118. Specializes in beef, fresh fish, duck, vegetarian dishes. Own baking. Hrs: 6-9 pm; Fri, Sat 5-9:30 pm. Closed Mon-Wed (Nov-mid-June). Res accepted. Bar. Semi-a la carte: dinner $16-$25. Parking. Intimate atmosphere in 1797 farmhouse. Cr cds: A, MC, V.

Sturbridge (C-5)

Settled ca 1730 **Pop** 7,775 **Elev** 619 ft **Area code** 508 **Zip** 01566-1057
Information Tourist Information Center, 380 Main St; 508/347-2761 or 888/788-7274.

What to See and Do

☑ **Old Sturbridge Village.** A living history museum that re-creates a rural New England town of the 1830s. The museum covers more than 200 acres with more than 40 restored buildings; costumed interpreters demonstrate the life, work and community celebrations of early 19th-century New Englanders. Working historical farm; many special events; picnic area. (Apr-Oct, daily; closed Dec 25) On US 20W, 2 mi W of jct I-84 exit 2 & MA Tpke (I-90) exit 9. Phone 508/347-3362, 508/347-5383 (TTY) or 800/SEE-1830. ¢¢¢¢¢

Annual Event

New England Thanksgiving. Old Sturbridge Village. Re-creation of early 19th-century Thanksgiving celebration. Includes turkey shoot, hearth cooking and meetinghouse service. Phone 508/347-3362 or 508/347-5383 (TTY). Late Nov.

Motels

✔★ **ECONO LODGE.** *682 Main St (US 20W), I-90 exit 9, I-84 exit 20W.* 508/347-2324. 52 rms, 7 suites. June-Oct: S, D $60-$90; each addl $5; lower rates rest of yr. Crib avail. TV; cable. Pool. Ck-out 11 am. Coin lndry. Some refrigerators. Cr cds: A, DS, MC, V.

★ ★ **OLD STURBRIDGE VILLAGE LODGES.** *US 20E, 2 mi W of jct I-84 exit 3B & MA Tpke (I-90) exit 9.* 508/347-3327; res: 800/733-1830; FAX 508/347-3018. E-mail osvlodge@asv.org; web www.osv.org. 59 rms in 7 bldgs, 1-2 story. May-Oct: S, D $80-$110; each addl $5; suites $90-$120; under 12 free; lower rates rest of yr. Crib $5. TV; cable. Pool. Restaurant adj 7 am-11 pm. Ck-out 11 am. Adj to Old Sturbridge Village. Cr cds: A, DS, MC, V.

★ ★ **QUALITY INN COLONIAL.** *1 1/2 mi E on US 20 at MA Tpke (I-90) exit 9.* 508/347-3306. 64 rms. May-Nov: S $72-$88; D $78-$88; each addl $10; under 18 free; lower rates rest of yr. TV; cable (premium), VCR avail. Pool. Playground. Restaurant adj 6:30 am-11 pm. Ck-out 11 am. Business servs avail. In-rm modem link. Sundries. Tennis. Spacious grounds; gardens, fountain. Cr cds: A, C, D, DS, ER, JCB, MC, V.

✔★ **STURBRIDGE COACH MOTOR LODGE.** *408 Main St (US 20), 2 mi W of jct I-84 exit 2 & MA Tpke (I-90) exit 9.* 508/347-7327; FAX 508/347-2954. 54 rms, 2 story. May-Oct: S $49-$62; D $60-$76; each addl $5; higher rates special events; lower rates rest of yr. Crib $5. TV; cable. Pool. Coffee in lobby. Restaurant nearby. Ck-out 11 am. Old Sturbridge Village opp. Cr cds: A, MC, V.

★ ★ ★ **STURBRIDGE HOST HOTEL & CONFERENCE CENTER.** *366 Main St (US 20).* 508/347-7393; FAX 508/347-3944; res: 800/582-3232. 241 rms, 3 story. Apr-Oct: S, D $109-$149; each addl $15; suites $195-$290; under 18 free; package plans; lower rates rest of yr. Crib free. TV. Indoor pool; whirlpool, poolside serv. Restaurant 7 am-11 pm. Rm serv. Bar to 1 am; entertainment Fri, Sat. Ck-out 11 am. Meeting rms. Bellhops. Valet serv. Sundries. Tennis. X-country ski 3 mi. Exercise rm; sauna. Lawn games. Miniature golf. Many bathrm phones. On lake; paddleboats, rowboats; dockage for small boats. Luxury level. Cr cds: A, C, D, DS, ER, MC, V.

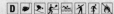

Inns

★ ★ **COLONEL EBENEZER CRAFTS INN.** *Fiske Hill Rd,* check in at PUBLICK HOUSE INN. 508/347-3313; FAX 508/347-5073. 8 rms, 3 story. June-Oct: S, D $90-$155; each addl $5; under 16 free; lower rates rest of yr. Crib $5. TV in sun rm; cable, VCR avail (movies). Pool. Restaurant adj 7 am-10 pm. Ck-out 11 am, ck-in 3 pm. Meeting rm. Business servs avail. Luggage handling. Tennis. X-country ski 2 mi. Lawn games. Built 1786; overlooks woods. Cr cds: A, C, D, MC, V.

⊠ 👟 ⩳ 🔥 **SC**

★ ★ **PUBLICK HOUSE.** *on the common, on MA 131, 1½ mi S of jct US 20, I-84 exit 2, off MA Tpke (I-90) exit 9.* 508/347-3313; FAX 508/347-5073. 17 rms, 2 story. June-Oct: S, D $90-$155; each addl $5; under 16 free; lower rates rest of yr. Crib $5. TV avail; VCR (movies). Playground. Restaurant 7 am-10 pm (also see PUBLICK HOUSE). Bar noon-midnight. Ck-out 11 am, ck-in 3 pm. Meeting rms. Business servs avail. Bellhops. Tennis. X-country ski 1 mi. Lawn games. Founded in 1771; originally a tavern. Colonial decor; antiques. Located on historic Sturbridge Common. Cr cds: A, C, D, MC, V.

⊠ 👟 🐾 🔥 **SC**

Restaurants

★ ★ **PUBLICK HOUSE.** *(See Publick House Inn)* 508/347-3313. Specializes in turkey, prime rib, lobster pie. Hrs: 7 am-10 pm. Res accepted. Bar. Semi-a la carte: bkfst $3.95-$12.95, lunch $7.95-$11.95, dinner $14.95-$27. Sun bkfst buffet: $10.95. Child's meals. Entertainment Fri, Sat. Outdoor dining. Open hearth. In original Colonial structure built in 1771. Located on historic Sturbridge Common. Cr cds: A, C, D, MC, V.

D **SC**

✔ ★ ★ **ROM'S.** *MA 131.* 508/347-3349. Web www.sturbridge.com. Italian, Amer menu. Specialties: veal parmigiana, chicken cacciatore. Own pasta. Hrs: 11 am-9 pm; Sat to 10 pm. Closed Thanksgiving, Dec 25. Res accepted. Serv bar. Semi-a la carte: lunch $3.95-$7.95, dinner $4.95-$12.95. Child's meals. Family-owned. Cr cds: A, D, DS, MC, V.

D

★ ★ ★ **THE WHISTLING SWAN.** *502 Main St.* 508/347-2321. Continental, Amer menu. Specializes in seafood, steak. Own baking. Hrs: Whistling Swan 11:30 am-2:30 pm, 5:30-9:30 pm; Sat to 10 pm; Sun noon-8 pm; res accepted. Ugly Duckling Loft 11:30 am-11 pm; Fri, Sat to 11:30 pm. Closed Mon; some major hols. Bar to 1 am. Semi-a la carte: lunch $4.95-$12.95, dinner $12.95-$23.95. Sun dinner $9.50-$12. Child's meals. Pianist, guitarist. Whistling Swan, on 1st floor, has 3 intimate dining areas; offers fine dining. Ugling Duckling Loft offers casual dining in 1 large dining area; bar. 1800s Greek-revival house with barn attached; many antiques. Cr cds: A, C, D, MC, V.

D

Sudbury Center (B-6)

(See also Boston)

Settled 1638 **Pop** 14,358 **Elev** 190 ft **Area code** 978 **Zip** 01776 **E-mail** sudburytm@msm.com **Web** www.ibeam-net.com/sudbury

Information Board of Selectmen, Loring Parsonage, 288 Old Sudbury Rd, Sudbury; 978/443-8891.

Sudbury, which has a number of 17th-century buildings, is best known for the Wayside Inn at South Sudbury, which was the scene of Longfellow's *Tales of a Wayside Inn* (1863).

What to See and Do

Great Meadows National Wildlife Refuge. Along with the Concord section (8 mi N), this refuge contains 3,400 acres of freshwater wetlands, open water and upland. More than 200 bird species have been recorded at this diverse habitat area. Visitor center/wildlife education center and HQ (May & Oct, daily; winter, Mon-Fri; closed hols in winter). Nature trail, hiking (daily). Office and visitor center off Lincoln Rd. Contact Refuge Manager, Weir Hill Rd; 978/443-4661. **Free.**

Longfellow's Wayside Inn (1702). A historical and literary shrine, this is America's oldest operating inn. Originally restored by Henry Ford, it was badly damaged by fire in Dec 1955, and restored again by the Ford Foundation. Period furniture. (Daily; closed July 4, Dec 25) Wayside Inn Rd, 3 mi SW, just off US 20. Phone 978/443-1776. (See INNS) Also on the property are

Martha Mary Chapel. Built and dedicated by Henry Ford in 1940, a nondenominational, nonsectarian chapel. No services; used primarily for weddings. (By appt)

Gristmill. With waterwheel in operation; stone grinds wheat and corn used by inn's bakery. (Apr-Nov, daily)

Redstone School (1798). "The Little Red Schoolhouse" immortalized in "Mary Had a Little Lamb." (May-Oct, daily)

Annual Events

Reenactment of March of Sudbury Minutemen to Concord on Apr 19, 1775. More than 200 costumed men muster on Common before proceeding to Old North Bridge in Concord. Phone 978/443-1776. Apr.

Fife & Drum Muster and Colonial Fair. Muster takes place on field across from Longfellow's Wayside Inn. Fife & drum corps from New England and surrounding areas compete. Colonial crafts demonstrations and sales. Last Sat Sept.

Motor Hotels

★ ★ ★ **BEST WESTERN ROYAL PLAZA.** *(181 Boston Post Rd W (MA 20), Marlborough 01752)* 1/2 mi W via MA 20 from I-495 exit 24B. 508/460-0700; res: 888/543-9500; FAX 508/480-8218. 429 rms, 6 story. S, D $89-$139; each addl $15; suites $150; under 18 free. Crib $5. TV; cable (premium). Indoor pool. Restaurant 6:30 am-10 pm. Rm serv. Ck-out 11 am. Convention facilities. Business servs avail. In-rm modem link. Game rm. Exercise equipt; sauna. Many refrigerators; microwave in suites. Cr cds: A, C, D, DS, JCB, MC, V.

D ⩳ 🐾 ⛄ 🔥 **SC**

✔ ★ ★ ★ **CLARION CARRIAGE HOUSE INN.** *(738 Boston Post Rd, Sudbury)* 978/443-2223; FAX 978/443-5830. 39 rms, 3 story, 5 suites. No elvtr. S, D $150-$175; suites $175; under 18 free; wkends (2-day min). Crib free. TV; cable (premium), VCR avail (movies). Complimentary full bkfst. Complimentary coffee in rms. Ck-out 11 am. Business servs avail. Valet serv. Free guest lndry. Exercise equipt. Microwaves avail. Cr cds: A, C, D, DS, ER, JCB, MC, V.

D 🐾 ⛄ 🔥 **SC**

✔ ★ ★ ★ **RADISSON.** *(75 Felton St, Marlborough 01752)* I-495, exit 24B (MA 20). 508/480-0015; FAX 508/485-2242. 206 rms, 5 story. S, D $89-$159; each addl $10; suites $195-$295; under 18 free; wkend rates. Crib free. TV; cable (premium), VCR avail (movies). Indoor pool; whirlpool. Restaurant 6:30 am-2 pm, 5:30-10 pm; wkend hrs vary. Rm serv. Bar 11:30-1 am. Ck-out noon. Meeting rms. Business servs avail. In-rm modem link. Sundries. Gift shop. Exercise rm; sauna. Raquetball courts. Some refrigerators; microwaves avail. Bathrm phone, wet bar in suites. Balconies in suites. Cr cds: A, C, D, DS, ER, JCB, MC, V.

D ⩳ 🐾 ⛄ 🔥 **SC**

Inns

★ ★ **ARABIAN HORSE.** *(277 Old Sudbury Rd, Sudbury)* 978/443-7400; res: 800/272-2426; FAX 978/443-0234. 4 rms, 2 with shower only, 3 story, 1 suite. June-Nov: S, D $149-$269; lower rates rest of yr. Pet accepted. TV; cable (premium). Complimentary full bkfst. Complimentary coffee in rms. Restaurant nearby. Ck-out 11 am, ck-in 3 pm. In-rm modem link. X-country ski on site. Some balconies. Built in 1886. Arabian horses, antique cars on site. Totally nonsmoking. Cr cds: MC, V.

★ ★ **LONGFELLOW'S WAYSIDE.** *Wayside Inn Rd. 978/443-1776; FAX 978/443-8041; res: 800/339-1776.* Web www.wayside.org. 10 rms, 2 story. Sept-Dec: S $72-$145; D $98-$145; lower rates rest of yr. Complimentary full bkfst. Restaurant (see LONGFELLOW'S WAYSIDE INN). Bar. Ck-out 11 am, ck-in 3 pm. Gift shop. Period furnishings. Historic inn (1716); self-guided tours through restored public rooms. National historic site; on grounds are Wayside Gristmill and Redstone School, built by former owner Henry Ford. Totally nonsmoking. Cr cds: A, C, D, DS, MC, V.

Restaurant

★ ★ **LONGFELLOW'S WAYSIDE INN.** *(See Longfellow's Wayside Inn)* 978/443-1776. Specializes in fresh seafood, prime rib. Hrs: 11:30 am-3 pm, 5-9 pm; Sun, hols, noon-8 pm. Closed Dec 25. Res accepted. Bar. Semi-a la carte: lunch $7.50-$10.50. Complete meals: dinner $16-$22. Child's meals. Totally nonsmoking. Cr cds: A, C, D, DS, MC, V.

Truro & North Truro (Cape Cod) (C-10)

Settled Truro: ca 1700 **Pop** Truro/N Truro: 1,573 **Elev** 20 ft **Area code** 508 **Zip** Truro 02666; North Truro 02652 **E-mail** info@capecodchamber.org **Web** www.capecodchamber.org

Information Cape Cod Chamber of Commerce, US 6 & MA 132, PO Box 790, Hyannis 02601-0790; 508/362-3225 or 888/33-CAPECOD.

Truro, named for one of the Channel towns of England, is today perhaps the most sparsely settled part of the Cape—with great stretches of rolling moorland dotted only occasionally with cottages. On the hill above the Pamet River marsh are two early 19th-century churches; one is now the town hall. The countryside is a favorite resort of artists and writers.

What to See and Do

Fishing. Surf casting on Atlantic beaches. Boat ramp at Pamet & Depot Rds; fee for use, harbor master on duty.

Pilgrim Heights Area. Interpretive display, self-guided nature trails, picnicking; rest rms. Cape Cod National Seashore (see). Off US 6.   **Free.**

Swimming. Head of the Meadow. A fine Atlantic beach (fee). N on US 6 & W of Chamber of Commerce booth. **Corn Hill Beach.** On the bay (fee). S on US 6, then E. A sticker for all beaches must be purchased from Truro Chamber of Commerce. No lifeguards. (Mid-June-Labor Day)

Truro Historical Society Museum. Collection of artifacts from the town's historic past, including shipwreck mementos, whaling gear, ship models, 17th-century firearms, pirate chest and period rms. (Mid-June-mid-Sept, daily) Highland Rd in N Truro. Phone 508/487-3397. ¢

Motels

★ **CROW'S NEST.** *(496 Shore Rd, North Truro 02652)* On MA 6A. *508/487-9031; res: 800/499-9799.* Web www.virtualcapecod.com/market/crowsnestmotel. 33 kit. units, 2 story. No A/C. Late June-Labor Day: S $76; D $90; each addl $10; wkly rates; lower rates Apr-late June, after Labor Day-Nov. Closed rest of yr. Crib free. TV; cable. Ck-out 10 am. Balconies. On beach. Cr cds: DS, MC, V.

★ **EAST HARBOUR.** *(618 Shore Rd, North Truro 02652)* On MA 6A. *508/487-0505; FAX 508/487-6693.* E-mail ehm@capecod.net; web ehm@capecod.net. rms, 7 kit. cottages. No A/C. Late June-Labor Day (2-day min): S, D $86-$110; cottages to 4, $825-$875/wk; lower rates mid-Apr-late June, after Labor Day-late Oct. Closed rest of yr. TV; cable. Complimentary coffee. Restaurant nearby. Ck-out 10 am. Coin lndry. Refrigerators, microwaves. Picnic tables, grills. Private beach. Cr cds: A, DS, MC, V.

★ **HARBOR VIEW VILLAGE.** *(168 Shore Rd, North Truro 02652)* On MA 6A. *508/487-1087; FAX 508/487-6269.* E-mail hbrview@capecod.net; web www.capecod.net/hbrview. 17 rms, 9 kits, 3 cottages. No A/C. No rm phones. Late June-Labor Day: S, D $65-$75; each addl $10-$15; kits., cottages $545-$745/wk; wkly rates; lower rates rest of yr. Children over 7 yrs only (in season). TV. Restaurants nearby. Ck-out 10 am. Refrigerators. Overlooking private beach. Cr cds: MC, V.

★ **SEA GULL.** *(Box 126, North Truro 02652)* 508/487-9070. 26 rms, 5 kit. apts. Late June-Labor Day: S, D $78-$100; each addl $10; cottages $820/wk; each addl $70/wk; lower rates mid-Apr-late June, after Labor Day-Oct. Closed rest of yr. TV. Restaurant nearby. Ck-out 10:30 am. Refrigerators, microwaves avail. Sun deck. Private beach. Picnic tables, grills. Cr cds: A, DS, MC, V.

Cottage Colony

★ ★ **KALMAR VILLAGE.** *(Shore Rd (MA 6A), North Truro 02652)* 508/487-0585. Web www.virtualcapecod.com/kalmarvillage. 42 kit. cottages. No A/C. July-Labor Day: kit. cottages $725-$1,595/wk; each addl $100-$150/wk; lower rates late May-June, after Labor Day-early Oct. Closed rest of yr. Crib free. TV; cable. Pool. Restaurant nearby. Ck-out 10 am, ck-in 3 pm. Coin lndry. Microwaves avail. Picnic tables, grills. On private beach. Cr cds: A, DS, MC, V.

Restaurants

★ **ADRIAN'S RESTAURANT.** *(535 MA 6, North Truro 02652)* 4¹/₂ mi N on MA 6. *508/487-4360.* Web www.capecod.com/adrians. Regional Italian menu. Specialties: shrimp pizza, linguine alle vongole, cayenne-crusted salmon. Hrs: 8 am-noon, 5:30-10 pm. Closed mid-Oct-mid-May. Bar. Semi-a la carte: bkfst $3.95-$7.50, dinner $6.95-$19.95. Child's meals. Outdoor dining. Overlooks Provincetown and bay. Cr cds: A, MC, V.

D   ➜

★ ★ **BLACKSMITH SHOP.** *(MA 6A, Truro Center)* ¹/₄ mi N on MA 6A. *508/349-6554.* Specializes in local seafood, free-range chicken, pasta. Hrs: 7 am-1 pm, 5-10 pm; Sun brunch 9 am-2 pm. Closed Dec 25; also Mon-Tues off-season. Res accepted. No A/C. Bar to midnight. Semi-a la carte: bkfst $3-$9, dinner $10-$21. Sun brunch $3-$11. Child's meals. Antiques; carousel horse. Cr cds: A, MC, V.

D   ➜

★ **MONTANO'S.** *(481 MA 6, North Truro)* 508/487-2026. Italian, Amer menu. Specialties: veal saltimbocca, seafood Fra Diavolo, baked stuffed lobster. Hrs: 4:30-10 pm; early-bird dinner 4:30-6 pm. Closed Dec 25. Res accepted. Serv bar. Semi-a la carte: dinner $8.95-$18.95. Child's meals. Nautical decor. Cr cds: A, DS, MC, V.

D   ➜

★ **PAPARAZZI.** *(518 Shore Rd, North Truro 02652) at Beach Point.* 508/487-7272. Italian, seafood menu. Specializes in local seafood, prime rib. Salad bar. Hrs: noon-10 pm; Mon, Tue from 4:30 pm. Closed Dec. Serv bar. Semi-a la carte: dinner $10-$30. Child's meals. Nautical decor. Overlooks bay. Cr cds: A, DS, MC, V.

Uxbridge
(see Worcester)

Waltham (B-7)

(See Boston)

Settled 1634 **Pop** 57,878 **Elev** 50 ft **Area code** 781 **Zip** 02154 **E-mail** wwscc@walthamchamber.com **Web** www.walthamchamber.com/advantage.html

Information Waltham West Suburban Chamber of Commerce, 1 Moody St, Ste 301; 781/894-4700.

The name Waltham, taken from the English town of Waltham Abbey, means "a home in the forest," and is still appropriate today, due to the town's many wooded and forested areas. Originally an agricultural community, Waltham is now an industrial center. It is also the home of Bentley College and Regis College.

What to See and Do

Brandeis University (1948). (3,700 students) The first Jewish-founded nonsectarian university in the US. Its 250-acre campus includes Three Chapels, Rose Art Museum (Sept-May; daily exc Mon; closed hols; free); Spingold Theater Arts Center (plays presented Oct-May; fee); and Slosberg Music Center, with classical and jazz performances (Sept May). 415 South St. Phone 781/736-4300.

Cardinal Spellman Philatelic Museum. Exhibition gallery; library. (Tues-Thurs, Sat, Sun; closed hols) 4 mi W on US 20, in Weston, at 235 Wellesley St. Phone 781/894-6735. **Free.**

Gore Place. A living history farm, Gore Place may be New England's finest example of Federal-period residential architecture; changing exhibits; 40 acres of cultivated fields. The mansion, designed in Paris and built in 1805, has 22 rms filled with examples of early American, European and Oriental antiques. (Mid-Apr-mid-Nov, daily exc Mon) On US 20 at the Waltham-Watertown line. Phone 781/894-2798. ¢¢

Lyman Estate "The Vale" (1793). Designed by Samuel McIntire for Boston merchant Theodore Lyman. Enlarged and remodeled in the 1880s, the ballroom and parlor retain Federal design. Landscaped grounds. Five operating greenhouses contain grape vines, camellias, orchids and herbs. House open by appt for groups only. Greenhouses (Mon-Sat, also Sun afternoons). 185 Lyman St. Phone 781/893-7232 (house); 781/891-7095 (greenhouses). ¢¢

Motor Hotels

★★ **BEST WESTERN TLC.** *477 Totten Pond Rd (02451), I-95 exit 27A.* 781/890-7800; FAX 781/890-4937. 100 rms, 6 story. S $129-$159; D $139-$169; each addl $10; under 12 free; higher rates special events. Crib free. TV; cable (premium), VCR avail. Indoor pool. Complimentary coffee in rms. Restaurant 7 am-10 pm; Sat, Sun 7-11 am, 5-11 pm. Rm serv. Bar 11 am-11 pm. Ck-out 11 am. Meeting rms. Business servs avail. In-rm modem link. Sundries. Exercise equipt; sauna. Health club privileges. Refrigerators, microwaves avail. Balconies. Cr cds: A, C, D, DS, JCB, MC, V.

★★ **HOME SUITES INN.** *455 Totten Pond Rd (02451), I-95 (MA 128) exit 27A.* 781/890-3000; FAX 781/890-0233; res: 800/424-4021. 116 rms, 3 story. Sept-Oct: S $75-$115; D $75-$155; each addl $10; suites $89-$169; kit. unit $169; under 18 free; wkly, wkend, hol rates; higher rates special events; lower rates rest of yr. Crib free. TV; cable (premium), VCR (movies). Pool. Complimentary continental bkfst. Complimentary coffee in rms. Restaurant 11 am-11 pm. Bar to midnight. Ck-out 11 am. Coin lndry. Business servs avail. In-rm modem link. Valet serv. Sundries. Health club privileges. Many refrigerators, microwaves. Picnic tables. Cr cds: A, C, D, DS, MC, V.

✔★ **SUSSE CHALET.** *385 Winter St (02451), I-95/128 exit 27A.* 781/890-2800; res: 800/824-2538; FAX 781/890-1021. 149 rms, 2 & 5 story. S $63.70-$115.70; D $68.70-$119.70; each addl $10; under 18 free. Crib free. TV; cable (premium), VCR avail. Complimentary continental bkfst. Restaurant 11:30 am-11:30 pm. Bar. Ck-out 11 am. Business servs avail. In-rm modem link. Microwaves avail. Cr cds: A, C, D, DS, MC, V.

Hotels

★★★ **DOUBLETREE GUEST SUITES.** *550 Winter St (02451), I-95 (MA 128) exit 27B.* 781/890-6767; FAX 781/890-8917. 275 suites, 8 story. Suites $99-$199; under 18 free. Crib free. TV; cable (premium), VCR avail. Indoor pool; whirlpool. Coffee in rms. Restaurant (see GRILLE AT HOBBS BROOK). Bar 11:30 am-midnight. Ck-out noon. Coin lndry. Convention facilities. Business center. In-rm modem link. Gift shop. Exercise equipt; sauna. Health club privileges. Game rm. Wet bars; refrigerators, microwaves avail. Cr cds: A, C, D, DS, ER, JCB, MC, V.

★★★ **WESTIN.** *70 Third Ave (02451), on MA 128, I-95 exit 27A.* 781/290-5600; FAX 781/290-3626. 346 rms, 2-8 story. S, D $89-$275; each addl $15; family, wkly, wkend rates. Crib free. TV; cable, VCR avail. Indoor pool; whirlpool. Restaurant 6:30 am-10 pm. Rm serv 24 hrs. Bar; entertainment. Ck-out 1 pm. Convention facilities. Business center. In-rm modem link. Gift shop. Free garage parking. Airport transportation. Exercise equipt; sauna, steam rm. Cr cds: A, C, D, DS, ER, JCB, MC, V.

★★★ **WYNDHAM GARDEN.** *420 Totten Pond Rd (02451), I-95 (MA 128) exit 27A.* 781/890-0100; FAX 781/890-4777. 148 rms, 6 story. S, D $139-$149; each addl $10; under 18 free; wkend rates. Crib free. TV; cable (premium). Indoor pool; poolside serv. Complimentary bkfst. Coffee in rms. Restaurant 6:30 am-10 pm. Bar 4 pm-midnight. Ck-out noon. Meeting rms. Business servs avail. In-rm modem link. No bellhops. Exercise equipt. Some refrigerators; microwaves avail. Cr cds: A, D, DS, ER, JCB, MC, V.

Restaurants

★★★ **GRILLE AT HOBBS BROOK.** *(See Doubletree Guest Suites Hotel)* 781/890-6767, ext. 7163. Specializes in grilled dishes. Hrs: 6:30 am-2 pm, 5-9:30 pm; Sat 7 am-2 pm, 5-10 pm; early-bird dinner to 6:30 pm; Sun brunch 7 am-2 pm. Res accepted. Bar 11:30 am-midnight. Wine list. Semi-a la carte: bkfst $6-$12.95, lunch $8-$20, dinner $13-$27. Sun brunch $12.95. Child's meals. Pianist evenings. Spacious, elegant rms offer views of chef's herb and vegetable gardens. Cr cds: A, C, D, DS, ER, MC, V.

★★★ **IL CAPRICCIO.** *888 Main St (MA 20) (02451), 1 mi E on I-95, exit 26.* 781/894-2234. Italian menu. Specializes in baccala gnocchi, roast trout. Own pasta. Hrs: 5-10 pm. Closed Sun; major hols. Bar. Wine list. Semi-a la carte: dinner $17-$26. Complete meals: dinner $38. Fine dining. Totally nonsmoking. Cr cds: A, C, D, DS, MC, V.

★ ★ **R PLACE.** *53 Prospect St (02453). 781/893-8809.* Eclectic menu. Specialties: Southwestern Caesar salad, Louisiana crab cakes. Hrs: 11:30 am-2:30 pm, 5:30-10 pm. Closed Mon; Jan 1, Thanksgiving. Wine, beer. Semi-a la carte: lunch $4-$12, dinner $16-$23. Street parking. Fine dining; original artwork. Cr cds: A, C, D, MC, V.

★ ★ **TUSCAN GRILL.** *361 Moody St (02453). 781/891-5486.* E-mail jb0649@aol.com. Italian menu. Specializes in wood-grilled dishes, seasonal items. Own baking, pasta. Hrs: 5:30-10 pm; Sun 5-9 pm. Closed July 4, Thanksgiving, Dec 24, 25. Res accepted. Bar. A la carte entrees: dinner $13.95-$17.95. Parking. Modern Italian trattoria with open kitchen. Cr cds: DS, MC, V.

Wellesley (B-7)

(See also Boston)

Settled 1661 **Pop** 26,615 **Elev** 141 ft **Area code** 781 **Zip** 02181 **E-mail** jl.wcc@worldnet.att.net **Web** www.wellesleyweb.com/chamber.htm
Information Chamber of Commerce, One Hollis St, Suite 111; 781/235-2446.

This Boston suburb was named after an 18th-century landowner, Samuel Welles. It is an educational and cultural center. There are four widely known institutions here: Dana Hall, girls' preparatory school; Babson College, a business school; Massachusetts Bay Community College; and Wellesley College.

What to See and Do

Map and Globe Museum. Coleman Map Bldg features largest physical map of America, with natural vegetation coloring. From viewing balcony one sees the same scene an astronaut would see from 700 mi above the Earth's surface. Switches operable by public pinpoint cities and other points of interest with special lights. (Tues-Fri, afternoons; also Sat & by appt) On Babson College Campus, Babson Park, Forest St and Wellesley. Phone 781/239-4232. **Free.**

Wellesley College (1870). (2,200 women) Founded by Henry F. Durant. 500 wooded acres bordering Lake Waban. On campus are Davis Museum and Cultural Center and Margaret C. Ferguson Greenhouses (daily). Central & Washington Sts, on MA 16/135. Phone 781/283-1000.

Motor Hotel

★ ★ **WELLESLEY INN ON THE SQUARE.** *576 Washington St. 781/235-0180; FAX 781/235-5263.* 70 rms, 3-4 story. S $82-$90; D $92-$110; each addl $10; suites $150; under 18 free. Crib free. TV; cable (premium). Restaurant 7-11 am, 11:30 am-2:30 pm; 5:30-9:30 pm; Sun hrs vary. Rm serv. Bar 11:30 am-11:30 pm. Ck-out 11 am. Meeting rms. Business servs avail. Valet serv. Cr cds: A, C, D, DS, MC, V.

Wellfleet (Cape Cod) (C-10)

Settled ca 1725 **Pop** 2,493 **Elev** 50 ft **Area code** 508 **Zip** 02667 **E-mail** wellfleet@capecod.net **Web** www.capecod.net/wellfleetcc
Information Chamber of Commerce, PO Box 571; 508/349-2510.

Once a fishing town, Wellfleet dominated the New England oyster business in the latter part of the 19th century. It is now a summer resort and an art gallery town, with many tourist homes and cottages. Southeast of town is the Marconi Station Area of Cape Cod National Seashore (see). Fishermen here can try their luck in the Atlantic surf or off deep-sea charter fishing boats.

What to See and Do

Historical Society Museum. Marine items, whaling tools, Marconi memorabilia, needlecraft, photograph collection, marine and primitive paintings. (Late June-mid-Sept, Tues-Sat; schedule may vary, phone ahead) Main St. Phone 508/349-9157. ¢

Sailing. Rentals at Wellfleet Marina; accommodates 150 boats; launching ramp, facilities.

Swimming. At numerous bayside and ocean beaches on marked roads off US 6. Freshwater ponds with swimming are scattered through woods E of US 6. Parking sticker necessary mid-June to Labor Day.

Wellfleet Bay Wildlife Sanctuary. Operated by the Massachusetts Audubon Society. Self-guiding nature trails. Natural history summer day camp for children. Guided nature walks, lectures, classes, Monomoy Island natural history tours. Sanctuary (Memorial Day-Columbus Day, daily; rest of yr, daily exc Mon). In South Wellfleet, on W side of US 6. Contact PO Box 236, South Wellfleet 02663; 508/349-2615. ¢¢

Motels

★ ★ **EVEN'TIDE.** *(South Wellfleet 02663)* 4 mi S on US 6. *508/349-3410; FAX 508/349-7804; res: 800/368-0007 (MA).* E-mail eventide@capecod.net; web www.capecod.net/eventide/. 31 rms, 2 story, 8 suites, 3 kits. Mid-June-mid-Sept (2-day min wkends): S, D $76-$97; each addl $7-$10; suites $89-$107; kit. units (3-day min) $110; wkly rates; lower rates rest of yr. Crib $5-$15. TV; cable. Indoor pool. Playground. Complimentary coffee in rms. Coin lndry. Refrigerators. Picnic tables, grills. Cr cds: A, C, D, DS, MC, V.

✔★ **OCEAN PINES.** *(Box 604, South Wellfleet 02663)* 5 mi S on US 6, at entrance to Marconi Beach National Seashore. *508/349-2774.* 10 motel rms, 7 cottages. No A/C in cottages. No rm phones. July-Labor Day: S, D $64-$75; each addl $10; cottages $425-$600/wk; lower rates late-May-June, after Labor Day-late Oct. Closed rest of yr. Children over 5 yrs only in motel. TV; cable. Ck-out 10 am. Refrigerators; microwaves avail in cottages. Picnic tables, grills. Cr cds: MC, V.

★ **SOUTHFLEET MOTOR INN.** *(South Wellfleet 02663)* on MA 6 across from Marconi National Seashore Entrance. *508/349-3580; FAX 508/349-0250; res: 800/334-3715.* 30 rms, 2 story. Late June-Labor Day (2-day min): S, D $88-$110; each addl $10; lower rates Apr-late June, after Labor Day-Oct. Closed rest of yr. Crib free. TV; cable (premium). 2 pools, 1 indoor; whirlpool. Complimentary morning coffee in office. Restaurant adj 8 am-10 pm in season. Bar noon-1 am. Ck-out 11 am. Meeting rm. In-rm modem link. Game rm. Refrigerators. Cr cds: A, C, D, DS, MC, V.

★ ★ **WELLFLEET MOTEL & LODGE.** *(Box 606, South Wellfleet 02663)* 5 mi SE on MA 6. *508/349-3535; FAX 508/349-1192; res:*

800/852-2900. Web www.virtualcapecod.com/. 65 rms, 1-2 story. Late June-Labor Day: S, D $76-$125; each addl $8-$10; suites $109-$180; lower rates rest of yr. Crib $6. TV; cable (premium). 2 pools, 1 indoor; whirlpool. Complimentary coffee in rms. Restaurant 7 am-noon in season. Bar. Ck-out 11 am. Meeting rm. Refrigerators; microwaves avail. Picnic tables, grills. Cr cds: A, C, D, MC, V.

Inns

✓★ **HOLDEN INN.** *140 Commercial St, on Wellfleet Bay, on road to the pier.* 508/349-3450. 27 rms, 13 with bath, 4 A/C, 2 story. No rm phones. May-mid-Oct: S $47; D $60-$70. Closed rest of yr. Children over 14 yrs only. Restaurant nearby. Ck-out 10 am, ck-in 2 pm. Picnic tables. Built 1840. No cr cds accepted.

★ ★ **THE INN AT DUCK CREEK.** *70 Main St.* 508/349-9333; FAX 508/349-0234. E-mail duckinn@capecod.net. 25 rms, 17 with bath, 4 A/C, 2-3 story. No rm phones. July-Aug: D $65-$95; each addl $15; lower rates mid-May-June, Sept-mid-Oct. Closed rest of yr. Crib $10. Complimentary continental bkfst. Restaurant (see DUCK CREEK TAVERN ROOM). Ck-out 11 am, ck-in 1 pm. Former sea captain's house (1815) furnished with period antiques. Sitting porch overlooks Duck Creek. Cr cds: A, MC, V.

Restaurants

★ ★ ★ **AESOP'S TABLES.** *Main St.* 508/349-6450. Specialties: fresh pasta Neptune, uptown marinated duck, Aesop's oysters. Own baking. Hrs: noon-3 pm, 5:30 pm-1 am. Closed mid-Oct-mid-May. Res accepted. No A/C. Bar. Wine cellar. A la carte entrees: lunch $10-$15, dinner $13-$24. Outdoor dining, 6 dining rms in restored house (1805). Cr cds: A, C, D, MC, V.

★ ★ **DUCK CREEK TAVERN ROOM.** *(See The Inn At Duck Creek)* 508/349-7369. E-mail duckinn@capecod.net. Specializes in seafood. Own coffee roaster. Hrs: 5:30-11 pm; early-bird dinner 5:30-7 pm. Closed mid-Oct-mid-May. Res accepted. Bar. Semi-a la carte: dinner $11-$17. Child's meals. Entertainment. Nautical decor; duck decoys. Colonial tavern atmosphere. Cr cds: A, MC, V.

✓★ ★ **VAN RENSSELAER'S.** *(1019 US 6, South Wellfleet)* 2 mi S on US 6, opp Marconi Station. 508/349-2127. E-mail yrhall@capecod.net. Specializes in creative pasta, fresh seafood, black Angus steaks. Salad bar. Hrs: 8 am-noon, 4:30-10 pm. Closed Dec-Mar. Res accepted. Bar 4-11 pm. Semi-a la carte: bkfst $2.75-$7.95, dinner $8-$19.95. Child's meals. Outdoor dining. Family-owned. Cr cds: A, C, D, DS, JCB, MC, V.

Unrated Dining Spot

BAYSIDE LOBSTER HUTT. *Commercial St.* 508/349-6333. Specializes in fresh native seafood, lobster, lobster salad roll. Salad, raw bar. Hrs: 11:30 am-10 pm. Closed Oct-May. No A/C. A la carte entrees: lunch $5.95-$15.95, dinner $6.95-$22. Child's meals. Nautical decor; indoor picnic tables. Family-owned. No cr cds accepted.

Williamstown (A-2)

Settled 1749 **Pop** 8,220 **Elev** 638 ft **Area code** 413 **Zip** 01267

A French and Indian War hero, Colonel Ephraim Williams, Jr, left a bequest in 1755 to establish a "free school" in West Hoosuck, provided the town be renamed after him. In 1765 the town name was changed to Williamstown, and in 1793 the school became Williams College. The life of this charming Berkshire Hills town still centers around the college.

What to See and Do

Sterling and Francine Clark Art Institute. More than 30 paintings by Renoir, other French Impressionists; old-master paintings; English silver; American artists Homer, Sargent, Cassatt, Remington. Extensive art library (Mon-Fri). Museum shop. Picnic facilities on grounds. (July-Labor Day, daily; rest of year, daily exc Mon; closed Jan 1, Thanksgiving, Dec 25) 225 South St. Phone 413/458-9545 for fees.

Williams College (1793). (1,950 students) Private liberal arts college; campus has wide variety of architectural styles, ranging from colonial to Gothic. Chapin Library of rare books is one of nation's finest, housing the 4 founding documents of the US. Hopkins Observatory, the nation's oldest (1836), has planetarium shows. Adams Memorial Theatre presents plays. The Paul Whiteman Collection houses Whiteman's recordings and memorabilia. 1 blk E of central green, US 7. Phone 413/597-3131. Also here is

Williams College Museum of Art. Considered one of the finest college art museums in the country. Houses approx 11,000 pieces. Exhibits emphasize contemporary, modern, American and non-Western art. Museum shop. (Tues-Sat, also Sun afternoons & Mon hols; closed Jan 1, Thanksgiving, Dec 25) Main St. Phone 413/597-2429. **Free.**

Motels

✓★ ★ ★ **THE 1896 HOUSE-BROOKSIDE & PONDSIDE.** *Cold Spring Rd, 2 mi S on US 7 & MA 2.* 413/458-8125. Web www.1896house.com. 29 rms in 2 bldgs. Memorial Day-Columbus Day: S, D $58-$108; each addl $10; apt $100-$125; ski, golf rates; under 8 free; higher rates: college events, special wkends; lower rates rest of yr. Crib $5. TV; cable. Heated pool. Complimentary continental bkfst. Coffee in rms. Restaurant (see THE 1896 HOUSE NEW ENGLAND TABLE). Ck-out 11 am. Business servs avail. Downhill/x-country ski 10 mi. Refrigerators avail. On brook & pond. Cr cds: A, D, DS, MC, V.

★ ★ **BERKSHIRE HILLS.** *US 7, 3 mi S on US 7.* 413/458-3950; res: 800/388-9677. 20 rms, 2 story. June-Oct: S, D $59-$129; each addl $10; under 3 free; lower rates rest of yr. Crib free. TV; cable. Heated pool. Complimentary buffet bkfst. Restaurant adj 5-10 pm. Ck-out 11 am. Downhill/x-country ski 5 mi. Gazebo in garden; wooded grounds bordering brook. Cr cds: A, DS, MC, V.

★ ★ **FOUR ACRES.** *213 Main St (MA 2).* 413/458-8158. E-mail foura@bcn.net; web www.fouracresmotel.com. 31 rms, 1-2 story. May-Oct: S, D $55-$110; each addl $10; higher rates special events; lower rates rest of yr. Crib $10. TV; cable. Pool. Complimentary continental bkfst. Restaurant adj 11 am-10 pm. Ck-out 11 am. Downhill ski 15 mi. Lawn games. Refrigerators avail. Some balconies. Picnic tables. Cr cds: A, C, D, DS, MC, V.

★ ★ **WILLIAMS INN.** *1090 Main St, at Williams College, jct US 7 & MA 2.* 413/458-9371; FAX 413/458-2767; res: 800/828-0133. 100 rms, 3 story. May-Oct: S $100-$120; D $120-$175; each addl $15; under 14 free; package plan; lower rates rest of yr. Crib free. Pet accepted, some restrictions; $10. TV; cable. Indoor pool; whirlpool. Restaurant 7 am-10 pm. Rm serv. Bar 11-1 am; entertainment Fri, Sat. Ck-out 11 am. Meeting rms. Business servs avail. Valet serv. Sundries. Downhill/x-country ski 6 mi. Sauna. Refrigerators avail. Picnic tables. Cr cds: A, C, D, DS, MC, V.

D ♥ ⤢ ≈ ⚲ 🔥 ✕

Inn

★ ★ ★ **ORCHARDS.** *222 Adams Rd.* *413/458-9611; FAX 413/458-3273; res: 800/225-1517 (exc MA).* 49 rms, 3 story. Mid-May-mid-Nov: S, D $165-$230; each addl $30; MAP avail; lower rates rest of yr. Crib $10. TV; cable (premium), VCR (movies). Pool; whirlpool. Dining rm (see THE ORCHARDS). Afternoon tea 3:30-4:30 pm. Rm serv. Bar noon-11:30 pm. Ck-out noon, ck-in 4 pm. Business servs avail. In-rm modem link. Luggage handling. Concierge serv. Tennis privileges. 18-hole golf privileges, pro, greens fee $55-$75. Downhill/x-country ski 6 mi. Exercise equipt; sauna, steam rm. Bathrm phones; many refrigerators; some fireplaces. Library. Cr cds: A, C, D, MC, V.

D ⤢ 🎿 ⛷ ⚲ ✈ ≈ 🔥 ✕

Restaurants

✔★ ★ **THE 1896 HOUSE NEW ENGLAND TABLE.** *(See The 1896 House-Brookside & Pondside Motel)* *413/458-1896.* Specializes in fresh fish, roast turkey, prime rib. Hrs: 4:30 pm-close; Sun from noon; early-bird dinner to 5:30 pm. Res accepted. Bar. Semi-a la carte: dinner $6.96-$19.96. Parking. Pianist Sat. Outdoor dining. Cr cds: A, D, DS, MC, V.

★ ★ **LE JARDIN.** *777 Cold Spring Rd (US 7).* *413/458-8032.* Continental menu. Specializes in fresh seafood, lamb chops, steak. Own baking. Hrs: 5-9 pm; Sat to 10 pm. Closed Tues Sept-June. Res accepted. Bar. Semi-a la carte: dinner $15-$25. Parking. Converted 19th-century estate overlooking trout ponds, waterfall. Guest rms avail. Cr cds: A, DS, MC, V.

★ ★ **THE ORCHARDS.** *(See Orchards Inn)* *413/458-9611.* Continental menu. Menu changes daily. Own baking. Hrs: 7-10 am, noon-2 pm, 5:30-9 pm; Sun 7 am-2 pm; Sun brunch 10 am-2 pm. Res accepted. Bar noon-11:30 pm. Wine cellar. A la carte entrees: bkfst $6-$12, lunch $8-$16, dinner $17-$30. Sun brunch $7-$20. Child's meals. Parking. Outdoor dining in season. Scenic view of fountain pond with exotic fish, mountains. Totally nonsmoking. Cr cds: A, C, D, MC, V.

D SC

★ ★ **WATER STREET GRILL.** *123 Water St.* *413/458-2175.* Continental menu. Specialties: fajitas, fresh seafood, pasta. Hrs: 11:30 am-11 pm. Closed Easter, Thanksgiving, Dec 25. Res accepted. Bar. A la carte entrees: lunch $4-$8, dinner $7-$14. Buffet: lunch Mon-Fri $5.95. Child's meals. Entertainment Fri, Sat. Parking. Locally popular; semi-formal atmosphere. Cr cds: A, MC, V.

D ⤓

★ ★ **WILD AMBER GRILL.** *101 North St, on US 7.* *413/458-4000.* Contemporary Amer menu. Specialties: sesame-seared tuna, seared scallops with roasted pepper sauce, osso bucco a la Milanaise. Own desserts. Hrs: 11:30 am-2 pm, 5:30-10 pm; Sun 11 am-2 pm, 5:30-9 pm. Closed Tues Sept-mid-June; also Jan 1, Thanksgiving, Dec 25. Res accepted. Bar. Semi-a la carte: lunch $5-$9, dinner $14-$22. Child's meals. Entertainment Fri, Sat in summer. Terrace dining. Colonial atmosphere. Totally nonsmoking. Cr cds: A, MC, V.

Woods Hole (Cape Cod) (E-8)

(See also Martha's Vineyard, Nantucket Island)

Pop 1,100 (est) **Elev** 15 ft **Area code** 508 **E-mail** info@capecodchamber.org **Web** www.capecodchamber.org

Information Cape Cod Chamber of Commerce, US 6 & MA 132, PO Box 790, Hyannis 02601-0790; 508/362-3225 or 888/33-CAPECOD.

A principal port of Cape Cod in the town of Falmouth (see), ferries leave here for Martha's Vineyard. The Oceanographic Institution and Marine Biological Laboratories study tides, currents and marine life (closed to the public).

What to See and Do

Bradley House Museum. Model of Woods Hole Village (ca 1895); audiovisual show of local history; restored spritsail sailboat; model ships. Walking tour of village. (July-Aug, Tues-Sat; June & Sept, Wed, Sat; schedule may vary, phone ahead) Woods Hole Rd. Phone 508/548-7270. **Free.**

Car/passenger boat trips. Woods Hole, Martha's Vineyard Steamship Authority conducts trips to Martha's Vineyard (all yr). Schedule may vary; phone ahead. Phone 508/477-8600. ¢¢¢

Motels

★ ★ **NAUTILUS MOTOR INN.** *539 Woods Hole Rd (02543), 3³/₄ mi S of MA 28.* *508/548-1525; FAX 508/457-9674; res: 800/654-2333 (MA).* E-mail jpnautilus@aol.com; web www.nautilusinn.com. 54 rms in 3 bldgs, 2 story. Late June-late Aug: S, D $98-$150; each addl $6; package plans; lower rates mid-Apr-late June, late Aug-late Oct. Closed rest of yr. TV; cable (premium). Pool. Restaurant adj 5:30-10 pm (also see THE DOME). Ck-out 11 am. Meeting rms. In-rm modem link. Tennis. Refrigerators avail. Balconies. Opp beach. Cr cds: A, D, DS, MC, V.

⚲ ≈ ✕ ✕ 🔥 SC

★ **SLEEPY HOLLOW MOTOR INN.** *527 Woods Hole Rd (02543).* *508/548-1986.* 24 rms, 1-2 story. Late June-Labor Day: D $85-$125; lower rates Apr-late June, Labor Day-mid-Nov. Closed rest of yr. Crib $6. TV. Pool. Complimentary coffee in rms. Restaurant nearby. Ck-out 11 am. Refrigerators avail. Cr cds: A, C, D, MC, V.

≈ 🔥

Inn

★ ★ ★ **THE MARLBOROUGH.** *320 Woods Hole Rd (05243).* *508/548-6218; FAX 508/457-7519; res: 800/320-2322.* 5 rms, 1 cottage, 2 story. Some phones. Late May-mid-Oct: S, D $85-$135; higher rates wkends, hols (2-day min); lower rates rest of yr. TV in sitting rm, cottage. Pool. Complimentary full bkfst; afternoon refreshments. Ck-out 11 am, ck-in 2-6 pm. In-rm modem link. Luggage handling. Concierge serv. Free ferry terminal transportation. Cape Cod reproduction built 1942; gardens. Cr cds: A, MC, V.

≈ ✕ 🔥 ✕

Restaurants

★ ★ **DOME.** *(See Nautilus Motor Inn Motel)* *508/548-0800.* Specialties: char-broiled swordfish, duck a la Chambord, prime rib. Hrs: 5:30-10 pm. Closed mid-Oct-mid-Apr. Res accepted. Bar. Semi-a la carte: dinner $8.95-$19.95. Child's meals. Entertainment Fri-Sun. Dining inside oldest geodesic dome in the world (1953), designed by Buckminster Fuller. Harbor view. Cr cds: A, C, D, DS, MC, V.

★★ **LANDFALL.** *2 Luscombe Ave (02543). 508/548-1758.* Specializes in lobster, swordfish, steak. Hrs: 11 am-10 pm; Sun brunch to 3 pm. Closed Dec-Apr. Res accepted. No A/C. Bar to 1 am. Semi-a la carte: lunch $6-$10, dinner $11-$21. Sun brunch $4-$10. Child's meals. Outdoor dining. Nautical atmosphere; maritime artifacts, old dory. On dock; overlooks harbor. Family-owned. Cr cds: A, MC, V.

✔★ **LEESIDE BAR & GRILL.** *Luscombe Ave, adj to steamship docks. 508/548-9744.* Specializes in seafood. Hrs: 11-1 am; Sun from noon. Closed Thanksgiving, Dec 25. Bar to 1 am. Semi-a la carte: lunch, dinner $4.95-$10.95. Child's meals. Entertainment Wed-Sun. Nautical decor. Harbor view. Family-owned. Cr cds: A, MC, V.

Worcester (B-5)

Settled 1673 **Pop** 169,759 **Elev** 480 ft **Area code** 508 **Web** www.worcester.org

Information Worcester County Convention & Visitors Bureau, 33 Waldo St, 01608; 508/755-7400 or 800/231-7557.

The municipal seal of Worcester (WUS-ter) calls it the "Heart of the Commonwealth." One of the largest cities in New England, it is an important industrial center. Also a cultural center, it has some outstanding museums and twelve colleges.

What to See and Do

American Antiquarian Society. Research library is the largest collection of source materials pertaining to the first 250 yrs of American history. Specializing in the period up to 1877, the library has two-thirds of all pieces known to have been printed in this country between 1640 and 1821. (Mon-Fri; closed hols) Guided tours (Wed afternoons). 185 Salisbury St. Schedule may vary, phone ahead; 508/755-5221. **Free.**

Blackstone River Valley National Heritage Corridor. This 250,000-acre region extends southward to Providence, RI (see) and includes myriad points of historical and cultural interest. Visitor center at Massachusetts Audubon Society's Broad Meadow Brook Wildlife Sanctuary, tours and interpretive programs. 414 Massasoit Rd. Phone 508/754-7363 or 508/755-8899.

Higgins Armory Museum. Large exhibition of medieval-Renaissance and feudal Japan's arms and armor; paintings, tapestries, stained glass. Armor demonstrations and try-ons. (Tues-Sat, also Sun afternoons; closed hols) 100 Barber Ave. Phone 508/853-6015. ¢¢

New England Science Center. Contains museum with environmental science exhibits; solar/lunar observatory, multimedia planetarium theater; African Hall. Indoor-outdoor wildlife, aquariums; train ride; picnicking. (Daily; closed some hols) 222 Harrington Way, 1½ mi E. Phone 508/791-9211. ¢¢¢

Salisbury Mansion (1772). House of leading businessman and philanthropist Stephen Salisbury. Restored to 1830s appearance. Guided tours. (Thurs-Sun afternoons; closed hols) 40 Highland St. Phone 508/753-8278. ¢

Worcester Art Museum. Fifty centuries of paintings, sculpture, decorative arts, prints, drawings and photography from America to ancient Egypt; changing exhibits; tours, films, lectures. Cafe, gift shop. (Wed-Sun; closed hols) 55 Salisbury St. Phone 508/799-4406. ¢¢

Worcester Common Outlets. More than 100 outlet stores can be found at this indoor outlet mall. Food court. (Daily) I-290, exit 16, at 100 Front St. Phone 508/798-2581.

Seasonal Event

Worcester Music Festival of the Worcester County Music Assn. Mechanics Hall. The country's oldest music festival; folkdance companies; choral masterworks; symphony orchestras, guest soloists; young people's program. Seven to 12 concerts. Phone 508/754-3231. Sept-Mar.

Motels

✔★ **DAYS INN.** *(426 Southbridge, Auburn 01501) 8 mi S on I-290, exit 9. 508/832-8300; FAX 508/832-4579.* 70 rms, 3 story. June-Oct: S $64-$104; D $71-$114; each addl $10; under 18 free; wkly rates; lower rates rest of yr. Crib free. TV; cable. Complimentary continental bkfst. Ck-out 11 am. Coin lndry. Meeting rms. Valet serv. Some refrigerators. Cr cds: A, C, D, DS, MC, V.

★ **DAYS INN.** *50 Oriol Dr (01605), I-290 exit 20W or 21E. 508/852-2800; res: 800/932-3297; FAX 508/852-4605.* 114 rms, 3 story. May-Oct: S, D $49-$95; each addl $5; under 18 free; lower rates rest of yr. Crib free. TV; cable. Pool. Playground. Complimentary continental bkfst. Restaurant nearby. Ck-out 11 am. Coin lndry. Meeting rms. Sundries. Lighted tennis. Health club privileges. Some refrigerators. Cr cds: A, D, DS, MC, V.

Motor Hotels

★★★ **BEECHWOOD HOTEL.** *363 Plantation St (01605). 508/754-5789; FAX 508/752-2060; res: 800/344-2589.* 58 rms, 5 story, 18 suites. S, D $89-$109; each addl $10; suites $119-$139; family rates; higher rates college graduation. Crib free. TV; cable. Restaurant 6:30 am-10 pm. Rm serv. Ck-out 11 am. Business servs avail. RR station, bus depot transportation. Downhill/x-country ski 15 mi. Lake 2 blks. Cr cds: A, C, D, DS, MC, V.

★★★ **CROWNE PLAZA HOTEL.** *10 Lincoln Square (01608), jct I-290 & MA 9. 508/791-1600; FAX 508/791-1796.* 250 rms, 9 story. S $135; D $155; each addl $10; studio rms $135-$155; suites $250-$350; under 18 free. Crib free. TV; cable. 2 pools, 1 indoor; whirlpool, poolside serv. Restaurant 6:30 am-11 pm. Rm serv. Bar 11-2 am. Ck-out noon. Convention facilities. Bellhops. Valet serv. Free airport transportation. Downhill/x-country ski 18 mi. Exercise equipt; sauna. Private patios, balconies. Cr cds: A, C, D, DS, ER, MC, V.

✔★ **HAMPTON INN.** *110 Summer St (01608). 508/757-0400; FAX 508/831-9839.* 99 rms, 5 story, 10 kits. (no equipt) S, D $55-$85; suites $125. Crib free. Pet accepted. TV; cable (premium). VCR avail. Complimentary bkfst buffet. Restaurant nearby. Ck-out 11 am. Meeting rms. Business servs avail. In-rm modem link. Sundries. Downhill ski 20 mi. Some refrigerators. Lake 3 blks. Cr cds: A, C, D, DS, MC, V.

Restaurant

★★★ **CASTLE.** *(1230 Main St, Leicester 01524) 5 mi W on MA 9. 508/892-9090.* E-mail nika.1248@worldnet.att.net; web www.castlerestaurant.com. Continental menu. Hrs: 11:30-1 am. Closed Mon; Jan 1, Thanksgiving, Dec 25. Res accepted. Bar. Wine list. Semi-a la carte: lunch $8-$25, dinner $20-$45. Child's meals. Patio dining overlooking lake. Stone replica of 16th-century castle complete with medieval decor. Family-owned. Cr cds: A, C, D, DS, MC, V.

New Hampshire

Population: 1,109,252
Land area: 8,992 square miles
Elevation: 0-6,288 feet
Highest point: Mount Washington (Coos County)
Entered Union: Ninth of original 13 states (June 21, 1788)
Capital: Concord
Motto: Live free or die
Nickname: Granite State
State flower: Purple lilac
State bird: Purple finch
State tree: White birch
Time zone: Eastern
Web: www.visitnh.gov

New Hampshire is a year-round vacation state, offering a variety of landscapes and recreational opportunities within its six unique regions. The lush Lakes Region, dominated by Lake Winnipesaukee, and the Seacoast Region, with its beaches, bays and historic waterfront towns, are ideal for water sports. The rugged, forested White Mountains offer hiking, camping, dazzling autumn foliage and excellent skiing. The "little cities" of the Merrimack Valley—Nashua, Manchester and Concord—are centers of commerce, industry, government and the arts. Rural nineteenth-century New England comes alive in the small towns of the Monadnock Region, and many features of these areas come together in the Dartmouth-Lake Sunapee Region, home of Dartmouth College.

The mountains in New Hampshire are known for their rugged "notches" (called "gaps" and "passes" elsewhere), and the old valley towns have a serene beauty. Some of the best skiing in the East can be found at several major resorts here. The state's many parks, antique shops, art and theater festivals and country fairs are also popular attractions, and more than half of New England's covered bridges are in New Hampshire.

David Thomson and a small group of colonists settled on the New Hampshire coast near Portsmouth in 1623. These early settlements were part of Massachusetts. In 1679, they became a separate royal province under Charles the Second. In 1776, the Provincial Congress adopted a constitution making New Hampshire the first independent colony, seven months before the Declaration of Independence was signed.

Although New Hampshire was the only one of the thirteen original states not invaded by the British during the Revolution, its men fought long and hard on land and sea to bring about the victory. This strong, involved attitude continues in New Hampshire to this day. The New Hampshire presidential primary is the first in the nation, and the town meeting is still a working form of government here.

Manufacturing and tourism are the principal businesses here. Electrical and electronic products, machinery, plastics, fabricated metal products, footwear, other leather goods and instrumentation are manufactured. Farmers sell poultry and eggs, dairy products, apples, potatoes, garden crops, maple syrup and sugar. Nicknamed the "Granite State," about 200 types of rocks and minerals, including granite, mica and feldspar, come from New Hampshire's mountains.

When to Go/Climate

New Hampshire experiences typical New England weather—four distinct seasons with a muddy month or so between winter and spring. Snow in the mountains makes for great skiing in winter; summer temperatures can push up into the 90s.

AVERAGE HIGH/LOW TEMPERATURES (°F)

CONCORD

Jan 30/7	**May** 69/41	**Sept** 72/46
Feb 33/10	**June** 77/51	**Oct** 61/35
Mar 43/22	**July** 82/57	**Nov** 47/27
Apr 56/32	**Aug** 80/55	**Dec** 34/14

MT WASHINGTON

Jan 12/-5	**May** 41/29	**Sept** 46/35
Feb 13/-3	**June** 50/38	**Oct** 36/24
Mar 20/5	**July** 54/43	**Nov** 27/14
Apr 29/16	**Aug** 52/42	**Dec** 17/-6

Parks and Recreation Finder

Directions to and information about the parks and recreation areas below are given under their respective town/city sections. Please refer to those sections for details.

NATIONAL PARK AND RECREATION AREAS

Key to abbreviations: I.H.S. = International Historic Site; I.P.M. = International Peace Memorial; N.B. = National Battlefield; N.B.P. = National Battlefield Park; N.B.C. = National Battlefield & Cemetery; N.C. = National Conservation Area; N.E.M. = National Expansion Memorial; N.F. = National Forest; N.G. = National Grassland; N.H. = National Historical Park; N.H.C. = National Heritage Corridor; N.H.S. = National Historic Site; N.L.

CALENDAR HIGHLIGHTS

MAY

Lilac Time Festival (Franconia). 8 mi W on NH 117, then 4 mi S on US 302, in Lisbon. Celebration of the state flower and observance of Memorial Day. Parade, carnival, vendors, entertainment, special events. Phone 603/431-5388.

JUNE

Portsmouth Jazz Festival (Portsmouth). Two stages with continuous performances on the historical Portsmouth waterfront. For schedule, phone 603/436-7678.

Market Square Days (Portsmouth). Summer celebration with 10K road race, street fair, entertainment. Phone 603/431-5388.

JULY

The Old Homestead (Keene). Potash Bowl in Swanzey Center. Drama of life in Swanzey during 1880s based on the Biblical story of the Prodigal Son; first presented in 1886. For schedule, phone 603/352-0697.

AUGUST

Mt Washington Valley Equine Classic (North Conway). Horse jumping. Phone Chamber of Commerce, 603/356-3171 or 800/367-3364.

Lakes Region Fine Arts and Crafts Festival (Meredith). Juried show featuring more than 100 New England artists. Music, children's theater, food. Phone Chamber of Commerce 603/279-6121.

League of New Hampshire Craftsmen's Fair (Sunapee). Mt Sunapee State Park. Over 200 craftsmen and artists display and sell goods. Phone 603/224-3375.

SEPTEMBER

New Hampshire Highland Games (Lincoln). Loon Mt. Largest Scottish gathering in Eastern US. Bands, competitions, concerts, workshops. Phone 800/358-SCOT.

Riverfest (Manchester). Outdoor festival with family entertainment, concerts, arts & crafts, food booths, fireworks. Phone 603/625-6915.

= National Lakeshore; N.M. = National Monument; N.M.P. = National Military Park; N.Mem. = National Memorial; N.P. = National Park; N.Pres. = National Preserve; N.R. = National Recreational Area; N.R.R. = National Recreational River; N.Riv. = National River; N.S. = National Seashore; N.S.R. = National Scenic Riverway; N.S.T. = National Scenic Trail; N.Sc. = National Scientific Reserve; N.V.M. = National Volcanic Monument.

Place Name	Listed Under
Saint-Gaudens N.H.S.	HANOVER
White Mountain N.F.	same

STATE PARK AND RECREATION AREAS

Key to abbreviations: I.P. = Interstate Park; S.A.P. = State Archaeological Park; S.B. = State Beach; S.C. = State Conservation Area; S.C.P. = State Conservation Park; S.Cp. = State Campground; S.F. = State Forest; S.G. = State Garden; S.H.A. = State Historic Area; S.H.P. = State Historic Park; S.H.S. = State Historic Site; S.M.P. = State Marine Park; S.N.A. = State Natural Area; S.P. = State Park; S.P.C. = State Public Campground; S.R. = State Reserve; S.R.A. = State Recreation Area; S.Res. = State Reservoir; S.Res.P. = State Resort Park; S.R.P. = State Rustic Park.

Place Name	Listed Under
Coleman S.P.	COLEBROOK
Crawford Notch S.P.	BRETTON WOODS
Echo Lake S.P.	NORTH CONWAY
Franconia Notch S.P.	same
Greenfield S.P.	PETERBOROUGH
Hampton Beach S.P.	HAMPTON BEACH
Miller S.P.	PETERBOROUGH
Monadnock S.P.	JAFFREY
Moose Brook S.P.	GORHAM
Mt Sunapee S.P.	SUNAPEE
Silver Lake S.P.	NASHUA
Wentworth S.P.	WOLFEBORO
White Lake S.P.	CENTER OSSIPEE

Water-related activities, hiking, riding, various other sports, picnicking and visitor centers, as well as camping, are available in many of these areas. There is an admission charge at most state parks; children under 12 in family groups are admitted free. Tent camping $12-$20/night; RV camp sites $24-$30/night. For further information contact the New Hampshire Division of Parks & Recreation, PO Box 1856, Concord 03302; 603/271-3556 or -3628 (camping res).

SKI AREAS

Place Name	Listed Under
Attitash Bear Peak Ski Resort	BARTLETT
Balsams/Wilderness Ski Area	DIXVILLE NOTCH
Black Mt Ski	JACKSON
Bretton Woods Ski Area	BRETTON WOODS
Cannon Mt Ski Area	FRANCONIA NOTCH STATE PARK
Dartmouth Skiway Ski Area	HANOVER
Gunstock Recreation Area	LACONIA
Jackson Ski Touring Foundation	JACKSON
King Pine Ski Area	CENTER OSSIPEE
Loon Mt Recreation Area	LINCOLN/NORTH WOODSTOCK
McIntyre Ski Area	MANCHESTER
Mt Cranmore Ski Area	NORTH CONWAY
Mt Sunapee S.P.	SUNAPEE
Pats Peak Ski Area	CONCORD
Ragged Mountain Ski Area	NEW LONDON
Snowhill at Eastman Ski Area	SUNAPEE
Waterville Valley Ski Area	WATERVILLE VALLEY
Wildcat Ski & Recreation Area	PINKHAM NOTCH

FISHING & HUNTING

Nonresident season fishing license: $35.50; 15-day, $27.50; 7-day, $23.50; 3-day, $18.50. Nonresident hunting license: $70.50; small game, $36.50; small game 3-day, $17.50; muzzleloader, $28. Combination hunting and fishing license, nonresident: $96. Fees subject to change. For further information and for the *New Hampshire Freshwater and Saltwater Fishing Digests,* pamphlets that summarize regulations, contact the NH Fish & Game Department, 2 Hazen Dr, Concord 03301; 603/271-3422 or 603/271-3211.

Driving Information

Passengers under 18 years must be in an approved passenger restraint anywhere in vehicle. Children under 4 years must be in an approved safety seat anywhere in vehicle. For further information phone 603/271-2131.

INTERSTATE HIGHWAY SYSTEM

The following alphabetical listing of New Hampshire towns in *Mobil Travel Guide* shows that these cities are within 10 miles of the indicated Interstate highways. A highway map should, however, be checked for the nearest exit.

Highway Number Cities	Towns within 10 miles
Interstate 89	Concord, Hanover, New London, Sunapee.
Interstate 91	(in Vermont): Hanover.

| Interstate 93 | Concord, Franconia, Franconia Notch State Park, Franklin, Holderness, Laconia, Lincoln/North Woodstock, Littleton, Manchester, Meredith, Plymouth, Salem. |
| Interstate 95 | Exeter, Hampton Beach, Portsmouth. |

Additional Visitor Information

The *New Hampshire Guidebook,*with helpful information on lodging, dining, attractions and events, is available from the New Hampshire Office of Travel & Tourism, 172 Pembroke Rd, PO Box 1856, Concord 03302; 603/271-2666, 603/271-2343 or 800/FUN-IN-NH. For recorded information about events, foliage and alpine ski conditions phone 800/258-3608.

The League of New Hampshire Craftsmen Foundation offers information on more than 100 galleries, museums, historic sites, craft shops and craftsmen's studios. Send stamped, self-addressed, business-size envelope to 205 N Main St, Concord 03301.

There are several welcome centers in New Hampshire; visitors who stop by will find information and brochures most helpful in planning stops at points of interest. Open daily: on I-93 at Hooksett, Canterbury, Salem and Sanborton Boulder; on I-89 at Lebanon, Springfield and Sutton; on I-95 at Seabrook; and on NH 16 at North Conway. Open Memorial Day-Columbus Day: on NH 9 at Antrim; on US 3 at Colebrook; on US 4 at Epsom; on NH 25 at Rumney; and on US 2 at Shelburne.

Bartlett (D-5)

(See also Bretton Woods, Jackson, North Conway)

Pop 2,290 **Elev** 681 ft **Area code** 603 **Zip** 03812
Information Mt Washington Valley Chamber of Commerce, N Main St, PO Box 2300, North Conway 03860; 603/356-3171.

What to See and Do

Attitash Bear Peak Ski Resort. 2 high-speed quad, quad, 3 triple, 3 double chairlifts; 2 surface lifts; patrol, school, rentals; snowmaking; nursery; cafeteria; bar. Longest run 1³/₄ mi; vertical drop 1,750 ft. (Mid-Nov-late Apr, daily) **Summer recreation:** Alpine Slide, water slides, scenic chairlift, horseback riding, mountain biking, hiking, driving range (mid-June-Labor Day, daily; Memorial Day-mid-June & early Sept-mid-Oct, wkends; fees). On US 302. Phone 603/374-2368. ¢¢¢¢

White Mountain National Forest (see).

Motel

✔★★ **ATTITASH MOUNTAIN VILLAGE.** *US 302. 603/374-6500; FAX 603/374-6509; res: 800/862-1600.* E-mail stay@attitashmtvillage.com; web www.attitashmtvillage. 253 rms, 3 story. S, D $39-$119; studio rms $99-$169; 2-3 bedrm units for 2-8, $139-$379; kit. units for 2-4, $79-$139; hol wks (3-day min). TV; cable, VCR avail. 3 pools, 1 indoor; whirlpool, sauna. Playground. Restaurant 11 am-10 pm. Bar 11:30-1 am. Ck-out 11 am. Coin lndry. Meeting rms. Business servs avail. Tennis. Downhill/x-country ski on site. Ice skating. Hiking trails. Game rm. Lawn games. Refrigerators. Private patios; many balconies. Picnic tables. Cr cds: A, DS, MC, V.

Bretton Woods (D-5)

(See also Franconia, Littleton, Twin Mountain)

Settled 1791 **Pop** 10 (est) **Elev** 1,600 ft **Area code** 603 **Zip** 03575

Bretton Woods is located in the heart of the White Mountains, on a long glacial plain in the shadow of Mt Washington (see) and the Presidential Range. Mt Washington was first sighted in 1497; however, settlement around it did not begin until 1771, when the the Crawford Notch, which opened the way through the mountains, was discovered. In the 1770s, Governor Wentworth named the area Bretton Woods for his ancestral home in England. This historic name was set aside in 1832 when all the tiny settlements in the area were incorporated under the name of Carroll. For a time, a railroad through the notch brought as many as 57 trains a day and the area grew as a resort spot. A string of hotels sprang up, each more elegant and fashionable than the last. In 1903 the post office, railroad station and express office reverted to the traditional name—Bretton Woods. Today, Bretton Woods is a resort area at the base of the mountain.

In 1944 the United Nations Monetary and Financial Conference was held here; it established the gold standard at $35 an ounce, organized plans for the International Monetary Fund and World Bank and chose the American dollar as the unit of international exchange.

What to See and Do

Bretton Woods Ski Area. Quad, triple, 2 double chairlifts, T-bar; patrol, school, rentals, snowmaking; restaurant, cafeteria, bar; child care; lodge. Longest run 2 mi; vertical drop 1,500 ft. (Thanksgiving-Easter, daily) Night skiing (early Dec-Mar, Fri & Sat). 48 mi of cross-country trails. 5 mi E on US 302. Phone 603/278-5000 or 603/278-3333 (snow conditions). ¢¢¢¢

Crawford Notch State Park. One of state's most spectacular passes. Mts Nancy and Willey rise to the west; Mts Crawford, Webster and Jackson to the east. Park HQ is at the former site of the Samuel Willey house. He, his family of six and two hired men died in a landslide in 1826 when they rushed out of their house, which the landslide left untouched. Fishing, trout-feeding pond. Hiking, walking trails of the Appalachian system. Picnicking, concession. Camping (standard fees). Interpretive center. (Late May-mid-Oct) Approx 8 mi SE on US 302. Phone 603/374-2272. In park are

Silver Cascade. A 1,000-ft cataract. N end of Crawford Notch.

Flume Cascade. A 250-ft fall. 3 mi N.

Arethusa Falls. Highest in state; 50-min walk from parking area. 1¹/₂ mi SW of US 302, 6 mi N of Bartlett.

Inns

★★★ **BRETTON ARMS.** *US 302E. 603/278-1000; FAX 603/278-8838; res: 800/258-0330 exc NH.* 31 rms, 3 suites. No A/C. S, D $89.95-$169; suites $119-$209; ski plans. Crib $10. TV; VCR. 3 pools, 2 indoor. Playground. Supervised child's activities (June-Labor Day); ages 5-12. Dining rm 7-9 am, 6-9 pm. Ck-out 11 am, ck-in 3 pm. Business servs avail. Airport, bus depot transportation. Tennis privileges. Golf privileges. Downhill ski adj; x-country ski on site. Sleigh rides. Exercise equipt. Restored Victorian inn (1896); antiques. Cr cds: A, DS, MC, V.

★★ **THE NOTCHLAND.** *(US 302, Harts Location 03812) S on US 302. 603/374-6131; FAX 603/374-6168; res: 800/866-6131.* 11 rms, 2 story. 4 suites. Some A/C. No rm phones. MAP: S $120-$140; D $170-$230; each addl $50; EP avail; 2-3-day min hols; higher rates foliage. Complimentary coffee in library. Complimentary bkfst. Dining rm (public by res) 7 pm sitting. Ck-out 11 am, ck-in 4 pm. Luggage handling. Downhill ski 7 mi; x-country ski on site. Granite mansion built in 1862; front parlor designed by Gustav Stickley. Totally nonsmoking. Cr cds: A, DS, MC, V.

Resort

★ ★ ★ **MOUNT WASHINGTON HOTEL.** *US 302. 603/278-1000; FAX 603/278-8838; res: 800/258-0330 (exc NH).* Web www.mtwashington.com. 200 rms, 4 story. MAP: S $170-$455; D $210-$495; each addl $70; suites avail; family rates; golf plan. Closed mid-Oct-mid-May. Crib $10. TV avail; VCR avail. 2 pools, 1 indoor; sauna, poolside serv. Playground. Supervised child's activities (June-Sept; also wkends Spring & Fall) ages 5-12. Dining rms 7-9 am, 11:30 am-4 pm, 6-9 pm (also see FABYAN'S STATION). Bars 11:30-1 am; entertainment. Ck-out 11 am, ck-in 3 pm. Meeting rms. Business servs avail. Concierge. Gift shop. Bus depot transportation. Sports dir. Tennis; pro. 27-hole golf, greens fee $25-$35, pro, putting green. Hiking trails. Bicycle rentals. Lawn games. Rec rm. Game rm. On river. Renovated hotel built 1902; view of Mt Washington. Cr cds: A, DS, MC, V.

Restaurant

✔★ **FABYAN'S STATION.** *(See Mount Washington Hotel Resort)* 603/278-2222. Specializes in nachos, hamburgers, fresh fish. Hrs: 11:30 am-10 pm; hrs vary Apr-mid-June, Oct-late Dec. Bar to 12:30 am. A la carte entrees: lunch $5-$8, dinner $7-$14. Child's meals. Converted railway station. Railroad artifacts. Cr cds: A, DS, MC, V.

Center Ossipee (F-5)

(See also Wolfeboro)

Pop 500 (est) **Elev** 529 ft **Area code** 603 **Web** www.ossipeevalley.org
Information Greater Ossipee Area Chamber of Commerce, 127 NH 28, Ossipee, 03864-7300; 603/539-6201 or 800/382-2371.

The communities in Ossipee Area are part of a winter and summer sports region centering around Ossipee Lake and the Ossipee Mountains. The mountains also harbor a volcano (extinct for 120 million years) that is considered to be the most perfectly shaped volcanic formation in the world and is rivaled only by a similar formation in Nigeria. A hike up Mt Whittier gives an excellent view of the formation. In the winter, the area comes alive with snowmobiling, dog-sledding, cross-country skiing and other activities.

What to See and Do

King Pine Ski Area. Triple, double chairlifts; 2 J-bars; snowmaking; patrol, school, rentals; night skiing; nursery; snack bar; bar. (Early Dec-late Mar, daily) 11 mi NE via NH 25, 153. Phone 603/367-8896 or 800/367-8897. ¢¢¢¢¢

Swimming. Ossipee Lake, N & E of village; Duncan Lake, S of village.
Sailing. Silver Lake, N & E of village; also Ossipee Lake. Marinas with small boat rentals.

White Lake State Park. Sandy beach on tree-studded shore. Swimming; trout fishing. Hiking. Picnicking, concessions. Tent camping. (Mid-May-mid-Oct) Snowmobile trails (Dec-Mar). Standard fees. 6 mi N on NH 16. Phone 603/323-7350. June-Aug   ¢¢

Colebrook (B-5)

(See also Dixville Notch)

Settled 1770 **Pop** 2,444 **Elev** 1,033 ft **Area code** 603 **Zip** 03576
Information North Country Chamber of Commerce, PO Box 1; 603/237-8939.

At the west edge of the White Mountains, Colebrook is the gateway to excellent hunting and fishing in the Connecticut Lakes region. The Mohawk and Connecticut rivers join here. Vermont's Mt Monadnock adds scenic beauty.

What to See and Do

Beaver Brook Falls. A scenic glen. 2 mi N on NH 145.

Coleman State Park. On Little Diamond Pond in the heavily timbered Connecticut Lakes region. Lake and stream fishing; picnicking; primitive camping. (Mid-May-mid-Oct) Standard fees. 7 mi E on NH 26, then 5 mi N on Diamond Pond Rd. Phone 603/237-4520.

Columbia Covered Bridge. 75 ft high. 4 mi S on US 3.

Shrine of Our Lady of Grace. Oblates of Mary Immaculate. More than 50 Carrara marble and granite devotional monuments on 25 acres. Special events throughout season. Guided tours (Mother's Day-2nd Sun Oct, daily). 2 mi S on US 3. Phone 603/237-5511.   **Free.**

Motel

✔★ **NORTHERN COMFORT.** *1 mi S on US 3. 603/237-4440.* E-mail comfort@ncia.net. 19 rms. S, D $56-$68; each addl $8-$10. Crib free. Pet accepted. TV; cable. Heated pool; whirlpool. Playground. Complimentary continental bkfst June-Sept. Restaurant nearby. Ck-out 11 am. Gift shop. Downhill/x-country ski 12 mi. Exercise equipt. Cr cds: A, DS, MC, V.

Concord (G-5)

(See also Manchester)

Settled 1727 **Pop** 36,006 **Elev** 288 ft **Area code** 603 **Zip** 03301 **E-mail** info@concordnhchamber.com **Web** www.concordnhchamber.com
Information Chamber of Commerce, 244 N Main St; 603/224-2508.

New Hampshire, one of the original 13 colonies, entered the Union in 1788—but its capital was in dispute for another 20 years. Concord finally won the honor in 1808. The state house, begun immediately, was finished in 1819. The legislature is the largest (more than 400 seats) of any state. Concord is the financial center of the state and a center of diversified industry as well.

What to See and Do

Capitol Center for the Arts. Renovated historic theater (1920s) is state's largest. Presents musicals, concerts, dance performances, symphonies and family entertainment all yr. For schedule and tickets, contact 44 S Main St; 603/225-1111.

Canterbury Shaker Village. Historic Shaker buildings; living museum of Shaker crafts, architecture and inventions. Guided tour of 6 historic buildings and museum. Restaurant. Gift shop. (May-Oct, daily; Apr & Nov-Dec, Fri-Sun) 15 mi N on I-93 to exit 18, follow signs. Phone 603/783-9511. ¢¢¢

Christa McAuliffe Planetarium. Official state memorial to nation's first teacher in space. Changing programs. (Daily exc Mon; closed some major hols, also Apr 12) 3 Institute Dr. I-93 exit 15E. Phone 603/271-7827. ¢¢

⭐ **League of New Hampshire Craftsmen.**

Concord Arts & Crafts. High-quality traditional and contemporary crafts by some of New Hampshire's finest craftsmen; monthly exhibits. (Daily exc Sun; closed most hols) 36 N Main St. Phone 603/228-8171. **Free.**

Foundation Headquarters. Craft gallery with changing exhibits. Library and resource center for League Foundation members. (Mon-Fri; closed hols) 205 N Main St. Phone 603/224-1471. **Free.**

Museum of New Hampshire History. Historical museum (founded 1823) with permanent and changing exhibits, including excellent examples of the famed Concord Coach; museum store. (Tues-Sat, also Sun afternoons). 6 Eagle Sq. Phone 603/226-3189. ¢¢

Pats Peak Ski Area. Triple, 2 double chairlifts, 2 T-bars, J-bar, pony lift; patrol, school, rentals, ski shop; snowmaking; cafeteria, lounge; nursery. (Dec-late Mar, daily; closed Dec 25) 8 mi W on I-89 to US 202, then 8 mi W to NH 114, then 3 mi S, near Henniker. Phone 603/428-3245. ¢¢¢¢

Pierce Manse. Home of President Franklin Pierce from 1842-1848. Reconstructed and moved to present site; contains many original furnishings and period pieces. (Mid-June-mid-Sept, Mon-Fri; also by appt; closed July 4, Labor Day) 14 Penacook St, 1 mi N of State House. Phone 603/224-0094, 603/224-7668 or 603/225-2068. ¢

State House. Hall of Flags; statues, portraits of state notables. (Mon-Fri; closed hols) Main St; entrance for disabled on Park St. Phone 603/271-2154. **Free.**

Motels

✔⭐ **BRICK TOWER MOTOR INN.** *414 S Main St. 603/224-9565; FAX 603/224-6027.* 51 rms. May-Oct: S $52; D $59-$64; each addl $5; under 12 free; higher rates special events; lower rates rest of yr. Crib free. Pet accepted. TV; cable. Pool. Complimentary continental bkfst. Ck-out 11 am. Some in-rm saunas. Cr cds: A, DS, MC, V.

🐾 🏊 🔥 **SC**

⭐⭐ **DAYS INN.** *406 S Main St, I-93, exit 125. 603/224-2511; FAX 603/224-6032.* 40 rms, 2 story. July-Sept: S $75; D $85; each addl $10; higher rates: special events, Oct; lower rates rest of yr. Crib free. TV; cable (premium). Pool. Playground. Complimentary continental bkfst. Business servs avail. Ck-out 11 am. Some in-rm whirlpools. Cr cds: A, C, D, DS, ER, JCB, MC, V.

🏊 🛇 🔥 **SC**

Motor Hotels

⭐⭐ **COMFORT INN.** *71 Hall St. 603/226-4100; FAX 603/228-2106.* 100 rms, 3 story. S, D $72-$130; each addl $10; suites $175; under 18 free. Crib free. Pet accepted. TV; cable. Indoor pool; whirlpool. Complimentary continental bkfst. Restaurant nearby. Ck-out noon. Meeting rms. Business servs avail. In-rm modem link. Valet serv. Sauna. Game rm. Some bathrm phones, in-rm whirlpools, refrigerators. Cr cds: A, C, D, DS, ER, JCB, MC, V.

D 🐾 🏊 🛇 🔥 **SC**

⭐⭐ **HAMPTON INN.** *(515 South St, Bow 03304) on I-89 exit 1, near jct I-93. 603/224-5322; FAX 603/224-4282.* 145 rms, 4 story. S, D $75-$150; under 18 free; higher rates special events. Crib free. TV; cable (premium), VCR avail. Indoor pool; whirlpool. Complimentary continental bkfst. Restaurant opp 7 am-10 pm. Ck-out noon. Coin lndry. Meeting rms. Refrigerators avail. Picnic tables. Cr cds: A, C, D, DS, MC, V.

D 🏊 🛇 🔥 **SC**

Inn

⭐⭐⭐ **COLBY HILL.** *(3 The Oaks, Henniker 03242) 17 mi W via US 202 to Henniker, ½ mi W on Western Ave. 603/428-3281; FAX 603/428-9218; res: 800/531-0330.* E-mail info@colbyhillinn.com; web www.colbyhillinn.com. 16 rms, 11 with shower only, 2 story. S $75-$155; D $85-$165; suites $290-$325. Children over 8 yrs only. TV in library; cable. Pool. Complimentary full bkfst. Dining rm (see COLBY HILL INN). Ck-out 11 am, ck-in 2 pm. Downhill/x-country ski 1½ mi. Meeting rm. Business servs avail. In-rm modem link. Lawn games. Some fireplaces. Historic farmhouse (ca 1800) used as tavern, church, meeting house and private school; sitting rm, antiques. On 5 acres. Totally nonsmoking. Cr cds: A, C, D, DS, MC, V.

🏊 🏊 🛇 🔥 🍴

Restaurants

⭐⭐ **COLBY HILL INN.** *(See Colby Hill Inn) 603/428-3281.* E-mail info@colbyhillinn.com; web www.colbyhillinn.com. Continental menu. Specialties: tournados Oscar, chicken Colby Inn, seafood. Hrs: 5:30-8:30 pm; Sun 4:30-7:30 pm. Closed Dec 24, 25. Res accepted. Serv bar. Semi-a la carte: dinner $17-$27. View of garden. Totally nonsmoking. Cr cds: A, C, D, DS, MC, V.

✔⭐ **GRIST MILL.** *(520 South St, Bow 03304) N on I-89, exit 1. 603/226-1922.* Specializes in pasta, seafood, bread bowls. Hrs: 6:30 am-9:30 pm; Sat, Sun from 7 am; Sun brunch 8-11:30 am. Closed Dec 25. Bar. Semi-a la carte: bkfst $1.50-$7.95, lunch, dinner $3.99-$12.95. Sun brunch $7.99. Child's meals. Outdoor dining. On Turkey River. Cr cds: A, MC, V.

D 🛇

⭐ **TIO JUAN'S.** *1 Bicentennial Square. 603/224-2821.* Mexican menu. Specialties: chimichangas, burritos, nachos. Hrs: 4-10 pm. Closed Thanksgiving, Dec 25. Bar to 12:30 am. Semi-a la carte: dinner $4.95-$10.50. Child's meals. Guitarist Tues, Thurs. Old Concord police station; cells converted to private rms. Cr cds: A, DS, MC, V.

SC 🛇 ♥

Dixville Notch (B-5)

(See also Colebrook)

Pop 30 (est) **Elev** 1,990 ft **Area code** 603 **Zip** 03576

The small village of Dixville Notch shares its name with the most northerly of the White Mountain passes. The Notch cuts through the mountain range between Kidderville and Errol. At its narrowest point, east of Lake Gloriette, is one of the most impressive views in the state. Every four years Dixville Notch is invaded by the national news media, who report the nation's first presidential vote tally shortly after midnight on election day.

What to See and Do

Balsams/Wilderness Ski Area. Chairlift, 2 T-bars; patrol, school, rentals; restaurant, cafeteria; nursery, resort (see). Longest run 2 mi; vertical drop 1,000 ft. (Dec-Mar, daily) Cross-country trails. On NH 26. Phone 603/255-3400 or 800/255-0600 (exc NH), 800/255-0800 (NH) for snow conditions. ¢¢¢¢

Table Rock. Views of New Hampshire, Maine, Vermont and Québec. ¾ mi S of NH 26, ½ mi E of village of Dixville Notch.

Resort

⭐⭐⭐⭐ **THE BALSAMS.** *On NH 26. 603/255-3400; FAX 603/255-4221; res: 800/255-0600 (exc NH), 800/255-0800 (NH).* E-mail thebalsams@aol.com; web www.thebalsams.com. This lavish turn-of-the-century resort occupies a 15,000-acre estate amid mountains and meadows. 208 rms, 3-6 story. No A/C. AP, July-Labor Day: S $230-$245; D $345-$650; family rates; MAP, ski plans avail late Dec-late Mar. 15% serv charge (late May-June, Sept-mid-Oct). Closed rest of yr. Crib avail. TV rm; cable, VCR avail (movies). Heated pool; attendant. Free supervised child's activities (July-Aug); ages 5-13. Dining rm 8-9:30 am, 12:30-2 pm, 6:30-8 pm. Box lunches, snacks. Rm serv. Bars 11:30-12:45 am. Ck-out noon, ck-in 4 pm. Business servs avail. In-rm modem link. Bellhops. Shopping arcade. 6 tennis courts, pro. 27-hole golf, pro, 2 putting greens. Private lake, boats, paddleboats, canoes. Downhill/x-country ski on site. Snowmobile trails, ice-skating. Mountain bikes. Horse-drawn hay rides. Hiking trails. Lawn games. Game rm. Rec rm. Exercise rm. Library. Soc dirs; dancing, entertainment, lectures; movies; theater. Stocked trout pond. Natural history program; naturalist on site. Cr cds: A, DS, MC, V.

Dover (G-6)

(See also Portsmouth)

Settled 1623 **Pop** 25,042 **Elev** 57 ft **Area code** 603 **Zip** 03820 **E-mail** info@dovernh.org **Web** www.dovernh.org

Information Chamber of Commerce, 299 Central Ave; 603/742-2218.

With its historic trails and homes, Dover is the oldest permanent settlement in New Hampshire. The town contains the only known existing colonial garrison.

What to See and Do

Woodman Institute. The Garrison House (1675), only garrison in New Hampshire now visible in nearly its original form. Woodman House (1818), residence of the donor, is now a natural history museum with collections of minerals, Native American artifacts and displays of mammals, fish, amphibians, reptiles, birds, insects; war memorial rms. Senator John P. Hale House (1813) contains articles of Dover history and antique furniture. (Apr-Jan, Wed-Sun afternoons; closed major hols) 182-190 Central Ave, ¹/₂ mi S on NH 108. Phone 603/742-1038. ¢¢

Seasonal Event

Cocheco Arts Festival. Mid-July-late Aug.

Motel

✔★ **DAYS INN.** *481 Central Ave. 603/742-0400; FAX 603/742-7790.* Web www.daysinn.com. 50 rms, 2 story, 13 kit. suites. June-Oct: S $64-$94; D $66-$98; each addl $5-$8; kit. suites $85-$160; under 12 free; lower rates rest of yr. Crib avail. Pet accepted. TV; cable. Pool; whirlpool. Continental bkfst. Restaurant nearby. Ck-out 11 am. Coin lndry. Business servs avail. Cr cds: A, C, D, DS, JCB, MC, V.

Motor Hotel

★★★ **NEW ENGLAND CENTER.** *(15 Strafford Ave, Durham 03824)* Approx 2 mi S on NH 108, 3 mi W on US 4, 1 mi S on Madbury Rd to Edgewood Rd, on University of NH campus. *603/862-2801; FAX 603/862-4351.* 115 rms, 8 story. July-Oct: S $70-$90; D $80-$110; suites $120-$150; lower rates rest of yr. TV; cable (premium), VCR avail. Indoor/outdoor pool privileges. Restaurant 7 am-10 pm. Bar 11 am-11 pm. Ck-out noon. Meeting rms. Business servs avail. Sundries. Tennis privileges. Health club privileges. On 10 wooded acres. Cr cds: A, C, D, MC, V.

Inn

★★ **SILVER STREET.** *103 Silver St. 603/743-3000; FAX 603/749-5673.* 10 rms, 2 share bath, 3 story. May-mid-Oct: S $79; D $89; each addl $10; under 15 free; lower rates rest of yr. Crib free. TV; cable. Complimentary full bkfst. Restaurant nearby. Ck-out 11 am. Business servs avail. Victorian house built ca 1880 for local businessman. Cr cds: A, C, D, DS, MC, V.

Restaurants

★★ **FIREHOUSE ONE.** *1 Orchard St. 603/749-3636.* Specializes in seafood, prime rib, vegetarian dishes. Hrs: 11:30 am-9 pm; Sat from 5 pm; Sun 10 am-8 pm; Sun brunch 10 am-2 pm. Closed Dec 25. Res accepted; required hols. Bar to midnight. A la carte: lunch $4-$8, dinner $8-$18. Sun brunch $8.95. Child's meals. Outdoor dining. Old restored firehouse (1840), arched doors and windows, tin walls and ceilings, overstuffed chairs. Cr cds: A, C, D, DS, MC, V.

★ **NEWICK'S LOBSTER HOUSE.** *431 Dover Point Rd. 603/742-3205.* Specializes in seafood. Hrs: 11 am-9 pm; hrs vary off season. Closed Thanksgiving, Dec 25. Serv bar. Semi-a la carte: lunch, dinner $1.95-$16.95. Seafood market. Gift shop. Nautical accents. Overlooks Great Bay. Cr cds: A, DS, MC, V.

Exeter (H-6)

(See also Hampton Beach, Portsmouth)

Settled 1638 **Pop** 12,481 **Elev** 40 ft **Area code** 603 **Zip** 03833 **E-mail** eacc@nh.ultranet.com **Web** www.exeterarea.org

Information Exeter Area Chamber of Commerce, 120 Water St; 603/772-2411.

A venerable preparatory school and colonial houses belie Exeter's radical history. It had its beginnings in religious nonconformity, led by Rev. John Wheelwright and Anne Hutchinson, both of whom were banished from Massachusetts for heresy. There was an anti-British scuffle in 1734 and by 1774 Exeter was burning Lord North in effigy and talking of liberty. It was made the capital of the state during the Revolution, since there were too many Tories in Portsmouth. Exeter is the birthplace of Daniel Chester French and John Irving.

What to See and Do

American Independence Museum. Site of Revolutionary War-era state treasury building; grounds house Folsom Tavern (1775). (May-Oct, Wed-Sun) 1 Governors Lane. Phone 603/772-2622. ¢¢

Gilman Garrison House (1676-1690). Built as a fortified garrison with hewn logs; pulley arrangement to raise and lower door still in place. Substantially remodeled in mid-18th century; wing added with 17th- & 18th-century furnishings. (June-mid-Oct, Tues, Thurs, Sat & Sun) 12 Water St. Phone 603/436-3205. ¢¢

League of New Hampshire Craftsmen/Exeter. Work in all media by New Hampshire's finest artisans. (Daily exc Sun) 61 Water St. Phone 603/778-8282. **Free.**

Phillips Exeter Academy (1781). (990 students) On 400 acres with more than 100 buildings. Co-ed school for grades 9-12. Founded by John Phillips, who sought a school for "students from every quarter"; known for its student diversity. On campus are a contemporary library (1971), designed by Louis I. Kahn, the Frederick R. Mayer Art Center and the Lamont Art Gallery. Phone 603/772-4311.

Inn

★ ★ **EXETER.** *90 Front St.* 603/772-5901; FAX 603/778-8757; res: 800/782-8444. 46 rms, 3 story. Mid-June-mid-Nov: S $69-$105; D $79-$125; each addl $15; suites $165; lower rates rest of yr. Crib $7.50. TV; cable. Dining rm 7 am-9 pm; Sat, Sun to 10 pm. Bar 11:45 am-midnight. Ck-out 11 am, ck-in 2 pm. Meeting rm. Business servs avail. Valet serv. On campus of Phillips Exeter Academy. Cr cds: A, D, DS, MC, V.

D ⊠ SC

Franconia (D-4)

(See also Littleton)

Pop 811 **Elev** 971 ft **Area code** 603 **Zip** 03580
Information Franconia Notch Chamber of Commerce, PO Box 780; 603/823-5661.

What to See and Do

Franconia Notch State Park (see). Approx 7 mi SE via NH 18 & I-93 (Franconia Notch State Pwky.)

Frost Place. Two furnished rms of Robert Frost's home open to public; memorabilia; poetry trail; 25-min video show. (July-Columbus Day, Wed-Mon afternoons; Memorial Day-June, Sat & Sun afternoons) 1 mi S on NH 116 to Bickford Hill Rd, right over bridge, left at fork, on to Ridge Rd. Phone 603/823-5510. ¢¢

New England Ski Museum. Details the history of skiing in the east; exhibits feature skis and bindings, clothing, art and photographs; vintage films. Gift shop. (Late May-mid-Oct, daily; Dec-late Mar, Fri-Tues; closed Dec 25) Franconia Notch Pwky (US 3) exit 2, near Cannon Mt Tramway. Phone 603/823-7177. **Free.**

White Mountain National Forest (see). SE on NH 18.

Annual Event

Lilac Time Festival. 8 mi W on NH 117, then 4 mi S on US 302, in Lisbon. Celebration of the state flower and observance of Memorial Day. Parade, carnival, vendors, entertainment, special events. Phone 603/431-5388. Late May.

Motels

✔★ **GALE RIVER.** *1 Main St, 1/2 mi N on NH 18.* 603/823-5655; res: 800/255-7989. 10 rms, 2 kit. cottages (2 bedrm). No A/C. July-mid-Oct & hol ski wks: S, D $55-$75; each addl $5-$10; cottages $110-$150 (5-day min); package plans, wkly rates (cottages); higher rates: wkends, fall foliage; lower rates rest of yr. Crib free. TV; cable. Heated pool; whirlpool. Playground. Complimentary coffee in rms. Ck-out 11 am. Downhill ski 4 mi. Lawn games. Refrigerators. Picnic tables, grills. Cr cds: A, DS, MC, V.

⊠ ⊠ ≋ ⊠ ⊠

★ ★ ★ **RED COACH INN.** *Wallace Hill Rd, I-93 exit 38.* 603/823-7422; FAX 603/823-5638; res: 800/262-2493. 60 rms, 2 story. S $55-$65; D $70-$110; under 12 free; ski plan; lower rates off season. Crib $5. TV; cable (premium), VCR avail. Indoor pool; whirlpool. Complimentary continental bkfst. Restaurant 6-10:30 am, 5:30-9 pm; hrs vary off season. Rm serv. Meeting rms. Business servs avail. Gift shop. Beauty shop. Downhill ski 4 mi; x-country ski 3 mi. Exercise equipt; sauna. Game rm. Cr cds: A, DS, MC, V.

D ⊠ ≋ ⊼ ⊠ ⊠ SC

✔★ **STONYBROOK MOTEL & LODGE.** *1 1/4 mi S on NH 18.* 603/823-8192; FAX 603/823-8196; res: 800/722-3552. Web www.stonybrookmotel.com. 23 rms. Some A/C. S, D $59-$75; each addl $7; under 18 free; wkly rates; ski plan; higher rates: fall foliage, hol wkends. Crib free. TV; cable. 2 pools, 1 indoor. Playground. Complimentary coffee in rms.

Ck-out 11 am. Downhill/x-country ski 2 mi. Game rm. Rec rm. Lawn games. Some refrigerators. Picnic tables, grills. Pond, stream. Cr cds: DS, MC, V.

⊠ ⊠ ≋ ⊠ ⊠ SC

Inns

★ ★ **FOX GLOVE.** *(Main St, Sugar Hill 03585) N on NH 18 to NH 117, 3 mi W on NH 117.* 603/823-8840; res: 888/343-2220; FAX 603/823-5755. E-mail foxgloveinn@compuserve.com. 6 rms, 2 story. No A/C. Rm phone avail. S $75; D $85-$125; ski plans; higher rates foliage season. Children over 12 yrs only. Cable TV avail. VCR avail. Complimentary full bkfst; afternoon refreshments. Ck-out 10 am, ck-in 3 pm. Business servs avail. Downhill ski 5 mi; x-country ski 1 mi. Renovated turn-of-the-century house with cozy rms. Totally nonsmoking. Cr cds: MC, V.

⊠ ⊁ ⊠ ⊠ ⊠

★ ★ ★ **THE FRANCONIA INN.** *Easton Rd, 2 1/8 mi S on NH 116.* 603/823-5542; FAX 603/823-8078; res: 800/473-5299. E-mail info@franconiainn.com; web www.franconiainn.com. 34 rms, 3 story. No A/C. No elvtr. No rm phones. S $71-$131; D $81-$146; each addl $10; suites $146; family, wkend rates; package plans; lower rates off season. Closed Apr-mid-May. Crib avail. TV rm; cable. Heated pool; whirlpool. Restaurant (see THE FRANCONIA INN). Bar from 4 pm. Ck-out 11 am, ck-in 3 pm. Tennis. Downhill ski 3 mi; x-country ski on site. Game rm. Rec rm. Lawn games. Trail rides. Sleigh rides, hayrides. Ice-skating; rentals. Library. On river; swimming. Cr cds: A, MC, V.

⊠ ⊁ ⊠ ⊁ ≋ ⊠ ⊠

✔★ **HILLTOP.** *(Main St, Sugar Hill 03585) 2 1/4 mi W on NH 117.* 603/823-5695; FAX 603/823-5518; res: 800/770-5695. 6 rms, 2 story, 1 suite. No A/C. No rm phones. S $60-$70; D $70-$95; each addl $15-$25; suite $90-$130; wkly rates; higher rates fall foliage (2-day min). Pet accepted; $10/day. TV in sitting rm; cable. Complimentary full bkfst; afternoon refreshments. Rm serv. Ck-out 11 am, ck-in 2-6 pm. Downhill ski 8 mi; x-country ski on site. Built 1895; antiques, quilts. Cr cds: DS, MC, V.

⊠ ≋ ⊠ ⊠

★ **HORSE & HOUND.** *205 Wells Rd.* 603/823-5501; res: 800/450-5501. 10 rms, 2 share bath, 2 story. No A/C. S $79.95; D $92.25; under 6 free; ski plans; hols (2-day min). Closed Apr. Crib $10. Pet accepted; $8.50. TV; VCR in common rm. Complimentary full bkfst. Restaurant (see HORSE & HOUND). Ck-out 11 am, ck-in 4 pm. Downhill ski 2 mi; x-country ski on site. Secluded country inn near Cannon Mt. Cr cds: A, C, D, DS, MC, V.

⊠ ≋ ⊠ ⊠

★ ★ **INN AT FOREST HILLS.** *NH 142.* 603/823-9550; FAX 603/823-8701; res: 800/280-9550. E-mail mobil@innfhills.com; web www.innatforesthills.com. 7 rms, 2 with shower only, 3 story. No A/C. No rm phones. S $85-$105; D $90-$110; each addl $25; ski plans; hols (2-day min); higher rates foliage season. Children over 11 yrs only. TV; cable, VCR avail (movies). Complimentary full bkfst. Ck-out 11 am, ck-in 3-6 pm. Tennis. Downhill ski 5 mi; x-country ski on site. Cottage built in 1890; large front porch, solarium. Totally nonsmoking. Cr cds: MC, V.

⊠ ⊠ ≋ ⊁ ⊠ ⊠

★ **LOVETT'S INN BY LAFAYETTE BROOK.** *Rte 18, 2 mi S at jct NH 18 & 142.* 603/823-7761; res: 800/356-3802 (exc NH). 6 rms, 5 with bath, 2 story; 16 guest cottages. Some A/C. S $100-$150; D $140-$190; MAP avail; package plans. Closed Apr. Crib avail. Pet accepted. TV. Pool. Restaurant (see LOVETT'S INN BY LAFAYETTE BROOK). Bar 6-10 pm. Box lunches. Ck-out 11 am, ck-in after 2 pm. Free bus depot transportation. Downhill ski 3 mi; x-country ski on site. Game rm. Rec rm. Lawn games. Fireplaces in cottages. Historic resort-type inn (1784); on 10 acres with trout pond, streams. Cr cds: A, MC, V.

D ⊱ ⊠ ≋ ⊠ ⊠

★ ★ **SUGAR HILL.** *1/2 mi W on NH 117.* 603/823-5621; res: 800/548-4748. 10 rms in inn; 6 cottage rms. No A/C in rms. S, D $115-$145. Afternoon refreshments. Dining rm (public by res). Bar. Ck-out 11 am, ck-in 3 pm. Downhill ski 3 mi; x-country ski 2 mi. Some fireplaces. Converted farmhouse (ca 1789). Totally nonsmoking. Cr cds: A, MC, V.

★ ★ **SUNSET HILL HOUSE.** *(Sunset Hill Rd, Sugar Hill 03585) 2 mi W on NH 117. 603/823-5522; FAX 603/823-5738; res: 800/786-4455.* 30 rms, 2 story. No A/C. No rm phones. S $60-$130; D $75-$145; each addl $20-$30; ski, golf plans; wkend rates; 2-day min hols; higher rates fall foliage. Crib $20. TV in common rm; cable. Heated pool. Complimentary full bkfst. Dining rm 5:30-9 pm. Ck-out 11 am, ck-in 3 pm. Business servs avail. 9-hole golf. Downhill ski 5 mi; x-country ski on site. Lawn games. Built in 1882; beautiful view of mountains, attractive grounds. Totally nonsmoking. Cr cds: A, DS, MC, V.

Restaurants

★ ★ ★ **THE FRANCONIA INN.** *(See The Franconia Inn) 603/823-5542.* E-mail info@franconiainn.com; web www.franconiainn.com. Continental menu. Specialties: bouillabaisse, rack of lamb, seafood. Own desserts. Hrs: 7:30-10 am, 6-9 pm; hrs vary off season. Closed Apr-mid-May. Res accepted. No A/C. Bar. Semi-a la carte: bkfst $5-$10, dinner $17-$21. Child's meals. Totally nonsmoking. Cr cds: A, MC, V.

★ ★ **HORSE & HOUND.** *(See Horse & Hound Inn) 603/823-5501.* Continental menu. Specializes roast duckling, chicken, veal. Hrs: 6-9 pm. Closed Sun-Wed. Res accepted. No A/C. Bar 5-10 pm. Semi-a la carte: dinner $14-$21. Child's meals. Family-owned. Totally nonsmoking. Cr cds: A, C, D, DS, MC, V.

SC

★ ★ **LOVETT'S INN BY LAFAYETTE BROOK.** *(See Lovett's Inn By Lafayette Brook) 603/823-7761.* Specialties: salmon dijon, pork roulade. Own baking. Hrs: 6-8:30 pm. Closed Apr, mid-Oct-mid-Nov. Res required. Bar 6-10 pm. Prix fixe: dinner $35. Historic building. Cr cds: A, DS, MC, V.

★ ★ **POLLY'S PANCAKE PARLOR.** *(NH 117, Sugar Hill 03585) I-93 exit 38. 603/823-5575.* Specializes in whole grain pancakes, waffles, sandwiches. Own soups, sausage, desserts. Hrs: 7 am-3 pm; wkends only Nov & Apr, hrs vary. Closed Dec-Mar. Res accepted. No A/C. A la carte entrees: bkfst, lunch, dinner $6-$18. Child's meals. In converted carriage shed (1840). Early American decor; antiques. Family-owned. Totally nonsmoking. Cr cds: A, DS, MC, V.

D

Franconia Notch State Park (D-4)

(See also Franconia, Lincoln/North Woodstock Area)

(Approx 7 mi SE of Franconia via NH 18 & I-93/Franconia Notch State Pkwy)

This seven-mile pass and state park, a deep valley of 6,440 acres between the Franconia and Kinsman ranges of the White Mountains, has been a top tourist attraction since the mid-19th century. Mts Liberty (4,460 ft), Lincoln (5,108 ft) and Lafayette (5,249 ft) loom on the east, and Cannon Mt (4,200 ft) presents a sheer granite face. The Pemigewasset River follows the length of the Notch.

The park offers various recreational activities, including swimming at sandy beach; fishing and boating on Echo Lake (jct NH 18 and I-93 exit 3); hiking; 8-mile paved bike path through Notch; skiing; picnicking; camping. Fees for some activities. For further information contact Franconia Notch State Park, Franconia 03580; 603/823-5563.

What to See and Do

Cannon Mt Ski Area. Tramway, quad, triple, 2 double chairlifts, pony lift; patrol, school, rentals; snowmaking; cafeterias, bar (beer & wine); nursery. New England Ski Museum. Longest run 2 mi; vertical drop 2,146 ft. (Late Nov-mid-Apr, daily; closed Dec 25) Tramway, rising 2,022 ft vertically over a distance of 1 mi in 6 min, also operates Memorial Day-mid-Oct, daily and on wkends rest of yr (weather permitting). 5 mi S of Franconia via NH 18 & I-93 (Franconia Notch State Pkwy), exit 2 or 3. Phone 603/823-5563; snow conditions 800/552-1234. Winter ¢¢¢¢¢; Summer ¢¢¢

Flume Gorge & Park Information Center. Narrow, natural gorge and waterfall along the flank of Mt Liberty, accessible by stairs and walks; picnicking. Mountain flowers and mosses, Liberty Gorge, the Cascades, covered bridges. Information Center offers 15-min movie introducing park every 1/2-hr. Interpretive exhibits. Gift shop, cafeteria. (Mid-May-late Oct, daily) 15 mi S of Franconia, I-93 (Franconia Notch State Pkwy), exit 1. Phone 603/745-8391. ¢¢¢

Lafayette Campground. Fishing. Hiking on Appalachian trail system. Picnicking. Camping. Fees for some activities. (Mid-May-mid-Oct, daily) 9 mi S of Franconia Village, off I-93 (Franconia Notch State Pkwy). Phone 603/823-9513. ¢¢¢¢

Old Man of the Mountains. Discovered in 1805, this craggy likeness of a man's face is formed naturally of 5 layers of granite and is 40 ft high; also known as the "Great Stone Face." 1,200 ft above Profile Lake, W of I-93 (Franconia Notch State Pkwy), exit 2.

The Basin. Deep glacial pothole, 20 ft in diameter, at foot of a waterfall, polished smooth by sand, stones and water. W of I-93 (Franconia Notch State Pkwy), S of Profile Lake.

Franklin (G-4)

(See also Laconia)

Settled 1764 **Pop** 8,304 **Elev** 335 ft **Area code** 603 **Zip** 03235

Franklin was named in 1828 for Benjamin Franklin; until then it was a part of Salisbury. It is the birthplace of Daniel Webster, lawyer, senator and statesman. The Pemigewasset and Winnipesaukee rivers, joining to form the Merrimack, provide the city with abundant water power.

What to See and Do

Congregational Christian Church (1820). Church that Daniel Webster attended; tracker action organ. A bust of Webster by Daniel Chester French is outside. (Wed & Thurs mornings, Sun, also by appt) 47 S Main St, on US 3. Phone 603/934-4242. **Free.**

Lakes Region Factory Stores. More than 45 outlet stores. (Daily) Approx 5 mi E on US 3, in Tilton. Phone 603/286-7880.

Motel

✔ ★ **SUPER 8.** *(US 3, Tilton 03276) 3 mi E on US 3. 603/286-8882; FAX 603/286-8788.* 62 rms, 2 story. July-mid-Oct: S $56.88; D $59.88; under 12 free; higher rates special events; lower rates rest of yr. Crib free. TV; cable, VCR avail (movies). Complimentary coffee in lobby. Restaurant adj 6 am-11 pm. Ck-out 11 am. Business servs avail. Sundries. Downhill ski 5 mi. Cr cds: A, C, D, DS, MC, V.

D **SC**

Inns

★ ★ **ATWOOD.** *(71 Hill Rd (NH 3A), West Franklin) N of jct US 11 & NH 3A. 603/934-3666.* 7 rms, 3 story. No rm phones. S $65; D $80-$90; each addl $25; under 12 free. TV in sitting rm; cable. Complimentary full bkfst. Restaurant nearby. Ck-out 11 am, ck-in 3 pm. Business servs avail. Downhill ski 10 mi; x-country ski on site. Fireplaces. Federal-style house built 1830; many antiques. Totally nonsmoking. Cr cds: A, D, DS, MC, V.

★ ★ ★ **HIGHLAND LAKE.** *(Maple St, East Andover 03231) 5 mi W on NH 11. 603/735-6426; FAX 603/735-5355.* 10 rms, shower only, 3 story. No rm phones. S, D $85-$100; each addl $20; 2-day min wknds; higher rates: racing wknds, fall foliage, graduation. Children over 8 yrs only. TV in parlor; cable, VCR avail (movies). Complimentary full bkfst. Ck-out 11 am, ck-in 3 pm. Business servs avail. Downhill/x-country ski 5 mi. Lawn games. Picnic tables. On lake. Farm house built in 1767. Totally nonsmoking. Cr cds: A, DS, MC, V.

Restaurants

★ **MR. D'S.** *(428 N Main St, West Franklin) At jct US 11 & NH 3A. 603/934-3142.* Specializes in seafood, steak, own soups. Hrs: 6 am-8 pm; Sun from 8 am. Closed some major hols. Serv bar. Semi-a la carte: bkfst $1.75-$5.95, lunch $3-$9, dinner $5-$12. Child's meals. Collection of old-fashioned photographs on walls. Cr cds: A, C, D, DS, MC, V.

★ ★ **OLIVER'S.** *(4 Sanborn Rd, Tilton 03276) Approx 3 mi E on NH 11/US 3, at NH 132. 603/286-7379.* Specializes in veal, pasta, fresh seafood. Hrs: 11 am-9 pm; Fri, Sat to 10 pm; Sun 8:30 am-9 pm, brunch to 2 pm. Res accepted. Bar to 12:30 am. Semi-a la carte: lunch $5.95-$8.95, dinner $9.95-$16.95. Sun brunch $5.95-$9.95. Child's meals. Entertainment Thurs. Country decor; some antiques. Cr cds: A, C, D, DS, MC, V.

Gorham (D-5)

Settled 1805 **Pop** 3,173 **Elev** 801 ft **Area code** 603 **Zip** 03581 **E-mail** nwmcc@northernwhitemountains.com **Web** www.northernwhitemountains.com

Information Northern White Mt Chamber of Commerce, 164 Main St, PO Box 298, Berlin 03570; 603/752-6060.

Commanding the northeast approaches to the Presidential Range of the White Mountains, at the north end of Pinkham Notch (see), Gorham has magnificent views and is the center for summer and winter sports. The Peabody River merges with the Androscoggin in a series of falls. A Ranger District office of the White Mt Natl Forest (see) is located here.

What to See and Do

Dolly Copp Campground. 176 campsites; fishing, hiking, picnicking. 6 mi S on NH 16 in White Mt Natl Forest (see). Contact the District Ranger, USDA Forest Service, 80 Glen Rd; 603/466-2713 or -3984 (camping). ¢¢¢-¢¢¢¢

Libby Memorial Pool & Recreation Area. Natural pool, bathhouses; picnicking. (Summer, daily, weather permitting) 1/4 mi S on NH 16. Phone 603/466-9401. ¢

Moose Brook State Park. Views of the Presidential Range of the White Mts; good stream fishing area. Swimming, bathhouse; picnicking; camping. Hiking to Randolph Range. (Late May-early Sept) Standard fees. 2 mi W on US 2. Phone 603/466-3860.

Moose Tours. Daily tours leave each evening from the Gorham Informational Booth on a specified route to locate moose for sighting. (Late May-mid-Oct) Main St. Phone 603/752-6060. For departure times phone 603/466-3103. ¢¢¢

Mt Washington (see). 10 mi S on NH 16.

Motels

✔ ★ **GORHAM MOTOR INN.** *324 Main St. 603/466-3381; res: 800/445-0913.* 39 rms. S $38-$72; D $42-$84; each addl $6; higher rates fall foliage. Crib free. Pet accepted, some restrictions; $6. TV; cable (premium). Pool. Restaurant nearby. Ck-out 11 am. Downhill/x-country ski 8 mi. Some refrigerators. Cr cds: A, DS, MC, V.

★ ★ **MOUNT MADISON.** *365 Upper Main St, on US 2. 603/466-3622; res: 800/851-1136.* E-mail madison@ncia.net. 33 rms, 2 story. May-Oct: S, D $52-$70; each addl $5; higher rates foliage season. Closed rest of yr. Crib $5. TV; cable. Heated pool. Playground. Restaurant opp. Ck-out 11 am. Some refrigerators. Balconies. Cr cds: A, DS, MC, V.

★ ★ **ROYALTY INN.** *130 Main St. 603/466-3312; FAX 603/466-5802; res: 800/437-3529.* E-mail innkeeper@royaltyinn.com; web www.royaltyinn.com. 90 rms, 1-2 story. July-Labor Day, mid-Sept-Oct: S, D $56-$78; each addl $6; kit. units $82; lower rates rest of yr. Crib $5. Pet accepted. TV; cable, VCR avail. 2 pools; 1 indoor. Restaurant 6-10:30 am, 5-9 pm. Bar 5-11 pm; Fri, Sat to 1 am. Ck-out 11 am. Coin lndry. Meeting rm. Business servs avail. Downhill ski 9 mi; x-country ski 7 mi. Exercise equipt. Health club privileges. Game rm. Some refrigerators. Cr cds: A, C, D, DS, MC, V.

✔ ★ ★ **TOWN & COUNTRY MOTOR INN.** *1/2 mi E on US 2. 603/466-3315; res: 800/325-4386 (NH).* 160 rms, 2 story. June-Oct: S $48-$64; D $56-$70; each addl $6; suites $70-$82; golf & ski plans; lower rates rest of yr. Crib $6. Pet accepted. TV; cable, VCR avail. Indoor/outdoor pool; whirlpool. Restaurant 6-10:30 am, 5:30-10 pm. Bar 4:00 pm-12:30 am; entertainment Wed-Sat. Ck-out 11 am. Meeting rms. Business servs avail. Sundries. Golf privileges, putting green. Downhill/x-country ski 6 mi. Snowmobile trails. Exercise equipt; sauna. Game rm. Refrigerators avail. Some in-rm whirlpools. Private patios, balconies. Cr cds: A, C, D, DS, MC, V.

Inn

★ ★ ★ **PHILBROOK FARM.** *(881 North Rd, Shelburne) 6 mi E on NH 2 to Meadow Rd, left 1 mi to North Rd, then right. 603/466-3831.* Web www.journeysnorth.com. 18 inn rms, 9 share bath, 3 story; 2 1-rm cottages, 5 kit. cottages. No A/C. No elvtr. No rm phones. MAP: S $85-$100; D $115-$145; cottages $600/wk; wkly rates. Closed Oct 31-Dec 25; also Apr. Crib $3. Pool. Full bkfst. Dining rm: dinner (1 sitting). Ck-out 11 am (cottages 10 am), ck-in after noon. Downhill ski 15 mi; x-country ski on site. Rec rm. Lawn games. Antiques; sitting rm. Originally a farmhouse (1834), the inn has been in business since 1861. No cr cds accepted.

Restaurant

★ ★ **YOKOHAMA.** *288 Main St. 603/466-2501.* Japanese, Amer menu. Specialties: sukiyaki, oyako donburi, habachi platter. Hrs: 11:30 am-9 pm. Closed Mon; Thanksgiving, Dec 25; also 3 wks in Apr. Res accepted. Serv bar. Semi-a la carte: lunch $4.50-$6.50, dinner $5.75-$13.25. Child's meals. Family-owned. Cr cds: A, C, D, MC, V.

Hampton Beach (H-6)

(See also Portsmouth)

Settled 1638 **Pop** 900 (est) **Elev** 56 ft **Area code** 603 **Zip** 03842

Information Chamber of Commerce, 490 Lafayette Rd, Ste 1, PO Box 790; 603/926-8717 or 800/GET-A-TAN.

What to See and Do

Fishing. Charter boats at Hampton Beach piers.

Fuller Gardens. Former estate of the late Gov Alvan T. Fuller featuring extensive rose gardens, annuals, perennials, Japanese garden and conservatory. (May-Oct, daily) 10 Willow Ave, 4 mi NE via NH 1A, just N of NH 111 in North Hampton. Phone 603/964-5414. **¢¢**

Hampton Beach State Park. Sandy beach on Atlantic Ocean. Swimming, bathhouse. Also here is the Sea Shell, a band shell and amphitheater. Camping (hookups). (Late May-Labor Day, daily) Standard fees. 3 mi S on NH 1A. Phone 603/926-3784.

Tuck Memorial Museum. Home of Hampton Historical Society. Antiques, documents, photographs, early postcards, tools and toys; trolley exhibit; memorabilia of Hampton history. Restored one-rm schoolhouse; fire station. (Mid-June-mid-Sept; Tues-Fri & Sun, afternoons; rest of yr, by appt) 40 Park Ave, on Meeting House Green, 4 mi N via NH 1A in Hampton. Phone 603/929-0781. **Free.**

Seasonal Events

Hampton Playhouse. 357 Winnacunet Rd, between Hampton and Hampton Beach, Route 101E. Performances in 200-yr-old modernized ox barn. Nightly exc Mon; matinee Wed, Fri; children's shows Sat. Phone 603/926-3073. Mid-June-Labor Day.

Band concerts. On beach. Evenings. Late June-Labor Day.

Motels

★ ★ **HAMPSHIRE INN.** *(NH 107, Seabrook 03874)* I-95 & NH 107. 603/474-5700; FAX 603/474-2886; res: 800/932-8520. 35 rms, 3 story. June-Oct: S, D $98-$118; suites $158; each addl $10; under 6 free; lower rates rest of yr. Crib $10. TV; cable (premium). Indoor pool; whirlpool. Complimentary continental bkfst. Restaurant nearby. Ck-out 11 am. Coin lndry. Meeting rms. Business servs avail. In-rm modem link. Valet serv. Airport transportation. Exercise equipt. Refrigerators; some in-rm whirlpools. Cr cds: A, D, DS, MC, V.

★ ★ **HAMPTON FALLS INN.** *(11 Lafayette Rd (US 1), Hampton Falls 03844)* W on NH 101, S on US 1. 603/926-9545; FAX 603/926-4155; res: 800/356-1729. 47 rms, 3 story. Mid-June-mid-Oct: S, D $89-$109; each addl $10; suites $129; under 12 free; wkly, wknd, hol rates (2-day min wknds, hols); lower rates rest of yr. Crib free. Pet accepted, some restrictions; $25 refundable. TV; cable, VCR avail. Indoor pool; whirlpool. Complimentary coffee in lobby. Restaurant. Ck-out 11 am. Meeting rms. Business servs avail. Bellhops. Valet serv. Sundries. Health club privileges. Game rm. Refrigerators, microwaves. Balconies. Picnic tables. Cr cds: A, C, D, DS, MC, V.

★ ★ **INN OF HAMPTON.** *(815 Lafayette Rd (US 1), Hampton)* 3 mi N on US 1. 603/926-6771; FAX 603/929-2160; res: 800/423-4561. 71 rms, 2 story. June-early Sept: S, D $105-$125; each addl $10; suites $180; under 12 free; lower rates rest of yr. Crib $10. TV; cable (premium), VCR avail. Indoor pool; whirlpool. Coffee in rms. Restaurant 6:30 am-2 pm, 5-9 pm; Mon to 2 pm; Sun 8 am-noon. Ck-out 11 am. Coin lndry. Meeting rm. Business servs avail. In-rm modem link. Exercise equipt. Refrigerators, microwaves. On 6 acres. Cr cds: A, C, D, DS, MC, V.

★ **REGAL INN.** *162 Ashworth Ave.* 603/926-7758; res: 800/445-6782. 36 rms, 3 story. No elvtr. July-Labor Day: S $85-$95; D $95-$105; kit. suites $129; each addl $8; under 13 free; family rates; lower rates rest yr. Crib $8. TV; cable. Heated pool; whirlpool. Complimentary continental bkfst. Restaurant nearby. Ck-out 11 am. Business servs avail. Game rm. Refrigerators; some in-rm whirlpools. Balconies. Cr cds: A, DS, MC, V.

Hotel

★ ★ **ASHWORTH BY THE SEA.** *295 Ocean Blvd.* 603/926-6762; FAX 603/926-2002; res: 800/345-6736. Web www.ashworth-hotel.com. 105 rms, 4 story. July-Sept: S, D $95-$189; each addl $20; under 18, $5; lower rates rest of yr. Crib $10. TV; cable (premium); VCR avail. Heated pool; poolside serv. Restaurant 6:30 am-11 pm; dining rm 8-11 am (summer), 11:45 am-2:30 pm, 5-10 pm. Bar; entertainment. Ck-out noon. Meeting rms. Business servs avail. In-rm modem link. Gift shop. Beauty shop. Valet parking. Sun deck. Many balconies. Cr cds: A, C, D, DS, MC, V.

Inns

★ ★ **LAMIE'S.** *(490 Lafayette Rd, Hampton)* on US 1 at jct NH 27. 603/926-0330; FAX 603/929-0017; res: 800/850-5050. 32 rms, 2 story, 1 suite. Late June-Labor Day: S $89-$99; D $109; each addl $10; under 17 free; lower rates rest of yr. Crib free. TV; cable (premium). Restaurant (see LAMIE'S TAVERN). Rm serv. Bar 4 pm-midnight; entertainment Fri, Sat (in season). Ck-out noon, ck-in 3 pm. Meeting rms. Business servs avail. Valet serv. Airport transportation. Refrigerators avail. Cr cds: A, C, D, MC, V.

★ ★ ★ **OCEANSIDE HOTEL.** *365 Ocean Blvd.* 603/926-3542. E-mail oceanside@nh.ultranet.com; web www.hamptonbeach.org. 10 rms, 2 story. No rm phones. July-Aug: D $95-$140; each addl $30; wkly rates; lower rates mid-May-June; Sept-mid-Oct. Closed rest of yr. TV; VCR (free movies) in library. Complimentary bkfst. Ck-out 11 am, ck-in 2 pm. Historic building (1880). Antiques; opp ocean beach; swimming, sun decks. Totally nonsmoking. Cr cds: A, DS, MC, V.

Restaurants

★ ★ **LAMIE'S TAVERN.** *(See Lamie's Inn)* 603/926-0330. Specializes in native seafood, prime rib. Hrs: 6:30 am-9 pm; Fri, Sat to 10 pm. Res accepted. Bar. Semi-a la carte: bkfst $1.95-$5.95, lunch $2.95-$8.50, dinner $9.95-$18.95. Child's meals. Entertainment Fri, Sat. Original Hampton homestead (1700s); Colonial decor; fireplace. Cr cds: A, C, D, MC, V.

★ **NEWICK'S FISHERMAN'S LANDING.** *(845 Lafayette Rd, Hampton)* 3 mi N on US 1. 603/926-7646. Specializes in fresh seafood. Hrs: 11:30 am-9 pm. Closed Thanksgiving, Dec 25; Mon, Tues (winter). Serv bar. Semi-a la carte: lunch, dinner $2.95-$18.95. Child's meals. Nautical theme; large ship models, artwork. Cr cds: A, DS, MC, V.

Hanover (F-3)

Settled 1765 **Pop** 9,212 **Elev** 531 ft **Area code** 603 **Zip** 03755
Information Chamber of Commerce, PO Box 5105, 216 Nugget Building; 603/643-3115.

Established four years after the first settlers came here, Dartmouth College is an integral part of Hanover. Named for the Earl of Dartmouth, one of its original supporters, the school was founded by the Rev. Eleazar Wheelock "for the instruction of the youth of Indian tribes . . . and others."

What to See and Do

Dartmouth College (1769). (5,400 students) Main & Wheelock Sts. Phone 603/646-1110. On campus are

Dartmouth Row. Early white brick buildings including Wentworth, Dartmouth, Thornton and Reed halls. Parts of Dartmouth Hall date from 1784. E side of Green.

Baker Memorial Library (white spire). Two million volumes; notable frescoes by the Mexican artist José Clemente Orozco. (Academic yr, daily) Guide service during vacations (Mon-Fri). Wentworth & College Sts.

Hood Museum and Hopkins Center for the Arts. Concert hall, theaters, changing art exhibits. Gallery (daily; free). Performing arts events all yr (fees). Opp S end of Green.

League of New Hampshire Craftsmen. Work by some of New Hampshire's finest craftspeople. (Daily exc Sun; closed major hols) 13 Lebanon St. Phone 603/643-5050.   **Free.**

⭐ **Saint-Gaudens National Historic Site.** Former residence and studio of sculptor Augustus Saint-Gaudens (1848-1907); "Aspet," built ca 1800, was once a tavern. Saint-Gaudens' famous works, *The Puritan*, *Adams Memorial* and *Shaw Memorial*, are among the 100 works on display. Also formal gardens and works by other artists; sculptor-in-residence; interpretive programs. (Memorial Day-Oct, daily) Approx 5 mi S on NH 10, then 12 mi S off NH 12A, in Cornish, across river from Windsor, VT. Contact Superintendent, RR 3, Box 73, Cornish 03745; 603/675-2175.   ¢¢

Skiing.

Dartmouth Skiway. Two double chairlifts; patrol, school; snack bar. Longest run 1 mi; vertical drop 900 ft. (Mid-Dec-Mar, daily) 10 mi N on NH 10 to Lyme, then 3 mi E. Phone 603/795-2143.   ¢¢¢¢¢

Webster Cottage (1780). Residence of Daniel Webster during his last year as a Dartmouth College student; colonial & Shaker furniture, Webster memorabilia. (June-mid-Oct, Wed, Sat & Sun afternoons) 32 N Main St. Phone 603/643-6529.   **Free.**

Motels

⭐ **CHIEFTAIN.** 84 Lyme Rd. 603/643-2550; FAX 603/643-5265; res: 800/845-3557. 22 rms, 2 story. June-Oct: S $74; D $84; each addl $10; lower rates rest of yr. TV. Continental bkfst. Ck-out 11 am. Picnic tables. View of Connecticut River. Cr cds: A, C, D, DS, MC, V.

[icons] SC

✔⭐ **LOCH LYME LODGE.** (70 Orford Rd, Lyme 03768) 11 mi N on NH 10. 603/795-2141; res: 800/423-2141. Web www.dartbook.com. 24 cottages, 12 kits. units, 4 rms in inn, all share bath. No A/C. No rm phones. S, D $42 $00; cottages $420-$725/wk; under 4 free; MAP avail. Cottages closed Sept-May. Crib $6. Pet accepted, some restrictions. Playground. Ck-out 10 am. Tennis privileges. Downhill ski 4 mi; x-country ski 10 mi. Lawn games. Fireplaces; some refrigerators. On Post Pond; swimming beach. Picnic tables, grills. No cr cds accepted.

[icons]

Motor Hotel

⭐⭐⭐ **HANOVER INN AT DARTMOUTH COLLEGE.** *PO Box 151, at Main & Wheelock Sts. 603/643-4300; FAX 603/646-3744; res: 800/443-7024 (exc NH).* E-mail hartson@dartmouth.edu; web www.dartmouth.edu/inn. 92 rms, 5 story, 22 suites. S, D $207-$217; suites $217-$287; ski, golf plans. Crib free. Pet accepted. Covered parking $5; free valet parking. TV; cable, VCR avail. Indoor pool privileges; sauna. Restaurant 7 am-10 pm. Rm serv. Bar 11:30 am-midnight. Ck-out noon. Meeting rms. Business servs avail. Free airport transportation. Bellhops. Valet serv. Gift shop. Lighted tennis privileges, pro. 18-hole golf privileges, greens fee $33, pro, putting green, driving range. Downhill ski 7 mi. Exercise equipt. Health club privileges. Bathrm phones. Georgian-style brick structure owned by college; used as guest house since 1780. Cr cds: A, D, DS, MC, V.

[icons] SC

Inns

⭐⭐ **ALDEN COUNTRY INN.** *(The Common, Lyme 03768) 10 mi N on NH 10 (Lyme Rd), E to The Common. 603/795-2222; FAX 603/795-9436.* 15 rms, 4 story. No elvtr. June-Oct: S $95-$130; D $115-$145; each addl $20; lower rates rest of yr. Complimentary full bkfst. Restaurant 7:30-9:30 am, 5:30-9:30 pm; Sun 5-8 pm. Bar to 9 pm. Ck-out 11 am, ck-in 3 pm. Downhill ski 3 mi; x-country ski 15 mi. Original inn and tavern built 1809; antique furnishings. Cr cds: A, D, DS, MC, V.

[icons] SC

⭐⭐⭐ **DOWD'S COUNTRY INN.** *(On The Common, Lyme 03768) 8 mi N on NH 10. 603/795-4712; res: 800/482-4712; FAX 603/795-4220.* E-mail dowds.inn@valley.net; web gather@dowdsinn.com. rms, 2 story. June-Oct: S $70-$125; D $80-$155; lower rates rest of yr. Crib $10. TV in common rm. Complimentary full bkfst. Ck-out 11 am, ck-in 3 pm. Business servs avail. RR station, bus depot transportation. Downhill ski 2 mi. Built 1780. Totally nonsmoking. Cr cds: D, DS, MC, V.

[icons]

⭐ **MOOSE MOUNTAIN LODGE.** *(PO Box 272, Etna 03750) E Wheelock St to Etna Center to Etna Rd, follow signs. 603/643-3529; FAX 603/643-4119.* E-mail meeze@aol.com. 12 rms, 5 share bath, 2 story. No A/C. No rm phones. Jan-mid-Mar, AP: $85-$90/person; Mid-June-late Oct, Dec 26-late Mar, MAP: $80; family rates. Closed rest of yr. Complimentary coffee in lobby. X-country ski on site. Totally nonsmoking. Cr cds: MC, V.

[icons]

⭐⭐ **WHITE GOOSE.** *(Orford 03777) 15 mi N on I-91, exit 15 to Orford. 603/353-4812; res: 800/358-4267; FAX 603/353-4543.* Web whitegooseinn@connriver.net 5 rms, 2 share bath, 8 A/C. No rm phones. May-Oct: S $75; D $85-$105; lower rates rest of yr. Children over 8 yrs only. TV in lobby. Complimentary full bkfst. Ck-out 11 am, ck-in 2 pm. Main building (1833) attached to original structure (ca 1770). Circular porch. Totally nonsmoking. Cr cds: MC, V.

[icons]

Restaurants

⭐⭐ **JESSE'S.** *Box 665, 1½ mi S on NH 120. 603/643-4111.* Specializes in steak, seafood, Maine lobster. Salad bar. Hrs: 5-10 pm; Fri, Sat to 11 pm; Sun 4:30-9:30 pm. Bar 4:30 pm-midnight. Semi-a la carte: dinner $8.95-$17.95. Child's meals. Outdoor dining. Victorian decor. Open-hearth cooking; mesquite grill. Cr cds: A, MC, V.

✔⭐ **MOLLY'S BALLOON.** *43 Main St. 603/643-2570.* Specializes in burgers, creative sandwiches, pasta. Hrs: 11:30 am-10 pm; Fri, Sat to 11 pm; Sun brunch 10 am-1 pm. Closed Thanksgiving, Dec 25. Bar. Semi-a la carte: lunch $5.95-$8.95, dinner $6.95-$14.95. Sun brunch $5.95-$7.50. Greenhouse-type decor; brass railings, Southwestern motif. Cr cds: A, MC, V.

Holderness (F-5)

(See also Meredith, Plymouth)

Settled 1770 **Pop** 1,694 **Elev** 584 ft **Area code** 603 **Zip** 03245

Holderness is the shopping center and post office for Squam Lake (second-largest lake in the state) and neighboring Little Squam. Fishing, boating, swimming, water sports and winter sports are popular in this area. The movie *On Golden Pond* was filmed here. A Ranger District office of the White Mountain National Forests(see) is located here.

What to See and Do

League of New Hampshire Craftsmen-Sandwich Home Industries. Work by some of New Hampshire's finest craftspeople. (Mid-May-mid-Oct, daily) 12 mi NE via NH 113, on Main St in Center Sandwich. Phone 603/284-6831. **Free.**

Science Center of New Hampshire. A 200-acre wildlife sanctuary with animals in natural enclosures; features bears, deer, bobcat, otter and birds of prey; nature trails; animal presentations. Picnicking. (May-Oct, daily) On NH 113. Phone 603/968-7194. ¢¢¢

Squam Lake Tours. Two-hr boat tours of area where *On Golden Pond* was filmed. (May-Oct, 3 tours daily) ¹/₂ mi S on US 3. Contact PO Box 185; 603/968-7577. ¢¢¢

Inns

★ ★ ★ **GLYNN HOUSE.** *(43 Highland St, Ashland 03217) 4 mi S on US 3.* 603/968-3775; FAX 603/968-3129; res: 800/637-9599. E-mail glynnhse@lr.net; web www.bbonline.com/nh/glynnhouse/. 9 rms, 2 story, 4 suites. No rm phones. S $75-$85; each addl $10; suites $125-$145; wkly rates; hols, wkends (2-day min); higher rates fall foliage. Children over 7 yrs only. TV; VCR (movies). Complimentary full bkfst. Ck-out 11 am, ck-in 3 pm. Luggage handling. Tennis privileges. Downhill ski 17 mi; x-country ski 3 mi. Lawn games. Refrigerators. Picnic tables. Built in 1896; gingerbread wraparound porch. Totally nonsmoking. Cr cds: A, D, DS, MC, V.

★ ★ **INN ON GOLDEN POND.** *Box 680 Rt 3, 4 mi SE of I-93 exit 24, on US 3.* 603/968-7269; FAX 603/968-9226. E-mail innongp@lr.net. 8 rms, 3 story, 1 suite. No rm phones. Mid-May-Nov: S $80; D $115; each addl $30; suite $140; lower rates rest of yr. Children over 12 yrs only. TV in sitting rm; cable. Complimentary full bkfst. Ck-out 11 am, ck-in 3 pm. Gift shop. Downhill ski 17 mi. Game rm. Lawn games. Built 1879; fireplace; rms individually decorated. On 50 wooded acres; hiking trails, nearby lake. Totally nonsmoking. Cr cds: A, MC, V.

★ ★ ★ **THE MANOR ON GOLDEN POND.** *US 3, Shepard Hill, ¹/₂ mi SE on US 3, NH 25.* 603/968-3348; FAX 603/968-2116; res: 800/545-2141. E-mail manorinn@lr.net; web www.manorongoldenpond.com. 17 inn rms, 3 story, 4 rms in carriage house, 4 cottages. S, D $210-$350, cottages $950-$1,725/wk. Serv charge 15%. Children over 12 yrs only. TV; cable, VCR avail (free movies). Pool. Complimentary afternoon refreshments. Restaurant (see MANOR ON GOLDEN POND). Bar 5-11:30 pm. Ck-out 11 am, ck-in 3-6 pm. Meeting rms. Business servs avail. Luggage handling. Valet serv. Concierge serv. Gift shop. Lighted tennis. Downhill ski 18 mi. Lawn games. Some in-rm whirlpools, fireplaces. Some balconies. On lake; canoes, paddleboats, private beach. English country house (1903). Totally nonsmoking. Cr cds: A, MC, V.

Restaurants

✔★ ★ **COMMON MAN.** *(Main St, Ashland) 1 mi E of I-93 exit 24.* 603/968-7030. Specialties: baked stuffed shrimp, lobster bisque, roast prime rib. Hrs: 11:30 am-2 pm, 5:30-9 pm. Closed Thanksgiving, Dec 24,

25. Bar 4-11 pm. Semi-a la carte: lunch $3.50-$7.95, dinner $10.95-$16.95. Child's meals. Antiques; rustic decor. Family-owned. Cr cds: A, DS, MC, V.

★ ★ **CORNER HOUSE INN.** *22 Main St (03227), 12 mi NE on NH 113.* 603/284-6219. Specialties: lobster & mushroom bisque, shellfish sauté. Hrs: 11:30 am-2:30 pm, 5:30-9:30 pm; early-bird dinner 5:30-6:30 pm. Closed Thanksgiving, Dec 25; also Mon Nov-May. Serv bar. Semi-a la carte: lunch $4.50-$11.95, dinner $10.95-$18.95. Victorian-style inn (1849), originally house and attached harness shop; guest rms avail. Totally nonsmoking. Cr cds: A, DS, MC, V.

★ ★ ★ **MANOR ON GOLDEN POND.** *(See The Manor On Golden Pond Inn)* 603/968-3348. Menu changes daily. Hrs: 5:30-8:30 pm. Res required. Bar from 5 pm. Wine list. Prix fixe: dinner $38 & $50. Fireplace. Overlooks Squam Lake, mountains. Totally nonsmoking. Cr cds: A, MC, V.

Jackson (D-5)

(See also Bartlett, North Conway)

Settled 1790 **Pop** 678 **Elev** 971 ft **Area code** 603 **Zip** 03846
Information Mt Washington Valley Chamber of Commerce, N Main St, PO Box 2300, North Conway 03860; 603/356-3171.

At the south end of Pinkham Notch (see), Jackson is a center for skiing and a year-round resort. The Wildcat River rushes over rock formations in the village; Wildcat Mt is to the north. A covered bridge (ca 1870) spans the Ellis River.

What to See and Do

Heritage-New Hampshire. Path winds among theatrical sets and takes visitors on a walk through 30 events during 300 yrs of New Hampshire history. Each set has animation, sounds and smells to re-create the past, from a stormy voyage to the New World to a train ride through autumn foliage in Crawford Notch. (Late May-early Oct, daily) 2 mi S on NH 16 in Glen. Phone 603/383-9776. ¢¢

Skiing.

Black Mt. Triple, double chairlifts, J-bar; patrol, school, rentals; cafeteria; nursery. Longest run 1 mi; vertical drop 1,200 ft. 2¹/₂ mi N on NH 16B. Phone 603/383-4490. ¢¢¢¢¢

Jackson Ski Touring Foundation maintains 95 mi of cross-country trails, connecting inns and ski areas. Instruction, rentals, rescue service. (Dec-mid-Apr, daily; closed Dec 25) Phone 603/383-9355. ¢¢¢

Story Land. Village of storybook settings; Cinderella's castle, Heidi's grandfather's house; themed rides, including raft ride, on 35 acres. (Mid-June-early Sept, daily; early Sept-early Oct, wkends) 2 mi S on NH 16 in Glen. Phone 603/383-4186. ¢¢¢¢¢

White Mountain National Forest (see). N & S on NH 16.

Motels

★ ★ ★ **BEST WESTERN STORYBOOK.** *(Glen 03838) 2 mi S at jct US 302 & NH 16.* 603/383-6800; FAX 603/383-4678. 78 rms, 1-2 story. July-late Oct: S $69-$99; D $89-$119; each addl $8; wkly rates; ski plans; higher rates special events; lower rates rest of yr. Crib $7. TV; cable. 3 pools, 1 indoor; wading pool, whirlpools. Playground. Restaurant 8-10 am, 6-9 pm. Bar from 5 pm. Ck-out 11 am. Coin lndry. Meeting rms. Business servs avail. Bellhops. Gift shop. Tennis. Downhill/x-country ski 3 mi. Exercise equipt; sauna. Game rm. Rec rm. Lawn games. Some refrigerators, microwaves. Private patios, balconies. Picnic tables, grills. Cr cds: A, C, D, DS, MC, V.

★ ★ **LODGE AT JACKSON VILLAGE.** *NH 16. 603/383-0999; FAX 603/383-6104; res: 800/233-5634.* 32 rms, 2 story. S $64-$134; D $69-$139; under 17 free; ski, golf plans; higher rates fall foliage. Crib $10. TV; cable. Pool. Complimentary coffee in lobby. Restaurant nearby. Ck-out 11 am. Coin lndry. Sundries. Tennis. Downhill ski 3 mi; x-country ski on site. Refrigerators. Private patios, balconies. Sitting rm with stone fireplace. On river. Cr cds: A, DS, MC, V.

✅ 🛶 🎿 ⛷ 🏊 🎿 🧺 SC

✔ ★ ★ **RED APPLE INN.** *(NH 302, Glen 03838) 3 mi S & W on US 302. 603/383-9680.* Web www.theredappleinn.com. 16 rms. S, D $39-$125; each addl $10; under 13 free; ski plans. Closed 2 wks Apr & 3 wks Nov. Crib $10. TV; cable. Pool. Playground. Ck-out 11 am. Downhill ski 2 mi; x-country ski 2 mi. Game rm. Some refrigerators, fireplaces. Picnic tables, grills. In wooded area. Cr cds: A, DS, MC, V.

🎿 🏊 🎿 🔥

Inns

★ ★ **CHRISTMAS FARM.** *¼ mi N on NH 16B. 603/383-4313; FAX 603/383-6495; res: 800/443-5837.* 33 rms, 8 A/C, 2 story, 7 cottages. MAP: S $93-$140; D $156-$250; family rates. Serv charge 15%. TV in some rms. Pool; whirlpool, poolside serv. Playground. Afternoon refreshments. Restaurant (see CHRISTMAS FARM INN). Bars from noon. Ck-out 11 am, ck-in after 3 pm. Meeting rm. Business servs avail. Gift shop. Putting green. Golf privileges. Downhill ski 1 mi; x-country ski on site. Sauna. Rec rm. Lawn games. Some in-rm whirlpools. Historic buildings from late 1700s, including town's first church and early jail; rms vary. Cr cds: A, MC, V.

🎿 🏊 ⛷ 🎿 🧺 SC

★ ★ **DANA PLACE.** *NH 16 Pinkham Notch, 5 mi N on NH 16 in Pinkham Notch. 603/383-6822; FAX 603/383-6022; res: 800/537-9276.* E-mail dpi@ncia.net; web www.danaplace.com. 35 rms, 4 share bath, 3 story. S $75-$155; each addl $25; under 18 free; MAP avail; package plans. Crib avail. Pet accepted, some restrictions. TV rm; VCR. Indoor pool; whirlpool. Complimentary bkfst; afternoon refreshments. Restaurant hrs vary. Bar 4-11 pm. Ck-out 11 am, ck-in 3 pm. Business servs avail. Tennis. Downhill ski 5 mi; x-country ski on site. Picnic tables. Historic farm house (1890) situated on 300 wooded acres, bordered by White Mtn National Forest & Ellis River. Cr cds: A, C, D, DS, MC, V.

🛶 🛶 🎿 ⛷ 🏊 🎿 🔥

★ ★ ★ **INN AT THORN HILL.** *Thorn Hill Rd, ¼ mi E of NH 16A. 603/383-4242; FAX 603/383-8062; res: 800/289-8990.* E-mail thornhill@ncia.net; web www.innatthornhill.com. 10 rms in 3-story inn, 6 rms in carriage house, 3 cottages. Some rm phones. MAP: S $95-$145; D $80-$155/person; package plans. Children over 10 yrs only. TV in parlor of main bldg & in cottages; cable. Pool; whirlpool. Dining rm 8-9:30 am, 6-9 pm (public by res). Bar. Ck-out 11 am, ck-in after 3 pm. Business servs avail. Downhill ski 2 mi; x-country ski on site. Lawn games. Some in-rm whirlpools, wet bars, fireplaces. Antique furnishings. Totally nonsmoking. Cr cds: A, D, DS, MC, V.

🛶 ⛷ 🎿 🏊 🎿 🔥 SC

★ ★ **NESTLENOOK FARM.** *Dinsmore Rd. 603/383-9443; res: 800/659-9443.* 7 rms, 2 A/C, 3 story, 2 suites. S, D $145-$275; 2-day min wkends. Children over 12 yrs only. TV in game rm; cable, VCR avail. Heated pool. Complimentary full bkfst; afternoon refreshments. Ck-out 11 am, ck-in 3 pm. Downhill ski 3 mi; x-country ski on site. Ice-skating; sleigh rides. Game rm. Lawn games. Picnic tables. Restored Victorian building, one of oldest in Jackson (1770); antiques, Tiffany lamps, 18th-century parlor stoves. Sitting rm with riverstone fireplace. 65 acres with screened gazebo, animal barn, open-air chapel, apple orchard, gardens and pond. On river. Totally nonsmoking. Cr cds: MC, V.

🛶 ⛷ 🎿 🏊 🎿 🔥

✔ ★ ★ **PRINCE PLACE AT THE BERNERHOF.** *(Glen 03838) 3 mi S on NH 16, then 1½ mi W on US 302. 603/383-4414; FAX 603/383-0809; res: 800/548-8007.* 9 rms, 3 story. S $55-$139; D $69-$139; package plans. Crib avail. TV; cable. Complimentary full bkfst. Restaurant (see PRINCE PLACE AT THE BERNERHOF). Rm serv. Ck-out 10 am, ck-in after 2 pm. Downhill ski 1 mi; x-country ski 4 mi. Some in-rm whirlpools. Victorian-style house (1890) with European accents; sitting rm, antiques. Cr cds: A, DS, MC, V.

🛶 🎿 🎿 🔥 🧺

★ ★ ★ **THE WENTWORTH.** *NH 16A. 603/383-9700; FAX 603/383-4265; res: 800/637-0013.* E-mail wentworth@nxi.com; web thewentworth.com. 60 rms, 2 story. S $135-$235; suites $205-$235 (MAP); under 12 free; package plans; wkly rates; higher rates: hol wks, fall foliage. TV; cable. Pool. Restaurant 7:30-11 am, 6-10 pm. Bar 5 pm-12:30 am; entertainment wkends (in season). Ck-out 11 am. Meeting rms. Bus depot transportation. Tennis. Downhill ski 2 mi; x-country ski on site. Lawn games. Some fireplaces. Private patios. Historic building (1860). View of river, mountains. Cr cds: A, C, D, DS, ER, JCB, MC, V.

✅ 🛶 ⛷ 🎿 🏊 🎿 🔥

Resort

★ ★ **EAGLE MOUNTAIN HOUSE.** *1 mi N on Carter Notch Rd. 603/383-9111; res: 800/966-5779.* 94 rms, 5 story, 30 suites. No A/C. S, D $69-$119; each addl $15; suites $89-$149; under 18 free; wkly rates; ski, golf plans; higher rates fall foliage. Crib avail. TV; cable (premium), VCR avail. Heated pool; whirlpool, poolside serv. Playground. Dining rm 7 am-10 pm. Bar 11:30-12:30 am. Ck-out 11 am. Meeting rms. Business servs avail. Concierge. Lighted tennis. 9-hole golf, greens fee $12-$18. Downhill ski 1 mi; x-country ski on site. Exercise equipt; sauna. Game rm. Rec rm. Lawn games. Spectacular view of mountains and forest. Cr cds: A, C, D, DS, ER, MC, V.

✅ 🛶 🎿 ⛷ 🏊 🏃 🎿 🔥 SC

Restaurants

★ ★ **CHRISTMAS FARM INN.** *(See Christmas Farm Inn) 603/383-4313.* Specialties: vegetable-stuffed chicken breast, veal basilico, shrimp scampi. Own baking. Hrs: 8-9:30 am, 5:30-9 pm; wkend hrs vary. Bar from 4 pm. Semi-a la carte: bkfst $2.45-$4.50, dinner $10.25-$17.25. In historic building (1786). Cr cds: A, MC, V.

★ ★ ★ **PRINCE PLACE AT THE BERNERHOF.** *(See Prince Place At The Bernerhof Inn) 603/383-4414.* Continental menu. Specialties: délices de gruyère, Wienerschnitzel. Own desserts. Hrs: 5:30-9:30 pm; July-Oct from 11:30 am. Res accepted. Wine list. Semi-a la carte: lunch $3.50-$9.95, dinner $13-$22. Child's meals. Parking. Host of "A Taste of the Mountains" cooking school. Cr cds: A, DS, MC, V.

✅ 🍴

★ **RED PARKA PUB.** *(Glen 03838) 3 mi S on US 302. 603/383-4344.* Specializes in barbecued pork spare ribs, prime rib. Salad bar. Hrs: 4:30-10 pm; Sat, Sun from 4 pm. Closed Thanksgiving, Dec 24, 25. Bar 3:30 pm-1 am. Semi-a la carte: dinner $5.95-$18.95. Child's meals. Entertainment wkends. Parking. Outdoor dining. One rm in 1914 railroad car. Cr cds: A, C, D, DS, MC, V.

SC

★ ★ **WILDCAT TAVERN.** *NH 16A, in Jackson Village. 603/383-4245.* Specializes in fresh seafood, veal. Hrs: 7:30-9:30 am, 11:30 am-3 pm, 6-9 pm; Fri, Sat to 10 pm; mid-Apr-mid-June from 6 pm. Bar 3 pm-12:30 am. Semi-a la carte: bkfst $3-$7, lunch $4-$9, dinner $12-$19. Child's meals. Parking. Outdoor dining. In historic inn (1896). Cr cds: A, D, MC, V.

✔ ★ **YESTERDAY'S.** *Main St. 603/383-4457.* Specializes in fresh meats, homemade soups & breads. Hrs: 6:15 am-3 pm. Closed Thanksgiving, Dec 25. Wine, beer. Semi-a la carte: bkfst $1.50-$6.50, lunch $2.25-$6.25. Child's meals. No cr cds accepted.

Jaffrey (J-4)

(See also Keene, Peterborough)

Settled 1760 **Pop** 5,361 **Elev** 1,013 ft **Area code** 603 **Zip** 03452 **E-mail** jaffreycoc@topmonad.net **Web** www.jaffreycoc.org
Information Chamber of Commerce, PO Box 2; 603/532-4549.

Jaffrey, on the eastern slopes of Mt Monadnock, has been a summer resort community since the 1840s.

What to See and Do

Barrett House "Forest Hall" (1800). Federal mansion with a 3rd-floor ballroom. Twelve museum rms contain some of the most important examples of 18th- and 19th-century furniture and antique musical instruments in New England. Extensive grounds with Gothic-revival summer house on terraced hill behind main house. Guided tours. (June-mid-Oct, Thurs-Sun) 10 mi SE on NH 124, then ¼ mi S on NH 123A (Main St) in New Ipswich. Phone 603/878-2517. ¢¢

⭐ **Cathedral of the Pines.** International nondenominational shrine. National memorial for all American war dead; Memorial Bell Tower dedicated to women who died in service. Outdoor altar, gardens, museum. (May-Oct, daily) 3 mi E on NH 124, then 3 mi S, in Rindge. Phone 603/899-3300. **Free.**

Monadnock State Park. Hikers mecca; 40-mi network of well-maintained trails on Mt Monadnock (3,165 ft). Summit views of all New England states. Picnicking, camping. Ski touring (Dec-Mar). Standard fees. 2 mi W on NH 124, then N. Phone 603/532-8862.

Jefferson (C-5)

Settled 1772 **Pop** 965 **Elev** 1,384 ft **Area code** 603 **Zip** 03583 **E-mail** nwmcc@northernwhitemountains.com **Web** www.northernwhitemountains.com
Information Northern White Mt Chamber of Commerce, 164 Main St, PO Box 298, Berlin 03570; 603/752-6060.

On the slopes of Mt Starr King in the White Mountains, this resort area is referred to locally as Jefferson Hill.

What to See and Do

Santa's Village. Santa and tame deer; unique rides; live shows, computerized animation. Playground; picnic area. (Father's Day-Labor Day, daily; after Labor Day-Columbus Day, Sat & Sun) 1 mi NW on US 2, ½ mi W of jct NH 116. Phone 603/586-4445. ¢¢¢¢

Six Gun City. Western frontier village; cowboy skits, frontier show, fort, Native American camp, homestead, carriage and sleigh museum, general store, snack bar; miniature horse show; pony & burro rides; bumper boats, water slides and other rides; miniature golf, games, animals and antiques. (Mid-June-Labor Day, daily; after Labor Day-Columbus Day, Sat & Sun) 4 mi E on US 2. Phone 603/586-4592. ¢¢¢

Annual Event

Lancaster Fair. 6 mi NW in Lancaster. Agricultural exhibits, horse show, entertainment. Labor Day wknd.

Motels

⭐ **EVERGREEN.** *W on US 2, opp Santa's Village. 603/586-4449.* 18 rms. July-Labor Day: S, D $50-$60; each addl $5; higher rates fall foliage; lower rates May-June, after Labor Day-Oct. Closed rest of yr. Crib free. TV; cable. Heated pool. Restaurant 8 am-8 pm; hrs vary off-season.

Ck-out 11 am. Picnic area. Camping, trailer facilities. Cr cds: A, DS, MC, V.

✓⭐ **LANTERN RESORT.** *US 2. 603/586-7151.* 30 rms. S, D $35-$59; each addl $4. Closed Nov-Apr. Crib $3. TV; cable. Pool; whirlpool. Playground. Coffee in lobby. Ck-out 11 am. Coin lndry. Gift shop. Game rm. Lawn games. On wooded grounds. Cr cds: A, D, DS, MC, V.

Inn

⭐ **JEFFERSON INN.** *US 2. 603/586-7998; FAX 603/586-7808; res: 800/729-7908.* E-mail jeffinn@ncia.net; web www.jefferson-inn.com. 11 rms, 3 story, 2 suites. No A/C. Some rm phones. S, D $75-$110; each addl $15; suites $120-$165; ski, golf plans; wkends, hols (2-day min). Crib free. TV in common rm. Complimentary full bkfst. Ck-out 11 am, ck-in 3 pm. Luggage handling. Concierge serv. Business servs avail. 18-hole golf privileges, greens fee $20. Downhill ski 15 mi; x-country ski opp. Lawn games. Some refrigerators. Renovated Victorian house; wraparound porch. Totally nonsmoking. Cr cds: A, DS, MC, V.

Restaurant

⭐⭐ **SEASONINGS.** *1 mi W via US 2. 603/586-7133.* Specializes in seafood, beef, desserts. Hrs: 7 am-9 pm. Res accepted. Semi-a la carte: bkfst $1.95-$4.95, lunch, dinner $2.95-$14.95. Child's meals. Sun rm gives view of mountains. Cr cds: MC, V.

Keene (H-3)

(See also Peterborough)

Settled 1736 **Pop** 22,430 **Elev** 486 ft **Area code** 603 **Zip** 03431 **E-mail** keenechamber@monad.net **Web** www.keenechamber.com
Information Chamber of Commerce, 48 Central Sq; 603/352-1303.

A modern commercial city, Keene is the chief community of the Monadnock region. Its industries manufacture many products including furniture, machinery, textiles and toys.

What to See and Do

Colony Mill Marketplace. Restored 1838 textile mill now transformed into regional marketplace with dozens of specialty shops, an antiques center, numerous dining options and varied entertainment. (daily) 222 West St. Phone 603/357-1240.

Horatio Colony House Museum. Stately Federalist home (1806) of son of prominent Keene mill owners. Features treasures collected from Colony's world travels; books, art, antique furniture. (June-mid-Oct, Tues-Sat; rest of year, Sat) 199 Main St. Phone 603/352-0460. **Free.**

Wyman Tavern (1762). Scene of first meeting of the Dartmouth College trustees in 1770; now furnished in 1820s style. (June-Sept, Thurs-Sat) 339 Main St. Phone 603/352-1895. ¢

Annual Events

The Old Homestead. 4 mi S on NH 32, at Potash Bowl in Swanzey Center. Drama of life in Swanzey during 1880s based on the Biblical story of the Prodigal Son; first presented in 1886. For schedule phone 603/352-0697. Mid-July.

Cheshire Fair. Fairgrounds, S on NH 12 in North Swanzey. Exhibits; horse and ox pulling contests; entertainment. Phone 603/357-4740. 1st wk Aug.

Motel

★ ★ **BEST WESTERN SOVEREIGN HOTEL.** *401 Winchester St. 603/357-3038; FAX 603/357-4776.* 131 rms, 2 story. S, D $55-$115; each addl $10; studio rms $90; under 18 free. Crib free. Pet accepted. TV; cable. Indoor pool. Complimentary full bkfst. Coffee in rms. Restaurant 6:30 am-10 pm. Bar 3 pm-12:30 am; entertainment. Ck-out noon. Meeting rms. Business servs avail. In-rm modem link. Game rm. Balconies. Picnic tables. Cr cds: A, C, D, DS, ER, JCB, MC, V.

D ⚓ ≈ ⊠ 🔥 SC

Inn

★ ★ ★ **CHESTERFIELD.** *HCR 10, Box 59 West Chesterfield (03466), 12 mi W on NH 9. 603/256-3211; FAX 603/256-6131; res: 800/365-5515.* 15 rms, 2 story. S, D $125-$200; each addl $15; higher rates fall foliage. Pet accepted. TV; cable. Complimentary full bkfst. Dining rm 5:30-9 pm. Ck-out 11 am, ck-in 2 pm. Business servs avail. In-rm modem link. Refrigerators; some fireplaces. Some balconies. In renovated farmhouse and barn (1787). Overlooks Green Mts and Connecticut River. Cr cds: A, D, DS, MC, V.

⚓ ⊠ 🔥 SC

Restaurants

★ ★ **176 MAIN.** *176 Main St. 603/357-3100.* E-mail ossm@176main.com; web www.176main.com. Specializes in Mexican, Italian and seafood dishes. Hrs: 11:30 am-11 pm; Fri to midnight; Sat 11 am-midnight; Sun 11 am-10 pm. Closed some major hols. Bar. Semi-a la carte: lunch $4.95-$6.95, dinner $9.95-$16.95. Child's meals. Outdoor dining. Rustic decor; exposed beams. Local artwork. Cr cds: A, D, DS, MC, V.

D

✔★ **THE PUB.** *Winchester & Ralston Sts. 603/352-3135.* Continental menu. Specializes in lamb, seafood, prime rib. Hrs: 7 am-10:30 pm. Res accepted. Bar 11 am-11 pm. Semi-a la carte: bkfst $1.25-$3.95, lunch $3.95-$6.95, dinner $5.95-$12.95. Child's meals. Family-owned. Cr cds: A, C, D, DS, MC, V.

D SC ⊡

Laconia (F-5)

(See also Franklin, Meredith, Wolfeboro)

Settled 1777 **Pop** 15,743 **Elev** 570 ft **Area code** 603 **Zip** 03246
Information Chamber of Commerce, 11 Veterans Sq; 603/524-5531.

On four lakes (Winnisquam, Opechee, Pauqus Bay and Winnipesaukee), Laconia is the commercial center of the area known as the "Lakes Region." Besides the resort trade, it has more than a score of factories whose products include knitting machinery, hosiery, knitted fabrics, ball bearings and electronic components. The headquarters of the White Mountain National Forest (see) is also located here.

What to See and Do

Cruises on Lake Winnipesaukee.

Queen of Winnipesaukee. This 46-ft sloop sails from M/S *Mount Washington* dock in Weirs Beach. 1 1/2-hr cruises (July-Labor Day, daily; mid-May-June & early Sept-early Oct, wkends). Two-hr evening, moonlight cruises (July-Aug, Tues-Sat). For reservations phone 603/366-5531. ¢¢¢¢¢

M/S *Mount Washington.* Leaves Weirs Beach and Wolfeboro on 3 1/4-hr cruises with stops at Center Harbor or Alton Bay. (Mid-May-late Oct, daily) US Mail boat leaves Weirs Beach on 2-hr cruises (mid-June-

mid-Sept). Moonlight Cruises, dinner and dancing (July-Labor Day, Tues-Sat evenings). Theme cruises (selected dates, June-Oct). Phone 603/366-5531. ¢¢¢¢¢

Gunstock Recreation Area. A 2,400-acre county-operated park. 7 mi E on NH 11A in Gilford. Phone 603/293-4345 or 800/GUNSTOCK.

Summer. Picnic and camp sites (Memorial Day wkend-Columbus Day wkend; fee; hookups addl; includes swimming privileges; fireplaces; stocked pond, blazed trails, playground; special events.

Winter. Skiing. Five chairlifts, 2 handle tows; patrol, school, rentals; snowmaking; cafeteria, lounge; nursery. Longest run 2 mi; vertical drop 1,400 ft. Cross-country trails. (Nov-Mar, daily; closed Dec 25) ¢¢¢¢¢

Recreation. The Weirs. Swimming, boating, fishing, sailing, waterskiing. Endicott Memorial Stone with initials of 1652 explorers, S end of beach. (Mid-June-Labor Day, daily) 5 mi N on US 3 at Weirs Beach on Lake Winnipesaukee. Phone 603/524-5046. Parking ¢¢

Surf Coaster. Family water park with wave pool, water slides, "Crazy River" inner tube ride, "Boomerang" rides inside translucent glass tubes; raft rentals, sun decks, showers, children's play areas. Snack bar. (Mid-June-Labor Day, daily; Memorial Day-mid-June, wkends) 6 mi N on US 3, then E on NH 11B, in Weirs Beach. Phone 603/366-4991. ¢¢¢¢¢

Winnipesaukee Railroad. Scenic train rides along Lake Winnipesaukee; can board in Weirs Beach or Meredith (see).

Seasonal Event

New Hampshire Music Festival. Gilford Middle High School, 5 mi E in Gilford. Symphony/pop concerts. Contact 88 Belknap Mt Rd, Gilford, 03246. Phone 603/524-1000. Fri, July-Aug.

Motels

★ ★ **B. MAE'S RESORT INN & SUITES.** *(17 Harris Shore Rd, Gilford) 6 mi E on NH 11 at jct NH 11B; 14 mi E of I-93 exit 20. 603/293-7526; FAX 603/293-4340; res: 800/458-3877.* E-mail bmaes@bmaesresort.com; web www.bmaesresort.com. 82 rms, 2 story. S, D $78-$116; each addl $12; suites $125-$165; under 12 free; ski plan. Crib free. TV; cable, VCR avail (movies). 2 pools, 1 indoor; whirlpool. Complimentary coffee in lobby. Restaurant 7-11 am, 5-10 pm; Sat 7-11 am, 5-10 pm; Sun 7-11 am, 4-9 pm. Bar from 4 pm. Ck-out 11 am. Meeting rm. Business servs avail. Sundries. Downhill/x-country ski 4 mi. Exercise equipt. Game rm. Private patios, balconies. Cr cds: A, C, D, DS, MC, V.

D ⚓ ≈ ⊠ ⊠ 🔥 SC

★ **BARTON'S.** *1330 Union Ave (NH 107N). 603/524-5674.* 37 rms, 4 kit. cottages. Some rm phones. Mid-June-mid-Sept: S, D $80-$90; each addl $7-$15; kit. units, cottages $145-$150; lower rates rest of yr. Crib free. TV; cable. Heated pool. Restaurant adj 6 am-10 pm. Ck-out 11 am. On lake; row boats; dockage, private beach. Cr cds: A, MC, V.

≈ 🔥

★ ★ **BELKNAP POINT.** *(107 Belknap Point Rd, Gilford) 5 mi E on NH 11. 603/293-7511; FAX 603/528-3552.* E-mail hblinn@bpmotel.com; web www.bpmotel.com. 16 rms, 1-2 story, 8 kits. Late June-Labor Day: S, D, kit. units (3-day min for kits.) $78-$98; each addl $10; suites $98-$108; lower rates rest of yr. Crib free. TV; cable. Restaurant nearby. Ck-out 10 am. Private patios, balconies. Picnic tables, grill. On lake; boat rentals; dockage; private beach. Cr cds: A, DS, MC, V.

⚓ 🔥

✔★ **BIRCH KNOLL.** *867 Weirs Blvd (03247). 603/366-4958.* E-mail birchknl@worldpath.net. 24 rms, 1-2 story. Late June-Labor Day: S, D $65-$89; each addl $8; higher rates special events; lower rates rest of yr. Closed Nov-Mar. Crib $6. TV; cable. Pool. Complimentary coffee. Ck-out 11 am. Business servs avail. Exercise equipt. Rec rm. Some refrigerators avail. Opp beach, boating & canoeing. Picnic tables, grill. Cr cds: A, DS, MC, V.

⚓ ≈ ⊠ 🔥 SC

✔★ **LORD HAMPSHIRE.** *(885 Laconia Rd, Winnisquam 03289)* I-93, exit 20, 4 mi NE on US 3/NH 11. 603/524-4331; FAX 603/524-8266. 8 rms, 12 kit. cottages. July-Labor Day: S $55-$75; D $70-$125; each addl $15; kit. units (2-day min) $12 addl; 1-2 bedrm cottages for 2-6 persons, $525-$1035/wk; family rates; lower rates Apr-June & after Labor Day-early Nov. Closed rest of yr. Crib $3. TV; cable. Ck-out 11 am; cottages 10:30 am. Business servs avail. Lawn games. Boat rentals. Some fireplaces. Picnic tables, grills. Some cottages with screened porches. On lake; private beach, sun deck. Cr cds: A, MC, V.

★★ **ST MORITZ TERRACE MOTEL & CHALET RESORT.** *937 Weirs Blvd, 5½ mi N on US 3.* 603/366-4482. 12 rms, 2 kits. (showers only, no ovens), 6 kit. chalets (no ovens). Mid-June-Labor Day: S, D $65-$70; suites $90-$115; chalets for 2-4 persons $600-$700/wk; lower rates mid-May-mid-June & after Labor Day-mid-Oct. Closed rest of yr. TV; cable. Pool. Restaurant nearby. Ck-out 10:30 am. Lawn games. Refrigerators. Private patios. Picnic tables, grills. Overlooks lake; private beach, dock opp. Cr cds: MC, V.

Inn

★★ **FERRY POINT HOUSE.** *(100 Lower Bay Rd, Sanbornton 03269)* I-93 exit 20, 4½ mi E on US 3/NH11. 603/524-0087; FAX 603/524-0959. E-mail ferrypt@together.net; web www.tiac.net/users/berg. 7 rms, 2 story. No A/C. No rm phones. May-Oct: S, D $85-$110; each addl $20. Closed rest of yr. TV in sitting rm, VCR (free movies). Complimentary full bkfst; afternoon refreshments. Ck-out 11 am, ck-in 2 pm. Swimming beach; boats. Early 19th-century Victorian summer home on Lake Winnisquam. Totally nonsmoking. No cr cds accepted.

Restaurant

★★ **HICKORY STICK FARM.** *(60 Bean Hill Rd, Belmont 03220)* I-93, exit 20, 5 mi E on US 3/NH 11, Union Rd 2 mi, follow signs. 603/524-3333. Web www.hickorystickfarm.com. Specializes in roast duckling. Own baking. Hrs: 5-9 pm; Sun from noon; winter hrs vary. Closed Mon. Res accepted. Serv bar. Semi-a la carte: dinner $12.95-$21.95. Outdoor dining. Converted colonial farmhouse, barn. Gift shop. Guest rms avail. Family-owned. Totally nonsmoking. Cr cds: A, DS, MC, V.

D

Lincoln/North Woodstock Area *(E-4)*

Pop Lincoln, 1,229; North Woodstock, 600 (est) **Elev** Lincoln, 811 ft; North Woodstock, 738 ft **Area code** 603 **Zip** Lincoln, 03251; North Woodstock, 03262 **E-mail** info@linwoodcc.org **Web** www.linwoodcc.org

Information Chamber of Commerce, NH 112, PO Box 358MO, Lincoln; 603/745-6621 or 800/227-4191.

In a spectacular mountain setting, the villages of Lincoln and Woodstock lie at the junction of the road through Franconia Notch State Park (see) and the scenic Kancamagus Scenic Byway (NH 112).

What to See and Do

Clark's Trading Post. Entertainment park has trained New Hampshire black bears, haunted house, replica of 1884 firehouse; 30-min ride on White Mt Central RR. Museum features early Americana, photo parlor, maple cabin, nickelodeons, ice cream parlor. Bumper boats. (July-Labor Day, daily; Memorial Day-June & early Sept-Columbus Day, wkends) 1 mi N of North Woodstock on US 3. Phone 603/745-8913. ¢¢¢

Franconia Notch State Park (see). 2 mi N on US 3.

Hobo Railroad. Fifteen-mi scenic excursions along the Pemigewasset River. Features restored Pullman Dome dining car. (Daily) Railroad St, off Main. Phone 603/745-2135. ¢¢¢

Lost River Gorge. Natural boulder caves, largest known granite pothole in eastern US; Paradise Falls; boardwalks with 1,900-ft glacial gorge; nature garden with 300 varieties of native shrubs and flowers; geology exhibits; cafeteria, picnicking. (Mid-May-mid-Oct, daily) Appropriate outdoor clothing recommended. 6 mi W of North Woodstock on NH 112, Kinsman Notch. Phone 603/745-8031. ¢¢¢

Skiing. Loon Mt Recreation Area. 7,100-ft gondola, 2 triple, 4 double chairlifts, 1 high-speed quad chairlift, pony lift; patrol, school, rentals, shops, snowmaking; restaurant, cafeterias, bar; nursery; lodge (see LODGE). Longest run 2½ mi; vertical drop 2,100 ft. (Late Nov-mid-Apr, daily) Cross-country trails (Dec-Mar). **Summer activities** include: mountain biking (rentals), bike tours, in-line skating, horseback riding, archery, wildlife theater. Gondola also operates Memorial Day-mid-Oct (daily). (See ANNUAL EVENT) 3 mi E of Lincoln off NH 112 (Kancamagus Hwy). Phone 603/745-8111. ¢¢¢¢¢ ; Summer ¢¢¢¢

Whale's Tale Water Park. Wave pool, water slides, "lazy river," children's activity pool; playground; concession, gift shop. (Mid-June-Labor Day, daily; Memorial Day-mid-June, Sat & Sun) N on I-93, exit 33, then N on US 3. Phone 603/745-8810. ¢¢¢¢¢

White Mt Natl Forest (see).

Annual Event

New Hampshire Highland Games. Loon Mt. Largest Scottish gathering in Eastern US. Bands, competitions, concerts, workshops. Phone 800/358-SCOT. 3 days Sept.

Motels

★★ **BEACON.** *(US 3, Lincoln 03251)* N on US 3. 603/745-8118; FAX 603/745-3783; res: 800/258-8934. 132 rms, 1-2 story, 26 suites, 24 cottages, 47 kits. July-mid-Oct, ski season & hol wkends (3-day min): S, D $65-$150; each addl $10; suites $150; cottages for 2-6, $65-$125; package plans; lower rates rest of yr. Crib $4. TV; cable. 4 pools, 2 indoor; wading pool, whirlpools, saunas. Restaurant 7:30-10:30 am, 5-8:30 pm; summer, wkends & hols to 9 pm. Bar from 5 pm; entertainment. Ck-out 11 am; cottages 10 am. Coin lndry. Meeting rm. Gift shop. Indoor tennis. Downhill ski 4 mi. Game rm. Lawn games. In-rm whirlpool, fireplace in suites. Screened porch on many cottages. Cr cds: A, DS, MC, V.

★★ **DRUMMER BOY.** *(US 3, Lincoln 03251)* 3 mi N on US 3 at I-93 exit 33. 603/745-3661; FAX 603/745-9829; res: 800/762-7275 (exc NH). 53 rms, 8 kits., 2 kit. cottages. May-Oct: D $70-$160; each addl $5; kit. units $10 addl; suites, kit. cottages for 2-4, $70-$110; 4-bedrm house $250; ski plan; lower rates rest of yr. Crib $5. TV; cable, VCR avail. 2 heated pools, 1 indoor; whirlpool, sauna. Playground. Complimentary continental bkfst (in season). Restaurant nearby. Ck-out 11 am. Coin lndry. Meeting rm. Sundries. Downhill/x-country ski 3 mi. Game rm. Some refrigerators, in-rm whirlpools. Patios, balconies. Picnic tables, grill. Cr cds: A, DS, MC, V.

D SC

★★ **INDIAN HEAD RESORT.** *(US 3, Lincoln 03251)* ½ mi N on US 3 at I-93 exit 33. 603/745-8000; FAX 603/745-8414; res: 800/343-8000. E-mail info@indianheadresort.com; web www.indianheadresort.com. 98 rms, 2 story. S, D $99-$129; each addl $10; under 12 free; ski plans; higher rates hol wkends. Crib free. TV; cable (premium). 2 pools, 1 indoor; whirlpools, sauna. Restaurant 7 am-9 pm. Bar noon-1 am. Ck-out 11 am. Coin lndry. Meeting rms. Sundries. Gift shop. Lighted tennis. Downhill/x-country ski 5 mi. Game rm. Rec rm. Lawn games. Refrigerators; some in-rm whirlpools. Private patios, balconies. Stocked pond. View of mountains. Cr cds: A, C, D, DS, MC, V.

D

✔★ ★ **KANCAMAGUS MOTOR LODGE.** (*Kancamagus Hwy, Lincoln 03251*) *1 mi E on NH 112 at I-93 exit 32.* 603/745-3365; FAX 603/745-6691; res: 800/346-4205. 34 rms, 2 story. Late June-mid-Oct, hol ski wks & wkends: S, D $64-$74; each addl $5-$10; under 12, $2; package plans; lower rates rest of yr. Crib free. TV; cable. Heated pool. Restaurant 7-11 am. Ck-out 11 am. Coin lndry. Downhill/x-country ski 2 mi. Lawn games. In-rm steam baths. Balconies. Cr cds: DS, MC, V.

✔★ **MOUNT COOLIDGE.** (*US 3, North Woodstock 03262*) *3 mi N on US 3, ¼ mi N of I-93 exit 33.* 603/745-8052. 18 rms. July-Nov: S $36-$62; D $42-$72; each addl $5; lower rates Apr-June. Closed rest of yr. Crib free. TV; cable. Heated pool. Restaurant adj 7:30 am-8:30 pm; closed mid-Oct-mid-May. Ck-out 11 am. On mountain stream. Cr cds: A, DS, MC, V.

★ **RED DOORS.** (*US 3, Lincoln 03251*) 603/745-2267; FAX 603/745-3647; res: 800/527-7596. E-mail englers@aol.com; web www.nettx.com/reddrs.htm. 30 rms. May-Oct, hol ski wks & wkends: S, D $63-$76; each addl $5; under 18 free; lower rates rest of yr. Crib $5. TV; cable (premium). Heated pool. Playground. Complimentary coffee in rms. Restaurant opp 7:30 am-8:30 pm; closed mid-Oct-mid-June. Ck-out 10 am. Coin lndry. Downhill/x-country ski 5 mi. Game rm. Lawn games. Picnic tables, grills. Cr cds: A, DS, MC, V.

★ ★ **WOODWARD'S MOTOR INN.** (*US 3, Lincoln 03251*) *1 mi N of I-93 exit 33.* 603/745-8141; FAX 603/745-3408; res: 800/635-8968. Web www.nettx.com/woodwards. 80 rms, 1-2 story. S, D $60-$109; each addl $5; 2-bedrm cottages for 3-6, $100-$140; MAP avail; ski plan. Crib free. TV; cable. 2 pools, 1 indoor; whirlpool. Playground. Restaurant 7:30-10:30 am, 5-8:30 pm. Bar from 4 pm. Ck-out 11 am. Coin lndry. Meeting rm. Tennis. Downhill ski 5 mi. Sauna. Game rm. Lawn games. Refrigerators. Some balconies. Duck pond. On mountain stream. Cr cds: A, C, D, DS, MC, V.

Lodge

★ ★ **MOUNTAIN CLUB ON LOON.** (*, Lincoln 03251*) *3 mi E of I-93 exit 32, on NH 112 (Kancamagus Hwy).* 603/745-2244; FAX 603/745-2317; res: 800/229-STAY. 234 rms, 4-6 story, 117 kit. suites. Dec-mid-Apr: S, D $109-$190; each addl $20; kit. suites $169-$399; ski plans; lower rates rest of yr. Crib free. TV; cable. 2 pools, 1 indoor; whirlpool. Supervised child's activities (July-Aug); ages 5-12. Dining rm 7:30-10:30 am, 11:30 am-2 pm, 5:30-9 pm. Bar; entertainment Tues-Sat (ski season). Ck-out 11 am. Coin lndry. Meeting rms. Bellhops (ski season). Concierge. Tennis. Downhill/x-country ski on site. Exercise equipt; sauna. Game rm. Rec rm. Some in-rm whirlpools. Balconies. Picnic tables. Nature trail. Cr cds: A, DS, MC, V.

Motor Hotel

★ ★ **MILL HOUSE INN.** (*Kancamagus Hwy, Lincoln 03251*) *1 mi E of I-93 exit 32.* 603/745-6261; FAX 603/745-6896; res: 800/654-6183. E-mail info@millatloon.com; web www.millatloon.com. 96 rms, 4 story. Late June-mid-Oct: S, D $89-$99; suites $99-$160; under 17 free; ski, golf plans; lower rates rest of yr. TV; cable. VCR avail. 2 pools, 1 indoor; whirlpools. Restaurant 7 am-10 pm. Ck-out 11 am. Meeting rms. Shopping arcade. Downhill ski 2 mi. Exercise equipt; sauna. Private patios, balconies. Cr cds: A, D, DS, MC, V.

Inns

✔★ **WILDERNESS.** (*US 3, North Woodstock 03262*) *I-93 exit 32.* 603/745-3890; res: 800/200-9453. E-mail wildernessinn@juno.com; web www.musar.com/wildernessinn/. 7 rms in house, 2 share bath, 3 with shower only, 2 story, 1 cottage. No rm phones. S $40-$80; D $45-$105; each addl $10; under 6 free; ski plan; higher rates: hols (2-day min), fall foliage. Crib free. TV in sitting rm; cable. Complimentary full bkfst; afternoon refreshments. Restaurant nearby. Rm serv. Ck-out 11 am, ck-in 3 pm. Downhill/x-country ski 3 mi. Croquet. Built 1912; view of Lost River & mountains. Totally nonsmoking. Cr cds: A, MC, V.

✔★ ★ **WOODSTOCK.** (*Main St, North Woodstock 03262*) *N on US 3.* 603/745-3951; FAX 603/745-3701; res: 800/321-3985. 19 rms, 11 with bath, 8 share bath, 3 story. June-Oct: S $35-$125; D $45-$135; under 12 free (up to 2), each addl child $8; MAP avail; ski packages; higher rates: fall foliage, some wkends; lower rates rest of yr. TV; cable, VCR avail. Complimentary full bkfst. Dining rm 7 am-10 pm (also see WOODSTOCK INN). Bar 11:30 am-midnight. Ck-out 11 am, ck-in 2 pm. Gift shop. Downhill/x-country ski 3 mi. Some in-rm whirlpools, refrigerators, gas fireplaces. Balconies. Victorian house (1890); antique furnishings. Some rms with view of river. Cr cds: A, DS, MC, V.

Resort

★ ★ **JACK O'LANTERN.** (*US 3, Woodstock 03293*) *5½ mi S on US 3, just W of I-93 exit 30.* 603/745-8121; FAX 603/745-8197; res: 800/227-4454 (exc NH). 23 motel rms, 30 cottages (1-3 bedrm), 20 condos. Mid-May-mid-Oct: S, D $66-$110; cottages $64-$108; condos (all-yr) $136-$220; under 12 free; MAP avail in season; golf packages. Closed rest of yr. Crib $12. TV; cable, VCR avail. 2 pools, 1 indoor; wading pool, whirlpool, sauna, poolside serv in summer. Playground. Dining rm 7:30-11 am, 5:30-9 pm. Bar in season. Ck-out 11 am, ck-in 3 pm. Grocery 2 mi. Package store 4 mi. Gift shop. Tennis. 18-hole golf. Swimming beach. Lawn games. Entertainment. Game rm. Rec rm. 300 wooded acres on Pemigewasset River. Cr cds: A, DS, MC, V.

Restaurants

★ ★ **COMMON MAN.** (*Pollard Rd, Ashland 03217*) *1 mi E of I-93 exit 32.* 603/745-3463. Specializes in prime rib, fresh seafood, pasta. Hrs: 5-9 pm. Closed Dec 24, 25. Bar. Semi-a la carte: dinner $9.95-$16.95. Child's meals. Parking. Converted farmhouse; one of oldest structures in city. Rustic decor; fireplace, antiques. Cr cds: A, DS, MC, V.

★ ★ **GORDI'S FISH AND STEAK HOUSE.** (*Kancamagus Hwy, Lincoln 03251*) *at The Depot.* 603/745-6635. Specializes in Maine lobster, prime rib, seafood. Salad bar. Hrs: 5-9 pm; Fri, Sat 4:30-9:30 pm; June-Oct noon-9 pm. Closed Thanksgiving, Dec 25. Res accepted. Bar. Semi-a la carte: lunch $4-$8, dinner $6.95-$18.95. Child's meals. Parking. Contemporary building with Victorian accents. Olympic ski motif. Cr cds: A, DS, MC, V.

★ ★ **GOVONI'S.** (*Lost River Rd (NH 112), North Woodstock 03262*) 603/745-8042. Italian menu. Specialties: scallop-stuffed scampi, veal parmigiana, homemade desserts. Hrs: 4:30-9 pm. Closed Labor Day-Memorial Day; also Mon-Wed in June. Bar. Semi-a la carte: dinner $6.95-$15.95. Child's meals. Parking. White clapboard building, formerly a schoolhouse, constructed over mountain stream. Cr cds: MC, V.

★ ★ **TAVERN AT THE MILL.** (*Main St, Lincoln 03251*) *At Millfront Marketplace.* 603/745-6635. Specializes in seafood, steak. Hrs: 5-9 pm; Sun from 11:30 am; Fri to 10 pm; Sat 11:30 am-10 pm. Bar to 1 am. Semi-a la carte: lunch, dinner $10-$19. Outdoor dining. Entertainment wkends. Converted mill drying shed (1926). Cr cds: A, DS, MC, V.

✔★ **TRUANTS TAVERNE.** (*96 Main St, North Woodstock 03262*) *at jct US 3 & NH 112.* 603/745-2239. Specializes in seafood, steak. Hrs: 11:30 am-10 pm; Fri, Sat to 11 pm. Closed Thanksgiving, Dec 25. Bar. Semi-a la carte: lunch $4.95-$10.25, dinner $4.95-$15.50. Child's meals. Parking. Rustic decor with old schoolhouse motif. Cr cds: A, DS, MC, V.

★ ★ **WOODSTOCK INN.** *(See Woodstock Inn)* 603/745-3951. Specializes in seafood, veal. Hrs: 7-11:30 am, 5:30-9:30 pm; Sun 7 am-1 pm; 5:30-9:30 pm. Closed Dec 25. Res accepted. Bar 11:30 am-midnight. Semi-a la carte: bkfst $2.50-$8.50, dinner $12-$24. Child's meals. Entertainment wkends in season. In Victorian house (1890). Cr cds: A, DS, MC, V.

Littleton (D-4)

(See also Franconia)

Chartered 1784 **Pop** 5,827 **Elev** 822 ft **Area code** 603 **Zip** 03561 **E-mail** chamber@moose.ncia.net **Web** www.littletonareachamber.com

Information Chamber of Commerce, 120 Main St, PO Box 105; 603/444-6561 or 888/822-2687.

Littleton is a resort area a few miles northwest of the White Mountain National Forests(see), which maintains a Ranger District office in nearby Bethlehem. Littleton is also a regional commercial center; its industries produce abrasives and electrical component parts. The Ammonoosuc River falls 235 feet on its way through the community.

What to See and Do

Littleton Historical Museum. Photographs, arts and crafts, stereographs, local memorabilia. (July-Sept, Wed, Sat afternoons; rest of yr, Wed afternoons) 2 Union St. Phone 603/444-6586 or 603/444-2637. **Free.**

Samuel C. Moore Station. Largest conventional hydroelectric plant in New England; 2,920-ft dam across Connecticut River forms Moore Reservoir, which extends nearly 11 mi and covers an area of 3,490 acres. Visitor center has exhibits (daily). Recreation areas offer hunting, fishing, boat launching, waterskiing, picnicking and nature studies. (Memorial Day-Columbus Day, daily) 8 mi W on NH 18, 135. Phone 603/638-2327. **Free.**

Motel

✔★ ★ **EASTGATE MOTOR INN.** *335 Cottage St, I-93 exit 41.* 603/444-3971. Web www.eastgatemotorinn.com. 55 rms. S $44-$64; D $50-$70; each addl $7; under 6 free. Pet accepted. TV; cable (premium). Heated pool; wading pool. Playground. Complimentary continental bkfst. Restaurant (see EASTGATE). Bar. Ck-out 11 am. Meeting rms. Business servs avail. Downhill ski 7 mi; x-country ski 6 mi. Lawn games. Cr cds: A, C, D, DS, MC, V.

Inns

★ ★ ★ **ADAIR.** *(80 Guider Ln, Bethlehem 03574)* I-93 exit 40, at US 302. 603/444-2600; FAX 603/444-4823; 800 888/444-2600. E-mail adair@connriver.net; web www.adairinn.com. 8 rms, some A/C, 3 story, 1 suite. No rm phones. S, D $135-$220; each addl $28. TV in lounge; VCR. Complimentary full bkfst; afternoon refreshments. Dining rm 5:30-9 pm. Ck-out 11 am, ck-in 3 pm. Luggage handling. Tennis. Downhill ski 5 mi; x-country ski 2 blks. Billiards. Some gas fireplaces. Built 1927. 200 landscaped acres designed by Olmsted Brothers. Totally nonsmoking. Cr cds: A, MC, V.

★ **MULBURN INN AT BETHLEHEM.** *(2370 Main St, Bethlehem 03574)* 6 mi E on US 302. 603/869-3389; res: 800/457-9440. Web www.mulburninn.com. 7 rms, 2 story. No A/C. No rm phones. S, D $70-$97; each addl $10; wkly rates; ski, golf plans; higher rates fall foliage. Closed Dec 24, 25. Crib $10. TV in lobby. Playground. Complimentary full bkfst. Restaurant nearby. Ck-out 10 am, ck-in 3 pm. Downhill/x-country ski 10 mi. Exercise equipt. Lawn games. Built 1913 by F.W. Woolworth as

summer home. Antiques. Sitting rm. Totally nonsmoking. Cr cds: A, MC, V.

✔★ ★ **THAYERS.** *111 Main St.* 603/444-6469; res: 800/634-8179. E-mail don@thayersinn.com; web thayersinn.com. 40 rms, 24 with bath, 4 story, 6 suites (2-bedrm). No elvtr. Some rm phones. S, D $39-$89; suites $69-$89; under 6 free; ski, spring break plans. Crib free. TV; cable (premium). Pool privileges. Ck-out 11 am, ck-in 2 pm. Downhill/x-country ski 10 mi. Some refrigerators. Historic inn (1843); antiques, library, sitting rm. Cupola open to public. Cr cds: A, C, D, DS, MC, V.

★ ★ **WAYSIDE.** *(US 302 at Pierce Bridge, Bethlehem 03574)* 6 mi SE on US 302. 603/869-3364; FAX 603/869-5769; res: 800/448-9557. Web www.waysideinn.com. 14 rms in inn, 2 story; 12 rms in motel, 2 story. Mid-May-late Oct, Dec-late Mar: S $58; D $68-$78; each addl $5; under 12 free; MAP avail; golf, ski plans; lower rates rest of yr. Crib avail. TV in motel rms; living rm of inn; cable. Dining rm 7:30-9:30 am, 6-9 pm. Bar. Ck-out 11 am, ck-in 3 pm. Tennis. 18-hole golf privileges. Downhill ski 8 mi; x-country ski on site. Lawn games. Some in-rm whirlpools, refrigerators. Balconies in motel. Originally four-rm homestead (1825) for the family of President Franklin Pierce. On Ammonoosuc River; natural sand beach. Cr cds: A, DS, MC, V.

Restaurants

★ ★ **CLAM SHELL.** US 302. 603/444-6445. Specializes in fresh seafood, prime rib. Salad bar. Own desserts. Hrs: 11:30 am-4 pm, 5-9:30 pm; Fri, Sat to 10 pm; Sun noon-9 pm. Closed Dec 24 (eve), 25. Bar to midnight. Semi-a la carte: lunch $4-$8.50, dinner $6.95-$15.95. Child's meals. Cr cds: A, DS, MC, V.

★ **EASTGATE.** *(See Eastgate Motor Inn Motel)* 603/444-3971. Web www.eastgatemotorinn.com. Continental menu. Specializes in seafood, chicken, prime rib au jus. Hrs: 5-9 pm; Fri, Sat to 9:30 pm. Closed Dec 24. Res accepted. Bar to midnight. Semi-a la carte: dinner $5.95-$15.95. Gazebo with fountain; view of Mt Eustis. Cr cds: A, C, D, DS, MC, V.

✔★ ★ **ITALIAN OASIS.** *106 Main St, in Parker's Marketplace.* 603/444-6995. Specializes in Italian dishes, steak, seafood. Hrs: 11:30 am-10 pm; Fri, Sat to 11 pm. Closed Easter, Thanksgiving, Dec 25. Res accepted. Bar. A la carte entrees: lunch $2.95-$6.95, dinner $4.95-$14.95. Outdoor dining. Converted Victorian home (ca 1890). Cr cds: A, DS, MC, V.

★ ★ **ROSA FLAMINGO.** *(Main St, Bethlehem 03574)* 6 mi E on US 302. 603/869-3111. Italian menu. Specialties: tortellini carbonara, fettucine rosa. Hrs: 11:30 am-11 pm. Closed Easter, Thanksgiving, Dec 25. Res accepted. Bar to 1 am. Semi-a la carte: lunch $3.95-$7.50, dinner $5.75-$16.75. Child's meals. Outdoor dining. Cr cds: A, MC, V.

Lyme

(see Hanover)

Manchester (H-5)

(See also Concord, Nashua)

Settled 1722 **Pop** 99,567 **Elev** 225 ft **Area code** 603 **E-mail** info@manchester-chamber.org **Web** www.manchester-chamber.org

Information Chamber of Commerce, 889 Elm St, 03101-2000; 603/666-6600.

Manchester is a city that has refused to bow to economic adversity. When the Amoskeag Manufacturing Company (cotton textiles), which had dominated Manchester's economy, failed in 1935, it left the city poverty-stricken. With determination worthy of New Englanders, a group of citizens bought the plant for $5,000,000 and revived the city. Now Manchester is northern New England's premier financial center.

What to See and Do

Currier Gallery of Art. One of New England's leading small museums; 13th-20th-century European and American paintings and sculpture; New England decorative art; furniture, glass, silver and pewter; changing exhibitions, concerts, films, other programs. Tours of Zimmerman House (Frank Lloyd Wright). (Daily exc Tues; closed hols) 201 Myrtle Way. Phone 603/669-6144. ¢¢

Manchester Historic Association. Museum and library with collections illustrating life in Manchester from pre-colonial times to present; firefighting equipment; decorative arts, costumes, paintings; changing exhibits. (Tues-Sat; closed hols) 129 Amherst St, 2 blks E of Elm St. Phone 603/622-7531. **Free.**

McIntyre Ski Area. 2 double chairlifts, pony lift; patrol, school, rentals, snowmaking; snack bar. Vertical drop 169 ft. (Dec-Mar, daily) Kennard Rd. Phone 603/624-6571. ¢¢¢¢

Palace Theatre. Productions in vintage vaudeville/opera house. 80 Hanover St. For schedule phone 603/669-8021.

Science Enrichment Encounters Museum. More than 60 interactive, hands-on exhibits demonstrate basic science principles. (July-Aug, daily; rest of yr, Thurs eves, Sat & Sun, school vacations; closed major hols) 324 Commercial St. Phone 603/669-0400. ¢¢

Annual Event

Riverfest. Outdoor festival with family entertainment, concerts, arts & crafts, food booths, fireworks. Phone 603/625-6915 or 603/623-2623. Labor Day wkend.

Motel

✔★ **SUSSE CHALET INN.** *860 S Porter St (03103), I-293, exit 1.* 603/625-2020; FAX 603/623-7562. 102 rms, 4 story. S, D $56.70-$63.70; each addl $7. TV; cable (premium). Pool. Complimentary continental bkfst. Restaurant opp 6 am-11 pm. Ck-out 11 am. Coin lndry. Business servs avail. In-rm modem link. Sundries. Valet serv. Refrigerators avail. Cr cds: A, C, D, DS, MC, V.

Motor Hotels

★★ **COMFORT INN & CONFERENCE CENTER.** *208 Queen City Ave (03102), I-293 exit 4.* 603/668-2600. 100 rms, 5 story. S $62.90-$84.90; D $68.90-$89.90; each addl $5; suites $135-$250; under 18 free; higher rates some wkends. Crib free. Pet accepted. TV; cable (premium). Indoor pool. Complimentary continental bkfst. Ck-out 11 am. Coin lndry. Meeting rms. Business servs avail. In-rm modem link. Bellhops. Free airport, bus depot transportation. Exercise equipt; sauna. Some refrigerators, microwaves. Cr cds: A, C, D, DS, JCB, MC, V.

✔★ **ECONO LODGE.** *75 W Hancock St (03102), I-293 exit 4.* 603/624-0111; FAX 603/623-0268. 120 rms, 5 story. S $40; D $45; each addl $5; under 18 free; wkly, monthly rates. Crib free. Pet accepted. TV; cable. Complimentary coffee in lobby. Restaurant opp 6:30 am-9 pm. Ck-out 11 am. Coin lndry. Business servs avail. Some refrigerators. Cr cds: A, C, D, DS, MC, V.

★★ **FOUR POINTS BY SHERATON.** *55 John Devine Dr (03103), I-293 exit 1.* 603/668-6110; res: 800/325-3535; FAX 603/668-0408. 119 rms, 4 story. S, D $67-$109; each addl $10; under 18 free; higher rates fall foliage. Crib free. TV; cable (premium). Indoor pool; whirlpool. Coffee in rms. Restaurant 6-10 am, 5-10 pm. Rm serv. Bar. Ck-out noon. Meeting rms. Business servs avail. Valet serv. Sundries. Airport transportation. Health club privileges. Mall of New Hampshire opp. Refrigerator, microwave avail. Cr cds: A, C, D, DS, ER, JCB, MC, V.

✔★ **SUPER 8.** *2301 Brown Ave (03103), I-293 exit 2, near Municipal Airport.* 603/623-0883; FAX 603/624-9303. 85 rms, 4 story. June-Labor Day: S $48.88-$74.88; D $55.88-$79.88; each addl $5; suites $84.88-$89.88; higher rates fall foliage; lower rates rest of yr. Crib free. TV; cable, VCR avail (movies). Complimentary coffee. Restaurant nearby. Ck-out 11 am. Meeting rms. Business servs avail. Valet serv. Free airport transportation. Refrigerator, whirlpool in some suites. Cr cds: A, C, D, DS, ER, JCB, MC, V.

★★★ **WAYFARER INN.** *(121 S River Rd, Bedford 03110)* 3 mi S at jct US 3 & NH 101, 1 blk N of Everett Tpke, Bedford exit. 603/622-3766; FAX 603/625-1126; res: 800/843-8272. 194 rms, 2-3 story. No elvtr. S, D $79-$115; each addl $10; suites $175; under 18 free; package plans. Crib free. TV; cable (premium). 2 pools, 1 indoor; whirlpool, poolside serv, lifeguard. Coffee in rms. Restaurant 6:30 am-10 pm; Sat, Sun 7 am-10:30 pm. Rm serv. Bar 11:30-12:30 am; entertainment Thurs-Sat. Ck-out noon. Meeting rms. Business servs avail. In-rm modem link. Valet serv. Sundries. Free airport transportation. Exercise equipt; sauna, steam rm. Some refrigerators. Balconies. Country-inn decor. Cr cds: A, C, D, DS, ER, MC, V.

Hotel

★★ **HOLIDAY INN-THE CENTER.** *700 Elm St (03101).* 603/625-1000; FAX 603/625-4595. Web cnh.hi.sales@grolen.com 2 rms, 12 story. S $98-$129; D $103-$134; suites $195-$495; under 19 free; wkend rates. Crib free. TV; cable (premium). Indoor pool; whirlpool. Coffee in rms. Restaurant 6:30 am-10 pm. Bar from noon; entertainment Fri, Sat. Ck-out 11 am. Convention facilities. Business servs avail. In-rm modem link. Gift shop. Validated indoor parking. Airport transportation. Exercise equipt; sauna. Bathrm phone in suites. Cr cds: A, C, D, DS, JCB, MC, V.

Inn

★★★ **BEDFORD VILLAGE.** *(2 Village Inn Ln, Bedford 03110)* 8 mi SW via NH 101; 5 mi W of I-293, Bedford exit. 603/472-2001; FAX 603/472-2379; res: 800/852-1166. 14 suites, 3 story, 2 kits. Suites $155-$195; kits. $250-$375. Crib $15. TV; cable (premium). Afternoon refreshments. Restaurant (see BEDFORD VILLAGE INN). Ck-out 11 am, ck-in 3 pm. Meeting rms. Business servs avail. In-rm modem link. Gift shop. In-rm whirlpools; some wet bars. Some balconies. Converted barn built early 1800s; antique furnishings, rms individually decorated. Cr cds: A, C, D, MC, V.

Restaurants

★ ★ ★ **BEDFORD VILLAGE INN.** *(See Bedford Village Inn)* *603/472-2001.* Specializes in New England-style dishes. Own baking. Hrs: 7-10:30 am, 11:30 am-2 pm, 5:30-9:30 pm; Sat 8 am-2 pm, 5:30-9:30 pm; Sun 8 am-2 pm, 5:30-9:30 pm; Sun brunch 8 am-2 pm. Closed Dec 25. Res accepted. Bar from 11:30 am. Wine list. Semi-a la carte: bkfst $4.50-$10.50, lunch $4.95-$18, dinner $17.50-$31. Sun brunch $6.50-$12.50. Gift shop. Yellow clapboard structure originally part of homestead (1790). Cr cds: A, C, D, MC, V.

★ **PURITAN BACKROOM.** *245 Hooksett Rd (03104).* *603/669-6890.* Specializes in chicken tenders, barbecued lamb. Own ice cream. Hrs: 11 am-11:30 pm; Wed-Sat to 12:30 am. Closed Thanksgiving, Dec 25. Bar. Semi-a la carte: lunch, dinner $3.95-$18. Child's meals. Stained-glass windows; many paintings. Cr cds: A, C, D, DS, MC, V.

Meredith (F-5)

(See also Holderness, Laconia, Plymouth)

Founded 1768 **Pop** 4,837 **Elev** 552 ft **Area code** 603 **Zip** 03253 **E-mail** meredith@lr.net **Web** www.meredithcc.org
Information Chamber of Commerce, PO Box 732; 603/279-6121.

Between Lakes Winnipesaukee and Waukewan in the Lakes Region, Meredith is a year-round recreation area.

What to See and Do

League of New Hampshire Craftsmen-Meredith/Laconia Arts & Crafts. Work by some of New Hampshire's finest craftsmen. (Daily) On US 3. Phone 603/279-7920. **Free.**

⭐ **Winnipesaukee Scenic Railroad.** Scenic train rides along shore of Lake Winnipesaukee. Board in Meredith or Weirs Beach. (Memorial Day-Columbus Day) Fall foliage trains to Plymouth. Phone 603/279-5253 or 603/745-2135. Excursion ¢¢¢; Dinner train ¢¢¢¢¢

Annual Events

Great Rotary Fishing Derby. 2nd wkend Feb.

Lakes Region Fine Arts and Crafts Festival. Juried show featuring more than 100 New England artists. Music, children's theater, food. Last wkend Aug.

Altrusa Annual Antique Show and Sale. 3rd Sat Sept.

Motels

★ **MATTERHORN MOTOR LODGE.** *(Box 123, NH 25, Moultonboro 03254)* 6 mi NE on NH 25 at Moultonboro Neck Rd. *603/253-4314.* 28 rms, 2 story. No rm phones. Memorial Day-Columbus Day: S, D $85-$110; each addl $10; wkly rates; higher rates special events; lower rates rest of yr. Crib $5. TV; cable. Heated pool. Restaurant adj 6 am-10 pm. Ck-out 11 am. Picnic tables, grill. Beach nearby. Cr cds: A, C, D, DS, MC, V.

✔★ **MEADOWS LAKESIDE.** *(Box 204, NH 25, Center Harbor 03226)* 5 mi NE on NH 25. *603/253-4347.* 35 rms, 4 story. Some rm phones. June-Sept: S $69-$120; D $79-$120; each addl $10; kit. units $120; under 4 free; wkly rates; lower rates May, Oct. Closed rest of yr. Crib $10. Pet accepted; $7/day. TV; VCR avail (movies). Complimentary coffee

in lobby. Restaurant nearby. Ck-out 11 am. Private patios, balconies. Picnic tables. On lake; beach, dockage. Cr cds: A, DS, MC, V.

Inns

★ ★ ★ **INN AT BAY POINT.** *NH 25. 603/279-7006; FAX 603/279-6797; res: 800/622-6455.* E-mail millfalls-baypoint@worldnet.att.net; web www.millfalls.baypoint.com. 24 rms, 4 story. June-Oct: S, D $139-$249; each addl $15; under 12 free; wkly, wkend rates; ski plans; wkends, hols (2-3-day min); lower rates rest of yr. Crib free. TV; cable, VCR avail (movies). Pool privileges. Whirlpool. Complimentary continental bkfst. Complimentary coffee in rms. Restaurant 11:30 am-9 pm. Rm serv. Bar. Ck-out 11 am. Meeting rms. Business servs avail. Luggage handling. Gift shop. Downhill ski 12 mi; x-country ski on nearby lake. Exercise equipt; sauna. Some refrigerators. Balconies. Picnic tables. On lake; private dock, beach. Cr cds: A, C, D, DS, MC, V.

★ ★ ★ **INN AT MILL FALLS.** *312 Daniel Webster Hwy (US 3), on US 3 at Dover St. 603/279-7006; FAX 603/279-6797; res: 800/622-6455.* E-mail millfalls.baypoint@worlnet.att.net; web www.millfalls-baypoint.com. 54 rms, 5 story. June-Oct: D $89-$195; each addl $15; ski plans; lower rates rest of yr. Crib free. TV; cable, VCR avail (movies). Indoor pool; whirlpool. Complimentary coffee in lobby. Restaurant nearby. Rm serv. Ck-out 11 am, ck-in 3 pm. Meeting rms. Business servs avail. Sauna. Some fireplaces; refrigerators avail. Balconies. On lake. Antique furnishings; some rms with lake view. Adj to historic Mill Falls Marketplace. Cr cds: A, C, D, DS, MC, V.

★ ★ ★ **OLDE ORCHARD INN.** *(Lee Rd, Moultonborough 03254)* Approx 7 mi N on NH 25. *603/476-5004; FAX 603/476-5419; res: 800/598-5845.* E-mail innkeep1@aol.com; web www.oldeorchardinn.com. 9 rms, 4 with shower only, 2 share bath. No rm phones. S, D $70-$125; each addl $15; kit. unit $80; wkends (2-day min); higher rates: summer, fall foliage. Crib $5. 1 TV; cable, VCR avail (movies). Complimentary full bkfst. Complimentary coffee in rms. Restaurant opp 5-9:30 pm. Ck-out 11 am, ck-in 3 pm. Luggage handling. Downhill ski 15 mi; x-country ski on site. Lawn games. Refrigerators. Picnic tables. Built in 1812. Totally nonsmoking. Cr cds: MC, V.

★ ★ **RED HILL.** *(NH 25B and College Rd, Centre Harbor 03226)* 3 mi N on US 3, E on NH 25B. *603/279-7001; FAX 603/279-7003; res: 800/573-3445.* E-mail info@redhillinn.com; web www.redhillinn.com. 26 rms, 9 suites. D $105-$175; suites $135. Crib $10. TV in sitting rm; VCR (free movies). Complimentary full bkfst. Dining rm noon-2 pm, 5-10 pm. Bar. Ck-out 11 am, ck-in 3 pm. Business servs avail. Pool; whirlpool. X-country ski on site. Lawn games. Some fireplaces. Built 1904 as summer estate; antiques. Cr cds: A, C, D, DS, MC, V.

Restaurants

★ ★ **HART'S TURKEY FARM.** *Jct NH 3 & 104. 603/279-6212.* Specializes in turkey, seafood, prime rib. Hrs: 11:15 am-9:30 pm. Semi-a la carte: lunch $3.95-$9.75, dinner $7.95-$15.95. Child's meals. Gift shop. Cr cds: A, C, D, DS, MC, V.

★ ★ **MAME'S.** *8 Plymouth St. 603/279-4631.* Specializes in prime rib, seafood, chicken. Hrs: 11:30 am-9 pm; wkends to 9:30 pm. Bars. Wine list. Semi-a la carte: lunch $4-$8.95, dinner $7-$18. Sun brunch $3.95-$6.95. Child's meals. Converted brick house and barn (1825). Cr cds: A, DS, MC, V.

Mt Washington (D-5)

(See also Bretton Woods, Gorham, Jackson)

E-mail info@4seasonresort.com **Web** www.4seasonresort.com or www.mountwashington.org

Information Mt Washington Valley Chamber of Commerce, N Main St, PO Box 2300, North Conway 03860; 603/356-5701 or 800/367-3364.

(10 mi S of Gorham on NH 16)

Mt Washington is the central peak of the White Mountains and the highest point in the northeastern United States (6,288 feet). At the summit is a 54-acre state park with an information center, first aid station, restaurant and gift shop. The mountain has the world's first cog railway, completed in 1869; a road to the top dates from 1861. P.T. Barnum called the view from the summit "the second-greatest show on earth."

The weather on Mt Washington is so violent that the timberline is at about 4,000 feet; in the Rockies it is nearer 10,000 feet. In the treeless zone are alpine plants and insects, some unique to the region. The weather station here recorded a wind speed of 231 miles per hour in April, 1934—a world record. The lowest temperature recorded was -49°F; the year-round average is below freezing. The peak gets nearly 15 feet of snow each year.

What to See and Do

Auto road. Trip takes approx 30 min each way. *Note:* Make sure your car is in good condition; check brakes before starting. (Mid-May-mid-Oct, daily, weather permitting) Guided tour service avail (daily). Approaches from the E side, in Pinkham Notch, 8 mi S of Gorham on NH 16. Phone 603/466-3988. ¢¢¢¢¢ Opp is

Great Glen Trails. All-season, non-motorized recreational trails park featuring biking programs (rentals), fly-fishing instruction and programs, hiking programs (guide or unguided), kayak and canoe tours and workshops in summer; cross-country skiing, snow shoeing and snow tubing in winter. (Daily; closed Apr) For detailed brochure with schedule and fees, contact NH 16, Pinkham Notch, Gorham 03581; 603/466-2333. ¢¢¢

Cog railway. Allow at least 3 hrs for round trip. (May-Memorial Day wkend, wkends; after Memorial Day wkend-Nov, daily) Base station road, off US 302, 4 mi E of jct US 3, 302; on W slope of mountain. For schedule, reservations phone 603/846-5404 or 800/922-8825. ¢¢¢¢¢

Hiking trails. Many crisscross the mountain; some reach the top. Hikers should check weather conditions at Pinkham Notch headquarters before climbing. Phone 603/466-2725. **Free.**

Mt Washington Summit Museum. Displays on life in the extreme climate of the summit; rare flora and fauna; geology, history. (Memorial Day-Columbus Day, daily) Top of Mt Washington. Phone 603/466-3388. ¢

Pinkham Notch (see). SE of Mt Washington on NH 16.

White Mountain Natl Forest (see).

Nashua (J-5)

(See also Manchester, Salem)

Settled 1656 **Pop** 79,662 **Elev** 169 ft **Area code** 603 **E-mail** chamber@nashuachamber.com **Web** www.nashuachamber.com

Information Greater Nashua Chamber of Commerce, 146 Main St, 2nd flr, 03060; 603/881-8333.

Originally a fur-trading post, Nashua's manufacturing began with the development of Merrimack River water power early in the 19th century. The city, second-largest in New Hampshire, has more than 100 diversified industries ranging from computers and tools to beer.

What to See and Do

Anheuser-Busch, Inc. Guided tours of brewery; sampling rm; gift shop. Children only with adult; no pets. 221 Daniel Webster Hwy (US 3) in Merrimack, Everett Tpke exit 10. For schedule phone 603/595-1202. **Free.** Adj is

Clydesdale Hamlet. Buildings modeled after a 19th-century European-style farm are the living quarters for the famous Clydesdales (at least 15 are here at all times); carriage house contains vintage wagons. **Free.**

Silver Lake State Park. 1,000-ft sand beach on a 34-acre lake; swimming, bathhouse; picnicking. (Late June-Labor Day) Standard fees. 8 mi W on NH 130 to Hollis, then 1 mi N off NH 122. Phone 603/465-2342.

Seasonal Event

American Stage Festival. 5 mi NW off NH 101 in Milford. Five plays; music events, children's series. For schedule phone 603/886-7000. June-Sept.

Motels

★ ★ **COMFORT INN.** *10 St Laurent St (03060), at jct NH 101A, Everett Tpke (US 3) exit 7E.* 603/883-7700; FAX 603/595-2107. 103 rms, 2 story. S $59-$89; D $64-$99; under 18 free. Crib free. TV; cable (premium), VCR avail (movies). Pool. Complimentary continental bkfst. Restaurant adj 11:30 am-10:30 pm; Sun from noon. Bar. Ck-out noon. Meeting rm. Business servs avail. Valet serv. Health club privileges. Refrigerators avail. Cr cds: A, C, D, DS, ER, JCB, MC, V.

D ⌲ ≈ ✕ ♨ SC

✔ ★ **FAIRFIELD INN BY MARRIOTT.** *(4 Amherst Rd, Merrimack 03054) 6 mi N on Everett Tpke (US 3) exit 11, 1 blk W.* 603/424-7500. 116 rms, 3 story. June-Labor Day: S $62; D $69; each addl $7; under 18 free; higher rates: wkends, fall foliage; lower rates rest of yr. TV; cable (premium). Pool. Complimentary continental bkfst. Restaurant nearby. Ck-out noon. Meeting rm. Business servs avail. In-rm modem link. Valet serv. Sundries. Cr cds: A, C, D, DS, MC, V.

D ⌲ ≈ ✕ ♨ SC

★ ★ **HOLIDAY INN.** *9 Northeastern Blvd (03062), W at US 3 exit 4.* 603/888-1551; FAX 603/888-7193. 218 rms, 3-4 story, 34 suites. May-Nov: S, D $89-$99; each addl $4; suites $99-$129; under 19 free; package plans; lower rates rest of yr. Crib free. Pet accepted. TV; cable (premium), VCR avail. Heated pool. Restaurant 6:30 am-10 pm. Rm serv. Bar 11:30-12:30 am; entertainment. Ck-out noon. Coin lndry. Meeting rms. Business servs avail. Valet serv. Exercise equipt. Some refrigerators. Private patios, balconies. Cr cds: A, C, D, DS, ER, JCB, MC, V.

D ⌲ ⌲ ≈ ✕ ⌲ ♨ SC

✔ ★ **RED ROOF INN.** *77 Spit Brook Rd (03060), at US 3 exit 1.* 603/888-1893; FAX 603/888-5889. 115 rms, 3 story. S $39.99-$69.99; D $44.99-$79.99; under 19 free. Crib free. Pet accepted. TV; cable (premium). Complimentary coffee in lobby. Ck-out noon. Business servs avail. Picnic table. Cr cds: A, C, D, DS, MC, V.

D ⌲ ⌲ ♨ ⌲

★ ★ **RESIDENCE INN BY MARRIOTT.** *(246 Daniel Webster Hwy, Merrimack 03054) 5 mi N on US 3.* 603/424-8100; FAX 603/424-3128. 129 kit. suites, 2 story. Kit. suites $102-$160. Crib free. Pet accepted; $50 & $5/day. TV; cable (premium). Pool; whirlpool. Complimentary continental bkfst. Ck-out noon. Coin lndry. Meeting rms. Business servs avail. In-rm modem link. Valet serv. Health club privileges. Sport court. Many fireplaces. Grills. Cr cds: A, C, D, DS, MC, V.

D ⌲ ≈ ✕ ♨ SC

Hotels

★ ★ ★ **CROWNE PLAZA.** *2 Somerset Pkwy (03063), just off Everett Tpke (US 3) exit 8.* 603/886-1200; res: 800/962-7482; FAX 603/595-4199. 213 rms, 8 story. S, D $89-$129; each addl $10; suites $150-$250;

under 18 free; wkend package plans. Crib free. TV; cable. Indoor pool; whirlpool. Complimentary coffee in rms. Restaurant 6 am-10 pm; dining rm from 5:30 pm. Bar 11:30-12:30 am. Ck-out noon. Meeting rms. Business servs avail. In-rm modem link. Gift shop. Beauty shop. Garage parking. Free airport transportation. Tennis. Exercise rm; saunas. Massage. Some in-rm whirlpools; refrigerators avail. 48-seat amphitheater. Luxury level. Cr cds: A, C, D, DS, ER, JCB, MC, V.

★ ★ ★ **MARRIOTT.** *2200 Southwood Dr (03063), Everett Tpke (US 3) exit 8.* 603/880-9100; FAX 603/886-9489. 251 rms, 4 story. Mar-mid-Sept: S, D $89; wkend rates; higher rates mid-Sept-Nov; lower rates rest of yr. Crib free. TV; cable (premium). Indoor pool; whirlpool. Play-ground. Coffee in rms. Restaurant 6:30 am-10 pm. Bar from noon; pianist Sat. Ck-out 1 pm. Convention facilities. Business servs avail. In-rm modem link. Concierge. Gift shop. Airport transportation. Exercise equipt. Lawn games. Refrigerators avail. Czechoslovakian chandeliers and Oriental objets d'art accent lobby. Luxury level. Cr cds: A, C, D, DS, ER, JCB, MC, V.

★ ★ ★ **SHERATON.** *Tara Blvd (03062), 2 mi S on US 3, at Everett Tpke exit 1.* 603/888-9970; FAX 603/888-4112. 337 rms, 7 story. S $79-$149; D $89-$169; each addl $10; under 18 free; wkend rates. Crib free. TV; cable (premium), VCR avail. 2 pools, 1 indoor; whirlpool, poolside serv, lifeguard. Supervised child's activities. Coffee in rms. Restaurant 6:30 am-10 pm. Bars 11:30-1 am; entertainment Fri, Sat. Ck-out noon. Convention facilities. Business center. In-rm modem link. Gift shop. Exercise rm; sauna, steam rm. Lawn games. Some bathrm phones, in-rm whirlpools; refrigerators avail. Luxury level. Cr cds: A, C, D, DS, ER, JCB, MC, V.

Restaurants

★ ★ **COUNTRY GOURMET.** *(438 Daniel Webster Hwy (NH 3), Merrimack 03054) 6 mi N on US 3, 1½ mi N of Everett Tpke exit 11.* 603/424-2755. French, continental menu. Specializes in seafood, beef, lamb. Hrs: 5:30-9 pm; Sun 4-8:30 pm. Closed some major hols. Res accepted. Bar to 11 pm. Semi-a la carte: dinner $15-$22. Child's meals. Entertainment Thurs-Mon. Originally built 1700s as a tavern; unique pump-kin-pine wainscoting, original fireplaces & mantels, beamed ceilings. Cr cds: A, C, D, DS, MC, V.

★ **HANNAH JACK TAVERN.** *(Merrimack 03054) E of Everett Tpke exit 11.* 603/424-4171. Specialties: prime rib, Alaskan king crab legs. Hrs: 11:30 am-2 pm, 5-9:30 pm; Sat from 4:30 pm; Sun from 4 pm. Closed July 4, Dec 25. Res accepted. Bar. Semi-a la carte: lunch $5.50-$8.50, dinner $12-$22. Child's meals. Parking. In Colonial building over 200 yrs old. Cr cds: A, D, MC, V.

★ **MODERN.** *116 W Pearl St (03060).* 603/883-8422. Specializes in steak, seafood, chicken. Hrs: 11 am-8:30 pm; Fri, Sat to 9 pm. Semi-a la carte: lunch $2.99-$6.99, dinner $4.99-$17.99. Child's meals. Cr cds: A, C, D, DS, MC, V.

★ **NEWICK'S.** *(696 Daniel Webster Hwy (US 3), Merrimack 03054) 6 mi N on US 3 exit 12.* 603/429-0262. Specializes in fresh seafood. Hrs: 11:30 am-8:30 pm; Fri, Sat to 9 pm. Closed Thanksgiving, Dec 25. Bar. Semi-a la carte: lunch, dinner $5.95-$19.95. Child's meals. Nautical decor. Cr cds: A, DS, MC, V.

New London (G-4)

(See also Sunapee)

Pop 3,180 **Elev** 825 ft **Area code** 603 **Zip** 03257
Information Chamber of Commerce, Main St, PO Box 532, 603/526-6575.

What to See and Do

Skiing.

Ragged Mountain. Three double chairlifts, T-bar; patrol, school, rent-als, snowmaking; cafeteria, bar. Longest run 1½ mi; vertical drop 1,250 ft. (Mid-Nov-Mar, daily) Cross-country skiing. 10 mi E on NH 11, then 7 mi N on US 4 to Danbury, then 1½ mi E on NH 104 to access road. Phone 603/768-3475. ¢¢¢¢

Seasonal Event

Barn Playhouse. Main St, off NH 11. Live theater presentations nightly; Wed matinees. Also Mon children's attractions. Phone 603/526-4631 or 603/526-6710. Mid-June-Labor Day.

Motels

★ **FAIRWAY.** *Country Club Lane (NH 11E), at Lake Sunapee Country Club.* 603/526-6040; FAX 603/526-9622. 12 rms. S, D $55-$70; each addl $8.50; under 13 free (with 2 adults). Crib free. TV; cable. Pool. Ck-out 11 am. Tennis privileges. Downhill ski 12 mi; x-country ski on site. Cr cds: DS, MC, V.

✔★ **LAMPLIGHTER MOTOR INN.** *6 Newport Rd.* 603/526-6484. 14 rms, 2 story. S, D $55-$65; kit. units $65-$70; each addl $5. TV; cable, VCR avail. Complimentary continental bkfst. Restaurant nearby. Ck-out 11 am. Business servs avail. Downhill/x-country ski 10 mi. Refrig-erators avail. Cr cds: A, C, D, DS, MC, V.

Inns

★ ★ ★ **FOLLANSBEE INN.** *(Box 92, North Sutton 03260) 4 mi SE on NH 114.* 603/927-4221; res: 800/626-4221. Web www.follansbee-inn.com. 23 rms, 12 share bath, 3 story. No rm phones. S $75-$105; D $80-$110; each addl $25. Closed 2 wks Nov & Apr. Children over 8 yrs only. Complimentary full bkfst. Serv bar. Ck-out, ck-in flexible. Downhill ski 14 mi; x-country ski on site. Restored 1840 New England farmhouse. On Kezar Lake; boats; private beach, pier. Bikes. Sitting rms with fireplaces. Totally nonsmoking. Cr cds: MC, V.

★ ★ ★ **INN AT PLEASANT LAKE.** *125 N Pleasant St.* 603/526-6271; res: 800/626-4907; FAX 603/526-4111. E-mail bmackenz@kear.tds.net; web www.innatpleasantlake.com. 12 rms, some A/C, 3 story. No rm phones. S, D $95-$145; each addl $25; suite $145; wkly rates. Complimen-tary full bkfst. Dining rm dinner sitting 6:30 pm. Ck-out 11 am, ck-in 3 pm. Meeting rm. Downhill ski 12 mi; x-country ski 3 mi. Exercise equipt. Some fireplaces. Original Cape farmhouse (1790) converted to summer resort in late 1800s; country antique decor. On Pleasant lake; private sand beach. Cr cds: DS, MC, V.

✔★ ★ **NEW LONDON.** *140 Main St (NH 114), I 89 exit 11, in center of town.* 603/526-2791; FAX 603/526-2749; res: 800/526-2791. E-mail nlinn@srnet.com; web www.newlondoninn.com. 28 rms, 10 with shower only, 3 story. June-mid-Oct: S $85-$125; D $110-$140; each addl $20; lower rates rest of yr. TV in sitting rm; VCR (free movies). Complimen-tary continental bkfst. Restaurant (see NEW LONDON INN). Bar from 5 pm. Ck-out 11 am, ck-in 3 pm. Meeting rm. Business servs avail. Down-hill/x-country ski 3 mi. Health club privileges. Lawn games. Built 1792. Cr cds: A, MC, V.

Restaurants

★ ★ **MILLSTONE.** *On Newport Road (NH 11W).* 603/526-4201. Specializes in veal, seafood, pasta. Own desserts. Hrs: 11:30 am-2:30 pm, 5-9 pm; Sun brunch 11 am-3 pm. Closed Dec 25. Res accepted. Semi-a la carte: dinner $5.95-$18.95. Child's meals. Casual, garden-view dining. Cr cds: A, C, D, DS, MC, V.

♥

★ ★ **NEW LONDON INN.** *(See New London Inn)* 603/526-2791. E-mail nlinn@srnet.com; web www.newlondoninn.com. Specialties: garlic-scented New York strip, grilled vegetables and shiitake mushroom sampler, herb-crusted Atlantic salmon. Hrs: 5-9 pm. Closed Sun. Res accepted; required Fri, Sat. Semi-a la carte: dinner $13-$22. Child's meals. Colonial decor. Overlooks village green, flower gardens. Totally nonsmoking. Cr cds: A, MC, V.

★ ★ **POTTER PLACE INN.** *(88 Depot St, Andover 03216)* 8 mi E on NH 11, at jct NH 4. 603/735-5141. Specializes in veal, roast duckling, fresh seafood & game. Hrs: 5:30-9 pm. Closed Mon Nov-Apr. Res accepted. Serv bar. Semi-a la carte: dinner $12-$18. House built 1790s; country atmosphere. Cr cds: A, MC, V.

D

Newport (G-3)

(See also Sunapee)

Settled 1765 **Pop** 6,110 **Elev** 797 ft **Area code** 603 **Zip** 03773
Information Chamber of Commerce, 2 N Main St; 603/863-1510.

Newport is the commercial headquarters for the Lake Sunapee area. Its industries include machine tools, woolens, clothing and firearms. The Town Common Historic District has many churches and colonial and Victorian houses.

What to See and Do

Fort at No. 4. Reconstructed French & Indian War log fort, complete with stockade, Great Hall, cow barns and living quarters furnished to reflect 18th-century pioneer living. Exhibits include Native American artifacts, demonstrations of colonial crafts and an audiovisual program. (Memorial Day-Labor Day, daily exc Tues; after Labor Day-Columbus Day, Sat & Sun) 10 mi W on NH 11/103, then 11 mi S on NH 11/12, near Charlestown. Phone 603/826-5700. ¢¢¢

Motel

✔★ **NEWPORT.** *467 Sunapee St (NH 11/103), 2 mi E on NH 11/103.* 603/863-1440; res: 800/741-2619. 18 rms. June-Oct: S, D $59.95-$74.95; each addl $7; lower rates rest of yr. TV; cable. Pool. Complimentary coffee. Ck-out 11 am. Downhill ski 5 mi; x-country ski 14 mi. Refrigerators avail. Cr cds: A, C, D, MC, V.

Inn

★ ★ ★ **THE EAGLE INN AT COIT MOUNTAIN.** *523 N Main St, 2 mi N on NH 10.* 603/863-3583; FAX 603/863-7816; res: 800/367-2364 *(exc NH).* 5 air-cooled rms, 2 share bath, 3 story. No rm phones. May-Oct: S, D $79-$129; each addl $20; wkly, wkend rates; ski plans; lower rates rest of yr. Crib free. Pet accepted. TV; VCR in library (free movies). Complimentary full bkfst. Restaurant 5-10:30 pm; Sun noon-9 pm. Ck-out 11 am, ck-in 2 pm. Downhill ski 8 mi. Lawn games. Refrigerators; some fireplaces. Historic house (1790); antiques. Library, sitting rm. Cr cds: A, MC, V.

North Conway (E-5)

(See also Bartlett, Jackson)

Settled 1764 **Pop** 2,100 (est) **Elev** 531 ft **Area code** 603 **Zip** 03860
E-mail info@4seasonresort.com **Web** www.4seasonresort.com
Information Mt Washington Valley Chamber of Commerce, N Main St, PO Box 2300; 603/356-5701 or 800/367-3364.

Heart of the famous Mt Washington Valley region of the White Mountains, the area also includes Bartlett, Glen, Jackson, Conway, Redstone, Kearsarge and Intervale. Mt Washington, seen from the middle of Main St, is one of the great views in the East.

What to See and Do

Conway Scenic Railroad. Steam and diesel trains depart from restored Victorian station (1874) for 11-mi (55-min) round trip. Valley Train explores the Saco River Valley (mid-May-Oct, daily; mid-Apr-mid-May, Nov & Dec, wkends); Notch Train travels through Crawford Notch (mid-Sept-mid-Oct, daily; late June-mid-Sept, Tues-Sat). Railroad museum. Depot on Main St. Phone 603/356-5251. ¢¢¢

Covered bridges. In Conway, Jackson and Bartlett.

Downeast Whitewater Rafting. Specializes in rafting, canoeing, kayak touring and paddling school. Programs include guided whitewater rafting trips, whitewater canoe and kayak school, calmwater and whitewater canoe rentals. (May-Oct) US 302, 2 mi E of Center Conway. Phone 603/447-3002. ¢¢¢¢

Echo Lake State Park. Mountain lake in the shadow of White Horse Ledge. Scenic road to 700-ft Cathedral Ledge, dramatic rock formation; panoramic views of the White Mts and the Saco River Valley. Swimming, picnicking. (Late June-Labor Day) Standard fees. 2 mi W, off NH 302. Phone 603/356-2672.

Factory outlet stores. Many outlet malls and stores can be found along NH 16. Contact Chamber of Commerce for more information.

League of New Hampshire Craftsmen. Work by some of New Hampshire's finest craftsmen. (Daily) On NH 16 (Main St). Phone 603/356-2441. **Free.**

Skiing. Mt Cranmore. Express quad, triple, double chairlift to summit, 3 double chairlifts to N, S & E slopes; patrol, school, rentals; snowmaking; restaurant, bar, cafeterias; day care. Longest run 1¾ mi; vertical drop 1,200 ft. (Dec-Mar, daily) 1 mi E off US 302 (NH 16). Phone 603/356-5543 or 800/786-6754. ¢¢¢¢¢

White Mt Natl Forest (see). N & S on NH 16; W on US 302.

Annual Events

Mt Washington Valley Equine Classic. Horse jumping. Mid-Aug.

Mud Bowl (football). Hog Coliseum. Sept.

Seasonal Event

Eastern Slope Playhouse. Main St, on grounds of Eastern Slope Inn Resort (see MOTELS). Mt Washington Valley Theatre Co presents four Broadway musicals. Daily exc Mon. Phone 603/356-5776. Late June-early Sept.

Motels

★ ★ **EASTERN SLOPE INN RESORT.** *2760 Main St (NH 16).* *603/356-6321; FAX 603/356-8732; res: 800/862-1600.* E-mail stay@eas terslopeinn.com; web www.easternslopeinn.com. 146 rms, 3 story. S, D $86-$95; each addl $15; townhouse suites $142-$172; under 12 free; ski plans; higher rates: fall foliage, hols. TV; cable, VCR avail. Indoor pool; whirlpool. Restaurant noon-midnight; entertainment Fri, Sat. Ck-out 10 am. Coin lndry. Meeting rms. Tennis. Downhill ski 1 mi; x-country ski on site. Sauna. Rec rm. Lawn games. Trout pond. Picnic tables, grills. Golf course adj. Cr cds: A, DS, MC, V.

⊡ ☛ ☀ ⚒ ≈ 🔥 SC

★ ★ **FOX RIDGE.** *NH 16. 603/356-3151; FAX 603/356-0096; res: 800/343-1804.* E-mail foxridge@redjacketinns.com; web www.red-jacketinns.com. 136 rms, 2 story. July-late Oct: S, D $90-$135; each addl $10; under 16 free; package plans; higher rates hol wkends; lower rates rest of yr. Closed late Oct-mid-May. Crib free. TV; cable. 2 pools, 1 indoor; poolside serv. Playground. Supervised child's activities (July-Aug); ages 6-12. Restaurant 7:30-11 am. Ck-out 11 am. Tennis. Game rm. Lawn games. Refrigerators. Private patios, balconies. Picnic tables. Cr cds: A, MC, V.

⊡ ☂ ≈ ≈ 🔥

★ ★ **GREEN GRANITE INN & CONFERENCE CENTER.** *Jct US 302 & NH 16. 603/356-6901; res: 800/468-3666.* 88 rms, 2 story. S, D $57-$129; each addl $10; suites $150-$175; kit. units $79-$149; condos $129-$199; under 16 free; family rates; package plans. Crib $5. TV; cable, VCR avail. Pools, 1 indoor. Playground. Complimentary continental bkfst. Meeting rms. Sundries. Downhill/x-country ski 4 mi. Refrigerator, whirlpool in suites. Private patios, balconies. Picnic tables, grill. Cr cds: A, DS, MC, V.

⊡ ☛ ≈ ≈ 🔥 SC

☛ ★ ★ **JUNGE'S.** *US 302 (NH 16). 603/356-2886.* Web www.jour neysnorth.com/junges. 28 rms, 1-2 story. Mid-June-Oct: S, D $65-$90; each addl $5-$10; higher rates special events; lower rates rest of yr. Crib $2-$5. TV; cable. Heated pool. Playground. Restaurant nearby. Ck-out 11 am. Downhill/x-country ski 2 mi. Rec rm. Lawn games. Picnic tables, grills. Cr cds: A, D, DS, MC, V.

☛ ≈ ≈ 🔥

★ ★ **NORTH CONWAY MOUNTAIN INN.** *Main St. 603/356-2803.* 32 rms, 2 story. S $59-$129; D $69-$139; higher rates fall foliage; lower rates off season. Crib free. TV; cable. Restaurant opp 6 am-9 pm. Ck-out 10 am. Downhill/x-country ski 2 mi. Balconies. Totally nonsmoking. Cr cds: A, MC, V.

⊡ ☛ ≈ 🔥

☛★ **SWISS CHALETS VILLAGE INN.** *(NH 16A, Intervale 03845) 3 mi N on NH 16A. 603/356-2232; res: 800/831-2727.* E-mail stay@swisschaletsvillage.com; web www.swisschaletsvillage.com. 42 rms, 1-3 story. S $69-$99; D $79-$139; each addl $10; suites $109-$179; under 18 free; ski plans; higher rates fall foliage. Crib free. Pet accepted; $10/day. TV; cable. Heated pool. Complimentary continental bkfst. Ck-out 11 am. Downhill ski 4 mi; x-country ski on site. Game rm. Refrigerators; some in-rm whirlpools, fireplaces. Some balconies. Picnic tables. Rms in Swiss chalet-style buildings; on 12 acres. Cr cds: A, DS, MC, V.

☛ ☛ ≈ ≈ 🔥

★ **SYLVAN PINES.** *S Main St (US 302/NH 16), 1½ mi S on US 302 (NH 16). 603/356-2878; FAX 603/356-9094.* E-mail janni boy@landmarknet.net. 39 rms, 1-2 story. Late June-mid-Oct: S, D $65-$95; each addl $5; lower rates rest of yr. TV; cable (premium). Heated pool. Complimentary coffee. Restaurant nearby. Ck-out 11 am. Downhill/x-country ski 2 mi. Patios, balconies. Cr cds: A, DS, MC, V.

☛ ≈ ≈ 🔥

★ **WHITE TRELLIS.** *3245 N Main St. 603/356-2492.* 22 rms. June-mid-Oct & hol ski wks: S, D $55-$110; each addl $5; some lower rates rest of yr. Crib free. TV; cable. Complimentary coffee in lobby. Restaurant nearby. Ck-out 10 am. Downhill/x-country ski 3 mi. Cr cds: DS, MC, V.

☛ ≈ 🔥

Lodge

★ ★ ★ **BEST WESTERN RED JACKET MOUNTAIN VIEW.** *White Mt Hwy (NH 16). 603/356-5411; FAX 603/356-3842; res: 800/752-2538.* E-mail redjacketmtn@redjacketinns.com; web www.redjacket-inns.com/redjacketmtn. 152 rms, 3 story, 12 kit. apts (2-bedrm). Mid-Dec-mid-Mar & Memorial Day-late Oct: S, D $99-$219; suites, 2-bedrm apts $235; family rates; package plans; higher rates hols; lower rates rest of yr. Crib free. TV; cable, VCR avail. 2 heated pools, 1 indoor; poolside serv in summer. Playground. Free supervised child's activities (late-June-Labor Day); ages 4-12. Dining rms 7:30-10 am, noon-9 pm. Rm serv. Bars noon-1 am; entertainment. Ck-out 11 am. Coin lndry. Meeting rms. Business servs avail. Bellhops. Sundries. Gift shop. Valet parking. Lighted tennis. Downhill ski 2 mi; x-country ski on site. Exercise equipt. Game rm. Lawn games. Refrigerators, some in-rm whirlpools. Many private patios, balconies. Cr cds: A, C, D, DS, MC, V.

⊡ ☛ ⚒ ≈ 🏃 ≈ 🔥

Hotel

★ ★ ★ **FOUR POINTS BY SHERATON.** *NH 16 at Settlers' Green. 603/356-9300.* 200 rms, 4 story. S, D $79-$165; suites $155-$215; under 18 free; MAP avail; ski plans. Crib $10. TV; cable (premium). Indoor pool; whirlpool. Restaurant 7 am-10:30 pm. Bar 11-1 am; entertainment wkends. Ck-out 11 am. Coin lndry. Meeting rms. Business servs avail. In-rm modem link. Downhill ski 3 mi; x-country ski 5 mi. Exercise equipt; sauna. Game rm. Bathrm phone, refrigerator, minibar in suites. Cr cds: A, C, D, DS, ER, JCB, MC, V.

⊡ ☛ ≈ 🏃 ≈ 🔥 SC

Inns

☛ ★ **1785.** *3582 White Mountain Hwy, 2 mi N on NH 16. 603/356-9025; FAX 603/356-6081; res: 800/421-1785.* E-mail the1785 inn@aol.com; web www.the1785inn.com. 17 rms, 5 share bath, 12 A/C, 3 story. No rm phones. S $49-$89; D $69-$109; each addl $10-$20; MAP avail; family rates; ski plans; higher rates fall foliage. Crib free. TV in some rms, sitting rm; cable, VCR avail. Pool; poolside serv. Playground. Complimentary full bkfst. Restaurant (see 1785 INN). Rm serv. Bar. Ck-out noon, ck-in 2 pm. Luggage handling. Downhill ski 2 mi; x-country ski on site. Lawn games. Picnic tables, grills. Colonial-style building (1785); original fireplaces, Victorian antiques. On 6 acres; river, view of Mt Washington. Totally nonsmoking. Cr cds: A, C, D, DS, MC, V.

☛ ☛ ≈ ≈ 🔥

★ ★ **BUTTONWOOD.** *Mt Surprise Rd, off Hurricane Mt Rd. 603/356-2625; FAX 603/356-3140; res: 800/258-2625.* E-mail but ton_w@moose.ncia.net; web www.buttonwoodinn.com. 10 rms, 2 story. No A/C. S $75-$165; D $85-$200; each addl $25. TV in sitting rm; cable. Pool. Complimentary full bkfst. Ck-out 11 am, ck-in 3 pm. Downhill ski 1 mi; x-country ski on site. Cape Cod-style building (1820s); antiques, library. Seventeen wooded acres on mountainside. Totally nonsmoking. Cr cds: A, DS, MC, V.

⊡ ☛ ≈ ≈ 🔥

☛★ **CRANMORE.** *Kearsarge St, ¼ mi E of US 302 (NH 16). 603/356-5502; res: 800/526-5502.* 18 rms, 3 story. No A/C. Late June-mid-Sept: S $52-$70; D $62-$80; suites $104-$118; wkly, family rates; package plans; higher rates fall foliage; lower rates rest of yr. Crib free. TV rm; cable. Pool. Complimentary bkfst. Dining rm 8-9 am. Ck-out 11 am, ck-in 3 pm. Downhill ski ⅓ mi; x-country ski on site. Health club privileges. Lawn games. In operation since 1863. Cr cds: A, MC, V.

☛ ≈ ≈ 🔥

★ ★ **CRANMORE MT LODGE.** *Kearsarge Rd, off NH 16. 603/356-2044; FAX 603/356-8963; res: 800/356-3596.* E-mail c-u@cml1.com; web www.cml1.com. 16 rms, 6 A/C, 2-3 story; 40 units in bunkhouse. No rm phones. S, D $69-$125; each addl $10-$15; bunkhouse units $17; suite $150-$225; 2-bedrm townhouse $220; MAP avail winter; wkly rates; ski plans; some lower rates off-season. Crib free. TV in some rms; cable. Pool; whirlpool. Playground. Complimentary full bkfst. Dining rm hrs vary. Ck-out 11 am, ck-in 3 pm. Coin lndry. Tennis. Downhill ski 1 mi; x-country ski on site. Ice-skating. Game rm. Lawn games. Picnic tables, grills. Historic guest house (1860); once owned by Babe Ruth's daughter. Library, sitting rm, antiques. Located on 12 acres; pond. Farm animals. Cr cds: A, D, DS, MC, V.

★ ★ **DARBY FIELD.** *(Bald Hill Rd, Conway 03818) 5½ mi S on NH 16, then approx 2 mi W & N on Bald Hill Rd. 603/447-2181; FAX 603/447-5726; res: 800/426-4147 (exc NH).* E-mail marc@darbyfield.com; web www.darbyfield.com. 16 rms, 2 share bath, 4 A/C, 3 story. No rm phones. MAP: S $110-$130; D $140-$240; each addl $45; ski, canoeing plans; higher rates fall foliage. Children over 2 yrs only. TV in lobby; cable, VCR. Pool. Complimentary bkfst. Dining rm 6-9 pm. Ck-out 9-11 am, ck-in 2-6 pm. Downhill ski 10 mi; x-country ski on site. Lawn games. Originally a farmhouse (1826); library, sitting rm; large fieldstone fireplace, rustic decor. View of Presidential Mts. Cr cds: A, MC, V.

★ ★ **EASTMAN.** *Main St (NH 16). 603/356-6707; res: 800/626-5855; FAX 603/356-7708.* E-mail eastman@eastmaninn.net; web www.eastmaninn.com. 14 rms, some A/C, 3 story. S, D $89-$129; higher rates fall foliage; lower rates off season. TV; cable. Complimentary full bkfst. Restaurant nearby. Ck-out 11 am, ck-in 3 pm. Downhill/x-country ski 1 mi. Built 1777. Antiques. Sitting rm with fireplace. Wrap-around porch. Totally nonsmoking. Cr cds: DS, MC, V.

✔ ★ ★ **THE FOREST.** *(NH 16A, Intervale 03845) 3¼ mi N on NH 16A. 603/356-9772; FAX 603/356-5652; res: 800/448-3534.* E-mail forest@ncia.net; web www.forest-inn.com. 11 rms, 1-3 story. July-mid-Oct, Dec-mid-Apr: S $75; D $80-$170; package plans; lower rates rest of yr. TV rm; cable. Heated pool. Complimentary full bkfst; afternoon refreshments. Ck-out 11 am, ck-in 3 pm. Downhill ski 4 mi; x-country ski on site. Lawn games. Tennis adj. Some fireplaces. Picnic table, grill. Operating as an inn since 1890. Totally nonsmoking. Cr cds: A, DS, MC, V.

★ ★ **MERRILL FARM.** *428 White Mt Hwy (NH 16). 603/447-3866; FAX 603/447-3867; res: 800/445-1017.* E-mail info@merrillfarm; web www.merrillfarm.com. 33 rms, 2 story, 17 suites; 11 cottages, 7 with kits. S, D $49-$99; each addl $12; suites $79-$149; cottages $69-$139; under 18 free; wkend rates; package plans; higher rates fall foliage. Crib free. TV; cable. Heated pool; whirlpool, sauna. Complimentary bkfst. Restaurant adj 6:30 am-10 pm. Ck-out 11 am. Coin lndry. Meeting rms. Downhill ski 3 mi; x-country ski 4 mi. Lawn games. Many refrigerators, in-rm whirlpools; some fireplaces. Picnic tables, grills. Converted farmhouse (1885) and cottages on Saco River. Dock. Cr cds: A, C, D, DS, MC, V.

✔ ★ ★ **SNOWVILLAGE.** *(Stuart Rd, Snowville 03832) 5 mi S on NH 16, then 6 mi S on NH 153, then 1½ mi E. 603/447-2818; FAX 603/447-5268; res: 800/447-4345.* E-mail snowvill@nxi.com; web www.snowvillageinn.com. 18 rms. No A/C. S, D $49-$99/person, each addl $45; MAP avail; extended stay rates. Dining rm 6-9 pm (public by res). Serv bar. Business servs avail. Downhill ski 6 mi; x-country ski on site. Hiking trails. Sauna. Lawn games. Some fireplaces. Secluded, on 10 acres. Panoramic view of mountains. Totally nonsmoking. Cr cds: A, D, DS, MC, V.

Resorts

★ ★ ★ **PURITY SPRING.** *(NH 153, East Madison 03849) 9 mi S on NH 153. 603/367-8896; FAX 603/367-8664; res: 800/373-3754.* E-mail info@purityspring.com; web www.purityspring.com. 48 rms, 4 share bath; 3 cottages (2-bedrm). AP: S $88-$117; D $73-$102/person; each addl $48; EP, MAP avail; wkly rates; ski plans. TV in common areas. Indoor pool; whirlpool. Playground. Supervised child's activities (late June-Labor Day); ages infant-6. Dining rm 7:30-9:30 am, noon-1:30 pm, 5:30-7:30 pm; Apr & Nov 8-9:30 am only. Bar 5-11 pm. Ck-out 11 am, ck-in 3 pm. Coin lndry. Business servs avail. Grocery, package store 9 mi. Sports dir. Tennis, pro. Private beach; waterskiing, rowboats, canoes, sailboats. Downhill ski on site. Sledding. Ice-skating. Exercise equipt. Lawn games. Rec rm. Game rm. Fish clean & store. Picnic tables. Cr cds: A, DS, MC, V.

★ ★ ★ **WHITE MOUNTAIN HOTEL & RESORT.** *West Side Rd. 603/356-7100; res: 800/533-6301.* E-mail dkelly@whitemountainhotel.com; web www.whitemountainhotel.com. 80 rms, 3 story, 13 suites. July-Oct: S, D $109-$159; suites $149-$199; under 18 free; wkly rates; ski, golf plans; lower rates rest of yr. Crib avail. TV; cable. Heated pool; whirlpool, poolside serv. Dining rm 7-10 am, 11:30 am-9 pm. Rm serv. Bar 11:30-1 am; entertainment, wkends (nightly in season). Ck-out 11 am, ck-in 3 pm. Coin lndry. Meeting rms. Business servs avail. Bellhops. Tennis. 9-hole golf, pro, putting green. Downhill ski 2½ mi. Exercise equipt; sauna. Game rm. Surrounded by White Mt Natl Forest and Echo Lake State Park. Cr cds: A, DS, MC, V.

Restaurants

★ ★ ★ **1785 INN.** *(See 1785 Inn) 603/356-9025.* E-mail the1785inn@aol.com; web www.the1785inn.com. French, Amer menu. Specialties: rack of lamb, raspberry duckling, veal chop morel. Own baking. Hrs: 8-9:30 am, 5-9 pm; wkends 7:30-10 am, 5-10 pm. Closed Dec 25. Res accepted. Bar 4 pm-midnight. Wine list. Complete meals: bkfst $9. Semi-a la carte: dinner $15-$23. Child's meals. Built by Revolutionary War veteran (1785); Colonial atmosphere, view of Mt Washington, antique fireplaces. Totally nonsmoking. Cr cds: A, C, D, DS, MC, V.

★ **BELLINI'S.** *33 Seavey St. 603/356-7000.* E-mail angelo@landmarknet.net; web www.bellinis.com. Italian menu. Specialties: rigatoni broccoli chicken, veal Marsala, fresh grilled seafood. Hrs: 5-10 pm; Fri, Sat to 11 pm. Closed Tues. Bar. Semi-a la carte: dinner $7.95-$17.95. Child's meals. Tuscan country atmosphere. Cr cds: A, C, D, DS, MC, V.

✔ ★ **HORSEFEATHERS.** *Main St. 603/356-2687.* Specializes in wood-grilled foods. Hrs: 11:30 am-11:45 pm. Closed Thanksgiving, Dec 25. Bar. Semi-a la carte: lunch, dinner $6.50-$17.95. Neighborhood nostalgia; landmark restaurant. Cr cds: A, MC, V.

★ ★ ★ **SCOTTISH LION.** *1¼ mi N on US 302 (NH 16). 603/356-6381.* Scottish, Amer menu. Specialties: Scottish trifle, Highland game pie, steak & mushroom pie. Own baking. Hrs: 11:30 am-2 pm, 5:30-9 pm; Sat to 9:30 pm; Sun brunch 10:30 am-2 pm. Closed Dec 24 eve, Dec 25. Res accepted. Bar. Wine list. Semi-a la carte: lunch $3.95-$7.95, dinner $9.95-$17.95. Sun brunch $12.95. Child's meals. Guest rms avail. Former residence of Erastus Bigelow, founder of Bigelow Carpet Co (ca 1872). Cr cds: A, C, D, DS, MC, V.

Unrated Dining Spot

PEACH'S. *Main St. 603/356-5860.* Specializes in home-made soups, desserts, salad dressings. Hrs: 6 am-2:30 pm. Closed Thanksgiving, Dec 25. Semi-a la carte: bkfst $1.25-$5.95, lunch $2-$5.95. Totally nonsmoking. No cr cds accepted.

North Woodstock

(see Lincoln/North Woodstock Area)

Peterborough (H-4)

(See also Jaffrey, Keene, Nashua)

Settled 1749 **Pop** 5,239 **Elev** 723 ft **Area code** 603 **Zip** 03458
InformationGreater Peterborough Chamber of Commerce, PO Box 401; 603/924-7234.

This was the home of composer Edward MacDowell (1861-1908). Edward Arlington Robinson, Stephen Vincent Benét, Willa Cather and Thornton Wilder, among others, worked at the MacDowell Colony, which made Peterborough famous.

What to See and Do

Greenfield State Park. 401 acres. Swimming, bathhouse; fishing. Picnicking, concessions. Camping (dump station) with separate beach. (Mid-May-mid-Oct) Standard fees. 9 mi N on NH 136, then W on unnumbered road, near Greenfield. Phone 603/547-3497.

Miller State Park. First of the New Hampshire parks. Atop 2,288-ft Pack Monadnock Mt; walking trails on summit; scenic drive; picnicking. (June-Labor Day, daily; May & Labor Day-Nov, Sat, Sun & hols) Standard fees. 4 mi E on NH 101.

New England Marionette Opera. Largest marionette facility in country devoted to opera. (Mid-May-late Dec, Sat eves, also Sun matinee; closed July 4, Thanksgiving) Main St. For reservations phone 603/924-4333.

Peterborough Historical Society. Exhibits on the history of the area; historical and genealogical library. (Mon-Fri; also Sat afternoon July-Aug) 19 Grove St. Phone 603/924-3235. July-Aug   ¢¢

Sharon Arts Center. Gallery and crafts center. (Daily) 5 mi SE on NH 123, in Sharon. Phone 603/924-7256.   **Free.**

Motel

★ **JACK DANIELS MOTOR INN.** *Rte 202 N, 2 mi N on US 202. 603/924-7548; FAX 603/924-7700.* 17 rms, shower only, 2 story. S $69; D $84; each addl $10; under 12 free; higher rates fall foliage season. TV; cable. Complimentary coffee in lobby. Ck-out 11 am. Business servs avail. Downhill ski 10 mi. On river. Cr cds: MC, V.

Inns

★ ★ **GREENFIELD.** *(Rte 31, Forest Rd, Greenfield 03047) 3 mi N on US 202, 6 mi NE on NH 136, in center of town. 603/547-6327; FAX 603/547-2418; res: 800/678-4144.* E-mail innkeeper@greenfieldinn.com; web www.greenfieldinn.com. 13 rms, 6 with bath, 2 story. D $49-$89; each addl $20; suite $119-$149, cottage $159; wkly rates. TV; cable, VCR (free movies). Complimentary full bkfst. Restaurants nearby. Ck-out 11 am, ck-in 4 pm. Business servs avail. Downhill/x-country ski 6 mi. Cr cds: A, MC, V.

★ ★ ★ **HANCOCK INN.** *(33 Main St, Hancock 03449) 3 mi N on US 202. 603/525-3318; FAX 603/525-9301; res: 800/525-1789.* 11 rms, 3 story. S $88-$110; D $106-$172. Children over 12 yrs only. TV; cable. Complimentary full bkfst; afternoon refreshments. Restaurant (see HANCOCK INN). Ck-out 11 am, ck-in 2 pm. Business servs avail. In-rm modem link. Luggage handling. Built 1789. Original art by Moses Eaton and Rufus Porter; antiques. Totally nonsmoking. Cr cds: A, C, D, DS, MC, V.

Restaurants

★ ★ ★ **HANCOCK INN.** *(See Hancock Inn) 603/525-3318.* Specialties: Shaker cranberry pot roast, roast duckling, apple braised salmon. Hrs: 6-9 pm. Closed Dec 25. Res required. Serv bar. Semi-a la carte: dinner $15-$22.50. Country decor; antiques. Totally nonsmoking. Cr cds: A, C, D, MC, V.

★ ★ **LATACARTA.** *6 School St. 603/924-6878.* Specialties: baked salmon with fresh herbs, tofu vegetarian dinner. Hrs: noon-2 pm, 5-8:30 pm; Fri, Sat to 9 pm; Sun 5-8 pm. Closed Mon; Dec 25. Res accepted. Bar. Semi-a la carte: lunch $4.75-$12, dinner $10-$16.95. Prix fixe: lunch $15, dinner $50. Child's meals. Former movie theater. Totally nonsmoking. Cr cds: A, MC, V.

Pinkham Notch (D-5)

(See also Gorham, Jackson, North Conway)

Elev 2,000 ft (at highest point) **E-mail** info@4seasonresort.com **Web** www.4seasonresort.com
Information Mt Washington Valley Chamber of Commerce, N Main St, PO Box 2300, North Conway 03860; 603/356-5701 or 800/367-3364.

Named for Joseph Pinkham, a 1790 settler, this easternmost White Mountain pass is closest to Mt Washington (see). Headquarters for the Appalachian Mountain Club Hut System is here.

What to See and Do

Glen Ellis Falls Scenic Area. E of NH 16, 12 mi N of Glen in White Mountain National Forests(see).

Skiing.

Wildcat Ski & Recreation Area. Detachable quad, 3 triple, double chairlifts, patrol, school, rentals; snowmaking; cafeteria, nursery. Longest run 2³/₄ mi; vertical drop 2,100 ft. Gondola. (Mid-Nov-late Apr, daily; closed Thanksgiving, Dec 25) Gondola also operates Memorial Day-late Oct (daily); picnicking. 10 mi N of Jackson on NH 16 in White Mt Natl Forest (see). Phone 603/466-3326.   ¢¢¢¢

Plymouth (F-4)

(See also Holderness, Meredith, Waterville Valley)

Settled 1764 **Pop** 5,811 **Elev** 660 ft **Area code** 603 **Zip** 03264 **E-mail** staff@plymouthnh.org **Web** www.plymouthnh.org
Information Chamber of Commerce, PO Box 65; 603/536-1001 or 800/386-3678.

Since 1795, Plymouth's varied industries have included lumber, pig iron, mattresses, gloves and sporting goods. It has been a resort center since the mid-19th century.

What to See and Do

Mary Baker Eddy Historic House. Residence of Mary Baker Eddy from 1860-1862, prior to the founding of the Christian Science Church. (May-Oct, daily exc Mon; closed hols) Approx 7 mi W via NH 25 to Stinson Lake Rd, then approx 1 mi N to N side of the Village of Rumney. Phone 603/786-9943.   ¢

Plymouth State College (1871). (3,200 students) A member of the Univ System of New Hampshire. Art exhibits in galleries and Lamson Library. Music, theater and dance performances in Silver Cultural Arts Center (some fees). Planetarium shows. Tours. 1 blk W of business center. Phone 603/535-5000.

Polar Caves Park. Glacial caves; animal exhibits; local minerals; scenic rock formations; maple sugar museum; gift shops, picnicking. (Early May-late Oct, daily) 5 mi W on Tenney Mt Hwy (NH 25). Phone 603/536-1888. ¢¢¢

Motel

★ **SUSSE CHALET.** *US 3, I-93 exit 26. 603/536-2330; FAX 603/536-2686.* 38 rms, 2 story. S $63.95; D $73.95; each addl $5; suite $83; family rates; ski, golf, bicycle plans. Crib free. Pet accepted. TV; cable, VCR avail. Pool. Complimentary continental bkfst. Restaurant opp 6 am-11 pm. Ck-out 11 am. Coin lndry. Meeting rm. Business servs avail. In-rm modem link. Downhill/x-country ski 15 mi. Some refrigerators. Picnic tables. Cr cds: A, D, DS, MC, V.

Restaurants

✔★ **JIGGER JOHNSON'S.** *75 Main St. 603/536-4386.* Specialties: chicken Dijon, steak Diane. Hrs: noon-10 pm; Thurs-Sat to midnight. Closed Dec 25. Bar. Semi-a la carte: lunch $2.95-$5.95, dinner $6.95-$11.95. Child's meals. Some street parking. Lively, informal atmosphere. Eclectic decor. Cr cds: A, DS, MC, V.

★ **TREE HOUSE.** *3 S Main St. 603/536-4084.* E-mail treehous@worldpath.net. Specializes in chicken, steak, seafood. Hrs: 11:30 am-2:30 pm, 4:30-9 pm. Closed Thanksgiving, Dec 25. Res accepted. Bar. Semi-a la carte: lunch $3.95-$8.95, dinner $8.95-$14.95. Child's meals. Musicians Fri, Sat. Rustic atmosphere; large stone fireplace, vintage items decorate rm. Cr cds: A, D, DS, MC, V.

Portsmouth (H-6)

(See also Dover, Exeter, Hampton Beach)

Settled 1630 **Pop** 25,925 **Elev** 21 ft **Area code** 603 **Zip** 03801
Information Greater Portsmouth Chamber of Commerce, 500 Market St, PO Box 239, 03802-0239; 603/436-3988 or 603/436-1118.

A tour of Portsmouth's famous houses is like a tour through time, with Colonial and Federal architecture from 1684 into the 19th century. Onetime capital of New Hampshire, Portsmouth was also the home port of a dynasty of merchant seamen who grew rich and built accordingly. The old atmosphere still exists in the narrow streets near Market Square.

The US Navy Yard, located in Kittery, Maine (see), on the Piscataqua River, has long been Portsmouth's major "industry." The peace treaty ending the Russo-Japanese War was signed at the Portsmouth Navy Yard in 1905.

What to See and Do

Children's Museum of Portsmouth. Arts and science museum featuring mock submarine, space shuttle, lobster boat, exhibits and gallery. (Summer & school vacations, daily; rest of yr, Tues-Sat, also Sun afternoons) 280 Marcy St. Phone 603/436-3853. ¢¢

Ft Constitution (1808). The first cannon was placed on this site in 1632; in 1694 it was known as Ft William and Mary. Information about a British order to stop gun powder from coming into the colonies, brought by Paul Revere on Dec 13, 1774, caused the Sons of Liberty from Portsmouth, New Castle and Rye to attack and capture the next day a fort that held 5 tons of gun powder. Much of this powder was used at Bunker Hill by the patriots. This uprising against the authority of the King was one of the first overt acts of the Revolution. Little remains of the original fort except the base of its walls. Ft Constitution had been built on the same site by 1808; granite walls were added during the Civil War. (Mid-June-early Sept, daily;

late May-mid-June, late Sept-mid-Oct, wkends, hols only) 4 mi E on NH 1B in New Castle. **Free.**

Ft Stark State Historic Site. A former portion of the coastal defense system dating back to 1746, exhibiting many of the changes in military technology from the Revolutionary War through World War II. The fort is situated on Jerry's Point, overlooking the Piscataqua River, Little Harbor and Atlantic Ocean. (Late May-mid-Oct; Sat & Sun) Wild Rose Lane, approx 5 mi E off NH 1B in New Castle. Phone 603/433-8583. ¢¢

InSight Tours. Specialized tours of Historic Portsmouth and the New Hampshire coastline including garden, history, nature and antique tours. 24-hr advance res requested. Phone 603/436-4223. ¢¢¢¢¢

Old Harbour Area. Features craftsmen, unique shops, bookstores, restaurants. Located on Historic Waterfront; NH 95 exit 7.

Portsmouth Harbor Cruises. Narrated historical tours aboard the 49-passenger M/V *Heritage.* 1¹/₂-hr harbor, 2¹/₂-hr Isles of Shoals, 1-hr cocktail, 1¹/₂-hr sunset cruises, 2¹/₂-hr inland river cruise, fall foliage cruise. (Mid-June-Oct) 64 Ceres St, Old Harbor District. For information and res phone 603/436-8084 or 800/776-0915. ¢¢¢-¢¢¢¢

⭐ **Portsmouth Historic Homes.** The Historic Associates, part of the Greater Portsmouth Chamber of Commerce, has walking-tour maps for 6 historic houses; maps are avail free at the Chamber of Commerce, 500 Market St; 603/436-1118.The houses include

Moffatt-Ladd House (1763). Built by Capt John Moffatt; later the home of Gen William Whipple, his son-in-law, a signer of the Declaration of Independence. Many original 18th- and 19th-century furnishings. Formal gardens. (Mid-June-mid-Oct, daily) 154 Market St. Phone 603/436-8221. ¢¢

Warner House (1716). One of New England's finest Georgian houses, with scagliola in the dining rm, restored mural paintings on the staircase walls, beautiful paneling, a lightning rod on the west wall said to have been installed by Benjamin Franklin in 1762, five portraits by Joseph Blackburn, appropriate furnishings. (June-mid-Oct, daily exc Mon) 150 Daniel St, at Chapel St. Phone 603/436-5909. ¢¢

John Paul Jones House (1758). Where the famous naval commander twice boarded; now a museum containing period furniture, collections of costumes, china, glass, documents, weapons. Guided tours (mid-May-mid-Oct, daily). 43 Middle St, at State St. Phone 603/436-8420. ¢¢

Governor John Langdon House (1784). John Langdon served 3 terms as governor of New Hampshire and was the first president *pro tempore* of the US Senate. House's exterior proportions are monumental; interior embellished with excellent woodcarving and fine Portsmouth-area furniture. George Washington was entertained here in 1789. Architect Stanford White was commissioned to add the large wing at the rear with dining rm in the Colonial-revival style. Surrounded by landscaped grounds with gazebo, rose and grape arbor and restored perennial garden beds. Tours (June-mid-Oct, Wed-Sun; closed hols). 143 Pleasant St. Phone 603/436-3205. ¢¢

Rundlet-May House (1807). Federal-style, 3-story mansion. House sits on terraces and retains its original 1812 courtyard and garden layout; landscaped grounds. House contains family furnishings and accessories, including many fine examples of Federal-period craftsmanship and the latest technologies of its time. (June-mid-Oct, Wed-Sun afternoons) 364 Middle St. Phone 603/436-3205. ¢¢

Wentworth-Gardner House (1760). Excellent example of Georgian architecture. Elaborate woodwork, scenic wallpaper, magnificent main staircase. (Mid-June-mid-Oct, Tues-Sun afternoons) 50 Mechanic St. Phone 603/436-4406. ¢¢

Star Island and Isles of Shoals. The M/V *Thomas Laighton* and the M/V *Oceanic* make cruises to historic Isles of Shoals, Star Island walkabouts, whale watch expeditions, lobster clambake river cruises, fall foliage excursion and others. (Mid-June-Labor Day, daily) Depart from Barker's Wharf, 315 Market St. For reservations phone 603/431-5500. ¢¢¢¢

⭐ **Strawbery Banke Museum.** Restoration of 10-acre historic waterfront neighborhood; site of original Portsmouth settlement. 42 buildings, dating from 1695-1950. Nine houses—Capt Keyran Walsh House (1796), Gov Goodwin Mansion (1811), Chase House (1762), Capt John Wheelwright House (1780), Thomas Bailey Aldrich House (1790), and Drisco House (1790s), Rider-Wood House (1840s), Abbott Grocery Store (1943)—and the William Pitt Tavern (1766) are restored with period furnishings. Shops, architectural exhibits, craft shops and demonstrations; tool, photo, archaeological and house construction exhibits; family programs and activities, special events, tours; picnicking, coffee shop. (May-Oct, daily) Hancock & Marcy Sts, downtown, follow signs. Phone 603/433-1100. ¢¢¢

Annual Events

Market Square Days. Summer celebration with 10K road race, street fair, entertainment. Phone 603/431-5388. June.

Portsmouth Jazz Festival. Two stages with continuous performances on the historical Portsmouth waterfront. For schedule phone 603/436-7678. Last Sun June.

Motels

★ ★ **COMFORT INN.** 1390 Lafayette Rd, 1390 Lafayette Rd, 3 mi S on US 1. 603/433-3338; FAX 603/431-1639. 121 rms, 6 story. June-Labor Day: S, D $89-$115; under 18 free; lower rates rest of yr. Crib free. TV; cable (premium). Indoor pool; whirlpool. Complimentary continental bkfst. Restaurant adj 11 am-8 pm. Ck-out 11 am. Coin lndry. Meeting rms. Business servs avail. In-rm modem link. Sundries. Gift shop. Exercise equipt. Refrigerators avail. Cr cds: A, C, D, DS, ER, JCB, MC, V.

[D] [pool] [exercise] [X] [N] [fire] [SC]

✓ ★ **PINE HAVEN.** (183 Lafayette Rd, North Hampton 03862) 5 mi S on US 1. 603/964-8187. 19 rms, 4 kits. (no oven). Mid-June-Labor Day (2-day min hols & wkends): S $59; D $65-$75; each addl $5; kit. units $78; lower rates rest of yr. Crib $3. TV; cable. Complimentary coffee in rms. Restaurant nearby. Ck-out 11 am. Refrigerators. Cr cds: A, DS, MC, V.

[fire]

✓ ★ **PORT MOTOR INN.** 505 US 1 Bypass, at Portsmouth Circle, I-95 exit 5. 603/436-4378; FAX 603/436-4378, ext. 200; res: 800/282-7678. 56 rms, 1-2 story, 20 studios. July-early Sept: S $62.95-$99.95; D $68.95-$99.95; each addl $6; studios $79.95-$119.95; under 13 free; lower rates rest of yr. Crib free. Pet accepted. TV; cable (premium). Pool. Complimentary continental bkfst. Ck-out 11 am. Refrigerator in studios. Picnic tables. Cr cds: A, C, D, DS, MC, V.

[P] [pool] [N] [fire] [SC]

★ **SUSSE CHALET.** 650 Borthwick Ave, I-95 exit 5. 603/436-6363; FAX 603/436-1621. 105 rms, 4 story. June-Labor Day: S, D $69.70-$100.70; under 18 free; lower rates rest of yr. Crib free. TV; cable (premium). Pool. Complimentary continental bkfst. Complimentary coffee. Restaurant nearby. Ck-out 11 am. Coin lndry. Business servs avail. Refrigerators avail. Cr cds: A, C, D, DS, MC, V.

[D] [pool] [N] [fire] [SC]

Motor Hotels

★ ★ **HOLIDAY INN.** 300 Woodbury Ave, I-95 exit at Portsmouth Cir. 603/431-8000; FAX 603/431-2065. 130 rms, 6 story. July-Labor Day: S, D $105.95-$150; suites $190; under 20 free; lower rates rest of yr. Crib free. TV; cable (premium). Indoor pool. Restaurant 6:30 am-9:30 pm. Rm serv. Bar 11:30-1 am; entertainment Tues-Sat. Ck-out 11 am. Meeting rms. Valet serv. Sundries. Exercise equipt. Game rm. Refrigerators avail. Cr cds: A, C, D, DS, JCB, MC, V.

[D] [pool] [X] [N] [fire] [SC]

★ ★ **SHERATON.** 250 Market St (03885). 603/431-2300; res: 800/325-3505; FAX 603/433-5649. 181 rms, 5 story, 24 suites. Mid-Apr-late Oct: S, D $135-$185; each addl $10; suites $275-$450; under 18 free; lower rates rest of yr. Crib avail. Garage parking $6. TV; cable (premium). Indoor pool. Complimentary coffee in rms. Restaurant 6:30 am-2:30 pm, 5:30-10 pm. Rm serv. Bar; entertainment. Ck-out 11 am. Meeting rms. Business center. Bellhops. Sundries. Valet serv. Free airport transporta-tion. Exercise equipt; sauna. Minibars; refrigerator in suites. On Piscataqua River. Cr cds: A, C, D, DS, MC, V.

[D] [pool] [X] [N] [N] [SC] [A]

Inns

★ **INN AT CHRISTIAN SHORE.** 335 Maplewood Ave. 603/431-6770. 5 rms, 2 story. No rm phones. June-Labor Day: S $75; D $95; each addl $15; lower rates rest of yr. TV; cable (premium). Complimentary full bkfst. Restaurant nearby. Ck-out 11 am, ck-in 2 pm. Free bus depot transportation. Fireplace. Restored Federal-style house (ca 1800); antiques, oil paintings. Totally nonsmoking. Cr cds: A, MC, V.

[N] [N] [SC]

★ ★ ★ **SISE.** 40 Court St. 603/433-1200; FAX 603/433-1200; res: 800/267-0525. 34 rms, 4 story, 9 suites. May-Nov: S $105-$175; D $115-$175; each addl $10; suites $150-$175; under 6 free; lower rates rest of yr. Crib $5. TV; cable (premium), VCR (movies $3). Complimentary continental bkfst. Restaurant nearby. Ck-out 11 am, ck-in 4 pm. Meeting rms. Business servs avail. Some in-rm whirlpools. Picnic tables, grills. Built 1881; antiques. Cr cds: A, C, D, MC, V.

[D] [N] [fire] [SC]

Restaurants

★ ★ ★ **METRO.** 20 High St, off Market Sq. 603/436-0521. Specializes in clam chowder, fresh seafood, veal Metro. Hrs: 11:30 am-2:30 pm, 5:30-10 pm. Closed Sun; Thanksgiving, Dec 25. Bar. Semi-a la carte: lunch $6-$12, dinner $12-$24. Entertainment Fri, Sat. Cr cds: A, MC, V.

[D] [⌐]

✓ ★ **PIER II.** 10 State St, at Memorial Bridge. 603/436-0669. Specializes in lobster, steak, seafood. Salad bar. Hrs: 11:30 am-11 pm. Closed Thanksgiving, Dec 25; also Jan. Res accepted. Bar to 1 am. Semi-a la carte: lunch $3-$6.50, dinner $8-$15. Child's meals. Entertainment Sun-Fri. Valet parking. Outdoor dining. Overlooks harbor; dockage. Cr cds: A, C, D, DS, MC, V.

[D] [⌐] [♥]

★ ★ **YOKEN'S THAR SHE BLOWS.** 1390 Lafayette Rd, 3 mi S of Traffic Circle on US 1. 603/436-8224. Specializes in steak, native seafood. Hrs: 11 am-8 pm; July & Aug to 9 pm. Res accepted. Serv bar. Semi-a la carte: lunch $3.25-$6.50, dinner $7.95-$12.95. Complete meals: lunch $4.95-$6.50. Child's meals. Nautical decor. Cr cds: A, C, D, DS, MC, V.

[D]

Salem (J-5)

Pop 25,746 **Elev** 131 ft **Area code** 603 **Zip** 03079 **E-mail** gscofc@ix.netcom.com **Web** www.salemnhchamber.org

Information Greater Salem Chamber of Commerce, 220 N Broadway, PO Box 304; 603/893-3177.

What to See and Do

⊠ **America's Stonehenge.** A megalithic calendar site dated to 2000 B.C., with 22 stone buildings on more than 30 acres. The main site features a number of stone-constructed chambers and is surrounded by miles of stone walls containing large, shaped monoliths that indicate the rising and setting of the sun at the solstice and equinox, as well as other astronomical alignments, including lunar. (Late Mar-late Dec, daily) 5 mi E of I-93, just off NH 111 in North Salem. Phone 603/893-8300. ¢¢¢

Canobie Lake Park. Family amusement park; giant roller coaster, log flume, pirate ship, giant ferris wheel, haunted mine ride; entertainment; lake cruise, fireworks; games, pool; concessions, restaurant. (Memorial

Day-Labor Day, daily; Apr-late May, wkends) 1 mi E of I-93, exit 2. Phone 603/893-3506. ¢¢¢¢¢

Robert Frost Farm. Home of poet Robert Frost from 1900-1911; period furnishings; audiovisual display; poetry-nature trail. (June-Labor Day, daily; after Labor Day-mid-Oct, wkends only) 1 mi SW on NH 38, then NW on NH 28 in Derry. Phone 603/432-3091. ¢¢

Rockingham Park. Thoroughbred horse racing. Live and simulcast racing (daily). Exit 1 off I-93. Phone 603/898-2311.

Motels

✔★ **PARK VIEW INN.** *109 S Broadway (NH 28). 603/898-5632; FAX 603/894-6579.* 58 rms, 28 kits. May-Dec: S $46-$56; D, kit. units (4-day min) $59; each addl $6; under 12 free; wkly rates; lower rates rest of yr. Crib free. TV; cable (premium). Complimentary continental bkfst. Restaurant nearby. Ck-out 11 am. Coin lndry. In-rm modem link. Refrigerators. Cr cds: A, C, D, DS, MC, V.

★ **SUSSE CHALET.** *8 Keewaydin Dr, I-93, exit 2. 603/893-4722; FAX 603/893-2898; res: 800/524-2538.* 104 rms, 4 story. S, D $64.70; under 18 free; seasonal rates. Crib free. TV; cable (premium). Pool. Continental bkfst. Restaurant opp 6 am-11 pm. Ck-out 11 am. Coin lndry. Meeting rm. Business servs avail. In-rm modem link. Cr cds: A, C, D, DS, MC, V.

Hotel

★★ **HOLIDAY INN.** *1 Keewaydin Dr, I-93 exit 2. 603/893-5511; FAX 603/894-6728.* 83 rms, 6 story. May-Oct: S, D $99-$109; lower rates rest of yr. Pet accepted. TV; cable (premium). Pool; poolside serv. Complimentary continental bkfst. Complimentary coffee in rms. Restaurant 6:30 am-10 pm. Ck-out 11 am. No bellhops. Meeting rms. Business servs avail. In-rm modem link. Exercise equipt. Health club privileges. Refrigerator avail. Cr cds: A, C, D, DS, ER, JCB, MC, V.

Sunapee (G-3)

(See also New London, Newport)

Pop 2,559 **Elev** 1,008 ft **Area code** 603 **Zip** 03782 **E-mail** sunapeevacations@sugar-river.net **Web** www.sunapeevacations.com

Information Lake Sunapee Business Association, PO Box 400; 603/763-2495 or 800/258-3530.

This is a year-round resort community on beautiful Lake Sunapee.

What to See and Do

Lake cruises.

M/V *Mt Sunapee II* Excursion Boat. 1½-hr narrated tours of Lake Sunapee. (Mid-June-Labor Day, daily; mid-May-mid-June & after Labor Day-mid-Oct, Sat & Sun) Lake Ave, Sunapee Harbor, off NH 11. Phone 603/763-4030. ¢¢¢

M/V *Kearsarge* Restaurant Ship. Buffet dinner while cruising around Lake Sunapee. Phone 603/763-5477. ¢¢¢¢¢

Mt Sunapee State Park. 2,714 acres. 1 mi S off NH 103. Phone 603/763-2356.

Summer. Swimming beach, bathhouse (fee); mountain biking (fee); trout pool; picnicking, playground, concession; chairlift rides (fee). Displays by artists & craftsmen (see ANNUAL EVENT). (Memorial Day wkend; mid-June-early Sept, daily; early Sept-Columbus Day, wkends)

Winter. Skiing. 3 triple, 3 double chairlifts, pony lift; patrol, school, rentals; cafeteria; snowmaking; nursery. 38 slopes and trails. Snowboarding. (Dec-Mar, daily; closed Dec 25) For snow conditions phone 800/552-1234. ¢¢¢¢¢

Snowhill at Eastman Ski Area. 1 chairlift; patrol, school; concession. Longest run ½ mi; vertical drop 243 ft. (Dec-Mar, Sat, Sun & hols exc Dec 25) Ski Touring Center has 30 km of cross-country trails; patrol, school, rentals; bar, restaurant (Dec-Mar, Wed-Sun; closed Dec 25). Summer facilities include Eastman Lake (swimming, boating, fishing); 18-hole golf, tennis; indoor pool; hiking. 4 mi N on NH 11, then 6 mi N on I-89, exit 13. Phone 603/863-4500 or 603/863-4240. Cross-country skiing ¢¢¢; Downhill ¢¢¢¢

Annual Event

League of New Hampshire Craftsmen's Fair. Mt Sunapee State Park (see). Over 200 craftsmen and artists display and sell goods. Phone 603/224-3375. Aug.

Motel

★ **BURKEHAVEN.** *179 Burkehaven Hill Rd, 1½ mi E of NH 11. 603/763-2788; FAX 603/763-9065; res: 800/567-2788.* E-mail boundbrook@cyberportal.net. 10 air-cooled rms, shower only, 5 kits. S, D $73; each addl $5; kit. units $85; wkly rates; ski packages. Crib free. Pet accepted. TV. Pool. Complimentary coffee in rms. Restaurant nearby. Ck-out 11 am. Business servs avail. Tennis. Some refrigerators. Cr cds: A, DS, MC, V.

Inns

✔★★ **CANDELITE INN.** *(5 Greenhouse Lane, Bradford 03221) Approx 10 mi W on NH 103, N on NH 114. 603/938-5571; res: 888/812-5571; FAX 603/938-2564.* Web www.virtualcities.com/ons/nh/nhyb601.htm. 6 rms, 2 with shower only, 3 story. No rm phones. S, D $70-$95; wkends (2-day min); higher rates: fall foliage, graduation. Complimentary full bkfst. Ck-out 11 am, ck-in 3 pm. Luggage handling. Downhill ski 7 mi. Lawn games. Built in 1897; gazebo porch. Totally nonsmoking. Cr cds: A, DS, MC, V.

★★ **DEXTER'S INN AND TENNIS CLUB.** *258 Stagecoach Rd, I-89 exit 12, 5 mi W on NH 11, left on Winhill Rd to Stagecoach Rd. 603/763-5571; res: 800/232-5571.* E-mail dexters@kear.tds.net; web www.bbhost.com/dextersinn/. 10 rms in lodge, 7 rms in annex, 2 story. No rm phones. MAP, May-Nov (2-day min wkends): S $95-$140; D $135-$180; each addl $45; kit. cottage (up to 4) $385; EP, golf, tennis plans. Closed rest of yr. Crib $5. Pet accepted; $10. TV in lobby. Pool. Dining rm 8-10 am, 6:30-8:30 pm. Rm serv 24 hrs. Bar 5-10 pm. Ck-out 11 am, ck-in 3 pm. Meeting rms. Business servs avail. Tennis, pro. Lawn games. On 20 acre estate. Cr cds: DS, MC, V.

Twin Mountain (D-5)

(See also Bretton Woods, Franconia, Littleton)

Pop 760 (est) **Elev** 1,442 ft **Area code** 603 **Zip** 03595 **Web** www.twinmountain.org

Information Chamber of Commerce, PO Box 194; 800/245-8946.

What to See and Do

Mt Washington (see). E off US 302.

White Mt Natl Forest (see). E on US 302; SW on US 3.

Motels

★ ★ **FOUR SEASONS MOTOR INN.** *US 3, exit 35.* 603/846-5708; *res: 800/228-5708.* Web www.4seasonsmotorinn.com. 24 rms, 2 story. No rm phones. S $40; D $47-$65; each addl $5; under 12 free; ski plans. Crib free. TV; cable. Pool. Playground. Restaurant nearby. Ck-out 11 am. Sundries. Downhill/x-country ski 4 mi. Game rm. Lawn games. Some refrigerators. Balconies. Picnic tables, grills. Cr cds: DS, MC, V.

🐾 🏊 ⛷ 🎿 SC

✔★ ★ **PAQUETTE'S MOTOR INN.** *US 3.* 603/846-5562. 33 rms, 2 story. S $37-$42; D $40-$62; wkly rates. Closed Apr-May, Nov-Dec. Crib $10. TV; cable. Pool. Restaurant 4:30-9 pm. Ck-out 10:30 am. Tennis. Golf privileges. Downhill/x-country ski 5 mi. Balconies. At base of White Mts. Cr cds: A, MC, V.

🐾 🧗 🏃 🏊 🎿 🔥 SC

★ **PROFILE DELUXE.** *US 3.* 603/846-5522; *res: 800/682-7222.* 13 rms, 12 A/C. S $50; D $65; each addl $5; under 12 free; wkly rates. Crib $5. TV; cable. Heated pool. Playground. Restaurant opp 6 am-10 pm. Ck-out 11 am. Downhill ski 5 mi; x-country ski on site. Some refrigerators. Cr cds: A, DS, MC, V.

🐾 🏊 🎿 🎿 🔥

Inn

✔★ ★ **NORTHERN ZERMATT.** *US 3, 1 mi N of jct US 302.* 603/846-5533; *FAX 603/846-5664; res: 800/535-3214.* 17 rms, 9 A/C, 2-3 story. No rm phones. S $32; D $40-$57; each addl $6; kit. units $57-$79; under 16 free; wkly rates. TV in some rms; cable. Pool. Playground. Complimentary continental bkfst. Restaurant nearby. Ck-out 11 am, ck-in after 3 pm. 18-hole golf privileges. Lawn games. Picnic tables, grills. Former boarding house (ca 1900) for loggers and railroad workers. Cr cds: DS, MC, V.

🐾 🧗 🏃 🏊 🔥 SC

Waterville Valley (E-5)

(See also Lincoln/North Woodstock Area, Plymouth)

Founded 1829 **Pop** 151 **Elev** 1,519 ft **Area code** 603 **Zip** 03215
Information Waterville Valley Region Chamber of Commerce, RFD 1, Box 1067, Campton 03223; 603/726-3804.

Although the resort village of Waterville Valley was developed in the late 1960s, the surrounding area has been attracting tourists since the mid-19th century, when summer vacationers stayed at the Waterville Inn. Completely encircled by the White Mountain National Forests, the resort, which is approximately 11 miles northeast of Campton, offers a variety of winter and summer activities, as well as spectacular views of the surrounding mountain peaks.

What to See and Do

Waterville Valley Ski Area. 5 double, 3 triple chairlifts, quad chairlift, T-bar, J-bar, platter pull; patrol; school; retail, rental and repair shops; snowmaking; restaurants, cafeterias, lounge; nursery. 48 ski trails; longest run 3 mi; vertical drop 2,020 ft. Limited lift tickets; half-day rates. (Mid-Nov-mid-Apr, daily) Ski Touring Center with 46 mi of cross-country trails; rentals, school, restaurants. Summer facilities include 9-hole golf, 18 clay tennis courts, small boating, hiking, fishing, bicycling, rollerblading, horseback riding; entertainment. Indoor sports center (daily). 11 mi NE of Campton on NH 49. Contact Waterville Valley Resort, Town Square; 800/468-2553. ¢¢¢¢¢

Lodge

★ ★ ★ **SNOWY OWL.** *Village Rd.* 603/236-8383; *FAX 603/236-4890; res: 800/766-9969.* 83 rms, 4 story. No A/C. Dec-Mar: S, D $79-$169; each addl $10; ski, golf, tennis plans; higher rates hol ski wk; lower rates rest of yr. Crib free. TV; cable (premium), VCR avail. Pool. Complimentary continental bkfst; afternoon refreshments. Restaurant nearby. Ck-out 11 am. Coin lndry. Meeting rms. Business servs avail. 9-hole golf privileges, greens fee $12-$18. Downhill ski 1 mi; x-country ski on site. Whirlpool. Rec rm. Health club privileges. Some in-rm whirlpools, minibars. Shopping arcade adj. Cr cds: A, D, DS, MC, V.

D 🧗 🏊 🏃 🏊 🔥 SC

Hotel

★ ★ **BLACK BEAR LODGE.** *NH 49, off Village Rd.* 603/236-4501; *FAX 603/236-4114; res: 800/349-2327.* E-mail wvlodge@together.net; web users.aol.com/wvlodge. 107 kit. suites, 78 A/C, 6 story. Suites $78-$229; ski plans; higher rates hol wkends; lower rates off season. Crib free. TV; cable (premium). Indoor/outdoor pool; whirlpool. Complimentary coffee in lobby. Restaurant opp 8 am-9 pm. No rm serv. Ck-out 11 am. Coin lndry. Meeting rms. Business servs avail. Downhill ski 2 mi; x-country ski 1/2 mi. Sauna. Health club privileges. Game rm. Fieldstone fireplace in lobby. Near pond. Cr cds: A, D, DS, MC, V.

🐾 🏊 🏊 🎿 🔥 SC

Resort

★ ★ **VALLEY INN.** *Tecumseh Rd.* 603/236-8336; *FAX 603/236-4294; res: 800/343-0969.* 52 rms, 5 story (enter on 2nd level). Mid-Dec-Mar, MAP: S, D $79-$169; under 12 free; package plans; lower rates summer & fall. Crib $5. TV; cable. Indoor/outdoor pool; whirlpool. Dining rm 8-11 am, 6-10 pm. Rm serv. Bar 4 pm-1 am; entertainment Fri, Sat (in season). Ck-out 11 am, ck-in 4 pm. Coin lndry. Meeting rms. Business servs avail. In-rm modem link. Tennis privileges, pro. 9-hole golf privileges, greens fee $8-$15, pro. Downhill/x-country ski 1 mi. Rec rm. Exercise equipt; sauna. Refrigerators, wet bars, in-rm whirlpools. Cr cds: A, C, D, DS, MC, V.

D 🧗 🏃 🏊 🎿 🔥

Restaurants

★ **CHILE PEPPERS.** *Town Square.* 603/236-4646. Mexican, Amer menu. Specialties: BBQ ribs, chile rellenos, fajitas. Hrs: noon-9 pm; Fri, Sat noon-9:30 pm. No A/C. Bar. Semi-a la carte: lunch $3.95-$7.95, dinner $6.95-$13.95. Outdoor dining. View of mountains, Snows Brook waterfall. Cr cds: A, C, D, MC, V.

D 🍽

★ ★ **THE WILLIAM TELL.** *(Waterville Valley Rd (NH 49), Thornton 03223) 3 mi E on NH 49.* 603/726-3618. Swiss, Amer menu. Specializes in fresh seafood, venison, veal. Hrs: 5-10 pm; Sun brunch noon-3 pm. Closed Wed. Res accepted. Bar. Semi-a la carte: dinner $10.50-$20. Sun brunch $6.25-$9.50. Child's meals. Patio dining overlooking duck pond. Swiss atmosphere. Family-owned. Cr cds: A, D, MC, V.

D

White Mountain National Forest (E-4 - C-5)

This national forest and major New Hampshire recreation area includes the Presidential Range and a major part of the White Mountains. There are more than 100 miles of roads and 1,128 miles of foot trails. The Appalachian Trail, with eight hostels, winds over some spectacular peaks. Eight peaks tower more than a mile above sea level; the highest is Mt Washington (6,288 feet). 22 mountains rise more than 4,000 feet. There are several well-defined ranges, divided by deep "notches" and broader valleys. Clear streams rush through the notches; mountain lakes and ponds dot the landscape. Deer, bear, moose and bobcat roam the wilds; trout fishing is good.

The US Forest Service administers 23 campgrounds with more than 700 sites ($12-$16/site/night), also picnicking sites for public use. There is lodging within the forest; for information, reservations contact the Appalachian Mountain Club, Pinkham Notch, Gorham 03581; 603/466-2727. There are also many resorts, campsites, picnicking and recreational spots in private and state-owned areas. A visitor center (daily) is at the Saco Ranger Station, 33 Kancamagus Hwy, Conway 03818; 603/447-5448. Information stations are also located at exits 28 and 32 off I-93 and at Franconia Notch State Park Visitor Center. For further information contact the Supervisor, White Mountain National Forests, 719 Main St, Laconia 03246; 603/528-8721.

The following cities and villages in and near the forest are included in the *Mobil Travel Guide*: Bartlett, Bretton Woods, Franconia, Franconia Notch State Park, Gorham, Jackson, Lincoln/North Woodstock Area, Mt Washington, North Conway, Pinkham Notch, Twin Mountain and Waterville Valley. For information on any of them, see the individual alphabetical listing.

Wolfeboro (F-5)

(See also Center Ossipee, Laconia)

Settled 1760 **Pop** 4,807 **Elev** 573 ft **Area code** 603 **Zip** 03894 **E-mail** chamber@wolfeboro.com **Web** www.wolfeboro.com-chamber

Information Chamber of Commerce, PO Box 547; 603/569-2200 or 800/516-5324.

Wolfeboro has been a resort area for more than two centuries; it is the oldest summer resort in America. In the winter it is a ski touring center with 40 miles of groomed trails.

What to See and Do

Clark House. Wolfeboro Historical Society is housed in Clark family homestead (1778), a one-rm schoolhouse (ca 1820) and a firehouse museum. Clark House has period furnishings, memorabilia; firehouse museum contains restored firefighting equipment dating from 1842. (July-Aug, daily exc Sun) S Main St. Phone 603/569-4997. **Donation.**

Lake Winnipesaukee cruises. (See LACONIA)

Wentworth State Park. On Lake Wentworth. Swimming; bathhouse. Picnicking. (Late June-Labor Day) Standard fees. 6 mi E on NH 109. Phone 603/569-3699.

Wright Museum. Showcases American enterprise during WWII. Collection of tanks, jeeps and other military vehicles, period memorabilia. (Daily) 77 Center St. Phone 603/569-1212.

Motels

★ ★ **LAKE.** *280 S Main St (US 28), 1 mi S on NH 28, 3/4 mi S of jct NH 109.* 603/569-1100; FAX 603/569-1620. 30 rms, 5 kit. units. July-Labor Day: S, D $89-$98; each addl $6; kit. units for 2, $630/wk; each addl $8; lower rates mid-May-June & after Labor Day-mid-Oct. Closed rest of yr. Pet accepted, some restrictions. TV; cable. Playground. Coffee in lobby. Restaurant adj 7:30 am-10 pm in summer. Ck-out 11 am. Business servs avail. Sundries. Tennis. Lawn games. On Crescent Lake; private beach, dockage. Cr cds: DS, MC, V.

★ ★ **LAKEVIEW INN & MOTOR LODGE.** *200 N Main St (NH 109).* 603/569-1335. 14 motel rms, 3 rms in inn, 2 story, 4 kits. July-Oct: S $80; D $90; each addl $5; kit. units $5 addl; lower rates rest of yr. Crib free. TV; cable. Complimentary continental bkfst. Complimentary coffee in rms. Restaurant 5-9 pm. Bar; entertainment Fri in season. Ck-out 11 am. Business servs avail. Some private patios, balconies. Inn built 1768 on king's land grant. Cr cds: A, MC, V.

🔥

↙★ **PINE VIEW LODGE.** *(NH 109, Melvin Village 03850)* approx 10 mi N on NH 109. 603/544-3800; res: 800/211-2620. 11 rms, showers only. No rm phones. July-Aug: S, D $69; lower rates rest of yr. TV. Complimentary coffee in lobby. Restaurant (June-Sept) 7-11 am, 5-9 pm. Bar 5 pm-1 am. Ck-out 11 am. Downhill ski 10 mi; x-country ski 2 mi. Picnic tables. Overlooks lake. Cr cds: MC, V.

Inn

★ ★ ★ **WOLFEBORO INN.** *90 N Main St (NH 109).* 603/569-3016; FAX 603/569-5375; res: 800/451-2389. Web www.wolfeboroinn.com. 44 rms, 3 story, 3 suites, 1 kit. unit. S, D $119-$129; suites $169-$219; kit. $200; under 8 free; wkly rates; higher rates major hols. Crib $10. TV; cable, VCR avail. Complimentary continental bkfst. Dining rm 7 am-11:30 pm. Rm serv. Ck-out 11 am, ck-in 3 pm. Business servs avail. Luggage handling. Valet serv. Sundries. Downhill ski 20 mi; x-country ski on site. Balconies. On Lake Winnipesaukee. Original building from 1812. Gardens. Cr cds: A, MC, V.

D ⊠ 🦘 🔥 SC

Cottage Colony

★ ★ **CLEARWATER LODGES.** *704 N Main St.* 603/569-2370. 15 kit. cottages (1-2 bedrm), 3-bedrm lodge. No A/C. No rm phones. July-Labor Day: cottages up to 2, $655/wk; cottages up to 4, $850/wk; each addl $80; daily rates; lower rates late May-late June & after Labor Day-late Sept. Closed rest of yr. Crib free. TV in rec rm. Ck-out 10 am, ck-in 3 pm. Coin lndry. Business servs avail. Grocery, package store 3 mi. Private waterfront; boats, motors. Rec rm. Barbecue, picnic areas. Rustic cottages, with fireplaces, porches, in tall pines on Lake Winnipesaukee. No cr cds accepted.

🦘 🔥

New York

Population: 17,990,456
Land area: 47,379 square miles
Elevation: 0-5,344 feet
Highest point: Mount Marcy (Essex County)
Entered Union: Eleventh of original 13 states (July 26, 1788)
Capital: Albany
Motto: Ever upward
Nickname: Empire State
State flower: Rose
State bird: Bluebird
State tree: Sugar maple
State fair: Late August-early September 1999, in Syracuse
Time zone: Eastern
Web: iloveny.state.ny.us

Largest of the northeastern states, New York stretches from the Great Lakes to the Atlantic. The falls at Niagara; the gorge of the Genesee, the "Grand Canyon" of the East; the Finger Lakes, carved by glaciers; the Thousand Islands of the St Lawrence; the Catskills, where Rip Van Winkle is said to have slept for 20 years; the white sand beaches of Long Island; the lakes and forested peaks of the Adirondacks; the stately traprock bluffs along the Hudson—these are a few of the features that attract millions of tourists and vacationers every year.

When Giovanni da Verrazano entered New York Harbor in 1524, the Native Americans of the state were at constant war with each other. But about 1570, under Dekanawidah and Hiawatha, they formed the Iroquois Confederacy (the first League of Nations) and began to live in peace. They were known as the Five Nations and called themselves the "Men of Men."

In 1609 Samuel de Champlain explored the valley of the lake that bears his name, and Henry Hudson sailed up the river that bears his. There was a trading post at Fort Nassau (Albany) in 1614. New Amsterdam (now New York City) was founded in 1625.

Wars with the Native Americans and French kept the area in turmoil until after 1763. During the Revolution, New York's eastern part was a seesaw of military action and occupation. After the war, Washington was inaugurated president in 1789, and the seat of federal government was established in New York City. As late as 1825, much of New York's central area was swampy wilderness.

Governor DeWitt Clinton envisioned a canal extending from the Hudson River at Albany to Buffalo to develop the state and give needed aid to its western farmers. Started in 1817 and finished in 1825, the Erie Canal became the gateway to the West and was the greatest engineering work of its time, reducing the cost of freight between Buffalo and New York City from $100 to $5 a ton. Enlarged and rerouted, it is now part of the New York State Canal system, 527 miles used mainly for recreational boating.

Industry grew because water power was available; trade and farming grew because of the Erie Canal and its many branches. The state has given the nation four native-born presidents (Van Buren, Fillmore and both Roosevelts) and two who built their careers here (Cleveland and Arthur).

In addition to being a delightful state in which to tour or vacation, New York has New York City, one of the great cosmopolitan centers of the world.

When to Go/Climate

New York State is large and the weather is varied. The northern and western parts of the state experience more extreme temperatures—cold, snowy winters and cool summers. Winters are long, especially near the Great Lakes. The Adirondacks, too, can have frigid winters, but fall foliage is magnificent, and summer temperatures and humidity are ideal. Spring thunderstorms frequently travel the Hudson River Valley, and summer here, as well as in New York City and environs, is hot and humid.

AVERAGE HIGH/LOW TEMPERATURES (°F)

NEW YORK CITY

Jan 38/25	**May** 72/54	**Sept** 76/60
Feb 40/27	**June** 80/63	**Oct** 65/50
Mar 50/35	**July** 85/68	**Nov** 54/41
Apr 61/44	**Aug** 84/67	**Dec** 43/31

SYRACUSE

Jan 31/14	**May** 68/46	**Sept** 72/51
Feb 33/15	**June** 77/54	**Oct** 60/41
Mar 43/25	**July** 82/59	**Nov** 48/33
Apr 56/36	**Aug** 79/58	**Dec** 35/21

Parks and Recreation Finder

Directions to and information about the parks and recreation areas below are given under their respective town/city sections. Please refer to those sections for details.

CALENDAR HIGHLIGHTS

MARCH

St Patricks Day Parade (Manhattan). Along Fifth Ave. New York's biggest parade; approximately 100,000 marchers. Phone Convention and Visitors Bureau, 212/397-8200.

APRIL

Central New York Maple Festival (Cortland). A variety of events showing the process of making maple syrup; also arts and crafts, hay rides and entertainment. Phone 607/849-3278 or 607/849-3812.

MAY

Tulip Festival (Albany). Washington Park. Three-day event. Includes crowning of Tulip Queen. Arts, crafts, food, vendors, children's rides, entertainment. Over 50,000 tulips throughout the park. Phone 518/434-5132.

Long Island Mozart Festival (Oyster Bay). Plantings Fields Arboretum. Outdoor musical festival, arts and crafts, lectures, garden tours. Phone 516/671-6263.

JULY

Stone House Day (Kingston). In Hurley. Tour of ten privately owned colonial stone houses, led by costumed guides; old Hurley Reformed Church and burying ground; antique show; re-creation of Revolutionary War military encampment; country fair. Phone 914/331-4121.

Time Warner American Music Fest (Rochester). Brown Square Park. Three-day celebration of American music. Nationally and internationally known jazz, blues, country, folk musicians. Phone 800/677-7282.

AUGUST

Erie County Fair (Buffalo). One of the oldest and largest fairs in the nation. Entertainment, rides, games, exhibits, agricultural and livestock shows. Phone 716/649-3900.

US Open Tennis (Queens). One of the bigger tennis tournaments of the year. Box office phone 718/760-6200.

New York State Fair (Syracuse). State Fairgrounds. The only state fair in New York. Agricultural, animal and commercial exhibits; midway concerts. Phone 315/487-7711.

SEPTEMBER

Adirondack Canoe Classic (Saranac Lake). Ninety-mile race from Old Forge to Saranac Lake for canoe, kayak, guideboat. Phone Chamber of Commerce 518/891-1990 or 800/347-1992.

NOVEMBER

NYC Marathon (Manhattan). Major city marathon with more than 25,000 runners. Phone New York Road Runners Club, 212/860-2280.

Thanksgiving Day Parade (Manhattan). An R.H. Macy production. Down Broadway to 34th St, from W 77th St & Central Park W. Floats, balloons, television and movie stars. Phone Macy's Special Events, 212/494-5432.

Festival of Lights (Niagara Falls). Downtown. Colored lights, animated displays, decorations; entertainment. Lighting of the Christmas tree. Phone 716/285-2400.

NATIONAL PARK AND RECREATION AREAS

Key to abbreviations: I.H.S. = International Historic Site; I.P.M. = International Peace Memorial; N.B. = National Battlefield; N.B.P. = National Battlefield Park; N.B.C. = National Battlefield & Cemetery; N.C. = National Conservation Area; N.E.M. = National Expansion Memorial; N.F. = National Forest; N.G. = National Grassland; N.H. = National Historical Park; N.H.C. = National Heritage Corridor; N.H.S. = National Historic Site; N.L. = National Lakeshore; N.M. = National Monument; N.M.P. = National Military Park; N.Mem. = National Memorial; N.P. = National Park; N.Pres. = National Preserve; N.R. = National Recreational Area; N.R.R. = National Recreational River; N.Riv. = National River; N.S. = National Seashore; N.S.R. = National Scenic Riverway; N.S.T. = National Scenic Trail; N.Sc. = National Scientific Reserve; N.V.M. = National Volcanic Monument.

Place Name	Listed Under
Castle Clinton N.M.	MANHATTAN
Federal Hall N.Mem.	MANHATTAN
Fire Island N.S.	same
Fort Stanwix N.M.	ROME
Gateway N.R.	BROOKLYN
General Grant N.Mem. (Grant's Tomb)	MANHATTAN
Hamilton Grange N.Mem.	MANHATTAN
Roosevelt-Vanderbilt N.H.S.	HYDE PARK
Sagamore Hill N.H.S.	OYSTER BAY
Saratoga N.H.	same
Statue of Liberty N.M. and Ellis Island	MANHATTAN
Theodore Roosevelt Birthplace N.H.S.	MANHATTAN
Theodore Roosevelt Inaugural N.H.S.	BUFFALO

STATE PARK AND RECREATION AREAS

Key to abbreviations: I.P. = Interstate Park; S.A.P. = State Archaeological park; S.B. = State Beach; S.C. = State Conservation Area; S.C.P. = State Conservation Park; S.Cp. = State Campground; S.F. = State Forest; S.G. = State Garden; S.H.A. = State Historic Area; S.H.P. = State Historic Park; S.H.S. = State Historic Site; S.M.P. = State Marine Park; S.N.A. = State Natural Area; S.P. = State Park; S.P.C. = State Public Campground; S.R. = State Reserve; S.R.A. = State Recreation Area; S.Res. = State Reservoir; S.Res.P. = State Resort Park; S.R.P. = State Rustic Park.

Place Name	Listed Under
Adirondack Park	same
Allan H. Treman S.M.P.	ITHACA
Allegany S.P.	same
AuSable Point S.P.	PLATTSBURGH
Bear Mountain S.P.	PALISADES INTERSTATE PARKS
Bethpage S.P.	BETHPAGE
Bowman Lake S.P.	NORWICH
Burnham Point S.P.	CLAYTON
Buttermilk Falls S.P.	ITHACA
Catskill Park	same PARK
Cayuga Lake S.P.	SENECA FALLS
Cedar Point S.P.	CLAYTON
Chenango Valley S.P.	BINGHAMTON
Chittenango Falls S.P.	CAZENOVIA
Coles Creek S.P.	MASSENA
Crown Point Reservation State Campground	CROWN POINT
Cumberland Bay S.P.	PLATTSBURGH
Delta Lake S.P.	ROME
DeWolf Point S.P.	ALEXANDRIA BAY
Evangola S.P.	DUNKIRK
Fair Haven Beach S.P.	OSWEGO
Fillmore Glen S.P.	CORTLAND
Fish Creek Pond S.P.C.	TUPPER LAKE
Fort Niagara S.P.	NIAGARA FALLS
Four Mile Creek S.P.	NIAGARA FALLS
Gilbert Lake S.P.	ONEONTA
Glimmerglass S.P.	COOPERSTOWN
Grass Point S.P.	CLAYTON

Green Lakes S.P.	SYRACUSE
Hamlin Beach S.P.	ROCHESTER
Harriman S.P.	PALISADES INTERSTATE PARKS
Hither Hills S.P.	MONTAUK
Jacques Cartier S.P.	OGDENSBURG
James Baird S.P.	POUGHKEEPSIE
Jones Beach S.P.	same
Keuka Lake S.P.	PENN YAN
Kring Point S.P.	ALEXANDRIA BAY
Lake Eaton S.P.C.	TUPPER LAKE
Lake Erie S.P.	DUNKIRK
Lake Taghkanic S.P.	HUDSON
Letchworth S.P.	same
Long Point on Lake Chautauqua S.P.	BEMUS POINT
Long Point S.P.	WATERTOWN
Mills-Norrie S.P.	HYDE PARK
Mine Kill S.P.	STAMFORD
Montauk Point S.P.	MONTAUK
Niagara Reservation S.P.	NIAGARA FALLS
Old Erie Canal S.P.	CANASTOTA
Pixley Falls S.P.	BOONVILLE
Reservoir S.P.	NIAGARA FALLS
Robert H. Treman	ITHACA
Robert Moses S.P.	MASSENA
Robert Moses S.P.	same
Rogers Rock State Public Campground	HAGUE
Rollins Pond State Public Campground	TUPPER LAKE
Sampson S.P.	GENEVA
Selkirk Shores S.P.	OSWEGO
Seneca Lake S.P.	GENEVA
Stony Brook S.P.	HORNELL
Sunken Meadow S.P.	HUNTINGTON
Taconic S.P.	HILLSDALE
Taughannock S.P.	ITHACA
Verona Beach S.P.	ONEIDA
Waterson Point S.P.	ALEXANDRIA BAY
Watkins Glen S.P.	WATKINS GLEN
Wellesley Island S.P.	ALEXANDRIA BAY
Westcott Beach S.P.	SACKETS HARBOR

Water-related activities, hiking, riding, various other sports, picnicking and visitor centers, as well as camping, are available in many of these areas. There are more than 200 outdoor state recreation facilities, including state parks, forest preserves and similar areas. Contact the Department of Environmental Conservation, 50 Wolf Rd, Albany 12233-4790, for information on recreation areas within the Adirondack and Catskill forest preserves; phone 518/457-2500. For other state parks and recreation areas contact Office of Parks, Recreation and Historic Preservation, Albany 12238; 518/474-0456. The state also provides funds for maintenance of 7,300 miles of trails for snowmobiling. Reservations for all state-operated campgrounds and cabins can be made by calling 800/456-CAMP. There is a $4 fee for boat launching at some state parks. Pets on leash where allowed. The basic fee for camping is $13/night; additional charges for amenities and hookups (electric and sewer). Phone or write for detailed information on individual parks.

SKI AREAS

Place Name	Listed Under
Belleayre Mt Ski Area	SHANDAKEN
Big Tupper Ski Area	TUPPER LAKE
Bristol Mt Ski & Snowboard Resort	CANANDAIGUA
Catamount Ski Area	HILLSDALE
Cortina Valley Ski Area	SAUGERTIES
Garnet Hill Ski Lodge	NORTH CREEK
Gore Mt Ski Area	NORTH CREEK
Greek Peak Ski Area	CORTLAND
Hickory Ski Center	WARRENSBURG
Holiday Mt Ski Area	MONTICELLO
Hunter Mt Ski Area	HUNTER
Kissing Bridge Ski Area	EAST AURORA
Labrador Mt Ski Area	CORTLAND
McCauley Mt Ski Area	OLD FORGE
Mt Pisgah Municipal Ski Center	SARANAC LAKE
Scotch Valley Resort	STAMFORD
Ski Windham	WINDHAM
Snow Ridge Ski Area	BOONVILLE
Song Mt Ski Area	CORTLAND
Swain Ski Center	HORNELL
Thunder Ridge Ski Area	BREWSTER
Titus Mt Ski Area	MALONE
Toggenburg Ski Center	CAZENOVIA
West Mt Ski Resort	GLENS FALLS
Whiteface Mt Ski Center	WILMINGTON
White Birches Cross-Country Ski Center	WINDHAM
Willard Mt Ski Area	GREENWICH
Woods Valley Ski Area	ROME

FISHING & HUNTING

New York state offers excellent fishing and hunting opportunities, with a wide variety of lengthy seasons. Write or phone for detailed information on fees and regulations. Contact NYS Dept of Environmental Conservation, License Sales Office-Rm 151, 50 Wolf Rd, Albany 12233-4790, 518/457-3521, for the most current fees and a mail order license application and fishing/hunting regulations guides. *The Conservationist* is the department's official illustrated bimonthly periodical on New York State natural resources; contact PO Box 1500, Latham, NY 12110-9983 for subscription ($10/yr).

Driving Information

Safety belts are mandatory for all persons in front seat of vehicle. Children under 10 years of age must be in an approved passenger restraint anywhere in vehicle: ages 4-9 may use a regulation safety belt; age 3 and under must use an approved safety seat. For further information phone 518/474-5111.

INTERSTATE HIGHWAY SYSTEM

The following alphabetical listing of New York towns in *Mobil Travel Guide* shows that these cities are within 10 miles of the indicated Interstate highways. A highway map should, however, be checked for the nearest exit.

Highway Number	Cities/Towns within 10 miles
Interstate 81:	Alexandria Bay, Binghamton, Clayton, Cortland, Syracuse, Watertown.
Interstate 84:	Brewster, Fishkill, Middletown, Newburgh, Port Jervis.

Interstate 87:	Albany, Ausable Chasm, Bolton Landing, Catskill, Diamond Point, Glens Falls, Hartsdale, Hudson, Kingston, Lake George Village, Lake Luzerne, Monroe, Newburgh, New Paltz, New York City, Nyack, Plattsburgh, Poughkeepsie, Rouses Point, Saratoga Springs, Saugerties, Schroon Lake, Spring Valley, Stony Point, Tarrytown, Troy, Warrensburg, Woodstock, Yonkers.
Interstate 88:	Bainbridge, Binghamton, Oneonta.
Interstate 90:	Albany, Amsterdam, Auburn, Batavia, Buffalo, Canaan, Canajoharie, Canandaigua, Canastota, Dunkirk, Geneva, Herkimer, Ilion, Johnstown, Oneida, Palmyra, Rochester, Rome, Schenectady, Seneca Falls, Syracuse, Troy, Utica, Victor, Waterloo.
Interstate 95:	Mamaroneck, White Plains.

Additional Visitor Information

I LOVE New York Winter Travel & Ski Guide and the *I LOVE New York Travel Guide* (covering upstate New York, Long Island and New York City) may be obtained from the State Department of Economic Development, Division of Tourism, PO Box 2603, Albany 12220-0603; 518/474-4116 or toll-free, 800/CALL-NYS.

Adirondack Park (B-7 - C-8)

(See also Blue Mountain Lake, Lake George Village, Lake Placid, Long Lake, Old Forge)

(14 mi NW of Amsterdam on NY 30)

The Adirondack Mountains are protected under an 1885 law establishing the forest preserve and an 1892 law creating Adirondack Park. The state now owns more than 2½ million of the nearly 6 million acres of the park, a wilderness mountain area with streams and lakes. There are 42 public campgrounds of varying size, a 125-mile canoe route from Old Forge to the Saranacs and 750 miles of marked foot trails among the pines and spruces. Hunting and fishing are permitted under state regulations. Detailed camping information may be obtained from the Department of Environmental Conservation, Bureau of Recreation, 50 Wolf Rd, Rm 679, Albany 12233-5253; 518/457-2500. Standard fees.

Albany (E-8)

(See also Schenectady, Troy)

Settled 1624 **Pop** 101,082 **Elev** 150 ft **Area code** 518 **E-mail** accvb@albany.org **Web** www.albany.org

Information Albany County Convention & Visitors Bureau, 52 S Pearl St, 12207, phone 518/434-1217 or 800/258-3582; or contact the Visitor Center, 25 Quackenbush Square, 12207, phone 518/434-0405.

Albany is situated on the Hudson River, where Henry Hudson ended the voyage of the *Half Moon* in 1609. It was settled by Dutch-speaking Walloons from Holland, Norwegians, Danes, Germans and Scots, during the patronship of Kiliaen Van Rensselaer, and was named in honor of the Duke of Kent and Albany when the British took over the city in 1664.

Despite the French and Indian War, Albany was a thriving fur-trading center in 1754. Albany's General Philip Schuyler commanded the northern defenses in the Revolution and according to Daniel Webster was "second only to Washington in the services he performed for his country."

Albany has been a transportation center since Native American trail days. Robert Fulton's steamboat, the *Clermont,* arrived here from Jersey City in 1807. The Erie Canal opened in 1825; by 1831, 15,000 canal boats and 500 ocean-going ships crowded Albany's docks.

Politics is a colorful part of the business of New York's capital city. Located on the western bank of the Hudson River and at the crossroads of major state highways, Albany is now a hub of transportation, business, industry and culture.

What to See and Do

Albany Institute of History and Art. Regional silver, ceramics, pewter, furniture and 18th and 19th-century Hudson-Mohawk Valley paintings and sculpture; textiles and clothing; contemporary art; changing exhibits and programs promote fine arts as well as regional history; research library with archival material. Tours (daily exc Mon, by appt). Galleries (Wed-Sun; closed hols); library (Tues-Fri); luncheon gallery (mid-Sept-late May, Tues-Fri). Free admission Wed. 125 Washington Ave, 1 blk W of capitol. Phone 518/463-4478. ¢¢

Crailo State Historic Site. Eighteenth-century Dutch house, now a museum of Dutch culture in the Hudson Valley. Exhibits and audiovisual presentation explain the history and development of Dutch settlements in America. (Mid-Apr-Oct, Wed-Sun) 9½ Riverside Ave in Rensselaer, 1½ blks S of US 9 & 20. Phone 518/463-8738. ¢¢

Dutch Apple Cruises Inc. Scenic cruises on the Hudson River with view of the Capital District. Sightseeing, dinner/entertainment and Sun brunch cruises (by appt). (May-Oct, daily) Broadway at Quay. Contact PO Box 395, 12201-0395; 518/463-0220. ¢¢¢

Empire State Plaza. A 98½-acre, 11-bldg complex providing office space for state government, cultural and convention facilities; New York State Modern Art Collection on view. On 42nd floor is the Tower Bldg observation deck (daily). NY State Thrwy, exit 23. Phone 518/474-2418. **Free.**

Historic Cherry Hill (1787). Georgian-style farmhouse built for Philip Van Rensselaer, a prominent merchant farmer. Lived in by four generations of descendants until 1963. Nine period rms of original furnishings and personal belongings from the 18th to the 20th centuries. Gardens. Tours (daily exc Mon; closed major hols and month of Jan). 523½ S Pearl St. Phone 518/434-4791. ¢¢

New York State Museum. Life-size dioramas, photo murals and thousands of objects illustrate the relationship between people and nature in New York State. Three major halls detailing life in Metropolitan New York, the Adirondacks and Upstate New York. Special exhibits of photography, art, history, nature, science and Native Americans. Entertainment, classes and films. (Daily; closed Jan 1, Thanksgiving, Dec 25) Empire State Plaza, Cultural Education Center. Phone 518/474-5877. **Free.**

Rensselaerville. Village, est in 1787, has restored homes, inns, churches, gristmill. Nature preserve and biological research station. Also here is the Rensselaerville Institute, offering cultural programs and a conference center for educational and business meetings. 27 mi SW via NY 443 to end of NY 85. Phone 518/797-3783.

Schuyler Mansion State Historic Site (1761). Georgian mansion, home of Philip Schuyler, general of the Revolutionary War and US senator. Alexander Hamilton married Schuyler's daughter here, and other prominent early leaders visited here. Exhibit at interpretation center. Tours (fee). (Mid-Apr-Oct, Wed-Sat, also Sun afternoons; closed hols exc Memorial Day, July 4, Labor Day) 32 Catherine St. Phone 518/434-0834. ¢¢

Shaker Heritage Society. Located on the site of the first Shaker settlement in America. Grounds, 1848 Shaker Meeting House, orchard and cemetery where founder Mother Ann Lee is buried. Tours (by appt). (Tues-Sat) Albany-Shaker Rd. Phone 518/456-7890. ¢

State Capitol. A $25,000,000 granite "French" chateau. Legislative session begins the week after the first Mon in Jan. Guided tours (daily, phone ahead for hrs; no tours Jan 1, Thanksgiving, Dec 25). State St. Phone 518/474-2418. **Free.**

Ten Broeck Mansion (1798). Brick Federal house with Greek-revival additions; built by General Abraham Ten Broeck, it was also the home of the prominent Olcott family. Contains collection of period furniture, fine arts, 3 period bathrms (1890s) and changing exhibits of the Albany County Historical Association; also lawn and herb garden during summer. (Apr-Dec, Wed-Sun afternoons; closed hols) Phone 518/436-9826. ¢¢

Univ at Albany, State Univ of New York (1844). (17,000 students) Complex of 13 bldgs under one continuous roof designed by Edward Durell Stone. A 382-acre campus; art gallery; performing arts center; one million-volume library; nuclear accelerator; atmospheric science research center; carillon tower. Between Washington & Western Aves, E of NY State Thrwy exit 24.

Annual Events

Tulip Festival. Washington Park. Willett St between State St & Madison Ave. Early May.

First Night. Celebration of the arts with music performances and fireworks to welcome the new yr. Dec 31.

Motels

★ ★ **BEST WESTERN AIRPORT INN.** *200 Wolf Rd (12205), near County Airport, I-87 exit 4.* 518/458-1000; res: 800/458-1016; FAX 518/458-2807. E-mail bwaai@crisny.org; web crisny.org/~bwaai. 153 rms, 2 story. S, D $65-$109; each addl $10; under 18 free; wkly, wkend, hol rates. Crib free. TV; cable (premium), VCR avail. Indoor pool. Restaurant 6:30 am-10 pm. Rm serv. Bar 2:30 pm-midnight. Ck-out noon. Meeting rms. Business servs avail. In-rm modem link. Bellhops. Health club privileges. Free airport transportation. Cr cds: A, C, D, DS, JCB, MC, V.

D ≅ ✈

★ ★ **COMFORT INN.** *1606 Central Ave (12205).* 518/869-5327; res: 800/233-9444; FAX 518/456-8971. 53 rms. S, D $75; suite $99-$125; under 15 free. Crib free. TV; cable (premium). Complimentary continental bkfst. Restaurant nearby. Meeting rms. Business servs avail. In-rm modem link. Sundries. Exercise equipt. Some refrigerators; microwaves avail. Cr cds: A, C, D, DS, MC, V.

D ✗ ≅ 🔥 SC

★ ★ ★ **COURTYARD BY MARRIOTT.** *168 Wolf Rd (12205), near County Airport.* 518/482-8800; FAX 518/482-0001. Web www.courtyard.com. 78 rms, 3 story. S, D $79-$119; under 18 free. Crib free. TV; cable (premium). Indoor pool. Complimentary coffee in rms. Ck-out noon. Coin lndry. Meeting rms. Business servs avail. In-rm modem link. Valet serv. Sundries. Free airport transportation. Exercise equipt. Refrigerator avail. Cr cds: A, C, D, DS, MC, V.

D ≅ ✗ ✈ ≅ 🔥 SC

✔★ **ECONO LODGE.** *(110 Columbia Tpke, Rensselaer 12144) I-87 exit 23 on US 9 & 20.* 518/472-1360; FAX 518/427-2924; res: 800/477-3123. 35 rms, 3 kits. S $35-$74; D $39-$89; kit. units $165-$300/wk; higher rates special events. Crib free. TV; cable (premium). Complimentary continental bkfst. Restaurant adj. Ck-out 11 am. Coin lndry. Business servs avail. In-rm modem link. Refrigerators. Cr cds: A, D, DS, MC, V.

≅ 🔥

★ ★ **HAMPTON INN.** *10 Ulenski Dr (12205), I-87 exit 4.* 518/438-2822; FAX 518/438-2931. Web www.hampton-inn.com/hampton-docs/mkts/ny-alba/abul/abul-3.html. 154 rms, 5 story. S, D $87-$94; under 18 free; higher rates special events. Crib free. TV; cable (premium). Pool. Complimentary continental bkfst. Restaurant adj 6 am-midnight. Ck-out noon. Coin lndry. Business servs avail. In-rm modem link. Free airport transportation. Health club privileges. Cr cds: A, C, D, DS, MC, V.

D ≅ ≅ 🔥 SC

★ ★ **HOWARD JOHNSON.** *416 Southern Blvd (12209), US 9W at I-87 exit 23.* 518/462-6555; FAX 518/462-2547. 135 rms, 1-2 story. S $65; D $75; each addl $8; suites $95; under 18 free. Crib free. Pet accepted, some restrictions. TV; cable (premium). Pool; lifeguard. Restau-rant open 24 hrs. Bar from 11 am. Ck-out noon. Coin lndry. Meeting rms. Business servs avail. Valet serv. Indoor tennis privileges, pro. Exercise rm. Private patios, balconies. Cr cds: A, C, D, DS, MC, V.

D ✔ ≅ ≅ ✗ ≅ 🔥 SC

★ ★ ★ **INN AT THE CENTURY.** *(997 New Loudon Rd (NY 9), Latham 12110) near I-87N exit 7.* 518/785-0931; res: 888/674-6873; FAX 518/785-3274. Web www.centuryhouse.inter.net. 68 rms, 2 story. S $85; D $95; each addl $12; suites $125-$225; under 12 free; higher rates: Saratoga racing season, special events. Crib avail. Pet accepted, some restrictions; $5. TV; cable (premium). Pool. Complimentary bkfst buffet. Restaurant 11 am-9:45 pm; Sat 4-10 pm; Sun noon-9 pm. Rm serv 4-9:30 pm. Bar 11 am-11 pm. Ck-out noon. Meeting rms. Business servs avail. In-rm modem link. Valet serv. Tennis. Exercise equipt. Nature trail. Some refrigerators; microwaves avail. Cr cds: A, D, DS, MC, V.

D ✔ ✗ ≅ ✗ ≅ 🔥

✔★ **MICROTEL.** *(7 Rensselaer Ave, Latham 12110) 5 mi N on I-87, exit 6.* 518/782-9161; FAX 518/782-9162; res: 800/782-9121. 100 rms, 2 story. S $36.95-$55.95; D $40.95-$59.95; under 14 free. Crib free. Pet accepted, some restrictions. TV; cable (premium). Complimentary coffee in lobby. Restaurant nearby. Ck-out noon. Meeting rm. Business servs avail. In-rm modem link. Sundries. Some refrigerators; microwaves avail. Cr cds: A, C, D, DS, MC, V.

D ✔

★ ★ **RAMADA LIMITED.** *1630 Central Ave (12205), 8 mi W on NY 5 to I-87 exit 2W, near County Airport.* 518/456-0222; res: 800/354-0223; FAX 518/452-1376. 105 rms, 2 story. July-Aug: S, D $79-$99; under 18 free; lower rates rest of yr. Crib free. Pet accepted; $50 deposit. TV; cable (premium), VCR (movies). Complimentary continental bkfst. Complimentary coffee in rms. Restaurant nearby. Ck-out noon. Meeting rms. Business servs avail. Beauty shop. Exercise equipt. Some in-rm whirl-pools, refrigerators, microwaves. Cr cds: A, D, DS, MC, V.

D ✔ ✗ ≅ 🔥 SC

Motor Hotels

★ ★ ★ **THE DESMOND.** *660 Albany-Shaker Rd (12211), at I-87 exit 4, near County Airport.* 518/869-8100; res: 800/448-3500; FAX 518/869-7659. Web www.desmondny.com. 321 rms, 1-4 story. S, D $99-$139; suites $139-$219; under 18 free; wkend rates. Crib free. TV; cable (premium). 2 indoor pools; whirlpool. Coffee in rms. Restaurant 6:30 am-midnight (also see SCRIMSHAW). Rm serv. Bar 11:30-2 am. Ck-out noon. Convention facilties. Business servs avail. In-rm modem link. Bell-hops. Valet serv. Concierge. Sundries. Gift shop. Free airport transportation. Exercise equipt; sauna. Game rm. Refrigerators avail. Private patios, balconies. Cr cds: A, C, D, DS, MC, V.

D ≅ ✗ ✈ ≅ 🔥

★ ★ ★ **HOLIDAY INN-TURF.** *205 Wolf Rd (12205), I-90 exit 24 to I-87 exit 4, near County Airport.* 518/458-7250; FAX 518/458-7377. 309 rms, 2-6 story. S, D $79-$129; suites $150; under 19 free; some wkend rates; higher rates: Aug, special events. Crib free. TV; cable. 2 pools, 1 indoor; whirlpool, lifeguard. Restaurant 6 am-midnight. Rm serv 6 am-10 pm. Bar 11:30-2 am. Ck-out noon. Meeting rms. Convention facilities. Business servs avail. In-rm modem link. Bellhops. Valet serv. Sundries. Gift shop. Barber, beauty shop. Airport transportation. Lighted tennis. Exercise equipt; sauna. Game rm. Some in-rm whirlpools; refrigerators avail. Cr cds: A, C, D, DS, JCB, MC, V.

D ✔ ≅ ✗ ✈ ≅ 🔥 SC

✔★ ★ ★ **RAMADA INN.** *1228 Western Ave (12203), I-90 exit 24; I-87 exit 1.* 518/489-2981; FAX 518/489-8967. E-mail ramadaonwestern@msn.com; web www.ramada.com/ramada.html. 195 rms, 5 story. S $69-$85; D $69-$95; each addl $10; suites $150-$195; under 18 free; wkend plan; higher rates special events. Crib free. Pet accepted. TV; cable (premium). Indoor pool. Complimentary full bkfst. Coffee in rms. Restaurant 6:30 am-10 pm. Rm serv 5-9 pm. Bar. Ck-out noon. Meeting rms.

Business servs avail. In-rm modem link. Valet serv. Beauty shop. Exercise equipt; sauna. Microwave in suites. Cr cds: A, C, D, DS, MC, V.

[D] [icons] SC

Hotels

★ ★ **MARRIOTT.** *189 Wolf Rd (12205), near County Airport, I-87 exit 4.* 518/458-8444; res: 800/443-8952; FAX 518/458-7365. 359 rms, 7-8 story. S, D $84-$168; suites $250-$350; wkend rates. Crib free. Pet accepted. TV; cable (premium), VCR avail (movies). 2 heated pools, 1 indoor; whirlpool, poolside serv, lifeguard. Restaurant 6:30 am-10 pm. Bar; entertainment wkends. Ck-out noon. Coin lndry. Convention facilities. Business center. In-rm modem link. Gift shop. Free airport transportation. Exercise equipt; sauna. Health club privileges. Refrigerators avail. Luxury level. Cr cds: A, C, D, DS, ER, JCB, MC, V.

[D] [icons] SC [icon]

★ ★ **OMNI.** *Ten Eyck Plaza (12207).* 518/462-6611; FAX 518/462-2901. 386 rms, 15 story. S $95-$155; D $95-$185; each addl $20; suites $125-$450; family, wkend rates. Crib free. Pet accepted; $50. TV; cable, VCR avail. Indoor pool; whirlpool. Coffee in rms. Restaurant 7 am-2 pm, 5-10 pm. Rm serv to noon. Bar 11:30-1 am. Ck-out noon. Meeting rms. Business servs avail. In-rm modem link. Shopping arcade. Covered parking. Free airport, RR station, bus depot transportation. Exercise equipt. Some refrigerators. Cr cds: A, C, D, DS, MC, V.

[D] [icons] SC

Inns

★ ★ **GREGORY HOUSE.** *(Averill Park 12018) I-90 exit 8 to NY 43E.* 518/674-3774; FAX 518/674-8916. E-mail gregoryhse@aol.com; web members.aol.com/gregoryhse. 12 rms, 2 story. S $80-$90; D $85-$95; each addl $5-$10. TV in common rm; cable. Pool. Complimentary continental bkfst. Restaurant (see GREGORY HOUSE). Bar. Ck-out 11 am, ck-in 2 pm. Fireplace in common rm; Oriental rugs, antiques. Some balconies. Cr cds: A, C, D, DS, MC, V.

[icons]

★ ★ **MANSION HILL.** *115 Philip St (12202), at Park Ave.* 518/465-2038; res: 888/299-0455; FAX 518/434-2313. E-mail inn@mansionhill.com; web www.mansionhill.com. 8 rms, 2 story. S $115; D $125; under 17 free; wkend rates. Crib free. Pet accepted. TV; cable (premium), VCR avail (movies). Complimentary full bkfst. Restaurant (see MANSION HILL INN). Rm serv 5-9 pm. Ck-out 11:30 am, ck-in 4 pm. Luggage handling. Valet serv. Concierge serv. RR station, bus depot transportation. Health club privileges. Cr cds: A, C, D, DS, MC, V.

[icons] SC

Restaurants

✓★ **BONGIORNO'S.** *23 Dove St (12210).* 518/462-9176. Italian menu. Specialties: scaloppine, saltimbocca, pollo cacciatore. Hrs: 11:30 am-2:30 pm, 5-9 pm; Thurs-Sat to 10 pm. Closed Sun; most major hols. Res accepted. Bar. Semi-a la carte: lunch $4.75-$9.50, dinner $8.95-$20. Child's meals. Cr cds: A, MC, V.

★ ★ **CRANBERRY BOG.** *56 Wolf Rd (12205).* 518/459-5110. Web www.cranbog.com. Specializes in steak, fresh seafood, veal. Hrs: 11:30 am-10 pm; Sun 10:30 am-1:30 pm, 4-9 pm; Sun brunch to 1:30 pm. Closed Jan 1, July 4. Res accepted. Bar to 1 am. Semi-a la carte: lunch $5.95-$12.95, dinner $12.95-$29.95. Sun brunch $13.95. Child's meals. Entertainment Mon-Sat. Parking. Outdoor dining. Family-owned. Cr cds: A, C, D, DS, MC, V.

[D]

★ ★ **DAKOTA.** *(579 Troy Schnectedy Rd, Latham 12110) approx 5 mi N on I-87, exit 6, at Latham Farms Mall.* 518/786-1234. Specializes in steak, seafood. Salad bar. Hrs: 4:30-10 pm; Fri to 11 pm; Sat 4-11 pm; Sun 1-9 pm. Bar. Semi-a la carte: dinner $7.95-$21.95. Child's meals.

Rustic decor with hunting lodge theme. Native American artifacts. Cr cds: A, C, D, DS, MC, V.

[D] [icons]

★ ★ ★ **GREGORY HOUSE.** *(See Gregory House Inn)* 518/674-3774. Continental menu. Specializes in veal, lamb, seafood. Own baking. Hrs: 5-9 pm; Sun 4-8 pm. Closed Mon; Dec 24-26. Res accepted; required wkends. Bar. Semi-a la carte: dinner $15.95-$23.95. Parking. Built 1830. Cr cds: A, C, D, DS, MC, V.

[D]

✓★ ★ ★ **JACK'S OYSTER HOUSE.** *42 State St (12207).* 518/465-8854. Specializes in seafood, vegetarian dishes, Angus beef. Hrs: 11:30 am-10 pm. Res accepted. Bar. A la carte entrees: lunch $4.95-$9.95, dinner $10.95-$17.95. Child's meals. Parking. Albany's oldest landmark restaurant. Family-owned. Cr cds: A, C, D, DS, MC, V.

★ ★ **L'ECOLE ENCORE.** *337 Fuller Rd (12203).* 518/437-1234. Continental menu. Specialties: artichokes French, chicken broccoli strudel, angel hair shrimp fra diavalo. Hrs: 11:30 am-3 pm, 5-10 pm; Sat from 5 pm; Sun 4-9 pm. Closed most major hols. Res accepted. Bar. Semi-a la carte: lunch $6.95-$9.95, dinner $14.95-$20.95. Jazz Thurs. Parking. Outdoor dining. Casual dining with intimate atmosphere. Cr cds: A, D, DS, MC, V.

★ ★ **LA SERRE.** *14 Green St (12207).* 518/463-6056. Continental menu. Specialties: medallions of veal, rack of lamb, fresh grilled fish. Own baking. Hrs: 11:30 am-2:30 pm, 5-9 pm; Sat, Sun from 5 pm. Res accepted Sat, Sun (dinner). Bar. Semi-a la carte: lunch $6.95-$9.95, dinner $12.95-$22.95. Child's meals. Outdoor dining. Built 1829; formerly a stove factory. Cr cds: A, C, D, MC, V.

[D]

★ ★ ★ **MANSION HILL INN.** *(See Mansion Hill Inn)* 518/465-2038. Specializes in seasonal, vegetarian and pasta dishes. Hrs: 5-9 pm. Closed Sun; some major hols. Res accepted. Bar. Wine list. Semi-a la carte: dinner $13-$21. Child's meals. Outdoor dining. In 1861 bldg. Cr cds: A, C, D, DS, MC, V.

★ ★ ★ **OGDEN'S.** *42 Howard St (12207).* 518/463-6605. Continental menu. Specializes in fresh seafood, veal, aged Angus steak. Hrs: 11:30 am-9 pm; Sat from 5:30 pm. Closed Sun; major hols. Res accepted. Bar. Wine list. Semi-a la carte: lunch $5.95-$11.95, dinner $15.95-$24.95. Restored historic building (1903); oak woodwork. Cr cds: A, MC, V.

★ ★ ★ **SCRIMSHAW.** *(See The Desmond Motor Hotel)* 518/869-8100. Web www.desmondny.com. Continental menu. Specialties: steak au poivre, shrimp scampi, veal Oscar. Hrs: 5:30-10 pm. Closed Sun; Memorial Day, July 4, Labor Day, Dec 25. Res accepted. Bar. Wine list. Semi-a la carte: dinner $16-$25. Child's meals. Pianist. Parking. Nautical theme; colonial atmosphere. Jacket. Cr cds: A, C, D, DS, MC, V.

[D]

★ ★ ★ **SHIPYARD.** *95 Everett Rd (12205).* 518/438-4428. Specializes in fresh fish, rack of lamb, beef tenderloin. Hrs: 5-9:30 pm; Sat, Sun 5-9 pm. Closed some major hols. Res accepted. Bar. Wine list. Semi-a la carte: dinner $12.95-$23. Prix fixe: dinner $20-$25. Parking. Country garden elegence. Cr cds: A, C, D, DS, MC, V.

★ **VEEDER'S.** *2020 Central Ave (12205), I-90 exit 24; I-87 exit 2W.* 518/456-1010. Continental menu. Specializes in leg of lamb, prime rib, scallops. Hrs: 11:30 am-9 pm; Sun noon-8 pm; early-bird dinner 4-7 pm. Closed Mon; Dec 24. Res accepted. Semi-a la carte: lunch $4.95-$7.50, dinner $8.50-$18. Child's meals. Parking. Family-owned. Cr cds: A, MC, V.

[D]

★ ★ ★ **YONO'S.** *289 Hamilton (12210).* 518/436-7747. Indonesian, continental menu. Specialties: saté, shrimp simmered in coconut milk, chicken au pistaches. Own desserts. Hrs: 5:30-10 pm. Closed Sun; Thanksgiving, Dec 25. Res accepted. Bar to midnight. Semi-a la carte: dinner $13.95-$21.95. Complete meals: dinner $32.50. Entertainment Fri. Outdoor dining. Cr cds: A, C, D, MC, V.

Alexandria Bay (Thousand Islands) (B-6)

(See also Clayton; also see Gananoque and Kingston, ON, Canada)

Pop 1,194 **Elev** 284 ft **Area code** 315 **Zip** 13607
Information Chamber of Commerce, Market St, Box 365; 315/482-9531, 800/541-2110 or 888-432-7884.

Resort center of the Thousand Islands, Alexandria Bay overlooks a cluster of almost 1,800 green islands divided by intricate waterways. The islands range in size from a few square inches, a handful of rocks with a single tree, to several miles in length.

What to See and Do

Boat trips.

Rockport Boat Lines. A 1-hr tour through the islands. (May-Oct, daily) 2 mi E of Thousand Islands International Bridge, off Thousand Islands Pkwy E in Rockport, Ontario. Phone 613/659-3402 or 800/563-8687. ¢¢¢¢

Uncle Sam Boat Tours. Two-hr cruises wind through scenic islands; dinner & luncheon cruises (May-Oct). All tours stop at Boldt Castle. James St. Phone 315/482-2611 or 800/ALEX-BAY. Two-hr cruise ¢¢¢¢;   Lunch & dinner cruises ¢¢¢¢¢

Boldt Castle. George C. Boldt came from Prussia in the 1860s and became the most successful hotel magnate in America, managing the Waldorf-Astoria in NYC and owning the Bellevue-Stratford in Philadelphia. The castle was a $2,500,000 present to his wife, who died in 1904; the castle was never completed. Other structures here incl the dove-cote, which housed fancy fowl; Italian garden, Alster Tower power house and the yacht house. Slide show in main castle; craft demonstrations and exhibits on 1st floor. **Note:** Structure and grounds now being restored. (Mid-May-early Oct) On Heart Island. Phone 315/482-2501 or 800/8-ISLAND.   ¢¢

Kring Point State Park. Swimming beach, bathhouse; fishing, boating (launch, dock); recreation programs, picnicking; cabins, tent & trailer sites; cross-country skiing. (Early May-Columbus Day) Standard fees. 6 mi NE on NY 12, then W on unnumbered road. Phone 315/482-2444.

Thousand Islands Skydeck. Between the spans of the Thousand Islands International Bridge, on Hill Island, Lansdowne, Ontario. (See GANANOQUE, ONTARIO)

Wellesley Island. On the island are three state parks: **Wellesley Island.** Swimming beach, bathhouse; fishing; boating (ramp, marina); nature center, hiking; golf; cross-country skiing, snowmobiling; picnicking, playground, concession; trailer sites. Standard fees. **DeWolf Point.** Swimming; fishing; boating (ramp); tent & trailer sites, cabins. Standard fees. **Waterson Point.** Accessible only by boat. Fishing, boat anchorage, camping; picnicking. Across Thousand Islands International Bridge. For info on these parks phone 315/482-2722.

Motels

★ ★ **CAPT. THOMSON'S.** *James St, I-81 exit 50N.* 315/482-9961; *FAX* 315/482-2611; *res:* 800/253-9229 (NY). 117 rms, 2 story, 2 kits. Mid-June-Labor Day: S $65-$104; D $86-$120; each addl $10; kit. units $165; under 12 free; lower rates May-mid-June & after Labor Day-Oct. Closed rest of yr. Crib free. TV; cable, VCR avail. Pool; wading pool. Restaurant 7 am-10 pm. Ck-out 11 am. Balconies. On seaway; dock. Cr cds: A, C, D, DS, MC, V.

★ **EDGEWOOD RESORT.** *¼ mi S of jct NY 12 & NY 26.* 315/482-9922; *FAX* 315/482-5210. 160 rms, 1-2 story. Mid-May-Labor Day: S, D $79-$149; each addl $10; suites $250; lower rates rest of yr. Crib free. TV. Pool; poolside serv. Playground. Restaurant 7 am-10 pm. Bar noon-2 am; entertainment. Meeting rms. Ck-out 11 am. Business servs

avail. Sundries. Gift shop. Lawn games. Many balconies; some private patios. Built 1886; extensive grounds on riverfront; boat tours. Cr cds: A, D, MC, V.

★ **LEDGES RESORT.** *17 Anthony St, 1 mi NE of NY 12, 3 mi NE of I-81 exit 50N.* 315/482-9334. 27 rms. Late June-Labor Day: D $88-$108; each addl $8; lower rates early May-late June & after Labor Day-mid-Oct. Closed rest of yr. Crib $8. Pet accepted. TV; cable. Heated pool. Restaurant adj 7:30-11 am, noon-2 pm, 5-10 pm. Ck-out 11 am. Free bus depot transportation. Refrigerators avail. Picnic tables, grills. Private dock. Cr cds: A, C, D, DS, MC, V.

✔ ★ **NORTHSTAR INN.** *NY 12, just W of jct NY 26.* 315/482-9332; *FAX* 315/482-5825. Web www.northstarresort.com. 70 rms. S $29-$89; D $39-$109; each addl $10. Crib $10. Pet accepted. TV; cable. Pool. Playground. Restaurant 6 am-9 pm. Ck-out 11 am. Some refrigerators. Boat launch, docks. Cr cds: A, DS, MC, V.

★ ★ **PINE TREE POINT.** *Anthony St, 1 mi NE of NY 12, on St Lawrence.* 315/482-9911; *FAX* 315/482-6420; *res:* 800/253-9229. 83 rms in resort & chalets. July-Labor Day: S, D $65-$145; each addl $10; suites $190; under 12 free; lower rates May-June & after Labor Day-Oct. Closed rest of yr. Crib free. TV; cable, VCR avail (movies). Pool; whirlpool. Restaurant 7 am-2 pm, 6-10 pm. Rm serv. Bar noon-2 am; entertainment. Ck-out 11 am. Meeting rms. Business servs avail. Bellhops. Sundries. Gift shop. Valet parking. Sauna. Lawn games. Many balconies. Dockage. Cr cds: A, C, D, DS, MC, V.

✔ ★ **ROCK LEDGE.** *NY 12, ¼ mi W on NY 12.* 315/482-2191. E-mail rockledge@1000islands.com; web www.1000islands.com/rock-ledge/rockledge.htm. 14 motel rms, 6 cabins. Late June-mid-Sept: S $30-$68; D $40-$68; cabins $35-$55; lower rates mid-Apr-late June & mid-Sept-mid-Oct. Closed rest of yr. TV; cable. Complimentary continental bkfst. Restaurant nearby. Ck-out 11 am. Cr cds: DS, MC, V.

Resorts

★ ★ ★ **BONNIE CASTLE.** *Holland St.* 315/482-4511; *FAX* 315/482-9600; *res:* 800/955-4511. 129 rms, 1-3 story. No elvtr. Mid-May-Labor Day: S, D $89-$185; each addl $10; suites $119-$275; under 12 free; lower rates rest of yr. TV; cable (premium). 2 pools, 1 indoor; whirlpool. Complimentary coffee in rms. Restaurant 7 am-2 pm, 5-10 pm (also see BONNIE CASTLE MANOR). Rm serv. Bar noon-2 am; entertainment. Ck-out 11 am, ck-in 2 pm. Business servs avail. Bellhops. Concierge. Sundries. Gift shop. Airport transportation. Tennis. Golf privileges, driving range. Exercise equipt; sauna. Miniature golf. Refrigerators, bathrm phones; some in-rm whirlpools. Private patios, balconies. Built circa 1875; extensive grounds; on river, boat dockage. Cr cds: A, C, D, DS, ER, MC, V.

★ ★ ★ **RIVEREDGE.** *17 Holland St.* 315/482-9917; *FAX* 315/482-5010; *res:* 800/365-6987. E-mail Enjoyus@riveredge.com; web www.riveredge.com. 129 rms, 4 story. June-Labor Day: S, D $126-$218; each addl $20; suites $178-$238; under 12 free; AP, MAP avail; ski, golf plans; lower rates rest of yr. Crib free. Pet accepted. TV; cable. 2 pools, 1 indoor; whirlpool, poolside serv. Dining rm 6:30 am-10 pm (also see JACQUES CARTIER). Rm serv. Bar 11-2 am; entertainment. Ck-out 11 am, ck-in 3 pm. Grocery, package store 1 blk. Coin lndry. Convention facilities. Business servs avail. Bellhops. Valet serv. Concierge. Gift shop. 9-hole golf privileges. Boats, dockage, waterskiing. X-country ski 5 mi. Snowmobiling, sleighing. Hiking. Lawn games. Exercise equipt; sauna. Massage. Fishing/hunting guides. Bathrm phones, minibars. Balconies. On river. Luxury level. Cr cds: A, C, D, DS, MC, V.

Restaurants

★ ★ **ADMIRALS' INN.** *20 James St. 315/482-2781.* E-mail barbres@northnet.org. Specializes in prime rib, fresh fish, fresh roasted turkey. Hrs: 11 am-10 pm; Fri, Sat to 11 pm; Sun to 9 pm. Closed Oct-Mar. Res accepted. Bar to 2 am. Semi-a la carte: lunch $3.50-$8.95, dinner $8.95-$25.95. Child's meals. Outdoor dining. Victorian house; nautical theme, antiques. Cr cds: A, DS, MC, V.

D

★ ★ ★ **BONNIE CASTLE MANOR.** *(See Bonnie Castle Resort) 315/482-4511.* Continental menu. Specializes in prime rib, seafood, veal. Own baking. Hrs: 7 am-2 pm, 5-10 pm; Fri, Sat to 11 pm. Closed Dec 25. Res accepted. Bar noon-2 am. Wine list. Semi-a la carte: bkfst $4.95-$12.95, lunch $5.95-$12.95, dinner $13.95-$21.95. Child's meals. Entertainment. Outdoor dining (lunch). View of river. Cr cds: A, C, D, DS, ER, MC, V.

D SC

★ ★ **CAVALLARIO'S STEAK & SEAFOOD HOUSE.** *24 Church St. 315/482-9867.* Continental menu. Specializes in prime rib, live Maine lobster, veal. Hrs: 5-10 pm; Sat to 11 pm; Sun 3-10 pm; early-bird dinner Mon-Fri 4-6 pm. Closed early Nov-mid-Apr. Res accepted; required Sat & hols. Bar to 2 am. Semi-a la carte: dinner $12.95-$28.50. Child's meals. Entertainment Fri-Sat. Valet parking. Medieval decor. Family-owned. Cr cds: A, D, MC, V.

★ ★ ★ **JACQUES CARTIER.** *(See Riveredge Resort) 315/482-9917.* E-mail enjoyus@riveredge.com; web www.riveredge.com. Specializes in veal, seafood. Own pastries. Hrs: 6-10 pm; Sun brunch 10:30 am-2:30 pm. Closed Dec 25. Res accepted. Wine cellar. Semi-a la carte: dinner $21-$25. Prix fixe: dinner $45. Sun brunch $15.95. Child's meals. Harpist. Valet parking. On St Lawrence River. Cr cds: A, C, D, DS, MC, V.

D SC

Allegany State Park (E-2 - F-2)

(See also Olean)

(At Salamanca on NY 17)

This 65,000-acre park is one of the most complete recreation areas in the US. It borders on the Allegany Indian Reservation and the Kinzua Reservoir in New York and the Allegheny National Forests in Pennsylvania. It has more than 85 miles of hiking trails and many scenic drives through rolling hills. The park is open all year and has a museum, seasonal stores and two restaurants. Swimming at Quaker and Red House lakes, bathhouses; hunting, fishing; boat rentals; sports fields, tennis; 25 miles of groomed cross-country ski trails; 55 miles of snowmobile trails; tobogganing; picnicking, refreshment stands; tent & trailer sites (Apr-Dec, most with electricity), cabins. Standard fees. Contact Allegany State Park Region, Salamanca 14779; 716/354-9121.

Amagansett, L.I. (A-5)

(See also East Hampton, Montauk, Sag Harbor)

Pop 2,180 (est) **Elev** 40 ft **Area code** 516 **Zip** 11930 **Web** www.peconic.net/community/eh-chamber

Information East Hampton Chamber of Commerce, 79A Main St, East Hampton 11937; 516/324-0362.

What to See and Do

Miss Amelia's Cottage Museum (1725). Built by Jacob Schellinger; preserved and furnished to allow visitors a glimpse of of how people lived from the earliest colonial times through the early 19th century. A changing series of exhibits show specific aspects of everyday life in the area. (June-Sept, Sat afternoons; phone for hrs) Main St & Windmill Lane. Phone 516/267-3020 or 516/267-8989. **Donation.**

Town Marine Museum. Exhibits on commercial and sport fishing, offshore whaling from colonial times to present; underwater archaeology, sailing, aquaculture, commercial-fishing techniques; garden; picnicking. Programs administered by the East Hampton Historical Society. (July-Aug, daily; June & Sept, wkends only) Bluff Rd, ½ mi S of NY 27 on ocean. Phone 516/267-6544 or 516/324-6850. ¢

Motel

★ ★ **SEACREST.** *Montauk Hwy, 6 mi E on NY 27. 516/267-3159; FAX 516/267-6840.* E-mail duneresort@aol.com; web www.webscope.com/hotel/dune. 74 kit. units, 2 story. S, D $60-$110. Crib $15. TV; cable (premium). Heated pool; lifeguard. Restaurant nearby. Ck-out 11 am. Coin lndry. Business servs avail. Tennis privileges. Refrigerators. Private patios, balconies. Picnic tables, grills. On ocean, beach. Cr cds: DS, MC, V.

D

Inn

★ ★ **MILL GARTH.** *Windmill Lane, off NY 27, near East Hampton Airport. 516/267-3757.* 12 kit. units, 3 A/C, 2 story, 4 suites, 5 cottages. Memorial Day-Oct: S, D $135-$465; each addl $25; suites $165-$300; studio rms $145-$185; cottages $225-$300; family, wkly rates; lower rates rest of yr. Crib avail. TV in sitting rm. Complimentary continental bkfst. Ck-out 11 am, ck-in 3 pm. Business servs avail. Health club privileges. Lawn games. Private patios. Picnic tables, grills. Antiques. Built 1840, became inn late 1800s; stone originally from ancient windmill. Cr cds: MC, V.

D SC

Restaurants

★ ★ **GORDON'S.** *Main St. 516/267-3010.* Continental menu. Specializes in seafood, veal. Hrs: noon-2:30 pm, 6-10 pm; July-Aug from 6 pm. Closed Mon; Thanksgiving, Dec 25; Feb. Bar. A la carte entrees: lunch $11.75-$15.75, dinner $15.75-$23.75. Complete meals: lunch $12.50, dinner $21. Cr cds: A, D, DS, MC, V.

D

 ★ **LOBSTER ROLL.** *1980 Montauk Hwy (NY 27) at Napeague Beach. 516/267-3740.* Web www.lobsterroll.com. Specialties: char-broiled fish, clam chowder, lobster rolls. Hrs: 11:30 am-10 pm. Closed Nov-Apr; also wkdays May & Oct. Wine, beer. A la carte entrees: lunch $5-$10, dinner $10-$15. Child's meals. Outdoor dining. Nautical decor. Family-owned. Cr cds: MC, V.

D

Amityville, L.I. (B-3)

Pop 9,286 **Elev** 25 ft **Area code** 516 **Zip** 11701 **Web** www.amityville.com

Information Chamber of Commerce, PO Box 885; 516/789-9505.

Amityville is a town on the Great South Bay noted for antiques, craftspeople and its many restored houses.

What to See and Do

Lauder Museum. Permanent and changing exhibits reflect Amityville's heritage and that of surrounding communities; research library, genealogical files. (Tues, Fri & Sun) 170 Broadway. Phone 516/598-1486. **Free.**

Restaurant

★ ★ ★ **AMATO'S.** *330 Merrick Rd, Southern State Pkwy exit 32S, E on Merrick Rd (NY 27A). 516/598-2229.* Italian, Amer menu. Specialties: chicken Shoemaker, lobster Fra Diavolo. Own pastries. Hrs: 11:30 am-9:30 pm; Fri to 10 pm; Sat 1-4 pm, 5-10:30 pm; Sun 1-9 pm; Sun brunch to 5 pm. Closed Mon; July 4, Thanksgiving, Dec 25. Serv bar. Wine cellar. Semi-a la carte: lunch, dinner $9.75-$40. Complete meals: lunch $9-$15, dinner $17.95-$35. Sun brunch $14-$17.50. Cr cds: A, C, D, DS, MC, V.

Amsterdam (D-8)

(See also Johnstown, Schenectady)

Settled 1785 **Pop** 20,714 **Elev** 450 ft **Area code** 518 **Zip** 12010
Information Montgomery County Chamber of Commerce, 366 W Main St, PO Box 309; 518/842-8200 or 800/743-7337.

Located on the Mohawk River and New York Barge Canal, this city manufactures clothing, novelties, toys and electronic equipment.

What to See and Do

Erie Canal. Site of last remaining section of original canal (built in 1822). 6 mi W on NY 5S at Ft Hunter. **Free.**

Guy Park State Historic Site (1773). Former home of Guy Johnson, Superintendent of Indian Affairs, who remained loyal to King George III; abandoned by Johnson in 1775. Served as a tavern for many yrs. Exhibits on Native Americans and on Erie Canal and its impact on westward expansion. (Mon-Fri; closed major hols) 366 W Main St. Phone 518/842-8200. **Free.**

National Shrine of the North American Martyrs. Site of Ossernenon, 17th-century Mohawk settlement, where Father Isaac Jogues and companions, the first canonized martyrs of the US, were put to death. Birthplace of Blessed Kateri Tekakwitha. Coliseum-type chapel seats 6,500. Native American museum; cafeteria. (Early May-Nov 1, daily) 6 mi W on NY 5S in Auriesville, Dewey Thrwy exit 27. Phone 518/853-3033. **Free.**

Schoharie Crossing State Historic Site and Visitors Center. Seven arches of the Schoharie Aqueduct; remains of original canal locks; canals from 1825 and 1840s and barge canal can be seen. Park, boat launch; historic site markers, picnic tables; hiking paths; wagon rides; tours. (Mid-May-Oct, Wed-Sat, also Sun afternoons) 5 mi W, just off NY 5S, in Ft Hunter. Contact PO Box 140, Ft Hunter 12069; 518/829-7516. **Free; Tours ¢¢**

Walter Elwood Museum. Exhibits of history, natural science and ethnology; changing exhibits in gallery; research library. (July-Aug, Mon-Thurs, also Fri mornings; rest of yr, Mon-Fri; closed hols) 300 Guy Park Ave. Phone 518/843-5151. **Donation.**

Motel

✔★ **SUPER 8.** *NY 30, S of I-90 exit 27. 518/843-5888; FAX 518/843-5888, ext. 172.* 67 rms, 2 story. S $48.88-$60.88; D $54.88-$64.88; each addl $4; under 12 free; higher rates: Aug, special events. Crib $4. TV; cable, VCR avail (movies). Complimentary continental bkfst. Restaurant adj 6 am-11 pm. Ck-out 11 am. Meeting rms. Business servs avail. Cr cds: A, C, D, DS, MC, V.

Motor Hotel

★ ★ **BEST WESTERN.** *10 Market St, just off NY 30N. 518/843-5760; FAX 518/842-0940.* 125 rms, 5 story. S $55-$72; D $58-$89; each addl $6; under 18 free; wkly rates; higher rates Aug. Crib $6. Pet accepted, some restrictions. TV; cable, VCR avail (movies). Indoor pool. Restaurant 6:30 am-10 pm. Rm serv. Bar 11-12:30 am. Ck-out noon. Meeting rms.

Business servs avail. In-rm modem link. Valet serv. Sundries. Refrigerator avail. Cr cds: A, C, D, DS, MC, V.

Restaurant

★ ★ ★ **RAINDANCER STEAK PARLOUR.** *4582 NY 30, 3 mi N on NY 30, 4 mi N of I-90, NY 30 exit 27N. 518/842-2606.* Specializes in steak, chops, seafood. Salad bar. Own baking. Hrs: 11:30 am-10 pm; Sun 1-9 pm; early-bird dinner Mon-Sat 4:30-6 pm, Sun 1-3 pm. Closed Super Bowl Sun, Dec 24, 25. Res accepted; required hols. Bar. Semi-a la carte: lunch $4.95-$12.95, dinner $10.50-$28.95. Child's meals. Country decor; garden rm. Cr cds: A, C, D, DS, MC, V.

Arcade (E-3)

Pop 3,938 **Elev** 1,497 ft **Area code** 716 **Zip** 14009

What to See and Do

Arcade and Attica Railroad. Steam train ride (1½-hr) through scenic countryside; Grover Cleveland's Honeymoon Car. (Late May-Oct, Sat, Sun & hols; July-Aug, also Wed) 278 Main St. Phone 716/496-9877. **¢¢**

Inn

★ ★ **INN AT HOUGHTON CREEK.** *(9722 Genesee St, Houghton 14744) 22 mi S on NY 243, 3 mi N on NY 19A. 716/567-8400; FAX 716/567-4842.* 17 rms, 2 story. S $54; D $59; each addl $5; under 5 free; higher rates college events (2-day min). Crib $5. TV; cable. Ck-out 11 am, ck-in 3 pm. Business servs avail. Luggage handling. X-country ski on site. Health club privileges. Country decor. Totally nonsmoking. Cr cds: A, DS, MC, V.

Auburn (D-5)

(See also Seneca Falls, Syracuse)

Settled 1793 **Pop** 31,258 **Elev** 708 ft **Area code** 315 **Zip** 13021 **E-mail** cctourism@relex.com **Web** www.cayuganet.org
Information Cayuga County Office of Tourism, 131 Genesee St; 315/255-1658 or 800/499-9615.

On Owasco Lake, Auburn is one of the largest cities in the Finger Lakes region. Harriet Tubman, whose home was a link in the Underground Railroad, lived here. A resort and farm center, Auburn's products include electronics, auto parts, air conditioners, wire, plastics, diesel engines, steel, bottles and aviation spark plugs.

What to See and Do

Cayuga Museum/Case Research Lab Museum. The Cayuga Museum is housed in Greek-revival Willard-Case Mansion (1836); 19th-century furnishings; local industrial history; Bundy Monumental clock; Civil War exhibit. The Case Research Lab Museum is the restored lab where T. W. Case and E. I. Sponable invented sound film; permanent exhibits of lab, Fox Movietone, and sound studio. (Tues-Sun afternoons; also open Mon hols; closed Jan) 203 Genesee St. Phone 315/253-8051. **Donation.** Adj is

Schweinfurth Memorial Art Center. Classical and contemporary fine art, photography, folk art & crafts; concerts, lectures, museum shop.

(Feb-Dec, daily exc Mon, afternoons; closed hols) 205 Genesee St. Phone 315/255-1553. ¢

Emerson Park. Swimming; boating (launch). Ball fields, playground. Picnicking. Kiddie rides. Agricultural museum. (Mid-May-mid-Sept, daily) 3 mi S on NY 38A, at head of Owasco Lake. Phone 315/253-5611.Parking ¢ In park is

Owasco Teyetasta Native American Museum. Permanent and changing exhibits on traditional Northeast Woodlands Native people's arts and culture; emphasis on Iroquois cultures of central New York. (Memorial Day-Labor Day, Wed-Sun) Phone 315/253-8051. **Free.**

Fort Hill Cemetery. Site was used for burial mounds by Native Americans as early as 1100 A.D. Burial sites of William Seward and Harriet Tubman are here. (Daily) 19 Fort St. Phone 315/253-8132. **Free.**

Harriet Tubman Home. Born a slave, Harriet Tubman escaped in 1849 and rescued more than 300 slaves via the Underground Railroad. She later assisted the Union Army during the Civil War and, settling in Auburn after the war, continued to pursue other humanitarian endeavors. (Tues-Sat; also Jan, by appt only) 180 South St. Phone 315/252-2081. **Donation.**

Hoopes Park Flower Gardens. Band concerts (July & Aug, Mon & Wed eves); ice-skating (winter). Park (daily). E Genesee St, on US 20. Phone 315/252-9940. **Free.**

Seward House (1816-1817). Home of William Henry Seward, governor of New York, US senator and Lincoln's and Andrew Johnson's secretary of state, who was instrumental in purchasing Alaska. Civil War relics, original Alaskan artifacts, costumes, furnishings. (Apr-Dec, Tues-Sat afternoons; closed hols) 33 South St. Phone 315/252-1283. ¢¢

Willard Memorial Chapel & Welch Memorial Bldg (1894). These grey and red stone Romanesque Revival bldgs were once part of the Auburn Theological Seminary. The chapel's interior was designed and handcrafted by the Tiffany Glass and Decoration Co, and is the only complete and unaltered Tiffany chapel known to exist. Tiffany Concert Series in the chapel (July & Aug, Wed noon). Tours (Tues-Fri afternoons or by appt; closed hols). 17 Nelson St. Phone 315/252-0339. Tours ¢

Motels

★ **DAYS INN.** 37 William St. 315/252-7567; FAX 315/252-7567, ext. 190. 51 rms, 2 story. May-Sept: S $52; D $62; each addl $5; under 12 free; higher rates graduation; lower rates rest of yr. Crib free. Pet accepted. TV; cable. Complimentary continental bkfst. Restaurant nearby. Ck-out 11 am. Coin lndry. Meeting rms. Business servs avail. In-rm modem link. Health club privileges. Cr cds: A, C, DS, MC, V.

D ⚐ ⊠ 🔥 SC

★ **SUPER 8.** 9 McMaster St. 315/253-8886; FAX 315/253-8329. 48 rms, 2 story. May-Oct: S $45.88; D $59.88; each addl $5; under 18 free; higher rates special events. Crib free. TV; cable. Complimentary continental bkfst. Restaurant nearby. Ck-out 11 am. Meeting rms. Business servs avail. In-rm modem link. Cr cds: A, C, D, DS, MC, V.

D ⊠ 🔥 SC

Motor Hotel

★ ★ ★ **HOLIDAY INN.** 75 North St. 315/253-4531; FAX 315/252-5843. 166 rms, 5 story. S, D $69-$139; suites $150-$300; under 19 free; higher rates special events. Crib free. TV; cable (premium). Indoor pool. Coffee in rms. Restaurant 6:30 am-2 pm, 5-10 pm; Sat, Sun from 6:30 am. Rm serv. Bar 11:30-2 am; entertainment Fri, Sat. Ck-out 11 am. Coin lndry. Meeting rms. Business servs avail. Bellhops. Beauty shop. Exercise equipt. Many balconies. Cr cds: A, C, D, DS, ER, JCB, MC, V.

D ≈ 🏋 ⊠ 🔥 SC

Inn

★ ★ **SPRINGSIDE.** Box 327, W Lake Rd (NY 38 S). 315/252-7247. 8 rms, 5 with bath, 3 story. No rm phones. S $47; D $65; each addl $10; wkend rates. Complimentary continental bkfst. Restaurant (see

SPRINGSIDE INN). Ck-out noon, ck-in 2 pm. Built in 1830 as a boy's school; antiques, sitting rm. Cr cds: A, MC, V.

⊠ 🔥

Restaurants

★ ★ **LASCA'S.** 252 Grant Ave. 315/253-4885. Italian, Amer menu. Specializes in fresh seafood, steak, veal. Hrs: 11:30 am-2 pm, 5-9 pm; Fri, Sat to 10 pm; Sun from 4 pm. Closed Mon; most major hols; also 1st 2 wks Feb. Res accepted. Bar. Semi-a la carte: lunch $2.75-$5.95, dinner $7.95-$18.95. Child's meals. Cr cds: C, D, DS, MC, V.

D ⊡

★ ★ **SPRINGSIDE INN.** (See Springside Inn) 315/252-7247. Continental menu. Specialties: duckling flambé, lobster Newburg, prime rib. Hrs: 5-10 pm; Sun 1-6 pm; Sun brunch 10:30 am-2 pm. Closed most major hols; also Mon, Tues Jan-Feb. Res accepted. Bar. Semi-a la carte: dinner $8.95-$21.95. Sun brunch $10.99. Child's meals. Entertainment Sat; jazz Wed. Colonial decor. Built in 1830. Owasco Lake opp. Family-owned. Cr cds: A, C, MC, V.

Ausable Chasm (B-8)

(See also Plattsburgh)

(1 mi N of Keeseville; 12 mi S of Plattsburgh off I-87)

Information Ausable Chasm Co, US 9, PO Box 390, 12911; 518/834-7454 or 800/537-1211 (NY & VT).

This scenic gorge, accessible from US 9, was opened to the public in 1870. It is one of the oldest tourist attractions in the United States. Ausable (Aw-SAY-bl) Chasm leads eastward toward Lake Champlain for about a mile and a half. This spectacular gorge is 20 to 50 feet wide and from 100 to 200 feet deep. The Ausable River plunges in falls and rapids past curious rock formations, each with its own name: Pulpit Rock, Elephant's Head, Devil's Oven, Jacob's Well, the Cathedral. Paths and bridges crisscross the chasm. Camping is available on the grounds.

What to See and Do

Activities. Miniature golf, game rm, glassblower's shop, craft shops, picnic area and playground. (July-Aug, daily) Cross-country ski center (winter).

☆ **Self-guided walking tour** to mid-way point of stream & guided boat ride through "flume" rapids. (Memorial Day wkend-Columbus Day wkend, daily) ¢¢¢¢

Avon (D-3)

(See also Geneseo, Rochester)

Pop 2,995 **Elev** 651 ft **Area code** 716 **Zip** 14414

Originally a health resort with sulphur springs, Avon has since become a farming, food processing and horse-breeding center.

What to See and Do

Genesee Country Village and Museum. A 19th-century village representing life in the Genesee River valley. Fifty-seven bldgs, incl a log cabin and a Greek-revival mansion. Small-scale farm, blacksmith, pottery, print and tinsmith shops and a general store are in daily operation by museum guides dressed as 19th-century villagers. Permanent exhibits of antique horse carriages. Gallery of Sporting Art has over 700 pieces of wildlife art. (Mid-May-mid-Oct, daily exc Mon) 8 mi NW via NY 5 to NY 36 in Mumford, on Flint Hill Rd. Phone 716/538-6822. ¢¢¢¢

Inn

★ ★ **AVON.** *55 E Main St. 716/226-8181; FAX 716/226-8185.* 15 rms, 2 story. S, D $65-$75; suites $85; family rates; package plans. TV. Complimentary continental bkfst. Dining rm Wed, Thurs 4:30-9 pm; Fri, Sat 5-10 pm; Sun 9 am-8 pm. Rm serv. Ck-out 11 am, ck-in 3 pm. Business servs avail. Historic inn (1820); antiques; fireplace. Gazebo & fountain in rear. Cr cds: A, C, D, DS, MC, V.

Bainbridge (E-6)

(See also Deposit, Oneonta)

Pop 1,550 **Elev** 1,006 ft **Area code** 607 **Zip** 13733
Information Chamber of Commerce, PO Box 2: 607/967-8700.

Annual Event

General Clinton Canoe Regatta. World championship flat water canoe race, arts and crafts show. Phone 607/967-8700. Late May.

Motel

✔ ★ **SUPER 8.** *(4 Mang Dr, Sidney 13838) 5 mi E on I-88.* 607/563-8880; FAX 607/563-8889. 39 rms, 2 story. Apr-Sept: S $48.88; D $54.88; under 12 free; higher rates: Regatta, graduation, Baseball Hall of Fame events; lower rates rest of yr. Crib free. TV; cable, VCR avail (movies). Complimentary coffee in lobby. Restaurant adj 6:30 am-10 pm. Ck-out 11 am. Business servs avail. Cr cds: A, C, D, DS, JCB, MC, V.

Restaurants

✔ ★ **JERICHO TAVERN.** *4 N Main Street, at jct NY 7 & NY 206.* 607/967-5893. Hrs: 11:30 am-2 pm, 5-8 pm; Sun noon-7 pm. Closed Mon, Tues; Dec 25. Res accepted. Bar. Semi-a la carte: lunch $5.95-$10.95, dinner $10.95-$25.95. Buffet: lunch $6.50; dinner (Fri-Sun) $13.95. Child's meals. Early Amer decor. In 1793 tavern; player piano, nickelodeon. Family-owned. Cr cds: MC, V.

★ ★ **RIVER CLUB.** *(1 Maple St, Afton 13730) 6 mi W on NY 41; I-88 exit 7.* 607/639-3060. Continental menu. Specializes in prime rib, fresh seafood, steak. Own desserts. Hrs: 4-11 pm; Sun 11:30 am-6 pm. Closed Mon, Tues; Dec 25. Res accepted. Bar. Semi-a la carte: dinner $9.95-$18.95. Child's meals. Outdoor dining. Converted railroad depot overlooking river. Cr cds: A, MC, V.

★ ★ **THE SILO.** *(NY 206, Greene 13778) 6 mi E on NY 206.* 607/656-4377. Specializes in veal, seafood, chicken. Salad bar. Hrs: 4-10 pm; Fri, Sat to 10:30 pm; Sun 10 am-8 pm; Sun brunch to 2 pm. Closed most major hols. Res accepted. Bar. Semi-a la carte: dinner $9.95-$25.95. Sun brunch $13.95. Folk guitarist Fri. Country setting; view of gardens. Overnight stays avail. Cr cds: A, C, D, DS, MC, V.

★ **UNADILLA HOUSE.** *(63 Main St, Unadilla) approx 7 mi E on NY 7.* 607/369-7227. Continental menu. Hrs: 11 am-2 pm, 5-9 pm; Fri, Sat to 9:30 pm. Closed Sun; most major hols. Res accepted. Bar to 1 am; wkends to 2 am. Semi-a la carte: lunch $4.50-$7.95, dinner $9.95-$20.95. Child's meals. Country decor, many antiques. Restored 19th-century hotel. Cr cds: A, MC, V.

Barryville (F-7)

(See also Middletown, Port Jervis)

Pop 600 (est) **Elev** 600 ft **Area code** 914 **Zip** 12719

What to See and Do

Ft Delaware Museum of Colonial History. Replica of 1755 stockade, cabins, blockhouses, gardens; exhibits, film and demonstrations depict life of early settlers. Colonial military encampments (July-Aug). Picnic area; snacks. (Last wk June-Labor Day, daily; Memorial Day-late June, Sat & Sun only) On NY 97 in Narrowsburg. Phone 914/252-6660. ¢¢

Lander's Delaware River Trips. Canoe, raft & kayak trips on white water & calm water; campground along river. (Mid-Apr-mid-Oct, daily) One- and 2-day package plans. 2 mi N via NY 97 in Minisink Ford. Contact 1336 Rte 97, Dept M, Narrowsburg 12764; 800/252-3925. ¢¢¢¢

✪ **Zane Grey Museum.** Former home of author; items incl Grey's books, photographs, oil paintings for book jackets; original furnishings and utensils. Guided tours (Memorial Day-Labor Day, Wed-Sun May & Sept-Oct, Sat & Sun; rest of yr, by appt) 4 mi NW on NY 97, left across Roebling Bridge then right, in Lackawaxen, PA. Phone 717/685-4871. ¢

Batavia (D-3)

(See also Buffalo, Rochester)

Founded 1801 **Pop** 16,310 **Elev** 895 ft **Area code** 716 **Zip** 14020 **E-mail** chamber@iinc.com **Web** www.iinc.com/gencounty
Information Genesee County Chamber of Commerce, 220 E Main St; 716/343-7440 or 800/622-2686.

Established at the crossing of two Native American trails by Joseph Ellicott, an agent of the Holland Land Co, which purchased 3,300,000 acres from Robert Morris, Batavia was named for a province of the Netherlands. The brisk rate of sales of this western New York State land is said to have inspired the phrase "doing a land-office business." Batavia today is a lively farm area producing potatoes, onions, fruit and dairy products. Industrial items include heat exchange equipment, alloy castings and shoes. The New York State School for the Blind is here.

What to See and Do

Batavia Downs Race Track. Oldest pari-mutuel harness track in North America. Clubhouse, open-air and enclosed grandstands. (Early Aug-late Nov, daily) Park Rd, I-90 to exit 48. Phone 716/343-3750. ¢

Darien Lake Theme Park & Camping Resort. Family entertainment complex is NY's largest. Features 5 roller coasters, a million-gallon wave pool and sun deck, 40,000-sq-ft water adventure park and performing arts center; 2,000-site campground. (Late May-early Sept, daily; rest of Sept, wkends) I-90 to exit 48A, S on NY 77 in Darien Center. Phone 716/599-4641. ¢¢¢¢¢

Holland Land Office Museum (1815). Bldg from which deeds to the lands in the Holland Purchase were issued. This stone office was built by Joseph Ellicott, land agent. Local Native American and pioneer artifacts, period furniture and costumes; Civil War, medical & surgical collections (Tues-Sat; closed hols). The annex houses the County Historian's Office and historical research library (Mon-Thurs). 131 W Main St. Phone 716/343-4727. **Donation.**

Iroquois Natl Wildlife Refuge. Migratory waterfowl, especially geese, visit here in large numbers during the spring migration. Overlooks, trails, illustrated talks (res); fishing, hunting (in season). Office (mid-Mar-Apr, daily; rest of yr, Mon-Fri; closed hols). 15 mi NW of town via NY 63, on Casey Rd in Alabama, NY. Phone 716/948-5445. **Donation.**

Le Roy House. Early 19th-century house with furnishings of the period; 9 rms open to the public. Also home of Le Roy Historical Society. (Tues-Fri, mid-morning-mid-afternoon; also Sun afternoons; closed hols) ½ mi E of jct NY 19 & 5; 7 mi S of NY State Thrwy exit 47, at 23 E Main St in Le Roy. Phone 716/768-7433. **Donation.**

Annual Events

Genesee County Agricultural Fair. Tractor pull, demolition derby, livestock show, entertainment. Phone 716/344-2424. Late July-early Aug.

Wing Ding Weekend. Ethnic festival, block party, food, games, entertainment. 3rd wkend Aug

Motels

★★ **BEST WESTERN.** *8204 Park Rd. 716/343-1000; res: 800/228-2842; FAX 716/343-8608.* 75 rms, 2 story. Mid-June-mid-Sept: S $74-$84; D $79-$99; each addl $6; under 18 free; lower rates rest of yr. Crib free. Pet accepted, some restrictions. TV; cable (premium), VCR avail. Heated pool; poolside serv, lifeguard. Restaurant 6:30 am-2 pm, 5-9 pm. Rm serv. Bar 11-2 am; entertainment Fri, Sat. Ck-out noon. Meeting rms. Business servs avail. In-rm modem link. Valet serv. Lawn games. Cr cds: A, C, D, DS, MC, V.

D ⬧ ≈ ⬙ ⬙ SC

★★ **DAYS INN.** *200 Oak St, just off I-90. 716/343-1440; res: 800/329-7466; FAX 716/343-5322.* 120 rms, 2 story. May-Sept: S $62-$82; D $69-$99; each addl $7; under 18 free; lower rates rest of yr. Crib free. Pet accepted. TV; cable (premium). Pool; lifeguard. Complimentary continental bkfst. Restaurant nearby. Ck-out noon. Meeting rms. Business servs avail. Health club privileges. Cr cds: A, C, D, DS, JCB, MC, V.

D ⬧ ≈ ⬙ ⬙ SC

✔★ **PARK OAK.** *301 Oak St. 716/343-7921; FAX 716/343-6701.* 23 rms, 2 story. S $30-$48; D $45-$68; each addl $6-$15; higher rates special events. TV; cable. Complimentary continental bkfst. Restaurant adj 6:30 am-8:30 pm. Ck-out 11 am. Business servs avail. Totally nonsmoking. Cr cds: A, DS, MC, V.

⬙ ⬙ SC

Restaurant

★★ **SUNNY'S.** *Genesee Country Mall, 1 mi E of I-90 exit 48. 716/343-4578.* Italian, Amer menu. Specializes in seafood, steak. Hrs: 11-2 am; early-bird dinner 4-6 pm. Closed Sun; some major hols. Res accepted. Bar. Semi-a la carte: lunch $4.25-$5.50, dinner $5.85-$17.95. Child's meals. Family-owned. Cr cds: A, C, D, DS, MC, V.

D ⬩

Bath (E-4)

(See also Hammondsport)

Pop 12,724 **Elev** 1,106 ft **Area code** 607 **Zip** 14810

Motels

✔★ **CABOOSE.** *(8620 NY 415, Avoca 14809) 8 mi NW on NY 415. 607/566-2216; FAX 607/566-3817.* 23 units, 1 story, 5 caboose rms. Mid-Apr-mid-Oct: S, D $45-$70; each addl $7; higher rates: college events, racing season; lower rates mid-Oct-Nov & May-late June. Closed Nov-Mar. Crib $5. Pet accepted, some restrictions. TV; cable (premium). Heated pool. Playground. Complimentary coffee in rms. Restaurant opp 6 am-8 pm. Ck-out 11 am. Business servs avail. In-rm modem link. Gift shop. Lawn games. Refrigerators avail. Picnic tables, grills. Five antique cabooses (1916), set on track laid adj to motel, provide unique accommoda-

tions; interiors, including intact bunks, air brakes, torpedo boxes, are in near-original condition. Cr cds: MC, V.

⬧ ≈ ⬙ ⬙

★ **HOLLAND AMERICAN.** *6632 NY 415, NY 17 exit 39. 607/776-6057.* 15 rms. S $32; D $36-$38; each addl $5; under 18 free. Crib $5. TV; cable. Coffee in lobby. Ck-out 11 am. Cr cds: A, DS, MC, V.

⬙ ⬙

★ **SUPER 8.** *333 W Morris St. 607/776-2187; FAX 607/776-3206.* 50 rms, 3 story. No elvtr. June-Aug: S $42.88-$47.88; D $48.88-$53.88; each addl $5; under 12 free; lower rates rest of yr. Crib free. TV; cable (premium), VCR avail (movies). Complimentary continental bkfst. Complimentary coffee in lobby. Restaurant nearby. Ck-out 11 am. Business servs avail. Cr cds: A, D, DS, MC, V.

D ⬙ ⬙ SC

Motor Hotel

★★ **DAYS INN.** *330 W Morris St. 607/776-7644; FAX 607/776-7650.* 104 rms, 5 story. June-Oct: S $55-$70; D $65-$75; each addl $5; under 18 free; lower rates rest of yr. Crib free. Pet accepted. TV; cable (premium), VCR avail (movies). Indoor pool. Restaurant 11 am-10 pm. Bar. Ck-out 11 am. Coin lndry. Meeting rms. Business servs avail. Cr cds: A, C, D, DS, JCB, MC, V.

D ⬧ ≈ ⬙ ⬙ SC

Restaurant

✔★ **THE LOAFIN' TREE.** *143 Geneva St. 607/776-7734.* Specializes in chicken, steak. Hrs: 11 am-10 pm; Sun from 7:30 am. Closed Thanksgiving, Dec 25. Bar. Semi-a la carte: bkfst $1.95-$7.25, lunch $1.99-$5.99, dinner $5.50-$13.49. Child's meals. Gift shop. Family-owned. Cr cds: A, DS, MC, V.

D ⬩

Bay Shore, L.I. (B-3)

(See also Sayville)

Founded 1708 **Pop** 11,553 **Elev** 15 ft **Area code** 516 **Zip** 11706

What to See and Do

Bayard Cutting Arboretum. Approx 690 acres; many broadleaf and coniferous evergreens, wildflowers, shrubs; aquatic birds; nature walks. (Daily exc Mon; closed Jan 1, Dec 25) 6 mi E on Montauk Hwy (NY 27A). Phone 516/581-1002. Per vehicle ¢¢

Robert Moses State Park. (see).

Sagtikos Manor. Apple Tree Wicke (1692), served as headquarters for Gen Henry Clinton; original kitchen, parlor; Thompson Music Rm and dining rm added ca 1890; antiques. (July-Aug, Wed, Thurs & Sun; June & Sept, Sun only) 3 mi W on Montauk Hwy (NY 27A). Phone 516/665-0093. ¢¢

Motel

★★ **HAMPTON INN.** *(1600 Veterans Memorial Hwy, Islandia 11722) E on NY 27 to NY 454 N; I-495 exit 57S. 516/234-0400; FAX 516/234-0415.* 121 rms, 4 story. S, D $99-$115; under 18 free. Crib free. TV; cable (premium). Complimentary continental bkfst. Restaurant nearby. Ck-out noon. Business servs avail. Valet serv Mon-Fri. Free airport, RR station transportation. Exercise equipt. Health club privileges. Cr cds: A, C, D, DS, MC, V.

Restaurant

★ **PORKY'S & GLENN'S FISH HOUSE.** *28 Cottage Ave. 516/666-2899.* Specializes in fresh seafood, prime rib. Hrs: 11:30 am-9 pm; Fri, Sat to 10 pm; summer 11:30 am-10 pm; Fri, Sat to 11 pm; Closed Dec 25. Res accepted. Bar. A la carte entrees: lunch $7.95-$9.95, dinner $12.95-$30. Child's meals. Outdoor dining. Deck overlooks Great South Bay. Family-owned. Cr cds: A, C, D, DS, MC, V.

D

Bear Mountain
(see Palisades Interstate Parks)

Bemus Point (E-2)

(See also Chautauqua, Jamestown)

Pop 383 **Elev** 1,320 ft **Area code** 716 **Zip** 14712

What to See and Do

Long Point on Lake Chautauqua State Park. Swimming; fishing; boating (marina). Snowmobiling, ice fishing, cross-country skiing. Picnicking. (Mid-May-Columbus Day) 1 mi W off NY 17. Phone 716/386-2722. Per vehicle ¢¢

Hotel

★ ★ **HOTEL LENHART.** *22 Lakeside Dr. 716/386-2715; FAX 716/386-5404.* 54 rms, 34 with bath, 4 story. MAP, late May-mid-Sept: S $47-$90; D $91-$140; family rates. Closed rest of yr. Restaurant 8:30-10 am, 12:30-1:30 pm, 6:30-7:30 pm; closed off-season. Bar. Ck-out 2 pm. Meeting rms. Business servs avail. Airport transportation. Tennis. Opp lake, swimming beach. Boat dockage. Family-owned since 1880. No cr cds accepted.

D

Restaurant

★ ★ **YE HARE 'N HOUNDS INN.** *64 Lakeside Dr, on Lake Chautauqua. 716/386-2181.* Continental menu. Specializes in seafood, beef, veal. Own desserts. Hrs: 5-10 pm; Sun to 9 pm; Sun in winter from 4 pm. Closed Labor Day, Dec 24, 25. Res accepted. Bar. Semi-a la carte: dinner $12.95-$24.95. Outdoor dining. English-style inn (1915); fireplaces. Cr cds: A, DS, MC, V.

Bethpage, L.I. (B-3)
(See also Plainview)

Pop 16,840 (est) **Elev** 106 ft **Area code** 516 **Zip** 11714

What to See and Do

Bethpage State Park. 1,475 acres. Hiking, biking; golf (five 18-hole courses), tennis, bridle paths, game fields; picnicking. Cross-country skiing. Standard fees. E off Bethpage Pkwy. Phone 516/249-0700. **Free.**

Old Bethpage Village Restoration. More than 25 pre-Civil War bldgs incl blacksmith, carpentry and hat shops, general store, tavern, schoolhouse, church, homes; working farm and craftsmen depict life of mid-1800s; film. Picnic area. (Mar-Dec, Wed-Sun; closed major hols) Round Swamp Rd, 1 mi S of L.I. Expy, exit 48. Phone 516/572-8401. ¢¢¢

Restaurant

★ **56TH FIGHTER GROUP.** *(NY 110, Republic Airport Gate 1, East Farmingdale 11735)* S on NY 135, E on NY 24 to NY 110. *516/694-8280.* Continental menu. Specializes in seafood. Hrs: 11 am-3 pm, 4-10 pm; Fri, Sat to midnight; Sun from 4 pm; Sun brunch noon-2 pm. Res required. Bar 11 am-midnight; wkends to 3:30 am. A la carte entrees: lunch $5.95-$9.95, dinner $10.95-$29.95. Sun brunch $19.95. Child's meals. Outdoor dining. World War II theme; airplanes, jeeps and pictures. Cr cds: A, C, D, DS, MC, V.

D

Binghamton (E-6)

(See also Endicott)

Settled 1787 **Pop** 53,008 **Elev** 860 ft **Area code** 607 **E-mail** bchamber@spectra.net **Web** www.spectra.net/broomechamber/

Information Broome County Convention and Visitors Bureau, 49 Court St, Box 995, 13902; 607/772-8860 or 800/836-6740. For recording of activities phone 607/772-8945.

Largest of the Triple Cities (Johnson City and Endicott branched off later), Binghamton lies at the junction of the Chenango and the Susquehanna rivers. Completion of the Chenango Canal in 1837 made it an important link between the coal regions of Pennsylvania and the Erie Canal.

What to See and Do

Binghamton Univ, State Univ of New York (1946). (12,000 students) Anderson Center for the Arts (phone 607/777-ARTS) offers performing arts events incl dance, music and theater. Foreign films, lectures, art museum (academic yr, daily exc Mon; closed hols). Tours of campus. 2 mi W on Vestal Pkwy E, NY 434. Phone 607/777-2000 (univ info) or 607/777-3535 (recording of events).

Chenango Valley State Park. Swimming beach, bathhouse; fishing; boat rentals; hiking, biking, nature trails; 18-hole golf (fee). Cross-country skiing. Picnicking, playground. Concession. Tent & trailer sites, cabins (closed winter). Standard fees. 13 mi NE via I-88. Phone 607/648-5251.

"Day of a Playwright." Theater has exhibit honoring Syracuse-born Rod Serling (1925-1975), who grew up in Binghamton and created "The Twilight Zone" TV series; incl photos & documents highlighting his career in TV and films. (Mon-Fri & during Forum performances) The Forum, 236 Washington St. Phone 607/778-2480. **Free.**

Discovery Center of the Southern Tier. Hands-on museum allows children to experience a simulated flight in an airplane, crawl through a culvert and stand inside a bubble, in addition to exploring other interactive exhibits.

(July & Aug, daily; rest of yr, daily exc Mon) 60 Morgan Rd. Phone 607/773-8661. ¢¢

Roberson Museum and Science Center. Regional museum with collections in art, history, folk art and science. Incl turn-of-the-century mansion; changing exhibits; planetarium (fee). (Daily; closed hols) 30 Front St. Phone 607/772-0660. ¢¢

Ross Park Zoo. Operated by the Southern Tier Zoological Society. A 75-acre park (free); 25-acre zoo, with Wolf Woods, tiger, Snow Leopard, spectacled bear exhibits, petting zoo and aviary. (Mar-Nov, daily) Playground; picnicking. 185 Park Ave. Phone 607/724-5461. ¢¢

Annual Events

Carousel Festival. Music, crafts, carousel carvers, fireworks. Late June.

Balloon Rally. Early Aug.

B.C. Open PGA Golf Tournament. Phone 607/754-2482. Sept.

Seasonal Events

Broome County Veterans Memorial Arena & Convention Center. Professional hockey (B.C. Icemen, UHL; winter); national shows and concerts. Phone 607/778-6626.

Broome County Performing Arts Theater, the Forum. Broadway shows, center for dramatic and musical comedy productions by professional performers. Phone 607/778-1369.

Motels

✓★ ★ **COMFORT INN.** *1156 Front St (13905). 607/722-5353; res: 800/528-5150; FAX 607/722-1823.* 67 rms, 2 story. S $40-$75; D $45-$85; each addl $10; kit. suites $60-$105; under 18 free; higher rates special events. Crib $8. Pet accepted; deposit. TV; cable (premium). Complimentary continental bkfst. Restaurant adj 7 am-11 pm. Ck-out noon. Coin lndry. Meeting rm. Business servs avail. In-rm modem link. Microwave in suites. Cr cds: A, C, D, DS, ER, JCB, MC, V.

D ✦ ⩭ ⋈ ⚒ SC

★ ★ **DAYS INN.** *1000 Front St (13905). I-81 exit 5. 607/724-3297; FAX 607/771-0206.* 106 rms, 4 story. S $65-$100; D $75-$110; each addl $8; under 18 free; some wkend rates; higher rates college events. Crib free. TV; cable (premium), VCR avail. Pool; lifeguard. Complimentary continental bkfst. Restaurant adj open 24 hrs. Ck-out 11 am. Meeting rms. Business servs avail. In-rm modem link. Valet serv. Sundries. Refrigerators avail. Picnic tables, grills. Cr cds: A, C, D, DS, ER, JCB, MC, V.

D ⩭ ⋈ ⚒ SC

★ **HOWARD JOHNSON EXPRESS.** *690 Old Front St (13905). I-81 exit 5. 607/724-1341; FAX 607/773-8287.* 107 rms, 2 story. S $40-$60; D $46-$70; each addl $5; higher rates special events. Crib free. Pet accepted, some restrictions. TV; cable, VCR. Complimentary continental bkfst. Coffee in rms. Restaurant nearby. Ck-out noon. Meeting rms. Business servs avail. Health club privileges. Balconies. Cr cds: A, C, D, DS, MC, V.

D ✦ ⩭ ⚒ SC

✓★ ★ **PARKWAY.** *(900 Vestal Pkwy E, Vestal 13851) NY 17 exit 67S, NY 434E, turn right. 607/785-3311; res: 800/754-4961; FAX 607/785-8117.* 58 rms, 10 kits. S $30-$45; D $38-$60; each addl $5-$10; family, wkly, wkend rates. Crib $5-$8. TV; cable. Pool. Restaurant nearby. Bar 11 am-midnight. Ck-out 11 am. Health club privileges. Refrigerators, microwaves avail. Cr cds: A, C, D, DS, MC, V.

D ⩭ ⋈ ⚒ SC

Motor Hotel

★ ★ ★ **BEST WESTERN REGENCY HOTEL.** *225 Water St (13901). I-81 & NY 17W exit 5, I-88 exit 5, at 1 Sarbro Square. 607/722-7575; res: 800/723-7676; FAX 607/724-7263.* E-mail concierge@bingregency.com; web bingregency.com. 204 rms, 9 story. S, D $68-$77; each

addl $10-$25; suites $109-$169; under 12 free; wkend rates. TV; cable (premium). Indoor pool; lifeguard. Restaurant 7 am-9 pm. Rm serv. Bar. Ck-out noon. Meeting rms. Business center. In-rm modem link. Bellhops. Valet serv. Sundries. Free covered parking. Exercise equipt. Health club privileges. Some bathrm phones, refrigerators. Cr cds: A, C, D, DS, MC, V.

D ⩭ ⚔ ⋈ ⚒ SC ⚲

Hotels

★ ★ ★ **HOLIDAY INN-ARENA.** *2-8 Hawley St (13901), I-88 exit 5; I-81 exit 3; NY 17 exit 72; NY 81 S exit 5. 607/722-1212; FAX 607/722-6063.* 241 rms, 8 story. S, D $93-$99; each addl $10; suites $130; under 19 free; wkend plans. Crib free. Pet accepted; $15. TV; cable (premium). Indoor pool; lifeguard. Coffee in rms. Restaurant 6:30 am-10 pm. Rm serv. Bar noon-1 am; Fri, Sat to 2 am; entertainment wkends. Ck-out noon. Coin lndry. Convention facilities. Business servs avail. In-rm modem link. Shopping arcade. Airport transportation. Health club privileges. Some refrigerators. Cr cds: A, C, D, DS, JCB, MC, V.

D ✦ ⩭ ⋈ ⚒ SC

★ ★ **HOTEL DE VILLE.** *80 State St (13901). 607/722-0000; res: 800/295-5599; FAX 607/722-7912.* 61 rms, 6 story. S $75-$95; D $85-$95; each addl $7; suites $150; under 18 free. Crib avail. Pet accepted, some restrictions. TV; cable (premium). Complimentary bkfst. Bar. Ck-out noon. Meeting rms. Business servs avail. In-rm modem link. Valet parking. X-country ski 5 mi. Health club privileges. Renovated city hall (1897). Cr cds: A, C, D, DS, ER, JCB, MC, V.

D ✦ ⚘ ⚑ ⋈ ⚒ SC

Restaurants

✓★ **ARGO.** *117 Court St (13901). 607/724-4692.* Specializes in seafood, Greek & Italian dishes. Own desserts. Hrs: 6 am-9 pm. Closed Jan 1, Thanksgiving, Dec 25. Wine, beer. Semi-a la carte: bkfst $1.75-$7.25, lunch $3-$14, dinner $6.50-$14.95. Child's meals. Family-owned. Cr cds: A, D, DS, MC, V.

★ ★ **NUMBER FIVE.** *33 S Washington. 607/723-0555.* Continental menu. Specializes in steak, seafood, poultry. Hrs: 4-10 pm; Fri, Sat to 11 pm; Sun noon-9 pm; early-bird dinner 4-5:45 pm, Sun to 5 pm. Closed Dec 25. Res accepted. Bar. Wine list. Semi-a la carte: dinner $17-$21. Child's meals. Entertainment Fri, Sat. Former fire station (1897); firehouse memorabilia. Cr cds: A, C, D, DS, MC, V.

★ **THE SPOT.** *1062 Front St (13905), I-81 exit 5, 6. 607/723-8149.* Greek, Amer menu. Specializes in seafood, prime rib, pastries. Open 24 hrs. Res accepted. Bar 8-1 am. Semi-a la carte: bkfst $2-$8.25, lunch $4.95-$9, dinner $6.50-$27.95. Child's meals. Cr cds: A, C, D, DS, MC, V.

D ⌁

Blue Mountain Lake (C-7)

(See also Long Lake)

Pop 250 (est) **Elev** 1,829 ft **Area code** 518 **Zip** 12812

This central Adirondack resort village has mountain trails, splendid views, interesting shops, water sports, good fishing and hunting.

What to See and Do

Adirondack Lakes Center for the Arts. Concerts, films, exhibitions, theater, community center. In village, next to Post Office. Phone 518/352-7715.

Adirondack Museum. On slope of Blue Mt overlooking lakes, mountains and village. Noted for landscaping; indoor and outdoor displays. Exhibits explore logging, transportation, boating, mining, schooling, outdoor recreation and rustic furniture. (Memorial Day-mid-Oct, daily) 1 mi N on NY 30. Phone 518/352-7311. ¢¢¢

Adirondack Park (see).

Blue Mt. Three-mi trail to 3,800-ft summit; 35-ft observation tower overlooks Adirondack Park (see). Blue Mt Lake Assn has map of trails. 1½ mi N.

Motel

★ ★ **HEMLOCK HALL.** 1½ mi N, 1 mi W of NY 28N, 30. 518/352-7706. 22 rms in lodge, motel & cottages, 20 baths, 10 kits. No A/C. No rm phones. MAP, mid-June-Oct: D $92-$115; each addl $35, under 8, $25; kit. cottages for 2, $125-$135; lower rates late-May-mid-June. Closed rest of yr. Serv charge 12%. Crib free. Playground. Dining rm (public by res) sittings 8:30 am & 6 pm. Ck-out 11 am. Game rm. Rec rm. Lawn games. Some private patios. Library. Many antiques. Secluded; resort inn near woods on lakeshore. Private sand beach. No cr cds accepted.

[symbols]

Bolton Landing (Lake George Area) (C-8)

(See also Diamond Point, Glens Falls, Warrensburg)

Pop 1,600 (est) **Elev** 360 ft **Area code** 518 **Zip** 12814
Information Chamber of Commerce, Lakeshore Dr, PO Box 368; 518/644-3831.

Bolton Landing, on the shores of Lake George, has been home to musicians, artists, authors and people of great wealth. Today most of the estates are resorts, but the cultural atmosphere lives on.

What to See and Do

Recreation. Veterans Memorial Park. ½ mi N on NY 9N. **Rogers Memorial Park.** Center of town on NY 9N. Beaches (parking fee), tennis, picnicking, arts & crafts instruction; swimming lessons (all free). Phone 518/644-3831.

Motels

★ **BONNIE VIEW RESORT.** 4654 Lake Shore Dr, 1½ mi S on NY 9 N, 8½ mi N of I-87 exit 22. 518/644-5591; FAX 518/644-3611. E-mail bonnieview@global2000.net. 22 rms, 28 kit. cottages (1-3 bedrm). Mid-July-late Aug: D $86-$101; each addl $7; kit. units for 2-8, $545-$1,117/wk; 3-4-day min stay July-Aug; lower rates mid-May-mid-July, late Aug-mid-Sept. Closed rest of yr. Crib avail. TV; cable. Heated pool. Playground. Complimentary coffee in motel rms. Restaurant nearby. Ck-out 10 am. Tennis. Lawn games. Some fireplaces. Picnic tables, grills. Private beach; boats. Cr cds: DS, MC, V.

[symbols]

★ ★ **MELODY MANOR.** Lake Shore Dr, 2 mi S on NY 9 N, 6 mi N of I-87 exit 22. 518/644-9750. E-mail mail@melodymanor.com; web www.melodymanor.com. 40 rms, 1-3 story. Late June-Labor Day: D $107-$125; each addl $10; wkly rates; lower rates mid-May-late June, after Labor Day-Oct. Closed rest of yr. TV; cable. Heated pool. Restaurant 8 am-noon, 5-10 pm. Bar 5-11 pm. Ck-out 11 am. Tennis. Rec rm. Lawn games. Rowboat, paddleboat. Some balconies. Picnic tables, grills. On 9 acres, 300-ft lakefront; private sand beach. Cr cds: A, MC, V.

[symbols]

★ **NORTHWARD HO.** Lake Shore Dr, 1½ mi S on NY 9 N, 6 mi N of I-87 exit 22. 518/644-2158; FAX 518/644-3117. 17 motel rms, 10 kits., 8 kit. cottages. Early July-Labor Day: motel: S, D $71-$81; each addl

$10; kits. $90-$95; kit. cottages $810-$960/wk; wkends (3-day min); lower rates after Labor Day-Nov, Apr-early July. Closed rest of yr. Crib avail. TV; cable. Pool. Playground. Ck-out 11 am. Game rm. Lawn games. Sun deck. Refrigerators. Picnic tables, grills. Private beach. Cr cds: MC, V.

[symbols]

✔ ★ ★ **VICTORIAN VILLAGE.** Lake Shore Drive, 1 mi S on NY 9N, 6½ mi N of I-87 exit 22. 518/644-9401. 33 rms. No A/C. Late June-Labor Day (3-day min): D $69-$77; each addl $12; lower rates mid-Apr-late June, after Labor Day-Nov. Closed rest of yr. TV; cable. Restaurant nearby. Ck-out 11 am. Tennis. Lawn games. Rec rm. Private sand beach. Cr cds: MC, V.

[symbols]

Resort

★ ★ ★ **THE SAGAMORE.** 110 Sagamore Rd, ¼ mi E on NY 9N, 6 mi E of I-87 exit 24. 518/644-9400; FAX 518/644-2604; res: 800/358-3585. E-mail saq_sales@global2000.net; web www.thesagamore.com. 100 rms in main hotel bldg, 3 story. 130 suites in lodge, 2 story. July-Aug: S, D $215-$345; each addl $12; 6-17 yrs $5; under 6 free; suites $360-$430; MAP avail; package plans; lower rates rest of yr. Serv charge $5/person. Crib free. TV; cable (premium). Indoor pool; whirlpool. Playground. Supervised child's activities (July-Aug; rest of yr wkends only); ages 3-12. Dining rm (public by res) 6:30 am-11 pm (also see TRILLIUM). Box lunches. Rm serv 24 hrs (summer). Bar 11 am-midnight. Ck-out noon, ck-in 4 pm. Package store nearby. Convention facilities. Business center. In-rm modem link. Bellhops. Concierge. Gift shop. Beauty shop. Valet parking. Airport, RR station, bus depot transportation; horse-drawn carriages. Lighted & indoor tennis, pro. 18-hole golf privileges, pro, putting green. Private beach. Boats, motors; sightseeing boats, dinner cruises avail; dockage. Downhill ski 18 mi; x-country ski on site. Ski store, rentals; ice skating. Nature trail. Bicycles. Soc dir; entertainment. Game rm. Racquetball court. Exercise rm; sauna, steam rm. Spa. Many refrigerators, wet bars, fireplaces; microwaves avail. Some private patios, balconies. Cr cds: A, C, D, DS, JCB, MC, V.

[symbols]

Restaurant

★ ★ ★ **TRILLIUM.** (See The Sagamore Resort) 518/644-9400. Web www.thesagamore.com. Own baking, ice cream. Hrs: 6-9:30 pm. Res required. Bar 11-1 am. Wine cellar. A la carte entrees: dinner $18-$32. Serv charge 17%. Valet parking. Elegant Greek-revival decor, furnishings. Two-level dining area; view of lake. Jacket. Cr cds: A, D, DS, MC, V.

[symbols]

Boonville (C-6)

(See also Rome)

Pop 5,000 (est) **Elev** 1,146 ft **Area code** 315 **Zip** 13309 **E-mail** bacc@borg.com **Web** www.cybervillage.com/bac
Information Boonville Area Chamber of Commerce, 122 Main St, PO Box 163; 315/942-5112 or 315/942-6823(recording).

This rural community is nestled in the divide between the Mohawk and Black rivers on the southeastern portion of the Tug Hill Plateau. Pioneers cleared the forests of this area for their dairy farms; it has since become the dairy center of the region.

What to See and Do

Constable Hall (ca 1820). Limestone Georgian residence built by William Constable, son of one of New York's most prominent merchants; he joined Alexander MaComb and William McCormick in the MaComb Purchase, which consisted of one-tenth of the state. Memorabilia of 5 generations of

Constable family. (June-mid-Oct, daily exc Mon) 7 mi NW via NY 12D, unnumbered road. Phone 315/397-2323. ¢

Dodge-Pratt-Northam Art and Community Center. Victorian mansion (1875) features changing art exhibits; tour and a variety of workshops and courses. Gift shop. (Mar-late Dec, Tues-Sat; closed Thanksgiving, Dec 25) 106 Schuyler St. Phone 315/942-5133. **Free.**

Erwin Park. Swimming pool (July-Aug). Tennis and basketball courts. Picnicking, playground. (Mid-May-mid-Oct) On NY 12. Phone 315/942-4402. **Free.**

Pixley Falls State Park. Fishing; hiking. Picnicking, playground. Tent & trailer sites. (May-Sept) Standard fees. 6 mi S on NY 46. Phone 315/942-4713 or 315/337-4670 (off season). Per vehicle ¢¢

Snow Ridge Ski Area. Four chairlifts, 2 T-bars, rope tow; patrol, school, ski shop, rentals, babysitting; restaurant, cafeteria, bar. (Dec-Apr, daily) Cross-country trails. 11 mi N via NY 12D, 26, in Turin. Phone 315/348-8456 or 800/962-8419 for snow conditions. ¢¢¢¢¢

Annual Events

Oneida County Fair. Phone 315/942-2251. 4th wk July.

NY State Woodsmen's Field Days. Forest industry exhibits; competition. Phone 315/942-4593. 3rd wkend Aug.

Fall Arts Fest. Craft fair, demonstrations, art show. 2nd wkend Oct.

Motel

✔★ ★ **HEADWATERS MOTOR LODGE.** 13524 NY 12, ¼ mi N on NY 12. 315/942-4493; FAX 315/942-4626. 37 rms, 1-2 story, 4 kits. S $45; D $55; each addl $8; under 12 free. Crib $5. Pet accepted, some restrictions. TV; cable (premium). Complimentary continental bkfst. Restaurant nearby. Ck-out 11 am. Meeting rms. In-rm modem link. Game rm. Downhill/x-country ski 9 mi. Health club privileges. Refrigerators. Cr cds: A, DS, MC, V.

D ✔ ⚞ ⚟ ⛷ SC

Restaurants

★ **BUFFALO HEAD.** (North Lake Rd, Forestport 13338) 2 mi S of NY 28. 315/392-2632. E-mail buffalohead@aol.com. Specializes in prime rib, steak, seafood. Own pastries. Hrs: 8 am-10 pm. Closed Dec 25. Res accepted. Bar. Semi-a la carte: bkfst $1.75-$8.25, lunch $3.25-$4.95, dinner $5.95-$22.95. Child's meals. Fireplace. Cr cds: A, DS, MC, V.

D ⛷

✔★ **HULBERT HOUSE.** 106 Main St, 1 blk W on NY 12D. 315/942-4318. Specializes in prime rib, seafood. Salad bar. Hrs: 11:30 am-2 pm, 5-9 pm; Sun 11:30 am-8 pm; Fri buffet (seasonal) 5-9 pm. Closed Election Day, Dec 25. Res accepted. Bar from 11 am. Semi-a la carte: lunch $2-$5, dinner $9.95-$15. Buffet: dinner $8.75. Child's meals. Early Amer decor; antiques; established 1812. Cr cds: A, MC, V.

Brewster (F-8)

(See also Mahopac, Mt Kisco, White Plains; also see Danbury, CT)

Settled 1730 **Pop** 1,566 **Elev** 395 ft **Area code** 914 **Zip** 10509 **E-mail** brewster@computer.net **Web** www.brewsterchamber.com

Information Chamber of Commerce; 914/279-2477.

What to See and Do

Southeast Museum. Located in the 1896 Old Town Hall of Southeast. Borden dairy condensary, circus and RR artifacts; Trainer collection of minerals from Tilly Foster Mine; seasonal exhibits and activities. (Apr-Dec, Wed, Sat & Sun afternoons; closed hols) Main St. Phone 914/279-7500. **Free.**

Thunder Ridge Ski Area. Three chairlifts, rope tow, Mighty mite; patrol, school, ski & snowboard rentals; snowmaking; cafeteria, bar. Longest run 1 mi; vertical drop 500 ft. (Dec-Mar, daily; closed Dec 25 morning) Half-day rates. 10 mi N on NY 22. Phone 914/878-4100. ¢¢¢¢

Restaurants

★ ★ ★ **THE ARCH.** On NY 22; E via I-84, exit 20N, then 1 mi N. 914/279-5011. French, continental menu. Specializes in seafood, veal, lamb. Hrs: noon-2:30 pm, 6-10 pm; Sat from 6 pm; Sun 2:30-8 pm; Sun brunch noon-2:30 pm. Closed Mon, Tues; Jan 1. Res accepted. Bar. Wine cellar. Complete meals: $54. Sun brunch $28. Child's meals. Outdoor dining. Elegant french country inn; stone fireplace. Family-owned. Cr cds: A, C, D, DS, MC, V.

D

★ ★ **AUBERGE MAXIME.** (NY 116, Ridgefield Rd, North Salem 10560) 6 mi SE of I-684 exit 7; at jct NY 116, 121. 914/669-5450. French menu. Specializes in duck, soufflés. Hrs: noon-3 pm, 6-9 pm; Sun noon-9 pm. Closed Wed. Res accepted. Bar. Prix fixe: 3-course lunch $19.95. Complete meals: dinner $29.98. Child's meals. Valet parking. Outdoor dining in season. Cr cds: A, D, MC, V.

D ⛷

Bronx, Brooklyn

(Follows New York City)

Buffalo (D-2)

(See also East Aurora, Niagara Falls, NY; also see Niagara Falls, ON, Canada)

Pop 328,123 **Elev** 600 ft **Area code** 716 **E-mail** info@buffalocvb.org **Web** www.buffalocvb.org

Information Greater Buffalo Convention & Visitors Bureau, 617 Main St, Ste 400; 716/852-0511.

Buffalo, at the eastern end of Lake Erie, is New York's second-largest city and one of the largest railroad centers in America. Fifteen freight depots and one passenger terminal handle more than 25,000 trains annually. Major products are metal alloys and abrasives; automobile parts and tires; aerospace and defense products; medical, dental and pharmaceutical devices and products; chemicals and dyes; and food products.

Planned by Joseph Ellicott (agent of the Holland Land Co) in 1803-1804, the city was modeled after Washington, DC, which his brother, Major Andrew Ellicott, had laid out. Buffalo radiates from Niagara Square, dominated by a monument to President William McKinley, who was assassinated here while attending the Pan-American Exposition in 1901. The area also includes a $7 million city hall, state and federal buildings. The Buffalo Philharmonic Orchestra, Albright-Knox Art Gallery and many nightclubs cater to the varied interests of residents and visitors. The city is ringed with 3,000 acres of parks, which offer swimming, boating, tennis, golf and riding.

In 1679, when Buffalo was claimed by the French, La Salle built the first boat to sail the Great Lakes, the wooden *Griffon.* During the War of 1812, Buffalo was burned by the British, but its 500 citizens returned a few months later and rebuilt. In 1816, *Walk-on-the-Water,* the first steamboat to ply the Great Lakes, was launched here. The opening of the Erie Canal in 1825 made Buffalo the major transportation hub between east and west and brought trade and prosperity. Joseph Dart's invention in 1843 of a steam-powered grain elevator caused Buffalo's grain-processing industry to boom.

Since completion of the St Lawrence Seaway in 1959, Buffalo has been one of the top Great Lakes ports in import-export tonnage.

Transportation

Buffalo/Niagara Intl Airport: Information 716/632-3115; lost and found 716/632-3115; weather 716/844-1717; cash machines, East & West Terminals, 2nd levels.

Car Rental Agencies: See IMPORTANT TOLL-FREE NUMBERS.

Public Transportation: Buses & trains (Metro), phone 716/855-7211.

Rail Passenger Service: Amtrak 800/872-7245.

What to See and Do

Albright-Knox Art Gallery. Eighteenth-century English, 19th-century French and American, 20th-century American and European paintings; works by Picasso, Matisse, Miró, Mondrian and Pollock; sculpture from 3000 B.C. to present. Changing exhibits. (Daily exc Mon; closed Jan 1, Thanksgiving, Dec 25) 1285 Elmwood Ave. Phone 716/882-8700. ¢¢

Allentown. Historic preservation district containing Victorian-era structures of every major style. Many restaurants, antique stores, art galleries and boutiques.

⭐ **Architecture in Buffalo.** Among the works of famous figures in American architecture are

Frank Lloyd Wright houses. 125 Jewett Pkwy, 118 Summit, 285 Woodward, 57 Tillinghast Pl and 76 Soldiers Pl.

Guaranty Bldg (1895-1896). Designed by Dankmar Adler and Louis Sullivan, the Guaranty Bldg is an outstanding example of Sullivan's ideas of functional design and terra-cotta ornament; one of America's great skyscrapers. 30 Church St.

Boat trips. Buffalo Charter Cruises. *Miss Buffalo II* (200 capacity) leaves Naval & Military Park, foot of Main St, for afternoon or eve cruise of harbor, Niagara River and Lake Erie. (July & Aug, daily; June & Sept, Sat & Sun; also eve cruises) Also *Niagara Clipper* leaves from North Tonawanda for lunch, brunch and dinner cruises around Grand Island. (Memorial Day-Dec) Phone 716/856-6696. ¢¢¢-¢¢¢¢¢

Buffalo & Erie County Botanical Gardens. A 150-acre park with Victorian conservatory and outdoor gardens. Eleven greenhouses with desert, rainforest and Mediterranean collections. Seasonal shows. (Daily) 4 mi SE, 2 mi off NY State Thrwy I-90, exit 55 West Ridge Rd, to South Park Ave. Phone 716/696-3555. **Free.**

Buffalo & Erie County Historical Society. A Pan-American Exposition bldg (1901). Exhibits incl history of western New York, pioneer life; 1870 street. (Daily exc Mon) 25 Nottingham Ct, at Elmwood. Phone 716/873-9644. ¢¢

Buffalo & Erie County Naval & Military Park. Largest inland naval park in the nation. Cruiser USS *Little Rock,* destroyer USS *The Sullivans;* and submarine USS *Croaker,* aircraft, PT boat, tank and other World War II equipment; museum, video presentations; gift shop. (Apr-Oct, daily; Nov, wkends) 1 Naval Park Cove. Phone 716/847-1773. ¢¢¢

Buffalo Museum of Science. Birds of western New York, endangered species, Gibson Hall of Space, Bell Hall of Space Exploration, Dinosaurs & Co, Insect World, exhibits on astronomy, botany, geology, zoology, anthropology and natural sciences; research library, Discovery Room for children. Kellogg Observatory (Sept-May, Fri); sun show (July-Aug, Mon-Fri). Nature walks, lectures. (Daily exc Mon; closed major hols) 1020 Humboldt Pkwy. Phone 716/896-5200. ¢¢¢

Buffalo Raceway. Pari-mutuel harness racing (Oct-Feb & Apr-July). Erie County Fairgrounds, 5600 McKinley Pkwy, Thrwy (I-90) exit 56 in Hamburg. Phone 716/649-1280. ¢¢

Buffalo Zoological Gardens. More than 2,200 animals in 23½-acre park; indoor and outdoor exhibits; gallery of Boehm wildlife porcelains; tropical gorilla habitat; outdoor lion & tiger exhibit; children's zoo. (Daily; closed Thanksgiving, Dec 25) Jewett & Parkside Aves, in Delaware Park. Phone 716/837-3900. ¢¢¢

City Hall/Observation Tower. Panoramic view of western New York, Lake Erie and Ontario, Canada. (Mon-Fri; closed hols) Niagara Square, 28th floor. Phone 716/851-5891. **Free.**

Gray Line bus tours. 3466 Niagara Falls Blvd, North Tonawanda 14120; 716/694-3600.

Professional sports.

NFL (Buffalo Bills). Rich Stadium, Abbott Rd & US 20, 15 mi SE in Orchard Park. Phone 716/649-0015.

NHL (Buffalo Sabres). Marine Midland Arena, 1 Main St. Phone 716/855-4100.

Q-R-S Music Rolls. World's largest and oldest manufacturers of player-piano rolls. Tours two times a day (Mon-Fri). Several steep stairways may pose a problem for some visitors. 1026 Niagara St. Phone 716/885-4600. ¢

Shea's Buffalo Theater (1926). Performing arts center; Broadway shows, theater, dance, opera, music and family programs. (Sept-June) 646 Main St. Phone 716/847-0850. ¢¢¢¢-¢¢¢¢¢

State Univ College at Buffalo (1867). (12,000 students) On campus are Burchfield Penney Art Center (daily exc Mon; Aug, Sun only; closed hols; phone 716/878-6011); Upton Gallery in Upton Hall (academic yr, Mon-Fri). 1300 Elmwood Ave. Phone 716/878-4000.

State Univ of NY at Buffalo (1846). (25,362 students) Buffalo Materials Research Center, Natl Center for Earthquake Research, rare library collections; art exhibits. Music, theater, dance performances. Campus tours. I-90 to Millersport Hwy, N to SUNY-Buffalo exit. Also at 3435 Main St, near Bailey Ave in Buffalo. Phone 716/645-2000.

Studio Arena Theatre. Regional professional theater presents world premieres, musicals, classic dramas and contemporary works. (Sept-May, nightly exc Mon) 710 Main St. Phone 716/856-5650. ¢¢¢¢-¢¢¢¢¢

Theodore Roosevelt Inaugural Natl Historic Site (Wilcox Mansion). Theodore Roosevelt was inaugurated in this classic Greek-revival house in 1901 following the assassination of President McKinley. Audiovisual presentation; tours; Victorian herb garden. Self-guided 2-mi architectural walking tours (fee). (Apr-Dec, daily; rest of yr, daily exc Sat) 641 Delaware Ave. Phone 716/884-0095. ¢¢

Annual Event

Taste of Buffalo. Main St. July.

Erie County Fair. 12 mi S, off I-90 exit 56 in Hamburg. Phone 716/649-3900. Aug.

Seasonal Event

Buffalo Philharmonic Orchestra. Kleinhans Music Hall, 370 Pennsylvania St (box office). Classical and pop concert series; children's & family programs. Summer season also. Phone 716/885-5000.

Motels

★ ★ **COMFORT SUITES.** *901 Dick Rd (14225), near Greater Buffalo Intl Airport.* 716/633-6000; FAX 716/633-6858. 100 suites, 2 story. S $67-$80; D $72-$88; each addl $7; family rates; ski plan; higher rates sporting events. Crib free. TV; cable (premium), VCR avail. Indoor pool; whirlpool, lifeguard. Complimentary continental bkfst. Complimentary coffee in rms. Restaurant nearby. Ck-out noon. Coin lndry. Meeting rms. Business servs avail. In-rm modem link. Sundries. Valet serv. Free airport, RR station transportation. Tennis privileges. Golf privileges. Downhill/x-country ski 20 mi. Exercise equipt. Game rm. Refrigerators, microwaves. Cr cds: A, C, D, DS, ER, JCB, MC, V.

D 🏂🏌️🏊🍴✈️🐾🧖 SC

★ ★ **HAMPTON INN.** *(10 Flint Rd, Amherst 14226) I-290 to exit 5B, left at Flint Rd.* 716/689-4414; FAX 716/689-4382. Web www.hart hotels.com. 198 rms, 4 story. S $67-$76; D $76-$85; under 18 free. Crib free. TV; cable (premium). Indoor pool. Complimentary continental bkfst. Restaurant opp 8 am-11 pm. Ck-out noon. Meeting rms. Business servs avail. In-rm modem link. Free airport, RR station transportation. Exercise equipt. Cr cds: A, D, DS, JCB, MC, V.

D 🏊🍴🐾🧖 SC

✔ ★ ★ **HERITAGE HOUSE COUNTRY INN.** *(8261 Main St, Williamsville 14221) I-90 exit 49, E on NY 5, near Intl Airport.* 716/633-4900;

res: 800/283-3899; FAX 716/633-4900. Web www.wnybiz.com/heritage. 53 rms, 2 story, 9 kit. units. S $52.95-$68.95; D $58.95-$75.95; kit. units $58.95-$88.95; each addl $7; under 18 free. Crib $7. Pet accepted, some restrictions. TV; cable. Complimentary continental bkfst. Ck-out noon. Valet serv. Free airport, RR station transportation. Refrigerator, microwave in kit. units. Picnic tables. Cr cds: A, C, DS, MC, V.

★ **MICROTEL.** (1 Hospitality Centre Way, Tonawanda 14150) I-290 to Delaware Ave exit, Crestmount Ave. 716/693-8100; FAX 716/693-8750; res: 800/227-6346. 100 rms, 2 story. Mid-June-early Sept: S $45.95-$60.95; D $50.95-$65.95; under 18 free; lower rates rest of yr. Crib free. Pet accepted, some restrictions. TV; cable. Complimentary continental bkfst. Ck-out noon. Cr cds: A, D, DS, MC, V.

✔ ★ **RED ROOF INN-AMHERST.** (42 Flint Rd, Amherst 14226) NE on I-290, Millersport exit 58 to Flint Rd. 716/689-7474; FAX 716/689-2051. 108 rms. June-Aug: S $69.99-$79.99; D $79.99-$89.99; under 18 free; higher rates special events; lower rates rest of yr. Crib free. Pet accepted, some restrictions. TV; cable (premium). Complimentary coffee. Restaurant nearby. Ck-out noon. Business servs avail. Cr cds: A, C, D, DS, MC, V.

★ ★ **RESIDENCE INN BY MARRIOTT.** (100 Maple Rd, Williamsville 14221) NE via I-290, NY 263 exit to Maple Rd. 716/632-6622; FAX 716/632-5247. Web www.residenceinn.com. 112 kit. suites, 2 story. Kit. suites $89-$159. Crib free. Pet accepted, some restrictions; $6/day. TV; cable, VCR avail. Heated pool. Complimentary continental bkfst. Ck-out noon. Coin lndry. Business servs avail. In-rm modem link. Valet serv. Free airport transportation. Exercise equipt. Health club privileges. Microwaves. Cr cds: A, C, D, DS, JCB, MC, V.

★ **SUPER 8.** (1 Flint Rd, Amherst 14226) E on NY 5, N on I-290, exit 5B. 716/688-0811; FAX 716/688-2365. 103 rms, 4 story. S $49.88; D $57.88; each addl $5; under 12 free; higher rates special events. TV; cable (premium), VCR avail (movies). Complimentary continental bkfst. Restaurant nearby. Ck-out 11 am. Microwaves avail. Cr cds: A, C, D, DS, MC, V.

★ ★ **VILLAGE HAVEN.** (9370 Main St, Clarence 14031) E on NY 5. 716/759-6845; FAX 716/759-6847. 30 rms, 4 kits. Late May-early Sept: S $55-$67; D $62-$72; each addl $7; wkly rates off-season; higher rates hols; lower rates rest of yr. Crib $7. TV. Pool; lifeguard. Playground. Complimentary continental bkfst. Complimentary coffee in rms. Restaurant nearby. Ck-out 11 am. Business servs avail. Some fireplaces; refrigerators, microwaves avail; whirlpool in suites. Picnic tables. Cr cds: A, MC, V.

Motor Hotels

★ ★ **BEST WESTERN INN DOWNTOWN.** 510 Delaware Ave (14202), I-190 exit N-9 Niagara St. 716/886-8333; FAX 716/884-3070. 61 rms, 5 story. S $69-$79; D $71-$95; each addl $7; suites $198-$250; under 18 free. Crib $7. TV; cable. Ck-out noon. Meeting rm. Business servs avail. Valet serv. Health club privileges. Wet bar in suites. Cr cds: A, C, D, DS, JCB, MC, V.

★ ★ **DAYS INN.** 4345 Genesee St (14225), near Greater Buffalo Intl Airport. 716/631-0800; FAX 716/631-7589. 130 rms, 6 story. S $55-$75; D $65-$85; each addl $8; family rates. Crib free. TV; cable (premium). Pool; lifeguard. Complimentary continental bkfst. Complimentary coffee in rms. Restaurant 6:30 am-10:30 pm. Rm serv. Ck-out noon. Meeting rms. Business center. In-rm modem link. Free airport, RR station

transportation. Health club privileges. Microwaves avail. Cr cds: A, C, D, DS, JCB, MC, V.

★ ★ **HOLIDAY INN-DOWNTOWN.** 620 Delaware Ave (14202). 716/886-2121; FAX 716/886-7942. E-mail buffdt@buffnet.net; web www.harthotels.com. 168 rms, 8 story. S, D $84-$99; each addl $10; under 18 free. Crib free. Pet accepted, some restrictions. TV; cable (premium). Heated pool; wading pool, lifeguard. Complimentary bkfst. Restaurant 6:30 am-10 pm. Rm serv. Bar 11 am-midnight. Ck-out noon. Coin lndry. Meeting rms. Business servs avail. In-rm modem link. Bellhops. Valet serv. Free airport transportation. Health club privileges. Cr cds: A, C, D, DS, JCB, MC, V.

★ **LORD AMHERST.** (5000 Main St, Amherst 14226) E on NY 5 to jct I-290, near Greater Buffalo Intl Airport. 716/839-2200; res: 800/544-2200; FAX 716/839-1538. 101 rms, 2 story. May-Sept: S $59-$69; D $69-$79; each addl $7; suites $95-$160; kit. units $75-$150; under 18 free; lower rates rest of yr. Crib free. Pet accepted, some restrictions. TV; cable. Heated pool; lifeguard. Complimentary full bkfst. Restaurant 7 am-midnight. Bar 11 am-2 am. Ck-out 1 pm. Coin lndry. Meeting rms. Business servs avail. In-rm modem link. Valet serv. Game rm. Exercise equipt. Microwaves avail. Colonial decor. Cr cds: A, C, D, DS, MC, V.

★ ★ ★ **MARRIOTT-NIAGARA.** (1340 Millersport Hwy, Amherst 14221) N on I-290, exit Millersport. 716/689-6900; res: 800/334-4040; FAX 716/689-0483. Web www.marriott.com. 356 rms. S $79-$142; D $89-$152; each addl $10; suites $250; under 18 free; wkend plans. Crib free. Pet accepted, some restrictions; $50. TV; cable (premium). Indoor/outdoor pool; whirlpool, poolside serv. Restaurant 6:30 am-10:30 pm; Fri, Sat 7 am-11 pm; Sun 7 am-10:30 pm. Bar noon-3 am, Tues, Fri, Sat to 4 am, Sun noon-midnight. Convention facilities. Business servs avail. In-rm modem link. Valet serv. Concierge. Gift shop. Free airport transportation. Exercise equipt; sauna. Game rm. Some bathrm phones. Refrigerators, microwaves avail. Some poolside patios. Luxury level. Cr cds: A, C, D, DS, ER, JCB, MC, V.

Hotels

★ ★ ★ **ADAM'S MARK.** 120 Church St (14202), I-190 exit Niagara or Church. 716/845-5100; res: 800/444-2326; FAX 716/845-5377. Web www.adamsmark.com. 483 rms, 9 story. S $99-$159; D $119-$179; each addl $16; suites $225-$925; family, wkend rates. Crib free. Garage parking (fee). TV; cable (premium), VCR avail. Indoor pool; poolside serv. Restaurants 6:30 am-midnight. Bars; entertainment. Ck-out 11 am. Convention facilities. Business center. In-rm modem link. Concierge. Gift shop. Exercise equipt. Refrigerator avail in some suites. Some private patios, balconies. Cr cds: A, C, D, DS, ER, JCB, MC, V.

★ ★ ★ **HYATT REGENCY BUFFALO.** Two Fountain Plaza (14202), corner of Pearl & Huron Sts. 716/856-1234; FAX 716/852-6157. E-mail hyattbfl@localnet.com; web www.hyatt.com. 400 rms, 16 story. S $89-$145; D $89-$164; each addl $25; suites $225-$450; under 18 free; wkend rates. Crib free. Garage $5.95. TV; cable (premium), VCR avail. Restaurant 6:30-11 pm. Bar 11:30-2 am, Sat, Sun from noon. Ck-out noon. Convention facilities. Business center. In-rm modem link. Gift shop. Beauty shop. Health club privileges. Microwaves avail. Bathrm phone, whirlpool in suites. Cr cds: A, C, D, DS, ER, JCB, MC, V.

✔ ★ **LENOX.** 140 North St (14201), just off Delaware Ave, I-190 exit N-9. 716/884-1700; FAX 716/885-8636. 149 rms, 9 story, 129 kits. S $59; D $69; each addl $10; suites $70-$100; under 12 free; wkly, monthly rates. Crib free. TV; VCR avail. Ck-out noon. Coin lndry. Meeting rms.

Business center. In-rm modem link. Microwaves avail. Built in late 1800s. Cr cds: A, C, D, DS, MC, V.

★ ★ ★ **RADISSON.** (4243 Genesee St, Cheektowaga 14225) I-90, exit 51 E, near Greater Buffalo Intl Airport. 716/634-2300; FAX 716/632-2387. Web www.moran.com/. 274 rms, 4 story, 54 suites. S $134; D $144; each addl $10; suites $154; under 18 free; wkend rates. Crib free. TV; cable (premium), VCR avail. Indoor pool; whirlpool, poolside serv; lifeguard. Restaurant 6 am-midnight. Bar noon-4 am; entertainment. Ck-out noon. Convention facilities. Business center. In-rm modem link. Concierge. Gift shop. Free airport, RR station transportation. Exercise equipt; sauna. Many bathrm phones; some wet bars. Luxury level. Cr cds: A, C, D, DS, ER, JCB, MC, V.

★ ★ **RADISSON SUITES.** 601 Main St (14203). 716/854-5500; res: 800/333-3333; FAX 716/854-4836. Web radisson-dt.afterfive.com. 146 suites, 7 story. S, D $140-$170; each addl $10; under 18 free; family rates. Crib free. TV; cable (premium). Complimentary continental bkfst. Complimentary coffee in rms. Restaurant 6 am-midnight. Bar 11-2 am. Ck-out noon. Meeting rms. Business servs avail. In-rm modem link. Downhill/x-country ski 15 mi. Exercise equipt. Health club privileges. Refrigerators; some microwaves. Cr cds: A, C, D, DS, JCB, MC, V.

Inn

★ ★ ★ **ASA RANSOM HOUSE.** (10529 Main St, Clarence 14031) E on NY 5. 716/759-2315; FAX 716/759-2791. E-mail asaransom@aol.com; web www.asaransom.com. 6 rms, 1 with shower only, 2 story, 3 suites. Apr-Oct: S $75-$135; D $95-$150; each addl $15; suites $145; higher rates Sat, hols; lower rates Nov-Dec, Feb-Mar. Closed Jan. Crib free. TV; cable. Complimentary full bkfst. Restaurant (see ASA RANSOM HOUSE). Ck-out 11 am, ck-in 3 pm. Free RR station transportation. Business servs avail. Many fireplaces, refrigerators. Many balconies. Built 1853; antiques. Each rm decorated to distinctive theme. Totally nonsmoking. Cr cds: DS, MC, V.

Restaurants

★ ★ ★ **ASA RANSOM HOUSE.** (See Asa Ransom House Inn) 716/759-2315. E-mail asaransom@aol.com; web www.asaransom.com. Specialties: grilled salmon steak, roast chicken, smoked corned beef with apple raisin sauce. Own baking, ice cream. Hrs: 4-8 pm; Wed 11:30 am-2:30 pm, 4-8 pm; early-bird dinner Mon-Thurs 4-5:30 pm. Closed Dec 25; also Jan-mid-Feb. Res accepted; required hols. Semi-a la carte: lunch $7-$13, dinner $9.95-$22.95. Child's meals. Parking. Outdoor dining. Built in 1853; Early Amer decor; library-sitting rm, antiques. Fresh herb garden. Braille menu. Cr cds: DS, MC, V.

★ ★ **DAFFODIL'S.** (930 Maple Rd, Williamsville 14221) NE via I-290, NY 263 exit. 716/688-5413. Specializes in seafood, beef, lamb. Hrs: 11:30 am-2:30 pm, 5-11 pm; Sun 4-9 pm. Res accepted. Bar. A la carte entrees: lunch $6.95-$11.95, dinner $14.95-$39.95. Child's meals. Pianist Fri, Sat. Valet parking. Victorian decor. Cr cds: A, D, MC, V.

★ ★ ★ **LORD CHUMLEY'S.** 481 Delaware St (14202), in Allentown Historic District. 716/886-2220. Web www.lordchumleys.com. Continental menu. Specialties: filet Monaco, swordfish, veal Oscar. Own pastries. Hrs: 5-9 pm; Fri, Sat to 10 pm; Sun 4-8 pm. Closed major hols. Res accepted. Wine cellar. Complete meals: dinner $29.95-$49.95. Entertainment. Indoor courtyard; cobblestone floor, marble fireplace, silk-screened wall coverings. Family-owned. Totally nonsmoking. Cr cds: C, D, DS, MC, V.

★ ★ **OLD RED MILL INN.** (8326 Main St, Williamsville 14221) E on I-90, exit 49. 716/633-7878. Specializes in prime rib, steaks, seafood combination plates. Hrs: 11:30 am-9 pm; Sun 11 am-9 pm; Sun brunch to 2 pm. Closed Mon; also Dec 25. Res accepted. Bar. Semi-a la carte: lunch $5.29-$9.95, dinner $10.29-$19.95. Sun brunch $13.95. Child's meals. Parking. Fireplaces; country inn built in 1858. Caboose & Union Pacific dining cars. Cr cds: A, C, D, DS, MC, V.

★ ★ ★ **RUE FRANKLIN WEST.** 341 Franklin St (14202), I-190 Church St exit. 716/852-4416. French menu. Seasonal specialties. Own pastries, sauces, soups. Hrs: 5:30-10 pm. Closed Sun, Mon; July 4, Thanksgiving, Dec 25. Res accepted. Bar to 12:30 am. Wine list. A la carte entrees: dinner $16-$22. Parking. Outdoor dining in summer. Built 1880s. Family-owned. Cr cds: A, C, D, MC, V.

★ ★ ★ **SALVATORE'S ITALIAN GARDENS.** 6461 Transit Rd (14043), I-90 exit 49, near airport. 716/683-7990. Italian, Amer menu. Specializes in steak, prime rib, lobster. Own pastries. Hrs: 5-11 pm; Sun from 3 pm. Closed Dec 24, 25. Res accepted. Bar. Wine list. Semi-a la carte: dinner $12.95-$45. Child's meals. Entertainment Fri, Sat. Parking. Courtyard & gardens. Family-owned. Cr cds: A, C, D, MC, V.

✔ ★ **SIENA.** (4516 Main St, Amherst 14226) 716/839-3108. Italian menu. Specializes in wood-oven pizza, fresh pasta. Hrs: 11:30 am-3 pm, 5-10 pm; Fri, Sat to midnight; Sun 4:30-9 pm. Closed some major hols. Bar. A la carte entrees: lunch $6.25-$8.75, dinner $8.50-$18.95. Parking. Italian bistro decor. Cr cds: A, MC, V.

Unrated Dining Spots

JENNY'S ICE CREAM. (78 E Spring St, Williamsville) 1 mi E of I-290/90 exit 50. 716/633-2424. Specializes in homemade ice cream creations, yogurt, sorbet. Hrs: 11 am-9:30 pm; July-Aug to 11 pm. Closed Nov-Mar. Former stable, built in 1807. Old-fashioned decor. Totally nonsmoking. No cr cds accepted.

OLD MAN RIVER. (375 Niagara St, Tonawanda) I-190 N exit River Rd. 716/693-5558. Specialties: charcoal-broiled hot dogs, chicken & sausage, sweet potato french fries. Clam & lobster bar in summer. Own apple dumplings, soups, cookies. Hrs: 8 am-11 pm; Oct-Apr to 9 pm. Closed Jan 1, Thanksgiving, Dec 25. A la carte entrees: bkfst, lunch, dinner $3-$6. Child's meals. All counter serv. Parking. Overlooks Niagara River; reproduction of 18th-century sailing ship for children to play on. No cr cds accepted.

PRIMA PIZZA PASTA. 396 Pearl St (14202), at Chippewa. 716/852-5555. Italian, Amer menu. Specializes in pizza, calzones, chicken wings. Hrs: 9:30 am-midnight; Thurs 9-1 am; Fri, Sat to 3 am; Sun 3-9 pm. Closed Dec 25. Serv bar. A la carte entrees: lunch, dinner $2.75-$10. Two-story; cafe style downstairs, upstairs dining area overlooking street. Cr cds: DS, MC, V.

Cairo (E-8)

(See also Catskill, Windham)

Pop 5,418 **Elev** 380 ft **Area code** 518 **Zip** 12413

What to See and Do

Durham Center Museum. Schoolhouse used from 1830-1940; displays of progress of the Catskill Valley; Native American artifacts; fossils; minerals; railroad and turnpike relics; antiques, household and business equipment.

(June-Aug, Wed, Thurs, Sat & Sun; other times by appt) 8 mi NW via NY 145, past East Durham. Phone 518/239-8461. ¢

Zoom Flume Waterpark. Featuring water slides and other rides and attractions. Gift shop; restaurant, snack bar. (Mid-June-Labor Day, daily) Exit 21 off NY State Thrwy, W on NY 23 to NY 145W, 1 mi off NY 145 on Shady Glen Rd in East Durham. Phone 518/239-4559. ¢¢¢¢¢

Motel

★ **GAVIN'S GOLDEN HILL RESORT.** (Golden Hill Rd, East Durham 12423) 7 mi N on NY 145. 518/634-2582; FAX 518/634-2531; res: 800/272-4591. 60 rms, 2 story. July-Aug, AP: S, D $75-$95/person; family, wkend, wkly rates; lower rates Sept-Oct, May-June. Closed rest of yr. Crib free. TV; cable, VCR avail (movies). Pool. Playground. Complimentary full bkfst. Restaurant sittings 8:30-10 am, 12:30 pm, 5:30-6:30 pm. Bar; entertainment seasonal. Ck-out 11 am. Downhill ski 20 mi. Lawn games. Cr cds: A, MC, V.

Inns

★ ★ ★ **GREENVILLE ARMS.** (Greenville 12083) 9 mi N on NY 32. 518/966-5219; FAX 518/966-8754. E-mail ny1889inn@sprintmail.com; web www.artworkshops.com/page5.html. 13 rms, 2 story. No rm phones. Jan-Nov: S $80-$120; D $110-$150; each addl $30; wkly rates (MAP); hols (2-day min). Closed Dec. Children over 12 yrs only. TV in sitting rm; cable. Pool. Complimentary full bkfst. Rm serv. Ck-out 11 am, ck-in 3 pm. Business servs avail. Luggage handling. Downhill ski 20 mi. Lawn games. Built 1889 for William Vanderbilt. Original artwork. On seven acres; flower gardens. Cr cds: MC, V.

★ ★ **WINTER CLOVE.** (Round Top 12473) 15 mi W of I-87 exit 20, 12 mi N on NY 32, NW on Heart's Content Rd, then 3 mi W on Winter Clove Rd. 518/622-3267. 40 rms, 4 story. No A/C. No elvtr. No rm phones. AP: $72-$82/person; under 4 free; wkly rates; wkends (2-day min). Closed first 3 wks Dec. Crib avail. TV in sitting rm. Indoor/outdoor pools. Playground. Supervised child's activities in season. Dining rm (public by res) 8 am-9 am, 12:30-1:30 pm, 6-7 pm. Ck-out 11 am, ck-in 1 pm. Free RR station transportation. Lighted tennis. 9-hole golf course. Downhill ski 15 mi; x-country ski on site. Game rm. Rec rm. Lawn games. Bowling alley. Inn since 1838; antiques. Cr cds: MC, V.

Resort

★ **PICKWICK LODGE.** (Round Top 12473) 12 mi N via NY 32, NW on Heart's Content Rd, then 4 mi W on Winter Clove Rd; 15 mi W of I-90 exit 20. 518/622-3364. 50 rms, 42 with bath, 3 story. No elvtr. No rm phones. AP, Apr-Nov: S $255-$395/person/wk; $120-$140/person for 2 days; family rates; Closed rest of yr. Crib free. TV in some rms. Pool. Dining rm (public by res) 8-9:15 am, 12:30-2 pm, 6-7:30 pm. Bar 11:30 am-midnight. Ck-out, ck-in 11 am. Meeting rms. Gift shop. Tennis. Putting green. Hiking trails. Lawn games. Rec rm. Large private stocked pond and creeks. Cr cds: MC, V.

Canaan (E-8)

(See also Albany, Coxsackie; also see Pittsfield, MA)

Pop 1,773 **Elev** 847 ft **Area code** 518 **Zip** 12029

Inns

★ ★ **INN AT SILVER MAPLE FARM.** NY 295, NY Thruway exit B3 N, NY 22 to NY 295W. 518/781-3600. Web www.silvermaplefarm.com. 9 rms. Some rm phones. S, D $95-$155; each addl $20. Children over 12 yrs only. TV; cable, VCR avail. Whirlpool. Complimentary full bkfst. Ck-out 11 am, ck-in 3 pm. Luggage handling. Gift shop. Downhill ski 11 mi; x-country ski 5 mi. Lawn games. Refrigerators. Converted barn and carriage house. Totally nonsmoking. Cr cds: A, DS, MC, V.

★ ★ **MILL HOUSE.** (01237). 10 mi N on NY 22, 1 mi E on NY 43. 518/733-5606; FAX 518/733-6025. E-mail fxt2@taconic.net. 12 rms, 2 story, 5 suites. S $75; D $88-$95; each addl $15; suites $105-$140; package plans; 2-day min stay hols, wkends July-Aug. Closed mid-Mar-mid-May, Sept & Nov. Crib free. TV in some rms, sitting rm. Pool. Complimentary continental bkfst. Ck-out 11 am, ck-in 2:30 pm. Early 1900s saw mill redone in central European manner; many antiques. Totally nonsmoking. Cr cds: A, DS, MC, V.

★ ★ ★ ★ **OLD CHATHAM SHEEPHERDING COMPANY INN.** (99 Shaker Museum Rd, Old Chatham 12136) 8 mi W on Shaker Museum Rd, adj Shaker Museum. 518/794-9774; FAX 518/794-9779. E-mail old-sheepinn@worldnet.att.net; web www.oldsheepinn.com. This 1790 Georgian-colonial manor house is set on 500 acres conveniently located between the Hudson River, the Berkshires and Saratoga Springs, NY. Guest rooms feature four-poster beds, unique artwork and private baths; views from each room include ancient maples, pastoral hills and a neighboring sheep pasture. 11 rms, 1 with shower only, 2 story, 4 suites. S, D $185-$500; wkends 2-day min, hols 3-day min. Closed Jan. Children by arrangement only. Complimentary full bkfst exc Sun. Restaurant (see OLD CHATHAM SHEEPHERDING COMPANY INN). Ck-out noon, ck-in 3 pm. Luggage handling. Tennis. X-country ski on-site. Some fireplaces. Some balconies. Totally nonsmoking. Cr cds: A, MC, V.

Restaurants

★ ★ ★ **OLD CHATHAM SHEEPHERDING COMPANY INN.** (See Old Chatham Sheepherding Company Inn) 518/794-9774. E-mail old-sheepinn@worldnet.att.net; web www.oldsheepinn.com. Regional Amer menu. Specialties: fresh camembert crisp, roast leg of farm-fresh lamb. Own baking, pastas. Hrs: from 5:30 pm; Sun brunch 10 am-2 pm. Closed Tues; also Jan. Res required. Bar. Wine cellar. Semi-a la carte: dinner $18-$27. Sun brunch $8-$12. Outdoor dining. In 1790 Georgian manor house; shaker-style woodwork, ornate fireplaces. Largest sheepherding dairy in the United States; herb gardens, greenhouse. Totally nonsmoking. Cr cds: A, MC, V.

★ ★ **SHUJI'S.** New Lebanon (12125), 5 mi N of I-90 at jct US 20 & NY 22 exit B3. 518/794-8383. Japanese menu. Specializes in sushi, sukiyaki, tempuri. Hrs: 6-9 pm; Fri to 10 pm; Sat 5-10 pm; Sun 5-9 pm. Res required wkends. Closed Mon; also mid-Nov-Apr. Serv bar. Semi-a la carte: dinner $15-$40. Complete meals: dinner $33. Parking. Former house (1897) of Governor Tilden of NY. Family-owned. Cr cds: MC, V.

Canajoharie (D-7)

Settled 1730 **Pop** 3,909 **Elev** 311 ft **Area code** 518 **Zip** 13317

Located on the south bank of the Mohawk River, Canajoharie is in the center of the scenic and industrial Mohawk Valley. Named for a native word meaning "pot that washes itself," the town is near Canajoharie Gorge, which has a creek that winds down to a waterfall. There are many interesting buildings in the area.

What to See and Do

Ft Klock (1750). Restored farmhouse (1750) and Native American trading post fortified during the Revolution; also Dutch barn schoolhouse, blacksmith shop, carriage house, herb garden; picnicking. (Memorial Day-mid-Oct, daily exc Mon) 1 mi N, then 8 mi W of NY Thrwy exit 29 on NY 5, in St Johnsville. Phone 518/568-7779. ¢

Ft Plain Museum. Site of fort and blockhouse (1780-1786) used in defense of the Mohawk Valley during the Revolutionary War. Museum contains local history and archaeological artifacts. (May-Sept, Wed-Sun; rest of yr, by appt) 4 mi W on NY 5S in Ft Plain. Phone 518/993-2527. **Free.**

Library and Art Gallery. Paintings by Sargent, Inness, Whistler, the Wyeths, Stuart; large Winslow Homer collection; Korean ceramics. (Daily exc Sun; closed hols) 2 Erie Blvd. Phone 518/673-2314. **Free.**

Motel

★ **RODEWAY INN.** *(East Grand St (Rte 5), Palatine Bridge 13428) just E of Palatine Bridge on NY 5, opp I-90 exit 29.* 518/673-3233; FAX 518/673-5011. 30 rms, 3 kits. May-Oct: S $50-$95; D $55-$125; each addl $8; kit. units $60-$125; family, wkly rates; lower rates rest of yr. Crib $5. TV; cable. Complimentary continental bkfst. Complimentary coffee in rms. Restaurant nearby. Ck-out 11 am. Business servs avail. Downhill/x-country ski 10 mi. Overlooks Mohawk River. Cr cds: A, C, D, DS, JCB, MC, V.

🐾 🏊 🎿 🐕 SC

Canandaigua (D-4)

(See also Geneva, Naples, Rochester, Victor)

Pop 10,725 **Elev** 767 ft **Area code** 716 **E-mail** chamber@canandaigua.com **Web** www.canandaigua.com/chamber **Information** Chamber of Commerce, 113 S Main St, 14424; 716/394-4400.

This is a resort city on Canandaigua Lake (westernmost of the Finger Lakes).

What to See and Do

Bristol Mt Ski & Snowboard Resort. Two double, 2 triple chairlifts, tow rope; patrol, school, rentals; snowmaking; cafeteria, bar. Longest run 2 mi, vertical drop 1,200 ft. (Mid-Nov-Apr, daily) 12 mi SW on NY 64. Phone 716/374-6000 or 716/987-5000 for ski conditions. ¢¢¢¢¢

Canandaigua Lady. Replica of 19th-century paddlewheel steamboat offers variety of cruises, incl lunch, brunch, dinner and special events. (May-Oct, daily exc Mon) 169 Lakeshore Dr. For details phone 716/394-5365. ¢¢¢¢¢

Finger Lakes Race Track. Thoroughbred racing (Apr-Nov, Fri-Tues). 7 mi NW on NY 332 at jct NY 96; I-90, exit 44. Phone 716/924-3232. ¢¢

Granger Homestead (1816) and **Carriage Museum.** Home of Gideon Granger, Postmaster General under presidents Jefferson and Madison; 9 restored rms; original furnishings. Carriage museum in 2 bldgs; more than 50 antique horse-drawn vehicles; incl coaches, cutters, surreys, sleighs, hearses. Tours (by appt). (June-Aug, daily exc Mon; mid-May-late May & Sept-mid-Oct, Tues-Fri) 295 N Main St. Phone 716/394-1472. ¢¢

Ontario County Historical Society. Museum and archives relating to the history of Ontario County; children's discovery area; research library for genealogical studies. Bookstore. (Tues-Sat; closed most major hols) 55 N Main St. Phone 716/394-4975. ¢

Sonnenberg Gardens. A 50-acre Victorian garden estate with 1887 mansion; conservatory; 9 formal gardens incl Italian, Japanese, colonial, rock and rose. Tours. (Mid-May-mid-Oct, daily) Off NY 21 N. Phone 716/394-4922. ¢¢¢

Annual Events

Ontario County Fair. Hopewell Townline Rd. July.

Pageant of Steam. 3 mi E on Gehan Rd. Working steam engines and models; parade. 4 days Aug.

Ring of Fire. Re-enactment of Native American ceremony. Sat before Labor Day.

Seasonal Event

SummerMusic '99. Rochester Philharmonic Orchestra, Finger Lakes Performing Arts Center. Symphonic, classical and pops concerts, special events. Indoor/outdoor seating. Picnic sites. Contact 108 East Ave, Rochester 14604; phone 716/454-2620. July.

Motels

🏊 ★ ★ **ECONO LODGE.** *170 Eastern Blvd (14424).* 716/394-9000; res: 800/797-1222; FAX 716/396-2560. 65 rms, 2 story. May-Oct: S $52; D $73; each addl $10; under 18 free; lower rates rest of yr. Crib free. Pet accepted, some restrictions. TV; cable (premium), VCR avail (movies). Complimentary coffee in lobby. Restaurant adj open 24 hrs. Ck-out 11 am. Coin lndry. Business servs avail. Downhill ski 12 mi. Opp lake. Cr cds: A, C, D, DS, JCB, MC, V.

D 🐾 🏊 🎿 🐕 SC

★ ★ **INN ON THE LAKE.** *770 S Main St (14424), off US 20.* 716/394-7800; FAX 716/394-5003; res: 800/228-2801. 134 rms, 2 story. 44 suites. May-Nov: S $98-$145; D $108-$155; each addl $10; suites $152-$295; under 18 free; package plans; lower rates rest of yr. Crib free. Pet accepted. TV; cable, VCR avail (movies). 2 heated pools, 1 indoor; whirlpool, lifeguard. Restaurant 6:30 am-9 pm; wknds to 10 pm. Rm serv. Bar 11-1 am. Ck-out 11 am. Coin lndry. Meeting rms. Business servs avail. In-rm modem link. Exercise equipt. Downhill ski 20 mi. Refrigerators in suites. Some balconies. Picnic tables. On lake. Cr cds: A, D, DS, MC, V.

D 🐾 🏊 🏊 🍴 🏋 🎿 🐕 SC

Inns

★ ★ **THE ACORN INN.** *(4508 Bristol Valley Rd, Bristol Center 14424-9309) 9 mi on I-90 exit 43-44.* 716/229-2834; FAX 716/229-5046. 4 rms, 2 story. May-Oct: S $105-$175; D $115-$175; each addl $25; ski plans; wknds 2-day min; higher rates hols; lower rates rest of yr. Children over 14 yrs only. TV; cable (premium), VCR (movies). Complimentary full bkfst; refreshments. Ck-out 11 am, ck-in 3 pm. Business servs avail. Luggage handling. Downhill/x-country ski 5 mi. Some fireplaces. Built in 1795; originally was a stagecoach inn. Federal style; antiques. Totally nonsmoking. Cr cds: A, DS, MC, V.

🎿 🐕 🔥 SC

★ ★ **ENCHANTED ROSE.** *(7479 NY 5 & 20, East Bloomfield 14443) 8 mi W on NY 5 & 20.* 716/657-6003; res: 888/657-6003; FAX 716/657-4405. E-mail enchrose@servtech.com; web www.servtech.com/public/enchrose. 2 rms, 2 story, 1 suite. May-Oct: S $90; D $95; each addl $10; suite $135; under 5 free; lower rates rest of yr. TV; VCR avail (movies). Complimentary full bkfst; afternoon refreshments. Restaurant nearby. Ck-out 11 am, ck-in 2 pm. Business servs avail.

Luggage handling. Lawn games. Picnic tables. Federal-style house built circa 1820; antiques. Totally nonsmoking. Cr cds: A, DS, MC, V.

★ ★ ★ **THE GREENWOODS.** *(8136 Quayle Rd, Honeoye 14471) W on US 20/NY 5, 4 mi S on NY 64, 5 mi W on NY 20A, right on Quayle Rd.* 716/229-2111; *res:* 800/914-3559. Web www.dreamscape.com/greenwoods. 5 rms, 3 story. No rm phones. S $60-$90; D $85-$135; each addl $15; ski plans. Children over 12 yrs only. TV. Whirlpool. Complimentary full bkfst. Ck-out 11 am, ck-in 3 pm. Business servs avail. Downhill ski 7 mi; x-country ski 8 mi. Picnic tables. Log bldg in rural setting with 3 porches. Totally nonsmoking. Cr cds: A, DS, MC, V.

★ ★ **MORGAN-SAMUELS BED & BREAKFAST.** *2920 Smith Rd (14424).* 716/394-9232; *FAX* 716/394-8044. 5 rms, 2 story, 1 suite. Mid-May-mid-Nov, wkend rates: S, D $119-$169; each addl $20; suite $195; lower rates rest of yr. Crib free. TV; VCR avail. Complimentary full bkfst. Ck-out 11 am, ck-in 3 pm. Business servs avail. Tennis. Downhill ski 11 mi; x-country ski on site. Health club privileges. Balconies. Stone and brick farmhouse (1810); library, fireplaces, antiques, original artwork. Extensive grounds. Totally nonsmoking. Cr cds: DS, MC, V.

★ ★ **SUTHERLAND HOUSE INN.** *3179 NY 21S (14424).* 716/396-0375; *res:* 800/396-0375; *FAX* 716/396-9281. E-mail goodnite@frontiernet.net; web www.sutherlandhouse.com. 5 rms, 1 suite. Some rm phones. S $75; D $95-$170; each addl $20; suites $170; package plans. TV; cable, VCR (movies). Complimentary full bkfst; afternoon refreshments. Ck-out 11 am, ck-in 3-6 pm. Business servs avail. Luggage handling. Concierge serv. Gift shop. Donwhill ski 10 mi; x-country ski 20 mi. Many fireplaces; some in-rm whirlpools, refrigerators. Built in 1885; country Victorian inn. Antiques. Totally nonsmoking. Cr cds: A, DS, MC, V.

Restaurants

★ ★ ★ **HOLLOWAY HOUSE.** *East Bloomfield (14443), 8 mi W on US 20 (NY 5).* 716/657-7120. Specialties: Sally Lunn bread, roast turkey. Own baking. Hrs: 11:30 am-2 pm, 5-8:30 pm; Sat to 9 pm; Sun noon-7:30 pm. Res accepted. Closed Mon; also late Dec-Mar. Bar. Semi-a la carte: lunch $6.95-$10.95, dinner $11.95-$22.95. Child's meals. Parking. Inn & stagecoach stop established 1808. Family-owned. Cr cds: A, MC, V.

✔★ **KELLOGG'S PAN-TREE INN.** *130 Lakeshore Dr (14424).* 716/394-3909. Specialties: griddle cakes, chicken pie, creamed codfish. Own baking. Hrs: 7:30 am-7:30 pm; Sun from 8 am. Closed Nov-mid-Apr. Semi-a la carte: bkfst $4-$6.25, lunch $4.50-$14.95, dinner $8-$14.25. Child's meals. Parking. Overlooks park, lake. Family-owned. Cr cds: MC, V.

★ ★ **LINCOLN HILL INN.** *3365 E Lake Rd (14424).* 716/394-8254. Continental menu. Specializes in seafood, beef, chicken. Hrs: 5-10 pm. Closed Sun & Mon mid-Oct-mid-Apr; Dec 25. Res accepted. Bar. Semi-a la carte: dinner $9.95-$20.95. Child's meals. Outdoor dining. Early Finger Lakes homestead, built 1804. Cr cds: A, MC, V.

✔★ **MANETTI'S.** *Parkway Plaza (14424).* 716/394-1915. Italian, Amer menu. Specializes in veal, pasta. Salad bar. Hrs: 4-10 pm; Sun from noon; 4-11 pm summer. Closed Thanksgiving, Dec 25. Res accepted. Bar to 1 am; Sat to 2 am. Semi-a la carte: dinner $7.25-$21.95. Child's meals. Parking. Solarium. Cr cds: A, D, MC, V.

Canastota (D-6)

(See also Rome, Syracuse, Utica)

Settled 1810 **Pop** 4,700 (est) **Elev** 420 ft **Area code** 315 **Zip** 13032

In 1820, when the first packetboat run was established on the Erie Canal from here to Rome, Canastota became a canal town. Some of the original structures still exist along the canal, which bisects the village.

What to See and Do

Canastota Canal Town Museum. Displays trace growth of Erie Canal and its effect on Canastota and western New York. Adj to state park. (Tues-Sat; closed most major hols) 122 Canal St. Phone 315/697-3451. **Free.**

Chittenango Landing Canal Boat Museum. Located on a remaining section of the Erie Canal and dedicated to the preservation of a 19th-century boat building and repair industry. Historic site has guided and self-guided walking tours, excavations, interpretive center, hands-on activities and exhibits. (July-Aug, daily; Apr-Jun & Sept-Oct, wkends; rest of yr, by appt only; closed Jan 1, Dec 25) 7 mi W via NY 5, on Lakeport Rd in Chittenango. Phone 315/687-3801. ¢¢

International Boxing Hall of Fame. In honor of those who have excelled in boxing and preservation of boxing heritage. (Daily; limited hrs hols; closed Easter, Thanksgiving, Dec 25) 1 Hall of Fame Dr. Phone 315/697-7095. ¢¢

Old Erie Canal State Park. This 35-mi strip of canal runs from Dewitt (canoe launching and picnicking at Cedar Bay Area) to Rome. Many features of original canal remain, incl towpath, aqueducts, change bridges, culverts. Fishing; canoeing. Hiking, bicycling. Horseback riding. Snowmobiling. Accessible from NY 5 & 46 and I-90 exits 33, 34. Phone 315/687-7821.

Canton (B-6)

(See also Ogdensburg, Potsdam)

Pop 11,120 **Elev** 380 ft **Area code** 315 **Zip** 13617
Information Chamber of Commerce, Municipal Bldg, PO Box 369; 315/386-8255.

Canton, which lies on the Grass River, was settled in the early 1800s by Vermonters. Canton College of Technology is located here.

What to See and Do

Silas Wright House and Museum (St Lawrence Co Historical Assn). Greek-revival residence (1832-1844) of the US senator and New York governor. First floor restored to 1830-1850 period; 2nd floor gallery for temporary exhibits on local history. Library, archives, museum (Tues-Sat; closed hols). 3 E Main St. Phone 315/386-8133. **Free;** archives ¢¢

St Lawrence Univ (1856). (2,200 students) On campus are the Griffiths Arts Center, Gunnison Memorial Chapel, Owen D. Young Library, Augsbury-Leithead Physical Education Complex. Campus tours. Phone 315/229-5261.

Annual Event

Rushton Canoe Races. Early May.

Motels

★ ★ **BEST WESTERN UNIVERSITY INN.** *90 Main St E, adj to St Lawrence University.* 315/386-8522; *res:* 800/528-1234; *FAX* 315/386-1025. E-mail sales@bwcanton.com; web www.bwcanton.com. 98 rms, 3 story. No elvtr. May-Oct: S $59; D $65-$75; under 12 free; golf plan; lower rates rest of yr. Crib free. Pet accepted. TV; cable (premium). Pool. Coffee in rms. Restaurant 6:30 am-9 pm. Rm serv. Bar 11-2 am. Ck-out noon. Meeting rms. Business servs avail. X-country ski on site. Exercise equipt. Some refrigerators, microwaves. Cr cds: A, C, D, DS, ER, MC, V.

✔★ **CLEARVIEW.** *(US 11, Gouverneur 13642) 20 mi S on US 11.* 315/287-2800. 34 rms. S $41-$47; D $45-$58; each addl $6; under 12 free. Crib free. TV; cable. Pool. Complimentary coffee in lobby. Restaurant adj 11 am-11 pm. Ck-out 11 am. Meeting rms. Sundries. 18-hole golf privileges, pro. Picnic tables, grills. Cr cds: A, DS, MC, V.

Restaurants

✔★ **McCARTHY'S.** *1 mi S on US 11.* 315/386-2564. Specializes in chicken and biscuits, soups. Own cinnamon rolls. Salad bar. Hrs: 7 am-9 pm. Closed some major hols. Res accepted. Bar. Semi-a la carte: bkfst $3.75-$6.50, lunch $2.95-$9.50, dinner $8.25-$12.95. Sun brunch $6.25. Child's meals. Cr cds: C, D, DS, MC, V.

★★ **RIB TRADER.** *Canton-Potsdam Rd.* 315/379-0113. Specializes in seafood, prime rib. Salad bar. Hrs: 5-9 pm; Sat, Sun 4:30-10 pm. Closed most major hols. Bar. Semi-a la carte: dinner $9.95-$19.95. Child's meals. Cr cds: DS, MC, V.

Catskill (E-8)

(See also Hillsdale, Hudson, Hunter)

Settled 1662 **Pop** 11,965 **Elev** 47 ft **Area code** 518 **Zip** 12414 **Web** www.greene-ny.com
Information Greene County Promotion Dept, NY Thrwy exit 21, PO Box 527; 518/943-3223 or 800/355-CATS.

This is the eastern entrance to the Catskill Mountains resort area. The town is at the west end of the Rip Van Winkle Bridge, over the Hudson River across from the manufacturing town of Hudson (see). The legendary Rip is said to have slept for twenty years near here.

What to See and Do

Catskill Game Farm. Children may feed tame deer, antelope, llamas, other animals. Rides; picnic grounds; cafeteria. (May-Oct, daily) 8 mi W on NY 23, 5 mi S on NY 32. Phone 518/678-9595. ¢¢¢¢

Zoom Flume Waterpark. Catskill's largest water park. (Mid-June-Labor Day) 7 mi W on NY 23, 7 mi N on NY 145, Stone Bridge Rd to Shady Glen Rd, in East Durham. Phone 518/239-4559 or 800/888-3586. ¢¢¢¢

Motels

✔★★ **CARL'S RIP VAN WINKLE.** *(Leeds 12412) on Old NY 23B, ¼ mi W of I-87 exit 21.* 518/943-3303; FAX 518/943-2309. 41 units, 27 cabins, 6 kits. Many rm phones. July-Aug: S, D $48-$65; each addl $5-$15; kit. units to 4, $425-$450/wk; lower rates mid-Apr-June, Sept-mid-Nov. Closed rest of yr. Crib $5. TV; cable (premium). Pool; wading pool. Playground. Restaurant adj 7:30-11 am, 4:30-9 pm. Ck-out 11 am. Hiking trails. Lawn games. Some refrigerators; fireplace in some cabins. Picnic tables, grill. On 160 wooded acres. Cr cds: A, MC, V.

★★ **CATSKILL MOUNTAIN LODGE.** *(HCR 1, Box 52, Palenville 12463) 10 mi W on NY 32A.* 518/678-3101; res: 800/686-5634; FAX 518/678-3103. Web www.thecatskills.com/catmtldg.htm. 42 units, 2 kit.

units, 2 cottages. Late-June-Labor Day: S, D $60-$95; kit. units $425/wk; cottages $625/wk; under 6 free; family, wkly rates (min stay required); higher rates hols; lower rates rest of yr. Crib $7.50. TV; cable. Restaurant adj 7 am-10 pm. Bar. Ck-out 11 am. Valet serv. Sundries. RR station transportation. Pool; wading pool. Playground. Game rm. Lawn games. Some refrigerators. Cr cds: A, C, D, DS, MC, V.

★★ **RED RANCH.** *4555 NY 32, ¼ mi S of jct NY 32 & 23A.* 518/678-3380; res: 800/962-4560. 39 rms, 2 story, 4 kits. July-Labor Day: S, D $45-$68; kit. units up to 6, $72-$90; wkly rates; ski plans; higher rates: Hunter Mt festivals, hol wkends; lower rates rest of yr. Crib $6. TV; cable (premium). Pool; wading pool. Playground. Restaurant adj 7:30 am-10 pm. Ck-out 11 am. Downhill/x-country ski 10 mi. Game rm. Lawn games. Refrigerators avail. Picnic tables. Cr cds: A, C, D, DS, MC, V.

Inn

★★ **STEWART HOUSE INN.** *(2 N Water St, Athens 12015) 4 mi N via NY 385.* 518/945-1357; res: 800/339-4622. 5 rms, 4 with shower only, 2 story. No rm phones. S, D $90; higher rates Dec 31. Complimentary full bkfst. Restaurant (see STEWART HOUSE). Ck-out noon, ck-in after 3 pm. On Hudson River. Built in 1883; antiques. Cr cds: A, MC, V.

Resorts

★★★ **FRIAR TUCK INN.** *4858 NY 32N.* 518/678-2271; FAX 518/678-2214; res: 800/832-7600. 525 rms, 2-5 story. MAP, June-Aug: D $95-$145/person; suites $150-$250/person; under 12 free; wkly rates; ski, golf plans; lower rates rest of yr. Crib free. TV; cable (premium). 3 pools, 1 indoor; whirlpool, lifeguard. Playground. Supervised child's activities (summer, winter). Dining rm 8 pm-midnight. Rm serv. Bar from 11 am; entertainment. Ck-out noon, ck-in 3 pm. Coin lndry. Convention facilities. Business center. Bellhops. Gift shop. Airport, bus depot transportation. Lighted tennis. Downhill/x-country ski 12 mi. Soc dir. Game rm. Rec rm. Exercise rm; sauna, steam rm. Theater. On lake. Cr cds: A, C, D, DS, MC, V.

★★ **WOLFF'S MAPLE BREEZE.** *360 Cauterskill Rd (12412), 2 mi E of NY 32.* 518/943-3648; res: 800/777-9653. 42 rms, 1-2 story. MAP, July-Aug: S, D $65-$80/person; suites $75-$95; wkly: $362-$415/person; family rates; lower rates May-June, Sept-Oct. Closed rest of yr. Crib free. TV; cable (premium). Pool; lifeguard. Playground. Supervised children's activities. Dining rm (public by res) 8:30-10 am, 5:30-6:30 pm. Snack bar. Bar; entertainment. Ck-out 11 am, ck-in 1 pm. Business servs avail. Grocery, coin lndry, package store 3 mi. Tennis. Boats, rowboats. Lawn games. Soc dir. Game rm. Refrigerators. Spacious grounds. Three lakes. Hayrides. No cr cds accepted.

Restaurants

★★ **FERNWOOD.** *(Malden Ave, Palenville 12463) 10 mi W on Malden Ave.* 518/678-9332. Continental menu. Specialties: chicken Rebecca, shrimp scampi, linguini bucaniera. Hrs: 5-10 pm. Closed Mon, Tues; Dec 25. Res accepted. Bar. Semi-a la carte: dinner $11.50-$30. Child's meals. Outdoor dining. Family-owned since 1966. No cr cds accepted.

★★ **LEGENDS.** *31 Brooks Lane, on grounds of Catskill Country Club.* 518/943-0920. Specializes in fresh seafood, chicken, beef. Hrs: 10 am-9 pm; Fri, Sat to 11 pm; Sun from 8 am. Res accepted. Bar. A la carte entrees: lunch $3.95-$6.95, dinner $9.95-$16.95. Child's meals. Outdoor dining. Country club setting. Cr cds: A, MC, V.

★ ★ **STEWART HOUSE.** *(See Stewart House Inn)* 518/945-1357. Specializes in steak, seasonal game, fish. Hrs: 5:30-10 pm; Fri, Sat to 11:30 pm; Sun 12:30-10 pm. Closed Mon; Thanksgiving, Dec 25. Res accepted. Bar. Semi-a la carte: dinner $12-$22. Musicians Thurs. Antique clock collection. Cr cds: A, MC, V.

🖼

Catskill Park (E-7 - F-7)

(See also Cairo, Hunter, Shandaken, Woodstock)

The 705,500-acre Catskill Park includes some of the wildest country south of Maine. More than 200 miles of marked trails wind through its woods. More than 272,000 acres are owned by the state and comprise the Forest Preserve. This includes seven campgrounds: **North/South Lake,** off NY 23A, 3 miles NE of Haines Falls, 518/589-5058; **Devil's Tombstone,** NY 214, 4 miles S of Hunter, 914/688-7160; **Woodland Valley,** off NY 28, 6 miles SW of Phoenicia, 914/688-7647; **Mongaup Pond,** off NY 17, 3 miles N of DeBruce, 914/439-4233; **Little Pond,** off NY 17, 14 miles NW of Livingston Manor, 914/439-5480; **Beaverkill,** off NY 17, 7 miles NW of Livingston Manor, 914/439-4281; **Kenneth L. Wilson,** off NY 28, 4 miles E of Mount Tremper on County 40, 914/679-7020. Nearby is **Bear Spring Mountain** (outside Catskill Park), 5 miles SE of Walton off NY 206, 607/865-6989. Standard fees. Skiing at Belleayre Mt (see SHANDAKEN), chairlift operating to 3,400 feet. For info phone 914/254-5600.

Cazenovia (D-6)

(See also Syracuse)

Pop 6,514 **Elev** 1,224 ft **Area code** 315 **Zip** 13035

What to See and Do

Chittenango Falls State Park. Has 167-ft waterfall. Fishing; hiking. Picnicking, playground. Tent & trailer sites. Standard fees. (May-Oct, daily) 4 mi N on NY 13. Phone 315/655-9620.

Lorenzo State Historic Site (1807). Elegant Federal-period mansion built by John Lincklaen; original furnishings; garden, arboretum. (May-Oct, Wed-Sun) ¾ mi S on NY 13. Phone 315/655-3200. **¢¢**

Toggenburg Ski Center. Triple, double chairlifts, 2 beginners' lifts, 2 T-bars; patrol, ski school, rentals; snowmaking; cafeteria, bar; nursery. (Dec-early Apr, daily; closed Dec 25) Cross-country trails in Highland Forest, approx 2 mi W on NY 80. 6 mi W on US 20, then 6 mi S on Pompey Center Rd. Phone 315/683-5842. **¢¢¢¢**

Inns

★ ★ **BRAE LOCH.** 5 Albany St, on NY 20 E. 315/655-3431; FAX 315/655-4844. 14 rms. S, D $80-$130; each addl $15; under 12 free. Crib free. TV. Complimentary continental bkfst. Restaurant (see BRAE LOCH INN). Ck-out 11 am, ck-in 2 pm. Gift shop. Located opp a swimming beach. Inn built ca 1805; many antiques. Cr cds: A, MC, V.

🖼 SC

★ ★ **BREWSTER.** 6 Ledyard Ave, on US 20 near jct NY 13, on S shore of Cazenovia Lake. 315/655-9232; FAX 315/655-2130. 17 rms, 3 story. S, D $75-$225; each addl $10. TV; cable (premium). Complimentary continental bkfst. Restaurant (see BREWSTER INN). Bar 5 pm-midnight. Ck-out 11 am, ck-in 2 pm. Business servs avail. 18-hole golf privileges. Exercise equipt. Victorian summer home (1890); elegant antique furnishings; library; fireplaces. Extensive grounds; elaborate landscaping. Cr cds: D, MC, V.

★ ★ ★ **LINCKLAEN HOUSE.** 79 Albany St, on NY 20. 315/655-3461; FAX 315/655-5443. Web www.cazenovia.com/lincklaen. 18 rms, 3 story. S, D $99-$140; suites $120-$140. Crib free. Pet accepted. TV. Complimentary continental bkfst. Ck-out 11 am, ck-in 2 pm. Meeting rms. Business servs avail. Built in 1835. Cr cds: A, MC, V.

D 🖼 🖼 🖼 SC

Restaurants

★ ★ **BRAE LOCH INN.** *(See Brae Loch Inn)* 315/655-3431. E-mail braeloch1@aol.com; web www.cazenovia/braeloch. Continental menu. Specialties: Angus Dundee, prime rib. Own baking. Hrs: 5-9:30 pm; Sat to 10 pm; Sun 11 am-9 pm; Sun brunch (Sept-June) to 2 pm. Closed Dec 24, 25. Res accepted. Bar. Semi-a la carte: dinner $9.95-$18.95. Sun brunch $12.95. Child's meals. Scottish pub atmosphere; downstairs pub dining. Family-owned. Cr cds: A, MC, V.

★ ★ ★ **BREWSTER INN.** *(See Brewster Inn)* 315/655-9232. Continental menu. Specializes in roast duck, fresh seafood, lamb. Own baking. Hrs: 5-9 pm; Sun brunch 11 am-2 pm. Closed some major hols. Res accepted. Bar. Wine list. Semi-a la carte: dinner $17-$20. Sun brunch $17. Outdoor dining. Victorian mansion; many antiques, 4 fireplaces. Overlooks lake. Cr cds: C, D, MC, V.

Chautauqua (E-1)

(See also Bemus Point, Jamestown)

Founded 1874 **Pop** 4,554 **Elev** 1,360 ft **Area code** 716 **Zip** 14722

Chautauqua Institution is a lakeside summer center for the arts, education, religion and recreation. Programs are offered to adults and children. Summer population swells to more than 10,000.

The community began as a Sunday school teachers' training camp and developed into a cultural center that originated nationwide book clubs and correspondence schools. It has provided a platform for presidents and political leaders, as well as great musical artists and popular entertainers.

What to See and Do

Boat cruise. *Chautauqua Belle.* Replica of a 19th-century paddlewheel steamboat cruises on Chautauqua Lake; incl narrative of history of the area and wildlife around the lake. (Memorial Day-Labor Day, most wkends, phone ahead for schedule) 3 mi NW via NY 394 in Mayville. Phone 716/753-2403 or 800/753-2506. **¢¢¢¢**

 The Chautauqua Institution. Summer center for arts, education, religion and recreation. Nine-wk season (late June-late Aug, daily) features a lecture platform as well as performing arts events. Along NY 394 on the W shore of Chautauqua Lake. For further info and fees phone 716/357-6200 or 800/836-ARTS.

Chautauqua Amphitheater. Contains 6,500 seats, home of Chautauqua Symphony Orchestra; recitals, ballet, lectures, special popular musical events.

Norton Memorial Hall. Four operatic productions are presented in English each season by the Chautauqua Opera Company.

Palestine, Park. Outdoor walk-through model of the Holy Land. Tours Sun afternoon Mon eve. **Free.**

Miller Bell Tower. Campanile on the shore of Chautauqua Lake. **Free.**

Recreation. Swimming, boating, sailing, fishing, tennis, windsurfing, 27-hole golf (fee), cross-country skiing (winter).

Motel

★ ★ **WEBB'S YEAR-ROUND RESORT.** (NY 394, Mayville 14757) 2 mi NW on NY 394. 716/753-2161; FAX 716/753-1383. Web www.webbsworld.com. 52 rms, 2 story. S, D $69-$249. Crib $5. TV.

Heated pool. Restaurant 11:30 am-2 pm, 5-10 pm; Sun noon-9 pm. Rm serv. Bar to midnight. Ck-out 11 am. Coin lndry. Meeting rm. Business servs avail. Sundries. Exercise equipt. Game rm. Lawn games. Open-air deck 11 am-midnight. Cr cds: A, MC, V.

Motor Hotel

★ ★ ★ **ST ELMO ACCOMMODATIONS.** *1 Pratt Ave, on grounds of Chautauqua Institution.* 716/357-3566; res: 800/507-5005; FAX 716/357-3317. E-mail careelmo@epix.net; web www.chautauquaarea.com. 25 kit. suites, 4 story. Kit. suites $66-$210; wkly rates; ski plans. Gate fee for Institution grounds (late June-late Aug). Crib free. TV; cable, VCR avail. Ck-out 10 am. Coin lndry. Meeting rms. Business servs avail. Shopping arcade. Tennis. 36-hole golf course, greens fee $15-$30, pro, putting green, driving range. Downhill ski 20 mi; x-country ski on site. Microwaves. Balconies. Victorian hotel on Chautauqua Lake. Cr cds: DS, ER, MC, V.

Hotel

★ ★ ★ **ATHENAEUM.** *On W shore of Chautauqua Lake, on grounds of Chautauqua Institution.* 716/357-4444; FAX 716/357-2833; res: 800/821-1881. Web www.chautauqua-inst.org. 157 rms. AP, late June-late Aug: S $143-$176; D $215-$317; each addl $75; suites $300-$420. Closed rest of yr. Gate fee for Institution grounds (late June-late Aug). Crib free. Valet parking. Supervised child's activities (June-Sept). Restaurant (see ATHENAEUM). Ck-out 10 am. Meeting rms. Business servs avail. Tennis. Golf. Lawn games. Nature walks. Sun deck. Concerts. Restored Victorian hotel (1881). Cr cds: MC, V.

Inn

★ ★ ★ **WILLIAM SEWARD.** *(6645 S Portage Rd, Westfield 14787) I-90E to NY 394S (exit 60).* 716/326-4151; FAX 716/326-4163; res: 800/338-4151. 12 rms, 7 with shower only, 2 story. No rm phones. S $60-$170; D $70-$180; each addl $15; wkends, hols (2-day min). Children over 12 yrs only. Complimentary full bkfst; afternoon refreshments. Ck-out 11 am, ck-in 2 pm. Downhill ski 20 mi; x-country ski 7 mi. Some fireplaces, in-rm whirlpools. Some balconies. 3 mi to lake. Restored Greek-revival mansion built 1837; antiques. Totally nonsmoking. Cr cds: A, DS, MC, V.

Restaurants

★ ★ ★ **ATHENAEUM.** *(See Athenaeum Hotel)* 716/357-4444. Continental menu. Specializes in seafood, veal. Hrs: 7-9:30 am, noon-1:30 pm, 5-7:30 pm. Closed Sept-May. Res required. Complete meals: bkfst $13.50, lunch $17, dinner $30.50. Child's meals. Valet parking. Outdoor dining. Victorian dining rm with many antiques. Jacket (dinner). Cr cds: MC, V.

★ **SADIE J'S CAFE.** *15-17 Ramble Ave, on grounds of Chautauqua Institute.* 716/357-5245. Specializes in vegetarian sandwiches, soup, muffins. Hrs: 9 am-4 pm; June-Aug 7 am-11 pm. Closed Easter, Thanksgiving, Dec 25. A la carte entrees: bkfst $2.25-$3.25, lunch, dinner $1.95-$3.75. Totally nonsmoking. No cr cds accepted.

✔ ★ ★ **WEBB'S-THE CAPTAIN'S TABLE.** *(NY 394, Mayville 14757) 2¼ mi NW on NY 394.* 716/753-3960. Specializes in beef, seafood, chicken. Hrs: 11 am-3 pm, 5-9 pm; wkends noon-10 pm. Res accepted. Bar. Semi-a la carte: lunch $5.95-$10.95, dinner $8.95-$22.95. Child's meals. Parking. Outdoor dining on deck. Intimate dining. Family-owned. Cr cds: A, DS, MC, V.

Clayton (Thousand Islands) (B-5)

(See also Alexandria Bay; also see Gananoque and Kingston, ON, Canada)

Pop 4,629 **Elev** 260 ft **Area code** 315 **Zip** 13624 **E-mail** ccoc@gisco.net **Web** www.thousandislands.com/claytonchamber

Information Chamber of Commerce, 510 Riverside Dr; 315/686-3771 or 800/252-9806.

Clayton juts into the St Lawrence River in the midst of the Thousand Islands resort region. Pleasure boats line the waterfront docks.

What to See and Do

Burnham Point State Park. Fishing; boating (launch, dock). Picnicking. Playground. Camping. (Mid-May-Labor Day) Standard fees. 10 mi W on NY 12E. Phone 315/654-2522.

Cedar Point State Park. Swimming beach, bathhouse; fishing; boating (ramp, marina). Picnicking. Playground, recreation programs. Camping. (Mid-May-mid-Oct) Standard fees. 6 mi W on NY 12 E. Phone 315/654-2522.

Grass Point State Park. Swimming beach, bathhouse; fishing; boating (launch, marina). Picnicking. Playground. Camping. (Mid-May-mid-Sept) Standard fees. 6 mi E on NY 12, 1 mi W of I-81. Phone 315/686-4472.

The Antique Boat Museum. Displays of antique boats and motors; nautical exhibits. (Mid-May-mid-Oct, daily) 750 Mary St. Phone 315/686-4104. ¢¢¢

Thousand Islands Museum. History of the region; replica of turn-of-the-century Clayton. (Mid-May-Labor Day, daily) Old Town Hall, 403 Riverside Dr. Phone 315/686-5794. **Donation.**

Uncle Sam Boat Tours. A 40-mi cruise of the Thousand Islands, traveling through Canadian & American waters, the St Lawrence Seaway; stop at Boldt Castle and Alexandria Bay. (Mid-May-Oct, daily) 604 Riverside Dr. Phone 315/686-3511. ¢¢¢¢

Annual Events

Duck, Decoy and Wildlife Art Show. East Line Rd, Recreation Park Arena. 3rd wkend July.

Antique Boat Show. The Antique Boat Museum. More than 150 restored antique craft; sailing race; boat parade. 1st wkend Aug.

Model Train Show. Recreation Park Arena. 2nd wkend Sept.

Motels

★ **BERTRAND'S.** *229 James St.* 315/686-3641; res: 800/472-0683. E-mail bertrand@gisco.net. 28 rms, 1-2 story, 5 kits. July-Labor Day: S $50; D $60-$62; each addl $7; kit. units $65-$70; family, wkly rates off-season; lower rates rest of yr. Crib free. TV; cable. Restaurant opp 6 am-10 pm. Ck-out 11 am. Picnic tables, grills. Cr cds: A, C, D, DS, MC, V.

★ **BUCCANEER.** *(Point St, Cape Vincent 13618) W on NY 12E, 1 blk off Seaway Trail.* 315/654-2975. 10 rms. Mid-June-Labor Day: S, D $75-$85; each addl $10; under 12 free; lower rates rest of yr. Crib free. TV; cable. Restaurant nearby. Ck-out 11 am. On river; dockage. Cr cds: MC, V.

✔ ★ **FAIR WIND LODGE.** *38201 NY 12E, St Lawrence Seaway, 2½ mi SW on NY 12E.* 315/686-5251; res: 800/235-8331. 10 rms, 8 cottages, 6 kit. cottages. Mid-June-early Sept: S, D $48-$66; each addl $6;

kit. cottages for 2, $495/wk; each addl $25; lower rates mid-May-mid-June, early Sept-mid-Oct. Closed rest of yr. Crib free. TV; cable (premium). Heated pool. Complimentary coffee in lobby. Restaurant nearby. Ck-out 10 am. Picnic tables. 45-ft dock. Cr cds: DS, MC, V.

✔★ **WEST WINDS.** *38267 NY 12E, 2 mi W on NY 12E, on shore of St Lawrence Seaway.* 315/686-3352; res: 888/937-8963; FAX 607/625-2297. E-mail hhurley@ibm.net; web www.thousandislands.com/westwinds/. 12 motel rms, 5 kit. cabins, 4 kit. cottages. Late June-early Sept: S $38-$60; D $48-$67; each addl $6; kit. cabins for 2, $520/wk; kit. cottages for 2, $760-$880/wk; each addl $50; lower rates mid-May-late June, early Sept-mid-Oct. Closed rest of yr. Crib $5. Pet accepted; fee. TV; cable (premium). Heated pool. Complimentary coffee. Restaurant nearby. Ck-out 10 am. Game rm. Picnic tables, grills. Boats; dockage. On 5 acres; gazebo. Cr cds: MC, V.

Restaurants

★★ **CLIPPER INN.** *126 State St (NY 12), opp Clayton Golf Course, 5 mi W of I-81 exit 50S.* 315/686-3842. Continental menu. Specializes in veal scampi, fresh fish. Hrs: 5-10 pm; early-bird dinner 5-6 pm. Closed Nov-Mar. Res accepted. Bar 4 pm-2 am. Semi-a la carte: dinner $10.95-$21.95. Child's meals. Nautical decor. Cr cds: A, DS, MC, V.

D

★★ **THOUSAND ISLANDS INN.** *335 Riverside Dr, on St Lawrence riverfront.* 315/686-3030. E-mail tiinn@1000-islands.com; web www.1000-islands.com. Specializes in prime rib, quail, seafood. Hrs: 7 am-1:30 pm, 5:30-9 pm; Sat, Sun to 10 pm; early-bird dinner 5:30-6 pm. Closed Oct-mid-May. Res accepted. Bar from 11 am. Semi-a la carte: bkfst $2.50-$6.95, lunch $2.95-$6.50, dinner $8.95-$24.95. Child's meals. Inn since 1897; thousand island dressing first created and served here. Cr cds: A, C, D, DS, MC, V.

Cooperstown (E-7)

(See also Oneonta)

Founded 1786 **Pop** 2,180 **Elev** 1,264 ft **Area code** 607 **Zip** 13326
E-mail info@cooperstownchamber.org **Web** www.cooperstownchamber.org
Information Chamber of Commerce, 31 Chestnut St; 607/547-9983.

Founded by James Fenimore Cooper's father, Judge William Cooper, Cooperstown is in the center of the "Leatherstocking" country. Here in 1839, on the south end of Otsego Lake, legend has it that Abner Doubleday devised modern baseball. The National Baseball Hall of Fame and Museum is located here, on Main Street.

What to See and Do

Fenimore House. Museum and HQ of NY State Historical Assoc. Large American folk art collection, exhibits of Native American art and artifacts, James Fenimore Cooper memorabilia, academic and decorative arts of Romantic Era, 1800-1850; research library. (May-Oct, daily; Nov-Dec, daily exc Mon) Inquire about combination ticket with Farmers' Museum and/or Natl Baseball Hall of Fame. 1 mi N on NY 80. Phone 607/547-1400. ¢¢¢

Glimmerglass State Park. Swimming beach, bathhouse; fishing; hiking, biking. Cross-country skiing, snowmobiling. Picnicking, playground. Tent & trailer sites. (Daily; closed Jan 1, Dec 25) Standard fees. 6 mi N on E Lake Rd. Phone 607/547-8662. Hyde Hall, Clarke family mansion with view of Otsego Lake; Classical-revival architecture (summer wkends). Per vehicle ¢¢

Lake Otsego Boat Tours. One-hr narrated cruises aboard wooden lake launches detailing points of historic interest. (Mid-May-mid-Oct, daily) Foot of Fair St. Phone 607/547-5295. ¢¢¢

★ **Natl Baseball Hall of Fame and Museum.** Nationally known museum dedicated to the game and its players. The Hall of Fame Gallery contains plaques honoring the game's all-time greats. The museum features displays on baseball's greatest moments, the World Series, All-Star Games, ballparks and a complete history of the game. Theater presents special multimedia show. Gift shop. Inquire about combination ticket with Farmers' Museum and/or Fenimore House. (Daily; closed Jan 1, Thanksgiving, Dec 25) Main St. Phone 607/547-7200. ¢¢¢

The Farmers' Museum and Village Crossroads. Outdoor museum of rural life in early times. Craftspeople present printing, weaving and blacksmithing in historic setting. Village of historic bldgs and barn filled with exhibits. Famous "Cardiff Giant," a 10-ft statue presented to the public in 1869 as a petrified prehistoric man, is here. (May-Oct, daily; Apr & Nov-Dec, daily exc Mon; closed Thanksgiving, Dec 25) Special events held throughout the yr. Inquire about combination ticket with Fenimore House and/or Natl Baseball Hall of Fame and Museum. 1 mi N on NY 80. Phone 607/547-2533. ¢¢¢

Annual Event

Autumn Harvest Festival. The Farmers' Museum and Village Crossroads. Mid-Sept.

Seasonal Events

Glimmerglass Opera. Alice Busch Opera Theater. Four productions, 28 performances. Phone 607/547-2255. July-Aug.

Cooperstown Concert Series. Sterling Auditorium, Cooperstown High School. Several performances per season by classical and jazz musicians, folk artists, dancers, actors. Phone 607/293-6124. Sept-May.

Motels

★ **BAY SIDE MOTOR INN.** *7 mi N on NY 80, on Otsego Lake.* 607/547-2371; FAX 607/547-5856. E-mail bayside@juno.com; web www.cooperstown.net/bayside. 19 rms, 1-2 story, 10 kit. cottages. Late June-Labor Day: S, D $99-$137; kit. cottages $650-$1,200/wk; lower rates after Labor Day-Oct, May-mid-June. Closed rest of yr. Crib $10. TV; cable (premium). Ck-out 11 am. Game rm. Lawn games. Microwave in cottages. Picnic tables, grills. Sand beach, marina. Cr cds: A, DS, MC, V.

D

★★ **BEST WESTERN INN AT THE COMMONS.** *50 Commons Dr, 3½ mi S on NY 28.* 607/547-9439; FAX 607/547-7082. 62 rms, 2 story. June-Sept: S $135-$155; D, suites $155-$185; each addl $10; under 12 free; higher rates special events; lower rates rest of yr. Crib free. TV; cable (premium), VCR avail (movies). Indoor pool; whirlpool. Playground. Complimentary continental bkfst. Restaurant adj 6 am-midnight. Ck-out 11 am. Coin lndry. Meeting rm. Business servs avail. In-rm modem link. Shopping arcade adj. Barber shop. Exercise equipt. Game rm. Refrigerator, microwave in suites. Picnic tables. Cr cds: A, C, D, DS, MC, V.

D

★★ **DEER RUN.** *7480 NY 80, 9 mi NE on NY 80.* 607/547-8600; res: 888/838-3337. Web www.cooperstown.net/deerrun. 30 rms. June-Labor Day: S $98-$108; D $108-$118; each addl $8; lower rates Apr-May, after Labor Day-Oct. Closed rest of yr. Crib $7. TV; cable. Indoor pool; sauna. Restaurant 7-10 am. Ck-out 11 am. Tennis. 9-hole golf adj, greens fee $15-$20. Lawn games. On 46 acres. Cr cds: A, DS, MC, V.

✔★ **HICKORY GROVE MOTOR INN.** *Lake Rd, 6 mi N on NY 80, on Otsego Lake.* 607/547-9874; FAX 607/547-8567. E-mail hgmi@telenet.net; web www.cooperstown.net/hickorygrove/. 12 rms. Mid-June-Labor Day: S, D $88-$110; each addl $5; higher rates special events; lower rates mid-Apr-mid-June, Sept-mid-Oct. Closed rest of yr. TV; cable.

Complimentary coffee. Restaurant nearby. Ck-out 11 am. Picnic tables, grills. Boat rentals. Cr cds: A, DS, MC, V.

★ ★ **LAKE 'N PINES.** *7 mi N on NY 80, on Otsego Lake.* 607/547-2790; FAX 607/547-5671; res: 800/615-5253. 24 rms, 1-2 story, 3 cottages. June-Labor Day: S $90; D $122; each addl $7; cottages $150; wkend rates; wkly rates off-season; lower rates Apr-May, after Labor Day-late Nov. Closed rest of yr. TV; cable (premium). 2 heated pools, 1 indoor; whirlpool. Complimentary coffee. Restaurant nearby. Ck-out 11 am. Sauna. Game rm. Refrigerators, microwaves in cottages. Some balconies. Picnic tables, grill. Observation deck. Rowboats, paddleboats. View of lake. Cr cds: A, DS, MC, V.

★ ★ **LAKE FRONT.** *10 Fair St.* 607/547-9511; FAX 607/547-2792. Web www.cooperstown.net/lakefront. 44 rms, 15 with shower only, 2 story. Late June-Aug: S, D $90-$130; lower rates rest of yr. TV; cable (premium). Restaurant May-Oct: 7:30 am-9 pm. Bar. Ck-out 11 am. Business servs avail. Sundries. Gift shop. On lake. Cr cds: MC, V.

★ ★ **LAKE VIEW.** *6 mi N on NY 80, on Otsego Lake.* 607/547-9740; FAX 607/547-5080; 800 888/452-5384. E-mail lakeview@magnum.wpe.com; web www.wpe.com/~lakeview. 19 rms, 7 kit. cottages. June-Aug: S, D $88-$135; each addl $7; kit. cottages $160; lower rates Apr-May, Sept-mid-Nov. Closed rest of yr. TV; cable (premium). Complimentary coffee. Ck-out 11 am. Some microwaves. Patios. Private beach; swimming. Free paddle boats, row boats, dockage. Cr cds: A, DS, MC, V.

Inn

★ ★ **INN AT COOPERSTOWN.** *16 Chestnut St, 1 blk off Main St.* 607/547-5756; FAX 607/547-8779. E-mail theinn@telenet.net; web www.cooperstown.net/theinn. 18 rms, 3 story. No A/C. No rm phones. May-Oct: S $98-$120; D $98-$130; each addl $20; lower rates rest of yr. TV in sitting rm. Complimentary continental bkfst; afternoon refreshments. Restaurants nearby. Ck-out 11 am, ck-in early afternoon. Business servs avail. Trolley stop nearby. Former annex to Fenimore Hotel, built 1874. Some antiques. Common rm with fireplace, Victorian furnishings. Cr cds: A, D, DS, MC, V.

Restaurants

✔ ★ ★ **GABRIELLA'S ON THE SQUARE.** *161 Main St.* 607/547-8000. Specialties: rack of lamb with encrusted dijon mustard and mushroom risotto, tuna steak au poivre. Own desserts. Hrs: 5-9 pm; hrs vary June-Oct. Closed Mon, exc summer. Res accepted. Semi-a la carte: dinner $14.95-$19.95. Child's meals. Wine cellar. Outdoor dining. Formal dining. Cr cds: A, D, MC, V.

★ ★ **PEPPER MILL.** *NY 28.* 607/547-8550. Specializes in beef, chicken, seafood. Own pastries. Hrs: 4-10 pm. Closed Dec 25; Jan-Mar. Res accepted. Bar. Semi-a la carte: dinner $6.95-$24.95. Child's meals. Cr cds: A, DS, MC, V.

Corning (E-4)

(See also Elmira, Watkins Glen)

Settled 1833 **Pop** 11,938 **Elev** 937 ft **Area code** 607 **Zip** 14830 **E-mail** chamber@upstate-ny.com **Web** www.corning-chamber.org

Information Chamber of Commerce, 42 E Market St; 607/936-4686.

This world glass center began to grow when completion of the Chemung Canal brought plentiful Pennsylvania anthracite. In 1868 lower fuel and materials costs attracted the Brooklyn Flint Glass Works, incorporated in 1875 as the Corning Glass Works. Mass production of bulbs for Thomas A. Edison's electric light soon began. Dresser-Rand makes compressors at Painted Post, near Corning. The city's central shopping district has been restored to its 1890s appearance.

What to See and Do

Benjamin Patterson Inn Museum Complex. Central attraction is restored and furnished 1796 inn, built to encourage settlement in the Genesee Country. Includes ladies' parlor, public rm and kitchen on 1st floor; ballrm and two bedrms on 2nd floor. Also on site is DeMonstoy Log Cabin (ca 1785), Browntown one-rm schoolhouse (1878), Starr Barn with agricultural exhibit (ca 1860) and blacksmith shop (ca 1820). (Daily exc Sun) 59 W Pulteney St. Phone 607/937-5281. ¢¢

✪ **Corning Glass Center.** Industrial showplace with 3 touring areas. **The Corning Museum of Glass** has more than 25,000 objects on display, incl outstanding pieces of both antique and modern Steuben and an 11-ft-high leaded glass window designed by Tiffany Studios in 1905. Library has most complete collection of materials on glass in the world. **The Hall of Science and Industry** has exhibits that reveal the unexpected properties of glass; glassmaking demonstrations and an audiovisual presentation on the future of fiber optics. **The Steuben Factory** features skilled craftsmen transforming hot molten glass into fine crystal; only factory in the world that produces Steuben crystal. Retail stores. (Daily; closed Jan 1, Thanksgiving, Dec 24-25) On Centerway. Phone 607/974-8173. ¢¢¢; Family rate ¢¢¢¢¢

The Rockwell Museum. Largest collection of American Western art in the East, incl paintings by Remington, Russell, Bierstadt, Catlin, others; antique firearms and toys; more than 2,000 pieces of Frederick Carder Steuben glass. Changing exhibits. (Daily; closed Jan 1, Thanksgiving, Dec 24-25) 111 Cedar St. Phone 607/937-5386. ¢¢

Motels

★ ★ **COMFORT INN.** *66 W Pulteney St, Rt 17, exit 46.* 607/962-1515; FAX 607/962-1899. 62 rms, 2 story. May-Oct: S $57-$95; D $75-$125; each addl $6; under 18 free; higher rates: LPGA Corning Classic, racing events; lower rates rest of yr. Crib free. TV; cable. Indoor pool. Complimentary continental bkfst. Restaurant nearby. Ck-out 11 am. Business servs avail. In-rm modem link. Exercise equipt; sauna. Some refrigerators. Cr cds: A, C, D, DS, ER, JCB, MC, V.

✔ ★ ★ **DAYS INN.** *23 Riverside Dr.* 607/936-9370; FAX 607/936-0513. 56 rms, 2-3 story. May-Oct: S $52-$72; D $58-$78; each addl $5; suites $85-$95; under 18 free; lower rates rest of yr. Crib free. TV; cable (premium). Indoor pool. Coffee in rms. Restaurant 7 am-10 pm. Ck-out 11 am. Business servs avail. In-rm modem link. Parking. Health club privileges. Cr cds: A, D, DS, MC, V.

★ **GATE HOUSE.** *145 E Corning Rd.* 607/936-4131. 20 rms, 6 with shower only. Mid-May-mid-Nov: S $33-$40; D $38-$52; each addl $6; under 21 free; higher rates: auto races, LPGA; lower rates rest of yr. Crib free. TV; cable. Restaurant 6 am-11 am. Ck-out 11 am. Coin lndry. Cr cds: A, MC, V.

KNIGHTS INN. *(2707 Westinghouse Rd, Horseheads 14815)* 10 mi on NY 17E exit 52. 607/739-3807; FAX 607/796-5293. 40 rms. Apr-Oct: S, D $32.95-$95.95; under 12 free; family rates; package plans; wkends 2-day min; higher rates special events; lower rates rest of yr. Crib free. Pet accepted, some restrictions; $5 and $25 deposit. TV; cable (premium), VCR avail (movies). Complimentary continental bkfst. Restaurant nearby. Business servs avail. In-rm modem link. Valet serv. Coin lndry. Pool. Some refrigerators, microwaves. Picnic tables, grills. Cr cds: A, DS, MC, V.

✔★ **STILES.** *(9239 Victory Hwy, Painted Post 14870)* 4 mi N on NY 415, 1/2 mi W of NY 17 exit 42. 607/962-5221; FAX 607/962-7299; res: 800/331-3920. E-mail stimot@servtech.com. 15 rms. May-Nov: S $32-$36; D $36-$47; each addl $5; family rates; wkly rates Dec-Apr; lower rates rest of yr. Crib $1. TV; cable. Playground. Complimentary coffee in rms. Ck-out 10:30 am. Refrigerators avail. Picnic tables. Country surroundings. Gazebo. Cr cds: DS, MC, V.

Motor Hotel

★★★ **RADISSON.** 125 Denison Pkwy E, on NY 17 (Denison Pkwy), downtown. 607/962-5000; FAX 607/962-4166. 177 rms, 3 story. S $107-$141; D $117-$151; each addl $10; suites $175-$255; under 18 free; wkend rates. Crib free. Pet accepted, some restrictions. TV; cable. Indoor pool; lifeguard. Coffee in rms. Restaurant 7 am-9:30 pm. Rm serv. Bar 11-12:30 am; entertainment Fri, Sat. Ck-out 1 pm. Meeting rms. Business servs avail. Bellhops. Cr cds: A, D, DS, MC, V.

Inn

★★★ **ROSEWOOD.** 134 E First St. 607/962-3253. E-mail rinn@stny.lrun.com. 7 rms, 2 story. S $85-$115; D $90-$125; each addl $20; suite $145; off-season rates. TV in some rms. Complimentary full bkfst. Ck-out 11 am, ck-in 3 pm. Restored Victorian home (1855); antiques. Rms individually decorated. Fireplace in parlor. Totally nonsmoking. Cr cds: A, C, D, DS, MC, V.

Restaurants

✔★ **BOOMERS.** 35 E Market St. 607/962-6800. Specializes in pasta, seafood, hamburgers. Hrs: 8 am-11 pm; Sun 8 am-8 pm. Closed Thanksgiving, Dec 25. Beer, wine. Semi-a la carte: bkfst .65¢-$4.45, lunch $2.95-$5.45, dinner $5.45-$11.95. Child's meals. 19th-century building; memorabilia, antique tools on display. Cr cds: A, C, D, DS, MC, V.

★★ **LONDON UNDERGROUND CAFE.** 69 E Market St. 607/962-2345. Continental menu. Specialties: marinated ostrich steak, fresh seafood, house-baked desserts. Hrs: 11:30 am-9 pm; Sun noon-5 pm. Closed most major hols. Res accepted. Beer, wine. A la carte entrees: lunch $5.75-$8.25. Semi-a la carte: dinner $15.25-$22.95. Child's meals. Pianist Sat evenings. Outdoor dining. Cr cds: A, C, D, MC, V.

★ **SPENCER'S.** 359 E Market St. 607/936-9196. Italian, Amer menu. Specializes in pasta. Own desserts. Hrs: 11 am-10 pm; early-bird dinner 4-6:30 pm (Mon-Thurs). Closed Thanksgiving, Dec 25. Res accepted. Bar. A la carte entrees: lunch $1.75-$5.95. Semi-a la carte: dinner $6.45-$23.95. Child's meals. Parking. Outdoor dining. Rustic decor. Unique gift shop. Cr cds: A, DS, MC, V.

Cortland (E-5)

(See also Ithaca)

Settled 1791 **Pop** 19,801 **Elev** 1,120 ft **Area code** 607 **Zip** 13045 **E-mail** cortcvb@mail.odyssey.net **Web** www.embark.com/fingerlakes/members/cortlandcounty.html

Information Cortland County Convention & Visitors Bureau, 34 Tompkins St; 607/753-8463 or 800/859-2227.

Cortland lies in the midst of rich farming country. This is the home of the State University College at Cortland.

What to See and Do

1890 House Museum. Former mansion of industrialist Chester F. Wickwire. Built in a style known as Victorian chateauesque, the bldg has 4 stories and 30 rms. Hand-carved cherry and oak woodwork, stained and painted glass windows, parquet floors and elaborate stenciling. The house remained in the Wickwire family until 1974. (Daily exc Mon; closed most major hols) 37 Tompkins St. Phone 607/756-7551. ¢¢

Country Music Park. Hall of Fame museum, memorial garden, concerts, playground, camping. On NY 13 N. For schedule and fees phone 607/753-0377.

Fillmore Glen State Park. Replica of President Millard Fillmore's birthplace cabin. Flow-through natural pool, bathhouse; hiking trails. Picnicking, playground area. Cross-country skiing, snowmobiling. Tent & trailer sites, cabins (mid-May-mid-Oct). Standard fees. 14 mi W on NY 90, then 3 mi N on NY 38, near Moravia. Phone 315/497-0130.

Skiing.

Greek Peak. Eight chairlifts, 2 T-bars; patrol, school, rentals; snowmaking; cafeteria, restaurants, lounges; ski shop, nursery. Lodging (yr-round). Longest run 1 1/2 mi; vertical drop 900 ft. Cross-country trails. (Dec-Apr, daily, depending on weather conditions) 6 mi S on NY 392, off I-81. Phone 607/835-6111, 800/955-2754 or 800/365-7669 (for ski conditions). ¢¢¢¢¢

Labrador Mt. Triple, 2 double chairlifts, T-bar; patrol, school, rentals; snowmaking; cafeterias, restaurant, bar; nursery. Longest run 1 1/2 mi; vertical drop 700 ft. 20 slopes. (Dec-Mar, daily; closed Dec 25) 10 mi NE on NY 13 to Truxton, then 2 mi N on NY 91. Phone 607/842-6204 or 800/446-9559 (for ski conditions). ¢¢¢¢¢

Song Mt. Double and triple chairlifts, 2 T-bars, J-bar; patrol, school, rentals; snowmaking; restaurant, cafeteria, bar; nursery. Longest run 1 mi; vertical drop 750 ft. (Dec-Mar, daily) Summer: 3,000-ft Alpine Slide (mid-June-Labor Day, daily; late May-mid-June and rest of Sept, wkends only); miniature golf; water slide; some fees. Approx 15 mi N off I-81, near Preble. Phone 315/696-5711 or 800/677-7664. ¢¢¢¢-¢¢¢¢¢

Suggett House Museum and Kellogg Memorial Research Library. HQ of the Cortland County Historical Society; museum (ca 1880) houses vignettes of home arts of 1825-1900; 1882 kitchen; military memorabilia, local art, children's rm and changing exhibits. Library has local history and genealogy material (addl fee per hr). (Tues-Sat, afternoons; other times by appt; closed most hols) 25 Homer Ave. Phone 607/753-6161. Museum ¢

Annual Events

Central New York Maple Festival. 14 mi S, I-81, exit 9, in Marathon. A variety of events showing the process of making maple syrup; also arts & crafts, hay rides and entertainment. Phone 607/849-3278 or 607/849-3812. Early Apr.

YWCA's Antiques Show & Sale. Benefits YWCA. Held annually since 1933. Phone 607/753-9651. June.

Seasonal Event

Cortland Repertory Theatre. Dwyer Memorial County Park Pavilion Theatre, 10 mi N on NY 281 in Little York. Musicals, comedies and drama. Phone 607/756-2627. Tues-Sun eves. Mid-June-late Aug.

Motels

★ ★ **COMFORT INN.** 2¹/₂ Locust Ave. *607/753-7721; FAX 607/753-7608.* 66 rms, 2 story. May-Nov: S, D $59-$89; under 18 free; ski plans; higher rates special events; lower rates rest of yr. Crib free. Pet accepted. TV; cable. Complimentary continental bkfst. Restaurant nearby. Ck-out 11 am. Business servs avail. In-rm modem link. Exercise equipt. Game rm. Microwaves avail. Cr cds: A, C, D, DS, ER, MC, V.

[D] [symbols] SC

✔ ★ **DOWNES.** 10 Church St. *607/756-2856; res: 800/800-0301.* 42 rms, 2 story. S, D $36-$52; each addl $8; kit. units $126-$136/wk; under 12 free; higher rates: wkends, special events. Crib free. TV; cable (premium), VCR avail (free movies). Complimentary coffee in lobby. Restaurant nearby. Ck-out 11 am. Business servs avail. Downhill/x-country ski 9 mi. Some refrigerators; microwaves avail. Patios, balconies. Cr cds: A, D, DS, MC, V.

[D] [symbols] SC

Inn

★ ★ ★ **BENN CONGER.** *(206 W Cortland St, Groton 13073) 10 mi E, just off NY 222. 607/898-5817; FAX 607/898-5818.* 5 rms. S, D $90-$220; each addl $25. TV; cable (premium), VCR avail (movies). Complimentary full bkfst; afternoon refreshments. Dining rm (public by res) 5:30-9 pm. Bar. Ck-out 11 am, ck-in 2 pm. Airport, bus depot transportation. Golf privileges. Downhill ski 15 mi; x-country ski on site. Health club privileges. Greek-revival mansion (1921); former home of Benn Conger, founder of Smith Corona. Antiques; handmade quilts. Winding staircase; library; glass-enclosed conservatory. Located on 18 acres, hiking trails. Cr cds: A, C, D, MC, V.

[symbols]

Restaurants

★ ★ ★ **BENN CONGER INN.** *(See Benn Conger Inn) 607/898-5817.* Mediterranean menu. Specialties: grilled pork tenderloin; shrimp, scallops and mussels with tomatoes; rack of lamb. Hrs: 5:30-9 pm. Closed Mon, Tues. Res required. Bar. Wine cellar. Semi-a la carte: dinner $14-$24. Child's meals. Antique decor. Cr cds: A, C, D, MC, V.

✔ ★ **ROCCI'S.** 294 Tompkins St *(NY 13W). 607/753-0428.* Italian, Amer menu. Specializes in pasta, beef, seafood. Salad bar. Hrs: 11:30 am-9 pm; Sun brunch 11:30 am-2:30 pm. Closed Jan 1, Dec 25. Res accepted. Bar. Semi-a la carte: lunch $5-$7, dinner $10-$15. Sun brunch $6.50. Greenhouse/solarium atmosphere. Cr cds: A, C, D, MC, V.

[D]

★ **RUSTY NAIL.** 3993 West Rd. *607/753-7238.* Specializes in fresh cut prime rib, steak, fresh seafood. Salad bar. Hrs: 11:30 am-10 pm; Fri, Sat to 11 pm; Sun 4-9 pm. Closed Jan 1, Thanksgiving, Dec 25. Res accepted. Bar. Semi-a la carte: lunch $3.50-$8.25, dinner $8.95-$29.95. Child's meals. Entertainment Sat. Rustic country decor. Cr cds: A, D, DS, MC, V.

[D]

Coxsackie (E-8)

(See also Albany, Catskill, Hudson)

Pop 7,633 **Elev** 50 ft **Area code** 518 **Zip** 12051

What to See and Do

Bronck Museum (1663). Built by Pieter, brother of Jonas Bronck, whose 500-acre "bouwerie" became New York City's Bronx. Complex of early Dutch houses dated 1663, 1685 and 1738 with outbuildings, incl 13-sided barn. Antique furniture, china, glass, silver, paintings, quilts and agricultural equipment. (Memorial Day wkend-mid-Oct, daily exc Mon) 4 mi S of Coxsackie Thrwy exit 21B on US 9W, then right on Pieter Bronck Rd. Phone 518/731-8862 or 518/731-6490. ¢¢

Restaurant

★ ★ **RED'S.** *(West Coxsackie 12192) on NY 9W, 2 mi S of I-87 exit 21B. 518/731-8151.* Specializes in fresh seafood, shellfish-pasta, hand-cut steak. Hrs: 11:30 am-9 pm; Sun brunch 10:30 am-2 pm. Closed Mon. Bar. Semi-a la carte: lunch $4.90-$10.90, dinner $9.90-$29. Sun brunch $12.95. Parking. Lobster tank. Family-owned. Cr cds: A, C, D, DS, MC, V.

[D]

Crown Point (C-8)

(See also Hague, Ticonderoga)

Pop 1,963 **Elev** 200 ft **Area code** 518 **Zip** 12928
Information Ticonderoga Area Chamber of Commerce, 108 Lake George Ave, Ticonderoga 12883; 518/585-6619.

Located on a peninsula that forms the northernmost narrows of Lake Champlain, the Point was a strong position from which to control the trade route between New York and Canada during the French and Indian War. In the 19th century, agriculture and ironworks dominated the area.

What to See and Do

Crown Point Reservation State Campground. Camping (fee), fishing, boating (launch); hiking, picnic area. (Mid-Apr-mid-Oct) Across highway from Crown Point State Historic Site. Phone 518/597-3603. Day use per vehicle ¢¢

Crown Point State Historic Site. Preserved ruins of fortifications occupied by French, British and American forces during the French and Indian and Revolutionary wars: Ft St Frederic (1734) and Ft Crown Point (1759). Visitor center with exhibits & audiovisual presentation on history of area. Self-guided tours; events. (Grounds: May-Oct, Mon-Fri; Visitor Center by appt) N on NY 9N/22, 4 mi E at Champlain Bridge. Phone 518/597-3666. **Free.**

Penfield Homestead Museum. Site of first industrial use of electricity in US. Museum of local history, Adirondack iron industry; self-guided tour through ironworks ruins. (Mid-May-mid-Oct, daily) 6 mi W, in Ironville Historic District. Phone 518/597-3804. **Donation.**

Inn

★ ★ **CROWN POINT BED & BREAKFAST.** *Main St (NY 9N). 518/597-3651; FAX 518/597-4451.* E-mail mail@crownpointbandb.com; web crownpointbandb.com. 5 rms, 1 with shower only, 2 story, 1 suite. No A/C. No rm phones. D $60-$75; each addl $12; suite $120; hols (2-day min). Closed Thanksgiving, Dec 25. Crib free. TV in parlor; cable. Complimentary continental bkfst. Restaurant nearby. Ck-out 11 am, ck-in 4 pm.

Victorian house built 1886 for banker; many antiques. Totally nonsmoking. Cr cds: A, DS, MC, V.

Deposit (F-6)

(See also Bainbridge, Binghamton)

Settled 1789 **Pop** 1,824 **Elev** 991 ft **Area code** 607 **Zip** 13754
Information Chamber of Commerce, PO Box 222; 607/467-2556.

Lodge

★ ★ **CHESTNUT INN.** *498 Oquaga Lake Rd, 4¹/2 mi S on Oquaga Lake Rd.* 607/467-2500; FAX 607/467-5911; res: 800/467-7676. 30 rms, 20 share bath, 3 story, 5 suites. No rm phones. S, D $69-$149; each addl $15; suites $99-$209; under 12 free; golf plans. Crib free. TV, cable. Lake swimming. Dining rm 7 am-2 pm, 5-10 pm. Bar. Ck-out 11 am. Meeting rm. Business servs avail. Bellhops. Tennis privileges. Golf privileges. Lawn games. Massage. Valet parking. Built 1928; antiques. On Oquaga Lake. Cr cds: A, D, DS, MC, V.

Resort

★ ★ **SCOTT'S OQUAGA LAKE HOUSE.** *4 mi SW, 3 mi S of NY 17 exits 82W, 84E, on Oquaga Lake.* 607/467-3094; FAX 607/467-2370. Web www.tempotek.com/cybertown/scotts.htm. 148 rms, 138 baths, 3 story, 4 cottages. No A/C. AP, late May-mid-Oct: S $117-$135; D $101-$111/person; cottages (EP) $185-$269/day; family, wkly rates. Closed rest of yr. Crib avail. Supervised child's activities. Dining rm 8-9 am, 12:45-1:30 pm, 6:15-7:15 pm. Soda fountain. Wkly cookouts. Ck-out 2 pm, ck-in 4 pm. Coin lndry. Grocery 2 mi. Meeting rms. Bellhops. Free bus depot transportation. Sports dir. Indoor/outdoor tennis. 18-hole golf, putting green, pitch & putt. Private waterfront; speedboats, canoes, sailboats, waterskiing. Lawn games. Bicycles. Soc dir. Stage entertainment. Rec rm. Tours. Showboat cruises; concerts, bowling. Some fireplaces. On 1,000-acre estate. Family-owned since 1869. Cr cds: DS, MC, V.

Diamond Point (Lake George Area) (C-8)

(See also Glens Falls, Lake Luzerne, Warrensburg)

Pop 400 (est) **Elev** 354 ft **Area code** 518 **Zip** 12824

This town is located on the southwestern shore of Lake George (see).

Motels

★ **JULIANA.** *3842 Lake Shore Dr, ¹/4 mi N on NY 9N, 3 mi NE of I-87 exit 22.* 518/668-5191; FAX 518/668-3294. E-mail bdw@capital.net; web www.capital.net/com/bdw. 26 motel rms, 1-2 story, 9 kit., 7 kit. cottages. Late June-Labor Day: S, D $71; each addl $5; kit. units $82-$97; kit. cottages $500-$625/wk; lower rates late May-late June. Closed rest of yr. Crib avail. TV; cable (premium). Pool. Playground. Restaurant nearby. Ck-out 10 am. Rec rm. Picnic tables, grills. Sun deck. Private beach; rowboat. Cr cds: MC, V.

★ **TREASURE COVE.** *Lake Shore Dr, 5 mi N of I-87 exit 22.* 518/668-5334; FAX 518/668-9027. Web www.treasurecoveresort.com. 50

rms, 14 kit. cottages, A/C in some cottages. July-Labor Day: S, D $90-$121; each addl $10; kit. units $100-$121; kit. cottages (to 4 persons) $975-$1,160/wk; lower rates mid-Apr-June, after Labor Day-mid-Oct. Closed rest of yr. Crib $5. TV; cable. Pools. Playground. Complimentary coffee. Restaurant nearby. Ck-out 10 am. Game rm. Lawn games. Boat rentals; fishing charters. Refrigerators; some fireplaces. Picnic tables, grills. Private beach. No cr cds accepted.

Resort

★ ★ ★ **CANOE ISLAND LODGE.** *Lake Shore Dr, ¹/2 mi N on NY 9N, 4 mi NE of I-87 exit 22, on Lake George.* 518/668-5592; FAX 518/668-2012. Web www.mediausa.com/ny/canoeis/. 30 rms in cottages, 18 rms in 2-story lodges, 6 mini-chalets, 67 A/C. MAP, May-Oct: D $85-$160/person; family rates. Closed rest of yr. Crib avail. TV; cable. Playground. Supervised child's activities (July-Aug); ages 3 & up. Dining rm 8-10 am, noon-2:30 pm, 6:30-8:30 pm. Box lunches. Bar 5 pm-midnight. Ck-out 11 am, ck-in 1-4 pm. Business servs avail. Free bus depot transportation. Tennis. Beach; waterskiing, boats, sailboats, rides; dockage. Lawn games. Rec rm. Entertainment; dancing. Barbecues on island. Some fireplaces in cottages. Some balconies. Rustic atmosphere. No cr cds accepted.

Dunkirk (E-2)

Pop 13,989 **Elev** 598 ft **Area code** 716 **Zip** 14048 **E-mail** nccc@netsync.net **Web** www.clweb.com/nccc
Information Northern Chautauqua Chamber of Commerce, 212 Lake Shore Dr W; 716/366-6200.

A pleasant industrial and vacation city southwest of Buffalo on the shore of Lake Erie, about 35 miles from the Pennsylvania border, this was the birthplace of author-historian Samuel Hopkins Adams.

What to See and Do

Boating. One of 3 small boat harbors of refuge on Lake Erie between Erie, PA and Buffalo, NY. Launch; protected inner harbor; mooring. Breakwater.

Dunkirk Lighthouse (1875). Built in 1875; 10 rms in lighthouse with a rm dedicated to each branch of the military service, lighthouse keeper's rm, Victorian furnishings in kitchen and parlor. Guided tour incl tower and history of the Great Lakes. (June-Aug, daily; Apr-May & Sept-Dec, Mon-Tues & Thurs-Sat) Off NY 5, on Point Dr N. Phone 716/366-5050. ¢¢

Evangola State Park. Swimming, 4,000-ft sand beach, bathhouse, lifeguards; fishing. Nature trails, hiking. Cross-country skiing, snowmobiling. Picnicking (fee), playground, game areas. Tent & trailer sites (fee). 17 mi N on NY 5. Phone 716/549-1802 or 716/549-1760 (camping). ¢¢

Historical Museum of the Darwin R. Barker Library. Period furniture, 1880s parlor; exhibits on Fredonia & Pomfret; documents, photos, portraits and genealogical material; children's museum, education programs. (Tues & Thurs-Sat afternoons) 20 E Main St, 3 mi S in Fredonia. Phone 716/672-2114. **Free.**

Lake Erie State Park. Fishing. Nature trails, hiking. Cross-country skiing, snowmobiling. Picnicking, playground. Tent & trailer sites, cabins (fee). (May-mid-Oct, daily) 7 mi W on NY 5. Phone 716/792-9214. ¢¢

Swimming. Point Gratiot Park Beach & Wright Park Beach. (Mid-June-Labor Day, daily) Bathhouses. Phone 716/366-6901.

Annual Event

Chautauqua County Fair. Last wk July.

Motels

★ ★ **DAYS INN.** *(10455 Bennett Rd, Fredonia 14063)* ¼ mi S, I-90 exit 59. 716/673-1351; FAX 716/672-6909. 132 rms, 2 story. Apr-Sept: S $51-$69; D $59-$79; each addl $7; under 18 free; lower rates rest of yr. Crib free. Pet accepted, some restrictions. TV; cable (premium), VCR avail. Ck-out 11 am. Lndry facilities. Meeting rms. Business servs avail. Valet serv. Downhill/x-country ski 20 mi. Cr cds: A, C, D, DS, JCB, MC, V.

✔ ★ **SOUTHSHORE.** 5040 W Lake Shore Drive. 716/366-2822. 9 rms, 7 kits., 12 kit. cottages. July-Aug: D, kit. units, kit. cottages $48-$95; wkly rates; lower rates rest of yr. Pet accepted, some restrictions. TV; VCR avail. Heated pool. Playground. Ck-out 10 am. Guest lndry. Lawn games. Refrigerators. Picnic tables, grill. Cr cds: MC, V.

★ ★ **VINEYARD.** 3929 Vineyard Dr, I-90 exit 59. 716/366-4400; res: 716/366-2200; FAX 716/366-3375. 38 rms in 2 buildings. July-early Sept: S $49-$69; D $59-$79; each addl $4; under 18 free; lower rates rest of yr. Crib free. Pet accepted. TV; cable (premium). Pool; lifeguard. Playground. Restaurant 6 am-11 pm. Bar 10 am-midnight, Sun noon-9 pm. Ck-out noon. Meeting rms. Business servs avail. Health club privileges. Cr cds: A, D, DS, MC, V.

Motor Hotel

★ ★ ★ **FOUR POINTS BY SHERATON.** 30 Lake Shore Dr E. 716/366-8350; res: 800/525-8350; FAX 716/366-8899. 132 rms, 4 story. June-mid-Sept: S, D $82-$100; each addl $10; suites $121-$131; under 17 free; ski plans; lower rates rest of yr. Crib free. Pet accepted. TV; cable. Indoor/outdoor pool; whirlpool, poolside serv, lifeguard. Complimentary coffee in lobby. Restaurant 7 am-10 pm. Rm serv. Bar 11 am-midnight. Ck-out noon. Meeting rms. Business servs avail. In-rm modem link. Downhill/x-country ski 15 mi. Exercise equipt; sauna. Some refrigerators, wet bars. On Lake Erie. Cr cds: A, C, D, DS, MC, V.

Inn

★ ★ ★ **THE WHITE INN.** *(52 E Main St, Fredonia 14063)* S on NY 60, right on E Main St. 716/672-2103; res: 888/373-3664; FAX 716/672-2107. E-mail inn@whiteinn.com; web www.whiteinn.com. 12 rms, 3 story, 11 suites. S, D $59-$169; each addl $10; under 13 free. Crib free. TV; cable, VCR avail. Complimentary full bkfst. Restaurant (see THE WHITE INN). Bar 11:30 am-11 pm, Fri, Sat to 2 am. Ck-out 11 am, ck-in 3 pm. Meeting rms. Business servs avail. Health club privileges. Some refrigerators. Built 1868; Victorian atmosphere. Antiques. Cr cds: A, D, DS, MC, V.

Restaurant

★ ★ ★ **THE WHITE INN.** (See The White Inn) 716/672-2103. E-mail inn@whiteinn.com; web www.whiteinn.com. Specialties: loin of lamb Wyoming, tenderloin filet. Hrs: 7-10 am, 11:30 am-2 pm, 5-8:30 pm; Fri, Sat to 9 pm; Sun 8-11 am, 12:30-8 pm. Res accepted. Bar. A la carte entrees: bkfst $2.75-$7.95, lunch $3.95-$8.25, dinner $12.95-$19.95. Buffet lunch $5.95. Outdoor dining. Authentic Victorian decor. Cr cds: A, D, DS, MC, V.

East Aurora (D-2)

(See also Arcade, Buffalo)

Pop 13,000 **Elev** 917 ft **Area code** 716 **Zip** 14052 **E-mail** info@eanycc.com **Web** www.eanycc.com
Information Greater East Aurora Chamber of Commerce, 431 Main St; 716/652-8444 or 800/441-2881.

East Aurora lies very close to the large industrial and commercial center, Buffalo. In the early 1900s, Elbert Hubbard, author of *A Message to Garcia*, lived here and made it the home of the Roycrofters, makers of fine books, copper and leather ware and furniture. The Roycroft campus is still operating, and it is the only continuous operation of its kind in America today. East Aurora is also the headquarters of Fisher-Price toys. The Baker Memorial Methodist Church, which has hand-signed Tiffany windows, is located here.

What to See and Do

Kissing Bridge Ski Area. Two quad, 4 double chairlifts, 2 T-bars, J-bar and handle tow; patrol, school, rentals; snowmaking; bars, cafe; nursery. Longest run 3,500 ft; vertical drop 550 ft. Night skiing. (Dec-Mar, daily) 9 mi W on US 20A, then 17 mi S on US 219 Expy S, exit at Armor Duells Rd to NY 240 S; follow signs. Phone 716/592-4963 or 716/592-4961 (for ski report). ¢¢¢¢¢

Millard Fillmore Museum. House (ca 1825) Fillmore built for his wife contains memorabilia, furnishings. 1830s herb and rose garden. Carriage house (ca 1830) built of lumber from the former Nathaniel Fillmore farm; antique tools, Fillmore sleigh. (June-mid-Oct, Wed, Sat & Sun; rest of yr, by appt) 24 Shearer Ave. Phone 716/652-0167. ¢

The Elbert Hubbard Museum. A 5-bedrm, 1910 Craftsman period home built by and for the Roycrofters. Contains Roycroft furniture, modeled leather, hammered metal, leaded glass, books, pamphlets and other artifacts from 1895-1938. Also here is material on Elbert Hubbard, author of the famous essay *The Message to Garcia*. (June-mid-Oct, Wed, Sat & Sun afternoons; tours by appt) 363 Oakwood Ave, located in the ScheideMantel House. Phone 716/652-4735 or 716/652-1424. ¢

Annual Events

Roycroft Summer Festival of Arts & Crafts. Roycroft artisans and members of the art society display their arts & crafts. Phone 716/655-4080. Last wkend June.

Toy Festival. Celebration commemorating Fisher-Price Toy Co's establishment here in the 1930s. Last wkend Aug.

Hotel

★ ★ ★ **ROYCROFT INN.** 40 S Grove St, NY 90 to NY 400, exit Maple St. 716/652-5552; res: 800/267-0525; FAX 716/655-5345. 22 suites, 3 story. Suites $120-$210; under 12 free; ski plans. Crib free. TV; cable, VCR. Complimentary continental bkfst. Restaurant (see ROYCROFT INN). Bar 11:30 am-9 pm. Ck-out 11 am. Meeting rms. Business servs avail. In-rm modem link. Downhill/x-country ski 10 mi. Health club privileges. In-rm whirlpools. Totally nonsmoking. Cr cds: A, D, DS, MC, V.

Inn

★ ★ **GREEN GLEN.** 898 E Main St. 716/655-2828. 4 rms, 3 with bath, 2 story. 3 A/C. No rm phones. S, D $65-$75; each addl $15. TV in lounge; VCR avail. Complimentary full bkfst. Restaurant nearby. Ck-out noon, ck-in 3 pm. Luggage handling. Downhill ski 8 mi; x-country ski 7 mi. Health club privileges. Queen Anne-style house (1890); many antiques. No cr cds accepted.

Restaurants

★ ★ ★ **OLD ORCHARD INN.** 2095 Blakeley Rd. 716/652-4664. Specializes in fish, roast beef, chicken fricassee with biscuits. Own dressings. Hrs: 11:30 am-2:30 pm, 5-9 pm; Sun noon-9 pm; early-bird dinner 5-6 pm; Sun noon-2 pm. Closed Dec 25. Res accepted. Bar. Semi-a la carte: lunch $6.95-$12.85, dinner $12.95-$26.25. Child's meals. Outdoor dining. Fireplaces. Duck pond; wooded countryside. Family-owned. Cr cds: A, D, DS, MC, V.

✔★ ★ ★ **ROYCROFT INN.** (See Roycroft Inn) 716/652-5552. E-mail mbaugat@roycroftinn.com; web www.someplacesdifferent.com. Specialties: rack of lamb, penne and smoked Salmon, chocolate terrine. Hrs: 11:30 am-9 pm; Fri to 10 pm; Sat 2-10 pm; Sun 10 am-9 pm; Sun brunch to 2 pm. Res accepted. Wine list. Semi-a la carte: lunch $5.95-$11.95, dinner $11.95-$21.95. Sun brunch $13.95. Outdoor dining. Restored to 1905 arts-and-crafts style. Totally nonsmoking. Cr cds: A, C, D, DS, MC, V.

D

East Hampton, L.I. (A-5)

(See also Amagansett, Sag Harbor, Southampton)

Settled 1648 **Pop** 16,132 **Elev** 36 ft **Area code** 516 **Zip** 11937 **Web** www.peconic.net/community/eh-chamber
Information East Hampton Chamber of Commerce, 79A Main St; 516/324-0362.

East Hampton is an old Long Island village, founded in 1648 by a group of farmers. Farming was the main livelihood until the mid-1800s, when the town began to develop into a fashionable resort.

What to See and Do

Guild Hall Museum. Regional art exhibits; changing shows. Art and poetry lectures, classes. Library covering art and artists of the region. (June-Sept, daily; rest of yr, Wed-Sun; closed some hols) 158 Main St. Phone 516/324-0806. **Donation.** Also here is

John Drew Theater at Guild Hall. A 400-seat theater for films, plays, concerts, lectures, children's performances. Phone 516/324-4050 or 516/324-0806.

Historic Mulford Farm (1680). Living history farm museum; 18th-century New England architecture; colonial history; period rms; costumed interpretation. (Afternoons: July & Aug, daily; June & Sept, wkends only; rest of yr, by appt) James Lane, adj to Payne House. Phone 516/324-6850. ¢
Nearby is

Historic Clinton Academy (1784). First preparatory school in New York. Now museum housing collection of artifacts of Eastern Long Island. (Afternoons: July & Aug, daily; June & Sept, wkends only) 151 Main St. Phone 516/324-6850. ¢

"Home Sweet Home" House (1680) **and Windmill** (1804). Childhood home of John Howard Payne (1791-1852), who wrote "Home, Sweet Home." Three centuries of American furniture, 18th- and 19th-century English china, mementos. Gallery with special and changing exhibits. Windmill in rear. Tours. (Daily; Feb by appt) 14 James Lane. Phone 516/324-0713. ¢¢

Hook Mill. 36 N Main St, on Montauk Hwy. Completely equipped 1806 windmill. Guided tours. (Late June-Sat after Labor Day, daily) ¢¢

Pollock-Krasner House and Study Center. Jackson Pollock's studio and house plus a reference library on 20th-century American art. (May-Oct, Thurs-Sat, by appt only) 830 Fireplace Rd. Phone 516/324-4929. ¢¢

Motel

★ ★ **EAST HAMPTON HOUSE.** 226 Pantigo Rd. 516/324-4300; FAX 516/329-3743. 52 rms, 2 story, 32 kits. July-Labor Day: D $125-$220; each addl $15; lower rates rest of yr. TV; cable (premium). Heated pool; wading pool, lifeguard. Ck-out 11 am. Business servs avail. Tennis. Private patios, balconies. Grill. Cr cds: A, DS, MC, V.

Inns

★ ★ **1770 HOUSE.** 143 Main St. 516/324-1770; FAX 516/324-3504. 7 rms, 2 story. S, D $120-$250. Children over 12 yrs only. Complimentary full bkfst. Restaurant. Ck-out 11:30 am, ck-in 2 pm. Business servs avail. Restored 18th-century house; antique furnishings. Cr cds: A, MC, V.

★ ★ ★ **CENTENNIAL HOUSE.** 13 Woods Lane. 516/324-9414; FAX 516/324-0493. 4 rms, 2 story, 1 cottage. May-Oct: D $225-$395; cottage $500; higher rates wkends & hols (3-6-day min); lower rates rest of yr. Children over 12 yrs only. Pet accepted. TV; cable. Pool. Complimentary full bkfst. Restaurant nearby. Ck-out 11 am, ck-in 2 pm. Business servs avail. Exercise equipt. Some fireplaces. Built 1876 by local craftsman. Period furnishings. Totally nonsmoking. Cr cds: MC, V.

★ ★ **THE HEDGES' INN.** 74 James Lane. 516/324-7100; FAX 516/324-5816. 11 rms, 3 story. No rm phones. May-Sept: D $145-$195; higher rates: wkends (3-day min), hols (5-day min); lower rates rest of yr. TV; cable (premium) in main rm. Complimentary continental bkfst. Restaurant (see JAMES LANE CAFE). Ck-out noon, ck-in 2 pm. Business servs avail. Tennis privileges. 9-hole golf privileges, pro, putting green, driving range. Victorian house built (ca 1870) with wraparound porch. Cr cds: A, C, D, MC, V.

★ ★ **HUNTTING INN.** 94 Main St, on NY 27. 516/324-0410; FAX 516/324-8751. 19 rms, 3 story. May-Sept: S $125; D $150-$250; each addl $15; suites $300; wkends; 5-day min July 4, Labor Day; lower rates rest of yr. TV. Complimentary continental bkfst. Dining rm (see PALM). Ck-out noon, ck-in 2 pm. Business servs avail. Luggage handling. Tennis privileges. Established in 1751; English country garden. Cr cds: A, C, D, MC, V.

★ ★ ★ **J. HARPER POOR COTTAGE.** (181 Main St, East Hampton) 516/324-4081; FAX 516/329-5931. 4 rms, 2 story. May-Oct (2-day min): D $275-$350; 3-day min July-Labor Day; lower rates rest of yr. TV; cable. Pool. Complimentary full bkfst. Restaurants nearby. Ck-out 11:30 am, ck-in 2 pm. Business servs avail. Original house built 1650. English garden. Cr cds: A, MC, V.

★ ★ ★ **MAIDSTONE ARMS.** 207 Main St (11963). 516/324-5006; FAX 516/324-5037. E-mail maidarms@aol.com; web www.themaidstonearms.com. 12 rms, 3 story, 4 suites, 3 cottages. D $195-$225; each addl $25; suites $265; cottages $325-$350; lower rates off season. Complimentary continental bkfst. Dining rm (see MAIDSTONE ARMS). Rm serv 8 am-10 pm. Bar noon-midnight. Ck-out 11 am, ck-in after 3 pm. Sitting area. Cr cds: A, D, MC, V.

Restaurants

★ ★ ★ **EAST HAMPTON POINT.** 295 Three Mile Harbor/Hog Creek Rd. 516/329-2800. Specializes in seafood. Hrs: noon-midnight; to 11 pm summer. Res required. A la carte entrees: lunch $9-$16, dinner

$19-$30. Child's meals. Valet parking. Outdoor dining. Sunset views. Cr cds: A, MC, V.

★ ★ **JAMES LANE CAFE.** *(See The Hedges' Inn)* 516/324-7100. Italian, Amer menu. Specializes in fresh local produce. Hrs: 5-10 pm. Closed Tues & Wed (Oct-May). Res accepted. A la carte entrees: dinner $15-$30. Valet parking. Outdoor tented dining. In 1870s Victorian home. Cr cds: A, MC, V.

★ ★ **LAUNDRY.** *31 Race Lane.* 516/324-3199. Specializes in fish. Hrs: 5:30 pm-midnight; winter to 11 pm. Closed Wed after Labor Day; Thanksgiving, Dec 25. A la carte entrees: dinner $16.50-$24. Parking. Once operated as a commercial laundry; courtyard, garden. Cr cds: A, C, D, DS, MC, V.

D

★ ★ **MAIDSTONE ARMS.** *(See Maidstone Arms Inn)* 516/324-5006. E-mail maidarms@aol.com; web www.themaidstonearms.com. Own baking. Hrs: 8-10:30 am, noon-2:30 pm, 6-10 pm; wknds to 10:30 pm; Sun brunch noon-2:30 pm. Res accepted wknds. Bar. Wine cellar. A la carte entrees: bkfst $6-$10, lunch $9.50-$16.50, dinner $17-$30. Sun brunch $10.50-$16. Parking. Cr cds: A, D, MC, V.

★ ★ **MARYJANE'S IL MONASTERO.** *(128 N Main St, East Hampton)* 516/324-8008. Italian, Amer menu. Hrs: 5-10 pm. Closed Thanksgiving, Dec 25. Res accepted. Bar. A la carte entrees: dinner $11.95-$18.95. Child's meals. Parking. 3 dining rms. Original art, Tiffany-style lamps. Cr cds: A, MC, V.

D

✔★ ★ **MICHAEL'S.** *28 Maidstone Park Rd.* 516/324-0725. Continental menu. Specializes in fresh seafood, marinated boneless steak. Hrs: 5-10 pm; wknds to 11 pm. Closed Wed off season; Dec 25. Res accepted. Bar. Semi-a la carte: dinner $9.95-$18.95. Casual, country atmosphere. Cr cds: A, MC, V.

★ ★ **NICK AND TONI'S.** *136 N Main St.* 516/324-3550. Mediterranean menu. Wood-burning oven specials. Own baking. Hrs: 6-10:30 pm; Fri, Sat to 11:30 pm; off season to 9:30 pm; Sun brunch 11:30 am-2:30 pm. Closed Dec 25. Res required. Bar. A la carte entrees: dinner $15-$28. Sun brunch $14. Parking. Contemporary decor, folk art. Cr cds: A, MC, V.

D

★ ★ **PALM.** *(See Huntting Inn)* 516/324-0411. Continental menu. Specializes in steak, lobster, seafood. Hrs: 5-11 pm. Bar. A la carte entrees: dinner $15-$30.Turn-of-the-century decor. Cr cds: A, D, MC, V.

★ ★ **SAPORE DI MARE.** *(Wainscott Stone Rd, Wainscott) 3 mi W on Montauk Hwy (NY 27).* 516/537-2764. Italian menu. Specializes in fish, coastal Mediterranean cuisine. Own baking. Hrs: 6-11:30 pm; Fri to 1 am; Sat noon-3 pm, 6 pm-1 am; Sun noon-3 pm, 6-11:30 pm. Closed Mon & Tues in winter. Res required. Bar 5:30 pm-closing. A la carte entrees: lunch $15-$26, dinner $18-$32. Valet parking. Outdoor dining. Trattoria with enclosed patio on pond. Cr cds: A, C, D, MC, V.

D

Ellenville (F-7)

(See also Kingston, Liberty, New Paltz)

Pop 4,422 **Elev** 330 ft **Area code** 914 **Zip** 12428
Information Chamber of Commerce, PO Box 227; 914/647-4620.

Center of the Ulster County resort area, Ellenville offers abundant scenic beauty. Hang gliding is popular here.

Resorts

★ ★ **HUDSON VALLEY.** *(445 Granit Rd, Kerhonkson 12446)* 6 mi N on US 209; 3 mi E off US 44 (NY 55). 914/626-8888; FAX 914/626-2595; 800 888/684-7264. Web www.hudsonvalleyresort.com. 296 rms, 8 story. AP: D $77-$118/person; MAP avail July-Aug; higher rates: wkends, hols. TV; cable. 2 pools, 1 indoor; whirlpool, poolside serv, lifeguard. Supervised child's activities; ages 4-13. Restaurants 7-11 am, noon-3 pm, 6-11 pm. Rm serv. Bar 11-3 am. Ck-out 11 am, ck-in 4 pm. Meeting rms. Business servs avail. Bellhops. Valet serv. Sports dir. Tennis. 18-hole golf, greens fee $23. Rowboats. Downhill/x-country ski on site. Indoor/outdoor games. Soc dir; nightclubs; entertainment. Exercise rm; sauna, steam rm. Cr cds: A, C, D, DS, MC, V.

★ ★ **THE NEVELE GRANDE.** 1½ mi S on US 209. 914/647-6000; FAX 914/647-9884; res: 800/647-6000. Web www.nevelle.com/new. 700 rms in main building & annexes, 10 story. AP (2-day min wkends, hols, or $10 addl), late June-early Sept: D $97-$148/person; family rates; varied rates rest of yr. Crib free. TV; cable, VCR avail (movies). 6 pools, 2 indoor; whirlpools, poolside serv, lifeguard. Supervised child's activities (July-early Sept, also wkends); ages 3-12. Dining rm (hrs flexible). Rm serv. Snack bar. Bar noon-4 am. Ck-out 1 pm, ck-in 3 pm. Coin lndry 1½ mi. Business center. In-rm modem link. Bellhops. Valet serv. Shopping arcade. Bus depot transportation. Sports dir. Lighted tennis, pro. 36-hole golf, greens fee $35-$50, pro, indoor miniature golf. Private lakes; boats, rowboats. Downhill/x-country ski on site. Ice rink, tobogganing, sleighing. Lawn games. Ball fields. Soc dir; stage productions, entertainment, dancing. 2 rec rms. Exercise rm; sauna, steam rm. Spa. Contemporary design, decor; on 1,000-acre estate. Cr cds: A, C, D, JCB, MC, V.

Elmira (E-5)

(See also Corning, Watkins Glen)

Settled 1788 **Pop** 33,724 **Elev** 859 ft **Area code** 607 **E-mail** ccommerc@stny.lrun.com **Web** www.chemungchamber.org
Information Chemung County Chamber of Commerce, 400 E Church St, 14901; 607/734-5137 or 800/627-5892.

Elmira is on both shores of the Chemung River—on a site where, in 1779, the Sullivan-Clinton expedition found a Native American village. By the mid-19th century the railroads and canals were opening new fields of industry; first lumber, later metalworking and textiles.

Samuel Clemens (Mark Twain) spent more than 20 summers at Quarry Farm, the Elmira country home of his wife's sister, Susan Crane. Elmira also was the birthplace of noted filmmaker Hal Roach, first United States woman space pilot Eileen Collins and fashion designer Tommy Hilfiger.

What to See and Do

Arnot Art Museum. An 1833 mansion with 3-story wing. Includes 17th-and 19th-century European paintings displayed in 1880 gallery; 19th-century American gallery; also changing exhibits. (Daily exc Mon; closed hols) 235 Lake St. Phone 607/734-3697. ¢

Chemung Valley History Museum. Local history displays, Mark Twain exhibit, research library; special events. (Tues-Sat; closed hols) 415 E Water St. Phone 607/734-4167. **Donation**

Elmira College (1855). (1,100 students) Liberal arts. Coeducational since 1969, Elmira College was the first (1855) to grant women degrees equal to those of men. Mark Twain Study at Park Place was presented to the college by Samuel Clemens' in-laws in 1952; Clemens did much of his writing here, incl *The Adventures of Huckleberry Finn*. Mark Twain exhibit in Hamilton Hall has memorabilia and a 20-min video. Study and exhibit (summer, daily; rest of yr, by appt). Park Place. Phone 607/735-1941. **Free.**

National Warplane Museum. Dedicated to preserving the planes, engines and memories of those who molded aviation heritage. Museum houses interactive displays, exhibits, aircrafts, library. Gift shop. (Daily) Elmira-Corning Regional Airport, off NY 17 exit 51. Phone 607/739-8200. ¢¢

Natl Soaring Museum and Harris Hill Soaring Site. "Soaring Capital of America." Museum has collection of historic and contemporary sailplanes; meteorology, aerodynamic & aviation exhibits; films; soaring memorabilia and World War II gliders. Sailplane rides (June-early Sept, daily; Apr-May & early Sept-Oct, wkends only; addl fee). Pool; playground, kiddie rides, picnicking and golf (early May-late Sept, daily). Museum (daily; closed Jan 1, Thanksgiving, Dec 25). 8 mi NW in Harris Hill Park, off NY 17 exit 51. Phone 607/734-3128. ¢¢

Replica Trolley Tours. Guided tours (90 min) of Chemung County's tourist attractions aboard a replica trolley. (Mid-June-Labor Day; Tues-Sat) 400 E Church St. Phone 607/734-5137. ¢

Woodlawn Cemetery. Graves of Samuel Clemens (Mark Twain) and Hal Roach. N end of Walnut St.Nearby is

> **Woodlawn Natl Cemetery.** Graves of 2,000 Confederate prisoners of war who died in Elmira.

Annual Events

Chemung County Fair. In Horseheads. Early Aug.

NASCAR Race Day. Contests, drivers, entertainment. Early Aug.

Seasonal Event

Baseball. Elmira Pioneers. Affiliate of the Northeast League. Mid-June-Labor Day.

Motels

✔★★ **BEST WESTERN MARSHALL MANOR.** (3527 Watkins Rd, Horseheads 14845) on NY 14, 5 mi N of NY 17 exit 52. 607/739-3891. 40 rms. S $36-$59; D $38-$66; each addl $5; under 18 free; higher rates special events. Crib $2. Pet accepted; $4. TV; cable, VCR avail. Pool. Complimentary continental bkfst. Complimentary coffee in rms. Restaurant 4-10 pm. Bar to 1 am. Ck-out 11 am. In-rm modem link. Refrigerators, microwaves avail. Cr cds: A, C, D, DS, MC, V.

 D ✔ ≈ ⊠ ⋀ SC

★ **COACHMAN MOTOR LODGE.** 908 Pennsylvania Ave (NY 14S) (14904). 607/733-5526; FAX 607/733-0961. 18 kit. units, 2 story. Apr-Nov: S $49-$55; D $60-$65; under 18 free; each addl $5; wkly rates; lower rates rest of yr. Crib free. Pet accepted. TV; cable. Complimentary coffee in rms. Restaurant nearby. Ck-out noon. Coin lndry. Business servs avail. Sundries. Health club privileges. Microwaves avail. Some balconies. Picnic table, grill. Cr cds: A, C, DS, MC, V.

D ✔ ⊠ ⋀ SC

★★ **ECONO LODGE.** 871 NY 64 (14903), near Regional Airport, Rte 17 exit 51. 607/739-2000; FAX 607/739-3552. 48 rms, 2 story. May-Oct: S $51-$67; D $62-$79; each addl $7; under 18 free; higher rates: racing events, college graduation; lower rates rest of yr. Crib free. TV; cable. Whirlpools. Complimentary continental bkfst. Ck-out 11 am. Coin lndry. In-rm modem link. Health club privileges. Refrigerators, microwaves. Cr cds: A, C, D, DS, MC, V.

D ⊠ ⋀ SC

★★★ **HOLIDAY INN-RIVERVIEW.** 1 Holiday Plaza (14901). 607/734-4211; FAX 607/734-3549. E-mail ELMDT@prodigy.net; web www.holiday-inn.com. 150 rms, 2 story. S, D $70-$100; under 19 free; higher rates special events. Crib free. Pet accepted. TV; cable (premium), VCR avail. 2 pools, 1 indoor (winter); wading pool. Restaurant 6:30 am-2 pm, 5-10 pm; wkends from 7 am. Rm serv. Bar 4 pm-midnight. Ck-out noon. Coin lndry. Meeting rms. Business servs avail. In-rm modem link.

Valet serv. Sundries. Exercise equipt. Health club privileges. Refrigerators, microwaves avail. Cr cds: A, C, D, DS, ER, MC, V.

D ✔ ≈ ⊼ ⊠ ⋀ SC

★★ **HOWARD JOHNSON.** (2671 Corning Rd, Horseheads 14845) off NY 17 exit 52 at NY14. 607/739-5636; FAX 607/739-8630. 76 rms, 1-2 story. May-mid-Nov: S $48-$70; D $58-$80; each addl $8; studio rms avail; under 18 free; lower rates rest of yr. Crib free. Pet accepted. TV; cable (premium). Pool. Coffee in rms. Restaurant 6:30 am-11 pm; Fri, Sat to midnight. Rm serv. Ck-out noon. In-rm modem link. Valet serv. Sundries. Some refrigerators; microwaves avail. Private patios, balconies. Cr cds: A, C, D, DS, JCB, MC, V.

✔ ≈ ⊠ ⋀ SC

Restaurant

★★ **HILL TOP INN.** 171 Jerusalem Hill Rd (14901), 2½ mi E, NY 17 Jerusalem Hill exit 57. 607/732-6728. E-mail hilltop@stny.lrun.com; web www.hill-top-inn.com. Specializes in lamb, steak, fresh seafood. Hrs: 5-10 pm. Closed some major hols; also 4 wks in Feb. Res accepted. Bar to 1 am. Semi-a la carte: dinner $8.95-$19.95. Child's meals. Outdoor dining in season. View of Elmira. Family-owned. Cr cds: A, C, D, DS, MC, V.

D ⇥ ♥

Endicott (E-5)

(See also Binghamton, Owego)

Settled 1795 **Pop** 13,531 **Elev** 840 ft **Area code** 607 **Zip** 13760

Endicott is a center of industry. With Binghamton (see) and Johnson City it makes up the "Triple Cities."

Motel

★★ **KINGS INN.** (2603 E Main St, Endwell) ¼ mi E on NY 17C. 607/754-8020; FAX 607/754-6768; res: 800/531-4667. E-mail kingsinn@spectra.net. 60 rms, 1-2 story. S $52.50; D $57-$62; each addl $7; under 12 free; higher rates B.C. Open. Crib free. TV; cable (premium). Indoor pool. Restaurant 7-9:30 am; Sat, Sun to 11 am. Ck-out noon. Business servs avail. In-rm modem link. Valet serv. Sundries. Exercise equipt; sauna. Health club privileges. Cr cds: A, C, D, DS, MC, V.

D ≈ ⊼ ⊠ ⋀ SC

Motor Hotel

★ **EXECUTIVE INN.** 1 Delaware Ave. 607/754-7570. 135 rms, 40 suites, 60 kits. S $44-$59; D $54-$59; suites $59-$89; kits. $79-$89; under 16 free; wkly, wkend, hol rates; higher rates special events. Crib free. Pet accepted, some restrictions; $50 refundable. TV; cable (premium), VCR avail (movies). Restaurant adj. Ck-out noon. Meeting rms. Business servs avail. Some refrigerators; microwaves avail. Cr cds: A, C, D, DS, MC, V.

D ✔ ⊠ ⋀ SC

Finger Lakes (E-4 - D-5)

(See also Auburn, Canandaigua, Corning, Cortland, Elmira, Geneseo, Geneva, Hammondsport, Ithaca, Owego, Penn Yan, Rochester, Skaneateles, Syracuse, Waterloo and Watkins Glen)

E-mail fingrlake@flare.net **Web** www.fingerlakes.org
Information Finger Lakes Assn, 309 Lake St, Penn Yan 14527; 315/536-7488 or 800/548-4386.

Scientists say the Finger Lakes were scooped out by glaciers, resulting in one of the most delightful landscaping jobs in America. There are 11 lakes in all; Canandaigua, Keuka, Seneca, Cayuga, Owasco and Skaneateles are the largest. The smaller lakes also have the characteristic finger shape. Seneca is the deepest at 630 feet and Cayuga the longest at 40 miles. The region has many glens and gorges with plunging streams. Hundreds of recreation spots dot the shores, offering every imaginable sport. The famous New York State wine grapes grow in the many miles of vineyards in the area.

This scenic area boasts 25 state parks, many waterfalls, camping and picnicking areas and other features.

Fire Island National Seashore (B-3)

(See also Bay Shore, Riverhead)

Five areas of the Fire Island National Seashore are open. **Otis Pike Wilderness Visitor Center,** reached via William Floyd Parkway and Smith Point Bridge (phone 516/281-3010); self-guided nature walk and board-walk trail for the disabled. Parking (May-Sept, fee) and swimming at adj county park. **Sailors Haven/Sunken Forest,** reached by ferry (begins running mid-May, phone 516/589-8980) from Sayville, has swimming, lifeguards, marina, picnicking, concession, visitor center, nature walk, self-guided tours, naturalist programs (June-Labor Day). **Watch Hill,** reached by ferry from Patchogue (phone 516/475-1665), offers the same facilities as Sailors Haven plus 26 family campsites (lottery res required, phone 516/597-6633 after May 1). **Fire Island Lighthouse** (1858) area, reached by Robert Moses Causeway, has boardwalk leading to light-house; nature trail (all yr); former lightkeeper's quarters are a visitor center with exhibits (Apr-June & Labor Day-Dec, Sat & Sun; July-Labor Day, Wed-Sun; phone 516/661-4876). Parking at adj Robert Moses State Park (field #5). Headquarters is at 120 Laurel St, Patchogue 11772; 516/289-4810.

Located on Washington Ave in Mastic Beach is the restored estate of one of the signers of the Declaration of Independence, William Floyd (July 4-Labor Day, wkends). Phone 516/399-2030 for tour schedule. No pets allowed.

Fishkill (F-8)

(See also Newburgh, Poughkeepsie)

Pop 17,655 **Elev** 223 ft **Area code** 914 **Zip** 12524 **E-mail** dctpa@idsi.net **Web** www.dutchesstourism.com
Information Dutchess County Tourism Promotion Agency, 3 Neptune Rd, Ste M-17, Poughkeepsie 12601; 914/463-4000 or 800/445-3131.

What to See and Do

Madam Brett Homestead (1709). Oldest standing structure in Dutchess County. Period furnishings of 7 generations, from Dutch Colonial through Federal and Victorian eras. Garden. Occupied by same family from 1709-1954. (May-Dec, 1st Sun every month, afternoons or by appt) SW on I-84, exit NY 52, then W 3 mi at 50 Van Nydeck Ave in Beacon. Phone 914/831-6533 or 914/896-6897. ¢¢

Mount Gulian Historic Site (1730-1740). HQ of Baron von Steuben during the final period of the Revolutionary War; birthplace of the Order of the Society of Cincinnati—the first veteran's organization. (Apr-Dec, Wed & Sun afternoons or by appt) 145 Sterling St, off NY 9D N at Chelsea Ridge Park, in Beacon. Phone 914/831-8172. ¢

Van Wyck Homestead Museum (1732). Once requisitioned by the Continental Army as HQ, orders for the army were issued from the house. Also site of court-martials, incl that of Enoch Crosby, counterspy for the American forces. Notables incl Washington, Lafayette and von Steuben visited here. Library. Collection of Hudson Valley Folk Art; also changing exhibits. (Memorial Day-Labor Day, Sat & Sun, also by appt) S of town, at jct US 9, I-84.Phone 914/896-9560. ¢¢

Motels

★ ★ ★ **RESIDENCE INN BY MARRIOTT.** *2481 US 9, at I-84 exit 13, US 9N.* 914/896-5210; FAX 914/896-9689. 136 suites, 2 story. Suites $150-$279. Crib free. Pet accepted; $150. TV; cable (premium), VCR avail (movies). Pool; whirlpool. Complimentary continental bkfst. Restaurant adj. Ck-out noon. Coin lndry. Meeting rm. Business servs avail. In-rm modem link. Coin lndry. Valet serv. Sundries. Exercise equipt. Health club privileges. Lawn games. Refrigerators, microwaves. Basketball, volleyball. Cr cds: A, C, D, DS, ER, JCB, MC, V.

D 🐾 🛏 🏋 🛬 🛶 🔥 SC

↙★ ★ **WELLESLEY INN.** *2477 US 9, I-84 exit 13.* 914/896-4995; FAX 914/896-6631; res: 800/444-8888. 82 rms, 4 story. Apr-Oct: S, D $60-$85; each addl $2; suites $95-$150; under 17 free; wkly rates; package plans; higher rates special events; lower rates rest of yr. Crib $5. Pet accepted; $5. TV; cable (premium). Complimentary continental bkfst. Complimentary coffee in rms. Restaurant adj open 24 hrs. Bar noon-11 pm. Ck-out 11 am. In-rm modem link. Health club privileges. Sundries. Some refrigerators; microwaves avail. Cr cds: A, C, D, DS, MC, V.

D 🐾 🛏 🔥 SC

Restaurants

★ ★ ★ ★ **HARRALDS.** (*3110 NY 52, Stormville 12582*) *2½ mi NW of I-84 exit 17; 5½ mi E of Taconic Pkwy, on NY 52.* 914/878-6595. This pleasant, rural, ma-and-pa gourmet restaurant occupies an attractive, timbered, country cottage decorated with period furnishings, wooden beams and a fireplace. The extensive wine list covers many modestly priced choices. Traditional international menu. Specialties: truite au bleu, Zürcher rahm schnitzel, poached fresh North Atlantic salmon. Own baking. Hrs: 6 pm-midnight. Closed Sun-Tues; Dec 24, 25; also Jan. Res required. Bar. Wine cellar. Prix fixe: dinner $65. Chef-owned. Jacket. No cr cds accepted.

D

★ ★ **HUDSON'S RIBS & FISH.** *2014 US 9, 3 mi N of I-84, exit 12.* 914/297-5002. E-mail hrf@aol.com. Seafood menu. Specializes in fresh seafood, hand-cut meat, babyback ribs. Own baking. Hrs: 4-10 pm; Fri, Sat to 11 pm; Sun to 9 pm. Bar. Semi-a la carte: dinner $12-$18. Child's meals. New England nautical decor; lobster traps, fish nets and picture windows abound. Cr cds: A, D, DS, MC, V.

D 🍽

★ ★ ★ **INN AT OSBORNE HILL.** *150 Osborne Hill Rd.* 914/897-3055. E-mail chefnola@aol.com. Specialties: breast of duck, loin of veal. Hrs: 11:30 am-2:30 pm, 5-9 pm; Fri, Sat 5-10 pm. Closed Sun; major hols. Res accepted. Bar. Wine list. Semi-a la carte: lunch $6-$9.95, dinner $11.95-$21.95. Child's meals. Outdoor dining. Built in 1935 as summer boarding house. Cr cds: A, D, MC, V.

D SC 🍽

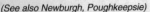

Floral Park, L.I.

(D-5 see New York City map)

(See also Garden City, Hempstead, New York City)

Pop 15,947 **Elev** 95 ft **Area code** 516

John Lewis Childs started a florist and seed business here in the 1870s. He planted the village with acres of flowers, which even lined the railroad tracks for over a mile, and had the town's name changed from East Hinsdale to Floral Park.

Motel

★★ **FLORAL PARK MOTOR LODGE.** *30 Jericho Tpke (11001), ¾ mi E of Cross Island Pkwy exit 27E. 516/775-7777; FAX 516/775-0451; res: 800/255-9680.* E-mail fpmotorlodge@mindspring.com; web www.floralparkmotorlodge.com. 107 rms, 3 story. S $87-$109; D $97-$140; under 18 free; higher rates Belmont races. Crib free. TV; cable (premium), VCR avail. Complimentary continental bkfst. Restaurant nearby. Ck-out noon. Meeting rms. Business servs avail. Health club privileges. Cr cds: A, C, D, DS, JCB, MC, V.

Restaurants

★★ **ARTURO'S.** *(246-04 Jericho Tpke, Bellerose 11001) 3 blks E of Cross Island Pkwy exit 27E. 516/352-7418.* Italian menu. Specialties: rigatoni with porcini mushrooms, Dover sole, veal chop. Own baking. Hrs: noon-3 pm, 5:30-10 pm; Fri, Sat to 11:30 pm; Sun 3-9:30 pm. Closed Easter, Thanksgiving, Dec 25. Res accepted. Bar. Semi-a la carte: lunch, dinner $9-$26. Cr cds: A, C, D, DS, MC, V.

★★ **CRABTREE'S.** *226 Jericho Tpke (11001). 516/326-7769.* Specializes in fish, fresh pasta, fresh seafood. Hrs: noon-10 pm; Fri, Sat to 11 pm; Sun brunch noon-4 pm. Closed Mon; Jan 1, Thanksgiving, Dec 25. Res accepted. Bar to midnight. A la carte entrees: lunch $5.95-$11.95, dinner $9.95-$18.95. Outdoor dining. Cr cds: A, C, D, MC, V.

★★ **MAGNOLIA GRILLE.** *(230 Jericho Tpke, Floral Park 11001) 516/354-8185.* Specialties: chicken pot pie, pot roast, seared salmon. Own baking. Hrs: noon-10:30 pm; Fri, Sat to 11:30 pm; Sun brunch 11:30 am-3:30 pm. Closed July 4, Dec 25. Res accepted. Bar. Semi-a la carte: lunch $5.95-$12.95, dinner $8.95-$17.95. Sun brunch $9.95. Child's meals. Entertainment Thurs, Sat. Two-level dining with many plants, skylights. Cr cds: A, D, DS, MC, V.

★ **STELLA RISTORANTE.** *152 Jericho Tpke. 516/775-2202.* Italian menu. Specialty: osso buco. Own pasta. Hrs: 11:30 am, 4-10 pm; Fri to 11 pm; Sat 4-11 pm; Sun 1-9:30 pm. Closed Mon; Thanksgiving, Dec 25. Res accepted. Bar. A la carte entrees: dinner $8.95-$22.95. Parking. Italian artwork. Family-owned. Cr cds: A, C, D, MC, V.

★ **VICTOR KOENIG'S.** *86 S Tyson Ave (11001), 1 mi E of Cross Island Pkwy exit 27E. 516/354-2300.* German, Amer menu. Specialties: sauerbraten, Wienerschnitzel, L.I. duckling. Hrs: noon-11 pm; Fri, Sat to 1 am. Res required wkends. Bar. A la carte entrees: lunch $4.25-$8.50. Complete meals: dinner $9.25-$18. Child's meals. Parking. Cr cds: A, C, D, MC, V.

Fulton (D-5)

(See also Oswego, Syracuse)

Pop 12,929 **Elev** 360 ft **Area code** 315 **Zip** 13069
Information Chamber of Commerce, 41 S Second St, Box 148; 315/598-4231.

What to See and Do

Battle Island State Park. N on NY 48. 18-hole golf (fee). Cross-country skiing. Concession. Phone 315/593-3408.

Motel

✓★★ **FULTON MOTOR LODGE.** *163 S 1st St, at Academy St, on river. 315/598-6100; FAX 315/592-4738; res: 800/223-6935.* 70 rms, 2 story. S $48-$79; D $55-$90; each addl $8; suites $72-$92. Crib free. Pet accepted. TV; cable (premium). Pool. Complimentary full bkfst. Ck-out noon. Meeting rms. Business servs avail. Valet serv. Exercise equipt. Business servs avail. Bathrm phones, refrigerators. Cr cds: A, D, DS, MC, V.

Restaurant

✓★★ **LOCK III.** *24 S 1st St. 315/598-6900.* Continental menu. Specializes in steak, chicken, seafood. Salad bar. Hrs: 11:30 am-2:30 pm, 4:30-10 pm; Sun noon-9 pm; early-bird dinner Mon-Sat 4:30-6 pm. Closed Memorial Day, July 4, Dec 25. Res accepted; required hols. Bar to 2 am. Semi-a la carte: lunch $3.95-$5.95, dinner $10.95-$14.95. Child's meals. Jazz Fri. Outdoor dining. Dining rm has view of river; overlooks Barge Canal. Cr cds: A, C, D, MC, V.

Garden City, L.I. (B-2)

(See also Floral Park, Hempstead, New York City, Westbury)

Pop 21,686 **Elev** 90 ft **Area code** 516 **Zip** 11530
Information Chamber of Commerce, 230 Seventh St; 516/746-7724.

Annual Event

Antique Car Parade. Franklin Ave. More than 300 antique and vintage cars. Easter Sun.

Hotels

★★★ **THE GARDEN CITY.** *45 Seventh St, 2 mi N of Southern State Pkwy exit 19N; 5 mi S of Northern State Pkwy exit 26; across from L. I. Railroad station. 516/747-3000; FAX 516/747-1414; res: 800/547-0400 (exc NY).* Web www.gch.com. 273 rms, 16 kits. S $225-$385; D $205-$385; each addl $20; suites $485-$1,650; under 12 free; wkly, wkend rates. Crib free. Pet accepted. TV; VCR avail. Indoor pool; lifeguard. Restaurant 6:30 am-11 pm. Rm serv 24 hrs. Bar 11:30-2 am; entertainment. Ck-out noon. Convention facilities. Business servs avail. In-rm modem link. Concierge. Shopping arcade. Beauty shop. Free parking. Exercise rm; sauna. Massage. Bathrm phones; some refrigerators. Balconies. Cr cds: A, C, D, DS, JCB, MC, V.

★★★ **LONG ISLAND MARRIOTT.** *(101 James Doolittle Blvd, Uniondale 11553) off Meadowbrook Pkwy exit M4. 516/794-3800; FAX*

516/794-5936. 617 rms, 11 story. S, D $159-$229; each addl $20; suites $350-$650; under 18 free; wknd rates. Crib free. Pet accepted, some restrictions. TV; cable (premium), VCR avail. Indoor pool; whirlpool, poolside serv, lifeguard. Restaurant 6:30 am-11 pm. Rm serv to midnight. Bar 11-2 am. Ck-out noon. Convention facilities. Business center. In-rm modem link. Barber, beauty shop. Exercise equipt; sauna. Game rm. Refrigerators, microwaves avail. Balconies. Adj Nassau Coliseum. Cr cds: A, C, D, DS, ER, JCB, MC, V.

Restaurants

★ ★ **AKBAR.** *One Ring Rd West, at Roosevelt Field.* 516/248-5700. Northern Indian menu. Hrs: noon-3 pm, 5:30-10 pm; Fri, Sat to 11 pm; Sun noon-3 pm, 5-10 pm; Sun brunch to 3 pm. Res required. Serv bar. Buffet: lunch $8.99, dinner (Sun) $15.99. A la carte entrees: dinner $9.95-$21.95. Indian decor. Cr cds: A, D, DS, MC, V.

★ ★ **ORCHID.** *730 Franklin Ave.* 516/742-1116. Chinese menu. Specializes in Hunan and Szechwan dishes. Hrs: 11:30 am-10 pm; Fri to 11 pm; Sat noon-11 pm; Sun 1-10 pm. Closed Thanksgiving. Res required. Bar. A la carte entrees: lunch $6.25-$8.95, dinner $15-$20. Elaborate decor; etched glass and murals. Cr cds: A, D, MC, V.

Garrison (A-2)

(See also Fishkill, Mahopac, Peekskill)

Pop 800 (est) **Elev** 21 ft **Area code** 914 **Zip** 10524

What to See and Do

Foundry School Museum. Old-fashioned schoolrm; West Point Foundry memorabilia, paintings, Native American artifacts, antiques; changing exhibits; genealogy and historical research library. Maintained by the Putnam County Historical Society. (Mar-Dec, Tues-Thurs & Sun, also by appt) 4 mi N on NY 9D, at 63 Chestnut St in Cold Spring. Phone 914/265-4010. **Free.**

Inns

★ ★ **THE BIRD & BOTTLE.** *Old Albany Post Rd (US 9), I-84 exit 13, 8 mi S on US 9.* 914/424-3000; res: 800/782-6837; FAX 914/424-3283. E-mail birdbottle@aol.com. 4 rms, 1-2 story. No rm phones. MAP: S, D $210-$240. Children over 12 yrs only. Complimentary full bkfst. Restaurant (see THE BIRD & BOTTLE INN). Ck-out noon, ck-in 2 pm. Business servs avail. Restored Colonial building (1761); many antique furnishings. Cr cds: A, MC, V.

★ ★ **HUDSON HOUSE.** *(2 Main St, Cold Spring 10516)* N on US 9 to 301 W. 914/265-9355; FAX 914/265-4532. E-mail hudhouse@computer.net; web www.hudsonhouseinn.com. 13 rms, 2 story, 1 suite. No rm phones. Apr-Dec, MAP: D $150; each addl $15; suite $180; lower rates rest of yr. Crib free. TV in sitting rm; cable, VCR avail. Complimentary full bkfst. Restaurant (see HUDSON HOUSE). Ck-out 11 am, ck-in 3 pm. Business servs avail. X-country ski 10 mi. Balconies. Picnic tables. Country inn (1832) on banks of Hudson River. Cr cds: A, MC, V.

Restaurants

★ ★ **THE BIRD & BOTTLE INN.** *(See The Bird & Bottle Inn)* 914/424-3000. E-mail birdbottle@aol.com. Continental menu. Specializes in fresh fish, chicken. Hrs: noon-3 pm, 6-9 pm; Sat 2 sittings 6 & 9 pm; Sun 4:30-7 pm; Sun brunch noon-2 pm. Closed Mon, Tues. Res accepted. Bar.

Complete meal: dinner $36.95-$51.95. Sun brunch $16.95-$23.95. Outdoor dining. Fireside dining in restored 18th-century tavern. Cr cds: A, MC, V.

★ ★ **HUDSON HOUSE.** *(See Hudson House Inn)* 914/265-9355. E-mail hud house @computer.net; web www.hudsonhouseinn.com. Specializes in fresh fish, game, smoked foods. Own desserts. Hrs: 11:30 am-3:30 pm, 5:30-9 pm; Fri, Sat to 10 pm; Sun 11:30 am-8 pm. Closed Dec 25. Res accepted; required wknds. Bar. Semi-a la carte: lunch $7.50-$16.95, dinner $17.50-$26.75. Child's meals. Built 1832. Overlooks river. Cr cds: A, MC, V.

★ ★ **PLUMBUSH INN.** *(NY 9D, Cold Spring 10516)* 8 mi N Bear Mt Bridge, or 1/2 mi S NY 301. 914/265-3904. Continental menu. Specialties: trout, Swiss apple fritters, medallions of veal. Own baking. Hrs: noon-2 pm, 5:30-9:30 pm; Sun noon-8 pm; Sun brunch to 3 pm. Closed Mon, Tues. Res accepted; required wknds. Bar. Semi-a la carte: lunch $8.50-$11.95. Complete meals: dinner from $32.50. Sun brunch $16.50. Valet parking. Fireplaces. Paintings by local artists displayed. 3 guest rms avail. Cr cds: A, MC, V.

★ ★ ★ **XAVIAR'S.** *NY 9D, at Highland Country Club,* 4 1/2 mi N of Bear Mt Bridge on Rt 9D. 914/424-4228. E-mail xavairs@weddings.com. Extensive floral arrangements give a romantic touch to this elegant dining room. Outdoor dining on a large terrace affords a view of a golf course. Continental menu. Specializes in contemporary cuisine. Hrs: 6-9 pm; Sun brunch 11:30 am-2 pm. Closed Mon-Thurs; some major hols; also mid-Jan-mid-Feb. Res required. Serv bar. Wine cellar. Prix fixe: dinner $75. Sun brunch $32. Child's meals. Entertainment Fri, Sat. No cr cds accepted.

Geneseo (D-3)

(See also Avon)

Pop 7,187 **Elev** 800 ft **Area code** 716 **Zip** 14454

What to See and Do

Letchworth State Park (see). 5 mi SW on I-390.

Livingston County Historical Museum. Pioneer exhibits, antique toys, Native American artifacts housed in Cobblestone School (1838); Shaker Colony Fountain Stone, farm items; antique fire equipment. (May-Oct, Sun & Thurs afternoons; summer, also Tues eves) 30 Center St. Phone 716/243-9147. **Donation.**

Motel

★ ★ **DAYS INN.** *4242 Lakeville Rd.* 716/243-0500; FAX 716/243-9007. 76 rms, 1-2 story. S $59-$74; D $65-$80; each addl $8; under 18 free; ski plan. Crib free. TV; cable (premium). Pool. Restaurant adj open 24 hrs. Ck-out noon. Meeting rms. Business servs avail. Sundries. X-country ski 6 mi. Cr cds: A, C, D, DS, JCB, MC, V.

Geneva (D-4)

Settled 1788 **Pop** 14,143 **Elev** 460 ft **Area code** 315 **Zip** 14456 **E-mail** gencham@epix.net **Web** www.genevany.com

Information Chamber of Commerce, 35 Lakefront Dr, Box 587; 315/789-1776.

In the 19th century Geneva attracted large numbers of retired ministers and spinsters and became known as "the saints' retreat and old maids' paradise." Today, Geneva is known as a "fisherman's paradise." Located at the foot of Seneca Lake, the deepest of the Finger Lakes, the town is surrounded by rich farmland with nurseries on the outskirts of the city.

What to See and Do

Geneva Historical Society Museum (Prouty-Chew House). 1829 Federal-style home with items of local history; changing exhibits. (July & Aug, daily exc Mon; rest of yr, Tues-Sat; closed hols) 543 S Main St. Phone 315/789-5151. **Free.**

Rose Hill Mansion (1839). Elegant country estate; Greek-revival architecture; Empire furnishings. Guided tours (May-Oct, Mon-Sat, also Sun afternoons). 3 mi E on NE shore of Seneca Lake on NY 96A, just S of US 20, use NY Thrwy exit 41 or 42. Phone 315/789-3848. **¢¢**

Sampson State Park. Swimming beach, bathhouse; fishing; boating (launch, marina); hiking; tennis. Picnicking, playground. Tent & trailer sites (mid-Apr-late Nov). 11 mi S on NY 96A. Phone 315/585-6392. Per vehicle (mid-May-Labor Day, wkends & hols) **¢¢**

Seneca Lake State Park. Swimming beach, bathhouse; fishing; boating (launch, marina). Picnicking, playground. 1 mi E on US 20 (NY 5). Phone 315/789-2331. Per vehicle **¢¢**

Smith Opera House for the Performing Arts (1894). Alternates films with theater, concerts, children's shows. Tours. (Mon-Fri) 82 Seneca St. Phone 315/781-LIVE. **¢¢**

Annual Events

National Trout Derby. Memorial Day wkend.

Seneca Lake Whale Watch. Lakeshore Park. 3 days of music, arts & crafts, food. Aug.

Inns

★ ★ ★ **BELHURST CASTLE.** Box 609, Lochland Rd, on NY 14. 315/781-0201. Web www.genevany.com. 13 rms, 3 story. May-Oct: S, D $105-$220; suites $240-$315; lower rates rest of yr. Crib $10. TV; cable. Restaurant (see BELHURST CASTLE). Bar 11-1 am. Ck-out 11 am, ck-in 3 pm. Balconies. Turreted, Romanesque mansion (1885) on Seneca Lake; extensive grounds, elaborate landscaping. Elegant antique furnishings; stained-glass windows. Cr cds: MC, V.

★ ★ ★ **GENEVA ON THE LAKE.** 1001 Lochland Rd (Rte 14S). 315/789-7190; FAX 315/789-0322; res: 800/343-6382. Web www.genevaonthelake.com. 30 kit. suites, 3 story. June 1-Nov 21: kit. suites $193-$495; each addl over 18, $30; 13-17, $10; under 12 free; wkly rates; lower rates rest of yr. Crib avail. TV; cable (premium), VCR avail (movies). Pool. Complimentary continental bkfst. Ck-out noon, ck-in 3 pm. Meeting rms. Business servs avail. Luggage handling. Valet serv. Gift shop. Tennis privileges. 18-hole golf privileges. Health club privileges. Private lakefront, sailboats. Refrigerators; some fireplaces. Some private patios, balconies. Picnic tables, grills. Italianate Renaissance villa (1912) overlooks Seneca Lake. Many antiques. Cr cds: A, DS, MC, V.

Restaurants

★ ★ ★ **BELHURST CASTLE.** (See Belhurst Castle Inn) 315/781-0201. Continental menu. Specializes in veal, seafood, prime rib. Hrs: 11 am-2 pm, 5-9:30 pm; Sun 3:30-9 pm; Sun brunch 11 am-2 pm. Res accepted. Bar to 1 am. Wine list. Semi-a la carte: lunch $5.95-$7.95, dinner $16-$30. Sun brunch $14.95. Child's meals. 19th-century Romanesque mansion with view of lake and gardens; was speakeasy & casino during Prohibition. Cr cds: MC, V.

★ ★ **EMILE'S.** 3 mi E on US 20 (NY 5). 315/789-2775. Continental menu. Specializes: prime rib, baby back ribs. Salad bar. Hrs: 11 am-2 pm, 5-9 pm; Fri, Sat to 10 pm. Closed Mon; Thanksgiving, Dec 25. Res accepted. Bar. Semi-a la carte: lunch $3-$5.95, dinner $7.95-$17.95. Child's meals. Casual dining. Cr cds: A, MC, V.

Glen Cove, L.I. (B-2)

(See also Jericho, Oyster Bay, Port Washington)

Pop 24,149 **Elev** 133 ft **Area code** 516 **Zip** 11542 **Web** www.glencove-li.com

Information Chamber of Commerce, 14 Glen St, Ste 303, PO Box 721; 516/676-6666.

What to See and Do

Garvies Point Museum and Preserve. Exhibits devoted to regional geology and Native American archaeology. The preserve incl 62 acres of glacial moraine covered by forest; high cliffs along the shoreline of Long Island Sound. There are 5 mi of trails throughout the preserve. (Daily exc Mon; closed hols) Barry Dr . Phone 516/571-8010. **¢**

Restaurants

★ ★ **BARNEY'S.** (315 Buckram Rd, Locust Valley 11560) 2 mi E on Forest Ave E, at Buckram & Bayville Sts. 516/671-6300. Specialties: L.I. duck, rack of lamb, crab cakes. Hrs: 5:30-10 pm; Fri, Sat to 11 pm; Sun 5-9 pm. Closed Mon; Dec 25. Res accepted Sat. Bar 5-10 pm, wkends to 1 am. A la carte entrees: dinner $20-$30. Prix fixe: 3 courses $25. Menu changes seasonally. Firehouse antiques and memorabilia. Cr cds: A, MC, V.

★ ★ **LA BUSSOLA.** 40 School St. 516/671-2100. Italian menu. Specializes in veal, pasta, seafood. Hrs: noon-10 pm; Sat 5-11 pm; Sun 3-9 pm. Closed some major hols. Res accepted. Bar. A la carte entrees: lunch $7-$19.50, dinner $11-$25. Cr cds: A, C, D, DS, MC, V.

★ ★ ★ **LA PACE.** 51 Cedar Swamp Rd. 516/671-2970. Northern Italian menu. Own baking. Hrs: noon-2:30 pm, 6-10 pm; Sat 6-11 pm; Sun 4-10 pm. Closed Easter, Dec 25. Res accepted. Bar. Wine cellar. A la carte entrees: lunch, dinner $14.95-$21.95. Prix fixe: dinner $25. Valet parking. Fireplaces. Cr cds: A, C, D, MC, V.

★ ★ ★ **VERANDA.** 75 Cedar Swamp Rd. 516/759-0394. Northern Italian menu. Specializes in chicken, veal, fish. Hrs: noon-3 pm, 5:30-10 pm; Sat to 11 pm; Sun 2-10 pm. Closed Jan 1, Dec 25. Res required. Bar. Wine list. A la carte entrees: lunch $7.95-$13.95, dinner $14.95-$26.95. Complete meals (exc Sat): dinner $20-$25. Valet parking. Fireplace, artwork. Cr cds: A, C, D, MC, V.

Glens Falls (D-8)

(See also Lake George Village, Lake Luzerne, Saratoga Springs)

Settled 1763 **Pop** 15,023 **Elev** 340 ft **Area code** 518 **Zip** 12801
Information Adirondack Regional Chambers of Commerce, 136 Warren St; 518/798-1761.

The Iroquois called what is now Glens Falls "Chepontuc," a word meaning "a difficult place to get around." Surrounded by the Adirondack Mountains and adjacent to the 60-foot drop in the Hudson River, the area was settled by Abraham Wing, a Quaker.

What to See and Do

Cross-country skiing. Glens Falls Intl Cross-Country Ski Trails, contact Recreational Dept; 518/761-3813.   **Free.**

Hyde Collection. Art museum in original collector's home. Emphasis on 15th-20th century art, incl Rembrandt, Rubens, Picasso, El Greco; sculptures, antique furniture; films and lectures. (Daily exc Mon; closed major hols) 161 Warren St. Phone 518/792-1761.   **Free.**

The Chapman Historical Museum. Victorian/Second Empire home (1868). Major portion has been redecorated as a period home reflecting 1865 & 1910. Gallery with rotating exhibits on Glens Falls, Queensbury and the southern Adirondacks. Large photographic library featuring collection of Seneca Ray Stoddard. (Tues-Sat; closed hols) 348 Glen St. Phone 518/793-2826.   ¢

West Mt Ski Resort. Triple, 2 double chairlifts, 2 rope tows, J-bar; night skiing; patrol, school, rentals; snowmaking; cafeterias, bar; shop, lodge. Longest run 7,800 ft; vertical drop 1,010 ft. (Dec-Apr, daily; closed Dec 25) I-87 exit 18, 3 mi W on Corinth Rd, then ¼ mi N on West Mt Rd. Phone 518/793-6606.   ¢¢¢¢¢

Seasonal Event

Lake George Opera Festival. Productions range from standard fare to new American works. Performances in English, with full orchestra. Cruises on Lake George (Sun eve). Contact Box 2172; 518/793-3858. Late July-early Aug.

Motels

✔★ **ALPENHAUS.** *851 Lake George Rd (Rte 9) (12804), I-87 exit 19.* 518/792-6941. 15 rms. Late June-early Sept: S $65-$80; D $72-$88; each addl $5; higher rates racing season; lower rates rest of yr. Crib $5. TV; cable. Restaurant nearby. Ck-out 11 am. Downhill ski 5 mi; x-country ski 1 mi. Alpine decor. Cr cds: A, MC, V.

[D] [≈] [⊠] [⛷]

★ **BROWN'S WELCOME INN.** *(53 Lake George Rd, Queensbury 12804)* N on I-87, exit 19, N on US 9. 518/792-9576; res: 800/780-7047. 20 rms, 5 with shower only. July-Labor Day: S $65-$85; D $65-$95; each addl $5; lower rates mid-May-June, Labor Day-mid-Oct. Closed rest of yr. Crib $5. TV; cable (premium). Pool. Playground. Complimentary coffee in rms. Restaurant adj 8 am-10 pm. Ck-out 10:30 am. Some refrigerators. Picnic tables. Cr cds: A, DS, MC, V.

[D] [≈] [⛷] [SC]

★★ **GRAYCOURT.** *(1082 US 9, Queensbury 12804)* 3½ mi N on US 9. 518/792-0223; FAX 518/792-2003. 25 units, 4 with shower only, 5 cottages. July-Labor Day: S $75; D $95; each addl $5; cottages $120-$140; under 12 free; lower rates rest of yr. Closed late Sept-Memorial Day. Crib $5. TV; cable. Complimentary coffee in rms. Restaurant adj 7 am-5:30 pm. Ck-out 11 am. Heated pool. Playground. Many refrigerators. Picnic tables, grills. Cr cds: A, DS, MC, V.

[≈] [⛷]

★★ **LANDMARK.** *Box 376, 5½ mi S on US 9, 1 mi N of I-87 exit 17N.* 518/793-3441; FAX 518/761-6909; res: 800/541-3441. 74 rms. Mid-July-Aug: S $85-$90; D $95-$105; each addl $5; higher rates hols, racing season; lower rates rest of yr. Crib $3-$5. TV; cable (premium). 2 pools, 1 indoor; whirlpool. Playground. Restaurant adj 6 am-11 pm. Ck-out 11 am. Meeting rm. Business servs avail. Airport, bus depot transportation. Putting green. Downhill ski 6 mi; x-country ski 3 mi. Rec rm. Exercise equipt. Game rm. Lawn games. Refrigerators avail. Picnic tables, grills. Cr cds: A, C, D, DS, MC, V.

[D] [≈] [✈] [⛷] [⊠] [⛷] [SC]

✔★ **SUPER 8.** *(191 Corinth Rd, Queensbury 12804)* I-87 exit 18. 518/761-9780; FAX 518/761-1049. 59 rms, 2 story. July: S $48-$50; D $55-$57; each addl $6; under 12 free; higher rates: wknds, special events; lower rates rest of yr. Crib free. TV; cable, VCR avail (movies). Complimentary coffee in lobby. Restaurant nearby. Ck-out 11 am. Downhill/x-country ski 10 mi. Cr cds: A, D, DS, MC, V.

[D] [⛷] [⊠] [⛷] [SC]

Motor Hotel

★★ **RAMADA INN.** *(Abby Ln, Queensbury 12804)* 1 mi N on NY 254 at I-87 exit 19, ⅛ mi W of US 9. 518/793-7701; FAX 518/792-5463. 110 rms, 2 story. Late July-early Sept: S, D $69-$125; each addl $10; under 17 free; higher rates racing season; lower rates rest of yr. Crib free. TV; cable (premium). Indoor pool. Complimentary coffee in rms. Restaurant 6:30 am-10 pm. Rm serv. Bar 5 pm-midnight. Ck-out noon. Meeting rms. Business servs avail. In-rm modem link. X-country ski 2 mi. Health club privileges. Microwaves avail. Picnic tables. Cr cds: A, C, D, DS, ER, JCB, MC, V.

[D] [≈] [⊠] [⛷] [SC]

Hotel

★★★ **QUEENSBURY.** *88 Ridge St, on NY 9L.* 518/792-1121; FAX 518/792-9259; res: 800/554-4526. E-mail queensbury-hotel@global2000.net; web www.queensburyhotel.com. 126 rms, 5 story. Aug: S, D $135-$195; suites $215-$325; under 18 free; lower rates rest of yr. Crib $10. TV; cable. Indoor pool; whirlpool. Restaurant 7 am-9 pm. Bar 11:30-1 am. Ck-out noon. Meeting rms. Business servs avail. Barber. Downhill ski 4 mi; x-country ski 1 mi. Exercise equipt. Massage. Health club privileges. Cr cds: A, C, D, DS, MC, V.

[D] [⛷] [≈] [✈] [⊠] [⛷] [SC]

Goshen (F-7)

(See also Monroe, Newburgh)

Settled 1714 **Pop** 11,500 **Elev** 440 ft **Area code** 914 **Zip** 10924
Information Chamber of Commerce, 44 Park Place, PO Box 506; 914/294-7741 or 800/884-2563.

This town, in the center of dairying and onion-growing country, has long been famous for harness racing.

What to See and Do

Brotherhood Winery (America's Oldest Winery). Tours, wine tasting. (May-Oct, daily; rest of yr, wknds; closed Jan 1, Dec 25) NY Thrwy to exit 16, NY 17W to exit 130, NY 208N to Washingtonville. Phone 914/496-9101.   ¢¢

Goshen Historic Track. Harness racing's oldest track dates to 1838. Self-guided walking tour. (Daily) (See SEASONAL EVENT) 44 Park Pl. Phone 914/294-5333.   **Free.**

Harness Racing Museum and Hall of Fame. Home of the Hall of Fame of the Trotter; incl Currier & Ives trotting prints; paintings; statues; dioramas of famous horses; library. Harness racing simulator; interactive exhibits. Tours by appt. (Daily; closed Jan 1, Thanksgiving, Dec 25) 240 Main St. Phone 914/294-6330. **¢¢¢**

Annual Event

Great American Weekend. Arts & crafts, entertainment, rides, races. July 3-4.

Seasonal Event

Racing. Goshen Historic Track. Grand Circuit; County Fair Sire Stakes; matinee racing. Phone 914/294-5333. 3 Sat June & 4 days early July.

Great Neck, L.I.

(C-5 see New York City map)

(See also New York City, Port Washington)

Pop 8,745 **Elev** 100 ft **Area code** 516
Information Chamber of Commerce, 643 Middleneck Rd, 11023; 516/487-2000.

Consisting of nine villages and an unincorporated area, the population would be approximately 41,500 if added together.

What to See and Do

US Merchant Marine Academy (1943). (950 midshipmen) Memorial Chapel honoring war dead. Visitors welcome (daily; closed federal hols & July). Regimental Reviews (spring & fall, Sat; schedule varies). The American Merchant Marine Museum is open (Tues, Wed, Sat & Sun). At Kings Point. Phone 516/773-5000. **Free.**

Restaurants

✔★ BRUZELL'S. 451 Middle Neck Rd (11023). 516/482-6600. Continental menu. Specializes in steak, fresh fish. Hrs: noon-2:30 pm, 5-10 pm; wkend hrs vary; Mon from 5 pm; early-bird dinner 5-6 pm. Closed Jan 1, Dec 25. Res accepted. Bar. A la carte entrees: lunch $9.95-$11.95, dinner $13.95-$24.95. Complete meals: lunch $10.95, dinner $16.50. Child's meals. Valet parking wkends. Bi-level dining with art deco decor. Cr cds: A, C, D, DS, MC, V.

D

★★ MILLIE'S PLACE. 25 Middle Neck Rd. 516/482-4223. Continental menu. Specializes in pasta with seafood. Hrs: 11:30 am-11 pm; Sun brunch to 4 pm. Closed Thanksgiving, Yom Kippur. Bar. Semi-a la carte: lunch $10-$23, dinner $12-$23. Outdoor dining. Antique mirrors, paintings. Cr cds: A, MC, V.

★★ NAVONA. 218 Middle Neck Rd (11021). 516/487-5603. Italian menu. Specializes in pasta, seafood, steak. Own baking. Hrs: noon-3 pm, 5:30-10 pm; Fri to 11 pm; Sat 5:30-11 pm; Sun 5:30-10 pm. Closed some major hols. Res required. Bar. A la carte entrees: lunch $9-$12, dinner $15.25-$24.75. Cr cds: A, C, D, MC, V.

D

★★ RISTORANTE BEVANDA. 570 Middle Neck Rd (11023). 516/482-1510. Italian menu. Specialties: cold & hot antipasto, chicken giardino, salmon dijon. Own pasta. Hrs: Sat 4:30-10:30 pm; Sun 3-9:30 pm. Res required. Bar. A la carte entrees: lunch $10-$16, dinner $15.50-$22.50. Complete meals: lunch $14.95. Old World atmosphere; traditional paintings. Cr cds: A, C, D, MC, V.

D

Greenport, L.I. (A-5)

(See also Riverhead, Shelter Island, Southold)

Pop 2,070 **Elev** 10 ft **Area code** 516 **Zip** 11944

Greenport is a bit of New England on Long Island. There are clean, uncrowded beaches visitors can enjoy as well as several wineries.

What to See and Do

Orient Point, NY-New London, CT, Ferry. 1½-hr crossing. (Daily; closed Dec 25) 1-day round trips. Reservation required for vehicle. 8 mi NE at end of NY 25 in Orient Point. Phone 516/323-2525 or 860/443-5281. **¢¢¢**

Annual Event

Greenport Maritime Festival. Wooden boat regatta, fishing tournament, whale boat race; clam chowder tasting contest. Phone 516/477-0004. Late Sept.

Motels

★ SILVER SANDS. Silvermere Rd, NY 25 to Silvermere Rd. 516/477-0011; FAX 516/477-0922. 35 rms, 15 kit. cottages. Mid-June-mid-Sept: S, D $100-$150; each addl $15; kit. cottages $850-$1,500/wk; wkly rates; lower rates rest of yr. Crib avail. TV; cable. Heated pool; lifeguard. Complimentary continental bkfst. Restaurant nearby. Ck-out 11 am. Game rm. Picnic tables, grills. On bay. Cr cds: A, D, DS, MC, V.

★★ SOUNDVIEW INN. Southold Rd. 516/477-1910; FAX 516/477-9436. 49 rms, 1-2 story. 31 kit. suites. Late June-early Sept: S, D $99; each addl $10; kit. suites $130-$275; lower rates rest of yr. TV; cable, VCR avail. Pool. Restaurant noon-10 pm. Bar; entertainment wkends, dinner theater Wed evenings in season. Ck-out noon. Meeting rms. Tennis. Golf privileges. Sauna. Refrigerators. On beach. Cr cds: A, C, D, DS, MC, V.

★ SUNSET. 62005 County Rd 48. 516/477-1776. 11 rms, 1-2 story, 11 kits. Mid-June-mid-Sept, Memorial Day wkend (3-day min; hol wkends 4-day min): D $95-$160; each addl $10; kit. units $115-$160; lower rates mid-Apr-mid-June, mid-Sept-Oct. Closed rest of yr. Crib free. TV; cable. Restaurant nearby. Ck-out 11 am. Tennis privileges. Lawn games. Porches. Picnic tables, grills. Private beach. Cr cds: DS, MC, V.

Restaurants

✔★ CHOWDER POT PUB. 104 Third St. 516/477-1345. Specialties: New England and Manhattan chowders. Hrs: noon-2:30 pm, 5-9 pm; Fri, Sat to 10 pm. Closed Mon; also winter wkdays. Res accepted. Bar. Semi-a la carte: lunch $3.75-$12.50, dinner $12.95-$15.75. Outdoor dining. Cr cds: A, MC, V.

D

★★ CLAUDIO'S. 111 Main St. 516/477-0627. Specializes in seafood, steak. Hrs: 11:30 am-10 pm; Fri, Sat to 11 pm. Res accepted. Bar. Semi-a la carte: lunch $9.95-$12.95, dinner $14.95-$22.95. Entertainment. Parking. Outdoor dining. Clam bar on dock. Souvenirs of America's Cup defenders decorate walls. View of fishing harbor. Family-owned for more than 100 yrs. Cr cds: MC, V.

Greenwich (D-8)

(See also Saratoga Springs)

Pop 4,557 **Elev** 360 ft **Area code** 518 **Zip** 12834

What to See and Do

Bennington Battlefield State Historic Site. Battlefield where militiamen under Brigadier General John Stark stopped a force of British sharpshooters, mercenaries, Loyalists and Native Americans in August 1777. Hilltop view; relief map, picnic tables. View of monument in Vermont. (May-Oct, daily) 7 mi SE via NY 372, 6 mi S on NY 22, & 2 mi E on NY 67, E of N Hoosick, in the town of Walloomsac. Phone 518/686-7109. **Free.**

Willard Mt Ski Area. Chairlift, T-bar, pony lift; patrol, school, rentals; snowmaking; bar & snack bar; ski shop. Longest run 3,500 ft; vertical drop 505 ft. (Early Dec-late Mar, daily; closed Thanksgiving, Dec 25) 6 mi S on NY 40.Phone 518/692-7337. ¢¢¢¢-¢¢¢¢¢

Restaurant

★ **WALLIE'S OF GREENWICH.** *56 Main St.* 518/692-7823. Specializes in prime rib, seafood. Hrs: 4-9 pm; Fri, Sat to 10 pm; Sun noon-9 pm; early-bird dinner Wed-Sat 4-6 pm. Closed Mon; Dec 24, 25. Bar. Complete meals: dinner $9.95-$23.95. Child's meals. Cr cds: MC, V.

Hague (Lake George Area) (C-8)

(See also Crown Point)

Pop 699 **Elev** 328 ft **Area code** 518 **Zip** 12836
Information Chamber of Commerce; 518/543-6353.

Hague is a resort community on the western shore of Lake George, near its northern tip.

What to See and Do

Rogers Rock State Public Campground. Camping (dump station; fee); boating (launch, motors); fishing; swimming, bathhouse, lifeguards; picnicking. (Early May-mid-Oct) 3 mi N on NY 9N, in Adirondack Park (see). Phone 518/585-6746. Day use per vehicle ¢¢

Motel

★ ★ **TROUT HOUSE VILLAGE.** *Lake Shore Dr (NY 9N), 1 blk N on NY 9N, opp lake.* 518/543-6088; res: 800/368-6088. Web www.trouthouse.com. 22 rms in motel, lodge, 3 kits., 5 kit. cottages, 10 kit. chalets, 1-3 story. No A/C. Mid-June-mid-Sept: S, D $65-$94; each addl $5; kit. units to 4, $92-$300; cabins $750-$2,100/wk; ski rates; lower rates rest of yr. Crib free. TV; cable. Ck-out 11 am. Putting green. X-country ski 2 mi. Rec rm. Lawn games. Some fireplaces, in-rm whirlpools. Picnic tables, grill. 400-ft swimming beach; dockage. View of lake. Cr cds: A, DS, MC, V.

 🏂 ⛷️ 🎣 🎿 🖕 **SC**

Hamilton (D-6)

(See also Cazenovia, Oneida)

Settled ca 1794 **Pop** 6,221 **Elev** 1,126 ft **Area code** 315 **Zip** 13346

What to See and Do

Colgate Univ (1819). (2,650 students) A handsome campus with bldgs dating from 1827. The Charles A. Dana Arts Center, designed by Paul Rudolph, houses the Picker Art Gallery (academic yr, daily; closed Jan 1, Easter, Thanksgiving, Dec 25). Broad St & Kendrick Ave. Campus tours, contact Admission Office, Administration Bldg; 315/228-1000.

Rogers Environmental Education Center. Approx 570 acres; visitor center, 350 mounted birds, outdoor exhibits, 3 mi of nature trails, cross-country skiing; trout ponds; observation tower; picnicking. Bldgs (June-Aug, daily; rest of yr, daily exc Sun). Center (daily; closed most major hols). Approx 12 mi S on NY 12 or NY 12B to Sherburne, then 1 mi W on NY 80. Phone 607/674-4017. **Free.**

Inn

★ ★ **COLGATE.** *1-5 Payne St, NY 12B on Village Green.* 315/824-2300; FAX 315/824-4500. 46 rms, 3 story. S $79-$109; D $89-$119; each addl $10; suites $150-$175; under 11 free. Crib free. TV; cable. Complimentary continental bkfst. Restaurant (see PAYNE STREET CORNER). Bar 11:30 am-midnight. Ck-out 11 am, ck-in 3 pm. Meeting rms. Business servs avail. Recreational facilities of Colgate University avail to guests. Some in-rm whirlpools. Cr cds: A, C, D, MC, V.

D 🖕 🖕

Restaurant

★ ★ **PAYNE STREET CORNER.** *(See Colgate Inn)* 315/824-2300. Specializes in fresh seafood, hand-cut steaks. Hrs: 11:30 am-8:30 pm; Fri, Sat to 9:30 pm; Sun brunch 10 am-1 pm. Res accepted. Bar 11:30 am-midnight. Semi-a carte: lunch $4.95-$8.95, dinner $9.95-$15.95. Buffet: lunch $5.95. Sun brunch $12.95. Child's meals. Outdoor dining. Early American tavern; fireplace. Cr cds: A, C, D, MC, V.

D

Hammondsport (E-4)

(See also Bath, Penn Yan)

Pop 929 **Elev** 743 ft **Area code** 607 **Zip** 14840

This is the center of the New York State wine industry, at the southern tip of Keuka Lake. The grape growers are mainly of German and Swiss origin. They have more than a century of viticulture in New York State behind them, dating from 1829, when the Rev. William Bostwick planted the first vineyard. Glenn H. Curtiss, a pioneer aviator, was born here; most of his early experimental flights took place in this area.

What to See and Do

Glenn H. Curtiss Museum. Curtiss memorabilia; historical aircraft; local history exhibits 1860-1948. Changing exhibits, restoration shop. (Apr-Dec, daily; winter hrs vary; closed most major hols) NY 54. Phone 607/569-2160. ¢¢

Wine & Grape Museum of Greyton H. Taylor. Vineyard equipment, exhibits on early champagne, wine and brandy production; presidential wine glass collection; barrel-making housed in old area winery (1880-1920). Tours. (May-Oct, daily) G.H. Taylor Memorial Dr, 1 mi N off NY 54A, W side of Keuka Lake. Phone 607/868-4814. **Donation.**

Winery tours. There are 9 wineries around Keuka Lake that have tasting rms and/or tours. For more info contact the Wine Country Tourism Assn, 607/569-2474.

Motel

✔★ **HAMMONDSPORT.** *William St, 2 blks N on NY 54A, on lake. 607/569-2600.* 17 rms. Apr-mid-Nov: S $55; D $60; each addl $9. Closed rest of yr. Crib $9. TV; cable. Ck-out 11 am. Dock, boat launch. On Keuka Lake; swimming. Cr cds: MC, V.

SC

Inn

★★ **THE BLUSING ROSÉ.** *11 William St. 607/569-3402; res: 800/982-8818; FAX 607/569-2504.* 4 rms, 3 with shower only. No rm phones. S $75-$85; D $85-$105; each addl $15; wkends 2-day min. Children over 12 yrs only. TV in common rm; cable (premium), VCR avail. Complimentary full bkfst; afternoon refreshments. Restaurant nearby. Ck-out 11 am, ck-in 3 pm. Luggage handling. Built in 1843; antiques. Totally nonsmoking. No cr cds accepted.

SC

Restaurant

★★★ **SNUG HARBOR.** *144 W Lake Rd. 607/868-3488.* Modern Amer menu. Specializes in steaks, seafood. Hrs: 11 am-10 pm; early-bird dinner 4-6 pm. Closed Dec 24, 25. Res accepted. Bar. Wine list. Semi-a la carte: lunch $2.50-$6.95, dinner $12.95-$21.95. Child's meals. Outdoor dining overlooking Keuka Lake. 5 dining areas in 1890 house. Overnight stay avail. Cr cds: A, DS, MC, V.

D

Hampton Bays, L.I. (B-4)

(See also Riverhead, Southampton, Westhampton Beach)

Pop 7,893 **Elev** 50 ft **Area code** 516 **Zip** 11946

Motel

★★★ **HAMPTON MAID.** *East Montauk Hwy, 1½ mi S on NY 27A, just E of Shinnecock Canal. 516/728-4166; FAX 516/728-4250.* 30 rms, 1-2 story. July-Aug: D $135-$165; each addl $25-$35; under 3 free; wkly rates off-season; higher rates hol wkends; lower rates mid-Apr-June, Sept-Oct. Closed rest of yr. TV; cable. Pool; lifeguard. Playground. Ck-out 11 am. Business servs avail. Health club privileges. Lawn games. Refrigerators. Private patios, balconies. Picnic tables. Opp bay. Antique shop. Cr cds: A, MC, V.

D

Restaurant

★★ **VILLA PAUL.** *162 Montauk Hwy. 516/728-3261.* Italian, Amer menu. Hrs: 4:30-10 pm. Closed Dec 25. Res accepted. Bar. A la carte entrees: dinner $11.50-$20.95. Late 1800s building; original woodwork in dining area. Family-owned. Cr cds: A, D, MC, V.

D

Hartsdale (A-2)

(See also White Plains)

Pop 9,587 **Elev** 182 ft **Area code** 914 **Zip** 10530

Restaurant

★★★ **AUBERGE ARGENTEUIL.** *42 Healy Ave, NY 287 exit 4. 914/948-0597.* French menu. Specialties: rack of lamb, filet with peppercorn, lobster bisque. Own baking. Hrs: noon-2 pm, 6-9 pm; Sat 6-10 pm; Sun 1-8 pm. Closed Mon; Jan 1, 2. Res accepted; required Fri, Sat. Bar. A la carte entrees: lunch $6.75-$20. Prix fixe: dinner $38. Country French decor. Cr cds: A, D, DS, MC, V.

Hawthorne (A-2)

(See also White Plains)

Pop 4,764 **Elev** 258 ft **Area code** 914 **Zip** 10532

Restaurants

★★ **GASHO OF JAPAN.** *2 Saw Mill River Rd (NY 9A). 914/592-5900.* Japanese menu. Specialties: teriyaki swordfish with broccoli, filet mignon and hibachi chicken combination. Hrs: 11:30 am-2:30 pm, 5-9:30 pm; Fri to 10 pm; Sat noon-2:30 pm, 5-10:30 pm; Sun noon-9 pm. Res required. Bar. Semi-a la carte: lunch $5.95-$19.95, dinner $12.95-$24.75. Child's meals. Tableside cooking. Building moved from Japan; Japanese gardens. Cr cds: A, D, DS, MC, V.

D

★★ **TACONIC BRAUHAUS.** *15 Commerce St, off Taconic State Pkwy. 914/769-9842.* German, Amer menu. Specialties: sauerbraten, Wienerschnitzel. Hrs: noon-3 pm, 5-9 pm; Fri, Sat 5-10 pm. Closed Mon. Res accepted. Bar. A la carte entrees: lunch $6.95-$10, dinner $12.95-$18.95. Child's meals. Entertainment Fri, Sat. German brauhaus atmosphere. Family-owned. Cr cds: A, C, D, DS, MC, V.

SC

Hempstead, L.I. (B-2)

(See also Bethpage, New York City, Rockville Centre)

Pop 49,453 **Elev** 60 ft **Area code** 516

Information Chamber of Commerce, 80 N Franklin, 11550; 516/483-2000.

What to See and Do

African-American Museum. Depicts the scope and depth of the story of African-American people on Long Island and their contributions to the development of its history. Collection of African-American artifacts; changing exhibits. Workshops, seminars, films. (Daily exc Mon; closed major hols) 110 N Franklin St. Phone 516/485-0470. **Free.**

Hofstra Univ (1935). (12,000 students) The Hofstra Museum presents exhibitions in the Emily Lowe Gallery, David Filderman Gallery, Hofstra's Cultural Center and in 9 other areas on campus. (Daily; closed hols) Concerts, lectures, drama productions, arboretum tours and sports events. Campus tours (Mon-Fri). Phone 516/463-6600.

Nassau Veterans Memorial Coliseum. Arena seats 17,000; 60,000 sq ft of exhibition space. Home of the New York Islanders (hockey) and New York Saints (lacrosse); facilities for basketball; ice shows; concerts, stage shows. 2 mi E, on Hempstead Tpke (NY 24). For schedule phone 516/422-9222 or 516/794-9300.

Herkimer (D-7)

(See also Ilion, Utica)

Settled 1725 **Pop** 10,401 **Elev** 407 ft **Area code** 315 **Zip** 13350 **E-mail** hcccomm@ntcnet.com **Web** www.herkimercountyinfo.com

Information Herkimer County Chamber of Commerce, 28 W Main St, PO Box 129, Mohawk 13407; 315/866-7820.

Herkimer is a town that retains pride in its history. General Nicholas Herkimer marched from the fort here to the Battle of Oriskany, one of the Revolution's bloodiest, which took place August 4, 1777. The Gillette trial, basis for Theodore Dreiser's *An American Tragedy,* was held in the Herkimer County Courthouse.

What to See and Do

Herkimer County Historical Society. Mansion contains exhibits of county history. (Mon-Fri; closed hols) 400 N Main St at Court St, on site of Ft Dayton (1776). Phone 315/866-6413. **Free.** Also avail tour of 1834 County Jail (Mon-Fri; closed hols)

Herkimer Home State Historic Site (1752). Gen Nicholas Herkimer lived here; period furnishings. Family cemetery and Gen Herkimer Monument. Visitor center; picnic area. 8 mi E on NY 169 off NY 5S. Phone 315/823-0398 for schedule. **Free.**

Motels

★ ★ **BEST WESTERN-LITTLE FALLS.** (20 Albany St, Little Falls 13365) Approx 7 mi E on NY 5. 315/823-4954; FAX 315/823-4507. 56 rms, 2 story. May-Sept: S $59; D $65; each addl $6; under 12 free; lower rates rest of yr. Crib free. Pet accepted, some restrictions; $10 refundable. TV; cable. Restaurant 6:30 am-2 pm, 5-9 pm; Sun 7 am-1 pm, 5-9 pm. Bar 11 am-2 pm, 5-11 pm. Ck-out noon. Meeting rms. Business servs avail. Game rm. Cr cds: A, C, D, DS, MC, V.

[D] [symbols] SC

✔★ **HERKIMER.** 100 Marginal Rd, adj I-90 Exit 30. 315/866-0490; FAX 315/866-0416. 61 rms, 2 story, 16 kits. July-early Sept: S $46-$68; D $56-$73; each addl $7; kit. units, studio rms $75-$83; under 13 free; wkly rates; lower rates rest of yr. Crib free. Pet accepted, some restrictions. TV; cable. Heated pool. Restaurant adj open 24 hrs. Ck-out 11 am. Coin lndry. Meeting rms. Business servs avail. Sundries. Downhill/x-country ski 7 mi. Picnic tables. Cr cds: A, C, D, DS, MC, V.

[D] [symbols] SC

Restaurant

★ ★ **CANAL SIDE INN.** (395 S Ann St, Little Falls 13365) 5 mi E, off NY 5, adj NY Barge Canal; or 2 mi N of I-90 exit 29A. 315/823-1170. French provincial, continental menu. Specializes in duck, seafood, lamb. Own pastries. Hrs: 5-10 pm. Closed Sun, Mon; most major hols; also Feb-mid-Mar. Res accepted. Bar. Wine list. Semi-a la carte: dinner $14.50-$19. Chef-owned. Cr cds: C, D, MC, V.

[D]

Hillsdale (E-8)

(See also Catskill, Coxsackie, Hudson)

Pop 1,648 **Elev** 700 ft **Area code** 518 **Zip** 12529

Information Columbia County Tourism Department, 401 State St, Hudson 12534; 800/724-1846.

What to See and Do

Catamount Ski Area. Four chairlifts, tow, J-bar; patrol, school, rentals; snowmaking; cafeteria, bar; nursery. Longest run 2 mi; vertical drop 1,000 ft. (Dec-Mar, daily) Half-day rates. 2 mi E of NY 22 on NY 23. Phone 518/325-3200, 413/528-1262 or 800/342-1840 (ski conditions). ¢¢¢¢

Taconic State Park. More than 4,800 acres. Bash Bish Stream and Ore Pit Pond are in the park. Swimming beach, bathhouse; fishing; hiking. Picnicking (all yr). Cross-country skiing. Tent & trailer sites. At Rudd Pond, also boating (launch, rentals). Ice-skating. S edge of town. Phone 518/789-3059. At Copake Falls Area, also nature trails; cabin units; nature & recreation programs. Standard fees. Phone 518/329-3993 or 800/456-CAMP (camping res). Memorial Day-Labor Day ¢¢; Rest of yr **Free.**

Inns

★ ★ ★ **LINDEN VALLEY.** NY 23, 2 mi E on NY 23. 518/325-7100; FAX 518/325-4107. 7 rms, 6 with shower only. July-Aug: S, D $125-$145; wkends (3-day min); lower rates rest of yr. Pet accepted, some restrictions. TV; cable. Complimentary full bkfst. Complimentary coffee in rms. Restaurant adj 6-9 pm. Ck-out 1 pm, ck-in 1 pm. Tennis. Downhill ski adj. Refrigerators, minibars. Some balconies. Large spring-fed pond with sand beach; swimming. Cr cds: A, MC, V.

[symbols]

★ ★ ★ **SIMMON'S WAY VILLAGE INN.** (33 Main St, Millerton 12546) 19 mi S via NY 22 to US 44E (Main St). 518/789-6235; FAX 518/789-6236. E-mail swvi@taconic.net. 10 rms, 3 story. No rm phones. S, D $145-$175 (2-day min wkends); Nov-May: MAP $125/person; ski plans. Crib free. TV in sitting rm; cable. VCR. Complimentary bkfst; afternoon refreshments. Restaurant (see SIMMON'S WAY). Rm serv. Ck-out noon, ck-in 2 pm. Business servs avail. Concierge. X-country skiing. Game rm. Lawn games. European-style inn (1854); original antique furnishings, fireplaces, library. Village setting. Cr cds: A, D, MC, V.

[symbols] SC

★ ★ **SWISS HUTTE.** NY 23, just off NY 23, adj Catamount Ski area. 518/325-3333; FAX 413/528-6201. E-mail 8057@msn.com; web www.swisshutte.com. 15 rms, 2 story. MAP: S $95-$140; D $150-$200; lodge suites $95/person; EP avail; wkly rates; lower rates Mar-Apr, Nov. Pet accepted, some restrictions. TV; cable. Heated pool. Restaurant (see SWISS HUTTE). Bar noon-11:30 pm. Ck-out 11 am, ck-in 2 pm. Meeting rms. Business servs avail. Tennis. Downhill/x-country ski adj. Lawn games. Refrigerators avail. Private patios, balconies. Cr cds: MC, V.

Restaurants

★ ★ ★ ★ **AUBERGINE.** Jct NY 22 & 23. 518/325-3412. Web ww.aubergine.com. This comfortable restaurant has a country French atmosphere with fireplaces, antiques and a garden. French, Amer menu. Specialties: Maine scallop cakes, hot soufflés, seasonal specialties. Own baking. Hrs: from 5:30 pm. Closed Mon, Tues. Res accepted. Bar. Wine cellar. A la carte entrees: dinner $17-$23. Guest rms avail. Chef-owned. Cr cds: MC, V.

★ ★ ★ **SIMMON'S WAY.** (See Simmon's Way Village Inn) 518/789-6235. E-mail swvi@taconic.net. Eclectic, international menu. Specializes in regional dishes, seasonal game. Own baking. Menu changes frequently. Hrs: 6-8 pm; Fri, Sat 5:30-9:30 pm; Sun brunch 11:30 am-2:30 pm. Closed Mon, Tues. Res accepted. Bar. Wine cellar. Semi-a la carte: dinner $16.95-$27.95. Sun brunch $7.50-$12.95. Outdoor dining. Former industrialist's house (1854) with country inn ambience. Cr cds: A, D, MC, V.

★ ★ ★ **SWISS HUTTE.** (See Swiss Hutte Inn) 518/325-3333. Hrs: noon-2 pm, 5:30-9 pm; Mon-Wed from 5:30 pm; Sat to 9:30 pm; Sun noon-3 pm, 5-9 pm. Closed Mon, Tues in winter; also 1 wk in Nov & 1 wk in Mar. Res accepted. Continental menu. Semi-a la carte: lunch $8.50-$14, dinner $17-$28. Child's meals. Specialties: Wienerschnitzel, rack of lamb, steak au poivre. Own baking. Outdoor dining. Swiss alpine decor; brick fireplace. Cr cds: MC, V.

Hornell (E-4)

(See also Bath)

Settled 1799 **Pop** 9,877 **Elev** 1,160 ft **Area code** 607 **Zip** 14843 **E-mail** hacckiwa@servtech.com

Information Hornell Area Chamber of Commerce, 40 Main St; 607/324-0310. A Tourist Information booth is located just off NY 17 at exit 34 and jct NY 36 & 21.

Also known as the "Maple City," Hornell is a scenic and popular gateway to the Finger Lakes Region. Fishing, hunting and outdoor recreation contribute to the town's offerings. Fall foliage is especially brilliant in September and October, in and around Hornell.

What to See and Do

Almond Dam Recreation Area. Incl a 125-acre lake; provides swimming; fishing, boating; hunting; camping facilities. Just W of town, accessible by NY 21 & 36, just off County Rd 66. Contact Chamber of Commerce for details. **Free.**

Stony Brook State Park. Swimming beach, bathhouse. Hiking; tennis. Cross-country skiing. Picnicking, playground, concession. Tent & trailer sites (mid-May-mid-Oct). Standard fees. 13 mi N on NY 36, 3 mi S of Dansville. Phone 716/335-8111. ¢¢

Swain Ski Center. Three quad, double chairlift; patrol, school, rentals; snowmaking; night skiing; restaurants, cafeteria, bar. Longest run 1 mi; vertical drop 650 ft. (Nov-Apr, daily) 8 mi N on NY 36, then 7 mi NW on NY 70 in Swain.Phone 607/545-6511. ¢¢¢¢¢

Motels

★ ★ **COMFORT INN.** 1 Canisteo Square. 607/324-4300; FAX 607/324-4311. 62 rms, 2 story. S $52-$75; D $59-$85; each addl $5; suites $76-$101; under 18 free; higher rates auto racing. Crib free. TV; cable (premium). Indoor pool. Complimentary continental bkfst. Restaurant nearby. Ck-out 11 am. Coin lndry. Meeting rm. Business servs avail. Valet serv. Downhill ski 15 mi. Exercise equipt. Refrigerators avail. Cr cds: A, D, DS, JCB, MC, V.

★ ★ **ECONO LODGE.** 7462 Seneca Rd N, 1½ mi N on Old NY 36; ½ mi S of NY 17 Hornell exit. 607/324-0800; FAX 607/324-0905; res: 800/698-0801. 67 rms, 2 story. S $39-$45; D $45-$55; each addl $3. Pet accepted. TV; cable, VCR avail (movies). Complimentary continental bkfst. Restaurant 5-10 pm; Sun brunch 11 am-3 pm. Bar from 4:30 pm. Ck-out 11 am. Meeting rms. Business servs avail. In-rm modem link. Downhill ski 10 mi. Picnic tables. Cr cds: A, D, DS, MC, V.

★ ★ **SAXON INN.** (One Park Street, Alfred 14802) W on NY 17, exit 33, on campus of Alfred University. 607/871-2600; FAX 607/871-2650. 26 rms, 2 story, 6 suites. S, D $85-$110; each addl $10; suites $110; under 12 free; higher rates university events. Crib free. TV; cable. Pool privileges.

Complimentary continental bkfst. Ck-out 11 am. Meeting rms. Business servs avail. Tennis privileges. Some refrigerators. Cr cds: A, D, DS, MC, V.

Howes Cave (E-7)

(See also Albany, Schenectady, Stamford)

Pop 150 (est) **Elev** 801 ft **Area code** 518 **Zip** 12092

What to See and Do

Howe Caverns. Elaborately developed series of caverns with underground river and lake, unique rock formations 160-200 ft below the surface; reached by elevators; 52°F in caverns. (Daily; closed Jan 1, Thanksgiving, Dec 25) Tour combined with boat trip. Snack bar. Restaurant (May-Oct). Picnic area. On NY 7. Phone 518/296-8990. ¢¢¢¢

Old Stone Ft Museum Complex. Church built in 1772 was fortified against raids by Tories and Native Americans during the Revolution and became known as Lower Fort. Major attack came in 1780; bldg restored to house of worship in 1785; now houses exhibits on Revolution and Schoharie Valley history; firearms, Native American artifacts and period furniture; local historical and genealogical library. Badgley Museum & Carriage House, annex built in style of fort. Furnishings, tools, farm implements, 1901 Rambler, fire engines. (May-Oct, daily exc Mon) 8 mi SE via NY 7, 30 in Schoharie. Phone 518/295-7192. ¢¢

Secret Caverns. Cave with natural entrance, 100-ft underground waterfalls, fossilized sea life; 50°F in caverns. (Late Apr-Oct, daily) ½-mi tour. On Secret Caverns Rd. Phone 518/296-8558. ¢¢¢

Motels

★ ★ ★ **BEST WESTERN INN OF COBLESKILL.** (12 Campus Drive, Cobleskill 12043) 3 mi SE on NY 7, Campus Dr extension. 518/234-4321; FAX 518/234-3869. E-mail bwcoby@midtel.net. 76 rms, 2 story. S, D $70-$139; under 12 free. Crib free. Pet accepted, some restrictions. TV; cable (premium), VCR avail (movies $7). Indoor pool; wading pool. Coffee in rms. Restaurant 7 am-9 pm. Rm serv. Bar 4-10 pm. Ck-out 11 am. Meeting rms. Business servs avail. Game rm. Bowling lanes. Refrigerators, microwaves avail. Cr cds: A, C, D, DS, MC, V.

★ **HOWE CAVERNS.** 3 mi E of Cobleskill on NY 7, on Howe Caverns Estate. 518/296-8950; FAX 518/296-8992. E-mail fun@howecaverns.com; web www.howecaverns.com. 21 rms. July-Labor Day: S, D $83-$46; each addl $10; lower rates late Apr-June, after Labor Day-Oct. Closed rest of yr. TV. Pool. Coffee in rms. Restaurant hrs vary. Ck-out 10:30 am. On hillside with view of valley. Cr cds: DS, MC, V.

Restaurant

★ ★ **BULLS HEAD INN.** (2 Park Place, Cobleskill 12043) I-88 exit 22 or 23, on Village Green (Rte 7). 518/234-3591. Specializes in steak, prime rib, seafood. Hrs: 11:30 am-2 pm, 5-9 pm; Fri to 10 pm; Sat 5-10 pm; Sun 1-8 pm. Closed Mon; Jan 1, Dec 25. Res accepted. Bar to midnight. Semi-a la carte: lunch $3.95-$8.75, dinner $10.95-$26.95. Open hearth cooking, brewery on premises. Historic building (1802). Cr cds: A, MC, V.

Hudson (E-8)

(See also Cairo, Catskill, Coxsackie, Hillsdale)

Settled 1783 **Pop** 8,034 **Elev** 80 ft **Area code** 518 **Zip** 12534
Information Columbia County Tourism Department, 401 State St; 800/724-1846.

What to See and Do

American Museum of Fire Fighting. Antique fire-fighting equipment incl 1725 Newsham fire engine; memorabilia, art gallery. (Daily; closed major hols) Harry Howard Ave. Phone 518/828-7695. **Free.**

Clermont State Historic Site. The ancestral home of Robert R. Livingston, one of 5 men elected to draft the Declaration of Independence, who later, as chancellor of New York, administered the oath of office to George Washington. Lived in by 7 generations of the Livingston family, the grounds and mansion retain their 1930 appearance, illustrating 200 yrs of changing tastes. Centerpiece of a 485-acre estate on the eastern shore of the Hudson River, the home features period furnishings, restored gardens, guided tours, nature trails and special events. Visitor center, museum store (May-Oct, daily exc Mon). Grounds open all yr for hiking, riding, cross-country skiing, picnicking. 16 mi S on NY 9G, then W on County Rte 6. Phone 518/537-4240. ¢¢

James Vanderpoel House. Federal period house built around 1820, now a museum with 19th-century furnishings and art. Maintained by the Columbia County Historical Society. (Memorial Day-Labor Day, Wed-Sun) 11 mi N on US 9 in Kinderhook. Phone 518/758-9265. ¢¢ The society also maintains

Luykas Van Alen House (1737). Restored house is a museum of Dutch domestic culture during the 18th century. 3 mi S of Kinderhook on NY 9H. ¢¢

Lake Taghkanic State Park. 1,569 acres. Swimming beaches, bathhouses; fishing; boating (launch, rentals); hiking trails. Cross-country skiing, snowmobiling, ice-skating. Picnicking, playground, concession. Tent and trailer sites, cabins, cottages. 177-acre lake. 11 mi SE via NY 23, 82. Phone 518/851-3631 or 800/456-CAMP (camping res). Memorial Day-Labor Day ¢¢; Rest of yr **Free.**

Martin Van Buren Natl Historic Site. Retirement house of America's eighth president. The estate, Lindenwald, was purchased by Van Buren from General William Paulding in 1839. The house, on 20 acres, contains 36 rms. Tours (May-Oct). 2 mi S of Kinderhook on NY 9H. Phone 518/758-9689. House ¢

Olana State Historic Site (1870). A 250-acre hilltop estate with views of the Hudson River and Catskill Mts, incl Persian/Moorish mansion and grounds landscaped in Romantic style, all designed by Hudson River school artist Frederic Edwin Church as a multi-dimensional work of art. Decorative Oriental arts and furnishings collected by the artist; also paintings by Church. Carriage roads for walking with views planned by the artist. Grounds (daily). House Museum (Apr-Oct, Wed-Sun): entrance by guided tour only—tours limited. Res recommended. 5 mi S on NY 9G. Phone 518/828-0135. Museum ¢

Shaker Museum and Library. One of the largest collections of Shaker culture; 26 galleries in 3 bldgs. Exhibits incl furniture, crafts, basketry, agricultural and industrial tools. Library (by appt only). Picnic area, cafe. Gift shop. (Late Apr-Oct, daily exc Tues) 88 Shaker Museum Rd, 18 mi NE via NY 66, County 13. Phone 518/794-9100. ¢¢¢

Hotel

✔★★★ **ST CHARLES.** *16 Park Pl. 518/822-9900; FAX 518/822-0835.* 34 rms, 3 story, 6 suites. S, D $69-$89; each addl $10; suites $99; under 18 free; ski plans. Crib free. Pet accepted. TV; cable, VCR avail. Complimentary continental bkfst. Restaurants 11:30 am-10 pm (also see REBECCA'S). No rm serv. Bar to midnight; entertainment. Ck-out noon.

Meeting rms. Business servs avail. No bellhops. Tennis privileges. Health club privileges. Cr cds: A, C, D, DS, MC, V.

[D] [🐾] [🏂] [🏊] [🛶]

Restaurant

★★ **REBECCA'S.** *(See St Charles Hotel) 518/822-9900.* Hrs: 4:30-10 pm. Closed Sun-Tues; Jan 1, Thanksgiving, Dec 25. Res accepted. Continental menu. Bar 11:30 am-midnight. Semi-a la carte: dinner $12.95-$22.95. Child's meals. Specialties: beef Wellington, salmon en croute, herb-encrusted spring lamb chops. Colonial decor with fireplace. Totally nonsmoking. Cr cds: A, C, D, DS, MC, V.

[D] [SC]

Hunter (E-8)

(See also Cairo, Catskill Park, Shandaken, Windham, Woodstock)

Pop 429 **Elev** 1,603 ft **Area code** 518 **Zip** 12442 **Web** www.greene-ny.com
Information Greene County Promotion Dept, NY Thrwy exit 21, PO Box 527, Catskill 12414; 518/943-3223 or 800/355-CATS.

What to See and Do

Hunter Mt Ski Resort. Offers 47 slopes and trails. Patrol, school, rentals; snowmaking; bar, restaurant, cafeteria; nursery. Longest run 2 mi; vertical drop 1,600 ft. (Early Nov-late Apr, daily) NY 23A. Phone 518/263-4223. ¢¢¢¢

Motel

★★ **HUNTER INN.** *Main St (NY 23 A). 518/263-3777; FAX 518/263-3981.* Web www.hunterinn.com. 41 rms, 2-3 story. No elvtr. Mid-Nov-mid-Apr: S, D $79-$165; each addl $10-$15; suites $115-$185; under 17 free; hols (3-day min); wkend, package plans; higher rates hols; lower rates rest of yr. Crib free. Pet accepted; $10. TV; cable. Whirlpool. Complimentary continental bkfst. Ck-out 11 am. Meeting rm. Business servs avail. Sundries. Exercise equipt. Downhill/x-country ski ½ mi. Cr cds: A, DS, MC, V.

[D] [🐾] [🚲] [🎿] [🏊] [🛶]

Lodge

★★★ **SCRIBNER HOLLOW.** *Main St (Rt 23A). 518/263-4211; FAX 518/263-5266; res: 800/395-4683.* Web www.scribnerhollow.com. 38 rms, 3 story, 22 suites, 36 townhouses. MAP, Thanksgiving-Mar: S $128-$180; D $170-$240; suites $200-$450; townhouses $200-$350; family, wkly rates; ski, golf plans; higher rates some hols, special events; lower rates rest of yr. Closed Apr-mid May. Crib free. TV; cable. 2 pools; 1 indoor pool; wading pool, whirlpool, poolside serv. Restaurant (see THE PROSPECT). Rm serv. Bar; entertainment. Ck-in 3 pm, ck-out noon. Meeting rms. Business servs avail. Bellhops. Valet serv. Concierge. Sundries. Free bus depot transportation. Tennis. Downhill ski adj; x-country ski on site. Sauna. Rec rm. Lawn games. Refrigerators. Rustic atmosphere blended with modern facilities; features "underground" grotto with waterfalls, alcoves, fireplace. Cr cds: A, DS, MC, V.

[🚲] [🎿] [🏊] [🛶] [SC]

Inn

★★ **EGGERY.** *(County Rd 16, Tannersville 12485) On County Rd 16, approx 11/4 mi S off NY 23A. 518/589-5363; FAX 518/589-5774.* 15 rms, 3 story. 9 A/C. July-Mar: S, D $90-$110; each addl $20-$30; wkends, fall season (2-day min); special events (3-day min); lower rates rest of yr. TV; cable. Complimentary full bkfst. Ck-out 11 am, ck-in 1 pm.

Lawn games. Antique furnishings. Restored farmhouse inn built 1900. Facing Hunter Mt. Cr cds: A, MC, V.

Restaurants

★ ★ ★ **CHATEAU BELLEVIEW.** *(Rte 23A, Tannersville 12485) 4 mi E on NY 23A.* 518/589-5525. Hrs: 5-10 pm; Sun from 1 pm. Closed Tues; also 2 wks Apr, 2 wks Nov. Res accepted. French menu. Bar. Semi-a la carte: dinner $14.95-$22.95. Child's meals. Specialties: fish with herbs or Cajun spices, duckling, beef bourguignon. Outdoor dining. View of Catskills. Cr cds: A, DS, MC, V.

★ ★ **MOUNTAIN BROOK DINING & SPIRITS.** *Main St.* 518/263-5351. Hrs: 5-10:30 pm; Sun brunch 11 am-3 pm (Mid-Dec-mid-Mar). Closed Tues in ski season, July, Aug; also Dec 25. Res required Sat. Some A/C. Bar. A la carte entrees: dinner $10.75-$18.75. Child's meals. Specialties: radicchio & endive salad with melted goat cheese; homemade meatloaf with rich veal stock gravy; grilled filet of tuna, wasabi soy ginger marinade. Sun brunch prices vary. Parking. Outdoor dining. Cr cds: MC, V.

★ ★ **THE PROSPECT.** *(See Scribner Hollow Lodge)* 518/263-4211. Web www.scribnerhollow.com. Hrs: 8-10 am, 5-10 pm; wknds 8 am-11 pm. Res accepted. Continental, contemporary Amer menu. Bar. Semi-a la carte: bkfst $7.95-$9, dinner $13.95-$19.95. Specializes in fresh fish, vegetarian specials, wild game. Child's meals. Jazz wknds. Wine tasting dinner. Overlooks Hunter Mt. Family-owned. Cr cds: A, DS, MC, V.

✔★ ★ **VESUVIO.** *(Goshen Rd, Hensonville 12439) 7 mi N, just off NY 296.* 518/734-3663. Regional Italian menu. Specializes in veal, lobster steak, fresh pasta. Own pastries, pasta. Hrs: 4-10 pm; Fri, Sat to 11 pm; early-bird dinner 4-8 pm, Sat to 6 pm. Res accepted. Bar. A la carte entrees: dinner $10.95-$21.95. Complete meals (Sun-Fri): dinner $10.95. Child's meals. Pianist wknds. Outdoor dining. Fireplace. Family-owned. Cr cds: A, MC, V.

Huntington, L.I. (B-3)

(See also Northport, Oyster Bay, Plainview)

Settled 1653 **Pop** 191,474 **Elev** 60 ft **Area code** 516 **Zip** 11743
Information Huntington Township Chamber of Commerce, 151 W Carver St; 516/423-6100.

Although the expanding suburban population of New York City has reached Huntington, 37 miles east on Long Island, it still retains its rural character. Huntington is a township including 17 communities, in which there are more than 100 industrial plants. The area has five navigable harbors and 51 miles of shorefront.

What to See and Do

Cold Spring Harbor Whaling Museum. Fully equipped 19th-century whale boat from the brig *Daisy* is on display. Marine paintings, scrimshaw, ship models, changing exhibit gallery. "Mark Well the Whale" permanent exhibit documents Long Island's whaling industry. Permanent exhibit "The Wonder of Whales" incl a hands-on whale bones display, a killer whale skull, sperm whale jaw and whale conservation info. (Memorial Day-Labor Day, daily; rest of yr, daily exc Mon) Main St, 2 mi W on NY 25A, in Cold Spring Harbor. Phone 516/367-3418. ¢

David Conklin Farmhouse (ca 1750). Four generations of Conklin family lived here. Period rms (colonial, Federal, Victorian). (Tues-Fri & Sun; closed hols) 2 High St at New York Ave. ¢¢ Other historic bldgs include

Huntington Trade School (1905). School bldg houses the offices of the Huntington Historical Society and a history research library. (Tues-Fri) 209 Main St. Phone 516/427-7045. ¢¢

Kissam House (1795). Federal house, barn, sheepshed and outbuildings; home of early Huntington physicians. Period rms (1800-1850). (Tues-Fri & Sun; closed hols) 434 Park Ave. ¢¢

Heckscher Museum of Art. Permanent collection of European and American art dating from 16th century; changing exhibits. (Daily exc Mon; closed Thanksgiving, Dec 25) Heckscher Park, Prime Ave & NY 25A (Main St). Phone 516/351-3250. **Donation.**

Joseph Lloyd Manor House (1767). Large colonial manor house, elegantly furnished; 18th-century garden. (Memorial Day-mid-Oct, Sat & Sun afternoons) Lloyd Lane, 3 mi N in Lloyd Harbor. Phone 516/941-9444. ¢

Sunken Meadow State Park. Swimming beach, bathhouse; fishing (all yr); nature, hiking, biking trails; three 9-hole golf courses (fee). Picnicking, playground, concession. Cross-country skiing. Recreation programs. Standard fees. Approx 9 mi E of town on NY 25A. Phone 516/269-4333. Per vehicle (Memorial Day-Labor Day) ¢¢

Target Rock Natl Wildlife Refuge. An 80-acre refuge with hardwood forest, pond and beach. Fishing, photography, nature trail, wildlife nature study and environmental education. (Daily) 8 mi N via West Neck Rd, follow onto Lloyd Harbor Rd. Phone 516/286-0485.

Walt Whitman Birthplace State Historic Site. Boyhood home of the poet; 19th-century furnishings; Whitman's schoolmaster's desk; his voice on tape; exhibits, sculpture; museum, research library (by appt); audiovisual presentation. Gift shop, picnic facilities. Guided tours, (groups by appt). Interpretive Center. (Wed-Sun; closed hols) 246 Old Walt Whitman Rd, across from Walt Whitman Mall. 1 mi from Long Island Expy. Phone 516/427-5240. **Free.**

Annual Event

Long Island Fall Festival at Huntington. Heckscher Park. Entertainment, carnival, sailboat regatta, food, wine tasting, family activities. Phone 516/423-6100. Mid-Oct.

Seasonal Event

Huntington Summer Arts Festival. Heckscher Park amphitheater. Local, national and international artists perform dance, folk, classical, jazz, theater and family productions. Phone 516/271-8442. Late June-mid-Aug, Tues-Sun.

Motels

★ ★ **HUNTINGTON COUNTRY INN.** *(270 W Jericho Tpke, Huntington 11746)* 516/421-3900; res: 800/739-5777; FAX 516/421-5287. 64 rms, 2 story. S $75-$85; D $85-$95; each addl $10; suite $150; under 16 free. Crib free. Pet accepted. TV; cable (premium). Pool; lifeguard. Complimentary continental bkfst. Complimentary coffee in rms. Restaurant adj noon-10 pm. Ck-out noon. Health club privileges. Some refrigerators, microwaves. Cr cds: A, C, D, DS, MC, V.

✔★ **RAMADA INN LIMITED.** *(8030 Jericho Tpke, Woodbury 11797) 4 mi S on NY 110 to South Huntington, then 5 mi W on NY 25 (Jericho Tpke).* 516/921-8500; FAX 516/921-1057. 102 rms, 2 story, 5 kit. suites. S, D $79-$129; suites $150-$225; kit. units $89-$129; under 17 free. Crib free. TV; cable (premium). Seasonal pool; lifeguard. Complimentary bkfst. Ck-out noon. Meeting rms. Business servs avail. In-rm modem link. Health club privileges. Some microwaves. Cr cds: A, C, D, DS, ER, JCB, MC, V.

Hotel

★ ★ ★ **HILTON.** *(598 Broad Hollow Rd, Melville 11747) S on NY 110, 1 mi S of I-495.* 516/845-1000; FAX 516/845-1223. 302 rms, 5 story. S $159; D $169; each addl $20; suites $225-$550. Crib free. TV; cable (premium), VCR avail (movies). 2 pools, 1 indoor; whirlpool, poolside serv; lifeguard. Restaurant 6:30 am-11 pm. Bar 11-2 am; entertainment. Ck-out noon. Convention facilities. Business servs avail. In-rm modem link. Concierge. Gift shop. Lighted tennis. Exercise equipt. Bathrm phones, minibars; wet bar in suites. Cr cds: A, C, D, DS, JCB, MC, V.

Restaurants

★ ★ **ABEL CONKLIN'S.** *54 New St. 516/385-1919.* Specializes in aged steak. Hrs: noon-10 pm; Fri to 11 pm; Sat, Sun 4:30-11 pm. Closed major hols. Res required. Bar. Complete meals: lunch $8-$12. A la carte entrees: dinner $10-$22. Built in 1830; etched glass, fireplace. Cr cds: A, C, D, MC, V.

★ ★ ★ **FOX HOLLOW.** *(7725 Jericho Tpke, Woodbury 11797)* 1/2 mi E of NY 135. 516/921-1415. Northern Italian menu. Hrs: 11:30 am-3 pm, 5-10 pm; Sat from 5 pm. Closed Sun; Dec 25. Res required. Bar. A la carte entrees: lunch $6.50-$16.25, dinner $14.75-$31. Piano bar. Valet parking. Patio dining (in season). Rustic surroundings in wooded area. Jacket. Family-owned. Cr cds: A, C, D, MC, V.

★ ★ **FREDERICK'S.** *(1117 Walt Whitman Rd, Melville 11747)* 10 mi S on NY 110. 516/673-8550. Continental menu. Blackboard specials change daily. Hrs: 11:30 am-2 pm, 5-9 pm; Sat 5-9 pm. Closed Sun. Res accepted. Serv bar. A la carte entrees: lunch $13.95-$24.75, dinner $14.95-$24.75. Parking. Cr cds: A, C, D, MC, V.

★ ★ **INN ON THE HARBOR.** *(105 Harbor Rd, Cold Spring Harbor 11724)* 2 mi W on NY 25A. 516/367-3166. French, continental menu. Own baking. Hrs: 11:30 am-2:30 pm, 4:30-9:30 pm; Fri, Sat to 10:30 pm; Sun brunch 11:30 am-2:45 pm. Closed Dec 25. Res accepted. Bar. A la carte entrees: lunch $6.95-$14.95, dinner $16.95-$26.95. Sun brunch $21.95. Valet parking. Fireplaces. Overlooks Cold Spring Harbor. Cr cds: A, C, D, MC, V.

✔★ **PETITE ON MAIN.** *328 Main St. 516/271-3311.* International menu. Specialties: grilled chicken with salsa, filet mignon, marinated skirt steak. Hrs: 5-9:30 pm; Fri, Sat to 10:30 pm; Sun to 8:45 pm. Closed Mon; major hols. Res required wkends. Setups. A la carte entrees: dinner $13-$23. Prix fixe Sun-Thurs: dinner $22. Casual country decor. Cr cds: A, C, D, MC, V.

Unrated Dining Spot

WYLANDS COUNTRY KITCHEN. *(55 Main St, Cold Spring Harbor)* 2 mi W on NY 25A. 516/692-5655. Specializes in flounder, shrimp. Own pastries. Hrs: 11 am-4:30 pm; Sat to 3:45 pm. Closed Sun, Mon; major hols; also late Feb-early Mar. Serv bar. A la carte entrees: lunch $6.50-$8.75. Child's meals. Casual dining. Family-owned. Cr cds: A, C, D, MC, V.

Hyde Park (F-8)

(See also New Paltz, Poughkeepsie, Rhinebeck)

Settled 1740 **Pop** 21,230 **Elev** 188 ft **Area code** 914 **Zip** 12538 **E-mail** dctpa@idsi.net **Web** www.dutchesstourism.com

Information Dutchess County Tourism Promotion Agency, 3 Neptune Rd, Ste M-17, Poughkeepsie 12601; 914/463-4000 or 800/445-3131.

Hyde Park was named for Edward Hyde, Lord Cornbury, provincial governor of New York, who in 1705 presented a parcel of land along the river to his secretary. Hyde's name was given to an estate on that property and later to the town itself. The area, noted for the varying scenery from rock outcroppings to scenic water views, is best known as the site of Springwood, the country estate of Franklin Roosevelt.

What to See and Do

Mills-Norrie State Park. Fishing; boat basin (marina, dock, launch); nature, hiking trails; 18-hole golf (fee). Cross-country skiing; picnicking, playground; tent & trailer sites, cabins. Environmental education programs, concert series. Standard fees. 4 mi N on US 9 in Staatsburg. Phone 914/889-4646. In park is

Mills Mansion State Historic Site. Built in 1832, the Greek-revival mansion was remodeled and enlarged in 1895 by prominent architect Stanford White into a 65-rm, neoclassical country residence for Ogden Mills. Furnished in Louis XIV, Louis XV and Louis XVI styles; tapestries, art objects, marble fireplaces, gilded plasterwork. Park overlooks the Hudson. (Mid-Apr-Oct, Wed-Sun; also last 2 wks in Dec) Phone 914/889-8851. ¢¢

✪ **Roosevelt-Vanderbilt Natl Historic Sites.** (Daily) 1 mi S on US 9. Phone 914/229-9115. Here is

Home of Franklin D. Roosevelt Natl Historic Site. The Hyde Park estate, Springwood, was President Roosevelt's birthplace and lifelong residence. The central part of the bldg, the oldest section, dates from about 1826. The house was bought in 1867 by FDR's father and was extensively remodeled and expanded in 1915 by FDR and his mother, Sara Delano Roosevelt. At that time the frame, Victorian house took on its present brick and stone, neo-Georgian form. The interior is furnished exactly as it was when FDR died. Roosevelt's grave and that of Anna Eleanor Roosevelt are in the rose garden. Home, library, and museum ¢¢¢ Adj is

Franklin D. Roosevelt Library and Museum. First of the public presidential libraries, it has exhibits covering the private lives and public careers of Franklin and Eleanor Roosevelt. Research library contains family artifacts and documents and presidential archives. Library, museum and home. Phone 914/229-8114.

Eleanor Roosevelt Natl Historic Site at Val-Kill. Dedicated as a memorial to Mrs. Roosevelt on Oct 11, 1984, the 100th anniversary of her birth, Val-Kill was her country residence from the 1920s until her death. The original house on the property, Stone Cottage (1924), is now a conference center. Her second house at Val-Kill was originally a furniture and crafts factory that Mrs. Roosevelt sponsored in an effort to stimulate rural economic development. After closing Val-Kill Industries, she had the factory remodeled to reflect her tastes and humanitarian concerns; here, she entertained family, friends and heads of state from around the world. Film; tour. 2 mi E of Roosevelt estate. ¢¢ Nearby is

Vanderbilt Mansion Natl Historic Site. Beaux-arts mansion (1898) designed by McKim, Mead and White for Frederick W. Vanderbilt is a prime example of the "American-millionaire palaces" typical of the period; the interior retains most of the original furnishings as designed by turn-of-the-century decorators. The grounds offer superb views up and down the Hudson River; many ancient trees; restored formal Italian gardens. Phone 914/229-9115. ¢¢¢

Motels

★ **ROOSEVELT INN.** *616 Albany Post Rd,* 1/4 mi S of NY 41 on US 9. 914/229-2443; FAX 914/229-0026. 26 rms, 2 story. May-Oct: S $45-$55; D $48-$68; each addl $4; under 17 free; lower rates rest of yr. TV; cable (premium), VCR avail. Restaurant 7-11 am. Ck-out 11 am. X-country ski 5 mi. Business servs avail. Some refrigerators. Balconies. Cr cds: A, DS, MC, V.

✔★ **SUPER 8.** *528 Albany Post Rd. 914/229-0088; res: 800/800-8000.* 61 rms, 2 story. Apr-Oct: S $47-$56; D $59-$62; each addl $4; higher rates special events; lower rates rest of yr. Crib $5. TV; cable (premium). Complimentary continental bkfst. Restaurant nearby. Business servs avail. In-rm modem link. Sundries. Microwaves, refrigerators avail. Cr cds: A, D, DS, MC, V.

Restaurants

★ ★ ★ **AMERICAN BOUNTY.** *433 Albany Post Rd (US 9), at Culinary Institute of America.* 914/471-6608. Regional Amer menu. Own baking. Hrs: 11:30 am-1 pm, 6:30-8:30 pm. Closed Sun, Mon; major hols; also 3 wks July, 2 wks Christmas. Res accepted. Bar 11:30 am-11 pm. Wine cellar. A la carte entrees: lunch $10.95-$14.95, dinner $16.50-$23. In former St Andrew-on-Hudson Jesuit Seminary on 150 acres, high above Hudson River. Cr cds: A, D, DS, MC, V.

D

★ **EASY STREET CAFE.** *489 Albany Post Rd (US 9).* 914/229-7969. Specializes in prime rib, veal, seafood. Hrs: 11 am-10 pm; Sun noon-9 pm. Closed Dec 25. Res accepted. Bar. Semi-a la carte: lunch $4.95-$9.50, dinner $9.50-$18.75. Country atmosphere. Cr cds: A, D, DS, MC, V.

D

★ ★ ★ **THE ESCOFFIER.** *433 Albany Post Rd (US 9), at Culinary Institute of America.* 914/471-6608. Classical French cuisine. Specialties: duck, Dover sole, crevette Madagascar. Own baking. Hrs: 11:30 am-1 pm, 6:30-8:30 pm. Closed Sun, Mon; major hols; also 3 wks July, 2 wks Christmas. Res accepted. Serv bar. Wine list. A la carte entrees: lunch $14.50-$18.50, dinner $20.50-$23. Table d'hôte: lunch $23. One of the four restaurants of the Culinary Institute of America, the country's foremost restaurant school. The student chefs prepare the dishes that their peers serve in the dining room. Some dishes prepared at table. Cr cds: A, D, DS, MC, V.

D

✔★ ★ **ST ANDREW'S CAFÉ.** *433 Albany Post Rd (US 9), at Culinary Institute of America.* 914/471-6608. Contemporary American menu. Own baking. Hrs: 11:30 am-1 pm, 6:30-8:30 pm. Closed Sat, Sun; major hols; also 3 wks July, 2 wks Dec. Bar. Semi-a la carte: lunch $8-$13.50, dinner $8.95-$17. Outdoor dining. Dining rm opens onto courtyard; original regional watercolors; fireplace. Cr cds: A, D, DS, MC, V.

D

Ilion (D-7)

Pop 8,888 **Elev** 410 ft **Area code** 315 **Zip** 13357

Restaurant

★ ★ **MOHAWK STATION.** *(95 E Main St, Mohawk 13407) ¹/₂ mi E on NY 55; NY S Thrwy (I-90) exit 30.* 315/866-1111. Specializes in prime rib, seafood, poultry. Salad bar. Hrs: 11 am-9 pm; Fri, Sat to 10 pm; Sun 10:30 am-8 pm. Sun brunch to 2:30 pm. Closed Dec 25. Res accepted. Bar. Semi-a la carte: lunch $3.95-$7.95, dinner $6.95-$26.95. Buffet: lunch $6.95. Sun brunch $9.95. Child's meals. Railroad theme; original caboose for dining area. Cr cds: MC, V.

D

Ithaca (E-5)

(See also Binghamton, Cortland)

Settled 1789 **Pop** 29,541 **Elev** 405 ft **Area code** 607 **Zip** 14850 **E-mail** cvbdesk@chamber.compcenter.com **Web** www.ithaca.ny.us/commerce
Information Ithaca/Tompkins County Convention & Visitors Bureau, 904 East Shore Dr; 607/272-1313 or 800/284-8422.

Ithaca climbs from the plain at the head of Cayuga Lake up the steep slopes of the surrounding hills. Creeks flow through town and cut picturesque gorges with cascading waterfalls. Named for Grecian Ithaca by Simeon De Witt, surveyor-general under Washington, Ithaca is a center of inland water transportation and an educational center of New York State.

What to See and Do

Cornell Univ (1865). (18,257 students) A 745-acre campus overlooks Cayuga Lake and incl Beebe Lake, gorges, waterfalls. Founded both as a land-grant and privately endowed college by Ezra Cornell (1807-1874) and Andrew Dickson White (1832-1918). There are 13 colleges, 4 of which are state supported; 11 schools and colleges are in Ithaca, 2 in New York City. E side of town. On campus are Willard Straight Hall; Laboratory of Ornithology (daily; phone 607/254-BIRD); Herbert F. Johnson Museum of Art (daily exc Mon; phone 607/255-6464); Olive Tjaden Hall Art Gallery (Sept-June, daily; closed hols, phone 607/255-3558); Cornell Plantations (daily; phone 607/255-3020); Visitor Info and Referral Center (daily exc Sun; phone 607/255-6200).

DeWitt Historical Society & Museum. Local historical exhibits; large photograph collection; local history library. (Tues-Sat; closed hols) 401 E State St. Phone 607/273-8284. **Free.**

Ithaca College (1892). (6,400 students) Liberal arts & professional programs. Music, art exhibits, drama, lectures and athletic programs. Handwerker Gallery. Campus overlooks city, Cayuga Lake. Tours of campus. ¹/₂ mi S on NY 96B. Phone 607/274-3011.

Recreation areas. Stewart Park. James L Gibbs Dr. Picnicking, tennis, playground, concession. **Cass Park.** 701 Taughannock Blvd. Pool, wading pool; ice-skating rink; tennis, ball fields (4 lighted), playground, picnicking, concession. Fees for some activities. Phone 607/273-1090 or 607/273-8364.

Sciencenter. Over 100 hands-on interactive science exhibits and outdoor science park; lectures; special events. (Daily exc Mon; closed major hols) 601 First St. Phone 607/272-0600. ¢¢On grounds is the

Sagan Planetwalk. Scaled model of the solar system built in remembrance of Carl Sagan. (Daily) 601 First St. Phone 607/272-0600. **Free.**

Six Mile Creek Vineyard. Family-operated winery. Tours, tastings. (Daily, afternoons) NY 79 E, 1551 Slaterville Rd. Phone 607/272-WINE. **Free.**

State parks.

Allan H. Treman State Marine Park. Fishing; boating (launch, marina). Picnicking. (Apr-late Oct) Standard fees. 3 mi N on NY 89. Phone 607/272-1460.

Buttermilk Falls. Swimming, bathhouse. Hiking trails. Cross-country skiing. Picnicking, playground, concession. Tent & trailer sites, cabins. (Mid-May-Columbus Day) Standard fees. 4 mi S on NY 13. Phone 607/273-5761.

Robert H. Treman. Swimming, bathhouse. Hiking trails. Picnicking, playground. Cabins. Recreation programs. Tent & trailer sites. (Mid-May-late Nov) Standard fees. 5 mi S on NY 13. Phone 607/273-3440. May-Oct ¢¢

Taughannock Falls. Swimming, bathhouse; fishing; boating (marina, launch). Nature trails, hiking trails. Cross-country skiing. Picnicking, playground, concession. Tent & trailer sites, cabins. Standard fees. 8 mi N on NY 89. Phone 607/387-6739.

Annual Events

Ithaca Festival. Ithaca Commons and Stewart Park. 1st wkend June.

Grassroots Festival. Trumansburg Fairground. 3rd wkend July.

Apple Harvest Festival. Downtown Ithaca Commons. 1st wkend Oct.

Finger Lakes Antique Show. Women's Community Bldg. Cayuga & Buffalo Sts. Early Oct.

Seasonal Event

Hangar Theatre. Professional summer theater in park setting adj to Treman Marina. Five main stage productions; dramas, comedies and musicals (Tues-Sat eves, also Sat & Wed afternoons). Children's theatre (Thurs-Sat mornings). For tickets phone 607/273-4497 or 800/724-0999. Late June-Labor Day wkend.

Motels

★ ★ ★ **BEST WESTERN UNIVERSITY INN.** 1020 Ellis Hollow Rd, East Hill Plaza. 607/272-6100; FAX 607/272-1518. 94 rms. S, D $79-$99; each addl $10; suites $109-$179; under 17 free; wkly rates. Crib free. Pet accepted, some restrictions; $10. TV; VCR (movies). Pool; lifeguard. Restaurant 7 am-5 pm; Sun to 2 pm. Ck-out noon. Meeting rms. Business servs avail. Valet serv. Airport transportation. Refrigerators; microwaves avail. Cr cds: A, C, D, DS, ER, JCB, MC, V.

★ ★ **CLARION UNIVERSITY.** 1 Sheraton Dr, at Triphammer Rd. 607/257-2000; FAX 607/257-3998. 106 rms, 3 story. S, D $89-$199; each addl $10; suites $135-$225; under 18 free; package plans; higher rates special events. Crib free. TV; cable. Indoor pool; lifeguard. Restaurant 7 am-2 pm. Rm serv. Ck-out noon. Meeting rms. Business servs avail. Bellhops. Valet serv. Free airport transportation. Sauna. Refrigerators avail. Cr cds: A, C, D, DS, MC, V.

✔★ **ECONO LODGE.** 2303 N Triphammer Rd, just off NY 13. 607/257-1400; FAX 607/257-6359. 72 rms, 2 story. May-Sept: S $51-$71; D $66-$76; each addl $5; suites $85-$102; under 18 free; lower rates rest of yr. Crib free. Pet accepted; $10. TV; cable. Continental bkfst. Restaurant nearby. Ck-out 11 am. Meeting rm. Business servs avail. In-rm modem link. Microwaves avail. Cr cds: A, D, DS, MC, V.

★ ★ ★ **RAMADA INN-AIRPORT.** 2310 N Triphammer Rd. 607/257-3100; FAX 607/257-4425. 121 rms, 2 story. S, D $55-$115; each addl $5; suites $95-$150; under 18 free; higher rates: wkends, special events. Crib free. Pet accepted, some restrictions. TV; cable, VCR avail (movies). 2 pools, 1 indoor; wading pool, whirlpool, poolside serv, lifeguard. Restaurant 6:30 am-2 pm, 5-10 pm. Rm serv. Bar 4:30 pm-1 am. Ck-out noon. Meeting rms. Business servs avail. In-rm modem link. Valet serv. Game rm. Free airport, bus depot, transportation. Exercise equipt; sauna. Refrigerators, microwaves avail. Cr cds: A, C, D, DS, ER, JCB, MC, V.

✔★ **SUPER 8.** 400 S Meadow. 607/273-8088; FAX 607/273-4832. 63 rms, 2 story. Apr-Sept: S $44.88-$75.88; D $55-$75.88; under 12 free; higher rates special events; lower rates rest of yr. Crib free. TV; cable (premium). Complimentary coffee. Ck-out 11 am. Cr cds: A, D, DS, MC, V.

Motor Hotel

★ ★ ★ **HOLIDAY INN EXECUTIVE TOWER.** 222 S Cayuga St, downtown. 607/272-1000; FAX 607/277-1275. Web www.harthotels.com. 178 rms, 10 story. S, D $99-$109; each addl $10; suites $120-$190; under 19 free; higher rates special events. Crib free. Pet accepted, some restrictions; $15. TV; cable (premium). Indoor pool. Coffee in rms. Restaurant

7-11 am, 5-10 pm. Rm serv. Bar 5 pm-1 am. Ck-out noon. Meeting rms. Business servs avail. Bellhops. Sundries. Free airport, bus depot transportation. Exercise equipt. Some bathrm phones. Cr cds: A, C, D, DS, JCB, MC, V.

Hotel

★ ★ ★ **STATLER.** 11 East Ave, on campus of Cornell University. 607/257-2500; FAX 607/257-6432; res: 800/541-2501. E-mail jh69@Cornell.edu; web www.hotelschool.cornell.edu/statler/rooms.html. 150 rms, 9 story, 18 suites. S $125-$160; D $135-$170; suites $175-$375. Crib free. Valet, lot parking in/out $5.50/day. TV; cable. Pool privileges. Coffee in rms. Restaurant 7 am-9 pm. Rm serv to 10 pm. Bar from 4:30 pm. Ck-out noon. Convention facilities. Business servs avail. In-rm modem link. Gift shop. Free airport transportation. Tennis privileges. 18-hole golf privileges. Downhill/x-country ski 17 mi. Health club privileges. Bathrm phones, refrigerators; microwaves avail. Access to recreational facilities of the university. Marriott Executive Education Center located on the 1st floor of the hotel. Cr cds: A, C, D, DS, MC, V.

Inns

★ ★ ★ **LA TOURELLE.** 1150 Danby Rd (NY 96B). 607/273-2734; FAX 607/273-4821; res: 800/765-1492. 35 units, 3 story. S, D $79-$129. Crib $10. Pet accepted, some restrictions. TV; cable, VCR (free movies). Restaurant adj. Ck-out noon, ck-in 3 pm. Meeting rm. Business servs avail. Tennis. X-country ski on site. Hiking trails. Refrigerators. European inn atmosphere. Located on 70 acres. Buttermilk Falls State Park adj. Cr cds: A, MC, V.

★ ★ ★ **ROSE INN.** (813 Auburn Rd, Groton 13073) 10 mi N on NY 34 N. 607/533-7905; FAX 607/533-7908. Guest rooms in this 19th-century Italianate mansion are individually decorated with period furnishings. The 20 landscaped acres include a pond and a garden. 15 rms, 2 story, 5 suites. S $100-$185; suites $200-$290. Children over 10 yrs only (or with advance arrangements). TV in public rm and in 2 suites. Complimentary full bkfst. Dining rm: 1 sitting (res required) Tues-Sat 7 pm. Rm serv on request. Bar, entertainment Fri, Sat. Wine cellar. Ck-out 11 am, ck-in 3 pm. Meeting rm (1850s carriage house). Business servs avail. In-rm whirlpool, fireplace in suites. Totally nonsmoking. Cr cds: MC, V.

Restaurants

★ ★ **CENTINI'S CODDINGTON.** 124 Coddington Rd, off 96 B. 607/273-0802. Hrs: 11 am-2 pm, 5-9 pm; Fri, Sat to 10 pm; Sun 4-9 pm. Closed Thanksgiving, Dec 25. Res accepted. Italian menu. Bar. Semi-a la carte: lunch $2.95-$9.95, dinner $7.50-$16.95. Child's meals. Specializes in homemade pasta & sauces. Parking. Outdoor dining. Italian decor. Terrace dining overlooks city and lake. Family-owned. Cr cds: A, D, DS, MC, V.

★ ★ **CHEF YEPPI PRESENTS.** 919 Elmira Rd (NY 13). 607/272-6484. Hrs: 11:30 am-9 pm; Fri, Sat to 10 pm; Sun brunch noon-3 pm; early-bird dinner Mon-Fri to 7 pm. Closed Dec 25. Res accepted. Bar. Semi-a la carte: dinner $10.95-$24.95. Sun brunch $10.95. Child's meals. Specializes in house-smoked products, local wines. Parking. In Victorian mansion (1852). Cr cds: A, DS, MC, V.

★ ★ **DANO'S.** 113 S Cayuga St. 607/277-8942. Web www.fingerlakes.net/danos. Continental menu. Specialties: chicken paprikash, house-smoked salmon with cabbage & potato piroghy, crème brûlée. Hrs: 5:30-10 pm. Closed Sun, Mon; some major hols. Res accepted. Bar. Wine list. A la carte entrees: dinner $12.95-$24.95. Formal dining. Artwork. Totally nonsmoking. Cr cds: A, D, MC, V.

✔★ ★ **JOE'S.** *602 West Buffalo St, at Meadow (NY 13). 607/273-2693.* Hrs: 4-10 pm; Fri, Sat to 11 pm. Italian, Amer menu. Bar. Semi-a la carte: dinner $8-$17. Child's meals. Specializes in pasta, steak, seafood. Parking. 1950s decor. Family-owned. Cr cds: A, C, D, DS, MC, V.

★ ★ ★ **JOHN THOMAS STEAK HOUSE.** *1152 Danby Rd (NY 96B). 607/273-3464.* Hrs: 5:30-10 pm; Fri, Sat to 11 pm. Closed Jan 1, July 4, Dec 25. Res accepted. Bar. A la carte entrees: dinner $12.95-$26.95. Specializes in prime dry-aged beef, fresh seafood. Own baking. Parking. Restored 1828 farmhouse with variety of dining rms. Pond with ducks. Cr cds: A, C, D, MC, V.

★ ★ **LEONARDO'S-WHAT'S YOUR BEEF?.** *East Hill Plaza, 2 mi E on Mitchell St; 1/2 mi S of NY 366 on Pine Tree Rd-E Hill Plaza. 607/272-2449.* Specializes in fresh cuts of beef, seafood, pasta. Hrs: 11 am-2 pm, 5-10 pm; Sat, Sun from 5 pm. Closed major hols. Res accepted. Bar from 3 pm. Semi-a la carte: dinner $8.95-$18.95. Child's meals. Parking. Early Amer decor. Fireplaces. Cr cds: A, D, DS, MC, V.

✔★ **MOOSEWOOD.** *215 N Cayuga St, at DeWitt Mall. 607/273-9610.* Gourmet vegetarian, seafood menu. Menu changes twice a day; daily vegan menu. Hrs: 11:30 am-4 pm, 5:30-9 pm; winter to 8:30 pm; summer wkends to 9:30 pm. Wine, beer. Semi-a la carte: lunch $4.50-$6, dinner $9.50-$13. Serv charge 15%. Outdoor dining. Totally nonsmoking. Cr cds: MC, V.

★ ★ **THE STATION.** *806 W Buffalo St. 607/272-2609.* Hrs: 4-9 pm; Sun noon-8 pm; early-bird dinner Tues-Fri 4-6 pm, Sun 12-4 pm. Closed Jan 1, Thanksgiving, Dec 25; also Mon Sept-June & 1st 2 wks Jan. Res accepted. Bar. Semi-a la carte: dinner $9.95-$18.95. Child's meals. Specializes in prime rib, seafood, veal. Salad bar. Parking. Converted 1886 railroad station. Ticket-punch menus. Family-owned. Cr cds: DS, MC, V.

Jamestown (E-2)

(See also Bemus Point, Chautauqua)

Settled 1811 **Pop** 34,681 **Elev** 1,370 ft **Area code** 716 **Zip** 14701 **E-mail** JACC@servtech.com
Information Chamber of Commerce, 101 W 5th St; 716/484-1101.

Jamestown made its mark early in the nineteenth century in the manufacture of metal products and furniture. These industries still flourish in this city at the southern end of Chautauqua Lake. Tourism and farming are important to the economy as well.

What to See and Do

Allegany State Park (see). Approx 30 mi E on NY 17.

Fenton Historical Center. Home of post-Civil War governor; memorabilia of Chautauqua Lake area, Fenton family, Victorian era; recreated Victorian drawing rm. Archival and genealogical library; Swedish and Italian heritage, Civil War exhibit. (Daily exc Sun; closed hols) 67 Washington St. Phone 716/483-7521. ¢¢

Lucy-Desi Museum. Interactive exhibits provide a look into the lives and careers of Lucille Ball and Desi Arnaz. Video presentation. Gift shop. (May-Oct, daily; Nov-Apr, Sat & Sun) 212 Pine St. Phone 716/484-7070. ¢¢

Panama Rocks Park. Massive rock outcrop (25 acres) of a primeval seashore formation; cliffs, caves, crevices and passages. Rare mosses, wildflowers, ferns; unusually shaped tree roots. Self-guided tours; hiking trail; picnicking. (May-mid-Oct, daily) (See ANNUAL EVENT) 6 mi W via NY 394, then 7 1/2 mi W off NY 474 near Panama. Phone 716/782-2845. ¢¢

Annual Event

Panama Rocks Folk Fair. Panama Rocks Park. 2nd Fri-Sun July.

Motel

★ ★ **COMFORT INN.** *2800 N Main St, I-17 exit 12. 716/664-5920; FAX 716/664-3068.* 101 rms, 2 story. June-mid-Sept: S from $69.95; D from $74.95; each addl $5; under 18 free; lower rates rest of yr. Crib free. Pet accepted, some restrictions. TV; cable (premium), VCR avail. Complimentary continental bkfst. Restaurant adj. Bar. Ck-out noon. Meeting rm. Business servs avail. Downhill ski 20 mi. Health club privileges. Some in-rm whirlpools. Microwaves avail. Cr cds: A, C, D, DS, ER, JCB, MC, V.

Motor Hotel

★ ★ ★ **HOLIDAY INN.** *150 W 4th St, I-17 exit 12. 716/664-3400; FAX 716/484-3304.* 146 rms, 8 story. S, D $79-$249; under 18 free; ski plans; wkend rates. Crib free. TV; cable (premium). Indoor pool. Complimentary coffee in rms. Restaurant 6:30 am-2 pm, 5:30-10 pm. Rm serv. Bars 5 pm-midnight. Ck-out noon. Coin lndry. Meeting rms. Business servs avail. In-rm modem link. Bellhops. Cr cds: A, C, D, DS, JCB, MC, V.

Restaurants

★ ★ **HOUSE OF PETILLO.** *382 Hunt Rd. 716/664-7457.* Continental menu. Specializes in veal, seafood, pasta. Hrs: 5 pm-midnight. Closed Sun, Mon; major hols. Res accepted. Bar. Semi-a la carte: dinner $8.95-$16. Child's meals. Fireplaces. Stein collection. Family-owned. Cr cds: A, C, D, DS, MC, V.

✔★ ★ **IRONSTONE.** *516 W 4th St. 716/487-1516.* Specializes in steak, seafood, rack of lamb. Hrs: 11:30 am-2 pm, 5-9 pm; Sat from 5 pm. Closed Sun; most major hols. Bar. Semi-a la carte: lunch $4.25-$6.95, dinner $12-$18. Victorian decor. In 1884 building. Family-owned. Cr cds: A, DS, MC, V.

★ ★ ★ **MacDUFF'S.** *317 Pine St. 716/664-9414.* E-mail macduffs@madbbs.com. Continental menu. Specialties: twin tournedoes of beef with port & stilton sauce, salmon stuffed with pike. Own baking, ice cream. Hrs: 5:30-10 pm. Closed Sun; most major hols. Res accepted. Bar. Wine list. Semi-a la carte: dinner $14.95- $24.95. Intimate dining. Cr cds: A, MC, V.

Jericho, L.I. (B-2)

(See also Oyster Bay, Plainview, Westbury)

Pop 13,141 **Elev** 180 ft **Area code** 516 **Zip** 11753

Restaurants

★ ★ **CAPRICCIO.** *399 Jericho Tpke, L.I. Expy exit 40E. 516/931-2727.* French, Italian menu. Specialties: chicken Riviera, roast L.I. duck, veal chop with fresh herbs. Own pastries. Hrs: 11:30 am-2:30 pm, 5:30-10 pm; Sat 5:30-11 pm. Closed Sun; some major hols. Bar. Wine list.

A la carte entrees: lunch $10.95-$18.95, dinner $16.95-$25.95. Valet parking. Cr cds: A, D, MC, V.

D

★ **FRANK'S STEAKS.** *4 Jericho Tpke. 516/338-4595.* Specializes in steak, chicken, seafood. Hrs: 11:30 am-10 pm; Fri to 11 pm; Sat 4-11:30 pm; Sun 4-9 pm. Closed Easter, Thanksgiving, Dec 25. Res accepted wkends. Bar. A la carte entrees: lunch $6.95-$15.95, dinner $14.95-$25. Cr cds: A, C, D, DS, MC, V.

D

★★ **MAINE MAID INN.** *Jericho Tpke, on NY 25; 1 blk E of jct NY 106. 516/935-6400.* Web www.516web.com/dining/maine-maid. Continental menu. Specialties: L.I. duckling, prime rib. Hrs: 11:30 am-10 pm; Fri, Sat to 11 pm; Sun to 9 pm; early-bird dinner Wed-Sat 4-6 pm. Closed Mon; some major hols. Res accepted. Bar. Complete meals: lunch $6.95-$14, dinner $12.95-$28.50. Child's meals. Built in 1789; Federal-period decor. Cr cds: A, C, D, DS, MC, V.

D

★★ **MILLERIDGE INN.** *Hicksville Rd, at jct NY 25, 106/107; 1/2 mi N of Northern State Pkwy exit 35N; L.I. Expy exit 41N. 516/931-2201.* Specialties: prime rib, pot roast, sauerbraten. Hrs: 11:30 am-9:30 pm; Fri to 10 pm; Sat to 11 pm; Sun to 9 pm; early-bird dinner Mon-Fri 3:30-6:30 pm. Closed Dec 25. Complete meals: lunch $9.95-$14.95, dinner $14.95-$22.95. Sun brunch $9.95-$14.95. Child's meals. Colonial inn (1672); fireplaces, antiques. Adj to Colonial Village. Family-owned. Cr cds: A, C, D, DS, MC, V.

D

Johnstown (D-7)

(See also Amsterdam, Canajoharie, Schenectady)

Founded 1723 **Pop** 9,058 **Elev** 691 ft **Area code** 518 **Zip** 12095 **E-mail** chamber@klink.net **Web** www.klink.net/~chamber/

Information Fulton County Regional Chamber of Commerce and Industry, 2 N Main St, Gloversville 12078; 518/725-0641 or 800/676-3858.

A center of leather tanning and related industries, Johnstown often is called a twin city to Gloversville, which it adjoins. A Revolutionary War battle was fought here six days after Cornwallis surrendered at Yorktown. Women's rights pioneer Elizabeth Cady Stanton was born here in 1815.

What to See and Do

Johnson Hall State Historic Site (1763). Residence of Sir William Johnson, first baronet of New York colony; Native Americans and colonists held meetings here. Site incl hall with period furnishings; stone blockhouse; interpretation center; dioramas depicting history of the estate; tours; special events. (Mid-May-Oct, Wed-Sat, also Sun afternoons) Hall Ave. Contact Site Manager, Hall Ave; 518/762-8712. ¢¢

Motel

✔★★ **HOLIDAY INN.** *308 N Comrie Ave (12095-1095), NY 30A N. 518/762-4686; FAX 518/762-4034.* 100 rms, 3 story. No elvtr. S $62-$72; D $68-$78; under 19 free; higher rates Aug. Crib free. Pet accepted, some restrictions. TV; cable (premium), VCR avail (movies). Heated pool. Coffee in rms. Restaurant 6:30 am-10 pm. Rm serv 8 am-10 pm. Bar 11 am-midnight; entertainment wkends. Ck-out 11 am. Coin lndry. Meeting rms. Business servs avail. In-rm modem link. Valet serv. Downhill/x-country ski 15 mi. Cr cds: A, C, D, DS, JCB, MC, V.

D ✔ ≈ ⊠ ≯ SC

Restaurant

★★ **UNION HALL INN.** *2 Union Place, at Main St (jct NY 67W & NY 29). 518/762-3210.* Continental menu. Specializes in seafood, vegetarian dishes. Hrs: 11:30 am-2 pm, 5 pm-closing; Sat from 5 pm; from 5 pm in July. Closed Sun; most major hols; also Mon. Res accepted; required hols. Bar. Semi-a la carte: lunch $4.50-$8.50, dinner $8.95-$15.95. Post-Revolutionary tavern (1798); early Colonial decor. Cr cds: A, MC, V.

Jones Beach State Park (B-3)

(See also New York City)

(On south shore of Long Island via pkwys)

For millions of New Yorkers, summer means Jones Beach, a fabulous recreation area that can accommodate hundreds of thousands of people on its more than 2,400 acres.

Recreational facilities include swimming in ocean, Zach's Bay and freshwater pools; bathhouses; fishing in ocean and bay; boating (dock). Nature, biking trails; 18-hole pitch-and-putt golf course, miniature golf, softball fields (with permit); shuffleboard; recreation programs. Restaurant, snack bars. Gift shop. Fees vary. Phone 516/785-1600.

Seasonal Event

Jones Beach Theatre. Concerts from country to rock; top entertainers. 11,000-seat outdoor theater. For info contact Box 1000, Wantagh 11793; box office phone 516/221-1000.

Kingston (F-8)

(See also New Paltz, Rhinebeck, Saugerties, Woodstock)

Settled 1652 **Pop** 23,095 **Elev** 200 ft **Area code** 914 **Zip** 12401 **Web** www.ulsterchamber.org
Information Chamber of Commerce of Ulster Co, 7 Albany Ave; 914/338-5100.

In more than 300 years, Kingston has had several names, including Esopus and Wiltwyck, and has been raided, burned and fought over by Native Americans, Dutch, British and Americans. It was the first capital of New York. The Delaware and Hudson Canal and then the railroads brought prosperity. A huge cement industry bloomed and died on Rondout Creek harbor in the 19th century.

What to See and Do

Delaware & Hudson Canal Museum. Dioramas, canalboat models, photographs and memorabilia. Tours. (June-Labor Day, Thurs-Sat & Mon, also Sun afternoons; May & Sept-Oct, Sat, also Sun afternoons) 15 mi S, NY Thrwy exit 19, then S on NY 209, turn left on NY 213 in High Falls. Phone 914/687-9311. ¢

Hudson River Maritime Museum. Models, photographs and paintings depict bygone era of river commerce; outdoor area features steam tug and a variety of antique and modern pleasure boats. (Daily) 1 Rondout Landing, at the foot of Broadway. Phone 914/338-0071. ¢

Hurley Patentee Manor. Dutch cottage (1696) expanded to 2-story English country mansion (1745); original furnishings, woodwork. Home of Hurley Patentee Lighting. (July-Labor Day, daily exc Mon; rest of yr, by appt) 4 mi SW of Kingston, NY Thrwy exit 19 to Old NY 209, then County Rd 29. Phone 914/331-5414. ¢

Old Dutch Church (congregation est 1659). A 19th-century church; buried on grounds is George Clinton, first governor of New York and vice president under Madison and Jefferson. Church and museum tours by appt. (Mon-Fri) Main & Wall Sts. Phone 914/338-6759. **Donation.**

Senate House State Historic Site (1676). Stone residence in which the first New York State Senate met in 1777. Furnished in 18th-century Dutch style; delft tiles, Hudson Valley furniture. Paintings by John Vanderlyn and others in adj museum; boxwood garden. Also library of regional history (by appt only), displays, special events. (Mid-Apr-Oct, Wed-Sat, also Sun afternoons) 312 Fair St, in Stockade District. Phone 914/338-2786. **Free.**

Ulster Performing Arts Center. Historic Vaudeville theater (1927) presents professional Broadway touring companies, dance, contemporary music, comedy and children's productions. 601 Broadway. Phone 914/339-6088 for schedule.

Annual Event

Stone House Day. Approx 1/2 mi NW on NY 28, then 2 mi S on US 209 in Hurley. Tour of 10 privately owned colonial stone houses, led by costumed guides; old Hurley Reformed Church and burying ground; antique show; re-creation of Revolutionary War military encampment; country fair. Phone 914/331-4121. 2nd Sat July.

Motels

★ ★ ★ **HOLIDAY INN.** *503 Washington Ave, just S of Dewey Thrwy exit 19.* 914/338-0400. 212 rms, 2 story. S, D $99-$139; suites $119-$149; under 19 free; higher rates wkends (May-Oct). Crib free. Pet accepted. TV. Indoor pool; wading pool, whirlpool. Coffee in rms. Restaurant 6 am-10 pm. Rm serv. Bar from 11:30 am; entertainment Wed-Sat. Ck-out noon. Coin lndry. Meeting rms. Business servs avail. Bellhops. Sundries. Sauna. Game rm. Refrigerators avail. Balconies. Cr cds: A, C, D, DS, JCB, MC, V.

D ⚡ ≈ ⊠ 🐾 SC

★ ★ **RAMADA INN.** *114 NY 28.* 914/339-3900; FAX 914/338-8464. 147 rms, 2 story. S, D $75-$130; each addl $10; suites $95-$130; under 18 free. Crib free. TV; cable (premium). Indoor pool; lifeguard. Restaurant 7 am-10 pm. Rm serv. Bar. Ck-out noon. Meeting rms. Business servs avail. Bellhops. Valet serv. Sundries. Downhill ski 20 mi. Exercise equipt. Health club privileges. Game rm. Refrigerators avail. Cr cds: A, C, D, DS, MC, V.

D ⚡ ≈ ✕ ⊠ 🐾 SC

✔ ★ **SUPER 8.** *487 Washington Ave.* 914/338-3078. 84 rms, 2 story. June-Oct: S $54.88; D $58.88-$63.88; each addl $6; under 12 free; lower rates rest of yr. Crib free. Pet accepted, some restrictions. TV; cable, VCR avail (movies). Complimentary continental bkfst. Restaurant adj open 24 hrs. Ck-out 11 am. Coin lndry. Sundries. Valet serv. Business servs avail. Refrigerators, microwaves avail. Cr cds: A, C, D, DS, MC, V.

D ⚡ ⊠ 🐾 SC

Restaurants

✔ ★ **CONCA D'ORO.** *11 Main St.* 914/340-4230. E-mail concadoro@hvi.net; web www.restaurantsamerica.com. Hrs: 11 am-10:30 pm; Sat 4-10 pm; Sun 4-10:30 pm. Closed some major hols. Res accepted. Sicilian seafood menu. Bar. Semi-a la carte: lunch $5-$9, dinner $7.95-$14.50. Child's meals. Specializes in beef, seafood, pasta. Band Thurs-Sat. Parking. Island atmosphere; tiki hut interior, wall aquarium. Cr cds: A, DS, MC, V.

D ➞

★ ★ **LE CANARD ENCHAÏNE.** *276 Fair St.* 914/339-2003. Hrs: 11:30 am-10 pm; Fri-Sun to 11 pm. Closed Dec 25. Res accepted. Classical French menu. Bar. A la carte entrees: lunch $5-$9, dinner $15-$21. Specialty: roasted duck. Street parking. French bistro atmosphere. Cr cds: A, MC, V.

D ➞

Lake George Area (C-8)

(See also Bolton Landing, Diamond Point, Hague, Lake George Village, Ticonderoga)

Early explorers and settlers knew Lake George as Lac du St Sacrement—the name given it when a Jesuit missionary, Father Isaac Jogues, reached the southern tip of the lake on the eve of Corpus Christi Day in 1646. In the foothills of the Adirondacks, the area is a center for winter as well as summer sports; there are many miles of snowmobile trails. The area is rich in memories of battles that played a major role in the future of the nation.

Lake George Village

(C-8)

(See also Glens Falls, Lake Luzerne)

Pop 3,211 **Elev** 353 ft **Area code** 518 **Zip** 12845
Information Chamber of Commerce, PO Box 272; 518/668-5755 or 800/705-0059.

This village, located on the 32-mile lake, is in a popular resort area well known for fishing, swimming, boating, golf and winter sports.

What to See and Do

🔲 **Ft William Henry Museum.** A 1755 fort rebuilt from original plans; French and Indian War relics; military drills, musket firings, bullet molding and cannon demonstrations. Movie, *Last of the Mohicans.* Tours (July & Aug). (May-Oct, daily) Canada St, S edge of village on US 9, NY 9N. Phone 518/668-5471. ¢¢¢

Lake excursions. MV *Mohican, Lac de Saint Sacrement* and the paddlewheeler *Minne-Ha-Ha* cruise Lake George. Trips vary from 1-hr shoreline cruise to 41/2-hr full-length cruise of Lake George; also lunch, dinner, moonlight and Sun brunch cruises (late June-Labor Day, daily; limited schedule spring & fall). Lake George Steamboat Co, Beach Rd. Phone 518/668-5777 or 800/553-BOAT. Scenic cruise ¢¢-¢¢¢; lunch, brunch, dinner cruises ¢¢¢¢¢

Lake George Battlefield Picnic Area. Site of Battle of Lake George (1755); ruins of Ft George. Picnic tables, fireplaces, charcoal grills, water. (Mid-June-Labor Day, daily; May-mid-June, wkends) 1 mi S off US 9. Phone 518/623-3671.

Prospect Mt State Pkwy (1969). A 51/2-mi paved road up Prospect Mt (2,100 ft); viewmobiles (free) from parking lot near top to crest. (Mid-May-mid-Oct, daily) 1/2 mi S on US 9. Phone 518/668-5198 or 518/623-3671. Toll per vehicle ¢¢

Swimming. Lake George Million Dollar Beach. In Adirondack Park (see). Bathhouse, lockers, lifeguards. (Mid-June-Labor Day, daily) 1/4 mi E off US 9. Beach ¢; Per vehicle ¢¢

The Great Escape and Splashwater Kingdom Fun Park. State's largest theme park has over 120 rides, live shows and attractions, incl numerous roller coasters, Raging River Raft Ride, All-American High-Dive Show, Storytown themed children's area. Splashwater Kingdom water park features giant wavepool, water slides, Adventure River and kiddie pools. (Memorial Day-Labor Day, daily) NY 9, between exits 19 & 20 off I-87. Phone 518/792-3500. ¢¢¢¢¢

Water Slide World. Water fun park incl wave pool, 13 water slides, Activity Pool, Lazy River and Toddler Lagoon play area. (Late June-Labor Day, daily) US 9. Phone 518/668-4407. ¢¢¢¢¢

Annual Events

Americade. Annual touring motorcycle event incl seminars, exhibits, shows, guided scenic tours. Phone 518/656-3696. 2nd wk June.

Family Festival. Shepard Park, Canada St. Craft show, family entertainment, game booths, music, food. Phone 518/668-5771. 3rd wk Aug.

Jazz Festival. Shepard Park Bandstand. Regional jazz bands; lawn seating. Phone 518/668-2616. Wkend after Labor Day.

Lakeside Festival. Beach Rd. Juried craft show; boat show with demo rides; food, music, fireworks. Phone 518/668-5771. 3rd wkend Sept.

Seasonal Event

Winter Carnival. Wkends Feb.

Motels

★ ★ **BAYFRONT HOUSEKEEPING COTTAGES.** *3226 Lake Shore Dr, I-87 exit 22.* 518/668-9579. 4 kit. units, 6 kit. cottages. Late June-Labor Day: up to 4, $850-$1,200/wk; lower rates Memorial Day wkend-late June, after Labor Day-mid-Oct. Closed rest of yr. Crib free. TV; cable (premium). Playground. Restaurant nearby. Ck-out 10 am. Porches. Picnic tables, grills. Beach, dockage. Rustic setting on lake. No cr cds accepted.

★ ★ **BEST WESTERN OF LAKE GEORGE.** *I-87 exit 21.* 518/668-5701; res: 800/234-0265; FAX 518/668-4926. E-mail reservations@bestwesternlakegeorge.com; web www.bestwesternlakegeorge.com. 87 rms, 2 story. July-Labor Day: S, D $99-$140; each addl $10; suites $166-$265; under 12 free; higher wkend rates in season; lower rates rest of yr. Crib free. TV; cable, VCR avail. 2 pools, 1 indoor; wading pool, whirlpool. Complimentary coffee. Ck-out 11 am. Business servs avail. Downhill ski 10 mi; x-country ski 8 mi. Fireplace in some suites. Balconies. Cr cds: A, C, D, DS, ER, MC, V.

★ **COLONEL WILLIAMS MOTOR INN.** *US 9.* 518/668-5727; res: 800/334-5727. E-mail colwilliam@aol.com. 40 rms. July-Labor Day: S, D $85-$125; each addl $8; suites $130-$160; family, wkly rates; lower rates mid-May-June, after Labor Day-late Oct. Closed rest of yr. Crib free. TV; cable. Indoor/outdoor pool; whirlpool. Playground. Restaurant nearby. Ck-out 11 am. Lndry facilities. Meeting rm. Exercise equipt; sauna. Game rm. Lawn games. Refrigerators, microwaves avail. Picnic tables, grill. Cr cds: A, DS, MC, V.

★ **COLONIAL MANOR.** *2200 NY 9, 1/4 mi S on US 9, NY 9N, 2 blks N of I-87 exit 21.* 518/668-4884. 35 motel rms, 1-2 story, 9 cottages, 17 kit. cottages (1-4-bedrm). Late June-Labor Day: S, D $68-$150; each addl $6-$10; under 12 free (motel only); kit. units to 4, $650-$1,450/wk; each addl $50-$100; lower rates May-late June, after Labor Day-mid-Oct. Closed rest of yr. Crib free. TV; cable. Heated pool; whirlpool. Playground. Restaurant opp open 24 hrs. Ck-out 11 am, kit. cottages 10 am. Lawn games. Refrigerators. Cottages with porches. Picnic tables, grill for kit. units. Shaded grounds. Cr cds: A, C, D, DS, MC, V.

★ **CREST HAVEN.** *Lake Shore Dr, 11/2 mi N on NY 9N; I-87 exit 22, on lake.* 518/668-3332; FAX 518/668-0324; res: 800/853-1632. 12 kit. units in motel (3-day min July-Aug), 15 kit. cottages, 20 cabins. Late June-Labor Day: S, D $105-$150; each addl $10-$20; kit. units, cottages (up to 4 persons) $950-$1,299/wk; lower rates mid-May-late June, after Labor Day-mid-Oct. Closed rest of yr. Crib free. TV; cable. Pool; wading pool. Playground. Restaurant 8 am-11 pm (in season). Ck-out 10 am. Private beach. Rec rm. Lawn games. Fireplace in cottages. Picnic tables, grills. Cr cds: MC, V.

★ ★ **DAYS INN.** *1454 NY 9, 3 mi S on NY 9, exit 20.* 518/793-3196; FAX 518/793-6028. Web www.daysinn.com. 109 rms, 2 story. July-Sept: S, D $78-$140; each addl $5; under 12 free; lower rates rest of yr. Crib free. TV; cable (premium). Indoor pool; whirlpool. Restaurant 7 am-11 pm. Ck-out 11 am. Business servs avail. Game rm. Some balconies. Cr cds: A, C, D, DS, MC, V.

★ **DUTCHESS.** *Lake Shore Dr, 1 mi N on NY 9N.* 518/668-5264; res: 800/785-9558. 14 rms, 1-2 story, 5 kits. July-Aug: S, D $65-$70; each addl $4-$8; kit. units $70-$75 ($460-$510/wk); lower rates rest of yr. Crib free. TV; cable. Pool. Playground. Coffee in lobby. Restaurant opp 8 am-9 pm. Ck-out 10 am. Tennis. Downhill/x-country ski 10 mi. Rec rm. Lawn games. Refrigerators. Picnic tables, grills. Cr cds: A, DS, MC, V.

★ ★ **ECONO LODGE.** *439 Canada St.* 518/668-2689; FAX 518/798-3455. E-mail econolodge@capital.net; web www.adirondack.net/tour/econolodge. 50 rms, 3 story. Mid-June-Labor Day: S, D $83-$110; each addl $10; under 18 free; lower rates May-mid-June, after Labor Day-Oct. Closed rest of yr. Crib free. TV; cable. 2 pools, 1 indoor; whirlpool. Restaurant opp 6 am-10 pm. Ck-out 10 am. Meeting rm. Business servs avail. Game rm. Refrigerators avail. Balconies. Cr cds: A, C, D, DS, MC, V.

★ ★ **FORT WILLIAM HENRY.** *48 Canada St, 1 mi N of I-87 exit 21, on lake.* 518/668-3081; res: 800/234-0267. E-mail reservations@fortwilliamhenry.com; web www.fortwilliamhenry.com. 99 rms, 2 story. Late June-Labor Day: S, D $140-$159; each addl $15; suite $200-$255; under 12 free; hol wkends (2-day min); lower rates rest of yr. Crib free. Pet accepted, some restrictions. TV; cable, VCR avail (movies). 2 pools, 1 indoor; whirlpool, poolside serv. Playground. Restaurant in season 7 am-10 pm. Bar noon-1 am, closed off-season. Ck-out 11 am. Meeting rms. Business servs avail. Downhill ski 20 mi; x-country ski 8 mi. Sauna. Bicycle rentals. Cr cds: A, C, D, DS, ER, MC, V.

★ **HERITAGE OF LAKE GEORGE.** *419 Canada St (US 9).* 518/668-3357; FAX 518/668-9784; res: 800/883-2653. Web www.heritageoflakegeorge.com. 38 rms, 7 with shower only, 2 story. July-Labor Day: S, D $65-$120; each addl $10; kit. units $775-$1,075; under 16 free; wkends, hols (2-day min); lower rates mid-May-June, Labor Day-mid-Oct. Closed rest of yr. Crib free. TV; cable. Heated pools. Complimentary coffee in lobby. Restaurant opp 6:30 am-10 pm. Ck-out 11 am. Business servs avail. Refrigerators; microwaves avail. Picnic tables, grills. Cr cds: A, DS, MC, V.

★ ★ **HOLIDAY INN.** *Canada St (US 9), I-87 exit 21.* 518/668-5781; FAX 518/668-9213. 105 rms, 2 story. July-Labor Day: S, D $135-$210; each addl $10; under 19 free; higher rates special events; lower rates rest of yr. Crib avail. TV; cable (premium). 2 pools, 1 indoor; wading pool, lifeguard in season. Playground. Restaurant 6:30 am-2 pm, 5-10 pm. Rm serv. Bar. Ck-out 11 am. Coin lndry. Meeting rms. Business servs avail. Gift shop. Exercise equipt. Game rm. Miniature golf. Refrigerators. Cr cds: A, C, D, DS, JCB, MC, V.

★ **HOWARD JOHNSON.** *2 Canada St.* 518/668-5744; res: 800/446-4656; FAX 518/668-3544. 110 rms, 2 story, 20 suites, 10 kit. units. July-Labor Day: S, D $109-$149; each addl $10; suites, kit. units $139-$199; under 18 free; hols (2-day min); lower rates rest of yr. Closed Dec-Mar. Crib $10. TV; cable (premium). 2 pools, 1 indoor; wading pool. Complimentary coffee in lobby. Restaurant 7 am-noon, 6-10 pm. Rm serv. Bar 5 pm-1 am; entertainment Thurs-Sun. Meeting rms. Business servs avail. Downhill/x-country ski 15 mi. Exercise equipt. Refrigerators avail. In-rm whirlpool in some suites. Picnic tables, grills. Cr cds: A, C, D, DS, MC, V.

★ ★ **LAKE CREST.** *366 Canada St, I-87 exits 21, 22, on lakeshore.* 518/668-3374; FAX 518/668-2273. 40 rms, 1-2 story. Late June-early Sept: S, D $98-$176; each addl $9; suites $158-$176; under 6 free; lower rates mid-Apr-late June, early Sept-mid-Oct. Closed rest of yr. Crib

$6. TV; cable. Heated pool. Restaurant 7:30 am-noon in season; closed rest of yr. Ck-out 11 am. Business servs avail. Sundries. Private sand beach. Terraces. Cr cds: MC, V.

✔★ **MOHAWK.** *435 Canada St, 1 blk from lake.* 518/668-2143. 60 rms, 8 kits., 7 kit. cottages. Late June-Labor Day: S, D $65-$119; each addl $8; kit. units (3-day min), cottages $650-$975/wk; lower rates rest of yr. Crib free. TV; cable. Indoor pool; whirlpool. Playground. Restaurant opp 9 am-11 pm. Ck-out 11 am, kit. units 10 am. Guest lndry. Downhill/x-country ski 8 mi. Game rm. Lawn games. Some in-rm whirlpools, fireplaces. Picnic tables, grills. Cr cds: DS, MC, V.

★ **MOHICAN.** *1545 NY 9, 1/2 mi N of I-87 exit 20.* 518/792-0474. 43 rms, 13 kit. units. Late June-Labor Day: S $98; D $115-$140; kit. units $140-$185; lower rates rest of yr. Crib $5. TV; cable (premium). 2 pools, 1 indoor; wading pools, whirlpools. Playground. Restaurant 7:30 am-4 pm. Ck-out 11 am. Coin lndry. Sundries. Downhill ski 15 mi; x-country ski 4 mi. Sauna. Game rm. Lawn games. Refrigerators. Picnic tables, grills. Cr cds: A, C, D, MC, V.

★ **NORDICK'S.** *2895 Lakeshore Dr.* 518/668-2697; FAX 518/668-4514; res: 800/368-2697. E-mail info@nordicks.com; web www.nordicks.com. 21 rms. Mid-July-Labor Day, hol wkends: S, D $69-$94; under 16 free; lower rates May-July 1, after Labor Day-late Oct. Closed rest of yr. Crib free. TV; cable. Heated pool. Complimentary coffee. Restaurant 7 am-10 pm. Bar. Ck-out 10 am. Health club privileges. Refrigerators avail. Patios, balconies. Cr cds: A, DS, MC, V.

★ **STILL BAY.** *NY 9 N, 2 3/4 mi N on NY 9N, 2 mi N of I-87 exit 22, on lakeshore.* 518/668-2584. E-mail stillbay@adrondaknet.com; web www.stillbay.com. 22 rms, 1-2 story, 4 kits., 2 kit. units (2-bedrm). July-Labor Day: D $98-$120; each addl $15; kit. units $115-$135; wkly rates; lower rates late May-June, Sept-mid-Oct. Closed rest of yr. Crib free. TV; cable. Complimentary buffet bkfst July-Labor Day. Restaurant nearby. Ck-out 11 am. Lawn games. Refrigerators avail. Picnic tables, grills. Private beach, boathouse, dockage, rowboats, paddle boats. Cr cds: MC, V.

★★ **SUN CASTLE VILLAS.** *Lake Shore Drive, 1 1/2 mi N on NY 9N; I-87 exit 22.* 518/668-2085; res: 518/745-7163; FAX 518/792-3072. 16 kit. villas (1-2 bedrm). Mid-June-Labor Day: villa (up to 4) $800-$1,375/wk; lower rates Memorial Day wkend-mid-June, after Labor Day-mid-Oct. Closed rest of yr. Crib free. Maid serv twice wkly (fee). TV; cable (premium). Heated pool. Restaurant nearby. Ck-out 11 am. Tennis. Wood-burning stoves (free firewood). Private patios, balconies. Picnic table, grills. Private beach; dock privileges, rowboats. Original mansion house on grounds. Cr cds: MC, V.

★★ **TALL PINES.** *US 9S, 1 3/4 mi S on US 9S.* 518/668-5122; FAX 518/668-3563; res: 800/368-5122. E-mail ncaple@aol.com; web www.mediausa.com/ny/tallpinesmotel. 26 rms, 1-2 story. Mid-July-Labor Day: S, D $108-$118; each addl $10; family, wkly rates; lower rates Memorial Day-mid-July. Closed rest of yr. Crib free. TV; cable. Pool; wading pool, whirlpool. Playground. Complimentary continental bkfst. Ck-out 11 am. Sauna. Refrigerators. Picnic table, grills. Cr cds: DS, MC, V.

Motor Hotel

★★ **THE GEORGIAN.** *(384 Canada St, Lake George)* 518/668-5401; FAX 518/668-5870; res: 800/525-3436. Web www.webny.com/georgian. 164 rms, 2 story. Late June-Labor Day: S, D $99-$199; each addl $10; suites $199-$299; under 5 free; wkend plans; lower rates rest of yr. Crib $7. TV; cable (premium), VCR avail. Underground garage parking. Heated pool; poolside serv, lifeguard. Coffee in rms. Restaurant 7am-9

pm. Rm serv. Bar 5 pm-1 am. Ck-out 11 am. Meeting rms. Business servs avail. Bellhops. Valet serv. Airport, RR station transportation. Downhill/x-country ski 8 mi. Game rm. Refrigerators in suites, avail for rms (fee). Some balconies. Cr cds: A, C, D, DS, MC, V.

Resorts

★★ **DUNHAM'S BAY LODGE.** *2999 SR 9L, 5 mi SE on NY 9L.* 518/656-9242; FAX 518/656-9250; res: 800/79-LODGE. E-mail vacation@dunhamsbay.com; web www.dunhamsbay.com. 20 rms in main building, 24 motel units, 1-2 story, 10 kit. cottages. No A/C in cottages. July-Labor Day: S, D $145-$160; each addl $20-$25; kit. cottages $850-$1,050; wkends (3-day min); family, wkly rates; lower rates mid-May-late June, after Labor Day-mid-Oct. Closed rest of yr. Crib free. TV; cable. Indoor pool; wading pool, whirlpool. Playground. Complimentary continental bkfst. Restaurant 8:30-10 am, Sun to 11 am. Bar. Ck-out 10 am, ck-in 3 pm. Business servs avail. Tennis. Boat rentals, dockage. Lawn games. Game rm. Some refrigerators. Some balconies. Picnic tables, grills. 150 acres on lake. Cr cds: A, MC, V.

★★★ **ROARING BROOK RANCH & TENNIS RESORT.** *3 mi SW on NY 9N, 1 mi W of I-87 exit 21.* 518/668-5767; res: 800/882-7665; FAX 518/648-4019. Web www.adirondack.net/tour/roaring. 142 rms, 2 story. MAP (2-day min) (riding optional): July-Labor Day: D $81-$86/person; suites $106/person; wkly rates 10% less; family rates; golf, tennis, riding plans; lower rates Jan-Feb, mid-May-June, after Labor Day-mid-Oct. Closed rest of yr. Crib free. TV. 3 pools, 1 indoor; poolside serv. Free supervised child's activities (summer); ages 4-7. Restaurant 8-10 am, 6-7:30 pm. Snack bar. Cookouts in summer season. Bars 11-3 am. Ck-out 11 am, ck-in 3 pm. Coin lndry. Meeting rms. Business servs avail. Free bus depot transportation. Sports dir. 5 tennis courts, pro in season. Golf privileges. Downhill ski 10 mi; x-country ski 6 mi. Snowmobile, nature trails. Lawn games. Entertainment; movies. Rec rm. Game rm. Exercise equipt; saunas. On 500 acres. Cr cds: MC, V.

Cottage Colonies

✔★ **ALPINE VILLAGE.** *Lake Shore Dr, 1 mi N on NY 9N; I-87 exit 22.* 518/668-2193. Web www.members.aol.com/alpinelg. 15 rms in lodge, guesthouse, 1-2 story; 24 rms in cabins, 18 A/C. Late June-Labor Day: D $72-$105; each addl $8-$10; cabins $460-$760/wk; under 3 free; wkly rates; 3-day min in season; lower rates rest of yr. TV. Heated pool. Playground. Snack bar. Ck-out 11 am, ck-in 3 pm. Package store 1/2 mi. Meeting rms. Free bus depot transportation. Tennis. Private beach, rowboats, canoes. Downhill/x-country ski 13 mi. Ice-skating. Lawn games. Rec rm. Entertainment. Grills. Fireplace in cabin units. Landscaped grounds; on lakeshore. Cr cds: A, DS, MC, V.

★★ **O'CONNOR'S RESORT COTTAGES.** *3454 Lake Shore Dr, 2 1/5 mi N on US 9, NY 9N; I-87 exit 22.* 518/668-3367. 32 kit. cottages (2-3 bedrm). Late June-Labor Day, wkly: from $860, kit. cottages for 2 from $644; lower rates rest of yr. Crib free. TV; cable. Playground. Restaurant nearby. Ck-out 10 am, ck-in 3:30 pm. Miniature golf. Private beach; float, dockage; paddleboats, rowboats. Lawn games. Picnic tables, grill. Wooded grounds. Cr cds: MC, V.

Restaurants

✔★ **BAVARIAN HOUSE.** *(3259 Lake Shore Dr, Lake George)* 2 1/2 mi N on NY 9N; I-87 exit 22. 518/668-2476. German, Amer menu. Specialties: Bavarian pot roast, sauerbraten, Wienerschnitzel. Hrs: 7:30 am-10 pm. Closed Mon off season; also mid-Sept-late May. Res accepted. Serv bar. Semi-a la carte: bkfst $1.95-$68.95, lunch $1.95-$10.95, dinner

$10.95-$16.95. Buffet: dinner $10.95. Child's meals. Terrace dining. Fireplace. Cr cds: A, MC, V.

★ ★ **THE COACHMAN.** *Lake George Rd, 3 mi S on US 9; I-87 exit 20.* 518/793-4455. Specializes in prime rib, veal, fresh seafood. Salad bar. Hrs: noon-10 pm; Sun to 9 pm. Closed Dec 25. Res accepted. Bar. Semi-a la carte: lunch $4.95-$9.95, dinner $10.95-$22.95. Buffet: (Mon-Sat) lunch $6.95. Child's meals. Cr cds: A, C, D, MC, V.

SC

★ ★ **THE LOG JAM.** *1484 NY 9, site 1, Jct US 9 & NY 149.* 518/798-1155. Specializes in steak, seafood, prime rib. Salad bar. Hrs: 11:30 am-9:30 pm; July, Aug: Fri, Sat to 10 pm. Closed Thanksgiving, Dec 25. Res accepted. Bar. Semi-a la carte: lunch $5.95-$10.50, dinner $13.95-$19.95. Child's meals. Lobster tank. Rustic decor. Cr cds: A, C, D, DS, MC, V.

D **SC**

★ ★ **MONTCALM SOUTH.** *1415 NY 9, 3¹/₂ mi S on US 9 at I-87 exit 20.* 518/793-6601. Web www.menumart.com. Continental menu. Specializes in veal, prime rib, seafood. Own baking. Hrs: 11:45 am-2:30 pm, 5-9:45 pm; Sun 11:45 am-9:30 pm. Closed some major hols. Res accepted. Bar. Wine list. Semi-a la carte: lunch $4.95-$7.95, dinner $11.95-$29.95. Child's meals. Fireplace. Family-owned. Cr cds: A, C, D, DS, MC, V.

D **SC**

Lake Luzerne (D-8)

(See also Glens Falls, Lake George Village)

Pop 2,816 **Elev** 610 ft **Area code** 518 **Zip** 12846
Information Chamber of Commerce, 79 Main St, PO Box 222; 518/696-3500.

Lumbering and papermaking formed the economic background of Lake Luzerne, now an all-year resort. In addition to being on the small lake for which it is named, it is near Great Sacandaga Lake, another popular area for summer and winter sports.

What to See and Do

Bow Bridge. Parabolic bridge (1895) spans the Hudson and Sacandaga rivers. The only remaining semideck lenticular iron truss bridge, typical of the late 19th-century iron bridges in New York State.

Rockwell Falls & Chasm. Hudson River flows over rocks causing a great rush of water; joins the Sacandaga River at the end of the falls and chasm. Viewed from bridge. SE of town via Northway, exit 21.

Swimming, boating, fishing. On Lake Vanare, Lake Luzerne and Great Sacandaga Lake. Boat launching sites (free) on the Hudson River, at Fourth Lake Campground and on the Sacandaga, North Shore Rd.

White water rafting. Down the Sacandaga River. Several outfitters operate in the area. Seasons usually Memorial Day-Labor Day; inquire locally.

Motels

★ **ISLAND VIEW.** *302 Lake Ave, I-87 exit 21.* 518/696-3079. 10 rms, 4 kits. June-Sept: S, D $60-$70; each addl $5; kit. units $70-$73; under 12 free; wkly rates; lower rates rest of yr. Crib free. TV; cable. Complimentary coffee. Restaurant nearby. Ck-out 11 am. Lawn games. Some refrigerators. Picnic tables, grills. Private beach, boats. Cr cds: DS, MC, V.

★ **PINE POINT COTTAGES.** *1369 Lake Ave, I-87 exit 21, on Lake Vanare.* 518/696-3015. 8 rms in motel, 7 A/C, 10 kit. cottages.

Mid-May-late Oct: S, D $57-$65; each addl $3-$5; kit. cottages for 2-4, $70-$96; wkly rates. Closed rest of yr. Crib free. TV; cable. Playground. Restaurant nearby. Ck-out 10 am. Free airport, bus depot transportation. Downhill ski 15 mi; x-country ski 1 mi. Lawn games. Many fireplaces. Porches. Picnic tables, grills. Private sand beach. Cr cds: MC, V.

Inns

★ ★ ★ **THE LAMPLIGHT.** *231 Lake Ave (NY 9N).* 518/696-5294; FAX 518/696-5256; res: 800/262-4668. E-mail lamp@nethaven.com; web www.lamplightinn.com. 15 rms, 2 story, 5 suites. MAP: S, D $89-$199; each addl $25; wkly rates. Children over 12 yrs only. TV in sitting rm; cable (premium). Complimentary full bkfst; afternoon refreshments. Dining rm Sun 10:30 am-1 pm. Ck-out 11 am, ck-in 3 pm. Meeting rm. Business servs avail. Gift shop. Lawn games. Some fireplaces, in-rm whirlpools. Picnic tables. Victorian house (1890) with 12-ft beamed ceilings, chestnut woodwork, chestnut keyhole staircase crafted in England; wrap-around porch; antiques; library. Lake, beach 1 blk. Cr cds: A, MC, V.

★ ★ **SARATOGA ROSE.** *(4274 Rockwell St, Hadley 12835)* 518/696-2861; res: 800/942-5025; FAX 518/696-5319. E-mail saratogarose@capital.net; web saratogarose.com. 6 rms, shower only, 2 story. No rm phones. Mid-June-Labor Day: S, D $85-$175; each addl $8.50-$17.50; ski, golf plans; wkends, hols (2-day min); lower rates rest of yr. Children over 10 yrs only. TV in common rm; VCR avail (movies). Complimentary full bkfst. Restaurant from 5 pm. Ck-out 11 am, ck-in 3 pm. Business servs avail. Downhill ski 12 mi; x-country ski 15 mi. Many in-rm whirlpools, fireplaces. Built in 1885 as wedding gift for a town founder's daughter. Antiques. Cr cds: DS, MC, V.

Restaurants

★ **CIRO'S.** *1439 Lake Ave, 5 mi E on NY 9N.* 518/696-2556. Italian, Amer menu. Specialties: fettucine Alfredo with frutti di mare, veal Anthony parmigiana. Soup bar. Hrs: 5-10 pm; winter 5-9 pm. Closed Thanksgiving, Dec 25; also Tues, Wed in winter. Res accepted. Bar. Semi-a la carte: dinner $6.95-$18.95. Child's meals. Cr cds: MC, V.

✔★ **DEFINO'S HERITAGE.** *61 Northwood Rd, 5 mi N on NY 9N then ¹/₈ mi on Northwood Rd.* 518/696-3733. Italian, Amer menu. Specialties: linguine with white or red clam sauce, stuffed cabbage, pot roast of beef. Hrs: 5-10 pm; Sun 4-9 pm. Closed Mon-Tues; mid-Oct-mid-May, Mon-Thurs in May & June and after Labor Day-Columbus Day. Res accepted. Bar. Semi-a la carte: dinner $7.95-$14.95. Child's meals. Candlelight dining; fireplaces. Chef-owned. Cr cds: MC, V.

★ **WATERHOUSE.** *¹/₂ mi S on NY 9N.* 518/696-3115. Specializes in prime rib, seafood. Own pies. Hrs: 11:30 am-9 pm; Fri, Sat to 10 pm; Sun from noon. Closed Thanksgiving, Dec 25. Res accepted. Bar. Semi-a la carte: lunch $1.95-$6.95, dinner $8.95-$18.95. Child's meals. Outdoor dining. Family-owned. Cr cds: MC, V.

Lake Placid (B-8)

(See also Saranac Lake, Wilmington)

Pop 2,485 **Elev** 1,882 ft **Area code** 518 **Zip** 12946 **E-mail** placidpr@northnet.org **Web** www.lakeplacid.com

Information Essex County Visitors Bureau, Olympic Center, 216 Main St; 518/523-2445 or 800/447-5224.

Mount Marcy, the highest mountain in New York State (5,344 ft) rises in the Adirondack peaks that surround the town. On Lake Placid, the village also partly surrounds Mirror Lake. This is one of the most famous all-year vacation centers in the East and the site of the 1932 and 1980 Winter Olympics. The Intervale Olympic Ski Jump Complex has 229-foot and 296-foot ski jumps constructed for the 1980 games, now open to the public and is used for training and competition.

What to See and Do

John Brown Farm Historic Site. Brown's final home; graves of the noted abolitionist, 2 sons and 10 others who died in the struggle to end slavery. (Late May-late Oct, Wed-Sun) John Brown Rd, 2 mi S, 1 mi off NY 73. Phone 518/523-3900.   **Free.**

Lake Placid Center For the Arts. Concerts, films, art exhibits. Gallery (July-Aug, daily exc Mon; rest of yr, Tues-Sat; free). Saranac Ave at Fawn Ridge. Phone 518/523-2512 for ticket prices.

Lake Placid Marina. 1-hr scenic cruises. (Mid-May-mid-Oct) Lake St, 1 mi N on NY 86 to Mirror Lake Dr. Phone 518/523-9704.   **¢¢¢**

Olympic Arena and Convention Center. Built for the 1932 Winter Olympics and renovated for the 1980 Winter games. Winter and summer skating shows, family shows, hockey; public skating, concerts. Main St. Phone 518/523-1655.

Olympic Sports Complex (Mt Van Hoevenberg Recreation Area). Site of 1980 Winter Olympic Games. Bobsled, luge, cross-country, biathlon events. Championship bobsled and luge races most wkends in winter. Cross-country trails (33 mi) open to the public when not used for racing. Bobsled rides (mid-Dec-early Mar, daily exc Mon; fee); luge rides (mid-Dec-early Mar, wkends; fee). 7 mi SE on NY 73. Phone 518/523-1655.   **¢¢**

Uihlein Sugar Maple Research-Extension Field Station. 4,000-tap sugar bush; maple syrup demonstrations, exhibits in Sugar House. Owned and operated by NY State College of Agriculture at Cornell Univ. (July-Labor Day, Tues-Fri; mid-Sept-mid-Oct, Fri; closed July 4) Schedule may vary. Bear Cub Rd. Phone 518/523-9337.   **Free.**

Motels

★ ★ **ADIRONDACK INN BY THE LAKE.** *217 Main St (NY 86). 518/523-2424; FAX 518/523-2425; res: 800/556-2424.* E-mail ad kinn@cencom.net; web trilakes.ny.us/lp/adkinn.html. 49 rms, 2 story. Wkends late Dec-mid-Mar, early July-Oct: S, D $90-$140; each addl $12; suites $150-$200; kit. unit $99-$130; ski, golf plans; lower rates rest of yr. Crib $10. TV; cable. 2 pools, 1 indoor; whirlpool. Playground. Restaurant 7 am-10 pm. Bar 5 pm-1 am in season. Ck-out 11 am. Meeting rms. Business servs avail. Downhill ski 8 mi; x-country ski 1 mi. Exercise equipt; sauna. Rec rm. Refrigerators. Many balconies. Opp Olympic Arena and Convention Hall. Cr cds: A, C, MC, V.

✓★ **ALPINE AIR.** *99 Saranac Ave. 518/523-9261; res: 800/469-3663; FAX 518/523-9273.* E-mail alpine@northnet.org. 24 rms, 6 with shower only, 1-2 story. Late-June-mid-Oct: S, D $46-$78; each addl $8; under 12 free; ski plans; wkends, hols (2-day min); lower rates rest of yr. Crib $8. TV; cable. Complimentary coffee in rms. Restaurant nearby. Ck-out 10:30 am. Downhill ski 8 mi; x-country ski 1 mi. Heated pool. Some balconies. Picnic tables. Cr cds: DS, MC, V.

★ ★ **ALPINE MOTOR INN.** *50 Wilmington Rd, 3/4 mi E of NY 86. 518/523-2180; FAX 518/523-1724; res: 800/257-4638.* 18 rms, 2 story. July-Aug, ski season: S, D $56-$78; kit. units $68-$82; under 12 free; lower rates rest of yr. Crib $3. TV; cable (premium). Heated pool. Restaurant 5-9:30 pm. Bar 3 pm-midnight. Ck-out 11 am. 45-hole golf privileges opp. Downhill ski 8 mi; x-country ski 1 mi. Sun deck. Some refrigerators. Balconies. Cr cds: A, D, DS, MC, V.

✓★ ★ **ART DEVLIN'S OLYMPIC.** *350 Main St, 1 blk S on NY 86, at jct NY 73. 518/523-3700; FAX 518/523-3893.* E-mail adevlin@capi tal.net; web lakeplacid.com. 40 rms, 2 story. S, D $48-$108; each addl $6; higher rates special events. Crib free. Pet accepted. TV; cable. Pool; wading pool. Complimentary continental bkfst. Ck-out 11 am. Airport, bus depot transportation. Downhill ski 8 mi; x-country ski 2 mi. Refrigerators; some in-rm whirlpools. Some balconies. Sun deck. Cr cds: A, DS, MC, V.

★ ★ **ECONO LODGE.** *Cascade Rd (NY 73). 518/523-2817; res: 800/553-2666.* Web www.econolodge.com/hotel/ny128. 61 rms, 2 story. Mid-June-mid-Oct, late Dec-Mar: S $65-$75; D $80-$90; each addl $5; under 18 free; lower rates rest of yr. Crib free. TV; cable. Indoor pool; whirlpool. Complimentary coffee in lobby. Restaurant nearby. Ck-out 11 am. Coin lndry. Meeting rm. Business servs avail. Downhill/x-country ski 1 mi. Game rm. Balconies. Picnic tables. Cr cds: A, C, D, DS, ER, JCB, MC, V.

★ ★ **HOWARD JOHNSON.** *Saranac Ave, 3/4 mi W on NY 86. 518/523-9555; FAX 518/523-4765.* 92 rms, 2 story. July-mid-Sept & mid-Dec-Mar: S, D $85-$140; each addl $10; suites $110-$150; under 18 free; golf plans; lower rates rest of yr. Crib free. Pet accepted. TV; cable (premium). Indoor pool; whirlpool. Coffee in rms. Restaurant 7 am-11 pm. Bar from noon. Ck-out noon. Coin lndry. Meeting rms. Business servs avail. Sundries. Tennis. Downhill ski 10 mi; x-country ski on site. Rec rm. Lawn games. Balconies. Picnic tables, grills. Cr cds: A, C, D, DS, ER, JCB, MC, V.

★ **MOUNTAIN VIEW INN.** *140 Main St, (NY 86). 518/523-2439; FAX 518/523-8974; res: 800/499-2668.* E-mail mtviewin@north net.org; web www.lakeplacidlodging.com. 18 rms, 2 story. July-Oct, ski season: S, D $68-$95; each addl $5-$10; higher rates hols, special events; lower rates rest of yr. Crib free. TV; cable. Restaurant nearby. Ck-out 11 am. Health club privileges. Refrigerators; microwaves avail. Balconies. Overlooks Lake Placid Village and Mirror Lake. Cr cds: A, MC, V.

✓★ **NORTHWAY.** *5 Wilmington Rd. 518/523-3500; res: 800/479-2135 (NY).* E-mail nmotel@aol.com. 14 rms. No A/C. Mid-June-mid-Oct, mid-Dec-Mar: S, D $65-$80; each addl $5; family units $75; under 14 free; lower rates rest of yr. Crib free. TV; cable. Pool. Playground. Complimentary coffee in lobby. Restaurant nearby. Ck-out 11 am. Downhill ski 9 mi; x-country ski adj. Lawn games. Cr cds: A, DS, MC, V.

✓★ **PLACID BAY INN.** *70 Saranac Ave. 518/523-2001.* E-mail placid-bay@worldnet.att.net; web www.spav.com/progc/placidbay. 20 rms, 2 story, 8 kit. units, 2 cottages. Late June-Labor Day, hol wks & winter wkends: S, D $60-$85; each addl $5; kit. units $68-$98; cottages (1-3 bedrm) $130-$200; family, wkly rates; lower rates rest of yr. Crib free. TV; cable. Heated pool. Playground. Restaurant nearby. Ck-out 11 am. Bus depot transportation. Downhill ski 8 mi; x-country ski 2 mi. Lawn games. Picnic tables, grill. Fishing charters & guide serv. Paddleboats, canoes. Cr cds: A, MC, V.

★ ★ **RAMADA INN.** *12 Saranac Ave, on NY 86. 518/523-2587; res: 800/741-7841; FAX 518/523-2328.* E-mail ramadalp@northnet.org; web www.lakeplacid.ny.us/ramada. 90 rms, 3 story. Mid-July-early Sept, late Sept-mid-Oct, late Dec-early Jan: S $55-$130; D $60-$140; each addl

$10; under 18 free; ski, golf plans; higher rates hols; lower rates rest of yr. Crib free. Pet accepted, some restrictions. TV; cable, VCR avail. Indoor pool; whirlpool. Coffee in rms. Restaurant 7 am-10 pm. Bar 4:30 pm-1 am. Ck-out noon. Business servs avail. In-rm modem link. Downhill ski 10 mi; x-country ski 1 mi. Exercise equipt. Game rm. Some balconies. Cr cds: A, C, D, DS, ER, JCB, MC, V.

★ **SCHULTE'S MOTOR INN.** *Cascade Rd (NY 73).* 518/523-3532. 30 units, 14 with shower only, 15 kit. cottages. Some A/C. Some rm phones. Mid-June-mid-Sept, mid-Dec-mid-Mar: S, D $68-$78; each addl $9; kit. cottages $48-$85; under 13 free; wkly rates; higher rates hols; lower rates rest of yr. Crib free. Pet accepted, some restrictions; $5. TV; cable. Restaurant nearby. Ck-out 11 am. Downhill ski 7 mi; x-country ski 2 mi. Pool. Playground. Lawn games. Many refrigerators. Some balconies. Picnic tables, grills. Cr cds: A, MC, V.

★ **TOWN & COUNTRY.** *67 Saranac Ave.* 518/523-9268; *res:* 888/523-6640; *FAX* 518/523-8058. E-mail info@tcmotorinn.com; web www.tcmotorinn.com. 24 rms, 2 story. June-Oct, Dec-Mar: S, D $56-$78; each addl $5; cottage/apt $140; family rates; golf plans; lower rates rest of yr. Crib $5. TV; cable. Heated pool. Complimentary bkfst. Restaurant nearby. Ck-out 11 am. Downhill ski 8 mi; x-country ski 1/2 mi. Refrigerators. Balconies. Picnic tables, grills. Cr cds: A, DS, MC, V.

★★ **WILDWOOD.** *88 Saranac Ave.* 518/523-2624; *FAX* 518/523-3248; *res:* 800/841-6378. 35 rms, 1-2 story, 6 kit. cottages. July-Oct: S, D $48-$88; suites, kit. units $58-$150; each addl $6; cottages $860-$900/wk; under 15 free; higher rates: hol wkends, special events; lower rates rest of yr. Crib free. TV; cable. Heated pool; outdoor natural pool, wading pool, whirlpool. Playground. Complimentary coffee in rms. Restaurant adj 6 am-10 pm; open 24 hrs in season. Ck-out 11 am. Downhill ski 10 mi; x-country ski 1/2 mi. Sauna. Lawn games. Rowboats, paddle boats, canoes free to guests. Refrigerators; some in-rm whirlpools, some fireplaces. Private patios, balconies. Picnic tables, grill. On beach. Cr cds: A, C, D, DS, MC, V.

Lodge

★★★★ **LAKE PLACID LODGE.** *Whiteface Inn Rd.* 518/523-2700; *FAX* 518/523-1124. Web www.lakeplacidlodge.com. Cedar branches, smooth-painted pine and diamond-paned windows mark the facade of this 1882 Adirondack lodge set in the shadow of Whiteface Mountain. Luxurious, rustic rooms and cabins are tastefully decorated with twig-and-bark furniture, richly colored fabrics and works by local artisans. 37 units, 9 A/C, 5 with shower only, 4 bldgs, 15 cabins. No elvtr. S, D $225-$500; each addl $50; cabins $300-$650; wkends (2-day min), hols (3-day min). Crib free. Pet accepted; $50/day. Complimentary full bkfst. Complimentary coffee in lobby. Restaurant (see LAKE PLACID LODGE). Box lunches. Bar. Ck-out noon. Meeting rms. Business servs avail. In-rm modem link. Bellhops. Concierge. Gift shop. Tennis privileges. Golf privileges. Downhill ski 10 mi; x-country ski on site. Game rm. Refrigerator, wet bar in cabins; some fireplaces. Some balconies. Picnic tables, fire pit. Cr cds: A, MC, V.

Motor Hotels

★★★ **BEST WESTERN GOLDEN ARROW.** *150 Main St, on Mirror Lake.* 518/523-3353; *FAX* 518/523-8063. E-mail info@golden-arrow.com; web www.golden-arrow.com. 125 rms, 2-4 story. July-mid-Oct, late Dec-Mar: S, D $89-$149; each addl $10; suites $99-$220; under 12 free; MAP avail; ski plans; lower rates rest of yr. Crib $6. Pet accepted; $25. TV; cable. Indoor pool; wading pool, whirlpool. Restaurant 7 am-9 pm. Bar 11-2 am; entertainment Wed-Sat (in season). Ck-out 11 am. Meeting rms. Business servs avail. In-rm modem link. Shopping arcade. Covered parking. Free airport transportation. Downhill ski 9 mi; x-country ski on site. Exercise rm; sauna. Racquetball. Paddle boats, canoes. Rec rm. Some

fireplaces; refrigerators avail. Private patios, balconies. Picnic tables, grill. Private beach. Cr cds: A, C, D, DS, ER, MC, V.

★★★ **HILTON-LAKE PLACID RESORT.** *1 Mirror Lake Dr.* 518/523-4411; *res:* 800/755-5598; *FAX* 518/523-1120. E-mail info@lphilton.com; web www.lphilton.com. 178 rms, 1-5 story. Mid-June-mid-Oct: S, D $99-$169; each addl $12; family rates; ski, golf plans; lower rates rest of yr. Pet accepted. TV. 4 pools, 2 indoor; whirlpools, poolside serv. Restaurant 7-10:30 am, noon-2 pm, 5:30-9 pm. Rm serv 7 am-9 pm. Bar 11-2 am; entertainment Fri, Sat. Ck-out noon. Meeting rms. Business servs avail. Bellhops. Covered parking. Downhill ski 8 mi; x-country ski 1 mi. Exercise equipt. Boats. Game rm. Rec rm. Many balconies. Some rms on beach. Cr cds: A, C, D, DS, ER, MC, V.

★★★ **HOLIDAY INN.** *One Olympic Dr, Olympic Arena adj.* 518/523-2556; *FAX* 518/523-9410. E-mail info@lpresort.com; web www.lpresort.com. 205 rms, 2-4 story. July-Aug: S, D $79-$229; each addl $10; under 19 free; MAP avail; wkend rates; ski, golf plans; lower rates rest of yr. Crib free. Pet accepted. TV; cable. Heated pool; whirlpool. Playground. Coffee in rms. Restaurant 7 am-10 pm. Rm serv. Bar 11-2 am. Ck-out 11 am. Meeting rms. Business servs avail. In-rm modem link. Gift shop. Rec rm. Tennis. Golf privileges, putting green. Downhill ski 9 mi; x-country ski on site. Exercise rm; sauna. Refrigerators, microwaves. Many balconies. On hilltop overlooking lake. Cr cds: A, C, D, DS, ER, JCB, MC, V.

★★★ **MIRROR LAKE INN.** *5 Mirror Lake Dr.* 518/523-2544; *FAX* 518/523-2871. E-mail 104522.3250@compuserve.com; web www.mirrorlakeinn.com. 128 inn rms, 4 story, 17 rms in lakeside bldg. S, D $95-$235; each addl $15; suites $275-$345; under 18 free; MAP avail; ski plans. Crib free. TV; cable. 2 heated pools, 1 indoor; wading pool, whirlpool. Complimentary coffee; afternoon refreshments. Dining rm (see AVERILL CONWELL DINING RM). Rm serv. Bar noon-2 am. Ck-out noon. Meeting rm. Business serv avail. Valet serv. Gift shop. Beauty shop. Tennis. Downhill ski 10 mi; x-country ski 1 mi. Row boats, paddle boats, canoeing. Exercise equipt; sauna. Rec rm. Refrigerators, fireplaces. Some balconies. Private sand beach. On 8 acres. Cr cds: A, C, D, DS, MC, V.

Inns

★ **BARK EATER.** *(Alstead Mill Rd, Keene 12942) 13 mi E via NY 73, then 1/2 mi on Alstead Mill Rd.* 518/576-2221; *FAX* 518/576-2071. Web www.barkeater@nuenet.com. rms, 7 share baths, 3 bldgs, 1-2 story. No rm phones. D $75-$136; each addl $36; under 3 free; MAP avail; wkly rates; ski, riding packages. Crib free. TV; cable (premium). Complimentary full bkfst. Dining rm 8-9 am, dinner (1 sitting) 7 pm. Box lunches. Setups. Ck-out 11 am, ck-in 1 pm. Business servs avail. Downhill ski 15 mi; x-country ski on site, rentals. Picnic tables, grills. Former stagecoach stop built in early 1800s; antiques. Spacious farm with 5-acre pond. Horse stables. Polo field. Family-owned since 1936. Totally non-smoking. Cr cds: A, DS, MC, V.

✔★ **INTERLAKEN.** *15 Interlaken Ave.* 518/523-3180; *FAX* 518/523-0117; *res:* 800/428-4369. Web www.inbook.com. 11 rms, 3 story. No A/C. No rm phones. S, D $80-$150; each addl $15; MAP avail; wkends (2-day min), hol wkends (3-day min). Children over 5 yrs only. Pet accepted, some restrictions. TV in sitting rm; cable. Complimentary full bkfst; afternoon refreshments. Dining rm 6-9 pm; closed Tues, Wed. Ck-out 11 am, ck-in 3 pm. Gift shop. Downhill/x-country ski 8 mi. Health club privileges. Some balconies. Picnic tables. Built in 1906; turn-of-the-century furnishings. Cr cds: A, MC, V.

Restaurants

★ ★ ★ **AVERILL CONWELL DINING ROOM.** *(See Mirror Lake Inn Motor Hotel)* 518/523-2544. E-mail info@mirrorlakeinn.com; web www.mirrorlakeinn.com. Specialties: roasted rack of lamb, venison sirloin saddleback, hickory-style home-smoked shrimp. Own baking. Hrs: 7:30-10 am, 5:30-9 pm; Sat, Sun 7:30-11 am, 5:30-9 pm. Res accepted. Bar. A la carte entrees: bkfst $3.50-$9.95, dinner $16.95-$29.95. Child's meals. Pianist Sat, Sun. Outdoor dining. Formal, early-American decor; view of lake. Family-owned. Totally nonsmoking. Cr cds: A, D, DS, MC, V.

★ ★ ★ **LAKE PLACID LODGE.** *(See Lake Placid Lodge)* 518/523-2700. Web www.lakeplacidlodge.com. Contemporary Amer menu. Hrs: 7:30-10:30 am, noon-2:30 pm, 6-9 pm; Fri, Sat 6-10 pm. Res accepted. Bar. A la carte entrees: bkfst $12.95, lunch $7.95-$14.95, dinner $16-$31. Outdoor dining. View of lake. Cr cds: A, MC, V.

★ ★ **LE BISTRO LALIBERTÉ.** *51 Main St.* 518/523-3680. French menu. Specialties in lamb, fresh seafood. Hrs: 5-10 pm; summer also 11:30 am-3 pm. Closed Easter, Thanksgiving, Dec 25; Mon in Nov; also Apr. Res accepted. Bar. Semi-a la carte: lunch $5.50-$8.95, dinner $15-$22. Child's meals. Street parking. Outdoor dining. Bistro atmosphere; open kitchen. Cr cds: MC, V.

Letchworth State Park (E-3)

(See also Avon, Geneseo)

(Entrances at Castile, Mt Morris, Perry and Portageville)

In this 14,344-acre park are 17 miles of the Genesee River Gorge, sometimes called the Grand Canyon of the East. Sheer cliffs rise 600 feet at some points, and the river roars over three major falls, one of them 107 feet high. The park has a variety of accommodations, including an inn and motel, a 270-site tent and trailer camping area and 82 camping cabins (ranging from one room to family size). Standard fees.

Swimming pools with bathhouses (mid-June-Labor Day); fishing; whitewater rafting; hot-air ballooning; nature and hiking (all yr) trails; outstanding fall foliage. Cross-country skiing, snowmobiling, snowtubing. Picnicking at eight areas with tables, fireplaces, shelters, rest rooms; playground. Recreation programs. No pets in cabin areas and part of camping area. Standard fees.

The William Pryor Letchworth Museum, the grave of Mary Jemison and a restored Seneca Indian Council House are in the park (mid-May-Oct, daily; donation).

For detailed information contact Letchworth State Park, 1 Letchworth State Park, Castile 14427; 716/493-3600.

Inns

✔★ **BROMAN'S GENESEE FALLS.** *NY 436 (14536), E of S park entrance on NY 436.* 716/493-2484; FAX 716/468-5654. 10 rms, 3 story. No rm phones. S, D $57-$77; each addl $15. Complimentary full bkfst. Restaurant (see BROMAN'S GENESEE FALLS INN). Bar. Ck-out 11 am, ck-in 2 pm. Inn since 1870s. Cr cds: MC, V.

★ ★ ★ **GLEN IRIS.** *(14427).* In park, 1 mi N of S park entrance. 716/493-2622. 14 rms in inn, 3 story, 7 kit. units in motel. No rm phones. Apr-Oct: S, D $70; each addl $7.50; suites $125-$135; kit. units for 2, $60. Closed rest of yr. TV in motel rms; also in library of main bldg; VCR avail. Playground. Restaurant (see GLEN IRIS). Serv bar. Ck-out noon, ck-in 2 pm. Meeting rms. Business servs avail. Gift shop. Some refrigerators.

Picnic tables, grill. Former residence of William Pryor Letchworth (1860s); antiques. Overlooks falls. Cr cds: A, MC, V.

✔★ ★ **JUST A "PLANE" BED 'N BREAKFAST.** *(11152 NY 19A, Fillmore 14735)* 10 mi S on NY 408, 5 mi S on NY 19A. 716/567-8338. 4 rms, 1 A/C, 3 with shower only, 3 story, 1 suite. No rm phones. S $45; D $57; each addl $12; suites $57; under 2 free. TV in common rm; VCR avail (movies). Complimentary full bkfst. Ck-out 11 am, ck-in 4 pm. X-country ski on-site. Picnic tables, grills. Built in 1926; family-owned farmhouse. Totally nonsmoking. Cr cds: A, MC, V.

Restaurants

✔★ **BROMAN'S GENESEE FALLS INN.** *(See Broman's Genesee Falls Inn)* 716/493-2484. Continental menu. Specializes in seafood, steak. Hrs: 8:30-1:30 am. Res accepted. Bar 11-2 am; Sun to 1 am. Semi-a la carte: bkfst $5, lunch $3.95-$8.95, dinner $11.95-$21. Child's meals. Victorian decor; antiques. Cr cds: MC, V.

★ ★ ★ **GLEN IRIS.** *(See Glen Iris Inn)* 716/493-2622. Continental menu. Specializes in prime rib, venison, seafood. Hrs: 8-10 am, noon-2 pm, 5:30-8 pm; Fri, Sat 9 pm. Closed 1st wkend Nov-Easter. Serv bar. Semi-a la carte: bkfst $5.95-$8.95, lunch $5.50-$9, dinner $15-$25. Child's meals. Cr cds: A, MC, V.

★ ★ **OLD HEIDELBERG.** *South Warsaw (14569), 2 1/2 mi S on NY 19, 9 mi N of S park entrance.* 716/786-5427. German, Amer menu. Specialties: Kasseler rippchen, rouladen, sauerbraten. Hrs: 11:30 am-2 pm, 5-9 pm; Fri to 10 pm; Sat 5-10 pm; Sun noon-7 pm. Closed Mon; Jan 1, Thanksgiving, Dec 24-25. Res accepted. Serv bar. Semi-a la carte: lunch $4.25-$8.50, dinner $10.50-$18.95. Child's meals. Extensive selection of German beers. Cr cds: A, MC, V.

Liberty (F-7)

(See also Catskill Park, Monticello, Roscoe)

Pop 9,825 **Elev** 1,509 ft **Area code** 914 **Zip** 12754
Information Chamber of Commerce, PO Box 147; 914/292-1878.

Near the junction of the Willowemoc and Beaverkill rivers and on the edge of the Catskill Forest Preserve, this area offers good hunting and trout fishing, camping, hiking and sightseeing.

What to See and Do

NY State Catskill Fish Hatchery. Ponds featuring trout of various sizes as well as breeder trout. (Daily; mid-June-mid Sept, mornings only; closed major hols) 11 mi NW on Fish Hatchery Rd near DeBruce. Phone 914/439-4328. **Free.**

Motel

★ **DAYS INN OF LIBERTY.** *25 Sullivan Ave, Just off NY 17 exit 100.* 914/292-7600; FAX 914/292-3303. 119 rms, 2 story. June-Sept: S, D $70-$85; each addl $6; under 12 free; lower rates rest of yr. Crib free. TV; cable (premium). 2 pools; 1 indoor. Complimentary continental bkfst. Restaurant 11:30 am-3 pm, 5-10 pm. Bar; entertainment Fri, Sat. Ck-out 11 am. Meeting rms. Business servs avail. Downhill/x-country ski 15 mi. Game rm. Cr cds: A, C, D, DS, MC, V.

Inn

★ **MOUNTAINVIEW INN.** *(913 Shandelee Rd, Livingston Manor 12758) Approx 10 mi N on NY 17.* 914/439-5070. 8 air-cooled rms, 2 story. No rm phones. S $54-$62; D $75-$84; each addl $15; under 5 free. TV in sitting rm. Complimentary full bkfst. Restaurant (see MOUNTAINVIEW). Ck-out, ck-in noon. Downhill ski 10 mi; x-country ski on site. Picnic tables. Built 1900; many antiques. Greenhouse sitting room. Cr cds: A, C, D, DS, MC, V.

Restaurants

★ **MOUNTAINVIEW.** *(See Mountainview Inn)* 914/439-5070. Italian, Amer menu. Specializes in veal, seafood. Hrs: 5-10 pm. Closed Sun, Mon. Res accepted. Bar. Semi-a la carte: dinner $6.50-$23. Child's meals. Country inn atmosphere. Cr cds: A, C, D, MC, V.

★ ★ **THE TROUT & BEAR.** *(Livingston Manor 12758) NY 17 exit 96.* 914/439-3999. Hrs: 5-10 pm. Closed Mon, Tues; also Thanksgiving, Dec 25. Res accepted Fri, Sat. Bar. A la carte entrees: dinner $18-$42. Child's meals. Specializes in beef, trout, duck. Parking. Adirondacks camp decor. Cr cds: A, DS, MC, V.

★ **VILLAGE SQUARE CAFE.** *70 NY 52 E.* 914/292-2233. Hrs: 11 am-3 pm. Closed Sun; also Jan 1, Thanksgiving, Dec 25. Res required July, Aug. Wine, beer. A la carte entrees: lunch $6.50-$10.25. Specializes in chicken, pasta. Child's meals. Parking. Outdoor dining. Totally nonsmoking. Cr cds: A, DS, MC, V.

Lockport (D-2)

(See also Batavia, Niagara Falls; also see Niagara Falls and Niagara-on-the-lake, ON, Canada)

Settled 1816 **Pop** 24,426 **Elev** 600 ft **Area code** 716 **Zip** 14094
Information Chamber of Commerce, 151 W Genessee St; 716/433-3828.

The town was originally settled around a series of locks of the Erie Canal, now the New York State Barge Canal.

What to See and Do

Canal Bridge. Claimed to be one of the widest single-span bridges (399¹/₂ ft) in the world. View of the locks' operation, raising and lowering barges and pleasure craft more than 60 ft. Cottage St.

Colonel William Bond House. Pre-Victorian home (1824) was built with bricks made on site. Restored, with 12 furnished rms; of special interest are the kitchen and the children's garret. (Mar-Dec, Thurs, Sat & Sun afternoons) 143 Ontario St. Phone 716/434-7433. **Free.**

Kenan Center. Art gallery and recreation/sports arena. Gallery (Sept-May, daily; June-Aug, Sun-Fri); Taylor Theater; garden and orchard, herb garden. 433 Locust St. Phone 716/433-2617. **Donation.**

Niagara County Historical Center. An 1860 brick house with antiques; Erie Canal artifacts. Pioneer Bldg contains Native American collection, pioneer artifacts; Washington Hunt Law Office (1835); Niagara Fire Co #1, with 1834 and 1836 pumpers. Nineteenth-century farming equipment. (Thurs-Sun; closed hols) 215 Niagara St. Phone 716/434-7433. **Free.**

Motel

✔★ ★ **LOCKPORT.** *315 S Transit St.* 716/434-5595; FAX 716/433-0105. 65 rms. S $54-$66; D $60-$80; each addl $2; suites $99-$150. Crib $5. TV; VCR avail (free movies). Pool; lifeguard. Complimentary

coffee. Restaurant opp 6 am-10 pm. Ck-out 11 am. Business servs avail. In-rm modem link. Refrigerators, microwaves. Whirlpool in suites. Cr cds: A, C, D, DS, MC, V.

Restaurant

★ **GARLOCK'S.** *35 S Transit St.* 716/433-5595. Specializes in prime rib, steak, seafood. Hrs: 5 pm-midnight; Sun 3-10 pm. Closed Thanksgiving, Dec 25. Res accepted. Bar to 1 am. Semi-a la carte: dinner $8.95-$29.95. Child's meals. In mid-1800s building. Collection of decanters. Cr cds: A, MC, V.

Long Island (B-2 - A-5)

Long Island stretches 118 miles east by northeast from the edge of Manhattan to the lonely dunes of Montauk. Much of the island is ideal resort country, with vast white beaches, quiet bays, coves and woods.

At the eastern tip, Montauk Light stands on its headland; on the southwestern shore is Coney Island. New York City sprawls over the whole of Long Island's two westernmost counties—Queens and Kings (boroughs of Queens and Brooklyn).

Nassau County, adjoining the city, is made up of suburbs filled with residential communities. Eastward in Suffolk County, city influence eases, and there are firms that have attracted substantial local populations. Potatoes and the famous Long Island duckling are still raised here alongside farms for horse-breeding and the vineyards producing Long Island wines.

Long Island has many miles of sandy barrier beaches along the south shore, with fine swimming and surf casting. The bays behind these make natural small-boat harbors. On the more tranquil waters of the north shore is a series of deeper harbors along Long Island Sound, many of them with beaches and offering good sailing opportunities. The island has played a major role in US history from the early seventeenth century; the record of this is carefully preserved in many buildings, some 300 years old. Few regions offer such varied interests in so small an area. The Long Island Railroad conducts tours to points of interest on the island (late May-early Nov). For information on these escorted day excursions, write to the Long Island Railroad, Sales and Promotion Dept, #1723, Jamaica 11435; phone 718/217-LIRR. For further information and special events contact the Long Island Convention & Visitors Bureau, 350 Vanderbilt Motor Pkwy, Suite 103, Hauppage 11788; 800/441-4601.

Long Island towns listed in *Mobil Travel Guide* are Amagansett, Amityville, Bay Shore, Bethpage, East Hampton, Fire Island National Seashore, Floral Park, Garden City, Glen Cove, Great Neck, Greenport, Hampton Bays, Hempstead, Huntington, Jericho, Jones Beach State Park, Massapequa Park, Montauk, Northport, Oyster Bay, Plainview, Port Jefferson, Port Washington, Riverhead, Robert Moses State Park, Rockville Centre, Roslyn, Sag Harbor, Sayville, Shelter Island, Smithtown, Southampton, Southold, Stony Brook, Westbury and Westhampton Beach.

Long Lake (C-7)

(See also Blue Mountain Lake, Tupper Lake)

Pop 935 (est) **Elev** 1,683 ft **Area code** 518 **Zip** 12847

Located in the heart of the Adirondack Park, this area is a wilderness setting for water sports, hunting, fishing, cross-country skiing and snowmobiling.

Motels

★ **LONG LAKE.** *Boat Landing Rd, 2 blks N, off NY 30.* *518/624-2613.* 8 motel rms, 9 cottages, 7 kits. No A/C. S, D $65-$80; each addl $10; kit. cottages for 2-4, $475-$800/wk. Closed mid-Oct-mid-May. Crib $7.50. TV; cable. Coffee in rms. Restaurant nearby. Ck-out 10:30 am; cottages 10 am. Lawn games. Picnic tables, grills. Private sand beach. Private screened patios overlook woods, lake. Cr cds: A, MC, V.

★ **SANDY POINT.** *2 mi S of jct NY 28 & NY 30. 518/624-3871.* 11 rms, 2 story, 6 kits. No A/C. Mid-June-Labor Day, fall foliage season: S, D $75; each addl $10; kit. units $12 addl (4-7-day min); higher rates special events; lower rates rest of yr. Crib free. TV; cable. Complimentary coffee in rms. Restaurant nearby. Ck-out 10:30 am. Sauna. Screened-in patios, balconies. Private sand beach, dockage, boat rentals. Cr cds: A, DS, MC, V.

★ **SHAMROCK.** (12847-0205). *1 mi S on NY 28, 30. 518/624-3861; FAX 518/624-9803.* 10 motel rms, 7 kit. cottages (3-day min). No A/C. Memorial Day-Labor Day: S, D $50-$65; each addl $10; cottages for 2-6, $475-$600/wk; family rates; higher rates special events; lower rates after Labor Day-Oct. Closed rest of yr. Crib $5. TV, some B/W. Playground. Complimentary coffee in rms. Ck-out 10:30 am. Coin lndry. Rec rm. Lawn games. Refrigerators. Picnic tables, grill. Private sand beach. Paddle boats, canoes. Cr cds: A, DS, MC, V.

Mahopac (A-2)

(See also Brewster, Garrison, Peekskill, Tarrytown, West Point, White Plains)

Pop 7,755 **Elev** 650 ft **Area code** 914 **Zip** 10541

What to See and Do

Mahopac Farm and Museum. Collection of antiques and memorabilia dating from 1800s to early 1900s displayed in a barn on a 31-acre working farm. (Daily; closed most major hols) NY 6 & Baldwin Place Rd, in Baldwin Place. Phone 914/628-9298. ¢ Adj and incl in admission is

Old Borden Farm. Country store, museum, farm animals. (Daily; closed most major hols)

Restaurants

★ ★ **CLAIRE'S.** *825 S Lake Blvd. 914/628-2702.* Hrs: 11:30 am-3 pm, 5-10 pm; Fri, Sat to 11 pm; Sun noon-9 pm. Closed Mon, Tues in Jan-early Apr; also Dec 25. Res accepted. Continental menu. Bar. A la carte entrees: lunch $5.50-$8.95, dinner $9.95-$21.95. Child's meals. Specializes in seafood, pasta. Dance band Fri, Sat (summer). Parking. Outdoor dining. Overlooks marina, lake. Cr cds: A, D, DS, MC, V.

★ **HEIDI'S BRAUHAUS.** *241 US 6N, 2 mi N of Talonic State Pkwy. 914/628-9795.* German, Amer menu. Specialties: sauerbraten, Wienerschnitzel, jägerschnitzel. Salad bar. Hrs: 5-9 pm; Fri, Sat from 4-10 pm; Sun 3-9 pm; Sun brunch 11:30 am-2:30 pm. Closed Mon, Tues. Res accepted; required hols. Bar. Semi-a la carte: dinner $10.95-$16.95. Sun brunch $9.95. Child's meals. German artifacts on walls. Cr cds: MC, V.

Malone (A-7)

(See also Adirondack Park)

Pop 12,982 **Elev** 722 ft **Area code** 518 **Zip** 12953 **Web** www.malone-ny.net/chamber.html
Information Chamber of Commerce, 170 E Main St; 518/483-3760.

What to See and Do

Franklin County Historical & Museum Society. Country store, craft rms; kitchen; exhibits, Victorian parlor. Kilburn Library, genealogical collection. (June-Labor Day, Tues-Sat; rest of yr, Sat only) 51 Milwaukee St. Phone 518/483-2750. **Donation.**

Titus Mountain Ski Area. Two triple, 5 double chairlifts, handle tow. Snow making. (Nov-Apr, daily) Duane Street Rd, 7 mi S. Phone 518/483-3740 or 800/848-8766. ¢¢¢¢¢

Annual Event

Franklin County Fair. Malone Fairgrounds. Early-mid-Aug.

Motels

✔★ ★ **CROSSROADS.** *(Moira 12957) 11 mi W on US 11. 518/529-7372; FAX 518/529-6755.* 43 rms. S $40-$52; D $48-$55; each addl $8; under 12 free; wkend rates; golf, ski plans. Crib $10. TV; cable. Pool. Restaurant 7 am-midnight. Bar 5 pm-1 am; entertainment, dancing exc Mon. Ck-out 11 am. Meeting rms. Gift shop. Barber, beauty shop. Downhill ski 15 mi; x-country ski 20 mi. Cr cds: A, C, D, DS, MC, V.

★ **ECONO LODGE.** *227 W Main. 518/483-0500.* 45 rms, 1-2 story. S $42-$47; D $48-$52; each addl $5. Crib $5. Pet accepted. TV; cable. Pool. Complimentary continental bkfst. Restaurant nearby. Ck-out 11 am. Meeting rms. Cr cds: A, D, DS, MC, V.

★ **FOUR SEASONS.** *W Main St, just W on US 11. 518/483-3490.* 26 rms. S $42-$52; D $45-$59; each addl $5; golf, ski plans. TV; cable (premium). Pool. Complimentary continental bkfst. Ck-out 11 am. 36-hole golf privileges. Downhill/x-country ski 4 mi. Cr cds: A, D, DS, MC, V.

Restaurant

★ **JAMMERS.** *E Main St (NY 11). 518/483-0711.* Specializes in prime rib, fresh seafood, steaks. Salad bar. Hrs: 11:30 am-10 pm; Fri to 11 pm; Sat 4-11 pm. Closed Jan 1, July 4, Dec 25. Res accepted. Bar. Semi-a la carte: lunch $3.49-$6.50, dinner $7.95-$17.95. Outdoor dining. Cr cds: A, MC, V.

Mamaroneck

(A-5 see New York City map)

(See also New Rochelle, New York City, White Plains, Yonkers)

Pop 27,706 **Elev** 50 ft **Area code** 914 **Zip** 10543

Restaurants

★ ★ **ABIS.** *406 Mamaroneck Ave. 914/698-8777.* Japanese menu. Specializes in sushi, steak, seafood. Hrs: 11:30 am-2:30 pm, 5:30-

9:30 pm; Fri to 10:30 pm; Sun brunch to 2:30 pm. Res accepted. Bar. Semi-a la carte: lunch $5.75-$10.50, dinner $9.95-$37. Sun brunch $16.95. Cr cds: A, D, MC, V.

★ ★ **CHEF ANTONIO.** *551 Halstead Ave.* 914/698-8610. Italian menu. Specializes in pasta, seafood. Own desserts. Hrs: 11:30 am-10:30 pm; Fri to 11:30 pm; Sat 4-11:30 pm; Sun 1-10 pm. Closed Thanksgiving, Dec 25. Res accepted. Bar. Semi-a la carte: lunch $5.95-$10.95, dinner $13.95-$20.95. Child's meals. Modern Italian decor; archways & artwork. Cr cds: A, C, D, DS, MC, V.

★ ★ **LE PROVENCAL.** *436 Mamaroneck Ave.* 914/777-2324. French menu. Specialties: sweetbread with olives & mushrooms, veal tenderloin, steak au poivre. Hrs: noon-2:30 pm, 6-10 pm; Fri to 11 pm; Sat 6-11 pm; Sun 5-9 pm. Closed Mon; also Jan 1, Dec 25. Res accepted. Bar. Semi-a la carte: lunch $7.50-$17.50, dinner $15.50-$24.50. Child's meals. Street parking. Outdoor dining. Totally nonsmoking. Cr cds: A, MC, V.

Manhattan
(Follows Yonkers at end of New York State)

Massapequa Park, L.I. (B-3)

(See also Amityville, Bethpage)

Pop 18,044 **Elev** 20 ft **Area code** 516 **Zip** 11762

What to See and Do

Tackapausha Museum & Preserve. Museum devoted to living things. Small collection of live animals. An 80-acre tract of glacial outwash plain maintained in natural state; many small mammals and birds. (Tues-Sat, also Sun afternoons; closed major hols) 4 mi SW on Washington Ave in Seaford. Phone 516/571-7443. ¢

Massena (A-7)

(See also Potsdam; also see Cornwall, ON, Canada)

Settled 1792 **Pop** 13,826 **Elev** 210 ft **Area code** 315 **Zip** 13662
Information Chamber of Commerce, 50 Main St; 315/769-3525.

This is the site of the largest power plant on the St Lawrence Seaway. Massena has two aluminum plants and a major foundry.

As far back as 1903, a canal linking the Grasse River and the St Lawrence Seaway has provided 90,000 horsepower for Massena-based Alcoa operations.

What to See and Do

Coles Creek State Park. Beach swimming; fishing (all yr); boating (launch, marina, dock). Picnicking, playground, concession. Tent & trailer sites. (Mid-May-Labor Day) Standard fees. 16 mi W on NY 37. Phone 315/388-5636. ¢¢

Eisenhower Lock. Visitors view vessels navigating the lock, lock operations, as well as the vehicular tunnel traffic under the lock. Interpretive center with films, photos. Viewing deck. Picnic tables. (May-Columbus Day, daily) E on NY 37, then N on NY 131, W end of Wiley-Dondero Ship Channel. Phone 315/769-2422. Viewing deck ¢

Robert Moses State Park. A different state park with the same name (see) is located on Fire Island, on the south shore of Long Island. Overlook

from which Moses-Saunders Power Dam can be viewed. Barnhart Island Power House at main dam. Visitors gallery and exhibit hall. Swimming beach, bathhouse; fishing; boating (launch, rentals, marina). Cross-country skiing. Picnicking, playground. Tent & trailer sites, cabins. Recreation programs. (Mid-May-mid-Oct, daily) Standard fees. E of town, 3 mi N of NY 37. Contact PO Box 548; 315/769-8663.

The St Lawrence Seaway. A joint project of the US and Canada, this is one of the world's great public works and provides a route for ocean ships from more than 60 countries around the world into mid-America—a "fourth coast." Ships traverse seaway from Apr-Dec. Locks can accommodate ships 730 ft long and 76 ft wide. Ocean and lake vessels carry bulk and general cargoes of iron ore, grain and coal to and from points along the seaway's 8,300-mi shoreline. The seaway was formally dedicated June 26, 1959, by Queen Elizabeth II and President Eisenhower.

Annual Events

Heritage Festival. Massena Arena, NY 37. Antique and craft show; parade, entertainment, casino. 1st Sat June.

Folklife Festival. Robert Moses State Park. Demonstrations, music, storytelling; ethnic foods. 2nd Sat Aug.

Massena Car Show. Robert Moses State Park. Classic and antique car show. 2nd Sat Sept.

Motels

★ ★ **ECONO LODGE MEADOW VIEW.** *15054 NY 37, 2 mi W on NY 37.* 315/764-0246; FAX 315/764-9615. 52 rms, 2 story. S $65-$90; D $75-$95; suites $80-$100; under 18 free. Crib free. TV; cable (premium). Coffee in rms. Restaurant in season 6:30-10:30 am, 5-10 pm; Sun 7 am-2 pm. Ck-out 11 am. Meeting rm. Business servs avail. In-rm modem link. Exercise equipt. Refrigerators. Cr cds: A, D, DS, JCB, MC, V.

🄳 🏋 ⊠ 🐾 SC

✔★ **SUPER 8.** *84 Grove St, at NY 37.* 315/764-1065; FAX 315/764-9710. 41 rms, 3 story. No elvtr. June-Sept: S $48; D $56; under 12 free; lower rates rest of yr. Crib free. TV; cable, VCR avail. Complimentary coffee in lobby. Ck-out 11 am. Meeting rm. Business servs avail. In-rm modem link. Cr cds: A, C, D, DS, JCB, MC, V.

🄳 ⊠ 🐾 SC

Restaurant

★ ★ **VILLAGE INN.** *181 Outer Maple St (NY 37B).* 315/769-6910. Continental menu. Specializes in fresh fish, veal, prime rib. Hrs: 11:30 am-10 pm; Sun 4-9 pm. Closed Mon, Tues; Dec 25. Res accepted. Bar 11 am-midnight. Semi-a la carte: lunch $4.25-$12, dinner $9.50-$19.50. Child's meals. Family-owned. Cr cds: A, MC, V.

🄳 ⊐

Middletown (F-7)

(See also Goshen, Monroe, Monticello, Newburgh, Port Jervis)

Pop 24,160 **Elev** 500 ft **Area code** 914 **Zip** 10940 **E-mail** octour@warwick.net **Web** www.orangetourism.org
Information Orange County Tourism, 30 Matthews St, Suite 111, Goshen 10924; 914/928-2946 or 800/762-8687.

Annual Event

Orange County Fair. Agricultural and industrial exhibits, stock-car races, entertainment. Phone 914/343-4826. Mid-late July.

Motel

★ **SUPER 8 LODGE.** *563 NY 211E. 914/692-5828.* 82 rms, 2 story. S $55.88-$65.88; D $64.88-$78.88; each addl $7; under 12 free; higher rates: special events, wkends. Pet accepted. TV. Complimentary continental bkfst. Ck-out 11 am. Downhill/x-country ski 15 mi. Some in-rm whirlpools. Cr cds: A, C, D, DS, MC, V.

Restaurants

★ **CASA MIA.** *NY 211E, off NY 17 exit 120, right for 2 mi. 914/692-2323.* Italian, Amer menu. Specializes in seafood, pasta, steak. Own desserts. Hrs: 11:30 am-10 pm. Closed Mon; Thanksgiving, Dec 24, 25. Res accepted. Bar. Semi-a la carte: lunch $3.50-$8.50, dinner $8.50-$22.95. Child's meals. Cr cds: A, C, D, MC, V.

★ **RUSTY NAIL.** *50 Dunning Rd. 914/343-8242.* Specializes in steak, seafood, pasta. Salad bar. Hrs: 11:30 am-10 pm; Fri, Sat to 11 pm; Sun 3-9 pm. Res accepted; required Fri, Sat. Bar to midnight; wkends to 3 am. Semi-a la carte: lunch $4.95-$9.95, dinner $11.95-$26.95. Child's meals. Entertainment Fri, Sat. Rustic decor; restored RR station. Cr cds: A, D, DS, MC, V.

Monroe (A-1)

(See also Goshen, Middletown, Newburgh, West Point)

Pop 23,035 **Elev** 679 ft **Area code** 914 **Zip** 10950

What to See and Do

Museum Village. Outdoor living history museum of over 25 bldgs depicting the crafts and technology of 19th-century America. Exhibit/demonstration bldgs incl print shop, log cabin, drug store, general store; schoolhouse. Broom maker, candle maker, blacksmith, weaver; farm animals; historical gardens. Shops, food service, picnic area. (Late May-early Dec, Wed-Sun; open Mon when federal hol; closed Thanksgiving) Museum Village Rd, W on NY 17M; US 6, NY 17 exit 129. Phone 914/782-8247. ¢¢¢

Montauk, L.I. (A-5)

(See also Amagansett, East Hampton)

Pop 3,001 **Elev** 18 ft **Area code** 516 **Zip** 11954
Information Chamber of Commerce, PO Box 5029; 516/668-2428.

This is a lively fishing town on Long Island, with a big business in deep-sea fishing (tuna, shark, marlin, striped bass and other varieties). Boats can be rented, and there are miles of uncrowded sandy beaches to enjoy.

What to See and Do

Hither Hills State Park. Swimming beach, bathhouse, lifeguards; fishing; nature, hiking trails. Picnicking, playground, concession. Tent & trailer sites (mid-Apr-Nov; res required). Standard fees. 3 mi W on NY 27. Phone 516/668-7600.

Montauk Point State Park. Barren moor with sea view. Montauk Lighthouse, built 1795; museum, tours (summer wkends; fee). Fishing; hiking, biking, picnicking, concession. Standard fees. 6 mi E on NY 27; easternmost tip of Long Island. Phone 516/668-2554.

Motels

★★ **BEACHCOMER RESORT.** *Old Montauk Hwy. 516/668-2894; FAX 516/668-3154.* E-mail beachtalks@aol.com; web beachcomber-montauk.com. 88 kit. suites, 2 story. Mid-June-Labor Day: S, D $155-$285; each addl $15; higher rates wkends & hols (3-day min); lower rates Apr-mid-June, Labor Day-late Oct. Closed rest of yr. Crib free. TV; cable (premium), VCR (movies). Heated pool. Sauna. Restaurant nearby. Ck-out 11 am. Coin lndry. Business servs avail. Swimming beach. Cr cds: A, C, D, DS, MC, V.

★★ **BURCLIFFE BY-THE-SEA.** *397 Old Montauk Hwy. 516/668-2880.* 7 kit. units, 5 with shower only. July-Sept: S, D $100-$120; each addl $20-$25; cottages $125-$225; wkly rates; higher rates wkends & hols (2-4-day min); lower rates rest of yr. Crib free. TV; cable (premium). Restaurant nearby. Ck-out 10 am. Tennis privileges. 18-hole golf privileges. Picnic tables, grills. Microwaves. Swimming beach. Cr cds: MC, V.

★★ **DRIFTWOOD ON THE OCEAN.** *Montauk Hwy. 516/668-5744; FAX 516/267-3081; res: 800/483-7438.* 57 units in 7 buildings, 1-2 story, 21 suites, 2 cottages. Late June-early Sept: S, D $143-$185; each addl $15; suites $163-$210; kit. units $148-$198; cottages $295; wkly plans; lower rates May-late June, early Sept-Oct. Closed rest of yr. TV; cable (premium), VCR avail (movies free). Heated pool; lifeguard. Playground. Complimentary coffee in rms. Restaurants opp. Ck-out 11 am. Coin laundry. Business servs avail. Tennis. Refrigerators. Balconies. Picnic tables, grills. On beach. Cr cds: A, DS, MC, V.

★ **MALIBU.** *88 S Elmwood Ave, 2 blks S of NY 27. 516/668-5233.* 32 rms, 2 story, 7 kits. S, D $85-$99; each addl $10; kit. units $95-$104; 3-day min wkends in season. Closed Jan-Mar. TV; cable (premium). Complimentary coffee. Restaurant nearby. Ck-out 11 am. Refrigerators. Picnic tables, grills. Cr cds: A, DS, MC, V.

★★ **ROYAL ATLANTIC BEACH RESORTS.** *S Edgemere St, off NY 27. 516/668-5103; FAX 516/668-4172.* 152 kit. units, 2 story. Mid-June-Labor Day: S, D $129-$165; each addl $10-$25; suites $155-$185; town houses $360; lower rates Apr-mid-June, after Labor Day-Oct. Most units closed rest of yr. TV; cable (premium). Heated pools; poolside serv, lifeguard. Restaurant 4-10 pm. Bar 4:30 pm-midnight. Ck-out 11 am. Business servs avail. Rec rm. Refrigerators. Balconies. Picnic tables. Private beach. Cr cds: A, C, D, DS, MC, V.

✔★ **SANDS.** *S Emery St, at Emerson Ave, off NY 27, opp ocean. 516/668-5100.* 42 rms, 1-2 story, 22 kits. June-Aug: S, D $99-$140; each addl $12-$25; suites $110-$185; kit. cottages $650-$1,195/wk; higher rates: wkends of Memorial Day, July 4, Labor Day; lower rates Sept-Nov, Apr-May. Closed rest of yr. Crib free. TV; cable (premium), VCR avail. Pool; lifeguard. Playground. Restaurants nearby. Ck-out 11 am. Business servs avail. Lawn games. Refrigerators. Some balconies. Picnic tables, grills. Cr cds: A, DS, MC, V.

★ **WAVECREST RESORT.** *Old Montauk Hwy. 516/668-2141; FAX 516/668-2337.* 65 kit. units, 2 story. No elvtr. July-Aug (wkends, 3-day min): S, D, studio rms $125-$155; each addl $15; suites $155; lower rates May-June, Sept-Oct. Closed rest of yr. Crib free. TV; cable (premium), VCR (movies). Indoor pool; lifeguard. Ck-out 11 am. Business servs avail. Private patios, balconies. On hilltop and dune, overlooking ocean, beach. Hither Hills State Park adj. Cr cds: A, DS, MC, V.

Motor Hotel

★ ★ **PANORAMIC VIEW.** *Old Montauk Hwy. 516/668-3000;
FAX 516/668-7870.* 118 kit. units, 1-3 story, 14 suites, 3 cottages. Late
June-early Sept: S, D $124-$172; each addl $15; suites $148-$198; cottages $398; wkend rates; lower rates Apr-late June, early Sept-Nov.
Closed rest of yr. Children over 10 yrs only. TV; cable (premium), VCR
avail. Pool; lifeguard. Restaurant nearby. Ck-out 11 am, ck-in 2 pm. Coin
lndry. Meeting rms. Business servs avail. In-rm modem link. Game rm.
Refrigerators. Grills. On beach. No cr cds accepted.

Resorts

★ ★ ★ **GURNEY'S INN RESORT, SPA & CONFERENCE CENTER.** *290 Old Montauk Hwy, 3 mi W. 516/668-2345; FAX 516/668-3576.*
Web www.gurneysweb.com. 109 rms, 1-4 story, 5 cottages. No elvtr.
MAP, Memorial Day-Labor Day, wkends: S, D $290-$340; each addl $90;
suites $340-$400; cottages (1-3 bedrm) $380-$1,080; serv charge 15%;
lower rates rest of yr. TV; cable (premium), VCR. Indoor sea water pool;
whirlpool; lifeguard. Dining rm 7:30-10 am, noon-3 pm, 6-10 pm. Rm serv.
Box lunches, snacks. Fisherman's bkfst from 4 am on request. Bar noon-4
am; entertainment. Ck-out 11:30 am, ck-in 3:30 pm. Meeting rms. Business servs avail. Bellhops. Drugstore. Barber, beauty shop. Airport, RR
station, bus depot transportation. Rec rm. Exercise rm; sauna, steam rm.
Refrigerators. Patios; many terraces. Resort-type inn on 1,000-ft private
beach. Cr cds: A, DS, MC, V.

★ ★ **MONTAUK YACHT CLUB.** *32 Star Island Rd, 1¹/₂ mi E on
NY 27, then N on NY 77 approx 2 mi to Star Island Road. 516/668-3100;
FAX 516/668-3303; res: 800/832-4200 (NY).* Web www.montaukyacht-club.com. 107 rms, 2 story, 23 villas. Late Apr-Oct: S, D $149-$299; each
addl $25; lower rates Apr, Oct. Closed rest of yr. Crib free. TV; cable
(premium). 3 pools, 1 indoor; lifeguard. Dining rms 7 am-11 pm. Rm serv.
Bar noon-2 am; entertainment Fri, Sat. Ck-out 11 am, ck-in 3 pm. Meeting
rms. Business servs avail. Bellhops. Local airport, RR station, bus depot
transportation. Tennis. Rec rm. Exercise equipt; sauna. Bathrm phones.
Private patios, balconies. Marina; sailing, waterskiing. Golf nearby. Cr cds:
A, C, D, DS, MC, V.

Restaurants

★ ★ **DAVE'S GRILL.** *468 W Lake Dr. 516/668-9190.* Specializes in seafood, pasta. Own pastries. Hrs: 5:30-10:30 pm. Closed Wed;
also Nov-Apr. Bar. A la carte entrees: dinner $14.95-$19.95. Parking.
Outdoor dining. Casual; located on fishing docks. Cr cds: A, DS, MC, V.

★ ★ **GOSMAN'S DOCK.** *500 W Lake Dr. 516/668-5330.* Specializes in fresh seafood. Own pastries. Hrs: noon-10 pm. Closed Nov-Mar.
Bar noon-2 am. A la carte entrees: lunch, dinner $13.95-$25. Child's
meals. Outdoor dining. On dock; view of boats. Cr cds: A, MC, V.

★ ★ **HARVEST ON FORT POND.** *11 S Emory St. 516/668-5574.* Specializes in fresh seafood, pasta, grilled pizzas. Hrs: Thurs 5:30-10 pm; Fri, Sat to 11 pm. Closed Thanksgiving, Dec 25. Res accepted. Bar.
A la carte entrees: dinner $16-$28. Parking. Outdoor dining in herb garden.
Bacci courts. Original artwork. Overlooks large pond with swans, rooftop
lounge overlooks ocean & pond. Cr cds: A, DS, MC, V.

★ ★ **RUSCHMEYER'S.** *(161 Second House Rd, Montauk) off
NY 27. 516/668-2877.* Menu changes daily. Hrs: 5-10 pm; May-Memorial
Day, mid-Sept-Columbus Day Fri-Sun 5-9 pm; early-bird dinner 5-6 pm.
Closed rest of yr. Res accepted. Bar. Semi-a la carte: dinner $12-$19.

Child's meals. Pianist Fri, Sat. Parking. Outdoor dining. Comfortable atmosphere. Cr cds: A, C, D, DS, JCB, MC, V.

★ **SHAGWONG TAVERN.** *774 Montauk Hwy. 516/668-3050.*
Menu changes daily. Specializes in fresh seafood. Hrs: noon-midnight;
early-bird dinner 4:30-6 pm; Sun 10 am-2 pm (brunch), 6-10 pm. Bar.
Semi-a la carte: lunch $6-$10, dinner $12-$20. Sun brunch $7-$10. Parking. Covered patio dining. Photographs of Old Montauk and celebrity
guests. Original tin ceiling (1927). Family-owned. Cr cds: A, C, D, DS, JCB,
MC, V.

Monticello (F-7)

(See also Barryville, Liberty)

Pop 6,597 **Elev** 1,520 ft **Area code** 914 **Zip** 12701 **Web**
www.co.sullivan.ny.ustg
Information Sullivan County Visitors Association, Inc, 100 North St;
914/794-3000 or 800/882-2287.

As the center of the Sullivan County Catskills resort region, Monticello
offers visitors a wide selection of activities: summer theaters, children's
camps, summer cottages, fishing, hunting, swimming, canoeing, skiing,
tennis, golf or just basking in the sun. Nearby lakes offer many water
sports.

What to See and Do

Holiday Mt Ski Area. Triple, 2 double chairlifts, pony lift, 2 T-bars, Pomalift, 2 rope tows; patrol, school, rentals; snowmaking; cafeteria, bar, ski
shop. Longest run 3,500 ft; vertical drop 400 ft. (Dec-Mar, daily) 3 mi E off
NY 17 exit 107. Phone 914/796-3161. ¢¢¢¢¢

Monticello Raceway. Harness racing. Pari-mutuel betting. 1 mi W on NY
17B, Quickway exit 104. Phone 914/794-4100 for schedule.

Woodstock Music Festival Monument. Monument to the 1969 music
festival, which was held here on Yasgur's farm. W on NY 17B to Hurd Rd
in Bethel.

Mt Kisco (A-2)

(See also New York City, Peekskill, Pound Ridge, White Plains)

Pop 9,108 **Elev** 289 ft **Area code** 914 **Zip** 10549
Information Chamber of Commerce, 3 N Moger Ave; 914/666-7525.

What to See and Do

Caramoor Center for Music and the Arts. European-style villa built
during 1930s with rms from European villas and palaces. Collections of
Chinese art, Italian Renaissance furniture; European paintings, sculptures
and tapestries dating from the Middle Ages through the 19th century;
formal gardens. Tours (June-mid-Nov, Thurs, Sat & Sun afternoons, also
Wed, Fri, by appt; rest of yr, by appt). Also Summer Music Festival (late
June-mid-Aug). 5 mi NE via Saw Mill River Pkwy to Katonah-Cross River
exit 6, then ¹/₂ mi E on NY 35, right onto NY 22 to jct with Girdle Ridge Rd;
follow signs. Phone 914/232-5035. ¢¢

John Jay Homestead State Historic Site. Estate of the first chief justice
of the US and four generations of his descendants; period furnishings,
American portrait collection, gardens, farm bldgs and grounds. Visits by
guided tour only. (May-Labor Day, Wed-Sun; phone for schedule after
Labor Day; closed most hols) Exit 6 off I-684, left on NY 35, E to NY 22 (Jay
St) between Katonah & Bedford Village. Phone 914/232-5651. **Free.**

Northern Westchester Center for the Arts. Home to a variety of programs and classes in music, dance, theater and visual arts. Participants in the various programs range from budding ballerinas to octogenarian actors all studying under faculty members who are accomplished in their fields; past performers incl Vanessa Williams, Alan Menken, Chevy Chase and Blythe Danner. 272 N Bedford Rd. For further info phone 914/241-6922.

Motel

★ ★ ★ **HOLIDAY INN.** *1 Holiday Inn Dr, 1 blk E of Saw Mill River Pkwy, exit 37.* 914/241-2600; FAX 914/241-4742. 122 rms, 2 story. S, D $139-$159; under 12 free; wkend plans. Crib. Pet accepted. TV; cable (premium), VCR avail. Pool; lifeguard. Coffee in rms. Restaurant 6:30 am-10 pm. Rm serv. Bar 2 pm-1 am, wkends to 3 am; entertainment. Ck-out 11 am. Coin lndry. Meeting rms. Business center. In-rm modem link. Beauty shop. Health club privileges. Refrigerators avail. Cr cds: A, C, D, DS, MC, V.

Restaurants

★ ★ ★ **CRABTREE'S KITTLE HOUSE.** *(11 Kittle Rd, Chappaqua 10514) 3 mi S on NY 117.* 914/666-8044. Specializes in game. Hrs: noon-2:30 pm, 5:30-9:30 pm; Fri to 11 pm; Sat 5:30-11 pm; Sun noon-2:30 pm (brunch), 3-9 pm. Closed Dec 25. Res accepted. Bar. Wine list. Semi-a la carte: lunch $7.50-$13.50, dinner $16.50-$26.50. Sun brunch buffet: $19.95. Child's meals. Valet parking. Elegant country decor. Picture windows overlook lawn. Cr cds: A, C, D, DS, MC, V.

D

★ ★ ★ **LA CAMELIA.** *234 N Bedford Rd.* 914/666-2466. Spanish menu. Specializes in tapas. Own desserts. Hrs: noon-3 pm, 6-9:30 pm; Sat, Sun 6-10 pm; Sun brunch noon-3 pm. Closed Mon; also Jan 1, Thanksgiving, Dec 25. Res accepted. Bar. Wine list. Semi-a la carte: lunch $12-$23, dinner $18-$30. Sun brunch $22. Child's meals. Parking. Elegant dining. Cr cds: A, DS, MC, V.

★ ★ ★ **TRAVELER'S REST.** *(NY 100, Ossining 10562) 5 mi N on NY 100, 2 mi N of Millwood.* 914/941-7744. German, Amer menu. Specialty: jaeger schnitzel. Hrs: 5-9:30 pm; Fri, Sat to 10 pm; Sun 1-9 pm. Closed Tues; Dec 24. Res accepted. Bar. Wine list. Complete meals: dinner $27.95-$32.95. Child's meals. Built 1880s; extensive grounds, gardens, waterfalls, pond; fireplaces. Family-owned. Cr cds: MC, V.

D

Naples (E-4)

(See also Canandaigua, Penn Yan)

Pop 2,559 **Elev** 800 ft **Area code** 716 **Zip** 14512

At the south end of Canandaigua Lake, one of the Finger Lakes, Naples is the center of a grape growing, winemaking area. Many of its residents are descendants of Swiss and German winemakers.

What to See and Do

Cumming Nature Center of the Rochester Museum & Science Center. A 900-acre living museum; nature trails, natural history programs; conservation trail with operating sawmill; cross-country skiing (rentals) & snowshoeing. Visitors bldg with theater and exhibit hall. (Late Dec-mid-Nov, Wed-Sun) 6472 Gulick Rd. Phone 716/374-6160. ¢¢

Widmer's Wine Cellars. Tours, wine tastings (Daily, afternoons). 1 Lake Niagara Lane. Phone 716/374-6311. ¢

Inn

★ ★ ★ **THE VAGABOND INN.** *3300 Sliter Rd.* 716/554-6271. 5 rms. No A/C. No rm phones. S, D $105-$192; each addl $25; package plans. Children over 13 yrs only. TV; VCR (movies). Complimentary full bkfst. Complimentary coffee in rms. Ck-out 11:30 am, ck-in 2:30 pm. 9-hole golf privileges, greens fee $8-$18. Downhill ski 12 mi; x-country ski 1/8 mi. Massage. Pool; whirlpool. Many in-rm whirlpools, fireplaces. Many balconies. Picnic tables, grills. Contemporary inn; antiques, art from around the world. On 65 acres. Totally nonsmoking. Cr cds: MC, V.

Restaurants

★ ★ **BOB'S & RUTH'S/THE VINEYARD.** *204 Main St, at jct NY 21 & NY 245.* 716/374-5122. Specializes in homemade soups and pies. Salad bar. Hrs: 6 am-8 pm. Closed Nov-Mar. Res accepted. Bar. Semi-a la carte: bkfst $2-$4.25, lunch $2.95-$10, dinner $9.95-$18.95. Child's meals. Wine wall. Outdoor dining. Family-owned. Cr cds: MC, V.

D

★ ★ **NAPLES HOTEL.** *111 S Main St.* 716/374-5630. German menu. Specialties: prime rib, sauerbraten, lobster bisque. Hrs: 11 am-2:30 pm; Fri, Sat to 9 pm; Sun noon-7 pm; hrs vary July-Labor Day. Res accepted. Bar to 1 am. Semi-a la carte: lunch $3.95-$5.95, dinner $8.50-$19.95. Child's meals. Pianist Fri, Sat evenings. Built in 1895; antiques. Guest rms avail. Cr cds: DS, MC, V.

SC

✔★ ★ **REDWOOD.** *Jct NY 21 & NY 53.* 716/374-6360. Specializes in steak, seafood. Salad bar. Hrs: 6 am-8 pm; Fri, Sat to 9 pm; Sun 7 am-8 pm. Closed Mon; Dec 24, 25. Res accepted. Bar from noon. Semi-a la carte: bkfst $1.85-$5.95, lunch $2.50-$6.95, dinner $6.95-$25.95. Child's meals. Cr cds: A, DS, MC, V.

D

Newburgh (F-8)

(See also Fishkill, New Paltz, Poughkeepsie, West Point)

Settled 1709 **Pop** 26,454 **Elev** 139 ft **Area code** 914 **Zip** 12550 **E-mail** orangeny@warwick.net **Web** www.orangeny.org

Information Chamber of Commerce of Orange County, Inc, 47 Grand St; 914/562-5100 or 914/782-2007 (Monroe office).

This manufacturing city was General George Washington's headquarters from April 1, 1782, until August 18, 1783. He announced the end of the American Revolution here, and officially disbanded the army.

Newburgh is the small urban center of eastern Orange County. West Point, the US Military Academy, lies 12 miles south of town (see).

What to See and Do

New Windsor Cantonment State Historic Site (1782). The Cantonment was the last winter encampment (1782-1783) of the Continental Army. Featured are demonstrations of 18th-century military life, incl muskets and artillery, woodworking, blacksmithing and camp life activities. Also exhibit bldgs and picnic area. (Mid-Apr-Oct, Wed-Sat, also Sun afternoons) Special events. On Temple Hill Rd (NY 300); 2 mi S of NY Thrwy exit 17 in Vails Gate. Phone 914/561-1765. **Free.**

Storm King Art Center. A 400-acre sculpture park and museum with permanent collection of 20th-century sculpture. Guided tours. (Apr-Nov, daily). 6 mi S via NY 32, Old Pleasant Hill Rd, in Mountainville. Phone 914/534-3115. ¢¢

Washington's Headquarters State Historic Site. Jonathan Hasbrouck house (1750); Gen George Washington's HQ for 16 1/2 months at the close of the Revolutionary War (Apr 1782-Aug 1783). Dutch vernacular field-stone house furnished as HQ. Adj museum has permanent and changing exhibits, audiovisual program. Tours, special events. (Mid-Apr-Oct, Wed-Sun; inquire for winter schedule) 84 Liberty St. Phone 914/562-1195. **Free.**

Motels

★ ★ **COMFORT INN.** *5 Lakeside Rd.* 914/567-0567; FAX 914/567-0582. 130 rms, 3 story, 2 suites. May-late Nov: S $59-$95; D $63-$125; each addl $10; under 18 free; higher rates West Point graduation; lower rates rest of yr. Crib $6. TV; cable, VCR avail (movies). Complimentary continental bkfst. Restaurant nearby. Ck-out 11 am. Coin lndry. Meeting rms. Business servs avail. In-rm modem link. Free airport, bus depot transportation. Cr cds: A, C, D, DS, MC, V.

★ ★ **HOLIDAY INN.** *90 NY 17, Jct I-84 & I-87.* 914/564-9020; FAX 914/564-9040. 122 rms, 2 story. S, D $85-$95; each addl $10; under 18 free. Crib free. TV; cable (premium). Pool; lifeguard. Coffee in rms. Restaurant 6:30 am-10 pm. Rm serv. Bar 4 pm-1 am; entertainment Fri, Sat. Ck-out noon. Meeting rms. Business servs avail. In-rm modem link. Free airport transportation. Exercise equipt. Some bathrm phones. Cr cds: A, C, D, DS, JCB, MC, V.

★ **HOWARD JOHNSON INN.** *95 Rte NY17K, I-87 exit 17.* 914/564-4000; FAX 914/564-0620. 74 rms, 2 story. May-Nov: S, D $89.95; each addl $8; under 18 free; higher rates special events; lower rates rest of yr. Crib free. Pet accepted. TV; cable (premium). Pool. Complimentary continental bkfst. Restaurant nearby. Ck-out noon. Coin lndry. Meeting rms. Business servs avail. Tennis. Downhill/x-country ski 15 mi. Health club privileges. Microwaves, refrigerators avail. Private patios, balconies. Cr cds: A, D, DS, MC, V.

★ ★ **RAMADA INN.** *1289 Rte 300, I-87 exit 17, follow sign to Rte 17 K West to Rte 300.* 914/564-4500; FAX 914/564-4524. 153 rms, 2 story, 40 suites. S, D $82-$92; each addl $10; suites $100-$130; under 18 free. Crib free. TV; cable. Pool; poolside serv. Complimentary full bkfst. Restaurant 6:30 am-10 pm. Rm serv. Bar 11-2 am; entertainment Wed, Fri, Sat. Ck-out noon. Meeting rms. Business servs avail. In-rm modem link. Free airport transportation. Exercise equipt. Game rm. Refrigerators, microwaves avail. Cr cds: A, C, D, DS, MC, V.

✔ ★ **SUPER 8.** *1287 NY 300.* 914/564-5700; FAX 914/564-7338. 108 rms, 2 story. S $52.88-$61.88; D $69.88; each addl $7; under 12 free. TV; cable (premium). Complimentary continental bkfst. Restaurant opp open 24 hrs. Ck-out 11 am. Business servs avail. Cr cds: A, C, D, DS, MC, V.

Restaurants

★ **BANTA'S STEAK & STEIN.** *(935 Union Ave, New Windsor)* NY 300, 1½ mi SW of I-87 exit 17. 914/564-7678. Specializes in steak, prime rib, seafood combo. Salad bar. Hrs: 4-10 pm; Fri, Sat to 11 pm; Sun from noon. Closed Thanksgiving, Dec 25. Bar. Semi-a la carte: dinner $7.95-$23.95. Child's meals. Family-owned. Cr cds: A, D, MC, V.

✔ ★ **COSIMO'S ON UNION.** *1217 NY 30.* 914/567-1556. Hrs: 11:30 am-10 pm; Fri, Sat to 11 pm; Sun from noon. Closed Easter, Thanksgiving, Dec 25. Res accepted. Italian menu. Wine, beer. Semi-a la carte: lunch $5.25-$8.95, dinner $7.95-$16.95. Child's meals. Specializes in wood-fired pizza, pasta, steak. Parking. Outdoor dining. Cr cds: A, MC, V.

★ ★ **SCHLESINGER'S STEAK HOUSE.** *(475 Temple Hill Rd, New Windsor 12553)* 2 mi S on NY 300. 914/561-1762. Specializes in steak, seafood, barbecue ribs. Hrs: 11:30 am-9 pm; Sat 4:30-10 pm; Sun 3-9 pm. Closed Thanksgiving, Dec 25. Bar. Semi-a la carte: lunch $4.95-$12, dinner $5.95-$29.95. Child's meals. Two dining rms in original Colonial building (1762). Cr cds: A, C, D, MC, V.

★ ★ ★ **YOBO.** *1297 NY 300, I-84 exit 7S.* 914/564-3848. Far Eastern menu. Specialties: Peking duck, hibatchi steak, sushi. Hrs: 11:30 am-10 pm; Fri to 11 pm; Sat 12:30-11 pm; Sun 12:30-10 pm. Closed Thanksgiving. Res accepted. Semi-a la carte: lunch $4.50-$8.50, dinner $9-$24.50. Japanese architect constructed building by hand; 5 dining rms; waterfalls, palm trees, teak statues. Cr cds: A, MC, V.

New Paltz (F-8)

(See also Kingston, Newburgh, Poughkeepsie)

Founded 1678 **Pop** 11,388 **Elev** 196 ft **Area code** 914 **Zip** 12561 **E-mail** npchamber@hvi.net **Web** www.kingston-ny.com/business/newpaltzchamber
Information Chamber of Commerce, 259 Main St; 914/255-0243 or 914/255-0411.

New Paltz was founded by a dozen Huguenots who were granted land by the colonial governor of New York. The town is surrounded by the fertile farmlands of the Wallkill River Valley, with apple orchards and vineyards.

What to See and Do

Huguenot St Old Stone Houses. Six original stone dwellings (1692-1712), a reconstructed French church (1717); Jean Hasbrouck House (1694) of medieval Flemish stone architecture. All houses furnished with heirlooms of descendants. (Early June-Labor Day, Wed-Sun) Visitor center at 6 Brodhead Ave. Phone 914/255-1660. ¢¢¢

Locust Lawn. Federal mansion of Josiah Hasbrouck (1814). Includes smokehouse, farmers' museum; Terwilliger Homestead (1738); bird sanctuary. (Early June-Labor Day, Wed-Sun) 4 mi S on NY 32. Phone 914/255-1660. ¢¢

State Univ of New York College at New Paltz (1828). (8,129 students) Art gallery (daily exc most Sat); concerts, plays. Language immersion program in 15 languages, summers and wkends; Music in the Mountains, contemporary music series (summer); Repertory Theatre (see SEASONAL EVENT). Campus tours by appt. On NY 32S, 1 mi W of NY State Thrwy exit 18. Phone 914/257-2121.

Annual Events

Ulster County Fair. Fairgrounds, 2 mi SW on Libertyville Rd. Contact Ulster Co Public Information Office, Box 1800, Kingston 12401; 914/340-3000. 1st wk Aug.

Apple Festival. Huguenot St. Oct.

Seasonal Event

SUNY College Summer Repertory Theatre. State Univ of New York College at New Paltz. Box office phone 914/257-3880. June-Aug.

Motel

✔ ★ **DAYS INN.** *601 Main St (NY 299).* 914/883-7373. 21 rms. S, D $49-$99; each addl $6; under 12 free; higher rates special events, wkends. Crib $6. TV; cable. Complimentary coffee. Restaurant nearby. Ck-out 11 am. X-country ski 5 mi. Cr cds: A, D, DS, MC, V.

Resort

★ ★ ★ **MOHONK MOUNTAIN HOUSE.** *Lake Mohonk, W on NY 299, cross bridge, turn right and follow signs.* 914/255-1000; FAX 914/256-2161; res: 800/772-6646. Web www.mohonk.com. 261 rms, 6-7 story. No A/C. AP: S $195-$475; D $315-$580; each addl $100; 4-12 yrs, $65; under 4 free; wkly, seasonal, special events rates. Crib free. Serv charge 13% per person. TV in lobby; cable. Supervised child's activities. Dining rm (public by res) 8-9:30 am, 12:30-2 pm, 6:30-8 pm; Fri to 10 pm. Rm serv. Box lunches, snack bar, picnics. Serv bar at lunch and dinner. Ck-out 2 pm, ck-in 4 pm. Coin lndry. Meeting rms. Bellhops. Valet serv. Gift shop. Resident doctor daily in summer, wkends rest of yr. Airport, RR station, bus depot transportation. Sports dir. Tennis. 9-hole golf, greens fee $12, putting green. Swimming from lake beach, lifeguard. Boats. X-country ski on site. Ice-skating. Lawn games. Hayrides, carriage rides, picnics. Soc dir. Movies, concerts, lectures, square dancing, theme wkends. Rec rm. Exercise rm; sauna. Many fireplaces. Many private balconies. Library. Resort since 1869; gardens, many gazebos. More than 2,000 mountainous acres, surrounded by 5,500-acre natural preserve. More than 90 mi of carriage roads, hiking trails. Cr cds: A, C, D, DS, MC, V.

★ ★ **ROCKING HORSE RANCH.** *(600 NY 44-45, Highland 12528)* 914/691-2927; res: 800/647-2624; FAX 914/691-6434. Web www.rhranch.com. 120 rms, 2 story. MAP, July-early Sept, wkly: S, D $725-$800; each addl $320-$345; under 4 free; package plans; wkends, hols (2-day min); lower rates rest of yr. Crib $5/day. Maid serv twice wkly. TV; cable, VCR avail (movies). Complimentary coffee in rms. Box lunches. Snack bar. Picnics. Bar noon-midnight; entertainment. Ck-out noon, ck-in 3 pm. Grocery 2 blks. Meeting rms. Business servs avail. Bellhops. Valet serv. Concierge. Aiport, RR station, bus depot transportation. Lighted tennis. 18-hole golf privileges, greens fee $45. Boats. Waterskiing. Downhill ski on site. Sleighing. Hiking. Lawn games. Soc dir. Rec rm. Game rm. Exercise rm; sauna, spa. Massage. Fishing guides. 3 pools, 1 indoor; wading pool, whirlpool, poolside serv, lifeguard. Playground. Supervised child's activities; ages 4-12. Some refrigerators. Picnic tables, grills. On lake. Cr cds: A, C, D, DS, MC, V.

Restaurants

✔ ★ **DOMINICK'S.** *30 N Chestnut St, N on NY 32.* 914/255-0120. Italian menu. Specializes in seafood, poultry, veal. Hrs: 11:30 am-10 pm; Sat from noon; Sun 11 am-8 pm; Sun brunch to 3 pm. Closed Mon, Tues; Thanksgiving, Dec 24-25. Res accepted. Bar. Semi-a la carte: lunch $5-$8.95, dinner $7.95-$17.95. Child's menu. Parking. Mediterranean decor. Family-owned for more than 50 yrs. Cr cds: A, C, D, DS, MC, V.

★ ★ **LOCUST TREE INN.** *215 Huguenot St.* 914/255-7888. Amer regional menu. Specialties: local produce, game, fish. Own desserts. Hrs: 11:30 am-2:30 pm, 5:30-10 pm; Sat 5:30-10 pm; Sun 3:30-8 pm; Sun brunch 11 am-2 pm. Closed Mon; Dec 25. Res accepted. Bar. Wine cellar. Semi-a la carte: lunch $6.95-$10.95, dinner $14.95-$21.95. Sun brunch $13. Parking. Outdoor dining. Dutch stone & frame house (portion dates from 1759) overlooking pond, 9-hole golf course; many antiques, fireplaces. Cr cds: A, C, D, DS, MC, V.

New Rochelle

(A-4 see New York City map)

(See also New York City, White Plains)

Pop 67,265 **Elev** 100 ft **Area code** 914
Information Chamber of Commerce, 514 Main St, 10801; 914/632-5700.

New Rochelle was founded in 1688 by a group of Huguenot families. Prior to the Europeans who settled here, the area was home to the Siwanoys, a part of the Mohegans stemming from the Algonquins. Boat building was the trade of many of the early settlers, and their boats carried goods to and from New York City and other towns and ports on the coast.

What to See and Do

Thomas Paine National Historical Association. Museum containing original writings and artifacts of Thomas Paine, author of *Common Sense;* also histories of the Huguenots and New Rochelle. (Fri, Sat & Sun, also by appt; closed winter) 983 North Ave. Phone 914/632-5376. ¢¢ Admission includes

Thomas Paine Cottage. This is the house where Paine lived upon his return from Europe. The cottage is now a museum containing Paine artifacts and memorabilia. (Fri, Sat & Sun, also by appt; closed winter) 20 Sicard. Phone 914/632-5376.

Motor Hotel

★ ★ ★ **RAMADA PLAZA.** *1 Ramada Plaza (10801), I-95 exit 16.* 914/576-3700; FAX 914/576-3711. 128 rms, 10 story. Apr-Oct: S $122; D $157; suites $225; under 18 free; wkly, wkend, hol rates; higher rates special events; lower rates rest of yr. Crib free. TV; cable (premium), VCR avail (movies). Pool; poolside serv, lifeguard. Complimentary coffee in lobby. Restaurant 6:30-10 pm; Sat from 7:30 pm; Sun 7:30-9 pm. Rm serv. Bar. Ck-out noon. Meeting rms. Business center. In-rm modem link. Bellhops. Valet serv. Sundries. Gift shop. Exercise equipt. Health club privileges. Some refrigerators. Cr cds: A, C, D, DS, ER, MC, V.

Restaurant

★ ★ **LA RISERVA-TRATTORIA.** *(2382 Boston Post Rd, Larchmont 10538)* 914/834-5584. Northern Italian menu. Specializes in veal, pasta, chicken. Hrs: noon-3 pm, 5-10 pm; Fri to 11 pm; Sat 4-11 pm; Sun brunch noon-3 pm. Closed Jan 1, Thanksgiving, Dec 25. Res accepted. Bar. Semi-a la carte: lunch $6.75-$12.75, dinner $10.95-$19.75. Child's meals. Cr cds: A, MC, V.

New York City
(Follows Yonkers at end of New York State)

Niagara Falls (D-2)

(See also Buffalo, Lockport; also see Niagara Falls and Niagara-on-the-Lake, ON, Canada)

Settled 1806 **Pop** 61,840 **Elev** 610 ft **Area code** 716 **E-mail** nfcvb@nfcvb.com **Web** www.nfcvb.com

Information Convention & Visitors Bureau, 310 4th St, 14303; 716/285-2400 or 800/421-5223.

There are higher falls, but Niagara still puts on a first-class performance. On the border with Canada, the American Falls are 184 feet high, the Canadian Horseshoe, 176 feet. The two are separated by Goat Island. For several hours in the evening the beauty of the falls continues in a display of colored lights playing over the water.

Originally, after the glacial period, the falls were seven miles downstream at the Niagara escarpment. Rocks have crashed from top to bottom causing the falls to retreat at a rate averaging about one foot per year.

With a flow of more than 200,000 cubic feet of water per second, Niagara has a power potential of about 4,000,000 horsepower. Electrical production is controlled by agreements between the US and Canada so that each receives a full share while the beauty of the cataracts is preserved.

The industries nourished by these waters include aircraft, aerospace equipment (Bell), abrasives (Carborundum), food products, paper, chemicals and a tremendous tourist business. (For Border Crossing Regulations see MAKING THE MOST OF YOUR TRIP.)

What to See and Do

Aquarium of Niagara Falls, NY. Dolphin & sea lion; more than 2,000 marine creatures, incl sharks, otters, piranha, penguins, exotic fish. Free outdoor sea lion pool; largest collection of freshwater gamefish in the Northeast. (Daily; closed Thanksgiving, Dec 25) 701 Whirlpool St. Phone 716/285-3575 or 716/692-2665. ¢¢¢

Artpark. A 200-acre state park and summer theater devoted to visual and performing arts. Events at 2,300-seat theater with lawn seating incl musicals, classical concerts by Buffalo Philharmonic Orchestra, dance programs and jazz and pop music concerts. 7 mi N on Robert Moses Pkwy, in Lewiston. For schedule, contact PO Box 371, Lewiston 14092; 716/754-9000 or 800/659-7275.

Devil's Hole State Park. View of Lower Rapids & Power Authority generating plant. Nature, hiking trail. Picnicking. 4½ mi N of falls. Phone 716/278-1770. **Free.**

Fantasy Island. An 80-acre family theme park with more than 100 attractions, incl water park, thrill rides, children's rides and western town; live shows; picnic area. (Mid-June-early Sept, daily; also wkends Mid-May-mid-June) 2400 Grand Island Blvd, S on I-190 in Grand Island. Phone 716/773-7591. ¢¢¢¢¢

Ft Niagara State Park. Swimming pool (fee), bathhouse; fishing; boating (launch); nature, hiking trails; tennis. Cross-country skiing, snowmobiling. (Daily; closed Jan 1, Thanksgiving, Dec 25) Standard fees. 14 mi N on Robert Moses Pkwy, in Youngstown. Phone 716/745-7273.Here is

Old Ft Niagara (1726). Restored fort played important role in French & Indian War and in War of 1812. Museum, French "Castle," other bldgs. Military drills, ceremonies in summer. (Daily) Phone 716/745-7611. ¢¢¢

Four Mile Creek State Park Campground. On Lake Ontario. Fishing; hiking. Playground. 266 tent & trailer sites. (Mid-Apr-Oct) Standard fees. Phone 716/745-7273.

Niagara Falls Convention & Civic Center. Sports events, concerts, conventions, trade shows. 305 4th St. Phone 716/286-4769.

Niagara Power Project Visitor Center. Glass-enclosed observation bldg with outdoor balcony; view of Niagara River Gorge, hydroelectric projects on both sides of river; displays explain power generation; Father Louis Hennepin mural; museum shows development of power and industry at Niagara Falls with hands-on displays. (Daily; closed hols) 5777 Lewiston Rd (NY 104), 4½ mi N of the falls. Phone 716/285-3211. **Free.**

★ **Niagara Reservation State Park.** Provides many views of Niagara Falls and the rapids above and below the cataract from Prospect and Terrapin Points, Luna Island and many other locations. Fishing; nature, hiking trails. Restaurant. Visitor center; recreation programs. Standard fees. 4 mi W of I-190 at Robert Moses Pkwy. Phone 716/278-1770. Per vehicle parking ¢¢ Includes

Boat ride. *Maid of the Mist* takes passengers close to the falls. (Mid-May-mid-Oct, daily, approx every 30 min) Fee incl use of waterproof clothing. Phone 716/284-4233. ¢¢¢

Cave of the Winds Trip. Elevators from Goat Island. Walk through the spray at the base of the American Falls. Waterproof garments supplied. (Mid-May-mid-Oct, daily) Phone 716/278-1770. ¢¢

Goat Island. Separates the Canadian Horseshoe and American Falls. Drives and walks in 70-acre park; closest possible views of falls and upper rapids. Picnic areas; restaurant, snack bar. Smaller Luna Island and Three Sister Islands can be reached by footbridge. Phone 716/278-1762.

Niagara Viewmobile. Miniature train ride from Prospect Point to Goat Island and return with stopovers at Cave of the Winds, Terrapin Point and Three Sister Islands. (Apr-Oct, daily) Phone 716/278-1730 or 716/278-1770. ¢¢

Prospect Park Visitor Center. Information desk, video displays; widescreen theater featuring movie *Niagara Wonders;* Great Lakes Garden; Virtual Reality Helicopter Simulator ride. (Daily) Phone 716/278-1796. Movie ¢; Simulator ride ¢¢

Prospect Point Observation Tower. The 282-ft tower rises adj to American Falls. Elevator to gorge below and *Maid of the Mist.* (Daily) Prospect Park. Phone 716/278-1770. ¢

Schoellkopf Geological Museum. Spiral-shaped bldg houses exhibits relating to geological formation and history of the falls. Audiovisual presentation. Rock garden, gorge overlook. (Memorial Day-Oct, daily; rest of yr, Thurs-Sun; closed Jan 1, Thanksgiving, Dec 25) Phone 716/278-1780. ¢

Niagara's Wax Museum of History. Life-size wax figures depict history of the area; historic items. (Daily) 303 Prospect St, at Old Falls St. Phone 716/285-1271. ¢¢

Reservoir State Park. Overlook at the Robert Moses Power Plant Reservoir. Tennis. Picnicking, playground, ball field. Cross-country skiing, snowmobiling. 4 mi NE at jct NY 31, 265. Phone 716/278-1762.

Whirlpool State Park. Splendid view of the famous Niagara River Gorge whirlpool and rapids. Ongiara Trail, nature, hiking trail. Picnicking, playground. 3 mi N of falls on Robert Moses Pkwy. Phone 716/278-1770.

Wintergarden. A seven-story indoor tropical park. Over 7,000 trees, shrubs and flowers; waterfall, glass elevators and elevated walkways. Adj to falls and Convention Center. (Daily; closed Dec 25) Rainbow Blvd. Phone 716/286-4940. **Free.**

Annual Event

Festival of Lights. Downtown. Colored lights, animated displays, decorations; entertainment. Lighting of the Christmas tree. Phone 716/285-2400. Mid-Nov-Dec.

Motels

★ ★ **BEST WESTERN SUMMIT INN.** *9500 Niagara Falls Blvd (14304).* 716/297-5050; FAX 716/297-0802. 88 rms, 2 story. July-early Oct: S $68-$88; D $88-$98; each addl $10; under 18 free; wkly & wkend rates; lower rates rest of yr. Crib free. Pet accepted, some restrictions. TV; VCR avail (movies). Indoor pool. Sauna. Restaurant 7-11 am, 4-9 pm. Bar 4-9 pm. Ck-out 11 am. Meeting rms. Business servs avail. Game rm. Cr cds: A, C, D, DS, MC, V.

✔★ **BUDGET HOST/AMERI-CANA MOTOR INN.** 9401 Niagara Falls Blvd (14304). 716/297-2660; FAX 716/297-7675. E-mail sandsmotel@wzrd.com. 45 rms. June-Labor Day: S $39-$69; D $45-$79; each addl $5-$10; kit. suites $45-$129; under 18 free; higher rates Amer & Canadian hols; lower rates rest of yr. Crib free. TV; cable (premium). Heated pool. Restaurant opp 7-3 am. Ck-out 11 am. Coin lndry. Business servs avail. Some in-rm whirlpools, refrigerators. Picnic tables. Cr cds: A, C, D, DS, MC, V.

[D] [≈] [¾] [🔥] [SC]

★ **CHATEAU MOTOR LODGE.** (1810 Grand Island Blvd, Grand Island 14072) S on I-190 exit 18A. 716/773-2868; FAX 716/773-5173. 17 rms, 4 kits. June-Sept: S $59; D $69; under 8 free; wkly rates; lower rates rest of yr. Crib free. Pet accepted, some restrictions. TV. Restaurant nearby. Ck-out 11 am. Refrigerators, microwaves avail. Cr cds: A, DS, MC, V.

[D] [🐾] [¾] [🔥] [SC]

✔★ **DRIFTWOOD.** 2754 Niagara Falls Blvd (14304). 716/692-6650; FAX 716/695-6428; res: 800/500-1765. 20 rms. S, D $32-$87. TV. Pool. Restaurants nearby. Ck-out 10 am. Some refrigerators, microwaves. Cr cds: A, C, DS, MC, V.

[≈] [¾] [🔥]

★ **ECONO LODGE.** 7708 Niagara Falls Blvd (14304). 716/283-0621; FAX 716/283-2121. Web www.choicehotels.com. 70 rms, 2 story. June-Labor Day: S, D $59-$99; each addl $7; under 18 free; wkly rates; higher rates hols; lower rates rest of yr. Crib $7. TV; VCR avail (movies). Heated pool. Complimentary coffee in lobby. Restaurants nearby. Ck-out 11 am. Business servs avail. Gift shop. Microwaves avail. Cr cds: A, C, D, DS, ER, JCB, MC, V.

[D] [≈] [¾] [🔥] [SC]

★ **PORTAGE HOUSE.** (280 Portage Rd, Lewiston 14092) 7 mi N on NY 104, at rear entrance to Artpark. 716/754-8295; FAX 716/754-1613. 21 rms, 2 story. No rm phone. May-Oct: S $57; D $64; each addl $7; under 12 free; lower rates rest of yr. Crib free. TV; cable. Restaurant nearby. Ck-out 11 am. Health club privileges. Cr cds: A, DS, MC, V.

[🔥] [SC]

✔★★ **RAMADA INN BY THE FALLS.** 219 4th St (14303). 716/282-1734; FAX 716/282-1881. Web www.ramada-ny.com/niagara_falls.html. 112 rms, 2 story. Apr-Oct: S, D $45-$120; each addl $8-$12; lower rates rest of yr. Crib free. TV. Indoor pool. Restaurant 6:30 am-11 pm. Ck-out 11 am. Coin lndry. Business servs avail. Cr cds: A, C, D, DS, ER, MC, V.

[D] [≈] [¾] [🔥] [SC]

Motor Hotels

★★ **BEST WESTERN INN ON THE RIVER.** 7001 Buffalo Ave (14304). 716/283-7612; FAX 716/283-7631. 150 rms, 8 story. Late May-Sept: S $78-$118; D $88-$128; each addl $10; under 18 free; mid-wk, wkend rates; lower rates rest of yr. Crib free. TV; VCR avail. Indoor pool. Sauna. Restaurant 7 am-2 pm, 4:30-9 pm. Rm serv. Bar noon-midnight; entertainment. Ck-out noon. Coin lndry. Meeting rms. Business servs avail. Game rm. Boat docking. On Niagara River. Cr cds: A, C, D, DS, ER, JCB, MC, V.

[≈] [¾] [🔥] [SC]

★★ **COMFORT INN-THE POINTE.** 1 Prospect Pointe (14303). 716/284-6835; res: 800/284-6835; FAX 716/284-5177. E-mail HotelFalls@aol.com. 118 rms, 6 story. June-Oct: S $82-$132; D $92-$142; each addl $10; suites $165-$300; under 18 free; lower rates rest of yr. Crib free. TV; cable (premium). Complimentary continental bkfst. Restaurant 7 am-11 pm. Ck-out 11 am. Meeting rms. Business servs avail. Sundries. Gift shop. Cr cds: A, C, D, DS, ER, JCB, MC, V.

[D] [¾] [🔥] [SC]

★★ **HOWARD JOHNSON AT THE FALLS.** 454 Main St (14301). 716/285-5261; FAX 716/285-8536. E-mail hojofalls@aol.com. 80 rms, 5 story. June-Labor Day: S $80-$140; D $90-$150; each addl $8-$10; under 18 free; wkly, wkend rates; higher rates: hols, special events; lower rates rest of yr. Crib free. TV; cable. Indoor pool. Sauna. Restaurant 6:30 am-11 pm. Ck-out noon. Coin lndry. Business servs avail. Sundries. Game rm. Some in-rm whirlpools. Near falls. Cr cds: A, C, D, DS, ER, JCB, MC, V.

[D] [≈] [¾] [🔥] [SC]

★★★ **THE NIAGARA.** 114 Buffalo Ave (14303). 716/285-2521; FAX 716/285-0963. 200 rms, 7 story. June-Aug: S $119-$149; D $129-$149; each addl $10; suites $175-$279; under 19 free; lower rates rest of yr. Crib free. TV; cable (premium). Indoor pool; whirlpool, lifeguard. Complimentary coffee in rms. Restaurant 6:30 am-10 pm. Rm serv. Bar noon-2 am. Ck-out noon. Coin lndry. Business servs avail. In-rm modem link. Bellhops. Valet serv. Exercise equipt; sauna. Game rm. Cr cds: A, C, D, DS, ER, JCB, MC, V.

[D] [≈] [✗] [¾] [🔥] [SC]

★★ **QUALITY INN RAINBOW BRIDGE AT THE FALLS.** 443 Main St (14301). 716/284-8801; FAX 716/284-8633. 168 rms, 8 story. Mid-June-mid-Sept: S, D $89-$129; each addl $10; under 18 free; wkend rates; lower rates rest of yr. Crib free. TV; cable. Indoor pool. Sauna. Restaurant open 24 hrs. Bar 4 pm-2 am. Ck-out 11 am. Coin lndry. Meeting rms. Business servs avail. Sundries. Game rm. Cr cds: A, C, D, DS, ER, MC, V.

[D] [≈] [¾] [🔥] [SC]

★★ **RAMADA INN AT THE FALLS.** 240 Rainbow Blvd (14303). 716/282-1212; FAX 716/282-1216. Web www.businessvillage.com/ramada.htm. 217 rms, 4 story, 8 suites. Memorial Day-Labor Day: S, D $69-$139; each addl $10; suites $90-$150; under 18 free; lower rates rest of yr. TV; VCR avail (movies). Indoor pool; whirlpool. Restaurant 6:30 am-10 pm. Bar 3 pm-1 am. Meeting rms. Business servs avail. Bellhops. Shopping mall adj. Cr cds: A, C, D, DS, MC, V.

[D] [≈] [¾] [🔥] [SC]

Hotels

★★★ **CLARION.** 3rd & Old Falls St (14303). 716/285-3361; FAX 716/285-3900. 401 rms, 6 story. Mid-June-mid-Sept: S, D $85-$139; each addl $10; suites $175-$375; lower rates rest of yr. Crib free. Pet accepted, some restrictions; $50 refundable. Free garage parking. TV; cable (premium), VCR avail. Indoor pool. Sauna. Restaurant 6:30 am-11 pm. Bar noon-midnight; Sat to 3 am. Ck-out noon. Convention facilities. Business servs avail. Gift shop. Exercise equipt. Game rm. Some refrigerators. Walkway to Intl Convention & Civic Center & Rainbow Center. Cr cds: A, C, D, DS, ER, JCB, MC, V.

[D] [🐾] [≈] [✗] [¾] [🔥] [SC]

★★ **DAYS INN FALLS VIEW.** 201 Rainbow Blvd (14303), 1 blk E of Falls. 716/285-9321; FAX 716/285-2539. 200 rms, 12 story. Mid-June-early Sept: S, D $59-$118; each addl $8; under 16 free; lower rates rest of yr. Crib free. Pet accepted. TV; VCR avail (movies). Restaurant 6:30 am-10 pm. Bar 11-2 am. Ck-out 11 am. Meeting rms. Business servs avail. Game rm. Some refrigerators; microwaves avail. Overlooks rapids. Cr cds: A, D, DS, MC, V.

[🐾] [¾] [🔥] [SC]

★★★ **HOLIDAY INN-GRAND ISLAND.** (100 White Haven Rd, Grand Island 14072) S on I-190, exit 19. 716/773-1111; FAX 716/773-9386. 262 rms, 6 story. Mid-June-early Sept: S, D $79-$140; each addl $10; under 19 free; wkend plan; lower rates rest of yr. Crib free. TV; cable (premium). 2 pools, 1 indoor; whirlpool, wading pool, lifeguard. Playground. Supervised child's activities (June-Sept). Complimentary coffee in rms. Restaurant 7 am-10 pm. Bar noon-2 am. Ck-out noon. Meeting rms. Business center. Gift shop. Exercise rm; sauna. Massage. Rec rm. Lawn games. Balconies. On Niagara River. Marina. Luxury level. Cr cds: A, C, D, DS, ER, JCB, MC, V.

Inn

★★★ **RED COACH INN.** *2 Buffalo Ave (14303).* 716/282-1459; FAX 716/282-2650; res: 800/282-1459. E-mail redcoach@wnyip.net; Web www.redcoach.com. 10 rms, 3 story, 8 kit. suites. S, D $99; kit. suites $119-$299; package plans. TV. Complimentary continental bkfst. Complimentary coffee in rms. Restaurant (see RED COACH INN). Rm serv. Bar. Ck-out 11 am, ck-in 3 pm. Meeting rms. Business servs avail. Microwaves avail. X-country ski 5 mi. View of Upper Rapids. Built 1923; authentic Old English atmosphere. Cr cds: DS, MC, V.

Restaurants

✔★ **ALPS CHALET.** *1555 Military Rd (14304).* 716/297-8990. Greek, Amer menu. Specializes in steak, seafood. Hrs: 11-2 am; Sat noon-3 am; Sun brunch 11 am-2 pm. Closed Mon. Res accepted. Bar. Semi-a la carte: lunch $3-$5, dinner $5.50-$13. Sun Brunch $7.95. Child's meals. Parking. Chalet-type decor. Family-owned. Cr cds: A, MC, V.

★★ **CLARKSON HOUSE.** *(810 Center St, Lewiston 14902)* N on Robert Moses Pkwy, Lewiston exit. 716/754-4544. Specializes in char-broiled steak, seafood, chicken. Hrs: 5-11 pm; Sun 3-9 pm. Closed Dec 25. Res accepted; required Sat, Sun. Bar. Semi-a la carte: dinner $10.50-$29.50. Child's meals. Parking. Open-hearth cooking. 1818 house. Family-owned. Cr cds: A, D, MC, V.

✔★★ **COMO.** *2220 Pine Ave (14301).* 716/285-9341. Web www.iaw.com/rosemelcomo/goose.html. Italian, Amer menu. Specialties: veal parmigiana, fettucine Alfredo, ravioli. Hrs: 11:30 am-11 pm; early-bird dinner Mon-Thurs 3-5 pm. Closed Dec 25. Res accepted. Bar. Semi-a la carte: lunch $4-$7, dinner $7-$12. Child's meals. Parking. Statuary reproductions. Family-owned. Cr cds: A, MC, V.

★★ **JOHN'S FLAMING HEARTH.** *1965 Military Rd (14304), 6 mi NE of Falls.* 716/297-1414. Specializes in steak, lobster. Own ice cream. Hrs: 11:30 am-10 pm; Sun noon-9 pm; early-bird dinner Mon-Fri 4-6 pm. Res accepted. Bar. Semi-a la carte: lunch $3-$7.50. Complete meals: dinner $11.95-$27.95. Child's meals. Entertainment Sat. Parking. Family-owned. Cr cds: A, C, D, DS, MC, V.

★ **MACRI'S PALACE.** *755 W Market St (14301).* 716/282-4707. Italian, Amer menu. Specializes in pasta, steak, seafood. Hrs: 11 am-11 pm; Fri, Sat to midnight. Closed most major hols. Res accepted. Bar 11:30-2:30 am; Fri, Sat to 3:30 am. Semi-a la carte: lunch $3.75-$6, dinner $7-$16.95. Child's meals. Contemporary decor. Cr cds: A, MC, V.

★★ **RED COACH INN.** *(See Red Coach Inn)* 716/282-1459. Specialty: prime rib. Hrs: 11:30 am-10 pm; Fri, Sat to 11 pm. Closed Dec 25. Bar. Semi-a la carte: lunch $3.95-$8.95, dinner $6.95-$19.95. Child's meals. Parking. Glassed-porch dining overlooking Upper Rapids. English inn decor & atmosphere. Cr cds: A, C, D, DS, MC, V.

★★ **RIVERSIDE INN.** *(115 S Water St, Lewiston 14902)* N on Robert Moses Pkwy, Lewiston exit. 716/754-8206. E-mail riverinn@local net.com; web www.riversideinn.net. Specializes in fresh seafood, steak, prime rib. Hrs: 11:30 am-3 pm, 4-11 pm; Fri & Sat to midnight; winter hrs vary; early-bird dinner 5:30 pm, Sun noon-8 pm. Res accepted. Bar. Semi-a la carte: lunch $4.95-$12.95, dinner $9.95-$29.95. Child's meals.

Entertainment Thurs-Sat; also Sun in summer. Parking. Outdoor dining. Built 1871; riverboat atmosphere. Family-owned. Cr cds: A, C, D, DS, JCB, MC, V.

★ **VILLA COFFEE HOUSE.** *(769 Cayuga St, Lewiston 14092)* N on NY 104, in shopping center. 716/754-2660. Specializes in egg dishes, pancakes, soup. Hrs: 7 am-2 pm. Closed Jan 1, Thanksgiving, Dec 25. Semi-a la carte: bkfst, lunch $2.95-$5.95. Child's meals. No cr cds accepted.

Niagara Falls, ON, Canada

(see Canada)

North Creek (C-8)

(See also Schroon Lake, Warrensburg)

Pop 950 (est) **Elev** 1,028 ft **Area code** 518 **Zip** 12853 **E-mail** goremtn@superior.net **Web** www.goremtnregion.org

Information Gore Mountain Region Chamber of Commerce Accommodation and Visitors Bureau, 295 Main St, PO Box 84; 518/251-2612 or 800/880-GORE.

What to See and Do

Adirondack Park (see).

Gore Mt Mineral Shop. Tours of open-pit garnet mine; opportunity to collect loose gem garnets. (Mid-June-Labor Day, daily) Barton Mine Rd. Phone 518/251-2706. ¢¢

Rafting. Sixteen-mi whitewater rafting trips from Indian Lake to North River. (Apr-Nov) Contact Gore Mt Region Chamber of Commerce.

Skiing.

Garnet Hill Ski Lodge & Cross-Country Ski Center. Approx 35 mi of groomed, cross-country trails adj state wilderness trails; tennis courts, hiking trails, fishing, beach and boat rentals on 13th Lake, site of abandoned garnet mine. Restaurant. (Daily; closed Thanksgiving) 5 mi NW via NY 28, at the top of 13th Lake Rd. Phone 518/251-2444 or 518/251-2821. **Free.**

Gore Mt. Gondola, triple, 5 double chairlifts, J-bar; cross-country trails; patrol, school, rentals; cafeteria, restaurant, bar; nursery; lodges; snow-making. Longest run 2½ mi; vertical drop 2,100 ft. (Nov-Apr, daily; also fall wkends for gondola) Approx 2 mi NW off NY 28. Phone 518/251-2411 or 800/342-1234 (snow conditions). ¢¢¢¢¢

Annual Events

White Water Derby. Hudson River. Canoe and kayak competition. First wkend May.

Adirondack Artisans Festival. Gore Mt Ski Area. 1st wkend Aug.

Teddy Roosevelt Celebration. Town-wide. Sept.

Motel

★★ **BLACK MOUNTAIN SKI LODGE.** *2999 NY 8, 4 mi W of jct NY 28.* 518/251-2800; FAX 518/251-4312. Web www.mediause.com/ny/blackmt. 25 rms. Mid-Dec-mid-May: S, D $41-$65; each addl $5; Apr-May: family, wkly rates; skiing, hiking, canoeing, rafting packages; lower rates rest of yr. Crib $5. Pet accepted. TV; cable. Pool. Playground. Restaurant

7-10 am. Ck-out 11 am. Sundries. Downhill/x-country ski 5 mi. Rec rm. Some refrigerators. Cr cds: A, DS, MC, V.

Inn

★ **GARNET HILL LODGE.** *North River (12856), 5 mi N on NY 28, then 5 mi on 13th Lake Rd, on 13th Lake. 518/251-2821; FAX 518/251-3089.* E-mail garnet@netheaven.com; web www.garnet-hill.com. 29 rms, 26 with bath, 2 story. MAP: S $82-$135; D $62-$95/person; each addl $45; family, wkly rates; skiing, rafting packages. TV rm; VCR (movies). Dining rm 7:30-9:30 am, noon-2:30 pm, 5-9 pm. Ck-out 11 am, ck-in 4 pm. Business servs avail. Airport transportation, free bus depot transportation. Tennis. Downhill ski 15 mi; x-country ski on site, instructor, rentals. Nature trails. Mountain bicycles. Rec rm. Exercise rm; sauna. Some balconies. Private beach; swimming. Fishing guides. Stocked lake. Rustic setting. Cr cds: MC, V.

North Salem

(see Brewster)

Northport, L.I. (A-3)

(See also Huntington, Smithtown, Stony Brook)

Settled 1656 **Pop** 7,572 **Elev** 100 ft **Area code** 516 **Zip** 11768

An early English Puritan settlement, the land in and around Northport was purchased from the Matinecock.

What to See and Do

Eaton's Neck Lighthouse (1798). Second lighthouse built in the US. A 73-ft-high beacon warns ships more than 17 mi out at sea. Lighthouse Rd.

Northport Historical Museum. Changing exhibits of local history; photographs, artifacts, costumes, and shipbuilding memorabilia. (Daily exc Mon; closed most major hols) Walking tours of village on some Sun afternoons in spring and summer. 215 Main St. Phone 516/757-9859. **Donation.**

Suffolk County Vanderbilt Museum. Marine science and natural history exhibits, habitat groups; original fine and decorative arts; Spanish-revival 21-rm mansion, 43 landscaped acres. (Daily exc Mon; closed most major hols) On Little Neck Rd in Centerport, about 1 mi N of NY 25A. Phone 516/854-5555. **¢¢¢** Also here is

Vanderbilt Museum Planetarium. Sky shows (daily exc Mon). Phone 516/854-5555. **¢¢¢;** Combination ticket **¢¢¢¢**

Norwich (E-6)

(See also Hamilton, Oneonta)

Pop 7,613 **Elev** 1,015 ft **Area code** 607 **Zip** 13815 **E-mail** chamber@norwich.net **Web** www.norwich.net/~chamber

Information Chenango County Chamber of Commerce, 19 Eaton Ave, 607/334-1400 or 800/556-8596.

What to See and Do

Bowman Lake State Park. This 660-acre park borders on 11,000 acres of state forest land. Swimming beach; fishing; rowboats (rentals); nature, hiking trails. Cross-country skiing, snowmobiling. Picnicking. Route 220W, in Oxford. Phone 607/334-2718. **¢¢**

Northeast Classic Car Museum. Features the largest collection of Franklin autos in the world; Duesenbergs, Cords, Auburns, Packards and more. All are restored, preserved and fully operational. (Daily; closed Jan 1, Thanksgiving, Dec 25) 24 Rexford St. Phone 607/334-AUTO. **¢¢¢**

Annual Events

General Clinton Canoe Regatta. General Clinton Park, Rt 7 in Bainbridge. Phone 607/967-8700. May 28-31.

Chenango County Fair. Chenango County Fairgrounds, W Main St. Phone 607/334-9198. Aug 10-15.

Motels

★★ **HOWARD JOHNSON HOTEL.** *75 N Broad St on NY 12. 607/334-2200; FAX 607/336-5619.* 87 units, 3 story. S $55-$75; D $65-$95; each addl $10; suites $75-$125; some wkend rates; higher rates special events. Crib free. Pet accepted, some restrictions; $5. TV; cable (premium). Indoor pool. Coffee in rms. Restaurant 8 am-11 pm. Bar. Ck-out 11 am. Meeting rms. Business servs avail. Health club privileges. In-rm whirlpools; some refrigerators; microwaves avail. Cr cds: A, D, DS, MC, V.

✔★ **SUPER 8.** *NY 12. 607/336-8880; FAX 607/336-2076.* 41 rms, 3 story, 4 suites. June-Aug: S, D $42.88-$62.88; each addl $5; suites $60-$99; under 12 free; wkend rates; higher rates special events; lower rates rest of yr. Crib free. TV; cable (premium). Complimentary continental bkfst. Restaurant opp 6 am-10 pm. Ck-out 11 am. Meeting rm. Refrigerator in suites. Picnic tables. Cr cds: A, C, D, DS, JCB, MC, V.

Restaurant

★★ **HANDS INN.** *S Broad St. 607/334-8223.* Specializes in steak, seafood, pasta. Hrs: 11 am-2 pm, 5-9:30 pm. Closed Sun; Memorial Day, July 4, Labor Day. Res accepted; required hols. Bar 11 am-10 pm. Semi-a la carte: lunch $4-$11.95, dinner $6.95-$25. Buffet: lunch $5.95. Child's meals. Family-owned. Cr cds: A, C, D, MC, V.

Nyack (A-2)

(See also White Plains)

Pop 6,558 **Elev** 70 ft **Area code** 914 **Zip** 10960
Information Chamber of Commerce, PO Box 677; 914/353-2221.

Many outstanding Victorian-style homes and an Edward Hopper art gallery grace this village.

What to See and Do

Antiques on the Hudson. A collection of more than 75 art, crafts and antique shops located in the village of Nyack on the Hudson. (Daily exc Mon) W side of Tappan Zee Bridge; NY State Thrwy N exit 10 or 11; or Thrwy S exit 11.

Hudson Valley Children's Museum. Interactive, hands-on exhibits focus on arts and sciences. Exhibits incl Early Childhood, Royal Bubble Factory, Gadget Garage, Creation Station and others with social and educational themes. Museum shop. (Daily exc Sun) 21C Burd St, Nyack Seaport. Phone 914/358-2191. **¢¢**

Motel

✔★ **SUPER 8.** *47 NY 59. 914/353-3880; FAX 914/353-0271.* 43 rms, 2 story. May-Sept: S $62.88; D $64.88; each addl $3; under 12 free;

higher rates: West Point graduation, some hols; lower rates rest of yr. Crib free. TV; cable (premium). Complimentary coffee in lobby. Restaurant adj 5 am-10 pm. Ck-out 11 am. Business servs avail. In-rm modem link. Cr cds: A, C, D, DS, JCB, MC, V.

D ⊠ ⚒ SC

Motor Hotel

★ **BEST WESTERN.** *26 NY 59, at NY Thrwy northbound exit 11.* 914/358-8100; FAX 914/358-3644. 80 rms, 2 story. S, D $95; each addl $5; under 18 free. Crib $10. TV; cable (premium). Restaurant open 24 hrs. Bar 4:30 pm-2 am; entertainment. Ck-out noon. Meeting rms. Business servs avail. In-rm modem link. Cr cds: A, C, D, DS, MC, V.

D ⊠ ⚒ SC

Restaurants

★ **ICHI RIKI.** *110 Main St.* 914/358-7977. Japanese menu. Specializes in sushi, Japanese dishes. Hrs: noon-2:30 pm, 5:30-10 pm; Fri to 11 pm; Sat 5-11 pm; Sun 5-9:30 pm. Closed Mon; Thanksgiving, Dec 25. Res accepted. Bar. Semi-a la carte: lunch $7.95-$18.95, dinner $12.50-$27.50. Cr cds: A, C, D, MC, V.

D

★ **THE KING AND I.** *93 Main St, US 87 exit 11.* 914/353-4208. Thai menu. Specialties: curried duck, whole crispy fish flambé, chicken with peanut sauce. Hrs: 11:30 am-3 pm, 5-10 pm; Fri to 11 pm; Sat 11:30 am-11 pm; Sun 11:30 am-10 pm. Closed some major hols. Res accepted. Bar. Semi-a la carte: lunch $7.50-$8.50, dinner $10.95-$17.95. Cr cds: MC, V.

D

★★ **THE MARINER.** *(701 Piermont Ave, Piermont 10968) 3 mi S of Tappanzee Bridge exit 10.* 914/365-1360. Seafood menu. Specializes in lobster. Own desserts. Hrs: 11:30 am-10 pm; Fri, Sat to 11 pm; Sun to 9 pm. Res accepted. Bar. A la carte entrees: lunch $3.95-$17.95, dinner $4.95-$17.95. Pianist Sat. Parking. Outdoor dining. Tiered dining rm overlooking the river; view of Tappan Zee Bridge. Cr cds: A, D, MC, V.

D ⤵

★★ **RESTAURANT X.** *(117 N NY 303, Congers 10920) NY Thrwy exit 12.* 914/268-6555. International menu. Own baking. Hrs: noon-2:30 pm, 5:30-10 pm; Sun 2-9 pm. Closed Mon; also Dec 25. Res accepted. Bar. Semi-a la carte: lunch $10-$15, dinner $17-$25. Parking. 3 fireplaces. Overlooks pond & gardens. Cr cds: MC, V.

D ⤵

✔★★ **RIVER CLUB.** *11 Burd St, on Hudson River.* 914/358-0220. Specializes in steak, seafood, ribs. Hrs: noon-midnight; Fri, Sat to 1 am; Sun brunch 11:30 am-3 pm. Closed Thanksgiving, Dec 25. Res accepted. Bar. A la carte entrees: lunch $6.95-$10.95, dinner $9.95-$21.95. Sun brunch $4.95-$9.95. Parking. Outdoor dining. Nautical decor; view of river, marina. Cr cds: A, C, D, DS, MC, V.

D

Ogdensburg (Thousand Islands) (B-6)

(See also Canton; also see Brockville, ON, Canada)

Settled 1749 **Pop** 13,521 **Elev** 280 ft **Area code** 315 **Zip** 13669 **E-mail** chamber@gisco.net **Web** www.ogdensburgny.com

Information Greater Ogdensburg Chamber of Commerce, Park St & Rte 37, PO Box 681; 315/393-3620.

On the St Lawrence Seaway, at the mouth of the Oswegatchie River, this busy port and industrial town had its beginnings as an outpost of New France, where the Iroquois were converted to Christianity. In 1837, it was the base from which American sympathizers worked "to free Canada from the yoke of England" in the abortive Patriots' War.

What to See and Do

Ft Wellington National Historic Site. Built during War of 1812 to protect communications link between Montreal and Kingston; rebuilt 1838-1839 in response to the Canadian Rebellions of 1837-1838. Restored blockhouse, officers' quarters, guides in period costume, demonstrations of 1846 life at the fort. Large military pageant with mock battles (3rd wkend July). (Mid-May-Sept, daily; rest of yr, by appt) 379 Van-Koughnet St in Prescott, Ontario, Canada, 4 mi W of International Bridge. Phone 613/925-2896. **Free.**

🌟 **Frederic Remington Art Museum.** Largest single collection of paintings, sculpture, drawings by Frederic Remington, foremost artist of the Old West; re-created studio; Belter furniture, glass, china, silver. (May-Oct, daily; rest of yr, Tues-Sat; closed legal hols) 303 Washington St. Phone 315/393-2425. ¢¢

Greenbelt Riverfront Park. Deep-water marina, launching ramp; picnicking, barbecue pits; lighted tennis courts. (Daily) Riverside Ave. Phone 315/393-1980.

Jacques Cartier State Park. Swimming beach, bathhouse; fishing; boating (launch, anchorage). Picnicking, playground, concession. Tent & trailer sites. (Late May-early Oct) Standard fees. 3 mi SW via NY 12, near Morristown. Phone 315/375-6371 or 315/375-8990.

Ogdensburg, NY-Johnstown, Ontario International Bridge. 13,510 ft long; opened Sept 1960. View of St Lawrence Valley and Seaway marine terminal. Travel Center, duty-free shop, bathing beach with concession on Bridge Plaza, just off bridge approach on US side. Connects NY 37 & 812 with Hwys 2, 16 & 401 in Canada. Contact Bridge Plaza; 315/393-4080. (For border crossing regulations, see MAKING THE MOST OF YOUR TRIP.) ¢

Swimming Beaches. Municipal Beach. At Bridge Plaza. **Lisbon Beach.** 5 mi N on NY 37. **Free.**

Upper Canada Village. (See MORRISBURG, ONTARIO, CANADA)

War of 1812 Battlefield Walking Tour. Walking tour along site of the Battle of Ogdensburg. 1/2 mi of paved walkways on waterfront; plaques located along the path detail the action. In Greenbelt Riverfront Park.

Annual Event

International Seaway Festival. Concerts, fireworks, parade, canoe race. Last full wk July.

Motels

★ **QUALITY INN GRAN-VIEW.** *Riverside Dr, 3 mi SW on NY 37.* 315/393-4550; FAX 315/393-3520. 48 rms, 2 story. Mid-May-mid-Sept: S $45-$55; D $57-$72; each addl $8; under 18 free; wkend plans; higher rates special events; lower rates rest of yr. Crib $5. TV; cable. Pool. Coffee in rms. Restaurant (see GRAN-VIEW). Bar 11-2 am; entertainment. Ck-out 11 am. Meeting rms. Business servs avail. In-rm modem link. Lawn games. Refrigerators avail. Private patios, balconies. Picnic tables, grills. Docking facilities. Overlooks river. Cr cds: A, C, D, DS, ER, JCB, MC, V.

★★ **RIVER RESORT.** *119 W River St. 315/393-2222; FAX 315/393-9602.* 78 rms, 2 story. July-mid-Oct: S $59; D $69-$79; each addl $10; suites $99; under 18 free; higher rates special events; lower rates rest of yr. Crib free. TV; cable (premium), VCR. Indoor pool; lifeguard. Restaurant 7 am-9 pm. Rm serv. Bar. Ck-out 11 am. Coin lndry. Meeting rms. Business servs avail. Exercise equipt. Game rm. Some refrigerators. Minibar in suites. On Oswegatchie River; dockage. Cr cds: A, C, D, DS, MC, V.

✔★ **RODEWAY INN.** *Riverside Dr, 5 mi SW on NY 37. 315/393-3730; FAX 315/393-3520.* 20 rms. July-Sept: S $35; D $45-$49; each addl $5; lower rates rest of yr. Crib $8. TV; cable. Pool. Ck-out 11 am. Sundries. Coffee in rms. Refrigerators avail. Picnic tables. Boat dockage. Overlooks St Lawrence Seaway. Cr cds: A, C, D, DS, MC, V.

★★ **STONE FENCE.** *7191 Riverside Dr. 315/393-1545; FAX 315/393-1749; res: 800/253-1545.* Web 1000islands.com/stonefence. 31 rms, 11 suites. May-Sept: S $63-$89; D $69-$99; each addl $5; suites $79-$145; wkly rates; lower rates rest of yr. Crib $6. Pet accepted; $12. TV; cable. Pool; whirlpool. Sauna. Complimentary coffee in rms. Restaurant 7 am-10 pm. Ck-out 11 am. Coin lndry. Tennis. Putting green. Many refrigerators; some wet bars. Whirlpool in suites. Picnic tables, grills. Gazebo. On river; dockage, boat rentals, beach. Cr cds: A, DS, MC, V.

Restaurants

★★ **GRAN-VIEW.** *(See Quality Inn Gran-View Motel) 315/393-4550.* Continental menu. Specializes in fresh seafood, veal, salad. Hrs: 7 am-11 pm; Sat from 8 am; Sun 8 am-9 pm; Sun brunch 10:30 am-1:30 pm. Closed Dec 24-30. Bar from 11 am. Semi-a la carte: bkfst $1.95-$4.95, lunch $3.95-$6.95, dinner $12.95-$38.50. Buffet lunch: (Tues-Fri) $4.95. Sun brunch $8.95. Child's meals. Entertainment wkends. Overlooks St Lawrence River. Cr cds: A, C, D, DS, ER, JCB, MC, V.

★ **PIER 37.** *1154 Paterson St (NY 37). 315/393-6093.* Specializes in fresh seafood, prime rib. Salad bar (lunch). Hrs: 11 am-10 pm; Sun 10 am-9 pm; Sun brunch to 2 pm. Closed Dec 25. Bar. Semi-a la carte: lunch $3.50-$11.95, dinner $8.95-$24.95. Sun brunch $9.95. Child's meals. Informal dining. Nautical decor. Cr cds: A, DS, MC, V.

★ **SHOLETTE'S STEAK & ALE.** *1000 Linden St. 315/393-5172.* Italian, Mexican, Amer menu. Specializes in steak, lasagne, seafood. Salad bar. Hrs: 10-2 am; Sat from 11 am; Sun from 11 am. Closed major hols. Res accepted. Bar. A la carte entrees: lunch $3-$7.50, dinner $6.50-$25.95. Child's meals. Family-owned. Cr cds: A, DS, MC, V.

Old Forge (C-7)

Pop 1,060 (est) **Elev** 1,712 ft **Area code** 315 **Zip** 13420
Information Visitor Information Center, Route 28, PO Box 68; 315/369-6983.

In almost any season there is fun in this Adirondack resort town, located in the Fulton Chain of Lakes region—everything from hunting, fishing, snowmobiling and skiing to basking on a sunny beach.

What to See and Do

Adirondack Park (see).

Canoeing. 86-mi canoe trip to the hamlet of Paul Smiths (N of the Saranac Lakes). For info on Adirondack canoe trips contact Dept of Environmental Conservation, Albany 12233-4255; 518/457-7433.

Enchanted Forest/Water Safari. A 60-acre water-theme park complex featuring 23 water attractions and 14 traditional amusement rides; circus performances. (June-Labor Day) ½ mi N on NY 28. Phone 315/369-6145. ¢¢¢¢¢

Forest Industries Exhibit Hall. Samples of products of forest industries; dioramas; film on managed forests. (Late May-Labor Day, daily exc Tues; after Labor Day-Columbus Day, wkends only) 1 mi N on NY 28. Phone 315/369-3078. **Free.**

Old Forge Lake Cruise. Cruises on Fulton Chain of Lakes (28 mi). (Memorial Day-Columbus Day) Also showboat and dinner cruises. Contact Box 1137; 315/369-6473. ¢¢¢

Public beach. Swimming; lifeguards, bathhouse. (Early June-Labor Day, daily) Tourist Information Center is located here (daily) On NY 28. ¢

Skiing. McCauley Mt. Double chairlift, 2 T-bars, rope tow, pony lift; patrol, rentals; snowmaking; cafeteria. Longest run ¾ mi; vertical drop 633 ft. (Dec-Apr, daily) Half-day rates. Chairlift to top of McCauley Mt also operates June-Oct (daily). Picnic area. 2 mi S off NY 28. Phone 315/369-3225 or 315/369-6983 for snow conditions. Maps of hiking and touring trails in the McCauley Mt area are at the Ski Information Center. ¢¢¢¢¢

Motels

✔★ **19TH GREEN.** *NY 28. 315/369-3575.* 13 rms. Late June-Sept, Dec-Mar: S, D $55-$80; each addl $5; lower rates rest of yr. Crib $5. TV; cable. Pool. Coffee in rms. Restaurant nearby. Ck-out 10 am. Downhill ski 3 mi; x-country ski adj. Game rm. Lawn games. Refrigerators, microwaves. Picnic tables. Golf course adj. Cr cds: A, DS, JCB, MC, V.

★★ **BEST WESTERN SUNSET INN.** *NY 28, 1 mi S on NY 28. 315/369-6836.* Web www.bestwestern.com. 52 rms, 1-2 story. Late June-Labor Day, late Dec-early Apr: S, D $79-$135; each addl $10, under 13 free; lower rates rest of yr. Crib $6. Pet accepted. TV; cable (premium). Indoor pool; whirlpool. Sauna. Playground. Complimentary continental bkfst. Restaurant nearby. Ck-out 11 am. Lndry facilities. Tennis. Golf opp. Downhill ski 3 mi; x-country ski opp. Some balconies. Picnic area, gazebo, grill. Cr cds: A, DS, MC, V.

★ **COUNTRY CLUB.** *Box 419, 1 mi S on NY 28. 315/369-6340.* 27 rms. Jan-Feb, late June-Labor Day: S, D $70-$85; each addl $5; wkly rates; under 12 free; lower rates rest of yr. Crib $5. TV; cable (premium). Heated pool. Complimentary coffee in rms. Restaurant nearby. Ck-out 11 am. Downhill ski 2 mi; x-country ski adj. Lawn games. Many refrigerators, microwaves. Cr cds: A, C, D, DS, JCB, MC, V.

★ **COVEWOOD LODGE.** *Eagle Bay (13331), 10 mi N on NY 28, 4 mi W on Big Moose Rd, on Big Moose Lake. 315/357-3041.* E-mail covewood@telenet.net; web www.covewoodlodge.com. 3 kit. apts (2-bedrm), 1-2 story, 17 kit. cottages. No A/C. No rm phones. Kit. apts $705-$810/wk; kit. cottages for 2-12, $600-$1,600/wk. Kit. apts and 3 cottages closed in winter. Crib free. Ck-out 10:30 am. Coin lndry. Tennis. Downhill ski 15 mi; x-country ski on site. Game rms. Lawn games. Lake swimming. Fireplaces. Library. Private porches. Grills. Dock. No cr cds accepted.

Restaurants

★ **BIG MOOSE INN.** *Eagle Bay (13331), 10 mi N on NY 28, then 5 mi W on Big Moose Rd, at Big Moose Lake. 315/357-2042.* E-mail www.bigmooseinn.com; web bigmoose@telenet.net. Continental menu. Specializes in prime beef, seafood. Own baking. Hrs: 11 am-10 pm; Sun 2-9 pm. Closed late Mar-mid May, mid-Nov-Dec 25. Res accepted. Bar. Semi-a la carte: lunch $2.95-$10.95, dinner $8.95-$32.50. Outdoor dining. Built 1903. Guest rms avail. Cr cds: A, MC, V.

★ ★ **OLD MILL.** *Box 578, ½ mi S on NY 28. 315/369-3662.* Specializes in steak, seafood. Hrs: 4:30-9:30 pm; Fri, Sat to 10 pm; Sun 1-9 pm. Closed 2nd wkend Mar; also Nov-Dec. Bar. Semi-a la carte: dinner $10.95-$17.95. Child's meals. Converted gristmill. Cr cds: MC, V.

Olean (E-3)

Settled 1804 **Pop** 16,946 **Elev** 1,451 ft **Area code** 716 **Zip** 14760 **E-mail** tourism@oleanny.com **Web** www.oleanny.com
Information Greater Olean, Inc, 120 N Union St; 716/372-4433.

Only seven years after the landing of the Pilgrims, a Franciscan father was led by Native Americans to a mystical spring near the present city of Olean. There he found what he called "thick water which ignited like brandy." It was petroleum. Olean (from the latin *oleum*, meaning "oil") was once an oil-boom town; now it is a manufacturing and retail center.

What to See and Do

Allegany State Park (see). 15 mi E on NY 17.

Friedsam Memorial Library. Paintings by Rembrandt, Rubens and Bellini; works by 19th-century and contemporary artists; American Southwest and pre-Columbian pottery, porelain collection; rare books. (Sept-mid-June, daily exc Sun; rest of yr, Mon-Fri; closed school hols) On campus of St Bonaventure Univ, St Bonaventure. Phone 716/375-2323 or 716/375-2000. **Free.**

Motel

✔★ **CASTLE INN.** *W State Rd, St Bonaventure Univ opp. 716/372-1050; FAX 716/372-4745; res: 800/422-7853.* 160 rms, 2 story. S $39-$69; D $59-$74; each addl $6; suites $71-$86; under 18 free; ski, wkend plans. Crib free. TV; cable. Heated pool. Complimentary full bkfst Sun-Thurs. Restaurant 6-11 am, 5-9 pm; Sat to noon; Sun 6 am-2 pm. Bar 5 pm-2 am; entertainment. Ck-out noon. Meeting rms. Business servs avail. Valet serv. 9-hole, par 3 golf. X-country ski 20 mi. Exercise equipt. Health club privileges. Bicycles. Lawn games. Some refrigerators. Private patios, balconies. Picnic tables. Cr cds: A, C, D, DS, MC, V.

❌ 🏌 ⛷ ✈ 🏔 🔥 **SC**

Inn

★ ★ ★ **OLD LIBRARY.** *120 S Union St. 716/373-9804; FAX 716/373-2462.* 7 rms, 3 story, 2 suites. S, D $65-$75; each addl $20; suites $115-$125. TV; cable, VCR avail. Complimentary full bkfst (see OLD LIBRARY). Ck-out 11 am, ck-in 3 pm. Meeting rm. Business servs avail. In-rm modem link. Health club privileges. House built in 1895. Antique furnishings; sitting rm with fireplace. Cr cds: A, DS, MC, V.

🔆 🔥

Restaurants

✔★ ★ **BEEF 'N BARREL.** *146 N Union St, on NY 16. 716/372-2985.* Specializes in beef, pie. Hrs: 11 am-10 pm; Fri, Sat to 11 pm. Closed Sun; major hols. Bar. Semi-a la carte: lunch $4.25-$9.95, dinner $4.95-

$18.95. Child's meals. Colonial decor. Family-owned. Cr cds: A, D, DS, MC, V.

★ ★ ★ **OLD LIBRARY.** *(See Old Library Inn) 716/372-2226.* Continental menu. Specializes in prime rib, scampi, veal. Own pastries. Hrs: 11 am-10 pm; Sun brunch to 2:30 pm. Closed some major hols. Res accepted. Bar. Wine cellar. Semi-a la carte: lunch $4.50-$9.95, dinner $9.95-$24.95. Sun brunch $9.95. Child's meals. Historic landmark; former Andrew Carnegie library (1909). Some original furnishings; many antiques; rotunda; marble frieze extends through the foyer; leaded glass. Cr cds: A, DS, MC, V.

Oneida (D-6)

(See also Canastota, Cazenovia, Herkimer, Ilion, Rome, Skaneateles, Syracuse, Utica)

Settled 1834 **Pop** 10,850 **Elev** 443 ft **Area code** 315 **Zip** 13421 **Web** www.oneidany.org
Information The Greater Oneida Chamber of Commerce, 136 Lenox Ave; 315/363-4300.

Perhaps the best known of the 19th-century American "Utopias" was established at Oneida (o-NYE-dah) in 1848 by John Humphrey Noyes, leader of the "Perfectionists." The group held all property in common, practiced complex marriage and undertook other social experiments. Faced with hostile attacks by the local population, the community was dissolved in 1880. In 1881 the Oneida Community became a stock corporation. The silverware factory it built remains a major industry, making "Community Plate" and William A. Rogers silver.

What to See and Do

Madison County Historical Society, Cottage Lawn Museum. An 1849 Gothic-revival cottage designed by Alexander Jackson Davis. Victorian period rms; historical and traditional craft archives; changing exhibits; 1862 stagecoach, 1853 gym and adj agricultural museum. (June-Aug, Tues-Sat afternoons; Sept-May, Mon-Fri afternoons) 435 Main St at Grove St. Phone 315/363-4136. **¢**

The Mansion House. The communal home built in the 1860s. Tours (Wed-Sat, morning & afternoon tours, also Sun afternoon tours). Phone 315/361-3671. **¢¢**

Vernon Downs. Harness racing; glass-enclosed grandstand and clubhouse. (Feb-early Nov) 8 mi E on NY 5, S of I-90 exit 33, on NY 31 in Vernon. For info and schedule phone 315/829-2201. Grandstand **¢**

Verona Beach State Park. Swimming beach, bathhouse; fishing; hiking (all yr). Cross-country skiing, snowmobiling. Picnicking, playground, concession. Tent & trailer sites. Standard fees. N on NY 46, W on NY 31, then N on NY 13, on Oneida Lake. Phone 315/762-4463. May-Aug **¢¢**

Annual Event

Craft Days. Madison County Historical Society Museum. Traditional craftsmen demonstrate their skills; food, entertainment. First wkend after Labor Day wkend.

Motels

✔★ **SUPER 8.** *215 Genesse St. 315/363-5168; FAX 315/363-4628.* 39 rms, 2 story. June-Sept: S $42-$50; D $45-$60; each addl $5; under 12 free; higher rates some wkends, special events; lower rates rest of yr. Crib free. TV; cable (premium). Complimentary continental bkfst in lobby. Restaurant adj 7 am-11 pm. Ck-out 11 am. In-rm modem link. Cr cds: A, C, D, DS, JCB, MC, V.

★ **SUPER 8.** *(5558 W Main St, Verona 13478) 1 mi N on NY 365.* 315/363-0096; FAX 315/363-2797. 63 rms, 2 story. S $45-$65; D $55-$80; each addl $5; under 12 free; wkend rates; higher rates special events. TV; cable (premium). Complimentary continental bkfst. Restaurant nearby. Ck-out 11 am. Cr cds: A, DS, MC, V.

🛇 ⛭ ♿ SC

Motor Hotel

★ ★ ★ **COMFORT SUITES.** *(4229 Stuhlman Rd (NY 31), Vernon 13476) 4 mi E, just off NY 5, at Vernon Downs.* 315/829-3400; FAX 315/829-3787. Web www.hotelchoice.com. 175 suites, 7 story. S, D $79-$225; under 16 free; higher rates wkends, special events. Crib free. TV; cable (premium). Indoor pool; whirlpool, lifeguard. Complimentary continental bkfst. Complimentary coffee in rms. Restaurant 6:30-10 am, 11:30 am-2:30 pm, 4:30-11 pm. Rm serv. Bar 4 pm-1 am. Ck-out noon. Meeting rms. In-rm modem link. Exercise rm; sauna. Gift shop. Game rm. Refrigerators, microwaves, some in-rm whirlpools. Cr cds: A, C, D, DS, JCB, MC, V.

D ⛱ ✈ ⊠ SC

Oneonta (E-7)

(See also Cooperstown, Norwich, Stamford)

Settled 1780 **Pop** 13,954 **Elev** 1,085 ft **Area code** 607 **Zip** 13820
Information Otsego County Chamber of Commerce, 12 Carbon St; 607/432-4500 or 800/843-3394.

Oneonta lies deep in the hills at the western edge of the Catskills. It was here in 1883 that the Brotherhood of Railroad Trainmen had its beginnings. A branch of the State University College of NY is located here.

What to See and Do

Gilbert Lake State Park. Swimming; fishing; boating. Picnicking, playground, concession. Tent & trailer sites, cabins. Standard fees. (Mid-May-mid-Oct, daily) 7½ mi N on NY 205 to Laurens, then County 12 to park. Phone 607/432-2114. Per vehicle (May-Aug) ¢¢

Hanford Mills Museum. Water-powered sawmill, gristmill and woodworking complex dating from ca 1840. Ten-ft diameter by 12-ft width overshot waterwheel drives machinery. Demonstrations of antique machine collection, tours. Special events. Picnicking. (May-Oct, daily) 11 mi E via NY 23, on County 10, in East Meredith. Phone 607/278-5744. ¢¢

Hartwick College (1797). (1,400 students) Library and archives house collections of works by Willard Yager, Judge William Cooper and John Christopher Hartwick papers. Hall of Science with display of fresh and saltwater shells and Hoysradt Herbarium. Anderson Center for the Arts. Yager Museum contains more than 10,000 Native American artifacts and the VanEss Collection of Renaissance and Baroque Art (Sept-May, daily; rest of yr, by appt only). Oyaron Hill. Phone 607/431-4200 or 607/431-4030.

National Soccer Hall of Fame. Displays and exhibits range from youth, amateur and collegiate to professional soccer; trophies, mementos, historical items, uniforms. Video theater with soccer films dating from 1930s. (Daily; closed some hols) 5-11 Ford Ave. Phone 607/432-3351. ¢¢

Motels

★ ★ ★ **HOLIDAY INN.** *NY 23, 1 mi E of I-88, exit 15.* 607/433-2250; FAX 607/432-7028. E-mail onhny@digital-marketplace.net; web www.holiday-inn.com/hotel/onhny. 120 rms, 2 story. S, D $79-$199; under 19 free; higher rates special events. Crib free. Pet accepted, some restrictions. TV; cable (premium). Pool; wading pool. Coffee in rms. Restaurant 7 am-9 pm. Rm serv. Bar noon-midnight; entertainment Wed, Fri, Sat.

Ck-out 11 am. Coin lndry. Meeting rms. In-rm modem link. Game rm. Refrigerators, microwaves avail. Picnic tables. Cr cds: A, C, D, DS, MC, V.

D ⛭ ⛱ ⊠ ♿ SC

✔★ **KNOTT'S.** *2306 NY 28, 5 mi N on NY 28, 1 mi N of I-88 exit 17, on lake.* 607/432-5948; FAX 607/433-2266. E-mail knotts@telenet.net; web www.cooperstownchamber.org/knotts. 25 rms, 10 kit. units. Some rm phones. S $54-$78; D $58-$82, kit. units $76-$94; each addl $4; wkly rates. Crib free. TV; cable. Complimentary coffee. Restaurant nearby. Ck-out 11 am. Tennis. Lawn games. Waterskiing; sailboats avail. Picnic tables, grill. Private beach. Cr cds: DS, MC, V.

D ⛭ 🚶 ⛱ ♿

★ **SUPER 8.** *4973 NY 23, ¼ mi S of I-88 exit 15.* 607/432-9505. 60 rms, 2 story. July-Aug: S $73.88-$83.88; D $78.88-$90.88; each addl $5; under 12 free; higher rates wkends, special events; lower rates rest of yr. Crib $3. Pet accepted, some restrictions. TV; cable, VCR avail (movies). Complimentary continental bkfst. Restaurant adj 7 am-10 pm. Ck-out 11 am. Coin lndry. Business servs avail. Cr cds: A, C, D, DS, JCB, MC, V.

D ⛭ ⛱ ♿ SC

Inn

★ ★ ★ **CATHEDRAL FARMS.** *NY 205, 1½ mi N of I-88, exit 13.* 607/432-7483; FAX 607/432-6368. 19 rms, 2 story, 4 suites. D $75-$125; suites $120-$250; under 18 free; wkly rates. Crib free. TV; cable. Heated pool; whirlpool. Complimentary coffee in rms. Restaurant (see CATHEDRAL FARMS). Rm serv. Ck-out noon, ck-in 3 pm. Business servs avail. Lawn games. Balconies. Inn was once servants' house built in the 1930s. Totally nonsmoking. Cr cds: A, C, D, MC, V.

D ⛭ ⛱ ⊠

Restaurants

★ ★ ★ **CATHEDRAL FARMS.** *(See Cathedral Farms Inn)* 607/432-7483. Continental menu. Specializes in fresh seafood, hand-cut prime beef, free-range chicken. Own baking, soups. Hrs: 3-9 pm; Fri, Sat to 10 pm; Sun 11 am-8 pm; Sun brunch 11 am-3 pm. Closed Mon, Tues. Res accepted. Bar to midnight. Wine cellar. Semi-a la carte: dinner $13.95-$22.95. Sun brunch $8.95-$16.95. Child's meals. Parking. Former estate (1915); extensive grounds. Peacocks on premises. Cr cds: A, C, D, MC, V.

D

✔★ **CHRISTOPHER'S.** *NY 23, ¼ mi W of I-88 exit 15 on Rte 23.* 607/432-2444. Continental menu. Specializes in steak, barbecued ribs, fresh seafood. Salad bar. Hrs: 11 am-10 pm; Sun noon-9 pm. Closed Dec 25. Res accepted. Bar to midnight. Semi-a la carte: lunch $4.50-$7.95, dinner $8.95-$18.95. Child's meals. Parking. Rustic decor. Fireplace. Guest rms avail. Cr cds: A, C, D, MC, V.

D

★ ★ **FARMHOUSE.** *1 mi E on NY 7; I-88 exit 16.* 607/432-7374. Continental menu. Specializes in prime rib, seafood, chicken. Salad bar. Hrs: 3-9 pm; Sun noon-9 pm; winter hrs vary; Sun brunch to 3 pm. Closed Dec 25. Res accepted. Serv bar. Semi-a la carte: dinner $10.95-$17.95. Sun brunch $6.95. Child's meals. Parking. Restored farmhouse built 1780s. Cr cds: A, MC, V.

D SC

★ **HOMESTEAD.** *(NY 7, Colliersville 13847) 3 mi E on NY 7, at jct NY 28.* 607/432-0971. Specializes in beef, seafood. Salad bar. Hrs: 3:30-closing; Sun noon-8 pm. Closed Mon; also Tues in winter. Res accepted; required hols, graduation. Bar. Semi-a la carte: dinner $8.95-$18.95. Buffet: lunch, dinner $7.95-$16.95. Child's meals. Parking. Late 18th-century stage coach stop; original fireplace. Cr cds: A, D, DS, MC, V.

D SC ♥

✔★ ★ **SABATINI'S LITTLE ITALY.** *NY 23. 607/432-3000.* Italian, American menu. Specializes in homemade mozzarella, authentic Italian dishes. Hrs: 4-9 pm; Fri, Sat to 10 pm. Closed Thanksgiving, Dec 25. Bar. A la carte entrees: dinner $8-$22.95. Parking. Italian decor. Cr cds: A, C, D, MC, V.

Oswego (C-5)

(See also Fulton)

Pop 19,195 **Elev** 298 ft **Area code** 315 **Zip** 13126
Information Chamber of Commerce, 156 W 2nd St; 315/343-7681.

Oswego's location on Lake Ontario, at the mouth of the Oswego River, made it an important trading post and a strategic fort as early as 1722. Today, as a seaway port and northern terminus of the State Barge Canal, Oswego carries on its industrial and shipping tradition. The town has the largest US port of entry on Lake Ontario.

What to See and Do

Fair Haven Beach State Park. Swimming beach, bathhouse; fishing; boating (rentals, launch, anchorage). Hiking trails. Cross-country skiing. Picnicking, playground; concession. Camping, tent & trailer sites, cabins. (Late Apr-early Nov) Standard fees. Approx 15 mi SW via NY 104, 104A. Phone 315/947-5205.

Ft Ontario State Historic Site. The original fort was built by the British in 1755, taken by the French and eventually used as a US Army installation (1840-1946). Strategic fort commanded the route from the Hudson and Mohawk valleys to the Great Lakes. Restored site re-creates life at a military installation during the 1860s. Exhibits; guided & self-guided tours. Picnic area. Drills (July-Labor Day). Special programs. Park (Memorial Day-Labor Day, Wed-Sun). Foot of E 7th St. Phone 315/343-4711. ¢¢

H. Lee White Marine Museum. Museum features 12 rms of artifacts, models, documents and paintings relating to 300 yrs of Oswego Harbor and Lake Ontario history. (Mid-May-Sept, daily) W First St at end of Pier. Phone 315/342-0480. **Donation.**

Oswego County Historical Society. Richardson-Bates Museum-Victorian House incl local historical material; period furnishings; changing exhibits. (Mon, by appt) 135 E 3rd St. Phone 315/343-1342. ¢

Selkirk Shores State Park. Beach; fishing; canoeing. Hiking. Cross-country skiing. Picnicking, playground, concession. Tent & trailer sites (fee), cabins. Standard fees. 17 mi NE via NY 104, 3. Phone 315/298-5737. May-Oct ¢¢

State Univ of New York (1861). (8,000 students) Campus overlooks Lake Ontario. On NY 104. Campus tours, contact Office of Admissions; 315/341-2250. Summer dinner theater, phone 315/341-2500.

Seasonal Event

Oswego Speedway. 300 E Albany, off Rte 104E. 5/8th’s asphalt racing facility. Short-track racing; supermodifieds and limited supermodifieds. Phone 315/342-0646. Early May-Labor Day.

Motels

★ ★ **BEST WESTERN CAPTAIN'S QUARTERS.** *26 E First St. 315/342-4040; FAX 315/342-5454.* 93 units, 4 story, 17 suites. S $76-$138; D $88-$150; each addl $12; under 12 free; higher rates: summer wkends, college events, Harbor Fest, Labor Day. Crib free. TV; cable. Indoor pool; whirlpool. Complimentary continental bkfst Mon-Fri. Complimentary coffee. Restaurant opp 11:30 am-10 pm; wkends from 8 am. Ck-out 11 am. Meeting rms. Business servs avail. In-rm modem link. Exercise equipt; sauna. View of river. Cr cds: A, C, D, DS, MC, V.

✔★ **DAYS INN.** *101 NY 104. 315/343-3136; FAX 315/343-6187.* 44 rms, 2 story. S $49-$70; D $59-$100; each addl $5; suites $89; under 13 free; wkly rates; higher rates special events. Crib avail. Pet accepted. TV; cable. Complimentary continental bkfst. Restaurant adj open 24 hrs. Ck-out 11 am. Business servs avail. Refrigerators. Cr cds: A, C, D, DS, MC, V.

Inn

✔★ **OSWEGO INN LTD.** *180 E 10th St. 315/342-6200; FAX 315/343-6234; res: 800/721-7341.* 13 rms, 2 story. May-Oct: S $45; D $55; each addl $10; under 12 free; wkly, monthly rates; higher rates special events; lower rates rest of yr. Crib $10. TV; cable (premium). Complimentary continental bkfst. Ck-out 11 am, ck-in 2 pm. Business servs avail. In-rm modem link. X-country ski 3 mi. Refrigerators. Totally nonsmoking. Cr cds: A, C, D, DS, MC, V.

Restaurant

✔★ ★ **VONA'S.** *W 10th & Utica Sts. 315/343-8710.* Italian, Amer menu. Specializes in veal, New York steak. Own pasta. Hrs: 11:30 am-2:30 pm, 4:30-10:30 pm; Sat, Sun 4-10 pm. Closed July 4, Thanksgiving, Dec 24-25. Res accepted. Bar 11:30-2 am. Semi-a la carte: lunch $5-$8, dinner $7.50-$15.95. Child's meals. Family-owned. Cr cds: A, C, D, MC, V.

Owego (E-5)

(See also Binghamton, Elmira, Endicott)

Pop 21,279 **Elev** 817 ft **Area code** 607 **Zip** 13827
Information Tioga County Chamber of Commerce, 188 Front St; 607/687-2020.

What to See and Do

Tioga County Historical Society Museum. Native American artifacts, folk art; pioneer crafts; exhibits on early county commerce, industry and military history. (Tues-Sat; closed most hols) 110 Front St. Phone 607/687-2460. **Free.**

Tioga Gardens. Tropical plant conservatory with solar dome. Greenhouses; 2-acre water garden with water lilies; Japanese garden. (Daily) NY 17C. Phone 607/687-5522. **Free.**

Tioga Scenic Railroad. Scenic rail excursions avail. (Early May-late Oct) Phone 607/687-6786. ¢¢¢¢

Annual Event

Owego Strawberry Festival. Phone 607/687-6305. Mid-June.

Tioga County Fair. Phone 607/687-1308. Mid-Aug.

Motels

✔★ **SUNRISE.** *3778 Wavery Rd, NY 17C W, exit 64. 607/687-5667; FAX 607/687-5666.* 20 rms. S $36; D $40-$42; each addl $4. Crib $3. Pet accepted, some restrictions; $5. TV; cable. Ck-out 11 am. Picnic tables. Cr cds: A, DS, MC, V.

★ ★ **TREADWAY INN & CONFERENCE CENTER.** *1100 NY 17C, adj Lockeed Martin. 607/687-4500; FAX 607/687-2456.* 96 rms, 2 story. S $60-$75; D $60-$95; each addl $5; under 18 free; wkend rates. TV; cable. Indoor pool. Restaurant 6:30 am-10 pm. Rm serv. Bar 11:30-1

am; entertainment Fri, Sat. Ck-out noon. Meeting rms. Valet serv (Mon-Fri). Sundries. 18-hole golf privileges, pro. Exercise equipt. Some private patios, balconies. On river. Cr cds: A, C, D, DS, MC, V.

D ♦ ♦ ≋ ♦ ♦ ♦ SC

Oyster Bay, L.I. (B-3)

(See also Glen Cove, Huntington, Jericho, New York City)

Settled 1653 **Pop** 6,687 **Elev** 20 ft **Area code** 516 **Zip** 11771
Information Chamber of Commerce, 120 South St, PO Box 21; 516/922-6464.

What to See and Do

Planting Fields Arboretum. A 400-acre estate of the late William Robertson Coe. Landscaped plantings (150 acres); large collections of azaleas and rhododendrons; self-guided tour; guided tours avail; nature trails; greenhouses. (May-Labor Day, daily; rest of yr, wkends) Planting Fields Rd, 1½ mi W, off NY 25A. Phone 516/922-9201 or 516/922-9200. Per vehicle parking ¢¢ Located in center of Arboretum is

Coe Hall (1918). Tudor-revival mansion (65 rms) was a country estate for Coe and his family. Various 16th- and 17th-century furnishings imported from Europe contribute to its atmosphere of a historic English country house. Guided tours. (Daily) Phone 516/922-0479. ¢¢

Raynham Hall Museum. Historic colonial house museum with Victorian wing. Home of Samuel Townsend, a prosperous merchant; HQ for the Queens Rangers during the American Revolution. Victorian garden. (Daily exc Mon) 20 W Main St. Phone 516/922-6808. ¢

★ **Sagamore Hill Natl Historic Site.** Theodore Roosevelt summer house has original furnishings and many historic items; summer White House from 1901 to 1909, the rambling Queen Anne/Victorian mansion incl famous trophy rm with mounted species and presidential memorabilia. Taped tour narrated by Roosevelt's daughter (fee). Film on Roosevelt's life shown at Old Orchard Museum on grounds. House (daily; closed most major hols). Golden Eagle Passport (see MAKING THE MOST OF YOUR TRIP). 2 mi NE via Cove Neck Rd. Contact the Superintendent, 20 Sagamore Hill; 516/922-4447. ¢

Theodore Roosevelt Memorial Bird Sanctuary & Trailside Museum. Owned by the National Audubon Society, the memorial contains 11 acres of forest and nature trails. The sanctuary serves as a memorial to Theodore Roosevelt's pioneering conservation achievements. Museum contains displays on Roosevelt and the conservation movement; bird exhibits. Adj in Young's Cemetery is Theodore Roosevelt's grave. Trails, bird-watching, library. (Daily) Cove Rd. Phone 516/922-3200. ¢

Annual Events

Long Island Mozart Festival. Planting Fields Arboretum. Outdoor musical festival, arts & crafts, lectures, garden tours. Phone 516/671-6263. Memorial Day wkend & 1st wkend June.

Oyster Festival. Street festival, arts & crafts. Phone 516/922-6464 or 516/624-8082. Usually wkend after Columbus Day.

Motel

★ ★ **EAST NORWICH INN.** (6321 Northern Blvd, East Norwich 11732) at jct NY 25A & NY 106; 4 mi N of L.I. Expy (exit 41N). 516/922-1500; FAX 516/922-1089; res. 800/334-4798. Web www.eastnorwichinn.com. 72 rms, 2 story. S $105; D $125; each addl $10; under 16 free. Crib free. TV; cable (premium). Heated pool; lifeguard. Complimentary continental bkfst. Ck-out noon. Meeting rms. Business servs avail. In-rm modem link. Valet serv. Exercise equipt; sauna. Cr cds: A, C, D, DS, MC, V.

 D ≋ ♦ ♦ ♦

Restaurants

★ ★ ★ **CAFE GIRASOLE.** (1053 Oyster Bay Rd, East Norwich) S on NY 106. 516/624-8330. Italian menu. Specializes in pasta, fresh fish. Hrs: noon-10 pm; Sat 5-11 pm; Sun 4-9 pm. Closed some major hols. Res required Fri, Sat. Bar. A la carte: lunch $11.50-$16.50, dinner $13-$24.50. Outdoor dining. Casual trattoria. Cr cds: A, C, D, MC, V.

D

★ **CANTERBURY ALES OYSTER BAR & GRILL.** 46 Audrey Ave. 516/922-3614. Specializes in mesquite-grilled seafood. Hrs: 11:30 am-11 pm; Fri, Sat to 1 am; Sun brunch to 3 pm. Closed Thanksgiving, Dec 25. Res accepted. Bar. Semi-a la carte: lunch $4.95-$13.95, dinner $7.50-$19.95. Sun brunch $5.95-$14.95. Child's meals. Parking. New England fish house atmosphere with bistro flair. Historic Teddy Roosevelt library in rear, includes photos. Cr cds: A, C, D, MC, V.

D

★ ★ ★ **MILL RIVER INN.** 160 Mill River Rd. 516/922-7768. Specializes in grilled fish, steak. Menu changes daily. Hrs: 6-10 pm; Sun 5-10 pm. Closed Dec 25. Res required. Bar. A la carte entrees (Sun-Thurs): $29-$38. Prix fixe: dinner (Fri) $48, (Sat) $58. Parking. Contemporary decor. Fireplace. Cr cds: A, D, MC, V.

★ ★ ★ **STEVE'S PIER I.** (33 Bayville Ave, Bayville 11709) 4 mi N of L.I. Expy exit 41N. 516/628-2153. Continental menu. Specializes in Nova Scotia lobster, seafood, steak. Own baking. Hrs: noon-10 pm; Mon to 9:30 pm; Fri to 11 pm; Sat to 11:30 pm; Sun & hols 1-9:30 pm. Bar. Wine cellar. Complete meals: lunch $11.95-$14.95, dinner $17.95-$23. Child's meals. Valet parking. Outdoor dining. On L.I. Sound. Cr cds: A, C, D, MC, V.

D

★ ★ **UWE'S.** (73 South St, Oyster Bay) 516/922-5044. Continental menu. Hrs: 11:30 am-2:30 pm, 5-10 pm; Sat from 5 pm. Closed Sun & Mon; major hols. Bar. A la carte entrees: lunch $5-$12.50, dinner $14.75-$26.50. Parking. Attractive decor and inviting atmosphere. Cr cds: A, C, D, MC, V.

D

Palisades Interstate Parks (A-2)

(See also New York City, Yonkers)

This system of conservation and recreation areas extends along the west side of the Hudson River from the George Washington Bridge at Fort Lee, NJ, to Saugerties, NY, and covers 81,008 acres. The main unit is the 51,680-acre tract of Bear Mountain and Harriman state parks. Included in the system are 17 parks and 6 historic sites.

Bear Mountain (5,067 acres) extends westward from the Hudson River opposite Peekskill. Only 45 miles from New York City via the Palisades Interstate Pkwy, this is a popular recreation area, with all-year facilities, mainly for one-day visits. Bear Mountain has picnic areas, hiking trails, swimming pool with bathhouse, boating on Hessian Lake, fishing and an artificial ice rink. Perkins Memorial Drive goes to the top of Bear Mountain, where there is a picnic area and a sightseeing tower. Near the site of Fort Clinton, just W of Bear Mountain Bridge is Trailside Museums and Wildlife Center, with native animals and exhibit buildings (daily). Phone 914/786-2701. ¢¢

Harriman (46,613 acres), southwest of Bear Mountain, consists of wilder country. Fishing, boating, scenic drives, lakes, bathing beaches at Lakes Tiorati, Welch and Sebago; tent camping at Lake Welch and cabins (primarily for family groups) at Lake Sebago. The **Silver Mine Area,** 4 mi west of Bear Mountain, has fishing, boating, picnicking. (All yr)

Charges for parking and for most activities change seasonally. Further information can be obtained from Palisades Interstate Parks Commission, Administration Building, Bear Mountain 10911-0427; 914/786-2701.

Motel

✔★★ **BEAR MOUNTAIN INN.** (Bear Mountain State Park, Bear Mountain 10911) on US 9W, 2 mi S of Highland Falls. 914/786-2731; FAX 914/786-2543. 12 rms in inn, 48 rms in 5 lodges. S, D $89; each addl $10. Crib $10. TV. Pool; lifeguard. Complimentary continental bkfst. Restaurant 11 am-3 pm, 5-9 pm; wkends to 10 pm. Bar 11 am-11 pm. Ck-out 11 am. Meeting rms. Business servs avail. Sundries. Balconies. Picnic tables. Cr cds: A, DS, MC, V.

Palmyra (D-4)

(See also Canandaigua, Rochester, Victor)

Founded 1789 **Pop** 7,690 **Elev** 472 ft **Area code** 315 **Zip** 14522

In 1820, in the frontier town of Palmyra, 15-year-old Joseph Smith had a vision that led to the founding of a new religious group—the Church of Jesus Christ of Latter-day Saints, better known as the Mormon Church.

What to See and Do

Alling Coverlet Museum. Largest collection of American Jacquard and handwoven coverlets in the country. (June-Sept, daily, afternoons, or by appt) 122 William St. Phone 315/597-6737. **Free.**

Mormon Historic Sites and Bureau of Information. Hill Cumorah, 4 mi S on NY 21, near I-90 exit 43. Guides. (Daily). Phone 315/597-5851. **Free.** Includes

Hill Cumorah. Where the golden plates from which Joseph Smith translated the *Book of Mormon* were delivered to him. A monument to the Angel Moroni now stands on the hill. Visitors center has religious exhibits and films. (Daily; also summer eves) Phone 315/597-5851.

Joseph Smith Home. Where Smith lived as a young man; period decor (1820-1830). Nearby is the Sacred Grove where he had his first vision. Stafford Rd. Phone 315/597-4383.

***Book of Mormon* Historic Publication Site.** Between June 1829 and March 1830, the first edition of 5,000 copies of the *Book of Mormon* was printed here at a cost of $3,000. (Daily; also summer eves) 217 E Main St. Phone 315/597-5982.

Palmyra Historical Museum. Display of 19th-century items incl furniture, toys and household items. (June-Sept, Sat & Sun afternoons, or by appt) 132 Market St. Phone 315/597-6981. **Free.**

Phelps General Store Museum. Contains displays of turn-of-the-century merchandise and household furnishings. (June-Sept, Sat & Sun afternoons, or by appt) 140 Market St. Phone 315/597-6981. **Free.**

Annual Event

The Hill Cumorah Pageant. At Hill Cumorah; seating for 6,500. Phone 315/597-6808. Early-mid-July.

Motels

★★ **QUALITY INN.** (125 N Main, Newark 14513) E on NY 31. 315/331-9500; FAX 315/331-5264. 107 rms, 2 story. S $68-$88; D $88-$108; each addl $10; under 18 free; monthly rates; ski plans. Crib free. Pet accepted. TV; cable (premium). Pool. Sauna. Restaurant 6:30 am-9 pm; wkend hrs vary. Bar 11-2 am. Ck-out 11 am. Meeting rms. Business servs avail. Downhill ski 8 mi; x-country ski 9 mi. Some refrigerators, microwaves. Picnic tables. On barge canal. Cr cds: A, D, DS, JCB, MC, V.

✔★ **WAYNE VILLA.** (344 NY 31, Macedon 14502) 6 mi W on NY 31. 315/986-5530; res: 800/564-8927. 14 rms, 1 kits, 2 apts. S $40; D $50. Crib free. TV; cable. Playground. Restaurant nearby. Ck-out 11 am. Picnic tables, grill. Cr cds: A, DS, MC, V.

Peekskill (A-2)

(See also Mahopac, Mt Kisco, Tarrytown, West Point)

Pop 19,536 **Elev** 132 ft **Area code** 914 **Zip** 10566 **Web** www.peekskillcortlandt.com
Information Peekskill/Cortlandt Chamber of Commerce, One S Division St; 914/737-3600.

This city is named for Jan Peek, a Dutchman who set up a trading post on the creek that runs along the northern edge of town.

Motel

★★ **PEEKSKILL INN.** 634 Main St. 914/739-1500; res: 800/526-9466; FAX 914/739-7067. Web www.peekskillinn.com. 53 rms, 2 story. S $70-$95; D $80-$105; suite $125-$150; higher rates West Point graduation. Crib free. Pet accepted, some restrictions. TV; cable (premium). Complimentary continental bkfst; full bkfst on wkends. Restaurant 11:30 am-10 pm; wkends 8 am-11 pm. Rm serv. Bar noon to 2 am. Ck-out 11 am. Business servs avail. Pool; lifeguard. Refrigerators avail. Some balconies. Grills. Cr cds: A, D, DS, MC, V.

Restaurants

★★ **CRYSTAL BAY.** 5 John Walsh Blvd, Charles Point Marina, NY 9 exit Louisa St. 914/737-8332. Eclectic menu. Specializes in seafood. Hrs: 11:30 am-3 pm, 5-10 pm; Sun brunch, 2 seatings, 11 am-1:30 pm. Closed Dec 25. Res accepted. Bar. A la carte entrees: lunch $7.95-$16.95, dinner $15-$30. Seafood buffet: dinner (Wed) $22.95. Sun brunch $18.95. Child's meals. Entertainment Fri, Sat. Outdoor dining. On the Hudson River. Cr cds: A, C, MC, V.

★★★ **MONTEVERDE AT OLDSTONE.** Rt 6 and 202 W. 914/739-5000. Continental menu. Specializes in French and Italian dishes. Hrs: noon-2:30 pm, 5:30-9:30 pm; Fri to 10:30 pm; Sat 5-11 pm; Sun noon-8:30 pm. Closed Tues. Res accepted; required Sat, hols. Bar. A la carte entrees: lunch $14.75-$17.75, dinner $16.75-$27.75. Outdoor dining. 18th-century mansion with outdoor terrace overlooking Hudson River. Victorian furnishings; wrought iron lamps and chandeliers. Cr cds: A, C, D, MC, V.

★★ **SUSAN'S.** 12 N Division St. 914/737-6624. Specialties: salmon strudel, chocolate dream cake. Hrs: noon-2:30 pm, 5:30-9 pm; Fri, Sat to 10 pm. Res accepted. Bar. Semi-a la carte: lunch $5.75-$8.50, dinner $12.50-$17.50. Child's meals. French country furnishings. Cr cds: A, D, MC, V.

Penn Yan (E-4)

(See also Canandaigua, Geneva, Hammondsport, Watkins Glen)

Founded 1787 **Pop** 5,248 **Elev** 737 ft **Area code** 315 **Zip** 14527 **E-mail** info@yatesny.com **Web** www.yatesny.com
Information Yates County Chamber of Commerce, 2375 Rte 14A; 315/536-3111 or 800/868-YATES.

Legend has it that the first settlers here, Pennsylvanians and Yankees, could not agree on a name for their town and finally compromised on Penn Yan. The town lies at the north end of Y-shaped Keuka Lake, in resort country; nearby is Keuka College.

What to See and Do

Fullager Farms Family Farm & Petting Zoo. Working dairy farm tour. Pony rides, hay rides, walking trails and picnic area. Petting zoo incl llamas, miniature donkey, rabbits, sheep and goats in addition to dairy cattle. (July-mid Sept, Tues-Sun; May-June & mid-Sept-Oct, wkends, also wkdays by appt) 3202 Bath Rd (County Rd 17). Phone 315/536-3545. ¢¢

Keuka Lake State Park. Swimming beach, bathhouse; fishing; boating (launch); hiking. Cross-country skiing. Playground. Tent & trailer sites (mid-May-Columbus Day). Standard fees. 6 mi SW off NY 54A. Phone 315/536-3666. Mid-May-Labor Day ¢¢

Oliver House Museum (1852). Brick house that originally belonged to the Oliver family, distinguished by 3 generations of physicians. Now HQ for the Yates County Genealogical & Historical Society, operated as a local history museum. Includes period rms, changing local history exhibits, research rm. (Mon-Fri; Sat by appt) 200 Main St. Phone 315/536-7318. **Donation.**

The Outlet Trail. Six-mi trail that follows an abandoned railroad path built in 1884. The Outlet drops almost 300 ft between Keuka and Seneca lakes, with waterfalls, wildlife and remains of early settlements and mills to be found along the way. Keuka St in Penn Yan to Seneca St, in Dresden.

Motel

✔★★ **VIKING RESORT.** 680 East Lake Rd. 315/536-7061; FAX 315/536-0737. E-mail viking@vikingresort.com; web www.vikingresort.com. 31 rms, 2 story, 24 kits. S, D $60-$140; each addl $15; kit. units $75-$160; family, wkly rates. Closed mid-Oct-mid-May. Crib free. Pet accepted; $20. TV; cable. Pool; whirlpool. Restaurant nearby. Ck-out 11 am. Lawn games. Refrigerators. Private patios, balconies. Picnic tables, grills. On Keuka Lake; private beach, daily cruises. Rental boats. No cr cds accepted.

Inn

★★★ **FOX INN.** 158 Main St. 315/536-3101; FAX 315/536-7612; res: 800/901-7997. E-mail mawhite@eznet.net; web www.yatesny .com/fox_inn. 5 rms, 1 with shower only, 2 story, 1 suite. No rm phones. June-Oct: S $70-$80; D $75-$85; each addl $15; suite $125; under 5 free; wkly rates; wkends (2-day min); lower rates rest of yr. Crib free. TV; cable, VCR avail (movies). Complimentary full bkfst. Restaurant adj 6 am-9 pm. Ck-out noon, ck-in 3 pm. Luggage handling. X-country ski ¼ mi. Picnic tables. Built in 1820. Totally nonsmoking. Cr cds: MC, V.

Plainview, L.I. (B-3)

(See also Bethpage)

Pop 26,207 **Elev** 180 ft **Area code** 516 **Zip** 11803

Motor Hotel

★★★ **MARRIOTT MELVILLE.** (1350 Old Walt Whitman Rd, Melville 11747) Long Island Expwy (I-495) exit 49, North Service Rd. 516/423-1600; FAX 516/423-1790. 374 rms, 4 story. S $149-$159; D $159; each addl $10; suites $169-$553; under 18 free; wkly, wkend & hol rates. Crib free. TV; cable. Indoor pool; whirlpool, lifeguard. Restaurant 6:30 am-10 pm; Sat to 11 pm. Rm serv. Bar; entertainment Fri, Sat. Ck-out 11 am. Convention facilities. Business center. In-rm modem link. Bellhops. Sundries. Gift shop. Exercise equipt. Game rm. Cr cds: A, C, D, DS, ER, JCB, MC, V.

Plattsburgh (B-8)

(See also Ausable Chasm, Rouses Point)

Pop 21,255 **Elev** 135 ft **Area code** 518 **Zip** 12901 **E-mail** chamber@westelcom.com **Web** northcountrychamber.com
Information Plattsburgh-North Country Chamber of Commerce, 101 West Bay Plaza, PO Box 310; 518/563-1000.

The Cumberland Bay area of Lake Champlain has been a military base since colonial days. Plattsburgh, at the mouth of the Saranac River, has a dramatic history in the struggle for US independence. The British won the Battle of Lake Champlain off these shores in 1776. Here, in 1814, Commodore Thomas Macdonough defeated a British fleet from Canada by an arrangement of anchors and winches that enabled him to swivel his vessels completely around, thus giving the enemy both broadsides. While this was going on, US General Alexander Macomb polished off the Redcoats ashore with the help of school boys and the local militia. Today, Plattsburgh accommodates both industry and resort trade.

What to See and Do

Adirondack Park (see). S on I-87.

Alice T. Miner Colonial Collection. Antiques, colonial household items and appliances in 1824 house; sandwich glass collection; gardens. (Tues-Sat; closed Jan, Dec 25) 12 mi N on NY 9 in Chazy. Phone 518/846-7336. ¢¢

Boat excursion. M/V *Juniper* leaves from ft of Dock St and cruises Lake Champlain, circling Valcour Island. (May-Sept, 2 daily departures; also sunset & dinner cruises nightly) Contact Heritage Adventures Inc, 69 Miller St; 800/388-8970. ¢¢¢-¢¢¢¢¢

Champlain Monument. Statue of the explorer. Cumberland Ave.

Kent-Delord House Museum (1797). Historic house; British officers' quarters during the Battle of Plattsburgh (War of 1812); period furnishings. Tours (Mar-Dec, Tues-Sat afternoons; rest of yr, by appt only; closed Jan 1, Thanksgiving, Dec 25). 17 Cumberland Ave. Phone 518/561-1035. ¢¢

Macdonough Monument. Obelisk commemorates the naval encounter. City Hall Place at City Hall.

State Univ of New York College at Plattsburgh (1889). (6,400 students) On campus is SUNY Plattsburgh Art Museum, comprised of Meyers Fine Arts Gallery and Winkel Sculpture Court; also Rockwell Kent Gallery, with extensive collection of paintings, drawings, prints and book engravings by American artist Rockwell Kent, famous for his illustrated Shakespeare and *Moby Dick* (daily exc Fri; phone 518/564-2813). Phone 518/564-2000.

Swimming. Municipal Beach. Bathhouse, lifeguard; picnicking, concession. 1¼ mi N on US 9, 1 mi E on NY 314. Phone 518/563-4431. **AuSable Point State Park.** 12 mi S on US 9. Beach; fishing; boating; camping. Phone 518/561-7080. **Cumberland Bay State Park.** Adj to Municipal Beach. Phone 518/563-5240. All areas (Memorial Day-mid-Sept). Admission fee. Phone 518/563-4431.

Motels

★ ★ **DAYS INN.** *8 Everleth Dr, opp Pyramid Mall. 518/561-0403; FAX 518/561-4192.* 112 rms, 3 story. Late June-mid-Oct: S $44-$79.99; D $46-$79.99; each addl $8; under 18 free; wkly rates off-season; higher rates college events; lower rates rest of yr. Crib free. TV; cable (premium). Indoor pool; whirlpool. Restaurant opp. Ck-out noon. Meeting rm. Business servs avail. Exercise equipt. Picnic table. Cr cds: A, C, D, DS, MC, V.

D ⚡ 🏊 🏋 🍴 🔥 SC

★ ★ **HOWARD JOHNSON.** *446 NY 3, 1½ mi W at jct NY 3 & I-87. 518/561-7750; FAX 518/561-9431.* 120 rms, 2 story. June-Labor Day: S, D $89-$99; each addl $10; under 18 free; higher rates some special events, hols; lower rates rest of yr. Crib free. Pet accepted. TV; cable (premium), VCR avail. Indoor pool; poolside serv. Coffee in rms. Restaurant 6 am-11 pm. Rm serv. Bar 3 pm-midnight, wkends to 1 am. Ck-out noon. Coin lndry. Meeting rms. Business servs avail. In-rm modem link. Exercise equipt. Rec rm. Refrigerators avail. Some private patios, balconies. Shopping mall adj. Cr cds: A, C, D, DS, JCB, MC, V.

D 🐾 🏊 🏋 🍴 🏊 🔥 SC

✔ ★ **STONEHELM.** *72 Spellman Rd, 4½ mi N on I-87 exit 40. 518/563-4800; FAX 518/562-1380; res: 800/443-4344.* 40 rms. July-Aug: S, D $49-$64; each addl $5; lower rates rest of yr. Crib free. TV; cable. Restaurant 7:30 am-2 pm. Ck-out 11 am. Many refrigerators. Picnic tables, grills. Cr cds: A, DS, MC, V.

🍴 🔥 SC

Motor Hotel

★ ★ **HOLIDAY INN.** *Jct I-87 & NY 3, I-87 exit 37. 518/561-5000; FAX 518/562-2974.* 102 rms, 4 story. Mid-June-mid-Oct: S, D $79-$99; each addl $10; under 19 free; lower rates rest of yr. Crib free. Pet accepted, some restrictions. TV; cable. Indoor pool; wading pool, whirlpool. Complimentary bkfst. Restaurant 6:30 am-1 pm, 5-9 pm. Rm serv. Bar from 4 pm. Ck-out noon. Meeting rms. Business servs avail. In-rm modem link. Sundries. Exercise equipt. Game rm. Cr cds: A, C, D, DS, JCB, MC, V.

D 🐾 🏊 🏋 🍴 🔥 SC

Restaurants

★ ★ **ANTHONY'S RESTAURANT & BISTRO.** *538 Rt 3. 518/561-6420.* Continental menu. Specialties: roast L.I. duckling, steak au poivre, roast rack of lamb. Hrs: 11:30 am-2:30 pm, 5-9:30 pm; wkends 5-10 pm. Closed some major hols. Res accepted. Bar to 11 pm. Semi-a la carte: lunch $4.95-$9.95, dinner $9.95-$23.95. Child's meals. Piano bar wkends. Country elegance. Cr cds: A, C, D, MC, V.

★ ★ **ROYAL SAVAGE INN.** *Lakeshore Rd, 5 mi S on US 9. 518/561-5140.* Specialties: baked stuffed shrimp, chicken Hawaiian. Hrs: 11:30 am-9 pm; Sun from noon. Closed Jan-Easter. Res accepted. Bar. Semi-a la carte: lunch $5.50-$9.95, dinner $8.95-$18.95. Complete meals: dinner $8.95-$14.95. Child's meals. Converted hay barn; many antiques. Fireplace in lobby, bar. Gift shop. View of Salmon River. Cr cds: A, C, D, DS, MC, V.

D

Port Jefferson, L.I. (A-3)

(See also Smithtown, Stony Brook)

Pop 7,455 **Elev** 50 ft **Area code** 516 **Zip** 11777 **Web** www.ptjeff.com/pjcoc
Information Greater Port Jefferson Chamber of Commerce, 118 W Broadway; 516/473-1414.

What to See and Do

Ferry to Bridgeport, CT. Car and passenger service. (Daily) For fees and schedule contact Bridgeport & Port Jefferson Steamboat Co, 102 W Broadway, phone 516/473-0286 or 888/44-FERRY(exc NY).

Thompson House (ca 1700). Historian Benjamin F. Thompson was born in this saltbox house in 1784; authentically furnished to depict 18th-century life on rural Long Island. Herb garden. (Memorial Day-mid-Oct, Fri-Sun) 4 mi W on NY 25A, on North Country Rd in Setauket. Phone 516/941-9444. ¢

Inn

★ ★ ★ **DANFORDS.** *25 E Broadway. 516/928-5200; FAX 516/928-3598; res: 800/332-6367.* 85 rms, 3 story, 7 suites, 3 kits. D $145-$300; each addl $10; suites $200-$400; kit. units $160; package plans. Crib free. TV; cable. Restaurant (see DANFORDS). Rm serv. Ck-out 11 am, ck-in 2 pm. Business servs avail. Bellhops. Valet serv. Concierge (wkends). Exercise equipt. Health club privileges. Balconies. On Long Island Sound. Library; Oriental rugs, antiques, fireplace. Cr cds: A, C, D, DS, MC, V.

D 🐾 🍴 🏊 🔥 SC

Restaurants

★ ★ **DANFORDS.** *(See Danfords Inn) 516/928-5200.* Specializes in fresh seafood, prime meats. Hrs: 7 am-10 pm; Fri, Sat to 11 pm; Sun 8 am-10 pm; Sun brunch 11:30 am-3 pm. Res accepted. Bars. A la carte: bkfst, lunch $7.50-$16.95, dinner $14-$24. Sun brunch $21.95. Child's meals. Entertainment Fri, Sat evenings. Outdoor dining. Built in 1890 as a chowder house. Cr cds: A, C, D, DS, MC, V.

D

★ **DOCKSIDE.** *111 W Broadway. 516/473-5656.* German, Amer menu. Specializes in German dishes, seafood. Hrs: noon-midnight. Res accepted. Bar. A la carte entrees: lunch $4.95-$17.95, dinner $12.50-$21.50. Child's meals. Pianist Fri-Sun. Outdoor dining overlooking harbor. Nautical theme. Cr cds: A, C, D, MC, V.

D

✔ ★ **VILLAGE WAY.** *106 Main St. 516/928-3395.* Specializes in seafood, beef, pasta. Hrs: 11-1 am; Fri, Sat to 2 am; early-bird dinner Mon-Fri 4-6 pm; Sun brunch 10 am-1 pm. Closed Thanksgiving, Dec 25. Res accepted. Bar. Semi-a la carte: lunch $5.50-$9.95, dinner $9.95-$15.95. Sun brunch $3.50-$9. Childs meals. Outdoor dining. Cr cds: A, C, D, DS, MC, V.

Port Jervis (A-1)

(See also Barryville, Middletown)

Pop 9,060 **Elev** 440 ft **Area code** 914 **Zip** 12771
Information Tri-State Chamber of Commerce, 5 S Broome St, PO Box 121; 914/856-6694 or 914/856-6695.

Port Jervis is a popular area for whitewater canoeing and rafting. Fishing, nature trails and hot-air ballooning are highlights of the area.

What to See and Do

Gillander Glass Museum and Factory Store. Observe skilled craftsmen at work as they transform molten glass into beautiful glass objects. Tours, museum, store. (Mon-Fri; wkends seasonal; closed hols) Erie & Liberty Sts. Phone 914/856-5375. ¢¢

Restaurants

★ ★ **CORNUCOPIA.** *176 US 209N, 2 mi N.* *914/856-5361.* Continental, German menu. Specializes in German dishes. Salad bar. Hrs: noon-2 pm, 5-9 pm; Sat from 5 pm; Sun 1-8 pm. Closed Mon. Res accepted. Bar. Semi-a la carte: lunch $4.95-$10.95, dinner $9.95-$25. Country inn built 1892; chalet decor. Guest rms avail. Cr cds: A, C, D, DS, MC, V.

SC

★ ★ **FLO-JEAN.** *2 Pike St, jct US 6 & US 209, at bridge over Delaware River.* *914/856-6600.* Specializes in prime rib, fresh seafood, roast turkey. Own desserts. Hrs: 11:30 am-9 pm; Fri, Sat to 10 pm. Closed Mon; Tues, Wed Oct-May. Res accepted. Bar. Semi-a la carte: lunch $3.95-$8.95, dinner $8.95-$18.95. Child's meals. Entertainment wkends. Outdoor dining. Overlooks Delaware River; antiques, doll collection. Cr cds: A, DS, MC, V.

Port Washington, L.I. (C-5 see New York City map)

(See also Glen Cove, Great Neck, New York City)

Pop 15,387 **Elev** 140 ft **Area code** 516 **Zip** 11050

Restaurants

★ ★ **DIWAN.** *37 Shore Rd.* *516/767-7878.* Indian menu. Specializes in tandoori, lamb, chicken. Hrs: noon-2:30 pm, 5:30-10 pm; wkends noon-3 pm, 5:30-10:30 pm; Sat, Sun brunch noon-3 pm. Res required. Bar. Complete meals: lunch $9.95. A la carte entrees: dinner $10.95-$19.95. India motif. Overlooks mill pond and marina. Cr cds: A, C, D, DS, MC, V.

D

★ ★ **LATITUDES.** *45 Orchard Beach Blvd.* *516/767-7400.* Specializes in seafood, pasta. Hrs: noon-10 pm; Fri, Sat to 11 pm; Sun brunch 11:30 am-3 pm. Closed Dec 25. Bar to midnight, wkends to 2 am. A la carte entrees: lunch $6.50-$12.95, dinner $12.95-$19.95. Outdoor dining. Patio overlooks marina and bay. Cr cds: A, C, D, MC, V.

D

★ **YAMAGUCHI.** *63 Main St, adj to train station.* *516/883-3500.* Japanese menu. Specializes in sushi, casseroles, meat dishes. Sushi bar. Hrs: noon-2:30 pm, 5:30-10 pm; Fri to 10:30 pm; Sat 5-10:30 pm; Sun 5-9:30 pm. Closed Mon; Jan 1, Thanksgiving, Dec 25. Res

required wkends. Bar. Semi-a la carte: lunch $6.50-$13.50, dinner $9.50-$22. Japanese lanterns and screens. Cr cds: A, C, D, MC, V.

D

Potsdam (B-7)

(See also Canton, Massena, Ogdensburg)

Founded 1802 **Pop** 16,822 **Elev** 433 ft **Area code** 315 **Zip** 13676 **E-mail** chamber@potsdam.ny.us **Web** www.potsdam.ny.us
Information Chamber of Commerce, PO Box 717; 315/265-5440.

What to See and Do

Adirondack Park (see). S on NY 56.

Potsdam College of the State Univ of New York (1816). (4,450 students) Founded as St Lawrence Academy. Gibson Art Gallery; Crane School of Music; planetarium; summer programs. Campus tours. Phone 315/267-2000.

Potsdam Public Museum. Collection of English pottery; local history and decorative arts displays; changing exhibits. Walking tour brochures avail. (Tues-Fri afternoons, also Sat mornings; closed major hols) Civic Center, Elm & Park Sts. Phone 315/265-6910. **Free.**

Motels

★ ★ ★ **CLARKSON INN.** *1 Main St.* *315/265-3050; res: 800/790-6970.* Web www.potsdam.ny.us/theclarksoninn. 40 rms, 2 story. S $69-$79; D $79-$89; higher rates college events. Crib $10. TV; cable. Restaurant 6:30-10 am; also opp 11 am-9 pm. Ck-out 11 am. Meeting rm. Business servs avail. In-rm modem link. Fireside sitting rm in lobby; turn-of-the-century atmosphere. Reproduced antique furnishings. Located along Racquette River & adj park. Cr cds: A, MC, V.

D

✔★ **SMALLING MOTEL.** *6775 NY 56, 2 mi N on NY 56.* *315/265-4640.* 15 rms. S $39; D $44-$49; each addl $5; under 5 free. Crib $5. TV; cable (premium). Pool. Complimentary coffee. Ck-out 11 am. Picnic tables. Cr cds: A, MC, V.

SC

✔★ **THE WEDGEWOOD INN.** *NY 56 North.* *315/265-9100.* 15 rms. S $44.50-$74.50; D $46.50-$86.50; each addl $8; wkly rates; higher rates major college events. Crib free. TV; cable, VCR (movies $3). Complimentary coffee in lobby. Restaurant nearby. Ck-out 11 am. Free bus depot transportation. Downhill/x-country ski 7 mi. Refrigerators. Cr cds: A, C, D, DS, MC, V.

SC

Restaurants

★ ★ ★ **FRENCH'S 1844 HOUSE.** *6885 US 11, 5 mi W on US 11.* *315/265-9896.* Continental menu. Specializes in veal, lamb, seafood. Hrs: 4 pm-closing. Closed Sun, Mon; Jan 1, Memorial Day, Dec 25. Res accepted. Bar. Semi-a la carte: dinner $12.95-$21.95. Child's meals. Outdoor dining. Restored house (1844); country French decor. Cr cds: A, C, D, DS, MC, V.

D

✔★ **TARDELLI'S.** *141 Market St.* *315/265-8446.* Italian menu. Specializes in veal, homemade pasta, prime rib. Hrs: 11:30 am-10 pm; Sat from 4 pm. Closed Sun; some major hols. Res accepted. Bar to 2 am. Semi-a la carte: lunch $2.75-$7.25, dinner $5.95-$12.95. Child's meals. Family-owned. Cr cds: A, C, D, MC, V.

SC

Poughkeepsie (F-8)

(See also Fishkill, Hyde Park, Newburgh, New Paltz)

Settled 1687 **Pop** 28,844 **Elev** 176 ft **Area code** 914 **E-mail** office@pokchamb.org **Web** www.pokchamb.org

Information Poughkeepsie Area Chamber of Commerce, 110 Main St, 12601; 914/454-1700.

Many people know this Hudson River town as the site of Vassar College, founded in 1861 by a brewer named Matthew Vassar. The Smith Brothers also helped put Poughkeepsie (p'KIP-see) on the map with their cough drops, once made here. For a brief time during the American Revolution, this town was the state capital; It was here in 1788 that New York ratified the Constitution.

What to See and Do

Bardavon Opera House (1869). Oldest operating theater in the state presents various dance, theatrical and musical performances; also Hudson Valley Philharmonic concerts. (Oct-May) 35 Market St. For schedule and ticket info, phone 914/473-5288 or -2072.

James Baird State Park. An 18-hole golf course & driving range, tennis. Hiking trails. Cross-country skiing. Picnicking (shelters), playground; restaurant. Nature center (June-Labor Day). Standard fees. 9 mi E on NY 55, then 1 mi N on Taconic Pkwy. Phone 914/452-1489.   **Free.**

★ Locust Grove (Young-Morse Historic Site) (ca 1830). Former house of Samuel F. B. Morse, inventor of the telegraph; remodeled by him into a Tuscan villa in 1847. Antiques; Morse Rm, telegraph equipment & memorabilia; alternating exhibits of dolls, fans, costumes, books and souvenirs acquired by Young family (owners following Morse); paintings, art objects and American furnishings. Wildlife sanctuary and park (150 acres) with hiking trails, picnic area. Tours (Memorial Day-Sept, Wed-Sun; Oct, wknds). 2 mi S of Mid-Hudson Bridge at 370 South Rd (US 9). Phone 914/454-4500.   **¢¢**

Mid-Hudson Children’s Museum. Interactive children’s museum featuring more than 50 exhibits; incl gravity roll, IBM’s Da Vinci inventions, optical odyssey, kids’ construction crane. (Tues-Sun, some Mon hols; closed most major hols) Located in South Hills Mall, Rte 9. Phone 914/297-5938.   **¢¢**

Vassar College (1861). (2,250 students) A 1,000-acre campus; coeducational (since 1969) liberal arts college. Art gallery (free). Raymond Ave. Phone 914/437-7000.

Windsor Vineyards. Makers of California and New York State wines and champagnes. Wine tasting. (Daily; closed most major hols) Approx 7¹/2 mi S on US 9 from Mid-Hudson Bridge, right on Western Ave, at Marlboro-on-the-Hudson. Phone 914/236-4233.   **Free.**

Motels

★ ★ ★ COURTYARD BY MARRIOTT. *408 South Rd (US 9) (12601).* 914/485-6336; FAX 914/485-6514. 149 rms, 2-3 story. S, D $69-$129; suites $129-$149; under 18 free; wkly rates. Crib free. TV; cable (premium), VCR avail. Indoor pool; whirlpool. Complimentary coffee in rms. Restaurant 6:30-10 am; Sat, Sun 7 am-noon. Bar 5-10 pm; closed Fri, Sat. Ck-out 1 pm. Coin lndry. Meeting rms. Business center. In-rm modem link. Valet serv (Mon-Fri). Exercise equipt. Refrigerator, microwave in suites. Balconies. Cr cds: A, D, DS, MC, V.

★ DAYS INN. *62 Haight Ave (12603).* 914/454-1010; res: 800/329-7466; FAX 914/454-0127. 41 rms, 2 story. S, D $65-$71; each addl $5; under 12 free. Crib free. TV; cable (premium). Pool; lifeguard. Complimentary continental bkfst. Restaurant nearby. Ck-out 11 am. Meeting rm. Business servs avail. In-rm modem link. Sundries. Refrigerators avail. Balconies. Vassar College nearby. Cr cds: A, C, D, DS, MC, V.

✔★ ECONO LODGE. *428 South Rd (US 9) (12601).* 914/452-6600; FAX 914/454-2210. 111 rms, 9 kit units, 1-2 story. S, D $99-$110; each addl $5; under 16 free; wkly rates. Crib $5. Pet accepted, some restrictions. TV; cable. Complimentary continental bkfst. Restaurant opp open 24 hrs. Ck-out 11 am. Coin lndry. Meeting rms. Business servs avail. In-rm modem link. Some refrigerators. Cr cds: A, C, D, DS, MC, V.

Motor Hotel

★ ★ HOLIDAY INN EXPRESS. *US 9 & Sharon Dr (12601), 1¹/2 mi S of Mid-Hudson Bridge.* 914/473-1151; FAX 914/485-8127. 121 rms, 4 story. S, D $89-$139; suite $175-$250; each addl $10; under 18 free; higher rates special events. Crib free. Pet accepted. TV; cable (premium). Pool; lifeguard. Complimentary continental bkfst. Ck-out noon. Guest lndry. Meeting rms. Business servs avail. Exercise equipt. Sundries. Cr cds: A, C, D, DS, ER, JCB, MC, V.

Hotel

★ ★ SHERATON CIVIC CENTER. *40 Civic Center Plaza (12601).* 914/485-5300; FAX 914/485-4720. 195 rms, 10 story. S, D $129; suites $250-$350; under 12 free. Crib free. TV; cable (premium). Restaurant 6:30 am-10:30 pm. Bar from noon. Ck-out noon. Meeting rms. Business servs avail. Free garage parking. Exercise equipt. Health club privileges. Cr cds: A, C, D, DS, MC, V.

Inns

★ ★ ★ INN AT THE FALLS. *50 Red Oaks Mill Rd (12603), 4 mi SE, just off NY 376.* 914/462-5770; res: 800/344-1466; FAX 914/462-5943. E-mail innatfalls@aol; web www.innatthefalls.com. 36 rms, 2 story. S, D $135-$140; suites $165-$170; under 13 free. Crib free. TV; cable, VCR avail. Complimentary continental bkfst. Rm serv (bkfst). Ck-out noon, ck-in 3 pm. Business servs avail. In-rm modem link. Refrigerators. Different period furnishings in every rm. Cr cds: A, D, DS, MC, V.

★ ★ ★ OLD DROVERS. *(Old US 22, Dover Plains 12522) US 44 E to Millbrook, US 343 to Dover Plains, S on US 22.* 914/832-9311; FAX 914/832-6356. Web www.olddroversinn.com. 4 rms. No rm phones. D $150-$230; MAP avail wkends $320-$395; higher rates May-Oct (2-day min). Closed Tues, Wed. Pet accepted, some restrictions; $25. TV; VCR avail (free movies). Complimentary full bkfst. Restaurant (see OLD DROVERS INN). Ck-out noon, ck-in 2 pm. Business servs avail. 18-hole golf privileges, greens fee $18-$24. Downhill ski 9 mi. Originally inn for cattle drovers (1750); antiques, fireplaces. Cr cds: MC, V.

★ ★ ★ TROUTBECK. *(Leedsville Rd, Amenia 12501) 20 mi NE via US 44 to Amenia, then continue straight at light onto NY 343 approx 2¹/4 mi to paved road beyond sign, turn right, cross bridge to first driveway on right.* 914/373-9681; res: 800/978-7688; FAX 914/373-7080. E-mail jbflahtery@att.net; web www.troutbeck.com. 42 rms, 2 story. AP $650-$1,050/couple/wkend. TV in sitting rm; VCR avail (movies). 2 pools, 1 indoor. Restaurant noon-2 pm, 6:30-9 pm Wed-Sat; brunch 11:30 am-3:30 pm. Open bar. Ck-out Sun 2 pm, ck-in Fri 5 pm. Meeting rms. Business center. In-rm modem link. Tennis. Downhill/x-country ski 10 mi. Exercise equipt; sauna. Game rm. Lawn games. Cr cds: A, D, MC, V.

Restaurants

★ ★ ★ ALLYN'S. *(US 44, Millbrook) 15 mi E on US 44.* 914/677-5888. Continental menu. Specialties: venison, roast duck with port wine & currants. Own baking. Hrs: 11:30 am-9:30 pm; Fri, Sat to 10:30 pm; Sun brunch to 3 pm. Closed Tues; Dec 25. Res accepted. Bar. Wine cellar. Semi-a la carte: lunch $4.95-$12.50, dinner $10.95-$21.95. Sun brunch $15.95. Child's meals. Parking. Outdoor dining. Renovated church (1790); hunt motif; fireplaces. Cr cds: A, C, D, DS, MC, V.

★ **BANTA'S STEAK & STEIN.** *(9 Mall Plaza, Wappingers Falls 12590) 6 mi S on US 9.* 914/297-6770. Specializes in steak, fresh fish, prime rib. Salad bar. Hrs: 4-10 pm; wkends to 11 pm; Sun from noon. Closed Thanksgiving, Dec 25. Bar 4-10 pm; wkends to 11 pm. Semi-a la carte: dinner $8.95-$26.95. Child's meals. Banjo band Mon. Parking. Fireplaces. Dutch colonial decor. Family-owned. Cr cds: A, D, MC, V.

D **SC**

✔★ **CAESAR'S.** *2 Delafield St (12601).* 914/471-4857. Web www.consorzi.com. Italian menu. Specializes in pasta, veal, chicken. Hrs: 5-9:30 pm; Sat to 10:30 pm, Sun 4-9 pm. Closed Jan 1, Easter, Memorial Day, Dec 25. Bar. A la carte entrees: dinner $12.95-$18.95. Child's meals. Parking. Cr cds: A, C, D, DS, MC, V.

★ ★ **CHRISTOS.** *155 Wilbur Blvd (12603), US 9 exit Spackenkill Rd E, on McCann golf course.* 914/471-3400. Web www.pojonews.com/christos. Continental menu. Specialties: filet of sole, châteaubriand bouquetière. Own baking. Hrs: 11:30 am-2:30 pm, 5-11 pm; Sat from 5 pm. Closed Sun, Mon; also Aug. Res accepted. Bar. Semi-a la carte: lunch $8-$15, dinner $17-$25. Child's meals. Parking. Outdoor dining. Cr cds: A, C, D, MC, V.

D

★ ★ **LE PAVILLON.** *230 Salt Point Tpke (12603).* 914/473-2525. Web www.lepavillionenjoy.com. French menu. Specializes in rack of lamb, seafood, sweetbreads. Own baking. Hrs: 5:30-10 pm. Closed Sun; major hols; also 2 wks July. Res accepted. Bar. Wine cellar. A la carte entrees: dinner $16-$19.95. Complete meals: Sat dinner $30. Child's meals. Parking. Patio dining. Brick farmhouse (1790); many antiques; spacious grounds. Cr cds: A, D, MC, V.

★ ★ **OLD DROVERS INN.** *(See Old Drovers Inn)* 914/832-9311. Specialties: brown turkey hash, double-cut lamb chops. Hrs: 5-9 pm; Fri noon-3 pm, 5-10 pm; Sat noon-10 pm; Sun noon-3:30 pm. Closed Tues, Wed; Dec 25. Res accepted. Bar. Wine cellar. A la carte entrees: lunch $15-$29, dinner $17-$35. Parking. Outdoor dining. Romantic dining. Colonial decor with stone fireplace and hurricane lamps. Cr cds: MC, V.

★ **RIVER STATION STEAK & SEAFOOD HOUSE.** *1 Water St (12601).* 914/452-9207. Specializes in steak, seafood, pasta. Hrs: 11:30 am-midnight; Fri, Sat to 2 am. Closed Dec 25. Res accepted; required hols. Bar. Semi-a la carte: lunch $5.50-$7.95, dinner $11.95-$23.95. Child's meals. Parking. Outdoor dining. Oldest food-and-drink establishment in city; view of river, Mid-Hudson Bridge. Cr cds: A, D, DS, MC, V.

D

Pound Ridge (A-3)

(See also Brewster, Mt Kisco, Stamford, White Plains; also see Norwalk, CT)

Pop 4,550 **Elev** 600 ft **Area code** 914 **Zip** 10576

What to See and Do

Muscoot Farm. This 777-acre park is a turn-of-the-century farm that incl farm animals, bldgs and a 28-rm main house. Demonstrations of sheepshearing, blacksmithing, beekeeping, harvesting, and bread-baking. Programs (Sun). Tours (groups only; phone for res and fees). NY 100, Somers. Phone 914/232-7118. **Free.**

Ward Pound Ridge Reservation. In 4,700-acre park is Trailside Nature Museum (Wed-Sun). Cross-country ski trails. Picnicking; playground. Camping in lean-tos (fee). Reservation (daily; closed Jan 1, Thanksgiving, Dec 25). About 4 mi NW on NY 137, then 3 1/2 mi N on NY 121S, just S of jct NY 35 in Cross River. Phone 914/763-3493. Per vehicle **¢¢¢**

Restaurants

★ ★ **INN AT POUND RIDGE.** *258 Westchester Ave, 8 mi N of Merritt Pkwy exit 35.* 914/764-5779. Specializes in rack of lamb, fresh fish, duck. Hrs: noon-2:30 pm, 6-9:30 pm; Fri, Sat 6-10:30 pm; Sun 4-9 pm; Sun brunch noon-3 pm. Res accepted; required wkends. Bar. A la carte entrees: lunch $8-$21, dinner $19-$29.50. Sun brunch $24. Child's meals. Valet parking. House built 1833; antiques, fireplaces. Cr cds: A, C, D, MC, V.

D

★ ★ ★ **L'EUROPE.** *(407 Smithridge Rd, South Salem 10590) 6 mi N on NY 123.* 914/533-2570. French, continental menu. Specializes in veal chops, rack of lamb, duck. Hrs: noon-2:30 pm, 6-9:30 pm. Closed Mon. Res accepted. Bar. Wine cellar. A la carte entrees: lunch $13-$22, dinner $21.50-$29.50. Prix fixe (Sat): dinner $51. Outdoor dining. Elegant dining in Country French atmosphere. Cr cds: A, C, D, MC, V.

D

Queens

(Follows New York City)

Rhinebeck (F-8)

(See also Hyde Park, Poughkeepsie)

Settled 1686 **Pop** 7,558 **Elev** 200 ft **Area code** 914 **Zip** 12572
Information Chamber of Commerce, 19 Mill St, Box 42; 914/876-4778.

Rhinebeck was once known as "violet town" because it claimed to produce more hothouse violets than any other town in the US.

What to See and Do

Hudson River Natl Estuarine Research Reserve. The Hudson River is an estuary, running from Manhattan to Troy, NY; over 4,000 acres of this estuarine land have been reserved for the study of its life and ecosystems. The Reserve incl Piermont Marsh and Iona Island in Rockland County, Tivoli Bays in Dutchess County and Stockport Flats in Columbia County. Reserve's HQ has lectures, workshops, special exhibits and public field programs. N on NY 9G to Annandale, 1 1/4 mi N of Bard College Main Gate. For schedule phone 914/758-5193. **Free.**

Montgomery Place. Estate along Hudson River. Mansion (1805) was remodeled in the mid-1800s in the Classical-revival style. Also on grounds are a coach house, visitor center, greenhouse with rose, herb, perennial and woodland gardens, museum and garden shop. Scenic trails and view of cataracts meeting the Hudson. (Apr-Oct, daily exc Tues; Mar & Nov-Dec, wkends) N on NY 9G to Annandale-on-Hudson. Phone 914/758-5461. Tours **¢¢¢**; Grounds **¢¢**

Old Rhinebeck Aerodrome. Museum of antique airplanes (1900-37). Planes from World War I and earlier are flown in air shows (mid-June-mid-Oct, Sat & Sun). Aerodrome (mid-May-Oct, daily). Picnicking. Barnstorming rides. About 3 mi NE via US 9, at 42 Stone Church Rd. Phone 914/758-8610. Admission **¢¢¢**

Annual Event

Dutchess County Fair. Fairgrounds. Harness racing, livestock shows, farm machinery exhibits. Late Aug.

Motel

✓★ ★ **VILLAGE INN.** *6 US 9S. 914/876-7000; FAX 914/876-4756.* 16 rms. S, D $56-$70; each addl $15; under 12 free; wkly rates. Crib free. TV; cable. Complimentary continental bkfst. Ck-out 11 am. Some refrigerators. Cr cds: DS, MC, V.

Inn

★ ★ ★ **BEEKMAN ARMS.** *4 Mill St, on US 9. 914/876-7077.* 59 rms, most A/C, 3 story. S, D $90-$120; each addl $10; suites $125-$150; under 12 free. Crib free. TV; cable. Restaurant (see BEEKMAN 1766 TAVERN). Bar 11-1 am. Ck-out 11 am, ck-in 3 pm. Meeting rms. Business servs avail. Historic inn, opened 1766. Antiques. Cr cds: A, C, D, MC, V.

Restaurants

★ ★ **BEEKMAN 1766 TAVERN.** *(See Beekman Arms Inn) 914/871-1766.* Specialty: cedar plank salmon. Hrs: 8-10 am, 11:30 am-3 pm, 5:30-9 pm; Fri, Sat to 9:30 pm; Sun 3:30-8 pm; Sun brunch 10 am-2 pm. Res accepted. Bar. Buffet: bkfst $5.25. Semi-a la carte: lunch $7.75-$10.95, dinner $10.50-$23.95. Sun brunch $19.95. Child's meals. Parking. Outdoor dining. Several small dining rms in historic inn. Cr cds: A, C, D, MC, V.

✓★ **LA PARMIGIANA.** *37 Montgomery St. 914/876-3228.* Italian menu. Specializes in pasta, pizza. Own pasta. Hrs: noon-10 pm; Wed, Thurs from 4 pm; Fri, Sat to 11 pm. Closed Tues; Thanksgiving, Dec 25. Bar. Semi-a la carte: lunch $5.50-$9.50, dinner $5.50-$16.50. Parking. Outdoor dining. Wood-burning brick oven. In renovated church; cathedral ceilings. Cr cds: A, D, MC, V.

✓★ **P. J. McGLYNN'S.** *(147 US 9, Red Hook 12571) 3½ mi N on US 9. 914/758-3102.* Specializes in freshly cut ribs and steaks. Hrs: 11 am-midnight; Sun brunch to 3 pm. Closed Thanksgiving, Dec 25. Res accepted. Bar; Fri, Sat to 2 am. Semi-a la carte: lunch $2.95-$6.95, dinner $8.95-$18.95. Sun brunch $4.95-$6.95. Child's meals. Outdoor dining. Casual, colonial decor in pre-1900 bldg. Cr cds: A, DS, MC, V.

✓★ ★ **RED HOOK INN.** *(31 S Broadway, Red Hook 12571) 5 mi N on US 9. 914/758-8445.* Regional Amer menu. Specialties: peppercorn-cured salmon with scallion pancakes, local free-range poultry. Own baking. Hrs: 5-10 pm; Sat 11:30 am-3 pm, 5-10 pm; Sun 11 am-3 pm (brunch), 4-9 pm. Closed Mon; Memorial Day, Labor Day; also 2 wks in winter. Res accepted. Bar 4-11 pm. Semi-a la carte: lunch $4.50-$10.95, dinner $11.95-$18.95. Sun brunch $11.95. Child's meals. Outdoor dining. Country inn (1842) with beamed ceiling, lantern lamps; guest rms avail. Cr cds: A, DS, MC, V.

Richfield Springs (D-7)

(See also Canajoharie, Cooperstown, Herkimer, Ilion)

Pop 1,565 **Elev** 1,315 ft **Area code** 315 **Zip** 13439

Motels

★ **FOUNTAIN VIEW.** *US 20, ½ mi E on US 20. 315/858-1360.* 16 rms. Mid-June-Nov: S, D $65-$75; each addl $5; higher rates:

wkends Sept-Nov, Hall of Fame wkend; lower rates wkdays Apr-mid-June. Closed rest of yr. Crib $5. TV; cable (premium). Restaurant nearby. Ck-out 11 am. Lawn games. On hillside. Overlooks illuminated fountain, park, pond. Refrigerators, microwaves. Cr cds: DS, MC, V.

✓★ **VILLAGE.** *E Main St (US 20). 315/858-1540.* 11 rms. June-Sept: S $65; D $75; each addl $5; higher rates hol wkends; lower rates rest of yr. Crib free. TV; cable (premium). Restaurant nearby. Ck-out 11 am. Downhill/x-country ski 15 mi. Picnic tables, grills. Cr cds: DS, MC, V.

Riverhead, L.I. (A-4)

(See also Hampton Bays)

Pop 23,011 **Elev** 19 ft **Area code** 516 **Zip** 11901
Information Chamber of Commerce, 542 E Main St, PO Box 291; 516/727-7600.

Suffolk County's thousands of acres of rich farmland, first cultivated in 1690, have made it one of the leading agricultural counties in the United States. Potatoes, corn and cauliflower are abundant here.

What to See and Do

Brookhaven Natl Laboratory. The Exhibit Center Science Museum is housed in the world's first nuclear reactor built to carry out research on the peaceful aspects of nuclear science. Participatory exhibits, audio-visual presentations and historic collections. Tours (July-Aug, Sun; closed hol wkends). 14 mi W of Riverhead via NY 24 and NY 495, in Upton. Phone 516/344-2345. **Free.**

Suffolk County Historical Society. Permanent and changing exhibits reflect the history of Suffolk County. Early crafts, ceramics, textiles, china, transportation, whaling and Native Americans on Long Island are highlighted. Research library specializes in area history and genealogy. Educational programs and tours by advance res. (Tues-Sat afternoons; closed hols) 300 W Main St. Phone 516/727-2881. **Free.**

Annual Event

Riverhead Country Fair. Downtown. Agricultural, needlecraft exhibits and competitions; farm animal exhibit; entertainment, midway, music. Phone 516/727-1215. Mid-Oct.

Motels

★ **BUDGET HOST INN.** *30 E Moriches Rd. 516/727-6200; FAX 516/727-6466.* 68 rms, 2 story, 12 kits. S $68-$102; D $80-$136; each addl $10; under 16 free; kits. $10 addl; higher rates: Memorial Day, July 4, Labor Day wkends; wkly rates. Crib $5. TV; cable (premium). Pool; lifeguard. Ck-out 11 am. Meeting rms. Business servs avail. Sundries. Lighted tennis. Picnic tables, grills. Cr cds: A, C, D, DS, MC, V.

★ **RAMADA INN EAST END.** *1830 NY 25, at L.I. Expy exit 72E. 516/369-2200; FAX 516/369-1202.* 100 rms, 2 story. Mid-May-Sept: S, D $89-$165; each addl $10; under 18 free; lower rates rest of yr. Crib free. TV; cable (premium). Pool; lifeguard. Restaurant 6:30 am-10 pm. Rm serv. Bar noon-midnight. Ck-out 11 am. Meeting rms. Business servs avail. Valet serv. Cr cds: A, C, D, DS, MC, V.

★ **WADING RIVER.** *(5890 Middle County Rd, Wading River 11792) 8 mi W on NY 25, 3 mi N of L.I. Expy exit 69. 516/727-8000.* 32 rms, 17 kits. Memorial Day wkend-mid-Sept: S, D $82-$92; each addl $10; kits. $16 addl; higher rates hol wkends; lower rates rest of yr. Crib $5. TV.

Heated pool. Ck-out 11 am. Lawn games. Picnic tables, grill. Sun deck. Cr cds: A, C, D, DS, MC, V.

Restaurant

★ **MEETING HOUSE CREEK INN.** *(Meeting House Creek Rd, Aquebogue 11931)* E on NY 25 to Edgar Ave S. 516/722-4220. Specializes in seafood. Hrs: 11:30 am-10 pm; Fri, Sat to 11 pm; Sun brunch to 3 pm. Closed Dec 25. Res accepted. Bar to 2 am. A la carte entrees: lunch $4.95-$9.95, dinner $12.95-$20.95. Sun brunch $12.95. Child's meals. Entertainment wkends. Outdoor dining. French country atmosphere. Overlooks marina. Cr cds: A, DS, MC, V.

D SC

Robert Moses State Park (B-3)

(See also Bay Shore, New York City)

(On Fire Island, off south shore of Long Island, reached via Pkwys)

Reached by the Robert Moses Causeway, the park consists of 875 acres of choice sand at the west end of a 50-mile barrier beach along the south shore of Long Island. Park includes beach swimming, bathhouses; picnic shelter, playground, surf and bay fishing and a pitch-putt golf course. Standard fees. Headquarters is at Belmont Lake State Park, Babylon, Long Island 11702. For information phone 516/669-1000.

Rochester (D-4)

(See also Avon, Canandaigua)

Founded 1803 **Pop** 231,636 **Elev** 515 ft **Area code** 716 **E-mail** grva@frontiernet.net **Web** www.visitrochester.com

Information Greater Rochester Visitors Association, 126 Andrews St, 14604; 716/546-3070 or 800/677-7282.

Rochester is a high-tech industrial and cultural center and the third largest city in the state. Its educational institutions include University of Rochester with its Eastman School of Music and Rochester Institute of Technology with its National Technical Institute for the Deaf. The Vacuum Oil Company, a predecessor of Mobil Oil Corporation, was founded here in 1866. The city also has a symphony orchestra and professional theatre.

Rochester has its share of famous citizens too: Susan B. Anthony, champion of women's rights; Frederick Douglass, black abolitionist and statesman; George Eastman, inventor of flexible film; Hiram Sibley, founder of Western Union; and musicians Mitch Miller, Cab Calloway and Chuck Mangione.

The city is on the Genesee River, near its outlet to Lake Ontario, in the midst of rich fruit and truck-gardening country.

Transportation

Greater Rochester Intl Airport: Information 716/464-6000; lost and found 716/464-6001; weather 716/235-0240; cash machines, Terminal Building.

Car Rental Agencies: See IMPORTANT TOLL-FREE NUMBERS.

Public Transportation: Buses (Regional Transit Service), phone 716/288-1700.

Rail Passenger Service: Amtrak 800/872-7245.

What to See and Do

Genesee Country Village & Museum 20 mi SW via NY 36, in Mumford (see AVON).

George Eastman House. Eastman's 50-rm mansion and gardens contain restored rms with their original 1920s furnishings and decor; exhibit on the house's restoration project; audiovisual shows about George Eastman and on film processes used by Eastman Kodak. Adj to house is the archive bldg; 8 exhibit spaces display extensive collection of 19th- and 20th-century photography representing major photographers of the past 150 yrs. Chronological display presents evolution of photographic and imaging industries. Interactive displays present history of imaging with touchscreens, video stations and programmed audiovisual shows. Museum tours (twice daily). (Daily exc Mon; closed Jan 1, Thanksgiving, Dec 25) 900 East Ave. Phone 716/271-3361. ¢¢¢

Hamlin Beach State Park. Swimming beach (mid-June-Labor Day); fishing; nature, hiking, biking trails. Cross-country skiing, snowmobiling. Picnicking, playground, concession. Tent & trailer area (early May-mid-Oct). Recreation programs. Pets allowed in some camping areas. Standard fees. 25 mi W on Lake Ontario State Pkwy. Phone 716/964-2462. Per vehicle ¢¢

★ **High Falls in the Brown's Race Historic District.** Area between Inner Loop and Platt & State Sts, along the Genesee River Gorge. One of Rochester's earliest industrial districts has been renovated to preserve the area where flour mills and manufacturers once operated and Eastman Kodak and Gleason Works originated. Today the district still houses businesses in renovated historic bldgs such as the Eastman Techologies Bldg. **Center at High Falls,** on Brown's Race St, is an interpretive museum with hands-on interactive exhibits on the history of the area as well as info on other attractions to visit in Rochester. **Brown's Race Market** has been transformed from a maintenance facility of the Rochester Gas and Electric Corp into 3 levels of viewing for a 30-min laser light and sound show that tells the story of Rochester's history and also illuminates the 96-ft High Falls. For more info on area, phone 716/325-2030.

Memorial Art Gallery (Univ of Rochester). Permanent collection spanning 50 centuries of art, incl masterworks by Monet, Matisse and Homer; changing exhibitions. Cafe, gift shop. (Daily exc Mon; closed major hols) 500 University Ave. Phone 716/473-7720. ¢¢

Rochester Historical Society. HQ is "Woodside," Greek-revival mansion (1839). Collection of portraits, memorabilia, costumes. Reference library, manuscript collection. Garden. (Mon-Fri, also by appt; closed hols) 485 East Ave. Phone 716/271-2705. ¢-¢¢

Rochester Institute of Technology (1829). (13,000 students) Eight colleges, National Technical Institute for the Deaf on campus. Also on campus are the **Bevier Gallery** (academic yr, daily; summer, Mon-Fri; phone 716/475-2646) and **Frank Ritter Memorial Ice Arena** (phone 716/475-2223). Tours of campus. Jefferson Rd at E River Rd. Phone 716/475-6736.

Rochester Museum & Science Center. Complex featuring regional museum of natural science, anthropology, history and technology. Changing and permanent exhibits. (Daily; closed Jan 1, Dec 25) 657 East Ave, at Goodman St. Phone 716/271-4320. ¢¢

Strasenburgh Planetarium of the Rochester Museum and Science Center. Star Theatre shows, CineMagic 870 screen with special shows (call for times), educational exhibits. (Daily exc Mon; closed Dec 24-25) Phone 716/442-7171. ¢¢

Seneca Park Zoo. Animals from all over the world; free-flight bird rm, reptiles, Children's Discovery Center. Rocky Coasts features underwater viewing of polar bears and seals. (Daily) 2222 St Paul St, at jct NY 104. Phone 716/266-6846. ¢

Stone-Tolan House (ca 1792). Restored pioneer homestead and tavern; 4 acres of gardens and orchards. (Fri-Sun, closed hols) 2370 East Ave, 4 mi SE off I-490 in Brighton. Phone 716/442-4606. ¢¢

Strong Museum. Children's learning center with hands-on exhibits and over 500,000 toys, dolls, miniatures and more. Three-dimensional, interactive exhibit based on the Children's Television Workshop program, *Can You Tell Me How To Get To Sesame Street?* Glass atrium features a historic street scene with operating 1956 diner and 1918 carousel. (Mon-Sat, also Sun afternoons; closed Jan 1, Thanksgiving, Dec 25) One Manhattan Sq. Phone 716/263-2700. ¢¢

Susan B. Anthony House. Susan B. Anthony lived here for 40 yrs; she was arrested here for voting illegally in the 1872 presidential election. Mementos of the women's suffrage movement; furnishings. (Thurs-Sat afternoons; closed hols) 17 Madison St. Phone 716/235-6124. ¢¢

The Landmark Center (Campbell-Whittlesey House Museum) (1835). Greek-revival home, Empire furniture. Also Hoyt-Potter House with gift shop and exhibit area. Tours (Fri & Sat, call for times). 133 S Fitzhugh St, at Troup St. Phone 716/546-7029. ¢¢

Univ of Rochester (1850). (7,700 students) Medical Center, 601 Elmwood Ave, off Mt Hope Ave. Seven colleges and schools. Tours by appt. River Campus, Wilson Blvd, on Genesee River. Phone 716/275-3221 or 716/275-3222.On campus are

C.E.K. Mees Observatory. On Gannett Hill, in the Bristol Hills.For info on Sat sunset tours contact the Physics & Astronomy Dept; 716/275-0539. **Free.**

Eastman School of Music of the Univ of Rochester. Concerts, recitals, opera in Eastman Theatre, Howard Hanson Recital Hall and Kilbourn Hall. 26 Gibbs St. Performances ¢¢¢

Laboratory for Laser Energetics. Pioneering multidisciplinary teaching and research unit in laser and energy studies. Tours by appt, phone 716/275-9517.

Rush Rhees Library. Univ of Rochester's central library on River campus. Extensive collection of rare books, manuscripts. (Mon-Thurs; closed hols) **Free.**

Victorian Doll Museum. More than 1,000 dolls from the mid-1800s to the present. Toy circus, puppet show and dollhouses. Gift shop. (Tues-Sat, also Sun afternoons; closed hols & Jan) W via I-490, exit 4 (NY 259), N to Buffalo Rd (NY 33), turn right (E) ½ blk, at 4332 Buffalo Rd in North Chili, adj to Roberts Wesleyan College.Phone 716/247-0130. ¢

Annual Events

Lilac Festival. In Highland Park, Highland Ave. More than 500 varieties of lilacs. Parade, art show, entertainment and tours. Phone 716/256-4960. Mid-May.

Monroe County Fair. Monroe County Fairgrounds, E Henrietta and Calkins Rds. Agricultural exhibits and displays, amusement rides, games, entertainment. Phone 716/334-4000. Late June.

Corn Hill Arts Festival. Arts and crafts; entertainment. Phone 716/262-3142 . Mid-July.

Clothesline Festival. Grounds of the Memorial Art Gallery, 500 University Ave. Outdoor art show. Phone 716/473-7720, ext 3007. Mid-Sept.

Seasonal Events

Comedies, dramas and musicals. GeVa Theatre. 75 Woodbury Blvd. Resident professional theater. Phone 716/232-1363. Nightly exc Mon; Sat, Sun matinees. Sept-June.

Rochester Philharmonic Orchestra. Eastman Theater, Main & Gibbs. Symphonic concerts. Phone 716/454-2620. Sept-July.

Motels

★ ★ **COMFORT INN-WEST.** 1501 Ridge Rd W (14615). 716/621-5700; FAX 716/621-8446. 83 rms, 5 story. S $48.55-$53.95; D $53.55-$58.95; each addl $5; suites $104.35-$115.95; under 18 free. Crib free. Pet accepted, some restrictions. TV; cable (premium). Continental bkfst. Restaurant nearby. Ck-out noon. Business servs avail. In-rm modem link. Valet serv. Some in-rm whirlpools. Cr cds: A, C, D, DS, ER, JCB, MC, V.

D ⌨ ⊱ ⟋ 🔥 SC

★ ★ **COURTYARD BY MARRIOTT.** 33 Corporate Woods (14623). 716/292-1000; FAX 716/292-0905. 149 rms, 3 story. S, D $99; suites $120; under 18 free; wkend rates. Crib free. TV; cable (premium), VCR avail. Indoor pool; whirlpool, lifeguard. Complimentary coffee in rms. Restaurant 6:30-10 am; Sat, Sun 7 am-noon. Bar. Ck-out 1 pm. Coin lndry. Meeting rms. Business servs avail. In-rm modem link. Sundries. Free

airport transportation. Exercise equipt. Balconies. Cr cds: A, C, D, DS, MC, V.

D ⌨ ⍓ ⟋ 🔥 SC

★ **DAYS INN-DOWNTOWN.** 384 East Ave (14607). 716/325-5010; FAX 716/454-3158. 128 rms, 60 with shower only, 2 story. S $50-$68; D $55-$79; each addl $5; suites $89-$150; under 18 free; family rates. Crib free. TV; cable (premium). Complimentary continental bkfst. Restaurant nearby. Ck-out 11 am. Meeting rms. Business servs avail. In-rm modem link. Valet serv. Free airport, RR station, bus depot transportation. Exercise equipt; sauna. Whirlpool. Cr cds: A, D, DS, MC, V.

⍓ ⟋ 🔥 SC

✔ ★ **ECONO LODGE.** 940 Jefferson Rd (14623). 716/427-2700; FAX 716/427-8504. 102 rms, 3 story. S, D $49.95-$68.95; each addl $5; suites $89.95-$109.95; under 18 free. Crib free. Pet accepted, some restrictions. TV; cable (premium). Continental bkfst. Restaurant nearby open 24 hrs. Ck-out 11 am. Coin lndry. Business servs avail. Valet serv. Free airport transportation. Some in-rm whirlpools. Cr cds: A, C, D, DS, ER, JCB, MC, V.

D ⌨ ⟋ 🔥 SC

★ **ECONO LODGE-BROCKPORT.** (Jct NY 19 & 31, Brockport 14420) 716/637-3157; FAX 716/637-0434. 39 rms, 2 story. S $49-$55; D $53-$60; each addl $5; kit. units $63; under 18 free. Crib $5. TV; cable (premium). Pool. Playground. Complimentary continental bkfst. Restaurant nearby. Ck-out 11 am. Coin lndry. Business servs avail. Cr cds: A, D, DS, JCB, MC, V.

D ⟋ 🔥 SC

★ ★ **HAMPTON INN.** 717 E Henrietta Rd (14623). 716/272-7800; FAX 716/272-1211. 113 rms, 5 story. S, D $89-$99; under 18 free. Crib free. Pet accepted, some restrictions. TV; cable. Complimentary continental bkfst. Restaurant adj 11:30 am-midnight. Ck-out noon. Meeting rms. Business servs avail. In-rm modem link. Valet serv. Health club privileges. Cr cds: A, C, D, DS, MC, V.

D ⌨ ⟋ 🔥 SC

★ ★ **MARKETPLACE INN.** 800 Jefferson Rd (14623), I-390 exit 14. 716/475-9190; FAX 716/424-2138; res: 800/888-8102. 144 rms, 3 story. S $62-$89; D $69-$99; each addl $7; under 18 free. Crib free. Pet accepted, some restrictions. TV; cable (premium), VCR (free movies). Pool; poolside serv, lifeguard. Complimentary bkfst buffet Mon-Fri. Restaurants noon-midnight. Rm serv. Bar. Ck-out noon. Meeting rms. Business servs avail. In-rm modem link. Free airport transportation. Health club privileges. Cr cds: A, C, D, DS, MC, V.

⌨ ⍓ ⟋ 🔥 SC

✔ ★ **RED ROOF INN.** (4820 W Henrietta Rd, Henrietta 14467) I-90 exit 46. 716/359-1100; FAX 716/359-1121. 108 rms, 2 story. S $29.99-$54.99; D $34.99-$65.99; each addl $7; under 18 free. Crib $5. Pet accepted. TV; cable (premium). Restaurant nearby. Ck-out noon. Business servs avail. Cr cds: A, C, D, DS, MC, V.

D ⌨ ⟋ 🔥 SC

★ ★ **RESIDENCE INN BY MARRIOTT.** 1300 Jefferson Rd (14623). 716/272-8850; FAX 716/272-7822. 112 kit. suites, 2 story. S $99-$135; D $145-$175; under 18 free; wkly, monthly rates. Crib free. Pet accepted, some restrictions; $125 & $6/day. TV; cable (premium), VCR avail (movies). Pool; whirlpool, lifeguard. Complimentary continental bkfst. Complimentary coffee in rms. Restaurant nearby. Ck-out noon. Coin lndry. Meeting rms. Business servs avail. In-rm modem link. Sundries. Downhill ski 20 mi. Health club privileges. Picnic tables, grills. Cr cds: A, C, D, DS, ER, JCB, MC, V.

D ⌨ ⍓ ⟋ 🔥 SC

★ **WELLESLEY INN-NORTH.** 1635 W Ridge Rd (14615), I-390 exit 24. 716/621-2060; FAX 716/621-7102; res: 800/444-8888. 97 rms, 1 with shower only, 4 story. Apr-Nov: S, D $55-$95; each addl $5; under 18 free; higher rates some special events; lower rates rest of yr. Crib free. Pet accepted, some restrictions; $3. TV; cable (premium). Complimentary continental bkfst. Complimentary coffee in rms. Restaurant adj 5:30 am-10:30 pm. Ck-out 11 am. Business servs avail. Health club privileges. Some refrigerators. Cr cds: A, C, D, DS, MC, V.

[D] [icons] SC

★ **WELLESLEY INN-SOUTH.** *797 E Henrietta Rd (NY 15A) (14623). 716/427-0130; FAX 716/427-0903.* 96 rms, 4 story. S $45-$70; D $50-$85; each addl $6; suites $80-$110; under 18 free. Crib free. Pet accepted, some restrictions; $3. TV; cable (premium). Complimentary continental bkfst. Complimentary coffee in rms. Ck-out 11 am. Business servs avail. In-rm modem link. Sundries. Health club privileges. Cr cds: A, C, D, DS, MC, V.

[D] [icons] SC

Motor Hotels

★ ★ ★ **BROOKWOOD INN.** *(800 Pittsford-Victor Rd, Pittsford 14534) 11 mi E on I-490, Bushnell's Basin exit. 716/248-9000; FAX 716/248-8569; res: 800/426-9995.* 108 rms, 4 story. S $93; D $101; each addl $8; suites $145-$225; under 18 free; wkend rates. Crib free. TV; cable (premium). Indoor pool; whirlpool, poolside serv, lifeguard. Restaurant 6:30 am-10 pm. Rm serv 6:30 am-10 pm. Bar. Ck-out noon. Meeting rms. Business servs avail. In-rm modem link. Bellhops. Valet serv. Sundries. Airport transportation. Downhill ski 20 mi. Exercise equipt; sauna. Bicycle path along Erie Canal; bike rentals. Cr cds: A, C, D, DS, ER, MC, V.

[D] [icons] SC

★ ★ **HAMPTON INN.** *500 Center Place (14615). 716/663-6070; res: 800/426-7866; FAX 716/663-9158.* 118 rms, 4 story. Apr-Sept: S $72-$139; D $75-$179; under 18 free; higher rates special events; lower rates rest of yr. Crib free. Pet accepted. TV; cable (premium). Complimentary continental bkfst. Complimentary coffee in rms. Restaurant nearby. Ck-out noon. Meeting rms. Business servs avail. In-rm modem link. Bellhops. Valet serv. Exercise equipt. Microwaves avail. Picnic tables. Cr cds: A, D, DS, MC, V.

[D] [icons] SC

★ ★ ★ **HOLIDAY INN-AIRPORT.** *911 Brooks Ave (14624). 716/328-6000; FAX 716/328-1012.* 280 rms, 2 story. S $99-$119; D $109-$129; each addl $10; suites $200-$250; under 19 free. Crib free. Pet accepted, some restrictions. TV; cable (premium). Indoor pool; whirlpool, lifeguard. Coffee in rms. Restaurant 6 am-2 pm, 5-10 pm. Rm serv. Bar 11-2 am; entertainment. Ck-out noon. Coin lndry. Meeting rms. Business center. In-rm modem link. Bellhops. Concierge. Gift shop. Valet serv. Free airport transportation. Exercise equipt; sauna. Cr cds: A, C, D, DS, ER, MC, V.

[D] [icons] SC

★ ★ **MARRIOTT THRUWAY.** *5257 W Henrietta Rd (14602), 8 mi S on NY 15; I-90 exit 46. 716/359-1800; FAX 716/359-1349.* 305 rms, 5 story. S, D $115-$125; each addl $15; suites $275-$425; under 18 free; wkend rates. Crib free. TV; cable (premium). 2 pools, 1 indoor; whirlpool, poolside serv, lifeguard. Sauna. Complimentary coffee. Restaurant 6:30 am-10 pm. Rm serv. Bar 11-2 am; entertainment. Ck-out noon. Convention facilities. Business center. Bellhops. Valet serv Mon-Fri. Sundries. Gift shop. Free airport transportation. Putting green. Some refrigerators. Some private patios. Luxury level. Cr cds: A, C, D, DS, ER, JCB, MC, V.

[D] [icons] SC

★ ★ **MARRIOTT-AIRPORT.** *1890 W Ridge Rd (14615). 716/225-6880; res: 800/228-9290; FAX 716/225-8188.* 210 rms, 7 story. S, D $60-$130; each addl $10; suites $185-$310; under 18 free; wkend rates. Crib free. Pet accepted, some restrictions. TV; cable (premium), VCR avail. Indoor pool; whirlpool, poolside serv. Restaurant 6:30 am-11 pm. Rm serv. Bar 11-2 am, Sun from noon. Ck-out noon. Meeting rms. Business servs avail. In-rm modem link. Bellhops. Valet serv. Concierge. Sundries. Free airport transportation. Exercise equipt; sauna. Cr cds: A, C, D, DS, ER, JCB, MC, V.

[D] [icons] SC

★ ★ ★ **RADISSON.** *175 Jefferson Rd (14623), I-90 exit 46, adj Rochester Institute of Technology. 716/475-1910; res: 800/333-3333; FAX*

716/475-9633. 171 rms, 4 story. S $79-$139; D $89-$149; each addl $10; family, wkend rates. Crib free. TV; cable (premium). Indoor pool; lifeguard. Restaurant 6 am-10 pm, wkend 7-10 pm. Rm serv. Bar 11-2 am; entertainment Fri, Sat. Ck-out noon. Meeting rms. Business servs avail. In-rm modem link. Bellhops. Valet serv. Sundries. Free airport transportation. Exercise equipt; sauna. Lawn games. Cr cds: A, C, D, DS, ER, MC, V.

[D] [icons] SC

Hotels

★ ★ ★ **CROWNE PLAZA.** *70 State St (14614). 716/546-3450; res: 800/243-7760; FAX 716/546-8712.* 369 rms, 7 story. S, D $99-$165; suites $199-$299; under 18 free; family rates; package plans. Crib avail. Pet accepted, some restrictions. Garage parking $3/day. TV; cable (premium). Complimentary coffee in rms. Restaurant 6 am-2 pm, 5-10 pm. Rm serv 24 hrs. Bar 3 pm-2 am. Convention facilities. Business servs avail. In-rm modem link. Concierge. Gift shop. Free airport, RR station, bus depot transportation. Downhill ski 20 mi. Exercise equipt. Heated pool; lifeguard. Game rm. Some minibars. On river. Luxury level. Cr cds: A, DS, MC, V.

[D] [icons]

★ ★ ★ **FOUR POINTS BY SHERATON.** *120 E Main St (14604). 716/546-6400; res: 800/325-3535; FAX 716/546-3908.* Web www.fourpoints.com. 466 rms, 15 story. S, D $99-$119; suites $125-$350; under 19 free. Crib free. Pet accepted, some restrictions. TV; cable (premium). Heated pool; poolside serv. Complimentary coffee in rms. Restaurant 7 am-10 pm. Bar 11-2 am. Ck-out noon. Coin lndry. Convention facilities. Business servs avail. In-rm modem link. Shopping arcade. Exercise equipt; sauna. Some balconies. On river. Cr cds: A, C, D, DS, MC, V.

[D] [icons] SC

★ ★ ★ **HYATT REGENCY.** *125 E Main St (14604). 716/546-1234; FAX 716/546-6777.* 337 rms, 25 story. S, D $99-$165; each addl $25; suites $240-$390; under 18 free; wkly rates. Crib free. Parking garage $3. TV; cable (premium), VCR avail (movies). Indoor pool; whirlpool, poolside serv, lifeguard. Restaurant 6:30 am-10 pm. Rm serv to midnight. Bar 11:30-1:30 am. Ck-out noon. Convention facilities. Business center. In-rm modem link. Gift shop. Free airport transportation. Exercise equipt. Bathrm phones. Refrigerator, wet bar in suites. Luxury level. Cr cds: A, C, D, DS, ER, JCB, MC, V.

[D] [icons] SC

★ ★ ★ **STRATHALLAN.** *550 East Ave (14607), I-490 Goodman St exit. 716/461-5010; FAX 716/461-3387; res: 800/678-7284.* 156 rms, 8-9 story. S, D, suites, kit. units $155-$375; under 18 free; wkend plans. Crib free. TV; cable (premium). Complimentary coffee in rms. Restaurant 6:30 am-9:30 pm. Rm serv to 11:30. Bar 5 pm-1 am; entertainment Fri, Sat. Ck-out noon. Meeting rms. Business servs avail. In-rm modem link. Beauty shop. Free valet parking. Free airport transportation. Exercise equipt; sauna. Health club privileges. Refrigerators, microwaves. Many balconies. In sedate residential area. Luxury level. Cr cds: A, C, D, DS, MC, V.

[D] [icons] SC

Inns

★ ★ ★ **DARTMOUTH HOUSE.** *215 Dartmouth St (14607). 716/271-7872; res: 800/724-6298; FAX 716/473-0778.* E-mail stay@dartmouthhouse.com; web www.dartmouthhouse.com. 4 rms, 2 story, 1 suite. S $68-$80; D $95-$100. Children over 12 yrs only. TV; VCR (movies). Complimentary full bkfst; afternoon refreshments. Ck-out 11 am, ck-in 3-6 pm. Business servs avail. Free airport, RR station, bus depot transportation. Library/sitting rm. Health club privileges. English Tudor house (1905); antiques, fireplace. Near International Museum of Photography (George Eastman House). Totally nonsmoking. Cr cds: A, C, D, MC, V.

[icons]

★ ★ ★ **GENESEE COUNTRY.** *(948 George St, Mumford 14511) 12 mi S via NY 383. 716/538-2500; FAX 716/538-4565; res: 800/697-8297.* Web www.geneseecountryinn.com. 9 air-cooled rms, 2 story. S $80-$110;

D $85-$140; each addl $15; some wkends (2-day min); package plans. TV. Complimentary full bkfst; afternoon refreshments. Restaurants nearby; dinner pkgs avail. Ck-out noon, ck-in 3 pm. Meeting rm. Gift shop. Picnic table, grill. Restored inn (1830) on 8 wooded acres; fishing in spring-fed trout stream; waterfall. Antiques; fireplaces. Totally nonsmoking. Cr cds: A, D, DS, MC, V.

⊡ ⊠ ⊠

★ ★ **OLIVER LOUD'S.** *(1474 Marsh Rd, Pittsford 14534) I-490 E to Bushnell's Basin exit.* 716/248-5200; FAX 716/248-9970. E-mail rchi@frontiernet.net; web www.frontiernet.net/rchi. 8 rms, 2 story. S $125; D $135-$145. Children over 12 yrs only. TV avail; cable. Complimentary continental bkfst in rms; afternoon refreshments. Restaurant (see RICHARDSON'S CANAL HOUSE). Ck-out 11 am, ck-in 3 pm. Business servs avail. In-rm modem link. On Erie Canal. Built 1812; stagecoach inn. Totally nonsmoking. Cr cds: A, C, D, MC, V.

D ⊠ ⊠

✔ ★ ★ **THE VICTORIAN.** *(320 Main St, Brockport 14420) N on US 490 to NY 104 W, approx 19 mi.* 716/637-7519; res: 800/836-1929. E-mail skehoe1@juno.com; web www.32.com/victorianbandb. 8 rms, 1 with shower only, 2 story. S $45-$70; D $59-$84; each addl $14; wkly rates; hols 2-day min. TV; cable, VCR avail (movies). Complimentary full bkfst. Restaurant nearby. Ck-out 11 am, ck-in 3 pm. Business servs avail. Golf privileges. Downhill ski/x-country ski 3 mi. Built in 1890; Queen Anne Victorian house. Totally nonsmoking. No cr cds accepted.

⊠ ⊠ SC

Restaurants

✔ ★ **BANGKOK.** *163 State St (14614).* 716/325-3517. Thai menu. Specializes in vegetarian dishes, seafood. Hrs: 11 am-10 pm; Fri, Sat to 11 pm. Closed Easter, Thanksgiving. Res accepted Fri, Sat. Wine, beer. Semi-a la carte: lunch $4.95-$6.25, dinner $6.50-$12.95. Parking (dinner). Thai decor. Cr cds: DS, MC, V.

D ⊡

★ ★ **BRASSERIE.** *387 E Main St (14604), at Eastman Place.* 716/232-3350. French, continental menu. Specializes in fresh fish, black Angus steak. Menu changes seasonally. Hrs: 11:30 am-4 pm, 5:30-10:30 pm. Closed Sun; most major hols. Res accepted. Bar. Wine list. A la carte entrees: lunch $12-$20, dinner $20-$30. Valet parking. Outdoor dining. 2 dining rms. Country French atmosphere. Cr cds: A, C, D, DS, MC, V.

D ⊡

★ ★ **CARTWRIGHT INN.** *(5691 W Henrietta Rd, W Henrietta 14586) I-90 exit 46.* 716/334-4444. Specializes in New England clam chowder, prime rib, lobster. Hrs: 11:30 am-10 pm; Sun from 12:30 pm; early-bird dinner 4:30-6:30 pm. Res accepted. Bar to 2 am. Semi-a la carte: lunch $3.50-$5.95, dinner $6.95-$18.95. Child's meals. Parking. In former stagecoach stop; built 1831. Cr cds: A, C, D, DS, MC, V.

D SC ⊡

★ ★ ★ **EDWARDS.** *13 S Fitzhugh (14614).* 716/423-0140. Specializes in seafood, beef, wild game. Own baking. Hrs: 11:30 am-2 pm, 5-9 pm; Fri, Sat to 10 pm. Closed Sun; major hols. Res accepted. Bar. Wine cellar. Complete meals: lunch $4.50-$12.50, dinner $12.50-$25.50. Pianist. Valet parking. Gourmet store on premises. Built 1873 as school; Edwardian decor. Cr cds: A, C, D, DS, MC, V.

⊡

★ ★ ★ **MARIO'S VIA ABRUZZI.** *2740 Monroe Ave (14618).* 716/271-1111. E-mail danielejd@aol.com; web www.5a/marios. Italian menu. Specializes in seafood, meats. Own pasta. Hrs: 5-10 pm; Fri to 11 pm; Sat 4-11 pm; Sun 4-9 pm; Sun brunch 11 am-2 pm. Closed some major hols. Res accepted. Bar. Wine cellar. Semi-a la carte: dinner $12.95-$23.95. Sun brunch $16.95. Child's meals. Strolling musicians Sat (dinner). Parking. Outdoor dining. Authentic central Italian architecture; original

paintings, sculptures. Family-owned since 1979. Totally nonsmoking. Cr cds: A, D, DS, MC, V.

D

★ ★ **OLIVE TREE.** *165 Monroe Ave (14607).* 716/454-3510. Greek menu. Specialties: seafood in filo, lamb, baklava. Hrs: 11:30 am-2 pm, 5-9 pm; Sat from 5 pm. Closed Sun; Jan 1, Thanksgiving, Dec 25. Res accepted. Bar. Semi-a la carte: lunch $4-$8.50, dinner $10.50-$17.50. Parking. Outdoor dining. Restored dry goods store (1864). Cr cds: A, MC, V.

✔ ★ **RAJ MAHAL.** *324 Monroe Ave (14607).* 716/546-2315. Indian menu. Specializes in tandoori and vegetarian dishes. Hrs: 11:30 am-2:30 pm. Closed some major hols. Res accepted wkends. Bar. Buffet lunch $6.99. Semi-a la carte: dinner $6.95-$14.95. Parking. Traditional Indian decor. Cr cds: A, C, D, DS, MC, V.

D SC ⊡

★ ★ **RICHARDSON'S CANAL HOUSE.** *(See Oliver Loud's Inn)* 716/248-5000. Contemporary American menu. Specializes in duckling, seafood, beef tenderloin. Own baking. Hrs: 6-9 pm. Closed Sun; Jan 1, Dec 25. Res accepted. Bar 4:30-11 pm; Fri, Sat to midnight. Wine list. Complete meals: dinner $35. Parking. Outdoor dining. Historic inn. Terrace overlooks Erie Canal. Cr cds: A, C, D, ER, MC, V.

D

★ ★ **THE RIO.** *282 Alexander St (14607).* 716/473-2806. Continental menu. Specialties: Dover sole, veal di Medici, rack of lamb. Hrs: 5-10 pm; early-bird dinner Mon-Fri 5-6:30 pm. Closed Sun; most major hols. Res accepted. Bar to midnight. Wine cellar. A la carte entrees: dinner $18-$27. Pianist Fri, Sat evenings. Valet parking. Intimate dining. Curved stairway in entry hall; antiques. Cr cds: A, C, D, DS, MC, V.

⊡

★ ★ **ROONEY'S.** *90 Henrietta St (14620).* 716/442-0444. Specializes in wood-grilled fish & game. Own baking. Hrs: 5-10 pm. Closed Thanksgiving, Dec 25. Res accepted. Wine cellar. Semi-a la carte: dinner $16-$24. Parking. In tavern built 1860, the original bar is still in use. Cr cds: A, D, DS, MC, V.

D ⊡

★ ★ **SCOTCH 'N SIRLOIN.** *3450 Winton Place (14623).* 716/427-0808. Specializes in steak, seafood. Salad bar. Hrs: 5-10 pm; Fri, Sat to 11 pm. Closed Mon; most major hols. Res accepted. Bar. Semi-a la carte: dinner $9-$25. Child's meals. Parking. Old West decor; antiques. Cr cds: A, C, D, MC, V.

SC ⊡

★ **TOKYO JAPANESE.** *2930 W Henrietta Rd (14623).* 716/424-4166. Japanese, vegetarian menu. Specializes in sushi, hibachi dishes. Hrs: 11:30 am-10 pm; Fri, Sat to 11 pm; Sun 4-10 pm. Closed Thanksgiving. Res accepted. Bar. Semi-a la carte: lunch $5.25-$8.95, dinner $7.50-$20.95. Child's meals. Parking. Traditional decor. Cr cds: A, DS, MC, V.

D SC ⊡ ♥

✔ ★ **VILLAGE COAL TOWER.** *(9 Schoen Place, Pittsford 14534) Approx 10 mi S on NY 96.* 716/381-7866. Specializes in hamburgers, chicken, salads. Hrs: 7 am-8 pm; wkends from 8 am. Semi-a la carte: bkfst $2-$4, lunch $2-$5, dinner $4-$6. Child's meals. Parking. Outdoor dining. In turn-of-the-century coal storage structure used to service boats on Erie canal. No cr cds accepted.

D SC ⊡

Unrated Dining Spot

TIVOLI PASTRY SHOP. *688 Park Ave.* 716/461-4502. Specializes in frozen yogurt, ice cream, bakery items. Hrs: 11 am-11 pm; Fri to midnight; Sat 10 am-midnight; Sun 10 am-11 pm. Closed Dec 25. A la carte entrees: $1-$3.25. Outdoor dining. Some antiques. Murals of Venice. No cr cds accepted.

Rockville Centre, L.I. (B-2)

(See also Hempstead, New York City)

Pop 24,727 **Elev** 25 ft **Area code** 516 **Zip** 11570
Information Chamber of Commerce, PO Box 226; 516/766-0666.

Incorporated in 1893, Rockville Centre maintains Long Island atmosphere in the midst of a thriving commercial district. The town boasts 200 acres of parkland and is a short ride from several fine beach areas.

What to See and Do

Rock Hall Museum (1767). Historic house with period furnishings and exhibits. (Apr-Nov, daily exc Tues) 5 mi SW on Broadway from Sunrise Hwy W, at 199 Broadway in Lawrence. Phone 516/239-1157.   **Free.**

Restaurants

★ ★ **BUON GIORNO.** *(476 Merrick Rd, Lynbrook 11563) S on Southern State Pkwy, exit 19 S.* 516/887-1945. Northern Italian menu. Specializes in veal scallopini, fish, chicken. Own pasta. Hrs: noon-3 pm, 5-10 pm; Sat 5-11 pm; Sun 4-9 pm. Closed Mon; most major hols. Res required wkends. Bar. Semi-a la carte: lunch $11-$15, dinner $11.95-$22.95. Formal dining. Original artwork. Cr cds: A, C, D, DS, MC, V.

D

★ ★ **COYOTE GRILL.** *(104 Waterview Rd, Island Park) 5 mi S on Long Beach Rd.* 516/889-8009. Southwestern menu. Specializes in fresh seafood, venison, rabbit. Hrs: noon-4 pm, 5-10 pm; Mon, Tues from 5 pm; Fri, Sat to 11 pm; Sun brunch to 3 pm. Closed Dec 25. Res accepted. Bar. A la carte entrees: lunch $6-$15, dinner $13-$22. Sun brunch $16-$18. Child's meals. Parking. Outdoor dining. Southwestern artifacts and decor. Cr cds: A, MC, V.

D

★ ★ **GEORGE MARTIN.** *65 N Park Ave.* 516/678-7272. Continental menu. Specializes in grilled meat and seafood. Hrs: 11:30 am-3 pm, 5-11 pm; Fri, Sat to midnight; Sun 5-10 pm. Closed Easter, Thanksgiving, Dec 25. A la carte entrees: lunch $4.95-$12.95, dinner $6.95-$24.95. Bistro-style decor and furnishings. Cr cds: A, MC, V.

D

★ **MAIER'S BRICK CAFE.** *(157 Lakeview Ave, Lynbrook 11563) Southern St Pkwy exit 17S, left fork on Ocean Ave, 1 mi right.* 516/599-9669. Specializes in steak. Hrs: 5-10 pm; Fri, Sat to midnight; Sun brunch noon-4 pm. Closed Thanksgiving, Dec 25. Res accepted. Bar. A la carte entrees: dinner $7.50-$19.75. Sun brunch $9.95. Pub atmosphere. Family-owned. Cr cds: A, D, DS, MC, V.

D

✔★ **RAAY-NOR'S CABIN.** *(550 Sunrise Hwy, Baldwin) E on Merrick Rd (NY 27) to Baldwin.* 516/223-4886. Specialties: barbecued chicken & ribs, Southern-fried chicken, sugar-cured ham steak. Hrs: noon-9 pm; Sat to 10 pm. Closed Dec 25. Res accepted. Bar. A la carte entrees: lunch $4.95-$7.95; dinner $8.95-$16.50. Child's meals. Parking. Family-style dining in log cabin. Rustic decor. Cr cds: A, D, MC, V.

★ ★ **SCHOONER.** *(435 Woodcleft Ave, Freeport) 3 mi E on Merrick Rd (NY 27), right on Guy Lombardo Ave, right on Front St.* 516/378-7575. Specializes in seafood, steak, chicken. Hrs: noon-9:30 pm; Fri, Sat to 11 pm; Sun 3-9:30 pm. Closed Dec 25; also 2nd & 3rd wks Jan.

Semi-a la carte: lunch $8.95-$16.95, dinner $13.95-$29.50. Valet parking. Nautical decor; overlooks Woodcleft Canal. Cr cds: A, D, MC, V.

D

Rome (D-6)

(See also Boonville, Canastota, Oneida, Utica)

Settled 1786 **Pop** 44,350 **Elev** 462 ft **Area code** 315 **Zip** 13440 **E-mail** info@romechamber.com **Web** www.romechamber.com
Information Rome Area Chamber of Commerce, 139 W Dominick St; 315/337-1700.

Originally the site of Fort Stanwix, where, during the Revolutionary War, tradition says the Stars and Stripes were first flown in battle. The author of the "Pledge of Allegiance," Francis Bellamy, is buried in Rome. Griffiss AFB is located here.

What to See and Do

Delta Lake State Park. Swimming beach (Memorial Day wknd-mid-June, limited days; mid-June-Labor Day, full-time), bathhouse; fishing; boating (ramp); tent & trailer sites; hiking, biking. Cross-country skiing. Picnicking, playground. Standard fees. 6 mi NE off NY 46. Phone 315/337-4670.

Erie Canal Village. Trips on restored section of the Erie Canal aboard mule-drawn 1840 canal packetboat, *The Chief Engineer*. Buildings of 1840s canal village incl church, blacksmith shop, train station, museums, schoolhouse, Victorian home, stable, settlers house; hotel; orientation center; picnic area & restaurant. (Mid-May-Labor Day, daily; call for extended schedule) 2¹/₂ mi W on NY 49. Phone 315/337-3999 or 888/374-3226.   ¢¢¢

Ft Rickey Children's Discovery Zoo. Restoration of 1700s British fort is site of a zoo that emphasizes animal contact. Wide variety of wildlife. Picnic facilities. (Memorial Day-Labor Day, daily; Sept, Sat & Sun only) 3 mi W via NY 49. Phone 315/336-1930.   ¢¢

Ft Stanwix National Monument. Reconstructed earth-and-log fort on location of 1758 fort; here the Iroquois signed a treaty opening territory east of Ohio River to colonial expansion. In 1777 fort was besieged by British; Gen Benedict Arnold forced their retreat. Costumed guides; film; museum. (Apr-Dec, daily; closed Thanksgiving, Dec 25) Phone 315/336-2090.   ¢

Tomb of the Unknown Soldier of the American Revolution. Designed by Lorimar Rich, who also designed the tomb at Arlington Natl Cemetery. 201 N James St.

Woods Valley Ski Area. Two double chairlifts, T-bar; patrol, snowmaking, school, rentals; bar, cafeteria. Longest run 3,700 ft, vertical drop 500 ft. (Dec-Mar, daily exc Mon; closed Dec 25) Some evening rates. 8 mi N on NY 46 in Westernville. Phone 315/827-4721 or 315/827-4206 (snow conditions).   ¢¢¢¢¢

Annual Event

World Series of Bocce. Italian lawn bowling. Mid-July.

Motels

★ ★ **PAUL REVERE LODGE.** 7900 Turin Rd. 315/336-1776; FAX 315/339-2636; res: 800/765-7251. Web www.thebeeches.com. 75 rms, 1-2 story, 6 kits. S $56-$63; D $62-$69; each addl $5; kit. units $85-$99; under 12 free; wkly rates; wkend rates. Crib free. Pet accepted, some restrictions; $20 deposit. TV; cable. Pool. Restaurant 6-10 am; Sat, Sun 8 am-noon. Ck-out 11 am. Business center. Downhill/x-country ski 8 mi. Lawn games. Refrigerator, microwaves avail. 52 acres with pond. Cr cds: A, C, D, DS, MC, V.

D

✔★★ QUALITY INN. *200 S James St, at Erie Blvd & S. James.* 315/336-4300; FAX 315/336-4492. 103 rms, 2 story. S, D $65-$78; each addl $10; suite $125; under 18 free. Crib free. TV; cable. Pool. Complimentary coffee in rms. Restaurant open 24 hrs. Ck-out 11 am. Coin lndry. Business servs avail. Game rm. Downhill/x-country ski 8 mi. Microwaves avail. Cr cds: A, C, D, DS, ER, JCB, MC, V.

Restaurants

★★ MICHELINA'S. *Turin Rd (NY 26), in The Beeches.* 315/336-1700. Specializes in fresh beef, veal, chicken. Hrs: 11:30 am-2:30 pm, 5-9:30 pm; Sat 5-10 pm; Sun brunch to 1:30 pm. Closed Mon; Jan 1, Dec 24, 25. Res accepted. Bar. Semi a la carte: lunch $4.25-$8, dinner $14-$29. Sun brunch $9.50. Child's meals. Original decor from '20s estate. Family-owned. Cr cds: A, C, D, DS, MC, V.

D

✔★★ SAVOY. *255 E Dominick St.* 315/339-3166. Italian, Amer menu. Specializes in own pasta, fresh seafood, steak. Hrs: 11:30 am-10 pm; Sat 5-11 pm; Sun 4-9 pm. Closed Thanksgiving, Dec 25. Res accepted. Bar. Semi-a la carte: lunch from $3.95, dinner $5.95-$15.95. Child's meals. Pianist Wed, Fri, Sat. Family-owned. Cr cds: A, C, D, DS, MC, V.

D

Roscoe (F-7)

(See also Liberty)

Pop 950 (est) **Elev** 1,300 ft **Area code** 607 **Zip** 12776 **E-mail** troutown **Web** www.chamber@roscoeny.com

Information Roscoe-Rockland Chamber of Commerce, Box 443; 607/498-6055.

Dutch settlers conquered the wilderness in this Catskill area, but in the process did not destroy it, a practice continued by those who followed. Small and large game abound in the area, and the Willowemoc and Beaverkill rivers provide excellent trout fishing. Four unusual and interesting covered bridges are located in the surrounding countryside.

What to See and Do

Catskill Fly Fishing Center & Museum. Fishing, hiking, demonstrations, programs and events. Interpretive exhibits featuring the heritage, science and art of the sport. Explore the lives of legendary characters who made angling history. Displays of rods, reels, flies, video rm, library, hall of fame. Visitor center; gift shop. (Apr-Oct, daily; Nov-Mar, Tues-Sat) Old Rte 17, between Roscoe & Livingston Manor. Phone 914/439-4810. ¢¢

Motel

✔★ ROSCOE. *Old Route 17, W on Old NY 17.* 607/498-5220. 18 rms. S $40; D $45-$55; each addl $10; kit. units $60; Apr-Oct wkends (2-day min). Crib free. Pet accepted. TV; cable. Pool. Complimentary continental bkfst. Ck-out 11 am. Some refrigerators. Picnic tables, grill. On Beaverkill River. Cr cds: MC, V.

Inn

★★★ THE GUEST HOUSE. *(223 Debruce Rd, Livingston Manor 12758) 3 mi E on Debruce Rd exit 96.* 914/439-4000; FAX 914/439-3344. 7 rms, 4 with shower only, 1-2 story, 2 suites, 1 guest house. Apr-Nov: S, D $145-$190; suites $290; guest house $260; package plans; wkends 2-day min; hols 3-day min; lower rates rest of yr. Pet accepted, some

restrictions. TV; cable (premium). Complimentary full bkfst. Complimentary coffee in rms. Restaurant nearby. Ck-out noon, ck-in 11 am. Business servs avail. Luggage handling. Airport transportation. Tennis. X-country ski on site. Exercise equipt. Massage. Indoor pool; whirlpool. On river. Country inn; antiques. Cr cds: A, MC, V.

Roslyn, L.I. (B-2)

(See also Floral Park, Westbury)

Pop 1,965 **Elev** 38 ft **Area code** 516 **Zip** 11576

Hotel

★★★ ROSLYN CLAREMONT. *1221 Old Northern Blvd, L.I. Expy (I-495) exit 37N, Roslyn Rd to Old Northern Blvd.* 516/625-2700; FAX 516/625-2731; res: 800/626-9005. 76 rms, 3 story. S $169-$199; D $189-$219; suites $275-$325. Crib $15. TV; cable (premium), VCR avail. Coffee in rms. Restaurant 7 am-10 pm. Rm serv 24 hrs. Bar; entertainment. Ck-out noon. Meeting rms. Business servs avail. In-rm modem link. Concierge. Exercise equipt; steam rm. Minibars. Cr cds: A, C, D, DS, MC, V.

D

Restaurants

★★★ BRYANT AND COOPER STEAK HOUSE. *Northern Blvd & Middle Neck Rd.* 516/627-7270. Specialties: prime steak, jumbo lobster, lamb & veal chops. Own breads. Hrs: noon-10 pm; Fri to 11 pm; Sat 5 pm-midnight; Sun 3-10 pm. Closed Dec 25. Res accepted. Bar. Wine cellar. Semi-a la carte: lunch $8-$15. A la carte entrees: dinner $14-$28. Valet parking. Cr cds: A, C, D, MC, V.

★★ CLASSICO. *(1042 Northern Blvd, Roslyn Estates) W on Northern Blvd.* 516/621-1870. Northern Italian menu. Specialties: coniglio al forno, trippa al classico, polenta con quaglie. Hrs: 4-11 pm; Wed-Fri from noon; Sun to 10 pm. Closed Jan 1, Dec 25. Res accepted. Bar. Semi-a la carte: lunch, dinner $12.50-$25. Complete meal: lunch $14.50. Own baking. Musicians Sat. Valet parking. Italian decor with murals, stucco walls, frosted glass. Cr cds: A, D, MC, V.

D

★★★ GEORGE WASHINGTON MANOR. *1305 Old Northern Blvd.* 516/621-1200. Specialties: country-style pot pie, Yankee pot roast. Hrs: 11:30 am-10 pm; Sun brunch 11:30 am-3 pm. Closed Dec 25. Res accepted. Bar. Wine list. Complete meals: lunch $10.95-$14.95, dinner $14-$21.95. Sun brunch $10.95-$14.95. Valet parking. Elegant dining in historic colonial mansion (1740). Cr cds: A, C, D, DS, MC, V.

D

★★ JOLLY FISHERMAN & STEAK HOUSE. *25 Main St.* 516/621-0055. Specializes in seafood, steak. Hrs: noon-9 pm; Fri, Sat to 11 pm; Sun 1-9 pm. Closed Mon; Yom Kippur, Thanksgiving. Res accepted. Bar. Semi-a la carte: dinner $15.95-$25.95. Complete meals: lunch $16.95, dinner $34.95. A la carte entrees: lunch $7.95-$16.95. Child's meals. Valet parking. Nautical decor. Overlooks lake. Family-owned. Cr cds: A, C, D, MC, V.

D

★★★ L'ENDROIT. *290 Glen Cove Rd.* 516/621-6630. French, continental menu. Specialties: foie de veau Bercy, lamb à l'endroit, salmon en crôute. Own baking. Hrs: 11:30 am-2:45 pm, 5-10 pm; Fri, Sat to 11 pm. Closed Sun; Jan 1, Thanksgiving, Dec 25. Res accepted; required wkends. Bar. Wine list. A la carte entrees: lunch $9.50-$22, dinner $14.95-$29.50. Valet parking. Original artwork. Cr cds: A, C, D, MC, V.

D

★ ★ ★ **LA COQUILLE.** *(1669 Northern Blvd, Manhasset 11030) 1 mi W on NY 25A (Northern Blvd).* 516/365-8422. French menu. Specializes in veal, chicken, lamb. Hrs: 5-10 pm; Fri, Sat to 11 pm; Sun 5-9 pm. Closed some major hols. Res required. A la carte entrees: dinner $20-$30. Valet parking. French villa decor. Jacket. Cr cds: A, C, D, JCB, MC, V.

[D]

★ ★ ★ **LA MARMITE.** *(234 Hillside Ave, Williston Park) S to I-495, exit 37S, E on NY 25B.* 516/746-1243. Continental menu. Specialties: roast rack of lamb; ravioli stuffed with shrimp, scallops and lobster. Own baking, pasta. Hrs: noon-3 pm, 5:30-10 pm; Sat 6-11 pm. Closed Sun; Jan 1, Dec 25. Res accepted. Bar. Wine cellar. A la carte entrees: lunch $5.25-$14.50, dinner $15.75-$25.75. Valet parking. Jacket. Cr cds: A, C, D, MC, V.

[D]

★ **LA PARMA.** *(707 Willis Ave, Williston Park)* 516/294-6610. Southern Italian menu. Specializes in lobster, pasta, veal. Hrs: noon-2:30 pm, 5-10 pm; Fri to midnight; Sat 4 pm-midnight; Sun 3-9 pm. Closed Mon. Res accepted hols. Bar. A la carte entrees: lunch $10-$15, dinner $20-$30. Valet parking. Family-style dining. Cr cds: A, C, D, MC, V.

[D]

★ ★ **RIVERBAY SEAFOOD BAR & GRILL.** *(700 Willis Ave, Williston Park) directly SW.* 516/742-9191. Specialties: sea bass, pompano, halibut. Hrs: noon-10 pm; Fri to 11 pm; Sat 5-11 pm; Sun 4-9:30 pm; Sun brunch 11:30 am-1:30 pm. Closed Thanksgiving, Dec 25. Bar. Semi-a la carte: lunch $5.50-$15, dinner $10-$17.50. Sun brunch $19.50. Valet parking. Cr cds: A, C, D, MC, V.

[D]

Rouses Point (A-8)

(See also Plattsburgh)

Pop 2,377 **Elev** 103 ft **Area code** 518 **Zip** 12979

A border town on a main route to Montreal, Rouses Point is a busy customs inspection point. A toll bridge across Lake Champlain goes to Vermont.

What to See and Do

Fort Lennox. Large stone fort built 1819-1829 on an island in the Richelieu River. Tours; picnic area, cafe; ferry (mid-May-early Sept, daily; fee). (For border-crossing regulations, see MAKING THE MOST OF YOUR TRIP.) St-Paul Île aux Noix, Quebec, Canada, 10 mi N off Hwy 223. Phone 514/291-5700. ¢¢

Sackets Harbor (C-5)

(See also Watertown)

Settled 1800 **Pop** 1,313 **Elev** 278 ft **Area code** 315 **Zip** 13685

This is a lakeside resort area for the eastern Lake Ontario region. Two major battles of the War of 1812 occurred here. In the first skirmish, the British warships invading the harbor were damaged and withdrew; a landing force was repulsed in the second battle.

What to See and Do

Sackets Harbor Battlefield State Historic Site. War of 1812 battlefield; Federal-style Union Hotel (1818); Commandant's House (1850) (fee); US Navy Yard (1812-1955); visitor center, exhibits; demonstrations; tours. (Mid-May-early Sept, daily) 505 W Washington St, overlooking lake. Phone 315/646-3634. **Free.**

Westcott Beach State Park. Swimming beach, bathhouse; fishing; boating (launch); hiking and nature trails. Cross-country skiing, snowmobiling. Picnicking, playground, concession. Tent & trailer sites. (Mid-May-Columbus Day wkend) Standard fees. 2 mi S on NY 3. Phone 315/938-5083.

Motor Hotel

★ ★ **ONTARIO PLACE.** *103 General Smith Dr.* 315/646-8000; FAX 315/646-2506. E-mail hotel@imcnet.net; web www.imcnet.net/Ontario_Place/Hotel.htm. 38 rms, 3 story, 13 suites. Mid-May-mid-Oct: D $69-$79; each addl $10; suites $125-$150; under 14 free; wkly rates; lower rates rest of yr. Crib free. Pet accepted, some restrictions. TV; cable, VCR avail. Restaurant nearby. Ck-out 11 am. Meeting rms. Business servs avail. In-rm modem link. Gift shop. Bicycles avail. Some bathrm phones. Refrigerators avail. Cr cds: A, D, DS, MC, V.

[D] [icons] [SC]

Restaurant

★ ★ **OLD STONE ROW.** *336 Brady Rd.* 315/646-2923. Continental menu. Specializes in fresh seafood, seasonal dishes. Hrs: 5-9 pm. Closed Mon; Thanksgiving, Dec 25. Res accepted. Bar. Semi-a la carte: dinner $9.95-$16.95. Patio dining. Former barracks built 1816; view of parade ground. Cr cds: A, C, D, DS, MC, V.

[D]

Sag Harbor, L.I. (A-5)

(See also Amagansett, East Hampton, Shelter Island, Southampton)

Settled 1660 **Pop** 2,134 **Elev** 14 ft **Area code** 516 **Zip** 11963
Information Chamber of Commerce, PO Box 2810, 516/725-0011.

This great whaling town of the 19th century provided prototypes from which James Fenimore Cooper created characters for his sea stories. Sheltered in a cove of Gardiners Bay, the economy of Sag Harbor is still centered around the sea.

What to See and Do

Custom House. Served as custom house and post office during the late 18th and early 19th centuries; antique furnishings. (July-Aug, daily exc Mon; May-June & Sept-Oct, Sat & Sun) Garden St. Phone 516/692-4664. ¢¢

Morton Natl Wildlife Refuge. A 187-acre sanctuary with sandy and rocky beaches and wooded bluffs. Nature trails; ponds and lagoon for wildlife observation, nature study, photography and environmental education. (Daily; beach closed Apr-Aug) 4 mi W on Noyack Rd. Phone 516/286-0485. Per vehicle ¢¢

Sag Harbor Whaling and Historical Museum. Relics of whaling days and historical artifacts in the former home of Benjamin Huntting, local ship owner. (Mid-May-Oct, daily) Garden & Main Sts. Phone 516/725-0770. ¢¢

Restaurants

★ ★ ★ **AMERICAN HOTEL.** *Main St.* 516/725-3535. French menu. Hrs: 5-10 pm; Sat, Sun also noon-4 pm. Closed Jan 1, Dec 24, 25. Res accepted. Bar. A la carte entrees: lunch $7.95-$18.50, dinner $17.95-$28.50. Inn built in 1846. Atrium rm. Cr cds: A, C, D, DS, MC, V.

[D]

✔★ ★ **IL CAPUCCINO.** *Madison St.* 516/725-2747. Northern Italian menu. Hrs: 5:30-10:30 pm; Fri, Sat to 11 pm; Sun 5-10 pm. Closed Thanksgiving, Dec 25. Serv bar. A la carte entrees: dinner $11.95-$15.95. Child's meals. Cr cds: A, MC, V.

★ ★ SPINNAKER'S. *(63 Main St, Sag Harbor) 516/725-9353.* Specializes in lobster, homemade desserts. Hrs: 11:30 am-10 pm; Fri, Sat to 11 pm. Closed Thanksgiving. Res accepted. Bar. A la carte entrees: lunch $5-$8, dinner $12-$20. Sun brunch $6-$9. Child's meals. Piano bar Sat evenings. Dining rm has dark wood and brass accents. Cr cds: A, D, MC, V.

D

Saranac Lake (B-8)

(See also Lake Placid, Tupper Lake)

Settled 1819 **Pop** 5,377 **Elev** 1,534 ft **Area code** 518 **Zip** 12983 **E-mail** besttown@northnet.org **Web** www.saranaclake.com

Information Chamber of Commerce, 30 Main St; 518/891-1990 or 800/347-1997.

Surrounded by Adirondack Park (see), the village of Saranac Lake was first settled in 1819 when one Jacob Moody, who had been injured in a sawmill accident, retired to the wilderness, built a log cabin at what is now Pine and River streets and raised a family of mountain guides. The qualities that attracted Moody and made the town a famous health resort in the 19th century continue to lure visitors in search of fresh, mountain air and a relaxing environment.

What to See and Do

Fishing. More than 130 well-stocked ponds and lakes plus 600 mi of fishing streams.

Meadowbrook State Public Campground. Tent sites, picnicking. (Mid-May-mid-Oct) 4 mi E on NY 86, in Adirondack Park (see). Phone 518/891-4351. Per site ¢¢¢

Mt Pisgah Municipal Ski Center. Five slopes, T-bar; patrol, snacks. Longest run 1,800 ft, vertical drop 300 ft. (Mid-Dec-mid-Mar, daily exc Mon) 3 mi NE on NY 86. Phone 518/891-0970. ¢¢¢¢¢

Robert Louis Stevenson Memorial Cottage. Where Robert Louis Stevenson lived while undergoing treatment for tuberculosis, 1887-1888; mementos. (July-mid-Sept, daily exc Mon) Schedule and fee may vary, phone ahead for confirmation. 11 Stevenson Lane. Phone 518/891-1462. ¢

Six Nations Indian Museum. Indoor and outdoor exhibits portray the life of the Native American, with a council ground, types of fires, ancient and modern articles; lecture on Native American culture and history. (July-Aug, daily exc Mon) On Buck Pond Rd, off NY 3, in Onchiota. Phone 518/891-2299. ¢¢

Annual Events

Winter Carnival. Parade; skating, ski, snowshoe and snowmobile racing. Early Feb.

Willard Hanmer Guideboat, Canoe & War Canoe Races. Lake Flower & Saranac River. Early July.

Adirondack Canoe Classic. Ninety-mi race from Old Forge to Saranac Lake for canoe, kayak, guideboat. 2nd wkend Sept.

Motels

★ ADIRONDACK. *23 Lake Flower Ave. 518/891-2116; res: 800/416-0117; FAX 518/891-1405.* 14 rms, 1-2 story, 4 kits. S, D $40-$85; each addl $5; kit. units $60-$100; wkly rates. Crib $5. Pet accepted. Complimentary continental bkfst. Restaurant nearby. Ck-out 11 am. Refrigerators. Picnic tables, grills. Paddle boats, canoes. On lake. Cr cds: A, C, DS, MC, V.

⇆ ⇆ ⊠ ⊠ SC

★ LAKE FLOWER INN. *15 Lake Flower Ave. 518/891-2310.* 14 rms. Late June-late Sept: S, D $58-$98; each addl $10; under 18 free; higher rates special events; lower rates rest of yr. Crib free. Pet accepted. TV; cable (premium). Pool. Ck-out 11 am. Downhill ski 20 mi; x-country ski 2 mi. Picnic tables. On lake. Cr cds: A, MC, V.

⇆ ⇆ ⊠ ⊠ ⊠ ⊠

★ LAKE SIDE. *27 Lake Flower Ave. 518/891-4333.* 22 rms. July-mid-Oct: S $59-$79; D $69-$89; each addl $5; kit. units $79-$99; higher rates: some hol wkends, special events; lower rates rest of yr. Crib free. Pet accepted. TV; cable (premium). Heated pool. Complimentary coffee in lobby. Restaurant nearby. Ck-out 11 am. Downhill ski 20 mi; x-country ski 2 mi. Canoes, rowboats, paddle boats avail. Patio. Picnic tables, grills. Overlooks lake; private sand beach. Cr cds: A, DS, MC, V.

⇆ ⇆ ⊠ ⊠ ⊠ ⊠ SC

✔★ ★ SARA-PLACID MOTOR INN. *120 Lake Flower Ave. 518/891-2729; FAX 518/891-5624; res: 800/794-2729.* Web www.capital.net/com/placid. 18 rms, 3 suites, 7 kits, 1 cottage. Some A/C. Mid-June-mid-Oct: S, D $58-$78; each addl $8; suites, kit. units $58-$175; higher rates: winter carnival, major hols; lower rates rest of yr. TV; cable (premium), VCR avail. Complimentary bkfst. Restaurant adj. Ck-out 11 am. Tennis. X-country ski on site. Ice-skating. Paddle boats. Picnic tables, grills. Opp lake. Cr cds: A, D, DS, MC, V.

D ⇆ ⊠ ⊠ ⊠ ⊠ SC

★ SARANAC INN GOLF AND COUNTRY CLUB. *HCR1, Box 16, 14 mi W, 5 mi S of jct NY 30, 86. 518/891-1402; FAX 518/891-1309.* E-mail JConnor@northnet.org. 10 rms. May-Oct: D $220 (incl golf & cart). Closed rest of yr. TV. Restaurant 7 am-3:30 pm. Bar. Ck-out 11 am. 18-hole golf, greens fee $50, putting green, driving range. Cr cds: MC, V.

⊠ ⊠ ⊠

Hotel

✔★ ★ HOTEL SARANAC OF PAUL SMITH'S COLLEGE. *101 Main St. 518/891-2200; FAX 518/591-5664; res: 800/937-0211.* E-mail hsaranac@paulsmiths.edu; web www.hotelsaranac.com. 92 rms, 6 story. Mid-June-mid-Oct: S, D $69-$79; each addl $10; under 18 free; golf, ski plans; lower rates rest of yr. TV; cable, VCR avail (movies). Restaurant (see A P SMITH). Bar 11-1 am. Ck-out 11 am. Meeting rms. Business servs avail. Gift shop. X-country ski 2 mi. Historic hotel (1927); lobby replica of foyer in Danvanzati Palace in Florence, Italy. Cr cds: A, C, D, DS, MC, V.

D ⊠ ⊠ ⊠ SC

Resort

★ ★ ★ ★ ★ THE POINT. *HCR 1, Box 65. 518/891-5674; FAX 518/891-1152; res: 800/255-3530.* E-mail thepoint@northnet.org; web www.pointny.com. This exclusive hideaway resort is located on a 10-acre wooded peninsula on Upper Saranac Lake. Built during the 1930s for William Avery Rockefeller, the buildings are made of local stone and wood. 11 units in 3 bldgs. Reservations & advance payment required. AP: S, D $850-$1,350; each addl $200; 2-day min wkends, 3-day min hols. Adults only. 15% serv charge. TV rm; VCR. Dining rm with gourmet meals, jacket & tie requested for dinner. Bar. Golf privileges. X-country ski on site; snowshoes avail. Bicycles. Lawn games. Game rm. Stone fireplace in each unit. Cr cds: A, MC, V.

⇆ ⊠ ⊠

Restaurant

★ ★ A P SMITH. *(See Hotel Saranac Of Paul Smith's College) 518/891-2200.* Web www.paulsmiths.edu/hsaranac. Hrs: 7 am-1:30 pm, 5-9 pm; Sun brunch 10 am-1:30 pm. Res accepted. Bar 11 am-9 pm; wkends to 10 pm. Semi-a la carte: bkfst $2.75-$6.25, lunch $3.95-$7.50, dinner $9.95-$14.95. Buffet (Thurs): dinner $12.95. Sun brunch $9.95.

Child's meals. Bakery. College-operated as training facility. Totally non-smoking. Cr cds: A, D, DS, MC, V.

Saratoga National Historical Park (D-8)

(See also Glens Falls, Saratoga Springs)

(30 mi N of Albany on US 4, NY 32)

In two engagements, September 19 and October 7, 1777, American forces under General Horatio Gates defeated the army of General John Burgoyne in the Battles of Saratoga. This brought France into the war on the side of the colonies. The battle is regarded as the turning point of the War of Independence. The scene of this historic event is the rolling hill country between US 4 and NY 32, five miles north of Stillwater. Park folders with auto tour information are available at the Visitor Center. (Daily; closed Jan 1, Thanksgiving, Dec 25). Phone 518/664-9821. Per vehicle ¢¢

What to See and Do

Battlefield. Living history demonstrations (Feb-Oct).

General Philip Schuyler House (1777). Home of patriot officer who commanded Northern Army before Gates. (Mid-June-Labor Day, Wed-Sun) 8 mi N on US 4 in Schuylerville.   **Free.**

John Neilson House. Restored American staff headquarters. (Usually June-Sept)

Saratoga Monument. Granite 155-ft obelisk commemorates surrender of Crown forces under Burgoyne to American forces under Gates on Oct 17, 1777. Burgoyne Rd, W of US 4 in Schuylerville.

Tour road. Self-conducted; 9 mi long; 10 stops where exhibits interpret history. (Early Apr-Nov, weather permitting)

Visitor Center and Museum. Visitor orientation. Exhibits and film program explain the battles.   **Free.**

Saratoga Springs (D-8)

(See also Glens Falls)

Settled 1773 **Pop** 25,001 **Elev** 316 ft **Area code** 518 **Zip** 12866 **E-mail** info@saratoga.org **Web** www.saratoga.org

Information Saratoga County Chamber of Commerce, 28 Clinton St; 518/584-3255.

Saratoga Springs is a resort city that is rural, yet cosmopolitan. Much of the town's Victorian architecture has been restored. Saratoga Springs boasts the springs, geysers and mineral baths that first made the town famous; internationally recognized harness and Thoroughbred racing and polo; respected museums; as well as the Saratoga Performing Arts Center.

What to See and Do

High Rock Spring. Now inactive; the original Saratoga Spring. Rock St at High Rock Ave.

Historic Congress Park. The Museum of the Historical Society and the Walworth Memorial Museum are housed in the old casino (1870). The museums trace the history of the city's growth, highlighting the springs, hotels, gambling and personalities; also Ann Grey Art Gallery; gift shop. Museums (Apr-Oct, daily; rest of yr, Wed-Sun afternoons; closed Thanksgiving, Dec 24-Jan 1). Park (daily). On Broadway. Phone 518/584-6920. ¢

National Bottle Museum. Antique bottles, jars, stoneware and related items; research library on bottle collecting. (June-Oct, daily; rest of yr,

Mon-Fri) 6 mi S via NY 50, at 76 Milton Ave in Ballston Spa. Phone 518/885-7589. ¢

National Museum of Dance. Dedicated to American professional dance. Exhibits, hall of fame, museum shop, cafe. (Late May-Labor Day, daily exc Mon) 99 S Broadway. Phone 518/584-2225. ¢¢

Petrified Sea Gardens. Reefs of fossilized organisms; glacial crevices and potholes; sundials, museum. Picnic, hiking and recreation areas. (Early May-Nov, daily) 3 mi W, off NY 29. Phone 518/584-7102 or 518/272-7844. ¢

Saratoga Lake. Boating, fishing, waterskiing. Fee. 3 mi E on NY 9P.

Saratoga Natl Historical Park (see).

Saratoga Equine Sports Center. Harness racing (Feb-Nov). Nelson Ave. Phone 518/584-2110. ¢

⭐**Saratoga Spa State Park.** This 2,200-acre park is home to the performing arts center, mineral bath houses, golf and many other recreational facilities. Visitor center. (Daily) S Broadway, 1 mi S on US 9 or SW on NY 50. Phone 518/584-2535. Per vehicle ¢¢

Lincoln and Roosevelt Baths. Treatments with the mineral waters. Baths, massage, hot packs. Roosevelt (all yr, Wed-Sun); Lincoln (July & Aug, daily). Phone 518/584-2011 or 518/583-2880.

Recreation Center. Swimming, diving, wading pools (June-Labor Day, daily). Victoria Pool; Peerless Pool complex; mineral springs and geysers; 2 golf courses (Mid-Apr-Nov). Picnicking.

Saratoga Performing Arts Center. Amphitheater in natural setting seats 5,000 under cover with space for more on the lawn. The Little Theatre is a 500-seat indoor showcase for chamber music. (See SEASONAL EVENTS)

Seasonal Events

Saratoga Performing Arts Center. Phone 518/587-3330. New York City Opera, June; New York City Ballet, July. The Philadelphia Orchestra and Saratoga Chamber Music Festival, Aug. Jazz festival, summer.

Saratoga Race Course. Union Ave, ¼ mi SW from exit 14 off I-87. Thoroughbred racing. Phone 518/584-6200. Late July-Labor Day.

Polo. Saratoga Polo Assoc. Saratoga Equine Sports Center. July & Aug. Also from Broadway St, W on Church St, then N on Seward. Phone 518/584-8108. Aug.

Motels

✔★ ★ **BEST WESTERN PLAYMORE FARMS.** *S Broadway,* 1½ *mi S on US 9;* ¾ *mi N of I-87 exit 13N.* 518/584-2350; FAX 518/584-2480. 36 rms. S $45-$75; D $50-$85; each addl $10; suites $75-$120; family, wkly rates (racing season). Crib $5. TV; cable (premium). Heated pool. Complimentary coffee in lobby. Restaurant nearby. Ck-out 11 am. X-country ski 2 mi. Refrigerators. State park nearby. Cr cds: A, C, D, DS, MC, V.

★ ★ **GRAND UNION.** *92 S Broadway.* 518/584-9000. 64 rms. S,D $45-$71; each addl $10; higher rates special events. Crib free. Pet accepted; $10. TV; cable. Pool; mineral bath spa. Sauna. Complimentary coffee in lobby. Restaurant adj 8 am-10 pm. Ck-out 11 am. Bellhops (seasonal). Sundries. Lawn games. Some refrigerators. Grill. Victorian-style lobby. Only private mineral bath spa in NY. Cr cds: MC, V.

★ ★ **ROOSEVELT SUITES.** *S Broadway, I-87, exit 13N.* 518/584-0980; FAX 518/581-8472; res: 800/524-9147. 34 rms, 2 story, 10 suites. June-mid-Oct: S, D $79.50-$89.50, each addl $10; suites $99.50-$109.50; higher rates special events; lower rates rest of yr. Crib $5. TV; cable (premium), VCR (movies $4). Heated pool. Complimentary continental bkfst. Restaurant 7 am-11 pm; Mon, Tues 11 am-10 pm. Rm serv. Bar. Ck-out 11 am. Meeting rms. Business servs avail. Tennis. Refrigerators; some in-rm whirlpools. Balconies. Picnic tables. Cr cds: A, DS, MC, V.

✔★ **THE SPRINGS.** *165 Broadway. 518/584-6336; FAX 518/587-8164.* 28 rms, 2 story. May-mid-July: S $44-$65; D $50-$68; each addl $5; under 16 free; higher rates special events (racing season); varied lower rates rest of yr. Crib $5. TV; cable. Pool. Complimentary coffee in rms. Restaurant nearby. Ck-out 11 am. Refrigerators. Cr cds: A, MC, V.

≈ 🏊 SC

Motor Hotel

★★ **HOLIDAY INN.** *232 Broadway. 518/584-4550; FAX 518/584-4417.* E-mail hisara@capital.net; web www.hisaratoga.com. 168 rms, 4 story. S, D $84-$249; each addl $10; suites $199-$459; under 19 free; wkly, ski rates. Crib free. Pet accepted. TV. Heated pool; poolside serv. Restaurant 6:30 am-10 pm. Rm serv. Bar 11-2 am. Ck-out 11 am. Coin lndry. Meeting rms. Business servs avail. In-rm modem link. Bellhops. Valet serv. Downhill ski 20 mi; x-country ski 1 mi. Exercise equipt. Health club privileges. Cr cds: A, C, D, DS, JCB, MC, V.

D 🐾 ≈ 🏊 🏋 🏊 🏊 SC

Hotels

★★ **ADELPHI.** *365 Broadway. 518/587-4688; FAX 518/587-0851.* Web www.adelphihotel.com. 39 rms, 3 story, 18 suites. S, D $95-$155; each addl $15; suites $130-$205; higher rates racing season (3-day min). Crib free. TV; cable (premium). Pool. Complimentary continental bkfst. Bar 5:30 pm-2 am. Ck-out noon. Meeting rm. Cr cds: A, MC, V.

≈ 🏊

★★★ **GIDEON PUTNAM.** *24 Gideon Putnam Rd, 1/2 mi S on US 9, located in Saratoga Spa State Park, adj Performing Arts Center. 518/584-3000; FAX 518/584-1354; res: 800/732-1560.* 132 rms, 5 story. Apr-Nov: S, D $130-$150; each addl $15; suites $170-$190; under 16 free; higher rates racing season; lower rates rest of yr. Crib free. TV; cable. Pool; lifeguard. Restaurant 7-10 am, noon-2 pm, 6-9 pm; Fri & Sat to 10 pm. Bar noon-closing; entertainment (seasonal). Ck-out noon. Meeting rms. Business servs avail. Gift shop. Downhill ski 15 mi; x-country ski on site. Lawn games. Some porches. Mineral bath. Cr cds: A, D, DS, MC, V.

D 🐾 ≈ 🏊 🏊 🏊 SC

★★ **THE INN AT SARATOGA.** *231 Broadway. 518/583-1890; res: 800/274-3573; FAX 518/583-2543.* E-mail info@theinnatsaratoga.com; web www.theinnatsaratoga.com. 38 rms, 3 story. Late June-late July: S, D $105-$145; each addl $15; suites $127-$147; under 12 free; higher rates special events (racing season); lower rates rest of yr. TV; cable. Complimentary continental bkfst. Dining rm 5-9 pm. Ck-out 11 am. Meeting rms. Business servs avail. Bellhops (in season). Downhill ski 15 mi; x-country ski 1 mi. Health club privileges. Some refrigerators. Established 1881. Cr cds: A, C, D, DS, MC, V.

D 🏊 🏊 🏊 SC

★★★ **SHERATON.** *534 Broadway, at City Center. 518/584-4000; res: 800/325-3535; FAX 518/584-7430.* 240 rms, 5 story. S, D $99-$130; each addl $10; suites $125-$275; under 18 free. Crib free. Pet accepted. TV; cable (premium); VCR avail. Indoor pool; lifeguard. Coffee in rms. Restaurant 7 am-10 pm. Bar 11-1 am; entertainment, Wed-Sat (summer). Ck-out noon. Meeting rms. Business center. Concierge. Gift shop. Tennis privileges. 18-hole golf privileges, pro. X-country ski 2 mi. Exercise equipt. Game rm. Some bathrm phones, refrigerators. Some balconies. Luxury level. Cr cds: A, C, D, DS, ER, JCB, MC, V.

D 🐾 ≈ 🏋 🏌 ≈ 🏊 🏊 🏊 SC 🏃

Inn

★★ **WESTCHESTER HOUSE.** *102 Lincoln Ave. 518/587-7613.* 7 rms, 2 story. No rm phones. S, D $80-$150; wkend rates; higher rates: Jazz Festival, racing season, special events. Closed Jan. Complimentary continental bkfst; afternoon refreshments. Restaurant nearby. Ck-out 11 am, ck-in 4 pm. In-rm modem link. Queen Anne Victorian house

(1885) in historical residential area. Oriental carpets, antiques. Garden. Totally nonsmoking. Cr cds: A, MC, V.

🏊

Restaurants

★★★ **CHEZ PIERRE.** *(340 US 9, Gansevoort 12831) 9 mi N on US 9. 518/793-3350.* E-mail chezpier@capital.net. French menu. Specialties: steak au poivre, veal Oscar, shrimp Madagascar. Hrs: 5-10 pm. Closed Dec 24-25. Res accepted. Bar. Semi-a la carte: dinner $14.95-$22.95. Child's meals. Family-owned. Cr cds: A, MC, V.

★ **THE OLD FIRE HOUSE.** *543 Broadway. 518/587-0047.* Specializes in seafood, steak. Hrs: 11:30 am-midnight; Sun from noon. Closed Thanksgiving, Dec 25. Res accepted. Bar. Semi-a la carte: lunch $4.50-$9.25, dinner $9.95-$20.95. Child's meals. Outdoor dining. Converted 1800s fire house; brick walls, exposed beams. Cr cds: A, C, D, MC, V.

D

★ **OLDE BRYAN INN.** *123 Maple Ave. 518/587-2990.* Specializes in fresh seafood, fettucine, prime rib. Hrs: 11 am-11 pm; Fri, Sat to midnight; Sun brunch to 1 pm. Closed Memorial Day, Thanksgiving, Dec 24, 25. Bar. Semi-a la carte: lunch $3.95-$6.95, dinner $10.95-$17.95. Sun brunch $5.95-$8.95. Child's meals. Outdoor dining. Stone house (1825); fireplaces. Cr cds: A, C, D, DS, MC, V.

D 🔲

Saugerties (E-8)

(See also Cairo, Hudson, Kingston, Woodstock)

Pop 18,467 **Elev** 155 ft **Area code** 914 **Zip** 12477

At the confluence of Esopus Creek and the Hudson River, Saugerties was a port of call for riverboats. The town was famous for building racing sloops and for the production of fine paper, leather and canvas.

What to See and Do

Cortina Valley Ski Area. Two double chairlifts, 2 pony lifts; patrol, school, rentals; all snow manufactured; restaurant, cafeteria, lodge, bar. Longest run 5,200 ft, vertical drop 625 ft. (Thanksgiving-Mar) Night skiing avail. 10 mi NW in Haines Falls. For days, hrs phone 518/589-6500. ¢¢¢¢¢

Opus 40 & Quarryman's Museum. Environmental sculpture rising out of an abandoned bluestone quarry. More than 6 acres of fitted bluestone constructed over 37 yrs by sculptor Harvey Fite. Site of Sunset Concert series and other programs. **Quarryman's Museum** houses collection of quarrymen's and other tools. (Memorial Day-Columbus Day, Fri-Sun; some Sat reserved for special events) 50 Fite Rd. Phone 914/246-3400. ¢¢

Motel

★ **COMFORT INN.** *2790 NY 32, I-90 exit 20. 914/246-1565; FAX 914/246-1631.* 66 rms. S $65-$89; D $65-$99; each addl $6; suites, kit. unit $69-$109; under 12 free. Crib free. TV; cable (premium). Complimentary continental bkfst. Restaurant adj 6 am-midnight. Ck-out 11 am. Meeting rms. Business servs avail. Whirlpool in suites. Some refrigerators, microwaves. Cr cds: A, C, D, DS, MC, V.

D 🏊 🏊 SC

Restaurant

✔★★★ **CAFE TAMAYO.** *89 Partition St. 914/246-9371.* French, Amer menu. Specialties: confit of duck, capellini pasta, crème brulée. Hrs: 5-9:30 pm; Thurs-Sat noon-2:30 pm; Sun brunch 11:30 am-3 pm. Closed

Mon, Tues; July 4, Dec 25. Bar. Wine list. Semi-a la carte: lunch $5.50-$9.50, dinner $12-$20. Outdoor dining. Victorian building (1864). Guest rms avail. Cr cds: DS, MC, V.

Sayville, L.I. (B-3)

(See also Bay Shore)

Pop 16,550 **Elev** 20 ft **Area code** 516 **Zip** 11782
Information Chamber of Commerce, Montauk Hwy & Lincoln Ave, PO Box 235; 516/567-5257.

What to See and Do

Long Island Maritime Museum. Local maritime exhibits; oyster cull house (ca 1870); Frank E. Penny Boatshop (1900); tug boat *Charlotte* (1888); oyster vessel *Priscilla* (1888); oyster sloop *Modesty* (1923). (Wed-Sun; closed most major hols) 1 mi W on Montauk Hwy, West Ave, in West Sayville. Phone 516/854-4974. **Free.**

Motels

★ ★ **HOLIDAY INN MAC ARTHUR AIRPORT.** *(3845 Veterans Memorial Hwy, Ronkonkoma 11741) 4 mi SE of I-495; L.I. Expy exit 57, at MacArthur Airport. 516/585-9500; FAX 516/585-9550.* E-mail holi ronk@aol.com; web www.holiday-inn.com/hotels/ronny. 289 rms, 2 story. S $145; D $155; each addl $10; suites $175-$225; under 19 free; wkend packages. Crib free. TV; cable (premium). Pool; lifeguard. Restaurant 6:30 am-10 pm. Rm serv. Bar 11:30-2 am; entertainment. Ck-out noon. Gift shop. Meeting rms. Business servs avail. In-rm modem link. Bellhops. Valet serv. Concierge. Airport, RR station, bus depot transportation. Exercise equipt. Refrigerators avail. Cr cds: A, C, D, DS, JCB, MC, V.

D ⊠ ✕ ✕ ✕ ⊠ SC

★ ★ **INN AT MEDFORD.** *(2695 NY 112, Medford 11763) S of LI Expy exit 64. 516/654-3000; FAX 516/654-1281; res: 800/626-7779.* 76 rms, 2 story. May-Sept: S $89-$99; D $99-$109; each addl $10; suites $140-$175; under 12 free; package plans; higher rates hols; lower rates rest of yr. Crib free. TV; cable, VCR avail (movies $4). Pool. Complimentary continental bkfst. Lounge 4:30 pm-midnight. Ck-out 11 am. Business servs avail. Bellhops. 18-hole golf privileges. Exercise equipt. Health club privileges. Game rm. Cr cds: A, C, D, DS, MC, V.

D ✕ ⊠ ✕ ✕ ⊠ SC

Hotel

★ ★ **BEST WESTERN MACARTHUR.** *(1730 N Ocean Ave, Holtsville 11742) Long Island Expwy exit 63. 516/758-2900; FAX 516/758-2612.* 134 rms, 3 story. S, D $99-$150; suites $179; under 12 free; lower rates in winter. Crib $5. TV; cable (premium). Indoor pool; whirlpool. Complimentary continental bkfst. Restaurant 11 am-11 pm. Bar. Ck-out noon. Meeting rms. Business servs avail. In-rm modem link. Refrigerators avail. Cr cds: A, C, D, DS, MC, V.

D ⊠ ⊠ ⊠ SC

Restaurants

★ ★ **BELLPORT.** *(159 S Country Rd, Bellport 11713) 5 mi E on County 85, 3 mi SE on County 36. 516/286-7550.* Specializes in crab cakes, rack of lamb. Hrs: 5:30-10 pm; Fri, Sat to 11 pm; Sun noon-9 pm; Sun brunch to 4:30 pm. Closed Tues; Dec 25. Res accepted. Bar. A la carte entrees: dinner $11.50-$19.50. Cr cds: MC, V.

D

★ **CHOWDER HOUSE.** *(19 Bellport Lane, Bellport) Sunrise Hwy exit 56, then 2 mi S on Station Rd. 516/286-2343.* Specializes in seafood. Hrs: 11:30 am-11 pm; Fri, Sat to midnight; Sun noon-11 pm; Sun

brunch to 3 pm. Closed Dec 25. Res accepted. Bar. A la carte entrees: lunch $5.95-$12.95, dinner $12.95-$24.95. Sun brunch $9.95. Parking. Outdoor dining. Cr cds: A, MC, V.

★ ★ **LE SOIR.** *(825 Montauk Hwy, Bayport 11705) 3 mi E on County 65. 516/472-9090.* French menu. Specializes in seasonal local fare. Own pastries. Hrs: 5-10 pm; Sat 2 sittings: 6:30 pm & 9:15 pm. Closed Mon; July 4, Thanksgiving, Dec 25. Bar. Complete meals: dinner $17.50-$24.95. Parking. Country French chalet. Cr cds: A, MC, V.

★ ★ ★ **RIVERVIEW.** *(Consuelo Place, Oakdale) 1 mi S of Montauk Hwy on Vanderbilt Blvd. 516/589-2694; FAX 516/589-2785.* Specializes in châteaubriand, live lobster. Hrs: noon-10 pm; Sat 6-11 pm; Sun brunch 11 am-2:30 pm. Res accepted wkends. Bar to 2 am. Wine list. A la carte entrees: lunch $8-$14, dinner $18.50-$26. Complete meals: dinner $19.95. Sun brunch $18.95. Child's meals. Patio dining. Reggae Fri, jazz Sun. Parking. View of Connetquot River. In Commodore Vanderbilt's "tea house." Deep water docking. Cr cds: A, C, D, MC, V.

D

★ ★ **SNAPPER INN.** *(500 Shore Dr, Oakdale 11769) 1½ mi S of Montauk Hwy. 516/589-0248.* Specializes in lobster, lamb chops. Hrs: noon-9:30 pm; Fri to 10 pm; Sat to 10:30 pm; Sun noon-9 pm; Sun brunch noon-3 pm. Closed Mon; Dec 25. Res accepted. Bar. Semi-a la carte: lunch $6.25-$12.50, dinner $15.25-$26.75. Sun brunch $17.75. Child's meals. Parking. Outdoor dining. Overlooks Connetquot River. Family-owned. Cr cds: A, C, D, MC, V.

D

Schenectady (D-8)

(See also Albany, Amsterdam, Saratoga Springs, Troy)

Settled 1661 **Pop** 65,566 **Elev** 224 ft **Area code** 518 **E-mail** ffazio@wsg.net **Web** www.schenectadychamber.org
Information Schenectady County Chamber of Commerce, 306 State St, 12305; 518/372-5656 or 800/962-8007.

Schenectady offers a unique blend of the old and the new, from row houses of the pre-Revolutionary War stockade area to the bustle and vitality of the downtown area.

What to See and Do

Proctor's Theatre (1926). Former movie/vaudeville palace is a regional performing arts center hosting Broadway touring shows, dance, opera and plays. 1931 Wurlitzer theater organ. Seats 2,700. Built by F.F. Proctor and designed by Thomas Lamb, its interior incorporates elegance and grandeur; pastoral mural by A. Lundberg. Free tours by appt. 432 State St. For ticket info, phone 518/346-6204.

The Historic Stockade Area. Privately owned houses, some dating to colonial times, many marked with historic plaques. **Schenectady County Historical Society**, 32 Washington Ave, offers guided tours of their building and folder describing walking tour. The society also maintains a historical museum with collection of Sexton and Ames paintings; also 19th-century dollhouse, Shaker collection, genealogical library. (Mon-Fri afternoons, also 2nd Sat of month). Downtown. Phone 518/374-0263. Individual ¢; Family ¢¢

The Schenectady Museum & Planetarium and Schenectady Heritage Area. Exhibits and programs on art, history, science and technology. (Daily exc Mon; closed major hols) Planetarium shows and children's planetarium shows (Sat & Sun) Nott Terrace Heights, off Nott Terr. Phone 518/382-7890. ¢¢

Union College (1795). (2,000 students) Country's first planned campus; original bldgs (1812-1814) by French architect Joseph Jacques Ramée. Nott Memorial (1875), only 16-sided bldg in the Northern Hemisphere. Also on campus is Jackson Garden, 8 acres of landscaped and informal plantings. Tours of campus. Union Ave & Union St. Phone 518/388-6000.

Annual Events

Festival of Nations. 3rd Sat May.

Walkabout. Walking tour of 6 houses and 3 churches in the Historic Stockade Area. Last wkend Sept.

Motels

★ ★ **BEST WESTERN ROTTERDAM.** *2788 Hamburg St (12303), Rt 7 to Rt 146.* 518/355-1111; FAX 518/356-3817. 50 rms, 2 story, 6 suites. Aug: S $87; D $93; each addl $10; suites $150; under 12 free; higher rates fall foliage season; lower rates rest of yr. Crib $10. TV; cable (premium). Indoor pool. Restaurant 5-10 pm; closed Sun, Mon. Rm serv. Bar from 4 pm. Ck-out 11 am. Meeting rms. Business servs avail. Sundries. Refrigerators avail. Cr cds: A, C, D, DS, MC, V.

D ⊠ ⊠ ⊠ SC

✔★ ★ **DAYS INN.** *167 Nott Terrace (12308).* 518/370-3297; FAX 518/370-5948. 68 rms, 3 story. Apr-Oct: S $75-$79; D $80-$85; each addl $5; under 18 free; lower rates rest of yr. Crib free. TV; cable (premium). Complimentary continental bkfst. Restaurant nearby. Ck-out noon. Business servs avail. Downhill/x-country ski 20 mi. Some in-rm whirlpools, refrigerators. Cr cds: A, C, D, DS, JCB, MC, V.

⊠ ⊠ ⊠ SC

Motor Hotels

★ ★ ★ **HOLIDAY INN.** *100 Nott Terrace (12308), at Franklin St.* 518/393-4141; FAX 518/393-4174. 184 rms, 4 story. S $69-$100; D $75-$125; suites $250; under 18 free; higher rates: college events, racing season. Crib free. Pet accepted, some restrictions. TV; cable (premium). Indoor pool; whirlpool. Complimentary bkfst. Restaurant 6:30-10 am, 5-10 pm. Rm serv. Bar 11-1 am; wkends noon-1 am. Ck-out noon. Meeting rms. Business servs avail. In-rm modem link. Valet serv. Coin lndry. Free airport, RR station transportation. Downhill/x-country ski 20 mi. Exercise equipt; sauna. Wet bar in suites. Cr cds: A, C, D, DS, JCB, MC, V.

D ⊠ ⊠ ⊠ ⊠ ⊠ ⊠ SC

★ ★ **RAMADA INN.** *450 Nott St (12308).* 518/370-7151; FAX 518/370-0441. Web www.ramada.com/ramada.html. 170 rms, 7 story. S, D $68-$78; each addl $10; suites $110; under 18 free; higher rates Aug. TV; cable, VCR avail (movies). Indoor pool; whirlpool, lifeguard. Restaurant 6:30 am-10 pm. Rm serv. Bar 5 pm-2 am; wkends from 11 am. Ck-out noon. Coin lndry. Meeting rms. Business servs avail. Valet serv. Sundries. Exercise equipt; sauna. Game rm. Refrigerators. Cr cds: A, C, D, DS, JCB, MC, V.

D ⊠ ⊠ ⊠ ⊠ SC

Inn

★ ★ ★ **GLEN SANDERS MANSION.** *(1 Glen Ave, Scotia 12302) 1/2 mi W on NY 5.* 518/374-7262; FAX 518/382-8348. E-mail gsmansion@aol.com; web www.glensandersmansion.com. 22 rms, 2 story, 2 suites. Aug: S, D $109; suites $175-$275; under 18 free; family rates; lower rates rest of yr. Crib $10. TV; cable (premium). Complimentary continental bkfst. Restaurant (see GLEN SANDERS MANSION). Ck-out 11 am, ck-in 3 pm. Business servs avail. In-rm modem link. Valet serv. Gift shop. Downhill/x-country ski 15 mi. In-rm whirlpool, fireplace in suites. Some balconies. On river. Mansion's kitchen was built in 1600s. Cr cds: A, C, D, DS, MC, V.

D ⊠ ⊠ ⊠

Restaurant

★ ★ ★ **GLEN SANDERS MANSION.** *(See Glen Sanders Mansion Inn)* 518/374-7262. Hrs: 11:30 am-2 pm, 5-10 pm; Sat 5-10 pm; Sun 4-9 pm; Sun brunch 10:30 am-1:30 pm. Closed major hols. Res required Sat, Sun. Continental menu. Bar. Wine cellar. Semi-a la carte: dinner $6.95-

$25.95. Sun brunch $15.95. Specializes in seafood. Parking. Cr cds: A, C, D, DS, MC, V.

Schroon Lake (C-8)

(See also Hague)

Pop 1,800 (est) **Elev** 867 ft **Area code** 518 **Zip** 12870 **E-mail** schroonlake@adirondack.net **Web** www.adirondack.net/orgs/slcc

Information Chamber of Commerce, PO Box 726; 518/532-7675 or 888/SCHROON.

The village extends for two miles along the west shore of Schroon Lake. A popular summer resort area, 70 lakes and ponds are within a five-mile radius. Outdoor recreation activities are popular all year long.

What to See and Do

Natural Stone Bridge and Caves. Self-guided tour; underground river, rock formations, caves; fishing, picnicking. (Memorial Day-Columbus Day, daily) 8 mi S on I-87, exit 26, then 2 mi W, in Pottersville. Phone 518/494-2283. ¢¢¢

Public campgrounds. Swimming, lifeguards; fishing, picnicking; boat ramp; camping. Phone 518/532-7675. ¢¢¢¢

Eagle Point. Also bathhouse. (Mid-May-early Sept) 8 mi S on US 9, N of Pottersville in Adirondack Forest Preserve. Phone 518/494-2220. Day use per vehicle ¢¢¢¢

Paradox Lake. Also boat launch, bathhouse. (Mid-May-mid-Nov) On NY 74, 2 mi E of Severance. Phone 518/532-7451. Day use per vehicle ¢¢¢

Motel

★ **DAVIS.** *Rd 1, 1/2 mi S of US 9.* 518/532-7583; FAX 518/532-0158. Web www.adirondack.net/tour/davis/index.. 20 rms, 4 kits. Late June-Labor Day: S, D $45-$55; each addl $5; kit. units $60; cottages $585-$660/wk; family, wkly rates; lower rates rest of yr. Crib $3. TV; cable. Heated pool. Playground. Restaurant nearby. Ck-out 11 am. Downhill ski 18 mi; x-country ski on site, rentals. Boat rentals. Lawn games. Picnic tables, grills. Cr cds: A, MC, V.

⊠ ⊠ ⊠

Seneca Falls (D-5)

(See also Auburn, Geneva, Waterloo)

Settled 1787 **Pop** 9,384 **Elev** 469 ft **Area code** 315 **Zip** 13148 **E-mail** windmill@seneca.org **Web** www.seneca.org

Information Seneca County Chamber of Commerce, NY 5 & 20 W; 315/568-2906 or 800/SEC-1848.

The first convention of the US Women's Suffrage Movement met in July 1848, in Seneca Falls. The town was the home of Amelia Jenks Bloomer, who drew international attention to women's rights by advocating and wearing the costume that bears her name. The two great leaders of the movement, Elizabeth Cady Stanton and Susan B. Anthony, also worked in Seneca Falls. The Stanton home has been preserved.

A 50-foot drop in the Seneca River provided power for local industry. The rapids have been replaced by the New York State Barge Canal.

What to See and Do

Cayuga Lake State Park. Swimming, beach, bathhouse; fishing; boating (launch, dock). Picnicking, playground. Tent & trailer sites, cabins (late Apr-late Oct). Standard fees. 3 mi E on NY 89. Phone 315/568-5163. **¢¢**

Montezuma Natl Wildlife Refuge. Federal wildlife refuge; visitor center. Peak migration for shorebirds (fall), Canadian geese and ducks (spring & fall). Refuge (daily). Office (Mon-Fri; closed hols). 5 mi E on US 20, NY 5.Phone 315/568-5987. **Free.**

Natl Women's Hall of Fame. Museum and education center honors famous American women, past and present. (May-Oct, daily; rest of yr, Wed-Sun) 76 Fall St. Phone 315/568-2936. **¢**

Seneca Falls Historical Society Museum. A 19th-century, 23-rm Victorian/Queen Anne mansion with period rm, local history exhibits; research library and archives. Museum shop. Tours (Mon-Fri, also Sat afternoons). 55 Cayuga St. Phone 315/568-8412. **¢**

State Barge Canal Locks #2 & #3. Observation point on S side, off E Bayard St to Seneca St. (May-early Nov)

Women's Rights Natl Historical Park. Visitor center with exhibits and film; talks scheduled daily during summer. 116 Fall St. Phone 315/568-2991.Included in the park are the Wesleyan Chapel and the

Elizabeth Cady Stanton House (ca 1830). House where Stanton worked and lived from 1847-1862. Artifacts incl original china, books and furniture. Tours (daily). 32 Washington St. **Free.**

Annual Event

Convention Days Celebration. Commemorates first women's rights convention, held July 19 & 20, 1848. Wkend closest to July 19 & 20.

Shandaken (E-7)

(See also Hunter, Kingston, Woodstock)

Pop 3,013 **Elev** 1,070 ft **Area code** 914 **Zip** 12480

This Catskill Mountain town carries the Iroquois name meaning "rapid waters." Shandaken is a town with the combination of being in the Catskills and having easy access to New York City. Shandaken is home of the highest peak in the Catskills, Slide Mt. It is also the home of Esopus Creek, one of the finest wild trout fisheries in the East, also noted for tubing. Skiing, hiking and hunting are popular in this area of mountains and streams.

What to See and Do

Catskill Park (see).

Skiing. Belleayre Mt. Triple, 3 double chairlifts, 2 T-bars, J-bar, tow bar; 32 runs; patrol, school, rentals; snowmaking; cafeterias; nursery. Longest run 1.3 mi; vertical drop 1,340 ft. (Nov-early Apr, daily) Half-day rates. Over 5 mi of cross-country trails. 8 mi W, just off NY 28 at Highmount. Phone 914/254-5600 or 800/942-6904 (ski conditions). **¢¢¢¢¢**

Lodge

★ ★ **AUBERGE DES 4 SAISONS.** *178 NY 42. 914/688-2223; res: 800/864-1877.* 30 rms, 10 with shower only. S, D $75-$185; hols (min stay required); higher rates hol wkends. Pet accepted, some restrictions. TV; cable. Complimentary full bkfst. Restaurant (see AUBERGE DES 4 SAISONS). Bar. Ck-out noon. Tennis. Pool. Playground. Rec rm. Lawn games. Many balconies. Picnic tables. On stream. Cr cds: A, MC, V.

Inns

★ ★ **BIRCHCREEK.** *(NY 28, Pine Hill 12465) 8 mi W on NY 28. 914/254-5222; FAX 914/254-5812.* 6 rms, 5 with shower only, 1 cottage, 2 story. No rm phones. Dec-Mar, June-Oct: S, D $75-$150; under 12 free; 2-day min wkends, 3-day min hols; ski plans; lower rates rest of yr. Crib free. TV in some rms; cable. Complimentary full bkfst. Complimentary coffee in rms. Restaurant nearby. Ck-out 11 am, ck-in 3 pm. Downhill ski 1/2 mi; x-country ski on site. Some refrigerators. Built in 1896; in Catskill Mountain forest. Totally nonsmoking. Cr cds: A, DS, MC, V.

★ ★ ★ **COPPER HOOD.** *7038 NY 28, 2 mi SE on NY 28. 914/688-2460; FAX 914/688-7484.* E-mail info@copperhood.com; web copper hood.com. 20 rms, 2 story. MAP: D $80-$160/person; children $35; wkly rates. Crib $15. TV; cable (premium), VCR avail. Indoor pool; whirlpool. Playground. Rm serv. Ck-out 11 am, ck-in 3 pm. Meeting rm. Business servs avail. Tennis. Downhill ski 8 mi; x-country ski on site. Exercise rm; sauna. Massage. Game rm. Lawn games. Picnic tables. On Esopus Creek surrounded by Catskills Park. Cr cds: A, MC, V.

★ **MARGARETVILLE MOUNTAIN INN.** *(Margaretville Mountain Rd, Margaretville 12455) 45 mi W on NY 28. 914/586-3933.* E-mail mmibnb@catskill.net; web www.catskill.net/mmibnb. 7 air-cooled rms, 2 story. A/C avail. No rm phones. S, D $50-$95; each addl $15; suites $115; under 12 free; ski plans; hols (2-3-day min). Crib free. Pet accepted; some restrictions; $10. TV in common rm; cable (premium), VCR avail (movies). Complimentary full bkfst. Ck-out 11 am, ck-in 4-6 pm. Downhill ski 9 mi; x-country ski on-site. Playground. Lawn games. Built in 1886; first commercial cauliflower farm in US. Totally nonsmoking. Cr cds: A, MC, V.

Restaurants

★ ★ ★ **AUBERGE DES 4 SAISONS.** *(See Auberge Des 4 Saisons Lodge) 914/688-2223.* French menu. Specialties: steak au poivre, roasted duck with wild rice. Hrs: 11:30 am-2:30 pm, 5:30-11 pm. Res accepted. Bar. Complete meals: lunch $7-$24, dinner $15-$38. Country setting in foothills of the Catskills. Cr cds: A, MC, V.

★ ★ **CATAMOUNT CAFE.** *(5638 NY 28, Mt Tremper 12457) 914/688-7900.* E-mail kaatsdevco@aol.com; web www.catskillcorners.com. Hrs: 5-10 pm; Sun brunch 11 am-2 pm. Closed Tues, Wed; also Dec 25. Res accepted. Contemporary Amer menu. Bar. Semi-a la carte: dinner $12.95-$21.95. Sun brunch $5.95-$8.95. Child's meals. Specialties: Long Island duck breast steak, venison loin and chop with juniper sauce, char-grilled salmon fillet. Jazz or classical music Fri-Sun. Parking. Outdoor dining. Adirondacks-style decor; oil paintings. Cr cds: A, DS, MC, V.

Shelter Island (A-5)

(See also East Hampton, Sag Harbor)

Settled 1652 **Pop** 2,263 **Elev** 50 ft **Area code** 516 **Zip** 11964
Information Chamber of Commerce, PO Box 598; 516/749-0399.

Quakers persecuted by the Puritans in New England, settled Shelter Island in Gardiners Bay off the east end of Long Island. The island is reached by car or pedestrian ferry from Greenport, on the north fork of Long Island, or from North Haven (Sag Harbor), on the south. There is a monument to the Quakers and a graveyard with 17th-century stones plus two historical museums; the 18th-century Havens House and the 19th-century Manhanset Chapel. Also 2,200-acre Nature Conservancy's Mashomack Preserve, with miles of trails for hiking and educational programs. The island offers swimming, boating off miles of sandy shoreline, biking, hiking, tennis and golfing.

Motels

★ ★ **DERING HARBOR INN.** *(13 Winthrop Rd, Shelter Island Heights 11965) 1 mi N on NY 114. 516/749-0900; FAX 516/749-2045.* 22 rms, 1-2 story. Memorial Day-Labor Day: S, D $165-$240; each addl $20; kit. cottages $240-$395; under 12 free; wkends (2-day min); lower rates May-Memorial Day & Labor Day-mid-Oct. Closed rest of yr. Crib free. TV; cable. Pool; lifeguard. Complimentary coffee in rms. Restaurant 6-9 pm. Ck-out noon. Coin lndry. Business servs avail. Tennis. Lawn games. Refrigerators. Picnic tables. Cr cds: A, DS, MC, V.

★ **PRIDWIN.** *Shore Rd, 1¹/₂ mi W of NY 114 Crescent Beach. 516/749-0476; FAX 516/749-2071; res: 800/273-2497.* 40 rms, 2-3 story, 8 kit. cottages. No elvtr. July-early Sept: S $79-$199; D $109-$229; each addl $19-$59; kit. cottages $179-$229; family rates; lower rates May-late June, early Sept-Oct. Only cottages open rest of yr. Crib $8. TV. Saltwater pool. Complimentary full bkfst. Restaurant 8-10 am, noon-3 pm, 6-10 pm. Bar noon-midnight; entertainment, dancing Wed, Sat in season. Ck-out noon. Meeting rm. Business servs avail. Tennis. Golf privileges. Game rm. Rec rm. Refrigerator in cottages. Private patios, decks on cottages. Private beach. Dockage. Cr cds: A, DS, MC, V.

★ ★ **SUNSET BEACH.** *(35 Shore Rd, Shelter Island Heights 11965) 1 mi W, off NY 114. 516/749-2001.* 20 rms, 2 story, 10 kits. Early July-Labor Day: S, D $125-$225; each addl $15-$25; kit. units $20 addl; family rates; lower rates rest of yr. Crib free. TV; cable. Complimentary continental bkfst. Restaurant 8 am-midnight (seasonal). Bar noon-1 am. Ck-out 11 am. Business servs avail. Tennis privileges. Golf privileges. Balconies. Picnic tables, grill. On beach. Cr cds: A, DS, MC, V.

Inn

★ ★ ★ **RAM'S HEAD.** *(Ram Island Dr, Shelter Island Heights 11965) 1 mi W. 516/749-0811.* 17 rms, 4 share bath, 2 story. No A/C. S, D $90-$125; each addl $15; suites $195. Crib free. Playground. Complimentary continental bkfst. Restaurant (see RAM'S HEAD INN). Bar 10 am-midnight. Ck-out noon, ck-in 3 pm. Meeting rms. Tennis. Sauna. Colonial-style inn (1929); extensive grounds; on beach. Totally nonsmoking. Cr cds: A, MC, V.

Restaurants

★ ★ ★ **CHEQUIT INN.** *23 Grand Ave. 516/749-0018.* Specializes in seafood, pasta. Hrs: noon-10 pm; wkends from 10 am. Closed Nov-mid-May. Res accepted. Bar noon-1 am. A la carte entrees: lunch $4-$9.50, dinner $15-$20. Entertainment wkends. Outdoor dining. Inn was originally built (ca 1870) around a maple tree that, now enormous, still shades the terrace that overlooks Dering Harbor. Cr cds: A, MC, V.

★ ★ ★ **RAM'S HEAD INN.** *(See Ram's Head Inn) 516/749-0811.* Specializes in duck, local seafood. Own baking. Hrs: 6-9:30 pm; Sun brunch (in season) 11:30 am-2 pm. Closed wkdays Nov-Apr. Res accepted. No A/C. Bar. Wine list. A la carte entrees: dinner $18-$24. Child's meals. Outdoor dining. Dining rm with fireplace, opens to veranda overlooking Coecles Harbor. Cr cds: A, MC, V.

Skaneateles (D-5)

(See also Auburn, Seneca Falls, Syracuse)

Settled 1794 **Pop** 7,526 **Elev** 919 ft **Area code** 315 **Zip** 13152

Skaneateles (skany-AT-les) was once a stop on the Underground Railroad. Today it is a quiet resort town at the north end of Skaneateles Lake.

What to See and Do

Boat trips. A 32-mi cruise along shoreline of Skaneateles Lake (July-Aug, daily exc Sun). Lunch cruise (Mon-Fri), dinner cruises (nightly), 4-hr excursion (Sun), sightseeing cruise (daily). (May-Sept) Depart Clift Park dock. Contact Mid-Lakes Navigation Co, PO Box 61-M; 800/545-4318 or 315/685-8500. ¢¢¢- ¢¢¢¢¢

Seasonal Event

Polo Matches. Skaneateles Polo Club Grounds. 1 mi S, just off NY 41A. Phone 315/685-7373. Sun July-Aug.

Motel

★ ★ **BIRD'S NEST.** *1601 E Genesee St. 315/685-5641.* 28 rms, 4 kits. Mid-May-Sept: S $40-$60; D $45-$95; each addl $5; kit. units $65-$85; under 5 free; wkly rates; lower rates rest of yr. Crib $5. Pet accepted. TV; cable. Pool. Playground. Complimentary coffee in rms. Restaurant nearby. Ck-out 11 am. Lawn games. Some refrigerators, whirlpools. Picnic tables, grill. Duck pond. Cr cds: A, C, D, DS, MC, V.

Inns

★ ★ ★ **HOBBIT HOLLOW FARM.** *3061 W Lake Rd. 315/685-2791; FAX 315/685-3426.* Web www.hobbithollow.com. 4 rms. S, D $150-$250; each addl $40. Children over 18 yrs only. TV; cable (premium), VCR avail (movies). Complimentary full bkfst; afternoon refreshments. Complimentary coffee in rms. Restaurant nearby. Ck-out noon, ck-in 3 pm. Business servs avail. In-rm modem link. Indoor tennis. X-country ski on site. Built in 1820; country decor. Totally nonsmoking. Cr cds: A, C, D, MC, V.

★ ★ ★ **SHERWOOD.** *26 W Genesee St, on US 20. 315/685-3405; res: 800/374-3796; FAX 315/685-8983.* 20 rms, 4 suites, 3 story. S, D $85-$160; each addl $10. Crib avail. Complimentary continental bkfst. Dining rm 5-10 pm; informal dining 11:30 am-10 pm. Bar 11:30-2 am. Ck-out noon, ck-in 3 pm. Meeting rms. Business servs avail. In-rm modem link. Gift shop. Public beach opp. Built 1807; former stage coach stop. Cr cds: A, C, D, MC, V.

Restaurants

✔★ **DOUG'S FISH FRY.** *8 Jordan St. 315/685-3288.* Specializes in fresh seafood. Hrs: 11 am-9 pm. Closed some major hols; also 3 wks in Jan. Beer. A la carte entrees: lunch, dinner $4-$10. Outdoor dining. No cr cds accepted.

★ ★ ★ **KREBS.** *53 W Genesee St, on US 20. 315/685-5714.* Specializes in prime rib, lobster Newburg, fried chicken. Own baking. Hrs: 6-9 pm; Fri, Sat to 10 pm; Sun 4-9 pm; Sun brunch 10:30 am-2 pm. Closed Nov-Apr. Res accepted. Bar from 4 pm; Sun from noon. Complete meals: dinner $31.95-$36.95. Sun brunch $11.50. Server recites menu. Formal

English garden. Early Amer decor; antiques. Established 1899. Cr cds: A, C, D, DS, MC, V.

★ ★ **MANDANA INN.** *RD 1, 5 mi S on NY 41A.* 315/685-7798. Specialties: Boston scrod, soft shelled crab. Hrs: 5-10 pm; Sun, hols 3-9 pm. Closed Tues; Dec 24-25; also Jan-Mar. Res accepted. Bar from 4 pm. Semi-a la carte: dinner $12.95-$22.95. Child's meals. Colonial decor. Inn since 1835. Family-owned. Cr cds: A, C, D, MC, V.

Smithtown, L.I. (B-3)

(See also Huntington, Stony Brook)

Pop 113,406 **Elev** 60 ft **Area code** 516 **Zip** 11787

Smithtown includes six unincorporated hamlets and three incorporated villages. The village of Smithtown is situated near several state parks.

Motels

★ **ECONO LODGE.** *755 NY 347.* 516/724-9000. 39 rms, 2 story. S $60-$65; D $65-$74; each addl $8; under 18 free. Crib $6. TV; cable (premium). Complimentary coffee in lobby. Restaurant nearby. Ck-out 11 am. Cr cds: A, C, D, DS, JCB, MC, V.

★ ★ **HAMPTON INN.** *(680 Commack Rd, Commack 11725)* approx 10 mi W on NY 25. 516/462-5700; FAX 516/462-9735. 144 rms, 5 story. S $94; D $110; under 18 free. Crib free. TV; cable (premium), VCR avail. Continental bkfst. Restaurant nearby. Ck-out noon. Meeting rm. Business servs avail. In-rm modem link. Airport transportation. Health club privileges. Some refrigerators, microwaves. Cr cds: A, C, D, DS, MC, V.

Motor Hotel

★ ★ ★ **SHERATON-LONG ISLAND.** *110 Vanderbilt Motor Pkwy (11788).* 516/231-1100; res: 800/325-3535; FAX 516/231-1143. 209 rms, 6 story. S, D $139; each addl $20; suites $208-$395; wkend rates. Crib avail. TV; cable (premium), VCR avail. Indoor pool; whirlpool, lifeguard. Restaurant 6:30 am-10:30 pm. Rm serv. Bar noon-1 am; entertainment. Ck-out noon. Meeting rms. Business servs avail. In-rm modem link. Bellhops. Valet serv. Sundries. Exercise equipt; sauna, steam rm. Game rm. Refrigerators avail. Cr cds: A, C, D, DS, MC, V.

Hotel

★ ★ ★ **MARRIOTT ISLANDIA.** *(3635 Express Dr N, Hauppauge 11788)* S to I-495 exit 58, on North Service Rd. 516/232-3000; res: 800/228-9290; FAX 516/232-3029. Web www.marriott.com. 280 rms, 10 story. S, D $115-$159. Crib free. TV; cable (premium). Indoor pool; whirlpool, lifeguard. Restaurant 6:30 am-2 pm, 5-11 pm. Bar 2 pm-midnight. Ck-out noon. Convention facilities. Business servs avail. Gift shop. Free airport, RR station transportation. Exercise equipt. Game rm. Refrigerators avail. Cr cds: A, C, D, DS, ER, MC, V.

Restaurants

★ ★ **BONWIT INN.** *(Commack Rd & Vanderbilt Pkwy, Commack)* 7 mi W on NY 25. 516/499-2068. Continental menu. Specializes in seafood, steak. Hrs: 11 am-midnight; Mon to 10 pm; Sun to 10 pm. Closed

Dec 25. Res accepted. Bar. A la carte entrees: lunch $4.95-$13.95, dinner $11-$29. Nautical theme. Fireplaces. Cr cds: A, C, D, MC, V.

★ ★ ★ **LA MASCOTTE.** *(3 Crooked Hill Rd, Commack 11725)* 3 mi SW at Vanderbilt Pkwy, off Commack Rd. 516/499-6446. French menu. Specialties: canard aux airelles, carré d'agneau. Own baking. Hrs: noon-3 pm, 5-10 pm; Fri to 11 pm; Sat, Sun 5-11 pm. Closed Dec 25. Res accepted. Bar. Wine cellar. A la carte entrees: lunch $11.50-$16.50, dinner $15-$26. Complete meals: lunch $15, dinner $24.95. Parking. Cr cds: A, C, D, DS, MC, V.

★ ★ **LOTUS EAST.** *(416 N Country Rd, St James 11780)* 5 mi N on NY 25A. 516/862-6030. Chinese menu. Specialties: General Tso's chicken, tangerine beef. Hrs: 11:30 am-10:30 pm; Fri, Sat to 11 pm; Sun 11 am-10 pm. Bar. Semi-a la carte: lunch $4.75-$6.95, dinner $7.75-$17.95. Chinese motif. Cr cds: A, C, D, MC, V.

★ ★ ★ **MIRABELLE.** *(404 N Country Rd, St James 11780)* 2 mi NE via NY 25A; 8 mi N of I-495 exit 56. 516/584-5999. French menu. Specialties: duck in two courses, ginger almond tarte. Hrs: noon-2 pm, 6-9:30 pm; Sat from 6 pm; Sun from 5 pm. Closed Mon; July 4, Thanksgiving, Dec 25. Res required. Bar. A la carte entrees: lunch $11-$21, dinner $21-$31. Complete meals: lunch $19.95. Parking. Cr cds: A, C, D, DS, MC, V.

Southampton, L.I. (A-4)

(See also East Hampton, Hampton Bays, Riverhead)

Settled 1640 **Pop** 44,976 **Elev** 25 ft **Area code** 516 **Zip** 11968 **E-mail** chamber@southampton.com **Web** www.southampton.com/chamber **Information** Chamber of Commerce, 76 Main St; 516/283-0402.

Southampton has many colonial houses. The surrounding dunes and beaches are dotted with luxury estates.

What to See and Do

Old Halsey House (1648). Oldest English frame house in state. Furnished with period furniture; colonial herb garden. (Mid-June-mid-Sept, daily exc Mon) S Main St. Phone 516/283-2494. ¢

Parrish Art Museum. Includes 19th- and 20th-century American paintings and prints; repository for William Merritt Chase and Fairfield Porter; Japanese woodblock prints; collection of Renaissance works; changing exhibits; arboretum; performing arts and concert series; lectures; research library. (Mid-June-mid-Sept, Mon-Tues & Thurs-Sat, also Sun afternoons; rest of yr, Thurs-Mon; closed most hols) 25 Job's Lane, town center. Phone 516/283-2118. ¢

Southampton Campus of Long Island Univ (1963). (1,200 students) Liberal arts, marine science research. Tour of campus. Montauk Hwy (NY 27A). Phone 516/283-4000.

Southampton Historical Museum. Main bldg formerly was whaling captain's home (1843). Period rms, costumes, china, toys. Large collection of Native American artifacts; one-rm schoolhouse; carriage house; farming and whaling collections. 18th-century barn converted to country store. (Mid-June-mid-Sept, daily exc Mon) 17 Meeting House Lane, off Main St. Phone 516/283-2494. ¢

Water Mill Museum. Restored gristmill, built in 1644, houses old tools, other exhibits; craft demonstrations. (Memorial Day-Labor Day, daily exc Tues) NE on Old Mill Rd, in Water Mill. Phone 516/726-4625. **Donation.**

Annual Event

Hampton Classic Horse Show. 240 Snake Hollow Rd, N of NY 27, in Bridgehampton. Horse show jumping event. Celebrities, food, shopping, family activities. Phone 516/537-3177. Last wk Aug.

Powwow. Shinnecock Indian Reservation, just off NY 27A. Dances, ceremonies, displays. Labor Day wkend.

Motels

★ **BAYBERRY INN.** *281 County Rd 39A. 516/283-4220; FAX 516/283-6496; res: 800/659-2020.* 30 rms, 3 suites. July-Aug: S $195; D $200; suites $225; under 18 free; wkend rates; higher rates: hol wkends, Hampton Classic; lower rates rest of yr. Pet accepted. TV; cable. Pool. Ck-out 11 am. Business servs avail. Some refrigerators. Cr cds: A, DS, MC, V.

★ **CONCORD INN.** *County Rd 39. 516/283-7600; FAX 516/283-4625; res: 800/321-4969.* 65 rms, 2 story, 32 kit. units. July-Aug: S, D, kit. units $115-$550; each addl $25; under 12 free; higher rates: hol wkends, horse show classic; lower rates rest of yr. Crib free. Pet accepted. TV; cable, VCR avail. Pool. Ck-out 10 am. Meeting rms. Business servs avail. Cr cds: A, MC, V.

★★ **CONCORD RESORT.** *161 Hill Station Rd. 516/283-6100; FAX 516/283-6102.* 40 kit. suites, 2 story. Memorial Day-Labor Day: S, D $149; higher rates wkends & horse show; 3-day min hol wkends; wkly rates; golf plan; lower rates rest of yr. Crib free. Pet accepted. TV; cable (premium), VCR avail. Pool; lifeguard. Complimentary continental bkfst. Restaurant nearby. Ck-out 11 am. Coin lndry. Meeting rms. Business servs avail. RR station transportation. Tennis. Golf privileges. Exercise equipt. Game rm. Lawn games. Balconies. Picnic tables. Cr cds: A, C, D, DS, JCB, MC, V.

★ **SOUTHAMPTON INN.** *91 Hill St, at First Neck Lane. 516/283-6500; FAX 516/283-6559; res: 800/832-6500.* 90 rms, 2 story. June-Sept: S, D $150-$225; each addl $25; wkend packages; lower rates rest of yr. Crib free. TV; cable (premium). Pool; poolside serv, lifeguard. Bar 5 pm-2 am (seasonal); entertainment, dancing Fri, Sat. Ck-out 11 am. Meeting rms. Business servs avail. In-rm modem link. Bellhops. Concierge. Tennis. Lawn games. Some refrigerators. Cr cds: A, MC, V.

★★ **VILLAGE LATCH INN.** *101 Hill St. 516/283-2160; FAX 516/283-3236; res: 800/545-2824.* 72 rms, 2 story. Memorial Day-Labor Day: S, D $195-$275; each addl $35; lower rates rest of yr. Crib $25. Pet accepted; $20/day. TV; cable (premium), VCR avail. Pool. Complimentary bkfst. Ck-out 11 am. Business servs avail. Tennis. Many refrigerators. Many private patios. Antique furnishings. Cr cds: A, C, D, DS, MC, V.

Inn

★★ **MAINSTAY.** *(579 Hill St, Southampton) 516/283-4375; FAX 516/287-6240.* 8 rms, 3 share baths, 3 story. No A/C. June-Sept: S, D $95-$350; wkends (2-day min); lower rates rest of yr. TV in some rms. Pool. Complimentary continental bkfst. Restaurant nearby. Ck-out 11 am, ck-in 3 pm. Business servs avail. Restored guest house (1870); antiques. Totally nonsmoking. Cr cds: A, MC, V.

Restaurants

★★★ **95 SCHOOL STREET.** *(95 School St, Bridgehampton 11932) approx 5 mi E on NY 27. 516/537-5555.* Regional Amer menu. Specialties: pan-roasted farm chicken, grilled duck breast, pasta with lobster and roasted corn. Hrs: 6-11 pm. Closed Mon, Tues (Labor Day-Memorial Day). Res accepted. Bar. A la carte entrees: dinner $16-$25. Atmosphere of country elegance. Cr cds: A, MC, V.

D

★★ **BASILICO.** *10 Windmill Lane. 516/283-7987.* Northern Italian menu. Specializes in pasta, fish, steak. Full vegetarian menu. Hrs: 6-11 pm; Fri-Sun noon-3 pm, 6 pm-midnight. Closed some major hols. Res required. Bar. A la carte entrees: lunch $11-$15, dinner $11-$26. Trattoria; wine racks on walls, many plants, herbs and flowers. Cr cds: A, C, D, DS, MC, V.

★★ **BOBBY VAN'S.** *(Montauk Hwy, Bridgehampton 11932) approx 5 mi E on NY 27. 516/537-0590.* Specializes in aged prime sirloin steak, veal chops, fresh seafood. Hrs: noon-10:30 pm. Res accepted. Bar. A la carte entrees: lunch $8-$19, dinner $16-$29. New York City-style chop house. Cr cds: A, C, D, DS, MC, V.

D

★★ **COAST GRILL.** *1109 Noyack Rd. 516/283-2277.* Specializes in grilled swordfish, lobster, clams. Own pastries. Hrs: 5 pm-2 am. Res accepted. Bar. Semi-a la carte: dinner $20-$25. Nautical theme; view of Wooley Pond. Cr cds: A, MC, V.

D

✔★★ **JOHN DUCK JR.** *15 Prospect St, at N Main St. 516/283-0311.* Specializes in L.I. duckling, steak, seafood. Own desserts. Hrs: 11:45 am-10:30 pm; Fri, Sat to midnight. Closed Mon; Dec 24, 25. Res accepted. Bar. Semi-a la carte: lunch $5.25-$13.50, dinner $14.75-$22. Complete meals: lunch $9.75-$13, dinner (Tues-Thurs) $14-$17.50. Child's meals. Valet parking wkends. Established 1900; 4th generation of ownership. Cr cds: A, C, D, DS, MC, V.

★★ **LE CHEF.** *75 Jobs Lane. 516/283-8581.* French, Amer menu. Specializes in grilled fish, French provincial cuisine. Hrs: 11:30 am-10 pm. Res accepted. Bar. Semi-a la carte: lunch $7-$15. Complete meals: dinner $16.75-$18. Cr cds: A, D, MC, V.

★ **LOBSTER INN.** *162 Inlet Rd, off NY 27. 516/283-1525.* Specializes in seafood, steak. Salad bar. Hrs: 11:30 am-11 pm. Closed Thanksgiving, Dec 24, 25. No A/C. Bar. Complete meals: lunch $5.75-$12.75, dinner $13.75-$25. Parking. Family-owned. Cr cds: A, MC, V.

★★ **MIRKO'S.** *(Water Mill Square, Water Mill) 5 mi NE on NY 27. 516/726-4444.* Continental menu. Specializes in pasta, veal chops. Hrs: 6-11 pm; winter to 10 pm. Closed Tues; Mon-Wed in winter; also Jan. Res required. Bar. A la carte entrees: dinner $17.50-$29. Outdoor dining. Fireplace. Cr cds: A, MC, V.

D

★★ **STATION BISTRO.** *(50 Station Rd, Water Mill 11976) 5 mi N on NY 27. 516/726-3016.* French menu. Specialties: herb-crusted bass, entrecote steak with roasted shallots, baked fruit tartes. Hrs: 6-10 pm; Sat, Sun noon-4 pm; winter hrs vary. Res accepted; required Fri, Sat. Bar. A la carte entrees: dinner $18-$25. In former railroad station (1903). Jacket. Cr cds: A, MC, V.

D

Unrated Dining Spot

GOLDEN PEAR. *97-99 Main St. 516/283-8900.* Specialties: pasta, chili, vegetable lasagne. Menu changes daily. Hrs: 8 am-5 pm; Fri-Sun to 6 pm. A la carte entrees: bkfst $4.95-$7.95, lunch $5.95-$10.95. Cr cds: A, MC, V.

Southold, L.I. (A-4)

(See also Greenport, Riverhead)

Settled 1640 **Pop** 19,836 **Elev** 32 ft **Area code** 516 **Zip** 11971
Information Greenport-Southold Chamber of Commerce, Main Rd, PO
Box 66, Greenport 11944; 516/477-1383.

What to See and Do

Horton Point Lighthouse & Nautical Museum. (Late May-Oct, Sat &
Sun late morning-mid-afternoon; other times by appt) Lighthouse Park,
54325 Main Rd. Phone 516/765-5500 or 516/765-3262. **Donation.**

The Old House (1649). Example of early English architecture; 17th and
18th-century furnishings. Also on Village Green are the **Wickham Farmhouse** (early 1700s) and the **Old Schoolhouse Museum** (1840). (July-
Labor Day, Sat-Mon; June & Sept, Sat & Sun) On NY 25, on the Village
Green in Cutchogue. Phone 516/734-7122. **¢**

Motel

★ **ALIANO'S BEACHCOMBER.** *(3800 Duck Pond Rd,
Cutchogue 11935) L.I. Expwy exit 71, N to NY 25, E to Depot Lane, Depot
Lane becomes Duck Pond Rd.* 516/734-6370. 50 rms, 2 story. 11 rm
phones. Memorial Day-Labor Day: D $115-$235; each addl $25; wkly
rates; 2-day min wkends; lower rates mid-Sept-mid-Oct. Closed rest of yr.
TV. Pool; wading pool. Complimentary coffee in rms. Ck-out 11 am. Game
rm. Refrigerators. Balconies. Swimming beach. Cr cds: A, DS, MC, V.

Restaurants

★ ★ ★ **ROSS' NORTH FORK.** *North Rd, NY 48.* 516/765-2111.
Specializes in seafood, L.I. duckling, fresh vegetables. Own baking. Hrs:
noon-2:30 pm, 5-10 pm; Sun 1-9 pm. Closed Mon; Dec 24, 25; also
Jan-mid-Feb. Res accepted. Bar. Wine cellar. A la carte entrees: lunch
$10-$14, dinner $17-$21. Complete meals: lunch $14-$18. Child's meals.
Cr cds: A, C, D, MC, V.

★ ★ **THE SEAFOOD BARGE.** *Main Rd.* 516/765-3010. Specializes in lobster, steamers, grilled fish. Hrs: noon-10 pm; mid-Sept-mid-
June, hrs vary. Res accepted. Bar. A la carte entrees: lunch $9.50-$13.50,
dinner $12-$28. Overlooks Peconic Bay and marina. Family-owned. Cr
cds: A, C, D, MC, V.

Spring Valley (A-2)

(See also Tarrytown)

Pop 21,802 **Elev** 420 ft **Area code** 914 **Zip** 10977

What to See and Do

Historical Society of Rockland County. Museum and publications on
county history; Jacob Blauvelt House (1832 Dutch farmhouse), barn.
(Tues-Sun afternoons; closed major hols) 3 mi N via NY 45, then 3 mi E on
New Hempstead Rd, then 2 mi N on Main St to 20 Zukor Rd in New City.
Phone 914/634-9629. **Free.**

Motels

★ ★ **HOLIDAY INN.** *(3 Executive Blvd, Suffern 10901)* I-87 exit
14B. 914/357-4800; FAX 914/368-0471. 241 rms, 3 story. S, D $99-$120;
kit. suites $175. Crib free. TV; cable (premium). Complimentary coffee in
lobby. Restaurant 7-10:30 am, noon-2 pm, 5-10 pm. Rm serv. Bar 3
pm-midnight. Ck-out noon. Meeting rms. Business center. Bellhops. Valet
serv. Sundries. Coin lndry. Exercise equipt; sauna. Indoor pool; whirlpool;
lifeguard. Game rm. In-rm whirlpool, refrigerator, microwave in kit. suites.
Cr cds: A, C, D, DS, MC, V.

★ **SUSSE CHALET.** *100 Spring Valley Marketplace,* I-87 and
I-287 exit 14. 914/426-2000; FAX 914/426-2008. 105 rms, 4 story. S
$73-$78; D $80-$85; each addl $3; under 18 free. Crib $10. TV; cable
(premium). Pool; lifeguard. Complimentary continental bkfst. Restaurant
nearby. Ck-out 11 am. Coin lndry. Health club privileges. Cr cds: A, C, D,
DS, MC, V.

✔ ★ **WELLESLEY INN.** *(17 N Airmont Rd, Suffern 10901)* I-
87/287 exit 14B. 914/368-1900; FAX 914/368-1927. 95 rms, 4 story.
Apr-Oct: S, D $82-$102; each addl $10; suites $110-$160; under 18 free;
higher rates: West Point graduation, Dec 31; lower rates rest of yr. Crib
free. Pet accepted, some restrictions; $5/day. TV; cable (premium). Com-
plimentary continental bkfst. Complimentary coffee in rms. Restaurant
nearby. Ck-out 11 am. Business servs avail. Refrigerators, microwaves
avail. Cr cds: A, C, D, DS, JCB, MC, V.

Hotel

★ ★ ★ **HILTON PEARL RIVER.** *(500 Veterans Memorial Dr, Pearl
River 10965)* Palisades Pkwy, exit 6W. 914/735-9000; FAX 914/735-9005.
150 rms, 5 story. S, D $124-$173; each addl $16; suites $300-$400; family,
wkend rates. Crib free. TV; cable (premium). Indoor pool; whirlpool, life-
guard. Restaurant 6:30 am-11 pm; Sat from 7 am. Bar 11-1 am; pianist.
Ck-out noon. Coin lndry. Meeting rms. Business center. In-rm modem link.
Exercise equipt; sauna. Refrigerators. French chateau style; on 17 acres.
Cr cds: A, C, D, DS, ER, JCB, MC, V.

Restaurant

★ ★ **RAMAPOUGH INN.** *(253 NY 59, Suffern 10901)* W on NY
59, in Cousins Shopping Center. 914/357-0500. Specializes in lobster,
steak, seafood. Hrs: 11:30 am-9:30 pm; Fri to 11 pm; Sat 4-11 pm; Sun
4-9:30 pm. Closed Mon; July 4, Thanksgiving, Dec 25. Res accepted. Bar
to 2 am. Semi-a la carte: lunch $4.95-$11.95, dinner $9.95-$19.95. Child's
meals. Cr cds: A, D, DS, MC, V.

Stamford (E-7)

Pop 2,047 **Elev** 1,827 ft **Area code** 607 **Zip** 12167

Stamford, located along the west branch of the Delaware River, has a large
historical district from the Victorian era.

What to See and Do

Lansing Manor. A 19th-century manor house depicting life of an Anglo-
Dutch household of the mid-1800s. (Memorial Day-Columbus Day, daily
exc Tues) 8 mi SE on NY 23, then 8 mi N on NY 30. Phone 607/588-6061,
518/827-6121 or 800/724-0309. **Free.** Adj is

Visitors Center. Remodeled dairy barn with hands-on exhibits, display on electricity, video presentation and computers. Powerhouse tours by appt. (Daily; closed Jan 1, Thanksgiving, Dec 24, 25 & 31) Phone 800/724-0309. **Free.**

Mine Kill State Park. Swimming pool (late June-early Sept; fee), bathhouse; fishing, boating (launch). Hiking, nature trails. Cross-country skiing, snowmobiling. Picnicking, playground, concession. Recreation programs. Standard fees. SE on NY 23, 4 mi N on NY 30. Phone 518/827-6111.

Scotch Valley Resort. Triple, 2 double chairlifts; patrol, school, rentals; snowmaking; restaurants, cafeteria, bar. Longest run 1¹/₂ mi; vertical drop 750 ft. Night skiing. Cross-country trails (30 mi; fee). Lodging. 3 mi N on NY 10.Phone 607/652-2470 or 888/640-7669 for snow conditions. ¢¢¢¢¢

Zaddock Pratt Museum. Period furnishings and memorabilia. Tours, exhibits. (Memorial Day-Columbus Day, Wed-Sun afternoons) 1828 Homestead, 13 mi SE via NY 23 in Prattsville. Phone 518/299-3395. ¢ Nearby is

Pratt Rocks. Relief carvings in the cliff face depicting Pratt, his son George and the tannery. Scenic climb; picnicking; pavilion.

Motels

✔★ **COLONIAL.** *(Main St, Grand Gorge 12434) 8 mi E via NY 23.* 607/588-6122. 14 rms, 3 A/C, 1-2 story, 3 kits. S $40-$50; D $55-$60; kits. $65. TV; cable (premium). Heated pool. Complimentary coffee. Restaurant adj 6 am-9 pm. Ck-out 11 am. Downhill/x-country ski 8 mi. Lawn games. Picnic tables, grills. Refrigerators. Family-owned. Cr cds: A, DS, MC, V.

★★★ **REXMERE LODGE.** *5 Lake St, at jct NY 10 & NY 23.* 607/652-7394; FAX 607/652-4765; res: 800/932-1090. 37 rms, 2 story. Mid-May-mid-Dec: S, D $50-$125; each addl $15; cottage $125; under 12 free; lower rates rest of yr. Pet accepted. TV; cable. Pool; whirlpool. Coffee in rms. Restaurant 11:30 am-9 pm; wkends to 10 pm. Rm serv. Bar. Ck-out noon. Meeting rms. Business servs avail. Downhill/x-country ski 3 mi. Refrigerators. Private patios, balconies. Cr cds: A, C, D, DS, MC, V.

Staten Island
(Follows New York City)

Stony Brook, L.I. (A-3)
(See also Port Jefferson, Smithtown)

Settled 1655 **Pop** 13,726 **Elev** 123 ft **Area code** 516 **Zip** 11790

Originally part of the Three Village area first settled by Boston colonists in the 17th century, Stony Brook became an important center for the shipbuilding industry on Long Island Sound in the 1800s.

What to See and Do

State Univ of New York at Stony Brook (1957). (17,500 students) Academic units incl College of Arts and Sciences, College of Engineering and Applied Sciences and Health Sciences Center. Museum of Long Island Natural Sciences has permanent displays on Long Island natural history. Art galleries in the Melville Library, Staller Center and the Student Union. Phone 516/689-6000. On campus is

Staller Center for the Arts. Houses 1,049-seat main theater, 3 experimental theaters, art gallery, 400-seat recital hall and electronic music studio. Summer International Theater Festival. Events all yr. Phone 516/632-7235, box office phone 516/632-7230.

The Museums at Stony Brook. Complex of 3 museums. The Melville Carriage House exhibits 90 vehicles from a collection of horse-drawn carriages. The Art Museum features changing exhibits of American art. The Blackwell History Museum has changing exhibits on a variety of historical themes as well as exhibits of period rms and antique decoys. Blacksmith shop, schoolhouse, other period bldgs. Museum store. (Wed-Sun & most Mon hols; closed Jan 1, Thanksgiving, Dec 24-25) On NY 25A.Phone 516/751-0066. ¢¢

Inn

★★★ **THREE VILLAGE INN.** *150 Main St.* 516/751-0555; FAX 516/751-0593. Web www.threevillageinn.com. 26 rms, 2 story, 6 cottages. S $95-$119; D $105-$139; each addl $10. Crib $10. TV; cable. Restaurant (see THREE VILLAGE INN). Bar. Ck-out noon, ck-in 3 pm. Meeting rm. Business servs avail. Picnic tables. Built in late 1700s; some fireplaces. Cr cds: A, C, D, MC, V.

Restaurants

★★★ **COUNTRY HOUSE.** *NY 25A, at Main St.* 516/751-3332. Specializes in creative American cuisine. Hrs: noon-3 pm, 5-10 pm. Closed Jan 1, July 4, Dec 25. Res accepted; required dinner. Bar. Prix fixe: lunch $16.75. A la carte entrees: dinner $16-$26. House built in 1710. Cr cds: A, C, D, MC, V.

★★ **THREE VILLAGE INN.** *(See Three Village Inn)* 516/751-0555. Web www.threevillageinn.com. Specializes in steak, seafood. Own baking. Hrs: 7-11 am, noon-4 pm, 5-10 pm; Fri, Sat to 11 pm; Sun brunch noon-3 pm. Closed Dec 25. Res accepted. Bar. A la carte entrees: bkfst $1.75-$7.95, lunch $8.95-$16.95. Complete meals: dinner $25.95-$33.95, Fri seafood dinner $23.95. Sun brunch $12.95-$16.95. Child's meals. Colonial homestead built in 1751. Attractive grounds; country dining. Near harbor. Cr cds: A, C, D, MC, V.

Stony Point (A-2)

(See also Monroe, Newburgh, Peekskill, West Point)

Pop 12,814 **Elev** 126 ft **Area code** 914 **Zip** 10980

What to See and Do

Stony Point Battlefield State Historic Site. Site of Revolutionary battle in which Gen "Mad Anthony" Wayne successfully stormed British fortifications, July 15-16, 1779, ending the last serious threat to Washington's forces in the North. Oldest lighthouse (1826) on the Hudson River. Museum with exhibits, audiovisual program. Musket demonstrations. Self-guided walking tour & guided tour. Special events (fee). Picnic area. (Mid-Apr-Oct, Wed-Sun) 2 mi N of town center, off US 9W, on Park Rd. Phone 914/786-2521. **Free.**

Stormville
(see Fishkill)

Suffern
(see Spring Valley)

Syracuse (D-5)

(See also Auburn, Cazenovia, Skaneateles)

Settled 1789 **Pop** 163,860 **Elev** 406 ft **Area code** 315 **E-mail** cvb@syracusecvb.net
Information Convention & Visitors Bureau, Greater Syracuse Chamber of Commerce, 572 S Salina St, 13202; 315/470-1800.

Syracuse began as a trading post at the mouth of Onondaga Creek. Salt from wells was produced here from 1796-1900. Industry began in 1793, when Thomas Wiard began making wooden plows. Shortly after 1800, a blast furnace was built that produced iron utensils and, during the War of 1812, cast shot for the Army. When the Erie Canal reached town in the late 1820s, Syracuse's industrial future was assured. Today the city has many large and varied industries.

What to See and Do

Beaver Lake Nature Center. A 600-acre nature preserve that incl 10 mi of trails and boardwalks, a 200-acre lake that serves as a rest stop for migrating ducks and geese and a visitor center that features exhibits. In the winter the preserve is also used for cross-country skiing and snowshoeing. Other programs incl maple sugaring and guided canoe tours. (Daily) 12 mi NW via I-690 at 8477 E Mud Lake Rd in Baldwinsville. Phone 315/638-2519. Per vehicle ¢

Burnet Park Zoo. Zoo traces origin of life from 600 million yrs ago; exhibits on animals' unique adaptations and animal/human interaction; gift shop. (Daily; closed Jan 1, Dec 25) S Wilbur Ave. Phone 315/435-8516. ¢¢

Erie Canal Museum. Indoor and outdoor exhibits detail the construction and operation of the Erie Canal; 65-ft reconstructed canal boat from which exhibits are seen; research library and archives. Museum also houses

Urban Cultural Park Visitor Center. Slide show and exhibits here introduce visitors to area attractions. (Daily; closed hols) Weighlock Bldg, Erie Blvd E & Montgomery St. Phone 315/471-0593. **Donation.** The museum also maintains

Canal Center. Located in Erie Canal State Park. Exhibits describe canal structures nearby, incl aqueducts and bowstring bridges. (Memorial Day-Labor Day, daily exc Mon) Lyndon Rd, 4 mi E at jct NY 5, 92. Phone 315/471-0593. **Free.**

Everson Museum of Art. First I.M. Pei Museum, permanent collection of American paintings, Asian art; collection of American ceramics; home of the Syracuse China Center for the Study of American Ceramics; changing exhibits. (Daily exc Mon; closed hols) 401 Harrison St. Phone 315/474-6064. **Free.**

Green Lakes State Park. Swimming beach, bathhouse; boat rentals, fishing. Hiking, biking trails; 18-hole golf. Cross-country skiing. Picnicking, playground, concession. Tent & trailer sites (late May-Columbus Day wkend), cabins. Standard fees. 10 mi E via NY 5 in Fayetteville. Phone 315/637-6111. Memorial Day-Labor Day ¢¢

Landmark Theatre. Built in 1928 as a Loew's State Theatre in the era of vaudeville-movie houses. The interior architecture is filled with carvings, chandeliers and ornate gold decorations. Theater houses concerts, comedy, plays, dance and classic movies. 362 S Salina St. For schedule phone 315/475-7979.

New York State Canal Cruises. Departs Albany, Syracuse and Buffalo (June-Oct). Also 3-hr dinner cruises (nightly), 4-hr excursions (Sun), sightseeing cruises (phone for schedule) depart from Liverpool (May-Oct). Contact Mid-Lakes Navigation Co, PO Box 61-M, Skaneateles 13152; 800/545-4318 or 315/685-8500.

Onondaga Historical Assoc Museum. Changing and permanent exhibits illustrate history of central New York. (Tues-Sat afternoons; closed most hols) 311 Montgomery St. Phone 315/428-1864. **Donation.**

Onondaga Lake Park. Picnicking, concession, bicycle rentals, exercise trail, tram rides, children's play area, boat launch and marina. 2 1/2 mi NW via I-81 to Liverpool exit. Phone 315/453-6712 or 315/451-7275. **Free.** On grounds are

Salt Museum. Re-created 19th-century salt "boiling block"; artifacts and exhibits of Onondaga salt industry. Starting point for history and nature trail around lake. (May-Oct, daily exc Mon) Phone 315/453-6767. ¢

Ste Marie Among the Iroquois. A 17th-century French mission living history museum. Blacksmithing, cooking, carpentry and gardening activities. Special programs. (May-Nov, Wed-Sun; Dec-Apr, daily exc Mon) Phone 315/453-6767. ¢¢

Syracuse Univ (1870). (16,720 students) Major, private graduate-level research and teaching institution. Noted for the Maxwell School of Citizenship and Public Affairs, Newhouse School of Public Communications, School of Computer & Information Science, College of Engineering and 50,000 seat Carrier Dome. University Ave at University Pl. Phone 315/443-3127.On the 650-acre campus is

Lowe Art Gallery. Shaffer Art Bldg. Shows, paintings, sculpture, other art. Phone 315/443-3127 for schedule. **Free.**

Annual Events

Balloon Festival. Jamesville Beach Park. Mid-June.

Onondaga Lake Waterfront Extravaganza. Onondaga Lake Park. Waterski show, musical entertainment, children's shows. July.

Scottish Games. Long Branch Park. Mid-Aug.

NY State Fair. State Fairgrounds. Phone 315/487-7711. Late Aug-early Sept.

Golden Harvest Festival. Beaver Lake Nature Center. Old-time harvest activities. Early Sept.

Seasonal Events

Open-air concerts. In city parks, downtown and throughout city. Mon-Fri. Phone 315/473-4330. Early July-late Aug.

Syracuse Stage. 820 E Genesee St. Original, professional theatrical productions. Phone 315/443-3275. Sept-May.

Motels

✔★ ★ **BEST WESTERN-MARSHALL MANOR.** *(US 11 & NY 80, Tully 13159)* 22 mi S on I-81 exit 14. 315/696-6061; FAX 315/696-6406. 44 rms, 2 story. S, D $44-$72; each addl $5; under 12 free; higher rates: state fair, Dirt wk. Crib $5. TV; cable. Restaurant 6 am-10 pm. Bar 4 pm-midnight. Ck-out 11 am. Meeting rms. Business servs avail. Downhill ski 2 1/2 mi; x-country ski 10 mi. Cr cds: A, C, D, DS, JCB, MC, V.

D ⚡ 🏊 🐾 📶 SC

★ **COMFORT INN.** 7010 Interstate Island Rd (13209). 315/453-0045; FAX 315/453-3689. 109 rms, 4 story. S, D $55-$60; each addl $5; under 18 free; higher rates: state fair, special events. Crib free. TV; cable, VCR avail (movies). Restaurant adj 6 am-11 pm. Ck-out 11 am. Meeting rms. Exercise equipt. Cr cds: A, C, D, DS, JCB, MC, V.

D 🏋 ✈ 🐾 📶 SC

★ ★ **COURTYARD BY MARRIOTT.** *(6415 Yorktown Circle, East Syracuse 13057)* E on I-690, exit 17. 315/432-0300; FAX 315/432-9950. 149 rms, 3 story. S, D $69-$94; suites $104; under 12 free; wkend rates. Crib free (with res). TV; cable (premium), VCR avail. Indoor pool; whirlpool, lifeguard. Complimentary coffee in rms. Restaurant 6:30-10 am. Bar 4-11 pm. Ck-out noon. Coin lndry. Meeting rms. Business servs avail. In-rm modem link. Valet serv. Sundries. Exercise equipt. Refrigerator in suites. Balconies. Cr cds: A, C, D, DS, MC, V.

D 🏊 🏋 🐾 📶 SC

✔★ ★ **ECONO LODGE.** *(401 7th North St, Liverpool 13088)* At jct I-81 exit 25 & I-90 exit 36. 315/451-6000; res: 800/553-2666; FAX 315/451-0193. 83 rms, 4 story. May-Sept: S $42-$59; D $49-$79; each addl $4; suites $49-$59; under 18 free; higher rates special events; lower rates rest of yr. Crib free. Pet accepted, some restrictions; $3. TV; cable. Complimentary continental bkfst. Restaurant adj 6 am-11 pm. Ck-out 11 am. Business servs avail. Cr cds: A, C, D, DS, MC, V.

D ✦ ⊠ 🔥 SC

✔★ ★ FAIRFIELD INN BY MARRIOTT. *6611 Old Collamer Rd (13057).* 315/432-9333. 135 rms, 3 story. June-Oct: S $54-$59; D $60-$70; under 18 free; lower rates rest of yr. Crib free. TV; cable (premium). Pool. Complimentary continental bkfst. Restaurants adj. Ck-out noon. Meeting rm. Business servs avail. In-rm modem link. Cr cds: A, D, DS, MC, V.

D ⊠ ⊠ 🔥 SC

★ ★ GENESEE INN. *1060 E Genesee St (13210).* 315/476-4212; FAX 315/471-4663; res: 800/365-HOME. 96 rms, 2 story. S $79-$99; D $89-$109; under 18 free; higher rates university special events. Crib free. Pet accepted. TV; cable. Restaurant 7 am-10 pm. Rm serv. Bar 11:30-1 am. Ck-out 11 am. Meeting rms. Business servs avail. Health club privileges. Cr cds: A, C, D, DS, MC, V.

D ✦ ⊠ 🔥 SC

★ HAMPTON INN. *6605 Old Collamer Rd (13057).* 315/463-6443; FAX 315/432-1080. 116 rms, 4 story. S, D $65.75; suites $85; under 18 free. Crib $10. TV; cable. Complimentary continental bkfst. Ck-out 1 pm. Meeting rm. Business servs avail. In-rm modem link. Valet serv (Mon-Fri). Health club privileges. Cr cds: A, D, DS, MC, V.

D ⊠ 🔥 SC

★ ★ HOLIDAY INN-EAST. *(6555 Old Collamer Rd S, East Syracuse 13057)* On NY 298 at I-90 exit 35. 315/437-2761; FAX 315/463-0028. 203 rms, 2 story. S, D $90-$119; under 19 free; wkend rates; higher rates special events. TV; cable. Indoor pool; whirlpool. Complimentary coffee in rms. Restaurant 6 am-2 pm, 5-10 pm. Rm serv. Bar 4 pm-2 am. Ck-out noon. Meeting rms. Business servs avail. In-rm modem link. Bellhops. Valet serv (Mon-Fri). Exercise equipt; sauna. Cr cds: A, C, D, DS, ER, JCB, MC, V.

D ⊠ ✗ 🔥 ⊠ SC

✔★ JOHN MILTON INN. *6578 Thompson Rd (13206),* I-90 exit 35, Carrier Circle. 315/463-8555; FAX 315/432-9240; res: 800/352-1061. 54 rms, 2 story. S $30-$70; D $37-$70; each addl $10; under 12 free; higher rates special events. Crib $5. Pet accepted. TV; cable (premium). Complimentary continental bkfst. Restaurant adj open 24 hrs. Ck-out 11:30 am. Business servs avail. Cr cds: A, C, D, DS, MC, V.

✦ ⊠ 🔥 SC

✔★ KNIGHTS INN. *(430 Electronics Pkwy, Liverpool 13088)* I-90 exit 37. 315/453-6330; FAX 315/457-9240; res: 800/843-5644. 82 air-cooled rms, 8 kits. S $35-$65; D $43.95-$75; each addl $5; under 18 free; wkly rates. Crib free. Pet accepted, some restrictions. TV; cable (premium), VCR (movies). Complimentary continental bkfst. Restaurant adj 11 am-10 pm. Ck-out 11 am. Meeting rms. Business servs avail. Downhill ski 20 mi; x-country ski 1 mi. Cr cds: A, C, D, DS, MC, V.

D ✦ ⊠ ⊠ 🔥 SC

★ ★ RAMADA INN. *1305 Buckley Rd (13212).* 315/457-8670; FAX 315/457-8633. E-mail sales@ramadasyracuse.com; web www.ramadasyracuse.com. 150 rms, 2 story. S $70-$89; D $80-$99; each addl $10; suites $129-$150; under 18 free; higher rates: state fair, university special events. Crib free. TV; cable (premium), VCR avail. Pool; lifeguard. Restaurant 6 am-10 pm. Rm serv. Bar 11:30 am-midnight. Ck-out noon. Meeting rms. Business servs avail. Valet serv. Sundries. Airport transportation. Exercise equipt. Cr cds: A, C, D, DS, ER, JCB, MC, V.

D ⊠ ✗ ✗ 🔥 SC

✔★ RED ROOF INN. *6614 N Thompson Rd (13206).* 315/437-3309; FAX 315/437-7865. 115 rms, 3 story. S $31.99-$64.99; D $35.99-$71.99; under 18 free. Crib free. Pet accepted. TV; cable (premium). Complimentary coffee in lobby. Restaurant opp open 24 hrs. Ck-out noon. Business servs avail. Cr cds: A, C, D, DS, MC, V.

D ✦ ⊠ 🔥 SC

★ ★ RESIDENCE INN BY MARRIOTT. *(6420 Yorktown Circle, East Syracuse 13057)* I-90 exit exit 35. 315/432-4488; FAX 315/432-1042. 102 kit. suites, 2 story. S $69-$114; D $89-$129; wkly, wkend rates; higher rates: hols, special events. Crib free. Pet accepted; $100. TV; cable (premium). Pool; whirlpool, lifeguard. Complimentary continental bkfst. Complimentary coffee in rms. Restaurant nearby. Ck-out noon. Coin lndry. Meeting rms. Business servs avail. Valet serv. Downhill ski 20 mi. Exercise equipt. Health club privileges. Picnic tables. Cr cds: A, C, D, DS, JCB, MC, V.

D ✦ ⊠ ✗ ⊠ 🔥 SC

✔★ SUPER 8. *(421 7th North St, Liverpool 13088)* I-90 exit 36 or I-81 exit 25. 315/451-8888; FAX 315/451-0043. 99 rms, 4 story. S $41-$46; D $39-$71; under 18 free; higher rates: state fair, university graduation, special events. Crib free. TV; cable. Complimentary continental bkfst. Restaurant nearby. Ck-out noon. Business servs avail. In-rm modem link. Downhill/x-country ski 20 mi. Picnic tables. Cr cds: A, C, D, DS, JCB, MC, V.

D ⊠ ⊠ 🔥 SC

Motor Hotels

★ ★ ★ FOUR POINTS BY SHERATON. *(Electronics Pkwy & 7th North St, Liverpool 13088)* I-90 exit 37, 1 mi NW off I-81 exit 25. 315/457-1122; FAX 315/451-1269. 280 rms, 6 story. S, D $75-$150; each addl $10; under 18 free; wkend rates. Crib free. Pet accepted. TV; cable. Indoor pool; whirlpool, lifeguard. Restaurant 6:30 am-11 pm. Rm serv. Bar 2 pm-2 am; entertainment (seasonal). Ck-out 1 pm. Business servs avail. In-rm modem link. Bellhops. Valet serv Mon-Fri. Sundries. Exercise equipt. Game rm. Patios. Cr cds: A, C, D, DS, ER, MC, V.

D ✦ ⊠ ✗ ⊠ 🔥 SC

★ ★ ★ MARRIOTT. *(6301 NY 298, East Syracuse 13057)* 8 mi NE on NY 298, 1/4 mi E of I-90 exit 35. 315/432-0200; FAX 315/433-1210. 250 units, 4-7 story. S $140; D $165; each addl $10; suites $275; studio rms $140; under 18 free; wkend rates. Crib free. TV; cable (premium). Indoor/outdoor pool; whirlpool, poolside serv. Restaurant 6 am-11 pm. Rm serv. Bar noon-2 am; entertainment Fri. Ck-out noon. Coin lndry. Convention facilities. Business servs avail. In-rm modem link. Bellhops. Valet serv. Sundries. Gift shop. Free airport transportation. Tennis privileges. Golf privileges. Exercise equipt; sauna. Game rm. Some refrigerators. Some private patios, balconies. Cr cds: A, C, D, DS, ER, JCB, MC, V.

D ✗ ✦ ⊠ ✗ ✗ ⊠ 🔥 SC

Hotels

★ ★ ★ EMBASSY SUITES. *6646 Old Collamer Rd (13057).* 315/446-3200; FAX 315/437-3302. 215 kit. suites, 5 story. S $109-$149; D $119-$169; each addl $10; under 18 free; higher rates: university events, state fair. Crib free. TV; cable (premium). Indoor pool; poolside serv, lifeguard. Complimentary full bkfst. Complimentary coffee in rms. Restaurant 11 am-10 pm. Bar to midnight. Ck-out noon. Coin lndry. Meeting rms. Business servs avail. In-rm modem link. Gift shop. Airport transportation. Exercise equipt; sauna. Wet bars. Cr cds: A, C, D, DS, MC, V.

D ⊠ ✗ ⊠ 🔥 SC

★ ★ ★ SHERATON UNIVERSITY HOTEL & CONFERENCE CENTER. *801 University Ave (13210),* at Syracuse Univ. 315/475-3000; FAX 315/475-3311. E-mail sales@syracuse.newcastlehotels.com; web www.syracusesheraton.com. 232 rms, 9 story. S $99-$149; D $99-$159; each addl $10; suites $290; under 18 free; higher rates university events. Crib $10. Pet accepted. TV; cable. Indoor pool; whirlpool, lifeguard. Coffee in rms. Restaurant 7 am-2 pm, 5-10 pm. Bar 11-2 am; entertainment. Ck-out noon. Convention facilities. Business center. In-rm modem link. Gift shop. Exercise equipt; sauna. Some refrigerators. Luxury level. Cr cds: A, C, D, DS, MC, V.

D ✦ ⊠ ✗ ⊠ 🔥 SC 🏃

Inns

★ ★ **THE DICKENSON HOUSE ON JAMES.** *1504 James St (13203).* 315/423-4777; res: 888/423-4777; FAX 315/425-1965. Web www.dereamscape.com/dickinsonhouse. 4 rms. S $95-$120; D $95-$135; each addl $15; hols 2-day min. TV avail; cable (premium), VCR avail (movies). Complimentary full bkfst. Restaurant nearby. Ck-out 11 am, ck-in 3 pm. Business servs avail. In-rm modem link. Luggage handling. Valet serv. Concierge serv. Downhill ski 15 mi; x-country ski 5 mi. Built in 1924; English Tudor decor. Totally nonsmoking. Cr cds: A, DS, MC, V.

★ ★ ★ **GREEN GATE.** *(2 Main St, Camillus 13031)* Approx 5 mi W via NY 5, then 1 mi W on NY 173. 315/672-9276. 6 rms. S, D $60-$175. TV; cable. Complimentary continental bkfst. Restaurant (see GREEN GATE INN). Rm serv. Ck-out 11 am, ck-in 3 pm. Business servs avail. Some whirlpools. Built 1861; first town wedding held here. Totally nonsmoking. Cr cds: A, C, D, DS, MC, V.

Restaurants

★ ★ **CAPTAIN AHAB'S.** *3449 Erie Blvd E (13214).* 315/446-3272. Specializes in seafood, steak, prime rib. Salad bar. Hrs: 11:30 am-10 pm; Fri, Sat to 11 pm. Closed Thanksgiving, Dec 25. Res accepted. Bar to 1 am. Semi-a la carte: lunch $4.95-$7.95, dinner $8.95-$26.95. Child's meals. Parking. Outdoor dining. Nautical decor. Saltwater aquarium. Family-owned since 1956. Cr cds: A, D, DS, MC, V.

★ ★ **COLEMAN'S.** *100 S Lowell Ave (13204).* 315/476-1933. Irish, Continental menu. Specializes in corned beef, steak, seafood. Own desserts. Hrs: 11:30 am-10 pm. Closed Dec 25. Res accepted. Bar 10-2 am. Semi-a la carte: lunch $4-$8, dinner $10-$17. Child's meals. Entertainment Fri, Sat. Parking. Outdoor dining. Authentic Irish pub; original tin ceiling, mahogany staircase. Family-owned since 1933. Cr cds: A, C, D, DS, MC, V.

✔★ **FRED GRIMALDI'S.** *6430 Yorktown Circle (13057).* 315/437-7608. Italian menu. Specializes in pasta, veal. Hrs: 5-10 pm. Closed Sun. Res accepted. Bar. Semi-a la carte: dinner $7.95-$19.95. Child's meals. Parking. Italian decor. Cr cds: A, D, DS, MC, V.

★ ★ **FRED GRIMALDI'S CHOP HOUSE.** *(6400 Yorktown Circle, East Syracuse 13057)* NY Thruway, exit 35. 315/437-1461. Continental menu. Specializes in steak, seafood, chops. Hrs: 11:30 am-10 pm; Fri, Sat to 11 pm; Sun 4-10 pm. Closed July 4, Dec 24, 25. Res accepted; required hols. Bar. Semi-a la carte: lunch $4.50-$12, dinner $12.95-$26.50. Child's meals. Parking. Antiques, objets d'art Cr cds: A, D, DS, MC, V.

★ ★ **GLEN LOCH MILL.** *(4626 North St, Jamesville 13078)* 10 mi S, I-481 exit 2, I-90 exit 34A. 315/469-6969. Continental menu. Specializes in seafood, veal, prime rib. Raw bar. Hrs: 5-10 pm; Sun 2-9 pm; Sun brunch 10 am-2 pm. Closed Dec 24-25. Res accepted. Bar 5 pm to midnight. Semi-a la carte: dinner $13.95-$18.95. Sun brunch $11.95. Child's meals. Dinner theater Fri-Sun. Parking. Outdoor dining. Glen setting, waterwheel. Converted feed mill; built in 1827. Family-owned. Cr cds: A, DS, MC, V.

★ ★ **GREEN GATE INN.** *(See Green Gate Inn)* 315/672-9276. Continental menu. Specializes in steak, seafood, veal. Hrs: 11:30 am-3 pm, 4-10 pm; Sat 4-10 pm; Sun 10 am-2 pm (brunch); 3-9 pm. Closed Dec 25. Res accepted. Bar 4 pm-midnight. Semi-a la carte: lunch $3.95-$7.95,

dinner $7.95-$22.50. Child's meals. Parking. Restored inn (1861) with fireplace, some antiques. 19th-century decor. Cr cds: A, C, D, MC, V.

★ ★ ★ **INN BETWEEN.** *(2290 W Genesee Tpke, Camillus 13031)* 10 mi W on NY 5, ¼ mi W of I-5 Auburn cut-off. 315/672-3166. Continental menu. Specialties: chicken Oscar, roast duckling, beef Wellington. Own baking. Hrs: 5-10 pm; Sun 2-9 pm. Closed Mon. Res accepted. Bar from 4 pm. Semi-a la carte: dinner $16.95-$21.95. Child's meals. Parking. Herb garden. In 1880 country house; elegant country decor. Cr cds: A, MC, V.

✔★ ★ **INN OF THE SEASONS.** *4311 W Seneca Tpke (13215).* 315/492-4001. Continental menu. Specializes in seafood, veal, steak. Hrs: 11:30 am-2 pm, 5-10 pm; Fri to 11 pm; Sat 5-11 pm; Sun noon-8 pm. Closed Mon. Res accepted. Bar. Semi-a la carte: lunch $4.75-$7.95, dinner $10.50-$19.95. Parking. Stone house (1812); colonial decor. Cr cds: A, MC, V.

★ ★ ★ **PASCALE.** *204 W Fayette St (13202).* 315/471-3040. Continental menu. Specializes in dishes prepared by wood-burning grill, oven and rotisserie. Hrs: 11:30 am-2:30 pm, 5:30-10 pm; Sat from 5:30 pm. Closed Sun; major hols. Res accepted. Bar. Wine cellar. Semi-a la carte: lunch $6-$8, dinner $10-$20. Outdoor dining (summer). Valet parking (dinner). Original paintings. Cr cds: A, C, D, MC, V.

★ **PHOEBE'S GARDEN CAFE.** *900 E Genesee St (13210).* 315/475-5154. Continental menu. Specializes in grilled steak, seafood, vegetarian choices. Own desserts. Hrs: 11:30 am-10 pm; Mon to midnight; Fri, Sat to 1 am; Sun 4-9 pm; Sun brunch 11 am-4 pm. Closed major hols. Res accepted. Bar. A la carte entrees: lunch $2.95-$10.95, dinner $5.95-$15.95. Sun brunch $10.95. Turn-of-the-century building; old gaslights. Cr cds: A, D, MC, V.

✔★ **PLAINVILLE FARMS.** *(8450 Brewerton Rd, Cicero 13039)* 15 mi N on US 11, ½ mi NW of I-81 exit 30. 315/699-3852. Specializes in turkey, steak, seafood. Salad bar. Hrs: 11 am-9 pm. Closed Dec 25. Semi-a la carte: lunch $2.95-$6.95, dinner $6.95-$9.95. Child's meals. Colonial decor. Totally nonsmoking. Cr cds: DS, MC, V.

★ ★ **TOP O' THE HILL.** *(5633 W Genesee St, Camillus 13031)* 6 mi W on W Genesee St. 315/488-2400. Continental menu. Specializes in prime rib, seafood. Own desserts. Hrs: 11:30 am-10 pm; early-bird dinner Tues-Sat 5-7 pm; Sun brunch 11 am-2:30 pm. Closed Mon. Res accepted. Bar to 1 am. Semi-a la carte: lunch $2.95-$7.95, dinner $7.95-$20. Sun brunch $9.95. Child's meals. Entertainment Fri, Sat. Parking. Country decor. Family-owned. Cr cds: A, C, D, DS, MC, V.

Unrated Dining Spots

BROOKLYN PICKLE. *2222 Burnet Ave (13206),* at Midler Ave. 315/463-1851. Deli menu. Specializes in sandwiches, soups, pickles. Hrs: 9 am-9 pm. Closed Sun; major hols. Semi-a la carte: bkfst $2-$4, lunch, dinner $3-$5. Parking. Outdoor dining. Family-owned. Totally nonsmoking. No cr cds accepted.

PASTABILITIES. *311 S Franklin St.* 315/474-1153. Continental menu. Specializes in homemade pasta, antipasto. Hrs: 11 am-3 pm, 5-10:30 pm; Fri, Sat to midnight. Closed Sun; major hols. Bar 5 pm-midnight; Fri, Sat to 2 am. A la carte entrees: lunch $4-$6, dinner $6-$18. Cafeteria-style serv at lunch, table-serv at dinner. Outdoor dining. In Old Labor Temple Bldg (1889). Extensive Italian & domestic wine list. Cr cds: A, C, D, MC, V.

TWIN TREES. *1100 Avery Ave (13204), off W Genesee St. 315/468-0622.* Italian, Amer menu. Specializes in pizza, Italian dishes. Hrs: 4-11 pm; Fri, Sat to 1 am. Closed Easter, Thanksgiving, Dec 25. Bar. Semi-a la carte: dinner $4-$22.95. Child's meals. Family-owned. Cr cds: A, C, D, DS, MC, V.

Tarrytown (A-2)

(See also New York City, White Plains, Yonkers)

Pop 10,739 **Elev** 118 ft **Area code** 914 **Zip** 10591 **Web** www.hudsonvalley.org
Information Sleepy Hollow Chamber of Commerce, 54 Main St, 10591-3660; 914/631-1705.

The village of Tarrytown and the neighboring villages of Irvington and Sleepy Hollow were settled by the Dutch during the mid-1600s. The name Tarrytown was taken from the Dutch word "Tarwe," meaning wheat. Here, on September 23, 1780, the British spy Major John André was captured while carrying the detailed plans for West Point given to him by Benedict Arnold. The village and the area were made famous by the writings of Washington Irving, particularly " *The Legend of Sleepy Hollow*," from which this region takes its name.

What to See and Do

Kykuit. This 6-story stone mansion was home to 3 generations of the Rockefeller family; principal first-floor rms open to the public. Extensive gardens with spectacular Hudson River views feature an important collection of 20th-century sculpture acquired by Gov. Nelson A. Rockefeller; carriage barn with collection of antique cars and horse-drawn vehicles. Scheduled tours lasting 2 1/2 hrs depart approx every 15 min from Philipsburg Manor (Mid-Apr-Oct, daily exc Tues; res advised). In Sleepy Hollow; accessible only by shuttle bus from Philipsburg Manor. Phone 914/631-9491. ¢¢¢¢¢

Lyndhurst (1838). Gothic-revival mansion built for William Paulding, mayor of New York City in the 1830s. Approx 67 landscaped acres overlooking the Hudson. Contains books, art and furnishings. Tours. (Mid-Apr-Oct, daily exc Mon; rest of yr, Sat & Sun) (See SEASONAL EVENT) 635 S Broadway, 1/2 mi S of Tappan Zee Bridge on US 9.Phone 914/631-4481. ¢¢¢

Marymount College (1907). (800 women) On 25-acre hilltop campus overlooking the Hudson River. Tours of campus. Phone 914/631-3200.

Music Hall Theater (1885). One of the oldest remaining theaters in the county; now serves as center for the arts. 13 Main St. Phone 914/631-3390.

Old Dutch Church of Sleepy Hollow (1685). Church bldg of Dutch origins built on what was the Manor of Frederick Philipse. Restored, including a replica of the original pulpit. Tours by appt. (May-Oct, daily exc Mon) Broadway & Pierson (US 9). Phone 914/631-1123.

Philipsburg Manor. Colonial farm and trading site (1720-1750); also departure point for tour of Kykuit. Manor house, barn, animals; restored operating gristmill, wooden millpond bridge across Pocantico River. A 15-min film precedes tours. Reception center; exhibition gallery; museum shop; picnic area. (Mar-Dec, daily exc Tues; closed Thanksgiving, Dec 25) (See ANNUAL EVENTS) In Sleepy Hollow, on US 9, 2 mi N of NY Thrwy exit 9. Phone 914/631-8200. ¢¢

Sleepy Hollow Cemetery. Graves of Washington Irving, Andrew Carnegie, William Rockefeller. Adj to Old Dutch Church in Sleepy Hollow.

Sunnyside. Washington Irving's Hudson River estate (1835-59). Contains much of his furnishings, personal property and library. Museum shop. Landscaped grounds; picnic area. (Mar-Dec, daily exc Tues; rest of yr, wkends; closed Jan 1, Thanksgiving, Dec 25) (See ANNUAL EVENTS) On W Sunnyside Lane, W of US 9, 1 mi S of NY Thrwy exit 9. Phone 914/631-8200. ¢¢¢

The Historical Society of the Tarrytowns. Victorian house incl parlor, dining rm; artifacts from archeological dig; Native American rm; library,

map and photograph collection; children's rm. (Tues-Sat afternoons; closed some hols) 1 Grove St. Phone 914/631-8374. **Donation.**

Van Cortlandt Manor. Post-Revolutionary War estate of prominent Colonial family. Elegantly-furnished manor house; ferry-house inn and kitchen bldg on old Albany Post Rd; "Long Walk" with flanking 18th-century gardens; picnic area. Frequent demonstrations of open-hearth cooking, brick-making, weaving. Museum shop. (Apr-Dec, daily exc Tues; closed Thanksgiving, Dec 25) (See ANNUAL EVENTS) In Croton-on-Hudson, at Croton Point Ave exit on US 9, 10 mi N of NY Thrwy exit 9.Phone 914/638-8200. ¢¢¢

Annual Events

Autumn Crafts & Tasks Festival. Van Cortlandt Manor. Demonstrations of 18th-century crafts and activities. Early Oct.

Candlelight Tours. At Sunnyside, Philipsburg Manor and Van Cortland Manor. English Christmas Celebration. Phone 914/631-8200 for res (Sunnyside & Philipsburg) or 914/631-4481 for res (Lyndhurst). Dec.

Seasonal Event

Sunset Serenades. On Lyndhurst grounds. Symphony concerts (Sat). Phone 914/631-4481. July.

Motels

★ ★ **COURTYARD BY MARRIOTT.** *475 White Plains Rd. 914/631-1122; FAX 914/631-1357.* Web www.courtyard.com. 139 rms, 2-3 story, 19 suites. S, D $149; suites $164-$169; family rates; package plans. Crib free. TV; cable. Indoor pool; whirlpool. Complimentary coffee in rms. Restaurant 6:30-10 am; Sat, Sun 6:30-midnight. Rm serv Mon-Fri 5-10 pm. Bar Mon-Thurs 4-11 pm. Ck-out noon. Coin lndry. Meeting rms. Valet serv. Exercise equipt. Refrigerator in suites; microwaves avail. Cr cds: A, C, D, DS, MC, V.

D 🏊 🏋 ⚓ 🐾 SC

★ ★ **RAMADA INN.** *(540 Saw Mill River Rd, Elmsford 10523)* E on NY 287, N on NY 9A. 914/592-3300; FAX 914/592-3381. 101 rms, 5 story. Mar-Oct: S $99-$144; D $99-$159; each addl $10; under 18 free. Crib free. Pet accepted, some restrictions. TV; cable (premium), VCR. Indoor/outdoor pool; lifeguard. Complimentary coffee in rms. Restaurant 6:30 am-10 pm. Rm serv. Bar noon-midnight; entertainment Fri, Sat. Ck-out noon. Meeting rms. Business servs avail. Health club privileges. Cr cds: A, C, D, DS, ER, JCB, MC, V.

D 🐾 🏊 ⚓ 🔥 SC

Lodges

★ ★ ★ **THE CASTLE AT TARRYTOWN.** *400 Benedict Ave. 914/631-1980; FAX 914/631-4612.* Web www.castleattarrytown.com. 39 rms, 4 story, 9 suites. S, D $300-$400; suites $375-$495; wkends 2-day min. TV; cable (premium), VCR (movies). Restaurant (see EQUUS). Rm serv 6 am-11 pm. Bar 11 am-10 pm. Ck-out noon. Meeting rms. Business center. In-rm modem link. Bellhops. Valet serv. Concierge. Airport transportation. Tennis privileges. 18-hole golf privileges. X-country ski 5 mi. Exercise equipt; sauna. Lawn games. Bathrm phones, refrigerators; some in-rm whirlpools, fireplaces. Cr cds: A, MC, V.

🎿 🏌 🏋 🔥

★ ★ ★ **TARRYTOWN HOUSE.** *E Sunnyside Lane, 1/2 mi off I-287, W off NY 9. 914/591-8200; FAX 914/591-7118; res: 800/553-8118 (NY).* E-mail threservations@erols.com; web www.dolce.com. 148 rms in two 2 story bldgs. S, D $139; each addl $15; under 12 free. Crib free. TV; cable (premium). 2 pools; 1 indoor, whirlpool. Complimentary full bkfst. Complimentary coffee in rms. Dining rm 6:30 am-10 pm. Ck-out 11 am. Business center. In-rm modem link. Concierge. Bellhops. Tennis. Racquetball. Exercise rm; sauna. Balconies. 26-acre estate includes two 19th-century mansions; Greek-revival King House and chateau-style Biddle House. Extensive gardens and wooded areas. Cr cds: A, D, DS, MC, V.

🄳 📺 🏊 ✈ 🕴 ⚡ 🐾 SC 🚶

Motor Hotel

★ ★ ★ **HILTON.** *455 S Broadway, at I-87 exit 9, on NY 9. 914/631-5700; res: 800/758-0781; FAX 914/631-0075.* 250 rms, 2 story. S, D $112-$172; each addl $20; suites $200-$430; family, wkend rates. Crib free. TV; cable (premium). 2 pools, 1 indoor; wading pool, whirlpool, poolside serv, lifeguard. Playground. Restaurant 6:30 am-11 pm. Rm serv. Bar 11:30-2 am; entertainment Fri, Sat. Ck-out noon. Meeting rms. Business center. In-rm modem link. Bellhops. Airport transportation. Tennis. Exercise equipt; sauna. Massage. Private patios. Cr cds: A, C, D, DS, ER, JCB, MC, V.

🄳 📺 🏊 ✈ 🕴 ⚡ 🐾 SC 🚶

Hotel

★ ★ ★ **MARRIOTT WESTCHESTER.** *670 White Plains Rd, off I-287 exit 1. 914/631-2200; FAX 914/631-7819.* 444 rms, 10 story. S, D $175-$195; suites $350-$500; family, wkly rates; wkend rates. Crib free. TV; cable (premium), VCR avail. Indoor/outdoor pool; whirlpool. Restaurant 6:30 am-11 pm. Bar 11-3 am; entertainment. Ck-out noon. Meeting rms. Business center. In rm modem link. Gift shop. Beauty shop. Exercise rm; sauna. Massage. Some balconies. Luxury level. Cr cds: A, C, D, DS, ER, JCB, MC, V.

🄳 🏊 🕴 ⚡ 🐾 SC 🚶

Inn

★ ★ ★ **ALEXANDER HAMILTON HOUSE.** *(49 Van Wyck St, Croton-on-Hudson 10520) N on US 9 to exit 9A/Rte 129. 914/271-6737; FAX 914/271-3927.* E-mail alexhmlths@aol.com; web www.alexanderhamiltonhouse.com. 7 rms, 3 story, 1 kit. unit. S $75-$150; D $95-$250; each addl child $10, adult $25; kit. unit $85-$95; family, wkly rates; wkends (2-day min). TV; cable (premium), VCR avail. Pool. Complimentary full bkfst. Ck-out 11 am, ck-in noon. Meeting rm. In-rm modem link. Free RR station transportation. Health club privileges. X-country ski 2 mi. Lawn games. Microwaves avail. Picnic tables, grills. Victorian house (1889). Victorian decor. Totally nonsmoking. Cr cds: A, D, DS, MC, V.

🏊 ⚡ 🐾 ⚡

Restaurants

★ ★ **CARAVELA.** *53 N Broadway, I-287 exit 9. 914/631-1863.* Web www.ezpages.com. Portuguese, Brazilian cuisine. Specialties: mariscada seafood combo, paella Valencia, roasted baby suckling pig. Hrs: 11:30 am-3 pm, 5-11 pm. Closed Thanksgiving, Dec 25. Res accepted; required wkends. Bar. Semi-a la carte: lunch $8.95-$12.95, dinner $12.50-$23. Child's meals. Parking. Outdoor dining. Tile floor. Cr cds: A, C, D, DS, MC, V.

🄳

★ ★ **EQUUS.** *(See The Castle At Tarrytown Lodge) 914/631-3646.* Web www.castleattarrytown.com. Continental menu. Specializes in beef, chicken, seafood. Hrs: 6:30-10 am, noon-2:30 pm, 6:30-10:30 pm; Sun 6:30-10 am, (brunch) noon-2:30 pm, 6:30-9 pm. Res accepted. Bar. Wine cellar. Semi-a la carte: bkfst $8-$25, lunch $23-$37, dinner $35-$50. Sun brunch $29. Child's meals. Valet parking. Outdoor dining. View of river. Cr cds: A, D, MC, V.

🄳

★ ★ **GAULIN'S.** *(86 E Main, Elmsford 10523) 2 mi SE on NY 119. 914/592-4213.* E-mail hashling2@aol.com; web www.townlink.com. Specializes in pasta, steak & chops, crab cakes. Own desserts. Hrs: 11:30 am-3:30 pm, 4-10:30 pm; Fri, Sat to 11 pm; Sun 2-9 pm. Res accepted. Bar. Semi-a la carte: lunch $5.50-$18.50, dinner $9.50-$23.50. Child's

meals. Parking. Outdoor dining. Fireplace. Family-owned. Cr cds: A, C, D, DS, MC, V.

🄳

★ ★ **ICHI RIKI.** *(1 E Main St, Elmsford 10523) 2 mi E on NY 119. 914/592-2220.* Japanese menu. Specializes in sushi. Hrs: 11:45 am-2:30 pm, 5:30-10 pm; Fri to 11 pm; Sat noon-2:30 pm, 5-11 pm; Sun 5-9:30 pm. Closed Mon; also Thanksgiving, Dec 25. Res accepted. Bar. Semi-a la carte: lunch $9-$13.25, dinner $14.25-$27.50.Parking. Japanese-style dining. Cr cds: A, C, D, MC, V.

🄳

★ ★ ★ **MAISON LAFITTE.** *(Chappaqua Rd, Briarcliff Manor 10510) Taconic State Pkwy, 9A N exit. 914/941-5787.* French continental cuisine. Specialties: crêpe Riviera, veal cordon bleu, duckling à l'orange. Hrs: noon-2:30 pm, 5-10 pm; Sat 5-11 pm; Sun noon-9 pm. Res accepted; required wkends. Bar. Wine cellar. A la carte entrees: lunch $9.50-$16. Complete meals: dinner $24-$29. Child's meals. Parking. Mansion (1902) overlooks garden, Hudson River; wrought iron doors, marble terrace. Family-owned. Cr cds: A, D, MC, V.

🄳

★ ★ **RUDY'S BEAU RIVAGE.** *(19 Livingston Ave, Dobbs Ferry 10522) 4 mi S of Tappanzee Bridge on Rte 9, right turn on Livingston Ave. 914/693-3192.* Continental menu. Specializes in seafood. Hrs: noon-3 pm, 5-9 pm; Fri, Sat to 10 pm; Sun noon-8 pm; Sun brunch to 3:30 pm. Closed Mon. Res accepted. Bar. Semi-a la carte: complete lunch $10, dinner $10.50-$20. Sun brunch $13.50-$16.95. Child's meals. Parking. Victorian decor. On Hudson River. Family-owned. Cr cds: A, MC, V.

🄳 🍽

✔★ ★ **SANTA FE.** *5 Main St, just W of NY 9. 914/332-4452.* Web www.e.z.pages.com/santefe. Mexican, Southwestern menu. Specializes in fajitas, taco baskets. Own desserts. Hrs: 11:30 am-10:30 pm; Fri, Sat to 11:15 pm; Sun 1-9:15 pm. Closed Easter, Thanksgiving, Dec 25. Res accepted. Bar. Semi-a la carte: lunch $3.95-$14.95, dinner $7.50-$16.95. Child's meals. Southwestern decor; artwork. Cr cds: A, C, D, DS, MC, V.

🄳

Thousand Islands (B-5)

(Along the eastern United States-Canadian border)

This group of more than 1,800 islands on the eastern US-Canadian border, at the head of the St Lawrence River, extends 52 miles downstream from the end of Lake Ontario. Slightly more than half the islands are in Canada. Some of them are five miles wide and extend more than 20 miles in length. These rocky slivers of land are noted for their scenery and numerous parks, including St Lawrence Islands National Park (see CANADA). The Thousand Islands Bridge and highway (7 miles long) between the New York and Ontario mainlands crosses several of the isles and channels. Many of the islands were settled during the early 1900s by American millionaires, whose opulent summer residences and private clubs made the area renowned throughout the world.

The Seaway Trail, a 454-mile national scenic byway, runs through the 1000 Islands region along the southeastern shore of Lake Ontario and beside the St Lawrence area.

Uncluttered villages, boat tours, museums, walks, water sports and abundant freshwater fishing make the Islands a popular vacation center. For details on recreational activities, contact the 1000 Islands Regional Tourism Development Corp, PO Box 400, Alexandria Bay 13607; 315/482-2520 or 800/8-ISLAND in US and Canada.

Listed here are the towns in the Thousand Islands included in *Mobil Travel Guide:* Alexandria Bay, Clayton, Ogdensburg in New York; Brockville, Gananoque, Kingston and St Lawrence Islands Natl Park in Ontario.

Ticonderoga (Lake George Area) (C-8)

(See also Crown Point, Hague)

Founded 1764 **Pop** 5,149 **Elev** 154 ft **Area code** 518 **Zip** 12883
Information Ticonderoga Area Chamber of Commerce, 108 Lake George Ave; 518/585-6619.

This resort area lies on the ancient portage route between Lake George and Lake Champlain. For almost two hundred years it was the site of various skirmishes and battles involving Native Americans, French, British, Canadians, Yankees and Yorkers.

What to See and Do

Boating. Launching sites, 2 mi E on NY 74, on Lake Champlain; Black Point Rd, on Lake George.

★ Ft Ticonderoga (1755). The fort was built in 1755 by the Quebecois, who called it Carillon, and was successfully defended by the Marquis de Montcalm against a more numerous British force in 1758. It was captured by the British in 1759 and by Ethan Allen and the Green Mountain Boys in 1775 (known as the first victory of the American Revolution). The stone fort was restored in 1909; the largest collection of cannons in North America is assembled on the grounds. The museum houses collections of weapons, paintings and articles of daily life of the soldiers garrisoned here during the Seven Year War and the American Revolution. Costumed guides give tours; cannon firings daily; fife and drum corps parade (July & Aug); special events. Museum shop; restaurant; picnic area. Scenic drive to the summit of Mt Defiance for 30-mi view. (Early May-mid-Oct, daily) 2 mi E on NY 74. Phone 518/585-2821. ¢¢¢

Ft Ticonderoga Ferry. (May-Oct, daily) Crosses Lake Champlain to Shoreham, VT. Phone 802/897-7999. One-way trip per car (incl driver and 4 passengers) ¢¢

Heritage Museum. Displays of civilian and industrial history of Ticonderoga. Children's Workshop. (Late June-Labor Day, daily; Labor Day-mid-Oct, wkends) Montcalm St. Phone 518/585-2696. **Donation.**

Putnam Pond State Public Campground. Tent & trailer sites; boating (launch); bathhouse, lifeguards; fishing; hiking; picnicking. (Mid-May-Labor Day) Standard fees. 6 mi W off NY 74, in Adirondack Park (see). Phone 518/585-7280.

Replica of Hancock House. The home of the Ticonderoga Historical Society is a replica of the house built for John Hancock on Beacon St in Boston. It is maintained as a museum and research library. The rms of the house display various period furnishings as well as exhibits presenting social and civil history from the 1700s through the present. (June-Sept, daily exc Sun; rest of yr, Wed-Sat; closed hols) 3 Wicker St, at Moses Circle. Phone 518/585-7868. **Donation.**

Annual Event

Fort Ticonderoga Celtic Music Festival. Early July.

Motel

★ **CIRCLE COURT.** *440 Montcalm St. 518/585-7660.* 14 rms. June-mid-Oct: S $51-$55; D $56-$59; each addl $5; wkly rates off-season; lower rates rest of yr. Pet accepted. TV; cable. Complimentary coffee in rms. Restaurant nearby. Ck-out 11 am. Refrigerators. Cr cds: A, MC, V.

Restaurant

✔★ **HOT BISCUIT DINER.** *428 Montcalm St. 518/585-3483.* Specializes in homemade biscuits, country dinner plates. Own desserts.

Hrs: 6 am-8 pm; Sun 7 am-2 pm. Closed some major hols. No A/C. Semi-a la carte: bkfst $1.45-$4, lunch $2.50-$5.95, dinner $6.95-$13.95. Child's meals. 1950s country diner decor; relaxed atmosphere. Cr cds: MC, V.

Troy (D-8)

(See also Albany, Schenectady)

Settled 1786 **Pop** 54,269 **Elev** 37 ft **Area code** 518 **E-mail** info@renscochamber.com **Web** www.renscochamber.com
Information Rensselaer County Chamber of Commerce, 31 Second St, 12180; 518/274-7020.

What to See and Do

Grave of Samuel Wilson, meat supplier to the Army in 1812. Because the initials "US" were stamped on his sides of beef that were shipped to Union soldiers, this supplier is regarded as the original "Uncle Sam." By an act of the 87th Congress, a resolution was adopted that saluted Wilson as the originator of the national symbol of "Uncle Sam." Oakwood Cemetery, Oakwood Ave.

Junior Museum. Science, natural history, Iroquois and art exhibits; settlers' cabin, marine aquarium, animals, diorama of beaver pond environment, planetarium shows, "Please Touch" family gallery plus other permanent and changing exhibits. Birthday parties and tours (by appt). (Wed-Sun, afternoons; closed hols) 282 5th Ave. Phone 518/235-2120. ¢¢

Rensselaer County Historical Society. An 1827 town house, the Hart-Cluett Mansion, has period rms furnished with decorative and fine arts; Troy stoves and stoneware. Research library, museum shop. Directions for walking tour of downtown area can also be obtained here. (Tues-Sat; closed major hols & Dec 23-Jan 31) 57-59 2nd St. Phone 518/272-7232. ¢

Rensselaer Polytechnic Institute (1824). (6,000 students) Tours begin at Admissions Office in Admissions and Financial Aid Bldg (Sept-Apr, daily exc Sun; rest of yr, Mon-Fri). 15th St, ¼ mi S off NY 7. Phone 518/276-6216.

Riverspark Visitor Center. Offers visitor info, hands-on exhibits, slide presentation. Driving and walking tour info avail. (Tues-Sat; also 1st Sun of month) 251 River St. Phone 518/270-8667. **Free.**

Russell Sage College (1916). (1,000 women) Established by Margaret Olivia Slocum Sage. Campus tours. Gallery features student art work and changing exhibits. The movie *The Age of Innocence* was filmed in part in the historic brownstones on the campus. 45 Ferry St, at 2nd St. Phone 518/270-2300.

Troy Savings Bank Music Hall (1875). Victorian showplace in Italian Renaissance bldg. Presents a wide variety of concerts. Tours by appt (Sept-May). State & 2nd St. Phone 518/273-0038.

Annual Event

Stars and Stripes Riverfront Festival. Concerts, fireworks, carnival rides, military equipt displays, arts and crafts, food. Phone 518/458-0547. Mid-June.

Motel

★ **SUSSE CHALET.** *(RD 2, Box 103, East Greenbush 12061)* Approx 8 mi S on US 4, at I-90 exit 9. 518/477-7984; FAX 518/477-2382. 105 rms, 4 story. May-Aug: S $58.70; D $65.70; each addl $3; lower rates rest of yr. Crib free. TV; cable (premium). Pool. Complimentary continental bkfst. Restaurant adj. Ck-out 11 am. Coin lndry. Business servs avail. Sundries. Cr cds: A, C, D, DS, MC, V.

Restaurants

★ ★ **CAPE HOUSE.** *254 Broadway (12180). 518/274-0167.* Specializes in mesquite swordfish, broiled seafood platter, fresh salmon. Hrs: 11:30 am-2 pm, 5-10 pm; Fri, Sat to 11 pm; Sun 3-9 pm. Closed Mon; also some major hols. Res accepted. Bar to midnight. Semi-a la carte: lunch $3.50-$5.95, dinner $10.95-$22.95. Built 1871; New England decor. Cr cds: A, C, D, DS, MC, V.

★ **ITALIA.** *24 4th St (12180). 518/273-8773.* Italian, Mediterranean menu. Specializes in veal, homemade pasta, seafood. Hrs: 11 am-10 pm; Sat 4-11 pm; Sun 3-9 pm. Closed some major hols. Res accepted. Bar. A la carte entrees: lunch $3.95-$6.95, dinner $8.50-$18.95. Buffet: lunch $4.95. Child's meals. Pianist Thurs-Sun evenings; jazz club wkends. In restored, turn-of-the-century ballroom. Cr cds: A, C, D, MC, V.

★ ★ ★ **TAVERN AT STERUP SQUARE.** *2113 NY 7 (12180). 518/663-5800.* Continental menu. Specializes in fresh seafood, veal, chicken. Hrs: 11 am-11 pm; Sun brunch 10 am-2 pm. Closed Dec 25. Res accepted. Bar. Semi-a la carte: lunch $7.95-$18.95, dinner $11.95-$37.95. Sun brunch $17.95. Child's meals. Outdoor dining. Modeled after Sterup Square in Sterup, Germany. Cr cds: A, C, D, DS, MC, V.

★ ★ ★ **VAN RENSSELAER ROOM.** *2113 NY 7 (12180), in Sterup Square. 518/663-5800.* French, Amer menu. Specialties: Dover sole, veal Wellington, Birds of a Feather. Hrs: 5-11 pm. Closed Dec 25. Res required. Bar. Wine cellar. A la carte entrees: dinner $22.95-$35.95. Prix fixe: dinner $50-$100. Own baking, pastas. Classical music wkends. Valet parking. Formal, elegant dining rm; ice sculptures. Jacket. Totally nonsmoking. Cr cds: A, C, D, DS, MC, V.

Tupper Lake (B-7)

(See also Lake Placid, Long Lake, Saranac Lake)

Settled 1890 **Pop** 4,087 **Elev** 1,600 ft **Area code** 518 **Zip** 12986 **E-mail** tuppercc@northnet.org **Web** www.tupperlakeinfo.com

Information Chamber of Commerce of Tupper Lake & Town of Altamont, 60 Park St; 518/359-3328 or 888/TUP-LAKE.

In the heart of the Adirondack resort country and surrounded by lakes, rivers and mountains, Tupper Lake offers hunting, fishing, boating, mountain climbing, skiing, camping, snowmobiling, golf, tennis and mountain biking amid magnificent scenery.

What to See and Do

Big Tupper Ski Area. Three chairlifts; patrol, school, rentals; snowmaking; bar, cafeteria. Longest run 2 mi; vertical drop 1,152 ft. (Dec-Apr, daily) 3 mi S off NY 30. Phone 518/359-7902 or 800/8-BIGSKI. ¢¢¢¢

Boating. State launching sites on NY 30, S of town, and on the Raquette River, via NY 3, 30. **Free.**

Camping. Fish Creek Pond State Public Campground. Tent & trailer sites; picnicking; boating (rentals; launch); swimming, bathhouse, lifeguards, fishing, hiking. (Apr-Nov) 12 mi E on NY 30, in Adirondack Park (see). Phone 518/891-4560. **Rollins Pond State Public Campground.** 288 campsites, most on waterfront. Same activities as Fish Creek. (Mid-May-early Sept) 12 mi E on NY 30, use Fish Creek entrance. Phone 518/891-3239. **Lake Eaton State Public Campground.** 141 campsites, half on waterfront. Boating (ramp, rentals); swimming, bathhouse, lifeguards; fishing. Fee for some activities. (Mid-May-early Sept) 20 mi S on NY 30. Phone 518/624-2641.

Historic Beth Joseph Synagogue. Built in 1905, this is the oldest synagogue in the Adirondacks, and the only synagogue outside of New York City listed in The Register of New York State Historic Bldgs. All fixtures and furnishings are the original contents of the bldg; the 2 stained-glass Rose Windows have been restored. (June-Sept, daily & hols; limited hrs) Lake St. Phone 518/359-7229. **Donation.**

Raquette River Outfitters. Canoe outfitting and rentals in the Adirondack Mts; guided tours. Contact Box PO 653; 518/359-3228.

Annual Events

Flatwater Weekend. Annual canoe races. 1st wkend June.

Woodsmen's Days. 2nd wkend July.

Tinman Triathlon. Swimming, biking, running. Mid-July.

Motels

✔★ **PINE TERRACE MOTEL & RESORT.** *94 Moody Rd, 2½ mi S on NY 30. 518/359-9258; res: 518/359-2146; FAX 518/359-8340.* Web www.adirondaczaues.com. 18 cottage units, 11 kits. No A/C. D $45-$80; each addl $5; kit. units $250-$450/wk; family rates. Crib avail. Pet accepted. TV; cable. Pool; wading pool. Ck-out 11 am. Lighted tennis. Lawn games. Refrigerators. Boats avail. Picnic tables, grills. Private beach opp. View of lake, mountains. Cr cds: A, DS, MC, V.

★ **SHAHEEN'S.** *310 Park St, ½ mi E on NY 3, 30. 518/359-3384; res: 800/474-2445.* E-mail shaheens@capital.net; web www.shaheensmotel.com. 31 rms, 15 A/C, 2 story. July, Aug: S $43-$67; D $58-$71; each addl $5; family units up to 6, $84; lower rates rest of yr. Crib $5. TV; cable (premium). Pool. Playground. Complimentary continental bkfst. Complimentary coffee in rms. Restaurant opp 3-10 pm. Ck-out 11 am. Miniature golf. Downhill/x-country ski 5 mi. Refrigerators. Balconies. Picnic tables. Cr cds: A, C, D, DS, MC, V.

✔★ **SUNSET PARK.** *71 De Mars Blvd, ½ mi W on NY 3. 518/359-3995.* 11 rms, 4 kits. No A/C. Mid-June-Oct: S, D $46-$60; each addl $4; kit. units $56-$62; lower rates rest of yr. Crib free. Pet accepted. TV; cable. Complimentary coffee in rms. Restaurant nearby. Ck-out 11 am. Downhill ski 3 mi. Lawn games. Picnic tables, grills. On Tupper Lake. Private sand beach, dock for small boats. Cr cds: A, DS, MC, V.

★ **TUPPER LAKE.** *259 Park St. 518/359-3381; res: 800/944-3585; FAX 518/359-8549; res: 800/944-3585.* E-mail tlmotel@north-net.org; web www.tvenet.com/tlmotel/. 18 rms. No A/C. Late June-mid-Oct: S $48; D $49-$61; each addl $5; lower rates rest of yr. Crib $5. TV; cable (premium). Pool. Complimentary continental bkfst. Complimentary coffee in rms. Restaurant nearby. Ck-out 11 am. In-rm modem link. Downhill ski 5 mi; x-country ski 10 mi. Refrigerators. Cr cds: A, DS, MC, V.

Utica (D-6)

(See also Herkimer, Ilion, Oneida, Rome)

Pop 68,637 **Elev** 423 ft **Area code** 315 **E-mail** oneidany@dreamscape.com **Web** www.oneidacountycvb.com

Information Oneida County Convention & Visitors Bureau, PO Box 551, 13503; 315/724-7221 or stop at the Information Booth, just off NY Thrwy exit 31.

Near the western end of the Mohawk Trail, Utica has been a manufacturing and trading center since its early days. By 1793 there was stagecoach service from Albany. The opening of the Erie Canal brought new business. The first Woolworth "five and dime" was opened here in 1879.

What to See and Do

Children's Museum. Hands-on exhibits teaching history, natural history and science. Iroquois exhibit incl section of Long House; local history displays; dress-up area; Childspace; outdoor RR display; special wkend programs. (July-Labor Day, daily exc Mon; rest of yr, Wed-Sun; closed major hols) 311 Main St. Phone 315/724-6128. ¢

F.X. Matt Brewing Co. Includes plant tour, trolley ride and visit to the 1888 Tavern. Free beer or root beer. (Daily; closed hols) Children only with adult. Court & Varick Sts. Phone 315/732-0022 or 800/765-6288(exc NY). ¢¢

Munson-Williams-Proctor Institute. Museum of Art has collection of 18th-20th-century American and European paintings and sculpture; European, Japanese and American prints; American decorative arts. Adj is **Fountain Elms**, a Victorian house museum, with five mid-19th-century rms; changing exhibits. (Daily exc Mon; closed hols) Also **School of Art Gallery** featuring exhibits by visiting artists, faculty and students. (Daily exc Sun; closed hols) 310 Genesee St. Phone 315/797-0000. **Free.**

Oneida County Historical Society. Museum traces Utica and Mohawk Valley history; reference library (fee); changing exhibits. (Tues-Fri; closed hols) 1608 Genesee St. Phone 315/735-3642. **Free.**

Utica College of Syracuse Univ (1946). (1,700 students) Campus tour (free). 1600 Burrstone Rd. Phone 315/792-3006.

Utica Zoo. More than 250 exotic and domestic animals. Children's Zoo (Apr-Oct, daily; incl with admission). Snack bar, picnicking. (All yr, daily) Steele Hill Rd. Phone 315/738-0472. ¢¢

Motels

★ ★ **BEST WESTERN GATEWAY ADIRONDACK INN.** *175 N Genesee St (13502).* 315/732-4121; FAX 315/797-8265. 89 rms, 1-2 story. S $79-$129; D $79-$149; each addl $10; under 12 free; higher rates special events. Crib free. Pet accepted, some restrictions. TV; cable. Complimentary continental bkfst. Coffee in rms. Restaurant adj 10-2 am. Ck-out 11 am. Business servs avail. Sundries. Gift shop. Exercise equipt. Game rm. Refrigerators avail. Cr cds: A, C, D, DS, MC, V.

✔★ **COUNTRY.** *1477 Herkimer Rd (NY 5E) (13502), 2 mi off Thruway exit 31.* 315/732-4628; FAX 315/733-8801. 25 rms. S $30-$36; D $42-$55; each addl $3; higher rates special events. Crib $6. TV; cable. Complimentary coffee in rms. Restaurant nearby. Ck-out 11 am. X-country ski 3 mi. Refrigerators avail. Picnic tables, grills. Cr cds: A, DS, MC, V.

★ ★ **HOLIDAY INN.** *(1777 Burrstone Rd, New Hartford 13413) S on NY 12, W on Burrstone Rd.* 315/797-2131; FAX 315/797-5817. 100 rms, 2 story. S, D $97-$129; under 18 free; higher rates some wkends. Crib free. Pet accepted. TV; cable. Pool; whirlpool. Coffee in rms. Restaurant 6:30 am-10 pm. Rm serv. Bar 4 pm-2 am; entertainment Fri, Sat. Ck-out noon. Coin lndry. Meeting rms. Business servs avail. In-rm modem link. Valet serv. Sundries. Gift shop. Exercise equipt. Game rm. Refrigerators avail. Cr cds: A, C, D, DS, JCB, MC, V.

✔★ ★ **RAMADA.** *(141 New Hartford St, New Hartford 13413) 5 mi S on New Hartford St.* 315/735-3392; FAX 315/738-7642. E-mail ramada@borg.com; web www.ramadanh.com. 104 rms, 2 story. S $79-$99; suites $125-$155; under 18 free; wkend rates; higher rates special events. Crib $10. TV; cable. Complimentary coffee in rms. Restaurant 6:30 am-10 pm. Rm serv. Bar to midnight; entertainment wkends. Ck-out noon. Meeting rms. Business servs avail. In-rm modem link. Valet serv. Sundries. Indoor tennis privileges. Exercise equipt. Health club privileges. Heated pool; lifeguard. Microwaves avail. Totally nonsmoking. Cr cds: A, C, D, DS, MC, V.

✔★ **RED ROOF INN.** *20 Weaver St at N Genesee St (13502).* 315/724-7128; FAX 315/724-7158. 112 rms, 2 story. S $42.99-$82; D $45.99-$82; each addl $7-$9; under 18 free. Crib free. Pet accepted, some restrictions. TV; cable (premium). Complimentary coffee in lobby. Restaurant nearby. Ck-out noon. Business servs avail. Sundries. Cr cds: A, C, D, DS, MC, V.

Hotel

★ ★ ★ **RADISSON-UTICA CENTRE.** *200 Genesee St (13502).* 315/797-8010; FAX 315/797-1490. 158 rms, 6 story. S, D $99-$124; suites $175; under 18 free; wkend rates. Crib free. Pet accepted. TV; cable. Indoor pool; lifeguard. Coffee in rms. Restaurant 6:30 am-2 pm, 5-10 pm; Sun 7 am-2 pm, 5-9 pm. Bar 3 pm-2 am; entertainment Fri-Sat. Ck-out noon. Meeting rms. Business servs avail. In-rm modem link. Shopping arcade. Gift shop. Barber, beauty shop. Garage parking. Downhill ski 10 mi; x-country ski 5 mi. Exercise rm. Game rm. Some refrigerators. Cr cds: A, C, D, DS, MC, V.

Inn

✔★ **SUGARBUSH BED & BREAKFAST.** *(8451 Old Poland Rd, Barneveld 13304) 10 mi N off NY 12, 28.* 315/896-6860; res: 800/582-5845. 6 air-cooled rms, 3 share bath, 2 story, 1 suite. No rm phones. S, D $50-$70; suites $125-$135. Crib $10. TV in some rms, common rm; cable (premium), VCR avail (movies). Complimentary full bkfst. Ck-out 10:30 am, ck-in 2:30 pm. X-country ski on site. Lawn games. Built in early 1800s as a school for boys. Totally nonsmoking. Cr cds: A, DS, MC, V.

Restaurants

★ ★ **HOOK, LINE & SINKER.** *(8471 Seneca Tpke, New Hartford 13413) 5 mi S via NY 5.* 315/732-3636. Specializes in seafood, steak, pasta. Salad bar. Own soups, desserts. Hrs: 11:30 am-3 pm, 4:30-10 pm; Fri, Sat to 11 pm; Sun 1-9 pm. Closed Thanksgiving, Dec 25. Res accepted; required hols. Bar to 2 am. Semi-a la carte: lunch $4.95-$7.95, dinner $7.95-$24.95. Child's meals. Entertainment Fri. Cape Cod decor. Cr cds: A, C, D, DS, MC, V.

★ ★ ★ **HORNED DORSET.** *(Main St, Leonardsville 13364) 15 mi S on NY 8.* 315/855-7898. French menu. Specialties: boneless loin of lamb with black currant sauce, veal Horned Dorset, salmon en croûte. Hrs: 6-9 pm; Sun 3-7:30 pm. Closed Mon; Jan 1, Dec 25. Res accepted. Serv bar. Wine cellar. Semi-a la carte: dinner $20-$30. Classical guitarist wkends. Former 19th-century grocery store with Palladian windows. 3 dining rms; Victorian decor, many antiques, view of garden. Recited menu. Overnight stays avail. Cr cds: A, MC, V.

✔★ **KITLAS.** *(Turner St, Frankfort 13340) E on NY 5S, I-90 exit 31.* 315/732-9616. Specializes in fresh seafood, babyback ribs, ethnic specials. Hrs: 11:30 am-2 pm, 4:30-8:30 pm; Mon to 2 pm. Closed Sun; major hols. Res accepted. Bar. Semi-a la carte: lunch $3.95-$5.95, dinner $9.50-$13.95. Child's meals. Family-owned. Cr cds: A, DS, MC, V.

♥

Victor _(D-4)

(See also Canandaigua, Palmyra, Rochester)

Pop 2,308 **Elev** 587 ft **Area code** 716 **Zip** 14564

What to See and Do

Valentown Museum. A 3-story structure built as a community center and shopping plaza in 1879. General store, harness maker and cobbler shops, bakery, schoolrm; Civil War artifacts. (May-Oct, Wed-Sun) 4 mi N on NY 96 to Valentown Sq, in Fishers; 1/4 mi N of I-90, exit 45, opp Eastview Mall. Phone 716/924-2645. ¢

Motels

✔★ **EXIT 45.** *7463 Victor-Pittsford Rd, 1/4 mi S of I-90 exit 45 on NY 96.* 716/924-2121; FAX 716/924-0468. 34 rms. S $45-$58; D $58-$79; each addl $5; wkly rates (winter only). TV; cable (premium). Restaurant adj 6 am-midnight. Bar from 11 am. Ck-out 11 am. Business servs avail. Rural setting. Cr cds: A, D, DS, MC, V.

★★ **HAMPTON INN & SUITES.** *7637 NY 96.* 716/924-4400. 123 rms, 3 story, 55 kit. units. May-Oct: S $85; D $95; kit. units $99-$106; under 18 free; lower rates rest of yr. Crib free. TV; cable (premium), VCR avail. Complimentary continental bkfst. Complimentary coffee in rms. Restaurant nearby 11-1 am. Ck-out noon. Meeting rms. Business servs avail. In-rm modem link. Valet serv. Gift shop. Coin lndry. Exercise equipt. Indoor pool; whirlpool. Some in-rm whirlpools, fireplaces. Grills. Cr cds: A, C, D, DS, ER, MC, V.

D ≈ ✕ ✕ 🔥 SC

★★ **SUNRISE HILL INN.** *(6108 Loomis Rd, Farmington 14425) I-90 exit 44.* 716/924-2131; res: 800/333-0536; FAX 716/924-1876. 89 rms, 2 story. Mid-June-mid-Sept: S, D $58-$68; each addl $8; suites $85; under 18 free; lower rates rest of yr. Crib free. Pet accepted, some restrictions. TV; cable, VCR avail (movies). Pool. Bar 5-10 pm Wed-Sat. Ck-out 11 am. Meeting rms. Business servs avail. In-rm modem link. Valet serv Mon-Sat. Health club privileges. Some balconies. Countryside view. Near race track. Cr cds: A, C, D, DS, ER, JCB, MC, V.

✈ ≈ ✕ 🔥 SC

Restaurant

★★★ **VICTOR GRILLING COMPANY.** *75 Coville St, in Whistlestop arcade.* 716/924-1760. Specialties: black Angus rib-eye steak, pasta with shrimp and sun-dried tomatoes. Hrs: 5:30-10 pm; Fri, Sat to 10:30 pm; Sun 4-9 pm. Closed Mon; some major hols; also 1 wk Jan. Res accepted Fri, Sat. Bar. Semi-a la carte: dinner $14-$24.95. Large microbrewery beer selection. Cr cds: A, D, DS, MC, V.

Warrensburg (C-8)

(See also Lake George Village, Lake Luzerne)

Pop 4,174 **Elev** 687 ft **Area code** 518 **Zip** 12885 **Web** www.adirondack.net/orgs/warrensburg.
Information Chamber of Commerce, 3847 Main St; 518/623-2161.

Warrensburg, near Lake George, is an old-time village in the heart of an all-year tourist area and is a center for campgrounds, dude ranches and antique shops. Activities include canoeing, fishing, golf, swimming, tubing, skiing, horseback riding and biking among others. The fall foliage is beautiful here.

What to See and Do

Hickory Ski Center. Two Pomalifts, T-bar, rope tow; school, rentals; snack bar. Longest run 1 1/4 mi; vertical drop 1,200 ft. (Dec-Apr, Sat, Sun, hol wks) 3 mi W on NY 418. Phone 518/623-2825. ¢¢¢¢¢

Warrensburg Museum of Local History. Exhibits detail the history of Warrensburg from the time it became a town to the present. Artifacts of livelihood, business, industry and general living of the residents. (July-Aug, Tues-Sat) 47 Main St. Phone 518/623-2928. **Free.**

Annual Events

Arts & Crafts Festival. Main St & Stewart Farrar Ave. July 4 wknd.

World's Largest Garage Sale and Foliage Festival. All of Main St & side sts. 1st wknd Oct.

Inn

★★★ **FRIENDS LAKE.** *(963 Friends Lake Rd, Chestertown 12817) N on US 9, then 5 mi NW on NY 28 to Friends Lake Rd.* 518/494-4751; FAX 518/494-4616. E-mail friends@netheaven.com; web www.friendslake.com. 16 rms, 3 story. S, D $120-$285; MAP: S, D $175-$325; ski, rafting packages. TV rm; cable (premium), VCR (movies). Outdoor whirlpool. Restaurant (see FRIENDS LAKE INN). Ck-out 11 am, ck-in 2 pm. Meeting rm. Business servs avail. X-country ski on site; rentals, instructor. Hiking trails. Restored Adirondack Inn (1860). Library. Beach. Cr cds: A, C, D, MC, V.

Restaurants

★★ **FRIENDS LAKE INN.** *(See Friends Lake Inn)* 518/494-4751. E-mail friends@netheaven.com; web www.friendslake.com. Specializes in veal, seafood, duck. Hrs: 8-10 am, 5-9 pm; Fri, Sat to 10 pm; Sun 8 am-noon, 4-9 pm. Bar. A la carte entrees: bkfst $3.25-$5.95, dinner $17-$32. Built 1860. Cr cds: A, C, D, MC, V.

★★★ **MERRILL MAGEE HOUSE.** *2 Hudson St.* 518/623-2449. E-mail mmhinn1@capital.net; web www.webny.com/merrillmageehouse. Specialties: rack of lamb, salmon Wellington, crisp roast duckling. Hrs: 11:30 am-2:30 pm, 5-9:30 pm; Sun, Mon from 5 pm. Closed Dec 25. Res accepted. Bar. Wine list. Semi-a la carte: lunch $6.95-$10.95, dinner $14.50-$21.95. Elegant dining in Victorian atmosphere. Overnight stays avail. Cr cds: A, DS, MC, V.

Waterloo (D-4)

(See also Canandaigua, Geneva, Seneca Falls)

Settled 1800 **Pop** 7,765 **Elev** 455 ft **Area code** 315 **Zip** 13165

The Church of Jesus Christ of Latter-day Saints was founded by Joseph Smith and five other men in a small log cabin here on April 6, 1830. The site is commemorated at the Peter Whitmer Farm.

What to See and Do

Peter Whitmer Farm. This site is where the Church of Jesus Christ of Latter-day Saints was organized in 1830; period furnishings. 20- to 30-min tours, video presentations. (Daily) 3 1/2 mi S via NY 96. Phone 315/539-2552. **Free.**

Terwilliger Museum. Historical museum housing collections dating from 1875; Native American displays; authentic full-size vehicles and a replica of a general store provides a glimpse of life as it was in the 1920s. Also 5 rms, each furnished to depict a specific era. (Mon afternoons & Wed eves) 31 E Williams St. Phone 315/539-0533. **Donation.**

The McClintock House (1835). Home of the McClintocks, a Quaker family who were active in the planning of the first Women's Rights Convention. 14 E Williams St. For schedule info phone 315/568-2991. ¢

Waterloo Memorial Day Museum. Mementos of Civil War, World Wars I and II, the Korean conflict, Vietnam and the first Memorial Day in this 20-rm mansion furnished in 1860-1870 period. (July-Labor Day, Mon & Thurs afternoons, also Sat late morning-early afternoon; closed July 4) Under 12 yrs only with adult. 35 E Main St. Phone 315/539-9611. **Donation.**

Motel

★ ★ ★ **HOLIDAY INN.** *2468 NY 414, 1 mi E on NY 414, just N of jct US 20, NY 5; 4 mi S of I-90 exit 41.* 315/539-5011; FAX 315/539-8355. 147 rms, 2 story. June-mid-Oct: S, D $79; higher rates special events; under 19 free; package plans; lower rates rest of yr. Crib free. Pet accepted. TV; cable (premium), VCR avail. Heated pool; whirlpool. Coffee in rms. Restaurant 6:30 am-10 pm. Rm serv. Bar 11:30-1 am; Fri, Sat to 2 am; Sun to midnight; entertainment Fri, Sat. Ck-out noon. Coin lndry. Meeting rms. Business servs avail. In-rm modem link. Valet serv (Mon-Fri). Tennis. Exercise equipt; sauna. Cr cds: A, C, D, DS, JCB, MC, V.

D 🦽 🏃 ≋ 🏊 ✕ 🛒 🔥 SC

Watertown (C-6)

(See also Clayton)

Settled 1799 **Pop** 29,429 **Elev** 478 ft **Area code** 315 **Zip** 13601 **E-mail** chamber@imcnet.net **Web** www.watertownny.com
Information Chamber of Commerce, 230 Franklin St; 315/788-4400.

Watertown lies along the Black River, 11 miles east of Lake Ontario and 22 miles south of the St Lawrence. Within the city, the river falls more than 100 feet, providing an opportunity for whitewater rafting. During a county fair here in 1878 young Frank W. Woolworth originated the idea of the five-and-ten-cent store.

What to See and Do

American Maple Museum. Displays of maple syrup production; equipment; history of maple production in North America; lumberjack display. (July-mid-Sept, daily exc Sun; mid-May-June & mid-Sept-mid-Oct, Mon, Fri, Sat; mid-Oct-Nov, by appt) 30 mi SE via NY 12 & NY 812, on Main St in Croghan. Phone 315/346-1107. ¢

Jefferson County Historical Society Museum. Paddock mansion (1876); Victorian mansion with period rms, military rms; Native American artifacts, changing and regional history exhibits; Victorian garden. (Mon-Fri; closed hols) 228 Washington St. Phone 315/782-3491. **Free.**

Long Point State Park. Fishing; boating (launch, dock). Picnicking. Tent & trailer sites. (May-mid-Sept) Standard fees. NW on Chaumont Bay, via NY 12E, 8 mi W of Three Mile Bay. Phone 315/649-5258.

Roswell P. Flower Memorial Library. Neo-classic marble bldg houses murals of local history, French furniture; miniature furniture; geneology and local history. (Mid-June-Labor Day, Mon-Fri; rest of yr, daily exc Sun; closed hols) 229 Washington St. Phone 315/788-2352. **Free.**

Sci-Tech Center. Hands-on science and technology museum for children. More than 40 exhibits, incl laser display and discovery boxes; science store. (Tues-Sat; closed major hols) 154 Stone St. Phone 315/788-1340. ¢

Annual Event

Jefferson County Fair. Agriculture, livestock, art exhibits; held annually for more than 150 yrs. Late July.

Motels

★ ★ **BEST WESTERN CARRIAGE HOUSE INN.** *300 Washington St.* 315/782-8000; FAX 315/786-2097. 160 rms, 3 story. S $62-$76; D $62-$81; each addl $5; suites $75-$140; under 19 free. Crib free. TV; cable. Indoor pool; poolside serv, sauna. Restaurant 6:30 am-10 pm. Rm serv. Bar 11-2 am; entertainment exc Sun. Ck-out noon. Meeting rms.

Business servs avail. Bellhops. Valet serv. Barber, beauty shop. Cr cds: A, C, D, DS, JCB, MC, V.

D ≋ 🏊 ✕ 🛒 SC

✔★ **DAVIDSON'S.** *26177 NY 3, 3 mi E on NY 3.* 315/782-3861. 20 rms. May-Sept: S, D $35-$49; each addl $4; lower rates rest of yr. Crib $5. TV; cable (premium). Heated pool. Complimentary coffee in lobby. Ck-out 10 am. Picnic table, grills. Shaded grounds; nature walk. Near Ft Drum. Cr cds: A, DS, MC, V.

≋ ✕ 🔥

★ **ECONO LODGE.** *1030 Arsenal St.* 315/782-5500; FAX 315/788-7608. 60 rms, 2 story. May-Sept: S $59.95-$64.95; D $69.95-$74.95; each addl $5; under 18 free; lower rates rest of yr. Crib free. Pet accepted; $5. TV; cable (premium). Indoor pool. Complimentary continental bkfst in lobby. Restaurant adj 11 am-9 pm. Ck-out 11 am. Coin lndry. Sundries. Refrigerators. Picnic tables, grills. Cr cds: A, C, D, DS, MC, V.

D 🦽 ≋ 🏊 🔥 SC

✔★ **NEW PARROT.** *Outer Washington St, 2 mi S on NY 11, 4 mi N of I-81 exit 44.* 315/788-5080; res: 800/479-9889. 26 rms. June-Oct: S $34-$36; D $45-$55; each addl $5; family rates off-season; lower rates rest of yr. Crib $5. Pet accepted; $3. TV; cable. Indoor pool. Restaurant adj 6 am-9 pm. Ck-out 11 am. Picnic tables, grills. Cr cds: A, D, DS, MC, V.

🦽 ≋ 🔥

★ ★ **QUALITY INN.** *1190 Arsenal St, on NY 3 at I-81 exit 45.* 315/788-6800; FAX 315/788-6800, ext. 298. 96 rms, 2 story. May-Oct: S $48-$56; D $60-$70; each addl $6; under 18 free; lower rates rest of yr. Pet accepted. TV; cable (premium). Pool. Ck-out noon. Coin lndry. Meeting rms. Game rm. Private patios, balconies. Health club privileges. Cr cds: A, C, D, DS, ER, JCB, MC, V.

🦽 ≋ 🏊 🔥 SC

✔★ **REDWOOD MOTOR LODGE.** *Utica Rd & Gifford St, 2 mi SE on NY 12.* 315/788-2850. 27 rms, 2 story. Some rm phones. May-Sept: S $34; D $42; each addl $3; under 12 free; wkly rates off-season; lower rates rest of yr. Crib $2. TV; cable. Pool. Ck-out 11 am. Cr cds: A, MC, V.

≋ 🔥 SC

Motor Hotels

★ ★ **DAYS INN-WATERTOWN/1000 ISLANDS.** *110 Commerce Park Dr.* 315/782-2700; FAX 315/782-7691. 135 units, 6 story. Mid-May-mid-Oct: S $55-$75; D $60-$80; each addl $5; suites $99; lower rates rest of yr. Crib avail. TV; cable. Indoor pool. Restaurant open 24 hrs. Rm serv 6 am-11 pm. Bar. Ck-out 11 am. Meeting rms. Business servs avail. Exercise equipt. Refrigerator, microwave in suites. Cr cds: A, C, D, DS, JCB, MC, V.

D ≋ ✕ 🏊 🔥 SC

★ ★ **RAMADA INN.** *6300 Arsenal St, at jct NY 3, I-81 exit 45.* 315/788-0700; FAX 315/785-9875. 145 rms, 4 story. S $64-$68; D $70-$74; each addl $6; suites $95; under 18 free; package plans. Crib free. TV; cable (premium). Pool. Restaurants 6:30-11 am, 11:30 am-11 pm; Fri to 1 am; Sat 8-1 am; Sun 8 am-11 pm. Rm serv. Bar 11:30-2 am; entertainment. Ck-out noon. Meeting rms. Business servs avail. In-rm modem link. Sundries. Free airport transportation. Exercise equipt. Cr cds: A, C, D, DS, JCB, MC, V.

D ≋ ✕ 🏊 🔥 SC

Restaurants

★ **BENNY'S STEAK HOUSE.** *1050 Arsenal St, on NY 3 at I-81 exit 45.* 315/788-4110. Italian, Amer menu. Specializes in steak, fresh seafood. Own pasta, desserts. Hrs: 11 am-11 pm; Sun from noon. Res accepted. Bar 9-2 am. A la carte entrees: lunch $2.50-$7.50, dinner

$6.95-$21. Child's meals. Entertainment Fri, Sat. Family-owned. Cr cds: A, C, D, DS, MC, V.

D SC

★ ★ **PARTRIDGE BERRY INN.** *26561 NY 3, 4 mi E on NY 3. 315/788-4610.* Continental menu. Specializes in prime rib, veal, fresh fish. Hrs: 6-9 pm; Sun 11:30 am-2:30 pm, 4-8 pm; Sun brunch to 2:30 pm. Res accepted. Bar; entertainment Fri, Sat. Semi-a la carte: dinner $7.95-$29.95. Sun brunch $10.95. Child's meals. Rustic decor; 3 large fireplaces. Cr cds: A, C, D, MC, V.

D SC

Watkins Glen (E-4)

(See also Corning, Ithaca, Penn Yan)

Pop 2,207 **Elev** 550 ft **Area code** 607 **Zip** 14891 **E-mail** chamber@schuylerny.com **Web** www.schuylerny.com
Information Schuyler County Chamber of Commerce, 1000 N Franklin St; 607/535-4300 or 800/607-4552.

Watkins Glen is situated at the southern end of Seneca Lake, where the famous tributary gorge for which it is named, emerges in the middle of the town. Several estate wineries offering tours and tastings are located on the southern shores of the lake, near town.

What to See and Do
Captain Bill's Seneca Lake Cruises. Two tour boats. Sightseeing, lunch, dinner & cocktail cruises. (Mid-May-mid-Oct, daily) First & Franklin Sts. Phone 607/535-4541. Sightseeing ¢¢¢; Dinner ¢¢¢¢¢

Montour Falls. Industrial community with 7 glens nearby; fishing for rainbow trout in Catharine Creek. Chequaga Falls (156 ft) plunges into a pool beside the main street. Municipal marina, N of town, has access to barge canal system. Trailer site (fee). 2 mi S on NY 14. Phone Village Hall, 607/535-7367.

Watkins Glen State Park. Stairs and bridges lead upward through Watkins Glen Gorge, past the cataracts and rapids, rising some 600 ft in 1½ mi. Pool (mid-June-Labor Day, daily), bathhouse; fishing. Picnicking, playground, concession. Tent & trailer sites. (Late May-Columbus Day) Franklin St; NY 14/414, past the lower entrance. Phone 607/535-4511. **Free.** Parking ¢¢¢On grounds is

Timespell. A sound and light show in the Watkins Glen Gorge. Laser images, panoramic sound and special effects present the history of this majestic wonder. (Mid-May-mid-Oct) Phone 607/535-4960. ¢¢¢

Winery tours. Twenty-two wineries dot the hillsides of Seneca Lake. Follow NY 14 or NY 414 for tastings and tours. Contact the Seneca Lake Wine Trail for more info; 315/563-9996.Includes

Glenora Wine Cellar. Winery on Seneca Lake; audiovisual presentation, tours, tastings. (Daily; closed some major hols) N on NY 14, in Dundee. Phone 607/243-5511. **Free.**

Seasonal Event
Watkins Glen International. 4 mi SW on County 16. IMSA and NASCAR Winston Cup racing. Phone 607/535-2481. Late May-Sept.

Motel
★ **BELLEVUE.** *3812 State, NY 14. 607/535-4232.* 7 rms, 5 cottages, 1 kit. unit. May-mid-Nov: S, D $59-$75; each addl $10; cottages $49-$65; kit. unit $75-$85; wkly rates. Closed rest of yr. TV. Complimentary continental bkfst. Restaurant nearby. Ck-out 11 am. Refrigerators. Picnic tables, grills. Overlooking lake. Cr cds: A, DS, MC, V.

Restaurants
★ ★ **CASTEL GRISCH.** *3380 County Rd 28. 607/535-9614.* Alpine, Amer menu. Specializes in Bavarian dishes, veal, steak. Hrs: 11 am-9 pm; Sun brunch to 2 pm. Closed Jan-Mar. Res accepted. Wine. A la carte entrees: lunch $3.95-$13.95, dinner $11.95-$21.95. German-Swiss buffet (Fri): dinner $17.95. Sun brunch $13.95. Terrace dining with view of lake. Winery on premises; gift shop. Guest rms avail. Overlooks Seneca Lake. Cr cds: A, DS, MC, V.

D

★ ★ **FRANKLIN ST GRILLE.** *413 Franklin St, on NY 14. 607/535-2007.* Specialties: London broil, vegan specials. Hrs: 11:30-10 pm. Closed Thanksgiving, Dec 25. Res accepted. Semi-a la carte: lunch $5.95-$7.95, dinner $7.95-$24.95. Child's meals. Outdoor dining. Family-owned. Cr cds: A, MC, V.

D

★ ★ **TOWN HOUSE.** *108 N Franklin St, on NY 14. 607/535-4619.* Specializes in char-broiled steak, seafood, gourmet dinner salads. Hrs: 11 am-10 pm. Closed Dec 25. Res accepted. Bar 11-1 am; Sun noon-9 pm. Semi-a la carte: lunch $3.95-$6.95, dinner $6.95-$20.95. Child's meals. Originally a hotel (1891). Cr cds: A, D, DS, MC, V.

★ ★ **WILDFLOWER CAFE.** *301 N Franklin St. 607/535-9797.* Contemporary Amer cuisine. Specializes in fresh seafood, vegetarian dishes, sautéed dishes. Own desserts, ice cream. Hrs: 11:30 am-10 pm; Fri, Sat to 11 pm. Closed some major hols. Res accepted. Bar 11:30-1 am. A la carte entrees: lunch $3.95-$8.95, dinner $11.95-$22.95. Totally non-smoking. Cr cds: A, MC, V.

D ♥

West Hempstead, L.I.
(see Hempstead)

West Point (US Military Academy) (F-8)

(See also Monroe, Newburgh, Peekskill, Stony Point)

Established 1802 **Pop** 8,024 **Elev** 161 ft **Area code** 914 **Zip** 10996

West Point has been of military importance since Revolutionary days; it was one of four points on the mid-Hudson fortified against the British. In 1778 a great chain was strung across the river to stop British ships. The military academy was founded by an act of Congress in 1802. Barracks, academic and administration buildings are closed to visitors.

What to See and Do
Battle Monument. Statue of Fame set on a single column, honoring Civil War officers and enlisted men killed in action. Inscribed on the column are names of the 2,230 men, by regiment. Nearby are some links from the chain used to block the river in 1778. Thayer & Washington Rds.

Cadet Chapel (1910). On hill overlooking the campus. Large pipe organ and stained glass. (Daily)

Michie Stadium. Seats 42,000. Army home football games.

Parades. Inquire at Visitors Center. (Late Apr-May, Sept-Nov) Phone 914/938-2638.

Visitors Center. Displays on cadet training, model cadet rm, films shown, tours. (Daily; closed Jan 1, Thanksgiving, Dec 25) Just outside Thayer Gate. Phone 914/938-2638.

West Point Museum. Exhibits on history and ordnance. (Daily; closed Jan 1, Thanksgiving, Dec 25) Near Visitors Center, just outside Thayer Gate. Phone 914/938-2203.

Motel

✔★ WEST POINT. *(156 Main St, Highland Falls 10928)* ¹/₂ mi S on NY 218, just off NY 9W. 914/446-4180. 51 rms, 2 story. S, D $60-$68; each addl $5; under 12 free; wkly rates; higher rates: hols, wkends, special events. TV; cable (premium). Complimentary continental bkfst. Restaurant opp 11 am-9 pm. Ck-out 11 am. Coin lndry. Some refrigerators. Cr cds: A, C, D, DS, MC, V.

Hotel

★★ THAYER. *(West Point)* US Military Academy, off NY 218. 914/446-4731; FAX 914/446-0338; res: 800/247-5047. Web www.hotelthayer.com. 189 rms, 5 story. S, D $89-$119; each addl $10; suites $110-$185. Crib $10. TV; VCR avail. Restaurant 7-10 am, 11:30 am-2 pm, 5:30-9 pm; Sun from 7:30-9 am. Bar 11:30 am-midnight. Ck-out 11 am (football wkends 10 am). Meeting rms. Business servs avail. Gift shop. Concierge. Downhill ski 2 mi. Outdoor terrace. Overlooks Hudson River. Cr cds: A, C, D, DS, MC, V.

Inn

★★ CROMWELL MANOR INN. *(Cornwall 12518)* 3 mi N on NY 9W exit Angola Rd. 914/534-7136. Web www.virtualcities.com/ny/cromwell.htm. 13 rms, 2 story, 3 suites, guest house. No rm phones. S, D $135-$190; suites $215-$275; guest house $650; wkends 2-day min. Premium cable TV in common rm. Complimentary full bkfst. Restaurant nearby. Ck-out 11 am, ck-in 4 pm. Free airport transportation. Many fireplaces. Built in 1820 by descendant of Oliver Cromwell; 7 acres of woodlands/gardens. Antiques. Cr cds: MC, V.

Restaurants

✔★★ CANTERBURY BROOK INN. *(331 Main St, Cornwall 12518)* 10 mi N on 9W exit Angola Rd. 914/534-9658. Continental menu. Specializes in veal, salmon, chicken. Hrs: 5-9 pm; Fri, Sat to 9:30 pm; Sun to 8 pm. Closed Mon, Tues; also Dec 25. Res accepted. Bar. Semi-a la carte: dinner $12.50-$19.95. Fireplaces. View of brook. Cr cds: A, MC, V.

★ PAINTER'S. *(266 Hudson St, Cornwall-on-Hudson)* 914/534-2109. E-mail painters85@aol.com; web winedine.com/painters. Specializes in pasta, seafood. Hrs: 11:30 am-10 pm; Fri, Sat to 10:30 pm; Sun brunch 10:30 am-3 pm. Closed major hols. Res accepted. Bar to 2 am. Semi-a la carte: lunch, dinner $5.50-$18. Sun brunch from $6.95. Child's meals. Outdoor dining. Cr cds: A, C, D, DS, MC, V.

Westbury, L.I. (B-2)

(See also Garden City, Jericho, New York City)

Pop 13,060 **Elev** 100 ft **Area code** 516 **Zip** 11590

What to See and Do

Clark Botanic Garden. The 12-acre former estate of Grenville Clark. Includes Hunnewell Rose Garden; ponds, streams; bulbs, perennials, annuals; wildflower, herb, rock, rhododendron, azalea and daylily gardens; children's garden; groves of white pine, dogwood and hemlock. (Daily) 193 I.U. Willets Rd, in Albertson. Phone 516/484-8600. **Free.**

Old Westbury Gardens. Charles II-style mansion on 88 acres of countryside with formal gardens, allées, ponds, pools and meadows. House has collection of 17th- and 18th-century English furniture, silver and paintings. Walled garden, rose garden, lilac and primrose walks. (Apr-Oct, daily exc Tues; Nov, wkends; Dec, select days) 71 Old Westbury Rd, in Old Westbury. Phone 516/333-0048. **¢¢¢**

Westbury Music Fair. Theater-in-the-round; musicals, concerts, children's shows. Brush Hollow Rd, between Northern State Pkwy & Jericho Tpke. Phone 516/334-0800.

Restaurants

★★ BENNY'S. *199 Post Ave. 516/997-8111.* Northern Italian menu. Specialties: osso bucco, Norwegian salmon, veal chop vadastana. Hrs: noon-3 pm, 5-10 pm; Fri, Sat to 11 pm. Closed Sun; major hols; also last 2 wks Aug. Res required. A la carte entrees: lunch $12.95-$25, dinner $10.50-$27. Parking. Formal atmosphere. Cr cds: A, C, D, MC, V.

★★ CAFE BACI. *1636 Old Country Rd. 516/832-8888.* Italian, Amer menu. Specializes in pasta, salad, pizza. Hrs: 11:30 am-10 pm; Fri, Sat to midnight; Sun 1-10 pm. Bar. A la carte entrees: lunch, dinner $7.95-$15.95. Parking. Casual dining. Cr cds: A, D, MC, V.

✔★★ CAFE SPASSO. *(307 Old Country Rd, Carle Place)* W on Old Country Rd. 516/333-1718. Italian menu. Specializes in pasta, veal, pizza. Hrs: 11:30 am-10 pm; Wed, Thurs to 11 pm; Fri, Sat to midnight; Sun 1-10 pm. Closed Thanksgiving, Dec 25. Bar. A la carte entrees: lunch, dinner $8-$16. Parking. Italian-style cafe. Cr cds: A, C, D, MC, V.

✔★★ CHURRASQUEIRA BAIRRADA. *(144 Jericho Tpke, Mineola 11510)* 3 mi W. 516/739-3856. Portuguese barbecue menu. Specializes in all-you-can-eat barbecue. Hrs: 11:30 am-10:30 pm. Closed Mon. Serv bar. Semi-a la carte: lunch $7.95-$12.95, dinner $8.95-$19.95. Hanging lamps, wall-to-wall mirrors. Cr cds: A, D, MC, V.

★★ GIULIO CESARE. *18 Ellison Ave, just off Old Country Rd. 516/334-2982.* Northern Italian menu. Specialties: chicken cacciatore, stuffed veal chop, pasta primavera. Hrs: noon-3 pm, 5-10 pm; Sat 5-10:30 pm. Closed Sun; major hols. Res accepted. Bar. A la carte entrees: lunch, dinner $10.95-$23. Parking. Cr cds: A, MC, V.

★★ RIALTO. *(588 Westbury Ave, Carle Place 11514)* just S of Westbury, between Glen Cove Rd and Post Ave. 516/997-5283. Northern Italian menu. Specialties: cold antipasta, rigatoni in vodka sauce, red snapper sorrentine. Hrs: noon-3 pm, 5-10 pm; Sat from 5 pm. Closed Sun; major hols. Res accepted. Bar. A la carte entrees: lunch $8.95-$16.50, dinner $9.50-$21. Parking. Comfortable, elegant atmosphere; many antiques. Cr cds: A, MC, V.

★★★ WESTBURY MANOR. *Jericho Tpke, off Meadowbrook Pkwy at Glen Cove Rd. 516/333-7117.* Web www.scottobros.com. Continental menu. Specialties: grilled fresh fish, roast rack of veal. Own baking, pasta. Hrs: noon-3 pm, 5-10:30 pm; Fri to midnight; Sat 5 pm-midnight; Sun 2:30-10 pm. Closed Dec 25. Res accepted. Bar. Wine cellar. A la carte entrees: lunch $8.95-$17.95, dinner $14.75-$28.50. Guitarist Tues; pianist Wed-Sun. Valet parking. On 6 acres of formal gardens that include fountains, waterfalls, ponds, gazebos. Cr cds: A, C, D, MC, V.

Westhampton Beach, L.I. (B-4)

(See also Riverhead)

Pop 1,571 **Elev** 10 ft **Area code** 516 **Zip** 11978
Information Greater Westhampton Chamber of Commerce, 173 Montauk Hwy, PO Box 1228; 516/288-3337.

Surrounded by water, this resort area offers fishing and water sports. Nearby are hiking and nature trails.

What to See and Do

Wertheim Natl Wildlife Refuge. A 2,400-acre refuge for wildlife incl deer, fox, raccoon, herons, hawks, ospreys and waterfowl. Walking trail; boating, canoeing, fishing and photography; environmental education. (Daily) Approx 10 mi W on NY 80 to Smith Rd S, in Shirley. Phone 516/286-0485. **Free.**

Restaurants

★★ **CASA BASSO.** *Montauk Hwy. 516/288-1841.* Italian menu. Specializes in veal, seafood. Hrs: 5 pm-midnight. Closed Mon. Res required. Bar. A la carte entrees: dinner $12-$22. Unusual outdoor sculptures; mermaids, horses, lions and 3 musketeers. Jacket. Cr cds: A, MC, V.

★★ **DORA'S.** *105 Montauk Hwy. 516/288-9723.* Specialties: shrimp Dora, L.I. duckling, marinated steak. Hrs: from 5 pm. Closed Thanksgiving, Dec 24, 25; also Mon-Wed Sept-June. Bar. A la carte entrees: dinner $13.45-$24.95. Child's meals. Cr cds: A, C, D, DS, MC, V.

★★ **PATIO.** *54 Main St. 516/288-4100.* Specializes in prime meats, fresh seafood. Hrs: 5:30-10:30 pm. Closed Dec 25; also Mon-Thurs mid-Sept-Dec. Bar. A la carte entrees: dinner $20-$32. Outdoor dining. Entertainment Sat (summer). Cr cds: A, C, D, MC, V.

★★★ **STARR BOGGS'.** *379 Dune Rd, at Dune Deck Hotel. 516/288-5250.* Specializes in local fish, seasonal vegetables. Hrs: noon-3 pm, 6-10 pm; Fri to 11:30 pm. Closed mid-Oct-mid-May. Res required. Bar. A la carte entrees: lunch $7-$14, dinner $20-$28. Lobster bake $40. Outdoor dining. Original art. Cr cds: A, D, MC, V.

White Plains (A-2)

(See also New Rochelle, New York City, Tarrytown, Yonkers; also see Stamford, CT)

Settled 1735 **Pop** 48,718 **Elev** 236 ft **Area code** 914
Information Westchester Convention & Visitor Bureau, 235 Mamaroneck Ave, 10605; 914/948-0047 or 800/833-9282.

In October 1776, General George Washington outfoxed General Lord Howe here. Howe, with a stronger, fresher force, permitted Washington to retreat to an impregnable position; Howe never could explain why he had not pursued his overwhelming advantage.

What to See and Do

Miller Hill Restoration. Restored earthworks from the Battle of White Plains (Oct 28, 1776). Built by Washington's troops. Battle diagrams. N White Plains.

Monument. Here the Declaration of Independence was adopted July 1776, and the state of New York was formally organized. S Broadway & Mitchell Place.

Washington's Headquarters (1776). Revolutionary War relics; demonstrations, lectures. (Wed-Sun) Virginia Rd, in N White Plains. Phone 914/949-1236. **Free.**

Hotels

★★★ **CROWNE PLAZA.** *66 Hale Ave (10601). 914/682-0050; FAX 914/682-7404.* Web www.hpncp.com. 401 rms, 12 story. S, D $174-$214; each addl $15; suites $475; under 12 free; wkend rates. Crib free. TV; cable (premium), VCR avail (movies). Indoor pool; whirlpool, lifeguard. Coffee in rms. Restaurant 6:30 am-11 pm. Bar noon-midnight. Ck-out noon. Coin lndry. Meeting rms. Business center. In-rm modem link. Gift shop. Garage parking. Free airport, RR station transportation. Exercise equipt. Health club privileges. Refrigerators avail. Luxury level. Cr cds: A, C, D, DS, JCB, MC, V.

★★★ **HILTON RYE TOWN.** *(699 Westchester Ave, Rye Brook 10573) E via I-287 exit 10, near Westchester County Airport. 914/939-6300; FAX 914/939-5328.* Web www.hilton.com. 437 rms. S $155-$230; D $175-$250, poolside rms $185; each addl $20; suites $310-$665; family, wkend rates. Crib $20. TV; cable (premium). 2 pools, 1 indoor; wading pool, whirlpool, lifeguard. Supervised child's activities (July 4-Sept 4); ages 3-15. Coffee in rms. Restaurant 6 am-11:30 pm. Bar 11-2 am. Ck-out 1 pm. Convention facilities. Business center. In-rm modem link. Concierge. Valet parking. Indoor & outdoor tennis. Exercise equipt; sauna. Lawn games. Private patios, balconies. Cr cds: A, C, D, DS, ER, JCB, MC, V.

★★ **RAMADA INN.** *(94 Business Park Dr, Armonk 10504) N on I-684, exit 3 S, in Westchester Business Park. 914/273-9090; FAX 914/273-4105.* 140 rms, 2 story. S, D $99-$189; each addl $10; suites $169-$225; under 18 free; wkend, hol rates; higher rates Dec 31. Pet accepted, some restrictions. TV; cable (premium). Pool; lifeguard. Complimentary coffee in rms. Restaurant 7 am-10 pm. Bar noon-2 am; entertainment wkends. Ck-out noon. Coin lndry. Meeting rms. Business servs avail. In-rm modem link. Free airport, RR station transportation. Exercise equipt. Some refrigerators; microwaves avail. Picnic tables. Cr cds: A, C, D, DS, ER, JCB, MC, V.

★★★ **RENAISSANCE WESTCHESTER.** *80 W Red Oak Lane (10604), at jct I-287, Hutchinson River Pkwy. 914/694-5400; FAX 914/694-5616.* 350 rms, 6 story. S $215-$235; D $225-$245; each addl $20; suites $375-$1,500; under 18 free; wkend rates. Crib free. TV; cable. Indoor pool; whirlpool, poolside serv, lifeguard. Complimentary coffee. Restaurant 6:30 am-10 pm. Rm serv 24 hrs. Bar noon-2 am. Ck-out 1 pm. Convention facilities. Business center. In-rm modem link. Concierge. Lighted tennis. Exercise equipt; sauna. Rec rm. Minibars; refrigerators avail. Private patios, balconies. Cr cds: A, C, D, DS, JCB, MC, V.

Resort

★★★ **DORAL ARROWWOOD.** *(Anderson Hill Rd, Rye Brook 10573) 3 mi E of I-287 exit 8E Westchester Ave; adj to SUNY-Purchase, near Westchester County Airport. 914/939-5500; FAX 914/323-5500.* Web www.arrowwood.com. 274 rms, 5 story. S, D $157-$459; golf plans; wkend rates. Crib free. TV; cable (premium). Indoor/outdoor pool; whirlpool, poolside serv, lifeguard. Dining rms (public by res) 6:30 am-10:30 pm. Rm serv 24 hrs. Box lunches, snack bar, picnics. Bar noon-2 am. Ck-out noon, ck-in 5 pm. Conference facilities. Business center. In-rm modem link. Bellhops. Airport, RR station, bus depot transportation. Sports dir. Indoor & lighted tennis, pro. 9-hole golf, greens fee, pro, putting green, driving range. Lawn games. Racquetball. Soc dir; entertainment. Rec rm. Exercise rm; sauna.

Massage. Refrigerators, microwaves avail. Some private patios, balconies. On 114 acres; duck pond; trails. Cr cds: A, C, D, DS, JCB, MC, V.

Restaurants

★ **CAFE MICHELANGELO.** *(208 Underhill Ave, West Harrison 10604)* 914/428-0022. Italian menu. Specializes in veal, seafood, pasta. Own desserts. Hrs: 11:30 am-3 pm, 4-10 pm; Fri to 11 pm; Sat noon-11 pm; Sun noon-9 pm. Closed most major hols. Res accepted. Semi-a la carte: lunch $7.95-$14.95, dinner $9.95-$24.95. Parking. Cr cds: A, D, DS, MC, V.

★ ★ **DAWAT.** *230 E Post Rd (10601), on NY 22S.* 914/428-4411. E-mail dawat/@aol.com; web www.westchestermenus.com. Indian menu. Specialties: leg of lamb, tandoori mixed grill. Hrs: noon-2:45 pm; 5:30-10:15 pm; Fri-Sat 5:30-10:45 pm; Sun 5-9:45 pm. Res accepted. Bar. A la carte entrees: dinner $12.95-$19.95. Lunch buffet $9.95. Parking. Contemporary decor with Indian influence. Cr cds: A, D, MC, V.

★ ★ ★ **LA PANETIERE.** *(530 Milton Rd, Rye 10580)* E on I-287 then S on I-95 exit 19, N on Milton Rd. 914/967-8140. This Westchester County restaurant has a formal atmosphere with many French objets d'art and antiques. The private dining room on the second floor features a greenhouse. Contemporary French menu. Specialties: Dover sole, roast breast of duckling, chessboard of dark and white chocolate mousse. Own baking. Hrs: noon-2:30 pm, 6-9:30 pm; Sat from 6 pm; Sun 1-8:30 pm. Res required. Bar. Wine list. A la carte entrees: lunch $16.50-$27, dinner $24-$32. Complete meals: dinner $80. Child's meals. Valet parking (dinner). Jacket. Cr cds: A, C, D, DS, MC, V.

✔★ **OLLIVER'S.** *15 S Broadway (10601),* I-287 E exit 6. 914/761-6111. E-mail olliverest@aol.com; web www.dinersgrapevine.com/ollivers. Specializes in chicken, black Angus steak. Salad bar. Hrs: 11:30-2 am; Sun brunch 11:30 am-3 pm. Closed Dec 25, some hols. Res accepted. Bar. Semi-a la carte: lunch $4.95-$10.95, dinner $7.95-$15.95. Sun brunch $10.95. Parking. Early Victorian decor. Cr cds: A, C, D, DS, MC, V.

★ ★ **REKA'S.** *2 Westchester Ave (10601),* I-287 E exit 6 or I-287 W exit 8. 914/949-1440. Thai menu. Specializes in seafood, crispy duck, wild boar. Hrs: noon-10 pm; Sat, Sun brunch noon-3 pm. Res accepted; required wkends. Bar. Semi-a la carte: lunch, dinner $9.95-$19.95. Sat, Sun brunch $14.95. Cr cds: A, C, D, MC, V.

Wilmington (B-8)

(See also Lake Placid, Saranac Lake)

Pop 1,020 **Elev** 1,020 ft **Area code** 518 **Zip** 12997 **E-mail** marketing.director@whiteface.net **Web** www.whiteface.net

Information Whiteface Mt Regional Visitors Bureau, NY 86, PO Box 277; 518/946-2255 or 888/944-8332.

Gateway to Whiteface Mountain Memorial Highway, Wilmington is made to order for skiers and lovers of scenic splendor.

What to See and Do

Adirondack Park (see).

High Falls Gorge. Deep ravine cut into the base of Whiteface Mt by the Ausable River. Variety of strata, rapids, falls and potholes can be viewed from a network of modern bridges and paths. Photography and mineral displays in main bldg. (Memorial Day-mid-Oct, daily) 5 mi S on NY 86. Phone 518/946-2278. ¢¢

Santa's Home Workshop. "Santa's home and workshop," Santa Claus, reindeer, children's rides and shows. (Late May-mid-Oct, daily) Reduced rates wkdays spring and fall. 1 1/2 mi W on NY 431, in North Pole. Phone 518/946-2211. ¢¢¢¢

Whiteface Mt Memorial Highway. A 5-mi toll road to top of mountain (4,867 ft). (Late May-mid-Oct, daily, weather permitting) Trail or elevator from parking area. Views of St Lawrence River, Lake Placid and Vermont. Elevator (begins late May). 3 mi W on NY 431. Phone 800/462-6236. Toll ¢¢

Whiteface Mt Ski Center. Two triple, 7 double chairlifts; snowmaking; patrol, school, rentals; cafeteria, bar, nursery. Longest run 2 1/2 mi; vertical drop 3,216 ft. Chairlift (mid-June-mid-Oct; fee). Lift-serviced mountain biking center; rental, repair shop, guided tours (late June-mid-Oct). (Mid-Nov-mid-Apr, daily) 3 mi SW on NY 86. Phone 800/462-6236 or 518/946-7171 (ski conditions). Skiing ¢¢¢¢¢; Biking ¢¢¢¢

Motels

★ ★ **HUNGRY TROUT.** *2 mi SW on NY 86, W branch of Ausable River.* 518/946-2217; FAX 518/946-7418; res: 800/766-9137. E-mail hungrytrout@whiteface.net; web www.hungrytrout.com. 20 rms. Dec-mid-Apr, late June-Labor Day: S, D $69-$89; suites $119-$139; ski, golf, fishing plans; lower rates rest of yr. Closed Apr, Nov. Crib $5. Pet accepted; $4. TV; cable. Pool; wading pool. Playground. Coffee in rms. Restaurant opp 7-10 am. Bar 5-10 pm. Ck-out 11 am. Downhill ski 1/2 mi; x-country ski 12 mi. On Ausable River. Cr cds: A, C, D, DS, MC, V.

★ ★ **LEDGE ROCK AT WHITEFACE MOUNTAIN.** *(Placid Rd, Whiteface Mountain)* 2 mi S on NY 86, opp Whiteface Mt Ski Center. 518/946-2302; FAX 518/946-7594; res: 800/336-4754. E-mail ledgerock@whiteface.net. 18 rms, 2 story. Mid-Dec-Mar, mid-June-late Oct: S, D $69-$120. Crib free. Pet accepted; $5. TV; cable. Heated pool; wading pool. Playground. Coffee in rms. Restaurant nearby. Ck-out 11 am. Rec rm. Game rm with fireplace. Refrigerators, microwaves. Some balconies. Picnic area, grills. Pond with paddleboats. Cr cds: A, DS, MC, V.

Inn

✔★ ★ **WHITEFACE CHALET.** *Springfield Rd, 1 1/2 mi S, 1/2 mi E of NY 86.* 518/946-2207; res: 800/932-0859. E-mail whiteface.chalet@whiteface.net; web lakeplacid.net/whitefacechalet/index.htm. 16 rms, 15 A/C. June-Oct, mid-Nov-Mar: S, D $45-$70; each addl $5; suites $55-$80; under 12 free; MAP avail; wkly rates; ski plans; lower rates rest of yr. Crib free. Pet accepted. TV; cable. Pool. Playground. Dining rm 8-10 am. Bar noon-1 am. Ck-out 11 am, ck-in 1 pm. Meeting rm. Airport, RR station, bus depot transportation. Tennis. Downhill ski 2 mi; x-country ski 3 mi. Lawn games. Rec rm. Balconies. Fireplace in lounge, living rm. Cr cds: A, DS, MC, V.

Restaurant

✔★ **WILDERNESS INN #2.** *1 1/2 mi SW on NY 86.* 518/946-2391. Specializes in fresh seafood, steak, pork chops. Salad bar. Hrs: 11 am-3 pm (summer & fall), 5-10 pm; winter to 9 pm. Closed Wed in winter; also first 3 wks Nov. Res accepted. Bar. Semi-a la carte: dinner $10.95-$16.95. Child's meals. Outdoor dining. Fireplace. Guest cottages avail. Family-owned. Cr cds: D, MC, V.

Windham (E-8)

(See also Cairo, Hunter)

Pop 1,660 (est) **Area code** 518 **Zip** 12496

What to See and Do

Ski Windham. High-speed detachable quad, double, 4 triple chairlifts, surface lift; patrol, ski school, rentals; snowmaking; nursery, ski shop, restaurant, 2 cafeterias, bar. Snowboarding. Longest run 12,500 ft; vertical drop 1,600 ft. (Early Nov-early Apr, daily) 25 mi W on NY 23, exit 21. Phone 518/734-4300; snow report, 800/729-4766 or 800/729-7549. ¢¢¢¢

White Birches Cross-Country Ski Touring Center. Approx 400 acres of Catskill Mt wilderness, lake. Over 15 mi of groomed trails; patrol, ski school, rentals; warming lodge. (Dec-Mar) Summer activities incl camping (hookups); lake swimming; canoes (rentals), paddleboats (fee); mountain bikes. Archery (fee). 2¹/₂ mi NE. Phone 518/734-3266. ¢¢¢

Motels

★ ★ **HOTEL VIENNA.** Rt 296. 518/734-5300; FAX 518/734-4749; res: 800/898-5308. Web www.pojonews.com/vienna. 30 rms, 2 story. S, D $80-$110; each addl $10-$20; higher rates: wkends (2-day min winter), hols. Closed Apr-mid-May. TV; cable. Indoor pool, whirlpool. Complimentary continental bkfst. Restaurant adj 4-10 pm. Ck-out 11 am. Ck-in 2 pm. Business servs avail. Downhill/x-country ski 1 mi. Balconies. Cr cds: MC, V.

★ ★ **WINDHAM ARMS.** NY 23. 518/734-3000; FAX 518/734-5900; res: 800/946-3476. 51 rms, some A/C, 2-3 story. No elvtr. Apr-early Oct, MAP: $400-$800/person/wk, summer $490-$920; EP: S, D $65-$250; each addl $10; lower rates rest of yr. Crib free. TV; cable. Heated pool. Playground. Restaurant 8-10 am, 5-8 pm. Ck-out 10 am. Coin lndry. Meeting rms. Business servs avail. Bellhops. Bus depot transportation. Tennis. Golf privileges, putting green. Downhill ski ¹/₂ mi; x-country ski 1 mi. Exercise equipt. Game rm. Rec rm. Lawn games. Many balconies. Theater. Cr cds: A, DS, MC, V.

Inn

★ ★ ★ **ALBERGO ALLEGRIA.** NY 296. 518/734-5560; FAX 518/734-5570; res: 800/625-2374. E-mail mail@albergousa.com; web www.albergousa.com. 15 rms, 2 story, 6 suites, 1 carriage house. Oct-mid-Mar: S, D $65-$145; each addl $25; suites $95-$225; package plans; lower rates rest of yr. TV; cable, VCR (free movies). Complimentary full bkfst; afternoon refreshments. Restaurant adj 4-10 pm. Ck-out 10:30 am, ck-in 1 pm. Business servs avail. Luggage handling. Valet serv. Gift shop. Tennis privileges. Downhill/x-country ski 1 mi. On river; swimming. Library/sitting rm; antiques. Some private decks. Two Queen Anne summer houses (1876) joined with Victorian-style addition. Cr cds: MC, V.

Restaurants

★ ★ ★ **LA GRIGLIA.** NY 296, just off NY 23. 518/734-4499. Italian menu. Specializes in fresh fish, own pasta, select beef. Own baking. Hrs: 4-10 pm; Sun brunch 11 am-3 pm. Closed Tues. Res accepted. Bar. Wine cellar. Semi-a la carte: dinner $11.95-$24. Sun brunch $14.95. Child's meals. Elegant atmosphere. Cr cds: A, D, MC, V.

★ ★ **THETFORD'S.** NY 23. 518/734-3322. Continental menu. Specializes in steak, fresh seafood, French sauces. Hrs: 4-10 pm; Fri to 11 pm; Sun 1-9 pm. Closed Mon, Tues Mar-June, Sept-Jan. Res accepted.

Bar. Semi-a la carte: dinner $10.95-$21.95. Child's meals. Colonial atmosphere. Family-owned. Cr cds: A, DS, MC, V.

Woodstock (F-8)

(See also Hunter, Kingston, Shandaken)

Pop 6,290 **Elev** 512 ft **Area code** 914 **Zip** 12498 **E-mail** wcoca@ulster.net **Web** www.woodstock-online.com
Information Chamber of Commerce and Arts, PO Box 36; 914/679-6234.

Woodstock has traditionally been known as an art colony. In 1902 Ralph Radcliffe Whitehead, an Englishman, came from California and set up a home and handcraft community (Byrdcliffe, north of town). The Art Students' League of New York established a summer school here a few years later. In 1916 Hervey White conceived the Maverick Summer Music Concerts, the oldest chamber concert series in the country. Woodstock was the original site chosen for the famous 1969 Woodstock Music Festival; however, when the event grew bigger than anyone imagined, it was moved 60 miles southwest to a farmer's field near Bethel (see MONTICELLO). Nevertheless, the festival gave Woodstock notoriety.

What to See and Do

Woodstock Artists Assoc Gallery. Center of the community since 1920. Changing exhibits of works by local and national artists. 28 Tinker St at Village Green. Phone 914/679-2940 for schedule. **Donation.**

Seasonal Event

Maverick Concerts. Maverick Rd, between NY 375 & 28. Chamber music concerts. Phone 914/679-8217. Sun June-early Sept.

Inns

★ ★ **THE DUTCHESS ANNE.** (Mt Tremper 12457) 10 mi W on NY 212, ¹/₃ mi N of NY 28. 914/688-5260; FAX 914/688-2438. 12 rms, 8 share bath, 2 story. No rm phones. S, D $60-$90; suite $120. Complimentary continental bkfst. Restaurant (see LA DUCHESSE ANNE). Bar. Ck-out noon, ck-in 2-11 pm. Built as a guest house 1850. Antique furnishings. Cr cds: A, DS, MC, V.

✔ ★ ★ **TWIN GABLES.** 73 Tinker St. 914/679-9479; FAX 914/679-5638. Web www.twingableswoodstockny.com. 9 rms, 6 share bath, 2 story. No rm phones. Memorial Day-Nov: S, D $48.49-$84.05; lower rates rest of yr. Restaurant adj. Ck-out 11:30 am, ck-in noon. Antique furnishings. Family-owned since 1940. Totally nonsmoking. Cr cds: A, DS, MC, V.

Restaurants

★ ★ **THE BEAR CAFE.** (295A Tinker St, Bearsville 12409) 2 mi W on NY 212, in Bearsville Theatre Complex. 914/679-5555. E-mail bearcafe@prodigy.com; web www.bearcafe.com. Specialties: ravioli with arugula & radicchio, filet mignon with port garlic sauce. Hrs: 5-10:30 pm; Fri, Sat to 11 pm. Closed Dec 25. Res accepted. Bar. Semi-a la carte: dinner $11.95-$20.50. Outdoor dining. Large windows in dining area overlook creek. Cr cds: MC, V.

✔ ★ ★ **CATSKILL ROSE.** (NY 212, Mt Tremper 12457) approx 10 mi W on NY 212. 914/688-7100. Contemporary Amer menu. Specialties: smoked duckling, chocolate fudge cake with white chocolate mousse. Hrs:

5-10 pm. Closed Mon, Tues. Res accepted. Bar. Semi-a la carte: dinner $13.75-$16.75. Child's meals. Pianist Sat. Parking. Outdoor dining. Cr cds: A, C, D, DS, MC, V.

★ ★ **JOSHUA'S.** *51 Tinker St. 914/679-5533.* Continental menu. Specialties: sesame chicken, vegetarian selections. Hrs: 11 am-10 pm; Fri, Sat to 11 pm; Sun from 10 am. Res accepted. Semi-a la carte: lunch $4-$12.95, dinner $10.95-$18.95. Guitarist Sat. Family-owned. Cr cds: A, MC, V.

★ ★ ★ **LA DUCHESSE ANNE.** *(See The Dutchess Anne Inn) 914/688-5260.* French menu. Specialties: rack of lamb, fish stew, roast duck. Own baking. Hrs: 5:30-9:30 pm; Fri, Sat to 11 pm; Sun from 11:30 am; Sun brunch to 3:30 pm. Closed Tues Feb-June, Wed & Thurs Feb-Mar. Res accepted. Bar. Wine list. A la carte entrees: dinner $14-$22. Sun brunch $7-$10. Country French atmosphere in 1850 guest house; original fixtures, antiques, large fireplace. Cr cds: A, DS, MC, V.

Yonkers (A-2)

Settled 1646 **Pop** 188,082 **Elev** 16 ft **Area code** 914 **E-mail** info@yonkerschamber.com **Web** www.yonkerschamber.com

Information Chamber of Commerce, 20 S Broadway, Ste 1207, 10701; 914/963-0332.

Yonkers, on the New York City line, was originally puchased by Adriaen Van Der Donck in the early 1600s. His status as a young nobleman from Holland gave him the nickname "DeJonkeer," which underwent many changes until it became "the Yonkers land" and finally Yonkers.

What to See and Do

St Paul's Church Natl Historic Site. Setting for historical events establishing basic freedoms outlined in the Bill of Rights. The event that made this site famous, the Great Election of 1733, led to the establishment of a free press in colonial America. Before completion, the fieldstone and brick Georgian St Paul's Church (1763) served as a military hospital for the British and Hessians during the American Revolution. Building was completed after the war and served not only as a church but also as a meeting house and courtrm where Aaron Burr practiced law on at least one occasion. Tours (Sat; Tues-Fri, by appt; closed Jan 1, Thanksgiving, Dec 25). 897 S Columbus Ave in Mount Vernon, 10 mi SE via Hutchinson River Pkwy exit 8 (Sandford Blvd). Phone 914/667-4116. **Free.**

Bill of Rights Museum. Exhibits incl working model of 18th-century printing press and dioramas depicting John Peter Zenger, whose trial and acquittal for seditious libel in 1735 helped establish freedom of the press in America. Series of panels detail history of site, incl the Anne Hutchinson story, the Great Election of 1733 and the Revolutionary period. (Same days as St Paul's Church) Phone 914/667-4116. **Free.**

The Hudson River Museum of Westchester. Includes Glenview Mansion (1876), an Eastlake-inspired Hudson River house overlooking the Palisades; Andrus Planetarium; regional art, history and science exhibits; changing exhibits of 19th- and 20th-century art in the Glenview galleries and contemporary wing. Changing exhibits, planetarium shows, lectures, jazz festival in summer. (Wed-Sun; closed major hols) 511 Warburton Ave. Phone 914/963-4550. Museum ¢¢; Planetarium ¢¢

Yonkers Raceway. Night harness racing; day simulcasting from NYRA. Yonkers & Central Aves in Yonkers, on I-87, between exits 2 & 4. For schedule phone 914/968-4200. ¢¢

Motel

★ ★ **HOLIDAY INN.** *125 Tuckahoe Rd (10710). 914/476-3800; FAX 914/423-3555.* 103 rms, 3 story. S $89-$99; D $89-$106; each addl $7; suites $195; under 18 free; wkend rates. Crib free. TV; cable (premium). Complimentary coffee in rms. Restaurant 7 am-10 pm. Rm serv. Bar 5 pm-midnight; wkends to 2 am; entertainment Thurs-Sat. Ck-out noon. Meeting rms. Business servs avail. In-rm modem link. Exercise equipt. Pool; poolside serv, lifeguard. Many balconies. Cr cds: A, D, DS, MC, V.

Restaurant

★ ★ **J.J. MANNION'S.** *640 McLean Ave (10705). 914/476-2786.* Hrs: 11-1 am; Sun brunch to 3 pm. Closed Dec 25. Bar. Semi-a la carte: lunch $4.50-$12, dinner $4.50-$22.95. Sun brunch $11.95. Street parking. Irish pub decor. Cr cds: A, C, D, DS, MC, V.

D

New York City

Settled: 1615
Population: 7,322,564
Elevation: 0-410 ft

New York is the nation's most populous city, the capital of finance, business, communications, theater and much more. It may not be the center of the universe, but it does occupy a central place in the world's imagination. Certainly, in one way or another, New York affects the lives of nearly every American. While other cities have everything that New York has—from symphonies to slums—no other city has quite the style or sheer abundance. Nowhere are things done in such a grandly American way as in New York City.

Giovanni da Verrazano was the first European to glimpse Manhattan Island (1524), but the area was not explored until 1609, when Henry Hudson sailed up the river that was later named for him, searching for a passage to India. Adriaen Block arrived here in 1613, and the first trading post was established by the Dutch West India Company two years later. Peter Minuit is said to have bought the island from Native Americans for $24 worth of beads and trinkets in 1626, when New Amsterdam was founded—the biggest real estate bargain in history.

In 1664 the Dutch surrendered to a British fleet, and the town was renamed New York in honor of the Duke of York. One of the earliest tests of independence occurred here in 1734, when John Peter Zenger, publisher and editor of the *New York Weekly-Journal,* was charged with seditious libel and jailed for making anti-government remarks. Following the Battle of Long Island in 1776, the British occupied the city through the Revolution, until 1783.

On the balcony of Federal Hall at Wall St, April 30, 1789, George Washington was inaugurated as first president of the United States, and for a time New York was the country's capital.

When the Erie Canal opened in 1825, New York City expanded vastly as a port. It has since consistently maintained its leadership. In 1898 Manhattan merged with Brooklyn, the Bronx, Queens and Staten Island. In the next half-century, several million immigrants entered the United States here, providing the city with the supply of labor needed for its growth into a major metropolis. Each wave of immigrants has brought new customs, culture and life, which makes New York City the varied metropolis it is today.

New York continues to capitalize on its image as the Big Apple, attracting more than 19 million visitors each year, and its major attractions continue to thrive in style. These, of course, are centered in Manhattan; however, vacationers should not overlook the wealth of sights and activities the other boroughs have to offer. Brooklyn has Coney Island, the New York Aquarium, the superb Brooklyn Museum, Brooklyn Botanic Garden, Brooklyn Children's Museum, and the famous landmark Brooklyn Bridge. The Bronx is noted for its excellent Botanical Garden and Zoo and Yankee Stadium. Flushing Meadows-Corona Park, in Queens, was the site of two World's Fairs; nearby is Shea Stadium, home of the New York Mets. Uncrowded Staten Island has Richmondtown Restoration, a re-creation of 18th-century New York, rural farmland, beaches, salt marshes and wildlife preserves.

Weather

The average mean temperatures for New York are 34°F in winter; 52°F in spring; 75°F in summer; and 58°F in fall. In summer the temperature is rarely above 90°F (maximum recorded: 106°F), but the humidity can be high. In winter the temperature is rarely lower than 10°F, but has gone as low as -14°F. Average mean temperatures are listed from surveys taken at the National Weather Bureau station in Central Park.

Theater

New York is theatrical headquarters of the United States, and theater here is an experience not to be missed. Broadway, a 36-square-block area (41st to 53rd Sts & 6th to 9th Aves), offers standard full-scale plays and musicals, more than 30 of them on any particular evening. Off-Broadway, not confined to one area, is less expensive and more experimental, giving new talent a chance at exposure and established talent an opportunity to try new and different projects, such as the New York Shakespeare Festival (see under SEASONAL EVENTS). Even less expensive and more daring is Off-Off-Broadway, consisting of dozens of small theaters in storefronts, lofts and cellars, producing every imaginable type of theater.

There are a number of ways to obtain tickets, ranging from taking a pre-arranged package theater tour to walking up to the box office an hour before curtain for returned and unclaimed tickets. Ticket Master outlets (phone 212/307-7171), hotel theater desks and ticket brokers will have tickets to several shows for the box office price plus a service charge. All Broadway theaters accept phone reservations charged to major credit cards. An On Stage Hotline can be reached at 212/768-1818.

The Times Square Ticket Center (a booth with large banners proclaiming "Tkts"), 47th St & Broadway, has same-day tickets at half price for most shows (daily) and for matinees (Wed, Sat, Sun). There is also a downtown branch located at the World Trade Center, open Mon-Sat, for same-day evening performances only. Same-day half-price tickets to music and dance events may be obtained at the Music & Dance Booth, at 42nd St & Avenue of the Americas in Bryant Park. *The New Yorker* and *New York* magazines carry extensive listings of the week's entertainment; the Friday edition of *The New York Times* also reports weekend availability of tickets.

Additional Visitor Information

Contact the New York Convention and Visitors Bureau, 810 7th Ave, 3rd floor, 10019; 212/484-1222. The bureau has free maps, "twofers" to Broadway shows, bulletins and brochures on attractions, events, shopping, restaurants and hotels. For events of the week, visitors should get copies

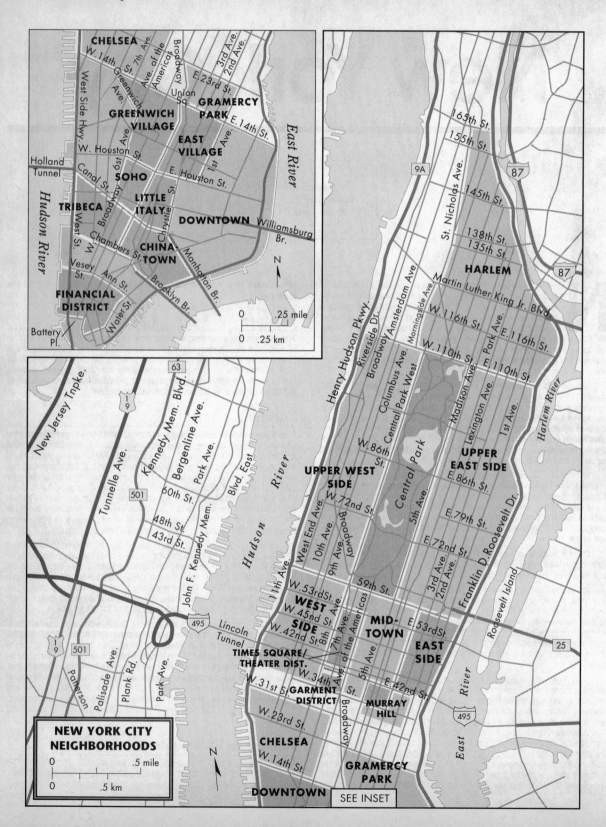

CHELSEA
W. 14th St.
7th Ave.
Ave. of the Americas
Broadway
3rd Ave.
2nd Ave.
E. 23rd St.
West Side Hwy.
Greenwich Ave.
Union Sq.
GRAMERCY PARK
GREENWICH VILLAGE
W. Houston St.
6th Ave.
5th Ave.
E. 14th St.
EAST VILLAGE
1st Ave.
W. Houston St.
E. Houston St.
SOHO
Holland Tunnel
Canal St.
Broadway
LITTLE ITALY
TRIBECA
West St.
W. Broadway
Chrystie St.
DOWNTOWN
Williamsburg Br.
Hudson River
Chambers St.
CHINA-TOWN
Manhattan Br.
Ann St.
Vesey St.
Brooklyn Br.
East River
FINANCIAL DISTRICT
Water St.
Battery Pl.
N
0   .25 mile
0   .25 km

New Jersey Tnpke.
63
19
Kennedy Mem. Blvd.
Bergenline Ave.
Park Ave.
Blvd. East
Hudson River
165th St.
155th St.
9A
St. Nicholas Ave.
145th St.
87
Tunnelle Ave.
501
60th St.
48th St.
43rd St.
John F. Kennedy Mem.
138th St.
135th St.
HARLEM
Martin Luther King Jr. Blvd.
Amsterdam Ave.
Broadway
Morningside Ave.
W. 116th St.
E. 116th St.
Park Ave.
87
W. 110th St.
E. 110th St.
Henry Hudson Pkwy.
Riverside Dr.
Columbus Ave.
Central Park West
Harlem River
495
Lincoln Tunnel
19
501
Palisade Ave.
Plank Rd.
Park Ave.
Paterson
11th Ave.
West End Ave.
10th Ave.
9th Ave.
Broadway
W. 86th St.
Central Park
5th Ave.
Madison Ave.
Lexington Ave.
1st Ave.
UPPER EAST SIDE
E. 86th St.
UPPER WEST SIDE
W. 72nd St.
E. 79th St.
E. 72nd St.
3rd Ave.
2nd Ave.
Franklin D. Roosevelt Dr.
Roosevelt Island
59th St.
W. 53rd St.
WEST SIDE
W. 45th St.
7th Ave.
Ave. of the Americas
E. 53rd St.
MID-TOWN
W. 42nd St.
8th Ave.
TIMES SQUARE/THEATER DIST.
EAST SIDE
25
W. 34th St.
5th Ave.
MURRAY HILL
W. 31st St.
GARMENT DISTRICT
E. 42nd St.
W. 23rd St.
East River
495
CHELSEA
W. 14th St.
GRAMERCY PARK
DOWNTOWN
SEE INSET

NEW YORK CITY NEIGHBORHOODS
0   .5 mile
0   .5 km
N

of *The New Yorker* and *New York* magazines and *The New York Times*. For those who intend to stay for some time and want to delve more deeply into the city, we suggest browsing in libraries and bookstores for the numerous guidebooks that detail what to see and do.

Transportation

Airports: *La Guardia,* in Queens 8 mi NE of Manhattan; *Kennedy Intl,* in Queens 15 mi SE of Manhattan (for both, see QUEENS—LA GUARDIA & JFK INTL AIRPORT AREAS); *Newark Intl,* 16 mi SW of Manhattan in New Jersey.

Car Rental Agencies: See IMPORTANT TOLL-FREE NUMBERS.

Public Transportation: Subway and elevated trains, buses (New York City Transit Authority), phone 718/330-3322 or 718/330-1234. The subway system, which carries more than four million people on weekdays, covers every borough except Staten Island, which has its own transportation system. Maps of the system are posted at every station and on every car.

Rail Passenger Service: Amtrak 800/872-7245.

Driving in New York

Vehicular traffic is heaviest during weekday rush hours and on both weekdays and weekends between Thanksgiving and Christmas week—a period of almost continuous rush hour. Most Manhattan avenues and streets are one-way. To assist tourists in finding cross streets nearest avenue addresses, telephone books and several tourist guides contain address locator tables. Because New York traffic is very heavy and parking is both scarce and expensive, many visitors find taxis more convenient and economical than driving.

Sightseeing Tours

For travelers desiring a general overview of the city, a variety of sightseeing tours are available using various forms of transportation (see SIGHTSEEING TOURS under MANHATTAN).

Manhattan (D-2 see New York City map)

Area code 212

When most people think of New York City, they think of Manhattan. When the first colonists arrived in 1626, Manhattan was a rugged, wooded island, inhabited only by a small band of Native Americans at its northern end. A mere three-and-a-half centuries later, it had become our most concentrated definition of the word "city." Only 12½ miles long and 2½ miles wide at its widest point, it is the center of American culture, communications and business, containing an enormous variety of restaurants, shops, museums and entertainment.

Many superlatives are needed to describe Manhattan—it has the largest banks, several of the finest streets and avenues, one of the greatest city parks (Central Park), an incredible skyline, the greatest theater district and the most sophisticated of almost everything. If Manhattanites sometimes forget that there is more to America than this tiny island, perhaps they may be forgiven. Their island is unique.

What to See and Do

American Bible Society Gallery/Library. Collection of Bibles and unusual current editions; replica of Gutenberg press; changing exhibits. (Mon-Fri; closed hols) Broadway & 61st St. Phone 212/408-1200.   **Free.**

American Museum of Natural History. Permanent exhibits include the Hall of Ocean Life, with its 94-ft great blue whale; the Hall of South American Peoples; Asian Peoples; Northwest Coast Indians; Eskimos; Mexico & Central America; African Peoples; Pacific Peoples; Hall of Reptiles and Amphibians; Habitat Groups of North America, Africa &Asia; skeletal constructions of dinosaurs and other prehistoric life. Changing exhibits. Museum Highlights Tour (daily; free). Demonstration lectures,

drama, dance, film. (Daily; closed Thanksgiving, Dec 25) IMAX film shown on huge indoor screen (phone 212/769-5034). Central Park W at 79th St. For general museum schedule and tour information phone 212/769-5100. ¢¢¢

Astro Minerals Gallery of Gems. Display of minerals, gems, jewelry; primitive and African art. (Daily; closed Jan 1, Thanksgiving, Dec 25) 185 Madison Ave, at 34th St. Phone 212/889-9000.   **Free.**

★ **Carnegie Hall.** Completed in 1891, the celebrated auditorium has been home to the world's great musicians for more than a century. Guided 1-hr tours (Mon, Tues, Thurs & Fri; fee). 154 W 57th St, at Seventh Ave. Phone 212/247-7800. Performances   ¢¢¢¢¢

Cathedral Church of St John the Divine (Episcopal). Under construction since 1892. When completed, this will be the largest Gothic Cathedral in the world, 601 ft long and 124 ft high. Bronze doors of the central portal represent scenes from the Old and New Testaments. The great rose window, 40 ft in diameter, is made up of more than 10,000 pieces of glass. Cathedral contains tapestry, painting and sculpture collection. The cathedral and 5 other buildings are on 13 acres with park and garden areas, including Biblical Garden. (Daily) Tours (Tues-Sat; also Sun following last morning service; no tours religious hols). Amsterdam Ave & 112th St. Phone 212/316-7490.   ¢

★ **Central Park.** Construction of this magnificent 843-acre park, designed by Frederick Law Olmsted and Calvert Vaux, began in 1857; it was the first formally planned park in the country. Topographically rugged, highlights include a lake with boat and gondola rentals; a lake for sailing miniature boats; a five-acre Central Park Wildlife Conservation Center (fee); two skating rinks; a swimming pool; a miniature golf course; a conservatory garden at Fifth Ave & 105th St; Strawberry Fields, given to the park by Yoko Ono in memory of John Lennon, at 72nd St & Central Park West; the Belvedere Castle; and the Delacorte Theater, where the summer Shakespeare Festival is staged (see SEASONAL EVENTS). Park drives running north and south are closed to vehicular traffic on Sat, Sun and hols, as well as certain hrs on wkdays (Apr-Oct). The entrances at 59th St and Fifth and Sixth Aves are known for the horse-drawn carriages, which can be hired for a ride through the park. Fifth Ave to Central Park W (Eighth Ave) and 59th St to 110th St. For information on Central Park SummerStage performances and concerts phone 212/360-2777. Park rangers conduct wkend tours; phone 212/427-4040.

   The Dairy. Exhibition/Visitor Information Center. Video on history of the park; time-travel video; gift and book shop. (Daily exc Mon) In the Park on 64th St, W of the Central Park Wildlife Conservation Center & the carousel. Phone 212/794-6564.   **Free.**

   Storytelling in the Park. At Hans Christian Andersen statue in Central Park, near the model boat pond, off 74th St at Fifth Ave (June-Sept, Sat). Recommended for children 5 & older; also in certain playgrounds (July-Aug). For details phone 212/360-3444.   **Free.**

Chrysler Building. New York's famous art deco skyscraper. The graceful pointed spire with triangular windows set in arches is lighted at night. The impressive lobby features beautiful jazz-age detailing. 405 Lexington Ave, at E 42nd St.

City Center. Landmark theater hosts world-renowned dance companies, including the Alvin Ailey American Dance Theater, Martha Graham Dance Company, the Paul Taylor Dance Company and Merce Cunningham Dance Company. Also presents American music and theater events. Downstairs, City Center Stages I and II host the Manhattan Theatre Club. 55th St between Sixth & Seventh Aves. Phone 212/581-1212.

City College of New York (1847). (14,660 students) One of the nation's best-known municipal colleges and the oldest in the city university system. Alumni include seven Nobel laureates, Supreme Court Justice Felix Frankfurter, and authors Upton Sinclair, Paddy Chayefsky and Bernard Malamud. Tours (Mon-Thurs, by appt). Convent Ave & W 138th St. Phone 212/650-6977.

Columbia University (1754). (18,499 students) This Ivy League university was originally King's College; classes were conducted in the vestry rm of Trinity Church. King's College still exists as Columbia College, with 3,073 students. The campus has more than 62 buildings, including Low Memorial Library, the administration building (which has the Rotunda and the Sackler Collection of Chinese Ceramics) and Butler Library, with more than 5 million volumes. The university numbers Alexander Hamilton, Gouverneur

Morris and John Jay among its early graduates and Nicholas Murray Butler, Dwight D. Eisenhower and Andrew W. Cordier among its former presidents. Barnard College (1889) (2,098 women) and Teachers College (1887) (5,433 students) are affiliated with Columbia. Multilingual guided tours. (Mon-Fri exc hols & final exam period) Broadway & 116th St. Phone 212/854-1754. **Free.**

Cooper Union (1859). (1,000 students) All-scholarship college for art, architecture and engineering. Great Hall, where Lincoln spoke in 1861, is auditorium for readings, films, lectures and performing arts. Home of the American Jazz Orchestra. Third Ave at 7th St. Phone 212/353-4195.

Dyckman House Park and Museum (ca 1783). Only 18th-century Dutch farmhouse still on Manhattan Island. Built by William Dyckman; refurnished with some original Dyckman pieces and others of the period. Replica of British officers' hut on landscaped grounds; smokehouse; garden. (Daily exc Mon; closed Jan 1, Thanksgiving, Dec 25) Children only with adult. 4881 Broadway, at 204th St. Phone 212/304-9422. **Free.**

El Museo del Barrio. Dedicated to Puerto Rican and other Latin American art, including paintings, photographs and sculpture; also films, theater, concerts and educational programs. Inquire about bilingual tours. (Wed-Sun; closed hols) 1230 Fifth Ave, between E 104th & 105th Sts. Phone 212/831-7272 or 212/831-7273. **¢¢**

⭐ **Empire State Building** (1931). The 1,454-ft-high 1930s- *moderne* skyscraper building that King Kong climbed in the movie classic. Open and enclosed observation platforms on 86th & 102nd floors (daily). 350 Fifth Ave, at 34th St. Phone 212/736-3100. **¢¢**

Fordham University. 60th St & Columbus Ave, across from St. Paul's Church. Phone 212/636-6000.

General Grant National Memorial. President and Mrs Ulysses S. Grant are entombed here. (Daily; closed hols) Riverside Dr & W 122nd St. Phone 212/666-1640.

Greenwich Village. An area reaching from Broadway west to Greenwich Ave between 14th St on the N and Houston St on the S. An extension of this area to the East River is known as the East Village. Perhaps most famous as an art and literary center, Greenwich Village was originally settled by wealthy colonial New Yorkers wishing to escape to the country. Many Italian and Irish immigrants settled here in the late 19th century. Among the famous writers and artists who have lived and worked in this area are Tom Paine, Walt Whitman, Henry James, John Masefield (he scrubbed saloon floors), Eugene O'Neill, Edna St. Vincent Millay, Max Eastman, Arctic explorer-writer Vilhjalmur Stefansson, Franz Kline, e.e. cummings, John Dos Passos and Martha Graham. It is a colorful area, with restaurants, taverns, book, print, art and jewelry shops.Greenwich Village is a fashionable and expensive place to live, particularly in the vicinity of

Washington Square. The Washington Arch, completed in 1895 as commemoration of Washington's first inauguration, is 86 ft high. The park is a local gathering place and the hub of the Village. The area is the site of outdoor art shows by artists from Greenwich Village and many other points (see SEASONAL EVENTS). E, N & S of the square is the main campus of New York University (see). At the S end of Fifth Ave.

The Church of the Ascension (Episcopal) (1840). English Gothic; redecorated 1885-1889 under the direction of Stanford White. John La Farge's mural, *The Ascension of Our Lord,*surmounts the altar; the sculptured angels are by Louis Saint-Gaudens. (Daily) 10th St & Fifth Ave. Phone 212/254-8620.

The Joseph Papp Public Theater. Complex of six theaters, where Shakespeare, new American plays, new productions of classics, films, concerts and poetry readings are presented. 425 Lafayette St, the former Astor Library. Phone 212/260-2400.

Hamilton Grange National Memorial (1802). Federal-style residence of Alexander Hamilton. (Wed-Sun) 287 Convent St, at W 141st St. Phone 212/283-5154. **Free.**

Harlem. An area reaching from 110th St to about 165th St, and from the Harlem River to Morningside Ave. Spanish Harlem is toward the east, although Harlem and Spanish Harlem overlap. Harlem has been called "the black capital of America." Tours: Harlem Spirituals, phone 212/757-0425.

International Center of Photography. Changing exhibits represent a wide range of photographic expression; audiovisual presentations; work-

shops, seminars, lectures. (Daily exc Mon; closed major hols) 1130 Fifth Ave, at 94th St. Phone 212/860-1777. **¢¢** Midtown branch is

ICP/Midtown. Changing exhibits; gallery tours; lectures, screening room; bookstore. 1133 Ave of the Americas. **¢¢**

Intrepid **Sea-Air Space Museum.** The famous aircraft carrier *Intrepid*was converted into a museum with gallery space devoted to histories of the ship itself, the modern navy, and space technology. Also on display is a nuclear guided submarine and a Vietnam-era destroyer (avail for boarding). Exhibits and film presentations. (Memorial Day-Labor Day, daily; rest of yr, Wed-Sun) Foot of W 46th St; at Pier 86, Hudson River. Phone 212/245-0072. **¢¢¢**

Jacob K. Javits Convention Center. One of the world's largest, most technically advanced exposition halls; 900,000 sq-ft of exhibit space and more than 100 meeting rms can accommodate 6 events simultaneously. The center is easily recognized for its thousands of glass cubes that mirror the skyline by day. The architect was I.M. Pei. Cafe. 34th-39th Sts, along Hudson River on 22-acre site SW of Times Square. Phone 212/216-2000.

Jewish Museum. Devoted to Jewish art & culture, ancient and modern. Historical exhibits; contemporary painting and sculpture. (Sun-Thurs afternoons; closed hols) Fifth Ave at 92nd St. Phone 212/423-3200. **¢¢¢**

Jewish Theological Seminary of America. Extensive collection of Judaica; rare book rm; courtyard with sculpture by Jacques Lipchitz. Special programs. Kosher cafeteria. Tours avail. (Daily exc Sat; closed hols) 3080 Broadway at 122nd St. Phone 212/678-8000.

Lincoln Center for the Performing Arts. America's premier performing arts center includes Avery Fisher Hall (symphony), New York State Theater (ballet, opera), Vivian Beaumont and Mitzi E. Newhouse Theaters (drama), Metropolitan Opera House and the Juilliard School, which also houses Alice Tully Hall (films, concerts). 70 Lincoln Center Plaza.

Lincoln Center Guided Tours. Includes Metropolitan Opera House, New York State Theater and Avery Fisher Hall. Tour Desk is located on the Concourse Level, downstairs from the Plaza. (Daily; no tours Jan 1, July 4, Thanksgiving, Dec 25). Phone 212/875-5350. **¢¢¢**

New York Public Library for the Performing Arts. Books, phonograph record collection; exhibits and research library on music, theater and dance; concerts, films, dance recitals. 40 Lincoln Center Plaza. Phone 212/870-1630. **Free.**

Madison Square Garden. The Garden has been the site of major sports, entertainment and special events for well over a century. The present Garden, the fourth building bearing that name, was opened in 1968. (The original Garden was actually on Madison Square.) It is the home of the New York Knickerbockers basketball team and New York Rangers hockey club. The Garden complex includes the 20,000-seat Arena, Exposition Rotunda and Bowling Center. Pennsylvania Plaza, above Pennsylvania Station, between Seventh & Eighth Aves, W 31st to W 33rd St. Phone 212/465-6000 for ticket information.

⭐ **Metropolitan Museum of Art.** More than 3 million objects from a period of more than 5,000 yrs make this the most comprehensive collection in America. Egypt, Greece, Italy, the Near and Far East, Africa, the Pacific Islands, pre-Columbian and Native America, Europe and America are represented. Twentieth-century art galleries, including rooftop sculpture garden, and Japanese art galleries. To see the entire collection would take days. Special exhibits and programs for children. No strollers Sun or special exhibits. (Daily exc Mon; closed Jan 1, Thanksgiving, Dec 25) Recorded tour (fee). Cafeteria; parking (fee). Free lectures, concerts, films, gallery talks. Fifth Ave at 82nd St. Phone 212/535-7710. **¢¢¢**

Morris-Jumel Mansion (1765). Built by Colonel Roger and Mary Philipse Morris, this was George Washington's headquarters in 1776 and later became a British command post and Hessian headquarters. Purchased by French merchant Stephen Jumel in 1810, house was the scene of the marriage of his widow, Madame Eliza Jumel, to Aaron Burr in 1833. The mansion is the only remaining colonial residence in Manhattan. Period furnishings. (Wed-Sun; closed major hols) 1765 Jumel Terrace at W 160th St, 1/2 blk E of St Nicholas Ave. Phone 212/923-8008. **¢¢**

Museum of the City of New York. Museum on the history of New York City, with paintings, prints, photographs, ship models, theatrical memorabilia, collection of 10 New York doll houses dating from 1769 to present, firefighting equipment, costumes and decorative arts. Dutch Gallery covers life in the early Dutch settlement; reconstructed portion of Ft Amsterdam. Multimedia "Big Apple" presentation. Walking tours of the city (Sun, springfall; fee). Concerts, gallery talks and other wkend programs (fee for some). Museum (Wed-Sat, also Sun afternoons; closed hols). 1220 Fifth Ave, between E 103rd &104th Sts. Phone 212/534-1672. ¢¢-¢¢¢

New York City Post Office. Guided 1¹/₂-hr tours (Tues-Fri, upon written request to Postmaster, or phone 212/330-2300; 1-wk advance reservation required). No cameras. Eighth Ave & 33rd St.

New York Public Library. One of the best research libraries in the world, with more than 10 million volumes. Exhibits of rare books, art materials; free programs at branches. One-hr tours of central building (daily exc Sun). Astor, Lenox & Tilden Foundations. 42nd St & Fifth Ave. Phone 212/930-0501 or 212/661-7220. **Free.** Many interesting collections on display at the Central Research Library and The New York Public Library for the Performing Arts (also tours) and the

> **Schomburg Center for Research in Black Culture.** The center's collection covers every phase of black activity wherever black people have lived in significant numbers. Books, manuscripts, periodicals, art and audiovisual materials. 515 Malcolm X Blvd, at 135th St. Phone 212/491-2200. **Free.**

New York University (1831). (33,973 students) One of the largest private universities in the country, NYU is known for its undergraduate and graduate business, medical and law schools, school of performing arts and fine arts programs. The university has graduated a large number of "Fortune 500" company executives. Most programs, including the Graduate Business Center, are located on the main campus surrounding Washington Square Park; the medical and dental schools are on the East Side. Tours (Mon-Fri exc hols, from Admissions Office at 22 Washington Square N). Phone 212/998-4524. In Main Bldg at northeast corner of Washington Square is Grey Art Gallery and Study Center, with paintings, drawings, sculpture; changing exhibits (Tues-Sat). Renaissance musical instrument collection in Waverly Bldg (by appt), phone 212/998-8300.

Pierpont Morgan Library. Museum/rare book library designed by McKim, Mead and White; holdings include medieval and Renaissance manuscripts, early printed books, bookbindings, old master drawings, autograph and musical manuscripts, historical documents, early children's books and manuscripts. Changing exhibits; permanent exhibits include Gutenberg Bible, Renaissance paintings and sculpture, medieval gold objects. Glass-enclosed Garden Court. (Daily exc Mon; closed hols, also last 2 wks Aug) 29 E 36th St. Phone 212/685-0610or 212/685-0008. ¢¢

Police Museum. Exhibits of police uniforms, badges and equipment. (Mon-Fri; closed hols; schedule may vary) 235 E 20th St, between Second & Third Aves; Police Academy Bldg, 2nd fl. By advance appt only, phone 212/477-9753. **Free.**

Professional sports.

> **American League baseball (New York Yankees).** Yankee Stadium (see BRONX). Phone 718/293-4300.

> **National League baseball (New York Mets).** Shea Stadium (see QUEENS). Phone 718/507-6387.

> **NBA (New York Knickerbockers).** Madison Square Garden, 4 Penn Plaza. Phone 212/465-6741.

> **NFL (New York Giants).** Giants Stadium, NJ 3 in East Rutherford, NJ. Phone 201/935-8111.

> **NFL (New York Jets).** Giants Stadium, NJ 3 in East Rutherford, NJ. Phone 516/560-8100.

> **NHL (New York Islanders).** Nassau Veterans Memorial Coliseum (see HEMPSTEAD, L.I., NY). Phone 800/882-4753.

> **NHL (New York Rangers).** Madison Square Garden, 4 Penn Plaza. Phone 212/465-6485.

✖ **Rockefeller Center.** The largest privately owned business and entertainment center in the world is made up of 19 buildings on 22 acres. The graceful GE (formerly RCA) Bldg, designed by Raymond Hood, is the highest structure and centerpiece of the complex, which has more than 1,200 tenant firms, 34 restaurants and 200 shops. The Channel Gardens, at Fifth Ave between 49th & 50th streets, has seasonal floral displays, including a spectacular Christmas tree. The gardens terminate at the gilded Prometheus Fountain. There is an outdoor cafe around the foun-

tain's pool, which in winter is used as an ice rink, where visitors may order food and drink and watch the skaters. Radio City Music Hall Entertainment Center, home of the Rockettes, with a capacity of 6,000, is the world's largest indoor theater (phone 212/247-4777 for event information). The buildings east of the Avenue of the Americas were completed in the 1930s; the Center buildings to the west were primarily completed in the 1960s. Self-guided tours; brochure avail at GE Bldg or Visitors Bureau. Fifth Ave to Avenue of the Americas and beyond, 47th St to 51st St with some buildings stretching to 52nd St. Phone 212/698-2950.

Shopping.

> **Bloomingdale's.** Flagship of famous department store chain. (Daily; closed major hols) 1000 Third Ave, at 59th St & Lexington Ave. Phone 212/705-2000.

> **Macy's Herald Square.** "The world's largest store" has everything from international fashion collections for men and women to antique galleries. (Daily; closed Easter, Thanksgiving, Dec 25) 34th St at Broadway. Phone 212/695-4400.

> **South Street Seaport.** Festival marketplace with more than 100 shops and 40 restaurants in Seaport Plaza, Schermerhorn Row and Museum Block and the multi-floored Pier 17, which extends into the East River. Fulton & Water Sts, at East River. Phone 212/732-7678.

> **World Financial Center.** The center includes more than 40 shops and restaurants on and around the Winter Garden, a 120-ft-high, vaulted glass and steel atrium, which affords views of the harbor and Hudson River; free performances, public events & art exhibits. (Daily; shops closed major hols) West St between Liberty & Vesey Sts, opp World Trade Center. Phone 212/945-0505.

Sightseeing tours.

> **Adventure on a Shoestring.** Walking tours of various neighborhoods, including SoHo artist area and Chinatown. Contact 300 W 53rd St, 10019; 212/265-2663. ¢¢

> **Circle Line Sightseeing Yachts.** Narrated cruises around Manhattan (3 hrs) offer unique views of city (daily). Two-hr express cruise (Mar-Dec, daily). Harbor Lights cruise (May-Oct, nightly; Nov-Dec, wkend evenings); refreshments. Boats depart from Pier 83, W 43rd St at Twelfth Ave & the Hudson River. Phone 212/563-3200. ¢¢¢¢¢

> **Gray Line.** For information on a variety of sightseeing tours, contact Gray Line of New York, 254 W 54th St, 10019; 212/397-2600.

> **Island Helicopter.** Offers 4 pilot-narrated tours: United Nations, Statue of Liberty, Skyscraper and Ultimate Delight (a combination of all flights). Multilingual staff avail. (Daily; no tours Dec 25) Depart from Heliport at 34th St & East River. Phone 212/683-4575. ¢¢¢¢¢

> **Shortline Tours.** Narrated tours of Manhattan aboard glass-top motor coaches. Length of tours range from 2¹/₂ hrs to a full day. Also day trips to Atlantic City, NJ. Also complete city packages with hotel, theater, dinner and airport transfers. Departs from 46th St office. Free shuttle service from several NYC hotels. 166 W 46th St; 10036. Phone 212/736-4700. ¢¢¢¢¢

SoHo. (For "South of Houston" Street). A neighborhood bounded by Broadway, Sixth Ave, Houston (HOUSE-ton) & Canal Sts. The brothel section of the city in the early 1800s, the area was later razed and hundreds of loft buildings used for light manufacturing and warehouses were built. Zoning changes in 1970 permitted residences in the area. The spacious buildings of this district, many with cast iron facades, are ideal for artists' lofts and galleries. Although still a commercial area, many artists have moved into the 50-blk area, making it another art colony. Contact Friends of Cast Iron Architecture, 235 E 87th St, Room 6C, 10128; 212/369-6004. Galleries, boutiques and restaurants can be found throughout the area, especially on W Broadway, Prince, Spring & Greene Sts.

> East of here is **Little Italy**, with Mulberry its main street. The colorful festival of San Gennaro (mid- or late Sept) is held here (see ANNUAL EVENTS).

Solomon R. Guggenheim Museum. This unique building, designed by Frank Lloyd Wright, has been restored. A ten-story tower, based on an earlier Wright design, was constructed for new galleries. Museum houses 19th- & 20th-century paintings and sculpture along a spiral ramp more than ¹/₄-mi in length. Wright's intention was that patrons take the elevator to the top and then leisurely descend the gently-pitched spiral. Restaurant. Performance art series. (Daily exc Thurs; closed some hols) 1071 Fifth Ave, between E 88th & 89th Sts. Phone 212/423-3500. Fri evenings by donation. ¢¢ Branch museum includes

Guggenheim Museum SoHo. Facility has 30,000 sq ft of exhibition space; also here are offices. (Wed-Sun; closed some hols) 575 Broadway, at Prince St. Phone 212/423-3500. ¢¢

South Street Seaport Museum. Eleven-blk area restored to display the city's maritime history, with emphasis on South St in the days of sailing vessels. Museum piers now moor the *Ambrose*, a lightship (1907); the *Lettie G. Howard*, a Gloucester fishing schooner (1893); the fully-rigged *Wavetree* (1885); the *Peking*, a German four-masted bark (1911); and the *Pioneer*, a schooner (1885). Permanent and changing maritime exhibits include models, prints, photos and artifacts. Tours. Harbor excursions. Children admitted only when accompanied by adult. (Apr-Oct, daily; rest of year, daily exc Tues; closed Jan1, Thanksgiving, Dec 25) South & Fulton Sts, at the East River. Phone 212/748-8600. Exhibition vessels ¢¢¢

Neighborhood. Rows of 19th- and early 20th-century buildings house almost 100 specialty shops and museum galleries and more than 40 restaurants and eateries. (Daily) Along South, Fulton & Water Sts.

South Street Seaport Events. Throughout the yr, concerts, festivals and special events are staged in the seaport area; weather permitting, passengers are taken for a sail around the harbor aboard the *Pioneer*; the museum's Children's Center hosts a variety of special programs, workshops and exhibits. In the fall, a fleet of classic sailing vessels is assembled to compete in a race for the Mayor's Cup.

St Patrick's Cathedral. This famous Gothic-revival cathedral is 330 ft high. The interior can seat 2,400 people. (Daily) Fifth Ave & 50th St.

✪ **Statue of Liberty National Monument.** Given by the French people, this statue by Frederic Bartholdi is 152 ft high, on a pedestal of about the same height. Made of 3/32 inch-thick copper, on a framework designed by Gustav Eiffel (designer of the Eiffel Tower in Paris), there are 354 steps to the crown. Snacks, souvenirs on island (daily). Boats leave from Castle Clinton on the Battery (southern tip of Manhattan, parking fee) every half-hr in summer; rest of yr, every 45 min (daily; closed Dec 25). In summer, boats also depart from Liberty State Park, NJ, at NJ Tpke exit 14B. Liberty Island. Contact Interpretive Staff, Liberty Island, 10004; 212/363-3200.Round trip ¢¢¢ At the base of the statue is the

Statue of Liberty Exhibit. Photographs, personal possessions, dioramas with light and sound effects depict the construction of the Statue of Liberty and the lifestyles and struggles of immigrants. Same hrs as Statue of Liberty. Near Liberty Island is

Ellis Island Immigration Museum. The most famous port of immigration in the country. From 1892 to 1954, more than 12 million immigrants began their American dream here. The principle structure is the Main Bldg, with its Great Hall, where the immigrants were processed; exhibits; audiovisual theater; snack bar. Same hrs as Statue of Liberty. Boat from Castle Clinton on Battery to Statue of Liberty includes stop at Ellis Island. Ellis Island has been incorporated into the monument.

Staten Island Ferry. Famous ferry to St George, Staten Island, offers passengers a close look at both the Statue of Liberty and Ellis Island, as well as extraordinary views of the lower Manhattan skyline. Departs from the ferry terminal at intersection of Whitehall, State & South Sts, just E of Battery Park. Phone 718/390-5253. Round trip (paid on Staten Island side only) ¢

Temple Emanu-El. Largest Jewish house of worship in the US; Reform Congregation founded in 1845. Romanesque-type Temple seats 2,500; Beth-El Chapel seats 350. (Daily; no visiting on High Holy Days) Tours (by appt, upon written request). Mail requests to 1 E 65th St, 10021. Fifth Ave & 65th St. Phone 212/744-1400.

The Asia Society Galleries. Presents exhibitions of ancient, modern and contemporary art assembled from public and private collections in Asia and the West; includes as a permanent collection The Mr. and Mrs. John D. Rockefeller 3rd Collection of Asian Art. (Daily exc Mon; closed major hols) Free admission Thurs evenings (limited hrs). 725 Park Ave, at 70th St. Phone 212/517-NEWS. ¢¢

The Cloisters. This branch of the Metropolitan Museum of Art has parts of five medieval monasteries, a Romanesque chapel, a 12th-century Spanish apse, extensive gardens and many examples of sculpture, painting, stained glass and other art from the 9th-15th centuries. (Daily exc Mon; closed Jan 1, Thanksgiving, Dec 25) In Fort Tryon Park, off Henry Hudson Pkwy, 1 exit N of George Washington Bridge. Phone 212/923-3700. ¢¢¢

The Frick Collection. European paintings, bronzes, sculpture, furniture, porcelains, enamels from the 14th-19th centuries exhibited in the Henry Clay Frick mansion. Unusual museum surroundings. (Daily exc Mon; closed most major hols) No children under 10; under 16 only with adult. 1 E 70th St, at Fifth Ave. Phone 212/288-0700. ¢¢

The Garment District. This crowded area, heart of the clothing industry in New York, has hundreds of small shops, factories and streets jammed with trucks and hand-pushed delivery carts. In this area is Macy's. Sixth Ave to Eighth Ave and from 34th St to 39th St.

The Museum of Modern Art (MOMA). Comprehensive survey of twentieth-century paintings, sculptures, drawings, prints, photographs, architectural models and plans, design objects, films and videos; changing exhibits; free gallery talks; daily films; two restaurants set alongside museum's Abby Aldrich Rockefeller Sculpture Garden. (Daily exc Wed, extended hrs Fri; closed Thanksgiving, Dec 25) Touch tours for visually impaired. (See SEASONAL EVENTS) 11 W 53rd St. Phone 212/708-9480 (exhibition and film information). ¢¢¢

The Museum of Television & Radio. Exhibits feature programs from the past and present, news and documentaries, entertainment and international TV. Collection of more than 40,000 radio and television programs; theaters; library; lectures and seminars; educational seminars. (Daily exc Mon; closed Jan 1, July 4, Thanksgiving, Dec 25) 25 W 52nd St. Phone 212/621-6800. ¢¢¢

The New York Historical Society. Variety of exhibits on American history with emphasis on New York (Wed-Sun). Research library (Wed-Fri). 170 Central Park W, between W 76th & 77th Sts. Phone 212/873-3400.

The Studio Museum in Harlem. One of the finest collections of African-American art. Changing exhibits feature master, mid-career and emerging black artists from the US, the Caribbean and Africa. Yrly exhibits showcase permanent collection. Workshops, lectures, seminars. (Wed-Sun; closed hols) 144 W 125th St. Phone 212/864-4500. ¢¢

Theodore Roosevelt Birthplace National Historic Site. The reconstructed birthplace of the 26th president, who lived here from 1858 to 1872. Tours of five rms restored to 1865 appearance. Audiovisual presentation, concerts and special events. (Wed-Sun) 28 E 20th St. Phone 212/260-1616. ¢

Times Square and the Theater District. Entertainment center of the city and theatrical headquarters of the country, offering plays, musicals, concerts, movies and exotic entertainments; named for the Times Tower at One Times Square, originally the home of the *New York Times*. (See THEATER in introductory copy.) Sixth to Eighth Aves & 40th to 53rd Sts.

Ukrainian Museum. Changing exhibits of Ukrainian folk art, fine art and history; workshops on wkends in folk crafts. (Wed-Sun; closed major hols, Jan 7, Easter, Orthodox Easter) 203 Second Ave, between 12th & 13th Sts. Phone 212/228-0110. ¢

United Nations. Four buildings, designed under the direction of Wallace K. Harrison, were completed 1950-1952. Regular sessions of the General Assembly start on the third Tues in Sept. Tickets are occasionally avail to certain official meetings on a first-come basis. Entrance is on First Ave at 46th St, at the north end of the General Assembly Bldg. In the lobby is an information desk and ticket booth; in the basement are the UN book and gift shops and the UN Post Office, where one can mail letters bearing United Nations stamps. On the fourth floor is the UN Delegates Dining Rm. The Conference Bldg is where the various UN Councils meet. The Secretariat Bldg is a rectangular glass-and-steel building that is 550 ft high; here the day-to-day work of the UN staff is performed. The fourth building is the Dag Hammarskjold Library, open only to UN staff and delegations, or by special permission for serious research. Guided tours (45 min) leave the public entrance lobby (1st Ave & 46th St) at frequent intervals (daily; closed Thanksgiving and several days during yr-end hol season; also wkends Jan-Feb); no children under 5. (Buildings, daily) 1st Ave from 42nd St to 48th St. Phone 212/963-1234. Tours ¢¢¢

Walk through downtown Manhattan. Allow at least 3 hrs. Start at Battery Park, in which is

t, this later
here Jenny
1855 it was
New York.
1855 and
e New York
d at Coney
ns to serve
e of Liberty
n, Statue of
Superinten-
0. Walk up
oldest park,
ttan for $24
side is the
neo-classic
ith statuary,
the rotunda,

eum of the
of the native
One Bowling
Whitehall St

the historic
Fraunces Tavern (1719) and four adjacent 19th-century buildings. The museum interprets history and culture of early America through permanent collection of prints, paintings, decorative arts and artifacts, changing exhibitions and two period rms, one of which, the Long Rm, is the site of George Washington's farewell to his officers at the end of the Revolutionary War (1783). The museum offers a variety of programs and activities, including tours, lectures, films, theatrical performances and concerts. Dining rm (see RESTAURANTS). (Daily) 54 Pearl St. Phone 212/425-1778. **¢¢** Retrace steps and continue N on Broadway to

Trinity Church (1846). The third building to occupy this site; original was built in 1697. Its famous graveyard, favorite lunchtime spot of workers in the financial district, contains the graves of Robert Fulton and Alexander Hamilton. The brownstone church is Gothic-revival and contains a museum. Parish center with dining rm open to the public. Services (daily). Broadway at Wall St. Phone 212/602-0800. **Free.** Directly behind the church is

Wall St. Walk one blk E to the corner of Broad St (which goes S) and Nassau St (which goes N). At this corner is

Federal Hall National Memorial (1842). Greek-revival building on the site of the original Federal Hall, where the Stamp Act Congress met (1765), George Washington was inaugurated (Apr 30, 1789) and the first Congress met (1789-1790). Originally a custom house, the building was for many years the sub-treasury of the US. The J.Q.A. Ward statue of Washington is on the Wall St steps. (Mon-Fri) Contact the Superintendent, Manhattan Sites, 26 Wall St, 10005; 212/825-6888. **Free.** S of here, on the W side of Broad St, is the

New York Stock Exchange. View of the exchange floor in action from the Visitors' Gallery. Audiovisual exhibits and film. Limited number of free admission tickets avail, distributed daily starting at 9 am. (Mon-Fri; closed hols) 20 Broad St, 3rd floor. Phone 212/656-5167. **Free.** Walk 2 blks N up Broad St & through narrow Nassau St to Liberty St. On the N side is the

Federal Reserve Bank of New York. Approx one third of the world's supply of gold bullion is stored here in a vault 80 ft below ground level; cash handling operation and historical exhibit of bank notes and coins. Tours (Mon-Fri exc hols). 16 yrs and older only; no cameras. Tour res required at least one wk in advance. 33 Liberty St. Phone 212/720-6130. **Free.** Walk 2 blks W on Liberty St to Church St. On the right is the

World Trade Center. Twin, 110-story complex 1,350 ft high on a 16-acre site, focusing on international trade and finance. Observation deck at 2 World Trade Center with rooftop open-air promenade, 1,377 ft above ground, is one of the highest in the world. (Daily) Phone 212/323-2340. Observation deck **¢¢¢** West, across West St, is the World

Financial Center. Walk N 3 blks to Fulton St and turn right 1 blk to Broadway to

St Paul's Chapel. A chapel of Trinity Church, this example of Georgian architecture, finished in 1766, is the oldest public building in continuous use on Manhattan Island. George Washington's pew is in the north aisle; chancel ornamentation by L'Enfant; Waterford chandeliers. Concerts (Mon & Thurs at noon). (Daily) Fulton St & Broadway; chapel faces Church St. 2 blks N is the

Woolworth Building. This neo-Gothic skyscraper by Cass Gilbert was the tallest building in the world (792 ft, 60 stories) when built. Frank W. Woolworth, the dime-store king, paid cash, $13.5 million, for his "cathedral of commerce" when it was completed in 1913. 233 Broadway. Cross Broadway from here and enter

City Hall Park. Architecturally, City Hall is a combination of American Federal-period and English Georgian, with Louis XIV detailing. It is built of marble and brownstone. Directly E is the

Brooklyn Bridge. The first bridge across the East River to Brooklyn, it was a remarkable engineering feat when opened in 1883. Fine view from bridge of the East River (actually a tidal estuary between Long Island Sound and New York harbor). In this area, at the foot of Fulton St and the East River, is the South Street Seaport Museum. From City Hall walk about 4 blks NE to Chatham Square and turn left on Mott St to

Chinatown. This colorful area has Chinese shops and restaurants. We suggest you walk back to Brooklyn Bridge and City Hall Park, from which a number of subways will take you wherever you wish to go. Mainly on Mott, Pell & Doyers Sts.

Washington Heights Museum Group (Audubon Terrace). Broadway & 155th St.Clustered around a central plaza and accessible from Broadway, this group includes the American Geographical Society, the American Academy and Institute of Arts and Letters, as well as the

Hispanic Society of America. Art of the Iberian Peninsula from prehistoric times to present. Paintings, sculpture, ceramics, drawings, etchings, lithographs, textiles, and metalwork. (Daily exc Mon; closed hols) Broadway between W 155th & 156th Sts. Phone 212/926-2234. **Free.**

American Numismatic Society. Society headquarters; numismatic library; "World of Coins" exhibit; changing exhibits. (Daily exc Mon; closed hols) Broadway at 155th St. Phone 212/234-3130. **Free.**

Whitney Museum of American Art. Collection of 20th-century American art, founded by Gertrude Vanderbilt Whitney; changing exhibits; film and video programs; restaurant. (Wed-Sun; Tues scheduled education programs only; closed natl hols) Free admission Thurs evenings. 945 Madison Ave, at E 75th St. Phone 212/570-3676. **¢¢¢** Branch museums include

Whitney Museum of American Art at Philip Morris. Gallery and sculpture court. Changing exhibits annually; free lectures, performances. Gallery talks (Mon, Wed, Fri). Gallery (Mon-Fri). Sculpture court (daily). 120 Park Ave at 42nd St. Phone 212/878-2550. **Free.**

Yeshiva University (1886). (7,000 students) America's oldest and largest university under Jewish auspices. Joseph and Faye Tanenbaum Hall, historic main building, has elaborate stone facade and Byzantine domes. The Mendel Gottesman Library houses many specialized collections (academic yr, daily exc Sat; closed legal & Jewish hols; tours by appt). 500 W 185th St. Phone 212/960-5400. On campus is

Yeshiva University Museum. Teaching museum devoted to Jewish art, architecture, history, and culture has permanent exhibits, including scale models of synagogues from the 3rd to 19th centuries; reproduction of frescoes from the Dura-Europos Synagogue; ceremonial objects, rare books; audiovisual presentations; theater; changing exhibits. (Academic yr, Tues-Thurs & Sun; closed legal & Jewish hols) 2520 Amsterdam Ave. Phone 212/960-5390. **¢¢**

Annual Events

Chinese New Year. In Chinatown, Mott, Pell & Doyers Sts. Parade with lions, dragons, costumes, firecrackers. Early-mid-Feb.

USA/Mobil Indoor Track & Field Championships. Madison Square Garden. Usually last Fri Feb.

St Patrick's Day Parade. Along Fifth Ave. New York's biggest parade; approx 100,000 marchers.

Ninth Avenue International Food Festival. Mid-May.

JVC Jazz Festival-New York. World-famous musicians perform in Avery Fisher Hall, Carnegie Hall, Town Hall and other sites throughout the city. Contact Box 1169, 10023; 212/501-1390. June 19-27.

Harbor Festival. Wkend of July 4.

San Gennaro Festival. Little Italy. Mid- or late Sept.

Columbus Day Parade. Upper Fifth Ave.

Hispanic Day Parade. Fifth Ave. Mid-Oct.

NYC Marathon. Usually Nov.

Thanksgiving Day Parade (an R. H. Macy production). Down Broadway to 34th St, from W 77th St & Central Park W. Floats, balloons, television and movie stars.

Seasonal Events

Live TV shows. For information regarding availability of regular and/or standby tickets contact NBC's ticket office at 30 Rockefeller Plaza, 10112 (phone 212/664-4000); CBS at 524 W 57th St, 10019 (phone 212/975-2476); or ABC, 77 W 66th St, 10023 (phone 212/456-7777). On the day of the show, the New York Convention and Visitors Bureau at 2 Columbus Circle often has tickets for out-of-town visitors on a first-come, first-served basis. Except for NBC productions, many hotels can get tickets for guests on reasonable notice. (To see an important production, write 4-6 wks in advance; the number of tickets is usually limited.) Most shows restricted to persons over 18 yrs.

Washington Square Art Show. Washington Square and nearby streets. Outdoor art show. Wkends, late May & early Sept.

Central Park Concerts. Free performances by the New York Philharmonic and the Metropolitan Opera Company on the Great Lawn, mid-park at 81st St. Phone 212/360-3456. June-Sept.

New York Shakespeare Festival & Shakespeare in the Park. At the 2,000-seat outdoor Delacorte Theater in Central Park, near W 81st St. Tues-Sun. Free tickets distributed evening of performance. Phone 212/861-PAPP. June-Sept.

Summergarden. Free music concerts at the Abby Aldrich Rockefeller Sculpture Garden of The Museum of Modern Art. Wkends. July-Aug.

Special Christmas Star Show. Hayden Planetarium. Late Nov-early Jan.

Christmas season. Rockefeller Center tree, carols, church music, animated store displays.

Horse racing:

Aqueduct (see QUEENS).

Belmont Park (see QUEENS).

Meadowlands Sports Complex. Off NJ 3 in East Rutherford, NJ.

Yonkers Raceway (see YONKERS, NY).

La Guardia & JFK Intl Airport Areas

For additional attractions and accommodations, see QUEENS (LA GUARDIA & JFK INTL AIRPORT AREAS),which follows BROOKLYN.

City Neighborhoods

Many of the restaurants, unrated dining establishments and some lodgings listed under Manhattan include neighborhoods as well as exact street addresses. Geographic descriptions of these areas are given, followed by a table of restaurants arranged by neighborhood.

Chelsea: Area of West Side south of 31st St, west of Sixth Ave, north of 14th St and east of the Hudson River.

Chinatown: Area of Downtown south of Canal St and east and west of Bowery; along Bayard, Pell and Mott Sts east of Bowery.

Downtown: South of 14th St, west of the East River and east of the Hudson River; also refers to the Financial District.

East Side: Area of Midtown south of 59th St, west of the East River, north of 42nd St and west of Lexington Ave.

East Village: Area of Downtown south of 14th St, west of First Ave, north of E Houston St and east of Broadway.

Financial District: Area of Downtown south of Vesey and Ann Sts, west of the East River, north of Water St and Battery Park and east of the Hudson River.

Garment District: Area of Midtown south of 42nd St, west of 6th Ave, north of 34th St and east of Eighth Ave.

Gramercy Park: Area of Midtown on and around Gramercy Park; south of E 23rd St, west of First Ave, north of 14th St and east of Broadway.

Greenwich Village: Area of Downtown south of 14th St, west of Broadway, north of W Houston St and east of Greenwich Ave.

Harlem: South of 165th St, west of the Harlem River, north of 110th St and east of Morningside Ave and St Nicholas Ave.

Little Italy: Area of Downtown south of Houston St, west of Chrystie St and the Sara Delano Roosevelt Pkwy, north of Canal St and east of Broadway.

Midtown: Between 59th St and 34th St and the East and Hudson rivers; south of 59th St, west of Eighth Ave, north of 34th St and east of Lexington Ave.

Murray Hill: Area of Midtown south of 42nd St, west of Second Ave, north of 32nd St and east of Fifth Ave.

SoHo: Area of Downtown south of Houston St, west of Broadway, north of Canal St and east of Avenue of the Americas (Sixth Ave).

Times Square/Theater District: Area of Midtown; intersection of Broadway and Seventh Ave; south of 53rd St, west of Avenue of the Americas (Sixth Ave), north of 40th St and east of Eighth Ave.

Tribeca: Area of Downtown south of Canal St, west of Broadway, north of Chambers St and east of the Hudson River.

Upper East Side: South of 110th St, west of the East River, north of 59th St and east of Central Park.

Upper West Side: South of 110th St, west of Central Park, north of 59th St and east of the Hudson River.

West Side: Area of Midtown south of 59th St, west of Eighth Ave, north of 34th St and east of the Hudson River.

No city in the United States has as many fine restaurants serving as many different and exciting international dishes as New York. Eating here is an adventure as well as an art. With thousands of restaurants to choose from, it can also be bewildering. The list that follows is organized alphabetically under each neighborhood/area heading.

MANHATTAN RESTAURANTS BY NEIGHBORHOOD AREAS

(For full description, see alphabetical listings under Restaurants)

CHELSEA
Caffe Bondi. 7 W 20th St
Cal's. 55 W 21st St
Campagna. 24 E 21st St
Chelsea Bistro & Bar. 358 W 23rd St
The Crab House. Pier 61
Da Umberto. 107 W 17th St
Empire Diner. 210 Tenth Ave
Follonico. 6 W 24th St
Gascogne. 158 Eighth Ave
Hot Tomato. 676 6th Ave
La Traviata. 461 W 23rd St
Le Madri. 168 W 18th St
Lola. 30 W 22nd St
Luma. 200 9th Ave
Periyali. 35 W 20th St
Steak Frites. 9 E 16th St
Trois Canards. 184 Eighth Ave
Zucca. 227 10th Ave

CHINATOWN
20 Mott Street. 20 Mott St
Harmony Palace. 94 Mott St

Hunan Garden. 1 Mott St
Shanghai Cuisine. 89-91 Bayard St

DOWNTOWN
Fraunces Tavern. 54 Pearl St
Mirezi. 59 Fifth Ave

EAST SIDE
Ambassador Grill (Regal U.N. Plaza Hotel). 1 UN Plaza
Dawat. 210 E 58th St
Delegates Dining Room. In United Nations General Assembly Bldg
Felidia. 243 E 58th St
Hosteria Fiorella. 1081 Third Ave
Il Nido. 251 E 53rd St
La Mangeoire. 1008 Second Ave
Le Colonial. 149 E 57th St
P.J. Clarke's. 915 Third Ave
Palm. 837 Second Ave
Rosa Mexicano. 1063 First Ave
Shun Lee Palace. 155 E 55th St
Smith & Wollensky. 797 Third Ave
Tatou. 151 E 50th St

EAST VILLAGE
First. 87 First Ave
Hasaki. 210 E 9th St
Helena's. 432 Lafayette St
Japonica. 100 University Place
Riodizio. 417 Lafayette St
Second Ave Deli. 156 Second Ave
Soba-Ya. 229 E 9th St

FINANCIAL DISTRICT
American Park. In Battery Park
Coco Marina. 2 World Financial Center
Edward Moran Bar And Grill. 250 Vesey St
Fulton Street Cafe. 11 Fulton St
Gemelli. 4 World Trade Center
The Grill Room. 225 Liberty St
Harbour Lights. Fulton Pier 17
Hudson River Club. 250 Vesey St
Wall Street Kitchen & Bar. 70 Broad St
Windows On The World. 1 World Trade Center
Yankee Clipper. 170 John St

GRAMERCY PARK
Alva. 36 E 22nd St
Angelo And Maxie's Steakhouse. 233 Park Ave S
Bolo. 23 E 22nd St
Da Vittorio. 43 E 20th St
Gramercy Tavern. 42 E 20th St
The Lemon. 230 Park Ave S
Mesa Grill. 102 Fifth Ave
Moreno. 65 Irving Place
Novita. 102 E 22nd St
Patria. 250 Park Ave S
Republic. 37 Union Square W
Union Pacific. 111 E 22nd St

GREENWICH VILLAGE
Café Loup. 105 W 13th St
Cafe De Bruxelles. 118 Greenwich Ave
Chez Michallet. 90 Bedford St
Clementine. 1 Fifth Ave
Cuisine De Saigon. 154 W 13th St
Da Silvano. 260 Sixth Ave
Drovers Tap Room. 9 Jones St
Elephant & Castle. 68 Greenwich Ave
Florent. 69 Gansevoort St
Gotham Bar And Grill. 12 E 12th St
Home. 20 Cornelia St
Indigo. 142 W 10th St
Ithaka. 48 Barrow St
La Metairie. 189 W 10th St
Marylou's. 21 W 9th St
Mi Cocina. 57 Jane St

One If By Land, Two If By Sea. 17 Barrow St
Pó. 31 Cornelia St
Village Grill. 518 LaGuardia Pl

LITTLE ITALY
Il Cortile. 125 Mulberry St
Sal Anthony's SPQR. 133 Mulberry St
Taormina. 147 Mulberry St

MIDTOWN
21 Club. 21 W 52nd St
American Festival. 20 W 50th St
An American Place. 2 Park Ave
Aquavit. 13 W 54th St
Artos. 307 E 53rd St
Barbetta. 321 W 46th St
Ben Benson's. 123 W 52nd St
Bice. 7 E 54th St
Box Tree (Box Tree Inn). 250 E 49th St
Brooklyn Diner USA. 212 W 57th St
Bryant Park Grill. 25 W 40th St
Bull & Bear Steakhouse (Waldorf-Astoria & Waldorf Towers Hotel). 301 Park Ave
Cafe Pierre (The Pierre Hotel). 2 E 61st St
Carnegie Deli. 854 Seventh Ave
Castellano. 138 W 55th St
Christer's. 145 W 55th St
Cibo. 767 Second Ave
Cité. 120 W 51st St
Comfort Diner. 214 E 45th St
David Ruggerio. 106 E 57th St
Domingo. 209 E 49th St
Estiatorio Milos. 125 W 55th St
Fantino (The Westin Central Park South Hotel). 112 Central Park South
Fifty Seven Fifty Seven (Four Seasons Hotel). 57 E 57th St
The Four Seasons. 99 E 52nd St
Harley-Davidson Cafe. 1370 Ave of the Americas
Harry Cipriani. 781 Fifth Ave
Il Toscanaccio. 7 E 59th St
Jean Georges (Trump International Hotel & Tower). 1 Central Park W
Jubilee. 347 E 54th St
Judson Grill. 152 W 52nd St
Keens Steakhouse. 72 W 36th St
Kuruma Zushi. 7 E 47th St
La Bonne Soupe. 48 W 55th St
La Côte Basque. 60 W 55th St
La Caravelle. 33 W 55th St
La Maison Japonaise. 125 E 39th St
La Reserve. 4 W 49th St
Le Cirque 2000 (The New York Palace Hotel). 455 Madison Ave
Le Perigord. 405 E 52nd St
Les Célébrités (Essex House Hotel Nikko). 160 Central Park South
Lespinasse (The St Regis Hotel). 2 E 55th St
Lutèce. 249 E 50th St
Maloney & Porcelli. 37 E 50th St
Manhattan Ocean Club. 57 W 58th St
Med Grill Bistro & Cafe. 725 5th Ave
Michael Jordan's-The Steakhouse. 23 Vanderbilt Ave
Michael's. 24 W 55th St
Mickey Mantle's. 42 Central Park South
Monkey Bar. 60 E 54th St
Morton's Of Chicago. 551 Fifth Ave
Mr K's. 570 Lexington Ave
Nadaman Hakubai (The Kitano Hotel). 66 Park Ave
Oak Room (The Plaza Hotel). Fifth Ave at 59th St & Central Park South
Oceana. 55 E 54th St
Osteria Laguna. 209 E 42nd St
Osterio Del Circo. 120 W 55th St
Otabe. 68 E 56th St
Oyster Bar. At Grand Central Station
Palm Court (The Plaza Hotel). Fifth Ave at 59th St & Central Park South
The Park (The Lombardy Hotel). 109 E 56th St
Patroon. 160 E 46th St
Peacock Alley (Waldorf-Astoria & Waldorf Towers Hotel). 301 Park Ave

Petrossian. 182 W 58th St
Planet Hollywood. 140 W 57th St
Rainbow Room. 30 Rockefeller Plaza
Raphael. 33 W 54th St
Redeye Grill. 890 Seventh Ave
Remi. 145 W 53rd St
The Rotunda (The Pierre Hotel). 2 E 61st St
Ruth's Chris Steak House. 148 W 51st St
San Domenico. 240 Central Park South
San Martin's. 143 E 49th St
San Pietro. 18 E 54th St
Savories. 30 Rockefeller Center
Sea Grill. 19 W 49th St
Shaan. 57 W 48th St
Sparks Steak House. 210 E 46th St
Stage Deli. 834 Seventh Ave
Sushisay. 38 E 51st St
Trattoria Dell'arte. 900 7th Ave
Tuscan Square. 16 W 51st St
Typhoon Brewery. 22 E 54th St
Union Square Cafe. 21 E 16th St
Vong. 200 E 54th St
Water Club. 500 E 30th St
Zarela. 953 2nd Ave

MURRAY HILL
Belluno. 340 Lexington Ave
I Trulli. 122 E 27th St
Meli Melo. 110 Madison Ave
Park Bistro. 414 Park Ave S
Sonia Rose. 150 E 34th St

SOHO
Alison On Dominick Street. 38 Dominick St
Aquagrill. 210 Spring St
Balthazar. 80 Spring St
Baluchi's. 193 Spring St
Barolo. 398 W Broadway
Blue Ribbon. 97 Sullivan St
Blue Ribbon Sushi. 119 Sullivan St
Boom. 152 Spring St
Cub Room. 131 Sullivan St
I Tre Merli. 463 W Broadway
L'ulivo. 184 Spring St
Manhattan Bistro. 129 Spring St
Mezzogiorno. 195 Spring St
Monzù. 142 Mercer
Penang Malaysian. 109 Spring St
Provence. 38 MacDougal St
Quilty's. 177 Prince St
Raoul's. 180 Prince St
Savore. 200 Spring St
Savoy. 70 Prince St
Soho Steak. 90 Thompson St
Zoë. 90 Prince St

TIMES SQUARE/THEATER DISTRICT
Becco. 355 W 46th St
Chez Napoleon. 365 W 50th St
Churrascaria Plataforma. 316 W 49th St
Coco Pazzo Teatro. 235 W 46th St
Firebird. 365 W 46th St
Frico Bar. 402 W 43rd St
Gallagher's. 228 W 52nd St
Joe Allen. 326 W 46th St
Le Bernardin. 155 W 51st St
Le Madeleine. 403 W 43rd St
Marlowe. 328 W 46th St
Orso. 322 W 46th St
Osteria Al Doge. 142 W 44th St
Palio. 151 W 51st St
Pierre Au Tunnel. 250 W 47th St
René Pujol. 321 W 51st St
Sardi's. 234 W 44th St

Siam Grill. 586 Ninth Ave
Siam Inn. 916 8th Ave
Trionfo. 224 W 51st St
Victor's Cafe 52. 236 W 52nd St
The View (Marriott Marquis Hotel). 1535 Broadway
Virgil's Real Barbecue. 152 W 44th St

TRIBECA
2 Seven 7 Church St. 277 Church St
Arqua. 281 Church St
Barocco. 301 Church St
Bouley Bakery. 120 W Broadway
Bubby's. 120 Hudson St
Capsouto Frères. 451 Washington St
Chanterelle. 2 Harrison St
City Wine & Cigar Co. 62 Laight St
Duane Park Cafe. 157 Duane St
El Teddy's. 219 W Broadway
Gigino Trattoria. 323 Greenwich St
Layla. 211 W Broadway
Montrachet. 239 W Broadway
Nobu. 105 Hudson St
Noor's. 94 Chambers
The Odeon. 145 W Broadway
Salaam Bombay. 317 Greenwich St
Screening Room. 54 Varick St
Spartina. 355 Greenwich St
Tribeca Grill. 375 Greenwich St

UPPER EAST SIDE
540 Park (The Regency Hotel). 540 Park Ave
Aureole. 34 E 61st St
Baraonda. 1439 Second Ave
Bistro Du Nord. 1312 Madison Ave
Cafe Boulud. 20 E 76th St
Cafe Nosidam. 768 Madison Ave
Cafe Trevi. 1570 First Ave
Carlyle (Carlyle Hotel). Madison Ave at E 76th St
Coco Pazzo. 23 E 74th St
Contrapunto. 200 E 60th St
Coté Sud. 181 E 78th St
Demi. 1316 Madison Ave
Gertrude's. 33 E 61st St
Il Monello. 1460 Second Ave
Jackson Hole. 1611 Second Ave
Jo Jo. 160 E 64th St
Kings' Carriage House. 251 E 82nd St
Le Boeuf à La Mode. 539 E 81st St
Le Régence (Plaza Athénée Hotel). 37 E 64th St
Le Refuge. 166 E 82nd St
Lenox Room. 1278 Third Ave
Lobster Club. 24 E 80th St
Lumi. 963 Lexington Ave
Lusardi's. 1494 Second Ave
Manhattan Grill. 1161 First Ave
March. 405 E 58th St
Matthew's. 1030 Third Ave
Maya. 1191 First Ave
Mezzaluna. 1295 Third Ave
Nino's. 1354 1st Ave
Our Place. 1444 Third Ave
Paola's. 245 E 84th
Parioli Romanissimo. 24 E 81st St
Park Avenue Cafe. 100 E 63rd St
Park View At The Boathouse. In Central Park
Payard Patisserie & Bistro. 1032 Lexington Ave
Pig Heaven. 1540 Second Ave
Post House. 28 E 63rd St
Primavera. 1578 First Ave
Red Tulip. 439 E 75th St
Serendipity 3. 225 E 60th St
Shabu-Tatsu. 1414 York Ave
Table d'hote. 44 E 92nd St
Trippletail. 322 E 86th St

Willow. 1022 Lexington Ave
Yellowfingers. 200 E 60th St
UPPER WEST SIDE
Cafe Des Artistes. 1 W 67th St
Cafe Fiorello. 1900 Broadway
Cafe Luxembourg. 200 W 70th St
Carmine's. 2450 Broadway
Coco Opera. 58 W 65th St
Diane's Downtown. 249 Columbus Ave
Gabriel's. 11 W 60th St
Merlot. 48 W 63rd St
Panevino Ristorante/Cafe Vienna. In Avery Fisher Hall
Picholine. 35 W 64th St
Rain. 100 W 82nd St
Sarabeth's. 423 Amsterdam Ave
Shark Bar. 307 Amsterdam Ave
Shun Lee. 43 W 65th St
Tavern On The Green. Central Park at W 67th St
Terrace. 400 W 119th St
Two Two Two. 222 W 79th St
Vince & Eddie's. 70 W 68th St

Motor Hotel

★ ★ **EAST SIDE INN.** *201 E 24th St (10011), between 2nd Ave & 3rd Aves, in Gramercy Park.* 212/696-3800; FAX 212/696-0077. Web www.nyhotels.com. 43 rms, 5 story. Jan-June, Sept-Dec: S $165-$185; D $205-$225; under 18 free; lower rates rest of yr. Crib free. TV; cable (premium), VCR (movies). Complimentary continental bkfst. Restaurant noon-midnight. Rm serv. Bar. Ck-out noon. Business servs avail. In-rm modem link. Valet serv. Concierge. Health club privileges. Bathrm phones; refrigerators avail. Cr cds: A, D, DS, MC, V.

⊠ 🔥

Hotels

★ ★ **ALGONQUIN.** *59 W 44th St (10036), between Fifth Ave and Avenue of the Americas, Midtown.* 212/840-6800; FAX 212/944-1419; res: 800/555-8000. Web www.camberleyhotels.com. 165 rms, 12 story. S, D $209-$329; suites $329-$529; wkend rates. Crib free. Garage parking $25. TV; cable (premium). Complimentary full bkfst. Restaurant 7-1 am; Sun from 11:30 am. Bar from 11 am; entertainment. Ck-out 1 pm. Meeting rms. Business center. Exercise equipt. Refrigerator in suites. Visited by numerous literary and theatrical personalities. Cr cds: A, C, D, DS, ER, JCB, MC, V.

D 🕱 ⊠ 🔥 🏃

★ ★ **AMERITANIA.** *230 W 54th St (10019), between Broadway & 8th Sts, Midtown.* 212/247-5000; res: 800/922-0330; FAX 212/247-3313. Web www.ameritaniahotel.com. 207 rms, 30 with shower only. S, D $175-$215; each addl $15; suites $275; under 12 free. Crib free. Garage parking $15. TV; cable (premium). Restaurant 6:30 am-11 pm. Bar noon-1 am. Ck-out noon. In-rm modem link. Concierge. Exercise equipt. Health club privileges. Cr cds: A, D, DS, MC, V.

🕱 🔥

★ ★ ★ **THE AVALON.** *16 E 32nd St (10016), between Fifth & Madison Aves, Midtown.* 212/299-7000. 100 rms, 12 story, 80 suites. S, D $195-$350; each addl $20; suites $250-$600. Crib free. Valet parking $23. Garage parking $23. TV; cable, VCR avail. Complimentary continental bkfst. Complimentary coffee in rms. Restaurant 6:30 am-11 pm. Bar 11:30 am-11 pm. Ck-out noon. Meeting rms. Business servs avail. In-rm modem link. Concierge. Exercise equipt. Bathrm phones, refrigerators; some in-rm whirlpools. Cr cds: A, C, D, DS, JCB, MC, V.

D 🕱 ⊠ 🔥 SC

★ ★ **BARBIZON.** *140 E 63rd St (10021), between Third & Lexington Aves, Upper East Side.* 212/838-5700; FAX 212/888-4271; res: 800/223-1020. 300 rms, 22 story. S $210-$280; D $230-$370; each addl $20; suites $425-$500; under 12 free; wkend rates. Garage parking $29.

TV; cable (premium). Pool; whirlpool. Ck-out noon. Business servs avail. In-rm modem link. Concierge. Exercise rm; sauna. Minibars. Some balconies. Landmark bldg known around the world as the Barbizon Hotel for Women from mid-1920s to mid-1970s. Cr cds: A, C, D, DS, JCB, MC, V.

D ⊠ 🏊 🕱 ⊠ ⊠ SC

✔ ★ ★ **BEACON.** *2130 Broadway (10023), Upper West Side at W 75th St.* 212/787-1100; res: 800/572-4969; FAX 212/724-0839. E-mail info@beaconhotel.com; web www.beaconhotel.com. 216 kit. units, 25 story. S $140-$150; D $160-$180; each addl $15; suites $195-$425; under 17 free. Crib free. Garage parking $20. TV; cable, VCR avail. Complimentary coffee in rms. Restaurant adj open 24 hrs. Ck-out noon. Coin lndry. Meeting rms. Health club privileges. Microwaves avail. Cr cds: A, C, D, DS, JCB, MC, V.

D ⊠ 🕱 ⊠ SC

★ ★ **BEDFORD.** *118 E 40th St (10016), between Park & Lexington, Midtown.* 212/697-4800; FAX 212/697-1093; res: 800/221-6881. E-mail bedfordhotel@pobox.com; web www.bedfordhotel.com. 200 rms, 17 story, 137 suites. S $170-$190; D $180-$200; each addl $10; suites $250-$300; under 13 free; wkend rates. Crib free. Garage $18. TV; cable (premium). Complimentary continental bkfst. Restaurant noon-11 pm. Bar. Ck-out noon. Coin lndry. Business servs avail. Cr cds: A, C, D, JCB, MC, V.

⊠ 🕱 ⊠ SC

★ ★ ★ **BEEKMAN TOWER.** *Three Mitchell Place (10017), at 49th St and First Ave, on the East Side.* 212/355-7300; FAX 212/753-9366; res: 800/637-8483. E-mail beckman@mesuite.com; web www.mesuite.com. 175 kit. suites, 26 story. S, studio suites $239; D $259-$299; each addl $20; 2-bedrm suites $499; under 12 free; wkend rates; lower rates June-Aug. Crib free. Garage $23. TV; cable, VCR avail. Complimentary coffee in rms. Restaurant 7 am-10:30 pm. Bar 5 pm-2 am; entertainment Tues-Sat. Ck-out noon. Coin lndry. Meeting rms. In-rm modem link. Concierge. Exercise equipt; sauna. Microwaves. Some private patios, balconies. Restored art-deco landmark completed in 1928. Cr cds: A, C, D, JCB, MC, V.

🕱 ⊠ 🕱 ⊠ SC

★ ★ **BENTLEY.** *500 E 62nd St (10021), at York Ave, Upper East Side.* 212/644-6000; FAX 212/207-4800. Web www.nyhotels.com. 196 rms, 21 story, 40 suites. S, D $255-$375; each addl $15; suites $425-$700; under 16 free. Crib free. Garage parking $25. TV; cable, VCR avail. Complimentary coffee in lobby. Restaurant 7 am-10 pm. Bar noon-10 pm. Ck-out noon. In-rm modem link. Concierge. Health club privileges. Bathrm phones, minibars; refrigerators avail. Cr cds: A, D, DS, JCB, MC, V.

⊠ 🔥

★ ★ **BEST WESTERN.** *17 W 32nd St (10001), between Fifth Ave & Broadway, Midtown.* 212/736-1600; FAX 212/790-2760. 176 rms, 14 story, 33 suites. S, D $119-$229; each addl $10; suites $149-$319; under 12 free. Crib free. Garage parking $16-$20. TV; cable (premium). Complimentary continental bkfst. Complimentary coffee in rms. Restaurant open 24 hrs. Bar 11-2 am. Ck-out noon. Meeting rms. Business center. Concierge. Gift shop. Barber, beauty shop. Exercise equipt. Some in-rm whirlpools. Cr cds: A, D, DS, ER, JCB, MC, V.

D 🕱 ⊠ 🔥 SC 🏃

★ ★ **BEST WESTERN SEAPORT INN.** *33 Peck Slip (10038), at Front St, in Financial District.* 212/766-6600; FAX 212/766-6615. E-mail bwseaportinn@juno.com. 72 rms, 7 story. S, D $149-$204; each addl $10; under 18 free; wkend rates; higher rates special events; lower rates rest of yr. Crib free. Garage parking $20. TV; VCR (movies $6.95). Complimentary continental bkfst. Restaurant nearby. Ck-out 11 am. Business servs avail. In-rm modem link. No bellhops. Health club privileges. Refrigerators. Some balconies. Located in historic district in restored 19th-century building. Cr cds: A, C, D, DS, MC, V.

D ⊠ 🕱 🔥 SC

★ ★ **BEST WESTERN-WOODWARD.** *210 W 55th St (10019), between Broadway & 7th Ave, Midtown.* 212/247-2000; FAX 212/581-

2248. 140 rms, 20 with shower only, 14 story, 40 suites. S, D $180-$210; each addl $20; suites $220-$350; under 12 free; wkend, hol rates. Crib free. Garage parking $24. TV; cable (premium), VCR avail. Complimentary coffee in rms. Restaurant 6:30 am-midnight. Rm serv to 3 am. Ck-out noon. Business servs avail. Concierge. Health club privileges. Cr cds: A, C, D, DS, ER, JCB, MC, V.

★ ★ ★ ★ ★ **CARLYLE.** *Madison Ave at E 76th St (10021), Upper East Side.* 212/744-1600; FAX 212/717-4682; res: 800/227-5737. The fabled Carlyle has hosted world leaders and the very, very rich for years and continues to be a symbol of European graciousness. And it's just steps away from the tony boutiques of Madison Avenue. 196 rms, 35 story. S, D $375-$650; suites (1-2 bedrm) $600-$2,500; under 18 free. Crib avail. Pet accepted, some restrictions. Garage $39. TV; cable (premium), VCR (movies). Restaurant (see CARLYLE). Rm serv 24 hrs. Bar from noon; Café Carlyle from 6 pm; entertainment (cover charge). Ck-out 1 pm. Meeting rms. Business center. In-rm modem link. Concierge. Exercise rm; sauna, steam rm. Massage. Bathrm phones, refrigerators, wet bars, mini-bars; microwaves avail. Many in-rm whirlpools, serv pantries. Grand piano in many suites. Some terraces. Cr cds: A, C, D, JCB, MC, V.

★ ★ ★ **CASABLANCA.** *147 W 43rd St (10036), between Broadway & Sixth, Times Square/Theater District.* 212/869-1212; res: 888/922-7225; FAX 212/391-7585. E-mail casahotel@aol.com; web www.casablancahotel.com. 48 rms, 8 with shower only, 6 story. S $225-$245; D $245; each addl $20; suites $325; under 12 free; wkend, hol rates. Crib free. Garage parking $24. TV; cable (premium), VCR (movies). Complimentary continental bkfst; afternoon refreshments. Restaurant 11 am-11 pm. Ck-out noon. Meeting rms. Business center. In-rm modem link. Concierge. Health club privileges. Bathrm phones, refrigerators. Cr cds: A, D, JCB, MC, V.

✔★ **COMFORT INN.** *42 W 35th St (10001), between 5th & 6th Aves, Murray Hill.* 212/947-0200; FAX 212/594-3047. E-mail acw64@aol.com; web www.comfortinnmanhattan.com. 131 rms, 12 story. S $119-$229; D $129-$229; each addl $20; under 18 free. Crib free. TV; cable (premium). Complimentary continental bkfst. Coffee in rms. Restaurant 7 am-8 pm. Ck-out noon. Business servs avail. In-rm modem link. Some refrigerators, microwaves. Cr cds: A, C, D, DS, MC, V.

★ ★ ★ **CROWNE PLAZA MANHATTAN.** *1605 Broadway (10019), at 49th St, Midtown.* 212/977-4000; FAX 212/333-7393. 770 rms, 46 story. S, D $209-$409; each addl $20; under 19 free. Crib avail. Garage $34. TV; cable (premium), VCR avail (movies). Indoor pool; lifeguard. Coffee in rms. Restaurant 6:30 am-2 pm, 5 pm-2 am; Sun hrs vary. Rm serv 24 hrs. Bar from 11:30 am. Ck-out noon. Convention facilities. Business center. In-rm modem link. Concierge. Exercise rm; sauna, steam rm. Minibars; refrigerators avail. Luxury level. Cr cds: A, C, D, DS, JCB, MC, V.

★ ★ **CROWNE PLAZA-UNITED NATIONS.** *304 E 42nd St (10017), between 2nd and 1st Aves, Midtown.* 212/986-8800; FAX 212/986-1758; res: 800/879-8836. E-mail nycun@aol.com. 300 rms in 2 towers, 17 & 20 story. S $289-$347; D $312-$347; each addl $25; suites $405-$695; under 12 free; wkend rates. Crib free. Garage parking $20-$23. TV; cable (premium), VCR avail. Restaurant 6:30 am-10:30 pm; Sat, Sun 7 am-11 pm. Rm serv 24 hrs. Bar. Ck-out noon. Meeting rms. Business servs avail. In-rm modem link. Concierge. Exercise equipt; saunas. Massage. Minibars. Some balconies. Cr cds: A, C, D, DS, ER, JCB, MC, V.

✔★ ★ **DAYS HOTEL.** *790 Eighth Ave (10019), at 49th St, Times Square/Theater District.* 212/581-7000; FAX 212/974-0291. 367 rms, 15 story. S $155-$197; D $167-$209; each addl $20; suites $240-$365; under

18 free. Crib free. TV. Restaurant 7 am-midnight. Bar noon-2 am. Ck-out 1 pm. Meeting rm. Business servs avail. Cr cds: A, C, D, DS, JCB, MC, V.

★ ★ **DELMONICO.** *502 Park Ave (10022), at 59th St, Midtown.* 212/355-2500; FAX 212/755-3779; res: 800/821-3842. 125 kit. suites, 32 story. Suites $310-$575; each addl $30; under 12 free; monthly, wkend rates. Crib free. Valet parking $36. TV; cable (premium), VCR avail. Bar noon-1 am. Ck-out noon. Business servs avail. In-rm modem link. Concierge. Exercise rm; sauna. Microwaves. Some balconies. Restored 1929 building. Cr cds: A, D, DS, MC, V.

★ ★ ★ **DORAL PARK AVENUE.** *70 Park Ave (10016), at E 38th St, Murray Hill.* 212/687-7050; FAX 212/808-9029; res: 800/223-6725. E-mail doralpark@aol.com. 188 rms, 17 story. S $195-$225; D $260-$380; each addl $20; suites $400-$1,000; under 12 free; wkend rates. Crib free. Parking $25. TV; cable. Restaurant 7-10:30 am, noon-2 pm, 5-10 pm. Bar noon-midnight. Ck-out noon. Business servs avail. Health club privileges. Minibars. Neo-classical decor. Cr cds: A, C, D, DS, ER, JCB, MC, V.

★ ★ **DOUBLETREE GUEST SUITES.** *1568 Broadway (10036), at 47th St & 7th Ave, Times Square/Theater District.* 212/719-1600; FAX 212/921-5212. Web www.doubletreehotels.com. 460 suites, 43 story. S $210-$350; D $350-$750; each addl $20; under 12 free; wkend rates; higher rates special events. Crib free. Garage; valet parking $30/day. TV; cable (premium) VCR avail. Complimentary coffee in rms. Restaurant 6:30 am-11 pm. Bar to 1 am. Ck-out noon. Coin lndry. Meeting rms. Business servs avail. In-rm modem link. Concierge. Gift shop. Exercise equipt. Bathrm phones, refrigerators, minibars, wet bars. Cr cds: A, C, D, DS, JCB, MC, V.

★ ★ **DUMONT PLAZA.** *150 E 34th St (10016), near Lexington Ave, Murray Hill.* 212/481-7600; FAX 212/889-8856; res: 800/637-8483. 247 kit. suites, 37 story. S $259-$309; D $279-$329; each addl $20; suites $499-$519; under 12 free; wkend rates. Crib free. TV; cable, VCR avail. Complimentary coffee in rms. Restaurant 7 am-10 pm. Rm serv 24 hrs. Ck-out noon. Coin lndry. Meeting rms. Business servs avail. In-rm modem link. Exercise equipt; sauna. Microwaves. Plaza with fountain. Cr cds: A, C, D, DS, ER, JCB, MC, V.

★ ★ **EASTGATE TOWER SUITES.** *222 E 39th St (10016), between Third & Second Aves, Murray Hill.* 212/687-8000; FAX 212/490-2634; res: 800/637-8483 (NY). Web www.mesuite.com. 188 kit. suites, 25 story. S $269-$309; D $289-$329; each addl $20; wkly rates. Garage; valet parking $22. TV; cable (premium). Restaurant 7:30-2 am. Rm serv 7:30 am-11 pm. Bar. Ck-out noon. Business center. In-rm modem link. Exercise equipt. Microwaves. Landscaped plaza with fountain. Cr cds: A, C, D, ER, JCB, MC, V.

✔★ ★ **EDISON.** *228 W 47th St (10036), Times Square/Theater District.* 212/840-5000; FAX 212/596-6850; res: 800/637-7070. E-mail edisonnyc@aol.com; web www.edisonhotelnyc.com. 1,000 rms, 22 story. S $125; D $140-$170; each addl $10; suites $160-$230; family rms $185-$230. Crib free. Garage $18. TV; cable (premium). Restaurant 6:15 am-midnight, Sun to 7 pm. Bar noon-2 am. Ck-out 1 pm. Meeting rm. Business servs avail. Gift shop. Beauty shop. Airport transportation. Cr cds: A, C, D, DS, JCB, MC, V.

★ ★ ★ **ELYSEE.** *60 E 54th St (10022), between Park & Madison Aves, Midtown.* 212/753-1066; FAX 212/980-9278; res: 800/535-9733. 99 rms, 15 story. S, D $265-$295; suites $325-$775; under 12 free. Crib free. TV; cable, VCR (free movies). Complimentary continental bkfst; afternoon refreshments. Restaurant noon-midnight. Rm serv 7 am-10:30 pm. Bar noon-2 am. Ck-out 1 pm. Meeting rms. Business servs avail. Health club privileges. Refrigerators, bathrm phones. Microwaves avail. Country French decor, antiques. Cr cds: A, C, D, JCB, MC, V.

[D] [icons]

★ ★ ★ ★ **ESSEX HOUSE HOTEL NIKKO NEW YORK.** *160 Central Park South (10019), between 6th & 7th Aves, Midtown.* 212/247-0300; res: 800/645-5687; FAX 212/315-1839. Web www.essexhouse.com. This New York landmark (1931) overlooks Central Park and exemplifies classic art-deco style. The spacious guest rooms are traditional with marble baths. Many have park views. 597 units, 40 story, 81 suites. S $375-$450; D $400-$475; each addl $25; suites $450-$3,000; under 18 free; wkend rates. Crib free. Garage parking, valet $40. TV; cable (premium), VCR. Restaurants 7 am-11 pm (also see LES CÉLÉBRITÉS). Rm serv 24 hrs. Bar noon-1 am. Ck-out noon. Convention facilities. Business center. In-rm modem link, fax. Concierge. Gift shop. Exercise rm; saunas, steam rms. Spa. Minibars. Cr cds: A, C, D, DS, ER, JCB, MC, V.

[D] [icons]

★ ★ ★ **FITZPATRICK MANHATTAN.** *687 Lexington Ave (10022), 57th St on the East Side.* 212/355-0100; FAX 212/355-1371; res: 800/367-7701. E-mail fitzusa@aol.com. 92 rms, 17 story, 52 suites. S $265; D $295; suites $350-$380; each addl in suite $30 wkday, $50 wkend; under 12 free; wkend, hol rates. Crib free. Garage $35. TV; cable (premium), VCR avail. Restaurant 7 am-10:30 pm. Rm serv 24 hrs. Bar noon-2 am. Ck-out noon. Meeting rms. Business servs avail. In-rm modem link. Concierge. Airport transportation. Health club privileges. Many refrigerators, wet bars. Cr cds: A, C, D, DS, MC, V.

[icons]

★ ★ ★ ★ **FOUR SEASONS.** *57 E 57th St (10022), between Madison & Park Aves, on the East Side.* 212/758-5700; res: 800/332-3442; FAX 212/758-5711. Web www.fshr.com. The elegant, five-year-old, 52-story hotel—New York's tallest—offers large guest rooms, meticulous service and spectacular views of the city skyline and Central Park. The huge, multilevel marble lobby seems almost like an Egyptian monument. 370 rms, 52 story, 61 suites. S $495-$630; D $540-$700; each addl $50; suites $975-$9,000; under 12 free; wkend rates. Crib free. Pet accepted, some restrictions. Garage, valet parking $35. TV; cable (premium), VCR. Restaurant 7 am-10:30 pm (also see FIFTY SEVEN FIFTY SEVEN). Rm serv 24 hrs. Bar 11:30-1 am. Ck-out noon. Convention facilities. Business center. In-rm modem link. Concierge. Extensive exercise rm; sauna, steam rm. Whirlpool. Massage. Health club privileges. Bathrm phones, minibars. Some terraces. Cr cds: A, C, D, ER, JCB, MC, V.

[D] [icons]

✔ ★ ★ **THE FRANKLIN.** *164 E 87th St (10128), between Lexington & 3rd Aves, Upper East Side.* 212/369-1000; FAX 212/369-8000; res: 800/600-8787. E-mail info@franklinhotel.com; web www.franklinhotel.com. 50 rms, 9 story. S, D $199-$219. Garage parking free, in/out $10. TV; cable, VCR (free movies). Complimentary continental bkfst. Restaurant nearby. Ck-out 1 pm. Refrigerators avail. Renovated boutique hotel. Cr cds: A, MC, V.

[icons]

★ ★ **GORHAM NEW YORK.** *136 W 55th St (10019), between 6th & 7th Aves, Midtown.* 212/245-1800; FAX 212/582-8332; res: 800/735-0710. E-mail reservations@gorhamhotel.com; web www.gorhamhotel.com. 114 kit. units, 17 story. S, D $210-$400; each addl $20; suites $235-$425; under 16 free. Crib free. TV; cable (premium), VCR avail. Ck-out noon. Business servs avail. In-rm modem link. Exercise equipt. Microwaves. Cr cds: A, C, D, JCB, MC, V.

[D] [icons]

★ ★ **GRAND HYATT.** *Park Ave at Grand Central (10017), 42nd St between Lexington & Vanderbilt, Midtown.* 212/883-1234; FAX 212/697-3772. Web www.hyatt.com. 1,347 rms, 30 story. S $300-$325; D $325-$350; each addl $25; suites $450-$2,000; under 18 free; wkend rates. Crib free. Garage $34. TV; cable (premium). Restaurant 6:30 am-midnight. Rm serv 24 hrs. Bar 11-2 am; entertainment. Ck-out noon. Convention facilities. Business center. Exercise equipt. Health club privi-

leges. Refrigerator in suites. Luxury level. Cr cds: A, C, D, DS, ER, JCB, MC, V.

[D] [icons]

★ ★ **HELMSLEY MIDDLETOWNE.** *148 E 48th St (10017), Midtown.* 212/755-3000; FAX 212/832-0261; res: 800/843-2157 (exc NY). Web hrlmsleyhotels.com. 192 rms, 17 story. S $165-$230; D $185-$250; each addl $20; suites $215-$375; under 12 free; wkend rates. Crib free. Garage; valet parking $30. TV; cable (premium), VCR avail. Complimentary coffee in lobby. Restaurant nearby. Ck-out 1 pm. Business servs avail. In-rm modem link. Health club privileges. Bathrm phones, refrigerators, microwaves, wet bars. Many balconies. Cr cds: A, C, D, DS, JCB, MC, V.

[D] [icons]

★ ★ ★ **HELMSLEY PARK LANE.** *36 Central Park South (10019), between 5th & 6th Aves, Midtown.* 212/371-4000; FAX 212/319-9065; res: 800/221-4982. E-mail sales@helmsleyparklane.com; web www.helmsleyhotel.com. 640 rms, 46 story. S, D $350-$450; each addl $30; suites $700-$950; under 12 free; wkend rates. Crib free. Garage parking $34. TV; VCR avail (movies). Restaurant 7 am-midnight. Rm serv 24 hrs. Bar 11-2 am. Ck-out 1 pm. Business center. In-rm modem link. Health club privileges. Refrigerators. Cr cds: A, C, D, DS, JCB, MC, V.

[D] [icons]

★ ★ **HELMSLEY WINDSOR.** *100 W 58th St (10019), at Avenue of the Americas, Midtown.* 212/265-2100; FAX 212/315-0371. 245 rms, 15 story. S $160-$200; D $170-$210; each addl $20; suites $260-$600; summer, wkend rates. Crib free. Garage $21. TV; cable (premium). Complimentary continental bkfst. No rm serv. Ck-out 1 pm. Business servs avail. Health club privileges. Serv pantry in suites. Cr cds: A, C, D, DS, JCB, MC, V.

[D] [icons]

✔ ★ **HERALD SQUARE.** *19 W 31st St (10001), between 5th Ave & Broadway, near Macy's, south of Midtown.* 212/279-4017; FAX 212/643-9208; res: 800/727-1888. E-mail hersquhtl@aol.com. 114 rms, some share bath, 9 story. S $50-$95; D $95-$125; each addl $5; under 10 free. Crib free. Garage $13-$21. TV; cable. Restaurant nearby. Ck-out noon. No bellhops. In landmark beaux-arts building (1893) designed by Carrere and Hastings; was once lived in by Charles Dana Gibson, illustrator who created the Gibson girl; was original headquarters of Life magazine. Hotel interior decorated with Life covers & graphics. . Cr cds: A, DS, JCB, MC, V.

[icons]

★ ★ ★ **HILTON AND TOWERS AT ROCKEFELLER CENTER.** *1335 Avenue of the Americas (10019), between W 53rd & 54th Sts, Midtown.* 212/586-7000; FAX 212/315-1374. E-mail nyhilton@hilton.com; web www.travelweb.com. 2,040 rms, 46 story. S $209-$395; D $239-$425; each addl $30; suites $545-$2,750; family rates; package plans. Crib free. Pet accepted. Garage $35. TV; cable (premium), VCR avail. Restaurant 6 am-midnight. Bar 11-2 am. Ck-out noon. Convention facilities. Business center. In-rm modem link. Shopping arcade. Barber, beauty shop. Exercise rm; sauna. Minibars. Refrigerators avail. Luxury level. Cr cds: A, C, D, DS, ER, JCB, MC, V.

[D] [icons]

★ ★ **HOLIDAY INN-DOWNTOWN.** *138 Lafayette St (10013), at Howard St, in Chinatown.* 212/966-8898; FAX 212/966-3933. E-mail holinnsoho@aol.com. 227 rms, 14 story. S, D $175-$209; each addl $15; suites $199-$229; under 12 free. Crib free. Valet parking $25. TV; cable. Complimentary coffee in rms. Restaurant 6:30 am-11 pm. Bar noon-midnight. Ck-out noon. Business servs avail. In-rm modem link. Concierge. Health club privileges. Renovated landmark building. Cr cds: A, C, D, DS, JCB, MC, V.

[D] [icons]

✔ ★ ★ **HOWARD JOHNSON PLAZA.** *851 Eighth Ave (10019), between 51st and 52nd Sts, Midtown.* 212/581-4100; FAX 212/974-7502. Web www.hojo.com. 300 rms, 11 story. S $140-$202; D $152-$214; each addl $20; under 17 free; wkend rates. Crib free. Garage $15. TV; cable.

Restaurant 6 am-midnight. Bar 11-2 am. Ck-out 1 pm. Business servs avail. Gift shop. Cr cds: A, C, D, DS, JCB, MC, V.

⊠ ⊠ SC

★ ★ ★ **INTER-CONTINENTAL.** *111 E 48th St (10017), between Lexington & Park Aves, Midtown.* 212/755-5900; FAX 212/644-0079; res: 800/327-0200. E-mail newyork@interconti.com; web www.interconti.com. 683 rms, 14 story. S, D $285-$385; each addl $40; suites $475-$4,000; under 14 free; wkend rates. Crib free. Garage parking $35; valet. TV; cable (premium). Restaurant 7 am-midnight. Bar 11:30-1 am. Ck-out noon. Meeting rms. Business center. In-rm modem link. Concierge. Gift shop. Exercise equipt; sauna, steam rm. Health club privileges. Massage. Mini-bars. Microwaves avail. Cr cds: A, C, D, DS, ER, JCB, MC, V.

D ⊠ ⊠ ⊠ ⊠ ⊠

★ ★ **THE IROQUOIS.** *49 W 44th St (10036), between 5th & 6th Aves, Midtown.* 212/840-3080; res: 800/332-7220; FAX 212/398-1754. 114 rms, 12 story. S, D $225; suites $350; under 12 free; wkend rates; hols 3-day min; higher rates Dec 31. Crib avail. Pet accepted, some restrictions. Valet parking $26. TV; cable (premium), VCR (movies). Complimentary continental bkfst. Restaurant 7 am-midnight. Rm serv 24 hrs. Bar to 1 am. Ck-out noon. Meeting rms. Business center. In-rm modem link. Concierge. Exercise equipt. Bathrm phones. Cr cds: A, C, D, JCB, MC, V.

D ⊠ ⊠ ⊠ ⊠ ⊠

★ ★ **JOLLY MADISON TOWERS.** *22 E 38th St (10016), at Madison Ave, Midtown.* 212/802-0600; FAX 212/447-0747; res: 800/225-4340. 225 rms, 18 story. S, D $180-$220; each addl $30; suites $350; under 12 free. Crib free. TV; cable (premium). Restaurant 6:30 am-11 pm. Bar 10-1 am. Ck-out noon. Business servs avail. In-rm modem link. Concierge. Cr cds: A, C, D, JCB, MC, V.

⊠ ⊠ SC

★ ★ **KIMBERLY.** *145 E 50th St (10022), between Lexington & 3rd Ave, Midtown.* 212/755-0400; FAX 212/486-6915; res: 800/683-0400. Web www.citysearch.com/nycity. 186 suites, 30 story. S $219-$325; D $234-$350; suites $265-$780; 2-bedrm $409-$675; under 18 free. Crib free. Garage parking $23. TV; cable (premium), VCR avail. Complimentary coffee in rms. Restaurant 7 am-11 pm. Bar noon-midnight; entertainment Thurs-Sat. Ck-out noon. Coin lndry. Business servs avail. Concierge. Health club privileges. Minibars. Terraces. Cr cds: A, C, D, DS, JCB, MC, V.

D ⊠ ⊠

★ ★ ★ **THE KITANO.** *66 Park Ave (10016), at 38th St, in Murray Hill.* 212/885-7000; res: 800/548-2666; FAX 212/885-7100. E-mail reservations@kitano.com. 149 rms, 18 story, 18 suites. S, D $315-$410; each addl $25; suites $500-$1,350; under 12 free; wkend rates. Crib free. Valet parking $26-$30. TV; cable (premium), VCR avail. Complimentary green tea in rms. Restaurants 7 am-11 pm (also see NADAMAN HAKUBAI). Bar noon-12:30 am; entertainment. Ck-out noon. Meeting rms. Business servs avail. In-rm modem link, fax. Concierge. Gift shop. Health club privileges. Minibars. Cr cds: A, C, D, DS, JCB, MC, V.

D ⊠ ⊠ SC

✔★ ★ **LEXINGTON.** *511 Lexington Ave (10017), at E 48th St, Midtown.* 212/755-4400; FAX 212/751-4091; res: 800/448-4471. 700 rms, 27 story. S, D $185-$265; each addl $15; suites $325-$550. Crib free. TV; cable (premium). Restaurant 6:30 am-midnight; entertainment. Bar noon-midnight. Ck-out noon. Meeting rm. Business center. Exercise equipt. Refrigerators, microwaves. Near Grand Central Station. Cr cds: A, C, D, DS, ER, JCB, MC, V.

⊠ ⊠ ⊠ SC ⊠

★ ★ ★ **LOEWS NEW YORK.** *569 Lexington Ave (10022), at E 51st St, Midtown.* 212/752-7000; FAX 212/758-6311. Web www.loewshotels.com. 722 rms, 20 story. S, D $199-$299; each addl $25; suites $250-$750; under 16 free; wkend rates. Crib free. Pet accepted, some restrictions. Garage $25. TV; cable (premium). Restaurant 7 am-midnight. Bar 11-2 am. Ck-out noon. Meeting rms. Business center. In-rm

modem link. Barber. Exercise rm; sauna. Bathrm phones, refrigerators; microwaves avail. Luxury level. Cr cds: A, C, D, DS, JCB, MC, V.

D ⊠ ⊠ ⊠ SC ⊠

★ ★ ★ **THE LOMBARDY.** *111 E 56th St (10022), between Park & Lexington Aves, Midtown.* 212/753-8600; res: 800/223-5254; FAX 212/754-5683. Web www.primahotels.com. 105 kit. units, 21 story, 60 suites. S, D $265; each addl $20; suites $360-$500; under 12 free; wkend rates (summer). Crib free. Garage parking $18. TV; cable (premium), VCR avail. Restaurant (see THE PARK). Rm serv from 6 am. Bar noon-midnight. Ck-out 1 pm. Meeting rms. Business servs avail. In-rm modem link. Concierge. Exercise equipt. Refrigerators; many microwaves. Some balconies. Cr cds: A, C, D, DS, JCB, MC, V.

D ⊠ ⊠ ⊠ ⊠

★ ★ ★ ★ **LOWELL.** *28 E 63rd St (10021), between Madison & Park Aves, Upper East Side.* 212/838-1400; FAX 212/319-4230; res: 800/221-4444. E-mail lowellhtl@aol.com; web www.preferredhotels.com/preferred.html. Accommodations are elegant, decorated with French and Oriental period furnishings, in this New York institution. 65 rms, 17 story, 56 kit. suites. S, D $345-$445; each addl $30; kit. suites $545-$2,600; under 12 free; wkend rates. Crib free. Valet parking $35. TV; cable (premium), VCR (movies). Restaurants 7 am-11 pm. Afternoon tea 3:30-6:30 pm. Bar noon-midnight. Ck-out 1 pm. Meeting rm. Business servs avail. In-rm modem link. Concierge. Exercise equipt. Health club privileges. Bathrm phones, refrigerators, minibars; many fireplaces; microwaves avail. Some balconies. Cr cds: A, C, D, DS, ER, JCB, MC, V.

D ⊠ ⊠ ⊠

★ ★ **THE LUCERNE.** *201 W 79th St (10024), Upper West Side.* 212/875-1000; res: 800/492-8122; FAX 212/362-7251. Web www.nyhotel.com. 250 rms, 14 story, 100 suites. S $135-$170; D $145-$180; each addl $15; suites $175-$325; under 16 free; family rates; package plans. Crib avail. Garage parking $16. TV; cable (premium), VCR avail. Complimentary coffee in rms. Restaurant 7-10:30 am, 5 pm-midnight. Bar 5 pm-2 am; entertainment from 8 pm. Ck-out noon. Meeting rms. Business servs avail. In-rm modem link in suites. Concierge. Exercise equipt. Health club privileges. Microwaves avail; refrigerator, microwave, wet bar in suites. Cr cds: A, C, D, DS, ER, JCB, MC, V.

⊠ ⊠ ⊠ ⊠ SC

★ ★ **LYDEN GARDENS.** *215 E 64th St (10021), between Second & Third Aves, Upper East Side.* 212/355-1230; FAX 212/758-7858; res: 800/637-8483. 133 kit. suites, 13 story. S $239-$259; D $259-$279; each addl $20; 1-bedrm $289-$309; 2-bedrm $499-$519; under 12 free; wkend rates. Crib free. Garage $18.50. TV; cable (premium). Complimentary coffee in rms. Restaurant nearby. No rm serv. Ck-out noon. Business servs avail. Concierge. Exercise equipt. Microwaves. Terraces, gardens. Cr cds: A, C, D, ER, JCB, MC, V.

D ⊠ ⊠ ⊠ ⊠

★ ★ **LYDEN HOUSE.** *320 E 53rd St (10022), Midtown, between 1st & 2nd Aves.* 212/888-6070; FAX 212/935-7690; res: 800/637-8483. E-mail gdrepaol@mesuite.com; web www.mesuite.com. 81 suites, 11 story. S, D $239-$269; 2-bedrm $499; under 12 free; wkend rates. Crib free. TV; cable (premium), VCR. Coffee in rms. Ck-out noon. Coin lndry. Health club privileges. Microwaves. Cr cds: A, C, D, DS, ER, JCB, MC, V.

D ⊠

★ ★ **THE MANSFIELD.** *12 W 44th St (10036), between 5th & 6th Aves, Midtown.* 212/944-6050; FAX 212/764-4477; res: 800/255-5167. E-mail mansfield@gothamhotels.com; web www.gothamhotels.com. 124 rms, 36 with shower only, 13 story, 27 suites. S, D $195-$245; suites $275; wkend rates. Crib free. TV; cable (premium), VCR (free movies). Complimentary continental bkfst. Ck-out noon. Business servs avail. Concierge. Free garage parking. Health club privileges. Refrigerators. Cr cds: A, MC, V.

⊠ ⊠

★ ★ ★ **THE MARK.** *25 E 77th St (10021), between Madison & 5th Aves, Upper East Side.* 212/744-4300; FAX 212/744-2749; res: 800/843-

6275. Web www.themark.com. 120 rms, 16 story, 60 suites. S $355-$405; D $380-$430; each addl $25; suites $550-$2,500; under 15 free; wkend, hol rates. Crib free. Garage $35. TV; cable (premium), VCR (movies). Restaurant 7 am-10:30 pm. Rm serv 24 hrs. Bar 12:30 pm-midnight. Ck-out 1 pm. Meeting rms. Business servs avail. In-rm modem link. Concierge. Exercise equipt; sauna, steam rm. Health club privileges. Bathrm phones. Cr cds: A, C, D, DS, ER, JCB, MC, V.

★ ★ ★ **MARRIOTT MARQUIS.** *1535 Broadway (10036), between 45th & 46th Sts, Times Square/Theater District.* 212/398-1900; FAX 212/704-8930. Web www.marriott.com. 1,919 rms, 50 story. S $225-$390; D $245-$415; each addl $15; suites $425-$3,500; under 18 free; wkend, package plans. Covered parking, valet $30. TV; cable (premium). Complimentary coffee in rms. Restaurants 7 am-midnight (also see THE VIEW). Rm serv 24 hrs. Bars. Ck-out noon. Convention facilities. Business center. In-rm modem link. Concierge. Gift shop. Exercise equipt; sauna, steam rm. Whirlpool. Minibars. Luxury level. Cr cds: A, C, D, DS, ER, JCB, MC, V.

★ ★ ★ **MARRIOTT-EAST SIDE.** *525 Lexington Ave (10017), between E 48th and 49th Sts, Midtown.* 212/755-4000; FAX 212/751-3440. Web www.marriott.com. 650 rms, 34 story. S, D $189-$299; suites $600-$900; under 18 free; wkend packages. Crib free. TV; cable (premium). Restaurant 7 am-10 pm. Bar noon-1 am. Ck-out noon. Business center. In-rm modem link. Concierge. Exercise equipt. Bathrm phones, minibars. Designed by Arthur Loomis Harmon, architect of Empire State Bldg; hotel was subject of Georgia O'Keefe cityscapes. Cr cds: A, C, D, DS, ER, JCB, MC, V.

★ ★ ★ **MARRIOTT-FINANCIAL CENTER.** *85 West St (10006), at Albany St, Financial District.* 212/385-4900; FAX 212/227-8136. Web www.marriott.com. 504 rms, 38 story. S, D $289; each addl $20; suites $349-$1,500; under 18 free; wkend rates. Crib free. Garage parking $25. TV; cable (premium). Indoor pool. Restaurant 6:30 am-10 pm. Bar 11:30-2 am. Ck-out 11 am. Convention facilities. Business center. In-rm modem link. Concierge. Gift shop. Exercise rm; sauna, steam rm. Walking distance to Wall St, ferry to Statue of Liberty. Cr cds: A, C, D, DS, ER, JCB, MC, V.

★ ★ ★ **MARRIOTT-WORLD TRADE CENTER.** *3 World Trade Center (10048), main entrance West St at Liberty St, in Financial District.* 212/938-9100; FAX 212/444-3100. Web www.marriott.com. 820 rms, 23 story. S, D $289-$395; each addl $25; suites $369-$1,700; under 12 free; wkend rates. TV; cable, VCR avail (movies). Indoor pool; lifeguard. Restaurant 6:30 am-11 pm. Rm serv 24 hrs. Bar noon-1 am. Ck-out 1 pm. Convention facilities. Business center. In-rm modem link. Concierge. Gift shop. Raquetball court. Exercise rm; sauna. Massage. Minibars. Cr cds: A, C, D, DS, ER, JCB, MC, V.

★ ★ **THE MAYFLOWER.** *15 Central Park West (10023), at 61st St, Upper West Side.* 212/265-0060; FAX 212/265-5098; res: 800/223-4164. 365 rms, 18 story, 200 suites. S $165-$205; D $180-$220; each addl $20; suites $270-$295; under 16 free; package plans; lower rates July, Aug & mid-Dec-Mar. Pet accepted. Garage parking, valet $28. TV; cable (premium). Restaurant 7 am-10 pm. Bar 11:30-1 am. Ck-out noon. Meeting rms. Business servs avail. In-rm modem link. Concierge. Exercise equipt. Many refrigerators. Some terraces. Cr cds: A, C, D, DS, ER, JCB, MC, V.

★ ★ ★ **THE MICHELANGELO.** *152 W 51st St (10019), between 6th & 7th Aves, Times Square/Theater District.* 212/765-1900; FAX 212/541-6604; res: 800/237-0990. 178 rms, 7 story, 52 suites. S, D $295-$395; each addl $30; suites $425-$950; under 16 free; wkend rates. Crib free. Valet parking $30/day. TV; cable (premium), VCR avail (movies $5). Complimentary continental bkfst. Restaurant 7 am-2:30 pm, 5:30-11:30 pm. Rm serv 24 hrs. Bar. Ck-out 1 pm. Meeting rms. Business center. In-rm modem link. Concierge. Exercise equipt. Health club privileges.

Bathrm phones; minibars. Refrigerators avail. Cr cds: A, C, D, DS, ER, JCB, MC, V.

★ **THE MILBURN.** *242 W 76th St (10023), between Broadway and West End Aves, Upper West Side.* 212/362-1006; res: 800/833-9622; FAX 212/721-5476. E-mail milburn@cris.com; web www.milburnhotel.com. 106 kit. units, 15 story, 55 suites. Mar-Dec: S $109-$135; D $119-$145; suites $165-$185; under 12 free; lower rates rest of yr. Crib free. Garage parking $16. TV; cable, VCR avail (movies). Complimentary coffee in rms. Restaurant nearby. Ck-out noon. Meeting rms. Business servs avail. In-rm modem link. Concierge. Coin lndry. Health club privileges. Bathrm phones; microwaves avail. Cr cds: A, C, D, MC, V.

★ ★ ★ **MILLENIUM HILTON.** *55 Church St (10007), Dey & Fulton Sts, Financial District.* 212/693-2001; res: 800/445-8667; FAX 212/571-2316. Web www.hilton.com. A high-rise hotel with a high-tech look, this property has amenities for both business and pleasure. 561 units, 55 story. S $290-$350; D $300-$350; each addl $30; suites $450-$1,500; under 18 free; wkend rates; package plans. Crib free. Garage; valet parking $35. TV; cable (premium), VCR avail. Indoor pool; lifeguard. Restaurants 6:30 am-11 pm. Rm serv 24 hrs. Bar 11:30-12:30 am; pianist Mon-Fri. Ck-out noon. Meeting rms. Business center. In-rm modem link. Concierge. Gift shop. Exercise rm; sauna. Massage. Bathrm phones, minibars. Cr cds: A, D, DS, ER, JCB, MC, V.

★ ★ ★ **MILLENNIUM BROADWAY.** *145 W 44th St (10036), between Sixth Ave & Broadway, Times Square/Theater District.* 212/768-4400; FAX 212/789-7688; res: 800/622-5569. E-mail mb.club.@mill.cop.com; web www.mill.bdwy.com. 627 rms, 52 story. S $250-$300; D $270-$320; suites $495-$3,500; under 18 free; wkend rates. Crib free. Valet parking $35. TV; cable (premium), VCR avail. Restaurant 6:30 am-11 pm. Bar 11-1 am. Ck-out noon. Convention facilities. Business center. In-rm modem link. Concierge. Gift shop. Exercise equipt; steam rm. Massage. Health club privileges. Minibars. Bathrm phone in suites. Post-modern skyscraper, with moderne setbacks, deco detailing, incorporates landmark, beaux-arts Hudson Theatre (1903), which has been restored. Cr cds: A, C, D, DS, ER, JCB, MC, V.

★ ★ ★ **MORGANS.** *237 Madison Ave (10016), between 37th & 38th Sts, Murray Hill.* 212/686-0300; FAX 212/779-8352; res: 800/334-3408. 113 rms, 19 story. S $250-$305; D $275-$335; each addl $30; suites $465-$600; under 12 free; wkend rates. Garage, valet parking $32. TV; cable (premium). Complimentary continental bkfst. Rm serv 24 hrs. Bar 5 pm-4 am; Sun, Mon to 2 am. Ck-out noon. Business servs avail. In-rm modem link. Concierge. Health club privileges. Bathrm phones, refrigerators, minibars. Andree Putman designed interiors; combines high-tech ultra-modern look with 1930s moderne styling. Cr cds: A, C, D, ER, JCB, MC, V.

★ ★ ★ **NEW YORK HELMSLEY.** *212 E 42nd St (10017), between Second and Third Aves, on the East Side.* 212/490-8900; FAX 212/986-4792; res: 800/221-4982. Web www.helmsleyhotels.com. 800 rms, 41 story. S $230-$270; D $255-$295; each addl $30; suites $500-$875; under 12 free; wkend rates. Crib free. Garage $33. TV; cable, VCR avail (movies). Restaurant 7 am-11:30 pm. Bar 11-1 am; entertainment. Ck-out noon. Meeting rms. Business center. In-rm modem link. Gift shop. Health club privileges. Bathrm phones; some refrigerators. 2 blks E of Grand Central Station. Cr cds: A, C, D, DS, JCB, MC, V.

★ ★ ★ **THE NEW YORK PALACE.** *455 Madison Ave (10022), at 50th St, Midtown.* 212/888-7000; FAX 212/303-6000; res: 800/697-2522. E-mail hrihotel@idt.ios.com; web www.newyorkpalace.com. Rooms in this centrally located New York institution have it all—from large desks for the business traveler to plush, pillow-covered beds for the vacationer. The dramatically renovated lobby leads out to one of the most famous areas of

Manhattan. 896 rms, 55 story, 104 suites. S, D $450-$550; suites $800-$10,000; under 18 free; wkend rates. Crib free. Garage parking $46. TV; cable, VCR avail (movies). Restaurants 6:30 am-11 pm (also see LE CIRQUE 2000). Rm serv 24 hrs. Bars 11:30-1 am. Ck-out 1 pm. Meeting rms. Business center. In-rm modem link. Concierge. Exercise rm; steam rm. Massage. Health club privileges. Refrigerators. Cr cds: A, C, D, DS, JCB, MC, V.

D ⊀ ⇤ ⊠ 🔥 👫

✔★★ **NEW YORK'S HOTEL PENNSYLVANIA.** 401 Seventh Ave (10001), at 33rd St, opp Madison Square Garden, in Garment District. 212/736-5000; FAX 212/502-8712; res: 800/223-8585. Web www.hotelpennsylvania.com. 1,705 rms, 22 story. S, D $139-$169; suites $180-$800; each addl $25; under 16 free. Crib free. Garage $26. TV. Restaurant 6:30-1 am. Bar noon-2 am, entertainment. Ck-out noon. Convention facilities. Business servs avail. Shopping arcade. Barber, beauty shop. Health club privileges. Cr cds: A, C, D, DS, ER, JCB, MC, V.

D SC

★★ **NOVOTEL.** 226 W 52nd St (10019), at Broadway, Midtown. 212/315-0100; FAX 212/765-5369; res: 800/221-3185. Web www.hotelweb.fr. 478 rms, 33 story. S, D $325; each addl $20; under 16 free. Crib $10. Pet accepted. TV; cable (premium). Restaurant 6 am-midnight. Bar 3:30 pm-1 am; entertainment exc Sun. Ck-out 1 pm. Meeting rm. Business center. In-rm modem link. Exercise equipt. Cr cds: A, C, D, ER, JCB, MC, V.

D ⚡ ⇤ ⊀ 🔥 SC 👫

★★ **OMNI BERKSHIRE PLACE.** 21 E 52nd St (10022), between Madison and 5th Aves, in Midtown. 212/753-5800; FAX 212/754-5020. Web www.omnihotels.com. 396 rms, 21 story, 64 suites. S, D $355-$395; each addl $30; suites $800-$1,200; under 17 free; wkend rates (2-day min). Valet parking $32. TV; cable (premium), VCR avail. Restaurant 6:30 am-9 pm; wkend hrs vary, entertainment. Rm serv 24 hrs. Bar 11-1:30 am. Ck-out noon. Meeting rms. Business center. In-rm modem link. Concierge. Gift shop. Exercise equipt. Health club privileges. Minibars. Balconies. Cr cds: A, C, D, DS, ER, JCB, MC, V.

D ⊀ ⇤ ⊠ SC 👫

★★ **PARAMOUNT.** 235 W 46th St (10036), between Broadway & Eighth Ave, Times Square/Theater District. 212/764-5500; FAX 212/354-5237; res: 800/225-7474. 600 rms, 20 story. S $180-$270; D $205-$285; each addl $20; suites $425-$550; under 16 free; monthly rates; wkend packages. Crib free. Garage $20. TV; cable (premium), VCR (movies). Restaurant 7-1 am; Fri, Sat to 2 am. Bar 4 pm-4 am; Sun to 3 am. Ck-out noon. Meeting rms. Business center. In-rm modem link. Concierge. Exercise equipt. Public areas and guest rms designed in a high-tech, futuristic style. Cr cds: A, D, DS, JCB, MC, V.

D ⊀ ⇤ ⊠ 🔥 👫

★★ **PARKER MERIDIEN.** 118 W 57th St (10019), between 6th & 7th Aves, Midtown. 212/245-5000; FAX 212/708-7477; res: 800/543-4300. Web www.parkermeridien.com. 700 rms, 42 story. S $325-$365; D $350-$390; each addl $30; suites $395-$2,500; under 12 free; wkend rates. Crib free. Pet accepted. Garage parking, valet $32. TV; VCR avail. Indoor pool; whirlpool. Restaurant 6:30 am-10:45 pm. Rm serv 24 hrs. Bar 3 pm-midnight. Ck-out 1 pm. Business center. In-rm modem link. Exercise rm; sauna. Microwaves avail. French ambience; Italian marble flooring, French tapestries. Cr cds: A, C, D, DS, ER, JCB, MC, V.

D ⚡ ≋ ⊀ ⇤ ⊠ 🔥 👫

★★★★ **THE PIERRE.** 2 E 61st St (10021), at Fifth Ave, Midtown. 212/838-8000; FAX 212/940-8109; res: 800/743-7734. Web www.fourseasons.com. Personal service and traditional style are hallmarks of this landmark at Central Park. 202 rms, 42 story. S $425-$625; D $475-$675; suites $695-$1,100; under 12 free. Crib free. Garage $37. TV; cable (premium), VCR avail. Restaurants 7-1 am (also see CAFE PIERRE; and see THE ROTUNDA, Unrated Dining). Rm serv 24 hrs. Bar from 11 am; entertainment from 8 pm. Ck-out noon. Meeting rms. Business servs avail. In-rm modem link. Concierge. Barber, beauty shop. Exercise equipt. Massage. Health club privileges. Minibars. Serv pantry in suites. Cr cds: A, C, D, DS, ER, JCB, MC, V.

D ⊀ ⇤ ⊠ 🔥

★★★★ **PLAZA ATHÉNÉE.** 37 E 64th St (10021), between Madison & Park Aves, Upper East Side. 212/734-9100; FAX 212/772-0958; res: 800/447-8800. Marble, reproductions of fine antiques, and Oriental rugs add style to this tastefully decorated hotel in the mode of the Paris original. The property is grand, but on an intimate scale. 153 rms, 17 story. S, D $370-$560; each addl $35; suites $790-$3,000. Crib free. Parking $42/day. TV; cable (premium), VCR avail. Restaurant 7 am-9:30 pm (also see LE RÉGENCE). Rm serv 24 hrs. Bar 11 am-midnight. Ck-out 1 pm. Meeting rm. Business servs avail. In-rm modem link. Concierge. Exercise equipt. Health club privileges. Refrigerators. Some suites with private dining rm. Some private patios, glassed-in balconies. Cr cds: A, C, D, ER, JCB, MC, V.

D ⊀ ⇤ ⊠ 🔥

★★★ **PLAZA FIFTY.** 155 E 50th St (10022), between Lexington & 3rd Aves, Midtown. 212/751-5710; FAX 212/753-1468; res: 800/637-8483. E-mail info@mesuite.com; web www.mesuite.com. 211 rms, 22 story, 137 suites. S $229; D $249; each addl $20; suites $279-$459; under 12 free; wkend rates. Crib free. TV; cable (premium). Coffee in rms. Ck-out noon. Business servs avail. In-rm modem link. Exercise equipt. Refrigerators, microwaves. Some balconies. Cr cds: A, C, D, DS, ER, JCB, MC, V.

D ⊀ ⇤ ⊠ 🔥

★★★★ **THE PLAZA HOTEL.** Fifth Ave at 59th St & Central Park South (10019), Midtown. 212/759-3000; FAX 212/759-3167; res: 800/759-3000. E-mail plaza@fairmont.com; web www.fairmont.com. Set on the southwest corner of Central Park West and Fifth Avenue, the world-renowned Plaza occupies one of the most valuable pieces of real estate in Manhattan. Spacious guest rooms are furnished in fine period details, including marble fireplaces and crystal chandeliers. A drink at the Oak Bar or brunch at Palm Court are New York experiences that should not be missed. 805 rms, 18 story. S, D $275-$725; each addl $35; suites $500-$4,000; under 18 free; wkend rates. Crib free. Garage $35. TV; cable (premium), VCR avail. Restaurants (see OAK ROOM and PALM COURT). Rm serv 24 hrs. Bar 11-2 am. Ck-out noon. Business center. In-rm modem link. Concierge. Gift shop. Barber, beauty shop. Exercise equipt. Health club privileges. Refrigerators, minibars. Cr cds: A, C, D, DS, ER, JCB, MC, V.

D ⊀ ⇤ ⊠ 🔥 SC 👫

★ **QUALITY HOTEL FIFTH AVENUE.** 3 E 40th St (10016), between Fifth & Madison Aves, Midtown. 212/447-1500; FAX 212/213-0972. 189 rms, 30 story. S, D $225-$275; each addl $15; wkend rates; under 18 free. Crib free. Garage parking $19. TV; cable (premium). Complimentary coffee in rms. Restaurant nearby. Ck-out noon. Business servs avail. In-rm modem link. Health club privileges. Cr cds: A, C, D, DS, ER, JCB, MC, V.

D ⇤ 🔥 SC

★★ **RADISSON EMPIRE.** 44 W 63rd St (10023), at Lincoln Center, Upper West Side. 212/265-7400; FAX 212/315-0349. 375 rms, 11 story. S, D $220-$290; each addl $20; suites $350-$650; under 17 free. Crib free. Garage $29. TV; cable (premium), VCR (movies). Restaurant 6:30-11 am, 5 pm-midnight. Rm serv 24 hrs. Bar 11 am-midnight. Ck-out noon. Business servs avail. In-rm modem link. Health club privileges. Cr cds: A, C, D, DS, ER, JCB, MC, V.

D ⇤ 🔥 SC

✔★★ **RAMADA MILFORD PLAZA.** 270 W 45th St (10036), at Eighth Ave, Times Square/Theater District. 212/869-3600; FAX 212/944-8357. 1,300 rms, 28 story. S $109-$225; D $124-$240; each addl $15; suites $200-$450; under 14 free. Crib free. Garage $14. TV; cable (premium). Restaurant 7 am-11 pm. Bar from noon. Ck-out noon. Convention facilities. Business servs avail. In-rm modem link. Exercise equipt. Refrigerators avail. Cr cds: A, C, D, DS, ER, JCB, MC, V.

⊀ 🔥 SC

★ ★ ★ ★ **REGAL U.N. PLAZA HOTEL.** *1 UN Plaza (10017), at First Ave & E 44th St, on the East Side.* 212/758-1234; res: 800/228-9000; FAX 212/702-5051. Web www.regal-hotels.com/newyorkcity. Guest rooms in this modern chrome-and-glass tower offer fine views of UN Headquarters and the surrounding area. 427 rms on floors 28-38, 45 suites. S, D $350; each addl $35; suites $500-$1,500; under 18 free; wkend rates. Crib free. Garage; valet parking $27, wkends $20. TV; cable (premium), VCR avail. Indoor pool; lifeguard. Restaurant (see AMBASSADOR GRILL). Bar noon-1 am. Ck-out noon. Meeting rms. Business center. In-rm modem link. Indoor tennis. Exercise rm; sauna, steam rm. Massage. Minibars, bathrm phones; some refrigerators; microwaves avail. Cr cds: A, C, D, DS, ER, JCB, MC, V.

★ ★ ★ ★ **THE REGENCY HOTEL.** *540 Park Ave (10021), at E 61st St, Upper East Side.* 212/759-4100; FAX 212/826-5674; res: 800/233-2356. Web www.loewshotels.com. The graceful guest rooms here are decorated with period furniture, and suites have marble foyers. 362 rms, 21 story, 185 kit. suites. S, D $335-$415; suites $470-$2,500; under 18 free; wkend rates. Crib free. Garage $40. TV; cable (premium), VCR. Restaurant (see 540 PARK). Rm serv 24 hrs. Ck-out 1 pm. Meeting rms. Business center. In-rm modem link. Concierge. Barber, beauty shop. Exercise rm; sauna. Massage. Refrigerators, bathrm TVs. Cr cds: A, C, D, DS, MC, V.

★ ★ ★ **RENAISSANCE NEW YORK.** *714 7th Ave (10036), Times Square/Theater District, between 47th & 48th Sts.* 212/765-7676; FAX 212/765-1962. Web www.renaissancehotels.com. 305 rms, 26 story. S, D $275-$330; each addl $20; suites $425-$475; under 12 free; wkend rates. Crib free. Garage $29-$39. TV; cable (premium), VCR. Complimentary coffee in rms. Restaurant 6:30 am-11 pm. Rm serv 24 hrs. Bar; pianist. Ck-out noon. Meeting rms. Business servs avail. In-rm modem link. Concierge. Massage. Exercise equipt. Minibars. Cr cds: A, C, D, DS, ER, JCB, MC, V.

★ ★ ★ **RIHGA ROYAL.** *151 W 54th St (10019), between Sixth and Seventh Aves, Midtown.* 212/307-5000; FAX 212/765-6530; res: 800/937-5454. E-mail debbie@rihga.com; web www.rihga.com. 496 suites, 54 story. 1-bedrm $425-$575; 2-bedrm $900-$1,900; each addl $25; Crown suites $1,600; Grand Royal suites S, D $2,800-$3,100; family; package plans. Crib free. Garage, valet parking $37. TV; cable, VCR. Restaurant 6:30-1 am. Rm serv 24 hrs. Bar 11:30-2 am; entertainment. Ck-out 1 pm. Meeting rms. Business center. In-rm modem link. Concierge. Exercise rm; sauna. Bathrm phones, refrigerators, minibars. Architecturally reminiscent of the classic skyscrapers of the 1920s and 1930s. Cr cds: A, C, D, DS, ER, JCB, MC, V.

★ ★ **ROGER WILLIAMS.** *131 Madison Ave (10016), in Murray Hill.* 212/448-7000; FAX 212/448-7007. 200 rms, 20 with shower only, 15 story. S, D $205-$275; each addl $15; suites $375; under 12 free. Crib free. TV; cable (premium), VCR (movies). Complimentary continental bkfst; afternoon refreshments. Restaurant nearby. Ck-out 1 pm. Business servs avail. In-rm modem link. Concierge. Health club privileges. Bathrm phones. Cr cds: A, D, MC, V.

★ ★ **ROOSEVELT.** *45 E 45th St (10017), between 45th St & Madison Ave, Midtown.* 212/661-9600. Web www.theroosevelthotel.com. 1,013 rms, 100 with shower only, 19 story. S $219-$259; D $239-$279; each addl $20; suites $275-$1800; under 18 free. Crib free. Pet accepted, some restrictions; $50. Valet parking $36. TV; cable, VCR avail. Restaurant 6:30 am-11 pm. Bar noon-2 am. Ck-out noon. Convention facilities. Business center. In-rm modem link. Concierge. Gift shop. Beauty shop. Exercise equipt. Cr cds: A, C, D, DS, ER, JCB, MC, V.

★ ★ ★ **ROYALTON.** *44 W 44th St (10036), between Fifth & Sixth Aves, Midtown.* 212/869-4400; FAX 212/869-8965; res: 800/635-9013. 205 rms, some with shower only, 16 story. S $305-$410; D $340-$475;

each addl $30; suites $475; wkend rates. Crib $25. Pet accepted, some restrictions. Valet parking $38. TV; cable (premium), VCR (movies). Restaurant 7-1 am. Rm serv 24 hrs. Bar. Ck-out 1 pm. Meeting rm. Business servs avail. In-rm modem link. Concierge. Exercise equipt. Bathrm phones, refrigerators, minibars; some fireplaces. Some balconies. Ultra-modern rm decor. Cr cds: A, C, D, ER, JCB, MC, V.

★ ★ **SALISBURY.** *123 W 57th St (10019), between 6th & 7th Aves, Midtown.* 212/246-1300; res: 888/223-5757; FAX 212/977-7752. E-mail nycsalisbury@worldnet.att.net; web www.nycsalisbury.com. 320 rms, 17 story. S $219; D $239; each addl $20; suites $269-$399; under 15 free; wkend rates. Crib free. TV; cable, VCR avail. Complimentary continental bkfst. Ck-out noon. Meeting rms. Business servs avail. In-rm modem link. Concierge. Health club privileges. Many refrigerators, microwaves. Cr cds: A, C, D, JCB, MC, V.

★ ★ **SAN CARLOS.** *150 E 50th St (10022), Midtown, between Lexington & 3rd.* 212/755-1800; FAX 212/688-9778; res: 800/722-2012. E-mail sancarlos@pobox.com; web www.sancarloshotel.com. 200 rms, 18 story, 138 kits. S $170-$190; D $180-$195; each addl $10; suites $225-$350; under 14 free; wkend rates. Crib free. TV, cable (premium). Complimentary continental bkfst. Restaurant 6 am-11 pm. Ck-out 11 am. Coin lndry. In-rm modem link. Microwaves. Cr cds: A, C, D, JCB, MC, V.

★ ★ ★ **SHELBURNE MURRAY HILL.** *303 Lexington Ave (10016), between 37th & 38th Sts, Murray Hill.* 212/689-5200; FAX 212/779-7068; res: 800/637-8483. Web www.mesuite.com. 258 suites, 16 story. Suites $259-$500; under 12 free; wkend rates. Garage parking $27. TV; cable (premium), VCR avail. Restaurant 7 am-11 pm. Bar. Ck-out noon. Coin lndry. Convention facilities. Business servs avail. In-rm modem link. Concierge. Exercise equipt; sauna. Microwaves. Private patios, balconies. Cr cds: A, C, D, DS, JCB, MC, V.

★ ★ ★ **SHERATON MANHATTAN.** *790 Seventh Ave (10019), between W 51st & 52nd Sts, Midtown.* 212/581-3300; FAX 212/262-4410. 663 rms, 22 story. S, D $209-$299; each addl $30; suites $575-$770; under 17 free; wkend rates. Crib free. Garage $25. TV; cable (premium), VCR avail. Indoor pool; lifeguard. Complimentary continental bkfst. Complimentary coffee in rms. Restaurant noon-11 pm; Sat, Sun from 4 pm. Rm serv 24 hrs. Bar 11 am-11 pm. Ck-out noon. Business center. In-rm modem link. Concierge. Exercise rm. Minibars. Refrigerators, microwaves avail. Cr cds: A, C, D, DS, ER, JCB, MC, V.

★ ★ ★ **SHERATON NEW YORK HOTEL & TOWERS.** *811 Seventh Ave (10019), between 52nd & 53rd Sts, Midtown.* 212/581-1000; FAX 212/262-4410. Web www.sheraton.com. 1,746 rms, 50 story. S, D $199-$289; each addl $30; suites $450-$965; under 17 free; wkend rates. Crib free. Garage $35. TV; cable (premium), VCR avail. Pool privileges. Complimentary coffee in rms. Restaurant 6:30 am-midnight. Bars 11:30-4 am. Ck-out noon. Convention facilities. Business center. In-rm modem link. Gift shop. Exercise rm; sauna. Minibars. Luxury level. Cr cds: A, C, D, DS, ER, JCB, MC, V.

★ ★ ★ **SHERATON RUSSELL.** *45 Park Ave (10016), in Murray Hill.* 212/685-7676; res: 800/537-0075; FAX 212/889-3193. Web sheraton hotelsofny.com/ittsheraton.com. 146 rms, 10 story, 26 suites. S, D $260-$425; suites $395-$595; under 17 free; wkend rates. Crib free. Valet, garage parking $35. TV; cable (premium), VCR avail. Complimentary continental bkfst. Complimentary coffee in rms. Rm serv 24 hrs. Bar from 5 pm. Ck-out 5 pm. Meeting rm. Business center. In-rm modem link. Concierge. Exercise equipt. Health club privileges. Pool privileges. Bathrm phones, minibars; many fireplaces. Cr cds: A, C, D, DS, ER, JCB, MC, V.

★ ★ **THE SHOREHAM.** *33 W 55th St (10019), between Fifth & Sixth Aves, Midtown.* 212/247-6700; FAX 212/765-9741; res: 800/553-3347. E-mail shorehotel@aol.com; web www.vacation-inc.com. 84 rms, 11 story, 37 suites. S, D $275; suites $335; wkend, hol rates. Crib free. Valet parking $18. TV; cable (premium), VCR (free movies). Complimentary continental bkfst. Restaurant nearby. Ck-out noon. Business servs avail. In-rm modem link. Concierge. Health club privileges. Refrigerators. Renovated hotel built 1930. Cr cds: A, D, MC, V.

D ⌧ ⟲ SC

★ ★ **SOHO GRAND.** *310 W Broadway (10013), between Grand & Canal St, in SoHo.* 212/965-3000; res: 800/965-3000; FAX 212/965-3200. Web www.sohogrand.com. 369 rms, 17 story. S $259-$369; D $279-$389; each addl $20; suites $1,049-$1,249; under 12 free. Crib free. Pet accepted. Garage parking $25. TV; cable (premium), VCR avail. Restaurant 6 am-midnight; Sat, Sun from 7 am. Rm serv 24 hrs. Bar noon-2 am; Sat, Sun from 1 pm. Ck-out noon. Meeting rms. Business center. In-rm modem link. Concierge. Free valet parking. Exercise equipt. Massage. Minibars. Cr cds: A, D, DS, JCB, MC, V.

D ⤢ ⌨ ⌧ ⟲

★ ★ ★ **SOUTHGATE TOWER SUITE.** *371 Seventh Ave (10001), at 31st St, south of Midtown.* 212/563-1800; FAX 212/643-8028; res: 800/637-8483. Web www.mesuite.com. 522 kit. suites, 28 story. S $189-$229; D $219-$279; each addl $20; suites $399-$439; wkend, wkly, monthly rates. Crib free. TV; cable (premium). Complimentary coffee. Restaurant 7 am-midnight. Ck-out noon. Coin lndry. Meeting rms. Business servs avail. Concierge. Barber. Exercise equipt. Some balconies. Cr cds: A, C, D, DS, ER, JCB, MC, V.

D ⌨ ⌧ ⟲

★ ★ ★ ★ ★ **THE ST REGIS HOTEL.** *2 E 55th St (10022), at Fifth Ave, Midtown.* 212/753-4500; FAX 212/787-3447; res: 800/759-7550. Web www.ittsheraton.com. Even in big, brash New York in the turbulent '90s, elegant tradition can be maintained. The St Regis, built by John Jacob Astor in 1904, has been restored to its Louis XV style. 313 rms, 20 story, 92 suites. S, D $520-$640; suites $895-$9,500; wkend rates. Crib free. Garage parking, valet, in/out $38. TV; cable (premium), VCR. Restaurant (see LESPINASSE). Afternoon tea in Astor Court 3-5:30 pm; harpist. Rm serv 24 hrs. Bar 11:30-1 am; Fri, Sat 11:30-2 am; Sun noon-midnight. Ck-out noon. Meeting rms. Business center. In-rm modem link. Concierge. Extensive shopping arcade. Barber, beauty shop. Exercise rm; sauna. Massage. Health club privileges. Bathrm phones. Cr cds: A, C, D, DS, ER, JCB, MC, V.

D ⌨ ⌧ ⟲ SC ⚲

✔ ★ **STANFORD.** *43 W 32nd St (10001), between Fifth Ave & Broadway, near Macy's, south of Midtown.* 212/563-1480; FAX 212/629-0043; res: 800/365-1114. E-mail stanfordny@aol.com. 121 rms, 12 story, 30 suites. S $90-$110; D $120-$150; each addl $20; suites $180-$200. Crib free. TV; cable. Complimentary continental bkfst. Restaurant 7 am-10 pm. Ck-out noon. Business servs avail. In-rm modem link. Refrigerators. Near Madison Square Garden. Cr cds: A, C, D, JCB, MC, V.

D ⟲ SC

★ ★ ★ **THE STANHOPE.** *995 Fifth Ave (10028), at 81st St, opp Metropolitan Museum of Art, Upper East Side.* 212/288-5800; FAX 212/517-0088; res: 800/828-1123. This stylish 1926 landmark hotel is across the street from Central Park. Many rooms offer views of the Manhattan skyline. 140 units, 17 story, 48 suites, some with kits. S, D $350-$425; suites $450-$1,350; under 12 free; wkend rates; package plans. Crib free. Garage $38. TV; cable (premium), VCR (movies). Restaurant 7 am-11 pm. Rm serv 24 hrs. Bar noon-1 am. Ck-out 1 pm. Meeting rms. In-rm modem link. Exercise equipt; sauna. Bathrm phones, minibars; some wet bars; microwaves avail. Cr cds: A, C, D, DS, JCB, MC, V.

D ⌨ ⌧ ⟲

★ ★ **SURREY.** *20 E 76th St (10021), Upper East Side.* 212/288-3700; res: 800/637-8483; FAX 212/628-1549. Web www.mesuite.com. 131 rms, 16 story. S $290-$310; D $310-$330; each addl $20; suites $345-$655; under 12 free; wkly, monthly rates; wkend rates. Crib avail.

Valet parking $35. TV; cable (premium), VCR (movies). Restaurant noon-3 pm, 5:30-11 pm. Bar. Ck-out noon. Coin lndry. Meeting rms. Business servs avail. In-rm modem link. Concierge. Exercise equipt. Health club privileges. Refrigerators, microwaves avail. Cr cds: A, C, D, DS, JCB, MC, V.

D ⌨ ⌧ ⟲

★ ★ ★ **SWISSÔTEL NEW YORK-THE DRAKE.** *440 Park Ave (10022), at E 56th St, Midtown.* 212/421-0900; FAX 212/371-4190; res: 800/372-5369. Web premierhotels.com. 495 units, 108 suites, 21 story. S $325-$345; D $345-$375; each addl $30; 1-, 2-bedrm suites $475-$1,500; under 12 free; wkend rates. Crib free. Garage $36. TV; cable (premium), VCR avail. Restaurant 6:30 am-11 pm. Rm serv 24 hrs. Bar noon-1 am. Ck-out noon. Conference facilities. Business center. In-rm modem link. Concierge. Exercise rm; sauna, steam rm. Spa. Health club privileges. Bathrm phones, minibars. Wet bar in suites. Cr cds: A, C, D, DS, ER, JCB, MC, V.

D ⌨ ⌧ ⟲ ⚲ ⚲

★ ★ ★ ★ ★ **TRUMP INTERNATIONAL HOTEL & TOWER.** *1 Central Park W (10023), at Columbus Circle, Midtown.* 212/299-1000; res: 888/448-7867; FAX 212/299-1150. Web www.preferredhotels.com; E-mail kruble@trumpintl.com. Offering stunning views of Central Park and Hudson River, this hotel is one of the newest to grace the skyline in New Yourk City. 68 kit. units, 52 story, 130 suites. S, D $395-$475; suites $625-$1,325; wkend rates. Crib free. Valet parking $42. TV; cable (premium), VCR (movies). Restaurant (see JEAN GEORGES). Rm serv 24 hrs. Bar. Ck-out noon. Business center. In-rm modem link. Concierge. Exercise rm; sauna, steam rm. Massage. Indoor pool. Bathrm phones, in-rm whirlpools, refrigerators, microwaves, minibars. Cr cds: A, C, D, JCB, MC, V.

D ⌧ ⟲ ⌨ ⌧ ⟲ ⚲

★ ★ **"W".** *541 Lexington Ave (10022), between 49th & 50th Sts, Midtown.* 212/755-1200; FAX 212/319-8344; res: 800/223-6725 (NY). 652 rms, 18 story. S, D $249-$279; each addl $15; 1-2 bedrm suites $425. Crib free. Garage parking $27, valet. TV; cable (premium), VCR. Ck-out noon. Business servs avail. Concierge. Exercise rm; sauna. Minibars. Cr cds: A, C, D, DS, ER, JCB, MC, V.

D ⌨ ⌧ ⟲ SC

★ ★ ★ **"W" COURT.** *130 E 39th St (10016), between Park & Lexington Aves, Murray Hill.* 212/685-1100; FAX 212/889-0287; res: 800/223-6725. 199 rms, 16 story, 53 kit. suites. S $175-$275; D $195-$295; each addl $20; kit. suites $250-$500; under 12 free; wkend rates. Crib free. Garage $25; wkends $19. TV; cable (premium). Restaurant 7-10 am, noon-2 pm, 5-10 pm. Rm serv 24 hrs. Bar 5 pm-midnight. Ck-out 1 pm. Meeting rms. Business servs avail. Concierge. Health club privileges. Refrigerators. Some balconies. Restored hotel in quiet residential neighborhood. Cr cds: A, C, D, DS, JCB, MC, V.

⌧ ⟲ SC

★ ★ ★ **"W" TUSCANY.** *120 E 39th St (10016), between Park & Lexington Aves, Murray Hill.* 212/686-1600; FAX 212/779-7822; res: 800/22-DORAL. 121 rms, 17 story. S $185-$285; D $205-$305; each addl $20; suites $400-$850; under 12 free. Crib free. Garage $25. TV; cable (premium). Restaurant 7-10:30 am, noon-2:30 pm, 5 pm-midnight. Rm serv 6 am-10 pm. Bar 5 pm-midnight. Ck-out 1 pm. Business servs avail. Bathrm phones, refrigerators, minibars. Cr cds: A, C, D, DS, JCB, MC, V.

⌧ ⟲ SC

★ ★ ★ **WALDORF-ASTORIA & WALDORF TOWERS.** *301 Park Ave (10022), between E 49th & 50th Sts, Midtown.* 212/355-3000; FAX 212/872-7272; res: 800/925-3673. Web www.hilton.com. This art-deco masterpiece personifies New York at its most lavish and powerful. The richly tinted, hushed lobby serves as an interior centerpoint of city life. 1,219 rms, 42 story. S $310-$390; D $350-$430; each addl $40; suites $460-$1,875; children free; wkend rates. Crib free. Garage $37-$45/day. TV; cable (premium), VCR avail (movies). Restaurant 7 am-11:45 pm (also see BULL & BEAR STEAKHOUSE and PEACOCK ALLEY). Rm serv 24 hrs. Bars 10:30-2:30 am; Sun noon-1 am. Ck-out noon. Convention facilities. Business center. In-rm modem link. Concierge. Barber, beauty shop.

Shopping arcade. Extensive exercise rm; steam rm. Massage. Refrigerators, minibars. Luxury level. Cr cds: A, C, D, DS, ER, JCB, MC, V.

★ ★ **WALES.** *1295 Madison Ave (10128), between 92nd & 93rd Sts, Upper East Side.* 212/876-6000; FAX 212/860-7000; res: 800/428-5252 (exc NYC). E-mail hotelwales@aol.com; web www.vacations-inc.com. 92 units, 10 story, 40 suites. S, D $195; each addl $25; suites $279. Crib free. Valet parking $28. TV; cable (premium), VCR (free movies). Complimentary continental bkfst; afternoon refreshments. Restaurant 8 am-11 pm. Harpist 5-6 pm Mon-Fri, chamber music 6-8 pm Sun, pianist 8-10 am. Ck-out 1 pm. Business servs avail. Health club privileges. Refrigerators avail. Restored 1902 hotel; original fireplaces. Cr cds: A, MC, V.

★ ★ ★ **WARWICK.** *65 W 54th St (10019), at 6th Ave, Midtown.* 212/247-2700; FAX 212/957-8915; res: 800/223-4099. E-mail sales.ny@warwickhotels.com; web www.warwickhotels.com. 425 rms, 33 story. S $255-$300; D $280-$325; each addl $25; suites $500-$1,200; under 12 free; wkend rates. Crib free. Garage $26-$40. TV; cable (premium). Restaurant 6:30 am-11 pm. Bar 11-1 am. Ck-out 1 pm. Meeting rms. Business center. Exercise equipt. Health club privileges. Microwaves avail. Many terraces. Cr cds: A, C, D, JCB, MC, V.

★ ★ ★ **THE WESTIN CENTRAL PARK SOUTH.** *112 Central Park South (10019), near 6th Ave, Midtown.* 212/757-1900; res: 800/937-8461; FAX 212/757-9620. Web www.westin.com. 208 rms, 25 story. S, D $199-$529; suites $595-$4,000. Crib free. Garage $39. TV; cable (premium), VCR avail. Restaurant (see FANTINO). Rm serv 24 hrs. Bar noon-1 am. Ck-out noon. Business center. In-rm modem link. Exercise equipt; sauna. Massage. Health club privileges. Some refrigerators. Cr cds: A, C, D, DS, ER, JCB, MC, V.

✔★ ★ **WYNDHAM.** *42 W 58th St (10019), off 5th Ave, Midtown.* 212/753-3500; FAX 212/754-5638. 204 rms, 16 story. S $125-$140; D $140-$155; suites $180-$210. Crib free. TV. Restaurant 7:30 am-10:30 pm. Bar from noon. Ck-out 1 pm. Business servs avail. In-rm modem link. Garage adj. Refrigerator, serv pantry in suites. Cr cds: A, D, MC, V.

Inns

★ ★ **BOX TREE.** *250 E 49th St (10017), at Second Ave, Midtown.* 212/758-8320; FAX 212/308-3899. 13 suites in 2 townhouses, 3 story. MAP (Fri & Sat): D $330-$350; lower rates (AP) wkdays. TV. Complimentary continental bkfst. Restaurant (see BOX TREE). Fri, Sat dining credit $100 per night included in MAP rates. Ck-out 11:30 am, ck-in 3 pm. Concierge. Bathrm phones, fireplaces. 1840s brownstones; antique furnishings; imported French amenities; rms individually decorated. Cr cds: A, D, MC, V.

✔★ **BROADWAY INN.** *264 W 46th St (10036).* 212/997-9200; FAX 212/768-2807; res: 800/826-6300. E-mail broadwayinn@att.net; web www.broadwayinn.com. 41 rms, 15 with shower only, 3 story. S $85-$185; D $115-$195; each addl $10; suites $195; under 12 free. TV; cable. Complimentary continental bkfst. Restaurant noon-4 am. Rm serv 24 hrs. Ck-out noon, ck-in 3 pm. Luggage handling. Some refrigerators, microwaves. Cr cds: A, D, DS, MC, V.

★ ★ ★ **INN AT IRVING PLACE.** *56 Irving Place (10003), between 17th & 18th Sts, in Gramercy Park.* 212/533-4600; FAX 212/533-4611; res: 800/685-1447. E-mail irving56@aol.com; web www.slh.com. 12 rms, 2 with shower only, 4 story. S $275; D $325-$350; each addl $25; suite $375; monthly rates. Children over 12 yrs only. TV; cable (premium), VCR (movies). Complimentary continental bkfst; afternoon refreshments. Dining rm noon-3 pm, 5-10 pm. Bar. Rm serv 24 hrs. Bar. Ck-out noon, ck-in 3 pm. Luggage handling. Business servs avail. In-rm modem link. Health

club privileges. Refrigerators, minibars. Elegant country-style inn with all modern conveniences. Cr cds: A, C, D, MC, V.

Restaurants

★ ★ **2 SEVEN 7 CHURCH ST.** *277 Church St (10013), between White & Franklin, in Tribeca.* 212/625-0505. Web www.277church.com. Hrs: 6 pm-1 am; Thurs, Fri, Sun to 2 am. Closed major hols. Res accepted. Eclectic menu. Bar. A la carte entrees: $19-$39. Specialties: seared Dartagnan duck, ginger snap-crusted rack of lamb, grilled New Zealand vension loin with rhubarb chutney. Street parking. Sophisticated decor. Totally nonsmoking. Cr cds: A, MC, V.

✔★ ★ **20 MOTT STREET.** *20 Mott St (10013), between Pell & Bowery Sts, in Chinatown.* 212/964-0380. Chinese menu. Specialties: dim sum, baked conch with curry sauce, filet mignon with black pepper sauce. Hrs: 9 am-11 pm; Sat, Sun from 8:30 am. A la carte entrees: dim sum from $1.90, lunch, dinner $7.95-$20. Fish tank. Cr cds: A, DS, JCB, MC, V.

★ ★ ★ **21 CLUB.** *21 W 52nd St (10019), between Fifth & Sixth Aves, Midtown.* 212/582-7200. Specialties: steak tartare, "21" burger. Own pastries. Hrs: noon-11 pm. Closed Sun; major hols; also Sat (July 4-Labor Day). Res accepted. Bar. Wine cellar. A la carte entrees: lunch $21-$39, dinner $24-$39. Prix fixe: lunch $25. Pre-theater dinner $29. Jacket. Cr cds: A, C, D, DS, JCB, MC, V.

★ ★ ★ **540 PARK.** *(See The Regency Hotel)* 212/339-4050. Web www.loewshotels.com. Specialties: cornmeal crusted cedar planked salmon, chicken fried lobster, BBQ duck & black bean quesadilla. Hrs: 7 am-10 pm; Sat, Sun brunch 11 am-3 pm. Res accepted. Bar noon-1 am. Wine cellar. A la carte entrees: bkfst $8-$20, lunch $13.50-$25, dinner $19-$30. Sun brunch $18-$24. Child's meals. Cr cds: A, C, D, DS, MC, V.

★ ★ ★ **ALISON ON DOMINICK STREET.** *38 Dominick St (10013), between Hudson & Varick Sts, in SoHo.* 212/727-1188. Country French menu. Specialties: grilled rabbit sausage, roast rack of lamb, sautéed halibut. Hrs: 5:30-10:30 pm; Fri, Sat to 11 pm; Sun to 9:30 pm; pre-theater dinner to 6:15 pm. Closed Labor Day, Dec 25; 1st wk July. Res accepted. Bar. Wine cellar. A la carte entrees: dinner $24-$35. Pre-theater dinner $34. Intimate and romantic dining. Cr cds: A, D, MC, V.

★ ★ ★ **ALVA.** *36 E 22nd St (10010), in Gramercy Park area.* 212/228-4399. E-mail alvausa@onepine.com. Specialties: grilled lamb chops, salmon gravlox club, grilled mahi mahi. Own desserts. Hrs: noon-3 pm, 5:30-midnight; Sat, Sun from 5:30 pm. Res accepted. Bar. A la carte entrees: lunch $10-$20, dinner $15-$24. Cr cds: A, D, MC, V.

★ ★ ★ **AMBASSADOR GRILL.** *(See Regal U.N. Plaza Hotel)* 212/702-5014. Specialties: rotisserie special, grilled shrimp, grilled double veal chop. Hrs: 7 am-2:30 pm, 5-10:30 pm; Sun brunch sittings: 11:30 am & 1:45 pm. Res accepted. Bar to midnight, Sat to 2 am. Wine list. A la carte entrees: lunch $14-$24, dinner $23-$27. Buffet: bkfst $19. Sun brunch $48. Child's meals. Valet parking. Modern decor. Jacket. Cr cds: A, C, D, DS, ER, JCB, MC, V.

★ ★ **AMERICAN FESTIVAL.** *20 W 50th St (10019), between Fifth & Sixth Aves, at Rockefeller Center, Midtown.* 212/332-7621. Web www.restaurantassoc.com. Regional Amer menu. Hrs: 7:30 am-11 pm; Fri to midnight; Sat 8:30 am-midnight; Sun 8:30 am-10 pm; Sat, Sun brunch 11 am-3 pm (Nov-Apr). Res accepted. Bar noon-11 pm. A la carte entrees: bkfst $6.95-$12.95, lunch, dinner $14-$28; Sat, Sun brunch $19.98. Prix fixe: dinner $23.95, $26.95. Seasonal dishes. Parking (after 5 pm; wkends after 11 am). Outdoor dining (May-Oct). Overlooks Rockefeller Center's famous Prometheus fountain and sunken pool (summer); skating rink (winter). Cr cds: A, C, D, JCB, MC, V.

★ ★ ★ **AMERICAN PARK.** *(10004), in Battery Park off State St, in Financial District. 212/809-5508.* Hrs: 11:45 am-3 pm, 5-10 pm; Sat brunch 11:45-3:30 pm; Sun (brunch) 11:45 am-5 pm. Closed major hols. Res accepted. Seafood menu. Bar. Wine list. A la carte entrees: lunch $18-$23, dinner $19-$26. Sat, Sun brunch $12.50-$15. Specialties: grilled mahi-mahi, grilled baby octopus. Valet parking. Outdoor dining. Raw bar. Wraparound vistas of Statue of Liberty, bridges and ferries. Cr cds: A, D, DS, MC, V.

★ ★ ★ **AN AMERICAN PLACE.** *2 Park Ave (10016), on 32nd St, Midtown. 212/684-2122.* Specializes in seafood, game. Hrs: 11:45 am-3 pm, 5:30-9:30 pm; Sat from 5:30 pm. Closed Sun; major hols. Res accepted. Bar. Wine cellar. A la carte entrees: lunch $15-$22, dinner $25-$32. Art deco dining rm with Prairie School-style furniture. Cr cds: A, D, DS, MC, V.

★ ★ ★ **ANGELO AND MAXIE'S STEAKHOUSE.** *233 Park Ave S (10003), at 19th St, in Gramercy Park. 212/220-9200.* Specialties: Angelo and Maxie's 28-oz ribeye steak, porterhouse steak deluxe for two, grilled veal chop with lemon-parsley butter. Own desserts. Hrs: 11:30 am-4 pm, 5 pm-midnight; Fri to 1 am; Sat 5 pm-1 am; Sun 5-11 pm. Closed Dec 25. Res accepted. Bar. Wine list. A la carte entrees: lunch, dinner $9-$24. Complete meals: lunch $19.99. Bustling steakhouse; murals of cows in back rm. Cr cds: A, MC, V.

★ ★ ★ **AQUAGRILL.** *210 Spring St (10012), at 6th Ave, in SoHo. 212/274-0505.* Specializes in seafood. Hrs: noon-3 pm, 6-10:45 pm; Fri to 11:45 pm; Sat noon-4 pm, 6-11:45 pm; Sun 6-10:30 pm; Sat, Sun brunch noon-4 pm. Closed Mon; major hols. Res accepted. Bar. A la carte entrees: lunch $8.50-$18, dinner $18-$25. Sat, Sun brunch $8.50-$18. Outdoor dining. Casual decor. Totally nonsmoking. Cr cds: A, MC, V.

★ ★ ★ ★ **AQUAVIT.** *13 W 54th St (10019), between Fifth & Sixth Aves, Midtown. 212/307-7311.* A towering glass-walled atrium and indoor waterfall accent this cooly elegant restaurant set in a townhouse once owned by Nelson Rockefeller. The extensive wine list is accompanied by New York's largest selection of aquavits. Scandinavian menu. Specialties: Scandinavian shrimp, game salmon. Hrs: noon-2:45 pm, 5:30-10:15 pm; Sun brunch noon-2:45 pm. Closed major hols. Res accepted. Bar. Wine cellar. A la carte entrees: lunch, dinner $13-$18. Prix fixe: lunch $29, dinner $25-$62. Cr cds: A, D, MC, V.

★ ★ ★ **ARQUA.** *281 Church St (10013), at White St, in Tribeca. 212/334-1888.* Italian menu. Specializes in homemade pastas, Venetian cuisine, desserts. Hrs: noon-3 pm, 5-10 pm; Fri, Sat to 11:30 pm, Sun from 5 pm. Closed major hols; also last 2 wks Aug. Res accepted. Bar. A la carte entrees: lunch, dinner $16-$28. Prix fixe: (Mon-Fri): lunch $19.99, (Sat, Sun) dinner $30. Cr cds: A, D, MC, V.

★ ★ ★ **ARTOS.** *307 E 53rd St (10022), between 1st & 2nd Aves, Midtown. 212/838-0007.* Hrs: noon-3 pm, 5-10:30 pm; Fri to 11 pm; Sat 5-11 pm; early-bird dinner 5-6:30 pm. Closed Sun; also Jan 1, Dec 25. Res accepted. Greek, Mediterranean menu. Bar. Wine list. A la carte entrees: lunch $14.50-$18.95, dinner $16-$29. Specialties: mousaka, whole charbroiled striped bass, baby lamb chops with thyme & vegetables. Street parking. Colorful murals. Cr cds: A, D, MC, V.

★ ★ ★ ★ **AUREOLE.** *34 E 61st St (10021), between Madison & Park Aves, Upper East Side. 212/319-1660.* Charles Palmer's fashionable restaurant is one of the toughest reservations in town. The elegant townhouse location with lovely outdoor garden offers a lush, romantic setting. Contemporary Amer menu. Specializes in fish, game. Own baking. Hrs: noon-2:30 pm, 5:30-11 pm; Sat from 5:30 pm. Closed Sun; some major hols. Res required. Bar. Wine list. A la carte entrees: lunch $18-$28. Prix fixe: lunch $32, dinner $65. Tasting menu: dinner $85. Street parking. Jacket. Cr cds: A, C, D, JCB, MC, V.

★ ★ ★ **BALTHAZAR.** *80 Spring St (10012), between Broadway & Crosby, in SoHo. 212/965-1414.* Hrs: 7:30 am-5 pm, 6 pm-2 am; Fri, Sat to 3 am; Sun 7:30-11:30 am; Sat, Sun brunch 11:30 am-4 pm. Res required Sat (dinner). French menu. Bar. Wine cellar. A la carte entrees: bkfst $2.25-$6.50, lunch $9.50-$16, dinner $15.95-$25. Sat, Sun brunch $8.50-$19. Specialties: steak frites, chicken riesling sautéed with mushrooms, skate vigneronne sautéed with vegetables. Street parking. Traditional French brasserie. Raw bar. Cr cds: A, MC, V.

★ ★ **BALUCHI'S.** *193 Spring St (10012), between Sullivan & Thompson Sts, in SoHo. 212/226-2828.* Indian menu. Specialties: whole leg of lamb marinated, lamb curry in cardamun sauce, vegetable balls in tomato sauce. Hrs: noon-3 pm, 5-11 pm; Sat noon-11:30 pm; Sun noon-11 pm. Res accepted. Bar. Semi-a la carte: lunch, dinner $10.95-29.95. Own bread. Indian decor. Totally nonsmoking. Cr cds: A, D, JCB, MC, V.

★ ★ **BARAONDA.** *1439 Second Ave (10021), between 75th Ave & 2nd Ave, Upper East Side. 212/288-8555.* Hrs: noon-3 pm, 5:30 pm-1 am; Sun noon-midnight; Sun brunch noon-4 pm. Closed Dec 25. Res accepted. Italian menu. Bar. A la carte entrees: lunch $8-$20, dinner $12-$30. Sun brunch $8.50-$12.50. Specializes in pasta, fish, seafood. Street parking. Outdoor dining. Colorful art. Totally nonsmoking. Cr cds: A, C, MC, V.

★ ★ ★ ★ **BARBETTA.** *321 W 46th St (10036), between 8th & 9th Aves, Midtown. 212/246-9171.* E-mail barbetta90@aol.com; web www.barbettasrestaurant.com. An 18th-century Venetian harpsichord sets the mood in this venerable establishment, known for classic northern Italian cooking. The property comprises two elegant, antique-furnished townhouses and an enchanting garden with century-old trees, perfumed in season with magnolia, wisteria, jasmine and gardenia. Italian menu. Hrs: noon-2 pm, 5 pm-midnight. Closed Sun. Res accepted. A la carte entrees: lunch $14-$21, dinner (after 8 pm) $22-$29. Complete meal: pre-theater dinner $41. Cr cds: A, C, D, DS, JCB, MC, V.

★ ★ **BAROCCO.** *301 Church St (10013), between Walker & White Sts, in Tribeca. 212/431-1445.* Regional Italian menu. Specialties: ravioli verdi, calamari fritti, pappardelle noodles with squab. Own gelato. Hrs: noon-3 pm, 6-11 pm; Sat 6-11:30 pm; Sun 6-10:30 pm. Closed major hols. Res accepted. Bar. A la carte entrees: lunch $7-$20, dinner $13-$27. Casual trattoria dining in industrial loft space. Cr cds: A, D, MC, V.

★ ★ ★ **BAROLO.** *398 W Broadway (10012), between Spring & Broome Sts, in SoHo. 212/226-1102.* Northern Italian menu. Specialties: filet with barolo wine sauce, trenette with Genovese pesto, risotto with porcini mushrooms. Antipasto bar. Hrs: noon-midnight; Fri, Sat to 1 am. Res accepted. Bar to 2 am. A la carte entrees: lunch $11.50-$23, dinner $13.50-$28. Garden dining among cherry trees and fountain. Three levels of dining. Contemporary decor. Cr cds: A, D, MC, V.

★ ★ ★ **BECCO.** *355 W 46th St (10036), between 8th & 9th Aves, Times Square/Theater District. 212/397-7597.* Web www.lidiasitaly.com. Italian menu. Specialties: grilled rack of lamb, whole spicy free-range chicken, osso bucco. Hrs: noon-3 pm, 5 pm-midnight; Sun noon-10 pm. Closed Dec 25. Res accepted; required pre-theater dinner. Bar. A la carte entrees: lunch $13.95-$25.95, dinner $16.95-$27.95. Pre-theater dinner $21.95. Three dining rms on two levels. Rustic, Northern Italian atmosphere. Totally nonsmoking. Cr cds: A, C, D, DS, MC, V.

✔★ ★ **BELLUNO.** *340 Lexington Ave (10016), between 39th and 40th Sts, in Murray Hill. 212/953-3282.* Web www.newyork.side walk.com/bellunoristorante. Northern Italian menu. Specialties: chicken tenders wrapped in fettucine, pan-seared hanger steak, penne with shrimp and portobello. Hrs: noon-3 pm, 5-10 pm. Closed Sun; most major hols. Res accepted. Bar to midnight. A la carte entrees: lunch, dinner $13-$19. Tri-level; contemporary decor. Totally nonsmoking. Cr cds: A, C, MC, V.

★ ★ **BEN BENSON'S.** *123 W 52nd St (10019), between 6th & 7th Aves, Midtown. 212/581-8888.* Hrs: noon-11 pm; Fri to midnight; Sat 5 pm-midnight; Sun 5-10 pm. Closed most major hols. Res accepted. Steakhouse menu. Bar. A la carte entrees: lunch, dinner $17.75-$32.50. Specializes in steak, seafood. Garage parking. Outdoor dining. Cr cds: A, JCB, MC, V.

★ ★ **BICE.** *7 E 54th St (10022), just off Fifth Ave, Midtown. 212/688-1999.* Italian menu. Specialties: lobster salad with raspberry vinaigrette, marinated salmon and swordfish with celery root. Own pasta, desserts. Menu changes daily. Hrs: noon-3 pm, 6 pm-midnight. Closed Dec 25. Res accepted. Bar. A la carte entrees: lunch, dinner $20-$38. Outdoor dining. Branch of original restaurant in Milan. Cr cds: A, C, D, DS, JCB, MC, V.

★ ★ **BISTRO DU NORD.** *1312 Madison Ave (10028), Upper East Side at 93rd St. 212/289-0997.* French menu. Specialties: sautéed calves liver, 3 peppercorn sirloin steak. Hrs: noon-4 pm, 5-11:30 pm; Sat, Sun brunch noon-4 pm. Closed Dec 25. Res accepted. Bar. Semi-a la carte: lunch $10-$16, dinner $18-$25. Complete meal: lunch $12.95. Pre-theater: dinner $18.45. Sat, Sun brunch $13.95. French bistro decor. Totally nonsmoking. Cr cds: A, MC, V.

✔★ ★ **BLUE RIBBON.** *97 Sullivan St (10012), between Spring and Prince Sts, in SoHo. 212/274-0404.* French, Amer menu. Specialties: paella royale, chocolate bruno. Hrs: 4 pm-4 am. Closed Mon; major hols; also last 2 wk in Aug. Bar. A la carte entrees: dinner $9.50-$28.50. Casual decor. Totally nonsmoking. Cr cds: A, D, MC, V.

★ ★ **BLUE RIBBON SUSHI.** *119 Sullivan St (10012), between Prince & Spring Sts, in SoHo. 212/343-0404.* Hrs: 4 pm-2 am. Closed Mon; major hols; also last 2 wks Aug. Wine, beer. A la carte entrees: dinner $11.50-$25. Specialties: lobster with Miso butter; dragon roll with eel, avocado & radish sprouts; blue ribbon special. Street parking. Japanese decor; sushi bar. Cr cds: A, D, MC, V.

★ ★ **BOLO.** *23 E 22nd St (10010), between Broadway & Park Ave S, in Gramercy Park area. 212/228-2200.* Spanish menu. Specialties: individual shellfish paella, baby clams in green onion broth. Hrs: noon-2:30 pm, 5:30 pm-midnight; Sat from 5:30 pm; Sun 5:30-11 pm. Closed Dec 25. Res accepted. A la carte entrees: lunch $13-$18, dinner $22-$28. Eclectic decor. Cr cds: A, D, DS, MC, V.

★ ★ **BOOM.** *152 Spring St (10012), between W Broadway & Wooster, in SoHo. 212/431-3663.* International menu. Specialties: Vietnamese five-spiced grilled quail, pan-seared salmon, Chinese shrimp. Hrs: noon-4 am; Sat, Sun brunch noon-5 pm. Res accepted. Bar. A la carte entrees: lunch $7-$17, dinner $10-$19. Sat, Sun brunch $6-$12. Old World atmosphere; frescoed walls, hanging sculpture. Cr cds: A, D.

★ ★ ★ **BOULEY BAKERY.** *120 W Broadway (10013), at Duane St, in Tribeca. 212/964-2525.* Hrs: 11:30 am-3:30 pm, 5:30-11:30 pm. Closed Sun; also mjor hols. Res required (dinner). Serv bar. Wine list. A la carte entrees: lunch $24-$38, dinner $32-$44. Complete meal: 3-course lunch $35, 6-course dinner $90. Specialties: seared duck breast in honey glaze, pan-roasted salmon with fricasse of wild mushroom, lobster with marjoram sauce. Street parking. Elegant dining. Entrance through retail bakery. Totally nonsmoking. Cr cds: A, MC, V.

★ ★ ★ **BOX TREE.** *(See Box Tree Inn) 212/758-8320.* French, continental menu. Specializes in lobster, filet of beef, rack of lamb. Own baking. Hrs: noon-3 pm, 5:30-10 pm; Sat, Sun from 5:30 pm. Res required. Bar. Prix fixe: lunch $42, 5-course dinner $86. Pre-theater menu (5:30-7 pm) $65. Jacket. Cr cds: A, D, MC, V.

✔★ **BROOKLYN DINER USA.** *212 W 57th St (10019), in Midtown. 212/977-2280.* Specialtes: chicken pot pie, chicken noodle soup, chinese chicken salad. Own pastries, desserts. Hrs: 8 am-midnight; Fri, Sat to 1 am; Sun to 11 pm. Bar. A la carte entrees: bkfst $4.50-$12, lunch $9.95-$19.95, dinner $12.95-$19.95. Art-deco style diner. Cr cds: A, D, DS, MC, V.

★ ★ **BRYANT PARK GRILL.** *25 W 40th St (10018), in Midtown. 212/840-6500.* Contemporary Amer menu. Specialties: confit of duck burritos, Caesar salad with parmesan toast. Hrs: 11:30 am-3:30 pm, 5 pm-1 am. Res accepted. Bar. A la carte entrees: lunch $12.50-$20, dinner $15.50-$23.50. Pre-theater dinner 5-7 pm, $25. Outdoor dining. Windows overlook Bryant Park. Totally nonsmoking. Cr cds: A, D, DS, MC, V.

✔★ **BUBBY'S.** *120 Hudson St (10013), between Franklin & Moore, in Tribeca. 212/219-0666.* Hrs: 8 am-11 pm; Sat, Sun from 9 am; Sat, Sun brunch 9 am-4:45 pm. Closed Thanksgiving, Dec 25. Bar. A la carte entrees: bkfst $7.95-$9.95, lunch $7.95-$13.95, dinner $7.95-$20.95. Sat, Sun brunch $8.95-$14.95. Child's meals. Specialties: malt waffles with strawberries & bananas, grilled squid with citrus vinagrette, smoked trout & potato cakes. Street parking. Outdoor dining. Homestyle cooking and atmosphere. Totally nonsmoking. Cr cds: A, C, D, DS, MC, V.

★ ★ ★ **BULL & BEAR STEAKHOUSE.** *(See Waldorf-Astoria & Waldorf Towers Hotel) 212/872-4900.* Specializes in Maine lobster, Angus prime beef, grilled fish. Own baking. Hrs: noon-11:30 pm; Sat, Sun from 5 pm. Res accepted. Bar to midnight. A la carte entrees: lunch $17-$28, dinner $23-$42. Open kitchen. Jazz trio Thurs-Fri. Elegant club-like atmosphere. Jacket. Cr cds: A, C, D, DS, ER, JCB, MC, V.

★ ★ **CAFÉ LOUP.** *105 W 13th St (10011), between 6th & 7th Aves, Greenwich Village. 212/255-4746.* Hrs: noon-3 pm, 5:30 pm-midnight; Mon to 11:30 pm; Sat 5:30 pm-midnight; Sun (brunch) noon-3:30 pm, 5:30-11:30 pm. Res accepted. French bistro menu. Bar. A la carte entrees: lunch $8.50-$14.50, dinner $14.95-$22.50. Sun brunch $8.50-$14.50. Specialties: smoked brook trout, sautéed calf's brains, crepes au citron. Street parking. French bistro; black & white photographs. Family-owned since 1977. Cr cds: A, C, D, DS, MC, V.

CAFE BOULUD. *(To new to be rated) 20 E 76th St (10021), between Fifth & Madison Aves, Upper East Side. 212/772-2600.* French menu. Specialties: beef tournedos rossini, stuffed quail with figs & foie gras, duo of fresh cod and bacalao; seasonal cuisine. Hrs: noon-2:30 pm, 5:45-11 pm; Mon from 5:45 pm. Closed Sun; most major hols. Res required. Bar. Wine cellar. A la carte entrees: lunch $24-$32, dinner $26-$35. Complete meal: lunch $28, dinner $55. Outdoor sidewalk terrace dining. Chef-owned. Jacket. Cr cds: A, D, MC, V.

✔★ ★ **CAFE DE BRUXELLES.** *118 Greenwich Ave (10011), at W 13th St, Greenwich Village. 212/206-1830.* Belgium, French menu. Specialties: grilled pork chops with apples and mushrooms, seafood casserole, steamed mussels prepared six different ways. Hrs: noon-11:30 pm; Fri, Sat to 12:30 am; Sun noon-10:30 pm; Sun brunch to 3:30 pm. Closed most major hols. Res accepted. Bar. A la carte entrees: lunch $7.50-$12.50, dinner $13.50-$19.50. Sun brunch $7.50-$12.50. Contemporary decor. Cr cds: A, MC, V.

★ ★ ★ **CAFE DES ARTISTES.** *1 W 67th St (10023), Upper West Side. 212/877-3500.* Country French menu. Specialties: rack of lamb with basil crust, grilled fillet of tuna, grilled smoked salmon. Hrs: noon-3 pm, 5:30 pm-midnight; Sun 10 am-3 pm, 5:30-11 pm; Sat brunch 11 am-3 pm. Closed Dec 25. Res required. Bar. Wine list. A la carte entrees: lunch $15-$24, dinner $25-$40. Romantic, Old World decor; Howard Chandler Christy murals. Near Lincoln Center. Jacket (after 5 pm). Cr cds: A, D, JCB, MC, V.

★ ★ **CAFE FIORELLO.** *1900 Broadway (10023), between W 63rd & 64th Sts, across from Lincoln Center, Upper West Side. 212/595-5330.* Italian menu. Specialties: mixed antipasto, vitello alla parmigiana, grilled filet of tuna. Own pastries. Hrs: 11:30 am-11:30 pm; Fri 11-12:30 am; Sun 11 am-10:30 pm; Sat, Sun brunch 11 am 3 pm. Closed Dec 25. Res accepted. Bar. A la carte entrees: lunch $14.95-$25.75, dinner $15.75-$28.95. Sat, Sun brunch $13.75-$28.95. Outdoor dining. Glass-front Italian trattoria with contemporary art; antipasto bar. Family-owned. Totally nonsmoking. Cr cds: A, C, D, MC, V.

★ ★ **CAFE LUXEMBOURG.** *200 W 70th St (10023), at Amsterdam Ave, Upper West Side. 212/873-7411.* French, Amer menu. Specialties: country salad, steak frites, fresh fish. Hrs: noon-midnight; Sat brunch noon-3 pm; Sun brunch 11 am-3 pm. Res accepted. Bar. A la carte entrees: lunch $10-$19, dinner $17-$28. Prix fixe: lunch $19.99, dinner $34. Bistro atmosphere; art-deco decor. Near Lincoln Center. Cr cds: A, C, D, MC, V.

★ ★ **CAFE NOSIDAM.** *768 Madison Ave (10021), between 65th & 66th Sts, Upper East Side.* 212/717-5633. Italian, Amer menu. Specializes in pasta, fish, lamb. Hrs: 11:30 am-midnight; Sun to 11 pm; Sun brunch to 3 pm. Res accepted. Bar. A la carte entrees: lunch, dinner $13.95-$28. Complete meals: lunch, dinner $19.95. Sun brunch $19.95. Outdoor dining. Contemporary decor; original art. Cr cds: A, MC, V.

⊡

★ ★ ★ **CAFE PIERRE.** *(See The Pierre Hotel)* 212/940-8185. Web www.fourseasons.com. Contemporary, continental menu. Specializes in seasonal offerings. Own pastries. Hrs: 7 am-11 pm; Sun brunch noon-2:30 pm. Res required. Bar 11:30-1 am. Wine list. A la carte entrees: bkfst $9.50-$21, lunch $18-$36, dinner $30-$36. Prix fixe: lunch $30. 4-course tasting menu $60. Pre-theater menu (6-7 pm) $34. Sun brunch $34-$40. Entertainment. Jacket. Cr cds: A, C, D, DS, ER, JCB, MC, V.

D ♥

★ ★ **CAFE TREVI.** *1570 First Ave (10028), between 81st & 82nd Sts, in Yorkville section of Upper East Side.* 212/249-0040. Northern Italian menu. Specializes in veal, pasta, chicken. Hrs: 5:30 pm-midnight. Closed Sun. Res accepted. Bar. A la carte entrees: dinner $15.50-$24.75. Child's meals. Trattoria atmosphere. Cr cds: A, D, MC, V.

D

★ ★ ★ **CAFFE BONDI.** *7 W 20th St (10011), between 5th & 6th Aves, in Chelsea.* 212/691-8136. Sicilian menu. Specialties: pasta con sarde, wild game, seafood. Hrs: 11:30 am-11:30 pm; Sat, Sun brunch noon-5 pm. Bar. A la carte entrees: lunch $12-$21, dinner $14-$24. Complete meals: lunch $19.99, dinner $29. Sat, Sun brunch $6.95-$15. Outdoor dining. Tapestries and changing photographic exhibits add to the casual elegance of this restaurant. Cr cds: A, D, DS, JCB, MC, V.

SC ⊡

★ ★ **CAL'S.** *55 W 21st St (10010), between 5th & 6th St, in Chelsea.* 212/929-0740. Mediterranean menu. Specializes in seafood, duck, steak. Hrs: 11:30 am-midnight; Sat from 5 pm; Sun 5-10:30 pm. Closed Jan 1, July 4, Dec 25. Res accepted. Bar. A la carte entrees: lunch $12.50-$18, dinner $12.50-$24. Outdoor dining. Former warehouse; casual decor. Cr cds: A, C, D, MC, V.

D ⊡

★ ★ ★ **CAMPAGNA.** *24 E 21st St (10010), between Broadway and Park Ave South, in Chelsea.* 212/460-0900. Italian menu. Specialties: scallopine al telefono, ravioli primavera, Florentine rib-eye steak. Hrs: noon-2:30 pm, 6-11:45 pm; Sat from 6 pm; Sun 5:30-10:45 pm. Closed some major hols. Res required. Bar. Wine cellar. A la carte entrees: lunch $13-$18.50, dinner $16-$29.50. Child's meals. Warm, comfortable atmosphere. Cr cds: A, C, D, MC, V.

D

★ ★ ★ **CAPSOUTO FRÈRES.** *451 Washington St (10013), 1 blk S of Canal St, near Hudson River, in Tribeca.* 212/966-4900. Contemporary French menu. Specialties: poached salmon, roast duckling, filet of beef with Madeira sauce. Own baking. Hrs: noon-3:30 pm, 6-11 pm; Mon from 6 pm; Fri to midnight; Sat 6-11 pm; Sat, Sun brunch noon-3:30 pm. Res accepted. Bar to midnight. Wine cellar. A la carte entrees: lunch $9-$22, dinner $14-$24. Prix fixe: lunch $19.99. Sat, Sun brunch $8.50-$20. Outdoor dining. In converted neo-Flemish, landmark warehouse (1891). Cr cds: A, C, D, MC, V.

★ ★ ★ **CARLYLE.** *(See Carlyle Hotel)* 212/744-1600. French, continental menu. Specializes in seasonal entrees. Own baking. Hrs: 7-10:30 am, noon-2:30 pm, 6 pm-1 am; Sun from 7:30 am. Sun brunch noon-2 pm. Res accepted. Bar noon-2 am. Wine list. A la carte entrees: bkfst $9.50-$22.50, lunch $25-$38.50, dinner $27-$39.50. Buffet: bkfst $26.50, lunch $35. Sun brunch $45. Valet parking. Cr cds: A, C, D, JCB, MC, V.

♥

★ ★ **CARMINE'S.** *2450 Broadway (10024), between 90th & 91st Sts, Upper West Side.* 212/362-2200. Southern Italian menu. Specialties: country-style rigatoni with sausage, cannellini beans and broccoli; porterhouse steak for four; chicken scarpariello. Hrs: 11:30 am-11 pm; Fri, Sat to midnight; Sun 2-10 pm. Bar. A la carte entrees: lunch $5.50-$12.50, dinner $16-$46. Complete meals (Mon-Fri): dinner $10.95 5-6:30 pm. Single entrees served family-style for 2-4 people. Outdoor dining. Dining rm, originally a hotel ballroom, is re-creation of 1940s neighborhood Italian restaurant. Cr cds: A, MC, V.

★ ★ **CASTELLANO.** *138 W 55th St (10019), between 6th & 7th Aves, Midtown.* 212/664-1975. Tuscan, Italian menu. Specialties: grilled calamari, fegato Castellano, risotti. Hrs: noon-11 pm; Sat, Sun from 5:30 pm. Closed some major hols. Res accepted. Bar. A la carte entrees: lunch, dinner $17-$29. Outdoor terrace dining. 3 dining areas on 2 levels. Tuscan decor. Cr cds: A, C, D, JCB, MC, V.

★ ★ ★ ★ ★ **CHANTERELLE.** *2 Harrison St (10013), in Mercantile Exchange Bldg, at Hudson St, in Tribeca.* 212/966-6960. Web www.newyorkeats.com/chanterelle. A gem of a restaurant tucked away in the formerly grim but gentrified neighborhood of Tribeca, Chanterelle offers top-quality contemporary French cuisine and excellent service, with a painstakingly selected menu that changes monthly. French menu. Specialty: grilled seafood sausage. Hrs: noon-2:30 pm, 5:30-11 pm; Mon from 5:30 pm. Closed Sun; major hols; also 2 wks July. Res required. Bar. Wine cellar. A la carte entrees: lunch $18.50-$25. Prix fixe: lunch $35, dinner $75 & $89. Chef-owned. Cr cds: A, C, D, DS, JCB, MC, V.

D

★ ★ ★ **CHELSEA BISTRO & BAR.** *358 W 23rd St (10011), between 8th & 9th Aves, in Chelsea.* 212/727-2026. Web www.nyloday.com/chelseabistro. French bistro menu. Specialties: roasted Atlantic salmon, Hanger steak, roasted duck. Hrs: 5:30-11 pm; Fri, Sat to midnight; Sun 5-10:30 pm. Res accepted. Bar. Wine list. A la carte entrees: dinner $17.50-$22. Glass-enclosed terrace. Cr cds: A, MC, V.

D

★ ★ **CHEZ MICHALLET.** *90 Bedford St (10014), at Grove St, in Greenwich Village.* 212/242-8309. French menu. Specialties: steak au poivre, poulet grille a la marocaine. Hrs: 5:30-11 pm; Sun to 10:30 pm. Closed Jan 1, Dec 25. Res accepted. Wine, beer. A la carte entrees: dinner $17.50-$23.95. Pre-theater dinner 5:30-6:30 pm, $19.95. Bistro decor. Totally nonsmoking. Cr cds: A, MC, V.

★ ★ **CHEZ NAPOLEON.** *365 W 50th St (10019), between Eighth & Ninth Aves, in Theater District.* 212/265-6980. French menu. Specialties: bouillabaisse, steak au poivre, duck à l'orange. Hrs: noon-2:30 pm, 5-10 pm; Fri to 11 pm; Sat 5-11 pm. Closed Sun; major hols. Res accepted. Bar. A la carte entrees: lunch $8-$15, dinner $13-$20.50. Pre-theater dinner 5-6:30 pm, $19.75. Small French bistro. Family owned. Cr cds: A, DS, MC, V.

⊡

★ ★ ★ **CHRISTER'S.** *145 W 55th St (10019), between 6th & 7th Aves, Midtown.* 212/974-7224. Scandinavian, Amer menu. Specialties: gravlax with mustard sauce, smoked serrano salmon, baked salmon on oak board. Hrs: noon-2:30 pm, 5:30-11 pm; Sat from 5:30 pm. Closed Sun; also major hols. Res accepted. Bar. A la carte entrees: lunch $14.50-$24, dinner $17.50-$29.50. Complete meals: lunch $19.99. Pre-theater menu $29-$36. Rustic fishing camp atmosphere with colorful decor. Cr cds: A, C, D, MC, V.

D ⊡

★ ★ **CHURRASCARIA PLATAFORMA.** *316 W 49th St (10019), between 8th & 9th Aves, Times Square/Theater District.* 212/245-0505. Hrs: noon-midnight. Closed Thanksgiving, Dec 25. Res accepted. Brazilian menu. Bar. Complete meal: lunch $25, dinner $29. Specializes in serving Brazilian rodizio-style. Brazilian music Wed-Sat (night). Street parking. Elegant dining. Totally nonsmoking. Cr cds: A, D, MC, V.

D

★ ★ ★ **CIBO.** *767 Second Ave (10017), between 41st & 42nd Sts, Midtown.* 212/681-1616. E-mail ciboat42nd@aol.com; web www.citysearch.com/nyc/cibo. Contemporary Amer menu. Specializes in wild game, seafood, pasta. Own baking, pasta. Hrs: 11:30 am-3 pm, 5:30-10 pm; Fri, Sat to 11 pm; Sat, Sun brunch to 3:30 pm. Closed some major hols. Res accepted. Bar. Wine list. Semi-a la carte: lunch $13-$29, dinner $19-$29. Complete meals: dinner $24.95. Sat, Sun brunch $7-$19.98. Outdoor dining. In landmark Daily News bldg; contemporary pastel decor. Cr cds: A, C, D, DS, MC, V.

★ ★ ★ CITÉ. 120 W 51st St (10020), between Sixth & Seventh Aves, In Time/Life Bldg, Midtown. 212/956-7100. French, Amer menu. Specialties: spit-roasted chicken, swordfish, steak au piovre. Own baking. Hrs: 11:30 am-midnight. Closed most major hols. Res accepted. Bar. Wine list. A la carte entrees: lunch, dinner $19.50-$29.50. Prix fixe: dinner $39.50 & $59.50. Zinc-covered bar. One rm informal bistro. Cr cds: A, C, D, DS, JCB, MC, V.

★ ★ ★ CITY WINE & CIGAR CO. 62 Laight St (10013), corner of Greenwich St, in Tribeca. 212/334-2274. Web www.cuisine.com. Contemporary Amer menu. Specialties: seared salmon, rack of lamb, grilled spicy hangar steak. Own pastries. Hrs: 5:30-11:30 pm; Thurs-Sat to 1 am; Fri noon-2:45 pm, 5:30 pm-1 am. Closed Sun; Dec 25. Res accepted. Bar 4:30 pm-2 am; Thurs-Sat to 3:30 am. Wine cellar. A la carte entrees: lunch, dinner $19-$27. Outdoor dining. Landmark bldg now contemporary restaurant with copper-topped tables, leather banquettes. Cr cds: A, C, D, MC, V.

★ ★ CLEMENTINE. 1 Fifth Ave (10003), at 8th St, Greenwich Village. 212/253-0003. Hrs: noon-4 am; Sat, Sun 6 pm-4 am. Res accepted. Eclectic menu. Bar. A la carte entrees: lunch $7-$15, dinner $15-$25. Complete meal: lunch $19.99. Specialties: buffalo mahi mahi, roasted cod, chili-rubbed pork loin. Street parking. Stone fountain in center of dining room. Cr cds: A, D, DS, MC, V.

★ ★ COCO MARINA. 2 World Financial Center (10281), in Financial District. 212/385-8080. Hrs: 11:45 am-3:30 pm, 5:30-10 pm; Sat noon-6 pm; Sun noon-4 pm. Closed major hols. Res accepted. Seafood menu. Bar noon-10 pm. A la carte entrees: lunch $9-$19.50, dinner $14-$28. Specialties: potato and crab salad, wood grilled & smoked lobster, coco mare & grande coco mare. Street parking. Sophisticated atmosphere; hand-painted murals of ocean life. Totally nonsmoking. Cr cds: A, C, D, DS, MC, V.

★ ★ COCO OPERA. 58 W 65th St (10023), between Columbus and Central Park S, Lincoln Center, Upper West Side. 212/873-3700. Hrs: 11:30 am-3 pm, 5-11 pm; Thurs-Sat to midnight. Closed major hols. Res accepted. Regional Tuscan (Italian) menu. Bar. A la carte entrees: lunch $12-$22, dinner $14-$32. Specialties: risotto made with farro, linguini alla pirata, campari orange ice cream soda. Street parking. Contemporary decor; cosmopolitan elegance. Totally nonsmoking. Cr cds: A, C, D, DS, MC, V.

★ ★ COCO PAZZO. 23 E 74th St (10021), between Fifth Ave & Madison Ave, Upper East Side. 212/794-0205. Italian menu. Specializes in Tuscan Italian cuisine. Hrs: noon-3 pm, 6 pm-midnight; Sun 5:30-11:30 pm; Sun brunch 11:30 am-3 pm. Closed most major hols. Res required. Bar. Wine cellar. A la carte entrees: lunch $12.50-$18, dinner $21-$28.50; Sun brunch $12.50-$18. Decor features large still-life frescoes in the Morandi style. Jacket. Cr cds: A, D, MC, V.

★ ★ ★ COCO PAZZO TEATRO. 235 W 46th St (10019), between Broadway & 8th Ave, in Times Square/Theater District. 212/827-4222. Italian menu. Specialties: Florentine steak with Coco Pazzo fries, lobster with saffron pasta, mastro raviolo con aragosta. Own pastries. Hrs: 11:30 am-3 pm, 5:30 pm-midnight; Sun 11 am-3 pm, 5:30-11:30 pm. Closed major hols. Res accepted; required dinner. Bar to 1 am. Wine list. A la carte

entrees: lunch $12.50-$16, dinner $15.50-$32. Informal Italian decor with marble columns, soft lighting. Cr cds: A, D, MC, V.

✔ ★ COMFORT DINER. 214 E 45th St (10017), between 2nd & 3rd Aves, Midtown. 212/867-4555. Specialties: Mom's meatloaf, wild mushroom potato pancakes, cobb salad sandwich. Own desserts. Hrs: 7:30 am-10 pm; Sat, Sun from 9 am. Closed Dec 25. Semi-a la carte: bkfst $1.99-$9.95, lunch $5.75-$10.95, dinner $5.75-$11.95. Child's meals. 1950s-style diner. Totally nonsmoking. Cr cds: A, D, DS, MC, V.

★ ★ CONTRAPUNTO. 200 E 60th St (10022), at Third Ave, Upper East Side. 212/751-8616. Italian menu. Specialties: tagliarini "forte" with smoked bacon, papparadelle with mushrooms, roast rack of lamb. Hrs: noon-11 pm; Fri, Sat to midnight; Sun to 10 pm. Serv bar. A la carte entrees: lunch $15-$21, dinner $13-$25. Open kitchen. Cr cds: A, D, DS, MC, V.

★ ★ COTÉ SUD. 181 E 78th St (10021), between Lexington & 3rd Aves, Upper East Side. 212/744-1800. Provencal menu. Specialties: roasted quail stuffed with curried apples, seared crisp codfish, grilled lavender chicken. Own pastries. Hrs: 6-11 pm; Fri, Sat to midnight. Closed Dec 25. Res accepted. Beer, wine. A la carte entrees: dinner $13-$18. Minimalist decor with open kitchen; large front windows. Cr cds: A.

★ THE CRAB HOUSE. Pier 61 (10011), 23rd St & 12th Ave, in Chelsea. 212/835-2722. Hrs: noon-10 pm; Fri, Sat to 11 pm. Closed Thanksgiving, Dec 25. Seafood menu. Bar. A la carte entrees: lunch $5.99-$9.99, dinner $11.99-$34.98. Complete meal: lunch $15, dinner $40. Buffet: lunch $7.99, dinner $20.99. Child's meals. Specialties: Maryland steamed blue crabs, Alaskan trio-king snow Dungeness crab, crab house broiled platter. Jazz band Fri, Sat. Parking. Outdoor dining. Raw bar. Overlooks Hudson River. Totally nonsmoking. Cr cds: A, C, D, DS, JCB, MC, V.

★ ★ ★ CUB ROOM. 131 Sullivan St (10012), in SoHo. 212/677-4100. Web www.cubroom.com. Specialties: lobster strudel, chateaubriand with wild mushrooms, yellowfin tuna on bed of Asian greens. Hrs: noon-midnight. Closed Dec 25. Res accepted. Bar to 2 am. Wine list. A la carte entrees: lunch, dinner $10-$16. Contemporary decor. Totally nonsmoking. Cr cds: A.

★ ★ CUISINE DE SAIGON. 154 W 13th St (10011), between 6th St & 7th Ave, in Greenwich Village. 212/255-6003. Vietnamese menu. Specialties: shrimp wrapped with sugar cane, Vietnamese spring roll, Saigon famous pasta (steamed wide noodles rolled with minced pork). Hrs: 5-11 pm; Fri, Sat to 11:30 pm; Sun to 10:30 pm. Closed most major hols. Res accepted; required wkends. Bar. A la carte entrees: dinner $7.95-$15.95. Cr cds: A, C, D, MC, V.

★ ★ ★ DA SILVANO. 260 Sixth Ave (10014), between Houston and Bleecker Sts, in Greenwich Village. 212/982-2343. Italian menu. Specialties: boneless quails al radicchio, seasonal Florentine dishes, stewed tripes. Hrs: noon-11:30 pm; Fri, Sat to midnight; Sun 2-10:30 pm. Res accepted. Serv bar. A la carte entrees: lunch, dinner $12.50-$36. Outdoor dining. Cr cds: A, MC, V.

★ ★ DA UMBERTO. 107 W 17th St (10011), between Sixth & Seventh Aves, in Chelsea. 212/989-0303. Northern Italian menu. Specializes in antipasto buffet, wild game, pasta. Hrs: noon-3 pm, 5-11 pm; Sat from 5:30 pm. Closed Sun; Jan 1, Dec 25; also wk of July 4. Res accepted. Bar. A la carte entrees: lunch $15-$26, dinner $18-$32. Complete meal: lunch $19 & $22. Florentine decor. Cr cds: A.

★ ★ DA VITTORIO. 43 E 20th St (10003), Gramercy Park. 212/979-6532. Italian menu. Specialties: potato gnocchi with gorgonzola and rosemary, risotto del gorno. Hrs: noon-3 pm, 5:30-11 pm; Fri to 11:30 pm; Sat 5:30-11:30 pm. Closed Sun; major hols. Res accepted. Bar. A la carte entrees: lunch, dinner $15.50-$35. Rustic Italian decor. Cr cds: A.

★ ★ ★ **DAVID RUGGERIO.** *106 E 57th St (10022), between Lexington & Park Aves, Midtown.* 212/751-2931. Murals of the château of Chantilly, fresh flowers and comfortable banquettes set a French mood at this New York institution. French menu. Specialties: grilled red snapper, roasted loin of rabbit, composition of Maine lobster with crispy noodle cake. Daily specials. Own baking. Hrs: noon-3 pm, 5:30-10:30 pm; Sat 5:30-11 pm; Sun 5-9:30 pm. Res required. Bar. Wine list. A la carte entrees: lunch $18-$24, dinner $18-$30. Prix fixe: lunch $20-$30, dinner $55. 7-course tasting menu: dinner $75. Street parking. Cr cds: A, JCB, MC, V.

D

★ ★ **DAWAT.** *210 E 58th St (10022), between Second & Third Aves, on the East Side.* 212/355-7555. Indian menu. Specialties: curried shrimp, salmon in coriander chutney. Hrs: 11:30 am-3 pm, 5:30-11 pm; Fri, Sat to 11:15 pm; Sun from 5:30 pm. Res required. Bar. A la carte entrees: lunch, dinner $12.95-$22.95. Complete meals: lunch $13.95 & $14.95, dinner $23.95. Parking (dinner). Contemporary East Indian decor. Cr cds: A, C, D, MC, V.

D

★ ★ **DELEGATES DINING ROOM.** *In United Nations General Assembly Bldg (10017), 4th floor, at First Ave & 46th St, visitors entrance, on the East Side.* 212/963-7625. International menu. Specializes in ethnic food festivals, seasonal salads, fresh seafood. Hrs: 11:30 am-2:30 pm. Closed Sat, Sun; some major hols. Res required. Serv bar. A la carte entrees: lunch $17.50-$25. Buffet: lunch $20.50. Panoramic view of East River. Open to public; identification with photograph required. Jacket. Cr cds: A, C, D, JCB, MC, V.

D ⌐

★ ★ **DEMI.** *1316 Madison Ave (10128), at 93rd St, Upper East Side.* 212/534-3475. Continental menu. Specialties: glazed duck breast, sautéed breast of chicken. Own baking. Hrs: 11:30 am-11 pm; Sun 5-10 pm. Closed July 4, Labor Day, Dec 25. Res accepted. Bar. A la carte entrees: lunch $9-$25, dinner $16-$27. Terrace dining. Attractive restaurant in townhouse; romantic atmosphere. Cr cds: A, MC, V.

⌐

★ ★ ★ **DOMINGO.** *209 E 49th St (10017), between 2nd & 3rd Aves, Midtown.* 212/826-8154. Spanish menu. Specialties: tapas, paella Valenciana, monkfish a la Catalana. Own baking. Hrs: noon-2:30 pm, 5:30-10:30 pm; Mon-Thurs from 5:30 pm. Closed Sun. Res accepted. Bar. Wine list. A la carte entrees: lunch, dinner $6-$28. Entertainment Mon, Tues, Thurs. Outdoor dining. Spanish Colonial decor; handcarved woodwork, large skylight, Spanish mural. Cr cds: A, D, MC, V.

⌐

★ ★ **DROVERS TAP ROOM.** *9 Jones St (10014), between Bleecker & 4th, Greenwich Village.* 212/627-1233. Hrs: 4 pm-midnight; Fri, Sat to 1 am; Sat, Sun brunch 11 am-4 pm. Res accepted. Bar. A la carte entrees: dinner $9-$17. Sat, Sun brunch $5-$12. Specialties: iron skillet macaroni & cheese, slow smoked beef ribs, buttermilk fried chicken. Street parking. Country-style decor; 1930's hanging lamps. Cr cds: A, MC, V.

⌐

★ ★ ★ **DUANE PARK CAFE.** *157 Duane St (10013), between Hudson & W Broadway, in Tribeca.* 212/732-5555. Italian, Amer menu. Specialties: seared tuna with savoy cabbage, crispy skate with ponzu, grilled miso marinated duck salad. Hrs: noon-2:30 pm, 5:30-10 pm; Fri to 10:30 pm; Sat 5:30-10:30 pm. Closed Sun; most major hols; also first wk July. Bar. A la carte entrees: lunch $14-$16, dinner $18-$26. Prix fixe: lunch $19.99. Intimate atmosphere with Italian accents. Cr cds: A, C, D, DS, JCB, MC, V.

★ ★ **EDWARD MORAN BAR AND GRILL.** *250 Vesey St (10281), in Bldg 4 of World Financial Center, in Financial District.* 212/945-2255. Specializes in hamburgers, sandwiches, seafood. Hrs: 11:30 am-10 pm; Sat, Sun brunch 11 am-4 pm. Res accepted. Bar. A la carte entrees: lunch, dinner $8.50-$15.95. Sat, Sun brunch: $9.95-$16.95. Outdoor dining. Pub-like atmosphere. Nautical decor. View of Ellis Island and Statue of Liberty. Cr cds: A, C, D, DS, MC, V.

D ⌐

★ ★ **EL TEDDY'S.** *219 W Broadway (10013), between Franklin & White Sts, in Tribeca.* 212/941-7070. Contemporary Mexican menu. Specializes in grilled seafood. Hrs: noon-3 pm, 6-11:30 pm; Thurs, Fri to 1 am; Sat 6 pm-1 am; Sun 6-11 pm. Closed Jan 1, Dec 25. Res accepted. Bar. A la carte entrees: lunch $7-$13, dinner $14-$19. Outdoor dining. Wild, eccentric decor spans styles from 1920s to the present. Located in white building with replica of Statue of Liberty's spiked crown on roof. Cr cds: A, D, MC, V.

⌐

★ ★ ★ **ESTIATORIO MILOS.** *125 W 55th St (10019), between 6th & 7th Aves, Midtown.* 212/245-7400. Hrs: noon-3 pm, 5:30 pm-midnight; Sat 5:30 pm-midnight; Sun 5-11 pm. Closed Jan 1, Dec 25. Res required (dinner). Mediterranean menu. Bar. Wine list. A la carte entrees: lunch, dinner $22-$32. Complete meal: lunch $29.50. Specializes in fresh line caught fish from around the world. Street parking. Cr cds: A, D, MC, V.

D

★ ★ ★ **FANTINO.** *(See The Westin Central Park South Hotel)* 212/757-1900. Web www.westin.com. American menu. Specialties: Mediterranean seafood risotto with saffron, roasted rack of lamb, pepper crusted sirloin. Hrs: 7-10:30 am, 5:30-11 pm; Mon noon-2 pm; Sat 7:30-11:30 am, 5:30-11 pm; Sun 7:30 am-2 pm, 5:30-11 pm. Res accepted. Bar noon-1 am. A la carte entrees: dinner $24.95-$30. Buffet: bkfst $23.75. Complete meal: lunch $24.95. Pre-theater dinner (5:30-7 pm) $29. Sun brunch $33. Traditional European decor; fireplaces. Cr cds: A, C, D, DS, ER, JCB, MC, V.

D

★ ★ ★ **FELIDIA.** *243 E 58th St (10022), between Second & Third Aves, on the East Side.* 212/758-1479. Web www.lidiasitaly.com. Italian menu. Specializes in homemade pasta, veal, seafood. Own baking. Menu changes daily. Hrs: noon-3 pm, 5-11 pm; Sat 5-11:30 pm. Closed Sun; major hols. Res accepted. Bar. Wine cellar. A la carte entrees: lunch $20-$29, dinner $21-$25. Complete meals: lunch $28.50. Hanging tapestry, plants are found throughout the different dining rms. Family-owned. Jacket. Cr cds: A, C, D, DS, MC, V.

★ ★ ★ **FIFTY SEVEN FIFTY SEVEN.** *(See Four Seasons Hotel)* 212/758-5700. Web www.fshr.com. Housed in the Four Seasons Hotel, designed by I.M. Pei, this is a spectacular, open, airy variation on a brasserie, with 22-foot coffered ceilings, bare maple floors with walnut inlays, bronze chandeliers and art-deco touches. Dining is sophisticated, luxurious and comfortable. Specialties: Maryland crab cakes, thyme-seared Atlantic salmon, herb-roasted rack of lamb. Hrs: 7 am-2 pm, 6-10:30 pm. Bar to 1 am; Fri, Sat to 2 am; Sun to midnight. A la carte entrees: bkfst $11-$18.50, lunch $19-$29, dinner $24-$32. Complete meals: lunch $39, dinner $49. Sun brunch $18-$29. Child's meals. Pianist Thurs-Sat to 1 am. Valet parking. Jacket. Cr cds: A, C, D, ER, JCB, MC, V.

D ♥

★ ★ ★ **FIREBIRD.** *365 W 46th St (10036), between 8th & 9th Aves, in Times Square/Theater District.* 212/586-0244. Russian menu. Specialties: caviar with sour cream and blini, herring under a blanket, grilled marinated lamb loin. Own baking. Hrs: 11:45 am-2:30 pm, 5-11 pm; Sun, Mon from 5 pm; Fri, Sat to 11:30 pm. Closed major hols. Res accepted. Bar. Wine cellar. Semi-a la carte: lunch $13.75-$16.75, dinner $17.25-$23.75. Complete meals: dinner $19.50. Opulent replica of Czarist mansion (1912); two-level dining with ornate decor, antique furnishings. Totally nonsmoking. Cr cds: A, C, D, DS, JCB, MC, V.

D

★ ★ ★ **FIRST.** *87 First Ave (10003), between 5th and 6th Sts; in East Village.* 212/674-3823. Specialties: Tokyo roast, paella, roast suckling pig. Hrs: 6 pm-2 am; Fri, Sat to 3 am; Sun 4 pm-1 am; Sun brunch 11 am-3 pm. Closed Dec 25. Res accepted. Bar. A la carte entrees: dinner $13-$21.

5 course tasting $34. Sun brunch $12.95. Stylish industrial decor. Cr cds: A, MC, V.

★ ★ ★ **FOLLONICO.** 6 W 24th St (10010), between 5th & 6th Aves, in Chelsea. 212/691-6359. Italian menu. Specialties: wood-roasted calamari, herb-printed fazzoletto over wild mushroom ragout, whole red snapper in rock-salt crust. Hrs: noon-3 pm, 6-10:30 pm; Fri, Sat 6-11 pm. Closed most major hols. Res accepted. Bar. Wine cellar. A la carte entrees: lunch $12-$18, dinner $16-$26. Tuscany farm house decor with wood-burning oven, beamed ceilings and original art. Cr cds: A, D, MC, V.

D

★ ★ ★ ★ **THE FOUR SEASONS.** 99 E 52nd St (10022), Seagram Bldg, between Park & Lexington Aves, Midtown. 212/754-9494. Web www.citysearch/fourseasons.com. Designed by Philip Johnson, this New York favorite is now a designated local landmark. Menu changes with the season. Own baking. Hrs: Pool Dining Room: noon-2:30 pm, 5-9:30 pm; Sat to 11:15 pm. Grill Room: noon-2 pm, 5:30-9 pm; Sat 5-10 pm. Closed Sun; major hols. Res accepted. Bar. Wine cellar. A la carte entrees: Pool Dining Room: lunch $29.50-$48, dinner $32.50-$45. Grill Room: a la carte entrees: lunch $25-$38.50, dinner $37-$48. Jacket. Cr cds: A, C, D, DS, JCB, MC, V.

★ ★ **FRAUNCES TAVERN.** 54 Pearl St (10005), at Broad St, downtown. 212/269-0144. Specializes in fish from Fulton fishmarket. Hrs: 7-10 am, 11:30 am-4 pm, 5-9:30 pm. Closed Sat, Sun; major hols. Res accepted. Bar. Prix fixe: bkfst $14.95. A la carte entrees: lunch, dinner $15-$25. Child's meals. Historic landmark built 1719; George Washington bade farewell to his officers here in 1783. Museum. Family-owned since 1937. Cr cds: A, C, D, MC, V.

★ ★ **FRICO BAR.** 402 W 43rd St (10036), 9th Ave & 43rd St, in Times Square/Theater District. 212/564-7272. Hrs: noon-3 pm, 5-11:30 pm; Sat 5-11:30 pm; Sun 4-10 pm. Closed Dec 25. Res required (dinner). Regional Italian menu. Bar. A la carte entrees: lunch $10-$24, dinner $10-$26. Complete meal: lunch $19.99, dinner $40. Specialties: frico tradizionale, krafi, osso bucco di vitello. Street parking. Outdoor dining. Casual Italian decor. Totally nonsmoking. Cr cds: A, C, D, DS, MC, V.

D

✔★ **FULTON STREET CAFE.** 11 Fulton St (10038), in South Street Seaport, in Financial District. 212/227-2288. Specializes in seafood. Raw bar. Hrs: 11:30 am-midnight. Bar. A la carte entrees: lunch, dinner $5-$18.95. Outdoor dining. Nautical decor. Cr cds: A, D, MC, V.

D

★ ★ **GABRIEL'S.** 11 W 60th St (10023), between Broadway & Columbus Ave, Upper West Side. 212/956-4600. Italian menu. Specialties: wood pan-roasted snapper in white wine, slow-roasted kid with white wine and rosemary, wood-grilled sturgeon. Hrs: noon-3 pm, 5:30-11 pm; Fri to midnight; Sat 5:30 pm-midnight. Closed Sun; most major hols. Res required. Bar. Wine list. A la carte entrees: lunch $12-$16, dinner $16-$27. Mahogany bar; original art. Cr cds: A, D, DS, MC, V.

D

★ ★ **GALLAGHER'S.** 228 W 52nd St (10019), at Broadway, Times Square/Theater District. 212/245-5336. Specializes in prime beef, sirloin steak, seafood. Hrs: noon-midnight. Res accepted. Bar. A la carte entrees: lunch $12.75-$42, dinner $14.95-$43. Street parking. Open kitchen. Photographs of sports & theater personalities. Cr cds: A, C, D, DS, JCB, MC, V.

✔★ ★ **GASCOGNE.** 158 Eighth Ave (10011), at 18th St, in Chelsea. 212/675-6564. French menu. Specialties: roasted quail with fresh spicy peaches, cassoulet bean stew with duck confit and sausages, warm fresh foie gras with seasonal fruit. Hrs: noon-3 pm, 6-10:30 pm; Fri, Sat to 11 pm; Sun noon-3 pm, 5-10 pm. Closed some major hols. Res accepted. Bar. A la carte entrees: lunch $8.75-$18, dinner $21-$23. Sun brunch $8.75-$18. Pre-theatre dinner $27. Garden dining. French country-style decor; farmhouse ambiance. Cr cds: A, MC, V.

★ ★ **GEMELLI.** 4 World Trade Center (10048), on plaza level of World Trade Center, in Financial District. 212/488-2100. E-mail gemelli@tonymay.com; web www.gemelli.com. Hrs: 11:30 am-2:30 pm, 5-9 pm. Closed Sun; also major hols. Res accepted. Regional Italian menu. Bar. A la carte entrees: lunch $16-$28, dinner $16-$32.50. Specializes in pasta, fish, steaks. Street parking. Outdoor dining. Rustic contemporary decor. Cr cds: A, D, MC, V.

D

★ ★ ★ **GERTRUDE'S.** 33 E 61st St (10021), between Madison and Park Aves, Upper East Side. 212/888-9127. French country menu. Specialties: ravioli of foie gras, roasted monkfish Basque-style, grilled veal chop. Hrs: noon-3 pm, 6-11:30 pm. Res accepted. Bar to 1 am. Wine list. A la carte entrees: lunch $19-$24, dinner $24-$34. Prix fixe: dinner $70. Outdoor dining. French country decor. Cr cds: A, D, MC, V.

★ ★ **GIGINO TRATTORIA.** 323 Greenwich St (10013), between Duane & Reade Sts, in Tribeca. 212/431-1112. Southern Italian menu. Specialties: thin pizza, linguini alla Vongole, spaghetti Padrino. Hrs: 11:30 am-11 pm; Fri to midnight; Sat 4 pm-midnight; Sun from 4 pm. Closed Jan 1, Memorial Day, Dec 25. Res accepted. Bar. A la carte entrees: lunch $10-$18, dinner $12-$21. Outdoor dining. Country farmhouse atmosphere. Cr cds: A, C, D, MC, V.

★ ★ ★ ★ **GOTHAM BAR AND GRILL.** 12 E 12th St (10003), between Fifth Ave & University Place, in Greenwich Village. 212/620-4020. E-mail gotham@aol.com. Chef Alfred Portale originated the vertical style of food presentation here—each plate is an artful, edible tower. Multi-leveled and post-modern in design, the Gotham was the prototype for the new-style New York restaurant. Specializes in game, seafood, lamb. Own pastries. Menu changes seasonally. Hrs: noon-2 pm, 5:30-10 pm; Fri to 11 pm; Sat 5:30-11 pm; Sun from 5:30 pm. Closed most major hols. Res required. Bar. A la carte entrees: lunch $15.50-$19, dinner $26-$34. Prix fixe: lunch $19.99. Cr cds: A, C, D, MC, V.

★ ★ ★ ★ **GRAMERCY TAVERN.** 42 E 20th St (10003), between Park Ave S & Broadway, in Gramercy Park. 212/477-0777. A 91-foot-long mural of fruit and vegetables wraps around the bar of this cozy colonial-decor tavern. Elegant dining is available in three rooms; furnishings include a blend of antiques, quilts and modern art. Specialties: salt-baked salmon, roast rabbit with black olives and sherry vinegar, lobster and artichoke salad. Hrs: 5:30-10 pm; Fri, Sat to 11 pm. Closed major hols. Res required. Bar to midnight. Wine cellar. A la carte entrees: lunch $15-$21. Complete meal: lunch $33, dinner $58. Street parking. Totally nonsmoking. Cr cds: A, D, MC, V.

D

★ ★ ★ **THE GRILL ROOM.** 225 Liberty St (10281), at World Financial Center, in Financial District. 212/945-9400. Specialties: roasted corn & seafood chowder, cowboy prime rib steak, James Beard's traditional fresh berry shortcake. Own baking. Hrs: noon-4 pm, 5:30-8:30 pm. Closed Sat, Sun; July 4, Labor Day, Dec 25. Res accepted. Bar noon-11 pm. Wine cellar. A la carte entrees: lunch $19.50-$32, dinner $22-$32. Glass-fronted bldg overlooks Hudson River, offers views of Statue of Liberty and marina. Cr cds: A, DS, MC, V.

D

★ ★ **HARBOUR LIGHTS.** Fulton Pier 17 (10038), South Street Seaport, in Financial District. 212/227-2800. Continental, Amer menu. Specializes in seafood, steak. Hrs: 11-1 am; Sun brunch to 3:30 pm. Closed Dec 25. Res accepted. Bar. A la carte entrees: lunch $15-$29, dinner $24-$34. Parking. Outdoor dining. Glass greenhouse-style building; large wraparound outdoor terrace. Overlooks East River; view of Brooklyn Bridge. Cr cds: A, D, DS, JCB, MC, V.

D

✔★ ★ **HARMONY PALACE.** 94 Mott St (10013), between Canal & Hester Sts, in Chinatown. 212/226-6603. Chinese menu. Specializes in Cantonese banquet dishes. Hrs: 8 am-10:30 pm. Res accepted. A la carte entrees: dim sum $1.95-$6.50, lunch, dinner from $8.50. Original Oriental art and objets d'art. Cr cds: A, MC, V.

★ ★ ★ **HARRY CIPRIANI.** *781 Fifth Ave (10022), at 59th St, Midtown.* 212/753-5566. Italian menu. Specialties: risotto alla primavera, calf's liver veneziana, baked green noodles with ham. Hrs: 7-10:30 am, noon-3 pm, 6-10:45 pm. Res accepted. Bar. Wine cellar. A la carte entrees: bkfst $15-$25, lunch $23.95-$37.95, dinner $23.95-$46.95. Complete meals: lunch $25.95-$42.95, dinner $51.95-$64.95. Understated decor; display of photos, posters and lithographs, reminiscent of Hemingway in Harry's Bar in Venice. Family-owned since 1931. Jacket. Cr cds: A, C, D, DS, MC, V.

🖼

✔★ ★ **HASAKI.** *210 E 9th St (10003), between 2nd and 3rd Aves; East Village.* 212/473-3327. Japanese menu. Specialties: sushi, sashimi. Sushi bar. Hrs: 5-11:30 pm. Closed Jan 1, July 4, Dec 25. Wine, beer. A la carte entrees: dinner $15-$27. Complete meals: dinner: $17. Rock wall entrance with wooden benches. Totally nonsmoking. Cr cds: A, D, DS, MC, V.

★ ★ **HELENA'S.** *432 Lafayette St (10003), between Astor & 4th St, in East Village.* 212/677-5151. Hrs: noon-midnight; Fri, Sat to 1 am; Sat, Sun brunch noon-4 pm. Closed Dec 25. Spanish menu. Bar. A la carte entrees: lunch, dinner $6.95-$12.95. Complete meal: dinner $13-$25. Sat, Sun brunch $6.50-$8.50. Specialties: tapas, paella, parrilladas. Salsa Mon, Wed, Thurs. Street parking. Outdoor dining. Colorful decor; garden. Cr cds: A, MC, V.

🖼

✔★ ★ **HOME.** *20 Cornelia St (10014), between Bleeker & 4th Sts in Greenwich Village.* 212/243-9579. Specialties: blue cheese fondue, roasted chicken sautéed greens with ketchup. Hrs: 9 am-3 pm, 6-11 pm; Sun 5:30-10 pm; Sat, Sun brunch 11 am-4 pm. Closed 2 wks in Jan, July. Res accepted. Wine, beer. A la carte entrees: bkfst $2-$6, lunch $6-$9, dinner $13-$17. Sat, Sun brunch $5-$10. Outdoor dining. Contemporary decor. Totally nonsmoking. Cr cds: A.

★ ★ **HOSTERIA FIORELLA.** *1081 Third Ave (10021), between 63rd & 64th Sts, East Side.* 212/838-7570. Italian menu. Specialties: mixed antipasto, homemade pizzas, mixed seafood grill. Own pastries. Hrs: 5-11:30 pm; Sat from 11 am; Sun 11 am-11 pm; Sat, Sun brunch to 3 pm. Closed Thanksgiving. Res accepted. Bar. A la carte entrees: dinner $15.95-$26.75. Sat, Sun brunch $12.50-$16. Casual Tuscan decor with nautical theme; two-level dining. Cr cds: A, D, MC, V.

🖼

★ **HOT TOMATO.** *676 6th Ave (10010), at W 21st St, in Chelsea.* 212/691-3535. Specialties: free-range bison burger, "best" Yankee meatloaf, "best" macaroni & cheese. Own pastries. Hrs: 11:30-1 am; Thurs to 2 am; Fri to 4 am; Sat 10-4 am; Sun 10 am-10 pm; Sat, Sun brunch to 5 pm. Closed Dec 25. Bar. A la carte entrees: lunch $6.95-$13.95, dinner $7.95-$18.95. Sat, Sun brunch $5.95-$14.95. Outdoor dining. Casual decor with tomato fixtures. Totally nonsmoking. Cr cds: A, C, D, MC, V.

★ ★ ★ **HUDSON RIVER CLUB.** *250 Vesey St (10281), in building 4 of World Financial Center, lobby level, Financial District.* 212/786-1500. Web www.hudsonriverclub.com. As its name suggests, this spacious and clubby dining room has river views of New York Harbor and the Statue of Liberty. Rotating art is displayed on walls. Hudson River Valley produce is showcased, and the towering desserts are like edible sculptures. Specialties: foie gras duo, roasted oysters with leeks, Hudson River Valley dishes. Own pastries. Hrs: 11:30 am-2:30 pm, 5-9:30 pm; Fri to 10 pm; Sat 5-10 pm; Sun brunch 11:30 am-2:30 pm. Closed Memorial Day, Labor Day, Dec 25; also Sun July-Aug. Res required. Bar. Wine cellar. A la carte entrees: lunch $24-$29, dinner $29-$36. Menu dégustation: 6-course dinner $60. Sun brunch $32. Street parking. Jacket. Cr cds: A, C, D, DS, MC, V.

Ⓓ

✔★ **HUNAN GARDEN.** *1 Mott St (10013), at Bowery St, in Chinatown.* 212/732-7270. Chinese menu. Specialties: Peking duck, lobster in ginger & garlic, sautéed chicken with shrimp. Hrs: 11 am-11 pm; Fri, Sat to midnight. Bar. A la carte entrees: lunch, dinner $6-$15. Enclosed sidewalk cafe. Cr cds: A, MC, V.

★ ★ ★ **I TRE MERLI.** *463 W Broadway (10012), between Prince & Houston Sts, in SoHo.* 212/254-8699. Web itremerli@com.sprint. Northern Italian menu. Specialties: herb ravioli with walnut sauce, focaccia sandwiches, sea bass with artichoke. Hrs: noon-1 am; Fri, Sat to 2 am. Res required Fri-Sun dinner. Bar to 4 am. Wine cellar. A la carte entrees: lunch $10-$23, dinner $12-$25. Outdoor dining. Over 1,000 wine bottles line exposed brick walls in converted warehouse bldg. Cr cds: A, D, JCB, MC, V.

★ ★ ★ **I TRULLI.** *122 E 27th St (10016), in Murray Hill.* 212/481-7373. Italian menu. Specialties: baked oysters, pancetta, grilled baby octopus. Hrs: noon-3 pm, 5:30-11 pm; Fri to midnight; Sat 5:30 pm-midnight. Closed Sun; major hols. Res accepted. Bar. A la carte entrees: lunch, dinner $16-$28. Outdoor dining. Wood-burning oven in the shape of a domed stone structure. Cr cds: A, MC, V.

✔★ ★ **IL CORTILE.** *125 Mulberry St (10013), between Canal & Hester Sts, in Little Italy.* 212/226-6060. Web www.menusonline.com. Italian menu. Specialties: capellini piselli e prosciutto, rack of veal sautéed in wine sauce, shrimp and seppioline grilled with garlic. Own pasta. Hrs: noon-midnight; Fri, Sat to 1 am. Closed Thanksgiving, Dec 24, 25. Res accepted. Bar. A la carte entrees: lunch, dinner $12.50-$26. Dining in skylighted garden rm. Cr cds: A, C, D, MC, V.

★ ★ ★ **IL MONELLO.** *1460 Second Ave (10021), between 76th & 77th Sts, Upper East Side.* 212/535-9310. Northern Italian menu. Specialties: combination pasta, stuffed veal chop. Own breads. Hrs: noon-3 pm, 5-11 pm; Fri, Sat to midnight; Sun 5-10 pm. Closed major hols. Res accepted. Bar. Wine cellar. A la carte entrees: lunch $21-$31, dinner $25-$35. Print collection by renowned 20th-century artists. Cr cds: A, C, D, MC, V.

★ ★ ★ **IL NIDO.** *251 E 53rd St (10022), between Second & Third Aves, on the East Side.* 212/753-8450. Northern Italian menu. Specializes in seasonal dishes. Own pastries. Hrs: noon-3 pm, 5:30-11 pm. Closed Sun; major hols. Res required. Bar. Wine cellar. A la carte entrees: lunch $21-$30, dinner $21-$38. Cr cds: A, C, D, MC, V.

★ ★ **IL TOSCANACCIO.** *7 E 59th St (10022), between Fifth & Madison Aves, Midtown.* 212/935-3535. Italian menu. Specializes in rustic Tuscan cuisine. Hrs: noon-3 pm, 5:30-11:30 pm; Sat, Sun from 5:30 pm. Closed some major hols. Res accepted. Bar. A la carte entrees: lunch $18-$22, dinner $19-$32. Photographs of Tuscan countryside and marketplace. Outdoor dining. Cr cds: A, D, MC, V.

Ⓓ

✔★ ★ **INDIGO.** *142 W 10th St (10014), between Greenwich Ave and Waverly Pl in Greenwich Village.* 212/691-7757. Web www.lumaindigo.com. Contemporary Amer menu. Specialties: wild mushroom strudel, roast leg of lamb, grilled salmon. Hrs: 6-11 pm; Fri, Sat to 11:30 pm; Sun 5:30-10:30 pm. Closed major hols. Res accepted. Bar. A la carte entrees: dinner $13-$16. Jazz on Sun. Contemporary decor. Cr cds: A.

🖼

✔★ ★ **ITHAKA.** *48 Barrow St (10014), between Bleeker St and 7th Ave S, in Greenwich Village.* 212/727-8886. Greek menu. Specialties: baked shrimp, baby lamb, stuffed eggplant. Hrs: 5 pm-midnight; Fri from 5 pm; Sat, Sun noon-1 am. Res accepted. Bar. A la carte entrees: lunch $7.95-$13.95, dinner $13.95-$18.95. Outdoor dining. Greek taverna decor. Cr cds: A, D, MC, V.

🖼

★ **JAPONICA.** *100 University Place (10003), at 12th St, East Village.* 212/243-7752. Japanese menu. Specialties: sushi, tataki, vegetable dumplings. Hrs: noon-10:30 pm; Fri, Sat to 11 pm; summer hrs vary. Closed Jan 1, Dec 25. Wine, beer. A la carte entrees: lunch $9-$26, dinner $14-$33. Japanese decor. Cr cds: A.

★ ★ ★ ★ **JEAN GEORGES.** *(See Trump International Hotel & Tower)* 212/299-3900. Opened in 1997 in the lobby of the Trump International Hotel and Towers, this newest venue of acclaimed chef Jean-Georges Vongerichten's fabulous French cuisine is a bright star in New York's culinary scene. The food is a study in herbs and spices that even experienced diners may not have tried. The sleek ultramodern Adam Tihany decor, floor-to-ceiling windows, and seamless service are the complement to Vongerichten's innovative flavors and creations. French menu. Specialties: Arctic char baked with wood sorrel, lobster tartine with pumpkin seed and pea shoots, muscovy duck steak with spices. Own baking. Hrs: noon-2:30 pm, 5:30-11 pm. Closed Sun. Res required. Bar. Wine list. A la carte entrees: lunch, dinner $29-$36. Complete meals: lunch $45, dinner $78. Elegant decor, high ceilings; glass walls surround restaurant and overlook Central Park. Jacket. Cr cds: A, C, D, JCB, MC, V.

D

★ ★ ★ **JO JO.** *160 E 64th St (10021), between Lexington & 3rd Aves, Upper East Side.* 212/223-5656. French menu. Specialties: codfish sautéed; roasted duck breast; chicken roasted in ginger, olive and coriander. Hrs: noon-2:30 pm, 6-11 pm; Sat 5:30-11:30 pm. Closed Sun; Jan 1, July 4, Dec 25. Res required. Serv bar. A la carte entrees: lunch, dinner $19-$30. Complete meals: lunch $25, dinner $40-$60. 2-story townhouse; casual French bistro atmosphere. 1 dining area on main floor, 2 dining rms on 2nd floor. Cr cds: A, D, MC, V.

★ ★ **JOE ALLEN.** *326 W 46th St (10036), between 8th & 9th Aves, in Times Square/Theater District.* 212/581-6464. Web www.joeallen orso.com. Specialties: Caesar salad, sautéed calf's liver, meatloaf with mashed potatoes. Hrs: noon-11:45 pm; Sun, Wed, Sat from 11:30 am; Sun brunch to 4 pm. Closed Thanksgiving, Dec 25. Res accepted; required dinner. Bar. A la carte entrees: lunch $9-$19.50, dinner $12.50-$19.50. Sun brunch $9-$19.50. Casual, American pub atmosphere; posters of failed Broadway shows line walls. Family-owned. Cr cds: MC, V.

★ ★ **JUBILEE.** *347 E 54th St (10022), between 1st & 2nd Aves, Midtown.* 212/888-3569. French bistro menu. Specialties: snails with garlic and parsley butter, mussels prepared five different ways, grilled shell steak with green peppercorn sauce. Own pastries. Hrs: noon-3 pm, 5:30-11 pm; Sat from 5:30 pm; Sun 5:30-10:30 pm. Closed Sun in summer; Jan 1, Dec 24, 25. Res accepted; required dinner. Bar. A la carte entrees: lunch $13-$16.50, dinner $14.50-$23.50. Complete meal: lunch $18. Jazz Thurs. Intimate French country bistro in townhouse bldg. Cr cds: A, D, MC, V.

★ ★ ★ **JUDSON GRILL.** *152 W 52nd St (10019), between 6th & 7th Aves, Midtown.* 212/582-5252. Web www.citysearch.com/nyc/judson grill. Specialties: peekytoe crab cocktail, Jamison farm's organic loin of lamb, spring vegetable plate. Hrs: noon-2:30 pm, 5:30-11 pm; Fri to 11:30 pm; Sat 5:30-11:30 pm. Closed Sun. Closed major hols. Res accepted. Bar. A la carte entrees: lunch $17-$24.50, dinner $19.50-$32. Vaulted ceiling; all glass 2-story front. Circular mahogany bar. Cr cds: A, D, DS, MC, V.

D

★ ★ **KEENS STEAKHOUSE.** *72 W 36th St (10018), between Fifth & Sixth Aves, Midtown.* 212/947-3636. Specialties: aged Porterhouse steak for 2 or 3, mutton chops. Hrs: 11:45 am-3 pm, 5:30-10 pm; Sat from 5 pm. Closed Sun; some major hols; also Sat, Sun in summer. Res accepted. Bar. A la carte entrees: lunch $13.50-$20, dinner $16.50-$32.50. Historic restaurant, established 1885; dark oak paneling, leaded-glass windows, famous clay pipe collection on ceiling. Famous patrons have included Teddy Roosevelt, Albert Einstein and Lillie Langtry, who sued to enter the once all-male premises. Cr cds: A, C, D, MC, V.

★ ★ **KINGS' CARRIAGE HOUSE.** *251 E 82nd St (10028), between 2nd & 3rd Aves, Upper East Side.* 212/734-5490. Irish, English menu. Specialties: grilled loin of lamb, pan-seared wild salmon, grilled filet mignon. Own pastries. Hrs: noon-3 pm, 6-10:30 pm; Sun 2-9 pm; high tea Mon-Fri 3-4 pm. Closed Dec 25. Res required high tea & Fri, Sat dinner. Bar. Prix fixe: lunch $12.95, dinner $39. High tea $14. Turn-of-the-century carriage house; romantic, intimate atmosphere. Totally nonsmoking. Cr cds: A, MC, V.

D

★ ★ **KURUMA ZUSHI.** *7 E 47th St (10017), between 5th & Madison Aves, on 2nd floor, Midtown.* 212/317-2802. Hrs: noon-2 pm,

5:30-10 pm. Closed major hols; also wk of July 4. Res accepted. Japanese menu. Bar. A la carte entrees: lunch, dinner $6-$18. Complete meal: lunch $20-$50, dinner $45-$100. Specializes in sushi, sashimi. Street parking. Japanese decor; sushi bar. Family-owned since 1977. Totally nonsmoking. Cr cds: A, JCB, MC, V.

★ ★ **L'ULIVO.** *184 Spring St (10012), between Sullivan & Thompson Sts, in SoHo.* 212/343-1445. Hrs: noon-3:30 pm, 5 pm-midnight; Sat, Sun noon-midnight. Closed Dec 25. Res accepted. Italian menu. Bar. A la carte entrees: lunch $6-$12, dinner $8-$14. Child's meals. Specializes in wood-burning oven pizzas, pasta, salads. Street parking. Outdoor dining. Contemporary Italian decor. Totally nonsmoking. No cr cds accepted.

✔ ★ **LA BONNE SOUPE.** *48 W 55th St (10019), Midtown.* 212/586-7650. French menu. Seasonal specialties. Hrs: 11:30 am-midnight; Sun to 11 pm; Sun brunch 11:30 am-3 pm. Closed some major hols. Bar. A la carte entrees: lunch, dinner $8.75-$18.95. Complete meals: lunch, dinner $18.95. Sun brunch $12.75. Child's meals. Limited outdoor balcony dining. Open kitchen. French bistro decor. Cr cds: A, MC, V.

★ ★ ★ ★ **LA CÔTE BASQUE.** *60 W 55th St (10019), Midtown.* 212/688-6525. Murals of the Basque coast, dark wooden cross beams and faux windows are just some of the elements that have followed this restaurant to its new home. Dramatic presentation—such as the signature roast duckling carved at tableside, or the glazed pumpkin custard served with a flaming candle inside a pumpkin lantern—adds to the dining experience here. French menu. Own pastries. Hrs: noon-2:30 pm, 5:30-10:30 pm; Fri to 11:30 pm; Sat 5:30-11:30 pm; Sun 5-10 pm. Closed major hols. Res required. Bar. Prix fixe: lunch $34, dinner $62. Chef-owned. Jacket. Cr cds: A, C, D, MC, V.

D

★ ★ ★ **LA CARAVELLE.** *33 W 55th St (10019), between 5th & 6th Aves in Midtown.* 212/586-4252. Murals of Parisian scenes decorate the walls, and light peach banquettes provide seating in this spacious and comfortable dining room. Classic and contemporary French menu. Specialties: truffeled pike quenelles in lobster sauce, crispy duck with cranberries, souffles. Own baking. Hrs: noon-2:30 pm, 5:30-10 pm. Closed Sun; major hols; also 1 wk prior to Labor Day. Res required. Bar. Wine cellar. A la carte entrees: lunch $25-$36, dinner from $44. Prix fixe: 3-course lunch $36, 3-course dinner $65, 5-course tasting menu $85. Child's meals. Cr cds: A, C, D, JCB, MC, V.

D

✔ ★ ★ ★ **LA MAISON JAPONAISE.** *125 E 39th St (10016), at Lexington Ave, Midtown.* 212/682-7375. French, Japanese menu. Specialties: chicken flambé, filet of sole chinoise, filet of tuna "La Maison Japonaise." Hrs: 11:45 am-2:30 pm, 5:30-10:30 pm; Sat from 5:30 pm. Closed Sun; major hols. Res accepted. Bar. Semi-a la carte: lunch $10.95-$16.75, dinner $10.95-$16.95. Complete meals: lunch $18.95, dinner $20.95. Cr cds: A, C, D, DS, MC, V.

✔ ★ ★ ★ **LA MANGEOIRE.** *1008 Second Ave (10022), between 53rd & 54th Sts, on the East Side.* 212/759-7086. Southern French menu. Specialties: Mediterranean-style fish soup, roasted rack of lamb, lavender scented crème brûlée. Hrs: noon-2:30 pm, 5:30-10:30 pm; Fri to 11 pm; Sat 5:30-11 pm; Sun brunch 11:30 am-3 pm. Closed major hols. Res accepted. Serv bar. A la carte entrees: lunch $7.95-$21, dinner $14.95-$26. Prix fixe: lunch $19.76, dinner 5:30-6:45 pm $19.76-$25. Sun brunch $13.95. Street parking. Country French inn atmosphere. Cr cds: A, C, D, MC, V.

★ ★ ★ **LA METAIRIE.** *189 W 10th St (10014), west of 7th Ave S, in Greenwich Village.* 212/989-0343. French menu. Specialties: filet mignon, rack of lamb. Hrs: noon-3 pm, 5-11 pm; Fri, Sat to midnight; Sun to 10 pm; Sat, Sun brunch noon-3 pm. Res required. A la carte entrees: lunch $12-$19, dinner $18-$29. Sat, Sun brunch $12-$19. French country atmosphere. Cr cds: A, D, DS, MC, V.

D

★ ★ ★ **LA RESERVE.** *4 W 49th St (10019), between Fifth & Sixth Aves, Midtown.* 212/247-2993. Web www.kerrymenu.com. French haute cuisine. Specialties: lobster and scallops in basil sauce, sautéed squab in foie gras wine sauce, grilled baby chicken with lemon olive oil and rosemary. Own pastries. Hrs: noon-3 pm, 5:30-10:30 pm; Fri, Sat to 11 pm. Closed Sun; major hols; also 1st wk July. Res required. Bar. Prix fixe: lunch $32, dinner $54. Pre-theater dinner $39.50. Wood paneled dining rm with wildlife murals, Venetian glass sconces, chandeliers. Jacket. Cr cds: A, D, JCB, MC, V.

D

✔★ ★ **LA TRAVIATA.** *461 W 23rd St (10011), between 9th & 10th Ave, in Chelsea.* 212/243-5497. Italian menu. Specialties: veal medallions with prosciutto, filet of red snapper, penne with spicy tomato sauce. Hrs: 11:30 am-10:30 pm; Fri to 11 pm; Sat 4:30-11 pm; Sun brunch 1-9 pm. Closed Sun (Memorial Day-Labor Day); July 4. Res accepted. Bar. Semi-a la carte: lunch, dinner $11.50-$23.95. Sun brunch $11.50-$23.95. Entertainment Wed-Sat. Northern Italian decor. Cr cds: A, D, DS, MC, V.

D ⊠

★ ★ ★ **LAYLA.** *211 W Broadway (10013), at Franklin St, in Tribeca.* 212/431-0700. Web www.cuisine.com. Mediterranean menu. Specialties: grilled chicken tagine, Moroccan spiced monkfish kebob, grilled salmon wrapped in grape leaves. Hrs: 5:30-10:45 pm; Fri noon-2:30 pm, 5:30-11:30 pm; Sat to 11:30 pm; Sun to 9:45 pm. Closed most major hols. Res accepted. Bar to midnight. A la carte entrees: lunch $12-$18, dinner $20-$27. Prix fixe: lunch $19.99. Outdoor dining. Arabian nights decor. Totally nonsmoking. Cr cds: A, D, MC, V.

★ ★ ★ ★ **LE BERNARDIN.** *155 W 51st St (10019), in Equitable Life Tower, between Sixth & Seventh Aves, Times Square/Theater District.* 212/489-1515. Web www.le-bernardin.com. Huge seascapes fill the paneled walls of this polished, high-ceilinged restaurant, where fish and seafood dinners are as delicious and well prepared as you can get anywhere. French, seafood menu. Specialties: monkfish with cabbage, thyme and pepper rare-seared yellowfin tuna, crispy Chinese-spiced red snapper. Own pastries. Hrs: noon-2:30 pm, 5:30-10:30 pm; Fri, Sat to 11 pm; Mon from 6 pm. Closed Sun; major hols. Res accepted. Bar. Prix fixe: lunch $42, dinner $70. Street parking. Jacket. Cr cds: A, C, D, JCB, MC, V.

D

★ ★ ★ **LE BOEUF À LA MODE.** *539 E 81st St (10028), near East End Ave, in Yorkville section of Upper East Side.* 212/249-1473. French menu. Specialties: fresh grilled salmon, châteaubriand with béarnaise sauce, roasted duck. Hrs: 5:30-11 pm. Closed major hols; also Sun in July, Aug. Res accepted. Bar. A la carte entrees: dinner $19-$30. Prix fixe: dinner $34. Outdoor dining. Intimate dining rm with colorful murals. Cr cds: A, D, MC, V.

★ ★ ★ ★ ★ **LE CIRQUE 2000.** *(See The New York Palace Hotel)* 212/303-7788. A meal at Le Cirque is a culinary event—a unique experience filled with excellent food served in extravagant surroundings. The futuristic Adam Tihany decor and boldly colored geometric patterns are at odd juxtaposition to the original, gilded, coffered ceilings, creating visual chaos or aesthetic interest, depending on one's point of view. Table settings are exquisite with custom china, Venetian glass goblets, delicate linen and sprays of peach and red roses. Chef Sotta Khunn's classic French-Italian and Jacques Torres's over-the-top desserts are uniformly wonderful and service is professional and accommodating. French menu. Specialties: sea bass wrapped in crisp potatoes with barolo sauce, braised veal shank, lobster roasted with young artichokes. Hrs: 11:30 am-3 pm, 5:30-11 pm; Fri, Sat to midnight. Res required. Bar to 1 am. Wine list. A la carte entrees: lunch $26-$34, dinner $28-$38. Complete meals: lunch $40, dinner $90. Jacket, tie. Cr cds: A, C, D, MC, V.

D

★ ★ ★ **LE COLONIAL.** *149 E 57th St (10022), between Third & Lexington Aves, on the East Side.* 212/752-0808. Vietnamese menu. Specialties: whole red snapper with spicy sour sauce, roast duck with tamarind sauce, sautéed jumbo shrimp with curried coconut sauce. Hrs: noon-2:15 pm, 5:30-10:30 pm; Fri to midnight; Sat 5:30-11 pm; Sun from 5:30 pm. Closed July 4, Thanksgiving, Dec 25. Res accepted. Bar 4:30

pm-1 am. A la carte entrees: lunch $12.50-$19.50, dinner $14.50-$29.50. Multi-level dining. Bamboo furniture, bird cages. Cr cds: A, D, MC, V.

D

★ ★ **LE MADELEINE.** *403 W 43rd St (10036), between 9th & 10th Aves, Times Square/Theater District.* 212/246-2993. Web www.new york.sidewalk.com.madeleine. Hrs: noon-3 pm, 5-11 pm; Fri, Sat to 11:30 pm. Closed Dec 25. Res accepted. French menu. Bar. A la carte entrees: lunch $8-$22, dinner $16-$23. Child's meals. Specialties: grilled slices of Maine salmon, roasted organic duck with sundried cranberries, grilled leg of lamb. Street parking. Outdoor dining. Casual bistro; enclosed garden. Family-owned since 1979. Totally nonsmoking. Cr cds: A, C, D, DS, MC, V.

D

★ ★ ★ **LE MADRI.** *168 W 18th St (10011), at 7th Ave, in Chelsea.* 212/727-8022. Italian menu. Specializes in regional Italian cuisine, seasonal dishes. Hrs: noon-3 pm, 5:30-11:30 pm; Sun to 10:30 pm; Sun brunch 11:30 am-3:30 pm. Closed some major hols. Res accepted. Bar. A la carte entrees: lunch $12-$18, dinner $19-$28.50. Sun brunch $21.50. Valet parking. Outdoor dining. Vaulted ceiling supported by columns; colorfully tiled wood-burning pizza oven. Jacket. Cr cds: A, D, MC, V.

★ ★ ★ **LE PERIGORD.** *405 E 52nd St (10022), between First Ave & Sutton Place, Midtown.* 212/755-6244. Modern French cuisine. Specialties: confit of duck, grilled Dover sole, boneless quails stuffed with vegetables. Own desserts. Hrs: noon-3 pm, 5:15-10:30 pm; Sat, Sun 5:15-10:30 pm. Res accepted. Bar. Wine cellar. A la carte entrees: lunch $18-$30, dinner $22-$38. Prix fixe: lunch $32, dinner $52. Street parking. Family-owned. Cr cds: A, C, D, DS, MC, V.

★ ★ ★ **LE RÉGENCE.** *(See Plaza Athénée Hotel)* 212/606-4647. French menu. Specialties: squab breast, Quebec foie gras, veal cheek and tongue terrine. Own pastries. Hrs: 7-10 am, noon-2:30 pm, 6-9:30 pm; Sun brunch noon-2:30 pm. Res accepted. Bar 11 am-midnight. Wine cellar. A la carte entrees: bkfst $9.50-$16.50, lunch $27-$32, dinner $28-$34. Prix fixe: bkfst $25, lunch $34. Sun brunch $42.50. Child's meals. Elegant decor. Cr cds: A, C, D, ER, JCB, MC, V.

D

★ ★ ★ **LE REFUGE.** *166 E 82nd St (10021), between Lexington & Third Aves, Upper East Side.* 212/861-4505. French menu. Specialties: roast duck with fresh fruit sauce; grilled salmon with red wine vinaigrette, garlic and olive oil; loin of lamb stuffed with spinach. Own baking. Hrs: noon-3 pm, 5-11 pm; Sun noon-4 pm, 5-9:30 pm; Sat brunch to 3 pm; Sun brunch to 4 pm. Closed major hols. Res accepted. Serv Bar. A la carte entrees: lunch $12.50-$15.50, dinner $17.50-$24.50. Sat, Sun brunch $17.50. Garden terrace dining (summer). French country inn decor. Cr cds: A.

✔★ ★ **THE LEMON.** *230 Park Ave S (10003), at 19th St, Gramercy Park.* 212/614-1200. Specialties: crispy duck spring rolls, five spice Chilean sea bass. Hrs: 11:30 am-3:30 pm, 5:30 pm-midnight; Thurs-Sat to 2 am; Sun brunch 11:30 am-4 pm. Closed Jan 1, Dec 25. Res accepted. Bar to 3 am. Semi-a la carte: lunch $7-$15, dinner $11-$22. Sun brunch $7-$15. Bistro decor. Cr cds: A, D, MC, V.

D

★ ★ **LENOX ROOM.** *1278 Third Ave (10021), between 73rd & 74th Sts, Upper East Side.* 212/772-0404. Web www.lenoxroom.com. Specializes in progressive American cuisine, fresh seafood. Hrs: noon-2:30 pm, 6-11 pm. Closed Jan 1. Res accepted. Bar. A la carte entrees: lunch $12-$17, dinner $19-$32. Complete meals: lunch $19.99. Raw bar. Several intimate dining areas. Cr cds: A, C, D, MC, V.

D

★ ★ ★ ★ ★ **LES CÉLÉBRITÉS.** *(See Essex House Hotel Nikko New York)* 212/484-5113. Web www.essexhouse.com. The superb French menu is complemented by the elegant surroundings, in which paintings by Hollywood celebrities adorn the walls. French menu. Specialties: filet of Dover sole, braised rack of veal, crispy duck braised in honey. Hrs: 6-10 pm; Sat to 10:30 pm. Closed Sun, Mon; also mid-Aug-mid-Sept. Res required. Bar. Wine cellar. A la carte entrees: dinner $38-$45. Table d'hôte:

dinner $75 & $105. Valet parking. Jacket. Cr cds: A, C, D, DS, ER, JCB, MC, V.

D

★ ★ ★ ★ ★ **LESPINASSE.** *(See The St Regis Hotel)* 212/339-6719. Web www.ittsheraton.com. A high, gilded ceiling, crystal chandelier, plush rugs, murals and large armchairs characterize this grand and spacious Louis XV dining room. An outstanding continental culinary experience features the best of the season. French menu. Specialties: crisped black bass, pan-seared rack of lamb, braised rib of beef. Hrs: 7-10:30 am, noon-1:45 pm, 5:30-9:45 pm; Fri, Sat to 10:15 pm; Sun 7-11:30 am. Res required. Bar 11:30-1 am; Fri, Sat to 2 am; Sun noon-midnight. Extensive wine list. A la carte entrees: bkfst $14.50-$21, dinner $32-$38. Complete meals: lunch $48, dinner $78-$130. Valet parking. Jacket. Cr cds: A, C, D, DS, ER, JCB, MC, V.

D

★ ★ **LOBSTER CLUB.** 24 E 80th St (10021), Upper East Side. 212/249-6500. Eclectic Amer menu. Specialties: matzo brei with wild lilies, Mom's meatloaf, almond-crusted banana split with malted milkball. Hrs: 11:30 am-3 pm, 5:30-10:30 pm; Fri, Sat to 11 pm; Sun to 10 pm. Closed major hols. Res accepted. Bar. A la carte entrees: lunch $15-$24.50, dinner $16.50-$29. Bi-level dining room with fireplace. Totally nonsmoking. Cr cds: A, D, MC, V.

★ ★ **LOLA.** 30 W 22nd St (10010), between 5th & 6th Aves, in Chelsea. 212/675-6700. Contemporary Amer menu. Specialties: Lola fried chicken with Cuban black beans, pineapple-glazed salmon with noodle cake, corn and rock shrimp. Own pastries. Hrs: noon-3 pm, 6 pm-12:30 am; Sat from 6 pm; Sun brunch sittings: 9:30 am, 11:30 am & 1:45 pm. Closed major hols. Res accepted. Bar noon-1 am. Wine list. A la carte entrees: lunch $15-$20.50, dinner $22-$32.50. Sun brunch $29.75. Entertainment. Elegant decor; French doors; black and white prints of city. Cr cds: A, D, MC, V.

★ ★ **LUMA.** 200 9th Ave (10011), between 22nd & 23rd Sts, in Chelsea. 212/633-8033. E-mail luma@interport.net; web www.lumaindigo.com. Hrs: 6-11 pm; Sun 5:30-10 pm. Closed most major hols. Res accepted. Contemporary Amer menu. Serv bar. A la carte entrees: dinner $16-$24. Specialties: pan-fried oysters, grilled filet mignon, whole roasted snapper. Street parking. Contemporary decor. Totally nonsmoking. Cr cds: A, D, DS, MC, V.

★ ★ **LUMI.** 963 Lexington Ave (10021), at 70th St, Upper East Side. 212/570-2335. Italian menu. Specialties: stripped roasted bass, osso bucco con risotto all' ortolana. Hrs: noon-11 pm. Res accepted. Bar. A la carte entrees: lunch $12.50-$22, dinner $14-$29. Outdoor dining. Contemporary decor. Cr cds: A, D, MC, V.

★ ★ **LUSARDI'S.** 1494 Second Ave (10021), between 77th & 78th Sts, Upper East Side. 212/249-2020. Northern Italian menu. Specialties: risotto with truffles or with wild mushrooms. Hrs: noon-3 pm, 5 pm-midnight. Closed most major hols. Res accepted. Bar. A la carte entrees: lunch, dinner $14-$26. Italian-style trattoria. Seasonal menu. Totally nonsmoking. Cr cds: A, C, D, DS, MC, V.

D

★ ★ ★ ★ **LUTÈCE.** 249 E 50th St (10022), between 2nd & 3rd Aves, Midtown. 212/752-2225. Dining at this New York City culinary favorite is in four different rooms: an airy, high-ceilinged main room in a covered garden, a quiet room decorated with stenciled foliage and two upstairs rooms subtly lighted by crystal chandeliers and hung with original oil paintings. French haute cuisine. Specialties: snails and wild mushroom in phyllo, sautéed turbotin in a tarragon broth, roast rack of lamb with a mustard honey glaze. Hrs: noon 2 pm, 5:30 10 pm; Mon from 5:30 pm; Fri to 10:30 pm; Sat 5:30-10:30 pm. Closed Sun. Res required. Bar. Wine cellar. Table d'hôte: lunch $38. Prix fixe: dinner $65. Cr cds: A, C, D, DS, MC, V.

★ ★ ★ **MALONEY & PORCELLI.** 37 E 50th St (10022), between Madison & Park Aves, Midtown. 212/750-2233. Specialties: angry lobster, crackling pork shank, drunken donuts. Own desserts. Hrs: noon-11:30 pm; Sat, Sun brunch to 3 pm. Closed Jan 1, Dec 25. Res accepted. Bar. Wine list. A la carte entrees: lunch $18.50-$28.75, dinner $19.50-$29.75. Sat,

Sun brunch $12.50-$19.50. Two-story restaurant with grand staircase, skylights. Cr cds: A, C, D, JCB, MC, V.

✔ ★ ★ **MANHATTAN BISTRO.** 129 Spring St (10012), between Wooster & Greene, in SoHo. 212/966-3459. Specialties: steak frites, cassoulet, black Angus steak au poivre. Hrs: 11:30 am-midnight; Fri, Sat to 2 am; Sat, Sun brunch 11:30 am-4:30 pm. Closed Memorial Day, Dec 25. Res accepted. Bar from 11:30 am. A la carte entrees: lunch $8.50-$15, dinner $13-$24.95. Complete meals: lunch $13.95, dinner $21.95. Sat, Sun brunch $8.50-$15. Intimate storefront bistro in area of studios, art galleries. Family-owned. Cr cds: A, MC, V.

★ ★ ★ **MANHATTAN GRILL.** 1161 First Ave (10021), between 63rd & 64th Sts, Upper East Side. 212/888-6556. Web www.dinette.com. Specializes in steak, lobster. Hrs: noon-11 pm; Sun brunch 11:30 am-3:30 pm. Closed Thanksgiving, Dec 25. Res accepted. Bar from 4 pm. Prix fixe: lunch, pre-theater dinner $17.95-$28.95. A la carte entrees: lunch $8.50-$19, dinner $18.75-$35.75. Sun brunch $17.95. Club-like atmosphere; paneling, Oriental rugs, 1920s period lighting. Cr cds: A, C, D, DS, JCB, MC, V.

★ ★ ★ **MANHATTAN OCEAN CLUB.** 57 W 58th St (10019), off Sixth Ave, Midtown. 212/371-7777. Specialties: red snapper with a leek crust, roasted blackfish, mahi-mahi marinated in Moroccan spices. Own pastries. Hrs: noon-11:30 pm; Sat, Sun from 5 pm. Closed Jan 1, Thanksgiving, Dec 25. Res required. Bar. Wine list. A la carte entrees: lunch, dinner $19.50-$29.50. Atmosphere of luxury ocean liner; broad sweeping staircase connects 2 floors. Cr cds: A, C, D, DS, JCB, MC, V.

★ ★ ★ ★ **MARCH.** 405 E 58th St (10022), between First Ave & Sutton Place, Upper East Side. 212/754-6272. Elegantly understated, the three dining rooms in this romantic townhouse are filled with antiques, a travertine floor and burled wood wainscoting. Service is polished, and there are hints of Asian influences in the cuisine. Specialties: confit de foie gras de canard, rack of Colorado lamb, seared rare bluefin tuna. Hrs: 6-10:30 pm. Closed major hols. Res required. Bar. Tasting menu: 4-course dinner $68, 7-course dinner $90. Outdoor dining. Jacket. Cr cds: A, C, D, JCB, MC, V.

★ ★ **MARLOWE.** 328 W 46th St (10036), between 8th & 9th Aves, Times Square/Theater District. 212/765-3815. Specialties: spiced seared yellow fin tuna, black Angus sirloin with caramelized shallot confit, grilled leg of lamb with ragout of woodland mushrooms. Hrs: noon-3 pm, 5 pm-midnight; Sun brunch noon-3 pm. Closed Dec 25. Res accepted. Bar. A la carte entrees: lunch $6-$13, dinner $9-$24. Complete meals: lunch $10, dinner $19. Sun brunch $4.95-$12.95. Outdoor dining. French country inn atmosphere. Totally nonsmoking. Cr cds: A, C, D, MC, V.

★ ★ **MARYLOU'S.** 21 W 9th St (10011), between Fifth & Sixth Aves, in Greenwich Village. 212/533-0012. Continental menu. Specialties: crispy whole red snapper, sesame-crusted swordfish, triple-thick lamb chops. Hrs: 5:30 pm-midnight; Fri, Sat to 1 am; Sun 5:30-11 pm; Sun brunch noon-4 pm. Closed some major hols. Res accepted. Bar. A la carte entrees: dinner $14-$24. Sun brunch $13.95. In 19th-century town house; fireplace, library, changing art exhibits. Cr cds: A, C, D, DS, MC, V.

★ ★ **MATTHEW'S.** 1030 Third Ave (10021), at 61st St, on the upper East Side. 212/838-4343. Specialties: crispy red snapper, Maine crab cakes, lamb shank. Hrs: noon-11 pm. Res accepted. Bar. A la carte entrees: lunch $14-$24, dinner $20-$27. Pre-theater dinner 5:30-6:45 pm, $35. Mediterranean atmosphere; white tented ceilings. Cr cds: A, C, D, MC, V.

D

★ ★ **MAYA.** 1191 First Ave (10021), between 64th & 65th Sts, Upper East Side. 212/585-1818. Hrs: 5:30-11 pm; Fri, Sat to midnight; Sun brunch 11 am-2 pm. Closed Jan 1, Dec 25. Res accepted. Mexican menu. Bar. A la carte entrees: dinner $16.95-$23.50. Sun brunch $34.95. Specialties: pan-seared red snapper with achiote paste, grilled butterflied filet mignon, chile relleno. Own tortillas. Street parking. Adobe-style decor; art, sculptures. Totally nonsmoking. Cr cds: A, D, DS, MC, V.

D

★ **MED GRILL BISTRO & CAFE.** *725 5th Ave (10022), between 56th & 57th Sts, in Trump Tower, Midtown.* 212/751-3526. Continental, Italian menu. Specializes in salad, pasta, risotto. Hrs: Cafe 8:30 am-6:30 pm, Bistro 11:30 am-4 pm. Closed some major hols. Res accepted. Bar 11:30 am-4 pm. A la carte entrees: lunch $9.95-$21.23. Contemporary decor with prints & oils on display; overlooks wall with cascading water. Cr cds: A, D, DS, MC, V.

D

★ ★ **MELI MELO.** *110 Madison Ave (10016), between 29th & 30th Sts, in Murray Hill.* 212/686-5551. Hrs: 11 am-11 pm. Closed Sun; also major hols. Res accepted. Eclectic menu. Bar. A la carte entrees: lunch $10.95-$13.95, dinner $12.95-$18.95. Specialties: roasted duck with barley risotto & mango sauce, sautéed monkfish with sweet corn salsa, South Mouth marinated double pork chop with corn haystack. Complete meal: dinner $28.50. Street parking. Outdoor dining. Contemporary decor; Mediterranean mural, exotic floral arrangements. Cr cds: A, D, MC, V.

D

★ ★ ★ **MERLOT.** *48 W 63rd St (10023), between Broadway & Columbus Ave, Upper West Side.* 212/582-2121. Web www.iridiumjazz.com. Specialties: pan-roasted wild striped bass, bone-in filet mignon. Jazz club on lower level. Hrs: 5 pm-1 am; Sun brunch 11:30 am-4 pm. Res accepted. Bar. A la carte entrees: dinner $16-$28; prix fixe jazz brunch $19.95. Eccentric, colorful decor based on question: what would music look like if it could be seen? Unique architectural design emphasizes curves. Cr cds: A, C, D, DS, MC, V.

★ ★ ★ **MESA GRILL.** *102 Fifth Ave (10011), between 15th & 16th Sts, in Gramercy Park area.* 212/807-7400. Contemporary Southwestern menu. Specialties: shrimp and roasted garlic corn tamale, blue corn tortilla-crusted red snapper, black Angus steak. Hrs: noon-2:30 pm, 5:30-10:30 pm; Fri to 11 pm; Sat 5:30-11 pm; Sun 5:30-10:30 pm; Sat, Sun brunch 11:30 am-3 pm. Closed some major hols. Res accepted. Bar. A la carte entrees: lunch $12-$17, dinner $18-$28. Industrial designed loft. Cr cds: A, D, DS, MC, V.

D

★ **MEZZALUNA.** *1295 Third Ave (10021), between 74th & 75th Sts, Upper East Side.* 212/535-9600. Italian menu. Specializes in pizza baked in wood-burning oven. Own pasta. Hrs: noon-3:30 pm, 6 pm-12:30 am. Closed Dec 25. Wine, beer. A la carte entrees: lunch $13.50-$21, dinner $15-$30. Outdoor dining. Trattoria atmosphere. Antique marble top tables and bar. Cr cds: A, MC, V.

✔ ★ ★ **MEZZOGIORNO.** *195 Spring St (10012), near Sullivan St, in SoHo.* 212/334-2112. Northern Italian menu. Specializes in brick-oven pizza. Hrs: noon-3:30 pm, 6 pm-1 am; Sat, Sun noon-1 am. Closed Dec 25. Res accepted. Bar. A la carte entrees: lunch, dinner $13-$16. Outdoor dining. Cr cds: A.

✔ ★ ★ **MI COCINA.** *57 Jane St (10014), at Hudson St, in Greenwich Village.* 212/627-8273. Mexican menu. Specialties: pechuga con rajas, camarones enchipotlados, enchiladas de mole poblano. Hrs: 5:30-10:45 pm; Fri, Sat to 11:30 pm; Sun 4:30-10:15 pm; Sun brunch 11:30 am-2:45 pm. Closed Dec 24, 25; also 2 wks Aug. Res accepted. Bar. A la carte entrees: dinner $9.95-$17.95. Sun brunch $7.95-$13.95. Child's meals. Modern Mexican atmosphere; colorful decor with yellow stucco walls, red tile floors. Outdoor dining. Cr cds: A, C, D, JCB, MC, V.

★ ★ **MICHAEL JORDAN'S-THE STEAKHOUSE.** *23 Vanderbilt Ave (10017), Grand Central Station, Midtown.* 212/655-2300. Hrs: 11:30 am-midnight. Res accepted. Steakhouse menu. Bar. A la carte entrees: lunch, dinner $11-$31. Specializes in chicken, seafood, steak. Street parking. Train decor. Cr cds: A, C, D, MC, V.

⊡

★ ★ ★ **MICHAEL'S.** *24 W 55th St (10019), between Fifth & Sixth Aves, Midtown.* 212/767-0555. Specialties: Florida red snapper with mango and vidalia sweets, Atlantic swordfish with tomato basil vinaigrette, Canadian salmon with grilled peppers and onions. Own baking. Hrs: 7:30-9:30 am, noon-3 pm, 5:30-10:30 pm; Sat from 5:30 pm. Closed Sun; some major hols. Res accepted. Bar. Wine cellar. A la carte entrees: bkfst $5-$15, lunch $19.50-$24.50. Serv charge 15%. Child's meals. Original artwork throughout. Cr cds: A, D, MC, V.

✔ ★ **MICKEY MANTLE'S.** *42 Central Park South (10019), between Fifth & Sixth Aves, Midtown.* 212/688-7777. Specializes in chicken-fried steak, seafood, hickory-smoked ribs. Hrs: noon-11 pm; Sat to midnight. Res accepted. Bar to 12:30 am; Sun to midnight. A la carte entrees: lunch, dinner $10.95-$22.95 Child's meals. Outdoor dining. Rotating collection of baseball memorabilia; original sports art. Cr cds: A, C, D, DS, MC, V.

D ⊡

★ ★ **MIREZI.** *59 Fifth Ave (10003), betweeen 12th & 13th Sts, downtown.* 212/242-9710. Web www.mirezi.com. Hrs: 6-10 pm; Fri, Sat to 11 pm; early-bird dinner 6-7 pm. Closed Sun; also major hols. Res accepted. Pan-Asian menu. Bar 5-11 pm; Thurs-Sat to midnight. A la carte entrees: dinner $17-$27. Complete meal: dinner $48. Specialties: lobster with steamed rice noodle spring roll, red snapper in crispy rice paper, grilled hanger steak marinated Seoul-style. Garage parking. Asian decor. Totally nonsmoking. Cr cds: A, D, JCB, MC, V.

★ ★ ★ **MONKEY BAR.** *60 E 54th St (10022), between Park & Madison Aves, Midtown.* 212/838-2600. Specialties: Salmon with asparagus, East Coast halibut, Colorado rack of lamb. Hrs: noon-2:30 pm, 6-11 pm; Fri to 11:30 pm; Sat 5:30-11:30 pm; Sun 6-10 pm. Closed Dec 25. Res accepted. Bar to 2 am; Fri, Sat to 3 am. A la carte entrees: lunch $19-$24, dinner $23-$34. 5-course tasting menu: dinner $65. Pianist. Monkeys hang from lighting; murals of monkeys decorate the bar. Jacket. Cr cds: A, D, MC, V.

✔ ★ ★ ★ **MONTRACHET.** *239 W Broadway (10013), between Walker & White Sts, in Tribeca.* 212/219-2777. Web www.cuisine.com. French menu. Specialties: farfalle with escargots, turbot with porcini and asparagus. Own pastries. Hrs: 6-11 pm; Fri also noon-2:45 pm. Closed Sun; major hols. Res required. Bar. Wine list. A la carte entrees: lunch $16-$24, dinner $23-$30. Prix fixe: lunch $19.99, dinner $34, $42, tasting $75. Cr cds: A, MC, V.

D

★ ★ ★ **MONZÙ.** *142 Mercer (10012), Mercer & Prince, in SoHo.* 212/343-0333. Hrs: noon-3:30 pm, 6-11 pm; Fri to 2 am; Sat (brunch) noon-4 pm, 6 pm-2 am; Sun brunch noon-4 pm. Res required Sat (dinner). Italian menu. Bar. Wine cellar. A la carte entrees: lunch $9-$18, dinner $14-$26. Sat, Sun brunch $8-$18. Specialties: antipasti; hazelnut-crusted foie gras; linguine with bottarga di tonno, cauliflower, currants & pinenuts. Street parking. Mediterranean-style decor. Cr cds: A, D, JCB, MC, V.

D ⊡

★ ★ **MORENO.** *65 Irving Place (10003), at E 18th St, in Gramercy Park area.* 212/673-3939. Contemporary Italian menu. Specializes in seafood, pasta. Seasonal menu. Hrs: noon-3 pm, 5:30 pm-midnight; Sat from 5:30 pm; Sun noon-10:30 pm. Res accepted. Bar. A la carte entrees: lunch $15-$20.95, dinner $16.50-$24.95. Prix fixe: Sun $19.95. Child's meals. Outdoor dining. Cr cds: A, D, DS, MC, V.

D

★ ★ ★ **MORTON'S OF CHICAGO.** *551 Fifth Ave (10017), at 45th St, Midtown.* 212/972-3315. Specializes in steak, lobster. Hrs: 11:30 am-2:30 pm, 5 pm-midnight; Sat from 5 pm; Sun 5-11 pm. Closed most major hols. Res accepted. Bar. A la carte entrees: lunch, dinner $19.95-$31.95. Counterpart of famous Chicago steak house. Cr cds: A, D, JCB, MC, V.

★ ★ ★ **MR K'S.** *570 Lexington Ave (10022), Lexington & 51st St, Midtown.* 212/583-1668. Hrs: 11:30 am-11 pm; Sat, Sun from midnight. Res accepted. Chinese menu. Bar. Wine list. Semi-a la carte: lunch $16.95-$32.95, dinner $17.95-$37.97. Complete meal: lunch $25, dinner $45. Specialties: chicken supreme, firecracker fish, seared beef medallion with scallion & oyster sauce. Street parking. Art deco Chinese decor; elegant furnishings. Jacket. Totally nonsmoking. Cr cds: A, D, MC, V.

D

★ ★ ★ **NADAMAN HAKUBAI.** *(See The Kitano Hotel)* 212/885-7111. E-mail reservations@kitano.com. Japanese menu. Specializes in traditional Kaiseki dishes. Hrs: 11:45 am-2:30 pm, 6-10 pm. Res accepted. Bar. A la carte entrees: lunch, dinner $12-$25. Complete meals: lunch $32, dinner $60-$150. Elegant Japanese decor. Totally nonsmoking. Cr cds: A, C, D, DS, JCB, MC, V.

D

★ ★ **NINO'S.** *1354 1st Ave (10021), between 72nd & 73rd Sts, Upper East Side.* 212/988-0002. Northern Italian menu. Specialties: char-grilled yellow-fin tuna, pick-your-own live lobster, rack of veal. Own pastries. Hrs: 5 pm-midnight; Sun 3-11 pm. Closed Jan 1, Memorial Day, Dec 25. Res required. Bar to 2 am. Wine cellar. A la carte entrees: dinner $17.95-$40. Complete meals: dinner $24.95. Tasting menu: dinner $60. Entertainment. Valet parking. Italian decor. Cr cds: A, C, D, DS, MC, V.

★ ★ ★ ★ **NOBU.** *105 Hudson St (10013), at Franklin St, in Tribeca.* 212/219-0500. A curved wall of river-worn black pebbles, bare-wood tables, birch trees and a hand-painted beech floor create a dramatic setting that invites conversation. Sake is the drink of choice; the clientele is as interesting as the menu, which features such tours de force as rock-shrimp tempura and black cod with miso. Japanese menu. Sushi bar. Hrs: 11:45 am-2:15 pm, 5:45-10:15 pm; Sat, Sun from 5:45 pm. Closed some major hols. Res accepted. Serv bar. A la carte entrees: lunch $12-$30, dinner $18-$30. Complete meals: lunch $19.99. Tasting menu: dinner $70. Cr cds: A, D, MC, V.

✔ **NOOR'S.** *94 Chambers (10007), between Broadway & Church, in Tribeca.* 212/732-5011. Indian menu. Specialties: chicken tikka masalla, tandoori mixed grill. Hrs: 11 am-11 pm; Sat, Sun from noon. Res accepted. Bar. A la carte entrees: lunch, dinner $7.95-$21.95. Buffet (Mon-Fri): lunch $8.75. Casual decor. Cr cds: A, D, DS, MC, V.

D

★ ★ **NOVITA.** *102 E 22nd St (10010), Gramercy Park.* 212/677-2222. Italian menu. Specialties: porcini ravioli in black truffle sauce, roasted duck with barolo sauce, tuna carpaccio with capers. Hrs: noon-3 pm, 6-11 pm; Fri, Sat 6 pm-midnight; Sun 5-10 pm. Closed major hols. Res accepted. Bar. A la carte entrees: lunch $12-$20, dinner $13-$21. Complete meals: lunch $19.99. Outdoor dining. Casual decor. Totally nonsmoking. Cr cds: A, C, D, MC, V.

★ ★ **OAK ROOM.** *(See The Plaza Hotel)* 212/759-3000. E-mail plaza@fairmont.com; web www.fairmont.com. Traditional European, Amer menu. Specialties: black Angus beef, roasted rack of lamb, surf and turf. Seasonal menu. Own baking. Hrs: 11:30 am-3 pm, 5:30-11:30 pm; Sun 5:30-10:30 pm. Pre theatre 5:30-7:30 pm. Res accepted. Bar to 1:30 am; Sun to 12:30 am. Wine list. A la carte entrees: lunch $14-$26, dinner $24-$34. Pre-theater dinner $44, includes free transportation to theaters. Pianist. Valet parking. Historic grand dining rm (1907) with hand-painted murals and 25-ft ceilings. Jacket. Cr cds: A, C, D, DS, ER, JCB, MC, V.

D

★ ★ ★ **OCEANA.** *55 E 54th St (10022), between Park & Madison Aves, Midtown.* 212/759-5941. Hrs: noon-2:30 pm, 5:30-10:30 pm; Sat from 5:30 pm. Closed Sun; most major hols. Res accepted. Wine cellar. Complete meals: lunch $40, dinner $62. Located in 2-story townhouse; spacious, bi-level dining rm. Elegant decor. Jacket. Cr cds: A, C, D, DS, JCB, MC, V.

★ ★ **THE ODEON.** *145 W Broadway (10013), between Thomas & Duane Sts, in Tribeca.* 212/233-0507. E-mail theodeon@aol.com. French, Amer menu. Specializes in seafood, grilled dishes. Hrs: noon-2 am; Fri, Sat to 3 am; Sun brunch 11:30 am-4 pm. Res accepted. Bar to 4 am. Complete meals: lunch $17. A la carte entrees: lunch $8.50-$21.50,

dinner $14-$23. Sun brunch $8.50-$21.50. Child's meals. Outdoor dining. Brasserie in 1930s, cafeteria-style art deco. Cr cds: A, D, DS, MC, V.

★ ★ ★ **ONE IF BY LAND, TWO IF BY SEA.** *17 Barrow St (10014), between Seventh Ave S & West Fourth, in Greenwich Village.* 212/228-0822. French, Amer menu. Specialties: open-faced Maine crab ravioli, citrus-marinated halibut, tenderloin of veal. Own pastries. Hrs: 5:30 pm-midnight. Closed most major hols. Res required. Bar 4 pm-2 am. Wine cellar. A la carte entrees: dinner $22-$39. Prix fixe: dinner $62. Pianist; vocalist Fri-Sat. In restored 18th-century carriage house once owned by Aaron Burr; many framed historical documents; dining rm overlooks courtyard garden. Jacket. Cr cds: A, D, MC, V.

★ ★ ★ **ORSO.** *322 W 46th St (10036), between Eighth and Ninth Aves, Time Square/Theater District.* 212/489-7212. E-mail orso.com; web www.joeallen-orso.com. Regional Italian menu. Hrs: noon-11:45 pm; Wed, Sat from 11:30 am. Res required (1 wk in advance). Bar. A la carte entrees: lunch, dinner $12.50-$22. Italian-style trattoria with skylighted, vaulted ceiling; celebrity photo collection. Cr cds: MC, V.

★ ★ **OSTERIA AL DOGE.** *142 W 44th St (10036), between 6th Ave & Broadway, Times Square/Theater District.* 212/944-3643. Italian menu. Specializes in Venetian dishes, seafood, pizza. Hrs: noon-11:30 pm; Fri, Sat to midnight; Sun 4:30-10:30 pm. Closed Jan 1, Dec 25. Res accepted. Bar. A la carte entrees: lunch $12.50-$19.50, dinner $13.50-$25. Cr cds: A, D, DS, MC, V.

★ ★ **OSTERIA LAGUNA.** *209 E 42nd St (10017), between Second & Third Aves, Midtown.* 212/557-0001. Web www.nyside walk.com. Hrs: 11:45 am-11 pm; Fri to 11:30 pm; Sat 5-11:30 pm; Sun 5-10:30 pm. Closed Easter, Dec 25. Res accepted. Italian menu. Bar. A la carte entrees: lunch $12.50-$25, dinner $13.50-$25. Specialties: osso bucco di vitello, astice americano, grigliata mista di pesce. Street parking. Italian decor. Cr cds: A, D, MC, V.

D

★ ★ ★ **OSTERIO DEL CIRCO.** *120 W 55th St (10019), Midtown.* 212/265-3636. E-mail nycirco@aol.com; web www.newyorkside walk.com.osteriodelcirco. Italian menu. Specialties: Tuscan fish soup, homemade pastas. Hrs: 11:30 am-2:30 pm, 5:30-11 pm; Fri, Sat to 11:30 pm; Sun 5-10:30 pm; Sat brunch 11:30 am-2 pm. Closed major hols. Res accepted. Bar. A la carte entrees: lunch $10-$24.75, dinner $15.50-$28. Sat brunch $25. Outdoor dining. Pseudo circus tent made of red and yellow panels of cloth. Cr cds: A, D, MC, V.

D

★ ★ ★ **OTABE.** *68 E 56th St (10022), Between Park and Madison Aves, midtown.* 212/223-7575. Complete dinners, which change monthly to reflect the seasons, are served in the traditional Japanese dining room. In the Teppan Grill Room, personal chefs prepare steak, fish and other seafood on steel griddles built onto a large semicircular counter and into tables in secluded alcoves. Japanese menu. Specialties: swordfish teriyaki, eel teriyaki, traditional Kaiseki tasting menu including sashimi and tempura. Hrs: Teppan Grill: noon-2:30 pm, 5:30-10:30 pm; Sat, Sun from 5:30 pm. Japanese dining room: noon-10:30 pm; Sat, Sun from 5:30 pm. Res accepted. A la carte entrees: lunch, dinner $15-$26. Complete meal: dinner $50-$70. Cr cds: A, C, D, JCB, MC, V.

D

★ ★ **OUR PLACE.** *1444 Third Ave (10028), at 82nd St, Upper East Side.* 212/288-4888. Chinese menu. Specialties: tangerine beef, Peking duck, Grand Marnier prawns. Hrs: noon-10:30 pm; Fri, Sat to 11 pm; Mon-Sat early-bird dinner 5-7 pm. Closed Thanksgiving. Res accepted. Bar. A la carte entrees: lunch $6.95-$8.95, dinner $11.95-$33. Interior designed by protégé of I.M. Pei. Cr cds: A, C, D, MC, V.

D

★ ★ ★ **OYSTER BAR.** *At Grand Central Station (10017), Vanderbilt Ave at 42nd St, Midtown.* 212/490-6650. Specializes in fish, shellfish, smoked salmon. Hrs: 11:30 am-9:30 pm. Closed Sat, Sun; major hols. Res accepted. Bars. Wine list. A la carte entrees: lunch, dinner $8.95-$25.95.

In landmark railroad station; Gustivino tiled vaulted ceilings, mahogany paneling. Cr cds: A, C, D, JCB, MC, V.

[D] [symbol]

★ ★ ★ **PALIO.** *151 W 51st St (10019), at Equitable Center, Times Square/Theater District.* 212/245-4850. Italian menu. Menu changes daily. Own baking. Hrs: noon-2:30 pm, 5:30-11 pm; Sat from 5:30 pm. Closed Sun; major hols. Res accepted. Bar 11:30 am-midnight; Sat from 4:30 pm. Wine cellar. A la carte entrees: lunch, dinner $19-$38. Murals. Cr cds: A, C, D, DS, JCB, MC, V.

[D]

★ ★ **PALM.** *837 Second Ave (10017), between 44th & 45th St, on the East Side.* 212/687-2953. Specializes in steak, seafood, veal. Hrs: noon-11:30 pm; Sat 5-11 pm. Closed Jan 1, Thanksgiving, Dec 25. Bar. A la carte entrees: lunch, dinner $14-$29.50. Complete meals: lunch $19.99. Menu recited. Valet parking after 6:30 pm. Original murals; celebrity caricatures. Popular with writers and artists. Family-owned. Cr cds: A, C, D, MC, V.

★ ★ ★ **PALM COURT.** *(See The Plaza Hotel)* 212/546-5350. E-mail plaza@fairmont.com; web www.fairmont.com. Specialties: fresh raspberry Napoleon, scones with Devonshire cream, Brazilian cake. Own baking. Hrs: 6:30 am-midnight. Sun brunch 10 am-2 pm. Res required Sun brunch. Serv bar. A la carte entrees: bkfst $12-$17, lunch, dinner $20-$26. Complete meals: bkfst $19.50-$24. Sun brunch $55. Piano, violinist; harpist. Valet parking. Edwardian, columned court off lobby; a New York tradition. Cr cds: A, C, D, DS, ER, JCB, MC, V.

[D]

★ ★ **PAOLA'S.** *245 E 84th St (10028), between 2nd & 3rd Aves, Upper East Side.* 212/794-1890. Hrs: 5-11 pm. Closed most major hols. Res accepted. Italian menu. Bar. A la carte entrees: dinner $14.95-$28.95. Specialties: pan-seared baby artichokes, veal stuffed with spinach & prosciutto, ravioli stuffed with spinach. Street parking. Outdoor dining. Intimate dining; romantic atmosphere. Totally nonsmoking. Cr cds: A.

★ ★ ★ **PARIOLI ROMANISSIMO.** *24 E 81st St (10028), between Madison & Fifth Aves, Upper East Side.* 212/288-2391. At this townhouse restaurant with neo-Renaissance architecture, seating is inside in an elegant dining room or outside in the striking garden. Northern Italian menu. Specialties: fetuccine with white truffles, venison, roasted rack of lamb. Own baking. Hrs: 5:30-11 pm; Fri, Sat to 11:30 pm. Closed Sun; major hols; also 2 wks in Aug. Res required. Bar. Wine cellar. A la carte entrees: dinner $29.50-$36. Jacket. Cr cds: A, D, MC, V.

[symbol]

★ ★ ★ **THE PARK.** *(See The Lombardy Hotel)* 212/750-5656. Hrs: noon-3 pm, 5-11 pm; Fri to midnight; Sat 5 pm-midnight. Closed Sun; also major hols. Res accepted. Bar. Wine cellar. A la carte entrees: lunch $16-$26, dinner $16-$37. Specialties: seared seasame tuna steak, prime rib steak with red wine sauce, marinated baby chicken. Piano, jazz Tues-Sat. Street parking. Elegant dining. Jacket. Totally nonsmoking. Cr cds: A, C, D, MC, V.

[D]

★ ★ ★ **PARK AVENUE CAFE.** *100 E 63rd St (10021), at Park Ave, Upper East Side.* 212/644-1900. Specialties: tuna & salmon tartare with cavier, swordfish chop, Mrs. Ascher's steamed vegetable torte. Hrs: 11:30 am-2:30 pm, 5:30-11 pm; Fri to midnight; Sat 5:30 pm-midnight; Sun 5:30-10:30 pm; Sat, Sun brunch 11 am-2:30 pm. Closed Jan 1, Dec 25. Res accepted. Bar. A la carte entrees: lunch $19.50-$26, dinner $24.50-$33.50. Complete meals: dinner $58-$67. Authentic American antiques, folk art, mix and match plates. Cr cds: A, C, D, DS, JCB, MC, V.

★ ★ ★ **PARK BISTRO.** *414 Park Ave S (10016), between 28th & 29th Sts, in Murray Hill.* 212/689-1360. French Provençale menu. Specialties: warm potato salad with goat cheese and herbs, fresh codfish with mashed potato and fried leeks in onion sauce, braised lamb shank with dry fruits sauce. Hrs: noon-3 pm, 5:30-11 pm; Sat, Sun from 5:30 pm. Closed major hols. Res accepted. Bar. A la carte entrees: lunch $17-$22.50,

dinner $22-$28.50. Casual dining; Parisian bistro decor and atmosphere. Cr cds: A, D, MC, V.

[symbol]

★ ★ **PARK VIEW AT THE BOATHOUSE.** *In Central Park (10028), enter at 72nd St & 5th Ave, at lake, Upper East Side.* 212/517-2233. Specialties: Maine monkfish, coriander spiced tuna loin, saddle of rabbit. Hrs: noon-4 pm, 5:30-10 pm; Sat, Sun from 11 am; Sat, Sun brunch to 4 pm. Bar. A la carte entrees: lunch $18-$26, dinner $18-$30. Sat, Sun brunch $11-$20. Child's meals. Outdoor dining overlooking lake. View of Bethesda Fountain. Cr cds: A, MC, V.

★ ★ ★ **PATRIA.** *250 Park Ave S (10003), at 20th St, in Gramercy Park.* 212/777-6211. Latin American menu. Specialties: Ecuadorian ceviche, Nicaraguan skirt steak, sugar cane tuna with malanga puree. This trendy, tri-level Caribbean cafe is painted in striking earth tones and decorated in colorful mosaics and Latin American art. The signature dessert is a chocolate-filled cigar with edible matches. Hrs: noon-2:45 pm, 6-11 pm; Fri to midnight; Sat 5:30 pm-midnight; Sun 5:30-10:30 pm. Closed Thanksgiving, Dec 25. Res accepted. Bar to 1 am. A la carte entrees: lunch $10-$21. Complete meals: lunch $25, dinner $52. Cr cds: A, D, MC, V.

★ ★ ★ **PATROON.** *160 E 46th St (10017), between Lexington & 3rd Aves, Midtown.* 212/883-7373. Specialties: lobster and cod cake with snow pea shoots, wood-grilled porterhouse steak for two, spit-fired roasted chicken for two. Own pastries. Hrs: noon-2:30 pm, 5:30-11 pm; Mon, Tues to 10 pm; Sat from 5:30 pm. Closed Sun; major hols; also Sat in Aug. Res accepted. Bar noon-11:30 pm. Wine cellar. A la carte entrees: lunch $21-$36, dinner $26-$36. Outdoor dining. Three-level dining rm with rooftop garden; contemporary decor. Jacket. Cr cds: A, D, DS, MC, V.

[D] [symbol]

★ ★ **PAYARD PATISSERIE & BISTRO.** *1032 Lexington Ave (10021), between 73rd & 74th Sts, Upper East Side.* 212/717-5252. Hrs: noon-2:30 pm, 6-10:30 pm. Closed major hols. Res accepted. French menu. Bar 11 am-midnight. A la carte entrees: lunch $19-$22, dinner $19-$25. Specialties: bouillabaisse, New York steak with homemade french fries, braised short ribs in red wine. Street parking. French bistro decor; soaring ceilings, framed mirrors. Totally nonsmoking. Cr cds: A, D, MC, V.

★ ★ ★ **PEACOCK ALLEY.** *(See Waldorf-Astoria & Waldorf Towers Hotel)* 212/872-4895. This very luxurious Waldorf-Astoria salon has always offered professional service, fine china, a comprehensive wine cellar, soothing lighting and cushy seating. Recently, however, it's added an updated classical decor and such interesting culinary offerings as theme dinners, showcasing famous chefs and cuisines from around the world. Continental menu. Specialties: seared wild grouper, veal loin, rack of lamb. Own baking. Hrs: 7-10:30 am, noon-2:30 pm, 5:30-10:30 pm; Sat 7:30-10:30 am, 5:30-10:30 pm; Sun brunch 11 am-2:30 pm; Mon to 2:30 pm. Res accepted. Bar. Wine cellar. A la carte entrees: bkfst $14-$23, lunch $18-$29.50, dinner $27-$36. Complete meals: lunch $32 & $37, dinner $80. Sun brunch $50. Entertainment Fri, Sat. Valet parking. Cr cds: A, D, MC, V.

[D]

★ ★ **PENANG MALAYSIAN.** *109 Spring St (10012), between Mercer and Green Sts, in SoHo.* 212/274-8883. Malaysian menu. Specialties: roti canai, sotong goreng, udang halia. Hrs: noon-midnight; Fri, Sat to 1 am. Bar. A la carte entrees: lunch $5.95-$19, dinner $7.95-$19. Exotic plants and a waterfall add to the rain forest atmosphere of this restaurant. Cr cds: A, D, MC, V.

[symbol]

★ ★ ★ **PERIYALI.** *35 W 20th St (10011), between Fifth & Sixth Aves, in Chelsea.* 212/463-7890. Nouvelle Greek menu. Specializes in charcoal-grilled fish, octopus, lamb chops. Own pastries. Hrs: noon-3 pm, 5:30-11 pm; Sat 5:30-11:30 pm. Closed Sun. Res required. Bar. A la carte entrees: lunch $15-$22, dinner $17-$25. Dining in glass-enclosed garden courtyard. Greek taverna decor. Cr cds: A, C, D, MC, V.

★ ★ ★ **PETROSSIAN.** *182 W 58th St (10019), at 7th Ave, Midtown. 212/245-2214.* French, Amer menu. Specialties: caviar, smoked salmon, foie gras. Own pastries. Menu changes quarterly. Hrs: 11:30 am-3 pm, 5:30-11:30 pm; Sat, Sun brunch 11:30 am-3 pm. Res accepted. Bar 11:30-1 am. A la carte entrees: lunch $19, dinner $26-$34. Prix fixe: lunch $22-$39, dinner $35. Sat, Sun brunch $12-$25. Art-deco dining room is decorated with Erté murals and Lalique crystal panels. Jacket. Cr cds: A, C, D, JCB, MC, V.

★ ★ ★ **PICHOLINE.** *35 W 64th St (10023), at Broadway & Central Park West, Upper West Side. 212/724-8585.* French, Mediterranean menu. Specialties: grilled octopus, wild mushroom and duck risotto, Morrocan spiced loin of lamb. Hrs: 11:45 am-2 pm, 5:30-11:45 pm; Mon from 5:30 pm; Sun 5-10 pm. Closed major hols. Res accepted. Bar. Wine cellar. A la carte entrees: lunch $12-$20, dinner $23-$35. Complete meal: dinner $58-$85. Provençale farmhouse atmosphere. Totally nonsmoking. Cr cds: A, D, MC, V.

★ ★ ★ **PIERRE AU TUNNEL.** *250 W 47th St (10036), between Eighth Ave & Broadway, Times Square/Theater District. 212/575-1220.* French menu. Hrs: noon-3 pm, 5:30-11:30 pm; Wed, Sat noon-2:30 pm, 4:30-11:30 pm. Closed Mon; major hols. Res accepted. Bar. A la carte entrees: lunch $10-$20. Complete meals: dinner $32. French-country dining rm decor; fireplace. Family-owned. Cr cds: A, MC, V.

★ ★ **PIG HEAVEN.** *1540 Second Ave (10028), at 80th St, Upper East Side. 212/744-4333.* Chinese menu. Specializes in pork dishes, seafood, poultry. Hrs: noon-midnight; Sat, Sun brunch to 4:30 pm. Res required. Bar. A la carte entrees: lunch $4.95-$6.25, dinner $10.95-$19.95. Cr cds: A, C, D, DS, MC, V.

D

✔ ★ **P.J. CLARKE'S.** *915 Third Ave (10022), at 55th St, on the East Side. 212/759-1650.* Specializes in hamburgers, steak, veal. Hrs: noon-4 am. Res accepted. Bar. A la carte entrees: lunch, dinner $6.90-$22. Juke box. Traditional, old New York-style pub (1864). Cr cds: A, C, D, MC, V.

✔ ★ **PÓ.** *31 Cornelia St (10014), between Bleecker & W 4th Sts in Greenwich Village. 212/645-2189.* Italian menu. Specialties: goat cheese truffle, marinated quail. Hrs: 11:30 am-2:30 pm, 5:30-11 pm; Fri, Sat to 11:30 pm; Sun 11:30 am-2:30 pm, 5-10 pm. Closed Mon; major hols; 2 wks in Feb & Sept. Res accepted. Bar. A la carte entrees: lunch $8-$10, dinner $10-$15. Prix fixe: lunch $21, dinner $35. Outdoor dining. Italian decor. Totally nonsmoking. Cr cds: A.

D

★ ★ ★ **POST HOUSE.** *28 E 63rd St (10021), Upper East Side. 212/935-2888.* Specialties: grilled Atlantic salmon, Maryland crab cakes, Cajun rib steak. Hrs: noon-11 pm; Fri to midnight; Sat 5:30 pm-midnight; Sun 5:30-11 pm. Closed Jan 1, Thanksgiving, Dec 25. Res accepted. Bar. Wine list. A la carte entrees: lunch $18.50-$28.50, dinner $22.50-$34. Own pastries. Club atmosphere. Cr cds: A, C, D, DS, JCB, MC, V.

★ ★ ★ **PRIMAVERA.** *1578 First Ave (10028), at 82nd St, Upper East Side. 212/861-8608.* Northern Italian menu. Specialties: baby goat, primavera pasta, risotto ai porcini. Hrs: 5:30 pm-midnight; Sun from 5 pm. Closed major hols. Res required. Bar. Wine cellar. A la carte entrees: dinner $19.75-$32.50. Tuscan decor. Jacket. Cr cds: A, C, D, MC, V.

✔ ★ **PROVENCE.** *38 MacDougal St (10012), at Avenue of the Americas (Sixth Ave), in SoHo. 212/475-7500.* Web www.citysearch.com/nyc-provence. Southern French menu. Specializes in seafood, bouillabaisse. Hrs: noon-3 pm, 6-11:30 pm; Fri, Sat to midnight; Sun 5:30-11 pm. Closed major hols. Res required. Bar. A la carte entrees: lunch $10-$18, dinner $15.50-$19.50. Sat brunch $10-$18. Cr cds: A.

★ ★ **QUILTY'S.** *177 Prince St (10012), between Thompson & Sullivan, in SoHo. 212/254-1260.* Web www.citysearch.com.-nyc-quilty's. Contemporary Amer menu. Specialties: char-grilled baby artichoke skewer, peppered yellowfin tuna steak frites, rack of Colorado lamb brushed with anise. Hrs: noon-11 pm; Mon from 6 pm; Sun 11 am-10 pm; Sun brunch to 3 pm. Closed Jan 1, Thanksgiving, Dec 25. Res required

(dinner). Bar to 1 am. Wine list. A la carte entrees: lunch $9-$18.50, dinner $18-$29. Sun brunch $8-$18.50. Outdoor dining. Simple decor with antique florist rack, plants, wood floors. Cr cds: A, C, D, DS, MC, V.

★ ★ **RAIN.** *100 W 82nd St (10024), between Amsterdam & Columbus, Upper West Side. 212/501-0776.* Thai menu. Specialties: green curry chicken, crispy whole fish, Thai-style duck fajitas. Hrs: noon-3 pm, 6-11 pm; Fri to midnight; Sat noon-4 pm, 5 pm-midnight; Sun noon-4 pm, 5-10 pm. Closed Dec 25. Res accepted. Bar. A la carte entrees: lunch $6-$14, dinner $11-$22. Thai decor. Cr cds: A, D, DS, MC, V.

★ ★ ★ ★ **RAINBOW ROOM.** *30 Rockefeller Plaza (10112), 65th floor of GE Bldg, Midtown. 212/632-5000.* At the top of a restored landmark skyscraper (1934) is this famous restaurant with a revolving dance floor under a domed ceiling. It boasts views of midtown Manhattan through two-story, floor-to-ceiling windows. Continental menu. Specialties: seafood extravaganza, lobster Thermidor, baked Alaska. Own baking. Hrs: 5 pm-1 am; Sun 6 pm-midnight; Sun brunch 11 am-2 pm. Closed Mon. Res required. Bar. Wine cellar. A la carte entrees: dinner $26-$42. Sun brunch $42. Cover charge $25/person (exc pre-theater & brunch). Entertainment. Street parking. Jacket. Cr cds: A, C, D, MC, V.

D

★ ★ **RAOUL'S.** *180 Prince St (10012), between Sullivan & Thompson St, in SoHo. 212/966-3518.* E-mail raoul@raouls.com; web www.raouls.com. French menu. Specialty: steak au poivre. Own desserts. Hrs: 5:30 pm-2 am. Res accepted. Bar. Wine list. Semi-a la carte: dinner $16-$30. Casual French bistro; original artwork, objets d'art. Cr cds: A, D, MC, V.

★ ★ ★ **RAPHAEL.** *33 W 54th St (10019), between Fifth & Sixth Aves, Midtown. 212/582-8993.* French menu. Specialties: loin of lamb scented with thyme & rosemary; pan-seared foie gras with mango; grilled loin of tuna. Own baking. Hrs: noon-2:30 pm, 6-10 pm; Sat 6-11 pm. Closed Sun; major hols. Res accepted. Bar. A la carte entrees: lunch $20-$24, dinner $23-$36. Complete meals: lunch $30. Tasting menu: dinner $70 & $90. Outdoor dining. In turn-of-the-century town house; fireplace; murals from Provence. Jacket. Cr cds: A, C, D, MC, V.

✔ ★ **RED TULIP.** *439 E 75th St (10021), between York & First Aves, Upper East Side. 212/734-4893.* Hungarian menu. Specialties: roasted pheasant, venison steak hunter, roasted quail. Hrs: 6 pm-midnight; Sun 5-11 pm. Closed Mon, Tues. Res accepted. Bar. A la carte entrees: dinner $14.50-$23. Strolling violinist; Gypsy music. European folk art; Hungarian antiques. Family-owned. Cr cds: A, D, MC, V.

D

★ ★ ★ **REDEYE GRILL.** *890 Seventh Ave (10019), at 56th St, Midtown. 212/541-9000.* Contemporary Amer menu. Specialties: twelve dancing shrimp, clay pot red gulf snapper, ribeye steak frites with redeye potatoes. Hrs: 11:30-1 am; Fri, Sat to 2 am; Sun, Mon to 11:30 pm; Sat, Sun brunch to 3 pm. Res accepted. Bar. Wine cellar. A la carte entrees: lunch $13.50-$26.75, dinner $13.50-$36.95. Jazz Tues-Sat, Sun brunch. Outdoor dining. Copper shrimp statues pirouette over raw seafood bar; colorful murals, toy airplanes decorate two separate dining rms. Cr cds: A, C, D, DS, JCB, MC, V.

D

★ ★ ★ **REMI.** *145 W 53rd St (10019), between Sixth & Seventh Aves, Midtown. 212/581-4242.* Venetian menu. Specialties: rack of lamb with pistachio herb crust, seared rare tuna with spinach & shallot sauce, calf's liver in black truffle butter. Hrs: noon-2:30 pm, 5:30-11:30 pm; Sat from 5 pm; Sun 5:30-10 pm. Closed major hols. Res required. Bar. A la carte entrees: lunch $14-$22, dinner $16-$27. Outdoor dining. Venetian-style trattoria with high, vaulted ceiling, Gothic detailing and room-length, fantasy mural of Venice. Cr cds: A, C, D, JCB, MC, V.

D

★ ★ ★ **RENÉ PUJOL.** *321 W 51st St (10019), between 8th & 9th Aves, Times Square/Theater District. 212/246-3023.* French menu. Specialties: onion tart, roasted rack of lamb with herb crust, roasted Atlantic salmon with green lentils. Own pastries. Hrs: noon-3 pm, 5-10:30 pm; Fri,

Sat to 11:30 pm. Closed Sun; major hols. Res accepted. Bar. Wine cellar. A la carte entrees: lunch $17-$27, dinner $20-$35. Complete meals: lunch $26, dinner $38. Informal country-French atmosphere. Cr cds: A, C, D, MC, V.

★ ★ ★ **RIODIZIO.** 417 Lafayette St (10003), between Astor Pl and E 4th St, in East Village. 212/529-1313. South American menu. Specialties: rodizio, coconut flan. Hrs: noon-3 pm; 5:30 pm-midnight; Mon to 11 pm; Sat from 5:30 pm; Sun, 5:30-11 pm. Closed Thanksgiving, Dec 25. Res accepted. Bar. A la carte entrees: lunch $5.95-$14.95, dinner $12.95-$24.95. Prix fixe: lunch $14.95, dinner $24.95. Outdoor dining. Cr cds: A, MC, V.

D

★ ★ **ROSA MEXICANO.** 1063 First Ave (10022), at 58th St, on the East Side. 212/753-7407. Mexican menu. Specialties: enchiladas de mole poblano, crepas camerones. Own guacamole. Hrs: 5 pm-midnight. Closed Thanksgiving. Res accepted. Bar. A la carte entrees: dinner $16-$27. Casual dining. Totally nonsmoking. Cr cds: A, C, D, DS, MC, V.

★ ★ **RUTH'S CHRIS STEAK HOUSE.** 148 W 51st St (10019), between 6th & 7th Aves, Midtown. 212/245-9600. Specializes in steak, lobster. Hrs: noon-midnight; Sat from 4 pm; Sun 4-10 pm. Closed some major hols. Res accepted. Bar. A la carte entrees: lunch $10.95-$26, dinner $17.50-$33.95. Men's club decor. Cr cds: A, C, D, MC, V.

✈

★ ★ **SAL ANTHONY'S SPQR.** 133 Mulberry St (10013), between Hester & Grand Sts, in Little Italy. 212/925-3120. Italian menu. Specialties: linguini with fresh clams, whole boneless trout, calamari. Hrs: noon-11 pm; Fri, Sat to midnight. Res accepted. Bar. Complete meals: lunch $9.95, dinner (until 6:30 pm) $18.95. A la carte entrees: dinner $14.75-$21. Parking. Outdoor dining. Spacious, elegant dining area. Cr cds: A, C, D, JCB, MC, V.

✔ ★ ★ **SALAAM BOMBAY.** 317 Greenwich St (10013), between Duane & Reade, in Tribeca. 212/226-9400. Indian menu. Specialties: rack of lamb marinated with ginger and lemon, chicken cooked with roasted coconut and spices, undhiyu. Hrs: noon-3 pm, 5:30-11 pm. Res accepted. Bar. A la carte entrees: dinner $9.95-$22.95. Buffet: lunch $10.95. Sitar music wkends. Colorful Indian canopy in middle of room. Totally nonsmoking. Cr cds: A, DS, MC, V.

★ ★ ★ **SAN DOMENICO.** 240 Central Park South (10019), Midtown. 212/265-5959. E-mail sandomny@aol.com; web www.food#2go.com. The setting overlooking Central Park is like a private villa, with terra-cotta and Italian marble floors, Florentine stucco walls, sumptuous leather chairs and lots of warm, earthy hues. Italian menu. Specialties: soft egg yolk-filled ravioli with truffle butter, Alaskan prawns with beans, roasted veal loin with bacon cream sauce. Hrs: noon-2:30 pm, 5:30-11 pm; Sat from 5:30 pm; Sun 5:30-10 pm. Closed Jan 1, Thanksgiving, Dec 25. Res accepted. Bar. Wine cellar. A la carte entrees: lunch $15.50-$32, dinner $16.50-$42.50. Tasting menu: dinner $75. Jacket. Cr cds: A, C, D, MC, V.

★ ★ **SAN MARTIN'S.** 143 E 49th St (10017), between 3rd & Lexington Aves, Midtown. 212/832-9270. Continental menu. Specialties: rack of baby lamb, paella Valenciana, roast suckling pig. Hrs: noon-midnight. Res accepted. Bar. A la carte entrees: lunch, dinner $9-$26. Complete meals: lunch $16, dinner $21. Outdoor dining. Family-owned. Cr cds: A, C, D, DS, MC, V.

★ ★ **SAN PIETRO.** 18 E 54th St (10022), between Fifth & Madison Aves, Midtown. 212/753-9015. Southern Italian menu. Specializes in fish, pasta. Hrs: noon-midnight. Closed Sun; major hols. Res required. Bar. A la carte entrees: lunch, dinner $7-$30. Outdoor dining. 2 large dining areas; massive ceramic scene of Amalfi coast. Jacket. Cr cds: A, D, MC, V.

D

★ ★ **SARABETH'S.** 423 Amsterdam Ave (10024), between 80th & 81st Sts, Upper West Side. 212/496-6280. Specialties: pumpkin waffles, farmer's omelette, warm berry bread pudding. Hrs: 8 am-3:30 pm, 5:30-10:30 pm; Fri to 11 pm; Sat 5:30-11 pm; Sun 5:30-9:30 pm; Sat, Sun brunch 9 am-4 pm. Closed Dec 25. Res accepted (dinner). Serv bar. A la

carte entrees: bkfst $6-$10, lunch $8.50-$14, dinner $10-$19. Sat, Sun brunch $8-$15. New England atmosphere. Totally nonsmoking. Cr cds: A, C, D, MC, V.

★ ★ **SARDI'S.** 234 W 44th St (10036), between Broadway & 8th Ave, Times Square/Theater District. 212/221-8440. E-mail max@sardis.com; web www.sardis.com. Specialties: shrimp a la Sardi, canneloni, chicken a la Sardi. Hrs: 11:30-12:30 am; Fri, Sat to 1 am. Res accepted. Bar. A la carte entrees: lunch $11-$28, dinner $20-$32. Prix fixe: lunch $29.50, dinner $41.50. Established 1921. Famous gathering place of theatrical personalities, columnists, publishers, agents; popular for before and after-theater dinner or drinks. Family-owned. Cr cds: A, C, D, MC, V.

★ ★ ★ **SAVORE.** 200 Spring St (10012), at Sullivan St, in SoHo. 212/431-1212. Italian menu. Specialties: corn mousse with wild boar sauce; salad of beets, zucchini, carrots and potatoes marinated in Balsamic vinegar. Own baking, pasta. Hrs: noon-3 pm, 5:30 pm-midnight; Sat, Sun noon-midnight. Closed Dec 25. Res accepted. Bar. Wine cellar. A la carte entrees: dinner $12-$26. Complete meals: lunch $19.99. Outdoor dining. Elegant decor with polished wood, antique furniture, alabaster chandeliers. Totally nonsmoking. Cr cds: A, MC, V.

D

★ ★ **SAVOY.** 70 Prince St (10012), at Crosby St in SoHo. 212/219-8570. French, Mediterranean menu. Specializes in seafood, duck, chicken. Hrs: noon-3 pm, 6-10:30 pm; Fri, Sat to 11 pm; Sun to 10 pm. Closed most major hols. Res accepted. Bar. A la carte entrees: lunch $8-$12, dinner $18-$29. Contemporary decor. Cr cds: A, DS, MC, V.

★ ★ **SCREENING ROOM.** 54 Varick St (10003), jct Varick & Laight, in Tribeca. 212/334-2100. Specialties: pan-fried artichokes, macaroni with spinach, cedar-planked salmon. Own pastries. Hrs: noon-3 pm, 6-11 pm; Sun, Mon from 6 pm; Fri to 11:30 pm; Sat 6-11:30 pm; Sun brunch 11:30 am-3 pm. Res accepted. Bar. A la carte entrees: lunch $9-$22, dinner $17-$24. Complete meal: dinner $30. Sun brunch $6-$17. Casual decor with movie theater. Cr cds: A, D, DS, MC, V.

D ✈

★ ★ ★ **SEA GRILL.** 19 W 49th St (10019), at Rockefeller Plaza, Midtown. 212/332-7610. Specialties: Maryland crab cakes with stone ground mustard, roasted Chilean sea bass, roasted cod with cous cous. Own pastries. Hrs: noon-3 pm, 5-10 pm; Sat from 5 pm. Closed Sun. Res required. Bar. Wine cellar. A la carte entrees: lunch $19-$28, dinner $23-$30. Complete meals: dinner $39. Outdoor dining. Floral, garden displays. Overlooks Prometheus fountain and pool (summer); ice-skating rink (winter). Jacket (dinner). Cr cds: A, C, D, ER, JCB, MC, V.

D

★ ★ **SHAAN.** 57 W 48th St (10020), between 5th & 6th Aves; Midtown. 212/977-8400. Indian menu. Specialties: chicken makhani, prawns bengali, paneer pasanda. Hrs: noon-3 pm, 5:30-11 pm. Res accepted. Bar. A la carte entrees: lunch, dinner $10.95-$29.95. Complete meals: lunch $15.95-$18.95, dinner $21.95-$25.95. Buffet: lunch $13.95. Entertainment Fri, Sat. Framed Indian tapestries on walls. Totally nonsmoking. Cr cds: A, D, MC, V.

D

★ **SHABU-TATSU.** 1414 York Ave (10021), at 75th St, Upper East Side. 212/472-3322. Japanese menu. Specialties: shabu-shabu (tabletop cooking), sukiyaki (hot pot with sauce), yakiniku (Japanese barbecue). Hrs: noon-2:30 pm, 5-10:30 pm; Fri to 11:30 pm; Sat noon-11:30 pm; Sun noon-10:30 pm; Sat, Sun brunch to 5 pm. Closed some major hols. Res accepted. Bar. A la carte entrees: lunch $5.95-$11.95, dinner $8-$17. Complete meals: dinner $28-$38. Sat, Sun brunch $7-$12. Cook your own meal; each table surrounds a stovetop. Totally nonsmoking. Cr cds: A, D, DS, JCB, MC, V.

✔ ★ **SHANGHAI CUISINE.** 89-91 Bayard St (10013), at Mulberry St, in Chinatown. 212/732-8988. Shanghai menu. Specialties: crispy duck, steamed tiny buns, yellow fish in sweet & sour sauce. Hrs: 10:30 am-10:30 pm. Res accepted. Bar. A la carte entrees: lunch, dinner $4.95-$19.95. No cr cds accepted.

★ **SHARK BAR.** 307 Amsterdam Ave (10023), between 74th & 75th Sts, Upper West Side. 212/874-8500. Regional Amer menu. Specialties: Louisiana deep-fried crab cakes, Georgia bank farm-bred catfish, honey-dipped southern fried chicken. Own baking. Hrs: noon-3 pm, 5-11:30 pm; Mon, Tues from 5 pm; Wed to midnight; Thurs to 12:30 am; Fri to 1:30 am; Sat 11:30 am-3 pm (brunch), 5 pm-1:30 am; Sun 11:30 am-3 pm (brunch), 5-11:30 pm. Closed Dec 25. Res accepted. Bar. A la carte entrees: lunch, dinner $10.95-$17.95. Sat, Sun brunch $15.95. Harlem Renaissance-era decor; red velvet, extensive woodwork; multi-level dining. Totally nonsmoking. Cr cds: A, D, DS, MC, V.

★ ★ **SHUN LEE.** 43 W 65th St (10023), between Central Park West & Columbus Ave, Upper West Side. 212/595-8895. Chinese menu. Specialties: jumbo prawns with broccoli in curry sauce, Peking duck, Norwegian salmon (Szechwan or Mandarin style). Hrs: noon-midnight; Sat from 11:30 am; Sun to 10:30 pm. Closed Thanksgiving. Bar. A la carte entrees: lunch $11.50-$22.95, dinner $15.95-$36. Contemporary decor. Jacket. Cr cds: A, C, D, MC, V.

★ ★ **SHUN LEE PALACE.** 155 E 55th St (10022), between Third & Lexington Aves, on the East Side. 212/371-8844. Chinese menu. Specializes in Cantonese, Hunan and Szechwan dishes. Hrs: noon-11:30 pm; Sun to 11 pm. Closed Thanksgiving. Res required. Bar. Wine cellar. A la carte entrees: lunch $16.50-$24.95, dinner $18.95-$37.95. Complete meals (Mon-Fri): lunch $19.99. Cr cds: A, C, D, MC, V.

D ♥

✔★ **SIAM GRILL.** 586 Ninth Ave (10036), between 42nd & 43rd Sts, in Times Square/Theater District. 212/307-1363. Thai menu. Specialties: sautéed chicken with cashew nuts & chili paste sauce, homemade red & green Thai curry, garlic duck. Hrs: 11:30 am-10:30 pm; Fri to 11 pm; Sat 1-11 pm; Sun 4-10:30 pm. Closed some major hols. Res accepted. Serv bar. A la carte entrees: lunch, dinner $7.95-$13.95. Complete meals: dinner $8.95. Cr cds: A, MC, V.

★ ★ **SIAM INN.** 916 8th Ave (10019), between W 54th & 55th Sts, Times Square/Theater District. 212/489-5237. Thai menu. Specialties: deep-fried whole fish, emerald shrimp, duck with ginger sauce. Hrs: noon-3 pm, 5-11:30 pm; Sat from 4 pm; Sun 5-11 pm. Closed most major hols. Res accepted Mon-Thurs; required Fri, Sat. Bar. A la carte entrees: lunch $8.25-$15.95, dinner $8.95-$15.95. Thai decor; artifacts displayed, photos of Bangkok, statues, plaques. Cr cds: A, D, MC, V.

★ ★ **SMITH & WOLLENSKY.** 797 Third Ave (10022), at 49th St, on the East Side. 212/753-1530. Specializes in steak, seafood. Hrs: noon-midnight; Sat, Sun from 5 pm. Closed Jan 1, Thanksgiving, Dec 25. Res accepted. Bar. Wine cellar. A la carte entrees: lunch $14.50-$27.75, dinner $18-$42. Built 1897; turn-of-the-century decor; old New York steakhouse atmosphere. Outdoor dining. Cr cds: A, C, D, DS, JCB, MC, V.

★ ★ **SOBA-YA.** 229 E 9th St (10003), between 2nd & 3rd Aves, in East Village. 212/533-6966. Hrs: noon-11 pm; early-bird dinner 5-6:30 pm (Tues-Fri). Closed Mon; also major hols. Res accepted. Japanese menu. Wine, beer. A la carte entrees: lunch, dinner $6.50-$14. Specializes in cold and hot noodle entrees. Street parking. Small fountain at entrance. Totally nonsmoking. Cr cds: A, D, DS, MC, V.

SC

★ **SOHO STEAK.** 90 Thompson St (10012), between Spring & Prince Sts, in SoHo. 212/226-0602. Hrs: 6:30-11 pm; Fri, Sat to midnight; Sun 6-10:30 pm; Sat, Sun brunch noon-4 pm. Closed major hols. Continental, Amer menu. Bar. A la carte entrees: dinner $14-$16. Sat, Sun brunch $4.50-$12. Specialties: braised oxtail raviolo, grilled hangar steak, double cut pork chop with organic barley. Street parking. Bistro atmosphere. No cr cds accepted.

⌐

✔★ ★ **SONIA ROSE.** 150 E 34th St (10016), between 28th and 29th Sts, Murray Hill. 212/545-1777. French menu. Specialty: warm asparagus puff pastry tenderloin of beef with chanterelle, black trumpet, and morel sauce. Hrs: 7-10 am, noon-3 pm, 5-9:30 pm; Sat 5:30-10:30 pm; Sun 5-9 pm. Res accepted. Bar. Complete meals: bkfst, lunch $25, dinner $41. Contemporary decor. Jacket. Totally nonsmoking. Cr cds: A, D, MC, V.

★ ★ ★ **SPARKS STEAK HOUSE.** 210 E 46th St (10017), between 2nd & 3rd Aves, Midtown. 212/687-4855. Specializes in steak, lobster, seafood. Hrs: noon-3 pm, 5-11 pm; Fri to 11:30 pm; Sat 5-11:30 pm. Closed Sun; major hols. Res required. Bar. Wine list. A la carte entrees: lunch, dinner $19.95-$31.75. Early Amer decor; etched glass, wood paneling. Jacket. Cr cds: A, C, D, MC, V.

D ⌐

✔★ ★ **SPARTINA.** 355 Greenwich St (10013), at Harrison St, in Tribeca. 212/274-9310. Mediterranean menu. Specialties: lamb shank Catalan-style, pepper-crusted tuna, grilled pizza. Hrs: 11:30 am-3 pm, 5:30-11:30 pm; Mon to 11 pm; Fri to midnight; Sat 5:30 pm-midnight. Closed most major hols. Bar. A la carte entrees: lunch $12.50-$21, dinner $16-$27. Outdoor dining. Custom-made Mission-style chairs, wood floors, contemporary art. Cr cds: A, D, MC, V.

★ ★ **STEAK FRITES.** 9 E 16th St (10003), between Fifth Ave & Broadway, in Chelsea. 212/463-7101. French menu. Specializes in black Angus steak. Hrs: noon-11:30 pm; Fri-Sat to 12:30 pm; Sun to 10 pm; Sun brunch noon-4 pm. Closed Jan 1, Dec 25. Res accepted. Bar. A la carte entrees: lunch $8.50-$17.50, dinner $12.50-$19. Sun brunch $7-$17.50. Outdoor dining. French bistro-style atmosphere; murals of Paris scenes. Cr cds: A, D, MC, V.

D

★ ★ **SUSHISAY.** 38 E 51st St (10022), between Park and Madison Aves, in Midtown. 212/755-1780. Japanese menu. Specialties: sushi, bento. Hrs: noon-2:15 pm, 5:30-10 pm; Sat 5-9 pm. Closed Sun; also major hols. Res required. Bar. A la carte entrees: lunch $18-$33, dinner $19.50-$33. Traditional and serene Japanese decor. Totally nonsmoking. Cr cds: A, D, MC, V.

★ ★ **TABLE D'HOTE.** 44 E 92nd St (10028), between Madison & Park Aves, Upper East Side. 212/348-8125. French menu. Specialties: seared tuna with Japanese rice cake, rack of lamb shank with spring pea risotto, bistro-style hanger steak. Hrs: noon-3 pm, 5:30-10:30 pm; Sat 11 am-4 pm; Sun 10:30 am-4 pm. Closed Dec 25. Res accepted. Wine, beer. A la carte entrees: lunch $8.75-$15, dinner $14.50-$26. Sun brunch $8.50-$15. Small, intimate bistro-style dining rm. Totally nonsmoking. Cr cds: A, D, MC, V.

✔★ ★ **TAORMINA.** 147 Mulberry St (10013), between Grand & Hester Sts, in Little Italy. 212/219-1007. Italian menu. Specializes in seafood, pasta. Hrs: 11 am-11:30 pm; Sat to 1 am; Sun to 11 pm. Closed Thanksgiving, Dec 25, 31. Res required. Bar. A la carte entrees: lunch, dinner $9.90-$19. Valet parking. Modern Italian decor. Cr cds: A, C, D, MC, V.

★ ★ **TATOU.** 151 E 50th St (10022), between Lexington & 3rd Aves, on the East Side. 212/753-1144. Specialties: pan-seared red snapper, rack of lamb, seared filet mignon. Hrs: noon-3 pm, 5:30-10:30 pm; Sat from 5:30 pm. Closed Sun; some major hols. Res required. Bar. A la carte entrees: lunch $15-$22, dinner $17-$29. Entertainment Tues-Sat. Terrace dining. Old theater setting; former nightclub from the 1940s. Jacket. Cr cds: A, D, MC, V.

⌐

★ ★ ★ **TAVERN ON THE GREEN.** Central Park at W 67th St (10023), Upper West Side. 212/873-3200. Web www.tavernonthegreen.com. Contemporary Amer menu. Own baking. Specialties: sautéed jumbo lump crab cakes, braised breast of veal, crab-crusted Maine halibut. Hrs: noon-3:30 pm, 5:30-10:45 pm; Fri, Sat to 11:30 pm; Sat, Sun brunch 10 am-3 pm. Res accepted. Bar. A la carte entrees: lunch $14.25-$28.50, dinner $22-$33. Table d'hôte: lunch $19.98-$27.75, Sat, Sun brunch $17.50-$28.75. Entertainment (exc Mon) in Chestnut Room. Valet parking. Garden terrace. Gift shop. Elaborate decor; in 1874 building within Central Park. Cr cds: A, C, D, JCB, MC, V.

D

★ ★ ★ **TERRACE.** 400 W 119th St (10027), between Amsterdam & Morningside Dr, on rooftop of Butler Hall, Columbia University, Upper West Side. 212/666-9490. Web laterrace.com. French menu. Specializes in seafood, game. Own pastries. Hrs: noon-2:30 pm, 6-10 pm; Sat from 6 pm. Closed Sun, Mon; Dec 25. Res accepted. Bar to 11 pm. Wine cellar. A la carte entrees: lunch $8.50-$25, dinner $24-$32. Prix fixe: lunch $25, dinner $45. Classical harpist evenings. Valet parking (dinner). Outdoor terrace. Panoramic view of Hudson River, George Washington Bridge and Manhattan skyline. Cr cds: A, C, D, DS, MC, V.

★ ★ **TRATTORIA DELL'ARTE.** 900 7th Ave (10019), at 57th St, Midtown. 212/245-9800. Italian menu. Specializes in pizza, veal chops, seafood. Own pastas. Hrs: 11:45 am-2:45 pm, 5-11:30 pm; Fri, Sat to 12:30 am; Sun to 10:30 pm; Sat, Sun brunch 11 am-3 pm. Closed Thanksgiving, Dec 25. Res accepted. Bar. A la carte entrees: lunch, dinner $17-$37.50. Sat, Sun brunch $13.75-$24. Authentic Italian antipasto bar. Modern Italian atmosphere. Opp Carnegie Hall; frequented by celebrities. Cr cds: A, D, DS, MC, V.

★ ★ ★ **TRIBECA GRILL.** 375 Greenwich St (10013), at Franklin St, in Tribeca. 212/941-3900. Web www.interactivegourmetsite.cui sine.com. Specialties: rare seared tuna, crab-crusted seabass, rack of lamb. Hrs: 11:30 am-3 pm, 5:30-11 pm; Fri to 11:30 pm; Sat 5:30-11:30 pm; Sun 5-10 pm; Sun brunch 11:30 am-3 pm. Res accepted. Bar. A la carte entrees: lunch $12-$20, dinner $19-$29. Prix fixe: lunch $19.99. Casual dining in converted warehouse. Cr cds: A, D, MC, V.

 D

✔★ ★ **TRIONFO.** 224 W 51st St (10019), Times Square/Theater District. 212/262-6660. Italian menu. Specialties: osso bucco "Trinofo," beef carpaccio with arugula and parmigiano, lobster-filled ravioli. Hrs: 11:30 am-11:30 pm; Sat from 5 pm; Sun to 10:30 pm. Closed major hols. Res accepted. Bar. A la carte entrees: lunch, dinner $12.50-$20.95. Outdoor dining. Italian decor with murals of Chianti. Cr cds: A, C, D, MC, V.

★ ★ **TRIPPLETAIL.** 322 E 86th St (10028), between 1st & 2nd Aves, Upper East Side. 212/717-5875. Hrs: 5-11 pm; Fri to midnight; Sat 11:30 am-3:30 pm, 5 pm-midnight; Sun 11:30 am-3:30 pm, 5-10 pm. Closed July 4, Thanksgiving, Dec 25. Res accepted. Seafood menu. Bar. A la carte entrees: dinner $7.95-$19.95. Child's meals. Specialties: seafood cocktails, fish bowls. Street parking. Raw bar. Totally nonsmoking. Cr cds: A, MC, V.

✔★ ★ **TROIS CANARDS.** 184 Eighth Ave (10011), between 19th & 20th Sts, Chelsea. 212/929-4320. French menu. Specialties: Dover sole, roast duckling with seasonal fruit sauce, filet mignon with pearl onions and wild mushrooms. Hrs: noon-3 pm, 5-11 pm; Fri to midnight; Sat 5 pm-midnight; Sat, Sun brunch 11 am-4 pm. Res accepted. Bar. A la carte entrees: lunch $6.95-$12.95, dinner $14.95-$21.95. Pre-theater dinner $21.95. Sat, Sun brunch $10.95. Duck motif. Contemporary decor. Totally nonsmoking. Cr cds: A, MC, V.

D

★ ★ **TUSCAN SQUARE.** 16 W 51st St (10020), between 5th & 6th Aves, at Rockefeller Center, Midtown. 212/977-7777. Hrs: 11:30 am-11 pm; Sat, Sun to 10:30 pm; Sat, Sun 11:30 am-3:30 pm. Closed major hols; also Sun brunch in summer. Res accepted. Italian menu. Bar. A la carte entrees: lunch, dinner $13-$20. Complete meal: 3-course dinner $32.50. Sat, Sun brunch $13-$20. Specialties: ricotta & spinach gnocchi with wild boar sauce, slow roasted veal marinated in lemon and sage, assorted antipasti. Street parking. Tuscan villa decor. Totally nonsmoking. Cr cds: A, D, MC, V.

D

★ ★ ★ **TWO TWO TWO.** 222 W 79th St (10024), between Amsterdam & Broadway, Upper West Side. 212/799-0400. Continental menu. Specialties: medallions of Canadian salmon, prime rack of Colorado lamb, Japanese Kobe sirloin steak. Hrs: 5-11 pm. Res accepted. Bar. Wine list. A la carte entrees: dinner $29-$42. Complete meal: pre-theater dinner $42.50. Cr cds: A, C, D, DS, MC, V.

★ ★ ★ **TYPHOON BREWERY.** 22 E 54th St (10022), between Madison & 5th Aves, Midtown. 212/754-9006. Thai menu. Specialties: crispy duck with sweet & sour five-spice sauce, grilled rare tuna, pan-seared monkfish. Own baking. Hrs: noon-2:30 pm, 5:30-10:30 pm; Fri to 11:30 pm; Sat in summer 5:30-11:30 pm. Closed Sun; major hols. Res

accepted. Bar. Wine list. Semi-a la carte: lunch $12-$18, dinner $13.75-$21. Industrial decor with metal tabletops, brick walls; large beer vats at entrance. Totally nonsmoking. Cr cds: A, D, DS, JCB, MC, V.

D

★ ★ ★ **UNION PACIFIC.** 111 E 22nd St (10010), between Park Ave S & Lexington, Gramercy Park. 212/995-8500. Hrs: noon-2 pm, 6 pm-midnight. Res accepted. Contemporary Amer menu. Bar. Wine list. Complete meal: lunch $23-$29, dinner $54. Specialties: Taylor Bay scallops, sea bass with endive & tarragon, salmon in salt crust. Street parking. Arched bridge leads to dining room with a small pond and waterfall. Totally nonsmoking. Cr cds: A, C, D, MC, V.

★ ★ ★ **UNION SQUARE CAFE.** 21 E 16th St (10003), between Fifth Ave & Union Square W, Midtown. 212/243-4020. Italian, Amer menu. Specialties: grilled marinated filet of tuna, fried calamari with spicy anchovy mayonnaise. Own pastries. Hrs: noon-2:15 pm, 6-10:15 pm; Fri, Sat to 11:15 pm; Sun 5:30-9:45 pm. Closed major hols. Res required. Bar. Wine list. A la carte entrees: lunch $16.50-$18.50, dinner $23-$27. Contemporary American bistro. Cr cds: A, D, MC, V.

★ ★ **VICTOR'S CAFE 52.** 236 W 52nd St (10019), between Broadway and 8th Ave, Times Square/Theater District. 212/586-7714. Cuban, Caribbean menu. Specialties: black bean soup, red snapper with plantain, suckling roast pig. Hrs: noon-midnight. Res accepted. Bar. A la carte entrees: lunch $7.95-$18.95, dinner $9-$29. Entertainment. Skylight; garden. Cr cds: A, C, D, MC, V.

★ ★ ★ **THE VIEW.** (See Marriott Marquis Hotel) 212/704-8900. Continental menu. Own baking. Hrs: 5:30-11 pm; Fri, Sat 5 pm-midnight; Sun brunch 10:30 am-2 pm. Res required. Bar. Wine cellar. A la carte entrees: dinner $24.95-$33. Prix fixe: pre-theater dinner $39.95, $49.95. Sun brunch $34.95. Valet parking. Revolving rooftop restaurant, lounge and ballroom. Braille menu. Jacket. Cr cds: A, C, D, DS, ER, JCB, MC, V.

D

✔★ ★ **VILLAGE GRILL.** 518 LaGuardia Pl (10014), at Bleecker St, in Greenwich Village. 212/228-1001. Contemporary Amer menu. Specialties: pan-seared peppered tuna, Phuket-style steamed mussels, grilled steak. Hrs: noon-2 am; Fri, Sat to 3 am; Sat, Sun brunch to 4 pm. Closed Thanksgiving, Dec 25. Res accepted. Bar to 4 am. A la carte entrees: lunch, dinner $9.75-$20.95. Sat, Sun brunch $9.75-$13.75. Outdoor dining. 1904 bldg with 30-ft-high ceilings, stainless-steel open kitchen; candid photos of Jack Kerouac, Allen Ginsberg and more. Cr cds: A, C, D, MC, V.

✔★ ★ **VINCE & EDDIE'S.** 70 W 68th St (10023), Upper West Side. 212/721-0068. Regional Amer menu. Specialties: Chesapeake crab cakes, fried calamari with lime juice, pan-roasted chicken. Hrs: noon-midnight. Res accepted. Bar. A la carte entrees: lunch $8.95-$14.95, dinner $17.50-$20.95. Outdoor dining. New England country inn decor. Cr cds: A, C, D, DS, MC, V.

★ **VIRGIL'S REAL BARBECUE.** 152 W 44th St (10036), between 6th Ave & Broadway, Times Square/Theater District. 212/921-9494. Specialties: barbecued Memphis pork ribs, pulled pork sandwiches, grilled catfish filet. Hrs: 11:30 am-midnight; Mon to 11 pm; Sun to 10 pm. Closed Dec 25. Res accepted. Bar. A la carte entrees: lunch, dinner $6.50-$24.95. Child's meals. Multi-level Southern-style restaurant. Walls lined with Americana. Totally nonsmoking. Cr cds: A, MC, V.

D

★ ★ ★ **VONG.** 200 E 54th St (10022), between 2nd & 3rd Aves, Midtown. 212/486-9592. Thai, French menu. Specialties: crab spring roll, fresh fish with wok-fried Napa cabbage, lobster with Thai herbs. Hrs: noon-2:30 pm, 6-11 pm; Sat 5:30-11:30 pm; Sun 5:30-10 pm. Closed major hols. Res required. Bar. Wine cellar. A la carte entrees: lunch, dinner $19-$32. Prix fixe: lunch $28. Outdoor dining. Exotic decor of Southeast Asia; ceiling and walls covered with gold leaf collage; Thai-style seating (sunken seating) in one area of dining rm. Cr cds: A, D, MC, V.

D

✔★ ★ **WALL STREET KITCHEN & BAR.** *70 Broad St (10004), at Beaver St, in Financial District.* 212/797-7070. Specializes in pizza, steak, hamburgers. Hrs: 11:30 am-11:30 pm. Closed Thanksgiving, Dec 25. Bar. A la carte entrees: lunch, dinner $6.75-$19.50. Restored 1908 bldg has vaulted ceiling, overhanging balcony, tiered seating. Cr cds: A, D, DS, MC, V.

D ⌐

★ ★ ★ **WATER CLUB.** *500 E 30th St (10016), at the East River, Midtown.* 212/683-3333. Specializes in lobster, oysters, tuna. Hrs: noon-2:30 pm, 5:30-11 pm; Sun 5:45-10 pm; Sun brunch 11 am-3 pm. Res required. Bar. A la carte entrees: lunch $15-$19, dinner $22-$34. Prix fixe: lunch $19.99, dinner $28. Sun brunch $33. Piano bar. Free valet parking. Outdoor dining (Memorial Day-Labor Day). Located on barge in the East River. Jacket. Cr cds: A, C, D, JCB, MC, V.

D

★ ★ **WILLOW.** *1022 Lexington Ave (10021), at 73rd St, Upper East Side.* 212/717-0703. French menu. Specialties: seared Atlantic salmon, rack of lamb, warm chocolate cake with Tahitian ice cream. Hrs: noon-4 pm, 5:30-10:30 pm; Sun brunch 11 am-4 pm. Closed Dec 25. Res accepted. Bar. A la carte entrees: lunch $9-$16, dinner $16.50-$28. Sun brunch $14.50. Outdoor dining. French decor. Totally nonsmoking. Cr cds: A, D, MC, V.

★ ★ ★ **WINDOWS ON THE WORLD.** *1 World Trade Center (10048), on 107th floor, in Financial District.* 212/524-7011. Web www.windowsontheworld.com. Upon exiting the elevator onto the top floor of the World Trade Center, you can't help but notice the spectacular panoramic views of Manhattan, Brooklyn, Queens & New Jersey. Once you are seated, however, the extremely attentive staff is a wonderful start to a most enjoyable lunch or dinner. Specialties: Maine lobster with truffles, North Carolina roasted quail, grilled black Angus sirloin. Hrs: noon-2:30 pm, 5-10:30 pm; Fri to 11:30 pm; Sat 5-11:30 pm; Sun 11 am-3 pm, 5-10 pm. Res accepted. Bar noon-1 am; Fri, Sat to 2 am; Sun to 11 pm. Wine cellar. Buffet: lunch $47.50. A la carte entrees: dinner $25-$35. Pre theater dinner $35. Dance band Wed-Sat. Valet parking. Panoramic views. Jacket. Cr cds: A, C, D, DS, JCB, MC, V.

D

★ ★ ★ **YANKEE CLIPPER.** *170 John St (10038), at South St, in Financial District.* 212/344-5959. Specializes in jumbo shrimp, pan-seared tuna, Norwegian salmon. Hrs: 11:30 am-10 pm; Sun noon-9 pm. Closed Thanksgiving, Dec 25. Res accepted. Bar. A la carte entrees: lunch, dinner $11-$24. Prix fixe: lunch, dinner $23. Three dining areas; main dining rm resembles dining salon on a luxury liner; display of ship models and prints of ships. Cr cds: A, C, D, DS, MC, V.

⌐

✔★ **YELLOWFINGERS.** *200 E 60th St (10022), at Third Ave, Upper East Side.* 212/751-8615. Continental menu. Specializes in grilled fish and meat, salads, gourmet individual pizza. Own desserts. Hrs: 11:30-1 am; Fri, Sat to 2 am; Sun to midnight. Bar. A la carte entrees: lunch, dinner $10-$19. Sun brunch $9.50-$19.50. Outdoor dining. Cr cds: A, D, DS, MC, V.

★ ★ **ZARELA.** *953 2nd Ave (10022), between 50th & 51st Sts, Midtown.* 212/644-6740. Mexican menu. Specialties: roasted duck, snapper hash. Hrs: noon-3 pm, 5-11 pm; Fri to 11:30 pm; Sat 5-11:30 pm; Sun 5-10 pm. Closed major hols. Res accepted. Bar. A la carte entrees: lunch $11-$16, dinner $13-$16.95. Entertainment Tues-Sat. Colorful Mexican decor; paper lanterns, masks, toys, piñatas. Cr cds: A, D.

⌐

★ ★ ★ **ZOË.** *90 Prince St (10012), between Broadway and Mercer St, in SoHo.* 212/966-6722. Contemporary Amer menu. Hrs: noon-3 pm, 6-10:30 pm; Mon from 6 pm; Fri to 11 pm; Sat 5:30-11:30 pm; Sun 5:30-10 pm; Sat brunch noon-3 pm, Sun 11:30 am-3 pm. Closed July 4, Dec 25. Res accepted. Bar. Wine list. A la carte entrees: lunch $9.50-$14, dinner $16-$25. Sat, Sun brunch $9.50-$14. Eclectic decor. Totally nonsmoking. Cr cds: A, C, D, MC, V.

D

★ ★ **ZUCCA.** *227 10th Ave (10011), between 23rd & 24th Sts, in Chelsea.* 212/741-1970. Mediterranean menu. Specialties: zuppa di Zucca, golden beet salad, Portuguese fish soup. Own pastries. Hrs: 11:30 am-2:30 pm, 5:30-10:30 pm; Mon from 5:30 pm; Fri to midnight; Sat 5:30 pm-midnight. Closed Jan 1, Dec 25. Res accepted (dinner). Bar 5:30 pm-midnight; Fri, Sat to 1 am. A la carte entrees: lunch $8-$12, dinner $16-$24. Complete meals: dinner $19.99. Casual decor; limestone-topped bar. No cr cds accepted.

⌐

Unrated Dining Spots

CARNEGIE DELI. *854 Seventh Ave (10019), off 55th St, Midtown.* 212/757-2245. Kosher deli menu. Specializes in sandwiches, corned beef, cheesecake. Hrs: 6:30-3:45 am. Semi-a la carte: bkfst $5-$7, lunch $7-$12, dinner $8-$15. Traditional Jewish-style New York deli. No cr cds accepted.

D

DIANE'S DOWNTOWN. *249 Columbus Ave, between 71st & 72nd Sts, Upper West Side.* 212/799-6750. Specializes in hamburgers, sodas, ice cream sundaes. Hrs: Noon-midnight; Fri to 1 am; Sat 11:30-1 am; Sun 11:30 am-midnight. Closed Thanksgiving, Dec 24-25. Wine, beer. A la carte entrees: bkfst, lunch, dinner from $2.50. Totally nonsmoking. No cr cds accepted.

ELEPHANT & CASTLE. *68 Greenwich Ave (10011), Seventh Ave & 11th St, in Greenwich Village.* 212/243-1400. Specializes in salads, hamburgers, Indian puddings. Daily specials. Hrs: 8:30 am-midnight; Sat, Sun from 10 am. Wine, beer, setups. A la carte entrees: bkfst $2.75-$7, lunch, dinner $2.75-$11.50. Totally nonsmoking. Cr cds: A, C, D, MC, V.

EMPIRE DINER. *210 Tenth Ave (10011), between 22nd & 23rd Sts, in Chelsea.* 212/243-2736. Specializes in sandwiches, omelettes, meatloaf. Own muffins, scones. Open 24 hrs; Sun brunch noon-4 pm. Bar. A la carte entrees: bkfst $1.50-$8.50, lunch, dinner $4.25-$14.95. Sun brunch $9.50. Pianist. Outdoor dining. Authentic chrome and stainless steel art-deco diner. Cr cds: A, D, DS, MC, V.

FLORENT. *69 Gansevoort St (10014), between Washington & Greenwich Sts, in Greenwich Village.* 212/989-5779. French, Amer menu. Specialties: mussels, own french fries, fresh fish. Open 24 hrs. Closed Dec 25. Res accepted. Bar. A la carte entrees: bkfst $3.95-$10.50, lunch $3.95-$13.95, dinner $9.50-$17.95. Chrome- & aluminum-trimmed diner attached to meat market in warehouse area of the Village. No cr cds accepted.

D

HARLEY-DAVIDSON CAFE. *1370 Ave of the Americas (10019), at 56th St, Midtown.* 212/245-6000. E-mail staff@harley-davidsoncafe.com; web www.harley-davidsoncafe.com. Specializes in seafood, barbecue chicken, Harley Hog sandwich. Hrs: 11:30 am-midnight; Fri, Sat to 1 am. Semi-a la carte: lunch, dinner $7.50-$19.95. Child's meals. Outdoor dining on wrap-around terrace. Extensive Harley-Davidson motorcycle memorabilia; multi-media displays. Cr cds: A, D, DS, JCB, MC, V.

D

JACKSON HOLE. *1611 Second Ave (10028), between 83rd & 84th Sts, Upper East Side.* 212/737-8788. Specializes in sandwiches, hamburgers. Hrs: 10-1 am; Fri, Sat to 4 am; Sat, Sun brunch 10:30 am-3 pm. Closed Thanksgiving, Dec 25. Bar. A la carte entrees: bkfst $4-$6, lunch, dinner $6-$10. Outdoor dining. Chrome and stainless steel art deco diner; juke box. Cr cds: A, MC, V.

D

PANEVINO RISTORANTE/CAFE VIENNA. *In Avery Fisher Hall, Lincoln Center, Broadway & 64th St, Upper West Side.* 212/874-7000. Italian menu at Panevino Ristorante; Viennese dessert & coffee menu at Cafe Vienna. Hrs: Panevino Ristorante 11:30 am-8 pm; Cafe Vienna 11:30 am-11 pm. Bar. A la carte entrees at Panevino: lunch

$10-$14, dinner $13-$21. A la carte desserts at Cafe Vienna: $5-$7. Outdoor dining. Cafe is authentic Viennese coffee house. Both establishments overlook Lincoln Center plaza. Cr cds: A, D, MC, V.

PLANET HOLLYWOOD. *140 W 57th St, Midtown.* *212/333-7827.* Specializes in pizza, hamburgers. Hrs: 11-1 am. Closed Dec 25. Bar to 1:45 am. Semi-a la carte: lunch, dinner $6.95-$16.95. Music videos and movie clips are shown daily. Authentic Hollywood memorabilia displayed. Cr cds: A, C, D, DS, JCB, MC, V.

REPUBLIC. *37 Union Square W (10003), in Gramercy Park. 212/627-7172.* Asian menu. Specialties: salmon sashimi salad, fried wontons. Hrs: noon-midnight. Closed Memorial Day, Dec 25. Bar. Semi-a la carte: lunch, dinner $6-$9. Former warehouse converted to noodle shop. Totally nonsmoking. Cr cds: A, D, MC, V.

THE ROTUNDA. *(See The Pierre Hotel) 212/940-8195.* Web www.fourseasons.com. Hrs: 8 am-midnight, tea 3-5:30 pm. A la carte entrees: bkfst, lunch $6.50-$32. Prix fixe: tea $26. Beaux-arts architecture with marble columns & pilasters. Murals by Edward Melcarth. Cr cds: A, C, D, ER, JCB, MC, V.

SAVORIES. *30 Rockefeller Center, downstairs, Midtown. 212/332-7630.* Web www.restaurantassociates.com. Specializes in and cold pasta, desserts. Hrs: 7 am-6 pm. Closed Sun May-Nov. Wine, beer. A la carte entrees: bkfst $2.50-$3.95, lunch $5-$13. Outdoor garden dining. Afternoon tea after 3 pm. Bistro atmosphere. Cr cds: A, C, D, MC, V.

SECOND AVE DELI. *156 Second Ave (10003), at 10th St, in the East Village. 212/677-0606.* Kosher menu. Specialties: pastrami, corned beef, chopped liver. Hrs: 8 am-midnight; Fri, Sat to 2 am. Closed Rosh Hashanah, Yom Kippur, Passover. Semi-a la carte: bkfst, lunch, dinner $7.95-$15. Complete meals: dinner $13.40-$20.45. Kosher deli; full menu served all day. Family-owned. Cr cds: A, D, DS, MC, V.

SERENDIPITY 3. *225 E 60th St, Upper East Side. 212/838-3531.* E-mail serendip3@aol.com; web www.serendipity3.com. Specializes in burgers. Hrs: 11:30-12:30 am; Fri to 1 am; Sat to 2 am; Sun to midnight. Closed Dec 25. Res accepted. A la carte entrees: lunch, dinner $4.50-$15. Art nouveau decor; Tiffany lamps; marble-top tables. Famous for ice cream specialties, pies, chocolate blackout cake. Enter restaurant through gift shop. Favorite of celebrities. Family-owned. Cr cds: A, C, D, DS, MC, V.

STAGE DELI. *834 Seventh Ave (10019), at 53rd St, Midtown. 212/245-7850.* E-mail stagedeli@msn.com; web www.stagedeli.com. Kosher deli menu. Specialties: corned beef, pastrami, brisket. Hrs: 6-2 am. Bar. A la carte entrees: bkfst $2.95-$7.50, lunch $4.50-$13.95, dinner $5.50-$20. Deli counter. Well-known New York deli; pickles own meats. Enclosed sidewalk dining. Celebrity photos. Cr cds: A, MC, V.

Bronx (C-4 see New York City map)

Area code 718
Information Chamber of Commerce, 2885 Schley Ave, 10465; 718/829-4111.

Jonas Bronck, a Swedish settler, bought 500 acres of land from the Dutch in 1639, lending his name to the future borough. Locally it is always referred to as "the Bronx," never simply "Bronx." It is the only borough in New York City on the North American continent (the others are all on islands).

What to See and Do

Bronx Museum of the Arts. Changing exhibits with a focus on contemporary art and current cultural subjects pertaining to the Bronx. Concerts, family workshops and special events. (Wed-Fri, also Sat & Sun afternoons) Free admission Sun. 1040 Grand Concourse, at 165th St. Phone 718/681-6000. ¢¢

Bronx Zoo. The largest metropolitan wildlife park in the US. Collection includes rare and exotic animals living in simulated naturalistic habitats. "JungleWorld" re-creates a Southeast Asian rain forest, mangrove swamp and scrub forest on a grand scale. "Wild Asia," a 40-acre habitat for Asian animals, offers a new concept in zoo land use. "Bengali Express" monorail carries visitors on 25-min trip to view Siberian tigers, elephants and other Asian wildlife. "Zoo Center" provides yr-round home for Asian elephant and Malayan tapirs. "Himalayan Highlands" features remote Asian mountaintops with snow leopards, red pandas and other native animals. "World of Darkness" is the home of nocturnal animals. "World of Birds" exhibits many species in varied natural habitats; walk-through aviary. "Big Birds" features ostriches, emus, cassowaries. South American Sea Bird Colony. Baboon Reserve with Ethiopian mountain range. Children's Zoo (Apr-Oct, daily) allows active participation. Zoo shuttle train starts near Zoo Center (Apr-Oct, daily). Aerial Skyfari ride (Apr-Oct, daily). Bengali Express (May-Oct, daily). Picnic tables, restaurants. (Daily) Free admission Wed. Fordham Rd & Bronx River Pkwy. Phone 718/367-1010. Parking ¢¢¢; Admission: Apr-Oct ¢¢¢; Rest of yr ¢¢

City Island. E of Hutchinson River Pkwy, through Pelham Bay Park, via City Island Bridge. Referred to as "a bit of New England in the city," City Island is devoted to shipping and ship building. Seafood restaurants; City Island Historical Nautical Museum (Sun);and

North Wind Undersea Museum. (Daily) 610 City Island Ave. Phone 718/885-0701. ¢¢

Edgar Allan Poe Cottage (1812). Poe wrote "Annabel Lee," "The Bells" and "Ulalume" while living here (1846-1849). Period furniture; exhibits about the poet and his wife. Films, tours (Sat & Sun). Located at Grand Concourse & E Kingsbridge Rd. Phone 718/881-8900. ¢

Fordham University (1841). (13,000 students) All four original Gothic-style structures of the Rose Hill campus are designated landmarks, in tribute to their historical and architectural interest: Univ Chapel (St John's Church), St John's Residence Hall, Administration Bldg & Alumni House. A second campus is at 60th & Columbus Ave, across from the Lincoln Center for the Performing Arts (see MANHATTAN). Fordham Rd, in N Bronx. Phone 718/817-1000.

Museum of Bronx History. Valentine-Varian House (1758), site of Revolutionary War activities; exhibits on Bronx history. (Sat & Sun) 3266 Bainbridge Ave, at E 208th St. Phone 718/881-8900. ¢

Pelham Bay Park. The city's largest park (2,764 acres) has Orchard Beach, two golf courses (18-hole), wildlife refuge, environmental center, nature trail, visitor center, tennis courts, ball fields, running track, riding stables and bridle paths, picnicking, 13 mi of saltwater shoreline and fishing. Hutchinson River & Hutchinson River Pkwy (W); the city's N limits; Pelham Pkwy, Burr Ave, Bruckner Expy & Watt Ave (S); and Eastchester Bay & Long Island Sound (E) at NE corner of Bronx. Phone 718/430-1832.Also here near S boundary is

Bartow-Pell Mansion Museum and Gardens. Greek-revival stone mansion (ca 1840) furnished in the Empire period; gardens (Tues-Sun, seasonal) carriage house. (Wed, Sat & Sun afternoons) Guided tours & luncheon tours (by appt). Free admission 1st Sun of each month. 895 Shore Rd N, in Pelham Bay Park. Phone 718/885-1461. ¢¢

The Hall of Fame for Great Americans. A 630-ft, open-air colonnade provides framework for bronze busts of great Americans; exhibits. Hall of Fame Terrace, on campus of Bronx Community College, W 181st St between Sedgwick & University Aves. Phone 718/289-5161 **Free.**

The New York Botanical Garden. One of the largest and oldest in the country, this botanical garden consists of 250 acres of natural terrain, 16 demonstration gardens, and many specialty gardens. Garden also has the last 40 acres of the forest that once covered New York City. Enid A. Haupt Conservatory is 11 distinct plant environments of changing exhibits and permanent displays including the Fern Forest, Palm Court and Desert Houses. Tours. Education courses. (Daily exc Mon) Free admission Sat mornings (mid-morning-noon). Bronx Park, entrance on Southern Blvd, S of Moshulu Pkwy. Phone 718/817-8705. Parking ¢¢; Grounds ¢¢; Conservatory ¢¢

Van Cortlandt House Museum (1748). Georgian-style house museum is furnished in 18th-century Dutch-English manner. (Daily exc Mon) In Van Cortlandt Park, Broadway at 246th St. Phone 718/543-3344. ¢

Wave Hill. Hudson River estate that was, at various times, home to such notables as Mark Twain and Arturo Toscanini, is now a public garden and cultural center, featuring Wave Hill House (1843), gardens, four greenhouses, nature trails, woods and meadows; grounds consist of 28 acres overlooking the Hudson. Special events include concerts, dance programs, art exhibits and education and nature workshops. (Daily exc Mon; closed Jan 1, Dec 25) Free admission Tues, also Sat mornings & Fri evenings. 249th St & Independence Ave. Phone 718/549-3200. ¢¢

Yankee Stadium. Home of the New York Yankees. 161st St & River Ave.

Inn

★ ★ **LE REFUGE.** *620 City Island Ave (10464), NY 95 to City Island, exit 8B. 718/885-2478; FAX 718/885-1519.* 8 rms, 4 share baths, 3 story, 2 suites, 1 cottage. Rm phones in suites, cottage. S $65; D $75; each addl $15; suites $140; cottage $175. TV; cable. Playground. Complimentary continental bkfst; afternoon refreshments. Dining rm 6-9 pm. Ck-out, ck-in by arrangement. Luggage handling. Picnic tables. Victorian house (1880) with individually decorated rms featuring many antiques. On Long Island Sound with views of Manhattan. Totally nonsmoking. Cr cds: A.

Restaurants

★ ★ **EMILIA'S.** *2331 Arthur Ave (10458), Between 184th & 186th Sts. 718/367-5915.* Italian menu. Specialties: fettuccine marinara, eggplant parmigiana, chicken Daniella with mushrooms. Hrs: noon-10 pm. Closed Mon, Tues; Thanksgiving, Dec 25. Res accepted. Bar. Semi-a la carte: lunch $9.95-$16.95, dinner $9.95-$25. Family-style restaurant. Cr cds: A, MC, V.

★ ★ **LOBSTER BOX.** *34 City Island Ave (10464), on City Island. 718/885-1952.* Specializes in lobster, shrimp, fresh fish. Hrs: noon-11 pm; Fri, Sat to 1 am. Closed Jan, Feb. Bar. Semi-a la carte: lunch $9.95-$15.95, dinner $14.95-$30.95. Valet parking. Terrace dining overlooks L.I. Sound. Family-owned. Cr cds: A, C, D, DS, MC, V.

★ ★ ★ **MARIO'S.** *2342 Arthur Ave (10458), between 184th & 186th Sts. 718/584-1188.* Italian menu. Specializes in pasta, veal, seafood. Hrs: noon-11 pm; Fri, Sat to 11:30 pm. Closed Mon; Dec 25; also first wk Jan, last 2 wks Aug, first wk Sept. Res accepted. Semi-a la carte: lunch, dinner $13-$28. Valet parking. Family-owned. Cr cds: A, C, D, DS, MC, V.

D

★ ★ **SEA SHORE.** *591 City Island Ave (10464), on City Island. 718/885-0300.* Specializes in fresh seafood, jumbo lobster. Hrs: 11 am-midnight; Fri, Sat to 2 am. Res accepted. Bar. A la carte entrees: lunch $9.95-$18.95, dinner $16.95-$38.95. Child's meals. Valet parking. Outdoor dining. Greenhouse dining rm & dock area overlooking L.I. Sound; marina. Family-owned. Cr cds: A, C, D, DS, MC, V.

Brooklyn *(E-2 see New York City map)*

Area code 718

Information Brooklyn Historical Society, 128 Pierrepont St, 11201, phone 718/624-0890; or the NYC Convention & Visitors Bureau.

Many of the novels, plays, films and television shows about New York City—ranging from *Death of a Salesman* to *The Honeymooners*—are set in Brooklyn rather than Manhattan, perhaps because of widely differing characters of these two boroughs. While Manhattan is world-class in

sophistication and influence, Brooklyn, famous for such things as the hot dogs on Coney Island, is and always has been quintessentially American.

Yet there is much more to Brooklyn than the popular stereotype. Manhattanites flock to performances at the renowned Brooklyn Academy of Music, and the Egyptology collection at the Brooklyn Museum compares with those in London and Cairo. Brooklyn's beautiful Prospect Park was designed by Olmsted and Vaux, who considered it more beautiful than another park they designed—Central Park in Manhattan.

The most heavily populated borough, Brooklyn handles about 40 percent of New York City's vast shipping. Brooklyn was pieced together from 25 independent villages and fought valiantly before allowing itself to be taken into New York City in 1898.

What to See and Do

Brooklyn Academy of Music (1907). Founded in 1859, BAM is the oldest performing arts center in America, presenting original productions in contemporary performing arts in the Next Wave Festival each fall, noted national and international theater, dance and opera companies and classical & contemporary music programs. 30 Lafayette Ave, Ft Greene/Clinton Hill. Phone 718/636-4100 for schedule and ticket information.

Brooklyn Children's Museum. Founded in 1899, this is the world's oldest children's museum. Interactive exhibits, workshops and special events. "The Mystery of Things" teaches children about cultural and scientific objects. "The Music Studio" welcomes young virtuosos. Many other hands-on exhibits. (Wed-Sun afternoons; also most school hols) 145 Brooklyn Ave, at St Marks Ave. Phone 718/735-4400. **Donation**

Brooklyn Heights. Centering around Borough Hall, Cadman Plaza. This 50-blk historic district, where Brooklyn started, has a wealth of Victorian architecture and beautiful streets. Henry Ward Beecher preached at the **Plymouth Church of the Pilgrims** (Orange St between Hicks & Henry Sts), a stop on the Underground Railroad during the Civil War. The **Esplanade** along the East River offers spectacular views of the Brooklyn Bridge, lower Manhattan and the Statue of Liberty.

Brooklyn's History Museum. Since 1881, headquarters of the Brooklyn Historical Society. Permanent and changing exhibits deal with Brooklyn history. Displays cover Coney Island, Brooklyn Dodgers, Brooklyn Bridge, Brooklyn Navy Yard; original set of "The Honeymooners" TV show; baseball cards; wax figures. Two-tiered library. (Tues-Sat; closed major hols) 128 Pierrepont St. Phone 718/624-0890. ¢¢

Coney Island. Originally a quiet resort community for wealthy New Yorkers, Coney Island was at one time so uncrowded that its dunes were used to represent the Sahara in Valentino's *The Sheik.* Now this 3-mi sand bar on the Atlantic Ocean is probably the best-known beach, boardwalk and amusement park in the country, with four roller coasters, a Wonder Wheel and many other amusements (fee for each). It is known for its amusement park food, especially the hot dogs at Nathan's Famous (Surf and Stillwell). Coney Island is easily reached from any part of the city by any of four subway lines. Swimming is good, but very crowded on pleasant days. (Easter Sun-2nd wkend Sept, daily) Surf Ave from Ocean Pkwy to 37th St. Phone 718/266-1234. **Free.** Also in the area are

Astroland Amusement Park. Theme park, featuring such rides as Astrotower, Log Flume and famous Cyclone roller coaster, has been in operation since 1927. (Mid-June-Labor Day, daily; Easter-mid-June, wkends) 1000 Surf Ave, at W 10th St, Coney Island. Phone 718/372-0275. General admission free. Individual ride tickets avail. Major ride ticket ¢¢¢¢¢

New York Aquarium. "Sea Cliffs" exhibit; also varied collection of marine life includes seals, sharks, beluga whales, invertebrates, penguins, sea otters, walrus; dolphin feedings (Apr-Oct, outdoors). Restaurant. (Daily) Parking (fee). Boardwalk & W 8th St, Coney Island. Phone 718/265-FISH. ¢¢¢

Sheepshead Bay. This area has all the requisites of an ocean-fishing community: seafood restaurants, clam bars, tackle shops, fishing boats and some lovely views. Just E and slightly N of Coney Island via Ocean Pkwy or Shore Pkwy.

Gateway National Recreation Area. One of the nation's first two urban national parks. A barrier peninsula across Rockaway Inlet from Coney Island via Flatbush Ave and the Marine Pkwy Bridge. This sprawling, urban recreation area consists of approximately 26,000 acres of land and water in 2 states—New York and New Jersey: Floyd Bennett Field in Brooklyn (Jamaica Bay in Brooklyn and Queens), Breezy Point on the Rockaway Peninsula in Queens, Miller Field and Great Kills Park on southeastern Staten Island and the Sandy Hook Unit in New Jersey (see). Jamaica Bay Wildlife Refuge in Broad Channel, Queens (9,000 acres) offers wildlife observation and hiking trails. Floyd Bennett Field has nature observation opportunities. Jacob Riis Park in Queens, with a mi-long board walk, offers beach and waterfront activities. Fort Tilden in Queens offers exhibits, nature walks, guided and self-guided tours of old defense batteries, sporting events and fishing. Canarsie Pier in Brooklyn offers free wkend summer concerts and restaurants. The Staten Island Unit offers hiking trails, organized athletic programs and recreational activities. Concession services at some units. Contact Public Affairs Office, Floyd Bennett Field, Bldg 69, Brooklyn 11234; 718/338-3688.

New York Transit Museum. Exhibits on the history of the New York City transit system displayed within a 1930s subway station. Subway cars on display, including a 1903 "El" car. Photographs, maps, antique turnstiles. (Daily exc Mon; closed hols) Beneath Boerum Place & Schermerhorn St. Phone 718/243-3060. ¢¢

Prospect Park. Planned by Olmsted and Vaux, designers of Central Park, its 526 acres include the impressive Grand Army Plaza with Memorial Arch (N end of park), the 90-acre Long Meadow and a 60-acre lake. Boathouse Visitor Center has information on park history and design; art shows (Apr-Nov); phone 718/965-8900. Ball fields, boating, ice rink, bridle paths, tennis courts, bandshell, historic carousel and the Lefferts Homestead, a 1783 Dutch Colonial farmhouse. Bounded by Parkside Ave, Ocean Ave, Flatbush Ave & Prospect Park W & SW. Park rangers conduct weekend tours; phone 718/438-0100.Directly across Flatbush Ave is

Brooklyn Botanic Garden. More than 50 acres with a conservatory complex; fragrance garden for the visually impaired; Japanese Hill-and-Pond Garden (Apr-Oct; fee wknds & hols); Cranford Rose Garden (June-Oct). One-hr guided tour (Sat &Sun, one departure each day; no tours certain hols). Steinhardt Conservatory with tropical, temperate and desert pavilions and the C.V. Star Bonsai Museum. (Daily exc Mon; also all hols) Children under 16 admitted only with adult. Free admission Tues. Eastern Pkwy, Washington & Flatbush Aves, opp Prospect Park. Phone 718/622-4433. ¢¢   Nearby is

Brooklyn Museum of Art. Outstanding collection of art from Egypt, Pacific Islands, North, South and Central America, the Orient and Middle East; painting, sculpture, prints, drawings; American and European decorative arts and furnished period rms; costumes, textiles; changing exhibits. Sculpture garden with architectural ornaments from buildings demolished in New York City area. Concerts, gallery talks, lectures, films. Cafeteria; gift shops. (Wed-Sun; closed Jan 1, Thanksgiving, Dec 25) 200 Eastern Pkwy. Phone 718/638-5000. ¢¢

Sightseeing tour. Discovery Tour of Brooklyn. Bus tour (6 hrs) to many of Brooklyn's sites and neighborhoods. (May-Oct, Thurs & Sat) Departs from Gray Line Bus Terminal in Manhattan. Phone 212/397-2600. ¢¢¢¢

Restaurants

★ ★ **ABBRACCIAMENTO ON THE PIER.** *2200 Rockaway Pkwy (11236), at Canarsie Pier, in Canarsie area. 718/251-5517.* Northern Italian, Amer menu. Specialties: veal scaloppini with artichoke champagne sauce, chicken breast stuffed with fontina cheese, pasta seafood bianco. Hrs: 11:30 am-midnight; Fri, Sat to 1 am; Sun brunch 11:30 am-3 pm. Closed Jan 1, Dec 25. Res required. Bar. A la carte entrees: lunch $9-$15, dinner $12-$25. Complete meals: dinner $19.95-$22.50. Sun brunch $15.95. Entertainment. Outdoor dining. On Canarsie Pier; overlooks Jamaica Bay; docking facilities. Cr cds: A, C, D, MC, V.

D

★ ★ **CUCINA.** *256 5th Ave (11215), between Carrol & Garfield Place, Park Slope area. 718/230-0711.* Italian menu. Specialties: roast rack of lamb, osso bucco & pappardelle. Antipasto bar. Hrs: 5:30-10:30 pm; Fri, Sat to 11 pm; Sun 5-10 pm. Closed Mon, Thanksgiving, Dec 25.

Res accepted. Bar. A la carte entrees: dinner $10-$25. Child's meals. Two dining rms; gold leaf wall montage by New York artist. Cr cds: A, D, MC, V.

D

★ ★ **EMBERS.** *9519 Third Ave (11209), between 95th & 96th Sts, in Bayridge area. 718/745-3700.* Specializes in pasta, T-bone steak. Hrs: noon-2:45 pm, 5-10:30 pm; Fri to 11:30 pm; Sat noon-1:45 pm, 4:30-11:30 pm; Sun 2-9:30 pm. Closed Thanksgiving, Dec 24, 25. Bar. A la carte entrees: lunch $4.50-$7.95, dinner $10.95-$16.95. Adj to meat market. No cr cds accepted. No cr cds accepted.

D

★ ★ **GIANDO ON THE WATER.** *400 Kent Ave (11211), under Williamsburg Bridge, Kent Ave at Broadway. 718/387-7000.* Italian menu. Specializes in seafood, fish. Hrs: noon-11 pm; Sat from 4 pm; Sun 3-9 pm; early-bird dinner 5-7 pm, Sat 4-6 pm, Sun 3-6 pm. Res accepted. Bar. Prix fixe: lunch $19.95, dinner $29.95. A la carte entrees: dinner $12-$27. Pianist Fri, Sat. Valet parking. On East River overlooking Williamsburg & Brooklyn bridges and Manhattan skyline from Empire State Bldg to Statue of Liberty. Cr cds: A, C, D, DS, MC, V.

D

✔★ ★ **GREENHOUSE CAFE.** *7717 Third Ave (11209), between 77th & 78th Sts, in Bayridge area. 718/833-8200.* Web www.greenhouse cafe.com. Specialties: roast Long Island duckling, seafood festival platter. Hrs: 11:30 am-11 pm; Fri, Sat to midnight; Sun 4-10 pm; Sun brunch noon-3 pm. Closed Dec 25. Res accepted. Bar. A la carte entrees: lunch $5.25-$13. Semi-a la carte: dinner $10.95-$17.95. Child's meals. Garden atrium. Cr cds: A, C, D, DS, MC, V.

D 🖘

★ ★ **PETER LUGER'S.** *178 Broadway (11211), at foot of Williamsburg Bridge. 718/387-7400.* Specializes in steak, lamb chops. Hrs: 11:30 am-9:45 pm; Fri, Sat to 10:45 pm; Sun 1-9:45 pm. Res accepted. Bar. Semi-a la carte: lunch $12.95. A la carte entrees: dinner $28.95-$60. Established in 1887; in 19th-century riverfront building. No cr cds accepted.

D

★ ★ **PONTE VECCHIO.** *8810 Fourth Ave (11209), between 88th & 89th Sts, in Bayridge area. 718/238-6449.* Italian menu. Specializes in pasta, veal, seafood. Hrs: noon-10:30 pm; Fri, Sat to 11:30 pm. Closed July 4, Thanksgiving, Dec 25. Res accepted. Serv bar. A la carte entrees: lunch $14-$22, dinner $27-$32. Valet parking. Cr cds: A, MC, V.

D

★ ★ ★ **RIVER CAFE.** *1 Water St (11201), on East River at foot of Brooklyn Bridge, in Brooklyn Heights area. 718/522-5200.* Specializes in lamb. Own chocolate desserts. Own baking. Hrs: noon-2:30 pm, 6-11:30 pm; Sun brunch 11:30 am-2:30 pm. Res required. A la carte entrees: lunch $20-$26. Prix fixe: dinner $68, tasting menu $85. Sun brunch $13-$26. Pianist. Valet parking. Jacket. Cr cds: A, C, D, MC, V.

★ ★ **TOMMASO.** *1464 86th St (11228), in Bayridge area. 718/236-9883.* Italian menu. Specializes in regional Italian dishes. Hrs: 4-11 pm; Sat to midnight; Sun 1-10 pm. Closed Dec 25. Res accepted. Bar. A la carte entrees: dinner $8-$20. Opera Thurs-Sun evenings. Family-owned. Cr cds: A, C, D, MC, V.

D 🖘

Queens (La Guardia & JFK Intl Airport Areas) (D-4 see New York City map)

Area code 718

By far the largest borough geographically, Queens occupies 121 square miles of Long Island. Like Brooklyn, it was assembled from a number of small towns, and each of these neighborhoods has retained a strong sense of identity. Parts of the borough are less densely settled than Brooklyn, and the majority of Queens' population are homeowners. Many manufacturing plants, warehouses and shipping facilities are in the portion called Long Island City, near the East River. Forest Hills, with its West Side Tennis Club, at Tennis Place and Burns St, is a world-famous center for tennis. Flushing Meadows Corona Park has been the site of two world's fairs; many facilities still stand.

Transportation

Car Rental Agencies: See IMPORTANT TOLL-FREE NUMBERS.

Public Transportation: Subway and elevated trains, buses (New York Transit Authority), phone 718/330-3322 or 718/330-1234.

Rail Passenger Service: Amtrak 800/872-7245.

Airport Information

Services: *At La Guardia*—information 718/476-5000; lost and found 718/533-3988; weather 900/976-1212; cash machines, upper level Main Terminal, Finger 4, Delta Terminal. *At Kennedy*—information 718/656-4444; lost and found 718/244-4225; weather 900/976-1212.

Airlines, *At La Guardia:* Air Canada, America West, American, Canadian Arlns Intl, Carnival Arlns, Colgan Air, Continental, Delta, Midway Arlns, Midwest Express, Northwest, TWA, United, USAir. *At Kennedy Intl:* Aer Lingus, Aeroflot, Aerolineas Argentinas, Aeromexico, Aeroperu, Air Afrique, Air China, Air Europa, Air France, Air India, Air Jamaica, Air South, Air Ukraine, Alitalia, All Nippon, America West, American, Asiana Arlns, Austrian, Avianca, Balkan-Bulgarian, Biman Bangladesh, British Airways, BWIA, Canadian Arlns Intl, Carnival Arlns, Cathay Pacific, China Arlns, Delta, Ecuatoriana, Egyptair, El Al, Eva Airways, Finnair, Ghana Airways, Gulf Air, Guyana Airways, Iberia, Icelandair, Japan Arlns, KLM, Korean Air, Krasnoyarsk Arlns, Kuwait Airways, LACSA, LAN Chile, LOT, LTU Intl, Lufthansa, Malev, Northwest, Olympic, Pakistan Intl Arlns, Pan Am Air Bridge, Qantas, Royal Air Maroc, Royal Jordanian, SABENA, SAETA, Saudi Arabian Arlns, Servivensa, Singapore Arlns, South African Airways, Swissair, TACA, TAP Air Portugal, Tarom, Transbrasil, Turkish Arlns, TWA, United, USAir, Uzbekistan Arlns, Varig, VASP, Virgin Atlantic.

What to See and Do

American Museum of the Moving Image. On site of historic Astoria Studios, where many classic early movies were filmed. Museum devoted to art and history of film, television and video and their effects on American culture. Permanent and changing exhibitions; two theaters with film and video series (screenings wkends). (Daily exc Mon; closed major hols) Free admission Tues-Fri afternoons. 35th Ave at 36th St, in Astoria. Phone 718/784-0077. ¢¢¢

Bowne House (1661). One of the oldest houses in New York City was built by John Bowne, a Quaker who led a historic struggle for religious freedom under Dutch rule; 17th-19th-century furnishings. (Tues, Sat & Sun afternoons; closed Easter & mid-Dec-mid-Jan) Under 12 admitted only with adult. 37-01 Bowne St. Phone 718/359-0528. ¢¢

Flushing Meadow Corona Park. Originally a marsh, this 1,255-acre area became the site of two world's fairs (1939-1940 and 1964-1965). It is now the home of the United States Tennis Association National Tennis Center, where the US Open is held annually (phone 718/760-6200). The park is also the site of some of the largest cultural and ethnic festivals in the city.

Facilities include an indoor ice rink, carousel, 87-acre Meadow Lake and the Playground for All Children, designed for disabled and able-bodied children. Grand Central Pkwy to Van Wyck Expy & Union Tpke to Northern Blvd. Park rangers conduct occasional wkend tours; phone 718/353-2460. **Free.** Also on the grounds are

The Queens Museum of Art. Interdisciplinary fine arts presentations, major traveling exhibitions; permanent collection includes 9,000-sq-ft panorama of New York City, which is the world's largest 3-dimensional architectural model. (Wed-Fri, also Sat & Sun afternoons; closed Jan 1, Thanksgiving, Dec 25) New York City Building. Phone 718/592-5555. ¢¢

New York Hall of Science. Exhibition Hall with hands-on science and technology exhibits. (Daily) Free admission Thurs & Fri afternoons. 111th St & 48th Ave in Flushing Meadows Corona Park. Phone 718/699-0005. ¢¢¢

Shea Stadium. Home of the New York Mets. 126th St & Roosevelt Ave. Phone 718/507-6387. ¢¢¢-¢¢¢¢¢

Isamu Naguchi Sculpture Museum. Former studio space of Japanese sculptor Isamu Naguchi, now holds 12 galleries filled with his stone work and stage-set designs. A small but evocative sculpture garden adjoins the museum. (Daily; closed Nov-Mar) 32-61 Vernon Blvd, entrance on 33rd Rd. Phone 718/204-7088. ¢¢¢

John F. Kennedy International Airport. The airport's 4,930 acres cover an area roughly one-third the size of Manhattan. Much of the air traffic going overseas is handled through here. (See AIRPORT INFORMATION) Van Wyck Expy, S of Southern Pkwy.

La Guardia Airport. Located at Grand Central Pkwy & 94th St. (See AIRPORT INFORMATION)

Queens Botanical Garden. Collections include large rose, herb, Victorian wedding, bee, woodland and bird gardens; arboretum. (Daily exc Mon) 43-50 Main St. Phone 718/886-3800. **Donation.**

Annual Event

US Open Tennis. Box office phone 718/760-6200. Late Aug-early Sept.

Seasonal Events

Thoroughbred horse racing.

Aqueduct. Near Cross Bay Blvd just off Belt Pkwy. IND Subway, Rockaway Beach train. Thoroughbred racing. Equestris dining complex (proper dress required); children admitted only with parent or guardian. Phone 718/641-4700. Jan-May & Oct-Dec.

Belmont Park. Just outside of Queens, in Nassau County, on Cross Island Pkwy, via Hempstead Tpke & Plainfield Ave, in Elmont, L.I. Thoroughbred racing. Home of the Belmont Stakes, the third leg of racing's Triple Crown. Reserved seats. Terrace Dining Complex (proper dress required); children admitted only with parent or guardian. Phone 718/641-4700. Mid-May-late July.

Hotels

★ ★ ★ **CROWNE PLAZA LA GUARDIA.** *(104-04 Ditmars Blvd, East Elmhurst 11369)* Grand Central Pkwy exit 94th St, near La Guardia Airport. 718/457-6300; FAX 718/899-9768. E-mail crownelga@world net.att.net; web www.ccconnect.com/fla/lagcp.htm. 358 rms, 200 with shower only, 7 story. S $175-$195; D $195-$205; each addl $20; suites $199-$600; under 19 free; wkly, wkend & hol rates. Crib free. Garage parking $5. TV; cable (premium), VCR (movies avail). Indoor pool; whirl pool, poolside serv. Complimentary coffee in rms. Restaurant 6 am-midnight. Bar 4 pm-2 am. Ck-out noon. Coin lndry. Convention facilities. Business center. In-rm modem link. Concierge. Gift shop. Free airport transportation. Tennis privileges. Exercise rm; sauna. Many refrigerators. Luxury level. Cr cds: A, C, D, DS, JCB, MC, V.

D ⚽ ≋ ✗ ✈ ⌦ ⚓ SC ⛹

★ ★ **HILTON JFK AIRPORT.** *138-10 135th Ave (11436),* at Kennedy Intl Airport. 718/322-8700; FAX 718/529-0749. E-mail jfk3@l.i.net; web www.hilton.com. 333 rms, 9 story. S $179-$240; D $189-$250; each addl $25; suites $289-$650; under 18 free. Crib free. TV; cable (premium), VCR avail. Restaurant 6 am-11:30 pm. Bar noon-2 am. Ck-out noon. Convention facilities. Business servs avail. In-rm modem link. Free airport transportation. Exercise equipt. Luxury level. Cr cds: A, C, D, DS, ER, JCB, MC, V.

★ ★ **HOLIDAY INN-JFK.** *(144-02 135th Ave, Jamaica (La Guardia & JFK Intl Airport Areas) 11430) near Kennedy Intl Airport. 718/659-0200; FAX 718/322-2533.* 360 rms, 12 story. S, D $189; each addl $15; suites from $239; under 18 free. Crib free. TV; cable, VCR avail (movies). Indoor/outdoor pool; whirlpool, lifeguard. Restaurant 6 am-10 pm. Bar 11:30-1 am. Ck-out noon. Convention facilities. Business servs avail. Free airport transportation. Exercise equipt, sauna. Cr cds: A, C, D, DS, JCB, MC, V.

★ ★ **MARRIOTT LAGUARDIA.** *102-05 Ditmars Blvd (11369), opp La Guardia Airport, in East Elmhurst area. 718/565-8900; FAX 718/898-4995.* Web www.marriot.com/lgaap. 436 rms, 9 story. S $150; D $170; suites $350-$650; under 18 free; wknd rates; wkend plans. Crib free. Pet accepted. Covered parking $5. TV; cable (premium), VCR avail. Indoor pool; whirlpool, lifeguard. Restaurants 6:30 am-11 pm. Bar 11-1 am. Ck-out 1 pm. Convention facilities. Business center. In-rm modem link. Gift shop. Free airport transportation. Exercise equipt, sauna. Microwaves avail. Luxury level. Cr cds: A, C, D, DS, ER, JCB, MC, V.

Restaurants

★ ★ **IL TOSCANO.** *(42-05 235th St, Douglaston 11363) in Douglaston area. 718/631-0300.* Italian menu. Specialties: sweetbreads sautéed with fresh thyme, green peppercorn and sherry; grilled brook trout with raspberry lemon. Hrs: 5-10 pm. Closed Sun. Res required. Bar. A la carte entrees: dinner $14-$24. Casual, trattoria atmosphere. Cr cds: A, C, D, MC, V.

★ ★ **MANDUCATIS.** *13-27 Jackson Ave (11101), at 47th Ave, in Long Island City. 718/729-9845.* E-mail 103752.2264@compuserve.com. Italian menu. Specialties: pappardelle Casertana, eggplant Napoletana. Hrs: noon-3 pm, 5-10 pm; Sat 5-11 pm; Sun 2-8 pm. Closed Sun July-Aug; last 2 wks in Aug; also most major hols. Res accepted. Bar. A la carte entrees: lunch $5-$18, dinner $7-$18.50. Attractive, comfortable neighborhood restaurant. Cr cds: A, C, D, MC, V.

★ ★ **MARBELLA.** *220-33 Northern Blvd (11361), 2 blks W of Cross Island Pkwy, in Bayside area. 718/423-0100.* Spanish, continental menu. Specialties: paella, rack of lamb, duckling Valenciana. Hrs: noon-midnight; Sat to 1 am. Res accepted. Bar. A la carte entrees: lunch $6.95-$10.95, dinner $8.95-$17.95. Harpist Fri-Sun. Parking. Spanish artifacts. Family-owned. Cr cds: A, D, MC, V.

★ ★ **PARK SIDE.** *107-01 Corona Ave (11368), at 51st St, in Corona area. 718/271-9274.* Italian menu. Specializes in pasta, veal, fish. Hrs: noon-11:30 pm. Res accepted. Bar. A la carte entrees: lunch $10-$18, dinner $10-$21. Valet parking. The five dining areas include a glass-enclosed garden rm. Cr cds: A, C, D, MC, V.

★ ★ **PICCOLA VENEZIA.** *42-01 28th Ave (11103), at 42nd St, Astoria area. 718/721-8470.* Northern Italian menu. Specializes in seafood, rack of lamb, pasta. Hrs: noon-11 pm; Sat 4:30-11:30 pm; Sun 2-10:30 pm. Closed Tues; Jan 1, Dec 25, also July 24-Aug 24. Res accepted. A la carte entrees: lunch $15-$35, dinner $15-$40. Complete meals: dinner $38.95-$46.95. Valet parking. Attractive restaurant with exposed brick walls and etched mirrors. Family-owned. Cr cds: A, C, D, MC, V.

★ ★ ★ **WATER'S EDGE.** *(44th Drive, Long Island City 11101) at East River. 718/482-0033.* Specializes in seafood, lobster. Own baking. Hrs: noon-3 pm, 5-11 pm; Fri, Sat 5:30-11:30 pm. Closed Sun. Res required. Bar. Wine cellar. A la carte entrees: lunch $10-$16, dinner $22-$31. Pianist. Valet parking. Complimentary river boat transportation to and from Manhattan. Outdoor dining. European decor. On riverfront opp United Nations complex; views of New York City midtown skyline. Cr cds: A, C, D, JCB, MC, V.

Staten Island

(E-1 see New York City map)

Area code 718

Information Staten Island Chamber of Commerce, 130 Bay St, 10301, phone 718/727-1900; or the NYC Convention & Visitors Bureau.

Staten Island, twice the size of Manhattan with only one twenty-fourth the population, is the most removed, in distance and character, from the other boroughs. At one time, sightseers on the famous Staten Island Ferry rarely disembarked to explore the almost rural character of the island. The completion of the Verrazano Bridge to Brooklyn, however, brought growth and the beginning of a struggle between developers and those who would preserve the island's uncrowded appeal.

Transportation

Staten Island Ferry: From Manhattan to St George, Staten Island. Phone 718/390-5253.

Verrazano-Narrows Bridge. The main span of this beautiful suspension bridge, which connects Staten Island with Brooklyn, is 4,260 ft; the total length is 13,700 ft. Westbound vehicles ¢¢

What to See and Do

Conference House. Built in the mid-1680s by an English sea captain, this was the site of an unproductive meeting on Sept 11, 1776, between British Admiral Lord Howe, Benjamin Franklin, John Adams and Edward Rutledge to discuss terms of peace to end the Revolutionary War. The meeting helped to produce the phrase the "United States of America." Rose, herb gardens; open-hearth cooking and spinning; weaving demonstrations. (Mar-Dec, Wed-Sun). 7455 Hylan Blvd, in Tottenville. Phone 718/984-2086 or 718/984-6046. ¢

Historic Richmond Town. Outdoor museum complex depicts three centuries of the history and culture of Staten Island and its surrounding region. The daily life and work of a rural community comes alive through trade demonstrations and tours of shops and buildings. Among the restoration's 27 historic structures are the Historic Museum, Voorlezer's House (ca 1695), the oldest surviving elementary school in the US, general store; trademen's shops. Special events and demonstrations. (Wed-Sun afternoons; extended hrs July &Aug; closed Jan 1, Thanksgiving, Dec 25) 441 Clarke Ave, Richmond &Arthur Kill Rds. Phone 718/351-1611. ¢¢

Jacques Marchais Museum of Tibetan Art. Collection of Tibetan and Oriental art in setting resembling Himalayan mountain temple. Terraced sculpture gardens, goldfish pond. (Apr-Nov, Wed-Sun afternoons; rest of yr, by appt) 338 Lighthouse Ave, between New Dorp & Richmondtown. Phone 718/987-3500. ¢¢

Snug Harbor Cultural Center. Founded in 1833 as a seamen's retirement home, Snug Harbor is now a performing and visual arts center with 28 historic buildings featuring Greek-revival and Victorian architecture; art galleries (Wed-Sun, fee); children's museum (daily exc Mon, afternoons); botanical garden, sculpture, 83 acres of parkland. (Daily; closed Thanksgiving, Dec 25) 1000 Richmond Terr. Phone 718/448-2500. Grounds **Free.**

Staten Island Zoo. Maintained by the Staten Island Zoological Society. Large collection of native and exotic reptiles, varied species of rattlesnakes, amphibians, marine reef fishes, mammals, birds. Children's center includes a miniature farm. (Daily; closed Jan 1, Thanksgiving, Dec 25) Free admission on Wed afternoon, inquire for hrs. Barrett Park, between Broadway & Clove Rd in W New Brighton. Phone 718/442-3100. ¢¢

The Greenbelt/High Rock. An 85-acre nature preserve in a 2,500-acre park. Visitor center, trails. Environmental programs, workshops. Self-guided tours. Urban park ranger-guided tours (by appt). (Daily) No picnicking or camping. Nevada Ave in Egbertville, 7 mi from Verrazano Bridge via Richmond Rd. Phone 718/667-2165. **Free.**

Rhode Island

Population: 1,003,464
Land area: 1,054 square miles
Elevation: 0-812 feet
Highest point: Jerimoth Hill (Providence County)
Entered Union: Thirteenth of original 13 states (May 29, 1790)
Capital: Providence
Motto: Hope
Nickname: Ocean State
State flower: Violet
State bird: Rhode Island Red Hen
State tree: Red Maple
Time zone: Eastern
Web: www.visitrhodeisland.com

Giovanni da Verrazano, a Florentine navigator in the service of France, visited the Narragansett Bay of Rhode Island in 1524; however, it wasn't until 1636 that the first permanent white settlement was founded. Roger Williams, a religious refugee from Massachusetts, bought land at Providence from the Narragansetts. Williams fled what he considered puritanical tyranny and established a policy of religious and political freedom in his new settlement. Soon others began similar communities, and in 1663, King Charles II granted them a royal charter, officially creating the "State of Rhode Island and Providence Plantations."

Although the smallest state in the nation, smaller than many of the counties in the US, Rhode Island is rich in American tradition. It is a state of firsts. Rhode Islanders were among the first colonists to take action against the British, attacking British vessels in its waters. On May 4, 1776, the state was the first to proclaim independence from Great Britian, two months before the Declaration of Independence was signed. In 1790, Samuel Slater's mill in Pawtucket became America's first successful water-powered cotton mill, and in 1876 polo was played for the first time in the US, in Newport.

Rhode Island has a tradition of manufacturing skill. The state produces machine tools, electronic equipment, plastics, textiles, jewelry, toys and boats. The famous Rhode Island Red Hen was developed by farmers in Little Compton. Rhode Island is also for those who follow the sea. With more than 400 miles of coastline, visitors can swim, sail, fish or relax in the many resort areas.

When to Go/Climate

The weather in Rhode Island is more moderate than in other parts of New England. Breezes off Narraganset Bay make summer humidity bearable and winter temperatures less bitter than elsewhere in the region.

AVERAGE HIGH/LOW TEMPERATURES (°F)
PROVIDENCE

Jan 37/19	**May** 67/47	**Sept** 74/54
Feb 38/21	**June** 77/57	**Oct** 64/43
Mar 46/29	**July** 82/63	**Nov** 53/35
Apr 57/38	**Aug** 81/62	**Dec** 41/24

Parks and Recreation Finder

Directions to and information about the parks and recreation areas below are given under their respective town/city sections. Please refer to those sections for details.

NATIONAL PARK AND RECREATION AREA

Key to abbreviations: I.H.S. = International Historic Site; I.P.M. = International Peace Memorial; N.B. = National Battlefield; N.B.P. = National Battlefield Park; N.B.C. = National Battlefield & Cemetery; N.C. = National Conservation Area; N.E.M. = National Expansion Memorial; N.F. = National Forest; N.G. = National Grassland; N.H. = National Historical Park; N.H.C. = National Heritage Corridor; N.H.S. = National Historic Site; N.L. = National Lakeshore; N.M. = National Monument; N.M.P. = National Military Park; N.Mem. = National Memorial; N.P. = National Park; N.Pres. = National Preserve; N.R. = National Recreational Area; N.R.R. = National Recreational River; N.Riv. = National River; N.S. = National Seashore; N.S.R. = National Scenic Riverway; N.S.T. = National Scenic Trail; N.Sc. = National Scientific Reserve; N.V.M. = National Volcanic Monument.

Place Name	Listed Under
Roger Williams National Memorial	PROVIDENCE

STATE PARK AND RECREATION AREAS

Key to abbreviations: I.P. = Interstate Park; S.A.P. = State Archaeological Park; S.B. = State Beach; S.C. = State Conservation Area; S.C.P. = State Conservation Park; S.Cp. = State Campground; S.F. = State Forest; S.G. = State Garden; S.H.A. = State Historic Area; S.H.P. = State Historic Park; S.H.S. = State Historic Site; S.M.P. = State Marine Park; S.N.A. = State Natural Area; S.P. = State Park; S.P.C. = State Public Campground; S.R. = State Reserve; S.R.A. = State Recreation Area; S.Res. = State Resevoir; S.Res.P. = State Resort Park; S.R.P. = State Rustic Park.

Place Name	Listed Under
Burlingame S.P.	CHARLESTOWN

Casimir Pulaski S.P.	GLOUCESTER
Colt S.P.	BRISTOL
Ft Adams S.P.	NEWPORT
Goddard Memorial S.P.	EAST GREENWICH
Lincoln Woods S.P.	PROVIDENCE
Misquamicut State Beach Park	WESTERLY
Salty Brine Beach, Roger	NARRAGANSETT
Wheeler Beach and Scarborough Beach S.P.	

Water-related activities, hiking, riding, various other sports, picnicking and visitor centers, as well as camping, are available in many of these areas. State parks are open sunrise to sunset. Parking fee at beaches: wkdays, $4-$8/car; wkends, hols, $5-$10/car. Camping, $8-$12/night; with electric & water, $10-$14; plus sewer $12-$16. No pets allowed. A map is available at the Division of Parks & Recreation, Dept of Environmental Management, 2321 Hartford Avenue, Johnston 02919. Phone 401/222-2632.

FISHING & HUNTING
No license is necessary for recreational saltwater game fishing. Freshwater fishing license: nonresident, $31; 3-day tourists' fee, $16. Both largemouth bass and northern pike can be found in Worden Pond; trout can be found in Wood River.

Hunting license: nonresident, $41. Resident licenses and regulations may be obtained at city and town clerks' offices and at most sporting goods shops. Non-resident licenses may be obtained by contacting DEM-Licensing, 22 Hayes St, Providence 02908; 401/222-3576. For further information write Division of Fish & Wildlife, Dept of Environment Management, Government Center, Wakefield 02879. Phone 401/222-2284.

Driving Information
Children ages 4-12 must be in an approved passenger restraint anywhere in vehicle; age 3 and under must use an approved safety seat. For further information phone 401/222-3024.

INTERSTATE HIGHWAY SYSTEM
The following alphabetical listing of Rhode Island towns in *Mobil Travel Guide* shows that these cities are within 10 miles of the indicated Interstate highway. A highway map, however, should be checked for the nearest exit.

Highway Number	Cities/Towns within 10 miles
Interstate 95	East Greenwich, Pawtucket, Providence, Warwick, Westerly.

Additional Visitor Information
Contact the Rhode Island Economic Development Corporation Division of Marketing & Communications, 1 W Exchange St, Providence 02903; 401/222-2601 or 800/556-2484. The *Providence Journal-Bulletin Almanac* is an excellent state reference book, and may be obtained from the Providence *Journal*, 75 Fountain St, Providence 02902.

There are several information centers in Rhode Island; visitors will find information and brochures most helpful in planning stops at points of interest. Two of the information centers are located: off I-95 in Richmond (daily); and 7 miles S of Providence in Warwick, at T. F. Green Airport.

Block Island (F-6)

(See also Newport, Westerly)

Settled 1661 **Pop** 620 (est) **Elev** 9 ft **Area code** 401 **Zip** 02807 **E-mail** bichamber@biri.com
Information Chamber of Commerce, Water St PO Drawer D; 401/466-2982 or 800/383-2474.

(By ferry from Providence, Newport and Point Judith; by air from Westerly. Also by ferry from New London, CT and Montauk, Long Island.)

Block Island, Rhode Island's "air-conditioned" summer resort, covers 21 square miles. Lying 12 miles out to sea from Point Judith, it received its nickname because it is 10 to 15 degrees cooler than the mainland in summer and consistently milder in winter. Although Verrazano saw the island in 1524, it was named for the Dutch explorer, Adriaen Block, who landed here in 1614. Until the resort trade developed, this island community was devoted to fishing and farming. Settler's Rock on Corn Neck Road displays plaques on the boulder listing the first settlers.

In recent years Block Island has become a favorite "nature retreat" for people seeking to escape fast-paced city living. More than 40 rare and endangered species of plants and animals can be found on the island, of which one-quarter is in public trust. The Nature Conservancy has designated Block Island as "one of the 12 last great places in the Western Hemisphere."

What to See and Do
Ferry service. For fares and schedules phone 401/783-4613.

Block Island/Montauk, Long Island. (Mid-June-Labor Day, 1 trip daily) Phone 516/668-5009.

Block Island/New London, CT. Two-hr trip. (Mid-June-Labor Day, 1 trip daily, extra trips Fri)

Block Island/Point Judith. Advance reservations for vehicles; all vehicles must be on pier 45 min before sailing. (Mid-June-mid-Sept, 8 round trips daily; early May-mid-June, mid-Sept-Oct, 4 round trips daily; rest of yr, 1 round trip daily)

Block Island/Providence, RI/Newport, RI. Departs from either Providence or Newport. (Late June-Labor Day, 1 trip daily) Non-vehicular ferry.

Fishing. Surf casting from most beaches; freshwater ponds for bass, pickerel, perch; deep-sea boat trips for tuna, swordfish, etc, from Old Harbor.

Fred Benson Town Beach. Swimming, bathhouse, lifeguards. Picnicking, concession. Parking. 1/2 mi N to Crescent Beach.

Natural formations. Mohegan Bluffs, west of Southeast Light lighthouse off Mohegan Trail, are 185-ft clay cliffs that offer a fine sea view. **New Harbor,** 1 mi W on Ocean Ave, is a huge harbor made by cutting through sand bar into Great Salt Pond.

New England Airlines. Twelve-min scheduled flights between Westerly State Airport and Block Island State Airport; also air taxi and charter service to all points. (Daily) For fares and schedules phone 401/466-5881, 401/596-2460 or 800/243-2460.

North Light. Lighthouse built 1867 at tip of island near Settler's Rock, now houses maritime museum. Bordering dunes are seagull rookery and wildlife sanctuary.

Hotels

★ ★ **SPRING HOUSE.** *52 Spring St. 401/466-5844; res: 800/234-9263.* 49 rms, most with shower only, 3 story, 14 suites. No A/C. Mid-June-early Sept: S, D $149-$250; each addl $20; suites $175-$250; under 12 free; wkly, wkend rates; 2-day min wkends, 3-day min hols; lower rates early Sept-Oct, May-mid-June. Closed rest of yr. Crib free. Playground. Complimentary continental bkfst. Restaurant noon-4 pm, 6-10 pm. Bar 6 pm-12:30 am. Ck-out 11 am. Meeting rms. Free airport transportation. Lawn games. On ocean. Cr cds: A, MC, V.

★ ★ **THE SURF.** *Dodge St. 401/466-2241.* 47 rms, 44 share bath, 4 story. No A/C. No rm phones. Late June-early Sept: S $55-$80; D $70-$140; each addl $15; wkly, wkend rates; wkends, hols (2-day min); lower rates early Sept-Oct, May-late June. Closed rest of yr. Crib $10-$15. TV in lobby. Complimentary continental bkfst. Restaurant nearby. Ck-out 11 am. Free airport transportation. Lawn games. Refrigerators avail. Grills. On ocean. Wrap-around porch. Cr cds: MC, V.

Inn

★ ★ ★ **THE 1661 INN & GUEST HOUSE.** *1 Spring St. 401/466-2063; FAX 401/466-2858; res: 800/626-4773.* 21 units, 6 with shower only, 4 share bath, 2 story, 2 suites, 2 kit. units. No A/C. Many rm phones. July-Sept: S, D $115-$248; suites $229-$325; kit. units $250; wkend rates; 3-day min wkends & hols; lower rates rest of yr. Crib free. Some cable TVs; VCR avail. Playground, petting zoo. Complimentary coffee in rms. Complimentary full bkfst; afternoon refreshments. Restaurant nearby. Ck-out 11 am, ck-in 1 pm. Luggage handling. Free airport transportation. Tennis. Lawn games. Refrigerators. Sun decks. Picnic tables. On ocean. Built 1890; restored Colonial with Early American art and antiques. Cr cds: A, MC, V.

Restaurants

★ ★ **FINN'S.** *Water St, at ferry landing. 401/466-2473.* E-mail dhoward@netsense.net. Specializes in seafood, lobster. Hrs: 11:30 am-10 pm; Fri, Sat to 11 pm. Closed Nov-Apr. No A/C. Bar. A la carte entrees: lunch, dinner $4.80-$34.50. Outdoor dining. View of town and harbor. Cr cds: A, MC, V.

★ ★ ★ **HOTEL MANISSES DINING ROOM.** *Spring St. 401/466-2836.* Continental menu. Specialties: herb-encrusted salmon, grilled swordfish with tomatilla salsa, filet mignon with shiitake mushroom demi-glacé. Hrs: 5:30-10 pm; Sat, Sun from 11:30 am. Closed Mon-Fri mid-Feb-Apr; also Dec-mid-Feb. No A/C. Bar. Wine cellar. Semi-a la carte: lunch $9-$21, dinner $15-$25. Prix fixe: dinner $29-$39. Child's meals. Outdoor dining. Stone-walled dining rm and glass-enclosed garden rm. Totally nonsmoking. Cr cds: A, MC, V.

★ ★ **MOHEGAN CAFE.** *Water St, opp ferry landing in historic downtown district. 401/466-5911.* Specializes in seafood. Hrs: 11 am-10:30 pm; Jan-Mar Sat & Sun 11 am-9 pm; Oct-Dec, Apr hrs vary. Closed Thanksgiving, Dec 25. Bar. Semi-a la carte: lunch $3.95-$9.95, dinner $8.95-$18.95. Child's meals. Panoramic view of Old Harbor. Cr cds: A, MC, V.

Bristol (D-7)

(See also Portsmouth, Providence)

Settled 1669 **Pop** 21,625 **Elev** 50 ft **Area code** 401 **Zip** 02809 **E-mail** info@bristolcountychamber.org **Web** www.bristolcountychamber.org
Information Bristol County Chamber of Commerce, 654 Metacom Ave, PO Box 250, Warren 02885-0250; 401/245-0750.

King Philip's War (1675-1676) began and ended on the Bristol peninsula between Mt Hope and Narragansett bays; King Philip, the Native American rebel leader, headquartered the Wampanoag tribe in the area. After the war ended, Bristol grew into an important port, and by the turn of the 18th century the town was the fourth-busiest port in the US. Bristol was the home of General Ambrose Burnside, Civil War officer and sometime governor and senator. The town was the site of the famous Herreshoff Boatyard, where many America's Cup winners were built. Roger Williams University (1948) is located in Bristol.

What to See and Do

Blithewold Mansion and Gardens. Former turn-of-the-century summer estate; 45-rm mansion surrounded by 33 acres of landscaped grounds; many exotic trees and shrubs including a giant sequoia. Grounds (open all yr; fee). Mansion and grounds tour (Apr-Oct, daily exc Mon; closed hols). 2 mi S on RI 114 (Ferry Road); on Bristol Harbor overlooking Narragansett Bay. Phone 401/253-2707. Guided tour ¢¢¢

Colt State Park. Three-mi scenic drive around shoreline of former Colt family estate on east side of Narragansett Bay. Fishing; boating. Hiking, bridle trails. Picnicking. 2 1/2 mi NW off RI 114. Per vehicle ¢ In park is

Coggeshall Farm Museum. Working farm from 18th-19th century; vegetables, herbs, animals; colonial craft demonstrations. (Daily exc Mon; closed Jan) (See ANNUAL EVENT) Phone 401/253-9062. ¢¢

Haffenreffer Museum of Anthropology. Brown Univ museum features Native American objects from North, Central and South America; Eskimo collections; African and Pacific tribal arts. (June-Aug, daily exc Mon; rest of yr, Sat & Sun) 1 mi E of Metacom Ave, RI 136, follow signs; overlooks Mt Hope Bay. Phone 401/253-8388. ¢

Herreshoff Marine Museum. Herreshoff Mfg Co produced some of America's greatest yachts, including 8 winners of the America's Cup. Exhibits include yachts manufactured by Herreshoff, steam engines, fittings; photographs and memorabilia from "golden age of yachting." (May-Oct, Mon-Fri afternoons; also Sat & Sun, late morning-mid-afternoon) 7 Burnside St. Phone 401/253-5000. ¢¢

Hope Street. Famous row of colonial houses. On RI 114.

Prudence Island. Ferry from Church St dock.

Annual Event

Harvest Fair. Coggeshall Farm Museum. Wkend mid-Sept.

Seasonal Events

Blithewold Mansion and Gardens. Concerts. Phone 401/253-2707. June-Aug.

Colt State Park. Concerts in Stone Barn. Sun & Wed, early July-Aug.

Motel

★ **KING PHILLIP INN.** *400 Metacom Ave (RI 136). 401/253-7600; FAX 401/253-5890; res: 800/253-7610.* 45 rms. Mid-May-mid-Oct: S, D $60-$79; each addl $5; under 12 free; higher rates special events; lower rates rest of yr. Crib free. TV; VCR avail. Restaurant 6-11 am, Sat-Sun 7 am-1 pm. Ck-out 11 am. Meeting rms. Business servs avail. Refrigerators. Cr cds: A, D, DS, MC, V.

[⊠] [🐾] **SC**

Inns

★ ★ **ROCKWELL HOUSE.** *610 Hope St, in historic downtown waterfront district. 401/253-0040; FAX 401/253-1811; res: 800/815-0040.* E-mail rockwellinn@ids.net. 4 rms, 1 with shower only, 2 story. No A/C. No rm phones. May-Oct: S, D $125; each addl $25; wkday rates; wkends, hols (2-day min); higher rates July 4th; lower rates rest of yr. Children over 12 yrs only. TV in parlor; VCR. Complimentary full bkfst. Restaurant nearby. Ck-out 11 am, ck-in noon-8 pm. Concierge serv. Luggage handling. Business servs avail. Lawn games. Refrigerator avail. Picnic tables. Federal-style house (circa 1809); fireplaces, hand stenciling in many rms. Cr cds: A, DS, MC, V.

[⊠] [🐾]

★ **WILLIAM'S GRANT INN.** *154 High St. 401/253-4222; res: 800/596-4222.* 5 rms, 2 share bath, 2 story. No A/C. No rm phones. May-Oct: S, D $85-$125; wkly rates; wkends, hols (2-day min); lower rates rest of yr. Children over 12 yrs only. Complimentary coffee in rms. Complimentary full bkfst. Restaurant nearby. Ck-out 11 am, ck-in noon-10 pm. Luggage handling. House built 1808; original fireplaces, artwork, many antiques. Totally nonsmoking. Cr cds: A, D, DS, MC, V.

[⊠] [🐾] **SC**

Restaurants

★ ★ **THE LOBSTER POT.** *119-121 Hope St. 401/253-9100.* Specializes in lobster, seafood. Hrs: noon-9 pm. Closed Mon. Bar. Semi-a la carte: lunch $4.75-$12.95, dinner $7.75-$23.95. Child's meals. Pianist wkends. On waterfront; view of harbor. Family-owned. Cr cds: A, MC, V.

[D]

★ ★ **NATHANIEL PORTER INN.** *(125 Water St, Warren 02885) 4 mi N on RI 114. 401/245-6622.* Specialties: filet with bernaise sauce, seafood. Hrs: 5-9 pm; Sun 4-8 pm; Sun brunch 10:30 am-2 pm. Res accepted. Bar. Semi-a la carte: dinner $12.95-$21.95. Child's meals. House built 1795; colonial decor, antiques. Guest rms avail. Cr cds: A, D, DS, MC, V.

Charlestown (E-6)

(See also Narragansett, Westerly)

Pop 6,478 **Elev** 20 ft **Area code** 401 **Zip** 02813 **E-mail** sctc@netsense.net **Web** www.southcountyri.com
Information South County Tourism Council, Stedman Government Center, 4808 Tower Hill Road, Wakefield 02879; 401/789-4422 or 800/548-4662.

Charlestown, named for King Charles II of England, was originally called Cross Mills for two gristmills that once stood here. Charlestown was first settled along the coast by summer residents, and by permanent residents after World War II. The town's past can be seen in Fort Ninigret, the historic Native American church and the Royal Indian Burial Ground.

What to See and Do

Burlingame State Park. More than 2,000 acres with wooded area. Swimming, lifeguard; fishing; boating. Picnicking, concession. Tent & trailer camping (mid-Apr-Oct). Standard fees. 2 mi SW via US 1, Kings Factory Rd. Phone 401/322-7337 or 401/322-7994(Nov-mid-Apr).

Kimball Wildlife Refuge. Thirty-acre refuge on S shore of Watchaug Pond has nature trails and programs. 2¹/₂ mi SW on US 1, Windswept Farm exit, left onto Montauk Rd.

Swimming; fishing. At several Block Island Sound beaches; S of US 1 on Charlestown Beach Rd; Green Hill Rd; Moonstone Rd. **Free.**

Annual Event

Seafood Festival. Seafood vendors, amateur seafood cook-off, helicopter rides, antique car show. Phone 401/364-3878. 1st Sat & Sun Aug.

Seasonal Event

Theatre-by-the-Sea. Historic barn theater (1933) presents professionally-staged musicals. Restaurant, bar, cabaret. Nightly exc Mon; matinees Thurs; children's shows July-Aug, Fri only. 7 mi NE via US 1, then S off Matunuck Beach Rd exit to Cards Pond Rd in Matunuck. Contact 364 Cards Pond Rd, Matunuck 02879; 401/782-8587. June-Sept.

East Greenwich (D-6)

(See also Warwick)

Pop 11,865 **Elev** 64 ft **Area code** 401 **Zip** 02818 **E-mail** egcc@aol.com **Web** www.eastgreenwichchamber.com
Information Chamber of Commerce, 5853 Post Rd, Suite 106, PO Box 514, 02818-0514; 401/885-0020.

Sometimes referred to as "the town on four hills," East Greenwich, on Narragansett Bay, is a sports and yachting center. In East Greenwich, in 1774, Nathanael Greene and James M. Varnum organized the Kentish Guards, who protected the town during the Revolution. The Guards are still active today.

What to See and Do

Goddard Memorial State Park. Approx 490 acres with swimming at Greenwich Bay Beach (bathhouse); fishing; boating. Bridle trails; 9-hole golf (fee). Ice-skating. Picnicking, concessions. Playing fields and fireplaces (fee). E side of Greenwich Cove, E of town via Forge Rd and Ives Rd. Phone 401/884-2010. Per vehicle ¢

Kentish Guards Armory (1843). HQ of the Kentish Guards, local militia chartered in 1774 and still active; Gen Nathanael Greene was a charter member. (By appt only) 92 Pierce St. Phone 401/821-1628. ¢

Old Kent County Court House (1750). Remodeled in 1909 & 1995. 125 Main St. Phone 401/886-8606.

Varnum House Museum. (1773). Mansion of Revolutionary War officer and lawyer; period furnishings, colonial items, gardens. (June-Sept, by appt) 57 Pierce St. Phone 401/884-4110. ¢

Varnum Memorial Armory and Military Museum (1913). The museum displays uniforms and armaments from the Revolutionary through the Vietnam Wars. (By appt) 6 Main St. Phone 401/884-4110. **Donation.**

Glocester (C-6)

(See also Putnam, CT)

Pop 5,011 **Elev** 422 ft **Area code** 401 **Zip** 02859 **E-mail** bvtourism@aol.com
Information Blackstone Valley Tourism Council, 171 Main St, Pawtucket 02860; 401/724-2200 or 800/454-2882 (Outside RI).

What to See and Do

Brown & Hopkins Country Store (1799). Nation's oldest continuously operating country store; inside are antiques, gourmet food, penny candy and a cafe. (Wed-Sun; closed hols) 3 mi SE on RI 100 to US 44 (Main St) in Chepachet. Phone 401/568-4830.

Casimir Pulaski State Park. Park has 100 acres with lake. Swimming beach. Cross-country skiing. Picnicking. Pavilion (res). (Late May-early Sept) 3 mi SE on RI 100, 6 mi W on US 44. Phone 401/568-2085 or -2013.

George Washington State Campground. Swimming beach; fishing; boating. Hiking trail. Picnicking. Camping (no fires). Standard fees. (Mid-Apr-mid-Oct) 3 mi SE on RI 100, 4 mi W on US 44. Phone 401/568-2013. ¢

Jamestown (E-6)

(See also Newport)

Settled ca 1670 **Pop** 4,999 **Elev** 8 ft **Area code** 401 **Zip** 02835 **E-mail** info@gonewport.com **Web** www.gonewport.com
Information Newport County Convention & Visitors Bureau, Newport Gateway Center, 23 America's Cup Ave, Newport 02840; 401/849-8048 or 800/976-5122.

Jamestown is centered around the Jamestown Ferry landing, but technically the town also includes all of Conanicut—one of three main islands in Narragansett Bay. The island is connected by bridges to Newport on the east (toll) and to the mainland on the west (free). While much of Jamestown was burned by the British in 1775, some old houses do remain.

The restored Conanicut Battery, a Revolutionary redoubt two miles south on Beavertail Road, is open to the public and is the second-highest point on the island.

What to See and Do

Fishing. Striped bass, tuna, flounder, bluefish. For boat charter inquire at East Ferry slip.

Jamestown Museum. Photos and displays pertain to town and old Jamestown ferries. (Late June-Labor Day, Tues-Sat afternoons) 92 Narragansett Ave. Phone 401/423-3771 or 401/423-0784. **Donation.** The Jamestown Historical Society also maintains the

Old Windmill (1787). Restored to working order. (Mid-June-mid-Sept, Sat & Sun afternoons) 1½ mi N on North Rd. Phone 401/423-1798. **Donation.**

Sydney L. Wright Museum. Exhibits of Native American and early colonial artifacts from Conanicut Island. (Daily exc Sun) 26 North Rd, located in the library. Phone 401/423-7280. **Free.**

Watson Farm (1796). This 280-acre farm on Conanicut Island is being worked as a typical New England farm. Self-guided tour of farm and pastures with focus on land-use history. (June-mid-Oct, Tues, Thurs & Sun, afternoons) North Rd, S of RI 138. Phone 401/423-0005. ¢¢

Inn

★ ★ **BAY VOYAGE.** *150 Conanicus Ave.* 401/423-2100; FAX 401/423-3209; res: 800/225-3522. Web www.easternresorts.com. 32 kit. suites, 3 story. May-Sept: S, D $165-$235; wkly rates; lower rates rest of yr. Crib $15. TV; cable (premium). Pool; whirlpool. Complimentary coffee. Dining rm 6-10 pm; closed Sun, Mon off-season. Ck-out 11 am, ck-in 4 pm. Sauna. Balconies. On Narragansett Bay. Cr cds: A, C, D, DS, MC, V.

Kingston (E-6)

(See also Narragansett, Newport, North Kingstown)

Pop 6,504 **Elev** 242 ft **Area code** 401 **Zip** 02881 **E-mail** sctc@netsense.net **Web** www.southcountyri.com
Information Chamber of Commerce, 328 Main St, PO Box 289, Wakefield 02880, phone 401/783-2801; or the South County Tourism Council, Stedman Government Center, 4808 Tower Hill Rd, Wakefield 02879, phone 401/789-4422 or 800/548-4662.

Known as Little Rest until 1825, Kingston was once forest land bought from the Narragansett. Early settlers were farmers and built a water-powered mill in an area still known as Biscuit City. Here, the state constitution was ratified, and a law was passed abolishing slavery in the state. Kingston overlooks a fertile flood plain, which geologists believe was an ancient river. Kingston is the home of the Univ of Rhode Island.

What to See and Do

Helme House (1802). Gallery of the South County Art Association. (Wed-Sun) Kingstown Rd. Phone 401/783-2195. **Free.**

Kingston Library (1776). Visited by George Washington and Benjamin Franklin, this building housed the Rhode Island General Assembly at the time the British occupied Newport. (Daily exc Sun) Kingstown Rd. Phone 401/783-8254.

Museum of Primitive Art and Culture. In 1856 post office building; prehistoric artifacts from New England, North America, South Seas, Africa, Europe and Asia. (Tues, Wed & Thurs; limited hrs; also by appt) 2 mi S via RI 108 in Peace Dale at 1058 Kingstown Rd. Phone 401/783-5711. **Donation.**

Night Heron **Nature Cruises.** Offers snorkeling, nature, sunrise, sunset and undersea nightlife cruises. Each cruise offers 2 or more departures daily; phone for schedule. Res recommended. (Late May-Oct, daily) Departs Snug Harbor Marina, at end of Gooseberry Rd, in South Kingstown. Phone 401/783-9977 or 888/644-8476 . ¢¢¢¢-¢¢¢¢¢

Annual Event

Hot-Air Balloon Festival. Univ of Rhode Island. Two-day event features hot-air balloon rides, parachute demonstrations, arts & crafts, music. Phone 401/783-1770. Late July or early Aug.

Motor Hotel

★ ★ **HOLIDAY INN-SOUTH KINGSTON.** *(3009 Tower Hill Rd, S Kingstown 02874)* At jct US 1, RI 138W. 401/789-1051; FAX 401/789-0080. 105 rms, 4 story. May-Oct: S, D $75-$150; each addl $10; under 18 free; lower rates rest of yr. Crib free. TV; cable (premium). Pool; lifeguard. Bar 4 pm-1 am. Ck-out 11 am. Meeting rms. Business servs avail. In-rm modem link. Cr cds: A, C, D, DS, MC, V.

Inn

✔★★ **LARCHWOOD.** *(521 Main St, Wakefield 02879)* *401/783-5454; FAX 401/783-1800; res: 800/275-5450.* 18 rms, 12 with bath, 3 story. Some A/C. Some rm phones. S, D $35-$130; each addl $10. Crib $10. Pet accepted; $5. TV in sitting rm. Restaurant (see LARCHWOOD INN). Bar 11-1 am; entertainment. Ck-out, ck-in noon. Meeting rms. Business servs avail. Private patio. Built 1831. Cr cds: A, C, D, DS, MC, V.

D ✔ ⊠ ⚲

Restaurant

✔★★ **LARCHWOOD INN.** *(See Larchwood Inn) 401/783-5454.* Specializes in prime rib, seafood. Hrs: 7:30 am-2:30 pm, 5:30-9 pm; wkends to 10 pm; early-bird dinner Mon-Fri 5:30-6:30 pm. Res accepted. Bar 11-1 am. A la carte entrees: bkfst $1.50-$7, lunch $4-$9, dinner $8.95-$13.95. Complete meals: bkfst $2.95-$6.95, lunch $3.95-$6.75, dinner $4.50-$13.95. Country inn. Scottish decor. Family-owned. Cr cds: A, C, D, DS, MC, V.

D

Little Compton (E-7)

(See also Portsmouth)

Pop 3,339 **Area code** 401 **Zip** 02837 **E-mail** info@gonewport.com **Web** www.gonewport.com
Information Town Hall, PO Box 523, phone 401/635-4400; or the Newport County Convention and Visitors Bureau, 23 America's Cup Ave, Newport 02840, phone 401/849-8048 or 800/976-5122.

In Little Compton's old burial ground lie the remains of the first white woman born in New England, Elizabeth Alden Pabodie, the daughter of John and Priscilla Alden.

What to See and Do

Gray's Store (1788). First post office in area (1804) features antique soda fountain; wheeled cheese; candy and tobacco cases. (Daily; closed Sun & hols in winter) 4 Main St in Adamsville, 7 mi NE on local road. Phone 401/635-4566.

Sakonnet Point. Swimming beaches; fishing. Harbor with lighthouse. West Main Rd.

Sakonnet Vineyards. Tour of winery and vineyard. Wine tasting (daily). 162 West Main. Phone 401/635-8486. **Free.**

Wilbor House (1680). Seventeenth-century house with 18th- and 19th-century additions was restored in 1956 by local historical society; period furnishings, antique farm and household implements. Display of carriages and sleighs in 1860 barn. Also one-rm schoolhouse, artist's studio. (Mid-June-mid-Sept, Wed-Sun, also by appt) 1 mi S on RI 77 at West Rd. Phone 401/635-4035 **¢¢**

Narragansett (E-6)

(See also Block Island, Kingston, Newport)

Settled 1675 **Pop** 14,985 **Elev** 20 ft **Area code** 401 **Zip** 02882 **E-mail** sctc@netsense.net **Web** www.southcountyri.com
Information South County Tourism Council, Stedman Government Center, 4808 Tower Hill Rd, Wakefield 02879; 401/789-4422 or 800/548-4662.

Part of the township of South Kingstown until 1901, Narragansett was named after the indigenous people who sold their land to the first settlers in the area. Once a center for shipbuilding, the town's center is still referred to as Narragansett Pier. Between 1878 and 1920, Narragansett was a well-known, elegant summer resort with many fine "cottages" and hotels. The most prominent landmark of that time was the Narragansett Casino. The casino's main entrance and covered promenade, "the Towers" on Ocean Road, is the only surviving element of that complex; the rest was lost in a devastating fire in 1900. Today, Narragansett's most important industries are commercial fishing and tourism. It is also the home of the University of Rhode Island's renowned Graduate School of Oceanography, located at the Bay Campus on South Ferry Rd.

What to See and Do

Block Island Ferry. Automobile ferries to Block Island from Point Judith and New London, CT. (Summer, daily) 5 mi S on Ocean Rd, 1 mi W on Sand Hill Cove Rd. Phone 401/783-4613.

Fishing. Wide variety of liveries at Narragansett Pier and the waterfront villages of Jerusalem, opposite side of the Point Judith Pond entrance, and Jerusalem, west of Point Judith. Fishing tournaments are held throughout summer.

Point Judith. Fine sea view. 6 mi S of center on Ocean Ave, to Coast Guard Station and Lighthouse.

South County Museum. Antiques representing rural life in 19th-century Rhode Island; costumes, vehicles and nautical equipment. Farm and blacksmithing displays; toys. Country kitchen, general store, cobbler's shop. Also complete turn-of-the-century letterpress print shop. (May-Oct, Wed-Sun) Located on Canonchet Farm, Boston Neck Rd (RI 1A). Phone 401/783-5400. **¢¢**

Swimming. Public beaches at **Narragansett Pier.** Pavilion; fees. **Scarborough State Beach,** 1½ mi S on Ocean Ave. **Salty Brine Beach,** Ocean Ave. Protected by seawall; fishing. **Roger Wheeler State Beach,** W of Point Judith. Playground, picnic tables, concession; parking (fee). Similar facilities at other beaches.

★ **The Towers.** This Romanesque entrance arch flanked by rounded, conical-topped towers is a grandiose and sad reminder of McKim, Mead and White's 19th-century casino, destroyed by fire in 1900, and Narragansett's own past as summer mecca for the rich and fashionable. Today, the Tourist & Information Center is located here. ¼ mi S on US 1.

Annual Event

Mid-winter New England Surfing Championship. Narragansett Town Beach. For information contact the Eastern Surfing Association, 126 Sayles Ave, Pawtucket, 02860; 401/789-1954. 3rd Sat Feb.

Motel

★★ **VILLAGE INN.** *1 Beach St. 401/783-6767; FAX 401/782-2220; res: 800/843-7437 (northeastern states).* 58 rms, 3 story. Mid-June-Labor Day: S $100-$120; D $115-$168; each addl $10; under 12 free; higher rates some hols; lower rates rest of yr. TV; cable, VCR. Indoor pool; whirlpool, lifeguard. Restaurant 6 am-10 pm; Sat to 11 pm. Bar noon-1 am. Ck-out 11 am. Meeting rms. Business servs avail. Some balconies. Opp ocean; beach. Cr cds: A, D, DS, MC, V.

D ≋ ⚲ SC

Restaurant

★ ★ **COAST GUARD HOUSE.** *40 Ocean Rd. 401/789-0700.* Continental menu. Specializes in seafood, prime rib, swordfish. Hrs: 11:30 am-3 pm, 5-10 pm; Fri-Sun to 11 pm; Sun brunch 10 am-2 pm. Closed Dec 24, 25. Bar 11:30-1 am; Sun from noon. Semi-a la carte: lunch $6-$10, dinner $13-$20. Sun brunch $13.95. Child's meals. Outdoor dining. Former Coast Guard station (1888); ocean view. Cr cds: A, C, D, DS, MC, V.

D **SC**

Newport (E-7)

(See also Jamestown, Portsmouth)

Founded 1639 **Pop** 28,227 **Elev** 96 ft **Area code** 401 **Zip** 02840 **E-mail** info@gonewport.com **Web** www.gonewport.com

Information Newport County Convention & Visitors Bureau, 23 America's Cup Ave; 401/849-8048 or 800/976-5122.

Few cities in the country have a history as rich and colorful as that of Newport, and fewer still retain as much evidence of their great past. The town was founded by a group of men and women who fled the religious intolerance of Massachusetts. They established the first school in Rhode Island the following year. Shipbuilding, for which Newport is still famous, began in 1646. The first Quakers to come to the New World settled in Newport in 1657. They were followed in 1658 by 15 Jewish families who came here from Holland. Newport produced the state's first newspaper, the *Rhode Island Gazette.*

Newport took an active part in the Revolution; local residents set fire to one British ship and continued to fire on others until the British landed 9,000 men and took possession. The city was occupied for two years; it was not until the French fleet entered the harbor that the British withdrew their forces.

Newport's fame as a summer resort began after the Civil War, when many wealthy families, including the August Belmonts, Ward McAllister, Harry Lehr, Mrs. William Astor and Mrs. Stuyvesant Fish, made the town a center for lavish and sometimes outrageous social events. Parties for dogs and one for a monkey were among the more bizarre occasions. Hostesses spent as much as $300,000 a season entertaining their guests. Although less flamboyant than it was before World War I, the summer colony is still socially prominent.

Today, Newport is famous for its boating and yachting, with boats for hire at many wharves. A bridge (toll) connects the city with Jamestown to the west.

What to See and Do

Artillery Company of Newport Military Museum. Military dress of many nations and periods. (June-Sept, Wed-Sat, also Sun afternoons; rest of yr, by appt) 23 Clarke St. Phone 401/846-8488.

Brick Market. Home of the Newport Historical Society. Built by Peter Harrison, architect of Touro Synagogue, in 1762 as a market and granary. The restored building and surrounding area house boutiques and restaurants. (Daily) Long Wharf & Thames St. Phone 401/846-0813.

CCInc Auto Tape Tours. This 90-min cassette offers a mile-by-mile self-guided tour of Newport. Written by experts, it provides information on history and points of interest. Avail at Paper Lion, Long Wharf Mall and Gateway Visitor Information Center (next to Marriott Hotel). Includes tape and recorder rental. Tape also may be purchased directly from CCInc, PO Box 227, 2 Elbrook Dr, Allendale, NJ 07401; 201/236-1666. ¢¢¢

⭐ **Cliff Walk.** Scenic walk overlooking Atlantic Ocean adjoins many Newport "cottages." Designated a National Recreational Trail in 1975. Begins at Memorial Blvd. **Free.**

Friends Meeting House (1699). Site of New England Yearly Meeting of the Society of Friends until 1905; meeting house, expanded in 1729 and 1807, spans 3 centuries of architecture and construction. Guided tours through Newport Historical Society. (By appt) Farewell & Marlborough Sts. Phone 401/846-0813. **Free.**

Ft Adams State Park. Park surrounds Ft Adams, the second-largest bastioned fort in the US between 1799 and 1945. The rambling 21-acre fort, constructed of stone over a 33-yr period, is closed due to unsafe conditions; park remains open. Beach swimming; fishing; boating (launch, ramps, hoist). Soccer, rugby fields. Picnicking. Standard fees. (Memorial Day-Labor Day, daily) Harrison Ave & Ocean Dr. Phone 401/847-2400. Per vehicle ¢¢

⭐ **Historic Mansions and Houses.** Combination tickets to the Elms, the Breakers, Rosecliff, Marble House, Hunter House, Chateau-sur-Mer, Kingscote and Green Animals topiary gardens (see PORTSMOUTH) are avail at any of these houses. (See ADDITIONAL VISITOR INFORMATION)

Astors' Beechwood. Italianate summer residence of Mrs. Caroline Astor, *the* Mrs. Astor. Theatrical tour of house includes actors portraying Mrs. Astor's servants and society guests. (Mid-May-mid-Dec, daily; rest of yr, wkends only) For schedule phone 401/846-3772. ¢¢¢

Belcourt Castle (1891). Designed by Richard Morris Hunt in French-château style, 62-rm house was residence of Oliver Hazard Perry Belmont and his wife, Alva Vanderbilt Belmont, who built Marble House when married to William K. Vanderbilt. Belcourt is unique for inclusion of stables within main structure; Belmont loved horses. Contains largest collection of antiques and objets d'art in Newport; gold coronation coach; large collection of stained-glass windows. Tea served. Special events scheduled throughout yr. (Daily; closed Thanksgiving, Dec 25, also Jan) Bellevue Ave, 2 mi S on RI 138A. Phone 401/846-0669. ¢¢¢

The Breakers (1895). Seventy-rm, Northern Italian palazzo designed by Richard Morris Hunt is the largest of all Newport cottages and is impressive by its sheer size; contains original furnishings. Children's playhouse cottage has scale-size kitchen, fireplace, playroom. Built for Mr. and Mrs. Cornelius Vanderbilt. (Apr-Oct, daily) Ochre Point Ave. Phone 401/847-1000. ¢¢¢ Also here is **The Breakers Stable and Carriage House.** Houses several carriages, including Vanderbilts' famous coach *Venture.* (July-Labor Day, wkends & hols) ¢¢

Chateau-sur-Mer (1852). Victorian mansion remodeled in 1872 by Richard Morris Hunt has landscaped grounds with Chinese moon gate. Built for William S. Wetmore, who made his fortune in the China trade. (May-Oct, daily; rest of yr, wkends) Bellevue Ave. Phone 401/847-1000. ¢¢¢

Edward King House (1846). Villa by Richard Upjohn is considered one of the finest Italianate houses in the country. Used as senior citizens' center. Tours. (Mon-Fri) 35 King St, Aquidneck Park. Phone 401/846-7426.

The Elms (1901). Modeled after 18th-century Chateau d'Asnieres near Paris, this restored "cottage" from Newport's gilded age boasts elaborate interiors and formal, sunken gardens that are among the city's most beautiful. Built for Edward J. Berwind, Philadelphia coal magnate. (May-Oct, daily; Nov-Mar, Sat & Sun) Bellevue Ave. Phone 401/847-1000. ¢¢¢

Hammersmith Farm. The unofficial summer White House during Kennedy Administration, farm dates back to 1640; 28-rm, shingle-style summer house was added in 1887 by John Auchincloss; descendant Hugh D. Auchincloss married Janet Lee Bouvier, mother of Jacqueline Bouvier Kennedy; rambling cottage was site of wedding reception of John and Jacqueline Kennedy. Gardens designed by Frederick Law Olmsted. Gift shop in children's playhouse. Guided tours. (May-Oct, daily) Ocean Dr. Phone 401/846-0420 or 401/846-7346. ¢¢¢

Hunter House (1748). Outstanding example of colonial architecture features gambrel roof, 12-on-12 pane windows, broken pediment doorway. Furnished with pieces by Townsend and Goddard, famous 18th-century cabinet makers. (May-Oct, daily; Apr, wkends) 54 Washington St. Phone 401/847-6543. ¢¢¢

Kingscote (1839). Gothic-revival cottage designed by Richard Upjohn; in 1881, McKim, Mead and White added the "aesthetic" dining rm, which features Tiffany-glass wall and fixtures. Outstanding Chinese-export paintings and porcelains. Built for George Noble Jones of Savannah, GA, Kingscote is considered the nation's first true summer "cottage."

(May-Sept, daily; Apr & Oct, wkends) Bellevue Ave. Phone 401/847-1000. ¢¢¢

Marble House (1892). French-style palace designed by Richard Morris Hunt is the most sumptuous of Newport cottages. Front gates, entrance, central hall are modeled after Versailles. House is named for the many kinds of marble used on interior, which also features lavish use of gold and bronze. Original furnishings include dining rm chairs made of gilded bronze. Built for Mrs. William K. Vanderbilt. On display are yachting memorabilia and restored Chinese teahouse where Mrs. Vanderbilt held suffragette meetings. (Apr-Oct, daily; rest of yr, wkends) Bellevue Ave. Phone 401/847-1000. ¢¢¢

Rosecliff (1902). Designed by Stanford White after the Grand Trianon at Versailles, Rosecliff boasts largest private ballroom in Newport and famous heart-shaped staircase. Built for socialite Mrs. Hermann Oelrichs. (Apr-Oct, daily) Bellevue Ave. Phone 401/847-6543. ¢¢¢

Samuel Whitehorne House (1811). Features exquisite furniture, silver and pewter made by 18th-century artisans; Chinese porcelain, Irish crystal and Pilgrim-era furniture; garden. (May-Oct, Fri-Mon & hols; or by appt, 24-hr advance notice necessary) 416 Thames St. Phone 401/849-7300. ¢¢

Wanton-Lyman-Hazard House (ca 1675). Oldest house in Newport, one of the finest Jacobean houses in New England, was site of 1765 Stamp Act riot; restored; 18th-century garden; guided tours. (Mid-June-late Aug, Tues-Sat; closed hols) 17 Broadway. Phone 401/846-0813. ¢

Whitehall Museum House (1729). Restored, hip-roofed country house built by Bishop George Berkeley, British philosopher and educator; garden. (July-Aug; daily; June, by appt only) 3 mi NE on Berkeley Ave in Middletown. Phone 401/846-3116. ¢¢

⭐ **International Tennis Hall of Fame & Museum.** World's largest tennis museum features interactive and dynamic exhibits detailing the history of the sport. Tennis equipment, fashions, trophies and memorabilia on display in the famous Newport Casino, built in 1880 and designed by McKim, Mead and White. (Daily; closed Thanksgiving, Dec 25) Grass courts avail (May-Oct, phone for reservation; fee). Professional tennis tournaments in season. Newport Casino, 194 Bellevue Ave. Phone 401/849-3990. ¢¢¢

The Newport Aquarium. Touch tank allows hands-on exploration of marine life. Sharks, ocean pout, native sealife from Narragansett Bay. (Memorial Day-Labor Day, daily) Easton's Beach . Phone 401/849-8430. ¢¢

Newport Art Museum and Art Association. Changing exhibitions of contemporary and historical art are housed in 1864 mansion designed by Richard Morris Hunt in the "stick style" and in 1920 beaux arts building. Lectures, performing arts events, evening musical picnics; tours. (Daily exc Mon, afternoons; closed hols) 76 Bellevue Ave, opp Touro Park. Phone 401/848-8200. ¢¢

Newport Historical Society Museum. Colonial art; Newport silver and pewter, china, early American glass, furniture. (Tues-Sat; closed hols) Walking tours of colonial Newport (Mid-June-Sept, Fri & Sat; fee). 82 Touro St, adj to Seventh Day Baptist Meeting House. Phone 401/846-0813. Free.

Newport Jai Alai. Parimutuel wagering. (Daily) Fronton & Civic Center, 150 Admiral Kalbfus Rd, at base of Newport Bridge. Phone 401/849-5000.

Old Colony and Newport Railroad. Vintage 1-hr train ride along scenic route to Narragansett Bay. (July-early Sept, Sat & Sun; May-June & mid-Sept-Nov, Sun; also Christmas season) Terminal, America's Cup Ave. Phone 401/624-6951or 401/683-4549. ¢¢¢

Old Stone Mill. Origin of circular stone tower supported by arches is unknown. Although excavations (1948-1949) have disproved it, some people still believe structure was built by Norsemen. Touro Park, Mill St off Bellevue Ave. Free.

Redwood Library and Athenaeum. Designed by master colonial architect Peter Harrison, this is thought to be oldest library building (1750) in continuous use in US; used by English officers as a club during Revolution. Collections include part of original selection of books and early portraits. (Daily exc Sun; closed hols) 50 Bellevue Ave. Phone 401/847-0292. Free.

Seventh Day Baptist Meeting House (1729). Historical church built by master builder Richard Munday. 82 Touro St, adj to Newport Historical Society. For schedule phone 401/846-0813.

Swimming. Easton's Beach. Well-developed public beach has bathhouse, snack bar, antique carousel, picnic area, designated surfing area. (Mid-June-Labor Day, daily; early June, wkends) Memorial Blvd, RI 138. Parking ¢¢¢ **King Park and Beach.** Restrms, picnic area. (Mid-June-Labor Day, daily) Wellington Ave. Phone 401/846-1398.

Touro Synagogue National Historic Site. Oldest synagogue (1763) in America, a Georgian masterpiece by country's first architect, Peter Harrison, contains oldest torah in North America, examples of 18th-century crafts, letter from George Washington; worship services follow Sephardic Orthodox ritual of founders. 72 Touro St. For schedule phone 401/847-4794.

Tours.

Newport Navigation. One-hr narrated cruise of Narragansett Bay and Newport Harbor aboard the *Spirit of Newport.* (May-Oct, daily) Newport Harbor Hotel & Marina. Phone 401/849-3575. ¢¢

Oldport Marine Harbor Tours. One-hr cruise of Newport Harbor aboard the *Amazing Grace.* (May-mid-Oct, daily) America's Cup Ave. Phone 401/847-9109. ¢¢¢

Viking Boat Tour. One-hr narrated trip includes historic Newport, yachts, waterfront mansions; also avail is extended trip with tour of Hammersmith Farm (see). (May-Oct) *The Viking Queen* leaves Goat Island Marina off Washington St. Phone 401/847-6921. ¢¢¢-¢¢¢¢

Viking Bus Tour. Two-, three- and four-hr narrated trips cover 150 points of interest, including mansions and restored areas. (Schedules vary) Three-hr trips include admission to one mansion; four-hr trip includes admission to two mansions. Leaves from Gateway Tourist Center, America's Cup Ave. Phone 401/847-6921. ¢¢¢¢

Trinity Church (1726). First Anglican parish in state (1698), Trinity has been in continuous use since it was built. George Washington and philosopher George Berkeley were communicants. Interior features Tiffany windows and an organ tested by Handel before being shipped from London. Tours. Queen Anne Sq. Phone 401/846-0660. **Free.**

White Horse Tavern (1673). Oldest operating tavern in the nation. (Daily) 42 Marlborough St. Phone 401/849-3600.

Annual Events

Newport Winter Festival. 23 America's Cup Ave. Ten days of food, festivities, music. More than 200 cultural and recreational events and activities. Phone 401/849-8048 or 800/326-6030. Late Jan-early Feb.

Newport Irish Heritage Month. Throughout the town. A variety of Irish heritage and theme events; films, concerts, plays, arts & crafts, exhibits; food and drink; parade, road race. Phone 401/849-8048. Mar.

Newport Music Festival. Chamber and Romantic music, held in Newport's fabled mansions. Phone 401/847-7090. 3 concerts daily, Mid-July.

JVC Jazz Festival. Ft Adams. Phone 401/847-3700. Mid-Aug.

Additional Visitor Information

The Preservation Society of Newport County publishes material on all Society properties. It sells combination tickets at all buildings under its administration and provides sightseeing information. Phone 401/847-1000.

The Newport County Convention and Visitor's Bureau maintains an information center at 23 America's Cup Ave (daily). Tickets to most tourist attractions are offered for sale. An eight minute video, maps, general tourist information and group tours and convention information are available. For further information phone 401/849-8048 or 800/976-5122.

Motels

★ ★ **BEST WESTERN MAINSTAY INN.** 151 Admiral Kalbfus Rd. 401/849-9880; FAX 401/849-4391. 165 rms, 2 story. July-Aug: S, D $95-$169; each addl $7.50; suites $125-$295; under 12 free; lower rates rest of yr. Crib avail. TV; cable. Pool; poolside serv. Restaurant 6:30 am-10 pm. Rm serv. Bar 11:30-1 am. Ck-out 11 am. Meeting rms. Business servs avail. Some refrigerators. Balconies. Cr cds: A, C, D, DS, MC, V.

D ⊠ ⊠ ⊠ SC

★ ★ COURTYARD BY MARRIOTT. (9 Commerce Dr, Middletown 02842) 3 mi N on RI 114. 401/849-8000; FAX 401/849-8313. 148 rms, 3 story. May-Oct: S, D $99-$175; suites $119-225; lower rates rest of yr. Crib free. TV; cable. Indoor/outdoor pool; whirlpool. Complimentary coffee in rms. Restaurant 6:30-11 am. Ck-out noon. Coin lndry. Meeting rms. Business center. In-rm modem link. Exercise equipt. Refrigerator in suites. Balconies. Cr cds: A, C, D, DS, MC, V.

D ⊠ ⊀ ⊠ ⊠ SC ⊁

✔★ ★ HOWARD JOHNSON INN. (351 W Main Rd, Middletown 02842) on RI 138 at jct RI 114. 401/849-2000; FAX 401/849-6047. 155 rms, 2 story. Late May-mid-Oct: S $59-$144; D $69-$159; each addl $5; suites $138-$318; studio rms $84-$164; under 18 free; some wkend rates; lower rates rest of yr. Crib free. Pet accepted. TV; cable (premium) VCR avail. Heated pool; whirlpool, lifeguard. Restaurant. Bar 5 pm-1 am. Ck-out 11 am. Meeting rms. Business servs avail. Valet serv. Sundries. Tennis. Sauna. Some refrigerators. Private patios, balconies. Cr cds: A, C, D, DS, MC, V.

D ⊷ ⊁ ⊠ ⊠ ⊠ SC

★ ★ ★ NEWPORT HARBOR HOTEL & MARINA. 49 America's Cup Ave, on RI 138 at the harbor. 401/847-9000; FAX 401/849-6380; res: 800/955-2558. Web www.nhhm.com. 133 rms, 4 story. May-Oct: S, D $129-$259; each addl $15; suites $219-$679; under 17 free; lower rates rest of yr. Crib free. TV; cable, VCR avail. Indoor pool. Sauna. Coffee in rms. Ck-out 11 am. Meeting rms. Business servs avail. Cr cds: A, C, D, DS, MC, V.

⊠ ⊠ SC

★ ★ RAMADA INN. (936 W Main Rd, Middletown) 3 mi N on RI 114. 401/846-7600; FAX 401/849-6919. 155 rms, 2 story. Mid-June-Sept: S, D $125; under 18 free; lower rates rest of yr. Crib free. Pet accepted $10. TV; cable (premium). Indoor pool. Complimentary continental bkfst. Bar 2-11 pm. Ck-out noon. Coin lndry. Meeting rms. Business servs avail. In-rm modem link. Gift shop. Cr cds: A, C, D, DS, ER, JCB, MC, V.

D ⊷ ⊠ ⊠ ⊠ SC

★ ★ ROYAL PLAZA HOTEL. (425 E Main Rd, Middletown 02842) 2 mi N on RI 138. 401/846-3555; FAX 401/846-3666; res: 800/825-7072. 75 rms, 2 story, 13 suites. May-Sept: S, D, suites $119-$189; under 14 free; lower rates rest of yr. Crib avail. TV; cable (premium), VCR avail. Complimentary continental bkfst. Ck-out 11 am. Meeting rm. Airport transportation. Cr cds: A, D, DS, MC, V.

D ⊠ ⊠ SC

✔★ ★ WEST MAIN LODGE. (1359 W Main Rd, Middletown 02842) approx 3½ mi N on RI 114. 401/849-2718; FAX 401/849-2798; res: 800/537-7704. 55 rms, 2 story. Mar-Dec: S, D $39-$139; each addl $15; under 12 free; higher rates hols; lower rates rest of yr. TV; cable. Restaurant nearby. Ck-out 11 am. Refrigerators avail. Some balconies. Cr cds: A, C, D, DS, ER, MC, V.

D ⊠ ⊠ SC

Motor Hotels

★ ★ ★ DOUBLETREE ISLANDER. Goat Island, by causeway from Washington St. 401/849-2600; FAX 401/846-7210. 253 rms, 9 story. Late May-early Sept: S, D $159-$254; each addl $15; suites $275-$550; under 17 free; lower rates rest of yr. Crib free. TV. 2 pools, 1 indoor; poolside serv. Restaurant 6:30 am-10 pm. Rm serv. Bar 10-1 am; entertainment. Ck-out noon. Convention facilities. Business center. In-rm modem link. Airport transportation. Bellhops. Valet serv. Sundries. Gift shop. Beauty shop. Tennis. Exercise equipt; sauna. Some bathrm phones. Some

private patios, balconies. Heliport for guests. Marina adj. Cr cds: A, C, D, DS, MC, V.

D ⊷ ⊠ ⊠ ⊀ ⊠ ⊠ ⊁

★ ★ HOTEL VIKING. 1 Bellevue Ave. 401/847-3300; FAX 401/848-4864; res: 800/556-7126 (exc RI). E-mail salemany@hotelviking.com; web www.hotelviking.com. 184 rms, 5 story. S, D $49-$299; suites $249-$999. Crib free. TV; cable. Indoor pool; whirlpool. Restaurant 7-11 am, 5-9 pm. Bar 11-1 am. Ck-out 11 am. Meeting rms. In-rm modem link. Bellhops. Concierge. Sundries. Tennis privileges. Golf privileges, pro, putting green, driving range. Exercise equipt; sauna. Health club privileges. Rooftop bar overlooks harbor. Cr cds: A, C, D, DS, MC, V.

D ⊀ ⊱ ⊠ ⊠ ⊀ ⊠ ⊠ SC

★ ★ INN ON LONG WHARF. 142 Long Wharf. 401/847-7800; FAX 401/845-0127; res: 800/225-3522 (exc RI). Web www.easternresorts.com. 40 kit. suites, 5 story. May-Sept: S, D $180-$225; higher rates Jazz Festival; lower rates rest of yr. Crib $15. TV; cable (premium). Restaurant 5-11 pm. Bar 4 pm-1 am. Ck-out 11 am. Valet serv. Concierge. Gift shop. Some covered, valet parking. In-rm whirlpools, wet bars. Overlooks harbor. Cr cds: A, D, DS, MC, V.

D ⊷ ⊠

✔★ ★ INN ON THE HARBOR. 359 Thames St. 401/849-6789; FAX 401/849-2680; res: 800/225-3522 (exc RI). Web www.easternresorts.com. 58 kit. suites, 6 story. May-Sept: S, D $140-$250; wkly rates; higher rates: Jazz Festival, major hols; lower rates rest of yr. Crib $15. TV; cable (premium). Restaurant, hrs vary. Bar; entertainment Fri-Sun. Ck-out 11 am. Valet serv. Concierge. Gift shop. Some covered parking; valet. Exercise equipt; sauna. Whirlpool. Overlooks harbor. Cr cds: A, C, D, DS, MC, V.

D ⊷ ⊀ ⊠ ⊠

Hotel

★ ★ ★ MARRIOTT. 25 America's Cup Ave. 401/849-1000; res: 800/228-9290; FAX 401/849-3422. Web www.marriott.com. 317 rms, 7 story. Mid-June-Sept: S, D $189-$269; suites $300-$600; under 18 free; wkly rates; wkend packages (Nov-Mar); lower rates rest of yr. Crib free. Garage parking, valet $12. TV; cable, VCR avail. Indoor pool; whirlpool, poolside serv. Restaurant 6:30 am-11 pm. Bar 11-1 am. Ck-out noon. Coin lndry. Convention facilities. Business servs avail. Concierge. Gift shop. Exercise equipt; sauna. Racquetball. On harbor. Cr cds: A, C, D, DS, ER, JCB, MC, V.

D ⊠ ⊀ ⊠ ⊠ SC

Inns

★ BRINLEY VICTORIAN INN. 23 Brinley St. 401/849-7645; FAX 401/845-9634; res: 800/999-8523. 17 rms, 4 with shower only, 3 story. No rm phones. May-Oct: S, D $115-$199; each addl $15; lower rates rest of yr. Children over 8 yrs only. Complimentary continental bkfst. Restaurant nearby. Ck-out 11 am, ck-in 2 pm. Courtyard with tables. Victorian inn built 1860. Library; antiques; several fireplaces. Rms individually decorated. Cr cds: A, MC, V.

⊠ ⊠ SC

★ ★ CASTLE HILL INN & RESORT. 590 Ocean Ave, 4 mi S. 401/849-3800; res: 888/466-1355; FAX 401/849-3838. E-mail castlehill@edgnet.net; web www.castlehillinn.com. 21 rms, 10 rms in 3 story inn, 11 rms adj, some share bath. S, D $95-$325; each addl $25. Children over 12 yrs only. Complimentary continental bkfst. Dining rm noon-3 pm, 6-9 pm. Ck-out 11 am, ck-in 3 pm. Victorian house (1874) was summer residence of naturalist Alexander Agassiz; antique furnishings. On ocean; swimming beach. Cr cds: A, DS, MC, V.

D ⊷ ⊠ ⊠

★ ★ ★ CLIFFSIDE. 2 Seaview Ave. 401/847-1811; FAX 401/848-5850; res: 800/845-1811. 15 rms, 2 with shower only, 3 story. S, D $185-$450; each addl $30; 2-day min wkends. Children over 13 yrs only.

TV; cable (premium), VCR. Complimentary full bkfst; afternoon refreshments. Ck-out 11 am, ck-in 3 pm. Antiques; some in-rm fireplaces, whirlpools. Victorian atmosphere. Built 1880 for Maryland Governor Thomas Swann and later the home of artist Beatrice Turner. Totally nonsmoking. Cr cds: A, D, DS, MC, V.

★ ★ ★ **FRANCIS MALBONE HOUSE.** *392 Thames St. 401/846-0392; FAX 401/848-5956; res: 800/846-0392.* E-mail inkeeper@malbone.com; web www.malbone.com. 18 rms, 6 with shower only, 3 story. 1 rm phone. May-Oct: S, D $175-$355; July-Oct (3-day min); lower rates rest of yr. TV; cable. Complimentary full bkfst; afternoon refreshments. Restaurant nearby. Ck-out 11 am, ck-in 2 pm. Concierge serv. Luggage handling. Business servs avail. In-rm modem link. Beautifully restored early American house built in 1760; many fireplaces. Cr cds: A, MC, V.

★ ★ **HAMMETT HOUSE.** *505 Thames St. 401/848-0593; FAX 401/848-2258; res: 800/548-9417.* 5 rms, 3 story. May-Oct: S, D $99-$165; each addl $15; under 5 free; higher rates: Jazz, Folk Festivals; lower rates rest of yr. TV; cable (premium). Complimentary continental bkfst. Dining rm 6-10 pm. Rm serv. Ck-out 11 am, ck-in 2 pm. Luggage handling. Georgian-style inn (1785) furnished with antique reproductions. Totally nonsmoking. Cr cds: A, DS, MC, V.

★ ★ **INN AT NEWPORT BEACH.** *30 Wave Rd. 401/846-0310; FAX 401/847-2621; res: 800/786-0310.* 50 rms, 3 story. S, D $59-$229; each addl $20; suites $99-$250; under 12 free; wkend rates (2-day min June-Oct). TV; cable (premium). Complimentary continental bkfst. Dining rm 11:30 am-9 pm. Rm serv. Ck-out 11 am, ck-in 3 pm. Business servs avail. Refrigerators. On beach. Cr cds: A, C, D, DS, MC, V.

★ ★ ★ **IVY LODGE.** *12 Clay St. 401/849-6865.* 8 rms, 3 story. No rm phones. May-Oct: S, D $100-$165; each addl $15; under 16 free; higher rates wkends & hols (2-, 3-day min); lower rates rest of yr. Crib free. Complimentary full bkfst. Ck-out 11 am, ck-in 2 pm. Balconies. Built 1886; Victorian decor. Totally nonsmoking. Cr cds: A, MC, V.

★ ★ ★ **MELVILLE HOUSE.** *39 Clarke St. 401/847-0640; FAX 401/847-0956.* E-mail innkeeper@ids.net; web www.melvillehouse.com. 7 rms, 2 share bath, 2 story. No rm phones. Early May-early Nov: S, D $115-$145; lower rates rest of yr. Children over 12 yrs only. Complimentary full bkfst; afternoon refreshments. Restaurant nearby. Ck-out 11 am, ck-in after 2 pm. Concierge serv. Sitting rm. Colonial inn (ca 1750); antiques. Cr cds: A, DS, MC, V.

★ ★ **MILL STREET INN.** *75 Mill St. 401/849-9500; FAX 401/848-5131; res: 800/392-1316.* 23 suites, 3 story. June-Sept: suites $125-$253; under 16 free; wkend, wkly, hol rates; higher rates: Jazz Festival, Folk Festival; lower rates rest of yr. Crib free. TV; cable (premium). Complimentary continental bkfst; afternoon refreshments. Restaurant nearby. Ck-out 11 am, ck-in 3 pm. Luggage handling. Concierge serv. Guest lndry. Business servs avail. Tennis privileges. Health club privileges. Minibars; some refrigerators. Some balconies. Contemporary restoration of historic mill building (1890). Cr cds: A, C, D, MC, V.

★ ★ **PILGRIM HOUSE.** *123 Spring St. 401/846-0040; FAX 401/846-8373; res: 800/525-8373.* Web www.pilgrimhouse.com. 11 rms, 2 share bath, 3 story. No rm phones. May-Oct: S, D $65-$155; each addl $25; higher rates: Jazz Fest, some hols; lower rates rest of yr. Children over 12 yrs only. TV in sitting rm. Complimentary continental bkfst; afternoon refreshments. Restaurant nearby. Ck-out 11 am, ck-in after 3 pm. Concierge serv. Victorian inn (ca 1810) near harbor. Rooftop deck. Cr cds: MC, V.

★ ★ **VICTORIAN LADIES.** *63 Memorial Blvd. 401/849-9960.* Web www.victorianladies.com. 11 rms, 3 story. Some rm phones. S, D $85-$185. Closed Jan. Children over 10 yrs only. TV. Complimentary full bkfst. Restaurant nearby. Ck-out 11 am, ck-in 2 pm. Built 1841; antiques, library, sitting rm. Near ocean. Cr cds: MC, V.

★ ★ ★ **THE WILLOWS.** *8 Willow St. 401/846-5486; FAX 401/849-8215.* Web www.newportri.com/users/willows. 5 rms in 2 bldgs, 3 with shower only, 3 story. No rm phones. Apr-Jan: S, D $98-$225 (2-, 3-day min); closed rest of yr. Complimentary continental bkfst in rm. Restaurant nearby. Ck-out 11 am, ck-in 3 pm. Concierge serv. Lawn games. Minibars. Sitting rm. Townhouses built 1740 & 1840; antiques. No cr cds accepted.

Restaurants

★ ★ ★ **CANFIELD HOUSE.** *5 Memorial Blvd. 401/847-0416.* Specialty: châteaubriand. Hrs: 5-10 pm; Sun 8 am-2 pm, 5-9 pm. Closed Mon; Thanksgiving, Dec 25. Res accepted. Bar 4 pm-closing. Semi-a la carte: dinner $14-$23. Parking. Cr cds: A, C, D, DS, MC, V.

★ ★ **CHRISTIE'S OF NEWPORT.** *351 Thames St. 401/847-5400.* Specialties: swordfish, fresh lobster, châteaubriand. Hrs: 11:30 am-10 pm; Sat to 11 pm; winter to 9 pm, Sat to 10 pm. Closed Dec 25. Res accepted. Bar to 1 am. Semi-a la carte: lunch $5.50-$12, dinner $13-$28. Child's meals. Parking. Outdoor dining. View of the water. Dockside bar; entertainment. Family-owned. Cr cds: A, C, D, DS, MC, V.

★ ★ **LA FORGE CASINO.** *186 Bellevue Ave. 401/847-0418.* French, Amer menu. Specializes in fresh native seafood dishes. Hrs: 11 am-10 pm; Sun brunch 10 am-3 pm. Closed Thanksgiving, Dec 25. Res accepted. Bar noon-1 am. Semi-a la carte: lunch $5.50-$13.50, dinner $14.50-$24. Sun brunch $5.25-$11.95. Child's meals. Pianist Fri, Sat evenings. Sidewalk cafe. Built in 1880. Adj to International Tennis Hall of Fame and Tennis Museum. Family-owned. Cr cds: A, MC, V.

★ ★ ★ **LA PETITE AUBERGE.** *19 Charles St. 401/849-6669.* Web www.mswebpros.com/auberge. French menu. Specializes in seafood. Hrs: 6-10 pm; Sun 5-9 pm. Closed Jan 1, Thanksgiving, Dec 25. Res accepted. Bar. Wine list. A la carte entrees: dinner $20-$38. Outdoor dining. House (1714) of naval hero Stephen Decatur; colonial decor, fireplaces. Cr cds: A, MC, V.

★ ★ ★ **LE BISTRO.** *41 Bowen's Wharf, off America's Cup Ave. 401/849-7778.* E-mail bistroman@aol.com; web www.lebistro.com. French menu. Specializes in seafood, Angus beef, fine pastry. Own baking. Hrs: 11:30 am-11 pm. Res accepted. Bar to 1 am. Wine cellar. Semi-a la carte: lunch $5.50-$12.95, dinner $9.95-$26.95. Parking. Cr cds: A, C, D, DS, MC, V.

★ ★ **THE MOORING.** *Sayer's Wharf. 401/846-2260.* Specializes in seafood. Hrs: 11:30 am-10 pm; Sat, Sun from noon. Closed Mon, Tues Nov-Mar; also Thanksgiving, Dec 25. Bar. A la carte entrees: lunch $6-$15, dinner $8.50-$21. Child's meals. Outdoor dining. View of harbor, marina. Cr cds: A, C, D, DS, MC, V.

★ **MUSIC HALL CAFE.** *250 Thames St. 401/848-2330.* Southwestern menu. Specializes in barbecued ribs, grilled meats, seafood. Hrs: noon-2:30 pm, from 5:30 pm. Closed Dec 25. Res accepted. Bar. A la carte entrees: lunch $4.75-$9.75, dinner $10.25-$19.75. Child's meals. Outdoor dining. Mexican decor in 1894 music hall. Cr cds: A, D, DS, MC, V.

★ ★ **PIER.** *W Howard, off Thames St. 401/847-3645.* Specialties: prime rib, baked stuffed lobster shipyard style, Pier clambake. Hrs: 11:30 am-10 pm; wkends to 10:30 pm. Closed Dec 25. Res accepted. Bar noon-1 am. Semi-a la carte: lunch $5.25-$11.95, dinner $9.75-$29.95.

Child's meals. Entertainment Fri, Sat. Patio dining. On Narragansett Bay, overlooking Newport Harbor. Family-owned. Cr cds: A, D, DS, MC, V.

★ ★ ★ **WHITE HORSE TAVERN.** *26 Marlborough St. 401/849-3600.* Web www.whitehorsetavern.com. Specialties: rack of lamb, beef Wellington. Own baking. Hrs: noon-3 pm, 6-10 pm. Closed Jan 1, Dec 25. Res accepted. Bar to 1 am. Wine cellar. A la carte entrees: lunch $8-$14, dinner $18-$32. Sun brunch $14-$19. Parking. Oldest operating tavern in America; building (est 1673) originally constructed as a residence. Jacket (dinner). Cr cds: A, C, D, DS, MC, V.

North Kingstown (E-6)

(See also Providence, Warwick)

Settled 1641 **Pop** 23,786 **Elev** 51 ft **Area code** 401 **Zip** 02852 **E-mail** sctc@netsense.net **Web** www.southcountyri.com

Information South County Tourism Council, Stedman Government Center, 4808 Tower Hill Rd, Wakefield 02879; 401/789-4422 or 800/548-4662.

North Kingstown was originally part of a much larger area named for King Charles II. The settlement was divided in 1722, creating North Kingstown and South Kingstown, as well as other townships.

What to See and Do

Casey Farm (ca 1750). Once the site of Revolutionary War activities, this farm was built and continuously occupied by the Casey family for 200 yrs. Views of Narrangansett Bay and Conanicut Island. Restored and operating farm with animals, organic gardens; 18th-century farmhouse with family paintings, furnishings; outbuildings. (June-Oct, Tues, Thurs & Sat afternoons) 3½ mi S on RI 1A (past Jamestown Bridge approach), on Boston Neck Rd in Saunderstown. Phone 401/295-1030. ¢¢

Gilbert Stuart Birthplace. Birthplace of portraitist Gilbert Stuart (1755-1828). Antique furnishings; snuffmill powered by wooden waterwheel; partially restored gristmill. Guided tours (½ hr). (Apr-Oct, daily exc Fri) 5 mi S off RI 1A, 815 Gilbert Stuart Rd, NW of Saunderstown. Phone 401/294-3001. ¢¢

Main Street, Wickford Village. There are 20 houses built before 1804; on side streets are 40 more. E from center.

Old Narragansett Church (Episcopal) (1707). Tours. (Mid-June-Labor Day, Fri-Sun) St Paul's Church. Church Lane. Phone 401/294-4357.

Smith's Castle (1678). Blockhouse (ca 1638), destroyed by fire in 1676 and rebuilt in 1678, is one of the oldest plantation houses in the country and the only known existing house where Roger Williams preached; 17th- and 18th-century furnishings; 18th-century garden. (June-Aug, Thurs-Mon, afternoons; May & Sept, Fri-Sun, afternoons; also by appt) 1½ mi N on US 1. Phone 401/294-3521. ¢¢

Annual Events

Wickford Art Festival. In Wickford Village. About 250 artists and artisans from around the country. Phone 401/294-6840. 2nd wkend July

Festival of Lights. House tours, hayrides. 1st wkend Dec.

Pawtucket (D-6)

(See also Providence)

Settled 1671 **Pop** 72,644 **Elev** 73 ft **Area code** 401 **E-mail** bvtourism@aol.com
Information Blackstone Valley Tourism Council, 171 Main St, 02860; 401/724-2200 or 800/454-2882 (outside RI).

This highly concentrated industrial center, first settled by an ironworker who set up a forge at the falls on the Blackstone River, is recognized by historians as the birthplace of the Industrial Revolution in America. It was here in Pawtucket, named for the Native American phrase, "falls of the water," that Samuel Slater founded the nation's first water-powered cotton mill. The town has since become one of the largest cities in the state and a major producer of textiles, machinery, wire, glass and plastics.

What to See and Do

Slater Memorial Park. Within 200-acre park are sunken gardens; Rhode Island Watercolor Assn Gallery (daily exc Mon); historical Daggett House (fee); carousel (July-Aug, daily; May-June & Sept-Oct, wkends only; fee). Tennis; playing fields. Picnicking. Newport Ave off US 1A. Phone 401/728-0500. **Free.**

Slater Mill National Historic Site. Nation's first water-powered cotton mill (1793) was built by Samuel Slater; on site are also Wilkinson Mill (1810) and Sylvanus Brown House (1758). Mill features restored water-power system, including raceways and 8-ton wheel; operating machines; spinning and weaving demonstrations; slide show. (June-Labor Day, daily exc Mon; Mar-May & after Labor Day-mid-Dec, wkends; closed most hols) Roosevelt Ave at Main St. Phone 401/725-8638. ¢¢

Annual Events

St Patrick's Day Parade. First wkend Mar.

Octoberfest Parade and Craft Fair. First wkend Oct.

Seasonal Events

Pawtucket Red Sox. McCoy Stadium. AAA farm team of the Boston Red Sox. For schedule contact PO Box 2365, 02861; 401/724-7303 or 401/724-7300. Apr-Sept.

Arts in the Park Performance Series. Slater Memorial Park. Tues-Thurs & Sun, July-Aug.

Motor Hotel

★ ★ **COMFORT INN.** *2 George St (02860), I-95 exit 27. 401/723-6700; FAX 401/726-6380.* 135 rms, 5 story. S $68-$100; D $72-$100; under 18 free; wkend rates. Crib free. TV; cable (premium). Pool. Restaurant 6:30-12:30 am. Bar. Ck-out noon. Meeting rms. Business servs avail. Health club privileges. Sundries. Balconies. Cr cds: A, C, D, DS, MC, V.

D ⌧ ⊠ ⚒ **SC**

Portsmouth (D-7)

(See also Bristol, Newport)

Founded 1638 **Pop** 16,857 **Elev** 122 ft **Area code** 401 **Zip** 02871 **E-mail** info@gonewport.com **Web** www.gonewport.com

Information Newport County Convention and Visitor's Bureau, 23 America's Cup Ave, Newport 02840; 401/849-8048 or 800/976-5122.

Originally called Pocasset, Portsmouth was settled by a group led by John Clarke and William Coddington, who were sympathizers of Anne Hutchinson of Massachusetts. Soon after the town was first begun, Anne Hutchinson herself, with a number of fellow religious exiles, settled in the town and forced Clarke and Coddington to relinquish control. Coddington then went south and founded Newport, with which Portsmouth temporarily united in 1640. Fishing, shipbuilding and coal mining were the earliest sources of revenue. Today, Portsmouth is a summer resort area.

What to See and Do

⭐ **Green Animals.** Topiary gardens planted in 1880 with California privet, golden boxwood and American boxwood sculptured into animal forms, geometric figures and ornamental designs; also rose garden, formal flower beds. Children's toy collection in main house. (May-Oct, daily) Off RI 114. Phone 401/847-6543. ¢¢¢

Prescott Farm and Windmill. Restored buildings include an operating windmill (ca 1810), General Prescott's guard house and a country store stocked with items grown on the farm. (Apr-Nov, daily) Tours (Mon-Fri). 2009 W Main Rd (RI 114), Middletown. Phone 401/847-6230 or 401/849-7300. ¢

The Butterfly Zoo. The only New England operation that breeds, raises, releases and sells butterflies. View a wide variety of butterflies, including a preserved specimen of one that is believed to be the world's largest. (Daily exc Mon) 594 Aquidneck Ave, in Middletown. Phone 401/849-9519. ¢¢

Motels

✓⭐ ★ **BEST WESTERN BAY POINT INN.** *144 Anthony Rd. 401/683-3600; FAX 401/683-6690.* 85 rms, 2 story. May-Oct: S $85-$89; D $109-$119; each addl $10; suites $150; under 16 free; lower rates rest of yr. Crib free. TV; cable (premium), VCR avail. Indoor pool; lifeguard. Restaurant 6:30 am-9:30 pm; wkends to 10 pm. Rm serv. Bar 4 pm-1 am; entertainment Fri-Sat. Ck-out 11 am. Meeting rms. Business servs avail. In-rm modem link. 18-hole golf privileges. Exercise equipt; sauna. Near beach. Cr cds: A, C, D, DS, ER, JCB, MC, V.

🛉 🏊 🎿 🐾 SC

★ **FOUNDER'S BROOK.** *314 Boyd's Lane. 401/683-1244; FAX 401/683-9129; res: 800/334-8765.* 32 units, 24 kit. suites. Early July-early Sept: S, D $60-$109; kit. suites $80-$129; under 18 free; wkly rates; lower rates rest of yr. Crib $10. Pet accepted. TV; cable, VCR avail. Complimentary continental bkfst (wkends). Ck-out 11 am. Coin lndry. Picnic tables, grills. Cr cds: A, C, D, DS, MC, V.

D 🐾 ⛱ 🔥 SC

Restaurant

★ ★ ★ **SEAFARE INN.** *3352 E Main Rd (02801). 401/683-0577.* Specializes in seafood, regional Amer cuisine. Hrs: 5-9 pm. Closed Sun, Mon; Jan 1, Dec 24, 25. Res accepted. Semi-a la carte: dinner $13.95-$22.95. In renovated 1887 Victorian mansion furnished with period pieces. Jacket. Cr cds: A, MC, V.

 D

Providence (D-6)

(See also Pawtucket, Warwick)

Settled 1636 **Pop** 160,728 **Elev** 24 ft **Area code** 401 **E-mail** provcvb1@wsii.com **Web** providencevb.com

Information Providence Warwick Convention & Visitors Bureau, One W Exchange St, 3rd Floor, 02903; 401/751-1177 or 800/233-1636.

Grateful that God's providence had led him to this spot, Roger Williams founded a town and named it accordingly. More than three and one-half centuries later, Providence is the capital and largest city of the State of Rhode Island and Providence Plantations, the state's official title.

In its early years, Providence was a farm center. Through the great maritime epoch of the late 18th century and first half of the 19th century, clipper ships sailed from Providence to China and the West Indies. During the 19th century, the city became a great industrial center, which today still produces widely known Providence jewelry and silverware. In addition, Providence is an important port of entry.

Providence's long history has created a blend of old and new; modern hotels and office buildings share the streets with historic houses. Benefit St, overlooking Providence's modern financial district, has one of the largest concentrations of colonial houses in America. The city's location along the upper Narragansett Bay and numerous cultural opportunities each provide many varied attractions for the visitor. In addition, Providence is the southern point of the Blackstone River Valley National Heritage Corridor, a 250,000-acre region that extends to Worcester, MA (see).

What to See and Do

Brown University (1764). (7,500 students) Founded as Rhode Island College, school was renamed for Nicholas Brown, major benefactor and son of a founder, in 1804. Brown is the seventh-oldest college in the US. Pembroke College for Women (1891), named for the Cambridge, England *alma mater* of Roger Williams, merged with the men's college in 1971. Head of College St on Prospect. Phone 401/863-1000. Here are

Annmary Brown Memorial (1907). Paintings; Brown family memorabilia. (Mon-Fri afternoons, by appt) 21 Brown St, N of Charlesfield St. Phone 401/863-1994. **Free.**

David Winton Bell Gallery (1971). Historical and contemporary exhibitions. (Late Aug-May, daily exc Mon; closed hols) 64 College St, in List Art Center. Phone 401/863-2932. **Free.**

John Carter Brown Library (1904). Library houses exhibits, books and maps relating to exploration, settlement of America. (Daily exc Sun; closed school vacations) S side of campus green on George St. Phone 401/863-2725. **Free.**

John Hay Library (1910). Named for Lincoln's secretary John Hay (Brown, 1858), library houses extensive special collections, including Lincoln manuscripts, Harris collection of American poetry and plays, university archives. (Mon-Fri) 20 Prospect St, across from Van Wickle gates. Phone 401/863-3723. **Free.**

Rockefeller Library (1964). Named for John D. Rockefeller, Jr (Brown, 1897), library houses collections in the social sciences, humanities and fine arts. (Daily; closed school vacations) College & Prospect. Phone 401/863-2167 or 401/863-2162. **Free.**

University Hall (1770). The original "college edifice" serves as main administration building.

Wriston Quadrangle (1952). Square named for president-emeritus Henry M. Wriston. On Brown St near John Carter Brown Library.

Cathedral of St John (Episcopal) (1810). This Georgian structure with Gothic detail was built on the site of King's Church (1722). (Daily exc Sat; closed hols) Tour (after Sun services). 271 N Main St, at Church St. Phone 401/331-4622. **Free.**

First Baptist Church in America. Oldest Baptist congregation in America, established 1638, erected present building, by Joseph Brown, in 1775.

Sun morning services. (Mon-Fri; closed hols) 75 N Main St, at Waterman St. Phone 401/454-3418. **Free.**

First Unitarian Church (1816). Organized as First Congregational Church, 1720, the church was designed by John Holden Greene and has the largest bell ever cast by Paul Revere. (Sept-June, Mon-Fri, wkends by appt; rest of yr, Mon-Fri by appt; closed hols) Benefit & Benevolent Sts. Phone 401/421-7970. **Free.**

Governor Stephen Hopkins House (1707). House of signer of Declaration of Independence and 10-time governor of Rhode Island; 18th-century garden; period furnishings. (Apr-Dec, Wed & Sat afternoons, also by appt) Children only with adult. Benefit & Hopkins Sts, opp courthouse. Phone 401/421-0694. **Donation.**

John Brown House (1786). Georgian-style masterpiece by Joseph Brown, brother of John. George Washington was among the guests entertained in house. Museum of 18th-century china, glass, Rhode Island antiques, paintings; John Brown's chariot (1782), perhaps the oldest American-made vehicle extant. Guided tours. (Mar-Dec, daily exc Mon; rest of yr, Sat & Sun; closed hols) Combination ticket for Museum of Rhode Island History at Aldrich House. 52 Power St, at Benefit St. Phone 401/331-8575. **¢¢** The Historical Society also maintains a

Library. One of the largest genealogical collections in New England; Rhode Island imprints dating from 1727; newspapers, manuscripts, photographs, films. (Sept-May, Wed-Sat; rest of yr, Tues-Fri; closed hols) 121 Hope St, at Power St. **Free.**

Johnson & Wales University (1914). (8,000 students) Two- and four-yr degree programs offered in business, hospitality, food service and technology. Tours avail by appt (free). 8 Abbott Park Pl. Phone 401/598-1000 or 800/DIAL-JWU. On campus is the

Culinary Archives & Museum. Dubbed the "Smithsonian of the food service industry," this museum contains over 200,000 items related to the fields of culinary arts and hospitality collected and donated by Chicago's Chef Louis Szathmary. Includes rare US Presidential culinary autographs; tools of the trade from the third millennium B.C.; Egyptian, roman and Asian spoons over 1,000 yrs old; gallery of chefs; original artwork; hotel and restaurant silver; and periodicals related to the field. Guided tours. (Daily exc Sun; closed major hols) Trade Center at Harborside Campus, 315 Harborside Blvd. Phone 491/598-2805. **¢**

Lincoln Woods State Park. More than 600 acres. Swimming, bathhouse, freshwater ponds; fishing; boating. Hiking, bridle trails. Ice skating. Picnicking, concession. Fees for some activities. 5 mi N via RI 146, just S of Breakneck Hill Rd. Phone 401/723-7892. Per vehicle **¢**

Museum of Rhode Island History at Aldrich House. Exhibits on Rhode Island's history. Headquarters for Rhode Island Historical Society. (Daily exc Mon; closed Jan 1, Thanksgiving, Dec 25) Combination ticket for John Brown House. 110 Benevolent St. Phone 401/331-8575. **¢¢¢**

North Burial Ground. Graves of Roger Williams and other settlers. 1 mi N of Market Sq on N Main (US 1).

Old State House. Where General Assembly of Rhode Island met between 1762 and 1900. Independence was proclaimed in Old State House 2 months before declaration signed in Philadelphia. (Mon-Fri; closed hols) 150 Benefit St. Phone 401/222-2678. **Free.**

Providence Athenaeum Library (1753). One of the oldest subscription libraries in the US is housed in Greek-revival building designed by William Strickland in 1836. Rare-book rm includes original Audubon elephant folios; small art collection. (Daily exc Sun; summer, Mon-Fri; closed hols, also 2 wks early Aug) Tours. 251 Benefit St. Phone 401/421-6970. **Free.**

Providence Children's Museum. Many hands-on, dynamic exhibits including: a time-traveling adventure through Rhode Island's multi-cultural history; a wet and wild exploration of the ways of water; and a hands-on geometry lab. Traveling exhibits. Wkly programs. Gift shop. (Sept-June, daily exc Mon; rest of yr, daily) 100 South St. Phone 401/273-KIDS. **¢¢**

Rhode Island School of Design (1877). (1,960 students) One of the country's leading art and design schools. Tours. 2 College St. Phone 401/454-6345(recording) or -6100.On campus are

RISD Museum. Collections range from ancient to contemporary. (Daily exc Mon; closed most hols) 224 Benefit St. **¢**

Woods-Gerry Gallery. Mansion built 1860-1863 has special exhibits by students, faculty and alumni. (Daily) 62 Prospect St.

Rhode Island State House. Capitol by McKim, Mead and White was completed in 1901. Building contains a Gilbert Stuart full-length portrait of George Washington and the original parchment charter granted to Rhode Island by Charles II in 1663. *Independent Man* statue on dome. Guided tours. Building (Mon-Fri; closed hols & 2nd Mon Aug). Smith St. Phone 401/222-2357. **Free.**

Roger Williams National Memorial. This 4.5-acre park, at site of old town spring, commemorates the founding of Providence and contributions made by Roger Williams to civil and religious liberty; slide presentation, exhibit. Visitor information. (Daily; closed Jan 1, Dec 25) 282 N Main St. Phone 401/521-7266. **Free.**

Roger Williams Park. Park has 430 acres of woodlands, waterways and winding drives. Japanese garden, Betsy Williams' cottage, greenhouses. (Daily; closed Jan 1, Thanksgiving, Dec 25) 3 mi S on Elmwood Ave. Phone 401/785-9450. **Free.** Also in the park are

Museum of Natural History. Anthropology, geology, oceanography, astronomy and biology displays; educational and performing arts programs. (Daily; closed Jan 1, Thanksgiving, Dec 25) Elmwood Ave. Phone 401/785-9450. **¢**

Zoo. Children's nature center, tropical building, African plains exhibit; over 600 animals. Educational programs; tours. (Daily; closed Dec 25) Phone 401/785-3510. **¢¢**

The Arcade (1828). First indoor shopping mall with national landmark status. More than 35 specialty shops; restaurants. Westminster St. Phone 401/598-1049.

Walking tours. The Providence Preservation Society offers daily walking tours and tour booklets of several historic Providence neighborhoods. (Mon-Fri) 21 Meeting St, 02903. Phone 401/831-7440. **¢¢¢**

Annual Event

Spring Festival of Historic Houses. Sponsored by the Providence Preservation Society, 21 Meeting St, 02903. Tours of selected private houses and gardens. Phone 401/831-7440. 2nd wkend June.

Motels

✔★ HI-WAY MOTOR INN. *(1880 Hartford Ave, Johnston 02919)* jct US 6A & I-295. 401/351-7810. 35 rms. S $42; D $50; each addl $5; suites $60-$70. TV; cable (premium). Restaurant nearby. Ck-out 11 am. Cr cds: A, MC, V.

D ⊠ 🔥

★ ★ JOHNSON & WALES INN. *(MA 114A & US 44, Seekonk 02771)* I-195E, exit 1 in MA, left onto MA 114A to jct US 44, turn right on US 44. 508/336-8700; FAX 508/336-3414. Web www.jwinn.com. 86 units, 2-3 story, 39 suites. S, D $79-$99; suites $109-$139. TV; cable (premium), VCR avail. Restaurant 6:30 am-10 pm. Rm serv. Bar. Ck-out 11 am. Meeting rms. Business center. Bellhops. Valet serv. Sundries. Health club privileges. Wet bar, whirlpool in suites. Cr cds: A, C, D, DS, MC, V.

D ⊠ 🛥 SC 🔥

★ RAMADA INN. *(940 Fall River Ave, Seekonk MA 02771)* 4 mi E at exit 1, jct I-195 & MA 114A. 508/336-7300; FAX 508/336-2107. 128 rms, 2 story. S $61-$82; D $66-$85; each addl $10; suites $107-$134; under 18 free; wkend rates. Crib free. TV; cable (premium). Indoor pool; whirlpool. Sauna. Playground. Restaurant 7 am-10 pm. Rm serv. Bar noon-1 am; entertainment. Ck-out noon. Meeting rms. Business center. Tennis. Putting green. Lawn games. Cr cds: A, D, DS, MC, V.

D 🏌 🛥 ⊠ 🔥 SC 🔥

Motor Hotel

★ ★ ★ MARRIOTT. 1 Orms St (02904). 401/272-2400; FAX 401/273-2686. 345 rms, 6 story. S, D $99-$179; suites $250; family, wkend rates; higher rates special events. Crib free. Pet accepted. TV; cable (premium), VCR avail. Indoor/outdoor pool; whirlpool, poolside serv, lifeguard. Coffee in rms. Restaurant 6:30 am-11 pm. Rm serv. Bar; entertainment. Ck-out noon. Convention facilities. Business center. In-rm modem link. Bellhops. Sundries. Gift shop. Airport transportation. Exercise equipt; sauna. Game rm. Balconies; some private patios. Cr cds: A, C, D, DS, ER, JCB, MC, V.

⊡ ≋ ✈ 🍴 ⋈ 🔥 SC 🚶

Hotels

★ ★ ★ **THE BILTMORE.** *Kennedy Plaza (02903). 401/421-0700; res: 800/294-7709; FAX 401/455-3050.* E-mail pvdblt@ix.netcom.com; web www.grandheritage.com/htmlcode/hus_provbilt.html. 244 rms, 18 story. S $120-$190; D $140-$220; each addl $20; suites $199-$750; under 18 free; wkend rates. Crib free. Pet accepted. TV; cable (premium), VCR avail. Restaurant 6:30 am-midnight. Bar noon-1 am; wkends to 2 am. Ck-out noon. Convention facilities. Business center. In-rm modem link. Beauty shop. Garage parking; valet. Exercise equipt. Refrigerators, microwaves avail. Cr cds: A, C, D, DS, JCB, MC, V.

⊡ ✦ ✈ 🍴 ⋈ 🔥 SC 🚶

★ ★ **DAYS HOTEL ON THE HARBOR.** *220 India St (02903), 2 mi E on RI 195, exit 3. 401/272-5577; FAX 401/272-5577, ext. 199.* 136 rms, 6 story. Apr-Oct: S $89-$149; D $99-$159; each addl $10; under 12 free; lower rates rest of yr. Crib avail. TV; cable (premium). Restaurant 6:30 am-2 pm, 5-10 pm. Bar 11-1 am. Ck-out 11 am. Meeting rms. Business center. In-rm modem link. Free airport, RR station, bus depot transportation. Exercise equipt. Overlooks harbor. Cr cds: A, C, D, DS, MC, V.

⊡ 🍴 ⋈ 🔥 SC 🚶

★ ★ ★ **WESTIN.** *1 W Exchange St (02903). 401/598-8000; FAX 401/598-8200.* Web proviwestin.com 3 rms, 25 story, 22 suites. S, D $189-$260; each addl $25; suites $260-$1200; under 18 free. TV; cable (premium), VCR avail (movies). Restaurant 6 am-10 pm. Bar to midnight. Ck-out noon. Convention facilities. Business center. In-rm modem link. Concierge. Exercise equipt; sauna. Indoor pool; whirlpool. Minibars; some bathrm phones, refrigerators. Cr cds: A, C, D, DS, MC, V.

⊡ ≋ 🍴 ⋈ 🔥 SC 🚶

Inns

★ ★ **OLD COURT.** *144 Benefit St (02903). 401/751-2002; FAX 401/272-4830.* E-mail reserve@oldcourt.com; web www.oldcourt.com. 10 rms, 3 story, 1 suite. May & Sept-Oct: S, D $120-$140; suites $250; wkly rates; lower rates rest of yr. TV; cable, VCR avail. Complimentary full bkfst. Restaurant nearby. Ck-out 11:30 am, ck-in 2-11 pm. Built 1863 as a rectory. Overlooks Old State House. Sitting rms. Antique furnishings, chandeliers and memorabilia from 19th century. Cr cds: DS, MC, V.

🔥

✔★ **STATE HOUSE.** *43 Jewett St (02908), near State Capitol Bldg. 401/351-6111; FAX 401/351-4261.* Web www3.edgenet.net/state housein. 10 rms, 3 story. S, D $79-$119; each addl $10; family rates. Crib avail. TV; cable, VCR avail. Complimentary full bkfst. Restaurant nearby. Ck-out 11 am, ck-in 3 pm. Built 1890. Sitting rm. Antiques, fireplaces. Totally nonsmoking. Cr cds: A, DS, MC, V.

⋈ 🔥

Restaurants

★ ★ **ADESSO.** *161 Cushing St (02906). 401/521-0770.* Contemporary Italian menu. Specializes in pasta dishes, duck, California style wood-oven pizzas. Hrs: 11:45 am-10:30 pm; Fri, Sat to 11:30 pm. Closed July 4, Thanksgiving, Dec 25. Bar. A la carte entrees: lunch $6.95-$15.95, dinner $9.95-$23.95. Parking. Modern decor; open kitchen. Cr cds: A, MC, V.

⊡ 🔥

★ ★ ★ **AL FORNO.** *577 S Main St (02903). 401/273-9760.* Italian menu. Specializes in grilled pizza appetizers, made-to-order desserts. Hrs: 5-10 pm; Sat from 4 pm. Closed Sun, Mon; July 4; also Dec 25-Jan 1. Bar. Wine cellar. A la carte entrees: dinner $36-$45. Parking. Italian trattoria atmosphere. Totally nonsmoking. Cr cds: A, D, MC, V.

⊡

★ ★ **FEDERAL RESERVE.** *60 Dorrance St (02903). 401/621-5700.* Specializes in steak, seafood, regional dishes. Hrs: 11:30 am-3 pm, 5:30-9 pm; Fri to 11 pm; Sat 5:30-11 pm; Sun brunch 11 am-2 pm. Closed Dec 25; also Sun June-Aug. Res accepted. Bar. Semi-a la carte: lunch $4-$8, dinner $10-$24. Sun brunch $15.95. Child's meals. Street parking. Outdoor dining. In 1901 bank; tellers' counters, 13-ton exposed vault. Totally nonsmoking. Cr cds: A, C, D, JCB, MC, V.

⊡

★ ★ **HEMENWAY'S SEAFOOD GRILL.** *One Providence-Washington Plaza (02903), at S Main St. 401/351-8570.* Specializes in fresh seafood from around the world. Hrs: 11:30 am-3 pm, 5-10 pm; Fri, Sat to 11 pm; Sun noon-9 pm. Closed Thanksgiving, Dec 25. Bar to midnight. Semi-a la carte: lunch $5.45-$11.95, dinner $11.95-$21.95. Child's meals. Valet parking. Outdoor dining. Cr cds: A, D, DS, MC, V.

⊡ ⊣

★ ★ **OLD GRISTMILL TAVERN.** *(390 Fall River Ave, Seekonk MA) On MA 114A, I-195 exit 1 in MA. 508/336-8460.* Specializes in prime rib, sirloin, seafood. Salad bar. Hrs: 11:30 am-2:30 pm, 4:30-10 pm; Sun noon-9 pm. Closed Thanksgiving, Dec 25. Bar 11:30 am-11 pm. Semi-a la carte: lunch $4.75-$9.95, dinner $7.95-$18.95. Child's meals. Parking. In restored mill (1745); antiques; fireplace. Gardens, pond, wooden bridge over waterfall. Cr cds: A, C, D, DS, MC, V.

★ ★ ★ **POT AU FEU.** *44 Custom House St (02903). 401/273-8953.* French menu. Specializes in classic and regional French dishes. Hrs: 11:30 am-2 pm, 5:30-9 pm; Fri to 11 pm; Sat 5:30-11 pm; Sun 4-9 pm. Closed most major hols; also Sun June-Aug. Res accepted. Bar. A la carte entrees: lunch $4-$12, dinner $12-$29. Prix fixe: dinner $26-$39. Two tiers; bistro atmosphere on lower level, formal dining on upper level. Cr cds: A, C, D, MC, V.

Wakefield

(see Kingston)

Warwick (D-6)

(See also East Greenwich, Providence)

Chartered 1647 **Pop** 85,427 **Elev** 64 ft **Area code** 401 **Web** www.warwickri.com
Information Dept of Economic Development, City Hall, 3275 Post Rd, 02886; 401/738-2000, ext 6402 or 800/4-WARWICK.

Warwick, the second-largest city in Rhode Island, is the location of T. F. Green Airport, the state's largest commercial airport. With 39 miles of coastline on Narragansett Bay, the city has more than 15 marinas. Warwick is a major retail and industrial center. The geographic diversity of Warwick promoted a decentralized pattern of settlement, which gave rise to a number of small villages, for example, Pawtuxet, Cowesett and Conimicut.

What to See and Do

Shopping.

Catalog Fashion Outlet. Stop here for discounted brand-name clothing for men, women and children. (Daily) 1689 Post Rd. Phone 401/738-5145.

Historic Pontiac Mills. Portions of 1863 mill complex have been restored and now house approx 80 small businesses, artisans and shops. Also open-air market (Sat & Sun). (Daily) 334 Knight St. Phone 401/737-2700.

Warwick Mall. Renovated and expanded, this is the largest mall in the state. Over 80 specialty shops and 4 department stores. Outdoor patio, video wall, topiary gardens. Wkly special events. (Daily) Jct RI 2 & RI 5. Phone 401/739-7500.

Walking Tour of Historic Apponaug Village. More than 30 structures of historic and/or architectural interest are noted on walking tour brochure available through Department of Economic Development, Warwick City Hall, 3275 Post Rd, Apponaug 02886. Along Post Rd between Greenwich Ave & W Shore Rd. **Free.**

Annual Events

Gaspee Days. Celebration of the capture and burning of British revenue schooner *Gaspee* by Rhode Island patriots; arts and crafts, concert, foot races, battle re-enactment, muster of fife and drum corps, parade, contests. May-June.

Warwick Heritage Festival. Warwick City Park. Revisit history with this wkend reenactment. Phone 800/4-WARWICK. Nov, Veterans Day wkend.

Seasonal Event

Warwick Musical Theatre. 522 Quaker Lane, jct RI 2, 3. Outdoor theater-in-the-round; concerts. Also children's shows. Contact PO Box 206, 02887; 401/821-7300. July-early Sept.

Motels

★ ★ **COMFORT INN.** *1940 Post Rd (02886), near T.F. Green State Airport. 401/732-0470; res: 800/228-5150.* 196 rms, 4 story. May-Oct: S $79-$89; D $89-$99; each addl $10; under 18 free; lower rates rest of yr. Pet accepted, some restrictions; $50. TV; cable (premium). Complimentary continental bkfst. Restaurant nearby. Ck-out noon. Bellhops. Business center. In-rm modem link. Free airport transportation. Health club privileges. Game rm. Cr cds: A, C, D, DS, MC, V.

[D] [symbols] SC [symbol]

★ ★ ★ **RADISSON AIRPORT HOTEL.** *2081 Post Rd (02886), at T.F. Green State Airport. 401/739-3000; FAX 401/732-9309.* 111 units, 2 story, 39 suites. S, D $89-$150; each addl $15; suites $125-$170; under 18 free; wkend rates. Crib free. TV; cable (premium), VCR avail. Complimentary continental bkfst (Mon-Fri). Restaurant 6:30 am-11 pm. Rm serv. Bar noon-1 am. Ck-out noon. Business servs avail. Bellhops. Valet serv. Concierge. Sundries. Free airport transportation. Wet bar in suites. Cr cds: A, C, D, DS, JCB, MC, V.

[D] [symbols] SC

★ ★ **RESIDENCE INN BY MARRIOTT.** *500 Kilvert St (02886), near T.F. Green State Airport. 401/737-7100.* 96 kit. suites, 2 story. Kit. suites $140-$190. TV; cable (premium). Indoor pool; whirlpool. Playground. Complimentary continental bkfst. Ck-out noon. Business center. Lawn games. Balconies. Cr cds: A, D, DS, JCB, MC, V.

[D] [symbols] SC [symbol]

✔ ★ **SUSSE CHALET.** *36 Jefferson Blvd (02888), near T.F. Green State Airport. 401/941-6600; FAX 401/785-1260.* E-mail sussechalet@tellink.net; web www.sussechalet.com. 115 rms, 5 story. July-Oct: S $74.70; D $84.70; each addl $4-$7; under 18 free; lower rates rest of yr. Crib free. TV; cable (premium). Pool; lifeguard. Complimentary

continental bkfst. Restaurant adj open 24 hrs. Ck-out 11 am. Coin lndry. Valet serv. Airport transportation. Cr cds: A, D, DS, MC, V.

[symbols] SC

Motor Hotels

★ ★ ★ **HOLIDAY INN AT THE CROSSINGS.** *801 Greenwich Ave (02886). 401/732-6000; FAX 401/732-4839.* E-mail hiwarwick@aol.com. 266 rms, 6 story. S $149; D $159; suites $275-$525; under 18 free. Crib free. TV; cable. Indoor pool; whirlpool, poolside serv. Coffee in rms. Restaurant 6 am-11 pm. Rm serv. Bar 4 pm-1 am. Ck-out 11 am. Coin lndry. Convention facilities. Business center. In-rm modem link. Bellhops. Sundries. Gift shop. Free airport transportation. Exercise equipt; sauna. Many refrigerators, wet bars; bathrm phones avail. Cr cds: A, C, D, DS, JCB, MC, V.

[D] [symbols] SC [symbol]

★ ★ ★ **SHERATON INN-PROVIDENCE AIRPORT.** *1850 Post Rd (02886), near T.F. Green State Airport. 401/738-4000; FAX 401/738-8206.* 207 rms, 5 story. S, D $99-$209; each addl $15; suites $195; under 18 free; wkend rates. Crib free. Pet accepted. TV; cable (premium), VCR avail. Heated pool; lifeguard. Coffee in rms. Restaurant 6:30 am-11 pm. Bar noon-1 am. Ck-out noon. Meeting rms. Business servs avail. In-rm modem link. Bellhops. Valet serv. Free airport transportation. Exercise equipt; sauna. Cr cds: A, C, D, DS, ER, MC, V.

[D] [symbols] SC

Restaurants

★ ★ **LEGAL SEA FOODS.** *2099 Post Rd. 401/732-3663.* Specializes in fresh seafood. Hrs: 11:30 am-10 pm; Sat 5-11 pm; Sun noon-8 pm. Closed Thanksgiving, Dec 25. Bar. Semi-a la carte: lunch $5.95-$9.95, dinner $9.95-$16.95. Child's meals. Cr cds: A, C, D, DS, MC, V.

[D]

★ ★ **MR MARCO.** *5454 Post Rd. 401/885-2120.* Continental, Chinese menu. Specialties: Peking lobster, veal Eric, beef Wellington. Own baking. Hrs: 5-9 pm; Sun 1-8 pm. Closed Dec 25. Res accepted; required Sat, Sun. Bar 5 pm-1 am. Semi-a la carte: dinner $10.95-$17.95. Child's meals. Harpist Fri, Sat. Live trees, plants, waterfalls. Cr cds: A, C, D, DS, MC, V.

[D]

Westerly (E-5)

(See also Charlestown; also see Mystic and Stonington, CT)

Founded 1669 **Pop** 21,605 **Elev** 50 ft **Area code** 401 **Zip** 02891 **E-mail** sctc@netsense.net **Web** www.southcountyri.com

Information Westerly-Pawcatuck Area Chamber of Commerce, 74 Post Rd, Rte 1, phone 401/596-7761 or 800/SEA-7636; or the South County Tourism Council, Stedman Government Center, 4808 Tower Hill Rd, Wakefield 02879, phone 401/789-4422 or 800/548-4662.

Westerly, one of the oldest towns in the state, was at one time known for its nearby granite quarries. Today, local industries include textiles, the manufacture of fishing line and tourism.

What to See and Do

Babcock-Smith House (ca 1732). A 2-story, gambrel-roofed Georgian mansion, was residence of Dr. Joshua Babcock, Westerly's first physician and friend of Benjamin Franklin. Later, the house was home to Orlando Smith, who discovered granite on the grounds. Furniture collection covers 200 yrs; toys date from 1890s; colonial garden and culinary herb garden. (July-mid-Sept, Wed & Sun; May-June & mid-Sept-mid-Oct, Sun only) 124 Granite St. Phone 401/596-4424 or 401/596-5704. ¢

Misquamicut State Beach. Swimming, bathhouse (fee); fishing nearby. Picnicking, concession. (Mid-June-early Sept, daily) Parking fee. 5 mi S off US 1A. ¢¢¢

Watch Hill. Historical community of handsome summer houses, many dating from the 1870s; picturesque sea views. 6 mi S on Beach St, via Avondale. Located here are

Flying Horse Carousel. Original amusement ride built in 1867. Watch Hill Beach.

Lighthouse (1856). Granite lighthouse built to replace wooden one built in 1807; lit by oil lamp until 1933, when replaced by electric. Museum exhibit (Tues & Thurs, afternoons).

Motels

★ ★ **BREEZEWAY RESORT.** *(70 Winnapaug Rd, Misquamicut) approx 4 mi S on RI 1A, S on Winnapaug Rd. 401/348-8953; FAX 401/596-3207; res: 800/462-8872.* E-mail breezeway@edgenet.net. 50 rms, 2 story, 14 suites, 3 kit. units, 2 villas. Mid-June-Aug: S $114-$129; D $129; each addl $10-$25; suites $144-$189; kit. units $144; villas $1,540/wk; under 2 free; wkly, wkend rates; wkends, hols (3-day min); lower rates April-mid June, Sept-Oct. Closed rest of yr. Crib $10. TV; cable. Heated pool. Playground. Complimentary continental bkfst. Bar 11:30 am-10 pm. Ck-out 11 am. Meeting rms. Business servs avail. Refrigerators. Balconies. Picnic tables. Cr cds: A, C, D, DS, MC, V.

★ ★ **PINE LODGE.** *92 Old Post Rd, 3¹/₂ mi N on US 1. 401/322-0333; res: 800/838-0333.* 11 rms, 19 cottages, 30 kits. Mid-June-mid-Sept: S, D $72-$80; each addl $8; kit. cottages $70-$91; under 16 free; wkly rates; lower rates rest of yr. Crib free. TV. Playground. Restaurant nearby. Ck-out 11 am. Lawn games. Refrigerators. Picnic tables, grills. In wooded area. Cr cds: A, C, D, DS, MC, V.

★ ★ **WINNAPAUG INN.** *169 Shore Rd. 401/348-8350; FAX 401/596-8654; res: 800/288-9906.* 49 units. July-Labor Day: S, D $109-$189; villas $1,043-$1,393/wk; lower rates Mar-June & after Labor Day. Crib free. TV; cable (premium). Heated pool. Playground. Complimentary continental bkfst. Restaurant nearby. Ck-out 11 am. Game rm. Refrigerators. Winnapaug Pond adj. Cr cds: A, D, DS, MC, V.

Inns

★ ★ **SHELTER HARBOR.** *10 Wagner Rd. 401/322-8883; FAX 401/322-7907; res: 800/468-8883.* 23 rms, 3 with shower only, 2 story. May-Oct: S, D $92-$136; each addl $15-$25; lower rates rest of yr. Crib $15. TV; cable. Playground. Complimentary full bkfst. Restaurant 7:30-10:30 am, 11:30 am-3 pm, 5-10 pm. Bar. Ck-out 11 am, ck-in 2 pm. Meeting rms. Business servs avail. Lawn games. Some balconies. Picnic tables. Originally a farm built in the early 1800s; guest house and converted barn. Cr cds: A, C, D, DS, MC, V.

★ ★ ★ **THE VILLA.** *190 Shore Rd. 401/596-1054; FAX 401/596-6268; res: 800/722-9240.* E-mail villa@riconnect.com; web www.thevillaat westerly.com. 6 suites, 3 story. Some rm phones. Memorial Day-Columbus Day: S, D $120-$200; each addl $25; wkly rates; higher rates wkends, hols (2-day min); lower rates rest of yr. Pet accepted, some restrictions. TV; cable (premium), VCR avail. Pool; whirlpool. Complimentary continental bkfst. Complimentary coffee in rms. Restaurant adj 6 am-midnight. Ck-out 11 am, ck-in 1 pm. Business servs avail. Luggage handling. RR station transportation. Some in-rm whirlpools, refrigerators, fireplaces. Some antiques. Mediterranean-style grounds. Cr cds: A, D, MC, V.

Restaurant

★ ★ **VILLA TROMBINO.** *112 Ashway Rd. 401/596-3444.* Italian, Amer menu. Specializes in pasta, fresh veal, seafood. Hrs: 4-9 pm; Sun to 9 pm; early-bird dinner 4-6 pm. Closed Mon; Thanksgiving, Dec 24, 25. Res accepted. Bar to 1 am. A la carte entrees: dinner $3.95-$19.95. Child's meals. Cr cds: A, MC, V.

Vermont

Population: 562,758
Land area: 9,273 square miles
Elevation: 95-4,393 feet
Highest point: Mt Mansfield (Lamoille County)
Entered Union: March 4, 1791 (14th state)
Capital: Montpelier
Motto: Freedom and Unity
Nickname: Green Mountain State
State flower: Red clover
State bird: Hermit thrush
State tree: Sugar maple
State fair: Late August-early September, 1999, in Rutland
Time zone: Eastern
Web: www.travel.com

Vermont was the last New England state to be settled. The earliest permanent settlement date is believed to be 1724. Ethan Allen and his Green Mountain Boys made Vermont famous when they took Fort Ticonderoga from the British in 1775. Claimed by both New York and New Hampshire, Vermont framed a constitution in 1777. It was the first state to prohibit slavery and the first to provide universal male suffrage, regardless of property or income. For 14 years, Vermont was an independent republic, running its own postal service, coining its own money, naturalizing citizens of other states and countries and negotiating with other states and nations. Vermont became the 14th state in 1791.

Although Vermont is usually thought of as a farm state, more than 17 percent of the labor force is in manufacturing. Machinery, food, wood, plastic, rubber, paper, electrical and electronic products are made here. Dairy products lead the farm list, with sheep, maple sugar and syrup, apples and potatoes following. Vermont leads the nation in its yield of marble and granite; limestone, slate and talc are also quarried and mined.

Tall steeples dominate the towns, forests, mountains and countryside where one can walk the 260-mile Long Trail along the Green Mountain crests. Vermont has one of the highest concentrations of alpine ski areas and cross-country ski touring centers in the nation. Fishing and hunting are excellent; resorts range from rustic to elegant.

When to Go/Climate

Vermont enjoys four distinct seasons. Comfortable summers are followed by brilliantly colored falls and typically cold New England winters. Heavy snowfall makes for good skiing in winter, while spring thaws bring on the inevitable muddy months. Summer and fall are popular times to visit.

AVERAGE HIGH/LOW TEMPERATURES (°F)
BURLINGTON

Jan 25/8	**May** 67/45	**Sept** 69/49
Feb 28/9	**June** 76/55	**Oct** 57/39
Mar 39/22	**July** 81/60	**Nov** 44/30
Apr 54/34	**Aug** 78/58	**Dec** 30/16

Parks and Recreation Finder

Directions to and information about the parks and recreation areas below are given under their respective town/city sections. Please refer to those sections for details.

NATIONAL PARK AND RECREATION AREA

Key to abbreviations: I.H.S. = International Historic Site; I.P.M. = International Peace Memorial; N.B. = National Battlefield; N.B.P. = National Battlefield Park; N.B.C. = National Battlefield & Cemetery; N.C. = National Conservation Area; N.E.M. = National Expansion Memorial; N.F. = National Forest; N.G. = National Grassland; N.H. = National Historical Park; N.H.C. = National Heritage Corridor; N.H.S. = National Historic Site; N.L. = National Lakeshore; N.M. = National Monument; N.M.P. = National Military Park; N.Mem. = National Memorial; N.P. = National Park; N.Pres. = National Preserve; N.R. = National Recreational Area; N.R.R. = National Recreational River; N.Riv. = National River; N.S. = National Seashore; N.S.R. = National Scenic Riverway; N.S.T. = National Scenic Trail; N.Sc. = National Scientific Reserve; N.V.M. = National Volcanic Monument.

Place Name	Listed Under
Green Mountain N.F.	same

STATE PARK AND RECREATION AREAS

Key to abbreviations: I.P. = Interstate Park; S.A.P. = State Archaeological Park; S.B. = State Beach; S.C. = State Conservation Area; S.C.P. = State Conservation Park; S.Cp. = State Campground; S.F. = State Forest; S.G. = State Garden; S.H.A. = State Historic Area; S.H.P. = State Historic Park; S.H.S. = State Historic Site; S.M.P. = State Marine Park; S.N.A. = State Natural Area; S.P. = State Park; S.P.C. = State Public Campground; S.R. = State Reserve; S.R.A. = State Recreation Area; S.Res. = State Reservoir; S.Res.P. = State Resort Park; S.R.P. = State Rustic Park.

made by contacting park or Department of Forests, Parks, and Recreation, 103 S Main St, Waterbury 05671-0603, with full payment. Pets are allowed on leash only. Phone 802/241-3655.

CALENDAR HIGHLIGHTS

FEBRUARY

Winter Carnival (Brattleboro). Week-long festival includes ski races, parade, ice show, sleigh rides, road races. Phone 802/258-2511.

APRIL

Maple Sugar Festival (St Albans). A number of producers welcome visitors who join sugarhouse parties for sugar-on-snow, sour pickles and raised doughnuts. Continuing events; arts and crafts; antiques; wood-chopping contests. Phone 802/524-5800.

JUNE

Lake Champlain Balloon and Craft Festival (Burlington). Champlain Valley Exposition. Balloon launches, rides, crafts, food and entertainment. Phone Lake Champlain Regional Chamber of Commerce, 802/863-3489.

Mountain Bike World Cup Race (West Dover). Mt Snow. More than 1,500 cyclists from throughout the world compete in downhill, dual slalom and circuit racing events. Phone 800/245-7669.

JULY

Festival on the Green (Middlebury). Village green. Classical, modern and traditional dance; chamber and folk music; theater and comedy presentations. Phone 802/388-0216.

SEPTEMBER

Vermont State Fair (Rutland). Exhibits of arts and crafts, flowers, produce, home arts, pets, animals, maple sugaring. Entertainment, agricultural displays, hot-air ballooning. Daily special events. Phone 802/775-5200.

SKI AREAS

Place Name	Listed Under
Bolton Valley Ski/Summer Resort	BURLINGTON
Bromley Mt Ski Area	PERU
Burke Mt Ski Area	LYNDONVILLE
Grafton Ponds Cross-Country Ski Center	GRAFTON
Haystack Ski Area	WILMINGTON
Killington Resort	KILLINGTON
Mad River Glen Ski Area	WAITSFIELD
Middlebury College Snow Bowl	MIDDLEBURY
Mount Snow Ski Area	WEST DOVER
Mountain Top Cross Country Ski Resort	RUTLAND
Okemo Mt Ski Area	OKEMO STATE FOREST
Sherman Hollow Cross-Country Ski Center	BURLINGTON
Smugglers' Notch Ski Area	JEFFERSONVILLE
Stowe Mt. Resort	STOWE
Stratton Mountain Ski Area	STRATTON MOUNTAIN
Sugarbush Resort Ski Area	WARREN
Suicide Six Ski Area	WOODSTOCK
Wild Wings Touring Center	PERU

For brochures on cross-country and downhill skiing in Vermont contact the Vermont Travel Division, 134 State St, Montpelier 05602; 802/828-3236.

FISHING & HUNTING

Nonresident fishing license: season $38; 7-day $25; 5-day $20; 3-day $18; 1-day $7. Nonresident hunting license: $80; $25 for those under 18 yrs. In order for a nonresident to obtain a hunting license, he must prove that he holds a license in his home state. Bow and arrow license (hunting or combination license also required): nonresident $15. Combination hunting and fishing license: nonresident $100. For *Vermont Guide to Fishing* contact the Fish and Wildlife Dept, 103 S Main St, Waterbury 05671-0501; 802/241-3700.

Driving Information

All vehicle occupants must be secured in federally approved safety belts. Children ages 1-4 must be secured in an approved child safety device. When the number of occupants exceeds the number of safety belts, children take priority and must be secured. Under age 1 must use an approved safety seat. For further information phone 802/828-2665.

INTERSTATE HIGHWAY SYSTEM

The following alphabetical listing of Vermont towns in *Mobil Travel Guide* shows that these cities are within 10 miles of the indicated Interstate highways. A highway map should, however, be checked for the nearest exit.

Highway Number	Cities/Towns within 10 miles
INTERSTATE 89:	Barre, Burlington, Montpelier, St Albans, Swanton, Waterbury, White River Junction.
INTERSTATE 91:	Bellows Falls, Brattleboro, Fairlee, Grafton, Lyndonville, Newfane, Newport, St Johnsbury, Springfield, White River Junction, Windsor, Woodstock.

Place Name	Listed Under
Branbury S.P.	BRANDON
Burton Island S.P.	ST ALBANS
Button Bay S.P.	VERGENNES
Calvin Coolidge S.F.	PLYMOUTH
Elmore S.P.	STOWE
Emerald Lake S.P.	MANCHESTER
Gifford Woods S.P.	KILLINGTON
Groton S.F.	BARRE
Jamaica S.P.	NEWFANE
Lake Carmi S.P.	ST ALBANS
Little River S.P.	WATERBURY
Molly Stark S.P.	WILMINGTON
Mt Ascutney S.P.	WINDSOR
Mt Mansfield S.F.	STOWE
Mt Philo S.P.	SHELBURNE
North Hero S.P.	NORTH HERO
Okemo S.F.	same
Shaftsbury S.P.	BENNINGTON
Silver Lake S.P.	WOODSTOCK
Townshend S.F.	NEWFANE
Wilgus S.P.	WINDSOR
Woodford S.P.	BENNINGTON

Water-related activities, hiking, riding, various other sports, picnicking, camping and visitor centers are available in many of these areas. Day-use areas (Memorial Day wkend-Labor Day, daily); over age 14, $2/person; ages 4-13, $1.50; under 4 free. Boat rentals, $5/hr. Paddleboats, $5/half-hr. Canoe rentals, $5/hr.

Camping: $13/night, lean-to $17 at areas with swimming beaches; $11/night, lean-to $15 at areas without swimming beaches. Reservations of at least 2 days (3 days mid-May-Oct) and maximum of 21 days may be

Additional Visitor Information

Vermont is very well documented. The Vermont Official Transportation Map, as well as numerous descriptive folders, are distributed free by the

Vermont Dept of Tourism and Marketing, 134 State St, Montpelier 05601-1471; 802/828-3236 or 800/VERMONT. Visitor centers are located off I-89 in Guilford (daily); off I-89 in Highgate Springs (daily); off US 4 in Fair Haven (daily); and off I-93 in Waterford (daily).

The Vermont Chamber of Commerce, PO Box 37, Montpelier 05601, distributes *Vermont Traveler's Guidebook* of accommodations, restaurants and attractions. *Vermont Life,* one of the nation's best known and respected regional quarterlies, presents photo essays on various aspects of life in the state; available by writing *Vermont Life,* 6 Baldwin St, Montpelier 05602. Another excellent source of information on the state is *Vermont: An Explorer's Guide* (The Countryman Press, Woodstock, VT, 1994) by Christina Tree and Peter Jennison; a comprehensive book covering attractions, events, recreational facilities, accommodations, restaurants and places to shop. Available in bookstores.

Various books on Vermont are also available from the Vermont Historical Society, Vermont Museum, Pavilion Bldg, 109 State St, Montpelier 05609.

For information regarding Vermont's Long Trail, along with other hiking trails in the state, contact the Green Mountain Club, RR 1, Box 650, VT 100, Waterbury Center 05677; phone 802/244-7037. The Department of Agriculture, 116 State St, Montpelier 05602, has information on farms offering vacations and maple sugarhouses open to visitors.

Several Vermont-based companies offer inn-to-inn bicycle tours from May through October (months vary). Tours range in length from two days to several weeks; most are designed to accommodate all levels of cyclists. Bicycling enthusiasts can obtain a brochure entitled *Bicycle Touring in Vermont* from the Vermont Dept of Tourism and Marketing, 134 State St, Montpelier 05601-1471; 802/828-3236.

Arlington (H-1)

(See also Bennington, Dorset, Manchester & Manchester Center)

Settled 1763 **Pop** 2,299 **Elev** 690 ft **Area code** 802 **Zip** 05250

What to See and Do

Candle Mill Village. Three buildings, including a gristmill built in 1764 by Remember Baker of the Green Mountain Boys; many music boxes, candles, cookbook & teddy bear displays. (Daily; closed Jan 1, Easter, Thanksgiving, Dec 25) 1½ mi E on Old Mill Rd. Phone 802/375-6068. **Free.**

Fishing. Trout and fly fishing on the Battenkill River.

Norman Rockwell Exhibition. Hundreds of magazine covers, illustrations, advertisements, calendars and other printed works displayed in historic 1875 church in the illustrator's hometown. Hosts are Rockwell's former models. Twenty-min film. (Daily; closed Easter, Thanksgiving, Dec 25) On VT Historic Rte 7A. Phone 802/375-6423. ¢

Motel

✔★ **CANDLELIGHT.** VT 7A. 802/375-6647; FAX 802/375-2566; res: 800/348-5294. 17 rms. Early Sept-mid-Oct: S, D $55-$85; each addl $10; lower rates rest of yr. TV; cable. Pool. Complimentary continental bkfst. Ck-out 11 am. Refrigerators. Cr cds: A, MC, V.

Inns

★★★ **ARLINGTON.** VT 7A. 802/375-6532; FAX 802/375-1528; res: 800/443-9442. 19 rms, 2 story. Some rm phones. D $70-$160; each addl $20; wkly rates. TV in game rm, some rms; cable, VCR avail. Complimentary full bkfst. Restaurant (see ARLINGTON INN). Bar 4-11 pm. Ck-out 11 am, ck-in 2 pm. Meeting rms. Business servs avail. Tennis.

Downhill ski 14 mi; x-country ski 1 mi. Game rm. Some private patios. Picnic tables. Greek revival mansion built in 1848 by railroad magnate, restored to capture charm of the mid-19th century. Cr cds: A, C, D, DS, MC, V.

✔★★ **HILL FARM.** Hill Farm Rd, 4 mi N on VT 7A, then ¼ mi E on Hill Farm Rd. 802/375-2269; FAX 802/375-9918; res: 800/882-2545. 13 rms, 5 share bath, 2 story, 2 suites, 4 cabins. No rm phones. S $55-$140; D $65-$150; each addl $10-$25; suites $110; cabins $70-$90; wkly rates. Cabins closed late Oct-late May. Crib $5. TV in sitting rm; cable. Playground. Complimentary full bkfst; afternoon refreshments. Beer, wine. Ck-out 11 am, ck-in 2 pm. Gift shop. Free bus depot transportation. Downhill ski 15 mi; x-country ski 5 mi. Lawn games. Inn buildings consist of historic guesthouse (1790) and farmhouse (1830); antiques. Library, sitting rm. On 50 acres, on Battenkill River. Cr cds: A, DS, MC, V.

★★★ **WEST MOUNTAIN.** ½ mi W on VT 313 off VT 7A. 802/375-6516; FAX 802/375-6553. 18 rms, 3 story, 4 kit. MAP: S $129-$159; D $169-$209; each addl $75; each addl child $10-$45. Serv charge 15%. Crib free. TV in library; cable. Playground. Dining rm (public by res) 8-10 am, 6-8:30 pm. Bar noon-11 pm. Ck-out, ck-in noon. Free bus depot transportation. X-country ski on site. Hiking. Game rm. Some refrigerators, fireplaces. Located on Battenkill River. Totally nonsmoking. Cr cds: A, DS, MC, V.

Restaurant

★★★ **ARLINGTON INN.** (See Arlington Inn) 802/375-6532. Specialties: pan-fried Maine crab cakes, roast duckling with apple calvados sauce, fresh seafood. Hrs: 6-9 pm. Closed Mon; Dec 24, 25. Res accepted. Bar from 4:30 pm. Wine cellar. A la carte entrees: dinner $16-$23. Child's meals. View of flower gardens. Totally nonsmoking. Cr cds: A, C, D, DS, MC, V.

Barre (D-3)

(See also Montpelier, Waitsfield, Warren, Waterbury)

Settled 1788 **Pop** 9,482 **Elev** 609 ft **Area code** 802 **Zip** 05641

Information Central Vermont Chamber of Commerce, PO Box 336; 802/229-4619 or 802/229-5711.

Barre (BA-rie) has a busy, industrial air. It is home to the world's largest granite quarries and a granite-finishing plant. Many highly-skilled European stonecutters have settled here. A popular summer area, Barre serves as an overflow area for nearby ski resorts in winter.

What to See and Do

Goddard College. (400 students) Several buildings designed by students; formal gardens. Theater, concerts. 5 mi N on VT 14, then 4 mi NE on US 2, in Plainfield. For schedule phone 802/454-8311.

Granite sculptures.

Hope Cemetery. "Museum" of granite sculpture. Headstones rival finest granite carvings anywhere. Carved by craftsmen as final tribute to themselves and their families. On VT 14 at N edge of town.

Robert Burns. Figure of poet stands near city park in downtown. Erected in 1899 by admirers of the poet; regarded as one of the world's finest granite sculptures.

Youth Triumphant. Erected Armistice Day, 1924. Benches around the memorial create a whisper gallery; whispers on one side of oval can be easily heard on other side. City park.

Groton State Forest. This 25,625-acre area includes 3-mi-long Lake Groton (elevation 1,078 ft) and 6 other ponds. Miles of trails have been established to more remote sections of the forest. Nine developed recreation areas. Swimming, bathhouse; fishing; boating (rentals). Nature trail. Snowmobiling. Picnicking, concession. Four campgrounds (dump station), lean-tos. (Memorial Day-Columbus Day) Standard fees. 19 mi E on US 302, then N on VT 232, near Groton. Phone 802/584-3822.

Rock of Ages Quarry and Manufacturing Division. Skilled artisans creating monuments; picnic area. Visitor center (May-Oct, daily). Manufacturing Divison (all yr, Mon-Fri). 30-min quarry shuttle tour (June-Oct, Mon-Fri; fee). Exit 6 from I-89 or 2 mi S on VT 14, then 3½ mi SE on Main St, in Graniteville. Phone 802/476-3119. **Free.**

Annual Event

Old Time Fiddlers' Contest. Barre Auditorium. Phone 802/476-0256. Usually last wkend Sept.

Motels

✔★★ **DAYS INN.** 173 S Main St. 802/476-6678; FAX 802/476-6678, ext. 61. 42 rms, 1-2 story. S $39-$70; D $49-$85; each addl $6; MAP avail; higher rates special events. Crib free. TV; cable (premium). Indoor pool; whirlpool. Restaurant 7-10 am, 5-9 pm. Bar 4:30 pm-midnight. Ck-out 11 am. Meeting rms. Business servs avail. X-country ski 8 mi. Refrigerators. Cr cds: A, C, D, DS, MC, V.

★★★ **HOLLOW INN.** 278 S Main St. 802/479-9313; FAX 802/476-5242; res: 800/998-9444. Web www.hollowinn.com. 26 motel rms, 15 inn rms, 2 story, 9 kits. Mid-Sept-late Oct: S, D (motel) $80-$85; S, D (inn) $91-$99; each addl $10; kit. units $80-$96; family, wkly rates; lower rates rest of yr. Crib free. Pet accepted. TV; cable (premium), VCR (movies $2.50). Heated pool; whirlpools. Coffee in rms. Complimentary continental bkfst. Ck-out 11 am. Meeting rm. Business servs avail. X-country ski 8 mi. Exercise equipt; sauna. Refrigerators. Some balconies. Picnic tables, grills. Cr cds: A, C, D, DS, MC, V.

Inns

★★ **GREEN TRAILS.** (Brookfield 05036) 14 mi S on I-89, exit 5, then E ½ mi to first road on right, then 5 mi S. 802/276-3412; res: 800/243-3412. 14 rms, 6 share bath, 2-3 story. No A/C. S, D $79-$161; ski plan. Children over 10 yrs only. TV in sitting rm; VCR (free movies). Complimentary coffee. Dining rm 8-9 am. Ck-out 11 am. Airport, RR station, bus depot transportation. X-country ski on site; rentals, instruction. Canoe. Lawn games. Buildings date from 1790 & 1830. On site of famed "Floating Bridge." Cr cds: DS, MC, V.

★★ **SHIRE INN.** (Main St, Chelsea 05038) approx 15 mi S on VT 110. 802/685-3031; FAX 802/685-3871; res: 800/441-6908. E-mail mtg@shireinn.com; web shireinn.com. 6 rms, 4 with shower only, 2 story. No A/C. No rm phones. S $80-$120; D $90-$130; each addl $25; hols (2-day min). Children over 7 yrs only. Crib avail. Complimentary full bkfst. Ck-out 11 am, ck-in 3 pm. Business servs avail. X-country ski 20 mi. Federal-style house built in 1832. Totally nonsmoking. Cr cds: DS, MC, V.

Bellows Falls (H-3)

(See also Brattleboro, Springfield)

Settled 1753 **Pop** 3,313 **Elev** 299 ft **Area code** 802 **Zip** 05101 **E-mail** gfrcc@sover.net **Web** www.virtualvermont.com/bellowsfalls.html
Information Chamber of Commerce, 34 The Square, PO Box 554; 802/463-4280.

The first construction work on a US canal was started here in 1792. Later, nine locks raised barges, rafts and small steamers over the falls. In 1983, a series of fish ladders, extending 1,024 feet, was constructed to restore Atlantic salmon and American shad to their migratory route up the Connecticut River. Power from the river helps make this an industrial town; wood products, paper and wire cord are among the chief products. Ben & Jerry's Ice Cream has a nationwide distribution center here.

What to See and Do

Adams Gristmill (1831). Former mill; museum contains early electrical equipment, implements used in paper manufacturing and farming. (By appt) End of Mill St. Phone 802/463-3706.

Green Mountain Railroad. Green Mountain Flyer offers scenic train rides through 3 river valleys. (Late June-Labor Day, daily exc Mon; mid-Sept-Columbus Day, daily) Depot St (at Amtrak station), ¼ mi N. Phone 802/463-3069. ¢¢¢

Native American Petroglyphs. Carvings on rocks, unique among Native American works, by members of an early American people; as early as 1,000 A.D. On riverbanks near Vilas Bridge.

Rockingham Meetinghouse (1787). Restored in 1907; colonial architecture, antique glass windows; old burying ground with quaint epitaphs. (Mid-June-Labor Day, daily) 5 mi N on VT 103; 1 mi W of I-91 exit 6 on Old Rockingham Rd in Rockingham. Phone 802/463-3964. ¢

Annual Event

Rockingham Old Home Days. Rockingham Meetinghouse. Celebrates founding of meetinghouse. Dancing, outdoor cafes, sidewalk sales, entertainment, fireworks; pilgrimage to meetinghouse last day. 1st wkend Aug.

Bennington (H-1)

(See also Arlington, Manchester & Manchester Center, Wilmington; also see Williamstown, MA)

Settled 1761 **Pop** 16,451 **Elev** 681 ft **Area code** 802 **Zip** 05201 **E-mail** benncham@sover.net **Web** www.bennington.com
Information Information Booth, Veterans Memorial Dr; 802/447-3311.

Bennington was headquarters for Ethan Allen's Green Mountain Boys, known to New Yorkers as the "Bennington Mob," in Vermont's long struggle with New York. On August 16, 1777, this same "mob" won a decisive battle of the Revolutionary War. Bennington has three separate areas of historic significance: the Victorian and turn-of-the-century buildings downtown; the colonial houses, church and commons in Old Bennington (1 mi W); and the three covered bridges in North Bennington.

What to See and Do

Bennington Battle Monument. A 306-ft monolith commemorates a Revolutionary War victory. Elevator to observation platform (mid-Apr-Oct, daily). Gift shop. 15 Monument Circle, in Old Bennington. Phone 802/447-0550. ¢

Bennington College (1932). (450 students) Introduced progressive methods of education; became coeducational in 1969. The Visual and Performing Arts Center has special exhibits. Summer programs and performances. On VT 67A. Phone 802/442-5401.

Bennington Museum. Early Vermont and New England historical artifacts, including American glass; paintings; sculpture; silver; furniture; Bennington pottery; Grandma Moses paintings; 1925 "Wasp" luxury touring car. Schoolhouse Museum contains Moses family memorabilia; Bennington flag; other Revolutionary War collections. (Daily; closed Thanksgiving, Dec 25) Genealogical library (by appt). 1 mi W on W Main St.Phone 802/447-1571. ¢¢

Long Trail. A path for hikers leading over the Green Mts to the Canadian border, crosses VT 9 approx 5 mi E of Bennington. A section of the trail is part of the Appalachian Trail.

Old First Church (1805). Example of early colonial architecture; original box pews; Asher Benjamin steeple. Guided tours. (Memorial Day-mid-Oct, daily) Monument Ave, in Old Bennington. Phone 802/447-1223 .Adj is

   Old Burying Ground. Buried here are poet Robert Frost and those who died in the Battle of Bennington.

Park-McCullough House Museum (1865). A 35-rm Victorian mansion with period furnishings; stable with carriages; costume collection; Victorian gardens; child's playhouse. (Early May-Oct, daily) Special events held throughout the yr. N via VT 67A, in North Bennington. Phone 802/442-5441. ¢¢

Shaftsbury State Park. The 26-acre Lake Shaftsbury, a former millpond, is surrounded by 101 acres of forests and wetlands. Swimming; fishing; boating (rentals). Nature, hiking trails. Picnicking. (Memorial Day-Labor Day) Standard fees. 10 1/2 mi N on US 7A, in Shaftsbury. Phone 802/375-9978 or 802/483-2001. ¢

Valley View Horses & Tack Shop, Inc. Full-service equestrian facility offers guided trail rides and horse rentals (by the hr). Also "Pony Express" pony rides at the stables for young riders. Western tack shop. (Daily) 9 mi S on US 7 at Northwest Hill Rd in Pownal. Phone 802/823-4649 for fees.

Woodford State Park. At 2,400 ft, this 400-acre park has the highest elevation of any park in the state. Swimming; fishing; boating (no motors; rentals). Nature, hiking trails. Picnicking. Tent & trailer sites (dump station), lean-tos. (Memorial Day-Columbus Day) Standard fees. Approx 10 mi E on VT 9. Phone 802/447-7169 or 802/483-2001. ¢

Annual Events

Mayfest. Sat of Memorial Day wkend.

Antique and Classic Car Show. 2nd wkend after Labor Day.

Motels

   ✔★ **BENNINGTON MOTOR INN.** *143 W Main St (VT 9). 802/442-5479; res: 800/359-9900.* E-mail zink@together.net; web www.thisisvermont.com/pages/bennmotorinn.html. 16 rms, 1-2 story. May-Oct: S $56-$80; D $58-$80; each addl $7; suites $68-$115; family rates; lower rates rest of yr. Crib $10. TV; cable. Restaurant adj 11 am-10 pm. Ck-out 11 am. Sundries. Downhill/x-country ski 10 mi. Some refrigerators. Balconies. Cr cds: A, DS, MC, V.

🏊 ⊠ 🔥

   ★★ **BEST WESTERN NEW ENGLANDER.** *220 Northside Dr (VT Historic Rte 7A). 802/442-6311.* 58 rms, 1-2 story. Mid-June-late Oct: S $62-$92; D $67-$97; each addl $7; suites $75-$120; under 12 free; lower rates rest of yr. Crib free. TV; cable (premium). Heated pool. Playground. Complimentary continental bkfst. Complimentary coffee in rms. Ck-out 11 am. Meeting rm. Business servs avail. Downhill/x-country ski 9 mi. Some in-rm whirlpools, refrigerators, microwaves. Picnic tables. Near Bennington College. Cr cds: A, C, D, DS, MC, V.

D 🏊 ⊠ 🔥 SC

   ★ **CATAMOUNT.** *500 South St (US 7). 802/442-5977; res: 800/213-3608.* 17 rms. S, D $42-$62; each addl $5. Crib free. TV; cable. Pool. Complimentary coffee in rms. Restaurant nearby. Ck-out 11 am. Lawn games. Picnic tables, grills. Cr cds: DS, MC, V.

🏊 ⊠ 🔥

   ✔★ **FIFE 'N DRUM.** *VT 7S, 1 1/2 mi S on US 7. 802/442-4074; FAX 802/442-8471.* E-mail toberua@sover.net; web www.sover.net/~toberua/. 18 rms, 1-2 story, 4 kits. May-Oct: S $39-$69; D $42-$82; each addl $7-$8; kit. units $49-$89; wkly rates off-season; lower rates rest of yr. Crib free. Pet accepted, some restrictions; $5. TV; cable (premium). Heated pool; whirlpool. Playground. Complimentary coffee in rms. Ck-out 11 am. Sundries. Gift shop. Free bus depot transportation. Downhill ski 20 mi; x-country ski 6 mi. Lawn games. Refrigerators. Picnic tables; some grills. Cr cds: A, DS, MC, V.

🐾 🏊 ⊠ 🔥 ⛵

   ✔★ **GOVERNOR'S ROCK.** *(VT 7A, Shaftsbury 05262) 7 mi N on VT 7A & 6 mi S of Arlington on Historic 7A. 802/442-4734.* E-mail govrock1@sover.net; web www.sover.net/~govrock/. 9 rms, shower only. No rm phones. S $39-$54; D $45-$59; each addl $6; under 12 free. Closed Nov-Apr. TV; cable. Complimentary continental bkfst. Ck-out 10 am. Refrigerators. Picnic tables. Cr cds: MC, V.

⊠ 🔥 SC

   ★ **IRON KETTLE.** *(VT 7A, Shaftsbury 05262) 6 mi N on VT Historic Rte 7A. 802/442-4316.* 20 rms. Aug-Oct: S, D $55-$65; each addl $5; lower rates rest of yr. Crib $5. TV. Pool. Complimentary coffee in rms. Ck-out 11 am. Coin lndry. Picnic tables. Cr cds: A, DS, MC, V.

🏊 ⊠ 🔥

   ✔★ **KNOTTY PINE.** *130 Northside Dr (VT Historic Rte 7A). 802/442-5487; FAX 802/442-2231.* E-mail kpine@sover.net; web www.bennington.com. 21 rms, 4 kits. May-Oct: S, D $48-$66; each addl $6; kit. units $56-$66; wkly rates off-season; lower rates rest of yr. Crib free. TV; cable; VCR avail. Pool. Complimentary coffee in rms. Restaurant nearby. Ck-out 11 am. Business servs avail. X-country ski 9 mi. Lawn games. Refrigerators. Picnic tables, grills. Cr cds: A, C, D, DS, MC, V.

🏊 ⊠ 🔥

   ✔★ **SERENITY.** *(VT 7A, Shaftsbury 05262) 7 mi N on VT 7A. 802/442-6490; FAX 802/442-5493; res: 800/644-6490.* E-mail serenity@sover.net; web www.thisisvermont.com/pases/serenity.html. 8 units, shower only. S $40-$45; D $45-$55; each addl $5; under 18 free; wkly rates. Closed Nov-Apr. Crib free. Pet accepted. TV; cable. Complimentary coffee in rms. Ck-out 11 am. Picnic tables, grills. Cr cds: A, D, MC, V.

🐾 🔥 SC

   ★★ **VERMONTER MOTOR LODGE.** *VT 9, Box 2377, West Rd, 3 mi W on VT 9. 802/442-2529; FAX 802/442-0879.* 31 air-cooled units, 18 motel rms, 13 cottages. June-Oct: S $53-$65; D $60-$72; each addl $10; cottages $50-$55; under 12 free; wkly rates; lower rates Nov-May. Crib $5. Pet accepted. TV; cable. Restaurant 7:30-11 am, 5-9 pm. Ck-out 11 am. Business servs avail. X-country ski 20 mi. Lawn games. Refrigerators avail. Picnic tables, grills. Swimming pond. Cr cds: A, D, DS, MC, V.

D 🐾 🏊 ⊠ 🔥 SC

Inns

   ★★★ **FOUR CHIMNEYS.** *21 West Rd (VT 9 W), 1 mi W on VT 9. 802/447-3500; res: 800/649-3503.* 11 rms, 3 story. S $85-$125; D $110-$185; each addl $15. TV. Complimentary continental bkfst. Restaurant (see FOUR CHIMNEYS). Ck-out 11 am, ck-in 2 pm. Business servs avail. Bus depot transportation. Tennis privileges, pro. Many in-rm whirlpools, fireplaces. Restored Georgian-revival mansion; antiques. Cr cds: A, C, D, DS, MC, V.

D ⊠ 🔥

   ★★★ **SOUTH SHIRE INN.** *124 Elm St. 802/447-3839; FAX 802/442-3547.* Web www.southshire.com. 9 rms, 2 story. July-mid-Oct: S, D $105-$180; each addl $15; lower rates rest of yr. Children over 12 yrs only. TV in carriage house. Complimentary full bkfst. Ck-out 11 am, ck-in 3 pm. Business servs avail. X-country ski 8 mi. Many fireplaces; some in-rm whirlpools. Built 1850; mahogany-paneled library. Totally nonsmoking. Cr cds: A, MC, V.

Restaurants

★ ★ **BENNINGTON STATION.** *150 Depot St, corner of River & Depot Sts.* 802/447-1080. Specializes in seafood, prime rib, turkey. Hrs: 11:30 am-4 pm, 4:30-9 pm; Fri, Sat to 10 pm; Sun 4-8 pm; early-bird dinner 4:30-6 pm; Sun brunch 11 am-2:30 pm. Res accepted. Bar. Semi-a la carte: lunch $4.95-$7, dinner $9.95-$16.95. Sun brunch $9.95. Child's meals. Old RR station (1898). Totally nonsmoking. Cr cds: A, D, MC, V.

★ ★ ★ **FOUR CHIMNEYS.** *(See Four Chimneys Inn)* 802/447-3500. Continental menu. Specializes in salmon with herbs, rack of lamb. Own pastries. Hrs: 11:30 am-2 pm, 5 pm-closing; Mon to 2 pm; Sun noon-2 pm, 5-9 pm. Res accepted. Bar. Wine list. A la carte entrees: lunch $6.95-$13.50. Prix fixe: dinner $33.50. Totally nonsmoking. Cr cds: A, C, D, DS, MC, V.

★ ★ **PUBLYK HOUSE.** *Harwood Hill, 1½ mi N on VT Historic Rte 7A.* 802/442-8301. Specializes in steak, fresh seafood. Salad bar. Hrs: 5-9 pm; Fri, Sat to 10 pm; Sun 4-9 pm. Closed Thanksgiving, Dec 24, 25. Bar from 4 pm. Semi-a la carte: dinner $9.95-$18.95. Child's meals. Outdoor dining. In converted barn; fireplace. Cr cds: A, MC, V.

Brandon (E-1)

(See also Middlebury, Rutland)

Settled 1761 **Pop** 4,223 **Elev** 431 ft **Area code** 802 **Zip** 05733 **E-mail** info@brandon.org **Web** www.brandon.org

Information Brandon Area Chamber of Commerce, PO Box 267; 802/247-6401.

Brandon is a resort and residential town located at the western edge of the Green Mountains. The first US electric motor was made in nearby Forestdale by Thomas Davenport.

What to See and Do

Branbury State Park. This 96-acre park has swimming, 1,000-ft sand beach; fishing; boating, sailing. Nature, hiking trails. Picnicking, concession. Camping (dump station), lean-tos. (Memorial Day-Columbus Day) Standard fees. 3 mi NE on VT 73, then N on VT 53, E shore of Lake Dunmore. Phone 802/247-5925 or 802/483-2001.

Green Mountain National Forests (see). E on VT 73.

Mount Independence. Wooded bluff on shore of Lake Champlain, part of Revolutionary War defense complex. Fort built in 1776 across from Ft Ticonderoga to house 12,000 troops and to protect colonies from northern invasion; evacuated in 1777. Least disturbed major Revolutionary War site in the country; 4 marked trails show ruins of fort complex. (Late May-early Oct, Wed-Sun) 16 mi W via VT 73 & 73A, in the town of Orwell. Phone 802/759-2412. **Donation.**

Stephen A. Douglas Birthplace. Cottage where the "Little Giant" was born in 1813. Douglas attended Brandon Academy before moving to Illinois in 1833. (By appt) 2 Grove St on US 7. Phone 802/247-6401. **Free.**

Motel

✓★ **ADAMS.** *US 7, 1 mi S.* 802/247-6644; res: 800/759-6537. 20 cottages (1-2 rm). No A/C. Mid-May-mid-Sept: S, D $55-$70; each addl

$5; MAP avail; wkly rates; higher rates fall foliage. Closed rest of yr. TV. Pool. Restaurant 7:30-9 am, 5:30-8:30 pm. Bar from 5 pm. Ck-out 10:30 am. Miniature golf. Lawn games. Pond; trout fishing. Fireplace in some rms, lobby. Cr cds: A, DS, MC, V.

Inns

★ ★ ★ **BLUEBERRY HILL.** *(Goshen)* 6 mi E on VT 73 to Goshen-Ripton Rd, then 4 mi N, follow signs. 802/247-6735; FAX 802/247-3983; res: 800/448-0707. E-mail info@blueberryhill.com; web www.blueberryhill inn.com. 12 rms, 2 story. No A/C. No rm phones. Mid-Dec-Mar, MAP: S $165; D $110/person; under 12 half price; EP avail; lower rates rest of yr. Dining rm (public by res); sitting: 7:30 pm. Setups. Ck-out 11 am. Business servs avail. X-country ski on site. Hiking trails. Lawn games. Sauna. Library. Many antiques, handmade quilts. Built in 1813 as an inn for loggers. Natural pond, stocked. Totally nonsmoking. Cr cds: MC, V.

★ ★ **BRANDON.** *20 Park St, on village green.* 802/247-5766; FAX 802/247-5768. Web www.brandoninn.com. 35 rms, 25 A/C, 3 story. S $60-$70; D $90-$100; suites $115-$190; mid-wk rates; ski plans; MAP avail; higher rates fall foliage season. Pool. Dining rm 8-9:30 am, 11:30 am-2 pm, 6-9 pm. Bar noon-midnight. Ck-out 11 am. Business servs avail. Downhill ski 20 mi; x-country ski 8 mi. Fireplace in lobby. Built in 1786. Cr cds: A, DS, MC, V.

★ ★ ★ **LILAC.** *53 Park St.* 802/247-5463; FAX 802/247-5499; res: 800/221-0720. E-mail lilacinn@sover.net. 9 rms, 2 story. Rm phones avail. S, D $105-$175; each addl $25; wknd rates; higher rates: fall foliage, hols. TV; cable, VCR avail. Complimentary full bkfst; afternoon refreshments. Restaurant (see LILAC INN). Ck-out 11 am, ck-in 3 pm. Business servs avail. In-rm modem link. Putting green. Downhill ski 20 mi; x-country ski 5 mi. Library. Greek-revival inn built 1909. Totally nonsmoking. Cr cds: A, DS, MC, V.

★ ★ **MOFFETT HOUSE.** *69 Park St.* 802/247-3843. 6 rms, 3 with shower only, 2 story. No A/C. No rm phones. S $65-$70; D $70-$110; each addl $15; under 2 free; ski plans; hols (2-day min); higher rates fall foliage. Closed Apr. Crib free. Pet accepted. TV; cable in some rms. Complimentary full bkfst. Restaurant nearby. Ck-out 11 am, ck-in 2 pm. Downhill ski 20 mi; x-country ski 5 mi. Built in 1856. Totally nonsmoking. Cr cds: MC, V.

Restaurant

★ ★ **LILAC INN.** *(See Lilac Inn)* 802/247-5463. Continental menu. Menu changes wkly. Hrs: 5:30-9 pm; Sun brunch 10 am-2 pm. Closed Mon, Tues. Res accepted. Bar. Semi-a la carte: dinner $10.95-$21. Sun brunch $13.95. Outdoor dining. Totally nonsmoking. Cr cds: A, D, MC, V.

Brattleboro (H-2)

(See also Bellows Falls, Marlboro, Newfane, Wilmington; also see Greenfield, MA and Keene, NH)

Settled 1724 **Pop** 12,241 **Elev** 240 ft **Area code** 802 **Zip** 05301 **E-mail** bratchmb@sover.net **Web** www.sover.net/~bratchmb/

Information Brattleboro Area Chamber of Commerce, 180 Main St; 802/254-4565.

The first settlement in Vermont was at Ft Dummer (2 mi S) in 1724. Rudyard Kipling married a Brattleboro woman and lived here in the 1890s. Brattleboro is a resort area and an industrial town.

What to See and Do

Brattleboro Museum & Art Center. Exhibits change periodically and feature works by New England artists; history exhibits; permanent display of Estey organ collection; frequent performances and lecture programs. (Mid-May-Nov, daily exc Mon; closed hols) Canal & Bridge Sts. Union Railroad Station. Phone 802/257-0124. ¢

Creamery Bridge (1879). One of Vermont's best preserved covered bridges. Approx 2 mi W on VT 9.

Harlow's Sugar House. Observe working sugarhouse (Mar-mid-Apr). Maple exhibit and products. Pick your own fruit in season: strawberries, blueberries, apples; also cider in fall. (Daily; closed Dec 25, also Jan-mid-Feb) 3 mi N via I-91, exit 4; on US 5 in Putney. Phone 802/387-5852. Sugarhouse **Free.**

Living Memorial Park. Swimming pool (mid-June-Labor Day). Ball fields, lawn games; tennis courts. Skiing (T-bar; Dec-early Mar), ice-skating (mid Nov-early-Mar). Picnicking, playground. Special events during summer. Fee for some activities. 2 mi W, just off VT 9. Phone 802/254-5808.

Santa's Land. A Christmas theme village; visit with Santa, railroad ride, carousel. Petting Zoo; gardens. Concessions. (Memorial Day wknd-Dec 24, daily; closed Thanksgiving) 12 mi N on US 5 or I-91, exits 4 or 5 in Putney. Phone 802/387-5550. ¢¢¢

Annual Event

Winter Carnival. Wk-long festival includes ski races, parade, ice show, sleigh rides, road races.Feb.

Seasonal Event

Yellow Barn Music Festival. 10 mi N via I-91 or US 5 in Putney, behind the Public Library. Five-week chamber music festival. Students and well-known guest artists at Yellow Barn perform concerts. Also Special Performance Series, children's concerts. Phone 802/387-6637 or 800/639-3819. Tues, Fri, Sat eves, some Thurs, Sun, July-Aug.

Motels

★ **QUALITY INN.** VT 5N, off I-91 exit 3. 802/254-8701; FAX 802/257-4727. 92 rms, 2 story. June-Oct: S, D $89-$109; each addl $10; under 18 free; lower rates rest of yr. Crib free. Pet accepted. TV; cable. 2 pools, 1 indoor; whirlpool, sauna. Complimentary full bkfst. Restaurant 6:30-10:30 am, 5-9:30 pm. Rm serv. Bar 4:30-11:30 pm. Ck-out 11 am. Meeting rms. Business servs avail. In-rm modem link. Cr cds: A, D, DS, MC, V.

D ✇ ≋ ⤬ ⋒ SC

★ **SUPER 8.** I-91, exit 3 to VT 5, then 1/4 mi S. 802/254-8889; FAX 802/254-8323. 64 rms, 2 story. S $43.88-$47.88; D $48.88-$52.88; each addl $5-$7; under 12 free. Crib free. TV; cable, VCR avail (movies). Complimentary coffee in lobby. Restaurant adj. Ck-out 11 am. Cr cds: A, C, D, DS, JCB, MC, V.

D ⤬ ⋒ SC

Restaurants

★ **JOLLY BUTCHER'S.** (254 Marlboro Rd, West Brattleboro 05303) 3 mi W on VT 9, 2¹/₂ mi W of I-91 exit 2. 802/254-6043. Specializes in steak, fresh seafood. Salad bar. Hrs: 11:30 am-2:30 pm, 5-10 pm; Sun noon-9 pm. Closed Thanksgiving, Dec 25. Bar from 11:30 am. Semi-a la carte: lunch $3.25-$7.95, dinner $7.95-$18.95. Child's meals. Open hearth. Lobster tank. Cr cds: A, C, D, MC, V.

D SC ♥

✔★ **MARINA ON THE WATER.** 28 Spring Tree Rd (Putney Rd). 802/257-7563. Specializes in fresh seafood. Hrs: 11:30 am-11 pm; Mon, Tues from 4 pm. Closed Mon, Tues in winter. Bar. Semi-a la carte: lunch $3.50-$6.75, dinner $6.75-$16.50. Child's meals. Entertainment Sun. Patio dining. Overlooks West River. Totally nonsmoking. Cr cds: A, C, D, DS, MC, V.

Burlington (C-1)

(See also Shelburne)

Settled 1773 **Pop** 39,127 **Elev** 113 ft **Area code** 802 **Zip** 05401 **E-mail** vermont@vermont.org **Web** www.vermont.org/chamber

Information Lake Champlain Regional Chamber of Commerce, 60 Main St, Suite 100; 802/863-3489.

Burlington, on Lake Champlain, is the largest city in Vermont. It is the site of the oldest university and the oldest daily newspaper (1848) in the state, the burial place of Ethan Allen and the birthplace of philosopher John Dewey. It has a diversity of industries. The lakefront area offers a park, dock and restaurants.

What to See and Do

Battery Park. View of Lake Champlain and Adirondacks. Guns here drove back British warships in War of 1812. VT 127 & Pearl St.

Bolton Valley Ski/Summer Resort. Resort has quad, 4 double chairlifts; 1 surface lift; school, patrol, rentals; snowmaking; cafeteria, restaurants, bar; nursery. 43 runs, longest run over 3 mi; vertical drop 1,600 ft. (Nov-Apr, daily) 62 mi of cross-country trails. Also summer activities. 20 mi E on Bolton Valley Access Rd, off US 2 in Bolton; I-89 exits 10, 11. Phone 802/434-2131. ¢¢¢¢¢

Burlington Ferry. Makes 1-hr trips across Lake Champlain to Port Kent, NY (mid-May-mid-Oct, daily). Refreshments. Leaves King St Dock. Phone 802/864-9804 for schedule, other trips. (See SHELBURNE) ¢¢¢¢-¢¢¢¢¢

Discovery Museum. "Hands-on" children's museum offers participatory exhibits in the physical & natural sciences, history, art. (Daily exc Mon; closed major hols) 51 Park St, on VT 2A in Essex Junction. Phone 802/878-8687. ¢¢

★ **Ethan Allen Homestead.** Allen's preserved pioneer homestead; re-created hayfield and kitchen gardens, 1787 farmhouse. One-hr guided tours; museum exhibits; audiovisual presentation. (Early May-late Oct, Tues-Sun; also Mon in summer) 2 mi N off VT 127. Phone 802/865-4556. ¢¢

Ethan Allen Park. Part of Ethan Allen's farm. Ethan Allen Tower (Memorial Day-Labor Day, Wed-Sun afternoons and eves) with view of Adirondacks and Lake Champlain to the west, Green Mts to the east. Picnicking. 2¹/₂ mi N on North Ave to Ethan Allen Pkwy. **Free.**

Excursion Cruises. *Spirit of Ethan Allen II*, Lake Champlain's largest excursion vessel a replica of a vintage sternwheeler, offers sightseeing sunset, moonlight, brunch and dinner cruises on Lake Champlain; both decks are enclosed and heated. Res required for dinner cruises. (June-Oct) Burlington Boathouse, College St. Phone 802/862-8300.

Green Mt Audubon Nature Center. Center has 230 acres with trails through many Vermont habitats, including beaver ponds, hemlock swamp, brook, river, marsh, old farm fields, woodland and sugar orchard. Educational nature center with classes, interpretive programs and special projects. Open all yr for hiking, snowshoeing and cross-country skiing. Grounds, office (hrs vary). Fee for some activities. 20 mi SE via I-89, Richmond exit, in Huntington near the Huntington-Richmond line. Phone 802/434-3068.

Lake Champlain Chocolates. View chocolates being made through large glass windows. Gift shop. (Daily exc Sun; closed hols) 431 Pine St. Phone 802/864-1807. **Free.**

Sherman Hollow Cross-Country Skiing Center. Area has 25 mi of groomed, one-way, double-tracked cross-country ski trails; more than 3 mi of lighted trails for night skiing; warming hut; rentals; restaurant. (Dec-Apr) 10 mi SE on I-89 to exit 11, then E on US 2, then S on Huntington Rd to Sherman Hollow Rd, then W. Phone 802/434-4553. ¢¢¢

St Michael's College (1904). (1,700 students) Chapel of St Michael the Archangel (daily). Also professional summer theater at St Michael's Playhouse. N via I-89 to exit 15, then 1/4 mi NE on VT 15, in Winooski-Colchester. Phone 802/654-2000 or 802/654-2535.

University of Vermont (1791). (10,000 students) Fifth-oldest university in New England. Graduate and undergraduate programs. Waterman Building, S Prospect St. Phone 802/656-3480. On campus are the **Billings Center**, of architectural significance; **Bailey-Howe Library**, largest in the state; Georgian design **Ira Allen Chapel**, named for the founder; and the **Old Mill**, classroom building with cornerstone laid by General Lafayette in 1825.Also here is

> **Robert Hull Fleming Museum.** American, European, African, pre-Columbian and Oriental art; changing exhibits. (Limited hrs) Colchester Ave. Phone 802/656-0750. **Donation.**

Annual Event

Lake Champlain Balloon and Craft Festival. Champlain Valley Exposition. Balloon launches, rides, crafts, food and entertainment. 3 days June.

Seasonal Events

St Michael's Playhouse. McCarthy Arts Center, St Michael's College. Summer theater. Professional actors perform 4 plays (2 wks each). Phone 802/654-2535. Tues-Sat, late June-late Aug.

Vermont Mozart Festival. Features 18 chamber concerts in picturesque Vermont settings, including the Trapp Family Meadow, Lake Champlain ferries, Basin Harbor Club in Vergennes, Waitsfield Round Barn and Shelburne Farms on Lake Champlain. Phone 802/862-7352. Mid-July-early Aug.

Motels

✔★★ **COMFORT INN.** (1285 Williston Rd, S Burlington 05403) 1/2 mi E of I-89 on US 2, near Intl Airport. 802/865-3150. E-mail comfort@together.net; web www.vtcomfortinn.net. 105 rms, 3 story. May-Labor Day: S $65-$95; D $74-$109; suites $89-$119; each addl $10; under 18 free; wkend rates; ski plans; higher rates fall foliage season. Crib free. TV; cable (premium). Pool. Complimentary continental bkfst. Restaurant adj 11 am-10 pm. Ck-out noon. Meeting rms. Business servs avail. In-rm modem link. Valet serv. Downhill ski 15 mi; x-country ski 5 mi. Exercise equipt. Some refrigerators. Cr cds: A, C, D, DS, ER, JCB, MC, V.

D ⚓ ≋ 🏋 ⛷ 🛷 SC

✔★★ **DAYS INN.** (23 College Pkwy, Colchester 05446) N on I-89, exit 15. 802/655-0900; FAX 802/655-6851. 73 rms, 4 story. July-mid Oct: S $49-$69; D $59-$85; under 16 free; suites $75-$120; higher rates special events; lower rates rest of yr. Crib free. Pet accepted; $50 deposit. TV; cable (premium). Indoor pool. Complimentary continental bkfst. Ck-out 11 am. Meeting rm. Business servs avail. Sundries. X-country ski 5 mi. Refrigerators; some in-rm whirlpools. Some balconies. Cr cds: A, D, DS, MC, V.

D ✤ ⚓ ≋ 🛷 🛠 SC

★★ **ECONO LODGE.** 1076 Williston Rd (US 2). 802/863-1125; FAX 802/658-1296. Web www.econolodge.com. 177 rms, 2 story. Late

June-mid-Sept: S $70-$110; D $80-$110; each addl $5; suites $80-$109; under 18 free; higher rates fall foliage; lower rates rest of yr. Pet accepted; $5. TV; cable (premium). Pool; whirlpool. Complimentary continental bkfst. Restaurant 11:30 am-2:30 pm, 5-10 pm; Sun 10 am-2:30, 4-9 pm. Ck-out 11 am. Coin lndry. Meeting rms. Business servs avail. Free airport transportation. Exercise equipt; sauna. Nature trail. Cr cds: A, C, D, DS, ER, JCB, MC, V.

D ✤ ≋ 🏋 🛫 🛷 🛠 SC

★ **HO-HUM.** (1660 Williston Rd, S Burlington 05403) 3 mi E on US 2, 1 mi E of I-89 exit 14E. 802/863-4551. 36 rms. Early June-late Oct: S $50-$70; D $65-$80; lower rates rest of yr. Crib free. TV; cable. Pool. Restaurant opp 7 am-11 pm. Ck-out 11 am. Free airport transportation. Cr cds: A, DS, MC, V.

≋ 🛷 🛠 SC

★★★ **HOWARD JOHNSON.** (1720 Shelburne Rd, S Burlington 05403) 3 mi S on US 7. 802/860-6000; FAX 802/864-9919. Web www.hojo.com. 121 rms, 3 story. Mid-June-Labor Day: S, D $80-$120; each addl $10; under 18 free; wknd rates; ski plans; higher rates: college graduation, fall foliage; lower rates rest of yr. Crib free. TV; cable. Indoor pool; whirlpool. Restaurant 6:30-9:30 am, 4:30-9:30 pm. Bar 4 pm-1 am. Ck-out noon. Coin lndry. Meeting rms. Business servs avail. In-rm modem link. Free airport transportation. Downhill ski 20 mi; x-country ski 8 mi. Exercise equipt; sauna. Cr cds: A, C, D, DS, ER, JCB, MC, V.

D ✤ ≋ 🏋 🛷 🛠 SC

★★ **RAMADA INN.** (1117 Williston Rd, S Burlington 05403) 2 mi E on US 2, I-89 exit 14E. 802/658-0250; FAX 802/863-0376. 130 rms, 2 story. S $60-$110; D $70-$115; each addl $5; under 18 free; higher rates fall foliage season. Crib free. TV; cable, VCR avail (movies). Pool; wading pool. Coffee in rms. Restaurant 6:30 am-10 pm. Rm serv to 9:30 pm. Bar 11-1 am; Sun to 11 pm. Ck-out noon. Meeting rms. Business servs avail. In-rm modem link. Sundries. Free airport transportation. Downhill ski 20 mi; x-country ski 6 mi. Exercise equipt. Cr cds: A, C, D, DS, ER, JCB, MC, V.

D ✤ ≋ 🏋 🛷 🛠 SC

★★ **RESIDENCE INN BY MARRIOTT.** (One Hurricane Lane, Williston 05495) jct I-89 exit 12 & VT 2A. 802/878-2001; res: 800/331-3131; FAX 802/878-0025. 96 kit. suites, 2 story. S, D $89-$149; wkly rates; higher rates: graduation, fall foliage. Crib free. Pet accepted. TV; cable (premium). Indoor pool; whirlpool. Playground. Complimentary continental bkfst. Ck-out noon. Coin lndry. Meeting rms. Business servs avail. In-rm modem link. Valet serv. Free airport transportation. Downhill/x-country ski 15 mi. Exercise equipt. Many fireplaces. Balconies. Cr cds: A, D, DS, MC, V.

D ✤ ≋ 🏋 🛷 🛠 SC

★★ **WILSON INN.** (10 Kellogg Rd, Essex Jct 05452) 5 mi N on I-89 exit 16, N on VT 7 to Severance Rd to Kellogg Rd. 802/879-1515; FAX 802/878-7950; res: 800/521-2334 (exc VT). 32 kit. suites, 3 story. No elvtr. S, D $74-$94, higher rates some wkends. Crib free. TV; cable (premium), VCR avail. Heated pool. Playground. Complimentary bkfst buffet. Complimentary coffee in rms. Ck-out 11 am. Coin lndry. Meeting rm. Business servs avail. In-rm modem link. Downhill ski 15 mi; x-country ski 8 mi. Health club privileges. Game rm. Lawn games. Microwaves. Cr cds: A, D, DS, MC, V.

D ✤ ≋ 🛷 🛠 SC

Motor Hotels

★★ **HAMPTON INN & CONFERENCE CENTER.** (8 Mountain View Dr, Colchester 05446) N on I-89 exit 16. 802/655-6177; FAX 802/655-4962. Web www.hampton-inn.com. 188 rms, 5 story. Aug-Oct: S, D $105; suites $125-$135; under 18 free; lower rates rest of yr. Crib free. Pet accepted. TV; cable (premium), VCR avail. Indoor pool; whirlpool. Complimentary continental bkfst. Coffee in rms. Restaurant 11:30 am-10 pm. Ck-out 11 am. Coin lndry. Meeting rms. Business center. In-rm modem link. Free airport transportation. Downhill ski 20 mi; x-country ski 5 mi. Exercise equipt. Refrigerators avail. Cr cds: A, C, D, DS, ER, MC, V.

[D] [icons] SC

★ ★ HOLIDAY INN. (1068 Williston Rd, S Burlington 05403) 1¹/₂ mi E on US 2, at I-89 exit 14E. 802/863-6363; FAX 802/863-3061. Web www.holiday-inn.com/hotels/btvvt. 174 rms, 4 story. May-Oct: S, D $85-$139; under 19 free; lower rates rest of yr. Crib free. Pet accepted. TV; cable. 2 pools, 1 indoor; whirlpool. Coffee in rms. Restaurant 6 am-10 pm. Rm serv. Bar noon-2 am, Sat to 1 am, Sun to 10 pm; entertainment Thurs-Sat. Ck-out noon. Meeting rm. Business servs avail. In-rm modem link. Bellhops. Sundries. Free airport transportation. Exercise equipt. Cr cds: A, C, D, DS, JCB, MC, V.

[D] [icons] SC

✔ ★ HOLIDAY INN EXPRESS. (1712 Shelburne Rd, S Burlington 05403) 3 mi S on US 7. 802/860-1112; FAX 802/860-1112. 78 suites, 3 story, 6 rms. Mid-June-mid-Sept: S, D $110-$150; under 18 free; higher rates: fall foliage, special events; lower rates rest of yr. Crib free. TV; cable. Pool privileges. Complimentary continental bkfst. Complimentary coffee in rms. Restaurant adj 7 am-11 pm. Ck-out noon. Coin lndry. Meeting rms. Business servs avail. Free airport, RR station, bus depot transportation. Downhill ski 20 mi; x-country ski 12 mi. Health club privileges. Refrigerators, microwaves. Near airport. Cr cds: A, D, DS, MC, V.

[icons] SC

★ ★ SHERATON HOTEL & CONFERENCE CENTER. (870 Williston Rd, S Burlington 05403) 1¹/₂ mi E on US 2, at I-89 exit 14W, near Intl Airport. 802/865-6600; FAX 802/865-6670. Web www.ITTsheraton.com. 309 rms, 2-4 story. May-Oct: S, D $99-$155; each addl $10; suites $250; under 17 free; wkend rates; ski plan; lower rates rest of yr. Crib free. Pet accepted. TV; cable (premium), VCR avail. Indoor pool; whirlpool. Coffee in rms. Restaurant 6:30 am-2:30 pm, 5-10:30 pm. Rm serv. Bar 11 am-midnight; entertainment Fri-Sat. Ck-out noon. Meeting rms. Business center. In-rm modem link. Bellhops. Gift shop. Free airport transportation. X-country ski 6 mi. Exercise rm. Game rm. Some refrigerators. Luxury level. Cr cds: A, C, D, DS, ER, JCB, MC, V.

[D] [icons] SC

Hotels

★ ★ ★ INN AT ESSEX. (70 Essex Way, Essex Junction 05452) I-89 exit 12, then N on VT 2A to VT 15E. 802/878-1100; FAX 802/878-0063; res: 800/727-4295 (exc VT). Web www.innatessex.com. 97 rms, 3 story. S, D $129-$199; each addl $10; under 12 free. Crib free. TV; cable (premium). Restaurant 5:30-10:30 pm. Rm serv 6 am-11 pm. Ck-out 11 am. Business servs avail. In-rm modem link. Concierge. Free airport, RR station, bus depot transportation. X-country ski 15 mi. Health club privileges. Some in-rm whirlpools, fireplaces. Each rm individually decorated with 18th-century, period-style furniture. Features food preparation by the New England Culinary Institute. Cr cds: A, C, D, DS, ER, MC, V.

[D] [icons] SC

★ ★ ★ RADISSON. 60 Battery St. 802/658-6500; FAX 802/658-4659. E-mail radisson@together.net. 255 rms. S, D $110-$179; each addl $10; suites $150-$450; under 18 free; higher rates: fall foliage, special events. Crib free. TV; cable (premium). Indoor pool; whirlpool. Coffee in rms. Restaurants 6:30 am-10 pm. Bar; comedy show Fri, Sat. Ck-out noon. Meeting rms. Business servs avail. Concierge. Gift shop. Free garage parking. Free airport transportation. Exercise equipt. View of lake. Luxury level. Cr cds: A, C, D, DS, MC, V.

[D] [icons] SC

Restaurants

✔ ★ CARBUR'S. 115 St Paul St. 802/862-4106. Specializes in sandwiches. Hrs: 11:30 am-11:30 pm; wkends to 1 am. Closed Thanksgiving, Dec 25. Bar. Semi-a la carte: lunch $5-$10, dinner $7-$15. Child's meals. Outdoor dining. Rustic decor, many antiques. Cr cds: A, C, D, DS, MC, V.

✔ ★ DAILY PLANET. 15 Center St. 802/862-9647. Continental menu. Specializes in rack of lamb, potato-crusted salmon, Thai pork loin chop. Hrs: 11:30 am-11 pm; Sat, Sun brunch 11 am-3 pm; May-Sept hrs vary. Closed some major hols. Res accepted. Bar to 2 am. Semi-a la carte: lunch $4.75-$7, dinner $6.75-$14.95. European-style cafe. Frequent art exhibits. Cr cds: A, D, MC, V.

[D]

★ ★ ICE HOUSE. 171 Battery St. 802/864-1800. Specializes in fresh seafood, steak. Own desserts. Hrs: 11:30 am-10 pm; early-bird dinner 5-6 pm; Sun brunch 10:30 am-2:30 pm. Res accepted. Semi-a la carte: lunch $4.95-$9.95, dinner $12.95-$20.95. Sun brunch $5.75-$8.95. Child's meals. Parking. Covered outdoor dining. Converted icehouse. Waterfront view. Cr cds: A, D, MC, V.

[D] [icon]

★ ★ ★ PAULINE'S. 1834 Shelburne Rd (US 7). 802/862-1081. Continental menu. Specializes in fresh seafood, local products. Own baking. Hrs: 11:30 am-2:30 pm; 5-10 pm; Sun to 2:30 pm, winter to 2 pm; early-bird dinner 5-6:30 pm. Closed Dec 24 evening, 25. Res accepted. Bar. Wine list. Semi-a la carte: lunch $6.95-$8.95, dinner $14.95-$22.95. Sun brunch $5.95-$9.95. Child's meals. Parking. Outdoor dining. Cherry, oak paneling; lace curtains; some antiques. Totally nonsmoking. Cr cds: A, C, D, DS, MC, V.

[D] [heart]

★ ★ PERRY'S FISH HOUSE. (1080 Shelburne Rd, S Burlington) 2¹/₂ mi S on US 7. 802/862-1300. E-mail fishhouse@juno.com. Hrs: 5-10 pm; Fri, Sat 4:30-11 pm; Sun 4-10 pm; early-bird dinner 5-6 pm. Closed Thanksgiving, Dec 25. Res accepted. Bar 4-11 pm. Semi-a la carte: dinner $9.95-$19.95. Child's meals. Specializes in fresh seafood, prime rib. Salad bar. Parking. Outdoor dining. Nautical decor; lobster tank. Cr cds: A, C, D, MC, V.

[D]

★ ★ SIRLOIN SALOON. (1912 Shelburne Rd, Shelburne) 4 mi S on US 7. 802/985-2200. Specializes in wood-grilled steak, chicken, fresh seafood. Salad bar. Hrs: 4:30-10 pm; Fri to 11 pm; Sat 4-11 pm; Sun 4-10 pm. Closed Thanksgiving, Dec 25. Res accepted. Bar 4-10 pm; Fri, Sat to 11 pm. Semi-a la carte: dinner $9.95-$18.95. Child's meals. Parking. Greenhouse dining. Open hearth. Native American artwork, artifacts. Totally nonsmoking. Cr cds: A, D, DS, MC, V.

[D] [heart]

★ ★ SWEETWATERS. 120 Church St. 802/864-9800. E-mail swi@middlebury.net. Specializes in salads, bison burgers, mesquite-broiled fish. Own desserts. Hrs: 11:30 am-10 pm; Fri, Sat to 11 pm; Sun brunch 10:30 am-2:30 pm. Closed Thanksgiving, Dec 25. Res accepted. Bar to 2 am. Semi-a la carte: lunch $3.95-$7.95, dinner $7.95-$14.95. Sun brunch $7.95-$8.95. Child's meals. Entertainment Thurs. Outdoor dining. Converted bank building (1882). Cr cds: A, D, DS, MC, V.

Charlotte

(see Shelburne)

Chester

(see Springfield)

Dorset (G-1)

(See also Manchester & Manchester Center, Peru)

Settled 1768 **Pop** 1,918 **Elev** 962 ft **Area code** 802 **Zip** 05251

This charming village is surrounded by hills 3,000 feet high. In 1776, the Green Mountain Boys voted for Vermont's independence here. The first marble quarry in the country was opened in 1785 on nearby Mt Aeolus.

Seasonal Event

Dorset Theatre Festival. Cheney Rd. Professional theater company presents 5 productions. Phone 802/867-5777. May-Labor Day.

Inns

★ ★ **BARROWS HOUSE.** *Rte 30, 1 blk S on VT 30.* 802/867-4455; FAX 802/867-0132; res: 800/639-1620. 28 rms in 9 houses, inn, 3 kits. No rm phones. June-Oct, MAP: S $125-$190; D $185-$235; each addl $30-$50; EP avail; lower rates rest of yr. Crib free. Pet accepted. TV in some rms; VCR avail. Heated pool; sauna, poolside serv. Restaurant (see BARROWS HOUSE INN). Bar 5-11 pm. Ck-out 11 am, ck-in early afternoon. Bus depot transportation. Meeting rm. Business servs avail. Tennis. Downhill ski 12 mi; x-country ski 6 mi. Bicycles. Lawn games. Game rm. Some refrigerators, fireplaces. Private patios. Picnic tables. Library. Antiques. Gardens. Built in 1804. Cr cds: A, DS, MC, V.

★ ★ ★ **DORSET INN.** *Church and Main Sts, center of town.* 802/867-5500; FAX 802/867-5542. 31 rms, 29 A/C, 3 story. No rm phones. S, D $75-$100. Adults only. TV in lounge. Restaurant (see DORSET INN). Bar 4 pm-midnight. Ck-out 11 am, ck-in 2 pm. Antique furnishings. Established in 1796; oldest continually operating inn in Vermont. Cr cds: A, MC, V.

★ ★ ★ **INN AT WESTVIEW FARM.** *Rte 30, 1/2 mi S on VT 30.* 802/867-5715; FAX 802/867-0468. E-mail westview@vermontel.com; web www.vtweb.com/innatwestviewfarm. 10 rms, 2 story. S, D $85-$140; each addl $25; MAP avail. TV in some rms; cable. Complimentary full bkfst. Restaurant (see VILLAGE AUBERGE). Bar 5-9 pm. Ck-out 11 am, ck-in after 2 pm. 18-hole golf privileges. Downhill ski 12 mi; x-country ski 5 mi. Antiques. Cr cds: A, MC, V.

Restaurants

★ ★ ★ **BARROWS HOUSE INN.** *(See Barrows House Inn)* 802/867-4455. Regional Amer menu. Specializes in crab cakes, fresh fish, fresh vegetables. Own desserts. Hrs: 7:30-9 am, 6-9 pm; Sat, Sun 8-9:30 am, 6-9 pm. Res accepted. Bar 5-11:30 pm. Semi-a la carte: bkfst $8.50. A la carte entrees: dinner $10.95-$23.95. Child's meals. Parking. Greenhouse dining. Totally nonsmoking. Cr cds: A, DS, MC, V.

★ ★ ★ **DORSET INN.** *(See Dorset Inn)* 802/867-5500. Specialties: rack of lamb, fresh fish, crispy duck confit. Own baking. Hrs: 7:30-10 am, 11:30 am-2 pm, 5:30-9 pm. Res accepted. Bar 4 pm-midnight. Wine list. Semi-a la carte: bkfst $7.50, lunch $5.50-$12.50, dinner $7.50-$19.50. Parking. Historic building (1796); colonial decor. Cr cds: A, MC, V.

★ ★ **VILLAGE AUBERGE.** *(See Inn At Westview Farm)* 802/867-5715. E-mail westview@vermontel.com; web www.vtweb.com/innatwestviewfarm. Continental menu. Specialties: rack of lamb à l'auberge, breast of duck. Own desserts. Hrs: 6-9 pm. Closed Sun-Tues; also Apr; 1st

2 wks Nov. Bar from 5 pm. A la carte entrees: dinner $15-$25. In converted 1850 farmhouse. Cr cds: MC, V.

Fairlee (E-3)

(See also White River Junction)

Pop 883 **Elev** 436 ft **Area code** 802 **Zip** 05045
Information Town Offices, Main St, PO Box 95; 802/333-4363.

Annual Events

Vermont State Open Golf Tournament. Lake Morey Inn Country Club (see RESORT). Mid-June.

Chicken Barbecue. On the Common, Main St. Phone 802/333-4363. July 4.

Lodge

✔ ★ **SILVER MAPLE.** *S Main St (VT 5).* 802/333-4326; res: 800/666-1946. E-mail silvermaple@connriver.net. 8 lodge rms, 2 share bath; 8 cottages. No A/C. No rm phones. S $49-$75; D $56-$82; each addl $6; cottages $69-$82; kit. cottages $75-$85. Pet accepted in cottages. TV in cottages. Complimentary continental bkfst. Restaurant nearby. Ck-out 11 am. Lodge built as farmhouse in 1790s. Wrap-around porch. Cr cds: A, DS, MC, V.

Resort

★ ★ **LAKE MOREY INN COUNTRY CLUB.** *Lake Morey Rd, 1 mi W of I-91 on Lake Morey Rd.* 802/333-4311; FAX 802/333-4536; res: 800/423-1211. E-mail lakemoreyinn@msn.com; web www.lakemoreyinn.com. 144 rms, 3 story, 22 cottages. MAP, mid-May-Oct: S, D $93-$127/person; each addl $20-$55; cottages (mid-May-mid-Oct only) $80-$99; golf, ski packages; lower rates rest of yr. Crib $10. TV. Indoor/outdoor pool; whirlpool. Supervised child's activities; ages 3-12. Dining rm (public by res) 7:30-9:30 am, 6:30-9:30 pm. Bar 4-11 pm. Ck-out 11 am, ck-in 2 pm. Business servs avail. In-rm modem link. Bellhops. Two tennis courts. 18-hole golf, greens fee, pro, putting green, driving range. Beach; swimming. Canoes, rowboats. Waterskiing. Windsurfing. Downhill ski 15 mi; x-country ski on site, rentals. Snowmobile trails, sleigh rides, tobogganing. Hiking. Lawn games. Rec rm. Game rm. Exercise equipt; sauna. Refrigerators avail. Balconies. Cr cds: MC, V.

Grafton (G-2)

(See also Bellows Falls, Londonderry, Newfane)

Pop 602 **Elev** 841 ft **Area code** 802 **Zip** 05146 **E-mail** gfrcc@sover.net
Web www.virtualvermont.com/chamber/greatfallscc/

Information Great Falls Regional Chamber of Commerce, 34 The Square, PO Box 554, Bellows Falls 05101; 802/463-4280.

This picturesque New England village is a blend of houses, churches, galleries, antique shops and other small shops—all circa 1800. Founded in pre-Revolutionary times under the patronage of George III, Grafton became a thriving mill town and modest industrial center after the damming of the nearby Saxton River. When water power gave way to steam, the town began to decline. Rescued, revived and restored by the Windham Foundation, it has been returned to its former attractiveness. A creek curling through town and the peaceful air of a gentler era contribute to the charm of this village, considered a paradise for photographers.

What to See and Do

Grafton Ponds Cross-Country Skiing Center. Featuring over 16 mi of groomed trails; school, rentals; concession, warming hut. (Dec-Mar, daily; closed Dec 25) In summer, walking and fitness trails (no fee). Townshend Rd. ¢¢¢¢

The Old Tavern at Grafton (1801). Centerpiece of village. Visited by many famous guests over the yrs, including several presidents and authors; names inscribed over the desk. Furnished with antiques, colonial decor. Former barn converted to lounge; annex is restored from 2 houses; dining by res. (May-Mar, daily; closed Dec 24, 25) (See INNS) Main St & Townshend Rd. Phone 802/843-2231.

Inns

★ ★ ★ **OLD TAVERN.** *Main St. 802/843-2231; FAX 802/843-2245; res: 800/843-1801.* E-mail tavern@sover.net; web www.old-tavern.com. 65 rms, 3 story, 7 houses. S, D $125-$295; each addl $30; kit. houses $580-$750. Closed Apr. Children over 7 yrs only (exc 3 houses). TV in sitting rm; cable. Complimentary full bkfst; afternoon refreshments. Dining rm 8-10 am, noon-2 pm, 6-9 pm. Bar. Ck-out 11 am, ck-in 4 pm. Coin lndry. Meeting rms. Tennis. Downhill ski 12 mi; x-country ski on site. Game rm. Porches, balconies. Restored inn (1801); Chippendale & Windsor furnishings. Many famous authors have stayed here. Natural swimming pond. Cr cds: MC, V.

[D] [symbols] SC

★ ★ **WOODCHUCK HILL FARM.** *Middletown Rd, 2 mi W of VT 35. 802/843-2398.* E-mail mmggabri@sover.net. 10 air-cooled rms, 8 with bath, 3 story. Rm phones in suites. S, D $89-$130; each addl $20; suites $120-$185. TV in sitting rm. Complimentary full bkfst; afternoon refreshments. Ck-out 11 am, ck-in 1 pm. Tennis privileges. Sauna. Canoes. Lawn games. Library, sitting rm; antiques. 1st farmhouse in town (1790). On 200 acres; pond, gazebo. Totally nonsmoking. Cr cds: A, DS, MC, V.

[D] [symbols]

Green Mountain National Forest (J-1 - D-2)

(See also Bennington, Manchester & Manchester Center, Rutland, Warren)

(Extends northward from the Massachusetts border, along the backbone of the Green Mountains)

This 360,000-acre tract lies along the backbone of the Green Mountains, beginning at the Massachusetts line. Its high point is Mt Ellen (4,083 ft). The 260-mile Long Trail, a celebrated hiking route, extends the length of the state; about 80 miles of it are within the forest.

Well-maintained gravel roads wind through the forests of white pine, hemlock, spruce, yellow birch and sugar maple; there are many recreation areas and privately-owned resorts. Hunting and fishing are permitted in the forest under Vermont regulations. There are white-tailed deer, black bear, ruffed grouse and other game, plus brook, rainbow and brown trout.

Developed and primitive camping, swimming and picnicking are found throughout the forest, as are privately operated alpine ski areas and ski touring centers. Fees charged at some recreation sites and at developed campsites. Phone 802/747-6700.

What to See And Do

Moosalamoo Recreation Area. 20,000 acres feature trails from which all of the forest's diverse natural beauty can be viewed. Winter activities include cross-country skiing on groomed, specially marked trails; also

alpine skiing. The nation’s oldest long-distance hiking trail, the Long Trail, runs the Moosalamoo border for nearly 15 mi. Biking allowed on roads and some trails. Camping facilities abound in the area. (Daily) Within Green Mt Natl Forest. Phone 802/747-6700 or 802/247-6401.

Jeffersonville (C-2)

(See also Stowe)

Pop 462 **Elev** 459 ft **Area code** 802 **Zip** 05464

What to See and Do

Smugglers' Notch. Resort has 5 double chairlifts, 3 surface lifts; school, rentals; snowmaking; concession area, cafeteria, restaurants; nursery, lodge (see RESORT). 60 runs, longest run over 3 mi; vertical drop 2,610 ft. (Thanksgiving-mid-Apr, daily) More than 25 mi of cross-country trails (Dec-Apr, daily; rentals). Ice skating. Summer activities include: 10 swimming pools, 3 water slides; tennis, miniature golf, driving range. 5 mi S on VT 108. Phone 802/644-8851 or 800/451-8752. ¢¢¢¢¢

Motel

✔★ **HIGHLANDER.** *Rte 108, 1½ mi S on VT 108. 802/644-2725; res: 800/367-6471.* 15 rms. No A/C. Late Dec-Apr & late June-Oct: S $58-$64; D $64-$72; each addl $5; dorm rates; higher rates some hols; lower rates rest of yr. Crib free. Pet accepted. TV; cable. Pool; sauna. Playground. Restaurant 7:30-9 am. Ck-out 11 am. Downhill/x-country ski 3 mi. Lawn games. Rec rm. Refrigerators avail. Picnic tables, grill. View of mountains. Cr cds: MC, V.

[symbols]

Inns

✔★ ★ **MANNSVIEW INN.** *NY 108 S, at Smugglers N. 802/644-8321; res: 888/937-6266; FAX 802/644-2006.* Web www.mannsview.com. 6 rms, 4 share bath, 2 with shower only, 3 story. No A/C. No rm phones. S $40-$65; D $65-$85; each addl $10-$15; ski plans; hols (2-day min); higher rates fall foliage. Children over 7 yrs only. Premium cable TV in common rm. Complimentary full bkfst. Restaurant nearby. Ck-out 11 am, ck-in 2 pm. Downhill/x-country ski 3 mi. Rec rm. View of mountains. Built in 1865; Victorian-style farmhouse. Totally nonsmoking. Cr cds: A, MC, V.

[symbols] SC

★ ★ **SINCLAIR INN.** *(389 VT 15, Jericho 05465) I-89 N, off exit 12, N 5 mi to Essex Junction on Vt 2A, E on Vt 15 10.5 mi. 802/899-2234; res: 800/433-4658.* Web www.virtualcities.com/ons/vt/j/vtj96010.htm. 6 rms, 4 with shower only, 3 story. No rm phones. Apr-Nov: S, D $80-$115; each addl $10; ski plans; wknds, hols, fall foliage (2-day min); higher rates special events; lower rates rest of yr. Children over 12 yrs only. Complimentary full bkfst. Ck-out 11 am, ck-in 3 pm. Downhill ski 18 mi; x-country ski 5 mi. Exercise equipt. Lawn games. Grills. Built in 1890; restored Queen Ann Victorian inn. Totally nonsmoking. Cr cds: DS, MC, V.

[D] [symbols]

★ **SMUGGLERS' NOTCH INN.** *Church St. 802/644-2412; res: 800/845-3101.* E-mail smuginn@pwshift.com; web www.smugglers-notch-inn.com. 11 rms, 2 story. No A/C. S $50; D $60-$125; each addl $10-$15; MAP avail. TV in sitting rm; cable. Pool; whirlpool. Complimentary full bkfst. Dining rm 5-9 pm. Ck-out 11 am, ck-in 2 pm. Downhill ski 4 mi; x-country ski 2 mi. Picnic tables. Old country inn (1789) with large porch. Library; many handmade quilts; antiques. Cr cds: A, MC, V.

[symbols]

★ **STERLING RIDGE.** *RR 2, Box 5780. 802/644-8265; res: 800/347-8266.* Web www.pbpub.com/smugglers/logcabins.html. 13 rms, 4 share bath, 5 kit. cabins. No A/C. No rm phones. Dec-mid-Apr, June-Labor

Day: S $50; D $62-$72; kit. cabins $90-$125; under 2 free; ski plans; hols (2-day min); higher rates special events; lower rates rest of yr. Crib free. TV in cabins; cable (premium); VCR avail. Complimentary full bkfst. Ck-out 11 am, ck-in 3 pm. Downhill ski 3 mi; x-country ski on site. Heated pool. Microwave, fireplace in cabins. Picnic tables, grills. On mountain. Totally nonsmoking. Cr cds: MC, V.

Resort

★ ★ ★ **SMUGGLERS' NOTCH RESORT.** *4323 VT 108S, 5 mi S on VT 108.* 802/644-8851; FAX 802/644-1230; res: 800/451-8752. E-mail smuggs@smuggs.com; web www.smuggs.com/. 525 rms, 113 A/C, 1-3 story, 400 kits. Mid-Dec-Mar: S $99-$225; D $109-$249; kit. units $109-$159; 1-5 bedrm apts avail; under 7 free; wkly rates; tennis, ski, golf plans; higher rates hols; lower rates rest of yr. Crib $20. TV; cable (premium), VCR avail (movies). Heated pool; whirlpool, lifeguard. Playgrounds. Supervised child's activities (summer, winter); ages 6 wks-17. Dining rm 7:30 am-10 pm. Bar 11-1 am; entertainment. Ck-out 10 am, 11 am in summer; ck-in 5 pm. Free lndry facilities. Convention facilities. Business servs avail. Grocery, sport shop. Airport, RR station, bus depot transportation. 12 tennis courts, 2 indoor. Downhill/x-country ski on site. Outdoor ice skating, sleighing. Water slides. Miniature golf; driving range. Lawn games. Bicycles. Hiking. Soc dir; entertainment, movies. Teen rec rm. Exercise equipt; sauna. Massage. Washers in most rms; some fireplaces; microwaves avail. Some balconies. Cr cds: A, C, D, MC, V.

Restaurant

★ ★ ★ **WINDRIDGE INN.** *Main St, center of village.* 802/644-5556. Specialties: rack of lamb, red beans & wild rice, duck with dijon sauce. French menu. Hrs: 5-9 pm. Closed Mon; Dec 25. Res accepted. Bar from 5 pm. A la carte entrees: dinner $10.95-$29.95. Elegant, formal dining in early American atmosphere. Totally nonsmoking. Cr cds: MC, V.

Killington (F-2)

(See also Plymouth, Rutland, Woodstock)

Pop 50 (est) **Elev** 1,229 ft **Area code** 802 **Zip** 05751

What to See and Do

Gifford Woods State Park. This 114-acre park has fishing at nearby pond; boat access to Kent Pond. Foot trails (Appalachian Trail passes through park). Virgin forest with picnic facilities. Tent & trailer sites (dump station), lean-tos. (Memorial Day-Columbus Day) Standard fees. On VT 100, 1 mi N of jct US 4. Phone 802/775-5354 or 802/886-2434 (off season).

Skiing. Killington Resort. Comprises 1,200 acres with 7 mountains (highest elev 4,241 ft). 3 gondolas, 6 high-speed quad, 6 quad, 6 triple, 4 double chairlifts, 8 surface lifts; patrol, school, rentals; snowmaking; mountaintop restaurant (with observation decks), 6 cafeterias, bars; children’s center, nursery; lodging. 212 runs; longest run 10 mi, vertical drop 3,150 ft. Snowboarding; snow tubing. (Oct-June, daily) 5 mi SW of jct US 4 & VT 100, N on Killington Rd. Phone 800/621-6867 or 802/422-3261 (ski reports). ¢¢¢¢¢

Summer activities at the resort include a tennis school (Memorial Day-Sept); 18-hole golf; mountain biking (rentals), in-line skating/skateboarding park; gondola rides to view foliage; 2 water slides (July 4-Sept)Also

Pico Alpine Slide and Scenic Chairlift. Chairlift to top of mountain slope; control speed of own sled on the way down. Sports center and restaurant below. (Late May-mid-Oct) Phone 802/621-6867. ¢¢

Motels

★ ★ ★ **CORTINA INN.** *On US 4, 4 mi W of jct VT 100.* 802/773-3333; FAX 802/775-6948; res: 800/451-6108. E-mail cortina1@aol.com; web www.cortinainn.com. 91 rms, 6 suites. S, D $99-$169; each addl $19-$35; suites $179-$259; under 14 free (exc Dec 25, Presidents wk); wkly, wkend rates; ski, golf, tennis plans; higher rates some hols. Crib $5. TV; cable, VCR avail. Indoor pool; whirlpool. Playground. Complimentary full bkfst. Restaurant (see ZOLA'S GRILLE). Rm serv. Bar 4 pm-1 am; entertainment. Ck-out 11 am. Meeting rms. Business servs avail. In-rm modem link. Bellhops. Gift shop. Free airport, bus depot transportation. Tennis, pro. Downhill ski 2 mi; x-country ski 4 mi. Ice skating, sleigh rides, snowmobiling. Exercise equipt; sauna. Massage. Hiking trail. Rec rm. Lawn games. Bicycle rentals. Some bathrm phones, refrigerators, wet bars, fireplaces. Private patios, balconies. Picnic tables, grills. Art gallery. Cr cds: A, C, D, DS, ER, JCB, MC, V.

★ ★ **GREY BONNET INN.** *On VT 100, 1/2 mi N of jct US 4.* 802/775-2537; FAX 802/775-3371; res: 800/342-2086. 40 rms, 3 story. No elvtr. MAP, Dec-Mar: S, D $48-$75; each addl $30; EP avail; family, wkly rates; golf plans; lower rates mid-June-mid-Sept. Closed Apr-May, late-Oct-late Nov. Crib $3. TV. 2 pools, 1 indoor; whirlpool. Playground. Restaurant 7:30-9:30 am, 6-9 pm. Bar. Ck-out 11 am. Meeting rm. Tennis. Downhill ski 2 mi; x-country ski adj. Exercise equipt; sauna. Game rm. Rec rm. Lawn games. Balconies. Cr cds: A, DS, MC, V.

✔ ★ **KILLINGTON PICO MOTOR INN.** *HC 34, on US 4.* 802/773-4088; FAX 802/775-9705; res: 800/548-4713. Web www.killingtonpico.com. 29 rms. Mid-Dec-mid-Mar: S $59-$94; D $65-$104; each addl $10-$15; wkly rates; higher rates hol wks; lower rates mid-Apr-Aug. Crib avail. TV; cable. Pool; whirlpool. Complimentary full bkfst (winter), continental bkfst (summer). Dining rm mid-June-Columbus Day 7-9:30 am. Bar. Ck-out 11 am. Business servs avail. Downhill/x-country ski 1 mi. Game rm. Lawn games. Refrigerators. Cr cds: A, DS, MC, V.

★ ★ **SHERBURNE-KILLINGTON.** *Box HCR 34, on US 4, 2 blks W of jct VT 100.* 802/773-9535; res: 800/366-0493. 20 rms. Oct-Apr: S, D $55-$115; each addl $16; under 12 free; ski plan; higher rates winter hol wks; lower rates rest of yr. Crib free. TV; cable, VCR (free movies). Heated pool. Playground. Ck-out 11 am. Downhill/x-country ski 1/2 mi. Lawn games. Refrigerators. Picnic tables, grills. View of mountains. Cr cds: A, DS, MC, V.

✔ ★ ★ **VAL ROC.** *On US 4, 1/2 mi W of jct VT 100S.* 802/422-3881; res: 800/238-8762. Web www.killingtoninfo.com/valrock. 24 rms, 16 A/C, 1-2 story, 2 kits. Mid-Dec-mid-Apr: D $60-$94; each addl $12-$14; kit. units $74-$98; under 12 free; family, wkly rates; higher rates wk of Dec 25; lower rates rest of yr. Crib free. Pet accepted. TV; cable (premium), VCR avail. Heated pool; whirlpool. Complimentary continental bkfst. Complimentary coffee in rms. Ck-out 11 am. Tennis. Downhill ski 1/4 mi; x-country ski 3 mi. Game rm. Lawn games. Refrigerators. Some balconies. Picnic tables. Cr cds: A, C, D, MC, V.

Lodge

✔ ★ **CASCADES LODGE.** *RR 1, Box 2848.* 802/422-3731; FAX 802/422-3351; res: 800/345-0113. E-mail cascades@vermontel.com; web www.genghis.com/cascades/lodge/htm. 46 rms, 3 story. No A/C. No elvtr. S $55-$141; D $59-$188; each addl $5-$35; suites $118-$267; family rates; golf, package plans; higher rates: winter hols, wkends. Crib free. TV; cable, VCR avail (movies $2.95). Indoor pool; whirlpool. Complimentary full bkfst. Dining rm (see CASCADES LODGE). Rm serv. Bar from noon; entertainment. Ck-out 11 am. Meeting rms. Business servs avail. In-rm modem link. Downhill/x-country ski on site. Exercise equipt; sauna. Game rm. Lawn games. Balconies. Cr cds: A, DS, MC, V.

Inns

★ ★ ★ **RED CLOVER.** *(RR 2, Box 7450, Mendon 05701) W on US 4 to Woodward Rd.* 802/775-2290; res: 800/752-0571. E-mail red-clover@vermontel.com. 14 rms, 2 story. MAP, Dec-Mar: S, D $140-$300; each addl $55; higher rates hols; lower rates rest of yr. Children over 8 yrs only. TV; VCR in parlor (movies). Pool. Complimentary coffee. Dining rm (see RED CLOVER). Ck-out 11 am, ck-in 2 pm. Downhill/x-country ski 6 mi. Antiques. Some in-rm whirlpools. Library/sitting rm. Built 1840; former general's residence. Totally nonsmoking. Cr cds: A, D, MC, V.

★ ★ **VERMONT.** *US 4, 4 mi W of jct VT 100.* 802/775-0708; res: 800/541-7795. Web www.vermontinn.com. 18 rms, 2 story. Some A/C. Mid-Dec-mid-Apr, MAP: S, D $90-$205; each addl $30-$40; EP avail; family, wkly plans; ski plan; higher rates hols; lower rates Memorial Day-mid-Dec. Children over 6 yrs only. TV in sitting rm. Pool; whirlpool. Restaurant (see VERMONT INN). Bar from 5 pm. Ck-out 11 am, ck-in 2 pm. Exercise equipt; sauna. Tennis. Downhill ski 2 mi; x-country ski 6 mi. Game rm. Rec rm. Lawn games. Some fireplaces. Picnic tables. Built 1840. Totally nonsmoking. Cr cds: A, MC, V.

Resorts

★ ★ ★ **INN OF THE SIX MOUNTAINS.** *Killinton Rd, 4 mi S of jct US 4, VT 100.* 802/422-4302; FAX 802/422-4321; res: 800/228-4676 (exc VT). E-mail iosm@vermontel.com. 103 air-cooled rms, 3 story. Jan-mid-Mar: S, D $139-$179; suites $179-$239; under 12 free; MAP avail; wkly, wkend rates; higher rates hols; lower rates rest of yr. TV; cable (premium). Indoor/outdoor pool; whirlpool. Complimentary full bkfst (winter). Coffee in rms. Dining rm (public by res) 7-10 am, 6-9 pm. Bar 4 pm-closing. Ck-out noon, ck-in 4 pm. Grocery 1/4 mi. Package store 4 mi. Convention facilities. Business servs avail. In-rm modem link. Gift shop. Ski area transportation. Tennis. Downhill ski 1/2 mi; x-country ski 3 mi. Hiking. Game rm. Exercise equipt; sauna. Massage. Refrigerators. Balconies. Fireplace in lobby. 18-hole golf adj. Cr cds: A, C, D, DS, MC, V.

★ ★ **SUMMIT LODGE.** *PO Box 119M, 2 mi S of jct US 4 & VT 100, N on Killington Ski Area Access Rd.* 802/422-3535; FAX 802/422-3536; res: 800/635-6343. E-mail summitlodge@killingtoninfo.com; web www.killingtoninfo.com/summit. 45 rms, 2-33 story. No A/C. No elvtr. S $63-$128; D $88-$146; each addl $15; family rates; MAP avail; package plans; higher rates some hols. Serv charge 15% (MAP). Crib free. TV; VCR avail (movies $6). 2 pools, 1 heated; whirlpool, poolside serv. Playground. Dining rm 7:30-9:30 am, 6-9 pm; summer 8-10 am, 6-9 pm. Bar from noon; winter from 4 pm. Ck-out 11 am. Business servs avail. Grocery, package store 2 mi. Tennis, pro. Airport transportation. Downhill ski 1 mi; x-country ski 1 mi. Ice-skating. Lawn games. Sauna, steam rm. Massage. Entertainment. Game rm. Rec rm. Racquetball courts. Fireplaces. Balconies. Library. Cr cds: A, C, D, MC, V.

Restaurants

✔★ ★ **CASCADES LODGE.** *(See Cascades Lodge)* 802/422-3731. E-mail cascade@vermontel.com; web www.cascadeslodge.com. Continental menu. Specialties: roast duck with sauce du jour, Caribbean-style crab cakes, paella. Own desserts. Hrs: 7-10 am, 5-9 pm. Closed May. Res accepted (dinner). No A/C. Bar. Semi-a la carte: bkfst $2.95-$6.95, dinner $10.95-$22.95. Child's meals. Greenhouse-style decor; large picture window offers views of mountains. Totally nonsmoking. Cr cds: A, DS, JCB, MC, V.

★ ★ ★ ★ **HEMINGWAY'S.** *On US 4, between jct US 100N & US 100S.* 802/422-3886. E-mail hemwy@sover.net; web www.hemingwayrestaurant.com. Antique mixes with modern in these three dining rooms in a renovated 19th-century house. The less formal garden room has a fireplace. European, Amer menu. Specializes in Vermont lamb and game birds, lobster ravioli, pan-roasted striped bass. Own pasta, pastries. Hrs: from 6 pm. Closed most Mon & Tues; also mid-Apr-mid-May. Res accepted. Wine cellar. Prix fixe: dinner $50. Tasting menu: dinner $72. Chef-owned. Cr cds: A, C, D, MC, V.

★ ★ ★ **RED CLOVER.** *(See Red Clover Inn)* 802/775-2290. E-mail redclover@vermontel.com. Specializes in fresh Vermont game, rack of lamb, garlic basil millefiore pasta. Own baking. Menu changes daily. Hrs: 6-9 pm. Closed Sun (inn guests only); also day after Easter-day after Memorial Day. Res accepted. Bar. Wine cellar. Semi-a la carte: dinner $17-$26. Country decor. Totally nonsmoking. Cr cds: DS, MC, V.

★ ★ **VERMONT INN.** *(See Vermont Inn)* 802/775-0708. Web www.vermontinn.com. Specializes in fresh seafood, veal, lamb. Hrs: 5:30-9:30 pm. Closed mid-Apr-Memorial Day. Res accepted. Bar from 5 pm. Semi-a la carte: dinner $12.95-$20.95. Child's meals. Parking. Fireside dining. View of Green Mts. Totally nonsmoking. Cr cds: A, MC, V.

★ ★ **ZOLA'S GRILLE.** *(See Cortina Inn Motel)* 802/773-3331. Specializes in fresh seafood. Hrs: 7-10 am, 5:30-9:30 pm; Sun brunch 10:45 am-1:30 pm. Res accepted; required hols. Bar. Bkfst buffet $9. Semi-a la carte: dinner $9.95-$21.95. Sun brunch $13.95. Child's meals. Parking. Totally nonsmoking. Cr cds: DS, MC, V.

Londonderry (G-2)

(See also Grafton, Peru, Stratton Mountain, Weston)

Founded 1770 **Pop** 1,506 **Elev** 1,151 ft **Area code** 802 **Zip** 05148

Motels

✔★ **BLUE GENTIAN.** *Magic Mountain Rd.* 802/824-5908; FAX 802/824-3531; res: 800/456-2405. E-mail kenalberti@csi.com. 13 rms, 3 with shower only, 2 story. No A/C. No rm phones. S $40-$65; D $50-$90; each addl $20; under 5 free; ski plans; higher rates: fall foliage, ski season; lower rates rest of yr. Crib free. TV; cable. Pool. Complimentary full bkfst. Complimentary coffee in lobby. Ck-out 11 am. Business servs avail. Downhill/x-country ski 1 mi. Rec rm. Picnic tables. Totally nonsmoking. Cr cds: MC, V.

★ ★ **DOSTAL'S.** *Magic Mountain Rd, 3 mi SE, off VT 11 on Magic Mt access road.* 802/824-6700; FAX 802/824-6701; res: 800/255-5373. 50 rms, 2 story. A/C in dining rm, main bldg. Mid-Dec-Mar, MAP: S $76-$99; D $57-$79/person; each addl $34-$44; under 6 free in summer & fall; EP avail; ski plan; some wkend rates; lower rates mid-June-Oct. Closed rest of yr. Serv charge 15%. Crib $12. TV; cable. 2 pools, 1 indoor; 2 whirlpools. Restaurant 8-10 am, 6:30-8:30 pm. Bar from 4 pm. Ck-out 11 am. Tennis. Downhill ski 8 mi; x-country ski 1 mi. Game rm. Cr cds: A, DS, MC, V.

✔★ ★ **SNOWDON.** *VT 11, 1 1/2 mi E on VT 11.* 802/824-6047; res: 800/419-7600. 12 air-cooled rms, 1-2 story. Mid-Dec-mid-Apr: S $40-$45; D $50-$75; each addl $15; family, wkly rates; ski plan; higher rates fall foliage season; lower rates rest of yr. TV; cable (premium). Restaurant 8-9 am. Ck-out 11 am. Business servs avail. Golf privileges. X-country ski 1 mi. Balconies. Picnic tables, grills. No cr cds accepted.

★ ★ **SWISS INN AND RESTAURANT.** *VT 11, 1¹/₂ mi W on VT 11. 802/824-3442; FAX 802/824-3442; res: 800/847-9477.* E-mail swissinn @sover.net; web www.swissinn.com. 19 rms, 2 story. June-Oct, Dec-Mar: S, D $50-$90; each addl $10; lower rates rest or yr. Crib free. TV; cable. Pool. Complimentary full bkfst. Restaurant 5:30-8:30 pm. Bar. Ck-out 11 am. Meeting rms. Tennis. Downhill ski 6 mi; x-country ski 1¹/₂ mi. Lawn games. Cr cds: MC, V.

Inns

★ ★ **HIGHLAND HOUSE.** *1¹/₂ mi N on VT 100. 802/824-3019; FAX 802/824-3657.* 17 rms, 15 with bath, 1-2 story, 4 suites. No A/C. No rm phones. S, D $65-$95; each addl $15; suites $93-$103; wkly rates; ski plans. Closed 3 wks Apr & 1 wk Nov. Children over 5 yrs only. TV in sitting rm; cable. Heated pool. Complimentary continental bkfst. Dining rm (public by res), 4 dinner sittings: 6, 6:30, 8 & 8:30 pm. Ck-out 11 am, ck-in 2 pm. Tennis. Downhill ski 15 mi; x-country ski on site, rentals avail. Game rm. Lawn games. In historic building (1842); antiques. Situated on 32 wooded acres. Cr cds: A, MC, V.

★ ★ **LONDONDERRY.** *(VT 100, South Londonderry 05155) 3 mi S on VT 100. 802/824-5226; FAX 802/824-3146.* E-mail londinn @sover.net; web bestinns.net/usa/vt/london.html. 25 air-cooled rms, 20 baths, some share bath, 3 story. No rm phones. Mid-Dec-Mar: S $49-$69; D $59-$79; each addl $13-$19; higher rates: hols, fall foliage, winter wkends, Dec 25-31; lower rates rest of yr. Crib $5. TV in sitting rm; cable. Pool. Complimentary continental bkfst. Dining rm 5:30-8:30 pm; wkends/ hols in-season. Ck-out 11 am, ck-in 2 pm. Business servs avail. Downhill ski 10 mi; x-country ski 4 mi. Lawn games. Former farmhouse (1826). No cr cds accepted.

Ludlow (G-2)

(See also Plymouth, Springfield, Weston)

Chartered 1761 **Pop** 2,302 **Elev** 1,067 ft **Area code** 802 **Zip** 05149
E-mail heartout@ludl.tds.net **Web** www.virtualvermont.com/chamber /ludlow

Information Ludlow Area Chamber of Commerce, Okemo Market Pl, PO Box 333; 802/228-5830.

What to See and Do

Crowley Cheese Factory (1882). Oldest cheese factory in the US; still makes cheese by hand as in the 19th century. Display of tools used in early cheese factories and in home cheesemaking. Watch process and sample product. (Mon-Fri; phone ahead for best time to view cheesemaking; closed major hols) A gift shop (daily; closed some major hols) is located 2 mi E of factory on VT 103. 5 mi W via VT 103 in Healdville. Phone 802/259-2340. **Free.**

Green Mountain Sugar House. Working maple sugar producer on shore of Lake Pauline. Shop offers syrup, candies, crafts and gifts. (Daily) 4 mi N on VT 100N. Phone 802/228-7151. **Free.**

Okemo Mt Ski Area. (See OKEMO STATE FOREST)

Inns

★ ★ ★ **ANDRIE ROSE.** *13 Pleasant St. 802/228-4846; FAX 802/228-7910; res: 800/223-4846.* E-mail andrierose@aol.com; web members.aol.com/andrierose. 23 rms, 6 A/C, 2 story, 9 suites. Some rm phones. Sept-Mar: S, D $110-$160; suites $215-$290; package plans; lower rates rest of yr. TV; cable (premium), VCR avail (free movies). Complimentary full bkfst. Ck-out 11 am, ck-in 3 pm. Business servs avail. Gift shop. Downhill ski ¹/₂ mi; x-country ski 1 mi. Some in-rm whirlpools,

refrigerators; fireplace in suites. Picnic tables. Grills. Elegant country inn (1829); furnished with antiques. Totally nonsmoking. Cr cds: A, DS, MC, V.

★ ★ **COMBES.** *RFD 1, Box 275, 5 mi N via VT 103, VT 100, follow signs. 802/228-8799.* E-mail billcfi@aol.com; web www.combesfa milyinn.com. 11 units, 2 story. No rm phones. Mid-Sept-mid-Apr: S $58-$69; D $82-$106; each addl $10-$21; MAP avail; family, wkly rates; golf, ski, theater package plans; higher rates last wk of Dec 25, hols; lower rates mid-May-mid-Sept. Closed rest of yr. Pet accepted. Dining rm (public by res) 8-9:30 am, 7 pm sitting. Rm serv 8-9:30 am. Ck-out 11 am, ck-in 2 pm. Bus depot transportation. Downhill ski 4 mi; x-country ski 3 mi. Game rm. Rec rm. Lawn games. Picnic tables, grills. Restored farmhouse (1891) on 50 acres; near Lake Rescue. Cr cds: A, DS, MC, V.

✔ ★ **ECHO LAKE.** *VT 100, 5 mi N on VT 100. 802/228-8602; FAX 802/228-3075; res: 800/356-6844.* Web www.vermontlodging.com .echolake.htm. 24 air-cooled rms, 17 baths, some share bath, 4 suites, 7 condos, 3 story. July-mid-Oct: S, D $119-$155; suites $150-$170; kit. units $100-$170 (2-day min); MAP avail; family, wkly rates; ski plan; wkends fall foliage season (2-day min); lower rates rest of yr. Serv charge 15%. Closed Apr. TV in sitting rm; cable. Pool; wading pool, whirlpool, poolside serv. Steam rm. Dining rm 8-10 am, 6-9 pm; outdoor porch dining (dinner). Rm serv to 9:30 am. Bar from 4 pm. Ck-out 11 am, ck-in 2 pm. Business servs avail. Bus depot transportation. Lighted tennis. Downhill ski 6 mi; x-country ski 5 mi. Lawn games. Whirlpool in suites. Picnic tables. Private dock, canoes. 1840 Victorian. Cr cds: A, DS, MC, V.

★ ★ **GOLDEN STAGE.** *(Proctorsville 05153) 3 mi S on VT 103 to VT 131. 802/226-7744; FAX 802/226-7882; res: 800/253-8226.* E-mail gldstgin@ludl.tds.net; web www.virtualvermont.com. 9 rms, 2 share bath. No A/C. July-late Oct, mid-Dec-mid-Mar: S, D $90-$105; each addl $10; MAP avail; wkly rates; lower rates rest of yr. Pool. Dining rm (public by res), 1 sitting 7 pm. Bar. Ck-out 11 am. Free bus depot transportation. Downhill/x-country ski 3 mi. Lawn games. Totally nonsmoking. Cr cds: DS, MC, V.

★ ★ ★ **GOVERNOR'S.** *86 Main St. 802/228-8830; res: 800/468-3766.* Web www.innbook.com. Built as the summer residence of former Vermont governor William Wallace Stickney, this house is quintessentially late Victorian. Each room is individually decorated with antiques. 9 rms, 3 story. No rm phones. MAP: S $180-$220; D $190-$230; B & B rates avail; higher rates: late Dec, fall foliage season. Adults only. Complimentary afternoon refreshments. Dining rm 8-9:30 am sitting, 7 pm sitting. Ck-out 11 am, ck-in flexible. Bus depot transportation. Downhill ski 1 mi; x-country ski ¹/₂ mi. Library, sitting rm. Totally nonsmoking. Cr cds: MC, V.

Restaurants

✔ ★ **HARRY'S CAFE.** *On VT 103, 3 mi N of jct VT 100. 802/259-2996.* Varied menu. Specializes in Thai cuisine. Hrs: 5-10 pm. Closed Mon, Tues; Easter, Thanksgiving, Dec 24, 25; also last wk Apr-1st wk May. Res accepted. No A/C. Bar. Semi-a la carte: dinner $10.95-$16.95. Child's meals. Casual ambience. Totally nonsmoking. Cr cds: A, C, D, MC, V.

★ ★ **MICHAEL'S SEAFOOD & STEAK TAVERN.** *S Main St (VT 103). 802/228-5622.* Specializes in steak, seafood. Salad bar. Hrs: 5-9:30 pm; Fri, Sat to 10 pm. Bar from 5 pm. Semi-a la carte: dinner $10-$18.95. Child's meals. Lobster pool. Early Amer decor. Braille menu. Cr cds: A, D, DS, MC, V.

★ ★ **NIKKI'S.** *44 Pond St (VT 103). 802/228-7797.* Specializes in steak au poivre, fresh seafood, black Angus beef. Hrs: 5-9:30 pm; Fri, Sat to 10 pm; summer hrs from 5:30 pm. Closed Thanksgiving. Bar. Wine cellar. A la carte entrees: dinner $9.95-$21.95. Child's meals. Cathedral ceiling. Totally nonsmoking. Cr cds: A, D, MC, V.

Lyndonville (C-4)

(See also St Johnsbury)

Settled 1781 **Pop** 1,255 **Elev** 720 ft **Area code** 802 **Zip** 05851

Home of small industries and trading center for the surrounding dairy and stock-raising farms, Lyndonville lies in the valley of the Passumpsic River. Five covered bridges, the earliest dating from 1795, are located within the town limits.

What to See and Do

Burke Mt Ski Area. Area has 2 chairlifts, 1 Pomalift, J-bar; school, rentals; snowmaking. 2 cafeterias, 2 bars; nursery. 30 runs, longest run approx 2.5 mi; vertical drop 2,000 ft. Over 57 mi of cross-country trails. (Mid-Nov-mid-Apr, daily) 1 mi N on US 5, then 6 mi NE on VT 114, in Darling State Park. Phone 802/626-3305or 800/541-5480. ¢¢¢¢¢

Lake Willoughby. Beaches, water sports; fishing. Hiking trails to summit of Mt Pisgah at 2,741 ft. 18 mi N on VT 5A.

Motel

★ **DAYS INN.** *I-91 exit 23.* 802/626-9316; FAX 802/626-1023. 40 rms, 2 story. S $42-$52; D $45-$65; each addl $5; under 12 free. TV; cable (premium). Complimentary continental bkfst. Restaurant nearby. Ck-out 11 am. Downhill/x-country ski 9 mi. Balconies. Cr cds: A, C, D, DS, MC, V.

Inns

✔★ **OLD CUTTER.** *(RR 1, Box 62, East Burke 05832) 1 mi N on US 5 to VT 114, then 4 mi N to Burke Mountain Rd.* 802/626-5152. Web www.pbpub.com/cutter.htm. 10 rms, 2 story. S $44-$56; D $54-$66; each addl $10-$12; kit. suite $120-$140; under 12 free; MAP avail. Closed Apr, Nov. Crib free. Pet accepted. TV in lobby. Pool. Dining rm (see OLD CUTTER INN). Ck-out 11 am, ck-in 1 pm. Downhill/x-country ski ½ mi. Lawn games. Picnic tables. Sitting rm. In restored farmhouse (ca 1845) & renovated turn-of-the-century carriage house. Cr cds: MC, V.

★★ **WILDFLOWER.** *Darling Hill Rd, 1 mi N on US 5 to VT 114, then N to Darling Hill Rd.* 802/626-8310; FAX 802/626-3039; res: 800/627-8310. 22 rms in 4 bldgs, 2 share bath, 2 story, 9 kit. suites. No A/C. No rm phones. S $74-$84; D $89-$105; suites $120-$200; higher rates fall foliage season. Closed 2 wks Apr & Nov. TV in sitting rm. Heated pool; wading pool, whirlpool, sauna. Free supervised child's activities (Memorial Day-Labor Day); ages 3-12. Complimentary full bkfst. Dining rm (public by res) 5-9 pm. Ck-out 11 am, ck-in 3 pm. Business servs avail. Gift shop. Art gallery. Free bus depot transportation. Tennis on site. Downhill ski 5 mi; x-country ski on site. Hay, sleigh rides. Game rm. Lawn games. Some balconies. Family-oriented inn on 500 acres; barns, farm animals; sledding slopes. Totally nonsmoking. Cr cds: MC, V.

Restaurant

★★ **OLD CUTTER INN.** *(See Old Cutter Inn)* 802/626-5152. Web www.pbpub.com/cutter.html. Swiss, continental menu. Specialties: tournedos of beef, rack of lamb, rahmschnitzel. Hrs: 5:30-9 pm; Sun brunch 11 am-1:30 pm. Closed Wed; also Apr, Nov. Res accepted. Bar.

Semi-a la carte: dinner $13-$18.50. Sun brunch $10.50. Child's meals. Converted 1845 farmhouse. Cr cds: DS, MC, V.

Manchester & Manchester Center (G-1)

(See also Arlington, Dorset, Londonderry, Peru, Stratton Mountain)

Settled 1764 **Pop** 3,622 **Elev** 899 & 753 ft **Area code** 802 **Zip** Manchester 05254; Manchester Center 05255 **E-mail** mmchambr@sover.net **Web** www.manchesterandmtns.com

Information Manchester-and-the-Mountains Regional Chamber of Commerce, 3451 Manchester Center; 802/362-2100.

These towns have been among Vermont's best-loved year-round resorts for 100 years. The surrounding mountains make them serenely attractive, and the ski business has added to their following. Bromley Mountain, Stratton Mountain and other areas lure thousands each year. A Ranger District office of the Green Mountain National Forests(see) is located here.

What to See and Do

American Museum of Fly Fishing. Collection of fly fishing memorabilia; tackle of many famous persons, including Dwight D. Eisenhower, Ernest Hemingway, Andrew Carnegie, Winslow Homer, Bing Crosby and others. (Apr-Nov, daily; Dec-Mar, Mon-Fri; closed major hols) Corner of VT Historic Rte 7A & Seminary Ave. Phone 802/362-3300. ¢

Emerald Lake State Park. This 430-acre park has rich flora in a limestone-based bedrock. Swimming beach, bathhouse; fishing (also in nearby streams); boating (rentals). Nature, hiking trails. Picnicking, concession. Tent & trailer sites (dump station), lean-tos. (Memorial Day-Columbus Day) Standard fees. 6 mi N on US 7, in North Dorset. Phone 802/362-1655 or 802/483-2001.

★ **Equinox Sky Line Drive.** A spectacular 5-mi paved road that rises from 600 to 3,835 ft; parking and picnic areas along road; view from top of Mt Equinox. Fog or rain may make mountain road dangerous and travel inadvisable. (May-Oct, daily) No large camper vehicles. 5 mi S on VT Historic Rte 7A. Phone 802/362-1114. Toll ¢¢¢

Factory outlet stores. Many outlet stores can be found in this area, mainly along VT 11/30 & at the intersection of VT 11/30 and VT 7A. Contact the Chamber of Commerce for a complete listing of stores.

Historic Hildene (1904). The 412-acre estate of Robert Todd Lincoln (Abraham Lincoln's son) includes a 24-rm Georgian manor house, held in the family until 1975; original furnishings; carriage barn; formal gardens; nature trails. Tours. (Mid-May-Oct, daily) 2 mi S via VT Historic Rte 7A, in Manchester Village. Phone 802/362-1788. ¢¢¢

Merck Forest & Farmland Center. Includes 2,800 acres of unspoiled upland forest, meadows, mountains and ponds; 26 mi of roads and trails for hiking and cross-country skiing. Fishing. Picnicking. Camping (res required). Educational programs. Fees for some activities. 8 mi NW on VT 30 to East Rupert, then 2½ mi W on VT 315. Phone 802/394-7836.

Southern Vermont Art Center. Painting, sculpture, prints; concerts; music festivals; botany trail; cafe. Gift shop. (Late May-mid-Oct, daily exc Mon) 1 mi N off West Rd. Phone 802/362-1405. ¢¢

Vermont Wax Museum. Three Victorian buildings house 85 life-size wax figures from JFK to Mark Twain. Changing audio & video presentations. On-site wax-casting studio. Fine Art Gallery features Vermont artist’s work in various media. Museum store. (Daily; closed Jan 1, Easter, Thanksgiving, Dec 25) VA 11/30 between VA 7 & 7A. Phone 802/362-0609. ¢¢

Motels

★ ★ **ASPEN.** *(Manchester Center 05255) 1 mi N on VT 7A. 802/362-2450.* Web www.thisisvermont.com/aspen. 24 rms, 1 cottage (2-bedrm). Mid-June-Oct, mid-Dec-Mar: S, D $58-$90; each addl $10; cottage $150-$180; ski plan; July (2-day min); lower rates rest of yr. Crib $5. TV; cable. Pool. Complimentary coffee in rms. Ck-out 11 am. Free bus depot transportation. Tennis privileges. Golf privileges, greens fee, pro. Downhill ski 8 mi; x-country ski 3 mi. Lawn games. Refrigerators avail. Picnic tables. Cr cds: A, DS, MC, V.

[D] [icons]

★ **BARNSTEAD INNSTEAD.** *(Manchester Center) on VT 30, 2 blks N of jct US 7, VT 30. 802/362-1619.* 14 rms, 1-3 story. S, D $65-$85; each addl $8; ski plan; higher rates special events. TV; cable. Heated pool. Complimentary coffee in rms. Restaurant nearby. Ck-out 11 am. Tennis privileges. Golf privileges, pro. Downhill ski 10 mi; x-country ski 7 mi. Converted barn (1830s). Fairgrounds opp. Totally nonsmoking. Cr cds: MC, V.

[icons]

✔★ **BRITTANY INN.** *(VT 7A, Manchester Center 05255) 802/362-1033.* 12 rms. Jan-mid-Mar, mid-June-mid-Sept: S, D $59-$64; each addl $7; higher rates fall foliage; lower rates rest of yr. Crib free. TV; cable. Complimentary coffee in rms. Ck-out 11 am. Downhill ski 10 mi; x-country ski 2 mi. Refrigerators. Picnic tables, grill. Cr cds: A, DS, MC, V.

[icons]

★ ★ **EYRIE.** *(US 7 & Bowen Hill Rd, E Dorset 05253) 7 mi N, just E of US 7. 802/362-1208; res: 888/397-4388; FAX 802/362-2948.* E-mail eyrie@together.net; web www.thisisvermont.com/eyriemotel. 12 rms. June-Oct, late Dec-mid-Mar (wkends): S, D $65-$85; each addl $10; wkday rates; lower rates rest of yr. TV. Pool. Complimentary continental bkfst. Ck-out 11 am. Downhill ski 10 mi; x-country ski on site. Hiking. Lawn games. Refrigerators. Picnic tables. Early Amer decor. On 23 acres; sweeping views. Cr cds: A, DS, MC, V.

[icons]

★ ★ **FOUR WINDS.** *(7379 Main St, Manchester Center) on VT 7A, 2¹/₂ mi N of jct VT 30. 802/362-0905.* E-mail fwmotel@sovernet.com. 18 rms. Mid-June-mid-Oct: S, D $78-$112; each addl $10; lower rates rest of yr. TV; cable. Pool. Coffee in rms. Complimentary continetal bkfst. Ck-out 11 am. Meeting rm. Tennis privileges opp. 18-hole golf privileges opp, greens fee, pro. Downhill ski 6 mi; x-country ski 2 mi. Health club privileges. Rec rm. Refrigerators. Private patios. Colonial atmosphere; many antiques. Cr cds: A, MC, V.

[icons] SC

★ ★ **MANCHESTER VIEW.** *(Manchester Center 05255) 2 mi N on VT 7A at High Meadow Way. 802/362-2739; FAX 802/362-2199.* E-mail manview@vermontel.com; web www.manchesterview.com. 35 rms, 1-2 story. S, D $74-$150; each addl $10; suites $155-$190; wkly rates; ski plan; higher rates hols (3-day min). Crib $10. TV; cable, VCR avail. Heated pool. Restaurant 8-9:30 am. Ck-out 11 am. Meeting rm. Business servs avail. In-rm modem link. Tennis privileges. Golf privileges, greens fee, pro. Downhill ski 7 mi; x-country ski 3 mi. Exercise equipt. Refrigerators, fireplaces; some in-rm whirlpools. Private patios, balconies. Cr cds: A, C, D, DS, MC, V.

[D] [icons]

★ ★ **NORTH SHIRE.** *(VT 7A, Manchester 05254) 2¹/₂ mi S on VT 7A. 802/362-2336.* 14 rms. May-late Nov: S, D $65-$90; each addl $5-$10. Closed rest of yr. Crib $3. TV; cable (premium). Pool. Continental bkfst (in season). Ck-out 11 am. Downhill ski 12 mi; x-country ski 2¹/₂ mi. Private patios. Extensive grounds. Cr cds: A, MC, V.

[icons]

★ **OLYMPIA MOTOR LODGE.** *(7259 Main St, Manchester Center 05255) 2¹/₂ mi N on US 7A. 802/362-1700; FAX 802/362-1705.* E-mail oml@compuserve.com; web olympia-vt.com. 24 rms, 2 story. Mid-June-Oct: S, D $70-$105; each addl $10; ski plan; lower rates rest of yr.

TV; cable (premium). Heated pool. Bar noon-11 pm. Ck-out 11 am. Business servs avail. In-rm modem link. Tennis. Golf privileges, greens fee, pro. Downhill ski 7 mi; x-country ski 3¹/₂ mi. Private patios, balconies. Cr cds: A, MC, V.

[icons]

★ ★ ★ **PALMER HOUSE.** *(Main St (VT 7A), Manchester Center 05255) 802/362-3600.* E-mail resort@palmerhouse.com; web www.palmerhouse.com. 40 rms. Mid-May-Oct: S, D $90-$125; each addl $10; lower rates rest of yr. TV; cable. Heated pool; whirlpool. Continental bkfst. Coffee in rms. Restaurant adj. Ck-out 11 am. Business servs avail. Tennis. Downhill ski 6 mi; x-country ski 2 mi. Refrigerators. Picnic tables. Grill. Surrounded by 22 acres of lawn and gardens; view of Green Mts. Lobby furnished with antiques; artwork. Antique doll collection. Cr cds: A, DS, MC, V.

[D] [icons]

✔★ **STAMFORD.** *(VT 7A North, Manchester Center) US 7. 802/362-2342.* 14 rms, 1-2 story. July-mid-Oct & winter wkends: S, D $56-$65; each addl $6; family, wkly rates; ski plan; lower rates rest of yr. Crib free. TV; cable. Heated pool. Coffee in rms. Ck-out 11 am. Tennis privileges. Golf privileges, greens fee, pro. Downhill ski 6 mi; x-country ski 2¹/₂ mi. Some refrigerators. Balconies. Picnic tables. Cr cds: A, C, D, DS, MC, V.

[icons]

★ ★ **TOLL ROAD MOTOR INN.** *(VT 11-30, Manchester Center 07628) 2¹/₄ mi E on VT 11/30; ¹/₄ mi E of US 7 exit 4. 802/362-1711; FAX 802/362-1715.* 16 rms, 2 story. No rm phones. S, D $70-$95; each addl $10; wkly rates in winter; ski; golf plans. TV. Pool. Complimentary coffee. Restaurant nearby. Ck-out 11 am. Tennis privileges. 18-hole golf privileges, greens fee, pro. Downhill ski 5 mi; x-country ski 3 mi. Refrigerators. Cr cds: A, DS, MC, V.

[icons]

★ ★ ★ **WEATHERVANE.** *(Historic Rt 7A, Manchester 05254) 2¹/₂ mi S on VT 7A. 802/362-2444; FAX 802/362-4616; res: 800/262-1317.* 22 rms. Memorial Day-late Oct, Dec-late Mar: S, D $79-$125; each addl $10; mid-wk rates (winter); higher rates: foliage season, Washington's Birthday, wk of Dec 25; lower rates rest of yr. TV; cable (premium). Heated pool. Complimentary coffee in rms. Restaurant nearby. Ck-out 11 am. Business servs avail. In-rm modem link. Sundries. Tennis privileges. Golf privileges, greens fee, pro, putting green. Downhill ski 7 mi; x-country ski ¹/₄ mi. Refrigerators avail. Private patios. Fireplace in lobby. Cr cds: A, MC, V.

[D] [icons] SC

✔★ **WEDGEWOOD.** *(VT 7A, Manchester Center 05255) 802/362-2145; FAX 802/362-0190; res: 800/254-2145.* E-mail ejwmike@sover.net; web thisisvermont.com/wedgewood/. 12 units. D $42-$88. TV; cable. Heated pool. Complimentary continental bkfst. Refrigerators. Picnic tables, grill. Cr cds: A, C, DS, MC, V.

[icons] SC

Hotel

★ ★ ★ **EQUINOX.** *(VT 7A, Manchester Village) 1 mi S on VT 7A, center of village. 802/362-4700; FAX 802/362-4861; res: 800/362-4747.* 183 units, 3-4 story, 21 kits. EP: S $159-$289; D $169-$299; each addl $30; suites $369-$559, kit. units $359-$899; under 12 free; MAP avail; ski, golf plans. Crib $10. TV; cable (premium), VCR avail. 2 pools, 1 indoor. Restaurant 7 am-9:30 pm; Sun brunch 11 am-2:30 pm. Bar noon-midnight, wkends to 1 am; entertainment Fri-Sat. Ck-out 11 am. Meeting rms. Business servs avail. Concierge. Gift shop. Tennis, pro. 18-hole golf, greens fee $60-$65, pro, putting green. Downhill ski 6 mi; x-country ski on site. Exercise rm; sauna, steam rm. Private patios, balconies. Library. 1700s building; Green Mountain Boys met here. On 2,000 acres. Cr cds: A, C, D, DS, MC, V.

[D] [icons] SC

Inns

★ ★ ★ **1811 HOUSE.** *(VT 7A, Manchester 05254) 1 mi S on VT 7A. 802/362-1811; FAX 802/362-2443; res: 800/432-1811.* 14 rms, 2 story. S $110-$210; D $120-$230; foliage season (2-day min). Children over 16 yrs only. TV avail; cable. Complimentary full bkfst. Bar 5:30-8 pm. Ck-out 11 am, ck-in 2 pm. Tennis privileges. 18-hole golf privileges, pro. Downhill ski 8 mi; x-country ski ½ mi. Game rm. Some fireplaces. Library. Restored 1770 farmhouse; inn since 1811. Canopied beds; antiques; original artwork. Adj to golf course. Cr cds: A, DS, MC, V.

★ ★ **BATTENKILL INN.** *(VT 7A, Sunderland 05254) 3 mi S on VT 7A. 802/362-4213; res: 800/441-1628.* 11 air-cooled rms, 2 story. No rm phones. D $75-$135; each addl $25; family rates; ski plans; higher rates hols. Complimentary full bkfst; afternoon refreshments. Ck-out 11 am, ck-in 3 pm. Downhill ski 10 mi; x-country ski 4 mi. Some fireplaces. Balconies. Victorian house (1840); antiques. Library, sitting rms. On river. Cr cds: A, D, MC, V.

★ ★ **EQUINOX MOUNTAIN INN.** *(Skyline Dr, Manchester 05254) 802/362-1113; res: 800/868-6843.* 18 rms, 2 story. No A/C. No rm phones. S $85-$135; D $90-$140; each addl $20; 2-day min wkends. Closed late Oct-early May. Children over 12 yrs only. Complimentary full bkfst. Restaurant 5:30-9 pm; closed Wed. Ck-out 11 am, ck-in 3 pm. Business servs avail. Picnic tables. Bldg on mountain top has 360-degree panoramic view of Vermont. Cr cds: MC, V.

★ ★ ★ **INN AT MANCHESTER.** *(VT 7A, Manchester 05254) 1 mi S on VT 7A. 802/362-1793; res: 800/273-1793; FAX 802/362-3218.* E-mail iman@vermontel.com; web www.innatmanchester.com. 18 rms in 2 bldgs, 3 story. Mid-June-Labor Day, mid-Dec-late Mar: D $119-159; each addl $25; wkly rates; package plans; higher rates hols; lower rates rest of yr. Children over 8 yrs only. Serv charge 15%. TV in sitting rm; cable. Pool. Complimentary full bkfst; afternoon refreshments. Dining rm 8-9:30 am. Ck-out 11 am, ck-in 2 pm. Downhill ski 7 mi; x-country ski 2 mi. Private patio. Picnic tables. Antique furnishings. Inn, carriage house (1880). Cr cds: A, DS, MC, V.

★ **LAKE ST CATHERINE.** *(Cones Point Rd, Poultney 05764) 15 mi E on US 4, then 5 mi N on VT 30. 802/287-9347; res: 800/626-5724.* E-mail innkeepers@lakesstcatherineinn.com; web www.lakestcatherine-inn.com. 35 rms, 11 with shower only, 19 A/C, 1-2 story. No rm phones. MAP, mid-June-mid-Oct: S $95, D $80-$86 per person; wkly, wkend rates; lower rates mid-May-mid-June. Closed rest of yr. Crib free. TV in sitting rm; cable; VCR. Complimentary full bkfst. Complimentary coffee in rms. Dining rm (public by res). Ck-out 11 am, ck-in 1 pm. Business servs avail. Rec rm. Lawn games. On lake; boats avail. Totally nonsmoking. No cr cds accepted.

★ ★ **MANCHESTER HIGHLANDS.** *(Highland Ave, Manchester 05255) 802/362-4565; FAX 802/362-4028; res: 800/743-4565.* E-mail innkeeper@highlandsinn.com; web www.highlandsinn.com. 15 rms, 10 with shower only, 3 story. No rm phones. Mid-June-Oct: D $105-$135; each addl $20; under 5 free; ski plans; hols (2-day min). Crib free. TV in common rm. Pool. Complimentary full bkfst. Restaurant nearby. Ck-out 11 am, ck-in 2 pm. Luggage handling. Business servs avail. Downhill ski 6 mi; x-country ski 1 mi. Game rm. Picnic tables. Built in 1898. Totally nonsmoking. Cr cds: A, MC, V.

★ ★ ★ **RELUCTANT PANTHER.** *(West Rd, Manchester Village 05254-0678) Off VT 7A. 802/362-2568; FAX 802/362-2586; res: 800/822-2331.* E-mail panther@sover.net; web www.reluctantpanther.com. 13 rms, 6 suites. MAP, mid-Sept-Oct: S, D $168-$450; wkends (2-day min), hols (3-day min); lower rates rest of yr. Adults only. TV; cable. Complimentary bkfst. Dining rm 6-9 pm; closed Tues, Wed. Ck-out 11 am, ck-in 3 pm.

Downhill ski 15 mi; x-country ski 2 mi. Health club privileges. Many fireplaces; whirlpool in suites. Sitting rm. Built 1850. Cr cds: A, MC, V.

✔ ★ ★ **SILAS GRIFFITH.** *(S Main St, Danby 05739) 12 mi N on US 7, then W on Main St. 802/293-5567; FAX 802/293-5559; res: 800/545-1509.* 17 air-cooled rms, 1-3 story. No rm phones. S $57-$79; D $72-$109; each addl $20; under 10 free; wkly rates; ski plans. TV in sitting rm; cable. Pool. Complimentary full bkfst. Dining rm (public by res) 6-8:30 pm. Ck-out 11 am, ck-in 2 pm. Free bus depot transportation. Downhill ski 15 mi; x-country ski 16 mi. Game rm. Home of Vermont's 1st millionaire (1891); antiques. Library, sitting rm. Totally nonsmoking. Cr cds: MC, V.

★ ★ ★ **VILLAGE COUNTRY.** *(VT 7A, Manchester 05254) 1 mi S at jct VT 11, 30 & US 7. 802/362-1792; res: 800/370-0300.* E-mail vci@vermontel.com; web www.villagecountyinn.com. 33 rms, 3 story. No elvtr. MAP: S, D $150-$215; each addl $65; suites $215-$350; ski, golf, fishing plans. Children over 12 yrs only. Serv charge 15%. Some TV. Pool. Complimentary full bkfst. Dining rm 8-9:30 am, 6-9 pm. Bar from 4 pm. Ck-out 11 am, ck-in 2 pm. Gift shop. Free bus depot transportation. Golf privileges, greens fee, pro. Downhill ski 6 mi; x-country ski ½ mi. Cr cds: A, DS, MC, V.

★ ★ ★ **WILBURTON.** *(Manchester 05254) 1½ mi S on VT 7A to River Rd, then ½ mi SE. 802/362-2500; FAX 802/362-1107; res: 800/648-4944.* 35 rms, 1-3 story. Aug-Oct: S, D $120-$215; suites $175; wkly, family rates; higher rates: hols; lower rates rest of yr. TV in most rms. Pool. Complimentary full bkfst. Dining rm (public by res) 8-10 am, 6-9 pm. Rm serv (in season). Bar from 5 pm. Ck-out 11 am, ck-in 1 pm. Business servs avail. Tennis. Golf privileges, greens fee. Downhill ski 6 mi; x-country ski ½ mi. Some refrigerators. Spacious grounds; sculptural displays. Early 1900s Victorian-style inn with mountain view. Cr cds: A, MC, V.

Restaurants

★ ★ ★ **BLACK SWAN.** *(VT 7A, Manchester) 1 mi S on VT 7A. 802/362-3807.* Continental menu. Specializes in fresh fish, pasta, veal. Own desserts. Hrs: 5:30-9 pm. Closed Dec 24, 25; 2 wks in Nov; also Tues, Wed Dec-May, Wed June-Oct. Res accepted. Bar. Semi-a la carte: dinner $11.75-$24. Parking. Converted farmhouse built in 1800s. Fireplaces. Cr cds: A, MC, V.

★ ★ ★ **CHANTECLEER.** *(VT 7A, Manchester Center) 3½ mi N on VT 7A. 802/362-1616.* Continental menu. Specializes in rack of lamb, sweetbreads, fresh seafood. Own desserts. Hrs: 6-10 pm. Closed Tues; Thanksgiving, Dec 25; Apr, mid-Nov-mid-Dec; also Mon in winter. Res accepted. Bar. Wine list. Semi-a la carte: dinner $19.95-$26. Parking. Tableside cooking. Former dairy barn. Fireplace. Cr cds: A, C, D, MC, V.

★ ★ **GARLIC JOHN'S.** *(VT 11/30, Manchester Center) 1 mi E on VT 11, 30, adj to US 7 exit 4. 802/362-9843.* Italian menu. Specializes in seafood, pasta, veal dishes. Hrs: 4:30-9:30 pm; Fri, Sat to 10 pm. Closed Thanksgiving, Dec 24. Bar. Semi-a la carte: dinner $7.95-$17.95. Child's meals. Parking. Totally nonsmoking. Cr cds: A, MC, V.

★ ★ **MARK ANTHONY'S YE OLDE TAVERN.** *(US 7 (N Main St), Manchester 05255) ½ mi N on US 7. 802/362-0611.* Specializes in poultry & veal dishes, fresh seafood. Hrs: 11:30 am-3 pm, 5-10 pm. Res accepted. Bar. Semi-a la carte: lunch $5.25-$12, dinner $12-$24.95. Parking. Historic 200-yr-old tavern. Cr cds: A, D, MC, V.

★ ★ **SIRLOIN SALOON.** *(VT 11, Manchester Center) ¼ mi E on VT 11, 30. 802/362-2600.* Specializes in wood-grilled steak, chicken, seafood. Salad bar. Hrs: 5-10 pm; Fri, Sat to 11 pm. Closed Thanksgiving. Res accepted. Bar from 4 pm. Semi-a la carte: dinner $7.95-$19.95.

Child's meals. Parking. Open hearth. Converted mill; antiques. Southwestern theme; Native American artwork, artifacts. Cr cds: A, C, D, MC, V.

Marlboro (H-2)

(See also Brattleboro, Wilmington)

Settled 1763 **Pop** 924 **Elev** 1,736 ft **Area code** 802 **Zip** 05344

What to See and Do

Marlboro College (1946). (275 students) Arts and sciences, international studies. On campus is Tyler Art Gallery (Mon-Fri; closed hols). 2¹/₂ mi S of VT 9. Phone 802/257-4333.

Seasonal Event

Marlboro Music Festival. Marlboro College campus. Chamber music concerts. Phone 215/569-4690. Mid-July-mid-Aug.

Inn

✔★ **WHETSTONE INN.** *South Rd, ¹/₂ mi off VT 9 (South Rd), follow Marlboro College signs. 802/254-2500.* 11 rms, 3 share bath, 2 story, 3 kits. No A/C. S $35-$60; D $55-$80; each addl $10; kit. units $75-$85; wkly rates. Crib $2. Pet accepted. Restaurant 8-10 am, 7-8 pm (public by res). Ck-out 2 pm, ck-in after 2 pm. Some refrigerators. Picnic tables. 18th-century country inn was originally a stagecoach stop; fireplaces in public rms. Swimming pond. No cr cds accepted.

Restaurant

✔★ **SKYLINE.** *13 mi W on VT 9. 802/464-3536.* Specializes in New England dishes. Hrs: June-mid-Apr 7:30 am-9 pm; mid-Apr-Memorial day 7:30 am-3 pm. Closed Thanksgiving, Dec 25. Serv bar. Semi-a la carte: bkfst $2.50-$7.95, lunch, dinner $5.25-$15.95. Child's meals. Early Amer decor; fireplace. On Hogback Mt; 100-mi view from dining rm. Cr cds: A, C, D, DS, MC, V.

SC

Middlebury (E-1)

(See also Brandon, Vergennes)

Settled 1761 **Pop** 8,034 **Elev** 366 ft **Area code** 802 **Zip** 05753 **E-mail** accoc@sover.net **Web** www.midvermont.com

Information Addison County Chamber of Commerce Information Center, 2 Court St; 802/388-7951.

Benjamin Smalley built the first log house here just before the Revolution. In 1800, the town had a full-fledged college. By 1803, there was a flourishing marble quarry and a female academy run by Emma Hart Willard, a pioneer in education for women; today, it is known as Middlebury College. A Ranger District office of the Green Mountain National Forests(see) is located here and has a map and guides for day hikes on Long Trail.

What to See and Do

Congregational Church (1806-1809). Built after a plan in the *Country Builder's Assistant*, and designed by architect Lavius Fillmore. Architecturally, one of finest in Vermont. (Mid-June-Aug, Fri & Sat) On the Common. Phone 802/388-7634.

Green Mountain National Forest (see).

Historic Middlebury Village Walking Tour. Contact the Addison County Chamber of Commerce Information Center for map and information. Phone 802/388-7951.

Middlebury College (1800). (1,950 students) Famous for the teaching of arts and sciences; summer language schools; Bread Loaf School of English and Writers' Conference. W of town on VT 125. Phone 802/443-5000.

Bread Loaf. Site of nationally known Bread Loaf School of English in July and annual Writers' Conference in Aug. Also site of Robert Frost's cabin. In winter, it is the Carroll and Jane Rikert Ski Touring Center. 10 mi E on VT 125.

Emma Willard House. Location of first female seminary (1814), now admissions and financial aid offices.

Middlebury College Museum of Art. (Daily exc Mon; closed Jan 1, Thanksgiving, Dec 25) Phone 802/443-5007. **Free.**

Middlebury College Snow Bowl. Area has triple, 2 double chairlifts; patrol, school, rentals; snowmaking; cafeteria. 15 runs. (Early Dec-early Apr, daily; closed Dec 25) 13 mi E on VT 125, just E of Bread Loaf. Phone 802/388-4356. ¢¢¢¢¢

Old Stone Row includes Painter Hall (1815), oldest college building in state.

Starr Library has collection of works by Robert Frost and other American writers. (Daily; closed some major hols)

Sheldon Museum. Comprehensive collection of 19th-century "Vermontiana" in brick house (1829) with black marble fireplaces. Authentic furnishings range from hand-forged kitchen utensils to country and high-style furniture. Museum also features oil portraits, pewter, Staffordshire, clocks, pianos, toys, dolls and local relics. Guided tours. (June-Oct, Mon-Fri; rest of yr, Wed & Fri; closed hols) 1 Park St. Phone 802/388-2117. ¢¢

UVM Morgan Horse Farm. Breeding and training farm for internationally acclaimed Morgan horses; owned by the Univ of Vermont. Daily workouts and training can be viewed. Guided tours, slide presentations. (May-Oct, daily) 2¹/₂ mi NW off VT 23. Phone 802/388-2011. ¢¢

Vermont State Craft Center at Frog Hollow. Restored mill overlooking Otter Creek Falls houses an exhibition and sales gallery with works of more than 300 Vermont craftspeople. Special exhibitions, classes and workshops. (Spring-fall, daily; rest of yr, daily exc Sun; closed some major hols) 1 Mill St. Phone 802/388-3177. **Free.**

Annual Events

Winter Carnival. Middlebury College Snow Bowl. Late Feb.

Addison County Home and Garden Show. Exhibits, demonstrations. Usually last wkend Mar.

Festival on the Green. Village green. Classical, modern and traditional dance; chamber and folk music; theater and comedy presentations. Early July.

Motels

✔★ **BLUE SPRUCE.** *RD 3, Box 376, 3 mi S on US 7. 802/388-4091; FAX 802/388-3003.* E-mail stpadd@sover.net. 17 rms, 6 cottages, 3 kits. S, D $58-$75; each addl $10; suites $95-$135; kit. units $10 addl; higher rates in fall. TV; cable. Ck-out 10 am. Downhill ski 8 mi; x-country ski 6 mi. Cr cds: A, C, D, DS, MC, V.

★ **GREY STONE.** *RD 4, Box 1284, 2 mi S on US 7. 802/388-4935.* 10 rms. Mid-May-Oct: S $52-$57; D $60-$70; each addl $8; lower rates rest of yr. TV; cable. Restaurant nearby. Ck-out 10 am. Downhill ski 11 mi; x-country ski 9 mi. Picnic tables. Cr cds: A, DS, MC, V.

Inns

★ ★ **MIDDLEBURY.** *Box 798, Court Square, on US 7. 802/388-4961; FAX 802/388-4563; res: 800/842-4666.* E-mail midinnut@sover.net; web www.middleburyinn.com. 45 rms in inn, 20 motel rms, 2-3 story. S $86-$160; D $90-$200; each addl $8; suites $144-$275. Crib free. Pet accepted, some restrictions; $8. TV; cable. Complimentary continental bkfst; afternoon refreshments. Coffee in motel rms. Restaurants 7:30-10 am, 11:30 am-2 pm, 5:30-9 pm (winter to 8 pm); Sun brunch 10:30 am-2 pm. Bar. Ck-out 11 am, ck-in 3 pm. Meeting rms. Business servs avail. Bellhops. Gift shop. Downhill/x-country ski 13 mi. Bathrm phones. Antiques. Porch dining in summer. Established in 1827. Cr cds: A, C, D, DS, MC, V.

[D] [symbols] [SC]

★ ★ ★ **SWIFT HOUSE.** *25 Stewart Lane. 802/388-9925; FAX 802/388-9927.* 21 rms in 3 bldgs, 2 story. S, D $90-$195; each addl $20. Crib free. TV in some rms; cable. Complimentary continental bkfst. Restaurant (see SWIFT HOUSE). Rm serv. Business servs avail. Downhill/x-country ski 10 mi. Sauna, steam rm. Some in-rm whirlpools, fireplaces. Built 1815; each rm individually decorated; four-poster beds, handmade quilts, antiques. Cr cds: A, C, D, DS, MC, V.

[D] [symbols]

★ ★ **WAYBURY.** *(VT 125, East Middlebury 05740) 5 mi SE on VT 125, 1 mi E of US 7. 802/388-4015; FAX 802/388-1248; res: 800/348-1810.* 14 rms, 5 A/C. No rm phones. Jan-Feb, May-Oct: S $50-$85; D $80-$115; each addl $10; lower rates rest of yr. TV in lobby; VCR. Complimentary full bkfst. Restaurant (see WAYBURY INN). Bar 4-11 pm. Ck-out 11 am, ck-in 3 pm. Meeting rms. Downhill/x-country ski 10 mi. Hiking trails nearby. Constructed as a stagecoach stop; inn since 1810. Parlor, porch. Sun deck. Near Middlebury College. Cr cds: DS, MC, V.

[symbols] [SC]

Restaurants

★ ★ **DOG TEAM.** *Dog Team Rd, 4 mi N off US 7. 802/388-7651.* Specializes in sticky buns, baked ham with fritters, fresh seafood. Hrs: 5-9 pm; Sat from 4 pm; Sun noon-9 pm. Closed Dec 24, 25. Bar. Semi-a la carte: dinner $9.95-$14.95. Child's meals. Parking. Country atmosphere. Totally nonsmoking. Cr cds: C, D, MC, V.

★ ★ **FIRE & ICE.** *26 Seymour St. 802/388-7166.* Specializes in steak, seafood. Salad bar. Hrs: 11:30 am-8:30 pm; Mon 5-8:30 pm; Sat to 9 pm; Sun 1-8:30 pm. Closed Dec 25. Res accepted. Bar. Semi-a la carte: lunch $8.95-$11.95, dinner $12.95-$20.95. Child's meals. Parking. Eclectic decor, casual. Totally nonsmoking. Cr cds: A, C, D, DS, MC, V.

[D]

✔ ★ **MISTER UP'S.** *Bakery Lane, just off Main St, adj to municipal parking lot. 802/388-6724.* Continental menu. Specializes in fresh seafood. Salad bar. Hrs: 11:30 am-midnight; Sun brunch 11 am-2 pm. Closed Thanksgiving, Dec 24 eve, 25. Res accepted. Bar. A la carte entrees: lunch $5.25-$7.95, dinner $9.25-$13.95. Child's meals. Parking. Outdoor dining on river. Cr cds: A, D, DS, MC, V.

★ ★ **SWIFT HOUSE.** *(See Swift House Inn) 802/388-9925.* Specializes in fresh seafood, breast of chicken, rack of lamb. Hrs: 6-9:30 pm. Res accepted. Bar. A la carte entrees: dinner $6.95-$21.95. Child's meals. Parking. In 1815 inn; 3 dining rms, Colonial decor, fireplaces. Totally nonsmoking. Cr cds: A, C, D, DS, MC, V.

[D]

★ ★ **WAYBURY INN.** *(See Waybury Inn) 802/388-4015.* E-mail thefolks@wayburyinn.com; web www.wayburyinn.com. Specializes in fresh fish, steak, rack of lamb. Hrs: 5-9 pm; Sun brunch 11 am-2 pm. Res accepted. Bar. Semi-a la carte: dinner $12.95-$21.95. Sun brunch $12.95. Child's meals. Parking. Porch dining in summer. Old colonial stagecoach stop. Totally nonsmoking. Cr cds: D, DS, MC, V.

[D]

Montpelier (D-2)

(See also Barre, Waitsfield, Waterbury)

Settled 1787 **Pop** 8,247 **Elev** 525 ft **Area code** 802 **Zip** 05602

Information Central Vermont Chamber of Commerce, PO Box 336, Barre 05641; 802/229-5711.

The state capital, on the banks of the Winooski River, is also a life insurance center. Admiral Dewey, victor at Manila Bay, was born here. A popular summer vacation area, Montpelier absorbs the overflow from the nearby ski areas in winter.

What to See and Do

Hubbard Park. A 110-acre wooded area with picnic area (shelter, fireplaces, water). Stone observation tower (1932). 1 mi NW, on Hubbard Park Dr. Phone 802/223-5141. **Free.**

Morse Farm. Maple sugar and vegetable farm in rustic, wooded setting. Tour of sugar house; view sugar-making process in season (Mar-Apr); slide show explains process off-season. Gift shop. (Daily; closed Easter, Dec 25) 3 mi N via County Road (follow signs on Main St) Phone 802/223-2740 or 800/242-2740. **Free.**

State House (1859). Made of Vermont granite; dome covered with gold leaf. (Mon-Fri, also Sat late morning-early afternoon July-mid-Oct) State St. Phone 802/828-2228. **Free.**

Thomas Waterman Wood Art Gallery. Oils, watercolors and etchings by Wood and other 19th-century American artists. Also American artists of the 1920s and ‘30s; changing monthly exhibits of works of contemporary local and regional artists. (Tues-Sun afternoons; closed major hols) In Vermont College Arts Center, at College St. Phone 802/828-8743. **¢**

Vermont Department of Libraries. Local and state history collections. (Mon-Fri; closed hols) Pavilion Office Bldg. 109 State St. Phone 802/828-3261. **Free.**

Vermont Historical Society Museum, Library. Historical exhibits. (Daily exc Mon; closed most hols) Pavilion Office Bldg, adj State House. Phone 802/828-2291. **¢¢**

Motels

★ ★ **COMFORT INN AT MAPLEWOOD LTD.** *on VT 62, 1/2 mi E of I-89 exit 7. 802/229-2222.* E-mail comfortin@aol.com; web www.comfortinnsuites.com. 89 rms, 3 story, 19 kit. suites. No elvtr. S, D $69-$79; each addl $10; kit. suites $89-$220; under 18 free; wkly rates; higher rates fall foliage. Crib free. TV; cable, VCR (movies). Complimentary continental bkfst. Restaurant adj 6 am-11 pm. Bar 5-10 pm. Ck-out 11 am. Coin lndry. Meeting rms. Business servs avail. In-rm modem link. Free airport transportation. Some refrigerators. Cr cds: A, C, D, DS, ER, MC, V.

[D] [symbols] [SC]

✔ ★ **LA GUE INNS.** *3 mi N on VT 62, opp Central VT Hospital, near E. F. Knapp Airport. 802/229-5766; FAX 802/229-5766.* 80 units, 2 story. S $50-$100; D $60-$120; each addl $10; under 6 free; wkly rates; higher rates: hols, fall foliage. Crib free. TV; cable (premium), VCR (movies $5). Indoor pool. Restaurant 6:30 am-9 pm. Bar. Ck-out 11 am. Meeting rms. Business servs avail. Free airport transportation. X-country ski 4 mi. Some refrigerators. Picnic tables. Cr cds: A, DS, MC, V.

[D] [symbols] [SC]

Hotel

★ ★ ★ **CAPITOL PLAZA.** *100 State St. 802/223-5252; FAX 802/229-5427; res: 800/274-5252.* E-mail capplaza@plainfield.bypass.com; web capitolplaza.com. 47 rms, 3 with shower only, 4 story. S, D $82-$92; each addl $10; under 16 free; higher rates: wkends, fall foliage. Crib free. TV; cable. Coffee in rms. Restaurant 7 am-9 pm; Sat, Sun from

8 am. Bar noon-11 pm. Ck-out 11 am. Meeting rms. Business servs avail. In-rm modem link. Gift shop. Barber, beauty shop. Health club privileges. Renovated 1930s hotel. Cr cds: A, DS, MC, V.

D ⊠ ⚠ SC

Inns

★ **BETSY'S BED & BREAKFAST.** *74 East State St. 802/229-0466; FAX 802/229-5412.* E-mail betsybb@plainfield.bypass .com; web www.central-vt.com/business/betsybb. 12 rms, 2 story, 5 kit. units. No A/C. S $50-$70; D $55-$75; kits. $95; higher rates May-Oct. Crib free. TV; cable. Complimentary full bkfst. Restaurant nearby. Ck-out 11 am, ck-in 5 pm. Exercise equipt. Built 1895; Victorian decor with many antiques. Cr cds: A, DS, MC, V.

⌁ ⊠ ⚠

★ ★ ★ **THE INN AT MONTPELIER.** *147 Main St. 802/223-2727; FAX 802/223-0722.* 19 rms, 2 story. S $89-$139; D $99-$149; each addl $10; higher rates fall foliage. TV; cable. Complimentary continental bkfst. Ck-out 11 am, ck-in 2-10 pm. Business servs avail. In-rm modem link. Some fireplaces. Federal-style buildings with large front porch (1828); sitting rms; paintings. Cr cds: A, C, D, MC, V.

⚠ SC

★ ★ ★ **INN ON THE COMMON.** *(Main St, Craftsbury Common 05827) 7 mi E on US 2, 30 mi N on VT 14. 802/586-9619; FAX 802/586-2249; res: 800/521-2233.* E-mail info@innonthecommon.com; web www.innonthecommon.com. 16 rms in 3 bldgs, 2 story. No A/C. No rm phones. MAP: S $150-$160; D $230-$250; suites $250; package plans; higher rates fall foliage. Serv charge 15%. Crib free. Pet accepted. TV in sitting rm; VCR. Heated pool. Afternoon refreshments. Dining rm 8-9:30 am, dinner (2 sittings) 6:30, 8 pm. Bar. Ck-out 11 am, ck-in 1 pm. Business servs avail. Tennis. Golf privileges. X-country ski on site. Bicycle rentals. Health club privileges. Lawn games. Antiques. Library. Some fireplaces. Restored Federal-period houses in scenic Vermont village; landscaped gardens. Extensive film collection. Cr cds: A, MC, V.

⛷ ⛷ ⚓ 🏃 🚴 ⚓ 🏊 ⚠

★ ★ **NORTHFIELD.** *(27 Highland Ave, Northfield 05663) 10 mi S on VT 12, near Norwich University. 802/485-8558.* 28 rms, 3 story, 2 suites. No A/C. S $65-$85; D $85-$95; suites $130. Children over 15 yrs only. TV, VCR avail (free movies). Complimentary full bkfst; afternoon refreshments. Ck-out 11 am, ck-in 3 pm. Business servs avail. Game rm. Lawn games. Built 1901; furnished with period pieces. Totally nonsmoking. Cr cds: MC, V.

⊠ ⚠

Restaurants

★ ★ **CHEF'S TABLE.** *118 Main St. 802/229-9202.* Continental menu. Hrs: 6-9:30 pm. Closed Sun; most major hols. Res accepted. Bar 4-11 pm. A la carte entrees: dinner $13.50-$18.75. Prix fixe: $30, $45 with wines. Serv charge 15%. Owned and operated by New England Culinary Institute. Totally nonsmoking. Cr cds: A, C, D, DS, MC, V.

D SC

★ **LOBSTER POT.** *313 Barre. 802/476-9900.* Specializes in seafood, steak. Salad bar in converted rowboat. Hrs: 11 am-9 pm; Sun brunch 10 am-2 pm. Closed Mon; major hols; also 4th wk Oct. Res accepted. Bar to 9 pm. Semi-a la carte: lunch $3.95-$7.25, dinner $8.50-$18. Sun brunch $7.47. Child's meals. Family-owned. Cr cds: A, C, D, DS, MC, V.

D SC ♥

★ ★ **MAIN STREET GRILL AND BAR.** *118 Main St. 802/223-3188.* Hrs: 7-10 am, 11:30 am-2 pm, 5:30-10 pm; Sat from 8 am. Sun brunch 10 am-2 pm. Closed major hols. Bar. Semi-a la carte: lunch $4.50-$6.50, dinner $6.95-$11.50 (serv charge 15%). Sun brunch $11.95.

Outdoor dining. Training restaurant for 1st and 2nd year students of New England Culinary Institute. Totally nonsmoking. Cr cds: A, DS, MC, V.

D SC

Mt Mansfield

(see Stowe)

Newfane (H-2)

(See also Brattleboro)

Settled 1774 **Pop** 1,555 **Elev** 536 ft **Area code** 802 **Zip** 05345
Information Town Clerk, PO Box 36; 802/365-7772.

Originally settled high on Newfane Hill, this is a charming, sleepy town. American poet Eugene Field spent many summer holidays here.

What to See and Do

Jamaica State Park. 758 acres. Old railroad bed along West River serves as trail to Ball Mt Dam. Fishing. Hiking trails. Picnicking. Tent & trailer sites (dump station), lean-tos. Whitewater canoe races on river. (May-Columbus Day) Standard fees. 13 mi W on VT 30, in Jamaica. Phone 802/874-4600 or 802/886-2434.

Scott Covered Bridge (1870). Longest single span in state (166 ft), built with lattice-type trusses. Together, the 3 spans total 276 ft. Other 2 spans are of king post-type trusses. Over the West River in Townshend, 5 mi N via VT 30.

Townshend State Forest. A 1,690-acre area with foot trail to Bald Mt (1,580 ft). Hiking trails. Picnic sites. Tent & trailer sites. Swimming at nearby Townshend Reservoir Recreation Area. (May-Columbus Day) Standard fees. 6 mi N, off VT 30. Phone 802/365-7500 or 802/886-2434.

Windham County Courthouse (1825). On the green.

Windham County Historical Society Museum. Contains artifacts from the 21 towns of Windham County; exhibits on the Civil War and the Vermont Regiment. (Memorial Day-Columbus Day, Wed-Sun & hols) Main St. Phone 802/365-4148. **Donation.**

Inns

★ ★ ★ **FOUR COLUMNS.** *230 West St, on Village Green. 802/365-7713; res: 800/787-6633; FAX 802/365-0022.* E-mail frcolinn @sover.net; web www.fourcolumnsinn.com. 15 rms, 4 suites. S, D $110-$125; each addl $25; suites $140-$225. Pet accepted. TV in lounge; cable (premium). Pool. Complimentary full bkfst. Dining rm 6-9 pm, except Tues (guests only) 8-9:30 am (also see FOUR COLUMNS). Bar from 4 pm. Ck-out 11 am, ck-in 2 pm. Business servs avail. Stately 19th-century house; colonial furnishings. On 150 wooded acres; walking paths, gardens. Totally nonsmoking. Cr cds: A, C, D, DS, MC, V.

⚓ ⚓ ⊠ ⚠

★ ★ **OLD NEWFANE.** *On VT 30, on Village Green. 802/365-4427.* 10 rms, 9 baths, 3 story. No A/C. No elvtr. No rm phones. S, D $95-$155; each addl $25; 2-day min wkends; 3-day min hols. Closed Mon; also Apr-late May, Nov-mid-Dec. Children over 10 yrs only. Complimentary continental bkfst. Restaurant (see OLD NEWFANE). Bar. Ck-out 11 am, ck-in 4 pm. Downhill ski 2 mi; x-country ski 12 mi. Some fireplaces. Established in 1787; authentic colonial furnishings. No cr cds accepted.

⊠ ⚠

★ ★ ★ **WINDHAM HILL.** *(311 Lawrence Dr, West Townshend 05359) 12 mi N on VT 30, off Windham Hill Rd. 802/874-4080; FAX 802/874-4702; res: 800/944-4080.* E-mail windham@sover.net; web wind hamhill.com. 21 rms, 3 story. MAP: S $190-$315; D $245-$370; wkend, wkly rates; higher rates fall foliage. Closed Apr. Children over 12 yrs only. TV in sitting rm. Heated pool. Dining rm (public by res). Ck-out 11 am, ck-in 2 pm. Business servs avail. Tennis court. Downhill ski 15 mi; x-country ski on site. Some fireplaces. Sun deck. Built 1825; many antiques. Situated on 160-acre mountainside location; views. Totally nonsmoking. Cr cds: A, DS, MC, V.

Restaurants

★ ★ ★ **FOUR COLUMNS.** (See Four Columns Inn) 802/365-7713; res: 800/787-6633; FAX 802/365-0022. E-mail frcolinn@sover.net; web www.fourcolumnsinn.com. Mediterranean menu. Specializes in local lamb, fresh game, fresh fish. Own baking. Hrs: 6-9 pm. Closed Tues; Dec 25; also 2 wks Apr. Res accepted. Bar. Wine list. A la carte entrees: dinner $20-$26. Colonial decor. Totally nonsmoking. Cr cds: A, DS, MC, V.

D

★ ★ ★ **OLD NEWFANE.** (See Old Newfane Inn) 802/365-4427. Continental menu. Specialties: frogs' legs, wild game. Own baking. Hrs: 6-9 pm; Sun 5-8:30 pm. Closed Mon; Apr-late May, Nov-mid-Dec. Res accepted. Bar. Wine list. Semi-a la carte: dinner $16.95-$28. Historical landmark (1787); colonial decor. No cr cds accepted.

Newport (B-3)

Settled 1793 **Pop** 4,434 **Elev** 723 ft **Area code** 802 **Zip** 05855
Information Chamber of Commerce, The Causeway; 802/334-7782.

Just a few miles from the Canadian border, Newport lies at the southern end of Lake Memphremagog. Rugged Owl's Head (3,360 ft) guards the western shore of the lake. Recreational activities in the area include swimming, fishing, boating, camping, skiing and snowmobiling.

What to See and Do

Goodrich Memorial Library. Artifacts of old Vermont in historic building; animal display. (Daily exc Sun; closed major hols) 70 Main St. Phone 802/334-7902. **Free.**

Haskell Opera House & Library. Historic turn-of-the-century building owned jointly by local Canadian and US residents. First floor houses library with reading rm in US, book stacks in Canada. Second floor is replica of the old Boston Opera House (seats 300) with audience in US, stage in Canada. Summer concert series (fee). 8 mi N via US 5, on Caswell Ave in Derby Line, Vermont, and Rock Island, Quebec, Canada. Phone 802/873-3022.

Newport's *Princess.* Cruise Lake Memphremagog, in both US and Canadian waters, aboard sternwheeler with turn-of-the-century decor. Cruises include Sightseeing (1 ½ hrs), **Pizza** (1 ½ hrs, res required), **Buffet Dinner** (2 hrs, res required), **Moonlight** (1 ½ hrs), and **Weekend Brunch** (1 ½ hrs, res required). (May-Oct, daily; departures vary) City Dock. For schedule and res, phone 802/334-6617. ¢¢¢-¢¢¢¢¢

Northeast Kingdom Tours. Escorted bus tours depart from Newport Municipal Bldg and local motels. Narrated trips (2 & 4 hrs) explore international border region (Vermont/Canada); includes stops at dairy farm and Old Stone House museum. Cruises on Lake Memphremagog and trips to Montréal also avail. 3 Clough St. For res, schedule and fee information phone 802/334-8687.

Old Stone House (1836). Museum housed in 4-story granite building with antique furniture; early farm, household and military items; 19th-century schoolbooks. (July-Aug, daily; mid-May-June, Sept-mid-Oct, Fri-Tues) 11 mi SE via US 5S or I-91 S to Orleans, then 2 mi NE on unnumbered road to Brownington Village. Phone 802/754-2022. ¢¢

Motels

★ ★ **NEWPORT CITY.** 974 E Main St (US 5). 802/334-6558; FAX 802/334-6557; res: 800/338-6558. 64 rms, 2 story. S, D $58-$75. Crib $6. TV; cable. Indoor pool; whirlpool. Coffee in rms. Restaurant opp 5:30 am-2 pm. Ck-out 11 am. Meeting rm. Business servs avail. In-rm modem link. Sundries. Downhill/x-country ski 15 mi. Exercise equipt. Some refrigerators. Balconies. Cr cds: A, C, D, DS, MC, V.

✔ ★ **SUPER 8.** 974 E Main St (05829), I-91 exit 25. 802/334-1775; FAX 802/334-1994. 52 rms, 2 story. S $45.88; D $58.88; each addl $6; suites $106; under 12 free. Crib $6. TV; cable. Complimentary continental bkfst. Restaurant nearby. Ck-out 11 am. Business servs avail. Cr cds: A, C, D, DS, JCB, MC, V.

D SC

Restaurant

★ ★ **THE EAST SIDE.** Lake St. 802/334-2340. Continental menu. Specializes in fresh seafood, steak, prime rib. Own desserts. Hrs: 7:30 am-10 pm; Sun from 7 am. Closed Mon (winter); Dec 25. Bar. Semi-a la carte: bkfst $3.25-$5.95, lunch $3.95-$6.95, dinner $7.50-$15. Outdoor dining. On lake; dockage. Cr cds: DS, MC, V.

D SC

North Hero (B-1)

Pop 502 **Elev** 111 ft **Area code** 802 **Zip** 05474 **E-mail** ilandfun@together.net **Web** www.champlainislands.com
Information Champlain Islands Chamber of Commerce, PO Box 213; 802/372-5683.

What to See and Do

North Hero State Park. A 399-acre park located in the N part of the Champlain Islands; extensive shoreline on Lake Champlain. Swimming; fishing; boating (ramps). Hiking trails. Playground. Tent & trailer sites (dump station), lean-tos. (Memorial Day-Labor Day) Standard fees. 6 mi N, off US 2 near South Alburg. Phone 802/372-8727 or 802/879-5674.

Seasonal Event

Royal Lippizan Stallions of Austria. Summer residence of the stallions. Performances Thurs & Fri eves, Sat & Sun afternoons. For ticket prices, contact Chamber of Commerce. July-Aug.

Motels

★ **RUTHCLIFFE LODGE.** (Old Quarry Rd, Isle La Motte 05463) N on US 2, W on VT 129, follow signs. 802/928-3200; FAX 802/928-3200. E-mail rcliffe@together.net; web www.virtualcities.com/ virtual. 9 rms, shower only, 3 share bath, 2 story. No A/C. No rm phones. Mid-June-mid-Oct: S, D $65-$96.50; each addl $15; lower rates mid-May-mid-June. Closed rest of yr. Crib free. TV avail. Complimentary full bkfst. Complimentary coffee in rms. Restaurant 8:30-11 am, noon-2 pm, 5-9 pm. Ck-out 11:30 am. Bicycle rentals. Lawn games. Picnic tables, grills. On lake, dockage; boats, canoes avail. Totally nonsmoking. Cr cds: A, DS, MC, V.

★ ★ **SHORE ACRES INN AND RESTAURANT.** US 2. 802/372-8722. E-mail info@shoreacres.com; web www.shoreacres.com. 23 rms, 9 A/C. Mid-June-mid-Oct: S, D $79.50-$129.50; lower rates rest of yr; limited rms avail mid-Oct-May. Pet accepted. TV; cable. Restaurant 7:30-10 am, 5-9 pm. Bar. Ck-out 10:30 am. Driving range. Lawn games.

Two tennis courts. Some refrigerators. 50 acres on Lake Champlain; panoramic view. Cr cds: DS, MC, V.

Inns

★ ★ ★ **NORTH HERO HOUSE.** *Champlain Islands, In center of village on US 2.* 802/372-4732; res: 888/525-3644; FAX 802/372-3218. E-mail nhhlake@aol.com; web www.northherohouse.com. 26 rms, 3 story. May-late Oct: S, D $79-$285; each addl $5-$45. Closed rest of yr. TV. Complimentary continental bkfst. Restaurant (see NORTH HERO HOUSE). Bar 5-11 pm. Ck-out 11 am, ck-in 2 pm. Tennis. Game rm. Lawn games. Some private patios, balconies. Rms vary in size, decor. Built in 1800; fireplace in lobby. On lake; beach, dockage. Cr cds: MC, V.

★ ★ **THOMAS MOTT HOMESTEAD.** *(Blue Rock Rd, Alburg 05440-9620)* 14 mi S, off VT 78. 802/796-3736; res: 800/348-0843. Web www.go-native.com/inns/0162.html. 5 rms, 2 story. No A/C. S, D $75-$95; each addl $10. Children over 6 yrs only. TV in sitting rm. Complimentary full bkfst; afternoon refreshments. Ck-out 11 am, ck-in 3 pm. X-country ski on site. Rec rm. Complimentary gourmet ice cream. Restored farmhouse (1838); overlooks lake. Totally nonsmoking. Cr cds: A, C, D, DS, MC, V.

Restaurant

★ ★ **NORTH HERO HOUSE.** *(See North Hero House Inn)* 802/372-4732. E-mail nhhlake@aol.com; web www.members.aol.com/nhhlake/. Specializes in fresh seafood, homemade desserts. Hrs: 8-9:30 am, 5:30-9 pm; Sun brunch 10 am-1:30 pm. Closed late Oct-mid May. Res accepted. Bar. Semi-a la carte: dinner $9.95-$14.95. Bkfst buffet $3.95-$6.95 (wkends). Sun brunch $11.95. Outdoor dining. Totally nonsmoking. Cr cds: A, DS, MC, V.

Okemo State Forest (G-2)

(See also Ludlow, Weston)

Information Okemo Mt Resort, 77 Okemo Ridge Rd, Ludlow 05149; 802/228-4041 or 800/78-OKEMO (lodging res).

Mt Okemo (3,372 ft), almost a lone peak in south central Vermont near Ludlow, commands splendid views of the Adirondacks, the White Mountains, the Connecticut Valley and Vermont's own Green Mountains. A road goes to within one-half-mile of the mountain top (summer, fall; free); from there, it's an easy hike to the fire tower at the top. Surrounding Mt Okemo is the 4,527-acre state forest, which is primarily a skiing area.

Area has 7 quad, 3 triple chairlifts, 2 Pomalifts, J-bar; patrol, school, rentals; snowmaking; cafeteria, restaurants, bar; nursery; 96 runs, longest run 4¹/₂ mi; vertical drop 2,150 ft. (Early Nov-mid-Apr, daily) Phone 802/228-4041; snow conditions, 802/228-5222; for information about area lodging phone 802/228-5571. ¢¢¢¢¢

Peru (G-2)

(See also Londonderry, Manchester & Manchester Center)

Settled 1773 **Pop** 324 **Elev** 1,700 ft **Area code** 802 **Zip** 05152

This small mountain village has many fine examples of classic New England architecture, such as the Congregational Church (1846). Spec-

tacular views of the Green Mountains surround this skiing center; also a popular area for fishing, hunting and hiking.

What to See and Do

Bromley Mt Ski Area. Area has 2 quad, 5 double chairlifts, 2 Mitey-mites, J-bar; patrol, school, rentals; snowmaking; 2 cafeterias, restaurant, 2 lounges; nursery; 41 runs, longest run over 2 mi; vertical drop 1,334 ft. (Mid-Nov-mid-Apr, daily) 2 mi SW on VT 11. Phone 802/824-5522. ¢¢¢

Summer activities Include miniature golf, thrill sleds, children's theater. (Mid-June-mid-Oct) Also

Bromley Alpine Slide. Speed-controlled sled ride and scenic chairlift; cafe, picnic area. Outdoor deck. Multistate view. (Late May-mid-Oct, daily, weather permitting) Phone 802/824-5522. ¢¢¢

Hapgood Pond Recreation Area. Swimming; fishing; boating. Picnicking. Camping. Fee for various activities. 2 mi NE on Hapgood Pond Rd, in Green Mt Natl Forest (see). Phone 802/824-6456. Per vehicle ¢¢

J.J. Hapgood Store (1827). General store featuring interesting old items; also penny candy, maple syrup, cheese. (Daily) Main St. Phone 802/824-5911.

Wild Wings Ski Touring Center. School, rentals; warming rm; concession. Twelve mi of groomed trails. 2¹/₂ mi N on North Rd.Phone 802/824-6793. ¢¢¢

Plymouth (F-2)

(See also Killington, Ludlow, Woodstock)

Pop 440 **Elev** 1,406 ft **Area code** 802 **Zip** 05056
Information Town of Plymouth, HC 70, Box 39A; 802/672-3655.

Seemingly unaware of the 20th century, this town hasn't changed much since July 4, 1872, when Calvin Coolidge was born in the back of the village store, still in business today. A country road leads to the cemetery where the former president and six generations of his family are buried. Nearby is the Coolidge Visitor's Center and Museum, which displays historical and presidential memorabilia.

What to See and Do

Calvin Coolidge State Forest. A 16,165-acre area. Hiking, snowmobile trails. Picnic facilities. Tent & trailer sites (dump station), primitive camping, lean-tos. (Memorial Day-Columbus Day) Standard fees. 1 mi N off VT 100A, Calvin Coolidge Memorial Hwy. Phone 802/672-3612 or 802/886-2434.

Plymouth Cheese Corp. Cheese, canned products, maple syrup and honey. Cheese processed Mon-Wed. (Facility open late May-Nov, daily; rest of yr, Mon-Fri; closed Jan 1, Thanksgiving, Dec 25) Phone 802/672-3650. **Free.**

President Calvin Coolidge Homestead. Restored to its early 20th-century appearance, Calvin Coolidge was sworn in by his father in the sitting rm in 1923. The Plymouth Historic District also includes the General Store that was operated by the President's father, the house where the President was born, the village dance hall which served as the 1924 summer White House office, the Union Church with its Carpenter-Gothic interior, the Wilder House (birthplace of Coolidge's mother), the Wilder Barn with 19th-century farming equipment, a restaurant and a visitors center with museum. (Late May-mid-Oct, daily) 1 mi NE on VT 100A, in Plymouth Notch. Phone 802/672-3773. ¢¢

Motel

✔★ **FARMBROOK.** *Box 139, 3 mi NE on VT 100A.* 802/672-3621. 12 rms, 1-2 story, 2 kits. No rm phones. S, D $45-$55; each addl $7; kit. units $60-$69; wkly rates; higher rates fall foliage. TV. Complimentary coffee in rms. Ck-out 11 am. Picnic tables, grill. Stream, water wheel. Near birthplace of Calvin Coolidge. No cr cds accepted.

Resort

★ ★ ★ **HAWK INN & MOUNTAIN RESORT.** *Box 64 Rte 100, 8 mi S of US 4 on VT 100.* *802/672-3811; FAX 802/672-5582; res: 800/685-4295.* Web www.hawkresort.com. 150 houses, townhouses, 50 inn rms. Late Dec-Feb: 2-4 bedrm houses, townhouses $250-$700/house; inn rms (includes bkfst): S, D $169-$279; wkly, monthly rates; ski plans; MAP & EP avail; lower rates rest of yr. Crib free. Maid serv $25/hr (houses, townhouses). TV; cable (premium), VCR (movies $3.50). 2 pools; 1 indoor; whirlpool. Playground. Supervised child's activities (June-Aug); ages 5-12. Full bkfst. Coffee in rms. Dining rm 6-10 pm. Rm serv (inn rms). Box lunches, picnics. Chef for hire. Bar. Ck-out 11 am, ck-in 4 pm. Grocery 2 mi. Package store 8 mi. Meeting rms. Business servs avail. In-rm modem link. Valet serv. Airport, RR station, bus depot transportation. Tennis. Swimming in natural pond. Boats, rowboats, canoes, sailboats, paddleboats. Downhill ski 10 mi; x-country ski on site. Tobogganing, ice skating. Horse-drawn sleigh rides. Hiking. Bicycles. Lawn games. Entertainment, movies. Exercise rm; sauna. Massage. Fishing guides. Refrigerators, minibars, fieldstone fireplaces. Private patios, balconies. Picnic tables, grills. Nature trails. Custom-designed vacation homes. Cr cds: A, C, D, DS, MC, V.

Rutland (F-2)

(See also Brandon, Killington)

Settled 1761 **Pop** 18,230 **Elev** 648 ft **Area code** 802 **Zip** 05701 **E-mail** rrccvt@aol.com **Web** www.rutlandvermont.com

Information Chamber of Commerce, 256 N Main St; 802/773-2747.

This is Vermont's second-largest city. Its oldest newspaper, the *Rutland Herald*, has been published continuously since 1794. The world's deepest marble quarry is in West Rutland. The office of the supervisor of the Green Mountain National Forests(see) is located here.

What to See and Do

Chaffee Center for the Visual Arts. Continuous exhibits of paintings, graphics, photography, crafts, sculpture. Print rm; gallery shop; annual art festivals (mid-Aug, Columbus Day wkend); other special events. (Daily exc Tues; closed major hols) 16 S Main St, on US 7, opp Main St Park. Phone 802/775-0356. **Free.**

Hubbardton Battlefield and Museum. On July 7, 1777, the Green Mountain Boys and colonial troops from Massachusetts and New Hampshire stopped British forces pursuing the American Army from Ft Ticonderoga. This was the only battle of the Revolution fought on Vermont soil and the first in a series of engagements that led to the capitulation of Burgoyne at Saratoga. Visitor Center with exhibits. Battle monument; trails; picnicking. (Memorial Day-Columbus Day, Wed-Sun) 7 mi W via US 4, exit 5. Phone 802/759-2412. **¢**

Mountain Top Cross Country Ski Resort. Patrol, school, rentals; snowmaking; concession area, restaurant at inn. 68 mi of cross-country trails. Ice-skating, horse-drawn sleigh rides. (Nov-Apr, daily) N via US 7, then 10 mi NE on unnumbered road, follow signs. Phone 802/483-2311 or 800/445-2100. **¢¢¢¢**

New England Maple Museum. One of largest collections of antique maple sugaring artifacts in the world; 2 large dioramas featuring more than 100 hand-carved figures; narrated slide show; demonstrations, samples of Vermont foodstuffs; craft and maple product gift shop. (Mid-Mar-Dec 24, daily; closed Thanksgiving) 7 mi N on US 7, in Pittsford. Phone 802/483-9414. **¢¢**

Norman Rockwell Museum. More than 2,000 pictures and Rockwell memorabilia spanning 60 yrs of artist's career. Includes the *Four Freedoms,* Boy Scout series, many magazine covers, including all 323 from the *Saturday Evening Post,* and nearly every illustration and advertisement. (Daily; closed Jan 1, Easter, Thanksgiving, Dec 25) Gift shop. E on US 4. Phone 802/773-6095. **¢¢**

 Vermont Marble Exhibit. Exhibit explains how marble is formed and the process by which it is manufactured. Displays; sculptor at work; balcony view of factory; "Gallery of the Presidents"; movie on the marble industry; marble market, gift shop. (June-Oct, daily; rest of yr, daily exc Sun) 61 Main St, 2 mi W on US 4, then 4 mi N on VT 3 in Proctor, adj to Vermont Marble Co factory. Phone 802/459-3311 or 800/451-4468, ext 436. **¢¢**

Wilson Castle. This 32-rm, 19th-century mansion, on a 115-acre estate, features 19 open proscenium arches, 84 stained-glass windows, 13 imported-tile fireplaces, a towering turret and parapet; European and Oriental furnishings; art gallery; sculpture; 15 other buildings. Picnic area. Guided tours. (Late May-mid-Oct, daily) 2¹/₂ mi W on US 4, then 1 mi N on West Proctor Rd. Phone 802/773-3284. **¢¢¢**

Annual Events

Green Mountain International Rodeo. PRCA rodeo. Free pony rides, petting zoo. Bands, dancing. Phone 802/773-2747. Mid-June.

Vermont State Fair. Exhibits of arts and crafts, flowers, produce, home arts, pets, animals, maple sugaring. Daily special events. Late-Aug-early-Sept.

Motels

★ ★ ★ **BEST WESTERN HOGGE PENNY.** *3 mi E on US 4.* *802/773-3200.* 112 units, 2 story, 56 kits. S, D $59-$99; each addl $8; suites for 2-8, $79-$210; under 12 free; wkly rates; ski plan; higher rates: special events, fall foliage. Crib free. TV; cable, VCR avail (movies $6). Heated pool. Complimentary continental bkfst. Coffee in rms. Restaurant 7-11 am, 5-10 pm. Bar 4 pm-midnight. Ck-out 11 am. Coin lndry. Meeting rms. Business servs avail. In-rm modem link. Sundries. Tennis. Downhill/x-country ski 12 mi. Private patios, balconies. Fireplace in lobby. Cr cds: A, C, D, DS, MC, V.

★ ★ **COMFORT INN.** *19 Allen St.* *802/775-2200.* E-mail comfort@vermontel.com; web www.comfortinn.com. 104 rms, 3 story. S, D $64.95-$89.95; each addl $10; under 18 free; higher rates: hols, fall foliage. Crib free. TV; cable. Indoor pool; whirlpool, sauna. Complimentary continental bkfst. Coffee in rms. Restaurant adj 11:30 am-10 pm. Ck-out 11 am. Meeting rms. Downhill/x-country ski 15 mi. Business servs avail. In-rm modem link. Refrigerators avail. Cr cds: A, C, D, DS, ER, JCB, MC, V.

★ ★ ★ **HOLIDAY INN CENTRE OF VERMONT.** *S Main St (US 7).* *802/775-1911; FAX 802/775-0113.* Web www.holidayinn-vermont.com. 151 rms. S, D $99-$111; MAP avail; ski plan; higher rates: wkends Jan-Mar, hols. Crib free. TV; cable (premium). Indoor pool; whirlpool, poolside serv. Coffee in rms. Restaurant 6:30 am-9 pm. Rm serv. Bar noon-1 am; entertainment. Ck-out noon. Coin lndry. Meeting rms. Business center. In-rm modem link. Bellhops. Sundries. Free airport, bus depot transportation. Downhill/x-country ski 10 mi. Exercise rm; sauna. Game rm. Lawn games. Fireplace in lobby. Cr cds: A, C, D, DS, JCB, MC, V.

✓★ ★ **HOWARD JOHNSON.** *S Main St, on US 7.* *802/775-4303; FAX 802/775-6840.* 96 rms, 2 story. S, D $42-$100; each addl $8; under 18 free. Crib free. TV; cable (premium), VCR avail (movies $2). Indoor pool; sauna. Complimentary continental bkfst. Ck-out noon. Guest lndry. Meeting rms. Business servs avail. Downhill/x-country ski 16 mi. Health club privileges. Game rm. Private patios, balconies. Cr cds: A, C, D, DS, ER, JCB, MC, V.

✔★ ★ **RAMADA LIMITED.** *253 S Main St (US 7).* 802/773-3361; *FAX 802/773-4892.* E-mail ramada@vermontel.com. 76 rms, 2 story, 3 kits. S, D $49-$89; each addl $6-$10; kit. units $89-$129; family rates; higher rates: hol wks. Crib free. TV; cable (premium). Indoor pool; sauna. Bkfst avail. Ck-out noon. Meeting rm. Downhill/x-country ski 16 mi. Health club privileges. Balconies. Cr cds: A, D, DS, MC, V.

[D] [symbols] SC

Inns

★ **FINCH & CHUBB.** *(82 N Williams St, Whitehall 12887)* 24 mi E on NY 4. 518/499-2049; FAX 518/499-2049. E-mail finch_chubb@msn.com. 8 rms, 1 shower only, 2 story. July-Aug: S $39-$59; D $59-$89; each addl $10; under 13 free; lower rates rest of yr. Crib free. TV; cable. Complimentary continental bkfst. Restaurant 11:30 am-2 pm, 4:30-9:30 pm. Ck-out 11:30 am, ck-in 3 pm. Pool. Built 1810 as an ammunition warehouse for US Navy during the war of 1812. Cr cds: A, C, D, DS, MC, V.

[symbols]

★ ★ **THE INN AT RUTLAND.** *70 N Main St.* 802/773-0575; *FAX 802/775-3506; res: 800/808-0575.* Web www.innrutland@vermontel.com. 2 rms, 4 with shower only, 3 story. Mid-Dec-Mar: S $69-$169; D $79-$179; each addl $10; under 6 free; ski plans; hols, fall foliage (2-day min); lower rates rest of yr. TV; cable, VCR in common rm. Complimentary full bkfst. Restaurant nearby. Ck-out 11 am, ck-in 3 pm. Business servs avail. In-rm modem link. Downhill/x-country ski 10 mi. Health club privileges. Built in 1890; furnished with Victorian decor. Totally nonsmoking. Cr cds: A, C, D, DS, MC, V.

[symbols]

★ ★ **MAPLEWOOD.** *(Rte 22A S, Fair Haven 05743)* 18 mi W on US 4 to VT 22A, then S, 1 mi past Fair Haven. 802/265-8039; *FAX 802/265-8210; res: 800/253-7729.* 5 rms, 2 story. Phones avail. S, D $75-$89; each addl $20; suites $115-$125. Children over 5 yrs only. TV; cable (premium). Complimentary continental bkfst. Setups. Ck-out 11 am, ck-in 2 pm. Business servs avail. Some fireplaces. Historic building (1843) part of dairy farm; antiques. Cr cds: A, C, D, DS, MC, V.

[symbol]

★ ★ **TULIP TREE.** *(Chittenden Dam Rd, Chittenden 05737)* 10 mi NE on US 7 to Chittenden Rd, follow signs. 802/483-6213; *res: 802/483-2623; res: 800/707-0017.* Web www.tuliptreeinn.com. 8 rms, 2 story. No rm phones. MAP: S, D $130-$299; wkly, wkend rates; ski plans; higher rates hol wkends. Closed Apr-mid May & 1st two wks Nov. Children over 17 yrs only. Dining rm 7 pm sitting. Bar 3 pm-midnight. Ck-out 11 am, ck-in 3 pm. Downhill ski 16 mi; x-country ski 1½ mi. Wooded grounds, trout stream. Previous home of William Barstow (1842), partner with Thomas Edison; antiques. Library, sitting rm. Cr cds: MC, V.

[symbols]

Resort

★ ★ **MOUNTAIN TOP INN AND RESORT.** *(Mountain Top Rd, Chittenden 05737)* 4 mi N on VT 7, then 6 mi NE via Chittenden Rd. 802/483-2311; *FAX 802/483-6373; res: 800/445-2100.* Web www.mountaintopinn.com. 60 units. EP: S, D $90-$115/person; each addl $60; cottages $105/person; MAP avail. Closed Apr & 1st 3 wks Nov. Crib free. TV in lobby; VCR (free movies). Heated pool; sauna, poolside serv. Complimentary coffee in rms. Dining rm (public by res) 8-10 am, noon-2 pm, 6-8:30 pm; Fri, Sat 6-9 pm. Rm serv. Bar noon-11:30 pm. Business servs avail. Gift shop. Bus depot transportation. Tennis. Par-3 golf course, putting green, golf school. Boats, rowboats, canoes. Fly fishing instruction. Downhill ski 8 mi; x-country ski on site; lessons, rental, snow making equipt. Sleigh rides. Hiking trails. Lawn games. Rec rm. Movie rm. Homemade maple syrup. On mountain top; 1,300 acres; scenic views. Cr cds: A, MC, V.

[symbols]

Restaurants

✔★ ★ **CASA BIANCA.** *76 Grove St.* 802/773-7401. Italian menu. Hrs: 5-10 pm; early-bird dinner Tues-Fri to 6:30 pm. Closed Mon; Dec 25. Res accepted. Bar. Semi-a la carte: dinner $9.95-$14.95. Child's meals. 4 dining rms in house, Italian country atmosphere. Cr cds: A, D, DS, MC, V.

[D]

★ ★ **COUNTRYMAN'S PLEASURE.** *(Townline Rd, Mendon)* 3 mi E off US 4 near Killington-Pico ski area. 802/773-7141. German, Austrian menu. Specialties: roast duck with raspberry sauce, sauerbraten, wild game. Own baking. Hrs: 5-9 pm; Sat to 10 pm; early-bird dinner 5-6 pm. Closed Dec 24, 25. Res accepted. Bar. Semi-a la carte: dinner $11.95-$22.95. Child's meals. Restored farmhouse (1824). Sun-porch dining. Cr cds: A, C, D, MC, V.

[D] SC [symbol]

★ ★ **ROYAL'S 121 HEARTHSIDE.** *37 N Main St (US 7), at jct US 4.* 802/775-0856. Specializes in New England dishes, popovers, fresh seafood. Own desserts. Hrs: 11 am-10 pm; Sun noon-9 pm; early-bird dinner Mon-Fri 5-6:30 pm. Res accepted; required hols. Bar. Semi-a la carte: lunch $5.25-$10.95, dinner $11.95-$19.95. Open-hearth charcoal cooking. Fireplaces. Cr cds: A, C, D, DS, MC, V.

[D] SC [symbol]

★ ★ **SIRLOIN SALOON.** *200 S Main St (US 7).* 802/773-7900. Specializes in wood-grilled steak, chicken, seafood. Salad bar. Hrs: 5-10 pm; Fri, Sat to 11 pm. Closed Thanksgiving. Res accepted. Bar 4-10 pm; Fri, Sat to 11 pm. Semi-a la carte: dinner $7.95-$18.95. Child's meals. Native American artwork, artifacts. Cr cds: A, D, DS, MC, V.

[D] [symbols]

Shelburne (D-1)

(See also Burlington, Vergennes)

Settled 1763 **Pop** 5,871 **Elev** 148 ft **Area code** 802 **Zip** 05482 **E-mail** shelbvt@together.net **Web** www.vermont.towns.org/shelburne
Information Town Hall, 5376 Shelburne Rd, PO Box 88; 802/985-5116.

Shelburne is a small, friendly town bordering Lake Champlain. West of town are the Adirondack Mountains; to the east are the Green Mountains. The Shelburne Museum has one of the most comprehensive exhibits of early American life.

What to See and Do

Charlotte-Essex Ferry. Makes 20-min trips across Lake Champlain to Essex, NY (Apr-Jan, daily). 5 mi S on US 7 to Charlotte, then 2 mi W to dock. Phone 802/864-9804 for schedule. (See BURLINGTON) One way, individual ¢; vehicle ¢¢¢

Mt Philo State Park. A 648-acre mountain-top park offering beautiful views of the Lake Champlain Valley. Picnicking. Camping, lean-tos. Entrance and camp roads are steep; not recommended for trailers. (Memorial Day-Columbus Day) Standard fees. 5 mi S on US 7, then 1 mi E on local road. Phone 802/425-2390 or 802/483-2001.

Shelburne Farms. Former estate of Dr. Seward Webb and his wife, Lila Vanderbilt, built at the turn of the century; beautifully situated on the shores of Lake Champlain. The grounds, landscaped by Frederick Law Olmstead and forested by Gifford Pinchot, once totalled 3,800 acres. Structures include the Webbs' mansion, Shelburne House, a 110-rm summer "cottage" built in the late 1800s on a bluff overlooking the lake; a 5-story farm barn with a courtyard of more than 2 acres; and the coach barn, once the home of prize horses. Tours (Memorial Day-mid-Oct, daily; closed hols). Also hay rides; walking trail. Visitor center, 802/985-8442. Cheese shop (all yr, daily). Overnight stays avail. Harbor & Bay Rds. Phone 802/985-8686. Tours ¢¢¢

⭐ **Shelburne Museum.** Founded by Electra Webb, daughter of Sugar King H.O. Havemeyer, this stupendous collection of Americana is located on 45 acres of park-like setting with 37 historic buildings containing items such as historic circus posters, toys, weather vanes, trade signs, and an extensive collection of wildfowl decoys and dolls. American and European paintings and prints (including works by Monet and Grandma Moses) are on display as well. Also here is the 220-ft sidewheel steamboat *Ticonderoga,* which carried passengers across Lake Champlain in the early part of the century and is now the last vertical beam passenger and freight sidewheel steamer intact in the US; a working carousel and a 5,000-piece hand-carved miniature traveling circus; a fully intact lighthouse; one-rm schoolhouse; authentic country store; the only 2-lane covered bridge with footpath in Vermont; blacksmith shop; printing & weaving demonstrations; farm equipment and over 200 horse-drawn vehicles on display. Visitor orientation film; free jitney; cafeteria; museum stores; free parking. (Late May-late Oct, daily; rest of yr, limited hrs) On US 7, in center of town. Phone 802/985-3346. ¢¢¢¢¢

Vermont Teddy Bear Company. Guided tour of "bear" factory shows process of handcrafting these famous stuffed animals. Gift shop. (Mon-Sat, also Sun afternoons) 6655 Shelburne Rd (VT 7). Phone 802/985-3001. ¢

Vermont Wildflower Farm. Acres of wildflower gardens, flower fields and woodlands; pond and brook. Changing slide/sound show (every 1/2-hr). Gift shop. (May-late Oct, daily) 5 mi S via US 7. Phone 802/425-3500. ¢¢

Motels

★ ★ **DAYS INN.** *1976 Shelburne Rd, 1¹/₂ mi N on US 7. 802/985-3334; res: 800/329-7466; FAX 802/985-3419.* 58 rms, 2 story. July-mid-Sept: S, D $65-$75; each addl $7; higher rates: fall foliage season, Labor Day, Columbus Day; lower rates rest of yr. Crib free. TV; cable. Pool. Complimentary continental bkfst. Ck-out 11 am. Downhill ski 20 mi. Cr cds: A, D, DS, JCB, MC, V.

🏊 〰 ⬜ 🐾 SC

✔★ **ECONO LODGE.** *1961 Shelburne Rd. 802/985-3377; res: 800/825-1882; FAX 802/985-3377.* 51 rms, 1-2 story, 20 suites. S $39.95-$69.95; D $59.95-$79.95; each addl $5; suites $84.95; under 17 free; higher rates fall foliage season; lower rates rest of yr. Crib avail. Pet accepted; $50 deposit. TV; cable. Complimentary continental bkfst. Restaurant adj 4-9:30 pm. Ck-out 11 am. Meeting rms. Business servs avail. Coin lndry. Downhill/x-country ski 20 mi. Pool. Refrigerator, microwave in suites. Picnic tables, grills. Cr cds: A, D, DS, MC, V.

〰 SC

✔★ **T-BIRD.** *2062 Shelburne Rd, ³/₄ mi N on US 7. 802/985-3663; res: 800/335-5029.* 24 rms. May-Oct: D $48-$88; each addl $6-$8; higher rates: fall foliage season, hol wkends, graduations. Closed Nov-mid May. Crib $5. TV; cable. Pool. Complimentary continental bkfst. Restaurant nearby. Ck-out 11 am. Lawn games. Some refrigerators. Picnic tables. Cr cds: A, MC, V.

〰 🔥 SC

Inn

★ ★ ★ **INN AT SHELBURNE FARMS.** *102 Harbor Rd. 802/985-8498; FAX 802/985-1233.* 26 rms, 7 share bath, 3 story. No A/C. No elvtr. Sept-mid-Oct: S, D $195-$350; each addl $30; cottages $240-$300; wkends, hols (2-day min); lower rates rest of yr. Crib avail. Cable TV in common rm. Restaurant 7:30-11:30 am, 5:30-9:30 pm. Ck-out 11 am, ck-in 3 pm. Business servs avail. In-rm modem link. Luggage handling. Gift shop. Tennis. Downhill/x-country ski 20 mi. Rec rm. Lawn games. On lake. Built in 1887; still a working farm. Totally nonsmoking. Cr cds: A, DS, MC, V.

🐾 🏊 🎿 〰 🔥

Restaurant

★ ★ ★ **CAFE SHELBURNE.** *5 mi S on US 7. 802/985-3939.* French, continental menu. Specializes in fillet of lamb, fresh seafood. Hrs: 5:30-9 pm. Closed Sun, Mon. Res accepted. Bar. Wine cellar. A la carte entrees: dinner $16-$21. Porch dining. Provincial bistro atmosphere. Chef-owned. Cr cds: A, C, D, MC, V.

Springfield (G-3)

(See also Bellows Falls, Grafton)

Settled 1761 **Pop** 9,579 **Elev** 410 ft **Area code** 802 **Zip** 05156 **E-mail** spfldcoc@vermontel.com
Information Chamber of Commerce, 14 Clinton St; 802/885-2779.

The cascades of the Black River once provided power for the machine tool plants that stretch along Springfield's banks. Lord Jeffrey Amherst started the Crown Point Military Road to Lake Champlain from here in 1759. Springfield has been the home of many New England inventors. It is also the headquarters of the Amateur Telescope Makers who meet at Stellafane, an observatory site west of VT 11.

What to See and Do

Eureka Schoolhouse. Oldest schoolhouse in the state; built in 1790 and recently restored. Nearby is a 100-yr-old lattice-truss covered bridge. (Memorial Day-Columbus Day, daily) On VT 11 (Charleston Rd). Phone 802/885-2779. ¢¢

Reverend Dan Foster House & Old Forge. Historic parsonage (1785) contains antique furniture, textiles, utensils, farm tools; old forge has working machinery and bellows. Guided tours. (Late June-Sept, Thurs-Mon or by appt) 6 mi N on Valley St to Weathersfield Center Rd in Weathersfield. For further information contact the Chamber of Commerce.

Springfield Art and Historical Society. American art and artifacts. Collections include Richard Lee pewter; Bennington pottery; 19th-century American paintings; costumes; dolls; toys; Springfield historical items. Changing exhibits. (May-Nov, Tues-Fri; closed hols) 9 Elm Hill. Phone 802/885-2415. **Free.**

Annual Event

Vermont Apple Festival and Craft Show. Family activities, cider pressing, apple pie bake-off, entertainment, crafts. Phone 802/885-2779. Columbus Day wkend.

Motel

★ ★ **HOLIDAY INN EXPRESS.** *818 Charlestown Rd. 802/885-4516; FAX 802/885-4595.* E-mail hixpress@aol.com. 88 rms, 2 story. July-mid-Oct: S, D $79-$109; each addl $5; suites $159-$179; under 19 free; higher rates graduation wk; lower rates rest of yr. Crib free. Pet accepted. TV; cable. Indoor pool. Complimentary continental bkfst. Restaurant 6 am-11 pm. Bar 4-11 pm. Ck-out noon. Meeting rms. Business servs avail. In-rm modem link. Valet serv. Downhill ski 20 mi; x-country ski 14 mi. Exercise equipt. Refrigerators, microwaves avail. Picnic tables. Cr cds: A, C, D, DS, JCB, MC, V.

D ✦ 〰 🏊 ✈ 🍴 🔥 SC

Inns

★ ★ **HARTNESS HOUSE.** *30 Orchard St. 802/885-2115; FAX 802/885-2207.* E-mail carolynh@together.net; web www.sover.net/avt-store/hart1.html. 40 rms in 2 bldgs, 3 story, 29 motel units. D $87-$120; suites $150; under 14 free; wkly rates; package plans. Crib free. TV. Pool. Complimentary full bkfst. Restaurant (see HARTNESS HOUSE INN). Rm serv. Ck-out 11 am, ck-in 3 pm. Business servs avail. Downhill ski 20 mi.

Built 1903; an underground tunnel connects main house to an historic observatory with operational telescope. Cr cds: A, D, MC, V.

★ **HUGGING BEAR.** (Main St, Chester 05143) 8 mi SW on US 91. 802/875-2412; res: 800/325-0519. 6 rms, 2 story. No A/C. No rm phones. S $55-$65; D $75-$85; each addl $10-$25; higher rates fall foliage. Closed Thanksgiving. Crib free. TV in sitting rm; VCR (free movies). Complimentary full bkfst. Restaurant opp 7 am-8 pm. Ck-out 11 am, ck-in 3 pm. Gift shop featuring extensive collection of teddy bears. Downhill ski 15 mi; x-country ski 7 mi. Victorian house (ca 1850) furnished with antiques and teddy bears. Totally nonsmoking. Cr cds: A, DS, MC, V.

★★★ **INN AT WEATHERSFIELD.** (VT 106, Weathersfield 05151) N on VT 106, approx ½ mi S of Perkinsville; look for sign. 802/263-9217; FAX 802/263-9219; res: 800/477-4828. Web www.weathersfieldinn.com. 12 rms, 2 story, 3 suites. No A/C. MAP: D $175-$250; each addl $75. Children over 8 yrs only. TV in game rm. Complimentary full bkfst; afternoon refreshments. Dining rm 6-9 pm. Ck-out 11 am, ck-in 1 pm. Downhill ski 20 mi. Game rm. Lawn games. Many fireplaces. On 21 acres at base of Hawks Mt. Original bldg dates back to 1795. Swimming pond. Cr cds: A, C, D, DS, MC, V.

✔★★ **STONE HEARTH.** (VT 11, Chester 05143) I-91 exit 6, then 12 mi W on VT 11. 802/875-2525; FAX 802/875-4688. E-mail shinn@vermontel.com; web www.virtualvermont\countryinn\shinn. 9 rms, 3 story. No A/C. No rm phones. S $45-$60; D $70-$130; each addl $12-$40; wkly rates; ski plans. MAP avail. Crib $6. TV in lounge. Complimentary full bkfst. Dining rm 7:30-9 am, 6-7:30 pm. Bar from 4 pm. Ck-out 11 am, ck-in 3 pm. Gift shop. Downhill ski 7 mi; x-country ski 6 mi. Whirlpool. Game rm. Lawn games. Some fireplaces. Picnic tables, grills. Restored farm house (1810); antiques. Cr cds: DS, MC, V.

Restaurant

★★ **HARTNESS HOUSE INN.** (See Hartness House Inn) 802/885-2115. Continental menu. Specializes in fresh seafood. Hrs: 7-9 am, 11:30 am-2 pm, 5-9 pm; Sat, Sun 8-10 am. Res accepted. Bar from 5 pm; Fri, Sat to midnight. Semi-a la carte: bkfst $5.95, lunch $4.50-$6.95, dinner $11.95-$19.95. Outdoor dining. Historic building (1900). Tours. Totally nonsmoking. Cr cds: A, D, MC, V.

St Albans (B-1)

(See also Swanton)

Settled 1785 **Pop** 7,339 **Elev** 429 ft **Area code** 802 **Zip** 05478 **E-mail** stalbans@together.net **Web** www.together.net/~stalbans/chamber.htm

Information Chamber of Commerce, 2 N Main St, PO Box 327; 802/524-2444.

This small city is a railroad town (Central Vermont Railway) and center of maple syrup and dairy interests. It was a stop on the Underground Railroad and has had a surprisingly violent history. Smugglers used the city as a base of operations during the War of 1812. On October 19, 1864, the northernmost engagement of the Civil War was fought here when a small group of Confederates raided the three banks in town and fled to Canada with $200,000. In 1866, the Fenians, an Irish organization pledged to capture Canada, had its headquarters here.

What to See and Do

Brainerd Monument. A father's revengeful commemoration of his son's death in Andersonville Prison. Greenwood Cemetery, S Main St.

Burton Island State Park. This 253-acre park offers swimming beach; fishing; canoeing (rentals), boating (rentals, marina with electrical hookups). Nature, hiking trails. Picnicking, concession. Tent sites, lean-tos. (Memorial Day-Labor Day) Standard fees. On island in Lake Champlain; 5 mi W on VT 36, then 3 mi SW on unnumbered road to Kamp Kill Kare State Park access area, where passenger ferry service (fee) is avail to island; visitors may use their own boats to reach the island. Phone 802/879-5674.

Chester A. Arthur Historic Site. Replica of second house of 21st president; nearby is brick church (1830) where Arthur's father was preacher. Exhibit of Chester A. Arthur's life and career. Rural setting; picnic area. (Mid-June-mid-Oct, Wed-Sun) 10 mi W via VT 36 to Fairfield, then unpaved road to site. Phone 802/828-3226.

Lake Carmi State Park. This 482-acre park features rolling farmland; 2-mi lakefront, swimming beach, bathhouse; fishing; boating (ramps, rentals). Nature trails. Picnicking, concession. Tent & trailer sites (dump station), lean-tos. (Memorial Day-Labor Day) Standard fees. 15 mi NE on VT 105 to North Sheldon, then 3 mi N on VT 236. Phone 802/879-5674.

St Albans Historical Museum. Toys, dolls; clothing; railroad memorabilia; farm implements; St Albans Confederate Raid material; photographs; library and reference rm; re-created doctor's office with medical and X-ray collections; items and documents of local historical interest. (June-Sept, Tues-Sat, also by appt) Church St. Phone 802/527-7933. ¢

Annual Events

Maple Sugar Festival. A number of producers welcome visitors who join sugarhouse parties for sugar-on-snow, sour pickles and raised doughnuts. Continuing events; arts and crafts; antiques; wood-chopping contests. Usually last wkend Apr.

Bay Day. Family activity day. Great Race, one-legged running, family games; volleyball, canoeing and bicycling. Concessions. Fireworks. July 4 wkend.

Civil War Days. Taylor Park. A 3-day event depicting scenes of the Civil War in St Albans, the northernmost point where the war was fought. Reenactment of major battle, entertainment, antiques. Mid-Oct.

Motels

★ **CADILLAC.** 213 Main St (US 7). 802/524-2191; FAX 802/527-1483. E-mail cadmotel@together.net; web www.motel-cadillac.com. 54 rms, S $43-$60; D $49-$75; each addl $7. Crib $7. TV; cable (premium). Heated pool. Restaurant 7 am-9 pm. Ck-out 11 am. Meeting rm. Sundries. Lawn games. Refrigerators. Picnic tables, grills. Cr cds: A, C, D, DS, MC, V.

★★ **COMFORT INN & SUITES.** 167 Fairfax Rd, I-89 exit 19. 802/524-3300. E-mail comfort2@together.net; web www.vtcomfortinn.com. 63 rms, 3 story, 17 suites. July-mid-Sept: S, D $69-$79; each addl $5; suites $95-$114; under 18 free; higher rates fall foliage; lower rates rest of yr. Crib free. TV; cable (premium). Complimentary continental bkfst. Restaurant nearby. Ck-out noon. Meeting rms. Business servs avail. In-rm modem link. Coin lndry. Exercise equipt. Indoor pool. Game rm. Refrigerator, microwave in suites. Picnic tables. Cr cds: A, C, D, DS, ER, JCB, MC, V.

St Johnsbury (C-4)

(See also Lyndonville)

Settled 1787 **Pop** 7,608 **Elev** 588 ft **Area code** 802 **Zip** 05819 **E-mail** nekinfo@vermontnekchamber.org **Web** www.vermontnekchamber.org
Information Northeast Kingdom Chamber of Commerce, 30 Western Ave; 802/748-3678 or 800/639-6379.

This town was named for Ethan Allen's French friend, St John de Crève-coeur, author of *Letters from an American Farmer.* The town gained fame and fortune when Thaddeus Fairbanks invented the platform scale in 1830. Fairbanks Scales, maple syrup and manufacturing are among its major industries.

What to See and Do

Fairbanks Museum and Planetarium. Exhibits and programs on natural science, regional history, archeology, anthropology, astronomy and the arts. More than 4,500 mounted birds and mammals; antique toys; farm, village and craft tools; Northern New England Weather Broadcasting Center; planetarium; Hall of Science; special exhibitions in Gallery Wing. (Mon-Sat, also Sun afternoons; closed Jan 1, Dec 25) Planetarium (July-Aug, daily; rest of yr, Sat & Sun only). Museum and planetarium closed some major hols. Main & Prospect Sts. Phone 802/748-2372. ¢¢

Maple Grove Farm of Vermont. Antique sugar house museum. Gift shop. Maple candy factory tours (Mon-Fri; closed hols). Res requested for tours. E edge of town on US 2; I-91, exit 20 or I-93, exit 1. Phone 802/748-5141. Tours ¢

St Johnsbury Athenaeum and Art Gallery. Works by Albert Bierstadt and artists of the Hudson River School. (Daily exc Sun; closed hols) 30 Main St (public library and art gallery). Phone 802/748-8291. **DONATION**

Seasonal Event

St Johnsbury Town Band. Courthouse Park. One of the oldest continuously performing bands (since 1830) in the country plays weekly outdoor evening concerts. Contact the Chamber of Commerce for further information. Mon, mid-June-late Aug.

Motels

✔★ **AIME'S.** *RFD 1, Box 332, 3 mi E at jct US 2, VT 18; I-93 exit 1. 802/748-3194.* E-mail aimmotel@hcr.net. 17 rms. D $37-$70; each addl $5. Crib free. TV; cable. Ck-out noon. Screened porches. Near brook. Cr cds: A, DS, MC, V.

★★ **FAIRBANKS INN.** *32 Western Ave, I-91 exit 21. 802/748-5666; FAX 802/748-1242.* E-mail p.j.murphy@plainfield.bypass.com. 46 rms, 3 story. S $55-$85; D $65-$95; each addl $10; package plans; higher rates fall foliage. TV; cable (premium). Heated pool. Complimentary continental bkfst. Ck-out 11 am. Business servs avail. In-rm modem link. Putting green. Downhill/x-country ski 15 mi. Health club privileges. Balconies. Picnic tables. On 2 acres along river. Cr cds: A, DS, MC, V.

✔★ **HOLIDAY.** *25 Hastings St, at jct US 2, 5. 802/748-8192; FAX 802/748-1244.* 34 rms. Mid-June-mid-Oct: S $48-$75; D $55-$89; each addl $5; higher rates: fall foliage season, some hols; lower rates rest of yr. TV; cable. Heated pool. Coffee in lobby. Restaurant opp 7 am-9 pm. Ck-out 11 am. Picnic tables. Cr cds: A, DS, MC, V.

Inn

★★★★ **RABBIT HILL.** *(VT 18, Lower Waterford 05848)* 10 mi S on VT 18; I-93 exit NH 44, then 1½ mi N on VT 18. 802/748-5168; FAX 802/748-8342; res: 800/762-8669. E-mail rabbit.hill.inn@connriver.net; web www.rabbithillinn.com. This restored inn (ca 1795-1825) has a country atmosphere. 21 rms, 1-3 story. 17 A/C. No rm phones. MAP: S $170-$315; D $210-$355; each addl $70; higher rates fall foliage season. Children over 12 yrs only. Complimentary afternoon refreshments. Coffee in rms. Restaurant (see RABBIT HILL). Bar. Ck-out 11 am, ck-in after 2 pm. Gift shop. Pond, canoes. Golf privileges. X-country ski on site. Lawn games. Some in-rm whirlpools, fireplaces. Porches. Gazebo. Totally nonsmoking. Cr cds: A, MC, V.

Restaurants

★★ **CREAMERY.** *(Hill St, Danville)* 7 mi W on US 2. 802/684-3616. Specializes in fresh seafood. Own baking, soups. Menu changes daily. Hrs: 11:30 am-2 pm, 5-8 pm; Sat from 5 pm. Closed Sun, Mon; Jan 1, Dec 24, 25. Res accepted. Bar from 4 pm. Semi-a la carte: lunch $5-$8, dinner $12-$17. Child's meals. Renovated creamery (1891); antiques, vintage photographs. Cr cds: A, MC, V.

★★ **RABBIT HILL.** *(See Rabbit Hill Inn)* 802/748-5168. E-mail rabbit.hill.inn@conriver.net; web www.rabbithillinn.com. Contemporary Amer menu. Own baking. Menu changes seasonally. Hrs: 6-8:45 pm. Res required. Bar. Wine cellar. Complete meals: dinner $37. On grounds of historic inn. Totally nonsmoking. Cr cds: A, MC, V.

Stowe (C-2)

(See also Waterbury)

Settled 1794 **Pop** 3,433 **Elev** 723 ft **Area code** 802 **Zip** 05672 **E-mail** stowe@sover.net **Web** www.stoweinfo.com
Information Stowe Area Association, PO Box 1320; 802/253-7321 or 800/24-STOWE.

Stowe is a year-round resort area with more than half of its visitors coming during the summer. Mt Mansfield, Vermont's highest peak (4,393 ft), offers skiing, snowboarding, snowshoeing and skating in the winter. Summer visitors enjoy outdoor concerts, hiking, biking, golf, tennis and many events and attractions, including a Ben & Jerry’s ice cream tour.

What to See and Do

Alpine Slide. Chairlift takes riders to 2,300-ft slide that runs through the woods and open field. Speed controlled by rider. (Memorial Day-mid-June, wkends & hols; mid-June-Labor Day, daily; after Labor Day-mid-Oct, wkends & hols) VT 108, N of Stowe Village. ¢¢¢

Elmore State Park. This 709-acre park offers swimming beach, bathhouse; fishing; boating (rentals). Hiking trails (1 trail to Elmore Mt fire tower). Picnicking, concession. Tent & trailer sites (dump station), lean-tos. Excellent views of Green Mt Range; fire tower. (Memorial Day-Columbus Day) Standard fees. N on VT 100, then S on VT 12, at Lake Elmore. Phone 802/888-2982 or 802/479-4280.

Mt Mansfield State Forest. This 38,000-acre forest can be reached from Underhill Flats, off VT 15, or from Stowe, N on VT 108, through Smugglers Notch, a magnificent scenic drive. The Long Trail leads to the summit of Mt Mansfield from the north and south. There are three state recreation areas in the forest. **Smugglers Notch** (phone 802/253-4014 or 802/479-4280) and **Underhill** (phone 802/899-3022 or 802/879-5674) areas offer hiking. Skiing, snowmobiling. Picnicking. Camping (dump station). **Little River Camping Area** (phone 802/244-7103 or 802/479-4280), NW of Waterbury, offers swimming; fishing; boating (rentals for campers only). Hiking. Camping. (Memorial Day-Columbus Day) Standard fees.

Stowe Mt Auto Road. A 4¹/₂-mi drive to summit. (Mid-May-mid-Oct, daily) Approx 6 mi NW of Stowe off VT 108.   ¢¢¢¢

Stowe Mt Resort. Resort has 8-passenger gondola, quad, triple, 6 double chairlifts; Mighty-mite handle tow; patrol, school, rentals; snowmaking; cafeterias, restaurants, bar, entertainment; nursery. 45 runs, longest run over 4 mi; vertical drop 2,350 ft. (Mid-Nov-mid-Apr, daily) Summer activities include alpine slide (mid-June-early Sept, daily); mountain biking (rentals); gondola rides; in-line skate park; fitness center, spa; recreation trail; three outdoor swimming pools; tennis, golf. NW via VT 108.Phone 802/253-3000 or 800/253-4754.   ¢¢¢¢¢   Nearby is

Mt Mansfield Gondola. An 8-passenger enclosed gondola ride to the summit of Vermont's highest peak. Spectacular view of the area. Restaurant and gift shop. (Late May-mid-June, wkends; mid-June-mid-Oct, daily) VT 108, N of Stowe Village.   ¢¢¢

Stowe Recreation Path. An approx 5-mi riverside path designed for nature walks, bicycling, jogging and in-line skating. Stowe Village.   **Free.**

Annual Event

Stoweflake Balloon Festival. Stoweflake Resort Field, Rte 108. Over 20 balloons launched continuously. Phone 802/253-7321. 2nd wkend July.

Seasonal Event

Trapp Family Meadow Concerts. Classical concerts in the Trapp Family Lodge Meadow. Phone 802/253-7321. Sun eves, late June-mid-Aug.

Motels

★ ★ **BUCCANEER COUNTRY LODGE.** *3214 Mountain Rd. 802/253-4772; FAX 802/253-4752; res: 800/543-1293.* E-mail buccaneer@compuserve.com; web www.stoweinfo.com/buccaneer. 12 rms, 2 story, 4 kit. suites. Mid-Dec-Mar, mid-Sept-mid-Oct: S, D $75-$99; each addl $10-$15; kit. suites $95; under 5 free; wkly rates; ski plans; wkends (2 day min); higher rates: hol wkends, wks of Washington's birthday, Dec 25; lower rates rest of yr. Crib free. TV; cable. Heated pool; whirlpool. Complimentary full bkfst (continental bkfst off-season). Restaurant nearby. Ck-out 11 am. Downhill ski 3 mi; x-country ski 1 mi. Rec rm. Refrigerators. Balconies. Picnic tables, grills. Fireplace. Library. Cr cds: MC, V.

✔★ ★ **COMMODORES INN.** *PO Box 970, VT 100S. 802/253-7131; FAX 802/253-2360; res: 800/44-STOWE.* E-mail commodores@mtmansfield.com; web www.stoweinfo.com/saa/commodores. 50 rms, 2 story. Mid-Sept-mid-Oct, mid-Dec-mid-Mar: S $78-$98; D $98-$120; each addl $10; under 12 free; wkend rates; higher rates wk of Dec 25; lower rates rest of yr. Crib free. Pet accepted; $10. TV; cable, VCR avail. 2 pools, heated, 1 indoor; wading pool, whirlpools. Complimentary continental bkfst off season. Restaurant 7-10:30 am, 6-9:30 pm. Ck-out 11 am. Meeting rm. Business servs avail. In-rm modem link. Downhill ski 9 mi; x-country ski 6 mi. Exercise equipt; saunas. Game rm. Refrigerators avail. Cr cds: A, C, D, DS, MC, V.

★ ★ **GOLDEN EAGLE.** *PO Box 1090, ¹/₂ mi NW on VT 108. 802/253-4811; FAX 802/253-2561; res: 800/626-1010.* E-mail stoweagle@aol.com; web www.stoweagle.com. 90 rms, 12 kits. Dec-Mar, late June-Oct: S, D $89-$159; each addl $10; suites $119-$199; kit. units $129-$299; under 12 free; family rates; ski, golf, package plans; higher rates: hols, special event wkends; lower rates rest of yr. Crib $5. TV; cable (premium), VCR avail (movies $7). 3 heated pools, 1 indoor; whirlpool. Playground. Supervised child's activities (summer & winter); ages 4 & up. Complimentary coffee in rms. Restaurant 7-11 am, 5:30-9:30 pm. Rm serv 7-11 am. Bar 5-9:30 pm. Ck-out 11 am. Meeting rms. Business servs avail. Sundries. Free RR station, bus depot, ski slope transportation. Tennis. Downhill ski 5 mi; x-country ski 3 mi. Exercise rm; sauna. Massage. Rec rm. Lawn games. Refrigerators; some in-rm whirlpools, fireplaces; microwaves avail. Some

balconies. Picnic tables, grills. Library, lounge. Stocked trout ponds on grounds; nature trails. Cr cds: A, C, D, DS, MC, V.

★ ★ **HOB KNOB INN.** *2364 Mountain Rd, 2¹/₂ mi NW on VT 108. 802/253-8549; res: 800/245-8540; FAX 802/253-7621.* Web www.stoweinfo.com/saa/hobknob. 20 rms, 6 kits. Ski season: D $85-$145; each addl $15; kit. units $10 addl; MAP avail; wkly rates; golf, ski plans; higher rates hols, special events; some lower rates off-season. Closed Nov. Crib free. TV. Pool. Complimentary full bkfst (winter), continental bkfst (summer). Restaurant 6-9 pm. Bar. Ck-out 11 am. Downhill ski 5 mi; x-country ski 1¹/₂ mi. Some refrigerators, fireplaces. Balconies. Cr cds: A, C, DS, MC, V.

★ ★ **HONEYWOOD COUNTRY LODGE.** *4527 Mountain Rd, 5 mi NW on VT 108. 802/253-4124; FAX 802/253-7050; res: 800/659-6289.* E-mail honeywd@aol.com; web www.stoweinfo.com/saa/honeywood. 13 rms, 4 kits. Mid-Dec-mid-Apr: D $74-$114; each addl $15; kit. units $76-$133; under 12 free; higher rates: hols, fall foliage; lower rates rest of yr. TV. Pool; whirlpool. Complimentary continental bkfst. Restaurant adj 8 am-10 pm. Ck-out 10 am. Downhill/x-country ski 1¹/₂ mi. Lawn games. Refrigerators; some wood stoves. Balconies. Picnic tables, grill. Fireplace in lounge. View of Mt Mansfield. Cr cds: A, MC, V.

★ ★ ★ **INN AT THE MOUNTAIN.** *5781 Mountain Rd, 6 mi NW on VT 108. 802/253-7311; FAX 802/253-3659; res: 800/253-4754.* E-mail skistowe@souer.net; web www.stowe.com/smr. 33 rms. MAP: Dec 25-mid-Apr: S, D $145-$180; suites $190-$230; under 12 free; condos $200-$600; learn-to-ski wk rates; golf plans; lower rates rest of yr. Crib $10. TV; cable. Heated pool; whirlpool. Restaurant 7:30-10 am, 5:30-9 pm. Rm serv. Bar 11-2 am. Ck-out 11 am. Meeting rm. Business servs avail. Bellhops. Tennis. Golf privileges. Downhill/x-country ski on site. Snowboarding; lessons, rentals. In-line skate park. Mountain bike center. Exercise equipt; sauna. Rec rm. Refrigerators, in-rm steam baths. Balconies. Sun deck. Ride attractions. Rms overlook ski slopes. Cr cds: A, C, D, DS, MC, V.

★ ★ **INNSBRUCK INN.** *Mt Mansfield Rd, 4 mi W on VT 108. 802/253-8582; FAX 802/253-2260; res: 800/225-8582.* 28 rms, 2 story, 4 kits. Mid-Dec-mid-Apr: S $65-$79; D $74-$119; each addl $15; under 12 free; higher rates hol wks; lower rates rest of yr. Crib $10. Pet accepted, some restrictions; $8. TV; cable, VCR avail (movies). Heated pool; whirlpool. Coffee in rms. Restaurant 7:30-9:30 am. Bar (winter only) 3:30 pm-1 am. Ck-out 11 am. Business servs avail. Ski shuttle. Indoor tennis privileges. Downhill ski 2 mi; x-country ski adj. Exercise equipt; sauna. Game rm. Refrigerators. Balconies. Picnic tables. Cr cds: A, DS, MC, V.

★ ★ ★ **MOUNTAIN ROAD.** *VT 108, 1 mi NW on VT 108. 802/253-4566; FAX 802/253-7397; res: 800/367-6873.* E-mail stowevt@aol.com; web www.stowevtusa.com. 30 rms, 7 suites (some with kit.), 7 kit. units. June-Oct, late Dec-Mar: D $89-$175; each addl $8-$20; suites $185-$335; kits. $125-$199; MAP avail; family, wkly rates; golf, ski plans; higher rates: hols, special events; lower rates rest of yr. Crib $5. Pet accepted; $15. TV; cable (premium), VCR avail. 2 pools, 1 indoor; whirlpool. Playground. Coffee in rms. Restaurant opp 7 am-9 pm. Ck-out 11 am. Business servs avail. Coin lndry. Sundries. RR station, bus depot transportation. Tennis. Downhill ski 4 mi; x-country ski 2¹/₂ mi. Bicycles. Exercise equipt; saunas. Rec rm. Lawn games. Refrigerators; some in-rm whirlpools; microwaves avail. Some balconies. Picnic tables, grills. Cr cds: A, C, D, DS, MC, V.

★ ★ **MOUNTAINSIDE RESORT AT STOWE.** *Mountain Rd, 2 mi NW on VT 108. 802/253-8610; FAX 802/253-7838; res: 800/458-4893.* E-mail mtside@together.net. 88 kit. apts, 3 story. No A/C. No elvtr. D $165-$200; 2-6, $220-$275; 2-3 bedrm apts to 8, $220-$275; wkly rates; golf, ski, mid-wk plans; higher rates: Washington's Birthday wk, Christmas wk. Crib $10/stay. TV; VCR (movies $2). Indoor pool; whirlpool. Playground. Ck-out 10 am. Guest lndry. Business servs avail. Tennis. Downhill ski 3 mi; x-country ski 1 mi. Lawn games. Exercise equipt; saunas. Many fireplaces. Balconies; many sun decks. Picnic tables, grills. Cr cds: A, MC, V.

⊠⛷🏊🎿🏃🎿⛵ SC

★ ★ **NOTCH BROOK.** *1229 Notch Brook Rd, 6 mi N; 1¹/₂ mi N of VT 108.* 802/253-4882; FAX 802/253-4882; res: 800/253-4882. E-mail nbrook@sover.net. 66 units, 33 kits. No A/C. Mid-Dec-Apr: S, D $72-$99; each addl $15; kit. units $119-$299; townhouse $189; wkly rates; ski plan; higher rates winter hols; lower rates rest of yr. Crib $5. Pet accepted. TV; cable. Heated pool; saunas. Complimentary continental bkfst (in season). Ck-out 11 am. Coin lndry. Business servs avail. Some garage parking. Tennis. Downhill/x-country ski 4 mi. Some fireplaces. Balconies. On 16 acres. Cr cds: A, C, D, MC, V.

⛷🎿🏊🎿⛵

✔★ ★ **STOWE INN & TAVERN AT LITTLE RIVER.** *123 Mountain Rd, Mt Mansfield Rd at Bridge St, just N on VT 108.* 802/253-4836; FAX 802/253-7308; res: 800/227-1108 (eastern US). 43 rms in motel, lodge, 4 kits., 8 condos (1-bedrm). Dec-Apr: D $55-$155; each addl $10; condos $150-$285; ski plan; higher rates special events; lower rates rest of yr. Crib $10. Pet accepted, some restrictions. TV; cable. Pool; whirlpool. Continental bkfst. Restaurant 11:30 am-9 pm. Bar. Ck-out 11 am. Business servs avail. Downhill ski 6 mi; x-country ski 4 mi. Rec rm. Some refrigerators. Cr cds: A, MC, V.

⛷🎿🏊🎿⛵ SC

✔★ ★ **STOWE/SNOWDRIFT.** *2043 Mountain Rd, 2 mi NW on VT 108.* 802/253-7629; res: 800/829-7629. E-mail stowemotel@aol.com; web www.stoweinfo.com/saa/stowe/hotel. 59 units, 28 kit. units, 4 chalets. D $76-$86; kit. units $86-$115; each addl $8; chalets to 10, $1,000-$1,800/wk; under 6 free; higher rates some hols; ski season; lower rates rest of yr. Crib $6. TV; cable. 2 heated pools; whirlpool. Restaurant nearby. Ck-out 11 am. Business servs avail. Tennis. Downhill ski 4¹/₂ mi; x-country ski 2¹/₂ mi. Lawn games. Bicycles; snowshoes. Refrigerators; some fireplaces. Picnic tables, grills. View of mountains; on 16 acres. Cr cds: C, D, DS, MC, V.

⛷🎿🏊⛵

★ ★ **STOWEFLAKE INN & RESORT.** *1746 Mountain Rd, 1¹/₂ mi NW on VT 108.* 802/253-7355; FAX 802/253-4419; res: 800/253-2232. E-mail stoweflk@sover.net; web www.stoweinfo.com/saa/stoweflake. 98 rms, 1-2 story, 24 townhouses. July-mid-Oct, late Dec-mid-Mar: S $126-$186; D $136-$196; each addl $10; suites, townhouses $195-$575; studio rms $165-$195; under 12 free; MAP avail; golf, tennis, ski plans; 2-day min hols; lower rates rest of yr. Crib free. TV; cable, VCR avail. 2 heated pools, 1 indoor; whirlpool, poolside serv. Restaurant 7:30-10:30 am, 4-10 pm. Summer lunch noon-3 pm. Rm serv. Bar 3 pm-1 am. Ck-out 11 am. Meeting rms. Business servs avail. In-rm modem link. Bellhops. Concierge. Gift shop. Tennis, pro. Golf privileges, putting green, driving range, lessons. Downhill ski 3¹/₂ mi; x-country ski 1¹/₂ mi. Exercise rm; sauna. Game rm. Lawn games. Sleigh and hay rides. Some refrigerators, microwave in suites; fireplace in townhouses. Library. Shopping mall adj. Cr cds: A, C, D, DS, MC, V.

D⛷🏃🎿🏊🎿🏔⛵ SC

★ ★ **SUN & SKI.** *1613 Mountain Rd, 1¹/₂ mi N on VT 108.* 802/253-7159; res: 800/448-5223. E-mail greyfoxinn@aol.com; web www.stowe-sunandski.com. 25 rms. S, D $63-$85; each addl $5-$16; suites $112-$145; ski plan; higher rates: hols, fall foliage, special events. Crib free. TV; cable. Heated pool; sauna. Complimentary continental bkfst 8-10 am. Coffee in rms. Restaurant opp 7:30 am-9:30 pm. Ck-out 11 am. Downhill ski 3 mi; x-country ski 2 mi. Lawn games. Bicycles. Trout stream. Refrigerators. Private patios. Picnic tables. Cr cds: A, MC, V.

D⛷🎿🏊⛵

✔★ ★ **SUNSET.** *(160 VT 15W, Morrisville 05661) jct VT 15, 100 10 mi NE.* 802/888-4956; FAX 802/888-3698; res: 800/544-2347. 55 rms. Mid-Sept-mid-Oct, mid-Dec-mid-Mar: S $48-$68; D $54-$78; each addl $5-$10; under 12 free; higher rates hols; lower rates rest of yr. Crib $5. TV; cable (premium), VCR avail. Pool. Playground. Restaurant adj 6 am-10 pm. Ck-out 11 am. Free airport transportation. Downhill ski 9 mi; x-country

ski 4 mi. Some in-rm whirlpools, refrigerators. Picnic tables, grills. Cr cds: A, C, D, DS, ER, MC, V.

D⛷🎿🏊🎿⛵ SC

✔★ **TOWN & COUNTRY MOTOR LODGE.** *Mountain Rd, 1 mi N on VT 108.* 802/253-7595; FAX 802/253-4764; res: 800/323-0311. E-mail tnc@together.net; web www.tcstowe.com. 45 rms, 1-2 story. Late June-Labor Day, late Dec-Mar: S $72-$104; D $85-$120; each addl $8; under 13 free; MAP avail; ski plan; higher rates: winter hol wks, antique car rally; lower rates rest of yr. Crib $5. TV; cable. 2 pools, 1 indoor; wading pool, sauna. Restaurant 7:30-10 am, 5:30-9 pm. Bar 5 pm-1 am. Ck-out 11 am. Meeting rms. Business servs avail. Tennis. Downhill ski 5¹/₂ mi. Rec rm. Lawn games. Some refrigerators. Cr cds: A, C, D, DS, MC, V.

⛷🎿🏊🎿⛵ SC

✔★ **WALKABOUT CREEK.** *199 Edson Hill Rd.* 802/253-7354; FAX 802/253-8429; res: 800/426-6697. E-mail walkcreek@aol.com; web www.walkaboutcreeklodge.com. 20 rms, 5 with shower only, 2 story. Mid-Dec-mid-Mar, mid-June-Labor Day: S $55-$65; D $90-$110; each addl $35; 3-bdrm townhouse $350; family, wkly, wkend rates; ski plans; higher rates hols (2-day min); lower rates rest of yr. Crib free. Pet accepted; $10/day. 5 TVs; cable (premium). Pool; whirlpool. Complimentary full bkfst. Restaurant 4-9 pm mid-June-Labor Day. Bar 4-1 am. Ck-out 11 am. Business servs avail. Tennis. Downhill ski 3 mi; x-country ski on site. Rec rm. Some balconies. Picnic tables. Totally nonsmoking. Cr cds: A, MC, V.

⛷🎿🏊🎿⛵

Lodge

★ ★ ★ **TRAPP FAMILY LODGE.** *42 Trapp Hill Rd, 2 mi N on VT 108 then 2 mi W on Trapp Hill Rd.* 802/253-8511; FAX 802/253-5740; res: 800/826-7000. E-mail info@trappfamily.com; web www.trappfamily.com. 73 rms in main lodge, 20 rms in lower lodge, 4 story, 100 guest houses. No A/C. Ski season: S, D $145-$220; each addl $25; guest houses $800-$2,200/wk; under 12 free (off season & summer only); MAP avail; package plans; some higher rates hol wkends; lower rates rest of yr. Crib free. 3 pools, 1 indoor. Dining rm (public by res) 7:30-10:30 am, 5:30-9 pm; Austrian tea rm 10:30 am-5:30 pm. Bar 3:30-10 pm; entertainment, movies. Ck-out 11 am, ck-in 3 pm. Business servs avail. Bellhops. Gift shop. Tennis. Downhill ski 6 mi; x-country ski on site, equipt, instruction. Exercise equipt; sauna. Lawn games. Sleigh rides. Hiking trails; guided nature walks. Many balconies. Fireplaces in public rms. Library. Alpine lodge owned by Trapp family, whose lives were portrayed in The Sound of Music. Cr cds: A, C, D, DS, MC, V.

D⛷🎿🏊🏃🎿⛵

Inns

✔★ ★ **BUTTERNUT.** *RD 1, Box 950, 3 mi NW on VT 108.* 802/253-4277; res: 800/328-8837. 18 rms, 3 story. July-Labor Day, mid-Sept-mid-Oct, mid-Dec-Mar: D $45-$75/person; ski plan; lower rates rest of yr. Adults only. TV, some B/W; cable. Heated pool. Complimentary bkfst; afternoon refreshments in sitting rm. Dining rm 8-10 am. Ck-out 11 am, ck-in 3 pm. Downhill ski 4 mi; x-country ski on site. Rec rm. Nature trail. Picnic table, grills. Fireplaces in public areas. Antique furnishings. Library. Totally nonsmoking. Cr cds: MC, V.

⛷🎿🏊🎿⛵

★ ★ **EDSON HILL MANOR.** *Edson Hill Rd, 6 mi NW off VT 108, 1 mi on Edson Hill Rd.* 802/253-7371; res: 800/621-0284. 9 rms in lodge, 16 carriage house units, 25 baths. A/C in lodge rms only. Mid-Dec-mid-Apr, MAP: D $95-$125/person; each addl $55; under 4 free; ski, riding & mid-wk plans; lower rates rest of yr. Serv charge 15%. Crib free. Pool. Dining rm 8-10 am, 6-9:30 pm. Bar 4:30 pm-midnight; summer from 5 pm. Ck-out 11 am, ck-in 2 pm. Downhill ski 5 mi; x-country ski on site; marked trails, instruction, rentals. Sleigh rides. Carriage rides. Stocked trout pond. Lawn games. Many fireplaces. Varied accommodations. 225 acres on hillside; view of Green Mts. Cr cds: A, DS, MC, V.

⛷🏃🎿🏊🎿🏔⛵

★ ★ ★ **GREEN MOUNTAIN.** *PO Box 60, Main St, on VT 100.* *802/253-7301; FAX 802/253-5096; res: 800/786-9346.* E-mail grnmtninn@aol.com; web www.greenmountaininne.com. 72 rms in inn, motel, 1-3 story, 1 carriage house. S, D $89-$139; suites $125-$189; each addl $15; MAP avail; under 12 free; higher rates: hols, fall foliage. Crib free. Pet accepted. TV; cable, VCR (movies $3.50). Pool; whirlpool. Dining rm 7:30 am-9:30 pm. Rm serv. Bar noon-1 am. Ck-out 11 am, ck-in 2 pm. Meeting rm. Business servs avail. Downhill ski 6 mi; x-country ski 5 mi. Exercise equipt; sauna. Massage. Some fireplaces. Some balconies. Historic inn (1833); antiques, library, paintings by Vermont artist. Cr cds: A, DS, MC, V.

⎹D⎸ 🐾 ⛷ ≋ 🎿 🏂 🔥 SC

★ ★ ★ **GREY FOX.** *990 Mountain Rd, 1 mi W on VT 108. 802/253-8921; res: 800/544-8454.* E-mail greyfoxinn@aol.com; web www.stowe-greyfoxinn.com. 42 rms, 1-3 story, 7 kits. July-mid-Oct, ski season: S $59-$105; D $69-$175; each addl $5-$16; kits. $69-$275; under 3 free; MAP avail; wkly, golf, ski packages; higher rates: special events; lower rates rest of yr. Crib $5. TV; cable (premium), VCR avail (free movies). 2 pools, 1 indoor; whirlpool. Dining rm 8-10:30 am; dinner 5:30-8:30 pm. Ck-out 11 am, ck-in 2 pm. Coin lndry. Meeting rm. Business servs avail. In-rm modem link. Downhill ski 3 mi; x-country ski 1 mi. Game rm. Lawn games. Exercise equipt. Bicycle rental. Some microwaves, fireplaces. Picnic tables, grills. Late 19th-century farmhouse; library. Cr cds: A, DS, MC, V.

⎹D⎸ 🐾 ≋ 🎿 🏂 🔥

★ ★ **INN AT THE BRASS LANTERN.** *717 Maple St. 802/253-2229; res: 800/729-2980; FAX 800/253-7425.* E-mail brasslntrn@aol.com; web www.stoweinfo.com/saa/brasslantern. 9 rms, 2 story. No rm phones. Mid-Dec-early Apr, mid-June-mid-Oct: S, D $75-$150; each addl $25; ski, golf plans; higher rates: Christmas wk; lower rates rest of yr. TV avail. Complimentary full bkfst; afternoon refreshments. Restaurant nearby. Ck-out 10:30 am, ck-in 3 pm. Gift shop. Downhill ski 7 mi; x-country ski 6½ mi. Health club privileges. Antiques. Library/sitting rm. Some in-rm whirlpools, fireplaces. Built 1810; operating farmhouse. Totally nonsmoking. Cr cds: A, MC, V.

🎿 ≋ 🏂

★ ★ **SCANDINAVIA INN AND CHALETS.** *3576 Mountain Rd, 3³/₄ mi NW on VT 108. 802/253-8555; res: 800/544-4229.* E-mail scandi@plainfiell.bypass.com; web www.stoweinfo.com/saa/scandinavia. 18 rms, 12 A/C, 4 chalets, 2 story. Ski season: D $75-$119; chalets $210-$276; each addl $15; wkly rates; ski plans; lower rates rest of yr. Closed mid-Oct-late Nov. TV; cable (premium). Heated pool; whirlpool. Dining rm 7:30-10 am, wkends to 11 am. Setups. Ck-out 11 am, ck-in 2 pm. Coin lndry. Free ski shuttle. Downhill ski 2½ mi; x-country ski ⅛ mi. Exercise equipt; sauna. Game rm. Lawn games. Picnic tables, grills. Home of the trolls. Some refrigerators. Totally nonsmoking. Cr cds: A, DS, MC, V.

🎿 ≋ 🏂 🔥

★ ★ **STOWEHOF.** *3½ mi N on Edson Hill Rd, just off VT 108. 802/253-9722; FAX 802/253-7513; res: 800/932-7136.* 50 rms, 3 story. Ski season, July-Oct: D $69-$120/person; each addl $35; MAP avail; higher rates: Christmas wk, fall season. Serv charge 15%. Crib free. TV; cable, VCR avail (free movies). Heated pool; whirlpool, poolside serv, sauna. Complimentary full bkfst. Dining rm 8-10 am, 6-9:30 pm; summer also noon-2 pm. Bar 4 pm-1 am. Ck-out noon, ck-in 3 pm. Meeting rm. Business servs avail. Luggage handling. Tennis, pro. Downhill ski 4 mi; x-country ski on site. Rec rm. Lawn games. Sleigh rides. Fireplaces. Private patios, balconies. Library. Trout pond. Cr cds: A, D, DS, MC, V.

🐾 🎿 🏂 ≋ 🎿 🏂 🔥

★ ★ **THREE BEARS AT THE FOUNTAIN.** *1049 Pucker St. 802/253-7671; res: 800/898-9634; FAX 802/253-8804.* Web www.stowe-info.com/saa/3bears. 5 rms, 4 with full bathrm, 2 story. No A/C. S, D $115-$135; each addl $20; under 12 free; ski plans; fall foliage, hols 2-day min; higher rates: fall foliage, hols. Closed 1st 2 wks Nov. Crib avail. Premium cable TV in common rm. Complimentary full bkfst. Restaurant nearby. Ck-out 10:30 am, ck-in 3 pm. Downhill ski 7 mi; x-country ski 1 mi.

Built in 1826; one of the oldest guesthouses in Stowe. Outdoor fountain. Totally nonsmoking. Cr cds: MC, V.

🎿 🔥

★ ★ ★ **YE OLDE ENGLAND INNE.** *433 Mountain Rd, ¼ mi N on VT 108. 802/253-7558; res: 800/477-3771; FAX 802/253-8944.* E-mail englandinn@aol.com; web www.oldenglandinne.com. 30 rms, 3-5 story, 10 suites, 3 cottages. No elvtr. Mid-Sept-mid-Oct, ski season: S, D $118-$158; suites $225-$275; each addl $25; under 12 free; EP avail; wkly rates; ski, golf, gliding; higher rates late Dec-early Jan; lower rates rest of yr. Serv charge 10%, cottages 5%. Crib $5. TV; cable (premium), VCR avail. Pool; whirlpool. Complimentary afternoon refreshments. Complimentary coffee in rms. Dining rm 8 am-10 pm in season. Bar 11:30-2 am; entertainment Wed-Sat (winter). Ck-out 11:30 am, ck-in 3 pm. Business servs avail. Tennis privileges. Downhill ski 5 mi; x-country ski 2 mi. Some in-rm whirlpools. Balconies. Picnic tables, grill. Built 1893. Cr cds: A, MC, V.

⎹D⎸ 🎿 🎿 ≋ 🏂 🔥 SC

Resort

★ ★ ★ ★ **TOPNOTCH AT STOWE.** *4000 Mountain Rd, 4 mi NW on VT 108. 802/253-8585; FAX 802/253-9263; res: 800/451-8686.* Web www.topnotch-resort.com/spa. Located on 120 mountain acres, this polished resort has individually decorated rooms and an imposing lobby with a freestanding circular stone fireplace, floor-to-ceiling windows and a cathedral ceiling. 92 rms in main bldg, 15 kit. townhouses. Some A/C in townhouses, chalet. Late May-mid-Oct: S, D $210-$280; each addl $45; suites $335-$652; kit. townhouses $300-$625; tennis, golf, ski, spa plans; lower rates rest of yr. Crib free. TV; cable (premium), VCR avail (movies). 2 heated pools, 1 indoor; whirlpool. Supervised child's activities (July-early Sept); ages 5-12. Complimentary afternoon refreshments. Dining rms 7-10 am, 11:30 am-2 pm, 5:30-9:30 pm. Rm serv 6:30 am-9:30 pm. Box lunches. Bar noon-2 am; entertainment. Ck-out 11 am, ck-in 3:30 pm. Meeting rms. Bellhops. Valet serv. Concierge. Gift shop. Beauty shop. 14 tennis courts, 4 indoor, pro. Golf privileges. Downhill ski 2 mi; x-country ski on site. Ski equipt, instruction. Trail rides, instruction. Mountain bikes. Bike rentals. Movies Sun-Thurs. Exercise rm; sauna, steam rm. Spa. Some refrigerators, fireplaces; microwaves avail. Some balconies. Libraries. Sun deck. Cr cds: A, D, DS, MC, V.

⎹D⎸ 🐾 ⛷ 🎿 🏇 🏃 ≋ 🎿 🏂 🔥 SC

Restaurants

★ **CLIFF HOUSE.** *VT 108. 802/253-3665.* Eclectic menu. Specialties: rock cornish game hen, fresh seafood. Hrs: 11 am-3 pm, 5:30-9 pm; Sun, Wed to 2:30 pm. Closed Mon, Tues; Thanksgiving; also mid-Apr-late June, late Oct-mid-Dec. Res required dinner. No A/C. Serv bar. Buffet: lunch $12.10. Complete meals: dinner $42.50, includes gondola ride. Sun brunch $18.95. View of mountains. Totally nonsmoking. Cr cds: A, D, DS, MC, V.

★ ★ ★ **ISLE DE FRANCE.** *On Mountain Rd. 802/253-7751.* Hrs: 6-10 pm. Closed Mon. Res accepted. French menu. Bar. Wine list. A la carte entrees: dinner $14.50-$23. Specialties: lobster Newberg, Dover sole meuniere, chateaubriand pour deux. Own bread. Parking. French provincial decor; formal dining in elegant atmosphere. Cr cds: A, C, D, DS, MC, V.

★ ★ **PARTRIDGE INN.** *Mountain Rd, ½ mi NW on VT 108. 802/253-8000.* Specializes in Maine lobster, fresh Cape Cod seafood, pasta. Hrs: 5:30-9:30 pm. Closed first 3 wks Nov. Res accepted. Bar 5-11 pm. Semi-a la carte: dinner $14.50-$19.95. Child's meals. Parking. Fireplace. Totally nonsmoking. Cr cds: A, C, D, DS, MC, V.

⎹D⎸ ♥

★ ★ **THE SHED.** *1559 Mountain Rd. 802/253-4364.* Hrs: 11:30 am-10 pm; Sun brunch 10 am-2 pm. Res accepted. Bar. Semi-a la carte: lunch $4.95-$9.95, dinner $8.75-$15.95. Sun brunch $12.95. Child's meals. Specializes in baby back ribs, fresh seafood, calf's liver. Parking.

Outdoor dining. Brewery on premises. Family-owned. Totally nonsmoking. Cr cds: A, D, DS, MC, V.

★ **SWISSPOT OF STOWE.** *Main St.* 802/253-4622. Swiss, Amer menu. Specializes in fondue, pasta, quiche. Hrs: 11:30 am-10 pm. Closed mid-Apr-mid-June, mid-Oct-mid-Dec. Res accepted. Bar. Semi-a la carte: lunch $4.95-$8.95, dinner $5.95-$17.95. Child's meals. Patio dining in summer. Built for 1967 Montreal Expo, then moved here. Totally nonsmoking. Cr cds: A, C, D, DS, MC, V.

★★ **WHISKERS.** *Mountain Rd, 1½ mi NW on VT 108.* 802/253-8996. Continental menu. Specializes in fresh lobster, fresh seafood, prime rib. Salad bar (dinner). Own desserts. Hrs: 5-10 pm; summer 11:30 am-3:30 pm, 5-10 pm. Closed Mon-Fri during summer lunch hrs. Res accepted. Bar. Semi-a la carte: lunch $5.95-$12.95, dinner $8.95-$21.95. Child's meals. Parking. Outdoor & greenhouse dining. Old farm house, antiques. Lobster tanks. Flower garden. Totally nonsmoking. Cr cds: A, C, D, DS, MC, V.

Stratton Mountain (H-2)

(See also Londonderry, Manchester & Manchester Center, Peru)

Area code 802 **Zip** 05155

What to See and Do

Skiing. Stratton Mountain. A high-speed gondola, high-speed 6-passenger, 4 quad, 1 triple, 3 double chairlifts; patrol, school, rentals; snowmaking; cafeterias, restaurants, bars; nursery, sports center. Ninety runs, longest run 3 mi; vertical drop 2,003 ft. (Mid-Nov-mid-Apr, daily) Over 17 mi of cross-country trails (Dec-Mar, daily), rentals; snowboarding. Summer activities include gondola ride; horseback riding; tennis, golf (school); festivals; concert series. On Stratton Mt access road, off VT 30. Phone 802/297-2200, 802/297-4000 or 800/STRATTON. ¢¢¢¢¢

Annual Event

Labor Day Street Festival. Stratton Mountain. Festival with continuous entertainment, specialty foods, imported beer, activities for children. Phone 802/297-2200. Labor Day wkend.

Seasonal Event

Stratton Arts Festival. Stratton Mountain Base Lodge. Paintings, photography, sculpture and crafts; special performing arts events; craft demonstrations. Phone 802/297-2200. Mid-Sept-mid-Oct.

Motel

★★ **LIFTLINE LODGE.** *(Stratton Mountain Rd, Stratton)* 802/297-2600; FAX 802/297-2949; res: 800/597-5438. 91 rms, 2 story, 69 with A/C. Mid-Dec-mid-Mar: S, D $125-$135; each addl $15; kit. units $225-$275; under 16 free; wkly rates; ski, golf plans; higher rates fall foliage season; lower rates rest of yr. Crib free. TV; cable. Pool; whirlpools. Restaurant 7-11 am, 5:30-9 pm. Bar 4 pm-1 am; entertainment ski season. Ck-out 11 am. Meeting rms. Business servs avail. In-rm modem link. Lighted tennis. 27-hole golf privileges, greens fee $69, putting green, driving range. Downhill ski adj; x-country ski 1 mi. Exercise equipt; saunas. Rec rm. Cr cds: A, C, D, DS, MC, V.

Resort

★★★ **STRATTON MOUNTAIN.** *Stratton Mountain Rd, 1½ mi N of jct VT 100N.* 802/297-4000; FAX 802/297-2939; res: 800/787-2886. E-mail skistratton@intrawest.com; web www.stratton.com. 110 condominiums (1-4 bedrm), 1-4 story. S, D $90-$480; family rates; ski-wk, tennis, golf plans; higher rates hols. TV; cable (premium), VCR (movies $3.50). 4 pools, 1 indoor; whirlpool. Supervised child's activities; ages 1-12. Box lunches. Snack bar. Ck-out 10 am, ck-in 5 pm. Lndry facilities. Package store 5 mi. Meeting rms. Business servs avail. Shopping arcade. Ski shuttle service. Sports dir. 15 tennis courts; indoor lighted tennis, clinic, pro. 27-hole golf, greens fee $49-$82, pro, putting green, driving range. Downhill/x-country ski on site. Racquetball/squash. Bicycles. Game rm. Rec rm. Exercise rm; sauna. Mountain bicycles (rentals). Refrigerators, fireplaces. Private patios, balconies. Picnic tables. Gondola rides (in season). Resort covers 4,000 acres. Cr cds: A, C, D, DS, MC, V.

Swanton (B-1)

(See also North Hero, St Albans)

Pop 2,360 **Elev** 119 ft **Area code** 802 **Zip** 05488
Information Chamber of Commerce, PO Box 210; 802/868-7200.

The location of this town, just two miles east of Lake Champlain, makes it an attractive resort spot.

What to See and Do

Missisquoi National Wildlife Refuge. More than 6,400 acres, including much of the Missisquoi River delta on Lake Champlain; primarily a waterfowl refuge (best in Apr, Sept & Oct), but other wildlife and birds may be seen. Fishing, hunting; hiking and canoe trails. (Daily) 2½ mi W via VT 78. Phone 802/868-4781. **Free.**

Annual Event

Swanton Summer Festival. On Village Green. Band concerts, square dancing; rides, children’s events; parades; arts & crafts. Last wkend July.

Resort

★★★ **TYLER PLACE ON LAKE CHAMPLAIN.** *Old Dock Rd (05460), off I-89.* 802/868-3301; res: 802/868-4000; FAX 802/868-7602. E-mail tyler@together.net; web www.tylerplace.com. 12 suites in 1-2-story inn, 27 kit. cottages (3-6 rm). Late May-Labor Day, AP: $77-$198/person; children $35-$81. Closed rest of yr. Crib free. TV rm. 2 pools, 1 indoor pool; wading pool, lifeguard. Supervised child's activities (May-Sept); ages infant-16 yrs. Dining rm 7:30-10:30 am, 12:30-1:30 pm, 6:30-8 pm. Box lunches, buffets. Bar noon-midnight. Ck-out 10 am, ck-in 3 pm. Tennis. Sailing, canoeing, fishing boats, motors (fee). Waterskiing (fee), windsurfing. Nature trails. Soc dir. Rec rm. Exercise rm. Fireplace in cottages. Refrigerator in rms. On 165 acres; private lakeshore. Cr cds: DS, MC, V.

Vergennes (D-1)

(See also Middlebury, Shelburne)

Settled 1766 **Pop** 2,578 **Elev** 205 ft **Area code** 802 **Zip** 05491

Vergennes is one of the smallest incorporated cities in the nation (1 sq mi). It is also the oldest city in Vermont and the third oldest in New England.

What to See and Do

Button Bay State Park. This 236-acre park on a bluff overlooking Lake Champlain was named for the buttonlike formations in the clay banks; spectacular views of Adirondack Mts. Swimming pool; fishing; boating (rentals). Nature, hiking trails. Picnicking. Tent & trailer sites (dump station). Museum, naturalist. (Memorial Day-Columbus Day) Standard fees. 6 mi W on Button Bay Rd, just S of Basin Harbor. Phone 802/475-2377 or 802/483-2001.

Chimney Point State Historic Site (1700s). This 18th-century tavern was built on the site of a 17th-century French fort. Exhibits on the Native American and French settlement of Champlain Valley and Vermont. (Memorial Day-Columbus Day, Wed-Sun) 6 mi S via VT 22A, then 8 mi SW via VT 17, at the terminus of the Crown Point Military Rd on shoreline of Lake Champlain. Phone 802/759-2412. ¢

John Strong Mansion (1795). Federal-style house; restored and furnished in the period. (Mid-May-mid-Oct, Fri-Sun) 6 mi SW via VT 22A, on VT 17, in West Addison. Phone 802/759-2309. ¢¢

Kennedy Bros Factory Marketplace. Renovated 1920s brick creamery building features gifts, crafts and antique shops. Deli, ice-cream shop, picnic area. (Daily; closed Jan 1, Thanksgiving, Dec 25) 11 Main St. Phone 802/877-2975. **Free.**

Rokeby Museum (ca 1785). Ancestral home of abolitionist Rowland T. Robinson was a station for the Underground Railroad. Artifacts and archives of four generations of the Robinson family. Set on 85 acres, farmstead includes an ice house, a creamery and a stone smokehouse. Special events yr-round. Tours. (Mid-May-mid-Oct, Thurs-Sun) 2 mi N on US 7, 6 mi S of ferry route on US 7, Ferrisburg. Phone 802/877-3406. ¢¢

Motel

✔★ **SKYVIEW.** *(2956 Rt 7, Ferrisburg 05456) 2 mi N on US 7. 802/877-3410.* 15 rms, 3 kits. May-mid Sept: S $45-$55; D $55-$75; each addl $5; kit. units $8 addl; family rates; higher rates fall foliage; lower rates rest of yr. Crib $10. TV; cable. Playground. Complimentary coffee in rms. Restaurant adj 6 am-8 pm. Ck-out 11 am. X-country ski 15 mi. Lawn games. Refrigerators. Picnic tables, grills. Cr cds: A, DS, MC, V.

Inns

✔★ **EMERSON'S GUEST HOUSE.** *82 Main St. 802/877-3293.* 6 rms, 1 A/C, 1 with shower only, 4 rms share bath. No rm phones. S, D $60-$95; each addl $10-$15. Children over 8 yrs only. TV in common rm, VCR avail. Complimentary full bkfst. Restaurant nearby. Ck-out 10:30 am, ck-in 3 pm. Built in 1850; Victorian inn. Totally nonsmoking. Cr cds: MC, V.

★★★ **STRONG HOUSE.** *82 W Main. 802/877-3337; FAX 802/877-2599.* E-mail stronghi@together.net; web www.flinet.com/~bargieleer/shi_inn.htm. 8 rms, 2 story. Some rm phones. S, D $75-$175; each addl $20; higher rates: fall foliage, hols. Children over 8 yrs only. TV in some rms. Complimentary full bkfst. Dining rm (guests only). Rm serv. Ck-out 11 am, ck-in 3 pm. Gift shop. Some fireplaces. Historic federal-style house (1834); antiques, library. Views of the Green Mountains and Adirondack range. Totally nonsmoking. Cr cds: A, MC, V.

Resort

★★★ **BASIN HARBOR CLUB.** *Basin Harbor Rd, 6 mi W of US 7, VT 22A. 802/475-2311; FAX 802/475-6545; res: 800/622-4000.* E-mail res@basinharbor.com; web www.basinharbor.com. 40 rms in lodges, 77 cottages (1-3 bedrm). Mid-May-mid-Oct, AP: S $165; D $220-$405; each addl $5-$70; EP avail mid-May-mid-June, Sept-Oct; wkly rates. Closed rest of yr. Crib avail. Pet accepted, some restrictions. TV avail. Heated pool; poolside serv. Free supervised child's activities (July-Aug); ages 3-15. Dining rm 8 am-10 pm. Box lunches. Bar 11 am-midnight. Ck-out 11

am, ck-in 4 pm. Coin lndry. Business servs avail. Concierge. Gift shop. Airport, RR station, bus depot transportation. Rec dirs. Tennis. 18-hole golf, greens fee $42, putting green, driving range. Beach; motorboats, sailboats, canoes, kayaks, cruise boat; windsurfing, waterskiing. Exercise rm. Massage. Fitness, nature trails. Lawn games. Bicycles. Rec rm. Refrigerator in cottages. Family-owned since 1886; colonial architecture. Located on 700 acres, on Lake Champlain; dockage. 3,200-ft airstrip avail. Cr cds: MC, V.

Waitsfield (D-2)

(See also Montpelier, Warren, Waterbury)

Pop 1,422 **Elev** 698 ft **Area code** 802 **Zip** 05673
Information Central Vermont Chamber of Commerce, PO Box 336, Barre 05641; 802/496-3409 or 800/82-VISIT.

This region, known as "the Valley," is a popular area in summer, as well as in the winter ski season.

What to See and Do

Mad River Glen Ski Area. Area has 3 double chairlifts, 1 single chairlift; patrol, school, rentals; snowmaking; cafeterias, restaurant, bar; nursery, telemark program. 33 runs, longest run 3 mi; vertical drop 2,000 ft. (Dec-Apr, daily) On VT 17, 5 mi W of VT 100. Phone 802/496-3551 or 802/496-2001 (24-hr snow reports). ¢¢¢¢¢

Inns

★★ **1824 HOUSE.** *Rt 100, 3 mi N on VT 100. 802/496-7555; res: 800/426-3986; FAX 802/496-7559.* E-mail 1824@madriver.com; web www.1824house.com. 7 rms, 2 story. No rm phones. S, D $75-$135; higher rates: major hols, fall foliage. Complimentary full bkfst. Ck-out 11 am, ck-in 4 pm. Downhill ski 6 mi; x-country ski 5 mi. Whirlpool. Lawn games. Restored farmhouse (1824); feather beds, oriental rugs, down quilts. Totally nonsmoking. Cr cds: A, MC, V.

★★★ **INN AT THE ROUND BARN FARM.** *RR 1, Box 247, 1¹/₂ mi S of VT 100 on E Warren Rd. 802/496-2276; FAX 802/496-8832.* E-mail roundbarn@madriver.com; web www.innattheroundbarn.com. 11 rms, 4 A/C, 2 story. Some rm phones. S $105-$215; D $115-$225; each addl $25. TV in sitting rm. Indoor pool. Complimentary full bkfst. Ck-out 11 am, ck-in 3 pm. Business servs avail. Gift shop. Game rm. X-country ski on site, rentals. In restored farmhouse (ca 1810), named for its historic 12-sided barn (1910). On 235 acres with perennial gardens and 5 ponds. Totally nonsmoking. Cr cds: A, DS, MC, V.

★★ **LAREAU FARM COUNTRY INN.** *VT 100. 802/496-4949; FAX 802/296-7979; res: 800/833-0766.* 13 rms, 11 with bath, 2 story. No A/C. No rm phones. Ski and foliage season: S, D $70-$125; family, wkly rates; ski plan; lower rates rest of yr. TV in living rm. Complimentary full bkfst. Ck-out 11 am, ck-in 2 pm. Downhill ski 5 mi. Sleigh rides in winter. Picnic tables. Farmhouse & barn built by area's first physician; sitting rm; antiques. Cr cds: MC, V.

★★ **TUCKER HILL LODGE.** *1 mi S of VT 100, 1¹/₂ mi W on VT 17. 802/496-3983; FAX 802/496-3203; res: 800/543-7841.* E-mail tuckhill@madriver.com. 22 rms, 16 baths. No A/C. Ski season, mid-June-late Oct, MAP: D $60-$78/person; lower rates rest of yr. TV in sitting rm, bar. Pool. Restaurant (see GIORGIO'S CAFE). Bar. Ck-out 11 am, ck-in 2 pm.

Tennis; pro. Downhill ski 2 mi; X-country ski on site. Hiking trails. Handmade quilts. Cr cds: A, MC, V.

★ ★ **VALLEY.** *1 mi S on VT 100. 802/496-3450; res: 800/638-8466.* 20 rms. No rm phones. Ski season, MAP: S $90-$95; D $65-$70/person; higher rates: hols, fall foliage; lower rates rest of yr. Closed mid-Apr-mid-May. Crib $15. TV in game rm; cable. Complimentary full bkfst. Ck-out 10 am, ck-in after 2 pm. Downhill ski 3 mi; x-country ski 4 mi. Game rm. Rustic atmosphere; antiques. Totally nonsmoking. Cr cds: A, MC, V.

★ ★ **WAITSFIELD.** *Rt 100, 1 mi S on VT 100. 802/496-3979; FAX 802/496-3970.* Web www.site-works.com/waitsfield. 14 rms, 2 story. No rm phones. Fall foliage season, mid-Dec-early Apr: S $74-$114; D $89-$129; each addl $15; family, wkly rates; ski plans; lower rates rest of yr. Closed Apr, Nov. Ck-out 11 am, ck-in 3 pm. Meeting rms. Downhill ski 6 mi; x-country ski 3 mi. Antiques, handmade quilts. Totally nonsmoking. Cr cds: A, DS, MC, V.

★ **WHITE HORSE INN.** *German Flats Rd. 802/496-3260; res: 800/323-3260; FAX 802/496-2476.* Web whorse@plainfield.bys.com. 24 rms, 16 with shower only, 2 story. No A/C. No rm phones. Dec-Mar: S $50-$70; D $64-$94; each addl $15; ski plans; hols, wkends (2-day min); lower rates rest of yr. Pet accepted. TV in some rms; cable. Complimentary full bkfst. Ck-out noon, ck-in 3 pm. Downhill ski 1/2 mi; x-country ski 2 mi. Picnic tables, grill. Totally nonsmoking. Cr cds: A, DS, MC, V.

Restaurants

★ **DEN.** *VT 100, 1 mi S. 802/496-8880.* Specializes in steak, fresh seafood. Salad bar. Hrs: 11:30 am-11 pm. Closed Thanksgiving, Dec 25. Bar to midnight. Semi-a la carte: lunch $3.95-$6.95, dinner $8.95-$13.95. Outdoor dining. Cr cds: A, MC, V.

★ ★ **GIORGIO'S CAFE.** *(See Tucker Hill Lodge Inn) 802/496-3983.* E-mail tuckhill@madriver.com. Hrs: 8-10 am, 5-9:30 pm. Bar 5-11 pm. Complete meal: bkfst $7. Semi-a la carte: dinner $8-$14.95. Child's meals. Outdoor dining. Cr cds: A, MC, V.

Warren (D-2)

(See also Waitsfield, Waterbury)

Pop 1,172 **Elev** 893 ft **Area code** 802 **Zip** 05674 **E-mail** chamber@madriver.com **Web** www.sugarbushchamber.org

Information Sugarbush Chamber of Commerce, PO Box 173, Waitsfield 05673; 802/496-3409.

What to See and Do

Sugarbush Golf Course. An 18-hole championship course designed by Robert Trent Jones, Sr; driving range; 9-hole putting green; championship tees (6,524 yds). Restaurant. (May-Oct, daily) Res recommended. 3 mi NW via VT 100. Phone 802/583-2722. ¢¢¢¢¢

Sugarbush Resort. Area has 3 quad, 3 triple, 6 double chairlifts; 4 surface lifts; patrol, school, rentals; snowmaking; concession area, cafeteria, restaurant, bar; nursery. 107 runs, longest run over 2 mi; vertical drop 2,600 ft. (Early Nov-early May, daily) 3 mi NW, off VT 100. Phone 802/583-2381, 800/53-SUGAR or 800/583-SNOW (snow conditions). ¢¢¢¢¢

Sugarbush Soaring Association. Soaring instruction, scenic glider rides. Picnicking, restaurant. (May-Oct, daily) Res preferred. 2 mi NE via VT 100, at Sugarbush Airport. Phone 802/496-2290.

Sugarbush Sports Center. Complete sports & fitness facility with pools and whirlpools, steam rm, saunas, massage. Gym. Indoor/outdoor tennis courts, racquetball/handball & squash courts. Sports instruction. Fee for activities. (Daily) 3 mi NW via VT 100, in Sugarbush Village. Phone 802/583-2391. ¢¢¢¢

Motels

✔★ **GOLDEN LION RIVERSIDE INN.** *VT 100, 1 mi N. 802/496-3084; FAX 802/493-3874.* 12 rms, 2 kit. units. No A/C. Mid-Sept-mid-Apr: S, D $55-$83; each addl $10; under 6 free; higher rates wkends, hols; lower rates rest of yr. Crib free. Pet accepted. TV; cable. Complimentary full bkfst. Restaurant nearby. Ck-out 11 am. Downhill/x-country ski 3 mi. Picnic table, grill. Cr cds: A, DS, MC, V.

★ **POWDERHOUND INN.** *Rte 100, 1 1/4 mi N on VT 100, at jct Sugarbush Access Rd. 802/496-5100; FAX 802/496-5163; res: 800/548-4022.* E-mail phound@madriver.com; web www.powderhoundinn.com. 48 units, 44 kit. units, 1-2 story. No A/C. Dec-late Mar: S, D $80-$115; higher rates: wk of Washington's birthday, wk of Dec 25; lower rates rest of yr. Crib $5. Pet accepted; $5. TV; cable. Pool; whirlpool. Restaurant (in season only) 7:30-9:30 am. Ck-out 10 am. Tennis. Downhill/x-country ski 3 mi. Balconies. Picnic tables, grills. Restored, 19th-century farmhouse. Cr cds: A, DS, MC, V.

★ ★ **SUGARBUSH VILLAGE.** *3 mi N on VT 100, then 3 mi W on Sugarbush Access Rd. 802/583-3000; FAX 802/583-2373; res: 800/451-4326.* E-mail segares@madriver.com; web madriver.com. 150 1-5 bedrm kit. condos, 1-5 story. No A/C. Ski season: 1-2 bedrm $90-$330; 3-5 bedrm $335-$440; wkly rates; ski-wk, sports plans; lower rates rest of yr. Crib avail. TV; cable, VCR avail. Pool. Ck-out 10 am. Coin lndry. Downhill ski adj; x-country ski 2 mi. Refrigerators; some microwaves, fireplaces or wood stoves. Private patios, some balconies. Cr cds: A, DS, MC, V.

Inns

★ ★ ★ **SUGARBUSH.** *3 mi N on VT 100, then 2 mi W on Sugarbush Access Rd. 802/583-2301; FAX 802/583-3209; res: 800/53-SUGAR.* E-mail sugarbush@madriver.com; web www.sugarbush.com. 46 rms in inn, 196 kit. condos. No A/C in condos. Dec-Mar: S, D, suites $90-$150; each addl $20-$35; kit. condos $200-$400 (2-day min); ski, golf, tennis plans; higher rates hols; lower rates rest of yr. Crib $10. TV; cable (premium), VCR avail (movies $3.50). 2 pools, 1 indoor; whirlpool. Dining rm 7:30-10 am, 6-10 pm. Bar from 4:30 pm. Ck-out 11 am, ck-in 6 pm. Meeting rms. Business servs avail. Bellhops. Gift shop. Tennis, clinics, pro. 18-hole golf, putting green. Downhill ski 1/2 mi; x-country ski on site, rentals. Exercise equipt; sauna. Ice-skating. Rec rm. Lawn games. Some refrigerators. Some private patios, balconies. Cr cds: A, D, DS, MC, V.

★ ★ **SUGARTREE.** *Sugarbush Access Rd, 3 mi N on VT 100 to Sugarbush Access Rd. 802/583-3211; FAX 802/583-3203; res: 800/666-8907.* E-mail sugartree@madriver.com; web www.sugartree.com. 9 rms, some A/C, 3 story. Late Dec-Mar: S $80-$125; D $90-$135; each addl $20-$30; ski plans; higher rates: hols, fall foliage; lower rates rest of yr. Closed 3 wks Apr. Children over 7 yrs only. Complimentary full bkfst. Restaurant adj 5:30-10 pm. Ck-out 11 am, ck-in 2 pm. Business servs avail. Downhill/x-country ski 1/4 mi. Health club privileges. Antiques. Gazebo. Totally nonsmoking. Cr cds: A, D, MC, V.

Resort

★ ★ **BRIDGES RESORT & RACQUET CLUB.** *3 mi N off VT 100, 2 1/4 mi W on Sugarbush Access Rd. 802/583-2922; FAX 802/583-*

1018; res: 800/453-2922. E-mail bridges@madriver.com; web www.bridges-resort.com. 100 kit. units (1-3 bedrm), 2-3 story. No A/C. No elvtr. Dec-Mar: 1 bedrm $205; 2 bedrm $160-$285; 3 bedrm $240-$435; under 12 free; wkly rates; tennis plan; wkends (2-day min); lower rates rest of yr. Crib $18. TV; cable (premium), VCR (movies $3). 3 pools, 1 indoor; poolside serv. Playground. Supervised child's activities (July-Aug); ages 4 & up. Restaurant nearby. Ck-out 11 am, ck-in 6 pm. Grocery nearby. Meeting rms. Business servs avail. Ski area transportation. Indoor & outdoor tennis; 12 courts. Downhill/x-country ski ¼ mi. Nature trail. Lawn games. Rec rm. Exercise equipt; sauna. Fireplaces. Private patios, balconies. Grills, picnic tables. Cr cds: A, MC, V.

Restaurants

★ ★ **BASS.** 3 mi N on VT 100, then ¼ mi W on Sugarbush Access Rd. 802/583-3100. Specializes in prime rib, lobster, fresh seafood. Hrs: 5-10 pm; from 4 pm during ski season. Closed Wed June-Aug; also late Apr-mid-May. Bar. A la carte entrees: dinner $9.50-$17.50. Fireplace. Tri-level dining with view of mountains. Totally nonsmoking. Cr cds: A, DS, MC, V.

★ ★ ★ **THE COMMON MAN.** German Flats Rd. 802/583-2800. Continental menu. Specialties: lapin roti, carre d'agneau, escargot maison. Menu changes wkly. Hrs: 6:30-9 pm; Sat 6-10 pm; winter months from 5:30 pm. Closed Thanksgiving, Dec 25. Res accepted. Serv bar. A la carte entrees: dinner $10.25-$21. Child's meals. Casual dining in mid-1800s barn. Family-owned. Totally nonsmoking. Cr cds: A, DS, MC, V.

Ⓓ

★ ★ ★ **SAM RUPERTS.** 3 mi N on VT 100, 2½ mi W on Sugarbush Access Rd. 802/583-2421. Specializes in Amer, International cuisine. Own baking, desserts. Hrs: 6-9:30 pm; Fri, Sat to 10 pm. Closed Tues; also Easter, Dec 25. Res accepted. Bar. Wine list. Semi-a la carte: dinner $10-$21.95. Child's meals. Magician on wkends. Outdoor dining. Rustic, greenhouse atmosphere. Cr cds: A, D, DS, MC, V.

Waterbury (D-2)

(See also Barre, Montpelier, Stowe, Waitsfield, Warren)

Pop 4,589 **Elev** 428 ft **Area code** 802 **Zip** 05676

Information Central Vermont Chamber of Commerce, PO Box 336, Barre 05641; 802/229-5711.

Centrally located near many outstanding ski resorts, including Stowe, Mad River Valley and Bolton Valley, this area is also popular in summer for hiking, backpacking and bicycling.

What to See and Do

Ben & Jerry's Ice Cream Factory. One-half-hr guided tour, offered every 30 min through ice-cream factory, includes slide show, free samples. Gift shop. (Daily; closed Jan 1, Thanksgiving, Dec 25) I-89 exit 10, then N on VT 100. Phone 802/244-TOUR. ¢

Camel's Hump Mt. State's third-highest mountain. Trail is challenging. Weather permitting, Canada can be seen from the top. 8 mi SW of town on dirt road, then 3½-mi hike to summit.

Cold Hollow Cider Mill. One of the largest cider mills in New England features 43-inch rack and cloth press capable of producing 500 gallons of cider an hr; also jelly-making operations (fall). Samples are served. 3½ mi N on VT 100. Phone 802/244-8771 or 800/327-7537.   **Free.**

Little River State Park. This 12,000-acre park offers swimming; fishing. Nature, hiking trails. Tent & trailer sites (dump station), lean-tos. (Memorial Day-Columbus Day) Standard fees. 2 mi W off, US 2. Phone 802/244-7103 or 802/479-5280.

Long Trail. A 22-mi segment of backpacking trail connects Camel's Hump with Mt Mansfield (see STOWE), the state's highest peak. Primitive camping is allowed on both mountains. Recommended for the experienced hiker.

Winter recreation. Area abounds in downhill, cross-country and ski touring facilities; also many snowmobile trails.

Motel

★ ★ **HOLIDAY INN.** Blush Hill Rd, at jct of I-89 exit 10 & VT 100 N. 802/244-7822; res: 800/621-7822; FAX 802/244-7822. 79 rms, 2 story. S, D $70-$145; each addl $10; under 12 free; higher rates fall foliage. Crib free. Pet accepted. TV; cable. Pool. Restaurant 7 am-2 pm, 5:30-9 pm; Sat, Sun 7 am-2 pm, 5:30-10 pm. Rm serv. Bar. Ck-out noon. Coin lndry. Meeting rms. Business servs avail. In-rm modem link. Tennis. Downhill/x-country ski 12 mi. Exercise equipt; sauna. Game rm. Picnic tables. Covered bridge. Cr cds: A, C, D, DS, ER, JCB, MC, V.

Inns

★ ★ ★ **BLACK LOCUST.** (Waterbury Center 05677) 5 mi N on VT 100, I-89 exit 10. 802/244-7490; FAX 802/244-8473; res: 800/366-5592. E-mail blklocst@sover.net; web www.blacklocustinn.com. 6 rms, 2 story. No rm phones. S, D $89-$135; each addl $25. Children over 12 yrs only. TV in sitting rm. Complimentary full bkfst; afternoon refreshments. Ck-out 11 am, ck-in 2 pm. Downhill/x-country ski 7 mi. Restored 1832 farmhouse; individually decorated rms; antiques. Totally nonsmoking. Cr cds: A, D, DS, MC, V.

✔★ **GRÜNBERG HAUS BED & BREAKFAST.** RR 2, Box 1595, 4 mi S on VT 100. 802/244-7726; res: 800/800-7760. 11 rms, some share bath, 2 story, 2 cabins. No A/C. No rm phones. S $40-$110; D $59-$130; each addl $7; wkly rates; ski plan; Complimentary full bkfst; afternoon refreshments. Ck-out 11 am, ck-in 3 pm. Tennis. Downhill ski 12 mi; x-country ski on site. Whirlpool, sauna. Game rm. Balconies. Tyrolean chalet; fieldstone fireplace, grand piano. On 14 acres; gardens, trails. Cr cds: DS, MC, V.

★ **INN AT BLUSH HILL.** Blush Hill Rd, just N of I-89 on VT 100, then left ¾ mi. 802/244-7529; FAX 802/244-7314; res: 800/736-7522. E-mail inn@blush.com; web www.blushhill.com. 5 rms, 2 story. No A/C. No rm phones. S, D $65-$95; each addl $15; ski plans; higher rates: fall foliage, Christmas wk. TV in sitting rm; cable. Complimentary full bkfst; afternoon refreshments. Restaurant nearby. Ck-out 11 am, ck-in 3 pm. Downhill/x-country ski 10 mi. Picnic tables, grills. Library. Former stagecoach stop (1790); colonial antiques; fireplaces. Situated on five acres; gardens. 9-hole golf course opp. Cr cds: A, DS, MC, V.

★ ★ **THATCHER BROOK INN.** VT 100N. 802/244-5911; FAX 802/244-1294; res: 800/292-5911. E-mail thatcherinn@aol.com; web www.discover-vermont.com/banner/thatcher.htm. 24 rms, 3 with shower only, 2 story. No A/C. Sept-Mar: S, D $105-$175; each addl $20; under 12 free; ski plans; wkend rates; MAP avail; 2-day min hols; lower rates rest of yr. Crib free. TV; cable, VCR in common rm. Complimentary full bkfst. Restaurant (see THATCHER BROOK). Ck-out 10:30 am, ck-in 3 pm. Business servs avail. Downhill ski 13 mi; x-country ski 10 mi. Rec rm. Built in 1899; twin gazebos with front porch. Cr cds: A, D, DS, MC, V.

Restaurants

★ ★ ★ **THATCHER BROOK.** (See Thatcher Brook Inn) 802/244-5911. E-mail thatcherinn@aol.com; web www.discover-vermont.com/banner/thatcher.htm. French menu. Specialties: roasted rack of lamb, honey-glazed breast of duck, mushrooms á la Thatcher. Hrs: 5-9:30 pm. Res accepted. Bar. A la carte entrees: dinner $12.95-$24.95. Child's meals. Entertainment. Outdoor dining. Cr cds: A, D, DS, MC, V.

★ ★ ★ **VILLA TRAGARA.** *(VT 100, Waterbury Center 05677)* *802/244-5288.* E-mail tragara@aol.com. Northern Italian menu. Specializes in pasta, fish. Own baking, pasta. Hrs: 5:30-9:30 pm. Res accepted. Bar. Wine list. Semi-a la carte: dinner $12-$17.75. Converted 1820s farmhouse. Totally nonsmoking. Cr cds: A, MC, V.

♥

Weathersfield
(see Springfield)

West Dover (H-2)
(See also Wilmington)

Pop 250 (est) **Elev** 1,674 ft **Area code** 802 **Zip** 05356 **E-mail** info@visitvermont.com **Web** www.visitvermont.com/
Information Mt Snow Valley Region Chamber of Commerce, VT 9, W Main St, PO Box 3, Wilmington 05363; 802/464-8092.

What to See and Do
Mt Snow Ski Area. Area has 2 quad, 6 triple, 9 double chairlifts; patrol, school, rentals; snowmaking; cafeterias, restaurant, bars, entertainment; nursery. Over 100 trails spread over 5 interconnected mountain areas (also see WILMINGTON); shuttle bus. Longest run 2½ mi; vertical drop 1,700 ft. (Nov-early May, daily) Half-day rates. 9 mi N on VT 100, in Green Mt Natl Forest. Phone 802/464-8501; for snow conditions 802/464-2151; for lodging 800/2 45-SNOW. ¢¢¢¢

Annual Events
Mountain Bike World Cup Race. Mt Snow. More than 1,500 cyclists from throughout the world compete in downhill, dual slalom and circuit racing events. Phone 800/245-7669. Mid-June.

Mt Snow Foliage Craft Fair. Mt Snow Ski Area (see). New England area artisans exhibit pottery, jewelry, glass, graphics, weaving and other crafts; entertainment. Columbus Day wkend.

Inns
★ **INN AT QUAIL RUN.** *(106 Smith Rd, Wilmington 05363)* *802/464-3362; FAX 802/464-7784; res: 800/34-ESCAPE.* E-mail quail-runvt@aol.com; web www.bbonline.com/vt/quailrun. 14 rms, 2 story. No A/C. No rm phones. S, D $80-$125; each addl $25; ski plans; higher rates fall foliage, hols. Crib free. Pet accepted. TV in some rms; cable. Pool; sauna. Playground. Complimentary full bkfst. Ck-out 11 am, ck-in 3 pm. Business servs avail. Downhill ski 4.5 mi; x-country ski on site. Rec rm. Lawn games. Picnic tables. On 12 acres in Green Mountains, view of Deerfield Valley. Totally nonsmoking. Cr cds: A, DS, MC, V.

★ ★ ★ **INN AT SAWMILL FARM.** *Crosstown Rd.* *802/464-8131; FAX 802/464-1130.* 21 rms, 2 story, 4 suites. No rm phones. MAP: S $295-$355; D $320-$360; each addl $85; suites $370-$400; higher rates: fall foliage season, Thanksgiving, wk of Dec 25, Jan 1. Serv charge 15%. TV in library. Pool. Restaurant (see INN AT SAWMILL FARM). Bar 4:30 pm-midnight. Ck-out noon, ck-in 3 pm. Business servs avail. Gift shop. Tennis. Downhill ski 1½ mi; x-country ski on site. Fireplace in suites. Converted dairy farm (1790). Individually decorated rms. Stocked trout ponds. Cr cds: A, MC, V.

✔★ **RED CRICKET INN.** *VT 100.* *802/464-8817; FAX 802/464-0508; res: 800/733-2742.* E-mail redcrick@sover.net. 25 rms, 20 with shower only, 2 story. Mid-Dec-mid-Mar: D $56-$120; each addl $5-$15; under 12 free midwk; wkly, hol rates (2-3-day min hols); ski plans; lower rates mid-Mar-mid-Apr, mid-May-mid-Dec. Closed rest of yr. Crib free. Complimentary continental bkfst. Business servs avail. Downhill ski 3½ mi; x-country ski 3 mi. Picnic tables. Cr cds: A, DS, MC, V.

★ ★ **WEST DOVER INN.** *Rt 100.* *802/464-5207; FAX 802/464-2173.* E-mail wdvrinn@sover.net; web www.westdoverinn.com. 12 rms, 2 story, 4 suites. No A/C. No rm phones. D $90-$125; each addl $25-$35; suites $135-$200; higher rates: fall foliage, hol wkends. Closed mid-Apr-Memorial Day. Children over 8 yrs only. TV; cable. Complimentary full bkfst. Dining rm 6-9:30 pm. Ck-out 11 am, ck-in 2 pm. Downhill ski 3½ mi; x-country ski 1 mi. Built 1846; was stagecoach stop & general store. Many antiques. Cr cds: A, DS, MC, V.

Restaurant
★ ★ ★ **INN AT SAWMILL FARM.** *(See Inn At Sawmill Farm)* *802/464-8131.* Continental menu. Specializes in seafood, duck, rack of lamb. Own baking. Hrs: 6-9:30 pm. Res accepted. Bar. Wine cellar. A la carte entrees: dinner $27-$32. 34,000 bottles of wine, 1,300 selections. Chef-owned. Cr cds: A, MC, V.

Weston (G-2)
(See also Londonderry, Peru)

Pop 620 (est) **Elev** 1,295 ft **Area code** 802 **Zip** 05161

Once nearly a ghost town, Weston is now a serene village secluded in the beautiful hills of Vermont. Charming old houses are situated around a small common, and shops are scattered along Main St. Weston is listed on the National Register of Historic Places.

What to See and Do
Farrar-Mansur House Museum (1797). Restored house/tavern with 9 rms. Period furnishings; paintings. Guided tours. (July-Aug, Mon-Fri; Memorial Day-Columbus Day, wkends) N side of Common. ¢¢

Greendale Camping Area. Picnicking. Camping (fee). 2 mi N on VT 100, 2 mi W on Greendale Rd in Green Mt Natl Forest (see).

Old Mill Museum. Museum of old-time tools and industries; tinsmith in residence. Guided tours (July & Aug). (Memorial Day-Columbus Day, daily) On VT 100, in center of village. **Donation.**

Vermont Country Store. Just like those Granddad used to patronize—rock candy and other old-fashioned foodstuffs. (Daily exc Sun; closed Thanksgiving, Dec 25) On VT 100, S of Village Green. Phone 802/824-3184.

Weston Bowl Mill. Wooden bowls, other wooden household products made on premises. Seconds avail. (Daily; closed Easter, Thanksgiving, Dec 25) Just N of Common on VT 100. Phone 802/824-6219. **Free.**

Weston Playhouse. One of the oldest professional theater companies in the state. Restaurant; cabaret. Village Green. For schedule and fee information phone 802/824-5288.

Motel
✔★ ★ **COLONIAL HOUSE.** *287 VT 100.* *802/824-6286; res: 800/639-5033.* 6 rms in inn, 2 share bath, 9 rms in motel, 2 story. No A/C. No rm phones. Mid-Dec-Apr, fall foliage season: S $45-$60; D $60-$90; each addl $15; family rates; golf, theater plans; lower rates rest of yr. Crib free. TV in lounge; cable. Complimentary bkfst. Restaurant 8-9:30 am,

6-7:30 pm (public by res exc Sun, Wed). Ck-out 11 am. Downhill ski 10 mi; x-country ski on site. Game rm. Lawn games. Sun rm. Cr cds: DS, MC, V.

Inns

★ ★ **WILDER HOMESTEAD INN.** *25 Lawrence Hill Rd, near village green.* 802/824-8172; FAX 802/824-5054. E-mail innkeeper@wilderhomestead.com; web www.wilderhomestead.com. 7 rms, 5 with bath, 3 story. No A/C. No rm phones. S, D $70-$115; each addl $30; higher rates fall foliage, hol wks. Closed 2 wks Apr. Children over 6 yrs only. TV, cable in sitting rm; VCR (free movies). Complimentary full bkfst. Ck-out 11 am, ck-in 2 pm. Gift shop. Downhill ski 10 mi; x-country ski 3 mi. Federal-style country inn; built 1827. Player piano. Overlooks river. Totally nonsmoking. Cr cds: MC, V.

White River Junction (F-3)

(See also Windsor, Woodstock; also see Hanover, NH)

Settled 1764 **Pop** 2,521 **Elev** 368 ft **Area code** 802 **Zip** 05001

Appropriately named, this town is the meeting place of the Boston & Maine and Central Vermont railroads, the White and Connecticut rivers and two interstate highways.

What to See and Do

Quechee Gorge. Often referred to as Vermont's "Little Grand Canyon," the Ottauquechee River has carved out a mile-long chasm that offers dramatic views of the landscape and neighboring towns. About 8 mi W on US 4.

Motels

✔★ ★ **BEST WESTERN AT THE JUNCTION.** *1 mi S on US 5, 1 blk E of jct I-89, I-91.* 802/295-3015; FAX 802/296-2581. 112 rms, 2 story. Mid-May-Mid-Sept: S $59-$76; D $71-$99; each addl $10; under 18 free; higher rates: fall foliage, special events; lower rates rest of yr. Crib free. Pet accepted. $10. TV; cable (premium). Indoor pool; wading pool; whirlpool. Playground. Restaurant adj 6 am-10 pm; Sat to 1 am. Bar 4 pm-1 am. Ck-out 11 am. Coin lndry. Meeting rms. Sundries. Downhill ski 20 mi; x-country ski 14 mi. Exercise equipt; sauna. Game rm. Refrigerators, microwaves avail. Private patios, balconies. Cr cds: A, C, D, DS, JCB, MC, V.

✔★ ★ **RAMADA INN.** *Sykes Ave & Holiday Inn Dr, 2 mi SW on US 5; off Sykes Ave at jct I-89, I-91.* 802/295-3000; FAX 802/295-3774. 140 rms, 2 story. S $59-$81; D $59-$97; each addl $8; under 19 free; ski plan; wkend rates; higher rates fall foliage. Crib free. Pet accepted. TV; cable (premium). Indoor pool; whirlpool. Coffee in rms. Restaurants 7 am-10 pm. Rm serv. Bar 4 pm-1 am; entertainment. Ck-out noon. Meeting rms. Business servs avail. Sundries. Putting green. Downhill ski 15 mi. Exercise equipt; sauna. Game rm. Balconies. Cr cds: A, C, D, DS, ER, JCB, MC, V.

Motor Hotel

✔★ ★ **COMFORT INN.** *Sykes Ave, I-91 exit 11.* 802/295-3051; FAX 802/295-5990. 71 rms, 4 story. S $54-$99; D $65-$115; each addl $5; under 18 free; higher rates fall foliage. Crib free. TV; cable. Heated pool. Complimentary continental bkfst. Restaurant nearby. Ck-out 11 am. Coin

lndry. Meeting rms. Business servs avail. In-rm modem link. Health club privileges. Microwave in suites. Cr cds: A, C, D, DS, JCB, MC, V.

Inn

★ ★ **STONECREST FARM.** *(119 Christian St, Wilder 05088) 3 mi N on VT 5.* 802/296-2425; res: 800/730-2425; FAX 802/295-1135. E-mail stonefarm1@aol.com. 6 rms, 4 with shower only, 2 story. No A/C. No rm phones. Mid-May-mid-Nov: S $105-$120; D $120-$135; each addl $25; hols (2-day min); lower rates rest of yr. Closed wk of Dec 25. Children over 8 yrs only. Complimentary full bkfst. Ck-out 11 am, ck-in 3-7 pm. Business servs avail. Downhill ski 15 mi; x-country ski 3½ mi. Lawn games. Built in 1810; country Victorian atmosphere. Totally nonsmoking. Cr cds: A, MC, V.

Restaurant

★ ★ **A.J.'S.** *Sykes Ave, 4 blks E of I-89, I-91.* 802/295-3071. Specializes in steak, prime rib, fresh seafood. Salad, soup bar. Hrs: 5-10 pm; Sun 4-9 pm. Res accepted. Bar. Semi-a la carte: dinner $7.95-$16.95. Child's meals. Rustic decor; wood stoves, fireplace. Totally nonsmoking. Cr cds: A, C, D, MC, V.

Wilmington (H-2)

(See also Bennington, Brattleboro, Marlboro, West Dover)

Chartered 1751 & 53 **Pop** 1,968 **Elev** 1,533 ft **Area code** 802 **Zip** 05363
E-mail info@visitvermont.com **Web** www.visitvermont.com/
Information Mt Snow Valley Region Chamber of Commerce, VT 9, W Main St, PO Box 3; 802/464-8092.

What to See and Do

Haystack Ski Area. Resort has double, 3 triple chairlifts; patrol, school, rentals; snowmaking; concession, cafeteria, bar; nursery, lodges. Over 100 trails spread over 5 interconnecting mountain areas (also see WEST DOVER); shuttle bus. Longest run 1½ mi; vertical drop 1,400 ft. (Dec-Mar, daily) Golf, pro shop; restaurant, bar (early May-mid-Oct). 3 mi NW, off VT 100. Phone 802/464-8501 or 802/464-2151(snow conditions); 800/245-7669 (lodging). ¢¢¢¢

Molly Stark State Park. A 158-acre park named for wife of General John Stark, hero of Battle of Bennington (1777); on W slope of Mt Olga (2,438 ft). Fishing in nearby lake. Hiking trails. Tent & trailer sites (dump station), lean-tos. Fire tower with excellent views. (Memorial Day-Columbus Day) Standard fees. Approx 4 mi E on VT 9. Phone 802/464-5460 or 802/886-2434.

Annual Event

Deerfield Valley Farmers Day Exhibition. Pony pull, midway rides; horse show, livestock judging, entertainment. Late Aug.

Seasonal Event

The Nights Before Christmas. Throughout Wilmington & West Dover (see). Celebrates holiday season with caroling, torchlight parade, fireworks, tree lighting. Festival of Light, living nativity and children’s hayrides. Phone 802/464-8092. Late Nov-late Dec.

Motel

✔★★ HORIZON INN. *VT 9. 802/464-2131; res: 800/336-5513.* 27 rms, 2 story. Mid-Dec-mid-Apr: S, D $60-$115; each addl $10; under 12 free; ski plans; wknd, hol rates (2-day min hols); lower rates rest of yr. Crib avail. TV; cable (premium). Indoor pool; whirlpool. Complimentary coffee in rms. Ck-out 11 am. Meeting rms. Business servs avail. Downhill ski 7 mi; x-country ski 2.5 mi. Exercise equipt; sauna. Game rm. Lawn games. Grills, picnic tables. Cr cds: A, DS, MC, V.

Lodge

★★ NORDIC HILLS. *34 Look Rd, Rte 9 to Rte 100N, left on Coldbrook Rd. 802/464-5130; FAX 802/464-8248; res: 800/326-5130.* 27 rms, 3 story. No A/C. No elvtr. S, D $60-$136; each addl $10-$45; higher rates: Presidents wk, Christmas wk; winter wknds (2-day min.) Closed Apr-mid-May. Crib free. TV. Heated pool; whirlpool, sauna. Complimentary full bkfst. Ck-out 11 am. Downhill/x-country ski 1½ mi. Game rm. Lawn games. Family-owned. Cr cds: A, D, DS, MC, V.

Inns

★★ HERMITAGE INN. *Coldbrook Rd, 2½ mi N on VT 100 to Coldbrook Rd, then 3 mi W. 802/464-3511; FAX 802/464-2688.* E-mail hermitag@sover.net; web www.hermitageinn.com. 15 air-cooled rms, 2 story. MAP: S $160-$185; D $100-$113/person; each addl $70; wkly rates; hunting packages. Serv charge 15%. TV; cable, VCR. Restaurant (see HERMITAGE). Bar from 11 am. Ck-out 11 am, ck-in 2 pm. Meeting rm. Business servs avail. Tennis. Downhill ski ½ mi; x-country ski on site. Fireplaces. Private patios. Hunting preserve. Sporting clays. Art gallery. Cr cds: A, D, MC, V.

★★ TRAIL'S END. *5 Trail's End Lane. 802/464-2727; res: 800/859-2585.* E-mail trailsnd@together.net; web www.trailsendvt.com. 15 rms, 2 story. No A/C. No rm phones. S, D $105-$185; each addl $30; wkends (2-day min); hol wkends (3-day min); wkly rates. Crib avail. TV, VCR in some rms, sitting rm. Heated pool. Complimentary full bkfst; afternoon refreshments. Ck-out 11 am, ck-in 2 pm. Tennis. Downhill ski 4½ mi; x-country ski ½ mi. Some fireplaces. On 10 acres; stocked trout pond. Cr cds: A, DS, MC, V.

★★ WHITE HOUSE OF WILMINGTON. *178 VT 9 E, ½ mi E of VT 9. 802/464-2135.* E-mail whitehse@sover.net; web www.whitehouse-inn.com. 16 rms in inn, 7 rms in guest house. No A/C. No rm phones. S, D $118-$198; higher rates: wk of Washington's Birthday, fall foliage, wk of Dec 25. Children over 10 yrs only. TV in sitting rm; cable, VCR. 2 pools, 1 indoor; whirlpool, sauna. Complimentary bkfst. Restaurant (see WHITE HOUSE). Bar 3 pm-midnight. Ck-out 11 am, ck-in 1 pm. Downhill ski 8 mi; x-country ski on site. Rec rm. Lawn games. Balconies. Some fireplaces, in-rm whirlpools. View of valley. Built in 1915 as summer house for lumber baron Martin Brown. Cr cds: A, D, DS, MC, V.

Restaurants

★★★ HERMITAGE. *(See Hermitage Inn) 802/464-3511.* E-mail hermitag@sover.net; web www.hermitageinn.com. Continental menu. Specializes in Wienerschnitzel, fresh trout, own game birds, home raised venison. Own baking. Hrs: 5-11 pm; Sun brunch 11 am-2 pm. Res accepted. Bar 11-2 am. Wine cellar. Semi-a la carte: dinner $14-$25. Sun brunch $7-$15. Serv charge 15%. Wine collection spans over 2,000 varieties. Trout pond. Game pens. Family-owned. Cr cds: A, D, MC, V.

★★ WHITE HOUSE. *(See White House Of Wilmington Inn) 802/464-2135.* Continental menu. Specializes in boneless stuffed duck, veal dishes, fresh seafood. Own baking. Hrs: 8-10 am, 5:30-9 pm; Sun brunch 11 am-2:30 pm. Res accepted. No A/C. Bar 3 pm-midnight. Wine list. Semi-a la carte: bkfst $3.50-$10, dinner $13.95-$19.95. Sun brunch $13.95. Parking. Outdoor dining. Colonial-revival decor. Cr cds: MC, V.

Windsor (F-3)

(See also White River Junction)

Settled 1764 **Pop** 3,714 **Elev** 354 ft **Area code** 802 **Zip** 05089
Information White River Area Chamber of Commerce, PO Box 697, White River Jct 05001; 802/295-6200.

Situated on the Connecticut River in the shadow of Mt Ascutney, Windsor once was the political center of the Connecticut Valley towns. The name "Vermont" was adopted, and its constitution was drawn up here. Inventors and inventions flourished here in the 19th century; the hydraulic pump, a sewing machine, coffee percolator and various refinements in firearms originated in Windsor.

What to See and Do

American Precision Museum. Exhibits include hand and machine tools; illustrations of their uses and development. Housed in former Robbins and Lawrence Armory (1846). (Late May-Oct, daily; rest of yr, by appt) 196 Main St. Phone 802/674-5781. ¢¢

Constitution House. An 18th-century tavern where constitution of the Republic of Vermont was signed on July 8, 1777. Museum. (Mid-May-mid-Oct, Wed-Sun) 16 N Main St, on US 5. Phone 802/672-3773. ¢

Covered bridge. Crossing the Connecticut River; longest in US.

Mt Ascutney State Park. This 1,984-acre park has a paved road to summit of Mt Ascutney (3,144 ft). Hiking trails. Picnicking. Tent & trailer sites (dump station), lean-tos. (Memorial Day-Columbus Day) Standard fees. 3 mi S off US 5 on VT 44A; I-91 exit 8. Phone 802/674-2060 or 802/886-2434.

Vermont State Craft Center at Windsor House. Restored building features works of more than 250 Vermont craftspeople. (June-Dec, daily; rest of yr, daily exc Sun) Main St. Phone 802/674-6729. **Free.**

Wilgus State Park. This 100-acre park overlooks the Connecticut River. Canoe launching. Hiking trails. Wooded picnic area. Tent & trailer sites (dump station), lean-tos. (Memorial Day-Columbus Day) Standard fees. 6 mi S on US 5. Phone 802/674-5422 or 802/886-2434.

Inn

★★★ JUNIPER HILL. *Juniper Hill Rd, ½ mi N of jct US 5. 802/674-5273; FAX 802/674-2041; res: 800/359-2541.* Web www.juniperhillinn.com. 16 rms, 2-3 story. No elvtr. No rm phones. S, D $95-$170; each addl $25; MAP avail; wkly rates; package plans. Children over 12 yrs only. TV in front rm. Pool. Complimentary full bkfst. Dining rm 8-9:30 am, 7 pm sitting (by res only). Bar 3:30-11 pm. Ck-out 11 am, ck-in 3 pm. Downhill/x-country ski 7 mi. Lawn games. Many fireplaces. Antique furnished mansion; library. Totally nonsmoking. Cr cds: DS, MC, V.

Restaurant

★★ WINDSOR STATION. *Depot Ave. 802/674-2052.* Continental menu. Specializes in seafood, veal, pasta. Own desserts. Hrs: 5:30-9 pm. Closed Jan 1, Dec 25. Bar from 4 pm. Semi-a la carte: dinner $10.95-$16.95. Child's meals. Restored RR depot (1900). Cr cds: A, MC, V.

Woodstock (F-3)

(See also Killington, Plymouth, White River Junction)

Settled 1768 **Pop** 3,212 **Elev** 705 ft **Area code** 802 **Zip** 05091 **E-mail** woodstock@aol.com **Web** www.woodstockvt.com

Information Chamber of Commerce, 18 Central St, PO Box 486; 802/457-3555.

The antique charm of Woodstock has been preserved, at least in part, by determination. Properties held for generations by descendants of original owners provided built-in zoning long before Historic District status was achieved. When the iron bridge that crosses the Ottauquechee River at Union St was condemned in 1968 it was replaced by a covered wooden bridge.

What to See and Do

Billings Farm & Museum. Exhibits include operating dairy farm and an 1890s farm house. (May-late Oct, daily) ½ mi N on VT 12. Phone 802/457-2355. ¢¢

Covered bridge (1968). First one built in Vermont since 1895. Two others cross the Ottauquechee River; one 3 mi W (1877), another 4 mi E, at Taftsville (1836). Center of village.

Kedron Valley Stables. Hayrides, sleigh rides, picnic trail rides; indoor ring; riding lessons by appt. About 5 mi S on VT 106, in S Woodstock. Phone 802/457-1480.

Silver Lake State Park. This 34-acre park offers swimming beach, bathhouse; fishing; boating (rentals). Picnicking, concession. Tent & trailer camping (dump station), lean-tos. Within walking distance of Barnard Village. (Memorial Day-Labor Day) Standard fees. 10 mi NW via VT 12 to Barnard, on Silver Lake. Phone 802/234-9451 or 802/886-2434.

Suicide Six Ski Area. Area has 2 double chairlifts, J-Bar; patrol, PSIA school, rentals; snowmaking; cafeteria, wine & beer bar; lodge. 19 runs, longest run 1 mi; vertical drop 650 ft. Site of first ski tow in US (1934). (Early Dec-late Mar, daily) 3 mi N on VT 12 (S Pomfret Rd). Phone 802/457-1666. ¢¢¢¢¢

Vermont Institute of Natural Science. There is a 75-acre preserve with trails (daily). Raptor Center, an outdoor museum, has 26 species of hawks, owls and eagles (summer, daily; winter, daily exc Sun). Gift shop. 1½ mi SW on Church Hill Rd. Phone 802/457-2779.   ¢¢

Walking Tours Around Woodstock. There are 1-2-hr tours of Historic District, covering over 1 mi; depart from Chamber of Commerce information booth on the green. (Mid-June-mid-Oct, Mon, Wed & Sat) Phone 802/457-2450 or 802/457-3458.

Woodstock Country Club. An 18-hole championship golf course; 10 tennis courts, paddle tennis. Cross-country skiing center with over 35 mi of trails; rentals, instruction, tours. Restaurant, lounge. (Daily; closed Apr & Nov) Fee for activities. S on VT 106. Phone 802/457-2112 or 802/457-2114.

Woodstock Historical Society. Dana House (1807) has 11 rms spanning 1750-1900, including a children's rm; also silver; glass; paintings; costumes; furniture; research library; Woodstock-related artifacts, photographs. Farm and textile equipment. Gift shop. (Mid-May-late Oct, daily) 26 Elm St. Phone 802/457-1822.

Motels

★ **BRAESIDE.** *PO Box 411, 1 mi E on US 4. 802/457-1366.* E-mail braeside@vermontel.com. 12 rms. S, D $48-$88. Crib free. TV; cable (premium), VCR avail. Pool. Restaurant nearby. Ck-out 11 am. Downhill ski 6 mi; x-country ski 2 mi. Picnic table. Cr cds: A, MC, V.

★ **OTTAUQUECHEE MOTOR LODGE.** *4½ mi W on US 4. 802/672-3404.* 15 rms, 14 A/C. S, D $46-$96; each addl $5-$10; higher

rates: fall foliage, Christmas wk. TV; cable. Complimentary coffee in rms. Restaurant adj 6 am-9 pm. Ck-out 11 am. Downhill ski 10 mi; x-country ski 5 mi. Refrigerators. Cr cds: D, DS, MC, V.

✔★ **POND RIDGE.** *US 4, 1½ mi W. 802/457-1667.* 14 rms, 6 kits. S, D $39-$69; each addl $10; kit. units $69-$150; under 6 free; wkly rates; ski plans; higher rates fall foliage season. Crib $10. TV; cable (premium). Complimentary coffee in rms. Ck-out 10 am. Downhill ski 8 mi; x-country ski 3 mi. Lawn games. Picnic tables, grills. On river; swimming. Cr cds: A, C, D, ER, MC, V.

★★ **SHIRE.** *46 Pleasant St. 802/457-2211.* E-mail dotcall@aol.com. 33 rms. May-mid-Sept: S, D $68-$125; under 12 free; higher rates fall foliage. Crib $7. TV; cable. Coffee in lobby. Restaurant nearby. Ck-out 11 am. Business servs avail. Downhill ski 4 mi; x-country ski 1 mi. Refrigerators. Cr cds: A, DS, ER, MC, V.

Inns

✔★★ **APPLEBUTTER.** *Happy Valley Rd (05073), 3 mi E on US 4, then S on Happy Valley Rd. 802/457-4158; res: 800/480-1734.* E-mail aplbtrn@aol.com. 5 rms, 2 story. No rm phones. S, D $70-$135; each addl $15. TV in sitting rm; VCR (free movies). Complimentary full bkfst. Ck-out 10:30 am, ck-in 3 pm. Downhill ski 5 mi; x-country ski 3 mi. Restored Federal-style house (1850); period furnishings. Totally nonsmoking. Cr cds: MC, V.

★★ **CANTERBURY HOUSE.** *43 Pleasant St, on VT 4. 802/457-3077.* 8 rms, 4 with shower only, 3 story. No rm phones. S, D $90-$155. Children over 12 yrs only. TV in sitting rm; VCR. Complimentary full bkfst; afternoon refreshments. Restaurant adj 5-10 pm. Ck-out 11 am, ck-in 2 pm. Victorian home built 1880; antiques. Totally nonsmoking. Cr cds: A, DS, MC, V.

★★ **CHARLESTON HOUSE.** *21 Pleasant St. 802/457-3843; res: 888/475-3800.* E-mail nohl@together.net; web www.pbpub.com/woodstock/charlestonhouse.htm. 9 rms, 2 story. No rm phones. S, D $110-$175; hol wkend (2-day min). Complimentary full bkfst. Restaurant nearby. Ck-out 11 am, ck-in 3 pm. Downhill ski 3 mi; x-country ski 1 mi. Greek-revival house built 1835; many antiques. Totally nonsmoking. Cr cds: MC, V.

★★★ **COUNTRY GARDEN INN.** *(37 Main St, Quechee 05059) 10 mi E on VT 4. 802/295-3023; res: 800/859-4191; FAX 802/295-3121.* E-mail ctrygarden@aol.com; web country-garden-inn.com. 5 rms, 4 with shower only, 2 story. Rm phones avail. May-Oct: S, D $130-$200; each addl $40; wkends, hols (2-3 day min); lower rates rest of yr. Closed Mar & 1st 3 wks in Nov. Children over 10 yrs only. TV in common rm; VCR avail (free movies). Pool. Complimentary full bkfst; afternoon refreshments. Restaurant nearby. Rm serv 9 am-9 pm. Ck-out 10 am, ck-in 3-7 pm. Business servs avail. In-rm modem link. Luggage handling. Concierge serv. Downhill/x-country ski 1 mi. Exercise equipt. Health club privileges. Rec rm. Picnic tables, grills. Built in 1819; antiques. Totally nonsmoking. Cr cds: MC, V.

★★ **FOUR PILLARS.** *(Happy Valley Rd, Taftsville 05073) 2½ mi E on VT 4. 802/457-2797; FAX 802/457-5138.* E-mail fpillars@vermontel.com; web www.vermontel.com/~fpillars. 5 rms, 4 shower only, 2 story. No A/C. No rm phones. June-mid-Sept: S, D $78-$138; each addl $15; higher rates fall foliage season; lower rates rest of yr. Children over 10 yrs only. TV in common rm; VCR avail (movies). Complimentary full bkfst. Restaurant nearby. Ck-out 10:30 am, ck-in 3-6 pm. Business servs avail.

Tennis privileges. 18-hole golf privileges, putting green. Downhill/x-country ski 3 mi. Built in 1836. Totally nonsmoking. Cr cds: DS, MC.

★ ★ ★ **KEDRON VALLEY.** *South Woodstock (05071), 5 mi S on VT 106.* 802/457-1473; res: 800/836-1193; FAX 802/457-4469. E-mail kedroninn@aol.com. 26 inn rms, 1-3 story. 10 with A/C. No elvtr. No rm phones. S, D $120-$230; each addl $6.50; MAP avail; mid-wk rates; wkend riding plan; higher rates: fall foliage, Dec 25. Closed Apr. Crib free. Pet accepted. TV. Restaurant (see KEDRON VALLEY). Bar 5-11 pm. Ck-out 11:30 am, ck-in 3:30 pm. Business servs avail. Downhill ski 7 mi; x-country ski 3 mi. Many fireplaces, wood stoves. Some private patios. Natural pond. Cr cds: DS, MC, V.

★ ★ **LINCOLN.** *3 mi W on US 4.* 802/457-3312; FAX 802/457-5808. E-mail lincon2@aol.com; web www.lincolninn.com. 6 rms, 5 with shower only, 4 A/C, 2 story. 7 rms, 3 story. No A/C. S $100; D $125; MAP avail; higher rates fall foliage. TV; cable, VCR in parlor. Complimentary full bkfst. Restaurant 6-9 pm; closed Mon. Ck-out 11 am, ck-in 3 pm. Business servs avail. Sundries. Downhill ski 4 mi; x-country ski 3 mi. Library. Renovated farmhouse (ca 1869). Property bordered by Ottauquechee River and covered bridge. Totally nonsmoking. Cr cds: A, DS, MC, V.

★ ★ ★ **MAPLE LEAF.** *(VT 12, Barnard 05031) 9 mi N.* 802/234-5342; res: 800/516-2753. Web www.mapleleafinn.com. 7 rms, 3 story. No A/C. S, D $110-$175. TV; VCR (free movies). Complimentary full bkfst; afternoon refreshments. Restaurant nearby. Ck-out 11 am, ck-in 3-6 pm. Business servs avail. Gift shop. Tennis privileges. Downhill 5 mi; x-country ski on site. Many in-rm whirlpools, fireplaces. Replica of Victorian farmhouse with wrap-around porch on 16 wooded acres; many antiques; library. Totally nonsmoking. Cr cds: A, C, D, DS, JCB, MC, V.

★ ★ **PARKER HOUSE.** *(16 Main St, Quechee 05059) 5 mi E on US 4.* 802/295-6077. E-mail parker_house_inn@valley.net; web www.phpub.com\quechee\parkerhouse.htm. 7 rms, 3 A/C, 3 story. No rm phones. S, D $100-$130. TV in sitting rm. Complimentary full bkfst. Restaurant (see THE PARKER HOUSE). Ck-out 11 am, ck-in 3 pm. Health club privileges. Antiques. Library. Victorian home (1857); former senator's residence. Cr cds: MC, V.

★ ★ ★ **QUECHEE BED AND BREAKFAST.** *(753 Woodstock Rd, Quechee 05059) 6½ mi E on US 4.* 802/295-1776. 8 rms, 2 story. No rm phones. S, D $94-$139. Children over 13 yrs only. Dining rm 8-9 am. Ck-out 11 am, ck-in 3 pm. Gift shop. Golf privileges. Downhill ski 10 mi; x-country ski ½ mi. Health club privileges. Some refrigerators. Flower gardens. Former stagecoach stop (1795). Cr cds: MC, V.

★ ★ ★ **QUECHEE INN AT MARSHLAND FARM.** *(Clubhouse Rd, Quechee 05059) I-89 exit 1, then W on US 4 ½ mi to Clubhouse Rd, then 1 mi N.* 802/295-3133; FAX 802/295-6587; res: 800/235-3133. E-mail quecheeinn@pinnacle-inns.com; web www.pinnacle-inns.com/quechee-inn/. 24 rms, 2 story. No rm phones. Aug-late Oct, hols, MAP: S $160-$210; D $200-$240; each addl $42; wk-day rates; package plans; lower rates rest of yr. Crib $10. TV; cable. Swimming, sauna privileges. Complimentary full bkfst; afternoon refreshments. Restaurant 8-10 am, 6-9 pm (also see QUECHEE INN AT MARSHLAND FARM). Bar 5-11 pm. Ck-out 11 am, ck-in 2 pm. Meeting rms. Business servs avail. Tennis privileges. Golf privileges. Canoes. Fly fishing clinics. Downhill ski 2 mi; x-country ski on site; instructor, rentals. Bicycles. 1793 farmhouse. Cr cds: A, D, DS, MC, V.

★ ★ ★ ★ ★ **TWIN FARMS.** *(Stage Coach Rd, Barnard 05031) 9 mi N on VT 12.* 802/234-9999; FAX 802/234-9990; res: 800/894-6327. The former home of Dorothy Thompson and Sinclair Lewis, this inn occupies a 1795 house on 300 acres. Each room has a fireplace and is furnished with antiques. 9 cottages, 4 rms in 2-story inn. AP (advance payment required): D $800; cottages $950-$1,500; 2-day min wkends, 3-day min hols. Closed Apr. Adults only. TV. Complimentary afternoon refreshments. Dining rm for guests only. Rm serv. Ck-out 1 pm, ck-in 4 pm. Business servs avail. In-rm modem link. Tennis, pro. Downhill/x-country ski on site. Exercise rm; Japanese furo tubs. Massage. Hiking trails. Rec rm. Totally nonsmoking. Cr cds: A, MC, V.

★ ★ **WINSLOW HOUSE.** *38 US 4, W on US 4.* 802/457-1820. 4 rms, 2 story. S $65; D $75-$95; each addl $15; under 6 free; hols (2-day min); higher rates fall foliage. Pet accepted. TV; cable (premium). Complimentary full bkfst. Ck-out 11 am, ck-in 2 pm. Downhill ski 8 mi; x-country ski 3 mi. Lawn games. Refrigerators. Farmhouse built 1872; period furnishings. Totally nonsmoking. Cr cds: C, D, DS, MC, V.

★ ★ ★ **WOODSTOCKER.** *61 River St, US 4.* 802/457-3896; FAX 802/547-3897; res: 800/457-3896. 9 rms, 8 A/C, 2 story, 3 kits. No rm phones. D $85-$105; each addl $20; suites $115-$135; higer rates fall foliage, wk of Dec 25. TV in sitting rm; cable, VCR (free movies). Whirlpool. Complimentary full bkfst; afternoon refreshments. Restaurant nearby. Ck-out 11 am, ck-in 3 pm. Downhill ski 3 mi; x-country ski ½ mi. Built in 1830; individually decorated rms, antiques. Cr cds: MC, V.

Resorts

★ ★ ★ **QUECHEE LAKES.** *(Quechee 05059) 5 mi W on US 4.* 802/295-1970; FAX 802/296-6852; res: 800/745-0042. E-mail qlrc@valley.net; web www.pbpub.com/quecheelakes/. 100 kit. condo units. Late May-Feb: 2-8 persons, $315-$750; wkly rates $575-$1,350; higher rates some hols; lower rates rest of yr; 2-day min stay. TV; cable, VCR avail. 2 pools, 1 indoor; whirlpool. Playground. Supervised children's activities summer, winter hols. Dining rm 11:30 am-9 pm. Bar 11-1 am. Ck-out 11 am, ck-in 3 pm. Coin lndry. Meeting rms. Business servs avail. Grocery 1 mi. Package store 6 mi. Tennis, pro. Two 18-hole golf courses, greens fee $60, pro, putting green, driving range. Private beach, swimming; rowboats, canoes, sailboats. Downhill/x-country ski on site. Sleigh rides, tobogganing. Bicycles. Hiking trails. Soc dir; entertainment, movies. Rec rm. Game rm. Exercise rm; sauna. Massage. Health club privileges. Microwaves, fireplaces. Private patios, balconies. Cr cds: MC, V.

★ ★ ★ **WOODSTOCK INN.** *On Village Green.* 802/457-1100; FAX 802/457-6699; res: 800/448-7900. E-mail woodstock.resort@connriver.net; web www.woodstockinn.com. At this genteel resort, the lobby has a floor-to-ceiling fieldstone fireplace and a massive wood-beam mantel. The patchwork quilts on the beds dominate the modern guest rooms; some have a fireplace. Antiques are found throughout. 144 rms, 3 story. S, D $159-$303; each addl $20; suites $425-$525; under 14 free; MAP avail; ski, golf, tennis, other plans. Crib free. TV; cable, VCR avail (movies). 2 pools, 1 indoor; whirlpool. Dining rm (see WOODSTOCK INN). Box lunches, picnics. Rm serv. Bar noon-midnight; entertainment. Ck-out 11 am, ck-in 3 pm. Grocery, package store ½ mi. Meeting rms. Business servs avail. Bellhops. Concierge. Gift shop. Sports dir. Indoor, outdoor tennis, pro. 18-hole golf, greens fee $49, pro, putting green, driving range. Downhill ski 4½ mi; x-country ski ½ mi. Lawn games. Exercise rm; sauna, steam rm. Massage. Some refrigerators. Cr cds: A, MC, V.

Restaurants

★ ★ ★ **BARNARD INN.** *(VT 12, Barnard 05031) Approx 8 mi N on VT 12.* 802/234-9961. French menu. Specialties: noisettes of lamb Green Mountain, roast crisp duck. Hrs: 6-11 pm. Closed Sun, Mon (winter), Mon (summer); Thanksgiving, Dec 25. Res accepted. Bar. Wine list. A la carte entrees: dinner $19-$25. Child's meals. Parking. Original brick structure of house built ca 1796. Totally nonsmoking. Cr cds: A, D, MC, V.

★ ★ **BENTLEY'S.** *3 Elm St, center of town. 802/457-3232.* Specializes in gourmet hamburgers, steak, pasta. Hrs: 7-11 am, 11:30 am-9:30 pm; Fri, Sat to 10 pm; Sun brunch 11 am-3 pm. Closed Thanksgiving, Dec 25. Res accepted. Bar to 2 am. Semi-a la carte: bkfst $3.75-$6.95, lunch $4.95-$8.95, dinner $9.95-$17.95. Child's meals. Totally nonsmoking. Cr cds: A, C, D, MC, V.

★ ★ ★ **KEDRON VALLEY.** *(See Kedron Valley Inn) 802/457-1473.* E-mail kedroninn@aol.com. Specialties: salmon in puff pastry, grilled loin of lamb, confit of duck. Own sorbet. Hrs: 8-9:30 am, 6-9 pm; wkends 8-10 am, 6-9:30 pm. Closed Wed exc fall foliage season & wk of Dec 25; also Apr. Res accepted. Bar 5 pm-11 pm. Complete meals: bkfst $9. A la carte entrees: dinner $16-$24. Child's meals. Parking. Cr cds: DS, MC, V.

★ ★ ★ **THE PARKER HOUSE.** *(See Parker House Inn) 5 mi E on US 4. 802/295-6077.* E-mail parker_house_inn@valley.net; web www.phpub.com/quechee/parkerhouse.htm. Specialties: roast leg of lamb, grilled portobello mushrooms, Maine crab cakes. Own desserts. Hrs: 6-9 pm; off season hrs vary. Res accepted. Bar. Wine cellar. A la carte entrees: dinner $16.50-$21.95. Parking. Outdoor dining. Victorian inn. Totally nonsmoking. Cr cds: A, MC, V.

★ ★ ★ **PRINCE & THE PAUPER.** *24 Elm St. 802/457-1818.* Continental menu. Specialties: rack of lamb in puff pastry, crisp roast duck. Own baking. Hrs: 6-9 pm; Fri, Sat to 9:30 pm. Closed Thanksgiving, Dec 25. Res accepted. Bar from 5 pm. Wine list. A la carte entrees: dinner $21-$28. Prix fixe: dinner $35. Outdoor dining. French country atmosphere. Cr cds: DS, MC, V.

★ ★ ★ **QUECHEE INN AT MARSHLAND FARM.** *(See Quechee Inn At Marshland Farm) 802/295-3133.* E-mail quecheeinn@pinnacle-inns.com; web www.pinnacle-inns.com/quecheeinn/. Continental menu. Specializes in duck, fresh seafood, lamb. Own baking. Hrs: 6-9 pm. Res accepted. Bar 5-11 pm. Wine list. Semi-a la carte: dinner $17-$24. Child's meals. Pianist Fri, Sat. Parking. View of garden and lake. 1793 farmhouse. Totally nonsmoking. Cr cds: A, D, MC, V.

★ ★ ★ **SIMON PEARCE.** *(Main St, Quechee 05059) 5 mi E on US 4. 802/295-1470.* Continental menu. Specializes in duck, seafood, lamb. Own desserts. Hrs: 11:30 am-2:45 pm, 6-9 pm. Closed Thanksgiving, Dec 25. Serv bar. Wine cellar. A la carte entrees: lunch $8.75-$12.50, dinner $17-$25. Parking. Outdoor dining. In renovated mill; overlooks river. Glass-blowing, pottery shop. Totally nonsmoking. Cr cds: A, D, DS, MC, V.

★ ★ ★ **WOODSTOCK INN.** *(See Woodstock Inn) 802/457-1100.* E-mail woodstock.resort@connriver.net; web www.woodstockinn.com. Specialties: jumbo lump crabmeat cake, roast rack of lamb. Changing menu. Hrs: 6-9 pm; Sun brunch 11:30 am-1:30 pm. Res accepted. Bar. Wine cellar. A la carte entrees: dinner $19-$26. Sun brunch $23.95. Child's meals. Parking. Outdoor dining. Jacket (Memorial Day-Labor Day). Totally nonsmoking. Cr cds: A, MC, V.

D

Canada

Population: 28,114,000
Land area: 3,849,674 square miles (9,973,249 square kilometers)
Highest point: Mt Logan, Yukon Territory, 19,850 feet (5,951 meters)
Capital: Ottawa
Speed limit: 50 or 60 MPH (80 or 100 km/h), unless otherwise indicated

Just north of the United States, with which it shares the world's longest undefended border, lies Canada, the world's largest country in terms of land area. Extending from the North Pole to the northern border of the United States and including all the islands from Greenland to Alaska, Canada's area encompasses nearly 4 million square miles (10.4 million square kilometers). The northern reaches of the country consist mainly of the Yukon and Northwest territories, which make up the vast, sparsely populated Canadian frontier.

Jacques Cartier erected a cross at Gaspé in 1534 and declared the establishment of New France. Samuel de Champlain founded Port Royal in Nova Scotia in 1604. Until 1759 Canada was under French rule. In that year, British General Wolfe defeated French General Montcalm at Québec and British possession followed. In 1867 the British North America Act established the Confederation of Canada, with four provinces: New Brunswick, Nova Scotia, Ontario and Québec. The other provinces joined later. Canada was proclaimed a self-governing Dominion within the British Empire in 1931. The passage in 1981 of the Constitution Act severed Canada's final legislative link with Great Britain, which had until that time reserved the right to amend the Canadian Constitution.

Today, Canada is a sovereign nation—neither a colony nor a possession of Great Britain. Since Canada is a member of the Commonwealth of Nations, Queen Elizabeth II, through her representative, the Governor-General, is the nominal head of state. However, the Queen's functions are mostly ceremonial with no political power or authority. Instead, the nation's chief executive is the prime minister; the legislative branch consists of the Senate and the House of Commons.

Visitor Information

Currency. The American dollar is accepted throughout Canada, but it is advisable to exchange your money into Canadian currency upon arrival. Banks and currency exchange firms typically give the best rate of exchange, but hotels and stores will also convert it for you with purchases. The Canadian monetary system is based on dollars and cents, and rates in *Mobil Travel Guide* are given in Canadian currency. Generally, the credit cards you use at home are also honored in Canada.

Goods and Services Tax (GST). Most goods and services in Canada are subject to a 7% tax. Visitors to Canada may claim a rebate of the GST paid on *short-term accommodations* (hotel, motel or similar lodging) and on *most consumer goods* purchased to take home. Rebates may be claimed for cash at participating Canadian Duty Free shops or by mail. For further information and a brochure detailing rebate procedures and restrictions contact Revenue Canada, Customs and Excise, Visitors' Rebate Program, Ottawa, ON K1A 1J5; 613/991-3346 or 800/66-VISIT (in Canada).

Driving in Canada. Your American driver's license is valid in Canada; no special permit is required. In Canada the liter is the unit of measure for gasoline. One US gallon equals 3.78 liters. Traffic signs are clearly understood and in many cities are bilingual. All road speed limits and mileage signs have been posted in kilometers. A flashing green traffic light gives vehicles turning left the right-of-way, like a green left-turn arrow. The use of safety belts is generally mandatory in all provinces; consult the various provincial tourism bureaus for specific information.

Holidays. All Canada observes the following holidays, and these are indicated in text: New Year's Day, Good Friday, Easter Monday, Victoria Day (usually 3rd Mon May), Canada Day (July 1), Labour Day, Thanksgiving (2nd Mon Oct), Remembrance Day (Nov 11), Christmas and Boxing Day (Dec 26). See individual provinces for information on provincial holidays.

Liquor. The sale of liquor, wine, beer and cider varies from province to province. Restaurants must be licensed to serve liquor, and in some cases liquor may not be sold unless it accompanies a meal. Generally there are no package sales on holidays. Minimum legal drinking age also varies by province. **Note:** It is illegal to take children into bars or cocktail lounges.

Daylight Saving Time. Canada observes Daylight Saving Time beginning the first Sunday in April through the last Sunday in October, except for most of the province of Saskatchewan, where Standard Time is observed year-round.

Tourist information is available from individual provincial and territorial tourism offices (see Border Crossing Regulations in MAKING THE MOST OF YOUR TRIP).

Province of New Brunswick

Pop 714,800 **Land area** 28,354 sq mi (73,437 sq km) **Capital** Fredericton **Web** www.gov.nb.ca/tourism

Information Tourism New Brunswick, PO Box 12345, Woodstock E7M 5C3; 800/561-0123.

New Brunswick, discovered by Jacques Cartier in 1535, was one of the first areas in North America to be settled by Europeans. Established as a province in 1784, it became one of the original provinces of the Canadian Confederation (1867).

New Brunswick's rich historic past is reflected in major restorations such as the Acadian Historical Village near Caraquet, Kings Landing Historical Settlement near Fredericton, and MacDonald Historic Farm near Miramichi. The Acadian influence is found throughout the province, predominantly along the north and east coasts. Caraquet and Moncton are the major centers of Acadian culture.

But there is much more to New Brunswick than history—the Bay of Fundy to the south (featuring some of the highest tides in the world and a great variety of whales), the Reversing Falls in Saint John, Magnetic Hill in Moncton, Hopewell Cape Rocks at Hopewell Cape—and always the sea. Some of the finest beaches in Atlantic Canada provide excellent recreational possibilities, exquisite seafood and the warmest waters north of Virginia. The capital, Fredericton, offers a full range of big-city attractions. The weather is ideal for vacations, June through August being the warmest months. During September and October the fall foliage is a spectacular sight, while the winter months attract many outdoor enthusiasts to ski over 600 miles (1,000 km) of cross-country trails and snowmobile the 5,400 miles (9,000 km) of groomed trails. Angling enthusiasts will be drawn to the world-famous Atlantic salmon river, Miramichi.

Visitor Information Centres are located throughout the province. It is important to note that reservations are not accepted at national parks and only at some provincial parks.

Safety belts are mandatory for all persons anywhere in vehicle. Children under 5 years or under 40 pounds in weight must be in an approved safety seat anywhere in vehicle.

Edmundston

(See also Caribou, Fort Kent and Presque Isle, ME)

Pop 11,497 **Elev** 462 ft (141 m) **Area code** 506
Information Chamber of Commerce, 74 Canada Rd, PO Box 338, E3V 3K9; 506/737-1866.

The Madawaska County's origin revolves around a border dispute between England and the United States. From 1785 to 1845, the area around Edmundston, part of the state of Maine and part of the province of Quebec, were left without allegiance to any government. A large portion was ceded to the United States in 1842, but the Canadian section remained unattached, prompting the residents to issue the "proclamation of the Republic of Madawaska." Though eventually becoming a part of New Brunswick and despite never having been a reality, the mythical title has remained, with the coat of arms registered in 1949.

Acadian culture predominates with almost all of the population speaking French—but nearly all are bilingual. The first families to arrive in Edmundston were Acadian and French Canadian.

What to See and Do

Edmundston Golf Club. Challenging 18-hole course within the city attracts people from a large area. (May-Sept, daily) Victoria St. Phone 506/735-3086. ¢¢¢¢

Grand Falls. At 75 ft (23 m) high, one of largest cataracts east of Niagara. Fascinating gorge & scenic lookouts along trail; museum. Stairs to bottom of gorge (fee). (Late May-Oct, daily) 40 mi (64 km) SE, in town of Grand Falls. Phone 506/473-6013 (May-Oct) or 506/473-3080. ¢

Les Jardins de la République Provincial Park (Gardens of the Republic). Park of 107 acres (43 hectares) overlooking the Madawaska River. Amphitheater, scene of music and film performances; 20-acre (8-hectare) botanical garden. Heated swimming pool, tennis, volleyball, softball, horseshoes, bicycling, playground, indoor game room; boat dock, launch; snack bar. Various fees. 113 campsites (most with electricity; fee). Park (June-Sept). 5 mi (8 km) N via Trans-Canada Hwy 2. Phone 506/735-2525. ¢¢¢ In the park is

Antique Auto Museum. Impressive display of vintage vehicles and mechanical marvels of the past 70 yrs. (Mid-June-Labour Day, daily) Phone 506/735-2525. ¢¢

New Brunswick Botanical Garden. Conceived and designed by a team from the prestigious Montreal Botanical Garden, the garden covers over 17 acres. More than 30,000 annual flowers and 80,000 plants are on display. (June-mid-Oct, daily) Exit 8, 4½ mi (7 km) N on Trans-Canada Hwy. Phone 506/739-6335. ¢¢

New Denmark Memorial Museum. Museum building is on site of original immigrant house built in 1872 to house settlers. Household articles, documents, machinery belonging to original settlers from Denmark. (Mid-June-Labour Day, daily; rest of yr, by appt) 45 mi (72 km) SE in farming community of New Denmark, oldest Danish colony in Canada (1872). Phone 506/553-6724 or 506/553-6764. **Free.**

Saint Basile Chapel Museum. Parish church; replica of first chapel built in 1786. (July-Aug, daily) 321 Main St, 3 mi (5 km) E in St Basile. Phone 506/263-5971. **Free.**

Annual Events

International Snowmobilers Festival. Phone 506/737-1866. 1st wk Feb.

Jazz Festival. Phone 506/739-2104. 3rd wkend June.

Foire Brayonne. French heritage festival. Phone 506/739-6608. Late July-early Aug.

Fredericton (D-2)

Founded 1762 **Pop** 45,000 (est) **Elev** 24 ft (7 m) **Area code** 506 **Web** www.city.fredericton.nb.ca
Information Fredericton Tourism, PO Box 130, E3B 4Y7; 506/460-2041.

Over the past 40 years the benefactions of the late Lord Beaverbrook have raised Fredericton from a quiet provincial capital to a major cultural center. Born in Ontario, this British newspaper baron maintained a strong loyalty to New Brunswick, the province of his youth. Wander the elm tree-lined streets, through the Green, a lovely park along the St John River, and admire examples of Beaverbrook's generosity that heighten the beauty of the city. Nestled along the tree-shaded Green sits the Christ Church Cathedral, an 1853 example of decorated Gothic architecture.

What to See and Do

Beaverbrook Art Gallery. Collection includes 18th-20th-century British paintings, 18th- and early 19th-century English porcelains, historical and contemporary Canadian and New Brunswick paintings and Salvador Dali's *Santiago el Grande;* Hosmer-Pillow-Vaughan Collection of European fine & decorative arts from the 14th-20th centuries. (Daily; closed Jan 1, Dec 25) 703 Queen St. Phone 506/458-8545. ¢¢

City Hall (1876). Seat of municipal government. Guided tours of council chambers, town history depicted in tapestry form. Changing of the Guard (July-Labour Day, Tues-Sat). Tourist Information Centre (May-Sept, daily; rest of yr, Mon-Fri). Queen & York Sts. Phone 506/452-9616. **Free.**

Golf.

Fredericton. 18 holes, very picturesque. Golf Club Rd, off Woodstock Rd. Phone 506/458-0003. ¢¢¢¢¢

Mactaquac. 18-hole championship course. In Mactaquac Provincial Park. Phone 506/363-3011. ¢¢¢¢¢

Kings Landing Historical Settlement. Settlement of 50 buildings and costumed staff of 100. Carpenter's shop, general store, school, church, blacksmith shop, working sawmill and gristmill, inn; replica of a 19th-century wood boat (river craft). All restoration and work is done with tools of the period. Recalls Loyalist lifestyle of a century ago. Settlement (June-early Oct, daily). Tours; children's programs. Restaurants, snack bar. 23 mi (37 km) W on Trans-Canada Hwy at exit 259. Phone 506/363-5805. ¢¢¢

Mactaquac Fish Hatchery. Sixty-seven rearing ponds with a potential annual production of 340,000 smolts (young salmon ready to migrate). Visitors center (mid-May-mid-Oct). (Daily) 10 mi (16 km) W on Rte 2/Trans-Canada Hwy. Phone 506/363-3021. **Free.**

Mactaquac Generating Station. Hydroelectric dam has powerhouse with turbines and generators; fish collection facilities at foot of dam. Free guided tours (mid-May-Aug, daily; rest of yr, by appt). 12 mi (19 km) W on Rte 2/Trans-Canada Hwy, exit 274. Phone 506/363-3093.

Mactaquac Provincial Park. Approx 1,400 acres (567 hectares) of farm-land and forest overlooking headpond of Mactaquac Dam. Boating (launch, marinas), swimming beaches, fishing; hiking; camping (hookups, dump station); golf; picnicking, playgrounds; restaurant, store, laundry. Also in the vicinity are an historic village, fish culture station and a generating plant. Some fees. On Rte 105, 15 mi (24 km) W. Phone 506/363-3011. Per vehicle (summer only) ¢¢

New Brunswick Legislative Assembly. Seat of provincial government; public galleries. Guided tour. Library (Mon-Fri) includes hand-colored engravings of Audubon Birds of America. (Mid-June-Labour Day, daily; rest of yr, Mon-Fri) Queen & St John Sts. Phone 506/453-2527. **Free.**

Odell Park. Unique example of the primeval forest of New Brunswick; part of original land grant. Approx 400 acres (160 hectares) include lodge, picnicking, play area, walking paths through woods; deer & other animals; ski trails; arboretum with 1³/₄-mi (2.8 km) trail. End of Rookwood Ave. Phone 506/458-8530. **Free.**

Officers' Square. Park with Lord Beaverbrook statue; changing of the guard ceremonies (July-Labour Day); band concerts Tues & Thurs evenings (late June-Aug), theater in the park (July-Aug). Queen St. On grounds are

Old Officers' Quarters. Typical architecture of the Royal Engineers in the Colonial Period; stone arches, iron handrails and stone staircase. Older part (1839-1840), near the river, has thicker walls of solid masonry and hand-hewn timbers; later end (1851) has thinner walls and sawn timbers. ¢ Contains

York-Sunbury Historical Society Museum. Permanent and changing exhibits of military and domestic area history; seasonal exhibitions of history, New Brunswick crafts and fine arts; mounted 42-lb (16-kg) Coleman frog. (July-Aug, daily; May-June & Sept-mid-Oct, daily exc Sun; rest of yr, Mon, Wed & Fri or by appt) Phone 506/455-6041. ¢¢

The Playhouse Theatre. Home of the professional theater company Theatre New Brunswick. 686 Queen St. Contact PO Box 566, E3B 5A6; 506/458-8345.

University of New Brunswick (1785). (8,000 students) One of oldest universities in North America. Tours (by appt). University Ave. Phone 506/453-4793.

Wilmot Park. Wading pool; lighted tennis; ball diamond; picnicking, playground; bowling green. Woodstock Rd. **Free.** Opp is

Old Government House (1828). Former residence of colonial governors; more recently was headquarters of Royal Canadian Mounted Police. Not open to public. Woodstock Rd.

Annual Events

Canada Day Celebration. Last wk June-early July.

Atlantic Crew Classic. Early July.

Highland Games. Last wkend July.

Fredericton Exhibition. 1st wk Sept.

Harvest Jazz and Blues Festival. Mid-Sept.

Motels

★ ★ **FREDERICTON MOTOR INN.** (1315 Regent St, Fredericton NB E3C 1A1) 506/455-1430; FAX 506/458-5448; res: 800/561-8777. 199 rms, 1-3 story. July-Sept: S $65-$105; D $75-$105; each addl $10; suites $105; kit. unit $115; lower rates rest of yr. Crib $6. Pet accepted. TV; cable, VCR avail. Heated pool; wading pool, whirlpool, poolside serv. Restaurant 6:30 am-11 pm. Rm serv. Bar 4 pm-1 am. Ck-out 11 am.

Meeting rms. Business servs avail. In-rm modem link. Bellhops. Sundries. Some in-rm whirlpools. Refrigerators avail. Balconies. Cr cds: A, C, D, DS, ER, MC, V.

D ⇆ ≋ ⊠ ⊠ SC

★ ★ ★ **HOWARD JOHNSON.** (Fredericton NB E3B 5E3) N side of Princess Margaret Bridge, ¹/₈ mi E on Trans-Can Hwy 2. 506/472-0480; FAX 506/472-0170. 116 rms, 2 story. S $65-$76; D $74-$79; each addl $8; suites $136; under 18 free. Crib free. Pet accepted, some restrictions. TV; cable (premium), VCR avail. Heated pool; whirlpool, poolside serv. Restaurant 7 am-10 pm. Rm serv. Bar 4 pm-1 am. Ck-out noon. Coin lndry. Meeting rms. Business servs avail. In-rm modem link. Valet serv. Airport transportation. Indoor tennis. Downhill ski 10 mi; x-country ski 5 mi. Exercise equipt; sauna. Rec rm. Lawn games. Balconies. Cr cds: A, C, D, DS, ER, JCB, MC, V.

D ⇆ ≋ ⊀ ⊠ ⊀ ⊠ ⊠ SC

✔ ★ **KEDDY'S INN.** (368 Forest Hill, Fredericton NB E3B 5G2) 1 blk N of Trans-Can Hwy 2 exit 295. 506/454-4461; FAX 506/452-6915. 120 rms, 3 story. S $61.95; D $67.95; each addl $8; under 18 free. Pet accepted. TV; cable, VCR avail. Heated pool. Sauna. Restaurant 7 am-9 pm. Rm serv. Bar 11:30 am-midnight, Sun 11 am-midnight. Ck-out noon. Meeting rms. Business servs avail. Valet serv. Downhill ski 15 mi; x-country ski 10 mi. Balconies. Picnic tables. Cr cds: A, C, D, DS, ER, MC, V.

⇆ ≋ ≋ ⊠ ⊠ SC

Motor Hotel

★ ★ **AUBERGES WANDLYN INN.** (58 Prospect St W, Fredericton NB E3B 4Y9) 1 blk N of Hwy 2 Smyth St exit. 506/462-4444; res: 800/561-0000; FAX 506/452-7658. Web www.wandlyn.com. 100 rms, 3 story. S, D $70-$99; studio rms $75-$100; each addl $10; suites $125-$199; under 18 free. Crib free. Pet accepted. TV; cable (premium), VCR avail. 2 pools, 1 indoor; whirlpool, poolside serv. Sauna. Restaurant 7 am-2 pm, 5-9:30 pm. Bar 11-1 am. Ck-out 11 am. Coin laundry. Meeting rms. Business servs avail. Valet serv. Sundries. Refrigerators avail. Cr cds: A, C, D, DS, ER, MC, V.

⇆ ≋ ⊠ ⊠ SC

Hotels

★ ★ ★ **LORD BEAVERBROOK.** (659 Queen St, Fredericton NB E3B 5A6) 506/455-3371; FAX 506/455-1441; res: 800/561-7666. 168 rms, 7 story. S $80; D $85; each addl $10; suites $90-$150; under 19 free; package plans. Crib free. Pet accepted. TV; cable, VCR avail. Heated pool; wading pool, whirlpool, poolside serv. Sauna. Supervised child's activities. Restaurant 6 am-10 pm. Bar 11 am-2 am; entertainment, dancing; also sun deck bar. Ck-out noon. Meeting rms. Business servs avail. In-rm modem link. Concierge. Gift shop. Airport transportation. Bicycle, boat, canoe rentals. Docking facilities. Rec rm. Game rm. Minibars. Picnic tables. Cr cds: A, C, D, DS, ER, MC, V.

D ⇆ ≋ ⊀ ⊠ ⊠ SC

★ ★ ★ **SHERATON INN.** (225 Woodstock Rd, Fredericton NB E3B 2H8) 506/457-7000; FAX 506/451-6694. 223 rms, 7 story. S, D $145; each addl $10; suites $155-$575; under 17 free. Crib free. TV; cable (premium), VCR avail. 2 pools, 1 indoor; wading pool, whirlpool, poolside serv, lifeguard. Complimentary coffee in rms. Restaurant 6:30 am-11 pm. Bar 11-2 am. Ck-out noon. Meeting rms. Business servs avail. Gift shop. In-rm modem link. Free airport transportation. Downhill ski 15 mi; x-country ski 2 mi. Exercise equipt; sauna. Minibars. On St John River. Cr cds: A, D, ER, JCB, MC, V.

D ⊠ ≋ ⊀ ⊀ ⊠ ⊠ SC

Fundy National Park (E-3)

(See also Moncton, Saint John)

E-mail infofundy@pch.gc.ca **Web** www.parkscanada.pch.gc.ca/parks/new-brunswick/fundy/fundye.htm
Information Superintendent, Fundy National Park, PO Box 40, Alma E0A 1B0; 506/887-6000.

On the coast between Saint John and Moncton (see both), the park's 80 square miles (207 square kilometers) of forested hills and valleys are crisscrossed by miles of hiking trails. Cliffs front much of the rugged coastline. Fish are found in its lakes and streams and the woods are filled with wildlife. The beaches at Herring Cove, Point Wolfe and Alma are exceptional for viewing the tides. Since the ocean water is frigid, swimming is enjoyed in the heated saltwater pool or one of the lakes. Golf, tennis, lawn bowling, picnicking; camping (May-Oct); cross-country skiing. Programs in amphitheater. Some fees. Guided beach walks (June-Aug). The park and headquarters are open all year; visitor area (mid-May-Oct). Accommodations available in park.

Moncton (D-3)

Pop 55,700 (est) **Elev** 50 ft (15 m) **Area code** 506 **E-mail** tourism@moncton.org **Web** www.greater.moncton.nb.ca
Information Tourism Moncton, 655 Main St, E1C 1E8; 506/853-3590 or 800/363-4558.

This commercial and cultural center of the Atlantic provinces is located on the Petitcodiac River, which at low tide becomes a mud flat clustered with sea gulls. As the tide turns, a tidal bore (a small wave) runs upstream to herald the incoming waters. Just off the Trans-Canada Highway another phenomenon awaits the traveler—Magnetic Hill. The experience of sitting in your car, without power, seemingly rolling up the hill, is one remembered by many. There is nothing magnetic about the hill; it is just an optical illusion created by the contours of the countryside. Nearby are the Magnetic Hill Zoo with North American and exotic wildlife and Magic Mountain, an exciting water theme park.

Existing as an Acadian center where English and French cultures have flourished for centuries, Moncton is an excellent beginning for a tour to the northeast along the coast to beautiful Kouchibouquac National Park. Visit the Acadian Museum at the University of Moncton, the Free Meeting House (1821), oldest building in Moncton, which has served nearly every faith, its pioneer cemetery with stones dating to 1816, and the adjacent Moncton Museum.

Nearby Shediac, lobster capital of the world, has a lobster festival in July. From here, northward along the coast of the Northumberland Strait, saltwater fishing and camping provide the visitor with a chance to relax and enjoy the French heritage of the area.

Stretching along the coast are little fishing villages where French-speaking people offer their hospitality. Each year, for a few days in early August, the village of Cocagne has a bazaar and international regatta—a curious mixture of Acadian and North American cultures. Hydroplane races attract thousands for two days; visitors remain to enjoy the Acadian festival with its special food, handcrafts, dancing and singing.

What to See and Do

Crystal Palace Amusement Park. Indoor and outdoor attractions, include rides, miniature golf, Science Center, video games and go-carts. (Daily) 499 Paul St, E in Dieppe. Phone 506/859-4386.

Fort Beausejour National Historic Site. Approx 600 acres (225 hectares). Built by the French between 1751-1755 during their long struggle with England for possession of Acadia. Attacked in 1755, the fort was captured by the British under Colonel Monckton, who renamed it Fort Cumberland. Following its capture, the fort was strengthened and its defenses extended. During the American Revolution in 1776, it withstood an attack by revolutionaries under Jonathan Eddy. It was manned by a small garrison during the War of 1812. Three casemates and a massive stone curtain wall have been restored; displays on history and culture of Isthmus of Chignecto; outdoor paintings showing garrison as it existed in 18th century. Picnicking (shelters). Visitor center. Panoramic view of site and surrounding salt marshes. (June-mid-Oct, daily) Approx 37 mi (60 km) E on Hwy 2, exit 550. Contact Chief, Visitor Activities, Aulac E0A 3C0; 506/536-0720.

Magnetic Hill Zoo. Wild-animal park and petting zoo; many species represented, including wildfowl. (May-Oct, daily) Near Magnetic Hill. Phone 506/384-0303. ¢¢

"The Rocks" Provincial Park. Unique cliffs, caves and flowerpot-shaped pillars of conglomerate rock interspersed with shale and sandstone layers. The tourist information center has interpretive displays, tour guides available. Visitors are advised to watch for caution signs; avoid loose cliff sections; do not climb any flowerpot or cliff; return from beach by the time posted at the stairs to avoid problems with rising tide. Picnicking, restaurant. (May-Oct, daily) Across Petitcodiac River, then 28 mi (45 km) SE on Hwy 114, "Rocks" exit, just S of Hopewell Cape. Contact Parks Branch, Dept of Natural Resources, PO Box 6000, Fredericton E3B 5H1; 506/856-2940 or 800/561-0123 (US & CAN). ¢¢

Tidal bore. A small tidal wave running upstream to usher in the Bay of Fundy tides on the normally placid Petitcodiac River. Within one hour water level rises more than 25 ft. The bore arrives twice daily. Main St at Bore View Park.

Motels

★ ★ **COLONIAL INN.** *(42 Highfield St, Moncton NB E1C 8T6)* 1/2 blk off Hwy 6. 506/382-3395; FAX 506/858-8991; res: 800/561-4667. 61 rms, 1-2 story. S $62 D $68; each addl $5; studio rms $75; under 16 free. Crib $5. Pet accepted, some restrictions. TV; cable. Heated pool; whirlpool. Restaurant open 24 hrs. Rm serv. Bar 11 am-midnight. Ck-out noon-2 pm. Meeting rm. Business servs avail. Valet serv. Sundries. Sauna. Some refrigerators. Cr cds: A, D, ER, MC, V.

⊠ ≋ ⊠ ⊠ SC

✔★ **ECONO LODGE.** *(1905 W Main St (Rte 6), Moncton NB E1E 1H9)* 506/382-2587; FAX 506/858-5998; res: 800/465-7666. E-mail doobie@fax.com. 67 rms, 5 kit. units, 2 story. S $59; D $79; each addl $5; studio rms $79; kit. units $89; each addl $5; under 12 free; wkly rates. Pet accepted, some restrictions. TV; cable. Heated pool. Restaurant 7 am-9 pm; Sun to 2 pm. Bar. Ck-out 11 am. Business servs avail. Cr cds: A, C, D, DS, ER, MC, V.

⊠ ≋ ⊠ ⊠ SC

★ ★ **TRAVELODGE.** *(434 Main St, Moncton NB E1C 1B9)* adj Tidal Bore Park. 506/382-1664; FAX 506/855-9494; res: 800/565-7633. E-mail rodds@rodd-motels.ca; web www.rodd-hotels.ca. 97 rms, 4 story. S $79; D $99; each addl $10; under 19 free. Crib free. Pet accepted, some restrictions. TV; cable (premium). Heated pool. Complimentary coffee in rms. Restaurant 7 am-2 pm, 5-10 pm. Bar. Ck-out noon. Meeting rms. Business servs avail. Valet serv. Cr cds: A, C, D, DS, ER, MC, V.

⊠ ≋ ⊠ ⊠ SC

Hotel

★ ★ ★ **BEAUSEJOUR.** *(750 Main St, Moncton NB E1C 1E6)* 506/854-4344; FAX 506/858-0957; res: 800/441-1414. Web www.cp hotels.ca. 310 rms, 9 story. S, D $109-$151; each addl $15; suites $240-$950; under 18 free; wkend rates. Crib free. Pet accepted. TV; cable (premium). Pool; poolside serv, lifeguard. Coffee in rms. Restaurants 6:30 am-11 pm. Rm serv 24 hrs. Bar 4:30 pm-1 am, wkends from 6 pm, closed Sun. Ck-out noon. Meeting rms. Business servs avail. In-rm modem link. Concierge. Gift shop. Barber. Exercise equipt. Minibars; many bathrm phones; some refrigerators. Cr cds: A, C, D, DS, ER, JCB, MC, V.

D ⊠ ≋ ✗ ⊠ ⊠ SC

Inn

✔★ **BONACCORD HOUSE.** *(250 Bonaccord St, Moncton NB E1C 5M6) at John St.* 506/388-1535; FAX 506/853-7191. 5 rms, 2 share bath, 1 with shower only, 1 A/C, 3 story, 1 kit. suite. S $40-$45; D $50-$55; each addl $10. TV in sitting rm, suite; cable, VCR avail. Complimentary full bkfst. Restaurant nearby. Ck-out 10 am, ck-in 2 pm. Business servs avail. Some balconies. Victorian residence (1890) with columned wrap-around veranda. Totally nonsmoking. Cr cds: V.

⊠ ⊠

Saint John (E-2)

Founded 1785 **Pop** 78,000 (est) **Elev** 100 ft (31 m) **Area code** 506
E-mail visitsj@city.saint-john.nb.ca **Web** www.city.saint-john.nb.ca
Information Visitor & Convention Bureau, City Hall, 11th floor, PO Box 1971, E2L 4L1; 506/658-2990 or 888/364-4444.

The largest city in the province, this deep-sea port was founded by the United Empire Loyalists after the American Revolution. It is Canada's first incorporated city. The heart of the old town is King's Square, where many historic landmarks (including an ancient burial ground) are found.

The Reversing Falls, another of the phenomena caused by the 30-foot (9-meter) tides on the Bay of Fundy, are found near the eastern approach to the city center off Highway 1. Here the high tidewater is forced back upstream into the St John River, causing a whirling torrent. A deck, where the tourist bureau is located, overlooks the rapids.

What to See and Do

Barbour's General Store. Restored general store reflecting period 1840-1940; 2,000 artifacts and wide selection of old-fashioned grocery items, china, yard goods, farm implements, cooking tools; re-created post office; barbershop with wicker barber's chair, collection of shaving mugs; pharmacy with approximately 300 samples of "cure-all or kill-alls"; potbellied stove; staff outfitted in period costumes. (Mid-May-mid-Oct, daily) In Market Slip area, downtown. Phone 506/658-2939.

Carlton Martello Tower National Historic Park. Circular coastal forts built for War of 1812; used in World War II as fire command post for harbor defenses (when 2-story superstructure was added); restored powder magazine of 1840s; barrack rm (ca 1865). Panoramic view of city, harbor and surrounding landscape. Guided tours of tower (June-mid-Oct, daily). Grounds open all yr. Hwy 1, exit 107. Phone 506/636-4011. ¢¢

Ferry Service to Digby, NS. Car and passenger; 45 mi (72 km). (All yr) Reservations required. Contact Bay Ferries Ltd, Box 3427, Station B, E2M 4X9; 506/636-4048 or 888/249-7245 (US).

Irving Nature Park. Features winding coastal road and hiking trails. Harbor seals, porpoises and many species of migrating birds can be viewed offshore. Picnicking. (Daily) Off of Sand Cove Rd on W side of city. Phone 506/653-7367. **Free.**

Loyalist House (1810-1817). Built by David Daniel Merritt, a United Empire Loyalist from New York. Six generations have lived in the house; gracious Georgian mansion remains much as it was when built; excellent craftsmanship. (July-Aug, daily; June & Sept, Mon-Fri; also by appt) 120 Union St. Phone 506/652-3590. ¢¢

New Brunswick Museum. International fine art and decorative art objects; human and natural history of New Brunswick. Exhibits include skeleton of Right Whale and Mastodon, and geologic "trail through time." Also family discovery center. (Daily; closed Good Friday, Dec 25) 1 Market Sq. Phone 506/643-2300. ¢¢¢   The museum's archives and library (Mon-Fri, limited hrs; closed Good Friday, Dec 25) are at 277 Douglas Ave. Phone 506/643-2322. **Free.**

Old City Market. Centralized market, dating back to 1876, sells fresh meats and vegetables as well as indigenous baskets and handicrafts. Roof is wooden timbers, all wood pegs; fashioned like the hull of an old sailing ship. Magnificent iron gates of the market designed in 1880 by local blacksmiths. Bell rung at opening, closing and noon. (Daily exc Sun; closed hols) 47 Charlotte St. Phone 506/658-2820. **Free.**

Rockwood Park. Municipal park with 2,200 acres of woodlands, lakes and recreational areas, (including) golf course, aquatic driving range and campground. (Daily) Located off Mt Pleasant Ave in city center. Phone 506/658-2883, campground 506/652-4050.

"Trinity Royal" Heritage Preservation Area. A 20-blk heritage area, located in the city center; 19th-century residential and commercial architecture; handicrafts and specialty goods.

Annual Events

Loyalist Days' Heritage Celebration. Celebrates the arrival of the United Empire Loyalists in 1783 with reenactment of Loyalist landing; citizens in period costumes; parades, entertainment, sporting events. Phone 506/634-8123. 5 days early July.

Festival by the Sea. Ten-day performing arts festival features Canadian entertainers. Phone 506/632-0086. Mid-Aug.

Motel

✔★★ **COLONIAL INN.** *(175 City Rd, Saint John NB E2L 3T5)* 506/652-3000; FAX 506/658-1664. E-mail colmtm@fundy.net; web www.colonial-inns.com. 94 rms, 82 A/C, 2 story. S $65; D $71; each addl $6; suites $85; under 18 free. Crib free. Pet accepted. TV; cable. Heated pool; whirlpool. Sauna. Restaurant open 24 hrs. Rm serv. Bar 6 pm-2 am. Ck-out noon-2 pm. Meeting rms. Business servs avail. Valet serv. Cr cds: A, D, ER, MC, V.

D ✔ ⊠ ⊠ ⊠ SC

Motor Hotels

★★ **HOTEL COURTENAY BAY.** *(350 Haymarket Sq, Saint John NB E2L 3P1)* 506/657-3610; FAX 506/633-1773; res: 800/563-2489. 125 rms, 5 story. S $59-$69; D $69-$79; each addl $8; under 18 free. Pet accepted. TV; cable (premium). Heated pool. Restaurant 7 am-11 pm. Rm serv. Bar 11 am-11 pm. Ck-out 1 pm. Coin lndry. Meeting rms. Business servs avail. Bellhops. Valet serv. Sundries. Minibars. Some private patios; balconies. Cr cds: A, C, D, ER, JCB, MC, V.

✔ ⊠ ⊠ ⊠ SC

★★ **HOWARD JOHNSON.** *(400 Main St, Saint John NB E2K 4N5)* 506/642-2622; FAX 506/658-1529. 96 rms, 7 story. S $92; D $102; each addl $10; suites $150; studio rms $79; under 12 free; wkend rates. Crib free. TV; cable, VCR avail (movies). Heated pool; whirlpool. Sauna. Complimentary coffee in rms. Restaurant 7 am-10 pm. Bar. Ck-out 1 pm. Business servs avail. Barber, beauty shop. Game rm. On Bay of Fundy. Cr cds: A, C, D, DS, ER, JCB, MC, V.

D ⊠ ⊠ ⊠ SC

Hotels

★★★ **DELTA BRUNSWICK.** *(39 King St, Saint John NB E2L 4W3) above Brunswick Square Shopping Mall.* 506/648-1981; FAX 506/648-9670; res: 800/268-1133. Web www.deltahotels.com. 255 units, 5 story. May-mid-Oct: S, D $125-$135; each addl $10; suites $135-$500; studio rms $135-$145; under 18 free; lower rates rest of yr. Crib free. Pet accepted. Covered parking $8.50; valet $12. TV; cable. Indoor pool; whirlpool. Free supervised child's activities (wkends), over age 2. Restaurant 6:30 am-10 pm (June-Sept). Rm serv 24 hrs. Bar 11-1 am. Ck-out 1 pm. Convention facilities. Business servs avail. Shopping arcade. Exercise equipt; sauna, steam rm. Game rm. Rec rm. Minibars; refrigerators avail. Covered walkway to downtown offices, Market Square. Cr cds: A, D, ER, JCB, MC, V.

D ✔ ⊠ ✕ ⊠ ⊠ SC

★ ★ ★ **HILTON.** *(1 Market Square, Saint John NB E2L 4Z6)* *506/693-8484; FAX 506/657-6610.* E-mail hiltonnb@nbnet.nb.ca. 197 rms, 12 story. May-Sept: S, D $109-$149; each addl $15; suites $305-$439; lower rates rest of yr. Crib free. Pet accepted, some restrictions. Garage parking $11.44. TV; cable. Indoor pool; whirlpool. Complimentary coffee in rms. Restaurant 6:30 am-11 pm. Bar 11:30-1 am; entertainment. Ck-out noon. Meeting rms. Business center. Concierge. Shopping arcade. Barber, beauty shop. X-country ski 2 mi. Exercise equipt; sauna. Health club privileges. Game rm. Rec rm. Refrigerators, minibars. Harbor view. Underground access to Market Square shopping mall. Cr cds: A, C, D, DS, ER, JCB, MC, V.

St Andrews (E-1)

(See also Calais, ME)

Pop 1,760 **Elev** 23 ft (7 m) **Area code** 506 **E-mail** stachamb@nbnet.nb.ea **Web** www.townsearch.com/canada/nb/standrews
Information Chamber of Commerce Tourist Information Centre, 46 Reed Ave, PO Box 89, EOG 2X0; 506/529-3556.

Explored by Champlain and later settled in 1783 by Loyalists from New England, this popular seaside resort is a beautiful village rich in history. On a peninsula projecting into Passamaquoddy Bay, fishing, swimming, sailing and rockhounding are favorite pastimes. Feast on fresh lobster, watch the tides swirl in, visit the specialty shops, or wander down the streets past many buildings erected before 1800. The white-framed Greenock Church, begun in 1822, and the Court House (1840) and Gaol (1832) are worth special visits.

From the shore, the Fundy Isles dot the bay, the most famous of which is Campobello. Here, Franklin Delano Roosevelt spent his summers from 1905 to 1921 when he was stricken with infantile paralysis. Tours of Roosevelt's cottage in the International Park are available.

Northeast toward Saint John, the road to Blacks Harbour affords views of lighthouses, lovely beaches and covered bridges. From this village, a ferry leaves for Grand Manan Island, largest of the three islands. This is a popular vacation destination with picturesque lighthouses and tiny fishing villages nestled in the barren seaside cliffs.

What to See and Do

Algonquin Golf Courses. Opened in 1894, 18-hole championship course with wooded glades & breathtaking shoreline views (fee). Executive 9-hole woodland course (fee). (Late Apr-late Oct) Algonquin Hotel, Reed Ave. Phone 506/529-3062 (summer).

Blockhouse Historic Site. Sole survivor of coastal defenses built during War of 1812; restored 1967. (Mid-May-mid-Oct, daily) In Centennial Park, Joe's Point Rd. Phone 506/529-4270. **Free.**

Huntsman Marine Science Center/Aquarium-Museum. Displays of coastal and marine environments with many fish and invertebrates found in waters of Passamaquoddy Region; "Touch Tank" allows visitors to handle marine life found on local rocky beaches. Displays of live animals include local amphibians, reptiles and a family of harbor seals. Exhibits on local geology; seaweed collection. (May-early Oct, daily) Brandy Cove Rd. Phone 506/529-1202. ¢¢

The Henry Phipps & Sarah Juliette Ross Memorial Museum. Private antique furniture & decorative art collection of the Rosses. (July-Aug, daily; May-June & Sept-early Oct, Tues-Sat) 188 Montague St. Phone 506/529-1824. **Free.**

Motels

✔★ **BLUE MOON.** *(300 Mowatt Dr, St Andrews NB E0G 2X0)* *506/529-3245; FAX 506/529-3245.* 39 air-cooled rms, 2 kits. May-Oct: S $50-$55; D $50-$75; each addl $7; kit. units $5 addl; under 6 free. Closed

rest of yr. Crib free. Pet accepted, some restrictions. TV; cable. Ck-out 11 am. Business servs avail. 18-hole golf privileges. Cr cds: A, D, DS, ER, MC, V.

★ **PICKET FENCE.** *(102 Reed Ave, St Andrews NB E0G 2X0)* *506/529-8985; FAX 506/529-8985.* 17 rms. No A/C. May-Oct: S $55; D $75; each addl $8; under 6 free. Closed rest of yr. Crib free. Pet accepted, some restrictions. TV; cable. Restaurant nearby. Ck-out 11 am. Picnic tables. Cr cds: A, D, DS, ER, MC, V.

✔★ **SEASIDE BEACH RESORT.** *(339 Water St, St Andrews NB E0G 2X0)* *506/529-3846; FAX 506/529-4479.* E-mail davidsu@nbnet.nb.ca; web www.seaside.nb.com. 24 kit. units, 19 with shower only, 1-2 story, 4 cottages. No A/C. No rm phones. June-Labor Day: S, D $65-$75; each addl $5; wkly rates; lower rates May, early Sept-Oct. Closed rest of yr. Crib $5. Pet accepted. TV; cable. Restaurant nearby. Ck-out 11 am. Coin lndry. Microwaves avail. Balconies. Picnic tables, grills. Overlooks bay. Cr cds: MC, V.

★ **ST STEPHEN INN.** *(99 King St, St Stephen NB E3L 2C6)* N via Hwy 127, W via Hwy 1 (King St). *506/466-1814; res: 800/565-3088; FAX 506/466-6148.* 52 rms, 2 story. July-Dec: S $65; D $80; each addl $8; under 17 free; lower rates rest of yr. Crib free. Pet accepted. TV; cable, VCR avail. Restaurant 7 am-10 pm. Meeting rms. Business servs avail. Cr cds: A, D, ER, MC, V.

Lodge

★ ★ ★ **TARA MANOR INN.** *(559 Mowat Dr (Hwy 127), St Andrews NB E0G 2X0)* *506/529-3304; FAX 506/529-4755.* 26 rms, 1-3 story, 15 suites. June-late Sept: S, D $98-$148; each addl $10; under 13 free; lower rates May, mid-Sept-mid-Oct. Closed rest of yr. Crib free. TV; cable. Heated pool; whirlpool. Playground. Complimentary coffee in library. Dining rm 7:30-10 am, 6-9 pm. Rm serv. Ck-out 11:30 am. Tennis. Golf privileges. Sauna. Refrigerator in suites. Balconies. Former country estate (1871) of Sir Charles Tupper; antiques. Situated on 16 acres of woods, lawns and gardens. Cr cds: A, D, ER, MC, V.

Inns

★ ★ ★ ★ **KINGSBRAE ARMS.** *(219 King St, St Andrews NB E0G 2X0)* *506/529-1897; FAX 506/529-1197.* E-mail kingbrae@nbnet.nb.ca; web www.relaischateaux.fr/kingsbrae. This 1897 manor house was built for the pleasures of merchants working the trade routes betweeen North America and Shanghai. Spacious suites and grand guest rooms offer sweeping bay and garden views. Rooms are impeccably furnished in period detail and feature fireplaces, marble baths and many other comforts and luxuries. 9 rms, 3 story, 3 suites. Mid-Mar-mid-Oct: S, D $225; suites $250-$350; package plans; wkends 2-day min; lower rates rest of yr. Children over 9 yrs only. Pet accepted, some restrictions. TV; cable, VCR avail (movies). Heated pool. Complimentary full bkfst; afternoon refreshments. Rm serv 24 hrs. Bar. Ck-out noon, ck-in 3 pm. Business center. In-rm modem link. Luggage handling. Valet serv. Concierge serv. Airport transportation. Tennis privileges. Health club privileges. Lawn games. Fireplaces; some in-rm whirlpools. Some balconies. Totally nonsmoking. Cr cds: MC, V.

★ ★ ★ **PANSY PATCH.** *(59 Carleton St, St Andrews NB E0G 2X0)* *506/529-3834; res: 888/726-7972; FAX 506/529-9042.* E-mail pansy@nbnet.nb.ca. 9 rms, 5 with shower only, 2-3 story, 2 suites. No A/C. May-mid-Oct: S, D $120-$205; each addl $15; suite $170. Closed rest of yr. Cable TV avail and in common rm. Complimentary full bkfst; afternoon refreshments. Restaurant 11 am-3:30 pm, 5-9 pm. Ck-out 11 am, ck-in 3 pm. Business servs avail. In-rm modem link. Luggage handling. Gift shop.

Tennis privileges. Exercise equipt. Health club privileges. Lawn games. Refrigerator, microwave, fireplace in suite. Some balconies. Built in 1912. Norman cottage architecture; extensive gardens. Totally nonsmoking. Cr cds: MC, V.

Resort

★ ★ ★ **ALGONQUIN.** *(184 Adolphus St, St Andrews NB E0G 2X0)* *506/529-8823; FAX 506/529-7162; res: 800/441-1414.* E-mail sales@alg.cp hotels.ca. 250 rms, 54 A/C, 4 story, 42 kit. units. Mid-May-mid-Oct: S, D $119-$219; each addl $20; suites $189-$369; under 18 free. Crib free. Pet accepted. TV; cable, VCR avail. Heated pool; whirlpool, lifeguard. Playground. Supervised child's activities (mid-June-Aug); ages 12 and under. Coffee in rms. Restaurant 7 am-10 pm. Rm serv. Bar; entertainment. Ck-out noon, ck-in 4 pm. Coin lndry. Business servs avail. Bellhops. Valet serv. Concierge. Gift shop. Free parking. Tennis. 18-hole golf, greens fee $25-$39, pro, putting green. Bicycle rentals. Exercise rm; sauna. Lawn games. Aerobics. Some in-rm whirlpools, microwaves, fireplaces. On hill; view of water from most rms. Cr cds: A, C, D, DS, ER, JCB, MC, V.

Restaurant

★ ★ **ST ANDREWS LIGHTHOUSE.** *(1 Patrick St, St Andrews NB E0G 2X0)* by lighthouse. *506/529-3082.* E-mail jurabob@nbnet.nb.ca. Continental menu. Specializes in fresh seafood, steak, chicken. Hrs: 5-9 pm; mid-June-mid-Sept 11:30 am-2 pm, 5-9 pm. Closed mid-Oct-mid-May. Res accepted. Semi-a la carte: lunch $3-$19.50, dinner $9.95-$26.50. Child's meals. Lighthouse (1833) on Passamaquoddy Bay. Cr cds: A, D, MC, V.

Province of Nova Scotia

Pop 874,100 **Land area** 20,402 sq mi (52,841 sq km) **Capital** Halifax **Information** Tourism Nova Scotia, PO Box 130, Halifax B3J 2M7; 902/424-4248 or 800/565-0000.

After a century of struggle between the British and French for control of North America, Nova Scotia became a British possession in 1710, with the seat of government in Halifax. In 1867 it joined with New Brunswick, Ontario and Québec to form the Confederation of Canada.

Nova Scotia was settled by French, English, Irish, German, Scottish and African peoples, whose languages and traditions add to its flavor. Today, a recreational wonderland awaits the tourist with fishing, boating, camping, golf, swimming and charter cruising—since no part of Nova Scotia is more than 35 miles (56 kilometers) from the sea.

Major attractions include the Cabot Trail—often described as "the most spectacular drive in North America," the highlands of Cape Breton, the reconstructed Fortress of Louisbourg National Historic Site and Lunenburg, a World Heritage Site renowned for its colonial architecture and Fisheries Museum. The Greater Halifax area offers a variety of attractions including parks, noteworthy public gardens, art galleries, universities, theater, outdoor recreation, pubs, fine seafood dining, the world's second-largest harbor and the Citadel Fortress—Canada's most visited historic site. Nearby is the rugged beauty of Peggy's Cove.

The weather is cool in the spring and late fall; warm in the summer and early fall. East Nova Scotia enjoys relatively mild winters due to the proximity of the Gulf Stream. Nova Scotia observes Atlantic Standard Time.

Safety belts are mandatory for all persons anywhere in vehicle. Children under 40 pounds in weight must be in an approved safety seat anywhere in vehicle. Compliance of passengers under age 16 is the responsibility of the driver. For further information phone 902/424-4256.

Antigonish (E-5)

(See also Baddeck)

Pop 5,205 **Elev** 15 ft (5 m) **Area code** 902
Information Provincial Tourist Bureau, 56 W St, PO Box 1301, B2G 2L6; 902/863-4921.

This harbor town, named for a Micmac word meaning "the place where branches were broken off the trees by bears gathering beechnuts," was settled by Highland Scottish immigrants and American Revolutionary War soldiers and their families. West of the Canso Causeway, this town, intersected by rivers, is surrounded by hills from which may be seen the shores of Cape Breton.

What to See and Do

Keppoch Mt Ski Area. T-bar, Pomalift, triple chairlift; beginner, intermediate & expert slopes; 10 trails. Longest run 5,000 ft (1,524 m); vertical drop 500 ft (152 m). Patrol, night skiing, school, rentals, snowmaking. (Dec-Apr, daily; closed Dec 25) Half-day rates. 7 mi (11 km) W. Phone 902/863-3744. ¢¢¢¢¢

Sherbrooke Village. Restored 1860s village reflects the area's former status as a prosperous river port. Historic buildings of that era are being restored and refurnished, including family homes, a general store, drugstore, courthouse, jail & post office; demonstrations of blacksmith forging, water-powered sawmill operation; horse-drawn wagon rides. Visitors can watch or try spinning, weaving and quilting. Restaurant. (June-mid-Oct, daily) 40 mi S via Hwy 7, exit 32. Phone 902/522-2400. ¢¢

St Ninian's Cathedral (1874). Built in Roman Basilica style of blue limestone and granite from local quarries. Interior decorated by Ozias LeDuc, Paris-trained Québec artist. Gaelic words *Tigh Dhe* (House of God) appear inside and out, representing the large Scottish population in the diocese who are served by the cathedral. St Ninian's St. Phone 902/863-2338.

Annual Event

Highland Games. Scottish festival; pipe bands, Highland dancing, traditional athletic events, concert, massed pipe-band tattoo. Mid-July.

Motels

★ ★ **GREEN WAY CLAYMORE.** *(Church St, Antigonish NS B2G 2M5)* S off 104 exit 33. *902/863-1050; res: 888/863-1050.* Web www.grassroots.ns.ca/welcome.html. 76 rms, 3 story. July-mid-Oct: S $77-$85; D $99-$119; each addl $10; under 18 free; lower rates rest of yr. Crib free. Pet accepted. TV; cable. Indoor pool; whirlpool. Restaurant 7 am-2 pm; also 5:30-8 pm July-mid-Oct. Bar. Ck-out noon. Exercise equipt; sauna. Downhill/x-country ski 7 mi. Some minibars. Cr cds: A, D, ER, MC, V.

★ ★ **HEATHER HOTEL.** *(Foord St, Stellarton NS B0K 1S0)* just off Trans-Canada Hwy 104 exit 24. *902/752-8401; res: 800/565-4500; FAX 902/755-4580.* 77 rms, 2 story. S $59; D $74; each addl $6; studio rms $68; under 12 free. Crib free. Pet accepted. TV; cable. Restaurant 7 am-10 pm. Rm serv. Bar 11 am-11:30 pm. Ck-out noon. Meeting rms. X-country ski 5 mi. Refrigerators; minibars. Cr cds: A, C, D, ER, MC, V.

★ ★ **MARITIME INN.** *(158 Main St, Antigonish NS B2G 2B7)* *902/863-4001; res: 888/662-7484; FAX 902/863-2672.* 34 rms, 2 story. Mid-June-mid-Oct: S, D $75-$85; each addl $10; suites $89-$125; under

18 free; lower rates rest of yr. Crib free. Pet accepted. TV; cable. Restaurant 7 am-9 pm. Bar 4 pm-midnight. Ck-out 11 am. Sundries. Tennis privileges. Downhill ski 7 mi. Cr cds: A, D, ER, MC, V.

Restaurant

★ ★ LOBSTER TREAT. (241 Post Rd, Antigonish NS B2G 2K6) 902/863-5465. Hrs: 11 am-10 pm. Closed Jan-Apr. Res accepted. Bar. Semi-a la carte: lunch $5.50-$10, dinner $7.95-$25. Child's meals. Specializes in fresh local seafood, steak. Former schoolhouse. Cr cds: A, D, DS, ER, MC, V.

Baddeck (D-5)

Pop 972 Elev 100 ft (30 m) Area code 902 E-mail cward@tcb.ns.ca Web www.cbisland.com

Information Tourism Cape Breton, PO Box 1448, Sydney B1P 6R7; 902/563-4636 or 800/565-9464.

This tranquil scenic village, situated midway between Canso Causeway and Sydney, is a good headquarters community for viewing the many sights on the Cabot Trail and around the Bras d'Or lakes. Fishing, hiking, swimming and picnicking are among favorite pastimes along the beautiful shoreline.

What to See and Do

Alexander Graham Bell National Historic Park. Three exhibition halls dealing with Bell's numerous fields of experimentation, including displays on his work with the hearing impaired, the telephone, medicine, marine engineering and aerodynamics. Bell's original HD-4 hydrodrome (a forerunner of the hydrofoil) is on display; hundreds of original artifacts and photographs. Historical talks, audiovisual presentations, kite-making workshops. Expanded hours, guide service June-Sept. (Daily) Across Baddeck Bay is Bell's summer estate, Beinn Bhreagh, where he conducted many of his experiments, including those in powered flight. Chebucto St, E side of town. Phone 902/295-2069.

Cape Breton Highlands National Park (see). 57 mi N on Cabot Trail.

The Gaelic College. Dedicated to preservation of Gaelic traditions; special summer and winter programs. 13 mi (22 km) E, at exit 11 off Trans-Canada Hwy 105 in St Ann's. Phone 902/295-3411.On campus are

Craft Centre. Items of Scottish and Nova Scotian origins. Examples of handwoven blankets, ties, shopping bags, kilts, skirts.

The Great Hall of the Clans. Colorful historic display of the Scot—his origin, the clans, tartans and migrations. Genealogical & audiovisual section; life and times of Highland pioneers, relics of Cape Breton giant Angus MacAskill. ¢¢

Motels

★ ★ ★ GISELE'S COUNTRY INN. (387 Shore Rd (Hwy 205), Baddeck NS B0E 1B0) 902/295-2849; FAX 902/295-2033; res: 800/304-0466. 63 rms, 3 story. Late June-Dec: S, D $75-$99; each addl $9; suites for 2, $125-$175; kit. units $150 (up to 4); under 10 free; lower rates rest of yr. Crib free. Pet accepted. TV. Restaurant 7:30-9.30 am, 5.30-10 pm. Bar. Ck-out 10 am. Lndry facilities. Sauna. Cr cds: A, C, D, ER, MC, V.

✔ ★ SILVER DART LODGE. (Shore Rd, Baddeck NS B0E 1B0) 1/2 mi W on Shore Rd (Rte 205). 902/295-2340; FAX 902/295-2484. 88 rms, 20 A/C, 62 air-cooled, 2 story, 24 kits. Mid-June-mid-Oct: S $55-$85; D $59-$95; each addl $8; under 16 free; suites $180-$225; cottages, kit. units $85-$95; under 18 free; lower rates May-early June, late Oct. Closed rest or yr. TV. Pool. Dining rm 7-9:30 am, 5:30-9 pm. Rm serv. Bar; entertainment. Ck-out 11 am. Meeting rm. Gift shop. Tennis. Golf privileges. Lawn games. Balconies. Private beach, dock; boat tours. Cr cds: A, ER, MC, V.

✔ ★ ★ TELEGRAPH HOUSE. (Chebucto St, Baddeck NS B0E 1B0) 902/295-1100; FAX 902/295-1136. 42 rms, 2-3 story. No elvtr. July-Oct: S $57-$80; D $74-$95; each addl $8; under 6 free; lower rates rest of yr. Crib free. TV; cable. Restaurant 7:30 am-8:45 pm. Rm serv. Bar 11-2 am; entertainment. Ck-out 11 am. Meeting rms. Tennis privileges. Golf privileges, greens fee $5. Miniature golf. Some private patios, balconies. Grills. Family-operated since 1860. Cr cds: A, MC, V.

Resort

★ ★ ★ INVERARY. (Shore Rd, Baddeck NS B0E 1B0) 1/4 mi W on Hwy 205. 902/295-3500; FAX 902/295-3527; res: 800/565-5660. E-mail inverary@atcon.com; web www.inveraryresort.com. 124 rms in motel, inn, 14 cottages, 4 kits. June-mid-Oct: S, D $89-$175; each addl $10; kit. units $175; lower rates rest of yr. Crib $10. TV; cable. Indoor pool; whirlpool. Playground. 2 dining rms 7 am-3 pm, 5:30-8:30 pm; entertainment. Serv bar. Ck-out 10:30 am, ck-in 3 pm. Grocery, coin lndry, package store 2 blks. Convention facilities. Airport transportation. Tennis. Exercise equipt. Private beach. Canoes, paddleboats. Boat tours. Hiking tours. Lawn games. Sauna. Gift shop. Fireplace in some rooms. Balconies. Cr cds: A, D, DS, ER, MC, V.

Cape Breton Highlands National Park (D-5)

(See also Baddeck)

Information Cape Breton Highlands National Park, Ingonish Beach B0C 1L0; 902/224-2306.

In the northern part of Cape Breton Island, this park is bounded on the west by the Gulf of St Lawrence and on the east by the Atlantic Ocean. The famous Cabot Trail, a modern 184-mile (294-kilometer) paved highway loop, beginning at Baddeck, runs through the park, including the scenic 66 miles (106 kilometers) between Ingonish and Cheticamp offering visitors spectacular vistas.

Along the western shore, steep hills, to a height of over 1,116 feet (335 meters), rise sharply from the gulf, affording magnificent views of the gulf and the broad plateau covering most of the park interior. The eastern shore is also rocky, indented with numerous coves at the mouths of picturesque valleys. The interior, least seen by visitors, is an area similar to subarctic regions.

Except for the interior, the 370-square-mile (950-square-kilometer) park is covered with a typical Acadian forest of mixed conifers and hardwoods. The interior is covered with heath bogs, and along the seacoast headlands the trees are stunted and twisted into grotesque shapes.

The park is home to many types of wildlife. Moose are numerous and often seen along the highways. Other animals native to the region range from black bear and white-tailed deer to smaller species such as lynx, red fox and snowshoe hare. Among the approximately 200 species of birds to be seen are the red-tailed hawk and bald eagle.

The park is open all year, but many facilities operate only from mid-May-late October. Information centers are maintained at Ingonish and Cheticamp, the main park entrances along the Cabot Trail. You should plan to stop at these facilities as the staff on duty can provide the latest information on what to see and do within the park. Roadside picnic areas are provided, and a variety of self-guiding trails and interpretive events held during summer encourage visitors to learn more about the park's significant areas and features. All visitors require a park entry permit, which allows access to Cabot Trail, sightseeing facilities, beaches and trails. Permit ¢¢¢

One of the best ways to see the park is on foot. The hiking trail system is large and diverse, providing access to the area's remote interior as well as allowing you to explore its rugged coastline. After a hike, visitors can enjoy a refreshing saltwater swim or just relax on one of the several developed natural sand beaches located within the park.

Golf is another popular sport in the park. The Highlands Golf Links in Ingonish is one of the best 18-hole courses in Canada.

Deep-sea fishing is popular, with local fishermen providing transportation and equipment. For those interested in freshwater fishing, a national park permit can be obtained at park information centers; the season generally runs from mid-April through September. There are fully equipped campgrounds on the Cabot Trail as well as primitive campsites on the coast.

Resort

★ ★ ★ **KELTIC LODGE.** (Middle Head Peninsula, Ingonish Beach NS B0C 1L0) on Cabot Trail (Hwy 312). 902/285-2880; FAX 902/285-2859; res: 800/565-0444. 100 units, 32 in lodge, 2 story, 2-, 4-bedrm cottages. MAP: S $194-$209; D $263-$278; each addl $75; cottages $418-$556; golf plans. Closed Jan-May, Nov-Dec. TV; cable. Heated pool; lifeguard. Dining rm 7-9:30 am, noon-2 pm, 6-9 pm. Bar. Ck-out 11 am, ck-in 3 pm. Package store 1 mi. Grocery, coin lndry 5 mi. Convention facilities. Business servs avail. Gift shop. Tennis privileges. Golf privileges, pro, greens fee $55, putting green. Exercise equipt. Lawn games. Some fireplaces. National park adj. Cr cds: A, D, DS, ER, MC, V.

Dartmouth (F-4)

(See also Halifax)

Founded 1750 **Pop** 62,277 **Elev** 75 ft (23 m) **Area code** 902 **Web** www.ttg.sba.dal.ca/nstour/halifax
Information Halifax Regional Municipality Tourism Department, PO Box 1749, Halifax B3J 3A5; 902/490-5946.

On the eastern side of Halifax Harbour, Dartmouth is Canada's "newest" city (incorporated in 1961) whose history extends back to the 18th century. The opening of the Angus L. MacDonald Bridge in 1955, a direct link to Halifax, and the Murray A. MacKay Bridge helped to make this an industrial city—with the largest naval bases in Canada, oil refineries and the Bedford Institute of Oceanography. The 22 lakes within its borders make Dartmouth a swimmer's paradise.

What to See and Do

Black Cultural Centre. History and culture of African-Americans in Nova Scotia. Library; exhibit rms; auditorium. (Daily) 1149 Main St, Rte 7 at Cherrybrook Rd. Phone 902-/434-6223 or 800/465-0767. ¢¢

Quaker Whaler's House. Restored 1785 house. (July-Aug, daily) 59 Ochterloney St. Phone 902/464-2253. **Donation.**

Shearwater Aviation Museum. Extensive collection of aircraft and exhibits on the history of Canadian Maritime Military Aviation. Art gallery; photo collection. (Apr-June & Sept-Nov, Tues, Wed, Fri, daily; July-Aug Tues-Fri, daily, Sat, Sun afternoons; rest of yr by appt) 13 Bonaventure Ave, at Shearwater Airport. Phone 902/460-1083. **Donation.**

Swimming. Supervised beach, 12 mi (19 km) E on Marine Dr, Rte 207. Many others within city.

Annual Event

Dartmouth Natal Day. Lake Banook. Parade, sports events, rowing & paddling regattas, entertainment, fireworks. 1st Mon Aug.

Motels

★ ★ **BURNSIDE.** (739 Windmill Rd (Hwy 7), Dartmouth NS B3B 1C1) exit Bedford at MacKay Bridge. 902/468-7117; res: 800/830-4656; FAX 902/468-1770. E-mail smt@ns.sympatico.ca. 92 rms, 3 story. S $59; D, suites $79-$99; each addl $8; under 16 free. TV; cable (premium), VCR avail. Pool. Restaurant 7 am-2:30 pm, 5-8:30 pm. Bar 10-2 am. Ck-out noon. Meeting rms. Business center. Valet serv. Some minibars; microwaves avail. Cr cds: A, D, DS, ER, MC, V.

✔ ★ **SEASONS MOTOR INN.** (40 Lakecrest Dr, Dartmouth NS B2X 1V1) 902/435-0060; FAX 902/454-6110. 42 rms, 2 story. June-mid-Oct: S, D $51; each addl $3; under 16 free; wkly rates; lower rates rest of yr. Pet accepted. TV; cable, VCR avail (movies). Ck-out 11 am. Business servs avail. X-country ski 5 mi. Refrigerators avail. Cr cds: A, C, D, DS, ER, MC, V.

Motor Hotel

✔ ★ ★ **KEDDY'S DARTMOUTH INN.** (9 Braemer Dr, Dartmouth NS B2Y 3H6) 902/469-0331; FAX 902/466-6324; res: 800/561-7666. E-mail keddys@nbnet.nb.ca; web www.keddys.nb.ca. 115 rms, 3 story, 14 kits. S $49.95; D $62-$80; each addl $8; suites $150; studio rms $75; kit. units $65; under 18 free. Crib free. Pet accepted. TV; cable (premium), VCR avail (movies). Restaurant 6:30 am-10 pm. Bar 10-2 am. Ck-out noon. Meeting rms. Business servs avail. Valet serv. X-country ski 5 mi. Some refrigerators. Balconies. Picnic tables. Lake opp. Cr cds: A, C, D, DS, ER, MC, V.

Hotels

★ ★ ★ **HOLIDAY INN.** (99 Wyse Rd, Dartmouth NS B3A 1L9) on Plaza of MacDonald Bridge. 902/463-1100; FAX 902/464-1227. 196 rms, 7 story. May-Oct: S $89, D $99; each addl $10; suites $195-$395; under 19 free; wkend rates; lower rates rest of yr. Crib free. Pet accepted, some restrictions. TV; cable. Heated pool. Restaurant 7 am-10:30 pm. Bar 11-1 am. Ck-out noon. Business center. In-rm modem link. Airport transportation. X-country ski 15 mi. Health club privileges. Microwaves avail. Some balconies. Cr cds: A, C, D, DS, ER, JCB, MC, V.

★ ★ ★ **RAMADA RENAISSANCE.** (240 Brownlow Ave, Dartmouth NS B3B 1X6) 902/468-8888; FAX 902/468-8765. E-mail ramadartc@fox.nstn.ca. 178 rms, 5 story, 31 suites. May-Oct: S, D $89; each addl $10; suites $129; under 15 free; package plans; lower rates rest of yr. Crib $10. Pet accepted, some restrictions; $50 deposit. TV; cable. Indoor pool; wading pool, whirlpool, lifeguard. Complimentary coffee in rms. Restaurant 6:30 am-10 pm. Bar 11-1 am. Meeting rms. Business center. Gift shop. X-country ski 1 mi. Exercise equipt; sauna. Many minibars; microwaves avail. Cr cds: A, D, DS, ER, MC, V.

Restaurant

★ ★ **ROCCO'S.** (300 Prince Albert Rd, Dartmouth NS) 902/461-0211. Italian menu. Specializes in chicken, seafood, veal. Hrs: 11:30 am-2:30 pm, 5-11 pm; Sat 11:30 am-11 pm. Closed Sun; Jan 1, Dec 24, 25. Res accepted. Bar. A la carte entrees: lunch $6.50-$8.25, dinner $8.95-$17.95. Child's meals. View of lake. Cr cds: A, C, D, ER, MC, V.

Digby (E-2)

Pop 2,558 **Elev** 50 ft (15 m) **Area code** 902 **E-mail** townof.digby.tartannet.ns.ca
Information Tourist Information Bureau, 110 Montague Row, PO Box 579, B0V 1A0; 902/245-5714 or 902/245-4769 (winter) or 888/463-4429.

Best known for its delicious scallops and harbor sights, this summer resort has many historic landmarks which trace its founding in 1783 by Sir Robert Digby and 1500 Loyalists from New England and New York. This Annapolis Basin town is the ideal headquarters for a day drive southwest down the Digby Neck peninsula, whose shores are washed by the Bay of Fundy with the highest tides in the world. Off Digby Neck are two islands which may be reached by ferry: Long Island and Brier Island which are popular for rockhounding, whale-watching and bird-watching. Swimming along the sandy beaches and hiking along the shores are favorite pastimes in this area with its dashing spray, lighthouses and wildflower-filled forests. A 35-mile (11-kilometer) drive to the northeast ends in Annapolis Royal and Port Royal, the first permanent European settlements in North America. Marking this is the restored fur trading fort, the Habitation of Port Royal, built by Samuel de Champlain. This seacoast drive, with high imposing cliffs, gently rolling farmland and quiet woodland settings, creates a study in contrasts.

What to See and Do

Ferry Service to Saint John, NB. Car and passenger; all yr; summer, up to 3 times daily. Contact BAY Ferries, 94 Water St, PO Box 634, Charlottetown, PEI, C1A 7L3; 888/249-7245.

Fishermen's Wharf. View one of the largest scallop fleets in the world.

Fort Anne National Historic Site. Built between 1702 and 1708 in one of the central areas of conflict between the English and French for control of North America. Of the original site, only the 18th century earthworks and a gunpowder magazine (1708) remain. Museum in restored officers' quarters. On grounds is Canada's oldest English graveyard, dating from 1720. (Mid-May-mid-Oct, daily; rest of yr, Mon-Fri; closed major hols) 28 mi E on Hwy 1, Annapolis Royal exit. Phone 902/532-2397 or 902/532-2321. **Free.**

Pines Golf Course. 18-hole championship golf course on provincially owned and operated resort (see RESORTS).

Point Prim Lighthouse. Rocky promontory with view of Bay of Fundy. Lighthouse Rd.

Port Royal National Historic Site. Reconstructed, 17th-century fur-trading post built by Sieur de Mons; follows plans, building techniques of that era. (Mid-May-mid-Oct, daily) 23 mi (38 km) NE via Rte 1, then 6 mi (10 km) W on Port Royal exit in Annapolis Royal. Phone 902/532-2898. **¢¢**

Trinity Church. Only church in Canada built by shipwrights; church cemetery famous for inscriptions of pioneer settlers. (Mon-Fri) Queen St.

Annual Event

Scallop Days. Scallop shucking contests; grand parade, pet show, entertainment; sporting, fishing, water events. 2nd wk Aug.

Motels

★ ★ **ADMIRAL DIGBY INN.** (411 Shore Rd, Digby NS B0V 1A0) 902/245-2531; FAX 902/245-2533; res: 800/465-6262. E mail admdigby@clan.Tartannet.ns.ca; web www.grtplaces.com/ac/admiral. 46 rms, 2 kit. cottages. Mid-June-mid-Sept: S, D $71-$89; each addl $6-$10; kit. cottages $110; under 12 free; lower rates Apr-mid-June & mid-Sept-Oct. Closed rest of yr. Crib $6. Pet accepted. TV; cable, VCR avail (movies). Heated pool. Restaurant 7:30-10:30 am, 5-9 pm. Bar 5-10 pm. Ck-out 11 am. Coin lndry. Business servs avail. Sundries. Gift shop. Overlooks Annapolis Basin. Cr cds: A, C, D, DS, ER, MC, V.

D 🕏 ⩰ 🖎 🔥 SC

✔★ ★ **COASTAL INN KINGFISHER.** (111 Warwick St, Digby NS B0V 1A0) off Hwy 101 exit 26, near St John Ferry. 902/245-4747; res: 800/665-7829; FAX 902/245-4866. E-mail coastalinns@ns.sympatico.ca; web www.coastalinns.com. 36 rms. S $55; D $65; each addl $7; under 10 free; some lower rates. Crib free. Pet accepted. TV; cable. Playground. Restaurant 7 am-8:30 pm; Sat, Sun 8 am-8:30 pm. Ck-out noon. Coin lndry. Meeting rm. Business servs avail. Microwaves avail. Picnic tables. Beach 4 mi. Cr cds: A, C, D, DS, ER, MC, V.

🕏 🖎 🔥

Resorts

★ ★ **MOUNTAIN GAP RESORT.** (217 Hwy 1, Digby NS B0V 1A0) 4 mi E on Rte 1; Hwy 101 exits 24, 25. 902/245-5841; FAX 902/245-2277; res: 800/565-5020. E-mail mtngap@tartannet.ns.ca; web www.mountaingap.ns.ca. 96 rms, 12 cottages. No A/C. Mid-May-mid-Oct: S $69; D $69-$180; each addl $10; kit. units, kit. cottages $159-$199; under 18 free; wkly rates. Closed rest of yr. Crib free. Pet accepted. TV; cable, VCR avail (movies). Heated pool. Playground. Dining rms 7:30-9:30 am, noon-2 pm, 5:30-9 pm. Bar 5:30 pm-midnight. Ck-out 11 am, ck-in 2 pm. Grocery store 1 mi. Business servs avail. Gift shop. Private beach. Tennis. 18-hole golf privileges. Lawn games. Bicycle rentals. Soc dir. Game rm. Private patios, grills. Rustic setting on 45 acres. Cr cds: A, C, D, DS, ER, MC, V.

D 🕏 📶 🖼 ⩰ 🐟 🖎 🔥 SC

★ ★ **THE PINES RESORT.** (103 Shore Rd, Digby NS B0V 1A0) 1 mi N on Shore Rd. 902/245-2511; FAX 902/245-6133; res: 800/667-4637. E-mail pines.resort@ns.sympatico.ca; web www.gov.ns.ca/resorts/. 84 rms, 3 story, 30 cottages. May-mid Oct: S $140-$175; D $161-$198; each addl $20; suites $215-$285; MAP: $52/person addl; family rates. Closed rest of yr. Crib free. TV; cable, VCR avail (movies). Heated pool; poolside serv. Playground. Supervised child's activities (July-Aug); ages 5-12. Dining rm (public by res) 7-10 am, noon-2 pm, 6-9 pm. Limited rm serv. Bar 5-11 pm. Ck-out 11 am, ck-in 3 pm. Grocery store 2 mi. Gift shop. Meeting rms. Business servs avail. Bellhops. Lighted tennis. 18-hole golf, greens fee $35, pro, driving range; Exercise equipt; sauna. Lawn games. Nature trails. Bicycles (rentals). Soc dir. Movies. Fireplace in cottages. Balconies. Veranda. On 300 acres; overlooks Annapolis Basin of Bay of Fundy. Cr cds: A, C, D, DS, ER, JCB, MC, V.

D 🎿 🏃 ⩰ 🏌 🎿 🖎 🔥

Restaurant

★ ★ **FUNDY.** (34 Water St (Rte 101), Digby NS) 902/245-4950. E-mail fundy@moiena.1star.ca. Specializes in seafood. Hrs: 7 am-10 pm; winter from 11 am. Closed Jan 1, Dec 25. Res accepted. Bar 11-2 am. A la carte entrees: bkfst $3.50-$8, lunch $4.95-$13.90, dinner $8.95-$24.95. Child's meals. Outdoor dining. Solarium dining area. On Annapolis basin. Cr cds: A, C, D, DS, ER, MC, V.

➦

Fortress of Louisbourg National Historic Site (E-6)

(See also Baddeck)

E-mail louisbourg-info@pch.gc.ca **Web** www.fortress.uccb.ns.ca
Information Director, PO Box 160, Louisbourg B0A 1M0; 902/733-2280.

(On Cape Breton Island, 22 mi or 35 km south of Sydney, via Highway 22)

This 11,860-acre (4,800-hectare) park includes the massive Fortress erected by the French between 1720-1745 to defend their possessions in the New World. Under the terms of the Treaty of Utrecht (1713), France lost Newfoundland and Acadia but was permitted to keep Cape Breton Island (Isle Royale) and Prince Edward Island (Isle Saint-Jean). English Harbour, renamed Louisbourg, was then selected by the French as the most suitable point for an Atlantic stronghold. It served as headquarters for a large fishing fleet and became an important trading center. Later it was used as the base for French privateers preying on New England shipping.

In 1745, after a 47-day siege, Louisbourg was captured by a volunteer force from New England led by Colonel William Pepperrell and a British fleet under Commodore Warren. Three years later the colony was returned to France by the treaty of Aix-la-Chapelle. In the Seven Years War, Louisbourg, after being twice blockaded by British fleets, was finally captured in 1758. In 1760 its fortifications were demolished. Reconstruction of about one-fourth of 18th-century Louisbourg is complete.

On the grounds and open are the Governor's apartment, the soldiers barracks, the chapel, various guardhouses, the Dauphin Demi-Bastion, the King's storehouse, the Engineer's house, the residence of the commissaire-ordonnateur, several private dwellings and storehouses, and the royal bakery. At the Hôtel de la Marine, L'Epée Royale and the Grandchamps Inn, visitors can sample food in the manner of the 18th-century, while period pastries may be enjoyed at the Destouches house and soldiers' bread purchased at the bakery. Costumed guides interpret the town as it was in 1744 with tours in English and French. Exhibits at various points inside and outside the reconstructed area; walking tours. Park (June-Sept, daily; May & Oct, limited tours). An average visit takes 4-5 hrs; comfortable shoes and warm clothes are advised. ¢¢-¢¢¢

Restaurant

★ ★ **GRUBSTAKE.** *(1274 Main St, Fortress of Louisbourg National Historic Site NS) adj City Hall. 902/733-2308.* Specializes in seafood, steak. Hrs: noon-10 pm. Closed Oct-mid-June. Bar 8 pm-midnight; closed Sun. Semi-a la carte: lunch $5.95-$12, dinner $10.95-$35. Early 1800s building. At fishing wharf. Cr cds: A, MC, V.

Grand Pré (F-4)

Pop 305 **Elev** 125 ft (38 m) **Area code** 902
Information Tourism Nova Scotia, PO Box 130, Halifax B3J 2M7; 902/490-5946 or 800/565-0000.

Site of one of the earliest French settlements in North America, this was the setting for Henry Wadsworth Longfellow's poem "Evangeline," which describes the tragic tale of the expulsion of the Acadians by the British in 1755. Its name refers to the extensively diked lands and means "the great meadow." Wolfville, nearby, is the center of the land of Evangeline and the starting point to memorable historic places.

What to See and Do

Grand Pré National Historic Site. Memorial to the Acadian people. Museum (mid-May-mid-Oct). Grounds and gardens (all yr). Phone 902/542-3631. **Free.** On grounds is

Acadian Memorial Church. Display commemorating Acadian settlement and expulsion. Old Acadian Forge; bust of Longfellow; "Evangeline" statue; formal landscaped gardens with original French willows. Guides available. **Free.**

Motel

★ ★ **GREENSBORO INN.** *(9016 Commercial St, New Minas NS B4W 3E2) 8 mi W on Hwy 101, exit 12. 908/681-3201; res: 800/561-3201 NS & PEI; FAX 908/681-3399.* Web www.valleyweb.com/greensboro. 26 rms. 1 kit. unit. Mid-May-Oct: S $59; D $69-$79, kit. unit $100; under 18 free; each addl $6; lower rates rest of yr. Pet accepted. TV; cable. Indoor pool. Complimentary coffee in lobby. Restaurant adj 11 am-10 pm.

Ck-out 11 am. Golf privileges. Downhill/x-country ski 20 mi. Picnic tables. Cr cds: A, D, ER, MC, V.

🖨 🏊 🕴 🚣 🚡 🐾 SC

Motor Hotels

★ ★ ★ **AUBERGES WANDLYN INN.** *(7270 Hwy 1, Coldbrook NS B0P 1K0) 902/678-8311; FAX 902/679-1253; res: 800/561-0000.* 70 units, 3 story. Mid-June-Oct: S $68-$88; D $88-$100; each addl $10; suites $88-$125; under 18 free; lower rates rest of yr. Crib free. Pet accepted. TV; cable, VCR avail. Indoor pool. Restaurant 7 am-9:30 pm. Bar 10-2 am. Ck-out noon. Meeting rms. Business servs avail. Some refrigerators. Picnic tables. Cr cds: A, C, D, DS, ER, MC, V.

D 🐾 🏊 🚣 🐾 SC

✔★ **SLUMBER INN-NEW MINAS.** *(5534 Prospect Rd, New Minas NS B0P 1X0) Hwy 101 W, exit 12. 902/681-5000; res: 800/914-5005.* E-mail slumberinn@valleyweb.com; web www.valleyweb.com/slumberinn. 79 rms, shower only, 2 story. No elvtr. S, D $70-$85; under 12 free. TV; cable (premium); VCR (movies). Restaurant opp. Ck-out 11 am. Business servs avail. Downhill/x-country ski 20 mi. Cr cds: A, D, ER, MC, V.

D 🏊 🚣 🐾 SC

Inns

★ ★ ★ **BLOMIDON.** *(127 Main St, Wolfville NS B0P 1X0) off Hwy 101 exit 10 or 11. 902/542-2291; FAX 902/542-7461; res: 800/565-2291.* Web www.blomidon.ns.ca. 26 rms, 3 story, 5 suites. May-Oct: S $69-$129; D $79-$139; each addl $10; suites $139; lower rates rest of yr. Crib $12. Pet accepted, some restrictions. TV in sitting rm; cable, VCR avail. Complimentary continental bkfst; afternoon refreshments. Dining rm 11:30 am-2 pm, 5-9:30 pm. Ck-out 11 am, ck-in 3 pm. Meeting rms. Business servs avail. Health club privileges. Tennis. Shuffleboard. Library, 2 parlors; antiques. Sea captain's mansion (1879) on 4 acres; period decor. Cr cds: A, D, ER, MC, V.

D 🐾 🎿 🐾 SC

★ ★ ★ **TATTINGSTONE.** *(434 Main St, Wolfville NS B0P 1X0) Hwy 101 exit 9. 902/542-7696; FAX 902/542-4427; res: 800/565-7696.* E-mail tattingstone@ns.sympatico; web www.tattingstone.ins.ca. 10 rms, 2 story. Apr-Oct: S, D $85-$158; lower rates rest of yr. TV; cable. Heated pool; steam rm, poolside serv. Dining rm 5-9 pm. Ck-out 11 am, ck-in 3 pm. Business servs avail. Lighted tennis. Some in-rm whirlpools. Former residence (1874), landscaped with many unusual trees. Victorian and Georgian period antiques. Cr cds: A, D, ER, MC, V.

D 🚣 🏊 🚣 🔥

★ ★ ★ **VICTORIA'S.** *(416 Main St, Wolfville NS B0P 1X0) just off Hwy 101, exit 10 or 11. 902/542-5744; FAX 902/542-7794; res: 800/556-5744.* E-mail victoria.inn@ns.sympatico.ca; web www.valleyweb.com/victoriasinn. 15 rms, 3 story. May-Oct: S, D $89-$175; each addl $15; suite $175; lower rates rest of yr. Complimentary full bkfst. Rm serv. Ck-out 11 am, ck-in 3 pm. Business center. Some balconies. Historic inn built in 1893; period furnishings. Totally nonsmoking. Cr cds: A, D, ER, MC, V.

🕴 🚣 🕴

Resort

★ ★ **OLD ORCHARD INN.** *(Hwy 101, exit 11, Wolfville NS B0P 1X0) 902/542-5751; FAX 902/542-2276; res: 800/561-8090.* E-mail oldoinn@mail.atcon.com; web www.atcon.com/oldorchard. 105 rms, 3 story, 29 cabins, 10 kits. May-Oct: S, D $79-$88; each addl $8; suites $120; cabins $59-$64 (with kit. $15 addl); family rates; ski plans. Crib free. TV; cable. Indoor pool. Sauna. Playground. Supervised child's activities (winter); ages 5-12. Dining rm 7 am-9 pm. Box lunches. Bar to 2 am. Ck-out 11 am, ck-in 3 pm. Coin lndry 3 mi. Meeting rms. Business center. Grocery, package store 3 mi. Lighted tennis. 18-hole golf privileges. Downhill ski 20 mi; x-country ski on site. Sleigh rides. Lawn games. Some private patios. Picnic tables. Cr cds: A, D, ER, MC, V.

D ⚐ 🏊 🎿 ⛷ ⚓ 🎣 🛶 🏴 SC 🚶

Restaurant

✔★ **PADDY'S PUB & BREWERY.** (42 Aberdeen St, Kentville NS B4W 2N1) 10 mi W on Hwy 1. 902/678-3199. E-mail paddys@fox.ns.ca. Irish, continental menu. Specializes in fish & chips, steak, seafood. Hrs: 11 am-midnight; Sun to 11 pm; Sun brunch to 3 pm. Closed Dec 25, 26. Res accepted. Bar. Semi-a la carte: lunch $3-$7, dinner $5-$15. Sun brunch $3-$6. Child's meals. Entertainment Fri, Sat. Irish pub atmosphere. Cr cds: A, D, ER, MC, V.

D SC

Halifax (F-4)

(See also Peggy's Cove)

Founded 1749 **Pop** 340,000 **Elev** 25-225 ft (8-69 m) **Area code** 902
E-mail beatong@region.halifax.ns.ca **Web** www.ttg.sba.dal.ca/nstour/halifax
Information International Visitors Centre, 1595 Barrington St, B3J 1Z7; 902/490-5946 or 800/565-0000.

Capital of Nova Scotia, this largest city in the Atlantic provinces offers a delightful combination of old and new. Founded in 1749 to establish British strength in the North Atlantic, it is growing rapidly as a commercial, scientific and educational center while continuing to preserve its natural heritage. Centrally situated in the province, it is perfectly suited as the starting point for the Evangeline and Glooscap Trails, the Lighthouse Route and the Marine Drive with their scenic and historic sights. Located on Bedford Basin, the world's second-largest natural harbor, Halifax recently merged with the town of Dartmouth; this area lies across the harbor and is reached via the MacDonald and MacKay bridges.

What to See and Do

Art Gallery of Nova Scotia. More than 2,000 works on permanent display, including folk art; changing exhibits. (Tues-Sat, also Sun afternoons; closed major hols) Free admission Tues. 1741 Hollis-at-Cheapside. Phone 902/424-7542. ¢¢

Bluenose II. Exact replica of famed racing schooner depicted on Canadian dime; public cruises in Nova Scotia waters. At waterfront. Contact Bluenose Preservation Trust; 800/763-1963 or 800/565-0000. ¢¢¢¢

Chapel of Our Lady of Sorrows. Built in one day by 2,000 men; altar carvings date from 1750. South & S Park Sts.

Halifax Citadel National Historic Park. Star-shaped hilltop fort, built 1828-1856 on site of previous fortifications. Excellent view of city and harbor. Audiovisual presentation the "Tides of History" (50-min). Restored signal masts, library, barrack rms, powder magazine, expense magazine, defense casemate and garrison cell. Exhibits on communications, the four Citadels and engineering and construction. Army Museum; orientation center. Coffee bar serving typical 19th-century soldiers' food; sales outlet; guided tours, military displays by uniformed students, bagpipe music, changing of the guard (summer). (Daily; closed Jan 1, Good Friday, Dec 25) Entrances on Sackville St and Rainnie Dr. Phone 902/426-5080.Fee charged June 15-Labour Day ¢ On grounds are

Maritime Museum of the Atlantic. 1675 exhibits of nautical history including *Titanic: The Unsinkable Ship* and *Halifax, Halifax Wrecked: The Story of the Halifax Explosion.* (Mid-May-mid-Oct, daily; rest of yr, daily exc Mon; closed some hols) Lower Water St. Phone 902/424-7490. ¢¢

Town Clock (1803). Halifax's most recognized landmark. Built under supervision of Prince Edward, Duke of Kent, father of Queen Victoria.

Historic Properties (Privateers Wharf). Variety of clothing, specialty shops, restaurants and pubs housed in several restored 18th-century buildings along the waterfront. (Daily) 1869-70 Upper Water St. Phone 902/429-0530.

Neptune Theatre. Home of internationally recognized theater company; presents five main stage plays per season. Small intimate theater with excellent acoustics. Reservations advised. Corner of Argyle & Sackville Sts. Phone 902/429-7070 or 902/429-7300.

Nova Scotia Museum of Natural History. Permanent exhibits on man and his environment in Nova Scotia; changing exhibits. (June-mid-Oct, daily; rest of yr, daily exc Mon; closed Jan 1, Good Friday, Dec 25) 1747 Summer St. Phone 902/424-7353. ¢

Point Pleasant Park. Remains of several forts. Nature trail, monuments, public beach, picnic areas; cross-country skiing. (Daily) Point Pleasant Dr. Phone 902/421-6519. **Free.** On grounds is

Prince of Wales Tower National Historic Park (1796-1797). Built to protect British batteries; said to be first tower of its type in North America. Exhibits portray tower's history, architectural features and significance as a defensive structure. (July-Labour Day, daily) Phone 902/426-5080. **Free.**

Province House. Oldest provincial Parliament building in Canada; office of Premier; legislative library. Guided tours (Mon-Fri; special summer hrs). Hollis St. Phone 902/424-8967. **Free.**

Public Archives of Nova Scotia. Provincial government records; private manuscripts; maps, photos, genealogies; film and sound archives; library. (Tues-Sat; closed hols) 6016 University Ave, S end of town. Phone 902/424-6060. **Free.**

Public Gardens. A 16³/₄-acre (7-hectare) formal Victorian gardens with trees, flower beds, fountains; bandstand; duck ponds; concession. (See SEASONAL EVENT) (May-Nov, daily) Spring Garden Rd & South Park St. Phone 902/421-6550. **Free.**

Sightseeing tours.

Gray Line bus tours, phone 800/565-9662; **Cabana Tours,** PO Box 8683, Station A, B3K 5M4, phone 902/423-6066; Markland Tours, multilingual mini-van tours, phone 902/499-2939.

Murphy's on the Water. Three boats. Live narration and historical commentary; 2-hr tour. (May-mid-Oct, daily) Murphy's Pier next to Historic Properties. Phone 902/420-1015. ¢¢¢¢

St George's Round Church (1801). Anglican; Byzantine-style church built at the direction of Edward, Duke of Kent, father of Queen Victoria. Nearby is **St Patrick's Roman Catholic Church,** a Victorian Gothic building still largely untouched by change. **St Paul's Church** (1750). Barrington St. First church in Halifax and oldest Protestant church in Canada. "Explosion window" on Argyle St side; during 1917 explosion that destroyed a large portion of the city, the 3rd window of the upper gallery shattered, leaving the silhouette of a human head. Tours (summer; free). (June-Sept, daily) Brunswick & Cornwallis Sts.

York Redoubt National Historic Site (1793). A 200-yr-old fortification on high bluff overlooking harbor entrance. Features muzzle-loading guns, photo display, picnic facilities, information service. Grounds (daily). (Mid-June-Labour Day, daily) 6 mi (9.7 km) SW via Purcell's Cove Rd. Phone 902/426-5050. **Free.**

Annual Events

Winterfest. Feb.

Multicultural Festival. June.

Atlantic Jazz Festival. July.

Highland games. July.

International Buskerfest. Aug.

Nova Scotia Air Show. Sept.

Seasonal Event

Public Gardens Band Concerts. Sun afternoons. July-Aug.

Motels

★ ★ **AUBERGES WANDLYN MOTOR INN.** *(50 Bedford Hwy, Halifax NS B3M 2J2)* 902/443-0416; FAX 902/457-0665; res: 800/561-0000. Web www.wandlyn.com. 66 rms, 2 story. June-Sept: S $60-$85; D $65-$85; each addl $10; suites $95-$135; under 18 free; lower rates rest of yr. Pet accepted. TV, VCR avail (movies). Restaurant 7-11 am, 5-9 pm. Bar 4-11 pm. Ck-out noon. Meeting rms. Business servs avail. Sundries. Exercise equipt. Microwaves avail. Ocean view from some rms. Cr cds: A, D, DS, ER, MC, V.

D ✦ ✕ ⇔ ⚕ SC

★ ★ **BLUENOSE INN AND SUITE.** *(636 Bedford Hwy, Halifax NS B3M 2L8)* 902/443-3171; res: 800/565-2301; FAX 902/443-9368. 51 units, 1-2 story, 17 kit. suites. June-Oct: S, D $65; each addl $7; kit. suites $89; some wkly rates; lower rates rest of yr. Crib free. Pet accepted. TV; cable, VCR avail. Complimentary continental bkfst. Playground. Restaurant 7-10 pm (off-season). Bar. Ck-out 11 am. Meeting rms. Balconies. Picnic tables. Cr cds: A, D, DS, ER, JCB, MC, V.

D ✦ ⇔ ⚕ SC

✔ ★ **GRAND VIEW.** *(Black Point, Halifax County NS B0J 1B0)* W on Hwy 103, exit 5, then left ¼ mi on Hwy 213, turn right at flashing light and continue 10 mi on Hwy 3. 902/857-9776; FAX 902/857-9776; 800 888/591-5122. 14 rms, 10 kit. units, 2 cottages. No A/C. No rm phones. Mid-June-early Sept: S $47-$55; D $50-$60; each addl $7; cottages $85; under 5 free; wkly rates; lower rates rest of yr. Crib avail. Pet accepted. TV; cable. Playground. Coffee in rms. Ck-out 10:30 am. Near swimming beach; all rms have view of St Margaret's Bay. Cr cds: MC, V.

D ✦ ⚕

★ **SEASONS MOTOR INN.** *(4 Melrose Ave, Halifax NS B3N 2E2)* 902/443-9341; res: 800/792-2498; FAX 902/443-9344. E-mail bill.turvey@ns.sympatico.ca. 36 rms, 32 air-cooled, 4 story. June-Oct: S $48; D $51; each addl $3; under 12 free; lower rates rest of yr. Pet accepted, some restrictions. TV; cable. Complimentary continental bkfst. Ck-out 11 am. Meeting rm. Cr cds: A, C, D, DS, ER, MC, V.

✦ ⇔ ⚕ SC

✔ ★ ★ **STARDUST.** *(1067 Bedford Hwy, Bedford NS B4A 1B8)* 9 mi E on Hwy 2. 902/835-3316; FAX 902/835-4973. 50 rms, 25 A/C, 3 story, 32 kits. June-Oct: S $45; D $50; each addl $10; family rms $60; 2-bedrm apts $100; kit. units $35-$45 (equipt $10 addl); under 12 free; lower rates rest of yr. Crib $5. Pet accepted. TV; cable, VCR avail. Restaurant 7 am-10 pm. Serv bar. Ck-out 11 am. Sundries. Some refrigerators. On Bedford Basin. Cr cds: A, ER, MC, V.

✦ ⇔ ⚕ SC

★ ★ **STARDUST.** *(1791 St Margarets Bay Rd, Halifax NS B3T 1B8)* 902/876-2301; FAX 902/835-4973. 12 rms, 2 with shower only, 10 kit. units (no equipt.). No A/C. No rm phones. June-Oct: S $40-$50; D $60; each addl $10; kit. units $40-$50; under 12 free; wkly rates; lower rates rest of yr. TV; cable. Ck-out 11 am. Picnic tables. On lake. Cr cds: A, ER, MC, V.

🖨 ⇔ ⚕ SC

★ ★ **WINDJAMMER.** *(Box 240, Chester NS B0J 1J0)* approx 45 mi W on Hwy 3. 902/275-3567; FAX 902/275-5867. 18 rms, 6 A/C. Mid-June-mid-Sept: S $44-$54; D $49-$59 each addl $6; under 12 free; lower rates rest of yr. Crib $5. Pet accepted. TV; cable, VCR avail. Restaurant adj 7:30 am-9 pm. Ck-out 11 am. Miniature golf. Some refrigerators, microwaves avail. Picnic tables. On lake; swimming beach. Cr cds: A, C, D, DS, ER, MC, V.

✦ ✦ ⚕ SC

Motor Hotels

★ ★ ★ **AIRPORT HOTEL.** *(60 Bell Blvd, Enfield NS B2T 1K3)* Off Hwy 102 exit 6, near International Airport. 902/873-3000; FAX 902/873-3001; res: 800/667-3333. Web www.jwg.com/atlific/. 156 rms, 3 story. No

elvtr. May-Nov: S $98-$110; D, kit. units $97-$144; each addl $10; suites $140; under 18 free; lower rates rest of yr. Crib avail. Pet accepted. TV; cable. 2 pools, 1 indoor; whirlpool. Restaurant 6:30 am-10 pm. Rm serv. Bar. Ck-out noon. Meeting rms. Business servs avail. In-rm modem link. Free airport transportation. Exercise equipt; sauna. Some refrigerators, minibars; microwaves avail. Cr cds: A, C, D, DS, ER, JCB, MC, V.

D ✦ ⇔ ✕ ✈ ⇔ ⚕ SC

★ ★ ★ **DELTA BARRINGTON.** *(1875 Barrington St, Halifax NS B3J 3L6)* 902/429-7410; res: 800/268-1133; FAX 902/420-6524. Web www.deltahotels.com. 202 rms, 4 story. S, D $131-$142; each addl $15; suites $289-$475; under 18 free; wkend rates; some lower rates. Crib free. Pet accepted, some restrictions. Parking $15. TV; cable, VCR avail. Indoor pool; whirlpool. Free supervised child's activities (2 days/wk); ages 3-11. Restaurant 6:30 am-2:30 pm, 5-10 pm. Rm serv to 1 am. Bar. Ck-out 1 pm. Meeting rms. Business servs avail. In-rm modem link. Bellhops. Valet serv. Shopping arcade. Barber, beauty shop. Exercise equipt; sauna. Minibars; microwaves avail. Cr cds: A, C, D, ER, JCB, MC, V.

D ✦ ⇔ ✕ ⇔ ⚕ SC

★ ★ ★ **HOLIDAY INN SELECT-HALIFAX CENTRE.** *(1980 Robie St, Halifax NS B3H 3G5)* jct Quinpool St. 902/423-1161; res: 800/465-4329; FAX 902/423-9069. E-mail hiselect@holinnselect.hfx.com. 232 rms, 14 story. S, D $125-$145; each addl $10; suites $195-$225; under 19 free; wkend rates. Crib free. Pet accepted. TV; cable, VCR avail. Indoor pool; wading pool, whirlpool, poolside serv. Complimentary coffee in rms. Restaurant 6 am-11 pm. Rm serv. Bars noon-1 am. Ck-out 1 pm. Meeting rms. Business center. In-rm modem link. Sundries. Indoor parking. Exercise equipt; sauna. Health club privileges. Microwaves avail. Cr cds: A, C, D, DS, ER, JCB, MC, V.

D ✦ ⇔ ✕ ⇔ ⚕ SC 🚶

★ ★ **KEDDY'S.** *(20 St Margaret's Bay Rd, Armdale NS B3N 1J4)* on Hwy 3, ½ mi W of Armdale Traffic Circle. 902/477-5611; FAX 902/479-2150; res: 800/561-7666. E-mail ked.hfx@avr.com; web www.keddys.com. 135 rms, 9 story, 14 kits. June-Oct: S $73; D $78; each addl $8; suites $85-$125; kit. units $57-$99; under 19 free; lower rates rest of yr. Crib free. Pet accepted. TV; cable, VCR avail (movies). Indoor pool; whirlpool. Restaurant 7 am-9 pm. Bar 11-1 am. Ck-out 11 am. Meeting rms. Business servs avail. In-rm modem link. Valet serv. Sundries. Sauna. Microwaves avail. Cr cds: A, C, D, DS, ER, MC, V.

D ✦ ⇔ ⇔ ⚕ SC

Hotels

★ ★ ★ **CAMBRIDGE SUITES.** *(1583 Brunswick St, Halifax NS B3J 3P5)* 902/420-0555; FAX 902/420-9379; res: 800/565-1263. E-mail general@hfx.cambridgesuites.ns.ca; web centennialhotels.com/cambridge. 200 suites, 6 story. S, D $105-$135; under 18 free; wkend rates. Crib free. Garage $6. TV; cable, VCR avail. Complimentary continental bkfst. Restaurant 7 am-10 pm. Ck-out 2 pm. Coin lndry. Meeting rms. Business center. In-rm modem link. Exercise equipt; sauna. Whirlpool. Rec rm. Sun deck. Refrigerators, microwaves, minibars. Grills. Cr cds: A, C, D, DS, ER, MC, V.

D ✕ ⇔ ⚕ SC 🚶

★ ★ ★ **CITADEL.** *(1960 Brunswick St, Halifax NS B3J 2G7)* at foot of Citadel Hill. 902/422-1391; FAX 902/429-6672; res: 800/565-7162 (CAN). 264 rms, 7 & 11 story. S, D $89-$169; each addl $15; suites $250-$305; wkend rates; under 18 free. Crib free. Pet accepted, some restrictions. TV; cable. Indoor pool; whirlpool, poolside serv. Restaurant 7 am-3 pm, 5-11 pm. Bar 11-1 am. Ck-out 1 pm. Meeting rms. Business center. In-rm modem link. Exercise equipt; sauna. Minibars; some refrigerators. Private patios, balconies. Cr cds: A, C, D, ER, JCB, MC, V.

✦ ⇔ ✕ ⇔ ⚕ SC 🚶

★ ★ ★ **HOTEL HALIFAX.** *(1990 Barrington St, Halifax NS B3J 1P2)* in Scotia Square. 902/425-6700; FAX 902/425-6214; res: 800/441-1414. Web www.cphotels.ca. 300 rms, 8 story. S, D $129-$159; each addl $20; suites $195-$400; under 18 free. Crib free. Pet accepted, some restrictions. Valet parking $12.95. TV; cable. Heated pool; whirlpool. Restaurant 6:30 am-10 pm. Bars 11-1 am. Ck-out noon. Meeting rms. Business center. Shopping arcade. Beauty shop. Exercise equipt; sauna. Minibars. On Halifax Harbour. Cr cds: A, C, D, DS, ER, JCB, MC, V.

★ ★ **INN ON THE LAKE.** *(Hwy 102, Fall River NS B0N 2S0) N on Hwy 102 exit 5.* 902/861-3480; res: 800/463-6465; FAX 902/861-4883. E-mail innlake@newedge.net; web innonthelake.com. 41 rms, 3 story. May-Dec: S, D $90-$104; each addl $10; suites $235-$290; wkly; lower rates rest of yr. Crib free. TV; cable (premium), VCR avail (movies). Pool; poolside serv. Complimentary coffee in rms. Restaurant 7 am-10 pm. Bar 11-1 am. Ck-out 11 am. Meeting rms. Business servs avail. In-rm modem link. No bellhops. Gift shop. Free airport transportation. Tennis. Some refrigerators, microwaves. Some balconies. Picnic tables. On lake. Cr cds: A, D, ER, MC, V.

★ ★ **LORD NELSON.** *(1515 S Park St, Halifax NS B3J 2T3) across from Public Gardens.* 902/423-6331; res: 800/565-2020; FAX 902/423-7148. E-mail reservations@lordnelson.ns.ca. 200 rms, 9 story. S, D $79-$109; each addl $10; suites $99-$150; under 18 free; wkend rates. Crib free. TV; cable. Ck-out 1 pm. Meeting rms. Business servs avail. Shopping arcade. Many microwaves. Cr cds: A, D, ER, MC, V.

★ ★ ★ **PRINCE GEORGE.** *(1725 Market St, Halifax NS B3J 3N9)* 902/425-1986; res: 800/565-1567; FAX 902/429-6048. E-mail reservations@princegeorgehotel.ns.ca; web centennialhotels.com/princegeorge. 206 rms, 6 story. S, D $119-$160; suites $225-$350; under 18 free; wkend rates. Crib free. Pet accepted, some restrictions. Garage $11/night. TV; cable (premium), VCR avail. Indoor pool; poolside serv. Restaurant 6:30 am-11 pm. Rm serv 24 hrs. Bar 11-2 am. Ck-out 1 pm. Convention facilities. Business center. Concierge. Gift shop. Exercise equipt. Minibars; microwaves avail. Directly connected to the World Trade & Convention Centre and the Metro Centre by shuttle elvtr and underground walkway. Cr cds: A, C, D, DS, ER, JCB, MC, V.

★ ★ ★ **SHERATON.** *(1919 Upper Water St, Halifax NS B3J 3J5) downtown.* 902/421-1700; res: 800/325-3535; FAX 902/422-5805. 349 rms, 6 story. S, D $139-$200; each addl $20; suites $225-$850; under 18 free. Crib free. Pet accepted. Parking $10. TV; cable, VCR avail (movies). Indoor pool; whirlpool, poolside serv. Complimentary coffee in rms. Restaurant 6:30 am-11 pm. Bars 11-2 am; entertainment. Ck-out noon. Convention facilities. Business center. In-rm modem link. Concierge. Shopping arcade. Barber, beauty shop. Exercise equipt; sauna. Some bathrm phones; microwaves avail. On ocean, Halifax Harbor. Casino. Cr cds: A, C, D, DS, ER, JCB, MC, V.

Inns

★ ★ **DAUPHINEE INN.** *(167 Shore Club Rd, Hubbards NS B0J 1T0) 25 mi W on NS 103.* 902/857-1790; res: 800/567-1790; FAX 902/857-9555. E-mail lobster@ns.sympatico.ca; web www.cybernetone.com/d/dauphineeinn. 6 air-cooled rms, 2 suites. No rm phones. S, D $78-$86; each addl $10; suites $125; under 5 free. Closed Nov-Apr. TV in common rm; cable (premium). Complimentary continental bkfst. Restaurant 5-9 pm. Ck-out 11 am, ck-in 2 pm. Business servs avail. Gift shop. In-rm whirlpool in suites. On swimming beach. Built in 1900; panoramic views of Hubbards Cove. Totally nonsmoking. Cr cds: A, D, DS, ER, MC, V.

✔ ★ **FRESH START.** *(2720 Gottingen St, Halifax NS B3K 3C7)* 902/453-6616; FAX 902/453-6617; 800 888/453-6616. 8 rms, 6 share baths, 2-3 story. No A/C. Rm phones avail. May-Oct: S $55-$70; D $66-$70; each addl $10; wkly rates; lower rates rest of yr. Pet accepted, some restrictions. TV in sitting rm; cable, VCR avail. Complimentary full bkfst. Ck-out 1 pm, ck-in 4 pm. Business servs avail. Microwaves avail.

Victorian house (1880); antiques. Maritime Command Museum opp. Totally nonsmoking. Cr cds: A, D, ER, MC, V.

★ ★ ★ **HADDON HALL.** *(67 Haddon Hill Rd, Chester NS B0J 1J0) 35 mi W on NS 3.* 902/275-3577; FAX 902/275-5159. 9 rms, 2 story, 2 kit. units. June-Oct: S, D, kit. units $150-$400; each addl $15; under 16 free; mid-June-mid-Oct; 2 day min (main house); lower rates rest of yr. TV; cable, VCR avail. Complimentary continental bkfst. Complimentary coffee in rms. Restaurant 5:30-8:30 pm. Rm serv. Ck-out 10 am, ck-in 11 am. Business servs avail. Luggage handling. Valet serv. Tennis. Heated pool. Refrigerator, microwave in kit. units. Built in 1905; panoramic ocean view. Cr cds: MC, V.

★ ★ **WAVERLEY.** *(1266 Barrington St, Halifax NS B3J 1Y5)* 902/423-9346; FAX 902/425-0167; res: 800/565-9346. E-mail welcome@waverlyinn.com; web www.waverlyinn.com. 32 rms, 3 story. June-Oct: S, D $79-$149; each addl $15; under 12 free; lower rates rest of yr. Crib avail. TV; cable, VCR avail. Complimentary continental bkfst. Restaurant nearby. Ck-out noon, ck-in after noon. Business servs avail. Some in-rm whirlpools; microwaves avail. Historic inn (1876); antiques. Near Halifax Harbour. Cr cds: A, D, ER, MC, V.

Resort

★ ★ ★ **OAK ISLAND INN & MARINA.** *(Western Shore NS B0J 3M0) 45 mi W on Hwy 103, exit 9.* 902/627-2600; FAX 902/627-2020; res: 800/565-5075. E-mail oakislnd@istar.ca; web home.istar.ca/~oakislnd. 70 rms, 3 story. No elvtr. June-Sept: S, D $75-$95; each addl $10; suites $115-$140; under 16 free; wkend rates; lower rates rest of yr. Crib free. Pet accepted. TV; cable (premium), VCR avail. Indoor pool; whirlpool, poolside serv. Dining rm 7 am-2 pm, 5-9 pm. Rm serv. Bar. Ck-out noon, ck-in 3 pm. Convention facilities. Business center. Tennis. 18-hole golf privileges. Swimming beach. X-country ski 1 mi. Hiking. Lawn games. Fishing guides, charter boats. Balconies. Oceanfront resort overlooking Oak Island. Cr cds: A, D, DS, ER, MC, V.

Restaurants

✔ ★ **ALFREDO, WEINSTEIN & HO.** *(1739 Grafton St, Halifax NS B3J 2W1)* 902/421-1977. Hrs: 11 am-midnight; Fri, Sat to 4 am. Closed Jan 1, Dec 24-26. Bar. Continental menu. Semi-a la carte: lunch $5.95-$9.95, dinner $9-$15. Child's meals. Specializes in Italian, Chinese, and delicatessen dishes. Sundae bar. Cr cds: A, D, ER, MC, V.

★ ★ **FIVE FISHERMEN.** *(1740 Argyle St, Halifax NS B3J 2W1)* 902/422-4421. Specializes in seafood, steak. Salad bar. Own desserts. Hrs: 5-11 pm; Sun to 10 pm. Closed Jan 1, Dec 22-25. Res accepted. Bar. Semi-a la carte: dinner $16.95-$27.95. Specialty: steamed mussels. Former school building (1816). Cr cds: A, C, D, ER, MC, V.

★ ★ ★ **SALTY'S ON THE WATERFRONT.** *(1869 Upper Water St, Halifax NS B3J 1S9)* 902/423-6818. E-mail saltysn@aol.com. Continental menu. Specializes in lobster, steak. Hrs: 11:30 am-10 pm. Res accepted. Bar to 10 pm. A la carte entrees: lunch $6.95-$10.95, dinner $14-$22. Child's meals. Nautical decor. Patio dining on harbor. Historic building (1800) on waterfront. Cr cds: A, D, DS, ER, MC, V.

Peggy's Cove (F-3)

(See also Halifax)

Pop 54 **Elev** 25 ft (8 m) **Area code** 902

Information Tourism Nova Scotia, PO Box 130, Halifax B3J 2M7; 902/490-5946 or 800/565-0000.

Twenty-seven miles (forty-four kilometers) southwest of Halifax, this tiny, picturesque village lies nestled in a snug harbor where lobster fishermen live and work. This area is surrounded by bold granite outcroppings where, during a storm, the sea dashes against the shoreline.

Within St John's Anglican Church, two murals painted by the late William deGarthe, one of Canada's foremost artists, may be viewed. Additional works include carvings of the villagers at work scribed into the rock cliff behind deGarthe's home, now a gallery. One of the many lighthouses dotting the Lighthouse Route, extending southwest from Halifax to Yarmouth, may be seen in this artist's haven.

What to See and Do

Fisheries Museum of the Atlantic. Restored schooner *Theresa E. Connor* & trawler *Cape Sable* serve as floating museum, situated in an old fish plant; *Bluenose* schooner exhibit; aquarium; working dory shop; hall of inshore fisheries, demonstrations room, theatre, gift shop, gallery; restaurant. (Daily) Bluenose Dr, between Duke & Montague Sts in Lunenburg. Phone 902/634-4794. ¢¢

Town of Lunenburg (founded 1753). Walking tour of this historic town provides comprehensive information on town's history and unique architectural character. The Tourist Bureau is located on Blockhouse Hill Rd, near Townsend St. Approx 50 mi (80 km) W on Hwy 103.

Restaurant

✔★★ **SOU' WESTER.** *(NS 333, Peggy's Cove NS)* 902/823-2561. Specializes in seafood chowder, lobster, gingerbread. Own soups, sauces. Hrs: 8 am-10 pm; June-Oct from 10 am. Closed Dec 24, 25. No A/C. Serv bar. Semi-a la carte: bkfst $4.25-$7.25, lunch, dinner $3.25-$17.95. Child's meals. Gift shop. On oceanfront. View of lighthouse & cove. Family-owned. Cr cds: A, C, D, MC, V.

Truro (E-4)

Settled 1703 **Pop** 12,885 **Elev** 15 ft (5 m) **Area code** 902 **E-mail** tdcoc@auracom.com

Information Chamber of Commerce, 577 Prince St, B2N 1G2; 902/895-6328.

After the expulsion of the Acadians (following British acquisition of this territory), Truro was resettled in 1760 by 53 Loyalist families from New England. Other settlers followed, mainly from Northern Ireland and those fleeing the American Revolution. After the arrival of the railroad, Truro was incorporated as a town in 1875.

What to See and Do

Acres of the Golden Pheasant. Contains over 50 species of birds, including pheasants, peacocks, parakeets, finches and doves. (Daily) Queen St. Phone 902/893-2734. ¢

Colchester County Museum. Exhibits depict the human and natural history of the county; changing exhibits. Archives, genealogy library. (June-Sept, daily exc Mon; rest of yr, Tues-Fri; closed major hols) 29 Young St. Phone 902/895-6284. ¢

Little White Schoolhouse Museum. One-rm schoolhouse built in 1871, furnished with desks, artifacts and textbooks from 1867-1952. (June-Aug, daily; rest of yr, by appt) Arthur St, on grounds of Nova Scotia Teachers College. Phone 902/895-5347, ext 291. **Free.**

Tidal bore. A wave of water rushes *backward* up the Salmon River before high tide. Bores range in height from a ripple up to several feet. Viewing area on Tidal Bore Rd, just off Hwy 102, exit 14. A timetable can be obtained from the Chamber of Commerce or by phoning "Dial-a-Tide" at 902/426-5494.

Victoria Park. 1,000-acre national park with hiking trails, outdoor pool, playground, tennis courts, picnic grounds and baseball field. (Daily) Brunswick St & Park Rd. Phone 902/895-6328. **Free.**

Annual Event

International Tulip Festival. 577 Prince St. Over 250,000 tulips planted. Late May.

Motels

★★ **BEST WESTERN GLENGARRY.** *(150 Willow St, Truro NS B2N 4Z6)* 902/893-4311; res: 800/567-4276; FAX 902/893-1759. 90 rms, 3 story. June-Oct: S $86.96-$97.39; D $97.39-$115; each addl $10; suites $180; under 18 free; lower rates rest of yr. Pet accepted. TV; cable, VCR avail (movies). 2 pools, 1 indoor; wading pool, whirlpool, poolside serv. Restaurant 7 am-9 pm; Sun 8 am-8 pm. Rm serv. Bar 5 pm-1 am; entertainment. Ck-out 11 am. Meeting rms. Cr cds: A, C, D, DS, ER, JCB, MC, V.

D ✦ ≋ ⊠ ⦿ SC

★ **HoJo.** *(165 Willow St, Truro NS B2N 4Z9)* 902/893-9413; FAX 902/897-9937. 38 rms. May-Oct: S $49.95; D $59.95; each addl $10; under 18 free; wkly rates; lower rates rest of yr. TV; cable. Restaurant 6 am-10 pm. Ck-out noon. Coin lndry. Meeting rm. Business servs avail. Sundries. Microwaves avail. Cr cds: A, D, ER, MC, V.

D ⊠ ⦿ SC

✔★ **PALLISER.** *(Tidal Bore Rd, Truro NS B2N 5G6)* Hwy 102 exit 14. 902/893-8951; FAX 902/895-8475. E-mail palliser@auracom.com. 42 rms. No A/C. No rm phones. Early May-late-Oct: S $39; D $47; each addl $5; under 10, $5. Closed rest of yr. Crib $5. Pet accepted. TV; cable. Complimentary continental bkfst. Restaurant 7:30 am-8:30 pm. Bar from 11 am. Ck-out 11 am. Meeting rm. Business servs avail. Gift shop. Cr cds: A, D, ER, MC, V.

D ✦ ⦿

✔★ **WILLOW BEND.** *(277 Willow St, Truro NS B2N 5A3)* 902/895-5325; FAX 902/893-8375; 800 888/594-5569. 27 rms, 9 kits. Mid-June-mid-Sept: S $40-$45; D $42-$55; each addl $5; kits. $39-$49; wkly rates; lower rates rest of yr. Pet accepted. TV; cable (premium), VCR avail. Pool; poolside serv. Bar from 5 pm. Ck-out 11 am. Business servs avail. 18-hole golf privileges. Cr cds: MC, V.

✦ ⅄ ≋ ⊠ ⦿

Yarmouth (F-2)

Pop 7,475 **Elev** 140 ft (43 m) **Area code** 902 **E-mail** ycta@auracom.com **Web** www.yarmouth.org

Information Yarmouth County Tourist Assn, PO Box 477, B5A 4B4; 902/742-5355.

This historic seaport is the largest town southwest of Halifax and the gateway to Nova Scotia from New England. While the town of Yarmouth was first settled by New Englanders in 1761, the Yarmouth County area was previously inhabited by the MicMac and French Acadians. Today it serves as the hub of the fishing, shipping and transportation industries of western Nova Scotia.

During the days of sail in the 1800s, this was one of the major shipbuilding and ship owning ports in the world. There are many evidences of this "Golden Age of Sail" to be found in the architecture of many of its fine old homes as well as ship paintings and artifacts exhibited in museums. Travel north on the Evangeline Trail, which passes through French Acadian settlements, fishing centers and rich orchards and farmlands. South, follow the Lighthouse Route which parallels the Atlantic coastline and passes near many picturesque lighthouses and fishing ports.

What to See and Do

Cape Forchu Lighthouse. Entrance to Bay of Fundy and Yarmouth Harbour. Route travels along rocky coastline and through colorful fishing villages. County park, picnicking. (Daily) On Cape Forchu Island, 7 mi (11 km) SW, linked by causeway to mainland. **Free.**

Ferry terminal.

The CAT. Advance reservations required. Passenger and car ferry service to Bar Harbor, ME. (June-Oct) For reservations, rates, schedule, contact Bay Ferries, 888/249-7245.

MS Scotia Prince. Advance reservations recommended. Passenger and car service between Yarmouth, NS and Portland, ME. (May-Oct, daily) For rates, reservations, schedule, contact Prince of Fundy Cruises, PO Box 4216, Portland, ME 04101; 207/775-5616, 902/775-5611 or 800/341-7540 (Canada & US exc ME), 800/482-0955 (ME). ¢¢¢¢-¢¢¢¢¢

Firefighters' Museum of Nova Scotia. Permanent display of history of firefighting service, including hand pumps, steamers, horse-drawn apparatus. Gift shop. (July-Aug, daily; rest of yr, daily exc Sun) 451 Main St. Phone 902/742-5525. ¢ In the museum is

National Exhibit Centre. Traveling exhibits change every six wks. Contact museum for schedule.

Frost Park. First town cemetary. Gazebo, fountain. Picnicking. Overlooks Yarmouth Harbour, on Water St.

Isaak Walton Killam Library. Unique memorial wall in park behind building. 405 Main St, between Parade & Grand Sts. Phone 902/742-5040.

Public wharves. Center of fishing fleet where herring seiners, inshore and offshore scallop draggers, Cape Island boats can be seen. On Yarmouth Harbour, on each side of BAY Ferry Terminal.

Yarmouth Arts Regional Centre. Center for visual and performing arts for southwestern Nova Scotia (356-seat capacity). Summer theatre, drama, musical comedy, concerts, art shows, courses, workshops, seminars. 76 Parade St. Phone 902/742-8150. ¢¢¢¢

Yarmouth County Museum. Displays history of county with emphasis on Victorian period. Features marine exhibits, period rms, blacksmith shop, stagecoach. Of special interest is a runic stone, found near Yarmouth Harbour in 1812, bearing clear inscription alleged to be left by Leif Ericson on voyage in 1007; Yarmouth Lighthouse lens. (June-Sept, daily; rest of yr, Tues-Sat; closed hols) 22 Collins St. Phone 902/742-5539. ¢

Annual Events

Festival Acadien de Wedgeport. Parade, costumes. Talent show, concerts, music. During Canada Day wk.

Seafest. Sporting events, entertainment, cultural productions; parade, Queen's Pageant. Fish feast; dory races. Phone 902/742-7585. Mid-July.

Western Nova Scotia Exhibition. Exhibition grounds. Animal judging, equestrian events, agricultural displays, craft demonstrations and exhibits, midway and entertainment; Canada/US ox hauls. Early Aug.

Yarmouth Cup Races. International yacht race; dockside entertainment. Windsurfing races; small craft races. Labour Day wkend.

Motels

★ ★ **BEST WESTERN MERMAID.** (545 Main St, Yarmouth NS B5A 1J6) 902/742-7821; res: 800/772-2774; FAX 902/742-2966. E-mail kelley@fox.nstn.ca. 45 rms, 2 story, 5 kits. No A/C. June-Oct: S, D

$99-$110; each addl $8; kit. units $110-$135; under 18 free; lower rates rest of yr. Crib $6. Pet accepted, some restrictions. TV; cable. Heated pool. Restaurant nearby. Ck-out 11 am. Coin lndry. Business center. Some refrigerators. Deep-sea fishing arranged. Cr cds: A, C, D, DS, ER, JCB, MC, V.

🐾 ≋ ⋈ 🔥 SC 🚶

★ ★ **CAPRI.** (8 Herbert St, Yarmouth NS B5A 1J2) off Main St. 902/742-7168; FAX 902/742-2966; res: 800/772-2774. E-mail kelley@fox.nstn.ca. 35 rms, some A/C, 2 story. S, D $89-$99; each addl $6; suites $95-$135. Crib $6. TV; cable (premium). Pool privileges. Complimentary continental bkfst. Restaurant adj 11:30 am-10 pm. Bar to 2 am. Ck-out 11 am. Business servs avail. Refrigerators avail. Balconies. Cr cds: A, C, D, DS, ER, JCB, MC, V.

🐾 ≋ ⋈ 🔥 SC 🚶

★ **LA REINE.** (RR 1, Box 950, Yarmouth NS B5A 4A5) 2 mi N on NS 1. 902/742-7154; res: 800/565-5093. 23 rms. No A/C. July-Aug: S $54, D $60-$64; each addl $6; under 12 free; lower rates June, Sept-mid-Oct. Closed rest of yr. Crib free. TV; cable (premium). Heated pool. Complimentary coffee in lobby. Restaurant adj 8 am-10 pm. Ck-out 11 am. Business servs avail. Picnic tables. On Doctors Lake. Cr cds: A, D, DS, ER, MC, V.

≋ 🔥

✔ ★ **LAKELAWN.** (641 Main St, Yarmouth NS B5A 1K2) 902/742-3588; FAX 902/942-3588. 31 rms, 2 story. No rm phones. July-Sept: S $50; D $60; each addl $5; under 12 free; lower rates May-June, Oct. Closed rest of yr. Crib free. Pet accepted, some restrictions. TV; cable. Full bkfst avail. Ck-out 11 am. Business servs avail. Free airport transportation. Cr cds: A, D, DS, ER, MC, V.

🐾 ⋈ 🔥

★ ★ **RODD COLONY HARBOUR INN.** (6 Forest St, Yarmouth NS B5A 3K7) at ferry terminal. 902/742-9194; FAX 902/742-6291; res: 800/565-7633. E-mail rodds@rodd-hotels.ca; web www.rodd-hotels.ca. 65 rms, 4 story, 8 suites. May-Sept: S $80; D $90; under 16 free; suites $101; lower rates rest of yr. Pet accepted. TV; cable, VCR avail (movies). Restaurant 7 am-11 pm. Rm serv. Bar noon-midnight. Meeting rms. Business servs avail. Valet serv. Airport transportation. Health club privileges. Microwaves avail. Cr cds: A, D, DS, ER, MC, V.

D 🐾 ✈ ⋈ 🔥 SC

★ ★ **VOYAGEUR.** (RR1, Yarmouth NS B5A 4A5) 2½ mi NE on Hwy 1. 902/742-7157; FAX 902/742-1208; res: 800/565-5026. 33 rms, 4 kits. Mid-June-mid-Sept: S, D $64; each addl $8; kits. $62-$82; family rates; lower rates rest of yr. Crib $6. TV; cable. Restaurant 7 am-10 pm. Ck-out 11 am. Business center. Whirlpool. Microwaves avail. Overlooks Doctors Lake. Cr cds: A, DS, ER, MC, V.

D ⋈ 🔥 SC 🚶

Hotel

★ ★ ★ **RODD GRAND HOTEL.** (417 Main St, Yarmouth NS B5A 4B2) near Municipal Airport. 902/742-2446; FAX 902/742-4645; res: 800/565-7633. E-mail rodds@rodd-hotels.ca; web www.rodd-hotels.ca. 138 air-cooled rms, 7 story. June-Oct: S, D $95-$105; each addl $10; suites $120-$130; under 16 free; lower rates rest of yr. Crib free. Pet accepted. TV; cable. Indoor pool. Restaurants 6:30 am-9 pm. Bar 11-1 am. Ck-out 11 am. Meeting rms. Business center. In-rm modem link. Shopping arcade. Free airport, bus depot transportation. Exercise equipt. Microwaves avail. Cr cds: A, C, D, ER, MC, V.

D 🐾 ✈ ✈ ⋈ ⋈ SC 🚶

Inn

★ ★ ★ **THE MANOR.** (Hebron NS B0W 1X0) 5 mi N on Hwy 1E. 902/742-2487; res: 888/626-6746; FAX 902/742-8094. E-mail manor inn@fox.nstn.ca; web www.nsonline.com/manorinn. 54 rms, 2 story. Mid-June-Sept: S, D $72-$107; under 16 free; lower rates rest of yr. Crib $12.

Pet accepted. TV; cable, VCR avail (movies). Heated pool. Dining rm 7-11 am, 5:30-9:30 pm. Sun brunch 11 am-2 pm. Rm serv. Ck-out 11 am, ck-in 2 pm. Business servs avail. Tennis. Lawn games. Microwaves avail. Some balconies. Picnic tables. Rms in colonial-style inn (ca 1920), coach house and motel building; antiques. Nine landscaped acres on Doctor's Lake; private dock. Cr cds: A, C, D, DS, ER, MC, V.

Restaurants

★ ★ **AUSTRIAN INN.** *(3 mi E on Hwy 101, Yarmouth NS) exit 103.* 902/742-6202. Continental menu. Specializes in seafood, veal. Own desserts. Hrs: 11 am-10 pm; Mon, Tues, Sun to 9 pm; Sun brunch to 2 pm. Closed mid-Dec-Mar. Res accepted. No A/C. Bar. Semi-a la carte: lunch $5.35-$19.85, dinner $9.65-$19.85. Sun brunch $11.50. Child's meals. Cr cds: A, MC, V.

✔★ **CHINA COURT.** *(67 Starrs Rd, Yarmouth NS B5A)* 902/742-9128. Chinese menu. Hrs: 11 am-10 pm; Fri, Sat to midnight; Sun 11:30 am-9 pm; Sun brunch to 2:30 pm. Closed major hols. Res accepted. Bar. Semi-a la carte: lunch $3.99-$7.75, dinner $2-$14. Sun brunch $5.95-$10.95. Child's meals. Chinese decor. Cr cds: A, JCB, MC, V.

★ **PRINCE ARTHUR STEAK & SEAFOOD HOUSE.** *(73 Starrs Rd, Yarmouth NS B5A 2T6)* 902/742-1129. Canadian menu. Specializes in T-bone steak, shrimp, lobster. Hrs: 11 am-9:30 pm; Sun 11 am-2 pm, 5-9 pm. Closed Dec 25. Res accepted. Bar to 2 am. Semi-a la carte: bkfst, lunch $4.99, dinner $9.95-$24.95. Sun brunch $9.95-$11.95. Child's meals. Entertainment. Family-owned. Cr cds: A, D, DS, ER, MC, V.

Province of Ontario

Pop 9,101,690 **Land area** 412,582 sq mi (1,068,175 sq km)
Capital Toronto **Web** www.ontario-canada.com
Information Ministry of Economic Development, Trade and Tourism, Queen's Park, Toronto M7A 2E1; 800/ONTARIO.

Although first explored by Samuel de Champlain in the 17th century, the Ontario region was not heavily settled until the 18th century by Loyalist refugees from the American Revolution. British settled in what was to become Ontario while French populated Québec. Two territories were formed following the battle of 1759; in 1867 they became provinces in the Dominion of Canada.

This vast province can be divided into northern and southern Ontario; the far northern wilderness dominated by lakes, forests and logging camps; the southern agricultural and industrial section inhabited by nine-tenths of the population. The province is easily accessible from many points across the United States, with each area offering exciting and beautiful sights for the traveler.

Certainly one of the most spectacular sights is Niagara Falls. Cosmopolitan Toronto, the provincial capital, and Ottawa, the country's capital, offer the tourist a wide spectrum of experiences including theater, fine restaurants, galleries, museums and recreational facilities. The Stratford Festival in Stratford, the Shaw Festival in Niagara-on-the-Lake and Upper Canada Village in Morrisburg are not to be missed.

Ontario is also known for its many recreational areas, such as Algonquin and Quetico provincial parks and St Lawrence Islands National Park. To the north lie Sudbury and Sault Ste Marie; to the northwest, Thunder Bay, Fort Frances and Kenora, offering a variety of wilderness activities including canoeing, fishing and hunting. Perhaps more appealing than any one attraction is the vast, unspoiled nature of the province itself. More than 400,000 lakes and magnificent forests form a huge vacationland just a few miles from the US border, stretching all the way to Hudson Bay.

Ontario lies mostly within the Eastern Time Zone. Travelers should note that fees are charged at international bridges, tunnels and ferries.

In addition to national holidays, Ontario observes Simcoe Day (1st Monday in August).

Safety belts are mandatory for all persons anywhere in vehicle. Children under 40 pounds in weight must be in an approved safety seat anywhere in vehicle.

Brantford (E-6)

(See also Hamilton, Stratford)

Founded 1784 **Pop** 81,290 **Elev** 815 ft (248 m) **Area code** 519 **E-mail** tourism@city.brantford.on.ca
Information Tourism Brantford, 1 Sherwood Dr, N3T 1N3; 519/751-9900 or 800/265-6299.

Brantford is located in the heart of southwestern Ontario along Grand River, a Canadian Heritage River. Captain Joseph Brant, leader of the Iroquois First Nations, crossed the river in 1784. It was through Native and European settlements Brantford was born. Brantford is equally famous as the place where Alexander Graham Bell lived and invented the telephone.

What to See and Do

Bell Homestead. The house is furnished just as it was when Alexander Graham Bell lived here in the 1870s. Also located here are the first telephone office and artifacts housed in a display center. (Daily exc Mon; closed Tues following Mon hols) 94 Tutela Heights Rd. Phone 519/756-6220. ¢

Brant County Museum. Collection of Native American artifacts, life histories of Captain Joseph Brant and Pauline Johnson. Also displays of pioneer life in Brant County, including Brant Square & Brant Corners, where former businesses are depicted. (Wed-Sat; also Sun June-Aug; closed Jan 1, Thanksgiving, Dec 25) 57 Charlotte St. Phone 519/752-2483. ¢

Glenhyrst Art Gallery of Brant. Gallery with changing exhibits of paintings, sculpture, photography and crafts surrounded by 16-acre (7-hectare) estate overlooking the Grand River. Beautiful grounds and nature trail. (Daily exc Mon; closed major hols) 20 Ava Rd. Phone 519/756-5932. **Free.**

Her Majesty's Royal Chapel of the Mohawks (1785). The first Protestant church in Ontario, the "Mohawk Chapel" is the only Royal Native Chapel in the world belonging to Six Nations people. (May-June, Wed-Sun afternoons; July-Labour Day, daily; early Sept-mid-Oct, Sat & Sun afternoons) 190 Mohawk St. Phone 519/445-4528. ¢¢

Myrtleville House Museum (1837). Georgian-style house is one of the oldest in Brant County; original furniture of the Good family, who lived here for more than 150 yrs. On 5½ acres (2 hectares) of parkland. Picnicking. (Mid-Apr-mid-Sept, daily exc Mon; closed hols) 34 Myrtleville Dr. Phone 519/752-3216. ¢

Riverboat Cruises. Big Creek Boat Farm. Dinner cruises on the Grand River. (Mid-May-Sept; reservations required) ON 54, 4 mi (6.4 km) W of Caledonia. Phone 905/765-4107. ¢¢¢¢

Sanderson Centre for the Performing Arts. This 1919 vaudeville house has been restored and transformed to a theater featuring music, dance and dramatic performances. 88 Dalhousie St. Phone 519/758-8090 or 800/265-0710 for schedule and ticket information.

Woodland Cultural Centre. Preserves and promotes culture and heritage of First Nations of eastern woodland area. Education, research and museum programs; art shows, festivals. (Daily; closed major hols) 184 Mohawk St. Phone 519/759-2650. Museum ¢¢

Annual Events

Riverfest. Three-day festival celebrates the Grand River. Entertainment, fireworks, crafts. Children's activities. Phone 519/751-9900. Last wkend May.

International Villages Festival. Ethnic villages celebrate with ethnic folk dancing, pageantry and food. Early July.

Six Nations Native Pageant. Forest Theatre, Sour Springs Rd, at Six Nations reserve. Six Nations people reenact their history and culture in natural forest amphitheater. Phone 519/445-4528. Fri, Sat. First 3 wkends Aug.

Six Nations Native Fall Fair. Ohsweken Fairgrounds. Native dances, authentic craft and art exhibits. Phone 519/445-4528. Wkend after Labour Day.

Motels

★ ★ **BEST WESTERN-BRANT PARK INN.** (19 Holiday Dr, Brantford ON N3T 5W5) Park Rd exit. 519/753-8651; FAX 519/753-2619. E-mail kbrown@bfree.on.ca; web www.bestwestern.com/thisco/bw/66036/66036_b.html. 115 rms, 2 story. June-Sept: S $64.95; D $77.95; each addl $7; under 12 free; lower rates rest of yr. Crib free. TV; cable. Heated pool; wading pool, whirlpool, lifeguard. Playground. Restaurant 6:30 am-9:30 pm. Rm serv. Ck-out 11 am. Meeting rms. Business servs avail. In-rm modem link. Bellhops. Valet serv. Exercise equipt; sauna. Private patios; some balconies. Cr cds: A, D, DS, ER, MC, V.

★ ★ **DAYS INN.** (460 Fairview Dr, Brantford ON N3R 7A9) 519/759-2700; FAX 519/759-2089; res: 800/329-7466. Web www.daysinn.com/daysinn.html. 75 rms, 2 story. Apr-Oct: S $56.95; D $66.95; each addl $7; under 12 free; wkly, wkend rates; lower rates rest of yr. Crib free. Pet accepted. TV; cable (premium). Pool privileges. Complimentary coffee in rms. Restaurant 7-1 am. Ck-out 11 am. Meeting rms. Business servs avail. In-rm modem link. Health club privileges. Cr cds: A, D, DS, ER, JCB, MC, V.

★ ★ **RAMADA INN.** (664 Colborne St, Brantford ON N3S 3P8) 519/758-9999; res: 800/272-6232; FAX 519/758-1515. Web www.ramada.ca. 98 rms, 2-3 story. No elvtr. May-Sept: S, D $79-$105; each addl $5; under 18 free; family rates; package plans; lower rates rest of yr. Crib free. TV; cable (premium), VCR avail. Complimentary coffee in rms. Restaurant 6:30 am-10 pm. Rm serv. Bar 11-2 am. Ck-out noon. Meeting rms. Business servs avail. In-rm modem link. Bellhops. Valet serv. Sundries. Coin lndry. Tennis privileges. Golf privileges. Downhill ski 6 mi; x-country ski 1 mi. Exercise equipt; sauna. Indoor pool; poolside serv. Game rm. Microwaves avail. Many balconies. Cr cds: A, D, ER, JCB, MC, V.

Restaurant

★ ★ **OLDE SCHOOLHOUSE.** (Hwy 2W & Powerline Rd W, Brantford ON N3T 5M1) 519/753-3131. Canadian, European cuisine. Specializes in steak, seafood. Hrs: 11:30-1 am; Sat from 5 pm; Sun brunch 11 am-3 pm. Closed Dec 25. Res accepted; required Sat. Bar. Semi-a la carte: lunch $6.95-$12.95, dinner $18.95-$26.95. Complete meals: dinner (Mon-Fri) $12.95. Sun brunch $10.95. Piano lounge. Restored 1850s schoolhouse; antiques, pioneer and school memorabilia. Cr cds: A, D, ER, MC, V.

Brockville (C-10)

(See also Alexandria Bay (Thousand Islands) NY, and Ogdensburg (Thousand Islands), NY)

Settled 1784 **Pop** 21,000 (est) **Elev** 300 ft (91 m) **Area code** 613 **E-mail** dpaul.brockville.com **Web** www.brockville.com

Information Tourism Office, 1 King St West, PO Box 5000, K6V 7A5; 613/342-8772 ext 430.

Settled by United Empire Loyalists, the town was known as Elizabethtown until 1812 when it was named Brockville after Major General Sir Isaac Brock. It was incorporated as a town in 1832, the first in Ontario. Brockville is the eastern gateway to the Thousand Islands on the St Lawrence River. It is home to the oldest railway tunnel in Canada which runs one quarter of a mile under the city to the riverfront. The city features many Victorian homes along with a historic downtown business section with numerous buildings more than 100 years old.

What to See and Do

Brockville Museum. Devoted to history surrounding the city. Exhibits, workshops, afternoon teas. 5 Henry St. Phone 613/342-4397. ¢¢¢

Thousand Island Cruises. Aboard the *General Brock.* Shallow-draft boat makes trips (1 hr) through heart of the region, including Millionaires Row and many smaller channels inaccessible to larger boats. (May-late Oct, daily) 14 mi (23 km) W via Hwy 401 to 1000 Islands Pkwy. Phone 613/659-3402 or 800/563-8687. ¢¢¢¢

Annual Events

Great Balloon Rodeo. Mid-June.

Riverfest. Waterfront. Mid-June-early July.

Poker Run. Mid-Aug.

Motels

★ ★ **BEST WESTERN WHITE HOUSE.** (1843 Hwy 2 E, Brockville ON K6V 5T1) 1½ mi E on ON 2. 613/345-1622; FAX 613/345-4284. 56 rms. S $67; D $72-$77; each addl $5. Crib $5. Pet accepted. TV. Heated pool. Complimentary continental bkfst. Complimentary coffee in rms. Restaurant 6:30 am-2 pm, 5-9 pm. Ck-out 11 am. Meeting rms. Business servs avail. In-rm modem link. Sundries. Picnic tables. Cr cds: A, C, D, DS, ER, MC, V.

★ **DAYS INN.** (160 Stewart Blvd, Brockville ON K6V 4W6) Hwy 401 exit 696. 613/342-6613; FAX 613/345-3811. 56 rms, 2 story. Mid-June-mid-Oct: S $57-$64; D $72-$74; each addl $7; under 17 free; lower rates rest of yr. Crib free. TV; cable (premium). Pool. Complimentary coffee in rms. Restaurant 11 am-2 pm, 4:30-9 pm. Bar noon-1 am. Ck-out 11 am. Meeting rms. Business servs avail. Picnic tables. Cr cds: A, C, D, DS, ER, JCB, MC, V.

Hotel

★ ★ ★ **ROYAL BROCK.** (100 Stewart Blvd, Brockville ON K6V 4W3) off OT 401 on OT 29S exit 696. 613/345-1400; FAX 613/345-5402; res: 800/267-4428. 72 rms, 5 story. S $112-$128; D $124-$140; each addl $12; suites $235-$247; studio rms $121-$133; under 16 free. Crib free. TV; cable (premium). Indoor pool; whirlpool, poolside serv. Supervised child's activities. Restaurant 6:30 am-11 pm. Bar 11:30-2 am; entertainment exc Sun. Ck-out noon. Meeting rms. Business servs avail. In-rm modem link. Beauty shop. Tennis. Exercise rm; sauna, steam rm. Massage. Cr cds: A, C, D, DS, ER, JCB, MC, V.

Cornwall (C-10)

(See also Morrisburg; also see Massena, NY)

Pop 46,144 **Elev** 200 ft (62 m) **Area code** 613 **Web**
www.visit.cornwall.on.ca
Information Cornwall and Seaway Valley Tourism, Gray's Creek, PO Box
36, K6H 5R9; 800/937-4748.

Cornwall is a thriving community located on the banks of the St Lawrence
River. It is connected to Massena, New York (see) by the Seaway International Toll Bridge. The Robert H. Saunders Generating Station, one of the
largest international generating stations in the world, is here.

What to See and Do

Inverarden Regency Cottage Museum (1816). Retirement home of fur
trader John McDonald of Garth. Collection of Canadian & English Georgian furniture; houses local picture archives. Tea rm (Sun in summer).
(Apr-mid-Nov, daily; rest of yr by appt) Montreal & Boundary Rds. Phone
613/938-9585. **Free.**

Long Sault Parkway. Six-and-one-half-mi (10-km) causeway loop con-
nects 11 islands in the St Lawrence River between Long Sault and
Ingleside; 1,300 scenic acres (526 hectares) with beaches and campsites.
Toll. 8 mi (13 km) W off ON 2.

United Counties Museum. Old stone house has displays showing early
life of the United Empire Loyalists. (Apr-late Nov, daily) 731 Second St W.
Phone 613/932-2381. **Free.**

Upper Canada Village. 25 mi (40 km) W on ON 2 in Morrisburg (see).

Annual Events

Raisin River Canoe Races. On Raisin River. Mid-Apr.

Worldfest/Festimonde. Cornwall Civic Complex. International folk festival; ethnic music, dancing, displays, costumes. 6 days early July.

Williamstown Fair. Mid-Aug.

Awesome August Festival. Balloon lift-off, Cornfest, performances. Mid-
Aug.

Motel

★ ★ ★ **BEST WESTERN PARKWAY INN.** *(1515 Vincent Massey
Dr (Hwy 2), Cornwall ON K6H 5R6)* 613/932-0451; FAX 613/938-5479. 91
rms, 2 story. S $86; D $110-$145; each addl $6; suites $200; under 18 free.
Crib free. Pet accepted. TV; cable (premium). Pool; whirlpool. Coffee in
rms. Restaurant 6:30 am-10 pm; Sun to 9 pm. Bar 11-2 am. Ck-out noon.
Meeting rms. Business servs avail. In-rm modem link. Valet serv. X-coun-
try ski 2 mi. Exercise equipt; sauna. Refrigerators, some fireplaces. Cr cds:
A, C, D, ER, MC, V.

Fort Frances (F-1)

Pop 8,906 **Elev** 1,100 ft (335 m) **Area code** 807 **E-mail**
thefort@ff.lakeheadu.ca
Information Chamber of Commerce, 474 Scott St, P9A 1H2;
807/274-5773 or 800/820-FORT.

Across the river from International Falls, Minnesota, Fort Frances is a
prosperous paper town and an important border crossing point for visitors
from the United States heading for northwestern Canadian destinations.
"The Fort" is a popular summer resort town. It is also a major fly-in center
for the vast wilderness areas to the north and east, a region of 40,000
lakes.

What to See and Do

Fort Frances Museum. This small museum has changing displays deal-
ing with the indigenous era, the fur trade and later settlement. (Mid-June-
Labour Day, daily; rest of yr, daily exc Sun; closed major hols) 259 Scott
St. Phone 807/274-7891. Summer admission ¢

Industrial tour. Abitibi Consolidated. The paper manufacturing process
is followed from debarking of the logs to the finished paper. (June-Aug,
Mon-Fri by res only) Ages 12 yrs and over only; flat, closed-toe shoes
required. 145 3rd St W. Phone 807/274-5311. **Free.**

Noden Causeway. Excellent island views may be seen from this network
of bridges. E on ON 11.

Pither's Point Park. This beautiful park has a reconstructed fort, logging
tug boat and a lookout tower with a pioneer logging museum at its base.
Tower, fort and boat (mid-June-Labour Day, daily). Campground (fee) with
swimming beach; fishing; boating (rentals adj to park). Playground; fitness
trail; cafe. (Late June-Labour Day) On Rainy Lake. Phone 807/274-5087
or -5502. **Free. Museum** ¢

Annual Events

Culturama Festival. Early May.

Fun in the Sun Festival. Late June.

Motel

★ ★ **LA PLACE RENDEZ-VOUS.** *(1201 Idylwild Dr, Fort
Frances ON P9A 3N1)* 1 mi E on Hwy 11, adj Pither's Point Park.
807/274-9811; FAX 807/274-9553; res: 800/544-9435. 54 units, 1-2 story.
S $85-$90; D $92-$97; each addl $7; under 12 free. Crib free. TV; cable,
VCR avail. Restaurant (see LA PLACE RENDEZ-VOUS). Rm serv. Bar
11-1 am. Ck-out 11 am. Meeting rms. Business servs avail. In-rm modem
link. Whirlpool. Sauna. Some balconies. Picnic tables. On Rainy Lake;
swimming beach. Cr cds: A, MC, V.

Restaurant

★ ★ **LA PLACE RENDEZ-VOUS.** *(See La Place Rendez-Vous
Motel)* 807/274-9811. Specializes in prime rib, walleye. Hrs: 6 am-10 pm;
Fri, Sat to 11 pm. Closed Dec 25. Res accepted. Bar 11-1 am. Semi-a la
carte: bkfst $2.95-$9.95, lunch $4.95-$10.95, dinner $10.50-$19.95.
Child's meals. Outdoor dining. Overlooks Rainy Lake. Family-owned. Cr
cds: A, MC, V.

D

Gananoque (D-9)

(See also Kingston; also see Alexandria Bay, NY, Clayton, NY)

Pop 4,863 **Elev** 300 ft (91 m) **Area code** 613 **E-mail**
gan@post.kosone.com **Web** www.1000islands.on.calgon
Information 1000 Islands Gananoque Chamber of Commerce, 2 King St
E, K7G 1E6; 613/382-3250 or 800/561-1595.

What to See and Do

1000 Islands Camping Resort. Campground area with tent & trailer sites
(hookups, showers, dump station). Pool, playground; nature trails; miniature golf (fee). Store, snack bar. Coin lndry. (Mid-May-mid-Oct, daily)
1000 Islands Pkwy, 5 mi (8 km) E. Phone 613/659-3058. Within the park is

Giant Waterslide. A 175-ft (53-m) water slide. (Mid-June-Labour Day,
daily) Per hour ¢¢

1000 Islands Skydeck. Atop 400-ft (146-m) tower; elevator to three
observation decks. (Early May-late Oct, daily) Between the spans of the

Thousand Islands International Bridge, on Hill Island, Lansdowne. Phone 613/659-2335.   ¢¢¢

Arthur Child Heritage Centre. Historical displays. Gift shop; clothing outlets. Overlooks St Lawrence River. 125 Water St. 613/382-2535. **Free.**

Baskin Robbins-Putt 'N Play. 18-hole miniature golf course. (May-Oct, daily) 787 King St E. Phone 613/382-7888.   ¢¢¢

Gananoque Boat Line. Three-hr tours through the 1000 Islands with a stop at Boldt Castle; snack bar. (Mid-May-mid-Oct; 1-hr trips July-Aug) Water St. Phone 613/382-2146.   ¢¢¢¢

Gananoque Historical Museum. Former Victoria Hotel (1863); parlour, dining rm, bedrm, kitchen furnished in Victorian style. Military and indigenous artifacts; china, glass, 19th- and 20th-century costumes. (June-Oct, daily) 10 King St E. Phone 613/382-4024.   ¢

St Lawrence Islands National Park (see). 14 mi (30 km) E.

Motels

★ ★ **BEST WESTERN PROVINCIAL.** (846 King St E (Hwy 2), Gananoque ON K7G 1H3) 613/382-2038; FAX 613/382-8663. 78 rms. July-Labour Day: S $68-$80; D $78-$98; each addl $6; lower rates Mar-June, after Labour Day-Oct. Closed rest of yr. Crib $6. TV; cable. Heated pool. Restaurant 7:30 am-9:30 pm; off-season to 9 pm. Bar noon-10 pm. Ck-out 11 am. Sundries. Gift shop. Lighted tennis. Some in-rm whirlpools. Cr cds: A, C, D, DS, ER, MC, V.

D ⚐ ⚒ ≋ 🎣 SC

★ ★ **DAYS INN.** (650 King St E, Gananoque ON K7G 1H3) 613/382-7292; FAX 613/382-4387. E-mail daysinn@gananoque.com; web www.daysinn.com. 34 rms, 2 story. Late June-Labor Day: S, D $89-$139; suites $149-$189; under 18 free; lower rates rest of yr. Crib free. TV; cable, VCR avail (movies). Heated pool. Complimentary coffee in rms. Restaurant 8 am-10 pm; off season 11 am-9 pm. Serv bar. Ck-out 11 am. Meeting rms. Business servs avail. Fireplace, in-rm whirlpool in suites. Cr cds: A, C, D, DS, ER, JCB, MC, V.

D ≋ ⚒ ⚐ SC

★ ★ **GANANOQUE INN.** (550 Stone St S, Gananoque ON K7G 2A8) 613/382-2165; res: 800/465-3101; FAX 613/382-7912. 50 rms, 3 story. No elvtr. Early June-early Sept: S, D $95-$165; suites $120-$250; lower rates rest of yr. Crib free. TV; cable. Restaurant 7 am-11 pm. Rm serv. Bar 11:30-2 am, entertainment Thurs-Sat. Business servs avail. Ck-out 11 am. X-country ski 5 mi. Bicycle, boat rentals. Health club privileges. Some in-rm whirlpools. Balconies. Cr cds: A, ER, JCB, MC, V.

⚒ ⚐ ≋ ⚐

Inn

★ ★ ★ **TRINITY HOUSE.** (90 Stone St S, Gananoque ON K7G 1Z8) 613/382-8383; FAX 613/382-1599; res: 800/265-4871 (CAN). E-mail trinity@kingston.net; web www.trinityinn.com. 8 rms, 3 story, 2 suites. No rm phones. S, D $75-$150; suites $135-$190; MAP avail. TV; cable, VCR avail. Complimentary continental bkfst. Dining rm (public by res) sittings from 5:30 pm; closed Mon. Rm serv. Bar. Ck-out 10 am, ck-in 2 pm. Business servs avail. Victorian mansion (1859) built with bricks imported from Scotland. Victorian gardens. Sundeck overlooking waterfalls. Cr cds: MC, V.

≋ ⚐

Restaurant

★ ★ **GOLDEN APPLE.** (45 King St W PB 83 (Hwy 2), Gananoque ON) 613/382-3300. Specializes in prime rib, roast lamb, seafood. Hrs: 11 am-9 pm; Sun brunch to 3 pm. Closed Jan-Mar. Res accepted. Serv bar. A la carte entrees: lunch $5.95-$12.95. Complete meals: dinner $14.95-$29.95. Sun brunch $11.95. Child's meals. Patio dining. Converted 1830 mansion; antiques. Exposed stone walls. Cr cds: A, MC, V.

D ⚐

Hamilton (E-7)

(See also Brantford, Mississauga, St Catharines, Toronto)

Pop 306,434 **Elev** 776 ft (237 m) **Area code** 905 **Web** www.hamilton-went.on.ca
Information Greater Hamilton Visitor and Convention Services, 1 James St S, 3rd Floor, L8P 4R5; 905/546-4222.

Thriving both industrially and culturally, Hamilton is Canada's largest steel center. It is located on Hamilton Harbour, spanned by the majestic Skyway Bridge to Toronto, which offers excellent views of the city.

What to See and Do

African Lion Safari. Drive-through wildlife park; exotic animal and bird shows, demonstrations. Admission includes large game reserves, *African Queen* boat, shows, scenic railway; play areas. Camping (June-Sept, fee). Park (Apr-Oct, daily). W on Hwy 8 between Hamilton & Cambridge, on Safari Rd. Phone 519/623-2620.   ¢¢¢¢

Andrés Wines. Escorted tours and tastings. (Apr-Dec, daily; rest of yr, by appt) Wine shop. 5 mi (8 km) W at Kelson Rd & S Service Rd, in Grimsby. Phone 905/643-TOUR.   ¢

Art Gallery of Hamilton. Collection of more than 8,000 photographs, sculptures and photographs covering several centuries, by American, Canadian, British and European artists. Impressive building; many international, national and regional exhibitions. (Wed-Sun; closed statutory hols) Fee may be higher for some shows. 123 King St W. Phone 905/527-6610.   ¢

Battlefield House and Monument. Devoted to the "Battle of Stoney Creek," this 1795 settler's home and monument honors one of the most significant encounters of the War of 1812. Some rms furnished as a farm home of the 1830s. Guides in period costumes. (Open for tours; mid-May-June & early Sept-mid-Oct, daily exc Sat; July-Labour Day, daily; rest of yr, by appt) QEW exit at Centennial Pkwy, 77 King St in Stoney Creek. Phone 905/662-8458.   ¢

Ben Veldhuis Limited. More than 2 acres (1 hectare) of greenhouses; thousands of varieties of cacti, succulents, saintpaulias and hibiscus; flowering tropical plants. Hibisci bloom all yr. (Daily; closed Jan 1, Dec 25) 154 King St E, off ON 8, W in Dundas. Phone 905/628-6307.   **Free.**

Canadian Football Hall of Fame and Museum. Sports museum and national shrine tracing 120 yrs of history of Canadian football. (Daily; closed Sun in winter & spring) 58 Jackson St W. Phone 905/528-7566.   ¢

Children's Museum. Participatory learning center where children between the ages of 2-13 can expand their sensory awareness of the world. "Hands-on" exhibits; changing theme exhibits. (Daily exc Mon; closed Dec 25, 26, also Jan & Sept) 1072 Main St E. Phone 905/546-4848. Adults free with child. Per child   ¢

Dundurn Castle. Home of Sir Allan Napier MacNab, Prime Minister of the United Provinces of Canada (1854-1856). The 35-rm mansion is restored to its former splendor. Exhibits, programs, special events featured all yr. Castle (late May-Labour Day & Dec, daily; rest of yr, daily exc Mon; closed Jan 1, Dec 25). York Blvd. Phone 905/546-2872.   ¢¢

Hamilton Military Museum. Displays Canadian uniforms, equipment and weapons from ca 1800. (Late May-Labour Day & Dec, daily; rest of yr, daily exc Mon; closed Jan 1, Dec 25) Dundurn Park. Phone 905/546-4974.   ¢

Flamboro Downs. Harness racing (all yr). Grandstand seats 3,000; restaurants, lounges. Confederation Cup race for top 3-yr-old pacers in North America held here (Aug). 967 Hwy 5, W in Flamborough. Phone 905/627-3561.   ¢¢

Hamilton Place. Live theater and concerts featuring international artists in a spectacular cultural center. (All yr) Main St. Phone 905/546-3050.

Hamilton's Farmers' Market. Fresh produce, flowers, meat, poultry, fish, cheese and baked goods are brought from all over the Niagara garden belt. (Tues, Thurs-Sat) 55 York Blvd. Phone 905/546-2096.

Museum of Steam and Technology. An 1859 Pumping Station contains unique examples of 19th-century steam technology; gallery features permanent and temporary exhibits on modern technology; also special events. Guided tours (daily; closed Jan 1, Dec 25). 900 Woodward Ave. Phone 905/546-4797. ¢¢

Royal Botanical Gardens. Colorful gardens, natural areas and a wildlife sanctuary. Rock Garden with seasonal displays; Laking Garden (herbaceous perennials); Arboretum (world-famous lilacs in late May); Rose Garden; Teaching Garden; woodland, scented and medicinal gardens. At Cootes Paradise Sanctuary trails wind around more than 1,200 acres (486 hectares) of water, marsh and wooded ravines. Mediterranean Garden greenhouse wing has particularly interesting displays (fee). Guided tours (fee). Peak period for gardens: May-Sept. (All yr, daily) Information Centre. 680 Plains Rd W at ON 2, 6 & 403. Phone 905/527-1158. ¢¢

Whitehern. Former home of the McQuesten family; 19th-century Georgian-style mansion furnished with original family possessions. Landscaped gardens. (June-Labour Day, daily; rest of yr, Tues-Sun afternoons; closed Jan 1, Dec 25) Jackson St W & McNab Sts. Phone 905/522-2018. ¢¢

Annual Events

Around the Bay Road Race. Canada's oldest footrace (1894). Phone 905/624-0046. Late Mar.

Hamilton International Air Show. Hamilton Civic Airport. Large international air show. Phone 905/528-4425. Mid-June.

Festival of Friends. Musicians, artists, craftsmen, puppets, dance, mime, theater. Phone 905/525-6644. 2nd wkend Aug.

Festitalia. Opera, concerts, bicycle race, fashion shows, ethnic foods. Phone 905/546-5300. Mid-Sept.

Hamilton Mum Show. Gage Park, in greenhouses. More than 6,000 blooms. Phone 905/546-2866. 1st 2 wks Nov.

Motels

✔★ ★ **ADMIRAL INN.** (3500 Billings Ct, Burlington ON L7N 3H6) N via Hwy 2/6 or QEW. 905/639-4780; FAX 905/639-1967. 67 rms, 2 story. S $54.95; D $62.95; each addl $4; under 12 free. Crib free. TV; cable (premium). Restaurant 7 am-11 pm. Bar 11 am-11 pm. Ck-out 11 am. Meeting rms. Business servs avail. Valet serv. Cr cds: A, D, ER, MC, V.

D ⬛ ⬛ SC

✔★ ★ **ADMIRAL INN.** (149 Dundurn St N, Hamilton ON L8R 3E7) 905/529-2311; FAX 905/529-9100. 58 rms, 3 story. S $59.95; D $63.95; each addl $4; suites $79.95; under 12 free. Crib free. TV; cable (premium), VCR avail. Restaurant 7 am-11 pm. Rm serv. Ck-out 11 am. Meeting rms. Business servs avail. Valet serv. Downhill/x-country ski 10 mi. Microwaves avail. Cr cds: A, D, MC, V.

⬛ ⬛ ⬛ SC

★ **DAYS INN.** (1187 Upper James St, Hamilton ON L9C 3B2) 905/575-9666; FAX 905/575-1098. Web www.daysinn.com/daysinn.html. 30 rms, 2 story. Late May-late Sept: S $47-$69; D $55-$89; each addl $7; under 13 free; lower rates rest of yr. Crib free. TV; cable (premium), VCR avail. Complimentary coffee in lobby. Restaurant open 24 hrs. Bar. Ck-out 11 am. Meeting rms. Business servs avail. In-rm modem link. Downhill ski 7 mi. Health club privileges. Some refrigerators; microwaves avail. Cr cds: A, D, DS, ER, MC, V.

⬛ ⬛ ⬛ SC

★ ★ **QUALITY INN.** (175 Main St W, Hamilton ON L8P 1J1) 905/528-0611; FAX 905/528-1130. Web www.qualityinn.com. 57 rms, 2 story. Apr-Sept: S $54.95-$64.95; D $64.95-$74.95; each addl $8; suite $94.29; under 18 free; wkly, hol rates; higher rates wkends (2-day min);

lower rates rest of yr. Crib free. TV. Restaurant 7 am-9 pm. Meeting rms. Business servs avail. In-rm modem link. Downhill/x-country ski 15 mi. Microwaves avail. Cr cds: A, C, D, ER, MC, V.

⬛ ⬛ ⬛ SC

Motor Hotel

★ ★ **VENTURE INN-BURLINGTON.** (2020 Lakeshore Rd, Burlington ON L7S 1Y2) N via Hwy 2/6 or QEW. 905/681-0762; FAX 905/634-4398; res: 800/486-8873. Web www.ventureinns.com. 122 rms, 7 story. S $95; D $105; each addl $10; suites $159; under 18 free. Crib free. Pet accepted, some restrictions. TV. Indoor pool; whirlpool. Continental bkfst. Restaurant adj 7-2 am; Sat, Sun 9-midnight. Bar; entertainment. Meeting rms. Business servs avail. Valet serv. Sauna. Sun deck. Picnic tables. Opp lake, beach. Cr cds: A, D, DS, ER, MC, V.

D ⬛ ⬛ ⬛ ⬛ ⬛ ⬛ SC

Hotels

★ ★ **HOWARD JOHNSON ROYAL CONNAUGHT.** (112 King St E, Hamilton ON L8N 1A8) 905/546-8111; FAX 905/546-8144. 206 rms, 11 story. S $99; D $109; each addl $10; suites from $139; under 18 free; wkend rates. Crib free. Pet accepted. TV; cable (premium), VCR avail. Indoor pool; whirlpool. Coffee in rms. Restaurant open 24 hrs. Rm serv 24 hrs. Bars 11-2 am. Ck-out noon. Meeting rms. Business servs avail. Barber, beauty shop. Exercise equipt; sauna. Some refrigerators, mini-bars; microwaves avail. 124-ft (38-m) pool slide. Cr cds: A, C, D, DS, ER, MC, V.

D ⬛ ⬛ ⬛ ⬛ ⬛ SC

✔★ ★ **RAMADA.** (150 King St E, Hamilton ON L8N 1B2) 905/528-3451; FAX 905/522-2281. 215 rms, 12 story. S, D $69-$110; each addl $10; suites $187.50-$325; under 19 free. Crib free. Pet accepted. TV; cable, VCR avail. Heated pool; wading pool; whirlpool. Restaurant 7 am-9 pm. Bar Fri-Sat 5:30 pm-2 am. Ck-out 11 am. Meeting rms. Business servs avail. Shopping arcade. Barber, beauty shop. Exercise equipt; sauna. Health club privileges. Refrigerators, microwaves avail. Cr cds: A, C, D, DS, ER, MC, V.

D ⬛ ⬛ ⬛ ⬛ ⬛ SC

★ ★ **SHERATON.** (116 King St W, Hamilton ON L8P 4V3) in Lloyd D Jackson Sq. 905/529-5515; FAX 905/529-8266. E-mail shsales@netaccess.on.ca; web www.sheraton.com. 299 units, 18 story. S, D $185-$200; each addl $15; suites from $225; under 17 free; wkend rates. Crib free. Pet accepted. Parking $7.99. TV; cable (premium). Indoor pool; whirlpool. Complimentary coffee in rms. Restaurant 6:30 am-10.30 pm. Rm serv to 1 am. Bar 11-2 am; entertainment. Ck-out noon. Convention facilities. Business center. In-rm modem link. Shopping arcade. Barber, beauty shop. Downhill/x-country ski 4 mi. Exercise equipt; sauna. Health club privileges. Bathrm phones; microwaves avail. Direct access to Convention Centre & Hamilton Place Concert Hall. Cr cds: A, C, D, DS, ER, JCB, MC, V.

D ⬛ ⬛ ⬛ ⬛ ⬛ ⬛ SC ⬛

Restaurants

★ ★ **ANCASTER OLD MILL INN.** (548 Old Dundas Rd, Ancaster ON L9G 3J4) off ON 403 to Mohawk Rd, W, then ½ mi to Old Dundas Rd. 905/648-1827. Continental menu. Specializes in steak, prime rib, fresh seafood. Own baking. Hrs: 11:30 am-2:30 pm, 4:30-8:30 pm; Fri, Sat to 11 pm; Sun to 8 pm; Sun brunch 9 am-2 pm. Res accepted. Bar. Wine list. A la carte entrees: lunch $9.47-$12.97, dinner $16.95-$24.95. Sun brunch $22.97. Child's meals. Pianist wkends. Outdoor dining. Originally a gristmill (1792); tour. Cr cds: A, D, ER, MC, V.

D ⬛

★ ★ **L'ESCARGOT.** (1375 King St E, Hamilton ON L8M 1H6) 905/549-6212. French menu. Specializes in venison, salmon, duck. Hrs: 11:30 am-2 pm, 5:30-10:30 pm. Closed Sun, Mon; most major hols. Res accepted. Serv bar. A la carte entrees: lunch $5.95-$10.95, dinner $16.50-$20.95. French Provincial decor. Cr cds: A, MC, V.

★ ★ ★ **SHAKESPEARE'S DINING LOUNGE.** *(181 Main St E, Hamilton ON L8N 1H2)* 905/528-0689. Continental menu. Specializes in steak, seafood, wild game. Hrs: noon-2:30 pm, 5-10:30 pm; Sat 5-11 pm. Closed Sun; Jan 1, Dec 25. Res accepted. Bar. A la carte entrees: lunch $6.50-$18.95, dinner $13.95-$38.95. Elizabethan decor; antique reproductions. Family-owned. Cr cds: A, C, D, ER, JCB, MC, V.

★ ★ **SIRLOIN CELLAR.** *(14½ James St N, Hamilton ON L8R 2J9)* 905/525-8620. Specializes in steak, lobster, fresh seafood. Hrs: 11 am-2:30 pm, 4:30-10 pm; Sat, Sun from 4:30 pm. Closed most major hols. Res accepted. Bar. Semi-a la carte: lunch $7.95-$15.95, dinner $13.95-$33.95. Cr cds: A, D, ER, MC, V.

Kenora (E-1)

Founded 1882 **Pop** 9,817 **Elev** 1,348 ft (411 m) **Area code** 807 **E-mail** info@lakeofthewoods.com **Web** www.lakeofthewoods.com

Information Lake of the Woods Visitor Services, 1500 Hwy 17E, P9N 1M3; 807/467-4637 or 800/535-4549.

An attractive and prosperous pulp and paper town, Kenora is also a popular resort center and gateway to both the Lake of the Woods area to the south and the wilderness country to the north. Fishing, hunting, boating, sailing and excellent resort accommodations may be found here, along with 14,500 islands and 65,000 miles (104,600 km) of shoreline on the lake. Winter activities include ice fishing, snowmobiling, downhill and cross-country skiing, curling and hockey. The Harbourfront in downtown Kenora hosts weekend summer festivals. There are many indigenous pictographs in the area. As fly-in capital of the country, many visitors pass through Kenora on the way to the wilderness of the north.

What to See and Do

Lake cruises. Lake Navigation, Ltd. The MS *Kenora* makes three 18-mi (29-km) cruises through the many islands and channels of Lake of the Woods (daily). Included is Devil's Gap, with its "spirit rock" painting. Lunch, mid-afternoon and dinner cruises. Restaurant, bar. (Mid-May-early Oct, daily) Harbourfront Wharf. Phone 807/468-9124. ¢¢¢¢

Lake of the Woods Museum. Houses more than 15,000 articles reflecting local, native and pioneer history. (July-Aug, daily; Sept-June, Tues-Sat) 300 Main St. Phone 807/467-2105. ¢¢

Rushing River Provincial Park. Approx 400 acres (160 hectares). Beautiful natural setting with a long and photogenic cascade. Swimming; fishing; boating. Nature, cross-country skiing trails. Picnicking, playground. Camping (fee, reservations). Museum (summer, daily). Park (all yr). 12 mi (20 km) E on Hwy 17 & 4 mi (6 km) S on Hwy 71. Phone 807/468-2501 (winter) or 807/548-4351 (summer). Per vehicle (summer) ¢¢¢

Stone Consolidated. Paper manufacturing process is followed from debarking of logs to the finished product. Ages 12 yrs and over only. Flat, closed-toe shoes required. (June-Sept, Mon & Wed-Fri, by res only) 504 9th St N. Phone 807/467-3000. **Free.**

Annual Events

ESCAPE (Exciting, Scenic, Canadian/American Powerboat Excursion). Lake of the Woods. Four-day event for powerboats to explore the many channels, islands and historic features of the lake. Canadian & US participants meet in vicinity of Flag Island, MN. Early July.

Kenora International Bass Fishing Tournament. 3-day competition. Early Aug.

Kenora Agricultural Fair. Kenora Recreation Centre Complex. Three days of competitions and cultural exhibitions including a midway show. Mid-Aug.

Motels

★ **COMFORT INN.** *(1230 Hwy 17E, Kenora ON P9N 1L9)* 807/468-8845; FAX 807/468-1588. 77 rms, 2 story. Mid-June-mid-Sept: S $70-$90; D $75-$100; each addl $4; under 18 free; lower rates rest of yr. Crib free. Pet accepted. TV; cable. Restaurant nearby. Ck-out 11 am. Business servs avail. Cr cds: A, D, DS, ER, MC, V.

D ✋ ⊠ 🐾 SC

★ ★ **TRAVELODGE.** *(800 Hwy 17E, Kenora ON P9N 1L9)* 807/468-3155; FAX 807/468-4780. 42 rms, 1-2 story, 5 kits. Mid-June-mid-Sept: S $75-$80; D $75-$104; lower rates rest of yr. Crib $6. Pet accepted. TV; cable (premium). 2 pools, 1 indoor; whirlpool. Playground. Restaurant 6 am-11 pm. Rm serv. Bar 11-1 am. Ck-out noon. Meeting rms. Business servs avail. Valet serv. Downhill/x-country ski 6 mi. Exercise equipt; sauna. Health club privileges. Picnic tables. Cr cds: A, D, DS, ER, JCB, MC, V.

D ✋ ⊠ ≋ 🍴 ⊠ 🐾 SC

Hotel

★ ★ **BEST WESTERN LAKESIDE INN.** *(470 1st Ave S, Kenora ON P9N 1W5)* just off Hwy 17 on Lake of the Woods. 807/468-5521; FAX 807/468-4734. 94 rms, 11 story. S $96; D $106; each addl $10; suites $175-$225; under 12 free. TV; cable (premium). Indoor pool. Complimentary coffee in rms. Restaurant 7 am-10 pm. Bar 11:30-midnight. Ck-out 11 am. Meeting rms. Downhill/x-country ski 4 mi. Sauna. On lakeshore. Cr cds: A, C, D, ER, MC, V.

D ✋ ≋ ⊠ 🐾 SC

Kingston (D-9)

(See also Gananoque; also see Alexandria Bay (Thousand Islands), NY, Clayton, (Thousand Islands), NY)

Founded 1673 **Pop** 55,051 **Elev** 305 ft (93 m) **Area code** 613 **E-mail** tourism@kingstonarea.on.ca **Web** www.kingstonarea.on.ca

Information Visitor Welcome Centre, 209 Ontario St, K7L 2Z1; 613/548-4415 or 888/855-4555.

Kingston is a city rich in tradition, and Kingstonians are justly proud of their city's 300-year history. Since July of 1673, when Count Frontenac, Governor of New France, erected a fort on the site of present-day Kingston, the city has played an important part in Canadian history. It was here that the United Empire Loyalists relocated to begin their new life. Kingston also had the honor of being the capital of the United Provinces from 1841-1844. However, because Kingston was vulnerable to attack by water from the United States, the capital was moved to Montréal, and later to Ottawa. Although Kingston did not retain its position as the capital city, its citizens can boast that it was a Kingstonian, Sir John A. Macdonald, who was the first Prime Minister of Canada and who later became known as the Father of Confederation.

Since Fort Frontenac was built in 1673, Kingston has grown and prospered to become a flourishing city. Yet over the years, Kingston has not lost the charm and grace that are unique to the city. In honor of the centennial year a beautiful waterfront area was created in front of City Hall with a new yacht basin.

Located at the eastern end of Lake Ontario where it empties into the St Lawrence, Kingston is Canada's freshwater sailing capital.

What to See and Do

Bellevue House National Historic Site. Italianate villa (1840) was home of Sir John A. Macdonald, first Prime Minister of Canada. Restored and furnished with period pieces. Modern display and video presentation at Visitor Centre. (Apr-Oct, daily; rest of yr, by appt) 35 Centre St. Phone 613/545-8666. **¢¢**

Boat trips.

Canadian Empress. This replica of a traditional steamship cruises St Lawrence and Ottawa rivers on 6 different routes; trips span 4 or 5 nights, some reaching Montréal and Québec City. (Mid-May-Nov) Ages 12 & up. Departs from front of City Hall. Contact St Lawrence Cruise Lines, 253 Ontario St, K7L 2Z4; 613/549-8091 or 800/267-7868 (reservations). **¢¢¢¢¢**

Island Queen. Showboat of the 1,000 Islands. Offers 3-hr river cruises through the Islands. (May-Oct, daily) Departs from Kingston Harbour, downtown. For information and reservations contact Kingston & The Islands Boatline, 6 Princess St, K7L 1A2; 613/549-5544. **¢¢¢¢**

Military Communications & Electronics Museum. Displays history of Canadian Forces branch and aspects of military communications. Collection ranges from early radios to satellites and modern technology; excellent telephone collection. (Mid-May-Labour Day, daily; rest of yr, Mon-Fri; closed hols in winter) Vimy Barracks, 1 mi (1.6 km) E on ON 2. Phone 613/541-5395. **Free.**

City Hall. Built of limestone in 1843-44 while Kingston was the capital of the United Provinces of Canada. (Mon-Fri, daily) 216 Ontario St. Phone 613/546-4291. **Free.**

Confederation Tour Trolley. 50-min, 10-mi (16-km) narrated tour of Kingston. (Victoria Day-Labour Day, daily on the hour; charters avail) Leaves from Confederation Park, 209 Ontario St. Phone 613/548-4453. **¢¢¢**

Fort Henry. One of Ontario's most spectacular historic sites, the present fortification was built in the 1830s and restored during the 1930s. Guided tour; 19th-century British infantry & artillery drills; military pageantry; exhibits of military arms, uniforms, equipment; garrison life activities. Fort (mid-May-late Sept, daily). E at jct Hwys 2 & 15. Phone 613/542-7388. **¢¢¢**

Grand Theatre. Century-old, renovated theater. Live theater, dance, symphonic and children's performances by professional companies and local groups; summer theater (See SEASONAL EVENT). (Daily) 218 Princess St. Phone 613/530-2050.

International Ice Hockey Federation Museum. Displays trace history of hockey from its beginning in Kingston in 1885 to present day. (Mid-June-Labour Day, daily; rest of yr, by appt) 303 York St. Phone 613/544-2355. **¢**

MacLachlan Woodworking Museum (ca 1850). "Wood in the service of humanity" is theme of museum; highlights life of the pioneer farmer in both the field and kitchen, as well as workshops of a cooper, blacksmith, cabinetmaker. (Victoria Day-Labour Day, daily; Mar-mid-May, early Sept-Oct, Wed-Sun) 2993 Hwy 2, 10 mi (16 km) E in Grass Creek Park. Phone 613/542-0543. **¢¢**

Marine Museum of the Great Lakes at Kingston. Ships have been built in Kingston since 1678. This museum explores the tales, adventures and enterprise of "Inland Seas" history. Ship Building Gallery, 1889 Engine Room, with dry dock engines & pumps; artifacts; changing exhibits. Library & archives. The **Museum Ship** *Alexander Henry,* a 3,000-ton icebreaker, is open for tours and bed & breakfast accommodations (Victoria Day-Thanksgiving). (May-Dec, daily; rest of yr, Mon-Fri; closed Dec 25) 55 Ontario St, on the waterfront. Phone 613/542-2261. Each museum **¢¢** One blk away is

Pump House Steam Museum. Displays on steam technology, model trains, small engines. (June 1-Labour Day, daily) 23 Ontario St. Phone 613/542-2261. **¢¢**

Murney Tower Museum (1846). Martello tower is now a museum with exhibits of the area's military and social history. Changing exhibits. (Mid-May-Labour Day, daily) King St at Barrie. Phone 613/544-9925. **¢¢**

Queen's University (1841). (13,000 students) Between Barrie, Union, Collingwood & King Sts. For tours phone 613/545-2217. **Free.** On campus are

Agnes Etherington Art Centre. Changing exhibitions of contemporary and historical art. (Daily exc Mon; closed hols) University Ave & Queen's Crescent. Phone 613/545-2190. **¢**

Geology Museum. Collection of minerals from around the world. (Mon-Fri; closed hols) Miller Hall on Union St. Phone 613/545-6767. **Free.**

Royal Military College of Canada (1876). (800 students) Canada's first military college and first institution of its kind to achieve university status. E of Kingston Harbour on Hwy 2. On grounds is

Fort Frederick & College Museum. Exhibits depict the history of the college and the earlier Royal Dockyard (1789-1853); Douglas Collection of small arms and weapons that once belonged to General Porfirio Díaz, president of Mexico from 1886-1912. (Late June-Labour Day, daily) In large Martello Tower. Phone 613/541-6000 ext 6652 (office) or ext 6664 (museum). **Free.**

Seasonal Event

Kingston Summer Festival. Grand Theatre. Phone 613/530-2050 or 800/615-5666. Late June-Labour Day.

Motels

★ ★ ★ **BEST WESTERN FIRESIDE INN.** *(1217 Princess St (Hwy 2), Kingston ON K7M 3E1)* 613/549-2211; FAX 613/549-4523. 75 rms, 2 story. S, D $96.50-$139; each addl $10; under 17 free; suites $179-$429. Crib free. TV; cable (premium). Heated pool. Restaurant 7 am-11 pm. Rm serv. Bar 11:30-1 am. Ck-out noon. Meeting rms. Business servs avail. In-rm modem link. Valet serv. Sundries. Fireplaces; some in-rm whirlpools. Cr cds: A, C, D, DS, ER, MC, V.

▭ ▭ SC

✔★ **ECONO LODGE.** *(2327 Princess St (Hwy 2), Kingston ON K7M 3G1)* 613/531-8929. 32 rms, 8 kits. May-Labour Day: S $48; D $58-$78; each addl $4; kit. units $4 addl; lower rates rest of yr. Crib $4. Pet accepted; $12/day. TV; cable. Heated pool. Playground. Complimentary coffee in lobby. Restaurant adj 7 am-9 pm. Health club privileges. Ck-out 11 am. Refrigerators. Picnic tables. Grills. Cr cds: A, C, D, ER, MC, V.

▭ ▭ ▭ ▭ ▭ SC

★ ★ **FIRST CANADA INN.** *(First Canada Court, Kingston ON K7K 6W2)* Hwy 401 exit 617 S. 613/541-1111; FAX 613/549-5735; res: 800/267-7899. 74 rms, 2 story. June-Oct 1: S $53.95-$69.95; D $60.95-$76.95; each addl $5; suites $85.95-$125.95; under 12 free; lower rates rest of yr. Crib free. Pet accepted. TV; cable, VCR avail (movies). Complimentary continental bkfst. Complimentary coffee in rms. Restaurant opp 10-2 am. Bar 4 pm-1 am. Coin lndry. Meeting rms. Business servs avail. Refrigerators. Cr cds: A, D, ER, MC, V.

▭ ▭ ▭ ▭ SC

★ ★ **GREEN ACRES.** *(2480 Princess St (Hwy 2), Kingston ON K7M 3G4)* 613/546-1796; FAX 613/542-5521; res: 800/267-7889. 32 rms, 3 kits. July-Aug: S $74-$99; D $77-$115; each addl $6; kit. suites $175; lower rates rest of yr. Crib $6. TV; cable (premium), VCR. Heated pool. Playground. Continental bkfst. Coffee in rms. Ck-out 11 am. Coin lndry. Meeting rm. Valet serv. X-country ski 10 mi. Health club privileges. Lawn games. Refrigerators; fireplace, whirlpool in suites; some microwaves. Picnic tables, gas grill. Cr cds: A, MC, V.

▭ ▭ ▭ ▭ SC

★ **KINGSTON EAST.** *(1488 Hwy 15, Kingston ON K7L 5H6)* 1/2 mi S of ON 401 exit 623. 613/546-6674. 22 rms. Mid-June-mid-Sept: S, D $60-$75; each addl $5; kit. units $10 addl; lower rates rest of yr. Crib $5. TV. Heated pool. Playground. Restaurant 7 am-7 pm. Ck-out 11 am. Sundries. Some refrigerators. Picnic tables, grills. Cr cds: MC, V.

 ▭ ▭

★ **SEVEN OAKES.** *(2331 Princess St (Hwy 2), Kingston ON K7M 3G1)* 613/546-3655; FAX 613/549-5677. 40 rms. June-Oct 1: S $64; D $68-$74; each addl $5; package plans; lower rates rest of yr. Crib free. Pet accepted. Heated pool; whirlpool. Sauna. Playground. Bar. Ck-out 11 am. Coin lndry. Sundries. Lighted tennis. Refrigerators; some in-rm whirlpools. Picnic tables, grills. Cr cds: A, D, DS, ER, MC, V.

Lodge

★ ★ ★ **ISAIAH TUBBS RESORT.** *(RR 1, West Lake Rd, Picton ON K0K 2T0)* approx 40 mi W on Hwy 33 and County Rd 12. 613/393-2090; FAX 613/393-1291; res: 800/267-0525. 60 rms in lodge, inn, many A/C, 12 kit. cabins. No phone in cabins. July-Labor Day: S $95-$200; D $150-$220; each addl $10; kit. suites $150-$200; cabins $650-$900/wk; under 5 free; MAP, conference plan avail; lower rates rest of yr. Crib free. TV. 2 pools, 1 indoor; whirlpool. Playground. Free supervised child's activities (July-Aug); ages 4-12. Dining rm 8-1 am. Bar. Ck-out 11 am, ck-in 4 pm. Coin lndry. Meeting rms. Business servs avail. Tennis. Swimming beach. X-country ski 1 mi. Lawn games. Exercise equipt; sauna. Some refrigerators. Picnic tables, grills. On West Lake, adj Sandbanks Provincial Park. Cr cds: A, D, ER, MC, V.

Motor Hotels

★ ★ **HOWARD JOHNSON CONFEDERATION PLACE.** *(237 Ontario St, Kingston ON K7L 2Z4)* 613/549-6300; FAX 613/549-1508. 94 rms, 6 story. May-late Sept: S, D $99-$160; each addl $10; suites $225-$250; under 18 free; higher rates special events; lower rates rest of yr. Crib free. Pet accepted. TV; cable. Heated pool; whirlpool, poolside serv. Restaurant 7 am-10 pm. Rm serv. Ck-out 11 am. Meeting rms. Business servs avail. Underground free parking. X-country ski 3 mi. Exercise equipt. Health club privileges. On waterfront. Cr cds: A, D, DS, ER, MC, V.

✔★ ★ **TRAVELODGE HOTEL LA SALLE.** *(2360 Princess St (Hwy 2), Kingston ON K7M 3G4)* 613/546-4233; FAX 613/546-0867. 69 rms, 4 story. May-mid-Sept: S, D $72-$90; under 12 free; lower rates rest of yr. Crib free. TV; cable, VCR avail. Indoor pool; whirlpool. Restaurant 6 am-10 pm. Rm serv. Bar 11 am-11 pm. Ck-out noon. Meeting rms. Business servs avail. Sauna. Sundries. Balconies. Cr cds: A, D, DS, ER, JCB, MC, V.

Inns

★ ★ ★ **HOCHELAGA.** *(24 Sydenham St S, Kingston ON K7L 3G9)* 613/549-5534; FAX 613/549-5534; res: 800/267-0525. 23 rms, 3 story. S, D $135-$145; each addl $10; under 5 free; lower rates rest of yr. Crib free. TV; cable (premium). Complimentary continental bkfst. Restaurant nearby. Ck-out 11 am, ck-in 3 pm. Business servs avail. Some balconies. Renovated house (1872); period antiques. Cr cds: A, D, ER, MC, V.

★ ★ ★ **MERRILL.** *(343 Main St E, Picton ON K0K 2T0)* Approx 40 mi W on Hwy 33 to Hwy 49 (Main St). 613/476-7451; FAX 613/476-8283; res: 800/567-5969. 14 rms, 3 story, 2 suites. No elvtr. July-Sept: S, D $85-$125; each addl $10; suites $125; under 3 free; lower rates rest of yr. Crib free. TV; cable (premium). Complimentary continental bkfst. Restaurant 11 am-11 pm. Ck-out 11 am, ck-in 3 pm. Meeting rm. Lawn games. Rms individually decorated with period antiques. Brick Victorian house (ca 1878); built for Edwards Merrill, one of Canada's top barristers. Cr cds: A, D, ER, MC, V.

★ ★ ★ **ROSEMOUNT INN.** *(46 Sydenham St S, Kingston ON K7L 3H1)* 613/531-8844; FAX 613/531-9722. E-mail rosemt@adan.kingston.net.

8 rms, 2 story, 1 cabin. No A/C. No rm phones. S, D $109-$159; each addl $30-$50; cabin $225; wkends, hols (2-day min). Closed Mid-Dec-early Jan. Children over 13 yrs only. Complimentary full bkfst; afternoon refreshments. Ck-out 11 am, ck-in 4 pm. Business servs avail. Luggage handling. Valet serv. Concierge serv. Gift shop. Some street parking. X-country ski 5 mi. Massage. Fireplace. Built in 1850. Victorian decor; antiques. Totally nonsmoking. Cr cds: A, MC, V.

Restaurant

★ ★ **AUNT LUCY'S.** *(1399 Princess St (Hwy 2), Kingston ON)* 613/542-2729. Specializes in steak, seafood, pasta. Hrs: 11:30 am-11 pm. Bar. Semi-a la carte: lunch, dinner $5.95-$19.95. Sun brunch $10.99. Child's meals. Open-hearth grill. Family-owned. Cr cds: A, MC, V.

Kitchener-Waterloo (E-6)

Pop Kitchener, 139,734; Waterloo, 49,428 **Elev** Kitchener, 1,100 ft (335 m); Waterloo, 1,075 ft (328 m) **Area code** 519
Information Visitor & Convention Bureau, 2848 King St E, Kitchener N2A 1A5; 519/748-0800 or 800/265-6959.

The twin cities of Kitchener-Waterloo were settled in the early 1800s by Mennonites, Amish and Germans whose cultural heritage is still clearly visible. Not far to the north in Elmira is the heart of Ontario's Pennsylvania German country, with Maple Sugar Festival and tours of Mennonite country. Although Kitchener and Waterloo are separate cities, each takes pride in the achievements of the other. A vigorous spirit of youth and industry pervades both cities, making a visit to the Kitchener-Waterloo area a pleasure for any traveler.

What to See and Do

Bingeman Park. Recreation center on banks of Grand River; swimming (pool, wave pool), watersliding, bumper boats; go-cart track, arcade, roller skating, miniature golf, golf driving range; batting cages; cross-country skiing; picnicking, restaurant; playground; camping. Park (summer, daily; also spring & fall, weather permitting). Campgrounds & restaurant (all yr, daily). Fee for some activities. 1380 Victoria St N, Kitchener. Phone 519/744-1555.

Doon Heritage Crossroads. Re-creation of early 20th-century village (ca 1915) includes museum, grocery store, post office/tailor shop, blacksmith, church, two farms and several houses. (May-late Dec, daily; closed Dec 23) Hwy 401 exit 275, Homer Watson Blvd. Phone 519/748-1914 or 519/575-4530. ¢¢¢

Farmers' Market. More than 100 vendors sell fresh produce, meat, cheese and handicrafts. Mennonite specialties featured. (All yr, Sat; mid-May-mid-Oct, also Wed). Market Square, Frederick & Duke Sts, downtown Kitchener. Phone 519/741-2287. **Free.**

Glockenspiel. Canada's first glockenspiel tells fairy tale of Snow White. Twenty-three bells form the carillon. Performance lasts 15 min (4 times daily). King & Benton Sts.

Joseph Schneider Haus. Pennsylvania German Mennonite house (1820), one of area's oldest homesteads, restored and furnished; "living" museum with costumed interpreters; daily demonstrations. Adj Heritage Galleries, including Germanic folk art; exhibits change every 3 months. (Victoria Day-Labour Day, daily; rest of yr, daily exc Mon; closed Jan 1, Dec 25, 26) 466 Queen St S, Kitchener. Phone 519/742-7752. ¢

Kitchener-Waterloo Art Gallery. Six exhibition areas cover all aspects of the visual arts. Gift shop. (Daily exc Mon; closed major hols) 101 Queen St N, at The Centre in the Square. Phone 519/579-5860. **Free.**

Laurel Creek Conservation Area. Approx 750 acres (305 hectares) of multipurpose area. Dam, swimming beach, boating (no motors), hiking, sports fields, camping (fee), picnicking, reforested areas and bird-watching. (May-mid-Oct) NW corner of Waterloo, bounded by Westmount Rd, Conservation Dr & Beaver Creek Rd. Phone 519/884-6620. **¢¢**

■ **Museum & Archive of Games.** Collection includes over 3,500 games. Many "hands-on" exhibits drawn from collection ranging from Inuit bone games to computer games. Exhibits change every 4 months. Archive contains documents pertaining to games and game-playing. (Tues-Thurs & Sun; closed univ hols) B.C. Matthews Hall, University of Waterloo. Phone 519/888-4424. **Free.**

The Seagram Museum. Complex is housed in century-old, renovated barrel warehouse and is devoted to history and technology of the wine and spirits industry; restaurant. (May-Dec, daily; rest of yr, daily exc Mon; closed Jan 1, Dec 25) 57 Erb St W, Waterloo. Phone 519/885-1857 or 800/465-8747. **Free.**

Waterloo Park. Log cabin schoolhouse built 1820 surrounded by picnic area and lake; playground. Small zoo and band concerts in summer (Sun). Central St, Waterloo. Phone 519/747-8733. (See ANNUAL EVENTS) **Free.**

Woodside National Historic Site. 528 Wellington St N, Kitchener. Boyhood home of William Lyon Mackenzie King, Canada's 10th prime minister. 1890s Victorian restoration. Interpretive center has theater and display on King's early life and career. Picnicking. (May-Dec, daily; closed winter hols) Phone 519/742-5273. **Free.** Nearby is

Pioneer Memorial Tower. Tribute to industrious spirit of pioneers who first settled Waterloo County. Cemetery on grounds includes graves of several original founders. Excellent view of Grand River. (May-Oct) **Free.**

Annual Events

Waterloo County Quilt Festival. Quilt exhibits, displays, workshops and demonstrations. Phone 800/265-6959. 9 days mid-May.

Sounds of Summer Music Festival. Waterloo Park. 3 days mid-June.

White Owl Culture Pow-Wow. Celebration of North American Aboriginal Culture in Waterloo Park. Phone 519/743-8635. Mid-June.

Busker Carnival Festival. International showcase of street performers. Phone 519/747-8738. Late Aug.

Wellesley Apple Butter & Cheese Festival. Pancake breakfast, farmers' market; free tours of farms, cider mill; horseshoe tournament, quilt auction, smorgasbord dinner, model boat regatta, antique cars & tractors. Phone 519/656-2222. Last Sat Sept.

Motels

★ **COMFORT INN.** *(220 Holiday Inn Dr, Cambridge ON N3C 1Z4)* ON 401 exit ON 24N. 519/658-1100; FAX 519/658-6979; res: 800/228-5150. 84 rms, 2 story. S $59-$80; D $67-$95; each addl $4; under 18 free. Crib free. Pet accepted. TV; cable (premium). Complimentary coffee in lobby. Ck-out 11 am. Business servs avail. Sundries. Downhill/x-country ski 4 mi. Cr cds: A, C, D, DS, ER, JCB, MC, V.

⦿ 🏊 🏊 🦶 SC

★ **DAYS INN.** *(650 Hespeler Rd, Cambridge ON N1R 6J8)* S on ON 24, off Hwy 401. 519/622-1070; FAX 519/622-1512. 119 rms, 2 story. S $74.95; D $78.95; each addl $7; under 17 free. Crib free. Pet accepted. TV; cable (premium), VCR avail. Heated pool. Playground. Ck-out 11 am. Meeting rms. Business servs avail. Valet serv. Sundries. Game rm. Microwaves avail. Cr cds: A, D, ER, JCB, MC, V.

D ⦿ 🏊 🏊 🦶 SC

★ **NEWBURG INN.** *(Hwy 7 & 8 West, New Hamburg ON N0B 2G0)* 10 mi W on ON 7, at ON 8. 519/662-3990. 12 rms. S $50; D $75; each addl $5; suite $75; monthly rates. TV; cable. Complimentary coffee in lobby. Restaurant nearby. Ck-out 11 am. Some refrigerators. Cr cds: A, MC, V.

🔥

Motor Hotels

★★ **CLARION INN.** *(1333 Weber St E, Kitchener ON N2A 1C2)* 519/893-1234; FAX 519/893-2100. 102 rms, 2-4 story. S $89-$109; D $99-$129; each addl $10; under 18 free; higher rates Oktoberfest. Crib free. Pet accepted, some restrictions; $50 refundable. TV; cable. Heated pool; whirlpool, poolside serv. Sauna. Complimentary coffee in rms. Restaurant 7 am-9 pm. Rm serv. Bar 11-1 am; entertainment Thurs-Sat. Ck-out 11:30 am. Meeting rms. Business center. Sundries. Some refrigerators; microwaves avail. Balconies. Cr cds: A, C, D, DS, ER, JCB, MC, V.

D ⦿ 🏊 🏊 🦶 SC 🛩

★★ **HOLIDAY INN.** *(30 Fairway Rd S, Kitchener ON N2A 2N2)* 519/893-1211; FAX 519/894-8518. 182 rms, 2-6 story. S $125.95-$145.95; D $136.95-$156.95; each addl $10; suites $205.95-$305.95; under 19 free. Crib free. Pet accepted. TV; cable (premium). Indoor/outdoor pool; poolside serv. Supervised child's activities (July-Aug). Complimentary coffee in rms. Restaurant 6:30 am-10 pm. Bar 11-1 am. Ck-out noon. Meeting rms. In-rm modem link. Valet serv. Downhill/x-country ski 2 mi. Exercise equipt. Microwaves avail. Private patios, balconies. Cr cds: A, C, D, DS, ER, JCB, MC, V.

D ⦿ 🏊 🏊 🏋 🦶 🔥 SC

★★★ **WATERLOO INN.** *(475 King St N, Waterloo ON N2J 2Z5)* 1 mi N on ON 86. 519/884-0220; FAX 519/884-0321; res: 800/361-4708. Web www.nrzone.com/waterlooinn/. 155 rms, 4 story. S $93; D $103; each addl $12; suites from $125; under 16 free. Crib free. Pet accepted. TV; cable. Indoor pool; whirlpool, poolside serv. Complimentary coffee in rms. Restaurant 7 am-10 pm. Rm serv 24 hrs. Bar 11-1 am. Convention facilities. Business servs avail. In-rm modem link. Valet serv. Sundries. Downhill ski 10 mi; x-country ski 1/2 mi. Exercise equipt; sauna. Game rm. Balconies. Landscaped courtyard. Cr cds: A, D, DS, ER, JCB, MC, V.

D ⦿ 🏊 🏊 🏋 🦶 🦶 SC

Hotels

★★★ **FOUR POINTS BY SHERATON.** *(105 King St E, Kitchener ON N2G 2K8)* at Benton. 519/744-4141; FAX 519/578-6889. 201 rms, 9 story. S, D $119-$139; each addl $10; suites $130-$269; studio rms $79; under 18 free; wkend package. Crib free. Pet accepted, some restrictions. TV; cable. Pool; whirlpool, poolside serv. Complimentary coffee in rms. Restaurant 6:30 am-2 pm, 5:30-10:30 pm. Bar 5 pm-1 am. Ck-out noon. Meeting rms. Business center. In-rm modem link. Free covered parking. Downhill/x-country ski 4 mi. Exercise rm; sauna. Game rm. Miniature golf. Rec rm. Minibars; microwaves avail. Some balconies. Cr cds: A, C, D, ER, MC, V.

D ⦿ 🏊 🏊 🏋 🦶 🦶 SC 🚶

★★ **LANGDON HALL.** *(RR 33, Cambridge ON N3H 4R8)* E on Hwy 8 to Fountain St, turn right to Blair Rd then left to Langdon. 519/740-2100; FAX 519/740-8161; res: 800/268-1898. E-mail langdon@golden.net. 43 rms, 3 story. 2-day min: S, D $229-$269; suites $369; under 10 free. Crib free. Pet accepted, some restrictions; $25. TV; cable (premium), VCR avail. Heated pool; whirlpool, poolside serv. Complimentary continental bkfst. Restaurant (see LANGDON HALL). Rm serv 24 hrs. Bar. Ck-out noon. Meeting rms. Business servs avail. In-rm modem link. Gift shop. Tennis. Downhill ski 4 mi; x-country ski on site. Hiking trail. Exercise equipt; sauna, steam rm. Massage. Rec rm. Lawn games. Balconies. Antebellum-style building in rural setting. Cr cds: A, D, ER, MC, V.

D ⦿ 🏊 🏋 🏊 🏋 🔥

★★ **SUPER 8.** *(730 Hespeler Rd, Cambridge ON N3H 5L8)* S on Hwy 24, at Hwy 401. 519/623-4600; FAX 519/623-2688. 106 rms, 7 story, 11 suites. S $99.99; D $109; each addl $10; suites $119; under 12 free; wkly rates; higher rates Oktoberfest. Crib free. TV; cable (premium). Indoor pool; whirlpool. Sauna. Complimentary continental bkfst. Coffee in rms. Restaurant nearby. Ck-out 11 am. Coin lndry. Meeting rms. Business servs avail. In-rm modem link. Downhill/x-country ski 5 mi. Game rm. Refrigerators; microwaves avail. Cr cds: A, D, DS, ER, MC, V.

★ ★ **WALPER TERRACE.** *(1 King St W, Kitchener ON N2G 1A1) At Queen St.* 519/745-4321; res: 800/265-8749; FAX 519/745-3625. E-mail service@walper.com; web www.walper.com. 63 rms, 5 story, 22 suites. S, D $99; each addl $10; suites $110-$210; under 16 free; wkend rates. Crib free. TV; cable (premium), VCR avail. Complimentary coffee in rms. Restaurant 7:30-1 am. Bar from 11:30 am. Ck-out noon. Business servs avail. Barber, beauty shop. Free parking. Health club privileges. Restored landmark hotel in the heart of downtown; retains air of old-European elegance. Cr cds: A, D, DS, ER, MC, V.

Inn

★ ★ ★ **ELORA MILL.** *(77 Mill St W, Elora ON N0B 1S0) 12 mi N.* 519/846-5356; FAX 519/846-9180. 32 rms, 5 story. S, D $150-$170; each addl $50; suites $220; under 13, $25. TV; cable. Complimentary full bkfst. Restaurant (see ELORA MILL). Bar 4:30 pm-1 am. Ck-out 11:30 am, ck-in 4 pm. Meeting rm. Business servs avail. Valet serv. X-country ski 1 mi. Health club privileges. Some refrigerators, fireplaces. Located in historic pre-Confederation village. Cr cds: A, ER, MC, V.

Restaurants

★ **BARRELS.** *(95 Queen St S, Kitchener ON N2G 1W1)* 519/745-4451. Portuguese, Thai menu. Specialties: mussels, piglet, pepper steak. Hrs: 11:30 am-2 pm, 5-10 pm. Closed Mon; Dec 24, 25. Res accepted. Bar. A la carte entrees: lunch $6.95-$13.95, dinner $10.95-$19.95. Cr cds: A, D, ER, MC, V.

★ ★ **BENJAMIN'S.** *(17 King St, St Jacobs ON N0B 2N0) N on Hwy 86.* 519/664-3731. Contemporary menu. Specializes in beef, pasta, seafood. Hrs: 11:30 am-3 pm, 3-5 pm (tea), 5-9 pm; Thurs-Sat to 10 pm. Closed Jan 1, Dec 25, 26. Res accepted. Bar. A la carte entrees: lunch $6.95-$9.25, dinner $13.50-$21. Re-creation of 1850s country inn; fireplace, artifacts. Cr cds: A, D, ER, MC, V.

★ ★ **CHARCOAL STEAK HOUSE.** *(2980 King St E, Kitchener ON N2A 1A9)* 519/893-6570. Web www.cyberdineout.com. Specializes in steak, spareribs, pigtails. Own baking. Hrs: 11:30-1 am; Sat from noon; Sun 10 am-11 pm. Res accepted. Bar. Wine list. A la carte entrees: lunch $7-$16, dinner $12-$35. Child's meals. Parking. Cr cds: A, C, D, ER, MC, V.

★ ★ **ELORA MILL.** *(See Elora Mill Inn)* 519/846-5356. Regional menu. Own baking. Hrs: 8-10 am, 11:30 am-2 pm, 5-8 pm; Fri, Sat to 9 pm. Res accepted. Bar. A la carte entrees: bkfst $7.95, lunch $8.95-$13.95, dinner $19.95-$29.95. Parking. Restored gristmill (1859). Cr cds: A, MC, V.

★ ★ **LANGDON HALL.** *(See Langdon Hall Hotel)* 519/740-2100. E-mail langdon@golden.net. Specialties: goat cheeze quenelle, roasted veal with tarragon, twice-cooked duck. Hrs: 7-10 am, noon-2 pm, 6-9 pm. Res required. Bar noon-1 am. Wine cellar. A la carte entrees: bkfst $4.75-$7.25, lunch $13.75-$19.75, dinner $12.50-$30. Parking. Outdoor dining. Elegant dining rm overlooking park. Gardens. Cr cds: A, D, ER, MC, V.

★ ★ **STONE CROCK.** *(59 Church St W, Elmira ON N3B 1M8) 9 mi N on Hwy 86.* 519/669-1521. Specializes in spareribs, turkey, cabbage rolls. Salad bar. Hrs: 7 am-8:30 pm; Sun from 11 am. Closed Dec 25. Semi-a la carte: bkfst $1.75-$5.75, lunch $5-$9.50, dinner $8.50-$10.95.

Buffet: dinner $13.25. Sat, Sun brunch $10.95. Child's meals. Parking. Country atmosphere. Gift shop. Cr cds: A, ER, MC, V.

★ ★ ★ **SWISS CASTLE INN.** *(1508 King St E, Kitchener ON N2G 2P1)* 519/744-2391. Swiss, continental menu. Specializes in wienerschnitzel, lobster tail. Own baking. Hrs: 11:30 am-2:30 pm, 4:30-9:30 pm; Sat from 4:30 pm; Sun 4:30-8 pm; early-bird dinner 4:30-6 pm. Closed Mon; also major hols. Res accepted. Bar. Wine list. Semi-a la carte: lunch $6.95-$12.95, dinner $9.95-$17.95. Child's meals. Parking. Fireplace. Swiss bell collection. Cr cds: A, D, ER, MC, V.

★ ★ ★ **WATERLOT.** *(17 Huron St, New Hamburg ON N0B 2G0) 11 mi W via ON 8, behind Royal Bank.* 519/662-2020. E-mail waterlot@sympatico.ca. French menu. Specializes in crab crêpes, duckling. Own baking. Hrs: 11:30 am-2 pm, 5-8:30 pm; Sun 5-7:30 pm; Sun brunch (2 sittings) 11:30 am, 1:30 pm. Closed Mon; Good Friday, Dec 25. Res accepted. Bar. Wine list. A la carte entrees: lunch $7.95-$13.95, dinner $15.50-$28.50. Complete meals: dinner (Sun-Fri) $24. Sun brunch $16.95. Child's meals. Victorian house (1845); guest rms avail. Cr cds: A, D, ER, MC, V.

London (E-5)

Pop 300,000 (est) **Elev** 912 ft (278 m) **Area code** 519 **Web** www.city.london.on.ca
Information Tourism London, 300 Dufferin Ave, N6B 1Z2; 519/661-5000 or 800/265-2602.

Called the "Forest City," London is a busy modern city with charming small-town atmosphere. Located on the Thames River, its street names are similar to those of the other London. A contrast of Victorian architecture and contemporary skyscrapers is prevalent here.

What to See and Do

Double-decker Bus Tour of London. Two-hr guided tour aboard authentic double-decker English bus with stop at Storybook Gardens in Springbank Park and Regional Art Museum. Departs City Hall (Wellington St and Dufferin Ave). (July-Labour Day, daily) Reservations suggested. Phone 519/661-5000 or 800/265-2602. ¢¢¢

Eldon House (1834). Oldest house in town; occupied by same family until donated to the city. Furnished much as it was in the 19th century with many antiques from abroad. Spacious grounds, lawns, brick paths, gardens, conservatory-greenhouse. Guided tours (by appt). (Daily exc Mon; closed Dec 25) 481 Ridout St N. Phone 519/661-5169. ¢¢

Fanshawe Pioneer Village. Living history museum of 24 buildings moved to this site to display artifacts & re-create the life of a typical 19th-century crossroads community in southwestern Ontario. Log cabin, barns and stable; blacksmith, weaver, harness, gun, woodworking and barbershops; general store, church, fire hall, school and sawmill; costumed interpreters. (May-Oct, Wed-Sun; Nov-mid-Dec, daily) Also at Fanshawe Conservation Area is Ontario's largest flood-control structure; swimming, sailing, fishing (walleye), camping, various sports activities and nature trails. NE edge of town; E end of Fanshawe Park Rd. Phone 519/457-1296. ¢¢

Grand Theatre. Contemporary facade houses 1901 theater, built by Colonel Whitney of Detroit and Ambrose Small of Toronto. Restored interior, proscenium arch, murals and cast plasterwork. Professional stock theater (Oct-May). 471 Richmond St. Phone 519/672-8800.

Guy Lombardo Music Centre. Institution housing artifacts belonging to world-famous London-born musician. Exhibits on other big-band era greats. (Mid-May-Labor Day, Thurs-Mon, daily; other times by appt) 205 Wonderland Rd S, in Springbank Park. Phone 519/473-9003. ¢

London Museum of Archaeology. Traces prehistory of southwestern Ontario; more than 40,000 artifacts show how indigenous people lived thousands of yrs before Columbus was born; archaeological and ethnographic exhibits from southwestern Ontario. Gallery, theater and native gift shop. (May-Sept, daily; closed Good Friday, Dec 25) 1600 Attawandaron Rd. Phone 519/473-1360. ¢¢ Also here is

Indian Village. Ongoing excavation and reconstruction of authentic 500-yr-old Neutral village located on original site. (Admission included in Museum fee; May-Sept, daily)

London Regional Art and Historical Museums. Changing exhibits on art, history and culture of the London area; regional, national and international art. (Daily exc Mon; closed Dec 25) 421 Ridout St N. Phone 519/672-4580. **Free.**

London Regional Children's Museum. Hands-on galleries allow children to explore, touch and discover. There are artifacts to touch, costumes to put on, and crafts to make. Children learn about their world, past, present and future; also special events. (Sept-June, Tues-Sat; July-Aug, daily; closed Jan 1, Dec 25) 21 Wharncliffe Rd S. Phone 519/434-5726. ¢¢

Ska Nah Doht Indian Village. Re-created Iroquoian village depicting native culture in southwestern Ontario 800-1,000 yrs ago. Guided tours; slide shows, displays; nature trails; picnicking, group camping. Park (daily). Resource Centre & Village (Canada Day-Labour Day, daily; rest of yr, Mon-Fri). 20 mi (32 km) W via ON 2 in the Longwoods Road Conservation Area. Phone 519/264-2420. Per vehicle ¢¢¢

Storybook Gardens. Family-oriented theme park, children's playworld and zoo, 8 acres (3 hectares) within London's largest park of 281 acres (114 hectares). (Early May-mid-Oct, daily) Springbank Park, Thames River Valley. Phone 519/661-5770. ¢¢

The Royal Canadian Regiment Museum. Displays include artifacts, battle scenes from 1883 to present, weapons and uniforms. (Daily exc Mon; closed hols) Wolseley Hall, Canadian Forces Base. Phone 519/660-5102 or 519/660-5173. **Donation.**

Annual Events

The Air Ontario Air Show. Airport. Flying exhibitions (2-hr show); ground displays. 1st wkend June.

Royal Canadian Big Band Music Festival. Downtown & Wonderland gardens. Live and recorded big band music; part of the Great Canadian Celebration. 1st wkend July.

Home County Folk Festival. Victoria Park. 3-day outdoor music fest. Mid-July.

Dragon Boat Festival. Fanshawe Conservation area. Mid-Aug.

Western Fair. Western Fairgrounds. Entertainment and educational extravaganza; horse shows, musicians, exhibits, livestock shows. 10 days early Sept.

Panorama Ethnic Festival. Throughout city. Open house of ethnic clubs; music, dance, food, crafts. 3 days late Sept.

Motels

★ ★ **BEST WESTERN LAMPLIGHTER INN.** *(591 Wellington Rd, London ON N6C 4R3)* 519/681-7151; FAX 519/681-3271. 126 rms, 2 story. S $79; D $109; each addl $8; suites $119-$209; under 12 free. Pet accepted, some restrictions. TV; cable. Pool. Complimentary coffee in rms. Restaurant 6:30 am-9 pm; Sun to 8 pm. Bar 4 pm-midnight. Ck-out 11 am. Meeting rms. Business servs avail. Some in-rm whirlpools. Private patios, balconies. Picnic tables. Cr cds: A, D, DS, ER, MC, V.

D ✦ ⊠ ⊠ ⅏ SC

✔ ★ ★ **HOLIDAY INN EXPRESS.** *(800 Exeter Rd, London ON N6E 1L5)* exit ON 401 at Wellington Rd N. 519/681-1200; FAX 519/681-6988. 125 rms, 2-3 story, 32 suites. S, D $84; each addl $7; under 19 free; suites $92-$96. Crib free. TV; cable (premium), VCR. Complimentary bkfst. Restaurant adj open 24 hrs. Ck-out 11 am. Meeting rms. Business servs avail. Microwaves avail. Cr cds: A, D, DS, ER, MC, V.

D ⊠ ⅏ SC

★ ★ ★ **RAMADA INN-401.** *(817 Exeter Rd, London ON N6E 1W1)* at ON 401 interchange 186 N. 519/681-4900; FAX 519/681-5065. 124 rms, 2 story. S, D $99-$109; each addl $10; suites $175-$225; under 18 free.

Crib free. TV; cable. Indoor pool; lifeguard (wkends). Complimentary coffee in rms. Restaurant 6:30 am-10 pm; Sat, Sun from 7 am. Rm serv. Bar 11-1 am. Ck-out 1 pm. Meeting rms. Business servs avail. Valet serv. Sundries. Sauna. Health club privileges. Microwaves avail. Cr cds: A, D, DS, ER, JCB, MC, V.

D ⊠ ⊠ ⅏ SC

Hotels

★ ★ ★ **DELTA LONDON ARMOURIES.** *(325 Dundas St, London ON N6B 1T9)* 519/679-6111; FAX 519/679-3957. Web www.deltahotels.com. 250 rms, 20 story. S $189; D $199; each addl $10; suites $250-$450; under 18 free; wkend rates. Crib free. Pet accepted. TV; cable (premium), VCR avail (movies). Indoor pool; wading pool, whirlpool. Supervised child's activities (July & Aug; rest of yr, Fri-Sun); ages 5-12. Coffee in rms. Restaurant 6:30 am-10 pm. Bar to 2 am. Ck-out noon. Meeting rms. Business center. Concierge. Valet parking. Putting green. Exercise equipt; sauna. Health club privileges. Rec rm. Minibars. Some balconies. Luxury level. Cr cds: A, C, D, DS, ER, MC, V.

D ✦ ⊠ ✗ ⊠ ⅏ SC ✈

★ ★ ★ **WESTIN.** *(300 King St, London ON N6B 1S2)* 519/439-1661; FAX 519/439-9672. Web www.westin.com. 331 rms, 22 story. S, D $135-$155; suites $300; under 18 free; wkend rates. Crib free. Pet accepted. TV; cable, VCR avail. Heated pool; wading pool, whirlpool. Restaurant 7 am-11 pm. Bar 11:30-1 am; entertainment. Ck-out 1 pm. Convention facilities. Business servs avail. In-rm modem link. Concierge. Gift shop. Exercise equipt; sauna. Health club privileges. Minibars. Luxury level. Cr cds: A, C, D, DS, ER, JCB, MC, V.

D ✦ ⊠ ✗ ⊠ ⅏ SC

Inn

★ ★ ★ **IDLEWYLD.** *(36 Grand Ave, London ON N6C 1K8)* 519/433-2891; res: 800/267-0525. Web www./someplacedifferent.com. 27 rms, 8 suites. S, D $89-$119; each addl $10; suites $119-$179; under 18 free; wkly rates. Crib free. TV; cable (premium). Complimentary continental bkfst. Ck-out noon, ck-in 3 pm. Business servs avail. In-rm modem link. X-country ski 3 mi. Some balconies. Picnic tables. Victorian mansion (1878); some original decor. Cr cds: A, D, ER, MC, V.

D ⊠ ⊠ ⅏ SC

Restaurants

✔★ **FELLINI KOOLINI'S.** *(153 Albert St, London ON N6A 1L9)* 519/642-2300. Italian menu. Specializes in pizza, pasta. Hrs: 11 am-10 pm; Fri, Sat to midnight; Sun 4:30-10:30 pm. Closed Jan 1, Dec 25, 26. Bar to 1 am. Semi-a la carte: lunch, dinner $7.95-$16.95. Child's meals. Outdoor dining. Italian country inn decor. Cr cds: A, D, ER, MC, V.

⊡

★ ★ **MARIENBAD.** *(122 Carling St, London ON N6A 1H6)* 519/679-9940. Continental menu. Specialties: Wienerschnitzel, beef tartar. Hrs: 11:30 am-midnight. Closed Jan 1, Dec 25. Res accepted. Bar 11:30-1 am. A la carte entrees: lunch $5.95-$10.75, dinner $8.95-$18.95. Child's meals. Atrium dining. Original and reproduction 19th-century furnishings. Murder mystery & dinner 3rd Fri each month. Cr cds: A, MC, V.

D ⊡

★ ★ **MARLA JANE'S.** *(460 King St E, London ON N6B 1S9)* 519/858-8669. Specializes in Cajun dishes. Hrs: 11:30 am-11 pm; Sun 5-10 pm. Closed Mon; Dec 25. Res accepted (dinner). A la carte entrees: lunch $7.25-$12.95, dinner $12.95-$24.95. Herb garden; terrace. Former embassy (ca 1900), Victorian architecture. Stained glass; changing art displays. Cr cds: A, D, ER, MC, V.

⊡

★ ★ **MICHAEL'S-ON-THE-THAMES.** *(1 York St, London ON N6A 1A1)* 519/672-0111. Continental menu. Specializes in table side cooking, châteaubriand, fresh seafood. Hrs: 11:30 am-11 pm; Thurs, Fri to midnight; Sat 5 pm-midnight; Sun, hols 5-9 pm. Closed Jan 1, Labour Day, Dec 25. Res accepted. Bar. A la carte entrees: lunch $5.95-$9.95, dinner $9.95-$24.95. Child's meals. Pianist Sat, Sun. Cr cds: A, D, ER, MC, V.

[D] [symbol]

Mississauga (D-7)

(See also Hamilton, Toronto)

Pop 430,000 **Elev** 569 ft (173 m) **Area code** 905
Information City of Mississauga, 300 City Centre Dr, L5B 3C1; 905/896-5058 or 905/896-5000.

One of the fastest-growing areas in southern Ontario, Mississauga is a part of the greater Toronto area, bordering Lester B. Pearson International Airport.

Motels

✔★ **DAYS INN.** *(4635 Tomken Rd, Mississauga ON L4W 1J9)* 905/238-5480; FAX 905/238-1031. 61 rms, 3 story. No elvtr. S, D $60-$100; each addl $5; suites $150; under 18 free. Crib free. Pet accepted. TV; cable, VCR (movies). Complimentary continental bkfst. Complimentary coffee in rms. Restaurant opp 11:30 am-midnight. Ck-out 11:30 am. Business servs avail. Some refrigerators. Cr cds: A, C, D, DS, ER, JCB, MC, V.

[D] [symbols] SC

★ **HOWARD JOHNSON.** *(2420 Surveyor Rd, Mississauga ON L5N 4E6)* 905/858-8600; FAX 905/858-8574. 117 rms, 2 story. June-Sept: S $69-$74; D $74-$84; each addl $5; under 18 free; package plans; lower rates rest of yr. Crib free. Pet accepted, some restrictions. TV; cable (premium). Complimentary continental bkfst. Complimentary coffee in rms. Restaurant opp open 24 hrs. Ck-out 1 pm. Coin lndry. Meeting rms. Business servs avail. Downhill/x-country ski 15 mi. Game rm. Some refrigerators. Picnic tables. Cr cds: A, D, DS, ER, MC, V.

[symbols] SC

★★ **QUALITY INN-AIRPORT WEST.** *(50 Britannia Rd E, Mississauga ON L4Z 2G2)* 905/890-1200; FAX 905/890-5183. 108 rms, 2 story. S, D $78-$96; each addl $7; suites $123-$149; under 18 free; monthly rates. Crib free. TV; cable (premium). Restaurant 7 am-10 pm. Rm serv. Serv bar 11-1 am. Ck-out noon. Meeting rms. Business servs avail. Exercise equipt; sauna. Refrigerators avail. Cr cds: A, C, D, DS, ER, MC, V.

[D] [symbols] SC

✔★ **TRAVELODGE-TORONTO SOUTHWEST/CARRIAGE INN.** *(1767 Dundas St E, Mississauga ON L4X 1L5)* off Hwy 427. 905/238-3400; FAX 905/238-9457. 85 rms, 2 story. June-Sept: S $70; D $75; each addl $5; suites $125-$150; under 12 free; wkly rates; lower rates rest of yr. Crib $5. TV; cable (premium). Complimentary continental bkfst. Coffee in rms. Restaurant nearby. Ck-out 11 am. Meeting rms. Health club privileges. Many refrigerators. Cr cds: A, D, DS, ER, MC, V.

[D] [symbols] SC

Motor Hotels

★★ **DAYS INN-TORONTO AIRPORT.** *(6257 Airport Rd, Mississauga ON L4V 1E4)* near Lester B. Pearson Intl Airport. 905/678-1400; FAX 905/678-9130. Web www.daysinn.com. 202 rms, 7 story. S $159; D $178; each addl $10; suites $199; under 18 free; wkend rates. Crib free. TV; cable (premium). Indoor pool; whirlpool. Coffee in rms. Restaurant 7 am-midnight. Rm serv. Bar 11 am-1 am. Ck-out noon. Meeting rms. Business servs avail. Bellhops. Gift shop. Barber, beauty shop. Valet serv.

Airport transportation. 18-hole golf privileges. Downhill/x-country ski 20 mi. Exercise equipt; sauna. Balconies. Cr cds: A, C, D, DS, ER, JCB, MC, V.

[D] [symbols] SC

★★ **HOLIDAY INN.** *(2125 North Sheridan Way, Mississauga ON L5K 1A3)* QEW exit Erin Mills Pkwy. 905/855-2000; FAX 905/855-1433. E-mail holinn.miss.qew@sympatico.ca. 151 rms, 6 story, 80 suites. S, D, suites $140-$160; each addl $10; under 19 free. Crib free. TV; cable (premium), VCR avail. Heated pool; poolside serv. Coffee in rms. Restaurant 6:30 am-10 pm. Rm serv 7 am-midnight. Bar 11-1 am. Ck-out 1 pm. Meeting rms. Bellhops. Valet serv. Sundries. Airport transportation. Health club privileges. Wet bars; some in-rm whirlpools; refrigerators, microwaves avail. Cr cds: A, C, D, DS, ER, JCB, MC, V.

[D] [symbols] SC

★★ **HOLIDAY INN-TORONTO WEST.** *(100 Britannia Rd, Mississauga ON L4Z 2G1)* 905/890-5700; FAX 905/568-0868. Web www.holiday-inn.com. 132 air-cooled rms, 6 story. S, D $145; each addl $8; under 20 free. Crib free. Pet accepted, some restrictions. TV; cable (premium), VCR avail. Coffee in rms. Restaurant from 6:30 am. Rm serv. Bar. Ck-out noon. Meeting rms. Business servs avail. In-rm modem link. Valet serv. Free airport transportation. Exercise equipt; sauna. Whirlpool. Refrigerators avail. Cr cds: A, D, DS, ER, JCB, MC, V.

[D] [symbols] SC

★★ **RADISSON-TORONTO/MISSISSAUGA.** *(2501 Argentia Rd, Mississauga ON L5N 4G8)* 905/858-2424; FAX 905/821-1592. 207 rms, 8 story. S, D $155-$165; each addl $10; suites $185; under 18 free; wkend rates. Crib free. TV; cable (premium). Indoor pool; whirlpool. Coffee in rms. Restaurant. Rm serv. Bar 11-1 am. Ck-out noon. Coin lndry. Meeting rms. Business servs avail. In-rm modem link. Bellhops. Valet serv. Sundries. Gift shop. Free airport transportation. Exercise equipt; sauna. Refrigerators; bathrm phone in suites; microwaves avail. Picnic tables. Cr cds: A, D, DS, ER, JCB, MC, V.

[D] [symbols] SC

★ **TRAVELODGE-TORONTO WEST.** *(5599 Ambler Dr, Mississauga ON L4W 3Z1)* SW of jct ON 401, Dixie Rd. 905/624-9500; FAX 905/624-1382. 225 rms, 6 story. S $59; D $68; under 18 free; suites $89.95. Crib free. Pet accepted. TV; cable. Indoor pool; whirlpool. Complimentary coffee in rms. Restaurant 7-1 am. Bar from noon. Ck-out 11 am. Guest lndry. Meeting rms. Business servs avail. Valet serv. Sundries. Cr cds: A, D, DS, ER, JCB, MC, V.

[D] [symbols] SC

Hotels

★★★ **DELTA MEADOWVALE RESORT & CONFERENCE CENTER.** *(6750 Mississauga Rd, Mississauga ON L5N 2L3)* in Meadowvale Business Park. 905/821-1981; FAX 905/542-4036; res: 800/268-1133 (CAN), 800/877-1133 (US). Web www.deltahotels.com. 374 rms, 15 story. S, D $190-$205; each addl $15; suites $150-$300; under 18 free. Crib free. Pet accepted. TV; cable (premium), VCR avail. 2 pools, 1 indoor; whirlpool, poolside serv. Supervised child's activities. Restaurant 6:30 am-10 pm. Rm serv 24 hrs. Bar 11-1 am. Ck-out 1 pm. Meeting rms. Business servs avail. Barber, beauty shop. Airport transportation. Indoor tennis, pro shop. Golf privileges. Exercise rm. Minibars; some fireplaces. Microwaves avail. Balconies. Cr cds: A, D, DS, JCB, MC, V.

[D] [symbols] SC

★★★ **FOUR POINTS BY SHERATON.** *(5444 Dixie Rd, Mississauga ON L4W 2L2)* 1/4 mi S of ON 401 Dixie Rd S exit. 905/624-1144; FAX 905/624-9477. Web www.fourpoints.com/torontoairport. 296 rms, 10 story. S, D $99-$209; each addl $15; suites $225-$395; under 18 free; package plans. Crib free. Pet accepted, some restrictions. TV; cable (premium), VCR avail. Heated pool. Supervised child's activities; ages 2-12. Complimentary coffee in rms. Restaurant 6:30 am-10 pm; Sat, Sun from 7 am. Bars 11:30-1 am. Ck-out 1 pm. Meeting rms. Business center. In-rm modem link. Gift shop. Beauty shop. Garage parking. Free airport transportation. Exercise equipt; sauna. Game rm. Refrigerators, minibars. Cr cds: A, C, D, DS, ER, JCB, MC, V.

★ ★ ★ **HILTON INTERNATIONAL-TORONTO AIRPORT.** *(5875 Airport Rd, Mississauga ON L4V 1N1) 1 mi W of jct ON 427, Dixon Rd, near Lester B. Pearson Intl Airport.* 905/677-9900; FAX 905/677-5073. E-mail salestoronto-apt@hilton.com; web www.hilton.com. 413 rms, 11 story. S, D $165-$185; each addl $20; suites $185-$225; family rates; wknd packages. Crib free. Pet accepted, some restrictions. TV. Heated pool; poolside serv. Coffee in rms. Restaurant 6 am-midnight. Bars 11-2 am; entertainment. Ck-out noon. Meeting rms. Business center. Barber. Garage parking $6. Free airport transportation. Exercise equipt; sauna. Minibars; many bathrm phones. Cr cds: A, D, DS, ER, JCB, MC, V.

★ ★ **NOVOTEL.** *(3670 Hurontario St, Mississauga ON L5B 1P3) jct ON 10 & Burnhamthorpe Rd.* 905/896-1000; res: 800/668-6835; FAX 905/896-2521. E-mail missmail@aol.com; web novojack@aol.com -cooled rms, 14 story. S, D $169-$189; each addl $15; suite $250; under 16 free; wknd rates. Crib free. Pet accepted. TV; cable (premium). Indoor pool. Restaurant 6 am-midnight. Bar 11-1 am. Ck-out 11 pm. Meeting rms. Business servs avail. In-rm modem link. Shopping arcade. Beauty shop. Covered parking. Free airport transportation. Exercise equipt. Health club privileges. Minibars; some bathrm phones. Shopping center opp. Cr cds: A, C, D, DS, ER, JCB, MC, V.

★ ★ ★ **STAGE WEST.** *(5400 Dixie Rd, Mississauga ON L4W 4T4)* 905/238-0159; FAX 905/238-9820; res: 800/668-9887. E-mail reserva tions@stagewest.com. 224 suites, 16 story. Suites $175; family, wkly rates; package plans. Crib free. TV; cable (premium), VCR avail. Indoor pool; whirlpool, lifeguard, water slide. Supervised child's activities; ages 1-12. Restaurant 6:30 am-midnight. Bar 11-1 am. Ck-out noon. Meeting rms. Business center. In-rm modem link. Concierge. Shopping arcade. Barber, beauty shop. Valet parking $5/day. Free airport transportation. Downhill/x-country ski 20 mi. Exercise equipt. Microwaves avail. Complex includes Stage West Dinner Theatre. Cr cds: A, D, ER, MC, V.

Inn

★ ★ ★ **GLENERIN.** *(1695 The Collegeway, Mississauga ON L5L 3S7) off Mississauga Rd.* 905/828-6103; res: 800/267-0525. E-mail wersdl@connect.reach.net. 39 rms, 2½ story, 13 suites. S $115; D $165; each addl $10; suites $195-$375; under 18 free; wkly rates; wkend packages. Crib free. TV; cable (premium), VCR avail. Complimentary bkfst. Dining rm 7 am-11 pm. Rm serv. Ck-out 11 am, ck-in 4 pm. Meeting rms. Business servs avail. Downhill/x-country ski 10 mi. Health club privileges. Some fireplaces. English-style manor house (1927); antique and modern furnishings. Rms vary in size and style. Cr cds: A, D, ER, MC, V.

Restaurants

★ ★ ★ **CHERRINGTONS.** *(7355 Torbram Rd, Mississauga ON L4T 3W3)* 905/672-0605. Continental menu. Specializes in fresh fish, steak, pasta. Hrs: 11:30 am-3 pm, 5-10:30 pm; Sat from 5 pm. Closed Sun; Easter, Dec 25. Res accepted. Bar to 1 am. Semi-a la carte: lunch $9.95-$14.95, dinner $15.95-$31.95. Child's meals. Entertainment Fri, Sat. Parking. Elegant dining rm divided by bar. Cr cds: A, D, ER, MC, V.

★ ★ **CHERRY HILL HOUSE.** *(680 Silvercreek Blvd, Mississauga ON L5A 3Z1) in Silvercreek Mall.* 905/275-9300. French, continental menu. Specializes in rack of lamb, pasta with lobster. Hrs: 11:30 am-2:30 pm, 5:30-10 pm; Sat from 5:30 pm. Closed Sun; major hols. Res accepted. Bar. A la carte entrees: lunch $8.75-$13.25, dinner $13.50-$19.75. Con-

verted house (ca 1850) is a designated historic site. Cr cds: A, C, D, DS, ER, MC, V.

★ **DECKER-TEN.** *(1170 Burnhamthorpe Rd W, Mississauga ON L5C 4E6)* 905/276-7419. Japanese menu. Specialties: sashimi, beef teriyaki. Sushi bar. Hrs: 11:45 am-2:15 pm, 5:30-10 pm; Sat from 5:30 pm; Sun 5-9:30 pm. Closed Jan 1, July 1, Dec 24, 25. Res accepted. Bar. A la carte entrees: lunch $7-$15, dinner $9-$20. Complete meal: dinner $14-$28. Child's meals. Japanese art. Cr cds: A, MC, V.

★ ★ **LA CASTILE.** *(2179 Dundas St E, Mississauga ON L4X 1M3)* 905/625-1137. Steak and seafood menu. Specialties: shrimp cocktail, prime rib, barbecued ribs. Hrs: 11:30 am-2:30 pm, 5 pm-midnight; Mon, Tues to 11 pm. Closed Sun; Dec 25. Res accepted. Bar to 2 am. Semi-a la carte: lunch $9.95-$18.95, dinner $16.95-$36.95. Pianist Wed-Sat. Parking. 16th-century castle decor; cathedral ceiling, tapestries, original oil painting. Cr cds: A, D, ER, MC, V.

★ ★ ★ **MOLINARO.** *(50 Burnhamthorpe Rd W, Mississauga ON L5B 3C2)* 905/566-1330. Italian menu. Specializes in pasta. Hrs: 11:30 am-2:30 pm, 5:30-11 pm. Closed Sun; major hols. Res accepted; required Fri, Sat (dinner). Bar. Wine list. A la carte entrees: lunch $10.95-$14.95, dinner $12.95-$25.95. Entertainment Thurs-Sat. Large windows; city views. Cr cds: A, D, ER, MC, V.

★ ★ ★ **MON RÊVE.** *(1011 Eglinton Ave E, Mississauga ON L4W 1K4)* 905/238-8483. French, continental menu. Specializes in seafood, steak, veal. Hrs: noon-11 pm; Sat from 5 pm. Closed Sun; Jan 1, Dec 25. Res accepted. Bar. Wine list. Semi-a la carte: lunch $8.95-$14.95, dinner $16.95-$36.95. Parking. Old French Provincial decor. Cr cds: A, D, ER, MC, V.

★ ★ **MUSKY SUPPER HOUSE.** *(261 Lakeshore Rd E, Mississauga ON L5H 1G8)* 905/271-9727. Web musky@istar.ca. Continental menu. Specialty: hickory-smoked pork with sour cherries. Hrs: 5:30-10 pm; Fri, Sat to 11 pm. Closed Sun, Mon; some major hols. Res accepted. Bar. A la carte entrees: dinner $15-$24. Original art and carvings. Totally nonsmoking. Cr cds: A, DS, MC, V.

★ ★ ★ **OLD BARBER HOUSE.** *(5155 Mississauga Rd, Mississauga ON L5M 2L9)* 905/858-7570. Specializes in veal, pasta, lamb. Own pastries. Hrs: 11:30 am-3 pm, 5-11 pm; Sat from 5 pm. Closed Sun; Jan 1, Dec 25. Res accepted. Bar 11-1 am. A la carte entrees: lunch $9.95-$13.95, dinner $11.95-$34.95. Parking. Victorian house (1862). Cr cds: A, ER, MC, V.

★ ★ **OUTRIGGER STEAK & SEAFOOD.** *(2539 Dixie Rd, Mississauga ON L4Y 2A1)* 905/275-7000. Specializes in steak, seafood. Salad bar. Own baking. Hrs: noon-11 pm; Sat, Sun from 4 pm. Closed Dec 25. Res accepted. Bar 4 pm-1 am. A la carte entrees: lunch $6.95-$12.95, dinner $10.95-$36.99. Child's meals. Cr cds: A, MC, V.

★ ★ **SNUG HARBOUR.** *(14 Stavebank Rd S, Mississauga ON L5G 2T1)* 905/274-5000. Continental menu. Specializes in fresh seafood, pasta. Hrs: 11:30 am-11 pm. Closed Jan 1, Dec 24-26. Res accepted. Bar. Semi-a la carte: lunch, dinner $6.95-$18.50. Child's meals. Jazz Fri, Sat. Outdoor dining. On Lake Ontario. Cr cds: A, MC, V.

Morrisburg (C-10)

(See also Cornwall; also see Massena, NY, Ogdensburg (Thousand Islands), NY)

Pop 2,308 **Elev** 250 ft (76 m) **Area code** 613
Information Chamber of Commerce, PO Box 288, K0C 1X0; 613/543-3443.

Rising waters of the St Lawrence Seaway forced the removal of Morrisburg and many other towns to higher ground. This was one of the earliest settled parts of Canada, and homes, churches and buildings of historic note were moved and reconstructed on the Crysler Farm located in the Upper Canada Village, itself a historic spot.

What to See and Do

Crysler Farm Battlefield Park. Scene of a decisive battle of the War of 1812, where 800 British and Canadians defeated 4,000 American troops. Also here are Crysler Park Marina, Upper Canada Golf Course, Crysler Beach (fee), Battle of Crysler's Farm Visitor Centre and Memorial Mound, Pioneer Memorial, Loyalist Memorial, Air Strip and Queen Elizabeth Gardens. Varying fees. 7 mi (11 km) E on ON 2. Nearby is

Upper Canada Village. An authentic recreation of a rural 1860s riverfront village. Demonstrations by staff in period costumes. Historic buildings include an operating woolen mill, sawmill, gristmill; Willard's Hotel; blacksmith's, tinsmith's, dressmaker's, shoemaker's and cabinetmaker's shops; tavern, churches, school, bakery, working farms, canal. May be seen on foot, by carryall or *bateau*. (Mid-May-mid-Oct, daily; closed some hols) Phone 613/543-3704. ¢¢¢

Fort Wellington National Historic Site. Original British fort first built in 1813, rebuilt in 1838 after Canadian Rebellions of 1837-1838. Restored blockhouse, officers' quarters, latrine; guides in period costume depict life at the fort circa 1846. Underground stone tunnel designed to defend the flank of the fort. Large military pageant with mock battles (3rd wkend July). (Mid-May-Sept, daily; rest of yr, by appt) 33 mi (53 km) SW via Hwy 401, in Prescott. Phone 613/925-2896. **Free.**

Prehistoric World. Life-size reproductions of prehistoric animals along a 3/4-mi (1-km) nature trail. More than 40 exhibits completed, including Brontosaurus and Tyrannosaurus Rex; others in various stages of construction. (Late May-Labour Day, daily) 5 mi (7 km) E via Hwy 401, exit 758. Phone 613/543-2503. ¢¢

Motel

★ **LOYALIST HOTEL.** *(Hwy 2 & 31, Morrisburg ON K0C 1X0)* 613/543-2932; FAX 613/543-3316. 31 rms, 1-2 story. S $39-$49; D $49-$69; wkend rates. Pet accepted. TV; cable. Heated pool. Restaurant 11:30 am-2 pm, 5-9:30 pm. Bar noon-1 am. Ck-out 11 am. Cr cds: A, MC, V.

🐾 ⊠ ✕ 🛇 **SC**

Niagara Falls (E-7)

(See Niagara-on-the-Lake, St Catharines; also see Buffalo, NY, Niagara Falls, NY)

Pop 70,960 **Elev** 589 ft (180 m) **Area code** 905 **E-mail** nfcvcb@niagara.com **Web** tourismniagara.com/nfcvcb
Information Visitor & Convention Bureau, 5433 Victoria Ave, L2G 3L1; 905/356-6061 or 800/563-2557.

The Canadian side of Niagara Falls offers some viewpoints different from, and in many ways superior to, those on the American side. Center of a beautiful 35-mile (60-kilometer) stretch of parks and home of a tremendous range of man-made attractions, this area is popular all year with tourists from all over the world.

What to See and Do

Boat ride. *Maid of the Mist* leaves from foot of Clifton Hill on Niagara River Pkwy near Rainbow Bridge (see NIAGARA FALLS, NY). Phone 716/284-4233 (NY) or 905/358-0311 (CAN). ¢¢¢

Canada One Factory Outlets. Outlet Centre which sells many national recognized brands of merchandise. 7500 Lundy's Ln. Phone 416/323-3977.

Historic Fort Erie. Site of some of the fiercest fighting of the War of 1812; restored to period. Guided tours by interpreters dressed in uniform of the Glengarry Light Infantry. (Mid-May-mid-Sept) 21 mi (34 km) S via QEW, at 4330 River Rd in Fort Erie. Phone 905/356-2241. ¢¢

Great Gorge Adventure. Niagara River at its narrowest point. Elevator and 240-ft (73-m) tunnel takes visitors to the boardwalk at edge of whirlpool rapids. (Apr-Oct, daily) 2 mi (3 km) N at 4330 River Rd. Contact PO Box 150, L2E 6T2; 905/356-2241. ¢¢

Guinness World of Records Museum. Based on the popular book of records; hundreds of original exhibits, artifacts; laser video galleries; recreations of many of the world's greatest accomplishments. (Daily) 4943 Clifton Hill. Phone 905/356-2299. ¢¢¢

Journey Behind the Falls. Elevator descends to point about 25 ft (8 m) above river, offering excellent view of Falls from below and behind; waterproof garments are supplied. (Daily; closed Dec 25) 1 mi S of Rainbow Bridge on Niagara Pkwy in Queen Victoria Park. Phone 905/354-1551. ¢¢¢ Also in park is

Greenhouse. Tropical and native plants; animated fountain, garden shop. (Daily) Phone 905/354-1721. **Free.**

Louis Tussaud's Waxworks. Life-size, historically costumed wax figures of the past and present; Chamber of Horrors. (Daily; closed Dec 25) 4915 Clifton Hill. Phone 905/374-6601 or 905/374-4534. ¢¢¢

Lundy's Lane Historical Museum (1874). On the site of the Battle of Lundy's Lane (1814). Interprets early settlement and tourism of Niagara Falls; 1812 war militaria; Victorian parlor, early kitchen, toys, dolls, photographs; galleries and exhibits. (May-Nov, daily; rest of yr, Mon-Fri; closed Jan 1, Dec 25) 5810 Ferry St. Phone 905/358-5082. ¢

Marineland. Performing killer whales, dolphins, sea lions; wildlife displays with deer, bears, buffalo and elk; thrill rides, including one of the world's largest steel roller coasters; restaurants, picnic areas. Park (Mar-mid-Dec, daily); rides (mid-May-early Oct). 7657 Portage Rd. Phone 905/356-8250. ¢¢¢¢¢

Niagara Falls Museum. One of North America's oldest museums, founded in 1827. Twenty-six galleries of rare, worldwide artifacts, including "Niagara's Original Daredevil Hall of Fame"; Egyptian mummy collection; dinosaur exhibit. (Summer, daily; winter, schedule varies) 5651 River Rd. Phone 905/356-2151 or 716/285-4898 (US). ¢¢¢

Niagara Parks Botanical Gardens. Nearly 100 acres of horticultural exhibits. Nature shop. (Daily) Niagara Pkwy North. Phone 905/356-8554. **Free.** On grounds is the

Niagara Parks Butterfly Conservatory. Approx 2,000 butterflies make their home in this 11,000-sq-ft (1,022-sq-m), climate-controlled conservatory filled with exotic greenery and flowing water. Nearly 50 species of butterflies can be viewed from a 600-ft (180-m) network of walking paths. Outdoor butterfly garden (seasonal). Gift shop. (Daily) Phone 905/356-8119. ¢¢¢

Niagara Spanish Aero Car. The 1,800-ft (549-m) cables support a car that crosses the whirlpool and rapids of the Niagara River. Five-min trip each way. (Mid-Apr-mid-Oct, daily) 3 1/2 mi (5 km) N on Niagara Parkway. Phone 905/354-5711. ¢¢

⭐ **Observation towers.**

Minolta Tower Centre. This awesome 325-ft (99.06-m) tower offers a magnificent 360° view of the Falls and surrounding areas. Eight levels at top; specially designed glass for ideal photography; Minolta exhibit floor; "Waltzing Waters" water & light spectacle (free; seasonal); gift shops; incline railway to Falls (fee; free parking); "Top of the Rainbow" dining rms overlooking Falls (reservations suggested). (Daily; closed Dec 24, 25) 6732 Oakes Dr. For addl information contact 6732 Oakes Dr, Niagara Falls L2G 3W6; 905/356-1501. ¢¢¢

Skylon Tower. Stands 775 ft (236 m) above base of Falls. Three-level dome contains an indoor/outdoor observation deck and revolving and stationary dining rooms served by three external, glass-enclosed "Yellow Bug" elevators. Specialty shops at base of tower. (Daily) 5200 Robinson St. Phone 905/356-2651. ¢¢¢ Adj is

IMAX Theatre and Daredevil Adventure. Six-story-high movie screen shows *Niagara: Miracles, Myths and Magic*, a film highlighting the falls. Daredevil Adventure has displays, exhibits and some of the actual barrels used to traverse the falls. (Daily; closed Dec 25) 6170 Buchanan Ave. Phone 905/374-IMAX (recording) or 905/358-3611. ¢¢¢

Typhoon Lagoon. Family water park featuring waterslides, pools, hot tubs; arcade, restaurant, gift shop. (June-mid-Sept, daily) 7430 Lundy's Lane. Phone 905/357-3380. ¢¢¢¢

Motels

★ ★ **CARRIAGE HOUSE.** *(8004 Lundy's Lane (ON 20), Niagara Falls ON L2H 1H1)* ½ mi W of QEW. 905/356-7799; res: 800/267-9887. 120 rms, 2 story. July-Aug: S, D $65-$105; each addl $10; suites $100-$150; family rates special events; lower rates rest of yr. Crib free. TV. 2 pools, 1 indoor; whirlpool. Restaurant 7 am-noon. Ck-out 11 am. Business servs avail. Sundries. X-country ski 4 mi. Some in-rm whirlpools. Some balconies. Cr cds: A, C, D, DS, ER, MC, V.

D ⛆ ≈ ⛆ 🔥 SC

★ **CAVALIER.** *(5100 Centre St, Niagara Falls ON L2G 3P2)* 3 blks W of Falls. 905/358-3288; FAX 905/358-3299. 39 rms, 2 story. July-Aug: S, D $66-$94; under 5 free; lower rates rest of yr. Crib free. TV; cable (premium). Heated pool. Restaurant opp from 7 am. Ck-out 11 am. French provincial decor. Cr cds: A, JCB, MC, V.

≈ ⛆ 🔥 SC

★ **CRYSTAL.** *(4249 River Rd (Niagara River Pkwy), Niagara Falls ON L2E 3E7)* 905/354-0460; FAX 905/374-4972. 38 rms, 2 story. Mid-June-mid-Sept: S, D $68-$95; each addl $8; lower rates rest of yr. Crib $4. TV; cable (premium). Heated pool. Restaurant nearby. Ck-out 11 am. Refrigerators; some in-rm whirlpools. Some balconies. 1 blk N of Whirlpool Rapids Bridge. Cr cds: A, DS, MC, V.

≈ ⛆ 🔥 SC

✔ ★ **ECONO LODGE.** *(7514 Lundy's Lane (ON 20), Niagara Falls ON L2H 1G8)* 2¾ mi W of Falls at QEW. 905/354-1849. 45 rms. Late June-mid-Sept: S, D $45-$115; each addl $5; higher rates hol wkends; lower rates rest of yr. Crib free. TV. Heated pool. Restaurant nearby. Ck-out 11 am. X-country ski 3 mi. Picnic tables. On landscaped grounds; back from highway. Cr cds: A, D, DS, MC, V.

⛆ ≈ ⛆ 🔥 SC

★ **ECONO LODGE.** *(5781 Victoria Ave, Niagara Falls ON L2G 3L6)* at Lundy's Lane. 905/356-2034. 57 rms, 2 story. Late June-Sept: S, D $89.95-$156.95; each addl $10; suites $156.95-$199.95; under 18 free; lower rates rest of yr. Crib free. TV; cable. Indoor pool; whirlpool. Restaurant adj open 24 hrs. Ck-out 11 am. X-country ski 2 mi. Cr cds: A, D, DS, MC, V.

⛆ ≈ ⛆ 🔥 SC

✔ ★ ★ **FLAMINGO MOTOR INN.** *(7701 Lundy's Lane (ON 20), Niagara Falls ON L2H 1H3)* 1½ mi W of Falls. 905/356-4646. 95 rms, 2 story. Mid-June-Labour Day: S, D $72-$104; each addl $10; whirlpool rm $104-$200; lower rates rest of yr. Crib free. Pet accepted, some restrictions. TV; cable. Heated pool. Restaurant adj 7 am-10 pm. Ck-out 11 am. Gift shop. Picnic tables. Cr cds: A, C, D, DS, MC, V.

🐾 ≈ ⛆ 🔥 SC

★ ★ **HONEYMOON CITY.** *(4943 Clifton Hill, Niagara Falls ON L2G 3N5)* 905/357-4330; FAX 905/357-0423; res: 800/668-8840. Web www.niagara.com/falls/. 77 rms, 2 story. Mid-June-early Sept: S, D $48-

$169; suites, kits. $129-$239; under 12 free; wkend, hol rates; lower rates rest of yr. Crib free. Pet accepted, some restrictions. TV; cable, VCR avail (movies). Heated pool. Restaurant 7 am-11 pm. Ck-out 11 am. Business servs avail. Shopping arcade. X-country ski 2 mi. Some balconies. Cr cds: A, MC, V.

🐾 ≈ ⛆ 🔥 SC

★ **LIBERTY INNS.** *(6408 Stanley Ave, Niagara Falls ON L2G 3Y5)* 2 blks W of Falls. 905/356-5877; FAX 905/356-9452; res: 800/263-2522. 102 rms, 3 story, 4 suites. June-Sept: S, D $89-$165; each addl $10; suites $150-$180; under 13 free; lower rates rest of yr. Crib $10. TV. Indoor pool. Restaurant 7 am-midnight; hrs vary rest of yr. Bar from noon. Ck-out 11 am. X-country ski 5 mi. Sauna. Balconies. Picnic tables. Cr cds: A, D, ER, JCB, MC, V.

≈ ⛆ 🔥 SC

★ ★ **OLD STONE INN.** *(5425 Robinson St, Niagara Falls ON L2G 7L6)* 905/357-1234; FAX 905/357-9299. E-mail atiene@oldstone.on.ca. 114 rms, 3 story. May-Oct: S, D $125-$225; each addl $10; suites $195-$349; under 12 free; wkend rates; higher rates hols; lower rates rest of yr. Crib free. TV; cable. 2 pools, 1 indoor; whirlpool, poolside serv. Restaurant (see THE MILLERY). Rm serv. Bar 11-2 am. Ck-out 11 am. Meeting rms. Business servs avail. Bellhops. Gift shop. Valet serv. X-country ski 2 mi. Main bldg former flour mill built 1904. Cr cds: A, D, DS, ER, JCB, MC, V.

D ⛆ ≈ ⛆ 🔥 SC

★ **PILGRIM MOTOR INN.** *(4955 Clifton Hill, Niagara Falls ON L2G 3N5)* 905/374-7777; FAX 905/354-8086. 40 rms, 3 story. Mid-June-mid-Sept: S, D $58-$149.50; each addl $10; higher rates: hols, wkends; lower rates rest of yr. Crib free. TV; cable. Ck-out noon. Balconies. Sun deck. Cr cds: A, MC, V.

⛆ 🔥 SC

★ **SURFSIDE INN.** *(3665 Macklem St (Niagara River Pkwy), Niagara Falls ON L2G 6C8)* 905/295-4354; FAX 905/295-4374; res: 800/263-0713. E-mail surfside@niagarafalls.net; web www.niagara falls.net/motel. 31 rms. Mid-Apr-mid-Nov: D $55-$125; each addl $6; suites $99-$185; lower rates rest of yr. Crib free. TV. Pool. Coffee in rms. Restaurant nearby. Ck-out 11 am. Refrigerators; microwaves avail. Some whirlpools in suites. Bicycle trail. Cr cds: A, C, D, DS, ER, JCB, MC, V.

D ⛆ ≈ ⛆ 🔥 SC

★ ★ **TRAVELODGE BONAVENTURE.** *(7737 Lundys Lane, Niagara Falls ON L2H 1H3)* 905/374-7171; FAX 905/374-1151. 118 rms, 3 story, 16 suites. Mid-June-Sept: S, D $59.50-$159; each addl $8; whirlpool rm $139-$179; under 17 free; 2-day min wkends in season; lower rates rest of yr. Crib free. TV; cable (premium). 2 pools, 1 indoor. Complimentary coffee in lobby. Restaurant opp 7-1 am. Ck-out 11 am. X-country ski 4 mi. Cr cds: A, D, DS, ER, MC, V.

D ⛆ ≈ ⛆ 🔥 SC

★ **VILLAGE INN.** *(5685 Falls Ave, Niagara Falls ON L2E 6W7)* just off QEW Spur at Rainbow Bridge, in Maple Leaf Village Complex. 905/374-4444; FAX 905/374-0800; res: 800/263-7135. Web www.falls.net/skyline. 206 rms, 2 story. Late June-early Sept: S, D $119.99; lower rates rest of yr. Crib free. TV; cable. Playground. Complimentary continental bkfst. Restaurant 6:30-11 am. Business servs avail. Health club privileges. Microwaves avail. Cr cds: A, C, D, DS, ER, JCB, MC, V.

⛆ 🔥 SC

Motor Hotels

★ ★ ★ **BEST WESTERN CAIRN CROFT.** *(6400 Lundy's Lane (ON 20), Niagara Falls ON L2G 1T6)* 1¼ mi W of Falls. 905/356-1161; FAX 905/356-8664. E-mail bestwestern@niagara.net; web niagara.net/cairn croft. 165 rms, 5 story. Late June-Aug: S, D $99.50-$149.50; each addl $10; suites $150-$199; under 18 free; lower rates rest of yr. Crib free. TV. Playground. Indoor pool. Restaurant 7 am-2 pm, 5-8 pm. Rm serv. Bar 4 pm-1 am; entertainment Tues-Sat. Ck-out 11 am. Meeting rms. Business servs avail. Bellhops. Valet serv. X-country ski 3 mi. Health club privileges. Enclosed courtyard. Cr cds: A, C, D, DS, ER, MC, V.

★ ★ **BEST WESTERN FALLSVIEW.** *(5551 Murray St, Niagara Falls ON L2G 2J4)* 1 blk to Falls. 905/356-0551; FAX 905/356-7773. Web www.bestwestern.com. 244 rms, 4-6 story. June-Sept: S, D $79-$169; each addl $10; lower rates rest of yr. Crib $5. Pet accepted. TV; cable. Indoor pool; whirlpool. Sauna. Restaurant 6 am-10 pm. Bar 11-1 am. Ck-out 11 am. Coin lndry. Meeting rms. Business servs avail. Bellhops. Gift shop. Sundries. Game rm. Some in-rm whirlpools. Cr cds: A, C, D, DS, ER, JCB, MC, V.

★ ★ **CASCADE INN.** *(5305 Murray St, Niagara Falls ON L2G 2J3)* 1 blk W of Falls. 905/354-2796; FAX 905/354-2797; res: 800/663-3301. E-mail niagara@cascade.on.ca; web www.cascade.on.ca.. 65 rms, 3-6 story. Mid-May-Labour Day: D $98-$129; lower rates rest of yr. Crib free. TV. Pool. Restaurant 7-11 am. Ck-out 11 am. Gift shop. X-country ski 2 mi. Near Skylon Tower. Cr cds: A, DS, MC, V.

★ ★ **COMFORT SUITES IMPERIAL.** *(5851 Victoria St, Niagara Falls ON L2G 3L6)* 905/356-2648; FAX 905/356-4068. 104 suites, 10 story. July-Aug: S, D $104-$179; each addl $15; under 16 free; lower rates rest of yr. Crib $10. TV. Indoor pool; whirlpool. Restaurant adj 7 am-10 pm. Bar 11-2 am. Ck-out noon. Coin lndry. Meeting rms. Business servs avail. Gift shop. X-country ski 2 mi. Game rm. Refrigerators; microwaves avail. Cr cds: A, D, DS, ER, MC, V.

★ ★ **HAMPTON INN AT THE FALLS.** *(5591 Victoria Ave, Niagara Falls ON L2G 3L4)* 905/357-1626; FAX 905/357-5869. 127 units, 3-6 story. Mid-June-Labour Day: S, D $89-$189; suites $139-$269; under 18 free; lower rates rest of yr. Crib free. TV; cable (premium). Indoor pool; whirlpool. Sauna. Complimentary continental bkfst. Complimentary coffee in rms. Bar 4 pm-1 am (in season). Ck-out 11 am. Meeting rms. Business servs avail. In-rm modem link. Sundries. Game rm. Balconies. Cr cds: A, D, DS, ER, MC, V.

★ ★ ★ **HOLIDAY INN BY THE FALLS.** *(5339 Murray St, Niagara Falls ON L2G 2J3)* 2 blks W of Falls. 905/356-1333; FAX 905/356-7128. E-mail res@holidayinn.com; web www.holidayinn.com. 122 rms, 6 story. Mid-June-mid-Sept: S, D $95-$195; each addl $10; bridal suite $175-$225; lower rates rest of yr. Crib $5. Pet accepted. TV. 2 pools, 1 indoor; whirlpool. Restaurant 7 am-10 pm; winter from 8 am. Rm serv. Bar noon-2 am. Ck-out noon. Sundries. Sauna. Some in-rm whirlpools. Balconies. Cr cds: A, C, D, DS, ER, JCB, MC, V.

✔★ ★ **HOWARD JOHNSON BY THE FALLS.** *(5905 Victoria Ave, Niagara Falls ON L2G 3L8)* 905/357-4040; FAX 905/357-6202. 199 rms, 6-7 story. S, D $59-$299; each addl $10; under 18 free. Crib free. TV; cable, VCR avail. Indoor/outdoor pool; whirlpool. Restaurant open 24 hrs. Ck-out noon. Meeting rms. Business servs avail. Gift shop. X-country ski 2 mi. Sauna. Game rm. Some in-rm whirlpools. Some balconies. Cr cds: A, C, D, DS, ER, JCB, MC, V.

★ ★ ★ **MICHAEL'S INN.** *(5599 River Rd, Niagara Falls ON L2E 3H3)* just N of Rainbow Bridge. 905/354-2727; FAX 905/374-7706; res: 800/263-9390 (US). E-mail michaels@michaelsinn.com; web www.michaelsinn.com. 130 rms, 4 story. May-Oct: S, D $59-$228; suites $125-$375; lower rates rest of yr. Crib $5. TV; cable (premium). Indoor pool; wading pool; whirlpool, lifeguard in season. Restaurant 7 am-11:30 pm. Rm serv. Bar. Ck-out 11 am. Meeting rms. Business servs avail. Bellhops. Valet serv. Sauna. Some refrigerators. Overlooks the Falls. Cr cds: A, C, D, ER, JCB, MC, V.

★ ★ ★ **RAMADA-CORAL INN RESORT.** *(7429 Lundy's Lane (ON 20), Niagara Falls ON L2H 1G9)* 2 mi W of Falls. 905/356-6116; FAX 905/356-7204. E-mail ramada.niagara@sympatico.ca; web tourismnia gara.com/ramcoral. 130 units, 2-4 story. Mid-June-early Sept: S, D $89-$139; each addl $10; suites, studio rms $129-$169; under 18 free; package plans; higher rates: Sat in season, hols, special events; lower rates rest of yr. Crib free. TV. 2 heated pools, 1 indoor; whirlpool. Restaurant 7 am-10 pm. Ck-out 11 am. Meeting rms. Business center. Valet serv. Gift shop. Exercise equipt; sauna. Health club privileges. Playground. Game rm. Refrigerators, in-rm whirlpools; fireplace in suites. Cr cds: A, C, D, DS, ER, JCB, MC, V.

★ ★ **TRAVELODGE-NEAR THE FALLS.** *(5234 Ferry St, Niagara Falls ON L2G 1R5)* 905/374-7771. 81 rms, 4 story, 22 suites. July-Aug: S, D $99-$149; each addl $10; suites $129-$199; family, wkly rates; higher rates hol wknds, lower rates rest of yr. Crib free. TV; cable (premium). Indoor pool; whirlpool. Sauna. Complimentary coffee in lobby. Restaurant 7 am-3 pm. Ck-out 11 am. X-country ski 2 mi. Whirlpool in suites. Cr cds: A, D, MC, V.

Hotels

★ **DAYS INN.** *(6361 Buchanan Ave, Niagara Falls ON L2G 3V9)* 905/357-7377; FAX 905/357-9300. Web www.daysinn.com/daysinn.html. 193 rms, 15 story. Late June-late Sept: S, D $99-$499; each addl $10; under 17 free; lower rates rest of yr. Crib free. TV. Indoor pool; whirlpool. Complimentary coffee in rms. Restaurant adj open 24 hrs. No rm serv. Bar. Ck-out 11 am. Meeting rms. Business servs avail. No bellhops. Gift shop. X-country ski 2 mi. Sauna. Game rm. Cr cds: A, D, DS, ER, MC, V.

✔★ **DAYS INN NEAR THE FALLS.** *(5943 Victoria Ave, Niagara Falls ON L2G 3L8)* 905/374-3333. 117 rms, 7 story. S, D $99-$199; each addl $10; under 18 free. Crib free. TV; cable. Indoor pool; whirlpool. Restaurant adj open 24 hrs. No rm serv. Ck-out noon. No bellhops. Gift shop. X-country ski 2 mi. Sauna. Game rm. Cr cds: A, D, DS, ER, MC, V.

★ ★ **FOUR POINTS BY SHERATON .** *(6045 Stanley Ave, Niagara Falls ON L2G 3Y3)* 905/374-4142; FAX 905/358-3430. 112 rms, 8 story. Late June-mid-Sept: S, D $129-$269; each addl $10; under 14 free; wknds (2-day min); higher rates hol wknds; lower rates rest of yr. Crib free. TV; cable. Indoor pool; whirlpool, poolside serv. Restaurant 7 am-2 pm, 5-10 pm. Bar from 5 pm. Ck-out 11 am. Meeting rms. Business center. Gift shop. X-country ski 2 mi. Cr cds: A, D, DS, ER, JCB, MC, V.

★ ★ **OAKES INN.** *(6546 Buchanan Ave, Niagara Falls ON L2G 3W2)* 2 blks S of Falls. 905/356-4514; FAX 905/356-3651; res: 800/263-2577 (exc ON & PQ). 800/263-7134 (ON & PQ). E-mail ua. 167 units, 12 story. Mid-June-mid-Sept: S, D $89-$309; each addl $5; suites $209-$349; family units; lower rates rest of yr. Crib $10. TV; cable. 2 heated pools, 1 indoor; whirlpool. Restaurants 7 am-midnight; off-season 8 am-9 pm. Bar noon-1 am. Ck-out 11 am. Meeting rms. Business servs avail. Gift shop. X-country ski 2 mi. Exercise equipt; sauna. Some in-rm whirlpools. Some rms with view of Falls. Enclosed observation deck. Cr cds: A, C, D, DS, ER, JCB, MC, V.

✔★ ★ **QUALITY HOTEL.** *(5257 Ferry St, Niagara Falls ON L2G 1R6)* 905/356-2842; FAX 905/356-6629. Web www.hotelchoice.com. 80 rms, 8 story. Mid-June-mid-Sept: S, D $89.99-$249.99; each addl $10-$50; lower rates rest of yr. Crib free. TV; cable. Indoor pool; whirlpool. Restaurant 7 am-noon. No rm serv. Ck-out noon. Meeting rms. Business servs avail. No bellhops. Gift shop. X-country ski 2 mi. Sauna. Cr cds: A, C, D, DS, ER, JCB, MC, V.

★ ★ ★ **RAMADA SUITES-NIAGARA.** *(7389 Lundy's Lane, Niagara Falls ON L2H 2W9)* 905/356-6119; FAX 905/356-7204. Web www.ramada.com. 73 suites, 7 story. Mid-June-early Sept: S, D $109-$159; each addl $10; under 18 free; suites $129-$169; family rates; higher rates; hol wkends, Sat in season; lower rates rest of yr. Crib free. TV. Indoor pool; whirlpool. Restaurant 7 am-11 pm. No rm serv. Bar 11:30 am-midnight. Ck-out 11 am. Meeting rms. Business center. In-rm modem link. Exercise equipt; sauna. Refrigerators; whirlpool in suites. Cr cds: A, C, D, DS, ER, JCB, MC, V.

D ⚊ 🏊 ⚟ ⚟ ⚟ 🔥 SC ⚟

★ ★ ★ **RENAISSANCE FALLSVIEW.** *(6455 Buchanan Ave, Niagara Falls ON)* 905/357-5200; FAX 905/357-3422. E-mail renfalls@niagara.com; web www.niagara.com/nf-renaissance. 262 rms, 19 story. Mid-June-Sept: S, D $185-$309; each addl $20; under 18 free; lower rates rest of yr. Crib free. TV; cable. Indoor pool. Restaurants 7 am-11 pm. Bar 11-1 am. Ck-out 11 am. Meeting rms. Business servs avail. Exercise equipt; sauna. Cr cds: A, D, DS, ER, JCB, MC, V.

D ⚊ 🏊 ⚟ ⚟ ⚟ 🔥 SC

★ ★ **SKYLINE BROCK.** *(5685 Falls Ave, Niagara Falls ON L2E 6W7)* just off QEW Spur at Rainbow Bridge, in Maple Leaf Village Complex. 905/374-4445; FAX 905/357-4804; res: 800/263-7135. Web www.falls.net/skyline. 233 rms, 12 story. June-Sept: S, D $129-$369; each addl $10; suites $249-$429; under 18 free; lower rates rest of yr. Crib free. TV; cable. Parking $4-$6 (in season). Restaurant 7 am-10 pm. Bar in season 11-1 am. Ck-out 11 am. Meeting rms. Business servs avail. Health club privileges. Most rms overlook Falls. Cr cds: A, C, D, DS, ER, JCB, MC, V.

⚟ ⚟ SC

★ ★ **SKYLINE FOXHEAD.** *(5875 Falls Ave, Niagara Falls ON L2E 6W7)* in Maple Leaf Village complex. 905/374-4444; res: 800/263-7135; FAX 905/357-4804. Web www.falls.net/skyline. 399 rms, 14 story. June-Sept: S, D $119-$269; each addl $10; under 18 free; higher rates hol wkends; lower rates rest of yr. Crib free. Valet parking $12/day in season. TV; cable (premium). Pool. Restaurant 6:30 am-10 pm. Bar from 11 am. Ck-out 11 am. Meeting rms. Business center. Concierge. Shopping arcade. X-country ski 2 mi. Exercise equipt. Some balconies overlooking Falls. Cr cds: A, C, D, DS, ER, JCB, MC, V.

D ⚟ ⚊ 🏊 ⚟ ⚟ 🔥 SC ⚟

Restaurants

★ ★ **CAPRI.** *(5438 Ferry St, Niagara Falls ON L2G 1S1)* 905/354-7519. Italian menu. Specializes in seafood, steak, pasta. Hrs: 11 am-11 pm. Closed Dec 24-26. Res accepted. Bar. A la carte entrees: lunch $5.75-$12.50, dinner $8.95-$34.95. Child's meals. Parking. Family-owned. Cr cds: A, C, D, ER, JCB, MC, V.

D ⚊

★ **FOUR BROTHERS.** *(5283 Ferry St, Niagara Falls ON L2G 1R6)* 905/358-6951. Italian menu. Specializes in steak, seafood, gourmet pasta dishes. Hrs: 11 am-11 pm; summer 7-1 am. Closed Dec 24, 25. Res accepted. Bar. A la carte entrees: bkfst $1.99-$5.50, lunch $1.95-$10.95, dinner $7.95-$19.95. Child's meals. Parking. Old World decor. Family-owned. Cr cds: A, D, DS, ER, MC, V.

D ⚊

★ ★ **THE MILLERY.** *(See Old Stone Inn)* 905/357-1234. Continental menu. Specialties: prime rib, rack of lamb. Hrs: 7 am-3 pm, 4:30-10 pm; early-bird dinner 4:30-6 pm. Res accepted (dinner). Bar 11-2 am. Semi-a la carte: bkfst $1.95-$8.95, lunch $4.95-$9.95, dinner $15.50-$40. Child's meals. Outdoor dining. In historic mill. Cr cds: A, D, ER, JCB, MC, V.

D ⚊

★ ★ **QUEENSTON HEIGHTS.** *(14184 Niagara Pkwy, Niagara Falls ON L2E 6T2)* 6 mi N of falls. 905/262-4274. Specializes in prime rib, lamb, steak. Hrs: noon-3 pm, 5-9 pm; Sat to 10 pm; high tea 3-5 pm;

mid-June-Labour Day to 9:30 pm; Sun brunch 11 am-3 pm. Closed Jan 5-wk before Easter. Res accepted. Bar. A la carte entrees: lunch $9.25-$11.95, dinner $15.95-$24.95. Sun brunch $17.95. Child's meals. Parking. Enclosed balcony dining overlooks river, orchards. Patio. War of 1812 battle site. Cr cds: A, D, ER, MC, V.

D ⚊

★ ★ **VICTORIA PARK.** *(S on Niagara Pkwy, Niagara Falls ON)* in Queen Victoria Park. 905/356-2217. Canadian, Amer menu. Specializes in prime rib. Menu changes seasonally. Hrs: 11:30 am-9 pm; early-bird dinner 4-6:30 pm; late June-Aug to 10 pm. Closed mid-Oct-Apr. Res accepted. No A/C. Bar. Semi-a la carte: lunch $8.29-$12.49, dinner $16.99-$21.99. Child's meals. Victorian decor. Parking. Outdoor patio with view of Falls. Also cafeteria. Cr cds: A, D, ER, JCB, MC, V.

D

Niagara-on-the-Lake (E-7)

(See also Niagara Falls, St Catharines; also see Niagara Falls, NY)

Settled 1776 **Pop** 12,186 **Elev** 262 ft (80 m) **Area code** 905 **Web** www.niagara-on-the-lake.com
Information Chamber of Commerce, 153 King St, PO Box 1043, L0S 1J0; 905/468-4263.

Often called the loveliest in Ontario, this picturesque town has a long and distinguished history which parallels the growth of the province. Originally the Neutral village of Onghiara, it attracted Loyalist settlers after the American Revolution, many of whom were members of the feared Butler's Rangers. Pioneers followed from many European countries, and after a succession of names including Newark, the town finally received its present name. In 1792 it became the first capital of Upper Canada and remained so until 1796. Governor John Graves Simcoe, considering the proximity to the United States in case of war, moved the seat of government to York, near Toronto. The town played a significant role in the War of 1812, was occupied and eventually burned along with Fort George in 1813.

Once a busy shipping, shipbuilding and active commercial center, the beautiful old homes lining the tree-shaded streets testify to the prosperity of the area. The town's attractions now include major theater events, historic sites, beautiful gardens and Queen St with its shops, hotels and restaurants. Delightful in any season, this is one of the best-preserved and prettiest remnants of the Georgian era.

What to See and Do

Brock's Monument. Massive, 185-ft (56-m) memorial to Sir Isaac Brock, who was felled by a sharpshooter while leading his troops against American forces at the Battle of Queenston Heights in Oct 1812. Narrow, winding staircase leads to tiny observation deck inside monument. Other memorial plaques in park; walking tour of important points on the Queenston Heights Battlefield begins at the Brock Monument; brochure available here. Brock and his aide-de-camp, Lieutenant-Colonel Macdonell, are buried here. (Mid-May-Labour Day, daily) 7 mi (11 km) S in Queenston Heights Park. Phone 905/468-4257. **Free.**

Court House (1847). Built on site of original government house, 3-story building is now the home of the Court House Theatre. First home of the Shaw Festival (see SEASONAL EVENT). Queen St.Opp is

Clock Tower (1921). Erected in memory of those who died in world wars. Set in center of the road surrounded by floral displays.

Fort George National Historic Site (1797). Once the principal British post on the frontier, the fort saw much action during the War of 1812. 11 restored, refurnished buildings and massive ramparts. (Mid-May-Oct, daily; rest of yr, by appt; living history mid-May-Labour Day) Guided tours by appt. On Niagara Pkwy. Phone 905/468-3938. ¢¢

Laura Secord Homestead. Restored home of Canadian heroine is furnished with early Upper Canada furniture. After overhearing the plans of the Americans billetted in her home, Laura Secord made an exhausting and difficult 19-mi (30-km) walk to warn British troops, which resulted in a victory over the Americans at Beaverdams in 1813. (Victoria Day-Labour Day, daily) Partition St, 5 mi (8 km) S in Queenston. Phone 905/262-4851 or 905/357-4020. Tours ¢

McFarland House (1800). Georgian brick home used as a hospital in the War of 1812; furnished in the Loyalist tradition, 1835-1845. (July-Labour Day, daily; mid-May-June & after Labour Day-Sept, wkends only) McFarland Point Park, Niagara Pkwy, 1 mi (1.6 km) S. Phone 905/356-2241. ¢

Niagara Apothecary (ca 1820). Restoration of pharmacy which operated on the premises from 1866-1964. Has large golden mortar and pestle over the door; original walnut and butternut fixtures, apothecary glass & interesting remedies of the past. (May-Labour Day, daily) Queen & King Sts. Phone 905/468-3845. **Free.**

Niagara Historical Society Museum. Opened in 1907, the earliest museum building in Ontario. Items from the time of the United Empire Loyalists, War of 1812, early Upper Canada and the Victorian era. (Mar-Dec, daily; rest of yr, wkends or by appt; closed Jan 1, Good Friday, Dec 25-26) 43 Castlereagh St. Contact the Niagara Historical Society, PO Box 208, L0S 1J0; 905/468-3912. ¢¢

St Mark's Anglican Church (1805, 1843). Original church damaged by fire after being used as a hospital and barracks during the War of 1812. Rebuilt in 1822 and enlarged in 1843. Unusual 3-layer stained-glass window. Churchyard dates from earliest British settlement. (July-Aug, daily; rest of yr, by appt) 41 Byron St, opp Simcoe Park. Phone 905/468-3123.

St Vincent de Paul Roman Catholic Church (1835). First Roman Catholic parish in Upper Canada. Excellent example of Gothic-revival architecture; enlarged in 1965; older part largely preserved. Picton & Wellington Sts.

Seasonal Event

Shaw Festival. Shaw Festival Theatre, specializing in the works of George Bernard Shaw and his contemporaries, presents ten plays each yr in repertory. Housed in three theaters, including Court House Theatre. Staged by an internationally acclaimed ensemble company. Also lunchtime theater featuring one-act plays by Shaw. Queen's Parade & Wellington St. Contact PO Box 774, L0S 1J0; 800/724-2934 (US) or 800/267-4759 (Canada). Mid-Apr-Oct.

Motor Hotel

★ ★ ★ **WHITE OAKS CONFERENCE RESORT & SPA.** (RR 4, Niagara-on-the-Lake ON L0S 1J0) Taylor Rd (L0S 1J0), 10 mi NW on QEW, Glendale Ave exit. 905/688-2550; FAX 905/688-2220; res: 800/263-5766. E-mail hotel@whiteoaks.on.ca; web www.whiteoaks.on.ca. 150 rms, 3 story. S $115-$169; D $125-$189; each addl $10; suites $189-$279; under 13 free; wkend rates. TV; cable, VCR avail. Indoor pool; poolside serv. Playground. Supervised child's activities; to age 10. Complimentary coffee in rms. Restaurant 7 am-11 pm. Rm serv. Bar 11-1 am. Ck-out noon. Meeting rms. Business center. In-rm modem link. Concierge. Valet serv. Indoor, outdoor tennis, pro. Putting green. Exercise rm. Spa. Rec rm. Bathrm phones. Private patios, balconies. Cr cds: A, D, ER, MC, V.

Hotel

★ ★ ★ **PRINCE OF WALES.** (6 Picton St, Niagara-on-the-Lake ON L0S 1J0) 905/468-3246; FAX 905/468-1310; res: 800/263-2452. Web www.princeofwaleshotel.on.ca. 101 rms. May-Oct: S, D $129-$225; each addl $20; suites $275; wkend rates (winter); lower rates rest of yr. Crib free. TV; cable (premium). Indoor pool; whirlpool. Restaurant 11 am-midnight (also see PRINCE OF WALES). Bar 11:30-1 am. Ck-out 11 am. Meeting rms. Business servs avail. In-rm modem link. Exercise equipt; sauna. Health club privileges. Sun deck. Victorian building (1864). Cr cds: A, D, DS, ER, MC, V.

Inns

★ ★ ★ **GATE HOUSE HOTEL.** (142 Queen St, Niagara-on-the-Lake ON L0S 1J0) 905/468-3263; FAX 905/468-7400. 10 rms, 2 story. June-Sept: S, D $160-$180; each addl $10; under 12 free; lower rates Mar-May, Oct-Dec. Closed rest of yr. Crib free. TV; cable (premium). Complimentary continental bkfst. Dining rm noon-2:30 pm, 5-10 pm. Bar 11:30-2 am. Ck-out 11 am. X-country ski 2 mi. Minibars. Modern decor. Cr cds: A, D, ER, JCB, MC, V.

★ ★ **KIELY HOUSE HERITAGE INN.** (209 Queen St, Niagara-on-the-Lake ON L0S 1J0) 905/468-4588; FAX 905/468-2194. 11 rms, 2 story, 4 suites. No A/C. Mid-Apr-Oct: S $75; D $119; suites $145-$175; under 12 free; lower rates rest of yr. Restaurant 11:30 am-9 pm. Ck-out 11 am, ck-in 1 pm. Lighted tennis privileges, pro. X-country ski 1 mi. Balconies. Built 1832 as private summer residence; several screened porches. Cr cds: A, MC, V.

★ ★ **MOFFAT INN.** (60 Picton St, Niagara-on-the-Lake ON L0S 1J0) QEW via ON 55. 905/468-4116; FAX 905/468-4747. 22 rms, 2 story. May-Oct: S, D $79-$125; each addl $10; lower rates rest of yr. TV. Complimentary coffee in rms. Dining rm 8 am-midnight. Bar. Ck-out 11 am, ck-in 2 pm. Business servs avail. In-rm modem link. Some private patios. Historic inn (1835); individually decorated rms, many with brass bed; some with fireplace. Totally nonsmoking. Cr cds: A, MC, V.

★ ★ ★ **PILLAR & POST.** (48 John St, Niagara-on-the-Lake ON L0S 1J0) King & John Sts. 905/468-2123; res: 800/361-6788; FAX 905/468-3551. Web www.pillarandpost.com. 123 rms. S, D $170; each addl $20; suites $225-$375; under 12 free; winter packages. TV; cable (premium). Heated pool; whirlpool. Restaurant (see THE CARRIAGES). Rm serv. Bar 11-1 am. Ck-out 11 am, ck-in 3 pm. Meeting rm. Business center. In-rm modem link. Luggage handling. Gift shop. Bicycle rentals. Exercise rm; sauna. Spa. Minibars; some fireplaces. Turn-of-the-century fruit canning factory. Cr cds: A, D, DS, ER, MC, V.

★ ★ ★ **QUEEN'S LANDING.** (155 Byron St, Niagara-on-the-Lake ON L0S 1J0) at Melville. 905/468-2195; FAX 905/468-2227; res: 800/361-6645. Web www.queenslanding.com. 142 rms, 3 story. S, D $195-$255; each addl $20; suites $350-$450; under 18 free; some lower rates off-season. Crib free. TV; cable (premium), VCR avail. Indoor pool; whirlpool. Dining rm 7 am-10 pm. Rm serv to midnight. Bar 11-1 am. Ck-out 11 am, ck-in 3 pm. Meeting rms. Business servs avail. In-rm modem link. Bellhops. Valet serv. Concierge. Tennis privileges. 18-hole golf privileges. X-country ski 6 mi. Exercise equipt; sauna. Health club privileges. Minibars. Antique furnishings; distinctive appointments. Many in-rm whirlpools, fireplaces. Located at the mouth of the Niagara River, opp historic Fort Niagara. Bicycle rentals. Cr cds: A, D, DS, ER, MC, V.

Restaurants

★ ★ **BUTTERY THEATRE.** (19 Queen St, Niagara-on-the-Lake ON L0S 1J0) 905/468-2564. Continental menu. Specialties: spare ribs, roast leg of lamb, lobster Newburg. Hrs: 11-1 am; Fri, Sat to 1 am. Closed Dec 25. Res accepted. Bar. A la carte entrees: lunch $7.50-$15.50, dinner $15-$23. Child's meals. Medieval feast Fri, Sat. Patio dining. Family-owned. Cr cds: A, MC, V.

★ ★ ★ **THE CARRIAGES.** (See Pillar & Post Inn) 905/468-2123. E-mail www.pillarandpost.com. Continental menu. Specializes in rack of lamb. Hrs: 7:30-10:30 am, noon-2 pm, 5-9 pm. Res required. Bar 11-1 am. Wine list. Semi-a la carte: bkfst $1.95-$7.25, lunch $9-$14.95, dinner

$15.95-$26.95. Buffet: bkfst $11. Child's meals. Intimate dining. Cr cds: A, DS, ER, MC, V.

★ **FANS COURT.** (135 Queen St, Niagara-on-the-Lake ON L0S 1J0) 905/468-4511. Chinese menu. Hrs: noon-10 pm. Res accepted. Bar. A la carte entrees: lunch $5-$7.50, dinner $9-$15.80. Outdoor dining. Large display of antique Chinese vases, jade & figurines. Cr cds: A, D, JCB, MC, V.

★★★ **PRINCE OF WALES.** (See Prince Of Wales Hotel) 905/468-3246. Continental menu. Specializes in rack of lamb, fresh salmon. Own pastries. Hrs: 7-10:30 am, 11:30 am-2 pm, 5-10 pm; Fri, Sat to 10 pm; Sun brunch 11 am-2:30 pm; winter hrs vary. Res accepted. Bar. A la carte entrees: bkfst $5.50-$12.95, lunch $11.50-$14.95, dinner $17.50-$29.95. Sun brunch $21.95. Child's meals. Greenhouse dining. Victorian decor. Built 1864. Cr cds: A, D, DS, ER, MC, V.

Ottawa (C-9)

Founded 1827 **Pop** 295,163 **Elev** 374 ft (114 m) **Area code** 613 **Web** www.tourottawa.org
Information Tourism & Convention Authority, 130 Albert St, Suite 1800, K1P 5G4; 613/237-5150 or 800/363-4465.

The capital city of Canada, Ottawa is situated at the confluence of the Ottawa, Gatineau and Rideau rivers. A camp established by Champlain in 1615 served as headquarters for explorations from Québec to Lake Huron. For nearly two centuries, fur traders and missionaries used the Ottawa River—their only transportation route—for travel to the interior.

The first European settlement in the area was Hull, Québec, founded across the Ottawa River in 1800. In 1823 the Earl of Dalhousie secured ground for the crown on what is now Parliament Hill. Shortly after, two settlements bordered this: Upper Town and Lower Town.

The area was named Bytown in 1827, after Colonel John By, an engineer in charge of construction of the Rideau Canal, which bisects the city and connects the Ottawa River to Lake Ontario. In 1854 Bytown was renamed Ottawa. About this time four cities were rivals for capital of the United Provinces of Upper and Lower Canada: Montréal, Québec City, Kingston and Toronto. Queen Victoria, in anticipation of confederation, unexpectedly selected Ottawa as capital in 1857, because the city was a meeting point of French and English cultures. Ten years later confederation took place, and Ottawa became capital of Canada.

Today Ottawa is an important cultural center with few heavy industries. With its parks full of flowers and its universities, museums and diplomatic embassies, Ottawa is one of Canada's most beautiful cities.

What to See and Do

By Ward Market. Traditional farmers' market; building houses boutiques and art galleries; outdoor cafés. Exterior market (daily); interior market (Apr-Dec, daily; rest of yr, daily exc Mon). Bounded by Dalhousie & Sussex Dr, George & Clarence Sts. Phone 613/562-3325. **Free.**

Bytown Museum. Artifacts, documents and pictures relating to Colonel By, Bytown, and the history and social life of the region. Tours (by appt). (Early May-mid-Oct, daily; rest of yr, Mon-Fri or by appt) Commissariat Building, 50 Canal Lane, beside the Ottawa Locks, Rideau Canal. Phone 613/234-4570. ¢¢

✪ **Canadian Museum of Civilization.** This vast facility employs state-of-the-art exhibition technology to illustrate Canada's history and heritage over 1,000 yrs of settlement. Permanent attractions include **The Children's Museum**, offering a variety of hands-on displays, workshops and activities; **CINÉPLUS**, the world's first convertible IMAX/Omnimax theater; **History Hall**, a setting for many life-size reconstructions of various build-

ings and environments in Canada's past; and **The Grand Hall**, an expansive space housing six Pacific Coast indigenous houses as well as demonstrations, native ceremonies and participatory activities. Large galleries with changing exhibits; theater. Tours. (May-mid-Oct, daily; rest of yr, daily exc Mon; closed Jan 1, Dec 25) Free admission to museum Sun mornings. 100 Laurier St, Hull, PQ. Phone 819/776-7000. Museum ¢¢; CINÉPLUS ¢¢¢-¢¢¢¢

Canadian Parliament Buildings. Neo-Gothic architecture dominates this part of the city. House of Commons and Senate meet here; visitors may request tickets (free) to both chambers when Parliament is in session. 45-min guided tour includes House of Commons, Senate Chamber, Parliamentary Library. (Daily; closed Jan 1, July 1, Dec 25) (See SEASONAL EVENTS) Wellington St on Parliament Hill. Phone 613/996-0896. **Free.** Also here are the **Centennial Flame**, lit in 1967 as a symbol of Canada's 100th birthday, and **Memorial Chapel**, dedicated to Canadian servicemen who lost their lives in the Boer War, World Wars I & II and the Korean War. **Observation Deck** atop the Peace Tower.

Canadian Ski Museum. History of skiing; collection of old skis & ski equipment from Canada and around the world. (Daily; closed some hols) 1960 Scott St. Phone 613/722-3584. ¢

Canadian War Museum. Exhibits tracing Canada's military history include arms, aircraft, military vehicles, uniforms and action displays. (May-mid-Oct, daily; rest of yr, daily exc Mon; closed Dec 25) 330 Sussex Dr. Phone 819/776-8600. ¢¢

Central Experimental Farm. Approx 1,200 acres (486 hectares) of field crops, ornamental gardens, arboretum; showcase herds of beef and dairy cattle, sheep, swine, horses. Tropical greenhouse (daily). Agricultural museum (daily; closed Dec 25). Clydesdale horse-drawn wagon or sleigh rides. Picnicking. (May-mid-Oct) Grounds (daily). Some fees. Prince of Wales Drive. Phone 613/991-3044.

City Hall. Situated on Green Island, on the Rideau River. View of city and surrounding area from 8th floor. Guided tours (Mon-Fri, by appt; closed hols). 111 Sussex Dr. Phone 613/244-5464. Opp are the Rideau Falls. **Free.**

Currency Museum. Artifacts, maps and exhibits tell the story of money and its use throughout the world. (May-Labour Day, daily; rest of yr, daily exc Mon) 245 Sparks St. Phone 613/782-8914. ¢

Laurier House. Former residence of two prime ministers: Sir Wilfrid Laurier and W.L. Mackenzie King. Re-created study of Prime Minister Lester B. Pearson. Books, furnishings and memorabilia. (Daily exc Mon; closed Jan 1, Good Fri, Dec 25) 335 Laurier Ave E. Phone 613/992-8142. ¢¢

Museum of Canadian Scouting. Depicts the history of Canadian Scouting; exhibits on the life of Lord R.S.S. Baden-Powell, founder of the Boy Scouts; pertinent documents, photographs and artifacts. (Mon-Fri; closed hols) 1345 Base Line Rd, 8 mi (13 km) SW. Phone 613/224-5131. **Free.**

National Archives of Canada. Collections of all types of material relating to Canadian history. Changing exhibits. (Daily) 395 Wellington St. Phone 613/995-5183. **Free.** Opp is **Garden of the Provinces.** Flags representing all Canadian provinces and territories; fountain illuminated at night. (May-Nov)

National Arts Centre. Center for the performing arts that houses a concert hall and two theaters for music, dance, variety and drama; home of the National Arts Centre Orchestra; more than 800 performances each yr; canal-side cafe (see RESTAURANTS). Landscaped terraces with panoramic view of Ottawa. Guided tours (free). 53 Elgin St at Confederation Square. Phone 613/996-5051 or 613/755-1111(Ticketmaster).

✪ **National Gallery of Canada.** Permanent exhibits include European paintings from 14th century to present; Canadian art from 17th century to present; contemporary and decorative arts, prints, drawings, photos and Inuit art; video and film. Reconstructed 19th-century Rideau convent chapel with Neo-Gothic fan vaulted ceiling, only known example of its kind in North America. Changing exhibits (fee), gallery talks, films; restaurants, bookstore. Guided tours (daily). (May-mid-Sept, daily; rest of yr, Wed-Sun; closed statutory hols) 380 Sussex Dr, at St Patrick St. Phone 613/990-1985. **Free.**

National Museum of Science and Technology. More than 400 exhibits with many do-it-yourself experiments; Canada's role in science and technology is shown through displays on Canada in space, transportation, agriculture, computers, communications, physics and astronomy. Unusual open restoration bay allows viewing of various stages of artifact repair & refurbishment. Cafeteria. (May-Labour Day, daily; rest of yr, daily exc Mon; closed Dec 25) 1867 St Laurent Blvd. Phone 613/991-3044. ¢¢ The museum also maintains

National Aviation Museum. More than 100 historic aircraft, 49 on display in a "Walkway of Time." Displays demonstrate the development of aircraft in peace and war, emphasizing Canadian aviation. (Daily) Rockcliffe Airport, NE end of city. Phone 613/993-2010 or 800/463-2038. ¢¢

Nepean Point. Lovely view of the area; Astrolabe Theatre, a 700-seat amphitheater, is the scene of musical, variety and dramatic shows in summer. Just W of Sussex Dr & St Patrick. Phone 613/239-5000. **Free.**

Professional sports.

NHL (Ottawa Senators). Corel Center, 1000 Palladium Dr, in Kanata. Phone 613/755-1166.

Recreational facilities. For information on canoes, rowboats, docking and launching, swimming at outdoor beaches and pools, phone 613/239-5000. Gatineau Park, across the Ottawa River in Québec, offers swimming, fishing, bicycling, cross-country skiing, picnicking and camping. There are more than 87 mi (140 km) of recreational trails and approximately 50 golf courses in the area. Boats may be rented on the Rideau Canal at Dow's Lake, Queen Elizabeth Driveway & Preston St. Contact the National Capital Commission, 90 Wellington St, opposite Parliament Hill, phone 613/239-5000. Fishing licenses (required in Québec for nonresidents) may be obtained at the Québec Dept of Tourism, Fish & Game, 13 rue Buteau, J8Z 1V4 in Hull, PQ (wkdays, exc summer hols); 613/771-4840.

★ **Rideau Canal.** Constructed under the direction of Lieutenant-Colonel John By of the Royal Engineers between 1826-32 as a safe supply route to Upper Canada. The purpose was to bypass the St Lawrence River in case of an American attack. There are 24 lock stations where visitors can picnic, watch boats pass through the hand-operated locks and see wooden lock gates, cut-stone walls and many historic structures. During summer there are interpretive programs and exhibits at various locations. Areas of special interest include Kingston Mills Locks, Jones Falls Locks (off ON 15), Smith Falls Museum (off ON 15), Merrickville Locks (on ON 43) and Ottawa Locks. Boating is popular (mid-May-mid-Oct, daily) and ice-skating is available (mid-Dec-late Feb, daily). Runs 125 mi (202 km) between Kingston and Ottawa. Phone 613/283-5170. **Free.**

Royal Canadian Mint. Production of coins; collection of coins and medals. Guided tours and film; detailed process of minting coins and printing bank notes is shown. (Daily; tours by appt) 320 Sussex Dr. Phone 613/993-8990. ¢

Sightseeing tours.

Double-Decker bus tours. Capital Trolley Tours. Buses seen in service in Britain visit various highlights of the city. (Apr-mid-Nov, daily) Phone 613/729-6888. ¢¢¢¢

Gray Line bus tours. (May-Oct, daily) Phone 613/725-1441.

Ottawa Riverboat Company. Two-hr cruises on Ottawa River. Boats depart from Hull & Ottawa docks (daily). Also evening dinner/dance cruises (Wed-Fri). Phone 613/562-4888. ¢¢¢-¢¢¢¢

Paul's Boat Lines, Ltd. Rideau Canal sightseeing cruises depart from Conference Centre (mid-May-mid-Oct, daily). Ottawa River sightseeing cruises depart from foot of Rideau Canal Locks (mid-May-mid-Oct, daily). Phone 613/225-6781. ¢¢¢

Victoria Memorial Museum Building. Castle-like structure houses museum that interrelates man and his natural environment. Houses the **Canadian Museum of Nature.** Natural history exhibits from dinosaurs to present day plants and animals. Outstanding collection of minerals and gems. (Daily; closed Dec 25) Metcalfe & McLeod Sts. Phone 613/566-4700. ¢¢

Annual Events

Winterlude. Extravaganza devoted to outdoor concerts, fireworks, skating contests, dances, music, ice sculptures. Phone 613/239-5000 3 wkends Feb.

Canadian Tulip Festival. Part of a 2-wk celebration, culminated by the blooming of more than three million tulips presented to Ottawa by Queen Juliana of the Netherlands after she sought refuge here during World War II. Tours of flower beds; craft market and demonstrations, kite flying, boat parade. Phone 613/567-5757. May.

Canada Day. Celebration of Canada's birthday with many varied events throughout the city including canoe and sailing regattas, concerts, music and dance, art and craft demonstrations, children's entertainment, fireworks. Phone 613/239-5000. July 1.

Ottawa International Jazz Festival. Phone 613/594-3580. 10 days July.

Seasonal Events

Sound & Light Show on Parliament Hill. Phone 613/239-5000. Mid-May-Labour Day.

Changing the Guard. Parliament Hill. Phone 613/239-5000. Late June-late Aug.

Motor Hotel

★ ★ **SUPER 8.** (480 Metcalfe St, Ottawa ON K1S 3N6) Hwy 417 exit Metcalfe St. 613/237-5500; FAX 613/237-6705. 157 rms, 9 story. S, D $79; each addl $10; suites $110; under 18 free; wknd rates. Crib free. TV; cable. Indoor pool. Complimentary coffee in rms. Restaurant 7 am-2 pm, 5-10 pm; Sun to 2 pm. Ck-out noon. Meeting rms. Business servs avail. In-rm modem link. Valet serv. Downhill/x-country ski 10 mi. Cr cds: A, D, DS, ER, MC, V.

⊡ ≈ ⋈ 🔥 **SC**

Hotels

★ ★ ★ **ALBERT AT BAY.** (435 Albert St, Ottawa ON K1R 7X4) 613/238-8858; FAX 613/238-1433; res: 800/267-6644. E-mail info@ab-suites.com; web www.albertatbay.com. 195 kit. suites, 12 story. S, D $124-$144; under 16 free; wkend, monthly rates. Crib free. Garage $8.50. TV; cable. Restaurant 6:30 am-midnight; Sat, Sun from 11 am. Ck-out noon. Coin lndry. Meeting rms. Business servs avail. In-rm modem link. Downhill ski 8 mi; x-country ski 5 mi. Exercise equipt; sauna. Whirlpool. Microwaves. Balconies. Renovated apartment building. Roof-top garden with picnic tables, lawn chairs. Cr cds: A, C, D, DS, ER, JCB, MC, V.

⊡ ≈ ⋉ ⋈ 🔥 **SC**

✔★ **BEST WESTERN HOTEL JACQUES CARTIER.** (131 Laurier St, Hull (Québec) ON J8X 3W3) On N side of Alexandria Bridge (to Ottawa). 819/770-8550; res: 800/265-8550; FAX 819/770-9705. 144 rms, 9 story. Mid-May-mid-Oct: S, D $86-$125; each addl $10; kit. units $100-$125; under 18 free; lower rates rest of yr. Crib $10. TV; cable. Indoor pool; lifeguard. Restaurant 7 am-2 pm, 5-10 pm; wkend hrs vary. Bar 11-3 am; entertainment. Ck-out noon. Meeting rms. Business servs avail. Many refrigerators. Some balconies. Opp Museum of Civilization. Cr cds: A, C, D, DS, ER, MC, V.

≈ ⋈ 🔥 **SC**

★ ★ **BEST WESTERN VICTORIA PARK SUITES.** (377 O'Connor St, Ottawa ON K2P 2M2) 613/567-7275; FAX 613/567-1161. E-mail steph@vpsuites.com; web www.vpsuites.com. 100 kit. units, 8 story. May-Oct: S, D $100-$145; wkend rates; lower rates rest of yr. Crib free. Garage parking $7. TV; cable. Complimentary continental bkfst. Restaurant nearby. Ck-out noon. Coin lndry. Meeting rms. Business servs avail. Exercise equipt. Microwaves. Cr cds: A, D, DS, ER, MC, V.

⋉ ⋈ 🔥 **SC**

★ ★ ★ **CHÂTEAU LAURIER.** (1 Rideau St, Ottawa ON K1N 8S7) opp Rideau Canal from Parliament Hill. 613/241-1414; FAX 613/592-7030; res: 800/441-1414. 425 rms, 8 story. S, D $149-$249; each addl $25; suites $330-$550; under 18 free. Crib free. Garage parking (fee). TV; cable (premium). Indoor pool; lifeguard. Supervised child's activities (summer). Restaurant 5:30 am-11 pm; dining rm (summer) 11:30 am-11 pm. Rm serv 24 hrs. Bar noon-1 am. Ck-out noon. Convention facilities. Business center. In-rm modem link. Concierge. Shopping arcade. Downhill/x-country ski 12 mi. Exercise rm; sauna. Massage. Rec rm. Minibars. Built in 1912. Luxury level. Cr cds: A, C, D, DS, ER, JCB, MC, V.

★ ★ ★ **CITADEL-OTTAWA HOTEL AND CONVENTION CENTRE.** (101 Lyon St, Ottawa ON K1R 5T9) 613/237-3600; FAX 613/237-2351; res: 800/567-3600. 411 rms, 26 story. S, D $89-$155; each addl $12; suites $150-$450; under 18 free; package plans. Crib free. Garage (fee). TV; cable. Indoor pool. Restaurant 6:30 am-10 pm. Bar 11-1 am. Ck-out 1 pm. Meeting rms. Business center. Concierge. Gift shop. Downhill/x-country ski 12 mi. Exercise rm; sauna. Cr cds: A, C, D, DS, ER, MC, V.

★ ★ ★ **DELTA.** (361 Queen St, Ottawa ON K1R 7S9) off Lyon St. 613/238-6000; FAX 613/238-2290; res: 800/268-1133. E-mail jwilliams@deltahotels.com; web www.deltahotels.com. 328 units, 18 story. May-June, Sept-Oct: S, D $155-$175; each addl $15; suites $180-$200; under 18 free; wkend rates; special summer rates; lower rates rest of yr. Crib free. Pet accepted. Garage $11.50. TV; cable. Indoor pool; whirlpool. Restaurant 6:30 am-10 pm. Rm serv 6 am-11 pm. Bars 11-2 am. Ck-out noon. Meeting rms. Business center. In-rm modem link. Barber, beauty shop. Downhill/x-country ski 12 mi. Exercise rm; saunas. Minibars. Some balconies. Luxury level. Cr cds: A, D, ER, JCB, MC, V.

★ ★ **LORD ELGIN.** (100 Elgin St, Ottawa ON K1P 5K8) at Laurier Ave. 613/235-3333; FAX 613/235-3223; res: 800/267-4298. Web www.interconti.com. 311 rms, 11 story. S $109-$135; D $115-$141; each addl $5; suites $180-$200; under 18 free; wkend rates. Crib free. Pet accepted, some restrictions. Garage; valet, in/out $11.50. TV; cable. Coffee in rms. Restaurant 7 am-11 pm. Bar 11:30-1 am. Ck-out 1 pm. Meeting rms. Business servs avail. In-rm modem link. Gift shop. Downhill/x-country ski 12 mi. Exercise equipt. Originally opened 1941; completely renovated. Cr cds: A, C, D, ER, JCB, MC, V.

★ ★ **RADISSON-OTTAWA CENTRE.** (100 Kent St, Ottawa ON K1P 5R7) 613/238-1122; FAX 613/783-4229. 478 rms, 26 story. S, D $125-$155; each addl $10; suites $300-$400; under 19 free; wkend rates. Crib free. Pet accepted. Garage (fee). TV; cable (premium). Indoor pool; whirlpool. Restaurant 6:30 am-11 pm; revolving rooftop dining rm 11:30 am-2:30 pm, 6-11 pm; Sat from 6 pm. Bar 11-1 am. Ck-out 1 pm. Meeting rms. Business servs avail. In-rm modem link. Downhill ski 15 mi. Exercise rm; sauna. Minibars. Many balconies. Adj underground shopping mall. Luxury level. Cr cds: A, C, D, DS, ER, JCB, MC, V.

★ ★ ★ **SHERATON.** (150 Albert St, Ottawa ON K1P 5G2) 613/238-1500; FAX 613/235-2723. 236 rms, 18 story. S $200; D $215; each addl $20; suites $280-$450; family rates; package plans. Crib free. Garage (fee). Pet accepted. TV; cable. Indoor pool; poolside serv. Coffee in rms. Restaurant 6:30 am-11 pm. Ck-out noon. Meeting rms. Business center. In-rm modem link. Gift shop. Downhill/x-country ski 12 mi. Exercise equipt; sauna. Minibars. Luxury level. Cr cds: A, D, DS, ER, JCB, MC, V.

★ ★ ★ **WESTIN.** (11 Colonel By Dr, Ottawa ON K1N 9H4) connects with Ottawa Congress Center, Rideau Center. 613/560-7000; FAX 613/560-7359. 484 rms, 24 story. Mid-Apr-June, mid-Sept-mid-Nov: S, D $190-$211; each addl $20; suites $265-$700; under 18 free; wkend rates; lower rates rest of yr. Crib free. Pet accepted, some restrictions. TV; cable. Indoor pool; whirlpool. Restaurants 6:30 am-11 pm. Rm serv 24 hrs. Bar 11:30-2 am. Ck-out 1 pm. Convention facilities. Business center. Concierge. Shopping arcade adj. Barber, beauty shop. Valet parking. Downhill/x-country ski 12 mi. Exercise rm; sauna. Massage. Minibars; some bathrm phones. Opp Rideau Canal; near Parliament Hill. Cr cds: A, C, D, DS, ER, JCB, MC, V.

Inns

★ ★ ★ **GASTHAUS SWITZERLAND INN.** (89 Daly Ave, Ottawa ON K1N 6E6) 613/237-0335; FAX 613/594-3327; 800 888/663-0000. E-mail switzinn@magi.com; web infoweb.magi.com/~switzinn/. 22 rms, 3 story. May-Oct: S, D $78-$128; lower rates rest of yr. Children over 12 yrs only. TV; cable. Complimentary full bkfst. Restaurant nearby. Ck-out 11 am, ck-in 3 pm. In-rm modem link. Some in-rm whirlpools, fireplaces. Picnic tables. In restored 1872 house. Totally nonsmoking. Cr cds: A, D, ER, MC, V.

✔ ★ **VOYAGEUR'S GUEST HOUSE.** (95 Arlington Ave, Ottawa ON K1R 5S4) 613/238-6445; FAX 613/236-5551. Web www.bbcanada.com/897.html. 6 rms, 3 share bath, 2 story. No rm phones. S $34; D $44; each addl $10; higher rates Canada Day. TV; cable (premium). Complimentary full bkfst. Restaurant nearby. Ck-out 11 am, ck-in 11 am. Downhill ski 20 mi; x-country ski 3 mi. Totally nonsmoking. Cr cds: D, ER, MC, V.

Resort

★ ★ ★ **LE CHÂTEAU MONTEBELLO.** (392 Rue Notre Dame, Montebello, Quebec QE J0V 1L0) 40 mi E on Hwy 148. 819/423-6341; FAX 819/423-5283; res: 800/441-1414. Web www.cphotels.ca. 210 rms, 3 story. Mid-May-mid-Oct, MAP: S $186.50; D $238; each addl $71.50; under 4 free; lower rates rest of yr. Crib free. Pet accepted. TV; cable. 2 pools, 1 indoor; whirlpool, lifeguard. Playground. Supervised child's activities (mid-June-early Sept); ages 3-12. Dining rm (see AUX CHANTIGNOLES). Rm serv 7 am-11 pm. Bar 11-1 am; entertainment Fri-Sat. Ck-out noon, ck-in 3 pm. Meeting rms. Business center. In-rm modem link. Bellhops. Valet serv. Gift shop. Sports dir. Indoor & outdoor tennis. 18-hole golf, greens fee (incl cart) $62, pro, putting green. X-country ski on site (rentals). Sleighing. Curling. Bicycles. Lawn games. Soc dir. Rec rm. Game rm. Squash courts. Exercise rm; sauna, steam rm. Massage. Fishing, hunting guides. Minibars. Marina. On 65,000 acres. Cr cds: A, C, D, DS, ER, JCB, MC, V.

Restaurants

★ ★ ★ **AUX CHANTIGNOLES.** (See Le Château Montebello Resort) 819/423-6341. French, continental menu. Specializes in seafood, veal, game. Own baking. Hrs: 7 am-3 pm, 5:30-10 pm; Sun brunch 11 am-3 pm. Res accepted. Serv bar. Wine list. Buffet: bkfst $14.25. Complete meals: lunch $19.50. A la carte entrees: dinner $24.50-$29.50. Sun brunch $28.50. Child's meals. Parking. Outdoor dining. Rustic decor; fireplace. Cr cds: A, C, D, DS, ER, JCB, MC, V.

★ ★ **CHEZ BUNTHA.** (64 Queen St, Ottawa ON K1P 5C6) off Elgin St. 613/234-0064. Continental menu. Specialties: lamb with fine herbs, sirloin flambé, seafood. Hrs: 11:30 am-midnight; Sat, Sun from 5 pm. Res accepted. Wine list. Buffet: lunch $8.50. A la carte entrees: lunch $7.50-$12, dinner $12.95-$19.95. Child's meals. Entertainment Fri, Sat. Formal, contemporary decor. Cr cds: A, C, D, ER, MC, V.

★ **FULIWAH.** (691 Somerset St W, Ottawa ON K2A 2C2) in Chinatown area. 613/233-2552. Chinese menu. Specializes in Cantonese, Szechwan cuisine. Hrs: 11 am-midnight; Sat, Sun from 10 am. Res accepted. Bar. Semi-a la carte: lunch, dinner $6.50-$24. Dim sum $2.25-$3.25. Parking. Cr cds: A, D, MC, V.

★ ★ **LA GONDOLA.** (188 Bank St, Ottawa ON K2P 1W8) 613/235-3733. Continental, Italian menu. Specializes in veal, pasta. Hrs: 11:30 am-11:30 pm; Sun 10 am-10 pm; Sat, Sun brunch 10 am-3 pm.

Closed Dec 25. Res accepted. Bar. A la carte entrees: lunch $5.95-$12.95, dinner $8.95-$22. Sat, Sun brunch $3.25-$7. Child's meals. Outdoor dining. Cr cds: A, C, D, ER, MC, V.

✔★ **LAS PALMAS.** (111 Parent Ave, Ottawa ON K1N 7B3) 613/241-3738. Mexican menu. Specializes in fajitas, enchiladas. Hrs: 11:30 am-11 pm. Bar. A la carte entrees: lunch, dinner $6-$15.95. Mexican village setting. Outdoor dining. Cr cds: A, C, D, ER, JCB, MC, V.

★★ **LE CAFÉ.** (53 Elgin St (National Arts Centre), Ottawa ON K1P 5W1) Confederation Sq. 613/594-5127. Nouvelle Canadian menu. Own pastries. Hrs: noon-11 pm. Closed Jan 1, Dec 24, 25; also Sun Sept-May. Res accepted. Bar. A la carte entrees: lunch $7.95-$13.95, dinner $12.95-$22.95. Child's meals. Parking. Outdoor dining on terrace overlooking Rideau Canal. Totally nonsmoking. Cr cds: A, D, ER, MC, V.

D

★★ **MARBLE WORKS STEAKHOUSE.** (14 Waller St, Ottawa ON K1N 9C4) 613/241-6764. Specializes in steak. Hrs: 11:30 am-2 pm, 5-10 pm; Sat from 5 pm; Sun from 10:30 am. Closed Dec 25. Res accepted. Bar to 2 am. A la carte entrees: lunch $8-$16, dinner $12-$24. Sun brunch $11.95. Child's meals. Sat entertainment. Parking. Outdoor dining. In renovated 1866 building. Cr cds: A, C, D, ER, MC, V.

★★ **THE MILL.** (555 Ottawa River Pkwy, Ottawa ON K1P 5R4) Wellington Ave and Portage bridge. 613/237-1311. Continental menu. Specializes in prime rib, fish, chicken. Hrs: 11:30 am-2:30 pm, 4:30-10 pm; wkends from 4:30 pm; Sun brunch 10:30 am-1:30 pm. Closed July 1. Bar. A la carte entrees: lunch $5.95-$9.95, dinner $9.95-$17.95. Sun brunch $4.95-$9.95. Child's meals. Parking. Outdoor dining. Former mill (1850); mill structure visible through glass wall. Cr cds: A, D, ER, MC, V.

✔★ **SITAR.** (417A Rideau St, Ottawa ON K1N 5Y6) 613/789-7979. Indian menu. Specializes in tandoori-prepared dishes, vegetarian dishes. Own breads. Hrs: 11:45 am-2 pm, 5-10:30 pm; Sun 5-10:30 pm. Closed Jan 1, Dec 25. Complete meals: lunch $7.95, dinner $14.95-$18.75. Cr cds: A, C, D, ER, MC, V.

D

Quetico Provincial Park (F-2)

(See also Fort Frances, Thunder Bay)

Web www.ontarioparks.com

Information Superintendent, Ministry of Natural Resources, 108 Saturn Ave, Atikokan P0T 1C0; 807/597-2735.

Quetico is a wilderness park and as such is composed largely of rugged landscape. There are no roads in the park, but its vast network of connecting waterways allows for some of the best canoeing in North America. More than 900 miles (1,450 kilometers) of canoe routes are within Quetico's 1,832-square-mile (4,622-square-kilometer) area. Canoeing (no motor-powered craft allowed), fishing and swimming are primary activities in the park. Appropriate fishing licenses are required. Interior fee/person/night ¢¢¢¢¢

Car camping is permitted at 107 sites in two areas of the Dawson Trail Campgrounds. Permits can be obtained at Park Ranger Stations. Payments may be made in Canadian or US currency (no personal checks). For reservations phone 807/597-2737 (Canadian residents) or 807/597-2735 (nonresidents). Camping ¢¢¢¢-¢¢¢¢¢

Picnic facilities, trails and a large assortment of pictographs may be enjoyed. In winter the vacationer can ice-fish and cross-country ski, although there are no maintained facilities. Park (Victoria Day wkend-Thanksgiving wkend, daily). Day-use fee/vehicle ¢¢¢

Sarnia (E-5)

(See also London)

Founded 1856 **Pop** 50,892 **Elev** 610 ft (186 m) **Area code** 519

Information Convention and Visitors Bureau of Sarnia-Lambton, 224 N Vidal St, N7T 5Y3; 519/336-3232 or 800/265-0316.

Sarnia was originally known as "The Rapids" and was renamed Port Sarnia in 1836. The town grew because of timber stands in the area, the discovery of oil and the arrival of the Great Western Railway in 1858. Today it is Canada's most important petrochemical center.

Sarnia is located in the center of one of Canada's most popular recreation areas. Lake Huron offers beaches from Canatara Park to nearby Lambton County beaches; the St Clair River flows south of Sarnia into Lake St Clair. Facilities for water sports and boating are excellent. The city and surrounding area has many golf courses, campsites and trailer parks. Easy access to the United States is provided by the International Blue Water Bridge (toll) spanning the St Clair River between Sarnia and Port Huron, Michigan (see Border Crossing Regulations in MAKING THE MOST OF YOUR TRIP).

What to See and Do

Canatara Park. Information center housed in reconstructed 19th-century log cabin (Victoria Day wkend-Labour Day wkend, Mon-Fri afternoons; rest of yr, wkends). Facilities for swimming, picnicking, barbecuing. Also refreshments, beach and bathhouse; lookout tower; fitness trail, natural area, toboggan hill, playground equipment and ball diamond. (Daily) At Cathcart Blvd, off N Christina St. Phone 800/265-0316. **Free.** Also in the park are

Children's Animal Farm. Farm buildings; animals, poultry and waterfowl. (Daily) **Free.**

Log Cabin. Two-floor cabin with natural wooden peg flooring, two fireplaces; interpretive programs featured in summer. Adj are carriage shed, with farm implement artifacts from 1850, and a smokehouse. (Open for special events) **Free.**

Lambton Heritage Museum. Features more than 400 Currier & Ives prints, Canada's largest collection of antique pressed-glass water pitchers; two farm machinery barns; slaughterhouse, chapel and main exhibit center with a chronological natural & human history of Lambton County. (Mar-Oct, daily; rest of yr, Mon-Fri; closed Dec 25-Jan 1) Picnicking. 45 mi (72 km) NE via ON 21, Grand Bend, opp Pinery Provincial Park. Phone 519/243-2600. ¢¢

Moore Museum. Country store, early switchboard, late-1800s church organ in main building; Victorian cottage; log cabin; farm implements; one-rm schoolhouse; 1890 lighthouse. (Mar-June, Wed-Sun; July & Aug, daily; Sept-mid Dec, Mon-Fri) 12 mi (19 km) S in Mooretown, 94 Moore Line, 2 blks E of St Clair Pkwy (County Rd 33). Phone 519/867-2020. ¢

Oil Museum of Canada. On site of first commercialized oil well in North America; historic items and data regarding the discovery. Six acres (2 1/2 hectares) of landscaped grounds with blacksmith shop, pioneer home & post office, railroad station, working oil field using 1860 methods; picnic pavilion. Guided tours. (May-Oct, daily; rest of yr, Mon-Fri) 30 mi SE in Oil Springs on Kelly Rd. Phone 519/834-2840. ¢¢

Sombra Township Museum. Pioneer home with displays of household goods, clothes, books & deeds, marine artifacts, indigenous and military items, music boxes, photographic equipment and farming tools. (June-Sept, afternoons; May, wkends; also by appt) 3470 St Clair Pkwy, S in Sombra. Phone 519/892-3982. ¢

The Gardens. Wide variety of plant life. The park also offers facilities for tennis, lawn bowling, swimming (fee), horseshoes, baseball and soccer. Germain Park, East St. Phone 519/332-0330.

Annual Event

Sarnia Highland Games. Centennial Park. Caber & hammer tossing; stone throwing; haggis-hurling; clan village, bands, dancers. Phone 519/336-5054. Mid-Aug.

Seasonal Events

Sarnia Waterfront Festival. Centennial Park. More than 80 events including singers, dancers; children's shows. Phone 800/265-0316. Late Apr-Labour Day wkend.

Celebration of Lights. Seven-wk festive season featuring 60,000 lights in waterfront park. Residential, commercial displays. Phone 800/265-0316. Late Nov-Dec.

Motels

★ ★ **COMFORT INN.** *(751 N Christina St, Sarnia ON N7V 1X5)* ON 402 Exit Front St.. 519/383-6767; FAX 519/383-8710. 100 rms, 3 story. S $55-$75; D $65-$85; each addl $5; family rates. Crib free. TV; cable. Complimentary continental bkfst. Restaurant adj 6:30 am-midnight. Ck-out noon. Meeting rms. Business center. In-rm modem link. Exercise equipt. Refrigerators avail. Cr cds: A, D, DS, ER, MC, V.

D ✕ ≥ ⊠ ⚲ SC ☒

★ ★ ★ **DRAWBRIDGE INN.** *(283 N Christina St, Sarnia ON N7T 5V4)* 519/337-7571; FAX 519/332-8181; res: 800/663-0376. 97 rms, 3 story. S, D $82; each addl $9; suites $115-$135; under 12 free; wkend rates. Crib free. Pet accepted. TV; cable. Indoor pool. Sauna. Restaurant 7 am-2 pm, 5-9 pm; Fri-Sun 8 am-2 pm, 5-9 pm. Rm serv. Bar noon-11 pm. Ck-out noon. Meeting rms. Business center. In-rm modem link. Bellhops. Valet serv. Health club privileges. Cr cds: A, D, DS, ER, MC, V.

✒ ≥ ⊠ ⚲ SC ☒

✔★ ★ **HARBOURFRONT INN.** *(505 Harbour Rd, Sarnia ON N7T 5R8)* 1/2 mi SW of Bluewater Bridge. 519/337-5434; FAX 519/332-5882; res: 800/787-5010. 105 rms, 2 story. S $51-$58; D $59-$67; each addl $4; under 16 free. Crib free. Pet accepted, some restrictions. TV; cable, VCR avail. Restaurant adj 11-1 am. Ck-out 11 am. Valet serv. Picnic tables. On river. Cr cds: A, D, ER, JCB, MC, V.

D ✒ ✒ ≥ ⚲ SC

★ ★ ★ **HOLIDAY INN.** *(1498 Venetian Blvd, Sarnia ON N7T 7W6)* 519/336-4130; FAX 519/332-3326. E-mail hi-sarnia@bristolhotels.com; web www.hi-online.com. 151 rms, 2 story. S, D $69-$89; suites $180-$240; under 19 free; wkend rates. Crib free. Pet accepted. TV; cable (premium). 2 pools, 1 indoor; whirlpool. Playground. Restaurant 6:30 am-10:30 pm. Rm serv. Bar 11-1 am. Ck-out 1 pm. Meeting rms. Bellhops. Valet serv. Golf privileges, greens fee $10, putting green. Exercise equipt; sauna. Lawn games. Balconies. Cr cds: A, C, D, DS, ER, JCB, MC, V.

D ✒ ☡ ≥ ✕ ⊠ ⚲ SC

Sault Ste Marie (B-3)

Pop 83,300 (est) **Elev** 580 ft (177 m) **Area code** 705 **E-mail** ssmcoc@age.net **Web** www.sault-canada.com

Information Chamber of Commerce, 334 Bay St, P6A 1X1; 705/949-7152.

Founded and built on steel, Sault Ste Marie is separated from its sister city in Michigan by the St Mary's River. Lake and ocean freighters traverse the river, which links Lake Huron and Lake Superior—locally known as "the Soo."

What to See and Do

Agawa Canyon Train Excursion. A scenic day trip by Algoma Central Railway through a wilderness of hills and fjord-like ravines. Two-hr stop-over at the canyon. Dining car on train. (June-mid-Oct, daily; Jan-Mar, wkends only) Advance ticket orders avail by phone; over the counter ticket pickup recommended one day in advance. 129 Bay St. Contact Passenger Sales, Algoma Central Railway, PO Box 7000, P6A 1W7; 705/946-7300 or 800/242-9287. ¢¢¢¢ /DESC

Boat cruises. Two-hr boat cruises from Norgoma dock, next to Holiday Inn on MV *Chief Shingwauk* and MV *Bon Soo* through American locks; also three-hr dinner cruises. (June-mid-Oct) Contact Lock Tours Canada, PO Box 424, P6A 5M1; 705/253-9850. ¢¢¢¢

Sault Ste Marie Museum. Local and national exhibits in a building originally built as a post office. Skylight Gallery traces history of the region dating back 9,000 yrs; includes prehistoric artifacts, displays of early industries, re-creation of 1912 Queen St house interiors. Durham Gallery displays traveling exhibits from the Royal Ontario Museum and locally curated displays. Discovery Gallery for children features hands-on exhibits. (Mon-Sat, daily; Sun afternoons; closed hols) 690 Queen St E. Phone 705/759-7278. **Donation.**

Annual Events

Ontario Winter Carnival Bon Soo. Features more than 100 events: fireworks, fiddle contest, winter sports, polar bear swim, winter playground sculptured from snow. Last wkend Jan-1st wkend Feb.

Algoma Fall Festival. Visual and performing arts presentations by Canadian and international artists. Late Sept-late Oct.

Motel

★ ★ **QUALITY INN-BAY FRONT.** *(180 Bay St, Sault Ste Marie ON P6A 6S2)* 705/945-9264; FAX 705/945-9766. 109 rms, 7 story. Sept-mid-Oct: S $102-$165; D $112-$165; each addl $10; family rates; ski; package plans; lower rates rest of yr. Crib free. TV; cable (premium), VCR avail. Indoor pool; whirlpool. Coffee in rms. Restaurant 7 am-midnight. Rm serv. Bar from 11:30 am. Ck-out 1 pm. Meeting rms. Bellhops. Valet serv. Downhill/x-country ski 8 mi. Exercise equipt; sauna. Some refrigerators. Cr cds: A, C, D, DS, ER, JCB, MC, V.

D ≥ ✕ ⊠ ⚲ SC

Motor Hotels

★ ★ ★ **ALGOMA'S WATER TOWER INN.** *(360 Great Northern Rd, Sault Ste Marie ON P6A 5N3)* 705/949-8111; FAX 705/949-1912. E-mail awtinn@age.net; web watertowerinn.com. 180 rms, 5 story. S, D $79-$99; each addl $7; suites $130-$290; under 18 free; ski plans. Crib free. Pet accepted. TV; cable (premium), VCR avail. Heated pool; whirlpool. Restaurant 7 am-11 pm. Rm serv 7-11 am, 5-10 pm. Bar noon-1 am. Ck-out noon. Meeting rms. Valet serv. Airport transportation. Sundries. X-country ski 5 mi. Exercise equipt. Some refrigerators, microwaves; whirlpool in suites. Cr cds: A, C, D, DS, ER, JCB, MC, V.

D ✒ ≥ ≥ ✕ ⊠ ⚲ SC

★ ★ **HOLIDAY INN.** *(208 St Mary's River Dr, Sault Ste Marie ON P6A 5V4)* 705/949-0611; res: 888/713-8482; FAX 705/945-6972. E-mail yamca.071@sympatico.ca. 195 rms, 9 story. June-mid-Oct: S, D $92-$139; each addl $10; suites $175-$275; under 12 free; lower rates rest of yr. Crib free. Pet accepted. TV; cable (premium). Indoor pool; whirlpool. Restaurant 6:30 am-10 pm. Rm serv. Bar 11-1 am. Ck-out 4 pm. Meeting rms. In-rm modem link. Bellhops. Valet serv. Sundries. Gift shop. Airport transportation. Exercise equipt; sauna. Game rm. Refrigerator in some suites. Cr cds: A, C, D, DS, ER, JCB, MC, V.

D ✒ ≥ ✕ ⊠ ⚲ SC

★ ★ **RAMADA INN & CONVENTION CENTRE.** *(229 Great Northern Rd (Hwy 17 N), Sault Ste Marie ON P6B 4Z2)* 705/942-2500; res: 800/563-7262; FAX 705/942-2570. 211 units, 2-7 story. S $86-$109; D $96-$122; each addl $10; suites $150-$275; under 18 free; package plans.

Crib free. Pet accepted. TV; cable, VCR avail. 2 pools, 1 indoor; whirlpool. Restaurant 7 am-11 pm. Rm serv. Bar to midnight. Ck-out noon. Meeting rms. Business servs avail. Bellhops. Valet serv (Mon-Fri). Sundries. Downhill ski 20 mi; x-country ski 3 mi. Exercise equipt. Miniature golf; water slide. Bowling. Game rms. Some refrigerators. Cr cds: A, C, D, DS, ER, JCB, MC, V.

⊡ 🐾 🏊 ✗ 🍴 🔥 SC

Restaurants

✔★ **GIOVANNI'S.** *(516 Great Northern Rd, Sault Ste Marie ON P6B 4Z9)* 705/942-3050. Italian menu. Specializes in family-style dinners. Hrs: 11:30 am-midnight; Sun to 11 pm. Closed Jan 1, Labor Day, Dec 25. Res accepted. Bar. Semi-a la carte: lunch $5-$8, dinner $7-$15. Child's meals. Cr cds: A, MC, V.

⊡

★★ **NEW MARCONI.** *(480 Albert St W, Sault Ste Marie ON P6A 1C3)* 705/759-8250. Italian, Amer menu. Specialties: barbecued ribs, steak, seafood. Own pasta. Hrs: noon-11 pm. Closed Sun; Jan 1, Dec 25. Res accepted. Serv bar. Semi-a la carte: lunch $4.25-$8.50, dinner $8-$50. Complete meals: dinner $16.95. Family-owned. Cr cds: A, D, ER, MC, V.

St Catharines (E-7)

(See also Hamilton, Niagara-on-the-Lake, Niagara Falls, NY & ON)

Pop 124,018 **Elev** 321 ft (98 m) **Area code** 905 **Web** www.st.catharines.com
Information Tourism Marketing Coordinator, City Hall, 50 Church St, PO Box 3012, L2R 7C2; 905/688-5601, ext 1999.

St Catharines, "The Garden City of Canada," is located in the heart of the wine country and the Niagara fruit belt, which produces half of the province's entire output of fresh fruit. A historic city, originally a Loyalist settlement, it was also a depot of the Underground Railway. Located on the Welland Ship Canal, and the site of the first canal, St Catharines was also the home of the first electric streetcar system in North America.

What to See and Do

Brock University (1964). (6,000 students) A 540-acre (219-hectare) campus encompasses some of the finest woods and countryside in the Niagara region. Named in honor of General Sir Isaac Brock, commander of the British forces at the Battle of Queenston Heights in 1812. Tours (Mon-Fri, by appt). Glenridge Ave/Merrittville Hwy, at St David's Rd. Phone 905/688-5550, ext 3245.

Happy Rolph Bird Sanctuary & Children's Farm. Feeding station for native fowl and farm animals; three ponds; nature trail; picnicking; playground. (Victoria Day-Thanksgiving, daily; ponds all yr) Queen Elizabeth Way, Lake St exit N to Lakeshore Rd E, cross ship canal, then N on Read Rd. Phone 905/937-7210. **Free.**

Morningstar Mill. Waterpowered, fine old mill containing rollers and millstones for grinding flour and feed. Picnic area. (Victoria Day wkend-Thanksgiving wkend, daily; rest of yr, Sat, Sun) De Cew Rd, at De Cew Falls. Phone 905/937-7210. **Free.**

Old Port Dalhousie. An 18th century harborfront village, once the northern terminus of the first three Welland Ship Canals; now part of a larger recreation area with handcrafted wooden carousel, restaurants and shops. Ontario St, N of QEW to Lakeport Rd. Phone 905/935-7555.

Prudhomme's Wet "N" Wild Water Park. Park features wave pool, water and tube slides; rides, arcades. Roller rink; miniature golf; playground; beach; picnicking, snack bar, restaurant (June-Labour Day). 8 mi (13 km) W off Queen Elizabeth Way, Victoria Ave exit 57, near Vineland. Phone 905/562-7304 or 905/562-7121. Day pass ¢¢¢¢

Rodman Hall Arts Centre. Art exhibitions, films, concerts, children's theater. (Daily exc Mon; closed hols) 109 St Paul Crescent. Phone 905/684-2925. **Free.**

The Farmers' Market. Large variety of fruit and vegetables from the fruit belt farms of the surrounding area. (Tues, Thurs & Sat) Church & James Sts, behind City Hall. Phone 905/688-5601, ext 1999.

Welland Canal Viewing Complex at Lock III. Via Queen Elizabeth Way exit at Glendale Ave to Canal Rd then N. Unique view of lock operations from an elevated platform. Ships from over 50 countries can be seen as they pass through the canal. Arrival times are posted. Large information center; picnicking, restaurant. Phone 905/688-5601, ext 1999.Also here is

St Catharines Museum. Illustrates development, construction and significance of the Welland Canal; working scale model lock; displays on history of St Catharines. Exhibitions on loan from major museums. (Daily; closed Jan 1, Dec 25-26) 1932 Government Rd. Phone 905/984-8880. ¢¢

Annual Events

Salmon Derby. Open season on Lake Ontario for coho & chinook salmon; rainbow, brown & lake trout. Prizes for all categories. Phone 905/935-6700. Mid-Apr-mid-May.

Folk Arts Festival. Folk Art Multicultural Centre, 85 Church St. Open houses at ethnic clubs, concerts, ethnic dancing and singing. Art and craft exhibits; big parade. Phone 905/685-6589. 2 wks late May.

Can-Am Soapbox Derby. Jaycee Park, QEW N, exit Ontario St. More than 100 competitors from US and Canada. June.

Niagara Grape and Wine Festival. Wine and cheese parties, athletic events, grape stomping, arts & crafts, ethnic concerts and a parade with bands and floats to honor the ripening of the grapes. Grand Parade last Sat of festival. Phone 905/688-2570. 10 days late Sept.

Seasonal Events

Niagara Symphony Association. Professional symphony orchestra; amateur chorus; summer music camp. (Sept-May) 73 Ontario St, Unit 104. Phone 905/687-4993.

Royal Canadian Henley Regatta. Henley Rowing Course. Champion rowers from all parts of the world. Second in size only to the famous English regatta. Several nation- and continent-wide regattas take place on this world-famous course from Apr to Oct. Phone 905/935-9771.

Motels

✔★★ **HIGHWAYMAN MOTOR INN.** *(420 Ontario St, St Catharines ON L2R 5M1)* 905/688-1646. Web www.ont.net/highwayman/owerche. 50 rms, 2 story. Mid-May-Sept: S $51.95; D $99.95; each addl $5; under 12 free; lower rates rest of yr. Crib $5. TV; cable (premium). Heated pool. Restaurant 7 am-2 pm. Ck-out noon. Meeting rms. Business servs avail. In-rm modem link. Valet serv. Sundries. Cr cds: A, C, D, DS, ER, MC, V.

🏊 🔥 🐾 SC

★★★ **HOLIDAY INN.** *(2 N Service Rd, St Catharines ON L2N 4G9)* at QEW Lake St exit. 905/934-8000; FAX 905/934-9117. E-mail holiday@niagra.com; web www.niagra.com/holidayinn_stc. 140 rms, 2 story. July-Sept: S $105-$135; D $115-$145; each addl $10; under 18 free; lower rates rest of yr. Crib free. Pet accepted. TV; cable (premium) VCR avail (movies). Indoor/outdoor pool; lifeguard. Playground. Complimentary coffee in rms. Restaurant 6:30 am-9 pm. Rm serv. Bar 11-1 am. Ck out noon. Meeting rms. Business servs avail. In-rm modem link. Bellhops. Valet serv. Gift shop. Exercise rm; sauna. Balconies. Cr cds: A, C, D, DS, ER, JCB, MC, V.

⊡ 🐾 🏊 ✗ 🍴 🔥 SC

Motor Hotels

★ ★ ★ **EMBASSY SUITES.** *(3530 Schmon Pkwy, Thorold ON L2V 4Y6) 905/984-8484; FAX 905/984-6691.* Web www.embassy-suites.com. 128 kit. suites, 4 story. S, D $94-$200; each addl $10; under 18 free. Crib free. Pet accepted. TV; cable, VCR avail. Indoor pool. Complimentary full bkfst. Coffee in rms. Restaurant 11 am-11 pm. Rm serv. Bar. Ck-out noon. Guest lndry. Meeting rms. Business center. In-rm modem link. Valet serv. Sundries. Exercise equipt; sauna. Lawn games. Microwaves. Cr cds: A, D, DS, ER, MC, V.

[symbols]

✔ ★ **HOWARD JOHNSON.** *(89 Meadowvale Dr, St Catharines ON L2N 3Z8) just off QEW Lake St N exit. 905/934-5400; FAX 905/646-8700.* 96 rms, 5 story. S $69-$149; D $79-$159; each addl $10; under 18 free. Crib free. Pet accepted. TV. Indoor pool. Coffee in rms. Restaurant open 24 hrs. Bar 11-2 am. Ck-out noon. Coin lndry. Meeting rm. Business servs avail. In-rm modem link. X-country ski 10 mi. Exercise equipt; sauna. Microwaves avail. Cr cds: A, D, DS, ER, MC, V.

[symbols]

★ ★ **RAMADA PARKWAY INN.** *(327 Ontario St, St Catharines ON L2R 5L3) QEW exit 47 S. 905/688-2324; FAX 905/684-6432.* 125 rms, 5 story. Late June-Labor Day: S $89.99; D $149.99; each addl $10; under 18 free; wknd plan off-season; lower rates rest of yr. Crib free. TV; cable. Indoor pool; whirlpool. Sauna. Coffee in rms. Restaurant 6:30 am-11 pm. Bar 11-2 am. Ck-out 11 am. Meeting rms. Business servs avail. Health club privileges. Bowling alley. Refrigerators; some in-rm whirlpools. Plaza adj. Cr cds: A, C, D, DS, ER, MC, V.

[symbols]

Restaurant

★ ★ **CELLAR BENCH.** *(81 James St, St Catharines ON L2R 3H6) 905/641-1922.* Continental menu. Specializes in regional wine-country cuisine. Hrs: 11 am-11 pm; Mon to 9 pm; Fri, Sat to midnight; Sun 3-10 pm. Closed some major hols. Res accepted. Bar. A la carte entrees: lunch $6.50-$10.95, dinner $11.50-$17.95. Child's meals. Outdoor dining. Intimate atmosphere. Cr cds: A, D, ER, MC, V.

St Lawrence Islands National Park (D-9)

(See also Gananoque, Kingston; also see Alexandria Bay (Thousand Islands), NY, Clayton (Thousand Islands), NY)

Information Superintendent, 2 County Rd 5, RR 3, Mallorytown, ON, K0E 1R0; 613/923-5261.

Established in 1904, this park lies on a 50 mile (80 kilometer) stretch of the St Lawrence River between Kingston and Brockville. It consists of 21 island areas and a mainland headquarters at Mallorytown Landing. The park offers boat launching facilities, beaches, natural and historic interpretive programs, island camping, picnicking, hiking and boating. A visitor reception center and the remains of an 1817 British gunboat at Mallorytown Landing (mid-May-mid-Oct, daily; rest of yr, by appt).

The islands can be accessed by water taxi or by boat rentals at numerous marinas along both the Canadian and American sides.

Stratford (E-6)

(See also Brantford, Kitchener-Waterloo)

Pop 27,500 (est) **Elev** 119 ft (36 m) **Area code** 519
Information Tourism Stratford, 88 Wellington St, N5A 2L2; 519/271-5140 or 800/561-SWAN.

The names Stratford and Avon River can conjure up only one name in most travelers' minds—Shakespeare. And that is exactly what you will find in this lovely city. World-renowned, the festival of fine theater takes place in this city every year.

What to See and Do

★ **Shakespearean Gardens.** Fragrant herbs, shrubs and flowering plants common to William Shakespeare's time. Huron St. Phone 519/271-5140. **Free.**

The Gallery/Stratford. Public gallery in parkland setting; historical and contemporary works. Guided tours on request. (Daily) 54 Romeo St N. Phone 519/271-5271. Admission (June-mid-Nov) ¢¢ Adj is

Confederation Park. Features rock hill, waterfall, fountain, Japanese garden and commemorative court.

Annual Event

Kinsmen Antique Show. Stratford Arena. Late July-Aug.

Seasonal Event

Stratford Festival. Contemporary, classical and Shakespearean dramas and modern musicals. Performances at Festival, Avon and Tom Patterson theaters. Contact Box Office, Stratford Festival, PO Box 520, N5A 6V2; 519/273-1600, 416/363-4471 (Toronto) or 800/567-1600. May-Nov, matinees & evenings.

Motels

★ ★ ★ **FESTIVAL INN.** *(1144 Ontario St, Stratford ON N5A 6W1) 519/273-1150; FAX 519/273-2111; res: 800/463-3581.* 183 rms, 1-2 story. May-mid-Nov: S $74-$135; D $80-$139; each addl $10; suites $150; under 12 free; lower rates rest of yr. Crib free. TV; cable (premium), VCR avail. Indoor pool; whirlpool; poolside serv. Restaurant 7 am-9 pm; Sat from 7:30 am; Sun 7:30 am-9 pm. Bar 11:30-1 am. Ck-out 11 am. Meeting rms. Business servs avail. Exercise equipt; sauna. Lawn games. Many refrigerators. Cr cds: A, D, DS, ER, JCB, MC, V.

[symbols]

✔ ★ **MAJER'S.** *(2970 Ontario St E, Stratford ON N5A 6S5) 1¼ mi E on Ontario St (ON 7/8). 519/271-2010; FAX 519/273-7951; res: 800/561-4483.* 31 rms. May-Oct: S $57-$65; D $70-$75; each addl $10; lower rates rest of yr. Crib free. TV; cable (premium). Heated pool. Playground. Complimentary coffee in lobby. Restaurant adj 11 am-11 pm. Ck-out 10:30 am. Refrigerators. Picnic tables. Cr cds: A, MC, V.

[symbols]

★ ★ **STRATFORD SUBURBAN.** *(2808 Ontario St E, Stratford ON N5A 6S5) 2½ mi E on Ontario St (ON 7/8). 519/271-9650; FAX 519/271-0193; res: 800/387-1070.* 25 rms. S $58-$67; D $68-$79; each addl $10. TV; cable. Heated pool. Restaurant nearby. Ck-out 11 am. Tennis. Refrigerators. Cr cds: MC, V.

[symbols]

Motor Hotel

★ ★ **VICTORIAN INN.** *(10 Romeo St N, Stratford ON N5A 5M7) 519/271-4650; FAX 519/271-2030.* E-mail victorian-inn@orc.ca; web www.victorian-inn.on.ca. 115 rms, 4 story. Mid-May-mid-Nov: S, D $79-$139; each addl $10; under 12 free; lower rates rest of yr. Crib $10. TV; cable (premium), VCR avail. Heated pool; poolside serv. Complimentary coffee in rms. Dining rm 7 am-11 am, 5-9 pm. Ck-out noon. Meeting rms. Business servs avail. In-rm modem link. Valet serv. Sundries. Exercise equipt. Game rm. Balconies. On Lake Victoria. Cr cds: A, D, DS, ER, JCB, MC, V.

Inn

★ ★ ★ **QUEEN'S INN.** (161 Ontario St, Stratford ON N5A 3H3) 519/271-1400; res: 800/461-6450; FAX 519/271-7373. E-mail queens@strat ford.webgate.net. 32 rms, 3 story, 7 suites. May-Oct: S $75-$110; D $85-$120; each addl $25; suites $130-$200; kit. units $190-$200; under 12 free; ski plans; lower rates rest of yr. Crib free. Pet accepted, some restrictions. TV; cable, VCR avail (movies). Restaurant 7 am-10 pm. Rm serv. Ck-out 11 am, ck-in 2 pm. Business servs avail. Luggage handling. Valet serv. Concierge serv. Downhill ski 20 mi; x-country ski 10 mi. Exercise equipt. Microwaves avail. Built in 1850. Cr cds: A, D, ER, MC, V.

Restaurants

★ ★ ★ **THE CHURCH RESTAURANT & THE BELFRY.** (70 Brunswick St, Stratford ON N5A 6V6) at Waterloo St. 519/273-3424. French menu. Specialties: salmon monette, filet mignon, loin of lamb. Own baking. Hrs: 11:30 am-2 pm, 5-9 pm; Tues from 5 pm; Fri, Sat 1 am. Closed Mon; Jan 1, Dec 25. Res accepted. Serv bar. Wine cellar. A la carte entrees: lunch $9.95-$16.25, dinner $26.50-$33.50. Complete meals: dinner $49.50-$58.50. Child's meals. Parking. In 1870 Gothic church. Cr cds: A, D, ER, MC, V.

✔ ★ **GENE'S.** (81 Ontario St, Stratford ON) 519/271-9678. Chinese menu. Specializes in Cantonese, Szechwan dishes. Own pies. Hrs: 11 am-midnight; Thurs to 11 pm; Fri, Sat to 2:30 am; Sun noon-9 pm. Closed Dec 25, 26. Res accepted. Bar. A la carte entrees: lunch $6-$7.50, dinner $8.25-$16.95. Child's meals. Oriental decor. Family-owned. Cr cds: A, D, ER, MC, V.

★ ★ **HOUSE OF GENE.** (108 Downie St, Stratford ON) 519/271-3080. Chinese menu. Specializes in Cantonese, Szechwan dishes. Hrs: 11:30 am-8 pm; Fri, Sat to 9 pm; Sun from noon. Closed Dec 25, 26. Res accepted. Bar. A la carte entrees: lunch $6.25-$7.95, dinner $6.25-$16.75. Buffet: lunch $6.95, dinner $8.95. Child's meals. Modern Oriental decor. Cr cds: A, D, ER, MC, V.

★ ★ **KEYSTONE ALLEY CAFE.** (34 Brunswick St, Stradford ON N5A 3L8) 519/271-5645. Continental menu. Specializes in pasta, fresh fish. Hrs: 11:30 am-3 pm, 5-9 pm; Mon to 3 pm. Closed Sun; most major hols. Res accepted. Bar. A la carte entrees: lunch $7.95-$9.95, dinner $15.95-$24.95. Child's meals. Open kitchen. Cr cds: A, D, ER, MC, V.

✔ ★ **MADELYN'S DINER.** (377 Huron St, Stratford ON) 519/273-5296. Specialties: English fish & chips, homemade pies. Hrs: 7 am-8 pm; Sun 8:30 am-1:30 pm. Closed Mon; Dec 25. Res accepted. Bar from 11 am. Semi-a la carte: bkfst $2.50-$7.95, lunch $2.75-$7.25, dinner $6.95-$10.95. Parking. Cr cds: A, MC, V.

★ ★ **OLD PRUNE.** (151 Albert St, Stratford ON N5A 3K5) 519/271-5052. Web www.cyg.net/~oldprune. Specializes in seafood, lamb. Hrs: 11:30 am-1:30 pm, 5-10 pm; Tues from 5 pm. Closed Mon; also Nov-Apr. Res accepted. Bar. A la carte entrees: lunch $8.50-$14.95.

Complete meals: dinner $53.50. Child's meals. Parking. Restored Edwardian residence; enclosed garden terrace. Cr cds: A, MC, V.

Thunder Bay (F-3)

Pop 112,486 **Elev** 616 ft (188 m) **Area code** 807 **Web** www.city.thunder-bay.on.ca/tourism
Information Tourism Thunder Bay, 500 Donald St E, P7E 5V3; 800/667-8386 or 807/983-2041.

Thunder Bay was formed with the joining of the twin cities of Fort William and Port Arthur. It is located on Lake Superior and is a major grain shipping port. The history of Thunder Bay is tied very closely to the fur trade in North America. In the early 19th century, the North West Company had acquired most of the fur trade. Fort William became the inland headquarters for the company, and today much of the activity and spirit of those days can be relived at the fort.

Thunder Bay offers the vacationer outdoor recreation including skiing, parks, and historical attractions and serves as a starting point for a drive around Lake Superior.

What to See and Do

Amethyst Centre. Full lapidary shop and gem cutting operation; retail, gift and jewelry shop. Tours. (Daily exc Sun; closed hols) 400 E Victoria Ave. Phone 807/622-6908. **Free.**

Amethyst Mine Panorama. Open-pit quarry adj to Elbow Lake. The quarrying operation, geological faults, Canadian Pre-Cambrian shield and sample gem pockets are readily visible. Gem picking; tours. (Mid-May-mid-Oct, daily) 35 mi (56 km) NE, 5 mi (8 km) off Hwy 11/17 on East Loon Rd. Phone 807/622-6908. **¢**

Centennial Conservatory. Wide variety of plant life including banana plants, palm trees, cacti. (Daily; closed Jan 1, Good Friday, Dec 24-26) Balmoral & Dease Sts. Phone 807/622-7036. **Free.**

Centennial Park. Summer features include a reconstructed 1910 logging camp; logging camp museum. Playground. Cross-country skiing; sleigh rides (by appt; fee) in winter. (Daily) Near Boulevard Lake, at Centennial Park Rd. Phone 807/683-6511. **Free.**

International Friendship Gardens. Park is composed of individual gardens designed and constructed by various ethnic groups including Slovakian, Polish, German, Italian, Finnish, Danish, Ukranian, Hungarian and Chinese. (Daily) 2000 Victoria Ave. Phone 807/625-3166. **Free.**

Kakabeka Falls Provincial Park. Spectacular waterfall on the historic Kaministiquia River, formerly a voyageur route from Montréal to the West. The 128-ft (39-km) high falls may be seen from highway stop. Waterflow is best in spring and on wkends—flow is reduced during the wk. Sand beach in the park, hiking, interpretive trails. Camping (day-use, electrical hookups; fee). Playground; visitor service center. 20 mi (32 km) W via ON 11/17. Phone 807/475-1535 (Oct-Apr) or 807/473-9231 (May-Sept). Per vehicle **¢¢¢**

Old Fort William. Authentic reconstruction of the original Fort William as it was from 1803 to 1821. Visitors experience the adventure of the Nor'westers convergence for the Rendezvous (re-creation staged 10 days mid-July). Costumed staff populate 42 buildings on the site, featuring tradesmen's shops, farm, apothecary, fur stores, warehouses, Great Hall, voyageur encampment, indigenous encampment; historic restaurant. Gift shop. Walking tours (exc winter). (May-Oct, daily) 1 King Rd, off Hwy 61S. Phone 807/577-8461. **¢¢¢**

Quetico Provincial Park (see). 27 mi W on ON 11/17.

Thunder Bay Art Gallery. Changing exhibitions from major national and international museums; regional art; contemporary native art. Tours, films, lectures, concerts. Gift shop. (Daily exc Mon; closed some hols) On Confederation College Campus; use Harbour Expy from Hwy 11/17. Phone 807/577-6427. **Free.**

Motels

✔★ COMFORT INN. *(660 W Arthur St, Thunder Bay ON P7E 5R8) near Thunder Bay Airport.* 807/475-3155; FAX 807/475-3816. 80 rms, 2 story. S $70-$85; D $75-$93; each addl $8; under 19 free. Crib free. Pet accepted. TV; cable. Complimentary coffee in lobby. Restaurant adj 7 am-11 pm. Ck-out 11 am. Business servs avail. In-rm modem link. Cr cds: A, D, DS, ER, MC, V.

D ✔ ⌧ ⌧ 🔥 SC

★★★ VICTORIA INN. *(555 W Arthur St, Thunder Bay ON P7E 5R5) near airport.* 807/577-8481; res: 800/387-3331; FAX 807/475-8961. E-mail vicinn@tbaytel.net; web www.tbaytel.net/vicinn. 182 rms, 3 story. S $76.95-$155; D $86.95-$155; each addl $10; suites $179-$229; under 16 free. Crib free. Pet accepted; $5. Indoor pool; wading pool, whirlpool, poolside serv, lifeguard. TV; cable. Complimentary coffee in rms. Restaurant 7 am-11 pm. Rm serv. Bar 11:30-1 am. Ck-out noon. Meeting rms. Business servs avail. In-rm modem link. Valet serv. Sundries. Coin lndry. Free airport transportation. Downhill ski 8 mi; x-country ski 5 mi. Exercise equipt; sauna. Health club privileges. Some refrigerators. Cr cds: A, C, D, DS, ER, MC, V.

D ✔ ⌧ ⌧ 🗡 ✈ ⌧ 🔥 SC

Motor Hotels

★★★ AIRLANE HOTEL. *(698 W Arthur St, Thunder Bay ON P7C 5R8) near Thunder Bay Airport.* 807/577-1181; FAX 807/475-4852; res: 800/465-5003. E-mail inquire@airline.com; web www.airline.com. 160 rms, 2-3 story. S $79-$105; D $85-$110; each addl $5; wkend rates. Crib free. Pet accepted. TV; cable (premium), VCR avail. Indoor pool; whirlpool. Restaurants 7 am-11 pm. Rm serv. Bar 4 pm-1 am, closed Sun; entertainment. Ck-out 11 am. Meeting rms. Business center. In-rm modem link. Bellhops. Valet serv. Sundries. Free airport transportation. Exercise equipt; sauna. Minibars. Cr cds: A, C, D, ER, MC, V.

D ✔ ⌧ 🗡 ✈ ⌧ SC 🚶 ⌧

★ BEST WESTERN CROSSROADS. *(655 W Arthur St, Thunder Bay ON P7E 5R6) at jct ON 11/17 & ON 61, near Thunder Bay Airport.* 807/577-4241; FAX 807/475-7059. 60 rms, 2 story. May-Oct: S $73; D $78; under 12 free; lower rates rest of yr. Crib free. Pet accepted. TV; cable. Complimentary coffee. Restaurant opp 7 am-midnight. Ck-out 11 am. Business servs avail. In-rm modem link. Valet serv. Free airport transportation. Some refrigerators. Cr cds: A, C, D, DS, ER, MC, V.

✔ ✈ ⌧ 🔥 SC

★★ LANDMARK INN. *(1010 Dawson Rd, Thunder Bay ON P7B 5J4) jct Hwy 11/17 & 102, County Fair Plaza.* 807/767-1681; FAX 807/767-1439; res: 800/465-3950 (CAN & MI, WI, IN). Web www.landmark.thunder-bay.on.ca. 106 rms, 4 story. S $80; D $86; each addl $8; under 12 free. Crib free. Pet accepted; $50. TV; cable. Indoor pool; whirlpool, poolside serv. Sauna. Complimentary continental bkfst. Coffee in rms. Restaurant 7-1 am. Rm serv. Bar 11-1 am. Ck-out 11 am. Meeting rms. Business servs avail. In-rm modem link. Valet serv. Sundries. Free airport transportation. Downhill ski 20 mi. Cr cds: A, D, DS, ER, MC, V.

D ✔ ⌧ ⌧ ⌧ 🔥 SC

★★ PRINCE ARTHUR. *(17 N Cumberland, Thunder Bay ON P7A 4K8)* 807/345-5411; FAX 807/345-8565; res: 800/267-2675. E-mail pahotel@tbaytel.net; web www.princearthur.on.ca. 121 rms, 6 story. S $59-$77; D $67-$85; each addl $8; suites $115-$145; under 16 free. Crib free. Pet accepted. TV; cable. Indoor pool; wading pool, whirlpool. Saunas. Coffee in rms. Restaurant 6:30 am-10 pm. Bar 11-1 am. Rm serv. Ck-out noon. Meeting rms. Business servs avail. In-rm modem link. Valet serv. Sundries. Free airport transportation. Health club privileges. Some refrigerators; microwaves avail. Downhill ski 10 mi. Overlooks harbor. Shopping mall opp. Cr cds: A, C, D, ER, MC, V.

D ✔ ✔ ⌧ ⌧ ⌧ 🔥 SC

★★★ VALHALLA INN. *(1 Valhalla Inn Rd, Thunder Bay ON P7E 6J1) at jct ON 11/17 & ON 61, near Thunder Bay Airport.* 807/577-1121; res: 800/964-1121; FAX 807/475-4723. E-mail valbay@baynet.net; web www.valhallainn.com. 267 rms, 5 story. S $175-$190; D $185-$200; each addl $10; suites $295-$305; under 18 free; ski, wkend rates. Crib free. Pet accepted; $10. TV. Indoor pool; whirlpool. Complimentary coffee in rms. Restaurant 6:30 am-11:30 pm. Rm serv. Bar 4:30 pm-2 am. Ck-out 1 pm. Meeting rms. Business servs avail. In-rm modem link. Valet serv. Sundries. Free airport transportation. Downhill ski 3 mi; x-country ski 4 mi. Exercise equipt; sauna. Bicycle rentals. Game rm. Some bathrm phones, minibars; microwaves avail. Luxury level. Cr cds: A, C, D, DS, ER, MC, V.

D ✔ ⌧ ⌧ 🗡 ✈ ⌧ 🔥 SC

★★ VENTURE INN. *(450 Memorial Ave, Thunder Bay ON P7B 3Y7) adj to auditorium.* 807/345-2343; FAX 807/345-3246; 800 888/483-6887. Web www.jwg.com/ventureinns/. 93 rms, 3 story. S $75; D $85; each addl $10; under 20 free. Crib free. Pet accepted. TV; cable. Indoor pool. Sauna. Complimentary continental bkfst. Restaurant adj 11-1 am. Ck-out 1 pm. Meeting rms. Business servs avail. In-rm modem link. Sun deck. Downhill ski 15 mi. Cr cds: A, C, D, DS, ER, MC, V.

✔ ⌧ ⌧ ⌧ 🔥 SC

Restaurant

★★ THE KEG. *(735 Hewitson Ave, Thunder Bay ON P7B 6B5) Balmoral at Harbour Expy.* 807/623-1960. Specializes in steak, seafood. Salad bar. Own cheesecake. Hrs: 4 pm-1 am. Closed Dec 24, 25. Bar. Semi-a la carte: dinner $15.99-$32.99. Child's meals. Pub atmosphere. Cr cds: A, D, ER, MC, V.

D

Toronto (D-7)

(See also Hamilton, Mississauga)

Founded 1793 **Pop** 3,400,000 (metro) **Elev** 569 ft (173 m) **Area code** 416

Information Tourism Toronto, Queens Quay Terminal at Harbourfront, 207 Queens Quay W, M5J 1A7; 416/203-2500 or 800/363-1990.

Toronto is one of Canada's leading industrial, commercial and cultural centers. From its location on the shores of Lake Ontario, it has performed essential communications and transportation services throughout Canadian history. Its name derives from the native word for meeting place, as the area was called by the Hurons who led the first European, Etienne Brule, to the spot. In the mid-1800s, the Grand Trunk and Great Western Railroad and the Northern Railway connected Toronto with the upper St Lawrence, Portland, Maine and Chicago, Illinois.

After French fur traders from Québec established Fort Rouille in 1749, Toronto became a base for further Canadian settlement. Its population of Scottish, English and United States emigrants was subject to frequent armed attacks, especially during the War of 1812 and immediately thereafter. From within the United States, the attackers aimed at annexation; from within Canada, they aimed at emancipation from England. One result of these unsuccessful threats was the protective confederation of Lower Canada, which later separated again as the province of Québec, and Upper Canada, which still later became the province of Ontario with Toronto as its capital.

Toronto today is a cosmopolitan city with many intriguing features. Once predominantly British, the population is now exceedingly multicultural—the United Nations deemed Toronto the world's most ethnically diverse city in 1989. A major theater center with many professional playhouses, including the Royal Alexandra Theatre, Toronto is also a major banking center, with several architecturally significant banks. Good shopping can be found throughout the city, but Torontonians are most proud of their "Underground City," a series of subterranean malls linking more than 300 shops and restaurants in the downtown area. For professional sports fans, Toronto offers the Maple Leafs (hockey), the Blue Jays (baseball), Raptors (basketball), and the Argonauts (football). A visit to the Harbourfront, a boat tour to the islands or enjoying an evening on the town should round out your stay in Toronto.

What to See and Do

Art Gallery of Ontario. Changing exhibits of paintings, drawings, sculpture and graphics from the 14th-20th centuries including Henry Moore Collection; permanent Canadian Collection & Contemporary Galleries; films, lectures, concerts. (Daily exc Mon; winter months Wed-Sun; closed Jan 1, Dec 25) Free admission Wed evenings. 317 Dundas St W. Phone 416/977-0414. ¢¢ Behind gallery is

The Grange. A Georgian house (ca 1817) restored and furnished in early Victorian style (1835-1840). (Same hrs as Art Gallery) **Free** with admission to Art Gallery.

Black Creek Pioneer Village. More than 30 buildings, restored to re-create life in a rural Canadian village of mid-19th-century, include general store, printing office, town hall, church, firehouse, blacksmith shop; special events wkends. Visitor reception centre has exhibit gallery, theater, restaurant. (Early Mar-Dec, variable schedule; closed Dec 25) 1000 Murray Ross Pkwy. Jane St & Steeles Ave, 2 mi (3 km) N on Hwy 400, E on Steeles, then ½ mi (1 km) to Jane St. Phone 416/736-1733. ¢¢¢

Casa Loma. A medieval-style castle built by Sir Henry Pellatt between 1911 and 1914. Furnished rms, secret passages, underground tunnel and stables. Restored gardens (May-Oct). Gift shop; cafe. (Daily; closed Jan 1, Dec 25) One Austin Terrace, 1½ mi (2 km) NW of downtown. Phone 416/923-1171. ¢¢¢ Adj is

Spadina (ca 1865). Home of financier James Austin and his descendants; Victorian & Edwardian furnishings and fine art; restored gardens. (Daily exc Mon, afternoons; closed Jan 1, Good Fri, Dec 25, 26) 285 Spadina Rd. Phone 416/392-6910. ¢¢

City Hall (1965). Distinctive modern design features twin towers that appear to support round, elevated council chambers. Exhibits, concerts in Nathan Phillips Square in front of building. Self-guided tours; guided tours (summer). (Mon-Fri) 100 Queen St W. Phone 416/392-7341. **Free.**

City parks. Listed below are some of Toronto's many parks. Contact the Dept of Parks & Recreation, 416/392-1111.

Toronto Island Park. Accessible by ferry (fee; phone 416/392-8193) from foot of Bay St. Historic lighthouse, other buildings. Fishing, boating, swimming, bicycling; children's farmyard; scenic tram ride (free); amusement area (fee); mall with fountains and gardens; fine views of city and lake. (May-Oct, daily) S across Inner Harbour. Phone 416/392-8186. **Free.**

Riverdale Park. Summer: tennis, swimming, wading pools, playgrounds, picnicking, band concerts. Winter: skating; 19th-century farm. (Daily) W side of Broadview Ave, between Danforth Ave & Gerrard St E.

Allan Gardens. Indoor/outdoor botanical displays, wading pool, picnicking, concerts. (Daily) W side of Sherbourne St to Jarvis St between Carlton St & Gerrard St E. Phone 416/392-7288. **Free.**

Queen's Park. The Ontario Parliament Buildings are located in this park. (Daily) Queen's Park Crescent. **Free.**

Grange Park. Wading pool, playground. Natural ice rink (winter, weather permitting). (Daily) Dundas & Beverley Sts, located behind the Art Gallery of Ontario. **Free.**

High Park. The largest park in the city (399 acres or 161 hectares). Tennis, swimming, wading pool and playgrounds, picnicking, hiking, floral display and rock falls in Hillside Gardens, animal paddocks. Shakespeare performances at Dream Site outdoor theater. Restaurant, concessions; trackless tour train. Ice-skating. Also here is Colborne Lodge at S end of park. (Daily) Between Bloor St W & The Queensway at Parkside Dr, near lakeshore. **Free.**

Edwards Gardens. Civic garden center; rock gardens, pools, pond, rustic bridges. (Daily) NE of downtown, at Leslie Ave E & Lawrence St. Phone 416/392-8186. **Free.**

★ **CN Tower.** World's tallest free-standing structure (1,815 ft/553 m). Three observation decks (daily), revolving restaurant (see 360 REVOLVING

RESTAURANT) and nightclub. Also various activities (fees). 301 Front St W, just W of University Ave. Phone 416/360-8500 (information) or 416/362-5411 (dining reservations). ¢¢¢¢ Here is

Virtual World. Two virtual reality-based adventures, Battletech and Red Planet , allow users to navigate in a world of fantasy. Strap yourself into a high-tech cockpit and enter a universe populated by machines but controlled by humans; or sit at the controls of a modified hovercraft and race through Mars. (Daily) Phone 416/360-8500. ¢¢¢

Colborne Lodge (1837). Built by John G. Howard, architect and surveyor; restored to 1870 style; art gallery houses changing exhibits; artifacts of 1830s; artist's studio. (Daily exc Mon; closed Good Fri, Dec 25-26) Colborne Lodge Dr & The Queensway in High Park. Phone 416/392-6916. ¢¢

Exhibition Place. Designed to accommodate the Canadian National Exhibition (see ANNUAL EVENTS), this 350-acre (141-hectare) park has events yr-round, as well as the Marine Museum of Upper Canada. (Aug-Sept, daily) S off Gardener Expy, on Lakeshore Blvd. Phone 416/393-6000.

George R. Gardiner Museum of Ceramic Art. One of the world's finest collections of Italian majolica, English delftware and 18th-century continental porcelain. (Daily; closed Jan 1, Dec 25) 111 Queen's Park, opp Royal Ontario Museum. Phone 416/586-8080. **Donation.**

Gibson House. Home of land surveyor and local politician David Gibson; restored and furnished as it would have been in the 1850s. Costumed interpreters conduct demonstrations. Tours. (Daily; closed Jan 1, Good Fri, Dec 24-26) 5172 Yonge St (ON 11), in North York. Phone 416/395-7432. ¢¢

Harbourfront Centre. This 10-acre waterfront community is alive with theater, dance, films, art shows, music, crafts and children's programs. Most events free. (Daily) 235 Queens Quay West at foot of York St. Phone 416/973-3000.

Historic Fort York. Restored War of 1812 fort and battle site. Costumed staff provide military demonstrations; eight original buildings house period environments and exhibits. Tours. (Daily; closed Jan 1, Good Fri, Dec 25, 26) Garrison Rd, SE near jct Bathurst & Fleet Sts by Strachan Ave. Phone 416/392-6907. ¢¢

Hummingbird Centre for the Performing Arts. Stage presentations of Broadway musicals, dramas and concerts by international artists. Home of the Canadian Opera Company and the National Ballet of Canada. Pre-performance dining; gift shop. 1 Front St E at Yonge St. Phone 416/393-7469 or 416/872-2262 (tickets).

Huronia Historical Parks. Two living history sites animated by costumed interpreters. (Daily) 63 mi (101 km) N via Hwy 400, then 34 mi (55 km) N to Midland on Hwy 93. Phone 705/526-7838. ¢¢¢ Consists of

Sainte-Marie among the Hurons (1639-1649). Reconstruction of 17th-century Jesuit mission that was Ontario's first European community. Twenty-two furnished buildings include native dwellings, workshops, barn, church, cookhouse, hospital. Candlelight tours, canoe excursions. Cafe features period-inspired meals and snacks. Orientation center, interpretive museum. Free parking and picnic facilities. (Victoria Day wkend-Oct, daily) E of Midland on Hwy 12. ¢¢¢ World-famous Martyrs' Shrine (site of Papal visit) is located across the highway. Other area highlights include pioneer museum, replica indigenous village, Wye Marsh Wildlife Centre.

Discovery Harbour. Marine heritage center and reconstructed 19th-century British Naval dockyard. Established in 1817, site includes 19th-century military base. Now rebuilt, the site features eight furnished buildings and orientation center. Replica of 49-ft (15-m) British naval schooner HMS *Bee;* also HMS *Tecumseth* and *Perseverance.* Costumed interpreters bring base to life, ca 1830. Sail-training and excursions (daily). Audiovisual display; free parking, docking, picnic facilities. Theater; gift shop, restaurant. (Victoria Day-Labour Day, Mon-Fri; after Labour Day-Sept, daily) Church St, Penetanguishene. ¢¢¢

Kortright Centre for Conservation. Environmental center with trails, beehouse, maple syrup shack, wildlife pond and plantings. Naturalist-guided hikes (daily). Cross-country skiing (no rentals); picnic area, cafe; indoor exhibits and theater. (Daily; closed Dec 24 & 25) 9550 Pine Valley Dr, Klienberg; 12 mi (19.3 km) NW via Hwy 400, Major MacKenzie Dr exit, then 2 mi (3 km) W, then S on Pine Valley Dr. Phone 905/832-2289. ¢¢

Mackenzie House. Restored 19th-century home of William Lyon Mackenzie, first mayor of Toronto; furnishings and artifacts of the 1850s; 1840s print shop. Group tours (by appt). (Daily exc Mon, afternoons; closed Jan 1, Good Fri, Dec 25, 26) 82 Bond St. Phone 416/392-6915. ¢¢

Marine Museum of Upper Canada. Contains exhibits depicting waterways of central Canada, the Great Lakes-St Lawrence System; shipping memorabilia; marine artifacts; wireless rm; fur trade exhibit. Adj is 80-ft (24-m) steam tugboat preserved in dry berth; 12-ft (4-m) tall operating marine triple-expansion steam engine is also on display. (Daily exc Mon; closed Jan 1, Good Fri, Dec 25, 26) Exhibition Place. Phone 416/392-1765. ¢¢

McMichael Canadian Art Collection. Works by Canada's most famous artists—the Group of Seven, Tom Thomson, Emily Carr, David Milne, Clarence Gagnon and others. Also Inuit (Eskimo) and contemporary indigenous art and sculpture. Restaurant, book, gift shop. Constructed from hand-hewn timbers and native stone, the gallery stands in 100 acres (40 hectares) on the crest of the Humber Valley; nature trail. (June-early Nov, daily; rest of yr, daily exc Mon; closed Dec 25) N via ON 400 or 427, 10365 Islington Ave in Kleinburg. Phone 905/893-1121. ¢¢¢

★ **Metro Toronto Zoo.** Approx 710 acres (287 hectares) of native and exotic plants and animals in six geographic regions: Indo-Malaya, Africa, North and South America, Eurasia and Australia. The North American Domain can be seen on a 3-mi (5-km) A/C vehicle ride. The Zoomobile takes visitors on half-hr drive through Eurasian, South American, and African areas. Parking fee. (Daily; closed Dec 25) 10 mi (16 km) E of Don Valley Pkwy on Hwy 401, then N on Meadowvale Rd in Scarborough. Phone 416/392-5900. ¢¢¢¢

Ontario Parliament Buildings. Guided tours of the Legislature Bldg and walking tour of grounds. Gardens; art collection; historic displays. (Victoria Day-Labour Day, daily; rest of yr, Mon-Fri; closed some hols) Queen's Park. Phone 416/325-7500. Free.

Ontario Place. A 96-acre (39-hectare) cultural, recreational and entertainment complex on three man-made islands in Lake Ontario. Includes outdoor amphitheater for concerts, two pavilions with multimedia presentations, Cinesphere theater with IMAX films (yr-round; fee); children's village. Three villages of snack bars, restaurants and pubs; miniature golf; lagoons, canals, two marinas; 370-ft (113-m) water slide, showboat, pedal & bumper boats; Wilderness Adventure Ride. (Mid-May-early Sept; daily) Parking fee. 955 Lakeshore Blvd W. Phone 416/314-9900 (recording) or 416/314-9811. ¢¢¢¢¢

Ontario Science Centre. Hundreds of hands-on exhibits in the fields of space, technology, communications, food, chemistry and earth science. Demonstrations on electricity, papermaking, metal casting, lasers, cryogenics. OmniMax theater (fee). Special exhibitions. (Daily; closed Dec 25) 770 Don Mills Rd, at Eglinton Ave E, 6 mi (10 km) NE via Don Valley Pkwy, in Don Mills. Phone 416/429-4100 (recording). Per person ¢¢¢; Parking ¢¢

Paramount Canada's Wonderland. More than 125 attractions in 8 themed areas offer 11 live stage shows and 50 rides, including Vortex & Top Gun (suspended roller coasters). Splash Works, a 10-acre area offers 15 water-related rides and attractions (mid-June-Labour Day, weather permitting; free with Pay-One Price admission). Special events, fireworks displays, top-name entertainment. (May & Sept-, wkends; June-Aug, daily) 9580 Jane St, 18 mi (29 km) N on Hwy 400. Phone 905/832-7000. Pay-One-Price Passport ¢¢¢¢¢

Professional sports.

American League baseball (Toronto Blue Jays). SkyDome, 1 Blue Jays Way. Phone 416/341-1000.

NBA (Toronto Raptors). SkyDome, 1 Blue Jays Way. Phone 416/214-2255.

NHL (Toronto Maple Leafs). Maple Leaf Gardens, 60 Carlton St. Phone 416/977-1641.

Royal Ontario Museum (ROM). Extensive permanent displays of fine and decorative art, archaeology and earth and life sciences. The collection includes Chinese temple wall paintings; 12 dinosaur skeletons; the Ming Tomb Gallery; the hands-on Discovery Gallery; Greek, Etruscan, Chinese, European and Egypt and Nubia galleries; special programs. (Daily; closed Jan 1, Dec 25) 100 Queen's Park. Phone 416/586-5549 or -5736. ¢¢¢

Scarborough Civic Centre. Houses offices of municipal government. Guided tours (daily; closed Dec 25). Concert Sun afternoons. 150 Borough Dr in Scarborough. Phone 416/396-7216. **Free.**

Sightseeing tours.

Gray Line bus tours. Contact 184 Front St E, Ste 601, M5A 4N3; 416/594-3310 for schedule and fees.

Toronto Tours Ltd. Four different boat tours of Toronto Harbour. Phone 416/869-1372. ¢¢¢-¢¢¢¢¢

SkyDome. State of the art sports stadium with a fully retractable roof; contains a hotel (see HOTELS), a Hard Rock Cafe and North America's largest McDonald's restaurant. Guided tours (1 hr) begin with 15-min film *The Inside Story* and include visits to a skybox, media center, locker room and the playing field (all subject to availability). Tour (daily, schedule permitting). 1 Blue Jays Way, adj CN Tower. Phone 416/341-2770. ¢¢¢

St Lawrence Centre for the Arts. Performing arts complex features theater, music, dance, films and other public events. 27 Front St E. Phone 416/366-7723 (box office).

The Market Gallery. Exhibition center for Toronto Archives; displays on city's historical, social and cultural heritage; art, photographs, maps, documents and artifacts. (Wed-Sat, also Sun afternoons; closed hols) 95 Front St E. Phone 416/392-7604. **Free.**

Todmorden Mills Heritage Museum & Arts Centre. Restored historic houses; Parshall Terry House (1797) and William Helliwell House (1820). Also museum; restored 1899 train station. Picnicking. (May-Sept, daily exc Mon; Oct-Dec, Mon-Fri) 67 Pottery Rd, 2¼ mi (4 km) N, off Don Valley Pkwy in East York. Phone 416/396-2819. Museum **Free;** Tours ¢¢

Toronto Stock Exchange. Stock Market Place visitor has multimedia displays, interactive games and archival exhibits to aid visitors in understanding the market. The Exchange Tower, 2 First Canadian Pl (King & York Sts). For schedule phone 416/947-4676. **Free.**

Toronto Symphony. Classical, pops and children's programs; Great Performers series. Wheelchair seating, audio enhancement for hearing-impaired. Roy Thomson Hall, 60 Simcoe St. For schedule, information phone 416/593-4828.

University of Toronto (1827). (55,000 students) Largest university in Canada. Guided walking tours of magnificent Gothic buildings begin at Hart House and include account of campus ghost (June-Aug, Mon-Fri; free). Downtown, W of Queen's Park. Phone 416/978-5000 for tour information.

Woodbine Racetrack. Thoroughbred racing (late Apr-Oct, Wed-Sun afternoons; Queen's Plate race in mid-July). 15 mi (24 km) N via Hwy 427 in Etobicoke. Phone 416/675-RACE. ¢¢

Young People's Theatre. Local professional productions for the entire family. (Sept-May, daily; Aug, wkends only) 165 Front St E. Phone 416/862-2222.

Annual Events

International Caravan. Fifty pavilions scattered throughout the city present ethnic food, dancing, crafts. Phone 416/977-0466. 3rd wk June.

Chin International Picnic. At Paramount Canada's Wonderland. Contests, sports, picnicking. Phone 416/531-9991. 1st wkend July.

Outdoor Art Show. Nathan Phillips Sq. Phone 416/408-2754. Mid-July.

Caribana. Caribbean music, grand parade, floating nightclubs, dancing, costumes, food at various locations throughout city. Phone 416/465-4884. Late July-early Aug.

Canadian National Exhibition. Exhibition Place on the lakefront. This gala celebration originated in 1879 as the Toronto Industrial Exhibition for the encouragement of agriculture, industry and the arts, although agricultural events dominated the show. Today sports, industry, labor and the arts are of equal importance to CNE. The "Ex," as it is locally known, is so inclusive of the nation's activities that it is a condensed Canada. A special 350-acre (141-hectare) park has been built to accommodate the exhibition. Hundreds of events include animal shows, parades, exhibits, a midway, water and air shows. Virtually every kind of sporting event is represented, from frisbee-throwing to the National Horse Show. Phone 416/393-6000. Mid-Aug-Labour Day.

Toronto International Film Festival. Celebration of world cinema in downtown theaters; Canadian and foreign films, international movie makers and stars. Phone 416/967-7371. Early Sept.

Canadian International. Woodbine Racetrack. World-class Thoroughbreds compete in one of Canada's most important races. Mid-late Oct.

Royal Agricultural Winter Fair. Coliseum Bldg, Exhibition Place. World's largest indoor agricultural fair exhibits the finest livestock. Food shows; Royal Horse Show features international competitions in several catergories. Phone 416/393-6400. Nov 5-14.

Additional Visitor Information

For further information contact Tourism Toronto, Queens Quay Terminal at Harbourfront, 207 Queens Quay W, M5J 1A7; 416/203-2500 or 800/363-1990 (US & Canada). Toronto's public transportation system is extensive and includes buses, subways, streetcars and trolley buses; for maps phone 416/393-4636.

City Neighborhoods

Many of the restaurants, unrated dining establishments and some lodgings listed under Toronto include neighborhoods as well as exact street addresses. Geographic descriptions of these areas are given, followed by a table of restaurants arranged by neighborhood.

Cabbagetown: North of Gerrard St, east of Parliament St, south of Rosedale Valley Rd and west of the Don River.

Downtown: North of Inner Harbour, east of Spadina Ave, south of Bloor St and west of Sherbourne St. **North of Downtown:** North of Bloor St. **East of Downtown:** East of Sherbourne St. **West of Downtown:** West of Spadina Ave.

Harbourfront: North of Inner Harbour, east of Bathurst St, south of Gardiner Expy and west of Yonge St.

Yorkville: North of Bloor St, east of Avenue Rd, south of Davenport Rd and west of Yonge St.

TORONTO RESTAURANTS BY NEIGHBORHOOD AREAS
(For full description, see alphabetical listings under Restaurants)

CABBAGETOWN
Provence. 12 Amelia St

DOWNTOWN
360 Revolving Restaurant. 301 Front St W
Accents (Sutton Place Hotel). 955 Bay St
Accolade (Crowne Plaza Toronto Centre Hotel). 225 Front St W
Avalon. 270 Adelaide St W
Bangkok Garden. 18 Elm St
Barootes. 220 King St W
Bistro 990. 990 Bay St
Bumpkins. 21 Gloucester St
Cafe Victoria (King Edward Hotel). 37 King St E
Canoe. 66 Wellington St W
Carman's Club. 26 Alexander St
Chez Max. 166 Wellington St W
Chiaro's (King Edward Hotel). 37 King St E
Ed's Warehouse. 270 King St W
La Fenice. 319 King St W
Lai Wah Heen (Metropolitan Hotel). 108 Chestnut St
Le Papillion. 16 Church St
Le Paradis. 166 Bedford Rd
Matignon. 51 Ste Nicholas St
Mövenpick Of Switzerland. 165 York St
Old Spaghetti Factory. 54 The Esplanade
Pawnbrokers Daughter. 1115 Bay St
Rivoli Cafe. 332 Queen St W
Senator. 253 Victoria St
Shopsy's Delicatessen. 33 Yonge St
Splendido. 88 Harbord St
Sushi Bistro. 204 Queen St W
Take Sushi. 22 Front St W
Tiger Lily's Noodle House. 257 Queen St W

Truffles (Four Seasons Hotel). 21 Avenue Rd at Bloor St
Xango. 106 John St
Yamase. 317 King St W

NORTH OF DOWNTOWN
Arlequin. 134 Avenue Rd
Centro Grill. 2472 Yonge St
Grano. 2035 Yonge St
Grazie. 2373 Yonge St
Harvest Cafe (Inn On The Park Hotel). 1100 Eglinton Ave E
Kally's. 430 Nugget Ave
North 44 Degrees. 2537 Yonge St
Pronto. 692 Mount Pleasant Rd
Quartier. 2112 Yonge St
Scaramouche. 1 Benvenuto Place
Thai Flavour. 1554 Avenue Rd
United Bakers Dairy Restaurant. 506 Lawrence Ave W
Vanipha Lanna. 471 Eglinton Ave W

EAST OF DOWNTOWN
Ellas. 702 Pape Ave
Rosewater Supper Club. 19 Toronto St

WEST OF DOWNTOWN
Chiado. 864 College St
Happy Seven. 358 Spadina Ave
Old Mill. 21 Old Mill Rd

HARBOURFRONT
Pier 4 Storehouse. 245 Queen's Quay W

YORKVILLE
Boba. 90 Avenue Rd
Gilles Bistro. 1315 Bay St
Il Posto. 148 Yorkville Ave
Joso's. 202 Davenport Rd
Marketta Jazz Bar And Dining. 138 Avenue Rd
Mistura. 265 Davenport Rd
Monarch Bistro. 838 Yonge St
Opus. 37 Prince Arthur Ave
Pangaea. 1221 Bay St
Patachou. 1095 Yonge St
The Rosedale Diner. 1164 Yonge St

Note: When a listing is located in a town that does not have its own city heading, it will appear under the city nearest to its location. In these cases, the address and town appear in parenthesis immediately following the name of the establishment.

Motel

✔★ **SEA HORSE INN.** *(2095 Lakeshore Blvd W (ON 2), Toronto ON M8V 1A1)* jct QEW, west of downtown. 416/255-4433; FAX 416/251-5121; res: 800/663-1123. E-mail seahorse@simpatico.ca; web wwwtoronto.com/seahorseinn. 74 rms, 1-3 story. S $57-$72; D $57-$89; each addl $5; suites $85-$170; under 18 free. TV; cable (premium). Pool; whirlpool. Playground. Complimentary continental bkfst. Ck-out 11 am. Meeting rms. Sauna. Refrigerators. Picnic tables, grills. On Lake Ontario. Cr cds: A, C, D, DS, ER, MC, V.

⊠ ⊠ ⊠ SC

Motor Hotels

✔★★ **HOLIDAY INN EXPRESS.** *(50 Estates Dr, Scarborough ON M1H 2Z1)* at jct Hwys 48 & 401. 416/439-9666; FAX 416/439-4295. 138 rms, 2-3 story. No elvtrs. S $59; D $79; each addl $10; under 19 free; wkend rates. Crib free. TV; cable (premium). Complimentary continental bkfst. Restaurant adj 11:30-1 am, Sat, Sun from 4:30 pm. Ck-out 11 am. Meeting rms. Business servs avail. Health club privileges. Cr cds: A, C, D, DS, ER, JCB, MC, V.

D ⊠ ⊠ SC

★★ **HOWARD JOHNSON-EAST.** *(940 Progress Ave, Scarborough ON M1G 3T5)* 416/439-6200; FAX 416/439-5689. E-mail in quiry@hojotoronto.com. 186 rms, 6 story. S $109; D $119; each addl $10; under 18 free; wkend rates; package plan. Crib free. Pet accepted. TV; cable (premium). Heated pool; whirlpool. Restaurant 6:30 am-2 pm, 5-10 pm. Rm serv. Bar 4:30 pm-1 am. Ck-out noon. Coin lndry. Meeting rms. Business servs avail. Valet serv. Sundries. Gift shop. Exercise equipt; sauna. Health club privileges. Microwaves avail. Cr cds: A, C, D, DS, ER, JCB, MC, V.

★★ **RAMADA HOTEL-TORONTO AIRPORT.** (2 Holiday Dr, Etobicoke ON M9C 2Z7) near Lester B Pearson Intl Airport. 416/621-2121; FAX 416/621-9840. 179 rms, 2-6 story. June-Aug: S, D $150-$160; each addl $10; suites $250-$350; under 18 free; wkly, wkend rates; lower rates rest of yr. Crib free. Pet accepted. TV; cable (premium). Indoor/outdoor pool; whirlpool. Complimentary coffee in rms. Restaurant 6 am-11 pm. Rm serv. Bar 11:30-1 am. Ck-out noon. Business servs avail. In-rm modem link. Bellhops. Valet serv. Free airport transportation. Exercise equipt; sauna. Some minibars; microwaves avail. Cr cds: A, C, D, DS, ER, JCB, MC, V.

★ **TRAVELODGE-EAST.** (20 Milner Business Ct, Scarborough ON M1B 3C6) 416/299-9500; FAX 416/299-6172. Web www.travelodge.com. 156 rms, 6 story. S, D $71-$81; each addl $6; suites $85-$105; under 17 free. Pet accepted. TV; cable (premium). Indoor pool; whirlpool. Complimentary coffee in rms. Restaurant 11-2 am. Rm serv noon-11 pm. Ck-out 11 am. Meeting rms. Business servs avail. Sundries. Health club privileges. Microwaves avail. Cr cds: A, D, DS, ER, MC, V.

★★ **TRAVELODGE-NORTH.** (50 Norfinch Dr, North York ON M3N 1X1) N on Hwy 400 to Finch Ave, then E to Norfinch Dr. 416/663-9500; FAX 416/663-8480. Web www.travelodge.com. 184 rms, 6 story. S $89; D $97; each addl $8; under 17 free. Crib free. Pet accepted, some restrictions. TV; cable (premium). Indoor pool; whirlpool. Coffee in rms. Restaurant 7-1 am. Rm serv. Bar. Ck-out 11 am. Meeting rms. Business servs avail. Sundries. Cr cds: A, D, DS, ER, MC, V.

★★ **VALHALLA INN.** (1 Valhalla Inn Rd, Toronto ON M9B 1S9) west of downtown. 416/239-2391; FAX 416/239-8764; res: 800/268-2500. E-mail valhalla@globalserve.net; web www.valhalla-inn.com. 240 rms, 2-12 story. S $160; D $170; each addl $10; suites $150-$275; under 18 free; wkend rates. Crib free. Pet accepted. TV; cable (premium). Heated pool. Coffee in rms. Restaurant 6 am-11 pm; dining rm noon-2:30 pm, 6-10 pm. Rm serv. Bars 11-2 am; entertainment. Ck-out 1 pm. Meeting rms. Business center. In-rm modem link. Bellhops. Valet serv. Sundries. Free airport transportation. Health club privileges. Some bathrm phones. Private patios, balconies. Grills. Cr cds: A, C, D, DS, ER, MC, V.

★ **VENTURE INN-YORKVILLE.** (89 Avenue Rd, Toronto ON M5R 2G3) downtown. 416/964-1220; FAX 416/964-8692; res: 800/387-3933. E-mail venture.cro@sympatico.ca; web www.ventureinn.com. 71 rms, 8 story. S $124; D $134; each addl $10; under 19 free; wkend rates off-season. Crib free. Pet accepted, some restrictions. Parking $6.50/day. TV; cable (premium), VCR avail. Complimentary continental bkfst. Ck-out 1 pm. Meeting rms. Business servs avail. Health club privileges. Cr cds: A, D, DS, ER, MC, V.

Hotels

★★ **BEST WESTERN PRIMROSE.** (111 Carlton St, Toronto ON M5B 2G3) at Jarvis St, downtown. 416/977-8000; FAX 416/977-6323. Web www.bestwestern.com. 338 rms, 23 story. S, D $149; each addl $10; suites $275; under 16 free. Crib free. Garage $12.50. TV; cable. Pool. Complimentary coffee in rms. Restaurant 6:30 am-10 pm. Bar 11-1 am.

Ck-out 11 am. Meeting rms. Business center. Exercise equipt; sauna. Cr cds: A, C, D, DS, ER, JCB, MC, V.

★★★ **BEST WESTERN-TORONTO AIRPORT-CARLTON PLACE.** (33 Carlson Court, Toronto ON M9W 6H5) near Lester B. Pearson Intl Airport, west of downtown. 416/675-1234; FAX 416/675-3436. 524 rms, 12 story. S $160-175; D $175-$190; each addl $15; suites $250-$350; under 18 free; wkend, mid-wk rates. Crib free. Parking in/out $5/day. TV; cable (premium). Indoor pool; whirlpool. Complimentary coffee in rms. Restaurant 6:30-1 am. Rm serv 24 hrs. Bar 11-1 am. Ck-out 1 pm. Meeting rms. Business center. Gift shop. Airport transportation. Exercise equipt; sauna. Health club privileges. Minibars. Cr cds: A, D, DS, ER, JCB, MC, V.

★ **BOND PLACE.** (65 Dundas St E, Toronto ON M5B 2G8) east of downtown. 416/362-6061; FAX 416/360-6406; res: 800/268-9390. 286 rms, 18 story, 51 suites. May-Oct: S, D $89-$109; each addl $15; suites $104-$134; under 15 free; lower rates rest of yr. Crib free. Parking, in/out $11. TV; cable (premium), VCR avail. Restaurant 7 am-11 pm. Rm serv 11 am-10 pm. Bar 5 pm-1 am. Ck-out 11 am. Meeting rms. Business servs avail. Cr cds: A, C, D, DS, ER, MC, V.

★★★ **CLARION-ESSEX PARK.** (300 Jarvis St, Toronto ON M5B 2C5) downtown. 416/977-4823; FAX 416/977-4830. E-mail clarion@net.com.ca; web www.hotelchoice.com. 102 rms, 10 story, 44 suites. S $155; D $170; each addl $15; suites $185-$265; under 18 free. Crib free. Garage parking $15. TV; cable (premium). Indoor pool; whirlpool. Complimentary coffee in rms. Restaurant 7 am-2 pm, 5-9 pm. Bar from 11 am. Ck-out 11 am. Meeting rms. Business servs avail. Concierge. Downhill/x-country ski 10 mi. Exercise equipt; sauna. Rec rm. Refrigerators. Cr cds: A, C, D, DS, ER, JCB, MC, V.

✔★★ **COMFORT HOTEL-DOWNTOWN.** (15 Charles St E, Toronto ON M4Y 1S1) downtown. 416/924-1222; FAX 416/927-1369. 108 rms, 10 story. S $109; D $119; each addl $10; suites $129-$139; under 18 free; wkend rates. Crib $10. Parking $9. TV; cable (premium), VCR avail. Restaurant noon-10 pm. Piano bar. Ck-out 11 am. Meeting rms. Business servs avail. Health club privileges. Refrigerators; microwaves avail. Cr cds: A, C, D, DS, ER, MC, V.

★★★ **CROWNE PLAZA-TORONTO CENTRE.** (225 Front St W, Toronto ON M5V 2X3) downtown. 416/597-1400; FAX 416/597-8128. Web crowneplaza.com. 587 rms, 25 story. S, D $219-$259; each addl $15; suites $350-$495; under 18 free; wkend rates. Crib free. TV; cable (premium), VCR avail. Indoor pool; wading pool, whirlpool, poolside serv. Coffee in rms. Restaurant 6-2 am (also see ACCOLADE). Bar 11:30-2 am; entertainment. Ck-out 2 pm. Meeting rms. Business center. In-rm modem link. Concierge. Valet parking. Exercise rm; sauna. Massage. Minibars; microwaves avail. Formal decor. Cr cds: A, C, D, DS, ER, JCB, MC, V.

★ **DAYS INN-DOWNTOWN.** (30 Carlton St, Toronto ON M5B 2E9) adj to Maple Leaf Gardens, between Yonge & Church Sts, downtown. 416/977-6655; FAX 416/977-0502. Web www.daysinn.com/daysinn.html. 536 rms, 23 story. S, D $119-$135; each addl $15; under 16 free. Crib free. Pet accepted, some restrictions. Covered parking $15/day. TV; cable. Indoor pool. Restaurant 7 am-10 pm. Bar 11:30-2 am. Ck-out 11 am. Coin lndry. Meeting rms. Business servs avail. Sundries. Barber, beauty shop. Sauna. Some refrigerators. Sun deck. Cr cds: A, D, DS, ER, JCB, MC, V.

★★★ **DELTA CHELSEA INN.** (33 Gerrard St W, Toronto ON M5G 1Z4) between Bay & Yonge Sts, downtown. 416/595-1975; FAX 416/585-4362; res: 800/268-1133. E-mail reservations@deltachelsea.com; web www.deltahotels.com. 1,590 rms, 26 story. S $245-$275; D $265-$295; each addl $15; suites, kit. units $255-$375; under 18 free; wkend rates. Crib free. Pet accepted, some restrictions. Valet parking $22 in/out.

TV; cable, VCR avail. 2 heated pools; whirlpool. Supervised child's activities; ages 2-13. Restaurant 6:30-1 am. Rm serv 24 hrs. Bar 11-1 am; entertainment. Ck-out 11 am. Convention facilities. Business center. Gift shop. Exercise equipt; sauna. Health club privileges. Game rm. Refrigerator in some suites. Microwaves avail. Many balconies. Cr cds: A, C, D, DS, ER, JCB, MC, V.

★ ★ ★ **DELTA-TORONTO AIRPORT.** *(801 Dixon Rd, Etobicoke ON M9W 1J5) near Lester B. Pearson Intl Airport.* 416/675-6100; FAX 416/675-4022; res: 800/668-1444. E-mail delta@nbnet.nb.ca; web www.deltahotels.com. 251 rms, 8 story. S, D $115-$165; each addl $15; suites $170-$220; under 18 free; package plans. Crib free. Pet accepted, some restrictions. TV; cable (premium). Indoor pool. Supervised child's activities (June-Aug). Restaurant 6 am-11 pm. Rm serv 24 hrs. Bar 11:30-2 am. Ck-out 1 pm. Convention facilities. Business center. Bellhops. Valet serv. Gift shops. Exercise equipt; sauna. Health club privileges. Minibars; microwaves avail. Cr cds: A, C, D, DS, ER, JCB, MC, V.

★ ★ ★ **EMBASSY SUITES.** *(8500 Warden Ave, Markham ON L6G 1A5)* 905/470-8500; FAX 905/477-8611. 332 suites, 10 story. S, D $160-$180; each addl $20; wknd rates; under 18 free. Crib free. Valet parking $3. TV; cable (premium). Indoor pool; whirlpool. Complimentary full bkfst. Coffee in rms. Restaurant 6:30 am-midnight. Bar 11-2 am. Ck-out noon. Convention facilities. Business center. Shopping arcade. Barber, beauty shop. Exercise rm; sauna, steam rm. Game rm. Minibars; microwaves avail. Extensive grounds; elaborate landscaping. Elegant atmosphere. Cr cds: A, C, D, ER, MC, V.

★ ★ ★ ★ **FOUR SEASONS.** *(21 Avenue Rd at Bloor St, Toronto ON M5R 2G1) downtown.* 416/964-0411; FAX 416/964-2302; res: 800/268-6282 (CAN & NY). Web www.fourseasons.com. This fashionable, elegant hotel has a prime location in Toronto. 380 rms, 32 story. S $305-$445; D $345-$485; each addl $25; suites $715; under 18 free; wknd rates. Crib free. Pet accepted. Garage $18.75/day. TV; cable (premium), VCR avail (movies). Indoor/outdoor pool; whirlpool, poolside serv, lifeguard. Restaurants 6:30 am-11 pm (also see TRUFFLES). Rm serv 24 hrs. Bar 11:30-2 am; entertainment exc Sun. Ck-out noon. Convention facilities. Business center. In-rm modem link. Concierge. Barber, beauty shop. Valet parking. Exercise rm; sauna. Massage. Bathrm phones, minibars; microwaves avail. Some balconies. Cr cds: A, D, DS, JCB, MC, V.

★ ★ ★ **GRAND BAY.** *(4 Avenue Rd, Toronto ON M5R 2E8) at Bloor St, downtown.* 416/924-5471; FAX 416/924-6693; res: 800/977-4197. E-mail rheyd@grandbaytor.com; web www.grandbay@.com. 348 rms 2-18 story; 46 suites. S, D $239-$315; each addl $15; suites $350-$2000; family, wknd rates. Crib free. Pet accepted. Garage in/out $20. TV; cable (premium), VCR avail. Restaurant 6 am-10:30 pm. Bar 11:30-2 am. Ck-out noon. Meeting rms. Business center. Concierge. Minibars. Many antique furnishings in public areas. Royal Ontario Museum opp. Cr cds: A, C, D, DS, ER, JCB, MC, V.

★ ★ ★ **HILTON.** *(145 Richmond St W, Toronto ON M5H 2L2) at University Ave, downtown.* 416/869-3456; FAX 416/869-1478. Web www.hilton.com. 601 rms, 32 story. Apr-Nov: S, D $239-$259; each addl $20; suites $249-$1,600; family rates; package plans; lower rates rest of yr. Crib free. Garage $17.50. TV; cable (premium). Indoor/outdoor pool; whirlpool, poolside serv in summer. Restaurant 6:30 am-11 pm. Rm serv 24 hrs. Bar 11:30-2 am. Ck-out noon. Convention facilities. Business center. Exercise equipt; sauna. Massage. Minibars. Luxury level. Cr cds: A, C, D, DS, ER, JCB, MC, V.

★ ★ **HOLIDAY INN.** *(970 Dixon Rd, Etobicoke ON M9W 1J9) near Lester B. Pearson Intl Airport.* 416/675-7611; FAX 416/675-9162. Web hype.com/holiday_inn/airport/home.htm. 445 rms, 12 story. S, D $160-$175; suites $230-$430; wknd rates. Crib free. Pet accepted. TV; cable (premium). 2 heated pools, 1 indoor; whirlpool. Playground. Coffee

in rms. Restaurant 6 am-11 pm. Rm serv to 1 am. Bar 11-2 am; Sun noon-11 pm. Ck-out 1 pm. Meeting rms. Business center. Concierge. Barber, beauty shop. Free airport transportation. Exercise equipt; sauna. Rec rm. Minibars. Cr cds: A, C, D, DS, ER, JCB, MC, V.

★ ★ **HOLIDAY INN.** *(600 Dixon Rd, Etobicoke ON M9W 1J1)* 416/240-7511; FAX 416/240-7519. 186 rms, 2-5 story. S, D $89-$150; each addl $10; suites $129-$155; under 18 free. Crib free. Pet accepted, some restrictions. TV; cable. Heated pool; wading pool, poolside serv. Coffee in rms. Restaurant open 24 hrs. Ck-out 1 pm. Meeting rms. Business servs avail. Airport transportation. Exercise equipt. Cr cds: A, C, D, DS, ER, JCB, MC, V.

★ ★ ★ **HOLIDAY INN ON KING.** *(370 King St W, Toronto ON M5V 1J9) downtown.* 416/599-4000; FAX 416/599-7394. E-mail info@hiok.com; web www.hiok.com. 425 rms, 20 story. S, D $189; each addl $15; suites $269; family rates; package plans. Crib free. Garage $16. TV; cable, VCR avail. Heated rooftop pool; poolside serv, lifeguard. Complimentary coffee in rms. Restaurant 6:30 am-2 am. Bar from 11 am. Ck-out noon. Convention facilities. Business center. Concierge. Gift shop. Exercise equipt; sauna. Massage. Wet bars. Cr cds: A, C, D, DS, ER, JCB, MC, V.

★ ★ ★ **HOLIDAY INN-DON VALLEY.** *(1100 Eglinton Ave E, Toronto ON M3C 1H8) north of downtown.* 416/446-3700; res: 800/465-4329; FAX 416/446-3701. 298 rms, 14 story. S, D $115-$155; each addl $10; suites $175-$325; family, wknd, wkly rates. Crib free. Pet accepted, some restrictions. TV; cable (premium), VCR avail (movies). Complimentary coffee in lobby. Restaurant 6:30 am-11 pm. Rm serv. Bar 6 pm-2 am; entertainment Thurs-Sat. Ck-out noon. Convention facilities. Business center. In-rm modem link. Concierge. Shopping arcade. Barber, beauty shop. Free valet parking. Airport, RR station transportation. Indoor tennis, pro. X-country ski 1/4 mi. Exercise equipt; sauna. Indoor/outdoor pool; whirlpool, poolside serv, lifeguard. Playground. Supervised child's activities (June-Sept); ages 5-12. Game rm. Lawn games. Bathrm phones, refrigerators. Many balconies. Cr cds: A, C, D, DS, ER, JCB, MC, V.

★ ★ **HOLIDAY INN-YORKDALE.** *(3450 Dufferin St, Toronto ON M6A 2V1) 1 blk S of ON 401 Dufferin St exit, north of downtown.* 416/789-5161; FAX 416/785-6845. 365 rms, 12 story. S $149.95; D $164.95; each addl $15; suites $350; under 12 free; wknd rates. Crib free. TV; cable (premium). Heated pool; whirlpool. Supervised child's activities. Complimentary coffee in rms. Restaurant 6 am-11 pm. Bar 11-1 am. Ck-out noon. Meeting rms. Business center. Exercise equipt; sauna. Rec rm. Minibars. Some balconies. Cr cds: A, C, D, DS, ER, JCB, MC, V.

★ ★ ★ **HOTEL TORONTO-EAST.** *(2035 Kennedy Rd, Scarborough ON M1T 3G2)* 416/299-1500; FAX 416/299-8959. E-mail net@hte.cphotels.ca; web www.cphotels.ca. 368 rms, 14 story. S, D $219; each addl $15; suites $365-$620; under 18 free; wknd rates. Crib free. Pet accepted. TV; cable. Indoor pool; wading pool; whirlpool. Free supervised child's activities (wkends, school hols); ages 3-15. Restaurants 6:30-2 am. Rm serv 24 hrs. Bar 11-2 am. Ck-out noon. Convention facilities. Business servs avail. In-rm modem link. Concierge. Gift shop. Barber, beauty shop. Covered valet parking. Putting green. Exercise rm; sauna. Game rm. Luxury level. Cr cds: A, D, DS, ER, JCB, MC, V.

★ ★ ★ **HOWARD JOHNSON PLAZA.** *(2737 Keele St, North York ON M3M 2E9) N on Hwy 401, exit Keele St, then 1 blk N.* 416/636-4656; FAX 416/633-5637. Web www.hojo.com. 367 rms, most A/C, 10 story, 27 suites. S, D $129-$179; each addl $10; suites $175-$375; family rates; package plans. Crib free. Pet accepted. TV; cable (premium), VCR avail. Indoor pool. Supervised child's activities (June-Sept); ages 4-12. Complimentary coffee in rms. Restaurant 6:30 am-11 pm; Sun to 10 pm. Bar 11-1 am. Ck-out noon. Meeting rms. Business servs avail. Free garage parking.

Downhill/x-country ski 10 mi. Exercise equipt; sauna. Game rm. Rec rm. Some minibars; microwaves avail. Cr cds: A, C, D, DS, ER, JCB, MC, V.

[icons] D 🐾 ✈ 🏊 ✕ 🚶 🛏 🐾 SC

★ ★ ★ **INN ON THE PARK.** (1100 Eglinton Ave E, Toronto ON M3C 1H8) at Leslie St, north of downtown. 416/444-2561; FAX 416/446-3308; res: 800/268-6282 (CAN). 270 rms, 23 story. S, D $135-$195; each addl $20; suites $225-$750; under 18 free; wkend rates. Crib free. Pet accepted. TV; cable (premium), VCR avail. 2 heated pools, 1 indoor; whirlpool, lifeguards. Free supervised child's activities (June-Sept); ages 5-12. Restaurants 6:30 am-midnight (also see HARVEST CAFE). Bar 11:30-1 am; vocalist exc Sun. Ck-out noon. Business center. In-rm modem link. Concierge. Barber, beauty shop. Valet parking. Lighted tennis, pro. X-country ski ¼ mi. Exercise equipt; sauna, steam rm. Rec rm. Lawn games. Some minibars. Some private patios, balconies. Cr cds: A, C, D, DS, ER, JCB, MC, V.

[icons] D 🐾 ✈ 🏇 🏊 ✕ 🏋 🛏 🐾 SC

★ ★ ★ ★ **INTER-CONTINENTAL.** (220 Bloor St W, Toronto ON M5S 1T8) downtown. 416/960-5200; FAX 416/960-8269. Web www.interconti.com. Edwardian and art-deco touches embellish public spaces and guest rooms of this post-modern structure. 209 rms, 8 story. S $265-$345; D $225-$355; suites $400-$1,400. Crib free. Valet parking $22. TV; cable (premium), VCR avail (movies). Indoor pool. Restaurants 7 am-11 pm. Rm serv 24 hrs. Bar noon-1 am. Ck-out 1 pm. Meeting rms. Business center. In-rm modem link. Concierge. Gift shop. Exercise equipt; sauna. Massage. Bathrm phones, minibars. Cr cds: A, C, D, ER, JCB, MC, V.

[icons] D 🏊 ✕ ✈ 🛏 🔥 SC 🚶

★ ★ ★ **INTERNATIONAL PLAZA.** (655 Dixon Rd, Toronto ON M9W 1J4) near Lester B. Pearson Intl Airport, west of downtown. 416/244-1711; FAX 416/244-8031; res: 800/668-3656. E-mail sales@internationalplaza.com; web www.internationalplaza.com. 415 rms, 12 story. S, D $170; each addl $10; suites $350-$500; under 18 free; wkend rates. Crib free. Pet accepted. Valet parking $6. TV; cable (premium). Indoor pool; wading pool, poolside serv, lifeguard. Supervised child's activities; ages 3-12. Restaurant 6:30 am-11 pm. Rm serv 24 hrs. Bar 11 am-2 am. Ck-out noon. Convention facilities. Business center. Concierge. Gift shop. Beauty, barber shop. Exercise equipt; sauna. Massages. Game rm. Refrigerators. Minibars in suites. Cr cds: A, D, DS, ER, MC, V.

[icons] D 🐾 🏊 ✕ 🛏 🔥 🐾 SC

★ ★ ★ ★ **KING EDWARD.** (37 King St E, Toronto ON M5C 1E9) downtown. 416/863-9700; FAX 416/367-5515; res: 800/225-5843. Built in 1903 and remodelled in the early 1980s, this stately and attractive hotel has a vaulted ceiling, marble pillars and palm trees in its lobby. 294 rms, 9 & 16 story. S $205-$360; D $230-$385; suites $435-$510; under 12 free; wkend rates. Crib free. Covered parking, valet $24. TV; cable (premium), VCR avail. Restaurants 6:30 am-2:30 pm, 5-11 pm (see CHIARO'S, also see CAFE VICTORIA, Unrated Dining). Rm serv 24 hrs. Bars 11:30-1 am. Ck-out noon. Convention facilities. Business center. In-rm modem link. Concierge. Shopping arcade. Beauty shop. Exercise equipt; sauna. Whirlpools. Massage. Health club privileges. Bathrm phones, minibars; microwaves avail. Cr cds: A, C, D, ER, JCB, MC, V.

[icons] D ✕ 🛏 🐾 SC 🚶

★ ★ ★ **MARRIOTT-AIRPORT.** (901 Dixon Rd, Etobicoke ON M9W 1J5) near Lester B. Pearson Intl Airport. 416/674-9400; FAX 416/674-8292. 424 rms, 9 story. S, D $240; suites $300-$1,200; under 18 free; wkend rates. Crib free. TV; cable (premium). Indoor pool; whirlpool. Restaurants 6 am-11 pm. Bar noon-2 am. Ck-out noon. Convention facilities. Business center. Gift shop. Covered parking. Free airport transportation. Exercise equipt; sauna. Luxury level. Cr cds: A, C, D, ER, JCB, MC, V.

[icons] D 🏊 ✕ ✈ 🛏 🐾 SC 🚶

★ ★ ★ **MARRIOTT-EATON CENTRE.** (525 Bay St, Toronto ON M5G 2L2) downtown. 416/597-9200; res: 888/440-9300; FAX 416/597-9211. Web www.marriott.com/marriott/yyzec. 459 rms, 18 story. May-Oct: S, D $350; suites $600-$1800; family rates; package plans; higher rates special events; lower rates rest of yr. Crib free. Garage parking $14, valet $18. TV; cable (premium), VCR avail. Indoor pool; whirlpool, poolside serv.

Restaurant 6:30 am-10 pm. Rm serv 24 hrs. Bar 11-1 am. Ck-out noon. Convention facilities. Business center. Concierge. Shopping arcade. Drug store. Barber, beauty shop. Exercise equipt; sauna. Cr cds: A, D, DS, ER, JCB, MC, V.

[icons] D 🏊 ✕ ✈ 🛏 🐾 SC 🚶

★ ★ ★ **METROPOLITAN.** (108 Chestnut St, Toronto ON M5G 1R3) downtown. 416/977-5000; res: 800/668-6600; FAX 416/977-9513. E-mail reservations@metropolitan.com; web www.metropolitan.com. 469 rms, 26 story. S $180; D $210; each addl $20; suites $225-$1100; wkend rates. Crib free. Parking, in/out $15.87. Pet accepted, some restrictions. TV; cable (premium), VCR avail (free movies). Indoor pool; whirlpool. Restaurant 6:30 am-midnight (see also LAI WAH HEEN). Bar 11-1 am. Ck-out noon. Meeting rms. Business center. In-rm modem link. Concierge. Gift shop. Exercise equipt; sauna. Bathrm phones, minibars. Adj to City Hall. Eatons Centre 2 blks. Cr cds: A, D, DS, ER, JCB, MC, V.

[icons] D 🐾 🏊 ✕ ✕ 🛏 🐾 SC 🚶

★ ★ **NOVOTEL-AIRPORT.** (135 Carlingview Dr, Etobicoke ON M9W 5E7) near Lester B. Pearson Intl Airport. 416/798-9800; FAX 416/798-1237; res: 800/668-6835. E-mail tairmail@aol.com. 192 rms, 7 story. S $165; D $175; suites $175; family, wkly, wkend rates. Crib free. Pet accepted. TV; cable (premium). Indoor pool; whirlpool. Restaurant 6 am-11 pm. Bar 11-1 am. Ck-out 1 pm. Meeting rms. Business center. In-rm modem link. Gift shop. Garage parking. Free airport transportation. Downhill/x-country ski 20 mi. Exercise equipt; sauna. Minibars. Cr cds: A, D, DS, ER, JCB, MC, V.

[icons] D 🐾 ✈ 🏊 ✕ ✈ 🚶 🛏 🐾 SC 🚶

★ ★ ★ **NOVOTEL-TORONTO CENTRE.** (45 The Esplanade, Toronto ON M5E 1W2) downtown. 416/367-8900; FAX 416/360-8285; res: 800/668-6835. Web novotel-northamerica.com/welcome. 262 rms, 9 story. S, D $205; each addl $20; suites $215; under 16 free; wkend rates. Crib free. Pet accepted. Garage, in/out $13.50. TV; cable (premium). Indoor pool; whirlpool. Restaurant 6 am-midnight. Bar 11-2 am. Ck-out 1 pm. Meeting rms. Business servs avail. Exercise equipt; sauna. Minibars. Cr cds: A, D, DS, ER, JCB, MC, V.

[icons] D 🐾 🏊 ✕ 🚶 🛏 SC

★ **QUALITY.** (111 Lombard St, Toronto ON M5C 2T9) downtown. 416/367-5555; FAX 416/367-3470; res: 800/228-5151. 196 rms, 16 story. S $139; D $149; each addl $10; under 18 free. Crib free. Pet accepted. Garage $11.75/day. TV; cable. Ck-out 11 am. Business servs avail. Exercise equipt. Health club privileges. Cr cds: A, D, DS, ER, JCB, MC, V.

[icons] D 🐾 ✕ 🛏 🔥 SC

★ **QUALITY.** (280 Bloor St W, Toronto ON M5S 1V8) downtown. 416/968-0010; FAX 416/968-7765. 210 rms, 14 story. Mid-Mar-Oct: S $120-$145; D $130-$155; under 18 free; wkend rates; higher rates special events; lower rates rest of yr. Crib free. Pet accepted, some restrictions. Garage in/out $11.50. TV; cable. Restaurant 7 am-11 pm. Ck-out 11 am. Meeting rms. Business servs avail. No bellhops. Health club privileges. Cr cds: A, D, DS, JCB, MC, V.

[icons] D 🐾 🛏 🐾 SC

✔★ ★ **QUALITY SUITES.** (262 Carlingview Dr, Etobicoke ON M9W 5G1) near Lester B. Pearson Intl Airport. 416/674-8442; FAX 416/674-3088. Web hotelchoice.com. 254 suites, 12 story. S, D $120-$145; each addl $5; under 18 free; wkend, hol rates. Crib free. Pet accepted. TV; cable (premium). Complimentary coffee in rms. Restaurant 6:30-1 am. Bar. Ck-out 11 am. Meeting rms. Business servs avail. No bellhops. Gift shop. Downhill/x-country ski 15 mi. Exercise equipt. Health club privileges. Minibars; microwaves avail. Cr cds: A, D, DS, ER, JCB, MC, V.

[icons] D 🐾 🏊 ✕ 🛏 🐾 SC

★ **QUALITY-AIRPORT EAST.** (2180 Islington Ave, Toronto ON M9P 3P1) west of downtown. 416/240-9090; FAX 416/240-9944. E-mail quality@ica.net; web www.qualityinn.com. 198 rms, 12 story. S, D $89-$139; each addl $10; under 18 free; package plans; higher rates special events. Crib free. Pet accepted. TV; cable (premium). Restaurant 6 am-midnight. Bar from 11 am. Ck-out 11 am. Meeting rms. In-rm modem link. Microwaves avail. Near airport. Cr cds: A, D, DS, ER, JCB, MC, V.

⊡ ⛵ ✈ 🏊 🐾 SC

★ ★ ★ **RADISSON.** *(50 E Valhalla Dr, Markham ON L3R 0A3) N on Hwy 404, at jct Hwy 7.* 905/477-2010; FAX 905/477-2026. Web www.radissonmarkham@sympatico.ca.com 4 rms, 15 story, 26 suites. S, D $220; each addl $15; suites $250; under 19 free; wkly, wkend rates; golf plans; higher rates Dec 31. Crib free. Indoor pool; whirlpool. Complimentary continental bkfst. Complimentary coffee in rms. Restaurant 6:30 am-11 pm. Bar 11-2 am. Ck-out noon. Meeting rms. Business servs avail. Gift shop. Tennis privileges. 18-hole golf privileges. Downhill/x-country ski 12 mi. Exercise equipt; sauna. Rec rm. Minibars; microwaves avail. Picnic tables. Cr cds: A, C, D, DS, ER, JCB, MC, V.

⊡ ⛷ 🏃 🏊 ✈ ⛷ 🐾 SC

★ ★ ★ **RADISSON PLAZA.** *(90 Bloor St E, Toronto ON M4W 1A7) at Yonge St, downtown.* 416/961-8000; FAX 416/961-4635; res: 800/267-6116. Web www.radisson.com/torontoca_yorkville. 258 rms, 6 story. S $260; D $275; each addl $15; suites $540-$555; under 18 free. Crib free. Garage parking, valet $18.50. TV; cable (premium). Coffee in rms. Restaurant 6:30 am-11 pm. Bar 11:30-1 am. Ck-out noon. Meeting rms. Business center. Health club privileges. Minibars; bathrm phone in suites, microwaves avail. Luxury level. Cr cds: A, C, D, DS, ER, JCB, MC, V.

⊡ 🏊 🐾 SC ✈

★ ★ ★ **RADISSON PLAZA-HOTEL ADMIRAL.** *(249 Queens Quay W, Toronto ON M5J 2N5) downtown.* 416/203-3333; FAX 416/203-3100. 157 air-cooled rms, 8 story, 17 suites. Early-May-mid-Nov: S, D $265-$295; each addl $20; suites from $495; family, wkend rates. Crib free. Parking $15/day. TV; cable (premium). Heated pool; whirlpool; poolside serv. Complimentary coffee in rms. Restaurant 7 am-11 pm. Rm serv 24 hrs. Bar 11:30-1 am. Ck-out noon. Meeting rms. Business servs avail. Concierge. Gift shop. Health club privileges. Bathrm phones, minibars. On waterfront; nautical theme throughout. View of Harbour. Cr cds: A, C, D, DS, ER, JCB, MC, V.

⊡ 🏊 🐾 SC ✈

★ ★ ★ **RADISSON SUITE-TORONTO AIRPORT.** *(640 Dixon Rd, Etobicoke ON M9W 1J1) near Lester B. Pearson Intl Airport.* 416/242-7400; FAX 416/242-9888. Web www.radisson.com. 215 suites, 14 story. S, D $204-$216; under 18 free. Crib free. Pet accepted, some restrictions. TV; cable, VCR avail. Complimentary continental bkfst. Restaurant 6:30 am-11 pm. Bar 11-1 am. Ck-out noon. Meeting rms. Business center. In-rm modem link. Concierge. Gift shop. Free valet parking. Exercise equipt. Minibars, microwaves avail. Cr cds: A, C, D, DS, ER, JCB, MC, V.

⊡ ⛵ ✈ 🏊 🐾 SC ✈

★ ★ **RAMADA-DON VALLEY.** *(185 Yorkland Blvd, Toronto ON M2J 4R2) at jct ON 401, Don Valley Pkwy, north of downtown.* 416/493-9000; FAX 416/493-5729. Web www.ramada.com/ramada.html. 285 rms, 10 story. S, D $105-$165; each addl $15; suites $175-$300; under 18 free; wkend rates. Crib free. TV; cable (premium). Indoor pool. Coffee in rms. Restaurant 6:30 am-10:30 pm; Sat from 7 am. Bar 11-2 am; Sun to 11 pm. Ck-out noon. Meeting rms. Business center. In-rm modem link. Exercise equipt; sauna. Health club privileges. Game rm. Rec rm. Some in-rm whirlpools. Luxury level. Cr cds: A, C, D, DS, ER, JCB, MC, V.

⊡ 🏊 ✈ 🐾 SC ✈

★ ★ ★ **REGAL CONSTELLATION.** *(900 Dixon Rd, Etobicoke ON M9W 1J7) near Lester B. Pearson Intl Airport.* 416/675-1500; FAX 416/675-1737; res: 800/268-4838. Web www.regal-hotels.com. 710 rms, 8-16 story. S, D $95-$165; each addl $15; suites from $275; under 18 free; wkend package plan. Crib free. Pet accepted, some restrictions. Valet parking $9.25/day. TV; cable (premium), VCR avail. 2 heated pools, 1 indoor/outdoor; whirlpool, poolside serv in season. Restaurant 6:30 am-11 pm; dining rm 11 am-2 pm, 5:30-10 pm. Rm serv 24 hrs. Bar 11-1 am; entertainment Thurs-Sat. Ck-out noon. Concierge. Convention facilities.

Business center. Gift shop. Beauty shop. Airport transportation. Exercise equipt; sauna. Some balconies. Cr cds: A, C, D, DS, ER, MC, V.

⊡ ⛵ 🏊 🏃 ✈ 🐾 SC ✈

★ ★ ★ **ROYAL YORK.** *(100 Front St W, Toronto ON M5J 1E3) opp Union Station, downtown.* 416/368-2511; FAX 416/368-2884; res: 800/828-7447 (US). E-mail reserve@ryh.cphotels.ca; web www.cphotels.ca. 1,365 rms, 22 story. S, D $189-$289; each addl $20; suites $295-$1,750; under 18 free; package plans. Crib free. Pet accepted. Garage (fee). TV; cable. Pool; wading pool, whirlpool. Restaurant 6:30 am-10:30 pm. Rm serv 24 hrs. Bars noon-2 am; entertainment. Ck-out noon. Convention facilities. Business center. Concierge. Shopping arcade. Barber, beauty shop. Exercise rm; sauna. Massage. Health club privileges. Minibars; refrigerators, microwaves avail. Luxury level. Cr cds: A, D, DS, ER, JCB, MC, V.

⊡ ⛵ 🏊 🏃 🐾 SC ✈

★ ★ ★ **SHERATON CENTRE.** *(123 Queen St W, Toronto ON M5H 2M9) opp City Hall, downtown.* 416/361-1000; FAX 416/947-4854. Web www.sheratonctr.toronto.on.ca. 1,382 rms, 43 story. Late June-Dec: S $275; D $285; each addl $20; suites $450-$850; under 18 free; wkend rates; lower rates rest of yr. Covered parking, valet $22/day. TV; cable (premium), VCR avail. Indoor/outdoor pool; whirlpool, poolside serv (summer), lifeguard. Supervised child's activities (daily July-mid-Sept; wkends rest of yr). Complimentary coffee in rms. Restaurant 6 am-11 pm. Rm serv 24 hrs. Bars. Ck-out noon. Convention facilities. Business center. Concierge. Shopping arcade. Barber, beauty shop. Exercise equipt; sauna. Massage. Rec rm. Minibars; microwaves avail. Private patios, balconies. Waterfall in lobby; pond with live ducks. Cr cds: A, C, D, ER, JCB, MC, V.

⊡ 🏊 🏃 🐾 SC ✈

★ ★ ★ **SHERATON GATEWAY.** *(PO Box 3000, Toronto ON L5P 1C4) at Lester B. Pearson Intl Airport, west of downtown.* 905/672-7000; FAX 905/672-7100. Web www.sheraton.com. 474 rms, 8 story. S, D $190-$240; each addl $15; suites $420-$800; under 18 free; wkly, wkend rates. Crib free. Pet accepted. Garage parking $9.50; valet $18. TV; cable (premium), VCR avail. Indoor pool; whirlpool. Restaurant 6 am-11 pm. Rm serv 24 hrs. Bar 11-1 am. Ck-out noon. Convention facilities. Business center. Concierge. Shopping arcade. Barber, beauty shop. Free airport transportation. Exercise equipt; sauna. Massage. Minibars. Modern facility connected by climate-controlled walkway to Terminal 3. Cr cds: A, C, D, DS, ER, JCB, MC, V.

⊡ ⛵ 🏊 🏃 ✈ 🐾 SC ✈

★ ★ ★ **SKYDOME.** *(1 Blue Jays Way, Toronto ON M5V 1J4) adj CN Tower, downtown.* 416/341-7100; FAX 416/341-5091; res: 800/441-1414. Web www.cphotels.ca. 346 rms, 11 story, 26 suites. May-Oct: S, D $169-$179; each addl $30; suites from $299-$559; under 18 free; wkend rates; package plans; lower rates rest of yr. Crib avail. Pet accepted. Garage parking $16; valet $22. TV; cable, VCR avail. Indoor pool. Complimentary coffee in rms. Supervised child's activities (June-Sept). Restaurant 7-1 am. Rm serv 24 hrs. Bar. Ck-out 9:30 am-noon. Convention facilities. Business center. Concierge. Gift shop. Health club privileges. Massage. Minibars. Modern facility within SkyDome complex; lobby and some rms overlook playing field. Cr cds: A, C, D, DS, ER, JCB, MC, V.

⊡ ⛵ 🏊 🐾 SC ✈

★ ★ ★ **SUTTON PLACE.** *(955 Bay St, Toronto ON M5S 2A2) downtown.* 416/924-9221; res: 800/268-3790; FAX 416/924-1778. E-mail res@tor.suttonplace.com; web www.travelweb.com/sutton.html. 292 rms, 33 story, 62 suites. S, D $320; each addl $20; suites $390-$1,500; under 18 free; wkend rates. Crib free. Garage parking $18; valet $21. TV; cable (premium), VCR avail (movies). Indoor pool; poolside serv. Restaurant (see ACCENTS). Rm serv 24 hrs. Bar 11-1:30 am; entertainment Thurs-Sat. Ck-out noon. Convention facilities. Business center. Concierge. Gift shop. Barber, beauty shop. Exercise equipt; sauna. Health club privileges. Massage. Minibars. Cr cds: A, C, D, ER, JCB, MC, V.

⊡ 🏊 🏃 🐾 SC ✈

★ ★ **TOWN INN.** *(620 Church St, Toronto ON M4Y 2G2) downtown.* 416/964-3311; FAX 416/924-9466; res: 800/387-2755. E-mail mitch@towninn.com; web towninn.com/. 200 kit. units (1-2 bedrm), 26 story. June-Dec: S $95-$125; D $110-$135; each addl $15; under 12 free; monthly rates; lower rates rest of yr. Crib free. Pet accepted. Garage $14. TV; cable (premium). Heated pool. Complimentary continental bkfst. Restaurant 7-10 am. Ck-out 11 am. Meeting rms. Business servs avail. Tennis. Exercise equipt. Health club privileges; saunas. Refrigerators, microwaves. Balconies. Cr cds: A, C, D, ER, MC, V.

⊡ 🐾 🏂 ≋ ≍ ⊼ ⋊ ⋉ SC

✔★★ **TRAVELODGE.** *(55 Hallcrown Pl, North York ON M2J 4R1)* ON 401 exit 376, then N on Victoria Park Ave, off Consumer Rd. 416/493-7000; FAX 416/493-6577. Web www.travelodge.com. 228 rms, 9 story. S, D $98-$103; each addl $10; suites $225; under 17 free; wkend rates. Crib free. TV; cable (premium). Indoor pool; whirlpool. Complimentary coffee in rms. Restaurant 7 am-10 pm. Bar. Ck-out noon. Meeting rms. Business servs avail. Sauna. Cr cds: A, C, D, DS, ER, JCB, MC, V.

⊡ ≋ ≍ ⋉ SC

★ **VENTURE INN-AIRPORT.** *(925 Dixon Rd, Etobicoke ON M9W 1J8)* near Lester B. Pearson Intl Airport. 416/674-2222; res: 888/4-VENTURE; FAX 416/674-5757. Web www.ventureinn.com. 283 rms, 17 story. S $120; D $140; each addl $10; suites $140-$275; under 18 free; wkend rates. Crib free. Pet accepted. TV, cable (premium). Indoor pool; whirlpool. Complimentary continental bkfst. Restaurant 11-2 am. Bar. Ck-out 1 pm. Convention facilities. Business servs avail. In-rm modem link. Airport transportation. Sauna. Health club privileges. Gift shop. Cr cds: A, D, DS, ER, MC, V.

⊡ 🐾 ≋ ⊼ ≍ ⋉ SC

★★ **WESTIN PRINCE.** *(900 York Mills Rd, North York ON M3B 3H2)* N on Don Valley Pkwy, W on York Mills Rd. 416/444-2511; FAX 416/444-9597. E-mail toprince@idirect.com; web www.princehotels.co.jp. 381 rms, 22 story. S $210-$245; D $230-$265; each addl $20; suites $340-$1,800; under 18 free; wkend rates. Crib free. TV; cable (premium), VCR avail (movies). Pool; whirlpool, poolside serv. Playground. Restaurant 6:30 am-10 pm. Rm serv 24 hrs. Bar 11:30-2 am; entertainment Mon-Sat. Ck-out 1 pm. Convention facilities. Business center. In-rm modem link. Concierge. Shopping arcade. Barber, beauty shop. Tennis. 18-hole golf privileges. Exercise equipt; sauna. Health club privileges. Game rm. Refrigerators. Balconies. Cr cds: A, C, D, DS, ER, JCB, MC, V.

⊡ ⋊ 🏂 ≋ ⊼ ≍ ⋈ ⋊

★★ **WYNDHAM BRISTOL PLACE HOTEL.** *(950 Dixon Rd, Etobicoke ON M9W 5N4)* near Lester B. Pearson Intl Airport. 416/675-9444; FAX 416/675-4426; res: 800/268-4927. E-mail bristol@interlog.com; web www.wyndham.com. 287 rms, 15 story. S, D $215-$240; each addl $15; suites from $625; under 18 free; wkend rates; package plans. Crib free. TV; cable (premium). Indoor/outdoor pool; poolside serv. Restaurant 6:30 am-10 pm (also see ZACHARY'S). Rm serv 24 hrs. Bars 11-2 am; entertainment Mon-Fri. Ck-out 1 pm. Convention facilities. Business center. In-rm modem link. Concierge. Valet parking. Free airport transportation. Exercise equipt; sauna. Minibars; bathrm phone, whirlpool in some suites; microwaves avail. Some private patios. Cr cds: A, C, D, DS, ER, JCB, MC, V.

⊡ ≋ ⊼ ✈ ≍ ⋉ SC ⋈

Inns

✔★★ **GUILD.** *(201 Guildwood Pkwy, Scarborough ON M1E 1P6)* 416/261-3331; FAX 416/261-5675. 96 rms, 3-6 story. Apr-Dec: S, D $79; each addl $10; suites $140; under 18 free; AP, MAP avail; wkly rates; lower rates rest of yr. Crib free. TV; cable (premium). Pool. Restaurant (see GUILD INN). Ck-out noon, ck-in 3 pm. Business servs avail. Tennis. Balconies. Opened in 1923 as art community. On 90-acres overlooking Lake Ontario. Log cabin (1805) on grounds. Cr cds: A, C, D, DS, ER, MC, V.

⊡ 🐾 ≋ ≍ ⋉ SC

★★ **MILLCROFT.** *(55 John St, Alton ON L0N 1A0)* Hwy 10 to Hwy 24, W to Hwy 136, then N to John St. 519/941-8111; res: 800/383-3976 (ON only); FAX 519/941-9192. E-mail millcroft@millcroft.com; web www.millcroft.com. 52 rms, 2 story, 20 chalets. S, D $185-$275. Crib free.

Heated pool; whirlpool, poolside serv. Complimentary continental bkfst. Restaurant (see MILLCROFT INN). Bar. Ck-out noon, ck-in 4 pm. Guest lndry. Meeting rm. Business servs avail. Valet serv. Tennis. Golf privileges. X-country ski on site. Exercise equipt; sauna. Volleyball. Game rm. Some private patios. 100 acres on Credit River. Former knitting mill (1881). Cr cds: A, D, ER, MC, V.

⊡ 🐾 🏂 ⋈ ≋ ⊼ ⋉ 🏂

Restaurants

★★★ **360 REVOLVING RESTAURANT.** *(301 Front St W, Toronto ON M5V 2T6)* in CN Tower, downtown. 416/362-5411. Web www.cntower.ca. Continental menu. Specializes in fresh rack of lamb, prime rib, corn-fed free-range chicken. Own baking. Hrs: 11 am-2:30 pm, 5-10:30 pm; Sun from 10:30 am. Res accepted. Bar. Wine cellar. A la carte entrees: lunch, dinner $19-$38. Sun brunch from $35. Revolving restaurant; view of harbor and city. Cr cds: A, D, ER, MC, V.

⊡

★★★ **ACCENTS.** *(See Sutton Place Hotel)* 416/324-5633. Continental menu. Specializes in market fresh cuisine. Hrs: 6:30 am-11:30 pm. Res accepted. Bar. Wine cellar. A la carte entrees: bkfst $2.95-$10.50, lunch $11.50-$14.50, dinner $22-$36. Pianist Thurs-Sat. Parking. Continental atmosphere. Cr cds: A, C, D, DS, ER, JCB, MC, V.

⊡ ⋽

★★★ **ACCOLADE.** *(See Crowne Plaza Toronto Centre Hotel)* 416/597-1400. Web crowneplaza.com. Continental menu. Specialty: rack of lamb. Own baking. Hrs: 11:45 am-2 pm, 5:45-10 pm; Sat, Sun from 6 pm. Res accepted. Bar to 2 am. Wine list. Semi a la carte: lunch $11.95-$21.95, dinner $26-$32. Complete meals: dinner $34.95. Valet parking. Cr cds: A, C, D, DS, ER, JCB, MC, V.

⊡

★★ **ARKADIA HOUSE.** *(2007 Eglinton Ave E, Scarborough ON M1L 2M9)* approx 10 mi E on Hwy 2. 416/752-5685. Greek menu. Specialties: roast lamb, souvlaki. Hrs: 11:30 am-3 pm, 4 pm-midnight. Closed Dec 24. Res accepted. Bar. Wine list. A la carte entrees: lunch $6.95-$12.95, dinner $10.95-$19.95. Child's meals. Parking. Garden cafe atmosphere. Cr cds: A, D, ER, MC, V.

SC ⋽

★ **ARLEQUIN.** *(134 Avenue Rd, Toronto ON M5R 2H6)* north of downtown. 416/928-9521. French, Mediterranean menu. Hrs: 8:30 am-10 pm; Fri, Sat to 11 pm. Closed most major hols. Res accepted. Bar. A la carte entrees: lunch $7.95-$12.95, dinner $12.95-$18.95. Complete meals: dinner (Mon-Wed) $18.95, (Thurs-Sat) $22.95. Small bistro with harlequin motif. Cr cds: A, D, ER, MC, V.

⋽

★★ **AVALON.** *(270 Adelaide St W, Toronto ON M5H 1X6)* downtown. 416/979-9918. Specialties: wood-roasted chicken, yellow fin tuna steak, grilled dry-aged rib steak. Hrs: noon-2:30 pm, 5:30-10 pm; Mon, Tues from 5:30 pm; Fri to 11 pm; Sat 5:30-11 pm. Closed Sun; most major hols. Res accepted. Bar. Wine list. A la carte entrees: lunch $13-$22, dinner $20-$30. Artwork by local artists. Cr cds: A, D, ER, JCB, MC, V.

⋽

★★ **BANGKOK GARDEN.** *(18 Elm St, Toronto ON M5G 1G7)* downtown. 416/977-6748. Thai menu. Specializes in soup, curry dishes, seafood. Hrs: 11:30 am-2:30 pm, 5-10 pm; Sat, Sun from 5 pm. Res accepted. Bar. A la carte entrees: lunch $8.95-$10.95, dinner $14.95-$19.25. Complete meals: dinner $25.95-$39.95. Buffet (Mon, Fri): lunch $9.95. Child's meals. Thai decor; indoor garden. Cr cds: A, C, D, ER, MC, V.

⋽

✔★★ **BAROOTES.** *(220 King St W, Toronto ON M5H 1K4)* downtown. 416/979-7717. International menu. Specialties: fresh stir-fry, Thai satay combination, grilled marinated lamb tenderloin. Hrs: 11:30

am-2:30 pm, 5-10:30 pm. Closed Sun; Jan 1, Dec 25. Res accepted. Bar. A la carte entrees: lunch $8.95-$12.95, dinner $11.50-$24.95. Traditional dining rm. Cr cds: A, D, ER, MC, V.

★ ★ **BISTRO 990.** *(990 Bay St, Toronto ON M5S 2A5) downtown. 416/921-9990.* Specializes in lamb, fresh fish. Hrs: noon-10:30 pm; Sat from 5:30 pm. Closed Sun. Res accepted. Bar. A la carte entrees: lunch $13.50-$29, dinner $14-$32. Prix fixe: lunch, dinner $19.90. Outdoor dining. French bistro decor. Cr cds: A, D, ER, MC, V.

★ ★ ★ **BOBA.** *(90 Avenue Rd, Toronto ON M5R 2H2) in Yorkville. 416/961-2622.* Contemporary Amer menu. Specializes in vegetarian dishes, desserts. Hrs: 5:30-10 pm. Closed Sun; Jan 1, Dec 25, 26. Res required. Bar. A la carte entrees: dinner $19.50-$29.95. Patio dining. Intimate dining rm; bistro atmosphere. Totally nonsmoking. Cr cds: A, D, ER, MC, V.

★ ★ **BOY ON A DOLPHIN.** *(1911 Eglinton Ave E, Scarborough ON M1L 2L6) 416/759-4448.* Specializes in steak, seafood. Salad bar. Hrs: 11 am-midnight; Sat from 4 pm; Sun brunch 11 am-2:30 pm. Res accepted. Bar to 1 am. Semi-a la carte: lunch $7.95-$12.95, dinner $14.95-$29.95. Sun brunch $12.95. Child's meals. Parking. Mediterranean decor. Cr cds: A, D, ER, MC, V.

★ ★ **BUMPKINS.** *(21 Gloucester St, Toronto ON M4Y 1L8) between Church & Yonge Sts, downtown. 416/922-8655.* Web www.where mags.com. French, Amer menu. Specialty: shrimp Bumpkins. Hrs: noon-2:30 pm; Sat from 5 pm. Closed Sun. A la carte entrees: lunch $3.95-$8.50, dinner $8.75-$20.95. Child's meals. Outdoor dining. Cr cds: A, ER, MC, V.

★ ★ ★ **CANOE.** *(66 Wellington St W, Toronto ON M5K 1H6) downtown. 416/364-0054.* Specialties: Québec foie gras, Yukon caribou, roast sea scallops. Hrs: 11:30 am-2:30 pm, 5-10:30 pm. Closed Sat, Sun; major hols. Res accepted. Bar to 2 am. Wine cellar. Semi-a la carte: lunch $14-$23, dinner $25-$32. View of harbor and islands. Totally nonsmoking. Cr cds: A, D, ER, MC, V.

★ ★ ★ **CARMAN'S CLUB.** *(26 Alexander St, Toronto ON) downtown. 416/924-8558.* Web www.dine.net/visit/carmans. Specialities: rack of lamb, Dover sole. Own pastries. Hrs: 5:30 pm-midnight. Closed Good Friday, Dec 25. Res accepted. Serv bar. Wine cellar. Complete meals: dinner $31.95-$35.95. Child's meals. In pre-1900 house; fireplaces. Family-owned. Cr cds: A, MC, V.

★ ★ ★ ★ **CENTRO GRILL.** *(2472 Yonge St, Toronto ON M4P 2H5) north of downtown. 416/483-2211.* The facade of etched glass, granite and marble may seem hard-edged, but the interior is as warm as the folksy town of Asolo. Massive columns that seem to hold up a bright blue ceiling and salmon-colored walls lined with comfortable banquettes help to create an intimate setting. Italian, Amer menu. Specialty: rack of lamb with tomato, garlic, Spanish capers, eggplant and salsa. Own baking. Hrs: 5-11:30 pm. Closed Sun. Res accepted. Bar. A la carte entrees: dinner $24.95-$39.50. Pianist. Valet parking. Cr cds: A, D, ER, MC, V.

★ ★ ★ **CHEZ MAX.** *(166 Wellington St W, Toronto ON) downtown. 416/599-9633.* French menu. Specialties: filet mignon, roasted medallions of monkfish. Hrs: noon-2:30 pm, 5:30-10 pm; Sat from 5:30 pm. Closed Sun; major hols. Res accepted. Bar. A la carte entrees: lunch $8.95-$17.50, dinner $16.75-$28.95. Modern decor. Jacket. Cr cds: A, D, ER, MC, V.

★ ★ ★ **CHIADO.** *(864 College St, Toronto ON M6H 1A3) west of downtown. 416/538-1910.* Portuguese menu. Specializes in Portuguese classical cuisine. Hrs: noon-midnight. Closed Sun; Dec 24-26. Res accepted. Wine cellar. A la carte entrees: lunch $9.50-$14, dinner $17.75-$30. Child's meals. Oil paintings. Cr cds: A, C, D, ER, MC, V.

★ ★ ★ **CHIARO'S.** *(See King Edward Hotel) 416/863-9700.* Web toprestaurants.com/toronto/chiaros.htm. Continental menu. Specialties: rack of lamb, Dover sole. Hrs: 6-10 pm. Closed Sun. Res accepted. Bar to 1 am. Wine cellar. Semi-a la carte: dinner $24-$43. Child's meals. Valet parking. Cr cds: A, C, D, ER, JCB, MC, V.

★ ★ ★ **DAVID DUNCAN HOUSE.** *(125 Moatfield Dr, North York ON) 1 mi S of ON 401, Leslie St exit. 416/391-1424.* Specializes in steak, seafood, rack of lamb. Hrs: 11:30 am-3 pm, 5-11 pm; Sat, Sun from 5 pm. Res accepted. Bar. Wine list. Semi-a la carte: lunch $9.95-$14.95, dinner $17.95-$41.95. Valet parking. In restored, Gothic-revival house (1865) with elaborate gingerbread & millwork, antiques, stained-glass skylight. Jacket. Cr cds: A, D, ER, MC, V.

★ ★ ★ **THE DOCTOR'S HOUSE.** *(21 Nashville Rd, Kleinberg ON L0J 1C0) 20 mi N on Hwy 27/427 to Kleinburg, turn right on Nashville Rd to top of hill. 905/893-1615.* Continental menu. Hrs: 11-1 am; Sun brunch 10:30 am-3 pm. Res accepted; required Sun brunch. Bar. Semi-a la carte: lunch $13-$16.50; dinner $16-$36.50. Sun brunch $29.50. Child's meals. Pianist Fri, Sat. Parking. Outdoor dining. Early Canadian atmosphere; antique cabinets with artifacts. Cr cds: A, MC, V.

★ ★ ★ **ED'S WAREHOUSE.** *(270 King St W, Toronto ON M5V 1H8) downtown. 416/593-6676.* English, Amer menu. Specializes in roast beef, steak. Own baking. Hrs: 4:30-9 pm; Sun-Tues to 8 pm. Closed Dec 24, 25. Serv bar. Wine list. A la carte entrees: dinner $10.95-$20.95. Unusual theatrical decor; many French antiques & statues, Tiffany lamps. Family-owned. Cr cds: A, D, MC, V.

★ ★ ★ **ELLAS.** *(702 Pape Ave, Toronto ON) east of downtown. 416/463-0334.* E-mail eria@ellas.com; web www.ellas.com. Greek menu. Specializes in lamb, shish kebab, seafood. Own pastries. Hrs: 11-1 am; Sun to 11 pm. Closed Dec 25. Res accepted. Bar. Semi-a la carte: lunch $7.95-$9.95, dinner $9.95-$24.95. Ancient Athenian decor; sculptures. Family-owned. Cr cds: A, D, ER, MC, V.

★ **GILLES BISTRO.** *(1315 Bay St, Toronto ON M5R 2C4) in Yorkville. 416/923-1005.* French, continental menu. Specialties: Cajun crab cake, roast duck breast, veal liver. Hrs: 11:30 am-2:30 pm, 5:30-9:30 pm; Sat 5-10 pm. Closed Mon, Sun; also major hols. Res accepted. A la carte entrees: lunch $7.50-$13.50, dinner $8.95-$16.95. Street parking. Outdoor dining. Art-deco decor. Cr cds: A, D, ER, MC, V.

✔★ ★ **GRANO.** *(2035 Yonge St, Toronto ON M4S 2A2) north of downtown. 416/440-1986.* Italian menu. Specializes in pasta. Hrs: 10 am-11 pm. Closed Sun; major hols. Res accepted. Bar. Semi-a la carte: lunch $7.95-$13.95, dinner $8.95-$15.95. Outdoor dining. Italian street cafe ambience. Cr cds: A, D, ER, JCB, MC, V.

★ ★ **GRAZIE.** *(2373 Yonge St, Toronto ON M4P 2C8) north of downtown. 416/488-0822.* Italian menu. Specializes in pizza, pasta. Hrs: noon-11 pm; Fri, Sat to midnight. Closed some major hols. Res accepted. Bar. A la carte entrees: lunch, dinner $7.50-$14. Child's meals. Bistro atmosphere. Cr cds: A, MC, V.

★ ★ ★ **GUILD INN.** *(See Guild Inn) 416/261-3331.* Continental menu. Specialties: rack of lamb, prime rib. Salad bar. Own baking. Hrs: 7 am-10 pm; Sun brunch 10:30 am-2:30 pm. Res accepted. Bar. Wine list.

Semi-a la carte: bkfst $2.75-$8.50, lunch $6.50-$15.95, dinner $15.90-$29.50. Sun brunch $17.95. Child's meals. Garden setting in former artist colony. Cr cds: A, C, D, DS, ER, MC, V.

★ **HAPPY SEVEN.** *(358 Spadina Ave, Toronto ON M5T 2G4) west of downtown.* 416/971-9820. Chinese menu. Hrs: 11:30-5 am. Res accepted. Bar to 2 am. Wine, beer. Semi-a la carte: lunch, dinner $7.95-$8.95. A la carte entrees: lunch $4.75-$6.50, dinner $7.95-$14.99. Street parking. Fish, crab, lobster tanks. Cr cds: MC, V.

★ ★ ★ **HARVEST CAFE.** *(See Inn On The Park Hotel)* 416/444-2561. Continental menu. Own baking. Hrs: 6:30 am-11 pm. Res accepted. Wine list. A la carte entrees: bkfst $3.95-$11.95, lunch, dinner $8.50-$18.95. Child's meals. Valet parking. Cr cds: A, C, D, DS, ER, JCB, MC, V.

[D]

★ ★ **IL POSTO.** *(148 Yorkville Ave, Toronto ON M5R 1C2) in Yorkville.* 416/968-0469. Northern Italian menu. Specializes in liver & veal chops, pasta with lobster, carpaccio. Hrs: noon-2:30 pm, 6-10:30 pm. Closed Sun; hols. Res accepted. A la carte entrees: $12-$18.50, dinner $14-$33. Outdoor dining. Cr cds: A, D, ER, MC, V.

[⬈]

★ ★ ★ **JOSO'S.** *(202 Davenport Rd, Toronto ON M5R 1J2) in Yorkville.* 416/925-1903. Mediterranean menu. Specializes in Italian dishes, seafood. Hrs: 11:30 am-2:30 pm, 5:30-11 pm; Sat from 5:30 pm. Closed Sun; some major hols. Res accepted. A la carte entrees: lunch $7-$19, dinner $14-$27. Child's meals. Outdoor dining. Wine cellar. Cr cds: A, D, ER, MC, V.

[D] [⬈]

★ ★ **KALLY'S.** *(430 Nugget Ave, Toronto ON M1S 4A4) north of downtown.* 416/293-9292. Specializes in steak, ribs. Salad bar. Hrs: 11:30 am-10 pm; Sun 4-9 pm. Closed hols; also 1st Mon in Aug. Serv bar. A la carte entrees: lunch $4.45-$14.95, dinner $8.45-$14.95. Child's meals. Parking. Pyramid-shaped skylights. Cr cds: A, MC, V.

[D] [⬈]

★ ★ ★ **LA FENICE.** *(319 King St W, Toronto ON M5V 1J5) downtown.* 416/585-2377. Italian menu. Specializes in fresh seafood, pasta. Hrs: 11:30 am-2:30 pm, 5:30-10:30 pm; Sat from 5:30 pm. Closed Sun; major hols. Res accepted. Bar to 1 am. Wine list. A la carte entrees: lunch $10.50-$24, dinner $16.50-$26. Sleek Milan-style trattoria. Near theater district. Cr cds: A, D, ER, JCB, MC, V.

[⬈]

★ ★ ★ **LAI WAH HEEN.** *(See Metropolitan Hotel)* 416/977-9899. E-mail lwh@metropolitan.com. Specializes in Cantonese dishes. Hrs: 11:30 am-3 pm, 5:30-10:30 pm. Res accepted. Wine cellar. A la carte entrees: lunch $12-$20, dinner $14-$48. Complete meal: lunch $16-$32, dinner $32-$42. Chinese decor. Cr cds: A, D, DS, ER, JCB, MC, V.

[D]

✔★ ★ **LE PAPILLION.** *(16 Church St, Toronto ON M5E 1M1) downtown.* 416/363-0838. French menu. Specialties: crêpes Bretonne, French onion soup. Hrs: noon-2:30 pm, 5-10 pm; Fri, Sat to midnight; Sun brunch to 3 pm. Closed Mon. Res accepted. Bar. Semi-a la carte: lunch, dinner $7.75-$18.95. Sun brunch $18. Child's meals. French country kitchen decor. Braille menu. Cr cds: A, D, ER, JCB, MC, V.

[D] [⬈]

★ **LE PARADIS.** *(166 Bedford Rd, Toronto ON M5R 2K9) downtown.* 416/921-0995. Web www.leparidis.com. Hrs: noon-11 pm; Sat 5:30-11 pm; Mon, Sun 5:30-10 pm. Closed Jan 1, Dec 24, 25. Res required Fri, Sat (dinner). Bar. A la carte entrees: lunch $3.95-$14.95, dinner $8.50-$14.95. Specialties: steak frites, moules a la mariniére, cassoulet. Street parking. Outdoor dining. Dinner menu changes daily. Cr cds: A, D, ER, MC, V.

[⬈]

★ **MARKETTA JAZZ BAR AND DINING.** *(138 Avenue Rd, Toronto ON M5R 2H7) in Yorkville.* 416/924-4447. French, Asian menu. Specialties: grilled sirloin burger, black-grilled chicken. Hrs: 11:30 am-10 pm; Fri, Sat to 2 am; Sun brunch 11:30 am-3 pm. Closed Mon; most major hols. Res accepted. Bar. A la carte entrees: lunch $8.95-$16.95, dinner $14.95-$17.95. Sun brunch $9.95-$16.95. French bistro ambience. Cr cds: A, D, ER, MC, V.

[D] [⬈]

★ ★ **MATIGNON.** *(51 Ste Nicholas St, Toronto ON M4Y 1W6) downtown.* 416/921-9226. Specialties: rack of lamb, duck breast, la darne de saumon aux câpres. Hrs: 11:30 am-2:30 pm, 5-10 pm. Res accepted. Bar. A la carte entrees: lunch $8.25-$15.95, dinner $13.50-$17.95. French atmosphere. Cr cds: A, D, ER, MC, V.

[⬈]

★ ★ ★ **MILLCROFT INN.** *(See Millcroft Inn)* 519/941-8111. E-mail millcroft@millcroft.com; web www.millcroft.com. Continental menu. Specializes in game meat. Hrs: 7:30-10 am, noon-2 pm, 6-9 pm; Sat, Sun 8-10:30 am; Sun brunch noon-2:30 pm. Res accepted. Bar from 11 am. A la carte entrees: bkfst $6.95-$9.95, lunch $16.25-$18.50, dinner $23.50-$32. Sun brunch $27.95. Valet parking. Restored knitting mill (1881) on the Credit River. Cr cds: A, D, ER, MC, V.

[⬈]

✔★ **MILLER'S COUNTRY FARE.** *(5140 Dundas St W, Etobicoke ON M9A 1C2)* 416/234-5050. Specializes in ribs, chicken, beef stew. Hrs: 11 am-10 pm; Fri to 11 pm; Sat 10 am-11 pm; Sat, Sun brunch to 2:30 pm. Closed Dec 25. Bar from 11 am. Semi-a la carte: lunch, dinner $6.25-$13.95. Sat, Sun brunch $3.95-$10.95. Child's meals. Parking. Country decor. Cr cds: A, D, ER, MC, V.

[D] [⬈]

★ ★ **MISTURA.** *(265 Davenport Rd, Toronto ON M5R 1J9) in Yorkville.* 416/515-0009. Hrs: 5-11 pm. Closed Sun; major hols; also Victoria Day. Res accepted. Italian menu. A la carte entrees: dinner $18.50-$21.75. Specialties: beet risotto, veal chops, turkey breast. Parking. Cr cds: A, D, ER, MC, V.

[D] [⬈]

✔★ **MONARCH BISTRO.** *(838 Yonge St, Toronto ON M4W 2H1) in Yorkville.* 416/924-6514. Continental menu. Specialty: crepes. Hrs: 10 am-10 pm; Sat from 9 am; Sun to 6 pm. Closed Jan 1, Dec 25. Res accepted. Bar to 2 am. Wine list. A la carte entrees: bkfst $3.50-$7.95, lunch, dinner $8.95-$12.95. Outdoor dining. French bistro atmosphere. Cr cds: A, JCB, MC, V.

[⬈]

★ ★ **MÖVENPICK OF SWITZERLAND.** *(165 York St, Toronto ON M5H 3R8) downtown.* 416/366-5234. Continental menu. Specializes in Swiss dishes. Salad bar. Hrs: 7:30 am-midnight; Fri to 1 am; Sat 9-1 am; Sun 9 am-midnight. Res accepted. Bar. Semi-a la carte: bkfst $2.50-$13.80, lunch $6.50-$18.50, dinner $9.25-$22.50. Buffet: dinner (exc Sun) $16.80-$28.50. Sun brunch $27.80. Child's meals. Parking. Outdoor dining. European decor. Cr cds: A, D, ER, MC, V.

[D] [⬈] [♥]

★ ★ ★ **NORTH 44 DEGREES.** *(2537 Yonge St, Toronto ON M4P 2H9) north of downtown.* 416/487-4897. North 44, Toronto's latitude, is the restaurant's logo and an oft-repeated visual refrain. The trendy atmosphere is fostered by a metallic, modern look, but chef Mark McEwan's dishes more than hold their own in this singular decor. Specializes in mixed appetizer platters, angel hair pasta, rack of lamb. Hrs: 5 pm-1 am. Closed Sun; some major hols. Res accepted. Bar. A la carte entrees: dinner $14.95-$37.95. Child's meals. Entertainment Wed-Sat. Valet parking. Cr cds: A, D, ER, MC, V.

[D] [⬈]

★ ★ ★ **OLD MILL.** *(21 Old Mill Rd, Toronto ON M8X 1G5) west of downtown.* 416/236-2641. E-mail isto@oldmilltoronto.com; web www.oldmilltoronto.com. Continental menu. Specializes in roast beef, prime rib.

Own baking. Hrs: noon-2:30 pm, 3-5 pm, 5:30-10 pm; Sat 5:30-11 pm; Sun 5:30-9 pm; Sun brunch 10:30 am-2:30 pm. Closed Dec 24. Res accepted. Bar. A la carte entrees: lunch $10.95-$16.95, dinner $25.95-$34. Buffet: lunch (Mon-Fri) $19.95, dinner (Sun) $25.95. Sun brunch $23.95. Cover charge (Fri, Sat from 8 pm) $3.50. Child's meals. Entertainment exc Sun. Parking. Old English castle motif. Jacket (dinner). Cr cds: A, D, ER, MC, V.

✔★ OLD SPAGHETTI FACTORY. *(54 The Esplanade, Toronto ON M5E 1A6)* downtown. 416/864-9761. Italian menu. Specialties: fettucine with seafood, chicken parmigiana. Hrs: 11:30 am-11 pm; Fri, Sat to midnight. Closed Dec 24. Bar. Semi-a la carte: lunch $5.99-$9.49, dinner $7.99-$14.50. Child's meals. Outdoor dining. Bright decor; carousel effect. Family-owned. Cr cds: A, D, DS, ER, MC, V.

★ ★ ★ OPUS. *(37 Prince Arthur Ave, Toronto ON M5R 1B2)* in Yorkville. 416/921-3105. Web www.cook-book.com\opus. Continental menu. Hrs: 5:30-11:30 pm. Res accepted. Bar to 2 am. Wine list. Semi-a la carte: dinner $24-$32. Patio dining. Cr cds: A, D, ER, MC, V.

★ ★ ★ PANGAEA. *(1221 Bay St, Toronto ON M5R 3P5)* in Yorkville. 416/920-2323. Hrs: 11:30 am-11:30 pm. Closed Sun; also major hols. Res accepted. Continental menu. Bar. Wine list. A la carte entrees: lunch $12.50-$18.95, dinner $17.95-$29.95. Specialties: calamari, wild mushroom risotto, rack of lamb. Street parking. Skylite ceiling. Cr cds: A, D, ER, JCB, MC, V.

★ PAWNBROKERS DAUGHTER. *(1115 Bay St, Toronto ON M5S 2B3)* downtown. 416/920-9078. Hrs: 11-3 am. Res accepted. Bar. A la carte entrees: lunch, dinner $4.95-$14.95. Patio dining. Pub atmosphere; pool table, video games. Cr cds: A, MC, V.

★ ★ PIER 4 STOREHOUSE. *(245 Queen's Quay W, Toronto ON M5J 2K9)* Harbourfront. 416/203-1440. Specialties: pepper steak Peru, red snapper. Hrs: noon-2:30 pm; 4:30 pm-midnight; Sun 11:30-12:30 am. Closed Jan 1, Dec 25. Res accepted. Bar. Semi-a la carte: lunch $9.50-$14.95, dinner $16.50-$35.95. Child's meals. Patio dining. Located at water end of a quay on Toronto Bay. Cr cds: A, D, DS, ER, MC, V.

★ ★ PREGO. *(15474 Yonge St, Aurora ON L4G 1P2)* approx 30 mi (48 km) north of downtown Toronto. 905/727-5100. Italian menu. Specializes in baked rack of lamb, pasta. Hrs: 11:30 am-2:30 pm, 5:30-10:30 pm; Sat from 5:30 pm; Sun 5-9:30 pm. Closed Mon; Jan 1, Good Friday, Dec 25, 26. Res accepted. Bar. A la carte entrees: lunch $7.50-$11.95, dinner $9.50-$23.50. Parking. Casual atmosphere. Cr cds: A, D, ER, MC, V.

★ ★ ★ PRONTO. *(692 Mount Pleasant Rd, Toronto ON M4S 2N3)* north of downtown. 416/486-1111. Italian, continental menu. Hrs: 5-11:30 pm; Sun to 10:30 pm. Closed Jan 1, Dec 24, 25. Res accepted. Bar. A la carte entrees: dinner $12.95-$27.95. Valet parking. Elegant modern decor; local artwork. Cr cds: A, C, D, ER, MC, V.

✔★ ★ PROVENCE. *(12 Amelia St, Toronto ON M4X 1A1)* in Cabbagetown. 416/924-9901. French menu. Specialties: rack of lamb, duck confit, steak. Hrs: noon-1 am; Sat, Sun brunch noon-2 pm. Closed Dec 25. Res accepted. Bar to 1 am. Semi-a la carte: lunch, dinner $9.95-$32. Sat, Sun brunch $12.95. French country cottage decor; original artwork. Cr cds: A, MC, V.

★ ★ QUARTIER. *(2112 Yonge St, Toronto ON M4S 2A5)* north of downtown. 416/545-0505. Hrs: 11 am-2:30 pm, 5-10:30 pm; early-bird dinner 5-6 pm. Closed most major hols. Res required Sat (dinner). French

menu. Bar. A la carte entrees: lunch $7.50-$12, dinner $13-$19. Specializes in fresh fish, lamb. Street parking. Outdoor dining. Cr cds: A, D, ER, MC, V.

✔★ RIVOLI CAFE. *(332 Queen St W, Toronto ON M5V 2A2)* downtown. 416/596-1908. Web home.1star.cia/~rivoli. Asian, Caribbean menu. Specialties: Sri Malay Bombay, Laotian spring rolls. Hrs: 11:30-2 am. Bar. A la carte entrees: lunch $6.50-$8.75, dinner $8.75-$14.95. Patio dining. Adj club offers comedy/variety shows evenings. Totally nonsmoking. Cr cds: A, MC, V.

★ THE ROSEDALE DINER. *(1164 Yonge St, Toronto ON M4W 2L9)* in Yorkville. 416/923-3122. E-mail dubi@zeygezunt; web www.zeygezunt.com. Hrs: 11:30 am-midnight; Sat 11-1 am; Sun 11 am-11 pm; Sat, Sun brunch 11 am-3:30 pm. Closed Easter, Dec 25. Res accepted. Eclectic menu. Bar. A la carte entrees: lunch $9.50-$15, dinner $10-$28. Sat, Sun brunch $6.95-$15. Child's meals. Specialties: herb-crusted rack of lamb, fresh saffron spaghettini, slow roasted chicken dijonaise. Street parking. Outdoor dining. 1940s decor and music. Cr cds: A, MC, V.

★ ★ ★ ROSEWATER SUPPER CLUB. *(19 Toronto St, Toronto ON M5C 2R1)* east of downtown. 416/214-5888. Continental menu. Own baking. Hrs: noon-2:30 pm, 5:30-11 pm; Sat from 5:30 pm. Closed Sun; major hols; also July 1, Dec 26. Res accepted. Bar 11:30-2 am. Wine cellar. A la carte entrees: lunch $9.95-$15.95, dinner $19-$32. Pianist. Early-20th-century atmosphere; elaborate Victorian crown moldings and cathedral-style windows. Totally nonsmoking. Cr cds: A, D, ER, MC, V.

★ ★ ★ ★ SCARAMOUCHE. *(1 Benvenuto Place, Toronto ON M4V 2L1)* north of downtown. 416/961-8011. This is Toronto's most luxurious French restaurant. Superb service and delicious food are served up in an atmosphere of understated elegance. Continental, French menu. Specialties: grilled Atlantic salmon, roasted rack of lamb. Own baking. Hrs: 5:30-10 pm; Sat to 11 pm. Closed Sun; major hols. Res accepted. Bar to midnight. A la carte entrees: dinner $22.75-$36.75. Pasta bar $13.75-$22.75. Free valet parking. Cr cds: A, D, ER, MC, V.

★ SEA SHACK. *(2130 Lawrence Ave E, Scarborough ON M1R 3A6)* 416/288-1866. Continental menu. Specializes in seafood, steak. Hrs: 11 am-11 pm; Sat 4-11 pm; Sun 4-10 pm. Closed Jan 1, Dec 25. Res accepted. Bar. Semi-a la carte: lunch $5.25-$11.95, dinner $7.95-$34.95. Child's meals. Parking. Nautical theme. Cr cds: A, MC, V.

★ ★ SENATOR. *(253 Victoria St, Toronto ON M5B 1T8)* downtown. 416/364-7517. Specializes in steak, seafood. Hrs: 11:30 am-2:30 pm, 5 pm-midnight. Closed Mon; some major hols. Res accepted. Bar. A la carte entrees: lunch $13.95-$19.95, dinner $20.95-$36.95. Parking. 1920s decor; in heart of theatre district. Cr cds: A, D, ER, JCB, MC, V.

★ ★ SPLENDIDO. *(88 Harbord St, Toronto ON M5S 1G5)* downtown. 416/929-7788. Continental menu. Specialties: rack of veal with grilled tomatoes, grilled peppered beef tenderloin with crispy fries. Hrs: 5-11 pm. Closed Sun. Res accepted. Bar. Semi-a la carte: dinner $19.95-$28.95. Valet parking. Fashionable trattoria with inviting atmosphere. Cr cds: A, D, MC, V.

✔★ SUSHI BISTRO. *(204 Queen St W, Toronto ON M5V 1Z2)* downtown. 416/971-5315. Japanese menu. Specialties: shrimp and mushrooms, sushi rolls, sashimi. Hrs: noon-2:45 pm, 5-10 pm; Fri, Sat noon-midnight. Closed Sun; major hols. Res accepted. Bar. A la carte entrees: lunch $7.25-$11, dinner $8.50-$18. Child's meals. Traditional Japanese food in modern setting. Cr cds: A, D, JCB, MC, V.

★ **TAKE SUSHI.** *(22 Front St W, Toronto ON M5J 1N7)* *downtown.* 416/862-1891. Hrs: 11:45 am-2:30 pm, 5:30-10:30 pm; Sat 5:30-10:30 pm. Closed Sun; also major hols. Res accepted. Japanese menu. A la carte entrees: lunch, dinner $11-$29. Complete meal: lunch $9.50-$45, dinner $22-$30. Specialty: lobster sushi. Parking. Cr cds: A, D, JCB, MC, V.

★ **THAI FLAVOUR.** *(1554 Avenue Rd, Toronto ON M5M 3X5)* *north of downtown.* 416/782-3288. Thai menu. Specialties: cashew nut chicken, pad Thai, basil shrimp. Hrs: 11 am-3 pm, 5-11 pm; Sun 5-10 pm. Closed Jan 1, Dec 25. Res accepted. Serv bar. A la carte entrees: lunch, dinner $7.45-$9.50. Cr cds: A, MC, V.

★ ★ **TIGER LILY'S NOODLE HOUSE.** *(257 Queen St W, Toronto ON M5V 1Z4)* *downtown.* 416/977-5499. Pan-Asian menu. Specializes in home-style egg roll. Hrs: 11:30 am-9 pm; Wed to 10 pm; Thurs-Sat to 11 pm. Closed most major hols. A la carte entrees: lunch, dinner $7.95-$12.95. Totally nonsmoking. Cr cds: A, MC, V.

★ ★ **TRAPPER'S.** *(3479 Yonge St, North York ON M4N 2N3)* *north of downtown.* 416/482-6211. Web www.yongestreet.com. Continental menu. Specializes in fresh fish, steak, pasta. Hrs: 11:30 am-2:30 pm, 5-10:30 pm; Sat from 5 pm; Sun 5-9:30 pm. Closed Dec 25. Res accepted. Bar. A la carte entrees: lunch $8.50-$11.50, dinner $13.95-$25.95. Child's meals. Casual dining. Cr cds: A, D, ER, MC, V.

★ ★ ★ **TRUFFLES.** *(See Four Seasons Hotel)* 416/964-0411. The wine list offers rare European and North American vintages in this formal, contemporary restaurant with bay windows and a high ceiling. Ceramics by local artists decorate the room. Provençal cuisine. Specialties: spaghettini with Périgord, rack of lamb with mustard seed sauce. Own pastries. Hrs: 6-11 pm. Res accepted. Wine cellar. Semi-a la carte: dinner $28-$36. Child's meals. Parking. Jacket. Cr cds: A, C, D, ER, JCB, MC, V.

★ ★ **VANIPHA LANNA.** *(471 Eglinton Ave W, Toronto ON M5N 1A7)* *north of downtown.* 416/484-0895. Thai menu. Specializes in Northern Thai dishes. Hrs: noon-11 pm; Sat to midnight. Closed Sun; most major hols. Res accepted Fri, Sat. A la carte entrees: lunch $6.25-$9.95; dinner $8.25-$12.50. Thai decor. Totally nonsmoking. Cr cds: A, MC, V.

★ ★ **VILLA BORGHESE.** *(2995 Bloor St W, Etobicoke ON M8X 1C1)* 416/239-1286. Italian menu. Specializes in fresh fish, veal, pepper steak. Own pasta. Hrs: noon-midnight; Sat, Sun from 4 pm. Closed Mon; Easter, Dec 25. Res accepted. Bar. Semi-a la carte: lunch $8-$15, dinner $11.95-$23.95. Entertainment. Italian villa decor. Cr cds: A, D, MC, V.

★ ★ **XANGO.** *(106 John St, Toronto ON M5V 2E1)* *downtown.* 416/593-4407. South Amer menu. Specialty: raw fish marinated in lime juice. Hrs: 5 pm-2 am. Closed Mon; Dec 24-26. Res accepted. Bar. A la carte entrees: dinner $19-$28. Outdoor dining. Converted house with veranda. Cr cds: A, D, MC, V.

★ **YAMASE.** *(317 King St W, Toronto ON M5V 1J5)* *downtown.* 416/598-1562. Japanese menu. Specializes in sushi, teriyaki, tempura dishes. Hrs: noon-2:30 pm, 5:30-11 pm; Sat from 5 pm. Closed Sun; Jan 1. Res accepted. Bar. A la carte entrees: lunch $5.50-$14.50, dinner $7.50-$24.50. Complete meals: dinner $15-$50. Intimate atmosphere; Japanese decor, artwork. Cr cds: A, D, ER, JCB, MC, V.

★ ★ **ZACHARY'S.** *(See The Bristol Place Hotel)* 416/675-9444. E-mail bristol@interlog.com. Continental menu. Specialty: rack of lamb. Own baking. Hrs: noon-2:30 pm, 6-10 pm; Sat from 6 pm; Sun brunch 11 am-2:30 pm. Res accepted. Bar 11-1 am. Wine list. A la carte entrees: lunch $12.50-$16.95, dinner $22.50-$31.95. Complete meals: lunch

$19.75, dinner $29.50. Sun brunch $23.95. Valet parking. Modern decor with Chinese prints. Cr cds: A, C, D, DS, ER, JCB, MC, V.

Unrated Dining Spots

CAFE VICTORIA. *(See King Edward Hotel)* 416/863-9700. Continental menu. Specializes in scones, pastries, sandwiches. Own baking. Hrs: 6:30 am-2:30 pm, 5-9 pm; Fri to 11 pm; Sat, Sun 7:30 am-2:30 pm, 5-11 pm. Traditional English tea service $16. Cr cds: A, D, JCB, MC, V.

PATACHOU. *(1095 Yonge St, Toronto ON)* in Yorkville. 416/927-1105. French menu. Specialties: cafe au lait, croque Monsieur. Own baking. Hrs: 8:30 am-6 pm; Sun from 10:30 am. Closed statutory hols. Pastries, croissants, desserts, sandwiches, quiche $5-$10. Patio dining. No cr cds accepted.

SHOPSY'S DELICATESSEN. *(33 Yonge St, Toronto ON M5E 1G4)* *downtown.* 416/365-3333. Delicatessen, all-day bkfst menu. Hrs: 7-1 am. Bar 11-1 am. A la carte entrees: bkfst $2.10-$6.75, lunch $3.95-$8.95, dinner $3.75-$11.75. Outdoor dining. Cr cds: A, D, MC, V.

UNITED BAKERS DAIRY RESTAURANT. *(506 Lawrence Ave W, Toronto ON M6A 1A1)* in the Lawrence Plaza, north of downtown. 416/789-0519. Jewish menu. Specializes in cheese blintzes, soups, gefilte fish. Hrs: 7 am-10 pm; Fri to 8 pm; Sat, Sun to 9 pm. A la carte entrees: lunch $5-$10, dinner to $12. Parking. Bakery on premises. Family-owned. Cr cds: MC, V.

Windsor (F-4)

Pop 192,083 **Elev** 622 ft (190 m) **Area code** 519 **E-mail** cvb@city.windsor.on.ca **Web** www.city.windsor.on.ca/cvb

Information Convention & Visitors Bureau of Windsor, Essex County and Pelee Island, 333 Riverside Dr W, City Centre Mall, Suite 103, N9A 5K4; 519/255-6530 or 800/265-3633.

Windsor is located at the tip of a peninsula and is linked to Detroit, Michigan by the Ambassador Bridge and the Detroit-Windsor Tunnel. Because of its proximity to the United States, it is often referred to as the Ambassador City. Because of its many beautiful parks, Windsor is also known as the City of Roses. The Sunken Gardens and Rose Gardens in Jackson Park boast more than 500 varieties of roses. Coventry Garden & Peace Fountain has the only fountain floating in international waters. Whatever the nickname, for many people traveling from the United States, Canada begins here.

Windsor is a cosmopolitan city, designated a bilingual-bicultural area because of the French influence so much in evidence. Windsor also has a symphony orchestra, theaters, a light opera company, art galleries, nightlife and all the amenities of a large city. Within its boundaries are 900 acres (364 hectares) of parks giving the city the charm of a rural environment. With easy access to lakes Erie and St Clair, and such pleasure troves as Pelee Island, it is also the major city in Canada's "Sun Parlor," Essex County. Because of mild climate and beautiful beaches, it is an excellent place to visit all year.

What to See and Do

Casino Windsor. Games include Baccarat, Blackjack, Roulette and more than 2,700 slot machines. The casino overlooks the Detroit skyline and is easily accessible from a number of hotels. (Daily) Riverside Dr in City Centre. Phone 519/258-7878 or 800/991-7777.

Colasanti Farms, Ltd. "A tropical paradise under glass." Over 25 greenhouses with acres of exotic plants; large collection of cacti; farm animals, parrots and tropical birds; crafts; mini-putt; restaurant. (Daily; closed Jan 1, Dec 25) 28 mi (45 km) SE, on Hwy 3 near Ruthven. Phone 519/322-2301. **Free.**

⭐ **Coventry Gardens and Peace Fountain.** Riverfront park & floral gardens with 75-ft-high (23-m) floating fountain; a myriad of three-dimensional water displays with spectacular night illumination (May-Sept, daily). Concessions. (Daily) Riverside Dr E & Pillette Rd. Phone 519/253-2300. **Free.**

Fort Malden National Historic Park. Ten-acre (four-hectare) park with remains of fortification, original 1838 barracks and 1851 pensioner's cottage; visitor and interpretation centers with exhibits. (Daily) 100 Laird Ave, 18 mi (29 km) S via City Rd 20, in Amherstburg. Contact PO Box 38, 100 Laird Ave, N9V 2Z2; 519/736-5416. ¢¢

Heritage Village. Historical artifacts and structures on 54 acres (22 hectares). Log cabins (1826 & 1835), railway station (1854), house (1869), church (1885), schoolhouse (1907), barber shop (ca 1920), general store (1847); transportation museum. Special events. Picnic facilities. 20 mi (32 km) SE via ON 3, then 5 mi (8 km) S of Essex on County Rd 23. Phone 519/776-6909. ¢¢

Jack Miner Bird Sanctuary. Features Canada geese and other migratory waterfowl; ponds; picnicking; museum. Canada geese "air shows" during peak season (Mar and late Oct-Nov; daily). (Daily exc Sun) 27 mi (44 km) SE via ON 3 & 29S, 2 mi (3 km) N of Kingsville. Phone 519/733-4034. **Free.**

North American Black Historical Museum. Chronicles achievements of black North Americans, many of whom fled the US for freedom in Canada. Permanent exhibits on Underground Railroad; artifacts, archives, genealogical library. (Apr-Nov, Wed-Fri, also Sat & Sun afternoons) 18 mi (29 km) S on City Rd 20, exit Richmond St E, at 227 King St in Amherstburg. Phone 519/736-5433. ¢¢

Park House Museum. Solid log, clapboard-sided house (ca 1795), considered to be oldest house in area. Built in Detroit, moved here in 1799. Restored & furnished as in the 1850s. Demonstrations of tinsmithing; pieces for sale. (June-Aug, daily; rest of yr, Tues-Fri & Sun) 219 Dalhousie St, 18 mi (29 km) S via City Rd 20, on the King's Naval Yard, near Ft Malden in Amherstburg. Phone 519/736-2511. ¢

Point Pelee National Park. The park is a 6-sq-mi (16-sq-km) tip of the Point Pelee peninsula. Combination dry land and marshland, the park also has a deciduous forest and is situated on two major bird migration flyways. More than 350 species have been sighted in the park. A boardwalk winds through the 2,500 acres (1,011 hectares) of marshland. Fishing, swimming, picnicking, trails and interpretive center. Canoeing and biking (rentals), transit ride (free). (Daily) 30 mi (48 km) SE via ON 3, near Leamington. Contact Chief of Visitor Services, RR 1, Leamington, N8H 3V4; 519/322-2365; -2371 (migration line). Entrance fee ¢¢-¢¢¢

The Art Gallery of Windsor. Collections consist of Canadian art, including Inuit prints and carvings, with emphasis on Canadian artists from the late 18th century to the present. Children's gallery; gift shop. (Daily exc Mon; closed major hols) 3100 Howard Ave. Phone 519/969-4494. **Free.**

University of Windsor. (16,000 students) On campus is Essex Hall Theatre, featuring seven productions/season (Sept-Mar, fee; box office phone 519/253-4565). 401 Sunset Ave. Phone 519/253-4232, ext 3240.

Willistead Manor (1906). Restored English Tudor mansion built for Edward Chandler Walker, son of famous distiller Hiram Walker, on 15 acres (6 hectares) of wooded parkland; elegant interiors with hand-carved woodwork; furnished in turn-of-the-century style. (July-Aug, Sun & Wed; Sept-June, 1st & 3rd Sun of each month) 1899 Niagara St, at Kildare Rd. Phone 519/253-2365. ¢¢

Windsor's Community Museum. Exhibits and collections interpret the history of Windsor and southwestern Ontario. (Tues-Sat, also Sun after noons; closed hols) Located in the historic Francois Baby House. 254 Pitt St W. Phone 519/253-1812. **Free.**

Wreck Exploration Tours. Exploration of a 130-yr old wreck site. Shoreline cruise; artifact orientation. (May-Oct, res required) 303 Concession 5, Leamington, ON N8H 3V5. Phone 519/326-1566 or 888/229-7325.

Annual Event

International Freedom Festival. Two-wk joint celebration by Detroit and Windsor with many events, culminating in fireworks display over the river. Phone 519/252-7264. Late June-1st wk July.

Motels

⭐⭐ **BEST WESTERN CONTINENTAL INN.** *(3345 Huron Church Rd, Windsor ON N9E 4H5)* 519/966-5541; FAX 519/972-3384. 71 rms, 2 story. S $66-$76; D $70-$80; each addl $6-$10; under 12 free. TV; cable (premium), VCR avail. Heated pool. Restaurant 7 am-10 pm. Rm serv. Ck-out 11 am. Meeting rms. Cr cds: A, D, DS, MC, V.

🏊 🔼 🔥 SC

⭐⭐ **COMFORT INN.** *(1100 Richmond St, Chatham ON N7M 5J5) E on HWY 401 to exit 81.* 519/352-5500; FAX 519/352-2520. 81 rms, 2 story. May-Sept: S $57-$95; D $65-$105; each addl $4; under 19 free; wkend rates; lower rates rest of yr. Crib free. Pet accepted. TV; cable. Complimentary coffee in lobby. Restaurant adj 9 am-10 pm. Ck-out 11 am. Cr cds: A, C, D, DS, ER, JCB, MC, V.

D 🔼 🏊 🔥 SC

✔⭐⭐ **MARQUIS PLAZA.** *(2530 Ouellette Ave, Windsor ON N8X 1L7)* 519/966-1860; FAX 519/966-6619; res: 800/265-5021. 97 rms, 2 story. S $48-$150; D $60; each addl $5; suites $90-$150. Crib $5. Pet accepted, some restrictions; $10. TV; cable (premium), VCR avail. Ck-out noon. Meeting rms. Cr cds: A, D, ER, MC, V.

D 🔼 🏊 🔥 SC

⭐⭐⭐ **ROYAL MARQUIS.** *(590 Grand Marais E, Windsor ON N8X 3H4) near Intl Airport.* 519/966-1900; FAX 519/966-4689. 99 rms, 5 story, 14 suites. S $70; D $80; each addl $5; suites $90-$175; under 12 free; wkend rates; higher rates prom. Crib $5. Pet accepted, some restrictions; $10. TV; cable (premium), VCR avail. Indoor pool; whirlpool. Supervised child's activities; ages 5-10. Restaurant 6:30 am-10 pm. Rm serv. Bar; entertainment Thurs-Sun. Meeting rms. Valet serv. Concierge. Barber, beauty shop. X-country ski 5 mi. Exercise equipt; sauna. Luxurious furnishings, atmosphere. Cr cds: A, D, ER, MC, V.

D 🔼 🏊 🏊 🛷 🔥 🔽

Motor Hotel

⭐⭐⭐ **BEST WESTERN WHEELS INN.** *(615 Richmond St, Chatham ON N7M 5K8) NE on Hwy 2, at Keil Dr.* 519/351-1100; FAX 519/436-5541. Web www.wheelsinn.com. 350 rms, 2-10 story. S, D $102.88-$154.88; each addl $5; suites $188.88-$208.88; under 18 free; lower rates mid-wk. Crib free. TV; cable. 2 pools, 1 indoor/outdoor; whirlpools, waterslides. Restaurant 7-11 am. Rm serv 7-11 am, 5 pm-midnight. Bar noon-1 am; entertainment exc Sun. Ck-out 11:30 am. Convention facilities. Business center. Gift shop. Miniature golf. Exercise rm; sauna, steam rm. Bowling. Game rm. Rec rm. Some balconies. Resort atmosphere; more than 7 acres of indoor facilities. Atrium. Cr cds: A, C, D, DS, ER, JCB, MC, V.

D 🏊 🛷 🔽 🔥 SC 🔼

Hotel

⭐ **RADISSON.** *(333 Riverside Dr W, Windsor ON N9A 5K4)* 519/977-9777; FAX 519/977-1411. 207 rms, 19 story. S, D $95; under 12 free. Crib free. Pet accepted, some restrictions. Garage avail. TV; cable (premium). Indoor pool; whirlpool. Complimentary full bkfst. Restaurant nearby. Ck-out noon. Meeting rms. In-rm modem link. Exercise equipt; saunas. Minibars. Cr cds: A, D, DS, ER, MC, V.

D 🔼 🏊 🛷 🔽 🔥 SC

Restaurants

★ ★ **CHATHAM STREET GRILL.** *(149 Chatham St W, Windsor ON N9A 5M7)* 519/256-2555. Specializes in fresh seafood, certified Angus beef. Hrs: 11:30 am-midnight; Sat from noon; Sun 5-11 pm. Closed major hols; Good Friday. Res accepted. Bar. Semi-a la carte: lunch $5.95-$10, dinner $14.95-$24.95. Cr cds: A, D, ER, MC, V.

✔★ ★ **COOK SHOP.** *(683 Ouellette Ave, Windsor ON N9A 4J4)* 519/254-3377. Italian, continental menu. Specializes in pasta, steak, rack of lamb. Hrs: 5-10 pm; Fri, Sat to midnight. Closed Mon; Dec 24, 25; also Aug. Res required. Serv bar. Semi-a la carte: dinner $7.65-$16.85. Parking. Cr cds: A, MC, V.

✔★ ★ **PASTA SHOP.** *(683 Ouellette Ave, Windsor ON N9A 4J4)* 519/254-1300. Italian, continental menu. Specialties: steak Diane, veal scaloppini. Hrs: 5-10 pm; Fri, Sat to midnight. Closed Mon; Dec 24, 25; also Aug. Res required. Serv bar. Semi-a la carte: dinner $11.50-$16.85. Parking. Open kitchen; intimate dining. Cr cds: A, MC, V.

★ ★ **TOP HAT SUPPER CLUB.** *(73 University Ave E, Windsor ON N9A 2Y6)* 519/253-4644. Specializes in steak, seafood, baby-back ribs. Hrs: 11 am-midnight; Fri, Sat to 2 am. Res accepted. Bar. Semi-a la carte: lunch $4-$10, dinner $6.50-$25. Child's meals. Entertainment Fri, Sat. Parking. Fireplace. Family-owned. Cr cds: A, DS, JCB, MC, V.

★ ★ **TUNNEL BAR-B-Q.** *(58 Park St E, Windsor ON N9A 3A7)* at tunnel exit. 519/258-3663. Specializes in barbecued ribs, chicken, steak. Hrs: 8-2 am; Fri, Sat to 4 am. Closed Dec 25. Wine, beer. Semi-a la carte: bkfst $3.25-$5.95, lunch $4.25-$7.95, dinner $7.45-$18.95. Child's meals. Old English decor. Family-owned. Cr cds: D, MC, V.

[D]

★ ★ **TUNNEL BAR-B-Q'S OTHER PLACE.** *(3067 Dougall Ave, Windsor ON N9E 1S3)* 519/969-6011. Specializes in steak, seafood, veal. Salad bar (lunch). Hrs: 11 am-11 pm; Sat to 1 am; Sun to 10 pm; Sun brunch to 2:30 pm. Closed some major hols. Res accepted. Bar. Semi-a la carte: lunch $4.95-$10.95, dinner $9.95-$27.95. Sun brunch $15.95. Child's meals. Dinner music Fri, Sat. Valet parking. Old English-style banquet area. Cr cds: A, D, ER, MC, V.

[D] [SC] [⊐]

★ ★ **YE OLDE STEAK HOUSE.** *(46 Chatham St W, Windsor ON N9A 5M6)* 519/256-0222. Specializes in soup, charcoal-broiled steak, fresh seafood. Hrs: 11:30 am-10 pm; Fri to 11 pm; Sat 4-11 pm; Sun from 4 pm. Closed Jan 1, Good Friday, Dec 25. Res accepted. Bar to 1 am. Semi-a la carte: lunch $3.75-$12, dinner $11-$24. Child's meals. Old English decor. Family-owned. Cr cds: A, D, ER, MC, V.

Province of Prince Edward Island

Pop 122,506 **Land area** 2,186 sq mi (5,662 sq km) **Capital** Charlottetown **E-mail** tourpei@gov.pe.ca **Web** www.peiplay.com
Information Tourism PEI, PO Box 940, Charlottetown, C1A 7M5; 902/368-4444 or 888/734-7529.

Prince Edward Island is located in the Gulf of St Lawrence on Canada's east coast, off the shores of Nova Scotia and New Brunswick. Although it is the smallest province, it is known as the "Birthplace of Canada" because Charlottetown hosted the Charlottetown Conference in 1864. This laid the foundation for the Confederation in 1867.

The island is 40 miles (64 kilometers) wide at its broadest point, narrowing to only 4 miles (6 kilometers) wide near Summerside and 140 miles (224 kilometers) long. Famous for its red soil, warm waters, fine white beaches and deep-cut coves, it can be reached by air , ferry and the Confederation Bridge, an 8-mile (12.9-kilometer) link between Borden-Carleton, PE and Cape Jourimain, New Brunswick.

Prince Edward Island is divided into six daytour regions. The North by Northwest daytour region encompasses the northwestern parts of the province from North Cape to Cedar Dunes Provincial Park. It is an area of unspoiled beauty with secluded beaches, picturesque fishing and farming communities, and quaint churches. (Visitor Information Centre on Rte 2 in Portage.)

The Ship to Shore daytour region covers the southwest. It introduces the visitor to the history of shipbuilding and fox farming, and the Malpeque oysters. Also here is the city of Summerside, located on the Bedeque Bay, which is gaining a reputation for hosting international sporting events. (Visitor Information Centre on Rte 1A, east of downtown.)

The Anne's Land daytour region features the central north shore of the province. It is home to many sites related to *Anne of Green Gables,* the children's story written by Lucy Maud Montgomery. The stunning white sand beaches of Prince Edward Island National Park (see) are also here. (Visitor Information Centre at jct Rte 6 & 13 in Cavendish & on Rte 15 at Brackley Beach.)

The Charlotte's Shore daytour encompasses the south central region of Prince Edward Island. It is here that the visitor is introduced to Charlottetown, the provincial capital and birthplace of the Canadian Confederation. The scenic red cliffs and warm waters of the south shore beaches are also inviting. (Visitor Information Centre on Water St in Charlottetown & at Gateway Village in Borden-Carleton.)

The Bays & Dunes daytour region covers the northeastern corner of the province. It offers the island's best coastline views, with miles of uncrowded white-sand beaches and spectacular dunes bordering the scenic countryside. (Visitor Information Centre on Rte 2 in Souris.)

The Hills & Harbours daytour details the southeastern region. It is home to some of the most pleasing vistas and peaceful fishing villages in the province. (Visitor Information Centre at jct Rte 3 & 4 in Pooles Corner at the Wood Islands Ferry Terminal.)

Safety belts are mandatory for all persons anywhere in vehicle. Children under 40 pounds in weight must be in an approved safety seat anywhere in vehicle: children 20-39 pounds may face forward in seat, however, children under 20 pounds must face backward in seat. For further information phone 902/368-5200.

Cavendish (D-4)

(See also Charlottetown)

Pop 93 **Elev** 75 ft (23 m) **Area code** 902 **E-mail** tourpei@gov.pe.ca **Web** www.peiplay.com
Information Tourism PEI, PO Box 940; Charlottetown C1A 7M5; 800/463-4734.

Located near the western end of Prince Edward Island National Park (see), Cavendish encompasses more than 15 miles (24 kilometers) of beach area. World famous as the home of *Anne of Green Gables,* the area also boasts excellent recreational facilities.

What to See and Do

Birthplace of Lucy Maud Montgomery. A replica of the "Blue Chest"; the writer's personal scrapbooks, containing copies of her many stories and poems, and her wedding dress and veil are stored here. (May-Thanksgiving, daily) Jct Hwy 6, 20 in New London. Phone 902/436-7329 or 902/886-2099. ¢ Nearby is

Lucy Maud Montgomery's Cavendish Home. Site where Montgomery was raised by her grandparents from 1876-1911. Bookstore & museum houses the original desk, scales & crown stamp used in post office. (June-Sept, daily) ¢

Green Gables. Famous as the setting for Lucy Maud Montgomery's *Anne of Green Gables.* Surroundings portray the Victorian setting described in the novel. Tours avail off-season (fee). (May-Oct, daily) Prince Edward Island National Park, on Hwy 6. Phone 902/672-6350 (Bilingual Guide Service). ¢¢

The Great Island Science & Adventure Park. Science centre; space shuttle replica; dinosaur museum; planetarium. (Mid-June-Labor Day, daily) 2.5 mi (4km) W of Cavendish on Rte 6 at Stanley Bridge. Phone 902/886-2252. ¢¢¢

Prince Edward Island National Park (see).

Rainbow Valley Family Fun Park. Approx 40 acres of woodland, lakes and landscaped areas; children's farm with petting areas; playground, swan boats, flumes, water slides; entertainment; picnicking, cafe. Mono Rail ride. (June-Labour Day, daily) On Hwy 6 near Green Gables. Phone 902/963-2221. ¢¢¢

☒ **Woodleigh Replicas & Gardens.** Extensive outdoor display of large scale models of famous castles and buildings of legendary, historic and literary interest. Included are the Tower of London, Dunvegan Castle and Anne Hathaway Cottage. Several models are large enough to enter and are furnished. Flower, shrub garden; children's playground; food service. (Early June-mid-Oct, daily) 14 mi (23 km) SW via Hwy 6, right on Hwy 20, left on Hwy 234 to Burlington. Phone 902/836-3401. ¢¢¢

Motels

★ ★ **CAVENDISH.** (Green Gables PE, Cavendish PE C0A 1M0) at jct Hwys 6, 13. 902/963-2244; res: 800/565-2243. 38 rms, some A/C, 2 story, 3 kit. units, 8 kit. cottages. May-late Sept: S $72-$78; D $78-$88; each addl $3-$6; kit. units $88; cottages (1-4 persons) $81-$105. Closed rest of yr. TV; cable. Heated pool. Complimentary continental bkfst (June-Sept). Restaurant adj 8 am-10 pm. Ck-out 10 am. Picnic tables, grills. Cr cds: A, MC, V.

★ ★ **SILVERWOOD.** (Green Gables PE, Cavendish Beach, Cavendish PE C0A 1N0) 1 mi W of jct Hwys 6, 13. 902/963-2439; res: 800/565-4753. 50 rms, 35 A/C, 1-2 story, 23 kits. Mid-May-mid-Oct: S, D $82; each addl $8; kit. units $90-$120. Closed rest of yr. TV. Heated pool. Playground. Restaurant adj 7:30 am-9 pm. Ck-out 10 am. Meeting rms. Picnic tables, grills. Cr cds: A, MC, V.

Restaurants

★ ★ **IDLE OARS.** (North Rustico, Cavendish PE C0A 1X0) 3 mi E on Hwy 6. 902/963-2534. Specializes in seafood, steak, fried chicken. Hrs: 8 am-10:30 pm. Closed Thanksgiving, Apr. Res accepted. Semi-a la carte: lunch $4.95-$12, dinner $5-$18.95. Child's meals. Rustic decor. Overlooks harbor. Cr cds: A, C, D, ER, MC, V.

★ ★ **NEW GLASGOW LOBSTER SUPPER.** (Rt 258 New Glasgow, Cavendish PE C0A 1N0) 5 mi S off Hwy 13. 902/964-2870. Specializes in fresh fish chowder, mussels, lobster. Hrs: 4-8:30 pm. Closed Nov-May. Complete meals: dinner $15.95-$26.95. Child's meals. Lobster pound adj. View of river. Family-owned. Cr cds: A, C, D, ER, MC, V.

D SC ⇥

Charlottetown (D-4)

(See also Cavendish)

Pop 15,282 **Elev** 25 ft (8 m) **Area code** 902 **E-mail** tourpei@gov.pe.ca **Web** www.peiplay.com

Information Tourism PEI, PO Box 940, C1A 7M5; 902/368-4444 or 888/734-7529.

Named for Queen Charlotte, King George III's wife, Charlottetown was chosen in 1765 as the capital of colonial St John's Island, as it was then known. The name was changed to Prince Edward Island in 1799. The first settlement in the area was at Port la Joye across the harbour, and was ruled by the French until ceded to Great Britain after the fall of Louisbourg. Known as the birthplace of Canada, because the conference that led to confederation was held here in 1864, the city has many convention facilities, cultural and educational institutions and attractions located within easy reach. Encircled by a scenic natural harbour, boating, yachting, swimming, golf, other sports and a variety of seafood are all popular and readily available. Charlottetown is a main feature of the Charlotte's Shore daytour region; a Visitor Information Centre is here.

Prince Edward Island may be reached from the mainland at Caribou, NS, by car ferry to Wood Islands, PE, 38 mi (61 km) southeast of Charlottetown. Contact Northumberland Ferries, PO Box 634, Charlottetown, PE, C1A 7L3; 902/566-3838 or 888/249-7245. (Daily, May-mid-Dec; 1¼-hr crossing; fee) The island can also be reached from Cape Jourimain, New Brunswick, via the Confederation Bridge, an 8-mile bridge that leads to Borden-Carleton, PE (toll).

What to See and Do

Basin Head Fisheries Museum. Depicts history of fishing in the province. Fishing equipment, scale models showing methods; old photographs, fish charts & other marine articles. Film & slide projections. (Mid-June-late Sept, daily) 58 mi (93 km) E via Rte 2 to Souris, then Rte 16 to Kingsboro. Phone 902/357-2966 or 902/368-6600. ¢¢

Beaconsfield (1877). Mansard-style house built for Island shipbuilder is architecturally intact; guided tours. Headquarters of Prince Edward Island Museum & Heritage Foundation; bookstore. Regular and annual events. (Mid-June-Labour Day, daily; after Labour Day, Sun & Tues-Fri afternoons) 2 Kent St. Phone 902/368-6600. Museum ¢¢

Confederation Centre of the Arts (1964). Canada's National Memorial to the Fathers of Confederation; opened by Queen Elizabeth II in honor of the centennial of the 1864 Confederation Conference. Contains provincial library, Confederation Centre Museum and Art Gallery, theatres and the Robert Harris Collection of portraiture. Courtyard restaurant, gift shop. Home of the Charlottetown Festival (see SEASONAL EVENT). Gallery and museum (Tues-Sat, also Sun afternoons). Centre (daily; closed major hols). 145 Richmond St. Phone 902/628-1864, 902/566-1267 (tickets) or 800/565-0278 (information and reservations). ΧΟΔΕ ΧΟΔΕ=∀1ΧΕΝΤ∀

Fort Amherst/Port La Joye National Historic Park. Only earthworks of the former French fort, Port la Joye (built in 1720) are still visible. Captured by British in 1758, abandoned in 1768. Cafe, boutique. Interpretive center. (Mid-June-Labour Day, daily) Near Rocky Point, on Hwy 19 across the harbour mouth. Phone 902/672-6350.

Green Park Shipbuilding Museum. Former estate of James Yeo, Jr, whose family members were leading shipbuilders of the 19th century. House (1865) restored to reflect life during the prosperous shipbuilding era. Photos of famous ships and artifacts in interpretive center; audiovisual presentation in museum theater. Lecture series and concerts. Annual events. Camping, swimming at Malpeque Bay. (Mid-June-Labour Day, daily) 63 mi (101 km) NW via Hwy 2 to Hwy 132 just past Richmond, right to jct with Hwy 12, left to Port Hill. Phone 902/831-7947 or 902/368-6600 (off season). ¢¢

Orwell Corner Historic Village. Reconstructed rural crossroads community of late 19th century. Combined store, post office & farmhouse; school, church, cemetery and barns. Farming activities as they were practiced 100 yrs ago. Annual events. Ceilidhs (Wed evenings). (Late June-early Sept, daily; mid-May-late June, Mon-Fri; early Sept-late Oct, Tues-Sun) 18 mi (29 km) E via Trans Canada Hwy. Phone 902/651-2013 or 902/368-6600 (off season). ¢¢

Prince Edward Island National Park (see).

Province House (1847). Birthplace of the Canadian nation and a national historic site. Confederation room where delegates met in 1864 to discuss confederation. National memorial, seat of Provincial Legislature. Tours. (June-early Oct, daily; rest of yr, Mon-Fri; closed hols) Richmond St. Phone 902/566-7626.

Sightseeing tour. Abegweit Tours. Charlottetown tours on authentic London double-decker buses; also north and south shore tours. Bilingual guide service avail. Contact 157 Nassau St, C1A 2X3; 902/894-9966. ¢¢¢-¢¢¢¢¢

St Dunstan's Cathedral Basilica. Largest church on the island. Gothic style cathedral with distinctive triple towers contains beautiful stained glass windows and an impressive altar 37 ft (11 m) high made of many types of marble and crowned with a beautiful rose window. Audio loop for hearing impaired. Restoration in progress. (Daily) 45 Great George St. Phone 902/894-3486.

Annual Event

Festival of Lights. Charlottetown Waterfront. Buskers, children's concerts, Waterfront Magic, children's midway. Fireworks display over Charlottetown Harbour on July 1 (Canada Day). Late June-early July.

Seasonal Event

Charlottetown Festival. Confederation Centre of the Arts. Original Canadian musicals, including *Anne of Green Gables,* and other productions; special gallery presentations and theater. Box office 902/566-1267; information 902/628-1864. Late June-late Sept.

Motels

★ ★ **ISLANDER.** *(146-148 Pownal St., Charlottetown PE C1A 3W6)* 902/892-1217; FAX 902/566-1623. 49 rms, 2 story, 3 kits. Mid-May-mid-Oct: S, D $86-$96; each addl $8; suites, kit. units $96-$120; under 12 free; lower rates rest of yr. Crib $7. Pet accepted. TV; cable. Restaurant 7 am-8 pm. Ck-out 11 am. Meeting rms. Sundries. Microwaves avail. Cr cds: A, ER, MC, V.

D ✦ ⚒

✦ ★ **SUNNY KING.** *(Cornwall PE C0A 1H0)* On Trans-Canada Hwy 1. 902/566-2209; FAX 902/566-4209. 39 rms, 1-2 story, 30 kits. No A/C. Late June-early Sept: S $54-$64; D $60-$70; each addl $8; suites, kit. units $68-$92; under 16 free; lower rates rest of yr. Crib $6. Pet accepted. TV; cable. Heated pool. Playground. Free supervised child's activities (May-mid-Nov). Restaurant adj 8 am-11 pm. Ck-out 11 am. Coin lndry. Business servs avail. Valet serv. Many microwaves. Picnic tables, grills. Cr cds: A, C, D, DS, ER, MC, V.

D ✦ ≋ ⚒ ⚒ SC

★ ★ ★ **THRIFT LODGE.** *(Trans Canada Hwy, Charlottetown PE C1A 7L3)* 2 mi W on Hwy 1. 902/892-2481; FAX 902/368-3247; res: 800/565-7633. E-mail rodds@rodd-hotels.ca; web www.rodd-hotels.ca/. 62 rms, 2 story, 31 suites. Mid-June-Sept: S, D $85-$94; suites $99-$115; under 16 free; lower rates rest of yr. Crib free. Pet accepted. TV; cable. Heated pool. Restaurant 7-10 am, 5-9 pm. Bar 11-1 am; closed Sun. Ck-out 11 am. Health club privileges. Refrigerators, microwaves avail. Cr cds: A, C, D, DS, ER, JCB, MC, V.

✦ ≋ ⚒ ⚒ SC

Motor Hotels

★ ★ ★ **BEST WESTERN MACLAUCHLANS.** *(238 Grafton St, Charlottetown PE C1A 1L5)* 902/892-2461; FAX 902/566-2979. E-mail maclauchlans@pei.sympatico.ca; web www.bestwestern.com. 143 rms, 2-3 story, 26 kits. June-mid-Oct: S $139-$149; D $149-$159; each addl $10; studio rms $149-$159; suites $169-$209; kit. units $149-$159; under 18 free; lower rates rest of yr. Pet accepted, some restrictions. TV; cable. Indoor pool; whirlpool. Complimentary coffee in rms. Restaurants 7 am-9 pm; Sun from 8 am. Ck-out noon. Meeting rms. Valet serv. Exercise equipt; sauna. Sundries. Microwaves avail. Cr cds: A, C, D, DS, ER, JCB, MC, V.

D ✦ ≋ ⚒ ⚒ ⚒ SC

★ ★ **QUALITY INN ON THE HILL.** *(150 Euston St, Charlottetown PE C1A 1W5)* 902/894-8572; FAX 902/368-3556. 48 rms, 5 story. Late June-mid-Oct: S $116; D $127; each addl $9; studio rms $137-$142; suites $152-$174; under 16 free; lower rates rest of yr. Pet accepted. TV; cable. Coffee in rms. Restaurant 7 am-8 pm. Rm serv. Bar 11-1 am. Ck-out

noon. Meeting rms. Bellhops. Health club privileges. Sundries. Cr cds: A, C, D, DS, ER, MC, V.

✦ ⚒ ⚒

★ ★ ★ **TRAVELODGE HOTEL.** *(Charlottetown PE C1A 8C2)* at jct Trans-Canada Hwy 1, 2. 902/894-8566; res: 800/578-7878; FAX 902/892-8488. 132 rms, 1-3 story, 6 kits. June-Oct: S $87; D $99; each addl $10; suites $125-$175; under 16 free; lower rates rest of yr. Crib free. TV; cable. Indoor pool. Restaurant 7 am-10 pm. Rm serv. Bar 4:30 pm-1 am; closed Sun. Ck-out noon. Meeting rms. Bellhops. Sundries. Exercise equipt; sauna. Balconies. Indoor courtyard adj to pool area. Cr cds: A, C, D, ER, MC, V.

D ≋ ⚒ ⚒ ⚒

Hotels

★ ★ **THE CHARLOTTETOWN.** *(Charlottetown PE C1A 7K4)* jct of Kent & Pownal Sts. 902/894-7371; FAX 902/368-2178; res: 800/565-7633. E-mail rodds@rodd-hotels.ca; web www.rodd-hotels.ca/. 115 rms, 5 story. June-mid-Oct: S, D $135-$215; each addl $10; under 16 free; lower rates rest of yr. Crib free. Pet accepted. TV; cable. Indoor pool; whirlpool. Restaurant 7 am-2 pm, 5-10 pm. Bar 4 pm-1 am; closed Sun. Ck-out 11 am. Meeting rms. Exercise equipt; sauna. Cr cds: A, D, DS, ER, JCB, MC, V.

D ✦ ≋ ⚒ ⚒ ⚒ SC

★ ★ ★ **THE PRINCE EDWARD.** *(18 Queen St, Charlottetown PE C1A 8B9)* 902/566-2222; FAX 902/566-1745. E-mail vdowne@peh.cphotels.ca; web www.peisland.com/prince/edward.htm. 211 rms, 10 story. May-mid-Oct: S $139-$229; D $159-$249; each addl $20; suites $299-$799; lower rates rest of yr. Crib avail. Pet accepted. TV; cable. Indoor pool; wading pool, whirlpool. Restaurants 6:30 am-11 pm. Bar; entertainment. Ck-out noon. Meeting rms. Business center. Exercise rm; sauna. Massage. On waterfront in "Olde Charlottetown." Cr cds: A, D, DS, MC, V.

D ✦ ≋ ⚒ ⚒ ⚒ SC ⚒

Prince Edward Island National Park (D-4)

(See also Cavendish, Charlottetown)

Information Field Unit Superintendant, Department of Canadian Heritage/Parks Canada, 2 Palmer's Lane, Charlottetown, PEI, C1A 5V6; 902/566-7050 or 902/672-6350.

Valet serv. Prince Edward Island National Park, 25 square miles (40 square kilometers), is one of eastern Canada's most popular vacation destinations. Warm salt waters and sandy beaches abound. There are several supervised beach areas for swimmers and miles of secluded shoreline to explore. In addition to golf, tennis, bicycling and picnicking, the park offers an interpretation program highlighting the natural and cultural features and stories of the area; campfires; beach walks and more. Green Gables and its association with Lucy Maud Montgomery's *Anne of Green Gables* is a major attraction, with daily walks offered around the house and grounds (see CAVENDISH). Camping is also available (maximum stay 21 nights, reservations accepted). Dalvay-by-the-Sea offers hotel accommodations in a unique setting. Many private cabins, hotels and campgrounds are available bordering the park.

Prince Edward Island may be reached by a car ferry. For further information, contact Marine Atlantic Reservation Bureau, PO Box 250, North Sydney, NS, B2A 3M3; 800/341-7981 (US). Another ferry crosses in 1¼ hours at Caribou, NS to Wood Islands, PEI (see CHARLOTTETOWN, PEI).

Province of Québec

Pop 6,438,403 **Land area** 643,987 sq mi (1,667,926 sq km) **Capital**
Québec **E-mail** Info@tourisme.gouv.qc.ca **Web** www.tourisme.gouv.qc.ca
Information Tourisme/Québec, CP 979, Montréal H3C 2W3;
514/873-2015 or 800/363-7777.

The Québécois, whose ancestors came from France more than 400 years
ago, made their stronghold in the Saint-Lawrence River valley. These
ancestors also gave this province its decidedly French character.

The geography of Québec is largely determined by the St Lawrence
River, the Laurentian mountains, lakes that are really inland seas and
streams that swell into broad rivers.

These magnificent natural settings provide the tourist with year-round
vacation wonders. The Laurentians, only an hour's drive from Montréal,
have some of the finest skiing, outdoor recreation and restaurants in North
America.

Combine the natural beauty of the area, the cosmopolitan yet historic
ambience of Montréal and Québec City, and a tour of the unspoiled Gaspé
Peninsula, and you will have a vacation destination nonpareil.

When dining in Québec, travelers should be aware that there is a
15.2% federal and provincial tax on food and alcohol added to all restaurant checks.

In addition to national holidays, Québec observes Saint-Jean Bap-
tiste Day (June 24).

Safety belts are mandatory for all persons anywhere in vehicle.
Children under 5 years or under 40 pounds in weight must be in an
approved safety seat. Radar detectors are strictly forbidden. For further
information phone 800/361-7620.

Drummondville (E-5)

(See also Montréal, Sherbrooke)

Pop 27,347 **Elev** 350 ft (107 m) **Area code** 819
Information Bureau du Tourisme et des Congrès, 1350 Michaud St, J2C
2Z5; 819/477-5529.

Known as the "Center of Québec," this industrial and commercial center is
advantageously located on the Saint-Francois River where the Trans-Canada and Trans-Québec highways intersect.

What to See and Do

Le Village Québécois d'Antan. Historical village (1810-1910), typical of
the area. (June-Labour Day) N via Hwy 20, exit 181 on rue Montplaisir.
Phone 819/478-1441. **¢¢¢**

Manoir et Domaine Trent. Period home (1836) restored by artisans;
restaurant. Camping (late June-Aug). Parc des Voltigeurs. Phone 819/472-
3662. **Free.**

Annual Event

World Folklore Festival. One of the major folklore events in North America. International singers, dancers & musicians participate at four different
sites. Phone 819/472-1184. 10 days July.

Motor Hotel

★ ★ **HÔTEL UNIVERSEL.** *(915 Hains St, Drummondville QE
J2C 3A1) 819/478-4971; FAX 819/477-6604; res: 800/668-3521.* E-mail
aub-uni@9bit.qc.ca. 115 rms, 4 story. S $75.95; D $85.95; each addl $10;
suites $120-$150; under 15 free. Crib free. Pet accepted. TV; cable. Indoor

pool; poolside serv. Restaurant 7 am-10 pm. Rm serv. Bar 11-3 am;
entertainment Wed-Sat. Ck-out noon. Meeting rms. Business servs avail.
Cr cds: A, C, D, DS, ER, MC, V.

Restaurant

✔ ★ ★ **RESTAURANT DU BOIS-JOLI.** *(505 St Joseph Blvd W,
Drummondville QE J2E 1K8) 819/472-4366.* French, continental menu.
Specialty: rôti de boeuf au jus. Hrs: 11 am-10 pm; Sun brunch to 2 pm. Res
accepted. Serv bar. A la carte entrees: lunch, dinner $5.75-$15.50. Complete meals: lunch $5.50-$9.75, dinner $9.95-$15.50. Buffet $6.50. Sun
brunch $9.25. Child's meals. Cr cds: A, D, MC, V.

Gaspé Peninsula (B-10 - C-9)

E-mail info@tourisme.gouv.qc.ca **Web** www.tourisme.gouv.qc.ca
Information Tourism Québec, CP 979, Montréal H3C 2W3; 514/873-2015
or 800/363-7777.

Jutting out into the Gulf of Saint-Laurent, the Gaspé Peninsula is a region
of varying landforms, including mountains, plateaus, beaches and cliffs. It
is blessed with abundant and rare wildlife and some unique flora, including
12-foot-high (4-meter) centuries-old fir trees. Landscapes are incredibly
beautiful. The rivers, teeming with trout, flow to meet the salmon coming
from the sea. Called "Gespeg" (meaning "land's end") by the aborigines,
the area was settled primarily by Basque, Breton and Norman fishermen,
whose charming villages may be seen clinging to the shore beneath the
gigantic cliffs. The French influence is strong; English is spoken in few
villages.

With the exception of suggested side trips, the entire Gaspé Peninsula Auto Tour follows Highway 132, making it very easy to follow. Until this
highway was developed, access to most of the peninsula was only by boat,
accounting for much of its unspoiled character.

Auto Tour

RIVIÈRE-DU-LOUP

Rivière-du-Loup is an educational, administrative and commercial center
offering remarkable panoramas by virtue of its location on a rocky spur
overlooking the majestic St Lawrence River. In the center of town is a 98-ft
(30-m) waterfall, which for many years provided the town with electrical
power. Excursions to the islands of the St Lawrence River (or *Fleuve
Saint-Laurent*), whale-watching trips, the Musée du Bas-St-Laurent, and
the public beach and marina at the "Pointe" of Rivière-du-Loup constitute
points of particular interest in this region.

For further information contact Association Touristique du Bas Saint-
Laurent, 148, rue Froser, Rivière-du-Loup G5R 1C8; 418/867-3015 or
800/563-5268.

Hunting, freshwater and deep-sea fishing are popular activities.
Whale watching tours conducted by Croisières Navimex; phone 418/867-
3361. A ferry may be taken across the St Lawrence River to St-Siméon
from mid-Apr-early Jan. For schedule, fees phone 418/862-9545 or
514/849-4466. Travel 25 miles (40 km) to

TROIS-PISTOLES

Named for three old French coins, supposedly the price of a silver cup that
fell into the river here, this well-known resort is an important port for tourist
fishing. Found here are an imposing church built between 1882 and 1887,
and the **Musée Saint-Laurent,** at 552 rue Notre Dame O, displaying
antique cars, farm equipment and various antiques (mid-June-mid-Sept;
fee). For further information phone 418/851-2345.

Three islands off the coast are bird sanctuaries. ˆL'Ile-aup-
Basques, the largest, shows restored furnaces used long ago by the

Basque fishermen to extract oil from whales. ˆL'Ile-aup-Basques and the two smaller islands, the Îles Rasades, shelter blue herons, gulls, eider ducks, cormorants and many other birds. Naturalists, bird-watchers and photographers are allowed to visit ˆL'Ile-aup-Basques with permission of the warden, in groups of five or more (mid-June-mid-Oct; fee). Phone 418/851-1202. Whales and seals also visit off this coast each summer and autumn. ¢¢¢¢ Continue driving along the coast 38 miles (61 km) to

RIMOUSKI

Established in 1696, one quarter of this center of the Lower St Lawrence region was destroyed by fire in 1950, yet no traces of the damage remain today. Its large and important harbor is open all year. The beach at Sainte-Luce, and Lepage Park with its monument to Lepage, the first settler, are places to see, as is the covered bridge at Mont-Lebel on the Rivière Neigette.

The **Musée Régional de Rimouski,** 35 rue Saint-Germain O, is located in the third Catholic church of Rimouski (1824); it houses a National Arts Center with major national, local and regional events and expositions; arts, crafts. For schedule, fees phone 418/724-2272.

Inland via Road 232 and a local road, you may take a small side excursion to Réserve Faunique de Rimouski, approximately 30 miles (48 km) to the south. Here you will find 284 square miles (735 sq km) of beautiful area with camping, picnicking, nature interpretation, hunting, fishing and boating; phone 418/779-2212 or 800/665-6527. Return via the same routes to Hwy 132 and follow it 19 mi (31 km) to

SAINTE-FLAVIE

This farming and resort village is indeed the Gateway to Gaspé and the Atlantic provinces. From Sainte-Flavie, along Hwy 132, around to the town of Percé, is some of the most incredibly beautiful scenery to be found anywhere. Enjoying this remarkable landscape, follow the highway 208 miles (335 km) around to the very tip of the Gaspé to Forillon National Park.

A few interesting sights on your way include **Jardins de Métis** at Grand-Métis, a few miles east of Sainte-Flavie. The 40-acre (16-hectare) Reford Estate comprising Jardins de Métis is a British-style garden. There are alpine shrubs, perennial and annual plants, some exotic species and many native plants. A section of wild and aquatic plants has been started and a waterfall-fed stream meanders through the garden, spanned by small bridges. Expanses of green lawn accented by coniferous and deciduous trees complete the lovely setting, surrounding the Reford Villa, a distinctive 37-rm mansion now housing a museum, restaurant and craft shop. The gardens are unique in North America because more than 800 species and 100,000 plants have been successfully cultivated in this northern climate. Visits to mansion museum (fee), natural harbor and picnic grounds. (1st wkend June-Sept, daily) Phone 418/775-2221. ¢¢

Along Hwy 132, about 32 mi (51 km), you pass through the town of Matane, where you may see a salmon migration channel right in the middle of town, or stop at the lighthouses and tourist information office in Musée du Vieux Phare (Old Lighthouse) at 968 du Phare O (June-Labour Day, daily). At Sainte-Anne-des-Monts, 57 miles (91 km) farther, you reach the first access route, Road 299, to **Parc de la Gaspésie** (Gaspesian Park), a vast area noted for its rugged terrain, mountain excursions, panoramic mountain rides and summit climbs; also fishing, canoeing, hiking, cross-country skiing; phone 418/763-3301. Returning to Hwy 132, and traveling 70 miles (112 km), you will come to the town of Grande-Vallée. Watch for the many bread ovens along the highway. The final 38-mile (61 km) drive brings you to your intended destination.

PARC NATIONAL FORILLON

This 95-square-mile (245-sq-km) park was established in 1970 to protect a special region of highly varied plant and animal life and geological formations. Escarpments rising over 500 feet (15 m) on the eastern shore and the Monts Notre-Dame, an eastern arm of the Appalachians, rising to 1,700 feet (518 m), along with a rugged coastline, give the park a most varied topography. The area embraces the Lower Saint Lawrence forest region and the Boreal Forest, with abundant and varied wildlife and vegetation. Some unique plant ecosystems are found in the arctic alpine flora of Cap Bon-Ami and the pioneer (sand dune) plants at Penouille.

Forillon National Park was developed to reflect both the unique coastal environment and the rich human history of the Gaspé region.

Headquarters are at Gaspé, 146 boul. Gaspé, phone 418/368-5505. Camping is available at Cap-Bon-Ami, Des Rosiers and Petit-Gaspé. Visitors may enjoy nature walks, hiking trails, cross-country ski trails, snowshoeing, cycling and picnic areas. Cruising and deep-sea fishing expeditions (fee) also leave from here; whales and seals can be seen from the tip of the Forillon Peninsula.

Returning to the highway and rounding the tip of the peninsula for 42 miles (68 km), you will come to the deep seaport and large sheltered bay of

GASPÉ

Three salmon rivers (the Dartmouth, York and Saint-Jean) empty into the bay at Gaspé, site of **Piscicole de Gaspé,** a 100-year-old fish hatchery (the oldest in Canada) that raises and releases more than a million salmon and trout fry into the rivers of eastern Canada every year (mid-June-mid-Sept, daily). For fishing information contact Société de Gestion des rivières du Grand Gaspé, Inc, CP 826, Gaspé, G0C 1R0; 418/368-2324.

A religious, educational and administrative center, Gaspé has a college and **Cathédrale de Gaspé,** a remarkable wooden cathedral, the only one in North America. It contains some very beautiful stained-glass windows. In front of the cathedral is a granite cross, erected during the celebration of the 400th anniversary of the discovery of Canada to commemorate the cross planted here by Jacques Cartier on his first voyage in 1534.

The **Musée de la Gaspésie,** located on Jacques Cartiers's Point on Hwy 132, offers a panoramic view of the bay and Forillon Park. The museum presents a chronological history dating from the Gaspé. Exhibits feature traditional occupations and contemporary culture of the area. (Late June-Sept, daily; limited hrs rest of yr) Contact CP 680, G0C 1R0; 418/368-1534. ¢

Side trips available from Gaspé are by air to the picturesque and peaceful Magdalen Islands, 157 miles (253 km) to the east via Inter-Canadien. 40-min flight (Mon-Fri). For reservations phone Inter-Canadien (514/847-2211 or 800/363-7530). Deep-sea fishing excursions at the Forillon National Park are offered from late June to Labour Day. Gaspé is another of the entrances to Parc de la Gaspésie (Gaspesian Park) to the west, leading to Lake Madeleine.

Just before arriving at Percé, 47 miles (76 km) away, you pass through the village of Coin-du-Banc, where you may find agates on the beach which hugs the cliff, view fossilized tree trunks, and see a beautiful waterfall set in sedimentary rock.

PERCÉ

One of the most astonishingly beautiful and interestingly situated towns is Percé, with its colossal rock formation, Rocher Percé (Percé Rock). The village takes the form of a semicircle, surrounded left to right by Cap Blanc, 1,143-foot (375-m) Mont Sainte-Anne, 1,116-foot (340-m) Mont Blanc, Pic de l'Aurore (Peak of Dawn), Trois-Soeurs (Three Sisters) and Cap Barré and opening onto two bays, separated by two capes and Percé Rock. Jacques Cartier anchored his three ships behind this famed rock in July 1534.

Percé Rock, 288 feet (88 m) high, 1,421 feet (433 m) long and weighing approximately 400 million tons (406 million metric tons), is formed of siliceous limestone of the Devonian period, which means it contains many fossils. It resembles a large ship at anchor and is pierced by a large arch near one end, 18 feet (6 m) high, which gives the rock and town their names. Formerly joined to shore and providing shelter for a large cod fleet, the rock can now be reached at low tide across a gravel bar. Be sure to inquire about the tide schedule. Phone 418/782-2240.

Craft shops, painters' galleries and fine food abound in this area, and deep-sea fishing excursions leave from this harbor. A trail behind Mont Sainte-Anne leads to an area of great crevasses; lookout points are good from Pic de l'Aurore, and Côte Surprise and the southeast side of Mont Sainte-Anne.

Excursion boats leave daily (mid-May-early Oct) for trips around Percé Rock, landing at Bonaventure Island; phone 418/782-2974. L'Île-Bonaventure Park comprises the entire island, 2 miles (3.5 km), offshore. Rocky ledges and cliffs 250 feet (76 m) high give sanctuary to thousands of sea birds. The major inhabitants are kittiwakes, razor-billed auks, black guillemots, a few Arctic puffins and especially gannets, with the largest and most accessible of the 22 known colonies in the world here. The island has rich and diverse vegetation. Climbs may be made to the cliff and four guided nature trails are available from mid-June-mid-Oct. Phone Gaspé, 418/782-2240; Percé (summer only), 418/782-2721.

Returning to the highway, traveling southwest and then west, 161 mi (258 km), to Restigouche, more than a few points of interest may be noted on the way.

At **Cap-d'Espoir,** approximately 10 miles (16 km), and Anse-aux-Gascons, 33 miles (53 km) farther, agates may be found on the beautiful beaches. Striking red cliffs at Shigawake may be viewed about 18 miles (29 km) farther on. At Bonaventure, reached by proceeding 22 miles (38 km) and rounding the cape, are a church of granite built in 1960 and noteworthy Musée Acadien du Québec, on the highway.

Continuing along Hwy 132 for another 78 miles (126 km), you will come to the deep seaport and large sheltered bay of

RESTIGOUCHE

A reservation and site of an ancient Recollet mission (1620), served by the Capuchin Fathers, Restigouche Reserve is today the location of a Sainte-Anne Shrine and museum in the monastery of the Capuchin Fathers. The church of Sainte-Anne is the 12th built on the site, the previous 11 having burned.

Pointe-à-la-Croix is a work site of the **Historic National Park Batsille-de-la-Ristigouche.** Archaeologists are reclaiming the 18th-century French supply ship *Machault,* scuttled during a battle in 1760. It has been underwater in front of the mission. Some cargo and structural elements have been excavated and are exhibited. Phone 418/788-5676. ¢¢

Turning northwest from Restigouche, the highway enters the Matapédia River Valley, which is tightly ensconced between mountains. The river flows in a deep hollow with steep embankments, which separate the mass of the Chic-Chocs Mountains from the highland zone to the southwest. The most striking section of the valley begins at Causapscal, the earlier section of the road having followed the former Kempt military road, itself developed from an old indigenous track. Causapscal is noted for its covered bridges across the Matapédia River and its excellent salmon fishing. The Domaine Matamajaw, situated along the river, is the only historic Atlantic salmon sportfishing site in Québec; exhibitions are presented at the interpretation center, phone 418/756-5999.

Twenty-three miles (37 kilometers) beyond Causapscal you pass through the town of Val-Brillant (called "Queen of the Valley") with its Gothic church, one of the most beautiful religious structures in the region. Having traveled 94 miles (151 km), from Restigouche, you return again to Sainte-Flavie.

Granby (E-3)

(See also Montréal, Sherbrooke)

Pop 38,069 **Elev** 270 ft (82 m) **Area code** 450 **Web** tourisme.granby.qc.ca
Information Tourism Granby, 650 Principale St, J2G 8L4; 450/372-7273 or 800/567-7273.

Begun as a mission in 1824, with the first settlers arriving in 1813, Granby was named for an English nobleman, the Marquis of Granby. Only 45 miles (71 kilometers) east of Montréal, the town is a favorite excursion spot for Montréalers, with its 18 beautiful parks containing a collection of old European fountains, and its devotion to good food. Located on the north bank of the Yamaska River, Granby manufactures rubber products, candy, electrical products and cement. Because of the abundance of maple groves, sugaring-off parties are a popular activity.

What to See and Do

Granby Zoological Garden. More than 1,000 animals of 225 species from every continent; education & African pavillions, amusement park. (May-Sept, daily) 525 rue Bourget. Phone 450/372-9113. ¢¢¢¢

Nature Interpretation Centre of Lake Boivin. Guided walking tours through woodland and marsh; concentrations of waterfowl and nature exhibits. (Daily) 700 rue Drummond. Phone 450/375-3861. **Free.**

Yamaska Provincial Park. Newly developed park with swimming, hiking, fishing, boating (rentals), paths, cross-country skiing (fee), picnicking; snack bar. Parking (fee). 3 mi (5 km) E. Phone 450/372-3204.

Annual Event

Granby International. Antique car show. Phone 450/777-1330. Last wkend July.

Resort

★ ★ **AUBERGE BROMONT.** *(95 rue Montmorency, Bromont QE J2L 2J1) Hwy 139 to CAN 10E, exit 78 and follow tourist signs.* 514/534-1199; res: 800/276-6668; FAX 514/534-1700. 50 rms, 3 story. No elvtr. S, D $98-$118; MAP avail; family rates; ski, golf plans. Crib free. TV; cable (premium). Pool; poolside serv, lifeguard. Dining rm (public by res) 7 am-3 pm, 6-10 pm. Bar 11-3 am. Ck-out noon, ck-in 4 pm. Business servs avail. Concierge. Lighted tennis, pro. 18-hole golf, greens fee $26-$33. Downhill ski 1 mi; x-country ski on site (rentals). Exercise equipt. Some minibars. Cr cds: A, D, ER, MC, V.

Hull
(see Ottawa, Ontario)

The Laurentians (D-6 - E-4)

Information Laurentian Tourism Association, 14142 rue de la Chapelle, RR #1, St-Jérôme, PQ, J7Z 5T4; 450/436-8532 or 800/561-6673.

The Laurentian region, just 45 miles from Montreal, is a rich tourist destination. Surrounded by forests, lakes, rivers and the Laurentian Mountains, this area provides ample settings for open-air activities year-round. Water sports abound in summer, including canoeing, kayaking, swimming, rafting, scuba diving and excellent fishing. Hunting, golfing, horseback riding and mountain climbing are also popular in warmer months, as is bicycling along the 125-mile P'tit train du Nord trail. Brilliant fall colors lead into a winter ideal for snow lovers. The Laurentian region boasts a huge number of downhill ski centers, 600 miles of cross-country trails and thousands of miles of snowmobiling trails. The territory of the Laurentian tourist zone is formed on the south by the Outaouais River, des Deux-Montagnes Lake and the Milles-Iles River. On the east, its limits stretch from the limit of Terrebonne to Entrelacs. It is bounded on the north by Ste-Anne du Lac and Baskatong Reservoir and on the west by the towns of Des Ruisseaux, Notre-Dame de Pontmain and Notre Dame du Laus. Places listed are Mont Tremblant Provincial Park, St Jérôme and Saint-Jovite.

Montréal (F-5)

Settled 1642 **Pop** 1,005,000 **Elev** 117 ft (36 m) **Area code** 514 **E-mail** info@tourisme.gouv.qc.ca **Web** www.tourisme.gouv.qc.ca
Information Tourisme-Québec, CP 979, H3C 2W3; 514/873-2015 or 800/363-7777.

Blessed by its location on an island at the junction of the St Lawrence and Ottawa rivers, Montréal has served for more than three centuries as a gigantic trading post; its harbor can accommodate more than 100 ocean-going vessels. While it is a commercial, financial and industrial center, Montréal is also an internationally recognized patron of the fine arts, hosting several acclaimed festivals attended by enthusiasts world-wide.

A stockaded indigenous settlement called Hochelaga when it was discovered in 1535 by Jacques Cartier, the area contained a trading post by the early 1600s; but it was not settled as a missionary outpost until 1642 when the Frenchman Paul de Chomedey, Sieur de Maisonneuve, and a group of settlers, priests and nuns founded Ville-Morie. This later grew as an important fur trading center and from here men such as Jolliet, Marquette, Duluth and Father Hennepin set out on their western expeditions. Montréal remained under French rule until 1763 when Canada was surrendered as a possession to the British under the Treaty of Paris. For seven months during the American Revolution, Montréal was occupied by Americans, but it was later regained by the British.

Today Montréal is an elegantly sophisticated city. Two-thirds of its people are French-speaking, and its French population is the largest outside of Europe. It is made up of two parts: the Old City, in the same area as the original Ville-Morie, which is a maze of narrow streets, restored buildings and old houses, best seen on foot; and the modern Montréal, with its many skyscrapers, museums, theaters, nearly 7,600 restaurants and glittering nightlife.

There is an underground Montréal also, with miles of shops, galleries, restaurants and access to one of the most unique subway systems in the world. Each station has been decorated by a different architect in a different style, and visitors have called it "the largest underground art gallery in the world." Mont-Royal rises from the center of the island-city to a height of 764 feet (233 meters), affording a panoramic view. Calèches (horse-drawn carriages) provide tourists with a charming means of viewing the city and are, with the exception of bicycles, the only vehicles permitted in some areas of Mount Royal Park. Adjacent to the park is the Westmount area, a section of meandering roads and charming older homes of the early 1900s with delightful English-style gardens.

In 1967, Montréal hosted Expo '67, celebrating Canada's centennial. The summer Olympic games were held here in 1976.

What to See and Do

Angrignon Park. 262 acres (106 hectares) with more than 21,600 trees; lagoons, river; playground; picnicking, bicycling; ice-skating, cross-country skiing. Park (daily). 3400 des Trinitaires Blvd. Phone 514/872-3816. Zoo ¢¢

Byzantine Museum. Gallery for icons and other works by Romanian-born artist Rosette Mociornitza, produced in the unique style of the Byzantine period using old wood, traditional techniques, materials from Europe. Works may be purchased. (Daily, by appt) 6780 Biarritz Ave, Brossard. Phone ahead; 514/656-0188. **Free.**

Casino Montréal. The Casino de Montréal offers guests a variety of games—Blackjack, Roulette, Baccarat, Pai Gow Poker, Keno—112 gaming tables as well as 2,700 slot machines. (Open 24 hrs) 1 Ave du Casino, housed in Expo 67's famous French Pavilion. Phone 514/392-2746 or 800/665-2274.

Dorchester Square. In the center of Montréal, this park is a popular meeting place. Also here is Mary Queen of the World Cathedral, a one-third-scale replica of St Peter's in Rome. Also information centre of Montréal and Tourisme Québec. René-Lévesque Blvd O between Peel & Metcalfe Sts. **Free.**

Fort Lennox. 45 mi (72.4 km) SE. (See ROUSES POINT, NY)

La Fontaine Park. Illuminated fountain; playground; monuments; 2 lakes, paddleboats; cycling trail. (Mid-May-Oct, daily) Winter activities include ice-skating, cross-country skiing; hockey rink. Sherbrooke St & Papineau St. Phone 514/872-2644. **Free.**

Maison Saint-Gabriel. Built in late 17th century, originally as a farm; also served as school for Marguerite Bourgeoys, founder of the Sisters of the Congrégatun de Notre-Dame, who looked after young French girls who were to marry the early colonists. Period furnishings; altar built in 1700s; items of French-Canadian heritage including woodcuts from ancient churches and chapels. (Mid-Apr-mid-Dec, daily exc Mon) 2146 Dublin Pl. Phone 514/935-8136. ¢¢

McGill University (1821). (31,000 students) The 80-acre main campus is set between the lower slopes of Mt Royal and the downtown commercial district. Guided tours by appt (free). Welcome Centre at 805 Sherbrooke St O. Phone 514/398-4455.

☒ **Montréal Botanical Garden.** Within 180 acres (73 hectares) grow more than 26,000 species and varieties of plants; 30 specialized sections include rose, perennial plant, heath gardens, flowery brook, bonsai, carnivorous plants and arboretum; one of the world's largest orchid collections; seasonal flower shows. The bonsai and penjing collections are two of the most diversified in North America. Chinese and Japanese gardens; restaurant, tearoom. Parking (fee). (Daily) 4101 Sherbrooke St E. Phone 514/872-1400. ¢¢ Also here (and included in admission)is

Insectarium de Montreal. Collection of more than 350,000 insects in a building designed to resemble a stylized insect. Interactive and participatory concept takes visitors through aviaries and living displays in six geographically themed areas. Hands-on exhibits; Outside Gardens; butterfly aviary (summer); traveling exhibits; children's amusement center. (Daily)

Montréal Planetarium. Astronomy shows: projectors create all features of the night sky; special effects. (Daily exc Mon; phone for schedule) 1000 Saint-Jacques St O. Phone 514/872-4530. ¢¢

Mount Royal Park. 430 acres (174 hectares) in center of city; lake, picnicking, bicycling, calèche tours; winter sports (skating, downhill/cross-country skiing); observation point at chalet lookout. Permanent exhibits at Chalet de la Montagne, a nature-appreciation center (daily; phone 514/844-4928). Côte des Neiges & Remembrance Rds. **Free.**

Museum of Decorative Arts. Historic mansion Chateau Dufresne (1918), partially restored and refurnished, now houses international exhibitions of glass, textiles and ceramic art; changing exhibits. (Wed-Sun; closed Jan 1, Dec 25) 2200 rue Crescent. Phone 514/259-2575. ¢¢

☒ **Old (Vieux) Montréal.** The city of Montréal evolved from the small settlement of Ville-Marie founded by de Maisonneuve in 1642. The largest concentration of 19th-century buildings in North America is found here; several original dwellings remain, while many other locations are marked by bronze plaques throughout the area. The expansion of this settlement led to what is now known as Old Montréal. The area roughly forms a 100-acre (40-hectare) quadrangle which corresponds approximately to the area enclosed within the original fortifications. Bounded by McGill, Berri, Notre-Dame Sts & the St Lawrence River.Some major points of interest are

Place d'Armes. A square of great historical importance and center of Old Montréal. The founders of Ville-Marie encountered the Iroquois here in 1644 and rebuffed them. In the square's center is a statue of de Maisonneuve, first governor of Montréal, and at one end is the St Sulpice seminary (1685) with an old wooden clock (1710), oldest building in Montréal. St Sulpice & Notre-Dame Sts. At 119 St Jacques St is the **Bank of Montréal.** This magnificent building contains a museum with collection of currency, mechanical savings banks, photographs, reproduction of old-fashioned teller's cage. (Mon-Fri; closed legal hols) Phone 514/877-6810. Some of the most important financial houses of the city are grouped around the square. **Free.** Across the square is

Notre-Dame Basilica (1824). In 1672, a church described as "one of the most beautiful churches in North America" was erected on the present Notre-Dame St. When this became inadequate for the growing parish, a new church designed by a New Yorker, James O'Donnell, was built. It was completed in 1829 and two towers and interior decorations were added later. *Le Gros Bourdon,* a bell cast in 1847 and weighing

24,780 lbs is in Perseverance Tower; there is a 10-bell chime in Temperance Tower. Built of Montréal limestone, the basilica is Neo-Gothic in design with a beautiful main altar, pulpit and numerous statues, paintings and stained-glass windows. (Daily; concerts in summer) 110 Notre-Dame St O.   **Free.**

Notre-Dame Basilica Museum. Works of religious and historical art; old furniture, statues; local folklore paintings. (*closed for renovation*) 424 Saint Sulpice St. Phone 514/842-2925.   ¢

Saint-Paul St. Oldest street in Montréal. The mansions of Ville-Marie once stood here but they have been replaced by commercial houses and office buildings. Here is

Notre-Dame-de-Bonsecours Church (1773). Founded in 1657 and rebuilt 115 yrs later, this is one of the oldest churches still standing in the city; tower has view of the river and city; museum (fee) has objects pertaining to early settlers. Miniature ships suspended from vault in church are votive offerings from sailors who worshiped here.

Château Ramezay (1705). Historical museum, once the home of the governors of Montréal, the West Indies Co of France and the Governors-General of British North America. Furniture, paintings, costumes, porcelain, manuscripts, art objects of the 17th-19th centuries. (Daily exc Mon) 280 Notre-Dame E, in front of City Hall. Phone 514/861-3708.   ¢¢

Place Jacques-Cartier. Named for the discoverer of Canada, this was once a busy marketplace. Oldest monument in the city, the Nelson Column (1809) is in the square's upper section. Notre-Dame St.

Olympic Park. Stadium was site of 1976 Summer Olympic Games and is now home of Montréal Expos baseball team & les Alouettes de Montréal football team; observatory of world's tallest inclined tower. Cafeteria, souvenir shop. Tours (daily). 4141 Pierre de Coubertin St. Phone 514/252-8687. Tours (with tower)   ¢¢ Adj stadium is

Biodôme de Montréal. Former Olympic Velodrome has been transformed into an environmental museum that combines elements of botanical garden, aquarium, zoo and nature center. Four ecosystems—Laurentian Forest, Tropical Forest, Polar World and Saint-Laurent Marine—sustain thousands of plants and small animals. 500-meter Nature Path with text panels and maps, interpreters; and discovery rm "Naturalia." (Daily; closed Jan 1, Dec 25) 4777 Pierre de Coubertin St. Phone 514/868-3000.   ¢¢¢

Parc Safari. Features 750 animals, rides and shows, children's theater and play area, swimming beach; drive-through wild animal reserve; picnicking, restaurants, boutiques. (Mid-May-mid-Sept, daily) 33 mi (56 km) S on Hwy 15 to exit 6, then follow zoo signs. Phone 800/465-8724.   ¢¢¢¢¢

Parc des Îles. Two islands in the middle of the St Lawrence River; access via Jacques-Cartier Bridge or Metro subway. Île Sainte-Hélène (St Helen's Island) was the main anchor site for Expo '67; now a 342-acre (138-hectare) multipurpose park with 3 swimming pools; picnicking; cross-country skiing, snowshoeing. Île Notre-Dame (Notre Dame Island), to the south, was partly built up from the river bed and was an important activity site for Expo '67. Here is Gilles-Villeneuve Formula 1 race track (see ANNUAL EVENTS); also beach, paddle boats, windsurfing and sailing. Some fees. Phone 514/872-6093. (Daily) Located here are

The Old Fort (1820-1824). Oldest remaining fortification of Montréal, only the arsenal, powder magazine and barracks building still stand. Two military companies dating from the 18th century, La Compagnie Franche de la Marine and the 78th Fraser Highlanders, perform colorful military drills and parades (late June-Aug, Wed-Sun).   ¢¢ In the fort's arsenal is

David M. Stewart Museum. Artifacts trace Canadian history from the 15th century through maps, firearms, kitchen utensils, engravings, navigational and scientific instruments. (Daily exc Tues; closed Jan 1, Dec 25) Admission included with Fort. Phone 514/861-6701.

Floral Park. Site of Les Floralies Internationales 1980; now permanent, it displays collection of worldwide flowers and plants. Walking trails; pedal boats, canoeing; picnic area; snack bar and restaurant. Some fees. (3rd wk June-mid-Sept, daily) Île Notre-Dame.   **Free.**

Théâtre des Lilas. Open-air theater with a variety of shows, including music & dance. Île Notre-Dame.

La Ronde. A 135-acre amusement park with 35 rides, including 132-ft (40-m) high wooden roller coaster; arcades, entertainment on a floating stage; waterskiing; live cartoon characters, children's village; circus, boutiques and restaurants. (June-Labour Day, daily; May, wkends; closed 4 days late Aug) Île Sainte-Hélène. Phone 514/872-4537 or 800/797-4537.   ¢¢¢¢¢

Place des Arts. This 4-theater complex is the heart of Montréal's artistic life. L'Opéra de Montréal, the Montréal Symphony Orchestra, les Grands Ballets Canadiens and La Compagnie Jean-Duceppe theatrical troupe have their permanent home here. Other entertainment includes chamber music, recitals, jazz, folk singers, variety shows, music hall, theater, musicals and modern & classical dance. Corner of Ste-Catherine and Jeonne-Mance. Phone 514/790-2787 (recording) or 514/842-2112 (tickets).

★ **Pointe-à-Callière, the Montréal Museum of Archaeology and History.** Deals with the founding and development of the City of Montréal. Built in 1992, over the actual site of the founding of Montréal, the main museum building, the **Éperon,** actually rests on pillars built around ruins dating from the town's first cemetery and its earliest fortifications, which are now in its basement. Two balconies overlook this archaeological site and a 16-min multimedia show is presented using the actual remnants as a backdrop. From here, visitors continue underground, amid still more remnants, to the **Archaeological Crypt,** a structure that allows access to many more artifacts and remains; architectural models beneath a transparent floor illustrate five different periods in the history of Place Royale. The **Old Customs House (Ancienne-Douane)** houses thematic exhibits on Montréal in the 19th & 20th centuries. Permanent and changing exhibits. Cafe; gift shop. (Daily exc Mon; extended hrs summer) 350 Place Royale, corner of Place Youville in Old Montréal. Phone 514/872-9150.   ¢¢¢

Professional sports.

National League baseball (Montréal Expos). Olympic Stadium, 4549 Pierre de Coubertin St. Phone 514/790-1245.

NHL (Montréal Canadiens). Molson Center, 1260 La Gaucheti'ere O. Phone 514/932-2582.

Saint Joseph's Oratory. Chapel (1904), crypt-church (1916); museum. Main church is a famous shrine attracting more than 2 million pilgrims yearly; basilica founded 1924; built in Italian Renaissance style; dome towers over city. 56-bell carillon made in France is outstanding. (Daily) 3800 Queen Mary Rd, on N slope of Mt Royal. Phone 514/733-8211. **Free.**

Sightseeing tours.

Calèche tours (horse-drawn carriages) depart from Place d' Armes, Mount Royal Park or Old Port of Montréal.   ¢¢¢¢

Gray Line bus tours. Contact 1140 Wellington St, H3C 1V8; 514/934-1222.

Montréal Harbour Cruises. Various guided cruises and dinner excursions (1-4 hrs); bar service. Reservations advised. (May-mid-Oct, daily) Depart from Quai de L'Horloge in Old Montréal, at the foot of Berri St and from Quai Jacque Cartier. Contact Croisières Vieure-Port de Montréal, Quai de l'Horlage, C.P. 1085, Succ. Place d'Armes, H2Y 3J6; 514/842-9300 or 800/667-3131.   ¢¢¢¢¢

The Montréal Museum of Fine Arts (Musée des beaux-arts de Montréal). Canada's oldest art museum (founded 1860) has a wide variety of displays, ranging from Egyptian statues to 20th-century abstracts. Canadian section features old Québec furniture, silver and paintings. (Daily exc Mon; closed Jan 1, Dec 25) 1379-1380 Sherbrooke St O. Phone 514/285-2000. ¢¢¢

Université de Montréal (1920). (58,000 students) On N slope of Mt Royal. 2900 boul Édouord-Montpetit. Phone 514/343-6111.

Annual Events

Canadian Grand Prix. Parc des Îles. Formula 1 racing at Gilles-Villeneuve track, Île Notre-Dame. Phone 514/350-0000. Early June.

Antiques Bonaventure. East Exhibition Hall, Place Bonaventure. Exhibits of private and public collections for sale; more than 100 dealers participate. Phone 514/397-2222. Mid-June.

Fête Nationale. St-Jean-Baptiste, patron saint of the French Canadians, is honored with 3 days of festivities surrounding provincial holiday. Celebration includes street festivals, bonfire, fireworks, musical events. June 24.

Montréal Jazz Festival. Downtown. More than 1,200 musicians and a million music lovers from around the world gather to celebrate jazz. 10-day fest includes more than 500 indoor and outdoor concerts. Phone 514/871-1881 or 888/515-0515. 1st 2 wks July.

Just for Laughs. International comedy festival. Phone 514/845-2322. Mid-July.

World Film Festival. Contact 1432 Bleury St; 514/848-3883. 2 wks late Aug.

Additional Visitor Information

Québec Tourism, PO Box 979, Montréal, H3C 2W3; phone 800/363-7777 or in person at Infotouriste, 1001 rue du Square-Dorchester (between Peel & Metcalfe Sts); also office at Old Montréal, Place Jacques-Cartier, 174 Notre-Dame St E; all have helpful information for tourists. The Consulate General of the United States is located on 1155 rue St-Alexandre, at Place ´Felip-Martin, at the corner of René Levesque Blvd; phone 514/398-9695. Public transportation is provided by the Société de Transport de la Communauté Urbaine de Montréal (STCUM), phone 514/288-6287.

Motels

★ ★ **AUBERGES WANDLYN.** (7200 Sherbrooke St E, Montréal QE H1N 1E7) 514/256-1613; FAX 514/256-5150. 123 rms, 2 story. June-Oct: S $63-$89.50; D $63-$99.50; each addl $10; suites $99.50-$129.50; under 18 free; lower rates rest of yr. TV; cable. Heated pool; poolside serv; lifeguard. Restaurant 7 am-2 pm. Bar 4 pm-midnight. Ck-out noon. Meeting rms. Business servs avail. Balconies. Cr cds: A, C, D, DS, ER, MC, V.

★ **HÔTEL LE SAINT-ANDRÉ.** (1285 rue St-André, Montréal QE H2L 3T1) 514/849-7070; FAX 514/849-8167; res: 800/265-7071. 61 rms, 4 story. May-Oct: S $64.50; D $69.50; each addl $5; lower rates rest of yr. TV. Complimentary continental bkfst. Restaurant nearby. Ck-out noon. Business servs avail. Sundries. Small, contemporary hotel. Cr cds: A, D, DS, ER, MC, V.

★ ★ ★ **HOSTELLERIE LES TROIS TILLEULS.** (290 Richelieu Blvd, St-Marc-sur-Richelieu QE J0L 2E0) 26 mi SE on Hwy 20E, exit 112, then 5 mi N on Hwy 223. 514/856-7787; FAX 450/584-3146; res: 800/263-2230. E-mail host.3tilleuls@sympatico.ca; web saveurs.sympatico.ca/enc-roy/quebec/tilleuls.htm. 24 rms, 3 story. S $92-$125; D $110-$145; each addl $20; suites $225-$390. Crib free. TV; cable (premium). VCR. Heated pool. Restaurant (see LES TROIS TILLEULS). Rm serv. Bar 11-2 am. Ck-out noon. Meeting rms. Business center. In-rm modem link. Lighted tennis. X-country ski 10 mi. Hunting trips. Private marina. Boat tours. Some in-rm whirlpools. Balconies. Golf nearby. In 1880 farmhouse. On Richelieu River. Cr cds: A, C, D, ER, MC, V.

Motor Hotels

★ ★ ★ **HOSTELLERIE RIVE GAUCHE.** (1810 Richelieu Blvd, Beloeil QE J3G 4S4) CAN 20E exit 112, at jct Hwy 223. 514/467-4477; FAX 514/467-0525. 22 rms, 3 story. S $92-$110; D $125-$145; each addl $20; suites $225-$235. Crib free. TV; cable (premium). Pool. Restaurant 7:30 am-10:30 pm. Bar 11-midnight. Ck-out noon. Meeting rms. Business servs avail. Lighted tennis. X-country ski 8 mi. Balconies. View of Richelieu River & Mont St-Hilaire. Cr cds: A, D, ER, MC, V.

✔★ **HOTEL LA RÉSIDENCE DU VOYAGEUR.** (847 Sherbrooke East, Montréal QE H2L 1K6) 514/527-9515; FAX 514/526-1070.

E-mail twng@ican.net; web wworks.com/~resvoyager. 28 units, 4 story. June-mid-Sept: S $50-$90; D $65-$105; each addl $5; under 12 free; wkly rates winter; lower rates rest of yr. TV; cable. Complimentary continental bkfst. Restaurants nearby. Ck-out noon. Business servs avail. Free parking. Airport transportation. Refrigerators, microwaves avail. Cr cds: C, D, ER, MC, V.

★ ★ **QUALITY HOTEL DORVAL.** (7700 Côte de Liesse, Montréal QE H4T 1E7) near Dorval Intl Airport. 514/731-7821; FAX 514/731-1538. 159 rms, 4 story, 47 kits. S, D $98-$145; each addl $10; wkend rates. Crib free. Pet accepted. TV; cable (premium). Pool; whirlpool, lifeguard, poolside serv. Restaurant 6:30 am-2 pm, 6-11 pm. Rm serv. Bar 5 pm-1 am. Ck-out noon. Coin lndry. Meeting rms. Business servs avail. Concierge. Valet serv. Free airport transportation. Exercise equipt; sauna. Health club privileges. Massage. Minibars. Cr cds: A, C, D, DS, ER, JCB, MC, V.

✔★ ★ **QUALITY INN LE BOULEVARD.** (6680 Taschereau Blvd, Brossard QE J4W 1M8) E on Hwy 10, exit 8E (Taschereau Blvd). 514/671-7213; FAX 514/671-7041. 91 rms, 3 story, 9 suites. May-Oct: S, D $75-$85; each addl $10; suites $165; under 18 free; lower rates rest of yr. TV. Pool. Complimentary continental bkfst. Restaurant 11:30 am-10:30 pm. Bar. Ck-out noon. Meeting rms. Business servs avail. Health club privileges. Cr cds: A, D, ER, MC, V.

Hotels

★ ★ **CHÂTEAU ROYAL HOTEL SUITES.** (1420 Crescent St, Montréal QE H3G 2B7) 514/848-0999; FAX 514/848-1891; res: 800/363-0335. E-mail reservations@chateauroyal.com; web chateauroyal.com. 112 kit. suites, 21 story. S, D $89-$270; each addl $15; under 14 free; wkend rates. Crib free. Garage $12. TV; cable (premium). Complimentary coffee in rms. Restaurant 7-1 am. Ck-out noon. Coin lndry. Meeting rms. Business servs avail. Health club privileges. Microwaves avail. Balconies. Apartment-style units. Cr cds: A, C, D, DS, ER, MC, V.

★ ★ ★ **CHÂTEAU VAUDREUIL.** (21700 Trans-Canada Hwy, Vaudreuil QE J7V 8P3) W on Trans-Canada Hwy 40, exit 36. 514/455-0955; FAX 514/455-6617; res: 800/363-7896. 117 rms, 6 story, 103 suites. May-Dec: S, D $125-$165; each addl $20; suites $135-$400; under 16 free; wkend rates; higher rates special events; lower rates rest of yr. Crib free. TV; cable, VCR (movies). Indoor pool; whirlpool. Complimentary coffee in rms. Restaurant 6:30 am-11 pm. Bar 11-2 am; entertainment Tues-Sun. Ck-out noon. Meeting rms. Business servs avail. In-rm modem link. Concierge. Tennis. Downhill/x-country ski 15 mi . Exercise equipt; sauna. Minibars. Some balconies. On lake. Cr cds: A, D, DS, ER, MC, V.

★ ★ ★ **CHÂTEAU VERSAILLES.** (1659 Sherbrooke St W, Montréal QE H3H 1E3) at St-Mathieu. 514/933-3611; FAX 514/933-6867; res: 800/361-7199 (CN); 800 361-3664 (US). 176 rms, 3-14 story. S, D $107-$190; each addl $15; suites $325-$350; under 16 free. Crib free. Heated garage; valet $12.50. TV; cable. Coffee in rms. Restaurant (see CHAMPS ELYSÉES). Meeting rms. In-rm modem link. Some minibars. Comprised of 4 renovated Victorian houses and a 14-story tower. Cr cds: A, D, DS, ER, MC, V.

★ **DAYS INN-MIDTOWN.** (1005 Guy St, Montréal QE H3H 2K4) at René Lévesque Blvd W. 514/938-4611; res: 800/567-0880; FAX 514/938-8718. 205 rms, 7 story. May-Oct: S $129; D $139; each addl $10; suites $200-$350; under 12 free; wkend rates; lower rates rest of yr. Crib free. Parking (fee). TV; cable. Heated pool; lifeguard. Restaurant 7 am-10 pm; closed Nov-Apr. Ck-out noon. Meeting rms. Business servs avail. Gift shop. Cr cds: A, D, DS, ER, MC, V.

★ ★ ★ **DELTA.** *(475 President Kennedy, Montréal QE H3A 1J7) 514/286-1986; FAX 514/284-4342; res: 800/268-1133 (CN); 800/877-1133 (US).* 453 rms, 23 story. S, D $195-$210; each addl $15; suites $315-$880; under 18 free; wknd packages. Crib free. Pet accepted. Covered parking $12. TV; cable, VCR avail. 2 pools, 1 indoor; whirlpool. Supervised child's activities; ages 2-17, wkends only. Coffee in rms. Restaurant 7 am-9:30 pm. Rm serv to 1 am. Bar 11:30-1:30 am; entertainment exc Sun. Ck-out noon. Convention facilities. Business center. In-rm modem link. Concierge. Barber, beauty shop. Exercise rm; sauna. Massage. Minibars. Balconies. Luxury level. Cr cds: A, C, D, DS, ER, JCB, MC, V.

⬛ ❦ ≋ ⌁ ⋈ 🔥 SC ⛷

★ ★ **FOUR POINTS SHERATON.** *(475 Sherbrooke St W, Montréal QE H3A 2L9) 514/842-3961; FAX 514/842-0945.* 194 rms, 20 story, 89 suites. May-Oct: S $95-$105; D $110-$120; each addl $15; suites $125-$400; under 12 free; package plans; lower rates rest of yr. Crib $15. Pet accepted. Parking (fee). TV; cable. Restaurant 7 am-10 pm. Bar from 10 am. Ck-out noon. Meeting rms. Business center. In-rm modem link. Concierge. Exercise equipt; sauna. Some minibars. Cr cds: A, C, D, ER, MC, V.

❦ ⌁ ⋈ 🔥 SC ⛷

★ ★ **HOLIDAY INN SELECT CENTRE VILLE.** *(99 Viger Ave W, Montréal QE H2Z 1E9) 514/878-9888; FAX 514/878-6341.* 235 rms, 8 story. May-Oct: S $160-$185; D $170-$195; each addl $10; suites $399-$499; family, wkly, wknd plans; lower rates rest of yr. Crib free. Garage fee in/out. TV; cable. Indoor pool; whirlpool. Coffee in rms. Restaurant 6:30 am-11 pm. Bar 11-1 am. Ck-out noon. Meeting rms. Business center. In-rm modem link. Gift shop. Barber, beauty shop. Exercise equipt; saunas, steam rm. Massage. Some balconies. Pagoda-topped building in Chinatown area. Cr cds: A, C, D, DS, ER, JCB, MC, V.

⬛ ≋ ⌁ ⋈ 🔥 SC ⛷

★ ★ **HOTEL AUBERGE UNIVERSEL MONTREAL.** *(5000 Sherbrooke St E, Montréal QE H1V 1A1) 514/253-3365; FAX 514/253-9958; res: 800/567-0223.* 231 rms, 7 story. S $97; D $107; each addl $12; suites $175-$225; under 16 free. TV; cable (premium), VCR avail. 2 pools, 1 indoor; whirlpool. Sauna. Restaurant 7 am-11 pm. Bar; entertainment Tues-Sat. Ck-out noon. Meeting rms. Business servs avail. Valet serv. Free covered parking. Refrigerator in suites. Microwaves avail. Across from Olympic stadium, biodome, botanical gardens. Cr cds: A, C, D, ER, MC, V.

≋ ⋈ 🔥 SC

★ ★ ★ **HOTEL DU PARC.** *(3625 Parc Ave, Montréal QE H2X 3P8) 514/288-6666; res: 800/363-0735; FAX 514/288-2469.* E-mail rooms@duparc.com. 459 rms, 16 story. May-Oct: S, D $99-$139; each addl $15; suites $160-$350; under 18 free; wknd rates; lower rates rest of yr. Crib free. Pet accepted, some restrictions. Garage (fee). TV; cable, VCR avail. Complimentary coffee in rms. Restaurant 6:30 am-10:30 pm. Bar from noon. Ck-out noon. Meeting rms. Business center. Shopping arcade. Barber, beauty shop. Exercise rm. Health club privileges. Luxury level. Cr cds: A, C, D, DS, ER, JCB, MC, V.

⬛ ❦ ⌁ ⋈ 🔥 SC ⛷

★ ★ ★ **HÔTEL WYNDHAM.** *(4 Complexe Desjardins, Montréal QE H5B 1E5) at Jeanne Mance St, opp Place des Arts, downtown. 514/285-1450; res: 800/361-8234; FAX 514/285-1243.* Web www.hoteldesjardins.com. 600 rms, 12 story. S, D $139-$214; each addl $20; suites $340-$950; under 18 free; wknd rates. Crib free. Garage fee. Pet accepted. TV; cable (premium), VCR avail. Indoor pool; whirlpool, poolside serv. Restaurant 7 am-midnight (also see LE CAFE FLEURI). Rm serv. Bar 11:30-1 am; entertainment. Ck-out noon. Meeting rms. Business center. In-rm modem link. Concierge. Shopping arcade. Exercise rm; sauna. Health club privileges. Massage. Minibars. Cr cds: A, C, D, DS, ER, JCB, MC, V.

⬛ ❦ ≋ ⌁ ⋈ 🔥 SC ⛷

★ ★ **INTER-CONTINENTAL.** *(360 rue St-Antoine W, Montréal QE H2Y 3X4) at the World Trade Centre. 514/987-9900; res: 800/361-3600; FAX 514/847-8550.* 357 rms, 17 story. May-mid-Oct: S, D $235-$315; each addl $25; suites $360-$2,000; under 14 free; family, wknd rates; lower rates rest of yr. Crib free. Pet accepted. Garage (fee). TV; cable, VCR avail. Indoor pool. Restaurant 6:30 am-11:30 pm. Rm serv 24 hrs. Bar 11:30-1 am; entertainment. Ck-out 1 pm. Convention facilities. Business center. In-rm modem link. Concierge. Shopping arcade. Barber, beauty shop. Exercise rm; sauna, steam rm. Massage. Bathrm phones, minibars. Located on 10th-26th floors of 26-story building. Cr cds: A, C, D, DS, ER, JCB, MC, V.

⬛ ❦ ≋ ⌁ ⋈ 🔥 SC ⛷

★ ★ ★ **LE CENTRE SHERATON.** *(1201 Rene Levesque W, Montréal QE H3B 2L7) 514/878-2000; FAX 514/878-3958; res: 800/325-3535.* 824 rms, 37 story, 40 suites. S, D $210; each addl $25; suites $295-$395; under 17 free; wknd packages. Crib free. Covered, valet parking (fee). TV; cable (premium). Indoor pool; whirlpool, poolside serv (summer only), lifeguard. Complimentary coffee in rms. Restaurant 6:30 am-2 pm, 5:30 pm-midnight. 2 bars 11:30-2 am. Ck-out noon. Convention facilities. Business center. In-rm modem link. Concierge. Shopping arcade. Barber, beauty shop. Airport transportation. Exercise rm; sauna. Massage. Many minibars. Luxury level. Cr cds: A, C, D, DS, ER, JCB, MC, V.

⬛ ≋ ⌁ ⋈ 🔥 SC ⛷

★ ★ **LE NOUVEL HÔTEL.** *(1740 René Levesque Blvd W, Montréal QE H3H 1R3) 514/931-8841; FAX 514/931-3233; res: 800/363-6063.* 126 rms, 32 studios, 8 story. S, D $130-$150; each addl $10; studio $150-$170; under 12 free. Crib free. Indoor parking $9.50. TV; cable (premium). Pool; whirlpool. Restaurant 7 am-11 pm. Bar. Ck-out noon. Meeting rms. Business servs avail. In-rm modem link. Valet serv. Gift shop. Beauty shop. Game rm. Microwaves avail. Near Molson Centre. Cr cds: A, C, D, DS, ER, MC, V.

⬛ ≋ ⋈ 🔥 SC

★ ★ ★ **LE WESTIN MONT-ROYAL.** *(1050 Sherbrooke St W, Montréal QE H3A 2R6) at Peel St, downtown. 514/284-1110; FAX 514/845-3025.* 300 rms, 31 story. May-Oct: S $175-$350; D $200-$365; each addl $25; suites $335-$1,600; under 18 free; wknd rates; lower rates rest of yr. Crib free. Pet accepted, some restrictions. Garage (fee). TV; cable, VCR avail (movies). Heated pool; whirlpool, poolside serv, lifeguard. Complimentary continental bkfst. Restaurants (also see ZEN and OPUS II). Rm serv 24 hrs. Bar noon-1 am; pianist. Ck-out 1 pm. Meeting rms. Business center. In-rm modem link. Concierge. Shopping arcade. Barber, beauty shop. Exercise rm; sauna, steam rm. Massage. Bathrm phones, minibars. Cr cds: A, C, D, DS, ER, JCB, MC, V.

⬛ ❦ ≋ ⌁ ⋈ 🔥 ⛷

★ ★ ★ **LOEWS HÔTEL VOGUE.** *(1425 rue de la Montagne, Montréal QE H3G 1Z3) 514/285-5555; res: 800/465-6654; FAX 514/849-8903.* E-mail loewsvogue@loewshotels.com. This small luxury hotel in the heart of Montréal has an elegant facade of polished rose granite, trimmed in aqua, with tall windows. Guest rooms are decorated with satiny duvets on the beds and striped silk. 126 rms, 9 story, 16 suites. Mid-May-mid-Oct: S, D $195-$315; each addl $20; suites $425-$1,275; under 18 free; wknd rates; lower rates rest of yr. Crib free. Pet accepted. Garage; valet parking $15. TV; cable, VCR (movies). Restaurant 7 am-11 pm. Rm serv 24 hrs. Bar 3 pm-1 am. Ck-out 1 pm. Meeting rms. Business servs avail. In-rm modem link. Concierge. Gift shop. Exercise equipt. Massage. Health club privileges. In-rm whirlpools, minibars. Cr cds: A, C, D, ER, JCB, MC, V.

⬛ ❦ ⌁ ⋈ 🔥

★ ★ ★ **MARRIOTT CHÂTEAU CHAMPLAIN.** *(1 Place du Canada, Montréal QE H3B 4C9) 514/878-9000; res: 800/200-5909; FAX 514/878-6761.* 611 rms, 36 story. May-Dec: S, D $175; suites $238-$1,350; under 18 free; wknd rates; lower rates rest of yr. Crib free. Parking (fee). TV; cable (premium), VCR avail. Indoor pool; whirlpool, poolside serv, lifeguard. Restaurant 7 am-2:30 pm, 5:30-10:30 pm. Rm serv 6:30-1 am. Bars. Ck-out noon. Meeting rms. Business center. In-rm modem link. Shopping arcade. Barber, beauty shop. Exercise rm; sauna. Massage. Minibars. Luxury level. Cr cds: A, C, D, DS, ER, JCB, MC, V.

⬛ ≋ ⌁ ⋈ 🔥 SC ⛷

★ ★ ★ **NOVOTEL.** *(1180 rue de la Montagne, Montréal QE H3G 1Z1) 514/861-6000; FAX 514/861-0992; res: 800/668-6835.* E-mail no vomtl@aol.com. 199 rms, 9 story. May-Oct: S, D $180-$190; each addl

$15; suites $300; family, wkend & hol rates; higher rates during Grand Prix; lower rates rest of yr. Crib free. Pet accepted, some restrictions; $15. Parking garage $9.75. TV; cable (premium). Restaurant 6:30 am-10:30 pm. Bar noon-midnight. Ck-out 1 pm. Meeting rms. Business servs avail. In-rm modem link. Exercise equipt. Minibars. Cr cds: A, C, D, DS, ER, MC, V.

★ ★ ★ **QUEEN ELIZABETH.** *(900 Rene Levesque Blvd W, Montréal QE H3B 4A5)* 514/861-3511; FAX 514/954-2256; res: 800/441-1414. Web www.ephotels.ca. 1,020 rms, 21 story. S, D $120-$220; each addl $30; suites $225-$1,850; under 18 free; wkend rates. Crib free. Garage $14. TV; cable (premium). Indoor pool; whirlpool. Coffee in rms. Restaurant (see THE BEAVER CLUB). Rm serv 24 hrs. Bars from 11 am. Ck-out noon. Convention facilities. Business center. In-rm modem link. Shopping arcade. Beauty shop. Exercise rm. Massage. Minibars. Underground passage to Place Ville Marie. Luxury level. Cr cds: A, C, D, DS, ER, JCB, MC, V.

★ ★ ★ **THE RITZ-CARLTON, MONTRÉAL.** *(1228 Sherbrooke St W, Montréal QE H3G 1H6)* at Drummond, downtown. 514/842-4212; FAX 514/842-2268; res: 800/363-0366. E-mail ritz@citenet.net. Opened in 1912 by a group of local investors who wanted an elegant hotel in which to woo their rich European friends, the Ritz-Carlton Montréal has been the backdrop for many noteworthy events ever since. Guest rooms are decorated in Edwardian style; service is impeccable. 230 rms, 9 story. May-Oct: S, D $215-$240; each addl $35; suites $395-$770; under 14 free; wkend rates; lower rates rest of yr. Crib free. TV; cable. Restaurants 6:30 am-10 pm (also see CAFÉ DE PARIS). Rm serv 24 hrs. Bar 11:30 am-midnight; pianist. Ck-out noon. Meeting rms. Business servs avail. In-rm modem link. Barber. Valet parking. Exercise equipt. Massage. Health club privileges. Minibars. Cr cds: A, C, D, ER, JCB, MC, V.

Inns

★ ★ ★ **AUBERGE DE LA FONTAINE.** *(1301 rue Rachel E, Montréal QE H2J 2K1)* 514/597-0166; FAX 514/597-0496; res: 800/597-0597. E-mail info@aubergedelafountaine.com; web www.aubergedelafountaine.com. 21 rms, 3 story, 3 suites. May-Oct: S $115-$135; D $130-$150; each addl $15; suites $180; under 12 free. TV; cable, VCR avail. Complimentary bkfst buffet. Ck-out noon, ck-in 3 pm. Meeting rm. Business servs avail. In-rm modem link. Sun deck. Some in-rm whirlpools. Some balconies. Former residence; quiet setting in urban location; opp La Fontaine Parc. Cr cds: A, C, D, ER, MC, V.

★ ★ ★ **AUBERGE HANDFIELD.** *(555 Chemin du Prince, St-Marc-sur-Richelieu QE J0L 2E0)* 28 mi SE on Hwy 20, exit 112; 6 mi N on Hwy 223. 514/584-2226; FAX 514/584-3650; res: 800/667-1087 (CAN). 55 rms, 2 story. S $65; D $75-$185; each addl $10; under 4 free; theatre, winter package plans. Crib free. TV; cable (premium). Pool; whirlpool, poolside serv. Restaurant (see AUBERGE HANDFIELD). Bar 11 am-midnight. Ck-out, ck-in noon. Meeting rms. Business servs avail. Golf privileges. Tennis privileges. Downhill ski 15 mi. Exercise equipt; sauna. Theater-boat (late June-early Sept). Marina. Sugar cabin (late Feb-late Apr). Built in 1880. Cr cds: A, C, D, DS, ER, MC, V.

✔★ **LE BRETON.** *(1609 rue St-Hubert, Montréal QE H2L 3Z1)* 514/524-7273; FAX 514/527-7016. 13 rms, 11 with bath, 3 story. Some rm phones. S $35-$55; D $45-$70; each addl $8. TV; cable. Complimentary continental bkfst. Restaurant nearby. Ck-out noon, ck-in 2 pm. Business servs avail. Street parking. Cr cds: MC, V.

✔★ **MANOIR AMBROSE.** *(3422 Stanley St, Montréal QE H3A 1R8)* 514/288-6922; FAX 514/288-5757. 22 rms, 15 with bath, 8 A/C, 3 story. May-Oct: S $45-$75; D $50-$75; each addl $10; under 12 free; wkly rates; lower rates rest of yr. Crib free. Parking $5. TV; cable. Complimen-

tary continental bkfst. Restaurant nearby. Ck-out noon, ck-in 2:30 pm. Business servs avail. Victorian mansion (1883); large windows, high ceilings. Near Peel metro station. Cr cds: MC, V.

Restaurants

★ ★ **AUBERGE HANDFIELD.** *(See Auberge Handfield Inn)* 514/584-2226. Canadian, French menu. Specialties: lapin sauté, petit cochon de lait, ragoût de pattes. Hrs: 8 am-midnight; Sun brunch 10 am-3 pm. Res accepted. Bar. A la carte entrees: lunch, dinner $14-$25. Sun brunch $19.50. Child's meals. Parking. In 1880 building. Indoor terrace with view over Richelieu River. Family-owned. Cr cds: A, C, D, DS, ER, MC, V.

★ ★ ★ ★ ★ **THE BEAVER CLUB.** *(See Queen Elizabeth Hotel)* 514/861-3511. Founded by fur traders during Montréal's colonial days and serving as a social club for the city's elite during the 19th century, the Beaver Club maintains the august atmosphere of a men's club. Classic haute cuisine and an extraordinary wine cellar help make it one of the most unusual and best dining rooms in North America. Continental menu. Specialties: steak Charles, shrimp artichoke, pan-fried duckling foie gras. Hrs: noon-3 pm, 6-11 pm; Sat from 6 pm. Closed Sun & Mon eve; also July. Res accepted. Bar. Wine cellar. A la carte entrees: dinner $24-$32. Complete meal: lunch $19.25-$23.25, dinner $32-$38. Child's meals. Valet parking. Jacket. Cr cds: A, C, D, DS, ER, JCB, MC, V.

★ ★ ★ **CAFÉ DE PARIS.** *(See The Ritz-Carlton, Kempinski Montréal Hotel)* 514/842-4212. French menu. Specialties: feuilleté de saumon, scallops. Own pastries. Hrs: 6:30-11:30 am, noon-2:30 pm, 3:30-5 pm, 6-10 pm; Sun brunch 11 am-2:30 pm. Res accepted. Bar. Wine list. A la carte entrees: bkfst $10-$19, dinner $25-$40. Table d'hôte: lunch, dinner $23-$35. Sun brunch $39.50. Child's meals. Entertainment. Valet parking. Outdoor dining. Cr cds: A, C, D, DS, ER, JCB, MC, V.

✔★ **CAFE ST ALEXANDRE.** *(518 Duluth St E, Montréal QE H2L 1A7)* 514/849-4251. Greek menu. Specialties: pikilia, shish kebab. Hrs: 11 am-midnight. Res accepted. Setups. A la carte entrees: lunch, dinner $7.95-$15.95. Table d'hôte: dinner $15.95-$17.95. Child's meals. Salad bar. Outdoor dining. Cr cds: A, MC, V.

★ ★ ★ **CHAMPS ELYSÉES.** *(See Château Versailles Hotel)* 514/939-1212. French menu. Specialties: braised salmon, rib steak with fresh onions, crêpes suzette. Hrs: 7-10:30 am, noon-2:30 pm, 6-10 pm; Sat 7:30-11 am, 6-10 pm; Sun 7:30-11 am. Res accepted. Bar. Wine cellar. Complete meal: bkfst $7.25-$9.75, lunch $13.95-$35, dinner $19.50-$26.50. Valet parking. Jazz trio Fri, Sat. Elegant French bistro. Cr cds: A, D, DS, ER, MC, V.

★ ★ ★ **CHEZ LA MÈRE MICHEL.** *(1209 Guy St, Montréal QE H3H 2K5)* 514/934-0473. French, nouvelle cuisine. Specialties: suprême de pintade au vinaigre de framboises, homard soufflé. Own pastries. Hrs: noon-2:30 pm, 5:30-10:30 pm; Sat, Mon from 5:30 pm. Closed Sun. Res required. Bar. Wine cellar. Table d'hôte: lunch $14.50-$17.50. A la carte entrees: dinner $22-$30. French provincial decor. Family-owned. Cr cds: A, ER, MC, V.

★ ★ ★ **CHEZ PAUZÉ.** *(1657 rue St Catherine Ouest, Montréal QE H3H 1L9)* 514/932-6118. French menu. Specialties: lobster, scampi, smoked salmon. Hrs: 11:30 am-10 pm; Thurs to 10:30 pm; Fri to 11 pm; Sat 5-11 pm; Sun 5-10 pm. Res accepted. Bar. Wine list. Complete meals: lunch, dinner $11.95-$45. Pianist Thurs-Sat. Outdoor dining. Montréal theme. Cr cds: A, D, ER, JCB, MC, V.

★ ★ ★ **EXOTIKA.** *(400 Ave Laurier Ouest, Montréal QE H2V 2K7)* *514/273-5015.* Eclectic menu. Specialties: alligator, bar rayé Pacifiko, royal praline. Hrs: 7 am-midnight. Res accepted (formal dining rm only). Bar 11:30 am-midnight. Wine list. A la carte entrees: bkfst $2.50-$10, lunch $6.50-$10, dinner $13-$32. Jazz. Multi-sensory adventure with African decor; safari motif. Cr cds: A, D, ER, MC, V.

[D] [⊐]

★ ★ **KATSURA MONTRÉAL.** *(2170 Rue de la Montagne, Montréal QE H3G 1Z7) 514/849-1172.* Japanese menu. Specializes in sushi, steak, teriyaki. Sushi bar. Hrs: 11:30 am-2:30 pm, 5:30-10 pm; Fri, Sat to 10:30 pm; Sun 5:30-9 pm. Closed most major hols. Res accepted. Wine list. A la carte entrees: lunch $8.10-$14.50, dinner $14-$27. Complete meals: dinner $27-$37. Cr cds: A, D, ER, JCB, MC, V.

[⊐]

★ ★ **L'EXPRESS.** *(3927 Saint Denis, Montréal QE H2W 2M4)* *514/845-5333.* French, continental menu. Specialties: steak tartare, fresh salmon, chicken liver mousse with pistachio. Hrs: 8-2 am; Sat, Sun from 10 am. Closed Dec 25. Res accepted. Bar to 3 am. A la carte entrees: bkfst $2.45-$3.45, lunch, dinner $9.95-$16.50. Cr cds: A, D, ER, MC, V.

[D] [⊐]

★ ★ **LA CAVERNE GRECQUE.** *(105 Prince Arthur E, Montréal QE H2X 1B6) 514/844-5114.* Greek menu. Specializes in seafood, steak, chicken. Hrs: 11-midnight; Fri, Sat to 1 am. Res accepted. Setups. Complete meals: lunch $5-$10. A la carte entrees: dinner $8.95-$19.95. Child's meals. Cr cds: A, D, ER, MC, V.

[⊐]

★ ★ ★ **LA MARÉE.** *(404 Place Jacques Cartier, Montréal QE H2Y 3B2) in Old Montréal. 514/861-8126.* Housed in an 1808 building, this restaurant has two distinct dining areas: one small and intimate, the other larger and brightly lit. Service is impeccable and formal. French menu. Specialties: homard bruneterie, châteaubriand grille. Own pastries, sherbets. Hrs: noon-3 pm, 6-11 pm; Sat, Sun from 5:30 pm. Closed Jan 1, Dec 25. Res required. Serv bar. Wine cellar. Complete meals: lunch $13.50-$15.50. A la carte entrees: dinner $24-$33. Street parking. Cr cds: A, C, D, DS, ER, JCB, MC, V.

[⊐]

★ ★ ★ **LA RAPIÈRE.** *(1155 rue Metcalfe, Montréal QE H3B 2V6)* *514/871-8920.* French menu. Specialties: foie gras de canard, le confit de canard au vinaigre de framboise, le cassoulet à la Toulousaine. Hrs: noon-3 pm, 5:30-10 pm; Sat from 5:30 pm. Closed Sun; major hols; also mid-July-mid-Aug. Res accepted. Bar. Wine list. A la carte entrees: lunch $17.75-$26.50, dinner $24.25-$27.75. French decor. Jacket. Cr cds: A, C, D, ER, MC, V.

[D] [⊐]

★ ★ ★ **LE CAFE FLEURI.** *(See Hôtel Wyndham) 514/285-1450.* Web www.hoteldesjardins.com. French, continental menu. Specialties: marinated Canadian salmon, casserole of scallops, puffed pastry shell stuffed with wild mushrooms. Salad bar. Own pastries. Hrs: 6:30 am-10 pm. Res accepted. Serv bar. A la carte entrees: bkfst $9.75-$14.25, lunch $8.25-$18.75, dinner $18.50-$22.50. Buffet: bkfst $16.95. Sun brunch $19.95. Child's meals. Parking. Terrace. Cr cds: A, C, D, DS, ER, JCB, MC, V.

[D] [⊐] [♥]

★ ★ ★ **LE CAVEAU.** *(2063 Victoria St, Montréal QE H3A 2A3) between University & McGill Sts. 514/844-1624.* French menu. Specializes in fresh fish. Own pastries. Hrs: 11:30 am-11 pm; Sat, Sun from 5 pm. Res accepted. Bar. Wine cellar. A la carte entrees: lunch, dinner $11.95-$25. Complete meals: lunch $11.95-$25, dinner $14.95-$25. Chef's menu $25.50. Child's meals. Dinner parking. Family-owned. Cr cds: A, C, D, ER, MC, V.

[SC] [⊐]

★ ★ ★ **LE CHRYSANTHÈME.** *(1208 Crescent, Montréal QE H3G 2A9) 514/397-1408.* Chinese, Szechuan menu. Specializes in jumbo shrimp, beef. Hrs: noon-2:30 pm, 6-10:30 pm; Fri, Sat 6-11:30 pm; Sun from 6 pm; closed Mon; Jan 1, Dec 24, 25. Res accepted. Bar. A la carte entrees: lunch $10.80-$14. Complete meals: lunch $10-$13, dinner $12-$20. Chinese decor, artifacts. Cr cds: A, D, ER, MC, V.

[⊐]

★ ★ **LE JARDIN DE PANOS.** *(521 Duluth St E, Montréal QE H2L 1A8) 514/521-4206.* Greek, French menu. Specialties: calmars frits, cotelettes d'agneau, brochette de poulet. Hrs: noon-midnight. Res accepted. Complete meals: lunch $7-$15. A la carte entrees: dinner $9-$19. Outdoor dining. Mediterranean decor. Cr cds: A, MC, V.

[⊐]

★ **LE KEG/BRANDY'S.** *(25 St Paul E, Montréal QE H2Y 1G2) 514/871-9093.* Specializes in steak, chicken, seafood. Salad bar. Hrs: 11:30 am-2:30 pm; 5-10 pm; Thurs, Fri to 11 pm; Sat 4 pm-midnight; summer hrs vary. Closed Dec 24, 25. Res accepted. Bar 11:30-3 am. A la carte entrees: lunch $4.29-$14.99, dinner $11.99-$23.79. Child's meals. Cr cds: A, MC, V.

[⊐]

★ ★ **LE MITOYEN.** *(652 Place Publique Ste-Dorothée Laval, Montréal QE H7X 1G1) 514/689-2977.* Nouvelle cuisine. Specialties: medaillons de caribou aux framboises, Magrets de canard. Own pastries, baking. Hrs: 6-11 pm. Closed Mon. Res accepted. Wine list. A la carte entrees: dinner $20.50-$28.50. Complete meals: dinner $29.50-$58. Child's meals. Parking. Renovated 1870 house. Fireplace. Outdoor terrace. Cr cds: A, D, ER, MC, V.

[D] [⊐]

★ ★ **LE PARIS.** *(1812 St Catherine Ouest, Montréal QE H3H 1M1) 514/937-4898.* French menu. Specializes in fish, liver, steak. Hrs: noon-3 pm, 5-10 pm. Closed Sun; Dec 25. Res accepted. A la carte entrees: lunch, dinner $13-$20. Parisian atmosphere. Cr cds: A, D, ER, MC, V.

[⊐]

★ ★ ★ **LE PASSE-PARTOUT.** *(3857 Boul Décarie, Montréal QE H4A 3J6) 514/487-7750.* French menu. Specialties: smoked salmon, red snapper à la Provencale. Own baking. Hrs: 11:30 am-2 pm, 6:30-9:30 pm; Tues, Wed to 2 pm; Sat from 6:30 pm. Closed Mon, Sun; most major hols. Res accepted. Complete meals: lunch $18.50, dinner $40-$50. Classic French decor. Cr cds: A, D, ER, JCB, MC, V.

[D] [⊐]

★ ★ ★ **LES CAPRICES DE NICOLAS.** *(2072 rue Drummond, Montréal QE H3G 1W9) 514/282-9790.* Modern French menu. Frequently changing market menu. Hrs: noon-2 pm, 6-10 pm; Sat to 6-10 pm. Closed Sun; most major hols; also June 24. Res accepted. Bar. Wine list. A la carte entrees: lunch $16-$29, dinner $22-$34. Complete meals: lunch $26-$30. Courtyard; atrium. Antique bar. Cr cds: A, D, ER, MC, V.

[⊐]

★ ★ ★ **LES CHENÊTS.** *(2075 Bishop St, Montréal QE H3G 2E8) downtown. 514/844-1842.* French menu. Specialties: délice du Chambord, filet of beef Rossini, pheasant with cream and morel sauce. Own pastries. Hrs: 11:30 am-3 pm, 5:30-11 pm; Sat, Sun from 5:30 pm. Res accepted. Extensive cognac list. Wine cellar. A la carte entrees: lunch $12-$22.95, dinner $22.50-$35. Table d'hôte: lunch $14.50, dinner $35. Chef-owned. Cr cds: A, C, D, ER, MC, V.

[⊐]

★ ★ ★ **LES HALLES.** *(1450 Crescent St, Montréal QE H3G 2B6) 514/844-2328.* French menu. Own pastries. Hrs: 11:45 am-2:30 pm, 6-11 pm; Mon, Sat from 6 pm. Closed Sun. Res accepted. Bar. Wine cellar. Complete meals: lunch $13.50-$23. A la carte entrees: dinner $19.95-$32. Complete meals: dinner $32-$45. Murals. Family-owned. Jacket. Cr cds: A, C, D, DS, ER, JCB, MC, V.

[⊐]

★ ★ **LES TROIS TILLEULS.** *(See Hostellerie Les Trois Tilleuls Motel)* 514/856-7787. E-mail host.3tilleuls@sympatico.ca; web saveurs.sym patico.ca/enc-roy/quebec/tilleuls.htm. French menu. Specialties: ris de veau trois tilleuls, cuisse de canard confite et son aiguillette. Own baking. Hrs: 7:30 am-10 pm. Res accepted. Bar 11-2 am. Wine cellar. Complete meals: lunch $18.50-$22. A la carte entrees: dinner $32.50-$44.50. Child's meals. Parking. In 1880 farmhouse with garden, terrace; view of river. Cr cds: A, C, D, ER, MC, V.

★ **MOKUM.** *(5795 rue Sherbrooke Ouest, Montréal QE H4A 1X2)* 514/488-4827. Continental menu. Frequently changing international menu. Hrs: 11:30 am-2:30 pm, 5:30-9:30 pm; Tues, Wed, Sat from 5:30 pm. Closed Mon, Sun; Jan 1, Dec 25. Res accepted. No A/C. Semi-a la carte: lunch $11.75-$15.50, dinner $20.75-$29.50. Outdoor dining. Casual dining. Cr cds: MC, V.

★ ★ ★ ★ **NUANCES.** *(1 ave de Casino, Montréal QE H3C 4W7)* in Casino de Montréal. 514/392-2708. In a city noted for fine restaurants, this is one of the best. High ceilings, stunning views and exquisite contemporary French cuisine make for memorable dining. French menu. Specialties: roast loin of Québec lamb, duo of lobster and scallops, foie gras of duck. Hrs: 5:30-11 pm; Fri-Sun to 11:30 pm. Res required. Bar. Extensive wine cellar. Semi-a la carte: dinner $27-$33. Cr cds: A, D, ER, MC, V.

★ ★ **OPUS II.** *(See Le Westin Mont-Royal Hotel)* 514/849-6787. Hrs: 6:30-11 am, noon-2:30 pm, 6-10 pm; Sun brunch noon-2:30 pm. Res accepted. French menu. Bar noon-11 pm. Wine cellar. A la carte entrees: lunch, dinner $16-$29. Complete meal: bkfst $12.75-$18.50. Buffet: bkfst $12. Sun brunch $24-$29. Child's meals. Specializes in seasonal menus with market freshness. Parking. Atrium; urban setting. Cr cds: A, D, DS, ER, JCB, MC, V.

★ **PICCADELI.** *(3271 Taschereau Blvd, Greenfield Park QE J4V 2H5)* Hwy 10 exit 8E, Tacheran Blvd, N on Hwy 134. 514/462-1166. Specializes in seafood, steak, lasagna. Hrs: 7:30-2 am. Res accepted. Bar. Complete meal: bkfst $1.95-$2.95, lunch, dinner $4.95-$23.95. Child's meals. Entertainment Wed-Sun. Parking. Family-owned. Cr cds: A, C, D, ER, MC, V.

★ ★ **SAWATDEE.** *(457 Rue St Pierre, Montreal QE H2Y 2M8)* 514/849-8854. Hrs: 11:30 am-3 pm, 5-11 pm; Sat, Sun 5-11 pm. Res accepted. Thai menu. Bar. A la carte entrees: lunch, dinner $8.95-$15.95. Complete meal: lunch, dinner $18.50-$24.50. Buffet: lunch, dinner $8.95. Child's meals. Specialties: som tum, chicken/shrimp with peanut sauce. Thai decor; art. Cr cds: A, D, ER, MC, V.

★ ★ **SZECHUAN.** *(400 Notre Dame St W, Montréal QE H2Y 1V3)* 514/844-4456. Chinese menu. Specializes in Szechuan, Hunan dishes. Hrs: 11:30 am-3 pm, 5:30-10:30 pm; Sat 5:30-11 pm. Closed Sun; Jan 1, Dec 24, 25. Res accepted. Bar. Semi-a la carte: lunch $10.95-$15.95, dinner $15-$25. Cr cds: A, D, MC, V.

★ ★ **TOKYO SUKIYAKI.** *(7355 Mountain Sights Ave, Montréal QE H4P 2A7)* 514/737-7245. Japanese menu. Specialties: shabu shabu, sushi, sukiyaki. Hrs: 5:30-11:30 pm. Closed Mon; Jan 1, Dec 25. Res accepted. Japanese whiskey, wine, beer. Complete meals: dinner $27. Parking. Japanese decor; traditional Japanese seating. Family-owned. Cr cds: A, D, ER, MC, V.

★ ★ **TOQUÉ!.** *(3842 rue St-Denis, Montréal QE H2W 2M2)* 514/499-2084. French menu. Specialties: hot foie gras, salmon tartare, manjari chocolat crème brûlée. Hrs: 6-11 pm. Closed most major hols. Res required. Bar. Wine list. A la carte entrees: dinner $22-$26. Art deco decor. Cr cds: A, D, ER, MC, V.

★ ★ ★ **ZEN.** *(See Le Westin Mont-Royal Hotel)* 514/499-0801. Asian menu. Specialties: Szechuan duck, General Tao's chicken, sesame orange beef. Hrs: 11:30 am-2:30 pm, 5:30-10 pm. Closed Dec 25. Res required. A la carte entrees: lunch, dinner $10.50-$20. Complete meals: lunch $12-$25, dinner $27. Cr cds: A, D, ER, MC, V.

Unrated Dining Spots

BENS DELICATESSEN. *(990 De Maisonneuve Blvd, Montréal QE H3A 1M5)* W at Metcalfe. 514/844-1001. Specialties: pastrami, smoked meat, corned beef. Hrs: 7:30-3 am; Fri, Sat to 4 am; Dec 24 to 6 pm. Serv bar. Semi-a la carte: bkfst, lunch, dinner $3.60-$10.95. Family-owned. Cr cds: MC, V.

BIDDLE'S JAZZ & RIBS. *(2060 Aylmer, Montréal QE H3A 2E3)* 514/842-8656. Specializes in chicken, ribs. Hrs: 11:30-2:30 am; Sun from 5:30 pm. Res accepted. Bar. A la carte entrees: lunch $6.25-$11.95, dinner $7.95-$16.95. Jazz combo. Parking. Cr cds: A, C, D, DS, ER, MC, V.

PIZZA MELLA. *(107 Prince Arthur E, Montréal QE)* 514/849-4680. Italian menu. Specializes in 30 types of pizza. Hrs: 11:30-1 am; wkends to 2 am. Closed Dec 25. Setups. Semi-a la carte: lunch, dinner $5.25-$9.35. Outdoor dining. Cooking on 3 woodburning brick ovens; open kitchen. Cr cds: A, C, D, ER, MC, V.

Mont Tremblant Provincial Park (E-4)

(Approx 15 mi or 24 km N of Saint-Jovite on PQ 327)

In 1894, the provincial government of Québec established this 482-square-mile (1,248-square-kilometer) wilderness reserve as a park. A vast territory gifted with abundant wildlife and a large variety of plants, it is filled with 300 lakes, three rivers, three major hydrographical basins, innumerable streams, waterfalls and mountains reaching as high as 3,120 feet (960 meters). Today it is a leisure haven for thousands of people interested in fishing, hiking, canoeing, biking, swimming, sailing, snowmobiling, snowshoeing, cross-country and downhill skiing. Many come just to see the spectacular foliage in fall. Entrances are at Saint Donat, on Hwy 125, Saint-Faustin on Hwy 117 North or Saint-Côme on Hwy 343. Canoes & boats for rent. Reception areas, picnicking. Some facilities for the disabled; inquire for details.

Camping is available from mid-May to early Oct; some trailer hookups available (fee). Winter activities may be enjoyed mid-Nov-mid-Mar. Phone 819/688-2281 or 819/688-6176.

Hotel

★ ★ ★ **PINOTEAU VILLAGE.** *(126 Pinoteau St, Mont Tremblant QE J0T 1Z0)* 8 mi N of St-Jovite on Hwy 327. 819/425-2795; FAX 819/425-9177. 50 condominiums, 2 story. No A/C. Mid-June-mid-Sept & Nov-mid-Apr: 1-bedrm $125-$160; 2-bedrm $180-$210; 3-bedrm $260-$280; under 12 free; ski plans; lower rates rest of yr. TV; cable (premium). Heated pool. No rm serv. Ck-out noon. Tennis. Golf privileges. Downhill ski ¼ mi; x-country ski adj. Exercise equipt. Microwaves. Private patios. On lake, private beach; boat rentals. Ski shop; rentals. Cr cds: A, MC, V.

Resorts

★ ★ ★ **CLUB TREMBLANT.** *(121 Cuttle St, Mont Tremblant QE J0T 1Z0) 9 mi N of St-Jovite on Hwy 327.* 819/425-2731; FAX 819/425-5617; res: 800/567-8341. E-mail club@tremblant; web www.clubtremblant.com. 100 condos. No A/C. MAP, mid-July-mid-Aug: suites $250; wkly rates; ski plan; under 6 free; lower rates rest of yr. TV; cable. 2 pools, 1 indoor; whirlpool. Playground. Free supervised child's activities (July-Aug). Dining rm 7:30-9:30 am, 6-8:30 pm; wkends to 9 pm. Bar 4 pm-1 am. Ck-out noon, ck-in 4:30 pm. Meeting rms. Business servs avail. In-rm modem link. Tennis, pro. Canoes, rowboats, sailboats, kayaks. Downhill ski ¼ mi; x-country ski adj. Ski shop; equipt rental. Rec dir. Rec rm. Exercise rm; sauna. Massage. Fireplaces. On Lake Tremblant; beach club. Cr cds: A, D, ER, JCB, MC, V.

★ ★ ★ **GRAY ROCKS.** *(525 Chemin Principal, Mont Tremblant QE J0T 1Z0) on Hwy 327, 4 mi N of Hwy 117.* 819/425-2771; FAX 819/425-3474; res: 800/567-6767. E-mail info@grayrocks.com; web www.grayrocks.com. 56 rms in 5-story inn, 18 chalet suites, 39 deluxe rms, 2 cottages, 56 condos; 21 rms share bath, some A/C. AP: S $165-$230; D $125-$198/person; suites $198/person (4 min); condos $180-$420; family, wkly, wkend rates; ski, golf, tennis, package plans. Crib free. Pet accepted. TV; cable. Indoor pool; whirlpool, lifeguard. Playground. Supervised child's activities (late June-early Sept & late Nov-Mar). Dining rm (public by res) 7:30-9:30 am, noon-1:30 pm, 6:30-8:30 pm. Bar noon-1 am. Snack bar. Ck-out 1 pm; ck-in 3 pm. Coin lndry. Meeting rms. Business servs avail. Gift shop. Bellhops. Tennis. 18-hole golf, greens fee $25-$80, 2 putting greens, driving range. Private beach; beachside serv. Rowboats, canoes, sailboats, paddleboats, kayaks. Windsurfing lessons. Downhill/x-country ski on site. Lawn games. Entertainment. Movies. Rec rm. Exercise equipt; sauna. Fireplace in some rms. Many private patios, balconies. Terrace. Sea plane base. Cr cds: A, D, DS, ER, MC, V.

Québec City (E-6)

Founded 1608 **Pop** 166,474 **Elev** 239 ft (73 m) **Area code** 418 **E-mail** bit@clic.net **Web** www.quebec-region.crq.qc.ca

Information Greater Québec Area Tourism & Convention Bureau, 835 Ave Wilfrid-Laurier d'Auteuil, G1R 2L3; 418/649-2608.

The city of Québec, one of the most beautiful in the Western Hemisphere, is 150 miles (240 kilometers) northeast of Montréal. Nestled on an historic rampart, Québec is antique, medieval and lofty, a place of mellowed stone buildings and weathered cannon, horse-drawn calèches, ancient trees and narrow, steeply angled streets. Here and there the 20th century has intruded, but Québec has preserved the ambience of the past.

Québec is a split-level city. Above is the sheer cliff and rock citadel that once made Québec the Gibraltar of the north. The Upper Town, built high on the cliff and surrounded by fortresslike walls, has one of the city's best-known landmarks, Le Château Frontenac, a hotel towering so high it is visible from 10 miles (16 kilometers) away. The Lower Town is the region surrounding Cape Diamond and spreading up the valley of the St Charles River, a tributary of the St Lawrence. The two sections are divided by the Funicular, which affords magnificent views of the harbor, river and hills beyond.

In soul and spirit Québec is French; the population is nine-tenths French. Although French is the official language, English is understood in many places. The city streets are perfect for a casual stroll and many of the things you'll want to see are convenient to one another. Winters here are quite brisk.

The first known visitor to what is now Québec was Jacques Cartier, who spent the winter of 1535 at what was then the local village of Stadacone. Undoubtedly, Cartier recognized the strategic significance of this site, but a European colony was not established until 1608 when Samuel de Champlain, a French nobleman acting in the name of the King

of France, established Kebec (native for "the narrowing of the waters"). The French began to put down roots in 1617 when Louis Hebert, the first agricultural pioneer, arrived with his family. The first settlement was wiped out in 1629 by British seafarers, but was later ceded back to France. For more than a century, Québec thrived despite constant harassment and siege from both the English and the Iroquois.

The decisive date in Québec history—and in the history of the British colonies to the south—was September 13, 1759. After an heroic ascent up the towering cliffs, General James Wolfe led his British troops to the Plains of Abraham (named after an early settler) and engaged the forces of the brilliant French General, Louis Joseph, Marquis de Montcalm. In 15 minutes the battle was over, both generals were among the fatalities and French dreams of an empire in America were shattered. (The last siege of Québec took place in 1775, when American troops under the command of Benedict Arnold attacked and were repelled.)

From its earliest days, Québec has been a center for military, administrative, religious, educational and medical activities. Today the provincial capital, it still is a center for these endeavors and also for industry.

What to See and Do

Artillery Park, National Historic Site. A 4-acre (2-hectare) site built by the French to defend the opening of the St Charles River. By the end of the 17th century it was known as a strategic site, and military engineers began to build fortifications here. Until 1871 the park housed French and British soldiers, eventually becoming a large industrial complex. Dauphine Redoubt (1712-1748), gun carriage shed (1813-1815), officers' quarters (1818) and arsenal foundry (1903) have been restored. Interpretation center. (All yr; closed Jan 1, Easter, Dec 25) St Jean & D'Auteuil Sts. Phone 418/648-4205. Admission (June 24-Labour Day)   ¢¢

Basilica of Sainte-Anne-de-Beaupré (1923). Noted as the oldest pilgrimage in North America. First chapel was built on this site in 1658; the present basilica, built of white Canadian granite, is a masterpiece in Romanesque style. Capitals tell story of Jesus' life in 88 scenes; vaults decorated with mosaics; unusual technique used for 240 stained-glass windows outlined in concrete. 14 life-size Stations of the Cross & *Scala Santa* (Holy Stairs) on hillside. (Daily) 22 mi (35 km) NE on Hwy 138. Phone 418/827-3781.

Cartier-Brébeuf National Historic Site. Commemorates Jacques Cartier, first European known to have wintered in mainland Canada (1535-1536) and Jean de Brébeuf, a martyred Jesuit priest. The *Grande Hermine*, a full-size replica of Cartier's 16th-century flagship, is in dry dock; the hold and between deck can be viewed. Interpretation center with videotaped material. Guided tours by reservation. Indigenous habitation on site is open to visitors. (Feb-Nov, daily exc wkends in Apr; Dec-Jan by appt) 175 de l'Espinay St. Phone 418/648-4038.   **Free.**

Explore. High-tech sound and visual art are used to illustrate the founding of Québec and the beginnings of New France during the Golden Age of Exploration, when Columbus, Cartier, Champlain and others began to venture into the Americas. (Daily; closed Dec 1-26) 63 rue Dalhousie. Phone 418/692-1759.   ¢¢

Grand Théâtre. Ultramodern theater has giant mural by sculptor Jordi Bonet in lobby; home of the Québec Symphony Orchestra and Opera; theatrical performances, concerts. 269 Blvd Rene Levesque. Phone 418/643-4975.

Île d'Orléans. This 23-mi-long (37-km) island was visited by Champlain in 1608 and colonized in 1648. Old stone farmhouses and churches of the 18th century remain. Farms grow an abundance of fruits and vegetables, especially strawberries, for which the island is famous. Across bridge, in St Lawrence River.

Jacques-Cartier Park. Beautiful views in boreal forest valley. Fishing, rafting, canoeing; mountain climbing; wilderness camping; cross-country skiing; hiking, mountain biking; picnicking; magnificent nature trail; nature interpretation. (Late May-mid-Oct, mid-Dec-mid-Apr) 25 mi (40.2 km) N via Hwy 175. Phone 418/848-3169.   **Free.**

✖ **La Citadelle.** Forming the eastern flank of the fortifications of Québec, La Citadelle was begun in 1820 and work continued on it until 1850. Vestiges of the French regime, such as the Cap Diamant Redoubt (1693) and a powder magazine (1750), can still be seen. Panoramic views; 50-min guided tours. Changing of the Guard (mid-June-Labour Day, daily);

Beating the Retreat, re-creation of a 16th-century ceremony (late June-Labour Day, Tues, Thurs, Sat & Sun; fee). On Cap Diamant. Phone 418/648-5175. ¢¢ In La Citadelle is

Museum of the Royal 22e Régiment. Located in two buildings. Powder magazine (ca 1750), flanked on both sides by massive buttresses, contains replicas of old uniforms of French regiments, war trophies, 17th-20th-century weapons; diorama of historic battles under the French; old military prison contains insignias, rifle and bayonnet collections, last cell left intact. (Mid-Mar-Oct, daily) Changing of the guard (mid-June-Labour Day, daily at 10 am).

Laurentides Wildlife Reserve. Camping, canoe-camping; canoeing, fishing; cottages, lodges; picnicking; small- and big-game hunting; cross-country & back country skiing, snowshoeing. (Late May-Labour Day, mid-Dec-mid-Apr) Some fees. 35 mi (48 km) N via Hwy 175. Phone 418/686-1717 or 418/848-2422 (in season). **Free.**

Mont-Sainte-Anne Park. Gondola travels to summit of mountain (2,625 ft or 800 m), affording beautiful view of St Lawrence River (late June-early Sept, daily). Skiing (Nov-May), 12 lifts, 50 trails; 85% snowmaking; cross-country, full service. Two 18-hole golf courses; bicycle trail. 166 campsites (phone 418/826-2323). The migration of 250,000 snow geese occurs in spring and fall at nearby wildlife reserve Cap Tourmente. Park (daily; closed May). Some fees. 23 mi (37 km) NE via ON 138, then N 3 mi (5 km) on Hwy 360. Phone 418/827-4561 or 800/463-1568 (lodging information).

Montmorency Park. Montmorency Falls; Wolfe's Redoubt, historic house (June-early Sept, by appt), artifacts. Picnicking. (May-Oct) 10 mi (16 km) E via Hwy 138. Phone 418/663-2877.

Musée du Fort. Narrated historical re-creation of the six sieges of Québec between 1629-1775; sound & light show. (Daily; closed Dec 1-26) Place d'Armes, corner of Sainte-Anne & du Fort Sts. Phone 418/692-2175. ¢¢

Museum of Civilization (Musée de la Civilisation). At entrance is *La Débâcle*, a massive sculpture representing ice breaking up in spring. Separate exhibition halls present four permanent and several changing exhibitions dealing with history of Québec and the French Canadian culture as well as cultures of other civilizations from around the world. All narrative panels and signs are in French; bilingual guides on duty in most exhibit areas and English guide books are avail (fee). Guided tours (1 hr; fee). (Late June- Labour Day, daily; rest of yr, daily exc Mon; closed Dec 25) 85 rue Dalhousie, near Place-Royale. Phone 418/643-2158. ¢¢

National Assembly of Québec. Guided tours (30 min) of century-old Parliament Building. Dufferin Ave. For schedule phone 418/643-7239. **Free.**

National Battlefields Park. Entrances along Grand-Allée. 250 acres (101 hectares) along edge of bluff overlooking St Lawrence River from Citadel to Gilmour Hill. Also called the Plains of Abraham, park was site of 1759 battle between the armies of Wolfe and Montcalm and 1760 battle of Sainte-Foy between the armies of Murray and Lévis. Visitor reception & interpretation center presents history of the Plains of Abraham from the New France period to the present. Bus tour of the park. Phone 418/648-4071. ¢ In the park are two Martello towers, part of the fortifications, a sunken garden, many statues and the

Musée du Québec, Collection of ancient, modern and contemporary Québec paintings, sculpture, photography, drawings, decorative arts; changing exhibits. (Daily; closed Jan 1, Dec 25) Parc des Champs-de-Bataille. Phone 418/643-2150. ¢

Old Port of Québec Interpretation Centre. Located in an ancient cement works and integrated into harbor installations of Louise Basin. Permanent exhibit shows importance of city as a gateway to America in the mid-19th century; timber trade & shipbuilding displays; films, exhibits; guides. (Early May-early Sept, daily; rest of yr, daily exc Mon) 100 St-André St. Phone 418/648-3300. Admission (June 24-Labour Day) ¢¢

Place-Royale. Encompasses earliest vestiges of French civilization in North America; ongoing restoration of 17th-19th-century buildings, which make this the greatest concentration of such structures in North America. Notre-Dame-des-Victoires Church (1688), exhibit and several houses are open to the public; information center at 215 Marché Finlay, G1K 8R5. Lower Town along St Lawrence Riverfront. One-hr guided tours by appt; phone 418/643-6631.

Québec Aquarium. Extensive collection of tropical, fresh and saltwater fish, marine mammals and reptiles; overlooks St Lawrence River. Seal feeding (morning & afternoon); films (mid-May-Aug; daily). Cafeteria, picnicking. (Daily) 1675 des Hôtels Ave in Sainte-Foy. Phone 418/659-5264. ¢¢¢

★ **Québec City Walls and Gates.** Encompassing Old Québec. Eighteenth-century fortifications encircle the only fortified city in North America; includes Governor's Promenade and provides scenic view of The Citadel, St Lawrence River & Lévis. (All yr exc Governor's Promenade) **Free.**

Québec Zoo. More than 270 species of native and exotic animals and birds in a setting of forests, fields and streams; children's zoo, sea lion shows; gift shops; restaurant, picnicking. (Daily; closed Dec 25) 9300 Faune St, in Charlesbourg, 7 mi (11.3 km) NW on CAN 73/CAN 175. Phone 418/622-0312. ¢¢¢

Saint-Jean-Port-Joli. Tradition of wood sculpture began in this town about 1936, initiated by the famed Bourgault family. Other craftsmen came and made this a premier handicraft center; sculptures, enamels, mosaics in copper & wood, fabrics, paintings. Golf club (May-Sept); tennis courts, mountain bike trails, marina. Guided tour. Approx 60 mi (96.6 km) NE on Hwy 132 halfway to the Gaspé Peninsula (see). Phone 418/598-3084. Also here are

Church (1779). Designed and decorated by famous woodcarvers. Renowned for the beauty of its lines and interior decor; has not been altered since it was built. Sculpted wood vault, tabernacle and reredos all by different artisans. **Free.**

Musée des Anciens Canadiens. Wood sculptures by Saint-Jean artisans. Original carvings by the Bourgault brothers. (Mid-May-Oct, daily) Phone 418/598-3392. ¢¢

Sightseeing tours.

Baillairgé Cultural tours. Guided walking tours of Old Québec. Depart Musée du Séminaire. (Late June-mid-Oct, daily) Phone 418/692-5737. ¢¢¢¢

Calèches (horse-drawn carriages) leave Esplanade parking lot on d'Auteuil St, next to Tourist Bureau.

Gray Line bus tours. 1576 Ave des Hôtels G1W 3Z5; 418/653-9722.

Harbour Cruises. M/V *Louis Jolliet* offers daytime, evening dance and dinner cruises on the St Lawrence River. Bar service, entertainment. (May-Oct) Chouinard Pier, opp Place Royale. Contact Croisières AML, 124 rue St-Pierre G1K 4A7; 418/692-1159 or 800/563-4643. ¢¢¢¢¢

St Andrew's Presbyterian Church (1810). Serving the oldest English-speaking congregation of Scottish origin in Canada. Church interior is distinguished by a long front wall with a high center pulpit. Original petition to King George III asking for a "small plot of waste ground" on which to build a "Scotch" church; spiral stairway leading to century-old organ. Stained-glass windows, historic plaques. Guide service. (July-Aug, Mon-Fri) Sainte-Anne & Cook Sts. Phone 418/656-0625. **Free.**

Université Laval (1663). (35,900 students) Oldest French university on the continent, Laval evolved from Québec Seminary, which was founded in 1663 by Québec's first bishop, Msgr. de Laval. In 1950 the university moved from "Le Quartier Latin" in old Québec to a 470-acre (190-hectare) site in suburban Sainte-Foy, where it developed into the present, modern campus. Sir Wilfrid Laurier Blvd & Du Vallon Route, in Sainte-Foy. Guided tours by appt; phone 418/656-2571.

Annual Events

Carnaval Québec Kellogg's. Internationally acclaimed French Canadian festival celebrated throughout the city. Main attraction is the Snow Palace, a 2-story structure built of blocks of ice, open to visitors. Other highlights include snow and ice sculptures, parades, canoe race on the St Lawrence, fireworks, many special events. Contact Carnaval de Québec, Inc, 290 rue Joly, G1L 1N8; 418/626-3716. 11 days beginning 1st Thurs Feb.

du Maurier Québec Summer Festival. Outdoor festival held at 15 locations throughout Old Québec. International event of the performing arts; more than 400 shows, most free. Contact 160 rue St-Paul, CP 24, Succ B, G1K 7A1; 418/692-4540. 11 days beginning 1st Thurs July.

Expo Québec. Exhibition Park. Agricultural, commercial and industrial fair; shows, games. Phone 418/691-7110. Late Aug.

Additional Visitor Information

Information centers are located at Tourism Québec, 12 Sainte-Anne St, phone 800/363-7777 (US & Canada), (Mon-Fri); and at the Greater Québec Area Tourism & Convention Bureau, 835 Ave Wilfrid-Laurier, G1R 2L3; 418/649-2608 (Daily). The US Consulate is located at 2 Terrasse Dufferin, phone 418/692-2095. Public transportation is operated throughout the city by the Qu&acut e;ebec Urban Community Transportation Commission.

Motels

★ **DAYS INN.** (2250 Ste-Anne Blvd (Hwy 138), Québec City QE G1J 1Y2) 418/661-7701; FAX 418/661-5221; res: 800/463-5568 (E CAN). 62 rms, 2 story. Mid-June-mid-Sept: S $70; D $75; each addl $10; suites $130; under 12 free; wkly rates off-season; lower rates rest of yr. Crib free. TV; cable (premium). 2 pools, 1 indoor; poolside serv. Sauna. Coffee in rms. Restaurant 7-10 am; Sat, Sun to 11 am. Rm serv. Ck-out noon. Meeting rms. Business servs avail. Free parking. Some refrigerators. Balconies. Cr cds: A, C, D, DS, ER, MC, V.

⊠ ⊭ 🔥 SC

✔★ **MOTEL SPRING.** (8520 Boul Ste Anne, Chateau-Richer QE G0A 1N0) N on Hwy 138. 418/824-4953; FAX 418/824-4117; 800 888/824-4953. E-mail bcj@mail.accent.net; web www.accent.net/bcj. 25 rms, 12 with shower only. No rm phones. July-early Sept: S $40-$50; D $40-$70; wkly rates; higher rates major hols; lower rates mid-May-June, early Sept-late Oct. Closed rest of yr. Crib free. Pet accepted. TV; cable. Restaurant 7 am-9 pm. Ck-out noon. Picnic tables. On river. Family-owned. Cr cds: MC, V.

D ⊭ 🔥 SC

✔★ **ONCLE SAM.** (7025 W Hamel Blvd, Ste-Foy QE G2G 1B6) 5½ mi W on Hwy 138, jct Hwy 540. 418/872-1488; FAX 418/871-5519; res: 800/414-1488. 44 rms, 1-2 story. Mid-June-mid-Sept: S, D $49-$69; each addl $10; under 14 free; lower rates rest of yr. Pet accepted. TV; cable, VCR avail. Heated pool. Playground. Ck-out noon. Coin lndry. Business servs avail. X-country ski 5 mi. Picnic table. Cr cds: A, C, D, ER, MC, V.

D ⊭ ⊠ ⊠ 🔥 SC

★ **PAVILLON BONNE ENTENTE.** (3400 Chemin Ste-Foy, Québec City QE G1X 1S6) 6 mi W on Hwy 73, Duplessis exit, then Chemin Ste-Foy exit W, on grounds of Château Bonne Entente Motel. 418/653-4502; FAX 418/653-3098; res: 800/463-4390. 45 rms, 1-2 story, 3 kit. units; ck-in/ck-out service at Château Bonne Entente Hotel (see). Mid-May-mid-Oct: S $114; D $124; each addl $15; kit. units $114-$124; under 17 free; wkly, wkend rates; higher rates Carnaval de Québec; lower rates rest of yr. Crib free. Pet accepted. TV; cable, VCR avail. Supervised child's activities; ages 6 mo and up. Ck-out 1 pm. Business servs avail. Airport transportation. X-country ski 5 mi. Exercise equipt. Massage. Cr cds: A, D, DS, ER, MC, V.

⊭ ⊠ 🛫 🏃 ✈ ⊠ 🔥 SC

★ ★ **QUÉBEC INN.** (7175 W Hamel Blvd, Ste-Foy QE G2G 1B6) 6½ mi W on Hwy 138. 418/872-9831; FAX 418/872-1336; res: 800/463-5777 (PQ). E-mail hotel@jaro.qc.cq. 135 rms, 2 story. June-mid-Oct: S $76.95-$86.95; D $86.95-$96.95; each addl $10; family rates; package plans; lower rates rest of yr. TV; cable. Indoor pool; whirlpool, poolside serv. Restaurant 6:30 am-11 pm. Rm serv. Bar 11-3 am; entertainment Wed-Sun. Ck-out noon. Meeting rms. Business servs avail. In-rm modem link. Beauty, barber shop. X-country ski 5 mi. Exercise rm; sauna. Massage. Balconies. Indoor garden. Cr cds: A, D, ER, MC, V.

D ⊠ ⊠ 🏃 🔥

✔★ ★ **SELECTÔTEL ROND-POINT.** (53 Kennedy Blvd, Lévis QE G6V 6C7) At jct Rive-Sud Blvd (Hwy 132) & Hwy 173; 1 mi N of Autoroute Jean Lésage (Hwy 20), exit 325N. 418/833-4920; FAX 418/833-

0634; res: 800/463-4451 (US, CAN). 124 rms, 2 story. July-mid-Sept: S $62-$69; D $74-$89; each addl $10; suites $140; lower rates rest of yr. Crib $5. TV; cable. Indoor pool. Restaurant 7 am-2 pm, 4:30-9:30 pm. Rm serv. Bar 4:30 pm-midnight (winter only). Ck-out noon. Coin lndry. Meeting rms. Business servs avail. Barber. Downhill/x-country ski 20 mi. Massage. Miniature golf. Some refrigerators. Some balconies. Cr cds: A, C, D, DS, ER, MC, V.

⊠ ⊠ ⊠ 🔥 SC

★ ★ **UNIVERSEL.** (2300 Chemin Ste-Foy, Québec City QE G1V 1S5) 3 mi NE of Pierre-Laporte Bridge via Quatre Bourgeois exit from Hwy 73. 418/653-5250; FAX 418/653-4486; res: 800/463-4495 (E CAN, NE US). 127 rms, 3 story, 47 kits. S, D, suites $79; each addl $5; under 14 free. Crib free. TV; cable. Indoor pool. Sauna. Playground. Restaurant noon-11 pm. Rm serv. Bar 5 pm-1 am. Ck-out noon. Meeting rms. Business servs avail. Bellhops. X-country ski 3 mi. Some refrigerators. Balconies. Cr cds: A, D, DS, ER, MC, V.

⊠ ⊠ ⊠ 🔥 SC

Lodge

✔★ ★ **CHALETS MONTMORENCY.** (1768 ave Royale, St Ferréol les Neiges QE G0A 3R0) E on Hwy 138, E on Hwy 360. 418/826-2600; FAX 418/826-1123; res: 800/463-2612. Web www.holidayjunction.com. 35 rms, 3 story, 25 kit. suites. S $48-$51; D $64-$68; suites $79-$390; ski, golf plans. Crib $5. TV; cable, VCR avail. 2 pools, 1 indoor; whirlpool. Sauna. Restaurant adj 8 am-11 pm. Ck-out noon. Business servs avail. Coin lndry. 18-hole golf course. Downhill/x-country ski 1 mi. Rec rm. Microwaves. Balconies. Picnic tables. Cr cds: MC, V.

D ⊠ 🍴🏌 ⊠ 🔥 SC

Motor Hotels

★ ★ **BEST WESTERN L'ARISTOCRATE.** (3100 chemin Saint-Louis, Ste-Foy QE G1W 1R8) Hwy 20 exit Chemin Saint-Louis. 418/653-2841; FAX 418/653-8525; res: 800/463-4752. 100 rms, 2 story. July-Aug: S, D $89-$119; each addl $5; under 18 free; wknd rates; lower rates rest of yr. Crib free. TV; cable, VCR avail. Pool; poolside serv, lifeguard. Restaurant 7 am-10 pm. Rm serv. Bar noon-10 pm. Ck-out noon. Meeting rms. Business servs avail. In-rm modem link. Valet serv. Health club privileges. Some refrigerators. Cr cds: A, C, D, DS, ER, MC, V.

D ⊠ ⊠ ⊠ 🔥 SC

★ ★ ★ **GOUVERNEUR HOTEL SAINTE-FOY.** (3030 Laurier Blvd, Ste-Foy QE G1V 2M5) 5 mi SW on Hwy 73, ½ mi E of Laurier Blvd exit. 418/651-3030; res: 888/910-1111 (CAN & NE US); FAX 418/651-6797. 320 rms, 2-4 story. May-Sept: S, D $115-$135; each addl $15; suites $200-$275; under 18 free; wkend rates; lower rates rest of yr. Crib free. TV; cable. Heated pool; poolside serv, lifeguard in summer. Restaurant 7 am-1 pm, 5-10 pm. Rm serv. Bar 5 pm-midnight. Ck-out 1 pm. Meeting rms. Business servs avail. Bellhops. Valet serv. Sundries. X-country ski 2 mi. Health club privileges. Some minibars. Many balconies. Cr cds: A, C, D, ER, JCB, MC, V.

D ⊠ ⊠ ⊠ 🔥

★ ★ **HOTEL CHÂTEAU LAURIER.** (695 E Grand-Allée, Québec City QE G1R 2K4) 418/522-8108; FAX 418/524-8768; res: 800/463-4453 (E CAN, NE US). 57 rms, 4 story. May-Oct: S $79-$99; D $89-$109; each addl $10; under 12 free; lower rates rest of yr. Crib free. Pet accepted, some restrictions. TV; cable, VCR avail. Restaurant 7:30 am-3:30 pm. Bar 11-3 am. Ck-out noon. Business servs avail. Cr cds: A, C, D, DS, ER, JCB, MC, V.

⊭ ⊠ 🔥

Hotels

★ **CHÂTEAU BELLEVUE.** (16 rue Laporte, Québec City QE G1R 4M9) 418/692-2573; FAX 418/692-4876; res: 800/463-2617 (E CAN, E US). 58 rms, 4 story. May-Oct: S, D $109-$129; each addl $10; winter packages; under 12 free; higher rates special events; lower rates rest of yr. Crib free. TV; cable. Complimentary continental bkfst (Nov-Apr). Restaurant nearby. No rm serv. Ck-out noon. Business servs avail. Cr cds: A, C, D, DS, ER, JCB, MC, V.

★ ★ ★ **CHÂTEAU BONNE ENTENTE.** (3400 Chemin Ste-Foy, Québec QE G1X 1S6) 6 mi W on CAN 73, Duplessis exit, then Chemin Ste-Foy exit W. 418/653-5221; FAX 418/653-3098; res: 800/463-4390. 109 rms, 3 story. May-Oct: S $168-$188; D $174-$194; each addl $15; suites $298-$314; under 17 free; wkend rates; lower rates rest of yr. Crib free. TV; cable, VCR avail. Heated pool; poolside serv, lifeguard. Playground. Free supervised child's activities; ages 6 mo and up. Complimentary coffee in lobby. Restaurant 6:30-11 am, noon-2 pm, 5-10 pm; Sat, Sun from 7 am (see LE PAILLEUR). High tea service 2-4 pm. Rm serv. Bar 11-2 am. Ck-out 1 pm. Meeting rms. Business center. In-rm modem link. Valet serv. Sundries. Free airport, bus depot, RR station transportation. Tennis. X-country ski 5 mi. Exercise equipt. Massage. Rec rm. Lawn games. Whirlpool in suites. Picnic table. Stocked pond. Cr cds: A, D, DS, ER, MC, V.

★ ★ **CLARENDON.** (57 rue St-Anne, Québec City QE G1R 3X4) 418/692-2480; res: 888/554-6001; FAX 418/692-4652. Web www.familledufour.com. 151 rms, 7 story. June-mid-Oct: S, D $99-$119; each addl $20; suites $189-$199; under 12 free; lower rates rest of yr. Crib free. Parking $6. TV; cable. Restaurant 7-10:30 am, noon-2 pm, 6-10 pm. Bar 11-3 am; entertainment. Ck-out noon. Meeting rms. Business servs avail. Historic hotel (1870)-the oldest in Québec. Cr cds: A, C, D, DS, ER, MC, V.

★ ★ ★ **HÔTEL GERMAIN-DES-PRÉS.** (1200 ave Germain-des-Prés, Ste-Foy QE G1V 3M7) 3 mi W on Laurier Blvd. 418/658-1224; FAX 418/658-8846; res: 800/463-5253. 126 rms, 8 story. June-mid-Oct: S $130; D $140; each addl $15; wkend rates; lower rates rest of yr. Crib free. TV; cable, VCR avail. Coffee in rms. Restaurant 7-10 am, 5-11 pm; Mon-Fri lunch 11:20 am; Sat bkfst 8-11 am; Sun 8 am-2 pm (see BISTANGO). Bar 5-11 pm. Ck-out noon. Business servs avail. In-rm modem link. Some free covered parking. Free airport, RR station, bus depot transportation. Health club privileges. Bathrm phones, minibars. Cactus garden in lobby. Cr cds: A, C, D, ER, MC, V.

★ ★ ★ **HILTON.** (1100 Blvd René Lévesque E, Québec City QE G1K 7M9) 418/647-2411; res: 800/447-2411; FAX 418/647-3737. 571 rms, 25 story. Mid-May-mid-Oct: S $138-$187; D $160-$209; each addl $22; suites $355-$835; wkend rates. Crib free. Pet accepted, some restrictions. Parking $16. TV; cable. Pool; poolside serv, lifeguard. Coffee in rms. Restaurant 7 am-midnight. Bars 11 am-midnight. Ck-out noon. Meeting rms. Business center. Barber, beauty shop. Downhill ski 11 mi; x-country ski nearby. Exercise rm; sauna. Massage. Quebec convention center opp. Luxury level. Cr cds: A, C, D, DS, ER, JCB, MC, V.

★ ★ **HOTEL CLASSIQUE.** (2815 Blvd Laurier, Ste-Foy QE G1V 4H3) 1 mi E of Hwy 73, blvd Laurier exit. 418/658-2793; res: 888/463-0083; FAX 418/658-6816. 237 rms, 32 A/C, 12 story, 102 suites, 60 kit. units (no equipt.). May-Sept: S $80-$110; D $110-$140; each addl $10; suites, kit. units $110-$180; under 12 free; wkly rates; lower rates rest of yr. Crib $10. TV; cable. 2 pools, 1 indoor; lifeguard. Restaurant open 24 hrs. Bar 11-3 am. Ck-out noon. Coin lndry. Meeting rms. Business servs avail. In-rm modem link. Free indoor parking. Gift shop. Health club privileges. Balconies. Cr cds: A, C, D, ER, MC, V.

★ ★ **HOTEL PLAZA QUEBEC.** (3031 Blvd Laurier, Ste-Foy QE G1V 2M2) 6 mi W. 418/658-2727; FAX 418/658-6587; res: 800/567-5276. E-mail hotel@jaro.qc.ca. 231 rms, 7 story. May-Oct: S $105-$125; D $120-$140; each addl $10-$15; suites $150-$250; family, wkend rates; lower rates rest of yr. Crib free. Free garage parking. TV; cable. Indoor pool; lifeguard, whirlpool. Saunas. Restaurant 6 am-11 pm. Bar. Ck-out

noon. Meeting rms. Business center. Gift shop. Refrigerator in suites. Some balconies. Indoor garden. Cr cds: A, D, ER, MC, V.

★ ★ ★ **LE CHÂTEAU FRONTENAC.** (1 rue des Carrières, Québec City QE G1R 4P5) 418/692-3861; res: 800/441-1414; FAX 418/692-1751. Web www.cphotels.ca. 613 rms, 18 story. May-Oct: S, D $189-$359; each addl $25; suites $399-$1,000; under 18 free; lower rates rest of yr. Crib free. Garage parking $15.45. TV; cable, VCR avail. Indoor pool; whirlpool, wading pool, poolside serv. Restaurant 7 am-midnight (also see LE CHAMPLAIN). Bar 11-2 am; entertainment exc Sun. Ck-out noon. Meeting rms. Business center. In-rm modem link. Shopping arcade. Ice skating. Downhill ski 11 mi; x-country ski 3 mi. Exercise rm. Minibars. Landmark château-style hotel (1893); site of historic conferences during World War II. Cr cds: A, C, D, DS, ER, JCB, MC, V.

★ ★ ★ **LOEWS LE CONCORDE.** (1225 place Montcalm, Québec City QE G1R 4W6) on Grande Allée. 418/647-2222; FAX 418/647-4710. Web www.loewshotels.com. 404 rms, 26 story. May-Oct: S, D $99-$215; each addl $20; suites $180-$750; wkend, ski plans; lower rates rest of yr. Crib free. Pet accepted. Garage $14; valet parking $18. TV; cable. Heated pool; whirlpool, poolside serv, lifeguard. Restaurant 6:45 am-midnight (also see L'ASTRAL). Bars 11-3 am. Ck-out 1 pm. Meeting rms. Business center. In-rm modem link. Concierge. Downhill ski 11 mi; x-country ski on site. Tennis privileges. Exercise rm; sauna. Health club privileges. Refrigerators, minibars; fireplace in 2 bi-level suites. Luxury level. Cr cds: A, C, D, DS, ER, JCB, MC, V.

★ ★ ★ **RADISSON HOTEL GOUVERNEUR.** (690 E Rene-Lévesque Blvd, Québec City QE G1R 5A8) in Place Haute-Ville. 418/647-1717; FAX 418/647-2146. 377 rms, 12 story. May-Oct: S $145-$180; D $165-$200; each addl $15; suites $195-$275; under 18 free (max 2); wkend, ski plans; lower rates rest of yr. Crib free. Parking $11. TV; cable, VCR avail. Heated pool; whirlpool, poolside serv, lifeguard. Coffee in rms. Restaurant 7 am-10:30 pm. Bar 11 am-10 pm. Ck-out noon. Meeting rms. Business center. Shopping arcade. Barber, beauty shop. X-country ski 1/2 mi. Exercise rm; sauna. Some minibars. Parliament buildings, Quebec convention center opp. Luxury level. Cr cds: A, C, D, DS, ER, JCB, MC, V.

Inns

★ **AU CHÂTEAU FLEUR DE LYS.** (15 Ste-Geneviève Ave, Québec City QE G1R 4A8) 1 blk N of Citadel. 418/694-1884; FAX 418/694-1666. 18 rms, 3 story. May-Oct: S, D $75-$110; each addl $10. Crib free. Parking $6.25. TV; cable. Continental bkfst. Restaurants nearby. Ck-out noon, ck-in 1 pm. Coin lndry. Business servs avail. Refrigerators. Greystone house (1873) in "Old Québec." Cr cds: A, DS, MC, V.

★ ★ **AU MANOIR STE-GENEVIÈVE.** (13 Ste-Geneviève Ave, Québec City QE G1R 4A7) 1 blk N of Citadel. 418/694-1666. 9 rms, 3 story, 3 kits. No rm phones. May-Oct: S $87; D, kit. units $100; each addl $10; under 12 free; some lower rates rest of yr. Crib free. Parking $6. TV; cable. Continental bkfst. Ck-out noon, ck-in 1 pm. Business servs avail. Greystone house (1895) with outside deck on upper level. No cr cds accepted.

Resort

★ ★ ★ **MANOIR DU LAC DELAGE.** (40 ave du Lac, Ville du Lac Delage QE G0A 4P0) 13 mi N via Hwy 175 to Hwy 371, then W to Lac Delage & follow signs. 418/848-2551; FAX 418/848-1352; res: 800/463-2841 (PQ). Web www.lacdelage.com. 105 rms, 54 A/C, 1-3 story. MAP: S $119-$145; D $164-$190; each addl $60; EP avail. Crib free. TV; cable. 2 pools; 1 indoor, poolside serv. Playground. Dining rm 7-10 am, noon-2 pm, 6-9 pm. Bar 11-1 am; pianist. Ck-out noon, ck-in 3 pm. Meeting rms.

Business servs avail. Lighted tennis. Marina; canoes, paddleboats, sailboats, windsurfing. Downhill ski 2 mi; x-country ski on site. Snow shoe activities, sledding, skating. Bicycles. Lawn games. Exercise equipt; sauna. Massage. Some minibars. Balconies. On lake. Summer theater performances. Cr cds: A, D, MC, V.

Restaurants

★ **AU CAFE SUISSE.** (32 Ste-Anne St, Québec City QE G1R 3X3) in front of Château Frontenac. 418/694-1320. Hrs: 11 am-midnight. Summer from 8 am. Res accepted. Swiss menu. Bar. A la carte entrees: bkfst $3.95-$9.95, lunch, dinner $7.95-$24.95. Complete meals: dinner $19.95-$24.95. Specializes in fondues, seafood, steak. Pianist Sat evenings. Parking. Sidewalk terrace dining in summer. Turn-of-the-century greystone house. Cr cds: A, C, D, ER, JCB, MC, V.

★ ★ **AUX ANCIENS CANADIENS.** (34 rue St-Louis, Québec City QE G1R 4P3) 418/692-1627. Hrs: noon-10 pm; summer to 11 pm. Res accepted. French-Canadian cuisine. Bar. Wine list. A la carte entrees: dinner $20-$29. Table d'hôte: dinner $24.50-$35. Specialties: country-style meat pie, small game. Own pastries. In building reputedly used as headquarters by General Montcalm; antiques. Family-owned. Cr cds: A, D, ER, MC, V.

✔★ ★ **BISTANGO.** (See Hôtel Germain-Des-Prés) 418/658-8780. French menu. Specializes in light French and California-style cuisine. Hrs: 7-10 am, 11:30 am-2 pm, 5-11 pm; Sat 8-11 am, 5-11 pm; Sun 8 am-2 pm, 5-11 pm. Res accepted. Bar. A la carte entrees: lunch $9.95-$11.95. Complete meals: dinner $22-$25. Child's meals. Valet parking. French bistro decor. Cr cds: A, C, D, ER, MC, V.

★ **CAFÉ DE PARIS.** (66 rue St-Louis, Québec City QE G1R 3Z3) 418/694-9626. Hrs: 11:30 am-11:30 pm. Closed Nov-Mar. Res accepted. French, continental menu. Semi-a la carte: lunch $9.95-$12.95, dinner $18.95-$28.95. Child's meals. Specializes in seafood, veal. Entertainment. Free valet parking. Built in 1827. Rustic decor with many original oil paintings. Cr cds: A, C, D, DS, ER, MC, V.

★ ★ ★ **L'ASTRAL.** (See Loews Le Concorde Hotel) 418/647-2222. Hrs: 11:45 am-3 pm, 6-11 pm; Sun brunch 10 am-3 pm. Res required. Bar to 12:30 am. Wine cellar. French, continental menu. A la carte entrees: lunch $9.50-$16.50, dinner $19.50-$35.50. Buffet: lunch from $16.50, dinner $34.95. Sun brunch $21.75. Child's meals. Specialties: rack of lamb, filet of veal, duckling with maple syrup. Own pastries. Salad bar. Pianist. Valet parking. Revolving rooftop restaurant. Cr cds: A, C, D, DS, ER, JCB, MC, V.

★ **L'OMELETTE.** (64 rue St-Louis, Québec City QE G1R 3Z3) 418/694-9626. Hrs: 7 am-10:30 pm. Closed Nov-Mar. Res accepted. Semi-a la carte: bkfst $3.50-$5.25, lunch $3-$6.50, dinner $5-$12.75. Specializes in omelets. Valet parking. Cr cds: A, C, D, DS, ER, MC, V.

★ ★ **LA MAISON SERGE BRUYÈRE.** (1200 rue St-Jean, Québec City QE G1R 1S8) 418/694-0618. French, continental menu. Specializes in complete gourmet dinners, Caribou, poached salmon. Own pastries. Hrs: 9 am-10:30 pm. Res accepted. Bar. Wine list. Prix fixe: dinner $8.95-$100. Valet parking. Fireplaces, original oil paintings. Family owned. View of St John's gate and city hall. Cr cds: A, D, DS, ER, MC, V.

★ ★ **LA RIPAILLE.** (9 rue de Buade, Québec City QE G1R 3Z9) 418/692-2450. Hrs: 11:30 am-2:30 pm, 5-11 pm; Sun from 5 pm; early-bird dinner 5-7 pm. Res accepted. French menu. Serv bar. A la carte entrees: lunch $9-$13.50, dinner $16-$19.95. Complete meals: lunch $8.95-$13.50, dinner $23.95. Child's meals. Specializes in seafood, rack of lamb,

veal tenderloin. Own pastries. Valet parking. In 1835 building. Cr cds: A, C, D, DS, ER, MC, V.

★ ★ **LE BONAPARTE.** (680 E Grande-Allée, Québec City QE G1R 2K5) 418/647-4747. Hrs: 11 am-11 pm. Closed Sat, Sun mornings in winter. Res accepted. French, continental menu. Bar to 3 am. Complete meals: lunch $5.95-$14.95, dinner $20.95-$28.95. A la carte entrees: dinner $10.95-$24.95. Child's meals. Specializes in rack of lamb, steak, seafood. Own pastries. Patio dining. In 1823 building. French murder mystery dinner Fri nights. Cr cds: A, C, D, ER, MC, V.

★ ★ ★ **LE CHAMPLAIN.** (See Le Château Frontenac Hotel) 418/692-3861. Hrs: 6-10 pm; Sun brunch 10 am-2 pm. Res accepted. Classical French menu. Serv bar. A la carte entrees: dinner $26.50-$35. Menu dégustation $49.50. Sun brunch $28. Specializes: Québec smoked salmon, rack of lamb. Own baking. Harpist Fri, Sat. Valet parking. Classical French atmosphere. Jacket. Cr cds: A, C, D, DS, ER, JCB, MC, V.

★ ★ ★ **LE CONTINENTAL.** (26 rue St-Louis, Québec City QE G1R 3Y9) 1 blk W of Place d'Armes. 418/694-9995. Hrs: noon-11 pm; Sun from 5:30 pm. Closed Dec 24, 25. Res accepted. French, continental menu. Wine cellar. A la carte entrees: dinner $17.75-$25.50. Complete meals: lunch $9.75-$14, dinner $23.50-$31. Specialties: steak tartare, curried shrimp, orange ducking flambe. Own pastries. Valet parking. Tableside cooking. Family-owned. Cr cds: A, C, D, DS, ER, JCB, MC, V.

★ ★ **LE DEAUVILLE.** (3000 Laurier Blvd, Ste-Foy QE G1V 2M4) ½ mi E of Hwy 73, Laurier Blvd exit. 418/658-3644. Specializes in prime rib, lobster, filet mignon. Hrs: 11:30 am-11 pm. Res accepted. Bar. A la carte entrees: lunch $8.25-$15.95, dinner $12.95-$24.95. Child's meals; under 6 free. Parking. Outdoor dining in season. Cr cds: A, D, ER, MC, V.

★ **LE MANOIR DU SPAGHETTI.** (3077 chemin St-Louis, Ste-Foy QE G1W 1R6) 418/659-5628. French, Italian menu. Specializes in pasta, veal. Hrs: 11 am-11 pm. Res accepted. Serv bar. A la carte entrees: lunch, dinner $5.50-$15.95. Table d'hôte: lunch $5.49-$10.99, dinner $14.99-$21.98. Child's meals. Parking. Terrace dining in summer. Cr cds: A, C, D, ER, MC, V.

★ ★ ★ **LE PAILLEUR.** (See Château Bonne Entente Hotel) 418/653-5221. Regional menu. Specializes in grilled meats, seafood. Own pastries. Hrs: 7 am-10 pm; Sun brunch 10 am-2 pm. Res accepted. Bar 11-2 am. Wine list. A la carte entrees: bkfst $4.95-$9.95. Buffet: bkfst $7.95-$9.95, lunch $12.95. Table d'hote: dinner $19.95-$32.95. Child's meals. Menu changes monthly. Parking. Pianist Thurs-Sun. Cr cds: A, D, DS, ER, MC, V.

★ ★ ★ **LE SAINT-AMOUR.** (48 Sainte-Ursule, Québec City QE G1R 4E2) 418/694-0667. E-mail jocelyne@saint-amour.com; web www.saint-amour.com. Hrs: 11:30-2:30 pm, 6-11 pm; Mon, Sat, Sun 6-11 pm. Closed Dec 24. Res accepted. French menu. Serv bar. Wine cellar. A la carte entrees: lunch, dinner $19.50-$28.50. Child's meals. Specialties: foie gras, rack of lamb, royale chocolate. Valet parking. Outdoor dining. Family-owned since 1978. Cr cds: A, C, D, ER, MC, V.

★ ★ **LE VENDOÔME.** (36 Côte de la Montagne, Québec QE G1K 4E2) 418/692-0557. Hrs: 11 am-11 pm. Closed Dec 24. Res accepted. French menu. Bar. A la carte entrees: lunch $7.50-$12.50, dinner $14.50-$23. Child's meals. Specializes in steaks, seafood, veal. Valet parking. Outdoor dining. Parisian decor; murals. Family-owned since 1951. Cr cds: A, D, DS, ER, MC, V.

★ ★ ★ **RESTAURANT AU PARMESAN.** *(38 rue St-Louis, Québec City QE G1R 3Z1) 418/692-0341.* Hrs: noon-midnight. Closed Dec 24, 25. Res accepted. Italian, French menu. Serv Bar. Wine cellar. A la carte entrees: lunch, dinner $9.95-$31. Complete meals: lunch $9.50-$13.50, dinner $17.75-$26.95. Menu gastronomique $59. Child's meals. Specializes in own pasta, seafood, veal. Own pastries. Accordionist. Valet parking. 4,000 liqueur bottles displayed; many oil paintings. Chestnuts roasted in fireplaces in winter. Cr cds: A, D, DS, ER, MC, V.

Saint-Jovite (A-1)

Pop 3,841 **Elev** 790 ft (241 m) **Area code** 819 **Web** www.laurentides.com
Information Laurentian Tourism Association, 14142, rue de La Chapelle, RR 1, Saint-Jérôme, PQ, J7Z 5T4; 450/436-8532.

Nestled in the valley of the du Diable River and situated close to Mont Tremblant Provincial Park (see), this major all-year tourist area is one of the oldest in the Laurentians. Hunting, fishing, snowmobiling and skiing are among the many available activities. Three public beaches around Lac des Sables in Ste-Agathe make this a water sports paradise; international dogsled races on ice in nearby Ste-Agathe-des-Monts add to the excitement of the region. French summer theater, mountain climbing on Monts Condor and Césaire, antique shops and a Santa Claus Village are other options in Val-David, to the southeast.

What to See and Do

Antiques, arts & crafts. Interesting artisan's shops & galleries: **Le Coq Rouge,** an antique shop (phone 819/425-3205); **Alain Plourde, Artisan** (phone 819/425-7873).

Sherbrooke (F-6)

(See also Granby)

Pop 85,000 **Elev** 600 ft (183 m) **Area code** 819 **Web** www.sders.com/tourism
Information Office of Tourism, 3010 King W St, J1H 5G1; 819/821-1919 or 800/561-8331.

Nestled in a land of natural beauty at the confluence of the Magog and Saint-François rivers, Sherbrooke is a bilingual and bicultural community. Originally settled in 1791 by the French, an influx of Loyalist settlers and English colonists brought an English influence to the city, which remains today despite the 95 percent French population. More than 150 types of industries, including pulp and paper, textile and heavy machinery manufacturing, are carried on in this major railroad center. The principal city of Québec's Eastern Townships, Sherbrooke is the center of one of Canada's fastest developing winter sports areas. There are many beautiful open areas, such as the Howard Estate with its lovely pond and grounds and the Lake of Nations.

What to See and Do

Basilica of Saint Michel. Center of archbishopric.

Beauvoir Sanctuary. Setting of natural splendor on a hill. Church built in 1920. Statue of the Sacred Heart here since 1916, making it a regional pilgrimage site. Gospel scenes in outdoor mountain setting. (May-Oct, daily; Nov-Apr, Sun) Summer: picnic tables, restaurant, gift shop. 4 mi (6 km) N, exit 146 off Hwy 10. On the east bank of the Saint-François River. Phone 819/569-2535. **Free.**

Louis S. St-Laurent National Historic Site. Birthplace of Prime Minister Louis S. St Laurent (1882-1973); landscaped grounds; general store & adj

warehouse with sound and light show. (May-mid-Oct, daily) S on Hwy 147, at 6 Main St in Compton. Phone 819/835-5448. **Free.**

Mena'Sen Place. Many legends surround island and its original lone pine, destroyed in a storm in 1913 and replaced by the cross in 1934. Site of large illuminated cross.

⭐ **Mt Orford.** 2,800 ft (864 m) high with range stretching across the border into Vermont. Recreational park with campground, golf course, hiking, swimming, picnicking, lake and wildlife. Downhill and cross-country skiing in winter. 22 mi (35 km) SW near Hwy 10, exit 118. Phone 819/843-6233 or 800/462-5349(PQ); 819/462-9855 for campground res (7-14-day stay). Some fees.Here are

Orford Arts Centre. World renowned hall is one of the finest auditoriums anywhere. Pavilion with teaching and practice studios, 500-seat concert hall. Performances given by noted artists during Orford Summer Festival. Visual arts program. (May-Sept) Phone 819/843-3981 or 800/567-6155 (seasonal).

Ski Mont Orford. Outstanding area and some of the best facilities in Québec. 39 runs, 8 lifts; patrol, school, rentals; day care; cafeteria, restaurant, bar. Longest run 2 1/2 mi (4 km). (Nov-Apr, daily) 20 acres (8.09 hectares) of glade, 25 mi (40.2 km) of cross-country skiing. 18-hole golf (fee; rentals). Scenic chairlift (July-mid-Aug, daily; rest of summer, wkends only). 22 mi (36 km) SW. Phone 819/843-6548. ¢¢¢¢

Musée du Séminaire de Sherbrooke. More than 90,000 objects of natural history. (Tues-Sun afternoons) 195 rue Marquette. Phone 819/564-3200. ¢¢ Fee includes

Léon Marcotte Exhibition Centre. Presents traveling exhibitions from other museums and assembles others from the Seminary Museum. (Tues-Sun afternoons) 222 rue Frontenac. Phone 819/564-3200. ¢¢

Uplands Museum and Cultural Centre. This neo-Georgian home built in 1862 is located on four acres of beautifully wooded grounds. Changing exhibits interpret heritage of Lennoxville-Ascot and eastern townships. Museum contains period furniture. Red Barn, on grounds, is home to children's theater. Afternoon tea is served all yr (res required in winter). (Daily exc Mon; extended summer hrs) 50 Park St; S via Rte 143, W on Church to Park St in Lennoxville. For fees, phone 819/564-0409.

Motor Hotel

★ ★ ★ **HOTEL DES GOUVERNEURS.** *(3131 King St W (Hwy 112), Sherbrooke QE J1L 1C8) 1/4 mi E of jct Hwy 55. 819/565-0464; res: 888/910-1111; FAX 819/565-5505.* 124 rms, 4 story. May-Sept: S, D $60-$95; each addl $10; suites $155; under 18 free; wkend rates; lower rates rest of yr. Crib $10. TV; cable (premium). Heated pool; lifeguard. Restaurant 7 am-9 pm. Bar; entertainment. Ck-out 1 pm. Lndry facilities. Bellhops. Cr cds: A, C, D, ER, MC, V.

D ⚊ ⚊ ⚊ **SC**

Inn

★ ★ ★ **AUBERGE HATLEY.** *(325 Virgin St, North Hatley QE J0B 2C0) off Autoroute 10 exit 121. 819/842-2451; FAX 819/842-2907.* 25 rms, 3 story, 5 suites. MAP: D $245-$390; each addl $90; wkly, wkend rates; ski plans. Heated pool. Complimentary full bkfst. Dining rm 8-10 am, 6 pm-closing. Ck-out noon, ck-in 4 pm. Business servs avail. Downhill ski 1 mi; x-country ski on site. Many fireplaces; some in-rm whirlpools, balconies. Lake opp; swimming, boats avail for guest use. 1903 Victorian-style mansion. Cr cds: A, MC, V.

D ⚊ ⚊ ⚊

Resort

★ ★ **CHÉRIBOURG.** *(2603 chemin du Parc, Orford QE J1X 3W9) Hwy 10, exit 118, then Hwy 141 N 2 mi. 819/843-3308; FAX 819/843-2639; res: 800/567-6132 (CAN).* 97 rms, 3 story. Mid-June-early Sept, late Jan-late Mar: S $113-$121; D $144-$152; each addl $44; suites $184-$192; under 12 free; lower rates rest of yr. Crib free. TV; cable (premium), VCR avail. 2 pools, 1 indoor; whirlpool, poolside serv, lifeguard.

Playground. Restaurants 7:30 am-10 pm. Rm serv. Bar. Ck-out noon. Coin lndry. Meeting rms. Business servs avail. Concierge. Valet serv. Indoor tennis, pro. Downhill/x-country ski 2 mi. Exercise equipt; sauna. Massage. Game rm. Rec rm. Lawn games. Some balconies. Cr cds: A, D, DS, ER, MC, V.

D ⚡🏃🏊🏋🐾 SC

St Jérôme (F-4)

(See also Montréal, Saint-Jovite)

Pop 25,123 **Elev** 362 ft (110 m) **Area code** 450 **Web** www.laurentides.com
Information Laurentian Tourism Association, 14142, rue de Lachapelle, RR 1, J7Z 5T4; 450/436-8532 or 800/561-6673.

Founded in 1834 on the Rivière du Nord is the "Gateway to the Laurentians," St Jérôme. In this resort area, north of St Jérôme amid the magnificent setting of mountains, forests, lakes and rivers, summer sports and recreation are unlimited, fall colors spectacular and winter sports and festivals delightful. Outfitters are available to help plan a wilderness vacation, but visitors may also choose from over 200 accommodations of every price and type.

Under the fierce leadership (1868-1891) of Curé Labelle, a huge man and a near legendary figure, this area began to grow. Curé Labelle hoped to open the whole country, north and to the Pacific, which was nearly empty at that time. Making over 60 canoe and foot trips of exploration, he selected sites for new parishes and founded more than 20. By pen and pulpit he sought to stop the flow of labor to the United States, and in 1876, due to his inexhaustible efforts, the railroad came to St Jérôme, bringing new prosperity. Curé Labelle became the Minister of Agriculture and Colonization in 1888. A bronze monument honoring him is in the park opposite the cathedral.

What to See and Do

Centre d'exposition du Vieux Palais. Exhibition centre of visual arts. 185 rue du Palais, Hwy 15 N, exit 43. Phone 514/432-7171.

Trois-Rivières (E-5)

Pop 50,466 **Elev** 120 ft (37 m) **Area code** 819
Information Tourism Information Bureau, 1457 Notre Dame St, G9A 4X4; 819/375-1122.

Considered the second-oldest French city in North America, Trois-Rivières was founded in 1634. Many 17th- and 18th-century buildings remain, and the Old Town area is a favorite haunt for visitors. The St Maurice River splits into three channels here as it joins the St Lawrence, giving the name to this major commercial and industrial center and important inland seaport. Paper milling and shipment of cereals are some of the more important industries. Trois-Rivières is a cathedral and university (Université du Québec) center as well.

What to See and Do

De Tonnancour Manor (1723). Oldest house in city; housed soldiers in 1812; in 1852 became the bishop's home. Displays of painting, pottery, sculpture, engravings, serigraphy and jewelry. (Daily exc Mon) 864, rue des Ursulines, Place Pierre-Boucher. Phone 819/374-2355. **Free.**

Les Forges du Saint-Maurice National Historic Site. Remains of the first ironworks industry in Canada (1729-1883). Blast-furnace and Ironmaster's House interpretation centers; models, audiovisual displays.

Guided tours. (Mid-May-Labour Day, daily; after Labour Day-late Oct, Wed-Sun) 8 mi (13 km) N at 10,000 boul des Forges. Phone 819/378-5116. ¢¢

Notre Dame-du-Cap. Small stone church (1714), and large octagonal basilica, renowned for its stained-glass windows. Important pilgrimage site. (May-Oct, daily) Across the river, at 626 rue Notre Dame in Cap-de-la-Madeleine. Phone 819/374-2441. **Free.**

Old Port. Magnificent view of the St Lawrence River. Built over part of the old fortifications. Pulp and paper interpretation center; riverside park; monument to La Vérendrye, discoverer of the Rockies (1743). Off rue Saint-François-Xavier, overlooking river. Phone 819/372-4633. Interpretation center ¢

Sightseeing tour. M/S *Jacques-Cartier.* Around Trois-Rivières Harbour and on the St Lawrence River. 400-passenger ship. Orchestra on wkend evening cruises. (Mid-May-mid-Sept) Wharf on des Forges St. Contact 1515 rue du Fleuve, CP 64, G9A 5E3; 819/375-3000. ¢¢¢

St James Anglican Church (1699). Rebuilt in 1754; used at various times as a storehouse and court; rectory used as prison, hospital and sheriff's office. In 1823, it became an Anglican church, and it is now shared with the United Church; carved woodwork added in 1917; cemetery dates from 1808. Still used for church services. 811 rue des Ursulines. Phone 819/374-6010.

The Cathedral (1854). Built in Gothic Westminster style; contains huge stained-glass windows, brilliantly designed by Nincheri, considered finest of their kind in North America. Renovated in 1967. 362 rue Bonaventure.

Ursuline Convent (1700). Norman-style architecture; building has been enlarged and restored many times. Historic chapel; museum and art collection. (May-Aug, daily exc Mon; Oct-Apr, Wed-Sun) 734 rue des Ursulines. Phone 819/375-7922. ¢

Annual Event

Trois-Rivieres International Vocal Arts Festival. Downtown. A celebration of song. Religious, lyrical, popular, ethnic, traditional singing. Phone 819/372-4635. June 25-July 1.

Motel

★ **COCONUT.** *(7531 rue Notre Dame, Trois-Rivières-Ouest QE G9B 1L7)* 819/377-3221; FAX 819/377-1344; res: 800/838-3221. 39 rms. Mid-June-Sept: S $42-$65; D $42-$70; each addl $5; suites $118; under 18 free; lower rates rest of yr. TV; cable (premium). Ck-out noon. Meeting rms. Refrigerator avail. Cr cds: A, C, D, ER, MC, V.

🏊🔥 SC

Hotels

★ ★ **DELTA.** *(1620 Notre Dame St, Trois-Rivières QE G9A 6E5)* 819/376-1991; FAX 819/372-5975; res: 800/877-1133 (US), 800/268-1133 (CAN). Web www.deltahotels.com. 159 rms, 12 story. S, D $72-$150; each addl $15; suites $150-$300; under 18 free; higher rates Formula Grand Prix (Aug). Crib free. Pet accepted. TV; cable. Indoor pool; whirlpool. Coffee in rms. Restaurant 7 am-9:30 pm. Bar 4 pm-midnight. Ck-out noon. Meeting rms. Business servs avail. In-rm modem link. Gift shop. Free garage parking. Downhill ski 10 mi; x-country ski 5 mi. Exercise equipt; sauna. Massage. Minibars; some bathrm phones. Cr cds: A, D, DS, ER, JCB, MC, V.

D ⚡🏊🏋🏃🏄🐾 SC

★ ★ **HOTEL DES GOUVERNEURS.** *(975 Hart St, Trois-Rivières QE G9A 4S3)* 819/379-4550; res: 888/910-1111; FAX 819/379-3941. 122 rms, 5 story. S, D $49; each addl $10; suites $140; under 18 free; wkend rates. Crib free. TV; cable (premium). Pool; poolside serv, lifeguard. Complimentary continental bkfst. Ck-out 1 pm. Business servs avail. In-rm modem link. Some minibars. Cr cds: A, C, D, DS, ER, MC, V.

D 🏊🐾 SC

Index

Establishment names are listed in alphabetical order followed by a symbol identfying their classification, and then city, state and page number. Establishments affiliated with a chain appear alphabetically under their chain name, followed by the state, city and page number. The symbols for classification are: [H] for hotel; [I] for inns; [M] for motels; [L] for lodges; [MH for motor hotels; [R] for restaurants; [RO for resorts, guest ranches, and cottage colonies; [U] for unrated dining spots.

Notes

Mobil Travel Guide

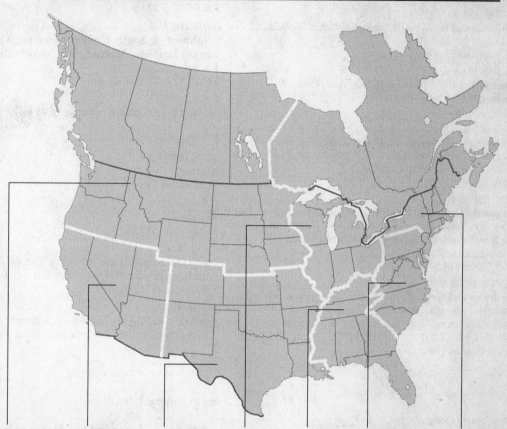

Northwest & Great Plains

Idaho
Iowa
Minnesota
Montana
Nebraska
North Dakota
Oregon
South Dakota
Washington
Wyoming

Canada:
Alberta
British Columbia
Manitoba

California & the West

Arizona
California
Nevada
Utah

Southwest & South Central

Arkansas
Colorado
Kansas
Louisiana
Missouri
New Mexico
Oklahoma
Texas

Great Lakes

Illinois
Indiana
Michigan
Ohio
Wisconsin

Canada:
Ontario

Southeast

Alabama
Florida
Georgia
Kentucky
Mississippi
Tennessee

Mid–Atlantic

Delaware
District of Columbia
Maryland
New Jersey
North Carolina
Pennsylvania
South Carolina
Virginia
West Virginia

Northeast

Connecticut
Maine
Massachusetts
New Hampshire
New York
Rhode Island
Vermont

Canada:
New Brunswick
Nova Scotia
Ontario
Prince Edward Island
Quebec

Mobil Travel Guide

Looking for the Mobil Guides . . . ?

**Call toll-free 800/533-6478 around the clock
or use the order form below.**

Please check the guides you would like to order:

☐ 0-679-00190-5
America's Best Hotels & Restaurants
$12.00 (Can $16.95)

☐ 0-679-00191-3
California and the West (Arizona, California, Nevada, Utah)
$16.95 (Can $23.50)

☐ 0-679-00194-8
Great Lakes (Illinois, Indiana, Michigan, Ohio, Wisconsin, Canada: Ontario)
$16.95 (Can $23.50)

☐ 0-679-00195-6
Mid-Atlantic (Delaware, District of Columbia, Maryland, New Jersey, North Carolina, Pennsylvania, South Carolina, Virginia, West Virginia)
$16.95 (Can $23.50)

☐ 0-679-00196-4
Northeast (Connecticut, Maine, Massachusetts, New Hampshire, New York, Rhode Island, Vermont, Canada: New Brunswick, Nova Scotia, Ontario, Prince Edward Island, Québec)
$16.95 (Can $23.50)

☐ 0-679-00198-0
Northwest and Great Plains (Idaho, Iowa, Minnesota, Montana, Nebraska, North Dakota, Oregon, South Dakota, Washington, Wyoming, Canada: Alberta, British Columbia, Manitoba)
$16.95 (Can $23.50)

☐ 0-679-00199-9
Southeast (Alabama, Florida, Georgia, Kentucky, Mississippi, Tennessee)
$16.95 (Can $23.50)

☐ 0-679-00200-6
Southwest & South Central (Arkansas, Colorado, Kansas, Louisiana, Missouri, New Mexico, Oklahoma, Texas)
$16.95 (Can $23.50)

☐ 0-679-00193-X
Major Cities (Detailed coverage of 45 major U.S. cities)
$18.95 (Can $26.50)

☐ 0-679-00241-3
Arizona
$12.00 (Can $16.95)

☐ 0-679-00192-1
Florida
$13.00 (Can $17.95)

☐ 0-679-00197-2
On the Road with Your Pet (More than 4,000 Mobil-rated Lodgings that Welcome Travelers with Pets)
$15.00 (Can $21.00)

☐ 0-679-00201-4
Southern California (Includes California south of Lompoc, with Tijuana and Ensenada, Mexico)
$13.00 (Can $17.95)

☐ My check is enclosed.

☐ Please charge my credit card

☐ VISA ☐ MasterCard ☐ American Express

Total cost of book(s) ordered $ _____

Shipping & Handling (please add $2 for first book, $.50 for each additional book) $ _____

Add applicable sales tax (In Canada and in CA, CT, FL, IL, NJ, NY, TN and WA.) $ _____

TOTAL AMOUNT ENCLOSED $ _____

Credit Card # _____

Expiration _____

Signature _____

Please ship the books checked above to:

Name _____

Address _____

City _____ State _____ Zip _____

Please mail this form to: Mobil Travel Guides, Random House, 400 Hahn Rd., Westminster, MD 21157

YOU CAN HELP MAKE THE *MOBIL TRAVEL GUIDE* MORE ACCURATE AND USEFUL

ALL INFORMATION WILL BE KEPT CONFIDENTIAL

Your Name _____
(Please Print)

Were children with you on trip? ☐ Yes ☐ No

Street _____

Number of people in your party _____

City, State, Zip _____

Your occupation _____

1. Establishment name _____
Hotel ☐ Resort ☐ Other ☐
Motel ☐ Inn ☐ Restaurant ☐

Street _____ City _____ State _____

Do you agree with our description? ☐ Yes ☐ No; if not, give reason _____

_____

Please give us your opinion of the following:

DECOR	CLEANLINESS	SERVICE	FOOD
☐ Excellent	☐ Spotless	☐ Excellent	☐ Excellent
☐ Good	☐ Clean	☐ Good	☐ Good
☐ Fair	☐ Unclean	☐ Fair	☐ Fair
☐ Poor	☐ Dirty	☐ Poor	☐ Poor

1999 *GUIDE* RATING _____ ★
CHECK YOUR SUGGESTED RATING BELOW:
☐ ★ good, satisfactory ☐ ★★★★ outstanding
☐ ★★ very good ☐ ★★★★★ one of best
☐ ★★★ excellent   in country
☐ ✓ unusually good value

Comments: _____

_____

Date of visit _____

First visit? ☐ Yes ☐ No

2. Establishment name _____
Hotel ☐ Resort ☐ Other ☐
Motel ☐ Inn ☐ Restaurant ☐

Street _____ City _____ State _____

Do you agree with our description? ☐ Yes ☐ No; if not, give reason _____

_____

Please give us your opinion of the following:

DECOR	CLEANLINESS	SERVICE	FOOD
☐ Excellent	☐ Spotless	☐ Excellent	☐ Excellent
☐ Good	☐ Clean	☐ Good	☐ Good
☐ Fair	☐ Unclean	☐ Fair	☐ Fair
☐ Poor	☐ Dirty	☐ Poor	☐ Poor

1999 *GUIDE* RATING _____ ★
CHECK YOUR SUGGESTED RATING BELOW:
☐ ★ good, satisfactory ☐ ★★★★ outstanding
☐ ★★ very good ☐ ★★★★★ one of best
☐ ★★★ excellent   in country
☐ ✓ unusually good value

Comments: _____

_____

Date of visit _____

First visit? ☐ Yes ☐ No

3. Establishment name _____
Hotel ☐ Resort ☐ Other ☐
Motel ☐ Inn ☐ Restaurant ☐

Street _____ City _____ State _____

Do you agree with our description? ☐ Yes ☐ No; if not, give reason _____

Please give us your opinion of the following:

DECOR	CLEANLINESS	SERVICE	FOOD
☐ Excellent	☐ Spotless	☐ Excellent	☐ Excellent
☐ Good	☐ Clean	☐ Good	☐ Good
☐ Fair	☐ Unclean	☐ Fair	☐ Fair
☐ Poor	☐ Dirty	☐ Poor	☐ Poor

1999 *GUIDE* RATING _____ ★
CHECK YOUR SUGGESTED RATING BELOW:
☐ ★ good, satisfactory ☐ ★★★★ outstanding
☐ ★★ very good ☐ ★★★★★ one of best
☐ ★★★ excellent   in country
☐ ✓ unusually good value

Comments: _____

_____

Date of visit _____

First visit? ☐ Yes ☐ No

FOLD AND TAPE (OR SEAL) FOR MAILING—PLEASE DO NOT STAPLE

CUT ALONG DOTTED LINE

66

Revised editions are now being prepared for publication next year:

California and the West: Arizona, California, Nevada, Utah.

Northeast: Connecticut, Maine, Massachusetts, New Hampshire, New York, Rhode Island, Vermont; Eastern Canada.

Mid-Atlantic: Delaware, District of Columbia, Maryland, New Jersey, North Carolina, Pennsylvania, South Carolina, Virginia, West Virginia.

Southeast: Alabama, Florida, Georgia, Kentucky, Mississippi, Tennessee.

Great Lakes: Illinois, Indiana, Michigan, Ohio, Wisconsin; Ontario, Canada.

Northwest and Great Plains: Idaho, Iowa, Minnesota, Montana, Nebraska, North Dakota, Oregon, South Dakota, Washington, Wyoming; Western Canada.

Southwest and South Central: Arkansas, Colorado, Kansas, Louisiana, Missouri, New Mexico, Oklahoma, Texas.

Major Cities: Detailed coverage of 45 Major Cities.

The Mobil Travel Guide is available at bookstores or by mail from the Mobil Travel Guide, Random House, 400 Hahn Rd., Westminster, MD 21157, or call toll-free, 24 hours a day, 1-800/533–6478.

HOW CAN WE IMPROVE *THE MOBIL TRAVEL GUIDE*?

Mobil Travel Guides are constantly being revised and improved. All attractions are updated and all listings are revised and evaluated annually. You can contribute to the accuracy and usefulness of the guides by sending us your reactions to the places you have visited. Your suggestions for improving the guides are also welcome. Just complete this form or address letters to: *Mobil Travel Guide,* 3225 Gallows Rd., Suite 7D 0407, Fairfax, VA 22037. Or, contact us online at www.mobil.com/travel. The editors appreciate your comments.

Have you sent us one of these forms before? ☐ Yes ☐ No

Please make any general comment here. Thanks! _____

_____

_____

_____